INDEX TO ILLUSTRATIONS

INDEX
TO
ILLUSTRATIONS

BY

JESSIE CROFT ELLIS

BOSTON

THE F. W. FAXON COMPANY

1966

Copyright by
The F. W. Faxon Company, Inc.
1967

LIBRARY OF CONGRESS CATALOG CARD NUMBER: 66-11619

PRINTED IN THE UNITED STATES OF AMERICA

To
THE MEMORY OF MY
FATHER AND MOTHER

GEORGE THOMAS CROFT
AND
MARGARET ELLEN (COX) CROFT

WHO GAVE ME
AN ENQUIRING MIND
AND OPENED THE WORLD TO ME
AS MY WORKSHOP

OTHER BOOKS

BY

JESSIE CROFT ELLIS

NATURE INDEX

TRAVEL THROUGH PICTURES

GENERAL INDEX TO ILLUSTRATIONS

MARY ANN OF OLD KENTUCKY

SMALL BUSINESS BIBLIOGRAPHY

NATURE AND ITS APPLICATIONS

PREFACE

This index is an entirely new addition to my series of indexes. It includes a far broader range of subjects as—world affairs, explorations, space, science subjects such as lazers, parts of the body, symbols, which are of much interest today. My work is to try to anticipate and provide answers to the many requests for material likely to be wanted, before it is wanted. To help teachers, lecturers, quiz programs, clubs, students, business and professional people, and very busy librarians save hours of searching for hard-to-find items which they might or might not be able to find without the aid of a ready reference book. It is suggested that librarians go through the index very carefully, to become familiar with the references and cross references, in order to be able to give fast service to all who come needing something in a hurry. It is chiefly for picture material but a large percent of them are included in articles about them and therefore it is possible to obtain much information about the subject from these references.

This book includes references to picture material in all fields, exclusive of nature. However you will find flowers and animals if you look under such headings as symbols, man, woman or other items with which they might be associated. If you want the symbol for something look for that which is wanted, such as snobbery, union, vanity, purification, rabbit's foot, radiology, quarantine, winged serpent. You will also find facial expressions and other emotions and ideas. Where there are several pages listed for the item you will find information about it. References are included to places of interest, such as mountains, lakes, places of scenic beauty. Teachers often ask their students to find pictures and biographies of authors for books they are reviewing. Just look for the author's name.

Have you ever said to yourself "where can I find it? I must have it at once." When such questions come over the librarians desk she offers a silent prayer for assistance of some kind to guide her search. And so I send this book forth with the hope that it may be the answer to that prayer and also be useful to many other people at home or business, and to everyone who needs help. There is practically no limit to the vast amount of material one can obtain from this index. While no index of this sort can be made perfect, careful selection of illustrations has made this book a valuable guide in answering many questions. A few issues of some of the periodicals have been omitted because they could not be obtained in nearby libraries and librarians do not like to send out their magazines on interlibrary loan.

Most of the periodicals cover a period of ten years, except *U.S. News* and *World Report* from which I have taken some special recent items and pictures of people of public interest.

I want to thank Mr. A. H. Davis, Jr., President of F. W. Faxon Co., for his patience and encouragement during the period of years while this index was being compiled, and thanks to the Chicago Public Library for special use of their books and periodicals while I was doing research there. I especially thank Miss Sue Montgomery, Head of the Reference Department, Evansville, Indiana, Public Library, and others in that department, who so willingly gave me their time and service in obtaining books and periodicals, and freedom to work in their book stacks as needed, and for calling my attention to new books of interest as they were received in the library.

JESSIE CROFT ELLIS

CONTENTS

BOOKS AND PERIODICALS USED IN THE INDEX

American heritage. Vol. 1-12 (1961).

Brooks, Emerson M. The growth of a nation. Pictorial review of the U.S. of America from colonial days to the present. 1956. Dutton & Co.

Ceram, C. W. The march of archaeology. 1958. Knopf.

Comstock, ed. Concise encyclopedia of American antiques. 1958.

Concise encyclopedia of antiques, compiled by the Connoisseur. Hawthorn Books, Inc.

Connoisseur (Amer. ed.) 1951-60.

Cooper, Martin, ed. Concise encyclopedia of music and musicians. 1958. Hawthorn Books, Inc.

Current biography. 1945-60.

Daniel, Dorothy. Cut and engraved glass 1771-1905. The collector's guide to American wares. 1950. M. Barrows & Co., N.Y.

Disney, Walt. People and places, by Jane Werner Watson and the staff of the Walt Disney studio. Golden Press, N.Y. 1959.

Durant, John and Alice. Pictorial history of the American circus. 1957. A. S. Barnes Co.

Gray, Henry. Anatomy of the human body, edited by Charles Mayo Goss. 1948. 25th ed. Reprinted 1953.

Holiday. 1949-60.

Horan, James D. and Sann, Paul. Pictorial history of the wild west. 1954. Crown Publisher, N.Y.

International graphic society. The Arts of mankind. Painting, architecture, music. The international pictorial treasury of knowledge. 1962. Esco Publishing Co.

Jensen, Amy La Follette. The White House and its thirty-three families. 1962. McGraw-Hill Co.

Jordan, E. L. Hammond's pictorial travel atlas of scenic America. 1955. Hammond & Company.

Junior book of authors, 2nd ed., rev., ed. by Stanley J. Kunitz and Howard Haycraft. 1951. H. W. Wilson Co.

Labande, Y. and E. R. Naples and its surroundings. Translated and adapted by J. H. Shaw, 1955. Nichols Kaye Co., London.

Lehner, Ernest. The picture book of symbols. 1956. Wm. Penn Publishing Corp., N. Y.

National geographic magazine.

Osward, Maxim. Asia Minor, with 160 pictures in photogravure, 8 colour plates and introduction by Maxim Osward, translated from the German by Norma Deane. 1957. Wm. Morrow & Co.

Pakula, Marvin H. Centennial album of the civil war in collaboration with Wm. J. Ryan and David K. Rothstein. 1960. Thomas Yoseloff, N. Y. and London.

The praeger picture encyclopedia of art. 1958. F. A. Praeger Publisher, N. Y.

Rawson, Marion Nicholl. The Antiquer's picture book. 1940. Dutton Co.

Saturday Evening Post, eds. The Face of America. 1957. Doubleday & Co.

Tilke, Max. Costume patterns & designs. A survey of costume patterns and designs of all periods and nations from antiquity to modern times. 1956. Illustrated in color. Frederick A. Praeger, N. Y.

Travel magazine.

Index to Illustrations

A

"A Kermess" (Brueghel). Con. 133: 257 Je '54.
Aalto, Hugo Alvar. Cur. biog. p. 1 (1948).
Aaltonen, Vaino (statue by). Travel 105: 35 Ap '56.
Aaltonen, Waino. Cur. biog. p. 1 (1954).
Aandahl, Fred G. Cur. biog. p. 1 (1958).
Aarhus, Denmark. Natl. geog. 105: 423 Mar '54.
Aaron, Henry. Cur. biog. p. 3 (1958).
abacus (sym.) Lehner: Pict. bk. of sym., p. 13.
Abbas, Ferhat. Cur. biog. p. 1 (1961).
Abbaye-Aux-Hommes (Caen). Holiday 27: 129 Jan '60.
Abbell, Maxwell. Cur. biog. p. 1 (1951).
Abbey, Arbroath. See Arbroath abbey.
Abbey, Edwin A. (work of). Amer. heri., vol. 6 no. 4 p. 38-9 (Je '55).
Abbey, Baden-Baden. Holiday 23: 86 (col.) Je '58.
Abbey, Bath (11th cent.). Holiday 26: 48 (col.) Aug '59.
Abbey, Bisham. See Bisham abbey.
Abbey, Fonthill. See Fonthill abbey.
Abbey, Jumieges (Normandy). Praeg.: Pict. ency., p. 187.
Abbey, Melrose. See Melrose abbey.
Abbey, Stoneleigh. See Stoneleigh abbey.
Abbey, Tintern. See Tintern abbey.
Abbey Benedictine of Maria Laach. Praeg.: Pict. ency., p. 234.
Abbey Centula (reconstruction). Praeg.: Pict. ency., p. 184.
Abbey church. See church, Norman abbey.
Abbey of Cluney, church of. Praeg.: Pict. ency., p. 222.
Abbey of Maria Laach, church of. Praeg.: Pict. ency., p. 234.
Abbey of Peterborough. See Peterborough cathedral.
Abbey theatre, (Dublin, Ireland). Holiday 6: 60-1 (col.) Dec. '49; 19: 41 Jan '56.
Abbot Archbishop George. Amer. heri., vol. 10 no. 4 p. 7 (Je '59).
Abbot (Greece). Natl. geog. 103: 383 (col.) Mar '53; 114: 773 (col.) Dec '58.
"Abbotsford" (home of Sir Walter Scott). Natl. geog. 112: 438-9 (col.) Oct '57.
—— (int.). Holiday 27: 75 (col.) May '60.
Abbott, Berenice. Cur. biog. p. 1 (1942).
Abbott, Bud. Cur. biog. p. 1 (1941).
Abbott, Douglas. Cur. biog. p. 1 (1949).
Abbott, Edith. Cur. biog. p. 3 (1941).
Abbott, L. F. (work of). Con. 135: 179-83 May 55.
Abbott, Lemuel F. (work of). Amer. heri. vol. 4 no. 4 p. 43 (summer '53).
abdomen. Gray's anatomy, p. 1191-3, 1377-91.

Abdullah, Mohammad. Cur. biog. p. 1 (1952).
Abdullah Al Salim Al Subah. Cur. biog. p. 1 (1957).
Abdullah Ibn Hussein (King of Trans-Jordan). Cur. biog. p. 4 (1948).
Natl. geog. 98: 745 (col.) Dec '50.
Abelson, Nathan. Cur. biog. p. 4 (1957).
Abend, Hallett. Cur. biog. p. 3 (1942).
Abercrombie, Sir Patrick. Cur. biog. p. 1 (1946).
Abercrombie, Thomas J. Natl. geog. 115: 830 Je '59.
Abetz, Otto. Cur. biog. p. 4 (1941).
Abildgaard, N. A. (work of). Con. 135: 49 Mar '55.
Abilene (Kansas). Holiday 21: 90-3 May '57.
—— (pioneer time). Horan: Pict. hist of wild west, p. 92.
Aborigines (Australia). Natl. geog. 103: 132-41 Jan '53.
Travel 108: 56 Oct '57.
—— (eating teredos). Natl. geog. 110: 565 Oct '56.
—— (Formosa). Natl. geog. 97: 166-7 (col.) Feb '50.
—— (harvesting teredos). Natl. geog. 110: 566 Oct '56.
"Abraham dividing the world" (Zanchi). Con. 144: 107 Nov '59.
Abrahams, Peter. Cur. biog. p. 5 (1957).
Abram, Jacques. Holiday 21: 42 Mar '57.
Abrams, Benjamin. Cur. biog. p. 4 (1954).
Abrams, Harry N. Cur. biog. p. 4 (1958).
abraxas (sym.) Lehner: Pict. bk. of sym., p. 66.
Absinthe house, old (New Orleans). Holiday 10: 10 Sept '51.
Abu Simbil, Temple of. See Temple of Abu Simbil.
Abul Kalam Azad, Maulana. Cur. biog. p. 5 (1942).
abundance (sym.). Lehner: Pict. bk. of sym., p. 27, 82.
Abusir pyramids. See Pyramids at Abusir.
Abyssinia (fortress). Int. gr. soc.: Arts . . . p. 85 (col.).
academic cap and gown. See cap & gown, college.
Academy of music. See music academy.
Academy of the Sacred Heart (New Orleans). Holiday 23: 85 Mar '58.
Acadia Natl. park. Natl. geog. 113: 648-9 (col.) May '58.
Acadian fisherman's home (La. bayou). Holiday 6: 61 (col.) Oct '49.
"Acadian house museum" (St. Martinville). Travel 102: 10 Aug '54.

1

Acadians (La. bayou country). Amer. heri. vol. 6 no. 1 p. 60-2 (col.) (fall '54). Holiday 6: 52-63 (col.) Oct '49.

Acadians. Travel 112: 32-3 Sept '59.

Acapulco (Mexico). Holiday 11: 52-7 (part col.) Mar '52; 26: 56-7 Nov '59.

Accademia of Villa Hadriana at Tivoli. Ceram: March. of arch., p. 15.

accelerator (atomic). Natl. geog. 114: 338 (col.) Sept. '58.

accordian (girl & man playing). Natl. geog. 111: 170-1 (col.) Feb '57.

—— (girl playing). Natl. geog. 101: 801 (col.) Je '52.

—— (man playing). Disney: People & places, p. 9, 73 (col.). Holiday 23: 40 (col.) Jan '58. Natl. geog. 113: 93 (col.) Jan '58.

—— (Swiss man playing). Natl. geog. 111: 785 (col.) Je '57.

—— (woman playing). Natl. geog. 99: 766 (col.) Je '51.

"Accordian player" (Lipchitz). Con. 145: 209 May '60.

Ace, Goodman. Cur. biog. p. 7 (1948).

Ace, Jane. Cur. biog. p. 7 (1948).

Achaemenian kings, tombs of. See tombs of Achaemenian kings.

Achelis, Elisabeth. Cur. biog. p. 5 (1954).

Acheson, Dean. Amer. heri. vol. 11 no. 2 p. 46 (Feb '60). Cur. biog. p. 6 (1941); p. 3 (1949). Holiday 7: 94 Feb '50.

achievement (sym.) Lehner: Pict. bk. of sym., p. 84.

"Achilles dipped in river Styx" (Rubens). Con. 126: 211 Dec '50.

"Achilles mourning the death of Patroclus." Con. 143: 245 Je '59.

"Achilles on Skyros" (Poussin). Con. 143: 127 Ap '59.

acid (sym.). Lehner: Pict. bk. of sym., p. 72.

Acker, Achille van. Cur. biog. p. 6 (1958).

Ackerman, Carl W. Cur. biog. p. 1 (1945).

Ackland, Sir Richard. Cur. biog. p. 1 (1944).

acorn cup, antique gold. Con. 139: 42 Mar '57.

acoustics (sym.). Lehner: Pict. bk. of sym., p. 10.

Acre (city wall). Travel 104: 11 Aug '55.

Acre, Israel (harbor). Holiday 16: 109 Nov '54. Natl. geog. 110: 754 (col.) Dec '56.

acrobat. Holiday 11: 150 Je '52.

acrobats. Holiday 19: 116 (col.) Jan '56; 22: 67 Oct '57.

—— (Cambodia). Natl. geog. 117: 550 (col.) Ap '60.

—— (circus). See circus acrobats.

—— (Egyptian). Durant: Pict. hist. of Amer. circus, p. 2.

—— (Grecian). Durant: Pict. hist. of Amer. circus, p. 3.

"Acrobats in the night-garden" (Miro). Praeg. pict. ency., p. 495.

Acropolis (Greece). Holiday 12: 52 (col.) Sept '52; 15: 56-7 (col.) Je '54; 20: 124 (col.) Oct 56. Natl. geog. 103: 354 Mar '53; 110: 744 (col.) Dec '56. Travel 113: 28 Ap. '60; 114: 25 Aug '60.

Acropolis (plan). Praeg. pict. ency., p. 145.

—— "Porch of the maidens." Natl. geog. 109: 48 (col.) Jan '56. Praeg. pict. ency., p. 154. Travel 114: 25 Aug '60.

Acropolis, Mr. Smith's Amer. Amer. heri. vol. 7 no. 4 p. 38-43, 104-5 (Je '56).

Acton, Thomas. Amer. heri. vol. 10 no. 4 p. 96 (Je '59).

actor, Greek (ancient times). Int. gr. soc.: Arts . . . p. 35 (col.)

——, Japanese. Holiday 12: 39 (col.) Aug '52.

——, painted (Red China). Natl. geog. 118: 218 (col.) Aug '60.

——, Roman (ancient times). Int. gr. soc.: Arts . . . p. 35 (col.).

actor & actress (caricature). Holiday 5: 43 Jan '49.

actors. Holiday 13: 76-7 Jan '53.

——, Greek. Natl. geog. 109: 54 (col.) Jan '56.

—— (make-up). Natl. geog. 97: 207 (col.) Feb. '50.

—— (outdoor stage). Natl. geog. 100: 61-4 (col.) Jl '51.

——, Shakespearian. Holiday 10: 94-5 (col.) Jl '51.

—— (Shakespeare, outdoor scene). Natl. geog. 102: 355 (col.) Sept '52.

actors & producers (movie). Holiday 5: 34-52 (col.) Jan '49.

actress, Chinese (opera). Natl. geog. 111: 343 (col.) Mar '57.

actresses. Holiday 24: 113 Dec '58.

——, (dressing room). Natl. geog. 100: 60 (col.) Jl '51.

——, Shakespearian. Holiday 10: 94-5 (col.) Jl '51.

Adair, Frank E. Cur. biog. p. 3 (1946).

"Adam & Eve" (Brancusi wood carving). Praeg. pict. ency., p. 458.

Adam architecture (Gothic). See architecture, Adam Gothic.

—— (Scotland). Con. 139: 140 (col.), 141-3 May '57.

Adams, Abigail Brooks (Mrs. Charles Francis Adams). Amer. heri. vol. 10 no. 3 p. 27 (col.) (Ap '59).

Adams, Abigail Smith (Mrs. John Adams). Amer. heri. vol. 10 no. 3 p. 42 (col.) (Ap '59). Jensen: The White House, p. 10.

Adams, Andy, Jun. bk. of auth., p. 1.

Adams, Arthur S. Cur. biog. p. 3 (1951).

Adams, Brooks. Amer. heri. vol. 10 no. 3 p. 27. (Ap '59).

Adams, Charles Francis. Amer. heri. vol. 8 no. 3 p. 41 (Ap '57); vol. 9 no. 5 p. 90 (Aug '58); vol. 10 no. 3 p. 27 (Ap '59).

Adams, Mrs. Charles Francis. See Adams, Abigail Brooks.

Adams, Diana. Cur. biog. p. 7 (1954).

Adams, Edith. Cur. biog. p. 9 (1954).

Adams, Eva B. Cur. biog. p. 1 (1962).

Adams, Lt. Comdr. F. M. Natl. geog. 115: 7 (col.) Jan '59.

Adams, Franklin P. Cur. biog. p. 7 (1941).

Adams, Sir Grantley H. Cur. biog. p. 8 (1958).

Adams, Henry. Amer. heri. vol. 7 no. 1 p. 43 (Dec '55); vol. 8 no. 5 p. 27 (Aug '57); vol. 10 no. 3 p. 27 (Ap '59).
Natl. geog. 97: 282 Mar '50.

Adams, Capt. Henry A. (by Japanese artist). Amer. heri. vol. 9 no. 3 cover (col.) (Ap '58).

Adams, James Truslow. Cur. biog. p. 9 (1941).

Adams, Jane. Amer. heri. vol. 12 no. 1 p. 13, 16 (Dec '60).

Adams, John. Amer. heri. vol. 6 no. 3 p. 45 (col.) (Ap '55); vol. 6 no. 6 p. 56 (Oct '55); vol. 7 no. 3 p. 30 (Ap '56); vol. 9 no. 4 p. 48 (col.) (Je '58).
Jensen: The White House, p. 4, 9.

—— **(head).** Holiday 14: 34 Nov '53.

—— **(mask).** Amer. heri. vol. 6 no. 4 p. 19 (Je '55).

—— **(portrait).** Natl. geog. 97: 282 Mar '50.

Adams, John Cranford. Cur. biog. p. 9 (1958).

Adams, John IV. Amer. heri. vol. 10 no. 3 p. 26 (col.) (Ap '59).

Adams, John Quincy. Amer. heri. vol. 7 no. 3 p. 30 (Ap '56); vol. 8 no. 1 p. 62 (Dec '56); vol. 9 no. 1 p. 128 (Dec '57); vol. 9 no. 2 p. 4 (Feb '58); vol. 10 no. 3 p. 27 (col.) (Ap '59); vol. 12 no. 1 p. 28 (col.) (Dec '60).

——. Jensen: The White House p. 40-1.

—— **(bust).** Holiday 14: 34 Nov '53.

—— **(by Chappel).** Amer. heri. vol. 6 no. 6 p. 6 (Oct '55).

Adams, Mrs. John Quincy. See Adams, Louisa Johnson.

Adams, John Quincy II. Amer. heri. vol. 10 no. 3 p. 29 (Ap '59).

Adams, Louisa Johnson (Mrs. John Quincy Adams). Amer. heri. vol. 10 no. 3 p. 32 (Ap '59).
Jensen: The White House, p. 42.

Adams, Randolph G. Cur. biog. p. 1 (1943).

Adams, Robert (int. work in library). Con. 138: 183 Dec '56.

—— **(Wedgwood).** Con. 133: XLVIII Mar '54.

Adams, Roger. Cur. biog. p. 1 (1947).

Adams, Samuel II. Amer. heri. vol. 10 no. 3 p. 28 (Ap '59).

Adams, Sherman Cur. biog. p. 4 (1952).
Jensen: The White House, p. 271.

Adams, Stanley. Cur. biog. p. 11 (1954).

Adams, William. Amer. heri. vol. 12 no. 1 p. 28 (col.) (Dec '60).

Adams family. Amer. heri. vol. 10 no. 3 p. 28-9 (part col.) (Ap '59).

Adams graves, John Q. & Abigail. Natl. geog. 97: 281 Mar '50.

Adams home, Henry. Amer. heri. vol. 7 no. 1 p. 44 (Dec '55).

Adams home, Pres. John. Amer. heri. vol. 10 no. 3 p. 31 (Ap '59).

Adams home, Pres. John Quincy. Amer. heri. vol. 10 no. 3 p. 31 (Ap '59).

Adams library, Charles Francis (int.) Amer. heri. vol. 10 no. 3 p. 26 (col.) (Ap '59).

Addams, Charles. Cur. biog. p. 13 (1954).

Adderley, Julian E. Cur. biog. p. 4 (1961).

Ade, George. Amer. heri. vol. 2 no. 1 p. 24 (fall '50).

Aden (Arabia). Natl. geog. 105: 506-7 (col.) Ap '54.

—— **(map).** Natl. geog. 111: 234 Feb '57.

Aden colony (Egypt). Natl. geog. 111: 230-54 Feb '57.

Adena pipe. Amer. heri. vol. 4 no. 3 p. 52 (col.) (spring '53).

Adenauer, Konrad. Cur. biog. p. 6 (1949); Cur. biog. p. 11 (1958).
Natl. geog. 115: 740 Je '59.

Aderemi, Adesoji. Holiday 25: 71 Ap '59.

Adirondack mt. region. Holiday 13: 5 (col.) Je '53.

Adkins, Bertha S. Cur. biog. p. 1 (1953).

Adkinson, Burton W. Cur. biog. p. 1 (1959).

Adler, Julius Ochs. Cur. biog. p. 9 (1948).

Adler, Larry. Cur. biog. p. 3 (1944).

Adler, Mortimer J. Cur. biog. p. 6 (1952).

Admiralty islands (tribesmen). Natl. geog. 112: 591 (col.), 592 Nov '57.

admiration (sym.). Lehner: Pict. bk. of sym., p. 28.

adobe apt. house. Holiday 23: 16 Feb '58.

adobe corn bins (Mexico). Natl. geog. 100: 798 (col.) Dec '51.

adobe houses (Nigeria). See house, adobe (Nigeria).

adobe hut (Mexico). Nation. geog. 100: 806 Dec '51.

adobe museum. See museum, adobe.

"Adoration of the infant Christ" (Santi). Con. 133: cover, opp. p. 3 (col.) Mar '54.

"Adoration of the kings." Con. ency. of ant. vol. 3 pl. 132.

—— **(Bruegel).** Con. ency. of ant. vol. 1 pl. 155.

—— **(Fabriano).** Praeg, pict. ency. p. 227 (col.).

—— **(15th cent.).** Con. ency. of ant. vol. 3 pl. 136.

—— **(Tintoretto).** Praeg. pict. ency. p. 302 (col.).

—— **(Van der Weyden).** Praeg. pict. ency. p. 262 (col.).

—— **(Veronese).** Praeg. pict. ency. p. 301 (col.).

"Adoration of the lamb" (Van Eyck). Con. 126: 213 Dec '50.

"Adoration of the Magi." Con. 133: 156-61 May '54.

—— **(evangelistary).** Praeg. pict. ency. p. 181 (col.).

—— **(Fra Angelico & Lippi).** Con. 135: 281 Je '55.

—— **(Hugo Van der Goes).** Con. 126: 6 Aug '50.

—— **(Missal).** Con. 141: 131 Ap '58.

—— **(Rubens).** Con. 140: 113 Nov '57.

—— **(detail, Batticelli).** Con. 139: 97 Ap '57.

—— **(whales bone relief of).** Con. 133: 156 May '54.

"Adoration of the shepherds" (Bassano). Con. 144: LIII Jan '60.

—— **(Van Dyck).** Con. 139: 248 Je '57.

—— **(Holzer ceiling).** Con. 145: 133 Ap '60.

—— **(Hugo Van der Goes).** Con. 126: 5 Aug '50.

—— **(Proost).** Con. 132: cover (col.) Jan '54.

Adoula, Cyrille. Cur. biog. p. 3 (1962).

Adrian, Lord Edgar. Cur. biog. p. 1 (1955).

Adrian, Gilbert. Cur. biog. p. 12 (1941).
Adriatic coast. Holiday 21: 50-5 (col.) Jan '57.
"Adventure town" (in Thousand Island region). Travel 104: 67 Jl '55.
advertisement (Tyrol). Natl. geog. 99: 789 Je '51.
—— **(1869, Mark Twain book).** Amer. heri. vol. 11 no. 1 p. 66 (Dec '59).
advertiser (drum). Natl. geog. 100: 15 (col.) Jl. '51.
advertising (18-19th cent.). Amer. heri. vol. 5 no. 4 p. 11-13 (Summer '54).
—— **(beginning of testimonial).** Jensen: The White House, p. 66.
advertising card (child, eggs, chicken). Amer. heri. vol. 7 no. 3 p. 50 (col.) (Ap '56).
—— **(boy, Victorian tricycle).** Amer. heri. vol. 8 no. 2 back cover (col.) (Feb '57).
—— **(clipper ship).** Amer. heri vol. 6 no. 6 p. 18-9 (col.) (Oct '55).
advertising cards (comic). Amer. heri. vol. 9 no. 6 p. 39 (col.) (Oct '58).
advertising poster. Amer. heri. vol. 7 no. 1 p. 48 (Dec. '55).
—— **(1834).** Amer. heri. vol. 11 no. 2 p. 83 (Feb '60).
—— **(Inn).** Amer. heri. vol. 11 no. 4 p. 60-3 (Je '60).
—— **(railroad).** Amer. heri. vol. 9 no. 1 p. 69 (col.), 71 (Dec '57).
advertising posters (antique). Amer. heri. vol. 7 no. 1 p. 32-41 (col.) (Dec '55).
—— *See* also election campaign posters.
advertising sign (Arabic). Natl. geog. 113: 507 Ap '58.
—— **(on barns).** Amer. heri., vol. 10 no. 4 frontis (Je '59).
adze. Rawson: Ant. pict. bk., p. 22, 61.
Aegean map. *See* map, Aegean.
Aegean sea. Travel 103: 40, 42 Ap '55.
Aegina (temple of Aphaea). *See* temple of Aphaea.
Aeolian harp (ancient). Int. gr. soc.: Arts . . . p. 27 (col.).
aerial car. Holiday 26: 46 Aug '59; 27: 186 (col.) May '60.
Travel 104: 21 Aug '55.
aerial chair lift. *See* chair lift, aerial; ski lift.
aerial troupe, circus. Durant: Pict. hist. of Amer. circus, p. 159, 166.
aerialists. Amer. heri., vol. 7 no. 1 p. 39 (Dec '55).
——, **circus.** Durant: Pict. hist. of Amer. circus, p. 191, 193, 201, 215, 257, 268-9.
Aerial (flying man). Durant: Pict. hist. of Amer. circus, p. 155.
aero cable (Niagara). Travel 111: 16 Je '59.
aeromancy (sym.). Lehner: Pict. bk. of sym., p. 67.
aeronautics (sym) Lehner: Pict. bk. of sym., p. 10.
Aesculapius (sym.) Lehner: Pict. bk. of sym., p. 30.
Aetna insurance office. Holiday 8: 32 Jl '50.
Afghan. Natl. geog. 114: 17, 20-1 (col.) Jl '58.
Afghan dancers. Natl. geog. 117: 81 (col.) Jan '60.
Afghan dinner (woman). Natl. geog. 114: 16 Jl '58.

Afghan girl (weaving). Natl. geog. 114: 21 (col.) Jl '58.
Afghanistan. Natl. geog. 98: 674-705 (part col.) Nov '50; 104: 418-32 Sept '53; 114: 8-9 (col.) Jl '58.
—— **(map).** Natl. geog. 104: 421 Sept. '53.
—— **(sculpture, marble head).** Con. 135: L Mar '55.
Africa. Holiday 12: 26, 32 Dec '52; 18: 145 (col.) Nov '55; 20: 56-61, 69 (part col.) Oct '56; 25: 22, 45, 49-94, 122, 129, 143-152 (part col.) Ap '59.
Natl. geog. 100: 264-81 Aug '51; 104: 146-98 (part col.) Aug '53; 106: 490-517 (part col.) Oct '54, 722-71 (part col.) Dec '54; 108: 774-79 (part col.) Dec '55; 110: 258-84 (part col.) Aug '56; 118: 304-409 (part col.) Sept. '60.
Travel 104: 29-55 Nov '55; 106: 34 Nov '56; 107: 52 Jan '57; 118: 304-409 (part col.) Sept '60.
—— **(Aden).** Natl. geog. 111: 230-54 Feb '57.
—— **(Belgian Congo).** Natl. geog. 101: 322-62 (part col.) Mar '52
—— **(cartoon).** Travel 111: 62 Mar '59.
—— **(central).** Natl. geog. 117: 116-36 (col.) Jan '60.
—— **(Dakar, hotel).** Holiday 25: 145 Ap '59.
—— **(east).** Natl. geog. 97: 312-78 (part col.) Mar '50.
—— **(French Morocco).** Natl. geog. 107: 148- (part col.) Feb '55.
—— **(French west).** Natl. geog. 112: 60-103 (col.) Jl '57.
—— **(jungle).** Holiday 23: 96 Je '58.
—— **(Kenya).** Natl. geog. 110: 537-41 (part col.) Oct '56.
—— **(map).** Holiday 15: 39 (col.) Mar '54.
Natl. geog. 104: 150-1 Aug '53; 106: 491 Oct '54; 110: 258 Aug '56, 330 Sept '56; 112: 586 Nov '57; 118: 422 (col.) Sept '60.
Travel 104: 32 Nov '55; 106: 34 Nov '56; 113: 21, 57 Jan '60.
—— **(map, Algeria, Sahara).** Natl. geog. 113: 680 May '58.
—— **(map, French west).** Natl. geog. 113: 390 Mar '58.
—— **(map, Nigeria).** Natl. geog. 116: 232 Aug '59.
—— **(map, northern).** Natl. geog. 112: 54 Jl '57.
—— **(map, outline).** Holiday 27: back cover (col.) Ap '60.
—— **(map, pictorial).** Holiday 25: 63 Ap '59.
—— **(mosque, Sidi Okba).** Holiday 24: 20 Oct '58.
—— **(Nigeria).** *See* Nigeria.
—— **(Nile).** Natl. geog. 107: 697-731 May '55.
—— **(Pygmyland).** Natl. geog. 117: 278-302 Feb '60.
—— **(a safari).** Holiday 15: 34-5 (col.) Mar '54
—— **(south).** Holiday 17: 72 (col.) Mar '55; 21: 34-43 (col.) Feb '57.
—— **(Tangier).** *See* Tangier.
—— **(Yemen).** Natl. geog. 101: 214-44 (part col.) Feb '52.
Africa U.S.A. (Florida). Travel 103: 31-2 Feb '55.

African. Holiday 8: 6, 8-9, 14 Dec '50; 13: 62 Jan '53; 14: 140 Jl '53, 13 Sept '53; 25: 64-94, 122, 143 (part col.) Ap '59; 27: 45 Je '60.

Natl. geog. 100: 268, 270-1, 275, 278, 281 Aug '51; 107: 714-5 May '55; 110: 259, 262, 274 Aug '56; 118: 304-88 (part col.) Sept '60.

Travel 102: 31-3 Aug '54; 104: 6-8 Nov '55; 108: 18-21 Oct '57; 113: 26-7 Jl '60.

—— (archer). Travel 102: inside cover Aug '54.

—— (beating drum). Travel 105: 42 Feb '56.

—— (camel). Natl. geog. 107: 728 May '55.

—— (child). Holiday 27: 41 Mar '60.

—— (children). Natl. geog. 107: 711 May '55.

—— (children, back view). Travel 106: 11 Dec '56.

—— (dance mask). Praeg. pict. ency. p. 548 (col.)

—— (dancer). Natl. geog. 118: 307, 325 (col.) Sept '60.

—— (drum, comic). Holiday 22: 8 Oct '57.

—— (girl). Holiday 25: cover (col.) Ap '59.

—— (man). Travel 113: cover Jan '60.

—— (woman). Holiday 21: 39 (col.) Feb '57.

—— (woman, bowl on head). Travel 104: 32 Nov '55.

—— (women playing musical instrument). Travel 105: 45 Feb '56.

African & zebra (cartoon). Travel 104: 70 Jl '55.

African chief. Holiday 12: 119 Sept '52, 28 Nov '52.

African hut. Int. gr. soc.: Arts . . . p. 11 (col.).

African jungle men (comic). Holiday 10: 141 Oct '51.

African merchant, sidewalk. Natl. geog. 108: 149 Jl '55.

African sculpture (primitive). Con. 145: IV Je '60.

African singers. Natl. geog. 100: 264-5 Aug '51.

African stockade (against Mau Mau). Natl. geog. 112: 98-9 (col.) Jl '57.

African village. Holiday 15: 41 Mar '54.

African waiter. Holiday 14: 161 Dec '53.

African warriors. See warriors, African.

Africans (comic). Holiday 6: 24 Jl '49; 22: 25 Sept '57.

—— (dancers). Holiday 27: 176 Ap '60. Natl. geog. 97: 317, 335 (col.) Mar '50.

—— (dancers, Gungu tribe). Holiday 25: 152 Ap '59.

—— (jungle). Natl. geog. 117: 118-36 (col.) Jan '60.

—— (men working). Natl. geog. 97: 319-21 (col.) Mar '50.

—— (seated). Holiday 12: 77 Aug '52.

—— (women). Travel 109: 48 Mar '58.

Afro. Cur. biog. p. 13 (1958).

"After the ball" (Garrido). Con. 144: XLIV Sept '59.

"After the ceremony" (Caballero). Con. 139: XXIV Je '57.

"After the christening" (Hamza). Con. 136: LV Jan '56.

Aga Kahn. Cur. biog. p. 5 (1946).

Aga Kahn Sir Sultan Mahomed Shah. Holiday 15: 57 May '54.

Agamemnon's mask. Ceram: March of arch., p. 51.

Agar, Herbert. Cur. biog. p. 5 (1944).

Agar, William. Cur. biog. p. 8 (1949).

"Agesander & his sons" (Laocoon group). Praeg. pict. ency., p. 158.

Aggstein castle (Danube). Natl. geog. 115: 202-3 (col.) Feb '59.

"Agony" (Gorky). Holiday 14: 61 (col.) Nov '53.

"Agony in the garden" (Sassetla). Con. 132: 207 Jan '54; 138: cover (col.) Sept '56.

Agora (market place). Osward: Asia Minor, pl. 34.

Agra (Itimad-Ud-Daula). See Itimad-Ud-Daula.

agricultural fair, world (Delhi). Natl. geog. 117: 622-3 (col.) May '60.

—— (U.S. pavillion). Travel 113: 44 Ap '60.

agriculture (sym). Lehner: Pict. bk. of sym., p. 10.

Agriculture commissioner. See Commissioner of agriculture.

Agrigento Greek temple. Natl. geog. 107: 22 (col.) Jan '55.

Agrippa's circle. Lehner: Pict. bk. of sym., p. 68.

Agrippa's seal. Lehner: Pict. bk. of sym., p. 74.

Aguinaldo, Emilio. Amer. heri. vol. 9 no. 2 p. 25 (Feb '58); vol. 12 no. 1 p. 71 (Dec '60).

Ahab, King (Palestine). Natl. geog. 118: 824 (col.) Dec '60.

Aherne, Brian. Cur. biog. p. 3 (1960).

Ahiram's coffin. See coffin, King Ahiram's.

Ahlgren, Mrs. Oscar A. Cur. biog. p. 9 (1952).

Ahmad, King of the Yemen. Cur. biog. p. 1 (1956).

Ahmadu, Alhaji. Cur. biog. p. 7 (1957).

Ahuramazda (winged god). Natl. geog. 98: 829 Dec '50.

"Aiding a comrade" (Remington). Amer. heri. vol. 4 no. 1 cover (col.), 1 (Fall '52).

aigrette, silver & jewel (18th cent.). Con. ency. of ant. vol. 1 pl. 95.

Aigues Mortes (France). Natl. geog. 109: 695 May '56.

Aiken, George David. Cur. biog. p. 3 (1947).

Aiken, Howard. Cus. biog. p. 6 (1947).

Aiken preparatory school. Holiday 19: 100-1 May '56.

Ainu (Japan). Travel 109: 36 Mar '58.

Ainu of Japan (head). Int. gr. Soc.: Arts . . . p. 183 (col.).

air boat (Florida Everglades). Natl. geog. 110: 835 (col.) Dec '56.

Air bridge monument (West Germany). Natl. geog. 115: 740 Je '59.

Air force, U.S. See U.S. Air force.

air mattress. See mattress, air.

air power (sym.). Lehner: Pict. bk. of sym. p. 94.

air traffic operators. Natl. geog. 104: 727 (col.) Dec '53.

air transport service, U.S. Natl. geog. 111: 284-317 (part col.) Mar '57.

aircraft (Dyna-Soar). See "Dyna-Soar."

airguide. Holiday 10: 135 Nov '51, 16 Dec '51.

airlift plane. Natl. geog. 112: 16 (col.) Jl '57.

airline emblems. Holiday 17: 121 (col.) Jan '55.

airline hostess (Japanese). Holiday 23: 19 (col.) Ap '58.

airline map of U.S. Holiday 7: 79 (col.) Je '50.

airline stewardess. See stewardess, airplane.

airman, U.S. war (sculpture). Natl. geog. 111: 740 Je '57.

airmen (emergency evacuation). Natl. geog. 103: 568 May '53.

—— (entertainment). Natl. geog. 111: 316-7 (col.) Mar '57.

—— (survival class room). Natl. geog. 103: 573 (col.) May '53.

—— (training for emergency). Natl. geog. 103: 570-602 (part col.) May '53.

—— (weightless in space flight). Natl. geog. 104: 779 (col.) Dec '53.

Airolo (Switzerland). Holiday 28: 42-3 (col.) Aug '60.

airplane. Amer. heri. vol. 10 no. 5 p. 101 (Aug '59).
Holiday (in almost every issue).
Int. gr. soc.: Arts . . . title p. (col.).
Jordan: Hammond's pict. atlas, p. 23 (col.).
Natl. geog. 97: 711, 818 Je '50; 99: 290 (col.) Mar '51, 744 (col.) Je '51; 102: 78 (col.) Jl '52, 391, 396 (col.) Sept '52; 104: 722-56, 758-80 (col.) Dec '53; 105: 727 (col.) Je '54; 106: 542 (col.) Oct '54; 107: 155 Feb '55, 573 Ap '55; 108: 250-1, 268-9 (col.) Aug '55, 420 (col.) Sept '55; 109: 642-3, 662 (col.) May '56; 110: 436 Oct '56; 111: 181, 204 (col.) Feb '57, 284, 294, 304-5, 312-4 (part col.) Mar '57; 112: 86 (col.) Jl '57; 113: 307 Mar '58; 115: 417 Mar '59; 116: 443 (col.) Oct '59; 117: 75 (col.) Jan '60; 118: 6-7 (col.) Jl '60.
Travel 101: 23 Jan '54, 27 Je '54; 102: 29 Jl '54, back cover Aug '54; 105: 73 Jan '56, 49 Feb '56; 106: 65 Nov '56; 107: 9 May '57, 65 Je '57; 110: 65 Sept '58; 111: 47 Jan '59, 65 Feb '59, 65 Mar '59, 63 Ap '59; 112: 56 Sept '59, 39, 61 Dec '59; 113: 63 Jan '60, 85 Ap '60, 65 May '60, 27 Je '60; 114: 55 Jl '60, 65 Sept '60, 39 Oct '60.

—— (Antarctic). Natl. geog. 112: 4, 7, 10, 12, 18-9, 24, 46 (part col.) Jl '57, 341-2, 391 (col.) Sept '57; 113: 468 (col.) Ap '58; 115: 30 Jan '59; 116: 556 (col.) Oct '59.

—— (Arctic). Natl. geog. 107: 568 (col.) Ap '55.

—— (B-24D). Holiday 27: 85 Mar '60.

—— (crash, jungle). Natl. geog. 117: 665 (col.) May '60.

—— (dinner). See man & woman (on plane, dinner).

—— (early model). Amer. heri. vol. 10 no. 4 p. 59 (col.) (Je '59).

—— (1874). Natl. geog. 115: 554 Ap '59.

—— (firing submarine). Natl. geog. 116: 296 (col.) Sept '59.

—— (int.). Holiday 13: 12-3 (col.) Jan '53; 18: 13 (col.) Aug '55.
Natl. geog. 104: 471 Oct '53, 724, 728, 730 (col.) Dec '53.
Travel 104: 55 Aug '55; 105: 50 Feb '56.

—— (int., comic). Holiday 23: 67 Je '58.

—— (int., prospectors). Natl. geog. 106: 552 (col.) Oct '54.

—— (landing on carrier ship). Natl. geog. 104: 546 Oct '53; 116: 290-1 (col.) Sept '59.

—— (monkey pilot). Natl. geog. 99: 130 (col.) Jan '51.

—— (1910). Amer. heri. vol. 7 no. 3 p. 4-7 (Ap '56).

—— (1910 Curtiss pusher). Natl. geog. 104: 724 (col.) Dec '53.

—— (1913). Amer. heri. vol. 10 no. 1 p. 96 (Dec '58).

—— (parachutes). Natl. geog. 110: 311 (col.) Sept '56.

—— (passengers alighting). Holiday 23: 137 (col.) Feb '58; 28: 141 (col.) Nov '60, 154 Dec '60.

—— (passengers boarding). Holiday 28: 12 (col.) Jl '60.

—— (passengers sleeping). Natl. geog. 111: 434 Mar '57.

—— (Piasecki 59K). See Piasecki 59K plane.

—— (ski wheels). Natl. geog. 110: 152, 154, 165, 177 (col.) Aug '56.

—— (sprays DDT). Natl. geog. 110: 320 Sept '56.

—— (wreck). Amer. heri. vol. 10 no. 4 p. 69 (Je '59).

airplane, amphibious (picnic). Natl. geog. 107: 223 (col.) Feb '55.

——, Canadian (1909). Natl. geog. 116: 255-67 (part col.) Aug '59.

——, combat transport. Natl. geog. 111: 309 Mar '57.

——, crop duster. See crop duster plane.

——, Delta (1954). Holiday 15: 17 Mar '54.

——, Douglas C-124. Natl. geog. 114: 138 Jl '58.

——, electra. Holiday 24: inside cover (col.) Jl '58.

——, "flying jeep." U.S. News & world report, p. 14 Aug 31 '64.

——, jet. Holiday 24: 12-3, 21 (col.) Aug '58, 115 (col.) Sept '58, 93 (col.) Oct '58, 39 (col.) Nov '58, 213 (col.) Dec '58; 25: 12-3 Jan '59, 116 (col.) Feb '59, 113 (col.) Mar '59, 2, 175 (col.) Ap '59, 2 (col.), 141 May '59, 12-3, 147, 179, inside back cover (part col.) Je '59; 26: 10 (col.) Jl '59, 13 (col.) Aug '59, 93, inside back cover (col.) Sept '59, 35, 47, 104-5, 132 Oct '59, 18 (col.), 167 Nov '59, 12-3, 145, 152, 233 (part col.) Dec '59; 27: 9, 112 (col.) Jan '60, 7, 136 (col.) Feb '60, 24, 130-1, 175, 180, 184, 186 (part col.) Mar '60, 12, 43, 138, 165 (col.), 169, 222 Ap '60, 2, 12, 155, 160, 211, 224 (part col.) May '60, 123 (col.), 142 Je '60; 28: 1, 5 (col.) Jl '60, 91, 107, 125 (part col.) Aug '60, 29, 97, 108 Sept '60, 20, 49, 140, 152, 173, 179 (part col.) Oct '60, 39, 51, 126, 136 (part col.) Nov '60, 121, 192, 205, 208, back cover (part col.) Dec '60.
Natl. geog. 97: 542 Ap '50; 98: 282-322 Sept '50, 654 Nov '50.

——, jet (int.). Holiday 27: 32-3 (col.) Jan '60; 28: 7 (col.) Oct '60.

——, **Kitty Hawk (1903).** Brooks: Growth of a nation, p. 229.

——, **Lilienthal (1890).** Amer. heri. vol. 5 no. 2 p. 40 (winter '54).

——, **Nieuport 28.** Holiday 27: 83 (col.) Mar '60.

——, **pontoon.** Natl. geog. 109: 750-1 (col.) Je '56.

——, **scorpion.** *See* scorpion airplane.

——, **ski-equipped.** Natl. geog. 106: 535 Oct '54.

——, **U.S. air force.** Natl. geog. 112: 277-94 Aug '57; 117: 650-71 (col.) May '60.

——, **U.S. navy.** Natl. geog. 104: 556, 562, 571 (part col.) Oct '53; 116: 284, 291-2, 304-5, 318-9, 327, 331 (part col.) Sept '59.

——, **Wright Bros.** Amer. heri. vol. 5 no. 2 p. 43 (winter '54); vol. 11 no. 2 p. 61, 63, 107 (Feb '60). Natl. geog. 112: 267-73 Aug '57; 117: 799 Je '60.

——, **X-20 Dyna-Soar.** Readers digest 81: 97 (col.) Sept '62.

——, **XB-70.** U.S. News & world report vol. LV no. 1 p. 26 Jl 1, 1963.

airplane captains. *See* captain, airline.

airplane carrier (ship). Natl. geog. 116: 290-1, 300-3, 326-9, 332-4 (part col.) Sept '59.

airplane equipment tester. Natl. geog. 99: 303 (col.) Mar '51.

airplane model (Vickers Spitfire). Con. 132: 112 Nov '53.

airplane signal. Natl. geog. 98: 383 (col.) Sept '50.

airplane signalers. Natl. geog. 104: 559 (col.) Oct '53.

airplane stewardess. *See* airline hostess; stewardess, airplane.

airplane symbols. Holiday 14: 69 (col.) Nov '53.

airplane vapor trails. *See* vapor trails, airplane.

airplanes. Int. gr. soc.: Arts . . . p. 161 (col.).

——, **(early).** Amer. heri. vol. 7 no. 3 p. 90-1 (Ap '56).

——, *See* also jetliners.

airport (Cal.). Holiday 26: 111 (col.) Jl '59.

——, **(N.Y. International).** Holiday 25: 87-9 (part col.) May '59.

—— **"Terminal city" (Idlewild, model).** Travel 103: 36 May '55.

—— **terminal (int., Wash., D.C.).** Natl. geog. 103: 27 (col.) Jan '53.

airways of U.S., commercial. Jordan: Hammond's pict. atlas, p. 12.

Aivasovsky, I. (work of). Amer. heri. vol. 11 no. 5 p. 63-5 (col.) (Aug '60).

Aiviliks (Hudson Bay). Natl. geog. 110: 671-87 (part col.) Nov '56.

Aix-la-Chapelle (int., chapel plan). Praeg. pict. ency., p. 183.

Aizpiri, Paul (work of). Con. 143: XVIII, 108 Ap '59.

Ajaccio water front. Travel 105: 43 Ap '56.

Ajanta temples (India). Natl. geog. 103: 666-82 May '53.

Akihito, Crown Prince of Japan. Cur. biog. p. 3 (1959).

Akko, Israel. Holiday 17: 42 Feb '55.

Ala, Hussein. Cur. biog. p. 5 (1951).

Alabama. Holiday 27: 50-9 (part col.) Mar '60. Jordan: Hammond's pict. atlas, p. 78-9 (col.).

—— **(boll weevil monument).** Brooks: Growth of a nation, p. 250.

—— **("Iron man" statue).** Brooks: Growth of a nation, p. 291.

—— **(state capitol).** Holiday 25: 8 Je '59.

Alabama gardens (Bellingrath). *See* Bellingrath gardens.

Alabama home ("Rosemont"). Holiday 27: cover (col.) Mar '60.

alabaster carving. Con. 133: 256 Je '54.

—— **(antique).** Con. 135: LVII Ap '55.

—— **(15th cent.).** Con. 143: LVII Ap '59.

—— **(lady).** Con. 139: XLIII Mar '57.

—— **(Nottingham).** Con. ency. of ant. vol. 3 pl. 129-36. Con. 133: 217-228 Je '54.

alabaster cave. Travel 109: 18 Feb '58.

alabaster figure. *See* figure, alabaster.

alabaster relief (Nineveh 669 B.C.). Praeg, pict. ency. p. 112.

alabaster tables, English mediaeval. Con. 135: 109-10 Ap '55.

Aladdin's gem of health (sym.). Lehner: Pict. bk. of sym., p. 47.

Aladdin lamp (genii, woman). Holiday 20: 84 (col.) Sept '56.

Alain, Daniel A. Cur. biog. p. 15 (1941).

Alaja Hoyuk (sphynx gateway). Osward: Asia Minor, pl. 10.

Alaja Hoyuk tomb gods. Osward: Asia Minor, pl. 3-5.

Alajalov, Constantin. Cur. biog. p. 8 (1942).

The Alamo. Amer. heri. vol. 1 no. 2 p. 25 (winter '50); vol. 4 no. 1 p. 21, 40-2 (part col.) (fall '52). Brooks: Growth of a nation, p. 131. Holiday 5: 127 (col.) Feb '49, 85 Ap '49; 7: 113 Je '50; 8: 130 Dec '50; 10: inside front cover (col.) Sept '51, 82 Dec '51; 12: 131 Jl '52; 15: 88 Je '54; 21: 10 (col.) Je '57; 23: 53 Feb '58; 24: 114 Nov '58; 25: 6 May '59; 28: 221 Dec '60. Jordan: Hammond's pict. atlas, p. 119 (col.). Natl. geog. 98: 7 Jl '50.

Alamo walkway. Jordan: Hammond's pict. atlas, p. 119 (col.).

Alanya (Mediterranean). Osward: Asia Minor, p. 118-9.

Alaska. Holiday 13: 9 Mar '53; 14: 100-7 Jl '53; 26: 27-45 (part col.) Aug '59. Natl. geog. 99: 551-62 Ap '51, 835-44 Je '51, 102: 58-86 (part col.) Jl '52; 105: 130-46 (part col.) Jan '54; 109: 738-808, 811-23 (part col.) Je '56; 116: 42-85 (part col.) Jl '59. Travel 101: 31-3 Je '54; 104: 33-4 Jl '55; 106: 39-41 Jl '56; 112: cover (col.), 16-29 Jl '59.

—— **(Arctic circle).** Natl. geog. 114: 128-46 Jl '58.

—— **(Barrow).** Holiday 28: 91 Jl '60.

—— **(map).** Holiday 26: 36 Aug '59. Natl. geog. 99: 552 Ap '51; 103: 766-7 (col.) Je '53.

—— **(Sitka, 1860).** *See* Sitka (Alaska).

—— **(snow fields).** Natl. geog. 109: 292-3 Feb '56.

Alaska (wild flowers). Natl. geog. 109: 811-23 (col.) Je '56.

Alaska university. See University of Alaska.

Alaska. See also Anchorage; Sitka.

Alaskan (man). Travel 104: 33 Jl '55.

Alaskans. Holiday 14: 102-3 Jl '53; 26: 30-45 (part col.) Aug '59.

Albanese, Licia. Cur. biog. p. 7 (1946).

Albani, Emma. Cooper: Con. ency. of music, p. 53.

Albani drawings, Cardinal. Con. 142: 165 Dec '58.

Albany (N.Y., air view). Natl. geog. 110: 592-3 Nov '56.

—— (night). Natl. geog. 110: 585 (col.) Nov '56.

—— (1757). Amer. heri. vol. 10 no. 1 p. 13 (Dec '58).

Albee, Edward. Cur. biog. (1963).

Albee, Fred H. Cur. biog. p. 3 (1943).

Alberghetti, Anna Maria. Cur. biog. p. 3 (1955).

Albers, Josef. Cur. biog. p. 5 (1962).

Albert, Prince. Holiday 16: 75 Aug '54; 19: 40 My '56.

Albert, Carl. Cur. biog. p. 10 (1957).

Albert, Eddie. Cur. biog. p. 15 (1954).

Alberta (Canada). Natl. geog. 118: 90-119 (part col.) Jl '60.

—— (map). Natl. geog. 118: 92 (col.) Jl '60.

Alberti, Jules. Cur. biog. p. 5 (1959).

Alberto, Alvaro. Cur. biog. p. 8 (1947).

Albertolli, Giocondo (Italian furniture). Con. 135: 28 Mar '55.

Albertson, Frank. Horan: Pict. hist. of wild west, p. 156.

Albi cathedral. Natl. geog. 100: 29 (col.) Jl '51.

Albion, Robert Greenhalgh. Cur. biog. p. 17 (1954).

Albright, Ivan Le Lorraine. Cur. biog. p. 9 (1944).

Albright, Tenley. Cur. biog. p. 3 (1956).

Albright, William F. Cur. biog. p. 6 (1955).

album, Victorian Christmas. Amer. heri. vol. 10 no. 1 p. 37-45 (col.) (Dec '58).

Albury park villa (England). Con. 127: 92-7 May '51.

Alcala (Spain, gateway). Natl. geog. 100: 718 (col.) Dec '51.

Alcan smelter (Canada). Natl. geog. 110: 388 (col.) Sept. '56.

Alcatraz. Holiday 20: 30 (col.) Aug '56.
Natl, geog. 110: 214 (col.) Aug '56.

The Alcazaba (Malaga, Spain). Holiday 23: 2 (col.) Jan '58.

Alcazar (Spain). Natl. geog. 97: 427 (col.) Ap '50.

—— castle (Segovia, Spain). Holiday 15: 43 Jan '54; 26: 116 (col.) Nov '59.
Travel 113: 69 Ap '60.

Alcazarquivir (Caliphs home). Travel 104: 60 Nov '55.

alchemic symbols. Lehner: Pict. bk of sym., p. 72-3.

Alcock, Norman Z. Cur. biog. (1963).

Alcora statuettes. See statuettes, Alcora (Spain).

Alcorn, Meade. Cur. biog. p. 12 (1957).

Alcott, Bronson. Amer. heri. vol. 8 no. 5 p. 33 (Aug '57).

Alcott, Mrs. Bronson. Amer. heri. vol. 8 no. 5 p. 32 (Aug '57).

Alcott home, Louisa May. Amer. heri. vol. 8 no. 5 p. 35 (Aug '57).
Natl. geog. 97: 305 (col.) Mar '50.

Alcott's desk, Louisa May. See desk, Louisa May Alcott's.

Aldagag hill. Osward: Asia Minor, pl. 49.

Alden, James M. (work of). Amer. heri. vol. 11 no. 3 p. 62 (col.) (Ap '60).

Alderson, Nannie Tiffany. Amer. heri. vol. 10 no. 2 p. 39 (Feb '59).

Aldis, Dorothy. Jun. bk. of authors, p. 2.

"Aldobrandini marriage" (Roman painting). Praeg pict. ency., p. 150 (col.).

Aldrich, Richard. Cur. biog. p. 7 (1955).

Aldrich, Thomas Bailey. Amer. heri. vol. 11 no. 1 p. 75 (Dec '59).

Aldrich, Winthrop W. Cur. biog. p. 3 (1953).

Aldridge, James. Cur. biog. p. 5 (1943).

Aldridge, John W. Cur. biog. p. 15 (1958).

ale glass, antique. Con. 135: XXXVI Je '55.

Alegria, Ciro. Cur. biog. p. 16 (1941).

alehouse (interior, colonial). Holiday 5: 57 (col.) Je '49.

—— (sign). Natl. geog. 108: 297 (col.) Sept '55.

Aleman, Miguel. Cur. biog. p. 10 (1946).

Aleppo. Travel 105: 21 Jan '56.

Alert (Arctic region). Natl. geog. 107: 566-7 (col.) Ap '55.

Alessandri, Jorge. Cur. biog. p. 7 (1959).

"Alessandro Alberti with a page." Natl. geog. 101: 88 (col.) Jan '52.

Aleut village. Natl. geog. 101: 509 Ap '52.

Alexander I, Czar of Russia. Amer. heri. vol. 9 no. 2 p. 7 (Feb '58); vol. 11 no. 3 p. 85 (Ap '60).
Con. 144: 277 Jan '60.

Alexander the Great (bust). Osward: Asia Minor, pl. 19.

—— (head, sculpture). Praeg. pict. ency., p. 159.

Alexander VI, Pope. Amer. heri. vol. 10 no. 3 p. 6 (Ap '59).

Alexander, Archie A. Cur. biog. p. 10 (1955).

Alexander, Madame Beatrice. Cur. biog. p. 13 (1957).

Alexander, Edward Porter. Pakula: Cent. album, p. 77.

Alexander, Franz. Cur. biog. p. 10 (1942).

Alexander, Franz G. Cur. biog. p. 5 (1960).

Alexander, Grover Cleveland. Amer. heri. vol. 10 no. 3 p. 22 (Ap '59).

Alexander, Gen. Harold R.L.G. Cur. biog. p. 12 (1942).

Alexander, Holmes. Cur. biog. p. 6 (1956).

Alexander, Ruth. Cur. biog. p. 6 (1943).

Alexander & wife, Viscount (Canada). Holiday 6: 36 Aug '49.

Alexanderson, Ernst F. W. Cur. biog. p. 11 (1955).

Alexandra, Queen of (Gt. Brit.). Amer. heri. vol. 6 no. 1 p. 47 (fall '54).

Alexandra Falls (Canada). Natl. geog. 108: 228-9 (col.) Aug '55.

Alexandria (Virginia). Natl. geog. 103: 20 Jan '53.

Alexei, Patriarch of Russia. Cur. biog. p. 5 (1953).

Alexis, Grand Duke. Amer. heri. vol. 7 no. 5 p. 36 (Aug '56).

Alfama (Lisbon's old quarter). Natl. geog. 118: 655 (col.) Nov '60.

Alfonso XIII, King of Spain. Amer. heri. vol. 6 no. 1 p. 46 (fall '54).

algaita (Nigerian trumpet). Natl. geog. 110: 332 (col.) Sept '56; 116: 251 Aug '59.

Algardi, Alessandro (marble bust by). Con. 139: 35 Mar '57.

Algardi, Alessandro (work by). Con. 138: 203-6 Dec '56.

Algeciras (Spain). Holiday 14: 44-5 (col.) Sept '53.

Algeria. Natl. geog. 117: 768-95 (col.) Je '60.
—— (map). Natl. geog. 113: 680 May '53; 117: 772 (col.) Je '60.

Algerian cavalrymen. Natl. geog. 114: 298-9 Aug '58.

Algerian costume (medieval). Int. gr. soc.: Arts . . . p. 69 (col.).

Algerian treaty (1815). Amer. heri. vol. 11 no. 2 p. 105 (Feb '60).

Alghero harbor (Sardinia). Holiday 23: 73 Jan '58.

Algiers. Holiday 5: 64-9 Feb '49; 16: 109 Nov '54.
Travel 104: 13-5 Nov '55.

Algonquian Bible, Eliot's. Amer. heri. vol. 9 no. 1 p. 6-7, 9 (Dec '57).

The Alhambra (Spain). Holiday 26: 85 Aug '59. Natl. geog. 97: 442-3, 454 (col.) Ap '50.
—— (Court of the lions). Praeg. pict. ency., p. 550.
—— (interior). Holiday 27: 128 Jan '60.
Travel 111: 39 May '59.

"Alhambra theatre" (London). Durant: Pict. hist. of Amer. circus, p. 39.

Al-Hassan, Prince of the Yemen. Cur. biog. p. 245 (1957).

Ali, Chaudhri Mohamad. Cur. biog. p. 7 (1956).

Ali, Mohammed. Cur. biog. p. 10 (1952).

Ali, tomb of. See Tomb of Ali.

Ali Iapu (Isfahan). Natl. geog. 100: 453 (col.) Oct '51.

Ali Kahn, Mahommed. Con. 145: 127 Ap '60.

"Alice in wonderland" (Alice Liddell). Holiday 15: 6 Je '54.
Natl. geog. 108: 319 Sept '55.
—— (book illus.) Amer. heri. vol. 8 no. 1 p. 32 (col.) (Dec '56).
—— (statue). Natl. geog. 118: 791 (col.) Dec '60.

alidade (man sighting). Natl. geog. 111: 205 (col.) Feb '57.

"Alinda" (by Ward). Con. ency. of ant., vol. 1 pl. 135.

Alkmaar market (Holland). Natl. geog. 98: 758 (col.) Dec '50.

Allah is king (talisman). Lehner: Pict. bk. of sym., p. 41.

"Allah is the past and future" (talisman). Lehner: Pict. hist. of sym., p. 41.

"Allah" (moslem). Natl. geog. 114: 728 Nov '58.

Allahverdi Khan bridge. Natl. geog. 114: 31 (col.) Jl '58.

Allan, John J. Cur. biog. p. 1 (1950).

Allatoona dam. Natl. geog. 105: 320 (col.) Mar '54.

Allee, Marjorie Hill. Jun. Bk. of authors. p. 3.

allegoric representation of months. Lehner: Pict. bk. of sym., p. 96.

allegoric symbols of mathematical science. Lehner: Pict. bk. of sym., p. 9.

allegory (Lafayette receives crown). Amer. heri. vol. 8 no. 1 p. 6 (Dec. '56).

allegory, sacred (Bellini). Praeg. pict. ency., p 269 (col.).

Allen, Arthur A. Cur. biog. p. 6 (1961).

Allen, Ethan. Cur. biog. p. 18 (1954).

Allen, Florence. Cur. biog. p. 17 (1941).

Allen, Florence E. Cur. biog. (1963).

Allen, Brig. Gen. Frank A. Cur. biog. p. 4 (1945).

Allen, Fred. Cur. biog. p. 19 (1941).
Holiday 7: 63 Mar '50.

Allen, George. Cur. biog. p. 76 (1951).

Allen, George E. Cur. biog. p. 13 (1946).

Allen, George V. Cur. biog. p. 11 (1948).

Allen, Gracie. Cur. biog. p. 76 (1951).

Allen, Jay. Cur. biog. p. 21 (1941).

Allen, Larry. Cur biog. p. 14 (1942).

Allen, Leo E. Cur. biog. p. 13 (1948).

Allen, Martha F. Cur. biog. p. 8 (1959).

Allen, Mel. Cur. biog. p. 3 (1950).

Allen, Ralph. Cur. biog. p. 16 (1958).

Allen, Raymond B. Cur. biog. p. 11 (1952).

Allen, Robert. Cur. biog. p. 659 (1941).

Allen, Steve. Cur. biog. p. 8 (1951)

Allen, Maj. Gen. Terry. Cur. biog. p. 9 (1943).

Allen, William L. Cur. biog. p. 7 (1953).

Allen, William M. Cur. biog. p. 9 (1953).

Alley, Rewi. Cur. biog. p. 11 (1943).

"Alley of giants" (Angkor Thom). Holiday 12: 44 Nov '52.

"The Alliance" ship. Amer. heri. vol. 11 no. 3 p. 11 (col.) (Ap '60).
—— (flag). Amer. heri. vol. 11 no. 3 p. 13 (col.) (Ap '60).

allied army. See U.S. allied army.

Allison, Clay. Horan: Pict. hist. of wild west. p. 70.

Allison, John M. Cur. biog. p. 9 (1956).

Allman, David B. Cur. biog. p. 17 (1958).

Allott, Gordon. Cur. biog. p. 14 (1955).

Allport, Gordon W. Cur. biog. p. 7 (1960).

"All-seeing eye" (sym). Lehner: Pict. bk. of sym., p. 61.

Allston, Washington (work of). Con. 141: 66 Mar '58.

Allyn, Stanley C. Cur. biog. p. 11 (1956).

Allyson, June. Cur. biog. p. 13 (1952).

almanac advertisement. See poster, almanac adv.

Almond, Lt. Gen. Edward M. Cur. biog. p. 9 (1951).

Almond, J. Lindsay, Jr. Cur. biog. p. 19 (1958).

alms beggar (Buddhist). Natl. geog. 117: 392 (col.) Mar '60.

alms dish, antique church. Con. 134: 13 Sept '54.
——, gilt. Con. 145: 242 Je '60.

Alonso, Alicia. Cur. biog. p. 16 (1955).
alpenhorn (Swiss). Travel 106: 32 Sept '56.
—— (man blowing). Disney: People & places, p. 44 (col.)
Holiday 16: 28 Aug '54; 23: 137 Mar '58, 118 Ap '58; 24: 4 Aug '58, 20, 77 Sept '58. Natl. geog. 98: 217 (col.) Aug '50; 110: 437 Oct '56.
Alpert, George. Cur. biog. p. 7 (1961).
Alpha & omega (sym.). Lehner: Pict. bk. of sym. p. 80.
alphabet, celestial (sym.). Lehner: Pict. bk. of sym., p. 23.
alphabet, magic. Lehner: Pict. bk. of sym., p. 71.
Alphand, Herve. Cur. biog. p. 11 (1951).
Alphonso XII, King (statue). Travel 107: 23 Ap '57.
Alphonso the magnanimous, King (bas relief). Lebande: Naples, p. 32.
Alpine castle. Holiday 26: 70-3 (part col.) Sept '59.
Alpine girl (with accordion). Holiday 13: 21 Jan '53.
Alpine horn. See Alpen horn.
Alpine hospice of St. Bernard. Amer. heri. vol. 11 no. 3 p. 24 (Ap '60).
Alpine man (comic). Holiday 22: 213 Dec '57.
Alpine village. Holiday 21: 33 (col.) Mar '57.
—— (on Lake George, N.Y.). Travel 106: 48-9 Jl '56.
Alps mts. Natl. geog. 98: 230 Aug '50; 118: 410-19 (col.) Sept '60.
—— (Austria). Natl. geog. 99: 771 Je '51; 115: 206 (col.) Feb '59; 118: 246-75 (part col.) Aug '60.
—— (Austria, skiers). Holiday 25: 72-7 (part col.) Jan '59.
—— (Bavaria). Holiday 25: cover, 50 (col.) May '59.
Natl. geog. 111: 786-7 (col.) Je '57; 115: 751-2 (col.) Je '59.
—— (French). Holiday 25: 72-7 (part col.) Mar '59.
Natl. geog. 101: 545-64 Ap '52.
—— (Salzburg). Holiday 25: 50 (col.) May '59.
—— (Switzerland). Holiday 7: 104 Jan '50; 14: 61 Dec '53; 15: 66 Jan '54. Natl. geog. 107: 826-48 (part col.) Je '55. Travel 113: 36 Je '60.
Als, Peder (work of). Con. 135: 48 Mar '55.
Alsace. Holiday 26: 98 Aug '59.
Alsace women (France). Holiday 5: 123 Ap '49.
Alsop, Joseph W., jr. Cur. biog. p. 16 (1952).
Alsop, Stewart. Cur. biog. p. 17 (1952).
Alstadt, William R. Cur. biog. p. 21 (1958).
Alston, Walter. Cur. biog. p. 20 (1954).
Alta (Utah, skiers). Face of Amer., p. 150-1 (col.).
altar, Buddhist. Natl. geog. 111: 350 (col.) Mar '57; 117: 393 (col.) Mar '60.
——, cathedral of Pistoria (silver). Con. 138: 148-54 Dec '56.
——, Catholic (outdoors). Face of Amer., p. 30-1 (col.).
——, chapel. Natl. geog. 108: 213 (col.) Aug '55.
——, church. Osward: Asia Minor, pl. II (col.).

——, church (Portugal). Con. 137: 36-9 Mar '56.
——, Issenheim. Natl. geog. 117: 761 (col.) Je '60.
——, portable (10th cent.). Con. 138: 237 Jan '57.
——, portable (Augsburg, 16th cent.). Con. 144: 83 Nov '59.
——, portable (of Albrecht V of Bavaria). Con. 144: 83 Nov '59
——, portable (Romanesque whale bone). Con. 142: 39 Sept '58.
——, Santo Tomas church. Natl. geog. 117: 415 (col.) Mar '60.
——, Valletta church of St. John. Con. 142: 147 Dec '58.
——, winged (St. Wolfgang 1480). Praeg. pict. ency., p. 98.
——, Wittingau. Praeg. pict. ency., p. 240 (col.).
altar boys (twins). Natl. geog. 115: 616 (col.) May '59.
altar carving (Rohr, Bavaria). Praeg. pict. ency., p. 331.
altar cross. See cross, altar.
altar dish, 17th cent. gilt. Con. 133: 152 May '54.
altar figure, terracotta (Bernini). Con. 145: XXXI Ap '60.
altar frontal (in wood by Plura). Con. 138: 176 Dec '56.
——, (tapestry, 16th cent.). Con. 129: LXIX Je '52.
altar panel (Durer). Praeg. pict. ency., p. 286 (col.)
——, "The nativity." Praeg. pict. ency., p. 239 (col.).
——, Portinari. See Portinari altar panel.
——, St. Columba. Praeg. pict. ency., p. 262 (col.).
——, St. Peter's cathedral. Praeg. pict. ency., p. 242 (col.).
altar piece. Con. 129: 41 Ap '52; 134: 160 Dec '54.
—— (alabaster carving). Con. 133: 225-8 Je '54.
—— (antique carving). Con. 140: 19-20 Sept '57.
—— (by Guercino). Con. 132: 13 Sept '53.
—— ("Descent from the cross"). Con. 142: 26 Sept '58.
——, Church of our Lady (Krakow). Natl. geog. 114: 384 (col.) Sept '58.
——, Church of our Lord (Creglingen). Praeg. pict. ency., p. 244.
——, Crucifixion. Praeg. pict. ency., p. 285 (col.).
——, Flemish (16th cent.). Con. 132: 66 Sept '53.
——, French school (1480). Con. 140: 277 Jan '58.
——, Italian (Tiepolo). Con. 135: 37 Mar '55.
——, Merode. Con. 141: 197 May '58.
——, Passion. Con. ency. of ant., vol. 3 pl. 130, 134.
——, "Resurrection." Con. ency. of ant., vol. 3, pl. 132.

——, Rococo Munich. Con. 142: 4 Sept '58.
altar pieces, Domenico Beccafumi. Con. 138: 155-9 Dec '56.
altar predella (Fra Andelico). Praeg. pict. ency., p. 251 (col.).
altar retable. Con. 138: 193 Dec '56.
altar screen (San Zaviers). Natl. geog. 104: 381 (col.) Sept '53.
altar set (Meissen). Con. 144: LXXIX, 199 Dec '59.
altar statuette (Taoist). Con. 129: LXXIII Je '52.
Altdorfer, Albrecht (work of). Con. ency. of ant., vol. 1, pl. 156.
Con. 126: 87 Oct '50.
Natl. geog. 110: 626 (col.) Nov '56.
Praeg. pict. ency., p. 287 (col.).
Altmeyer, Arthur J. Cur. biog. p. 15 (1946).
aluminum dishes. Holiday 20: 33 Dec '56.
aluminum making (man). Natl. geog. 113: 564 Ap '58.
aluminum molds. Natl. geog. 102: 589 Nov '52.
aluminum ore, red. Natl. geog. 105: 346 (col.) Mar '54.
aluminum pig molds. See pig molds, aluminum.
aluminum rods, coiled. Natl. geog. 117: 463 Ap '60.
Alvarez, Luis W. Cur. biog. p. 9 (1947).
Alvarez, Dr. Walter C. Cur. biog. p. 11 (1953).
Aly Khan, Prince. Cur. biog. p. 9 (1960).
"Ama" (Japanese diving girl). See diving girl.
Amalfi (Italy). Holiday 11: 124 (col.) Mar '52; 16: 13 (col.) Oct '54; 21: 152 (col.) Mar '57.
Natl. geog. 116: 472-509 (part col.) Oct '59.
Amalfi (cathedral). Lebande: Naples. p. 194-5.
Amalfi drive. Natl. geog. 116: 500-1 Oct '59.
Amalfi (night). Natl. geog. 116: 482-3 (col.) Oct '59.
Amalienburg (int., near Munich). Con. 142: 2 (col.) Sept '58.
Aman-Jean (Seurat). Con. 142: 61 Sept '58.
amalgam (sym.). Lehner: Pict. bk. of sym., p. 72.
Amazon. Disney: People & places, p. 99-112 (col.).
—— (jungle). Natl. geog. 115: 632-69 (part col.) May '59.
—— (man, woman & child). Travel 113: 58 Feb '60.
Ambassador bridge (U.S.-Canada). Natl. geog. 104: 823 Dec '53.
Ambassador hotel. Holiday 13: 118 Ap '53.
—— (Chicago). Holiday 14: 142 Oct '53.
—— (N.Y.). Holiday 13: 136 Je '53.
Ambedkar, B. R. Cur. biog. p. 13 (1951).
Ambergris Caye Island (Honduras). Travel 110: 36-7 Sept '58.
"Amberjack." See submarine.
Ambrogini, Angelo. See Politian.
Ambrosa, Laura. Holiday 26: cover (col.) Sept '59.
"Ambrose." See lightship "Ambrose."
ambulance. Travel 107: 62 Jan '57.
——, aerial. Natl. geog. 99: 301 Mar '51.
——, U.S. army. Natl. geog. 103: 674 May '53.

Amenophis III, King (statue). Holiday 25: 144 Ap '59.
the "America" (trading ship, 1805). Amer. heri. vol. 6 no. 2 p. 11 (col.) (winter '55).
the "America" schooner (1851). Amer. heri. vol. 9 no. 5 p. 4 (col.), 6 (Aug '58).
American ancient civilization map. See map (Amer. ancient civilization).
American express co. (Paris). Holiday 21: 82 Mar '57.
American Falls dam. See dam, American Falls.
"American Gothic" (Wood). Brooks: Growth of a nation, p. 237.
American museum natural hist. (entrance). Natl. geog. 118: 792 (col.) Dec '60.
American revolution (battles 1776). Amer. heri. vol. 3 no. 2 p. 30-1 (col.) (winter '52) vol. 7 no. 6 p. 77 (Oct '56); vol. 10 no. 6 p. 22-5 (Oct '59).
Holiday 16: 106-7 (col.) Jl '54.
Natl. geog. 117: 12-3 (col.) Jan '60.
—— (Hudson river). Amer. heri. vol. 10 no. 1 p. 14 (col.) (Dec '58).
—— (British soldiers, cartoon). Amer. heri. vol. 11 no. 6 p. 56-8 (Oct '60).
—— (British surrender). Natl. geog. 102: 154 (col.) Aug '52.
—— (Burgoyne surrender) (by Trumbull). Amer. heri. vol. 7 no. 4 p. 4-5 (col.) (Je '56).
—— (burning Wash., D.C.) Jensen: The White House, p. 26.
—— (cartoon). Jensen: The White House, p. 27.
American revolution map (historic places). Holiday 16: 106-7 (col.) Jl '54.
"The American school" (Pratt). Amer. heri. vol. 2 no. 2 p. 28 (winter '51).
American temples. See temples, American.
American univ. (Beirut). Travel 102: 34 Sept '54.
Americans land on Japan (1853). Natl. geog. 104: 89 Jl '53.
amerindic peace. See peace (amerindic).
amerindic war. See war (amerindic).
Amery, Leopold S. Cur. biog. p. 16 (1942).
Ames, Albert. Amer. heri. vol. 9 no. 2 p. 30 (Feb '58).
Ames, Ezra (work of). Con. 142: 66 Sept '58.
Ames, Louise. Cur. biog. p. 300 (1956).
Ames, Oakes. Amer. heri. vol. 8 no. 3 p. 52 (Ap '57).
Amhara women (dog). Natl. geog. 106: 753 (col.) Dec '54.
——, (water jugs). Natl. geog. 106: 751 (col.) Dec '54.
Amherst, Lord Jeffery. Amer. heri. vol. 2 no. 2 inside cover (winter '51); vol. 12 no. 1 p. 4, 8, 9 (col.), 89, 93 (Dec '60).
Con. 129: 137 Je '52.
Amiens cathedral (construction of). Praeg. pict. ency., p. 200.
Amies, Hardy. Cur. biog. p. 7 (1962).
Amigoni, Jacopo (work of). Cooper: Con. ency. of music, p. 95.
Amini, Ali. Cur. biog. p. 9 (1962).
Amis, Kingsley. Cur. biog. p. 23 (1958).
Amish family. Travel 105: cover Mar '56.
—— (buggy). Holiday 18: 103 (col.) Oct '55.

Amish man & woman (back view). Natl. geog. 104: 838 Dec '53.
Amish people. Amer. heri. vol. 3 no. 4 p. 4-8 (Summer '52).
Travel 105: cover, 19-23 Mar '56.
Amman (Holy Land). Natl. geog. 98: 713, 739 (col.) Dec '50; 102: 842 Dec '52.
Ammann, Othmar. Cur. biog. (1963).
ammoniac salt (sym). Lehner: Pict. bk. of sym., p. 72.
Amor (sym.). Lehner: Pict. bk. of sym., p. 92.
"Amorino" (statue by Canova). Con. 144: 229 Jan '60.
Amorite nomads (murals). Natl. geog. 112: 842-3 Dec '57.
Amory, Charles. Holiday 14: 53 Dec '53.
Amory, Cleveland. Holiday 26: 57 (col.) Jl '59.
Amory, Derick Heathcoat. Cur. biog. p. 24 (1958).
amphibious duck boat. Natl. geog. 113: 22 (col.) Jan '58.
amphicar (auto on land & water). Travel 114: 58 Aug '60.
amphitheater. Natl. geog. 103: 10-11 (col.) Jan '53.
——, **Arles.** Natl. geog. 109: 676-7 (col.) May '56.
——, **Aspendos.** See Aspendos amphitheatre.
——, **University of Richmond).** Holiday 10: 95 (col.) Sept '51.
——, **Denver open-air.** Natl. geog. 98: 38 Jl '50.
——, **Nimes (France).** Natl. geog. 100: 2 Jl '51.
——, **Roman.** See Roman amphitheater (Tunisia).
——, **Sevilla gladiator's (Spain).** Natl. geog. 99: 519 Ap '51.
amphitheatre (Rome). See Coliseum, Roman.
——, **circus.** Durant: Pict. hist. of Amer. circus, p. 49, 53.
amphitheatre of Side (Mediterranean). Osward: Asia Minor, pl., 106-7.
amphora, antique. Con. 132: 114 Nov '53.
——, **Attic.** See Attic amphora.
——, **Attic (540 B.C.).** Con. 145: 139 Ap '60.
—— **(7th cent. B.C.).** Con. 134: XLIX Dec '54.
amphorae, Rhodian (ancient). Natl. geog. 117: 694 (col.) May '60.
ampulla, British. Int. gr. soc.: Arts . . . p. 165 (col.).
ampulla & spoon. Natl. geog. 104: 325 (col.) Sept '53.
Amr-ibn-el-Aas mosque (corridor). Natl. geog. 114: 729 Nov '58.
Amritsar (temple, India). Holiday 26: 170 (col.) Nov '59.
Travel 111: 16 Jan '59.
Amsterdam. Holiday 23: 56 Jan '58, 150 (col.) Feb '58.
Natl. geog. 98: 756 Dec '50.
Travel 106: 32 Sept '56; 110: 33-6 Aug '58.
—— **(canal).** Travel 111: back cover Feb '59, back cover Mar '59, back cover Ap '59, back cover May '59.
—— **(city map).** Travel 110: 32 Aug '58.
—— **(Hilton hotel).** Travel 111: 53 Mar '59.
"Amsterdam" (Storck). Con. 136: IX Sept '55.
—— **(winter).** Con. 143: XXXV (col.) Je '59.

amulet. Con. 141: 119 Ap '58.
Amundsen-Scott (IGY South Pole station). Natl. geog. 112: 20 Jl '57.
"An event in the forest" (Landseer). Con. 129: XLIV Ap '52.
Anacapri (Italy). Labande: Naples, p. 213, 219.
Anaho Bay (Nuku Hiva). Natl. geog. 97: 30 (col.) Jan '50.
Ananias, chapel of. See chapel of Ananias.
Anatolia. Osward: Asia Minor, pl. 100.
anatomy (sym.). Lehner: Pict. bk. of sym., p. 10.
—— **(woman, comic).** Holiday 26: 77 Nov '59.
anchor, codfish boat. Rawson: Ant. pict. bk., p. 77.
——, **deep water.** Rawson: Ant. pict. bk., p. 77.
——, **Phoenician.** Natl. geog. 113: 504 Ap '59.
——, **ship.** Holiday 18: 26 (col.) Sept '55.
Amer. heri. vol. 11 no. 5 p. 56 (Aug '60).
Natl. geog. 108: 521 (col.) Oct '55.
anchor & seal (antique design). Natl. geog. 105: 33 Jan '54.
—— **(state seal).** Amer. heri. vol. 11 no. 3 cover (col.) (Ap '60).
—— **(sym.).** Lehner: Pict. bk. of sym., p. 35, 89.
——, **wrecked ship.** Natl. geog. 112: 765 Dec '57.
anchorage, Alaska. Holiday 26: 38 (col.) Aug '59.
Natl. geog. 109: 806 (col.) Je '56; 116: 47 (col.) Jl '59.
Travel 101: 21-4 Jan '54.
ancient Amer. civilisation map. See map (Amer. ancient civilisation).
"And the prayer of faith shall heal the sick." Con. 145: 267 Je '60.
Andalusia (cave dwellers). Natl. geog. 112: 572-82 Oct '57.
—— **(map).** Natl. geog. 112: 576 Oct '57; 13: 402 Mar '58.
Andalusian dancers. Natl. geog. 113: 422-4 (col.) Mar '58.
Andalusian marshes. Natl. geog. 113: 398-424 (part col.) Mar '58.
Andersen, Hans Christian. Int. gr. soc.: Arts . . . p. 137 (col.).
Jun. bk. auth., p. 5.
—— **(statue).** Travel 103: 11 May '55.
Andersen home, Hans Christian. Holiday 18: 34 (col.) Sept '55.
Travel 103: 14 May '55.
Andersen's "Little Mermaid", Hans C. Natl. geog. 108: 82 (col.) Jl '55.
Anderson, Mrs. Arthur Forrest. Cur. biog. p. 15 (1948).
Anderson, C. W. Jun. bk. of auth., p. 6.
Anderson, Carl D. Cur. biog. p. 16 (1951).
Anderson, Clinton P. Cur. biog. p. 6 (1945).
Anderson, Dame Judith. Cur. biog. p. 9 (1961).
Anderson, Dewey. Cur. biog. p. 7 (1950).
Anderson, Erica. Cur. biog. p. 15 (1957).
Anderson, Mrs. Eugenie. Cur. biog. p. 5 (1950).
Anderson, Maj. Gen. Frederick L. Cur. biog. p. 11 (1944).
Anderson, Gaylord W. Cur. biog. p. 12 (1953).

Anderson, Ad. George W., jr. Cur. biog. p. 11 (1962).
Anderson, Guy. Holiday 25: 40 Feb '59.
Anderson, Howard R. Cur. biog. p. 17 (1955).
Anderson, Sir John. Cur. biog. p. 23 (1941).
Anderson, Commodore John W. Cur. biog. p. 15 (1953).
Anderson, Judith. Cur. biog. p. 25 (1941); p. 9 (1961).
Anderson, Lt. Gen. Sir Kenneth A.N. Cur. biog. p. 13 (1943).
Anderson, Leroy. Cur. biog. p. 19 (1952).
Anderson, Marian. Cur. biog. p. 10 (1950). Holiday 10: 23 Sept '51.
Anderson, Mary E. (Hawaiian prayer). Amer. heri. vol. 11 no. 2 p. 87 (Feb '60).
Anderson, Maxwell. Cur. biog. p. 19 (1942); p. 16 (1953). Holiday 22: 149 Dec '57.
Anderson, Robert. Cur. biog. p. 22 (1954). Pakula: Cent. album, p. 79.
Anderson, Robert B. Cur. biog. p. 20 (1853).
Anderson, Samuel W. Cur. biog. p. 24 (1954).
Anderson, Sigurd. Cur. biog. p. 21 (1953).
Anderson, Victor E. Cur. biog. p. 13 (1956).
Anderson, W. F. Amer. heri. vol. 10 no. 6 p. 42-3 (Oct '59).
Anderson, Comdr. W. R. Natl. geog. 115: 7, 20 (col.) Jan '59.
Anderson, William (work of). Con. 140: LI Jan '58.
Anderson, Capt. William R. Cur. biog. p. 10 (1959).
Andes Indians. Natl. geog. 98: 472-3 (col.) Oct '50.
Andes mts. Holiday 12: 108 Oct '52.
—— (Peru) Natl. geog. 107: 136-45 Jan '55.
—— (surveyors). Natl. geog. 109: 354-5 (col.) Mar '56.
Andes mt. valley. Holiday 23: 116 (col.) Mar '58.
Andino, Tiburcio Carias. Cur biog. p. 136 (1942).
andiron, bronze (Louis XVI). Con. 145: LI Je '60.
——, 16th cent. Con. 133: 189 May '54.
andirons. Con. ency. of ant. vol. 3 pl. 165. Con. 129: LXXV Je '52.
——, Charles II (silver). Con. 141: 130 Ap '58.
——, Henry VIII. Con. 132: 113 Nov '53.
andirons. See also firedog.
Andorra. Holiday 21: 16 Jan '57.
Andover (Mass.). Holiday 7: 57-61 Mar '50 (part col.).
Andover (N.H.) Face of Amer. p. 110-11 (col.).
Andover college. Holiday 7: 60 (col.) Mar '50.
Andrade, Victor. Cur. biog. p. 23 (1953).
Andrae, Elisabeth (drawing by). Ceram: March of arch. p. 227.
Andre, Maj. John. Amer. heri. vol. 10 no. 1 p. 15 (Dec '58).
Andresen, August H. Cur. biog. p. 15 (1956).
Andrewes, Vice Adm. Sir William. Cur. biog. p. 20 (1952).
Andrews, Bert. Cur. biog. p. 17 (1948).
Andrews, Dana. Cur. biog. p. 11 (1959).
Andrews, Lt. Gen. Frank M. Cur. biog. p. 22 (1942).

Andrews, H. (work of). Con. 132: XXVII Sept '53.
Andrews, Julie. Cur. biog. p. 17 (1956).
Andrews, Roy Chapman. Cur. biog. p. 27 (1941), p. 25 (1953).
Andrews, S. P. Amer. heri. vol. 7 no. 4 p. 44 (Je '56).
Andrews, Stanley. Cur. biog. p. 21 (1952).
Andrews, Thomas Coleman. Cur. biog. p. 25 (1954).
Andric, Ivo. Cur. biog. p. 13 (1962).
Andriessen's memorial (to war dead). Natl. geog. 118: 546 (col.) Oct '60.
Andromeda constellation. Natl. geog. 115: 673 (col.) May '59.
Andromeda nebula. Natl. geog. 101: 255 Feb '52.
Andros club (Bahama is.). Travel 113: 23 Feb '60.
Andros island (Bahama). Holiday 23: 74-9 (col.) Mar '58.
—— (map). Natl. geog. 99: 639 May '51.
Andros reef (ocean hole). Natl. geog. 113: 200-1 (col.) Feb '58.
Angamis (India). Natl. geog. 107: 258 (col.), 260-1 Feb '55.
angel. Amer. heri. vol. 9 no. 6 p. 86 (Oct '58). Con. 132 LIX Sept '53, 143-4 Jan '54. Holiday 26: 21 Sept '59. Natl. geog. 110: 756 (col.) Dec '56; 114: 775 (col.) Dec '58.
"Angel" (carved wood). Con. ency. of ant., vol. 3 p. 54.
angel (Christmas gift). Holiday 18: 84 (col.) Dec '55.
—— (Christmas sym.) Lehner: Pict. bk. of sym., p. 50.
—— (flying). Holiday 26: 20 Oct '59.
—— (sculpture). Holiday 10: 62 Dec '51. Labande: Naples, p. 60.
——, guardian. See guardian angel.
——, seal of. Lehner: Pict. bk. of sym., p. 25.
angel & book (sym.). Lehner: Pict. bk. of sym., p. 38.
"Angel appearing to Hagar & Ishmael." Con. 145: 39 Mar '60.
—— (Assereto). Con. 132: 4 Sept '53.
—— (Guercino). Con. 132: 14 Sept '53.
"Angel appearing to St. Francis" (Carracci). Con. 132: 5 Sept '53.
angel candlesticks, polychrome. Con. 143: LXXV May '59.
"Angel Falls" (Venezuela). Holiday 15: 99 Ap '54. Travel 105: 21 Feb '56.
Angel of peace (sym.). Lehner: Pict. bk. of sym., p. 92.
"Angel of the Annunciation" (wood carving). Con. ency. of ant., vol. 3 pl. 53.
angel. See also angels.
Angeles, Victoria de Los. Cur. biog. p. 19 (1955).
"Angelica & the Hermit" (Rubens). Con. 127: 124 May '51.
Angelico, Fra (work of). Praeg. pict. ency., p. 251 (col.).
Angelini, Giuseppe (sculpture by). Con. 143: 243 Je '59.

Angell, Sir Norman. Cur. biog. p. 18 (1948).
Angelo, Valenti. Jun. bk. of authors, p. 8.
angels. Durant: Pict. hist. of Amer. circus, p. 194.
——, Gothic carved (church, St. Wolfgang). Natl. geog. 118: 267 (col.) Aug '60.
——, guardian. See guardian angels.
"Angels adoring" (Guardi). Con. 145: LXIV May '60.
angels. See also angel.
Angkor (Bangkok). Travel 111: 38 Feb '59.
Angkor Thom. Holiday 12: 44-7, 88 (part col.) Nov '52.
    Natl. geog. 102: 298 (col.) Sept '52; 116: 850 (col.) Dec '59.
—— (gate). Natl. geog. 117: 547 (col.) Ap '60.
—— (king's throne). Natl. geog. 117: 534-5 (col.) Ap '60.
Angkor wall carvings. Natl. geog. 98: 502 Oct '50.
Angkor warriors defeated. Natl. geog. 117: 560-1 (col.) Ap '60.
Angkor Wat. Holiday 12: 45-7, 87 (part col.) Nov '52.
——. Natl. geog. 99: 468 (col.) Ap '51; 116: 792-3 (col.) Dec '59; 117: 518-67 (col.) Ap '60.
—— (plan). Natl. geog. 117: 520 Ap '60.
Angle, Paul M. Cur. biog. p. 21 (1955).
anglers. See fishermen.
Angoff, Charles. Cur. biog. p. 22 (1955).
Angola (Africa). Travel 105: 42-5 Feb '56.
Angouleme cathedral (12th cent.). Praeg. pict. ency. p. 214.
Anguisciola, Sophonisba. Con. 144: 110 Nov '59.
Angular dancers. See dancers, Angular (Bangkok).
Angus, W. H. (Red). Horan: Pict. hist. of wild west, p. 185.
animal carvings (Faberge). Con. 145: XXXV Mar '60.
—— (Hitite ritual). Osward: Asia Minor, pl. 2.
animal god, Japanese burial (6th cent.). Con. 145: 289 Je '60.
animal sculpture. See sculpture, animal.
animal trainer (circus). Durant: Pict. hist. of Amer. circus, p. 32, 35, 137, 143, 165, 196, 253 (part col.).
—— (horse & man). Durant: Pict. hist. of Amer. circus, p. 303.
animal trap. See trap, animal.
animals (sym.). Lehner: Pict. bk. of sym.
Ankara (Turkey). Natl. geog. 117: 598-9 (col.) May '60.
    Osward: Asia Minor, pl. 148, 150-9.
—— (temple of Augustus). See Temple of Augustus.
Ankara department store. Natl. geog. 100: 182 Aug '51.
Ankh (sym.). Lehner: Pict. bk. of sym., p. 27.
ankle joint. Gray's anatomy, p. 1420.
"Ann, Countess of Bedford" (Van Dyck). Con. 126: 208 Dec '50.
Anna, Gen. Santa. See Santa Anna, Gen.
Annapolis (Maryland). Holiday 23: 78-83 (col.) Je '58.
"Anne, Countess of Chesterfield" (Gainsborough). Con. 144: III Dec '59.

"Anne, Countess of Chesterfield" (Guardi). Con. 144: 270 Jan '60.
"Anne of Brittany" (medal). See medal, bronze (Anne of Brittany).
Anne, Princess of England. Holiday 23: 68 Jan '58.
Anne, Queen. Con. 145: 127 Ap '60.
Annecy (French Alps). Holiday 5: 134 Mar '49.
Annemasse cafe (France). Holiday 23: 75 (col.) Jan '58.
"Annie & Mary" railroad (1897). Amer. heri. vol. 11 no. 3 p. 2 (Ap '60).
Annigoni, Pietro. Con. 135: VIII Je '55.
—— (work of). Con. 138: 53 Sept '56; 139: 6 Mar '57.
announcement (sym.). Lehner: Pict. bk. of sym., p. 84-5.
"Annunciation" (sculpture). Con. 144: 178 Dec '59.
"The annunciation" (Crivelli). Praeg. pict. ency., p. 37 (col.)
"Annunciation" (German woodcut). Con. 129: 143 Je '52.
"Annunciation" (Gunther). Con. 142: 6 Sept '58.
    Praeg. pict. ency., p. 332.
"The annunciation" (Italian ivory carving). Con. 142: 269 Jan '59.
"The annunciation" (Martini). Praeg. pict. ency., p. 230 (col.)
"Annunciation" (Pereda). Con. 133: XXV Mar '54.
"Annunciation" (Stoss, Nuremberg). Praeg. pict. ency., p. 247.
"Annunciation" (Veneziano). Con. 143: 104 Ap '59.
anointing spoon, British. Int. gr. soc.: Arts . . . p. 165 (col.).
Anouilh, Jean. Cur. biog. p. 27 (1954).
Anraadt, Pieter van. See Van Anraadt, Pieter.
Ansermet, Ernest. Cur. biog. p. 9 (1949).
Anslinger, Harry J. Cur. biog. p. 20 (1948).
Anspach, Charles L. Cur. biog. p. 19 (1956).
ant (sym.). Lehner: Pict. bk. of sym., p. 57.
Antalya (on Mediterranean). Osward: Asia Minor, pl. 106-11, 111, VI (col.).
    Travel 106: 56 Jl '56.
Antarctic. Amer. heri. vol. 6 no. 4 p. 51 (Je '55).
    Holiday 19: 134-5 May '56.
    Natl. geog. 110: 142-80 (part col.) Aug '56; 112: 2-48 (part col.) Jl '57, 340-98 (part col.) Sept '57; 113: 440-78 (part col.) Ap '58; 115: 26-47 (part col.) Jan '59; 116: 526-56 (part col.) Oct '59.
—— (map). Natl. geog. 109: 288 Feb '56; 110: 147 Aug '56; 112: 15 Jl '57, 380-1 (col.) Sept '57; 113: 475 Ap '58; 115 35 Jan '59; 116: 542-3 Oct '59.
Antarctic. See also costume (Antarctic).
Antarctic explorers, first. Natl. geog. 112: 9 (col.) Jl '57.
antenna. See television antenna.
antependium (16th cent.). Con. 135: LIII Je '55.
Antheil, George. Cur. biog. p. 30 (1954).
Anthony, John J. Cur. biog. p. 23 (1942).

Anthony, Susan B. Amer. heri. vol. 7 no. 4 p. 47 (Je '56); vol. 10 no. 6 p. 19 (Oct '59).

antiaircraft gun. Natl. geog. 99: 354 (col.) Mar '51.

"Anticipation" (Rotta). Con. 133: XXV Ap '54.

Antietam battle field. Amer. heri. vol. 9 no. 5 p. 56-7, 94 (part col.) (Aug '58).

"Antietam" carrier ship, U.S. Natl. geog. 104: 574 (col.) Oct '53.

Antietam creek. Amer. heri. vol. 12 no. 1, p. 18 (col.) (Dec '60).

"Antigallican" (Marshall). Con. 144: 270 Jan '60.

Antigua (Easter processions). Natl. geog. 117: 407-9 (col.) Mar '60.

—— (harbor). Natl. geog. 116: 449 (col.) Oct '59.

antimony (sym.). Lehner: Pict. bk. of sym. p. 72.

"Antinous" (sculpture). Ceram: March of arch. p. 9.

—— (sculpture by Foggini). Con. 141: 223 Je '58.

Antioch. Natl. geog. 110: 731 (col.) Dec '56.

—— (St. Peter's church). Osward: Asia Minor, pl. 25-6.

Antioch women. See women, Antioch.

antique sales. Natl. geog. 107: 786-7 (col.) Je '55.

antique shop (Mass.). Travel 109: 26 Je '58.

Antoine. Cur. biog. p. 23 (1955).

Antoine, Josephine. Cur. biog. p. 14 (1944).

Antoine's restaurant (New Orleans). Holiday 9: 106 Mar '51; 28: 109 Jl '60. Travel 110: 23 Aug '58.

Antrim, William Henry Harrison. Horan: Pict. hist. of wild west, p. 58, 68.

Antrim, Mrs. William (mother of "Billy the Kid"). Horan: Pict. hist of wild west, p. 58.

Antwerp. Con. 144: LIX Jan '60. Holiday 5: 139 Mar '49; 28: 138 Oct '60. Travel 103: 36 Ap '55; 113: 9 Je '60.

—— (guild houses). Holiday 23: 2 (col.) Jan '58.

anvil. Natl. geog. 102: 28 (col.) Jl '52. Natl. geog. 113: 867 Je '58. Rawson: Ant. pict. bk. p. 55.

—— (sym.). Lehner: Pict. bk. of sym. p. 28, 90.

"Anxious muses" (Chirico). Praeg. pict. ency. p. 453.

aorta. Gray's anatomy, p. 554, 606-16.

"Apache gun dancers" (Dewey). Natl. geog. 107: 366 (col.) Mar '55.

Apache Indian children. Natl. geog. 104: 372 (col.) Sept '53.

Apache Kid. Horan: Pict. hist. of wild west, p. 176.

Apache trail. Travel 106: 26 Oct '56.

Apartment bldgs. Natl. geog. 105: 247 (col.) Feb '54.

—— (Algiers). Natl. geog. 117: 770 (col.) Je '60.

—— (Chile). Natl. geog. 117: 189 (col.) Feb '60

—— (Italy). Natl. geog. 109: 835 Je '56

—— (Pakistan). Natl. geog. 102: 648 (col.) Nov '52.

—— (Rome). Natl. geog. 111. 453, 479 (col.) Ap '57.

—— (Rotterdam). Natl. geog. 118: 538-9 (col.) Oct '60.

—— (Sao Paulo). Holiday 18: 71 Oct '51.

—— (Singapore). Natl. geog. 103: 196 (col.) Feb '53.

apartment house (Africa). Holiday 22: 166 Dec '57.

—— (Chicago). Praeg.: Pict. ency., p. 441.

—— (on stilts, Marseilles). Travel 104: 54 Oct 55.

apartment houses (Russia). Natl. geog. 116: 744. 5 (col.) Dec '59.

apartments (Hamburg, Ger.). Natl. geog. 115: 770 (col.) Je '59.

——, adobe (Morocco). Natl. geog. 107: 178-9 (col.) Feb '55.

——, modern. Holiday 28: 77 (col.) Dec '60.

——, —— (Brasilia, Brazil). Natl. geog. 117: 708-9, 724 (col.) May '60.

——, —— (Puerto Rico). Holiday 5: 53 (col.) Feb '49.

——, —— (Rome). Holiday 27: 71 Ap '60.

——, nud-brick (Aden). Natl. geog. 117: 111 (col.) Jan '60.

——, serpentine (Paris). Natl. geog. 117: 763 Je '60.

Aphaea, temple of. See Temple of Aphaea.

"Aphrodite" (bronze 17th cent, by Susini). Con. 140: 206 Dec '57.

—— (bust). Holiday 23: 105 Ap '58.

—— (marble statue, headless). Con. 139: 124 Ap '57.

—— (sym.). Lehner: Pict. bk. of sym., p. 31.

Aphrodite of Arles (4th cent. statue). Con. ency. of ant., vol. 3, pl. 68.

Aphrodite of Cnidos. Praeg.: Pict. ency., p. 133.

"Apollo" (sculpture, Canova). Con. 144: 226 Jan '60.

—— (sym.). Lehner: Pict. bk. of sym., p. 31.

—— (Temple of Zeus). Praeg.: Pict. ency., p. 101.

——, temple of. See Temple of Apollo.

"Apollo & Marsyas" (Tintoretto). Con. 127: 116 May '51.

"Apollo & the seasons" (Wilson). Con. 138: XII (col.) Jan '57.

"Apollo Citharoedus" (bronze). Labande: Naples, p. 100

"Apollo of Belvedere". Praeg. Pict. ency., p. 14.

"Apollo on horseback". Durant: Pict. hist. of Amer. circus, p. 38.

"Apollo" (Parnassus ceiling, Mengs). Con. 144: 226 Jan '60.

Apollo's birthplace (legendary). Travel 101: 43 May '54.

Apollo's dolphin (sym.). Lehner: Pict. bk. of sym., p. 64.

Apollo's doric temple (Corinth). Natl. geog. 110: 752 (col.) Dec '56.

"Apostle Bartholomew" (Rembrandt). Con. 126: 127 Oct '50.

Apostle island. See Madeline island.

"Apostle St. James" (El Greco). Con. 144: , 128 Nov '59.

apostle spoon. See spoon, apostle.

apostolic clock (1878). Brooks: Growth of a nation, p. 220.

apothecaries jar. See drug jar.

apothecary cabinet. Con. 132: 32-3 Sept '53.
apothecary figure. Amer. heri. vol. 3 no. 3 p. 40 (col.) (Spring '52).
apothecary laboratory (17th cent.). Natl. geog. 117: 839 (col.) Je '60.
apothecary shop, Colonial. Natl. geog. 106: 465 (col.) Oct '54.
—— (1820). Amer. heri. vol. 8 no. 3 p. 50 (col.) (Ap '57).
"Apothecary shop" (Van Mieris). Con. 133: 127 (col.) Ap '54.
"Apotheosis of Francesca Barbaro" (Tiepolo). Con. 139: XLVIII Mar '57.
"Apotheosis of Homer" (Wedgewood plaque). Con. 135: 254 Je '55.
Appel, Karel. Cur. biog. p. 11 (1961).
Apperson auto. (1916). Int. gr. Soc.: Arts . . . p. 161 (col.).
Appian Way. Holiday 11: 44 Ap '52; 27: 77 Ap '60.
Natl. geog. 117: 663 (col.) May '60.
apple butter making. Natl. geog. 102: 513 (col.) Oct '52.
apple butter stirrer. Rawson: ant. pict. bk. p. 26.
apple-corer horse. Rawson: Ant. pict. bk. p. 32.
Appleton, Sir Edward. Cur. biog. p. 9 (1945.)
Appley, Lawrence A. Cur. biog. p. 11 (1950)
Appomattox courthouse. Amer. heri. vol. 6 no. 4 p. 88 (Je '55).
April fool day (sym.). Lehner: Pict. bk. of sym. p. 52.
agualunger. See diver.
aquamanile (13th cent.). Praeg pict. ency. p. 213.
aquascope (in Chesapeake Bay). Natl. geog. 107: 685-95 (part col.) May '55.
aqueduct (France). Natl. geog. 100: 20-1 Jl '51.
—— (Mexico). Travel 101: 17 Mar '54.
——, canal. Natl. geog. 117: 436 (col.) Mar '60.
——, Roman. See Roman aqueduct.
——, Spanish. Holiday 10: 85 Aug. '51.
Travel 105: 45 Ap '56.
aqueduct tower. Natl. geog. 100: 817 (col.) Dec '51.
arabesque wall decoration. Praeg pict. ency. p. 77.
Arab legion soldier. Natl. geog. 105: 487 (col.) Ap '54.
Arab refugee camp. Natl. geog. 102: 849 Dec '52.
Arabia. Holiday 20: 48-51 (part col.) Aug '56.
Natl. geog. 101: 214-44 (part col.) Feb '52; 110: 66-104 (part col.) Jl '56; 114: 714-32 Nov '58.
—— (map). Natl. geog. 114: 714-5 Nov '58.
Arabian. Holiday 15: 104 Feb '54.
—— (back view). Natl. geog. 110: 709 (col.) Dec '56.
—— (back view, prayer beads). Natl. geog. 115: 495 (col.) Ap '59.
—— (camel). Holiday 7: 96 (col.) Mar '50; 13: 19 Feb '53; 17: 16 Feb '55.
Natl. geog. 113: 691 (col.) May '58; 114: 726 Nov '58.
—— (drum). Natl. geog. 113: 671 (col.) May '58.
—— (falcon). Natl. geog. 114: 486 (col.) Oct '58.
—— (hat vendor). Holiday 5: 64 (col.), 122 Mar '49.

—— (planting tree). Natl. geog. 114: 732 Nov '58.
—— (seated). Amer. heri. vol. 10 no. 4 p. 57 (col.) (Je '59)
—— (sewing, smoking). Natl. geog. 108: 157 (col.) Aug '55.
Arabian nazaar street. Natl. geog. 115: 498-9 (col.) Ap '59.
Arabian boy. Natl. geog. 107: 156 (col.) Feb '55; 110: 67 (col.) Jl '56.
—— (shining shoes). Holiday 5: 65 Jan '49.
—— (seated on cushion). Natl. geog. 113: 231, 234 (col.) Feb '58.
Arabian boys (water buffalo). Natl. geog. 113: 227 (col.) Feb '58.
Arabian child. Holiday 5: 68 Jan '49.
—— (seated). Natl. geog. 114: 726 Nov '58.
—— (seated, doll). Natl. geog. 114: 726 Nov '58.
Arabian costume. Natl. geog. 104: 8 Jl '53.
Arabian desert. Natl. geog. 102: 784-802 (part col.) Dec '52.
Arabian desert camp. Natl. geog. 105: 500-1 (col.) Ap '54.
Arabian feast (Trans Jordan). Natl. geog. 117: 444 Mar '60.
Arabian girl. Natl. geog. 98: 727, 730 (col.) Dec '50.
Arabian man. Holiday 5: 69 Jan '49; 14: 135 Oct '53; 19: 99 (col.) May '56.
Natl. geog. 102: 463 (col.) Oct '52.
—— (milking camel). Natl. geog. 110: 70 Jl '56.
Arabian man & boy. Natl. geog. 107: 156 (col.) Feb '55.
Arabian marshmen. Natl. geog. 113: 204-39 (part col.) Feb '58.
Arabian men. Natl. geog. 98: 725, 744-5 (col.) Dec '50; 110: 66-7 (col.) Jl '56.
—— (camels). Natl. geog. 106: 744 (col.) Dec '54.
—— (dog fight). Natl. geog. 113: 235 Feb '58.
—— (seated, beach). Natl. geog. 110: 96-7 (col.) Jl '56.
Arabian merchant. Natl. geog. 111: 231 Feb '57.
"Arabian nights" costumes. See costumes, "Arabian nights".
Arabian nights court (Cal. fair). Natl. geog. 112: 703 (col.) Nov '57.
Arabian pearling vessel. Natl. geog. 105: 500 (col.) Ap '54.
Arabian prince. Natl. geog. 104: 35 Jl '53.
Arabian sheiks. See sheiks (Arabia).
Arabian woman. Holiday 5: 64 Jan '49.
Natl. geog. 102: 852 Dec '52.
—— (veiled head). Holiday 20: 48 (col.) Aug '56.
Arabian women. Natl. geog. 104: 863 (col.) Dec '53; 114: 722, 726 Nov '58.
—— (baskets on heads). Natl. geog. 110: 85 (col.) Jl '56; 115: 498 (col.) Ap '59.
—— (heads). Natl. geog. 107: 161 (col.) Feb '55.
—— (veiled). Natl. geog. 108: 162 (col.) Aug '55.
Arabians. Natl. geog. 101: 223, 226, 237, 241, 243-4 (col.) Feb '52; 102: 784-802 (part col.) Dec '52; 108: 159, 162-6 (col.) Aug '55; 114: 713-7, 721-32 (part col.) Nov '58.

—— (camels). Natl. geog. 102: 831 Dec '52; 106: 744 (col.) Dec. '54; 111: 300-1 (col.) Mar '57.

—— (dancing). Natl. geog. 110: 66, 72-3 (col.) Jl '56.

—— (drinking coffee). Int. gr. soc.: Arts . . . p. 179 (col.).

—— (eating). Natl. geog. 108: 163 (col.) Aug '55.

—— (horseback, battle). Natl. geog. 114: 716-7 Nov '58.

—— (Nomads). Holiday 20: 50-1 (col.) Dec '56.

—— (seated). Int. gr. soc.: Arts . . . p. 179 (col.) Natl. geog. 110: 714-5 (col.) Dec '56.

—— (shoppers). Natl. geog. 117: 771 (col.) Je '60.

Arachova (Greece). Holiday 27: 186 (col.) Je '60.

Arafa. Natl. geog. 104: 4-5 (col.) Jl '53.

Araki, Eikichi. Cur. biog. p. 23 (1952)

Aramburu, Maj. Gen. Pedro Eugenio. Cur. biog. p. 17 (1957).

Aramburu, Gen. Pedro. Natl. geog. 113: 306 Mar '58.

Aranha, Oswaldo. Cur. biog. p. 25 (1942).

Ararat, Mt. See Mt. Ararat.

Aras, Tevfik Rustu. Cur. biog. p. 27 (1942)

Arathron (seal of). Lehner: Pict. bk. of sym. p. 25.

Arbor day (sym.). Lehner: Pict. bk. of sym. p. 52.

Arbroath abbey (pageant, Scotland). Natl. geog. 112: 484-5 (col.) Oct '57.

Arc de Triomphe (Paris). Holiday 7: 23 May '50; 8: 171 Dec '50; 9: 93, 125 Mar '51; 13: 5 (col.) Mar '53, cover, 124 Ap '53; 15; 97, 148 May '54; 25: 80, 123 Jan '59; 27: 215 Ap '60, 179 Je '60. Natl. geog. 101: 773 (col.) Je '52; 114: 284 Aug '58; 117: 727 (col.) Je '60. Travel 111: back cover Mar '59, back cover Ap '59, back cover May '59.

—— (relief). Praeg pict. ency. p. 428.

arcade. Holiday 11: 112 May '52.

——, store. Natl. geog. 101: 325 Mar '52.

arcade street (Moscow). Natl. geog. 116: 722 (col.) Dec '59.

Arcadius the 1st (bust). Osward: Asia Minor, pl. 53.

Arcaro, Eddie. Cur. biog. p. 26 (1958)

Arcata & Mad river railroad. Amer. heri. vol. 11 no. 3 p. 2 (Ap '60).

Arce, Jose. Cur. biog. p. 11 (1947).

Arceneaux home, Louis (faithless lover of Evangeline). Amer. heri. vol. 6 mo. 1, p. 62 (col.) fall '54.

arch, Chinese memorial. Holiday 21: 77 (col.) Je '57.

——, Hadrian's. See Hadrian's arch.

——, Iranian street. Natl. geog. 100: 445 Oct '51.

——, memorial. See Memorial arch.

——, monumental (Syria). Travel 105: 20 Jan '56.

——, Renaissance. Holiday 23: 4 Ap '58.

——, Trajan. See Trajan arch.

——, triumphal (Bergen 1733). Con. 141: 153 May '58.

——, triumphal (to Greely). Amer. heri. vol. 11 no. 4 p. 106 (Je '60).

Arch du Carrousel (Paris). Natl. geog. 98: 62 (col.) Jl '50.

Arch of Constantine (Rome). Holiday 7: 10 (col.) Jan '50. Praeg. pict. ency. p. 141.

Arch of Ctesiphon (Near East). Natl. geog. 114: 38-9 (col.) Jl '58.

Arch of triumph (Paris). See Arc de Triomphe.

Arch of triumph, Constantine. See Arch of Constantine.

Arch of Triumphs. Holiday 8: 31 Sept '50.

archaeologists (working). Natl. geog. 103: 721 (col.), 732 Je '53. Travel 113: 46 Mar '60.

archaeology. Natl. geog. 118: 420, 424-35 (part col.) Sept '60.

—— (cave dwelling). Natl. geog. 116: 621-2 Nov '59.

—— (Eskimo graves). Natl. geog. 110: 672-85 (col.) Nov '56.

—— (Indian relics). Natl. geog. 110: 546-58 (part col.) Oct '56.

—— (Mexico). Natl. geog. 110: 366-74 (part col.) Sept '56.

—— (sea divers). Natl. geog. 117: 685, 687-8, 694 (col.) May '60.

—— (Sicily). Natl. geog. 107: 23 (col.) Jan '55.

archaeology excavation. Travel 113: 46 Mar '60.

—— (Assyria). Natl. geog. 99: 43-104 (col.) Jan '51.

—— (Old Testament life). Natl. geog. 118: 812-51 (part col.) Dec '60.

Archambault, Louis. Cur. biog. p. 13 (1959).

Archbishop Wendel (blessing people). Natl. geog. 115: 748 (col.) Je '59.

Archbishop Paul-Emile Leger. Holiday 10: 54 Aug '51.

Archbishop Paul Emile Cardinal Leger. Holiday 26: 52 Sept '59.

Archdeacon, Catholic. Natl. geog. 109: 631 (col.) May '56.

Archdruid of Wales. Holiday 25: 190 (col.) May '59.

"Archduke Leopold Wilhelm . . . in gallery" (Teniers). Natl. geog. 97: 752 Je '50.

Archer, Glenn LeRoy. Cur. biog. p. 12 (1949).

archer. Holiday 10: 21 Sept '51.

—— (crossbow). Natl. geog. 107: 648 (col.) May '55.

——, Assyrian. See Assyrian archer.

"The archers" (Raeburn). Con. 141: 62 Mar '58.

archers, Hitite carved. Osward: Asia Minor-pl. 6.

archery (Bhutan). Natl. geog. 102: 751 (col.) Dec '52.

——. (British Guiana). Natl. geog. 107: 333 (col.) Mar '55.

—— (girls). Holiday 8: 53 (col.) Dec '50. Natl. geog. 106: 229 (col.) Aug '54.

archery contest (medieval). Int. gr. soc.: Arts . . . p. 77 (col.).

arches, types of. Praeg. pict. ency., p. 35.

arches national monument (Utah). Holiday 23: 129 Ap '58; 26: 50 Jl '59. Jordan: Hammond's pict. atlas, p. 171 (col.). Natl. geog. 99: 742 (col.) Je '51; 108: 402-25 (col.) Sept '55.

——, (1858, houses). Amer. heri. vol. 8 no. 4 p. 112 (Je '57).

——, English. Con. 132: 3 Sept '53; 143: 68-74 (part col.) Ap '59; 144: 72, 74-7 (part col.) Nov '59.
Holiday 14: 55 Nov '53; 17: 12 (col.) Mar '55; 21: 18 (col.) Ap '57; 23: 82-90 (col.) Ap' 58; 25: 155 Ap '59, 97 May '59; 26: 48-53 (col.) Aug '59.
Int. gr. soc.: Arts . . . p. 101 (col.).
Natl. geog. 98: 195 (col.) Aug '50; 103: 809-29 (col.), 834-37 Je '53; 108: 297, 306-47 (part col.) Sept '55; 114: 47, 61 (col.) Jl '58.
Travel 107: 57 Ap '57.

——, English (int.). Con. 142: 70-4 (part col.) Nov '58.

——, English abbey (int. & ext.). Con. 141: 205-11 Je '58.

——, English abbey (int. & ext.). Con. 141: 205-11 Je '58.

——, English ("Coleshill", Berkshire, 1649-62). Con. 139: 243 Je '57.

——, English (Felbrigg Hall, Norfolk). Con. 141: 217 Je '58.

——, English home (int. & ext.). Con. 140: 74-9 (part col.) Nov '57, 210-17 (part col.), Jan '58.

——, English (pub). Holiday 26: 7 (col.) Nov '59.

——, English (16th cent.). Con. 144: 2-7 (part col.) Sept '59.

——, English village. Holiday 14: 92 (col.) Jl '53.

——, English. See also homes, English; house, English.

——, European. Holiday 27: 123-30 Jan '60.

——, Federal period type (18th cent.). Natl. geog. 103: 544 (col.) Ap '53.

——, Frank Lloyd Wright. Holiday 20: 37 Sept '56.

——, French. Holiday 21: 77, 82-4, 90 (part col.) Ap '57.
Natl. geog. 100: 29-35 (col.) Jl '51; 105: 175 (col.) Feb '54; 117: 733, 735-7, 752, 762-3 (part col.) Je '60.

——, French (Rhone river). Holiday 27: 69-73 Jan '60.

——, French type. Holiday 14: 34-5 (col.) Sept '53.

——, German. Holiday 25: 42-3 (col.) Jan '59, 50, 53-5, 63, 67 (part col.) May '59.
Natl geog. 111: 258-9, 262-3, 266-7 (part col.) Feb '57.

——, German (town hall). Praeg. pict. ency., p. 305.

——, Gothic. Amer. heri. vol. 6 no. 2 p. 22-3 (winter '55); vol. 7 no. 1 p. 4, 7, 9 (part col.) (Dec '55).
Travel 113: 34 Je '60.

——, Gothic (Belgium). Holiday 23: 2 (col.) Jan '58.

——, Gothic (cathedrals). Int. gr. soc.: Arts . . . p. 49 (col.).

——, Gothic (facade details). Con. 133: XLVIII-XLXI May '54.

——, Gothic (Ger. church). Int. gr. soc.: Arts . . . p. 47 (col.)

——, Greece. Natl. geog. 103: 370, 376, 387 (col.) Mar '53.

——, Greek style. Holiday 20: 36 Sept '56.

——, Iceland. Natl. geog. 100: 614 (col.) Nov '51.

——, Illinois (early). Travel 110: 57 Sept '58.

——, Inca. Int. gr. soc.: Arts . . . p. 51 (col.).

——, India. Holiday 14: 34 (col.) Oct '53.
Natl. geog. 118: 446, 450-1, 463, 470-1 (part col.) Oct '60.
Praeg pict. ency., p. 524.

——, Irish. Con. 145: 148-55 May '60.
Natl. geog. 99: 654, 657, 661, 663 May '51; 104: 118, 125, 128 (col.) Jl '53.

——, Ischia island. Natl. geog. 105: 541, 544 (col.) Ap '54.

——, Italian. Con. 142: 139 Dec '58.
Natl. geog. 100: 403, 406, 408-10 (col.) Sept '51; 109: 829, 835, 838-9, 842-3, 856-7 (part col.) Je '56; 116: 496-7, 502, 509 (col.) Oct '59.
Travel 103: 51 May '55.

——, Japanese. Holiday 23: 168 (col.) Mar '58.

——, (John Nash). Con. 145: 252-4 Je '60.

——, Kashmir. Natl. geog. 114: 613, 616, 618, 640-1 (col.) Nov '58.

——, Kentucky. See Kentucky arch.; Kentucky home.

——, Ladakh. Natl. geog. 99: 614-17 (col.) May '51.

——, La. bayou. Amer heri. vol. 6 no. 1 p. 62 (col.) (fall '54).

——, Luxembourg. Holiday 18: 128 (col.) Nov. '55.

——, Macau. Natl. geog. 103: 686 (col.) May '53.

——, Malaya. Natl. geog. 103: 188 Feb '53.

——, Mayan. Int. gr. soc.: Arts . . . p. 51 (col.).

——, Mecca. Natl. geog. 104: 24, 28 (col.) Jl '53.

——, Medieval. Int. gr. soc.: Arts . . . p. 75, 78 (col.).

——, Mexican. Holiday 26: 51-9 (col.) Nov '59.
Natl. geog. 103: 327, 334 Mar '53

——, Minorcan. Holiday 27: 53-5 (part col.) Jan '60.

——, Missouri. Natl. geog. 103: 713, 716 (col.) Je '53.

——, modern. Holiday 12: 48-53 (col.) Aug '52.
Int. gr. soc.: Arts . . . p. 125-9 (col.).

——, modern (Cal. homes). Holiday 10: 98-103 (col.) Sept '51.

——, Moorish. Natl. geog. 97: 454 (col.) Ap '50.

——, Morocco. Natl. geog. 107: 148, 150, 178-9 (col.) Feb '55.

——, Moslem. Int. gr. soc.: Arts . . . p. 45 (col.).
Natl. geog. 114: 2, 6, 14-5, 22, 31, 36, 38, 42 (part col.) Jl '58.

——, New Orleans. Amer. heri. vol. 12 no. 1 p. 125 (Dec '60).
Natl. geog. 103: 165 (col.) Feb '53.

——, N. Y. (Lever Bros.). Praeg. pict. ency., p. 436.

——, N Y. (1777-). Amer. heri. vol. 4 no. 1 p. 13-5 (fall '52).

——, N. Y. (Hudson Valley, 1855). Amer. heri. vol. 10 no. 1 p. 19-20 (Dec '58).

——, North Africa (medieval). Int. gr. soc.: Arts . . . p. 85 (col.).

architecture, Norwegian. Con. 145: 2 (col.) 3-6 Mar '60.
Holiday 12: 93 Sept '52.
Natl. geog. 106: 154, 163, 166, 170, 182, 186, 188 (part col.) Aug '54.
——, Ohio (early). Amer. heri. vol. 4 no. 3 p. 44-51 (part col.) (spring '53).
——, Palladio. Amer. heri. vol. 10 no. 5 p. 66, 70 (Aug '59).
Int. gr. soc.: Arts . . . p. 83 (col.).
——, Persian. Int. gr. soc.: Arts . . . p. 85 (col.).
——, Peruvian. Natl. geog. 98: 430-1 (col.) Oct '50.
——, Poland. Natl. geog. 114: 359, 362-3, 368-9 (col.) Sept. '58.
——, Portugal. Holiday 19: 35 (col.) Jan '56.
Natl. geog. 118: 628-9, 643, 651-2 (col.) Nov '60.
——, Rhode Island. Holiday 27: 102-7 (col.) May '60.
——, Rome. Holiday 27: 69-93 (part col.) Ap '60.
Natl. geog. 111: 441, 438, 453-4, 479 (part col.) Ap '57.
——, Romanesque. Int. gr. soc.: Arts . . . p. 47 (col.).
——, Rotterdam. Natl. geog. 118: 538-9, 543, 546-7 (col.) Oct '60.
——, Russian. Natl. geog. 116: 352, 354, 358-9, 365, 371, 384-7, 389 (part col.) Sept '59.
——, Russian (ext. & int.). Con. 142: 219, 221-5 Jan '59.
——, Saudi, Arabia. Natl. geog. 114: 722-3 Nov '58.
——, Scotch. Amer. heri. vol. 11 no. 5 p. 6-7 (Aug '60).
Con. 145: 70 (col.)-75 Ap '60.
Natl. geog. 110: 5-9, 15 (col.) Jl '56; 112: 438-9, 447, 450-1, 458, 460 (part col.) Oct '57.
——, Siamese. Int. gr. soc.: Arts . . . p. 85 (col.).
——, Sicily. Natl. geog. 107: 22, 31, 33-4 (col.) Jan '55.
——, Singapore. Natl. geog. 103: 202-3 (col.) Feb '53.
——, southern. See architecture, colonial; home, colonial.
——, Spanish. Natl. geog. 109: 307 (col.) Mar '56.
——, Swedish. Natl. geog. 98: 630, 638-43 (col.) Nov '50.
——, Swiss. Holiday 28: 31-43 (part col.) Aug '60.
Natl. geog. 98: 216, 218, 222, 240-1 (col.) Aug '50; 110: 440-78 (col.) Oct '56.
——, (symbol). Lehner: Pict. bk. of sym. p. 10.
——, Thailand (medieval). Int. gr. soc.: Arts . . . p. 85 (col.).
——, Tudor. Con. 127: 131 May '51; 143: 2, 4 Mar '59.
Int. gr. soc.: Arts . . . p. 101 (col.).
——, Tudor style (Va.). Natl. geog. 103: 789 Je '53
——, Turkey. Praeg. pict. ency., p. 516.
——, unusual. Travel 104: 54-5 Oct '55.

——, Venice. Holiday 18: 42-7 (part col.) Oct '55
——, Victorian. Amer. heri. vol. 6 no. 6 p. 34-41 (Oct '55).
——, Virginia. Natl. geog. 97: 554-91 (part col.) May '50.
——, arches. Praeg. pict. ency., p. 35.
——, capitals. Praeg. pict. ency., p. 43.
——, domes. Praeg. pict. ency., p. 53.
——, ornament (carving & engraving). Praeg. pict. ency., p. 76-7.
architecture. See also house, colonial; homes; houses.
Archway, colonial. Natl. geog. 109: 483 (col.) Ap '56.
Arciniegas, German. Cur. biog. p. 32 (1954).
Arco Felice (near Cumae, Italy). Labande: Naples, p. 146.
Arcos de la Frontera (Spain). Holiday 13: 140 (col.) Mar '53.
Natl. geog. 113: 418-9 (col.) Mar '58.
Arctic circle. Natl. geog. 114: 128-46 Jl '58.
—— (map). Natl. geog. 106: 521-32 Oct '54; 114: 136-7 Jl '58.
Arctic explorers. Natl. geog. 103: 491-2, 499, 501-3 Ap '53.
Arctic region. Natl. geog. 103: 491-502 Ap '53; 111: 526-45 (part col.) Ap '57; 115: 2-17 (part col.) Jan '59; 116: 2-41 (part col.) Jl '59.
—— (Canada). Natl. geog. 107: 544-71 (part col.) Ap. '55.
—— (map). Natl. geog. 103: 493 Ap '53; 104: 472 Oct '53; 107: 547 Ap '55; 111: 531 Ap '57; 115: 8-9 Jan '59; 116: 8-9 Jl '59.
Arctic settlement, Greely (1884). Amer. heri. vol. 6 no. 4 p. 44, 47-8 (col.) (Je '60).
Ardalan, Ali Gholi. Cur. biog. p. 34 (1954).
Arden, Elizabeth. Cur. biog. p. 19 (1957).
Arden, Eve. Cur. biog. p. 31 (1953).
Ardvreck castle (ruin in Scotland). Holiday 27: cover (col.) May '60.
Areilza, Count Jose Maria. Cur. biog. p. 26 (1955).
arena (Swiss festival). Natl. geog. 114: 565 (col.) Oct '58.
Arena chapel fresco (Padua). Praeg. pict. ency., p. 228 (col.)
Arena chapel (Madonna). Praeg. pict. ency., p. 244.
Arends, Leslie C. Cur. biog., p. 23 (1948).
Arendt, Hannah. Cur. biog. p. 15 (1959).
Arequipa (Peru, hotel). Holiday 14: 95 (col.) Nov '53.
Ares (sym.). Lehner: Pict. bk. of sym., p. 32.
Aretino, Spinello (work of). Con. 133: 99 Ap '54.
Argentina. Holiday 8: 12 (col.) Nov '50; 12: 106-11 (part col.) Oct '52; 13: 13 (col.) Ap '53, 13 (col.) May '53; 21: 12 (col.) May '57.
Natl. geog. 108: 756-7 (col.) Dec '55; 113: 298-351 (part col.) Mar '58.
Travel 102: 40-2 Sept. '54; 105: 12-5 Jan '56.
—— (Bariloche). Holiday 15: 13 (col.) Ap '54.
—— (gauchos). Holiday 16: 71 (col.) Jl '54.
—— (honor insignia). Int. gr. soc.: Arts . . . p. 167 (col.).

—— (lake). Holiday 22: 84-5 (col.) Sept '57.
—— (Lake Lacar). Holiday 25: 83 (col.) Feb '59.
—— (lake side). Holiday 24: 85 (col.) Oct '58.
—— (mts. & lake). Holiday 25: 101 (col.) Ap '59.
Argentina. See also Buenos Aires.
Argentine folk dancers. Natl. geog. 113: 333 (col.) Mar '58.
Argentine man (head). Holiday 26: 103 (col.) Nov '59.
—— (on horse). Holiday 26: 26 (col.) Oct '59.
Argentine stamps. See stamps, Argentine.
Argentines (play El Pato). Holiday 20: 78-9 Nov '56.
Argentinita (Encarnacion Lopez). Cur. biog. p. 29 (1942).
Arhan (sym.). Lehner: Pict. bk. of sym., p. 48.
"Ariadne" (Titian). Con. 126: 182 Dec '50.
Arias, Arnulfo. Cur. biog. p. 28 (1941).
"Aristide Bruant" (Toulouse-Lautrec). Con. 140: 81 Nov '57.
—— See also Bruant, Aristide.
arithmetic allegoric (sym). Lehner: Pict. bk. of sym., p. 9, 13.
Arizona. Holiday 15: 98-103 (col.) Mar '54; 25: 55-67 (part col.) Mar '59.
Natl. geog. 104: 344-84 (part col.) Sept '53. Travel 106: 26-7 Oct '56; 110: 40-1 Aug '58.
—— ("cook-out"). Travel 114: 30 Sept '60.
—— (desert). Holiday 12: 117 (col.) Jl '52; 13: 26-7, 30-3 (part col.) Jan '53.
—— (ghost town). See Jerome (Arizona).
—— (Grand Canyon). Face of Amer., p. 48-9 (col.).
—— (hikers). Travel 101: 31-4 Feb '54.
—— (hotel). Holiday 10: 115 (col.) Oct '51, 83 (col.) Nov '51; 12: 17 (col.) Nov '52.
—— (Oak Creek canyon). Travel 108: 40-2 Oct '57.
—— (Roosevelt dam). Brooks: Growth of a nation, p. 230.
—— (sheep trek). Natl. geog. 97: 463-78 (part col.) Ap '50.
Arizona, U.S.S. See U.S.S. Arizona memorial (Hawaii).
ark (sym.). Lehner: Pict. bk. of sym., p. 89.
ark, Noah's. See Noah's ark.
ark of Ishmael. Natl. geog. 112: 864 Dec '57.
Arkansas. Holiday 16: 34-43 (col.) Nov '54; 19: 69 (col.) Feb '56.
Arkwright, Sir Richard (Smith). Con. 145: 267 Je '60.
Arlen, Harold. Cur. biog., p. 27 (1955).
Arles (France). Natl. geog. 109: 666-99 (part col.) May '56.
"Arlington" (Robt. E. Lee home, Vir.). Amer. heri. vol. 1 no. 2 p. 25 (winter '50).
Hoilday 13: 52-5 (part col.) Jan '53.
—— (entrance, Union guard, 1864). Natl. geog. 103: 19 Jan '53.
Arlington amphitheater (Natl. cemetery). Natl. geog. 103: 10-11 (col.) Jan '53.
—— (soldier's memorial). Natl. geog. 114: 598-9 (col.) Nov '58.
Arlington memorial bridge. Natl. geog. 103: 9 (col.) Jan '53.

arm (holding hammer). Amer. heri. vol. 10 no. 2 p. 107 (Feb '59).
—— (lymphatic system). Gray's anatomy, p. 708.
—— (nervous system). Gray's anatomy, p. 964-5, 968-71.
arm & hand. Gray's anatomy, p. 1402-5, 1408, 1410.
arm bone (church of St. Paul). Natl. geog. 110: 757 (col.) Dec '56.
arm chair. See chair, arm.
Arma Virginis (syn.). Lehner: Pict. bk. of sym., p. 38.
Armada, The invincible. See Invincible Armada.
Armand, Louis. Cur. biog. p. 22 (1957).
Armenia. Holiday 19: 52-3 (col.) Feb '56.
—— (map). Holiday 19: 54 Feb '56.
Armenian "Washing-feet" pageant. Natl. geog. 98: 717 (col.) Dec '50.
Armer, Laura Adams. Jun. bk. of auth., p. 9.
"Armida falling in love with Rinaldo" (Gemignani). Con. 136: 282 Jan '56.
armillary sphere, antique. Con. 134: 87 Nov '54.
——, (1588). Con. 141: 163 May '58.
—— (sym.). Lehner: Pict. bk. of sym., p. 10.
Armistead, Brig. Gen. Lewis Addison. Amer. heri. vol. 9 no. 1 p. 45 (Dec '57).
armistice day (sym.). Lehner: Pict. bk. of sym., p. 52.
"Armistice signed" (N.Y. Times headline). Amer. heri. vol. 9 no. 4 p. 66-85 (Je '58).
Armitage, Kenneth. Cur. biog. p. 25 (1957).
armonica (B. Franklin playing). Amer. heri. vol. 10 no. 4 p. 103 (Je '59).
armor. See armour.
armorial dishes. See dishes, armorial.
Armour, Norman. Cur. biog. p. 11 (1945).
Armour, Richard. Cur. biog. p. 27 (1958).
armour (knight's armour). Amer. heri. vol. 8 no. 2 p. 108-9 (Feb '57).
Con. ency. of ant., vol. 1, p. 191-8, pl. 105-8.
Con. 144: 18-20 Sept '59.
Holiday 16: 65 Dec '54; 27: 75 (col.) May '60, 12, 71 (col.) Je '60.
Int. gr. soc.: Arts . . . p. 59, 73 (col.).
Natl. geog. 97: 757 (col.) Je '50; 103: 801 Je '53; 107: 194-5 (col.) Feb '55.
—— (knights horseback). Int. gr. soc.: Arts . . . p. 67, 73, 187 (col.).
Natl. geog. 97: 738 Je '50.
——, British (medieval). Int. gr. soc.: Arts . . . p. 73 (col.).
——, Byzantium. Int. gr. soc.: Arts . . . p. 73 (col.).
——, dog steel. Natl. geog. 107: 194 (col.) Feb '55.
——, 15th cent. Con. 132: 135 Nov '53.
——, foot-jousting. Con. 144: 43 Sept '59.
——, Genouilhac. Con. 144: 241-3 Jan '60.
——, Gothic (man, horse). Con. 142: 192 Dec '58.
——, Greenwich. Con. 141: 140-1 May '58.
——, Henry VIII. Con. 144: 241 Jan '60.
——, Italian. Con. 136: 193 Dec '55.

armour, Italian (medieval). Int. gr. soc.: Arts . . . p. 73 (col.).

——, Japanese. Con. 142: 68 Sept '58.

——, Japanese (medieval). Int. gr. soc.: Arts . . . p. 73 (col.).

——, knights (medieval). Int. gr. soc.: Arts . . . p. 73 (col.), 187 (col.).

——, Milanese (15th cent.). Con. 133: XLII Mar '54.

——, Nurnberg (16th cent.). Con. 143: 55 Mar '59.

——, Peruvian (medieval). Int. gr. soc.: Arts . . . p. 73 (col.).

——, tilting. Con. 143: LXII Je '59.

armour. See also knights (in armour).

armour laboratory. Natl. geog. 104: 814 Dec '53.

armour room (castle). Holiday 18: 17 (col.) Nov '55.

armourer's vise (Italian, 16th cent.). Con. 143: 201 May '59.

arms. See gun; firearms; pistols.

Armstrong, Charlotte. Cur. biog. p. 16 (1946).

Armstrong, David W. Cur. biog. p. 13 (1949).

Armstrong, Maj. Gen. George E. Cur. biog. p. 25 (1952).

Armstrong, Hamilton Fish. Cur. biog. p. 24 (1948).

Armstrong, Maj. Gen. Harry G. Cur. biog. p. 18 (1951).

Armstrong, James Sinclair. Cur. biog. p. 29 (1958).

Armstrong, Capt. John. Horan: Pict. hist. of wild west, p. 123.

Armstrong, Louis. Cur. biog. p. 16 (1944).

Armstrong-Jones, Antony. Cur. biog. p. 11 (1960).

army (Mass., 1645). Amer. heri. vol. 6 no. 5 p. 16-7 (col.) (Aug '56).

—— (Okinawa). Natl. geog. 97: 544 Ap '50.

——, Colonial. Holiday 16: 106-7 (col.) Jl. '54.

——, Nepalese. Natl. geog. 112: 140-1 (col.) Jl '57.

——, U.S. See U.S. army.

army camp (Civil war). Amer. heri. vol. 7 no. 2 p. 119 (Feb '56).

——, (1865). Amer. heri. vol. 11 no. 2 p. 66-7 (Feb '60).

—— (Wyo. ter.). Amer. heri. vol. 11 no. 2 p. 111 (Feb '60).

army commission, Meriwether Clark's. Natl. geog. 103: 749 Je '53.

army firing squad. See U.S. army firing squad.

army men & women (dine at waterside table). Natl. geog. 109: 807 (col.) Je '56.

army mess hall (dinner). Natl. geog. 109: 237 (col.) Feb '56.

army parade (Korea). Natl. geog. 97: 778 Je '50.

army sergeant. Holiday 28: 58 (col.) Sept '60.

Arnald, George (work of). Con. 133: 294 Je '54.

Arnall, Ellis. Cur. biog. p. 13 (1945).

Arnau, Bishop Narciso Jubany. Holiday 26: 107 (col.) Dec '59.

Arnavutkoy. Osward: Asia Minor, pl. 83.

Arnaz, Desi. Cur. biog. p. 35 (1952).

Arne, Sigrid. Cur. biog. p. 16 (1945).

Arne, Thomas Augustine (caricature by Bartolozzi). Cooper: Con. ency. of music, p. 54.

Arnest, Bernard (work of). Amer. heri. vol. 8 no. 5 p. 31 (Aug '57).

Arno, Peter. Cur. biog. p. 32 (1942).

"The Arno at Florence" (Bellotte). Con. 145: 162 May '60.

Arno river (Italy). Natl. geog. 111: 794-5 (col.) Je '57.

Arnold, Benedict. Amer. heri. vol. 7 no. 2 p. 31 (col.) (Feb '56); vol. 8 no. 6 p. 28 (Oct '57).

Arnold, Dorothy Harriet Camille. Amer. heri. vol. 11 no. 5 p. 25, 94 (Aug '60).

Arnold, Edwin G. Cur. biog. p. 14 (1947).

Arnold, Gen. Henry H. Cur. biog. p. 34 (1942).

Arnold, John. Horan: Pict. hist of wild west, p. 194.

Arnold, Gen. & Mrs. H. H. Natl. geog. 97: 400, 402, 405 Mar '50.

Arnold, Samuel. Amer. heri. vol. 8 no. 2 p. 57 (Feb '57).

Arnold, Rev. Mgr. William R. Cur. biog. p. 36 (1942).

Arnold monument. Holiday 6: 41 Sept '49.

Arnold's boot monument (Saratoga). Holiday 16: 106 Jl '54.

Arnold's home, Benedict. Amer. heri. vol. 8 no. 6 p. 28-9 (Oct '57).

"Arnolfini & his wife" (Van Eyck). Praeg. pict. ency. p. 261 (col.).

"Arnolfini marriage portrait" (Van Eyck). Con. 140: 274 Jan '58.

Arnon, Daniel I. Cur. biog. p. 29 (1955).

Arnow, Harriette. Cur. biog. p. 36 (1954).

Arnstein, Daniel. Cur. biog. p. 37 (1942).

Aron, Raymond. Cur. biog. p. 37 (1954).

Aronin, Jeffrey Ellis. Cur. biog. p. 31 (1955).

Aronson, John Hugo. Cur. biog. p. 39 (1954).

Arp. Jean. Cur. biog. p. 41 (1954).

—— (concrete figure). Praeg. pict. ency., p. 463.

arquebus, antique. Con. ency. of ant., vol. 1, pl. 112.

——, German. Con. 143: 267 Je '59.

Arquette, Cliff. Cur. biog. p. 13 (1961).

Arrau, Claudio. Cur. biog. p. 39 (1942). Holiday 22: 121 Sept '57.

"The Arrival" (Lesur). Con. 136: XLIV Nov '55.

"Arrival at the Isle of Love" (Pater). Con. 127: 27 (col.) Mar '51.

"Arrival of St. Paul at Malta" (Spada). Con. 142: 143 Dec '58.

arrow heads, Indian. Natl. geog. 110: 548 Oct '56.

Arrowhead Springs (Cal.). Holiday 8: 25-31 Oct '50.

arrows (woman fletching with feathers). Natl. geog. 99: 306 (col.) Mar '51.

arrows & yoke (sym.). Lehner: Pict. bk. of sym., p. 94.

arrows, bundle of (sym.). Lehner: Pict. bk. of sym., p. 83.

——, five (Five nations sym.). Amer. heri. vol. 6 no. 2 p. 29 (winter '55).

Arroyo Del Rio, Carlos Alberto. Cur. biog. p. 41 (1942).

arsenal, Colonial Va. Natl. geog. 106: 450 (col.) Oct '54.

arsenic sulphur (sym.). Lehner: Pict. bk. of sym., p. 72.

art (industry). Con. 138: 10-11 Sept '56.
——, **Amer.** Con. ency. of ant., vol. 3 pl. 89-96.
Holiday 10: 42-3 (col.) Nov '51.
——, **Amer. (early portrait).** Amer. heri. vol. 1 no. 4 p. 46-9 (part col.) (Summer '50).
——, **Amer. Indian.** Natl. geog. 107: 353-77 (part col.) Mar '55.
——, **Amer. primitive.** Amer. heri. vol. 2 no. 2 p. 44-5, 47, 75 (col.) (winter '51); vol. 6 no. 2 p. 38-47 (part col.) (winter '55).
——, **Assyrian.** Ceram: March of arch., p. 202.
——, **Byzantine.** See Byzantine art.
——, **Caribbean.** Holiday 19: 15 (col.) May '56; 20: 168 (col.) Nov '56; 22: 96 (col.) Sept '57, 146 (col.) Oct '57, 2 (col.) Nov '57.
——, **Catacombs.** See Catacombs art.
——, **cave.** See cave art.
——, **chalk & water color.** Int. gr. soc.: Arts . . . p. 133 (col.).
——, **children's.** Natl. geog. 111: 367-87 (part col.) Mar '57.
——, **church.** Holiday 25: 84 (col.) Mar '59.
——, **Dominican Republic.** Holiday 20: 68 (col.) Sept '56.
——, **Dutch.** Con. 126: 134-6 Oct '50; 127: 123 May '51; 135: 199 May '55; 136: 275 (col.) Jan '56; 139: 102-3 (col.) Ap '57, LXV (col.) May '57; 140: 116-8 (part col.) Nov '57.
——, **eclesiastical.** Con. 140: 172-5 Dec '57.
——, **Egyptian (tomb).** Natl. geog. 108: 622, 627, 630-1 (col.) Nov '55.
——, **18th cent.** Con. 135: 4-11 Mar '55; 140: 29-32 Sept '57.
——, **expressionism.** Praeg. pict. ency., p. 13.
——, **famous.** Int. gr. soc.: Arts . . . p. 133 (col.).
——, **Flemish.** Con. 133: 229 Je '54; 138: 216-7 Jan '57; 139: 102-3 (col.) Ap '57, 204 May '57.
——, **Flemish (primitive).** Con. 126: 3-10 Aug '50; 127: 45 Mar '51.
——, **folk.** See Penn. Dutch folk art.
——, **French.** Con. 135: 40-4 Mar '55; 137: 135-40 Ap '56; 141: 37-41 Mar '58.
——, **French (18th cent.).** Con. 133: 61-6 Mar '54; 140: 29-32 Sept '57.
——, **German.** Con. 138: 136-40 Nov '56.
——, **impressionists.** Con. 140: 80-1 Nov '57.
——, **India.** Con. 139: 78-81 Ap '57.
——, **Indian.** See art, Amer. Indian.
——, **Italian.** Con. 138: 118-20 Nov '56; 145: 39-40 Mar '60.
Holiday 19: 44-5 (col.) Jan '56.
——, **Italian (Palazzo Corsini).** Con. 138: 160-5 Dec '56.
——, **Japanese.** See Japanese art.
Japanese color prints
——, **modern.** Con. 145: XLV Ap '60, 207-8 May '60.
Holiday 25: 84 (col.) Mar '59.
Praeg. pict. ency., p. 453, 455, 463-4, 467, 478-9, 481-3, 486-8 (col.), 494-5, 504-6 (col.), 508-12 (col.) 514-5.
——, **New Guinea wood carving.** See New Guinea wood carving.
——, **19th cent.** Con. 139: IX-XI (col.) Je '57; 141: XXVI-XXVII Mar '58.
——, **Palestinian (carving 5th cent).** Con. 133: 269 Je '54.

——, **primitive (Hunter).** Holiday 19: 115 (col.) Mar '56.
——, **Puerto Rican.** See Puerto Rican art.
——, **Renaissance.** Natl. geog. 113: 264-5 (col.) Feb '58.
——, **revolution in.** Int. gr. soc.: Arts . . . p. 89 (col.).
——, **Roman (1600 yrs. old).** Natl. geog. 111: 210-28 (col.) Feb '57.
——, **Russian (13-20th cent).** Con. 143: 28-31 Mar '59.
——, **Scandinavian.** See Scandinavian art.
——, **Spanish-Indian religious.** Holiday 14: 57 (col.) Dec '53.
——, **Swedish.** See Swedish art.
——, **Venezuelan.** Holiday 20: 15 (col.) Aug '56.
——, **Veronese.** Con. 143: 36-8 Mar '59.
——, **western.** Amer. heri. vol. 6 no. 1 p. 33-41 (col.) (fall '54).
art. See also name of artist.
name of picture.
art carving. Rawson: Ant. pict. bk., p. 92.
art class (life models). Holiday 10: 52 (col.) Oct '51.
art collection. Holiday 12: 38-9 (col.) Oct '52.
"The Art dealers" (Vuillard). Con. 133: 287 Je '54.
art display. Holiday 22: 173-80 (part col.) Dec '57.
art exhibit. Holiday 27: 80 May '60.
——, **outdoor.** Holiday 20: 49 (col.) Oct '56.
——, **sidewalk.** Natl. geog. 103: 153 (col.) Feb '53.
——, **world-wide.** Holiday 22: 94-5 (col.) Nov '57.
art fakes. Con. ency. of ant., vol. 3 pl. 97-100.
art forgery. See art fakes.
art gallery (drawing by Smith). Amer. heri. vol. 7 no. 4 p. 40-3 (Je '56).
—— **(exhibits).** Natl. geog. 113: 252-76 (part col.) Feb '58.
——, **(int.).** Holiday 14: 153 Dec '53.
——, **Beaverbrook.** Con. 145: 179 May '60.
——, **Buffalo (N.Y.).** Travel 103: inside cover Mar '55.
——, **London.** Con. 140: XLIV Nov '57.
——, **Parke-Bernet (N.Y.).** Con. 140: LIV Nov '57; 141: LV Ap '58; 142: XLVIII Sept '58, LV Nov '58, LVIII Dec '58, LXX Jan '59; 143: LV Mar '59, LII Ap '59, LXXIII May '59, LXX Je '59; 144: LXIV Sept '59, LXI Nov '59, LXXVII Dec '59, LXXIX Jan '60; 145: LVII Mar '60, LXXXVIII May '60, LXXVI Je '60.
——, **Santa Fe.** Holiday 15: 147 (col.) Je '54.
——, **Washington Natl.** Natl. geog. 110: 620-57 (part col.) Nov '56.
art museum, Belgium. Natl. geog. 107: 646 (col.) May '55.
——, **Guggenheim** See Guggenheim museum of art.
art, museum of modern (N.Y.). Holiday 14: 56-63 Nov '53.
art museum, Philadelphia. See Philadelphia (art museum).
art studio. Holiday 11: 46 (col.) Ap '52; 22: 64-5 Jl '57.
—— See also Artist's floating studio.

Artaud, William (self portrait). Con. 137: 179 May '56.
—— (work of). Con. 137: 180-1 May '56.
Artemis (sym.). Lehner: Pict. bk. of sym., p. 32.
arteries, human. Gray's anatomy, p. 581-646.
Arthur, Chester A. Amer. heri. vol. 7 no. 3 p. 32 (Ap '56).
Holiday 8: 46 Aug '50.
Jensen: The White House, p. 129.
Arthur, J. A. (work of). Amer. heri. vol. 10 no. 2 p. 15 (Feb '59).
Arthur, Jean. Cur. biog. p. 17 (1945).
Arthur, Jean (as "Calamity Jane"). Amer. heri. vol. 11 no. 5 p. 38 (Aug '60).
artifacts (archaeology). Natl. geog. 118: 816 (col.) Dec '60.
artillery, antique. Holiday 13: 49 (col.) May '53.
artillery company, English. Natl. geog. 103: 824 (col.) Je '53.
artillerymen, Royal Scotch. Natl. geog. 112: 462 (col.) Oct '57.
artist. Holiday 18: 98-9 (col.) Aug '55; 25: 39 (col.) Jan '59.
—— (beard, comic. Holiday 28: 9 Aug '60.
—— (designing tapestry). Natl. geog. 113: 834 (col.) Je '58.
—— (drawing). Holiday 11: 46 (col.) Ap '52.
—— (drawing map). Natl. geog. 113: 271 (col.) Feb '58.
—— (exhibit). Travel 104: inside cover Oct '55.
—— (exhibit, sidewalk). Holiday 27: 167 (col.) Ap '60.
—— (girl, sand dunes). Natl. geog. 108: 524 (col.) Oct '55.
—— (model). Natl. geog. 117: 741 (col.) Je '60.
—— (needle painting). Natl. geog. 115: 187 (col.) Feb '59.
—— (painting). Holiday 10: 53 (col.), 62, 64 Oct '51, 95 Nov '51; 11: 40 Jan '52, 77 (col.) Feb '52; 12: 49, 73 (col.) Sept '52, 57 (col.) Oct '52; 13: 30, 88, 115 (col.), 147 Ap '53; 16: 25 (col.) Nov '54; 24: 2 (col.) Jl '58; 25: 74 Mar '59, 45 (col.) Ap '59.
Natl. geog. 99: 362 (col.) Mar '51; 100: 312 (col.) Sept '51, 623 (col.) Nov '51; 102: 31 (col.) Jl '52; 104: 380 (col.) Sept '53; 105: 542 (col.) Ap '54; 106: 795 (col.) Dec '54; 107: 15 (col.) Jan '55, 317 (col.), 351 Mar '55, 643 (col.) May '55; 111: 480 (col.) Ap '57; 112: 689 (col.) Nov '57; 118: 787 (col.) Dec '60.
Travel 101: 21 May '54; 106: 54 Nov '56; 109: 27 Je '58; 110: 19 Sept '58.
—— (painting, beach). Holiday 10: 41 (col.) Aug '51.
—— (painting, harbor). Natl. geog. 111: 628 (col.) May '57.
—— (painting, Harpers Ferry). Natl geog. 111: 412-3 (col.) Mar '57.
—— (painting miniatures). Natl. geog. 99: 755 (col.) Je '51.
—— (painting, Nigeria). Natl. geog. 116: 242 Aug '59.
—— (painting tiles). Natl. geog. 116: 494 (col.) Oct '59.
—— (renew pictures). Natl. geog. 113: 255 (col.) Feb '58.
—— (repair war damage). Natl. geog. 99: 755 (col.) Je '51.

—— (sand painting). Natl. geog. 112: 722 (col.) Nov '57.
—— (satellite picture). Natl. geog. 109: 489 (col.) Ap '56.
—— (showing picture). Amer. heri. vol. 11 no. 5 p. 10 (col.) (Aug '60).
—— (teaching boys). Natl. geog. 108: 756 (col.) Dec '55.
—— (wood chip worker). Natl. geog. 100: 138 Jl '51.
artist, Iranian. Natl. geog. 100: 455 (col.) Oct '51.
——, Mycenaean (painting vase, ancient). Int. gr. soc.: Arts . . . p. 19 (col.).
——, Negro (painting). Holiday 10: 152 Nov '51.
——, sidewalk. Natl. geog. 98: 50-1 (col.) Jl '50.
artists. Int. gr. soc.: Arts . . . p. 91 (col.).
—— (in bar, cartoon). Holiday 23: 48-9 Jan '58.
—— (life models). Holiday 10: 52 (col.) Oct '51.
—— (man & woman). Natl. geog. 109: 247 (col.) Feb '56.
artist's floating studio. Natl. geog. 106: 808 (col.) Dec '55.
artist's table (16th cent). Con. 126: 139 Oct '50.
arts (deity of). Lehner: Pict. bk. of sym., p. 49.
—— (goddess of). Lehner: Pict. bk. of sym., p. 30.
—— (symbols). Lehner: Pict. bk. of sym., p. 9-22.
——, triangle of. Lehner: Pict. bk. of sym., p. 70.
arts & crafts, Amer. (early). Amer. heri., vol. 2 no. 2 p. 32-3, 35 (winter '51).
Artzybasheff, Boris. Cur. biog. p. 19 (1945) Jun. bk of auth., p. 10.
Aruba Caribbean hotel-Casino. Travel 112: 49 Sept '59.
Aruba island. Travel 105: 15-9 Feb '56.
Arundel castle keep (England). Holiday 23: 90 (col.) Ap '58.
Aryton, Michael (work of). Cooper: Con. ency. of music, p. 149.
Asa, King (Mizpah). Natl. geog. 118: 818 (col.) Dec '60.
Asaf Ali. Cur. biog. p. 15 (1947).
Asakai, Koichiro. Cur. biog. p. 27 (1957).
Asam, Egid Quirin (work of). Con. 142: 4 Sept '58.
Praeg. pict. ency., p. 331.
Ascalon statues. Travel 104: 10 Aug '55.
ascension (sym.). Lehner: Pict. bk. of sym., p. 27.
Ascension Island. Natl. geog. 116: 458-9 (col.) Oct '59.
"Ascension of Virgin" (alter piece). Praeg. pict. ency., p. 244.
Asclepius (sym.). Lehner: Pict. bk. of sym., p. 30.
Ascoli, Max. Cur. biog. p. 43 (1954).
Ascot gold cup (1877). Con. 126: 224 Dec '50.
Asgeirsson, Asgeir. Cur. biog. p. 26 (1952).
ash tray. Holiday 28: 7 Sept '60.
—— (cigarettes). Holiday 12: 113 Dec '52; 19: 156 (col.) May '56; 20: 10 (col.) Sept '56; 27: 157 (col.) Je '60.
——, antique. Con. 141: XLVII Mar '58.
——, antique silver. Con. 132: XIII Sept '53.
Ashcroft, Dame Peggy. Cur. biog. (1963).

Asheville (N.C.). Holiday 24: 13 Jl '58. Travel 106: 21 Aug '56.
Ashford castle (Ireland). Travel 101: 32 May '54.
Ashida, Hitoshi. Cur. biog. p. 27 1948).
"Ashland" (home of Henry Clay). Amer. heri. vol. 7 no. 6 p. 29 (Oct '56).
Ashmore, Harry S. Cur. biog. p. 11 (1958).
Ashton, Frederick. Cur. biog. p. 20 (1951).
Ashton, Thomas (Reynolds). Con. 143: 84 Ap '59.
Ashur (gateway). Natl. geog. 99: 97 (col.) Jan '51.
Ashurbanipal (Assyrian king). Int. gr. soc.: Arts . . . p. 29 (col.).
Asia. Natl. geog. 117: 70-111 (part col.) Jan '60.
—— (architecture). Int. gr. soc.: Arts . . . p. 85 (col).
—— (Bhutan). Natl. geog. 102: 714-52 (part col.) Dec '52.
—— (dancers) *See* dancers (Asia).
"Asia" (Tiepolo). Praeg. pict. ency., p. 321 (col).
Asian temples, south-east *See* temples, southeast Asia.
Asimov, Isaac. Cur. biog. p. 34 (1953).
Askey, E. Vincent. Cur. biog. p. 15 (1961).
Aspen music festival headquarters (Colo.). Holiday 27: 242 May '60.
Aspendos amphitheatre (near Antalya). Osward: Asia Minor, pl. VI (col.).
Assam (Tibet). Natl. geog. 101: 410-16 Mar '52.
Assereto, Gioachino (work of). Con. 132: 4 Sept '53.
Assiniboin Indian. Amer. heri. vol. 6 no. 1 p. 34 (fall '54).
Assis Chateaubriand, Bandeira de Mello. Cur. biog. p. 29 (1957).
Assisi (church of St. Francis). Holiday 16: 98 Sept '54 (col.).
"Assumption" (Piazzetta). Con. 142: 5 Sept '58.
"Assumption of Blessed Virgin" (altar). Praeg. pict. ency., p. 331.
"Assumption of the Virgin" (Giordano). Con. 136: LXIII Dec '55.
Assyria. Natl. geog. 99: 43-104 (col.) Jan '51.
Assyrian archer (ancient). Int. gr. soc.: Arts . . . p. 33 (col.).
Assyrian art *See* art, Assyrian.
Assyrian costume (ancient). Int. gr. soc.: Arts . . . p. 29 (col.).
Assyrian relief *See* relief, Assyrian.
Assyrian winged bull *See* winged bull, Assyrian.
Astaire, Fred. Cur. biog. p. 19 (1945). Holiday 23: 149 Je '58.
asteroids (sym.). Lehner: Pict. bk. of sym., p. 20-1.
Astin, Allen V. Cur. biog. p. 21 (1956).
Astley, Philip (circus founder). Durant: Pict. hist. of Amer. circus, p. 16.
Astley's amphitheatre (18th cent.). Con. 126: 186-89 Dec '50.
Astor, John Jacob. Amer. heri. vol. 9 no. 5 p. 61 (Aug '58).
Astor, Col. John Jacob. Cur. biog. p. 45 (1954).
Astor, Mary. Cur. biog. p. 17 (1961).
Astoria (Oregon, 1813). Brooks: Growth of a nation, p. 97.
Astoria fort & fur trading post (Warre). Amer. heri. vol. 9 no. 5 p. 58-9 (col.) (Aug '58).

astrolabe. Natl. geog. 110: 9 (col.) Jl '56; 118: 627 (col.) Nov '60.
——, **antique.** Con. 139: 194 May '57.
——, **Flemish.** Con. 132: 124 Nov '53.
——, **16th cent.** Con. 139: XLVIII Ap '57, LXII May '57; 143: 104 Ap '59.
——, **13-19th cent.** Con. 134: 85-6 Nov '54.
astrology (sym.). Lehner: Pict. bk. of sym., 22-5, 67.
astronaut (weightless). Natl. geog. 118: 53 Jl 60.
astronauts, U. S. Natl. geog. 118: 54-5 (col.) Jl 60.
astronomical dial. Con. 136: 9 Sept '55.
astronomical instruments (India). Natl. geog. 100: 737 (col.) Dec '51.
astronomical ring (antique). Con. 134: 87 Nov '54.
astronomy. Natl. geog. 115: 670-8 (part col.) May '59.
—— (map). Natl. geog. 98: 406, 410-11, 414-5 Sept '50.
—— (muse of). Lehner: Pict. bk. of sym., p. 33.
—— (sky survey). Natl. geog. 110: 781-90 Dec '56.
—— (sym.). Lehner: Pict. bk. of sym., p. 9-10.
Aswell, James. Cur. biog. p. 22 (1951).
"At the altar" (Lahrtmann). Con. 134: 206 Dec '54.
"At the tavern" (Brouwer). Praeg. pict. ency., p. 343.
"At the window" (Boldini). Con. 134: 206 Dec '54.
"At the window" (Bonnard). Praeg. pict. ency., p. 462 (col.).
Atacama desert (Chile). Natl. geog. 117: 230-1 (col.) Feb '60.
"Atahualpa & retinue received by Spaniards". Amer. heri. vol. 6 no. 5 p. 103 (Aug '55).
Ataq (walled fort). Natl. geog. 111: 238 Feb '57.
Ataturk (statue). Osward: Asia Minor, pl. 153.
Ataturk's mausoleum. Osward: Asia Minor, pl. 149, 151.
Ataturk's sarcophagus (Ankara). Osward: Asia Minor, pl. 151.
Ataturk's tomb. Natl. geog. 117: 600-1 (col.) May '60.
Atcheson, George, jr. Cur. biog. p. 18 (1946).
"Athena" (head, Greek statue). Con. ency. of ant., vol. 3, pl. 67.
"Athena" (sculpture). Praeg. pict. ency., p. 133.
"Athena pouring wine for Hercules" (chalice). Praeg. pict. ency. p. 151 (col.).
Athenaeum library, Boston (int.). Natl. geog. 97: 304 (col.) Mar '50.
Athenagoras I, Patriarch. Cur. biog. p. 15 (1949).
Athena's temple (Greece). Holiday 12: 56 (col.) Sept '52.
Athene (sym.). Lehner: Pict. bk. of sym., p. 30.
Athene bearing arms (Greek vase). Ceram: March of arch., p. 30 (col.).
Athens (Greece). Holiday 12: 57 (col.) Sept '52; 20: 124 (col.) Oct '56.
Natl. geog. 100: 729-30 (col.) Dec '51; 109: 38 (col.) Jan '56; 110: 744-5 (col.) Dec '56; 117: 636- (col.) May '60.
Travel 113: 28- Ap '60; 114: 24-9 Aug '60.
—— (harbor). Travel 102: 36 Sept '54.
—— (Hilton hotel). Travel 114: 27 Aug '60.

Athens (map). Travel 114: 23 Aug '60.
—— (Parthenon) *See* Parthenon.
Atherton, Warren H. Cur. biog. p. 15 (1943).
athlete (horseback, comic). Holiday 21: 14 May '57.
—— (pole vaulter). Natl. geog. 113: 295 Feb '58.
—— (running). Holiday 18: 26 Jl '55; 28: 187 Nov '60.
——, Cretan (ancient). Int. gr. soc.: Arts . . . p. 29 (col.).
athletes, Ali follower. Natl. geog. 104: 17 (col.) Jl '53.
——, Greek. Natl. geog. 104: 704 (col.) Nov '53.
——, Greek (Olympic games, ancient). Int. gr. soc.: Arts . . . p. 39 (col.).
——, India (camels). Natl. geog. 118: 470 (col.) Oct '60.
——, Israeli. Natl. geog. 98: 746 (col.) Dec '50.
——, Peking. Natl. geog. 118: 206-7 (col.) Aug '60.
athletes kissing, French. Holiday 21: 55 Ap '57.
Atillan, Lake. *See* Lake Atillan.
Atkins, Dave. Horan: Pict. hist. of wild west, p. 195.
Atkins, Mary (portrait by Ramsay). Con. 138: XI Sept '56.
Atkinson, Brooks. Cur. biog. p. 44 (1942); p. 19 (1961).
Holiday 17: 95 Jan '55.
Atkinson, Edward. Amer. heri. vol. 11 no. 4 p. 33 (Je '60).
Atkinson, Lt. Gen. Joseph. Cur. biog. p. 23 (1956).
Atkinson, Oriana. Cur. biog. p. 35 (1953).
Atlanta (Ga). Natl. geog. 105: 296 (col.) Mar '54.
—— (Civil war battle). Amer. heri. vol. 7 no. 2 p. 32-43 (col.) (Feb '56).
Brooks: Growth of a nation, p. 145.
Natl. geog. 105: 309 Mar '54.
"Atlanta & a warrior" (Moitte terracotta). Con. 140: 6 Sept '57.
Atlantic City. Holiday 18: 14 Jl '55.
Natl. geog. 117: 42-5 (col.) Jan '60.
Travel 114: 37-8 Aug '60.
—— (beach). Holiday 12: 91 (col.) Aug '52.
—— (1815-). Amer. heri. vol. 5 no. 4 p. 4-9 (summer '54).
—— (skyline). Jordan: Hammond's pict. atlas, p. 43 (col.).
Atlas (holding world). Holiday 25: 27 Ap '59.
—— (sym.). Lehner. Pict. bk. of sym., p. 32.
ato (council hut). Holiday 18: 92 Aug '55.
atom. Natl. geog. 105: 72-90 Jan '54; 114: 304-53 (part col.) Sept '58.
—— (shattered). Natl. geog. 109: 289 Feb '56.
—— (sym.). Lehner: Pict. bk. of sym., p. 15.
atomic blasting. Natl. geog. 103: 842-48 Je '53.
atomic clock. *See* clock, atomic.
atomic cloud (stone formation). Natl. geog. 114: 503 (col.) Oct '58.
atomic laboratory (worker). Natl. geog. 105: 75 Jan '54.
atomic mushroom cloud (over Nagasaki). Natl. geog. 112: 288 Aug '57.
atomic power reactor. Natl. geog. 114: 316-7 (col.) Sept '58.
atomic projects (Cal.). Holiday 8: 50 Dec '50.

atomic show. Natl. geog. 107: 775 (col.) Je '55.
atomic submarine. Natl. geog. 112: 333 Sept '57.
atomic tanker. Natl. geog. 115: 22-3 Jan '59.
atomium tower (Brussels fair). Natl. geog. 113: 798 Je '58.
Atotonilco shrine (Mexico). Travel 101: 20 Mar '54.
atrium, Salerno cathedral. Labande: Naples, p. 188.
"Attack on Fort MacKenzie". Amer. heri. vol. 6 no. 1 p. 34 (col.) (fall '54).
"Attack on the supply train" (Remington). Amer. heri. vol. 6 no. 1 p. 39 (col.) (fall '54).
Attalea. *See* Antalaya.
Attanasio, N. (work of). Con. 132: LVIII Jan '54.
Attaway, William. Cur. biog. p. 30 (1941).
Attell, Abe. Amer. heri. vol. 11 no. 4 p. 26 (Je '60).
"Attentive nurse". Natl. geog. 101: 85 (col.) Jan '52.
Attic Amphora (800 B.C.). Praeg. pict. ency. p. 139 (col.).
Attlee, Clement Richard. Cur. biog. p. 17 (1947).
attributes, the six. *See* The six attributes.
Atwood, Donna. Cur. biog. p. 47 (1954).
Atzerodt, George A. Amer. heri. vol. 8 no. 2 p. 57 (Feb '57).
Auburn (Colonial home). Jordan: Hammond's pict. atlas, p. 87 (col.).
Auchincloss, Louis. Cur. biog. p. 48 (1954).
Auchinleck, Gen. Sir Claude. Cur. biog. p. 46 (1942).
Auckland univ. (clock tower). Natl. geog. 101: 429 (col.) Ap '52.
auction (antiques). Natl. geog. 109: 454 Ap '56.
—— (dog day). Natl. geog. 99: 817 Je '51.
auction room, flower (Holland). Natl. geog. 98: 748 Dec '50.
auctioneer stand, state fair. Natl. geog. 106: 307 (col.) Sept '54.
Audubon, J. J. L. (work of). Con. ency. of ant. vol. 3 pl. 81.
Audubon, John (by J. J. Audubon). Amer. heri. vol. 11 no. 1 p. 15 (col.) (Dec '59).
Audubon, John & Victor (work of). Natl. geog. 99: 191 (col.) Feb '51.
Audubon, John James (birds, animals, insects). Amer. heri. vol. 11 no. 1 p. 18-23 (col.) (Dec '59).
—— (by his sons). Amer. heri. vol. 11 no. 1 p. 12 (col.) Dec '59.
Natl. geog. 99: 191 (col.) Feb '51.
—— (landscape by). Amer. heri. vol. 11 no. 1 p. 16-7 (col.) (Dec '59).
—— (portraits by). Amer. heri. vol. 11 no. 1 p. 14-5 (part col.) (Dec '59).
Audubon, Lucy (Mrs. J. J. Audubon). Amer. heri. vol. 11 no. 1 p. 15 (col.) (Dec '59).
Audubon, Victor (by J. J. Audubon). Amer. heri. vol. 11 no. 1 p. 15 (col.) (Dec '59).
Audubon home, John James (N.Y. City). Amer. heri. vol. 11 no. 1 p. 94 (Dec '59).
Audubon shrine (Phila.). Natl. geog. 118: 164-5 Aug '60.
Auerbach-Levy, William. Cur. biog. p. 29 (1948).
auger, pod. Rawson: Ant. pict. bk., p. 21.

Augsburg town hall. Praeg. pict. ency., p. 305.
augury (sym.). Lehner: Pict. bk. of sym. p. 67.
Augusta of Saxe Gotha (Princess of Wales).
Amer. heri. vol. 11 no. 4 p. 10 (col.) (Je '60).
Augustinian hermits. Holiday 23: 54-5 (col.)
May '58.
Augustus, Emperor (1st cent. cameo). Praeg.
pict. ency., p. 193 (col.).
Augustus, William (bust). Con. 145: XXXIII
Ap '60.
Augustus, Temple of. See Temple of Augustus
(Ancyra).
Augustus of Primaporta. Praeg. pict. ency., p.
146.
Aulaire, Edgar d'. Jun. bk. of auth., p. 12.
Aulaire, Ingri d'. Jun. bk. of auth., p. 12.
Aurelius, Marcus (bust). Con. 144: 134 Nov '59.
Aurelius column, Marcus. See column, Marcus
Aurelius.
Auriol, Jacqueline. Cur. biog. p. 36 (1953).
Auriol, Vincent. Cur. biog. p. 22 (1947).
Aurobindo, Shri (India's Man-God). Holiday 6:
73 Sept '49.
Aurora Australia (South Pole). Natl. geog. 116:
532-3 (col.) Oct '59.
Aurora Borealis. Natl. geog. 109: 777 Je '56.
Auroral tube. Natl. geog. 112: 803 (col.) Dec
'57.
Ausable chasm (N.Y.). Jordan: Hammond's
pict. atlas, p. 39 (col.).
Austen, Alice (1st great woman photographer).
Holiday 12: 66 Sept '52.
Austin, Margretta. Cur. biog. p. 50 (1954).
Austin, Warren R. Cur. biog. p. 19 (1944).
Australia. Holiday 8: 98-108 (part col.) Nov '50.
Natl. geog. 109: 234-59 (part col.) Feb '56;
111: 2-48 (part col.) Jan '57.
—— (Aborigines). Natl. geog. 103: 130-41 Jan
'53.
—— (canoe race). Travel 107: 28-31 Mar '57.
—— (Great barrier reef). See Great barrier
reef.
—— (hotel). Travel 114: 56 Dec '60.
—— (Houses of Parliament, Canberra). Holiday
8: 99 (col.) Nov '50.
—— (lorikeets). Natl. geog. 110: 511-18 (col.)
Oct '56.
—— (map). Natl. geog. 109: 241 Feb '56, 425
Mar '56; 110: 690 Nov '56; 112: 587 Nov
'57; 114: 517 Oct '58.
Travel 105: 15 Mar '56.
—— (Melbourne). Holiday 20: 166 (col.) Dec
'56.
Natl. geog. 110: 688-93 Nov '56.
—— (Melville island). Natl. geog. 109: 418-40
(part col.) Mar '56.
—— (northern part). Travel 108: 56-7 Oct '57.
—— (Tasmania). Natl. geog. 110: 792-818
(part col.) Dec '56.
Austria. Disney: People & places, p. 53-6 (col.).
Holiday 19: 98-103 (part col.) Je '56.
Natl. geog. 99: 750-90 (part col.) Je '51; 115:
172-213 (col.) Feb '59.
Travel 105: 51 Ap '56; 109: 46-7 Ap '58.
—— (Alpine). Natl. geog. 118: 246-75 (part
col.) Aug '60.
—— (castle). Travel 111: 22 Ap '59.
—— (map). Holiday 19: 100 Je '56.
Natl. geog. 99: 750-1 Je '51; 115: 181 Feb
'59; 118: 250 (col.) Aug '60.

Travel 103: 22 Je '55.
—— (Oberndorf). Travel 108: 29-31 Dec '57.
—— (patron saint of). Lehner: Pict. bk. of
sym., p. 39.
—— (Russian zone). Travel 103: 22-5 Je '55.
—— (villages, Alps). Holiday 25: 73-7 (part
col.) Jan '59.
Austrian costume. Natl. geog. 99: 777, 780-4
(col.) Je '51.
—— dancers. Natl. geog. 115: 210-11 (col.)
Feb '59.
—— dancers (costumed). Travel 101: cover
Jan '54.
—— men & girls. Holiday 21: 116 Jan '57.
Austrian Tyrol. Holiday 12:: 110 (col.) Sept '52;
15: 146 (col.) Ap '54.
Austrians (heads). Natl. geog. 118: 272-3 (col.)
Aug '60.
authority, democratic (sym.). Lehner: Pict. bk.
of sym., p. 94.
——, monarchistic (sym.). Lehner: Pict. bk. of
sym., p. 94.
——, oriental (sym). Lehner: Pict. bk. of sym.,
p. 94.
——, Papal (sym.). Lehner: Pict. bk. of sym.,
p. 94.
authors. Cur. biog. (all issues).
Jun. bk. of authors (all issues).
Int. gr. soc.: Arts . . . p. 137 (col.).
autoharp. Holiday 19: 168 May '56; 20: 181
Nov '56.
automat, outdoor (Holland). Natl. geog. 98: 778
Dec '50.
automobile. Holiday (in most issues).
Natl. geog. 97: 821 Je '50; 100: 182, 194
(col.) Aug '51; 101: 154 (col.) Feb '52; 102:
362 (col.) Sept '52; 106: 540, 577 Oct '54,
838 (col.) Dec '54; 107: 239 (col.) Feb '55,
759 Je '55; 110: 199 (col.) Aug '56; 111:
777 (col.) Je '57; 113: 140 Jan '58, 662
May '58, 797 (col.) Je '58; 114: 444-5
(col.) Oct '58, 670 Nov '58; 115: 470 (col.),
501 Ap '59; 116: 608 (col.) Nov '59, 766
Dec '59; 117: 312 (col.) Mar '60.
Travel 101: 13 Mar '54; 103: cover, 8-9, 24
Jan '55, 32 May '55, 44 Je '55; 104: 39
Nov '55; 105: 45, 59 Jan '56, 73 Feb '56,
47, 61 Ap '56, 45 May '56; 106: 56 Nov
'56; 107: 57 Mar '57, 57 Je '57; 110: 14
Aug '58, 26 Oct '58; 111: 20 Mar '59, 27
May '59; 112: 20, 44 Aug '59.
—— (antique). Amer. heri. vol. 4 no. 3 back
cover (col.) (spring '53); vol. 5 no. 4 back
cover (col.) (summer '54); vol. 9 no. 1, p.
88 (Dec '57); vol. 10 no. 4 p. 58 (col.)
(Je '59).
Holiday 7: 75 Je '50.
Natl. geog. 104: 742 Dec '53.
Travel 103: 15 Ap '55; 108: 52 Dec '57;
111: 65 Je '59.
—— (antique, 43 yrs. old). Holiday 11: 32 May
'52.
—— (antique, 1906). Amer. heri. vol. 1 no. 2
p. 60 (winter '60).
—— (antique, 19th cent.). Holiday 12: 70 Sept
'52.
—— (antique, 36 yrs. old). Holiday 12: 140 Oct
'52.
—— (being pushed out of ruts). Natl. geog. 114:
18 (col.) Jl '58.

automobile (campers). Natl. geog. 113: 603 (col.) May '58.
—— (carried by Nepalese). Natl. geog. 97: 35 (col.) Jan '50.
—— (cartoon). Holiday 14: 124 Dec '53.
—— (children). Natl. geog. 108: 195 (col.) Aug '55.
—— (comic). Amer. heri. vol. 8 no. 4 p. 66 (Je '57).
Holiday 24: 45 Dec '58.
——, (dog on seat). Holiday 12: 117 (col.) Nov '52.
—— (family, comic). Holiday 21: 151 Ap '57.
—— (girl on hood). Natl. geog. 101: 784 Je '52.
—— (in flood). Natl. geog. 101: 484 (col.) Ap '52.
—— (in tree tunnel). Natl. geog. 105: 802 (col.) Je. '54.
—— (lions). Holiday 18: 145 (col.) Nov '55; 20: 69 (col.) Oct '56.
—— (man, comic). Holiday 20: 63 Aug '56.
—— (man, girls waving). Holiday 21: 17 (col.) Feb '57.
—— (man, woman cleaning). Natl. geog. 108: 214 (col.) Aug '55.
—— (men building). Natl. geog. 115: 799 (col.) Je '59.
—— (park, bears). Natl. geog. 109: 622 May '56.
—— (parking lot). Brooks: growth of a nation, p. 269.
—— (people, bears near). Holiday 23: 147 May '58.
—— (stuck in mud). Brooks: Growth of a nation, p. 240.
—— (swamp). Natl. geog. 113: 98 Jan '58.
—— (travelers). Travel 103: 60 May '55.
—— (tunnel). Natl. geog. 117: 756 (col.) Je '60.
—— (woman, child). Natl. geog. 108: 205 (col.) Aug '55.
—— (woman, mts., snow). Natl. geog. 109: 313 (col.) Mar '56.
—— (women). Natl. geog. 114: 5 (col.) Jl '58.
automobile types (Ambassador). Holiday 25: 124 Je '59; 26: 27 Jl '59, 87 Aug '59; 27: 86 (col.) Jan '60, 20 (col.) Mar '60; 28: 80 (col.) Jl '60, 7 (col.) Nov '60.
—— (Anglia). Holiday 26: 140-1 (col.) Dec '59; 28: 40 Oct '60.
—— (Austin). Holiday 5: 138 (col.) Ap '49; 23: 115 Mar '58, 16 Ap '58; 25: 164 Ap '59; 27: 141 Mar '60, 159 Ap '60.
—— (Austin-Healey). Holiday 26: 150 Dec '59.
—— (Austrian). Natl. geog. 115: 177 Feb '59; 118: 260-1 (col.) Aug '60.
—— (Bel Air). Holiday 21: inside cover Mar '57.
—— (Bentley). Holiday 18: 91 Dec '55.
—— (Bonneville). Holiday 23: 27 (col.) Feb '58; 27: 12 (col.) Feb '60.
—— (Buick). Holiday 13: 23 (col.) Ma' 53; 25: 145 May '59, 47 Je '59; 26: 105 Jl' 59; 27: 142 Feb '60, 49 Je '60; 28: 84 (col.) Sept '60.
Travel 103: 8 Jan '55.
—— (Buick, 1954). Holiday 15: 87 (col.) Mar '54.
—— (Cadillac). Holiday 10: 59 (col.) Aug '51, 7 (col.) Oct '51; 11: 25 (col.) Mar '52; 12:

7 (col.) Jl '52, 65 (col.) Sept '52; 13: 71 (col.) Mar '53, 7 (col.) May '53; 14: 31 (col.) Jl '53, 61 (col.) Aug '53, 15 (col.) Sept '53, 71 (col.) Nov '53; 18: 23 (col.) Jl '55, 63 (col.) Sept '55; 19: 13 (col.) Jan '56, 83 (col.) Mar '56, 15 (col.) Je '56; 20: 17 (col.) Aug '56, 7 (col.) Sept '56; 21: 7 (col.) Jan '57, 97 (col.) Mar '57, 7 (col.) Ap '57, 27 (col.) Je '57; 22: 7 (col.) Sept '57; 23: 15 (col.) Jan '58, 111 (col.) Mar '58, 2 (col.) May '58; 24: 23 (col.) Jl '58; 25: 5 (col.) Jan '59, 97 (col.) Feb '59, 26 (col.) Mar '59, 139 (col.) May '59; 26: 7 (col.) Jl '59, 15 (col.) Dec '59; 27: 123 (col.) Feb '60, 117 (col.) Mar '60, 7 (col.) Ap '60, 103 (col.) Je '60; 28: 13 (col.) Aug '60.
—— (Cadillac sport, 1904). Natl. geog. 114: 118 (col.) Jl '58.
—— (Chevrolet). Holiday 10: 15 (col.) Aug '51, inside cover (col.) Sept '51, 66 (col.) Oct '51; 11: 15 (col.) Ap '52, 101 (col.) May '52; 12: 77 (col.) Jl '52, 7 (col.) Aug '52, 25 (col.) Sept '52; 13: inside cover (col.) Mar '53, 82 (col.) Ap '53, 111 (col.) May '53, 94 (col.) Je '53; 14: 18 (col.) Jl '53, 83 (col.) Aug '53, 2 (col.) Oct '53; 18: 71 (col.) Jl '55, 7 (col.) Aug '55, 75 (col.) Sept '55; 19: 68 (col.) Mar '56, 64 (col.) May '56; 20: 15 (col.) Dec '56; 21: 79 (col.) Jan '57, 37 (col.) May '57, 100 (col.) Je '57; 22: 2 (col.) Dec '57; 23: 86 (col.) Jan '58, 22 (col.) Mar '58, 5 (col.) Ap '58, 138 (col.) May '58, 2, 43 (col.) Je '58; 24: inside cover (col.) Dec '58; 25: 2 (col.) Feb '59, 111 (col.) Ap '59, 28 (col.) May '59; 26: 20 (col.) Nov '59, 115 (col.) Dec '59; 27: 135 (col.) Mar '60, 191 (col.) Ap '60, inside cover (col.) May '60, 143 (col.) Je '60; 28: 12 (col.) Nov '60.
—— (Chile). Natl. geog. 117: 223 (col.) Feb '60.
—— (Chrysler). Holiday 11: 85 (col.) Feb '52, 33 (col.) May '52, 17 (col.) Je '52; 12: 25 (col.) Jl '52, 60 (col.) Aug '52, 7 (col.) Dec '52; 13: 73 (col.) Jan '53; 14: 40 (col.) Dec '53; 18: 2 (col.) Jl '55, 73 (col.) Aug '55, 20 (col.) Dec '55; 19: 24 (col.) Feb '56; 27: 16, 140-1 (col.), 193 Ap '60, 154 (col.) May '60, 97 Je '60; 28: 47 (col.) Dec '60.
—— (Citroen). Holiday 19: 123 Jan '56; 21: 128 Jan '57, 208 Ap '57; 25: 10 Jan '59, 112 Feb '59; 26: 186 Nov '59; 27: 120 Jan '60, 43 Mar '60, 33 May '60, 189 Je '60.
—— (Continental). Holiday 18: 2 (col.) Dec '55; 19: 63 (col.) Jan '56, 7, 75 (col.) Feb '56; 20: inside cover (col.) Oct '56; 23: inside cover (col.) Feb '58, 140 (col.) Mar '58, 110 (col.) May '58; 24: 5 (col.) Jl '58; 25: 102 (col.) May '59.
—— (Convertible). Holiday 11: 83 (col.) 155 Je '52; 12: 143 Jl '52, inside cover (col.) Aug '52, 8, 65 (col.) Sept '52; 18: 71 (col.) Jl '55, 15, 125 (col.) Sept '55, 76 (col.) Oct '55, 68 (col.), 122 Nov '55, 12, 29 (col.) Dec '55; 19: 7, 75, 83 (col.) Mar '56, 32 (col.) Je '56; 20: 107 Aug '56, 112 (col.) Nov '56; 21: 149, 151 Mar '57, 29, 39 (col.), 151, 176 Ap '57, 13 (col.) Je '57; 24: 24 Sept '58; 25: 43 (col.) Feb '59, 48, 128 (col.) Ap '59, 10 (col.), 22 May '59 26: 17, 24 (col.) Jl '59, 33 Nov '59, 150

Dec '59; 27: 113 (col.) Jan '60, 12 (col.) Feb '60, 57 Ap '60, 65 May '60; 28: 47, 168 Nov '60, 59 Dec '60. Natl. geog. 103: 3 Jan '53; 112 692 (col.) Nov '57.

—— (Corvair). Holiday 26: 21 (col.) Nov '59; 28: 14 (col.) Nov '60.

—— (Daimler). Holiday 18: 91 Dec '55; 28: 77 Aug '60.

—— (Datsum). Holiday 25: 121 Ap '59; 26: 131 Sept '59; 27: 32 Mar '60.

—— (Dauphine). Holiday 21: 44 (col.) Je '57; 22: 6 (col.) Oct '57, 148 Nov '57; 23: 105 Jan '58.

—— (Dauphine, Europe). Holiday 23: 166 Mar '58.

—— (DeSoto). Holiday 13: 2 (col.) May '53, 85 (col.) Je '53; 14: 67 (col.) Jl '53; 21: inside cover (col.) Feb '57, 110 (col.) Mar '57, 34 (col.) Ap '57, 98 (col.) May '57; 23: 7 (col.) Feb '58, 122 (col.) Mar '58; 25: 121 (col.) Je '59; 27: 47 (col.) Mar '60, 119 (col.) Ap '60.

—— (Dodge). Holiday 11: 25 (col.) Feb '52; 12: 1 Jl '52, 87 (col.) Dec '52; 13: 31 (col.) May '53, 13 (col.) Je '53; 14: 111 (col.) Jl '53, inside cover (col.) Dec '53; 19: 86 (col.) Feb '56, 78 (col.) May '56; 20: 39 (col.) Dec '56; 21: 96 (col.) Jan '57, 90 (col.) Feb '57, 2 (col.) Ap '57, 44-5 (col.) May '57, 112 (col.) Je '57; 23: 7 (col.) Jan '58; 24: 49 (col.) Nov '58; 27: 143 (col.) Mar '60, 26 (col.) Ap '60, 19, 115 (col.) May '60, 5, 109 (col.) Je '60; 28: 145 (col.) Dec '60.

—— (Duryea, early) Durant. Pict. hist. of Amer. circus. p. 156.

—— (English). Natl. geog. Holiday 27: 4, 15 (col.) Mar '60.

—— (English land-Rover). Natl. geog. 118: 366-7 (part col.) Sept '60.

—— (English-Ford). Holiday 23: 156 Mar. '58; 27: 233 May '60, 43 (col.) Je '60.

—— (Fiat). Holiday 24: 17 Jl '58, 90 Aug '58, 98 Sept '58, 10 Oct '58, 141 Nov '58; 25: 38 Ap '59, 164 May '59, 108 Je '59; 26: 135 Jl '59, 43 Oct '59, 172 Dec '59; 27: 160 Mar '60, 168 May '60; 28: 25 (col.) Jl '60, 168 Nov '60.

—— (Ford). Holiday 7: 15 (col.) Je '50; 8: inside cover (col.) Jl '50, 58 (col.) Aug '50, 95 (col.) Sept '50, 66 (col.) Oct '50; 10: 24 (col.) Aug '51; 12: 65 (col.) Jl '52, inside cover (col.) Aug '52, 73 (col.) Sept '52; 14: 2 (col.) Sept '53, 74 (col.) Oct '53, inside cover (col.) Nov '53; 16: 75 (col.) Oct '54, 5 (col.) Nov '54; 18: 15 (col.) Nov '55; 19: 117 Mar '56, 26 (col.), 118 May '56; 20: 72 (col.) Aug '56; 23: 18 (col.) Feb '58, 12-3 (col.) May '58; 24: 84-5 (col.) Jl '58, 124 Nov '58; 27: 35 (col.) Feb '60, 172 Ap '60, 232 May '60, 28: 119, 131 Jl '60, 22 (col.) Aug '60. Travel 103: 10 Jan '55.

—— (Ford, 1896, 1st built). Brooks: Growth of a nation, p. 224.

—— (Ford, 1896). Natl. geog. 101: 293 (col.) Mar '52; 114: 101 (col.) Jl '58.

—— (Ford, English). Holiday 23: 156 Mar '58; 27: 233 May '60, 43 (col.) Je '60.

—— (Ford, 1908). Natl. geog. 101: 293 (col.) Mar '52.

—— (Ford, model A, 1903). Holiday 21: 73 (col.) Je '57.

—— (Ford, model T). Brooks: Growth of a nation, p. 238. Holiday 18: 51 (col.) Dec '55.

—— (Ford, model T, 1910). Holiday 21: 73 (col.) Je '57.

——(Ford, model T, 1923). Holiday 26: 152 Nov '59.

—— (Ford, 1940). Int. gr. soc.: Arts . . . p. 161 (col.).

—— (Ford, 1954). Holiday 15: 82 (col.) Mar '54, 17 (col.) Ap '54, 82 (col.) Je '54; 16: 2 Aug '54, 5 (col.) Sept '54.

—— (French make). Holiday 27: 19 Mar '60.

—— (Gen. motors). Holiday 27: 26 May '60.

—— (German). Holiday 25: 6 Feb '59, 184 Mar '59, 176 Ap '59, 145 May '59, 47 Je '59; 26: 105 Jl '59, 19 Aug '59, 169 Nov '59, 254 Dec '59; 27: 32 Ap '60, 222 May '60.

—— (Hillman). Holiday 27: 167 Jan '60, 140 May '60.

—— (Hillman minx). Holiday 13: 18 Ap '53, 75 May '53.

—— (Imperial). Holiday 11: 33 (col.) May '52, 17 (col.) Je '52; 12: 25 (col.) Jl '52, 60 (col.) Aug '52; 22: 39 (col.) Dec '57; 23: 32 (col.) Feb '58, 48 (col.) Mar '58, 31 (col.) May '58, 144 (col.) Je '58; 24: 7 (col.) Aug '58; 25: 33 (col.) Mar '59, 127 (col.) May '59; 26: 83 (col.) Jl '59, 44 Nov '59, 164-5 Dec '59; 27: 44 Feb '60, 125 Ap '60, 124-5 May '60.

—— (Jaguar). Holiday 20: 44 (col.) Nov '56; 23: 9 Ap '58, 164 May '58, 125 Je '58.

—— (Lancia). Holiday 26: 121 Nov '59, 207 Dec '59.

—— (Landaulet). Holiday 18: 91 Dec '55.

—— (Lincoln). Holiday 19: 15 (col.) Feb '56, 81 (col.) Je '56; 20: 30 (col.) Dec '56; 21: 18 (col.) Mar '57, 98 (col.) Ap '57, 19 (col.) May '57; 23: inside cover (col.) Feb '58, 101 (col.) Mar '58, 27 (col.) Ap '58, 19 (col.) Je '58; 24: 103 (col.) Sept '58, 2 (col.) Oct '58; 25: 48 (col.) Ap '59.

—— (Martinique, tree fern). Natl. geog. 115: 272 Feb '59.

—— (Mercedes-Benz). Holiday 23: 133 Je '58; 26: 17 (col.) Jl '59, 162 Nov '59, inside cover (col.) Dec '59; 27: 90 (col.) Jan '60, 130 (col.) Feb '60, 181 (col.) Mar '60.

—— (Mercury). Holiday 11: 7 (col.) May '52, 83 (col.) Je '52; 13: :10 (col.) Mar '53, 67 (col.) Ap '53, 81 (col.) May '53, inside cover (col.) Je '53; 14: 87 (col.) Aug '53, 15 (col.) Oct '53.

—— (midget, racing. Holiday 5: 63 Jan '49.

—— (Nash). Holiday 13: 74 (col.) Mar '53; 14: inside cover (col.) Jl '53, 79 (col.) Sept '53.

—— (Oldsmobile). Holiday 10: 24 (col.) Jl '51, 13 (col.) Sept '51, 67 (col.) Nov '51; 11: 67 (col.) Mar '52, inside cover (col.) May '52; 12: 98 (col.) Jl '52, 17 (col.) Oct '52; 13: 15 (col.) Feb '53, inside cover (col.) Ap '53, 114 (col.) Je '53; 14: 4 (col.) Aug '53, 66 (col.) Oct '53; 18: 85 (col.) Sept '55, 7 (col.) Dec '55; 19: 58 (col.) Feb '56, 68 (col.) Je '56; 20: 49 (col.) Dec '56; 21: 81 (col.) Feb '57,

10 (col.) Ap '57, 2 (col.) Je '57; 22: 23 (col.) Dec '57; 23: 87 (col.) Feb '58, inside cover (col.) Mar '58, 116 (col.) Ap '58, 33 (col.) Je '58; 24: 5 (col.) Nov '58; 25: 90 (col.) Jan '59, 126 (col.) Mar '59, 38 (col.) May '59; 26: 2 (col.) Nov '59; 27: 146 (col.) Feb '60, 110 (col.) Mar '60, 15 (col.) May '60; 28: 15 (col.) Dec '60.

—— (Packard). Holiday 10: 2 (col.) Jl '51, 79 (col.) Oct '51; 13: 9 Feb '53, 91 (col.) Mar '53, 7 (col.) Ap '53; 18: 31 (col.) Jl '55; 19: 7 (col.) Feb '56, 165 May '56, 5 (col.) Je '56.

—— (Peugeot, French). Holiday 23: 110-11 Je '58; 24: 28 Jl '58, 103 Aug '58, 160 Nov '58; 27: 145 Mar '60, 41 Ap '60.

—— (Plymouth). Holiday 13: 5 (col.) Feb '53, 83 (col.) Mar '53, 103 (col.) May '53; 14: 23 (col.) Jl '53, 85 (col.) Dec '53; 18: 100-1 (col.) Dec '55; 19: 66 (col.) Feb '56; 20: 2 (col.) Dec '56; 21: 10 (col.) Jan '57, 44-5 (col.) Ap '57, 13 (col.) Je '57; 22: 15 (col.) Dec '57; 23: 5 (col.) Mar '58; 27: 20 (col.) May '60, 108 (col.) Je '60.

—— (Pontiac). Holiday 10: 7 (col.) Aug '51, 23 (col.) Oct '51; 11: 6 (col.) Ap '52; 12: 91 (col.) Jl '52, 13 (col.) Nov '52; 13: 18 (col.) Mar '53, 68 (col.) Je '53; 14: 59 (col.) Sept '53; 18: 86 (col.) Jl '55, 2 (col.) Aug '55, 15 (col.) Sept '55; 19: 7 (col.) Mar '56, 7 (col.) May '56; 20: 24 (col.) Je '56; 22: 167 (col.) Dec '57; 23: 32 (col.) Jan '58; 27: 12 (col.) Feb '60; 28: 3 (col.) Nov '60, 160 (col.) Dec '60.

—— (Rambler). Holiday 13: 23 (col.) May '53; 25: 1 Ap '59, 133 May '59.

—— (Rapier). Holiday 20: 95 (col.) Oct '56.

—— (Renault). Holiday 19: 78 Jan '56, 13 May '56; 21: 103 Jan '57, 124-5 Mar '57; 23: 133 Ap '58, 6, 159 (col.) Je '58; 24: 13 (col.) Sept '58, 110 (col.) Oct '58, 109 (col.) Nov '58; 25: 165 Mar '59, 17 Ap '59, 161 May '59, 16, 192 (col.) Je '59; 26: 30 Jl '59, 110 (col.) Oct '59, 178 Nov '59; 27: 106 (col.) Mar '60, 42 (col.) May '60; 28: 98 (col.) Jl '60, 46-7 Nov '60.

—— (Roadmaster). Holiday 10: 1 Oct '51.

—— (Rover). Holiday 28: 56 Nov '60, 157 Dec '60.

—— (Russia). Natl. geog. 116: 728 Dec '59.

—— (Saab). Holiday 27: 163 Ap '60.

—— (Scotland). Holiday 112: 477 Oct '57.

—— (Simca, France). Holiday 24: 131 Jl '58; 25: 17 Mar '59, 155 Je '59; 26: 101 (col.) Jl '59.

—— (Stanley). Amer. heri. vol. 10 no. 2 p. 40-5 (part col.) (Feb '59).

—— (Stanley Steamer, early). Amer. heri. vol. 10 no 2 p. 86-7 (Feb '59).

—— (Stanley, 1903). Natl. geog 114: 98 (col.) Jl '58.

—— (Studebaker). Holiday 13: 5 (col.) Mar '53, 88 (col.) May '53; 14: inside cover (col.) Aug '53, 88 (col.) Oct '53; 22: 9 Dec '57; 23: 109 Jan '58, 82 Feb '58, 17 Mar '58; 25: 90 (col.) Feb '59, 137 (col.) Mar '59, 33 (col.) Ap '59, 114 (col.) May '59; 26: 50 (col.) Dec '59; 27: 113 (col.) Jan '60, 103 (col.) Mar '60, 52 (col.) Ap '60, 164 (col.) May '60. Travel 101: 5 Feb '54.

—— (Taunus). Holiday 27: 37 May '60.

—— (Tempest). Holiday 28: 9 Dec '60.

—— (Thunderbird). Holiday 18: 29 (col.) Dec '55; 19: 75 (col.) Mar '56, 32 (col.) Je '56; 23: 36-7, 38 (part col.), 100 (col.) Mar '58, 140 (col.) Ap '58, 23 (col.) May '58; 24: 78 (col.) Aug '58; 25: 10 (col.) Feb '59, 118 (col.) Mar '59, 128 (col.) Ap '59, 10 (col.) May '59, 116 (col.) Je '59; 26: 153 Nov '59; 27: 26 (col.) Feb '60, 118 (col.) May '60; 28: 59 Dec '60.

—— (Triumph). Holiday 18: 89 Nov '55; 20: 9 Oct '56; 23: 43 Mar '58, 44, 120 May '58; 24: 30 Nov '58; 26: 32-3 Nov '59, 227 Dec '59; 27: 146-7 Jan '60, 112 Feb '60, 121 Mar '60, 57 Ap '60, 65 May '60, 173 Je '60; 28: 9 Jl '60.

—— (Valiant). Holiday 27: inside cover (col.) Mar '60, 144 (col.) May '60.

—— (Vauxhall). Holiday 24: 126 Jl '58, 19 Aug '58, 122 Dec '58; 25: 22 Jan '59, 128 Feb '59.

—— (Volkswagen). Holiday 18: 67 Nov '55; 19: 136 Jan '56, 138 Mar '56, 142 May '56; 21: 151 Jan '57, 179 Mar '57, 207 Ap '57; 26: 9 Sept '59, 100 Oct '59, 9 Nov '59; 27: 172 Mar '60, 132-3 Ap '60, 5 (col.), 183 May '60, 167 (col.) Je '60; 28: 33 Sept '60, 35 Oct '60, 132 (col.) Nov '60.

—— (Volvo). Holiday 26: 91 Sept '59.

—— (Woods). See Motor vehicles, Woods.

automobile, President's (cheering crowd). Natl. geog. 97: 61 Jan '50.

automobiles. See also station wagon.

automobile accident. Travel 103: 22 Jan '55; 106: 62 Nov '56, 62 Dec '56.

—— (cartoon). Travel 103: back cover Jan '55.

—— (overturned). Natl. geog. 117: 337 (col.) Mar '60.

automobile crash (comic). Holiday 13: 27 (col.) Je '53.

automobile design room. Natl. geog. 115: 461 (col.) Ap '59.

automobile driving (safety). Travel 106: 57 Nov '56.

—— (safety cartoons). Travel 112: 50-1 Jl '59.

automobile hitching post, electric (Alaska). Natl. geog. 109 762 (col.) Je '56.

automobile house trailer. See house trailer, auto.

automobile inn (Skyhost motel). Travel 114: 43 Jl '60.

automobile license plates. See license plates, auto.

automobile parking system. Travel 103: 15-7 Jan '55.

automobile race. Travel 103: 25 Jan '55.

—— (beach). Holiday 19: 164 (col.) May '56.

automobile seat. Holiday 10: 70 (col.) Jl '51, 86 (col.) Aug '51, 4 (col.) Sept '51, 146 (col.) Oct '51, 154 (col.) Nov '51, 94 (col.) Dec '51; 11: 80 (col.) Jan '52; 14: 142 (col.) Dec '53.

automobile show room (Russia). Natl. geog. 116: 362 (col.) Sept '59.

automobile symbol (Cadillac & Pontiac). Holiday 6: 5 (col.) Jl '49, 7 (col.) Sept '49; 7: 15 (col.) Mar '50, 79 (col.) May '50; 8: 63 (col.) Jl '50, 11 Aug '50, 7 (col.) Sept '50, 93 Oct '50, 71 Nov '50; 9: 79 (col.) Mar '51; 10: 7, 59 (col.) Aug '51; 16: 63 Aug '54, 75 Oct '54; 17: 7 (col.) Mar '55; 28: 60 (col.) Nov '60.

automobile test (G.M.). Holiday 18: 40 (col.) Dec '55.
automobile tire. Holiday 5: 158 Je '49; 6: 10 (col.), 95 Jl '49, 94 Aug '49, inside back cover (col.) Sept '49; 7: 110 Ap '50, 21 Je '50; 8: 53 Jl '50, 105 Aug '50, 30 Sept '50, 128 Nov '50; 13: 1, 96 May '53, 27 (col.) Je '53; 14: 25, inside back cover Jl '53, 73 Sept '53; 18: 184 (col.) Dec' 55; 20: 20-1 (col.) Nov '56; 21: 22 May '57, 177 (col.) Je '57; 22: 94 (col.) Jl '57, 110 (col.) Oct '57; 26: 15 Sept '59, 164 Oct '59; 27: 9, 39 (col.) Ap '60, 227 May '60, 33, 106 (col.) Je '60; 28: 32 Jl '60, 81 Sept '60.
automobile tire (damaged). Holiday 12: 80 (col.) Jl '52.
——— **(comic).** Holiday 23: 96 Mar '58, 97 May '58, 129 Je '58; 24: 107 Jl '58, 77 Aug '58; 26: 102 Jl '59, 22 Aug '59.
——— **(man repairing).** Natl. geog. 114: 23 (col.) Jl '58.
automobile tire tread. Holiday 24: 77 Aug '58.
automobile top press. See press, automobile top.
automobile trailer. See house trailer, auto.
automobile wreck. See automobile accident.
automobiles (African jungle). Natl. geog. 118: 390-1 (col.) Sept '60.
——— **(natl. park).** Natl. geog. 116: 178-9 (col.) Aug '59.
——— **(on beach).** Natl. geog. 113: 44-5 (col.) Jan '58.
——— **(types).** Int. gr. soc.: Arts . . . p. 161 (col.).
autopista highway (Venezuela). Travel 105: 22 Feb '56.
Autry, Gene. Cur. biog. p. 24 (1947).
"Autumn" (Boucher). Con. 139: 121 Ap '57.
autumn (trout stream). Natl. geog. 107: 762-3 (col.) Je '55.
autumn signs (Zodiac). Lehner: Pict. bk. of sym., p. 19.
Auvers (church). See church at Auvers.
"The Auxerre statuette" (17th cent.). Con. ency. of ant., vol. 3 pl. 65.
Avalon bay (Cal.). Holiday 15: 85 May '54.
Avdat (lost city, Israel). Holiday 26: 75 (col.) Dec '59.
"The Avenger" (sculpture). Praeg. pict. ency., p. 457.
"The Avenue, Middelharnis" (Hobbema). Con. 135: 164 May '55.
Praeg. pict. ency., p. 345 (col.)
"Avenue of trees" (Sisley). Praeg. pict. ency., p. 418 (col.).
Averill, Esther. Jun. bk. of auth., p. 13.
Averill, James. Horan: Pict. hist. of wild west, p. 182.
Averkamp, Hendrik (work of). Con. 140: cover (col.), 116 Nov '57.
Averoff-Tositsas, Evangelos. Cur. biog., p. 31 (1957).
Avery, Capt. John. Amer. heri. vol. 8 no. 2 p. 14 (Feb '57).
Avery, Milton. Cur. biog., p. 32 (1958).
Avery, Sewell. Cur. biog. p. 24 (1944).
Avignon (France.) Holiday 14: 81 (col.) Nov '53; 19: 60-1 (col.) Feb '56.
Natl. geog. 117: 746-7 (col.) Je '60.
Avignon bridge. Natl. geog. 108: 151 Jl '55.
Avila (Spain). Holiday 15: 47 (col.) May '54.
Natl. geog. 97: 420 Ap '50.

Avon river (Shakespeare theater, swans). Holiday 10: 97 Jl '51.
awl (sym.). Lehner: Pict. bk. of sym., p. 91.
Awolowo, Obafemi. Cur. biog. p. 8 (1957).
ax. Holiday 5: 115 Ap '49; 14: 81 Aug '53; 24: 67 (col.) Aug '58.
Travel 113: 29 Feb '60.
———, **battle.** Rawson: Ant. pict. bk., p. 25.
———, **broad.** Rawson: Ant. pict. bk., p. 21.
———, **double-headed (sym.).** Lehner: Pict. bk. of sym., p. 87.
———, **Minoan votive.** See votive ax, Minoan.
———, **Nepal.** Natl. geog. 117: 378 (col.) Mar '60.
———, **ritual.** See Olmec ax, ritual.
———, **stone age.** Natl. geog. 113: 436 Mar '58.
"Axel at grave of Maria" (Wickenberg). Con. 144: 32 Sept '59.
Ay Ay. See St. Croix (Virgin islands).
Aya Sofya cathedral. Natl. geog. 112: 405 Sept '57.
Ayala, Poma de (work of). Amer. heri., vol. 6 no. 5 p. 103 (Aug '55).
Ayasluk fortress. See fortress of Ayasluk.
Aydelotte, Frank. Cur. biog. p. 32 (1941); p. 28 (1952).
Aylward, W. J. (work of). Amer. heri., vol. 10 no. 6 p. 16 (col.), 17 (Oct '59).
Aymara Indians (Peru). Natl. geog. 107: 137-45 Jan '55.
Ayrton, Michael (work of). Con. 132: 109 Nov '53.
Cooper: Con. ency. of music, p. 306.
Ayub Khan, Mohammad. Cur. biog. p. 17 (1959).
Azande hunter (huts, dogs). Natl. geog. 114: 214 (col.) Aug '58.
Azikiwe, Nnamdi. Cur. biog. p. 9 (1957).
the Azores. Amer. heri., vol. 12 no. 1 p. 56-7 (col.) (Dec '60).
Holiday 21: 66-71 (col.) Jan '57.
——— **(volcanic eruption).** Natl. geog. 113: 736-57 (part col.) Je '58.
Aztec art. Amer. heri., vol. 10 no. 2 p. 46-57 (col.) (Feb '59).
Ceram: March of arch., p. 253-6, 261-2.
Aztec circus acts. Durant: Pict. hist. of Amer. circus, p. 20.
Aztec headdress. See headdress, Aztec feather.
Aztec human sacrifices. See sacrifices, Aztec.
Aztec king (costume). Natl. geog. 100: 819 (col.) Dec '51.
Aztec mask. Praeg.: Pict. ency., p. 548 (col.).
Aztec shield (mosaic of feathers). Ceram: March of arch., pl. XVI (col.).
Aztec skull (mosaic). Ceram: March of arch., p. 286 (col.).
Azuma IV, Tokuho. Cur. biog. p. 51 (1954).
Azzam, Abdul Rahman. Cur. biog. p. 27 (1947).

B

Baalbek (temples). Natl. geog. 105: 499 Ap '54; 113: 508-11 (part col.) Ap '58.
——— **(temple gate).** Ceram: March of arch., p. 67-8.
Babb, James T. Cur. biog. p. 33 (1955).
Babbitt, Milton. Cur. biog. p. 15 (1962).
Babcock, Orville E. Amer. heri. vol. 8 no. 3 p. 52 (Ap '57).
Babson, Naomi Lane. Cur. biog. p. 30 (1952).

Babson, Roger W. Cur. biog. p. 24 (1945).

baby. Holiday 7: 91 (col.) Feb '50; 8: 2 (col.) Jl' 50, 9 Aug '50, 25 Nov '50, 81 Dec '50; 10: 188 Dec '51; 22: 149 Nov '57. Travel 111: 59 Jan '59.

—— (Alaska). Natl. geog. 99: 557 Ap '51.

—— (asleep). Holiday 18: 87 (col.) Sept '55.

—— (asleep in cart). Natl. geog. 114: 118 (col.) Jl '58.

—— (sleep on beach). Natl. geog. 118; 635 (col.) Nov '60.

—— (back view). Holiday 27: 167 (col.) Mar '60.

——(ball). Travel 101: inside back cover Ap '54.

—— (crying). Holiday 7: 28 May '50.

——(crying, in cart). Natl. geog. 107: 574 Ap '55.

—— (dog). Natl. geog. 105: 115 Jan '54.

—— (head). Holiday 10: 134 Dec '51; 14: 82 Nov '53; 23: 8 Ap '58; 24: 170 Nov '58, 56 Dec '58.

—— (head, laughing). Holiday 10: 129 Nov '51.

—— (in basket on bearer's head). Natl. geog. 116: 225 (col.) Aug '59.

—— (in bathtub). Holiday 11: 27 Feb '52, 81 Ap '52.

—— (in carriage, Poland). Natl. geog. 114: 375 (col.) Sept '58.

—— (in carriage, woman). Natl. geog. 112: 457 (col.) Oct '57.

—— (in cart). Natl. geog. 117: 835 (col.) Je '60.

—— (in cart, comic). Holiday 25: 117 Je '59.

—— (in chair). Holiday 14: 23 Dec '53.

—— (in cradle). Holiday 23: 156 Feb '58, 171 Mar '58, 189 Ap '58; 24: 125 Aug '58, 191 Nov '58, 226 Dec '58.

—— (in washtub). Natl. geog. 112: 698 (col.) Nov '57.

—— (man's cap on). Holiday 23: 152 Mar '58.

—— (nurse). Holiday 21: 199 May '57.

—— ("peek a boo"). Holiday 22: 107 Sept '57.

—— (portable cradle). Natl. geog. 103: 352 Mar '53.

—— (seated). Holiday 27: 158 Je '60.

—— (sleepy). Holiday 5: 79 (col.) Je '49.

—— (stork bringing). Holiday 11: 141 May '52.

—— (Swiss mother). Natl. geog. 107: 840 Je '55.

—— (toys). Holiday 11: 22 Jan '52.

—— (wearing hat). Holiday 8: 63 Oct '50.

—— (woman bathing). Natl. geog. 107: 861 Je '55.

—— (woman holding). Natl. geog. 111: 305 (col.) Mar '57.

baby, African (on mother's back). Natl. geog. 118: 320 (col.) Sept '60.

——, Chinese. Natl. geog. 115: 430 Mar '59.

——, Indian. See Indian baby.

——. Lapp (in cradle). Natl. geog. 106: 253 (col.) Aug '54.

——, refugee. Natl. geog. 111: 433 Mar '57.

——, Rhodesian (on mother's back). Natl. geog. 111: 377, 382 (col.) Mar '57.

——, Turkey (woman holding). Natl. geog. 110: 751 (col.) Dec '56.

baby & mother. See mother & baby.

baby & stork. See stork (with baby).

baby buggy (woman pushing). Natl. geog. 105: 565 Ap '54.

baby. See also woman & baby; man & baby.

baby pen. Natl. geog. 118: 552 (col.) Oct '60.

"baby show". Face of Amer., p. 74-5 (col.).

Babylon. Ceram: March of arch., p. 163, 221, 227.

Natl. geog. 99: 58-104 (col.) Jan '51; 114: 469 (col.) Oct '58.

——, plan of. Ceram: March of arch., p. 188.

——, Processional way. See Processional way (Babylon).

Babylon excavations. Ceram: March of arch., p. 221.

Babylonian chronicle (597 B.C.). Natl. geog. 118: 842 Dec '60.

Babylonian costume (ancient). Int. gr. soc.: Arts . . . p. 29 (col.).

Babylonian king (ancient). Int. gr. soc.: Arts . . . p. 29 (col.).

Babylonian ruler (head). Int. gr. soc.: Arts . . . p. 181 (col.).

Babylonian temple (Hanging gardens). Int. gr. soc.: Arts . . . p. 13 (col.).

Babylonian temple (3000 yrs. old). Int. gr. soc.: Arts . . . p. 11 (col.)

Babylonian woman & king (ancient). Int. gr. soc.: Arts . . . p. 29 (col.).

Bacall, Lauren. Holiday 15: 12 Jan '54.

Baccaloni, Salvatore. Cur. biog. p. 26 (1944).

"The Baccanale" (Titian). Con. 126: 177 Dec '50.

"Bacchanal" (Pellegrini). Con. 145: 107 Ap '60.

"Bacchanalian revel . . ." (Poussin). Con. 126: 181 Dec '50.

Praeg. pict. ency., p. 329 (col.)

Bacchant (fresco, Pompeii). Labande: Naples, p. 106.

"Bacchante" (Le Brun). Con. 135: IX (col.) Mar '55.

Bacchus (sym.). Lehner: Pict. bk. of sym., p. 31.

Bacchus, temple of. See Temple of Bacchus.

"Bacchus & Ariadne" (de la Fosse). Con. 141: 39 Mar '58.

—— (Titian). Con. 126: 178 Dec '50.

"Bacchus & Midas" (Poussin). Con. 126: 179 Dec '50.

Bacchus temple carvings. Natl. geog. 113: 513 (col.) Ap '58.

Bach, J. S. Holiday 18: 9 Aug '55.

Bach, Johann Sebastian. Int. gr. soc.: Arts . . . p. 109 (col.).

—— (by Haussmann). Cooper: Con. ency. of music, p. 55.

Bachambeer society. Natl. geog. 103: 523 (col.) Ap '53.

Bacharach, Bertram. Cur. biog. p. 33 (1957).

Bacharach (Rhine river). Holiday 23: 37 (col.) Jan '58.

Bachauer, Gina. Cur. biog. p. 54 (1954).

Bache, Harold L. Cur. biog. p. 19 (1959).

bachelor chest. See chest, bachelor.

Bacher, Robert Fox. Cur. biog. p. 29 (1947).

Bachman, John (work by). Amer. heri. vol. 10 no. 6 p. 26-7 (Oct '59).

back, human. Gray's anatomy, p. 1365-6.

backgammon board. Con. ency. of ant., vol. 3 pl. 142-3.
Backhaus, Wilhelm. Holiday 21: 42 Mar '57; 22: 121 Sept '57.
Backman, Jules. Cur. biog p. 31 (1952).
Backstrand, Clifford J. Cur. biog. p. 56 (1954).
Bacoli. Labande: Naples, p. 142-3.
Bacon, Charles L. Cur. biog. p. 17 (1962).
Bacon, Sir Edmund (Walton). Con. 143: 88 Ap '59.
Bacon, Sir Francis. Amer. heri. vol. 8 no. 4 p. 93 (Je '57).
Con. 143: 5 Mar '59.
—— **(bust).** Con. 139: 7 Mar '57; 141: XVIII Ap '58.
Bacon, Francis. Cur. biog. p. 34 (1957).
Bacon, Leonard. Cur. biog. p. 34 (1941).
Bacon, Sir Nathaniel. Con. 143: 5 Mar '59.
—— **(self portrait).** Con. 137: 119 Ap '56.
—— **(work of).** Con. 137: 117 (col.) Ap '56; 143: 5, 7 Mar '59.
Bacon, Lady Nathaniel. Con. 143: 7 Mar '59.
Bacon, Nicholas. Con. 143: 4 Mar '59.
Bacon, Selden D. Cur. biog. p. 33 (1952).
Bad Ems (Germany). Travel 104: 54 Sept '55.
Baden-Baden (Germany). Holiday 23: 86-9 (part col.) Je '58.
Baden-Powell, Lady Olave. Cur. biog. p. 20 (1946).
badge, crown. See crown badge.
badge, hat. See hat badge.
badge of office (British antique dealers). Con. 143: 108 Ap '59.
Badger, Vice-Adm. Oscar C. Cur. biog. p. 17 (1949).
Badger Pass ski house. Natl. geog. 99: 492 Ap '51.
Badlands (Red Deer river, Alberta). Natl. geog. 118: 100 (col.) Jl '60.
Badlands (S.D.). Holiday 14: 98 Jl '53.
"Bad Lands" natl. monument. Amer. heri. vol. 6 no. 3 p. 29 (Ap '55).
Holiday 27: 129 Je '60.
Travel 113: 43 Mar '60.
Badshahi mosque. Natl. geog. 102: 656 (col.) Nov '52.
Baehr, George. Cur. biog. p. 48 (1942).
Baehr, George F. Amer. heri. vol. 11 no. 3 p. 61 (Ap '60).
Baez, Joan. Cur. biog. (1963).
Baffin island (Alaska). Natl. geog. 114: 128-9 Jl '58.
—— **(map).** Natl. geog. 100: 467 Oct '51.
bag (travel kit). See travel kit.
——, **airline.** Holiday 21: 15 (col.) Feb '57; 23: 15 (col.) Feb '58.
——, **bottle.** Holiday 23: 139 (col.) Jan '58.
——, **brief.** See brief case.
——, **camera.** Holiday 19: 130 (col.) May '56.
——, **loot.** Holiday 22: 177 Nov '57.
——, **stirrup.** Holiday 26: 200 Nov '59.
——, **straw shopping.** Natl. geog. 113: 170-1 (col.) Feb '58.
——, **traveling.** See traveling bag.
bag for charter seal, embroidered. Con. 143: 234 Je '59.
baggage. See luggage.
baggage porter (old train). Holiday 22: 77 Jl '57.

baggage porter (plane). Holiday 21: 1 Feb '57.
Baghdad (on Tigris river). Holiday 15: 102-3, 105 Feb '54.
Natl. geog. 114: 42 Jl '58, 444-54 (part col.) Oct '58; 115: 50 (col.) Jan '59.
—— **(royal mausoleum).** Travel 105: 20 Jan '56.
bagpipe (player). Disney: People & places, p. 11, 26-7 (col.).
Holiday 10: 143 (col.) Oct '51; 20: 30 (col.) Nov '56; 21: 160 (col.) Mar '57, 136 (col.) Ap '57.
Natl. geog. 101: 661 (col.) May '52; 102: 93-8 (col.) Jl '52; 112: 445 (col.) Oct '57; 114: 186 (col.) Aug '58.
——, **Breton.** Holiday 7: 103 (col.) Jan '50.
——, **Celtic (ancient).** Int. gr. soc.: Arts . . . p. 27 (col.).
Bahama island. Holiday 23: 74-9 (col.) Mar '58; 25: 112 (col.) May '59; 27: 116-7 (col.) Jan '60; 28: 158 (col.) Dec '60.
Natl. geog. 113: 148-203 (part col.) Feb '58.
Travel 103: 35-8 Jan '55; 108: 40-1 Nov '57; 111: 41-2 Jan '59; 113: 19-25 Feb '60.
—— **(beach).** Holiday 25: 26 (col.) Feb '59.
—— **(dancer).** Holiday 27: 201 Ap '60.
—— **(flamengo show).** Natl. geog. 112: 554-71 (part col.) Oct '57.
—— **(map).** Natl. geog. 113: 152 Feb '58; 117: 170-1 (col.) Feb '60; 118: 122 (col.) Jl '60.
Travel 105: 46 Mar '56.
Bahama islands . See also Eleuthera island.
Baharata dance. See dance of Baharata.
Bahia. Travel 103: 9 Mar '55.
Bahrein island (women washing clothes). Travel 113: 35 Feb '60.
Bahrein men. Natl. geog. 105: 503 (col.) Ap '54.
Baie de Tonerre harbor (Quebec). Travel 108: 51 Aug '57.
Baie St. Paul (Quebec). Holiday 6: 40-3 Aug '49.
Bailer, John C., jr. Cur. biog. p. 20 (1959).
bailer shells. See shells, bailer.
Bailey, Carolyn Sherwin. Cur. biog. p. 31 (1948) Jun. bk. of auth., p. 14.
Bailey, Consuelo Northrop. Cur. biog. p. 58 (1954).
Bailey, Sir Donald Coleman. Cur. biog. p. 27 (1945).
Bailey, John M. Cur. biog. p. 19 (1962).
Bailey, Josiah W. Cur. biog. p. 29 (1945).
Bailey, Liberty H. Cur. biog. p. 33 (1948).
Bailey, Pearl. Cur. biog. p. 35 (1955).
Baillie, Hugh. Cur. biog. p. 22 (1946).
Baines, Sir Thomas (Fuller). Con. 140: 232 Jan '58.
Bainton, Roland H. Cur. biog. p. 21 (1962).
Baird, Bil. Cur. biog. p. 60 (1954).
Baird, Cora. Cur. biog. p. 60 (1954).
Bakar (Croatia). Holiday 25: 85 (col.) Je '59.
bake oven (woman). Holiday 11: 102 (col.) Je '52.
bake shop. See bakery.
Baker, Carroll. Holiday 21: 93 Feb '57.
Baker, Dorothy. Cur. biog. p. 17 (1943).
Baker, Frank. Cur. biog. p. 34 (1948).
Baker, George. Cur. biog. p. 29 (1944).

Baker, George F. Amer. heri. vol. 8 no. 4 p. 35 (Je '57).

Baker, George T. Cur. biog. p. 38 (1953).

Baker, John H. Cur. biog. p. 18 (1949).

Baker, La Fayette C. Amer. heri. vol. 8 no. 2 p. 56 (Feb '57).

Baker, Louise. Cur. biog. p. 61 (1954).

Baker, Margaret. Jun. bk. of auth., p. 15.

Baker, Mary. Jun. bk. of auth., p. 15.

Baker, Melvin H. Cur. biog. p. 13 (1960).

Baker, Nina Brown. Cur. biog. p. 32 (1947). Jun. bk. of auth., p. 17.

Baker, Olaf. Jun. bk. of auth., p. 18.

Baker, Phil. Cur. biog. p. 25 (1946). Holiday 7: 68 Mar '50.

Baker, Roy G. Cur. biog. p. 36 (1948).

baker (decorating cake). Natl. geog. 118: 605 (col.) Nov '60.

—— (head). Holiday 28: 25 Dec '60.

—— (sym.). Lehner: Pict. bk. of sym., p. 90.

baker cart. Amer. heri. vol. 6 no. 4 p. 48 (col.) (Dec '54).

Baker's death, Col. Edward D. Amer. heri. vol. 6 no. 1 p. 18 (fall '54).

bakery. Natl. geog. 100: 563 Oct '51.

——, Colonial. Natl. geog. 106: 467 (col.) Oct '54.

——, Iranian. Natl. geog. 100: 431 Oct '51.

——, Turkish. Holiday 19: 52 (col.) Feb '56.

baking dish. See dish, baking.

Bakke, Edward Wight. Cur. biog. p. 40 (1953).

Bakshi Ghulam Mohammad. Cur. biog. p. 25 (1956).

Balaban, Barney. Cur. biog. p. 27 (1946).

balances (scales, sym). Lehner: Pict. bk. of sym., p. 17.

balances. See also scales.

Balanchine, George. Cur. biog. p. 63 (1954).

Balbi-Durazzo palace. See palace Balbi-Durazzo.

Balboa (Cal., harbor). Holiday 25: 36 Feb. '59.

Balboa park (San Diego). Travel 113: 35 May '60.

Balch, Emily Greene. Cur. biog. p. 33 (1947).

Balchen, Bernt. Cur. biog. p. 21 (1949).

balconies (iron railing). Jordan: Hammond's pict. atlas, p. 83 (col.)
Natl. geog. 103: 144, 151, 155 (part col.) Feb '53; 105: 175 (col.) Feb '54, 329 Mar '54; 107: 312 (col.) Mar '55.

——, (on building). Labande: Naoles, p. 62.

——, street (houses). Natl. geog. 107: 497 (col.) Ap '55.

balcony (woman at breakfast). Holiday 19: 57 (col.) May '56.

——, house (sea). Natl. geog. 113: 176 (col.) Feb '58.

——, window. Natl. geog. 102: 543 (col.) Oct '52.

balcony scene (Romeo & Juliet). Natl. geog. 100: 417 Sept '51.

Balderston, William. Cur. biog. p. 23 (1949).

Baldomir, Alfredo. Cur. biog. p. 51 (1942).

Baldwin, Calvin B. Cur. biog. p. 19 (1943).

Baldwin, Faith. Holiday 22: 148 Dec '57.

Baldwin, Hanson W. Cur. biog. p. 53 (1942).

Baldwin, James. Cur. biog. p. 21 (1959).

Baldwin, Raymond E. Cur. biog. p. 29 (1946).

Baldwin, Thurman. Horan: Pict. hist. of wild west, p. 148.

Baldwin, William H. Cur. biog. p. 31 (1945).

Balearic islands. Natl. geog. 111: 622-60 (part col.) May '57.

—— (harbor). Travel 101: 32-3 Mar '54.

—— (map). Natl. geog. 111: 624 May '57.

Balenciaga, Cristobal. Cur. biog. p. 65 (1954).

Balestra, Antonio (work of). Con. 134: 5 Sept '54.

Balewa, Abubakar Tafawa. Cur. Biog. p. 21 (1961).

Balewa, Alhaji Abubakar Tafawa. Holiday 25: 67 Ap '59.

Bali. Holiday 18: 52-7 (part col.) Jl '55.
Natl. geog. 99: 3-26 (col.) Jan '51; 116: 804-13 (col.) Dec '59.
Travel 108: 12-6 Nov '57.

—— (map). Natl. geog. 99: 6 Jan '51.

Bali funeral. Natl. geog. 99: 4 Jan '51; 116: 812-3 (col.) Dec '59.

Bali funeral pyre. Natl. geog. 108: 370-1 (col.) Sept '55.
Travel 108: 14 Nov '57.

Bali mask. Int. gr. soc.: Arts . . . p. 185 (col.).

Bali temple dancer. Travel 108: cover, 9, 12-5 Nov '57.

Balinese boy & girl. Holiday 18: 52-3, 56 (col.) Jl '55.

Balinese dancer. Natl. geog. 116: 810-11 (col.) Dec '59.

—— (dressing). Natl. geog. 108: 379 Sept '55.

Balinese dancers. Holiday 18: 54-5 Jl '55.
Natl. geog. 99: 9-13 (col.) Jan '51, 360-2 (col.) Mar '51.
Travel 102: 20 Nov '54.

Balinese man (training crickets). Natl. geog. 104: 388 Sept '53.

Balinese monkey dance. Holiday 18: 104 Sept '55.
Natl. geog. 116: 808-9 (col.) Dec '59.

Ball, Gorge W. Cur. biog. p. 23 (1962).

Ball, Joseph H. Cur. biog. p. 21 (1943).

Ball, Lucille. Cur. biog. p. 35 (1952).

Ball, Stuart S. Cur. biog. p. 38 (1952).

Ball, Zachary. Cur. biog. p. 41 (1953).

a ball (dance, California, 1836). Amer. heri. vol. 11 no. 6 p. 36 (col.) (Oct '60).

——, Confederate (Civil war). Jensen: The White House, p. 90.

——, Mardi Gras. Natl. geog. 103: 161-3 (col.) Feb '53.

——, Mardi Gras (costume). Natl. geog. 118: 730-1 (col.) Nov '60.

——, "Snow." See "Snow Ball" (Buffalo).

——, White House (1860). Jensen: The White House, p. 81.

ball (toy, child). Holiday 18: 71 (col.) Jl '55.

——, beach. Holiday 11: 77 (col.) Feb '52.

——, beach (boys). Natl. geog. 111: 809 (col.) Je '57.

——, Boz. See Boz ball.

——, golf. See golf ball.

——, water. Holiday 7: 93 (col.) Je '50.

——, water (child). Holiday 10: 74 (col.) Jl '51.

ball & chain (sym). Lehner: Pict. bk. of sym., p. 82.

ball bearing (sym.). Lehner: Pict. bk. of sym., p. 12.

ball game court, ancient Indian. Holiday 15: 101 Mar '54.

Ballantine, Ian. Cur. biog. p. 67 (1954).

ballerina, parody of (comic). Holiday 12: 134 Nov '52.

ballerinas. Holiday 22: 53 (col.) Jl '57.

ballet. Holiday 6: 27 Jl '49; 7: 116-20 Jan '50; 18: 112-3 Dec '55; 24: 57 Aug '58.
Travel 114: 12 Sept '60.
—— (beach). Holiday 10: 47 Jl '51.
—— (ice skater). Holiday 11: 44 (col.) Jan '52.
—— (training). Holiday 23: 68 Je '58.
——, Burmese. *See* Burmese ballet.
——, classical. Int. gr. soc.: Arts . . . p. 147 (col.).

ballet dancer. Amer. heri. vol. 7 no. 1 p. 41 (col.) (Dec '55).
Holiday 12: 97 Sept '52; 28: 3 Nov '60.
Int. gr. soc.: Arts . . . p. 123, 139 (col.).

ballet dancers. Holiday 5: 131 Ap '49; 12: cover, 106-11 (part col.) Nov '52; 21: 91 (col.) Je '57; 27: 132 (col.) Feb '60.
—— (children). Holiday 12: 109 Nov '52.
—— (girls). Holiday 13: 107 (col.) Mar '53; 28: 136 (col.) Oct '60.
—— (Boys & girls on beach). Natl. geog. 98: 335 (col.) Sept '50.

ballet dancers, Cambodia. Natl. geog. 102: 305 (col.) Sept '52.
——, Scandinavian. Travel 113: 46 Ap '60.

ballet figurines. Con. 139: XXII May '57.

ballet slippers. *See* slippers, ballet.

Balling, Ole Peter Hansen (work of). Amer. heri. vol. 7 no. 6 p. 30-1 (col.). (Oct '56).

balloon. Amer. heri. vol. 10 no. 1 p. 89 (Dec '58); vol. 11 no. 6 p. 16 (Oct '60).
Holiday 6: 74 (col.) Oct '49; 23: 127 (col.) Mar '58.
Natl. geog. 103: 100, 104, 110 Jan '53; 111: 277, 280 Feb '57.
—— (cornflake box). Amer. heri. vol. 8 no. 4 p. 67 (Je '57).
—— (1859). Amer. heri. vol. 6 no. 4 p. 10-3, 107 (part col.) (June '55).
—— (1890). Amer. heri. vol. 12 no. 1 p. 115 (Dec '60).
—— (Explorer II). Natl. geog. 112: 281 Aug '57.
—— (Japanese drawing, 1860). Jensen: The White House, p. 80.
—— (man). Amer. heri. vol. 1 no. 3 p. 31 (spring '50).
—— (man, beach). Natl. geog. 116: 456 (col.) Oct '59.
—— (1783). Natl. geog. 101: 798 (col.) Je '52.

balloon, helium-filled. Natl. geog. 110: 494 Oct '56.
——, old European. Con. 138: 268 Jan '57.
——, plastic. Natl. geog. 108: 272-3 Aug '55.
——, plastic rocket. Natl. geog. 111: 563, 565, 569 Ap '57.

balloon trip (men & woman). Natl. geog. 116: 123-45 (part col.) Jl '59.

balloonists. Natl. geog. 111: 270, 274-5 Feb '57.

balloons. Natl. geog. 113: 466 (col.) Ap '58.
——, toy. Holiday 11: 102 (col.) Mar '52; 24: 110 (col.) Oct '58, 109 (col.) Nov '58; 26: 97, 126 (col.) Jl '59, inside cover (col.) Sept '59.

Natl. geog. 114: 382 (col.) Sept '58; 118: 502 (col.) Oct '60.

ballot box (sym.). Lehner: Pict. bk. of sym., p. 94.

ballplayers. *See* baseball players; football players.

Balmain, Pierre. Cur. biog. p. 69 (1954).

Balmoral castle (Scotland). Holiday 16: 74 Aug '54.
Natl. geog. 110: 26 (col.) Jl '56.

"Balsam, Queen of Sheba, King Solomon" (Chartres cathedral). Praeg. pict. ency., 208.

Balten, Pieter (work of). Con. 144: XXXVII (col.) Nov '59.

"Balthazar" (Philpot). Con. 129: 121 Je '52.

Baltimore (Md.). Holiday 21: 88-93 Mar '57.
—— (battle at). Amer. heri. vol. 3 no. 2 p. 30-1 (col.) (winter '52).
—— (Ft. McHenry). *See* Fort McHenry.

Baluchistan armour (medieval). Int. gr. soc.: Arts . . . p. 73 (col.).

baluster measure, antique. Con. 132: XXXVI Nov '53; 140: XL Nov '57.

balustrade for minstrel gallery, Gothic. Con. 140: XLVI Sept '57.

Bamberg (Germany). Holiday 25: 63 (col.) May '59.

"Bamberger Reiter" (13th cent). Praeg. pict. ency., p. 219.

bamboo (sym.). Lehner: Pict. bk. of sym., p. 46.

"Bamboo & sparrows" (Satatsu, Japanese). Con. 133: 141 Ap '54.

bamboo arch. Natl. geog. 105: 313 Mar '54.

bamboo curtain. Holiday 26: 74 (col.) Jl '59.

Bamian's colossus. *See* Buddha (Bamian).

Banaras (India). Holiday 14: 34 (col.) Oct '53.

Banaras fakir. Holiday 19: 61 (col.) Je '56.

Bancroft, Anne. Cur. biog. p. 14 (1960).

Bancroft, Dr. Edward. Amer. heri. vol. 7 no. 3 p. 78 (Ap '56).

Bancroft, George. Amer. heri. vol. 8 no. 5 p. 27 (Aug '57).

Bancroft, Hubert Howe. Amer. heri. vol. 1 no. 3 p. 17 (spring '50).

band. Holiday 7: 12, 16 Je '50.
—— (at train). Holiday 27: 114 Feb '60.
—— (boys & girls). Holiday 20: 78 (col.) Dec '56.
—— (ceremonial, comic). Holiday 25: 11 Mar '59.
—— (circus). Durant: Pict. hist. of Amer. circus, p. 198.
—— (musicians). Holiday 26: 104 Aug '59; 27: 85 May '60.
—— (playing instruments). Holiday 16: 42-3 (col.) Dec '54.
——, Bermuda. Holiday 23: 72 Je '58.
——, busbied (Royal regiment). Holiday 11: 102 (col.) Je '52.
——, carnival. Holiday 11: 94 (col.) Feb '52.
——, Casanova steel. Holiday 11: 95 (col.) Feb '52.
——, Jamaican. Holiday 26: 169 (col.) Oct '59, 43 (col.) Dec '59.
——, jazz. *See* jazz band.
——, Negro (funeral procession). Holiday 11: 44 Mar '52.

band, Scottish. Natl. geog. 112: 462-3 (col.) Oct '57.

——, Turk Murphy. Holiday 18: 73 (col.) Sept '55.

——, U.S. marine. See U.S. marine band.

——, West India regiment. Holiday 5: 44 (col.) Feb '49.

band concert, high school. Holiday 10: 49 (col.) Dec '51.

band leaders, high school. Natl. geog. 100: 291 (col.) Sept '51.

band parade (early Amer.). Amer. heri. vol. 7 no. 1 p. 36-7 (col.) (Dec '55).

—— (Ohio). Holiday 6: 73 Nov '49.

band shell (Chicago). Natl. geog. 104: 790 Dec '53.

—— (Miami). Natl. geog. 98: 566 Nov '50.

band stand. Amer. heri. vol. 5 no. 2 p. 44 (col.) (winter '54).

—— (1912). Natl. geog. 116: 111 (col.) Jl '59.

Banda, Hastings. Cur. biog. (1963).

Banda dance (Haiti). Holiday 16: inside cover (col.) Aug '54.

Bandaranaike, Sirimavo. Cur. biog. p. 23 (1961).

Bandaranaike, Solomon W.R.D. Cur. biog. p. 26 (1956).

bandbox. Amer. heri. vol. 10 no. 5, frontis (col.) (Aug '59).

bandits (early west). Horan: Pict. hist. of wild west.

bandoleer. Natl. geog. 117: 88 Jan '60.

bandwagon, circus. Durant: Pict. hist. of Amer. circus, p. 36, 230.

Banff (Canada). Natl. geog. 102: 124 Jl '52; 118: 98 (col.) Jl '60.

Banff natl. park. Holiday 14: 42-3 (col.) Jl '53.

Banff Spring hotel (Alberta). Holiday 14: 44 Jl '53.

Bangkok. Natl. geog. 100: 739 (col.) Dec '51. Travel 102: 23-6 Nov '54.

—— (harbor). Natl. geog. 99: 359 (col.) Mar '51.

—— (lion temple guards). Travel 105: inside cover May '56.

—— (Mondop temple). Int. gr. soc.: Arts . . . p. 85 (col.).

—— (rice field). Travel 111: 59 Mar '59.

—— (Thailand). Natl. geog. 116: 846-52 (col.) Dec '59.

Bangkok's floating market. See floating market, Bangkok's.

Bangor, Bishop of (miniature). Con. ency. of ant., vol. 1 pl. 131.

Bangs, Gorge. Horan: Pict. hist. of wild west, p. 209.

banjo, Egyptian (ancient). Int. gr. soc.: Arts . . . p. 27 (col.).

bank (Conway, Mass., 1855). Amer. heri. vol. 8 no. 1 p. 51 (Dec '56).

bank, Victorian style. Amer. heri. vol. 6 no. 6 p. 38 (Oct '55).

——, piggy. See piggy bank.

——, savings. See "shoot the bear" coin bank.

——, U.S. 2nd (Phila.). Amer. heri. vol. 7 no. 4 p. 9 (col.) (Je '56).

bank failure cartoon (1833). Amer. heri. vol. 7 no. 4 p. 11 (Je '56).

bank interior (Pittsburgh). Holiday 6: 38 (col.) Oct '49.

Bankhead, John H. Cur. biog. p. 24 (1943).

Bankhead, Tallulah. Cur. biog. p. 37 (1941); p. 43 (1953). Holiday 5: 47 (col.) Ap '49.

bankmobile. Natl. geog. 106: 579 Oct '54.

Banks, Ernie. Cur. biog. p. 23 (1959).

Banks, Nathaniel P. Pakula: Cent. album, p. 81.

banner (wind blown). Natl. geog. 114: 534-5 (col.) Oct '58.

——, Chinese New Year. Travel 111: 34 Jan '59.

——, heraldic. Natl. geog. 107: 630 (col.) May '55.

"Banner-carrier of Lucerne" (Graf). Praeg. pict. ency., p. 284.

Bannerman, Helen. Jun. bk. of auth., p. 20.

Bannerman's castle. Holiday 6: 40 Sept '49.

banners, processional (medieval). Int. gr. soc.: Arts . . . p. 79 (col.).

Bannister, Constance. Cur. biog. p. 37 (1955).

Bannister, Roger. Cur. biog. p. 28 (1956).

Bannow, Rudolph F. Cur. biog. p. 16 (1960).

banquet (men's club). Amer. heri. vol. 6 no. 1 p. 28-9 (fall '54).

——, Roman. Int. gr. soc.: Arts . . . p. 179 (col.).

"Banquet at the Guild Hall" (Howard). Con. 132: XI Sept '53.

banquet hall. See Persian banquet hall.

"Banquet of Cleopatra" (Tiepolo). Con. 135: 34 Mar '55.

banquet table. Travel 105: 13 Mar '56.

——, (India). Natl. geog. 117: 618 (col.) May '60.

——, wedding. See wedding banquet.

Banteai Srei shrine (entrance). Natl. geog. 117: 564 (col.) Ap '60.

Banyar, Goldsbrow (Ames). Con. 142: 66 Sept '58.

Bao Dai. Cur. biog. p. 24 (1949).

baptising, ritual (Essenes). Natl. geog. 114: 789 (col.) Dec '58.

"Baptism in Andalusia" (Rosello). Con. 129: LII Je '52.

"Baptism of Christ" (Gassel). Con. 138: 19 (col.) Sept '56.

"Baptism of Christ" (Master). Natl. geog. 110: 627 (col.) Nov '56.

"Baptism of Christ" (Murillo). Con. ency. of ant., vol. 1 pl. 162-3.

"Baptism of Christ" (Poussin). Con. 143: 127 Ap '59.

"Baptism of Clovis." Natl. geog. 101: 90 (col.) Jan '52.

baptismal font (St. Mary's in Wismar). Praeg. pict. ency., p. 54.

—— (Van Tricht). Con. 139: 221 Je '57.

——, bronze. Con. 129: 38 Ap '52.

baptisterium, St. John. See St. John baptisterium.

baptistery (17th cent.). Con. 145: LIX Ap '60.

baptistery doors (Florence). Praeg. pict. ency., p. 298.

bar (cocktail, cartoon). Holiday 13: 114 Jan '53.

——, home. Holiday 14: 3 Dec '53.

——, recreation room. Holiday 10: 14 Oct '51.

Bar Harbor (Maine). Holiday 10: 40-47 (part col.) Jl '51.
bar tender. Holiday 26: inside back cover (col.) Dec '59.
Baranov, Alexander. Amer. heri. vol. 10 no. 3 p. 71 (Ap '59); vol. 11 no. 3 p. 8 (Ap '60).
Baranov's fort (1805). Amer. heri. vol. 10 no. 3 p. 69 (Ap '59).
Baratta, Giovanni (sculpture by). Con. 141: 222 Je '58.
—— **(work by).** Con. 142: 170 Dec '58.
Baratta, Pietro (sculpture by). Con. 142: 176-7 Dec '58.
Barbados island. Holiday 5: 104-5 Mar '49. Natl. geog. 101: 364-92 (part col.) Mar '52; 116: 142-3 (col.) Jl '59. Travel 103: 35-7 Mar '55.
—— **(harbor).** Holiday 23: 40 (col.) Feb '58.
—— **(man, comic).** Holiday 27: 225 Ap '60.
—— **(map).** Natl. geog. 101: 366 (col.) Mar '52.
Barbados natives (West Indies). Holiday 27: 22 Je '60.
Barbarossa brothers (pirates). Amer. heri. vol. 8 no. 2 p. 18 (col.) (Feb '57).
Barbary, states of (map, 1804). Amer. heri. vol. 11 no. 2 p. 28-9 (col.) (Feb '60).
barbecue cooker. Holiday 27: 10 (col.) Ap '60.
barbecue pit. Amer. heri. vol. 4 no. 2 p. 24 (winter '53).
barbecuing lambs. Natl. geog. 113: 322 Mar '58.
Barbed wire. Brooks: Growth of a nation, p. 186.
Barber, Jerry. Cur. biog. (1963).
Barber, Mary I. Cur. biog. p. 39 (1941).
Barber, Red. Cur. biog. p. 27 (1943).
Barber, Samuel. Cooper: Con. ency. of music, p. 56.
Barber, Cpl. Samuel. Cur. biog. p. 31 (1944); (1963).
barber. Holiday 6: 47 (col.) Nov '49.
—— **(cutting hair).** Natl. geog. 106: 21 (col.) Jl '54; 114: 747 (col.) Dec '58.
—— **(shaves woman's head).** Natl. geog. 104: 51 (col.) Jl '53.
—— **(sym.).** Lehner: Pict. bk. of sym., p. 90.
——, **Afghanistan.** Natl. geog. 104: 430 Sept '53.
——, **India.** Travel 111: 20 Jan '59.
——, **ship.** Natl. geog. 116: 801 Dec '59.
barber & wig shop, Colonial. Natl. geog. 106: 449 Oct '54.
barber pole. Lehner: Pict. bk. of sym., p. 90.
barber shop. Holiday 10: 87 Nov '51; 28: 80 Dec '59.
—— **(comic).** Holiday 8: 83 Oct '50.
—— **(frontier).** Travel 108: 30 Aug '57.
——, **India.** Natl. geog. 107: 256 Feb '55.
barbershop quartet. Amer. heri. vol. 5 no. 2 p. 48 (winter '54).
Barbey, Daniel E. Cur. biog. p. 33 (1945).
Barbieri, Fedora. Cur. biog. p. 36 (1957).
Barbieri, Giovanni Francesco. *See* Guercino.
Barbour, Ralph Henry. Jun. bk. of auth., p. 21.
Barca, Desert of (soldiers). Amer. heri. vol. 11 no. 2 p. 32 (Feb '60).
Barcelona (Spain). Holiday 24: 220 (col.) Dec '58; 26: 104-9 (part col.) Dec '59. Travel 105: 45 Ap '56.

Bard, Mary. Cur. biog. p. 30 (1956).
bard, German (11th cent.). Int. gr. soc.: Arts . . . p. 69 (col.).
Bardeen, John. Cur. biog. p. 38 (1959).
Barden, Graham A. Cur. biog. p. 26 (1949).
"Barden towers" (Wharfedale, Eng.) Travel 112: 46 Aug '59.
Bardot, Brigitte. Cur. biog. p. 18 (1960).
barge. Natl. geog. 102: 63 (col.) Jl '52; 112: 265 Aug '57; 114: 676, 688-9 (col.) Nov '58.
—— **(Amalfi, Italy).** Natl. geog. 116: 504 (col.) Oct '59.
—— **(England).** Natl. geog. 98: 193 (col.) Aug '50.
—— **(men).** Natl. geog. 106: 373 (col.) Sept '54.
——, **bamboo (Singapore).** Natl. geog. 103: 195 (col.) Feb '53.
——, **canal.** Natl. geog. 117: 434-5 (part col.) Mar '60.
——, **coal.** Natl. geog. 97: 208 (col.) Feb '50.
——, **freight.** Natl. geog. 110: 215 (col.) Aug '56.
——, **German.** Natl. geog. 111: 773 (col.) Je '57.
——, **grain.** Travel 102: 13 Oct '54.
——, **motor river.** Natl. geog. 109: 668 (col.) May '56.
——, **palace (Bangkok).** Natl. geog. 116: 788 (col.) Dec '59.
——, **pontoon.** *See* pontoon barge.
——, **river.** Brooks: Growth of a nation, p. 105.
Holiday 5: 38 Mar '49. Natl. geog. 97: 184, 188 (col.) Feb '50; 110: 127 Jl '56; 118: 688-9, 700-1 (col.) Nov '60.
barge & mules (model). Natl. geog. 117: 435 (col.) Mar '60.
barge. *See* also sailing barge; tugboat.
barge life, river (France to Belgium). Natl. geog. 108: 532-58 (part col.) Oct '55.
barge terminal (St. Louis). Natl. geog. 114: 683 (col.) Nov '58.
bargemaster, Queen's. *See* Queen's bargemaster.
Bargrave, Isaac (Johnson). Con. 140: 231 Jan '58.
Bariloche (Argentina). Holiday 8: 12 (col.) Nov '50.
Baring, Lady Mary. Holiday 25: 86 (col.) Ap '59.
bark painting (Tiwi). Natl. geog. 109: 430 Mar '56.
Barker, Eric. Holiday 25: 35 (col.) Feb '59.
Barkley, Alben W. (Vice Pres.). Cur. biog. p. 41 (1941); p. 27 (1949). Holiday 7: 46, 62 (col.) Feb '50; 19: 86 Mar '56. Natl. geog. 102: 146 Aug '52.
—— **(V. Pres. welcome).** Natl. geog. 97: 212 Feb '50.
Barlach, Ernst (sculpture by). Praeg. pict. ency., p. 457.
Barlow, Howard. Cur. biog. p. 71 (1954).
barn. Amer. heri. vol. 6 no. 2 p. 100 (winter '55); vol. 7 no. 2 p. 105 (Feb '56), vol. 7 no. 3 p. 48 (col.) (Ap '56). Face of Amer. p. 102, 114, 149, 152-3, 165 (col.).

Holiday 6: 43 (col.) Jl '49, 53 (col.) Nov '49; 10: cover (col.) Sept '51, 149 (col.) Oct '51; 11: 46, 61 (col.) Je '52; 12: 83 Dec '52; 22: 42-3 (col.) Jl '57, 63 Sept '57, 53 (col.) Nov '57; 24: 63 (col.) Oct '58.

Natl. geog. 100: 296 (col.) Sept '51; 102: 2, 9 (col.) Jl '52; 110: 586 (col.) Nov '56; 111: 113 (col.) Jan '57, 610 May '57; 112: 531 (col.) Oct '57, 115: 483 (col.) Ap '59, 593 (col.) May '59; 117: 198 (col.) Feb '60.

Rawson: Ant. pict. bk., p. 73.

Travel 101: 23 Feb '54; 112: 46 Sept '59.

—— (burning). Face of Amer., p. 36 (col.).

——, Dutch (Penn.). Travel 105: 22 Mar '56.

——, (1858). Amer. heri. vol. 4 no. 3 p. 22 (spring '53).

—— (Ste. Agathe des Monts, Quebec). Travel 107: 48 Feb '57.

——, sod roof (Iceland). Natl. geog. 100: 622 (col.) Nov '51.

——, tobacco. Holiday 8: 39 (col.) Jl '50.

barn adv. signs. See advertising signs (on barns).

barn & silo (Japan). Natl. geog. 118: 754 (col.) Dec '60.

Barnard, Chester I. Cur. biog. p. 35 (1945).

Barne, Kitty. Jun. bk. of auth., p. 23.

Barnes, Albert C. Cur. biog. p. 37 (1945).

Barnes, Henry A. Cur. biog. p. 38 (1955).

Barnes, Margaret Campbell. Cur. biog. p. 45 (1953).

Barnes, Judge Stanley N. Cur. biog. p. 47 (1953).

Barnes, Wendell B. Cur. biog. p. 39 (1957).

Barnett, Eugene E. Cur. biog. p. 42 (1941).

Barnett, M. Robert. Cur. biog. p. 13 (1950).

Barnett, Ross Robert. Cur. biog. p. 25 (1961).

Barnhart, Clarence L. Cur. biog. p. 73 (1954).

Barnum, Phineas T. Amer. heri. vol. 5 no. 1 p. 47 (col.) (fall '53).

Durant: Pict. hist. of Amer. circus, p. 50, 59, 63.

Barnum birthplace, P. T. Durant: Pict. hist. of Amer. circus, p. 51.

Barnum home, P. T. Durant: Pict. hist of Amer. circus, p. 57.

Barnum's museum, P. T. Durant: Pict. hist. of Amer. circus, p. 52.

barometer. Holiday 6: 7 Dec '49; 8: 125 Nov '50; 10: 16, 175 Dec '51; 11: 19 May '52; 12: 112, 140 Dec '52; 14: 26, 88 Dec '53; 18: 130, 198 Dec '55; 20: 138 Dec '56; 22: 39 Oct '57, 187 Dec '57; 24: 191 Nov '58, 212 Dec '58; 26: 3 Nov '59, 59 Dec '59, 28: 209 Nov '60, 19 Dec '60.

——, diagonal. Con. 136: LVI Jan '56.

——, ivory (17th cent.). Con. 143: XXVII Mar '59.

"Baronet" (Stubbs). Con. 143: 276 Je '59.

baroque architecture. Int. gr. soc.: Arts . . . p. 99 (col.).

baroque decoration (palace). Holiday 22: 60-1 (col.) Sept '57.

barque, cedar (burial boat, Egypt). Natl. geog. 114: 237 Aug '58.

Barr, Alfred Hamilton, jr. Cur. biog. p. 27 (1961).

Holiday 14: 61 Nov '53.

Barr, John Andrew. Cur. biog. p. 29 (1961).

Barr, Roger. Holiday 27: 26 Jan '60.

Barraband, J. (work of). Con. ency. of ant., vol. 3 pl. 85.

Barracuda, club, See Club Barracuda.

barracks, marine. See U.S. Marine barracks.

Barratt, Sir Arthur Sheridan. Cur. biog. p. 43 (1941).

Barraud, H. & W. (work of). Con. 145: XXXVI Je '60.

Barrault, Jean-Louis. Cur. biog. p. 48 (1953).

Barrault, Madeleine Renaud. Cur. biog. p. 49 (1953).

Barre, Col. (West). Amer. heri. vol. 11 no. 1 p. 30 (col.) (Dec '59).

barrel. Holiday 18: 24 Jl '55; 23: 36, 61 Je '58; 25: 132 (col.) Feb '59, 30 (col.) Mar '59, 114, 182 (col.) Ap '59, 116 (col.) May '59; 26: 21 (col.) Aug '59, 20 (col.) Sept '59, 161 (col.) Oct '59, 142 (col.) Nov '59, 23 (col.), 224 Dec '59; 27: 108 (col.), 157 Jan '60, 120 (col.) Feb '60, 183 (col.) Mar '60; 28: 155 (col.) Oct '60.

Lehner: Pict. bk. of sym., p. 82, 90.

Natl. geog. 101: 374 (col.) Mar '52; 103: 238-9 (col.) Feb '53; 106: 790 (col.) Dec '54; 115: 392 Mar '59.

Durant: Pict. hist. of Amer. circus, p. 138 (col.).

barrel (crackers). Amer. heri. vol. 6 no. 1 p. 22 (col.) (fall '54).

—— (going over waterfall). Holiday 10: 16 Aug '51.

—— (on cart). Holiday 19: 53 Jan '56.

—— (on dog's shoulder). Holiday 23: 113 Je '58.

——, fawcet. Holiday 22: 201 (col.) Dec '57.

——, money. Amer. heri. vol. 11 no. 1, frontis (col.) (Dec '59).

——, seaweed (Japan). Disney: People & places, p. 158 (col.).

——, water. Rawson: Ant. pict, bk., p. 61.

——, whiskey. See whiskey barrel.

——, top (painting, 1850). Amer. heri. vol. 10 no. 1, cover (col.) (Dec '58).

barrels. Holiday 23: 122 (col.) Je '58.

—— (stacked). Holiday 27: 97, 221 (col.) May '60; 28: 158 (col.) Nov '60, 63, 218 (col.) Dec '60.

"Barrels of Money" (V. Dubreuil). Amer. heri. vol. 11 no. 1, frontis (col.) (Dec '59).

Barrett, Mrs. Bryan (Stuart). Con. 142: 123 Nov '58.

Barrett, Edward Ware. Cur. biog. p. 35 (1947).

Barrett, Frank A. Cur. biog. p. 31 (1956).

Barrette, Antonio. Cur. biog. p. 20 (1960).

barrier reef. See Great barrier reef.

barroom. Holiday 13: 83 (col.) Jan '53.

—— (Scotland). Holiday 27: 158 (col.) Jan '60.

barroom. See also Pompeii (bar).

Barros Hurtado, Cesar. Cur. biog. p. 24 (1959).

Barrow (Alaska). Holiday 28: 91 Jl '60.

Barry, Gene. Amer. heri. vol. 11 no. 5 p. 44 (Aug '60).

Barry, James (work of). Con. 126: 25 Aug '50.

Barry, William F. Pakula: Cent. album, p. 83.

Barrymore, Ethel. Cur. biog. p. 45 (1941).

Holiday 7: 65 Mar '50.

Barrymore, Lionel. Cur. biog. p. 29 (1943).

Bart, Black. See Bolton, Charles E.

Barth, Karl. Cur. biog. p. 28 (1962).

Bartholdi (statue of Liberty, adv. on card). Amer. heri. vol. 8 no. 6 p. 40 (col.) (Oct '57).
Bartlett, Edward Lewis. Cur. biog. p. 23 (1951).
Bartlett, Mrs. Paul W. Holiday 7: 43 (col.) Feb '50.
Bartok, Bela. Int. gr. soc.: Arts . . . p. 139 (col.).
Bartolommeo, Fra (work of). Con. 141: 44 Mar '58.
Bartolozzi (work of). Cooper: Con. ency. of music, p. 54.
Barton, Bruce. Cur. biog. p. 31 (1961).
Barton, Clara. Holiday 19: 86 Mar '56.
Barton, George A. Cur. biog. p. 51 (1953).
Barton, Robert B. Cur. biog. p. 26 (1959).
Barton, William. Horan: Pict. hist. of wild west, p. 76.
Barton, Col. William (Rev. war). Amer. heri. vol. 11 no. 5 p. 28 (col.) (Aug '60).
Baruch, Bernard M. Cur. biog. p. 47 (1941); p. 16 (1950).
barway post. See post, barway.
Barzin, Leon. Cur. biog. p. 25 (1951).
Basaiti, Marco (work of). Con. 142: 126 Nov '58.
Basaldella, Afro. See Afro.
Baschet, Marcel (work of). Cooper: Con. ency. of music, p. 86.
bascinet, Italian. Con. 136: 194 Dec '55.
Basdevant, Jules. Cur. biog. p. 18 (1950).
baseball. Holiday 28: 138 Sept '60.
  Natl. geog. 98: 107 (col.) Jl '50.
—— **(cartoon).** Amer. heri. vol. 10 no. 3 p. 16-7, 19 (Ap '59).
baseball bat. See bat, baseball.
baseball batters. Holiday 5: 72-8 Je '49.
baseball boys. See boys, baseball; baseball players.
baseball catcher (college). Holiday 25: 191 May '59.
baseball equipment. Holiday 15: 80 (col.) May '54.
baseball game. Face of Amer., p. 12-3 (col.). Holiday 7: 46 (col.) Ap '50; 19: 108 Feb '56. Natl. geog. 118: 802 (col.) Dec '60.
—— **(boys, man).** Holiday 21: 106 Je '57.
—— **(comic).** Holiday 11: 32 (col.) Je '52.
—— **(on skis).** Natl. geog. 115: 252 (col.) Feb '59.
——, **Antarctica.** Natl. geog. 110: 152 (col.) Aug '56.
——, **Japan.** Natl. geog. 118: 768 (col.) Dec '60.
baseball game & players. Holiday 7: 43-59 (part col.) May '50.
baseball glove. Holiday 18: 104 Dec '55.
baseball ground, Florida. Holiday 17: 64 Mar '55.
baseball player. Holiday 19: 11 Je '56; 26: 107 (col.) Nov '59.
  Natl. geog. 99: 293 (col.) Mar '51.
—— **(head).** Holiday 27: 61 (col.) May '60.
—— **(standing on head).** Holiday 6: 75 Jl '49.
—— **(trophy).** Holiday 19: 145 (col.) May '56.
baseball players. Amer. heri. vol. 10 no. 3 p. 86 (Ap '59); vol. 11 no. 4 p. 24-5 (Je '60). Holiday 7: 136 (col.) Je '50; 11: 28 Je '52; 18: 62 Aug '55; 28: 79 (col.) Jl '60.

Travel 105: 52 May '56.
—— **(at car).** Holiday 27: 192 Mar '60.
—— **(comic).** Holiday 11: 95 Je '52; 15: 87 (col.) May '54; 27: 51 May '60.
—— **(girls).** Holiday 11: 50-1, 75, 80 Je '52.
——, **the Giants.** Holiday 23: 83-5 May '58.
baseball players & managers. Amer. heri. vol. 10 no. 3 p. 21-4 (Ap '59).
baseball stadium. Holiday 19: 102 Mar '56.
——, **Mich.** Holiday 10: 29 Jl '51.
——, **Wis.** Holiday 24: 65 Oct '58.
——, **Yankee.** Holiday 20: 54 Oct '56.
baseball team. Holiday 19: 64 (col.) May '56.
—— **(comic, 1845).** Holiday 26: 3 Dec '59.
Basharri (Lebanon). Natl. geog. 113: 500-1 (col.) Ap '58.
Basie, Count. Cur. biog. p. 55 (1942).
basilica (Monastery Montserrat). Travel 104: 45 Aug '55.
—— **(plan).** Praeg. pict. ency., p. 40.
——, **Franciscan (Holy Land).** Natl. geog. 98: 715 Dec '50.
basin, (15th cent.). Con. 132: 21 Sept '53.
——, **copper gilt Venetian (16th cent.).** Con. 144: 218 Jan '60.
——, **Elizabethan silver.** Con. 139: 29 Mar '57.
——, **Fiji ceremonial drink.** Holiday 28: 76 (col.) Oct '60.
——, **Sevres porcelain.** Con. ency. of ant., vol. 1 pl. 63.
——, **silver gilt (17th cent.).** Con. 139: 30 Mar '57.
——, **silver gilt Venetian (16th cent.).** Con. 144: 219 Jan '60.
"Basin of St. Mark's." Natl. geog. 101: 82 (col.) Jan '52.
Basin Springs (Banff Park). Travel 106: 42 Jl '56.
basin stand. See washing stand.
basket. Holiday 11: 1 May '52; 12: 14 Jl '52, 99 (col.) Sept '52; 21: 191 Je '57; 28: 194 Oct '60.
—— **(apples).** Con. 145: IX (col.) May '60. Natl. geog. 99: 138 Jan '51.
—— **(bottle).** Holiday 12: 128 Oct '52, 74 Nov '52, 97 (col.) Dec '52; 13: 26 Ap '53.
—— **(champagne).** Holiday 11: 21 Mar '52.
—— **(dolls).** Travel 112: inside back cover Dec '59.
—— **(Easter eggs).** Lehner: Pict. bk. of sym., p. 52.
Travel 113: 7 Mar '60, inside back cover Ap '60.
—— **(elephants).** Holiday 27: 59 May '60.
—— **(flowers).** Holiday 27: 18 (col.) May '60.
—— **(girl holding).** Natl. geog. 104: 367 (col.) Sept '53.
—— **(picnic).** Natl. geog. 110: 19 (col.) Jl '56.
—— **(toys).** Travel 112: 11 Dec '59.
—— **(truffles).** Natl. geog. 110: 420 Sept '56.
——, **bicycle.** Natl. geog. 105: 207, 217 (col.) Feb '54.
——, **cake.** See cake basket.
——, **dessert (antique silver).** Con. 139: 58 Mar '57.
——, **farm.** Natl. geog. 111: 649 (col.) May '57.
——, **fruit.** See fruit basket.

basket, Geo. II silver. Con. 135: III Ap '55; 136: XXIII Nov '55; 138: VII Dec '56.
——, ice bucket. Holiday 11: 142 Ap '52.
——, Indian. Amer. heri. vol. 7 no. 6 p. 15 (Oct '56).
——, Iraq. Natl. geog. 114: 454 (col.) Oct '58.
——, market. Holiday 23: 38 (col.) Feb '58. Natl. geog. 98: 759 (col.) Dec '50.
——, pygmy. Natl. geog. 117: 295 Feb '60.
——, reed (Cypress isle). Natl. geog. 101: 663 (col.) May '52.
——, shopping. Holiday 20: 114 (col.) Nov '56.
——, silver (Lamerie). Con. 144: 62 Sept '59.
——, silver (16th cent.). Con. 143: 51 Mar '59.
——, silver gilt (Storr, 1797). Con. 144: XXVII Dec '59.
——, Sudan. Natl. geog. 103: 265 (col.) Feb '53.
——, vegetable. Holiday 21: 42 (col.) Ap '57. Natl. geog. 97: 47 Jan '50.
——, wicker. Natl. geog. 103: 693 May '53.
——, woven. Natl. geog. 110: 741 Dec '56.
——, woven (Laos). Natl. geog. 117: 48, 69 (col.) Jan '60.
——, woven (Nepal). Natl. geog. 117: 382 (col.) Mar '60.
basket boat, bamboo. See boat, bamboo basket.
basket making (Ischia). Natl. geog. 105: 544 (col.) Ap '54.
basket of flowers (carved wood). Con. ency. of ant., vol. 3 pl. 103.
basket shop (Karachi). Natl. geog. 102 647 (col.) Nov '52.
basket weaving, Indian. Brooks: Growth of a nation, p. 25.
basket. See also baskets.
basketball. Holiday 10: 159 Dec '51; 18: 104 Dec '55.
basketball game. Holiday 10: 87 Aug '51. Travel 106: 4 Nov '56.
—— (on horses). Natl. geog. 113: 314-5 (col.) Mar '58.
—— (on horses, comic). Holiday 21: 14 May '57.
——, Chinese. Natl. geog. 111: 352 Mar '57.
baskets (fish). Holiday 16: 98 (col.) Nov '54.
—— (men, clams). Natl. geog. 107: 201 (col.) Feb '55.
—— (on women's heads). Natl. geog. 99: 39 (col.) Jan '51; 103: 42 (col.) Jan '53; 107: 413 (col.) Mar '55.
—— (tomatoes, men, trucks). Natl. geog. 98: 399 (col.) Sept '50.
—— (woman, tomatoes). Natl. geog. 98: 379 (col.) Sept '50.
——, Caribbean. Holiday 25: 45 (col.) May '59.
——, Chile (women). Natl. geog. 117: 213 (col.) Feb '60.
——, Java. Natl. geog. 99: 32 (col.) Jan '51.
——, Hong Kong (produce). Natl. geog. 105: 259 (col.) Feb '54.
——, shrimp. Natl. geog. 111: 700 (col.) May '57.
——, vegetables (on donkey). Natl. geog. 100: 151 (col.) Aug '51.
——, water (field irrigation, Iraq). Natl. geog. 114: 482-3 (col.) Oct '58.
baskets of fruit, Pitcairn islands. Natl. geog. 112: 779 (col.) Dec '57.

baskets of grapes (men carrying). Holiday 26: 13 (col.) Nov '59.
Basle (Switzerland). Con. 129: 82 Je '52.
Basofi men (Africa). Travel 104: 54-5 Nov '55.
bason & ewer, Portuguese silver (16th cent.). Con ency. of ant., vol. 3 p. 32.
Basque dancer (man). Holiday 27: 138 Je '60.
Basque dancers (Spain). Natl. geog. 109: 328-9 (col.) Mar '56.
Basque dances. Natl. geog. 105: 148-9, 161-3 (part col.) Feb '54.
Basque festival (France). Holiday 25: 142 (col.) May '59.
Basque harbor. Travel 106: 24 Oct '56.
Basques. Holiday 23: 88-9 Mar '58. Natl. geog. 105: 148-86 (part col.) Feb '54.
——, Lands of the (map). Natl. geog. 105: 153 Feb '54.
bas-relief (Abe Lincoln). Natl. geog. 101: 165 (col.) Feb '52.
—— (Folger library). Natl. geog. 100: 414 Sept. '51.
—— (4th cent.). Con. 144: 208 Dec '59.
—— (Hittite carving). Natl. geog. 115: 77 (col.) Jan '59.
—— (Marquette & Joliet). Brooks: Growth of a nation, p. 58.
—— (Saint Gaudens). Amer. heri., vol. 9 no. 4 p. 55 (Je '58).
—— (Santa Restitula, 13th cent.). Labande: Naples, p. 44.
——, Bavarian. Ceram: March of arch., p. 213.
——, cave (China). Natl. geog. 99: 397 (col.) Mar '51.
——, wall (Angkor). Natl. geog. 117: 536-7, 540-1, 557, 569 (part col.) Ap '60.
Bass, Sam. Horan: Pict. hist. of wild west, p. 85-6, 88.
bass drum. See drum, bass.
bass flute. See flute, bass.
bass violin, double. Cooper: Con. ency. of music, p. 345.
—— (by Forster, 1789). Cooper: Con. ency. of music, p. 351.
—— (internal case, 1853). Cooper: Con. ency. of music, p. 351.
Bassano (work of). Con. 138: 211 Dec '56.
Bassano, Francesco (work of). Con. 144: LIII Jan '60.
Bassano, Jacopo (work of). Con. 140: 164-5, 184 Dec '57; 144: LXXIII Dec '59.
basset horn (1880). Cooper: Con. ency. of music, p. 401.
Bassett, Charles E. Horan: Pict. hist. of wild west, p. 105.
Bassett, Sara Ware. Cur. biog. p. 33 (1956).
bassoon. Cooper: Con. ency. of music, p. 402-3. Int. gr. soc.: Arts . . . p. 141 (col.).
——, contra. Cooper: Con. ency. of music, p. 403.
——, Cor Anglais. Cooper: Con. ency. of music, p. 403.
Bastille Day parade. Natl. geog. 101: 774 (col.) Je '52.
Bastille, Paris storming. Amer. heri., vol. 8 no. 1 p. 108 (Dec '56).
Baston, T. (engraving by). Con. 140: XII Dec '57.
bat (sym.). Lehner: Pict. bk. of sym., p. 45.

bat, baseball. Holiday 15: 80 May '54. Natl. geog. 105: 299 (col.) Mar '54.
—— (boy). Holiday 21: 106 Je '57.
Batak homes. *See* homes, Batak.
Batalha church, 16th cent. (Portuguese Gothic). Con. 139: LI May '57.
Batcheller, Hiland G. Cur. biog. p. 30 (1949).
Bates, Edward. Amer. heri. vol. 11 no. 6 p. 46 (Oct '60).
Bates, Herbert E. Cur. biog. p. 33 (1944).
Bates, Marston. Cur. biog. p. 34 (1956).
Bates, Sanford. Cur. biog. p. 33 (1961).
Bath (England). Holiday 26: 48-53 (part col.) Aug '59.
Natl. geog. 108: 334 (col.) Sept '55.
bath, Roman. *See* Roman bath.
Bath Stone conservatory (near Guildford). Con. 138: XXXVIII Sept '56.
bath tub. *See* bathtub.
"Bather" (Matisse). Holiday 14: 60 (col.) Nov '53.
"the bathers." Praeg. pict. ency., p. 429 (col.).
bathers (lunch on beach). Holiday 21: 57 Ap '57.
"Bathers" (Renoir). Con. 134: 62 Sept '54.
bathers (swimming pool). Natl. geog. 113: 62-3 (col.) Jan '58.
bathers, health (Lake Urmia, Iran). Natl. geog. 115: 65 (col.) Jan '59.
"Bathers before a tent" (Cezanne). Con. 145: 184 (col.) May '60.
"Bathers with a turtle" (Matisse). Con. 133: 288 Je '54.
bathers. *See* also girls (bathing suits); men & girls (beach); swimming pool, etc.
bathing (Japan). *See* bathtub, communal.
bathing beauties (1924). Jensen: The White House, p. 227.
bathing boxes (Africa). Natl. geog. 104: 167 (col.) Aug '53.
bathing ghats. *See* ghat, bathing.
bathing suit (1875). Amer. heri. vol. 5 no. 4 p. 6 (summer '54).
—— (old fashioned). Holiday 23: 142 (col.) Je '58.
—— (1903). Amer. heri. vol. 10 no. 1 p. 92 (Dec '58).
—— *See* also girls (bathing suits).
"Bathing women" (Flemish-Italo, bronze). Con. 143: 216 Je '59.
bathrobe. Holiday 28: 220 Nov '60.
bathroom. Holiday 27: 149-54 (part col.) Mar '60.
"Bathsheba after the bath" (Rembrandt). Con. 138: 29 Sept '56.
bathtub, Japanese. Disney: People & places, p. 157 (col.).
——, Japanese communal. Natl. geog. 118: 752-3 (col.) Dec '60.
——, old style (woman & boy). Amer. heri. vol. 3 no. 4 p. 3 (summer '52).
——, Pres. Taft's (The White House). Jensen: The White House, p. 197.
——, wooden (antique). Rawson: Ant. pict. bk., p. 15.
bathynauts. Natl. geog. 118: 239 (col.) Aug '60.
bathyscaphe. Natl. geog. 106: 68-86 Jl '54; 107: 540 Ap '55; 113: 719, 722-4 May '58.
—— (men). Natl. geog. 117: 146-7 Jan '60.

—— (U.S. Navy Trieste). Natl. geog. 118: 224-36 (part col.) Aug '60.
batik making. Natl. geog. 99: 2 Jan '51.
——, Java (girls). Natl. geog. 108: 369 (col.) Sept '55.
Batista, Gen. Fulgencio. Cur. biog. p. 40 (1952).
Baton Rouge (La.). Natl. geog. 118: 710 (col.) Nov '60.
—— (capital bldg.). Holiday 15: 78 Feb '54. Jordan: Hammond's pict. atlas, p. 84 (col.).
batons (antique ivorylike bones). Natl. geog. 97: 233 Feb '50.
Batt, William L. Cur. biog. p. 58 (1942).
Batt, William L., jr. Cur. biog. p. 30 (1962).
Batta pipe. Amer. heri. vol. 6 no. 2 p. 17 (Feb '55).
Battalion monument, Mormon (Utah). Travel 101: 4 Ap '54.
Battersea enamel box. *See* enamel box, Battersea.
Battersea enamel wine label. Con. 143: 101 Ap '59.
battery, auto. Holiday 6: 17 Oct '49, 137 Nov '49, 103 Dec '49; 7: 157 Je '50; 8: 85 Jl '50; 10: 124 Oct '51, 85 Nov '51, 91 Dec '51.
battery element (sym.). Lehner: Pict. bk. of sym., p. 12.
Battistini, Mattia. Cooper: Con. ency. of music, p. 57.
Battle, John S. Cur. biog. p. 20 (1950).
battle (Ball's Bluff). Amer. heri. vol. 6 no. 1 p. 18 (fall '54).
—— (British & Amer.). Amer. heri. vol. 8 no. 5 p. 9 (col.) (Aug '57).
—— (British attack on Ft. Moultrie). Amer. heri. vol. 6 no. 6 p. 62-3 (col.) (Oct '55).
—— (Capt. Cook at Hawaii). Amer. heri. vol. 11 no. 2 p. 10 (col.) (Feb '60).
—— (Clivedon house). Natl. geog. 118: 176 (col.) Aug '60.
—— (Custer's last stand). Brooks: Growth of a nation, p. 181.
Holiday 8: 37 Sept '50.
—— (Fallen timbers, 1793). Amer. heri. vol. 9 no. 4 p. 58 (Je '58).
—— (Israelites, Philistines). Natl. geog. 112: 846-7 (col.) Dec '57.
—— (Khmers defeated, 1432). Natl. geog. 117: 560-1 (col.) Ap '60.
—— (Marines raise flag, Tripoli). Amer. heri. vol. 11 no. 2 p. 33 (Feb '60).
—— (Monitor & Merrimac). Amer. heri. vol. 8 no. 4 p. 10-11 (col.) (Je '57).
—— (Mormons, 1857). Amer. heri. vol. 7 no. 6 p. 22 (Oct '56).
—— ("Old Ironsides"). Amer. heri. vol. 6 no. 3 p. 57 (col.) (Ap '55).
—— (Pickett's charge, Gettysburg). Amer. heri. vol. 9 no. 1 p. 30 (col.) (Dec '57).
—— (Ruffin Walker attacks). Amer. heri. vol. 9 no. 1 p. 28-9 (Dec '57).
—— (1758). Amer. heri. vol. 6 no. 5 p. 12 (col.) (Aug '55).
—— (1777). Amer. heri. vol. 8 no. 1 p. 105 (Dec '56).
—— (1781). Amer. heri. vol. 7 no. 3 p. 35 (col.) (Ap '56).
—— (Spanish & Indians). Amer. heri. vol. 6 no. 1 p. 106 (fall '54).

battle (Ticonderoga). Amer. heri. vol. 12 no. 1 p. 7 (col.) Dec '60).

—— (Trenton). Amer. heri. vol. 8 no. 5 p. 63 (col.) (Aug '57).

—— (U.S. vs Mexico). Amer. heri. vol. 6 no. 4 p. 21, 23 (col.) (Je '55); vol. 9 no. 5 p. 16-7 (col.) (Aug '58).

—— (western pioneer). Horan: Pict. hist. of wild west, p. 63.

——, Amer. revolution. See Amer. revolution.

——, Civil war. See U.S. Civil war.

——, sea (1804). Amer. heri. vol. 11 no. 2 p. 30-1 (part col.) (Feb '60).

——, sea (1812). Amer. heri. vol. 7 no. 3 p. 13-21 (col.) (Ap '56).

"Battle Abbey" (Richmond, Va.). Amer. heri. vol. 5 no. 3 p. 40 (spring '54).

"Battle at Gettysburg" (by Philippoteaux). Amer. heri. vol. 9 no. 1 p. 30 (col.) (Dec '57).

battle-ax. See ax, battle.

"Battle between Alexander & Darius (Mosaic, Pompeii). Labande: Naples, p. 104.

battle camp (Harpers Ferry). See Harpers Ferry battle camp.

battle of Quebec (1759). See Quebec (battle, 1759).

battle map (Harpers Ferry). See Harpers Ferry region (map).

battle monuments. See monument, battle.

Battle of Alexander (Pompeii). Praeg. pict. ency., p. 149 (col.).

battle of Antietam (1862). Amer. heri. vol. 9 no. 5 p. 56-7, 94 (col.) (Aug '58).

"Battle of Atlanta" (Civil war). Amer. heri. vol. 7 no. 2 p. 32-43 (col.) (Feb '56).
Brooks: Growth of a nation, p. 145.
Natl. geog. 105: 309 Mar '54.

"Battle of Bunker Hill" (by Pyle). Amer. heri. vol. 10 no. 2 p. 16-7 (col.) (Feb '59).

battle of Hickory Point (1856). Amer. heri. vol. 7 no. 5 p. 7 (Aug '56).

"Battle of Lake Erie" (Garneray). Natl. geog. 99: 189 Feb '51.

"Battle of Lexington" (1775). Amer. heri., vol. 10 no. 5 p. 61 (col.), 63 (Aug '59).
Natl. geog. 102: 161 (col.) Aug '52.

Battle of Little Big Horn. Brooks: Growth of a nation, p. 181.
Holiday 8: 37 Sept '50.

"Battle of Manila Bay." Amer. heri. vol. 8 no. 2 p. 32 (col.) (Feb '57).

"Battle of Naseby" (1645). Amer. heri. vol. 6 no. 5 p. 16-7 (col.) (Aug '55).

Battle of New Orleans. Amer. heri. vol. 8 no. 5 p. 4-5 (col.) (Aug '57).

—— (war 1812). Holiday 23: 78-9 (col.) May '58.

Battle of San Jacinto (Texas). Jordan: Hammond's pict. atlas, p. 117 (col.).

"Battle of the Nile" (Anderson). Con. 140: LI Jan '58.

"Battle of the nudes" (Pollaiuolo). Con. 129: 73 Ap '52.

"Battle of the Saints" (Luny). Con. 140: VIII Jan '58.

—— (map of). See map (Battle of the Saints).

"Battle of Trafalgar" (Jeakes). Con. ency. of ant., vol. 1, pl. 140.

battle of Hudson Bay (1697). Amer. heri. vol. 2 no. 2 p. 51-5 (part col.) (winter '51).

battlefield, Gettysburg. See Gettysburg.

——, U.S. Civil war. See U.S. Civil war (battlefield).

battleship. Amer. heri. vol. 12 no. 1 p. 68-9 (Dec '60).
Holiday 26: 88-9 Dec '56.

—— (17th cent.). Con. 129: XLII Je '52.

—— (1778). Natl. geog. 116: 94-5 (col.) Jl '59.

—— (1812). Holiday 23: 74-5 (col.) May '58.

—— (1813). Amer. heri. vol. 10 no. 2 p. 29 (col.) (Feb '59).
Con. 141: XLV Mar '58.

—— (1815). Amer. heri. vol. 10 no. 4 p. 60 (col.) Je '59.

—— (1861). Amer. heri. vol. 10 no. 6 p. 66, 71 (col.) (Oct '59).

—— (18th cent.). Con. 132: 115 Nov '53.

—— (Scott). Con. 133: XIII Mar '54.

——, antique. Con. 132: LXVII Nov '53.

——, old. Con. 129: 111 Je '52.

battleship "Constitution," Con. 129: 140 Je '52.

battleships. Amer. heri. vol. 8 no. 4 p. 10-11 (col.) (Je '57); vol. 10, no. 6 p. 23 (Oct '59); vol. 11 no. 4 p. 28 (Je '60).

—— (1588). Amer. heri. vol. 10 no. 3 p. 14-5 (col.) (Ap '59).

—— (1782). Con. 140: VIII Jan '58.

—— (Revolution). Amer. heri. vol. 9 no. 4 p. 6-7 (col.) (Je '58).

—— (spring day festival). Natl. geog. 110: 599 (col.) Nov '56.

—— (Tripoli, 1804). Amer. heri. vol. 10 no. 2 p. 27 (Feb '59).

Baudouin, Prince royal of Belgium. Cur. biog. p. 21 (1950).

Bauer, Louis Hopewell. Cur. biog. p. 38 (1948).

the Bauhaus (Dessau). Praeg. pict. ency., p. 441.

Baum, Kurt. Cur. biog. p. 36 (1956).

Baumer, Marie. Cur. biog. p. 34 (1958).

Baumgartner, Leona. Cur. biog. p. 23 (1950).

Bavaria. Holiday 12: 136 (col.) Oct '52; 25: 50, 54 (col.) May '59.

—— (castle). Holiday 19: 40-1 (col.) Mar '56.

—— (festival). Holiday 10: 16-9, 22 Oct '51.

—— (Hall of liberation). Praeg. pict. ency., p. 423.

—— (girls dancing). Holiday 10: 16-7 Oct '51.

—— (man & woman). Holiday 16: 13 (col.) Nov '54.

—— (woman, harvest field). Travel 114: 8 Jl '60.

Bavarian Alps. See Alps, Bavarian.

Bavarian bas-relief. See bas-relief, Bavarian.

Bavarian folk dancers. Natl. geog. 115: 474 (col.) Ap '59.

Bax, Sir Arnold. Cur. biog. p. 32 (1943).

Baxter, Frank C. Cur. biog. p. 41 (1955).

Baxter, James P., 2d. Cur. biog. p. 37 (1947).

Baxter, James Phinney, 3d. Cur. biog. p. 37 (1947).

Bay, Mrs. Charles Ulrick. Cur. biog. p. 41 (1957).

"Bay of fire" (Puerto Rico). Natl. geog. 118: 122 (col.) Jl '60.

Bay of Fundy. Natl. geog. 112: 154-92 (part col.) Aug '57.

—— (map). Natl. geog. 112: 162 Aug '57.

Bay of Naples. Labande: Naples, p. 36.
——. Travel 103: 19 Ap '55.
"Bay of Naples" (Joli). Con. 141: XXV Mar '58.
Bayar, Celal. Cur. biog. p. 26 (1950).
Bayard, James Asheton, Amer. heri. vol. 12 no. 1 p. 28 (col.) (Dec '60).
Bayou, Louisiana. *See* Louisiana bayou.
Bayreuth festspielhaus. Cooper: Con. ency. of music, p. 450.
Bayreuth opera house. Int. gr. soc.: Arts . . . p. 123 (col.).
bazaar (Aswan). Natl. geog. 118: 352 (col.) Sept '60.
—— (Baghdad). Natl. geog. 114: 42 Jl '58.
——, outdoor (Kashmir). Natl. geog. 114: 616 (col.) Nov '58.
—— (Lebanon). Natl. geog. 113: 498 (col.) Ap '58.
—— (St. Veran mobile). Natl. geog. 115: 372 Ap '59.
—— (Saudi Arabia). Natl. geog. 104: 36 (col.) Jl '53.
bazaar street, Arabia. Natl. geog. 115: 498-9 (col.) Ap '59.
Bazin, Germain. Cur. biog. p. 27 (1959).
Beach, Capt. Edward. Cur. biog. p. 21 (1960).
Beach, Thomas (work of). Con. 135: 241 (Je '55).
beach. Holiday 6: 30 (col.) Dec '49; 8: 19 (col.) Sept '30; 13: 39 (col.) Feb '53, 88, 120 (col.) Mar '53, 5, 122, 151 (col.) Ap '53, 18, 20, 39, 40, 103, 167 (col.) May '53, 26, 49, 71, 87, 143 (col.) Je '53; 14: 96-7 (col.) Jl '53, 125 Oct '53, 13 (col.) Nov '53; 18: 75 (col.) Jl '55; 23: 98 (col.) Jan '58, 7 (col.) Ap '58, 143 (col.) May '58; 25: 119 Ap '59; 26: 142 (col.) Nov '59; 27: 110 (col.) Mar '60.
Travel 101: 8 Feb '54, 4, 12 Mar '54, 7 Ap '54; 102: 5, 11 Jl '54, 22, 52 Dec '54; 103: 36 Jan '55, 7, 11, 24, 26 Feb '55, 46 Mar '55, 58 May '55, inside cover, 30, 45 Je '55; 104: 17 Sept '55, 14 Oct '55, 62 Nov '55; 105: 12 Jan '56, 45, 49 Mar '56; 106: cover Sept '56; 112: 31 Aug '59.
—— (bathers). Holiday 23: 51 Jan '58.
Natl. geog. 105: 783 (col.) Je '54; 113: 779 (col.) Je '58; 118: 566-7 (col.) Oct '60.
—— (bathers, chairs, umbrellas). Natl. geog. 116: 481 (col.) Oct '59.
—— (bathers, sandy). Natl. geog. 111: 640 (col.) May '57.
—— (boy & girl). Holiday 12: 115 (col.) Sept '52.
—— (fisherman, waves). Natl. geog. 112: 296-7 (col.) Sept '57.
—— (man & girl at car). Holiday 25: 10 (col.) Feb '59.
—— (man, woman & children). Natl. geog. 98: 156 (col.) Aug '50.
—— (men, woman & children). Natl. geog. 109: 258 (col.) Feb '56.
—— (men & woman). Natl. geog. 113: 345 (col.) Mar '58.
—— (men & women). Holiday 28: 49 (col.) Nov '60.
—— (moonlight). Holiday 24: 75 (col.) Nov '58; 28: 20 (col.) Oct '60.

—— (ocean). Holiday 8: 57, 120 (col.) Oct '50, 31 (col.) Nov '50; 9: 98, 133 (col.) Mar '51.
Jordan: Hammond's pict. atlas, p. 68, 74 (col.).
Natl. geog. 108: 772-3 (col.) Dec '55.
—— (ocean, men fish). Natl. geog. 113: 630 (col.) May '58.
—— (people at table). Natl. geog. 111: 659 (col.) May '57.
—— (rocky). Face of Amer., p. 94-5 (col.).
Holiday 11: 79 (col.) Ap '52; 13: 103 (col.) Je '53; 14: 41, 89 (col.) Jl '53; 24: 107 (col.) Dec '58; 25: 41 Feb '59; 27: 29 (col.) Feb '60.
Natl. geog. 101: 384-5, 388 (col.) Mar '52; 105: 236 (col.) Feb '54; 107: 735 (col.) Je '55; 113: 649 (col.) May '58.
—— (rocky, picnic). Holiday 12: 111 (col.) Jl '52.
Natl. geog. 108: 122-3 (col.) Jl '55.
—— (sand & rocks). Holiday 20: 67 (col.) Aug '56.
—— (sandy). Natl. geog. 111: 846-7 (col.) Je '57; 114: 282 (col.) Aug '58; 116: 442 (col.) Oct '59.
—— (sandy, cliffs). Natl. geog. 107: 750 (col.) Je '55.
—— (storm, man, palm trees). Natl. geog. 113: 236-7 Feb '58.
—— (sunrise). Face of Amer., p. 168-9 (col.).
—— (winter, snow). Travel 107: inside back cover Feb '57.
—— (women). Amer. heri. vol. 8 no. 5 p. 48-9 (col.) Aug '57.
Natl. geog. 103: 41, 53, 62 (col.) Jan '53.
——, Africa (Cape Town). Natl. geog. 104: 162, 164-5 (col.) Aug '53.
——, Africa (Cape Town, rocky). Natl. geog. 104: 174-5 (col.) Aug '53.
——, Alaska (bathers). Natl. geog. 109: 750 (col.) Je '56; 116: 76 (col.) Jl '59.
——, Anaho Bay. Natl. geog. 97: 90 (col.) Jan '50.
——, Argentina (Mar de Plata). Travel 108: 51 Nov '57.
——, Australia. Travel 112: 30-1, 35 Dec '59.
——, Australia (Sydney). Holiday 8: 102 (col.) Nov '50.
——, Bahamas. Natl. geog. 113: 179 (col.) Feb '58.
——, Bahamas (man, girl). Holiday 25: 26 (col.) Feb '59.
——, Bahamas (sandy). Natl. geog. 113: 188-9 (col.) Feb '58.
——, Bermuda. Holiday 11: 12 (col.) Je '52; 21: 184 (col.) Ap '57; 23: 75 (col.) Je '58; 25: 40 (col.) Mar '59, 168 (col.) Ap '59; 26: 103 (col.) Oct '59; 27: 98 (col.) Mar '60; 28: 150 (col.) Oct '60.
Natl. geog. 105: 222-3 (col.) Feb '54.
Travel 111: 16 Feb '59.
——, Biarritz. Natl. geog. 109: 329 (col.) Mar '56.
——, Boca Raton. Holiday 26: 54 Dec '59.
——, Brazil. Holiday 12: 145 (col.) Oct '52; 27: 229 (col.) May '60.
Natl. geog. 108: 755 (col.) Dec '55.
——, Brazil (Rio de Janeiro). Holiday 11: in-

side cover (col.) Jan '52; 12: 92 (col.) Nov '52.

——, Brazil (Rio de Janeiro, man, girl). Holiday 18: 13 (col.) Dec '55.

——, Brazil (Rio de Janeiro, bathers). Natl. geog. 107: 308-9 (col.) Mar '55.

——, Brittany. Holiday 27: 79 (col.) Jan '60.

——, the Bronx. Natl. geog. 112: 304-5 Sept '57.

——, California. Holiday 11: 87 (col.) May '52; 12: 13, 115, 118 (col.) Dec '52; 21: 181 (col.) Ap '57; 24: 127 (col.) Dec '58; 26: 61 (col.) Jl '59. Natl. geog. 105: 756 (col.) Je '54.

——, California (La Jolla). Natl. geog. 102: 764-5, 768, 775, 778 (col.) Dec '52.

——, California (Pueblo beach). Travel 109: 46 Je '58.

——, California (rugged cliffs). Natl. geog. 105: 765 Je '54.

——, Caribbean. Holiday 25: 126 (col.) Feb '59.

——, Chicago (lake). Jordan: Hammond's pict. atlas, p. 97 (col.).

——, Colorado. Natl. geog. 106: 230 (col.) Aug '54.

——, Costa do Sol. Holiday 19: 34 (col.) Jan '56.

——, Cuba. Holiday 13: 72-3 Feb '53.

——, Delaware (Rehoboth). Holiday 17: 110 (col.) Mar '55.

——, England. Holiday 27: 85 Feb '60.

——, England (Bath). Natl. geog. 108: 334 (col.) Sept '55.

——, Falkland (rocky). Natl. geog. 109: 388 (col.) Mar '56.

——, Florida. Holiday 13: 7 (col.) Jan '53; 24: 155 (col.) Dec '58; 26: 87 (col.) Nov '59; 27: 7 (col.) Jan '60, 121 (col.) Ap '60, 31 (col.) May '60. Travel 114: 30, 32 Dec '60.

——, Florida (Daytona). Holiday 25: 176 Ap '59. Natl. geog. 113: 44-5 (col.) Jan '58.

——, Florida (Ft. Clinch). Travel 109: 20 Jan '58.

——, Florida (Ft. Lauderdale). Holiday 11: 34-5 (col.) Jan '52; 26: 53 (col.) Dec '59.

——, Florida (Ft. Myers). Travel 107: 25 Jan '57.

——, Florida (Miami). Brooks: Growth of a nation, p. 293. Holiday 11: 30-1 (col.) Jan '52. Natl. geog. 98: 563 Nov '50.

——, Formosa (rocky, mt.). Natl. geog. 97: 163 (col.) Feb '50.

——, France (cliffs). Natl. geog. 115: 629 (col.) May '59.

——, France (Deauville). Holiday 14: 95 (col.) Sept '53.

——, France (La Baule). Holiday 27: 86 (col.) May '60.

——, Greve de Lecq. Travel 101: 9 May '54.

——, Hawaii. Holiday 14: 82 (col.) Sept '53, 149 (col.) Oct '53; 19: 88 (col.) Mar '56; 21: 21 (col.) Mar '57; 22: 4 (col.) Nov '57; 24: 19 (col.) Jl '58, 75 (col.) Aug '58; 25: 97 (col.) Jan '59; 26: 18 (col.) Oct '59, 119 Nov '59; 27: 122 (col.) Feb '60, 152

(col.) Ap '60; 28: 109 Aug '60, 92 (col.) Sept '60, 185 (col.) Oct '60, 45 (col.) Nov '60, 118 (col.) Dec '60. Natl. geog. 115: 795 (col.) Je '59. Travel 102: 11-2, 14, 31 Nov '54; 107: 43 Jan '57.

——, Hawaii (Waikiki). Travel 113: 60 Mar '60.

——, Ischia. Natl. geog. 105: 532 (col.) Ap '54.

——, Isle of Pines. Holiday 27: 194 (col.) Ap '60.

——, Italy. Holiday 21: 51, 53 (col.) Jan '57. Labande: Naples, p. 25, 136.

——, Jamaica. Holiday 24: 122 (col.) Aug '58; 25: 62 (col.) Feb '59.

——, Jamaica (rocky). Natl. geog. 105: 351 (col.) Mar '54.

——, Jamaica (Montego Bay). Travel 109: 49 May '58.

——, Lake Mendota (swimmers, sail boat). Natl. geog. 111: 152 (col.) Feb '57.

——, Lake Ontario. Amer. heri. vol. 8 no. 3 p. 4, 10 (col.) Ap '57.

——, Mahe (tropical). Natl. geog. 116: 685 (col.) Nov '59.

——, Malaya. Natl. geog. 103: 215 (col.) Feb '53.

——, Malta, Holiday 27: cover (col.) Je '60.

——, Mar del Plata (bathers). Natl. geog. 113: 303 Mar '58.

——, Mediterranean. Natl. geog. 113: 480-1 (col.) Ap '58.

——, Mexico. Holiday 7: 30 (col.) Feb '50; 22: 22 (col.) Sept '57.

——, Michigan. Holiday 10: 38 (col.) Jl '51.

——, Montevideo. Holiday 8: 71 (col.) Dec '50.

——, Nantucket. Holiday 10: 44 (col.) Aug '51.

——, Naples. Labande: Naples, p. 89.

——, Nassau. Holiday 8: 12 (col.) Dec '50; 10: 26 (col.) Nov '51, 105 (col. Dec '51; 14: 83 (col.) Nov '53; 17: back cover (col.) Mar '55; 19: 18 (col.) Mar '56; 20: 42 (col.) Nov '56; 21: 137 (col.) Feb '57, 48 (col.) May '57; 23: 10 (col.) Feb '58, 174 (col.) May '58, 10 (col.) Je '58; 24: 122 (col.) Jl '58; 25: 108 (col.) Jan '59; 27: 74-5 (col.) Mar '60, 209 (col.) Ap '60.

——, Nassau (boy, girl). Holiday 26: 2 (col.) Jl '59.

——, New Hampshire. Holiday 10: 43 (col.) Sept '51.

——, New Jersey. Holiday 12: 98-9 (col.) Aug '52.

——, New Mexico (Bluewater lake). Travel 109: 21 Mar '58.

——, New Zealand. Holiday 24: 27 (col.) Sept '58.

——, Nile river. Natl. geog. 108: 636 (col.) Nov '55.

——, Oregon. Holiday 11: 15 (col.) Mar '52; 13: 115 (col.) Feb '53; 19: 121 (col.) Feb '56, 21 (col.) Mar '56; 24: 42-3 (col.) Jl '58.

——, Oregon (Ecola State park). Travel 113: 52 May '60.

——, Palmyra island. Travel 106: 10 Sept '56.

——, Peru. Disney: People & places, p. 112 (col.).

——, Pitcairn island. Natl. geog. 112: 750-1 (col.) Dec '57.

——, **Pondichery.** *See* Pondichery beach.

——, **Portugal.** Holiday 19: 34-5 (col.) Jan '56; 26: 106 (col.) Aug '59.

Natl. geog. 106: 688 (col.) Nov '54.

——, **Puerto Rico.** Holiday 21: 79 (col.) Mar '57; 23: 101 Jan '58; 24: 55 (col.) Dec '58.

——, **Russia (bathers).** Natl. geog. 116: 739 (col.) Dec '59.

——, **Salton sea (bathers).** Natl. geog. 112: 712 (col.) Nov '57.

——, **Samandag.** Osward: Asia Minor, pl. 30.

——, **Samoa.** Disney: People & places, p. 130 (col.).

Holiday 28: 54-5 (col.) Oct '60.

Travel 101: 34 Jan '54.

——, **South Seas.** Natl. geog. 97: 94 (col.) Jan '50.

——, **Tahiti.** Holiday 19: 132 (col.) Feb '56; 28: 68-9 (col.) Nov '60.

Natl. geog. 112: 726-7 (col.) Dec '57.

——, **Texas (Galveston).** Travel 103: 26 May '55.

——, **Virgin Islands.** Natl. geog. 109: 202-3, 225 (col.) Feb '56.

——, **Washington.** Holiday 27: 12 (col.) Mar '60.

——, **West Indies.** Holiday 14: 170 (col.) Nov '53.

——, **West Indies (Tobago).** Travel 109: 46 May '58.

beach guard stand. Holiday 27: 91 (col.) Mar '60.

beach picnic. *See* picnic, beach.

beach shelter. Natl. geog. 113: 179 (col.) Feb '58.

beach tents. *See* tents, beach.

beach umbrella. *See* umbrella, beach.

beach. *See* also boy & girl (beach); man & woman (beach).

beachcomber (Tahiti). Holiday 28: 68 Oct '60.

beacon. *See* light beacon.

Beacon Hill handbell ringers (Boston). Holiday 14: 38 (col.) Nov '53.

Beadle, George Wells. Cur. biog. p. 38 (1956).

Beadle's dime novels. *See* dime novels.

beaker. Lehner: Pict. bk. of sym., p. 16.

—— **(man pouring liquid).** Natl. geog. 114: 319 (col.) Sept '58.

——, **antique.** Con. 135: 177 May '55; 136: 28 Sept '55.

——, **antique German.** Con. 139: 231 Je '57.

——, **antique glass.** Con. 138: 65 Sept '56.

——, **antique horn.** Natl. geog. 97: 750 Je '50.

——, **Charles II silver.** Con. 127: 80 May '51; 133: X Ap '54, XXIV Mar '54, XVI May '54; 134: IX, XXVI Sept '54; 135: X May '55.

——, **Chelsea.** Con. 141: 247 Je '58.

——, **corded (Stone age, Rathmannsdorf).** Praeg. pict. ency., p. 19.

——, **Dutch 17th cent.** Con. 145: 244 Je '60.

——, **founder's silver gilt (14th cent.).** Con. 143: 167 May '59.

——, **George II silver.** Con. 139: 58 Mar '57.

——, **gladiator Roman glass.** Con. 140: 112 Nov '57.

——, **James I silver.** Con. 137: XI Ap '56.

——, **Norwegian (16th cent. silver).** Con. 145: 12 Mar '60.

——, **Norwich silver.** Con. 134: XV Dec '54.

——, **17th cent.** Con. 141: 151 May '58.

——, **silver (Berger).** Con. 143: 225 Je '59.

——, **silver gilt (German 15th cent.).** Con. ency. of ant., vol. 3 pl. 34.

——, **silver gilt double (16th cent.).** Con. 144: 14 Sept '59.

——, **Swedish (18th cent.).** Con. 135: XXIII Je '55; 141: 9-10 Mar '58.

——, **Swedish "peace."** Con. 141: 28 Mar '58.

——, **William III.** Con. 127: 81 May '51.

beaker & cover, gilt. Con. 145: 243 Je '60.

Beale, Oliver Howard. Cur. biog. p. 29 (1959).

"Beale's cut" (Fremont Pass). Amer. heri. vol. 11 no. 4 frontis (Je '60).

Beall, J. Glenn. Cur. biog. p. 43 (1955).

Beall, Lester. Cur. biog. p. 32 (1949).

Beals, Carleton. Cur. biog. p. 49 (1941); p. 61 (1942).

Beals, Ralph Albert. Cur. biog. p. 39 (1947).

Beam, Jacob D. Cur. biog. p. 31 (1959).

beams, ceiling. Natl. geog. 106: 403 (col.) Sept '54.

Bean, Louis H. Cur. biog. p. 39 (1948).

Bean, Roy. Horan: Pict. hist. of wild west, p. 138-9.

Bean, Judge Roy (holds court in early Texas). Amer. heri. vol. 4 no. 1 p. 48 (col.) (fall '52).

Bean, Stephen (Stuart). Con. 144: LXII Nov '59.

bean pots. Rawson: Ant. pict. bk., p. 88.

bear (Russian sym.). Lehner: Pict. bk. of sym., p. 60.

bear, Teddy. *See* Teddy bear.

"Bear hunt" (Herrera). Natl. geog. 107: 365 (col.) Mar '55.

Beard, Charles. Amer. heri. vol. 8 no. 5 p. 27 (Aug '57).

Beard, Charles A. Cur. biog. p. 52 (1941).

Beard, Charles Edmund. Cur. biog. p. 40 (1956).

Beard, Geoffrey W. (work of). Con. 138: 189 (col.) Dec '56.

Beard, Mary. Cur. biog. p. 53 (1941).

beards, men's (1862). Amer. heri. vol. 10 no. 1 p. 84 (Dec '58).

Beardsley, Aubrey (bk. illus.). Praeg. pict. ency., p. 409.

Beardsley, William S. Cur. biog. p. 27 (1950).

Beare, Charles (work of). Con. 140: 236 Jan '58.

bearer of burden (god of). Lehner: Pict. bk. of sym., p. 32.

beatniks. Holiday 26: 84-5 Oct '59.

Beaton, Cecil. Cur. biog. p. 35 (1944); p. 32 (1962).

Holiday 14: 52 Dec '53; 23: 149 Je '58.

"Beatrice addressing Dante." Praeg. pict. ency., p. 388 (col.).

Beatty, Bessie. Cur. biog. p. 37 (1944).

Beatty, Jim. Cur. biog. (1963).

Beatty, Warren. Cur. biog. p. 35 (1962).

Beau, Maj. Gen. Lucas Victor. Cur. biog. p. 75 (1954).

Beau Rivage motel (Miami Beach). Travel 108: 43 Dec '57.

Beaufort, Lady Margaret. Con. 139: 214 Je '57.

Beaufort castle (Scotland). Holiday 16: 43 Sept '54.

Beaulac, Willard L. Cur. biog. p. 35 (1958). Natl. geog. 113: 306 Mar '58.

Beaumont, Sir George. Con. 132: 97, 100 Nov '53.

Beauregard, Pierre G. T. Pakula: Cent. album, p. 85.

Beauregard's headquarters (Civil war). Brooks: Growth of a nation, p. 146.

beauty (goddess of). Lehner: Pict. bk. of sym., p. 31.

beauty contestants. Holiday 12: 37 Sept '52.

beauty make-up (women). Int. gr. soc.: Arts . . . p. 183 (col.).

beauty parlor (ancient Palestine). Natl. geog. 118: 840 (col.) Dec '60.

— — (exhibit). Natl. geog. 116: 720-1 (col.) Dec '59.

beauty queen. See queen, beauty.

beaver (sym.). Lehner: Pict. bk. of sym., p. 57.

Beaver lake lodge (Colo.). Travel 113: 26 Mar '60.

Beaverbrook art gallery. See art gallery, Beaverbrook.

Bebler, Ales. Cur. biog. p. 29 (1950).

Bech, Joseph. Cur. biog. p. 31 (1950).

Bechtel, Stephen D. Cur. biog. p. 43 (1957).

Beck, Bertram Maurice. Cur. biog. p. 35 (1961).

Beck, Dave. Cur. biog. p. 34 (1949).

Beck, Mildred Buchwalder. Cur. biog. p. 32 (1950).

Becker, Joseph (work of). Amer. heri. vol. 10 no. 1 p. 52 (col.) (Dec '58).

Becker, May Lamberton. Cur. biog. p. 55 (1941).

Becker, Ralph E. Cur. biog. p. 41 (1948).

Beckmann, Max. Praeg. pict. ency., p. 498 (col.).

Beckmann, Max (work of). Praeg. pict. ency., p. 13.

bed. Holiday 11: 151 (col.) Ap '52; 12: 121 Dec '52; 18: 66 Sept '55; 22: 24 (col.) Dec '57; 28: 39 (col.) Oct '60.

—— (dog on it). Holiday 24: 97 Aug '58.

—— (modern). Holiday 22: 107 (col.) Oct '57; 24: 95-102 (col.) Aug '58.

——, angel or half-tester. Con. 136: 241 Jan '56.

——, bunk. See bunk bed.

——, bus. Natl. geog. 111: 772 Je '57.

— —, canopy. See bed, fourposter.

— —, child's. Rawson: Ant. pict. bk., p. 15.

— —, Chippendale. Con. 144: LXIV Sept '59.

— —, Chippendale fourposter. Con. 143: LXXVII May '59.

——, Colonial type. Holiday 17: 105 (col.) Jan '55.

——, Combe Abbey state. Con. 135: XLIX Ap '55.

——, doll canopy. Holiday 26: 187 Oct '59.

——, double (ladder). Natl. geog. 98: 627 Nov '50.

——, Dutch (in closet). Natl. geog. 106: 382 (col.) Sept '54.

——, Elizabethan. Con. 139: LVII May '57.

——, Empire. Natl. geog. 118: 182 (col.) Aug '60.

——, field. See field bed.

——, 15th cent. Con. 133: 254 Je '54.

——, folding. See folding bed.

——, fourposter. Con. 139: 141 May '57; 140: 79 Nov '57, 216 Jan '58; 143: 73 Ap '59, 141 May '59.
Holiday 26: 61 (col.) Aug '59.
Jensen: the White House, p. 261.
Natl. geog. 97: 306 (col.) Mar '50; 104: 664 (col.) Nov '53; 106: 461 (col.) Oct '54; 118: 183 (col.) Aug '60.
Travel 113: 31 Mar '60.

——, fourposter (1850). Natl. geog. 113: 541 Ap '58.

——, fourposter (Henry Clay). Amer. heri. vol. 7 no. 6 p. 109 (Oct '56).

——, fourposter (Italian, 18th cent.). Con. 144: 143 Dec '59.

——, fourposter (James II). Con. 145: 167 May '60.

——, fourposter (middle ages). Int. gr. soc.: Arts . . . p. 53-4 (col.).

——, fourposter (modern). Holiday 24: 95, 99, 102 (col.) Aug '58.

——, fourposter (Portuguese, 17th cent.). Con. 143: 270 Je '59.

——, fourposter (royal). Amer. heri. vol. 8 no. 6 p. 6 (col.) (Oct '57).

——, fourposter (16th cent.). Con. 133: 176 My '54.

——, fourposter (16th cent.) Con. 144: 5 Sept '59.

——, fourposter (17th cent.). Con. 132: XIII Nov '53.

——, fourposter (18th cent.). Con. 145: 54 Mar '60.

——, fourposter (Viennese, 18th cent.). Con. ency. of ant., vol. 3 pl. 24.

——, inlaid (gilt shell). Con. 144: 216 Jan '60.

——, Jacob style (Louis XVI). Con. 144: 1 (col.) Nov '59.

——, Japanese (child asleep). Holiday 19: 105 Feb '56.

——, jungle. Natl. geog. 104: 284 (col.) Aug '53.

——, Louis XIV. Con. 127: 103 May '51.
Holiday 27: 20 (col.) Ap '60.

——, Maximilian's (1860). Natl. geog. 109: 848 (col.) Je '56.

——, swan. Holiday 15: 55 Feb '54.

——, Swiss. Natl. geog. 98: 242 (col.) Aug '50.

——, Swiss (woman). Natl. geog. 110: 453 (col.) Oct '56.

——, Thos. Jefferson. Natl. geog. 97: 567 (col.) May '50.

——, wicker. Holiday 23: 98 (col.) Mar '58.

bed alcove (Italian baroque). Con. 140: 205 Dec '57.

bed canopy (Greece). Natl. geog. 114: 737 (col.) Dec '58.

bed cording implements. See Jack & pegs for cording beds.

bed cover, passementerie. Con. 143: cover (col.) Ap '59.

bed coverlet (embroidered antique). Con. 143: 234 Je '59.

bed headboard, Chinese. Con. 145: LIX Ap '60.

bed headpiece (detail). con. ency. of ant., vol. 1 pl. 3.

——, Chippendale. Con. 145: LXXXIV May '60.

——, **French directoire.** Con. 144: LXXIX Jan '60.

——, **regency.** Con. 145: LXXVIII Je '60.

bed in wall, sink. See "sink bed."

bed of Samuel Clemens. Amer. heri. vol. 11 no. 1 p. 73 (Dec '59).

bed-step (early English). Con. 127: 15 Mar '51.

"bed warmer" stones. Rawson: Ant. pict. bk., p. 9.

Bedford (N. Y.). Holiday 8: 116 (col.) Dec '50.

Bedouin. Holiday 20: 50 (col.) Dec '56; 26: 75 (col.) Dec '59.

Natl. geog. 103: 555 Ap '53; 104: 42 (col.) Jl '53; 108: 857, 867 (col.) Dec '55; 110: 76, 102-4 Jl '56; 112: 106 (col.) Jl '57.

—— **(back view).** Natl. geog. 115: 500 Ap '59.

—— **(camel).** Holiday 13: 73 May '53.

—— **(seated, making coffee).** Natl. geog. 106: 840 Dec '54.

"Bedouin Arabs" (circus). Durant: Pict. hist. of Amer. circus, p. 31.

Bedouin boy (profile). Holiday 10: 119 Dec '51.

Bedouin hunter (hawk, child). Natl. geog. 110: 93 (col.) Jl '56.

Bedouin legion troops. Natl. geog. 111: 249 Feb '57.

Bedouin man. Natl. geog. 111: 242-3 Feb '57.

bedroom. Holiday 22: 119 (col.) Sept '57; 25: 211 (col.) Ap '59; 26: 119 (col.) Oct '59.

—— **(antiques).** Con. 143: 141 May '59.

——, **Colonial.** Natl. geog. 106: 460 (col.) Oct '54.

——, **George Washington's.** Natl. geog. 104: 664 (col.) Nov '53.

bedroom slippers. See slippers, bedroom.

bedspread (girls making designs). Natl. geog. 105: 315 Mar '54.

——, **applique (antique).** Amer. heri. vol. 2 no. 2 back cover (col.) (winter '51).

——, **India (18th cent.).** Con. 132: 77-8 Nov '53.

——, **Jacobean needlework.** Natl. geog. 108: 302 (col.) Sept '55.

——, **Penn. Dutch.** Holiday 18: 61 (col.) Jl '55.

Beebe, Lucius. Amer. heri. vol. 4 no. 3 p. 23 (spring '53).

Holiday 24: 62-5 Sept '58.

Beebe, William, Cur. biog. p. 57 (1941).

Beech, Olive Ann. Cur. biog. p. 42 (1956).

Beecham, Sir Thomas. Cooper: con. ency. of music, p. 58.

Cur. biog. p. 59 (1941); p. 27 (1951).

Beecham, Sir Thomas (bronze head). Con. 140: 129 Nov '57.

Beecher, Henry Ward. Amer. heri. vol. 4 no. 2 p. 20 (winter '53); vol. 7 no. 4 p. 44 (Je '56).

Holiday 25: 78 Feb '59.

Beecher, Henry Ward (gatepost). Rawson: Ant. pict. bk., p. 81.

Beecher, Henry Ward (in court). Amer. heri. vol. 7 no. 4 p. 88 (Je '56).

Beechey, Sir William (work of). Con. 127: opp. p. 120 (col.) May '51; 129: 79 Je '52.

Beeching, Richard. Cur. biog. (1963).

Beecroft, John. Cur. biog. p. 77 (1954).

"Beefeater" (England). See Yeoman of the guard (England).

beehive. Natl. geog. 103: 244 Feb '53.

Rawson: Ant. pict. bk., p. 28.

—— **(sym.).** Lehner: Pict. bk. of sym., p. 58.

beehive oven. See cooking oven, Beehive.

beer jug. See jug, beer.

beer mug. See mug, beer.

beer wagon. See wagon, beer.

Beethoven, Ludwig van. Cooper: Con. ency. of music, p. 17 (col.).

Int. gr. soc.: Arts . . . p. 109 (col.).

Begay, Harrison. Natl. geog. 107: 353 (col.) Mar '55.

beggar. Holiday 5: 67 Jan '49.

——, **blind Persian.** Natl. geog. 114: 39 (col.) Jl '58.

"Beggar & child" (Picasso). Con. 145: 256 (col.) Je '60.

"Beggar boy" (Piazzetta). Con. 143: 99 Ap '59.

Beggar's opera" (Hogarth). Con. 129: 44 Ap '52.

beginning (sym.). Lehner: Pict. bk. of sym., p. 80.

beginning & end (sym.). Lehner: Pict. bk. of sym., p. 80.

beginning—middle—end (sym.). Lehner: Pict. bk. of sym., p. 80.

Begley, Ed. Cur. biog. p. 44 (1956).

Begtrup, Bodil. Cur. biog. p. 32 (1946).

Behan, Brendan F. Cur. biog. p. 37 (1961).

Behan, Johnny. Horan: Pict. hist. of wild west, p. 113.

"Beheading of St. John" (Caravaggio). Con. 142: 147 Dec '58.

"Beheading of St. John the Baptist." Natl. geog. 101: 97 (col.) Jan '52.

"Beheading of St. John the Baptist" (Bassano). Con. 140: 165 Dec '57.

"Beheading of St. John the Baptist" (Caravaggio). Cur. biog. 139: 35 Mar '57.

Behistun inscription. Ceram: March of arch., p. 207.

Behn, Sosthenes. Cur. biog. p. 40 (1947).

Behrman, Samuel N. Cur. biog. p. 34 (1943).

Beidler, John X. (early vigilante). Horan: Pict. hist. of wild west, p. 25.

Beim, Jerrold. Jun. bk. of authors, p. 25.

Beim, Lorraine. Jun. bk. of authors, p. 26.

Beinum, Eduard van. Cur. biog. p. 45 (1955).

Beirne, Joseph A. Cur. biog. p. 33 (1946).

Beirut. Natl. geog. 105: 496-7 (col.) Ap '54; 113: 480-1, 484-5 (part col.) Ap '58.

Bekesy, George von. Cur. biog. p. 37 (1962).

"Bel air dancers at evening" (Cromwell). Holiday 21: 140 (col.) May '57.

Belafonte, Harry. Cur. biog. p. 46 (1956).

Belaunde, Victor Andres. Cur. biog. p. 23 (1960).

Belfast. Holiday 11: 48-51 (part col.) Jan '52.

Belfast Maine coast (haunted). Travel 110: 56 Oct '58.

belfry (Bruges). Natl. geog. 107: 652, 657, 664 (col.) May '55; 113: 810 (col.) Je '58.

—— **(Ghent).** Natl. geog. 113: 815 (col.) Je '58.

——, **mission.** Holiday 22: 52 Oct '57.

Belgian (pageant). Holiday 21: 191 May '57.

Belgian Congo. Holiday 21: 164 (col.) Je '57.

Natl. geog. 101: 322-62 (part col.) Mar '52;

106: 725, 737 (col.) Dec '54; 112: 82-96 (col.) Jl '57.
—— (map). Natl. geog. 101: 324 Mar '52; 117: 284 Feb '60.
Belgian Congo dancers. Natl. geog. 101: 327 (col.) Mar '52; 112: 84 (col.) Jl '57.
—— (Gungu tribe). Holiday 25: 152 Ap '59.
Belgian Congo man. Holiday 10: 28 Sept. '51, 144 Nov '51.
Belgian fisherman. Holiday 21: 41 Jan '57; 25: 45 Jan '59.
Belgian girl. Holiday 13: 79 Feb '53.
Belgian train (early). Int. gr. soc.: Arts . . . p. 161 (col).
Belgium. Holiday 11: 126 (col.) Je '52; 21: 34-5 Jan '57; 26: 19 Aug '59, 210 (col.) Dec '59. Natl. geog. 107: 630 May '55; 108: 541-58 (part col.) Oct '55; 113: 794-837 (part col.) Je '58.
Travel 113: 9 Je '60; 114: 12 Oct '60.
—— (Brussels). See Brussels.
—— (buildings). Holiday 26: 143 Nov '59.
—— (cathedral int.). Holiday 25: 47 (col.) Jan '59.
—— (chateau). Holiday 24: 23 (col.) Oct '58.
—— (Chateau de Beersel). Holiday 28: 33 Dec '60.
—— (Guild houses). Holiday 23: 2 (col.) Jan '58.
—— (map). Natl. geog. 113: 805 Je '58.
Belgium home. Travel 103: inside cover Feb '55.
Belgium insignia. Int. gr. soc.: Arts . . . p. 167 (col.).
—— (honor). Int. gr. soc.: Arts . . . p. 167 (col.).
Belgrade (Yugoslavia). Natl. geog. 99: 162 (col.), 167 Feb '51.
Belkin, Samuel. Cur. biog. p. 42 (1952).
Belknap, W. W. Amer. heri. vol. 8 no. 3 p. 52 (Ap '57).
Bell, Alexander Graham. Amer. heri. vol. 3 no. 1 p. 2-5 (fall '51).
Natl. geog. 110: 227-8 (col.), 251, 254, 256, 268 Aug '56; 116: 266 Aug '59.
Bell, Mrs. Alexander Graham. Natl. geog. 110: 235, 256 Aug '56.
Bell, Alexander Melville. Natl. geog. 103: 535 Ap '53.
Bell & grandchildren, Alexander Graham. Natl. geog. 110: 241-2 Aug '56.
Bell, Rev. Bernard Iddings. Cur. biog. p. 53 (1953).
Bell, Bert. Cur. biog. p. 34 (1950).
Bell, Daniel W. Cur. biog. p. 35 (1946).
Bell, David Elliott. Cur. biog. p. 39 (1961).
Bell, Elliott V. Cur. biog. p. 54 (1953).
Bell, John. Amer. heri. vol. 11 no. 5 p. 55 (Aug '60).
Bell, Lawrence D. Cur. biog. p. 63 (1942).
Bell, Margaret Elizabeth. Cur. biog. p. 44 (1952).
Bell, Marilyn. Cur. biog. p. 48 (1956).
bell. Holiday 6: 15, 113 Dec '49; 7: 77 Jan '50, 20 Feb '50, 112 Mar '50, 77 Ap '50; 8: 80 Nov '50, 135 Dec '50; 14: 21 Oct '53; 15: 131 Ap '54; 17: 119 Feb '55, 23 Mar '55; 19: 130 Mar '56, 113 May '56, 31

Je '56; 20: 90 Oct '56, 176 Dec '56; 21: 133 Jan '57, 138 May '57; 22: 11, 83 (col.) Jl '57, 145 Oct '57, 49 Dec '57; 24: 16 Oct '58.
Travel 108: 31 Aug '57.
—— (Chinese sym.). Lehner: Pict. bk. of sym., p. 46.
—— (Christmas). Lehner: Pict. bk. of sym., p. 50.
—— (in arch). Amer. heri. vol. 6 no. 4 p. 99 (Je '55).
—— (in tower). Holiday 27: 189 (col.) Mar '60.
—— (reflections). Holiday 26: 37 (col.) Oct '59; 27: 99 (col.) Jan '60, 187 (col.) May '60; 28: 95 (col.) Jl '60, 27 (col.) Sept '60, 203 (col.) Nov '60.
—— (reflections of people). Holiday 26: 187 (col.) Nov '59.
—— (silhouette). Holiday 12: 25 (col.) Nov '52.
——, antique table. Con. 134: XL Nov '54.
——, blessing of the church. Natl. geog. 115: 699 (col.) May '59.
——, call (glass). Travel 104: 3 Aug '55.
——, Chinese (bronze). Con. 141: LIV May '58.
——, cow. See cow bell.
——, crystal. Holiday 18: 9 Sept '55, 63 Nov '55.
——, diving. See diving bell.
——, glass. Travel 102: 5 Aug '54.
——, hand (antique). Holiday 18: 76 Sept '55, 126 Nov '55, 14 Dec '55; 28: 71 (col.) Jl '60.
——, horse. See horse bell.
——, Kettins. Natl. geog. 110: 47 (col.) Jl '56.
——, Liberty. See Liberty bell.
——, mission. Amer. heri. vol. 1 no. 3 p. 32 (spring '50).
Natl. geog. 116: 582 (col.) Nov '59.
——, old (ringing). Holiday 19: 83 Jan '56.
——, St. Patrick's. See St. Patrick's bell.
——, silver (1806). Con. ency. of ant., vol. 1 p. 153.
——, temple. Holiday 28: 217 Nov '60.
——, town crier's. See town crier's bell.
——, tubular. See tubular bells.
——, winged (Easter). Lehner: Pict. bk. of sym., p. 52.
——, world's largest (Kremlin). Natl. geog. 116: 356 Sept '59.
bell. See also bells.
bell boy. Holiday 12: 101 Sept '52.
——, hotel. Holiday 25: 116 Mar '59.
Bell home, Alexander Graham. Natl. geog. 110: 230 (col.) Aug '56.
Bell museum, A. G. See museum, Alexander Graham Bell.
bell-push, antique. Con. 141: XLVII Mar '58.
——, antique Faberge. Con. 134: XXXIII Nov '54.
——, Siberian jade. Con. 142: XLIX Nov '58.
——, Sphinx lapis lazuli. Con. 145: XXXV Mar '60.
bell ringer, mechanical. See man (mechanical bell ringer).
bell ringing (14th cent.). Holiday 11: 19 Feb '52, 135 Ap '52.
——, king (14th cent. music). Holiday 10: 11 Nov '51.

Bell Smith Springs (Eddyville, Ill.). Travel 113: 57 May '60.

bell tower (Austria). Natl. geog. 118: 252-3 (col.) Aug '60.

—— **(Bruges).** Natl. geog. 113: 810 (col.) Je '58.

—— **(Capri, Italy).** Labande: Naples, p. 212.

—— **(Giralda).** See Giralda bell tower.

—— **(Mexico).** Natl. geog. 107: 235 (col.) Feb '55.

—— **(Oxford).** Natl. geog. 114: 61 (col.) Jl '58.

—— **(Sant 'Eligio).** Labande: Naples, p. 65.

—— **(Tavira, Portugal).** Travel 110: 47 Sept '58.

——, **tetrahedral.** Natl. geog. 110: 243 Aug '56.

bell tower memorial, Robt. A. Taft. Natl. geog. 116: 755 (col.) Dec '59.

bell tower. See also carillon tower; campanile.

Bellamann, Henry. Cur. biog. p. 64 (1942).

Bellamy, Ralph. Cur. biog. p. 30 (1951).

Bellange, Jacques (work of). Con. 132: 134 Nov '53.

Belle, Alexis Simon (work of). Con. 140: 234 Jan '58.

"Belle Grove" plantation (La.). Amer. heri. vol. 4 no. 2 p. 26-7 (col.) (winter '53); vol. 7 no. 4 p. 61 Je '56.
Holiday 11: 47 (col.) Mar '52.

"Belle Helene" house (La.). Natl. geog. 113: 542 (col.) Ap '58.

"The Belle of the Winter" (Currier & Ives). Amer. heri. vol. 9 no. 1 back cover (col.) (Dec '57).

Belleroche, Albert de (work of). Con. 135: 114 Ap '55.

"Belles Heures" book, Duke of Berry's. Con. 139: 133 Ap '57.

Bellingrath gardens. Holiday 11: 56, 60-1 (col.) Feb '52.
Jordan: Hammond's pict. atlas, p. 78 (col).
Travel 109: 14 Mar '58.

Bellini, Gentile (work of). Con. 133: 98 Ap '54; 136: 136 Nov '55.

Bellini, Giovanni (work of). Con. 126: 175 Dec '50; 140: 240 Jan '58.
Praeg. pict. ency., p. 269 (col.).

Bellmon, Henry. Cur. biog. (1963).

Bellotto, B. (work of). Con. 145: 162 May '60.

bellows, blacksmith. Rawson: Ant. pict. bk., p. 56.

——, **fireplace.** Holiday 10: 124 Dec '51.

bells (ringing). Holiday 9: 135 Mar '51; 12: 97 (col.) Oct '52, 141 Dec '52.

——, **ceremonial.** Holiday 21: 30 Mar '57.

——, **crusader church.** Natl. geog. 105: 487 (col.) Ap '54.

——, **sleigh.** See sleigh bells.

——, **Swiss.** Disney: People & places, p. 42 (col.).

——, **wedding.** Lehner: Pict. bk. of sym., p. 56.

bells & holly, Christmas. Travel 106: inside cover Nov '56.

bells. See also bell.

Belluschi, Pietro. Cur. biog. p. 33 (1959).

Belmont, Mrs. August. Cur. biog. p. 41 (1944).

Belmont (Vermont). Holiday 6: 53 (col.) Nov '49.

Belmont castle (Scotland). Natl. geog. 110: 12 (col.) Jl '56.

Belo Horizonte, (Brazil). Holiday 13: 110 (col.) Feb '53.

Belson, George. Con. 145: 127 Ap '60.

Belt, Guillermo. Cur. biog. p. 43 (1947).

belt, coin studded. Natl. geog. 113: 327 (col.) Mar '58.

——, **ladies'.** Holiday 11: 69 (col.) Je '52; 25: 120-1 (col.) Ap '59.

——, **man's.** Holiday 10: 4 (col.) Oct '51, 102 (col.) Dec '51; 11: 117 Mar 52, 36 (col.) May '52; 13: 84 (col.) Feb '53, 4 (col.) Mar '53; 14: 24 (col.) Sept '53, inside cover (col.) Oct '53, 77 (col.) Nov '53; 18: 64 (col.) Sept '55, 16 (col.) Oct '55; 19: 29 (col.) May '56; 20: 110 (col.) Sept '56, 147 (col.) Oct '56; 21: 124 (col.) Ap '57, 36 (col.) May '57; 22: 153 (col.) Oct '57, 101 Nov '57; 24: 19 Sept '58, 15, 210 (col.) Nov '58; 25: 32 Mar '59, 34 Ap '59; 26: 177 (col.) Dec '59; 27: 8 Ap '60, 143 May '60; 28: 11 Oct '60, 34 (col.) Nov '60.

——, **man's (pistol holster).** Holiday 11: 69 (col.) Je '52; 12: 77 (col.) Dec '52.

——, **Sullivan championship.** Amer. heri. vol. 10 no. 5 p. 55 Aug '59.

Belvedere palace (Vienna). Praeg. pict. ency., p. 364.

Belward, Richard Fisher (Opie). Con. 143: 88 Ap '59.

Belzoni, Giovanni Battista (portrait). Ceram: March of arch., p. 83.

Bemelmans, Ludwig. Cur. biog. p. 61 (1941).

Bemelman's drawings, Ludwig. Holiday 6: 60-2 Nov '49, 126 (col.) Dec '49.

Bemelman's sketches, Ludwig (Europe). Holiday 6: 110-14 (part col.) Sept '49.

Bemis, Samuel Flagg. Cur. biog. p. 36 (1950).

Ben Bella, Ahmed. Cur. biog. p. 26 (1963).

Ben-Gurion, David. Cur. biog. p. 44 (1947); p. 45 (1957).
Holiday 28: 99 (col.) Dec '60.

"Ben Johnson" steamboat. Amer. heri. vol. 2 no. 1 p. 47 (fall '50).

Ben-Zvi, Isaac. Cur. biog. p. 57 (1953).

Benares (India). Holiday 6: 65-73 Jl '49.
Natl. geog. 118: 492-5 (col.) Oct '60.

—— **(bathing in Ganges).** Travel 111: 19 Jan '59.

Benavente, Jacinto. Cur. biog. p. 58 (1953).

Benbow, John (Kneller). Con. 127: 29 Mar '51.

bench. Holiday 21: 57 May '57.

—— **(man).** Holiday 18: 98 (col.) Oct '55.

——, **fireplace (18th cent.).** Natl. geog. 97: 577 (col.) May '50.

——, **hall (George IV).** Con. 143: 81 Ap '59.

——, **splat-backed.** Holiday 10: 137 Dec '51.

bench end, church. Rawson: Ant. pict. bk., p. 16.

Benchley, Bob. Holiday 17: 73 Mar '55.

Benchley, Nathaniel. Cur. biog. p. 61 (1953).

Benchley, Robert. Cur. biog. p. 63 (1941).

Bender, George H. Cur. biog. p. 44 (1952).

Bender, James F. Cur. biog. p. 35 (1949).

Bendetsen, Karl R. Cur. biog. p. 47 (1952).

Bendix, William, Cur. biog. p. 43 (1948).

Benedict, Commodore Elias C. Amer. heri. vol. 8 no. 6 p. 11 (Oct '57).

Benedict, Ruth. Cur. biog. p. 65 (1941).
Benedictine abbey (Fecamp, France). Travel 104: 45-6 Sept '55.
"The Benediction" (Y. Gill). Con. 126: II Aug '50.
Benefiale, Marcus (work of). Con. 135: 125 Ap '55.
beneficial spirits. See spirits, signs of beneficial (sym.).
Benes, Eduard. Cur. biog. p. 66 (1942).
Benesh, Joan. Cur. biog. p. 48 (1957).
Benesh, Rudolf. Cur. biog. p. 48 (1957).
Benet, Laura. Jun. bk. of auth., p. 27.
Benet, William Rose. Holiday 7: 49 (col.) Je '50.
Bengough, Percy R. Cur. biog. p. 31 (1951).
Benin bronze figure. Con. 133: 134 Ap '54.
Benin bronze head of a queen (XVIth cent.) Con. 133: 53 Mar '54.
Bennet, William (Stuart). Con. 143: 87 Ap '59.
Bennett, F. M. Con. 17: XLIX May '55.
Bennett, F. M. (work of). Con. 132: XL Sept '53.
Bennett, Lt. Gen. Henry Gordon. Cur. biog. p. 69 (1942).
Bennett, Henry G. Cur. biog. p. 34 (1951).
Bennett, Hugh H. Cur. biog. p. 37 (1946).
Bennett, Maj. Gen. Ivan L. Cur. biog. p. 49 (1952).
Bennett, James Gordon. Amer. heri. vol. 6 no. 2 p. 32 (winter '55).
Bennett, James V. Cur. biog. p. 37 (1949).
Bennett, John. Jun. bk. of auth., p. 28.
Bennett, John C. Cur. biog. p. 41 (1961).
Bennett, Rear Adm. Rawson, 2nd. Cur. biog. p. 37 (1958).
Bennett, Richard. Jun. bk. of auth., p. 29.
Bennett, Robert Russell. Cur. biog. p. 39 (1962).
Bennett, Russell. Cur. biog. p. 70 (1942).
Bennett, Wallace F. Cur. biog. p. 39 (1949).
Bennett, William A. C. Cur. biog. p. 62 (1953).
Bennett, William J. Cur. biog. p. 79 (1954).
—— (work of). Con. ency. of ant., vol. 3 pl. 92.
Bennett's grave, Jack. See grave of Jack Bennett.
Bennington battle monument. Holiday 16: 106 Jl '54.
Bennington pottery designs. See pottery designs, Bennington.
Benny, Jack. Cur. biog. p. 67 (1941); (1963). Holiday 7: 62 Mar '50.
Benoit-Levy, Jean. Cur. biog. p. 47 (1947).
Bensin, Basil M. Cur. biog. p. 46 (1948).
Benson, Ambrosius (work of). Con. 129: LVI Ap '52; 137: XI (col.) May '56.
Benson, Ezra Taft. Cur. biog. p. 63 (1953).
Benson, Robert F. Natl. geog. 113: 459 Ap '58.
Benson, Sally. Cur. biog. p. 69 (1941).
Benteen, Capt. Frederick W. Amer. heri. vol. 5 no. 4 p. 35 (summer '54).
Benten (deity). Lehner: Pict. bk. of sym., p. 49.
Bentley, Thomas. Con. 129: 133 Je '52.
Benton, Mrs. Henry. See "Mrs. Henry Benton."
Benton, Thomas (work of). Amer. heri. vol. 2 no. 2 p. 75 (col.) (winter '51).
Benton, Thomas Hart. Amer. heri. vol. 9 no. 2 p. 45 (Feb '58).
Holiday 22: 148 Dec '57.

Benton, William. Cur. biog. p. 41 (1945).
Benvenuto, Gerolamo di (work of). Con. 135: 55 Mar '55.
Benz auto (1903). Int. gr. soc.: Arts . . . p. 161 (col.).
Beppu's stone devil. Natl. geog. 104: 645 (col.) Nov '53.
Beranek, Leo L. Cur. biog. (1963).
Berber child (back view). Natl. geog. 107: 171 Feb '55.
Berber girl (Africa, head). Natl. geog. 107: 161 (col.) Feb '55.
Berber horsemen (North Africa). Holiday 25: 78-9 Ap '59.
Berber mothers (tattoos). Natl. geog. 117: 781 (col.) Je '60.
Berchem, Nicolaes (work of). Con. 138: 14 Sept '56; 143: XXX Ap '59; 145: 269 Je '60.
Berchtesgaden. Holiday 25: cover (col.) May '59.
Berding, Andrew H. Cur. biog. p. 25 (1960).
Berelson, Bernard R. Cur. biog. p. 43 (1961).
Berendsen, Sir Carl August. Cur. biog. p. 47 (1948).
Berenson, Bernhard (portrait by Annigoni). Con. 138: 53 Sept '56.
beret, French. Natl. geog. 115: 574 Ap '59.
Berg, Gertrude. Cur. biog. p. 71 (1941); p. 27 (1960).
Berge, Wendell. Cur. biog. p. 39 (1946).
Bergen, Edgar. Cur. biog. p. 43 (1945).
Bergen, John J. Cur. biog. p. 45 (1961).
Bergen, Polly. Cur. biog. p. 38 (1958).
Bergen & Charlie, Edgar. Holiday 10: 150 (col.) Dec '51.
Bergen (Norway). Natl. geog. 106: 154-59 (part col.) Aug '54. Travel 106: 34 Aug '56.
—— (hotel Orion). Travel 107: 49 Ap '57.
Berger, Meyer. Cur. biog. p. 37 (1943).
Berger, Oscar (work of). Amer. heri. vol. 10 no. 3 p. 88-93 (Ap '59).
Bergerac, Jacques. Holiday 21: 85 (col.) May '57.
bergeres (Napoleon 1). Con. 143: LXX May '59.
Bergeret, Madame (Fragonard). Con. 144: 55 Sept '59.
Berggrav, Bishop Eivind. Cur. biog. p. 38 (1950).
Bergman, Ingmar. Cur. biog. p. 29 (1960).
Bergman, Ingrid. Holiday 5: 40 (col.) Jan '49; 24: 79 Aug '58.
Bergquist, Maj. Gen. Kenneth P. Cur. biog. p. 47 (1961).
Bergson, Herbert A. Cur. biog. p. 40 (1950).
Beria, Lavrenti P. Cur. biog. p. 73 (1942).
Bering, Vitus (wrecked on Aleutian island). Amer. heri. vol. 7 no. 5 p. 70 (Aug '56).
Beriosova, Cvetlana. Cur. biog. p. 31 (1960).
Berkeley castle (England. int. & ext.). Con. 137: 240 (col.), 242-48 Je '56.
"Berkeley hundred" (Harrison plantation, Va). Amer. heri. vol. 8 no. 3 p. 58-63 (col.) (Ap '57).
"Berkeley" (entrance) (W. M. Harrison home). Natl geog. 103: 791 (col.) Je '53.
Berkner, Lloyd V. Cur. biog. p. 41 (1949).
Berkson, Seymour. Cur. biog. p. 43 (1949).

Berle, Adolf Augustus, jr. Cur. biog. p. 48 (1961).

Berle, Milton. Cur. biog. p. 44 (1949).
Holiday 7: 63 Mar '50.

Berlin, Ellin. Cur. biog. p .43 (1944).

Berlin, Irving. Cur. biog. p. 75 (1942); (1963).

Berlin (Germany). Holiday 18: 66-9 (part col.) Dec '55.
Natl. geog. 100: 692-703 Nov '51.
Travel 101: 12-4 May '54.

—(church). Praeg. pict. ency., p. 433.

— (Hilton hotel model). Travel 106: 49 Nov '56.

— (the Neue Wache). Praeg. pict. ency., p. 381.

— (night clubs). Holiday 25: 60-3 (part col.) Jan '59.

Berlin, West (Hansa quarter). Holiday 25: 53 May '59.

Berlin staatsoper. Cooper: Con. ency. of music, p. 449.

Berlioz, Hector. Cooper: Con. ency. of music, p. 59.

Berlitz, Charles F. Cur. biog. p. 51 (1957).

Bermejo, Bartolome (work of). Con. 126: 87 Oct '50.

Bermuda. Holiday 5: 89 (col.) Ap '49; 10: 20 (col.) Jl '51; 13: 102-7 (col.) Je '53; 15: 137 (col.) Mar '54; 16: 8 (col.) Oct '54, 66 (col.) Nov '54; 18: 113 (col.) Nov '55; 23: cover, 22, 70-5 (part col.) Je '58; 24: 155 (col.) Oct '58; 25: 40 (col.) Mar '59, 168 (col.) Ap '59, 102, 162 (col.) Je '59; 26: 103 (col.) Oct '59; 27: 98 (col.) Mar '60.
Natl. geog. 105: 204-38 (part col.) Feb '54.
Travel 101: 33 Ap '54; 102: 31-3 Sept '54; 111: cover (col.), 14-9 Feb '59.

— (beach). Holiday 14: 74 (col.) Sept '53; 27: 38 (col.) Je '60.

— (blockade runners). Amer. heri. vol. 6 no. 5 p. 38-9 (col.) (Aug '55).

— (Castle Harbour). Holiday 24: 143 Oct '58.

— (fortifications). Amer. heri. vol. 10 no. 4 p. 106-10 (Je '59).

— (harbor). Holiday 7: 94 (col.) Feb '50; 28: 150 (col.) Oct '60.
Travel 112: 5 Aug '59; 113: inside cover Mar '60.

— hotel. Holiday 27: 225 Ap '60; 28: 200 Oct '60.

— (house). Holiday 23: 138 (col.) Ap '58.

— (Lantana Colony club). Travel 109: 41 Mar '58.

— (map). Natl. geog. 105: 208-9 Feb '54.

Bernadotte, Count Folke. Cur biog. p. 45 (1945).

Bernard, S. (work of). Amer. heri. vol. 9 no. 2 p. 48-9 (col.) (Feb '58).

Bernardino, Minerva. Cur. biog. p .42 (1950).

Bernays, Edward L. Cur biog. p. 77 (1942); p. 33 (1960).

Berne (Switzerland). Holiday 28: 34-5 (col.) Aug '60.
Natl. geog. 98: 240-1 (col.) Aug '50; 110: 450 (col.) Oct '56.
Travel 108: 22-7 Nov '57; 111: 47 Je '59.

Bernhard, Prince of Netherlands. Cur. biog. p. 43 (1950).
Holiday 10: 53-4 (part col.) Nov '51.

Bernheim, Bertram M. Cur. biog. p. 39 (1943).

Bernie, Ben. Cur. biog. p. 73 (1941).

Bernini, Gian Lorenzo (bust). Holiday 27: 89 Ap '60.

— (altar group). Praeg. pict. ency., p. 332.

— (sculpture by). Con. 126: 133 Oct '50.
Praeg. pict. ency., p. 334.

— (terracotta work). Con. 145: XXXI, 89 Ap '60.

— (work of). Int. gr. soc.: Arts . . . p. 87 (col.).

Bernstein, Leonard. Cur. biog. p. 45 (1944); p. 35 (1960).
Holiday 21: 42 Mar '57; 26: 93 Oct '59.

Bernstein, Philip S. Cur. biog. p. 36 (1951).

Berra, Lawrence. Cur. biog. p. 51 (1952).

Berry, Erick. Jun. bk. of auth., p. 30.

Berry, George L. Cur. biog. p. 49 (1948).

Berry, Martha (with school children). Natl. geog. 105: 319 (col.) Mar '54.

Berry, Walter. Holiday 25: 64 (col.) Jan '59.

Berryman, James Thomas. Cur. biog. p. 45 (1950).

Berthoud, James (by Audubon). Amer. heri. vol. 11 no. 1 p. 14 (Dec '59).

Berthoud, Mrs. James (by Audubon). Amer. heri. vol. 11 no. 1 p. 14 (Dec '59).

Berthoud, Nicholas (by Audubon). Amer. heri. vol. 11 no. 1 p. 14 (Dec '59).

Bertoldo (bronze sculpture). Con. 142: 268 Jan '59.

Berwick-Upon-Tweed (England). Holiday 8: 74-9 Aug '50.

Beskow, Elsa. Jun. bk. of auth., p. 31.

Bess, Demaree. Cur. biog. p. 40 (1943).

bessemer converter. Lehner: Pict. bk. of sym., p. 14.

Best, Charles H. Cur. biog. p. 53 (1957).

Best, Edna. Cur. biog. p. 81 (1954).

Best, Herbert. Jun. bk. of auth., p. 32.

Beston, Henry. Jun. bk. of auth., p. 34.

Bestor, Arthur. Cur. biog. p. 40 (1958).

bet, lost. See lost bet.

Betancourt, Romulo. Cur. biog. p. 37 (1960).

Bethe, Hans A. Cur. biog. p. 47 (1950).

Bethlehem church of nativity. Natl. geog. 102: 852-5 Dec '52.

Bethor (seal of). Lehner: Pict. bk of sym., p. 25.

Bethune, Mary McLeod. Cur. biog. p. 80 (1942).

"The Betrothal" (Velarde). Natl. geog. 107: 369 (col.) Mar '55.

Betsy Ross home (Philadelphia). Amer. heri., vol. no. 3 back cover (spring '52).
Holiday 16: 55, 106 Jl '54.

— (int.). Jordan: Hammond's pict. atlas, p. 45 (col.).

Bettelheim, Bruno. Cur. biog. p. 51 (1961).

Bettis, Valerie. Cur. biog. p. 66 (1953).

Bettmann, Otto L. Cur. biog. p. 52 (1961).

Betts, Rome Abel. Cur. biog. p. 46 (1949).

Betty lamp. Rawson: Ant. pict. bk., p. 93.

"Between Chamonix & Martigny" (Cozens). Con. ency. of ant., vol. 1 p. 141.

Bevan, Aneurin. Cur. biog. p. 42 (1943).

beverage dispensers (Russia). Natl. geog. 116: 739 (col.) Dec '59.

Beveridge, Albert J. Amer. heri. vol. 11 no. 4 p. 32 (Je '60).

Beveridge, Sir William. Cur. biog. p. 45 (1943).

Beverly Hills (Cal.) Holiday 12: 34-42 (part col.) Oct '52.

Bevin, Ernest. Cur. biog. p. 48 (1949).

Bevis, Howard L. Cur. biog. p. 50 (1950).

Bevis, Palmer. Cur. biog. p. 68 (1953).

Beyen, Johan W. Cur. biog. p. 69 (1953).

Bhabha, Homi Jehanger. Cur. biog. p. 50 (1956).

Bhakra dam (India). Natl. geog. 118: 457 (col.) Oct '60.

Bharata dance. See dance of Bharata.

Bharata dancer (India). Holiday 27: 28 (col.) May '60.

Bhave, Vinoba. Cur. biog. p. 71 (1953).

Bhutan. Natl. geog. 102: 714-52 (part col.) Dec '52.

—— (map). Natl. geog. 102: 716 Dec '52.

Bhuvaneswar (India, temple). Praeg. pict. ency., p. 551.

Bialk, Elisa. Cur. biog. p. 82 (1954).

Bianchi, Peter V. (work of). Natl. geog. 114: 784 Dec '58.

Bianco, Margery Williams. Jun. bk. of auth., p. 35.

Biarritz (France). Travel 106: 23-4 Oct '56.

Biarritz beach. Natl. geog. 109: 329 (col.) Mar '56.

Bible, Alan. Cur. biog. p. 55 (1957).

Bible (sym.). Lehner: Pict. bk. of sym., p. 38.

—— (Indian, Guatemala). Natl. geog. 117: 406 (col.) Mar '60.

Bible cities (O.T.). Holiday 18: 68-9 Jl '55.

Bible costumes. See costume, Bible.

Bible for Indians, Eliot's (title page). Amer. heri. vol. 9 no. 1 p. 6-7, 9 (Dec '57).

Bible lands. Holiday 17: 38-45 (part col.) Feb '55.
Natl. geog. 110: 708-59 (part col.) Dec '56.
Osward: Asia Minor, pl. 30.

—— (map). Natl. geog. 118: 820-1 (col.) Dec '60.

Bible pages (English & Indian). Amer. heri. vol. 9 no. 1 p. 6-7, 9 (Dec '57).

Bible times, life in. Natl. geog. 112: 834-63 (col.) Dec '57.

Biblical scenes (O.T.). Amer. heri. vol. 7 no. 1 p. 54-61 (col.) (Dec '55).

—— (1000 yrs. before Christ). Natl. geog. 118: 812-51 (part col.) (Dec '60).

—— (by Soulen). Natl. geog. 112: 834-63 (col.) Dec '57.

Bibury (England). Holiday 23: 97 (col.) Ap '58.

bicycle. Holiday 5: 94, 132 Je '49; 6: 28, 70 Jl '49, 82 Aug '49; 7: 79, 144 Ap '50, 97 May '50, 103, 112 Je '50; 8: 60, 73 Jl '50, 96 Dec '50; 11: 134 Ap '52, 16, 143 May '52, 67 Je '52; 12: 27, 123 Jl '52, 5, 58 Aug '52; 14: 176 Dec '53.
Natl. geog. 106: 160, 178 Aug '54.
Travel 106: 16 Sept '56.

—— (boy). Natl. geog. 107: 633 (col.) May '55; 114: 359 (col.) Sept '58.

—— (boy & girl). Natl. geog. 105: 207, 225 (col.) Feb '54.

—— (boys). Holiday 10: 30 Sept '51.
Natl. geog. 108: 130-1 Jl '55.

—— (family). Holiday 13: 45 Ap '53.

—— (girl). Natl. geog. 105: 173 (col.) Feb '54.

—— (man). Natl. geog. 116: 61 (col.) Jl '59.

—— (man, comic). Holiday 16: 19 Aug '54.

—— (riders). Holiday 7: 108, 160 Je '50; 8: 30 Sept '50, 119 Dec '50; 13: 95 Ap '53; 15: 119 Ap '54, 119 May '54; 16: 26 Jl '54, 84 Sept '54, 80 Oct '54; 17: 4 Jan '55; 27: 98 Mar '60.

—— (riders, comic). Holiday 16: 26 Jl '54.

—— (riders, Holland). Natl. geog. 98: 773 Dec '50.

—— (riders, high wire, circus). Durant: Pict. hist. of Amer. circus, p. 208.

—— (stunt rider). Holiday 6: 17 Aug '49.

——, antique. Amer. heri. vol. 10 no. 1 p. 90-1 (Dec '58); vol. 12 no. 1 p. 115 (Dec '60).
Natl. geog. 99: 775 Je '51; 102: 773 (col.) Dec '52.

——, boy's. Holiday 10: 183 Dec '51; 19: 53 Mar '56.

——, double (men). Natl. geog. 117: 424-5 (col.) Mar '60.

——, girl's. Holiday 10: 174 Dec '51; 12: 14 Nov '52.

——, man's. Holiday 10: 100 Dec '51.

bicycle race. Travel 106: 53 Jl '56.

——, long distance (France). Natl. geog. 101: 793 (col.) Je '52.

"bicycle thieves" (movie). Int. gr. soc.: Arts . . . p. 151 (col.).

bicycle tire. See tire, bicycle.

bicycle wheel. Holiday 14: 108 Sept '53.

bicycles (boy & girl). See boy & girl (bicycles).

—— (riders). Amer. heri. vol. 8 no. 1 p. 68-75 (Dec '56).
Holiday 5: 2 (col.) Feb '49; 77 Ap '49; 6: 17, 77 Jl '49.
Natl. geog. 102: 288 Sept '52; 106: 379 (col.) Sept '54.

—— (riders, tour). Natl. geog. 108: 150, 154 Jl '55.

——, antique. Holiday 15: 119 Ap '54.

Bidault, Georges. Cur. biog. p. 48 (1945).

Biddle, Gen. Anthony Drexel. Holiday 23: 158 Je '58.

Biddle, Anthony J. Drexel, jr. Cur. biog. p. 75 (1941).

Biddle, Francis. Cur. biog. p. 76 (1941).

Biddle, George. Cur. biog. p. 83 (1942).

Biddle, Nicholas (Inman). Amer. heri. vol. 7 no. 4 p. 10 (Je '56).

Biederbick, Stewart Henry. Amer. heri. vol. 11 no. 4 p. 50 (Je '60).

Biedermann, Johann J. (work of). Con. 145: XL Ap '60.

Bienne (Switzerland). Holiday 6: 76 Aug '49.

bier, Bali funeral. Natl. geog. 99: 4 Jan '51.

Bierstadt, Albert (work of). Amer. heri. vol. 6 no. 1 p. 37 (col.) (fall '54).

Bierut, Boleslaw. Cur. biog. p. 51 (1949).

Biffle, Leslie L. Cur. biog. p. 41 (1946).

Big basin redwoods state park. Holiday 25: 39 (col.) Feb '59.

"Big Ben" clock (London). Holiday 11: 121 (col.) Mar '52; 18: 128 Jl '55; 21: 33 Mar '57; 25: 145 Jan '59. Natl. geog. 100: 715 (col.) Dec '51; 108, 127 Jl '55; 114: 47 col.) Jl '58. Travel 103: inside cover Feb '55.

"Big Bend" (New Mexico). Jordan: Hammond's pict. atlas, p. 121 (col.).

Big Bend natl. park. Travel 101: 18 Feb '54.

"The Big Blow" (Bohrod). Amer. heri. vol. 11 no. 5 p. 6-7 (col.) (Aug. '60).

Bigari, Vittorio (work of). Con. 135: 51 Mar '55.

Bigart, Homer. Cur. biog. p. 38 (1951).

Bigelow, Karl W. Cur. biog. p. 53 (1949).

Bigg, William Redmore (work of). Con. 141: CXII Je '58.

Biggers, John D. Cur. biog. p. 79 (1941).

Biggs, E. Power. Cur. biog. p. 51 (1950).

Bikel, Theodore. Cur. biog. p. 39 (1960).

Bilbo, Theodore G. Cur. biog. p. 48 (1943).

Bill, Alfred H. Jun. bk. of auth., p. 37.

Bill, Max (plaster figure). Praeg. pict. ency., p. 467.

bill, $3.00 (1860). Amer. heri. vol. 8 no. 6 p. 16 (col.) (Oct '57).

bill hook. Rawson: Ant. pict. bk., p. 21.

"bill of fare," steamboat. Amer. heri. vol. 8 no. 6 p. 23 (col.) (Oct '57).

billboard, cylindrical (Paris). Natl. geog. 100: 719 (col.) Dec '51.

billboards, Russian. Natl. geog. 116: 402 (col.) Sept '59.

billboards. See also posters.

"The billeting order" Conti). Con. 135: XLIV Mar '55.

billfold. Holiday 10: 1, 20, **41**, 172 (part col.) Dec '51; 11: 158 May '52, 59 (col.) Je '52; 12: 119 (col.) Nov '52, 100, 134 Dec '52; 18: 82 (col.) Nov '55, 169 (col.) Dec '55; 19: 2 (col.) Je '56; 20: 102 (col.) Dec '56; 22: 114, 183 (col.) Dec '57.

——, ladies. Holiday 14: 22 (col.) Dec '53.

billfold. See also wallet.

billiard game (cartoon). Jensen: the White House, p. 57.

billiard room (int.). Holiday 28: 43 Nov '60.

billiard table (Parham, 18th cent.). Con. 145: 1 Mar '60.

Billiken (sym.). Lehner: Pict. bk. of sym., p. 62.

Billingsley, John Sherman. Cur. biog. p. 43 (1946).

"Billy goat at the tree of life." See "Tree of life, Billy goat at."

"Billy the Kid." See Bonney, William H., II.

—— (grave of). See grave of "Billy the Kid."

Biloxi lighthouse (Miss.). Jordan: Hammond's pict. atlas, p. 81 (col.).

"Biltmore" (home of G. W. Vanderbilt, II). Amer. heri. vol. 6 no. 2 p. 21 (col.) (winter '55).

Biltmore hotel (Arizona). Holiday 8: 119 Nov '50, 11 Dec '50; 10: 115 (col.) (Oct '51), 83 (col.) Nov '51; 12: 17 (col.) Nov '52; 13: 129 Mar '53. Jordan: Hammond's pict. atlas, p. 178 (col.).

Bimini islands. Natl. geog. 101: 187-212 (part col.) Feb '52.

—— (map). Natl. geog. 101: 188 Feb '52.

Bimson, Carl A. Cur. biog. p. 54 (1961).

Binder, Carroll. Cur. biog. p. 40 (1951).

Bing, Rudolf. Cur. biog. p. 53 (1950). Holiday 8: 76 Nov '50.

Bingham, Barry. Cur. biog. p. 55 (1949).

Bingham, George Caleb (work of). Amer. heri. vol. 1 no. 4 p. 18-23 (part col.) (Summer '50); vol. 7 no. 5 p. 9 (col.) (Aug '56). Natl. geog. 99: 192 (col.) Feb '51. Praeg. pict. ency., p. 396 (col.).

Bingham, Hiram. Cur. biog. p. 42 (1951).

Bingham, J. A. Amer. heri. vol. 11 no. 1 p. 61 (Dec '59).

Bingham, Jonathan B. Cur. biog. p. 84 (1954).

Bingham, Millicent Todd. Cur. biog. p. 56 (1961).

Bingham falls (Vermont). Travel 102: 16 Aug '54.

Bingham's Melcombe home (int. & ext.). Con. 140: 74 (col.), 79 Nov '57.

Binns, Joseph Patterson. Cur. biog. p. 86 (1954).

binoculars. Amer. heri. vol. 10 no. 3 p. 52 (col.) (Ap '59). Holiday 5: 161 Je '49; 7: 144 Ap '50, 163 May '50; 8: 52, 113 Jl '50, 103 Aug '50, 18 Sept '50, 118 Oct '50, 127 Nov '50, 132, 164 Dec '50; 10: 12, 16, 60, 121 Jl '51, 76, 112 Aug '51, 14, 24 Sept '51, 27, 127, 130 Oct '51, 26, 86, 150 Nov '51, 127, 165 Dec '51; 11: 89 Jan '52, 78 Feb '52, 21, 23, 114 Mar '52, 116, 137, 142 Ap '52, 30, 126 May '52, 84, 135, 153 Je '52; 12: 13-4, 138 Jl '52, 12 Aug '52, 30, 114 Sept '52, 135 Oct '52, 95 Nov '52, 172, 174, 182 Dec '52; 13: 18 Feb '53, 29, 142 Mar '53, 150 Ap '53, 154, 166 May '53; 14: 15 Jl '53, 67 Aug '53, 18 Dec '53; 18: 87 Jl '55, 12, 106-7 Aug '55, 23, 116-8 Sept '55, 73 Oct '55, 160, 168 Nov '55, 197-8 Dec '55; 19: 128 Jan '56, 134 Feb '56, 166 Mar '56, 120 May '56, 31, 86 Je '56; 20: 112 Aug '56, 115 Sept '56, 94, 138 Oct '56, 14, 191, 206 Dec '56; 21: 164 Mar '57, 30 Ap '57, 154, 194 Je '57; 22: 90 Sept '57, 169 Oct '57, 165 Nov '57, 228 Dec '57; 23: 178 Je '58 24: 102 Jl '58, 24 Dec '58; 25: 124 Ap '59, 109, 169, 207 May '59, 29 Je '59; 26: 85 Aug '59, 97, 174 Oct '59, 189 Nov '59, 8, 59, 201 Dec '59; 27: 105, 166, 142 May '60, 48, 164 Je '60; 28: 14 Jl '60, 88 Aug '60, 77, 132 Sept '60, 37, 192 Oct '60, 63, 219 Nov '60, 51, 163, 181 Dec '60. Travel 111: 5 Mar '59; 112: 50 Dec '59; 113: 7 Jan '60, 53 Feb '60, 58 Mar '60, 42 Ap '60, 44 May '60.

—— (in case). Travel 114: 58 Oct '60, 66 Nov '60, 66 Dec '60.

—— (view in end). Holiday 11: 63 Ap '52, 136 May '52, 154 Je '52; 12: 101 Jl '52.

——, folding. Travel 108: back cover Jl '57; 109: back cover Je '58; 110: inside cover Aug '58, 52 Nov '58; 113: 7 Jan '60, 53 Feb '60, 58 Mar '60, 42 Ap '60, 19 Je '60; 114: 50 Jl '60, 66 Aug '60.

binoculars, infrared. Holiday 28: 58 Sept '60.
——, sport. Holiday 10: 130, 133 Dec '51.
Binoit, Peter (work of). Con. 145: XI (col.) Je '60.
biology experimental apparatus. Natl. geog. 107: 213 (col.) Feb '55.
Birch, Thomas (work of). Amer. heri. vol. 11 no. 6, cover (col.) (Oct '60).
   Con. ency. of ant., vol. 3 pl. 94.
Birch state park (Florida). Travel 107: 12 Je '57.
Bird, Will R. Cur. biog. p. 88 (1954).
bird, funeral. See funeral bird.
bird bath (kitten). Holiday 10: 106 Aug '51.
—— (Florentine). Natl. geog. 105: 542 (col.) Ap '54.
bird blind, photographers. See blind, bird.
bird cage. Con. 137: 128 Ap '56; 139: 193 May '57.
   Holiday 5: 70 Je '49; 8: 28 Dec '50; 10: 130 Oct '51; 11: 21 Jan '52; 12: 46 (col.) Sept '52; 18: 120 Jl '55, 106 Aug '55; 20: 79 Oct '56, 26, 93 Nov '56; 25: 71 (col.) Feb '59; 27: 168 Mar '60, 31 (col.) Je '60.
——, Russian. Con. 145: 187 May '60.
——, Swiss. Con. 141: 250 Je '58.
bird call whistle. Natl. geog. 106: 587 Nov '54.
bird feeder. See humming bird feeder.
bird feeding station. Holiday 6: 117 Dec '49.
bird house. Brooks: Growth of a nation, p. 275.
—— (sym.). Lehner: Pict. bk. of sym., p. 81.
bird prints. Con. ency. of ant., vol. 3 pl. 81-8.
"Bird watchers" (men, women). Natl. geog. 99: 299 Mar '51.
birds, porcelain (Doughty). See Doughty birds.
Birdseye, Clarence. Cur. biog. p. 45 (1946).
Birdwell, Russell. Cur. biog. p. 47 (1946).
biretto. Con. 136: 2 (col.), 3 Sept '55.
Birley, Sir Oliver (portrait by). Con. 127: 121-2 May '51.
Birley, Oswald (work of). Con. 134: 70 (col.) Sept '54; 144: 13 Sept '59.
birling match (British Columbia). Natl. geog. 114: 170 (col.) Aug '58.
birling. See also log rolling.
Birney, David B. Pakula: Cent. album, p. 87.
Birnie, William A. H. Cur. biog. p. 52 (1952).
Birren, Faber. Cur. biog. p. 51 (1956).
Birs, Nimrud. Ceram: March of arch., p. 192-3.
birth (sym.). Lehner: Pict. bk. of sym., p. 26.
——, animal. Natl. geog. 103: 410-11 Mar '53.
birth certificate (Pa. Dutch). Holiday 18: 60 (col.) Jl '55.
birth chart, U.S. Natl. geog. 116: 705 Nov '59.
birth of Brahma. Lehner: Pict. bk. of sym., p. 43.
"Birth of Orion" (Rosa). Con. 145: XXXII (col.) Ap '60.
"Birth of Scottish freedom" (pageant). Natl. geog. 112: 484-5 (col.) Oct '57.
"Birth of the Virgin" (Altdorfer). Con. ency. of ant., vol. 1, pl. 156.
"Birth of Venus" (Botticelli). Holiday 27: 197 (col.) Ap '60.
"Birth of Venus" (Redon). Con. 144: XXV Dec '59.
"Birth of Venus" (tropical painting). Holiday 27: 78 (col.) Mar '60.

birthday (sym.) Lehner: Pict. bk of sym., p. 56.
birthtree (sym.). Lehner: Pict. bk. of sym., p. 78.
Bisham abbey, (England). Natl. geog. 98: 195 (col.), 200 Aug '50.
Bishamon (sym.). Lehner: Pict. bk. of sym., p. 48.
"Bishop Alvise Grimani." Natl. geog. 101: 87 (col.) Jan '52.
Bishop, Claire Huchet. Jun. bk. of auth., p. 39.
Bishop, Hazel. Cur. biog. p. 57 (1957).
Bishop, Joey. Cur. biog. p. 41 (1962).
Bishop, William Avery. Cur. biog. p. 80 (1941).
bishop's staff. See staff, bishop's.
Bismarck. Holiday 19: 85 Mar '56.
Bisschop,, Cornelius (work of). Con. 140: 117 (col.) Nov '57.
Bisschop, Jan de (work of). Con. 127: 61 Mar '51.
Bissell, Claude T. Cur. biog. p. 35 (1959).
Bissell, Maj. Gen. Clayton L. Cur. biog. p. 51 (1943).
Bissell, George. Amer. heri. vol. 10 no. 2 p. 68 (Feb '59).
Bisset, Sir James G. P. Cur. biog. p. 49 (1946).
Bitar, Salah. Cur. biog. p. 42 (1958).
bits & bridle bosses, Horse. Con. 140: 138 Nov '57.
Bittner, Van Amberg. Cur. biog. p. 49 (1947).
biwa (Japan). Natl. geog. 118: 771 Dec '60.
Bjoerling, Jussi. Cur. biog. p. 51 (1947).
Bjornsson, Sveinn. Cur. biog. p. 48 (1944).
Black, Eugene R. Cur. biog. p. 55 (1950).
Black, Hugo. Cur. biog. p. 82 (1941).
Black, Hugo L. Holiday 7: 78 Feb '50.
"Black Ball liners" (ship). Amer. heri. vol. 6 no. 6 cover (col.) (Oct '55).
"Black Bart." See Bolton, Charles E.
Black Forest (Ger.). Disney: People & places, p. 47-56 (col.).
   Holiday 27: 66 (col.) Jan '60.
"Black Friday panic 1869." Amer. heri. vol. 8 no. 3 p. 54 (Ap '57).
The black hand. See hand, black.
"Black Hawk" (statue). Natl. geog. 101: 183 Feb '52.
The Black Hills (S.D.). Jordan: Hammond's pict. atlas, p. 106-7 (col.).
   Natl. geog. 110: 480-509 (part col.) Oct '56.
   Travel 113: 40-3 Mar '60.
—— (Borglum sculpture). See Mt. Rushmore memorial.
—— (map). Natl. geog. 110: 485 Oct '56.
the "Black Maria" studio, Edison's. Amer. heri. vol .11 no. 3 p. 104 (Ap '60).
"Black Point inn" (Prout's Neck, Me.). Travel 114: 42 Aug '60.
Black watch Sgt-Maj. (Scotland). Holiday 27: cover (col.) May '60.
Blackall, Frederick S., jr. Cur. biog. p. 73 (1953).
Blackbeard (Edward Teach). Amer. heri. vol. 8 no. 2 p. 10 (col.) (Feb '57).
Blackett, Patrick M. S. Cur. biog. p. 57 (1950).
"blackjack" mug. See mug. "blackjack."
blacksmith. Natl. geog. 113: 867 Je '58.
   Travel 113: 30 Mar '60.

—— (Austria). Natl. geog. 118: 255 (col.) Aug '60.

—— (medieval). Int. gr. soc.: Arts . . . p. 69 (col.).

—— (repairing axhead). Natl. geog. 103: 819 Je '53.

—— (shoeing horse). Holiday 11: 43 (col.) Je '52.
Natl. geog. 115: 581 Ap '59.

—— (sym.). Lehner: Pict. bk. of sym., p. 90.
blacksmith & boy (1850). Amer. heri. vol. 8 no. 1 p. 57 (Dec '56).
blacksmith shop. Natl. geog. 112: 309 (col.) Sept '57.

—— (ext. & int.). Rawson: Ant. pict. bk., p. 53-6.
Blackwater Falls (W. Va.). Travel 101: 14 Mar '54.
Blackwater Falls state park. Travel 110: 49 Oct '58.
Blackwell, Betsy Talbot. Cur. biog. p. 90 (1954).
Blackwell, Earl. Cur. biog. p. 41 (1960).
bladder, human. Gray's anatomy, p. 1277-9.

——, lymphatic system. Gray's anatomy, p. 723.
Blagonravov, Anatoli A. Cur. biog. p. 43 (1958).
Blaik, Col. Earl H. Cur. biog. p. 52 (1945).
Blain, Daniel. Cur. biog. p. 53 (1947).
Blaine, James G. Amer. heri. vol. 6 no. 5 p. 58 (Aug '55); vol. 8 no. 3 p. 52 (Ap '57).
Blair, David. Cur. biog. p. 58 (1961).
Blair, James T., jr. Cur. biog. p. 45 (1958).
Blair, Montgomery. Amer. heri. vol. 11 no. 6 p. 46 (Oct '60).
Blair castle (Scotland). Holiday 16: 42 Sept '54.
Blair House (Pres.' guest house). Holiday 20: 62-3 Oct '56.
Blaisdell, Thomas C., jr. Cur. biog. p. 59 (1949).
Blake, Doris. Cur. biog. p. 85 (1941).
Blake, Rev. Eugene Carson. Cur. biog. p. 47 (1955).
Blake, William (work of). Con. 129: 36 Ap '52; 140: 114 Nov '57; 144: 35 Sept '59; 145: 214 May '60.
Praeg. pict. ency., p. 388 (col.).
Blakeslee, Albert F. Cur. biog. p. 86 (1941).
Blalnik, John A. Cur. biog. p. 47 (1958).
Blalock, Alfred. Cur. biog. p. 51 (1946).
Blalock, Mrs. Richard W. Cur. biog. p. 56 (1950).
Blamey, Gen. Sir Thomas. Cur. biog. p. 84 (1942).
Blanch, Arnold. Cur. biog. p. 91 (1954).

—— (work of). Amer. heri. vol. 2 no. 4 p. 46 (col.) (summer '51).
Blanchard, Felix A. Cur. biog. p. 54 (1946).
Blanchard, Hazel A. Cur. biog. (1963).
Blanchfield, Col. Florence A. Cur. biog. p. 54 (1943).
Blancke, Harold. Cur. biog. p. 59 (1957).
Blandford, John B., jr. Cur. biog. p. 86 (1942).
Blandford, Marquis of (miniature). Con. 142: IV Dec '58.
Blanding, Donald. Cur. biog. p. 60 (1957).
Blanding, Sarah Gibson. Cur. biog. p. 56 (1946).
Blandy, Rear Adm. William H. P. Cur. biog. p. 87 (1942).

Blaney, Mrs. Charles. Amer. heri. vol. 12 no. 1 p. 16 (Dec '60).
Blank, Theodor. Cur. biog. p. 54 (1952).
Blankenhorn, Herbert. Cur. biog. p. 54 (1956).
blanket. Holiday 20: 128 (col.) Oct '56; 22: 128 (col.) Oct '57, 123 (col.) Dec '57; 24: 12 (col.) Dec '58, 168 (col.) Nov '58, 50 (col.) Dec '58; 26: 20 (col.) Dec' 59; 28: 12 (col.) Dec '60.

——, fur (women buying). Natl. geog. 113: 335 (col.) Mar '58.

——, plaid. Natl. geog. 110: 41 (col.) Jl '56.
Blanton, Dr. Smiley. Cur. biog. p. 56 (1956).
Blarney castle (Ireland). Holiday 6: 38 (col.) Dec '49; 21: 115 Jan '57.
blast-furnace towers. Natl. geog. 102: 35 (col.) Jl '52.
Blattenberger, Raymond. Cur. biog. p. 49 (1958).
Blaustein, Jacob. Cur. biog. p. 61 (1949).
"Blea tarn" (England). Natl. geog. 109: 540 (col.) Ap '56.
bleachers. See grandstand.
Blechen, Karl (work of). Praeg. pict. ency., p. 395 (col.).
Bled (Yugoslavia). Holiday 10: 72, 74-5 Jl '51.
blender, Waring. See Waring blender.
Blenheim palace (England). Holiday 15: 29 Je '54; 23: 85 Ap '58.
"Blessed Hermann Joseph adoring Virgin" (Van Dyck). Natl. geog. 97: 767 (col.) Je '50.
blessing circus. Durant: Pict. hist. of Amer. circus, p. 292.
blessing sign (Judaism sym.). Lehner: Pict. bk. of sym., p. 36.
Bligh, William. Natl. geog. 112: 734 Dec '57.
blimp. Natl. geog. 114: 350 (col.) Sept '58.
blind, bird (photographer's). Natl. geog. 116: 663 Nov '59.
blind man (factory worker). Natl. geog. 107: 473 (col.) Ap '55.

—— ("seeing eye dog"). Natl. geog. 114: 206 Aug '58.
blindness triangle (Sym.). Lehner: Pict. bk. of sym., p. 70.
Bliss, Henry E. Cur. biog. p. 75 (1953).
Bliss, Maj. Gen. Raymond W. Cur. biog. p. 45 (1951).
Blitch, Iris F. Cur. biog. p. 58 (1956).
Bliven, Bruce. Cur. biog. p. 88 (1941).
Bloch, Rear Adm. Claude C. Cur. biog. p. 88 (1942).
Bloch, Ernest. Cur. biog. p. 78 (1953).
Bloch, Felix. Cur. biog. p. 93 (1954).
Block, Herbert. Cur. biog. p. 95 (1954).
Block, Joseph L. Cur. biog. p. 59 (1961).
Block Island (map). Travel 102: 21-2 Aug '54.
block printing textiles. Natl. geog. 99: 577 (col.) May '51; 114: 37 (col.) Jl '58.
block tackle & knot. Rawson: Ant. pict. bk., p. 77.
block to stamp wallpaper. Rawson: Ant. pict. bk., p. 81.
blockade runners (ships at Bermuda). Amer. heri. vol. 6 no. 5 p. 38-9 (col.), 41 (Aug '55).
blockhouse (fort). Natl. geog. 100: 316 (col.) Sept '51; 103: 737 Je '53.

blockhouse (Ft. Pitt). Amer. heri. vol. 4 no. 3 p. 42 spring '53).
Holiday 6: 41 Oct '49; 18: 101 Oct '55.
—— (Ft. Recovery). Amer. heri. vol. 6 no. 3 p. 106 (Ap '55).
—— (frontier). Travel 101: 39 Je '54.
—— (Mackinac island). Travel 102: 42 Aug '54.
—— (Saratoga). Holiday 6: 41 Sept '49.
blockhouses (fort). Amer. heri. vol. 5 no. 4 p. 1 (summer '54).
Blodgett, Katherine Burr. Cur. biog. p. 56 (1952).
Bloemaert, Abraham (work of). Con. 142: 66 Sept. '58.
Bloemfontein (observatory). See Lamont Hussey observatory.
Blondin (hero of Niagara). Amer. heri., vol. 9 no. 5 p. 34, 37 (col.) (Aug '58).
blood vascular system, human. Gray's anatomy, p. 503-43, 552, 554, 558, 562.
bloodstone box, antique German. Con. 134: 42 Sept '54.
Bloom, Claire. Cur. biog. p. 60 (1956).
Bloom, Sol. Cur. biog. p. 56 (1943).
bloom (goddess of). Lehner: Pict. bk. of sym., p. 33.
Bloomgarden, Kermit. Cur. biog. p. 51 (1958).
Blosse, Capt. Tobias. Con. 141: 162 May '58.
blotter (Faberge). Con. 145: LXXIX May '60.
Blough, Roger M. Cur. biog. p. 49 (1955).
Blough, Roy. Cur. biog. p. 58 (1950).
Blount, Charles. Amer. heri. vol. 10 no. 4 p. 16 (col.) (Je '59).
blouses, women's. Holiday 10: 149 (col.) Dec '51.
blowgun (Indian blowing). Natl. geog. 111: 865 Nov '57.
Blucher, Franz. Cur. biog. p. 61 (1956).
Blue, Robert D. Cur. biog. p. 52 (1948).
"Blue Boy" (Gainsborough). Con. 140: 238 Jan '58.
Natl. geog. 113: 253 (col.) Feb '58.
Praeg. pict. ency., p. 374 (col.).
"Blue Duck" (Indian). Horan: Pict. hist. of wild west, p. 133.
Blue Grotto (Capri). Holiday 6: 30 (col.) Aug '49.
Labande: Naples, p. 211.
"The Blue Horse" (Marc). Praeg. pict. ency., p. 448 (col.).
Blue Mosque. Natl. geog. 100: 160 (col.) Aug '51.
Holiday 20: 52 (col.) Dec '56.
—— (ext. & int.). Osward: Asia Minor, pl. 86-7.
blue ribbon (sym.). Lehner: Pict. bk. of sym., p. 84.
Blue Ridge (N. C., map). Natl. geog. 113: 860-1 Je '58
Blue Ridge parkway. Jordan: Hammond's pict. atlas, p. 59 (col.).
"Blue seam" (Jamaican policeman). Holiday 5: 45 (col.) Feb '49.
Blueberry picking, girl. Natl. geog. 107: 792 (col.) Je '55.
"The bluff" (Croegaert). Con. 142: XXXIX Nov '58.

Blume, Peter. Cur. biog. p. 63 (1956).
Blundell, Michael. Cur. biog. p. 97 (1954).
Blunt, Katharine. Cur. biog. p. 58 (1946).
Bly, Nellie. Travel 103: inside back cover Ap '55.
—— (cartoon). Natl. geog. 100: 750 Dec '51.
Blyth, Benjamin (work of). Amer. heri. vol. 10 no. 3 p. 32 (col.) (Ap '59).
Blythe, David C. (work of). Natl. geog. 99: 200 (col.) Feb '51.
"Boar hunt" (Tiepolo). Con. 135: 277 Je '55.
Boardman, Mabel. Cur. biog. p. 49 (1944).
boat. Holiday 11: 16 Feb '52, 86 Mar '52, 84 Ap '52, 17 May '52, 154 Je '52; 12: 4, 100 Jl '52, 100 Aug '52, 72 (col.) Sept '52; 18: 121 Jl '55, 79 Sept '55, 100 Nov '55; 19: 70, 179 May '56, 7 (col.)—9 Je '56; 20: 115, 166-7 Nov '56; 21: 24-5 (col.), 111-6 Feb '57, 154-5, 163 Mar 57; 22: 28, 119 (col.) Jl '57.
Natl. geog. 112: 161 (col.) Aug '57; 113: 480-1 (col.) Ap '58; 115: 300-1, 313 (col.) 317, 332 Mar '59; 117: 479 (col.) Ap '60, 759 (col.) Je '60.
Travel 101: 28 Feb '54; 104: 12, 14-5 Aug '55; 105: 48 Mar '56; 108: 33 Jl '57; 112: 17 Jl '59, 5 Aug '59.
—— (burning). Amer. heri. vol. 6 no. 1 p. 15 (col.) (fall '54).
—— (cartoon). Holiday 21: 111 Feb '57.
—— (comic). Holiday 5: 29 Je '49.
—— (cup race). Natl. geog. 117: 502 (col.) Ap '60.
—— (deck). Holiday 6: 111 (col.) Jl '49.
—— (fisherman). Holiday 10: 1 Nov '51; 12: 40 (col.) Dec '52.
See also boat, fishing.
—— (in bottle). Holiday 28: 170 Nov '60.
—— (in canal lock). Natl. geog. 104: 848 (col.) Dec '53; 115: 310 (col.) Mar '59, 450 (col.) Ap '59.
—— (like basket). Holiday 14: 28 Jl '53.
—— (man & girl). Holiday 19: inside cover (col.) Feb '56; 20: 8 Aug '56.
—— (man & woman). Praeg. pict. ency., p. 416 (col.).
—— (man, woman fishing). Holiday 12: 93 (col.) Nov '52.
—— (man & woman). See also man & woman (boat).
—— (man, comic). Holiday 22: 98 Jl '57.
—— (man poling, swamp). Natl. geog. 105: 322 (col.) Mar '54; 114: 664 Nov '58.
—— (man, woman & child). Natl. geog. 117: 436 (col.) Mar '60.
—— (nature study). Natl. geog. 106: 594, 600-1, 606 (col.) Nov '54.
—— (on beach). Disney: People & places, p. 60-1 (col.).
—— (passenger, lake). Natl. geog. 109: 630 (col.) May '56.
—— (river, swans, village). Natl. geog. 114: 76-7 Jl '58.
boat, aluminum. Holiday 19: 123 Feb '56.
——, ancient. Travel 103: 15 Mar '55.
——, bamboo basket. Natl. geog. 102: 308 (col.) Sept '52.

——, **bamboo covered river.** Natl. geog. 104: 63 Jl '53.

——, **boom.** *See* boom boat.

——, **buffalo skin (Nepal).** Natl. geog. 117: 376 Mar '60.

——, **bulrush.** Natl. geog. 98: 483 (col.) Oct '50.

——, **bulrush (Peru).** Natl. geog. 107: 134 Jan '55.

——, **bunder.** *See* bunder boat.

——, **burial barque.** *See* barque, cedar.

——, **canal.** Travel 105: 25 Ap '56.

——, **canal (England).** Travel 106: 22-5 Aug '56.

——, **canal (Poland).** Natl. geog. 114: 389 Sept '58.

——, **canal (on portage railroad).** Amer. heri. vol. 5 no. 4 p. 45 (summer '54).

——, **canopied (Balearic island).** Natl. geog. 111: 653 (col.) May '57.

——, **ceremonial (Pescadores island).** Natl. geog. 109: 269 (col.) Feb '56.

——, **clam.** Natl. geog. 113: 352 (col.) Mar '58.

——, **coal burner.** Natl. geog. 108: 702 (col.) Nov '55.

——, **copra.** Travel 105: 60 Feb '56.

——, **crab.** *See* crab boat.

——, **cruiser.** *See* cruiser (boat).

——, **diving.** Natl. geog. 109: 158 Feb '56.

——, **excursion.** Natl. geog. 104: 656 Nov '53.

——, **expedition.** Natl. geog. 110: 56 (col.), 59 Jl '56.

——, **ferry.** *See* ferry boat.

——, **fishing.** Amer. heri. vol. 11 no. 2 p. 89 (Feb '60).
Holiday 6: 60 (col.) Jl '49; 12: 123 Oct '52; 24: 55 (col.) Aug '58.
Natl. geog. 99: 324 (col.) Mar '51; 108: 529 (col.) Oct '55; 112: 172-3, 176 (col.) Aug '57.
Rawson: Ant. pict. bk., p. 77-80.
Travel 101: 26 Je '54; 102: 35 Oct '54; 103: 36 Feb '55; 106: 26-9 Sept '56, 36 Oct '56, 38 Nov '56, 48 Dec '56; 107: 16 Je '57; 108: 25 Jl '57, 20 Dec '57; 112: 45 Aug '59.

——, **fishing (Alaska).** Natl. geog. 109: 744-5 (col.) Je '56.

——, **fishing (being repaired).** Travel 107: inside cover Je '57.

——, **fishing (Canary Islands).** Natl. geog. 107: 502 (col.) Ap '55.

——, **fishing (deck).** Holiday 6: 61 (col.) Sept '49.

——, **fishing (deep sea).** Natl. geog. 109: 858 (col.), 868 Je '56.

——, **fishing (Greece).** Natl. geog. 117: 641 (col.) May '60.

——, **fishing (Iceland).** Natl. geog. 100: 616 (col.) Nov '51.

——, **fishing (Italy).** Labande: Naples, p. 192. Natl. geog. 109: 842 (col.) Je '56.

——, **fishing (Japan).** Natl. geog. 104: 620 Nov '53.

——, **fishing (Kashmir).** Holiday 11: 97 Je '52.

——, **fishing (Lobos).** Holiday 20: 118 Dec '56.

——, **fishing (Laos).** Natl. geog. 117: 66 (col.) Jan '60.

——, **fishing (Malaya).** Natl. geog. 103: 222 (col.) Feb '53.

——, **fishing (Martinique).** Natl. geog. 115: 275 (col.) Feb '59.

——, **fishing (Mauritius).** Natl. geog. 109: 98-9 (col.) Jan '56.

——, **fishing (Mexico).** Natl. geog. 107: 222 (col.) Feb '55.

——, **fishing (night).** Natl. geog. 116: 488 (col.) Oct '59.

——, **fishing (Norway).** Natl. geog. 106: 154 (col.) Aug '54.
Travel 105: 52 Jan '56.

——, **fishing (Nova Scotia).** Travel 114: 40 Jl '60.

——, **fishing (Pescadores island).** Natl. geog. 109: 278 (col.) Feb '56.

——, **fishing (Portugal).** Holiday 16: 21 Aug '54.
Natl. geog. 106: 674-6, 683, 688, 695 (part col.) Nov '54; 118: 652-3 (col.) Nov '60.

——, **fishing (Quemoy, rotting, war).** Natl. geog. 115: 426-7 Mar '59.

——, **fishing (Sicily).** Natl. geog. 107: 20-1, 30, 46-7 (col.) Jan '55.

——, **fishing (Spain, women).** Natl. geog. 109: 319 (col.) Mar '56.

——, **flatbottom river.** Holiday 12: 102-3 (col.) Oct '52.

——, **freight.** Brooks: Growth of a nation, p. 273.
Natl. geog. 98: 330 (col.) Sept '50; 102: 591 Nov '52; 104: 637 Nov '53; 108: 205 (col.) Aug '55; 111: 164 (col.) Feb '57; 113: 6 Jan '58; 115: 316 (col.) Mar '59.
Travel 103: 10 May '55; 104: 9 Sept '55; 109: 32, 54 Jan '58.

——, **freight (Cairo).** Natl. geog. 106: 770 (col.) Dec '54.

——, **freight (Great Lakes).** Natl. geog. 101: 314 (col.) Mar '52.

——, **freight (Indonesia).** Natl. geog. 108: 356 Sept '55.

——, **freight (Iraq).** Natl. geog. 114: 484-5 (col.) Oct '58.

——, **freight (Japan).** Natl. geog. 108: 238 (col.) Aug '55.

——, **freight (Nigeria).** Natl. geog. 110: 356 (col.) Sept '56.

——, **freight (ocean).** Natl. geog. 105: 308 Mar '54.

——, **freight (Suez Canal).** Natl. geog. 111: 125 Jan '57.

——, **freight (Sweden).** Natl. geog. 104: 794 (col.) Dec '53.

——, **freight (Wales).** Natl. geog. 108: 568 Oct '55.

——, **funeral (Egypt).** Natl. geog. 108: 613 (col.) Nov '55.

——, **gasoline tanker.** Natl. geog. 108: 531 (col.) Oct '55.

——, **glass-bottom.** Travel 102: 6 Jl '54.

——, **house.** *See* house boat.

——, **icebreaker.** Natl. geog. 115: 490 Ap '59.

——, **keel.** *See* keelboat.

——, **landing craft (Viet Nam).** Natl. geog. 102: 316 Sept '52.

——, **lobster.** *See* lobster boat.

boat, long. *See* longboat.

——, market. *See* market boat.

——, motor. Holiday 13: 24 Mar '53, 155 May '53, 78 Je '53; 14: 28 Jl '53, 89 Aug '53; 24: 21 Jl '58; 25: back cover (col.) Jan '59, 19, 162, 181 Mar '59, 99, 131 Ap '59, 43 Je '59; 26: 22 Nov '59; 27: back cover (col.) Jan '60, 110 (col.) Feb '60, 134, 170, 199 (part col.) Mar '60, 42, 119 (col.) Ap '60; 28: 94, 99 (col.) Sept '60, 42, 117, 157 Nov '60.
Natl. geog. 107: 62 (col.) Jan '55.
Travel 105: 30 Ap '56.

——, motor (Finland). Natl. geog. 106: 250 (col.) Aug '54.

——, motor (fishermen). Holiday 24: 149, 155 (col.) Dec '58.

——, motor (girl). Holiday 25: cover (col.) Mar '59.

——, motor (men & girl). Holiday 24: 20-1 (col.) Nov '58; 25: 13 May '59; 26: 10 (col.) Nov '59, 114 (col.) Dec '59.

——, motor (men, woman & child). Holiday 25: 101 (col.) Jan '59.

——, motor (Norway). Natl. geog. 106: 182 Aug '54.

——, motor (pulling skiers). Holiday 27: 53 (col.) Ap '60.

——, oil tanker. Natl. geog. 117: 7 (col.) Jan '60.

——, ore carrier. Natl. geog. 98: 815, 817 Dec '50; 103: 51 (col.) Jan '53; 115: 448 Ap '59.

——, ore carrier (Great Lakes). Holiday 8: 90-3 (part col.) Aug '50.

——, outboard cruising. Holiday 22: 5 (col.) Sept '57.

——, outboard motor. Holiday 11: 90 (col.) Mar '52; 12: 29 (col.) Jl '52; 13: 65 Ap '53, 18, back cover (col.) Je '53; 19: 81 (col.) Mar '56, 66 (col.) May '56, 17 (col.) Je '56; 21: 112 Feb '57, 40 (col.) Mar '57, 192 (col.) May '57; 22: 41 (col.) Nov '57, 63 (col.), 92 Dec '57; 23: 28 (col.) May '58; 28: 206 (col.) Dec '60.
Natl. geog. 103: 111 Jan '53.

——, outboard motor (boy & girl). Holiday 23: 112 Mar '58; 27: 141 (col.) Je '60.

——, outboard motor (fishermen). Holiday 21: 97 Ap '57; 22: 13 (col.) Oct '57; 23: 2 (col.) Mar '58.

——, outboard motor (Hawaiians). Holiday 20: 12-3 (col.) Oct '56.

——, outrigger. *See* outrigger boat.

——, paddle. Holiday 10: 130 Dec '51.
Travel 106: 42 Nov '56.

——, paddle (boy & girl). Holiday 11: 57 (col.) Mar '52.
Travel 113: cover (col.) Ap '60.

——, paddle (girls). Natl. geog. 112: 246, 258-9, 261-2, 264 (col.) Aug '57.

——, paddle-wheel. Travel 102: 17 Jl '54; 109: 65 May '58, 52 Je '58; 112: 25-7 Aug '59.

——, paddle-wheel (Austria). Natl. geog. 118: 253 (col.) Aug '60.

——, plastic paddle (boy & girl). Holiday 11: 76 (col.) Je '52.

——, pleasure. Holiday 5: 14, 88, back cover (col.) Jan '49, 12, 23, 70, 136 (col.) Mar '49, 154 Ap '49, 53 (col.) Jl '49; 6: 121 Oct '49, 7 (col.) Dec '49; 7: back cover (col.) Jan '50, 4 Feb '50, 19, 83 (col.) Mar '50, 88 (col.) Ap '50, 126 (col.) May '50, 129 (col.) Je '50; 9: 76, 97 Mar '51; 15: 139 Mar '54, 1, 24, 85, 156 Ap '54, 66, 132 (col.) May '54, 125, back cover (col.) Je '54; 16: 24, 61 (col.) Jl '54, 114 Oct '54, 60 (col.) Nov '54; 17: 18, 42, 128 Jan '55, 67 Feb '55, 74, 87 Mar '55.
Natl. geog. 108: 303 (col.) Sept '55.

——, power. *See* powerboat.

——, pulpwood. *See* pulpwood boat.

——, racing shell. *See* racing shells.

——, river. Amer. heri. vol. 6 no. 2 p. 117 (winter '55); vol. 11 no. 5 p. 50 (col.) (Aug '60).
Holiday 5: cover, 36-9, 56 (col.), 85 Mar '49; 6: cover (col.) Sept '49, 16 Oct '49; 7: 44 Mar '50; 8: 31 (col.) Nov '50; 16: 34 (col.), 41 Oct '54; 17: 115 Jan '55, 116 Mar '55; 23: 125, 127 (col.) Jan '58, 129 Mar '58.
Natl. geog. 108: 342 (col.) Sept '55; 111: 548 (col.) Ap '57; 118: 691 (col.) Nov '60.
Travel 110: 29 Oct '58; 112: 37 Aug '59.

——, river (all steel). Natl. geog. 114: 685-7 (part col.) Nov '58.

——, river (int. saloon). Amer. heri. vol. 6 no. 1 p. 13 (col.) (fall '54).

——, river. *See* also steamboat.

——, row. *See* rowboat.

——, rubber. Natl. geog. 105: 384, 389 (col.) Mar '54.

——, shanty. *See* shanty boat.

——, show. *See* show boat.

——, shrimp. Amer. heri. vol. 6 no. 1 p. 63 (col.) (fall '54).
Jordan: Hammond's pict. atlas, p. 85 (col.).

——, sidewheeler. *See* steamboat, sidewheeler.

——, sight seeing. Travel 104: 43 Jl '55.

——, speed. *See* speedboat.

——, square-rigger (U.S. Coast Guard). Natl. geog. 108: 50-84 (col.) Jl '55.

——, sternwheeler. *See* steamboat, sternwheeler.

——, swan. *See* swan boat.

——, teak carrier. Natl. geog. 116: 796 Dec '59.

——, tow. *See* towboat.

——, trap. Rawson: Ant. pict. bk., p. 78.

——, tree trunk (Nile river). Natl. geog. 107: 706 May '55.

——, U.S. Destroyer. *See* U.S. Destroyer boat.

——, U.S. Navy. *See* U.S. Navy boat.

——, Viking. Holiday 21: 47 Je '57.

——, whale hunting. Natl. geog. 110: 60 (col.) Jl '56.

——, woodburning (Bolivia). Travel 104: 22 Oct '55.

——, wrecked. Natl. geog. 113: 22-3 (col.) Jan '58.

boat, Arabian dhow. *See* dhow.

——, Austria (man rowing). Natl. geog. 118: 256 (col.) Aug '60.

——, Bangkok. Natl. geog. 116: 788-9 (col.) Dec '59.

——, Belgium (men & woman). Natl. geog. 113: 810 (col.) Je '58.

——, **Borneo.** Natl. geog. 108: 384-5 (col.) Sept '55.

——, **Brazil.** Natl. geog. 117: 711 (col.) May '60.

——, **Canada.** Holiday 22: 245 Dec '57.

——, **China.** Con. 135: XLVII Ap '55. Travel 108: 38 Nov '57.

——, **China (marble).** Holiday 21: 80 (col.) Je '57.

——, **Corinth canal.** Natl. geog. 110: 753 (col.) Dec '56.

——, **Dieppe (France).** Natl. geog. 115: 626-7 (col.) May '59.

——, **England (Lake dist.).** Natl. geog. 109: 512-3 (col.) Ap '56.

——, **Eskimo.** Natl. geog. 108: 787 Dec '55.

——, **Farmington canal.** *See* Farmington canal boat.

——, **Florida (tourist).** Travel 107: 39 Mar '57.

——, **Formosa.** Natl. geog. 109: 266, 284 (col.) Feb '56.

——, **Greece.** Natl. geog. 103: 371 (col.) Mar '53.

——, **Greenland (explorers).** Natl. geog. 109: 120, 124 Jan '56.

——, **Ifalik (man making).** Natl. geog. 109: 568 (col.) Ap '56.

——, **India.** Travel 105: 53 Feb '56.

——, **India (tourists).** Travel 105: 54 Feb '56.

——, **Iraq, (river).** Natl. geog. 99: 56 Jan '51.

——, **Irish hooker.** Natl. geog. 108: 742 (col.) Dec '55.

——, **Key West.** Natl. geog. 111: 706 May '57.

——, **Mafia.** Travel 112: 42 Sept '59.

——, **Malta taxi.** Holiday 27: 67 (col.) Je '60.

——, **Newfoundland (fishermen).** Holiday 25: 5 (col.) Je '59.

——, **Nile river.** *See* Nile river boat.

——, **Norway.** Natl. geog. 111: 98 (col.) Jan '57.

——, **Pakistan.** Natl. geog. 107: 400, 418, 424 (part col.) Mar '55.

——, **Philippine.** Natl. geog. 118: 601 (col.) Nov '60.

——, **Philistine.** Natl. geog. 112: 846-7 (col.) Dec '57.

——, **Pondichery.** Natl. geog. 105: 519 (col.) Ap '54.

——, **Portugal.** Natl. geog. 118: 617, 629, 631-2 (col.) Nov '60.

——, **Portugal (oxen pull to shore).** Natl. geog. 118: 631 (col.) Nov '60.

——, **Rabelo (Portugal).** Holiday 6: 105 Sept '49.

——, **Rotterdam.** Natl. geog. 118: 548-9 Oct '60.

——, **Russia.** Holiday 18: 102 Jl '55.

——, **Sarawak.** Travel 109: 48, 51 Feb '58.

——, **Singapore (girl on it).** Holiday 23: 106 (col.) Mar '58.

——, **Tasmania.** Natl. geog. 110: 802 (col.) Dec '56.

——, **Turkey.** Natl. geog. 109: 75 (col.) Jan '56. Osward: Asia Minor, pl. V (col.).

boat. *See* also bumboat, bunder boat, canoe, catamaran, clipper ship, cruiser, dinghies, flat-boat, freight boat, heliboat, houseboat, kayak, ketch, launch, outrigger, punt, row-boat, sailboat, shikaras, ship, sloop, surfboat, steamboat, tug, yacht, yawl, boats, skiff.

boat basin (Cape May). Travel 104: 44 Sept '55.

boat building (men). Natl. geog. 113: 186 (col.) Feb '58.

boat "canal clipper." Natl. geog. 117: 420 (col.) Mar '60.

boat deck (ocean liner). Holiday 17: 28 (col.) Mar '55.

boat hooks. Natl. geog. 113: 17 (col.) Jan '58.

boat house. Con. 126: 27 Aug '50.

boat landing. Natl. geog. 108: 702 (col.) Nov '55; 109: 234 (col.) Feb '56; 115: 753 (col.) Je '59.

—— *See* also pier.

——, **launching, Japanese.** Natl. geog. 97: 631 (col.) May '50.

boat making, glass. Natl. geog. 114: 660 (col.) Nov '58.

boat models. Natl. geog. 101: 792 (col.) Je '52; 113: 779 (col.), 780 Je '58.

boat oar. Holiday 13: 156 May '53.

"Boat off Deer Isle" (Marin). Praeg. pict. ency., p. 476 (col.).

boat race (rough water). Travel 101: 31 Ap '54.

—— **(Wellesley college).** Holiday 15: 51 Ap '54.

boat race tragedy (1845). Amer. heri. vol. 10 no. 1 p. 17 (Dec '58).

boat steward. Holiday 13: 18 (col.) May '53.

"The boatman" (Carra). Praeg. pict. ency., p. 475 (col.).

boatman (Mukalla). Natl. geog. 111: 243 Feb '57.

Boatner, Maj. Gen. Haydon L. Cur. biog. p. 57 (1952).

boats (harbor). Face of Amer., p. 84-5 (col.). Holiday 24: 50 (col.) Aug '58.

——, **Arabian.** Natl. geog. 97: 323 (col.) Mar '50.

——, **bum.** *See* bumboats.

——, **canal.** Brooks: Growth of a nation, p. 113.

——, **fiesta.** Natl. geog. 105: 772-5 (col.) Je '54.

——, **fishing.** Face of Amer., p. 121 (col.).

——, **freight.** Natl. geog. 104: 562 (col.) Oct '53; 107: 473 (col.) Ap '55.

——, **Hong Kong.** Natl. geog. 116: 855 (col.) Dec '59.

——, **Japanese.** Disney: People & places, p. 147, 156, 158-9 (col.).

——, **Japanese (silhouettes).** Natl. geog. 118: 758-9 (col.) Dec '60.

——, **merchant (Kashmir).** Natl. geog. 114: 628 (col.) Nov '58.

——, **Mexican.** Holiday 14: 56-7 (col.) Jl '53.

——, **navy torpedo (Denmark).** Natl. geog. 108: 822 (col.) Dec '55.

——, **Normandy beach (war invasion).** Natl. geog. 115: 622-3 May '59.

——, **ore.** Natl. geog. 99: 723 Je '51.

——, **sardine & tuna.** Natl. geog. 105: 155 (col.) Feb '54.

"Boats becalmed" (Van Goyen). Con. 142: 111 (col.) Nov '58.

boats. *See* also boat.

"The boatswain" (Martin). Con. 135: 49 Mar '55.

Boaz & Ruth (Biblical scene). Natl. geog. 118: 847 (col.) Dec '60.

"Bob Cherry" (Smith). Con. 143: XLVI Ap '59.

bobbing for apples, students. Natl. geog. 114: 614 Nov '58.

Boboli gardens (16-17th cent.). Holiday 12: 46 (col.) Oct '52.

bobsled. Travel 105: 39-41 Jan '56.

Boca Raton hotel (Florida). Holiday 26: 161 Nov '59; 27: 114 Jan '60; 28: 23 (col.) Nov '60, 199 (col.) Dec '60.

Boccioni, Umberto (bronze statue). Praeg. pict. ency., p. 458.

"The Boche Looter" (Dunn). Amer. heri. vol. 10 no. 6 p. 15 (col.) (Oct '59).

Bock, Gen. Field Marshall Fedor von. Cur. biog. p. 90 (1942).

Bocklin, Arnold (self portrait with Death). Praeg. pict. ency., p. 410.

Bodeman, William (work of). Con. 145: XXXVIII Ap '60.

Bodhisattva (head). Con. 144: LXXVII Jan '30.

Bodhisattva (sculpture). Con. 134: 145 Nov '54.

bodkin holder, enamel. Con. ency. of ant., vol. 1 pl. 76.

Bodmer, Charles (work of). Amer. heri. vol. 7 no. 6 front cover (col.) (Oct '56).

Bodmer, Karl (work of). Amer. heri. vol. 6 no. 1 p. 34 (fall '54); vol. 9 no. 4 p. 59 (col.) (Je '58).

Bodo (Norway). Travel 111: 42 Ap '59.

bodyguard, Sultan's (Morocco). Natl. geog. 107: 158 (col.) Feb '55.

Boeschenstein, Harold. Cur. biog. p. 61 (1961).

Bogardus, Capt. Adam H. Durant: Pict. hist. of Amer. circus, p. 136.

Bogart, Humphrey. Cur. biog. p. 91 (1942). Holiday 12: 40 Oct '52.

Boggs, Hale. Cur. biog. p. 52 (1958).

Boggs, J. Caleb. Cur. biog. p. 65 (1956).

Bogota (Columbia). Travel 109: 32 Mar '58.

bog-shoe, horse. Rawson: Ant. pict. bk., p. 68.

Boheman, Erik. Cur. biog. p. 47 (1951).

Bohemia, patron saint of. Lehner: Pict. bk. of sym., p. 39.

"Bohemian musicians" (Dusart). Con. 129: LXX Ap '52.

"Bohemian with mandolin" (Corot). Con. 133: 259 Je '54.

Bohlen, Charles E. Cur. biog. p. 54 (1948); p. 43 (1960).

Bohr, Niels. Cur. biog. p. 55 (1945).

Bohrod, Aaron. Cur. biog. p. 51 (1955).

Bohrod, Aaron (work of). Amer. heri. vol. 11 no. 5 p. 6-7 (col.) (Aug '60).

Boilly, Louis-Leopold (work of). Con. 137: XII (col.) May '56; 141: VIII (col.) May '58.

Boisson, Pierre. Cur. biog. p. 59 (1943).

Bok, Judge William Curtis. Cur. biog. p. 99 (1954).

Bok singing tower (Florida). Holiday 13: 42 (col.) Feb '53; 14: 25 Aug '53. Jordan: Hammond's pict. atlas, p. 73 (col.). Travel 103: 10 Feb '55.

Boland, Frederick H. Cur. biog. p. 63 (1961).

Boldini, Giovanni (work of). Con. 134: 206 Dec '54.

Boldt castle (Heart Island). Travel 110: 35 Jl '58.

boleadora. Natl. geog. 113: 327 (col.) Mar '58.

Boles, Ewing T. Cur. biog. p. 80 (1953).

Boles, Paul Darcy. Cur. biog. p. 67 (1956).

Bolet, Jorge. Holiday 21: 42 Mar '57.

Bolger, Raymond W. Cur. biog. p. 93 (1942).

Bolivar (Teodoro Bource Herrera). Travel 102: 41 Oct '54.

Bolivia. Holiday 8: 52-8 (col.) Nov '50; 11: 16-9 Jan '52.
Natl. geog. 98: 481-96 (part col.) Oct '50.
Travel 104: 18-21 Oct '55.

Bolivian. Holiday 80: 85 Nov '56.
Travel 112: 17 Sept '59.

—— (child on back). Holiday 21: 12 (col.) May '57.

—— (woman). Holiday 8: 52, 56 (col.) Nov '50.

boll weevil monument (Alabama). Brooks: Growth of a nation, p. 250.

Bollee, Leon. Amer. heri. vol. 11 no. 2 p. 60 (Feb '60).

Bolling, Richard. Cur. biog. p. 45 (1960).

Bologna, Vitale de (work of). Con. 143: 265 Je '59.

Bolshoi dancers (opera). Natl. geog. 116: 376 (col.) Sept '59.

Bolshoi theater, Russian (int.). Natl. geog. 116: 376-7 (col.) Sept '59.

"Bolsover castle" (Chantrey). Con. 129: 82 Je '52.

Bolt, Richard H. Cur. biog. p. 101 (1954).

Bolt, Robert. Cur. biog. (1963).

Bolte, Charles G. Cur. biog. p. 57 (1945).

Bolte, Gen. Charles L. Cur. biog. p. 103 (1954).

Bolton, Charles E. ("Black Bart"). Horan: Pict. hist. of wild west, p. 82.
Natl. geog. 110: 219 (col.) Aug '56.

Bolton, Frances P. Cur. biog. p. 105 (1954).

Bolz, Lothar. Cur. biog. p. 37 (1959).

bomb (sym.). Lehner: Pict. bk. of sym., p. 95.

Bombay. Travel 106: 12 Nov '56.

"Bombay prowl court" (Van Ruith). Con. 133: XXXVII May '54.

bomber plane. Natl. geog. 99: 345 Mar '51; 112: 282-94 Aug '57.

bombs. Holiday 27: 85 Mar '60.

—— (dropped by airplane). Natl. geog. 112: 281 Aug '57.

——, aerial. Natl. geog. 104: 544 (col.) Oct '53.

——, U.S. Navy. Natl. geog. 116: 306 (col.) Sept '59.

Bonaire (Dutch island). Travel 104: 61 Sept '55.

Bonapart home, Napoleon (St. Helena). Natl. geog. 98: 272 Aug '50.

Bonavia, C. (work of). Con. 139: XIII Ap '57.

bonbonniere, Antique. Con. 133: LV Je '54.

——, enamel. Con. ency. of ant., vol. 1, pl. 73.

Bond, Horace Mann. Cur. biog. p. 107 (1954).

bondage (sym.). Lehner: Pict. bk. of sym., p. 82.

Bondone, Giotto di. See Giotto di Bondone.

bone cells. Gray's anatomy, p. 70.

bone lamp. See lamp, stone age bone.

bones, human. Gray's anatomy, p. 133-71, 186-205, 208-52.

Bonesteel, Maj. Gen. Charles H. Cur. biog. p. 95 (1942).

bonfire (lakeside). Natl. geog. 106: 190 (col.) Aug '54.

Bonheur-du-jour. Con. ency. of ant., vol. 3, pl. 124.
Con. 141: XXXVI Mar '58; 145: 109 Ap '60.
—— (18th cent.). Con. 143: LIX May '59.
——, antique. Con. 140: 101 Nov '57.
——, Coromandel. Con. 145: back cover May '60.
——, English. Con. 138: 263 Jan '57.
——, Louis XV. Con. 139: XXVII Je '57.
——, Regency. Con. 138: XXX Sept '56; 142: LXII Dec '58.
——, Sheraton. Con. 139: X Ap '57; 142: XXVII Dec '58; 144: inside back cover Jan '60.
——, secretaire. Con. 144: XL Sept '59.

Bonifacio (Mediterranean). Holiday 25: 19 Mar '59.

Bonington, Richard Parkes (work of). Con. ency. of ant., vol. 1, pl. 148, 168.
Con. 134: 203 (col.) Dec '54; 138: 55 (col.) Sept '56; 144: 127 Nov '59.

Bonnard, Pierre (work of). Con. 133 XXII Mar '54; 138: 190 (col.) Dec '56; 139: XV, XIX Ap '57; 140: 44 (col.) Sept '57, 91 (col.) Nov '57, 254 (col.) Jan '58; 141: X (col.) Je '58; 142: 1 (col.) Sept '58, 1 Nov '58; 143: XXXIV Ap '59, 146 May '59.
Praeg. pict. ency., p. 462 (col.).

Bonnell, John Sutherland. Cur. biog. p. 59 (1945).

Bonner, Herbert C. Cur. biog. p. 68 (1956).
Bonner, Mary Graham. Cur. biog. p. 60 (1950).
Bonner, Paul Hyde. Cur. biog. p. 52 (1955).
Bonnet, Henri. Cur. biog. p. 61 (1945).
Bonnet, Louis-Marie (work of). Con. 138: 48 Sept '56.
Bonnet, Austrian. Natl. geog. 115: 201 (col.) Feb '59.

bonnet, ceremonial (Angami, India). Natl. geog. 107: 262 Feb '55.
——, old. Natl. geog. 108: 521 (col.) Oct '55.
——, sun. See sunbonnet.

bonnet iron. Rawson: Ant. pict. bk., p. 12.

Bonneville Dam. Amer. heri. vol. 4 no. 4 p. 46 (summer '53).
Natl. geog. 102: 598 (col.) Nov '52.

Bonney, Therese. Cur. biog. p. 51 (1944).
Bonney, William H. II ("Billy the Kid"). Amer. heri. vol. 11 no. 5 p. 47 (Aug '60).
Brooks: Growth of a nation, p. 166.
Horan: Pict. hist. of wild west, p. 57, 67.
—— (reward poster). Horan: Pict. hist. of wild west, p. 62.

"Bonnie Prince Charlie." Holiday 18: 31 (col.) Dec '55.

Bonnier, Albert (wife & daughter). Holiday 24: 14 Dec '58.

Bonny, Anne (pirate). Amer. heri. vol. 8 no. 2 p. 14 (col.) (Feb '57).

Bonomi, Ivanoe. Cur. biog. p. 56 (1944).
Bonomi, Joseph (drawings by). Ceram: March of arch., p. 81.
Bonomi, Maria. Cur. biog. p. 47 (1960).
Bonsal, Philip Wilson. Cur. biog. p. 39 (1959).

Bonsal, Stephen. Cur. biog. p. 64 (1945).
Bontemps, Arna. Cur. biog. p. 60 (1946).
Jun. bk. of auth., p. 40.

bonzes. See monks, Siamese.

"Booby hut" sleigh. Amer. heri. vol. 7 no. 6 p. 94 (col.) (Oct '56).

book. Amer. heri. vol. 1 no. 2 p. 70 (winter '50); vol. 1 no. 4 p. 24 (summer '50); vol. 2 no. 4 p. 61 (summer '51).
Con. ency. of ant., vol. 3, pl. 77.
Con. 145: XXII Mar '60.
Holiday 10: 8 Dec '51; 11: 132 (col.) Mar '52, 134 Je '52; 12: 7 (col.) Nov '52, 25, 123 Dec '52; 18: 22 Nov '55; 19: 89 (col.) Jan '56; 21: 41 Ap '57, 151, 168 May '57, 45 Je '57; 22: 95 Sept '57; 25: 1 Mar '59; 26: 5 (col.) Nov '59; 27: 39 (col.) Je '60; 28: 153 Oct '60, 60, 124 (col.) Dec '60.
Natl. geog. 98: 795 (col.) Dec '50.
Travel 107: 55 Mar '57.
—— (860 B.C.). Natl. geog. 110: 459 (col.) Oct '56.
—— (girls reading). Natl. geog. 107: 458 (col.) Ap '55.
—— (man & woman). Holiday 12: 63 (col.) Nov '52.
—— (open). Amer. heri. vol. 8 no. 4 p. 57 (Je '57).
Con. ency. of ant., vol. 3 pl. 80.
Holiday 12: 104 Oct '52, 29 Nov '52.
Lehner: Pict. bk. of sym., p. 85.
Natl. geog. 113: 267 (col.) Feb '58.
——, chant. See chant book.
——, social register. Holiday 27: 93 May '60.

book. See also books.

book advertisement (1869). Amer. heri. vol. 11 no. 1 p. 66 (Dec '59).

book & candle (sym.). Lehner: Pict. bk. of sym., p. 58.

book & skull (sym). Lehner: Pict. bk. of sym., p. 10.

book cabinet. See bookcase.

book cover (18th cent.). Con. 133: 187 May '54.
—— (Hennepin). Amer. heri. vol. 8 no. 3 p. 80 (Ap '57).
—— (1022-1411). Praeg. pict. ency., p. 47-50 (col.).
——, Italian. Con. 144: 207 Dec '59.

book covers (dime novels). Amer. heri. vol. 7 no. 2 p. 50-5 (col.) (Feb '56).

book ends. Holiday 8: 15 Nov '50.

book illumination. Natl. geog. 113: 271 (col.) Feb '58.
Con. 140: 105-9 Nov '57.
Praeg. pict. ency., p. 48-9, 180 (col.).
—— (Ferrarese, 15th cent.). Con. 133: 18-24 Mar '54.
—— (medieval). Con. 134: 216-8 Dec '54.

book illumination. See also manuscript, illumination.

book illus. (children's). Amer. heri. vol. 8 no. 1 p. 26-37, 121-4 (part col.) (Dec '56).
—— (English, 1775-1850). Con. ency. of ant., vol. 3, pl. 73-80.
—— (15th cent.). Con. ency. of ant., vol. 1, pl. 113-8.
—— (Flemish). Con. 143: 54 Mar '59.

book illus. (French, 15th cent.). Con. 145: 189 May '60.

—— (Indian manuscript). Praeg. pict. ency., p. 533 (col.).

—— (Persian). Praeg. pict. ency., p. 521 (col.).

—— (13th cent.). Con. 145: 54-5 Mar '60.

book making (medieval). Int. gr. soc.: Arts . . . p. 63 (col.).

book market, sidewalk. Natl. geog. 98: 72 Jl '50.

"Book of Coming Forth by Day." See "Egyptian Book of the Dead."

"The Book of Hours" (illus.). Praeg. pict. ency., p. 49 (col.).

—— (open). Natl. geog. 113: 271 (col.) Feb '58.

—— (page from). Praeg. pict. ency., p. 218 (col.).

"Book of Hours of Virgin" (Flemish). Con. 143: 54 Mar '59.

Book of Kells (Ireland). Holiday 6: 35 (col.) Dec '49.

—— (illumi.). Praeg. pict. ency., p. 180 (col.).

book page ("Compleat Angler"). See "Compleat Angler."

book pages (1598). Amer. heri. vol. 11 no. 1 p. 47-8 (Dec '59).

—— (wild west). Amer. heri. vol. 11 no. 5 p. 32-3 (part col.) (Aug '60).

book title page (1670, hist. of Rome). Amer. heri. vol. 9 no. 5 p. 68 (Aug '58).

bookbinder (sym.). Lehner: Pict. bk. of sym., p. 90.

bookbinder shop. Con. 136: LXX Jan '56.

bookbinding, antique. Con. ency. of ant., vol. 3 pl. 153-6.

——, embroidered antique. Con. ency. of ant., vol. 1 pl. 119.

——, Gothic. Con. 142: 51 (col.) Sept '58.

——, Neapolitan. Con. 140: 280 Jan '58.

——, rare. Natl. geog. 100: 418 Sept '51.

bookcase. Holiday 21: 61 (col.) Feb '57; 22: 9 Oct '57; 25: 139 (col.) Je '59.
Natl. geog. 107: 312, 403 (col.) Mar '55.

——, Adam. Con. 136: LXI Nov '55; 138: XX-XXI Jan '57.

——, Adam breakfront. Con. 132: XXIX Sept '53; 135: XXIX May '55.

——, antique. Con. 133: XXX, XXXVIII Ap '54; 136: XLVI Nov '55; 140: 228 Jan '58.

——, antique breakfront. Con. 139: IV Ap '57; 142: VI Jan '59; 144: IV Sept '59.

——, bureau. See bureau bookcase.

——, Chinese Chippendale breakfront. Con. 140: 260 Jan '58.

——, Chippendale. Con. 132: XXXV Nov '53; 133: XXI May '54; 135: XXXV May '55; 136: IV, XLIII Sept '55; 137: LXVI Jan '56, XXVI Mar '56; 140: XXII Nov '57, XXXIV Jan '58.

——, Chippendale breakfront. Con. ency. of ant., vol. 1, pl. 43.
Con. 127: 43 Mar '51; 132: XLIV Nov '53; 134: XX Nov '54; 139: XLIV May '57; 140: XIV Dec '57; 141: XLV May '58, XIII Je '58; 143: XVI Mar '59, LI Je '59; 145: LXXXI May '60.

——, 18th cent. Con. 133: XIX May '54; 134: LIX Dec '54; 135: XXXVII Ap '55; 136: 56

Sept '55, XXVI, LXIII Nov '55; 138: LIV Jan '57; 143: LIII May '59; 144: XIV Sept '59.

——, 18th cent. breakfront. Con. ency. of ant., vol. 1, pl. 27.
Con. 134: XIX Sept '54; 135: LXIII Ap '55; 140: 55 Sept '57; 142: IV Nov '58.

——, English antique. Con. 126: 42, 45 Aug '50; 136: 243 Jan '56.

——, George I. Con. 135: XXVII Mar '55.

——, George II. Con. 132: XXXI Nov '53; 139: 125 Ap '57; 141: VI Je '58.

——, Hepplewhite. Con. 133: XXXVIII Mar '54; 135: V May '55; 136: XL Jan '56; 137: XVI Ap '56; 139: XXIV May '57; 145: LXXI Je '60.

——, Hepplewhite breakfront. Con. ency. of ant., vol. 1, pl. 42.
Con. 132: XLV Sept '53; 133: XI Je '54; 135: XX Mar '55, XXXIV Ap '55; 137: XXXVI Je '56; 138: IV Nov '56, LXXVII Jan '57; 139: XXXV Je '57; 141: XIV Mar '58; 142: LXIII Jan '59; 143: XIV, XXXVI May '59; 144: XXXIII Sept '59, LI Nov '59, LXV Jan '60; 145: XLI Mar '60.

——, Hepplewhite open. Con. 145: inside back cover Mar '60.

——, Queen Anne. Con. 136: X, XII Sept '55, LIII Dec '55; 138: XLIII Sept '56; 143: XXIX Ap '59.

——, Regency. Con. 135: XXXI Je '55 136: XXIV Jan '56; 138: XVIII Jan '57; 141: XLII Ap '58; 144: XLIV Jan '60.

——, Regency breakfront. Con. 143: XXI May '59.

——, Regency dwarf. Con. 144: XXXIV Sept '59.

——, secretaire. See secretaire bookcase.

——, Sheraton. Con. 136: XXVI Sept '55, LIX Nov '55; 137: XIX Ap '56; 138: XIX Nov '56; 139: XX Ap '57, XXV May '57; 143: VI Ap '59.

——, Sheraton breakfront. Con. 138: 60 Sept '56; 139: XXVI Ap '57; 140: XVI Dec '57; 142: XVI, LI Sept '58.

——, Sheraton double breakfront. Con. 144: LXIX Dec '59.

——, Sheraton revolving. Con. 142: VIII Dec '58.

——, Wm. & Mary. Con. 137: XIX Mar '56.

bookcase & bureau, Queen Anne. Con. 137: VI, XLVIII Ap '56.

bookcase & desk, blockfront. Con. 141: 65 Mar '58.

——, 18th cent. Con. 141: 128 Ap '58.

bookcases, wall. Natl. geog. 106: 668 (col.) Nov '54; 112: 330 (col.) Sept '57.

bookmobile (int., children). Natl. geog. 107: 200 (col.) Feb '55.

bookplate, Remington's. Amer. heri. vol. 6 no. 4 p. 109 (Je '55).

——, Rex Whistler. Con. 144: 87-90 Nov '59.

——, Washington's. Amer. heri. vol. 7 no. 2 p. 71 (Feb '57).

books. Holiday 19: 9 Feb '56, 104 Mar '56; 21: 9, 131, 143 Jan '57; 22: 9, 24 (col.) Oct '57, 57 Dec '57; 23: 8 Feb '58; 25: 55

(col.) Je '59; 26: 9 Jl '59, 9, 27 (col.) Oct '59; 27: 172 Jan '60, 176 Mar '60.
Int. gr. soc.: Arts . . . p. 133 (col.).
Natl. geog. 97: 310 (col.) Mar '50; 100: 591 (col.) Nov '51.
—— (on table). Con. 143: inside back cover Je '59.
—— (shelves). Natl. geog. 113: 270 (col.) Feb '58.
—— (stacked). Amer. heri. vol. 11 no. 6 p. 64 (Oct '60).
—— (standing). Holiday 28: 67 (col.) Jl '60.
books. See also book.
bookshelves. Holiday 22: 78 (col.) Dec '57; 28: 172 (col.) Dec '60.
——, English antique revolving. Con. 126: 45 Aug '50.
bookshop (int.). Natl. geog. 103: 514 Ap '53.
——, old (English). Natl. geog. 103: 837 Je '53.
bookstacks (in library). Natl. geog. 107: 213 (col.) Feb '55.
bookstall (Buenos Aires). Holiday 11: 74 (col.) Je '52.
——, Chinese. Natl. geog. 111: 344 (col.) Mar '57.
boom boat (logs). Natl. geog. 117: 471 (col.) Ap '60.
Boone, Daniel. Amer. heri. vol. 6 no. 6 p. 10-11 (part col.) (Oct '55).
—— (statue). Brooks: Growth of a nation, p. 72.
Boone, Vice-Adm, Joel T. Cur biog. p. 49 (1951).
Boone, Pat. Cur. biog. p. 40 (1959).
Boonesboro (Ky., early days). Brooks: Growth of a nation, p. 83.
boot. Holiday 5: 94, 128-9 Jan '49, 95 Feb '49; 6: 77 Sept '49; 11: 157 Je '52; 12: 174 Dec '52; 13: 155 May '53, 137 Je '53; 14: 9 Aug '53, 107 Sept '53; 15: 102 Je '54; 18: 100 Aug '55, 131 Oct '55, 169 Nov '55; 19: 170 May '56, 159 Je '56; 22: 174 Oct '57, 144 Nov '57; 23: 158 Feb '58.
——, Mexican. Natl. geog. 107: 231 (col.) Feb '55.
——, woman's. Holiday 24: 132 Nov '58; 25: 152 Jan '59; 28: 155 Nov '60, 163 Dec '60.
boot & spur. Amer. heri. vol. 11 no. 5 p. 32 (col.) (Aug '60).
Holiday 25: 36 Mar '59.
boot. See also boots.
boot cleaner. Amer. heri. vol. 6 no. 4 p. 47 (col.) (Je '55).
bootblack. Natl. geog. 100: 799 (col.) Dec '51.
—— (Mexico). Natl. geog. 107: 231 (col.) Feb '55.
Booth, Albie. Holiday 26: 65 Nov '59.
Booth, Arch N. Cur. biog. p. 65 (1961).
Booth, Evangeline. Cur. biog. p. 90 (1941).
Booth, John Wilkes. Amer. heri. vol. 3 no. 2 p. 67 (Winter '52).
Booth, Samuel (portrait by Highmore). Con. 138: 123 Nov '56.
Booth Shirley. Cur. biog. p. 96 (1942); p. 82 (1953).
Holiday 17: 90 (col.) Jan '55.
Boothe, Clare. Cur. biog. p. 98 (1942).
Bootjack. Rawson: Ant. pict. bk., p. 76.

boots. Holiday 5: 169 Ap '49; 6: 114 Aug '49; 8: 5 Nov '50; 10: 115 Nov '51; 12: 29 Sept '52; 19: 52-3 Mar '56; 20: 215 Dec '56; 22: 134 Sept '57; 24: 169, 228 Dec '58; 26: 247 Dec '59; 28: 86 Sept '60, 37 Oct '60, 187 Nov '60.
Lehner: Pict. bk. of sym., p. 64, 91.
——, woman's. Holiday 28: 119 Oct '60.
——, dude ranch. Natl. geog. 104: 352 (col.) Sept '53.
——, old. Rawson: Ant. pict. bk., p. 58.
——, snow. Holiday 6: 2 (col.) Dec '49.
boots. See also boot.
Bora Bora island. Holiday 28: 52-3 (col.) Oct '60.
Travel 102: 40 Nov '54.
borax (sym.). Lehner: Pict. bk. of sym., p. 72.
Borberg, William. Cur. biog. p. 60 (1952).
Borchardt, Ludwig (drawings of). Ceram: March of arch., p. 107.
Borden, Neil H. Cur. biog. p. 109 (1954).
Bordighera (Italy). Holiday 13: 56 (col.) Je '53.
Borge, Victor. Cur. biog. p. 62 (1946).
Borgese, Giuseppe Antonio. Cur. biog. p. 54 (1947).
Borghese, Cardinal Scipione (bust by Algardi). Con. 138: 204 Dec '56.
Borghese gallery (int.). Natl. geog. 111: 488-9 (col.) Ap '57.
Borglum, Gutzon (Lincoln head). Natl. geog. 101: 162 Feb '52.
—— (sculpture). Natl. geog. 102: 177 Aug '52.
—— (Black Hills sculpt.). See Mt. Rushmore memorial.
Borgnine, Ernest. Cur. biog. p. 70 (1956).
Boring, Edwin. Cur. biog. p. 43 (1962).
Boris III, King of Bulgaria. Cur. biog. p. 92 (1941).
Born, Max. Cur. biog. p. 53 (1955).
born (genealogy sym.). Lehner: Pict. bk. of sym., p. 12.
Borne, Mortimer. Cur. biog. p. 111 (1954).
Borneo. Natl. geog. 108: 384 (col.) Sept. '55; 109: 711-36 May '56.
—— (map). Natl. geog. 116: 777 Dec '59.
Borneo dancer. Natl. geog. 109: 718 May '56.
Borobudur (Java). Holiday 18: 107 (col.) Sept '55.
Borobudur temple. Natl. geog. 99: 30 (col.) Jan '51.
Borodin, Alexander Porfirevich (by Repin). Cooper: Con. ency. of music, p. 60.
Borromine, Il (work of). Con. 137: 48 Mar '56.
Borst, Lyle B. Cur. biog. p. 113 (1954).
Bortz, Edward Leroy. Cur. biog. p. 56 (1947).
Borzage, Frank. Cur. biog. p. 64 (1946).
Bosch, Hieronymus (work of). Praeg. pict. ency., p. 272 (col.).
Bosch, Juan. Cur. biog. (1963).
Bosch, Pepin. Holiday 27: 59 (col.) Feb '60.
Bosco-Gurin (Switzerland). Travel 110: inside cover Jl '58.
Bose, Subhas Chandra. Cur. biog. p. 59 (1944).
Bosin, F. Blackbear (work of). Natl. geog. 107: 354-5 (col.) Mar '55.
Bosone, Reva Beck. Cur. biog. p. 62 (1949).
Bosporus river. Natl. geog. 100: 156-7 (col.) Aug. '51; 115: 86-7 (col.) Jan '59.

Osward: Asia Minor, pl. 83, 93.
Bosschaert, Abraham (work of). Con. 144: XVII (col.) Sept '59.
Bosschaert, Ambrosius (work of). Con. 143: XLII (col.) Je '59; 145: X (col.) Je '60.
Bossi, Giovanni Domenico (work of). Con. 141: 19 Mar '58.
"Bossuet et le Grand Dauphin de France" (de Largilliere). Con. 133: 233 (col.) Je '54.
Boston (Mass.). Holiday 16: 14-5 Oct '54; 24: 92-101 Dec '58.
Jordan: Hammond's pict. atlas, p. 30-1 (col.). Natl. geog. 107: 773 (col.) Je '55.
—— **(historic places).** Travel 112: 53 Jl '59.
—— **(Old North Church).** Amer. heri. vol. 8 no. 1 p. 80 (Dec '56).
Holiday 11: 40 Je '52; 21: 117 (col.) Ap '57. Travel 106: 12 Dec '56.
—— **(Old North Church, int.).** Holiday 14: 43 (col.) Nov '53.
—— **(Old State House).** Holiday 11: 40 Je '52; 16: 106 (col.) Jl '54.
—— **(Paul Revere house).** Holiday 23: 52 Mar '58.
—— **(public garden).** Face of Amer., p. 70-1 (col.).
—— **(1721).** Amer. heri. vol. 8 no. 5 p. 40-1 (col.) (Aug '57).
—— **(Tremont St., 1840).** Con. 124: 69 Ap '52.
—— **(views by James Turner).** Con. 127: 113 May '51.
"Boston booby" sleigh. Amer. heri. vol. 7 no. 6 p. 94 (col.) (Oct '56).
Boston harbor (1768). Con. ency. of ant., vol. 3, pl. 89.
"Boston stump" tower (England). Natl. geog. 103: 809 (col.) Je '53.
Boston symphony hall. Cooper: Con. ency. of music, p. 451.
Bosustow, Stephen. Cur. biog. p. 54 (1958).
Boswell, James. Holiday 16: 6 Aug '54.
Boswell, N. K. Horan: Pict. hist. of the wild west, p. 209.
botany (sym). Lehner: Pict. bk. of sym., p. 11.
Botetourt, Lord (statue). See statue (Lord Botetourt).
Both, Jan (work of). Con. 145: XLIX May '60.
Bothe, Walther. Cur. biog. p. 56 (1955).
Bothwell, Jean. Cur. biog. p. 65 (1946).
Jun. bk. of auth., p. 41.
Botticelli, Sandro. Holiday 27: 197 (col.) Ap '60.
—— **(work of).** Con. ency. of ant., vol. 1, pl. 152.
Con. 129: 22 Ap '52; 136: 38 Sept '55; 139: 97-8 Ap '57; 145: 39 Mar '60.
Natl. geog. 110: 635 (col.) Nov '56.
Praeg. pict. ency., p. 256 (col.)
Botticini, Francesco (work of). Con. 137: XXVII Je '56.
bottle. Natl. geog. 110: 590 (col.) Nov '56.
—— **(pouring).** Holiday 21: 108 (col.) Jan '57, 114 (col.) Mar '57, 105 (col.) Je '57; 23: 130 (col.) Jan '58.
—— **(pouring cocktail).** Holiday 27: 47 (col.) May '60.
—— **(Yardley lotion).** Holiday 21: 139 Mar '57.

——, **Amer. antique glass.** Con. ency. of ant., vol. 3, p. 79.
——, **antique.** Con. ency. of ant., vol. 1, pl. 36, 47, p. 78.
Rawson: Ant. pict. bk., p. 84.
——, **antique engraved glass.** Con. 134: 99 Nov '54.
——, **antique whiskey flasks.** Amer. heri. vol. 11 no. 2 p. 90-3 (Feb '60).
——, **glass (on floating ice).** Holiday 28: 106 (col.) Jl '60.
——, **Irish antique glass.** Con. ency. of ant., vol. 3, pl. 45-6.
——, **Isnik.** Con. 145: 186 May '60.
——, **Meissen porcelain.** Con. 139: 230 Je '57; 145: 223 Je '60.
——, **milk.** See milk bottle.
——, **nail enamel.** See nail enamel bottle.
——, **onion.** Natl. geog. 117: 157 (col.) Feb '60.
——, **perfume.** Con. 133: XXXVI (col.) Je '54; 142: L Dec '58, LVI Jan '59; 144: LIV Nov '59, LXX Dec '59, LXIV Jan '60; 145: XXX May '60, XLVIII Je '60.
Holiday 10: 14, 119 Nov '51, 26, 39, 152 Dec '51; 11: 7 (col.) Feb '52, 125 Ap '52; 12: 3, 96 Oct '52, 11, 81 Nov '52, 39, 63, 71, 186 Dec '52; 13: 2 (col.), 143, 147 Mar '53, 65, 69, 81, 92, 136 Ap '53, 15, 20, 109, 140 May '53; 14: 30, 137 Jl '53, 16, 62 Aug '53, 137 (col.) Nov '53, 1, 5 (col.) Dec '53; 18: 123 (col.) Sept '55, 135 (col.) Nov '55, 8, 71 Dec '55; 19: 22 (col.), 66 (col.) Jan '56; 20: 26 Nov '56, 6, 10 (col.), 26, 32 (col.), 97 (col.), 117 (col.), 151 Dec '56; 21: 35, 64 (col.), 118 Ap '57, inside cover, 9 May '57, 183 Je '57; 22: 14 Oct '57, 25, 35 (col.) Nov '57, 1, 59, 143, 146, 201 (part col.) Dec '57; 23: 96 Jan '58, 164, 168 Ap '58, 1 Je '58; 24: 3, 28, 90 Oct '58, 15, 106 Nov '58, 1, 19, 121, 176, inside back cover (col.) Dec '58; 25: 146, 151 (col.) Jan '59, 30 Ap '59, 1, 11 May '59, 1 Je '59; 26: 41 Nov '59, 11, 25, 161 Dec '59; 27: 153 Jan '60, 51, 135, 198 Ap '60, 64 May '60, 22 Je '60; 28: 1, 26 Sept '60, 21, 118, 139 Oct '60, 53, 189 Nov '60, 1, 20 (col.), 36, 50 (col.), 64, 128, inside back cover (col.) Dec '60.
Natl. geog. 100: 163 (col.) Aug '51.
——, **salad dressing.** Holiday 25: 107 (col.) Je '59; 27: 117 (col.) Ap '60, 154 (col.) Je '60; 28: 7 (col.) Aug '60.
——, **Stiegel.** Rawson: Ant. pict. bk., p. 84.
——, **Syrian-Egyptian.** Int. gr. soc.: Arts . . . p. 177 (col.).
——, **Syrian glass (6th cent.)** Con. 133: 137 Ap '54.
——, **Venetian glass.** Holiday 22: 35 (col.) Nov '57.
bottle bag. Holiday 12: 175 Dec '52
bottle cartoon. Con. 133: XXXVIII May '54, XXXIV Je '54.
——, **wine.** Con. 133: LXII Ap '54.
bottle opener. Holiday 11: 30 Feb '52, 21 Mar '52; 12: 138 Nov '52, 176 Dec '52; 14: 162 Nov '53.
bottle stopper. See stopper.

"bottle tree." Natl. geog. 98: 52 (col.) Jl '50.
bottles. Holiday (practically all issues).
—— (sym.). Lehner: Pict. bk. of sym., p. 91.
——, medieval. Con. 139: 105-8 Ap '57.
——, pottery (Bedouin). Natl. geog. 108: 857 (col.) Dec '55.
Boucher, Anthony. Cur. biog., p. 46 (1962).
Boucher, Francoise (work of). Con. ency. of ant., vol. 1, pl. 160
Con. 133: 108-9 (col.) Ap '54, cover (col.), 192 May '54, 261 Je '54; 134: cover (col.) Sept '54, LI Dec '54; 135: cover (col.), 8, 41 Mar '55; 139: 121 Ap '57; 142: 109 Nov '58; 143: IX, 208 Je '59.
Praeg. pict. ency., p. 361 (col.).
Boudeau, Lou. Cur. biog., p. 101 (1942).
Boudin, Eugene (work of). Con. 138: X (col.) Nov '56, LI Jan '57; 140: 71 Sept '57; 142: XVII (col.) Dec '58; 143: XIII Ap '59; 145: XLIX Je '60.
Boughton House, Kettering (hall). Holiday 23: 87 (col.) Ap '58.
Bouguereau, William A. (work of). Con. 129: LXXV Je '52.
Boulanger, Nadia. Cur. biog. p. 48 (1962).
boulders. Natl. geog. 111: 689 (col.) May '57.
——, balanced. Natl. geog. 111: 670-1 May '57.
Boult, Sir Adrian. Cur. biog. p. 67 (1946).
the "Bounty mutiny." Natl. geog. 112: 730-1 Dec '57.
the "Bounty ship." Natl. geog. 112: 758-9 Dec '57.
"Bounty ship" model (children). Natl. geog. 118: 560 (col.) Oct '60.
Bouquet, Henry. Amer. heri. vol. 4 no. 3 p. 40 (col.) (spring '53).
Bouquet, Col. Henry. Amer. heri. vol. 8 no. 4 p. 62 (col.) (Je '57).
bouqet, bride's. Lehner: Pict. bk. of sym., p. 56.
Bouquet's battle route, Col. Henry (1763). Amer. heri. vol. 8 no. 4 p. 61 (Je '57).
Bourdon, Sebastian (work of). Con. 142: XLIX Dec '58.
Bourges cathedral (int., France). Int. gr. soc.: Arts . . . p. 49 (col.).
Bourges-Maunoury, Maurice. Cur. biog. p. 62 (1957).
Bourguiba, Habib Ben Ali. Cur. biog. p. 57 (1955).
Boutell, Clarence B. Cur. biog. p. 69 (1946).
Boutelle, Richard S. Cur. biog. p. 51 (1951).
Bouts, Dirk. Praeg. pict. ency., p. 264 (col.).
Boutwell, G. S. Amer. heri. vol. 11 no. 1 p. 61 (Dec '59).
Bovary, Emma. Con. 139: 25 Mar '57.
Bovary birthplace, Emma. Holiday 19: 53 Jan '56.
Bovet, Daniele. Cur. biog. p. 55 (1958).
bow, ribbon. Holiday 11: 65 (col.) Jan '52; 28: 50 (col.) Dec '60.
bow & arrow. Natl. geog. 107: 333 (col.) Mar '55, 595 May '57.
—— (hunter). Holiday 12: 53 (col.) Oct '52.
—— (Indian holding). Amer. heri. vol. 7 no. 6 p. 10 (col.) (Oct '56).
—— (Lama). Natl. geog. 99: 611 (col.) May '51.

—— (Philistine warriors). Natl. geog. 112: 846 (col.) Dec '57.
bow & quiver (sym.). Lehner: Pict. bk. of sym., p. 65.
Bow dish. Con. 132: 167 Jan '54.
bow drill. See drill, bow.
Bow figurine. Con. 129: LXV, 123, 130 Je '52; 132: XII, XXII Sept '53; 133: inside cover Ap '54, XIV May '54; 138: XXVIII Sept '56; 141: VI Mar '58, XXXIII Ap '58, 272 Je '58; 145: 69 Ap '60, XXIV Je '60.
Bow mug. Con. 132: 166 Jan '54.
Bow plate. Con. 133: 112 Ap '54.
Bowater, Sir Eric. Cur. biog. p. 72 (1956).
Bowditch, Mary (Mrs. Nathaniel Bowditch). Amer. heri. vol. 11 no. 5, p. 60 (Aug '60).
Bowditch, Nathaniel. Amer. heri. vol. 11 no. 5 p. 61 (col.) Aug '60.
Natl. geog. 97: 290 (col.) Mar '50.
—— (Osgood). Amer. heri. vol. 6 no. 2 p. 19 (col.) (winter '55).
Bowditch, Richard L. Cur. biog. p. 85 (1953).
Bowditch home, Nathaniel (Boston). Amer. heri. vol. 11 no. 5 p. 89 (Aug '60).
Bowditch monument, Nathaniel. Amer. heri. vol. 11 no. 5 p. 56 (Aug '60).
Bowen, Catherine Drinker. Cur. biog. p. 61 (1944).
Bowen, Ira Sprague. Cur. biog. p. 53 (1951).
Natl. geog. 108: 185 Aug '55.
Bowers, Claude G. Cur. biog. p. 95 (1941).
Bowers, Faubion. Cur. biog. p. 42 (1959).
Bowers, Mrs. Faubion. See Rama Rau, Santha.
Bowes, Edward. Cur. biog. p. 96 (1941).
Bowie, Jim. Holiday 23: 54 Feb '58.
bowie knife. See knife, bowie or hunting.
bowl. Holiday 12: 10 (col.) Oct '52, 173 Dec '52.
—— (custard). Holiday 24: 95 (col.) Oct '58.
—— (flowers). Con. ency. of ant., vol. 1, pl. 33.
Con. 140: XVII (col.) Sept '57, 110 Nov '57.
Holiday 18: 133 (col.) Nov '55; 19: 143 (col.) Mar '56, 13 (col.) Je '56; 22: 150 (col.) Dec '57; 23: 50 (col.) Ap '58; 24: 201 (col.) Dec '58.
—— (flowers) (Latour). Con. 142: XXIII (col.) Nov '58.
—— (fruit). Holiday 20: 89 (col.) Sept '56.
—— (olives). Holiday 12: 123 Nov '52.
—— (salad). Holiday 27: 31 (col.) Mar '60, 117 (col.) Ap '60; 28: 7 (col.) Aug '60.
—— (vegetables). Holiday 18: 41 (col.) Aug '55.
——, antique. Con. 134: XL Nov '54; 136: 44 Sept '55.
——, antique (on pedestal). Con. 140: inside cover (col.) Nov '57.
——, antique glass (on pedestal). Con. 140: XIV Nov '57.
——, antique gold. Con. 138: III Dec '56.
——, antique porcelain. Con. 141: 247 Je '58.
——, antique silver. Con. 138: 276 Jan '57.
——, antique silver (covered). Con. 139: 241 Je '57.
——, antique silver gilt. Con. 136: LXIX Jan '56.
——, antique stoneware. Con. 129: 49 Ap '52.

bowl, avanturine quaich. Con. 138: 126 Nov '56.

——, Bowcock. Con. 144: 28 (col.) Sept '59.

——, Canton. Con. 142: 56 Sept '58.

——, cedar. Natl. geog. 105: 235 (col.) Feb '54.

——, Chantilly. Con. 142: XXIII Dec '58.

——, Chinese. Con. ency. of ant., vol. 1, pl. 66, 70.

——, Chinese (antique). Con. 133: 138 Ap '54; 134: 39 Sept '54.

——, Chinese (Han). Con. 144: X Jan '60.

——, Chinese jade. Con. 133: 263 Je '54.

——, Chinese porcelain. Con. 129: LXVI Ap '52; 133: V May '54; 140: XXXVI Dec '57; 141: III Mar '58.

——, Chinese (antique). Con. 134: VI Nov '54.

——, Chinese (Ch'ien Lung, 18th cent.). Con. 142: LXVI Dec '58.

——, (Chih). Con. 145: XIV Ap '60.

——, Chinese silver. Con. 139: 275 Je '57.

——, Chinese stoneware (antique). Con. 142: X Dec '58.

——, Chinese temple. Natl. geog. 97: 216 Feb '50.

——, christening. See christening bowl.

——, craft. Con. 144: 31 Sept '59.

——, cut glass. Daniel: Cut & engraved glass.

——, Delft ship. Con. 145: XXVI Mar '60.

——, earthenware. Travel 110: 16 Nov '58.

——, Fiji island drinking. Holiday 28: 57 (col.) Oct '60.

——, finger. See finger bowl.

——, French (16th cent. silver). Con. 138: 271 Jan '57.

——, George I silver. Con. 138: XXVII Nov '56.

——, George III fruit (silver). Con. 144: XXIV Sept '59.

——, George III (silver gilt). Con. 143: XXII Je '59.

——, gilded silver (17th cent.). Int. gr. soc.: Arts . . . p. 95 (col.).

——, Hellenistic cut glass. Con. 145: 288 Je '60.

——, Henry VII (Mazer). Con. 129: III Je '52.

——, Hispano-moresque armorial. Con. 143: III Mar '59.

——, imperial emerald & jade. Con. 140: 258 Jan '58.

——, imperial Ju Yao narcissus. Con. 143: 122 Ap '59.

——, Indian. Natl. geog. 97: 239 (col.) Feb '50.

——, Irish antique silver. Con. 137: LXI May '56.

——, Irish fruit. Con. 139: XX May '57.

——, Irish glass. Con. ency. of ant., vol. 3, pl. 51.

——, Irish glass antique. Con. 139: XXXVI Ap '57.

——, Irish glass (18th cent.). Con. 142: XXII Sept '58.

——, Irish Monteith. Con. 132: XXIII Nov '53; 134: XXXV Dec '54.

——, Irish provincial silver. Con. 145: LVIII Je '60.

——, Islamic pottery. Con. 141: 190 May '58.

——, jade. See jade bowl.

——, James I fruit wood. Con. 139: 194 May '57.

——, James II. Con. 138: 128 Nov '56.

——, Kakiemon (Louis XVI). Con. 140: 58 Sept '57.

——, Lamerie silver. Con. 129: LXVI Ap '52.

——, Liverpool porcelain. Con. 139: XIV Ap '57.

——, Marquesan rosewood. Natl. geog. 97: 74 Jan '50.

——, Mazer. See Mazer bowl.

——, Meissen. See Meissen bowl.

——, Ming. Con. 137: 55 Mar '56.

——, Ming (Ch'eng Hua). Con. 144: 126 Nov '59.

——, Monteith. Con. 140: LIII Sept '57, V Nov '57, 181 Dec '57.

——, Monteith (17th cent.). Con. 132: 86 Nov '53.

——, Monteith silver. Con. ency. of ant., vol. 1, pl. 84.
Con. 145: V Ap '60.

——, Niobid. See Niobid bowl.

——, Peruvian pottery. Praeg. pict. ency., p. 553 (col.).

——, pewter (18th cent.). Con. 133: LXIV Je 54.

——, punch. See punch bowl.

——, Rostrand faience (18th cent.). Con. 144: 102 Nov '59.

——, salad. Holiday 26: 7 (col.) Aug '59, 144 (col.) Oct '59; 27: 154 (col.) Je '60.

——, salad (glass). Holiday 25: 107 (col.) Je '59; 27: 94 (col.) Jan '60.

——, Scandinavian (silver). Con. 137: 177 May '56.

——, Sevres. Con. 132: inside cover (col.) Sept '53.

——, Sheffield silver. Con. 141: XXIV Mar '58.

——, silver. Holiday 14: 117 Oct '53, 14 Dec '53.

——, silver (covered). Con. 134: 131 Nov '54.

——, Swedish (18th cent.). Con. 143: 239 Je '59.

——, Swedish (18th cent. silver). Con. 141: XXI Mar '58.

——, wassail. Con. 132: LXVI Jan '54.

——, white jade. Con. 132: XLVI Nov '53; 142: LXII Nov '58.

——, Worcester. Con. 132: 169 Jan '54; 133: 264 Je '54.

Bowl & cover, Irish hexagonal silver. Con. 145: LVIII Je '60.

—— (silver). Con. 144: 36 Sept '59.

bowler hat. Holiday 18: 105 Oct '55.

Bowles, Chester. Cur. biog. p. 63 (1943); p. 64 (1957).

bowling, lawn. Holiday 12: 101 Sept '52; 25: 90 (col.) Ap '59.
Natl. geog. 99: 304 (col.) Mar '51.

—— (New Guinea). Holiday 28: 104 (col.) Nov '60.

bowling alley. Holiday 28: 213 (col.) Dec '60. Travel 106: 50 Sept '56.

bowls (ancient pottery). Int. gr. soc.: Arts . . . p. 19 (col.).

—— (stacked on women's heads). Natl. geog. 114: 459 (col.) Oct '58.

Bowman, Isaiah. Cur. biog. p. 66 (1945).
Bowman, James Cloyd. Jun. bk. of auth., p. 43.
bow-pin, yoke. Rawson: Ant. pict. bk., p. 66.
Bowron, Fletcher. Cur. biog. p. 61 (1950).
bows (viola, violin, cello). Cooper: Con. ency. of music, p. 352-3.
Bowyer vase. See vase, Bowyer.
box. Travel 101: 5 Jan '54.
—— (kitten). Holiday 10: 107 Jl '51, 11 Sept '51, 148 Nov '51, 136 Dec '51; 11: 65 Jan '52.
—— (tied up). Travel 101: 5 Feb '54.
—— (wrapped). Holiday 14: 25 (col.), 27 Nov '53.
——, Battersea enamel. See enamel box, Battersea.
——, Chinese ivory. Con. 143: X Ap '59.
——, Chinese porcelain. Con. 144: XVI Nov '59.
——, enameled (18th cent.). Con. 143: XLVII Ap '59.
——, gift. Holiday 14: 10 (col.), 27 (col.) Dec '53; 23: 17 (col.) Jan '58.
——, golf ball. Holiday 26: 245 Dec '59.
——, Hispano. Arabic ivory. Con. 141: LXIV May '58.
——, lace. See lace box.
——, Louis XV gold jewel. Con. 140: XXXI Jan '58.
——, Mennecy (in form of a boar). Con. 143: 140 May '59.
——, Penn. clothes. See Penn. clothes box.
——, spice (17th cent.). Holiday 28: 19 Aug '60.
——, Swedish enamel. Con. 143: 121 Ap '59.
——, Vienese porcelain. Con. 143: LX May '59.
——, wood utility. Amer. heri. vol. 2 no. 2 p. 35 (col.) (winter '51).
box. See also boxes; casket.
box kite, powered. Natl. geog. 104: 751 Dec '53.
box sled, dog. Holiday 21: 114 Jan '57.
boxcar, flying. See flying boxcar.
boxers (Nigeria). Natl. geog. 116: 235 (col.) Aug '59.
boxes (in bag pulley). Holiday 23: 20 (col.) May '58.
——, Christmas (stacked). Holiday 28: 66 (col.) Dec '60.
——, Indian quill. Natl. geog. 98: 259 (col.) Aug '50.
boxing. Amer. heri. vol. 10 no. 5 p. 92-3, 95 (Aug '59).
Travel 107: 4 Jan '57.
—— (cartoon). Holiday 23: 113 Feb '58.
—— (early sport). Amer. heri. vol. 1 no. 4 p. 14 (summer '50).
——, West Point cadets. Natl. geog. 101: 611 May '52.
boxing match. Amer. heri. vol. 10 no. 5 p. 56 (col.) (Aug '59).
Con. 129: IV Ap '52.
Holiday 18: 50 Oct '55.
boxing ring. Holiday 10: 54 Oct '51.
boy. Amer. heri. vol. 6 no. 5 p. 55 (Aug '55).
Con. 145: 207 May '60.
Face of Amer., p. 27 (col.).

Holiday 14: 26 Oct '53; 23: 69 Jan '58.
Travel 104: 48 Sept '55.
—— (armload of pigs). Natl. geog. 101: 70 Jan '52.
—— (asleep in field). Holiday 27: 207 May '60.
—— (asleep with dog). Natl. geog. 105: 97 (col.) Jan '54.
—— (at party, comic). Holiday 21: 107 May '57.
—— (back view). Holiday 21: 168 Ap '57; 26: 23 (col.) Oct '59.
Natl. geog. 103: 740 (col.) Je '53.
—— (barefoot). Natl. geog. 97: 66 (col.) Jan '50.
—— (barefoot, cabin). Holiday 10: 93 Aug '51.
—— (baseball player). See baseball player (boy).
—— (baseball suit). Holiday 26: 107 (col.) Nov '59.
—— (basket on back). Natl. geog. 97: 246 Feb '50.
—— (bathing in pool). Natl. geog. 107: 607 (col.) May '55.
—— (bathing in waterfall). Natl. geog. 107: 605 (col.) May '55.
—— (beating drum). Disney: People & places, p. 47 (col.).
Holiday 28: 4 Sept '60.
—— (beside pagan god). Natl. geog. 97: 99 Jan '50.
—— (bicycle). Holiday 11: 154 May '52.
Natl. geog. 115: 786 (col.) Je '59.
—— (bicycle, dog). Natl. geog. 108: 664 (col.) Nov '55.
—— (binoculars). Holiday 18: 79 (col.) Oct '55.
—— (boat, comic). Holiday 26: 98 Jl '59.
—— (boxing). Amer. heri. vol. 7 no. 1 p. 40 (col.) (Sept '55).
—— (camp cooking). Holiday 23: 108 Je '58.
—— (cannon ball in wall). Natl. geog. 109: 447 (col.) Ap '56.
—— (cartoon). Holiday 28: 129 Jl '60.
—— (chapel). Natl. geog. 117: 232 (col.) Feb '60.
—— (cheering). Holiday 14: 129 Dec '53.
—— (chickens). Holiday 5: 81 (col.) Ap '49.
—— (Chinese book stall). Natl. geog. 111: 344 (col.) Mar '57.
—— (Christmas tree). Amer. heri. vol. 9 no. 1 p. 21 (col.) (Dec '57).
—— (climbing fence). Holiday 8: 23 Oct '50.
—— (climbing to house top). Natl. geog. 101: 142 Feb '52.
—— (cockatoo). Natl. geog. 111: 504 Ap '57.
—— (comic). Holiday 19: 143 May '56, 143 (col.) Je '56; 20: 86 Sept '56, 136 Dec '56; 26: 207 Nov '59; 27: 189 May '60, 161, 164 Je '60.
—— (cowboy suit). Natl. geog. 97: 699 Je '50; 101: 487 (col.) Ap '52.
—— (crippled by war). Holiday 18: 55 Aug '55.
—— (cripples, beggar). Holiday 18: 138 Dec '55.
—— (crutches). Travel 101: 8 Jan '54; 104: 47 Aug '55.
—— (digging). Con. 126: cover, opp. p. 83 (col.) Oct '50.

boy (diving). Holiday 12: 137 (col.) Jl '52, 22 Aug '52; 14: 115 Jl '53.
Natl. geog. 106: 813 Dec '54; 114: 63 (col.) Jl '58.
—— (dog). Holiday 14: 117 Dec '53; 16: 86 Aug '54; 27: 113 (col.) May '60.
—— (dog & basket). Amer. heri. vol. 6 no. 1 p. 25 (fall '54).
—— (dog, comic, artist). Holiday 23: 95 Feb '58.
—— (dog lying down). Amer. heri. vol. 9 no. 3 back cover (col.) (Ap '58).
—— (dog, sheep). Natl. geog. 110: 44 (col.) Jl '56.
—— (dog, sled, silhouette). Travel 112: 56 Dec '59.
—— (dog, wagon). Natl. geog. 98: 325 Sept '50.
—— (donkey). Holiday 26: 152 Oct '59.
Natl. geog. 104: 719 Nov '53.
—— (drawing on blackboard). Natl. geog. 116: 64 (col.) Jl '59.
—— (drawing on board). Holiday 12: 18 Oct '52.
—— (drinking coke). Holiday 25: 148 (col.) May '59.
—— (eating sea urchin). Natl. geog. 117: 214 (col.) Feb '60.
—— (eating sugar cane). Natl. geog. 99: 447 (col.) Ap '51.
—— (fish). Holiday 21: 10 (col.) Je '57.
Natl. geog. 117: 478 (col.) Ap '60.
Travel 109: 31 Jan '58; 111: 32 Mar '59, 34 May '59; 113: 28 Je '60.
—— (fishing). Holiday 8: cover (col.) Aug '50.
Natl. geog. 107: 487 Ap '55; 109: 624 (col.) May '56; 110: 468 (col.) Oct '56; 114: 56 (col.) Jl '58.
—— (fishing, comic). Holiday 19: 133 (col.) May '56.
—— (fishing, dog). Natl. geog. 112: 522 (col.) Oct '57.
—— (fishing, raft). Natl. geog. 116: 155 (col.) Aug '59.
—— (flower vendor). Holiday 27: 71 Ap '60.
—— (gathers flamingo eggs). Natl. geog. 99: 638 May '51.
—— (guitar). Natl. geog. 99: 425 Ap '51.
—— (head). Con. 142: 273 Jan '59, 137 Dec '58; 143: 105 Ap '59; 144: LX Nov '59.
Holiday 14: 20 Jl '53, 155 Nov '53; 24: 224 Dec '58; 26: 134 Sept '59, 188 Oct '59, 247 Dec '59; 27: 176 Feb '60, 204 Mar '60; 28: 60 (col.) Nov '60.
Travel 102: inside back cover Dec '54; 114: 14 Sept '60, 51 Nov '60.
—— (head, back view). Holiday 14: 38 Dec '53.
—— (head, ball on string). Natl. geog. 109: 503 Ap '56.
—— (head, cap). Holiday 12: 127 Nov '52.
—— (head, comic). Holiday 10: 33 Nov '51; 25: 206 Ap '59, 37 May '59.
—— (head, dog). Holiday 21: 19 Feb '57.
—— (head, laughing). Holiday 10: 6 Dec '51; 25: 149 Feb '59; 27: 50 (col.) May '60.
Natl. geog. 114: 870 Dec '58.
—— (head, marble). Con. 140: 58 Sept '57.

—— (head, silhouette). Natl. geog. 113: 124 Jan '58.
—— (head, Portuguese). Natl. geog. 118: 625 (col.) Nov '60.
—— (herd of cattle). Natl. geog. 114: 635 (col.) Nov '58.
—— (herons). Natl. geog. 115: 690 (col.) May '59.
—— (holding girl). Holiday 13: 78 May '53.
—— (holly & wishbone). Con. 144: LXIV Jan '60.
—— (horse). Holiday 10: 17 (col.) Jl '51.
—— (horse & colt). Holiday 10: 111 Dec '51.
—— (ice cream). Holiday 22: 128 Jl '57.
—— (in bed). Holiday 19: 93 Jan '56.
—— (in swing). Amer. heri. vol. 8 no. 5 p. 47 (Aug '57).
—— (kangaroo). Natl. geog. 108: 498 Oct '55.
—— (kisses woman's hand). Holiday 28: 53 Sept '60.
—— (lying on grass). Amer. heri. vol. 8 no. 5 p. 46 (col.) (Aug '57).
—— (medieval). Int. gr. soc.: Arts . . . p. 71 (col.).
—— (mosaic head). Osward: Asia Minor, p. 54.
—— (mowing lawn). Holiday 27: 111 (col.) Je '60.
Natl. geog. 116: 47 (col.) Jl '59.
—— (nailing flag to staff). Amer. heri. vol. 7 no. 2 back cover (col.) (Feb '56).
—— (on buffalo head). Natl. geog. 102: 315 Sept '52.
—— (on lawn mower). Holiday 25: 140 Ap '59.
—— (on windowsill). Natl. geog. 101: 543 Ap '52.
—— (picking fruit). Holiday 26: 243 (col.) Dec '59.
—— (pirate suit). Holiday 22: 157 Dec '57.
—— (plowing buffalo). Natl. geog. 102: 320 (col.) Sept '52.
—— (porcupine). Natl. geog. 98: 248 Aug '50.
—— (prize steer). Natl. geog. 100: 298 (col.) Sept '51.
—— (raking hay). Amer. heri. vol. 7 no. 3 p. 44 (Ap '56).
—— (red head). Natl. geog. 108: 299 (col.) Sept '55.
—— (rocking chair). Natl. geog. 97: 584 (col.) May '50.
—— (rolling hoop). Amer. heri. vol. 6 no. 4 p. 29 (col.) (Je '55).
Natl. geog. 101: 778 (col.) Je '52.
—— (rowing boat). Amer. heri. vol. 11 no. 5 p. 22 (col.) (Aug '60).
—— (running). Natl. geog. 105: 541 Ap '54.
—— (sailboat). Natl. geog. 113: 801 (col.) Je '58.
—— (Santa Claus). Holiday 12: 26 (col.) Dec '52.
—— (seal). Natl. geog. 101: 499 (col.) Ap '52.
—— (seated). Con. 140: 111 Nov '57; 143: 145 May '59.
Holiday 23: 111 May '58.
Travel 107: 47 Jan '57.
—— (seated, daguerreotype). Amer. heri. vol. 8 no. 1 p. 58 (Dec '56).

—— (seated, hillside). Natl. geog. 112: 448 (col.) Oct '57.

—— (seated, laughing). Natl. geog. 111: 618 (col.) May '57.

—— (selling lilies). Natl. geog. 99: 457 (col.) Ap '51.

—— (selling papers). Travel 109: back cover Feb '58.

—— (serving coffee, comic). Holiday 23: 137 Mar '58.

—— (17th cent.). Con. 145: XXXVIII (col.) May '60.

—— (shoe shiner). Holiday 5: 65, 130 Jan '49.

—— (shooting arrow). Holiday 25: 163 May '59.

—— (ski lift). Holiday 14: 26 (col.) Nov '53.

—— (skiing). Holiday 5: 20-1, 30 Jan '49, 7 Ap '49.

—— (sled). Holiday 20: 44 (col.) Dec '56.

—— (spotted moray). Natl. geog. 116: 802 (col.) Dec '59.

—— (standing on head). Durant: Pict. hist. of Amer. circus, p. 146.

—— (sticks finger in dike). See statue ("boy sticks finger in dike").

—— (stilts). Holiday 10: 130 Oct '51.

—— (stretching, happy). Holiday 19: 140 Feb '56.

—— (swimming). Holiday 12: 137 (col.) Jl '52.

—— (tennis). Holiday 13: 72 Je '53.

—— (tipping hat). Holiday 26: 8 Dec '59.

—— (toy boats, Arabia). Natl. geog. 110: 83 (col.) Jl '56.

—— (toys). Natl. geog. 112: 463 (col.) Oct '57.

—— (tractor, dog). Natl. geog. 105: 323 (col.) Mar '54.

—— (traveling). Holiday 20: 144 (col.) Dec '56.

—— (traveling, Colonial). Amer. heri. vol. 6 no. 4 p. 27 (Je '55).

—— (tropical birds). Travel 114: 52 Sept '60.

—— (violin). Natl. geog. 116: 279 Aug '59.

—— (volcanic lava). Natl. geog. 118: 506, 508 (col.) Oct '60.

—— (war cripple, beggar). Holiday 18: 138 Dec '55.

—— (water buffalo). Natl. geog. 111: 360 (col.) Mar '57.

—— (watering calf). Natl. geog. 107: 176 (col.) Feb '55.

—— (wheel chair). Natl. geog. 117: 335 Mar '60.

—— (writing, dog). Holiday 6: 92 Sept '49.

boy, African (donkey). Natl. geog. 118: 358 (col.) Sept '60.

——, African (jug on head). Holiday 25: 74 Ap '59.

——, African (lunch pan on head). Natl. geog. 108: 778 Dec '55.

——, Arabian. See Arabian boy.

——, Bengal. Natl. geog. 107: 415 (col.) Mar '55.

——, Borneo (learning to write). Natl. geog. 109: 721 May '56.

——, Cretan. Natl. geog. 104: 705 (col.) Nov '53.

——, Dutch. Holiday 25: 198 Je '59; 26: 189 Oct '59.

——, Dutch (dog). Con. 140: 118 (col.) Nov '57, XLVIII Dec '57; 142: 122 Nov '58.

——, Eskimo. Natl. geog. 109: 772 (col.) Je '56.

——, farm (playing violin). Amer. heri. vol. 7 no. 3 p. 46 (col.) (Ap '56).

——, India. Natl. geog. 109: 577 Ap '56.

——, India (headhunter). Natl. geog. 107: 249 (col.) Feb '55.

——, Indian. See Indian boy.

——, Lapland (reindeer). Holiday 18: 106 (col.) Dec '55.

——, Mexico. Holiday 23: 28 Je '58; 24: 109 Aug '58, 114 Oct '58, 136 Nov '58, 117 Dec '58.

——, Negro (backview). Holiday 25: 92 (col.) Ap '59.

——, Russia (rabbit). Natl. geog. 116: 383 (col.) Sept '59.

——, Siam (asleep). Disney: People & places, p. 167 (col.).

——, straw. Holiday 13: 100 May '53.

——, Victorian (trycicle). Amer. heri. vol. 8 no. 2 back cover (col.) (Feb '57).

boy & child (laughing). Holiday 10: 85 (col.) Sept '51, 68 Nov '51.

boy (child on shoulder). Natl. geog. 104: 426 Sept '53.

boy & dog (snow). Amer. heri. vol. 7 no. 1 p. 19 (Dec '55).

boy & girl. Holiday 13: 59 May '53, 51, 102, 106 (col.) Je '53; 14: 114 Jl '53; 18: 89 (col.) Jl '55; 19: 19 Mar '56; 23: 26, 122 Feb '58, 34, 159 (col.) Ap '58, 100 Je '58. Jordan: Hammond's pict. atlas, p. 139 (col.). Travel 101: 13 Mar '54; 103: 44 Mar '55; 104: 41 Sept '55.

—— (artists at beach). Natl. geog. 97: 69 (col.) Jan '50.

—— (at beach table). Holiday 14: 74 (col.) Sept '53.

—— (at football game). Holiday 26: 146 (col.) Dec '59.

—— (at game). Holiday 28: 137 (col.) Oct '60.

—— (at gate). Holiday 27: 125 (col.) Feb '60.

—— (at table). Holiday 13: 117, 122, inside back cover (col.) Ap '53, 75, 161 May '53, 74 (col.) Je '53; 14: 58 Nov '53; 23: 103 (col.) Mar '58.

—— (auto). Holiday 13: 12 (col.) Je '53; 22: 128 (col.) Dec '57; 23: 43 (col.) Je '58; 24: 25 Nov '58; 27: 52 (col.) Ap '60.

—— (auto, comic). Holiday 24: 99 Oct '58, 136 Dec '58.

—— (auto, lunch). Holiday 26: back cover (col.) Sept '59.

—— (back view). Amer. heri. vol. 3 no. 1 back cover (fall '51). Natl. geog. 102: 354 (col.) Sept '52.

—— (back view, beach). Natl. geog. 113: 352 (col.) Mar '58.

—— (back view, lake). Holiday 19: 141 (col.) Feb '56.

—— (back view, mt.). Natl. geog. 97: 718 (col.) Je '50.

—— (ball). Holiday 18: 7 (col.) Jl '55.

—— (bathing suits). Holiday 14: 8 Aug '53, 2 (col.), 85 Nov '53; 19: 4, 60 (col.) May '56;

23: 177 (col.) Je '58; 24: 85 (col.) Jl '58; 26: 99 (col.) Aug '59.

—— (bathing, beach). Holiday 10: 111 Jl '51, 75 Aug '51, 86 (col.) Dec '51; 11: 123 (col.) Ap '52; 11: 87, 127 (col.) May '52, 13 (col.) Je '52; 26; 10 (col.) Nov '59; 27: 243 May '60; 28: 163 Nov '60.
Travel 114: 64 Jl '60.

—— (bathing suits, running). Holiday 11: 66 Mar '52, 169 May '52, 74 (col.) Je '52; 23: 120 Je '58.

—— (bathing, ship deck). Holiday 20: 106 (col.) Nov '56.

—— (beach). Holiday 13: 20 (col.), 172 May '53, 49, 87, 143, 148 (col.) Je '53; 14: 82 (col.) Sept '53; 19: 25 (col.) Je '56; 20: 158 (col.) Nov '56, 120, 187 (col.) Dec '56; 21: 10 (col.) Feb '57.
Travel 106: cover Sept '56; 109: 60 Feb '58, 16, 50 Je '58.

—— (beach, silhouette). Holiday 12: 40 Dec '52.

—— (bears in park). Natl. geog. 98: 17 (col.) Jl '50.

—— (bicycles). Holiday 5: 77 Ap '49; 6: 96 Oct '49; 8: 31 Sept '50, 119 Dec '50; 10: 33, 60, 87 Jl '51, 9 Aug '51, 149 (col.) Oct '51, 57 (col.), 158 Dec '51; 11: 86 Ap '52, 67, 153 Je '52; 12: 25 Aug '52; 13: 95 Ap '53; 14: 129 Jl '53, 109 Aug '53, 55, 108 Sept '53, 176 Dec '53; 17: 4 Jan '55; 18: 7 (col.) Jl '55; 22: 117 (col.) Oct '57; 23: 138 (col.) Ap '58; 27: 98 Mar '60; 28: 104 Sept '60.
Natl. geog. 100: 15 (col.) Jl '51; 105: 207 (col.) Feb '54; 110: 8 (col.) Jl '56; 117: 744 (col.) Je '60.
Travel 111: cover (col.) Feb '59; 112: 15 Aug '59; 113: 45 Je '60.

—— (bicycles, books). Holiday 11: 127 Ap '52.

—— (bicycles, dog). Natl. geog. 99: 578 (col.) May '51.

—— (bicycles, travelers). Travel 113: 32, 34 Mar '60.

—— (boat). Holiday 11: 5 (col.) Je '52; 13: 18, 28 (col.) May '53, 74, 141 (col.) Je '53; 27: 38 (col.) Feb '60.

—— (boat, bathing suits). Holiday 23: 7, 101 (col.) May '58; 26: 92 (col.) Aug '59.

—— (boat, fishing). Holiday 26: 5 (col.) Oct '59.

—— (boat, shuffleboard). Holiday 13: 19 (col.) Je '53.

—— (boat, swimming pool). Holiday 13: 19 (col.) Je '53.

—— (boat, wheel). Holiday 13: 130 (col.) Je '53.

—— (buying flowers). Holiday 24: 84 (col.) Jl '58.

—— (carve name on plant). Natl. geog. 105: 752 (col.) Je '54.

—— (centennial parade). Natl. geog. 97: 204 (col.) Feb '50.

—— (cocktail table). Holiday 21: 8 May '57.

—— (cocoanut drink). Natl. geog. 99: 427 (col.) Ap '51.

—— (colonial). Holiday 13: 172 May '53.

—— (comic). Holiday 6: 95 Aug '49; 8: 106 (col.) Dec '50; 11: 149 Ap '52, 77 Je '52; 18: 97 Oct '55.

—— (cowboy). Holiday 23: 175 Mar '58.

—— (dancing). Holiday 11: 88, 118 Mar '52, 103 (col.) Ap '52, 42 (col.) Ap '53, 25, 155, 172 May '53; 14: 86 Jl '53; 19: 15 (col.) Mar '56; 20: 101 Sept '56; 22: inside cover (col.) Dec '57; 26: 101 (col.) Aug '59, 38 Dec '59; 27: 170 Ap '60.
Travel 101: 35 May '54.

—— (dancing, Sumatra). Natl. geog. 108: 390 (col.) Sept '55.

—— (dog, apples). Natl. geog. 99: 138 Jan '51.

—— (eloping). Holiday 13: 82 Mar '53.

—— (evening dress). Holiday 26: 30 Nov '59.

—— (fireplace). Holiday 20: 44 (col.) Dec '56.

—— (football game). Holiday 22: 15 (col.) Nov '57.

—— (fountain, drinking). Holiday 10: 15 Sept '51.

—— (fun car). Holiday 10: 73 Aug '51.

—— (garden). Holiday 22: 45 (col.) Dec '57.

—— (gift). Holiday 10: 168 Dec '51.

—— (golf). Travel 105: 54 May '56.

—— (heads). Holiday 10: 10 (col.) Jl '51, 109 Aug '51; 13: 110 Je '53; 24: 14 Nov '58; 26: 204 Nov '59, 238-40 Dec '59; 27: 71 Ap '60, 113 (col.) May '60.
Travel 107: inside back cover Mar '57.

—— (heads, clarinets). Holiday 20: 113 Sept '56.

—— (heads, comic). Holiday 27: 159 Jan '60.

—— (heads, Hawaii). Holiday 20: 158 (col.) Nov '56.

—— (heads, laughing). Holiday 20: 180 Nov '56.

—— (holding flags). Natl. geog. 97: 72 (col.) Jan '50.

—— (horses). Holiday 10: 42 (col.) Sept '51; 13: 172 May '53.

—— (horses running). Holiday 6: 60 (col.) Sept '49.

—— (hugging). Holiday 11: 52 (col.) Feb '52; 23: 168 (col.) Je '58.

—— (in buggy). Travel 103: 65 May '55, 29 Je '55; 104: 49 Jl '55, 51 Aug '55.

—— (in lake). Holiday 23: 37 May '58.

—— (jumping). Travel 107: 13 Feb '57.

—— (kissing). Holiday 23: 39 (col.) May '58; 24: 80 Jl '58, 61 Aug '58.

—— (lantern light). Natl. geog. 117: 859 Je '60.

—— (laughing). Holiday 26: 65 Dec '59.
Natl. geog. 97: 205 (col.) Feb '50.

—— (lawn chairs). Holiday 11: 25 (col.) Ap '52.

—— (lighting cigarette). Holiday 10: 105 Jl '51.

—— (looking at picture). Holiday 27: 37 Feb '60.

—— (lunch). Holiday 25: 18 (col.) May '59.

—— (lunch counter). Holiday 28: 117 (col.) Sept '60.

—— (lunch table). Natl. geog. 99: 493 (col.) Ap '51.

—— (motor boat). Holiday 26: 10 (col.) Nov '59.

—— (mt. climbers). Natl. geog. 99: 571 (col.) May '51.

—— (mt. hikers). Natl. geog. 109: 624 (col.) May '56.

—— (on cloud). Holiday 26: 80 Aug '59, 106 Sept '59, 157 Oct '59, 207 Nov '59, 62 Dec '59; 27: 136 Jan '60, 166 Feb '60, 164 Mar '60.

—— (on floor). Natl. geog. 97: 288 (col.) Mar '50.

—— (on train). Holiday 23: 150 Ap '58. Travel 112: 9 Dec '59, 9 Ap '60.

—— (outdoor table). Holiday 28: 117 (col.) Sept '60.

—— (ox, sledge, Greece). Natl. geog. 114: 743 Dec '58.

—— (paddle boat). Holiday 11: 57 (col.) Mar '52; 28: 8 Oct '60. Travel 113: cover (col.) Ap '60.

—— (party). Holiday 13: 51 Je '53; 23: 118 (col.) May '58; 26: 134 (col.) Nov '59.

—— (picnic). Holiday 12: 106, 111 (col.) Jl '52; 26: 110 (col.) Oct '59, 146 (col.) Dec '59.

—— (pier). Holiday 10: 41 (col.) Jl '51.

—— (porch). Natl. geog. 97: 591 (col.) May '50.

—— (presenting trophy). Holiday 19: 145 (col.) May '56.

—— (reading). Natl. geog. 97: 287 (col.) Mar '50.

—— (reading paper). Natl. geog. 105: 197 (col.) Feb '54.

—— (river, boat). Natl. geog. 110: 129 Jl '56.

—— (rocky beach). Holiday 18: 24 (col.) Sept '55.

—— (rowboat). Holiday 26: 34 (col.) Dec '59. Travel 103: 7 Je '55.

—— (running). Holiday 5: 18 Ap '49; 8: 145 Dec '50; 14: 24 Dec '53.

—— (running, beach). Holiday 23: 17 Ap '58. Travel 103: 45 Je '55; 107: 12 Jan '57.

—— (sailboat). Holiday 14: 61 Sept '53; 25: 148 (col.) May '59; 27: 42 (col.) Feb '60.

—— (seated). Holiday 14: back cover (col.) Sept '53, 167 (col.) Dec '53. Natl. geog. 99: 778 (col.) Je '51; 111: 616 (col.) May '57.

—— (seated, 1835). Amer. heri. vol. 11 no. 5 p. 15 (col.) (Aug '60).

—— (see the moon). Natl. geog. 113: 279 Feb '58.

—— (selling fruit). Natl. geog. 100: 326 Sept '51.

—— (shadow). Holiday 26: 31 (col.) Nov '59.

—— (ship deck). Holiday 14: 2 Aug '53, 7, 129 (col.) Oct '53.

—— (ship deck chair). Holiday 13: 113 (col.) Mar '53, 18 (col.) May '53; 18: 20 (col.) Oct '55. Travel 111: 54 Feb '59.

—— (ship deck, waving). Holiday 10: 96 Nov '51.

—— (shuffleboard). Holiday 18: 23 Nov '55. Travel 101: 52 May '54; 105: 55 May '56.

—— (Sicily, dancers). Natl. geog. 107: 12 (col.) Jan '55.

—— (silhouette). Holiday 14: 5 Aug '53.

—— (silhouette, boat deck). Travel 104: 10 Sept '55.

—— (skating). Holiday 11: 5 (col.) Feb '52; 18: 66 Jl '55.

—— (skating, comic). Holiday 10: 180 Dec '51.

—— (ski lift). Holiday 14: 39 Dec '53; 20: 35 Dec '56.

—— (skiers). Holiday 5: 23 Feb '49, 26 Mar '49; 13: 90 Mar '53.

—— (skiis). Holiday 5: 2 (col.), 86 Feb '49.

—— (sled). Holiday 6: 20 Dec '49.

—— (sport clothes). Holiday 10: 15 Sept '51; 20: 123 (col.) Dec '56.

—— (sport coats). Holiday 14: 76 Sept '53.

—— (stair railing). Natl. geog. 109: 444 Ap '56.

—— (surfboard). Holiday 13: 70 (col.) Feb '53, 155 May '53.

—— (swimming). Holiday 10: 34 (col.) Jl '51.

—— (swimming pool). Holiday 10: 98 (col.) Aug '51; 13: 138, inside back cover (col.) Ap '53, 139 (col.) May '53. Natl. geog. 113: 172 Feb '58.

—— (table tennis). Holiday 13: 104 May '53.

—— (taking pictures). Holiday 14: 165 Nov '53.

—— (tennis racquets). Holiday 20: 10 (col.) Sept '56, 111 (col.) Oct '56; 23: 43 (col.) Je '58.

—— (throwing rocks on cairn). Natl. geog. 97: 307 (col.) Mar '50.

—— (travelers, comic). Holiday 27: 22 Jan '60.

—— (under cannon). Natl. geog. 105: 293 Mar '54.

—— (volcanic lava). Natl. geog. 118: 507 (col.) Oct '60.

—— (wading in water). Travel 104: 9 Aug '55.

—— (water skiing). Holiday 18: 4 (col.) Jl '55; 21: 115 (col.) Je '57; 23: 174 Mar '58, 159 May '58, 182 Je '58; 25: 146 Feb '59.

—— (water skiing, comic). Holiday 18: 137 Oct '55; 23: 208 Je '58.

—— (water toys). Holiday 11: 76 (col.) Je '52.

—— (wind blown). Holiday 19: 151 May '56.

—— (woodland). Holiday 26: 173 (col.) Nov '59.

boy & girl, Balinese. Holiday 18: 52-3, 56 (col.) Jl '55.

——, college (reading, ice cream cones). Natl. geog. 97: 191 (col.) Mar '50.

——, Davak (Indochina). Natl. geog. 99: 475 (col.) Ap '51.

——, Dutch. Natl. geog. 107: 468 (col.) Ap '55.

——, Dutch (skating). Amer. heri. vol. 8 no. 1 p. 33 (col.) (Dec '56).

——, French. Holiday 13: 105 Ap '53.

——, Greek. Natl. geog. 109: 63 (col.) Jan '56.

——, Hawaiian. Holiday 24: 106 (col.) Oct '58.

——, Hawaii (beach). Holiday 20: 21 (col.) Sept '56.

——, West Indies (dancers). Holiday 26: 38 Dec '59.

boy & girl. *See* also teen-agers, boys, children, man & boys.

boy & girls. Natl. geog. 98: 331 (col.) Sept '50.

—— (totem pole). Natl. geog. 108: 231 (col.) Aug '55.

boy & girls, college. Natl. geog. 97: 194 (col.) Feb '50.

boy fireman (Currier & Ives). Amer. heri. vol. 6 no. 1 back cover (col.) (Dec '54).

boy scout. Natl. geog. 100: 646 (col.) Nov '51; 102: 146 Aug '52.

—— (cartoon). Holiday 23: 77 Feb '58.

Boy Scout, Eagle (Paul A. Siple). Natl. geog. 112: 2 Jl '57.

boy scouts. Holiday 8: 89 Jl '50. Natl. geog. 101: 483 (col.) Ap '52.

—— (camping). Natl. geog. 116: 154-5 (col.) Aug '59.

—— (camporee, Greenville, Ohio). Natl. geog. 107: 480-1 (col.) Ap '55.

—— enact Indian treaty, Ohio). Natl. geog. 107: 481 (col.) Ap '55.

—— (glacier). Natl. geog. 109: 610-11 (col.) May '56.

—— (identify trees & leaves). Natl. geog. 108: 653-91 (part col.) Nov '55.

—— (jamboree tent city, Valley Forge). Natl. geog .105 :194-6, 199 (col.) Feb '54.

—— (poster). Holiday 19: 19 Feb '56.

boy scouts ranch (Philmont). Natl. geog. 110: 400-15 (part col.) Sept '56.

"Boy with a dog" (Tiepolo). Con. 142: 179 (col.) Dec '58.

"Boy with squirrel" (Copley). Amer. heri. vol. 8 no. 1 cover (col.) (Dec '56).

Boyce, Col. Westray Battle. Cur. biog. p. 68 (1945).

Boyd, Bill. Cur. biog. p. 63 (1950).

Boyd, James. Cur. biog. p. 64 (1949).

Boyd, Louise A. Cur. biog. p. 49 (1960).

Boyd, Stephen. Cur. biog. p. 67 (1961).

Boyer, Charles. Cur. biog. p. 66 (1943). Holiday 22: 5 (col.) Oct '57.

Boyer, Harold Raymond. Cur. biog. p. 61 (1952).

Boyer, Isabella. *See* Singer, Mrs. Isaac.

Boyer, Marion W. Cur. biog. p. 54 (1951).

Boykin, Frank W. Holiday 27: 58 (col.) Mar '60.

Boylan, Robert P. Cur. biog. p. 65 (1950).

Boyle, Hal. Cur. biog. p. 70 (1945).

Boyle, Kay. Cur. biog. p. 102 (1942).

Boyle, William M., jr. Cur. biog. p. 65 (1949).

Boylston, Helen. Jun. bk. of auth., p. 44.

Boylston, Helen Dore. Cur. biog. p. 104 (1942).

Boys, T. Shotter (work of). Con. ency. of ant., vol. 1, pl. 140. Con. 141: 117 Ap '58.

boys (as soldiers). Con. 137: XII (col.) May '56.

—— (back view). Holiday 14: 153 Dec '53.

—— (ball game). Natl. geog. 105: 541 Ap '54.

—— (bicycles). Holiday 10: 30 Sept '51.

—— (bicycles). Natl. geog. 107: 633 (col.) May '55.

—— (big fish). Natl. geog. 97: 71 (col.) Jan '50.

—— (bob for apples). Natl. geog. 114: 614 Nov '58.

—— (bobsled). Travel 107: 4 Jan '57.

—— (burros). Natl. geog. 110: 404 Sept '56.

—— (card games). Natl. geog. 106: 835 (col.) Dec '54.

—— (cave). Natl. geog. 111: 403 (col.) Mar '57.

—— (cleaning fish nets). Natl. geog. 118: 117 (col.) Jl '60.

—— (college sports). Holiday 23: 91 (col.) May '58.

—— (dog, walking). Natl. geog. 98: 342 (col.) Sept '50.

—— (fighting). Amer. heri. vol. 12 no. 1 p. 26 (col.) Dec '60.

—— (flour mill). Natl. geog. 113: 787 (col.) Je '58.

—— (goats, Formosa). Natl. geog. 107: 587 Ap '57.

—— (heads, group). Natl. geog. 114: 380 Sept '58.

—— (heads, old lock & key). Natl. geog. 109: 450 Ap '56.

—— (horses). Natl. geog. 110: 401 (col.) Sept '56.

—— (hurdles). Natl. geog. 107: 386 (col.) Mar '55.

—— (in library). Natl. geog. 100: 578 Nov '51.

—— (laughing). Holiday 21: 123 Jan '57.

—— (marching, patriotism). Natl. geog. 107: 744 (col.) Je '55.

—— (on fence). Natl. geog. 110: 12 (col.) Jl '56.

—— (on fence, overalls). Natl. geog. 98: 336 (col.) Sept '50.

—— (on saddles in shop). Natl. geog. 100: 311 (col.) Sept '51.

—— (orchestra). Holiday 7: 28 (col.) Je '50.

—— (peeling sugar cane). Natl. geog. 115: 379 (col.) Mar '59.

—— (penguins). Natl. geog. 103: 782 (col.) Je '53.

—— (pets). Travel 106: 20 Sept '56.

—— (playing). Amer. heri. vol. 8 no. 5 p. 47 (col.) (Aug '57).

—— (playing ball). Holiday 7: 43 (col.) May '50.

—— (playing in pool). Natl. geog. 116: 281 Aug '59.

—— (raft). Holiday 25: 117 Mar '59. Natl. geog. 110: 128 Jl '56.

—— (reading). Natl. geog. 98: 14 Jl '50.

—— (river). Travel 112: 24 Aug '59.

—— (rocky beach). Travel 107: 43 Mar '57.

—— (rocky harbor). Holiday 28: 62 (col.) Sept '60.

—— (rowboat). Holiday 26: 116 (col.) Aug '59.

—— (sawing tree). Natl. geog. 110: 409 Sept '56.

—— (school room). Holiday 22: 8 Oct '57.

—— (search for sea life). Natl. geog. 107: 810 Je '55.

—— (seated, back view, ranch). Natl. geog. 110: 406-7 (col.) Sept '56.

—— (ship model). Natl. geog. 111: 582 (col.) May '57.

—— (snow balls). Natl. geog. 99: 688 (col.) May '51.

—— (snow suits). Holiday 20: 21 (col.) Nov '56.

—— (soccer). Natl. geog. 100: 178 (col.) Aug '51.

—— (stunts). Holiday 12: 90 Oct '52.

—— **(swimming).** Holiday 13: 41 Feb '53.

—— (volleyball). Natl. geog. 109: 273 (col.) Feb '56.

—— (watching towboat). Natl. geog. 97: 192 (col.) Feb '50.

boys, Aiken Prep. school. Holiday 19: 100-1 May '56.

——, Arabian. See Arabian boys.

——, Balinese (xylophone). Natl. geog. 99: 12 (col.) Jan '51.

——, baseball. Holiday 24: 15 (col.) Aug '58. Natl. geog. 110: 590 (col.) Nov '56.

——, college (rowboat). Holiday 26: 45 (col.) Sept '59.

——, cub scout. See cub scout.

——, delivery (marching). Holiday 26: 243 (col.) Dec '59.

——, English school. Holiday 19: 90-3 Jan '56.

——, Eton college. See Eton college.

——, Harvard college. Natl. geog. 97: 309 (col.) Mar '50.

——, Holland (soccer team). Natl. geog. 106: 385 (col.) Sept '54.

——, Lebanon (funeral procession). Holiday 20: 56 (col.) Dec '56.

——, Mexican (at library shelves). Natl. geog. 102: 539 (col.) Oct '52.

——, school (waving). Holiday 24: 22 (col.) Oct '58.

——, Seminole Indians (on fence). Natl. geog. 110: 835 (col.) Dec '56.

——, Tarascan. Natl. geog. 101: 139 Jan '52.

——, Univ. (band instruments). Natl. geog. 98: 576 (col.) Nov '50.

——, western (head, laughing). Holiday 19: 106 (col.) Feb '56.

——, Zanzibar. Natl. geog. 101: 275 Feb '52.

boys & girls. Travel 108: 60 Dec '57.

—— (art gallery). Natl. geog. 113: 261, 264-5, 273 (part col.) Feb '58.

—— (at table). Natl. geog. 100: 590 (col.) Nov '51.

—— (back view, mt.). Natl. geog. 110: 486 (col.) Oct '56.

—— (bathing suits). Travel 107: 53 Feb '57.

—— (bathing suits, beach). Holiday 23: 10 (col.) Feb '58, 128 Mar '58, 106 (col.) Ap '58, 174 (col.) May '58, 5, 10, 22, 24 (part col.) Je '58; 24: 85, 122 (col.) Jl '58.

—— (bathing suits, sailboat). Travel 113: cover (col.) Feb '60.

—— (beach). Holiday 13: 123 (col.) Mar '53, 15 (col.) Ap '53.

—— (beach, Hawaii). Holiday 14: 32 (col.) Nov '53.

—— (beach picnic). Travel 108: 53 Oct '57.

—— (bicycle tour). Natl. geog. 108: 150, 154 Jl '55.

—— (bicycles). Face of Amer., p. 162-3 (col.). Travel 107: 23 Je '57; 113: 32, 34 Mar '60.

—— (boat). Holiday 13: 65 (col.) Ap '53; 14: 100-3 Aug '53.

—— (camp fire). Holiday 23: 5 (col.) Je '58.

—— (college commencement). Holiday 13: 56-7 (col.) Mar '53.

—— (dancing). Holiday 23: 57 Mar '58.

—— (dancing, Caribbean). Holiday 18: inside cover (col.) Sept '55.

—— (dancing, Chile). Natl. geog. 117: 234-5 (col.) Feb '60.

—— (diving board). Holiday 6: 53 (col.) Jl '49.

—— (folkdance). Holiday 24: 44 (col.) Aug '58.

—— (hike). Natl. geog. 115: 814 (col.) Je '59.

—— (looking at the White House). Jensen: The White House, frontis.

—— (lower flag). Natl. geog. 108: 732 (col.) Dec '55.

—— (Maypole dance, medieval). Int. gr. soc.: Arts . . . p. 79 (col.).

—— (motor boat). Holiday 23: 117 Je '58.

—— (on fence). Natl. geog. 100: 296, 389 (col.) Sept '51.

—— (party). Holiday 14: 113 Jl '53.

—— (picnic). Holiday 14: 95 (col.) Aug '53.

—— (play on beach). Natl. geog. 111: 809 (col.) Je '57.

—— (sailboat). Holiday 23: 7 (col.) Je '58.

—— (seated). Travel 104: 10 Jl '55.

—— (seated, artists). Natl. geog. 98: 380 (col.) Sept '50.

—— (seated, back view). Holiday 10: 95 (col.) Sept '51.
Natl. geog. 99: 576 (col.) May '51.

—— (seated, steps). Holiday 10: 94 (col.) Sept '51.
Natl. geog. 108: 133 Jl '55.

—— (skiers). Jordan: Hammond's pict. atlas, p. 141 (col.).

—— (square dance). Holiday 23: 7 (col.) May '58.
Natl. geog. 106: 232 (col.) Aug '54.

—— (study outdoors). Holiday 22: 59 (col.) Nov '57.

—— (toy planetarium). Natl. geog. 112: 813 Dec '57.

—— (walking). Holiday 13: 94 (col.) Mar '53.

—— (winter sport). Holiday 23: 101 (col.) Mar '58.

——, Apache. Natl. geog. 104: 372 (col.) Sept '53.

——, Argentine (dancers). Natl. geog. 113: 333 (col.) Mar '58.

——, Chinese (opera). Travel 112: 27-9 Dec '59.

——, college. See college boys & girls.

——, Hawaiian (flag). Natl. geog. 116: 121 Jl '59.

——, school. Natl. geog. 99: 453 (col.) Ap '51.

boy's band, Dinkelsbuhl. Disney: People & places, p. 52 (col.).

boy's choir. Holiday 12: 37 Oct '52.

—— (Washington cathedral). Natl. geog. 111: 92 (col.) Jan '57.

boys. See also band; children; man & boy.

Boyton, Paul. Amer. heri. vol. 11 no. 3 p. 36, 39, 92-3 (Ap '60).

Boz ball (to welcome Charles Dickens). Amer. heri. vol. 9 no. 1 p. 10-11 (Dec '57).

Brace, Gerald Warner. Cur. biog. p. 58 (1947).

bracelet. Holiday 13: 73 (col.) Jan '53; 14: 115 Sept '53; 24: 60 Dec '58; 26: 92 Sept '59.

——, antique. Con. 140: 182 Dec '57.

——, charm. Holiday 19: 99 (col.) Mar '56; 20: 207 Dec '56; 28: 136 Sept '60.

——, Egyptian king's. Ceram: March of arch., p. 149.

bracelet, 18th cent. Con. 140: XXIV Dec '57.
Bracken, Brendan. Cur. biog. p. 98 (1941).
Bracken, Eddie. Cur. biog. p. 64 (1944).
bracket (Vivares etching, 1750). Con. 144: 223 Jan '60.
Brackett, Charles. Cur. biog. p. 56 (1951). Holiday 5: 42 (col.) Jan '49.
Brackman, Robert. Cur. biog. p. 86 (1953).
Bradbury, Norris E. Cur. biog. p. 67 (1949).
Bradbury, Ray. Cur. biog. p. 87 (1953).
Braddock, Gen. E. (wounded). Amer. heri. vol. 8 no. 4 p. 58 (col.) (Je '57).
Braddock, Elizabeth M. Cur. biog. p. 67 (1957).
Braddock's battle route (1755). Amer. heri. vol. 8 no. 4 p. 61 (Je '57).
Braden, Spruille. Cur. biog. p. 72 (1945).
Bradford, Gamaliel. Amer. heri. vol. 11 no. 4 p. 33 (Je '60).
Bradford, Robert F. Cur. biog. p. 56 (1948).
Bradford tombstone, William. Rawson: Ant. pict. bk., p. 92.
Bradley, David. Cur. biog. p. 69 (1949).
Bradley, Lt. Gen. Omar N. Cur. biog. p. 69 (1943).
Bradley, Gen. Omar N. & Mrs. Natl. geog. 103: 2 Jan '53.
Bradley, Dr. Preston. Cur. biog. p. 73 (1956).
"Bradshaw family" (Zoffany). Con.. 136; 21 Sept '55.
Brady, Diamond Jim. Holiday 25: 78 Feb '59.
Brady, Don Roberto. Horan: Pict. hist. of wild west, p. 56.
Brady, Mathew (work of). Amer. heri. vol. 8 no. 1 p. 20 (Dec '56).
Brady, William Thomas. Cur. biog. p. 69 (1961).
Braemar gathering (Scotland). Natl. geog. 110: 19 (col.) Jl '56.
Braffett, Mark. Horan: Pict. hist. of wild west, p. 206.
Bragdon, Helen D. Cur. biog. p. 58 (1951).
Bragg, Braxton. Pakula: Cent. album, p. 89.
Brahamism (philosophies). Lehner: Pict. bk. of sym., p. 43.
Brahma, birth of. See birth of Brahma.
Brahms, Johannes. Cooper: Con. ency. of music, p. 61.
Int. gr. soc.: Arts . . . p. 123 (col.).
Brahui tribesmen. Natl. geog. 105: 512 (col.) Ap '54.
braid weaving loom. See loom, braid weaving.
Brailowsky, Alexander. Cur. biog. p. 76 (1956).
brain, human. Gray's anatomy, p. 577, 824.
brain wave recorder. Natl. geog. 98: 570 (col.) Nov '50.
Brainard, D. L. Amer. heri. vol. 11 no. 4 p. 50 (Je '60).
Braine, John. Holiday 23: 92 Ap '58.
Bramante, Donato (sculpture). Holiday 27: 85 Ap '60.
Bramuglia, Juan A. Cur. biog. p. 70 (1949).
Brancusi, Constantin. Cur. biog. p. 59 (1955).
—— (wood carving). Praeg. pict. ency., p. 458.
Brand, Oscar. Cur. biog. p. 51 (1962).
Brandeis, Louis Dembitz. Amer. heri. vol. 9 no. 3 p. 25 (Ap '58).
Holiday 7: 75 Feb '50.
brander. Con. ency. of ant., vol. 3, p. 241.

branding iron. Rawson: Ant. pict. bk., p. 41.
Brando, Marlon. Cur. biog. p. 63 (1952).
Brandon, Duke Charles. Con. 143: 255 (col.) Je '59.
"Brandon" (house, 1715). Holiday 10: 38-9 (col.) Nov '51.
brands, cattle. See cattle brands.
Brandt, Paul (work of). Con. 145: 280 Je '60.
Brandt, Willy. Cur. biog. p. 57 (1958).
brandy warmer, Geo. I silver. Con. 135: X May '55; 141: XII Mar '58, XX Ap '58, XXVI May '58, XVIII Je '58; 142: XII Sept '58, XLVI Nov '58, XII Dec '58, XXXIV Jan '59.
——, Geo IV silver. Con. 133: XIV Ap '54.
Brandford college (Yale Univ.). Holiday 13: 60 May '53.
Braniff, T. E. Cur. biog. p. 64 (1952).
Brann, Esther. Jun. bk. of auth., p. 45.
Brannaman, Ray Harold. Cur. biog. p. 59 (1947).
Brannan, Charles F. Cur. biog. p. 57 (1948).
Bransome, Edwin D. Cur. biog. p. 66 (1952).
Brant, Joseph. Amer. heri. vol. 3 no. 3 cover (col.), 27 (spring '52); vol. 9 No. 4 p. 110 (Je '58); vol. 10 no. 3 p. 82 (Ap '59).
Branzell, Karin. Cur. biog. p. 71 (1946).
Braque, Georges. Cur. biog. p. 72 (1949).
—— (work of). Con. 133: 288 Je '54; 141: XI (col.) Je '58; 144: 41 Sept '59; 145: 182, 208 May '60.
Holiday 14: 61 (col.) Nov '53.
Praeg. pict. ency., p. 503 (col.).
Brasher, Rex (portfolio of birds). Amer. heri. vol. 7 no. 5 p. 44-51 (col.) (Aug '56).
Brasilia (Brazil, capitol). Holiday 27: back cover (col.) Ap '60, 234 (col.) May '60.
Int. gr. soc.: Arts . . . p. 127 (col.).
Natl. geog. 117: 704-24 (part col.) May '60.
—— (hotel). Travel 111: 44 Feb '59.
—— (plan). Natl. geog. 117: 720-1 (col.) May '60.
Brasiliano, Roche. Amer. heri. vol. 8 no. 2 p. 19 (Feb '57).
brass (sym.). Lehner: Pict. bk. of sym., p. 72
brass sculpture, Ife (Africa). Holiday 25: 71 Ap '59.
Brattain, Walter H. Cur. biog. p. 69 (1957).
Braun, Werner. Cur. biog. p. 70 (1957).
brazier, Chou. Con. 136: 70 Sept '55.
——, Italian Silver. Con. 144: 155 Dec '59.
Brazil. Holiday 12: 2 (col.) Dec '52; 13: 110 (col.) Feb '53, 13, 24, 151 (part col.) Ap '53; 26: 28 Sept' 59; 27: 229, 234 (col.) May '60, 20 (col.) Je '60.
Natl. geog. 108: 748-55 (col.) Dec '55; 117: 704-24 (part col.) May '60.
Travel 103: 7-10 Mar '55; 112: cover (col.), 20 Sept '59.
—— (Amazon jungle). Natl. geog. 102: 697-710 Nov '52; 115: 632-69 (part col.) May '59.
—— (Brasilia, capitol). See Brasilia.
—— (Indian girls "come of age") Natl. geog. 116: 628-49 (part col.) Nov '59.
—— (Kraho Indians). Natl. geog. 115: 340-62 (part col.) Mar '59.

—— (map). Natl. geog. 102: 699 Nov '52; 117: 706 May '60.

—— (President's palace). Holiday 25: 46 Mar '59.

—— (Rio de Janeiro). Holiday 19: 44-5 (col.) Mar '56; 24: 76-85 (col.) Dec '58. Natl. geog. 107: 290-328 (part col.) Mar '55.

Brazilian Republican guard. Int. gr. soc.: Arts . . . p. 159 (col.).

Brazzi, Rossano. Cur. biog. p. 71 (1961). Holiday 23: 9 Jan '58.

bread. Natl. geog. 114: 311 (col.) Sept '58.

—— (desert). Natl. geog. 114: 486 (col.) Oct '58.

—— (stacked on head tray, Greece). Natl. geog. 117: 639 (col.) May '60.

——, loaves of (child). Natl. geog. 117: 734 Je '60.

——, loaves (french). Natl. geog. 105: 173, 175 (col.) Feb '54.

——, loaves (strapped to bicycle, France). Natl. geog. 117: 744 (col.) Je '60.

break baking (Lebanon women). Natl. geog. 113: 521 (col.) Ap '58.

break basket, baked (Iran). Natl. geog. 100: 431 Oct '51

bread kneading trough. Rawson: Ant. pict. bk., p. 17.

bread makers, Indian. Natl. geog. 114: 822-3 (col.) Dec '58.

bread making (Canary Island cave). Natl. geog. 107: 506 Ap '55.

—— (Cypress Isle). Natl. geog. 101: 655 May '52.

—— (Old Testament days). Natl. geog. 118: 822-3 (part col.) Dec '60.

bread plate, Russian ceremonial. Con. 144: 277 Jan '60.

breadtray (19th cent.). Amer. heri. vol. 2 no. 2 p. 35 (winter '51).

"The Breakers" (home of Vanderbilt). Amer. heri. vol. 6 no. 2 p. 22 (winter '55).

Breakers hotel (Palm Beach, Fla.). Travel 105: 44 Jan '56; 107: 49 Jan '57.

breakfast food, Battle Creek (cartoons). Amer. heri. vol. 8 no. 4 p. 82-3, 85, Je '57.

breakfast table. See table breakfast.

breakfront bookcase. See bookcase, breakfront.

breast plate (ancient armour). Int. gr. soc.: Arts . . . p. 33 (col.).

——, Columbia (ancient). Praeg. pict. ency., p. 554 (col.).

——, Indian. See Indian beaded breastplate.

Breckenridge, John Cabell. Pakula: Cent. album, p. 91.

Breckinridge, Aide de Acosta. Cur. biog. p. 115 (1954).

Bredalbane, Duchess of (miniature). Con. ency. of ant., vol. 1, pl. 132.

Breech, Ernest R. Cur. biog. p. 61 (1955).

breechlock. Natl. geog. 117: 157 (col.) Feb '60.

Breen, Joseph I. Cur. biog. p. 67 (1950).

Brehm, Worth (book illus. by). Amer. heri. vol. 8 no. 1 p. 32 (col.) (Dec '56).

Brekelenkam, Quiryn (work of). Con. 140: 184 Dec '57.

Bremen harbor. Amer. heri. vol. 11 no. 5 p. 74-5 (col.) (Aug '60).

"Bremo" (home in Virginia). Natl. geog. 97: 582 (col.) May '50.

Brennan, Walter. Cur. biog. p. 99 (1941).

Brennan, Justice William J., Jr. Cur. biog. p. 73 (1957).

Brenner, E. (self-portrait). Con. 141: 20 Mar '58.

Brenner Pass (Italy). Natl. geog. 100: 381, 385 Sept '51.

Brent, James. Horan: Pict. hist. of wild west, p. 69.

Brentano, Heinrich von. Cur. biog. p. 64 (1955).

Brenton, Woodward Harold. Cur biog. p. 89 (1953).

Brentwood trailer park (Cal.). Travel 112: 49 Aug '59.

Brereton, Maj. Gen. Lewis H. Cur biog. p. 71 (1943).

Breslin, Howard. Cur. biog. p. 59 (1958).

Breton, Andre. Holiday 24: 61 Aug. '58.

Breton man (playing bagpipe). Holiday 7: 103 (col.) Jan '50.

Breton women (France). Holiday 15: 51 Jan '54.

Brett, Lt. Gen. George H. Cur biog. p. 106 (1942).

Brett, George P., Jr. Cur biog. p. 60 (1948).

Brett, Harold M. (book illus. by). Amer. heri. vol. 8 no. 1 p. 31 (col.) (Dec '56).

Breuer, Marcel. Cur. biog. p. 101 (1941); p. 50 (1960).

brew jug. See Penn's brew jug.

Brewer, David J. Amer. heri. vol. 11 no. 6 p. 55 (Oct '60).

Brewer, Roy M. Cur. biog. p. 91 (1953).

brewer (sym). Lehner: Pict. bk. of sym., p. 90.

brewery. Holiday 27: 171 (col.) Je '60.

—— (int.). Holiday 27: 61 Ap '60, 97, 221 (col.) May '60.

——, antique. Holiday 26: 21 (col.) Aug '59.

Brewster, Ellis Wethrell. Holiday 14: 44 Nov '53.

Brewster, John (work of). Amer. heri vol. 11 no. 3 p. 53 (col.) (Ap '60).

Brewster, Owen. Cur. biog. p. 62 (1947).

Brewster & Co. Carriage trade. Amer. heri. vol. 7 no. 6 p. 90-4 (col.) (Oct '56).

Brezhnev, Leonid I. Cur. biog. (1963).

Brice, Fanny. Cur biog. p. 74 (1946).

Brick, John. Cur biog. p. 93 (1953).

brick, glazed (processing way). Praeg. pict. ency., p. 113.

Brickell, Herschel. Cur. biog. p. 75 (1945).

Bricker, John W. Cur. biog. p. 73 (1943); p. 77 (1956).

Brickley, Charlie. Holiday 26: 64 Nov '59.

Brico, Antonia. Cur. biog. p. 62 (1948).

bridal crown, Norwegian. Con. 144: XXIV Nov '59.

bridal crown, silver (Norwegian 18th cent.). Con. 145: 14 Mar '60.

Bridal Veil Falls (Great Smoky Mts.). Travel 113: 37 Mar' 60.

Bridal Veil Falls (N.C.). Travel 106: 20 Aug '56.

bride. Holiday 7: 140-1 May '50; 8: 115 Aug 50.

bride (being dressed). Con. 145: XVIII (col.) Ap '60.
—— (being kissed). Holiday 25: 87 (col.) Jan '59.
—— (gifts). Holiday 21: 10 (col.) May '57.
—— (head). Holiday 10: 64 Aug '51.
"The Bride" (Solomon). Con. 145: XVIII (col.) Ap '60.
——, Greek. Holiday 25: 4 Jan '59.
——, Japanese. Natl. geog. 116: 858 (col.) Dec '59.
——, Kashgai (Iran). Natl. geog. 101: 815 (col.) Je '52.
——, Kazakh. Natl. geog. 106: 636 (col.) Nov '54.
——, Mogh. Natl. geog. 107: 416 (col.) Mar '55.
——, Nepal. Natl. geog. 97: 9 (col.) Jan '50.
——, New Guinea. Natl. geog. 108: 458 (col.) Oct. 55.
——, Palestine. Natl. geog. 106: 842 Dec '54.
——, Sardinia. Disney: People & places, p. 73 (col.).
——, Switzerland. Natl. geog. 110: 447 (col.) Oct '56.
bride & groom. Holiday 5: 121, 134 (col.) Je '49; 21: 11, 37 Je '57; 24: 101 (col.) Jl '58; 26: 30 Jl '59.
—— (army). Holiday 11: 71 Feb '52.
—— (at car). Holiday 28: 119 Jl '60.
—— (comic). Holiday 28: 96 Sept '60.
—— (cutting cake). Con. 139: XXXIII Ap '57.
—— (1800-). Amer. heri. vol. 3 no. 4 p. 60-2 (part col.) (summer '52).
—— (1889). Holiday 5: 121 Je '49.
—— (heads). Holiday 11: 14 Je '52; 27: 36 Je '60.
—— (leaving church). Holiday 27: 44 Feb '60.
—— (old fashioned). Holiday 13: 28 Mar '53.
——. (running). Holiday 13: 23 Je '53.
—— (wedding). Natl. geog. 107: 369 (col.) Mar '55.
—— (wedding, Hindu). Natl. geog. 117, 394 (col.) Mar '60; 118: 468 (col.) Oct '60.
—— (wedding, navy). Holiday 18: 204 Dec '55.
—— (wedding, Poland). Natl. geog. 114: 396-7 (col.) Sept '58.
——, West Point. Natl. geog. 101: 624 (col.) May '52.
——, Bhutan. Natl. geog. 102: 737-52 (col.) Dec '52.
——, France. Holiday 21: 55 Ap '57.
——, Hindu (wedding). Natl. geog. 117: 394 (col.) Mar '60; 118: 468 (col.) Oct '60.
——, Lhasa. Natl. geog. 108: 5 (col.) Jl '55.
——, Malay (heads). Natl. geog. 116: 784 (col.) Dec '59.
——, Morocco. Natl. geog. 107: 188 Feb '55.
——, Norway. Natl. geog. 111: 119 (col.) Jan '57.
——, Poland. Holiday 6: 56 (col.) Jl '49.
——, (wedding). Natl. geog. 114: 396-7 (col.) Sept '58.
——, Polynesian. Natl. geog. 97: 532 (col.), 537 Ap '50.
——, Russia. Natl. geog. 116: 390 (col.) Sept 59.

——, Sumatra. Natl. geog. 99: 20 Jan '51.
bride & groom. See also wedding.
bride-to-be (India, head). Natl. geog. 107: 257 Feb '55.
Bride's dowry. Natl. geog. 108: 459 (col.) Oct '55.
bridge. Amer. heri. vol. 9 no. 5 p. 54 (col.) (Aug '58).
Holiday 5: 13 Mar '49; 6: 11 Jl '49, 34, 36 Sept '49; 13: 101 May '53; 14: cover Nov 53; 21: 108 (col.) Je '57.
Nalt. geog. 98: 110 (col.) Jl '50; 105: 220 (col.) Feb '54.
Osward: Asia Minor, pl. 147.
Travel 103: 17 Feb '55, 16 May '55; 105: 19 May '56; 111: 21 Je '59; 112: 23 Jl '59.
—— (across street, shops, Moscow). Natl. geog. 116: 722 (col.) Dec '59.
—— (Brazil). Natl. geog. 107: 348 Mar '55.
—— (Cincinnati). Natl. geog. 97: 188 (col.) Feb '50.
—— (Dublin). Holiday 19: 38 (col.) Jan '56.
—— (early wooden). Amer. heri. vol. 1 no. 3 p. 5 (col.) (spring '50).
—— (flower garden). Natl. geog. 103: 319 (col.) Mar '53.
—— (Heidelberg). Natl. geog. 115: 756 (col.) Je '59.
—— (Hong Kong). Natl. geog. 100: 749 Dec '51; 105: 259 (col.) Feb '54.
—— (park). Face of Amer., p. 70-1 (col.).
——, Alaska railroad. Travel. 101: 31 Je '54.
——, Allahverdi Khan. See Allahverdi Khan bridge.
——, Antietam Creek. Natl. geog. 117: 270 (col.) Feb '60.
——, arched. Natl. geog. 106: 381 (col.) Sept '54.
——, arched rock (Scotland). Natl. geog. 110: 20 (col.) Jl '56.
——, Asian trade route. Natl. geog. 99: 612 (col.) May '51.
——, Avignon. Holiday 14: 81 (col.) Nov '53; 19: 61 (col.) Feb 56.
——, Avon river. Natl. geog. 108: 303 (col.) Sept '55.
——, Arlington memorial See Arlington memorial bridge.
——, bamboo. Natl geog. 100: 674 (col.) Nov '51.
——, bamboo swaying (Nepal). Natl. geog. 108: 590-1 (col.) Nov '55.
——, bay (Cal.) Natl. geog. 110: 215 (col.) Aug '56.
——, Goksu river. Osward: Asia Minor, pl. 121.
——, Bronx-Whitestone. Natl. geog. 99: 293 (col.) Mar '51.
——, Brooklyn. See Brooklyn bridge.
——, Buffalo river. Natl. geog. 110: 417 Sept '56.
——, camelback (Harrisburg). Amer. heri. vol. 3 no. 4 p. 22 (summer '52).
——, canal. Amer. heri. vol. 9 no. 2 p. 98, 100 (Feb '58).
Natl. geog. 107: 650 (col.) May '55.
——, (Venice). Holiday 25: 135 Mar '59.

——, **Capilano.** Natl. geog. 114: 181 Aug '58.

——, **Chesapeake Bay.** Natl. geog. 105: 437 Ap '54 111: 606 (col.) May '57

——, **Clifton suspension (1831).** Con. 135: 244 Je '55.

——, **covered.** Amer. heri. vol. 3 no. 4 p. 57 (col.) (summer '52); vol. 6 no. 2 p. 100 (winter '55), no 3 p. 104, 112 (Ap '55); vol. 10 no. 4 p. 30-7, 82-4 (part col.) (Je '59).
Holiday 6: 52 (col.) Nov '49; 10: 38 (col.) Sept '51; 13: 25 (col.) Je '53; 21: 17 Jan '57, 185 May '57, 184 (col.) Je '57; 23: 157 May '58; 27: 37 Je '60; 28: 6 Sept '60, 142 Oct '60.
Jordan: Hammond's pict. atlas, p. 27 (col.).
Natl. geog. 99: 600 (col.) May 51; 107: 734 (col.) Je '55.
Rawson: Ant. pict. bk., p. 46.
Travel 101: 15 Mar '54; 102: 16 Jl '54; 104: 17 Aug '55; 112: 27-9 Sept '59; 114; 23 Sept '60.

——, **(Switzerland).** Natl. geog. 110: 449 (col.) Oct '56.

——, **Delaware memorial.** Natl. geog. 102: 19 Jl '52.

——, **Donner Pass.** Jordan: Hammond's pict. atlas, p. 189 (col.).

——, **drawbridge (world's smallest).** Natl. geog. 105: 225 (col.) Feb '54.

——, **floating.** Jordan: Hammond's pict. atlas, p. 149 (col.).
Natl. geog. 117: 514 (col.) Ap '60.

——, **Florida to Key West.** Holiday 6: 118 (col.) Dec '49; 28: 177 (col.) Oct '60.
Natl. geog. 97: 49 (col.) Jan '50.

——, **Galata.** *See* Galata bridge.

——, **Galveston-Texas.** Travel 103: 24 May '55.

——, **garden.** Holiday 11: 60-1 (col.) Feb '52.

——, **George Washington.** *See* George Washington bridge (N.Y.).

——, **Golden Gate.** *See* Golden Gate bridge.

——, **humpbacked.** Natl. geog. 110: 20 (col.) Jl 56.
Rawson: Ant. pict. bk., p. 45.

——, **Japanese garden.** Int. gr. soc.: Arts . . . p. 121 (col.).

——, **Japanese (girls).** Natl. geog. 104: 641 (col.) Nov '53.

——, **kissing.** Rawson: Ant. pict. bk., p. 46.

——, **Lions Gate (Canada).** Natl. geog. 108: 238 (col.) Aug '55.

——, **log (Afghanistan).** Natl. geog. 98: 688 (col.) Nov '50.

——, **Mackinac Is.** *See* Mackinac bridge.

——, **Memphis (Ark.).** Travel 104: 13 Jl '55.

——, **Michigan, suspension.** Holiday 23: 25 (col.) Feb '58.

——, **moon.** Natl. geog. 113: 272 (col.) Feb '58.

——, **Natural.** *See* Natural bridge.

——, **New York Thruway.** Natl. geog. 110: 574 (col.) Nov '56.

——, **Niagara Falls.** Natl. geog. 117: 258 (col.) Feb '60.

——, **old double arch stone.** Rawson: Ant. pict. bk., p. 44.

——, **1000 islands international.** Travel 110: 32 Jl '58.

——, **Port Huron "Blue Water".** Travel 102: 43 Aug '54.

——, **Prague.** Praeg. pict. ency., p. 497 (col.).

——, **Pulteney (Bath, Eng.).** Holiday 26: 52 (col.) Aug '59.

——, **railroad.** Natl. geog. 107: 781 (col.) Je '55.
Travel 112: 20 Jl '59.

——, **railroad (Swiss).** Travel 111: 8 Ap '59.

——, **rainbow (rock).** *See* rainbow bridge.

——, **Richmond (Eng.).** Con. 137: 94-6 Ap '56.

——, **river** Amer. heri. vol. 9 no. 1 p. 68 (col.) (Dec '57).
Face of Amer., p. 40-1 (col.).
Holiday 13: 14 Jan '53.
Natl. geog. 102: 4, 9 (col.) Jl '52; 110: 126-7 Jl '56; 111: 162 (col.) Feb '57; 114: 73 (col.) Jl '58; 115: 446 (col.) Ap '59; 117: 422-3 (col.) Mar '60.

——, **river (Bhutan).** Natl. geog. 102: 723 (col.) Dec '52.

——, **river (France).** Natl. geog. 108: 536 (col.) Oct '55.

——, **river (India).** Natl. geog. 118: 500-1 (col.) Oct '60.

——, **river (Liffey).** Travel 110: 48 Jl '58.

——, **river (Merrimack).** Natl. geog. 99: 110 Jan '51.

——, **river (New Orleans).** Natl. geog. 118: 714-5 (col.) Nov '60.

——, **river (Nile).** Natl. geog. 107: 718 May '55.

——, **river (Ohio).** Amer. heri. vol. 3 no. 2 p. 58 (col.) (winter '52).

——, **river (Paris).** Holiday 14: back cover (col.) Sept '53.
Natl. geog. 108: 531 (col.) Oct '55; 98: 58 (col.) Jl '50.

——, **river (Ponte Vecchio, Florence).** Holiday 6: 135 (col.) Oct '49.
Natl. geog. 111: 794-5 (col.) Je '57.
Travel 114: 84 Jl '60.

——, **river (Potomac).** Natl. geog. 103: 516 Ap '53.

——, **river (Scotland).** Natl. geog. 110: 32 Jl '56.

——, **river (Tarn).** Natl. geog. 100: 32 (col.) Jl '51.

——, **river (Tiber).** Natl. geog. 111: 474 (col.) Ap '57.

——, **River Cam (Cambridge, Eng.).** Natl. geog. 108: 312 (col.) Sept '55.

——, **rock.** Con. 144: 92 Nov '59.
Natl. geog. 112: 191 (col.) Aug '57.

——, **river ("Brig o' Doon").** Natl. geog. 112: 456 (col.) Oct '57.

——, **river (Thames river).** Natl. geog. 114: 59 (col.) Jl '58.

——, **rock tower (Bryce Canyon).** Natl. geog. 114: 510 (col.) Oct '58.

——, **Roman.** Con. 144: LXVII (col.) Jan '60.
Natl. geog. 110: 742 (col.) Dec '56.
Travel 101: inside cover May '54.

——, **Roman (55 AD Pyrenees).** Holiday 5: 123 Ap '49.

bridge, Roman (near Issus). Osward: Asia Minor, pl. 29.

——, Roman style. Natl. geog. 105: 164 (col.) Feb '54.

——, Seine river (Paris). Travel 109: inside back cover Je '58.

——, seven- mile (Fla.-Key West). See bridge, Florida to Key West.

——, steel train. Natl. geog. 117: 470-1 (col.) Ap '60.

——, stone. Con. 144: LI Jan '60.
Holiday 12: 54 Oct '52; 19: 61 (col.) Feb '56.
Natl. geog. 99: 152 (col.) Feb '51.
Rawson: Ant. pict. bk., p. 44.

——, (England). Natl. geog. 109: 534 (col.) Ap '56.

——, suspension. Holiday 23: 25 (col.) Feb '58.
Natl. geog. 107: 617 May '55.

——, suspension (longest). Natl. geog. 105: 724-5, 727 (col.) Je '54.

——, suspension (world's highest). Natl. geog. 106: 235 (col.) Aug '54.

——, swamp (men & women). Natl. geog. 113: 111-12 (col.) Jan '58.

——, swinging. Travel 106: 19 Aug '56.

——, Tampa Bay. Natl. geog. 107: 75 Jan '55.

——, Tarn river. Natl. geog. 100: 32 (col.) Jl '51.

——, Tiber river. Natl. geog. 111: 474 (col.) Ap '57.

——, Tower. See London (Tower bridge).

——, U.S. to Canada. Natl. geog. 104: 822 Dec '53.

——, Venice. Con. 136: XVI Dec '55; 140: XXIX Nov '57.
Holiday 6: 33 Oct '49, 127 Nov '49; 15: 33 Jan '54.

——, Washington. Travel 102: cover Oct '54.

——, Williamsburg. Natl. geog. 99: 296 Mar '51.

——, wooden. Natl. geog. 115: 712-3 May '59.

——, (boys). Natl. geog. 108: 512 (col.) Oct '55.

——, Y (Zanesville). Travel 104: 18 Aug '55.

——, Yugoslavia. Holiday 25: 83 Je '59.
"Bridge at Rimini" (Wilson). Con. 145: 39 Mar '60.
bridge builders, river. Natl. geog. 118: 699 (col.) Nov '60.
"Bridge of Sighs" (Venice). Travel 101: 7 May '54.
"Bridge on the River Dee" (Wilson). Con. ency. of ant., vol. 1, pl. 133.
"Bridge Over the Po" (Bellotto). Con. 144: 192 Dec '59.
bridge towers. Holiday 13: 113 Je '53; 14: 62 Sept '53.

—— (Strasbourg). Holiday 10: 55 Jl '51.
bridge. See also bridges.
Bridger, Jim. Brooks: Growth of a nation, p. 98.
Holiday 27: 185 May '60.
Bridges, Harry. Cur. biog. p. 70 (1950).
Bridges, Styles. Cur biog. p. 64 (1948).
bridges, marble (China). Natl. geog. 118: 210-11 (col.) Aug '60.

——, old. Rawson: Ant. pict. bk., p. 50.
Bridgetown (Barbados Island). Holiday 23: 40 (col.) Feb '58.
Natl. geog. 101: 370-1, 378, 380, 383 (part col.) Mar '52.
Bridgman, Percy Williams. Cur. biog. p. 65 (1955).
bridle bosses & bits, horse. Con. 140: 138 Nov '57.
brief bag. Holiday 28: 113 Aug '60.
brief case. Holiday 6: 5 (col.), 6 Dec '49; 7: 152 Je '50; 8: 14 Sept '50; 11: 59, 69 (col.) Je '52; 12: 83 Nov '52; 13: 9 May '53; 19: 118 May '56.
Brienno (Lake Como, Italy). Holiday 25: 94 (col.) Mar '59.
Brier, Howard M. Cur. biog. p. 60 (1951).
"Brig O' Doon" (Scotland). Natl. geog. 112: 456 (col.) Oct '57.
Briggs, Eugene S. Cur. biog. p. 67 (1948).
Briggs, Maj. Gen. James E. Cur. biog. p. 75 (1957).
Brigham, Clarence S. Cur. biog. p. 43 (1959).
Brighton (England). Holiday 8: 52-5 (part col.) Sept '50; 24: 47-9 Aug '58.
Brighton royal pavilion. Holiday 27: 127 (col.) Feb '60.

—— (banquet room). Con. 139: 245 Je '57.
brilliance, goddess of. Lehner: Pict. bk. of sym., p. 33.
Brind, Adm. Sir. Patrick. Cur. biog. p. 68 (1952).
Briney, Nancy. Cur. biog. p. 117 (1954).
Brink, Carol. Cur. biog. p. 75 (1946).
Jun. bk. of auth., p. 46.
Brinkley, David. Cur. biog. p. 52 (1960).
Brinton, Crane. Cur. biog. p. 45 (1959).
Brinton, Howard H. Cur. biog. p. 75 (1949).
Brisbane (Australia). Natl. geog. 109: 248 Feb '56.
Briscoe, Robert. Cur. biog. p. 76 (1957).
Brislee tower. See tower, Brislee.
bristlecone pine (oldest living thing). Natl. geog. 113: 354-72 (part col.) Mar '58.
Bristol, Lee H. Cur. biog. p. 53 (1962).
"The Bristol" (river boat). Amer. heri. vol. 6 no. 1 p. 8, 10, 13 (col.), 14 (fall '54).
British armour. See armour, British.
"British attack Washington, D.C." (Ryland). Amer. heri. vol. 6 no. 1 p. 51 (fall '54).
British Colonial hotel (Nassau). Holiday 14: 6 Jl '53.
British Columbia (Canada). Holiday 23: 86 (col.) Feb '58.
Jordan: Hammond's pict. atlas, p. 144-5 (col.).
Natl. geog. 114: 148-89 (part col.) Aug '58.

—— (beach). Holiday 25: 123 (col.) Feb '59.

—— (fiords). Travel 104: 20-2 Jl '55.

—— (map). Natl. geog. 114: 156-7 Aug '58.

—— (mts.). Amer. heri. vol. 11 no. 6 p. 60-1 (col.) (Oct '60).
British Columbia mortuary mask. Int. gr. soc.: Arts . . . p. 185 (col.).
British Guiana. Natl. geog. 107: 330-46 (part col.) Mar '55; 111: 852-74 Je '57.
Travel 106: 33-5 Dec '56.

—— (map). Natl. geog. 111: 857 Je '57.

British Honduras. Travel 102: 24 Sept '54.
British Isles (map). Natl. geog. 110: 11 Jl '56.
British museum. Holiday 18: 48-53 (part col.)
    Sept '55.
British naval officer (time of Nelson). Int. gr.
    soc.: Arts . . . p. 115 (col.).
British royal coach (coronation). Int. gr. soc.:
    Arts . . . p. 163 (col.).
British royal jewels. Int. gr. soc.: Arts . . . p.
    165 (col.).
British school boys. Int. gr. soc.: Arts . . . p.
    153. (col.).
"British surrender at Yorktown" (Trumball).
    Amer. heri. vol. 9 no. 4 p. 46-7 (col.)
    (Je '58).
    Natl. geog. 102: 154 (col.) Aug '52.
British West Indies (man & woman). Holiday
    18: 73 Oct '55.
—— (man & woman, comic). Holiday 15: 125
    Je '54; 16: 93 Oct '54, 32 Dec '54.
British Yeoman of the Guard. See Yeoman of
    the Guard.
Brittany (France). Holiday 7: 98-103 (part col.)
    Jan '50; 27: 79-83, 131 (part col.) Jan '60.
"Brittany landscape" (Gauguin). Con. 140: 195
    (col.) Dec '57.
Britten, Benjamin. Cooper: Con. ency. of music,
    p. 62.
    Cur. biog. p. 108 (1942); p. 73 (1961).
    Holiday 23: 138 Ap '58.
    Int. gr. soc.: Arts . . . p. 139 (col.).
Britton, Edgar C. Cur biog. p. 69 (1952).
Bro, Margueritte Harmon. Cur biog. p. 71
    (1952).
Broadhurst, Air Vice Marshall Harry. Cur. biog.
    p. 78 (1943).
Broadmoor hotel (Col. Springs). Holiday 8: 63
    Nov '50, 169 Dec '50; 10: 146 Oct '51, 77
    (col.) Nov '51; 12: 26 Nov '52; 14: 52-3
    (col.) Sept '53, 85 Nov '53, 8 Dec '53; 18:
    38 Dec '55; 24: 59 Dec '58; 26: 56 (col.)
    Jl '59; 27: 23 Jan '60.
broadside, presidential campaign (1876). Amer.
    heri. vol. 11 no. 6 .p. 7 (Oct '60).
broadsword. See glaive.
Broadwell, Dick. Horan: Pict. hist. of wild
    west, p. 163.
brocade (man making). Natl. geog. 113: 499
    (col.) Ap '58.
——, Persian. See Persian brocade.
Brock, Emma L. Jun. bk. of auth., p. 47.
Brock, Leonard C. Horan: Pict. hist. of wild
    west, p. 153.
Brock, W. L. Horan: Pict. hist. of wild west,
    p. 153.
Brock, Wallace R. Cur. biog. p. 60 (1958).
Brode, Wildred H. Cur. biog. (1963).
Brogan, Denis William. Cur. biog. p. 63 (1947).
Broglie, Prince Louis De. Cur. biog. p. 68
    (1955).
Brokenshire, Norman. Cur. biog. p. 71 (1950).
brokerage office (Wall St.). Holiday 19: 77 Feb
    '56.
Bromfield, Louis. Cur. biog. p. 67 (1944).
Bromley, Dorothy Dunbar. Cur. biog. p. 77
    (1946).
Bronk, Detlev W. Cur. biog. p. 77 (1949).
Bronowski, Jacob. Cur. biog. p. 62 (1958).

Bronson, Wilfred S. Jun. bk. of auth., p. 49.
Bronte sisters. Con. 135: 107 Ap '55.
    Natl. geog. 108: 338 Sept '55.
Bronx zoo (N.Y.). Holiday 12: 60 (col.) Sept
    '52.
—— (school). Natl. geog. 110: 694-706 Nov
    '56.
bronz bust (Epstein). Praeg. pict. ency., p. 479.
bronze carving (Hartung). Praeg. pict. ency.,
    p. 463.
bronze centerpiece, antique. Con. 143: XXX
    Mar '59.
bronze doors (baptistery). Praeg. pict. ency., p.
    298.
bronze figure, antique. Con. 134: 60 Sept '54.
—— (man on horse, by Riccio). Con. 145: 223
    Je '60.
bronze figures. Con. 143: 214-7 Je '59.
——, antique. Con. 136: 28-9 Sept '55.
bronze griffin head, Greek. Con. 145: 139 Ap
    '60.
bronze sculpture. Con. 126: 60 Aug '50; 142:
    233-7 Jan '59.
—— (Bertoldo). Con. 142: 268 Jan '59.
—— (Matare). Praeg. pict. ency., p. 494.
—— (Nineveh, 2270 B.C.). Praeg. pict ency.,
    p. 110.
—— (Pollauiolo). Con. 142: 267 Jan '59.
—— (Rodin). Con. 143: 92 Ap '59.
—— ("Spirit of youth"). Natl. geog. 111: 748
    (col.) Je '57.
bronze statue. Con. 145: 283 Je '60.
—— (Egyptian). Con. 136: LIV Sept '55.
—— (by Houdon). Natl. geog. 113: 261 Feb
    '58.
—— (Italian). Natl. geog. 111: 797 (col.) Je
    '57.
—— (by Kolbe). Praeg. pict. ency., p. 489.
—— (Maillol). Con. 145: 55 Mar '60.
—— (19th cent.) Con. 145: 55 Mar '60.
bronze statues. Praeg. pict. ency., p. 458.
bronze statuette (Etruscan). Con. 143: 103 Ap
    '59.
bronze tablet (Nigeria, armed warrior). Praeg.
    pict. ency., p. 546.
bronzes of Tada, Nigeria. Holiday 25: 49 Ap
    '59.
bronzes, Shang dynasty. Con. 136: 65-70 Sept
    '55.
Bronzino, A. (work of). Con. 139: 100 Ap '57.
brooch, antique. Con. 143: 188 May '59; 144:
    VII Dec '59.
—— (Beuerl, 17th cent.). Con. 144: 84 Nov
    '59.
——, diamond. Con. 135: XXV Mar '55.
——, diamond (antique). Con. 145: 129 Ap '60.
——, diamond (18th cent.) Con. 145: III May
    '60.
——, 11th cent. Con. 138: 236 Jan '57.
——, Italian (500 A.D.). Praeg. pict. ency., p.
    152 (col.).
——, lyre. Con. 144: XLIII Dec '59.
Brook, Alexander. Cur biog. p. 103 (1941).
Brook, Peter. Cur. biog. p. 75 (1961).
Brook farm (1844). Amer. heri. vol. 10 no. 3
    p. 58-9 (col.) (Ap '59).
Brooke, Sir Alan. Cur. biog. p. 105 (1941).
Brooke, Sir Basil. Cur. biog. p. 68 (1948).

Brooke, G.A.G. (work of). Con. 140: 110 Nov '57.

Brooke, L. Leslie. Jun. bk., of auth., p. 50.

Brooke-Popham, Sir Robert. Cur. biog. p. 107 (1941).

Brookfield zoo (Chicago). Natl. geog. 104: 795 (col.) Dec '53.

"Brookhill" (home in Va.). Natl. geog. 97: 578 (col.) May '50.

Brooking, Charles. Con. 134: IX Dec '54.
—— (work of). Con. 141: 59 Mar '58.

Brooklyn (N.Y.). Holiday 7: 34-59 (part col.) Je '50.
—— 1817. Amer. heri. vol. 7 no. 1 p. 15 (col.) (Dec '55).

Brooklyn bridge. Amer. heri. vol. 7 no. 6 p. 69, 71, 73, 110, 112 (part col.) (Oct '56); vol. 10 no. 6 p. 30-1 (col.) (Oct '59). Holiday 25: 78 Feb '59, 125 Je '59.
—— (opening, 1883). Amer. heri. vol. 5 no. 1 p. 12 (col.) (fall '53).

Brooklyn college. Holiday 7: 57 (col.) Je '50.

Brooklyn heights. Holiday 25: 65-9 Feb '59.

Brooklyn terminal boat piers. Natl. geog. 106: 791 (col.) Dec '54.

Brooks, Charles Wayland. Cur. biog. p. 65 (1947).

Brooks, David W. Cur. biog. p. 61 (1951).

Brooks, Gwendolyn. Cur. biog. p. 73 (1950). Holiday 28: 80 Dec '60.

Brooks, James. Cur. biog. p. 47 (1959).

Brooks, Matilda M. Cur. biog. p. 109 (1941).

Brooks, Overton. Cur. biog. p. 79 (1957).

Brooks, Van Wyck. Cur. biog. p. 110 (1941); p. 54 (1960).

Brooks, Walter R. Jun. bk. of auth., p. 52.

Broom, Capt. Thomas. Amer. heri. vol. 9 no. 2 p. 57 (col.) (Feb '58).

broom. Natl. geog. 101: 289 (col.) Mar '52 Rawson: Ant. pict. bk. p. 13, 52.

broom machine, old. Rawson: Ant. pict. bk., p. 52.

broom making. Natl. geog. 104: 804 (col.) Dec '53.

broom making roller. Rawson: Ant. pict. bk., p. 52.

brooms (girls sweep for a game). Natl. geog. 104: 845 (col.) Dec '53.

Brophy, Thomas D'Arcy. Cur. biog. p. 72 (1952).

Broschi, Carlo (Farinelli). See Farinelli (Carlo Broschi).

Brosio, Manlio. Cur. biog. p. 70 (1955).

Brossard, Edgar B. Cur. biog. p. 119 (1954).

Broster, D. K. Jun. bk. of auth., p. 53.

Brough, Louise. Cur. biog. p. 70 (1948).

Brouwer, Adriaen (work of). Praeg. pict. ency., p. 343 (col.).

Browder, Earl. Cur. biog. p. 69 (1944).

Browdy, Benjamin G. Cur. biog. p. 65 (1951).

Browere, John (masks by). Amer. heri. vol. 6 no. 4 p. 14, 19 (Je '55).

Brown, Maj. Gen. Albert Eger. Cur biog. p. 73 (1948).

Brown, Alberta L. Cur. biog. p. 63 (1958).

Brown, Arapaho. Horen: Pict. hist of wild west, p. 189.

Brown, Cecil. Cur. biog. p. 110 (1942).

Brown, Charles H. Cur. biog. p. 113 (1941).

Brown, Vice Adm. Charles R. Cur. biog. p. 65 (1958).

Brown, Clarence J. Cur. biog. p. 67 (1947).

Brown, David M. Cur. biog. p. 74 (1950).

Brown, Edmund G. Cur. biog. p. 56 (1960).

Brown, Edna A. Jun. bk. of auth., p. 54.

Brown, Ford Madox (work of). Amer. heri. vol. 11 no. 5 cover (col.) (Aug '60).

Brown, George. Cur. biog. (1963).

Brown, George Loring (work of). Amer. heri. vol. 10 no. 1 p. 19 (col.) (Dec '58).

Brown, George T. Amer. heri. vol. 11 no. 1 p. 110 (Dec '59).

Brown, Gilmor. Cur. biog. p. 74 (1944).

Brown, Harold. Cur. biog. p. 77 (1961).

Brown, Harrison. Cur. biog. p. 71 (1955).

Brown, Irving. Cur. biog. p. 66 (1951).

Brown, J. (work of). Con. 132: IV Nov '53.

Brown, Joe E. Cur. biog. p. 77 (1945).

Brown, Mrs. Joe T. Ameri. heri. vol. 10 no. 2 p. 38 (Feb '59).

Brown, John (by Curry). Amer. heri. vol. 6 no. 2 p. 5 (col.) (winter '55).
—— (Civil war plot). Travel 112: 44-7 Jl '59.
—— (hanging of). Amer. heri. vol. 6 no. 2 p. 7 (winter '55).

Brown, John (western). Horan: Pict. hist. of wild west, p. 148.

Brown, Lt. John Mason. Cur. biog. p. 112 (1942).

Brown, John Nichols. Holiday 27: 104 May '60.

Brown, Lewis H. Cur. biog. p. 70 (1947).

Brown, Margaret Wise. Jun. bk. of auth., p. 55.

Brown, Mather (work of). Con. 141: 270 Je '58.

Brown, Melvin. Holiday 11: 112 Jan '52.

Brown, Moses. Amer. heri. vol. 9 no. 3 p. 37 (Ap '58.)

Brown, Neil. Horan: Pict. hist. of wild west, p. 105

Brown, Newell. Cur. biog. p. 49 (1959).

Brown, P. (work of). Con. ency. of ant., vol. 3, pl. 84.

Brown, Paul. Jun. bk. of auth., p. 56.

Brown, Perry. Cur. biog. p. 79 (1949).

Brown, Prentiss M. Cur. biog. p. 79 (1943).

Brown Palace hotel (Denver). Travel 107: 58 Mar '57.

Brown univ. graduation. Holiday 11: 116 May '52.

Browne, Coral. Cur biog. p. 50 (1959).

Browne, Orris. Amer. heri. vol. 10 no. 1 p. 51 (Dec '58).

Brownell, Herbert, jr. Cur. biog. p. 76 (1944); p. 121 (1954).

Brownell, Samuel Miller. Cur. biog. p. 123 (1954).

a brownie. Holiday 6: 117 (col.) Aug '49. Travel 102: 7 Nov '54.
—— (riding fish). Holiday 28: 204 Nov '60.

brownies. Holiday 14: 1 Oct '53.
—— (Christmas, comic). Holiday 18: 132-3 Dec '55.

Browning, Maj. Gen. Frederick A.M. Cur. biog. p. 82 (1943).

Brownlow, "Parson" **W. G.** Amer. heri. vol. 11 no. 5 p. 54 (Aug '60).

Brown's raid, John (Harpers Ferry). Natl. geog. 111: 408 Mar '57.

Brownson, Charles B. Cur. biog. p. 74 (1955).

Bruant, Aristide (Toulouse-Lautrec). Con. 140: 60 Sept '57.

—— *See* also "Aristide Bruant".

Brubeck, Dave. Cur. biog. p. 79 (1956).

Bruce, David K. E. Cur. biog. p. 81 (1949); 79 (1961).

Bruce, Howard. Cur. biog. p. 74 (1948).

Bruce, James. Cur. biog. p. 82 (1949).

Brucker, Wilber Marion. Cur. biog. p. 75 (1955).

Brueghel, Jan (work of). Con. 137: IX (col.) May '56; 138: XXII (col.) Jan '57, XIV Nov '56; 145: LXXV (col.) May '60.

Brueghel the elder, Jan (work of). Con. 135: 199 May '55, 261 (col.) Je '55; 141: 253 (col.), 264 Je '58.

Brueghel, Peter (work of). Con. 129: LXXVIII Ap '52.

Brueghel, Pieter. Int. gr. soc.: Arts . . . p. 91 (col.).

—— (work of). Con. 129: 129 Je '52, 132: 209 Jan '54.

Brueghel the elder, Pieter (work of). Con. ency. of ant., vol. 1, pl. 155.

Con. 133: 95 Ap '54; 144: LIV-LV (col.) Dec '59.

Natl. geog. 101: 83 (col.) Jan '52.

Praeg. pict. ency., p. 311 (col.)

Brueghel the younger, Pieter (work of). Con. 133: LIII Mar '54, 257 Je '54; 140: 61 Sept '57; 141: 254 (col.) Je '58; 142: 26 Sept '58; 143: 191 May '59.

Natl. geog. 113: 806-7 (col.) Je '58.

Bruges (Belgium). Holiday 6: 22 Sept '49, 91 Oct '49; 11: 126 (col.) Je '52.

Natl. geog. 107: 630-64 (col.) May '55; 113: 812-3 (col.) Je '58.

—— (canal). Holiday 13: 117 Mar '53.

—— (cathedral, int.). Holiday 25: 47 (col.) Jan '59.

Bruhn, Erik. Cur. biog. p. 52 (1959).

Brumel, Valeri. Cur. biog. (1963).

Brumidi, Constantino (work of). Natl. geog. 102: 160-1, 164-6, 184-90 (col.) Aug '52.

Brunauer, Esther Caukin. Cur. biog. p. 71 (1947).

Brundage, Avery. Cur. biog. p. 76 (1948).

Brundage, Percival F. Cur. biog. p. 81 (1957).

Brunei Town (Borneo). Natl. geog. 116: 784-5 (col.) Dec '59.

Brunelleschi (Capella Pazzi, Florence). Praeg. pict. ency., p. 260.

Brunery, Francois (work of). Con. 139: XXXV, 147 May '57.

Brunery, M. (work of). Con. 137: XL Je '56.

Brunery, Marcel (work of). Con. 139: LVIII, 147 May '57.

Brunner, Edmund De S. Cur. biog. p. 67 (1958).

Brunner, Jean Adam. Cur. biog. p. 79 (1945).

Bruns, Franklin R., jr. Cur. biog. p. 125 (1954).

Brunsdale, Clarence Norman. Cur. biog. p. 127 (1954).

Brunswick lion (bronze). Praeg. pict. ency., p. 220.

Brush, paint. *See* paint brush.

brushpot (18th cent., imperial). Con. 132: 201 Jan '54.

Brussels (Belgium). Holiday 13: 27 Ap '53; 28: 28 Sept '60.

Natl. geog. 101: 699, 701 May '52; 113: 794-801 (part col.) Je '58.

Travel 105: 21 Ap '56; 109: 19-21 Ap '58; 111: back cover Feb '59, back cover Mar '59, back cover Ap '59, back cover May '59.

—— (city map). Travel 109: 17 Ap '58.

—— (18th cent.). Con. 133: IX Je '54.

—— (memorial work of Meunier). Praeg. pict. ency., p. 425.

Brussels world's fair. Natl. geog. 113: 798 Je '58.

Travel 110: 23-7 Jl '58.

—— (sym.). Holiday 23: 30 Jan '58.

—— (U.S. pavilion). Holiday 23: 19 May '58. Travel 109: 21 Ap '58; 110: 23 Jl '58.

Bruton Parish church (Williamsburg, Va.). Natl. geog. 106: 476-7 (col.) Oct '54.

Travel 106: 12 Dec '56.

Brutt, Ferdinand (work of). Con. 139: 147 May '57.

Bryan, Ernest Rowlett. Cur. biog. p. 76 (1950).

Bryan, James E, Cur. biog. p. 55 (1962).

Bryan, William Jennings. Amer. heri. vol. 9 no. 2 p. 67 (Feb '58).

—— (campaign poster). Amer. heri. vol. 7 no. 4 p. 28 (col.) (Je '56).

Bryan home, Wm. Jennings. Amer. heri. vol. 12 no. 1 p. 117 (Dec '60).

Bryant, Com. Benjamin. Cur. biog. p. 83 (1943).

Bryant, C. Farris. Cur. biog. p. 81 (1961).

Bryant, Joseph. Amer. heri. vol. 8 no. 6 p. 10 (Oct '57).

Bryant, Louise. Amer. heri. vol. 11 no. 2 p. 9 (Feb '60).

Bryce, James. Amer. heri. vol. 7 no. 2 p. 22 (Feb '56).

Bryce canyon. Holiday 16: 49 Jl '54; 19: 66 (col.) Je '56.

Jordan: Hammond's pict. atlas, p. 173, 175 (col.).

Natl. geog. 99: 743 (col.) Je '51; 114: 491-510 (part col.) Oct '58.

—— (map). Natl. geog. 114: 500-1 Oct '58.

Bryn Mawr College. Holiday 11: 60-5 (col.) May '52.

Brynner, Yul. Cur. biog. p. 81 (1956).

Bryson, Lyman. Cur. biog p 69 (1951).

Brzeska, Henri Gaudier (sculpture). Con. 138: 244-7 Jan '57.

Buber, Martin. Cur. biog. p. 94 (1953).

Buchanan, Frank. Cur. biog. p. 71 (1951).

Buchanan, James. Amer. heri. vol. 7 no. 3 p. 31 (Ap '56); vol. 7 no. 5 p. 6 (Aug '56). Jensen: The White House, p. 76-7, 79.

—— (Eicholtz). Amer. heri. vol. 7 no. 1 p. 20. (col.) (Dec '55).

—— (message to Congress, 1861). Amer. heri. vol. 7 no. 5 p. 90 (Aug '56).

Buchanan, Scott. Cur. biog. p. 56 (1962).

Buchanan, Wiley T. jr. Cur. biog. p. 83 (1957).

Buchanan home, Pres. James. Amer. heri. vol. 5 no. 3 cover (col.), 44-9 (part col.) (spring '54).

Buchannan, Bessie A. (Negro, N.Y. Legislature). Holiday 27: 74 (col.) Je '60.

Bucher, Walter H. Cur. biog. p. 84 (1957).

Bucher-Tilton scandal. Amer. heri. vol. 7 no. 4 p. 88-9 (Je '56).

Buchholz, Horst. Cur. biog. p. 57 (1960).

Buchwald, Art. Holiday 25: 121, 140 Mar '59.

Buchwald, Arthur. Cur. biog. p. 59 (1960).

Buck, Frank. Cur. biog. p. 85 (1943).

Buck, Gene. Cur. biog. p. 115 (1941).

Buck, Mrs. James Lawrence. Cur. biog. p. 73 (1947).

Buck, Paul H. Cur. biog. p. 77 (1955).

Buck, Pearl. Cur. biog. p. 83 (1956).
  Jensen: The White House, p. 283.

Buck, Rufus. Horan: Pict. hist. of wild west, p. 144.

Buck, Solon Justus. Cur. biog. p. 75 (1947).

Buck Hills Falls (Penn.). Jordan: Hammond's pict. atlas, p. 47 (col.).

bucket. Holiday 26: 59 Oct '59.

——, maple syrup. Natl. geog. 105: 478-9 (col.) Ap '54.

——, marble quarry. Natl. geog. 107: 756 (col.) Je '55.

——, oaken. Rawson: Ant. pict. bk., p. 48.

——, sap. See sap bucket.

——, wooden. Holiday 22: 179 Nov '57.

bucket & cup, well (antique). Natl. geog. 110: 729 (col.) Dec '56.

bucket & dipper (grain). Natl. geog. 115: 468 (col.) Ap '59.

Buckingham house (England). Con. 144: XX-XVI (col.) Jan '60.

Buckingham palace (London). Travel 101: 38 May '54.

Buckland-in-the-moor (England). Holiday 27: 2 (col.) May '60.

buckle & mordant (15th cent.). Con. 132: 53 Sept '53.

buckle of Isis (sym.). Lehner: Pict. bk. of sym., p. 27.

buckles, antique. Con. 140: 138 Nov '57.

Buckley, William F., jr. Cur. biog. p. 58 (1962).

Buckmaster, Henrietta. Cur. biog. p. 79 (1946).

Buckner, Maj. Gen. Simon B. Cur. biog. p. 113 (1942).
  Pakula: Cent. album, p. 93.

Budd, Edward G., jr. Cur. biog. p. 84 (1949).

Buddha. Con. 145: LXIV Ap '60.
  Holiday 12: 30 Sept '52, 64 (col.) Oct '52; 14: 77 Aug '53, 49 Oct '53; 19: 1 Feb '56; 23: 15 (col.) May '58; 24: 91 Aug '58.
  Natl. geog. 105: 734 (col.) Je '54.
  Travel 101: 18 Ap '54; 112: cover Dec '59.

—— (head). Travel 111: 49 Jan '59.

—— (sym.). Lehner: Pict. bk. of sym., p. 42.

——, Bamian. Natl. geog. 114: 12 (col.) Jl '58.

——, bronze. Con. 133: LVI May '54.

——, Ceylon. Travel 111: 22 Jan '59.

——, child (Tibet). Natl. geog. 108: 32 Jl '55.

——, Chinese (antique wood). Con. 132: LVI Sept '53.

——, Chinese (cave). Natl. geog. 99: 386, 389, 398, 400-1 (part col.) Mar '51.

——, Chinese (head). Con. 138: XXVIII Dec '56.

——, Chinese (head, wood). Con. 139: VI May '57.

——, Emerald (Bangkok). Holiday 20: 12 Oct '56.

——, Gautama (sym.) Lehner: Pict. bk. of sym., p. 42.

——, gilded. Holiday 12: 55 (col.) Dec '52.

——, gold (Laos). Natl. geog. 117: 65 (col.) Jan '60.

——, gold (Thailand). Natl. geog. 116: 787 (col.) Dec '59.

——, The Grand. Lehner: Pict. bk. of sym., p. 49.

——, Great (Japan). Natl. geog. 104: 98 Jl '53; 118: 765 (col.) Dec '60.

——, holy disciple of (sym.). Lehner: Pict. bk. of sym., p. 48.

——, India (cave sculpture). Natl. geog. 103: 667, 669, 671 May '53.

——, Kamakura. Holiday 6: 13 Jl '49.

——, marble. Con. 138: LXVI Jan '57.

——, Nepal. Holiday 21: 71 May '57.

——, Nepal (lacquer). Con. 138: LI Nov '56.

——, new born. Lehner: Pict. bk. of sym., p. 48.

——, Sarnath (India). Holiday 6: 73 Jl '49.

——, Siam. Holiday 18: 31 Nov '55; 20: 200 Nov '56.

——, temple. See temple Buddha.

Buddha footprints (sym.). Lehner: Pict. bk. of sym., p. 42.

Buddha Sakyamuni (Japan). See Sakyamuni Buddha (Japan).

Buddha shrine. See shrine, Buddha.

Buddha statue. Holiday 6: 92 Nov '49.

Buddha tooth (elephant, procession). Holiday 20: 98 (col.) Aug '56.

Buddha worshipers. Natl. geog. 117: 64 (col.) Jan '60.

Buddhagaya temple. See temple of Buddhagaya.

Buddhist. Natl. geog. 118: 216-7 (col.) Aug '60.

—— (fire-walking, Japan). Natl. geog. 118: 760 (col.) Dec '60.

Buddhist double ax (divine). Lehner: Pict. bk. of sym., p. 42.

Buddhist god (Lhasa). Natl. geog. 108: 21 (col.) Jl '55.

Buddhist mace. See mace, Buddhist.

Buddhist monk. Con. 142: X Jan '59.

Buddhist novice (boy). Natl. geog. 117: 53 (col.) Jan '60.

Buddhist stupa (India). Praeg. pict. ency., p. 524.

—— (Java). Holiday 18: 107 (col.) Sept '55.

Buddhist temple (India). Travel 111: 18 Jan '59.

Budenny, Semyon M. Cur. biog. p. 117 (1941).

Budenz, Louis F. Cur. biog. p. 72 (1951).

Budge, Donald. Cur. biog. p. 119 (1941).

Budva (Yugoslavia). Natl. geog. 99 156 (col.) Feb '51.

Buechner, Frederick. Cur. biog. p. 53 (1959).

Buechner, Thomas S. Cur. biog. p. 83 (1961).

Buell, Don Carlos. Pakula: Cent. album, p. 95.

Buenos Aires (Argentina). Holiday 11: 102-11 (part col.) Mar '52; 13: 13 (col.) May '53; 14: 13 (col.) Jl '53, 115 (col.) Aug '53, 84 (col.) Oct '53; 15: 13 Ap '54; 20: 119 (col.) Sept '56; 21: 12 (col.) May '57; 22: 96 (col.) Jl '57; 24: 148 (col.) Dec '58; 25: 90-1 (col.) Je '59; 28: back cover (col.) Oct '60.
  Natl. geog. 108: 756-7 (col.) Dec '55; 113: 301 (col.) Mar '58.
  Travel 105: 13 Jan '56; 108: 50-1 Nov '57; 112: 17 Sept '59.

—— **(400th anniversary of Argentine's independence, obelisk).** Travel 101: cover Feb '54.

——. **(President's palace).** Holiday 27: 20 (col.) Je '60.

Buetow, Herbert P. Cur. biog. p. 61 (1960).
Buff, Conrad. Jun. bk. of auth., p. 58.
Buff, Mary March. Jun. bk. of auth., p. 59.
Buffalo (N.Y.). Holiday 18: 94-99 (part col.) Aug '55.
  Natl. geog. 110: 612-3 Nov '56; 115: 464-5 Ap '59.

—— **(skyway).** Natl. geog. 110: 417 Sept '56.
Buffalo Bill. See Cody, William Frederick.
"Buffalo calling" (Dupree). Natl. geog. 107: 372 (col.) Mar '55.
"Buffalo chase" (Catlin). Amer. heri. vol. 6 no. 1 p. 33 (col.) (fall '54).
buffalo chase (man on horse). Amer. heri. vol. 1 no. 4 p. 7 (summer '50).
"Buffalo hunt" (Catlin). Con. 144: 69 Sept '59.
"Buffalo hunt" (Ma-Pe-Wi). Natl. geog. 107: 357 (col.) Mar '55.
buffalo hunt, Indian. Brooks: Growth of a nation, p. 23.
"Buffalo hunter". Amer. heri. vol. 6 no. 1 cover (col.) (fall '54).
buffalo robe. Natl. geog. 107: 376 Mar '55.
buffalo sketch, French artist (16th cent). Amer. heri. vol. 12 no. 1 p. 79 (Dec '60).
"Buffalo stampede" (Jackson). Amer. heri. vol. 7 no. 5 p. 39 (col.) (Aug '56).
Buffet, Bernard. Cur. biog. p. 55 (1959).
  Holiday 21: 69 (col.) Ap '57.
  Praeg. pict. ency., p. 468.
buffet. Holiday 20: 13 (col.) Sept '56.
——, **James I.** Con. 132: XXV Sept '53.
——, **Kenilworth.** Con. 127: 99 May '51.
——, **Napoleonic empire.** Con. 145: LIV Mar '60.
——, **17th cent.** Con. 133: XXIX Ap '54.
——, **16th cent.** Con. 140: 112 Nov '57.
buffet-chest. Holiday 24: 133 Nov '58.
"Buffoon" (Goya). Con. 142: 258 Jan '59.
Buford, John. Pakula: Cent. album, p. 97.
Buford, John Lester. Cur. biog. p. 85 (1956).
Bugaboo mt. group (climbers). Natl. geog. 114: 188-9 (col.) Aug '58.
Bugas, John Stephen. Cur. biog. p. 77 (1947).
buggy. Holiday 16: 62 Dec '54.
—— **(Bermuda).** Holiday 23: 70 (col.) Je '58.
—— **(1860-).** Amer. heri. vol. 7 no. 6 p. 90-3 (col.) (Oct '56).
—— **(girls).** Holiday 25: 67 (col.) Je '59.

—— **(girls & man).** Holiday 21: 28 (col.) Jan '57.
—— **(horse).** Amer. heri. vol. 9 no. I p. 65 (col.) (Dec '57).
  Brooks: Growth of a nation, p. 70, 241, 244
  Holiday 6: 56 (col.) Oct '49; 12: 70 Sept '52, 131 Dec '52; 14: 63 Sept '53, 123 (col.) Oct '53, 109 Nov '53, 178 Dec '53; 23: 51 (col.) Mar '58; 26: 53 Oct '59.
  Jensen: The White House, p. 166.
  Jordan: Hammond's pict. atlas, p. 69 (col.).
  Travel 103: inside cover, 45 May '55; 105: 14, 29 May '56.
—— **(horse, boy & girl).** Holiday 27: 53 (col.) May '60.
—— **(horse & driver).** Holiday 11: 105 Mar '52; 19: 80 (col.) Mar '56; 20: 21 (col.) Oct '56; 22: 128 Sept '57, 117 (col.) Oct '57, 41, 63 (col.) Dec '57.
  Natl. geog. 113: 27 (col.) Jan '58; 118: 706 (col.) Nov '60.
—— **(horse, man, woman).** Natl. geog. 116: 110 (col.) Jl '59.
—— **(horse & men).** Holiday 10: 33 Jl '51.
  Natl. geog. 107: 645 (col.) May '55.
—— **(horse, people).** Holiday 21: 143 (col.) Mar '57; 23: 109 (col.) Mar '58.
—— **(horse, people, Poland).** Natl. geog. 114: 395 (col.) Sept '58.
—— **(horse, riders).** Natl. geog. 105: 230 (col.) Feb '54; 108: 193 (col.) (Aug '55).
—— **horse, snow).** Holiday 10: 58 Dec '51.
—— **(horse, man, western).** Holiday 24: 42 (col.) Oct '58.
——, **(horse, man, woman, old fashioned.** Holiday 18: 89 Sept '55.
——, **antique.** Travel 109: 31 Je '58.
——, **Canada.** Travel 114: 16 Jl '60.
——, **doll.** See doll carriage.
——, **Italy.** Labande: Naples, p. 199.
——, **Rome.** Natl. geog. 100: 720 (col.) Dec '51.
——, **salesman's (horses).** Brooks: Growth of a nation, p. 231.
——, **Turkey (horse).** Osward: Asia Minor, pl. IV (col.).
buggy. See also carriage.
buggy step. Rawson: Ant. pict. bk., p. 74.
Bugher, Dr. John C. Cur. biog. p. 97 (1953).
bugle, Civil war. Holiday 28: 57 Sept '60.
bugler. (Barbados). Natl. geog. 101: 387 (col.) Mar '52.
—— **(Poland).** Natl. geog. 114: 385 (col.) Sept '58.
Buick auto. See automobile, Buick.
buildings (burning). Amer. heri. vol. 7 no. 1 p. 68-9 (col.) (Dec '55).
Buley, Roscoe Carlyle. Cur. biog. p. 74 (1951).
Bulganin, Nikolai A. Cur. biog. p. 79 (1955).
Bulkeley memorial, Rev. Peter. See memorial tablet, Rev. Peter Bulkeley.
Bull, Ole. Amer. heri. vol. 4 no. 2 p. 12, 14 (winter '53).
bull, stone (guard, Persia's throne room). Natl. geog. 104: 787 Dec '53.
bull-dancer (Greek sculpture). Ceram: March of arch., p. 60.

bull head (caps on column, Persepolis). Travel 113: 32 Feb '60.

——, carved (Persia). Travel 113: 32 Feb '60.

bull Nandi, sacred (temple, Jaipur). Natl. geog. 118: 461 (col.) Oct '60.

bull of Persepolis (sculpture). Travel 105: 25 Jan '56.

Bullard, Sir. Edward. Cur. biog. p. 129 (1954).

bulldog, English (sym.). Lehner: Pict bk. of sym., p. 60.

bulldozer. Natl. geog. 113: 345 (col.) Mar '58; 117: 343 (col.) Mar '60.

bullet melting pan. See pan (for melting bullets).

bulletins, travel. Holiday 20: 129 Nov '56.

bullets, gun. Natl. geog. 107: 568 (col.) Ap '55.

bullfight. Holiday 10: 95 (col.) Dec '51; 11: 25, 52-5 (part col.) Jan '52, 55 Mar '52; 12: 33 Sept '52; 13: 94 (col.) Ap '53; 20: 80 (col.) Nov '56; 21: 64-5 Jan '57, 30 (col.) May '57; 22: 105 (col.) Oct '57; 23: 28 Je '58; 25: 173 Mar '59, 37 (col.) Ap '59; 28: 141 (col.) Oct '60.
Travel 106: 24 Oct '56.

—— (Arles, Fr.). Natl. geog. 109: 676-7 (part col.) May '56.

—— (Basque). Holiday 23: 90 Mar '58.

—— (comic). Holiday 13: 1 Ap '53.

—— (Mexico). Holiday 26: 61 (col.) Nov '59.

—— (Okinawa). Natl. geog. 107: 280 Feb '55.

—— (Portugal). Holiday 6: 106 (col.) Sept '49.

—— (Spain). Holiday 23: 65 Jan '58.
Travel 107: 22 Ap '57.

—— (statue). Holiday 12: 83 Sept '52.

bull fight arena (Savillia). Natl geog. 99: 512 (col.) Ap '51.

—— (Spain). Natl. geog. 97: 426 (col.) Ap '50.

bull fight arena & toreros. Holiday 15: 34-5, 65 (col.) May '54.

bullfight ring. Holiday 24: 110 (col.) Dec '58.

—— (Lisbon, Portugal). Holiday 22: 107 (col.) Nov '57.

—— (Spain). Holiday 26: 107 (col.) Dec '59.

bullfighter. Holiday 7: 49 (col.) Je '50; 24: 109 Aug '58; 26: 248 Dec '59; 27: 195 (col.) May '60.
Travel 114: 40-5 Nov '60.

—— (amateur). Natl. geog. 109: 324 Mar '56.

—— (lady). Holiday 20: 139 Nov '56.

—— (Mexico). Natl. geog. 100: 793 (col.) Dec '51; 107: 240 (col.) Feb '55.

—— (Spain). Natl. geog. 97: 435 Ap '50; 105: 180, 185 (col.) Feb '54.

bullfighter. See also matador, toreador, torero.

bullfighter's cape (Spain). Natl. geog. 99: 529 (col.) Ap '51.

Bullis, Harry A. Cur. biog. p. 81 (1946).

Bulloch, Sailing master Irvine. Amer. heri. vol. 10 no. 1 p. 50 (Dec '58).

Bulosan, Carlos. Cur. biog. p. 82 (1946).

bulrush boat. Natl. geog. 107: 134 Jan '55.

bumba (dugout boat, Haiti). Holiday 5: 61 (col.) Feb '49.

bumboats (Port Said, Egypt). Natl. geog. 105: 491 (col). Ap '54.

bump races (row boats). Holiday 7: 118 (col.) Je '50.

Bump tavern (Catskill turnpike). Amer. heri. vol. 3 no. 3 p. 34 (spring '52).

Bumpstead, Albert H. Natl. geog. 112: 38 Jl '57.

Bunche, Ralph J. Cur. biog. p. 77 (1948).

bunder boat (Karachi). Natl. geog. 105: 512 (col.) Ap '54.

Bundesen, Herman Niels. Cur. biog. p. 80 (1948).

Bundy, McGeorge. Cur. biog. p. 62 (1962).

bunk bed (girls). Natl. geog. 107: 766 (col.) Je '55.

—— (refugee ship). Natl. geog. 107: 866 Je '55.

Bunker, Ellsworth. Cur. biog. p. 131 (1954).

Bunker, George M. Cur. biog. p. 86 (1957).

Bunker Hill monument. Holiday 16: 106 Jl '54.
Natl. geog. 107: 746 (col.) Je '55.

bunkhouse, cowboy. See cowboy bunkhouse.

bunks, ship. Natl. geog. 116: 316 Sept '59.

Bunting, Earl. Cur. biog. p. 78 (1947).

Bunyan, Paul (folklore hero). Amer. heri. vol. 1 no. 3 p. 3, 79 (col.) (Spring '50).
Natl. geog. 114: 653 (col.) Nov '58.

—— (statue). Natl. geog. 105: 827 Je '54.

Bunyan, Paul (& Babe, blue ox). Holiday 7: 20 (col.) Ap '50; 14: 140 Jl '53; 18: 28 Aug '55.

Buontalenti, Bernardo (work of). Con. 142: 53 Sept '58.

buoy. Amer. heri. vol. 9 no. 6 p. 95 (Oct '58).
Natl. geog. 102: 338, 361. (col.) Sept '52; 106: 782 (col.) Dec '54.

—— (girls). Natl. geog. 98: 232 Aug '50.

——, life. Face of Amer., p. 57 (col.).

——, life (sym.). Lehner: Pict. bk. of sym., p. 64.

Burbank, Luther. Brooks: Growth of a nation, p. 205.

Burchard, John E. Cur. biog. p. 69 (1958).

Burchfield, Charles. Holiday 18: 98 (col.) Aug '55.

Burchfield, Charles Ephraim. Cur. biog. p. 115 (1942); p. 85 (1961).

Burdell, Edwin S. Cur. biog. p. 73 (1952).

Burdett, Winston M. Cur. biog. p. 89 (1943).

Burdick, Quentin N. Cur. biog. (1963).

Burdick, Usher L. Cur. biog. p. 76 (1952).

bureau, antique. Con. ency. of ant., vol. 1, p. 60.
Con. 133: VIII Ap '54; 141: XLIII May '58.

——, chippendale. Con. 134: XLVI Sept '54; 139: XXVIII May '57; 143: IV Mar '59.

——, 18th cent. Con. 135: XXII May '55; 140: LII Jan '58; 141: XIV Je '58.

——, George I. Con. 139: LVIII May '57.

——, George II. Con. 140: XXIX Dec '57.

——, Louis XV. Con. 140: 260 Jan '58.

——, Louis XVI. Con. 138: I Jan '57.

——, Queen Anne. Con. ency. of ant., vol. 1, pl. 13.
Con. 126: 69 Aug '50; 132: VI Nov '53; 136: XXV Sept '55; 140: XLV Sept '57; 142:

XXI Sept '58; 144: XX Sept '59; 145: XLIV Mar '60, XL May '60.

——, 17th cent. Con. ency. of ant., vol. 3, pl. 16.

——, tambour. *See* tambour bureau.

——, William & Mary. Con. 134: XLV Sept '54; 142: XXI Sept '58.

bureau à cylindre, Louis XVIII. Con. 143: 210, 213 Je '59.

bureau bookcase. Con. 132: XXII Nov '53.

——, breakfront chippendale. Con. 140: 183 Dec '57.

——, broom wood (Sandeman). Con. 145: 99-100 Ap '60.

——, chippendale. Con. 129: XX Ap '52; 132: VI Nov '53; 133: inside back cover May 54; 135: XXIX Mar '55; 138: XXXIX Jan '57; 140: XIII Dec '57; 142: VI Jan '59; 144: LVIII Jan '60.

——, 18th cent. Con. 133: XXXII May '54; 138: XXIV Nov '56, XLV Jan '57; 140: back cover Jan '58; 141: XVIII Ap '58; 142: XXVIII Nov '58; 145: XLI May '60.

——, George I. Con. 133: XXVII Ap '54; 139: I Mar '57.

——, George II. Con. 142: 57 Sept '58.

——, Queen Anne. Con. ency. of ant., vol. 1, pl. 14, p. 26.
Con. 129: XLIII Je '52; 132: XXXVIII Nov '53, 137: L Je '56; 139: XXXVIII Ap '57; 140: XXXIII Sept '57, LVI Dec '57; 143: 203 Je '59; 145: XXII May '60.

——, sheraton. Con. 134: XXIV Sept '54.

——, William & Mary. Con. 133: XXVI May '54; 135: XLIV May '55.

bureau cabinet, antique. Con. 129: 61 Ap '52; 134: 46 Sept '54; 143: XXXIX Mar '59, LIII Je '59.

—— (18th cent). Con. 132: L Nov '53; 141: XLI Mar '58.

bureau cabinet (18th cent.). Con. 145: XXII, XXXI Mar '60, 272 Je '60.

—— (lacquer). Con. 140: 180 Dec '57.

—— (lacquer, Granger) Con. 145: LXXXVI Je '60.

——, Queen Anne. Con. 139: 265 Je '57; 141: VIII-IX Mar '58.

——, William & Mary. Con. 129: XLI Ap '52.

bureau Capucin, Louis XV. Con. 139: 195 May '57, 265 Je '57.

——, Louis XV (marquetry). Con. 140: 57 Sept '57.

bureau-de-dame, Louis XV. Con. 135: 53 Mar '55; 137: 212 May '56; 143: 73 Ap '59.

bureau desk (18th cent.) Con. 142: XXXVII Jan '59.

bureau dos d' ane, Louis XV. Con. 144: XLII Dec '59.

bureau dressing table (18th cent.). Con. 138: 185 Dec '56.

Bureau of chemistry members (1884). Brooks: Growth of a nation, p. 208.

Bur. of labor building *See* U.S. Bur. of Labor building.

bureau on stand (18th cent.). Con. 142: XXXIV Nov '58.

bureau plat, English (19th cent.). Con. 144: 58 Sept '59.

——, English antique Con. 142: XXIX Jan '59.

——, Louis XV. Con. 133: 265 Je '54; 140: 115 Nov '57; 141: XIX Je '58; 143: 211, 265 Je '59; 144: IV Jan '60; 145: XXI May '60, XXI May '60, XXXIII Je '60.

bureau secretaire (17th cent.). Con. ency. of ant., vol. 3, pl. 16.

bureau table, Chippendale. Con. ency. of ant., vol. 1 pl. 41.

Burgenstock palace & hotel (Switzerland). Holiday 19: 56-61 (part col.) May '56.

Burgess, Carter L. Cur. biog. p. 88 (1957).

Burgess, G. H. (work of). Amer. heri. vol. 2 no. 3 p. 30 (col.) (spring '51).

Burgess, Robert W. Cur. biog. p. 63 (1960).

Burgess, Thonton W. Jun. bk. of auth., p. 60.

Burgess, Warren Randolph. Cur. biog. p. 85 (1949).

"Burghers of Calais" (Rodin). Praeg. pict. ency., p. 398.

Burghley, Lord David George B.C. Cur. biog. p. 87 (1956).

Burgis, William (work of). Con. ency. of ant., vol. 3, pl. 89.

Burgkmair, Hans (work of). Con. 133: 51 Mar '54.

burglar. Holiday 21: 26 Ap '57, 193 Je '57. Horan: Pict. hist. of wild west, p. 15.

Burglon, Nora. Jun. bk. of auth., p. 61.

burgomaster, German. Natl. geog. 111: 264 (col.) Feb '57.

"Burgomaster's room" (de Hooch). Con. 145: 278 Je '60.

Burgos cathedral. Holiday 15: 37 May '54.

Burgoyne, Gen. John. Amer. heri. vol. 7 no. 4 cover Je '56.

—— (portrait by Ramsay). Con. 139: 76 Ap '57.

Burgoyne coat of arms. *See* coat of arms, Gen. Burgoyne.

"Burgoyne surrenders to Gates, 1777" (Trumbull). Amer heri. vol. 7 no. 4 p. 4-5 (col.) (Je '56).

"Burgoyne talks to Indians". Amer. heri. vol. 7 no. 4 p. 6 (Je '56).

burial mound. *See* Indian burial mound.

burial shrine (Pakistan). Travel 108: 31 Nov '57.

Burke, Rear Adm. Arleigh A. Cur. biog. p. 81 (1955).
Natl. geog. 115: 590 Ap '59.

Burke, Billy. Durant: Pict. hist. of Amer. circus, p. 151.

Burke, Thomas A. Cur. biog. p. 133 (1954).

Burke, William R. Cur. biog. p. 87 (1961).

Burlacy, Sir John (Flemish art). Con. 126: 165 Dec '50.

Burleigh, Harry T. Cur. biog. p. 121 (1941).

Burma. Holiday 20: 44-7 (part col.) Sept '56; 25: 168 (col.) Mar '59.

—— (woman's head). Int. gr. soc.: Arts . . . p. 181 (col.).

Burmese ballet. Holiday 20: 47 Sept '56.

Burne-Jones, Sir. Edward (work of). Con. 140: XLV Dec '57; 141: cover (col.) Je '58; 142: 83 Nov '58.

Burnet, Sir Macfarlane. Cur. biog. p. 135 (1954).

Burnett, Carol. Cur. biog. p. 65 (1962).
Burnett, Frances Hodgson (book illus. by). Amer. heri. vol. 8 no. 1 p. 33 (Dec '56).
Burnett, Hallie Southgate. Cur. biog. p. 136 (1954).
Burnett, Whit. Cur. biog. p. 293 (1941).
Burney, Charles (Reynolds). Con. 133: 179 May '54.
Burney, Leroy E. Cur. biog. p. 90 (1957).
Burnham, Daniel H. Amer. heri. vol. 11 no. 6 p. 11 (Oct '60).
Burnham, James. Cur. biog. p. 122 (1941).
Burnham, T.O. H.P. (work of). Amer. heri. vol. 2 no. 4 p. 38 (col.) (summer '51).
"burning giraffe" (Dali). Praeg. pict. ency., p. 453.
Burns, Sir Alan. Cur. biog. p. 98 (1953).
Burns, Arthur F. Cur. biog. p. 101 (1953).
Burns, Edward M. Cur. biog. p. 137 (1954).
Burns, Eedson Louis M. Cur. biog. p. 83 (1955).
Burns, Eveline M. Cur. biog. p. 65 (1960).
Burns, George. Holiday 7: 62 Mar '50.
Burns, Hendry S.M. Cur. biog. p. 139 (1954).
Burns, James MacGregor. Cur. biog. p. 67 (1962).
Burns, John Horne. Holiday 5: 32 Feb '49.
Burns, John L. Cur. biog. p. 67 (1960).
Burns, Robert. Natl. geog. 112: 450 (col.), 478 Oct '57.
Burns, William J. Amer. heri. vol. 11 no. 1 p. 10 (Dec '59).
Burns country, Robert. Natl. geog. 112: 456-7 (col.) Oct '57.
Burns home, Robert. Holiday 5: 113 (col.) Feb '49; 8: 46 (col.) Dec '50.
Burnside, Ambrose E. Pakula: Cent. album, p. 99.
Burnside's bridge (Maryland). Amer. heri. vol. 9 no. 5 p. 54, 56 (col.) (Aug '58).
Burpees, David. Cur. biog. p. 85 (1955).
Burr, Raymond. Cur. biog. p. 89 (1961).
Burrini, Giovanni Antonio (work of). Con. 144: 24 Sept '59.
Burroughs, John. Amer. heri. vol. 10: no. 6 p. 41 (Oct '59).
Burrows, Abe. Cur. biog. p. 78 (1951).
Burrows, Jim. Horan: Pict. hist of wild west, p. 153.
Burrows, Millar. Cur. biog. p. 89 (1956).
Burrows, Rube. Horan: Pict. hist. of wild west, p. 153.
Burton, Alan C. Cur. biog. p. 91 (1956).
Burton, Harold. Holiday 7: 46 (col.) Feb '50.
Burton, Harold H. Cur. biog. p. 81 (1945). Holiday 7: 78 Feb '50.
Burton, James. Ceram: March of arch., p. 135.
Burton, Jean. Cur. biog. p. 82 (1948).
Burton, Richard. Cur. biog. p. 68 (1960).
Burton, Shakespeare (work of). Con. 139: XXII Mar '57.
Burton, Virginia Lee. Cur. biog. p. 90 (1943). Jun. bk. of auth., p. 62.
Bury, Adrian (work of). Con. 126: 217 Dec '50.
bus. Amer. heri. vol. 1 no. 3 p. 14 (Spring '50). Holiday 5: 19 (col.) Je '49; 6: 23 (col.) Nov '49; 7: 117, 123 (col.) Feb '50, 91 (col.)

Mar '50, 123 (col.) May '50, 111 (col.) Je '50; 8: 7 (col.) Oct '50, 79 (col.) Nov '50; 10: 149 (col.) Oct '51; 11: 15 (col.) Jan '52, 5 (col.) Feb '52, 140 Je '52; 12: 46 (col.) Jl '52, 105 Oct '52; 14: 133 Jl '53; 15: 27, 95 Jan '54, 23 Feb '54; 16: 68 (col.) Jl '54, 71 (col.) Nov '54, 145 Dec '54; 18: 136 (col.) Dec '55; 19: 4 (col.), 22 Feb '56, 92 May '56, 90 Je '56; 20: 119 (col.) Oct '56, 131 (col.) Dec '56; 21: 4 (col.) Mar '57, 123 Ap '57, 177 May '57, 39 Je '57; 23: 4 (col.) Jan '58.
  Natl. geog. 98: 4 Jl '50; 103: 9 (col.) Jan '53; 106: 540 Oct '54; 109: 248 Feb '56.
——. Travel 104: 70 Nov '55; 106: 56 Dec '56; 111: 25 Je '59.
—— (cartoon). Holiday 14: 54 Sept '53.
—— (int.). Holiday 13: 79 (col.) Mar '53.
—— (man washing). Natl. geog. 98: 37 Jl '50.
—— (1910). Holiday 12: 69 Sept '52.
—— (passengers boarding). Holiday 10: 87 (col.) Dec '51.
  Natl. geog. 98: 36 Jl '50.
——, Afghanistan. Natl. geog. 104: 419 Sept '53.
——, Austria. Natl. geog. 99: 771 Je '51.
——, Chile. Natl. geog. 117: 186-7, 189 (col.) Feb '60.
——, Corsica. Travel 105: 43 Ap '56.
——, Cyprus island. Natl. geog. 109: 877 Je '56.
——, Edinburgh. Natl. geog. 112: 476 Oct '57.
——, Egypt (double deck). Holiday 10: 120 (col.) Dec '51.
——, English. Natl. geog. 102: 39 Jl '52; 104: 292-3 (col.) Sept '53.
——, English (double deck). Natl. geog. 114: 61 (col.) Jl '58.
——, French. Natl. geog. 111: 771 (col.) Je '57.
——, Greece (bride's dowry). Natl. geog. 109: 65 (col.) Jan '56.
——, Greyhound. Holiday 5: 2 (col.) Feb '49, 86 (col.) Mar '49; 14: 139 (col.) Jl '53.
——, Haiti. Holiday 7: 99 (col.) Mar '50.
——, Hong Kong. Natl. geog. 105: 243 (col.) Feb '54.
——, Indonesia. Natl. geog. 108: 358 (col.) Sept '55.
——, Iranian. Natl. geog. 100: 444 Oct '51.
——, Isle of Skye. Natl. geog. 102: 99 (col.) Jl '52.
——, Mecca. Natl. geog. 104: 49 (col.) Jl '53.
——, Norway. Natl. geog. 104: 691 Nov '53; 111: 102 (col.) Jan '57.
——, open sightseeing. Natl. geog. 105: 777 (col.) Je '54.
——, Paris. Natl. geog. 100: 719 (col.) Dec '51; 101: 776 (col.) Je '52.
——, Peking. Natl. geog. 118: 212, 221. (col.) Aug '60.
——, Peruvian motor. Natl. geog. 98: 436 (col.) Oct '50.
——, Puerto Rico. Natl. geog. 99: 440 Ap '51.
——, school (park). Natl. geog. 108: 515 (col.) Oct '55.
——, sightseeing. Natl. geog. 110: 139 Jl '56.
——, Spain. Natl. geog. 97: 444 (col.) Ap '50.

——, **Sumatra.** Natl. geog. 108: 389 (col.) Sept '55.

——, **Switzerland.** Natl. geog. 110: 441 (col.) Oct '56.
Travel 113: 53 Je '60.

——, **tour.** Travel 106: 57 Oct '56.

——, **double deck.** Natl. geog. 106: 216 (col.) Aug '54.

bus driver (in bus). Natl. geog. 98: 3, 41 Jl '50.

bus lines of U.S. Jordan: Hammond's pict. atlas, p. 14.

bus terminal (Jerusalem). Natl. geog. 98: 720 (col.) Dec '50.

Busch, Augustus A. (children in goat cart). Amer. heri. vol. 10 no. 1 p. 86 (Dec '58).

Busch, Fritz. Cur. biog. p. 84 (1946).

Bush, Prescott S. Cur. biog. p. 117 (1942); p. 141 (1954).

Bush, Vannevar. Cur. biog. p. 80 (1947).

bushel measure (English). Natl. geog. 103: 819 Je '53.

bushman (Africa). Holiday 20: 56-61 (part col.) Oct '56.

Bushnell, Asa S. Cur. biog. p. 78 (1952).

Busiri, G. B. (work of). Con. 141: 218 Je '58.

Busoni, Ferruccio. Cooper: Con. ency. of music, p. 63.

Busoni, Rafaello. Jun. bk. of auth., p. 63.

Buss, Robert W. (work of). Con. 132: 41 Sept '53.

bust (Amenhotep III). Con. 144: 208 Dec '59.

—— **(Bustelli).** Con. 144: 65 Sept '54.

—— **(Cagliostro).** Natl. geog. 110: 657 Nov '56.

—— **(Pope Clement XIV, by Hewetson).** Con. 144: 228 Jan '60.

—— **(by Despiau).** Con. 142: XXIV Dec '58.

——. **(18th cent.).** Con. 145: 131 Ap '60.

—— **(C.G. Fisher).** Natl. geog. 98: 579 Nov '50.

—— **(Henry W. Longfellow).** Natl. geog. 97: 287 (col.) Mar '50.

—— **(Jefferson & Lee).** Holiday 28: 220 Nov '60.

—— **(John Paul Jones).** Natl. geog. 97: 282 Mar '50.

—— **(knowledge in man's head).** Holiday 27: 8 Je '60.

—— **(Louis XV).** See Louis XV (bust).

—— **(man).** Holiday 18: 63 (col.) Sept '55.

—— **(Empress Maria Fyodorovna).** Con. 144: 276 Jan '60.

—— **(Marietta Strozzi).** Praeg. pict. ency., p. 296.

—— **(Queen Nefertite).** Holiday 18: 191 Dec '55.

—— **(Vittorio Amedeo III).** Con. 142: 152 Dec '58.

—— **(woman).** Con. 145: XXXIV Ap '60.

——, **bronze.** Con. 142: 233 Jan '59; 145: 206 May '60.

——, **bronze (Lipchitz).** Con. 145: 230 Je '60.

——, **Chelsea porcelain.** Con. 145: XXXIII Ap '60.

——, **maiolica.** Con. 143: 105 Ap '59.

——, **marble.** Con. 143: 66 Mar '59.

——, **marble (Cellini).** Con. 143: 131 Ap '59.

——, **(176 A.D.).** Con. 144: 134 Nov '59.

——, **Roman (1st cent. B.C.-211 A.D.).** Praeg. pict. ency., p. 143.

——, **Roman sculpture.** Holiday 27: 83, 85-6, 89, 91 (col.), 101, 104 Ap '60.

——, **terracotta ceremonial (17th cent.).** Con. 143: 105 Ap '59.

——, **marble (child, by Houdon).** Con. 144: 128 Nov '59.

butcher. Holiday 18: 162 Nov '55, 195 Dec '55.
Natl. geog. 98: 64 (col.) Jl '50.

"The Butcher" (Banastre Tarleton). Amer. heri. vol. 9 no. 3 p. 47 (Ap '58).

butcher (sym.). Lehner: Pict. bk. of sym., p. 90.

——, **Arab.** Natl. geog. 98: 744 (col.) Dec '50.

butcher stall trade sign, antique. Amer. heri. vol. 6 no. 3 p. 32 (Ap '55).

Butler, Benjamin F. Amer. heri. vol. 7 no. 4 p. 47 (Je '56); vol. 8 no. 3 p. 52 (Ap '57); vol. 11 no. 1 p. 61 (Dec '59).
Pakula: Cent. album, p. 101.

Butler, Frank H. Amer. heri. vol. 11 no. 2 p. 62 (Feb '60).

Butler, Hugh. Cur. biog. p. 78 (1950).

Butler, John. Cur. biog. p. 87 (1955).

Butler, John Marshall. Cur. biog. p. 143 (1954).

Butler, Nevile. Cur. biog. p. 123 (1941).

Butler, Paul M. Cur. biog. p. 89 (1955).

Butler, Pierce. Amer. heri. vol. 9 no. 3 p. 25 (Ap '58).

Butler, Reginald (flexible iron sculpture). Praeg. pict. ency., p. 458.

Butler, Reginald C. Cur. biog. p. 93 (1956).

Butler, Richard Austen. Cur. biog. p. 78 (1944).

Butler, Sally. Cur. biog. p. 87 (1946).

butler (Negro). See Negro butler.

Butt, Archie. Jensen: The White House, p. 198.

Butte (Mont.). Holiday 8: 46 (col.) Sept '50.
Natl. geog. 97: 703 (col.) Je '50.

Buttenwieser, Benjamin J. Cur. biog. p. 79 (1950).

butter chips, china. Holiday 12: 145 Nov '52.

butter dish, glass. Daniel: Cut & eng. glass, pl. 104.

——, **Irish glass.** Con. ency. of ant., vol. 3, pl. 51.

butter making (woman). Amer. heri. vol. 3 no. 4 p. 14 (summer '52).

butter molds. Amer. heri. vol. 3 no. 4 p. 14-5, 77 (summer '52).
Rawson: Ant. pict. bk., p. 82.

butter roll. Rawson: Ant. pict. bk., p. 82.

Butterfield, Roger. Cur. biog. p. 84 (1948).

butterfly (sym.). Lehner: Pict. bk. of sym., p. 58.

butterfly net (Indian boy). Natl. geog. 115: 653 (col.) May '59.

butterfly table. See table, butterfly.

Buttersworth, James E. (work of). Amer. heri. vol. 6 no. 6 p. 20 (col.) (Oct '55).

Butterworth, James E. (work of). Natl. geog. 99: 194 (col.) Feb '51.

Button, Richard. Cur. biog. p. 88 (1949).
Holiday 15: 12 Jan '54.

Buttoni, Giovanni. Cur. biog. p. 61 (1962).

Buttons, Red. Cur. biog. p. 71 (1958).

buttons, 19th cent. Con. 133: 103-6 Ap '54.
——, sleeve *See* sleeve buttons.
Buttram, Frank. Holiday 13: 123 (col.) May '53.
Butts, Alfred M. Cur. biog. p. 145 (1954).
Büyük Ada. Osward: Asia Minor, pl. VII (col.).
Byas, Hugh. Cur. biog. p. 91 (1943).
Byblos (harbor). Natl. geog. 113: 504-5 Ap '58.
Byers, Margaretta. Cur. biog. p. 124 (1941).
Bygrave, William (work of). Amer. heri. vol. 6 no. 6 p. 16-7 (col.) (Oct '55).
Byington, Spring. Cur. biog. p. 95 (1956).
Byrd, Harry F. Cur. biog. p. 118 (1942); p. 90. (1955).
Byrd, Adm. Richard E. Cur. biog. p. 121 (1942); p. 96 (1956).
Natl. geog. 104: 754 Dec '53; 106: 65 H Jl '54; 110: 146, 148, 155, 166 (col.) Aug '56; 112: 2-3, 38, 40, 44-5, 47 Jl '57, 382 (col.) Sept '57.
Byrd, Mrs. Richard E. Natl. geog. 112: 40 Jl '57.
Byrd, Richard E., jr. Natl. geog. 112: 3, 48 Jl '57.
Byrd, Robert C. Cur. biog. p. 70 (1960).
Byrd, Samuel A. Cur. biog. p. 123 (1942).
Byrd, William II (Sir Godfrey Kneller). Amer. heri. vol. 11 no. 1 p. 4 (col.) (Dec '59).
Byrd coat of arms, William. *See* coat of arms (Wm. Byrd).
Byrd home, William (Virginia). Amer. heri. vol. 11 no. 1 p. 7 (col.) (Dec '59).
Byrnes, James F. Cur. biog. p. 125 (1941); p. 80 (1951).
Byrnes, Gov. & Mrs. James F. (flower garden). Natl. geog. 103: 297 (col.) Mar '53.
Byrnes, John W. Cur. biog. p. 72 (1960).
Byroade, Henry A. Cur. biog. p 80 (1952).
Byzantine architecture. *See* architecture, Byzantine.
Byzantine armour. *See* armour, Byzantine.
Byzantine art. Con. 142: 27-31 Sept '58.
Natl. geog. 103: 527 (col.) Ap '53.
Praeg. pict. ency., p. 182 (col.).
Byzantine column. *See* column, Byzantine.
Byzantine enamels. Con. 132: 104-5 Nov '53.
Byzantine ivory relief. Con. 126: 88 Oct '50.
Byzantine mosaic. *See* mosaic, Byzantine.
Byzantine sculpture *See* sculpture, Byzantine.
Byzantine walls, Nicaea. Natl. geog. 100: 177 (col.) Aug '51.
Byzantium chalice. *See* chalice, Byzantium.

C

cab (driver). Holiday 12: 67 Sept '52.
—— (horses) Holiday 8: 133 Oct '50.
——, hansom. Amer. heri. vol. 11 no. 5 p. 70 (col.) (Aug '60).
Holiday 5: 144 Je '49.
——, (English). Con. 137: 212 May '56.
cab driver, Canadian (dog). Natl. geog. 98: 337 (col.) Sept '50.
"Cabaclo" girl (Peru). Disney: People & places, p. 109 (col.).
Caballero, Maxim (work of). Con. 139: XXIV Je '57.

cabana (beach). Holiday 10: 19 Jl '51; 11: 35 (col.) Jan '52; 12: 93 Aug '52; 25: 8 (col.) Ap '59.
cabbala (sym.). Lehner: Pict. bk. of sym., p. 74.
caber (Gaelic pole). Natl. geog. 110: 18 (col.) Jl '56.
caber tossing (Isle of Skye, Scotland). Natl. geog. 102: 107 (col.) Jl '52.
Cabeza exploration map. Amer. heri. vol. 12 no. 1 p. 80 (Dec '60).
cabin. Horan: Pict. hist. of wild west, p. 39. Travel 102: 36 Jl '54.
—— (beside river). Con. 145: LXXIII (col.) May '60.
—— (campaign poster handkerchief). Amer. heri. vol. 7 no. 4 p. 27 (col.) (Je '56).
Cabin, Alpine. Holiday 26: 75 (col.) Sept '59.
——, Ky. mountain. Holiday 9: 48 Mar '51.
——, Lincoln log. *See* Lincoln log cabin, Abraham.
——, log *See* log cabin.
——, Negro. Amer. heri. vol. 2 no. 1 p. 44 (col.) (fall '50); vol. 8 no. 6. p. 20 (col.) (Oct '57).
——, thatch-roof. Holiday 8: 87 (col.) Dec '50.
——, western. Horan: Pict. hist of wild west, p. 133, 180, 202-3.
——, western (1857). Amer. heri. vol. 7 no. 5 p. 8 (Aug '56).
cabin. *See* also cabins; huts.
cabinet, Adam. Con. 126: 91 Oct '50.
——, antique. Con. 127: 103 May '51; 132: XXXVII Nov '53; 135: 107 Ap '55; 137: 108-9 Ap '56.
——, antique (Wm. Vile). Con. 139: 273 Je '57.
——, antique English. Con. 136: 82 Nov '55.
——, antique gilt wood. Con. 136: 257 (col.) Jan '56.
——, apothecary's *See* apothecary's cabinet.
——, backgammon (Victorian, Webb). Con. ency. of ant., vol. 3, pl. 3.
——, bow-front (19th cent.). Con. 143: XXXI Mar '59.
——, breakfront. Holiday 24: inside cover (col.) Nov '58.
——, Burgundian (16th cent.). Praeg. pict. ency., p. 319 (col.).
——, Charles II (lacquer). Con. 140: XXIII Sept '57.
——, china. *See* china cabinet.
——, Chinese chippendale. Con. 133: XLIV Je '54.
——, Chinese 18th cent. Con. 132: 159 (col.) Jan '54.
——, Chinese lacquer. Con. 140: 111 Jan '58.
——, Chinese (Ch'ien Lung). Con. 145: XXIX Je '60.
——, Chinese type (18th cent.). Con. 143: 81 Ap '59.
——, Chippendale. Con. 126: 69 Aug '50; 134: IV Sept '54; 136: 113 Nov '55, XXXIV Dec '55.
——, Chippendale (18th cent.). Con. 143: LXXIII May '59.

——, Chippendale breakfront. Con. 134: LXI Nov '54; 139: LXVIII May '57.

——, Chippendale display. Con. 145: 286 Je '60.

——, ebonized (1871). Con. ency. of ant., vol. 3, pl. 4.

——, (18th cent.). Con. 133: XXX May '54; 140: XVII Nov '57; 144: XXV, XXXVII Sept '59.

——, filigree paper work. Con. ency. of ant., vol. 3. pl. 124.

——, filigree miniature. Con. 141: 153 May '58.

——, French bureau. Con. 136: 126 Nov '55.

——, French ormolu. Con. 133: VI Je '54.

——, French, 17th cent. Con. 138: 77 Sept '56.

——, George II. Con. 140: 55 Sept '57.

——, George III. Con. 136: 219 Dec '55.

——, Japanese lacquer. Con. 145: 220 Je '60.

——, lacquer. Con. 137: LVIII-LIX May '56; 140: 113 Nov '57.

——, lacquer, 18th cent. Con. 140: IX Sept '57, XLIX Dec '57.

——, Louis XVI. Con. 133: LIII Je '54.

——, Louis XVI (brass inlaid). Con. 145: 75 Ap '60.

——, marquetry. Con. ency. of ant., vol. 3, pl. 123.

——, marquetry Tunbridge ware). Con. ency. of ant., vol. 3, pl. 121.

——, marquetry, English seawood (on stand). Con. 144: 211 Jan '60.

——, medal. See medal cabinet.

——, needlework cover (17th cent.). Con. ency. of ant., vol. 3, pl. 119.

——, papier-mache (19th cent.). Con. ency. of ant., vol. 3, pl. 123.

——, pietre dure. Con. 141: 215 Je '58.

——, Portuguese (17th cent.). Con. 143: 269-70 Je '59.

——, Queen Anne. Con. 133: XII Ap '54; 141: VIII Je '58.

——, Queen Anne (bureau). Con. 137: XV Mar '56.

——, Queen Anne double domed. Con. 142: XX Jan '59.

——, regency. Con. 129: LXV Je '52; 135: XVI Ap '55; 137: XXIII Mar '56; 140: XXXVI Sept '57; 141: LI, XLIX Mar '58. XXXII May '58; 142: XXXVIII Sept '58; 143: XLIII May '59; 144: XXXIII Dec '59.

——, regency black lacquer. Con. 143: XXX-III Mar '59.

——, regency coromandel wood. Con. 144: XXXV Nov '59.

——, regency dwarf. Con. 137: XII Mar '56.

——, regency inlaid. Con. 145: LXIII Je '60.

——, regency lacquer. Con. 140: XV Sept '57.

——, regency marble top. Con. 139: VI, XXXV Ap '57.

——, regency ormolu. Con. 140: inside back cover Jan '58.

——, renaissance (16th cent.). Con. 133: LIII Ap '54.

——, rock-crystal carved (16th cent.). Con. 144: 81 Nov '59.

——, seal (18th cent.). Con. 138: XXIV Dec '56.

——, 17th cent. Con. 144: XIV Sept '59.

——, Sheraton. Con. 145: LIX May '60.

——, Sheraton breakfront china. Con. 134: VIII Dec '54.

——, Sheraton dwarf. Con. 143: XXXVI Mar '59.

——, Sheraton dwarf breakfront. Con. 143: XL Mar '59.

——, table. See table cabinet.

——, Victorian. Con. ency. of ant., vol. 3, pl. 2-6.

——, Victorian (by Ashbee). Con. ency. of ant., vol. 3, pl. 6.

——, Victorian (Pugin & Grace). Con. ency. of ant., vol. 3, pl. 5.

——, Victorian ebonized wood (Godwin & Watt). Con. ency. of ant., vol. 3, pl. 4.

——, Victorian ivory inlay (Gimson). Con. ency. of ant., vol. 3, pl. 7.

——, Victorian (Wedgwood plaques). Con. ency. of ant., vol. 3, pl. 6.

——, Victorian (Wedgwood plaques). Con. ency. of ant., vol. 3, pl. 2.

——, William & Mary. Con. 135: IV Mar '55; 136: 293 Jan '56.

——, William & Mary (on stand). Con. 135: XLV May '55.

——, writing. See writing cabinet.

cabinet. See also china cabinet.

Cabinet members, Lincoln's. Amer. heri. vol. 11 no. 6 p. 46 (Oct '60).

cabinetmaker, Colonial. Natl. geog. 106: 465 (col.) Oct '54.

cabinets. Holiday 19: 13 (col.) Feb '56.

cabins (float in flood). Natl. geog. 117: 349 (col.) Mar '60.

——, ice fisherman's. See fishing huts, ice.

cabins. See also cabin.

cable, George Washington. Amer. heri. vol. 11 no. 1 p. 75 (Dec '59).

——, transatlantic (being laid). Amer. heri. vol. 9 no. 6 p. 40, 45-51, 86, 88, 91-2, 95 (part col.) (Oct '58).

cable car. Amer. heri. vol. 8 no. 6 p. 41 (col.) (Oct '57).

Holiday 10: 14 Aug '51; 12: 2 (col.), 23 Nov '52, 2 Dec '52; 14: 37 Sept '53; 21: 117 (col.) Ap '57; 28: 158 (col.) Oct '60.

Jordan: Hammond's pict. travel atlas, p. 201 (col.)

Natl. geog. 98: 75 Jl '50; 99: 588 (col.) May '51; 105: 244 Feb '54; 107: 324 (col.) Mar '55, 612 (col.) May '55; 115: 224-5 Feb '59.

Travel 107: 45 May '57.

—— (Alps). Natl. geog. 118: 411, 413-4, 416, 418-9 (col.) Sept '60.

—— (Austria-Alpine). Natl. geog. 118: 268-9 (col.) Aug '60.

—— (Austria). Travel 110: 50 Aug '58.

—— (Cal.). Natl. geog. 105: 730-1 (col.) Je '54; 110: 190, 192, 214 (col.) Aug '56.

—— (Cape Town). Natl. geog. 118: 305 (col.) Sept '60.

cable car (Colo.). Natl. geog. 106: 235 (col.) Aug '54.

—— (Norway). Natl. geog. 111: 120 (col.) Jan '57.

—— (Rotterdam). Natl. geog. 118: 528 (col.) Oct '60 .

—— (funicular). Natl. geog. 105: 244 Feb '54. Travel 104: 43 Aug '55.

cable lift (Belgium). Natl. geog. 108: 545 (col.) Oct '55.

cable railway. Holiday 15: 80 Mar '54.

Cabot, Godfrey Lowell. Holiday 14: 40 Nov '53.

Cabot, John M. Cur. biog. p. 103 (1953).

Cabot, John & Sebastian (discover Amer.). Brooks: Growth of a nation, p. 29.

Cabot, Sebastian. Amer. heri. vol. 10 no. 3 p. 6 (Ap '59).

Cabot, Thomas D. Cur. biog. p. 83 (1951).

Cabrillo, Juan Rodriguez. Brooks: Growth of a nation, p. 34.

Cabrillo memorial cross, Juan Rodriguez. Natl. geog. 114: 283 Aug '58.

Caccia, Sir Harold. Cur. biog. p. 92 (1957).

cache, nomad food. Holiday 12: 95 (col.) Sept '52.

cache-pot, porcelain (18th cent.). Con. 133: 3 Mar '54.

cache-pots, St. Cloud. Con. 143: 136 May '59.

cache-pots, Sevres. Con. 129: XLVIII Je '52.

——, Vincennes. Con. 139: XVI, 195 May '57; 143: XI May '59.

"cactus fancier". Praeg. pict. ency., p. 401 (col.).

"Cactus Jack" See Garner, John N. ("Cactus Jack").

caddy, car. See car caddy.

——, donkey golf. Natl. geog. 102: 131 Jl '52.

——, golf. Natl. geog. 105: 330 Mar '54.

caddy wagons (man & girls). Natl. geog. 112: 686 (col.) Nov '57.

Cadell, Elizabeth. Cur. biog. p. 85 (1951).

cadets (climb mizzenmast). Natl. geog. 108: 71 (col.) Jl '55.

——, Citadel College. Natl. geog. 113: 26 (col.) Jan '58.

——, English military. Holiday 23: 92-3 Mar '58.

——, girl (college). Holiday 22: 52 (col.) Sept '57.

——, military school (Canada). Natl. geog. 98: 355 (col.) Sept '50.

——, Navy (Denmark). Natl. geog. 108: 827 (col.) Dec '55.

——, plumed (St. Cyr military school). Natl. geog. 111: 744 (col.) Je '57.

——, sea. Natl. geog. 101: 520 (col.) Ap '52.

——, U.S. Coast Guard. See U.S. Coast Guard Cadets.

——, V.M.I. (patrol). Holiday 12: 35 (col.) Nov '52.

——, Valley Forge (marching). Natl. geog. 105: 189 Feb '54.

——, West Point. See West Point Cadets.

Cadillac auto. Holiday 5: 15 (col.) Feb '49, 74 (col.) Mar '49; 6: 5 (col.) Jl '49; 8: 63

(col.) Jl '50, 7 (col.) Sept '50, 71 (col.) Nov '50; 15: 7 Ap '54, 17 (col.) Je '54; 16: 63 (col.) Aug '54; 17: 7 (col.) Mar '55.

Travel 103: 8 Jan '55.

"Cadillac landing" (Detroit). Amer. heri. vol. 2 no. 4 p. 55 (summer '51).

Cadmus, Paul. Cur. biog. p. 125 (1942).

Cadogan, Sir. Alexander. Cur. biog. p. 80 (1944).

Ca d' Oro (Venice). Praeg. pict. ency., p. 207.

Caduceus (sym.). Lehner: Pict. bk. of sym., p. 13.

"Caen" (Prout). Con. ency. of ant., vol. 1, pl. 146.

"Caernarvon castle" (Turner). Con. ency. of ant., vol. 1, pl. 168.

Con. 129: cover, 33 (col.) Ap '52.

Holiday 14: 92 (col.) Jl '53; 28: 36-7 (col.) Sept '60.

Caesar, Julius. Int. gr. soc.: Arts . . . p. 25 (col.).

—— (marble bust). Praeg. pict. ency., p. 143.

Caesar, Sid. Cur. biog. p. 86 (1951).

Holiday 20: 71 Sept '56.

Caesarea. Osward: Asia Minor, pl. 67-70.

cafe (above surf, Syria). Natl. geog. 105: 494 (col.) Ap '54.

——, outdoor waterside (Berlin). Holiday 18: 68 Dec '55.

——, Pentagon open-air. Natl. geog. 103: 14 (col.) Jan '53.

——, sidewalk. Holiday. 13: 117 (col.) Ap '53.

——, sidewalk (France). Holiday 28: 47 (col.) Aug '60.

——, sidewalk (Israel). Holiday 26: 71 (col.) Dec '59.

——, sidewalk (Paris). Holiday 13: 43 (col.) Ap '53; 14: 75 (col.) Aug '53.

Natl. geog. 98: 47, 68 Jl '50; 101: 787 Je '52.

Cafe de la Paix (Paris, comic). Holiday 11: 72-3 Mar '52.

Cafe Filho, Joao. Cur. biog. p. 94 (1955).

"Caffe House" (Rome). Con. 141: 231 Je '58.

Cafferata, Private. Holiday 14: 58 Aug '53.

Cafferata, James H. (work of). Natl. geog. 99: 196 (col.) Feb '51.

Caffery, Jefferson. Cur. biog. p. 93 (1943).

Caffrey, James Joseph. Cur. biog. p. 83 (1947).

Cage, John. Cur. biog. p. 91 (1961).

cage, animal (circus). Durant: Pict. hist. of Amer. circus, p. 27.

——, bird. See bird cage.

——, carrying (dog). Holiday 11: 5 Mar '52.

——, lion tamer (circus). Durant: Pict. hist. of Amer. circus, p. 210-11.

——, sea turtle (men). Natl. geog. 116: 682-3 (col.) Nov '59.

——, tiger. Holiday 21: 65 (col.) May '57.

cages, rabbit. See rabbit cages.

Cagliostro, Count of (bust). Natl. geog. 110: 657 Nov '56.

Cagnacci, Guido (work of). Con. 144: 24 Sept '59.

Cagney, James. Cur. biog. p. 128 (1942). Holiday 10: 4 (col.) Nov '51.

Cahours, Henry Maurice. Holiday 24: 63 (col.) Aug '58.

Cain, Harry P. Cur. biog. p. 89 (1949).

Cain, James M. Cur. biog. p. 85 (1947).

"Cain cursed by the Lord" (Rubens). Con. 144: 43 Sept '59.

caique (Greek boat). Natl. geog. 103: 371, 374 (col.) Mar '53; 109: 59 (col.) Jan '56. Travel 113: 79 Ap '60.

caiques (Turkey). Natl. geog. 100: 149 (col.) Aug '51.

cairn (Arctic). Natl. geog. 101: 16 (col.) Jan '52.

—— (Australia). Natl. geog. 109: 255 (col.) Feb '56.

—— (Ft. Fork, Canada). Natl. geog. 108: 232 (col.) Aug '55.

—— (International peace garden). Natl. geog. 100: 289 Sept '51.

——, rock (Coats island). Natl. geog. 110: 682 (col.) Nov '56.

——, Scottish memorial. Natl. geog. 102: 95 (col.) Jl '52.

——, Thoreau rock. Natl. geog. 97: 307 (col.) Mar '50.

Cairo, Francesco. See del Cairo, Francesco.

Cairo (Egypt). Holiday 25: 50-5 (col.) Feb '59. Natl. geog. 106: 764-5, 768-71 (col.) Dec '54; 118: 353 (col.) Sept '60. Travel 104: 19 Nov '55.

—— (hotel). Holiday 26: 26 Jl '59.

—— (Medrese of Bey Kait). Praeg. pict. ency., p. 517.

—— (men on boat). Holiday 25: 50 (col.) Feb '59.

Cairo (Ill., air view). Natl. geog. 104: 806-7 (col.) Dec '53.

Cajun country (La.). Travel 108: 12-7 Oct '57.

—— (map). Holiday 18: 84 Oct '55.

Cajun cruise. Holiday 18: 84-5 Oct '55.

Cajun woman (head, laughing). Holiday 11: 48 Mar '52.

cake (North Pole celebration). Natl. geog. 115: 10 (col.) Jan '59.

—— (on dish). Holiday 27: 35 (col.) Je '60.

——, birthday (sym.). Lehner: Pict. bk. of sym., p. 56.

——, wedding. See wedding cake.

cake basket, antique silver. Con. 138: XV Nov '56; 140: XIX Jan '58.

——, George II (silver). Con. 129: inside cover, V Ap '52; 132: XXIV, XXVI Nov '53; 134: X Sept '54, XXXIX Nov '54; 137: XXI Mar '56; 141: XV May '58; 142: III Sept '58; 144: XXIV Sept '59.

——, George III (silver). Con. 135: XVIII Mar '55.

——, Lamerie (silver). Con. 142: 195 Dec '58.

——, silver (18th cent.) Con. ency. of ant., vol. 1, pl. 84. Con. 145: LXV Je '60.

cake decorating (baker). Natl. geog. 118: 605 (col.) Nov '60.

cake tray, Amer. glass (antique). Con. ency. of ant., vol. 3, pl. 43.

calabashes (on women's heads). Natl. geog. 110: 345 (col.) Sept '56.

calabashes. See also gourds, drinking.

"Calamity Jane". Amer. heri. vol. 11 no. 5 p. 38 (Aug '60). Horan: Pict. hist. of wild west, p. 127-29.

Calcutta (India). Travel 101: 4 Ap '54.

—— (river harbor). Natl. geog. 100: 738 (col.) Dec '51.

—— (temple) Travel 111: cover Jan '59.

Caldecott, Randolph. Jun. bk. of auth., p. 64.

Calder, Alexander. Cur. biog. p. 90 (1946). Holiday 26: 42 (col.) Sept '59.

—— (work). Praeg. pict. ency., p. 464.

Calder, Alexander Sterling (work of). Int. gr. soc.: Arts . . . p. 131 (col.).

Calder, Ritchie. Cur. biog. (1963).

Calderon Guardia, Rafael A. Cur. biog. p. 129 (1942).

Calderone, Frank A. Cur. biog. p. 82 (1952).

Caldwell, Arthur A. Cur. biog. p. 87 (1947).

Caldwell, Millard F. Cur. biog. p. 85 (1948).

Caldwell, Sarah C. Cur. biog. p. 105 (1953).

Caldy island (Monk's island). Natl. geog. 108: 564-77 Oct '55.

—— (map). Natl. geog. 108: 567 Oct '55.

calendar (allegoris representation). Lehner: Pict. bk. of sym., p. 96.

calf nose collar. See nose collar, calf.

Calgary stampede (Canada). Natl. geog. 118: 93-4 (col.) Jl '60.

Calhern, Louis. Cur. biog. p. 88 (1951). Holiday 10: 64 Dec '51.

Calhoun, John C. Amer. heri. vol. 6 no. 6 p. 56, 95 (Oct '55).

calico printing. Con. 143: 75 Ap '59.

California. Amer. heri. vol. 1 no. 3 cover, 19, 26-47 (part col.) (spring '50). Holiday 10: 108-15 (part col.) Dec '51; 12: 12-3 (col.) Dec '52; 13: 120 (col.) Mar '53, 91 (col.) Ap '53, 26 (col.) May '53; 14: 12-3 (col.) Nov '53; 16: 45-61 (col.) Dec '54; 21: 17 (col.) Feb '57, 80-5 (col.) May '57; 22: 20 (col.) Sept '57, 50-95 (part col.) Oct '57; 24: 127 (col.) Dec '58; 25: 15 (col.) Feb '59, 171 (col.) Ap '59; 26: 7 (col.) Dec '59; 27: 165 (col.) Feb '60, 44-5 (col.) Mar '60. 175 (col.) Ap '60; 28: 195 (col.) Dec '60. Jordan: Hammond's pict. travel atlas, p. 186-7, 194-207 (col.). Natl. geog. 105: 724-868 (part col.) Je '54; 116: 572-617 (col.). Nov '59. Travel 101: cover, 9-12 Mar '54; 109: 45-7 Je '58.

—— (Beverly Hills). Holiday 12: 34-42 (part col.) Oct '52.

—— (desert). Natl. geog. 112: 676-701 (part col.) Nov '57.

—— (desert area, map). Natl. geog. 112: 680-1 Nov '57.

—— (desert effigies). See effigies (desert mesas).

—— (Fisherman's wharf). Face of Amer., p. 84-5 (col.)

—— (gold rush). Holiday 24: 65-9 (part col.) Aug '58.

——(Huntington library). See Huntington library.

California (islands). Natl. geog. 114: 256-83 (part col.) Aug '58.

—— (La Jolla). Natl. geog. 102: 756-82 (part col.) Dec '52.

—— (Los Angeles). *See* Los Angeles.

—— (map, 17th cent.). Natl. geog. 105: 804 Je '54 .

—— (mission). *See* mission (Cal.)

—— (Monterey Peninsula). Face of Amer., p. 78-9 (col.).

Holiday 26: 82-7 (col.) Dec '59.

—— (Napa Valley) Holiday 12: 102-7 (part col.) Aug '52.

—— (natl. parks). Natl. geog. 116: 148-87 (part col.) Aug '59.

—— (Palm Springs). *See* Palm Springs.

—— (red-wood forest). Face of Amer., p. 72-3 (col.).

Travel 101: cover Mar '54.

—— (Sundown ranch). Face of Amer., p. 142-3 (col.).

—— (swimming pool, girls). Holiday 26: 74-9 (col.) Jl '59.

—— (upper Suisum Valley). Face of Amer., p. 52-3 (col.).

California militia co. (1856). Amer. heri. vol. 7 no. 5 back cover (col.) (Aug '56).

"California Republic" banner. Amer. heri. vol. 7 no. 2 p. 95 (Feb '56).

California trailer park. Travel 112: 49 Aug '59.

California university. *See* Univ. of California.

calipers (sym.). Lehner: Pict. bk. of sym., p. 17.

Caliphs house (Alcazarquivir). Travel 104: 60 Nov '55.

Calkins, Robert D. Cur. biog. p. 85 (1952).

Callander, William F. Cur. biog. p. 87 (1948).

Callas, Maria Meneghini. Cur. biog. p. 99 (1956).

—— (as Anna in "Anna Bolene"). Cooper: Con. ency. of music, p. 64.

Callender, John Hancock. Cur. biog. p. 96 (1955).

Callery, Mary. Cur. biog. p. 97 (1955).

calligraphy, Carolingian (9th cent.). Con. 143: 65 Mar '59.

"Calling of St. Matthew" (Caravaggio). Praeg. pict. ency., p. 327 (col.).

calliope (man playing, 1866). Amer. heri. vol. 11 no. 5 p. 49-50 (Aug '60).

—— (muse). Lehner: Pict. bk. of sym., p. 33.

——, steam. Natl. geog. 114: 674 (col.) Nov '58.

Callot, Jacques (etching). Praeg. pict. ency., p. 341.

Callot figures. Con. 138: 126 Nov '56, 193 Dec '56.

Callow, William (work of). Con. ency. of ant., vol. 1, pl. 148.

Calloway, Cab. Cur. biog. p. 85 (1945).

Calumet (sym.). Lehner: Pict: bk. of sym., p. 86.

"Calvary" (Brueghel the Elder). Con. 141: 253 (col.) Je '58.

"Calvary" (Signorelli). Natl. geog. 101: 78 (col.) Jan '52.

Calvary (sym.). Lehner: Pict. bk. of sym., p. 36.

"Calvary" (Van Valckenborch). Con. 141: 50 Mar '58.

"Calvary group" (Sweden, 14th cent.). Con. 145: 91-5 Ap '60.

Calverley embroideries, Lady. *See* embroideries, Calverley.

Calvin, Melvin. Cur. biog. p. 69 (1962).

Calyo, John A. (work of). Amer. heri. vol. 10 no. 2 p. 4 (col.) (Feb '59).

Calypso dancer. Holiday 27: 77 (col.) Mar '60.

——, Trinidad. Natl. geog. 103: 34, 65 (col.) Jan '53.

"Calypso Joe" (Trinidad singer). Holiday 5: 7-9 Jan '49.

"Calypso" research ship. Natl. geog. 113: 374-96 (part col.) Mar '58.

Calypso singers. Travel 103: 14 Mar '55.

Cam, Helen Maud. Cur. biog. p. 89 (1948).

Cam river (England). Holiday 7: 118 (col.) Je '50.

Camargue (France). Natl. geog. 109: 666-99 (part col.) May '56.

—— (map). Natl. geog. 109: 670 May '56.

Cambiaso, Luca (work of). Con. 138: 174 Dec '56.

Cambodia. Holiday 19: 91 Feb '56.

Natl. geog. 102: 291 Sept '52.

—— (map). Natl. geog. 117: 526 (col.) Ap '60.

—— (Nakhon-Wat). *See* Nakhon-Wat.

—— (temple). Natl. geog. 102: 303 (col.) Sept '52.

Cambodian acrobats. *See* acrobats, Circus.

Cambodian costume. Int. gr. soc.: Arts . . . p. 147 (col.)

Cambodian dancers Int. gr. soc.: Arts . . . cover, p. 147 (col.).

Natl. geog. 117: 516, 557 (col.) Ap '60.

Cambodian girl. Natl. geog. 99: 467 (col.) Ap '51.

Cambodian women (royal). Natl. geog. 117: 532 (col.) Ap '60.

Cambridge college portrait collection (Eng.). Con. 139: 213-8 Je '57.

Cambridge univ. (Eng.). Con. 141: XXXVII Ap '58.

Holiday 7: 114-20 (part col.) Je '50; 25: 72-7 (part col.) Je '59.

Natl. geog. 108: 312 (col.) Sept '55.

Cambridge war memorial, U.S. Natl. geog. 111: 741 (col) Je '57.

"Camden mt. across the bay" (Marin). Holiday 14: 61 (col.) Nov '53.

camel, marble (Chinese sculpt. on road to tombs). Natl. geog. 118: 218 (col.) Aug '60.

came; auction (Egypt). Natl. geog. 108: 646 (col.) Nov '55.

camel caravan (men, Iraq). Natl. geog. 114: 482-3 (col.) Oct '58.

—— (Morocco). Natl. geog. 107: 176-7 (col.) Feb '55.

camel cart *See* cart, camel.

camel pack train. Natl. geog. 113: 502 (col.) Ap '58.

camel patrol (Morocco). Natl. geog. 107: 159 (col.) Feb '55.

camel train (in U.S.). Brooks: Growth of a nation, p. 138.
cameleer, Bedouin. Natl. geog. 111: 242 Feb '57.
cameo. Holiday 28: 37 Oct '60.
cameo pendant (16th cent.). Con. ency. of ant., vol. 1, pl. 94.
cameos, glass (Portuguese). Con. 137: 32-4 Mar '56.
camera. Holiday (in practically all issues).
—— (comic). Holiday 10: 131 Nov '51.
—— (sym.). Lehner: Pict. bk. of sym., p. 17.
——, antique. Amer. heri. vol. 12, no. 1, p. 115-6, 118 (Dec '60).
Holiday 8: 95 Oct '50.
——, antique (as house). Holiday 28: 19 Sept '60.
——, antique (man taking pictures). Natl. geog. 106: 424-7 Sept '54.
——, graphic. Holiday 10: 68 Jl '51.
camera. See also kodak.
camera, motion picture. See camera, movie.
camera, movie. Holiday 10: 47 Jl '51, 2 (col.) Dec '51; 11: 22 Jan '52, 18, 73 Ap '52, 18 May '52; 13: 151 Je '53; 14: 71 (col.) Oc '53, 75 Nov '53, 193 Dec '53; 18: 4 (col.), 80 Jl '55, 11 Aug '55, 124 (col.) Nov '55, 79 (col.) Dec '55; 19: 91 (col.) May '56, 149 Je '56; 20: 61 (col.) Sept '56, 27 (col.) Nov '56, 20, 195 (col.) Dec '56; 21: 43, 96, 156 May '57, 115 (col.), 132, 167 Je '57; 22: 10 (col.), 100 Jl '57, 109, 127 Oct '57, 128 Nov '57, 20-1 (col.), 227 (col.) Dec '57; 23: 180 Ap '58, 23, 25, 105, 165 (part col.) Je '58; 24; inside cover Aug '58, 79 Oct '58, 124 (col.), 172 Dec '58; 25: 83 (col.) Jan '59, 97 (col.) May '59, 166 (col.) Je '59; 26: 85 Jl '59, 25, 81 Sept '59, 99 Nov '59; 27: 99 (col.) Feb '60, 101 (col.) Je '60; 28: 11, 81 (col.) Jl '60, 75 (col.) 87 Aug '60, 8 Sept '60, 43, 132 Oct '60, 118-9 (col.) 123, 129, 143 Nov '60, 114-5 (col.), 138-9 Dec '60.
——, movie (comic). Holiday 21: 136 Je '57.
camera, slide. Holiday 22: 36, 115 (col.) Dec '57; 26: 112 Nov '59, 6 Dec '59; 28: 183 Oct '60.
——, zoomatic movie. See zoomatic movie camera.
camera bag. See bag, camera.
camera film box. Holiday 12: 89 (col.) Dec '52.
camera lens. Holiday 14: 4 Sept '53.
Cameron, Basil. Cur. biog. p. 95 (1943).
Cameron, Dr. Charles S. Cur. biog. p. 147 (1954).
Cameron, Sir D.Y. (work of). Con. 138: XII (col.) Nov '56; 139: L Je '57; 145: XXVI May '60.
Cameron, Simon. Amer. heri. vol. 8 no. 3 p. 52 (Ap '57).
Cameroon dancers. Natl. geog. 116: 220 (col.) Aug '59; 118: 325 (col.) Sept '60.
Cameroons. Natl. geog. 116: 220-53 (part col.) Aug '59.
—— Moslem celebration). Natl. geog. 116: 240 (col.) Aug '59.
Camidge, John the younger. Con. 144: 8 Sept '59.

Camm, Sydney. Cur. biog. p. 131 (1942).
Camogli (Italy). Holiday 13: 61 (col.) Je '53.
Camp, Walter. Holiday 26: 65 Nov '59.
camp. Holiday 8: 65 Oct '50; 16: 25 Sept '54. Travel 103: 44 Je '55.
——, Antarctica. Natl. geog. 110: 155 (col.). 156, 174-5 (col.) Aug '56.
——, army. See army camp.
——, gypsy. Amer. heri. vol. 9 no. 6 p. 69 (Oct '58).
——, mt. Natl. geog. 106: 13, 18, 21, 26 (part col.) Jl '54.
——, mt. (Canada). See Canada (mt. camps).
——, Orcas island. Travel 105: 35 May '56.
——, Russia (girls). Natl. geog. 116: 742 (col.) Dec '59.
——, summer. Holiday 6: 39 (col.) Nov '49.
camp cooking (gauchos). Natl. geog. 113: 321 (col.) Mar '58.
camp equipment. Holiday 24: 111-114 (part col.) Jl '58.
camp fire. Amer. heri. vol. 2 no. 1 p. 68 (fall '50).
Holiday 10: 70 Nov '51; 26: cover (col.) Nov '59.
Natl. geog. 112: 135 (col.) Jl '57.
Travel 105: 37 Mar '56.
—— (Antarctic men). Natl. geog. 113: 467 (col.) Ap '58.
—— (Boy scouts). Natl. geog. 110: 413 (col.) Sept '56.
—— (girl cooking). Natl. geog. 106: 223 (col.) Aug '54.
—— (man & woman). Natl. geog. 112: 252 (col.), 254 Aug '57.
—— (men & women). Natl. geog. 116: 184-5 (col.) Aug '59.
—— (men cooking). Natl. geog. 114: 166 (col.) Aug '58.
—— (park group). Natl. geog. 116: 157 Aug '59.
—— (picnic). Natl. geog. 113: 603 (col.) May '58.
—— (picnic, river). Natl. geog. 114: 656 (col.) Nov '58.
—— (study group). Natl. geog. 102: 485-6 (col.) Oct '52.
——, Yosemite. Natl. geog. 113: 594-5 (col.) May '58.
camp fire girl. See campfire girl.
camp group (Natl. park). Natl. geog. 116: 160 (col.) Aug '59.
Camp Topridge lodge (int.). Holiday 21: 54-5 (col.) Je '57.
Campa, Miguel Angel. Cur. biog. p. 93 (1957).
Campagna, Girolamo (bronze figures). Con. 143: 216 Je '59.
campaign map (1862). Amer. heri. vol. 11 no. 2 p. 70-1 (Feb '60).
campaign poster, Govt. Amer. heri. vol. 4 no. 1 p. 2, 52 (fall '52).
——, political. Amer. heri. vol. 7 no. 4 p. 25-33 (part col.) (Je '56); vol. 10 no. 2 p. 107 (Feb '59).
——, political (1840). Amer. heri. vol. 4 no. 1 p. 2, 52 (fall '52).
——, political (Pompeian). Ceram: March of arch., p. 23.

campaign speaker, election. Amer. heri. vol. 9 no. 5 p. 112 (Aug '58).
Canpanella, Roy. Cur. biog. p. 106 (1953).
campanile (Cal. univ.). Natl. geog. 105: 732 Je '54; 110: 213 (col.) Aug '56.
—— (Venice. Natl. geog. 100: 398 Sept '51.
——, church. Natl. geog. 108: 142 Jl '55.
——, Lucca. Travel 107: 27 Ap '57.
campanile. See also bell tower.
Campbell, Archibald (Romney). Con. 145: 43 (col.) Mar '60.
Campbell, Boyd. Cur. biog. p. 101 (1956).
Campbell, Douglas. Cur. biog. p. 72 (1958). Holiday 27: 83 (col.) Mar '60.
Campbell, E. Simms. Cur. biog. p. 128 (1941).
Campbell, Sir Gerald. Cur. biog. p. 129 (1941).
Campbell, Grace. Cur. biog. p. 90 (1948).
Campbell, Sir. Malcolm. Cur .biog. p. 89 (1947).
Campbell, Patricia. Cur. biog. p. 95 (1957).
Campbell, Rev. (wooden statue). Amer. heri. vol. 3 no. 3 p. 33 (col.) (spring '52).
campers. Travel 110: 56 Aug '58.
—— (Canada). Natl. geog. 114: 166-7 (col.) Aug '58.
—— (eating at table). Natl. geog. 105: 54 (col.) Jan '54.
—— (Finland). Natl. geog. 106: 251 (col.) Aug '54.
—— (fire). Natl. geog. 99: 685 (col.) May '51.
—— (forest). Natl. geog. 110: 294-5 (col.) Sept '56.
——(mt.). Natl. geog. 118: 413 (col.) Sept '60.
—— (mt. climbers). Natl. geog. 105: 850-68 (part col.) Je '54.
—— (Nepal). Natl. geog. 117: 368 (col.) Mar '60.
—— (Nigeria). Natl. geog. 116: 222 (col.) Aug '59.
—— (Norway). Natl. geog. 111: 103 (col.) Jan '57.
—— (Norway, bicycles). Natl. geog. 106: 178 Aug '54.
—— (sleeping out). Natl. geog. 106: 223 (col.) Aug '54 .
——, girl. Natl. geog. 98: 92 (col.) Jl '50; 107: 790-1 (col.) Je '55 .
campers cooking. Natl. geog. 104: 104-5 Jl '53.
Campese (harbor). Travel 112: 40 Sept '59.
campfire girls. Jensen: The White House, p. 219.
—— (cartoon). Holiday 13: 95 Mar '53.
camphene lamp. See lamp, 1st camphene.
Campidoglio (Rome). Holiday 27: 129 Jan '60.
Campione (Italy). Holiday 27: 147 Jan '60.
Campney, Ralph Osborne. Cur. biog. p. 99 (1955).
Campora, Giuseppe. Cur. biog. p. 97 (1957).
Camrose, Lord William E.B. Cur. biog. p. 131 (1941).
can. Holiday 13: 19, 26 May '53, 120, 158 Je '53; 18: 88 (col.) Sept '55; 19: 130 Jan '56; 21: 28 (col.) Je '57; 22: 142 Sept '57.
——, oil (comic). Holiday 11: 16 Je '52; 12: 71 Jl '52, 101 Oct '52, 131 Nov '52.
——, oil (pouring). Holiday 18: 23 (col.) Sept '55, 115 (col.) Oct '55, 80 (col.) Nov '55; 23: 97 (col.) Mar '58.
——, tin. Holiday 14: 138 Jl '53, 112 Aug '53,

115 Sept '53, 130, 145 Oct '53, 161 Nov '53; 21: 109 Mar '57; 23: 135 Feb '58, 3 Mar '58, 34, 137, 172 Ap '58; 24: 29 Jl '58, 14 Sept '58; 25: 130 Feb '59, 6 Je '59; 26: 28 Jl '59, 86, 115 Aug '59, 3 Sept '59.
——, tin (comic). Holiday 11: 159 May '52.
can can dancers. See dancers, can can.
can opener Holiday 10: 125 Dec '51.
Canaanites & Philistines (battle). Natl. geog. 112: 846-7 (col.) Dec '57.
Canada. Holiday 5: 124 (col.) Ap '49, 90 (col.) Je '49; 6: 34-59 (part col.) Aug '49; 7: 106 (col.) Ap '50, 155 (col.) May '50, 71 (col.) Je '50; 13: 154 (col.) Ap '53, 10, 15, (col.) May '53, 87 (col.) Je '53; 14: 38-47, 134 (part col.) Jl '53, 98-106 (part col.) Sept '53; 17: 113 (col.) Mar '55; 18: 15 (col.) Jl '55; 21: 46-51 (part col.) Feb '57, 7 (col.) Ap '57; 23: 101 (col.) Feb '58, 163 (col.) Ap '58; 24: 112 (col.) Aug '58, 50-9 (col.) Nov '58; 25: 9 Jan '59, 12 (col.)—13 Feb '59; 26: 50-55 (part col.) Sept '59; 27: 140 (col.) Jan '60, 10 (col.) Feb '60, 223 (col.) May '60; 28: 114 (col.) Aug '60.
Jordan: Hammond's pict. travel atlas, p. 20-1, 144-5 (col.).
Natl. geog. 104: 822-52 (part col.) Dec '53; 108: 192-238 (part col.) Aug '55; 115: 824-9 (part col.) Je '59.
Travel 102: 13-8 Jl '54; 105: 13-5 May '56; 110: 14-9 Aug '58; 111: 21-3 Je '59; 114: 14-42 Jl '60.
—— (Alberta). Natl. geog. 118: 90-119 (part col.) Jl '60.
—— (British Columbia). Natl. geog. 114: 148-89 (part col.) Aug '58.
—— (harbor). Holiday 27: 146 (col.) Mar '60.
—— (Hudson's Bay). Natl. geog. 103: 100-15 Jan '53.
—— (Manitoba, beach) Holiday 25: 124 Feb '59.
—— (map). Natl. geog. 108: 198-9 (col.) Aug '55.
—— (mt. camps). Travel 103: 7-12 Je '55.
—— (19th cent.). Con. 133: 203-7 May '54.
—— (Ottawa). See Ottawa.
—— (Univ. of Toronto). See Univ. of Toronto.
—— (Victoria, Parliament bldg.). Travel 114: 4 Sept. '60.
——, French. Holiday 27: 51-9 (col.) Je '60.
Canada Bill. See Jones, William.
Canaday, Ward M. Cur. biog. p. 91 (1951).
Canadian coat of arms. See coat of arms, Canadian.
Canadian guards. Holiday 13: 29 (col.) Ap '53. Natl. geog. 115: 827 (col.) Je '59.
Canadian natl. parks. See natl. parks, Canadian.
Canadian police. See police, Canadian; Royal Canadian mounted police.
Canadian rocky mts. Holiday 6: 52-3 (col.) Aug '49; 7: 86 (col.) Mar '50; 16: 90-5 (part col.) Sept '54; 19: 122 (col.) Je '56. Travel 107: cover May '57.
Canady, John. Cur. biog. p. 71 (1962).
Canal, Antonio. See Canaletto.
canal. Travel 105: 25, 27-9 Ap '56.
—— (Amsterdam). Travel 105: 25 Ap '56.

—— (Antwerp). Natl. geog. 113: 810 (col.) Je '58 .

—— (Bangkok, market sampans). Natl. geog. 116: 847 (col.) Dec '59.

—— (Cape Cod). Travel 106: 34 Sept '56.

—— (England). Travel 106: 22-5 Aug '56.

—— (Holland). Holiday 15: 110 (col.) Jan '54; 21: 53 (col.) Mar '57.
Natl. geog. 98: 768 (col.) Dec '50.
Travel 102: inside cover Nov '54.

—— (Trieste). Natl. geog. 109: 829 (col.) Je '56.

—— (Venice). Holiday 18: 42-7 (part col.) Oct '55.
Natl. geog. 100: 408-9 (col.) Sept '51.

——, Albert (Belgium). Natl. geog. 108: 550 (col.) Oct '55.

——, Chesapeake & Ohio. See Chesapeake & Ohio canal.

——, Corinth. See Corinth canal.

——, Gowanus. Holiday 7: 54 (col.) Je '50.

——, Meuse. Holiday 21: 44 Jan '57.

——, Sault Ste. Marie. See Sault Ste. Marie.

——, Soo. See Sault Ste Marie canal.

——, swamp (Va. & N.C.). Natl. geog. 113: 20 (col.) Jan '58.

——, Welland. Travel 106: 22 Nov '56; 109: 54-7 Mar '58.

canal. See also name of canal.

canal boat. See boat, canal.

canal locks (Georgetown). Natl. geog. 117: 421 (col.) Mar '60.

—— (Sweden). Natl. geog. 98: 618-20 (col.) Nov '50.

——, Rideau (Canada). Natl. geog. 104: 848 (col.) Dec '53.

——, Sault Ste Marie. See Sault Ste Marie.

"Canale di Cannaregio" (Venice). Praeg. pict. ency., p. 362 (col.).

Canaletto, Antonio (work of). Con. 126: 39 (col.) Aug '50; 132: 111, 123 Nov '53, 195 (col.) Jan '54; 135: 53 Mar '55; 138: XXIX Jan '57; 139: XXVIII-XXIX Je '57; 140: 99 Nov '57; 142: 41 Sept '58; 143: 54 Mar '59, XXXVIII (col.) Je '59; 144: 44 Sept '59, 238 Jan '60; 145: 186 May '60.
Natl. geog. 101: 82 (col.) Jan '52.

Canaletto, Island of Torcello (Italy). Con. 135: LV Je '55.

"Canaletto" (Venice). Con. 141: 237 Je '58.

Canary islanders dancing. Travel 110: 23 Oct '58.

Canary islands. Holiday 12: 16-9 Aug '52.
Natl. geog. 107: 486-522 (part col.) Ap '55.

—— (map). Natl. geog. 107: 488 Ap '55.

Canaveral, Cape. See Cape Canaveral.

Canby, Edward R.S. Pakula: Cent. album, p. 101.

Canby, Henry Seidel. Cur. biog. p. 132 (1942).

cancer-fighting device. Natl. geog. 108: 210 (col.) Aug '55.

cancer treatment. Natl. geog. 105: 78 Jan '54.

Candau, Dr. Marcolino G. Cur. biog. p. 149 (1954).

Candee, Brig. Gen. Robert C. Cur. biog. p. 82 (1944).

Candela, Felix. Cur. biog. p. 74 (1960).

candelabra. Holiday 10: 39 (col.), 123 Nov '51;

14: 10 (col.) Dec '53; 20: 82 (col.) Dec '56; 25: 64 May '59; 27: 126 (col.) Ap '60, 24 Je '60.

—— (lighted). Holiday 23: 94 (col.) Mar '58.

—— (sym.). Lehner: Pict. bk. of sym., p. 55.

——, Adam. Con. 138: XXXVIII Nov '56.

——, Adam cut glass. Con. 141: 247 Je '58.

——, antique. Con. 127: 103 May '51; 136: LVI Sept '55, XVI Dec '55.
Holiday 20: 41 (col.) Aug '56.

——, antique Chelsea. Con. 135: XVI Ap '55.

——, antique crystal. Con. 141: XLIX May '58.

——, antique silver. Con. 132: XIII Sept '53; 136: XLIX Jan '56; 138: 274 Jan '57.

——, antique (Sondag). Con. 141: 49 Mar '58.

——, Boulton. Con. 142: LXIV Dec '58; 144: XIII Nov '59.

——, Boulton silver. Con. 145: XVIII May '60.

——, brass. Natl. geog. 106: 441, 452 (col.) Oct '54.

——, brass (18th cent.). Con. 144: LI Nov '59.

——, brass (19th cent.). Con. 144: back cover Sept '59.

——, crystal (18th cent.). Con. ency. of ant., vol. 3, pl. 115-6.

——, crystal regency. Con. 142: XLIII Jan '59.

——, early 19th cent. Con. 134: III Nov '54.

——, 18th cent. Con. 132: XL Nov '53, 189 Jan '54; 133: 263 Je '54; 137: XXXIII Ap '56; 139: XLVI Ap '57; 143: 192 May '59.

——, empire. Con. 143: VI May '59.

——, English cut glass. Con. 138: XXXII Jan '57.

——, figurine. Con. 140: V Sept '57.

——, Florentine bronze. Con. 142: 269 Jan '59.

——, French. Jensen: The White House, p. 32.

——, George II (silver). Con. 129: XI Ap '52; 139: 264 Je '57; 142: XI Nov '58.

——, George III. Con. 136: IX Dec '55, XIII, LVII Jan '56; 137: LVII Ap '56; 138: LXI Jan '57; 139: XVII Je '57; 143: XV Je '59; 144: VII, XXVII Sept '59.

——, George III-George IV (silver). Con. 143: XLII Mar '59.

——, Georgian. Con. 139: LVII Je '57; 143 XXVI Ap '59.

——, Georgian (18th cent.). Con. 132: LIV Nov '53.

——, gilt-bronze (Ladatte). Con. 142: 152-3 Dec '58.

——, glass. Con. ency. of ant., vol. 3, pl. 113-6.
Daniel: Cut & engraved glass, p. 136.

——, glass (18th cent.). Con. 144: 251 Jan '60.

——, Irish antique. Con. 136: XLII Jan '56.

——, Irish antique glass. Con. 133: LIV Je '54.

——, Irish glass. Con. ency. of ant., vol. 3, pl. 49.
Con. 137: XX May '56.

——, Irish reading. Con. 135: LV May '55; 142: LV Sept '58.

——, Irish silver. Con. 137: XXVII Mar '56.

——, Italian silver. Con. 145: XLII May '60.

——, Louis XV. Con. 135: LIII May '55.

——, canary glass (New England). Con. ency. of ant., vol. 3, pl. 39.

——, Charles II. Con. 140: 58 Sept '57; 127: 65 Mar '51.

——, Chelsea. Con. 129: LXXX Je '52; 132: XXXVII Sept '53; 133: 263 Je '54.

——, Chelsea "seasons". Con. 145: LII Ap '60.

——, Douai (18th cent.). Con. 142: 16 Sept '58.

——, Dutch silver. Con. ency. of ant., vol. 3, p. 61.

——, Dutch silver-gilt. Con. 136: 306 Jan '56.

——, figurine. Con. 140: V Sept '57.

——, George I silver. Con. 133: XXXVIII May '54, IV, LII Je '54; 134: XXII Sept '54; 136: LXI Jan '56; 142: LV Sept '58, XXI Dec '58.

——, George I & George II. Con. 136: LIII Nov '55.

——, George II silver. Con. 129: XXVI Ap '52; 132: XIX Nov '53; 133: XXXVIII May '54; 134: XLIV Sept '54; 135: VII Ap '55; 136: XX Jan '56; 137: V, XLIV Ap '56, VII Je '56; 138: LXV Sept '56, XIX Jan '57; 139: XXIX May '57, LI Je '57; 140: V Dec '57, XI Jan '58; 141: XLIX Je '58; 142: XI Nov '58, LXXI Jan '59; 143: XX Mar '59; 143: LXI Je '59; 144: X Sept '59; 145: XLIX Mar '60.

——, George III. Con. 129: XXVI Je '52; 132: VIII, IX Sept '53; 133: XXXI Mar' 54, XX, LII Je '54; 134: XXVIII Sept '54, V Nov '54; 135: XXXVII Mar '55; 136: XLV, 56 Sept '55, LVI, LX Nov '55, IX, XV Dec '55, LVII Jan '56; 138: XVI Sept '56; 140: 115 Nov '57, LV Jan '58; 141: VII Mar '58; 142: XLVIII Dec '58; 144: XX Sept '59, XXIII Nov '59.

——, Georgian silver. Con. 139: XXII Ap '57; 140: XVIII Nov '57, X Dec '57.

——, Georgian silver (18th cent.). Con. 143: XXIX May '59.

——, Harlequin. Con. 129: V Je '52.

——, hog scraper. Rawson: Ant. pict. bk., p. 94.

——, Irish antique. Con. 138: XLVI Nov '56.

——, Irish glass. Con. 145: XXXII Mar '60.

——, Irish silver. Con. 139: XLIX May '57.

——, Italian silver. Con. 140: XXIV Nov '57; 144: 156 Dec '59.

——, Italian silver gilt & crystal (16th cent.). Con. ency. of ant., vol. 3, pl. 34.

——, Jacobean pewter. Con. 133: XXII Ap '54.

——, James II silver. Con. 139: III Je '57.

——, Louis XV. Con. 133: LVII Je '54; 135: XXXI Ap '55.

——, Louis XV ormolu. Con. 133: 200 May '54, I Je '54.

——, Meissen. Con. 141: 251 Je '58; 142: 38 Sept '58.

——, 19th cent. gilt. Con. 133: 154 May '54.

——, Ormolu. Con. 133: 200 May '54, 1 Je '54; 135: LIX May '55.

——, pewter. Con. ency. of ant., vol. 1, pl. 78-9.

——, pewter antique. Con. 134: XXXIV Dec '54; 138: 44 Sept '56.

——, pewter (English octagon). Con. 132: XXVI Sept '53.

——, pewter (17th cent.). Con. 133: XXIV Mar '54; 137: LX, 182-4 May '56; 142: XXX Dec '58, XLII Jan '59.

——, pricket brass. Con. 140: 135 Nov '57.

——, pricket pewter. Con. 134: XXIV Sept '54; 140: XXX Jan '58; 142: LII Jan '59.

——, pricket (17th cent.) Con. 129: LXIII Je '52.

——, Queen Anne. Con. 129: V Je '52; 132: XXVIII Sept '53; 134: XXXVI Dec '54; 136: XXXII Sept '55, LI Dec '55; 137: XLVI Mar '56; 139: XLI Mar '57, 264 Je '57; 140: XXXV Dec '57, LIX Jan '58; 141: XXXI, LV Mar '58; 142: XXVII Dec '58, XXXIX, LXXI Jan '59; 143: XXV May '59; 144: XLIV Nov '59.

——, regency cut glass. Con. 143: XLVIII Mar '59.

——, rococo (Portuguese). Con. 144: XLVI Dec '59.

——, Sevres. Con. 143: inside cover May '59.

——, Sevres porcelain. Con. 133: inside cover Mar '54.

——, Sgraffito. Con. 140: 135 Nov '57.

——, Sheffield. Con. 140: XLII Dec '57, XXIV Jan '58; 141: XL Je '58; 142: LVII Jan '59.

——, silver. Natl. geog. 109 477 (col.) Ap '56.

——, silver (18th cent.). Con. ency. of ant., vol. 1, p. 83, 89.
Con. 132: LX Nov '53; 138: IV, 275 Jan '57; 139: 123 Ap '57. XX May '57; 142: XXXIV Sept '58; 144: XXX Nov '59, XII Dec '59, XIV, XLV Jan '60; 145: XX, XXVI Mar '60, LII Ap '60, XX May '60.

——, silver (Faberge). Con. 145: LXXVII Je '60.

——, silver (Harache, 17th cent.). Con. 145: LVIII Je '60.

——, silver (Henning, 18th cent.). Con. 143: 19 Mar '59.

——, silver (Hungarian). Con. 145: LIV Je '60.

——, silver (19th cent.). Con. 137: XLI Ap '56.

——, silver (Norwegian, 18th cent.). Con. 145: 16 Mar '60.

——, silver (Parker, 18th cent.). Con. 145: LXXVII May '60.

——, silver (Roettiers, 1784). Con. ency. of ant., vol. 3, pl. 30.

——, silver (17th cent.). Con. 138: V Sept '56, 272 Jan '57; 139: V Ap '57; 141: XXXIV, 247 Je '58.

——, silver (1734). Con. ency. of ant., vol. 1, p. 153.

——, silver (1701, 1743). Con. 142: XIV, XXVIII Dec '58.

——, 16th cent. Con. 140: LXXI Nov '57.

——, Staffordshire. Con. 142: LVI Nov '58.

——, Staffordshire enamel. Con. ency. of ant., vol. 1, pl. 74.

——, Swedish (18th cent.). Con. 141: 9-10, 12 Mar '58.

candlestick, Venetian glass. Holiday 22: 35 (col.) Nov '57.

——, **William III silver.** Con. 133: XXVII Mar '54; 135: XXXVII Je '55; 138: III, VII Jan '57; 139: XIII Je '57; 145: XVII Mar '60.

candlestick group, antique. Con. 139: X Ap '57.

candlesticks, Charles II silver. Con. 140: XX-XIX Nov '57.

——, **Chinese antique jade.** Con. 139: L Ap '57.

——, **crystal.** Daniel: Cut & engr. glass, pl. 135.

candy, peppermint stick. Natl. geog. 105: 299 (col.) Mar '54.

candy cane. Holiday 14: 2 (col.) Dec '53.

—— **(sym.).** Lehner: Pict. bk. of sym., p. 50.

candy display. Holiday 10: 70 (col.) Dec '51.

candy pulling. *See* taffy candy pulling.

cane, candy. *See* candy cane.

cane handle, porcelain (18th cent.). Con. 145: 250 Je '60.

Canfield, Cass. Cur. biog. p. 151 (1954).

Canham, Erwin D, Cur. biog. p. 87 (1945); p. 76 (1960).

Caniff, Milton A. Cur. biog. p. 83 (1944).

canister. Holiday 10: 19 Jl '51.

cannery, salmon (Kodiak, Alaska). Natl. geog. 109: 783, 786 (col.) Je '56.

Cannes (France). Holiday 17: 11 Feb '55. Travel 103: 46 Ap '55.

—— **(beach).** Holiday 7: 10 (col.) Jan '50; 23: 50 (col.) Jan '58. Natl. geog. 117: 752-3 (col.) Je '60.

Cannibal, Fijian. Natl. geog. 114: 536 Oct '58.

Canning, George. Amer. heri. vol. 6 no. 6 p. 7 (Oct '55).

Canning, Stratford. Con. 144: 10 Sept '59.

Cannon, Cavendish W. Cur. biog. p. 98 (1957).

Cannon, Clarence. Cur. biog. p. 91 (1949).

Cannon, Howard W. Cur. biog. p. 78 (1960).

Cannon, LeGrand, jr. Cur. biog. p. 96 (1943).

cannon. Amer. heri. vol. 8 no. 2 p. 31 (Feb '57); vol. 10 no. 6 p. 93 (Oct '59). Con. 140: XXXVI Jan '58. Holiday 9: inside cover Mar '51; 18: 79 (col.) Nov '55, 63 Dec '55; 28: 54 (col.) Sept '60. Natl. geog. 98: 335 (col.) Sept '50. Travel 109: 45 Feb '58, 36 May '58; 110: cover, 19-20 Jl '58.

—— **(antique).** Amer. heri. vol. 3 no. 3 p. 52 (col.) (spring '52); vol. 6 no. 3 p. 102 (Ap '55); vol. 7 no. 4 p. 109 (Je '56). Holiday 14: 37 (col.), 162 Dec '53. Travel 114: 21 Oct '60.

—— **(antique, men firing).** Amer. heri. vol. 6 no. 5 p. 95 (Aug '55).

—— **(cartoon, 1902).** Amer. heri. vol. 11 no. 6 p. 54 (Oct '60).

—— **(early 19th cent.).** Amer. heri. vol. 3 no. 2 p. 2 (col.) (winter '52).

—— **(1812).** Natl. geog. 115: 466 Ap '59. Travel 108: 34 Jl '57.

—— **(1829).** Jensen: The White House, p. 46.

—— **(fort, 1890).** Holiday 12: 71 Sept '52.

—— **("Rodman gun", 1863).** Amer. heri. vol. 5 no. 2 p. 27 (winter '53-54).

—— **(1775).** Holiday 21: 61 Je '57.

—— **(with eagle).** Amer. heri. vol. 11 no. 6 p. 51 (Oct '60).

——, **Canadian.** Holiday 19: 139 Mar '56.

——, **Civil war.** Amer. heri. vol. 5 no. 2 p. 29-37 (col.) (winter '53-54); vol. 5 no. 3 p. 39 (spring '54); vol. 6 no. 1 p. 2 (col.) (fall '54); vol. 9 no. 1 p. 49-50 (col.) (Dec '57); vol. 12 no. 1 p. 119 (Dec '60). Holiday 11: 60-1 (col.) Je '52; 12: 2 (col.) Aug '52; 13: 49 (col.) May '53; 18: 101 Oct '55. Natl. geog. 113: 31 Jan '58. Travel 113: 15 Ap '60.

——, **Civil war (men & women).** Natl. geog. 118: 703 (col.) Nov '60.

——, **Civil war (twin-barreled).** Natl. geog. 105: 293 Mar '54.

——, **Dutch (1620).** Con. 144: XLVIII Nov '59.

——, **Fort Niagara.** Amer. heri. vol. 4 no. 4 p. 35-6 (summer '53).

——, **Italian (San Marino).** Holiday 6: 78 Oct '49.

——, **"Molly Stark".** Natl. geog. 99: 135 (col.) Jan '51.

——, **Revolutionary war.** Holiday 16: 106 Jl '54. Travel 107: 17 Jan '57.

——, **Scotch.** Natl. geog. 110: 6 Jl '56.

——, **ships.** Natl. geog. 103: 75 Jan '53.

——, **Ticonderoga (1775).** Natl. geog. 107: 746 (col.) Je '55.

——, **Valley Forge.** Natl. geog. 105: 199 (col.) Feb '54.

cannon muzzles, German. Con. 140: LXI Nov '57.

canoe. Amer. heri. vol. 1 no. 3 p. 23 (spring '50); vol. 8 no. 3 p. 12, 15 (col.) (April '57); vol. 10 no. 1 p. 82 (Dec '58). Holiday 6: 13 (col.) Nov '49; 7: 20, 135 (col.) Ap '50, 161 May '50, 86 Je '50; 8: 23 Oct '50; 10: 31 (col.) Jl '51; 11: 79 (col.) Ap '52, 90 Je '52; 15: 163 May '54; 16: 106, 108 (col.) Aug '54, 23 Oct '54; 18: 28 Jl '55; 20: 23 Aug '56; 22: 127 Jl '57; 27: 165 (col.) Feb '60. Natl. geog. 98: 75, 82, 89, 115, 118 (part col.) Jl '50; 99: 320, 336-7 (col.) Mar '51; 100: 66, 82-6 (col.) Jl '51; 101: 28, 30 (col.) Jan '52; 103: 739 (col.) Je '53; 114: 666, 669 Nov '58. Travel 107: 13 Je '57; 108: 12 Aug '57; 114: 30 Oct '60.

—— **(boy & girl).** Travel 113: 26 Feb '60.

—— **(boy, girl, cyprus garden).** Natl. geog. 103: 313 (col.) Mar '53.

—— **(girl carrying).** Holiday 18: cover (col.) Aug '55.

—— **(girls).** Holiday 11: 65 Ap '52.

—— **(lake).** Holiday 22: 158-9 (col.) Oct '57.

—— **(man).** Holiday 21: 121 Feb '57; 27: 178 Feb '60.

—— **(man & girl).** Holiday 21: 35 (col.) Je '57; 25: 143 Feb '59.

—— **(man & woman).** Holiday 10: 26, 36, 120 (part col.) Jl '51, 36 Sept '51, 7 (col.) Nov

'51; 11: 120 (col.) Feb '52; 12: cover (col.) Oct '52.
Natl. geog. 114: 58 (col.) Jl '58.
Travel 113: 38 Mar '60; 114: 52 Aug '60.
—— (man, woman paddling). Face of Amer., p. 9 (col.).
—— (man carrying). Natl. geog. 99: 554 Ap '51.
—— (man, comic). Holiday 21: 109 Je '57.
—— (man paddling). Holiday 15: 30 Feb '54.
—— (man, woman, children). Travel 112: 39-41 Aug '59.
—— (men). Holiday 10: 61 (col.) Sept '51; 19: 97 Feb '56.
—— (men & women). Natl. geog. 117: 429 (col.) Mar '60.
—— (men carrying). Brooks: Growth of a nation, p. 59.
—— (men, Indian woman & baby). Natl. geog. 103: 730 (col.) Je '53.
—— (men pushing to water). Travel 106: 33 Nov '56.
—— (men, woman, child). Natl. geog. 99: 159 (col.) Feb '51.
—— (on top of station wagon). Natl. geog. 103: 740, 744 (col.) Je '53.
—— (rowers). Amer. heri. vol. 6 no. 3 p. 24 (Ap '55); vol. 6 no. 5 p. 5 (col.) (Aug '55).
Natl. geog. 100: 97 Jl '51.
Travel 102: 8 Jl '54; 112: 29 Jl '59.
—— (sails). Natl. geog. 107: 131 (col.) Jan '55.
—— (sails, Fiji). Natl. geog. 114: 556-7 Oct '58.
—— (sails). See also sailboat.
—— (soldiers). Amer. heri. vol. 6 no. 2 p. 52-3 (col.) (winter '55); vol. 6 no. 5 p. 24 (Aug '55).
—— (tilting contest). Natl. geog. 102: 11 (col.) Jl '52.
—— (woman rowing). Holiday 13: cover (col.) Mar '53.
——, African. Natl. geog. 108: 776 (col.) Dec '55.
——, African (dugout). Natl. geog. 110: 260, 275 Aug '56.
——, African bushman. Holiday 20: 56 (col.) Oct '56.
——, Arabian (Iraq). Natl. geog. 113: 212-3 Feb '58.
——, Bolivia. Holiday 8: 56 (col.) Nov '50.
——, Borneo. Natl. geog. 109: 724 May '56.
——, cargo Natl. geog. 99: 357, 359 (col.) Mar '51.
——, Chili. Holiday 20: 82 (col.) Nov '56.
——, Colombia. Natl. geog. 102: 376, 380, 385 (col.) Sept '52.
——, dugout. Natl. geog. 101: 334 (col.) Mar '52; 110: 260, 275 Aug '56; 112: 624-5 (col.) Nov '56.
——, Egyptian (man paddling, ancient). Int. gr. soc.: Arts . . . p. 43 (col.).
——, Eskimo. Natl. geog. 110: 678 (col.), 680 Nov '56.
——, Florida (Everglades). Natl. geog. 110: 821 (col.) Dec '56.
——, Hawaiian (men rowing). Holiday 28: 38 (col.) Jl '60.

——, Holland (man poling). Natl. geog. 106: 400 (col.) Sept '54.
——, Indian. Amer. heri. vol. 8 no. 6 p. 43 (col.) (Oct '57); vol. 9 no. 5 p. 46 (Aug '58).
Brooks: Growth of a nation, p. 41.
Holiday 7: 34-5 (col.) Mar '50.
——, Indian (girl). Natl. geog. 103: 724 (col.) Je '53.
——, Indian (night). Amer. heri. vol. 10 no. 5 p. 51 (col.) (Aug '59).
——, Iraq. Natl. geog. 113: 218, 229, 233, 239 (part col.) Feb '58.
——, Mexico. Natl. geog. 100: 810-11 (col.) Dec '51.
——, outrigger. See outrigger canoe.
——, Palembang. Natl. geog. 99: 37 (col.) Jan '51.
——, Panama jungle (men). Natl. geog. 104: 283 (col.) Aug '53.
——, Samoan. Disney: People & places, p. 130, 141 (col.).
——, South Seas. Holiday 27: 19 Je '60.
——, Sumatra. Natl. geog. 99: 33 (col.) Jan '51.
——, Yap Island. Natl. geog. 102: 824 (col.) Dec '52.
canoe building (man). Holiday 11: 57 (col.) May '52.
——, Seminole Indian. Natl. geog. 110: 832-3 (col.) Dec '56.
—— (Tahiti). Natl. geog. 112: 767 Dec '57.
canoe race, Australia. Travel 107: 28-31 Mar '57.
——, (carnival (snow). Natl. geog. 113: 86-7 (col.) Jan '58.
canoes (soldiers, 1759. Amer. heri. vol. 11 no. 1 p. 24-5 (col.) (Dec '59).
——, Admiralty island. Natl. geog. 112: 592-3 Nov '57.
——, British Guiana. Natl. geog. 107: 334 Mar '55.
——, fishermen. Natl. geog. 116: 670-1 (col.) Nov '59.
——, Indian racing war. Natl. geog. 117: 475 (col.) Ap '60.
——, Khmer war. Natl. geog. 117: 538-9 (col.) Ap '60.
——, Nigeria. Natl. geog. 110: 346-7 Sept '56.
"Canonchet" (home of Wm. Sprague, R. I.). Amer. heri. vol. 7 no. 5 p. 93 (Aug '56).
canopy bed. See bed, canopy.
Canova, Antonio (sculpture by). Amer. heri. vol. 8 no. 2 p. 46 (Feb '57).
Con. 140: 248 Jan '58; 143: 242, 245 Je '59; 144: 226-31 Jan '60.
Natl. geog. 116: 581 (col.) Nov '59.
Praeg. pict. ency., p. 411.
—— (Venus statue). Natl. geog. 111: 489 (col.) Ap '57.
Cantarini, Simone (work of). Con. 144: 22 Sept '59.
canteen, army. Amer. heri. vol. 10 no. 6 p. 4 (col.) (Oct '59).
——, 17th cent. military. Con. 141: XIV May '58.
Canterbury (England). Natl. geog. 108: 315 (col.) Sept '55.

Canterbury (King's school). Natl. geog. 108: 314 (col.) Sept '55.
Canterbury cathedral. Con. 129: XLII Ap '52.
—— chapel (int.). Holiday 23: 82 (col.) Ap '58.
Cantinflas, Mario M. Cur. biog. p. 108 (1953).
Canton, Frank M. Horan: Pict. hist of wild west, p. 187.
Canton (China, harbor). Amer. heri. vol. 6 no. 2 p. 16 (col.) (winter '55).
Canton island. Natl. geog. 107: 118-32 (part col.) Jan '55.
—— (map). Natl. geog. 107: 122 Jan '55.
Cantor, Eddie. Cur. biog. p. 133 (1941); p. 153 (1954).
Cantor, Eddie (black face). Holiday 7: 62 Mar '50.
canyon (Mexico). Travel 110: 27-8 Nov '58.
—— (Utah). Natl. geog. 108: 402-25 (col.) Sept '55.
—— Waimea. See Waimea canyon.
Canyon de Chelly. Holiday 13: 35 (col.) Jan '53.
"Canyon of the lost souls" (Colo.). Amer. heri. vol. 9 no. 1 p. 70 (Dec '57).
canyons. Natl. geog. 105: 375, 380, 384, 388, 390 (col.) Mar '54.
——. See also name of canyon.
Cao, Diogo (work of). Natl. geog. 108: 774 (col.) Dec '55.
cap. Holiday 19: 70 (col.) Mar '56; 21: 194 May '57; 28: 136 Sept '60.
——, Arabian. Natl. geog. 107: 156 (col.) Feb '55.
——, army officer's. Amer. heri. vol. 10 no. 6 p. 4 (col.) (Je '55).
——, aviator's. Holiday 13: 133 (col.) Je '53.
——, boat captain's. Holiday 13: 2 (col.) Ap '53.
——, chef. See chef cap.
——, college (comic). See owl (college cap, comic).
——, confederate officer's. Holiday 28: 57 Sept '60.
——, dunce. See dunce cap.
——, Dutch. Holiday 19: 98 (col.) Jan '56. Natl. geog. 98: 763 (col.) Dec '50.
——, graduation. See mortarboard; cap & gown, college.
——, Greek smoking. Amer. heri. vol. 9 no. 6 p. 23 (Oct '58).
——, hunting. Holiday 18: 105 Oct '55.
——, man's. Holiday 10: 21 Sept '51; 18: 79 (col.), 84 Jl '55; 27: 157 (col.) Mar '60, 28 (col.) Ap '60, 115 (col.) Je '60; 28: 121 (col.) Jl '60, 30 (col.) Sept '60, 146 (col.) Oct '60. Natl. geog. 107: 473 (col.) Ap '55.
——, man's (red). Natl. geog. 110: 56 (col.). Jl '56.
——, man's riding. Holiday 27: 159 Feb '60.
——, navy. Holiday 14: inside cover (col.) Sept '53.
——, Oriental pearl. Con. 142: XLIX Nov '58.
——, Phrygian. See Phrygian cap.
——, Russian fur (men). Natl. geog. 116: 383 Sept '59.
——, soldier's (1865). Amer. heri. vol. 6 no. 6 p. 48 (Oct '55).

——, swimming. Holiday 18: 30 Jl '55.
cap & gown (graduation procession). Face of Amer., p. 119 (col.).
——, academic (India). Natl. geog. 117: 620-1 (col.) May '60.
——, college graduate. Holiday 10: 92 (col.) Dec '51; 13: 56 Mar '53.
——, college graduate. Int. gr. soc.: Arts . . . p. 153 (col.).
caps & gowns, college style. Natl. geog. 102: 556 Oct '52.
cape, bullfighter's. See bullfighter's cape.
Cape Ann (Mass.). Travel 107: 17-9 May '57.
—— (map of Mass. coast). Travel 107: 18 May '57.
Cape Breton island (fort). Amer. heri. vol. 12 no. 1 p. 6-7 (col.) (Dec '60).
—— (harbor). Holiday 14: 46-7 (col.) Jl '53.
Cape Canaveral (Florida, missile test center). Natl. geog. 112: 790 (col.) Dec '57; 116: 424-70 (part col.) Oct '59.
Cape Cod (Mass.). Holiday 6: 56-63 (part col.) Sept '49.
Jordan: Hammond's pict. atlas, p. 33 (col.).
—— (air map). Natl. geog. 99: 710-11 Je '51.
—— (pier). Travel 109: 7 May '58.
—— (village). Holiday 28: 71 (col.) Jl '60.
Cape Cod cottages. Holiday 8: 52-7 (part col.) Aug '50.
Cape Cod Melody tent (Hyannis). Travel 113: 28 May '60.
Cape Cross (rocks, seals, ocean spray). Natl. geog. 108: 770-1 (col.) Dec '55.
Cape Kennedy. U.S. News & world report, p. 57 Aug 31 '64.
Cape Kiwanda coast. Holiday 23: 107 (col.) Feb '58.
Cape Orso. Lebande: Naples, p. 24, 193.
Cape Sabine (Arctic, 1884). Amer. heri. vol. 11 no. 4 p. 47-8 (col.) (Je '60).
Cape Thunder (Van Cleve). Amer. heri. vol. 9 no. 5 p. 46 (col.) (Aug '58).
Cape Town (Africa). Holiday 21: 34-5 (col.) Feb '57.
Travel 113: 29-31 Jan '60.
—— (Houses of Parliament). Natl. geog. 104: 166 (col.) Aug '53.
—— (resort Clifton). Holiday 25: 149 Ap '59.
—— (Sea Point). Holiday 25: 51 (col.) Ap '59.
Capehart, Homer Earl. Cur. biog. p. 90 (1947).
Capelinhos lighthouse (Azores). Natl. geog. 113: 746 (col.) Je '58.
Capelia Pazzi (Florence, Italy). Praeg. pict. ency., p. 260.
Capello, Vicenzo (Titian). Natl. geog. 110: 638 (col.) Nov '56.
Capilano bridge. See bridge, Capilano.
Capistrano mission. See mission, Capistrano.
capital (columns). Praeg. pict. ency., p. 43.
capitals, Romanesque. Int. gr. soc.: Arts . . . p. 47 (col.)
capitol bldg., Alabama. See Alabama (state capitol).
——, Argentina. Natl. geog. 113: 304-5 (col.) Mar '58.
——, Brazil. See Brasilia.
——, Cal. Natl. geog. 105: 750 (col.) Je '54.

——, **Colonial (Williamsburg, Va.).** Amer. heri. vol. 1 no. 2 p. 40 (winter '50).
Brooks: Growth of a nation, p. 65.
Holiday 18: 107 (col.) Nov '55.
Natl. geog. 106: 441, 453 (col.) Oct '54.
——, **Colo.** Holiday 18: 14 Sept '55; 19: 6 Jan '56.
Natl. geog. 100: 198 Aug '51; 106: 216 (col.) Aug '54.
——, **Confederate.** See Confederate capitol.
——, **Conn.** Amer. heri. vol. 3 no. 3 p. 60 (spring '52).
Holiday 26: 39 Sept '59.
——, **Del.** See Delaware capitol bldg.
——, **Ga.** Natl. geog. 105: 289, 296 (col.) Mar '54.
——, **Ill.** Natl. geog. 104: 815 Dec '53.
——, **Ill. old state.** See Illinois old state capitol.
——, **India.** Natl. geog. 118: 466-7 (col.) Oct '60.
——, **Indonesia.** Natl. geog. 108: 358-9 (col.) Sept '55.
——, **Iowa.** See Iowa state capitol.
——, **Korean.** Natl. geog. 97: 778 Je '50.
——, **La.** Jordan: Hammond's pict. atlas, p. 84 (col.).
Natl. geog. 118: 710 (col.) Nov '60.
——, **Minn.** See Minn. state capitol bldg.
——, **Mont.** Natl. geog. 97: 702 (col.) Je '50.
——, **N.H.** Natl. geog. 99: 108 Jan '51.
——, **N.Y. state.** See N. Y. state capitol.
——, **N.D.** Natl. geog. 100: 291, 293 (col.) Sept '51.
——, **Ohio (1st state).** Amer. heri. vol. 4 no. 3 p. 39 (spring '53).
——, **Ohio.** Natl. geog. 107: 444 Ap '55; 117: 266-7 (part col.) Feb '60.
——, **Ore.** Travel 101: 8 Ap '54; 108: 20 Nov '57.
——, **Puerto Rico.** Natl. geog. 99: 422 Ap '51.
——, **R. I.** Holiday 27: 102 (col.) May '60.
Natl. geog. 107: 777 Je '55.
——, **S.C.** Natl. geog. 103: 283 Mar '53.
——, **U.S.** See U.S. capitol.
——, **Utah.** Holiday 14: 33 Aug '53.
——, **Va.** Amer. heri. vol. 10 no. 5 p. 69 (Aug '59).
——. Holiday 10: 140 (col.) Oct '51.
——. See also Capitol. Colonial (Williamsburg, Va.).
——, **Wash. (D.C.).** See U.S. Capitol bldg.
——, **Wash. state.** See Wash. state capitol.
——, **Wis.** Jordan: Hammond's pict. atlas, p. 94 (col.).
Natl. geog. 111: 142 (col.) Feb '57.
Caplin, Mortimer M. Cur. biog. p. 93 (1961).
Capnomancy (sym.). Lehner: Pict. bk. of sym., p. 67.
Capo di Monte (sculpture). Con. 138: inside cover Sept '56.
Capodimonte, palace of. See palace of Capodimonte.
Capodimonte porcelain. See porcelain, Capodimonte.
Capogrossi, Giuseppe. Cur. biog. p. 100 (1957).
Capone, Al. Holiday 10: 97 Oct '51.
Capote, Truman. Cur. biog. p. 92 (1951).
Holiday 23: 63 (col.) Mar '58.

Capp, Al. Cur. biog. p. 93 (1947).
Cappadocia (Turkey). Natl. geog. 113: 122-46 Jan '58.
Osward: Asia Minor, pl. 72-5.
—— **(map).** Natl. geog. 113: 129 Jan '58.
Cappella dei principi (Florence, Italy). Con. 141: 214 Je '58.
Capper, Arthur. Cur. biog. p. 91 (1946).
Capra, Frank. Cur. biog. p. 91 (1948).
Capri, island of (Italy). Holiday 25: 52-7 (part col.) Jan '59.
Labande: Naples, p. 207-220.
—— **(drawings by Bemelman).** Holiday 6: 60-2 (col.) Nov '49.
—— **(market).** Holiday 6: 135 (col.) Oct '49.
"Capriccios" (Guardi). Con. 143: XXXVI-XXXVII (col.) Je '59.
Capsule, Mercury. Natl. geog. 118: 60-1 (part col.) Jl '60.
captain, airline. Holiday 22: 18 (col.) Nov '57; 24:: 78 Oct '58, 208 Nov '58, 159 Dec '58; 25: 12 (col.) Je '59.
——, **German airforce.** Holiday 25: 42 (col.) Jan '59.
——, **ship.** Holiday 13: 79 (col.) Ap '53; 24: 131 Oct '58, 112 Nov '58.
——, **ship (early days).** Holiday 27: 124 (col.) Je '60.
——, **ship (head).** Holiday 25: 117 May '59, 33-4 (col.) Je '59; 27: 204 May '60, 104 Je '60.
——, **ship (with boy).** Holiday 27: 134 Jan '60.
——, **Spanish.** Int. gr. soc.: Arts . . . p. 115 (col.).
captain & girl (on boat). Holiday 14: 80 (col.) Jl '53.
captain & stewardess, airline (back view). Holiday 25: 9 Ap '59.
"Capt. Charles Stewart". See Stewart, Capt. Charles (by Sully).
"Captain Read" (Kauffmann). Con. 127: 57 Mar '51.
captain's stool. See stool, captain's.
Capua (church of Santa Caterena ruins). Labande: Naples, p. 135.
Capua gate. Labande: Naples, p. 75.
car, aerial. See aerial car.
——, **root beer.** Amer. heri. vol. 6 no. 4 p. 46 (col.) (Je '55).
car body stamping press. Int. gr. soc.: Arts . . . p. 173 (col.).
car caddy. Travel 113. 11 Mar '60.
car. See also automobile.
Carabinieri (Italian police, Rome). Holiday 28: 30 Dec '60.
Nalt. geog. 111: 482-3 (col.) Ap '57.
Caracalla (Roman sculpture). Praeg. pict. ency., p. 143.
Caracas (Venezuela). Natl. geog. 117: 236 (col.). Feb '60.
Travel 101: 11-3 Ap '54; 105: 22 Feb '56.
—— **(Caracas Hilton hotel).** Travel 110: 41 Jl '58.
—— **(Mt. top hotel).** Travel 107: 45 May '51.
—— **(The Pantheon).** Holiday 6: back cover (col.) Oct '49.
carafe (bottle). Holiday 24: 33 Dec '58; 28: 32 Dec '60.

Caravaggio, Michelangelo (work of). Con. 126: 201 Dec '50; 142: 143-7 Dec '58.
Praeg. pict. atlas, p. 327 (col.).
Caravaggio signature, Michelangelo de. See signature, Caravaggio.
caravan (man & donkey). Natl. geog. 113: 140 Jan '58.
——, camel. Natl. geog. 102: 652-3 (col.) Nov '52.
——, Hindu (on horses). Natl. geog. 110: 526-7 Oct '56.
Caraway, Hattie W. Cur. biog. p. 90 (1945).
carbon filament lamp. See lamp, Edison, carbon filament.
Carboni, Bernardo Giovanni (work of). Con. 142: XIX Sept '58.
Carcassonne (France). Holiday 21: 86-7 (col.) Ap '57.
Natl. geog. 100: 34-5 (col.) Jl '51.
Carcassone city wall. Travel 107: 13 Ap '57.
card, adv. Amer. heri. vol. 6 no. 1 p. 27 (col.) (fall '54).
——, Italian playing. Con. 133: 54-60 Mar '54.
——, playing (sym.). Lehner: Pict. bk. of sym., p. 62, 65, 79.
——, trade See trade card.
card case, antique. Con. 142: 243-4 Jan '59.
card game (men & women). Holiday 10: 2 (col.) Oct '51.
"Card players" (Van Leyden). Natl. geog. 110: 653 (col.) Nov '56.
card shuffler. Holiday 10: 131 Oct '51.
card table (1800). Con. 142: 134 Nov '58.
——, Adam. Con. 144: XIX Dec '59.
——, antique. Con. 138: 45 Sept '56; 139: 243 Je '57; 141: inside back cover May '58; 142: IV Sept '58.
——, Baltimore hepplewhite. Con. 135: 69 Mar '55.
——, Chippendale. Con. ency. of ant., vol. 1, pl. 39.
Con. 133: XXXII May '54; 137: XIV Mar '56; 138: VI Dec '56; 141: VI Je '58.
——, Chippendale serpentine. Con. 135: XX-XIII Je '55; 141: XLVI Je '58.
——, 18th cent. Con. 133: XIX, XXII, LIII May '54; 134: LV Nov '54; 137: VI Ap '56; 138: 60, XLIV Sept '56; 142: 21 Sept '58.
——, 18th cent. serpentine. Con. 143: XXXIV Je '59.
——, George II serpentine. Con. 132: 140 Nov '53.
——, hepplewhite. Con. 134: XV Nov '54.
——, marble top. Con. 139: XXIV Je '57.
——, Queen Anne. Con. ency. of ant., vol. 1, pl. 23.
Con. 132: XLI Sept '53; 141: 73 Ap '58; 145: 280 Je '60.
——, regency. Con. 144: XL Jan '60; 145: XV Mar '60, XXVI, XXXVIII Ap '60.
——, Sheraton. Con. 129: XIX Je '52; 139: XXX Mar '57; 141: XXX Ap '58; 143: XXIV Mar '59.
——, William & Mary. Con. 144: 58 Sept '59.
card table & chairs. Holiday 21: 82 Feb '57; 28: 44 (col.) Oct '60.
"Cardiff giant" (petrified man, Cooperstown,

N. Y.). Amer. heri. vol. 3 no. 3 p. 35. (spring '52).
Durant: Pict. hist. of Amer. circus, p. 66.
Travel 103: 22 Mar '55.
Cardinal (Vatican). Holiday 23: 62 (col.) May '58.
"Cardinal Bandinello Sauli". Natl. geog. 101: 79 (col.) Jan '52.
Cardinal Doi Peter Tatsuo. See Doi, Peter Tatsuo, Cardinal.
Cardinal Meyer, Albert. See Meyer, Albert, Cardinal.
Cardinal Muench, Aloisius. See Muench, Aloisius, Cardinal.
Cardinal Rugambwa. See Rugambwa, Laurian, Cardinal.
Cardinal Santos, Rufino J. See Santos, Rufino J., Cardinal.
carding comb, wool. See wool carding comb.
Cardon, Philip V. Cur. biog. p. 155 (1954).
Cardozo, Benjamin N. Amer. heri. vol. 9 no. 3 p. 25 (Ap '58).
cards, adv. See advertising cards.
——, playing. See playing cards.
——, ship sailing. See ship sailing cards, clipper.
——Tarot. See Tarot cards.
Carew, Richard. Con. 143: 71 Ap '59.
Carey, Ernestine Gilbreth. Cur. biog. p. 225 (1949).
Carey, James B. Cur. biog. p. 135 (1941); p. 94 (1951).
Caribbean Indians. Holiday 5: 27 (col.) Feb '49.
Caribbean islands. Holiday 5: 34-63 (part col.) Feb '49; 23: 36-51 (col.) Feb '58; 25: 2 (col.) Jan '59.
Natl. geog. 105: 335-62 (part col.) Mar '54.
Travel 105: 9-14 Feb '56; 109: 22-3 May '58; 114: 38-57 Oct '60.
—— (beach). Holiday 5: 39 (col.) Feb '49; 25: 126 (col.) Feb '59.
—— (bean sorters). Holiday 24: 144 (col.) Oct '58.
—— (church ceremony). Holiday 24: 131 (col.) Nov '58.
—— (harbor). Holiday 27: 136 (col.) Feb '60.
—— (map). See map (Caribbean).
—— (night view). Holiday 26: 42 (col.) Nov '59.
—— art. See art, Caribbean.
Caribbean dancers. Holiday 15: 68 (col.) Je '54; 18: 71 (col.) Aug '55, inside front page (col.) Sept '55; 24: 94 (col.) Aug '58.
Caribbean life. Holiday 22: 96 (col.) Sept '57.
Caribbean man. Holiday 6: 30 (col.) Oct '49.
—— (beating drum). Holiday 18: 71 (col.) Aug '55.
—— (comic). Holiday 15: 127 Je '54.
—— (cutting cane). Holiday 5: 96 (col.) Ap '49.
Caribbean men & women. Holiday 25: 110 (col.) May '59.
Caribbean musicians. See musicians (Caribbean).
Caribbean people (caricatures). Holiday 16: inside cover (col.) Aug '54.
Caribbean sea. Travel 103: 11-7 Mar '55.

—— (map). Holiday 5: 35 (col.) Feb '49; 23: 34-5 (col.) Feb '58.
Natl. geog. 118: 122 (col.) Jl '60.
Travel 103: 11 Mar '55.
Caribbean woman. Holiday 24: 7 (col.) Sept '58; 26: 159 (col.) Oct '59.
—— (pushing child in cart). Holiday 14: 29 Dec '53.
—— (riding mule). Holiday 14: 29 Dec '53.
Caribe Hilton hotel (San Juan). Travel 109: 41 Jan '58.
caricature (P.T. Barnum). Durant: Pict. hist. of Amer. circus, p. 57.
caricatures (U.S. Presidents, by Berger). Amer. heri. vol. 10 no. 3 p. 88-93 (Ap '59).
——, Swedish (Sergel). Con. 141: 31-3 Mar '58.
——, transcendentalist (Cranch). Amer. heri. vol. 10 no. 3 p. 60-1 (Ap '59).
caricatures. See also cartoon.
carillon, aboriginal. Natl. geog. 97: 170 (col.) Feb '50.
Carillon hotel (Miami Beach). Travel 108: 43 Dec '57.
carillon tower. Natl. geog. 113: 815 (col.) Je '58.
—— (Ottawa). Natl. geog. 104: 829 (col.) Dec '53.
—— (White Springs, Fla.). Holiday 24: 141 (col.) Sept '58; 28: 49 (col.) Nov '60.
carillon. See also bell tower.
"Carlo & Ubaldo resisting enchantments". Con. 145: 40 Mar '60.
Carlsbad cavern (N.M.). Holiday 5: 85 Ap '49; 11: 45 Feb '52; 13: 137 (col.) May '53; 14: 142 (col.) Jl '53; 18: 68 (col.) Nov '55; 23: 4 (col.) Mar '58; 27: 44 Ap '60.
Jordan: Hammond's pict. atlas, p. 122-3 (col.).
Natl. geog. 101: 129 Jan '52; 104: 434-68 (col.) Oct '53.
Travel 101: 16 Ap '54; 106: 24 Dec '56; 109: cover, 11 Feb '58.
Carlsbad caverns natl. park. Holiday 19: 78 (col.) Feb '56; 21: 4 (col.) Ap '57.
Carlsbad hotel (Cal.). Travel 108: 47 Nov '57.
Carlson, Anton J. Cur. biog. p. 94 (1948).
Carlson, Lt. Col. Evans F. Cur. biog. p. 98 (1943).
Carlson, Frank. Cur. biog. p. 94 (1949).
Carlson, John Roy. Cur. biog. p. 101 (1943).
Carlson, William S. Cur. biog. p. 86 (1952).
Carlton hotel (Cannes, France). Holiday 26: 66-9 (part col.) Aug '59.
Carlyle, Thomas. Amer. heri. vol. 8 no. 5 p. 27 (Aug '57).
Carmel-Del Monte Pebble beach (Cal.). Holiday 26: 61 (col.) Jl '59.
Carmel mission. See mission, Carmel.
Carmen. Cooper: Con. ency. of music, p. 91.
Carmer, Carl. Holiday 6: 32 Sept '49.
Carmer's home, Carl (Irvington, N. Y.). Amer. heri. vol. 10 no. 1 p. 19 (Dec '58).
Carmichael, Hoagy. Cur. biog. p. 137 (1941).
Carmichael, J. W. (work of). Con. 134: 127 Nov '54.
Carmichael, Oliver C. Cur. biog. p. 94 (1946).

Carmona, Antonio Oscar de Fragoso. Cur. biog. p. 81 (1950).
Carmona, Marshal A. O. (Pres. of Portugal). Holiday 6: 100 Sept '49.
carnation (sym., Mother's Day). Lehner: Pict. bk. of sym., p. 54.
"Carnavon castle" (Wilson). Con. 139: 87 Ap '57.
Carnegie, Andrew. Amer. heri. vol. 8 no. 3 p. 46 (Ap '57); vol. 11 no. 5 p. 5 (Aug '60).
—— (cartoon). Amer. heri. vol. 11 no. 5 p. 8-9 (Aug '60).
Carnegie, Dale. Cur. biog. p. 139 (1941); p, 101 (1955).
Carnegie, Dorothy. Cur. biog. p. 102 (1955).
Carnegie, Hattie. Cur. biog. p. 137 (1942).
Carnegie birthplace, Andrew (Scotland). Amer. heri. vol. 11 no. 5 p. 8 (Aug '60).
Carnegie Hall, N. Y. Cooper: Con. ency. of music, p. 461.
—— (int.). Holiday 26: 93 (col.) Oct '59.
Carnegie home, Andrew. Amer. heri. vol. 11 no. 5 p. 7 (Aug '60).
Carnes, Capt. John. Amer. heri. vol. 6 no. 2 cover (col.) (winter '55).
Carnes, John. Holiday 18: 44 (col.) Aug '55.
Carney, Art. Cur. biog. p. 73 (1958).
Holiday 28: 125 Nov '60.
Carney, Adm. Robert B. Cur. biog. p. 97 (1951).
carnival (18th cent., Europe). Int. gr. soc.: Arts . . . p. 117 (col.).
—— (Havana). Holiday 12: 68 (col.) Dec '52.
—— (Lisbon, Portugal). Holiday 6: 106 (col.) Sept '49.
—— (masked). Holiday 26: 188 (col.) Dec '59.
—— (Rio de Janeiro). Holiday 17: 10 (col.) Feb '55.
—— (Trinidad). Holiday 11: 90, 94-5 (col.) Feb '52; 23: 46-7 (col.) Feb '58.
Natl. geog. 103: 60 Jan '53.
——, winter (Quebec). Natl. geog. 113: 73-96 (part col.) Jan '58.
——, winter stunts (St. Paul, Minn.). Travel 113: 39-40 Jan '60.
carnival actors. Holiday 24: 185 (col.) Nov '58.
carnival acts. (Virgin islands). Natl. geog. 109: 214-5 (col.) Feb '56.
carnival costumes (Brazil). Holiday 18: 10 (col.) Nov '55.
—— (Trinidad). Holiday 23: 46-7 (col.) Feb '58.
carnival crowd (Brazil). Natl. geog. 107: 302-3, 305-7 (col.) Mar '55.
carnival Queen (Trinidad). Holiday 11: 95 (col.) Feb '52.
carnival swing (Ischia island). Natl. geog. 105: 548 Ap '54.
carnival time (Spain). Natl. geog. 99: 524-30 (col.) Ap '51.
carnival, Veiled Prophet ball (St. Louis). Holiday 8: 38-9 (col.) Oct '50.
carol singers (sym.). Lehner: Pict. bk. of sym., p. 50.
carol singers. Natl. geog. 106: 140 (col.) Jl '54.
Travel 102: 11 Dec '54.
—— (heads). Holiday 26: 179, 180 Dec '59.

Caroline of Anspach, Queen. *See* "Queen Caroline".

Caron, Leslie. Cur. biog. p. 157 (1954).

Caron, Pierre Augustin. Amer. heri. vol. 7 no. 3 p. 86 (Ap '56).

"Carondelet". *See* gunboat "'Carondelet".

Caroselli, Angelo (work of). Con. 143: LIV Ap '59.

carp fish (sym.). Lehner: Pict. bk. of sym., p. 62.

Carpaccio, Vittorio (work of). Con. 135: 138 Ap '55; 142: 64 Sept '58, 206 Dec '58.

carpenter (sym.). Lehner: Pict. bk. of sym., p. 90.

Carpenter, Constance. Holiday 14: 49 Dec '53.

Carpenter, Dan. Amer. heri. vol. 10 no. 4 p. 96 (Je '59).

Carpenter, Francis B. (work of). Amer. heri. vol. 11 no. 6 p. 46 (Oct '60).

Carpenter, George L. Cur. biog. p. 104 (1943).

Carpenter, John Alden. Cur. biog. p. 95 (1947).

Carpenter, Julius H. Cur. biog. p. 105 (1943).

Carpenter, Malcolm Scott. Cur. biog. p. 73 (1962).

carpenter (Saar costume). Natl. geog. 105: 570 Ap '54.

Carpenter's Hall (Phila.). Amer. heri. vol. 1 no. 2 p. 20 (winter '50); vol. 3 no. 1 p. 43 (fall '51).
Holiday 26: 127 Jl '59.

carpenter's tools. *See* tools, carpenter's.

Carpentier, Lt. Gen. Marcel-Maurice. Cur. biog. p. 99 (1951).

carpet. Holiday 10: 20-1 (col.) Oct '51.

——, **Adam.** Con. 129: LXIII Ap '52.

——, **Ardabil.** Con. 144: 137 Nov '59.

——, **Aubusson.** Con. 142: XX Dec '58, 207 Jan '59; 145: XXVI Je '60.

——, **Aubusson (detail).** Con. 143: 262 Je '59.

——, **Aubusson. (Louis Quinze).** Con. 142: XLII Nov '58.

——, **Carabagh.** Con. 143: X Ap '59.

——, **Directoire.** Con. 133: XXX Je '54.

——, **English needlework (18th cent.).** Con. 141: XXXVI Je '58.

——, **French (19th cent.).** Con. 141: XLV Ap '58.

——, **Italian (18th cent.).** Con. 132: 211 Jan '54.

——, **Kabistan.** Con. 142: X Dec '58.

——, **Kashan.** Con. 143: XIV Mar '59.

——, **Kirman.** Con. 144: XXXII Sept '59.

——, **Kiz-Ghiordez (Asia Minor).** Con. 144: LV Nov '59.

——, **Louis XV.** Con. 143: VIII Ap '59.

——, **magic.** *See* magic carpet.

——, **needlework.** Con. 129: LXV Je '52; 133: XXI May '54.

——, **needlework (antique).** Con. 133: LX Je '54.

——, **needlework (English, 18th cent.).** Con. 141: XXXVI Je '58.

——, **needlework (French).** Con. 145: XXVI May '60.

——, **Persian.** *See* Persian carpet.

——, **Polonaise.** Con. 133: LII May '54.

——, **Savonnerie.** Con. 140: 68 Sept '57; 143: LXIV May '59, 204 (col.) Je '59.

——, **17th cent.** Con. 144: LXI, LXIII-LXIV (col.) Nov '59.

——, **Ukrainian.** Con. 139: LIII Ap '57.

——, **Wilton.** Con. 140: XX Dec '57.

carpet. *See* also rug.

carpet-rag needle. Rawson: Ant. pict. bk., p. 7.

carpet sweeper. Int. gr. soc.: Arts . . . p. 171 (col.).

carpet weavers (Isparta). Osward: Asia Minor, p. 140-1.

carpet weaving (India). Natl. geog. 118: 786 (col.) Oct '60.

—— **(Iran).** Natl. geog. 101: 826 (col.) Je '52

carpets, oriental. Con. ency. of ant., vol. 1, pl. 127-8.
Holiday 18: 60-1 (col.) Nov '55.

Carr, Emma P. Cur biog. p. 56 (1959).

Carr, Lt. K. M. Natl. geog. 115: 7 (col.) Jan '59.

Carr, Mary Jane. Jun. bk. of auth., p. 66.

Carr, Robert K. Cur. biog. p. 95 (1961).

Carr, William G. Cur. biog. p. 89 (1952).

Carra, Carlo (work of). Praeg. pict. ency., p. 475 (col.).

Carracci, Agostino (work of). Con. 143: 92 Ap '59.

Carracci, Annibale (work of). Con. 132: 5-6 Sept '53, 101 Nov '53; 135: XXVI Je '55; 138: 227-9 Jan '57; 142: 197 Dec '58.

Caraway, Gertrude S. Cur. biog. p. 159 (1954).

Carrera hotel (Santiago, Chile). Holiday 13: 12 (col.) May '53, 119 (col.) Je '53.

carriage (driver, women). Natl. geog. 101: 309 (col.) Mar '52.

—— **(1840, horses, driver).** Jensen: The White House, p. 66.

——, **baby.** *See* baby buggy.

——, **doll.** *See* doll carriage.

carriage, & sacred oxen (India). Holiday 7: 87 (col.) May '50.

carriage. *See* also buggy.

Carrick, Valery. Jun. bk. of auth., p. 67.

Carrickfergus castle (Ireland). Holiday 13: 131 (col.) Ap '53.

carrier-chair (Egyptian ceremonial, ancient). Int. gr. soc.: Arts . . . p. 43, 81 (col.).

carrier ship, U.S. Natl. geog. 104: 574 (col.) Oct '53.

Carriera, Rosalba (work of). Con. 138: LXIX Jan '57; 141: 237 Je '58.

Carrington, Elaine Sterne. Cur. biog. p. 86 (1944).

Carroll, Mrs. Daniel. *See* Darnall, Eleanor.

Carroll, Dishann. Cur. biog. p. 75 (1962).

Carroll, H. Bailey. Amer. heri. vol. 4 no. 1 p. 1 (fall '52).

Carroll, John. Cur. biog. p. 103 (1955).

Carroll, John A. Cur. biog. p. 75 (1958).

Carroll, Lt. Gen. Joseph F. Cur. biog. p. 77 (1962).

Carroll, Lewis (pseud.). *See* Dodgson, Charles Lutwidge.

Carroll, Madeleine. Cur. biog. p. 95 (1949).

Carroll, Thomas. Cur. biog. p. 79 (1962).

carrot carnival (Cal.). Natl. geog. 112: 706 (col.) Nov '57.

"Carrying of the Cross". Con. 126: 219 Dec '50.

cars, cable. *See* cable cars.

Carson, Kit. Amer. heri. vol. 7 no. 4 p. 19 (Je '56).
Brooks: Growth of a nation, p. 125.

Carson, Rachel. Cur. biog. p. 101 (1951).

Carson grave, Kit. (Taos, N.M.). Travel 109: 23 Mar '58.

Carson cave, Kit. Holiday 19: 78 (col.) Feb '56.

cart (horse). Travel 101: 4 Ap '54; 108: 27 Jl '57.

—— **(horse, boy).** Natl. geog. 112: 158 Aug '57.

—— **(horse, children).** Holiday 21: 77 Ap '57.

—— **(horse, man).** Natl. geog. 101: 144 Feb '52.

—— **(horse, man, woman).** Holiday 27: 55 (col.) May '60.

—— **(horse, people).** Holiday 28: 192 (col.) Oct '60.

—— **(mule, Negroes).** Natl. geog. 111: 618 (col.) May '57.

—— **(pepper loaded).** Natl. geog. 111: 643 (col.) May '57.

——, **antique (boys, horse, exhibit).** Natl. geog. 99: 139 Jan '51.

——, **Arabian (curtained).** Natl. geog. 104: 42 (col.) Jl '53.

——, **Barbados, W. I. (horse).** Holiday 27: 22 Je '60.

——, **Black Forest (horses, people).** Disney: People & places, p. 49 (col.).

——, **Brazil (man, horse).** Natl. geog. 117: 713 May '60.

——, **Burdur.** Osward: Asia Minor, p. 142.

——, **camel.** Natl. geog. 102: 646 (col.) Nov '52.

——, **Caraboo.** Travel 104: 6 Oct '55.

——, **Chile (horse).** Natl. geog. 117: 197 (col.) Feb '60.

——, **Cyprus road (horse, load).** Natl. geog. 112: 108 (col.) Jl '57.

——, **donkey.** Travel 102: 21 Sept '54.

——, **donkey (children).** Holiday 20: 52 Oct '56.
Natl. geog. 101: 778 (col.) Je '52; 111: 387 Mar '57.

——, **donkey (children, men).** Natl. geog. 115: 627 (col.) May '59.

——, **donkey (Cyprus island).** Natl. geog. 101: 643 (col.) May '52.

——, **donkey (movers, Greece).** Natl. geog. 103: 373 (col.) Mar '53.

——, **fire hose.** Natl. geog. 104: 680 (col.) Nov '53.

——, **France (horse, men).** Holiday 25: 38 (col.) Jan '59.

——, **goat (children).** Jensen: The White House, p. 147.

——, **Greece.** Natl. geog. 109: 51 (col.) Jan '56.

——, **grocery (women).** Natl. geog. 109: 748 (col.) Je '56.

——, **Holland (horse).** Natl. geog. 106: 381 (col.) Sept '54.

——, **Indonesia (horse).** Natl. geog. 99: 37 (col.) Jan '51.

——, **Irish.** Natl. geog. 104: 126, 130 (col.) Jl '53.

——, **Irish (horse, woman).** Holiday 24: 87 (col.) Dec '58.

——, **Irish pony.** Natl. geog. 99: 674 (col.) May '51.

——, **Italy (horse).** Labande: Naples, p. 75, 146.

——, **maple syrup.** *See* maple syrup cart.

——, **market (horse).** Natl. geog. 98: 636 (col.) Nov '50.

——, **Mexican burro (tourists).** Natl. geog. 105: 778 (col.) Je '54.

——, **Norwegian carved.** Con. 145: 35 Mar '60.

——, **ox.** Amer. heri. vol. 10 no. 5 p. 101 (Aug '59).
Disney: People & places, p. 74, 102 (col.)
Holiday 10: 13 (col.) Nov '51; 12: 158 (col.) Dec '52; 13: 106 (col.) May '53; 21: 92 (col.) Ap '57; 23: 34 (col.) Feb '58.
Natl. geog. 100: 10 (col.) Jl '51 105: 158, 160 (col.) Feb '54, 563 Ap '54.
Travel 101: 20 Ap '54.

——, **ox (animal cage, ancient).** Natl. geog. 111: 226-7 (col.) Feb '57.

——, **ox (Chile).** Holiday 11: 13 (col.) Mar '52.

——, **ox (Cyprus island).** Natl. geog. 101: 639 (col.) May '52.

——, **ox (Formosa, men).** Natl. geog. 109: 267 (col.) Feb '56.

——, **ox (Java).** Natl. geog. 99: 32 (col.) Jan '51.

——, **ox (Laos).** Natl. geog. 117: 56 (col.) Jan '60.

——, **ox (Malaya).** Natl. geog. 103: 208 Feb '53.

——, **ox (man).** Rawson: Ant. pict. bk., p. 70.

——, **ox (Negro driver).** Natl. geog. 103: 295 (col.) Mar '53.

——, **ox (Pescadores island, women.** Natl. geog. 109: 276 (col.) Feb '56.

——, **ox (Philippines).** Travel 113: 10 May '60.

——, **ox (Russia).** Natl. geog. 116: 393 (col.) Sept '59.

——, **ox (St. Efisio parade, Sardinia).** Holiday 23: 70 (col.) Jan '58.

——, **ox (Switzerland).** Natl. geog. 111: 786 (col.) Je '57.

——, **ox (Turkey).** Natl. geog. 100: 176 (col.) Aug '51.

——, **peddler's.** Holiday 26: 59 (col.) Oct '59.

——, **pony.** Jensen: The White House, p. 107

——, **Scotland (horse).** Disney: People & places, p. 29 (col.).

——, **Scotland (horse & driver).** Natl. geog. 110: 9 (col.) Jl '56.

——, **Sicily (horse, people, festival).** Natl. geog. 107: 15 (col.) Jan '55.

——, **Spain (men, straw).** Natl. geog. 109: 323 (col.) Mar '56.

cart, tea. *See* tea cart.

——, two-wheel. Natl. geog. 99: 171 Feb '51; 103: 37 Jan '53.

——, two-wheel (Afghanistan). Natl. geog. 104: 420 Sept '53.

——, two-wheel farm. Natl. geog. 111: 610 May '57.

——, two-wheel farm (Iceland). Natl. geog. 100: 622 (col.) Nov '51.

——, vegetable (vender). Holiday 10: 45 (col.) Dec '51.

——, Yugoslavia. Holiday 14: 47 Aug '53.

cart & plow, ox. Natl. geog. 103: 235, 240-1 (col.) Feb '53.

Cartagena (Spain). Holiday 24: 140 (col.) Oct '58.

—— (Holy week procession). Travel 107: 20 Ap '57.

Carte, Rupert D'Oyly. Cur. biog. p. 156 (1948).

Carter, Anne. Amer. heri. vol. 8 no. 3 p. 60 (Ap '57).

Carter, Boake. Cur. biog. p. 139 (1942).

Carter, Don. Cur. biog. (1963).

Carter, Elliott C. Cur. biog. p. 79 (1960).

Carter, Hodding, jr. Cur. biog. p. 96 (1946).

Carter, John. Cur. biog. p. 58 (1959).

Carthusian monastery (Capri, Italy). Labande: Naples, p. 215.

Cartier-Bresson, Henri. Cur. biog. p. 97 (1947).

Cartograph (Utah). Holiday 14: 29 Aug '53.

cartography (sym.). Lehner: Pict. bk. of sym., p. 11.

cartoon (Abraham Lincoln). Amer. heri. vol. 11 no. 6 p. 77 (Oct '60).

—— (Abraham Rueff). Amer. heri. vol. 11 no. 1 p. 102 (Dec '59).

—— (Amer. & John Bull). Amer. heri. vol. 9 no. 5 p. 105 (Aug '58).

—— (Andrew Carnegie). *See* Carnegie, Andrew (cartoon).

—— (Andrew Johnson as a parrot, 1868). Amer. heri. vol. 8 no. 1 p. 102 (Dec '56).

—— (bank failure, 1833). Amer. heri. vol. 7 no. 4 p. 11 (Je '56).

—— (baseball). Amer. heri. vol. 10 no. 3 p. 16-7, 19 (Ap '59); vol. 11 no. 4 p. 89 (Je '60).

—— (book agents). Amer. heri. vol. 9 no. 5 p. 79 (Aug '58).

—— (Boston, 1774). Amer. heri. vol. 2 no. 2 p. 27 (winter '51).

—— (British, 1861). Amer. heri. vol. 8 no. 3 p. 42 (Ap '57).

—— (British man & woman). Holiday 23: 123 Ap '58.

—— (buffalo hunt). Amer. heri. vol. 7 no. 5 p. 37 (Aug '56).

—— (by Art Young). Amer. heri. vol. 11 no. 2 p. 95, 99 (Feb '60).

—— (Carry Nation). Amer. heri. vol. 9 no. 1 p. 54 (Dec '57).

—— (clergymen, 1905). Amer. heri. vol. 6 no. 3 p. 76 (Ap '55).

—— (club life). Amer. heri. vol. 9 no. 5 p. 103 (Aug '58).

—— (cowboy). Holiday 14: 84 Nov '53, 30 Dec '53.

—— (Dickens farewell). Natl. geog. 108: 304 Sept '55.

—— (early radio). Amer. heri. vol. 6 no. 5 p. 81 (Aug '55).

—— (Father Neptune & Atlantic cable). Amer. heri. vol. 9 no. 6 p. 92 (Oct '58).

—— (football hero). Holiday 14: 66 (col.) Nov '53.

—— (Franklin D. Roosevelt). Amer. heri. vol. 6 no. 3 p. 109 (Ap '55); vol. 9 no. 3 p. 106 (Ap '58).

—— (hookworms & laziness). Amer. heri. vol. 6 no. 3 p. 83 (Ap '55).

—— (Indians sell Manhattan). Amer. heri. vol. 11 mo. 1 p. 62-3 (Dec '59).

—— (Jefferson Davis). Amer. heri. vol. 9 no. 4 frontis. (col.) (Je '58).

—— (John Hay, 1898). Amer. heri. vol. 11 no. 4 p. 76 (Je '60).

—— (John Pierpont Morgan). Amer. heri. vol. 8 no. 4 p. 98 (Je '57).

—— ("Join or die", Franklin Gazette, 1754). Amer. heri. vol. 7 no. 2 p. 7 Feb '56.

—— (King George III). Amer. heri. vol. 11 no. 4 p. 7 (col.) (Je '60).

—— (Lord Amherst, 1780). Amer. heri. vol. 12 no. 1 p. 93 (Dec '60).

—— (man). Holiday 5: 28 Feb '49; 9: 81 Mar '51; 13: 6 Jan '53, 9, 77 (col.), 80 Mar '53, 143 May '53, 67, 81, 94 Je '53; 14: 62 Sept '53; 23: 11, 27 Jan '58.

—— (man & steaming glass). Amer. heri. vol. 6 no. 5 p. 40 (Aug '55).

—— (man on bucking horse). Brooks: Growth of a nation, p. 80.

—— (man traveler. Travel 113: 10 Mar '60.

—— (Mark Hanna). Amer. heri. vol. 11 no. 1 p. 35 (Dec '59).

—— (men). Holiday 13: 64 (col.) Feb '53, 139 Je '53; 14: 21 Dec '53.

—— (men & women in bar, Venice). Holiday 23: 48-9 Jan '58.

—— (men crawling). Holiday 14: 90 Nov '53.

—— (New England-town meeting). Amer. heri. vol. 12 no. 1 p. 42-3 (Dec '60).

—— (Northwest passage). Amer. heri. vol. 3 no. 4 p. 45 (summer '52).

—— (outerspace life). Holiday 14: 73 Nov '53.

—— (people). Holiday 13: 9, 77 (col.) 80 Mar '53.

—— (political). Holiday 23: 124 Jan '58.

—— (political discussion). Amer. heri. vol. 11 no. 5 p. 102-3 (Aug '60).

—— (Pres. McKinley). Amer. heri. vol. 8 no. 2 p. 40 (col.) (Dec '57).

—— (Rockefeller gifts). Amer. heri. vol. 6 no. 3 p. 85 (Ap '55).

—— (Rockefeller-Gladden collision). Amer. heri. vol. 6 no. 3 p. 79 (Ap '55).

—— (Santa Claus). Holiday 14: 153 (col.) Nov '53.

—— (school freedom). Amer. heri., vol. 11 no. 2 p. 12-3 (col.) (Feb '60).

—— (Seward in Alaska). Amer. heri. vol. 12 no. 1 p. 103 (Dec '60).

—— (Theo. Roosevelt). Amer. heri. vol. 11 no. 6 p. 92 (Oct '60).

—— (Theo. Roosevelt resting). Amer. heri. vol. 7 no. 2 p. 97 (Feb '56).

—— (Uncle Sam & Cuba). Amer. heri. vol. 8 no. 2 p. 41 (col.) (Feb '57).

—— (Wall Street). Amer. heri. vol. 7 no. 4 p. 87 (Je '56).

—— (wedding). Amer. heri. vol. 11 no. 1 p. 106 (Dec '59).

—— (Wm. P. Frye, 1898). Amer. heri. vol. 11 no. 4 p. 77 (Je '60).

—— (woman at table). Holiday 14: 151 Nov '53.

—— (Yankee Doodle twits John Bull, 1851). Amer. heri. vol. 9 no. 5 p. 6 (Aug '58).

——, bottle. See bottle carton.

——, campaign. Amer. heri. vol. 7 no. 4 p. 29 (Je '56).

——, campaign (Wm. McKinley). Amer. heri. vol. 11 no. 1 p. 42-3 (Dec '59).

——, early. Amer. heri. vol. 10 no. 1 p. 124, 127 (Dec '58).

——, historical. Amer. heri. vol. 4 no. 4 p. 11-3 (summer '53).

——, Leslie's (cabinet officers). Amer. heri. vol. 8 no. 3 p. 55 (Ap '57).

——, Puck ("peace", 1905). Amer. heri. vol. 11 no. 4 p. 30 (Je '60).

——, Punch (Lincoln-Trent affair). Amer. heri. vol. 8 no. 3 p. 101 (Ap '57).

——, Thos. Nast. Amer. heri. vol. 7 no. 4 p. 46 (Je '56); vol. 9 no. 5 p. 90 (Aug '58).

——, Thos. Nast (political). Amer. heri. vol. 11 no. 6 p. 101 (Oct '60).

——, Thos. Nast. (ruin of speculators). Amer. heri. vol. 8 no. 3 p. 54 (Ap '57).

——, Thos. Nast. (U.S. frauds & scandals). Amer. heri. vol. 8 no. 3 p. 55 (Ap '57).

——, war (Quebec). Amer. heri. vol. 11 no. 1 p. 106-7 (Dec '59).

——, world war. Amer. heri. vol. 12 no. 1 p. 40 (Dec '60).

cartoon posters (1852-). Amer. heri. vol. 4 no. 3 p. 12-5 (spring '53).

cartoons. Holiday 13: 46-7, 64 (col.) Feb '53.

—— (breakfast food). Amer. heri. vol. 8 no. 4 p. 82-3, 85 (Je '57).

—— (man & woman traveling). Holiday 14: 160 Dec '53.

——, coal strike. Amer. heri. vol. 11 no. 3 p. 96-9 (Ap '60).

——, Currier, Ives (comic). Amer. heri. vol. 8 no. 4 p. 44-5 (col.) (Je '57).

——, French. Holiday 18: 50-1 Nov '55.

——, gold rush. Amer. heri. vol. 1 no. 3 p. 40-3 (col.) (spring '50).

——, Irish posters. Amer. heri. vol. 9 no. 5 p. 24-5 (Aug '58).

——, Police Gazette (1894). Amer. heri. vol. 11 no. 6 p. 105-12 (Oct '60).

——, restaurants. Holiday 28: 107, 110-12, 116 Jl '60.

——, society. Holiday 27: 93-5 May '60.

——, U.S. Civil war. Amer. heri. vol. 3 no. 2 p. 10-5 (winter '52).
Brooks: Growth of a nation, p. 144.

——, war. Amer. heri. vol. 9 no. 4 p. 77-81 (Je '58).

——, western. Holiday 27: 88-93 Je '60.

cartouche (given to Indians). Amer. heri. vol. 10 no. 3 p. 84 (Ap '59).

cartridge filler. Rawson: Ant. pict. bk., p. 35.

Cartuja sacristy (Granada). Praeg. pict. ency., p. 350.

Cartwright, Morse A. Cur. biog. p. 99 (1947).

Cartwright, Peter. Amer. heri. vol. 10 no. 4 p. 80 (Je '59).

Caruso, Enrico. Amer. heri. vol. 10 no. 3 p. 57 (Ap '59).
Holiday 8: 75 Nov '50.

carved rocks. See rock carvings.

Carvel, Elbert N. Cur. biog. (1963).

Carvel Hall hotel (Annapolis). Holiday 23: 83 (col.) Je '58.

Carver, Bill (Tod). Horan: Pict. hist. of wild west p. 199.

Carver, Geo. Washington. Brooks: Growth of a nation, p. 153.

Carver, Robert (work of). Con. 139: X Ap '57.

Carver, William. Horan: Pict. hist. of wild west, p. 220.

carving, antique coral. Con. 133: XLIV, Je '54.

carving, Iranian rock wall. Natl. geog. 100: 458 (col.) Oct '51.

carving, Sherpas rock. Natl. geog. 117: 390 (col.) Mar '60.

carving, wall (Grinling Gibbons). Con. 132: 44 Sept '53.

carving machine. Natl. geog. 100: 137 Jl '51.

carving meat. Holiday 18: 80-1 (col.) Dec '55.

carvings, alabaster. See alabaster carvings.

carvings, Bayon wall rock (India). Natl. geog. 116: 852 Dec '59.

——, Grinling Gibbons limewood. Con. 138: VIII-X, 147 Dec '56; 140: XLVI Dec '57; 141: LI May '58.

——, Indian. See Indian carvings.

Cary, Arthur Joyce. Cur. biog. p. 97 (1949).

Cary, Joyce. Holiday 16: 25 Aug '54; 23: 117 Ap '58.

Cary, William L. Cur. biog. (1963).

caryatid (Athens). Holiday 12: 55 Sept '52; 15: 69 Jan '54; 18: 16 Oct '55.
Int. gr. soc.: Arts . . . p. 17 (col.).
Natl. geog. 109: 48 (col.) Jan '56.
Praeg. pict. ency., p. 154.

——, James I (bedhead). Con. ency. of ant., vol. 1, pl. 3.

——, French. Con. 144: 216 Jan '60.

Casa Grande. Travel 101: 19 Feb '54.

Casa Grande tower (adobe ruins). Natl. geog. 104: 368 (col.) Sept '53.

Casa Loma castle (Toronto). Travel 105: 13 May '56.

Casablanca (French Morocco). Holiday 5: 64-70 Jan '49.
Natl. geog. 107: 150, 153 (col.) Feb '55.
Travel 104: 9-11 Nov '55.

Casadesus, Robert. Cur. biog. p. 92 (1945).

Casals, Pablo. Cur. biog. p. 83 (1950).
Holiday 19: 85 Mar '56; 23: 49 Feb '58.
Jensen: The White House, p. 282.

Casals, Pau. Cooper: Con. ency. of music, p. 65.

Casbah (Algiers). Travel 104: 64 Nov '55.
—— **(Arab shoppers).** Natl. geog. 117: 771 (col.) Je '60.
—— **(Tangier).** Holiday 23: 66 (col.) Mar '58.
Cascais (Portugal). Travel 107: 23 Je '57.
Case, Clifford P. Cur. biog. p. 105 (1955).
Case, Francis. Cur. biog. p. 98 (1946).
Caserta Vecchia (cathedral tower). Labande: Naples, p. 127.
Casey, Robert J. Cur. biog. p. 107 (1943).
cash registers. Natl. geog. 107: 457 (col.) Ap '55.
Cashman, Robert. Cur. biog. p. 90 (1952).
Casino (circular). Natl. geog. 105: 769 Je '54.
—— **(Enghien-les-Bains).** Con. 139: LIII May '57.
—— **(Monte Carlo).** Holiday 24: 36 Aug '58.
—— **(Ostend).** Natl. geog. 113: 822 (col.) Je '58.
—— **(int., France).** Holiday 27: 90 (col.) May '60.
casket (coffin). Lehner: Pict. bk. of sym., p. 79.
casket, Charles II silver. Con. 139: XXXIX Je '57.
——, **embroidered** (17th cent.). Con. ency. of ant., vol. 1, pl. 122.
——, **enamel trinket.** Con. ency. of ant., vol. 1, pl. 74.
——, **15th cent.** Con. 137: LXV May '56.
——, **French silver gilt.** Con. 137: XXXVII Je '56.
——, **George II silver.** Con. 134: XIX Nov '54.
——, **hobby (19th cent.).** Con. ency. of ant., vol. 3, pl. 120.
——, **Italian (Ormola & silver gilt, 16th cent.).** Con. 142: 205 Dec '58.
——, **Italian (16th cent.).** Con. 137: 214 May '56; 142: 267 Jan '59.
——, **jewel (Jamnitzer, 16th cent.).** Con. 144: 84 Nov '59.
——, **needlework.** See needlework casket.
——, **prayer book.** Con. 140: 65-6 Sept '57.
——, **Romanesque.** Con. 141: LXIV May '58.
——, **sacred relics (middle ages).** Int. gr. soc.: Arts . . . p. 57 (col.).
casket on stand (George II). Con. ency. of ant., vol. 3, pl. 16.
—— **(17th cent.).** Con. ency. of ant., vol. 3, pl. 16.
casket. See also coffin.
casks, rum. See rum casks.
Caspary, Vera. Cur. biog. p. 100 (1947).
Cass, Lewis. Amer. heri. vol. 8 no. 1 p. 63 (Dec '56).
Cassady, Vice-Adm. John H. Cur. biog. p. 92 (1952).
Cassatt, Mary (work of). Con. 143: X Je '59.
Casserley, Anne. Jun bk. of auth., p. 68.
casserole. Holiday 14: 136 Jl '53; 20: 135 Oct '56.
——, **antique clay.** Amer. heri. vol. 4 no. 1 p. 11 (fall '52).
Cassidy, Butch (Robt. LeRoy Parker). Horan: Pict. hist. of wild west, p. 196, 204, 234.
Cassidy, Claudia. Cur. biog. p. 107 (1955).
Cassidy, Henry C. Cur. biog. p. 110 (1943).

Cassiel (seal of). Lehner: Pict. bk. of sym., p. 25.
Cassini, Oleg L. Cur. biog. p. 96 (1961).
"Cassiobury Park" (house in England). Con. 141: 194-7 May '58.
cassolettes. Con. 141: 245 Je '58.
cassone, antique. Con. 136: 39 Sept '55.
——, **Gothic.** Con. 142: XLII Sept '58.
Castagnetta, Grace, Cur. biog. p. 161 (1954).
Castan, E. (work of). Con. 142: XXVI Jan '59.
Castaneda, Jorge Ubico. Cur. biog. p. 848 (1942).
Castaneda, Luciano (drawings by). Ceram: March of arch., p. 274.
Castel del Monte (Apulia). Praeg. pict. ency., p. 221.
Castel del 'Ovo (Naples). Holiday 20: 102 Oct '56.
    Labande: Naples, p. 84-5, 89.
Castel Sant' Angelo (Rome). Holiday 27: 19 Ap '60.
Castelbouc (Tarn gorge). Natl. geog. 100: 26 (col.) Jl '51.
Castello, Valerio (work of). Con. 132: 7 Sept '53.
Castello (Italy). Travel 112: 39 Sept '59.
Castelo (England). Con. 144: LXVII (col.) Jan '60.
caster, bed. Rawson: Ant. pict. bk., p. 15.
caster, Charles II (silver). Con. 133: XVI Ap '54.
——, **George I (silver).** Con. 133: IX Ap '54; 136: III, XVI Nov '55.
——, **George I (Georgian).** Con. 142: IX Dec '58.
——, **George II (silver).** Con. 138: XLII Dec '56; 143: XX Je '59.
——, **Queen Anne (silver).** Con. 133: XXXVIII Je '54; 140: 39 Sept '57, VIII Nov '57.
——, **silver (antique).** Con. 137: XIV, 227 Je '56; 140: XII Jan '58.
——, **silver (18th cent.).** Con. ency. of ant., vol. 1, pl. 86; 143: 275 Je '59.
——, **silver (Georgian).** Con. 137: XXIII May '56.
——, **silver (Laramie).** Con. 142: V Sept '58.
——, **silver (Lamerie, 18th cent.).** Con. 144: 16, 62 Sept '59.
——, **silver (Nash, 18th cent.)** Con. 141: 90 Ap '58.
——, **silver (17th cent.).** Con. 133: III May '54.
——, **silver (1715).** Con. ency. of ant., vol. 1, p. 153.
——, **sugar.** Con. 140: XII Dec '57.
——, **sugar (antique).** Con. 134: XL Nov '54.
——, **sugar (silver antique).** Con. 140: XXX Sept '57, XXX Nov '57.
——, **sugar (Charles II, silver).** Con. 134: L Dec '54.
——, **sugar (George I).** Con. 135: XXIV Ap '55.
——, **sugar (silver, 18th cent.).** Con. 144: XXX Nov '59, XII Dec '59, XIV Jan '60; 145: XX Mar '60, LII Ap '60, XX May '60.
——, **sugar (silver, urn-shaped).** Con. 145: 274 Je '60.

——, William III (silver). Con. 134: XII Nov '54; 139: 193 May '57; 140: XXXVI Nov '57.

caster cover, silver (1716). Con. ency. of ant., vol. 1, p. 153.

Castiella, Fernando Maria. Cur. biog. p. 77 (1958).

Castiglione (Capri, Italy). Labande: Naples, p. 209.

Castillo, Antonio. Cur. biog. p. 81 (1962).

Castillo Armas, Col. Carlos. Cur. biog. p. 109 (1955).

Castillo, Ramon S. Cur. biog. p. 141 (1941).

Castillo de San Marcos (1672). Amer. heri. vol. 4 no. 2 p. 64 (winter '53).
  Holiday 12: 99 (col.) Nov '52; 27: 177 (col.) Je '60.
  Natl. geog. 113: 43 (col.) Jan '58.

Castillo Najera, Francisco. Cur. biog. p. 101 (1946).

casting-bottle, silver gilt (Elizabethan). Con. 143: 51 Mar '59.

casting reel. Holiday 28: 162 Dec '60.

Castle, Lewis G. Cur. biog. p. 79 (1958).

castle. Con. 145: LXVIII May '60.
  Holiday 17: 12 (col.) Jan '55; 21: 124 (col.) Jan '57; 26: 191 Oct '59.
  Natl. geog. 100: 375 (col.) Sept '51.
  Travel 107: 23 Je '57.

—— (Austria). Natl. geog. 115: 172-3 (col.) Feb '59.
  Travel 111: 22 Ap '59.

—— (Austria, Alpine). Natl. geog. 118: 248-9 (col.) Aug '60.

—— (Bavaria). Holiday 12: 136 (col.) Oct '52; 19: 40-1 (col.) Mar '56.

—— (Carcassone). Natl. geog. 100: 34 (col.) Jl '51.

—— (Denmark). Holiday 28: 144 Jl '60, 182 Oct '60.

—— (Disneyland). Travel 104: 16 Jl '55.

—— (England). Con. 137: 240 (col.), 242-8 Je '56.
  Holiday 15: 28-9 (col.) Je '54; 16: 28 (col.) Jl '54; 17: 12 (col.) Mar '55; 25: 15 Mar '59.

—— (Greece). Natl. geog. 103: 354 Mar '53.

—— (Ireland). Holiday 6: 36, 38 (col.) Dec '49; 13: 131 (col.) Ap '53; 16: 6 Aug '54; 21: 14 Jan '57; 25: 20, 88 (col.) Mar '59.

—— (Italy). Holiday 26: 67 (col.) Sept '59.

—— (Japan). Holiday 12: 40 Aug '52.

—— (Malta). Holiday 27: 69 Je '60.

—— (Mt. peak). Natl. geog. 110: 464 (col.) Oct '56.

—— (Portugal). Natl. geog. 118: 643 (col.) Nov '60.

—— (Scandinavian). Holiday 27: 197 May '60.

—— (Scilla, Italy). Natl. geog. 104: 588 Nov '53.

—— (Scotland). Disney: People & places, p. cover, 25.
  Holiday 16: 74 Aug '54, 38-45 (part col.) Sept '54; 27: 69-75. May '60.
  Natl. geog. 112: 454-5 (col.) Oct '57.

—— (Segovia, Spain). Holiday 12: 19 Sept '52, 88 Nov '52.

—— (silhouette). Holiday 25: 7 (col.) Ap '59.

—— Spain). Holiday 11: 76 (col.) Feb '52; 15: 43 Jan '54; 23: back cover (col.) Ap '58; 26: 116 (col.) Nov '59.

—— (Switzerland). Holiday 16: 26 (col.), 36 Aug '54.

—— (Vadstena, Sweden). Travel 105: 29 Ap '56.

—— (Vienna). Holiday 16: 49 (col.) Nov '54.

—— (Wales, 1285). Holiday 11: 75 (col.) Mar '52.

—— (Wales). Holiday 14: 132 (col.) Nov '53.

——, Aggstein. See Aggstein castle.

——, Ardvreck. See Ardvreck castle.

——, Ashford. See Ashford castle.

——, Balmoral. See Balmoral castle.

——, Belmont. See Belmont castle.

——, Blarney, See Blarney castle.

——, Byzantine (Silifke). Osward: Asia Minor, pl. 120.

——, Caernavon (Wales). Holiday 14: 92 (col.) Jl '53; 28: cover (col.) Nov '60.

——, Caerphilly. See Caerphilly castle (Wales).

——, Cochem. See Cochem castle.

——, crusader's (Cyprus island). Natl. geog. 101: 660 (col.) May '52.

——, "Death Valley Scotty's". Jordan: Hammond's pict. atlas, p. 194 (col.).

——, Dunnottar. See Dunnottar castle.

——, Dunvegan (Scotland). Holiday 16: 38 (col.) Sept '54.
  Natl. geog. 102: 96 (col.), 112 Jl '52.

——, Edinburgh. See Edinburgh castle.

——, Estoril. See Estoril castle.

——, fairy (Belgium festival). Natl. geog. 113: 818-9 (col.) Je '58.

——, Floors. See Floors castle.

——, Fort Niagara. Amer. heri. vol. 4 no. 4 p. 33-7 (col.) (summer '53).

——, Gussing. See Gussing castle (Austria).

——, Gutenberg. See Gutenberg castle.

——, Gutenfels. See Gutenfels castle.

——, Harlech. See Harlech castle.

——, Heidelberg. See Heidelberg castle.

——, Hohenzollern. Disney, People & places, p. 50 (col.).

——, Howth. See Howth castle.

——, Hradcany. See Hradcany castle.

——, Kalmar. See Kalmar castle.

——, Katz See Katz castle.

——, Kronborg. See Kronborg castle.

——, Leeds. See Leeds castle.

——, Leira. See Leira castle.

——, Lullingstone. See Lullingstone castle.

——, Maiden's. See The Maiden's castle.

——, Marienburg. See Marienburg castle.

——, Mont Orgueill. See Mont Orgueill castle.

——, Morro. See Morro castle.

——, Niedzica. See Niedzica castle.

——, Nyborg. See Nyborg castle.

——, Oberhofen. See Oberhofen castle.

——, Osborn's. See Osborn's castle.

——, pirate (Virgin Island). Natl. geog. 109: 226 (col.) Feb '56.

——, Polignac. See Polignac castle.

——, Portchester. See Portchester castle.

——, Provencal. Natl. geog. 101: 553 Ap '52.

castle, Reifenstein. Natl. geog. 100: 382 Sept '51.

——, Rushen. *See* Rushen castle.

——, St. Angello. *See* St. Angello castle.

——, Schonburg. *See* Schonburg castle.

——, Sigmaringen (on the Danube). Holiday 17: 68 (col.) Mar '55.

——, Skibo. *See* Skibo castle.

——, "Swallow's nest" (near Yalta). Natl. geog. 116: 389 (col.) Sept '59.

——, Tattershall. *See* Tattershall castle.

——, Vianden (Luxembourg). Holiday 23: 150 (col.) Feb '58.

——, Warwick. *See* Warwick castle.

——, Windsor. *See* Windsor castle.

——, Alcazar. *See* Alcazar castle.

castle at Poitiers. Praeg. pict. ency., p. 49 (col.).

"Castle by the River" (Van Goyen). Con. 133: 257 Je '54.

Castle Casa Loma (Toronto, Canada). Travel 105: 13 May '56.

Castle Chillon. *See* Chillon castle.

Castle Combe (Wiltshire, Eng.). Holiday 14: 55 Nov '53.

"Castle Defiance" (home of Robert Morris). Amer. heri. vol. 7 no. 6 p. 88 (Oct '56).

"Castle Garden" (New York). Durant: Pict. hist. of Amer. circus, p. 58.

Castle Gillette. *See* Gillette castle.

"Castle Hill" (R.T. Crane home). Holiday 28: 62 (col.) Aug '60.

"Castle Hill" (home in Va.). Natl. geog. 97: 588 (col.) May '50.

Castle Hill (on Mediterranean). Osward: Asia Minor, pl. 118-9.

Castle Hochosterwitz (Austria). Holiday 19: 103 (col.) Je '56.
Travel 111: 22 Ap '59.

Castle hotel Hahnhof (Baden-Baden). Holiday 23: 89 Je '58.

Castle in 1320 (int., comic). Holiday 23: 84 Je '58.

castle interior (Ireland). Holiday 6: 42 (col.), 44-5 Dec '49.

—— (Scotland). Holiday 17: 73 (col.) Jan '55; 19: 63 (col.) Feb '56.

—— (Scotland, 16th cent.). Holiday 26: 95 (col.) Nov '59.

—— (Spain). Travel 111: 25 Ap '59.

"Castle Lawn" (Ky. home, Fayette co.). Holiday 6: inside back cover (col.) Nov '49; 7: 145 (col.) Ap '50; 15: inside back cover (col.) Mar '54.

Castle Miramare. *See* Miramare castle.

Castle Mittersill (Alpine). Holiday 26: 70-3 (part col.) Sept '59.

Castle Neuschwanstein. Holiday 19: 40-1 (col.) Mar '56; 21: 33 (col.) Mar '57.

Castle Nuovo. Labande: Naples, p. 40-1.

Castle of Baiae. Labande: Naples, p. 136.

Castle of Chillon. See Chillon castle.

Castle of Hollenfels (Luxembourg). Holiday 22: 107 (col.) Nov '57.

Castle of Invercauld (Scotland). Natl. geog. 110: 26 (col.) Jl '56.

"Castle of Love" (Chenonceaux). Holiday 27: 20-1 (col.) Jan '60.

See also Chateaux Chenonceaux.

Castle of Richard the Lion Hearted (Normandy, France). Holiday 17: 126 (col.) Mar '55.

Castle of St. George (Lisbon). Travel 108: 22 Aug '57.

Castle of San Giusto (Italy). Natl. geog. 109: 841 (col.) Je '56.

Castle of the sea (Sayda). Natl. geog. 113: 516-7 (col.) Ap '58.

Castle of Tourbillon (Switzerland). Natl. geog. 110: 464 (col.) Oct '56.

Castle on Beblowe Craig (Lindisfarne, Eng.). Natl. geog, 102: 560 Oct '52.

"Castle on the River" (Van Ruysdael). Con. 143: IX May '59.

castle ruins (Scotland). Natl. geog. 110: 45 (col.) Jl '56.

Castle Tirol (Alps). Holiday 27: 39 (col.) Jan '60.

castle tower, Crusader (Syria). Natl. geog. 106: 814 (col.) Dec '54.

Castlerigg stone circle. Natl. geog. 109: 538 (col.) Ap '56.

Castles (France). Holiday 15: 50 Jan '54.

—— (German). Natl. geog. 115: 756-8, 765 (col.) Je '59.

castor. *See* caster.

Castro, Fidel. Cur. biog. p. 80 (1958).
Holiday 27: 51 (col.) Feb '60.
U.S. News & world report, p. 53 Aug 31 '64.

Caswell, Hollis L. Cur. biog. p. 103 (1956).

cat, black (Halloween, sym.). Lehner: Pict. bk. of sym., p. 53.

"Cat & fiddle" pub. (England). Holiday 26: 7 (col.) Nov '59.

catacombs (art). Int. gr. soc.: Arts . . . p. 21 (col.).

Catafalque (A. Lincoln). Jensen: The White House, p. 95.

Catalan dance. Holiday 26: 106 (col.) Dec '59.

Catalina island. Holiday 7: 80, 87-8 Ap '50.
Travel 110: 27 Aug '58.

Catamaran boat. Holiday 26: 85 (col.) Dec '59.
Natl. gcog. 118: 23 (col.) Jl '60.

Cates, Gen. Clifton. Cur. biog. p. 85 (1950).

Catesby, M. (work of). Con. ency. of ant., vol. 3, pl. 87.

cathedral (Amalfi). Natl. geog. 116: 502 (col.) Oct '59.

—— (Barcelona). Travel 105: 45 Ap '56.

—— (Basel, Switzerland). Holiday 16: 37 Aug '54.

—— (Berlin). Holiday 18: 69 (col.) Dec '55.

—— (Candia, Crete). Natl. geog. 104: 694 Nov '53.

—— (Constantinople). Natl. geog. 112: 405 Sept '57.

—— (Cuzco). Holiday 21: 113 (col.) Je '57.

—— (Hermosillo, Mexico). Travel 103: 34 Jan '55.

—— (Lourenco, Marques). Travel 104: 26 Nov '55.

—— (Malaga, Spain). Travel 105: 48 Ap '56.

—— (Mexico City). Natl. geog. 100: 790, 795, 822 (col.) Dec '51.

—— (Port-au-Prince). Holiday 7: 100 Mar '50.

—— (Salerno, Italy). Labande: Naples, p. 188-9.

—— (Sitka, Russia). Natl. geog. 116: 63 (col.) Jl '59.

—— (Tunis). Travel 101: 41 Ap '54.

—— (Zocalo, Mexico). Holiday 11: 20 May '52.

—— (Zurich, Switzerland). Holiday 16: 31 (col.) Aug '54.

——, Amiens. See Amiens cathedral.

——, Angouleme. See Angouleme cathedral.

——, Asuncion de Maria Santisima (Mexico City). Holiday 13: 38-9 (col.) Mar '53.

——, Bourges. See Bourges cathedral.

——, Canterbury. See Canterbury cathedral.

——, Chartres. See Chartres cathedral.

——, Cologne. See Cologne cathedral.

——, Durham. See Durham cathedral.

——, Exeter. See Exeter cathedral.

——, Giralda tower. See Giralda tower, cathedral.

——, Gloucester. See Gloucester cathedral.

——, Gothic (Cyprus island). Natl. geog. 101: 634 (col.) May '52.

——, Gothic (entrance). Int. gr. soc.: Arts . . . p. 75 (col.).

——, Guadalajara. See Guadalajara cathedral.

——, Holy Trinity. See Holy Trinity cathedral.

——, Iona. Natl. geog. 106: 562 Oct '54.

——, Konigslutter. See Konigslutter cathedral.

——, Lincoln. See Lincoln cathedral.

——, Messina. See Messina cathedral.

——, Milan. See Milan cathedral.

——, Mountain-top (LePuy, France). Travel 107: 52 Ap '57.

——, Naumburg. See Naumburg cathedral.

——, Notre Dame. See Notre Dame cathedral.

——, Palma. See Palma cathedral (Majorca).

——, Peterborough. See Peterborough cathedral.

——, Pisa. See Pisa cathedral.

——, Rheims. See Rheims cathedral.

——, St. Clemens. See St. Clemens cathedral.

——, St. Francis Xavier (Vincennes). Holiday 8: 28 Aug '50.

——, St. Louis. See St. Louis cathedral.

——, St. Patrick's. See St. Patrick's cathedral.

——, St. Paul's. See St. Paul's cathedral.

——, St. Peter's. See St. Peter's cathedral (Mexico City); St. Peter's (Rome).

——, St. Stephen. See St. Stephen cathedral.

——, Salisbury. See Salisbury cathedral.

——, salt mine. See salt mine cathedral.

——, San Cristobal. See San Cristobal cathedral.

——, sand. Natl. geog. 103: 827 (col.) Je '53.

——, Siena. See Siena cathedral.

——, Speyer. See Speyer cathedral.

——, Strasbourg. Holiday 10: 54 Jl '51.

——, Suvaii. Travel 104: 24 Oct '55.

——, Ulm. See Ulm cathedral.

——, Washington. See Washington cathedral.

Wells. See Wells cathedral.

——, Worcester. Holiday 13: 131 (col.) Ap '53

——, Worms. See Worms cathedral

——, York. See York cathedral.

——, Zagreb (Yugoslavia). Natl. geog. 99: 146 Feb '51.

Cathedral De Beauvais (Dumont). Con. 133: 261 Je '54 .

cathedral entrance (festival). Holiday 27: 99 (col.) May '60.

cathedral floor plan. See floor plan.

cathedral interior (Russia). Holiday 18: 111 Jl '55.

Cathedral of Bruges (int.). Holiday 25: 47 (col.) Jan '59.

Cathedral of Holy Trinity (Jordanville, N. Y.). (tower). Holiday 27: 105 Mar '60.

Cathedral of Our Lord & Blessed Virgin. Holiday 18: 112 (col.) Aug '55.

Cathedral of Pines (Rindge, N. H.). Travel 106: 13 Dec '56.

Cathedral of St. Francis (Santa Fe). Amer. heri. vol. 8 no. 6 p. 32 (Oct '57).

Cathedral of St. George the Martyr (Ger., 13th cent.). Int. gr. soc.: Arts . . . p. 47 (col.).

Cathedral of San Gennaro (door). Labande: Naples . . . p. 43.

Cathedral of Santiago di Compostella (portico). Praeg. pict. ency., p. 197.

cathedral rocks (Yosemite valley). Holiday 24: 54-5 Jl '58.

Cathedral Santa Ana (Canary Island). Natl. geog. 107: 491 (col.) Ap '55.

cathedral spire, Ulm. See spire, Ulm cathedral.

cathedral spires, rock (S.D.). Natl. geog. 110: 480-1 (col.) Oct '56.

cathedral tower (Caserta Vecchia). Labande: Naples, p. 127.

—— (St. Pauls, London). Natl. geog. 108: 320 Sept '55.

Cathedral Valley (Utah). Natl. geog. 101: 708-9, 734 (col.) Je '52.
Travel 110: 24 Oct '58.

cathedral window, Chartres. See Chartres cathedral window.

——, Gothic. Amer. heri. vol. 7 no. 1 p. 4 (col.) (Dec '55).

cathedrals (Vatican & Rome). Holiday 7: 106-13 (part col.) May '50.

——, Gothic. Int. gr. soc.: Arts . . . p. 49 (col.).

cathedral's bell tower, Canterbury. Natl. geog. 108: 315 (col.) Sept '55.

Catherine de 'Medici talisman. Lehner: Pict. bk. of sym., p. 66.

Catherwood, Frederick (drawings by). Ceram: March of arch., p. 80, 284.

Catholic falsehoods (pamphlets, 1836). Amer. heri. vol. 10 no. 2 p. 58-9, 61 (Feb '59).

Catholic ordination (outdoors). Face of Amer., p. 30-1 (col.).

Catholic priest. Natl. geog. 98: 425 Oct '50.

—— (Holy blood). Natl. geog. 107: 662 (col.) May '55.

—— (mass in grotto). Natl. geog. 110: 720 (col.) Dec '56.

—— (statue). Natl. geog. 111: 657 May '57.

Catholic priests (sacred treasures). Natl. geog. 110: 757 (col.) Dec '56.

Catholic sister (nursery). Natl. geog. 109: 237 (col.) Feb '56.

Catholic sister. Holiday 23: 56 May '58.
Natl. geog. 110: 721 (col.) Dec '56.

Catholic sister (laughing). Natl. geog. 117: 590 (col.) May '60.

Catholic sister & boys. Natl. geog. 115: 732 May '59.

Catholic sister & child. Holiday 23: 85 Mar '58.

Catholic sister & children (walking). Holiday 22: 70-1 (col.) Dec '57.

Catholic sisters. Holiday 12: 93 Aug '52. Natl. geog. 114: 300 Aug '58.

—— (sewing). Natl. geog. 113: 814 Je '58.

Catholic sisters. See also Nun; Nuns.

Catholic university (Chile). Natl. geog. 117: 186-7 (col.) Feb '60.

Catlin, George. Amer. heri. vol. 8 no. 3 cover (col.) (Ap '57).

—— (work of). Amer. heri. vol. 6 no. 1 p. 33 (col.) (fall '54); vol. 7 no. 1 p. 26 (col.) (Dec '55); vol. 7 no. 2 frontis (col.) (Feb '56); vol. 7 no. 6 p. 17 (col.) (Oct '56); vol. 8 no. 3 cover, 4-19 (col.) (Ap '57); vol. 9 no. 1 frontis (col.) (Dec '57); vol. 9 no. 3 p. 11 (col.) (Ap '58).
Con. 139: 138 Ap '57; 144: 69 Sept '59.

Catroux, Gen. Georges. Cur. biog. p. 111 (1943).

"cat's eye" gem. Natl. geog. 98: 798 (col.) Dec '50.

Catskills. Holiday 24: 38-45 (col.) Aug '58.

cattle branding (Sudan). Natl. geog. 103: 263 (col.) Feb '53.

cattle brands. Amer. heri. vol. 7 no. 3 p. 104-7 (Ap '56).
Brooks: Growth of a nation, p. 170.
Holiday 21: 93 May '57.

cattle exhibit (Switzerland). Natl. geog. 110: 457 Oct '56.

cattle herder, Ethiopian. Natl. geog. 118: 305 (col.) Sept '60.

cattle pens, western. Natl. geog. 104: 371 (col.) Sept '53.

cattle respirator testing machine. See respiratory machine.

cattle round-up (King ranch). Natl. geog. 101: 42, 44 (col.), 58 Jan '52.

—— (Texas). Holiday 24: 44 (col.) Oct '58.

cattle show (New Zealand). Natl. geog. 101: 435 (col.) Ap '52.

cattle trail marker. Holiday 21: 92 May '57.

cattlemen (on fence). Holiday 5: 59 Je '49.

Catto, Thomas Sivewright. Cur. biog. p. 89 (1944).

Catton, Bruce. Con. biog. p. 163 (1954).

Catton house, Norwich. Con. 144: 232 Jan '60.

catwalk (bridge, Africa). Natl. geog. 112: 80-1 (col.) Jl '57.

——, log (river). Natl. geog. 117: 92 (col.) Jan '59.

——, Mt. birds-nest (men). Natl. geog. 117: 379 (col.) Mar '60.

Caucasus mts. Natl. geog. 116: 398-9 (col.) Sept '59.

Caudill, Rebecca. Cur. biog. p. 86 (1950).

caudle cup. Con. 137: 216 May '56.

—— (by Dummer). Con. 139: 65 Mar '57.

——, Charles II. Con. 137: 55 Mar '56; 138: XVIII Nov '56; 140: LXXII Nov '57.

——, Delft. Con. 138: 126 Nov '56.

——, 17th cent. Con. 133: XXVII Mar '54; 132: 86 Nov '53.

——, silver. Con. 145: 138 Ap '60.

caudle cup & cover, Charles II. Con. 142: 252 Jan '59; 144: V Nov '59.

Caulfield, Joan. Cur. biog. p. 165 (1954).

Caulaincourt, Armand Augustin Louis de. Amer. heri. vol. 9 no. 2 p. 85 (Feb '58).

Cavaceppi's workshop. Ceram: March of arch., p. 14.

cavalier, armoured (on horse, 16th cent.). Natl. geog. 107: 197 (col.) Feb '55.

Cavallet dance (Majorca). Natl. geog. 111: 646 (col.) May '57.

Cavallino, Bernardo (work of). Labande: Naples, p. 112.

cavalry, Colonial. Natl. geog. 106: 450 (col.) Oct '54.

——, English. Natl. geog. 103: 810-11 (col.) Je '53.

——, Pakistan. Natl. geog. 102: 643 (col.) Nov '52.

——, Polish winged. Con. 136: 4 Sept '55.

——, U.S. See U.S. cavalry.

"Cavalry Officer of the Guard" (Gericault). Con. ency. of ant., vol. 1, pl. 162.

cavalrymen, Algerian. See Algerian cavalrymen.

Cavanah, Frances Elizabeth. Cur. biog. p. 166 (1954).

Cavanaugh, Rev. John J. Cur. biog. p. 102 (1947).

Cavanna, Betty. Cur. biog. p. 87 (1950).

Cavaradossi. Cooper: Con. ency. of music, p. 190.

cave (Ala.). Natl. geog. 110: 543-58 (part col.) Oct '56.

—— (boys). Natl. geog. 111: 403 (col.) Mar '57.

—— (Carlsbad). See Carlsbad cavern.

—— (Dead Sea Scrolls). Natl. geog. 114: 800 Dec '58.

—— (int.). Holiday 27: 5 (col.) Feb '60.

—— (night club). Holiday 10: 95 (col.) Aug '51.

——, rock (men & women). Natl. geog. 112: 453 (col.) Oct '57.

cave. See also caverns; caves.

cave art, Maori. Natl. geog. 101: 460 Ap '52.

——, prehistoric (Altamira, Spain). Int. gr. soc.: Arts . . . p. 21 (col.).

——, stone age. Praeg. pict. ency., p. 105 (col.).

cave dwellers (Spain). Natl. geog. 97: 448 (col.), 456 Ap '50.

—— (stone age). Natl. geog. 113: 426-37 Mar '58.

cave dwelling, rock (Turkey). Natl. geog. 113: 131, 136-7 Jan '58.

—— (int., ancient). Int. gr. soc.: Arts . . . p. 15 (col.).

——, gypsy. Natl. geog. 112: 572-82 Oct '57.

cave entrance. Natl. geog. 112: 754 Dec '57.

cave grotto chapel (Andalusia). Natl. geog. 112: 577 Oct '57.

Cave-in-Rock park (Cairo, Ill.). Travel 113: 55 May '60.

Cave of St. John (Patmos Isle). Natl. geog. 103: 383 (col.) Mar '53.

Cave of the dragon. Natl. geog. 111: 630-1 May '57.

Cave of the Winds (Colo.). Travel 109: 16 Feb '58.

cave of the winds (Niagara). Travel 104: 23 Aug '55.

Cave temples (India). See Ajanta temples (India).

cavern (Ky.). Jordan: Hammond's pict. atlas, p. 104-5 (col.).

—— (Ore.). Holiday 21: 5 (col.) Mar '57.

—— (Spook cave, Iowa). Travel 110: 34 Sept '58.

—— (Va.). Holiday 8: 27 (col.) Sept '50; 28: 9 Sept '60.

Travel 113: 15 Ap '60.

——, Carlsbad. See Carlsbad cavern.

——, Lewis & Clark (Mont.). Natl. geog. 97: 717 (col.) Je '50.

Travel 108: 13 Jl '57.

——, Luray. See Luray cavern.

——, mine. Natl. geog. 97: 703 (col.) Je '50.

——, Shenandoah (Va.). Holiday 25: 31 (col.) Ap '59.

Caverns state park (Fla.). Travel 107: 15 Je '57.

caverns. See also cave; name of cavern.

Cavert, Samuel McCrea. Cur. biog. p. 103 (1951).

caves. Travel 109: 11-9 Feb '58.

—— (Fla.). Travel 107: 15 Je '57.

——, ice. See ice caves.

——, pictorial. Travel 106: 37-40 Dec '56.

"Caves of the 1000 Buddhas" (China). Natl. geog. 99: 386-401 (col.) Mar '51.

Cayton, Horace R. Cur. biog. p. 103 (1946).

Ceccarini, Sebastiano (work of). Con. 135: 52 Mar '55.

Cecil, Robert. Amer. heri. vol. 10 no. 4 p. 16 (col.) (Je '59).

Cecil, Lord William. Amer. heri. vol. 10 no. 3 p. 12 (Ap '59).

Cecil of Essendon, Lord Robert A. J. Cur. biog. p. 143 (1941).

Cedar Key Island (Fla.). Travel 110: 50-1 Jl '58.

Cedros island. Travel 105: 31-3 Jan '56.

ceiling, carved. Con. 142: 70 (col.), 72 Nov '58.

——, church (Wurttemberg). Praeg. pict. ency., p. 320 (col.).

——, decorated room. Natl. geog. 98: 87 (col.) Jl '50.

——, cathedral (St. Cecile). Natl. geog. 100: 31 (col.) Jl '51.

ceiling painting (Nogari). Con. 140: 155 Dec '57.

—— (Ringling museum, Fla.). Con. 145: 133 Ap '60.

—— (Sistine chapel, Michelangelo). Praeg. pict. ency., p. 7.

Celebrezze, Anthony J. Cur. biog. (1963).

Celeste, Celine. Jensen: The White House, p. 53.

celestial alphabet. See alphabet, celestial.

celestial sphere (sym.). Lehner: Pict. bk. of sym., p. 20.

"Celestina" (Picasso). Con. 145: LXXXI Je '60.

cellarette, Chippendale. Con. 134: IV Sept '54; 140: IV Sept '57.

——, 18th cent. Con. ency. of ant., vol. 3, pl. 10.

celler, Emanuel. Cur. biog. p. 99 (1949).

Cellini, Benvenuto (work of). Natl. geog. 97: 754 Je '50.

Praeg. pict. ency., p. 295.

—— (statue by). Natl. geog. 111: 797 (col.) Je '57.

cello. Cooper: Con. ency. of music p. 345.

Int. gr. soc.: Arts . . . p. 141 (col.).

—— (man playing). Cooper: Con. ency. of music, p. 65.

—— (woman playing). Cooper: Con. ency. of music, p. 170 (col.).

——, English (18th cent.). Cooper: Con. ency. of music, p. 349.

cells, bone. See bone cells.

——, cartilage. Gray's anatomy, p. 256.

Celsus' library. See library of Celsus.

Celtic cross. See cross, Celtic.

Celtic musicians (ancient). Int. gr. soc.: Arts . . . p. 27 (col.).

Celts (man, woman, ancient times). Int. gr. soc.: Arts . . . p. 31 (col.).

cement sculpture (Wotruba). Praeg. pict. ency., p. 515.

cemeteries, overseas war (map). Natl. geog. 111: 736-9 (col.) Je '57.

——, Mass. (Puritan). Amer. heri. vol. 11 no. 2 p. 38-43 (Feb '60).

cemetery. Face of Amer., p. 42-3 (col.).

Holiday 11: 36 Je '52.

——, Civil war. Amer. heri. vol. 12 no. 1 p. 118 (Dec '60).

——, Gettysburg battle field. Amer. heri. vol. 9 no. 1 p. 49 (col.) (Dec '57).

——, Memorial Day (Hawaii). Natl. geog. 118: 31 (col.) Jl '60.

——, natl. See Arlington amphitheater (Natl. cemetery).

——, old island. Natl. geog. 118: 582 Oct '60.

——, Tombstone. Natl. geog. 104: 357 (col.) Sept '53.

——, Trinity (N.Y.). Holiday 10: 47 (col.) Sept '51; 19: 76 Feb '56.

cemetery vaults (La Paz, Bolivia). Holiday 8: 54 Nov '50.

Cenerazzo, Walter W. Cur. biog. p. 111 (1955).

cenotaph, Alamo memorial. Amer. heri. vol. 4 no. 1 p. 43 (fall '52).

——, Auckland war memorial. Natl. geog. 101: 430 (col.) Ap '52.

——, Taj Mahal. Natl. geog. 118: 475 (col.) Oct '60.

Cenote Xlacah (Maya). Natl. geog. 115: 121 (col.) Jan '59.

censer (18th cent.). Con. 141: 107 Ap '58.

—— (sym.). Lehner: Pict. bk. of sym., p. 37.

——, Bavaria rococo silver. Con. ency. of ant., vol. 3 p. 62.

——, Italian silver. Con. 144: 154 Dec '59.

——, Tibetan (golden). Natl. geog. 108: 41 (col.) Jl '55.

censorship (sym.). Lehner: Pict. bk. of sym., p. 94.

census chart, U.S. (1790-1960). Natl. geog. 116: 700-1, 710-11 Nov '59.
census taking, U.S. (1790-1960). Natl. geog. 116: 696-713 Nov '59.
centaur (sym.). Lehner: Pict. bk. of sym., p. 32.
centaur's dance. See cavallet dance.
"center of Amer." (exhibit, Fla.). Travel 103: 47-9 May '55.
center table. See table, regency center.
centerpiece, silver antique. Con. 132: 188 Jan '54.
——, table. See table centerpiece.
Central Amer. Holiday 17: 34-47 (part col.) Mar '55.
Central Amer. art, ancient. Amer. heri. vol. 10 no. 2 p. 46- (col.) (Feb '59).
Central Pacific & Union Pacific railroads (join near Ogden). Amer. heri. vol. 9 no. 2 p. 21-3 (part col.) (Feb '58).
Central Park (N.Y.). Holiday 5: 66 Ap '49. Natl. geog. 118: 782-805 (col.) Dec '60.
centrifuge, Navy's. Natl. geog. 108: 242-3 (col.) Aug '55.
centrifuge instrument, ultra. Natl. geog. 97: 559 May '50.
Century club. Amer. heri. vol. 6 no. 1 p. 29 (fall '54).
ceramic figure (church of St. Catherine). Praeg. pict. ency., p. 493.
ceramics, Chinese (old). Con. 138: XXVI Sept '56.
——, English (earliest ceramic bird). Con. 144: 194 Dec '59.
——, Finnish. Travel 105: 37 Ap '56.
——, Greek (ancient). Int. gr. soc.: Arts . . . p. 19 (col.).
——, Kaj Franck's. See Franck's ceramics, Kaj.
cerberus (sym.). Lehner: Pict. bk. of sym., p. 61.
Cerda, Pedro Aguirre. Cur. biog. p. 13 (1941).
ceremonial chest. See chest, ceremonial.
"Ceremonial road" (Ephesus, mosaic). Osward: Asia Minor, pl. 57.
ceremonial staff. See Nigeria (ceremonial staff).
ceremonial vase, Chinese bronze. Con. 129: 146 Je '52.
Ceres (sym.). Lehner: Pict. bk. of sym., p. 30.
Ceres, temple of. See Temple of Ceres.
Cerf, Bennett A. Cur. biog. p. 145 (1941); p. 82 (1958).
Cerri, Carlo (bust by della Valle). Con. 144: 172 Dec '59.
Cervantes. Holiday 19: 86 Mar '56.
Cesare, Giulio (work of). Con. 138: 118 Nov '56.
Cescinsky furniture. See furniture, Cescinsky.
Ceylon. Holiday 20: 94-9 (col.) Aug '56; 22: 94 Sept '57.
Travel 101: 17-20 Ap '54; 111: 21-3 Jan '59.
—— (man, drum). Holiday 19: 148 Je '56.
—— (men on elephants in water). Natl. geog. 105: 520-1 (col.) Ap '54.
—— (woman praying). Holiday 20: 94 (col.) Aug '56.
Ceylon dancer. Holiday 27: 57 May '60, 120 Je '60.

Ceylon dancers. Natl. geog. 105: 522 (col.) Ap '54.
—— (headmen). Holiday 20: 99 (col.) Aug '56; 28: 104 (col.) Oct '60.
—— (Kandy). Holiday 9: 119 Mar '51; 28: 193 (col.) Nov '60.
Ceylon devil-dancer. See devil dancer.
Ceylon metal palace (100 B. C.). Int. gr. soc.: Arts . . . p. 11 (col.).
Cezanne, Paul. Con. 134: 205 Dec '54.
—— (work of). Con. 133: 16 Mar '54; 137: 138 Ap '56; 141: 250 Je '58; 142: 124 Nov '58, 194 Dec '58, 254 Jan '59; 143: 135 May '59, 273 Je '59; 144: 41 Sept '59, 271 Jan '60; 145: 184 (col.), 211 May '60, 234-5 Je '60.
Int. gr. soc.: Arts . . . p. 133 (col.).
Praeg. pict. ency., p. 437 (col.).
Cezanne, Madame Paul. Con. 144: 41 Sept '59.
Chaban-Delmas, Jacques. Cur. biog. p. 84 (1958).
chadar (Iran). Natl. geog. 104: 708 Nov '53.
—— (Iran woman's wrap). Natl. geog. 100: 429, 439, 450, 456 (col.) Oct '51.
chaderis (Afghanistan veils). Natl. geog. 114: 40-1 (col.) Jl '58.
Chadler, Winthrop (work of). Amer. heri. vol. 1 no. 4 p. 46-8 (part col.) (summer '50).
Chadwick, Florence. Cur. biog. p. 88 (1950). Holiday 22: 149 Dec '57.
Chadwick, Sir James. Cur. biog. p. 94 (1945).
chadwick, Lynn (iron figure). Praeg. pict. ency., p. 463.
Chaffee, Zech, jr. Cur. biog. p. 142 (1942).
Chafing dish. Holiday 13: 113 Jan '53; 14: 158 Nov '53; 19: 10 (col.) Mar '56; 22: 204 (col.) Dec '57.
——, antique silver. Con. 137: 215 May '56.
Chagall, Marc. Cur. biog. p. 81 (1960).
Praeg. pict. ency., p. 461 (col.).
—— (work of). Con. 142: 255, XLV Jan '59.
Chagla, Mahomed Ali Currim. Cur. biog. p. 60 (1959).
Chahar Bagh theological school (Isfahan). Natl. geog. 100: 433 (col.) Oct '51.
Chaim Soutine. See Soutine, Chaim.
chain. Brooks: Growth of a nation, p. 191.
—— (that bound St. Paul). Natl. geog. 110: 757 (col.) Dec '56.
——, logging. Rawson: Ant. pict. bk., p. 21.
chain & ball. See ball & chain.
chain store (int.). Brooks: Growth of a nation, p. 251.
chair. Holiday 18: 94 Oct '55; 19: 12-3 (col.) Feb '56, 83 (col.) May '56.
Natl. geog. 103: 537 (col.) Ap '53.
—— (ancient). Natl. geog. 112: 857 (col.) Dec '57.
—— (bentwood). Holiday 26: 149 Nov '59.
—— (upholstered). Holiday 10: 2, 123 (col.) Oct '51; 11: 71 (col.) Je '52; 12: 19 (col.) Oct '52, 125 (col.) Nov '52; 18: 173 Dec '55; 19: 129 (col.) Je '56; 20: 10 (col.) Oct '56, 163 (col.) Dec '56; 21: 155 May '57; 25: 139 (col.) Je '59; 26: 126 (col.) Dec '59; 28: 184 (col.) Oct '60, 137, 145, 150 (col.) Nov '60.

Natl. geog. 109: 463 (col.) Ap '56.

——, **Adam.** Con. 133: LXI Je '54; 139: X May '57; 140: XIX Dec '57, XLVIII Jan '58; 141: 43 Mar '58, XIII Ap '58; 142: XXIX Sept '58, inside back cover Nov '58; 143: XXIII Mar '59.

——, **Adam arm.** Con. ency. of ant., vol. 1, pl. 29.
Con. 143: XXXIII Mar '59.

——, **Adam gilt arm.** Con. 143: XXXIII Mar '59.

——, **Adam gilt wood.** Con. 142: XXXI Jan '59.

——, **Adam gothic.** Con. 142: 76 Nov '58.

——, **Amer. Hepplewhite.** Con. 135: 68 Mar '55.

——, **antique.** Con. 129: VI, 16 Ap '52; 132: 49 Sept '53; 133: 68 Mar '54, XIII Ap '54; 136: 44 Sept '55, VIII Nov '55, 171 Dec '55; 137: 144 Ap '56, 275 Je '56; 140: IV Sept '57, XV, 100 Nov '57, 227-8 Jan '58; 141: 126-7, XXIX Ap '58, XXV Je '58; 143: LIII Ap '59; 144: LIV Jan '60.
Holiday 13: 53 (col.) Jan '53; 14: 50-1 (col.) Dec '53.
Natl. geog. 97: 562 (col.) May '50; 102: 761 (col.) Dec '52.

——, **antique (1865).** Amer. heri. vol. 8 no. 1 p. 20 (Dec '56).

——, **antique arm.** Con. 133: 254 Je '54; 144: XLII Nov '59.
Holiday 21: 64 May '57.
Natl. geog. 97: 293 (col.) Mar '50.

——, **antique hall.** Con. 136: 245 Jan '56.

——, **antique style.** Travel 109: 25 Je '58.

——, **arm** Holiday 22: 109 (col.) Sept '57; 23: 21 Mar '58, 115 Je '58; 24: 30 (col.) Oct '58; 25: 119 Je '59; 26: 126, 129 Oct '59.

——, **arm (antique design).** Amer. heri. vol. 5 no. 4 p. 54 (summer '54).

——, **arm (back view).** Holiday 24: 91 (col.) Oct '58.

——, **arm (18th cent.).** Con. 144: 71, 77 Nov '59, XLVII, LXXVI Jan '60.
Con. ency. of ant., vol. 3, pl. 18.

——, **arm (1810).** Con. ency. of ant., vol. 3, pl. 12.

——, **arm (Louis XV).** Int. gr. soc.: Arts . . . p. 103 (col.).

——, **arm (modern).** Holiday 22: 68 (col.) Sept '57.

——, **arm (Napoleon).** Con. 143: LXX May '59.

——, **arm (Norwegian, 18th cent.).** Con. 145: 24 Mar '60.

——, **arm (17th cent.).** Con. 133: XXXII, 175 May '54.

——, **arm (1750).** Con. 144: 58 Sept '59.

——, **(back view).** Holiday 24: 130 Oct '58.

——, **barber (18th cent.).** Con. 134: VI Sept '54.

——, **beach.** Holiday 15: 38 Jan '54.
Natl. geog. 106: 402 (col.) Sept '54.

——, **bended-back (18th cent.).** Con. ency. of ant., vol. 1, pl. 17.

——, **Benjamin Randolph.** Con. 141: 127 Ap '58.

——, **Gov. Bradford's.** Con. 141: 126 Ap '58.

——, **Brewster.** Con. ency. of ant., vol. 1, p. 60.
Rawson: Ant. pict. bk., p. 16.

——, **cane bottom.** Holiday 27: 2 (col.) Je '60.
Natl. geog. 109: 449 (col.) Ap '56.

——, **Charles II.** Con. ency. of ant., vol. 1, pl. 16.
Con. 137: XXXI, 126 Ap '56; 142: LXI Nov '58.

——, **Charles Eames.** Holiday 26: 153 Nov '59.

——, **child's.** Holiday 10: 131 Oct '51.

——, **child's high.** Amer. heri. vol. 8 no. 4 p. 48-9 (col.) (Je '57).
Con. ency of ant., vol. 1, pl. 8.

——, **Chinese Chippendale.** Con. 134: XLV Nov '54.

——, **Chinese style (18th cent.).** Con. ency. of ant, vol. 1, pl. 29.

——, **Chinese style arm (1817).** Con. 143: 81 Ap '59.

——, **Chippendale.** Con. 127: 49 Mar '51; 129: XXV, XXIX, XXXVI, L Ap '52, XVI, 131 Je '52; 132: 51 Sept '53; 133: XI, 52 Mar '54, XV Ap '54, XII, 202 May '54; 134: XVI, 207 Dec '54; 135: IV, XLI, LIV May '55, 229-235 Je '55; 136: IV, L, 57 Sept '55, 81, 147 Nov '55, LXVI Jan '56; 137: VI Mar '56, IV, 212 May '56, LV Je '56; 139: IV, XVIII (col.), Ap '57: XXXIX May '57, LXV, Je '57; 140: XXIV Sept '57, 260 Jan '58; 141: XV Mar '58, XXXI May '58, XLVI Je '58; 142: VII, XXXVI Sept '58, XXXII, 131 Nov '58, 142, LIII Dec '58; 143: LXXII May '59, LIV Je '59; 144: XIV Sept '59, XXX Jan '60; 145: XXXI Je '60.
Int. gr. soc.: Arts . . . p. 105 (col.).

——, **Chippendale & Hepplewhite.** Con. 136: XLVII Dec '55.

——, **Chippendale arm.** Con. 132: 200 Jan '54; 136: VII Sept '55; 142: XV Dec '58, XXIV Jan '59; 144: XX Jan '60; 145: XVI, 56 Mar '60, XXXI Je '60.

——, **Chippendale director arm.** Con. 143: LIV Ap '59.

——, **Chippendale elbow.** Con. 132: XXXII Nov '53, 133: XVI Mar '54.

——, **Chippendale Gainsborough arm.** Con. 133: LXVII Je '54; 145: LXVIII Je '60.

——, **Chippendale Raeburn arm.** Con. 143: IV Mar '59; 145: XLVI May '60.

——, **contour.** Holiday 20: 156 Dec '56; 24: 37 (col.) Nov '58; 26: 143 (col.) Nov '59.

——, **coronation.** *See* coronation chair.

——, **debating** (head-hunters). Natl. geog. 108: 451 (col.) Oct '55.

——, **dining.** Holiday 20: 13 (col.) Sept '56, 122 (col.) Nov '56; 22: 127 (col.) Sept '57; 26: inside cover (col.) Nov '59; 28: 91, 93 (col.) Aug '60.

——, **dining (antique).** Holiday 26: 95 (col.) Nov '59.

——, **dining (Chinese Chippendale).** Natl. geog. 106: 460 (col.) Oct '54.

——, **directoire arm.** Con. 144: 212 (col.) Jan '60.

chair, drawing-room giltwood (18th cent.). Con. 144: XXI Nov '59.

——, early English arm. Con. 126: 145 Oct '50.

——, early English cane. Con. 127: 8-13 Mar '51, 83-91 May '51.

——, Egyptian style. Con. 140: 230 Jan '58.

——, 18th cent. Con. 129: LII Ap '52, XXXIII Je '52; 133: XLVII Ap '54, XIX May '54; 134: XXV Nov '54; 136: L Nov '55; 137: XLVII Ap '56, XX May '56; 138: LVII Dec '56; 139: XXXI May '57; 140: VIII Nov '57; 142: XXXV Sept '58; 144: LIV Sept '59, XLVII Jan '60.

——, 18th cent. arm. 133: LXXIII Je '54.

——, 18th cent. gilt. Con. 134: back cover Sept '54.

——, elbow (18th cent.). Con. 142: XXXV Dec '58.

——, English antique. Con. 126: 41 Aug '50.

——, English antique (17-18th cent.). Con. 136: XIV Sept '55.

——, English arm (18th cent.). Con. 144: 222 Jan '60.

——, English wing (1715). Praeg. pict. ency., p. 81 (col.).

——, exercising (18th cent.). Con. 135: LIII May '55.

——, Farthingale type (17th cent.). Con. ency. of ant., vol. 1, pl. 3.

——, French gilt arm. Con. 145: 110 Ap '60.

——, French transitional arm. Con. 145: 216 Je '60.

——, Gainsborough arm. Con. 143: LIII Je '59.

——, Genoese arm (18th cent.). Con. 144: 46 Sept '59.

——, George I. Con. 129: XXXII Ap '52; 133: XXXVI May '54; 138: XLIV Sept '56; 139: XL Mar '57, XXV Ap '57; 142: XVIII Sept '58, LXVIII Jan '59; 143: XIV May '59; 145: LXXXVI Je '60.

——, George I and Adam. Con. 136: 113 Nov '55.

——, George I arm. Con. 143: LI Ap '59.

——, George I master's arm. Con. 144: 267 Jan '60.

——, George I-II hoop-backed. Con. 133: XX May '54.

——, George II. Con. 129: XL Ap '52, LIII Je '52; 132: XLI Nov '53; 138: IV Sept '56; 140: XXIII Jan '58; 144: LXV Nov '59.

——, George II gilt wood. Con. 137: 277 Je '56.

——, Georgian. Con. 133: 29 Mar '54, XXX-VIII Je '54; 134: XLVII Sept '54; 139: 23-4 Mar '57, 91-4 Ap '57.

——, Georgian (18th cent.). Con. 142: 135 Nov '58.

——, gilt (Holland). Con. 144: XXVIII Jan '60.

——, gilt (Norwegian, 18th cent.). Con. 145: 24 Mar '60.

——, gilt arm (antique). Con. 145: back cover May '60.

——, gilt arm (18th cent.). Con. 143: 80, 121 Ap '59.

——, gilt arm (Holland). Con. 144: XXVIII Jan '60.

——, gilt regency arm. Con. 143: 262 Je '59.

——, gilt wood (antique). Con. 140: 149 Dec '57.

——, gothic. Con. 139: 223-4 Je '57.

——, gothic style Windsor. Con. 129: 42 Ap '52.

——, Granny. See Granny chair.

——, Greco-Roman style. Con. 140: 227 Jan '58.

——, harnessmaker's. See harnessmaker's chair.

——, Hepplewhite. Con. 129: I, XV Je '52; 132: XII, XXVIII Sept '53, VI Nov '53; 133: XV, XVI May '54; 134: XXX Sept '54; 135: LIII Ap '55; 137: XIV Ap '56, XIX May '56, XXXII Je '56; 138: XVIII, 60 Sept '56, LVII Dec '56, XXXV Jan '57; 139: XVII Mar '57, IV Ap '57, XXI Je '57; 140: 55 Sept '57, XXI Nov '57, 183 Dec '57; 141: XV, 45 Mar '58, inside back cover Ap '58, XXV May '58; 142: 127, 130 Nov '58; 143: XV Mar '59, XXXIX Ap '59; 144: LIII Nov '59, XX Dec '59; 145: XXXIV Mar '60.
Int. gr. soc.: Arts . . . p. 105 (col.).

——, Hepplewhite arm. Con. 133: XV Je '54; 142: XXXII Dec '58; 143: XXXIX Ap '59; 144: LIII Nov '59, XX Dec '59.

——, Hepplewhite elbow. Con. ency. of ant., vol. 1, pl. 29.
Con. 143: XIX Ap '59; 144: XI Sept '59; 145: XXXIV Mar '60.

——, Hepplewhite. Louis XV. Con. 134: XXI Dec '54.

——, hooded (Orkney islands). Natl. geog. 104: 523 Oct '53.

——, Hope. Con. 141: XXXVIII Mar '58.

——, iron wire (19th cent.). Con. ency. of ant., vol. 3, pl. 28.

——, Italian. Con. 135: 22, 24 Mar '55.

——, Italian (18th cent.). Con. 135: 20 Mar '55.

——, Italian regency. Con. 134: XIX Dec '54.

——, Italian wicker. Holiday 13: 93-5 (col.) Feb '53.

——, James I arm. Con. 133: XLIX Mar '54.

——, kitchen (old). Natl. geog. 101: 173 (col.) Feb '52.

——, ladderback (antique). Con. 139: 94 Ap '57.

——, leather (dog). Holiday 11: 108 (col.) May '52; 12: 82 (col.) Sept '52, 30 Oct '52, 96 (col.) Dec '52.

——, library (Chippendale). Con. 145: XLVI May '60.

——, library (18th cent.). Con. 143: XXIV Mar '59.

——, library (regency). Con. 144: XXXIII Jan '60.

——, Louis XIV. Con. 140: L Dec '57.

——, Louis XV. Con. 129: LXXIX Ap '52; 137: 214 May '56; 138: LXVII Jan '57; 139: 2 (col.) Mar '57; 141: LVI Je '58.
Natl. geog. 98: 601 (col.) Nov '50.

——, Louis XV arm. Con. 132: 70 Sept '53; 144: cover (col.) Sept '59, LXXI Jan '60.
Int. gr. soc.: Arts . . . p. 103 (col.).

——, Louis XV (Hepplewhite). Con. 134: XXI Dec '54.

chair, Louis XVI. Con. 138: VI Nov '56; 141: LVII May '58, XXXIX Je '58.
Int. gr. soc.: Arts . . . p. 105 (col.).
——, Louis XVI arm. Con. 144: XXII Nov '59; 145: 218 Je '60.
——, lounge. Holiday 14: 190 Dec '53.
——, Martha Washington. Con. ency. of ant., vol. 1, p. 70.
——, Mass. Chippendale. Con. 135: 64 Mar '55.
——, Morris (1866). Con. ency. of ant., vol. 3, pl. 4.
——, mortuary (17th cent.). Con. ency. of ant., vol. 1, pl. 4.
——, needlework (18th cent.). Con. 133: I Mar '54.
——, parcel-gilt arm (embroidered). Con. 143: 235 Je '59.
——, Phila. Chippendale. Con. 135: 68 Mar '55.
——, photographer's posing (1900). Amer. heri. vol. 12 no. 1 p. 128 (Dec '60).
——, Pilgrim. Con. ency. of ant., vol. 1, p. 66.
——, Portuguese. Con. 137: 72 Mar '56; 143: 195-6 May '59.
——, President's. See President's chair (Princeton, Univ.).
——, Queen Anne. Con. 126: 46 Aug '50; 132: XLI Sept '53, VI Nov '53; 133: 195 May '54; 137: XII Je '56; 138: XLIII, 194 Dec '56, 260 Jan '57; 142: LIX, 130 Nov '58.
Int. gr. soc.: Arts . . . p. 105 (col.).
——, Queen Anne wing. Con. ency. of ant., vol. 1, pl. 17, pl. 39.
Con. 132: XIV Sept '53; 133: XXXVI Mar '54; 143: XXIX Ap '59.
——, regency. Con. 134: XXIX, XXII Sept '54; 138: XII Dec '56, 260 Jan '57; 139: 262 Je '57; 144: X Jan '60.
——, regency arm. Con. 133: 259 Je '54; 142: LXV Jan '59; 143: 193 May '59; 144: X Jan '60; 145: LII May '60.
——, regency chinoiserie. Con. 145: XXI Mar '60.
——, Restoration type cane (1687-8). Con. ency. of ant., vol. 1, pl. 9.
——, rocking. See rocking chair.
——, Russian gilt arm (18th cent.). Con. 144: 272 Jan '60.
——, 17th cent. Con. 135: XLVII Mar '55; 139: 243 Je '57; 140: XLVIII Dec '57; 142: 128 Nov '58.
——, Sheraton. Con. ency. of ant., vol. 1, pl. 29.
Con. 129: VI Je '52; 133: XLV Mar '54; 138: XVI Nov '56; 140: XIX Dec '57; 141: XVI May '58; 142: IV Nov '58; 144: L Sept '59; 145: XXIV May '60.
——, Sheraton arm. Con. 144: XLI Nov '59, XXVII Dec '59.
——, Sheraton (white & gold). Con. 145: inside back cover Je '60.
——, side (Queen Anne). Con. 145: XLI Je '60.
——, snowshoe. Holiday 19: 157 Je '57.
——, Spanish (17th cent.). Con. 140: LXIII Nov '57.
——, steel (Victoria & Albert). Con. 142: 223 Jan '59.

——, Stuart arm. Con. 145: LXXXIII Je '60.
——, table (1668). Con. ency. of ant., vol. 1, pl. 8.
——, Tuscany (16th cent.). Con. 138: LXII Jan '57.
——, Victorian (by Mackintosh). Con. ency. of ant., vol. 3, pl. 7.
——, Victorian (by Voysey). Con. ency. of ant., vol. 3, pl. 7.
——, Victorian arm. (Morris adjustable). Con. ency. of ant., vol. 3, pl. 4.
——, Viennese arm (Josef II). Con. ency. of ant., vol. 3, pl. 21.
——, Viennese gilt arm. (18th cent.). Con. ency. of ant., vol. 3, pl. 21.
——, Viennese high-back arm. Con. ency. of ant., vol. 3, pl. 24.
—— Viennese side gilt (Josef II). Con. ency. of ant., vol. 3, pl. 21, 24.
——, wainscot (New Jersey). Con. 143: 66 Mar '59.
——, wainscot (17th cent.). Con. ency. of ant., vol. 1, pl. 4.
——, wheel. See wheel chair, Pres. Rosselelt's.
——, wheelback arm (18th cent.). Con 141: 247 Je '58.
——, wicker (antique). Holiday 26: 151 Nov '59.
——, William & Mary. Con. 129: XXXIV Ap '52; 136: 42 Sept '55, XXVIII Jan '56.
——, willow. Holiday 13: 142 Mar '53; 21: 189 Je '57.
——, Windsor. Con. ency. of ant., vol. 1, p. 70, pl. 16.
Con. 132: LII Nov '53; 135: IV Mar '55.
Int. gr. soc.: Arts . . . p. 105 (col.).
——, Windsor high. Holiday 22: 172 Oct '57.
——, Windsor side. Holiday 22: 134 Sept '57.
——, Windsor type. Con. ency. of ant., vol. 1, pl. 3.
——, wing (antique). Con. 133: VIII Mar '54.
——, wing (Chippendale). Con. 142: 130 Nov '58.
——, wing (Queen Anne). Con. 145: LXXIV Je '60.
——, wing arm. (18th cent.). Con. 133: XLIX Mar '54.
——, writing (antique). Con. 135: XXXVI Ap '55.
chair & steps (combined, 1810). Con. ency. of ant., vol. 3, pl. 12.
——, library elbow. Con. 145: XXVI Mar '60.
chair back (slat). Con. ency. of ant., vol. 1, p. 68.
——, Portuguese. Con. 143: 197 May '59.
chair-carrier. See carrier-chair.
chair foot, William & Mary. Con. ency. of ant., vol. 1, p. 69.
chairlift, aerial. Jordan: Hammond's pict. atlas, p. 189 (col.).
——, aerial (Mt.). Natl. geog. 109: 11 Jan '56. Travel: 104: 37 Aug '55.
——, aerial (skiers). Holiday 21: 47 (col.) Feb '57.
——, aerial (Vancouver). Natl. geog. 114: 148 (col.) Aug '58.
chairlift, aerial. See also ski lift.

chair-table (1668). Con. ency. of ant., vol. 1, pl. 8.

chairs. Holiday 22: 138-42 Nov '57.

——, antique. Con. 141: 126-7 Ap '58.

——, antique (at table). Con. 144: 72 (col.) Nov '59.

——, card table. Holiday 22: 105 (col.) Nov '57.

—— (1836). Holiday 20: 31 (col.) Sept '56.

——, Chippendale. Con. 126: 43 Aug '50.

——, Chippendale library. Con. 144: XVI Sept '59.

——, dining. See table & chairs.

——, elbow (18th cent.). Con. 140: XLVII Jan '58.

——, English (1700). Int. gr. soc.: Arts . . . p. 105 (col.).

——, lawn. Holiday 21: 80 (col.) May '57.

——, middle ages. Int. gr. soc.: Arts . . . p. 53-4 (col.).

——, modern. Holiday 20: 132-3 Nov '56.

——, rolling. See rolling chairs.

chaise lounge, Thos. Jefferson's. Natl. geog. 97: 564 (col.) May '50.

Chakma women (Pakistan). Natl. geog. 107: 417 (col.) Mar '55.

Chalcedony carvings (Wigstrom). Con. 145: 55 Mar '60.

chalet, Granite park. Natl. geog. 109: 606-7 (col.) May '56.

——, ski. See ski chalet.

——, Swiss. See Swiss chalet.

Chaliapin, Feodor Ivanovich (as Boris in "Boris Godunov"). Cooper. Con. ency. of music, p. 66.

chalice, antique. Con. 138: 113-5, 124 Nov '56.

——, antique church. Con. 134: 10-12 Sept '54.

——, antique Dutch plate. Con. 134: 160 Dec '54.

——, antique silver. Con. 132: VII Nov '53, LXXIII Jan '54.

——, Ardenno. Con. 142: 8 Sept '58.

——, Byzantium. Int. gr. soc.: Arts . . . p. 57 (col.).

——, Charles II. Con. 127: 77-8 May '51.

——, early crystal. Daniel: Cut & engraved glass, pl. 18, 23.

——, Flemish (15th cent.). Con. 142: 127 Nov '58.

——, Portuguese silver (12th cent.). Con. 137: 10 Mar '56.

——, Romanesque silver. Con. ency. of ant., vol. 3, p. 63.

——, Russian silver-gilt. Con. 144: 279 Jan '60.

——, silver (St. Edmund's college ware). Con. 142: 13 Sept '58.

——, silver (14th cent.). Con. 143: XXXVII Mar '59.

——, silver (17th cent.). Con. 141: inside cover Je '58.

——, silver Borsa. Con. 141: 107 Ap '58.

——, silver gilt & jewels (18th cent.). Con. ency. of ant., vol. 3 pl. 35.

——, Venetian silver (15th cent.). Con. ency. of ant. vol. 3, p. 63.

——, Tassilo. Praeg. pict. ency., p. 45.

——, Wilten. Natl. geog. 97: 775 Je '50.

chalice & cross (sym.). Lehner: Pict. bk. sym., p. 36.

chalice & paton (antique). Con. 145: 241-4 Je '60.

chalice of Duris. Praeg. pict. ency., p. 151 (col.).

chalice of Exekias. Praeg. pict. ency., p. 151 (col.).

chalifah dance (Africa). See dance, chalifah.

Chalf, O. Roy. Holiday 26: 55 (col.) Oct '59.

chalk cliffs (England). Holiday 23: 101 (col.) Ap '58.

challenge (sym.). Lehner: Pict. bk. of sym., p. 86.

Chalon, J.J. (work of). Con. 132: XVII Nov '53.

Chambord, Chateaux of. See Chateau de Chambord.

chamber of Deputies (Paris). Amer. heri. vol. 11 no. 3 p. 19 (col.) (Ap '60).

chamber organ. See organ, chamber.

Chamberlain, Francis L. Cur. biog. p. 61 (1959)

Chamberlain, Owen. Cur. biog. p. 84 (1960).

Chamberlain, Richard. Cur. biog. p. 65 (1963).

Chamberlain, Samuel. Cur. biog. p. 167 (1954).

Chamberlain, Wilton Norman. Cur. biog. p. 85 (1960).

Chambord chateau. See Chateau de Chambord.

Chamonix. Holiday 13: 125 (col.) Mar '53.

Chamoun, Camille N. Cur. biog. p. 105 (1956).

Champaigne, Philippe de (work of). Con. 137: 49 Mar '56.
Natl. geog. 101: 84 (col.) Jan '52.

Champion, George. Cur. biog. p. 99 (1961).

Champion, Gower. Cur. biog. p. 111 (1953).

Champion, Marge. Cur. biog. p. 111 (1953).

Champollion, Jean-Francois (portrait). Ceram: March of arch., p. 85.

Champ's route, John (war deserter). Amer. heri. vol. 8 no. 6 p. 26 (Oct '57).

chancel screen, Gothic. Con. 138: XLIX Nov '56.

Chancellor, Joe. Horan: Pict. hist. of wild west, p. 196.

Chancellor, John. Cur. biog. p. 82 (1962).

chandelier. Amer. heri. vol. 4 no. 1 p. 17 (col.) (fall '52).
Con. 140: 74 (col.) Nov '57.
Holiday 12: 46 (col.) Sept '52; 23: 59 (col.) Jan '58; 27: 85, 182 (col.) May '60; 28: 75 (col.) Sept '60.
Jensen: The White House, p. 102, 151.

—— (bag or tent shaped). Con. ency. of ant., vol. 3, pl. 114.

—— (candles). Holiday 10: 143 (col.) Dec '51; 27: 174 (col.) Je '60; 28: 95 (col.) Aug '60.
Natl. geog. 103: 168 Feb '53.

——, Adam. Con. ency. of ant., vol. 3, pl. 113.

——, Adam crystal. Con. 135: XXII May '55.

——, Adam cut glass. Con. 140: VIII Sept '57.

——, antique. Con. 135: L Ap '55, XVIII Je '55; 142: 2 (col.) Sept '58; 143: 72 Ap '59.
Holiday 13: 53 (col.) Jan '53.

——, brass (antique). Amer. heri. vol. 1 no. 2 p. 41 (winter '50).

Con. 145: XXXI May '60.

——, **brass (18th cent.).** Con. 133: XXIV Ap '54; 139: XXX Je '57; 143: XXVIII, LXX Je '59; 145: back cover Je '60.

——, **brass (17th cent.).** Con. 133: XVIII May '54; 140: XLVIII Jan '58.

——, **Chinese-Chippendale.** Con. ency. of ant., vol. 3, pl. 113.

——, **crystal.** Con. 136: I Sept '55; 144: 140 (col.) Dec '59.
Holiday 12: 53 (col.) Nov '52; 18: 53 (col.) Aug '55; 20: 63 Oct '56; 24: 71 (col.) Aug '58, 23 Dec '58; 25: 75 (col.) May '59, 18 (col.) Je '59.
Natl. geog. 98: 601 (col.) Nov '50; 102: 147 Aug '52; 103: 162-3 (col.) Feb '53, 794 (col.) Je '53; 105: 300 (col.) Mar '54; 109: 479-80 (col.) Ap '56; 113: 549 (col.) Ap '58; 114: 114 (col.) Jl '58; 116: 727 (col.) Dec '59.

——, **crystal (antique).** Con. 135: LII Mar '55; 136: L Nov '55.

——, **crystal (candles).** Holiday 27: 174 (col.) Je '60.

——, **crystal (18th cent.).** Con. 133: LII Ap '54; 134: LVIII Nov '54, LII Dec '54; 135: LXII Ap '55.

——, **crystal (1800).** Con. 145: XXXIX Ap '60.

——, **crystal (modern).** Holiday 26: 59 (col.) Nov '59.

——, **crystal (19th cent.).** Con. 143: XI Je '59.

——, **cut glass (19th cent.).** Con. 145: LII May '60.

——, **18th cent.** Con. 134: L Nov '54; 136: XLIV Jan '56; 137: L Je '56; 140: XLII Sept '57; 141: XL May '58; 142: XXXVI Nov '58.

——, **French (18th cent.).** Con. 145: 110 Ap '60.

——, **glass (antique).** Con. 133: LVI Mar '54.

——, **glass (colonial).** Natl. geog. 109: 449 (col.) Ap '56.

——, **glass (early).** Daniel: Cut & engraved glass, pl. 137-8.

——, **glass (18th cent.).** Con. 142: back cover Nov '58.

——, **glass (19th cent.).** Con. ency. of ant., vol. 3, pl. 114-6.

——, **glass lantern.** Natl. geog. 107: 460 (col.) Ap '55.

——, **Grecian (19th cent.).** Con. 143: 94-5 Ap '59.

——, **Italian (17th cent.).** Con. 141: LVIII May '58.

——, **19th cent.** Con. 138: back cover Dec '56.

——, **regency.** Con. 137: XXXII Mar '56; 139: XXVIII May '57; 141: XXXII May '58; 142: XXXIII Sept '58.

——, **regency crystal.** Con. 129: VI Mar '52; 135: 148 Ap '55, XLIV Je '55.

——, **regency cut glass.** Con. 133: XXXIV May '54.

——, **regency glass.** Con. 140: LXXI Jan '58; 142: XXVI Nov '58.

——, **Russian imperial.** Con. 132: 139 Nov '53.

——, **17th cent.** Con. 129: back cover Je '52. Holiday 20: 31 (col.) Sept '56.

——, **17-18th cent.** Con. 135: back cover Je '55.

——, **17th cent. silver.** Con. 134: 194 Dec '54.

——, **silver (antique).** Con. 134: XIII Sept '54.

——, **Venetian crystal (17th cent.).** Int. gr. soc.: Arts . . . p. 95 (col.).

——, **Venetian glass.** Con. 138: 169-73 Dec '56.

——, **Waterford.** Con. 132: LXXII Jan '54.

——, **Waterford crystal.** Con. 132: LXII Nov '53; 133: LXXIV Je '54; 134: LVI Sept '54.

"chandelier tree" base. Jordan: Hammond's pict. travel atlas, p. 198 (col.).

chandeliers. Holiday 14: 26-7 (col.) Sept '53.

—— **(antique).** Con. 138: 241-3 Jan '57.

Chandler, Albert B. Cur. biog. p. 118 (1943); p. 107 (1956).

Chandler, Dorothy Buffum. Cur. biog. p. 102 (1957).

Chandler, Norman. Cur. biog. p. 103 (1957).

Chandler, Raymond. Cur. biog. p. 107 (1946).

Chandy, Judge Anna. Cur. biog. p. 87 (1960).

Chanel, Grabrielle. Cur. biog. p. 169 (1954).

Chang, John M. Cur. biog. p. 101 (1949).

Changing of the Guard (London). Holiday 13: inside back cover (col.) Feb '53, 122 (col.) Je '53; 21: 136 (col.) Ap '57; 23: 150 (col.) May '58.
Natl. geog. 114: 80 (col.) Jl '58.

—— **(Quebec).** Natl. geog. 115: 312 (col.) Mar '59.

Channel Islands (Cal.). Natl. geog. 114: 256-83 (part col.) Aug '58.

Channing, Ellery (caricature). Amer. heri. vol. 10 no. 3 p. 60. (Ap '59).

Channing, William Henry. Amer. heri. vol. 8 no. 2 p. 23 (Feb '57).

Chant book (Illuminated). Natl. geog. 111: 789 (col.) Je '57.

Chantereau, J. F. (work of). Con. ency. of ant., vol. 1, pl. 175.

Chantrey, Sir Francis (work of). Con. 129: 82 Je '52.

Chapala (Mexico). Travel 110: 19-20 Nov '58.

chapel (Oberndorf, Austria). Travel 108: 30 Dec '57.

—— **(Okinawa, airfield).** Natl. geog. 107: 279 Feb '55.

—— **(Ruspoli castle).** Holiday 27: 98 (col.) Ap '60.

—— **(Russian fort, Cal.).** Brooks: Growth of a nation, p. 111.

——, **Aiquina (Chile festival).** Natl. geog. 117: 232 (col.) Feb '60.

——, **Alamo (Texas).** Amer. heri. vol. 4 no. 1 p. 42 (fall '52).

——, **cave grotto.** *See* cave grotto chapel.

——, **Cuttyhunk island.** Travel 107: 35 Je '57.

——, **fisherman's (Thira).** Natl. geog. 114: 759 (col.) Dec '58.

——, **Fishtown.** Amer. heri. vol. 3 no. 4 p. 54 (summer '52).

——, **hermit's (Ischia).** Natl. geog. 105: 533 (col.) Ap '54.

——, **Lutheran (Minden, Neb.).** Travel 109: 31 Je '58.

chapel, Notre-Dame-du-Haut. Holiday 21: 92 (col.) Ap '57.
Natl. geog. 117: 762 Je '60.
——, "Our Lady of Fatima". *See* "Our Lady of Fatima" chapel.
——, Pazzi. *See* Pazzi chapel.
——, Rockefeller memorial. *See* Rockefeller memorial chapel.
——, royal Tonga. Holiday 28: 79 Oct '60.
——, St. Michel. *See* St. Michel's chapel.
——, Sawston Hall (16th cent., int.). Con. 144: 7 Sept '59.
——, U.S. war memorial (overseas). Natl. geog. 111: 741, 750 (col.) Je '57.
——, West Point. Natl. geog. 101: 605 (col.) May '52.
chapel at Ronchamp (France). Int. gr. soc.: Arts . . . p. 125 (col.).
Chapel of Ananias. Natl. geog. 110: 725 (col.) Dec '56.
Chapel of Our Lady (Ephesus, int.). Osward: Asia Minor, pl. II (col.).
"Chapel of Transfiguration" (Teton mts.). Natl. geog. 109: 15 (col.) Jan '56.
Travel 104: 34 Aug '55.
chapel services, workmen religions. Natl. geog. 104: 799 (col.) Dec '53.
Chapin, Katherine G. Cur. biog. p. 121 (1943).
Chaplin, Charles Spencer (Charlie). (eating, comic). Int. gr. soc.: Arts . . . p. 151 (col.).
Chaplin, Charles S. Cur. biog. p. 101 (1961).
Chaplin, Charles S. Holiday 5: 36 (col.) Jan '49.
Chaplin, Charles Spencer (Charlie). Holiday 12: 35 Dec '52.
Chapman, Albert K. Cur. biog. p. 94 (1952).
Chapman, Charles F. Cur. biog. p. 86 (1958).
Chapman, Conrad Wise (work of). Con. 135: 251 (col.) Je '55; 137: 240 (col.) Je '56.
Natl. geog. 99: 199 (col.) Feb '51.
Chapman, Daniel A. Cur. biog. p. 63 (1959).
Chapman, Gilbert W. Cur. biog. p. 105 (1957).
Chapman, Oscar L. Cur. biog. p. 102 (1949).
Chapman, Sydney. Cur. biog. p. 107: (1957).
Chapman, Mrs. Theodore S. Cur. biog. p. 113 (1955).
Chappel, Alonzo (work of). Amer. heri. vol. 6 no. 6 p. 6 (Oct '55); vol. 8 no. 4 p. 58 (col.) (Je '57).
Chapultepec (battle, Mexico). Amer. heri. vol. 6 no. 4 p. 21 (col.) (Je '55); vol. 10 no. 2 p. 26 (Feb '59).
Chaqueneau, Mrs. Julien. Holiday 14: 52 Dec '53.
character expressions. *See* emotional expressions.
charcoal cart. Amer. heri. vol. 6 no. 4 p. 48 (col.) (Je '55).
charcoal iron. Rawson: Ant. pict. bk., p. 12.
Chardin, Jean (portrait). Ceram: March of arch., p. 172.
Chardin, Jean-Baptiste-Simeon (work of). Con. 133: XVIII, III Ap '54; 137: XIV (col.) May '56; 145: cover (col.) Je '60.
Natl. geog. 101: 85 (col.) Jan '52.
Praeg. pict. ency., p. 359 (col.).

charger (royal marriage of Charles II). Con. 145: 114 (col.) Ap '60.
——, George II silver. Con. 133: XLIX Ap '54.
——, Irish silver (old). Con. 135: LII Mar '55.
——, Lambeth delft. Con. 134: X, XIV Nov '54.
——, polychrome. Con. 134: XXX Dec '54.
chariot (horse, man). Natl. geog. 112: 840-1 (col.) Dec '57.
——, (horses, driver). Natl. geog. 112: 860 (col.) Dec '57.
——, Persian (ancient). Int. gr. soc.: Arts . . . p. 43 (col.).
——, Roman. Holiday 15: 114 Ap '54.
——, Roman ceremonial. Int. gr. soc.: Arts . . . p. 43 (col.).
——, Scandinavian (medieval). Int. gr. soc.: Arts . . . p. 81 (col.).
——, Sumerian (battle). Natl. geog. 99: 71 (col.) Jan '51.
——, sun. *See* sun chariot.
——, war. *See* war chariot.
chariot race. Holiday 27: 118 Mar '60.
Durant: Pict. hist. of Amer. circus, p. 68.
"Charioteer from Delphi" (sculpture). Praeg. pict. ency., p. 132.
chariots, Middle East (ancient). Int. gr. soc.: Arts . . . p. 43 (col.).
Charisse, Cyd. Cur. biog. p. 172 (1954).
charity (sym.). Lehner: Pict. bk. of sym., p. 34.
Charlemagne's chapel plan & choir (Aix-la-Chapelle). Praeg. pict. ency., p. 183.
Charles, Prince of Belgium. Cur. biog. p. 108 (1946).
Charles, Prince of England. Holiday 23: 68-9 Jan '58.
—— (climbing). Natl. geog. 104: 306 Sept '53.
Charles I. Con. 139: 217 Je '57.
"Charles I and Duke of York" (Lely). Con. 126: 26 Aug '50.
Charles II (bust). Con. 143: 105 Ap '59.
—— (de Miranda). Con. 141: LIII Ap '58.
—— (Lely). Con. 143: 6 Mar '59.
Charles III (statue). Labande: Naples, p. 79.
Charles V. Con. 134: 189 Dec '54.
Charles, Ezzard. Cur. biog. p. 104 (1949).
Charles, Lord Halifax (Closterman). Con. 144: 76 Nov '59.
"Charles bridge, Prague" (Kokoschka). Praeg. pict. ency., p. 497 (col.).
Charles-Roux, Francois. Cur. biog. p. 95 (1952).
"Charles W. Morgan" (whaling ship). Holiday 26: 35 (col.) Sept '59.
Charleston, (S.C.). Holiday 28: 70-5 (part col.) Sept '60.
Jordan: Hammond's pict. atlas, p. 62-3 (col.).
—— (air view). Natl. geog. 103: 306 Mar '53.
—— (1831). Amer. heri. vol. 9 no. 2 p. 48-61 (part col.) (Feb '58).
—— (1855). Amer. heri. vol. 9 no. 2 p. 89 (Feb '58).
—— (gardens). Holiday 11: 64-7 (part col.) Ap '52.
Natl. geog. 103: 307, 313-20 (col.) Mar '53.
Charleston (W. Va.). Holiday 14: 103 (col.) Oct '53.

Charleston housetops (Sumter bombardment). Amer. heri. vol. 9 no. 2 p. 93 (Feb '58).

Charlestown, Nevis island. Amer. heri. vol. 6 no. 4 p. 6, 8-9 (Je '55).

Charlesworth, James C. Cur. biog. p. 173 (1954).

Charlie & Bergen. See Bergen & Charlie, Edgar.

Charlot, Jean. Cur. biog. p. 96 (1945).

Charlotte, Grand Dutchess of Luxembourg. Cur. biog. p. 106 (1949).

Charlotte, Queen. Con. 132: 148 Jan '54. Amer. heri. vol. 11 no. 4 back cover, 5-6 (col.) (Je '60).

Charlotte, Queen of Gt. Brit. (cartoon). Amer. heri. vol. 11 no. 4 p. 19 (col.) (Je '60).

Charlotte & her baby, Queen (Cotes). Con. 126: 27 Aug '50.

Charlotte (N.C.). Holiday 6: 81-5 Dec '49.
—— (Manger motor inn). Travel 113: 14 May '60.

Charlotte Amalie (Virgin Islands). Natl. geog. 109: 208, 218, 223, 231 (part col.) Feb '56.

Charlotte Sophia, Consort of George III. Con. 135: 238 Je '55.

Charlottesville (Va.). Natl. geog. 97: 554-92 (part col.) May '50.

"Charpentier" (Van Gogh). Con. 141: V May '58.

chart, old school reading. Amer. heri. vol. 8 no. 5 p. 11 (Aug '57).

chart room, ship (skipper). Natl. geog. 116: 783 (col.) Dec '59.

Chaterhouse motor hotel (Wash., D.C.). Travel 110: 43 Nov '58.

"Charteris children" (Romney). Con. 134: 49 Sept '54.

Chartres cathedral. Holiday 18: 128-9 (col.). Dec '55; 25: 39 Jan '59; 27: 129 Jan '60. Natl. geog. 117: 736-7 (col.) Je '60.

Chartres cathedral (sculpture). Praeg. pict. ency., p. 208.

Chartres cathedral window. Natl. geog. 116: 837 (col.) Dec '59.
Praeg.: Pict. ency., p. 204 (col.).

Chase, Harry Woodburn. Cur. biog. p. 97 (1948).

Chase, Ilka. Cur. biog. p. 144 (1942).

Chase, Joseph Cummings. Cur. biog. p. 115 (1955).
—— (work of). Amer. heri. vol. 10 no. 6 p. 12-3 (col.) (Oct '59).

Chase, Kate. Amer. heri. vol. 7 no. 5 p. 41 (Aug '56).
Jensen: The White House, p. 88.

Chase, Lucia. Cur. biog. p. 104 (1947).

Chase, Margaret. See Smith, Margaret Chase.

Chase, Mary. Cur. biog. p. 99 (1945).

Chase, Salmon P. Amer. heri. vol. 7 no. 5 p. 42 (Aug '56); vol. 11 no. 6 p. 46 (Oct '60).

Chase, Maj. William C. Cur. biog. p. 97 (1952).

Chase, William Merritt (work of). Amer. heri. vol. 6 no. 2 p. 45 (Feb '55).
Con. 139: 267-70 (part col.) Je '57.

Chase-Loyd house (Annapolis). Holiday 23: 82 (col.) Je '58.

Chasins, Abram. Cur. biog. p. 89 (1960).

"Chasm at Delphi" (Cozens). Con. 139: 53 Mar '57.

Chastain, Madye Lee. Cur. biog. p. 89 (1958).

chasuble. Con. 140: 175 Dec '57.

chateau (int.). Holiday 21: 66 (col.) Ap '57; 27: 20 (col.) Ap '60.
—— (near Pau, Pyrenees). Amer. heri. vol. 11 no. 3 p. 23 (Ap '60).

chateau, Belgian (int.). Holiday 21: 43 (col.) Jan '57.
——, French. Holiday 13: inside back cover (col.) Ap '53.
——, French (St. Aubin-d-Ecrosville). Holiday 21: 83 (col.) Ap '57.
——, Norman. Amer. heri. vol. 10 no. 4 p. 100 (Je '59).
——, Walzin (Belgian). Holiday 21: 44 Jan '57.

Chateau Chanpremault (18th cent.). Con. 145: LIII Je '60.

Chateau Chenonceaux (Loire Valley, France). Holiday 15: 50 Jan '54.
Natl. geog. 117: 735 (col.) Je '60.
—— (moonlight). Holiday 27: 20-1 (col.) Jan '60.

Chateau d'Amour. Holiday 21: 62-3 (col.) Ap '57.

Chateau de Beersel (Belgium). Holiday 28: 33 Dec '60.

Chateau de Blois stairway. Natl. geog. 117: 733 (col.) Je '60.

Chateau de Chambord (France). Holiday 18: 116 (col.) Jl '55; 25: 167 Ap '59.
Int. gr. soc.: Arts . . . p. 83 (col.).
Praeg. pict. ency., p. 266.
—— (dining room). Holiday 24: 70 (col.) Oct '58.

Chateau de Chavaniac (home of Lafayette). Travel 107: 53 Ap '57.

Chateau de la Bretesche. Holiday 27: 89 May '60.

Chateau de la Roche-pot (15th cent.). Con. 145: LIII Je '60.

Chateau de Laerne. Holiday 24: 23 (col.) Oct '58.

Chateau de Langeais (Flanders). Con. 133: 33 Mar '54.

Chateau de Maintenon. Holiday 26: 59 Dec '59.
Travel 113: 56 Ap '60.

Chateau de Miromesnil. Holiday 19: 52 Jan '56.

Chateau de Montsoreau. Con. 143: 53 Mar '59.

Chateau du Clos de Vougeot. Holiday 26: 97 Aug '59.

Chateau d'Usse (France). Holiday 5: 134 Mar '49.

Chateau Frontenac (Quebec). Holiday 5: 124 (col.) Ap '49; 11: 99 (col.) Je '52.
Jordan: Hammond's pict. atlas, p. 21 (col.).
Natl. geog. 113: 70-1, 85 (col.) Jan '58; 115: 312 (col.) Mar '59.

Chateau Gaillard (Normandy). Natl. geog. 115: 596 May '59.

Chateau Laurier (Ottawa, Canada). Holiday 5: 124 Mar '49; 14: 119 (col.) Jl '53.

Chateau Mercues (France). Holiday 13: 125 (col.) Mar '53.

Chateau of Vianden. Con. 143: 165 May '59.

Chateau Sully (Loire Valley). Holiday 23: 13 (col.) Mar '58.

"Chateau-Thierry street barricade" (Alyward). Amer. heri. vol. 10 no. 6 p. 16. (col.) (Oct '59).

Chateaux, Loire. See Loire chateaux.

Chatham Island (Waitangi). Travel 112: 42 Dec '59.

Chattanooga (Tenn.). Holiday 8: 38-9 (col.) Nov '50.

Chauncey, Henry. Cur. biog. p. 105 (1951).

Chauvel, Jean. Cur. biog. p. 90 (1950).

Chavan, Y. B. Cur. biog. p. 67 (1963).

Chavannes, P. Puvis de (work of). Con. 142: 62 Sept '58.

Chavchadze, George. Cur. biog. p. 123 (1943).

Chavez, Carlos. Cur. biog. p. 107 (1949).

Chavez, Dennis. Cur. biog. p. 110 (1946).

Chayefsky, Paddy. Cur. biog. p. 109 (1957).

Cheatham, Benjamin F. Pakula: Cent. album, p. 105.

check (1889). Natl. geog. 113: 577 Ap '58.

——, traveler's. See traveler's check.

check mark (sym.). Lehner: Pict. bk. of sym., p. 85.

check to Mrs. U.S. Grant (for war memoirs book). Amer. heri. vol. 11 no. I p. 78 (Dec '59).

checker board. Holiday 11: 30 Feb '52.

—— (bottles as checkers). Holiday 28: 122 (col.) Dec '60.

checker game (Arabs). Natl. geog. 102: 794 (col.) Dec '52.

—— (country store). Holiday 18: 39 (col.) Jl '55.

cheer leaders (games). Holiday 15: 10 Jan '54.

cheese. Holiday 6: 44 (col.) Jl '49.

—— (in cave). Natl. geog. 114: 673 (col.) Nov '58.

——, Gouda. Holiday 24: 47 (col.) Dec '58.

——, Holland (men carrying). Natl. geog. 98: 759 (col.) Dec 50.

——, Holland (on barrows). Natl. geog. 106: 408 (col.) Sept '54.

——, Switzerland (on wagon). Natl. geog. 110: 467 (col.) Oct '56.

cheese bearers (Holland). Holiday 23: 57 Jan '58.

cheese cave (man, women). Natl. geog. 100: 39 (col.) Jl '51.

cheese cradle. See cradle, cheese.

cheese factory. Holiday 6: 44 (col.) Jl '49.

cheese jar. Holiday 21: 168 Mar '57.

cheese maker. Natl. geog. 100: 407 (col.) Sept '51.

cheese making. Natl. geog. 98: 243 (col.) Aug '50; 107: 468 (col.) Ap '55.

—— (men). Natl. geog. 111: 169 (col.) Feb '57.

cheese testing corer. Rawson: Ant. pict. bk., p. 8.

cheesepress. Rawson: Ant. pict. bk., p. 9.

chef. Holiday 6: 91 Nov '49; 7: 57, 59-62 Jan '50; 10: 52 (col.) Aug '51, 13 (col.), 127 Nov '51; 11: 57-8 Jan '52, 62-3 Feb '52, 13, 69, 121 (part col.) Mar '52, 97 Ap '52;

12: 56 (col.) Aug '52, 15 Sept '52, 73 Nov '52; 14: 64 Aug '53, 127 Nov '53; 19: 53 Jan '56; 20: 78 (col.) Aug '56; 21: 79 (col.), 104 Feb '57, 67 (col.) Ap '57, 24, 83 (col.) May '57, 17 (col.) Je '57; 22: 79 Jl '57, 77 (col.) Oct '57, 107 (col.) Dec '57; 23: 14, 94, 165 (part col.) Mar '58, 37 (col.) Je '58; 24: 2 Sept '58, 135 (col.) Oct '58; 25: 176 Je '59; 26: 58-9 Aug '59, 136 Oct '59; 27: 78 (col.) Feb '60, 62 Ap '60, 145 May '60; 28: 71 (col.) Aug '60, 58, 228 Nov '60.

Natl. geog. 98: 63 (col.) Jl '50; 99: 768 (col.) Je '51; 102: 176 Aug '52; 103: 158 (col.) Feb '53.

Travel 103: 53 Je '55.

—— (back view). Holiday 20: 106 (col.) Oct '56.

—— (comic). Holiday 11: 4 Feb '52; 18: 121 Sept '55; 19: 131 Mar '56; 21: 153 (col.) Je '57; 27: 193 May '60; 28: 107 Jl '60, 210 Nov '60.

Travel 108: 61 Nov '57.

—— (cooking). Natl. geog. 98: 155 (col.) Aug '50; 110: 425 Sept '56.

—— (decorating cake). Natl. geog. 99: 447 (col.) Ap '51.

—— (dinner table). Holiday 20: 2 (col.) Nov '56.

—— (food cooked). Holiday 20: 82 (col.) Dec '56.

—— (head). Holiday 13: 149 Mar '53; 18: 25 Sept '55; 19: 65 Je '56; 27: 113, 116, 130 (col.) Je '60.

—— (pie). Holiday 20: 158 (col.) Dec '56.

——, Austrian (kitchen). Natl. geog. 118: 259 (col.) Aug '60.

——, restaurant. Holiday 13: 57 Ap '53.

——, sidewalk (cooking crabs). Natl. geog. 110: 204 (col.) Aug '56.

chef cap. Holiday 14: 81 Jl '53; 18: 74 Jl '55.

chefs. (box lunches, service men's). Natl. geog. 111: 291 (col.) Mar '57.

Chelf, Frank L. Cur. biog. p. 99 (1952).

Chelan, Lake. See Lake Chelan.

Chelsea (England). Holiday 10: 70-5 Sept '51.

Chelsea candlestick. Con. 132: XXXVII Sept '53; 133: 262 Je '54.

Chelsea dishes. Con. 133: XII Je '54.

Chelsea figurine. See figurine, Chelsea.

Chelsea porcelain. See porcelain, Chelsea.

Cheltenham paddock (Munnings). Con. 135: VI Ap '55.

chemical plant. Natl. geog. 102: 34-5 (col.) Jl '52.

chemist (in lab.). Travel 106: inside back cover Aug '56.

chemistry (sym.) Lehner: Pict. bk. of sym., p. 11.

chemistry, Bur. of. See Bur. of chemistry members (1884).

chemistry lab. (Russian student). Natl. geog. 116: 364 (col.) Sept '59.

Chen Cheng. Cur. biog. p. 147 (1941).

Chen Yi. Cur. biog. p. 65 (1959).

Cheney, Brainard B. Cur. biog. p. 66 (1959).

Chennault, Brig. Gen. Claire L. Cur. biog. p. 147 (1942).
Holiday 22: 148 Dec '57.

Chenonceaux, Chateau. *See* Chateau Chenonceaux.

Cheops, pyramid of. *See* pyramid of Cheops.

Chephren pyramid. Ceram: March of arch., p. 91.

—— **(cross section).** Ceram: March of arch., p. 105.

Chepstow homes (England). Holiday 14: 132 (col.) Nov '53.

Chernyakhovsky, Gen. Ivan D. Cur. biog. p. 91 (1944).

"Cherokee Bill". *See* Cook, Bill.

Cherokee Indian dance. Natl. geog. 102: 495 (col.) Oct '52.

Cherry, Francis A. Cur. biog. p. 175 (1954).

cherry twins (sym.). Lehner: Pict. bk. of sym., p. 65.

cherubs. Con. 141: XVI Mar '58, XLII, 139 May '58.

Cherwell, Lord Frederick A.L. Cur. biog. p. 101 (1952).

the "Chesapeake", U.S.S. (battle ship, 1813). Amer. heri. vol. 7 no. 3 p. 17-19 (col.) (Ap '56); vol. 10 no. 2 p. 29 (col) (Feb '59).

Chesapeake & Ohio canal (1857). Amer. heri. vol. 9 no. I p. 68 (col.) (Dec '57). Natl. geog. 117: 418-39 (col.) Mar '60.

—— **(map).** Natl. geog. 117: 424-5 (col.) Mar '60.

Chesapeake Bay. Holiday 16: 26 (col.) Sept '54.

Chesapeake Bay country. Holiday 10: 34-51 (part col.) Nov '51.

Cheseman, Robert Holbein. Con. 127: 55 Mar '51.

Cheshire, Leonard. Cur. biog. p. 84 (1962).

chess board. Con. 143: 120 (Ap '59).

—— **(living chessmen, Italy).** Natl. geog. 110: 659-68 (col.) Nov '56.

chess game. Holiday 22: 161 Oct '57. Natl. geog. 117: 492 (col.) Ap '60.

—— **(soldiers).** Natl .geog. 117: 663 (col.) May '60.

—— **("The Turk").** Amer. heri. vol. 11 no. 2 p. 34-7 (Feb '60).

—— **(Russian).** Natl. geog. 116: 402 (col.) Sept '59.

chess men (antique). Con. ency. of ant., vol. 3, pl. 137-9.

—— **(medieval).** Int. gr. soc.: Arts . . . p. 77 (col.).

"The Chess Players" (Brunery). Con. 139: 147 May '57.

chess set. Con. 141: XXII Mar '58. Holiday 25: 23 (col.) Je '59.

——, **(Indian design).** Holiday 26: 115 Sept '59.

——, **Charles II.** Con. 134: XX Dec '54.

——, **George III silver.** 139: XLVII Ap '57.

——, **ivory.** Con. 139: 78 Ap '57.

——, **Meissen.** Con. 143: 266 Je '59.

chest, Amer. (18th cent. block & shell). Con. 135: 65 Mar '55.

—— **(1700).** Con. 141: 127 Ap '58.

chest, antique. Con. 136: 47, 74 Sept '55; 137: LIV May '56; 141: XXXV Mar '58.

——, **armorial (French 16th cent.).** Con. 133: LXII Je '54.

——, **bachelor.** Holiday 22: 159 (col.) Dec '57.

——, **bachelor antique.** Con. 133: VI May '54.

——, **bachelor Chippendale.** Con. 136: 292 Jan '56.

——, **bachelor (18th cent.).** Con. 136: XLV Sept '55;; 139: XVI Ap '57; 142: XXXI Sept '58.

——, **bachelor Queen Anne.** Con. 142: XXI Sept '58.

——, **blanket.** Con. ency. of ant., vol. 3, pl. 123, 126-8.

——, **block front (New England).** Con. 133: 264 Je '54.

——, **bow fronted (antique).** Con. 135: XLVI Ap '55.

——, **bridal (Medici-Strozzi).** Praeg. pict. ency., p. 294.

——, **caravan (Morocco).** Natl. geog. 107: 156 (col.) Feb '55.

——, **ceremonial (Norwegian, 18th cent.).** Con. 145: 23 Mar '60.

——, **Charles II (lacquer).** Con. 135: XXXIII Ap '55.

——, **Chippendale.** Con. 129: VI, XXXVI Ap '52; 136: IV Sept '55, 146 Nov '55; 138: IV, XLIII Sept '56.

——, **Chippendale serpentine.** Con. 132: L Sept '53.

——, **Chippendale style.** Holiday 20: 135 Oct '56.

——, **Connecticut.** Con. ency. of ant., vol. 1, p. 61.

——, **dower.** Holiday 12: 12 Jl '52. Rawson: Ant. pict. bk., p. 17.

——, **dower (Chinese).** Con. 132: X Sept '53.

——, **dower (Queen Anne).** Con. 142: XXII Dec '58.

——, **18th cent.** Con. 132: 51 Sept '53; 134: VI, VIII Sept '54; 136: LXII Jan '56; 142: XVI Jan '59; 144: XXXVIII Dec '59.

——, **Elizabethan.** Con. 136: XI Nov '55.

——, **English antique.** Con. 126: 41 Aug '50.

——, **15th cent.** Con. 133: 255 Je '54.

——, **14th cent. ('pas Saladin).** Con. 133: 253 Je '54.

——, **French gothic.** Con. 126: 53 Aug '50.

——, **French provincial style.** Natl. geog. 101: 299 Mar '52.

——, **Gaudreau.** Con. 138: 221 Jan '57.

——, **George I.** Con. 142: 56 Sept '58; 144: LVIII Jan '60.

——, **George II.** Con. 135: XXIV Mar '55; 138: XLIV Jan '57.

——, **Georgian.** Con. 138: 61 Sept '56.

——, **gothic.** Con. 134: LVII Dec '54.

——, **Greek.** Natl. geog. 114: 737 (col.) Dec '58.

——, **Hadley.** Con. ency. of ant., vol, 1, p. 64.

——, **Hepplewhite.** Con. 145: XXXVIII Je '60.

——, **Hepplewhite serpentine.** Con. 133: XVI Mar '54; 143: XXIV Je '59; 145: XVIII May '60.

chest, kneehole (18th cent.). Con. 132: XXXI, XXXV Sept '53.
——, kneehole (Queen Anne). Con. 139: XXIV May '57.
——, lacquer (18th cent.). Con. 140: 15 Sept '57.
——, liquor. See liquor chest.
——, Louis XV. Con. 139: LXVII Je '57.
——, mule. See mule chest.
——, 19th cent. Con. 140: XXXVI Nov '57.
chest, pirate. Holiday 23: 4 (col.) Feb '58.
——, plate. See plate chest.
——, Portuguese (17th cent.). Con. 143: 270 Je '59.
——, Queen Anne. Con. 133: VI Mar '54; 143: IV Ap '59.
——, Scottish antique. Con. 136: VI Jan '56.
——, serpentine (antique). Con. 144: XII Nov '59.
——, serpentine (18th cent.). Con. 141: LVIII Je '58; 142: 57 Sept '58; 143: XLII Mar '59; 144: XXXVI Nov '59.
——, 17th cent. Con. 129: XVI Ap '52, LXIII Je '52.
——, Sheraton. Con. 136: VI Jan '56.
——, Sheraton bowfront. Con. 133: XV Je '54.
——, Sheraton serpentine. Con. 141: XLV Je '58.
——, 13th cent. Con. ency. of ant., vol. 1, p. 16.
——, travel. Con. ency. of ant., vol. 3, pl. 123.
——, treasure. See treasure chest.
——, Tudor. Con. 139: LXIII Je '57; 144: 5 Sept '59.
——, Van Pelt high. Con. 141: 128 Ap '58.
——, Wells Fargo. Horan: Pict. hist. of wild west, p. 114.
——, Welsh (16th cent.). Con. 139: XLIV Ap '57.
——, William & Mary Con. 126: 47 Aug '50; 133: XIV Mar '54; 134: XLIII Nov '54; 135: XLVII Mar '55.
chest-bench. Holiday 24: 190 Nov '58.
chest design (19th cent.). Amer. heri. vol. 2 no. 2 p. 35 (col.) (winter '51).
chest of drawers. Holiday 10: 123 (col.) Oct '51, 2 (col.) Nov '51; 11: 151 (col.) Ap '52; 12: 125 (col.) Nov '52, 121 Dec '52.
——, antique. Con. 141: XXXVI Ap '58.
——, antique (18 cent.). Con. 141: IV Ap '58.
——, Chippendale. Con. 143: XIV May '59.
——, 18th cent. Con. 141: XXXVIII Ap '58.
——, modern. Holiday 21: 119 (col.) Ap '57.
——, Queen Anne. Con. 135: XLIV Je '55.
——, Sheraton. Con. 142: VI Jan '59.
——, William & Mary. Con. ency. of ant., vol. 1, pl. 15.
chest-on-chest, antique. Con. 133: 70 Mar '54.
——, Charleston. Con. 135: 70 Mar '55.
——, 18th cent. Con. ency. of ant., vol. 1, pl. 40.
——, 18th cent. Amer. Con. 137: 126 Ap '56.
——, kneehole. Con. 129: 147 Je '52.
——, Mass. Con. 135: 65 Mar '55.
——, Mass. blockfront (18th cent.). Con. 134: 206 Dec '54.

chest on stand, William & Mary. Con. ency. of ant., vol. 1, pl. 18.
Chester, Edmund. Cur. biog. p. 148 (1941).
Chester fife & drum corps (Conn.). Holiday 26: 37 (col.) Sept '59.
the "Chester W. Chapin" (river boat). Amer. heri. vol. 6, no. I p. 10 (col.) (Dec '54).
Chesterton G. K. Amer. heri. vol. 8 no. 5 p. 27 (Aug '57).
chests (18th cent.). Con. ency. of ant., vol. 3, pl. 117-28.
Chevalier, Elizabeth Pickett. Cur. biog. p. 125 (1943).
Chevalier, Maurice. Cur. biog. p. 100 (1948). Int. gr. soc.: Arts . . . p. 149 (col.).
"Chevalier of the Order of St. Esprit" (Nattier). Con. 141: 41 (col.) Mar '58.
Chevaliers du Tastevin. Holiday 21: 82-3 (col.) May '57.
Cheves, Mrs. Langdon. Amer. heri. vol. vol. 9 no. 2 p. 57 (col.) (Feb '58).
Chevrier, Lionel. Cur. biog. p. 103 (1952).
Chevrolet auto. Holiday 5: 7 (col.) Ap '49, 131 (col.) Je '49; 6: 10 (col.) Sept '49, 90 (col.) Oct '49, inside cover (col.) Nov '49; 7: 103 (col.) May '50, 69 (col.) Je '50; 8: 83 (col.) Jl '50, 22 (col.) Aug '50; 9: 15 (col.) Mar '51; 15: 4 Feb '54, 92 (col.) Mar '54, 68 (col.) Ap '54, 22 (col.) May '54; 16: 74 (col.) Jl '54, 15 (col.) Sept '54; 17: inside cover (col.) Feb '55, 77 (col.) Mar '55. Travel 103: 9 Jan '55.
Chew, Benjamin. Natl. geog. 118: 177 (col.) Aug '60.
Chew house (Phila.). Holiday 16: 106 Jl '54.
Cheyenne (Wyo.). Holiday 10: 39 (col.) Aug '51.
—— (in the 70's). Horan: Pict. hist. of wild west, p. 185.
"Chez le barbier" (Maillot). Con. 133: XLVII May '54.
Chiang Ching-Kuo. Cur. biog. p. 177 (1954).
Chiang Kai-Shek. Cur. biog. p. 113 (1953). Natl. geog. 107: 587 Ap '55.
Chaing Kai-Shek, Madame. Jensen: The White House, p. 244.
Chiappini St. (Cape Town, Africa). Travel 113: 29-31 Jan '60.
Chiappini wedding (Africa). See wedding, Chiappini (Africa).
Chiari, Roberto F. Cur. biog. p. 103 (1961).
Chiaroscuro (Mosque, Africa). Holiday 24: 20 Oct '58.
Chibcha breastplate (Columbia). Praeg. pict. ency., p. 554 (col.).
Chicago. Holiday 10: all issue (part col.) Oct '51; 14: 60-3 Oct '53; 20: 38-9 (col.) Sept '56; 28: 75-87 (part col.) Dec '60. Natl. geog. 99: 730-1 (col.) Je '51; 104: 782-97 (col.) Dec '53.
—— (air view). Holiday 14: 4 Jl '53.
—— (lake front). Natl. geog. 109: 663 (col.) May '56.
—— (motel). Travel 111: 47 May '59.
—— (motor hotel). See Oxford House (motor hotel).
—— (night). Holiday 10: 34-5 (col.) Oct '51. Natl. geog. 115: 472-3 (col.) Ap '59.

—— (Oxford House). *See* Oxford House (motor hotel).

—— (pictorial map). Holiday 10: 49 (col.) Oct '51.

—— (Sheraton Tel Aviv hotel). Travel 113: 51 Mar '60.

—— (Tel Aviv Inn). Travel 113: 51 Mar '60.

Chicago Columbian Exposition. Amer. heri. vol. 11 no. 6 p. 8-21 (part col.) (Oct '60).

Chicago fire (1871). Holiday 21: 14 Ap '57.

Chicago Loop. Holiday 8: 82-8 Nov '50.

Chicago Lyric opera (int.). Holiday 28: 79 (col.) Dec '60.

Chicago skyline. Jordan: Hammond's pict. atlas, p. 97 (col.).

Chicago symphony hall. Cooper: Con. ency. of music, p. 452.

Chicago world's fair. *See* Chicago Columbian Exposition.

Chichele, Archbishop (tomb of). *See* tomb of Archbishop Chichele.

Chichen-Itza (temple-pyramid). Praeg. pict. ency., p. 543.
Travel 103: 43 May '55.

—— carvings. Amer. heri. vol. 11 no. 4 p. 109-11 (Je '60).

chick, Easter (sym.). Lehner: Pict. bk. of sym., p. 52.

Chickahominy river. Natl. geog. 111: 598 (col.) May '57.

chickee (Seminole Indian house). Natl. geog. 110: 826-7 (col.) Dec '56.

——, Seminole style. Natl. geog. 113: 110 (col.) Jan '58.

Chidlaw, Gen. Benjamin W. Cur. biog. p. 117 (1955).

Chief Massasoit. *See* Massasoit, Chief.

Chief mountain (Canada). Holiday 24: 56 (col.) Nov '58.

Chieftan, Wagenia (Belgian Congo). Natl. geog. 112: 82-4 (col.) Jl '57.

Chieftans, Pakistan. Natl. geog. 102: 661 Nov '52.

Ch'ien Chu (work of). Praeg. pict. ency., p. 540 (col.).

Ch'ien Lung, Emperor. Con. 129: LXVIII Je '52.

Chiericati palace. *See* Palazzo Chiericati.

Chierici, Gaetano (work of). Con. 138: IX (col.) Nov '56.

chiffonier, antique. Con. 136: 245 Jan '56.

——, Louis XV. Con. 140: 57 Sept '57; 143: 190 May '59.

——, regency. Con. 140: XXXV Dec '57.

Chifley, Joseph B. Cur. biog. p. 101 (1945).

child. Con. 143: LXXI Je '59.
Holiday 6: 107 (col.) Nov '49; 14: 26 (col.) Jl '53, 63 Nov '53.
Labande: Naples, p. 113.
Natl. geog. 98: 641 (col.) Nov '50.
Travel 102: 50 Jl '54; 104: 28 Aug '55.

—— (antique coin machine). Natl. geog. 107: 754 (col.) Je '55.

—— (antique dolls). Natl. geog. 111: 323 Mar '57.

—— (asleep). Holiday 26: 146 (col.) Dec '59.

—— (asleep, dog). Natl. geog. 99: 832 Je '51.

—— (asleep in pedicab). Natl. geog. 111: 341 (col.) Mar '57.

—— (asleep on bench). Natl. geog. 98: 5 Jl '50.

—— (at desk). Travel 112: 60 Jl '59.

—— (at window). Amer. heri. vol. 10 no. 4 p. 56 (col.) (Je '59).

—— (basket of lemons). Natl. geog. 116: 485 (col.) Oct '59.

—— (basket on back). Holiday 24: 90 Oct '58. Travel 111: 45 Mar '59.

—— (basket on head). Natl. geog. 115: 383 (col.) Mar '59.

—— (beach). Holiday 14: 10 Jl '53.
Natl. geog. 107: 799 Je '55.
Travel 103: 26 Feb '55.

—— (bedtime, reading). Natl. geog. 116: 275 Aug '59.

—— (bedside kettle). *See* child (stirring kettle).

—— (bicycle seat). Natl. geog. 111: 341 (col.) Mar '57.

—— (big cabbage). Natl. geog. 116: 61 (col.) Jl '59.

—— (birthday cake). Holiday 22: 89 (col.) Jl '57.

——(blowing up balloon). Holiday 24: 129 Dec '58.

—— (book). Holiday 20: 180 Nov '56.

—— (building blocks). Natl. geog. 98: 61 (col.) Jl '50.

—— (buying wiener). Natl. geog. 99: 767 (col.) Je '51.

—— (calf). Holiday 8: 115 Oct '50.

—— (candy). Holiday 21: 38 Ap '57.

—— (carrying bread). Holiday 23: 122 Jan '58.

—— (cartoon). Holiday 21: 99 Jan '57.

—— (cat). Con. 142: XXXVIII Dec '58.

—— (chair). Holiday 10: 125 Nov '51.

—— (cheetah). Natl. geog. 103: 786 (col.) Je '53.

—— (comic). Holiday 22: 31, 38, 41 Sept '57.

—— (corn shuck doll). Holiday 9: 47 (col.) Mar '51.

—— (costume of Gen. in Civil War). Amer. heri. vol. 8 no. 5 back cover (col.). (Aug '57).

——(costume, Hawaiian). Holiday 23: 119 (col.) Je '58.

—— (costume, Indian suit). Holiday 23: 122 Mar '58.

—— (costume, pirate). Holiday 23: 140 Je '58.

—— (costume, Texas outfit). Holiday 21: 190 May '57.

—— (costume). *See* also children-costume; children (name of country).

—— (crawling under bed). Holiday 11: 11 Je '52.

—— (crippled). *See* boy (crutches); child, crippled.

—— (crying). Holiday 7: 107 Ap '50; 12: 103 (col.) Sept '52.

—— (curtsying). Holiday 26: 76 Oct '59.

—— (deer). Holiday 7: 31 (col.) Mar '50.
Travel 109: 38 Mar '58.

—— (diving). Holiday 13: 91 May '53.

—— (dodo bird). Natl. geog. 109: 91 Jan '56.

child (dog). Con. 140: XVII (col.) Dec '57. Travel 101: 26 Ap '54.

—— **(dog at fireplace).** Natl. geog. 105: 453 (col.) Ap '54.

—— **(dog, on donkey).** Natl. geog. 105: 496 (col.) Ap '54.

—— **(dog tugs to safety).** Natl. geog. 114: 218 Aug '58.

—— **(doll).** Holiday 20: 177 Nov '56. Natl. geog. 105: 463 (col.) Ap '54; 116: 816, 831 (col.) Dec '59.

—— **(doll carriage).** Natl. geog. 108: 294 Aug '54.

—— **(drawing).** Natl. geog. 116: 270 Aug '59.

—— **(drawing in sand).** Holiday 19: 94 (col.) Jan '56.

—— **(ducks, stream).** Natl. geog. 109: 534 (col.) Ap '56.

—— **(eating).** Holiday 7: 12 (col.) Je '50. Natl. geog. 109: 588 Ap '56. Travel 102: back cover Nov '54.

—— **(eating bread).** Natl. geog. 100: 23 Jl '51.

—— **(eating corn).** Travel 103: 66 May '55.

—— **(eating ice cream cone).** Holiday 8: 57 Jl '50.

—— **(eggs, chickens).** Amer. heri. vol. 7 no. 3 p. 50 (col.) (Ap '56).

—— **(Eloise comic).** Holiday 23: 166 Mar '58.

—— **(feeding bird).** Amer. heri. vol. 8 no. 4 p. 42 (col.) (June '57).

—— **(feeding goat).** Disney: People & places, p. 41 (col.). Travel 109: 44 Feb '58.

—— **(feeding pigeons).** Natl. geog. 118: 780 (col.) Dec '60. Travel 103: inside cover Mar '55; 107: 27 May '57.

—— **(feeding sheep).** Natl. geog. 114: 271 Aug '58.

—— **(feeding squirrel).** Holiday 6: 116 Aug '49.

—— **(feeding swans).** Natl. geog. 108: 303 (col.) Sept '55.

—— **(fish).** Travel 107: 34 Je '57.

—— **(flower).** Natl. geog. 111: 823 (col.) Je '57; 114: 179 (col.) Aug '58.

—— **(flower mart).** Natl. geog. 106: 400 (col.) Sept '54.

—— **(fountain, comic).** Holiday 11: 150 Ap '52.

—— **(going to school).** Travel 101: inside back cover May '54.

—— **(grocery cart).** Holiday 22: 86 Sept '57.

—— **(gun).** Natl. geog. 115: 308 Mar '59.

—— **(head).** Con. 140: 109 Nov '57, 142 LIX Nov '58, XXXVIII Dec '58; 144: 76 Nov '59 145: II (col.) May '60. Holiday 14: 4 Sept '53, 124 Dec '53 23: 44 Ap '58; 24: 116 Aug '58, 109 Dec '58 26: back cover (col.) Aug '59, 196 Nov '59, 208, 252 Dec '59 27: 138 Mar '60, 8, 229 Ap '60, 240 May '60; 28: 24 (col.) Jl '60. Praeg. pict. ency., p. 25 (col.). Travel 104: 53 Sept '55; 109: 4 Je '58; 110: 6 Jl '58.

—— **(head, butterflies).** Natl. geog. 102: 254 (col.) Aug '52.

—— **(head, comic).** Holiday 18: 92 Oct '55, 168 Dec '55.

—— **(head, crying).** Holiday 21: 168 May '57; 22: 112 Nov '57.

—— **(head, curls).** Natl. geog. 113: 260 Feb '58.

—— **(head, doll).** Holiday 22: 12 (col.) Dec '57.

—— **(head, hair braids).** Holiday 19: 92 May '56.

—— **(head, laughing).** Holiday 10: 81 (col.) Dec '51; 21: 195 Ap '57; 23: 124 Je '58; 25: 147 May '59; 27: 122 Ap '60; 28: 28 Aug '60, 193 (col.) Oct '60, 186 Nov '60.

—— **(head, sad).** Holiday 20: 133 Dec '56.

—— **(head, thinking).** Holiday 20: 81 Sept '56.

child (high chair). Natl. geog. 103: 98 Jan '53.

—— **(horse).** Holiday 10: 17 (col.) Jl '51.

—— **(horseback).** Con. 145: XXXVI Je '60. Holiday 10: 55 Nov '51; 25: 7 (col.) Je '59.

—— **(hunter).** Holiday 22: 130 Oct '57.

—— **(in baby cart, 1817).** Amer. heri. vol. 9 no. 2 p. 55 (col.) (Feb '58).

—— **(in bed drawing).** Amer. heri. vol. 8 no. 1 p. 29 (col.) (Dec '56).

—— **(in mother's lap).** Travel 107: 26 May '57.

—— **(in stroller).** Holiday 14: 94 (col.) Jl '53; 27: 6 Jan '60.

—— **(in woods).** Holiday 28: 116 (col.) Oct '60.

—— **(iris garden).** Natl. geog. 115: 704 (col.) May '59.

—— **(jumping).** Holiday 11: 155 May '52.

—— **(kilometer stone).** Natl. geog. 117: 197 (col.) Feb '60.

—— **(kitten, Africa).** Natl. geog. 112: 77 (col.) Jl '57.

—— **(lamb, duck).** Natl. geog. 109: 685 May '56.

—— **(laughing).** Holiday 20: 23 Nov '56. Travel 113: 57 Feb '60.

—— **(malnutrition).** Travel 101: 39 Jan '54.

—— **(mt. flower).** Natl. geog. 109: 636 (col.) May '56.

—— **(musical bottles).** Natl. geog. 118: 270 (col.) Aug '60.

—— **(nude, at beach).** Holiday 24: 19 (col.) Jl '58.

—— **(on back of bicycle).** Natl. geog. 98: 619 (col.) Nov '50.

—— **(on crutches).** *See* child, crippled.

—— **(on gate).** Natl. geog. 108: 337 (col.) Sept '55.

—— **(on swan boat).** Holiday 8: 112 (col.) Jl '50.

—— **(opossum).** Natl. geog. 103: 409 Mar '53.

—— **(pajamas).** Holiday 26: 199 (col.) Dec '59.

—— **(palsy victim).** Travel 113: 65 Jan '60.

—— **(pets).** Holiday 21: 185 Je '57.

—— **(picking flowers).** Natl. geog. 117: 431 (col.) Mar '60.

—— **(playing).** Holiday 21: 83 Mar '57. Natl. geog. 117: 731 (col.) Je '60.

—— **(playing accordion).** Natl. geog. 108: 534 (col.) Oct '55.

—— **(playing ball).** Holiday 18: 71 (col.) Jl '55.

—— (playing in water). Holiday 10: 30 Oct '51; 11: 17 (col.) Feb '52.
Natl. geog. 111: 2 (col.) Jan '57.
—— (playing on barge). Natl. geog. 108: 547 (col.) Oct '55.
—— (playing piano). Holiday 26: 104 Nov '59.
—— (playing, sand). Holiday 10: 94 Oct '51.
—— (playing with fish). Natl. geog. 102: 692 (col.) Nov '52.
—— (poor.) Holiday 19: 146 Je '56; 27: 14 Jan '60.
—— (praying). Travel 102: inside back cover Sept '54.
—— (puppies under bed). Holiday 28: 102 (col.) Sept '60.
—— (putting on clothes). Holiday 14: 165 Nov '53.
—— (reading book). Natl. geog. 116: 561 Oct '59.
—— (refugee). See refugee children.
—— (riding horse). See child (horseback).
—— (running). Holiday 11: 17 May '52; 18: 110 Sept '55.
—— (saucer sled). Natl. geog. 113: 97 Jan '58.
—— (school). Holiday 16: 67 (col.) Aug '54; 19: 97 Jan '56.
—— (school with old man). Holiday 17: 1 Jan '55.
—— (scrubs scooter). Natl. geog. 106: 398 Sept '54.
—— (seated). Holiday 24: 148 Oct '58, 227 Dec '58.
Travel 104: 27 Aug '55.
—— (seated, daguerreotype). Amer. heri. vol. 8 no. 1 p. 64 (Dec '56).
—— (seated, laughing). Travel 113: 57 Feb '60.
—— (seated on floor). Natl. geog. 114: 454 (col.) Oct '58.
—— (seated on pavement). Holiday 20: 100 Oct '56.
—— (seated in river bank, boat). Natl. geog. 114: 127 (col.) Jl '58.
—— (seated on table). Natl. geog. 100: 759 Dec '51.
—— (sheepdog). Natl. geog. 114: 219 Aug '58.
—— (shells). Natl. geog. 111: 38 (col.) Jan '57.
—— (skunk). Natl. geog. 108: 280 Aug '55.
—— (smiling). Natl. geog. 102: 572 Nov '52.
—— (snow man). Travel 109: 60 Jan '58.
—— (standing in man's hand). Durant: Pict. hist. of Amer. circus, p. 253.
—— (stirring kettle). Holiday 10: 32 (col.) Sept '51; 17: 72 (col.) Mar '55; 18: 145 (col.) Nov '55; 19: 10 (col.) Feb '56; 20: 69 (col.) Oct '56, 5 (col.) Nov '56; 21: 139 (col.) Jan '57; 22: 141 (col.) Sept '57; 23: 5 (col.) Jan '58; 25: 29 (col.) Jan '59, 125 Ap '59; 26: 131 Oct '59; 27: 41 Mar '60.
—— (stooping down). Travel 101: 38 Je '54.
—— (swans). Int. gr. soc.: Arts . . . p. 137 (col.).
—— (swimming, inner tube). Holiday 18: 67 (col.) Jl '55.
—— (swinging). Holiday 10: 55 Nov '51; 24: 86 (col.) Oct '58.
—— (taking picture, comic). Holiday 28: 29 Sept '60, 115 Oct '60.

—— (telephone). Holiday 8: 90 (col.) Dec '50; 17: 132 Jan '55; 21: 194 Ap '57; 22: 47 Oct '57 28: 2 (col.) Jl '60.
—— (tortoise). Natl. geog. 115: 689 May '59.
—— (toys). Holiday 10: 132 Dec '51.
Natl. geog. 112: 463 (col.) Oct '57.
Travel 101: 5 Ap '54.
—— (tricycle). Holiday 26: 193 Dec '59.
Natl. geog. 108: 311 (col.) Sept '55; 111: 456 (col.) Ap '57.
—— (umbrella). Holiday 21: 67 May '57.
—— (unhappy). Holiday 21: 19 Mar '57.
—— (walking). Natl. geog. 111:: 612 (col.) May '57.
—— (walking doll). Travel 114: 17 Nov '60, 7 Dec '60.
—— (walking, eating). Holiday 12: 90 Oct '52.
—— (washing dishes). Holiday 23: 40 May '58; 24: 14 Jl '58.
—— (waving, teddy bear). Holiday 28: 157 Oct '60.
—— (whispers to statue). Natl. geog. 118: 790 (col.) Dec '60.
child, Cabaclo (girl). Disney: People & places, p. 109 (col.).
——, Canada. Natl. geog. 115: 828 Je '59.
——, Chinese. Natl. geog. 118: 220 (col.) Aug '60.
——, Chinese. (basket on back). Holiday 24: 36 Nov '58; 25: 164 Mar '59; 26: 231 Dec '59.
Travel 112: 17 Dec '59.
——, Colonial. Holiday 23: 104 Ap '58.
——, Colonial (cradle). Natl. geog. 118: 183 (col.) Aug '60.
——, crippled. Travel 101: 8 Mar '54; 103: inside back cover Jan '55; 105: back cover Ap '56.
——, Ecuador. Holiday 20: 88 Nov '56.
——, France (loaves of bread). Natl. geog. 117: 734 Je '60.
——, France (1749). Con. 143: 208 Je '59.
——, Greece. Travel 109: 4 Ap '58.
——, Greece (poor). Holiday 21: 203 Ap '57; 25: 149 Jan '59.
——, Indian (armadillos). Natl. geog. 115: 361 (col.) Mar '59.
——, Indian (poor). Holiday 22: 156 Dec '57.
——, Iran. Natl. geog. 100: 459 (col.) Oct '51.
——, Isfahan. Natl. geog. 114: 37-8 (col.) Jl '58.
——, Italy (poor). Holiday 26: 141 Nov '59.
——, Italy (16th cent.). Int. gr. soc.: Arts . . . p. 111 (col.)
——, Japan. Holiday 12: 38 (col.) Aug '52.
Natl. geog. 97: 629 (col.) May '50.
——, Japan (praying). Natl. geog. 118: 764 (col.) Dec '60.
——, Japan (sleeping). Holiday 19: 105 Feb '56.
——, Jerusalem. Holiday: 7: 127 (col.) Ap '50.
——, Korea (peace banner). Natl. geog. 103: 650 May '53.
——, Korea (refugee). Holiday 25: 169 Ap '59.
——, Laos. Natl. geog. 117: 48 (col.) Jan '60.
——, Madeira island (firewood). Natl. geog. 115: 379 (col.) Mar '59.

child, medieval (playing). Int. gr. soc.: Arts . . . p. 77 (col.).

——, Mexico Holiday 22: 161 Nov '57, 241 Dec '57; 24: 91 Jl '58.

——, New Britain (listens to tape recorder). Natl. geog. 118: 886 Dec '60.

——, New Guinea. Holiday 28: 97 (col.) Nov '60.

——, 19th cent. Int. gr. soc.: Arts . . . p. 155 (col.).

——, Nomad (blankets). Natl. geog. 117: 84 (col.) Jan '60.

——, Sardinia. Disney: People & places, p. 79, 81 (col.).

——, Siam (head). Holiday 18: 49 (col.) Oct '55.

——, Tibet. Natl. geog. 108: 34 Jl '55.

——, Venice. Holiday 23: 198 May '58.

——, western (lasso). Holiday 27: 163 (col.) Ap '60.

——, Yap (crying). Holiday 28: 95 Oct '60.

child & Catholic Sister. Holiday 23: 85 Mar '58.

child & doll (wig maker). Natl. geog. 106: 474 (col.) Oct '54.

child & policeman. Holiday 18: 83 (col.) Oct '55.

child & Santa Claus. See Santa Claus & child.

"The Child Moses" (Poussin). Con. ency. of ant., vol. 1, pl. 158.

"Child with pomegranite" (Jordaens). Con. 129: cover (col.) Je '52.

child. See also girl; boy; man, woman & child.

children. Amer. heri. vol. 2 no. 3 p. 57, 59 (spring '51).

Con. 145: 238-9 Je '60.

Face of Amer., p. 52 (col.).

Holiday 6: 37 Sept '49; 7: 44-5 (col.) Jan '50, 42-3, 46 (col.) Ap '50; 8: 2 (col.) Jl '50, 49 (col.) Oct '50, 28 (col.) Dec '50; 12: 86 Nov '52; 13: 62 Ap '53, 27, 28 (col.), 84 (col.) May '53; 25: 105, 176 Ap '59; 26: 63 (col.) Aug '59, 179 Oct '59; 27: 161 Jan '60.

Jordan: Hammond's pict. atlas, p. 76 (col.).

Natl. geog. 97: 215 Feb '50, 583 (col.) May '50; 98: 718 (col.) Dec '50; 114: 776 (col.) Dec '58; 115: 800 Je '59; 118: 544-5 (col.) Oct '60.

Travel 109: 25 Jan '58.

—— (animals). Travel 101: 38-9 Je '54.

—— (art gallery). Natl. geog. 99: 179 Feb '51.

—— (asleep at table). Natl. geog. 100: 741 (col.) Dec '51.

—— (at car). Holiday 24: 13 (col.) Sept '58, 110 (col.) Oct '58, 109 (col.) Nov '58; 26: 126 (col.) Jl '59.

—— (at fair). Natl. geog. 106: 327 (col.) Sept '54.

—— (at Greek temple, back view). Natl. geog. 109: 48 (col.) Jan '56.

—— (at lobster table). Natl. geog. 102: 360 (col.) Sept '52.

—— (at soda fountain). Holiday 16: 68 (col.) Sept '54.

—— (at table). Travel 107: 27 May '57.

—— (at window). Natl. geog. 118: 161 (col.) Aug '60.

—— (at zoo). Natl. geog. 101: 318 (col.) Mar '52.

—— ("baby show"). Face of Amer., p. 74-5 (col.).

—— (back view). Natl. geog. 98: 358 (col.) Sept '50; 106: 777 (col.) Dec '54; 117: 452 (col.) Ap '60.

Travel 105: 33 May '56; 107: 47 Jan '57, 24 May '57; 109: 43 Feb '58; 111: 31 Feb '59.

—— (back view, balloons). Natl. geog. 114: 382 (col.) Sept '58.

—— (back view, Lincoln statue). Natl. geog. 111: 79 (col.) Jan '57.

—— (back view, seashore). Holiday 28: 86 (col.) Aug '60.

—— (back view, shadows). Travel 104: inside cover Sept '55.

—— (ballet dancers). Holiday 12: 109 Nov '52.

—— (bathed in Amazon). Disney: People & places, p. 104.

—— (beach). Disney: People & places, p. 59. Holiday 8: 57 (col.) Oct '50; 13: 167 (col.) May '53, 71 (col.) Je '53; 14: 25 Aug '53; 19: 162 (col.) Mar '56; 20: 195 (col.) Dec '56; 108: 334 (col.) Sept '55; 114: 859 (col.) Dec '58; 117: 455 (col.) Ap '60.

Travel 107: 25 Jan '57; 111: 34 Feb '59.

—— (beach, guard dog). Natl. geog. 114: 198 (col.) Aug '58.

—— (beach, playing). Holiday 12: 77 (col.) Jl '52; 19: 27 May '56; 21: 7 (col.) Ap '57; 23: 28 (col.) May '58.

Travel 103: 67 May '55; 105: 29 Jan '56.

—— (beach, running). Holiday 14: 115 Jl '53; 23: 153 Je '58.

Travel 114: 22 Oct '60.

—— (bookmobile). Natl. geog. 107: 200 (col.) Feb '55.

—— (Bronx zoo school). Natl. geog. 110: 694-706 Nov '56.

—— (burning house). Amer. heri. vol. 9 no. 3 p. 54 (col.) (Ap '58).

—— (carnival). Natl. geog. 113: 77 (col.) Jan '58.

—— (cart, dog). Natl. geog. 98: 343 (col.) Sept '50.

—— (cartoon). Travel 102: 14 Dec '54.

—— (cathedral). Natl. geog. 98: 742 (col.) Dec '50.

—— (Christmas). Holiday 8: 7 (col.) Dec '50; 10: 2 (col.) Dec '51; 22: 227 (col.) Dec '57; 24: 193 (col.) Dec '58.

—— (Christmas, peeking). Holiday 18: 79 (col.) Dec '55.

—— (Christmas, dog watching). Holiday 18: 95 (col.) Dec '55.

—— (clown & duck). Holiday 19: 113 (col.) Jan '56.

—— (comic). Holiday 6: 86 Oct '49; 10: 61 Jl '51, 161 Dec '51; 11: 133 May '52; 25: 8 Feb '59; 28: 115 Oct '60.

—— (cookies). Natl. geog. 113: 829 Je '58.

—— (costume, "dressing up"). Natl. geog. 111: 410 (col.) Mar '57.

—— (costume, "grown-up"). Natl. geog. 112: 488 (col.) Oct '57.

✓ —— (costume, 1836). Amer. heri. vol. 11 no. 2 p. 48-9 (col.) (Feb '60).

✓ —— (costume, 1862). Amer. heri. vol. 10 no. 1 p. 86-7 (Dec '58).

—— (costume, festival). Natl. geog. 111: 172-3 (col.) Feb '57.

—— (costume, wedding dresses). Holiday 21: 81 p. '57.

children (costume). See also children, name of country.

—— (dog). Con. 129: XIII Ap '52.

—— (doll buggy). Natl. geog. 108: 335 (col.) Sept '55.

—— (drinking at spring). Natl. geog. 103: 715 (col.) Je '53.

—— (drinking at stream). Natl. geog. 116: 158 (col.) Aug '59.

—— (drinking milk). Natl. geog. 107: 276 Feb '55.

—— (drum, horn). Holiday 27: 106 (col.) Mar '60.

—— (eagle). Natl. geog. 109: 18 (col.) Jan '56.

—— (eating). Travel 107: 27 May '57.

—— (eating at table). Travel 111: 45 Je '59.

—— (elephants, museum). Natl. geog. 118: 793 (col.) Dec '60.

—— (fawn). Holiday 11: 138 (col.) Je '52.

—— (feed mt. donkey). Natl. geog. 106: 237 (col.) Aug '54.

—— (field of flowers). Natl. geog. 105: 761 (col.) Je '54.

—— (ferryboat deck). Natl. geog. 115: 834-5 Je '59.

—— (fish). Travel 107: 13 Je '57.

—— (fishing). Natl. geog. 108: 345 (col.) Sept '55.

—— (fishing, dog). Natl. geog. 113: 622 (col.) May '58.

—— (flower garden). Holiday 21: 40 (col.) Je '57.

—— (Ford museum). Natl. geog. 114: 115 (col.) Jl '58.

—— (forest). Natl. geog. 108: 92, 96 (col.) Jl '55; 113: 630 (col.) May '58.

—— (fountain with birds). Face of Amer., p. 14 (col.).

—— (fried potato wagon). Natl. geog. 107: 638 (col.) May '55.

—— (gazing globe). Natl. geog. 98: 792 (col.) Dec '50.

—— (going swimming). Holiday 7: 81 Je '50.

—— (going to bed). Travel 102: 16 Dec '54.

—— (goslings). Natl. geog. 109: 8 (col.) Jan '56.

—— (group). Holiday 21: 127 Feb '57.

—— (Halloween). Holiday 20: 130 Oct '56.

—— (Halloween, Jack-o-lantern). Natl. geog. 106: 672 (col.) Nov '54.

—— (heads). Travel 110: inside cover Oct '58.

—— (heads, crowd). Natl. geog. 98: 45 Jl '50.

—— (heads, iguana). Natl. geog. 106: 667 (col.) Nov '54.

—— (heads, laughing). Holiday 18: 31 Oct '55; 20: 181 Nov '56.

—— (heads, terrarium). Natl. geog. 106: 653 (col.) Nov '54.

—— (horseback). Holiday 6: 49 (col.) Oct '49; 21: 90 (col.) Je '57.

Natl. geog. 106; 704 (col.) Nov '54.

—— (in art). Amer. heri. vol. 11 no. 3 p. 47-53 (col.) (Ap '60).

Con. 141: 72 Ap '58.

—— (in car trunk). Travel 112: 23 Aug '59.

—— (in cart). Amer. heri. vol. 12 no. 1 p. 121 (Dec '60).

—— (in cemetery). Face of Amer., p. 43 (col.).

—— (in overalls). Holiday 9: 46 (col.) Mar '51.

—— (inoculations). Natl. geog. 97: 245 Feb '50.

—— (jumping rope). Natl. geog. 118: 16 (col.) Jl '60.

—— (kissing). Holiday 25: 124 Ap '59.

Travel 104: 69 Nov '55.

—— (lamb, 1841). Amer. heri. vol. 7 no. 3 p. 53 (col.) (Ap '56).

—— (laughing). Holiday 18: 116 Aug '55.

—— (lean on yard wall). Natl. geog. 104: 125 (col.) Jl '53.

—— (looking at pictures). Natl. geog. 113: 615 (col.) May '58.

—— (marching, patriotism). Natl. geog. 107: 744 (col.) Je '55.

—— (merry-go-round). Holiday 24: 138 (col.) Dec '58.

Natl. geog. 98: 70 Jl '50.

—— (merry-go-round horse). Holiday 14: 131 (col.) Jl '53.

—— (mock polo team). Holiday 20: 35 (col.) Sept '56.

—— (model steamboat). Natl. geog. 97: 185 Feb '50.

—— (monastery altar). Natl. geog. 111: 656 (col.) May '57.

—— (mouse on clock). Natl. geog. 106: 669 (col.) Nov '54.

—— (museum). Natl. geog. 110: 212 (col.) Aug '56.

—— (N.Y. park). Natl. geog. 118: 786 (col.) Dec '60.

—— (nursery). Natl. geog. 109: 237 (col.) Feb '56.

—— (on boat). Travel 109: 33-5 Jan '58.

—— (on Brahma cow). Natl. geog. 101: 51 Jan '52.

—— (on camel). Natl. geog. 103: 782 (col.) Je '53.

—— (on doorstep). Natl. geog. 103: 804, 807 (col.) Je '53; 105: 182 (col.) Feb '54.

—— (on elephant). Natl. geog. 99: 131 (col.) Jan '51; 104: 127 (col.) Jl '53.

—— (on fence). Natl. geog. 101: 48 (col.) Jan '52, 170 (col.) Feb '52; 106: 22, 25 Sept '56.

Travel 112: 65 Jl '59.

—— (on ponies, horse show. Natl. geog. 104: 124 (col.) Jl '53.

—— (on tortoise). Natl. geog. 103: 783 (col.) Je '53.

children, (painting pictures). Natl. geog. 111: 376, 378, 387 Mar '57.

—— (park relief map). Natl. geog. 113: 598 (col.) May '58.

—— (pets). Travel 106: 20 Sept '56.

—— (picking flowers). Natl. geog. 108: 732 (col.) Dec '55.

—— (picnic). Natl. geog. 99: 126 (col.) Jan '51.

—— (pigeons, Paris). Natl. geog. 101: 797 (col.) Je '52.

—— (pine cones). Natl. geog. 110: 295 (col.) Sept '56.

—— (playground, N.Y.). Holiday 10: 46-7 Aug '51.

—— (playing). Con. 145: 238 Je '60. Holiday 14: 132 (col.) Nov '53; 23: 58 (col.) Jan '58. Natl. geog. 105: 199 (col.) Feb '54; 109: 452-3 (col.) Ap '56; 110: 391 (col.) Sept '56; 114: 375 (col.) Sept '58; 115: 699 (col.) May '59; 116: 110 (col.) Jl '59; 118: 540 (col.) Oct '60. Travel 105: 31 Feb '56.

—— (playing, comic). Holiday 25: 150 Je '59.

—— (playing, 1841). Amer. heri. vol. 7 no. 3 p. 53 (col.) (Ap '56).

—— (playing golf). Travel 102: 15 Dec '54.

—— (playing in lake). Natl. geog. 115: 444 Ap '59.

—— (playing in room). Natl. geog. 100: 589 (col.) Nov '51.

—— (playing in stream). Natl. geog. 98: 170 Aug '50.

—— (playing on sand dunes). Natl. geog. 112: 117, 129 (col.) Jl '57.

—— (playing recorder). Natl. geog. 97: 291 (col.) Mar '50.

—— (playing with dog). Amer. heri. vol. 8 no. 6 p. 41 (col.) (Oct '57).

—— (playroom). Holiday 14: 73 Oct '53.

—— (policeman, comic). Holiday 28: 29 Sept '60.

—— (pony cart). Holiday 25: 97 (col.) May '59.

—— (pool). Holiday 19: 83 May '56.

—— (poster display). Natl. geog. 106: 611 Nov '54.

—— (puffballs). Natl. geog. 109: 12 (col.) Jan '56.

—— (puppet show). Natl. geog. 101: 779 (col.) Je '52.

—— (putting wreath on statue). Travel 103: 11 May '55.

—— (pygmies). Natl. geog. 117: 280-1 Feb '60.

—— (reading). Holiday 22: 160 Oct '57, 148 Nov '57; 23: 68 Jan '58. Natl. geog. 101: 478 Ap '52; 109: 527 Ap '56.

—— (riding donkeys). Holiday 27: 127 (col.) Feb '60.

—— (river). Natl. geog. 115: 317 (col.) Mar '59.

—— (rowboat). Holiday 26: 116 (col.) Aug '59.

—— (running). Holiday 13: 71 (col.) Je '53; 16: 69, 74 (col.) Jl '54; 18: 34 (col.) Sept '55; 27: 167 (col.) Je '60.

—— (Santa Claus). Holiday 14: 30 (col.) Dec '53; 23: 124 Jan '58.

—— (school). Face of Amer., p. 112-3 (col.). Holiday 5: 48 (col.) Jan '49. Natl. geog. 98: 416 Sept '50.

—— (school, Japan). Natl. geog. 116: 856-8 (col.) Dec '59.

—— (school, pledge flag). Natl. geog. 116: 116 (col.) Jl '59.

—— (seashore). Holiday 28: 67 (col.) Aug '60. Natl. geog. 118: 436-44 Sept '60.

—— (seated). Holiday 7: 42, 47 (col.) Je '50; 19: 73 (col.) Je '56. Natl. geog. 97: 608 (col.) May '50. Travel 107: cover Feb '57.

—— (seated, back view). Natl. geog. 98: 395 (col.) Sept '50; 106; 822 (col.), 843 Dec '54; 112: 706-7 (col.) Nov '57.

—— (seated, back view, chapel). Natl. geog. 110: 725 (col.) Dec '56.

—— (seated, lady reading). Natl. geog. 105: 319 (col.) Mar '54.

—— (seated on grass). Travel 106: 16 Sept '56.

—— (on grass, playing). Natl. geog. 115: 607 (col.) May '59.

—— (seated, river bank). Holiday 14: cover Nov '53.

—— (seated with man). Amer. heri. vol. 6 no. 1 p. 55 (fall '54).

—— (secret stairway). Natl. geog. 97: 298 Mar '50.

—— (ship). Natl. geog. 106: 794 (col.) Dec '54.

—— (silhouette). Holiday 28: 61 Oct '60.

—— (skate, "mermaid's purse," beach). Natl. geog. 116: 412-20 (part col.) Sept '59.

—— (sled). Holiday 23: 101 (col.) Mar '58.

—— (snake). Natl. geog. 103: 783 (col.) Je '53.

—— (snowman). Natl. geog. 104: 824 Dec '53.

—— (snowshoes). Natl. geog. 110: 775 (col.) Dec '56.

—— (star fish). Travel 102: 36 Aug '54.

—— (swimming hole). Face of Amer., p. 82-3 (col.).

—— (swings). Travel 110: 22 Sept '58.

—— (teacher). Natl. geog. 99: 696 May '51.

—— (Thanksgiving table). Holiday 18: 7 (col.) Nov '55.

—— (toy sailboat). Holiday 19: 11 Mar '56; 23: 135 (col.) Mar '58. Natl. geog. 114: 296 Aug '58.

—— (toys). Natl. geog. 108: 325 (col.) Sept '55.

—— (traveling fun). Holiday 26: 107 (col.) Nov '59.

—— (traveling). *See* also man, woman & children (traveling).

—— (tree play house). Holiday 19: 20 (col.) Mar '56.

—— (tricycle). Holiday 7: 8 May '50. Travel 101: inside back cover Ap '54.

—— (turtles). Natl. geog. 101: 666 May '52.

—— (under fountain spray). Natl. geog. 108: 819 Dec '55.

—— (wading). Holiday 7: 46 (col.) Je '50; 14: 137 Oct '53.
Travel 107: 26 May '57.

—— (wading in ocean). Natl. geog. 108: 753 (col.) Dec '55.

—— (wading pool). Holiday 21: 116 Je '57.

—— (walking). Holiday 25: 123 (col.) Mar '59.

—— (walking, backview). Natl. geog. 110: 36 (col.) Jl '56; 113: 189 (col.) Feb '58.

—— (wash dishes). Natl. geog. 116: 274 Aug '59.

—— (water buckets). Travel 107: cover Je '57.

—— (water raft). Holiday 8: 112 (col.) Jl '50.

—— (water toys). Holiday 10: 74 (col.) Jl '51.

—— (working). Natl. geog. 106: 587 Nov '54.
children, Afghanistan. Natl. geog. 117: 610 (col.) May '60.

——, Africa. Holiday 18: 114-7 (part col.) Dec '55.

——, African jungle. Natl. geog. 100: 277 Aug '51.

——, African Masai. Natl. geog. 106: 501 Oct '54.

——, Akwaios (jungle). Travel 106: 35 Dec '56.

——, Alaska. Holiday 9: 77 Mar '51.

——, Andalusia. Natl. geog. 113: 424 (col.) Mar '58.

——, Arabia. See Arabian child.

——, Austria (backview, festival). Natl. geog. 115: 210 (col.) Feb '59.

——, Azores. Holiday 21: 71 (col.) Jan '57.

——, Bali. Natl. geog. 116: 811 (col.) Dec '59.

——, Bangkok. Natl. geog. 116: 846, 849 (col.) Dec '59.

——, Bedouin. Natl. geog. 112: 106 (col.) Jl '57.

——, Belgium (making lace). Natl. geog. 107: 647 (col.) May '55.

——, Borneo (learn to write). Natl. geog. 108: 383 (col.) Sept '55.

——, Canada. Natl. geog. 108: 195 (col.) Aug '55.

——, Canada Badlands. Natl. geog. 118: 100 (col.) Jl '60.

——, Canary islands. Natl. geog. 107: 519, 521 (col.) Ap '55.

——, Canton island. Natl. geog. 107: 132 Jan '55.

——, Chile. Natl. geog. 117: 202, 234 (col.) Feb '60.

——, Chinese. Natl. geog. 111: 341, 344-5, 350 (col.) Mar '57.

——, Colonial. Natl. geog. 106: 455 (col.) Oct '54.

——, Crete (group). Natl. geog. 104: 701 (col.) Nov. '53.

——, cripple (Easter seals). Travel 113: 4 Ap '60.

——, cripple (poster). Travel 113: 4 Ap '60.
children, crippled. See also child, crippled.

——, Cuba. Holiday 19: 94-7 (part col.) Jan '56.

——, Currier & Ives. Amer. heri. vol. 8 no. 4 p. 41 (col.) Je '57.

——, deaf. See deaf children.

——, Dutch. Natl. geog. 106: 376 (col.) Sept '54.

——, Dutch costume (tulip garden). Travel 109: 17 Mar '58.

——, English. Natl. geog. 103: 690 May '53.

——, English (1771). Amer. heri. vol. 11 no. 4 p. 5-6 (col.) Je '60.

——, Eskimo. See Eskimo children.

——, Formosa. Natl. geog. 107: 574 Ap '55.

——, France. Holiday 11: 88 Ap '52.
Natl. geog. 112: 60 (col.) Jl '57, 423 Sept '57.

——, Greece. Natl. geog. 117: 639 (col.) May '60.

——, Guatemala (baby on back). Natl. geog. 117: 412 (col.) Mar '60.

——, Hawaii. Holiday 23: 119 (col.) Je '58.

——, Hawaii (seated). Natl. geog. 116: 866 (col.) Dec '59.

——, Hindu. Natl. geog. 112: 200 (col.) Aug '57.

——, Hong Kong (refugees). Natl. geog. 116: 854 (col.) Dec '59.

——, Hunza. Natl. geog. 104: 511, 515 (col.) Oct '53.

——, Ifalik (beach). Natl. geog. 109: 568 (col.) Ap '56.

——, India. Natl. geog. 117: 631 (col.) May '60.

——, Indian. See children, Navajo Indian.

——, Iraq (playing). Natl. geog. 114: 474 (col.) Oct '58.

——, Irish (dancing). Holiday 17: 85 Feb '55, 22 Mar '55.

——, Ireland (drive ducks). Natl. geog. 108: 743 (col.) Dec '55.

——, Israeli (farm settlement). Natl. geog. 98: 746 (col.) Dec '50.

——, Israeli (Jewish orphans). Natl. geog. 98: 723 (col.) Dec '50.

——, Italy. Holiday 19: 100-3 Jan '56.

——, Japan. Disney: People & places, p. 156-7, 162 (col.).
Holiday 19: 102-5 (part col.) Feb '56.
Natl. geog. 117: 33 (col.) Jan '60.

——, Japan (heads, laughing). Natl. geog. 116: 832-3 (col.) Dec '59.

——, Japan (U.S. airman). Natl. geog. 117: 670 (col.) May '60.

——, Japan (U.S. sailors, dinner table). Natl. geog. 116: 322 (col.) Sept '59.

——, Jordan (Holy Land). Natl. geog. 114: 859 (col.) Dec '58.

——, Korea. Natl. geog. 97: 784 (col.) Je '50.

——, Korea (comic book). Natl. geog. 103: 649 May '53.

——, Korea (orphan). Holiday 17: 96 Jan '55.

——, Korea (waifs). Holiday 23: 170 Je '58.

——, Korea (woman bathing child in stream). Natl. geog. 103: 660 (col.) May '53.

——, Lapland. Disney: People & places, p. 18.
Holiday 18: 106-9 (part col.) Dec '55.
Natl. geog. 106: 253, 256-7 (col.) Aug '54.

——, Lichtenstein. Travel 106: 26 Jl '56.

——, Madeira island (5-6 yrs. old embroidering). Natl. geog. 115: 373 Mar '59.

children, Majorca (dancing). Natl. geog. 111: 647 (col.) May '57.

——, Maldive islands. Natl. geog. 111: 831 (col.) Je '57.

——, Mauritius island. Natl. geog. 109: 85 (col.) Jan '56.

——, Mexico. Natl. geog. 100: 810-11 (col.) Dec '51.

——, Moslem (water jugs on heads). Natl. geog. 106: 746 Dec '54.

——, Navajo Indian. Disney: people & places, p. 116-8 (col.).
Natl. geog. 114: 818, 820, 841 (part col.) Dec '58.

——, Nepal. Natl. geog. 117: 365 (col.) Mar '60.

——, Norway. Natl. geog. 100: 708 Dec '51; 106: 161, 164 (col.) Aug '54.

——, Okinawa. Natl. geog. 97: 551 Ap '50.

——, Pakistan. Natl. geog. 107: 411 (col.) Mar '55.

——, Paris (orphans). Natl. geog. 105: 172 (col.) Feb '54.

——, patron of. See patron of children.

——, Pescadores island. Natl. geog. 109: 269, 272, 279, 281-3 (col.) Feb '56.

——, Philippines. Holiday 18: 88 Aug '55.

——, Pilgrims. Int. gr. soc.: Arts . . . p. 113 (col.).

——, Polynesia Natl. geog. 97: 534 (col.) Ap '50.

——, Portugal (dancing). Natl. geog. 106: 685 (col.) Nov '54.

——, refugee. See refugee children.

——, Russia. Amer. heri. vol. 11 no. 5 p. 67 (Aug '60).
Holiday 23: 68-9 Je '58.

——, Saar. Natl. geog. 105: 576 Ap '54.

——, Samoan. See Samoan children.

——, Scotland. Natl. geog. 110: 8, 36 (col.) Jl '56; 112: 445 (col.) Oct '57.

——, South Seas. Natl. geog. 97: 92 (col.) Jan '50.

——, Spain (at Fair). Natl. geog. 99: 502, 505 Ap '51.

——, Spain (playing). Holiday 11: 53 (col.) Jan '52.

——, Sumatra. Natl. geog. 99: 38 (vol.) Jan '51.

——, Switzerland. Disney: People & places, p. 40 (col.).

——, Switzerland (at table). Natl. geog. 111: 783 (col.) Je '57.

——, Switzerland (in buggy). Natl. geog. 111: 170 (col.) Feb '57.

——, Switzerland (seated on bench). Natl. geog. 110: 471 (col.) Oct '56.

——, tiny (playroom). Natl. geog. 99: 293 (col.) Mar '51.

——, Tyrol. Natl. geog. 100: 394 (col.) Sept '51.

——, Venezuela. Natl. geog. 109: 348-9 (col.) Mar '56.

——, Victorian period. Amer. heri. vol. 10 no. 1 p. 36-45 (col.) (Dec '58).

——, Viet Nam (refugee). Natl. geog. 107: 870 Je '55.

——, West Germany. Natl. geog. 115: 748 (col.) Je '59.

——, The White House. Jensen: The White House.

——, world. Holiday 18: 105-17 (part col.) Dec '55; 19: 98-109 (part col.) Feb '56.

children & mother. Holiday 8: 105 (col.) Aug '50.

—— (fireplace). Natl. geog. 112: 315 (col.) Sept '57.

children & nurses (back view, harbor). Natl. geog. 113: 27 (col.) Jan '58.

children & teacher. See teacher & children.

children & U.S. airman (Japan). Natl. geog. 117: 670 (col.) May '60.

children dancing. Natl. geog. 117: 845 Je '60. Travel 102: 16 Dec '54.

——, Irish. Holiday 17: 85 Feb '55, 22 Mar '55.

——, Majorca. Natl. geog. 111: 647 (col.) May '57.

——, Portugal. Natl. geog. 106: 685 (col.) Nov '54.

——, Scotland. Natl. geog. 110: 36 (col.) Jl '56; 112: 445 (col.) Oct '57.

children dancing (class). Holiday 27: 84 May '60.

"Children Outside les Collettes" (Renoir). Con. 136: cover (col.) Sept '55.

children skiers. Natl. geog. 115: 232-7 (part col.) Feb '56.

children sleeping (porcelain). Con. 129: 35 Ap '52.

children's hotel (Florida). Travel 102: 14-6 Dec '54.

"Children's Hour" (bedtime stories). Natl. geog. 118: 709 (col.) Nov '60.

"Children's Hour" poem (illus. by Read). Natl. geog. 97: 289 (col.) Mar '50.

Children's orchestra (Switzerland). Natl. geog. 116: 278-9 Aug '59.

children's party. Holiday 28: 75 (col.) Aug '60.

children's party (birthday). Holiday 23: 144 May '58.

children's party (fancy). Holiday 23: 161 (col.) Je '58.

children's party (table). Holiday 18: 84 (col.) Aug '55.

"Children's pet" (Zampighi). Con. 139: XLIX Je '57.

children's village (Switzerland). Natl. geog. 116: 268-82 Aug '59.

children. See also child; school children; teacher & students; man, woman, children; woman & children.

Childs, Marquis W. Cur. biog. p. 127 (1943).

Childs, Richard S. Cur. biog. p. 119 (1955).

Chile. Holiday 10: 16-20 Nov '51; 26: 62-3 (col.) Aug '59.
Natl. geog. 108: 758-60 (col.) Dec '55; 117: 186-235 (col.) Feb '60.
Travel 102: 35 Dec '54.

—— (map). Natl. geog. 117: 190 (col.) Feb '60.

Chilian (wearing poncho). Travel 107: 17 Mar '57.

Chilian dancers. Natl. geog. 117: 234-5 (col.) Feb '60.
Chillon castle (Switzerland). Holiday 16: 36 Aug '54.
Natl. geog. 110: 431 (col.) Oct '56.
Travel 101: 16 May 54; 109: cover Ap '58; 113: cover (col.) Ap '60.
Chimbu (New Guinea). Natl. geog. 116: 781 (col.) Dec '59.
chimney piece. See fireplace; mantlepiece.
chimney pots. Holiday 11: 103 (col.) Je '52.
chimney rock (Neb.). Holiday 14: 61 (col.) Jl '53.
chimney sweep (man). Amer. heri. vol. 6 no. 4 p. 47 (col.) (Je '55).
—— (sym.). Lehner: Pict. bk. of sym., p. 62.
——, English. Holiday 23: 72 Ap '58.
——, Saar. Natl. geog. 105: 570 Ap '54.
China. Holiday 21: 74-81 (part col.) Je '57.
Natl. geog. 97: 381-95 Mar '50.
—— (harbors). Natl. geog. 103: 508-11 Ap '53.
—— (Peking). Natl. geog. 118: 194-222 (part col.) Aug '60.
—— (river ferryboat). Natl. geog. 100: 726 Dec '51.
—— (wingd lion). Praeg. pict. ency., p. 529.
China, Free (Quemoy). Natl. geog. 115: 414-38 Mar '59.
China, Great wall. See Great wall of China.
china cabinet. Holiday 10: 2 (col.) Nov '51; 28: 93-5 (col.) Aug '60.
——, Chippendale. Con. 141: XIII Je '58; 142: XIX Nov '58.
——, Chippendale breakfront. Con. 134: LXI Nov '54; 139: X Mar '57; 143: XI May '59.
——, 18th cent. Con. 141: 247 Je '58; 144: XIV Sept '59; 145: LXXXIII Je '60.
——, 18th cent. breakfront. Con. 141: LIII Ap '58.
——, George II. Con. 141: VI Je '58.
——, Hepplewhite breakfront. Con. 145: LI Ap '60.
——, Sheraton. Con. 144: 268 Jan '60.
china dishes (antique Amer.). Amer. heri. vol. 6 no. 5 p. 48-53 (col.) (Aug '55).
—— (girl painting). Natl. geog. 110: 602 (col.) Nov '56.
china painting. Natl. geog. 102: 26 (col.) Jl '52.
Chinard, Joseph (terracotta work). Con. 140: 7 Sept '57.
Chinatown (N.Y.) Holiday 5: 108 Ap '49; 12: 64-5 (col.) Oct '52.
—— (San Francisco). Brooks: Growth of a nation, p. 307.
Holiday 7: 71 (col.) Ap '50; 14: 37 Sept '53; 16: 98-103 (col.) Aug '54.
Natl. geog. 105: 728 Je '54.
Travel 110: 23 Aug '58; 114: 25 Sept '60.
—— (Singapore). Natl. geog. 103: 198 (col.) Feb '53.
Chinatown parade. Natl. geog. 110: 210-11 (col.) Aug '56.
chinaware. See china dishes.
Chinese (at table, circus). Durant: Pict. hist. of Amer. circus, p. 142 (col.).

—— (carrying firewood). Natl. geog. 105: 209 (col.) Feb '54.
—— (eating at table). Natl. geog. 118: 215 (col.) Aug '60.
—— (stewardess). Holiday 27: 98 (col.) Feb '60.
Chinese art. Praeg. pict. ency., p. 539-42 (col.).
Chinese biscuit joss-stick holders. Con. 139: V Mar '57.
Chinese bowl (early stoneware). Con. 142: X Dec '58.
——, Han (206 B.C.). Con. 144: X Jan '60.
——, Ming (Ch-eng Hua). Con. 144: 126 Nov '59.
Chinese boy. Holiday 21: 75 Je '57.
Chinese boys & girls (opera school). Travel 112: 27-9 Dec '59.
Chinese bronze bell. Con. 141: LIV May '58.
Chinese bronze cup. Con. 141: 6-7 Mar '58.
Chinese bronze food vessel. Con. 133: V Mar '54; 135: V May '55.
Chinese bronze jar. Con. 129: 148 Je '52.
Chinese bronze kuei. Con. 132: 208 Jan '54.
Chinese bronze ritual vessel. Con. 133: VIII Mar '54.
Chinese bronze sculpture. Con. 139: 135 Ap '57.
Chinese bronze wine jar. Con. 133: 258 Je '54.
Chinese bronze wine vessel. Con. 139: 135 Ap '57.
Chinese Buddha head (carved wood). Con. 139: VI May '57.
Chinese building. Con. 129: 99 Je '52.
Chinese cabinet, 18th cent. Con. 132: 159 (col.) Jan '54.
——, lacquer (Ch'ien Lung). Con. 145: XXIX Je '60.
Chinese casket, jade. Con. 141: XXI May '58.
Chinese ceramic Bactrian camels. Con. 145: XLVI Mar '60.
Chinese ceramic plate (K'ang Hsi). Con. 144: XXII Jan '60.
Chinese ceramics. Con. 145: XLIV Ap '60.
Chinese child (basket on head). Holiday 26: 231 Dec '59.
Chinese children (eating dinner). Natl. geog. 99: 408 Mar '51.
Chinese coromandel lacquer screen. Con. 145: VII Mar '60.
Chinese court & dragon robes. Con. 126: 95-105 Oct '50, 206 Dec '50.
Chinese court robes. Con. 126: 11-18 Aug '50.
Chinese crafts. Con. 134: 107 Nov '54.
Chinese dancer (head). Int. gr. soc.: Arts . . . p. 183 (col.).
Chinese dancing girls. Natl. geog. 111: 348 (col.) Mar '57.
Chinese dinner table. Natl. geog. 110: 196-7, 209, 216 (col.) Aug '56.
Chinese dower chest. Con. 132: X Sept '53.
Chinese figure. Con. 141: 251 Je '58; 142: LXII Jan '59.
—— (carved). Con. 132: V Nov '53.
—— (cloisonne). Con. 139: XXIV Mar '57; 144: XXIV Dec '59.
—— (Han). Con. 144: XVI Dec '59.
—— (ivory). Con. 132: LII Sept '53; 144: XII Dec '59.

Chinese figure (Ming bronze). Con. 129: LXX-VIII Je '52.
—— (porcelain). *See* Chinese porcelain figure.
—— (pottery). Con. 139: XIV Je '57.
—— (pottery, Han). Con. 141: VI Ap '58.
—— (terracotta). Con. 143: L Ap '59.
Chinese figures (Ch'ien Lung). Con. 138: XLIII Sept '56; 145: 128 Ap '60, 277 Je '60.
—— (T'ang dynasty). Con. ency. of ant., vol. 3, pl. 57-64.
—— (Tz-ii Chou). Con. 145: XLVIII Ap '60.
Chinese Fukien porcelain figure (Gov. Duf). Con. 144: LXXXI Jan '60.
Chinese games (ancient). Int. gr. soc.: Arts . . . p. 37 (col.).
Chinese girls (handicrafts). Natl. geog. 105: 250, 253, 256 (col.) Feb '54.
Chinese girls (heads). Natl. geog. 110: 185 (col.) Aug '56.
—— (library scrolls). Natl. geog. 99: 413 Mar '51.
—— (make firecrackers). Natl. geog. 103: 685 (col.) May '53.
Chinese glass painting. Con. 144: 46 Sept '59.
Chinese god Pu-tai. *See* Pu-tai.
Chinese "Goddess of Mercy" (lacquered). Con. 142: X Nov '58.
Chinese gold & silver dishes & ornaments. Con. 141: 2 Mar '58.
Chinese great wall. *See* wall, Chinese great.
Chinese head of Buddha. Con. 138 XXVIII Dec '56.
Chinese jade. Con. 129: 94-9 Je '52.
—— (Ming). Con. 142: 40 Sept '58.
Chinese jade bowl. Con. 133: 263 Je '54; 140: 258 Jan '58.
Chinese jade buffalo (17th cent.). Con. 145: XIX May '60.
Chinese jade candlesticks. Con. 139: L Ap '57.
Chinese jade carved head. Con. 139: XIV Mar '57.
Chinese jade carving. Con. 129: LXXI Je '52; 138: XVIII Jan '57.
Chinese jade cup. Con. 142: LXIV Jan '59.
Chinese jade figure. Con. 138: XIV Dec '56.
Chinese jade group. Con. 142: XXXVI Nov '58.
Chinese jade incense burner. Con. 145: XL Je '60.
Chinese jade Koro. Con. 138: LVIII Jan '57; 141: XXXVII Mar '58, XIII May '58.
Chinese jade mt. "Isle of the Blest". Con. 141: XV Je '58.
Chinese jade table screen. Con. 145: VIII Mar '60.
Chinese jade vase. *See* Chinese vase, jade.
Chinese jade vessel. Con. 129: XIV Ap '52.
Chinese jar, Tz'u Chou type. Con. 135: X May '55.
Chinese jar, antique. Con. 138: XXVI Sept '56.
Chinese laborers. Natl. geog. 111: 337, 355-61 (col.) Mar '57.
Chinese lacquer cabinet. Con. 140: III Jan '58.
Chinese lacquer corner cupboard. Con. 141: LV May '58.
Chinese lacquer screen. Con. 141: 42 Mar '58; 144: LXXXIV Jan '60.
Chinese lacquer tray. Con. 144: XII Nov '59.

Chinese man (banker's coat). Holiday 20: 22 Sept '56.
—— (on horse). Praeg. pict. ency., p. 540 (col.).
—— (seated). Amer. heri. vol. 6 no. 2 p. 17 (winter '55).
Chinese man & woman (donkey). Natl. geog. 99: 404 (col.) Mar '51.
Chinese mandarin (1838). Holiday 18: 45 (col.) Aug '55.
Chinese marble lions (T'ang, 618 A.D.). Con. 145: 210 May '60.
Chinese marble statue. Con. 139: XVIII Je '57.
Chinese men. Travel 108: 39 Nov '57.
—— (carry basket). Natl. geog. 100: 749 Dec '51.
—— (eat dinner). Natl. geog. 97: 393 Mar '50.
—— (sawing logs). Natl. geog. 111: 353 Mar '57.
—— (seated). Praeg. pict. ency., p. 542 (col.).
Chinese men & women (ancient costume). Praeg. pict. ency., p. 540-42 (col.).
Chinese minister to U.S. (1st., 1878). Jensen: The White House, p. 119.
Chinese mirror painting (18th cent.). Con. 145: XXXV May '60.
Chinese mirror picture. Con. 129: XLVI Ap '52. 145: 56 Mar '60.
Chinese mortuary figures. *See* mortuary figures.
Chinese official. Holiday 5: 80-2 Jan '49. Jensen: The White House, p. 119.
Chinese pagoda centerpiece (ant. Eng. silver). Con. 138: XXXIII Sept '56.
Chinese painting on silk. Praeg. pict. ency., p. 534, 540 (col.).
Chinese pilgrims. Natl. geog. 97: 213-26 Feb '50.
Chinese porcelain. Con. 137: V Je '56; 140: 61 Sept '57, LXX Nov '57; 141: XIV Ap '58, 246 Je '58.
—— (antique). Con. 140: X Dec '57.
—— (18th cent.). 138: 196 Dec '56.
—— (K'ang Hsi). Con. 142: V Dec '58.
—— (Ming dynasty). Con. 142: X Sept '58.
Chinese porcelain & pottery. Con. ency. of ant., vol. 1, pl. 65-72, p. 120-4.
Chinese porcelain birds. Con. 132: I Sept '53.
Chinese porcelain bowl. Con. 129: LXVII Ap '52; 133: V May '54; 139: 264 Je '57; 140: XXXVI Dec '57; 141: III Mar '58.
—— (Chih). Con. 145: XIV Ap '60.
—— (K'ang Hsi). Con. 144: V Jan '60.
Chinese porcelain box. Con. 144: XVI Nov '59.
Chinese porcelain dish. Con. 143: VI Ap '59.
Chinese porcelain figure. Con. 133: I Ap '54, LXIV Je '54; 139: LXII Je '57; 140: LX-III, 249 Jan '58; 141: IV Mar '58; 144: XL Sept '59.
—— (Kwan Yin). Con. 143: V May '59.
Chinese porcelain ginger jar. Con. 133: LVIII May '54; 145: LXIV Je '60.
Chinese porcelain hounds. Con. 138: V Dec '56.
Chinese porcelain jar. Con. 138: VI Nov '56, VI Jan '57; 139: LXIV Je '57; 141: XXXII Je '58.

—— (Ch'ang Hsi). Praeg. pict. ency., p. 547 (col.).

Chinese porcelain jardiniere. Con. 139: V May '57.

Chinese porcelain jug. Con. 139: 182 May '57.

Chinese porcelain marks. Con. ency. ant., vol. 1, p. 126-7.

Chinese porcelain plates. Con. 129: 60 Ap '52.

Chinese porcelain saucer. Con. 135: V Je '55.

—— (K'ang Hsi). Con. 144: V Dec '59.

Chinese porcelain saucer dish. Con. 134: III Dec '54.

Chinese porcelain tureen. Con. 134: I Dec '54; 138: XXXVI Nov '56.

Chinese pottery. Con. ency. of ant., vol. 1, p. 120-9.

—— (Han dynasty figurine). Con. 141: VI Ap '58.

—— (T'ang dynasty). Con. 142: VI Sept '58.

—— (T'ang figurine). Con. 142: VIII Dec '58.

—— (Wei dynasty, horse & rider). Con. 143: XXI Mar '59.

Chinese pottery horse. Con. 129: 145 Je '52; 140: XV Jan '58.

—— horse & rider (Wei). Con. 143: XXIV Ap '59.

—— horses. Con. 141: XX May '58.

—— unicorn. Con. 133: 69 Mar '54.

Chinese refugee children (at table, asleep). Natl. geog. 100: 741 (col.) Dec '51.

Chinese rice bearers. Natl. geog. 97: 150 (col.) Feb '50.

Chinese room (Claydon house). Con. 142: 73 Nov '58.

Chinese sacrificial bronze vessel. Con. 129: LXXIV Ap '52.

—— food vessel (Chou). Con. 145: 64 Mar '60.

Chinese sandstone figure of Buddha. Con. 145: XXVII May '60.

Chinese screen. Con. 145: XI May '60.

—— (by Sesshu) Con 132: 68 Sept '53.

Chinese sculpture. Con. 132: V Nov '53; 133: 135-7 Ap '54, XXXI Je '54; 141: LII May '58.

—— (bronze). Con. 139: 135 Ap '57.

—— (dogs on pedestal). Con. 129: XLIII Ap '52.

—— (stone). Con. 142: III Jan '59.

—— (wood). Con. 138: 280 Jan '57; 143: LV May '59.

—— (wood, 900 A.D.). Con. 138: 280 Jan '57.

Chinese seal box. Con. 132: VIII Nov '53.

Chinese shadow puppets. Con. ency. of ant., vol. 3, pl. 173.

Chinese silk painting (Lin Liang). Con. 143: LVIII Ap '59.

Chinese street (Macau). Natl. geog. 103: 681 (col.) May '53.

Chinese street market. See market, Formosa street.

Chinese stucco head (Kwan Yin). Con. 143: XVI May '59.

Chinese sun god. See sun-god, Chinese.

Chinese symbols. Lehner: Pict. bk. of sym., p. 44-6.

Chinese table (16th cent. lacquer). Con. 139: XII Ap '57.

Chinese Taoist. Praeg. pict. ency., p. 32.

Chinese tea cup. Con. 132: 202 Jan '54.

Chinese teapot. Con. 132: 209 Jan '54.

Chinese temples. See temples, Chinese.

Chinese terracotta figure. Con. 143: L Ap '59.

—— pack mule. Con. 141: LVII Je '58.

Chinese tomb guardian. See tomb guardian, Chinese.

Chinese vase. Con. 132: XLIII Sept '53.

—— (antique). Con. 139: 65 Mar '57.

——, bottle porcelain. Con. 143: LX Je '59.

——, bronze. Con. 139: XVI Mar '57.

——, bronze ceremonial. Con. 129: 146 Je '52.

——, Celadon. Con. 140: XXXIV Jan '58.

——. Ch'ien Lung (18th cent.). Con. 145: 269 Je '60.

——, enameled. Con. 139: XII May '57.

——, jade. Con. 129: LX Je '52; 133: 134 Ap '54; 141: VI Mar '58.

——, jade (Ch'ien Lung). Con. 142: LX Jan '59; 144: XV Jan '60.

——, K'ang Hsi. Con. 143: XXIV Mar '59; 145: VIII Ap '60.

——, porcelain. Con. 132: V Sept '53; 138: 128 Nov '56, 146 Dec '56; 139: XXII Ap '57, I, V, VIII Je '57; 140: 249 Jan '58; 141: LX May '58, LXIV, 246 Je '58; 143: XLVI Je '59; 145: XX May '60.

——, porcelain (Kuan ware). Con. 143: XXX May '59.

——, pottery (antique). Con. 129: VIII Je '52.

——, 16th cent. Con. 145: XXII Je '60.

——, Sung. Con. 145: LVI Je '60.

Chinese vase with chain (19th cent.). Con. 141: LVII Je '58.

Chinese wallpaper. See wallpaper, Chinese.

Chinese wine ewer. Con. 141: 42 Mar '58.

—— (Chia Ching). Con. 143: XXXII Mar '59.

Chinese woman. Holiday 25: 42 (col.) Feb '59.

—— (at toilet table). Praeg. pict. ency., p. 541 (col.).

—— (grain field). Natl. geog. 111: 359 (col.) Mar '57.

Chinese writing. Con. 132: 202 Jan '54.

Ching, Cyrus S. Cur. biog. p. 102 (1948).

chintz designs. Con. 140: 92-5 Nov '57.

—— (18th cent.). Con. 139: 175-8 May '57.

—— (wood-block). Con. 141: 93-5 Ap '58; 143: 23-7 Mar '59.

Chioggia, Italy. Travel 103: 52 May '55.

Chipperfield, Robert B. Cur. biog. p. 109 (1956)

Chiricahua natl. monuments. Natl. geog. 104: 361 Sept '53.

Chirico, Giorgio de. Cur. biog. p. 111 (1956).

—— (work of). Praeg. pict. ency., p. 453.

Chirico, J. de (work of). Con. 145: 188 May '60.

Holiday 14: 61 (col.) Nov '53.

Chiromancy (sym.). Lehner: Pict. bk. of sym., p. 67.

chisel (sym.). Lehner: Pict. bk. of sym., p. 17.

Chisholm, Brock. Cur. biog. p. 105 (1948).

Chisos mts. Travel 101: 18 Feb '54.

Chisum, John. Horan: Pict. hist. of wild west, p. 59.

Chisum, Sallie. Horan: Pict. hist. of wild west, p. 66.

"Chiswick from the river" (Varley). Con. ency. of ant., vol. 1, pl. 143.

Chittenden locks (canal). Natl. geog. 117: 506-7 (col.) Ap '60.

chivalry, orders of. Int. gr. soc.: Arts . . . p. 167 (col.).

chloris (sym.). Lehner: Pict. bk. of sym., p. 33.

Choco girl & boy. Holiday 13: 46-7 Jan '53.

chocolate jug, Queen Anne. Con. 144: 198 Dec '59.

chocolate pot, 18th cent. Con. 132: 87 Nov '53.

——, George II silver. Con. 139: XXVIII Ap '57.

——, jade. Natl. geog. 98: 796 (col.) Dec '50.

——, James II silver. Con. 135: LXII May '55.

——, Louis XV. Con. 141: LIV Je '58.

——, Queen Anne silver. Con. 136: LIII Nov '55; 138: XLVII Sept '56; 139: XLI Mar '57; 140: VII Sept '57, XXVII Nov '57; 142: 257 Jan '59; 143: LXXXVI May '59; 145: XLIII Ap '60.

——, silver (17th cent.). Con. 140: V Jan '58.

——, silver (18th cent.). Con. 142: 16 Sept '58.

——, silver (1709). Con. 142: XIV Dec '58.

——, William III. Con. 144: XIII Sept '59.

Chodorow, Edward. Cur. biog. p. 93 (1944).

choir (rehearsal). Holiday 6: 57 (col.) Jl '49.

—— (Switzerland). Disney: People & places, p. 44 (col.).

——, country (1900). Amer. heri. vol. 12 no. I p. 123 (Dec '60).

——, Episcopal church. Natl. geog. 106: 477 (col.) Oct '54.

——, Naumburg cathedral. Praeg. pict. ency., p. 236.

choir boy, British royal. Holiday 25: 190 (col.) May '59.

choir boys (Cambridge Univ.). Holiday 25: 72 (col.) Je '59.

"Choir practice" (Gallegos). Con. 133: LX May '54.

choir stall ("Holy Mass"). Con. 138: 63 Sept '56.

—— (Trier cathedral). Con. 145: 135 Ap '60.

Cholmondeley, Marquess of. Holiday 23: 83 (col.) Ap '58.

"Choosing wedding gown". (Mulready). Con. 144: 94 Nov '59.

chop dish, George IV silver. Con. 141: XLVIII May '58.

Chopin, Frederic. Cooper: Con. ency. of music, p. 36 (col.).
Int. gr. soc.: Arts . . . p. 123 (col.).

choral group. Natl. geog. 103: 523 (col.) Ap '53.

choreographic score. Int. gr. soc.: Arts . . . p. 147 (col.).

choreography (sym.). Lehner: Pict. bk. of sym., p. 11.

Choris, Louis (and work). Amer. heri. vol. 11 no. 2 p. 15-21 (col.) (Feb '60).

choristers (at a tomb). Holiday 18: 112 (col.) Aug '55.

"Choristers," group of (della Robbia). Int. gr. soc.: Arts . . . p. 87 (col.).

choristers, robed (girls). Natl. geog. 102: 556 Oct '52.

Chortens, Lama. Natl. geog. 99: 608, 629 (col.) May '51.

chorus girls. Holiday 11: 31 Ap '52.

—— (Japan, theater). Natl. geog. 118: 739 (col.) Dec '60.

Chotzinoff, Samuel. Holiday 16: 25 Sept '54.

Chou En-Lai, Gen. Cur. biog. p. 114 (1946); p. 111 (1957).

Chou sacrificial food vessel. Con. 145: 64 Mar '60.

Chretien, Felix (work of). Con. 133: opp. p. 147 (col.) May '54.

Chrisman, Arthur Bowie. Jun. bk. of auth., p. 69.

Christ (in church dome). Natl. geog. 101: 659 (col.) May '52.

—— (life 1000 years before). Natl. geog. 118: 812-51 (part col.) Dec '60.

—— (monogram). Lehner: Pict. bk. of sym., p. 34.

—— (porcelain figure). Con. 140: 200 Dec '57.

—— (sym.). Lehner: Pict. bk. of smy., p. 34.

——, Baptism of (Gassel or Van Helmond). Con. 138: 19 (col.) Sept '56.

"Christ among the doctors" (Ribera). Natl. geog. 97: 770 (col.) Je '50.

"Christ and cross", imitation (Antigua). Natl. geog. 117: 409 (col.) Mar '60.

"Christ and the fishermen" (Rouault). Praeg. pict. ency., p. 473 (col.).

"Christ and the Magdalene" (Lippi). Con. 135: 138 Ap '55.

"Christ & the woman taken in adultery" (Brueghel). Con. 129: 129 Je '52.

"Christ as a king" (15th cent.). Con. ency. of ant., vol. 3, pl. 132.

"Christ at Gethsemane" (El Greco). Con. 136: 134 Nov '55.

"Christ at the column" (marble by Parodi). Con. 139: 34 Mar '57.

"Christ at the column" (16th cent, wood). Con. ency. of ant., vol. 3, pl. 53.

"Christ being led before Caiaphas" (Van Ryn). Con. 129: LXVII Je '52.

"Christ blessing the universe" (Van Dyck). Con. 142: 258 Jan '59.

Christ church (int., Alexander). Natl. geog. 103: 16 (col.) Jan '53.

"Christ cleansing the temple" (El Greco). Natl. geog. 110: 633 (col.) Nov '56.

"Christ glorified in court of Heaven" (Fra Angelico). Praeg. pict. ency., p. 251 (col.).

"Christ healing woman" (Veronese). Natl. geog. 97: 769 (col.) Je '50.

"Christ in act of blessing" (Basaiti). Con. 142: 126 Nov '58.

"Christ in majesty" (Epstein lead figure). Con. 145: 277 Je '60.

"Christ of the Andes" monument. Holiday 12: 109 Oct 52; 14: 93 Oct '53.
Natl. geog. 113: 343 (col.) Mar '58.

"Christ on the cross" (15th cent.). Praeg. pict. ency., p. 217 (col.).
—— (Portuguese, sculpture, 14th cent.). Con. 136: 267 Jan '56.
—— (Schonguer). Con. 140: 58 Sept '57.
—— (wood, by Plura). Con. 138: 176 Dec '56.
"Christ on the cross". See also "Placing of Christ on the cross".
"Christ raising daughter of Jairus". (Mount). Amer. heri. vol. 11 no. 5 p. 13 (Aug '60).
"Christ taking leave of his mother" (El Greco). Con. 133: 96 Ap '54.
"Christ teaching" (sculpture, 4th cent.). Con. 138: 233 Jan '57.
"Christ the redeemer" (statue, Rio de Janeiro). Natl. geog. 107: 290 (col.), 295 Mar '55.
"Christ, the savior of man" (sym.). Lehner: Pict. bk. of sym., p. 34.
"Christ washing feet of Disciples" (Tintoretto). Con. 143: 52 Mar '59.
Christ. See also Jesus.
"Christ child at temple". See "Presentation of Christ child at temple".
Christenberry, Robert K. Cur. biog. p. 104 (1952).
christening bowl (Fahlstrom). Con. 144: 96 Nov '59.
"Christening feast" (le Nain). Con. 141: 38 Mar '58.
—— (Steen). Con. 144: 232 Jan '60.
christening font, Charles II. Con. 132: 52 Sept '53.
christening trousseau of Charles I. Con. 144: 197 Dec '59.
Christian X, King of Denmark. Amer. heri. vol. 6 no. 1 p. 46 (fall '54).
Cur. biog. p. 129 (1943).
Christian, Fred. Natl. geog. 112: 760, 777 (col.) Dec '57.
Christian, Parkin. Natl. geog. 112: 741, 753 (col.) Dec '57.
christian architecture (medieval). See architecture, christian.
Christian brothers novitiate (Cal.). Holiday 25: 157 Ap '59.
"Christian meets evangelist" (Blake). Con. 145: 214 May '60.
Christian Scientist church (Boston). Travel 106: 15 Dec '56.
christian sculpture. See scultpure, christian.
Christianborg castle. Holiday 18: 32 Sept '55.
christianity (sym.). Lehner: Pict. bk. of sym., p. 34-8.
Christians, Mady. Cur. biog. p. 103 (1945).
Christianso (harbor). Natl. geog. 98: 642 (col.) Nov '50.
Christie, Ned. Horan: Pict. hist. of wild west, p. 145.
"Christina of Denmark" (Holbein). Con. ency. of ant., vol. 1, pl. 157.
"Christine Buys a Gendarmerie". Con. 145: LIII Ap '60.
Christison, Lt. Gen. Sir Philip. Cur. biog. p. 105 (1945).
Christman, Elisabeth. Cur. biog. p. 105 (1947).

Christmas. Amer. heri. vol. 9 no. 1 p. 16 (col). (Dec '57).
—— (book illus., 1821). Amer. heri. vol. 12 no. 1 p. 23-6 (col.) (Dec '60).
—— (family). Holiday 18: inside cover (col.), 1 Dec '55.
—— (home). Amer. heri. vol. 9 no. 1 p. 18-21 (col.) (Dec '57).
—— (N.Y. City). Holiday 10: 58-69 (part col.) Dec '51.
—— (N.Y.C., Rockefeller Center). Holiday 10: 59 (col.) Dec '51.
—— (war refugees). Natl. geog. 111: 436 Mar '57.
—— (West Ger. home). Natl. geog. 115: 773 Je '59.
—— (jungle). Natl. geog. 102: 710 Nov '52.
Christmas candleholders. Rawson: Ant. pict. bk., p. 11.
Christmas cards. Amer. heri. vol. 3 no. 2 p. 50-2 (part col.) (winter '52).
Holiday 10: 83 Dec '51; 12: 155 Dec '52.
——, Victorian. Amer. heri. vol. 10 no. 1 p. 37-45 (col.) (Dec '58).
Christmas cookies. See cookies, Christmas.
Christmas cribs. See "Feast of Christmas in cribs."
Christmas decorations. Holiday 8: 57 (col.) Dec '50.
Christmas fable (Illus.). Holiday 26: 90-5 (col.) Dec '59.
Christmas gifts (Pitcairn island). Natl. geog. 112: 747 (col.) Dec '57.
Christmas greeting cards. See Christmas cards.
Christmas in the country. Amer. heri. vol. 9 no. 1 p. 16, 18-21 (col.) (Dec '57).
Christmas in Tyrol. Holiday 8: 64 Dec '50.
Christmas morning (1870). Amer. heri. vol. 12 no. 1 p. 121 (Dec '60).
Christmas ornament. Holiday 23: 135, 139 (col.) Jan '58.
Christmas procession (Mexico). Holiday 16: 22 Dec '54.
Christmas seals (1954). Travel 102: back cover Dec '54.
Christmas sock. Holiday 28: 207 (col.) Dec '60.
Christmas stamps. Natl. geog. 106: 140 (col.) Jl '54.
Christmas stockings (1890). Amer. heri. vol. 12 no. 1 back cover (col.) (Dec '60).
—— (sym.). Lehner: Pict. bk. of sym., p. 51.
Christmas symbols. Lehner: Pict. bk. of sym., p. 50-1.
Christmas tree (Australia). Natl. geog. 109: 242 (col.) Feb '56.
—— (South Pole). Natl. geog. 112: 35 (col.) Jl '57.
—— (sym.). Lehner: Pict. bk. of sym., p. 51.
—— (Victorian period). Amer. heri. vol. 10 no. 1 p. 42 (col.) (Dec '58).
Christmas wreath. See wreath, Christmas.
Christopher, George. Cur. biog. p. 90 (1958).
Christopher, George T. Cur. biog. p. 107 (1947).
Chriostophe's citadel (Haiti). Holiday 5: 62-3 Feb '49.

"Christ's agony in the garden" (Correggio). Con. 126: cover, opp. p. 155 (col.) Dec '50.

Christ's birthplace. Natl. geog. 98: 725 (col.) Dec '50; 106: 845 (col.) Dec '54.

"Christ's farewell to his mother" (Altdorfer). Con. 126: 87 Oct '50.

Christ's manger (Bethlehem). Natl. geog. 102: 855 Dec '52.

Christus, Petrus (work of). Con. 140: 271-3, 275 Jan '58.

Christus statue, Grant. (Cubilete Hill, Mexico). Travel 110: 39 Nov '58.

Christy, Howard Chandler (work of). Amer. heri. vol. 4 no. 3 p. 35 (spring '53). Natl. geog. 102: 159 (col.) Aug '52.

chromolithograph. Amer. heri. vol. 11 no. 3 p. 17 (col.) (Ap '60).

chromosome. Gray's anatomy, p. 17.

chronometer. Natl. geog. 106: 802 Dec '54.

Chrysler auto. Holiday 5: 71 (col.) Je '49; 6: 126 (col.) Jl '49, 82 (col.) Nov '49; 15: 32 (col.) Feb '54; 16: 79 (col.) Jl '54. Travel 103: 9 Jan '55.

Chu Teh. Cur. biog. p. 150 (1942).

Chubb, Lewis Warrington. Cur. biog. p. 109 (1947).

Chubb, Crater. Natl. geog. 101: 2-31 (part col.) Jan '52.

"Chuck wagon". Amer. heri. vol. 4 no. 3 p. 28 (col.) (spring '53). Holiday 17: 5 Jan '55; 25: 151 (col.) May '59. Jordan: Hammond's pict. atlas, p. 197 (col.). Natl. geog. 118: 94-5 (col.) Jl '60.

"'Chucky Jack" (pageant). Travel 111: 30 Je '59.

Church, Frank. Cur. biog. p. 91 (1958).

Church, Mrs. Marguerite Stitt. Cur. biog. p. 108 (1951).

church. Amer. heri. vol. 7 no. 1 p. 16-7 (col.) (Dec '55); vol. 8 no. 4 p. 46 (Je '57). Holiday 10: 63 Jl '51; 13: 64 Ap '53; 19: 31 (col.) May '56; 24: 93 Aug '58. Natl. geog. 106: 238 Aug '54, 332 (col.) Sept '54.

—— (Alamos, Mexico). Natl. geog. 107: 230 (col.) Feb '55.

—— (Austria, snow). Holiday 25: 77 (col.) Mar '59.

—— (Belgium). Holiday 26: 210 (col.) Dec '59.

—— (Bermuda). Travel 111: 17 Feb '59.

—— (Cajun country, La.). Travel 108: 13 Oct '57.

—— (Camogli, Italy). Holiday 13: 61 (col.) Je '53.

—— (Canada). Holiday 27: 54 (col.) Je '60. Natl. geog. 98: 338 (col.) Sept '50.

—— (Center Sandwich, N.H.). Travel 106: 34 Oct '56.

—— (Chorin). Praeg. pict. ency., p. 42.

—— (Davencourt, Eng.). Con. 143: XXXVII May '59.

—— (Delephaven, Holland). Amer. heri. vol. 10 no. 6 p. 50 (col.) (Oct '59).

—— (Denmark). Natl. geog. 108: 811 Dec '55.

—— (Germany). See German church.

—— (Guatemala). Holiday 17: 47 (col.) Mar '55.

—— (Italy). Travel 101: cover Je '54.

—— (Jamestown, Va.). Brooks: Growth of a nation, p. 39.

—— (Lapland). Disney: People & places, p. 21, 24 (col.). Natl. geog. 106: 276 (col.) Aug '54.

—— (lighted, snow). Holiday 10: 176 (col.) Dec '51; 12: 164 (col.) Dec '52.

—— (Litchfield, Conn.). Holiday 26: 47 (col.) Sept '59.

—— ("Little Brown Church in the Vale"). Brooks: Growth of a nation, p. 196.

—— (Lower Warterford, Ver.). Amer. heri. vol. 6 no. 4 p. 31 (col.) (Je '55).

—— (McIndoe Falls, Ver.). Amer. heri. vol. 6 no. 4 p. 29 (col.) (Je '55).

—— (Malta, Italy). Holiday 26: 88 (col.) Aug '59.

—— (Martha-Mary chapel). Natl. geog. 114: 98 (col.) Jl '58.

—— (Mass.). Travel 113: 29 Mar '60.

—— (Nevis). Amer. heri. vol. 6 no. 4 p. 8 (Je '55).

—— (New Canaan, Con.). Travel 108: 14 Dec '57.

—— (New England). Face of Amer., p. 110-11 (col.).

—— (night). Holiday 12: 147 (col.) Dec '52.

—— (Pfunds, Alps). Holiday 27: 46 (col.) Jan '60.

—— (Portsmouth, Eng.). Natl. geog. 101: 523 (col.) Ap '52.

—— (Portugal). Natl. geog. 118: 636 (col.) Nov '60.

—— (Puerto Rico). Natl. geog. 99: 443, 456 (col.) Ap '51.

—— (South America, 1732). Holiday 25: 156 (col.) May '59.

—— (S.C.). Amer. heri. vol. 9 no. 2 p. 58-9 (Feb '58).

—— (S.D.). Amer. heri. vol. 10 no. 1 frontis. (Dec '58).

—— (Sweden). Holiday 20: 42 Aug '56.

—— (Switzerland). Holiday 28: 41 Aug '60. Natl. geog. 111: 782 (col.) Je '57.

—— Switzerland (13th cent.). Natl. geog. 110: 465 (col.) Oct '56.

—— (Tallahassee, Fla., 1832). Holiday 23: 127 (col.) May '58.

—— (Tanganyika). Travel 104: 23 Nov '55.

—— (Tangier island). Travel 101: 12 Je '54.

—— (Teton mts.). Holiday 10: 35 (col.) Aug '51.

—— (Tunis). Travel 101: 40 Ap '54.

—— (Unterseen, Swiss Alps). Holiday 7: 106 Jan '50.

—— (Ver., old). Holiday 22: 53 (col.) Nov '57.

—— (Ver., 119 yrs. old). Natl. geog. 107: 744 (col.) Je '55.

—— (Vienna). Natl. geog. 115: 194 (col.) Feb '59.

—— (with pointing hand, Port Gibson, Miss.). Brooks: Growth of a nation, p. 157.

——, Abbey. See church, Norman abbey.

——, **Acadian (La. bayou).** Holiday 6: 55 Oct '49.

——, **America's 1st.** Travel 101: 36 Ap '54.

——, **baroque (Quito).** Holiday 20: 62 (col.) Nov '56.

——, **Benjamin (by Revere).** Amer. heri. vol. 10 no. 1 p. 69 (Dec '58).

——, **Bruton Parish.** See Bruton Parish church.

——, **Byzantine.** Natl. geog. 109: 72 (col.) Jan '56.

——, **Byzantine (Cyprus isle).** Natl. geog. 101: 658 (col.) May '52.

——, **Byzantine (1175).** Praeg. pict. ency., p. 194 (col.).

——, **Christ.** See Christ church.

——, **Christian Science.** See Christian Science church.

——, **City (N.Y.).** Holiday 10: 47-51 Sept '51.

——, **Colonial.** Amer. heri. vol. 9 no. 4 p. 50 (Je '58).
Holiday 11: 45, 124 Je '52; 12: 45 Jl '52; 25: 6 Mar '59.
Natl. geog. 99: 578 (col.) May '51; 102: 358 (col.) Sept '52; 106: 476-7 (col.) Oct '54; 107: 737, 738 (part col.) Je '55; 108: 659 Nov '55; 114: 317 (col.) Sept '58.

——, **Colonial (Mass.).** Travel 113: 29 Mar '60.

——, **Colonial (N.H.).** Natl. geog. 99: 600 (col.) May '51.

——, **Colonial (Peterborough, N.H.).** Face of Amer., p. 170-1 (col.).

——, **Colonial (S.C.).** Jordan: Hammond's pict. atlas, p. 63 (col.).

——, **Congregational (New Canaan, Conn.).** Travel 106: 15 Nov '56.

——, **Coptic.** See Coptic church (sym.).

——, **country.** See church, rural.

——, **Dutch (den Hoorn).** Travel 108: 57 Aug '57.

——, **Dutch Reformed.** Holiday 5: 120 Mar '49.

——, **Dutch Reformed (Willemstad).** Holiday 5: 121 (col.) Mar '49.

——, **early (Mass.).** Natl. geog. 107: 191 (col.) Feb '55.

——, **Gallarus (15th cent., Ireland).** Natl. geog. 99: 665 May '51.

——, **German (16th cent.).** Holiday 25: 50 (col.) May '59.

——, **gothic (Austria).** Natl. geog. 99: 763 (col.) Je '51.

——, **gothic (Normandy).** Natl. geog. 115: 614 (col.) May '59.

——, **Holy Trinity.** See Holy Trinity church (Palm Beach).

——, **Irongray (London).** Natl. geog. 98: 174 (col.) Aug '50.

——, **Isola San Michele.** Travel 103: 51 May '55.

——, **Kaiser Wilhelm memorial.** Holiday 18: 69 Dec '55.

——, **Laja Indian.** Natl. geog. 98: 486 (col.) Oct '50.

——, **Lutheran (Minden, Neb.).** Travel 109: 31 Je '58.

——, **Mary Magdalene's (France).** Natl. geog. 103: 237 (col.) Feb '53.

——, **Mennonite.** Amer. heri. vol. 10 no. 5 p. 33 (Aug '59).

——, **Mexican.** Natl. geog. 103: 327, 333, 340 (part col.) Mar '53.

——, **Mexican (Hidalgo).** Travel 101: 19 Mar '54.

——, **modern (France).** Praeg. pict. ency., p. 442.

——, **modern (Iceland).** Natl. geog. 100: 614 (col.) Nov '51.

——, **modern (Rome).** Holiday 27: 69 Ap '60.

——, **Morman.** See Morman church.

——, **mountain.** Natl. geog. 113: 871 Je '58.

——, **Norfolk island (St. Barnabas).** Travel 112: 36 Dec '59.

——, **Norman.** Natl. geog. 98: 178 (col.) Aug '50.

——, **Norman abbey (12th cent.).** Natl. geog. 106: 562 Oct '54.

——, **Norwegian stave.** Int. gr. soc.: Arts . . . p. 11 (col.)

——, **Old North** See Boston (Old North church).

——, **Old Swede's (Wilmington, Del.).** Con. 141: 63 Mar '58.

——, **open-air (boats, waterway).** Natl. geog. 115: 332 (col.) Mar '59.

——, **Orthodox (Alaska).** Natl. geog. 109: 788 (col.) Je '56.

——, **Park Street (Boston).** Holiday 11: 35 (col.) Je '52.

——, **Pilgrimage.** See Pilgrimage church.

——, **Riverside.** See Riverside church (N.Y.).

——, **rock (Göreme).** Osward: Asia Minor, pl. 74.

——, **Ronchamp (France).** Praeg. pict. ency., p. 442.

——, **rural.** Brooks: Growth of a nation, p. 289.
Holiday 10: 30, 34 (col.) 45 Sept '51; 18: 106 (col.) Nov '55.

——, **Russian.** Holiday 27: 164 Jan '60.

——, **Russian (doors).** Con. 144: 275 Jan '60.

——, **St. Helena's.** Amer. heri. vol. 10 no. 6 p. 52 (Oct '59).

——, **St. Irene (Turkey).** Natl. geog. 100: 155 (col.) Aug '51.

——, **St. John's.** See St. John's church.

——, **St. Kevin's.** See St. Kevin's church.

——, **St. Simeon (Canada).** Travel 110: 18 Aug '58.

——, **San Cayetano (Mexico).** Holiday 26: 51 (col.) Nov '59.

——, **San Felipe (Albuquerque).** Jordan: Hammond's pict. atlas, p. 127 (col.).

——, **San Gorman.** Travel 111: 42 Feb '59.

——, **Sandra.** Travel 111: 10 May '59.

——, **Santa Maria della Salute.** See Santa Marie della Salute church.

——, **Santo Tomas.** See Santo Tomas church.

——, **Santuario de Chimayo.** Holiday 11: 43 (col.) Feb '52.

——, **Stanford Univ. memorial.** Natl. geog. 110: 221 (col.) Aug '56.

——, **stave (Norway).** Int. gr. soc.: Arts . . . p. 11 (col.).
Praeg. pict. ency., p. 246.

church, Superga. *See* Superga church.

——, Trinity. *See* Trinity church.

——, Vettica Maggiore (Italy). Natl. geog. 116: 484 (col.) Oct '59.

——, village. Holiday 27: 10 (col.) Feb '60.

church altar. *See* altar.

church at Auvers. Praeg. pict. ency., p. 438 (col.).

church ceiling. *See* ceiling, church.

church ceremony (Trinidad). Holiday 24: 131 (col.) Nov '58.

church court (Dresden). Praeg. pict. ency., p. 357.

church entrance. Natl. geog. 103: 522 (col.) Ap '53.

church entrance (people). Holiday 27: 2 (col.) Feb '60.

church frescoes, rock-cut. Natl. geog. 113: 142-3 Jan '58.

church gateway (Sizun, Brittany). Holiday 27: 81 Jan '60.

church ground plan. Praeg. pict. ency., p. 324, 348.

church in Werder market (Berlin). Praeg. pict. ency., p. 433.

church interior. Amer. heri. vol. 4 no. 2 p. 41 (winter '53).
Holiday 27: 79 (col.) Je '60.

—— (Cal.). Holiday 19: 126 Mar '56.

—— (Canada, for police use). Natl. geog. 108: 213 (col.) Aug '55.

—— (Catholic, Kansas). Natl. geog. 101: 474 (col.) Ap '52.

—— (cave grotto). Natl. geog. 112: 577 Oct '57.

—— (colonial). Holiday 22: 70 (col.) Sept '57.

—— (colonial, 1773). Natl. geog. 103: 16 (col.) Jan '53.

—— (Denmark). Natl. geog. 101: 696 May '52.

—— (Dutch). Con. 145: IX Ap '60.

—— (English, historic). Con. 135: 167-9 May '55.

—— (English, Norfolk). Con. 138: 186 Dec '56.

—— (modern, Mexico). Holiday 26: 59 (col.) Nov '59.

—— (Nordlingen, St. George's, 15th cent.). Praeg. pict. ency., p. 63.

—— (Notre-Dame-du-Pont). Con. 138: 186 Dec '56.

—— (Old Swede's). Natl. geog. 102: 27 (col.) Jl '52.

—— (Peterborough, N.H.). Face of Amer., p. 170-1 (col.).

—— (Portuguese). *See* Portuguese church (int.).

—— (Russian). Natl. geog. 116: 384-5 (col.) Sept '59.

—— (St. James Goose Creek, Charleston). Holiday 28: 73 Sept '60.

—— (Santa Maria Tonantzintla, Mexico). Holiday 26: 58 (col.) Nov '59.

—— (Staunton Harold, Leicestershire). Con. 134: 128 Nov '54.

—— (Vezelay). Holiday 21: 89 (col.) Ap '57.

Church of Benedictine abbey of Cluny. Praeg. pict. ency., p. 222.

Church of Benedictine abbey of Maria Laach. Praeg. pict. ency., p. 234.

Church of Christ Scientist (memorial, Cambridge). Natl. geog. 97: 294 (col.) Mar '50.

Church of Nations (outside Jerusalem). Holiday 8: 5 Aug '50.

Church of Our Lady of Good Voyage. Natl. geog. 104: 78-9 (col.) Jl '53.

Church of Our Lady Pammakaristos (Istanbul). Int. gr. soc.: Arts . . . p. 45 (col.).

Church of St. Anthony (Trieste). Natl. geog. 109: 829 (col.) Je '56.

Church of St. Catherine (ceramic figure). Praeg. pict. ency., p. 493.

Church of St. Charles, floor plan (Vienna). Praeg. pict. ency., p. 24.

Church of St. Francis of Assisi. *See* Assisi (church of St. Francis).

Church of St. John, pedestal (Ephesus). Osward: Asia Minor, pl. 43.

Church of St. John the Baptist, Creole. Holiday 5: 112 Jan '49.

Church of St. John. *See* St. John's church.

Church of St. Nicholas. Holiday 25: 88 (col.) Je '59.

Church of St. Peter (Gallicantu). Natl. geog. 110: 720 (col.) Dec '56.

Church of St. Vulfran (Boudin). Con. 142: XVII (col.) Dec '58.

Church of San Francisco (Argentina). Natl. geog. 113: 338 (col.) Mar '58.

Church of San Juan (int.). Natl. geog. 100: 812 (col.) Dec '51.

Church of San Pedro. Holiday 8: 55 Nov '50.

Church of Santa Maria della Febbre. Natl. geog. 110: 652 (col.) Nov '56.

Church of Santa Maria della Salute. *See* Santa Maria della Salute.

Church of Santiago de Compostela. Int. gr. soc.: Arts . . . p. 99 (col.).

Church of the Dormition (Jerusalem). Natl. geog. 110: 754 (col.) Dec '56.

Church of the Evanghelismos (int., Rhodes). Natl. geog. 114: 744 (col.) Dec '58.

Church of the Holy Sepulcher (int.). Natl. geog. 115: 502-4 (col.) Ap '59.

Church of the Miraculous Medal (modern, int., Mexico). Holiday 26: 59 (col.) Nov '59.

Church of the Nativity (Bethlehem). *See* Bethlehem church of Nativity.

Church of the Redentore (Canaletto). Con. 142: 41 Sept '58.

Church of Trinita dei Monti. *See* Trinita dei Monti church.

Church of Wies (int., Bavaria). Int. gr. soc.: Arts . . . p. 99 (col).

church. *See* also meeting house.

church ornament. *See* altar piece; alabaster carvings (Nottingham); sculpture, religious.

church pedestal (Ephesus). Osward: Asia Minor. pl. 43.

church procession (Rome). Holiday 11: 39 (col.) Ap '52.

church pulpit (Portuguese). Con. 137: 39 Mar '56.

church pulpit (St. Wolfgang, Austria). Natl. geog. 118: 266 (col.) Aug '60.

church sculpture. *See* sculpture, Christian; sculpture, religious.
church spire. Holiday 27: 41 Jan '60.
church steeple, Charleston. Natl. geog. 103: 292 Mar '53.
church tower, St. Trophine. Natl. geog. 109: 666 (col.) May '56.
—— (Oxford, Eng.). Natl. geog. 108: 318 (col.) Sept '55.
—— (Scotland). Natl. geog. 110: 15 (col.) Jl '56.
church window. Travel 111: 56 Ap '59.
churches, American. Travel 106: 12-7 Dec '56.
——, Gothic. Int. gr. soc.: Arts . . . p. 49 (col.).
——, Romanseque. Int. gr. soc.: Arts . . . p. 47 (col.).
Churchill, Lady Clementine O.H.S. Cur. biog. p. 115 (1953).
Churchill, Edward D. Cur. biog. (1963).
Churchill, Gordon. Cur. biog. p. 93 (1958).
Churchill, Randolph. Cur. biog. p. 111 (1947).
Churchill, Sarah. Cur. biog. p. 121 (1955).
Churchill, Sir Winston. Amer. heri. vol. 6 no. 2 p. 89 (winter '55); vol. 8 no. 5. p. 27 (Aug '57).
    Cur. biog. p. 153 (1942); p. 117 (1953).
    Holiday 7: 54 Feb '50; 19: 84 Mar '56; 23: 149 Je '58.
—— (painting of). Con. 132: 48 Sept '53.
—— (Mcevoy). Con. 133: 115 Ap '54.
Churchill's victory sign (sym.). Lehner: Pict. bk. of sym., p. 86.
churchyard adobe entrance. Travel 101: 14 Feb '54.
churn, antique butter. Amer. heri. vol. 1 no. 3 p. 63 (spring '50); vol. 3 no. 4 p. 14 (summer '52).
    Natl. geog. 97: 732 (col.) Je '50; 100: 588 (col.) Nov '51.
    Rawson: Ant. pict. bk., p. 61, 88.
——, treadmill. Natl. geog. 110: 598 (col.) Nov '56.
churn dasher. Rawson: Ant. pict. bk., p. 7.
Churriguera, Jose de (architecture). Praeg. pict. ency., p. 350.
Chute, Charles Lionel. Cur. biog. p. 110 (1949).
Chute, Joy. Cur. biog. p. 91 (1950).
Chute, Marchette. Cur. biog. p. 92 (1950).
ciborium, copper gilt. Con. 136: 239 Jan '56.
——, miniature (890). Con. 144: 80 Nov '59.
——, silver gothic. Con. ency. of ant., vol. 3, p. 63.
Ciccolini, Aldo. Holiday 22: 121 Sept '57.
Cicognani, Archbishop Amleto G. Cur. biog. p. 109 (1951).
cider press. Rawson: Ant. pict. bk., p. 32.
cider press monument (San Francisco). Holiday 14: 37 Sept '53.
Cierplikowski, Antek. *See* Antoine.
cigar. Holiday 10: 131 Dec '51; 22: 189 Nov '57.
cigar. *See* also cigars.
cigar box tops (lithographs). Holiday 5: 41 (col.) Feb '49.
cigar store Indian (statue). Amer. heri. vol. 3 no. 3 p. 33 (col.) (spring '52).
    Natl. geog. 117: 504 (col.) Ap '60.

—— (1800s). Holiday 18: 60 (col.) Jl '55.
cigarette box, silver (modern). Con. 144: 36 Sept '59.
cigarette case. Con. 129: XXXVII Ap '52; 139: XXXV Mar '57, XLI Ap '57; 142: LXI Jan '59.
    Holiday 14: 11 (col.) Nov '53; 27: inside cover (col.) Je '60.
——, antique. Con. 135: XXI Mar '55.
——, antique jade. Con. 138: XXXVII Nov '56.
——, gold. Con. 138: XXXVII Dec '56.
——, ladies. Con. 144: LIII Sept '59.
——, Russian. Con. 135: XLVII May '55.
cigarette lighter. Holiday 10: 4, 16 Oct '51, 171 Dec '51; 20: 218 Dec '56; 22: 205 (col.) Dec '57; 24: 9 Nov '58, back cover (col.) Dec '58; 25: 115 (col.) 193, Je '59; 27: back cover (col.) May '60.
——, table. Holiday 27: 107 Jan '60.
cigarette package. Con. 129: LVIII Je '52; 132: LXVIII Nov '53.
    Holiday 10: 12 (col.) Oct '51; 11: 5 (col.) Mar '52, 84 (col.) Ap '52, 89 (col.) Je '52; 12: 124 (col.) Jl '52, 107 (col.) Sept '52, 5 (col.) Oct '52, 85 (col.) Nov '52; 13: 14 May '53; 18: 1, 81 Aug '55, 113 Oct '55, 74, 203 (col.) Dec '55; 19: 71 (col.) Jan '56, 115, 156 (col.) May '56; 21: 136 May '57, 11 Je '57; 22: 8 Sept '57, 96 Nov '57; 27: 23 (col.) Feb '60, 157 (col.) Je '60; 28: 87 (col.) Jl '60.
cigarettes. Holiday 23: 122 Feb '58; 27: 157 (col.) Je '60.
—— (ash tray). Holiday 12: 113 Dec '52; 19: 156 (col.) May '56; 20: 10 (col.) Sept '56.
—— (in box). Con. 138: XLI Nov '56, XLVII Dec '56; 139: XX Mar '57, XXXII Ap '57, XLII Je '57; 140: LVI Jan '58; 142: LV Jan '59; 143: XLIII Ap '59; 145: XI Mar '60, XVII Ap '60, XV (col.) May '60.
    Holiday 24: 179 (col.) Nov '58.
—— (in carton). Holiday 23: 32 Ap '58.
—— (in holder). Holiday 28: 197 Nov '60.
cigars. Holiday 28: 228 Dec '60.
—— (in box). Con. 141: XLI Ap '58; 142: L Nov '58.
cigars. *See* also cigar.
Cignani, Carlo (work of). Con. 144: 21 Sept '59; 145: XLVI Je '60.
Cincinnati (Ohio). Holiday 8: 102-11 (part col.) Sept '50.
—— (1853). Amer. heri. vol. 8 no. 1 p. 18 (col.) (Dec '56).
—— (harbor). Natl. geog. 97: 188 (col.) Feb '50; 107: 436-7 (col.) Ap '55.
"Cinderella in her coach" (mural). Natl. geog. 109: 833 (col.) Je '56.
cinema. *See* motion picture.
cinerary urn. *See* urn, sepulchral.
cinquefoil. Praeg. pict. ency., p. 248.
Cintra palace (Portugal). Holiday 19: 28 Jan '56.
Ciparis prison dungeon (Martinique). Natl. geog. 115: 282 (col.) Feb '59.
Cipriano, Nazzareno (work of). Con. 143: XXII Je '59.

circle of infinity (sym.). Lehner: Pict. bk. of sym., p. 80.

circles, magic (sym.). Lehner: Pict. bk. of sym., p. 68-70.

"Circumcision of St. John" (by Spada). Con. 142: 146 Dec '58.

circus. Holiday 14: 93 Jl '53.
Durant: Pict. hist. of Amer. circus.

—— (Angkor). Natl. geog. 117: 550-1 (col.) Ap '60.

—— (Aztecs of Mexico). Durant: Pict. hist. of Amer. circus, p. 20.

The Circus (Bath, England). Con. 134: 44 Sept '54.

circus (1832-). Amer. heri. vol. 5 no. 1 p. 49-51 (fall '53).

—— (India). Natl. geog. 116: 852 (col.) Dec '59.

—— (lion cage). Int. gr. soc.: Arts . . . p. 149 (col.).

—— (moving). Holiday 10: 22-3 Aug '51.

——, Roman. Int. gr. soc.: Arts . . . p. 35 (col.).
Durant: Pict. hist. of Amer. circus, p. 4-6.

circus acrobats. Holiday 10: 15 (col.) Nov '51, 140 (col.) Dec '51.

circus actors. Amer. heri. vol. 7 no. 1 p. 38-9 (Dec '55).

circus clown. Holiday 8: 45-51 (part col.) Jl '50; 15: 94 Feb '54; 16: back cover (col.) Aug '54.
Int. gr. soc.: Arts . . . p. 149 (col.).
Durant: Pict. hist. of Amer. circus.

circus clown. See also clown.

circus dwarfs. Jensen: The White House, p. 227.

circus fire. Durant: Pict. hist. of Amer. circus, p. 19.

circus ground (layout). Durant: Pict. hist of Amer. circus, p. 158.

circus man (walking tight thread). Amer. heri. vol. 8 no. 6 p. 41 (col.) (Oct '57).

Circus Maximus (Rome). Durant: Pict hist. of Amer. circus, p. 4.

circus parade. Durant: Pict. hist. of Amer. circus, p. 168-9.

circus posters. See posters, circus.

circus riders, Russian. Natl. geog. 116: 378 (col.) Sept '59.

circus stunt (pyramid riders, camels). Natl. geog. 118: 470 (col.) Oct '60.

circus stunts. Amer. heri. vol. 10 no. 1 p. 90-1 (Dec '58).

circus tricks. Travel 112: 28 Jl '59.

circus wagon carving. See Sparks circus wagon carving.

Ciry, Michel (work of). Con. 139: 25-8 Mar '57.

Cisler, Walker Lee. Cur. biog. p. 123 (1955).

Cistercian abbey nave (Portugual). Con. 139: LX Je '57.

cistern, lead rainwater (1725). Con. ency. of ant., vol. 3, pl. 27.

citadel (Dinant, Belgium). Holiday 26: 210 (col.) Dec '59.

—— (Mesopotamia). Natl. geog. 99: 46 Jan '51.

—— (Quebec). Holiday 11: 100 Je '52.

—— (S.C.). Holiday 20: 79 (col.) Dec '56.

—— (Spain). Holiday 13: 140 (col.) Mar '53.

——, hermetic (sym.). Lehner: Pict. bk. of sym., p. 72.

——, mud-brick (Afghanistan). Natl. geog. 114: 23 (col.) Jl '58.

citadel college (quadrangle). Natl. geog. 113: 26 (col.) Jan '58.

"The Citadel Plymouth" (Carmichael). Con. 134: 127 Nov '54.

cities, lost. Travel 108: 23-7 Dec '57.

Citrine, Sir Walter. Cur. biog. p. 149 (1941).

city, empire (being destroyed, Cole). Amer. heri. vol. 8 no. 6 p. 58-9 (col.) (Oct '57).

——, empire (ruins, Cole). Amer. heri. vol. 8 no. 6 p. 60 (col.) (Oct '57).

city, walled. See walled city.

City College stadium (N.Y.). Holiday 23: 94-5 Je '58.

city gates. See gateway, city.

city hall (Africa). Natl. geog. 104: 172 (col.) Aug '53.

—— (San Francisco). Natl. geog. 110: 202 (col.) Aug '56.

city hall. See also town hall.

city harbor, empire (Cole). Amer. heri. vol. 8 no. 6 p. 56-7 (col.) (Oct '57).

city island (N.Y.). Natl. geog. 112: 316-7 (col.) Sept '57.

city model (Rotterdam). Natl. geog. 118: 534 (col.) Oct '60.

"City of Havana" boat. Travel 111: 39 Je '59.

the "City of New York" (river boat). Amer. heri. vol. 6 no. 1 p. 11 (col.) (fall '54).

City of rocks park (near Deming, N.M.). Travel 109: 22 Mar '58.

"City of the Dead" (Thebes). Holiday 27: 69 (col.) Mar '60.

city plan. See town plan.

"City without a heart" (bronze memorial). Praeg. pict. ency., p. 464.

Ciudalela port. Travel 101: 29-30 Mar '54.

Civil air patrol (cadets). Natl. geog. 109: 639-57 (col.) May '56.

Civil war battlefield. See U.S. Civil war battlefield.

Civil war cartoons. See cartoon (Civil war); cartoons (Civil war).

Civil war prison camp. See prison camp, Civil war.

Civil war. See U.S. Civil war.

civilisation map. See map (Amer. ancient civilisation).

Claesz, Pieter (work of). Con. 143: XL (col.) Je '59.

Claflin, ("Buck") Reuben Buckman. Amer. heri. vol. 7 no. 4 p. 44 (Je '56).

Clague, Ewan. Cur. biog. p 112 (1947).

Clair, Rene. Cur. biog. p. 151 (1941).

Claire, Ina. Cur. biog. p. 179 (1954).

clairvoyant. See fortune teller.

clam (sym.). Lehner: Pict. bk. of sym., p. 83.

clam diggers. Natl. geog. 107: 798 Je '55.

Clandon Park (Surrey, Eng.). Con. 138: 91-4 Nov '56.

—— (1733). Con. 138: 189 (col.) Dec '56.

clansmen (Scotland). Natl. geog. 102: 93-8 (col.) Jl '52.

Clapp, Gordon Rufus. Cur. biog. p. 114 (1947).

Clapp, Margaret. Cur. biog. p. 106 (1948).

Clapp, Verner W. Cur. biog. p. 67 (1959).

Clapper, Olive Ewing. Cur. biog. p. 116 (1946).

Clarence, Duke of. Con. 142: IV Dec '58.

Claridge restaurant (London, cartoon). Holiday 27: 69 Mar '60.

clarinet. Int. gr. soc.: Arts . . . p. 141 (col.)
—— (man playing). Holiday 22: 113 Jl '57.
——, bass. Cooper: Con. ency. of music, p. 401.

Clark, Ann Nolan. Jun. bk. of Auth., p. 71.

Clark, Bennett Champ. Cur. biog. p. 153 (1941).

Clark, Bobby. Cur. biog. p. 111 (1949).

Clark, Charles E. Cur. biog. p. 69 (1959).

Clark, Dick. Cur. biog. p. 71 (1959).

Clark, Dorothy Park. Cur. biog. p. 347 (1957).

Clark, Edward. Amer. heri. vol. 9 no. 6 p. 37 (Oct '58).

Clark, Eugenie. Cur. biog. p. 121 (1953).
Holiday 17: 48-51 (part col.) Jan '55.

Clark, Evans. Cur. biog. p. 116 (1947).

Clark, Fred G. Cur. biog. p. 114 (1949).

Clark, Gen. George Rogers (statue). Brooks: Growth of a nation, p. 79.

Clark, Georgia Nesse. Cur. biog. p. 115 (1949).

Clark, John. Cur. biog. p. 106 (1952).

Clark, John D. Cur. biog. p. 118 (1947).

Clark, Vice-Adm. Joseph J. Cur. biog. p. 181 (1954).

Clark, Joseph S., jr. Cur. biog. p. 108 (1952).

Clark, Sir Kenneth. Cur. biog. (1963).

Clark, Leonard. Cur. biog. p. 113 (1956).

Clark, M. C. Horan: Pict. hist. of wild west, p. 105.

Clark, Lt. Gen. Mark W. Cur. biog. p. 158 (1942).

Clark, Meriwether. Natl. geog. 103: 709, 730 (col.) Je '53.

Clark, Paul F. Cur. biog. p. 125 (1955).

Clark, Robert L. Cur. biog. p. 109 (1952).

Clark, Sydney. Cur. biog. p. 115 (1956).

Clark, Tom. Holiday 7: 46 (col.) Feb '50.

Clark, Tom C. Cur. biog. p. 108 (1945).
Holiday 7: 78 Feb '50.

Clark, William. Natl. geog. 103: 709, 730 (col.) Je '53.
Travel 102: 13 Oct '54.

Clarke, Charles Walter. Cur. biog. p. 121 (1947).

Clarke, Walter. Cur. biog. p. 121 (1947).

Clarke school (deaf children). Natl. geog. 107: 378-97 (part col.) Mar '55.

Clark's army commission, Meriwether. See army commission, Meriwether Clark's.

clasped hands. See hands, clasped.

classroom (teacher & service men). Natl. geog. 103: 583 (col.) May '53.

classroom. See also schoolroom; teacher & students.

Claude Lorrain (work of). Con. ency. of ant., vol. 1, pl. 158.
Con. 127: 133 (col.) May '51; 138: 213 Dec

'56; 140: 53 Sept '57; 145: 57-63 Mar '60.
Praeg. pict. ency., p. 330 (col.).

Claudius, Emperor (bust). Holiday 23: 61 May '58.

"Claudius Civilis" (Rembrandt). Con. 138: 21-5 Sept '56.

clavichord, Louis XV. Con. 141: 249 Je '58.

Claxton, Brooke. Cur. biog. p. 123 (1947).

Clay, Cassius. Cur. biog. (1963).

Clay, Cassius Marcellus. Amer. heri. vol. 11 no. 4 p. 37 (Je '60).

Clay, Henry. Amer. heri. vol. 7 no. 6 p. 27 (col.) (Oct '56); vol. 12 no. 1 p. 28 (col.) (Dec '60).
Holiday 18: 24 Jl '55; 23: 158 (col.) May '58; 26: 21 (col.) Aug '59; 28: 188 (col.) Nov '60.

Clay, Lt. Gen. Lucius. Cur. biog. p. 111 (1945); (1963).

Clay battalion (Civil war). Jensen: The White House, p. 89.

Clay home, Cassius Marcellus. See "White Hall".

Clay home, Henry. Amer. heri. vol. 7 no. 6 p. 29 (Oct '56).

a clay industry (Ga.). Natl. geog. 105: 316 (col.) Mar '54.

clay pots. Int. gr. soc.: Arts . . . p. 177 (col.).

clay tablet, Pietro's. Ceram: March of arch., p. 177, 179.

Claydon House, (int., England). Con. 142: 70 (col.)-4 Nov '58.

Clayton, Rev. Philip T. B. Cur. biog. p. 127 (1955).

Clayton, Sir Robert (Gainsborough). Con. 126: 151 Oct '50.

Clayton, Sir William. See "Sir William Clayton" (Wright).

Clayton, William H. H. Horan: Pict. hist of wild west, p. 143.

Clayton, William L. Cur. biog. p. 95 (1944).

cleaver making machine (girls). Natl. geog. 98: 375 Sept '50.

Cleburne, Patrick R. Pakula: Cent. album, p. 107.

Clegg, Charles. Amer. heri. vol. 4 no. 3 p. 23 (spring '53).

Clemenceau, Georges. Amer. heri. vol. 8 no. 4 p. 25 (Je '57); vol. 9 no. 4 p. 67 (Je '58).

Clemens, Clara. Amer. heri. vol. 11 no. 1 p. 69, 71, 76 (Dec '59).

Clemens, Olivia L. (Mrs. Samuel L. Clemens). Amer. heri. vol. 11 no. 1 p. 76 (Dec '59).

Clemens, Samuel Langhorne. Amer. heri. vol. 4 no. 3 p. 23 (spring '53); vol. 8 no. 6 p. 62 (Oct '57).
Holiday 18: 24 Jl '55; 25: 161 (col.) Ap '59; 26: 8 Nov '59.
Natl. geog. 110: 124 Jl '56.
Travel 113: 48 May '60.
—— (bust). Holiday 14: 113 Nov '53.
Travel 104: 41 Aug '55.
—— (caricature). Amer. heri. vol. 11 no. 1 p. 79 (Dec '59).

Clemens, Mr. & Mrs. Samuel L. Natl. geog. 110: 132 Jl '56.

Clemens, Susy. Amer. heri. vol. 11 no. 1 p. 71, 76, 80 (Dec '59).

Clemens birthplace, Samuel L. Natl. geog. 110: 125 Jl '56.

Clemens home, Samuel L. Amer. heri. vol. 11 no. 1 p. 65, 67, 72-4, 76 (Dec '59).
Brooks: Growth of a nation, p. 156.
Jordan: Hammond's pict. atlas, p. 101 (col.).
Natl. geog. 110: 122-24 Jl '56.
Travel 104: 40-1 Aug '55.

Clemen's office, Samuel L. Natl. geog. 110: 134 Jl '56.

Clement XI, Pope. See Pope Clement XI.

Clement XIV, Pope. See Pope Clement XIV.

Clement, Frank G. Cur. biog. p. 129 (1955).

Clement, Martin W. Cur. biog. p. 118 (1946).

Clement, Rufus E. Cur. biog. p. 121 (1946).

Clements, Earle C. Cur. biog. p. 131 (1955).

Clements, Jo. Horan: Pict. hist. of wild west, p. 120.

Clements, John Gipson (Gyp.). Horan: Pict. hist. of wild west, p. 120.

Clements, Manning. Horan: Pict. hist of wild west, p. 118.

Cleopatra (Cagnacci). Con. 144: 24 Sept '59.

Cleopatra circle (sym.). Lehner: Pict. bk. of sym., p. 68.

Cleopatra's needle (New Mexico). Holiday 15: 93 (col.) May '54, 147 (col.) Je '54.

clergyman, Anglican. Natl. geog. 102: 554 Oct '52.

Clerisseau, Jacques Lewis (work of). Con. 142: XLII Dec '58.

"Clermont" steamboat. Amer. heri. vol. 10 no. 1 p. 17 (Dec '58).

Clesinger, J. B. (sculpture by). Con. 140: 247 Jan '58.

Cleveland, Frances Folsom (Mrs. Grover Cleveland). Amer heri. vol. 8 no. 6 p. 11 (Oct '57).
Jensen: The White House, p. 135, 169.

Cleveland, Grover Amer. heri. vol. 7 no. 3 p. 32 (Ap '56); vol. 7 no. 5 p. 103. (Aug '56); vol. 8 no. 6 p. 10 (Oct '57).
Jensen: The White House, p. 132.

—— (campaign ribbon). Amer. heri. vol. 7 no. 4 p. 26 (Je '56).

—— (wedding). Jensen: The White House, p. 136.

Cleveland, Harlan. Cur. biog. p. 105 (1961).

Cleveland home, Grover ("Oak View"). Jensen: The White House, p. 137.

Cleveland summer home, Grover. Amer. heri. vol. 8 no. 6 p. 103 (Oct '57).

Cleveland (Ohio). Natl. geog. 107: 452-5 (col.) Ap '55.

Cliburn, Van. Cur. biog. p. 95 (1958).
Holiday 24: 1 Sept '58.

cliff (near Trieste, Italy). Natl. geog. 109: 844 (col.) Je '56.

cliff coast road (Formosa). Natl. geog. 111: 362 (col.) Mar '57.

cliff dwellings. Holiday 23: 49 Mar '58.

—— (Alaska). Natl. geog. 102: 82 (col.) Jl '52.

—— (Nepal). Natl. geog. 117: 384-5 (col.) Mar '60.

——, Indian. Holiday 12: 41 Sept '52; 13: 137 (col.) May '53; 25: 24 Mar '59.

——, Indian (colo.). Natl. geog. 113: 642-3 (col.) May '58; 115: 154 Jan '59; 116: 618, 621-5 (part col.) Nov '59.

——, Indian (Mesa Verde). Jordan: Hammond's pict. atlas, p. 166, 176 (col.).
Natl. geog. 113: 642-3 (col.) May '58; 116: 618, 621-5 (part col.) Nov '59.

Cliff House (San Francisco). Holiday 14: 36 Sept '53.
Jordan: Hammond's pict. atlas, p. 201 (col.).

Cliff House restaurant. Natl. geog. 110: 198 (col.) Aug '56.

Clifford, Clark McAdams. Cur. biog. p. 124 (1947).

cliffs (Greenland). Natl. geog. 111: 526-7 (col.) Ap '57.

—— (Mass.). Natl. geog. 107: 750 (col.) Je '55.

—— (passage to Petra). Natl. geog. 110: 726-7 (col.) Dec '56.

—— (Portuguese village). Natl. geog. 106: 694 (col.) Nov '54.

——, chalk. See chalk cliffs.

cliffs, granite (Rio). Natl. geog. 107: 311 (col.) Mar '55.

——, riverside. Holiday 12: 102 (col.) Oct '52.

——, rock. Natl. geog. 105: 378, 384, 386-7, 390 (part col.) Mar '54.

——, rock (river). Natl. geog. 111: 158-9 (col.) Feb '57.

——, rock (Utah). Natl. geog. 108: 400-25 (col.) Sept '55.

——, sand & clay (bird nests, boys). Natl. geog. 112: 178 (col.) Aug '57.

——, sandstone (Cal.). Natl. geog. 102: 780 (col.) Dec '52.

"Cliffs & crags of Ross" (Cameron). Con. 138: XII (col.) Nov '56.

"Cliffs at Etretat" (Courbet). Con. 145: 137 Ap '60.

Clift, David H. Cur. biog. p. 111 (1952).

Clift, Montgomery. Cur. biog. p. 183 (1954).

Clifton, Dan. Horan: Pict. hist. of wild west, p. 168.

"Clifton" home (Colonial hallwat, Va.). Natl. geog. 109: 472 Ap '56.

climbers, pole (Tiwis). Natl. geog. 109: 432 (col.) Mar '56.

Clinchy, Rev. Everett R. Cur. biog. p. 156 (1941).

Cline, John Wesley. Cur. biog. p. 110 (1951).

Clinton's "dumbell code". Amer. heri. vol. 10 no. 3 p. 112 (Ap '59).

Clio (goddess). Lehner: Pict. bk. of sym., p. 33.

clip board. Holiday 12: 114 Sept '52.

clipper ship. See ship, clipper.

Clive, Lord Robert. Con. 145: XLIV Je '60.

"Cliveden" house (besieged). Natl. geog. 118: 157, 176-7 (col.) Aug '60.

cloak (woman models). Natl. geog. 98: 53 (col.) Jl '50.

——, Indian ceremonial. Amer. heri. vol. 10 no. 4 p. 5 (Je '59).

clock. Con. 137: XLIII Ap '56.

clock, Louis XV. Con. 129: LV Ap '52.

——, **Louis XV (ormolu).** Con. 138: 47 Sept '56.

——, **Louis XV (ormolu cartel).** Con. 145: 129 Ap '60, 186 May '60.

——, **Louis XV (parquetry regulator).** Con. 141: 187 May '58.

——, **Louis XV wall.** Con. 133: 258 Je '54; 141: 249 Je '58; 142: 56 Sept '58.

——, **Louis XV wall (bronze).** Con. 141: LVI May '58; 143: LX May '59.

——, **Louis XVI.** Con. 136: 86 Nov '55.

——, **Louis XVI (ormolu).** Con. 135: LIX May '55; 138: 44 Sept '56.

——, **mantle.** Holiday 20: 78 (col.) Aug '56.

——, **mantle (antique).** Natl. geog. 101: 175 (col.) Feb '52.

——, **mantle (18th cent.).** Con. 140: 13 Sept '57.

——, **Meissen porcelain.** Con. 129: LXXXII Ap '52; 137: 211 May '56; 139: XLV Ap '57; 145: XLIX Mar '60.

——, **Minerva.** *See* Minerva clock.

——, **"Nautilus" (given to Mrs. Eisenhower).** Natl. geog. 115: 5 (col.) Jan '59.

——, **night.** Con. 129: 102 Je '52.

——, **148 town hall.** Holiday 21: 58 (col.) Jan '57.

——, **pagoda bracket.** Con. 129: XLIV Je '52.

——, **Quare table.** Con. 141: 189 May '58.

——, **Russian circular.** Con. 139: 55 Mar '57.

——, **"Storyland".** Holiday 28: 77 Jl '60.

——, **street.** Con. 141: XLIII Ap '58. Holiday 10: 37 Oct '51; 22: 132 Sept '57.

——, **table.** 14: 148 Nov '53; 18: 23 Oct '55, 21 Nov '55, 19, 176 (col.) Dec '55; 20: 115 Dec '56; 22: 122 (col.) Dec '57; 23: 152 Jan '58; 26: 139 Dec '59. Travel 112: 5 Jl '59.

——, **table (antique).** Con. 142: XLVIII Dec '58.

——, **table (Chantilly).** Con. 143: inside cover Je '59.

——, **table (Faberge).** Con. 132: XLVII Sept '53; 143: XXXIII May '59.

——, **table (French, 18th cent.).** Con. 145: 281 Je '60.

——, **table. (Louis XV rococo).** Con. 144: LIV Nov '59.

——, **table (Louis XVI ormolu).** Con. 145: XLI May '60.

——, **table (19th cent.).** Con. 144: XLIII Nov '59.

——, **table (porcelain).** Holiday 27: 163 (col.) Jan '60.

——, **table (17th-18th cent.).** Con. ency. of ant., vol. 1, pl. 103.

——, **table 400 day.** Holiday 22: 1 Oct '57.

——, **table ormolu & marble (Cachard).** Con. 145: XXIII Mar '60.

——, **travel.** Con. 144: 271 Jan '61. Holiday 10: 127 Dec '51; 28: 134 Jl '60, 81 Aug '60, 12 Dec '60. Travel 113: 47 Feb '60.

——, **travel (17th cent.).** Con. 144: LVII Nov '59.

——, **wall.** Con. ency. of ant., vol. 3, p. 105.

Holiday 14: 10 (col.) Dec '53; 20: 138 Oct '56; 22: 122-3 (col.) Dec '57; 28: 44, 49 Dec '60. Natl. geog. 106: 94 Jl '54; 110: 42 (col.) Jl '56; 111: 574 Ap '57.

——, **wall (adv.).** Holiday 18: 94 (col.) Jl '55, 60 (col.) Sept '55, 15 (col.) Oct '55, 182 (col.) Dec '55.

——, **wall (antique).** Con. 139: XVIII May '57. Holiday 20: 64 (col.) Oct '56.

——, **wall (Dutch).** Natl. geog. 106: 383 (col.) Sept '54.

——, **wall (George Nelson).** Holiday 26: 153 Nov '59.

——, **wall (Willard 18th cent.).** Con. ency. of ant., vol. 1, pl. 38.

——, **William III.** Con. 129: 125 (col.) Je '52.

clock dials & works (17th-18th cent.). Con. ency. of ant., vol. 1, pl. 97-9, 102.

clock dome (Tompion). Con. 139: 43 Mar '57.

clock face. Holiday 23: 22 (col.) Feb '58, 150 (col.) Mar '58; 24: 86 (col.) Sept '58, 18 (col.) Oct '58, 139 (col.) Nov '58, 168 (col.) Dec '58.

clock tower. Holiday 7: 60 (col.) May '50; 11: 121 (col.) Mar '52, 45 Je '52; 19: 2 (col.) Feb '56; 20: 117 (col.) Nov '56, 29 Dec '56; 25: 175 (col.) Ap '59; 28: 12 (col.) Aug '60, 88-9 Sept '60, 161 (col.) Nov '60. Natl. geog. 104: 785 (col.) Dec '53; 105: 240 (col.) Feb '54; 106: 213 (col.) Aug '54, 440-1 (col.) Oct '54; 107: 33 (col.) Jan '55; 109: 212 (col.), 248 Feb '56, 336 (col.) Mar '56, 843 (col.) Je '56; 113: 815 (col.) Je '58; 116: 693 (col.) Nov '59; 118: 153 Aug '60.

—— **(Auckland, Univ.).** Natl. geog. 101: 429 (col.) Ap '52.

—— **(Bavaria).** Holiday 25: 54 (col.) May '59.

—— **(Berne, Switzerland).** Natl. geog. 98: 240 (col.) Aug '50. Travel 108: 22 Nov '57.

—— **("Big Ben", London).** Holiday 18: 128 Jl '55; 25: 145 Jan '59.

—— **(Cornell Univ.).** Holiday 18: 37 Nov '55. Natl. geog. 110: 599 (col.) Nov '56.

—— **(court house).** Holiday 25: 131 Je '59.

—— **(Edinburgh).** Natl. geog. 98: 182 Aug '50.

—— **(Fiji).** Natl. geog. 114: 537 Oct '58.

—— **("Gog & Magog").** Natl. geog. 114: 108 (col.) Jl '58.

—— **(Hartford, Conn.).** Holiday 27: 83 Feb '60.

—— **(Italy).** Natl. geog. 110: 659 (col.) Nov '56.

—— **(Oslo).** Natl. geog. 106: 188 (col.) Aug '54.

—— **(Ottawa, parliament).** Natl. geog. 108: 195 (col.) Aug '55; 115: 824 (col.) Je '59.

—— **(Penang island).** Travel 107: 44 Feb '57.

—— **(Poland).** Natl. geog. 114: 369 (col.) Sept '58.

—— **(Rouen).** Natl. geog. 115: 621 (col.) May '59.

—— (Singapore). Natl. geog. 103: 203 (col.) Feb '53.

clock vendor (Black Forest). Disney: People & places, p. 50 (col.).

clockmaker, German. Natl. geog. 111: 780 (col.) Je '57.

Clodion. See Michel, Claude.

"Cloelia and the Virgins" (Fontebasso). Con. 144: 191 Dec '59.

The Cloister (Sea island, Ga. coast). Travel 110: 49 Nov '58.

cloister, Amalfi cathedral. Labande: Naples, p. 194.

cloister, Konigslutter cathedral. Praeg. pict. ency., p. 232.

cloister, Monastery of San Martino. Labande: Naples, p. 117.

cloister, Mont-Saint-Michel. Holiday 11: 91 (col.) Jan '52.

cloister, Santa Chiara. Labande: Naples. p. 66-7.

cloistered corridor. Holiday 10: 100 Aug '51.

Clonney, James Goodwyn (work of). Amer. heri. vol. 8 no. 1 back cover (col.) (Dec '56); vol. 9 no. 4 back cover (col.) (Je '58).

Clooney, Rosemary. Cur. biog. p. 113 (1957).

"Clooty well" fence (good luck wishes). Natl. geog. 110: 12 (col.) Jl '56.

Close, Upton. Cur. biog. p. 99 (1944).

"Close of a hunting day" (Landseer). Con. 139: cover (col.) Je '57.

Closterman (work of). Con. 144: 76 Nov '59.

Clostermann. (work by). Cooper: Con. ency. of music, p. 242.

cloth dyeing (Africa). Natl. geog. 104: 158-9 (col.) Aug '53.

cloth hall & town hall (Ypres). Praeg. pict. ency., p. 207.

clothes (on line). See washing (on line).

clothes box (Penn.). See Penn. clothes box.

clothes brush. Holiday 24: 15 (col.) Nov '58. Rawson: Ant. pict. bk., p. 52.

clothes dryer. Holiday 13: 75 Ap '53, 121 Je '53.

clothes drying rack. Rawson: Ant. pict. bk., p. 13.

clothes exhibit. Holiday 19: 60-1 (col.) Jan '56.

—— (Paris). Holiday 19: 48-9 (part col.) Jan '56.

clothes exhibit. See also woman (clothes exhibit); women (winter coats); costume.

clothes pins, antique. Rawson: Ant. pict bk., p. 13.

clothes press (16th cent.). Con. 143: LXXV Je '59; 144: LXXXIII Jan '60.

—— (18th cent.). Con. ency. of ant., vol. 1, pl. 25.

——, rococo. Con. 137: 155 May '56.

clothes tree. Holiday 13: 120 Ap '53, 102 May '53.

——, Russian. Holiday 24: 60 Oct '58.

cloud formations. Holiday 11: 34-5 (col.) Feb '52, 31, 98-9 (col.) Ap '52.

clouds. Holiday 11: 115 (col.) Je '52; 12: 117 (col.) Jl '52, 94 (col.) Sept '52, 52-3, 102 (col.) Oct '52; 22: 191 (col.) Dec '57.

——, monsoon. See monsoon clouds.

Clouet, Francois (work of). Con. 133: XV Mar '54.

Natl. geog. 110: 642 (col.) Nov '56.

Clovelly (England). Holiday 21: 136 (col.) Ap '57; 27: 127 (col.) Feb '60.

Natl. geog. 108: 324-5 (col.) Sept '55.

clover, four-leaf (sym.). Lehner: Pict. bk. of

clover reaper. Rawson: Ant. pict. bk., p. 27.

clown. Holiday 8: 6 Oct '50; 11: 94 (col.) Je '52; 12: 20 (col.) Aug '52, 121 Nov '52; 19: 113 (col.) Jan '56.

Natl. geog. 106: 309 Sept '54; 117: 41 (col.) Jan '60.

—— (antique toy). Amer. heri. vol. 11 no. 1 p. 88 (col.) (Dec '59).

—— (head). Con. 143: XVIII Ap '59.

Holiday 10: 14 Oct '51; 11: 152 (col.) May '52; 12: 101 Dec '52; 27: 113 (col.) May '60.

—— (kissing woman). Travel 113: 40 Jan '60.

—— (on horse). Durant: Pict. hist. of Amer. circus, p. 187.

"Clown" (Rouault). Holiday 14: 51 (col.) Dec '53.

clown (Trinidad). Holiday 11: 94 (col.) Feb '52.

clown, circus. See circus clown.

——, Italian. Holiday 27: 65 (col.) Jan '60.

clown doll & child. Natl. geog. 116: 816 (col.) Dec '59.

clown skier. Natl. geog. 115: 242 (col.) Feb '59.

clowns (St. Thomas island carnival). Natl. geog. 109: 214-5 (col.) Feb '56.

club, beach (N.H.). Holiday 10: 43 (col.) Sept '51.

——, country. See country club.

——, Elbow beach surf. Holiday 12: 92 Oct '52.

——, Fiji war. Holiday 28: 81 (col.) Oct '60.

——, Iroquois Indian. Con. 141: 35 Mar '58.

——, Lima country. Holiday 11: 12 (col.) Mar '52.

——, tennis. See tennis club.

——, war. See war club.

——, yacht. See yacht club.

Club Barracuda. Holiday 10: 99 (col.) Nov '51.

Club de Pesca hotel (Mexico). Holiday 11: 54 Mar '52.

club house. Holiday 24: 113 (col.) Oct '58; 28: 160 (col.) Dec '60.

——, Penang island. Travel 107: 43 Feb '57.

——, Sea island. Natl. geog. 105: 325 (col.) Mar '54.

——, yacht (Larchmont). Natl. geog. 112: 324-5 (col.) Sept '57.

club house entrance (Christmas). Holiday 23: 15 (col.) Jan '58.

club life in America (cartoon). Amer. heri. vol. 9 no. 5 p. 103 (Aug '58).

club man (cartoon). Amer. heri. vol. 6 no. 1 p. 31 (fall '54).

club room interior (cartoon). Holiday 13: 76 Feb '53.

clubs, men's. Amer. heri. vol. 6 no. 1 p. 28-9 (fall '54).

Clum, John P. (with bodyguard). Horan: Pict. hist. of wild west, p. 115.

Clurman, Harold. Cur. biog. p. 73 (1959).

Clyde, George D. Cur. biog. p. 97 (1958).

Cnossus. Holiday 18: 34-5 (col.) Aug '55.

Cnossus palace gate. Natl. geog. 104: 703 (col.) Nov '53.

Cnossus palace throne room. Praeg. pict. ency., p. 125.

coach. Rawson: Ant. pict. bk., p. 71.
Travel 111: 49 Ap '59.
—— (driver, 18th cent.). Int. gr. soc.: Arts . . . p. 119 (col.).
—— (driver, horse). Durant: Pict. hist. of Amer. circus, p. 23, 55.
—— (hold up). Horan: Pict. hist. of wild west, p. 84.
—— (horses). Amer. heri. vol. 11 no. 3 p. 19 (col.) (Ap '60).
Holiday 6: 125 Sept '49, 129 Oct '49.
Jordan: Hammond's pict. atlas, p. 149 (col.).
——, Black Forest. Disney: People & places, p. 51 (col.).
——, British royal. Holiday 15: 12 Feb '54.
Int. gr. soc.: Arts . . . p. 163 (col.).
——, Concord. Horan: Pict. hist. of wild west, p. 82.
——, Empress Josephine's. Holiday 5: 87 (col.) Je '49.
——, state. Con. 140: 113 Nov '57.

coach house, Geo. Washington's. Natl. geog. 104: 667 Nov '53.

coach lamp, antique. Con. 143: LII May '59.

coachman (London). Holiday 13: 27 Ap '53.

coal exchange, court (London). Con. 136: 61 Sept '55.

coal miner's families. Amer. heri. vol. 11 no. 3 p. 56 (Ap '60).

coal miner's homes. Amer. heri. vol. 11 no. 3 p. 57 (Ap '60).

coal miner's strike (1902). Amer. heri. vol. 11 no. 3 p. 54-61, 96-9 (Ap '60).

coal mines (Saar). Natl. geog. 105: 566-67 Ap '54.

coal pit. Natl. geog. 104: 818 (col.) Dec '53.

Coanda, Henri. Cur. biog. p. 117 (1956).

coast guard. See U.S. coast guard.

coat, fur. See woman (fur coat).
——, Japanese. See "happi coat" (Japanese).
——, judo. Holiday 19: 30 May '56.
——, man's Holiday 19: 162 May '56; 21: 132 Jan '57; 22: 134 Sept '57; 23: 108 (col.) Mar '58; 28: 38 (col.) Dec '60.
——, padded. Holiday 24: 233 Dec '58.

coat display, Women's. Holiday 20: 92-3 (col.) (Oct '56).

coat hangers, antique. Rawson: Ant. pict. bk., p. 12.

coat of arms. Amer. heri. vol. 6 no. 2 p. 65 (col.) (winter '55); vol. 6 no. 3 p. 62 (col.) (Ap '55); vol. 8 no. 2 p. 17 (col.) (Feb '57); vol. 8 no. 4 cover (col.) (Je '57); vol. 9 no. 6 p. 29 (Oct '58).
Con. 140: XXIX, 42 Sept '57, XXIII Nov '57, V Dec '57; 141: XLIII Ap '58;

142: XI Sept '58, 144 Dec '58; 145: 273 Je '60.
Holiday 11: 21 (col.) May '52; 13: 15 Jan '53, 71, 91 (col.) Mar '53, 7 (col.) May '53; 14: 31 (col.) Jl '53, 20, 71 (col.) Nov '53, 135 (col.) Dec '53; 24: 143 (col.) Nov '58; 25: inside cover (col.) Jan '59, 129 (col.) Feb '59; 28: 95 (col.) Sept '60.
Int. gr. soc.: Arts . . . p. 67 (col.).
Natl. geog. 111: 591 May '57.
—— (Grimaldis). Int. gr. soc.: Arts . . . p. 67 (col.).
—— (industry). Con. 143: XLVII, LVI Ap '59, XXXIII May '59.
—— (sym.). Lehner: Pict. bk. of sym., p. 12.
—— (trade). Con. 144: LIII Sept '59; 145: XXX May '60, XX Ap '60, XXX Je '60.
——, Beresford plate. Con. 139: 179 May '57.
——, Gen. Burgoyne's. Amer. heri. vol. 7 no. 4 p. 84 (Je '56).
——, Canada's Natl. geog. 115: 826 (col.) Je '59.
——, Columbus. Amer. heri. vol. 7 no. 1 p. 94 (Dec '55).
——, compound. Int. gr. soc.: Arts . . . p. 67 (col.).
——, English. Amer. heri. vol. 11 no. 4 p. 7 (col.) (Je '60).
Con. 129: XI Je '52; 132: VI Sept '53, VII Nov '53; 133: VII Mar '54, VII, LIV Ap '54, VII May '54, VII, LXXIX Je '54.
——, Sir Ferdinando Georges. Amer. heri. vol. 10 no. 5 p. 23 (col.) (Aug '59).
——, George II. Natl. geog. 106: 458 (col.) Oct '54.
——, Holland royal. Holiday 10: 53 (col.) Nov '51.
——, Johnson. Amer. heri. vol. 10 no. 3 p. 47 (Ap '59).
——, Liechtenstein. Holiday 6: 107 (col.) Nov '49.
——, Napoleon III. Natl. geog. 111: 321 Mar '57.
——, Queen Elizabeth II. Natl. geog. 115: 828 Je '59.
——, Stuart period, Eng. Con. 132: LXIX Jan '54.
——, Trumbull. Amer. heri. vol. 9 no. 4 p. 41 (col.) (Je '58).
——, Washington. Holiday 19: 125 May '56.
——, Wm. Byrd. Amer. heri. vol. 11 no. 1 p. 117 (Dec '59).

coat of arms. See heraldry.

coat of mail. See armour.

coat rack, antique. Holiday 26: 151 Nov '59.

coats, winter. See women (winter coats).

Coat's thread adver. cards. Amer. heri. vol. 8 no. 6 p. 40-1 (col.) (Nov '57).

Coatsworth, Elizabeth. Jun. bk. of auth., p. 72.

Cobb, Howell. Amer. heri. vol. 11 no. 5 p. 55 (Aug '60).

Cobb, Jerrie. Cur. biog. p. 107 (1961).

Cobb, Lee J. Cur. biog. p. 91 (1960).

Cobb, Ty. Amer. heri. vol. 10 no. 3 p. 21 (Ap '59).
Cur. biog. p. 112 (1951).

cobbler, Turkish. Osward: Asia Minor, pl. 89.

cobbler's tools. Rawson: Ant. pict. bk., p. 58-9.
Cobham, Charles J. L. Cur. biog. p. 86 (1962).
cobirons. Con. ency. of ant., vol. 3 pl. 165.
Coblentz, Catherine Cate. Jun. bk. of auth., p. 74.
Coblentz, Stanton A. Cur. biog. p. 185 (1954).
Coblentz, William W. Cur. biog. p. 187 (1954).
Cobo, Albert E. Cur. biog. p. 114 (1951).
Coburn, Charles. Cur. biog. p. 101 (1944).
Coca, Imogene. Cur. biog. p. 116 (1951).
Coca Cola. Holiday 27: 10 (col.) Ap '60; 28: 2 (col.) Aug '60.
Coca Cola bottle & glass. Holiday 28: 106 (col.) Jl '60.
Coca Cola stand (Mecca). Natl. geog. 104: 45 (col.) Jl '53.
Coccorante, Leonardo (work of). Con. 142: 25 Sept '58.
Cochem castle Moselle river, Germany). Holiday 23: 34 Jan '58; 25: 42 (col.) Jan '59.
Cochin, C. N. (engravings). Con. 145: 219 Je '60.
Cochran, H. Merle. Cur. biog. p. 94 (1950).
Cochran, Jacqueline. Cur. biog. (1963).
Cochrane, Vice-Adm. Edward L. Cur. biog. p. 117 (1951).
cock, gallic (sym., France). Lehner: Pict. bk. of sym., p. 57.
"The Cock of the Family" (Hogarth). Con. 145: XXIII May '60.
cock fight. Holiday 11: 94 May '52.
Cockburn, Rear Adm. Sir George. Amer. heri. vol. 6 no. 1 p. 48 (col.) (fall '54).
Cockburn, Sir George. Jensen: The White House, p. 25.
Cockburn, James Pattison (work of). Con. 133: 203-7 May '54.
Cockcroft, Sir John. Cur. biog. p. 108 (1948). Holiday 23: 95 Ap '58.
Cocke, Charles Francis. Cur. biog. p. 113 (1952).
Cocke, Erle, jr. Cur. biog. p. 120 (1951).
cockney costermongers. See costermongers, King & Queen of London's cockney.
Cockrell, Ewing. Cur. biog. p. 121 (1951).
cocktail bar. Holiday 25: 71 Mar '59, 40 (col.) Ap '59.
cocktail, fruit. Holiday 28: 116 (col.) Sept '60.
cocktail glasses. Holiday (in practically all issues).
cocktail lounge, glacier. Natl. geog. 98: 208 Aug '50.
cocktail table. Holiday 10: 18 Jl '51, 96 Dec '51; 24: inside cover (col.) Nov '58.
cocktails. Holiday 23: 15 (col.) Je '58.
cocoanut cup. See cup, cocoanut.
Cocoanut Grove hotel (Los Angeles). Holiday 14: 110 Sept '53.
Cocos island woman (baby, bird cage). Holiday 12: 72 Nov '52.
Cocteau, Jean (Modigliani). Con. 145: 234 Je '60.
Codex Mendoza (sample page). Ceram: March of arch., p. 271.
Codman, Henry S. Amer. heri. vol. 11 no. 6 p. 11 (Oct '60).
Cody, William Frederick (Buffalo Bill). Amer. heri. vol. 7 no. 5 p. 36 (Aug '56).

Brooks: Growth of a nation, p. 180.
Horan: Pict. hist. of wild west, p. 48, 53-4.
Natl. geog. 101: 481 Ap '52.
Durant: Pict hist of Amer. circus, p. 134.
Coe, Frederick. Cur. biog. p 74 (1959).
Coe, George. Horan: Pict. hist. of wild west, p. 68.
Coeymans, Ariaantje. Amer. heri. vol. 10 no. 1 p. 11 (col.) (Dec '58).
Coffee, John M. Cur. biog. p. 123 (1946).
coffee & tea service, silver. Con. 126: inside cover Aug '50.
coffee bar (Rome). Natl. geog. 111: 472 (col.) Ap '57.
coffee boy, dining room. Holiday 24: 130 Oct '58.
——, hotel. Holiday 23: 17 Ap '58; 24: 137 Sept '58, 34 Dec '58.
——, hotel (comic). Holiday 23: 170 May '58; 24: 123 Aug '58, 137 Nov '58; 25: 146 Jan '59.
——, hotel (serving lady). Holiday 23: 106 Je '58.
——, restaurant (comic). Holiday 24: 20 Jl '58.
coffee cup & saucer. See cup & saucer.
coffee grinder, store (antique). Natl. geog. 112: 306 (col.) Sept '57.
coffee hottles. Holiday 11: 134 Je '52.
coffee maker. Holiday 22: 21 (col.) Oct '57; 24: 12 Dec '58; 28: 13 (col.) Dec '60.
coffee mill (antique). Amer. heri. vol. 6 no. 1 p. 22 (fall '54).
Holiday 20: 81 (col.) Oct '56.
coffee percolater. See percolater, coffee.
coffee pot. Holiday 6: 7 Jl '49, 71 Aug '49; 13: 17 Ap '53; 14: 148 Nov '53; 18: 121 Oct '55; 22: 166, 225 (col.) Dec '57; 24: 217 Dec '58; 25: 160 May '59; 26: 20 Dec '59.
—— (comic). Amer. heri. vol. 8 no. 4 p. 77 (Je '57).
——, Amer. (18th cent.). Con. 133: 265 Je '54; 145: 213 May '60.
——, antique. Amer. heri. vol. 3 no. 4 p. 37 (col.) (summer '52); vol. 8 no. 1 p. 99 (Dec '56).
Con. 136: XIII Sept '55, XLVI Dec '55.
——, antique Hennell. Con. 136: 264 Jan '56.
——, antique porcelain. Con. 133: XL Ap '54.
——, antique silver. Con. 133: XXXVI Ap '54; 135: XLIV Ap '55; 139: XLV May '57; 140: 221 Jan '58; 141: XX Mar '58.
——, antique (on stand). Con. 132: XIX Sept '53.
——, antique silver-gilt. Con. 142: 86 Nov '58.
——, Bateman (18th cent. silver). Con. 142: LXXI Je '59.
——, Chelsea. Con. 140: 258 Jan '58.
——, Dutch. Holiday 10: 132 Oct '51.
——, earthenware (Staffordshire). Con. ency. of ant., vol. 1 p. 49.
——, 18th cent. Con. 133: 265 Je '54; 135: XXXVIII Mar '55.
——, 18th cent. porcelain. Con. 132: 70 Sept '53.
——, 18th cent. silver. Con. ency. of ant., vol. 3 pl. 36.
Con. 132: LX Nov '53; 133: 212 May '54;

139: XXXVIII Mar '57; 142: 56 Sept '58; 143: 16-7 Mar '59, XIII Je '59; 145: XXII Je '60.

coffee pot, electric. Holiday 20: 1 Nov '56; 28: 134 Jl '60, 81 Aug '60, 23 Dec '60.

——, English antique silver. Con. 138: XLV Dec '56.

——, French. Holiday 26: 151 (col.) Nov '59.

——, Furstenberg. Con. 139: 231 Je '57.

——, George I silver. Con. 132: XVII Sept '53; 138: XXXIII Nov '56; 140: XXXVII Sept '57; 144: 43 Sept '59, VII Dec '59, XIII, LXIII Jan '60; 145: 229 Je '60.

——, George II silver. Con. 127: inside cover Mar '51; 129: XVI, LIII, LX Je '52; 132: XXIII, 51 Sept '53, LXI Nov '53; 133: XXXI May '54; 134: 129 Nov '54, 201 Dec '54; 136: III Sept '55, LIII Nov '55, LII Dec '55; 137: XXXVIII, XLVI Mar '56; 138: XXVI, XLII Dec '56; 139: XXVI, 57 Mar '57, XVI Je '57; 140: XLVIII Nov '57, 1 Dec '57; 141: XL, LII Mar '58, 121 Ap '58; 142: XV-XVI, XLIV, LVII Sept '58, XVI Dec '58, 255 Jan '59; 143: 188 May '59, LXI Je '59; 144: LXXIII Jan '60; 145: LVIII May '60, LXII Je '60.

——, George II silver, Queen Anne, George III. Con. 134: XXXIX Nov '54.

——, George III silver. Con. 137: XXXVI May '56; 139: XXXIV Ap '57; 140: XXX Sept '57, XXX Nov '57, XII Dec '57, XII Jan '58; 141: XXVIII Mar '58; 142: XVI Sept '58.

——, George IV silver. Con. 139: LI Je '57.

——, Grundy silver. Con. 144: 58 Sept '59.

——, Irish (antique). Con. 134: VII Sept '54.

——, Italian porcelain. Con. 135: 14, 16 Mar '55.

——, Italian silver. Con. 140: XXIV Nov '57; 144: 156 Dec '59.

——, Lamerie silver. Con. 144: XI Dec '59.

——, Leeds. Con. ency. of ant., vol. 1, pl. 51.

——, Meissen. See Meissen coffee pot.

——, 19th cent. Amer. heri. vol. 2 no. 2 p. 35 (col.) (winter '51).

——, Norwegian silver (18th cent.). Con. 145: LX, 15-6 Mar '60.

——, Penn. folk art. Con. 145: 290 Je '60.

——, porcelain. Holiday 28: 94 Aug '60.

——, Queen Anne silver. Con. 129: III Ap '52; 132: XXIII Jan '54; 134: LIV Sept '54; 145: XLIII Ap '60.

——, Rococo silver (1753). Con. ency. of ant., vol. 1, pl. 85.

——, Russian painted (19th cent.). Con. 144: 274 Jan '60.

——, Sheffield. Con. 141: XXVI Je '58.

——, silver. Con. 144: 129-33 Nov '59. Natl. geog. 99: 129 (col.) Jan '51.

——, silver (modern). Con. 144: 37 Sept '59.

——, Sorensen. Con. 141: 153 May '58.

——, Swedish (18th cent.). Con. 141: 9 Mar '58.

——, Worcester. Con. 141: inside cover Ap '58; 145: XLIV May '60.

——, Worcester porcelain. Con. 144: XXXIX Jan '60.

coffee pot & cup (pouring coffee). Holiday 23: 118 Ap '58, 14 May '58.

coffee roaster. Rawson: Ant. pict. bk., p. 7.

coffee service. Con. 136: LXIV Jan '56; 137: LVII Je '56. Holiday 10: 133 Oct '51; 22: 148 (col.) Oct '57.

——, antique. Con. 132: XIII Sept '53; 136: LXVII Jan '56.

——, antique silver. Con. 129: LIII Ap '52; 132: XIX Sept '53, XLIII Nov '53.

——, Bottger porcelain. Con. 143: 267 Je '59.

——, Danish. Holiday 28: 136 Sept '60.

——, 18th cent. silver. Con. 140: LXIX Nov '57; 141: 43 Mar '58; 143: XVIII Mar '59.

——, George I silver. Con. 140: XLVIII Nov '57.

——, George II silver. Con. 133: XLVIII Ap '54; 138: XXII Sept '56; 140: XL Jan '58.

——, George III silver. Con. 132: XLII Sept '53; 133: XII Ap '54; 139: LVII Je '57; 140: XIX Jan '58; 142: XXXIII Nov '58, LXXI Jan '59; 143: XXII Mar '59; 144: XXIII Sept '59, XXXII Jan '60.

——, George IV Con. 134: XXVII Dec '54.

——, Lisbon silver (18th cent.). Con. 145: XXII Mar '60.

——, Louis XV silver. Con. 143: XXVI Je '59.

——, Meissen. Con. 142: 124 Nov '58.

——, silver (19th cent.). Con. ency. of ant., vol. 1, pl. 88.

——, silver (on stand). Con. 143: 57 Mar '59.

——, 19th. cent. (in box). Con. 143: 223 Je '59.

coffee shop (Austria). Natl. geog. 118: 258 Aug '60.

—— (street tables). Natl. geog. 107: 66-7 (col.) Jan '55.

coffee urn. Holiday 13: 18 May '53.

——, electric. Holiday 28: 186 Oct '60.

——, George III silver gilt. Con. 132: IX Sept '53.

——, Georgian. Con. 138: XXXIV Dec '56.

——, silver (19th cent.). Con. ency. of ant., vol. 1, pl. 88.

coffer, enameled. Con. 140: 175 Dec '57.

——, French (16th cent.). Con. 134: IX Dec '54.

——, Gothic. Con. 136: XXVIII Sept '55.

——, 13th cent. Con. 133: 252 Je '54.

cofferdam (Colo. river). Natl. geog. 116: 627 Nov '59.

coffin, Frank M. Cur. biog. p. 76 (1959).

Coffin, Rev. Henry Sloane. Cur. biog. p. 103 (1944).

coffin, King Ahiram's stone. Natl. geog. 113: 489 Ap '58.

coffin, King Tutankhamen's. See Tutankhamen coffin, King.

coffin, Pres. Warren Harding's. Jensen: The White House, p. 223.

coffin. See also casket.

"Coffin notices" (coal strike). Amer. heri. vol. 11 no. 3 p. 95 (Ap '60).

Coffre, Benoit le (work of). Con. 135: 46 Mar '55.

cog railway. *See* railway engine, cog; train, cog-rail.

Cogdell, John S. Amer. heri. vol. 9 no. 2 p. 56 (col.) (Feb '58).

Coggeshall, George. Amer. heri. vol. 8 no. 6 p. 67, 71, 76, 85 (Oct '57).

cogwheel (sym.). Lehner: Pict. bk. of sym., p. 17.

Cohen, Arthur A. Cur. biog. p. 93 (1960).

Cohen, Barbara. Cur. biog. p. 115 (1957).

Cohen, Benjamin A. Cur. biog. p. 109 (1948).

Cohen, Benjamin V. Cur. biog. p. 158 (1941).

Cohn, Harry. Holiday 5: 38 (col.) Jan '49.

Cohu La Motte T. Cur. biog. p. 123 (1951).

coiffeuse, antique French. Con. 137: VI Je '56.

Coimbra Univ. (Portugal). Holiday 6: 100 Sept '49.

coin, Henry VIII gold sovereign. Con. 138: 262 Jan '57.

———, **oldest found in Palestine (500 B.C.).** Natl. geog. 118: 816 (col.) Dec '60.

———, **peseta (Spain).** Holiday 23: 136 Ap '58.

———, **"Pine tree" shilling.** Amer. heri. vol. 10 no. 6 p. 82 (Oct '59).

———, **Greek (antique).** Con. 126: 141 Oct '50.

coins. Holiday 11: 114 Feb '52; 19: 74 (col.) Je '56; 20: 117 (col.) Oct '56; 25: 144 Jan '59; 27: 144 (col.) May '60.

———, **antique.** Con. 133: 174 May '54; 138: 238-9 Jan '57; 143: 59-61 Mar '59.

———, **British.** Holiday 21: 2 Feb '57.

Coit, Margaret Louise. Cur. biog. p. 125 (1951).

Coit tower (San Francisco). Natl. geog. 105: 738 Je '54; 110: 222 Aug '56.

Coke, Sir Edward. Amer. heri. vol. 8 no. 4 cover, frontis (col.) (Je '57).
Con. 133: 25 Mar '54.

Coker, Elizabeth Boatright. Cur. biog. p. 78 (1959).

Coker, Mrs. James Lide, 3rd. *See* Coker, Elizabeth Boatright.

Colbert, Claudette. Cur. biog. p. 115 (1945).

Colbert, Lester L. Cur. biog. p. 127 (1951).

Coldwell, Michael J. Cur. biog. p. 134 (1943).

Cole, Albert M. Cur. biog. p. 189 (1954).

Cole, David L. Cur. biog. p. 117 (1949).

Cole, John (work of). Con. 144: 191 Dec '59.

Cole, Nat King. Cur. biog. p. 119 (1956).

Cole, Thomas (work of). Amer. heri. vol. 8 no. 6 p. 53-61 (col.) (Oct '57).

Cole, William S. Cur. biog. p. 191 (1954).

Cole, Lt. William S., jr. Natl. geog. 115: 7 (col.) Jan '59.

Cole, William Washington. Durant: Pict. hist. of Amer. circus, p. 155.

"Cole family of Frognal, London" (Downman). Con. 133: 213 May '54.

Coleman, Ann Caroline (Horner). Amer. heri. vol. 7 no. 1 p. 21 (col.) (Dec '55).

Coleman, James P. Cur. biog. p. 121 (1956).

Coleman, John S. Cur. biog. p. 123 (1953).

Coleman, Lonnie. Cur. biog. p. 99 (1958).

Coleman, Ornette. Cur. biog. p. 108: (1961).

Coleman, Peter Tali (Governor of Samoa). Holiday 28: 78 Oct '60.

Coleridge, Samuel Taylor. Con. 144: 8 Sept '59.
Cooper: Con. ency. of music p. 67.

"Coleshill" home (England). Con. 132: 3 Sept '53.

Collette. Holiday 13: 108 Ap '53.

Colfax, Schuyler. Amer. heri. vol. 8 no. 3 p. 52 (Ap '57).

Colina, Rafael de la. Cur. biog. p. 128 (1951).

coliseum, Roman. Natl. geog. 109: 835 Je '56.

collar, antique gold. Con. 141: 24-6 Mar '58.

collector's room. Holiday 19: 64 (col.) Mar '56.

College, Brooklyn. *See* Brooklyn college.

College, Fatima Jinnah. *See* Fatima Jinnah medical college.

College, Georgia state. *See* Georgia state college.

College, Holy Cross. *See* Holy Cross Catholic college.

College, Iowa state. *See* Iowa state college.

College, Kansas state. *See* Kansas state college.

College, Liahona Tonga. *See* Liahona Tonga.

College, N.Y. City. *See* N.Y. (City College).

College, Pakistan. *See* Fatima Jinnah medical college.

College, Penn state. *See* Pennsylvania state college.

College, Robert. *See* Robert college (Turkey).

College, Trinity. *See* Trinity college.

College, Union. *See* Union college.

College, Williams. *See* Williams college.

college boy & girl. Holiday 11: 48, 71 Feb '52.

college boys. Holiday 23: 91-5 (part col.) May '58.

——— **(Phillips Andover).** Natl. geog. 99: 121 (col.) Jan '51.

college boys & girls (Amherst college). Natl. geog. 97: 308 (col.) Mar '50.

college cap (graduation). *See* mortarboard.

college cap & gown. *See* academic cap & gown.

college chapel. Face of Amer., p. 118-9 (col.).

college commencement (Northwestern Univ.). Holiday 13: 56-7 (col.) Mar '53.

college fraternity initiations. *See* fraternity house (Initiations).

college girls. *See* girls, college.

———, **Skidmore.** *See* Skidmore college girls.

college graduate (Hawaii). Natl. geog. 118: 17 (col.) Jl '60.

college graduates. Face of Amer., p. 119 (col.).

college men (singing). Holiday 23: 95 May '58.

college professor (cap & gown). Holiday 10: 92 (col.) Dec '51.

——— *See* also university professor.

college sports. *See* sports, college.

college students *See* students, college.

colleges. Travel. 110: cover (col.), 14-7 Oct '58.

———, **Ivy league.** Holiday 18: 35-43 (part col.) Nov '55.

colleges. *See* also university.

Colleoni, Bartolommeo (statue, Venice). Con. 143: XVII Je '59.
Int. gr. soc.: Arts . . . p. 87 (col.).
Natl. geog. 101: 780 (col.) Je '52.
Praeg. pict. ency., p. 257.

——— **(Richter).** Con. 144: XLIII Jan '60.

Collet, John C. Cur. biog. p. 125 (1946).

Collier, Constance. Cur. biog. p. 191 (1954).

Collier, John. Cur. biog. p. 160 (1941).
Colliery, Huber. Natl. geog. 98: 93 (col.) Jl '50.
Collingwood, Charles. Cur. biog. p. 137 (1943).
Collins, Eddie. Amer. heri. vol. 10 no. 3 p. 23 (Ap '59).
Collins, Hugh (work of). Con. 132: XVIII Nov '53.
Collins, James. Cur. biog. (1963).
Collins, Gen. Joseph Lawton. Cur. biog. p. 119 (1949).
Collins, Leroy. Cur. biog. p. 123 (1956).
Collins, Seaborn P. Cur. biog. p. 133 (1955).
Collins, William (work of). Con. 133: XLVII Je '54; 138: XXVI Jan '57; 145: 114 Ap '60.
Collyer, John L. Cur. biog. p. 126 (1947).
Colman, Ronald. Cur. biog. p. 139 (1943).
Cologne (Ger.). Holiday 25: 58 (col.) May '59.
—— (Heyden). Con. 142: XXII (col.) Nov '58.
Cologne cathedral (Eng.). Amer. heri. vol. 7 no. 1 p. 9 (Dec '55).
Con. 141: 117 Ap '58.
Holiday 23: 45 Jan '58; 25: 58-9 (col.) May '59.
Cologne theater. Cooper: Con. ency. of music, p. 453.
Colombe, Jean. Con. 134: 35-8 Sept '54.
Colombia (Bogota). Holiday 20: 76-7 (col.) Nov '56.
Natl. geog. 102: 370-83 (part col.) Sept '52.
Travel 105: 41 Mar '56; 109: 32 Mar '58.
—— (S. Amer., natives). Travel 113: 58 Feb '60.
—— (salt mine cathedral). Travel 108: 29-31 Oct '57.
Colombia (Cartagena). See Cartagena.
Colombia (man on horse). Holiday 20: 54 (col.) Nov '56.
Colombo (Ceylon, Buddha). Travel 111: 22 Jan '59.
colon (lymphatic system). Gray's anatomy, p. 720.
Colonel, Ky. See Ky. Colonel.
colonial architecture. See architecture, colonial.
colonial costume. See costume (colonial).
colonial houses. See homes, colonial.
colonial man (on horse). Holiday 13: 149 Mar '53.
colonial men & Negro butler. Holiday 28: 55 (col.) Dec '60.
colonial natl. historical park (Jamestown). Natl. geog. 111: 582-620 (part col.) May '57.
colonnade (Palmyra). Travel 105: 20 Jan '56.
——, Bernini's (Vatican). Holiday 11: 37 Ap '52.
"The Colony" restaurant (N.Y.). Holiday 24: 71 Aug '58.
color guard, Valley Forge military academy. Natl. geog. 105: 200 (col.) Feb '54.
Colorado. Holiday 12: 34-51 (part col.) Sept '52; 16: 46 Jl '54.
Jordan: Hammond's pict. atlas, p. 162-5 (col.).
Natl. geog. 100: 188-214 Aug '51; 106: 206-48 (part col.) Aug '54.
Travel 104: 9-13 Oct '55; 112: 34-7 Sept '59; 113: 26-7 Mar '60.

—— (Denver, a mining camp). Brooks: Growth of a nation, p. 177.
—— (ghost town). Travel 114: 45 Sept '60.
—— (hotel). Holiday 10: 146 Oct '51, 77 Nov '51; 12: 26 Nov '52.
—— (lodges, Grand Mesa). Travel 113: 26 Mar '60.
—— (lost city). Travel 105: 60-2 Jan '56.
—— (mts. & lake). Face of Amer., p. 92-3 (col.).
—— (state capitol bldg.). See capitol bldg, Colorado state.
Colorado river. Holiday 16: 90-5 (part col.) Aug '54.
Jordan: Hammond's pict. atlas, p. 182 (col.).
Natl. geog. 111: 548-9 (col.) Ap '57.
Colorado springs. Holiday 23: 104 May '58.
Jordan: Hammond's pict. atlas, p. 164-5 (col.).
Natl. geog. 100: 203 Aug '51; 115: 864-5 (col.) Je '59.
—— (hotel). Holiday 18: 38 Dec '55; 26: 56 (col.) Jl '59.
colosseum, Roman. See Roman colosseum.
Colossus, Banian's. See Buddha, Banian.
Colossus of Memnon. Ceram: March of arch., p. 80.
Holiday 25: 144 Ap '59; 27: 63 (col.) Mar '60.
Natl. geog. 106: 768 (col.) Dec '54; 107: 727 May '55; 118: 304 (col.) Sept '60.
Colossus of Rameses II. Natl. geog. 106: 756 (col.) Dec '54; 108: 634, 639 (col.) Nov '55.
Colt gun factory. See gun factory, Colt.
Colum, Padraic. Jun. bk. of auth., p. 77.
Columbia (S. Amer.). Travel 113: 58 Feb '60.
"Columbia leads allied troops" (mosaic). Natl. geog. 111: 765 (col.) Je '57.
Columbia river. Holiday 5: 34-49 (col.) Je '49; 11: 74 (col.) May '52.
Natl. geog. 102: 579-610 (part col.) Nov '52.
Travel 102: 14 Oct '54.
Columbia river gorge (Oregon). Holiday 11: 15 (col.) Mar '52; 13: 42-3 (col.) Je '53; 14: 109 (col.) Sept '53; 21: 105 (col.) Feb '57.
Natl. geog. 103: 74-5 (col.) Je '53.
Travel 101: 8 Ap '54.
Columbia univ. Travel 101: 21 Ap '54.
—— (aerial view). Amer. heri. vol. 5 no. 1 p. 17 (fall '53).
Columbian exposition (Chicago 1893). Amer. heri. vol. 6 no. 2 p. 25 (winter '55).
Brooks: Growth of a nation, p. 222.
Columbus, Christopher. Amer. heri. vol. 7 no. 1 p. 73 (Dec '55).
Holiday 12: 75 (col.) Oct '52, 166 (col.) Dec '52.
Natl. geog. 102: 184 (col.) Aug '52.
—— (antique bust). Natl. geog. 111: 325 Mar '57.
—— (head). Holiday 13: 12 Feb '53.
—— (Tallyrand Columbus, by Sebastiano del Piombo). Amer. heri. vol. 6 no. 6 frontis (col.) (Oct '55).
"The Columbus" (ship, 1798). Amer. heri. vol. 11 no. 2 p. 28 (Feb '60).

"Columbus at Spanish Court" (theater play). Amer. heri. vol. 1 no. 3 p. 61 (spring '50).
Columbus coat of arms. Amer. heri. vol. 7 no. 1 p. 94 (Dec '55).
Columbus day (sym.). Lehner: Pict. bk. of sym., p. 52.
Columbus discovers a new world. Brooks: Growth of a nation, p. 28.
Columbus expeditions announcement (1659). Amer. heri. vol. 10 no. 5 p. 108 (Aug '59).
Columbus memorial (Santander, Spain). Natl. geog. 108: 68 (col.) Jl '55.
Columbus signature, Christopher. Amer. heri. vol. 7 no. 1 p. 93 (Dec '55).
column (sym.). Lehner: Pict. bk. of sym., p. 60.
——, broken (sym.). Lehner: Pict. bk. of sym., p. 79.
——, Byzantine. Int. gr. soc.: Arts . . . p. 45 (col.).
——, Ionic. Int. gr. soc.: Arts . . . title p. (col.).
——, Karnak temple. Int. gr. soc.: Arts . . . p. 11 (col.).
——, Marcus Aurelius. Natl. geog. 108: 146 Jl '55 .
——, Mexican stone (ancient). Int. gr. soc.: Arts . . . p. 11 (col.).
——, rostral (sym.). Lehner: Pict. bk. of sym., p. 87.
columns, Agora (ancient). Osward: Asia Minor, pl. 100.
——, castle gate. Holiday 12: 46 (col.) Oct '52.
——, classic. Int. gr. soc.: Arts . . . p. 17 (col.).
——, Corinthian. Osward: Asia Minor. pl. 126-7.
——, Doric porch. Natl. geog. 118: 187 (col.) Aug '60.
——, foyer (colonial). Natl. geog. 118: 177 (col.) Aug '60.
——, Greek classic. Amer. heri. vol. 10 no. 5 p. 65 (Aug '59).
Natl. geog. 105: 295 (col.) Mar '54.
Praeg. pict. ency., p. 76.
——, Harlequin. See Harlequin columns.
——, Ionic Holiday 18: 76 Jl '55; 22: 108 Sept '57; 25: 59 (col.) Je '59.
Int. gr. soc.: Arts . . . p. 17 (col.).
——, Luxor temple. Natl. geog. 106: 761 (col.) Dec '54.
——, porch. Holiday 27: 59 (col.) Mar '60.
Natl. geog. 105: 295 (col.) Mar '54; 118: 187 (col.) Aug '60.
——, Roman basilica. Natl. geog. 109: 841 (col.) Je '56.
——, stone (Persia). Travels 113: 34 Feb '60.
columns. See also pillars.
Colvin, Mrs. David Leigh. Cur. biog. p. 105 (1944).
Colwell, Eileen. Cur. biog. (1963).
combat transport plane. See airplane, combat transport.
combine (Canadian farm). Natl. geog. 108: 222 (col.) Aug '55.
——, grain. Natl. geog. 97: 698 Je '50; 114: 649 Nov '58.

——, grain (Russia). Natl. geog. 116: 393 (col.) Sept '59.
——, rice (man). Natl. geog. 113: 554 (col.) Ap '58.
——, wheat. Natl. geog. 100: 292-3 (col.) Sept '51.
Combs, Bertram T. Cur. biog. p. 94 (1960).
Combs, Mrs. Loula Long. Holiday 14: 108 Nov '53.
Comden, Betty. Cur. biog. p. 117 (1945).
comedy (goddess of). Lehner: Pict. bk. of sym., p. 33.
comet. Natl. geog. 112: 816 Dec '57.
—— (Sym.). Lehner: Pict. bk. of sym., p. 10. 20.
comic books (illus.). Amer. heri. vol. 10 no. 6 p. 101 (Oct '59).
comic characters. Holiday 23: 135 Je '58.
comic characters. See also Eloise.
comics. See also man (comic).
"Coming of age", Indian. See Indian girls coming of age.
Comiskey, Charles A. Amer. heri. vol. 11 no. 4 p. 27 (Je '60).
Commager, Henry Steele. Cur. biog. p. 127 (1946).
commencement (sym.). Lehner: Pict. bk. of sym., p. 85.
——, Robert College. Natl. geog. 112: 408 Sept '57.
commerce (god of). Lehner: Pict. bk. of sym., p. 30.
Commissioner of Agri., 1st (1862). Brooks: Growth of a nation, p. 198.
commode. Natl. geog. 110: 453 (col.) Oct '56.
commode, Adam. Con. 132: XXVII Nov '53; 137: XXXVI Ap '56; 139: XIII Mar '57; 140: XIX Sept '57.
——, Adam half round. Con. 144: XXXI Nov '59.
——, Adam-Hepplewhite. Con. 135: 129 Ap '55; 137: 1 Je '56; 144: 266 Jan '60.
——, antique. Con. 133: 238-9 Je '54; 134: XXV Sept '54, XLI Dec '54; 135: XXXII Mar '55; 140: LVII Jan '58; 141: XLVI Mar '58.
——, antique satinwood. Con. 140: 112 Nov '57.
——, bombe ormulo (18th cent.). Con. ency. of ant., vol. 3 pl. 17.
——, bombe shape. Con. 139: 18-9 Mar '57.
——, bombe shape (18th cent.). Con. 138: XXIV Jan '57; 140: 129 Nov '57.
——, Chippendale. Con. 129: XLV Je '52; 132: 1 Jan '54; 133: 202 May '54; 134: III Sept '54; 136: 45 Sept '55; 136: XXVII, XXXIV Dec '55; 137: 108 Ap '56; 138: XLIII Nov '56; 139: XXXVII Mar '57, 274 Je '57; 140: XXIV Sept '57, XXIV Nov '57, 183 Dec '57; 141: XV, LI Mar '58; 144: 136 Nov '59.
——, Chippendale (18th cent.). Con. 145: XIV Ap '60.
——, Chippendale serpentine front. Con. ency. of ant., vol. 1, pl. 30.
Con. 134: XXII Dec '54; 143: LII Mar '59.
——, 18th cent. Con. 132: XXI Sept '53, 124

Nov '53; 133: XIV Mar '54, 175 May '54; 134: XXXVIII, 43 Sept '54; 135: XXXV Ap '55; 136: 56 Sept '55, back cover Nov '55; 137: LI Je '56; 139: 17- 20, 54 Mar '57; 140: XXVI Dec '57, 260 Jan '58; 141: XXIX Mar '58, 73 Ap '58; 142: XVI, XXXVII Nov '58; 143: 105 Ap '59.

——, **English lacquer.** Con. 134: XXXI Dec '54.

——, **French antique.** Con. 133: LIX Je '54.

——, **French regency.** Con. 136: 84 Nov '55.

——, **French style.** Con. 143: 257-9 Je '59.

——, **George II.** Con. 129: 117 Je '52; 140: LIII Jan '58.

——, **German.** Con. 140: 180 Dec '57.

——, **Hepplewhite.** Con. 137: X Ap '56; 139: XXIX Mar '57, 123 Ap '57, LXIX May '57.

——, **Hepplewhite dining room.** Con. 143: XLIII Mar '59.

——, **Hepplewhite serpentine.** Con. 140: XX-XVI Sept '57; 142: LVIII Jan '59; 144: XX-XII Jan '60.

——, **inlaid (18th cent.).** Con. 143: XXXII May '59.

——, **inlaid (Norwegian, 18th cent.).** Con. 145: 25 Mar '60.

——, **Italian.** Con. 135: 23, 25-6 Mar '55; 144: XXXIV Dec '59.

——, **Italian (18th cent.).** Con. 135: 145 Ap '55; 143: XVI Ap '59.

——, **lacquer (antique black).** Con. 133: 259 Je '54.

——, **lacquer (18th cent.).** Con. 140: 69 Sept '57; 145: 109 Ap '60.

——, **Louis VII.** Con. 141: XXVII Ap '58.

——, **Louis XIV.** Con. 138: LXII Jan '57.

——, **Louis XV.** Con. 132: I Nov '53; 133: 265 Je '54; 134: I, 120 Nov '54; 135: LIX May '55; 136: XII, 82-3 Nov '55; 137; 54 Mar '56, 126 Ap '56, XXXVIII Je '56; 139: 262 Je '57; 140: I, 56-7, 60 Sept '57; 141: LX, 187 May '58; 142: 141, 195 Dec '58; 143: 55 Mar '59, 139 May '59, LXIX Je '59; 144: LXII Jan '60. Int. gr. soc.; Arts . . . p. 103 (col.).

——, **Louis XV (lacquer).** Con. 140: 56 Sept '57; 144: 65 Sept '59.

——, **Louis XV (lacquer, serpentine).** Con. 145: 55 Mar '60.

——, **Louis XV (marble top).** Con. 141: 249 Je '58.

——, **Louis XV (marquetry).** Con. 142: XXIX Nov '58.

——, **Louis XV (marquetry, 18th cent.).** Con. 135: 267 Je '55.

——, **Louis XV (ormolu).** Con. 133: 274 Je '54; 143: XXV Ap '59.

——, **Louis XVI.** Con. 134: 50, 60 Sept '54; 136: 147 Nov '55.

——, **Regency.** Con. 138: 127 Nov '56; 139: 110 Ap '57, 193 May '57; 142: inside back cover Dec '58; 143: 192 May '59; 144: 266 Jan '60.

——, **Riesener.** Con. 140: 56 Sept '57.

——, **Roussel.** Con. 144: XLIV Dec '59; 145: XLIX Ap '60.

——, **secretaire.** See secretaire commode.

——, **serpentine.** Con. 139: XXXII Je '57; 143: 80 Ap '59.

——, **serpentine (18th cent.).** Con. 132: LXIX Jan '54.

——, **Sheraton.** Con. 133: XXXV May '54; 134: inside back cover Sept '54; 136: XIV Nov '55; 138: XLVI Nov '56, XVI Jan '57; 140: XXII Nov '57, I, XLVII Jan '58.

——, **Sheraton (semi-circular).** Con. 145: XXX Je '60.

——, **Sheraton (semi-elliptical).** Con. 143: XIX Je '59.

——, **Sheraton (serpentine).** Con. 132: inside back cover Jan '54.

——, **ship's.** Con. 144: XXIV Jan '60.

——, **Viennese.** Con. 135: 187 May '55.

——, **Viennese (Josef II).** Con. ency. of ant., vol. 3, pl. 19.

commode chest, Sheraton. Con. 144: 43 Sept '59.

commode top, Florentine. Con. 142: XXXVIII Jan '59.

"Commodore Perry carrying 'Gospel of God' to heathens" (Evans). Natl. geog. 99: 195 (col.) Feb '51.

"The Commonwealth" (river boat). Amer. heri. vol. 6 no. 1 p. 14 (fall '54).

Communications service, air. Natl. geog. 111: 302 (col.) Mar '57.

communism (sym.). Lehner: Pict. bk. of sym., p. 94.

Como, Perry. Cur. biog. p. 129 (1947).

Como, Lake. See Lake Como.

compacts. Holiday 10: 29 (col.) Dec '51.

compass. Holiday 6: 88-9 Aug '49; 10: 36 Nov '51.

—— **(sym.)** Lehner: Pict. bk. of sym., p. 11.

——, **antique school.** Rawson: Ant. pict. bk., p. 19.

——, **geomancer's.** See geomancer's compass.

——, **Manjiro's.** Amer. heri. vol. 8 no. I p. 92 (Dec '56).

——, **mariner's.** Amer. heri. vol. 11 no. 5 p. 58 (Aug '60). Natl. geog. 116: 486 (col.) Oct '59.

compendium (19th cent.). Con. ency. of ant., vol. 3, pl. 119.

"Compleat angler" (page from the). Con. 144: 196 Dec '59.

composers, music. Int. gr. soc.: Arts . . . p. 139 (col.).

compote, glass. Daniel: Cut & engraved glass, pl. 72.

Compton, Arthur H. Cur. biog. p. 100 (1958).

Compton, Gen. Hatton (miniature). Con. 143: XXIV May '59.

Compton, Karl T. Cur. biog. p. 162 (1941).

Compton, Wilson. Cur. biog. p. 115 (1952).

"Compton Wynyates" (house in England). Holiday 15: 28 (col.) Je '54.

Comstock, Henry. Amer. heri. vol. 10 no. 3 p. 39 (col.) (Ap '59).

Comstock lode (mine). Amer. heri. vol. 10 no. 3 p. 39-42 (part col.) (Ap '59).

Conant, James Bryant. Cur. biog. p. 163 (1941); p. 130 (1951).

Conant, Pioneer Roger (statue). Holiday 15: 108 Mar '54.

Concarneau, Brittany (France). Holiday 7: 98-103 (col.) Jan '50.

conceit (god of). Lehner: Pict. bk. of sym., p. 31.

Concello, Art. Durant: Pict. hist. of Amer. circus, p. 307.

concert, Vienna See Vienna concert.

concert chamber (men & women, musicians). Int. gr. soc.: Arts., p. 109 (col.).

"Concert Champetre". Praeg. pict. ency., p. 299 (col.).

concert director. Holiday 19: 10 (col.) Jan '56.

concert hall. See music hall.

concert shell (Cal.). Holiday 27: 175 (col.) Ap '60.

——, jade. Con. 138: 194 Dec '56.

Concheso, Aurelio F. Cur. biog. p. 159 (1942).

Concordia tin mines. Horan: Pict. hist. of wild west, p. 233-4.

concourse, Pentagon (int.). Natl. geog. 103: 15 (col.) Jan '53.

Conde (bust). Int. gr. soc.: Arts . . . p. 87 (col.).

"Conde Duque Olivarez on horse" (Velazquez). Con. 140: 238 Jan '58.

conditions (sym.). Lehner: Pict. bk. of sym., p. 82-3.

Condon, Eddie. Cur. biog. p. 107 (1944).

Condon, Edward U. Cur. biog. p. 128 (1946).

conductor, train. See train conductor.

cone, nose. See nose cone, missile.

Conegliano, Cima da (work of). Natl. geog. 110: 630 (col.) Nov '56.

Conerly, Charles. Cur. biog. p. 96 (1960).

cones, rock (Cappadocia). Natl. geog. 113: 122-9, 134-5 Jan '58.

Conestoga wagon. See wagon, Conestoga.

Coney island. Holiday 18: 46-7 Sept '55.

—— (show posters). Amer. heri. vol. 9 no. 4 p. 15 (col.), 93-4 (Je '58).

Confederate capitol (Richmond). Amer. heri. vol. 6 no. 3 p. 39 (Ap '55).

Confederate monument (Charleston, S.C.). Holiday 16: 44 Oct '54.

Confederate soldier (return home). Brooks: Growth of a nation, p. 148.

—— See also costume, Confederate soldier.

Confederate submarine torpedo boat (Chapman). Natl. geog. 99: 199 (col.) Feb '51.

Confederate White House (Richmond). Holiday 12: 62 Sept '52; 13: 19 Mar '53.

conference, peace. See Dumbarton Oakes.

confession, Catholic girl at. Holiday 19: 33 Jan '56.

confessional, Catholic outdoor (Poland). Natl. geog. 114: 373 (col.) Sept '58.

configuration of the planets. See planets, configuration of the.

conflagration square (sym.). Lehner: Pict. bk. of sym., p. 70.

Congo, Belgian. See Belgian Congo.

Congo, French. See French Congo.

Congo dancer. Travel 104: 49 Nov '55.

Congo mask. Int. gr. soc.: Arts . . . p. 185 (col.).

Congo river. Holiday 25: 56-7 Ap '59.

Congress Hall (int., Phila.). Travel 110: 30 Jl '58.

"Congress of Vienna" (Isabey). Amer. heri. vol. 6 no. 6 p. 8-9 (Oct '55).

"Congress voting independence" (1794). Amer. heri. vol. 2 no. 2 p. 28 (winter '51). Con. ency. of ant., vol. 3, pl. 91.

congressmen, U.S. Natl. geog. 102: 145, 162-3 (col.) Aug '52.

Coningham, Air Marshall Sir Arthur. Cur. biog. p. 109 (1944).

"The Conjuror" (Lonza). Con. 133: XXIX Mar '54.

Conkling, Roscoe. Amer. heri. vol. 8 no. 3 p. 52 (Ap '57).

Conley, Eugene. Cur. biog. p. 197 (1954).

Conn, Billy. Cur. biog. p. 166 (1941).

Connally, John B. Cur. biog. p. 110 (1961).

Connally, Thomas T. Cur. biog. p. 167 (1941).

Connally, Tom. Cur. biog. p. 121 (1949).

Connecticut. Holiday 26: 34-47 (part col.) Sept '59; 27: 82-7 (col.) Feb '60.

—— (state parks). Travel 108: 32 Aug '57.

Connecticut general life ins. co. bldg. Holiday 26: 40 Sept '59.

Connecticut Governor's foot guard. Holiday 26: 36 (col.) Sept '59.

Connecticut homes, Colonial. Holiday 8: 41 (col.) Jl '50.

——, modern. Holiday 12: 48-53 (col.) Aug '52.

Connecticut Valley. Holiday 8: 38-43 (part col.) Jl '50.

Connell, Arthur J. Cur. biog. p. 199 (1954).

Connell, Maurice. Amer. heri. vol. 11 no. 4 p. 50 (Je '60).

Connell, Pat. Horan: Pict. hist. of wild west, p. 36.

Connemara (pageant). Amer. heri. vol. 9 no. 5 p. 26 (col.) (Aug '58).

Conner, Nadine. Cur. biog. p. 135 (1955).

Connolly, Cyril. Cur. biog. p. 130 (1947).

Connolly, Maureen. Cur. biog. p. 133 (1951).

Connor, John T. Cur. biog. p. 112 (1961).

Conover, Harry. Cur. biog. p. 123 (1949).

Conrad, Barnaby, jr. Cur. biog. p. 79 (1959).

Conrad, Noel. Cur. biog. p. 90 (1962).

Conroy, Pat. Cur. biog. p. 201 (1954).

Consagra, Pietro. Holiday 27: 108 (col.) Ap '60.

conscience (sym.). Lehner: Pict. bk. of sym., p. 26.

Conservatory, Bath Stone. Con. 138: XXXVIII Sept '56.

Considine, Bob. Holiday 13: 17 Mar '53.

Considine, Robert B. Cur. biog. p. 131 (1947).

console table. See table, console.

Constable, John (work of). Con. ency. of ant., vol. 1, pl. 134.
  Con. 127: 71-5 May '51; 129: 3-8, 24 Ap '52; 132: 19 (col.) Sept '53; 133: LI, 119 Ap '54; 134: 78-84, 138 (part col.) Nov '54; 135: 220 Je '55; 137: XVIII, 251-2, 254, 259-62, 283-4 Je '56; 138: XXX Nov '56, 249 Jan '57; 139: 56 Mar '57; 140: LVI Sept '57; 142: cover (col.), 37 Sept '58, 82

Nov '58, XVIII (col.) Jan '59; 143: XVII
(col.) May '59; 144: 35, 45 (col.) Sept '59,
XXVII Nov '59; 145: 278 Je '60.
Praeg. pict. ency., p. 378 (col.).
Constantine (barbwire fence). Natl. geog. 117:
775 (col.) Je '60.
——, **Arch of.** See Arch of Constantine.
"Constantinople from the sea of Marmora"
(R.S.). Con. 139: 121 Ap '57.
Constantinople. See also Istanbul.
constellation, Andromeda. See Andromeda con-
stellation.
"Constellation" ship (in storm). Amer. heri.,
vol. 7 no. 2 p. 18 (col.) (Feb '56).
"The Constitution" (battle ship-front). Natl.
geog. 107: 747 (col.) Je '55.
Constitution, U.S. frigate. See U.S. frigate Constitution.
"The Constitution" ship. Con. 129: 140 Je '52.
—— **(1804).** Amer. heri. vol. 10 no. 2 p. 27
(Feb '59).
—— **(1812).** Amer. heri. vol. 7 no. 3 p. 13-4
(col.) (Ap '56).
Constitutional convention (Phila., 1787). Natl.
geog. 102: 158 (col.) Aug '52.
containers (ancient crafts). Int. gr. soc.: Arts . . .
p. 19, 95, 177 (part col.).
Conti, Tito (work of). Con. 135: XLIV Mar
'55.
contortionist, circus. Durant: Pict. hist. of Amer.
circus, p. 243.
contour chair. See chair, contour.
contra-bassoon. See bassoon, contra.
convent (Cuba). Holiday 22: 72 (col.) Dec '57.
—— **(Vlacherna island).** Holiday 24: 70 Sept
'58.
convention, Democratic. See Democratic convention.
"Conversion of an Arian" (St. Remy). Natl.
geog. 101: 91 (col.) Jan '52.
"Conversion of Saint Paul" (Tintoretto). Natl.
geog. 110: 620-1 (col.) Nov '56.
conveyor belt, olive (girl inspectors). Natl.
geog. 100: 329 Sept '51.
convicts (escaping from jail). Horan: Pict. hist.
of wild west, p. 173.
convoy ship. Amer. heri. vol. 10 no. 6 p. 10
(Oct '59).
Conway, John (work of). Con. 142: IV Dec '58.
Conway, Sir Thomas (Flemish art). Con. 126:
164 Dec '50.
Conway (Wales, night). Holiday 28: 40-1 (col.)
Sept '60.
Conway castle (Wales). Holiday 15: 89 May
'54.
Conyngham, Capt. Gustavus. Amer. heri. vol.
7 no. 3 p. 82 (Ap '56).
Coogan, Jackie. Holiday 11: 54 Je '52.
Cook, Barbara. Cur. biog. (1963).
Cook, Bill ("Cherokee Bill"). Horan: Pict. hist.
of wild west, p. 146-8.
Cook, Capt. (boat, Tonga island). Holiday 28:
148 Oct '60.
Cook, Donald. Cur. biog. p. 203 (1954).
Cook, Donald C. Cur. biog. p. 117 (1952).
Cook, Fannie. Cur. biog. p. 130 (1946).

Cook, Lemuel. Amer. heri. vol. 9 no. 3 p. 33
(Ap '58).
cook (man, outdoor). Holiday 18: 1 Jl '55.
—— **(outdoor grill).** Holiday 20: 69 Aug '56.
—— **(sym.).** Lehner: Pict. bk. of sym., p. 90.
——, **Mexican sidewalk.** Natl. geog. 103: 343
(col.) Mar '53.
——, **Negro.** See Negro cook.
Cook islands. Travel 102: 36-7 Nov '54.
"A cook maid" (Metsu). Con. 137: 274 Je '56.
Cook marker, Capt. James' (Hawaii). Natl.
geog. 118: 33 Jl '60.
"cook-out", western. Travel 114: 30 Sept '60.
Cooke, Alistair. Cur. biog. p. 118 (1952).
Cooke, George (work of). Con. ency. of ant.,
vol. 3, pl. 94.
Cooke, Jay. Amer. heri. vol. 8 no. 3 p. 52 (Ap
'57).
Cooke, Leslie E. Cur. biog. pp.. 88 (1962).
Cooke, Morris Llewellyn. Cur. biog. p. 95
(1950).
cookhouse. Holiday 10: 108 Aug '51.
cookie cutter (antique). Rawson: Ant. pict. bk.,
p. 7.
cookie cutters. Amer. heri. vol. 5 no. 2 p. 20-5
(winter '53-4).
cookies, Christmas. Natl. geog. 108: 845-50
(col.) Dec '55.
cooking outdoors (man). Natl. geog. 99: 127
(col.) Jan '51.
cooking oven, beehive (yard). Amer. heri. vol.
4 no. 1 p. 10 (fall '52).
——, **rock.** Natl. geog. 112: 743 (col.) Dec '57.
cooking pots (on woman's head). Natl. geog.
99: 25 (col.) Jan '51.
cooking utensils (antique). Amer. heri. vol. 8 no.
1 p. 99 (Dec '56).
cooking vessel, Chinese bronze (antique). Con.
126: 50 Aug '50.
cooking ware. Holiday 26: 182 (col.) Dec '59.
cooks (comic). Holiday 18: 67 Aug '55.
—— **(prepare food).** Natl. geog. 98: 395 (col.)
Sept '50.
Cookworthy, William. Con. 134: 193 Dec '54.
cooler, wine-glass. Con. ency. of ant., vol. 1,
p. 83.
Cooley, Harold D. Cur. biog. p. 135 (1951).
Coolidge, U.S. Pres. Calvin. Amer. heri. vol. 6
no. 2 p. 67-8 (winter '55); vol. 6 no. 5 p.
54 (Aug '55); vol. 7 no. 3 p. 33, 47 (Ap
'56); vol. 7 no. 4 p. 26 (Je '56); vol. 9 no.
5 p. 31 (Aug '58).
Jensen: The White House, p. 224-6, 228.
Natl. geog. 112: 39 Jl '57.
—— **(cartoon).** Amer. heri. vol. 6 no. 2 p. 76
(winter '55).
—— **(presents medal to R.E. Byrd).** Natl. geog.
106: 65H Jl '54.
Coolidge, Mrs. Calvin. Amer. heri. vol. 6 no. 2
p. 67 (winter '55).
Jensen: The White House, p. 225, 228.
Coolidge, Elizabeth Sprague. Cur. biog. p. 169
(1941).
Coolidge, William D. Cur. biog. p. 133 (1947).
Coolidge family, U.S. Pres. Calvin. Jensen: The
White House, p. 225, 228.

coolies, Chinese (carrying produce). Natl. geog. 111: 358, 361 (col.) Mar '57.
——, Siam. Disney: People & places, p. 173 (col.).
Coombs, Elder M. Vernon (Mormon missionary). Holiday 28: 67 Oct '60.
Coon, Carleton S. Cur. biog. p. 137 (1955).
Cooney, Mrs. M. A. Amer. heri. vol. 10 no. 2 p. 38 (Feb '59).
Coons, Albert H. Cur. biog. p. 98 (1960).
Cooper, Abraham (work of). Con. 141: 20 Mar '58; 142: XLII Dec '58.
Cooper, Anthony Ashley. Amer. heri. vol. 4 no. 2 p. 56 (winter '53).
Cooper, Daniel (statue by Saint Gaudens). Amer. heri. vol. 10 no. 2 p. 11 (Feb '59).
Cooper, Gary. Cur. biog. p. 171 (1941).
Cooper, Gladys. Cur. biog. p. 125 (1956).
Cooper, John Sherman. Cur. biog. p. 98 (1950).
Cooper, Joseph D. Cur. biog. p. 120 (1952).
Cooper, Kent. Cur. biog. p. 111 (1944).
Cooper, Leon Jere. Cur. biog. p. 139 (1955).
Cooper, Louise Field. Cur. biog. p. 100 (1950).
Cooper, Peter (Calyo). Amer. heri. vol. 10 no. 2 p. 4 (col.) (Feb '59).
—— (political poster). Amer. heri. vol. 10 no. 2 p. 107 (Feb '59).
Cooper, R. Conrad. Cur. biog. p. 99 (1960).
Cooper, Samuel (work of). Con. ency. of ant., vol. 1, pl. 130.
Con. 138: 82 Nov '56; 142: IV Dec '58.
cooper home, Fenimore. Amer. heri. vol. 3 no. 3 p. 32 (spring '52).
cooperage tools. Rawson: Ant. pict. bk., p. 61.
Cooper's "Tom Thumb" locomotive. See "Tom Thumb" locomotive.
Cooper's union (1859). Amer. heri. vol. 10 no. 2 p. 8 (Feb '59).
Cooperstown (N.Y.). Amer. heri. vol. 3 no. 3 p. 32-41 (part col.) (spring '52).
—— (1885). Amer. heri. vol. 10 no. 1 p. 81-95 (Dec '58).
Copacabana (Rio, Brazil). Travel 112: cover (col.) Sept '59.
—— (beach). Holiday 8: 13 (col.) Nov '50.
Copacabana (Titicaca). Natl. geog. 98: 494 (col.) Oct '50.
Copan (jungle city, Honduras). Travel 104: 34 Sept '55.
—— (sculptured pillars). Ceram: March of arch., p. 281.
Cope, Austrian (18th cent.). Con. 142: 7 Sept '58.
Copeland, Lammot Du Pont. Cur. biog. (1963).
Copenhagen. Natl. geog. 101: 695 May '52. Travel 102: 34 Oct '54.
—— (city map). Travel 111: 45 Ap '59.
—— (harbor). Natl. geog. 98: 622 Nov '50; 100: 709 Dec '51.
—— (hotel Imperial). Travel 109: 41 Ap '58.
—— (Royal hotel). Travel 113: 58 Ap '60.
—— (stock exchange). Praeg. pict. ency., p. 316.
Copland, Aaron. Cooper: Con. ency. of ant., p. 68.
Cur. biog. p. 137 (1951).

Copley, John Singleton (work of). Amer. heri. vol. 6 no. 2 p. 39 (col.) (winter '55); vol. 9 no. 2 p. 54 (col.) (Feb '58).
Con. 126: 54 Aug '50; 135: 147 Ap '55; 140: XVII (col.) Jan '58; 141: 269 Je '58.
Natl. geog. 99: 184 (col.) Feb '51.
copper (sym.). Lehner: Pict. bk. of sym., p. 72.
——, molton. Natl. geog. 117: 228 (col.) Feb '60.
copper mill. See Kennecott copper mill.
copper mine. Brooks: Growth of a nation, p. 304.
Holiday 8: 46-8 (col.) Sept '50.
Natl. geog. 104: 378-9 (col.) Sept '53.
—— (Africa, night). Natl. geog. 118: 318-9 Sept '60.
—— (blast). Natl. geog. 117: 228 (col.) Feb '60.
copper sulphate (run from vats). Natl. geog. 117: 229 (col.) Feb '60.
copper urn, Egyptian. Holiday 18: 9 Sept '55, 63 Nov '55.
Coppers, George H. Cur. biog. p. 121 (1952).
coppersmith shop (Pakistan). Natl. geog. 102: 669 (col.) Nov '52.
Coppini, Pompeo (sculpture by). Amer. heri. vol. 4 no. 1 p. 18-9 (fall '52).
Coptic church (sym.). Lehner: Pict. bk. of sym., p. 34.
Coptic cross. See cross, Coptic.
Coques, Gonzales (work of). Con. 144: LXXI Dec '59.
cor anglais (musical instrument). Int. gr. soc.: Arts . . . p. 141 (col.).
cor anglais bassoon. See bassoon, cor anglais.
cor anglais oboe. See oboe, cor anglais.
coral. Natl. geog. 111: 5-6, 8-9, 18-9 (col.) Jan '57.
Coral Gables (Fla.). Holiday 22: 82-5 (part col.) Nov '57.
coral reefs (Fiji islands). Natl. geog. 114: 546-7 (col.) Oct '58.
Corbett, James. Amer. heri. vol. 10 no. 5 p. 58 (Aug '59).
Corbett, Jim. Cur. biog. p. 131 (1946).
Corbin, Molly ("Molly Pitcher"). Amer. heri. vol. 8 no. 1 p. 46 (Dec '56).
Corcovado Mt. (Brazil). Travel 103: 10 Mar '55.
cordage. Holiday 14: 44 Nov '53.
Cordellina villa. See Villa Cordellina.
cordial pot, William III silver. Con. 135: 129 Ap '55.
Cordier, Andrew W. Cur. biog. p. 101 (1950).
Cordiner, Ralph J. Cur. biog. p. 140 (1951).
Cordoba (Spain, mosque). See mosque, Mezquita.
Cordon, Guy. Cur. biog. p. 123 (1952).
Cordova mosque (int.). Praeg. pict. ency., p. 21.
core drill (men). Natl. geog. 109: 375 (col.) Mar '56.
Corea, Sir Claude. Cur. biog. p. 114 (1961).
Corfield, Colin (work of). Con. 145: 191 May '60.
Corfu island (Greek coast). Holiday 14: 112 Sept '53; 24: 70 (col.) Sept '58.

Cori, Carl F. Cur. biog. p. 136 (1947).
Cori, Gerty T. Cur. biog. p. 136 (1947).
coring tube, marine. Natl. geog. 113: 64 Jan '58.
Corinth, Lovis (work of). Praeg. pict. ency., p. 28 (col.).
Corinth canal. Natl. geog. 110: 753 (col.) Dec '56.
Corinthian columns. See columns, Corinthian.
cork extractor. Holiday 10: 125 Dec '51; 11: 21 Mar '52.
cork pile. Holiday 6: 104 Sept '49.
cork screw. Holiday 12: 97 Nov '52, 137 Dec '52; 21: 14 Ap '57.
Cormack, Maribelle. Jun. bk. of auth., p. 78.
corn (cooked, on cob). Holiday 11: 64 (col.) Je '52.
corn bins, adobe. See adobe corn bins.
"Corn dance" (Velarde). Natl. geog. 107: 359 (col.) Mar '55.
corn husker. Rawson: Ant. pict. bk., p. 27.
corn mill (200 yrs. old). Holiday 10: 44 (col.) Aug '51.
—— (Wales). Holiday 28: 39 (col.) Sept '60.
corn planter. Rawson: Ant. pict. bk., p. 27.
corn popper, Chinese. Natl. geog. 111: 355 (col.) Mar '57.
corn sheller. Rawson: Ant. pict. bk., p. 27.
corn shock & pumpkins (Thanksgiving). Lehner: Pict. bk. of sym., p. 55.
Cornelius, John C. Cur. biog. p. 101 (1960).
Cornelius, Robert. Amer. heri. vol. 8 no. 1 p. 50 (Dec '56).
Cornell, Ezra. Amer. heri. vol. 3 no. 3 p. 57 (spring '52).
Cornell, Katherine. Cur. biog. p. 172 (1941); p. 126 (1952).
Cornell college (Memorial chapel, Mt. Vernon, Iowa). Face of Amer., p. 118-9 (col.).
Cornell Univ. Natl. geog. 110: 598-9 (col.) Nov '56.
—— (campus). Travel 110: 14 Oct '58.
—— (clock tower). Holiday 16: 114 (col.) Sept '54.
—— ("spring day" festival). Natl. geog. 110: 599 (col.) Nov '56.
—— (students, party). Holiday 12: 114-5 Nov '52.
cornerstone, Ford museum. Natl. geog. 114: 115 (col.) Jl '58.
——, Washington's home (Mt. Vernon). Natl. geog. 104: 676 Nov '53.
cornerstone laying. Travel 105: 12 Mar '56.
cornet (man blowing). Durant: Pict. hist. of Amer. circus, p. 199, 401.
—— (17th cent.). Cooper: Con. ency. of music, p. 401.
cornflake poster. Amer. heri. vol. 8 no. 4 p. 65-7 (Je '57).
Corniglia (Italy). Travel 101: 7 Je '54.
Corning glass (man & girls). Natl. geog. 110: 607 (col.) Nov '56.
Corning glass center. Travel 106: 24 Nov '56; 110: 29-31 Sept '58.
Cornish miner's home. Natl. geog. 111: 176 (col.) Feb '57.

Cornopean (1830). Cooper: Con. ency. of music, p. 409.
cornucopia (fruit). Holiday 27: 95 (col.) Mar '60.
—— (sym.). Lehner: Pict. bk. of sym., p. 82.
Cornwall valley (Eng.). Holiday 23: 66-7 (col.) Ap '58.
"Cornwallis surrenders to Washington". Holiday 10: 42 (col.) Nov '51; 16: 107 (col.) Jl '54.
Cornwell, Dean (work of). Amer. heri. vol. 4 no. 4 p. 21 (col.) (summer '53).
"Coronado in Texas". Amer. heri. vol. 4 no. 1 p. 20 (col.) (fall '52).
coronary circle (sym.). Lehner: Pict. bk. of sym., p. 68.
coronation, Nepal (Katmandu). Natl. geog. 112: 138-52 (part col.) Jl '57.
coronation chair (Scotland). Con. 133: 81 Ap '54.
coronation of Queen Christina (1650). Con. 134: 196 Dec '54.
coronation of Elizabeth II. See Elizabeth II, Queen (coronation of).
"Coronation of the Virgin". Con. ency. of ant., vol. 3, pl. 133, 135.
—— (Carracci). Con. 132: 6 Sept '53.
—— (Gaddi). Con. 126: 173 (col.) Dec '50.
—— (Gerini). Con. 136: 201 (col.) Dec '55.
—— (Hugo Vander Goes). Con. 126: 3 Aug '50.
coronation parade (London). Holiday 13: 135 (col.) Je '53.
coronation ring (British). Int. gr. soc.: Arts . . . p. 165 (col.).
—— ("wedding"). Natl. geog. 104: 325 (col.) Sept '53.
coronation robes. Natl. geog. 103: 703 May '53; 104: 312 (col.) Sept '53.
Corot, Jean Baptiste Camille (work of). Con. 129: 70 Ap '52; 132: 103 Nov '53; 133: LXXV, 259 Je '54; 134: XI Nov '54; 138: X (col.) Nov '56, XLVIII Dec '56; 139: 54 Mar '57, XIX Je '57; 140: X (col.) Nov '57; 142: 41 Sept '58, 109 Nov '58, 196 Dec '58; 143: 1 May '59; 145: XLIII Je '60.
Praeg. pict. ency., p. 413 (col.).
Corpus Christi mass (Vienna). Natl. geog. 99: 764 (col.) Je '51.
corral, platform (Pakistan). Natl. geog. 107: 422 Mar '55.
——, ranch. Holiday 11: 40 Feb '52.
——, ranch (Texas). Holiday 24: 49 Oct '58.
——, western cattle. Travel 108: 10 Jl '57.
"Corral of the Sisters". See "Curral das Freiras" (Madeira island).
correct (sym.). Lehner: Pict. bk. of sym., p. 85.
Correggio, Antonio Allegri (work of). Con. 126: cover, opp. p. 155 (col.) Dec '50.
Praeg. pict. ency., p. 312 (col.).
Correll, Charles J. Cur. biog. p. 248 (1947).
corselet, antique. Con. 136: 2 (col.) Sept '55.
corset. Holiday 26: 122 Oct '59.

—— (19th cent.). Amer. heri. vol. 2 no. 4 p. 12 (summer '51).

—— (on form). Holiday 27: 41 May '60.

——, Queen Elizabeth I (girls trying it on). Natl. geog. 100: 423 Sept '51.

corset. See also girdle.

Corsica. Travel 105: 42-3 Ap '56.

—— (Calvi harbor). Holiday 16: 108 Nov '54.

Corsini palace (art in). Con. 138: 160-5 Dec '56.

Corson, Bishop Fred Pierce. Cur. biog. p. 116 (1961).

Cortelyou, George B. Amer. heri. vol. 8 no. 4 p. 35 (Je '57).

Cortes (meeting Moctezuma). Ceram: March of arch., p. 251.

——, Herman (portraits). Ceram: March of arch p. 252

Cortes & his mistress (in Mexico). Ceram: March of arch., p. 251.

Corti, Walter Robert. Natl. geog. 116: 270 Aug '59.

Cortines, Adolfo Ruiz. Cur. biog. p. 507 (1952).

Cortney, Philip. Cur. biog. p. 102 (1958).

Cory, John Mackenzie. Cur. biog. p. 124 (1949).

Cosa, Juan de la (map by). Amer. heri. vol. 7 no. 1 p. 75 (Dec '55).

Cosimo I (mosaic portrait by Ferrucci). Con. 141: 213 Je '58.

cosmic diagram (Hindu). Lehner: Pict. bk. of sym., p. 75.

cosmic vision. Con. 141: 191 May '58.

Cossa, Francesco (work of). Con. 142: 257 Jan '59.

Cossack (Russia). Holiday 18: 107 Jl '55.

——. Int. gr. soc.: Arts . . . p. 115 (col.).

Cost, March. Cur. biog. p. 103 (1958).

Costa Brava (Spain). Travel 108: 20-1 Jl '57.

Costa, Lorenzo (work of). Con. 127: 119 May '51; 140: 181 Dec '57.

Costa Rican girl. Holiday 20: 184 Dec '56.

Costain, Thomas B. Cur. biog. p. 125 (1953).

Costello, John A. Cur. biog. p. 112 (1948).

Costello, Lou. Cur. biog. p. 1 (1941).

Costermongers, King & Queen of London's cockney. Holiday 11: 33 Je '52.

costume (16th cent.). Con. 142: LIX Dec '58.

—— (17th cent.). Con. 144: LVII (col.) Dec '59.

—— (18th cent.). Con. 143: XVII (col.) May '59, XLIV (col.) Je '59.
Natl. geog. 97: 562-8 (col.) May '50; 113: 258-9 (col.) Feb '58.

—— (1769). Con. 145: VII (col.) May '60.

—— (1770). Holiday 18: 61 (col.) Jl '55.

—— (1785). Con. 143: 207 Je '59.

—— (19th cent.). Amer. heri. vol. 8 no. 5 p. 53 (col.) (Aug '57); vol. 9 no. 3 p. 54 (col.) 98-9, 102-3 (Ap '58).
Holiday 26: 94 (col.) Jl '59.
Int. gr. soc.: Arts . . . p. 155 (col.).

—— (1840). Amer. heri. vol. 4 no. 1 p. 3 (fall '52).

—— (1862). Amer. heri. vol. 10 no. 1 p. 83-95 (Dec '58).

—— (1874). Amer. heri. vol. 7 no. 4 p. 91 (Je '56).

—— 1800). Travel 111: 16 May '59.

—— (1888). Holiday 12: 66 Sept '52.
Travel 110: 60 Sept '58.

—— (1893). Amer. heri. vol. 11 no. 6 p. 19 (col.) (Oct '60).

—— (20th cent.). Int. gr. soc.: Arts . . . p. 155 (col.).

—— (1909). Natl. geog. 112: 268 Aug '57.

costume (armour). See armour.

—— (Boy Scouts as Indians). Natl. geog. 107: 480-1 (col.) Ap '55.

—— (carnival). See carnival costume.

—— (children, 1841). Amer. heri. vol. 7 no. 3 p. 53 (col.) (Ap '56).

—— (cowboy). Holiday 16: 34 (col.) Jl '54.

—— (family, 1836). Amer. heri. vol. 11 no. 2 p. 48-9 (col.) (Feb '60).

—— (fancy dress parade). Natl. geog. 99: 321 (col.) Mar '51.

—— (firemen, 1850). Amer. heri. vol. 8 no. I p. 54 (Dec '56).

—— (football suits, 1896). Amer. heri. vol. 6 no. 6 back cover (col.) (Oct '55).

—— (foreign lands). Holiday 6: 36-7 (col.) Jl '49.

—— (George & Martha Washington). Natl. geog. 103: 18 Jan '53.

—— (girl, 1847). Amer. heri. vol. 10 no. 2 back cover (col.) (Feb '59).

—— (girl's formal). Natl. geog. 103: 291 (col.) Mar '53.

—— (hooped skirt). Amer. heri. vol. 8 no. 2 p. 112 (Feb '57).

—— (ice skaters, 1862). Natl. geog. 118: 798 (col.) Dec '60.

—— (man, 1668). Holiday 21: 85 Feb '57.

—— (man, 1715). Amer. heri. vol. 11 no. 1 p. 4 (col.) (Dec '59).

—— (man, 1791). Con. 145: LIII Mar '60.

—— (man & woman, 1809). Amer. heri. vol. 4 no. 2 p. 7 (winter '53).

—— (man & woman, 1906). Holiday 21: 40 (col.) Mar '57.

—— (men & girl, 1835). Amer. heri. vol. 11 no. 5 p. 15 (col.) (Aug '60).

—— (men, 1890). Amer. heri. vol. 6 no. 3 p. 63 (Ap '55).

—— (men, 19-20th cent.). Int. gr. soc.: Arts . . . p. 155 (col.).

—— (men, sports & professional). Int. gr. soc.: Arts . . . p. 153 (col.).

—— (mid-Victorian men). Con. 135: XXVI Ap '55.

—— (military general, 1769). Con. 144: 264 (col.) Jan '60.

—— (patterns, designs . . .). Tilke: Costume patterns & designs, all periods. . . .

—— (pierot, party). Holiday 17: 10 (col.) Jan '55.

—— (pirate). Amer. heri. vol. 8 no. 2 p. 10, 15 (col.) (Feb '57).

—— (Pocahontas court dress). Natl. geog. 111: 619 (col.) May '57.

—— (priest). Amer. heri., vol. 8 no. 2 p. 110 (Feb '57).

costume (rebel & redcoat soldiers). Amer. heri. vol. 8 no. 2 p. 65-7, 73, 82, 89 (Feb '57).

—— (religious orders, medieval). Int. gr. soc.: Arts . . . p. 71 (col.).

—— (royal guard). Travel 111: 18-9 Ap '59.

—— (royal highlander). Holiday 26: 52 Sept '59.

—— (royal robes, ancient). Int. gr. soc.: Arts . . . p. 29 (col.).

—— (school girls, 1894). Amer. heri. vol. 11 no. 6 p. 107 (Oct '60).

—— (Victorian period). Amer. heri. vol. 10 no. 1 p. 37-45 (col.) (Dec '58).

—— (Victorian boy). Amer. heri. vol. 8 no. 2 back cover (col.) (Feb '57).

—— (widow, 19th cent.). Amer. heri. vol. 9 no. 3 p. 56 (Ap '58).

costume, Acadia. Jordan: Hammond's pict. atlas, p. 85 (col.).

——, Admiralty island. Natl. geog. 112: 591 (col.) Nov '57.

——, Afghanistan. Natl. geog. 98: 682-705 (part col.) Nov '50; 114: 20-1 (col.) Jl '58; 114: 20-1 (col.) Jl '58; 117: 610 (col.) May '60.

——, Africa. Holiday 21: 39 (col.) Feb '57; 25: 64-94 (part col.) Ap '59.
Natl. geog. 97: 319, 335, 337, 341, 347 (col.) Mar '50; 104: 146-59 (col.) Aug '53; 118: 307, 317, 320-1, 325, 372, 388 (col.) Sept '60.

——, Africa (Masai). Natl. geog. 106: 492-517 (part col.) Oct '54, 722-3 (col.) Dec '54.

——, Africa (south-west). Natl. geog. 108: 774 (col.) Dec '55.

——, Alaska. Holiday 9: 77 Mar '51.
Natl. geog. 99: 552-62 Ap '51; 105: 135-46 (part col.) Jan '54; 109: 778 (col.) Je '56; 116: 42, 71-2 (col.) Jl '59.

——, Algeria. Natl. geog. 117: 771 (col.) Je '60.

——, Algeria (Medieval). Int. gr. soc.: Arts . . . p. 69 (col.).

——, Alsace. Holiday 5: 123 Ap '49.

——, Amazon. Disney: People & places, p. 99-110 (col.).

——, Amer. (early). Natl. geog. 101: 471 (col.) Ap '52.

——, Amer. (1773). Amer. heri. vol. 6 no. 3 p. 40-1 (col.) (Ap '55).

——, Amer. (1820). Jensen: The White House p. 40.

——, Amer. (1877). Jensen: The White House, p. 112, 115.

——, Amer. Revolution. Amer. heri., vol. 11 no. 5 p. 28 (col.) (Aug '60).

——, Amer. (picnic, 1912). Natl. geog. 116: 101-11 (col.) Jl '59.

——, Amer. (1600's). Holiday 24: 36 (col.) Sept '58.

——, Amer. soldiers. See costume, U.S. soldiers.

——, Andalusian (festival). Natl. geog. 113: 422-4 (col.) Mar '58.

——, Antarctic. Natl. geog. 116: 526, 540 (col.) Oct '59.

——, Arabia. Holiday 20: 48-51 (part col.) Aug '56
Natl. geog. 98: 727, 730, 744-5 (col.) Dec '50; 101: 223, 237, 241, 243-4 (col.), 267, 269, 271-2 (col.) Feb '52; 102: 784-5, 789-96 (col.) Dec '52; 104: 22, 36 (col.) Jl '53, 863 (col.) Dec '53; 105: 508 Ap '54; 108: 159, 162-66 (col.) Aug '55; 110: 66-7, 69, 71-3, 76, 78-9, 86-8 (col.) Jl '56; 113: 204, 206-7, 220-2, 227, 231, 233-4 (part col.) Feb '58, 670-1 (col.) May '58; 114: 713, 717, 721-32 (part col.) Nov '58; 117: 662 (col.) May '60.

——, "Arabian nights". Natl. geog. 100: 435 (col.) Oct '51.

——, Arabian soldiers. Natl. geog. 101: 239 (col.) Feb '52.

——, Argentina. Holiday 21: 96 (col.) Feb '57.

——, Argentina gauchos. Natl. geog. 113: 320-1, 326-7, 332-3 (col.) Mar '58.

——, Asian dancers. Holiday 18: 65 (col.) Dec '55.

——, Austria. Holiday 26: 74 (col.) Sept '59.
Natl. geog. 99: 777, 780-4 (col.) Je '51; 115: 200-13 (col.) Feb '58.

——, Austria (Alpine). Natl. geog. 118: 249 (col.) Aug '60.

——, Austria (Tyrol). Holiday 21: 116 Jan '57.
Natl. geog. 100: 388, 391, 393 (col.) Sept '51.

——, Bahrein. Natl. geog. 105: 503 (col.) Ap '54.

——, Balearic islands. Natl. geog. 111: 646-7 (col.) May '57.

——, Bali. Holiday 18: 52-7 (part col.) Jl '55.
Natl. geog. 108: 370-1 (col.) Sept '55.

——, Bali dancers. Natl. geog. 99: 360-2 (col.) Mar '59.

——, Basque country. Holiday 25: 142 (col.) May '59.
Natl. geog. 105: 148-9, 158 (col.) Feb '54; 109: 328-9, 331 (col.) Mar '56.

——, Bavaria. Natl. geog. 115: 474 (col.) Ap '59.

——, Bavaria (Black Forest). Holiday 16: 13 (col.) Nov '54.

——, Bedouin. Natl. geog. 104: 42 (col.) Jl '53; 106: 840-1 (part col.) Dec '54; 108: 867 (col.) Dec '55; 110: 76, 81, 93 (col.) Jl '56; 111: 242-3 Feb '57.

——, Belgian Congo. Natl. geog. 106: 725, 737 (col.) Dec '54.

——, Belgium. Holiday 13: 79 Feb '53.
Natl. geog. 107: 651 (col.) May '55.

——, Belgium (16th cent.). Natl. geog. 113: 803, 806-7 (col.) Je '58.

——, Bhutan (Asia). Natl. geog. 102: 718-52 (col.) Dec '52.

——, Bible characters. Natl. geog. 112: 837-63 (col.) Dec '57.

——, Bible (Old Testament). Natl. geog. 118: 812-49 (col.) Dec '60.

——, Bible times. Natl. geog. 112: 842-3 Dec '57.

——, Bolivia (Indians). Natl. geog. 98: 486-7, 489 (col.) Oct '50.

costume, Bolivia (woman). Holiday 8: 52, 56 (col.) Nov '50.

——, Brahui. Natl. geog. 105: 512 (col.) Ap '54.

——, Breton men's. Holiday 27: 81 Jan '60.

——, British & Amer. soldiers (1776). Amer. heri. vol. 7 no. 4 p. 4-5 (col.) (Je '56).

——, British parliament. Natl. geog. 105: 228 (col.) Feb '54.

——, British royal marines. Natl. geog. 101: 538 (col.) Ap '52.

——, British royalty (1727-71). Amer. heri. vol. 11 no. 4 p. 4-20 (col.) (Je '60).

——, British soldiers (1645). Amer. heri. vol. 6 no. 5 p. 18-9 (col.) (Aug '55).

——, British uniforms. Holiday 25: 190 (col.) May '59.

——, British. See also Costume, England.

——, Brittany. Holiday 7: 100-3 (col.) Jan '50.

——, Burma. Holiday 20: 44-7 (part col.) Sept '56.

——, Cairo. Holiday 25: 53-4 (col.) Feb '59.

——, Cambodia. Int. gr. soc.: Arts . . . p. 147 (col.).
Natl. geog. 99: 467, 471 (col.) Ap '51; 102: 305, 309 (col.) Sept '52; 117: 532, 543 (col.) Ap '60.

——, Canada, French. Natl. geog. 98: 353 (col.) Sept '50.

——, Canadian govt. officials. Holiday 18: 61 (col.) Dec '55.

—— Canary Islands. Natl. geog. 107: 498, 518-9, 522 (col.) Ap '55.

——, Caribbean. Holiday 18: 71 (col.) Aug '55; 23: 38-9 (col.) Feb '58; 25: 110 (col.) May '59.

—— Cavaliers. Natl. geog. 97: 587 (col.) May '50.

——, Celtic. Holiday 23: 54 (col.) Je '58.
Int. gr. soc.: Arts . . . p. 27 (col.).

——, Central Amer. Holiday 17: 38-9 (col.) Mar '55.

——, Ceylon. Holiday 20: 94-9 (col.) Aug '56.
Travel 111: 21 Jan '59.

——, Chevaliers du Tastevin. Holiday 21: 82-3 (col.) May '57.

——, Chile. Holiday 26: 62-3 (col.) Aug '59.
Natl. geog. 117: 184, 210, 234-5 (col.) Feb '60.

——, China. Holiday 20: 22 Sept '56.
Natl. geog. 105: 250, 253, 256, 264, 270 (part col.) Feb '54; 110: 185 (col.) Aug '56.

——, China (ancient). Praeg. pict. ency., p. 540-42 (col.).

——, Chinese robes. Con. 126: 95-105 Oct '50.

——, Colonial. Amer. heri. vol. 11 no. 4 p. 108 Je '60.
Brooks: Growth of a nation, p. 76-9.
Holiday 6: 84 (col.) Jl '49; 8: 15 (col.) Aug '50, 131 (col.) Oct '50; 11: 43 (col.) Je '52; 12: 60 (col.) Oct '52; 15: 122, 125 May '54; 17: 104, 118 Feb '55; 20: 199 Dec '56; 21: 176 Mar '57; 22: 71 (col.) Sept '57; 26: 119 (col.) Sept '59.
Natl. geog. 103: 166, 184 (part col.) Feb '53, 522 (col.) Ap '53; 105: 447 (col.) Ap '54;

106: 441-86 (col.) Oct '54; 111: 584 (col.) May '57; 118: 706-7 (col.) Nov '60.

——, Colonial (girls). Holiday 25: 156 Feb '59.

——, Colonial (Jamestown). Natl. geog. 111: 604 (col.) May '57.

——, Colonial (man, 1726). Holiday 21: 120 Ap '57.

——, Colonial (man & woman). Holiday 9: 94 Mar '51.

——, Colonial (men). Amer. heri. vol. 3 no. 1 p. 26, 38-9 (col.) (fall '51); vol. 4 no. 4 p. 3, 28, 36-7 40 (part col.) (summer '53).
Holiday 10: 78 (col.) Nov '51, 97 (col.) Dec '51; 12: 143 (col.) Dec '52; 14: 126 (col.) Dec '53 16: 106 Aug '54, 84 (col.) Dec '54; 18: 105 Nov '55, 118 (col.) Dec '55; 20: 190 (col.) Dec '56; 26: 129 Sept '59; 28: 55 (col.) Dec '60.

——, Colonial (warriors). Holiday 9: 77 Mar '51.

——, Colonial (woman). Natl. geog. 102: 773 (col.) Dec '52.

——, Confederate soldier. Brooks: Growth of a nation, p. 148.

——, Conn. (Governor's foot guard). Holiday 8: 30 (col.) Jl '50.

——, Crete. Natl. geog. 104: 699, 705 (col.) Nov '53.

——, Crusaders. Holiday 20: 56 (col.) Dec '56.
Int. gr. soc.: Arts . . . p. 73 (col.).

——, Cuba (Havana mummers, dancers). Holiday 12: 68-9 (col.) Dec '52.

——, Currier & Ives (woman skating). Amer. heri. vol. 9 no. 1 back cover (col.) (Dec '57).

——, Cyprus island. Natl. geog. 101: 633, 636-48, 663-4 (col.) May '52.

——, Denmark. Natl. geog. 101: 697 May '52.

——, Dominican Republic. Holiday 18: inside cover (col.) Sept '55.

——, Druse. Natl. geog. 104: 18 (col.) Jl '53.

——, Dutch. See costume, Holland.

——, Egypt. Natl. geog. 106: 768 (col.) Dec '54; 108: 622, 628-32, 649. (col.). Nov '55; 112: 104 (col.) Jl '57.

——, Egypt (19th dynasty). Praeg. pict. ency., p. 116 (col.).

——, Egyptian king (18th dynasty). Praeg. pict. ency., p. 121 (col.).

——, Egyptian style. Amer. heri. vol. 2 no. 4 p. 11 (summer '51).

——, El Oued (burnoose-clad). Natl. geog. 117: 784-5 (col.) Je '57.

——, English (14-15th cent.). Int. gr. soc.: Arts . . . p. 69 (col.).

——, English (Lt. Gen., 18th cent.). Con. 145: 43 (col.) Mar '60.

——, English (man, 17th cent.). Con. 143: 6 Mar '59.

——, English (royal family, 1771). Amer. heri. vol. 11 no. 4 p. 5-6 (col.) (Je '60).

——, English (woman, 1607). Amer. heri. vol. 10 no. 5 p. 24-5 (col.) (Aug '59).

——, English. See also costume, British.

——, Eskimo. Natl. geog. 107: 558 (col.) Ap '55; 111: 542 (col.) Ap '57.
Travel 112: cover (col.) Jl '59.

costume, Eskimo. *See* also Costume, Greenland (Eskimo).

——, **Essenes.** Natl. geog. 114: 784, 789-90, 796, 798-9 (col.) Dec '58.

——, **Ethiopia.** Natl. geog. 106: 749, 752-3 (col.) Dec '54.

——, **Etruscan (ancient).** Int. gr. soc.: Arts . . . p. 31 (col.).

——, **European (medieval).** Int. gr. soc.: Arts . . . p. 69. (col.).

——, **European (1670).** Con. 136: 88-91 Nov '55.

——, **European (peasants, 16-18th cent.).** Int. gr. soc.: Arts . . . p. 113 (col.).

——, **Fiji island.** *See* Fijians.

——, **Formosa.** Natl. geog. 97: 166-7, 170 (col.) Feb '50; 111: 331, 338, 340-5, 348-61 (col.) Mar '57.

——, **France.** Holiday 10: 137 Nov 51; 15: 51 Jan '54; 23: 20 Mar '58.
Natl. geog. 115: 610-11 (col.) May '59.
Travel 112: 50 Sept '59.

——, **France (Arles festival).** Natl. geog. 109: 671 (col.) May '56.

——, **France (child, 1749).** Con. 143: 208 Je '59.

——, **France (18th cent.).** Int. gr. soc.: Arts . . . p. 93, 113 (col.).

——, **France (nobility, 18th cent.).** Int. gr. soc.: Arts . . . p. 111 (col.).

——, **France (Paris, 18th cent.).** Natl. geog. 101: 798 (col.) Je '52.

——, **France (peasant, 13th cent.).** Int. gr. soc.: Arts . . . p. 69 (col.).

——, **Frankish (about 900).** Int. gr. soc.: Arts . . . p. 69 (col.).

——, **Gambia.** Natl. geog. 112: 624-5 (col.) Nov '57.

——, **Georgian (man, 1700's).** Natl. geog. 113: 262 (col.) Feb '58.

——, **German.** Holiday 15: 48 Jan '54; 23: 37 (col.) Jan '58.
Natl. geog. 107: 458 (col.) Ap '55; 108: 132 Jl '55.

——, **German (bard, medieval).** Int. gr. soc.: Arts . . . p. 69 (col.).

——, **German (men).** Holiday 11: 150 Je '52.

——, **German (Rothenburg festival).** Natl. geog. 100: 717 (col.) Dec '51.

——, **Godey fashions.** Amer. heri. vol. 9 no. 6 p. 21-7 (col.), 98-100 (Oct '58).

——, **Greece fashions.** Int. gr. soc.: Arts . . . p. 19 (col.).
Natl. geog. 103: 365, 381-8 (col.) Mar '53; 109: 38, 50, 56, 69 (col.) Jan '56; 117: 639 (col.) May '60.

——, **Greece (ancient).** Int. gr. soc.: Arts . . . p. 31 (col.).

——, **Greenland (Eskimos).** Natl. geog. 100: 479, 480, 490-1, 507 (col.) Oct '51.

——, **Guatemala (Indians).** Natl. geog. 117: 407-16 (col.) Mar '60.

——, **Hawaii.** Holiday 15: 32 (col.) May '54; 24: 106 (col.) Oct '58; 25: 86 (col.) Feb '59.
Natl. geog. 118: 7 (col.) Jl '60.

——, **Hawaii.** *See* also Hawaiian (Hula dress); Hawaiian (Muumuu dress); Hawaiian dancers.

——, **Hebrew (ancient).** Int. gr. soc.: Arts . . . p. 31 (col.).

——, **Hindu.** Natl. geog. 107: 403, 406, 413 (col. Mar '55.

——, **Holland.** Con. 136: 275 (col.) Jan '56.
Holiday, 10: 74 (col.) Sept '51; 19: 98-9 (part col.) Jan '56; 21: 55 (col.) Mar '57; 23: 56 Jan '58.
Natl. geog. 98: 755, 761, 765, 770 (col.) Dec '50; 101: 287-9 (col.) Mar '52; 106: 382, 384-7, 396-7, 407 (col.) Sept '54; 107: 468 (col.) Ap '55; 108: 78 (col.) Jl '55.

——, **Holland (boy & girl).** Amer. heri. vol. 8 no. 1 p. 33 (col.) (Dec '56).

——, **Holland (early men & women).** Amer. heri. vol. 10 no. 1 p. 9, 11 (col.) (Dec '58).

——, **Holland (man, 1640).** Brooks: Growth of a nation, p. 49.

——, **Hunza.** Natl. geog. 104: 489-516 (col.) Oct '53.

——, **Hunza (school boys).** Natl. geog. 117: 96-7 (col.) Jan '60.

——, **Iceland.** Natl. geog. 100: 615 (col.) Nov '51.

——, **Ifalik atoll.** Natl. geog. 109: 546-76 (part col.) Ap '56.

——, **India.** Holiday 14: cover, 42, 44-5, 52-3 (col.) Oct '53; 16: 51 Sept '54; 22: 26 (col.) Dec '57; 27: 98 (col.) Jan '60.
Int. gr. soc.: Arts . . . p. 27 (col.).
Natl. geog. 102: 207, 226-7 (col.) Aug '52; 109: 577, 582 Ap '56; 113: 707-10 (col.) May '58; 117: 589, 617, 630-1, 666 (col.) May '60; 118: 453, 461-502 (col.) Oct '60.

——, **India (Naga Hills, headhunters).** Natl. geog. 107: 248, 251-2, 260-1 (col.) Feb '55.

——, **India (woman).** Holiday 23: 160 Mar '58; 24: 100 Sept '58.
Natl. geog. 103: 39, 56 (col.) Jan '53.

——, **Indian.** Holiday 13: 119, 122 (col.) May '53; 21: 4 (col.) Ap '57.
Natl. geog. 98: 249, 258 (col.) Aug '50.

——, **Indian (Tewa).** Natl. geog. 106: 244 (col.) Aug '54.

——, **Indian chiefs.** Amer. heri. vol. 6 no. 2 p. 27 (col.) (winter '55), vol. 7 no. 2 frontis (col.) Feb '56.
Holiday 9: 87 (col.) Mar '51.

——, **Indian chief & squaw.** Natl. geog. 110: 486 (col.) Oct '56.

——, **Indians (Navajo).** Natl. geog. 114: 813, 816-7, 820, 822-3, 825, 832, 837-41, 844, 846 (col.) Dec '58.

——, **Indians (San Blas).** Holiday 12: 57 (col.) Nov '52.

——, **Indians (Seminole).** Holiday 13: 43 (col.) Feb '53.
Natl. geog. 110: 820-38 (col.) Dec '56.

——, **Indians (Sibundoy).** Natl. geog. 98: 473 (col.) Oct '50.

——, **Indochina.** Natl. geog. 98: 508 Oct '50; 99: 464, 471 (col.) Ap '51.

——, **Indochina. (Davaks tribe).** Natl. geog. 99: 475 (col.) Ap '51.

costume, Indonesia. Natl. geog. 99: 9-13, 36 (col.) Jan '51.

——, Italy. Natl. geog. 100: 100-403 (col.) Sept '51.

——, Italy (men, medieval). Holiday 25: 34 (col.) Jan '59; 26: 62-3 (col.) Sept '59. Brooks: Growth of a nation, p. 28.

——, Italy (military police). Natl. geog. 111: 482-3 (col.) Ap '57.

——, Italy (nobility, 15th cent.). Int. gr. soc.: Arts . . . p. 111 (col.).

——, Iraq. Natl. geog. 114: 454, 459, 470-1, 475-7, 479, 482-3, 484-6 (col.) Oct '58; 115: 57 (col.) Jan '59.

——, Ischia. Natl. geog. 105: 535 (col.) Ap '54.

——, Jamaica. Holiday 25: 61 (col.) Feb '59.

——, Japan. Con. 137: 205 May '56. Disney: People & places, p. 147-62 (col.). Holiday 12: 34-5, 38-9 (col.) Aug '52; 16: 84 Sept '54; 24: 50 Dec '58; 25: 105 (col.) Feb '59; 26: 99 (col.) Aug '59. Natl. geog. 97: 601, 607, 616, 622-3 (col.) May '50; 104: 632, 640-1, 643 (col.) Nov '53; 116: 858, 861 (col.) Dec '59; 117: 668 (col.) May '60; 118: 734, 760, 766 (col.) Dec '60.

——, Japan (Geisha girl). Natl. geog. 100: 741 (col.) Dec '51.

——, Japanese. See also Japanese woman.

——, Java. Natl. geog. 99: 31 (col.) Jan '51. Travel 112: 24 Sept '59.

——, Kandyan. Holiday 20: 99 (col.). Aug '56.

——, Kashgai (Iran). Natl. geog. 101: 814-28 (col.) Je '52.

——, Kazakh. Natl. geog. 106: 627-44 (part col.) Nov '54.

——, knight. Holiday 21: 43 (col.) Jan '57.

——, Korea. Natl. geog. 97: 781, 783-805 (col.) Je '50.

——, Kurds. Natl. geog. 115: 62-3 (col.) Jan '59.

——, Ladakh (man & women). Natl. geog. 99: 609, 616, 618, 621-34 (part col.) May '51.

——, Lao. Natl. geog. 102: 325 (col.) Sept '52.

——, Laotia & Wouni (girls). Natl. geog. 107: 470 (col.) Ap '55.

——, Lapland. Disney: People & places, p. 13-24 (col.). Holiday 12: 91, 95 (col.) Sept '52; 18: 106-7 (col.) Dec '55. Natl. geog. 106: 253, 255-80 (part col.) Aug '54; 108: 114 (col.) Dec '55. Travel 108: 40, 42 Jl '57.

——, Latin Amer. (Colonial). Con. 133: 162-7 May '54.

——, Lebanese. Natl. geog. 113: 495, 499 (col.) Ap '58.

——, Lhasa. Natl. geog. 108: 5-48 (col.) Jl '55.

——, Lhasa (bride & groom). Natl. geog. 108: 5 (col.) Jl '55.

——, Malay. Natl. geog. 103: 218 (col.) Feb '53; 116: 784 (col.) Dec '59.

——, Maldive islands. Natl. geog. 111: 830-47 (col.) Je '57.

——, Malta. Holiday 27: 122 Jan '60.

——, Malta (woman). Holiday 27: 156 (col.) Ap '60.

——, Maori. Natl. geog. 101: 427, 440, 442 (col.) Ap '52.

——, Martinique. Travel 114: 51 Oct '60.

——, Martinique (colonial). Natl. geog. 115: 262-3 (col.) Feb '59.

——, Meo. Natl. geog. 99: 471 (col.) Ap '51; 102: 326 (col.) Sept '52.

——, Mesopotamia. Natl. geog. 99: 58-104 (col.) Jan '51.

——, Mesopotamia (ancient). Int. gr. soc.: Arts . . . p. 31 (col.).

——, Mesopotamia (royal, ancient). Int. gr. soc.: Arts . . . p. 29 (col.).

——, Mexico. Holiday 10: 99 (col.) Nov '51. Natl. geog. 103: 330, 344 (col.) Mar '53; 107: 220, 240-1 (col.) Feb '55. Travel 114: cover (col.) Nov '60.

——, Mexico (festival). Natl. geog. 100: 818-9 (col.) Dec '51.

——, Mexico (haciendo owner). Amer. heri. vol. 9 no. 5 p. 13 (col.) (Aug '58).

——, Mexico (rancho women). Amer. heri. vol. 9 no. 5 p. 12 (col.) (Aug '58).

——, Mexico (woman). Natl. geog. 102: 761 (col.) Dec '52.

——, Mohammed. Holiday 25: 80 (col.) Ap '59.

——, Mongolian. Natl. geog. 99: 399, 406 (col.) Mar '51.

——, Moorish (girls). Natl. geog. 112: 72 (col.) Jl '57.

——, Morocco. Disney: People & places, p. 83-98 (col.). Holiday 23: cover, 68-71 (col.) Mar '58. Natl. geog. 107: 148, 156, 158-9, 161, 166-7, 170, 175, 181 (col.) Feb '55; 112: 57 (col.) Jl '57; 117: 646-7 (col.) May '60.

——, Morocco (medieval). Int. gr. soc.: Arts . . . p. 69 (col.).

——, Moslem. Holiday 25: 76, 148 (col.) Ap '59. Natl. geog. 104: 19, 21 (col.) Jl '53; 114: 3, 29 (col.) Jl '58, 607, 609, 624, 630-39 (col.) Nov '58.

——, Napoleonic time. Int. gr. soc.: Arts . . . p. 155 (col.).

——, Nazarene. Natl. geog. 99: 450 (col.) Ap '51.

——, Nepal. Natl. geog. 97: 9, 11, 13, 16, 20-1, 25, 33, 36-9 (part col.) Jan '50; 108: 586, 588 (col.) Nov '55; 112: 138-43, 146 (col.) Jl '57; 117: 371, 380-2, 399-401 (col.) Mar '60.

——, New Guinea (highland warriors). Holiday 28: 84-5 (col.) Nov '60.

——, New Zealand (girl). Holiday 24: 32 Sept '58.

——, Nigeria. Natl. geog. 104: 146-52 (col.) Aug '53 110: 331-40, 350-1, 353, 359, 362 (col.) Sept '56.

——, Nigeria (jungle). Natl. geog. 116: 234-5, 238, 241-52 (col.) Aug '59.

——, Nomad (woman). Natl. geog. 117: 83-105 (col.) Jan '60.

costume, Nomad (woman & children). Natl. geog. 109: 71 Jan '56.

——, Norman (peasant). Int. gr. soc.: Arts . . . p. 69 (col.).

——, Normandy (France). Natl. geog. 115: 610-11 (col.) May '59.

——, Norway. Holiday 12: 91 (col.) Sept '52. Natl. geog. 106: 176 (col.) Aug '54; 111: 97, 104, 118-9 (col.) Jan '57.

——, Pacific islands. Holiday 28: 72-97 (part col.) Oct '60.

——, Pakistan. Natl. geog. 102: 643-76 (part col.) Nov '52; 107: 398-417 (part col.) Mar '55; 111: 80 Jan '57.

——, Pakistan (cavalryman). Natl. geog. 102: 643-4 (col.) Nov '52.

——, Pennsylvania (1812). Amer. heri. vol. 8 no. 3 p. 48-51 (col.) (Ap '57).

——, Pennsylvania Dutch. Natl. geog. 102: 504-13 (col.) Oct '52.

——, Pennsylvania German (farmer). Amer. heri. vol. 7 no. 3 p. 2 (col.) (Ap '56).

——, Persian (ancient royal). Int. gr. soc.: Arts . . . p. 29 (col.).

——, Peru. Holiday 11: 106 (col.) May '52. Natl. geog. 98: 438-9, 453, 455, 459 (col.) Oct '50. Travel 112: 58 Jl '59.

——, Peru (modern). Holiday 27: 110-11 (col.) May '60.

——, Peru, Indians. Holiday 21: 46 Ap '57. Natl. geog. 107: 137-8 Jan '55; 109: 351-2 (col.) Mar '56.

——, Pilgrims. Amer. heri. vol. 10 no. 6 p. 73 (Oct '59); vol. 11 no. 5 p. 81 (Aug '60); vol. 11 no. 6 p. 88 (Oct '60); vol. 12 no. 1 p. 109 (Dec '60). Natl. geog. 103: 830 (col.) Je '53; 112: 634, 665 (part col.) Nov '57.

——, pioneers. Amer. heri. vol. 7 no. 3 p. 108 (Ap '56; vol. 7 no. 5 p. 106 (Aug '56); vol. 7 no. 6 p. 98 (Oct '56); vol. 8 no. 1 p. 94 (Dec '56); vol. 8 no. 3 p. 94 (Ap '57); vol. 8 no. 4 p. 86 (Je '57); vol. 8 no. 5 p. 96 (Aug '57); vol. 9 no. 3 p. 82 (Ap '58); vol. 9 no. 4 p. 86 (Je '58); vol. 9 no. 5 p. 108 (Aug '58); vol. 9 no. 6 p. 112 (Oct '58); vol. 10 no. 1 p. 116 (Dec '58); vol. 10 no. 2 p. 108 (Feb '59); vol. 10 no. 3 p. 108 (Ap '59); vol. 10 no. 4 p. 99 (Je '59). Travel 108: 30-1 Aug '57.

——, Poland. Natl. geog. 114: 391-9 (col.) Sept '58.

——, Poland (trumpeter). Natl. geog. 114: 385 (col.) Nov '58.

——, Polynesia. Natl. geog. 97: 525-34 (part col.) Ap '50.

——, Portugal. Disney: People & places, p. 57-67 (col.). Holiday 19: 27 (col.) Jan '56.

——, Puerto Rico. Holiday 17: 56 (col.) Feb '55; 18: 64 (col.) Nov '55.

——, Puritans. Amer. heri. vol. 11 no. 1 p. 113 (Dec '59); vol. 11 no. 3 p. 108 (Ap '60). Natl. geog. 107: 741 (col.) Je '55.

——, Rome (ancient). Int. gr. soc.: Arts . . . p. 31, 37, 43 (col.).

——, Rumania. Natl. geog. 108: 720 Nov '55.

——, Russia. Holiday 25: 30 Jan '59.

——, Saar professions. Natl. geog. 105: 570 Ap '54.

——, St. Thomas island. Natl. geog. 109: 214 (col.) Feb '56.

——, Samarian. Natl. geog. 99: 451 (col.) Ap '51.

——, Samoa. Disney: People & places, p. 129-45 (col.).

——, Sardinia. Disney: People & places, p. 69-82 (col.). Holiday 13: 26 Feb '53; 23: 71 (col.) Jan '58.

——, Saudi Arabia (men). Natl. geog. 105: 493 Ap '54.

——, Scandinavian. Holiday 16: 134 Dec '54; 17: 16 Jan '55.

——, Scotland. Disney: People & places, p. 25-34 (col.). Holiday 8: cover (col.), 68 Dec '50; 14: 132 (col.) Nov '53; 15: 136 Ap '54, 25 (col.) Je '54; 16: 10, 15 (col.) Aug '54, 39-45 (part col.) Sept '54, 78 (col.) Oct '54, 100, 124 (col.) Dec '54; 17: 61, 66 (col.) Feb '55. Natl. geog. 110: 2-3, 17-9, 26, 47 (col.) Jl '56; 112: 444-5, 462-3 (col.) Oct '57.

——, Scotland (bagpipe). Holiday 9: inside cover (col.) Mar '51; 21: 160 (col.) Mar '57. Natl. geog. 107: 458 (col.) Ap '55.

——, Scotland (cartoon). Amer. heri. vol. 11 no. 5 p. 8 (Aug '60).

——, Siam. Disney: People & places, p. 163-75 (col.).

——, Siam (dancers). Natl. geog. 100: 739 (col.) Dec '51.

——, Siam (woman). Holiday 24: 32 Sept '58.

——, Sicily. Natl. geog. 107: 5, 29 (col.) Jan '55.

——, southern. Holiday 13: 23 Feb '53.

——, Spain. Amer. heri. vol. 9 no. 5 cover, 8 (col.) (Aug '58). Holiday 10: 84 Aug '51; 15: 38 (col.), 160 May '54; 27: 99 (col.) May '60. Natl. geog. 97: 424-5, 429-30, 439, 451, 454 (col.) Ap '50; 99: 523-30 (col.) Ap '51; 116: 592 (col.) Nov '59.

——, Spain (Anso). Natl. geog. 109: 305-7, 329 (part col.) Mar '56.

——, Spain (early explorers). Amer. heri. vol. 6 no. 1 p. 91 (fall '54).

——, Spain (men, 1513). Brooks: Growth of a nation, p. 32.

——, Spain (nobility, 16th cent.). Int. gr. soc.: Arts . . . p. 111 (col.).

——, Sudan. Natl. geog. 103: 260-1, 265 (col.) Feb '53.

——, Sweden. Natl. geog. 98: 635 (col.) Nov '50.

——, Switzerland. Disney: People & places, p. 37-46 (col.). Holiday 16: 28-9, 32-1 Aug '54; 21: 140 (col.) Feb '57.

costume. Natl. geog. 107: 826 (col.), 834-5 Je '55; 110: 440-78 (col.) Oct '56; 111: 170-1 (col.) Feb '57, 785 (col.) Je '57; 112: 706 (col.) Nov '57.

——, Switzerland (festival). Natl. geog. 114: 562, 564-9 (col.) Oct '58.

——, Switzerland (folk). Natl. geog. 98: 213, 215, 217, 220, 241 (col.) Aug '50.

——, Switzerland (Swiss guard). Holiday 23: cover (col.) May '58.

——, Switzerland (vine grower). Natl. geog. 114: 564 (col.) Oct '58.

——, Tahiti. Holiday 22: 116 Jl '57; 28: 69 (col.) Oct '60.
Natl. geog. 112: 729, 753 (col.) Dec '57.

——, Thailand. Natl. geog. 116: 795 (col.) Dec '59; 117: 669 (col.) May '60.

——, Thrace. Natl. geog. 109: 62-3 (col.) Jan '56.

——, Tibet. Holiday 12: 57 (col.) Dec '52. Natl. geog. 102: 217, 228-9 (col.) Aug '52; 117: 403 (col.) Mar '60.

——, Timbuktu. Natl. geog. 112: 66 (col.) Jl '57.

——, Tiwi (funeral). Natl. geog. 109: 424, 434 (col.) Mar '56.

——, Trinidad. Holiday 11: 90-5 (col.) Feb '52.

——, Tristan da Cunha. Natl. geog. 97: 115-6 (col.) Jan '50.

——, Trucial Oman. Natl. geog. 110: 88, 100 (col.) Jl '56.

——, Tuareg. Natl. geog. 112: 68-77 (col.) Jl '57.

——, Turkey Natl. geog. 110: 738, 751 (col.) Dec '56; 113: 128, 132-3 Jan '58; 115: 74-5, 77, 82 (part col.) Jan '59.

——, Turkey (girls). Natl. geog. 112: 415, 418 (col.) Sept '57.

——, Tuscany. Holiday 6: 30 (col.) Aug '49.

——, Tyrol. Natl. geog. 99: 753 (col.) Je '51; 100: 388-403 (part col.) Sept '51.

——, Tyrol (Alps, men). Holiday 27: 43 (col.) Jan '60.

——, Ukraine. Natl. geog. 108: 226 (col.) Aug '55; 116: 388 (col.) Sept '59.

——, U.S. admiral (1814). Amer. heri. vol. 6 no. 1 p. 48 (col.) (fall '54).

——, U.S. marines. Holiday 22: 74-5 (col.) Nov '57.

——, U.S. marines (1830—). Amer. heri. vol. 10 no. 2 cover (col.) (Feb '59).

——, U.S. marines (1840-). Amer. heri. vol. 10 no. 2 p. 24-35 (col.) (Feb '59).

——, U.S. Putnam's phalanx (Hartford, Conn.). Amer. heri. vol. 7 no. 5 p. 22 (Aug '56).

——, U.S. soldiers (Amer. Rev., Civil war, World war). Holiday 28: 54-5 (col.) Sept '60.

——, U.S. soldiers (Civil war). Pakula: Cent. album, (col.).

——, U.S. soldiers (17th cent.). Amer. heri. vol. 6 no. 5 back cover (col.) (Aug '55).

——, U.S. soldiers (1839). Amer. heri. vol. 7 no. 5 p. 18 (col.) (Aug '56).

——, U.S. soldiers (1860). Amer. heri. vol. 7 no. 5 p. 12, 15-23 (col.) (Aug '56).

——, Venezuela (dancers). Holiday 15: 22 (col.) Ap '54.

——, Viet Nam. Natl. geog. 102: 295 (col.), 314 Sept '52.

——, Wales. Holiday 21: 136 (col.) Ap '57. Natl. geog. 108: 566 Oct '55.

——, Watusi giants. Natl. geog. 112: 96 (col.) Jl '57.

——, western (man & boy). Natl. geog. 101: 463 Ap '52.

——, woodsman (1880). Amer. heri. vol. 11 no. 1 p. 12 (col.) (Dec '59).

——, Yugoslavia. Natl. geog. 99: 149, 154-5, 159 (col.) Feb '51.

——, Zouave band. Natl. geog. 105: 343 (col.) Mar '54.

——, Zouave cadet. Amer. heri. vol. 7 no. 5 p. 12 (col.) Aug '55.

costume making, German. Natl. geog. 111: 268 (col.) Feb '57.

costumes (bathing suits 1875). Amer. heri. vol. 5 no. 4 p. 6 (summer '54).

——, medieval. Int. gr. soc.: Arts . . . p. 53, 55, 61, 65, 69, 81 (col.).

——, modern. Holiday 28: 78-9 (col.) Sept '60.

——, national. Holiday 7: 56 (col.) Je '50.

——, sports (1894). Amer. heri. vol. 11 no. 6 p. 106, 108-9 (Oct '60).

——, street (middle 19th cent.). Amer. heri. vol. 6 no. 4 p. 46-9 (col.) (Je '55).

costumes. See also dresses; fashion.

Cosway, Richard (miniature by). Con. 138: 82 Nov '56; 144: XXX Sept '59.

Cot, Pierre. Cur. biog. p. 115 (1944).

Cote d'Azur (France). Travel 108: 57 Jl '57.

Cotes, Francis (work of). Con. 126: 27 Aug '50; 133: 181 (col.) May '54; 134: 49 Sept '54; 135: 51 Mar '55; 142: 26 Sept '58; 145: VII (col.) May '60.

Cotes, Samuel (work of). Con. ency. of ant., vol. 1, pl. 130.

Cothran, James W. Cur. biog. p. 126 (1953).

Cotman, John Sell (work by). Con. ency. of ant., vol. 1, pl. 143.
Con. 135: 220 Je '55; 142: 112 Nov '58.

Cotswold (England). Holiday 17: 26-31 (col.) Jan '55; 23: 157 (col.) Ap '58. Natl. geog. 98: 178 (col.) Aug '50.

—— (cottages, 300 yrs. old). Natl. geog. 114: 56, 58-9, 110-11 (col.) Jl '58.

cottage, farm. Amer. heri. vol. 11 no. 5 p. 20 (col.) (Aug '60).

——, summer (beach). Holiday 25: 10 (col.) Ap '59.

——, thatch roof. See house, thatch roof.

——, Worcestershire. Con. 144: XXVIII Jan '60.

"The Cottage Door" (Gainsborough). Con. 134: 111 (col.) Nov '54; 144: 234 Jan '60.

cottage on mountainside (Montreal). Holiday 7: 52 (col.) Jan '50.

"Cottage Ornee". See architecture, "Cottage Ornee".

cottages (Cotswold, Eng.). See Cotswold (England).

—— (1858.) Amer. heri. vol. 8 no. 4 p. 112 (Je '57).

cottages, Scotland. Natl. geog. 112: 466, 488 (part col.) Oct '57.

——, thatch roof. Travel 107: 57 Ap '57.

cottages. See also house; home.

Cotten, Joseph. Cur. biog. p. 142 (1943).

Cotterell, Geoffrey. Cur. biog. p. 204 (1954).

Cotton, John. Amer. heri. vol. 10 no. 6 p. 49 (Oct '59).

Cotton, Norris. Cur. biog. p. 127 (1956).

cotton (men weighing). Natl. geog. 105: 305 (col.) Mar '54.

cotton bales (Africa, wharf). Natl. geog. 97: 330 Mar '50.

cotton carding machine, first. Rawson: Ant. pict. bk., p. 33.

cotton carnival (Memphis, Tenn.). Holiday 15: 106-10 (part col.) May '54.
Natl. geog. 118: 692-3 (col.) Nov '60.

cotton gin, Whitney. Amer. heri. vol. 2 no. 3 p. 65 (spring '51); vol. 6 no. 3 p. 7 (col.) (Oct '55).
Brooks: Growth of a nation, p. 87.
Rawson: Ant. pict. bk., p. 33.

cotton harvester. Natl. geog. 118: 695 (col.) Nov '60.

cotton mill. Amer. heri. vol. 9 no. 3 p. 34 (col.), 38-9 (Ap '58).

—— (England). Amer. heri. vol. 9 no. 3 p. 36 (Ap '58).

cotton picker, Negro. Natl. geog. 105: 305 (col.) Mar '54.

cotton picker machine. Brooks: Growth of a nation, p. 286.
Natl. geog. vol. 104: 349 Sept '53; 105: 304 (col.) Mar '54.

cotton pickers. Holiday 20: 33 Sept '56.

cotton plantation. Amer. heri. vol. 6 no. 3 p. 4-5 (col.) (Ap '55).

cotton press. Rawson: Ant. pict. bk., p. 33.

cotton roller-gin. Rawson: Ant. pict. bk., p. 33.

"Cotton-wool castle" (near Hierapolis). Osward: Asia Minor, pl. 136-7, VIII (col.).

Cottrell, Ida Dorothy. Cur. biog. p. 141 (1955).

Coty, Rene (Pres. of France). Cur. biog. p. 206 (1954).
Natl. geog. 113: 717 May '58.

couch. Holiday 11: 151 (col.) Ap '52, 71 (col.) Je '52; 12: 19 (col.) '52, 125 (col.) Nov '52; 19: 12 (col.) Feb '56; 20: 134 Nov '56; 24: 91, 130 Oct '58; 27: 181 (col.) Je '60; 28: inside cover, 1 (col.) Oct '60, 145 (col.) Nov '60.

—— (African hunt). Holiday 20: 96 (col.) Oct '56.

—— (quilt). Holiday 12: 46 (col.) Sept '52.

—— (upholstered). Holiday 10: 123 (col.) Oct '51.

——, antique. Holiday 16: 38 (col.) Oct '54; 27: 28 (col.) Mar '60.
Natl. geog. 118: 188 (col.) Aug '60.

——, antique gilt carved. Con. 142: LX Nov '58.

——, Chippendale. Con. 143: 4 Mar '59.

——, Egyptian style. Con. 140: 230 Jan '58.

——, English cane (early). Con. 127: 88 May '51.

——, French antique. Con. 129: 21 Ap '52.

——, Louis XVI. Con. 133: 246 Je '54.

——, modern. Holiday 18: 56 (col.) Oct '55; 21: 115 (col.) Mar '57.

——, Queen Anne. Con. 127: 15 Mar '51.

——, regency. Con. 137: XXVI Je '56; 138: XII Dec '56.

——, 17th cent. Con. 135: LI Je '55.

couch. See also settee; sofa.

Coudenhove-Kalergi, Count Richard N. Cur. biog. p. 114 (1948).

Coudert, Frederic Rene, jr. Cur. biog. p. 175 (1941).

Coulter, Lt. Gen. John B. Cur. biog. p. 208 (1954).

"Council at Vincennes, Gen. Harrison & Tecumseh". Amer. heri. vol. 4 no. 1 p. 2 (fall '52).

Council hall, Samoa (int.). Holiday 28: 87 Oct '60.

Council hut (Ato, Philippines). Holiday 18: 93 Aug '55.

"Council of war after landing of Prince William of Orange at Torkay" (Glindoni). Con. 129: XXXIX Ap '52.

"Count Axel von Fersen" (Pasch). Con. 136: 33 Sept '55.

"Count Lowenstein" (Grien). Praeg. pict. ency., p. 289 (col.).

counter, Tudor. Con. 143: LIX Mar '59.

"Countess of Derby" (Lawrence). Con. 140: 239 Jan '58.

"Countess of Nottingham" (Lely). Con. 126: 36 Aug '50.

country club. Holiday 27: 139 Jan '60.

—— (Lima, Peru). Holiday 10: 12 (col.) Nov '51; 11: 106 (col.) May '52; 14: 13 (col.) Jl '53.

—— (Portland). Holiday 25: 70 (col.) May '59.

—— (Westchester, N.Y.). Holiday 8: 113 (col.) Dec '50.

"The country fair" (Woodside). Amer. heri. vol. 7 no. 3 p. 48-9 (col.) (Ap '56).

"Country school (Homer). Natl. geog. 99: 205 (col.) Feb '51.

country store. See store, country.

Counts, George S. Cur. biog. p. 177 (1941).

"County election day" (Bingham). Natl. geog. 99: 192 (col.) Feb '51.

Coup, W. C. Durant: Pict. hist. of Amer. circus, p. 67.

coupe (driver). Holiday 7: 10 (col.) Ap '50; 8: 74 (col.) Nov '50.

Couperin, Francois (Flupot). Cooper: Con. ency. of music p. 85.

courage (sym.). Lehner: Pict. bk. of sym., p. 57.

Courbet, Gustave (work of). Con. 133: 16 Mar '54; 138: 143 Nov '56; 139: LXVIII May '57; 144: XXIV, 263 (col.) Jan '60; 145: 137 Ap '60.
Cooper: Con. ency. of music, p. 59.
Praeg. pict. ency., p. 415 (col.).

Courchevel ski area (French Alps). Travel 113: 34-5 Jan '60.

Cournand, Andre F. Cur. biog. p. 118 (1957).

"The Course of the Empire" (Cole). Amer. heri. vol. 8 no. 6 p. 53-61 (col.) (Oct '57).

court, criminal (Chicago, early). Amer. heri. vol. 6 no. 5 p. 98 (Aug '55).

court, London, Old Bailey (cartoons). Holiday 28: 60-1 Aug '60.

"Court Ladies of the Queen of Sheba" (Francesca). Praeg. pict. ency., p. 59 (col.).

"Court of the Lions". See Alhambra (court of the lions).

"Court of Two Sisters" (New Orleans). Jordan: Hammond's pict. atlas, p. 82 (col.).

—— (diners, New Orleans). Natl. geog. 118: 713 (col.) Nov '60.

court scene (early western). Horan: Pict. hist. of wild west, p. 139.

courthouse (1837). Natl. geog. 117: 256 (col.) Feb '60.

——, Dayton (Ohio). Natl. geog. 107: 459 Ap '55.

——, Kingston (N.Y., 1777). Amer. heri. vol. 4 no. 1, p. 13 (fall '52).

——, Lincoln county (early). Horan: Pict. of wild west, p. 65.

——, New York (1777). Amer. heri. vol. 4 no. 1 p. 13 (fall '52).

——, Romney (W. Va.). Brooks: Growth of a nation, p. 258.

——, Springfield. Natl. geog. 117: 262-3 (col.) Feb '60.

——, Yorktown (1706). Natl. geog. 100: 570 Nov '51.

courtroom (1868). Amer. heri. vol. 8 no. 1 p. 24 (Dec '56).

—— (1736). Amer. heri. vol. 5 no. 1 p. 25 (col.) (fall '53).

——, Colonial (Mass.). Travel 104: 40 Oct '55.

——, Bank of England. Con. ency. of ant., vol. 3, pl. 104.

——, Colonial (Williamsburg, Va.). Natl. geog. 106: 453 (col.) Oct '54.

courtyard. Con. 143: 142 May '59.

—— (fountain, people). Holiday 23: 67 (col.) Mar '58.

—— (Mexico). Holiday 26: 54 (col.) Nov '59.

—— (museum). Holiday 14: 39 (col.) Nov '53.

—— (pirate's court). Holiday 28: 74 Sept '60.

—— (Spain). Holiday 15: 39 (col.) May '54.

——, hotel France et Choiseul. Travel 110: inside back cover Aug '58.

courtyard. See also patio.

Cousin Michael, Germany (sym.). Lehner: Pict. bk. of sym., p. 93.

Cousins, Frank. Cur. biog., p. 103 (1960).

Cousins, Margaret. Cur. biog. p. 210 (1954).

Cousins, Norman. Cur. biog. p. 144 (1943).

Cousteau, Jacques V. Cur. biog. p. 128 (1953).

Cousteau, Capt. & Mrs. Jacques Yves. Natl. geog. 108: 166 (col.) Aug '55.

Cousy, Bob. Cur. biog. p. 105 (1958).

Couture, Thomas (work of). Con. 139: XLIX Mar '57, XXXVIII Ap '57.

Couve de Murville, Maurice. Cur. biog. p. 142 (1955).

Covarrubias, Miguel. Natl. geog. 100: 813 (col.) Dec '51.

Covelly (harbor). Holiday 11: 75 (col.) Mar '52.

"Covent Garden" theatre (London). Con. 132: 108 Nov '53.

—— (int.). Cooper: Con. ency. of music, p. 456.

covered bridge. See bridge, covered.

covered wagon. Brooks: Growth of a nation, p. 112.

Rawson: Ant. pict. bk., p. 74.

Travel 101: 39 Je '54; 111: 19 May '59.

—— (attacked). Amer. heri. vol. 6 no. 1 p. 39 (col.) (fall '54).

—— (buffalo stampede). Amer. heri. vol. 7 no. 5 p. 39 (col.) (Aug '56).

—— (4 steers). Natl. geog. 110: 509 Oct '59.

—— (horses). Amer. heri. vol. 7 no. 3 p. 48 (col.) (Ap '56); vol. 7 no. 6 p. 88 (Oct '56); vol. 9 no. 3 p. 4-5 (col.) (Ap '58).

—— (mules). Brooks: Growth of a nation, p. 194.

—— (oxen). Brooks: Growth of a nation, p. 123.

Holiday 14: 59 Jl '53.

Natl. geog. 101: 177 (col.) Feb '52.

Travel 109: 25 Feb '58.

—— (oxen, people). Amer. heri. vol. 3 no. 2 p. 6 (winter '52).

Travel 113: 30 Feb '60.

—— (pigs, boy). Holiday 20: 45 Oct '56.

covered wagon train (oxen). Amer heri. vol. 6 no. 4 p. 60 (col.) (Je '55).

cow bell. Natl. geog. 111: 145 (col.) Feb '57.

Rawson: Ant. pict. bk., p. 68.

cow ear marks. Rawson: Ant. pict. bk., p. 64.

"Cow town" (1878). Brooks: Growth of a nation, p. 164.

"Cow towns" (old west, 1865-78). Horan: Pict. hist. of wild west, p. 100-2, 106, p. 109.

Cowan, Minna G. Cur. biog. p. 117 (1948).

Coward, Noel. Cur. biog. p. 179 (1941).

cowardice (sym.). Lehner: Pict. bk. of sym., p. 57.

cowboy. Holiday 5: 151 Ap '49; 13: 70 Je '53; 16: 34 (col.) Jl '54; 19: 49 (col.) Je '56; 22: 122 (col.) Oct '57.

—— (1880). Brooks: Growth of a nation, p. 169.

—— (bucking horse). Holiday 5: 140 Mar '49, 69 (col.), 146 Ap '49; 6: 30 (col.) Dec '49; 7: 7 Ap '50; 19: 23 Je '56.

Horan: Pict. hist of wild west, p. 96-7.

Natl. geog. 110: 505 (col.) Oct '56.

—— (bucking steer). Natl. geog. 101: 462 Ap '52.

—— (bull throwing). Natl. geog. 97: 705 (col.) Je '50.

—— (bull tosses). Natl. geog. 110: 504 (col.) Oct '56.

—— (cartoon). Holiday 14: 78 Sept '53, 84 Nov '53.

—— (cattle ranch, Hawaii). Natl. geog. 118: 34-5 (col.) Jl '60.

—— (cattle roundup). Natl. geog. 97: 725 (col.) Je '50.

—— (comic). Holiday 5: 61 (col.) Jan '49, 147 Ap '49; 10: 46 Jl '51, 156 Dec '51.

cowboy (France). Natl. geog. 109: 686, 688-9 (col.), 693 May '56.
—— (head & horse head). Natl. geog. 114: 163 (col.) Aug '58.
—— (horse). Holiday 10: 28, 32-3, 37 Aug '51; 15: 117 (col.) Jan '54; 16: 104 Sept '54.
—— (horse breaking). Natl. geog. 114: 163 (col.) Aug '58.
—— (horses, cattle). Holiday 12: 55 Oct '52.
—— (horse jumping). Natl. geog. 100: 284 Sept '51.
—— (horse running cattle). Amer. heri. vol. 4 no. 1 p. 32-3 (col.) (fall '52).
—— (packing horse). Holiday 7: 85 (col.) Je '50.
—— (Portugal). Disney: People & places, p. 66 (col.).
—— (resting, cartoon). Holiday 14: 30 Dec '53.
—— (riding). Holiday 16: 90 Jl '54.
—— (radio rider). Natl. geog. 114: 164 (col.) Aug '58.
—— (roping, on horse, Mexican). Natl. geog. 107: 237 (col.) Feb '55.
—— (roping steer). Amer. heri. vol. 8 no. 6 p. 40 (col.) Oct '57.
—— (South America). Holiday 22: 12 (col.) Oct '57.
—— (supper). Holiday 14: 21 (col.) Nov '53.
—— (supper party). Holiday 14: 77 Nov '53.
—— (thrown by bull). Holiday 19: 46-7 (col.) Je '56.
Natl. geog. 97: 705 (col.) Je '50; 110: 504 (col.) Oct '56.
cowboy ambush (western). Horan: Pict. hist. of wild west, p. 12.
cowboy & girl. Holiday 6: 139 Nov '49; 8: 27 Nov '50.
cowboy. See also statue (cowboy).
cowboy bunkhouse (int.). Brooks: Growth of a nation, p. 168.
cowboy hats. See hats, cowboy.
cowboys. Holiday 24: 35 (col.). Oct '58.
Natl. geog. 101: 45, 48, 67 (part col.) Jan '52.
—— (brand calf). Natl. geog. 104: 371 (col.) Sept '53.
—— (cattle herd). Amer. heri. vol. 11 no. 3 p. 65-80 (Ap '60).
Natl. geog. 108: 222-3 (col.) Aug '55.
—— (horses, cattle). Natl. geog. 100: 310-11 (col.) Sept '51.
—— (racing horses). Face of Amer., p. 58-9 (col.).
——, Argentina. See gaucho.
——, Mauriticas (truss up cattle). Natl. geog. 109: 104 (col.) Jan '56.
——, Mexican (cattle roundup). Natl. geog. 107: 226-7 Feb '55.
——, Mexican (roping on horse). Natl. geog. 107: 237 (col.) Feb '55.
——, western (on horses). Holiday 14: 125 Oct '53.
Cowden, Howard A. Cur. biog., p. 128 (1952).
Cowdry, Edmund V. Cur. biog. p. 119 (1948).
Cowen, Joshua Lionel. Cur. biog. p. 212 (1954).
cowgirl (Spain). Holiday 25: 37 Jan '59.

Cowles, Fleur. Cur. biog. p. 130 (1952).
Cowles, Gardner, jr. Cur. biog. p. 146 (1943).
Cowles, Mrs. Gardner (Fleur). Holiday 14: 42 (col.) Dec '53.
Cowles, John. Cur. biog. p. 214 (1954).
Cowles, Virginia. Cur. biog. p. 161 (1942).
Cowpens, battle of. Amer. heri. vol. 7 no. 3 p. 34 (col.) (Ap '56).
Natl. geog. 116: 97 (col.) Jl '59.
Cowtown. See Cow town.
Cox, Allyn. Cur. biog. p. 216 (1954).
Cox, Archibald. Cur. biog. p. 117 (1961).
Cox, David (work of). Con. ency. of ant., vol. 1, pl. 144.
Con. 144: 92 Nov '59.
Cox, Eugene. Cur. biog. p. 149 (1943).
Cox, Herald R. Cur. biog. p. 119 (1961).
Cox, Mary Peachey. Amer. heri. vol. 10 no. 2 p. 39 (Feb '59).
Cox, Wally. Cur. biog. p. 218 (1954).
Coxe, Howard. Cur. biog. p. 181 (1941).
Coy, Wayne. Cur. biog. p. 121 (1948).
Coymans, Joseph (Hals). Con. 143: 62 Mar '59.
Coyne, James E. Cur. biog. p. 144 (1955).
Coysevox, Antoine (work of). Int. gr. soc.: Arts . . . p. 87 (col.).
Cozens, Alexander (work of). Con. ency. of ant., vol. 1, pl. 133.
Con. 140: 127 Nov '57.
Cozens, J. R. (work of). Con. ency. of ant., vol. 1, pl. 141.
Con. 139: 53 Mar '57; 145: XXXVII May '60.
Cozumel island. Holiday 18: 13 (col.) Aug '55.
Travel 109: 37-9 Feb '58.
Cozzens, James Gould. Cur. biog. p. 126 (1949).
crab (sym.). Lehner: Pict. bk. of sym., p. 59.
crab boat. Holiday 20: 29 Aug '56.
—— (Japan). Natl. geog. 118: 756 (col.) Dec '60.
cracker stamp, antique. Rawson: Ant. pict. bk., p. 9.
cradle (1600). Rawson: Ant. pict. bk., p. 14.
—— (17th cent.). Natl. geog. 108: 302 (col.) Sept '55.
—— (sym.). Lehner: Pict. bk. of sym., p. 56.
——, antique. Con. 136: 172 Dec '55.
——, antique style. Holiday 24: 198 Nov '58.
——, baby chair. Holiday 18: 168 Nov '55; 20: 214 Dec '56; 22: 176 Oct '57, 186 Nov '57, 253 Dec '57.
——, cheese. Holiday 21: 56 (col.) Mar '57.
——, Colonial. Natl. geog. 105: 454 (col.) Ap '54; 118: 183 (col.) Aug '60.
——, doll. Holiday 25: 150 Feb '59.
Natl. geog. 115: 773 Je '59.
——, Indian. Amer. heri. vol. 7 no. 6 p. 15 (col.) (Oct '56).
——, Lapland (baby). Natl. geog. 106: 253 (col.) Aug '54.
——, Switzerland (baby). Natl. geog. 110: 444 (col.) Oct '56.
——, Tudor. Amer. heri. vol. 9 no. 6 p. 23 (Oct '58).
"cradle of Liberty". See Faneuill Hall (Boston).

cradling grain. Brooks: Growth of a nation, p. 103.
Craft, Col. Ida. Holiday 24: 68 Nov '58.
Crafts, Ebenezer (& son). Amer. heri. vol. 1 no. 4 p. 47 (col.) (summer '50).
crafts, modern & antique. Int. gr. soc.: Arts. . . .
crafts display (men). Holiday 22: 68 (col.) Sept '57.
craftsmen (India). Natl. geog. 116: 842 (col.) Dec '59.
—— (Moroccan). Natl. geog. 107: 163 (col.) Feb '55.
Craig, Cleo F. Cur. biog. p. 141 (1951).
Craig, Elizabeth May. Cur. biog. p. 127 (1949).
Craig, George N. Cur. biog. p. 103 (1950).
Craig, Gen. Malin. Cur. biog. p. 117 (1944).
Craigavon, Viscount James. Cur. biog. p. 181 (1941).
Craigie, Sir Robert. Cur. biog. p. 162 (1942).
Crain, Jeanne. Cur. biog. p. 143 (1951).
Cranach, Lucas (work of). Con. ency. of ant., vol. 1, pl. 155.
Con. 126: 86 Oct '50; 139: 260 Je '57.
Praeg. pict. ency., p. 288 (col.).
Cranach the elder, Lucas (work of). Con. 129: 67 Ap '52; 134: 93 Nov '54.
Cranach the younger, Lucas (work of). Con. 138: 137 Nov '56.
Cranbrook foundation (Mich.). Jordan: Hammond's pict. atlas, p. 99 (col.).
crane (hoists boat). Natl. geog. 114: 277 (col.) Aug '58.
—— (lifting load). Natl. geog. 115: 303 (col.) Mar '59.
—— (marble lifting). Natl. geog. 99: 597 (col.) May '51.
crane, gantry. See gantry crane.
cranes, harbor (Pakistan). Natl. geog. 107: 424 Mar '55.
cranes & pine tree (sym.). Lehner: Pict. bk. of sym., p. 44.
Cranston, Alan. Cur. biog. p. 104 (1950).
Crater lake (Ore.). Holiday 12: 39 (col.) Jl '52; 19: 21 (col.) Mar '56; 22: 54-5 (col.) Jl '57.
Natl. geog. 113: 619 (col.) May '58.
Travel 106: 25 Dec '56.
craters, moon. Natl. geog. 113: 292-3 Feb '58.
"Craters of the moon" natl. monument. Natl. geog. 118: 504-25 (col.) Oct '60.
—— (map). Natl. geog. 118: 509 (col.) Oct '60.
Cratloe castle (Ireland). Holiday 6: 36 Dec '49.
Craveiro Lopes, Francisco Higino. Cur. biog. p. 129 (1956).
Craven, Thomas. Cur. biog. p. 119 (1944).
"Craven bowl". Rawson: Ant. pict. bk., p. 89.
"The Craven children" (Vanderbanck). Con. 138: XXIII Nov '56.
Crawford, Broderick. Cur. biog. p. 106 (1950). Horan: Pict. hist. of wild west, p. 156.
Crawford, Cheryl. Cur. biog. p. 121 (1945).
Crawford, Frederick C. Cur. biog. p. 151 (1943).
Crawford, Joan. Cur. biog. p. 133 (1946).
Crawford, Phyllis. Jun. bk. of auth., p. 80.
cream ewer, George III (silver). Con. 142: XX-XIII Nov '58.

cream ewer. See also cream jug; cream pitcher.
cream jug, 18th cent. (silver). Con. ency. of ant., vol. 1, pl. 86, p. 153.
——, George I (silver). Con. 140: XLVIII Nov '57.
——, Irish glass. Con. ency. of ant., vol. 3, pl. 52.
——, Lamerie (silver). Con. 145: 126 Ap '60.
——, silver (1792). Con. 145: XL Je '60.
——, silver-gilt (antique). Con. 142: 85 Nov '58.
——, William Pether. Con. 144: 31 Sept '59.
cream pitcher, antique. Con. 132: LX Nov '53.
——, antique porcelain. Con. 141: inside cover Mar '58; 142: 11 Sept '58.
——, 18th cent. (silver). Con. 142: 134 Nov '58; 143: XVIII Mar '59.
——, George I (silver). Con. 140: XXXVII Sept '57.
——, George II (silver). Con. 144: LXVIII Dec '59; 145: XLIX Mar '60.
——, George III (silver). Con. 143 XXII, XL-VII Mar '59, XXXIV Ap '59, XVI May '59, XXXIV Je '59; 144: VII Nov '59.
——, George IV (silver). Con. 142: XXXVIII Nov '58.
——, Lamerie (silver). Con. 144: 64 Sept '59.
——, Louis XV (silver). Con. 143: XXVI Je '59.
——, Meissen. Con. 145: 56 Mar '60.
——, Paul Revere (silver). Con. 144: 70 Sept '59.
Creasey, Cassius. Cur. biog. (1963).
creation (sym.) Lehner: Pict. bk. of sym., p. 27-8.
——, octagram of. See octagram of creation.
——, serpent of. See "serpent of creation".
"Creation of man". Praeg. pict. ency., p. 7.
creation principle (sym.). Lehner: Pict. bk. of sym., p. 45.
creative power. See power, creative (sym.).
The Creator (Brahma). Lehner: Pict. bk. of sym., p. 43.
"Creator & his creatures" (from Holkham Bible pict. bk.). Con. 134: 211 Dec '54.
credence table, Elizabethan. Con. 132: XXIV Sept '53.
credit card. Holiday 28: 99 Jl '60.
Credle, Ellis. Jun. bk. of auth., p. 81.
Cree trappers (Canada). Natl. geog. 108: 196 Aug '55.
creek (children, swans). Holiday 10: 103 (col.) Aug '51.
"Creek ball game" (Deere). Natl. geog. 107: 357 (col.) Mar '55.
Creel, George. Cur. biog. p. 121 (1944).
cremation procession (Bali). Natl. geog. 116: 812-3 (col.) Dec '59.
cremation pyre, Buddhist (Cambodia). Natl. geog. 99: 472 (col.) Ap '51.
"Cremona" (Maryland home). Natl. geog. 105: 442 (col.) Ap '54.
Creole woman. Natl. geog. 109: 83 (col.) Jan '56.
Crerar, Gen. Henry D.G. Cur. biog. p. 123 (1944).
Cresap, Mark W., jr. Cur. biog. p. 81 (1959).

crescent (sym.). Lehner: Pict. bk. of sym., p. 62.

crescent & star (sym.). Lehner: Pict. bk. of sym., p. 36.

Crespi, Giuseppe-Maria. Con. 135: 5 Mar '55.

—— (work of). Con. 132: 7 Sept '53; 144: 24 Sept '59.

crests, European city. Natl. geog. 111: 816 (col.) Je '57.

——, railway. See railway crests.

Cret, Paul Philippe. Cur. biog. p. 166 (1942).

Cretan costume (ancient). Int. gr. soc.: Arts . . . p. 29 (col.).

Cretan man (head). Natl. geog. 104: 695 Nov '53.

Cretan palace (Knossos). See Palace of King Minos (Knossos).

Cretan woman. Natl. geog. 104: 699 (col.) Nov '53.

Crete. Holiday 18: 34-9 (part col.) Aug '55. Natl. geog. 104: 694-706 (part col.) Nov '53.

—— (map). Natl. geog. 104: 697 Nov '53.

Crete "snake goddess". See snake goddess, Crete.

crewel-work, antique. Con. ency. of ant., vol. 1 pl. 120.

cricket (sym.). Lehner: Pict. bk. of sym., p. 62.

cricket box, antique. Natl. geog. 104: 393 Sept '53.

cricket game (Delhi, India). Natl. geog. 116: 840 (col.) Dec '59.

—— (England). Natl. geog. 108: 348-9 Sept '55.

—— (Maldive islands). Natl. geog. 111: 836-7 (col.) Je '57.

cricket players (London). Holiday 24: 127 Oct '58.

cricketer. Holiday 21: 62 (col.) May '57.

Crider, John H. Cur. biog. p. 129 (1949).

criers, English. Natl. geog. 103: 812 (col.) Je '53.

Crillon hotel (Paris). Travel 108: 48 Jl '57.

criminology (sym.). Lehner: Pict. bk. of sym., p. 11.

Cripple Creek (Col., mining). Holiday 10: 90-3 (part col.) Jl '51.

crippled child. See boy (crutches); child, crippled; children, crippled.

Cripps, Sir. Richard Stafford. Cur. biog. p. 123 (1948).

Cripps, Stafford. Holiday 21: 89 May '57.

Crisler, Herbert Orin. Cur. biog. p. 126 (1948).

Crisp, Capt. Nicholas. Con. 141: 162 May '58.

Crispin, Edmund. Cur. biog. p. 130 (1949).

Crist, Brig. Gen. William E. Cur. biog. p. 123 (1945).

Crittenden, Dick. Horan: Pict. hist of wild west, p. 147.

Crittenden, Thomas T. Horan: Pict. hist. of wild west, p. 42.

Crittenden, Zeke. Horan: Pict. hist. of wild west, p. 147.

Crivelli, Carlo (work of). Praeg. pict. ency., p. 37 (col.).

Croatian. Natl. geog. 115: 210-11 (col.) Feb '59.

Croatian coast. Holiday 25: 85 (col.) Je '59.

Croatian wheel dance. Natl. geog. 115: 210 (col.) Feb '59.

Croce, Benedetto. Cur. biog. p. 128 (1944).

Crockett, Davy (ship figurehead). Rawson: Ant. pict, bk., p. 79.

Crockett, Lucy Herndon. Cur. biog. p. 130 (1953).

Crockett hotel (San Antonio). Jordan: Hammond's pict. atlas, p. 118 (col.).

crocodile (sym.). Lehner: Pict. bk. of sym., p. 58.

Croegaert, Georges (work of). Con. 142: XX-XIX Nov '58.

Croft, Arthur C. Cur. biog. p. 132 (1952).

Crome, John (work of). Con. 126: 190-1 Dec '50; 144: 234, 236-7 Jan '60.

Cromwell, Joseph (work of). Holiday 21: 140 (col.) May '57.

Cromwell, Oliver (Lely). Con. 135: 237 Je '55.

Cronin, Archibald J. Cur. biog. p. 168 (1942).

Cronkite, Walter Leland, jr. Cur. biog. p. 131 (1956).

Cronyn, Hume. Cur. biog. p. 133 (1956). Holiday 26: 64 Jl '59.

Crook, Gen. George. Amer. heri. vol. 11 no. 2 p. 55 (Feb '60). Pakula: Cent. album, p. 109.

"Croome court" (house, Worcestershire, Eng.). Con. 132: 74-6 Nov '53.

crop duster plane. Natl. geog. 110: 320 Sept '56; 115: 555 Ap '59.

cropsey, Jasper F. (work of). Con. 137: XXXV Je '56.

croquet. Holiday 10: 46 Jl '51.

—— (women & man playing). Holiday 26: 94 (col.) Jl '59.

croquet game. Holiday 12: 89 Aug '52.

Crosby, Bing. Cur. biog. p. 182 (1941); p. 131 (1953). Holiday 20: 69 Sept '56.

Crosby, John. Cur. biog. p. 134 (1953).

Crosby, Robert. Cur. biog. p. 220 (1954).

crosier, French (antique). Con. 140: 20 Sept '57.

Crosland, Anthony. Cur. biog. (1963).

Crosley, Powell, jr. Cur. biog. p. 138 (1947).

Cross, Beresford Hope. Con. 142: 30 Sept '58.

Cross, Burton N. Cur. biog. p. 222 (1954).

Cross, Lawrence (work of). Con. 145: 127 Ap '60.

Cross, Lothar. Con. 138: 237 Jan '57.

Cross, Sir Ronald H. Cur. biog. p. 184 (1941).

Cross, Waltham (work of). Con. 141: XVII May '58.

cross. Natl. geog. 111: 584 (col.) May '57; 113: 465 (col.) Ap '58.

—— (crucified rose). Lehner: Pict. bk. of sym., p. 73.

—— (crucifixion). Natl. geog. 100: 393 (col.) Sept '51: See also crucifixion.

—— (man carrying). Disney: People & places, p. 74 (col.).

—— (marker of 1st Spanish capitol). Amer. heri. vol. 2 no. 2 p. 8 (winter '51).

—— (men & woman). Travel 113: 42 Mar '60.

—— (on top mt. Matterhorn). Travel 101: 17 Jan '54.

—— (sym. of faith). Lehner: Pict. bk. of sym., p. 35.

—— (war cemetery). Natl. geog. 111: 734, 738, 758, 763 Je '57.

cross, altar (Flemish). Con. 143: V Ap '59.

——, altar (French, Carrand, Col.). Con. 140: 17 Sept '57.

——, Bishop's pectoral silver. Con. 144: 37 Sept '59.

——, Celtic (Ireland). Holiday 6: 35 Dec '49; 19: 129 (col.) Feb '56.
Natl. geog. 106: 563 Oct '54.

——, cemetery. Natl. geog. 98: 356 (col.) Sept '50.

——, Coptic (sym.). Lehner: Pict. bk. of sym., p. 34.

——, double-beam (sym.). Lehner: Pict. bk. of sym., p. 35.

——, 18th cent. Con. 132: XV Nov '53.

——, Episcopal (sym.). Lehner: Pict. bk. of sym., p. 34.

——, 15th cent. Con. 132: 126-8 Nov '53.

——, flower. Natl. geog. 107: 212 (col.) Feb '55.

——, Greek Orthodox church (sym.). Lehner: Pict. bk. of sym., p. 35.

——, green (sym.). Lehner: Pict. bk. of sym., p. 89.

——, infinite (sym.). Lehner: Pict. bk. of sym., p. 80.

——, Irish. Amer. heri. vol. 9 no. 5 p. 92 (Aug '58).

——, Italian processional. Con. 138: 121 Nov '56.

——, Latin. Natl. geog. 111: 732 (col.) Je '57.

——, Lutheran (sym.). Lehner: Pict. bk. of sym., p. 36.

——, "Magic square" (Pompeii). Ceram: March of arch., p. 30.

——, Maltese. Con. 132: XV Nov '53.

——, memorial (discoverer of San Miguel). Natl. geog. 114: 283 Aug '58.

——, memorial (to E. Shackleton). Natl. geog. 112: 618 (col.) Nov '57.

——, mission. Holiday 27: 49 Feb '60.

——, painted (Verona). Con. 143: 36 Mar '59.

——, Portuguese gold (antique). Con. 137: 11 Mar '56.

——, Portuguese reliquary. Con. 137: 14 Mar '56.

——, processional. Con. 140: 173 Dec '57.

——, Russian orthodox church. Lehner: Pict. bk. of sym., p. 37.

——, St. Cuthbert's retreat. Natl. geog. 102: 561 Oct '52.

——, San Salvador's (Columbus's 1st landing). Natl. geog. 113: 198 (col.) Feb '58.

——, 17th cent. (rose diamond). Con. 134: V Dec '54.

——, 17th cent. (silver). Con. 139: V Ap '57.

——, Spanish monument. Travel 111: 31 Ap '59.

——, Tav (sym.). Lehner: Pict. bk. of sym., p. 29.

——, Tibetan thunderbolt (sym.). Lehner: Pict. bk. of sym., p. 42.

——, war (France). Amer. heri. vol. 10 no. 6 p. 17 (Oct '59).

——, wheel. See wheel cross (sym.).

——, world's tallest (Bald Knob Mt.). Travel 103: 37 May '55.

cross & crown of thorns (sym.). Lehner: Pict. bk. of sym., p. 53.

cross & helmet (sym.). Lehner: Pict. bk. of sym., p. 54.

cross & sceptor (English). Natl. geog. 104: 325 (col.) Sept '53.

"Cross of Christ" (on ship's sails). Natl. geog. 118: 650 (col.) Nov '60.

Cross of Lothair (Aachen, 10th cent.). Praeg. pict. ency., p. 193 (col.).

Cross of St. George order (18th cent.). Con. 144: 85 Nov '59.

cross. See also crucifix.

crossbones & skull. See skull & crossbones.

crossbow (17th cent.). Con. ency. of ant., vol. 1, pl. 109.

crossbowmen (Italy, pageant). Natl. geog. 110: 663 (col.) Nov '56.

crossbows. Natl. geog. 107: 648 (col.) May '55.

Crosse, Richard (miniature by). Con. ency. of ant., vol. 1, pl. 131.

crossed fingers. See fingers, crossed.

Crosser, Robert. Cur. biog. p. 136 (1953).

cross-staff (man sighting). Natl. geog. 110: 9 (col.) Jl '56.

——, wood. Natl. geog. 111: 714 May '57.

crossing sign (sym.). Lehner: Pict. bk. of sym., p. 89.

——, railroad. Travel 106: 56 Sept '56.

Crossley, Archibald M. Cur. biog. p. 185 (1941).

Crossman, Richard H. S. Cur. biog. p. 140 (1947).

Crouse, Russel. Cur. biog. p. 187 (1941). Holiday 28: 64 Aug '60.

Crow, Carl. Cur. biog. p. 189 (1941).

Crow, James. Holiday 26: 102 (col.) Nov '59.

Crowley, Leo T. Cur. biog. p. 155 (1943).

crown. Holiday 11: 85 (col.) Feb '52, 33 (col.) May '52, 17 (col.) Je '52; 22: 24 (col.) Oct '57.
Natl. geog. 103: 703 May '53.

—— (sym.). Lehner: Pict. bk. of sym., p. 13.

——, bridal. See bridal crown.

——, British imperial. Int. gr. soc.: Arts . . . p. 165 (col.).
Natl. geog. 113: 575 Ap '58.

——, English (abstraction). Holiday 23: cover, 3 Ap '58.

——, English Queen's (14th cent.). Con. 144: 80 Nov '59.

——, English royal. Holiday 28: 108 (col.) Oct '60.

——, English state. Natl. geog. 104: 326 (col.) Sept '53.

——, Episcopal. Natl. geog. 103: 383 (col.) Mar '53.

——, George III. Amer. heri. vol. 11 no. 4 p. 95 (Je '60).

crown, German imperial (10th cent.). Praeg. pict. ency., p. 192 (col.).

——, golden (Christmas). Holiday 22: 174 Nov '57.

——, Hitite queen's. Osward: Asia Minor, pl. 16.

——, King of Bavaria. Con. 144: 84 Nov '59.

——, King's Holiday 13: 155 Ap '53.

——, mural (sym.). Lehner: Pict. bk. of sym., p. 87.

——, Norwegian bridal (silver-gilt). Con. 144: XXIV Nov '59.

——, Persian (jeweled). Natl. geog. 114: 26 (col.) Jl '58.

——, planetary. See planetary crown.

——, Queen's (11th cent.). Con. 144: 80 Nov '59.

——, royal. Holiday 10: 88 Aug '51; 12: 60 (col.) Aug '52, 33 (col.) Dec '52 22: 25 (col.) Dec '57.

——. St. Edward's. Natl. geog. 104: 302, 324 (col.) Sept '53.

——, Sweden royal. Holiday 20: 38 (col.) Aug '56.

crown & sceptor (sym.). Lehner: Pict. bk. of sym., p. 95.

crown & shield. See shield & crown.

crown & skull. See skull & crown.

crown badge (for cartridge box). Amer. heri. vol. 2 no. 4 p. 60 (summer '51).

crown jewels. Holiday 27: 20 Feb '60.

crown of Empress Anna (Russia). Int. gr. soc.: Arts . . . p. 165 (col.).

crown of Michael Feodorovitch. Int. gr. soc.: Arts . . . p. 165 (col.).

crown of Monomach (Russia). Int. gr. soc.: Arts . . . p. 165 (col.).

crown of thorns (sym.). Lehner: Pict. bk. of sym., p. 36.

"Crowning with thorns" (Van Dyck). Con. 129: pl. opp. p. 77 (col.) Je '52.

Crowninshield, George. Amer. heri. vol. 11 no. 5 p. 59 (Aug '60).

Crowninshield, Jacob. Amer. heri. vol. 6 no. 2 p. 15 (winter '55).

Crowninshield, Capt. Jacob. Durant: Pict. hist. of Amer. circus, p. 24.

Crowninshield wharf (Salem, 1805). Amer. heri. vol. 6 no. 2 p. 10-11 (col.) (winter '55).

crowns, Hawaiian king's. Natl. geog. 118: 14 (col.) Jl '60.

"Crow's nest" at top of ship (watch tower). Holiday 8: 59 Oct '50.

Crowther, Bosley. Cur. biog. p. 120 (1957).

crozier. Con. 140: 172 Dec '57.

—— (ivory). Int. gr. soc.: Arts . . . p. 57 (col.).

crucible (aluminum, making). Natl. geog. 113: 564 Ap '58.

crucified rose (sym.) Lehner: Pict. bk. of sym., p. 73.

crucified serpent (sym.). Lehner: Pict. bk. of sym., p. 72.

crucifix, El Greco. Con. 134: 176-9 Dec '54.

——, Italian (silver-gilt & crystal). Con. ency. of ant., vol. 3, pl. 34.

——, North Umbrian. Con. 132: 212 Jan '54.

——, Portuguese (14th cent., wood figure). Con. ency. of ant., vol. 3, pl. 53.

——, Romanesque. Con. 136: 151-3 Dec '55.

——, wood. Con. 136: 17 Sept '55.

crucifix. See also cross.

crucifix base, Italian silver. Con. 144: 154 Dec '59.

"Crucifixion" (Andrea di Bartolo of Siena). Con. 133: 214 May '54.

"Crucifixion" (David). Con. 127: 119 May '51; 139: 205 May '57.

"Crucifixion" (Holbien the younger). Con. 136: 239 Jan '56.

"Crucifixion" (medieval wooden sculpture). Con. 140: 168-9 Dec '57.

"Crucifixion" (Nicoletto, carved panel). Con. 137: 147 Ap '56.

"Crucifixion" (Niethardt). Praeg. pict. ency., p. 285 (col.).

"Crucifixion" (on Mass cloth). Praeg. pict. ency., p. 217 (col.).

"The Crucifixion" (Poilleve, enamel). Con. 143: 174 May '59.

"Crucifixion" (Ribera). Praeg. pict. ency., p. 31.

"Crucifixion with the Virgin & St. John" (Terbruggen). Con. 139: 56 Mar '57.

crucifixion cross. Natl. geog. 100: 393 (col.) Sept '53.

cruet. Natl. geog. 103: 346 Mar '53.

——, 18th cent. (silver). Con. 143: XLVIII Je '59.

——, George II (silver). Con. 139: XXXIV Ap '57.

——, Georgian (silver). Con. 137: XXXIII May '56; 143: XLII May '59.

——, glass. Daniel: Cut & engraved glass, pl. 149.

——, salad dressing. Holiday 27: 117 (col.) Ap '60.

cruet frame (Douai, 1771). Con. 142: 16 Sept '58.

cruet jug (Norwegian, 1763). Con. 145: 11 Mar '60.

cruet set, boat shaped (antique). Con. 145: 275 Je '59.

cruet stand, George II. Con. 142: XXVI Dec '58, V Jan '59.

——, Irish (antique). Con. 134: VII Sept '54.

——, Italian (silver). Con. 144: 156 Dec '59.

Cruger's store, Nicholas (St. Croix). Amer. heri. vol. 6 no. 4 p. 7 (Je '55).

cruiser (boat). Holiday 14: 61 (col.), 94-5 Oct '53; 19: 81 (col.) Jan '56; 21: 113 Feb '57, 182 May '57, 121 (col.) Je '57; 22: 124 (col.) Oct '57; 23: 12 (col.) Feb '58, 104, 126 Mar '58, 36 (col.) Ap '58; 25: inside cover (col.), 112 Feb '59, 113 (col.) Ap '59, back cover (col.) Je '59; 26: 98 Jl '59,, 18 Sept '59, 107 (col.) Oct '59; 27: 134 Feb '60; 28: 103 Sept '60, 163 Nov '60.

Natl. geog. 107: 101 Jan '55; 113: 21 (col.) Jan '58.

Travel 102: 12 Jl '54; 103: 22 Feb '55; 107: 33 Jan '57, 51 Feb '57; 112: 17 Aug '59; 113: inside cover Mar '60; 114: 33 Jl '60.

—— (being built). Holiday 10: 44-5 Nov '51.

—— **(girls).** Travel 107: 51 Mar '57.

—— **(girls & boys).** Natl. geog. 98: 151, 154 (col.) Aug '50.

——, **Canada.** Natl. geog. 114: 154 (col.) Aug '58.

——, **Santa Rosa.** Travel 113: 81 Ap '60.

——, **paddle-wheeler.** Natl. geog. 107: 69 (col.) Jan '55.

cruises, vacation (map, routes). Holiday 22: 139-44 Oct '57.

Crum, Bartley C. Cur. biog. p. 142 (1947).

Crump, Irving. Jun. bk. of auth., p. 84.

Crump, Jerry K. Natl. geog. 114: 599 (col.) Nov '58.

Crump, Norris. Cur. biog. p. 122 (1957).

Crusader castle of Judin (ruins). Holiday 17: 41 (col.) Feb '55.

Crusader costume. See costumes, Crusader.

Crusader lands. Natl. geog. 106: 814-51 (col.) Dec '54.

Crusaders, Penafiel (Portugal). Holiday 6: 107 (col.) Sept '49.

Crusader's castles. See castle, Crusader's.

Cruse (Crete, 3000 yrs. ago). Int. gr. soc.: Arts . . . p. 19 (col.).

Cruttenden sisters (Gainsborough). Con. 126: 125 Oct '50.

Cruzan, William. Horan: Pict. hist. of wild west, p. 192.

Cruzen, Rear Adm. Richard H. Cur. biog. p. 144 (1947).

crystal (sym.). Lehner: Pict. bk. of sym., p. 14.

crystal ball gazer (comic, fortune teller). Holiday 23: 42 Je '58.

crystal gazing globe. Lehner: Pict. bk. of sym., p. 67.

"Crystal palace" museum. Amer. heri. vol. 11 no. 3 p. 17 (col.) (Ap '60).

"Crystal palace theater" (London). Durant: Pict. hist. of Amer. circus, p. 40.

Ctesiphon, arch of. See Arch of Ctesiphon.

Cub Scout group & leader. Face of Amer., p. 122-3 (col.).

Cub Scouts. Face of America. p. 122-3 (col.).

Cuba. Holiday 5: 34-43 (col.) Feb '49; 12: 158 (col.) Dec '52; 13: 72-3 Feb '53; 22: 66-75 (col.) Dec '57; 27: 24-5 (part col.) Jan '60. Travel 106: 18-21 Dec '56.

—— **(Havana, "Plaza de Armes").** Con. 132: IV Jan '54.

—— **(map).** Natl. geog. 99: 639 May '51. Travel 106: 18 Dec '56.

—— **(war).** Amer. heri. vol. 8 no. 2 p. 42-5 (col.) (Feb '57).

"Cuba & Uncle Sam". Amer. heri. vol. 8 no. 2 p. 41 (col.) (Feb '57).

Cuban children. Holiday 19: 94-7 (part col.) Jan '56. Natl. geog. 97: 72 (col.) Jan '60.

Cuban dancers. See dancers, Cuban.

Cuban drummer (silhouette). Holiday 19: 74 Jan '56.

Cuban musicians (on raft). Holiday 25: 171 (col.) Je '59.

Cuban woman & market man. Holiday 5: 36 (col.) Feb '49.

Cubanos dancing. Holiday 10: 184 (col.) Dec '51; 11: 83 Jan '52; 22: 74 (col.) Dec '57.

Cubans. Holiday 27: 51-9 (part col.) Feb '60.

cuckoo clock. Holiday 15: 162 May '54; 16: 13 (col.), 143 Nov '54; 17: 115 Feb '55; 18: 107 Aug '55, 9, 117 Sept '55, 63 Nov '55; 21: 76 Jan '57. Travel 104: 3 Aug '55.

cuff links. Holiday 18: 68-9 (col.) Oct '55; 20: 134 (col.) Dec '56; 24: 60 (col.) Dec '58.

Cugat, Xavier. Cur. biog. p. 171 (1942).

cuirasses (helmets). Travel 113: 36 Ap '60.

Cukor, George. Cur. biog. p. 157 (1943).

Cullen, Bill. Cur. biog. p. 105 (1960).

Cullen, Hugh Roy. Cur. biog. p. 146 (1955).

Cullis, Winifred C. Cur. biog. p. 158 (1943).

Cullman, Howard S. Cur. biog. p. 145 (1951).

"Cumaean Sibyl" (Guercino). Con. 139: 35 Mar '57.

Cumberland Gap (Va., Ky., Tenn.). Brooks: Growth of a nation, p. 82. Travel 109: 36-40 Je '58.

—— **(tower on pinnacle).** Travel 104: 15 Jl '55.

Cumberland trail. Travel 108: 19 Jl '57.

Cummings, Robert. Cur. biog. p. 136 (1956).

Cundall, Charles (work of). Con. 135: 60 Mar '55.

Cuneiform carvings (Persia). Travel 113: 34 Feb '60.

Cuneiform inscription. Ceram: March of arch., p. 210.

Cuneiform script. Ceram: March of arch., p. 182, 184.

—— **(597 B.C.).** Natl. geog. 118: 842 Dec '60.

Cuneo, John F. Cur. biog. p. 108 (1950).

Cunningham, Sir Alan. Cur. biog. p. 136 (1946).

Cunningham, Sir Andrew B. Cur. biog. p. 191 (1941).

Cunningham, Sir Graham. Cur. biog. p. 132 (1949).

cup. Holiday 22: 222 (col.) Dec '57.

—— **(sym.).** Lehner: Pict. bk. of sym., p. 67.

——, **acorn.** See acorn cup.

——, **agate.** Con. 136: 9 Sept '55; 138: 126 Nov '56.

——, **Amer. Tying silver.** Con. 135: 75 Mar '55.

——, **antique silver.** Con. 134: LIX Nov '54, XXX Dec '54; 135; XIII, XIV Mar '55; 136: 261 Jan '56.

——, **antique silver-gilt.** Con. 134: V Sept '54, XXIX Dec '54.

——, **Ascot gold.** Con. 126: 224 Dec '50.

——, **bronze libation.** Con. 136: 66 Sept '55.

——, **Campion (1500).** Con. ency. of ant., vol. 1, p. 153.

——, **caudle.** See caudle cup.

——, **Charles II.** Con. 127: 81 May '51; 135: VII Je '55; 137: III Ap '56.

——, **Charles II (covered).** Con. 138: LX Nov '56.

——, **Chelsea.** Con. 135: LI Ap '55.

——, **Chinese (antique).** Con. 132: 202 Jan '54. Int. gr. soc.: Arts . . . p. 91 (col.).

——, **Chinese (bronze).** Con. 141: 6 Mar '58.

——, **Chinese (porcelain, 16th cent.).** Con. 138: 183 Dec '56.

cup, coconut. Con. 134: 161 Dec '54; 140: 131 Nov '57.

——, coconut (Scotch antique). Con. 135: 177 May '55.

——, coconut (silver). Con. ency. of ant., vol. 3, p. 64.

——, coconut (silver mounted, 1650). Con. ency. of ant., vol. 1, pl. 82.

——, columbine (Nuremberg). Con. ency. of ant., vol. 3, pl. 32.

——, covered (carved wood). Con. ency. of ant., vol. 3, pl. 107.

——, covered (18th cent. silver). Con. 138: XIII Dec '56, XIII Jan '57.

——, covered (Elizabethan, silver gilt). Con. 140: 255 Jan '58.

——, covered (George II, silver). Con. 138: XXXIV Sept '56.

——, covered (George III, gold). Con. 139: 192 May '57.

——, covered (George III, silver). Con. 138: XLI Jan '57.

——, covered (German renaissance). Con. 138: 48 Sept '56.

——, covered (Groth). Con. 142: 106 Nov '58.

——, Cretan. Ceram: March of arch., p. 60.

——, Doncaster. Con. 135: 227 Je '55; 139: 241 Je '57.

——, Drinking (18th cent.). Con. 133: 86 Ap '54.

——, drinking (James I, silver). Con. 141: XX-XV May '58.

——, drinking (Russian). Con. 141: XXXV Je '58.

——, drinking (16th cent.). Con. 133: 82 Ap '54.

——, Durham. Con. 135: 227 Je '55.

——, egg. Holiday 26: 24 Oct '59.

——, Egyptian faience. Con. 133: 37 (col.) Mar '54.

——, Egyptian gold (15th cent.). Con. 145: 213 May '60.

——, Elizabeth I (silver). Con. 142: XII Jan '59.

——, English (antique). Con. 137: 226-7 Je '56.

——, English (ivory & silver standing, early). Con. 126: 201 Dec '50.

——, Etruscan. Holiday 14: 116 Sept '53.

——, eye. Con. 132: 193 Jan '54.

——, Fairfax (enamel glass). Con. 143: 188 May '59.

——, Fairfax (seal on box). Con. 143: 32-3 (col.) Mar '59.

——, falcon (silver gilt, 16th cent.). Con. 143: 168 May '59.

——, George I (silver). Con. 135: LV May '55.

——, George II (silver). Con. 133: XXXII Mar '54; 135: LIII May '55; 137: XLVI Mar '56, V Ap '56, IX Je '56.

——, George III (gold). Con. 137: XXII Mar '56; 139: 167 May '57.

——, George III (silver). Con. 132: LXXI Jan '54; 138: 111 Sept '56.

——, George III (silver-gilt). Con. 127: inside cover May '51.

——, German double (silver). Con. ency. of ant., vol. 3, p. 64.

——, gold (18th cent.). Con. 142: 65 Sept '58.

——, Islamic lustre. Con. 145: 288 Je '60.

——, Italian gold (16th cent.). Holiday 27: 115 (col.) Feb '60.

——, James I. Con. 127: 76 May '51.

——, Lamerie. Con. 134: XXXI Sept '54; 145: 68 Mar '60.

——, measuring. See measuring cup.

——, mustache. Travel 110: 56 Sept '58.

——, nautilus. See nautilus cup.

——, 19th cent. (gilt & jewel). Con. 133: 155 May '54.

——, 19th cent. (standing). Con. 133: 155 May '54.

——, pineapple silver (German). Con. ency., of ant., vol. 3, p. 65.

——, Queen Anne. Con. 133: XLV Ap '54; 137: XLI May '56.

——, Queen Anne (gilt). Con. 132: XLIX Nov '53.

——, Queen's (to commemorate the coronation). Con. 132: 188 Jan '54.

——, racing. See racing cup.

——, Radziwil. Con. 144: 82 Nov '59.

——, Richmond. Con. 135: 227 Je '55.

——, silver (antique). Con. 132: 205 Jan '54.

——, silver (17th cent.). Con. 132: 22 Sept '53; 139: 30 Mar '57.

——, silver (1740). Con. 142: VII Jan '59.

——, silver-gilt. Con. 138: 145 Nov '56.

——, stag silver-gilt (16th cent.). Con. ency. of ant., vol. 3, pl. 33.

——, steeple. Con. 139: 243 Je '57.

——, steeple (James I). Con. 139: 31 Mar '57.

——, Strasbourg double (16th cent.). Con. 133: 263 Je '54.

——, sugar cane sirup. Natl. geog. 113: 551 (col.) Ap '58.

——, Sutton. Con. 140: 112 Nov '57.

——, Swaythling. See Swaythling cup.

——, trophy. See trophy cup.

——, two-handled. Con. 140: 131 Nov '57.

——, two-handled (silver, 18th cent.). Con. 141: 91 Ap '58.

——, wager silver (form of girl). Con. ency. of ant., vol. 3, p. 67.

——, wassail (antique). Con. 129: XXIV Ap '52.

——, welcome. See welcome cup.

——, William III (silver). Con. 132: XXVI Nov '53; 133: XXIV Mar '54, X Ap '54, XVI May '54, VIII Je '54; 137: XXXVII Mar '56.

——, windmill (silver, 17th cent.). Con. ency. of ant., vol. 3, pl. 33.

——, wine. See wine cup.

——, "Winged monster" (rock crystal). Con. 144: 40 Sept '59.

——, Zurich globe (silver). Con. ency. of ant., vol. 3, p. 65.

cup & cover, Ashburnham (silver-gilt, 18th cent.). Con. 143: 171 May '59.

——, Burleigh standing (silver-gilt). Con. 143: 170 May '59.

cup & cover, coconut (14th cent.). Con. 143: 167 May '59.
——, Elizabeth I (silver-gilt ostrich egg). Con. 144: 197 Dec '59.
——, Elizabethan crystal. Con. 140: XXIX Sept '57.
——, Elizabethan crystal high (silver-gilt). Con. 145: 128 Ap '60.
——, Emes (19th cent. silver). Con. 140: XX-XV Dec '57.
——, English pineapple. Con. 142: 227 Jan '59.
——, Flemish-Renaissance. Con. 140: 182 Dec '57.
——, George I (Irish silver). Con. 142: XLIV Jan '59.
——, George II (silver). Con. 140: 39 Sept '57.
——, George III (silver). Con. 144: XXVI Nov '59, XXXI Jan '60.
——, George III (silver-gilt). Con. 143: XXII May '59.
——, George III (Storr, silver). Con. 143: XIV May '59.
——, parcel-gilt. Con. 142: 252 Jan '59.
——, Queen's (modern). Con. 144: 36 Sept '59.
——, silver (1590). Con. ency. of ant., vol. 1, p. 153.
——, silver (modern). Con. 144: 36 Sept '59.
——, silver (16th cent.). Con. 141: 105 Ap '58.
——, silver (18th cent.). Con. ency. of ant., vol. 1, pl. 92. Con. 142: 230-1 Jan '59.
——, silver-gilt (19th cent.). Con. 144: VII Jan '60.
——, standing (silver-gilt, 17th cent.). Con. 143: 169 May '59.
——, standing (silver-gilt, 17th cent.). Con. 144: 15 Sept '59.
——, standing (16th cent.). Con. 143: 167 May '59.
cup & saucer. Amer. heri. vol. 3 no. 4 p. 37 (col.) (summer '52). Holiday 10: 122 Oct '51; 18: 110 Sept '55, 121 (col.) Oct '55, 136 Nov '55; 19: 19 Feb '56, 30 May '56, 156 Je '56; 20: 152 Nov '56; 22: 77 (col.) Sept '57; 23: 125 (col.) Mar '58; 24: 28 (col.) Dec '58; 25: inside cover (col.), 160 May '59; 26: 52 (col.) Dec '59; 27: 160 Jan '60; 28: 186 Oct '60, 224 Nov '60, 117 (col.) Dec '60.
——, antique. Amer. heri. vol. 2 no. 1 p. 50 (fall '50).
——, Capo di Monte. Con. 144: XXXIX Jan '60.
——, Doccia. Con. 135: 17 Mar '55.
——, James II (silver-gilt). Con. 141: 129 Ap '58.
——, Lenox china. Holiday 23: 115 Je '58.
——, Meissen. See Meissen cup & saucer.
——, New Hall (18th cent.). Con. ency. of ant., vol. 1, pl. 53.
——, Russian (19th cent.). Con. 144: 278 Jan '60.
——, Sevres. Con. 143: 224 Je '59.
——, Swedish. Natl. geog. 101: 694 May '52.

cup, saucer & plate (Lenox). Holiday 23: 133 Ap '58.
cupboard (1600). Rawson: Ant. pict. bk., p. 15.
——, 17th cent.). Con. 129: XVIII Ap '52.
——, (18th cent.). Con. 143: 80 Ap '59.
——, Amer. (1760). Int. gr. soc.: Arts . . . p. 105 (col.).
——, Baroque corner. Con. ency. of ant., vol. 3 pl. 17.
——, Chinese corner (18th cent.). Con. 141: LV May '58.
——, Chippendale. Con. 138: IV Sept '56.
——, Chippendale corner. Con. 129: VI Je '52.
——, Colonial corner. Holiday 8: 41 (col.) Jl '50. Natl. geog. 105: 465 (col.) Ap '54.
——, corner. Con. 145: 221 Je '60. Holiday 21: 5 (col.) Jan '57.
——, corner (18th cent.). Con. 143: XLVI Mar '59.
——, court (16th cent.). Con. 137: LX Ap '56.
——, Danzig. Praeg. pict. ency., p. 20.
——, dwarf regency. Con. 145: XV Je '60.
——, Elizabethan. Con. 139: 226-7 Je '57.
——, Elizabethan court. Con. 143: XII Mar '59, 202 May '59.
——, English (antique). Con. 126: 47 Aug '50.
——, Henry VIII. Con. 142: LXXIII Jan '59.
——, James I. Con. 132: XXV Sept '53.
——, Louis XV corner. Con. 135: 129 Ap '55.
——, Portuguese (17th cent.). Con. 143: 271 Je '59.
——, press. See press cupboard.
——, recess (18th cent.). Con. 145: LVII May '60.
——, Regency style. Int. gr. soc.: Arts . . . p. 105 (col.).
——, Sheraton. Con. 136: XXI Dec '55.
——, Sheraton bow-front. Con. 143: XXVIII Mar '59.
——, Sheraton corner. Con. 138: 61 Sept '56; 144: LII Sept '59.
——, Sheraton linen. Con. 132: VI Nov '53.
——, Swedish (antique). Con. 141: XXII Mar '58.
——, three-tier. Con. 141: 106 Ap '58.
——, wing (17th cent.). Con. ency. of ant., vol. 1, pl. 7.
cupboard. See also tridarn.
cupid. Con. 143: XXII Mar '59, XXX Ap '59, XXXIV May '59, XXXIV Je '59.
—— (head). Labande: Naples, p. 95.
"Cupid" (Julien terracotta). Con. 140: 7 Sept '57.
—— (seated in chair). Amer. heri. vol. 9 no. 1 p. 82, 94 (Dec '57).
—— (shooting arrow). Amer. heri. vol. 9 no. 1 p. 81 (Dec '57). Holiday 24: 26 Jl '58; 27: 90-1 (col.) (Ap '60).
—— (sym.). Lehner: Pict. bk. of sym., p. 65.
"Cupid & Psyche" (Canova statue). Con. 144: 230 Jan '60.
—— (Della Valle etching). Con. 144: 179 Dec '59.
—— (terracotta). Con. 140: 4 Sept '57.
cupids. Con. 142: LIV Dec '58.

cupids (eating ice cream). Amer. heri. vol. 8 no. 4 p. 48-9 (col.) (Je '57).
cupola. Travel 113: 31 Jan '60.
——, types of. Praeg. pict. ency., p. 85.
cupola of Santa Caterina a Formello. Labande: Naples, p. 75.
Curacao. Holiday 5: 118 Mar '49.
Travel 114: 94 Jl '60.
"Curassiers at the mosque" (Pasini). Con. 138: XXXIII Jan '57.
curb bit, Italian. Con. 136: 230 Dec '55.
curfew (metal fire cover). Con. ency. of ant., vol. 3, p. 242.
Curie, Madame Marie. Jensen: The White House, p. 217.
Curley, James Michael (in jail). Amer. heri. vol. 10 no. 4 p. 88 (Je '59).
Curley, Jim. Amer. heri. vol. 10 no. 4 p. 20-5 (Je '59).
curling iron, wig. See wig curling iron.
curling match (Scotland). Disney: People & places, p. 34. (col.).
curling stone game. Natl. geog. 104: 845 (col.) Dec '53; 109: 542-3 Ap '56; 113: 78-80 (part col.) Jan '58.
currach, Irish. Holiday 23: 62 (col.) Je '58.
"Curral das Freiras" (Madeira island). Natl. geog. 115: 382 (col.) Mar '59.
Curran, Joseph E. Cur. biog. p. 125 (1945).
currency. See coin.
Currie, Lauchlin. Cur. biog. p. 193 (1941).
Currier, Nathaniel (work of). Amer. heri. vol. 6 no. 1 p. 15 (col.) (Dec '54).
Currier & Ives (lithographs by). Amer. heri. vol. 2 no. 1 p. 44-5 (col.), 48 (fall '50).
—— (prints). Amer. heri. vol. 8 no. 4 p. 41-53 (col.) (Je '57).
—— ("woman's rights" cartoon). Amer. heri. vol. 10 no. 6 p. 20-1 (col.) (Oct '59).
Curry, Big Nose George. Horan: Pict. hist. of wild west, p. 210.
Curry, John Stewart. Cur. biog. p. 194 (1941).
—— (work of). Amer. heri. vol. 6 no. 2 p. 5 (col.) (Feb '55).
Curry, Kid. See Logan, Harvey.
Curry, Peggy Simson. Cur. biog. p. 107 (1958).
curry comb. Rawson: Ant. pict. bk., p. 67.
curtain, bamboo. See bamboo curtain.
Curtice, Harlow H. Cur. biog. p. 139 (1953).
Curtin, John. Cur. biog. p. 195 (1941).
Curtis, Ann. Cur. biog. p. 128 (1945).
Curtis, Cyrus H. K. Holiday 8: 24 Jl '50.
Curtis, Glenn H. Natl. geog. 116: 266 Aug '59.
Curtis, Tony. Cur. biog. p. 83 (1959).
Curusi, Ugo. Cur. biog. p. 96 (1948).
Curzon, Clifford. Cur. biog. p. 110 (1950).
Cusco (Peru). Natl. geog. 98: 422-26, 430-1, 442 (col.), 447 Oct '50.
Cushing, Alonzo H. Amer. heri. vol. 9 no. 2 p. 30 (Feb '58).
Cushing, Archbishop Richard J. Cur. biog. p. 133 (1952).
Cushing, William Barker. Pakula: Cent. album, p. 111.
Cushman, Pauline. Horan: Pict. hist. of wild west, p. 131.
cuspidor, brass. Holiday 26: 151 (col.) Nov '59.

Custer, Gen. George Armstrong. Amer. heri. vol. 5 no. 4 p. 32, 36 (summer '54); vol. 8 no. 2 cover, 4, 9 (col.) (Feb '57); vol. 9 no. 2 p. 30 (Feb '58).
Brooks: Growth of a nation, p. 182.
Holiday 8: 36 Sept '50.
Pakula: Cent. album, p. 113.
Custer battlefield memorials. Amer. heri. vol. 5 no. 4 p. 40-43 (summer '54).
Custer's battle route, Gen. G.A. Amer. heri. vol. 8 no. 2 p. 91 (Feb '57).
"Custer's last fight". Amer. heri. vol. 5 no. 4 p. 30-1, 37 (col.) (summer '54).
"Custer's last stand" (1876). Brooks: Growth of a nation, p. 181.
"Custer's last stand". (Remington). Amer. heri. vol. 8 no. 2 cover (col.) (Feb '57).
Custis, Gen. Washington Parke. Amer. heri. vol. 5 no. 3 p. 26 (spring '54).
Custis, Mary Anne Randolph. See Lee, Mrs. Robert E.
custode. Con. 136: 9-10 Sept '55.
custom house (Dublin, Ireland). Holiday 6: 56 (col.) Dec '49.
Travel 110: 49 Jl '58.
—— (Salem, Mass.). Travel 104: 40 Oct '55.
—— (Virgin islands). Natl. geog. 109: 229 Feb '56.
customs office (French). Natl. geog. 105: 173 (col.) Feb '54.
customs officer, Belgium. Natl. geog. 108: 542 (col.) Oct '55.
customs officer inspects luggage. Natl. geog. 106: 796 (col.) Dec '54.
cut glass trade-marks. Daniel: Cut & engraved glass, pl. 164-5.
Cuthbert, Margaret. Cur. biog. p. 145 (1947).
cutlass (1860). Brooks: Growth of a nation, p. 173.
cutlery. Con. 134: 165-73 Dec '54.
Holiday 20: 164 Dec '56.
cutlery making (man). Natl. geog. 113: 515 (col.) Ap '58.
cutouts (by C. Dana Gibson). Amer. heri. vol. 10 no. 4 p. 112 (Je '59).
"Cutter Zephyr racing in the Mersey" (Walters). Con. 144: XLV Nov '59.
cutting block, kitchen. Holiday 12: 145 Nov '52.
"Cutty Sark". See ship, clipper ("Cutty Sark").
Cuttyhunk island (Mass.). Travel 107: 32-5 Je '57.
Cuzco. Amer. heri. vol. 6 no. 5 p. 32 (col.) (Aug '55).
"Cuzco" (engraved by de Bry). Amer. heri. vol. 6 no. 5 p. 37 (Aug '55).
Cuzco dancers. See dancers, Cuzco.
cycle-buggy (riders). Natl. geog. 113: 48 (col.) Jan '58.
cyclorama bldg. (Atlanta). Travel 110: 18 Jl '58.
cyclorama of Battle of Atlanta. See Battle of Atlanta.
cyclotron. Natl. geog. 104: 789 (col.) Dec '53.
cyclotron room. Natl. geog. 114: 340-1 (col.) Sept '58.
cylix & serpent (sym.). Lehner: Pict. bk. of sym., p. 13.

cymbals (musical instrument). Int. gr. soc.: Arts . . . p. 141 (col.).
cymbium amphora shells. *See* shells, bailer (cymbium).
Cynthia Ann & baby (on horse). Amer. heri. vol. 7 no. 3 p. 38 (Ap. '56).
Cyprus, Isle of. *See* Isle of Cyprus.
Cyprus gardens (Charleston). Holiday 11: 65-6 (col.) Ap '52; 16: 42-3 (col.) Oct '54. Natl. geog. 103: 313, 319 (col.) Mar '53.
Cyprus gardens (Fla.). Jordan: Hammond's pict. atlas, p. 73 (col.).
Cyrankiewicz, Józef Cur. biog. p. 124 (1957).
Czechoslovakia (Prague). Holiday 21: 56-9 (col.) Jan '57.
Czettel, Lodislas. Cur. biog. p. 197 (1941).

D

Dabney, Virginius. Cur. biog. p. 128 (1948).
da Carravaggio, Michelangelo (work of). Con. 129: 47 Ap '52.
Dache, Lilly. Cur. biog. p. 198 (1941). Holiday 5: 130 Mar '49.
Daddi, Bernardo (work of). Con. 145: LXV (col.) May '60.
"Daedalus & Icarus" (statue by Canova). Con. 143: 242 Je '59.
Da Faenza, Giovanni B.U. (work of). Con. 140: 184 Dec '57.
da Firenze, Michele. *See* Michele da Firenze.
Da Gama, Vasco. Holiday 25: 75 Feb '59.
dagger. Holiday 28: 123 (col.) Dec '60.
—— (boy). Natl. geog. 110: 67 (col.) Jl '56.
—— (1500 B.C.). Natl. geog. 117: 860 Je '60.
——, Mycenae. Ceram: March of arch., p. 50.
——, Tuareg (on arm). Natl. geog. 112: 69 (col.) Jl '57.
dagger & skull. *See* skull & dagger (sym.).
daggers, antique. Con. 144: 195 Dec '59.
daguerreotype. Natl. geog. 106: 427 Sept '54.
—— (3rd oldest in U.S.). Amer. heri. vol. 2 no. 2 p. 57 (winter '51).
daguerreotypes (1850—). Amer. heri. vol. 8 no. 1 p. 55-64 (Dec '56).
Dahanayake, W. Cur. biog. p. 106 (1960).
Dahl, J. C. (work of). Con. 145: 26-9 Mar '60.
Dahl, Michael (self-portrait). Con. 133: 178 May '54.
Dahlberg, Rev. Edwin T. Cur. biog. p. 108 (1958).
Dahlgren, John A. Pakula: Cent. album, p. 115.
Dahlquist, Charles (work of). Amer. heri. vol. 4 no. 2 p. 14. (winter '53).
Daibutsu (Buddha). Lehner: Pict. bk. of sym., p. 49.
—— (Great Buddha). Natl. geog. 118: 765 (col.) Dec '60.
dairy ware, Wedgwood. Con. 140: 21 Sept '57.
dairyman (bicycle). Natl. geog. 104: 717 Nov '53.
dairymen (mechanical milking). Natl. geog. 117: 22-3 (col.) Jan '60.
dais (King of Bunyoro). Natl. geog. 118: 373 (col.) Sept '60.
——, Virgin's. *See* "Virgin's dais".

daisy (sym.). Lehner: Pict. bk. of sym., p. 65.
Dal Lake (India). Travel 105: 53 Feb '56.
Dalai Lama (Lhasa). Cur. biog. p. 148 (1951). Holiday 26: 32 Dec '59. Natl. geog. 99: 415 Mar '51.
Dale, Chester. Cur. biog. p. 110 (1958).
Dale, Sir Thomas (Flemish art). Con. 126: 164 Dec '50.
Daley, Arthur. Cur. biog. p. 137 (1956).
Daley, Richard J. Cur. biog. p. 148 (1955).
Dalgliesh, Alice. Jun. bk. of auth., p. 86.
Dali, Salvador. Cur. biog. p. 149 (1951). Holiday 13: 83 May '53; 23: 61 Jan '58; 24: 14 Dec '58.
—— (work of). Con. 144: 253 (col.) Jan '60. Praeg. pict. ency., p. 453.
Dallas, Charles Donald. Cur. biog. p. 133 (1949).
Dallas (Texas, Hall of state). Amer. heri. vol. 4 no. 1 p. 16-21 (part col.) (fall '52).
Dalmation coast. Holiday 14: 38 (col.) Aug '53.
—— (map). Travel 107: 36 Ap '57.
Dalmia, Ramkrishna. Cur. biog. p. 130 (1948).
Dalrymple, Jean. Cur. biog. p. 141 (1953).
Dalton, Bob. Horan: Pict. hist. of wild west, p. 157, 163.
Dalton, Emmett. Horan: Pict. hist. of wild west, p. 158, 165.
Dalton, Grat. Horan: Pict. hist. of wild west, p. 163.
Dalton, Hugh. Cur. biog. p. 130 (1945).
Dalton, J. Frank. Horan: Pict. hist. of wild west, p. 44.
Dalton, Julia. Horan: Pict. hist. of wild west, p. 156, 159.
Daly, James. Cur. biog. p. 84 (1959).
Daly, John. Cur. biog. p. 131 (1948).
Daly, Maureen. Cur. biog. p. 138 (1946).
Dam, Henrik. Cur. biog. p. 136 (1949).
dam, Allatoona. *See* Allatoona dam.
dam, Amer. falls (Idaho). Travel 104: inside cover Jl '55.
——, Bhakra. *See* Bhakra dam.
——, Bonneville. *See* Bonneville dam.
——, Dokan. *See* Dokan dam.
——, Fontana. *See* Fontana dam.
——, Fort Loudoun. *See* Fort Loudoun dam.
——, Fort peck. *See* Fort Peck dam.
——, Grand Coulee. *See* Grand Coulee dam.
——, Hebgen. *See* Hebgen dam.
——, Hoover. *See* Hoover dam.
——, Imperial. *See* Imperial dam.
——, Jackson lake. *See* Jackson lake dam.
——, Kaprum. *See* Kaprum dam.
——, Kariba. *See* Kariba dam (Africa).
——, Kentucky. *See* Kentucky dam.
——, Kerr. *See* Kerr dam.
——, Moses-Saunders power. *See* Moses-Saunders power dam.
——, Nakahodo. Natl. geog. 107: 274 Feb '55.
——, Norris. *See* Norris dam.
——, Owen Falls. *See* Owen Falls dam.
——, Pickwick. *See* Pickwick dam (Tenn.).
——, power (Puerto Rico). Natl. geog. 99: 437 Ap '51.

dam, river (Pakistan). Natl. geog. 102: 633 Nov '52.

——, Roosevelt. *See* Roosevelt dam.

——, Sault spillway. *See* Sault spillway dam.

——, Shasta. *See* Shasta dam.

Damascus. Natl. geog. 110: 723-4 (col.) Dec '56; 114: 730-1 Nov '58.

Damaskinos, Archbishop. Cur. biog. p. 133 (1945).

Damon, Ralph S. Cur. biog. p. 137 (1949).

Dampier, Robert (work of). Amer. heri. vol. 11 no. 2 cover (col.) (Feb '60).

Damrosch, Walter. Cur. biog. p. 132 (1944).

Dana, Charles A. Amer. heri. vol. 8 no. 3 p. 22 (Ap '57).

Dana, Richard Henry. Amer. heri. vol. 11 no. 6 p. 28 (Oct '60).

"Danae" (Titian). Con. ency. of ant., vol. 1, pl. 154.

Natl. geog. 97: 759 (col.) Je '50.

Dance, Nathaniel (work of). Con. 135: 286 Je '55; 138: XLVII Nov '56; 140: 236 Jan '58.

a dance. *See* "Snow Ball" (Buffalo).

dance (muse of). Lehner: Pict. bk. of sym., p. 33.

—— (Quadrille, Spanish Embassy). Natl. geog. 111: 88-9 (col.) Jan '57.

a dance (social). *See* a ball.

dance, African "baboon". Natl. geog. 97: 317 Mar '50.

——, Austrian. *See* "Schuhplattler".

——, Austrian "shoe clapper". Holiday 26: 73 Sept '59.

——, Balinese monkey. Holiday 18: 104 Sept '55.

Natl. geog. 116: 808-9 (col.) Dec '59.

——, Basque street. Holiday 25: 142 (col.) May '59.

——, Chalifah (Africa). Travel 113: 31 Jan '60.

——, Eskimo. Holiday 26: 43 Aug '59.

——, flamenco. *See* flamenco dance.

——, folk. *See* folk dance.

——, funeral. *See* funeral dance, Kaleri.

——, German sword. Natl. geog. 111: 265 (col.) Feb '57.

——, Hula. *See* Hawaiian dancer.

——, Indian. *See* Indian dance.

——, Jordan Valley (deity). Natl. geog. 112: 834-5 Dec '57.

——, Maypole. *See* Maypole dance; "Dance around the Maypole".

——, medicine men. *See* Indian medicine mask dance.

——, modern (college class). Holiday 11: 61 (col.) May '52.

——, monkey dance. *See* dance, Balinese monkey.

——, Morris. *See* Morris dance.

——, rain. *See* rain dance.

——, rustic (about 1830). Amer. heri. vol. 11 no. 3 p. 13 (col.) (Aug '60).

——, Samoa. Disney: People & places, p. 144-5 (col.).

——, Scandinavian festival. Holiday 27: 197 May '60.

——, Scotch highland. Travel 114: 37 Jl '60.

——, shepherd's (Kashmir). Natl. geog. 114: 634 (col.) Nov '58.

——, Spanish. *See* Sardana dance.

——, square. Holiday 10: 97 Aug '51, 41 Sept '51.

Natl. geog. 102: 497 (col.) Oct '52.

——, square (street). Natl. geog. 106: 232 (col.) Aug '54.

——, stick. *See* Trinidad "stick dance".

——, sword. *See* sword dance.

——, Tahitian. Natl. geog. 118: 18 (col.) Jl '60.

——, Tuareg. Natl. geog. 112: 74 Jl '57.

——, West Point. Natl. geog. 101: 623 (col.) May '52.

"Dance around the Maypole" (Brueghel). Con. 132: 209 Jan '54; 133: LIII May '54.

dance lessons. Holiday 11: 48 Je '52.

dance of Bharata (India). Holiday 26: 31 (col.) Dec '59; 27: 140 Feb '60.

Travel 113: 19 Jan '60.

"Dance of Salome". Natl. geog. 101: 97 (col.) Jan '52.

"Dance of the peasants" (Teniers). Con. 141: cover (col.) Ap '58.

"Dance of the soldier societies" (West). Natl. geog. 107: 358 (col.) Mar '55.

dancer (comic). Holiday 6: 81 Aug '49.

—— (girl). Holiday 22: 153 Nov '57; 27: 141 May '60.

—— (man). Holiday 19: 154 (col.) May '56; 26: 151 (col.) Dec '59; 27: 51 Ap '60, 64 May '60, 22 Je '60; 28: 26 Sept '60, 139 Oct '60, 189 Nov '60, 36 Dec '60.

—— (woman). Holiday 28: 21 Oct '60.

——, African. Natl. geog. 118: 307 (col.) Sept '60.

——, Bahama. Holiday 27: 201 Ap '60.

——, Bali temple. Travel 108: cover, 9, 12-15 Nov '57.

——, Balinese. Natl. geog. 116: 810-11 (col.) Dec '59.

——, Balinese (dressing). Natl. geog. 108: 379 Sept '55.

——, ballet. *See* ballet dancer.

——, Basque man. Holiday 27: 138 Je '60.

——, Bharata. Holiday 27: 28 (col.) May '60.

——, Borneo. Natl. geog. 109: 718 May '56.

——, Calypso. *See* Calypso dancer.

——, Ceylon. Holiday 27: 57 May '60, 120 Je '60.

——, child (headhunters). Natl. geog. 108: 460 (col.) Oct '55.

——, Cuban. Holiday 5: 84 Jan '49; 10: 184 (col.) Dec '51; 11: 83 Jan '52; 22: 74 (col.) Dec '57.

——, Devil. *See* Devil dancer (Nepal).

——, Eskimo. Natl. geog. 109: 772 (col.) Je '56.

——, Fijian. Natl. geog. 107: 126 (col.) Jan '55.

——, gypsy. Natl. geog. 112: 574 Oct '57.

——, Hawaiian. *See* Hula dancer.

——, Hindu. *See* Hindu dancer.

——, Hula. *See* Hula dancer.

——, India. Holiday 26: 31 (col.) Dec '59.

——, India (folk dancer). Natl. geog. 102: 195 Aug '52.

dancer, India (Naga girl). Natl. geog. 107: 255 (col.) Feb '55.

——, Indian. *See* Indian dancer; Navajo Indian dancer.

——, interpretive. Amer. heri. vol. 10 no. 1 p. 93 (Dec '58).

——, Japanese. *See* Japanese dancer.

——, Kandyan. *See* Kandyan dancer.

——, Kazakh (girl). Natl. geog. 106: 634 (col.) Nov '54.

——, Malay (girl). Natl. geog. 99: 332 Mar '51.

——, Mexican. Holiday 14: 78 Oct '53; 27: 138 Jan '60.

——, Nigerian stilt. Natl. geog. 110: 340 (col.) Sept '56.

——, Peruvian. Holiday 19: 20 (col.) May '56.

——, Puerto Rican. Holiday 27: 110 Je '60; 28: 105 Jl '60, 76 Aug '60, 88 Sept '60, 107 Oct '60, 134 Nov '60, 220 Dec '60.

——, Scotch. *See* Scotch dancer.

——, Siamese. Holiday 18: 49 (col.) Oct '55.

——, Spanish. Holiday 27: 178 Je '60.

——, Thailand. *See* Thailand dancer.

dancers. Holiday 5: 85 Feb '49, 4 Mar '49; 6: 27 Jl '49; 7: 89, 116-20 Jan '50, 23, 51, 81 (part col.) Feb '50, 32, 56 (col.) Mar '50, 7, 37 Ap '50, 64 (col.), 80, 154 (col.) May '50; 14: 86 Jl '53; 17: 114 Mar '55; 27: 29 (col.) Feb '60.
Int. gr. soc.: Arts . . . p. 139 (col.).
Natl. geog. 99: 576 (col.) May '51.

—— (air force cadets & girls). Natl. geog. 115: 863 (col.) Je '59.

—— (ballet). Holiday 5: 131 Ap '49; 27: 132 (col.) Feb '60.

—— (California). Travel 105: 18 May '56.

—— (children). Holiday 17: 117 Jan '55.

—— (Chinese mortuary figures). Con. ency. of ant., vol. 3, pl. 63.

—— (comic). Holiday 21: 126 Jan '57.

"The dancers" (from Herculaneum). Labande: Naples, p. 93.

dancers (in mid-air, Verne illus). Natl. geog. 113: 289 Feb '58.

—— (man & girl). Holiday 27: 125 (col.) Mar '60.

—— (men). Holiday 27: 91 (col.) May '60.

—— (men, comic). Holiday 21: 113 May '57.

—— (men on horses). Natl. geog. 99: 754 (col.) Je '51.

—— (outdoors). Holiday 8: 53 (col.) Dec '50.

—— (silhouette). Holiday 17: 62 Mar '55.

—— (square dance). Holiday 5: 68 Ap '49.

—— (television). Holiday 27: 193 Mar '60.

——, Afghanistan. Natl. geog. 98: 683 (col.) Nov '50.

——, Africa. Holiday 27: 176 Ap '60.
Natl. geog. 97: 335 (col.) Mar '50.

——, Amazon Indian. Natl. geog. 116: 631 (col.) Nov '59.

——, Ambalangoda (Ceylon). Holiday 18: 64 (col.) Dec '55.

——, Ami (Formosa). Natl. geog. 111: 348 (col.) Mar '57.

——, Andalusian. Natl. geog. 113: 422-4 (col.) Mar '58.

——, Angkor Wat. Natl. geog. 99: 469 (col.) Ap '51.

——, Argentina folk. Natl. geog. 113: 333 (col.) Mar '58.

——, Arles folk. Natl. geog. 109: 671 (col.) May '56.

——, Asia. Holiday 18: 64-5 (col.) Dec '55.

——, Austria. Natl. geog. 115: 210-11 (col.) Feb '59.

——, Austria (costumed). Travel 101: cover Jan '54.

——, Balinese. Holiday 18: 54-5 Jl '55.
Natl. geog. 99: 9-13 (col.) Jan '51, 360-2 (col.) Mar '51.

——, Bangkok (angular). Travel 102: 26 Nov '54.

——, Basque. Natl. geog. 109: 328-9 (col.) Mar '56.

——, Bavarian folk. *See* Bavarian folk dancers.

——, Belgian Congo. Natl. geog. 101: 327, 352, 355, 358 (col.) Mar '52; 112: 84 (col.) Jl '57.

——, Bhutan. Natl. geog. 102: 734 Dec '52.

——, Bhutan (masked). Natl. geog. 102: 749 (col.) Dec '52.

——, Bhutan (wedding). Natl. geog. 102: 748 (col.) Dec '52.

——, Bolivia Indian. Natl. geog. 98: 489, 493 (col.) Oct '50.

——, boogie, woogie. Holiday 5: 48 (col.) Mar '49.

——, Bugaku (Japan). Holiday 18: 65 (col.) Dec '55.

——, Cambodia. Int. gr. soc.: Arts . . . cover p. 147 (col.).
Natl. geog. 117: 516, 557 (col.) Ap '60.

——, Cameroon. Natl. geog. 116: 220 (col.) Aug '59; 118: 325 (col.) Sept '60.

——, can can. Holiday 10: 12 Jl '51.
Travel 101: 23 Jan '54.

——, Canary island. *See* Canary islanders dancing.

——, Caribbean. *See* Caribbean dancers; men, Caribbean (dancers).

——, Ceylon. *See* Ceylon dancers.

——, Cherokee Indian. Natl. geog. 102: 495 (col.) Oct '52.

——, Chilean. Natl. geog. 117: 234-5 (col.) Feb '60.

——, Cuban rumba. Holiday 5: 37 (col.) Feb '49.

——, Cuzco. Travel 112: 18 Sept '59.

——, Danish. Holiday 6: 37 (col.) Jl '49.

——, Dominican republic. Holiday 16: 60 (col.) Sept '54; 18: inside cover (col.) Sept '55.

——, English folk dance. Natl. geog. 98: 195 (col.) Aug '50.

——, Estonian polka. Natl. geog. 118: 805 (col.) Dec '60.

——, European. Holiday 17: 79 Jan '55.

——, Fijian. Travel 102: 31 Nov '54.

——, Fijian spear. Natl. geog. 114: 528-9 (col.) Oct '58.

——, France. Holiday 21: 71 (col.) Ap '57.

dancers. Natl. geog. 109: 666 (col.) May '56; 115: 910-11 (col.) May '59.

——, France (Arles). Natl. geog. 109: 671 (col.) May '56.

——, Geisha. See Geisha dancers.

——, German. Natl. geog. 111: 267 (col.) Feb '57; 115: 754-5 (col.) Je '59.

——, German teen age. Natl. geog. 115: 789 (col.) Je '59.

——, Greece. See Greek dancers.

——, Haiti. Holiday 16: inside cover (col.) Aug '54.

——, Hawaii. Amer. heri. vol. 11 no. 2 p. 19 (col.) (Feb '59). Holiday 25: 161 Je '59.

——, Hemis devil. See devil dancers, Hemis.

——, highland. See Scotch dancers.

——, Hindu. See Hindu dancer.

——, Hunza war. Natl. geog. 104: 502 (col.) Oct '53.

——, Ifalik. Natl. geog. 109: 562-3 (col.) Ap '56.

——, Inca Indian. Natl. geog. 98: 433 (col.) Oct '50.

——, India. Natl. geog. 102: 205 (col.) Aug '52; 117: 617 (col.) May '60.

——, India (war). Natl. geog. 107: 249 (col.) Feb '55.

——, Indian rain. See Indian rain dance.

——, Indochinese. Natl. geog. 99: 469 (col.) Ap '51; 108: 353 (col.) Sept '55.

——, Jamaica. Holiday 15: 50 Feb '54; 25: 118 (col.) May '59.

——, Jamaica street. Holiday 26: 21 (col.) Jl '59.

——, Javanese. See Javanese dancers.

——, Kolo (Yugoslavia). Int. gr. soc.: Arts . . . p. 147 (col.).

——, Lithuanian folk. See Lithuanian folk dancers.

——, Lotuka. See Lotuka dancers.

——, Madeira. See Madeira island dancers.

——, Majorca. Natl. geog. 111: 646-7 (col.) May '57.

——, Malaya. Holiday 27: 166 Feb '60.

——, Mexico. See Mexican dancers.

——, Morris (England). Holiday 17: 23 (col.) Jan '55.

——, Naga Hills. See Naga Hills dancers (India); dancer, India (Naga girls).

——, Nassau. Holiday 27: 77 (col.) Mar '60.

——, Nepal god. Natl. geog. 117: 398-9 (col.) Mar '60.

——, New Hebrides. See New Hebrides dancers.

——, Normandy. See Normandy dancers.

——, Oriental. Holiday 18: 64-5 (col.) Dec '55.

——, Papuan. Holiday 28: 88-9 (col.) Nov '60.

——, Peruvian Indian. Natl. geog. 107: 141 Jan '55.

——, Phnom Penh. Natl. geog. 102: 305 (col.) Sept '52.

——, Poland. Natl. geog. 114: 356-7 (col.) Sept '58.

——, Polish mountaineer. Natl. geog. 111: 171 (col.) Feb '57.

——, Portuguese folk. Natl. geog. 118: 647 (col.) Nov '60.

——, Puerto Rico. See Puerto Rican dancers.

——, pygmy. Natl. geog. 117: 290-3 Feb '60.

——, rumba. Holiday 10: 178 Dec '51.

——, rumba (Havana). Holiday 12: 69 (col.) Dec '52.

——, Russian opera. Natl. geog. 116: 376-7 (col.) Sept '59.

——, Scandinavian. See Scandinavian dancers.

——, Scotch. See Scottish dancers.

——, Siam. Holiday 25: 105 Je '59. Natl. geog. 100: 739 (col.) Dec '51.

——, Sicily. Natl. geog. 107: 12 (col.) Jan '55.

——, Spanish (girls). Natl. geog. 97: 445 (col.), 456 Ap '50.

——, Spanish Flamenco. Int. gr. soc.: Arts . . . p. 147 (col.).

——, stage. Holiday 11: 74 Jan '52.

——, street (theater). Holiday 26: 66-7 (col.) Jl 59.

——, Sumatra. See Sumatra dancers.

——, Swiss. Natl. geog. 111: 170-1 (col.) Feb '57, 785 (col.) Je '57; 114: 568-9 (col.) Oct '58.

——, Swiss-Amer. Natl. geog. 112: 706 (col.) Nov '57.

——, Tahiti. Holiday 9: 54 Mar '51.

——, Tahiti (girls). Holiday 28: 76 (col.) Nov '60.

——, Tahiti (torchlight, beach). Holiday 28: 81 Nov '60.

——, Taiyal aborigines. Natl. geog. 97: 169 (col.) Feb '50.

——, temple. Holiday 27: 152 (col.) May '60.

——, Tiwi. See Tiwi dancers.

——, Trinidad. Holiday 15: 145 (col.) May '54.

——, tropical island. Holiday 17: 21 (col.) Feb '55.

——, Turkey. Holiday 28: 25 Aug '60. Natl. geog. 115: 74-5 (col.) Jan '59.

——, Ukrane. See Ukranian folk dancers.

——, Venezuela. Holiday 15: 22 (col.) Ap '54.

——, Vienna. Natl. geog. 115: 178-9, 190-1 (col.) Feb '59.

——, Wai Wai Indians. Natl. geog. 107: 324-3 (col.) Mar '55.

——, Wales. Holiday 28: 35 (col.) Sept '60.

——, Watusi (Central Africa). Int. gr. soc.: Arts . . . p. 147 (col.). Travel 104: 49-50 Nov '55.

——, West Germany. Natl. geog. 115: 754-5 (col.) Je '59.

——, West Indies. Holiday 27: 156 Jan '60.

——, Yap women. Natl. geog. 102: 816-7 (col.) Dec '52.

——, Yugoslav Kolo. Int. gr. soc.: Arts . . . p. 147 (col.).

dancers. See also girl (dancing); girl (toe dancing).

dances, Basque. Natl. geog. 105: 148-9, 161-3 (col.) Feb '54.

——, traditional. Int. gr. soc.: Arts . . . p. 147 (col.).

dancing (1842). Amer. heri. vol. 9 no. 1 p. 10-11 (Dec '57).

—— (Jamaica). Holiday 25: 61 (col.) Feb '59.

—— (Portugal). Disney: People & places, p. 63 (col.).

—— (Schuhplattler). Disney: People & places, p. 53 (col.).

—— (Scotland, Highland fling). Disney: People & places, p. 32 (col.).

—— (Switzerland). Disney: People & places, p. p. 45 (col.).

—— (Thailand). Disney: People & places, p. 163, 172 (col.).

—— (Yugoslavia). See Yugoslav sword dance.

——, folk. Holiday 12: 105 Aug '52; 23: 37 (col.) Jan '58.

——, toe dancing. Holiday 26: 18 Aug '59. See also ballet.

——, boy & girl. Holiday 26: 101 (col.) Aug '59.

——, children (Portugal). Natl. geog. 106: 685 (col.) Nov '54.

——, college students (outdoors). Natl. geog. 113: 483 (col.) Ap '58.

——, girls. Con. 143: XXXII Je '59.

——, girls (Japanese theater). Natl. geog. 118: 739 (col.) Dec '60.

——, men & women. See men & women (dancing).

——, street. Holiday 18: 38 (col.) Oct '55; 25: 82 Je '59.

——, street (Nice, France). Holiday 25: 107 Feb '59.

——, street (Trucial Oman). Natl. geog. 110: 72-3 (col.) Jl '56.

——, western old time. Travel 101: 34 Feb '54.

dancing class. Holiday 27: 84 May '60.

—— class (boys & girls). Holiday 20: 80-1 Dec '56.

dancing faun (bronze). Labande: Naples, p. 103.

dancing giants, Watusi. Natl. geog. 112: 96 (col.) Jl '57.

"Dancing on the barn floor" (Mount). Amer. heri. vol. 7 no. 3 p. 46 (col.) (Ap '56).

dancing stump (Sequoia park). Natl. geog. 99: 684 (col.) May '51.

dancing woman (cartoon, 1894). Amer. heri. vol. 11 no. 6 p. 105 (Oct '60).

dancing. See also girl (dancing); girls (dancing).

"D'Andrade" (Slevogt). Praeg. pict. ency., p. 431 (col.).

Dandridge, Bartholomew (work of). Con. 137: XVIII (col.) Mar '56.

Dane, Nathan. Amer. heri. vol. 3 no. 3 p. 46 (spring '52).

danger (sym.). Lehner: Pict. bk. of sym., p. 88-9.

Dangerfield, George. Cur. biog. p. 143 (1953).

dangle-spit. See spit, dangle.

Dangolsheim madonna (1490). Praeg. pict. ency,. p. 205 (col.).

Daniel, Hawthorne. Jun. bk. of auth., p. 87.

Daniel, Price. Cur. biog. p. 139 (1956).

Daniel, Robert Prentiss. Cur. biog. p. 135 (1952).

Daniel, Wilbur C. Dan. Cur. biog. p. 125 (1957).

"Daniel Boone protecting his family." Amer. heri. vol. 6 no. 6 p. 11 (col.) (Oct '55).

"Daniel in the lion's den". Natl. geog. 118: 844-5 (col.) Dec '60.

"Daniel in the lion's den" (Zobel). Con. 135: 113 Ap '55.

Daniel-Rops, Henry. Cur. biog. p. 128 (1957).

Daniell, Raymond. Cur. biog. p. 137 (1944).

Daniell, Samuel. Con. 135: XXIX Ap '55.

Daniels, Bebe. Holiday 5: 47 (col.) Jan '49.

Daniels, Grace B. Cur. biog. p. 86 (1959).

Daniels, Jonathan. Cur. biog. p. 173 (1942).

Daniels, Josephus. Cur. biog. p. 139 (1944).

Danish dancers. Holiday 6: 37 (col.) Jl '49.

Danish royal guard. Int. gr. soc.: Arts . . . p. 159 (col.).

Danish woman (smoking). Holiday 25: 41 Jan '59.

"Danseuse sur la Scene" (Degas). Con. 144: 65 Sept '59.

Dante's Divine Comedy. Int. gr. soc.: Arts . . . p. 59 (col.).

Danube canal (sunset). Natl. geog. 115: 184-5 (col.) Feb '59.

Danube river. Disney: People & places, p. 47-56 (col.). Travel 103: 23 Je '55.

"Danube valley" (Altdorfer). Praeg. pict. ency., p. 287 (col.).

D.A.R. convention. Natl. geog. 100: 581-96 (col.) Nov '51.

D'Arcy, Rev. Martin. Cur. biog. p. 108 (1960).

Darden, Colgate W., jr. Cur. biog. p. 133 (1948).

Dargelas, A.H. (work of). Con. 141: XXVI Mar '58.

Darien, Henri (work of). Con. 142: XLIII Nov '58.

Darin, Bobby. Cur. biog. (1963).

Daringer, Helen Fern. Cur. biog. p. 152 (1951).

Dario, Rubin. Int. gr. soc.: Arts . . . p. 137 (col.).

Darius, King (rock carving). Natl. geog. 98: 836 Dec '50.

Darius I. Int. gr. soc.: Arts . . . p. 29 (col.).

"Darius carvings" (Iran). Natl. geog. 98: 826-42 Dec '50.

Darius monument. Natl. geog. 98: 839 Dec '50.

Darius relief. Ceram: March of arch., p. 205, 207.

Darlan, Jean. Cur. biog. p. 201 (1941).

Darling, Jay Norwood. Cur. biog. p. 175 (1942).

Darnall, Eleanor (later Mrs. Daniel Carroll I). Amer. heri. vol. 7 no. 1 cover (col.) (Dec '55).

Darnley, Lord (Eworth). Con. 142: 25 Sept '58.

Darre, Richard Walther. Cur. biog. p. 202 (1941).

Darrell, Robert D. Cur. biog. p. 149 (1955).

Darrow, Whitney, jr. Cur. biog. p. 111 (1958).

Dart, Justin W. Cur. biog. p. 140 (1946).

dart thrower. Natl. geog. 115: 484 Ap '59.

Dartmouth college. Travel 110: 16 Oct '58.

—— (students). Holiday 11: 48-53 (part col.). Feb '52.

Darwell, Jane. Cur. biog. p. 204 (1941).
Darwin, Charles Robert. Con. 144: 10 Sept '59.
"Dashwood children" (Beechey). Con. 127: 121 (col.) May '51.
D'Assia, Prince Enrico. Holiday 27: 100 (col.) Ap '60.
Daubigny, Charles Francois (work of). Con. 144: 114 (col.) Nov '59.
Daud Khan, Sardar Mohammed Cur. biog. p. 129 (1957).
Daugherty, Carroll R. Cur. biog. p. 139 (1949).
Daugherty, James. Jun. bk. of auth., p. 89.
daughters of Amer. rev. See D.A.R.
"Daughters of Louis XV" (Nattier). Con. 133: 12-3 Mar '54.
Daumier, Honore (work of). Con. 129: 25 Ap '52; 137: cover (col.) Je '56; 142: 60 Sept '58.
Praeg. pict. ency., p. 407.
Dauser, Capt. Sue S. Cur. biog. p. 142 (1944).
Davak boy & girl (Indochina). Natl. geog. 99: 475 (col.) Ap '51.
da Varallo, Tanzio. See Varallo, Tanzio da.
Davenport, Homer (cartoon by). Amer. heri. vol. 11 no. 1 p. 35 (Dec '59).
Davenport, Marcia. Cur. biog. p. 143 (1944).
Davenport, Russel W. Cur. biog. p. 145 (1944).
Davenport (Iowa, 1856). Amer. heri. vol. 8 no. 1 p. 15 (col.) (Dec '56).
David, Donald K. Cur. biog. p. 135 (1948).
David, Gerard (work of). Con. ency. of ant., vol. 1, pl. 160.
Con. 127: 119 May '51; 133: 30 Mar '54; 136: cover, 258 (col.) Jan '56; 139: 205 May '57; 143: 199 May '59; 144: 38 Sept '59.
David, Jacques Louis (work of). Natl. geog. 110: 647 (col.) Nov '56.
Praeg. pict. ency., p. 398.
David, Louis. Int. gr. soc.: Arts . . .p. 91 (col.).
David, Villiers (work of). Con. 144: 111 Nov '59.
"David" (Burrini). Con. 144: 24 Sept '59.
"David" (Michelangelo). Travel 107: 59 Ap '57.
"David" (Pasinelli). Con. 144: 23 Sept '59.
"David" (Tanzio da Varallo). Con. 138: 118 Nov '56.
"David playing on lyre" (Soulen). Natl. geog. 112: 853 (col.) Dec '57.
Davidson, Maj. Gen. Garrison H. Cur. biog. p. 131 (1957).
Davidson, George (work of). Amer. heri. vol. 7 no. 5 p. 85 (Aug '56).
Davidson, Irwin D. Cur. biog. p. 141 (1956).
Davidson, Jo. Cur. biog. p. 135 (1945).
Davidson, Rear Adm. John F. Cur. biog. p. 110 (1960).
Davidson, Roy E. Cur. biog. (1963).
Davidson, William L. Cur. biog. p. 137 (1952).
Davidson home, Maj. Gen. Howard C. Natl. geog. 105: 442 (col.) Ap '54.
Davies, Clement. Cur. biog. p. 111 (1950).
Davies, Ernest. Cur. biog. p. 154 (1951).
Davies, Joseph E. Cur. biog. p. 178 (1942).
Davies, Judge Ronald N. Cur. biog. p. 113 (1958).

Da Vinci, Leonardo. See Leonardo da Vinci.
da Vinci, Pierino (sculpture). Con. 142: 198 Dec '58.
Davis, Arthur (work of). Con. 144: 271 Jan '61.
Davis, Brig. Gen. Benjamin O. Cur. biog. p. 181 (1942).
Davis, Brig. Gen. Benjamin O., jr. Cur. biog. p. 151 (1955).
Davis, Bette. Cur. biog. p. 206 (1941); p. 145 (1953).
Holiday 5: 40 (col.) Jan '49.
Davis, David. Amer .heri. vol. 6 no. 2 p. 108 (winter '55).
Davis, Edward W. Cur. biog. p. 153 (1955).
Davis, Elmer. Amer. heri. vol. 2 no. 1 p. 6 (fall '50).
Davis, Gladys Rockmore. Cur. biog. p. 147 (1953).
Davis, Glenn. Cur. biog. p. 142 (1946).
Davis, Harvey N. Cur. biog. p. 147 (1947).
Davis, Henry Winter. Amer. heri. vol. 6 no. 4 p. 77 (Je '55).
Davis, James C. Cur. biog. p. 133 (1957).
Davis, Jefferson (Confed. Pres.). Amer. heri. vol. 6 no. 3 p. 36 (Ap '55); vol. 10 no. 6 p. 91 (Oct '59).
Pakula: Cent. album, following pl. 20.
—— **(cartoon).** Amer. heri. vol. vol. 3 no. 2 p. 15 (winter '52); vol. 9 no. 4 frontis (col.) (Je '58).
—— **(house where he married).** Brooks: Growth of a nation, p. 107.
Davis, Jess H. Cur. biog. p. 143 (1956).
Davis, Joan. Cur. biog. p. 138 (1945).
Davis, John W. Cur. biog. p. 149 (1953).
Davis, Joseph H. (work of). Amer. heri. vol. 6 no. 2 p. 38 (winter '55).
Davis, Joseph S. Cur. biog. p. 150 (1947).
Davis, Julia. Jun. bk. of auth., p. 90.
Davis, Lavinia R. Jun. bk. of auth., p. 91.
Davis, Lewis. Horan: Pict. hist. of wild west, p. 144.
Davis, Luckey. Horan: Pict. hist of wild west, p. 144.
Davis, Luther (movie writer). Holiday 5: 42 (col.) Jan '49.
Davis, Mary Gould. Jun. bk. of auth., p. 93.
Davis, Meyer. Cur. biog. p. 121 (1961).
Davis, Miles. Cur. biog. p. 92 (1962).
Davis, Nathanael V. Cur. biog. p. 87 (1959).
Davis, Richard Harding. Travel 108: inside back cover Oct '57.
Davis, Robert. Cur. biog. p. 141 (1949).
Jun. bk. of auth., p. 95.
Davis, Roy H. Cur. biog. p. 155 (1955).
Davis, Sammy, jr. Cur. biog. p. 145 (1956).
Davis, Stuart. Holiday 23: 59 (col.) Mar '58.
—— **(work of).** Praeg. pict. ency., p. 455.
Davis, Tobe Coller. Cur. biog. p. 89 (1959).
Davis, Watson. Cur. biog. p. 140 (1945).
Davis, William H. Cur. biog. p. 209 (1941).
Davis, William Rhodes. Cur. biog. p. 211 (1941).
Davis memorial, Tom J. Travel 113: 37 Mar '60.
Natl. geog. 109: 631 (col.) May '56.

Davison, Bill. Holiday 21: 143 May '57.
Davison, Brig. Gen. Frederick T. Cur. biog. p. 142 (1945).
dawn (bay, Japan). Natl. geog. 118: 758-9 (col.) Nov '60.
—— **(lava field).** Natl. geog. 118: 524 (col.) Oct '60.
Dawson, John A. Cur. biog. p. 139 (1952).
Dawson, William. Cur. biog. p. 212 (1941).
Dawson, William L. Cur. biog. p. 143 (1945).
Dawson (gold rush town). Natl. geog. 112: 262-3 (col.) Aug '57.
Day, Albert M. Cur. biog. p. 137 (1948).
Day, Doris. Cur. biog. p. 226 (1954).
Day, Dorothy. Cur. biog. p. 95 (1962).
Day, Edmund Ezra. Cur. biog. p. 144 (1946).
Day, J. Edward. Cur. biog. p. 97 (1962).
Day, Laraine. Cur. biog. p. 151 (1953).
"The Day of Decision" (Faulkner mural). Amer. heri. vol. 3 no. 1 p. 26 (col.) (fall '51).
Dayal, Rajeshwar. Cur. biog. p. 123 (1961).
Dayan, Maj. Gen. Moshe. Cur. biog. p. 135 (1957).
daybed, Charles II Con. 129: VI Ap '52.
——, **Chippendale.** Con. 139: XIV Mar '57.
——, **Queen Anne.** Con. 143: XXVIII Je '59.
"Daybreak" home (Delaware). Holiday 17: 107 (col.) Mar '55.
daylight hours (Alaska). Natl. geog. 116: 66-7 Jl '59.
days of the week, sym. of. Lehner: Pict. bk. of sym., p. 24.
Daytona beach. See beach, Daytona.
the dead, Judge of. See Judge of the dead.
"Dead Christ lamented by angels" (sculpture). Con. 144: 177 Dec '59.
"A dead man's prayer" (Egyptian tomb wall painting). Ceram: March of arch., opp. p. 142 (col.).
Dead river (fishing camp, Fla.). Face of Amer., p. 160-1 (col.).
Dead Sea scrolls. Natl. geog. 112: 839 Dec '57; 114: 802, 804-5 Dec '58.
—— **(fragment).** Int. gr. soc.: Arts . . . p. 25 (col.).
——, **men who hid the.** Natl. geog. 114: 784-99 (part col.) Dec '58.
deadfalls & snares (for game). Natl. geog. 103: 578-9 (col.) May '53.
Deadwood (S.D., 1876). Horan: Pict. hist. of wild west, p. 87.
deaf child (teacher). Natl. geog. 104: 811 Dec '53.
deaf children (being taught). Natl. geog. 107: 378-97 (part col.) Mar '55.
deaf children's school. See Clarke school (deaf children).
deaf teaching teachers. Natl. geog. 104: 811 Dec '53.
Deakin, Arthur. Cur. biog. p. 140 (1948).
Dean, Arthur H. Cur. biog. p. 228 (1954).
Dean, Dizzy. Cur. biog. p. 156 (1951).
Dean, Gordon. Cur. biog. p. 114 (1950).
Dean, Henry Trendley. Cur. biog. p. 137 (1957).
Dean, Sir Patrick. Cur. biog. p. 125 (1961).
Dean, Vera Micheles. Cur. biog. p. 161 (1943).

Dean, Maj. Gen. William F. Cur. biog. p. 230 (1954).
Dean, William F. Holiday 11: 112 Jan '52.
Deane, Silas. Amer. heri. vol. 7 no. 3 p. 75 (Ap '56).
De Angeli, Marguerite. Cur. biog. p. 152 (1947).
Jun. bk. of auth., p. 96.
Dearborn, Ned Harland. Cur. biog. p. 153 (1947).
Dearborn, Henry Ford. See Greenfield Village (Mich.).
Deasy, Mary. Cur. biog. p. 115 (1958).
Deat, Marcel. Cur. biog. p. 183 (1942).
"Death" (Böcklin). Praeg. pict. ency., p. 410.
death (skeleton with reaper). Lehner: Pict. bk. of sym., p. 76.
death (sym.). Lehner: Pict. bk. of sym., p. 28, 78-9, 92.
"Death & fire" (Klee). Praeg. pict. ency., p. 487 (col.).
"Death of Cleopatra" (terracotta). Con. 139: 34 Mar '57.
"Death of Dido" (Raimondi). Con. 138: 17 Sept '56.
"Death of Gen. Montgomery" (Trumbull). Amer. heri., vol. 9 no. 4 p. 45 (col.) (Feb '58).
"Death of Germanicus" (Poussin). Con. 143: 123 Ap '59.
"Death of St. Scholastica" (Restout). Con. 135: 42 Mar '55.
"Death of the Virgin" (German carving). Con. 144: 196 Dec '59.
—— **(Hugo Van der Goes).** Con. 126: 6-7 Aug '50.
"The Death of Wolfe" (West). Amer. heri. vol. 11 no. 1 p. 30-1 (col.) (Dec '59).
Con. 141: 60 Mar '58.
"death pit" of Ur. Ceram: March of arch., p. 239.
death ship. See ships of the dead, Egyptian.
Death Valley (Cal.). Holiday 28: 45 Aug '60.
Jordan: Hammond's pict. travel atlas, p. 194 (col.).
Natl. geog. 105: 761 (col.) Je '54.
de Ayala, Poma. See Ayala, Poma de.
debarkation net, ship. Natl. geog. 98: 655 Nov '50.
De Blaas, Eugene (work of). Con. 137: XXVI-XXVII May '56.
Debre, Michel. Cur. biog. p. 91 (1959).
De Brebeuf, Jean. Amer. heri. vol. 10 no. 6 p. 57 (col.) (Oct '59).
—— **(martyred).** Amer. heri. vol. 10 no. 6 p. 57 (Oct '59).
De Bry, Theodore (work of). Amer. heri. vol. 7 no. 6 p. 10-11 (part col.) (Oct '56).
Debucourt (work of). Con. 140: 53 Sept '57.
Debussy, Claude. Int. gr. soc.: Arts . . . p. 139 (col.).
Debussy, Claude Achille (Baschet). Cooper: Con. ency. of music, p. 86.
debutante cotillion. Holiday 10: 56 (col.) Oct '51.
"Debutante in blue" (Gainsborough). Con. 142: 52 (col.) Sept '58.

debutante. *See* also girls (debutantes).

Debutts, Harry A. Cur. biog. p. 154 (1953).

Debye, Peter J. W. Cur. biog. (1963).

decade ring (sym.). Lehner: Pict. bk. of sym., p. 37.

decanter. Con. 138: 142 Nov '56.
Holiday 10: 113 Aug '51.
Travel 113: inside back cover Je '60.

——, antique. Con. ency. of ant., vol. 1, p. 78, pl. 47.

——, antique Bristol. Con. 143: XVIII Je '59.

——, antique crystal. Con. 132: XIII Sept '53.

——, Beilby. Con. 127: 110 May '51.

——, Georgian. Con. 138: XXXVIII Jan '57; 142: XXVIII Jan '59.

——, Georgian glass. Con. 142: XX Sept '58.

——, glass. Daniel: Cut. & engraved glass, pl. 6, 11, 143-46.

——, Irish glass. Con. ency. of ant., vol. 3, pl. 46-7.

——, musical. Travel 113: inside back cover May '60.

——, porcelain figurine. Con. 134: LXI (col.) Sept '54.

De Castro, Morris F. Cur. biog. p. 116 (1950).

Decatur, Stephen. Amer. heri. vol. 7 no. 3 p. 12 (col.) (Ap '56).
Holiday 23: 77 May '58.

Deception Pass bridge (Wash.). Travel 102: cover Oct '54.

Deception Pass state park (Wash.). Holiday 25: 38 (col.) Feb '59.

de Chirico, J. *See* Chirico, J. de.

Decker, Gen. George H. Cur. biog. p. 127 (1961).

Decker, Jeremias de (poet). Con. 138: 31 Sept '56.

Decker, Fire chief John. Amer. heri. vol. 10 no. 4 p. 96 (Je '59).

Declaration of Independence. Amer. heri. vol. 6 no. 4 frontis. (Je '55).

——, drafting of. Amer. heri. vol. 3 no. 1 p. 38 (col.) (fall '51).

——, signers of. Amer. heri. vol. 9 no. 4 p. 48-9 (col.) (Je '58).

Declaration of Independence. *See* also "Signing of Declaration of Independence".

De Cort, Hendrik Frans (work of). Con. 144: XLIV Sept '59.

de Coter, Colin (work of). Con. 143: 65 Mar '59.

Decoursey, Brig. Gen. Elbert. Cur. biog. p. 232 (1954).

decoy, duck (19th cent.). Holiday 18: 61 (col.) Jl '55.

—— (man). Natl. geog. 98: 389 Sept '50.

De Creeft, Jose. Cur. biog. p. 184 (1942).

de Decker, Jeremias. *See* Decker, Jeremias de.

"Dedham mill" (Constable). Con. 144: XXVII Nov '59.

De Dreux, Alfred (work of). Con. 140: 127 Nov '57.

Dee, John. Amer. heri. vol. 10 no. 3 p. 12 (Ap '59).

deepfreeze huts. *See* huts, deepfreeze (Antarctica).

"Deer" (Ma-Pe-Wi). Natl. geog. 107: 371 (col.) Mar '55.

Deere, John. Amer. heri. vol. 6 no. 4 p. 34 (Je '55).

Deere, Noah (work of). Natl. geog. 107: 357 (col.) Mar '55.

Deering (Alaska). Natl. geog. 102: 66 (col.) Jl '52.

defeat (sym.). Lehner: Pict. bk. of sym., p. 86.

defense, patron saint of. Lehner: Pict. bk. of sym., p. 40.

Defoe, Daniel (1726). Holiday 21: 120 Ap '57.

De Forest, Lee. Cur. biog. p. 213 (1941).

Degas, Edgar (work of). Con. 133: 281-2 (col.) Je '54; 138: XXVII Dec '56; 139: XXXIII Mar '57; 140: cover (col.), 53, 59, LVI Sept '57; 141: XXVI May '58, X (col.) Je '58; 142: 63 Sept '58; 143: 145, 191 May '59; 144: 65 Sept '59; 145: 146 May '60, XXVI, LXII, 269 Je '60.
Praeg. pict. ency., p. 417 (col.).

de Gaulle, Charles. Cur. biog. p. 218 (1949); p. 157 (1960).

—— (head). Holiday 27: 62 (col.) Feb '60.

De Graaff, Johannes. Amer. heri. vol. 9 no. 6 p. 58 (col.) (Oct '58).

De Graff, Robert F. Cur. biog. p. 163 (1943).

De Hamilton family (work of). Con. 145: 226-7 Je '60.

de Heem, Cornelis (work of). Con. 144: cover (col.) Jan '60.

de Heem, Jan Davidsz (work of). Con. 145: XII (col.) Je '60.

Dehler, Thomas. Cur. biog. p. 157 (1955).

Dehn, Adolf. Cur. biog. p. 215 (1941).

—— (work of). Amer. heri. vol. 2 no. 4 p. 47, 67 (col.) (summer '51).

Dehn, Adolph (work of). Amer. heri. vol. 3 no. 2 p. 54 (col.) (winter '52).

de Hondecoeter, Melchior (work of). Con. 141: XXIX (col.) May '58.

De Hooch, Charles (work of). Con. ency. of ant., vol. 1, pl. 171.

de Hooch, Pieter (work of). Con. 132: opp. p. 73 (col.) Nov '53; 135: XII (col.) Ap '55; 136: 139 Nov '55; 142: 41 Sept '58; 144: LVII (col.) Dec '59; 145: 278 Je '60.
Praeg. pict. ency., p. 70 (col.).

Deir el-Bahri. Praeg. pict. ency., p. 153.

deities (Bhutan). Natl. geog. 102: 747 (col.) Dec '52.

——, Greek & Roman. Lehner: Pict. bk. of sym., p. 30-3.

——, Japanese (sym.). Lehner: Pict. bk. of sym., p. 48-9.

deity, Iranian. Natl. geog. 98: 829 Dec '50.

deity dance (Jordan valley). Natl. geog. 112: 834-5 (col.) Dec '57.

De Jong, David C. Cur. biog. p. 148 (1944).

De Jong, Dola. Cur. biog. p. 155 (1947).

Dejong, Meindert. Cur. biog. p. 140 (1952).

De Jonghe, Ludolf (work of). Con. 140: 118 (col.) Nov '57, XLVIII Dec '57; 142: 122 Nov '58.

De Keyser, Thomas (work of). Con. 142: LIX Dec '58.

De Kiewiet, Cornelis W. Cur. biog. p. 155 (1953).
Dekleine, William. Cur. biog. p. 217 (1941).
de Koninck, Andries (work of). Con. 133: XVII (col.). Mar '54.
De Kooning, William. Cur. biog. p. 159 (1955). Holiday 26: 91 (col.) Oct '59.
De Kruif, Paul. Cur. biog. p. 186 (1942); (1963).
de la Croix, Charles F. (work of). Con. 144: 123 Nov '59.
Delacroix, Eugene. Con. 134: XI Dec '54.
—— (work of). Con. 133: 260 Je '54; 137: 143 Ap '56, 253 Je '56; 138: 196 Dec '56; 139: 54 Mar '57; 140: 53 Sept '57, 247 Jan '58; 141: LIII Ap '58; 143: 144 May '59, 1 Je '59; 144: 198 Dec '59; 145: L Ap '60.
Cooper: Con. ency. of music, p. 36 (col.).
Int. gr. soc.: Arts . . . p. 133 (col.).
Praeg. pict. ency., p. 385 (col.).
de la Fosse, Charles (work of). Con. 141: 39 Mar '58.
De La Guardia, Ricardo A. Cur. biog. p. 188 (1942).
De La Mare, Walter. Jun. bk. of auth., p. 98.
Delaney, Shelagh. Cur. biog. p. 99 (1962).
Delano, Columbus. Amer. heri. vol. 8 no. 3 p. 52 (Ap '57).
Delany, Vice-Adm. Walter S. Cur. biog. p. 141 (1952).
De Largilliere, Nicolas (work of). Con. ency. of ant., vol. 1, pl. 159.
Con. 133: cover, 233 (col.) Je '54; 139: LII Ap '57.
De La Torre, Lillian. Cur. biog. p. 142 (1949).
de La Tour, Georges (work of). Con. 139: 34 Mar '57; 140: 70-1 Sept '57; 141: 37 Mar '58.
de la Tour, M. Quentin (work of). Con. 135: 41 Mar '55.
Delaware. Amer. heri. vol. 2 no. 4 p. 18-23 (part col.) (spring '51).
Holiday 17: 104-11 (col.) Mar '55.
Travel 106: 20-22 Oct '56.
—— (capitol bldg.). Natl. geog. 98: 380 (col.) Sept '50.
Travel 108: 35 Jl '57.
—— (map). Natl. geog. 98: 371 Sept '50; 102: 5 Jl '52; 105: 439 (col.) Ap '54.
—— (Trap Pond). Travel 110: 56 Aug '58.
Delaware river. Holiday 22: 65-71 (col.) Sept '57.
Delaware river route. Natl. geog. 102: 2-40 (part col.) Jl '52.
del Cairo, Francesco (work of). Con. 138: 119 Nov '56.
Del Cano, Juan Sebastian (statue). Natl. geog. 105: 169 (col.) Feb '54.
De Leeuw, Adele. Jun. bk. of auth., p. 98.
De Lery's castle. Amer. heri. vol. 4 no. 4 p. 39 (summer '53).
de Lesseps, Ferdinand Marie, viscount. See Lesseps, Ferdinand Marie, viscount de.
Delff, Willem (work of). Con. 138: 17 Sept '56.
Delft (Holland). Travel 104: 61 Aug '55.
Delhi. Natl. geog. 117: 614-25 (part col.) May '60.

Delhi's red fort. Natl. geog. 116: 839 (col.) Dec '59; 118: 470-1 (col.) Oct '60.
Deli throne room. See throne room, Sultan of Deli's.
Delibes, Leo. Cooper: Con. ency. of music, p. 87.
delicatessen, kosher. Holiday 10: 53 Sept '51.
"Delight makers" (Kabotie). Natl. geog. 107: 368 (col.) Mar '55.
"Delights of autumn" (Boucher). Con. 133: 109 (col.) Ap '54.
De Lima, Sigrid. Cur. biog. p. 116 (1958).
"De Lisle Hours" (Illus. from). Con. 141: 251 Je '58.
Delius, Frederick. Cooper: Con. ency. of music, p. 88.
delivery boy. Holiday 11: 142 (col.) May '52.
delivery man (Ischia island). Natl. geog. 105: 540 Ap '54.
Della Casa, Lisa. Cur. biog. p. 147 (1956).
Della Chiesa, Vivian. Cur. biog. p. 164 (1943).
della Francesca, Piero. See Francesca, della Piero.
Della Robbia, Giovanni (work of). Con. 139: XLV Mar '57.
—— (carving). Holiday 18: 91 Nov '55.
Della Robbia, Lucca (work of). Int. gr. soc.: Arts . . . p. 87 (col.).
Praeg. pict. ency., p. 310.
della Valle, Filippo (sculpture by). Con. 141: 224 Je '58; 144: 172-9 Dec '59.
Dello Joio, Norman. Cur. biog. p. 139 (1957).
Dells (Wis.). Jordan: Hammond's pict. atlas, p. 95 (col.).
Delmarva peninsula. Travel 108: 32 Jl '57.
Del-Mar-Va school room. Natl. geog. 98: 377 (col.) Sept '50.
de Lorrain, Claude. See Claude de Lorrain.
Delos (Greece, ruins). Holiday 24: 68 Sept '58. Natl. geog. 105: 32 (col.) Jan '54.
—— (harbor). Natl. geog. 114: 777 (col.) Dec '58.
Delphi (Greece). Natl. geog. 109: 54-5 (col.) Jan '56.
—— (theater). Natl. geog. 109: 54 (col.) Jan '56.
del Piombo, Sebastiano (work of). See Sebastiano del Piombo.
del Sarto, Andrea. (work of). Con. 132: 101 Nov '53; 136: 36 Sept '55.
Praeg. pict. ency., p. 280 (col.).
"Delta Queen" (river boat). Amer. heri. vol. 11 no. 5 p. 50 (col.) Aug '60.
De Luca, Giuseppe. Cur. biog. p. 156 (1947).
De Luce, Daniel. Cur. biog. p. 150 (1944).
"De Luna landing" (Fla., 1559). Holiday 23: 127 (col.) May '58.
de Lyon, Corneille. Con. 145: LIV Je '60.
de Medici, Giuliano (portrait). Con. 139: 98 Ap '57.
Demeter (sym.). Lehner: Pict. bk. of sym., p. 30.
demi-armoire. Louis XV marquetry. Con. 145: VI Ap '60, 186 May '60.
de Michelino, Domenico (work of). Int. gr. soc.: Arts . . . p. 59 (col.).

demigod. Holiday 12: 44 Nov '52.
—— (4 headed, Japan). Con. 143: 201 May '59.
Demikhov, Vladimir P. Cur. biog. p. 111 (1960).
De Mille, Agnes. Cur. biog. p. 166 (1943).
De Mille, Cecil B. Cur. biog. p. 191 (1942).
Holiday 5: 36 (col.) Jan '49; 19: 87 Mar '56.
Deming, Dorothy. Cur. biog. p. 168 (1943).
de Miranda, Juan Carreno. See Miranda, Juan Carreno de.
democracy (sym.). Lehner: Pict. bk. of sym., p. 94.
democratic authority. See authority, democratic (sym.).
Democrat Convention ribbon (approved, Jefferson, 1900). Amer. heri. vol. 7 no. 4 p. 23 (Je '56).
Democratic convention (1860). Amer. heri. vol. 11 no. 4 p. 56-9, 82-3, 85 (Je '60).
demon chaser, Chinese. Natl. geog. 97: 218 Feb '50.
demon statue (Siam). Disney: People & places, p. 172 (col.).
demons, temple. Travel 102: 23 Nov '54.
Demosthenes. Int. gr. soc.: Arts . . . p. 25 (col.).
—— (head, statue). Con. ency. of ant., vol. 3 pl. 67.
Demott, Richard H. Cur. biog. p. 158 (1951).
Dempsey, Jack. Cur. biog. p. 145 (1945).
Dempsey, John. Cur. biog. p. 129 (1961).
Dempsey, Lt. Gen. Miles C. Cur. biog. p. 152 (1944).
Dendramis, Vassili. Cur. biog. p. 159 (1947).
Denebrink, Vice-Adm. Francis C. Cur. biog. p. 149 (1956).
Denfeld, Adm. Louis E. Cur. biog. p. 160 (1947).
Holiday 7: 60 (col.) Feb '50.
Denham, Robert N. Cur. biog. p. 162 (1947).
"Denial of St. Peter" (Barbieri). Con. 132: 11 Sept '53.
Denmark. Holiday 18: 27-35 (part col.) Sept '55.
Natl. geog. 98: 642-44 (col.) Nov '50; 101: 695-7 May '52; 105: 420-29 Mar '54; 108: 810-28 (col.) Dec '55.
—— (castle). Holiday 28: 182 Oct '60.
—— (castle guards). Holiday 15: 108 Jan '54.
—— (fairy tale tour). Travel 103: 11-5 May '55.
—— (farmers, ancient times). Int. gr. soc.: Arts . . . p. 31 (col.).
—— (harbor). Natl. geog. 98: 642-3 (col.) Nov '50.
—— (honor insignia). Int. gr. soc.: Arts . . . p. 167 (col.).
—— (map). Travel 103: 15 May '55.
Denner, Balhasar (work of). Cooper: Con. ency. of music, p. 118 (col.).
Dennis (cartoon character). Cur. biog. p. 337 (1956).
Dennis, Eugene. Cur. biog. p. 143 (1949).
Dennis, Lawrence. Cur. biog. p. 219 (1941).
Dennis, Olive Wetzel. Cur. biog. p. 221 (1941).
Dennison, Adm. Robert Lee. Cur. biog. p. 113 (1960).

Denny, Charles R., jr. Cur. biog. p. 165 (1947).
Denny, George V., jr. Cur. biog. p. 117 (1950).
de Noailles, viscount. Amer. heri. vol. 3 no. 4 p. 27 (summer '52).
Densford, Katharine J. Cur. biog. p. 167 (1947).
dental design (book cover). Amer. heri. vol. 6 no. 4 p. 94 (Je '55).
dentist (at work). Natl. geog. 112: 409 Sept '57.
—— (comic). Holiday 28: 14 Oct '60.
——, mt. (child). Natl. geog. 113: 868 Je '58.
——, Russian. Natl. geog. 116: 405 (col.) Sept '59.
dentist office, ancient. Con. 129: IV Je '52.
dentistry clinic, Univ. Holiday 12: 63 Nov '52.
Denver (Colo.). Holiday 6: 106-11 (part col.) Aug '49.
Jordan: Hammond's pict. atlas, p. 162 (col.).
Natl. geog. 106: 213-7 (col.) Aug '54.
—— (mining camp). Brooks: Growth of a nation, p. 177.
—— (city & county bldg.). Natl. geog. 100: 201 Aug '51.
"The Departing coach" (Martin). Con. 139: XLI May '57.
"Departure of Enea Silvio Piccolomini" (Pinturicchio). Con. 136: 59 Sept '55.
Depinet, Ned E. Cur. biog. p. 119 (1950).
"Deposition from the cross" (Van der Weyden). Holiday 25: 66-7 (col.) Jan '59.
depot, railroad (girls). Holiday 22: 53 (col.) Sept '57.
——, railroad (Mass.). Travel 114: 47 Sept '60.
——, railroad (train, auto). Holiday 21: 112 (col.) Je '57.
de Predis, Ambrogio (work of). Con. 133: 211 May '54.
depth charges, destroyer. Natl. geog. 102: 612 Nov '52.
De Quille, Dan. Amer. heri. vol. 4 no. 3 p. 22 (spring '53).
Derain, Andre (work of). Con. 139: LXI Je '57; 140: LII Dec '57.
Praeg. pict. ency., p. 472 (col.).
Derby, Elias Hasket. Amer. heri. vol. 6 no. 2 p. 15 (col.) (winter '55).
Derby dessert service. Con. 133: 142 Ap '54.
Derby figurine. Con. 138: XXI Sept '56.
Derby figurine caudle sconces. Con. 129: XIII Je '52.
Derby figurine musician. Con. 129: 53 (col.) Ap '52.
derby hat. See hat, man's (derby).
Derby porcelain (19th cent.). Con. 133: X Ap '54.
Derby porcelain flower pot & pitcher. Con. 132: XL Sept '53.
Der Harootian, Koren. Cur. biog. p, 161 (1955).
DeRochemont, Louis. Cur. biog. p. 145 (1949).
De Rochemont, Richard. Cur. biog. p. 148 (1945).
derricks. Natl. geog. 103: 178, 180 (col.) Feb '53; 109: 831 Je '56.
derricks. See also oil derrick.
derringer gun (world's smallest). Natl. geog. 113: 875 Je '58.

Derthick, Lawrence G. Cur. biog. p. 141 (1957).
dervishes (Sufi sect). Natl. geog. 110: 86-7 (col.), 90-1 Jl '56.
Derwent, Clarence. Cur. biog. p. 167 (1947).
"Derwent Water" (Southey, Eng.). Natl. geog. 109: 510 (col.) Ap '56.
Desai, Morarji. Cur. biog. p. 117 (1958).
De Sapio, Carmine G. Cur. biog. p. 163 (1955).
"The Descent" (alabaster). Con. 133: 256 Je '54.
"Descent from the cross" (carvings). Con. 133: LXXI Je '54.
"Descent from the cross" (Delacroix). Con. 141: LIII Ap '58.
"Descent from the cross" (Hugo Van der Goes). Con. 126: 4 Aug '50.
"Desdemonde Maudite par son Pere" (Delacroix). Con. 140: 53 Sept '57.
desert. Holiday 11: inside cover (col.) Ap '52; 13: 26-7, 30-1, 32-3 (part col.) Jan '53; 24: 45 (col.) Oct '58.
Natl. geog. 101: 713 (col.) Je '52.
—— (Algeria). Natl. geog. 117: 782-3. 786 (col.) Je '60.
—— (Arabia, men, camel). Natl. geog. 110: 78-9 (col.) Jl '56.
—— (Libya, camel caravan). Holiday 25: 54-5 (col.) Ap '59.
—— (Monument valley). Disney: People & places, p. 113-28 (col.).
—— (Morocco). Disney: People & places, p. 91 (col.).
—— (New Mexico). Holiday 22: 38-9 (col.) Jl '57.
—— (N. M. way station). Face of Amer., p. 64-5 (col.).
desert, Sahara. See Sahara desert.
Desert Air hotel (Cal.). Holiday 26: 111 (col.) Jl '59.
desert directory, Amer. (map). Travel 107: 34 Mar '57.
desert farm, irrigated (award to war veteran). Natl. geog. 102: 604-7 (col.) Nov '52.
desert house. See house, desert.
desert tour, Amer. Travel 107: 33-5 Mar '57.
De Seversky, Alexander P. Cur. biog. p. 222 (1941).
De Sherbinin, Betty. Cur. biog. p. 141 (1948).
De Sica, Vittorio. Cur. biog. p. 141 (1952).
designs, perforated tin. Rawson: Ant. pict. bk., p. 20.
desk, Adam. Con. 137: XL Mar '56.
——, Amer. block front. Con. 135: 66 Mar '55.
——, antique. Con. 141: inside back cover May '58.
Natl. geog. 97: 293 (col.) Mar '50.
——, Chippendale. Con. ency. of ant., vol. 1, pl. 28.
Con. 136: XLI, XLVII Dec '55; 138: LIV Nov '56, LI Jan '57.
——, Chippendale partners. Con. 143: inside back cover Ap '59.
——, Chippendale pedestal. Con. 142: XXX Nov '58.
——, 18th cent. Con. 137: XXXVI May '56; 138: XV Sept '56; 141: XIV Ap '58.
——, English (antique). Con. 126: 45 Aug '50.

——, Georgian. Con. 137: XLI Je '56.
——, kneehole (antique). Con. 142: XXXI Jan '59.
——, kneehole Chippendale. Con. 140: XXXI Dec '57; 142: IV Nov '58.
——, kneehole (18th cent.). Con. 140: XXII Sept '57, XVI Dec '57; 144: LI Sept '59, XXX Jan '60.
——, kneehole Hepplewhite. Con. 144: XXII Dec '59.
——, library (18th cent.). Con. 134: back cover Dec '54 135: inside back cover Mar '55.
——, library serpentine. Con. 132: XVI Jan '54.
——, Louis XV. Con. 136: LXII Dec '55.
——, Louis XVI. Con. 132: 210 Jan '54; 134: 207 Dec '54; 135: 188-9 May '55; 136: 85 Nov '55.
——, Louisa May Alcott's. Natl. geog. 97: 305 (col.) Mar '50.
——, Pres. Monroe's. Jensen: The White House, p. 33.
——, oval (18th cent.). Con. 144: VI Sept '59.
——, pedestal (18th cent.). Con. 139: XL Ap '57.
——, pedestal (19th cent.). Con. 129: XLII Je '52; 140: XIV Jan '58.
——, Queen Anne kneehole. Con. 142: XVIII Sept '58.
——, Queen Victoria's. Holiday 21: 104 (col.) Jan '57.
——, regency. Con. 135: XXV Ap '55; 140: LXIX Jan '58.
——, regency bookcase. Con. 140: inside back cover Jan '58.
——, regency partners. Con. 141: XXIII May '58; 142: XIII Jan '59.
——, roll top (Louis XVIII). Con. 143: 210, 213 Je '59.
——, Sheraton. Con. 134: 47 Sept '54; 137: XXIII, XXX Ap '56.
——, Sheraton bow front. Con. 140: VII Nov '57.
——, Sheraton cylinder. Con. 139: 182 May '57.
——, Thos. Jefferson's. Natl. geog. 97: 564 (col.) May '50.
——, writing. See writing desk.
desk & chair. Holiday 22: 159 (col.) Dec '57.
desk set (antique). Con. 134: XXV Dec '54.
——, Faberge. Con. 142: L Jan '59.
desk with cupboards (18th cent.). Con. 135: back cover Mar '55.
Desmarees, George (work of). Con. 142: 7 Sept '58.
De Soto (discoverer). Holiday 6: 57 (col.) Nov '49.
De Soto auto. Holiday 5: 23 (col.) Ap '49, 138 (col.) Je '49; 6: 23 (col.) Jl '49, inside cover (col.) Aug '49, 66 (col.) Sept '49, 95 (col.) Oct '49, 15 (col.) Nov '49, 66 (col.) Dec '49; 8: 15 (col.) Oct '50.
Desportes, A. F. (work of). Con. 136: XVII (col.) Sept '55.
Despujols, Jean (with his work). Natl. geog. 99: 465, 467-82 (part col.) Ap '51.
Dessau (the Bauhaus). Praeg. pict. ency., p. 441.

dessert plate, George III silver. Con. 141: 43 Mar '58.

——, Irish glass. Con. ency. of ant., vol. 3, pl. 51.

dessert service, gold. Con. 152: 47 Sept '53.

dessert service, Swansea. Con. 144: 128 Nov '59.

——, Worcester. Con. 129: XLIV Je '52.

——, Worcester porcelain. Con. 145: XXX Ap '60.

Desses, Jean. Cur. biog. p. 150 (1956).

Destinn, Emmy (as Carmen in "Carmen"). Cooper: Con. ency. of music, p. 91.

de Stoeckl, Edouard. Amer. heri. vol. 12 no. 1 p. 47 (Dec '60).

the destroyer (sym.). Lehner: Pict. bk. of sym., p. 43.

De Sylva, Buddy. Cur. biog. p. 169 (1943).

detective. Holiday 24: 21 Oct '58.

—— (comic). Holiday 5: 79 (col.) Jan '49.

de Thyle, Baron. Con. 145: 44 Mar '60.

de Tocqueville, Alexis. Amer. heri. vol. 10 no. 4 p. 101 (Je '59).

Detroit. Amer. heri. vol. 2 no. 4 cover, p. 33-55 (summer '51).

—— (skyline). Holiday 27: 24 Ap '60. Natl. geog. 98: 820-1 Dec '50; 115: 460 (col.) Ap '59.

deuce of clubs card. Lehner: Pict. bk. of sym., p. 62.

Deuel, Wallace R. Cur. biog. p. 192 (1942).

Deupree, Richard R. Cur. biog. p. 146 (1946).

Deutsch, Julius. Cur. biog. p. 154 (1944).

de Valdes, Archbishop Fernando (Velasquez). Con. 145: 102-4 Ap '60.

De Valera, Eamon. Cur. biog. p. 160 (1951).

De Valois, Ninette. Cur. biog. p. 148 (1949).

de Vancy, Gaspard Duche (work of). Amer. heri. vol. 1 no. 3 p. 46 (spring '50).

"The Devastated City" (monument, Rotterdam). Int. gr. soc.: Arts . . . p. 131 (col.).

Dever, Paul A. Cur. biog. p. 149 (1949).

Devereux, Robert. Con. 139: 217 Je '57.

Devers, Lt. Gen. Jacob L. Cur. biog. p. 195 (1942).

Devil (on card). Lehner: Pict. bk. of sym., p. 77 (no. 15).

the Devil (sym.). Lehner: Pict. bk. of sym., p. 92.

Devil dance (Tibet). Holiday 12: 56 Dec '52.

Devil dancer. Holiday 9: 112 Mar '51.

—— (Ceylon). Holiday 11: 20 (col.) May '52.

—— (Nepal). Natl. geog. 112: 146 (col.) Jl '57.

—— (Hemis). Natl. geog. 99: 632 (col.) May '51.

devil's postpile. Holiday 13: 26 May '53.

"Devil's tower" (Wyo.). Natl. geog. 110: 506 (col.) Oct '56; 113: 621 May '58.

de Vinci, Leonardo. Int. gr. soc.: Arts . . . p. 91 (col.).

Devine, Andy. Horan: Pict. hist of wild west, p. 156.

Devine, Brig. Gen. John M. Cur. biog. p. 142 (1948).

Deviny, John J. Cur. biog. p. 144 (1948).

Devis, Arthur (work of). Con. 132: XXI (col.) Jan '54; 141: XXVII Je '58.

de Vlaminck, M. See Vlaminck, M. de.

Devoe, Brig. Gen. Ralph G. Cur. biog. p. 155 (1944).

Devonshire (England). Travel 105: 40 Ap '56.

de Vos, Cornelis (work of). Con. 136: 71 Sept '55.

De Vos, Cornetius (work of). Con. 140: XVII (col.) Dec '57.

devotional statues. See sculpture, church; statues, church.

De Voto, Bernard. Cur. biog. p. 171 (1943). Holiday 16: 33 Jl '54.

De Vries, Peter. Cur. biog. p. 92 (1959).

Dewey, Charles S. Cur. biog. p. 151 (1949).

Dewey, Adm. George. Amer. heri. vol. 6 no. 4 p. 34 (Je '55); vol. 12 no. 1 p. 70 (Dec '60).

Dewey, George Goodman. Amer. heri. vol. 2 no. 3 p. 51-3 (spring '51).

Dewey, John. Cur. biog. p. 158 (1944).

Dewey, Thomas E. Cur. biog. p. 162 (1944).

Dewey, Wilson (work of). Natl. geog. 107: 366 (col.) Mar '55.

Dewey's victory, Adm. George (at Manila). Amer. heri. vol. 11 no. 4 p. 28 (Je '60).

Dewhurst, James Frederic. Cur. biog. p. 146 (1948).

De Wint, Peter (work of). Con. ency. of ant., vol. 1, pl. 145. Con. 142: 258 Jan '59.

de Wit, Jacob (work of). Con. 132: XLIX Sept '53; 136: XXXIX Jan '56.

De Witt, Lt. Gen. John L. Cur. biog. p. 198 (1942).

de Witte, Emanuel (work of). Con. 145: 279 Je '60.

De Wohl. Louis. Cur. biog. p. 165 (1955).

de Wolf, John. Amer. heri. vol. 10 no. 3 p. 70 (Ap '59).

Dexheimer, Wilbur App. Cur. biog. p. 167 (1955).

Dhandi (Nepal). Holiday 21: 72 (col.) May '57.

D'Harnoncourt, Rene. Cur. biog. p. 145 (1952).

Dhebar, U.N. Cur. biog. p 169 (1955).

D'Hondecoeter, Melchior (work of). Con. 140: XXXV p. 58 Sept '57; 144: IX Sept '59; 145: cover (col.) May '60.

dhow, Arab (sail boat). Natl. geog. 97: 323 (col.) Mar '50; 101: 115 Jan '52; 105: 494 (col.) Ap '54; 108: 163 (col.) Aug '55.

——, Africa. Natl. geog. 97: 340 (col.) Mar '50.

——, Persian Gulf. Natl. geog. 117: 74, 102 (col.) Jan '60.

Dia, Mamadou. Holiday 25: 66 Ap '59.

diagrams (sym.). Lehner: Pict. bk. of sym., p. 75.

——, geomantic, Lehner: Pict. bk. of sym., p. 45.

Dial, Morse G. Cur. biog. p. 152 (1956).

dial, folding or diptych (antique). Con. 134: 90 Nov '54.

dials, equatorial (antique). Con. 134: 90 Nov '54.

Diamant, Gertrude. Cur. biog. p. 200 (1942).

Diamond, Harry O. Holiday 5: 32 Jan '49.

diamond. Holiday 14: 78 Nov '53.
Natl. geog. 98: 780 Dec '50; 113: 568-85 (part col.) Ap '58.
——, Hope. See Hope diamond.
——, step-cut. Con. 144: 42 Sept '59.
diamond drill. Amer. heri. vol. 2 no. 3 p. 42 (col.) (spring '51).
Diamond Head (Hawaii). Holiday 13: 34 (col.) May '53; 15: 70-1 Jan '54; 16: 72 Sept '54, 5 (col.) Oct '54, 126 (col.) Nov '54; 17: 71 (col.) Feb '55; 22; 4 (col.) Nov '57; 28: 109 Aug '60, 4 Oct '60, 118, 212 (col.) Dec '60.
Natl. geog. 118: 26 (col.) Jl '60.
Travel 113: 60 Mar '60.
Diamond Head volcano. Holiday 28: 55 Jl '60.
Diamond rock (Martinique). Natl. geog. 115: 266 (col.) Feb '59.
Diana (goddess). Lehner: Pict. bk. of sym., p. 32.
—— (bust). Con. 143: 66 Mar '59.
—— (Greek statue). Int. gr. soc.: Arts . . . p. 17 (col.).
—— (terracotta, 400 B.C.). Con. 143: 63 Mar '59.
"Diana & Callisto" (La Farge). Con. 140: 29 Sept '57.
"Diana & Endymion" (Italian porcelain). Con. 135: 15 Mar '55.
"Diana & Endymion" (marble by Plura). Con. 138: 179 Dec '56.
"Diana the huntress" (Houdon, statue). Natl. geog. 113: 261 Feb '58.
"Diane de Poitiers" (Clouet). Natl. geog. 110: 642 (col.) Nov '56.
diaphragm. Gray's anatomy, p. 389.
diary, Frances Seward's (page from). Amer. heri. vol. 10 no. 6 p. 61 (Oct '59).
diary, Schliemann's. See Schliemann's diary.
Diaz, N. (work of). Con. ency. of ant., vol. 1, pl. 175.
Con. 143: 117 Ap '59.
di Bartolo of Siena, Andrea (work of). Con. 133: 214 May '54 .
Dibelius, Bishop Otto F. K. Cur. biog. p. 157 (1953).
di Bicci, Neri (work of). Con. 145: 114 Ap '60.
di Bondone, Giotto. See Giotto di Bondone.
di Camaino, Tino (marble relief by). Con. 145: 53 Mar '60.
dice (sym.). Lehner: Pict. bk. of sym., p. 62.
dice of good luck (sym.). Lehner: Pict. bk. of sym., p. 47.
Dichter, Ernest. Cur. biog. p. 131 (1961).
Dickens, Charles. Holiday 24: 81 Oct '58.
Natl. geog. 108: 304-5 Sept '55.
——, (with wife & sister). Amer. heri. vol. 9 no. 1 p. 113 (Dec '57).
Dickens' characters (cartoon). Natl. geog. 108: 304 Sept '55.
Dickens' welcome to N.Y. (Boz Hall). Amer. heri. vol. 9 no. 1 p. 10-11 (Dec '57).
Dickey, Clifford R., jr. Natl. geog. 113: 458 Ap '58.
Dickey, John Sloan. Cur. biog. p. 170 (1955).
Dickinson, Edwin. Cur. biog. (1963).

Dickinson, Emily. Amer. heri. vol. 6 no. 3 p. 52 (Ap '55).
Holiday 16: 6 Sept '54.
Dickinson, John. Amer. heri. vol. 10 no. 1 p. 61 (Dec '58).
Dickinson, Mrs. Lafell. Cur. biog. p. 150 (1945).
Dickinson, Robert L. Cur. biog. p. 121 (1950).
Dickinson home (Amherst, Mass.). Amer. heri. vol. 6 no. 3 p. 54 (Ap '55).
Dickson, Lovat. Cur. biog. p. 101 (1962).
Dickson, Marguerite. Cur. biog. p. 148 (1952).
Dido (in "Dido & Aeneas"). Cooper: Con. ency. of music, p. 96.
Die Entfuhrung, Mozart (title page). Cooper: Con. ency. of music., p. 493.
died (genealogy sym). Lehner: Pict. bk. of sym., p. 12.
Diefenbaker, John G. Cur. biog. p. 143 (1957).
Diehl, Mrs. Ambrose N. Cur. biog. p. 170 (1947).
Dieppe (France). Natl. geog. 115: 626-7 (col.) May '59.
"Dieppe with boats & figures" (Stanfield). Con. 134: XVIII Sept '54.
Dieterle, William. Cur. biog. p. 175 (1943).
Dietrich, Marlene. Cur. biog. p. 159 (1953).
Dietz, Ferdinand (wood carving). Con. ency. of ant., vol. 3, pl. 55.
Diggs, Charles C., jr. Cur. biog. p. 145 (1957).
Dighton rock. Amer. heri. vol. 9 no. 4 p. 62-3, 91 (Je '58).
di Giorgio, Francesco (sculpture). Con. 138: 209 Dec '56.
—— (work of). Con. 145: cover (col.) Ap '60.
Dike, Phil. Cur. biog. p. 202 (1942).
Dill, Sir John G. Cur. biog. p. 224 (1941).
diligence (sym.). Lehner: Pict. bk. of sym., p. 57.
Dillingham, Walter F. Holiday 28: 49 Jl '60.
Dillman, Bradford. Cur. biog. p. 115 (1960).
Dillon, Clarence D. Cur. biog. p. 162 (1953).
Dilworth, Richardson. Holiday 23: 61 Mar '58.
Dimaggio, Joe. Cur. biog. p. 225 (1941); p. 163 (1951).
Holiday 12: 36 Oct '52.
Dimaio, Frank. Horan: Pict. hist. of wild west, p. 230.
dime (magnified). Natl. geog. 102: 56 Jl '52.
dime novels. Amer. heri. vol. 3 no. 3 p. 43-5 (spring '52); vol. 7 no. 2 p. 50-5, 115 (part col.) (Feb '56).
Dimechkie, Nadim. Cur. biog. p. 117 (1960).
Dimitrov, Georgi. Cur. biog. p. 153 (1949).
Dinant (Belgium). Holiday 26: 210 (col.) Dec '59.
Natl. geog. 108: 544 (col.) Oct '55.
Dingell, John D. Cur. biog. p. 155 (1949).
dinghies (boat). Natl. geog. 107: 790 (col.) Je '55; 114: 70-1 (col.) Jl '58; 118: 124 (col.) Jl '60.
Dingman's waterfalls. Holiday 12: 56 (col.) Oct '52.
dining hall (int., Cambridge univ.). Holiday 25: 77 (col.) Je '59.
——, communal (model, Peking). Natl. geog. 118: 214 Aug '60.

dining room. Holiday 22: 37 Nov '57.

—— **(antique).** Con. 143: 137 May '57; 144: LIV, 212 (col.) Jan '60.

—— **(int., antique).** Con. 144: 72 (col.) Nov '59.

—— **(int., modern).** Holiday 28: 44 (col.) Oct '60.

—— **(on ship).** Holiday 24: 94 (col.) Nov '58.

—— **(Provost's house, Dublin).** Con. 145: 155 May '60.

—— **(train).** Holiday 21: 165 Ap '57.

——, **Adam.** Con. ency. of ant., vol. 3, pl. 9. Con. 144: 60 Sept '59.

——, **Amer. (antique).** Con. 144: 280 Jan '60.

——, **Colonial.** Natl. geog. 106: 461 (col.) Oct '54.

——, **18th cent.** Con. 145: 160 May '60.

——, **hotel.** Holiday 10: 63 Oct '51; 14: 26-7 (col.) Sept '53.

——, **hotel (Riminis Grand, Italy).** Holiday 21: 50 Jan '57.

——, **palace.** Natl. geog. 107: 795 Je '55.

dining rooms, hotels (Chicago). Holiday 10: 102-4 (part col.) Oct '51.

dining table & chairs. See table & chairs, dining.

dining table. See table, dining.

dining tent, circus. Durant: Pict. hist. of Amer. circus, p. 235.

Dinkelsbuhl (Germany, pageant). Natl. geog. 111: 255-68 (part col.) Feb '57.

dinner service, Georgian silver. Con. 145: XX-XVI Mar '60.

——, **Hague & Meissen.** Con. 142: LVIII Dec '58.

——, **silver.** Con. 138: XXI Dec '56.

dinner table. See table, dining.

dinner ware. See dishes.

dinoflagellates (under microscope). Natl. geog. 118: 127 (col.) Jl '60.

dinosaur (model). Natl. geog. 105: 373 Mar '54.

Dinosaur Natl. Monument. Natl. geog. 105: 365-90 (part col.) Mar '54.

—— **(map).** Natl. geog. 105: 364 Mar '54.

Dinosaur park (S.D.). Natl. geog. 110: 492-3 (col.) Oct '56.

dinosaur skeleton (diplodocus). Natl. geog. 105: 367 Mar '54.

Diomede (Alaska). Natl. geog. 99: 552-9 Ap '51.

Dionysus (sym.). Lehner: Pict. bk. of sym., p. 31.

Dionysus theatre. See theatre (Dionysus).

Dior, Christian. Cur. biog. p. 147 (1948). Holiday 17: 46 Jan '55; 21: 64 Ap '57.

Dior dress (France). Holiday 17: 45 (col.) Jan '55.

di Pietro, Sano (work of). Con. 141: 45 Mar '58, 187 May '58.

diplodocus skeleton. Natl. geog. 105: 367 Mar '54.

diploma (sym.). Lehner: Pict. bk. of sym., p. 85.

Diplomat hotel (Hollwood-by-the-Sea, Fla.). Travel 111: 55 Feb '59.

dipper. Holiday 21: 137 Ap '57.

—— **(for melting lead).** Rawson: Ant. pict. bk., p. 35.

—— **(pouring).** Holiday 19: 16 Je '56.

Dipre, Nicholas (work of). Con. 132: LXIII Nov '53.

diptych, Andrew's (detail). Con. 142: 191 Dec '58.

——, **Byzantine art.** Con. 142: 27 Sept '58.

——, **ivory (antique).** Con. 135: 94 Ap '55.

——, **Memling.** Con. 134: 73 Sept '54.

——, **Wilton (1395).** Praeg. pict. ency., p. 206 (col.).

dirigible. Amer. heri. vol. 10 no. 2 p. 19-23 (Feb '59).

Dirksen, Everett M. Cur. biog. p. 227 (1941); p. 147 (1957).

Disalle, Michael V. Cur. biog. p. 165 (1951).

disciple of Buddha. See Buddha, Holy disciple of.

"Disciples at Emmaus" (Champaigne). Con. 137: 49 Mar '56.

disease, patron saint against. Lehner: Pict. bk. of sym., p. 40.

dish, altar (17th cent.). Con. 133: 152 May '54.

——, **antique.** Con. 136: XIII, XL Sept '55.

——, **antique leaf.** Con. 133: XX Mar '54.

——, **antique porcelain.** Con. 133: VIII Je '54.

——, **baking.** Holiday 11: 141 May '52; 27: 56 May '60.

——, **Bow.** Con. 132: 167 Jan '54.

——, **Byzantine art (silver).** Con. 142: 28 Sept '58.

——, **charger (Lambeth delft).** Con. 134: X, XIV Nov '54.

——, **Charles I silver.** Con. 137: XIII Je '56.

——, **Charles II silver.** Con. 138: XIII Nov '56.

——, **Charles II silver-gilt.** Con. 144: LII Jan '60.

——, **Chelsea.** Con. 139: LXIII Je '57; 140: LXXI Nov '57, XVI Jan '58; 142: L, 255, 257 Jan '59.

——, **Chelsea cabbage leaf.** Con. 144: LV Sept '59.

——, **Chelsea mulberry leaf.** Con. 138: 126 Nov '56.

——, **Chinese blue glazed (15th cent.).** Con. 135: 129 Ap '55.

——, **Chinese porcelain.** Con. 143: VI Ap '59.

——, **Cromwellian silver.** Con. 129: L Je '52.

——, **Deruta lustred (6th cent.).** Con. 143: III Mar '59.

——, **dessert (18th cent.).** Con. 140: 193 (col.) Dec '57.

——, **dessert Worcester.** Con. 129: XLIV Je '52.

——, **English broad rim (17th cent.).** Con. 145: XXXII Je '60.

——, **English silver (antique).** Con. 138: 107 Nov '56.

——, **entree.** See entree dish.

——, **Faberge.** Con. 132: XXXIX Nov '53.

——, **Faenza maiolica.** Con. 140: 161, 163 Dec '57.

——, **Fahlstrom (1739).** Con. 144: 96 Nov '59.

——, **French covered (silver).** Con. ency. of ant., vol. 3, p. 66.

dish, fruit (18th cent. silver). Con. 143: XIII Mar '59.
——, George I (silver). Con. 129: XXIII Je '52.
——, George II (2nd course). Con. 144: VII Dec '59.
——, George III (silver). Con. 141: VI Je '58.
——, Irish glass. Con. 136: XXXIV Sept '55.
——, Irish silver. Con. 136: XXVII Sept '55; 140: LV Jan '58.
——, Islamic pottery. Con. 143: VI May '59.
——, James I (silver). Con. 139: 55 Mar '57, XIII May '57.
——, Lamerie (shell-handled silver). Con. 144: 61 Sept '59.
——, Limoges enamels. Con. 143: 172-4 May '59.
——, Lyons faience. Con. 143: 186 May '59.
——, Majolica lusterware. Con. 142: 269 Jan '59.
——, Norwegian (1765). Con. 145: 10-11 Mar '60.
——, polychrome. Con. 141: LIII May '58.
——, Queen Anne (silver). Con. 129: VII Je '52.
——, renaissance crystal. Con. 129: 139 Je '52.
——, rosewater. See rosewater dish.
——, Russian silver gilt octagonal. Con. 142: 230 Jan '59.
——, Sevres porcelain. Con. 133: XXXV (col.) Je '54.
——, sideboard. Con. 133: XIX Je '54.
——, silver (for Pembroke college, 1951). Con. 143: 102 Ap '59.
——, silver (Napoleon's). Con. 143: 225 Je '59.
——, silver (Vianen, 1635). Con. ency. of ant., vol. 3, pl. 30.
——, silver-gilt. Con. 136: 2 Sept '55.
——, standing silver (16th cent.). Con. ency. of ant., vol. 3 p. 71.
——, William III (silver-gilt). Con. 142: 39 Sept '58.
——, Worcester porcelain. Con. 141: XLIII May '58.
dish & cover, faience (Swedish, 18th cent.). Con. 143: 240 Je '59.
——, rock crystal (Holbein design). Con. 144: 82 Nov '59.
dish rack (antique). Natl. geog. 112: 309 (col.) Sept '57.
dish ring, Irish silver. Con. 145: LVIII Je '60.
dishes. Holiday 22: 222 (col.) Dec '57; 26: 21 Oct '59.
——, aluminum. Holiday 21: 10 (col.) May '57.
——, antique. Amer. heri. vol. 6 no. 5 p. 49 (col.) (Aug '55).
Con. 136: XX Sept '55; 137: XXIX-XXXI May '56; 139: 15 Mar '57; 140: 114 Nov '57.
——, armorial service. Con. 142: 246-7 Jan '59.
——, Chelsea. Con. 133: XII Je '54; 144: XX-XIX Jan '60.
——, Chelsea-Derby. Con. 144: XLIV Jan '60.

——, Chelsea porcelain. Con. 134: 15-21 (part col.) Sept '54.
——, Chinese (gold & silver). Con. 141: 2 Mar '58.
——, Christmas. Holiday 10: 124 Dec '51; 26: 144 Nov '59.
——, Coalport dessert. Con. 141: XII Mar '58.
——, Derby. Con. 133: 142 Ap '54; 138: 258 (col.) Jan '57; 142: XLI Nov '58.
——, Dutch. Natl. geog. 106: 382-3 (col.) Sept '54.
——, 18th cent. Con. 144: XXXIX Jan '60.
——, entree (antique silver). Con. 138: X Sept '56.
——, Greece (ancient). Int. gr. soc.: Arts . . . p. 19 (col.).
——, Italian (15-16th cent.). Con. 143: III Mar '59.
——, Louis XV. Con. 133: 272 (col.) Je '54.
——, Meissen. See Meissen dishes.
——, metal. Holiday 19: 132 May '56.
——, orvieto (11th cent.). Con. 133: LXIII Je '54.
——, pewter. Con. 136: XXXVIII Sept '55.
——, pewter (antique). Con. 143: XLVIII Je '59.
——, porcelain. Holiday 20: 37 (col.) Dec '56.
——, Rostrand faience (18th cent.). Con. 144: 96-103 Nov '59.
——, Sevres. Con. 133: XXXIII May '54; 141: 208 Je '58.
——, silver (18th cent.). Con. 142: VII Nov '58.
——, Slipware. Rawson: Ant. pict. bk., p. 87, 90.
——, Swansea porcelain. Con. 132: XVI Nov '53.
——, Swedish modern stoneware. Con. 141: LXII Mar '58.
——, Vincennes porcelain. Con. 133: 4-8 Mar '54.
——, Wedgewood dairy ware. Con. 140: 21 Sept '57.
——, Worcester. Con. 132: 169 Jan '54; 133: LXIV Je '54; 139: XXXIII Mar '57; 140: LXVI Nov '57; 143: LXXII Je '59; 145: XXX Ap '60.
dishes. See also name of dish.
dishwasher. Holiday 13: 130 Mar '53, 9 May '53; 14: 20 Oct '53.
—— (girl & woman). Holiday 26: 183 (col.) Dec '59.
"Disillusioned souls" (Hodler). Praeg. pict. ency., p. 483.
disk, raised. See raised disk.
Disney, Doris Miles. Cur. biog. p. 234 (1954).
Disney, Walt. Cur. biog. p. 149 (1952).
Disney: People & places, p. 11 (col.).
Holiday 5: 38 (col.) Jan '49.
Disney, Walter E. Holiday 22: 57 Oct '57.
Disneyland (Cal.). Holiday 22: 57 Oct '57; 24: 19 Nov '58.
Travel 104: 16-9 Jl '55.
Disneyland (Ken-L-Land hotel). Travel 109: 41 Je '58.
Disney's "Snow White" (movie scene). Int. gr. soc.: Arts . . . p. 151 (col.).

"Dispute of the Holy Sacrament". Con. 145: LXXXIII May '60.
"Disrobing of Christ" (El Greco). Praeg. pict. ency., p. 314 (col.).
distaff (sym.). Lehner: Pict. bk. of sym., p. 57.
distillery. Holiday 27: 168 Ap '60.
—— (int.). Holiday 28: 158 (col.) Nov '60, 63 (col.) Dec '60.
——, Colonial. Holiday 26: 102 (col.) Nov '59.
——, Irish. Holiday 23: 61 Je '58.
——, old. Holiday 25: 15 (col.) Je '59.
——, Scotland. Holiday 27: 26 May '60; 28: 123 Sept '60, 138 Oct '60, 156 Nov '60, 40 Dec '60.
——, wine (int.). Holiday 28: 115 Sept '60.
distillery. See also brewery.
distilling vat, mint hay. Natl. geog. 102: 588 Nov '52.
distress (sym.). Lehner: Pict. bk. of sym., p. 88.
Ditchy, Clair W. Cur. biog. p. 235 (1954).
Ditmars, Raymond L. Jun. bk. of auth., p. 100.
diver. Holiday 23: 139 (col.) Feb '58.
Natl. geog. 116: 440, 470, 478 (part col.) Oct '59.
—— (cartoon). Holiday 23: 136 Feb '58.
—— (comic). Travel 110: 62 Aug '58.
—— (early). Amer. heri. vol. 1 no. 4 p. 26 (summer '50).
—— (feeding fish). Natl. geog. 102: 687 (col.) Nov '52.
—— (fish). Natl. geog. 107: 126 (col.) Jan '55.
—— (lobster catch). Natl. geog. 107: 789 (col.) Je '55.
—— (Maya ruins). Natl. geog. 115: 111, 115, 119, 124-5. 127 (part col.) Jan '59.
—— (under water). Ceram: March of arch., p. 303.
Travel 101: 46 Je '54; 104: 19-22 Sept '55.
—— (with shells). Natl. geog. 97: 63 Jan '50.
——, pearl. Natl. geog. 110: 98 (col.) Jl '56.
——, sea. Holiday 12: 73 (col.) Sept '52; 16: 52 Aug '54.
Natl. geog. 107: 524-41 Ap '55; 108: 170, 181-2 (col.) Aug '55; 117: 177, 182 (col.) Feb '60, 583 Ap '60.
Travel 101: 29 Feb '54; 105: 31 Mar '56; 113: 8 Mar '60.
——, sea (treasure recovery). Natl. geog. 117: 683-703 (part col.) May '60.
——, skin. Holiday 17: 66 Jan '55, 11 Mar '55; 20: 105 (col.) Aug '56; 25: 159 (col.) Je '59.
Natl. geog. 112: 756-7, 761-2, 764 (part col.) Dec '57; 113: 57 (col.) Jan '58, 192 Feb '58.
Travel 107: 32-5 Jan '57; 114: 45-6 Oct '60.
——, undersea explorer. Holiday 18: 94-7 (part col.) Sept '55.
diver & mermaid (comic). Holiday 14: 67 Aug '53.
divers. Natl. geog. 105: 2, 5-6, 8, 14-5, 23, 28-9, 36 (part col.) Jan '54.
—— (boat, lobsters). Natl. geog. 114: 259 (col.) Aug '58.

—— (caged against sharks). Natl. geog. 108: 177 (col.) Aug '55.
——, girl. (stage underwater show). Natl. geog. 107: 70-1 (col.) Jan '55.
——, Japanese. Natl. geog. 97: 630-1 (col.) May '50.
——, jungle tower. Natl. geog. 107: 78-91 (part col.) Jan '55.
——, skin. Holiday 25: 168 (col.) Ap '59.
Natl. geog. 102: 432-70 (part col.) Oct '52; 109: 150, 159-60, 162-3, 164-7, 170, 178, 187, 198, 200 (part col.) Feb '56.
——, treasure. Natl. geog. 117: 169 Feb '60.
divers. See also girl (diving); boy (diving).
divers discoveries. Natl. geog. 117: 155-7 (col.) Feb '60.
divider, Circle & triangle (sym.). Lehner: Pict. bk. of sym., p. 13.
divider & ruler (sym.). Lehner: Pict. bk. of sym., p. 11.
divinations (sym.). Lehner: Pict. bk. of sym., p. 67.
Divine comedy (Dante). See Dante's Divine comedy.
the divine hand (sym.). Lehner: Pict. bk. of sym., p. 88.
divine power (sym.). Lehner: Pict. bk. of sym., p. 28, 42.
divine protection (sym.). Lehner: Pict. bk. of sym., p. 27.
"Divine right" letter (coal strike, 1902). Amer. heri. vol. 11 no. 3 p. 61 (Ap '60).
diving, high. Holiday 11: 56 (col.) Mar '52.
——, scuba. See diving, skin.
——, skin (cartoon). Holiday 23: 64 May '58; 25: 78 Je '59.
diving bell (int.). Natl. geog. 97: 56 (col.) Jan '50.
diving girl, (Japan). Disney: People & places, p. 158-60 (col.).
Holiday 12: 35 (col.) Aug '52.
diving helmet. Natl. geog. 97: 63 Jan '50.
diving horses (riders). Natl. geog. 117: 41 (col.) Jan '60.
diving saucers. Natl. geog. 117: 570, 574-5, 577-86 (part col.) Ap '60.
diving suit (comic). Holiday 14: 133 Jl '53.
divinity (sym.). Lehner: Pict. bk. of sym., p. 34, 42.
—— (Tibetan sym.). Lehner: Pict. bk. of sym., p. 42.
"Division-Unite" (Kandinsky). Praeg. pict. ency., p. 488 (col.).
Dix, Beulah Marie. Jun. bk. of auth., p. 101.
Dixie orchestra (New Orleans). Int. gr. soc.: Arts . . . p. 143 (col.).
Dixon, Dean. Cur. biog. p. 177 (1943).
Dixon, Sir Owen. Cur. biog. p. 203 (1942).
Dixon, Sir Pierson. Cur. biog. p. 237 (1954).
Diziani, Gasparo (work of). Con. 135: XXXIV May '55.
Djanira (Djanira Paiva). Cur. biog. p. 133 (1961).
djellaba & veil (Moroccan woman). Natl. geog. 107: 187 Feb '55.
Djilas, Milovan. Cur. biog. p. 119 (1958).
Djuanda. Cur. biog. p. 121 (1958).

d'Medici, Piero (portrait). Con. 139: 100 Ap '57.
Doan, Leland L. Cur. biog. p. 152 (1952).
Dobbie, Gen. Sir William. Cur. biog. p. 151 (1945).
Dobbs, Mattiwilda. Cur. biog. p. 172 (1955).
Dobie, James Frank. Cur. biog. p. 154 (1945).
Dobrynin, Anatoly. Cur. biog. p. 103 (1962).
Dobson, William (work of). Con. 127: 96 May '51.
Dobzhansky, Theodocius G. Cur. biog. p. 105 (1962).
Doccia porcelain "Pieta". Con. 140: 196 (col.)-99 Dec '57.
Docking, George. Cur. biog. p. 123 (1958).
docks, iron-ore. See iron-ore docks.
doctor (head, stethoscope). Holiday 12: 5 (col.) Nov '52.
—— (operating on patient). Natl. geog. 99: 174 Feb '51.
—— (patient). Natl. geog. 107: 446 (col.) Ap '55.
—— (patient, comic). Holiday 12: 135 Nov '52.
—— (patients, India). Natl. geog. 109: 584 Ap '56.
—— (sick donkey, Morocco). Natl. geog. 107: 169 (col.) Feb '55.
—— (sick lady). Amer. heri. vol. 9 no. 1 p. 83 (Dec '57).
—— (treats man, Nepal). Natl. geog. 117: 367 (col.) Mar '60.
——, Chinese herb (head). Natl. geog. 97: 224 Feb '50.
——, early (on horse). Amer. heri. vol. 1 no. 2 p. 77 (winter '50).
"Dr. Dolittle's Puddleby" (book illus.). Amer. heri. vol. 8 no. 1 p. 36 (col.) (Dec '56).
document box, Penn. (18th cent.). Con. 145: 290 Je '60.
Dodd, Alvin E. Cur. biog. p. 172 (1947).
Dodd, Martha. Cur. biog. p. 148 (1946).
Dodd, Norris E. Cur. biog. p. 158 (1949).
Dodd, Thomas J. Cur. biog. p. 94 (1959).
Dodds, Gilbert L. Cur. biog. p. 173 (1947).
Dodds, Harold W. Cur. biog. p. 157 (1945).
Dodecanese islands. Natl. geog. 103: 358-90 (part col.) Mar '53.
Dodge, Bayard. Cur. biog. p. 149 (1948).
Dodge, Cleveland E. Cur. biog. p. 239 (1954).
Dodge, David. Cur. biog. p. 154 (1956).
Dodge, J. R. Brooks: Growth of a nation, p. 198.
Dodge, John V. Cur. biog. p. 119 (1960).
Dodge, Joseph M. Cur. biog. p. 176 (1947).
Dodge, Mabel. Amer. heri. vol. 11 no. 2 p. 9 (Feb '60).
Dodge, Ossian E. Durant: Pict. hist. of Amer. circus, p. 59.
Dodge auto. Holiday 5: 30 (col.) Ap '49, 82 (col.) Je '49; 6: 15 (col.) Jl '49; 8: inside cover (col.) Sept '50; 15: 74 Feb '54, 78 (col.) May '54; 16: 10 (col.) Jl '54; 17: 24 (col.) Feb '55.
Dodge City (Kan., 1878). Brooks: Growth of a nation, p. 164.
Dodgson, Charles Lutwidge (Lewis Carroll). Holiday 15: 6 Je '54.

Doenitz, Vice Adm. Karl. Cur. biog. p. 204 (1942).
dog, black (sym.). Lehner: Pict. bk. of sym., p. 62.
dog hotel (Disneyland). Travel 109: 41 Je '58.
dog monument. See monument, dog.
dog race. Natl. geog. 109: 524 Ap '56.
dog show. See Westminster kennel club dog show.
dog show judges. Natl. geog. 105: 101, 104 (col.) Jan '54.
dog sled. See sled, dog.
"Doge Grimani" (Bassano). Con. 140: 184 Dec '57.
Doge of Amalfi (rowing regatta). Natl. geog. 116: 504 (col.) Oct '59.
Dodge palace (Venice). Natl. geog. 100: 398, 410 (col.) Sept '51.
—— palace staircase. Con. 143: 54 Mar '59.
"Dogs of Fo", Chinese porcelain. Con. ency. of ant., vol. 1, pl. 72.
"dogwood festival" (Gordon Jr. high school). Natl. geog. 103: 543 (col.) Ap '53.
Doherty, Robert E. Cur. biog. p. 160 (1949).
Doi, Peter Tatsuo, Cardinal. Cur. biog. p. 120 (1960).
Doihara, Maj. Gen. Kenji. Cur. biog. p. 206 (1942).
Doisy, Edward A. Cur. biog. p. 161 (1949).
Dokan dam (Iraq). Natl. geog. 114: 488 Oct '58.
Dolan, Daniel Leo. Cur. biog. p. 155 (1956).
Dolbier, Maurice. Cur. biog. p. 157 (1956).
Dolci, Danilo B. P. Cur. biog. p. 135 (1961).
"Doldabarn castle" (Wilson). Con. 140: 114 Nov '57; XXVI Dec '57.
Dolin, Anton. Cur. biog. p. 150 (1946).
doll. Holiday 10: 129 Nov '51; 18: 166 Nov '55; 19: 130 Jan '56; 20: 184 Nov '56; 28: 222 Nov '60, 228 Dec '60.
—— (in cradle). Holiday 25: 150 Feb '59.
—— ("poppet", oldest known type in Amer.). Holiday 9: 47 Mar '51.
——, antique. Amer. heri. vol. 1 no. 2 p. 64 (winter '50).
Con. 136: 55 Sept '55.
Natl. geog. 105: 463 (col.) Ap '54.
——, antique (chair). Natl. geog. 109: 447 (col.) Ap '56.
——, fashion. Con. 143: LXIV May '59.
——, French (18th cent.). Con. 137: 294 Je '56.
——, German. Holiday 21: 21 (col.) Jan '57.
——, Japanese. Holiday 18: 190 Dec '55.
——, Kewpie. See Kewpie doll.
——, rag. Holiday 27: 160 Jan '60.
——, rope. Holiday 20: 211 Dec '56.
doll carriage. Holiday 27: 8 Ap '60.
doll heads. Natl. geog. 117: 9 (col.) Jan '60.
doll house. Natl. geog. 107: 391 (col.) Mar '55.
—— (children). Natl. geog. 110: 702 Nov '56.
——, Japanese. Natl. geog. 118: 770 (col.) Dec '60.
doll house for the dead (Indian groves). Natl. geog. 112: 256 (col.) Aug '57.
Dollard, Charles. Cur. biog. p. 151 (1948).

dolls. Holiday 13: 24 May '53; 18: 197 Dec '55; 26: 189, 191 (col.) Dec '59.

Natl. geog. 114: 841 (col.) Dec '58.

Travel 113: 6-7 Mar '60; 114: 11 Oct '60.

—— **(in basket).** Travel 110: back cover Nov '58.

——, **Dutch.** Travel 114: 17 Nov '60, 7 Dec '60.

——, **German.** Holiday 25: 153 Jan '59.

——, **Japanese.** Natl. geog. 97: 623 (col.) May '50.

——, **nested peasant.** Holiday 12: 139 Nov '52.

——, **Roman (ancient).** Int. gr. soc.: Arts . . . p. 37 (col.).

——, **world.** Natl. geog. 116: 816-31 (col.) Dec '59.

dolman, Brittany (prehistoric). Int. gr. soc.: Arts . . . p. 11 (col.).

The Dolomites (Hotel Elefante). Holiday 15: 27 May '54.

—— **(Italy).** Holiday 19: 148 (col.) May '56.

Dolores Hidalgo church (Mexico). Travel 101: 19 Mar '54.

dolphin, Apollo's. *See* Apollo's dolphin.

Domagk, Gerhard. Cur. biog. p. 125 (1958).

dombra (woman playing). Natl. geog. 106: 635 (col.) Nov '54.

dome, church (int.). Int. gr. soc.: Arts . . . p. 45 (col.).

——, **nylon (receiving antenna).** Natl. geog. 116: 446 (col.) Oct '59.

——, **plastic (meteorologist).** Natl. geog. 112: 352 (col.) Sept '57.

——, **stupa.** Int. gr. soc.: Arts . . . p. 13 (col.).

——, **U.S. capitol.** Natl. geog. 116: 765 (col.) Dec '59.

Dome of the Rock (Jerusalem). Natl. geog. 115: 493, 495 (col.) Ap '59.

——, **Islam's.** Natl. geog. 110: 715 (col.) Dec '56.

Domenichino (work of). Con. 132: 8 Sept '53.

Domergue, Jean Gabriel (work of). Con. 133: 236 Je '54.

—— **(art collection).** Con. 133: 229-36 Je '54.

domesticity (sym.). Lehner: Pict. bk. of sym., p. 57.

Dominican father. Holiday 11: 98 (col.) Je '52.

Dominican Republic (dancers). *See* dancers, Dominican Republic.

—— **(hotels).** Holiday 23: 35 (col.) May '58.

—— **(map).** Travel 103: 53 Je '55.

—— **art.** *See* art, Dominican Republic.

"Dominican Saint rescuing pilgrims . . ." (Guardi). Natl. geog. 97: 768 (col.) Je '50.

dominoes. Holiday 19: 132 May '56.

"Domremy" (home of Jeanne de Arc). Travel 111: 32 May '59.

"Don Balthasar Carlos" (as a hunter in Predo, by Velasquez). Con. 141: 72 Ap '58.

"Don Balthasar Carlos on horseback" (Prince, son of Philip IV, Spain). Praeg. pict. ency., p. 351 (col.).

"Don Carlos" (scene, Schiller's). Int. gr. soc.: Arts . . . p. 107 (col.).

Don Jose (as in "Carmen"). Cooper: Con. ency. of music, p. 99.

"Dona Antonia" (Goya). Con. 145: 160 May '60.

"Dona Isabel Cobos" (Goya). Praeg. pict. ency., p. 354 (col.).

"Dona Isabel de Bourbon" (Velasquez). Con. ency. of ant., vol. 1, pl. 161.

"Dona Polyxena Spinola Guzman". Natl. geog. 101: 86 (col.) Jan '52.

Donald, David H. Cur. biog. p. 137 (1961).

Donald, William H. Cur. biog. p. 152 (1946).

"Donald duck rock". Natl. geog. 101: 722 (col.) Je '52.

Donaldson, Jesse Monroe. Cur. biog. p. 152 (1948.).

Donatello (work of). Praeg. pict. ency., p. 273.

Donck, Henrik (work of). Con. 136: 275 (col.) Jan '56.

Donegan, Bishop Horace W. B. Cur. biog. p. 241 (1954).

Donelson, Emily. Jensen: The White House, p. 51.

Döner Kümbed mausoleum (Kayseri). Osward: Asia Minor, pl. 68.

Dongen, Kees van. *See* Van Dongen, Kees.

Donizetti, Gaetano (by Felix). Cooper: Con. ency. of music, p. 92.

donkey cart race (St. Croix, Virgin is.). Natl. geog. 109: 228 (col.) Feb '56.

donkey team (Africa). Natl. geog. 104: 170 (col.) Aug '53.

Donlevy, Brian. Horan: Pict. hist. of wild west, p. 156.

Donlon, Mary. Cur. biog. p. 163 (1949).

Donnell, Forrest C. Cur. biog. p. 165 (1949).

Donnelly, Phil M. Cur. biog. p. 158 (1956).

Donnelly, Walter J. Cur. biog. p. 153 (1952).

Donner, Frederic G. Cur. biog. p. 96 (1959).

Donner, Georg Raphael (work of). Con. 145: 131 Ap '60.

Praeg. pict. ency., p. 356.

Donner Pass (Cal.). Natl. geog. 105: 741 (col.), 745 Je '54.

Donner Pass bridge. Jordan: Hammond's pict. atlas, p. 189 (col.).

Donovan, James B. Cur. biog. p. 139 (1961).

Donovan, William J. Cur. biog. p. 229 (1941); p. 244 (1954).

Dons, Yankee. *See* Yankee Dons.

"Doodlebug" (oil prospector). Amer. heri. vol. 3 no. 1 p. 7 (fall '51).

"Dooley, Mr." *See* "Mr. Dooley".

Dooley, Ray. Holiday 7: 65 Mar '50.

Dooley, Dr. Thomas (playing piano). Natl. geog. 117: 67 (col.) Jan '60.

Dooley, Thomas A. Cur. biog. p. 149 (1957).

Doolittle, Major Gen. James H. ("Jimmy"). Cur. biog. p. 209 (1942).

Holiday 10: 110 Jl '51.

Doolittle, Lt. Gen. James H. Cur. biog. p. 151 (1957).

Doone Valley (Eng.). Natl. geog. 108: 328-9 (col.) Sept '55.

door (Tain's old tower, Scotland). Natl. geog. 110: 31 (col.) Jl '56.

——, **antique.** Con. 138: LVII Jan '57.

——, **carved (15th cent.).** Con. 140: XLVI Sept '57.

——, carved copper (Mexico). Natl. geog. 102: 529 (col.) Oct '52.

——, carved stone facade (Mexico). Natl. geog. 102: 532 Oct '52.

——, Colonial. Holiday 18: 73 (col.) Aug '55. Jensen: The White House, p. 257. Natl. geog. 105: 462 (col.) Ap '54; 109: 449, 470, 472, 483 (part col.) Ap '56.

——, India (house). Natl. geog. 109: 577 Ap '56.

——, Morocco (house). Holiday 23: cover (col.) Mar '58.

——, Venice. Con. 136: 174 Dec '55.

door bar (antique). Natl. geog. 105: 447 (col.) Ap '54.

door knocker. Holiday 11: 22 Jan '52; 14: 158 Nov '53; 24: 13 Jl '58; 26: 80 Aug '59, 106 Sept '59, 157 Oct '59, 207 Nov '59, 62 Dec '59; 27: 166 Feb '60; 28: 108 Aug '60, 101 Sept '60, 184 Oct '60, 219 Dec '60. Natl. geog. 111: 491 Ap '57.

——, brass. Holiday 27: 136 Jan '60.

——, brass (17th cent.). Con. 143: LIII May '59.

——, Colonial. Holiday 12: 143 Nov '52.

doors (fanlight). Natl. geog. 97: 562 (col.) May '50.

——, baptistery. See baptistery doors.

——, bronze carved (Pilgrim's Progress). Natl. geog. 108: 323 (col.) Sept '55.

——, Civil war. Natl. geog. 105: 447 (col.) Ap '54.

——, Colonial. Natl. geog. 104: 659 (col.) Nov '53.

——, Russian (royal church). Con. 144: 275 Jan '60.

——, Russian (royal church Byzantium, 16th cent.). Con. 142: 34 Sept '58.

doorway. Con. 141: 102 Ap '58.

—— (Christmas decoration). Holiday 14: back cover (col.) Dec '53.

—— (hotel Jules Cesar). Natl. geog. 109: 674 (col.) May '56.

—— (old). Holiday 18: 44 Jl '55.

—— (1707). Holiday 11: 44 Je '52.

—— (1730). Natl. geog. 112: 444 (col.) Oct '57.

——, arched (oldest in U.S.). Natl. geog. 105: 466 (col.) Ap '54.

——, baroque style. Holiday 22: 60 (col.) Sept '57.

——, carved baroque. Con. 142: 70 (col.), 72 Nov '58.

——, classic. Amer. heri. vol. 9 no. 1 p. 90 (Dec '57).

——, Colonial. Holiday 10: 42 Aug '51. Natl. geog. 103: 522 (col.) Ap '53; 106: 461 (col.) Oct '54; 118: 154, 180 (col.) Aug '60.

——, Figian house. Natl. geog. 114: 531 (col.) Oct '58.

——, German. Natl. geog. 115: 783 (col.) Je '59.

——, Gothic. Con. 133: XLX-XLXI May '54.

——, Holbein (1517). Con. 133: 78 Ap '54.

——, Italian. Natl. geog. 111: 797 (col.) Je '57.

——, Louis XV. Con. 133: 248 Je '54.

——, Moorish style house. Natl. geog. 105: 182 (col.) Feb '54.

——, Persian school. Natl. geog. 100: 433, 457 (col.) Oct '51.

——, Roman. Holiday 18: 102 (col.) Sept '55.

——, Rose. Amer. heri. vol. 2 no. 1 p. 15 (fall '50).

——, Spanish. Natl. geog. 109: 305 Mar '56.

——, triple arch. Holiday 23: 111 (col.) Mar '58.

Dooyeweerd, Herman. Cur. biog. p. 127 (1958).

Dorati, Antal. Cur. biog. p. 154 (1948). Holiday 22: 121 Sept '57.

Dore, Gustave (book illus.). Praeg. pict. ency., p. 407.

doric columns. See columns.

dories. Natl. geog. 101: 571, 582-3, 586, 588-92 (part col.) May '52.

Dormition, church of the. See church of the Dormition.

Doronne, Dina. Holiday 26: 71 (col.) Dec '59.

Dörpfeld, Wilhelm. Ceram: March of arch., p. 43.

Dorsey, Jimmy. Cur. biog. p. 210 (1942).

Dorsey, Tommy. Cur. biog. p. 211 (1942).

Dorticos, Osvaldo. Cur. biog. (1963).

dorymen. Natl. geog. 101: 577, 585, 590-2, 596 (part col.) May '52.

—— (with fish). Natl. geog. 101: 568 May '52.

Dostoievsky, F. M. Int. gr. soc.: Arts . . . p. 137 (col.).

double ax (sym.). See Buddhist double ax.

double boiler. Holiday 20: 190 Nov '56.

double-headed ax. See ax, double-headed.

Dougherty, Dora. Cur. biog. (1963).

Doughton, Robert L. Cur. biog. p. 213 (1942).

doughtray scraper. Rawson: Ant. pict. bk., p. 8.

Doughty birds (porcelain). Con. 145: LXXIX Je '60.

Douglas, Arthur F. Cur. biog. p. 122 (1950).

Douglas, Donald W. Cur. biog. p. 231 (1941); p. 124 (1950). Holiday 22: 56 Oct '57.

Douglas, Emily Taft. Cur. biog. p. 159 (1945).

Douglas, Helen Gahagan. Cur. biog. p. 169 (1944).

Douglas, James H., jr. Cur. biog. p. 153 (1957).

Douglas, Kirk. Cur. biog. p. 155 (1952).

Douglas, Lewis W. Cur. biog. p. 177 (1947).

Douglas, Marjory Stoneman. Cur. biog. p. 163 (1953).

Douglas, Melvyn. Cur. biog. p. 216 (1942).

Douglas, Paul H. Cur. biog. p. 168 (1949). Holiday 15: 60 Feb '54.

Douglas, Sir. Sholto. Cur. biog. p. 179 (1943).

Douglas, Stephen A. Amer. heri. vol. 6 no. 4 p. 34 (Je '55); vol. 7 no. 5 p. 4 (Aug '56); vol. 10 no. 2 p. 98 (Feb '59). Holiday 28: 41 (col.) Oct '60.

Douglas, William O. Cur. biog. p. 233 (1941); p. 126 (1950). Holiday 7: 78 Feb '50. Natl. geog. 114: 27 Jl '58; 115: 48, 78 Jan '59.

Douglas MacArthur park (Los Angeles). Jordan: Hammond's pict. atlas, p. 205 (col.).

Doulton miniatures. *See* miniatures, Royal Doulton.

Douro valley (Portugal). Disney: People & places, p. 62 (col.).

dovap (electric system). Natl. geog. 111; 577 Ap '57.

dove (sym.). Lehner: Pict. bk. of sym., p. 58.

dove & olive branch (sym.). Lehner: Pict. bk. of sym., p. 52, 86.

"Dove Cattage" (Wordsworth's home). Natl. geog. 109: 538 (col.) Ap '56.

dove, triangle, trefoil (sym.). Lehner: Pict. bk. of sym., p. 35.

doves & hearts (sym.). Lehner: Pict. bk. of sym., p. 65.

dovetailing (furniture). Con. ency. of ant., vol. 1, p. 30.

Dow, Willard H. Cur. biog. p. 173 (1944).

dower chest. *See* chest, dower.

Dowling, Eddie. Cur. biog. p. 154 (1946).

Dowling, Robert W. Cur. biog. p. 157 (1952).

Dowling, Walter C. Cur. biog. (1963).

Downey, Fairfax D. Cur. biog. p. 169 (1949).

Downey, Morton. Cur. biog. p. 170 (1949). Holiday 10: 64 Dec '51.

Downey, Sheridan. Cur. biog. p. 172 (1949).

down-hearth. Con. ency. of ant., vol. 3, pl. 167.

Downing, Samuel. Amer. heri. vol. 9 no. 3 p. 28 (Ap '58).

Downing home, Samuel (Edinburgh, N.Y.). Amer. heri. vol. 9 no. 3 p. 29 (col.) (Ap '58).

Downman, John (work of). Con. 133: 213 May '54.

Downs, Robert B. Cur. biog. p. 236 (1941); p. 159 (1952).

Doyle, Adrian Conan. Cur. biog. p. 247 (1954).

Doyle, Conan. Int. gr. soc.: Arts . . . p. 137 (col.).

Doyle, William M. S. (portrait by). Amer. heri. vol. 11 no. 2 p. 27 (Feb '60).

draft lottery capsule (1917). Holiday 28: 57 Sept '60.

draftsman (sym.). Lehner: Pict. bk. of sym., p. 90.

dragon (sym.). Lehner: Pict. bk. of sym., p. 44, 61.

"The dragon-killer" (Marees). Praeg. pict. ency., p. 402 (col.).

dragon of Babylon. Ceram: March of arch., p. 230.

dragon of the elements (sym.). Lehner: Pict. bk. of sym., p. 73.

dragon, snakes (China town parade). Natl. geog. 110: 210-11 (col.) Aug '56.

Dragon tree park (Canary is.). Natl. geog. 107: 513 (col.) Ap '55.

Drake, Alfred. Cur. biog. p. 175 (1944).

Drake, Edwin L. Amer. heri. vol. 10 no. 2 p. 69, 73 (Feb '59).

Drake, Sir Francis. Amer. heri. vol. 10 no. 3 p. 8 (col.) (Ap '59). Holiday 7: 149 (col.) Ap '50.

Drake, Frank D. Cur. biog. p. (1963).

Drake, St. Clair. Cur. biog. p. 105 (1946).

Drake univ. (Iowa). Holiday 6, 98-104 (part col.) Oct '49.

drama (sym.). Lehner: Pict. bk. of sym., p. 11.

——, Graeco-Roman. Holiday 19: 49 (col.) May '56.

drama. *See* also theatricals.

Draper, Dorothy. Cur. biog. p. 237 (1941).

Draper, Paul. Cur. biog. p. 177 (1944).

Draper, William H., jr. Cur. biog. p. 161 (1952).

drapery, window. *See* window drapery.

draughts, game of. Natl. geog. 110: 39 (col.) Jl '56.

drawbridge. Natl. geog. 110: 561 Oct '56.

drawer pull, antique. Con. 143: 258 Je '59. Rawson: Ant. pict. bk., p. 85.

drawing board (man & girl). Holiday 12: 73 (col.) Sept '52.

drawing room (antiques). Con. 143: 204 (col.), 211 Je '59.

drayman (on donkey, Iraq). Natl. geog. 114: 471 (col.) Oct '58.

dredge, harbor. Natl. geog. 113: 196 Feb '58.

——, hydraulic (clams). Natl. geog. 113: 9 (col.) Jan '58.

dredger, silver (George II). Con. 143: XXXIV Ap '59, XVI May '59, XXXIV Je '59.

Drees, Willem. Cur. biog. p. 174 (1949).

Dresden (court church). Praeg. pict. ency., p. 357.

dress, Mrs. Benjamin Harrison's Natl. geog. 100: 583 (col.) Nov '51.

——, child's. Holiday 27: 229 Ap '60, 239 May '60.

——, wedding (1769). Natl. geog. 100: 583 (col.) Nov '51.

——, woman's (1909). Natl. geog. 112: 268 Aug '57.

dress. *See* also costume; dresses.

dress display (store window). Natl. geog. 112: 683 (col.) Nov '57.

dress fashions. Holiday 28: 102-7 (part col.) Dec '60.

dress forms. Holiday 27: 41 May '60.

Dressen, Chuck. Cur. biog. p. 167 (1951).

Dresser, Frank. Amer. heri. vol. 8 no. 6 p. 39 (Oct '57).

dresser. Holiday 18: 66 Sept '55; 28: 39 (col.) Oct '60.

—— (antique). Con. 129: XXXII Je '52; 132: XIV Nov '53.

——, Charles II. Con. ency. of ant., vol. 1, pl. 11.

——, 18th cent. Con. 135: XVIII Mar '55, XXX Ap '55; 137: XLII Ap '56, XLII Je '56.

——, Jacobean. Con. 132: X Sept '53.

——, 17th cent. Con. 133: XLVII Ap '54; 140: VI Sept '57.

——, Victorian (by Lethaby). Con. ency. of ant., vol. 3, pl. 7.

——, Victorian inlaid. Con. ency. of ant., vol. 3, pl. 7.

——, Welsh oak (17th cent.). Con. ency. of ant., vol. 1, pl. 6.

dresser & rack (18th cent.). Con. 137: XVI May '56.

dresser service, English (antique). Con. 140: 253 (col.) Jan '58.

dresses (early Amer.). Natl. geog. 100: 586-7, 595-6 (col.) Nov '51.

—— (formal). Natl. geog. 105: 300 (col.) Mar '54.

—— (woman). Natl. geog. 104: 797 (col.) Dec '53.

dresses. *See* also costume; dress.

dressing board (17th cent.). Con. 145: XCI May '60.

dressing box, Tudor. Con. 132: LIX Nov '53.

dressing-commode (antique). Con. 126: 46 Aug '50.

dressing room, actress. Natl. geog. 117: 37 (col.) Jan '60.

"The Dressing table" (Picasso). Con. 145: 208 May '60.

dressing table (antique). Con. 126: 43-4 Aug '50; 134: XXXIIII Sept '54.

——, Chippendale. Con. 134: IV, XXXV Sept '54, 120 Nov '54; 139: 56 Mar '57.

——, Chippendale kneehole. Con. 133: VI May '54.

——, Duncan Phyfe. 141: 128 Ap '58.

——, early English. Con. 127: 113 May '51.

——, 18th cent. Con. 137: XXXII May '56; 141: 128 Ap '58.

——, George II Con. 144: 268 Jan '60.

——, New England kneehole. Con. 138: 260 Jan '57.

——, Sheraton. Con. 133: XXXIV Ap '54; 138: XXXI Nov '56; 143: IV Ap '59.

——, Sheraton fold-top. Con. 145: LXXXVI May '60.

——, Viennese (18th cent.). Con. ency. of ant., vol. 3, pl. 19.

dressmaker (fitting dress). Natl. geog. 109: 253 (col.) Feb '56.

—— (sym.). Lehner: Pict. bk. of sym., p. 90.

Dreux, Alfred de. *See* De Dreux, Alfred.

Drew, Charles R. Cur. biog. p. 179 (1944).

Drew, Daniel. Amer. heri. vol. 8 no. 3 p. 52 (Ap '57); vol. 10 no. 2 p. 7 (Feb '59).

Drew, George A. Cur. biog. p. 158 (1948).

Dreyfus, Camille. Cur. biog. p. 174 (1955).

Dreyfus, Pierre. Cur. biog. p. 128 (1958).

Dreyfuss, Henry. Cur. biog. p. 159 (1948); p. 98 (1959).

driftwood. Holiday 18: 71 (col.) Jl '55.

drill, bow. Natl. geog. 102: 68 (col.) Jl '52. Rawson: Ant. pict. bk., p. 24.

——, diamond. *See* diamond drill.

——, portable. Int. gr. soc.: Arts . . . p. 173 (col.).

driller, mine. *See* mine driller.

drillers, iron ore. Natl. geog. 100: 75 (col.) Jl '51.

——, snow (Greenland). Natl. geog. 109: 145 Jan '56.

——, sulphur. Natl. geog. 118: 113 (col.) Jl '60.

drinking glasses. *See* glasses, drinking.

drinking horn, Danish (copper-gilt). Con. ency. of ant., vol. 3, pl. 36.

——, English. Con. 138: 128 Nov '56.

——, Persian. Ceram: March of arch., opp. p. 190 (col.).

drinking table (antique). Con. 143: IV Ap '59.

——, 18th cent. Con. 132: back cover Jan '54.

——, Georgian. Con. 144: LXXX Jan '60.

——, Hepplewhite. Con. 139: XXIII Je '57.

drinks (outdoor tables, Argentina). Holiday 20: 89 Nov '56.

Driscoll, Alfred E. Cur. biog. p. 175 (1949).

drive-in hotel. *See* hotel, drive-in.

Droochsloot, Joost Cornelisz (work of). Con. 144: VIII-IX Dec '59; 145: XXIV Mar '60.

Drozniak, Edward. Cur. biog. p. 107 (1962).

drug jar, delft (antique). Con. 127: 21-2 Mar '51.

drug pot, Florentine armorial (15th cent.). Con. 143: III Mar '59.

drugstore (gold rush days). Natl. geog. 97: 732 (col.) Je '50.

—— (int., 1880). Natl. geog. 114: 119 (col.) Jl '58.

"Druid priest" (Halloween festival). Disney: People & places, p. 32 (col.).

Druid ritual (Eng.). Holiday 23: 98 Ap '58.

Druids. Natl. geog. 117: 864-5 Je '60.

Drum, Hugh A. Cur. biog. p. 239 (1941).

drum. Holiday 28: 4 Sept '60. Travel 102: 8 Dec '54.

—— (Ceylon). Holiday 19: 148 Je '56.

—— (head hunters). Natl. geog. 108: 459-85 (part col.) Oct '55.

—— (Negro playing). Int. gr. soc.: Arts . . . p. 143 (col.).

—— (primitive). Int. gr. soc.: Arts . . . p. 27 (col.).

—— (pygmy beating). Natl. geog. 117: 278 Feb '60.

—— (Santa playing). Holiday 12: 111 (col.) Dec '52.

—— (Scotsman). Holiday 19: 137 (col.) Feb '56.

—— (Tibetan woman). Holiday 12: 56 Dec '52.

—— (West Indies man). Holiday 18: 182 Dec '55.

——, Afghanistan. Natl. geog. 98: 683 (col.) Nov '50; 117: 81 (col.) Jan '60.

——, African. Holiday 8: 12 Dec '50. Natl. geog. 97: 317, 319 (col.) Mar '50; 118: 306 (col.) Sept '60.

——, Bali (man beating). Natl. geog. 116: 810 (col.) Dec '59.

——, bass. Int. gr. soc.: Arts . . . p. 141 (col.).

——, Belgian Congo. Natl. geog. 112: 84 (col.) Jl '57.

——, Bongo. Holiday 21: 198 Ap '57; 22: 173 Oct '57, 179 Nov '57.

——, Civil war. Amer. heri. vol. 3 no. 2 cover (col.) (winter '52).

——, Eskimo. Natl. geog. 109: 772 (col.) Je '56.

——, gaucho. Natl. geog. 113: 333 (col.) Mar '58.

——, Indian. Natl. geog. 107: 603 (col.) May '55; 116: 630 (col.) Nov '59.

——, jungle (Negro). Natl. geog. 113: 195 (col.) Feb '58.

——, kettle. Int. gr. soc.: Arts . . . p. 141 (col.).

——, Korean. Natl. geog. 118: 203 (col.) Aug '60.

——, Malaya. Natl. geog. 103: 221 (col.) Feb '53.

drum, military. Amer. heri. vol. 10 no. 6 cover (col.) (Oct '59).

——, Naga. Natl. geog. 117: 623 (col.) May '60.

——, Scotsman. Holiday 19: 137 (col.) Feb '56.

——, side. Int. gr. soc.: Arts . . . p. 141 (col.).

——, snare & bass. Cooper: Con. ency. of music, p. 412.

——, Swiss guard. Natl. geog. 114: 562 (col.) Oct '58.

——, timpani. See timpani.

drum & winged sticks (sym.). Lehner: Pict. bk. of sym., p. 84.

drum major (band leader). Lehner: Pict. bk. of sym., p. 93.

—— (Scotsman). Holiday 10: 21 (col.) Aug '51, 100 (col.) Dec '51; 11: 20 (col.) Ap '52; 12: 17 (col.) Aug '52, 185 (col.) Dec '52; 21: 104 (col.) Jan '57.

——, U.S. Civil war. Pakula: Cent. album, pl. 16 (col.).

drum top table. See table, drum top.

drummer. Durant: Pict. hist. of Amer. circus, p. 14.

—— (Bahamas). Natl. geog. 113: 195 (col.) Feb '58.

—— (Barbados). Holiday 28: 68 Aug '60.

—— (Puerto Rico). Holiday 28: 107 Oct '60.

drummer boy (panel in 1st private railroad car of a president). Amer. heri. vol. 7 no. 6 back cover (col.) (Oct '56).

—— (Brazil). Natl. geog. 107: 305 (col.) Mar '55.

drummers (Ceylon). Travel 111: 21 Jan '59.

——, Negro (Trinidad). Natl. geog. 103: 43 (col.) Jan '53.

Drummond, Roscoe. Cur. biog. p. 177 (1949).

"Drummond castle" Con. 132: 189 Jan '54.

"Drury Lane dentist" (Rowlandson). Con. 129: IV Je '52.

Druses at fountain. Natl. geog. 104: 18 (col.) Jl '53.

Dryden, Hugh L. Cur. biog. p. 99 (1959). Natl. geog. 118: 63 (col.) Jl '60.

Dryden, John (Kneller). Con. 140: 232 Jan '58.

Dryfoos, Orvil E. Cur. biog. p. 109 (1962).

Duart castle (Scotland). Holiday 16: 39 (col.) Sept '54.

d'Ubertino, Francesco (work of). Con. 135: 282 Je '55.

Dubilier, William. Cur. biog. p. 157 (1957).

Dubinsky, David. Cur. biog. p. 218 (1942); p. 158 (1957).

Dublin, Louis I. Cur. biog. p. 221 (1942).

Dublin (Ireland). Holiday 6: 52-63 (part col.) Dec '49; 19: 38-43 (part col.) Jan '56. Natl. geog. 99: 657 May '51; 104: 118, 129 (col.) Jl '53. Travel 110: 44-9 Jl '58.

Dublin tower. Holiday 19: 41 Jan '56.

Du Bois, Guy Pene. Cur. biog. p. 157 (1946).

Du Bois, William Pene. Jun. bk. of auth., p. 103.

Dubos, Rene J. Cur. biog. p. 164 (1952).

Dubreuil, V. (work of). Amer. heri. vol. 11 no. 1 frontis (col.) (Dec '59).

Dubridge, Lee Alvin. Cur. biog. p. 162 (1948).

Dubrovnik (Yugoslavia). Holiday 14: 39 (col.) Aug '53; 16: 109 Nov '54. Natl. geog. 99: 153 (col.) Feb '51. Travel 107: 39 Ap '57.

Dubuffet, Jean. Cur. biog. p. 111 (1962).

—— (work of). Con. 145: 207 May '60.

Dubuque (Iowa). Holiday 15: 80-1 Mar '54.

du Casse, Admiral. Holiday 8: 110 (col.) Oct '50.

Duchamp, Marcel. Cur. biog. p. 124 (1960).

—— (work of). Praeg. pict. ency., p. 455.

Duchamp-Villon (bronze figure). Praeg. pict. ency., p. 478.

"Duchess of Cleveland" (Lely). Con. 126: 33 Aug '50.

Duchess of Windsor. Holiday 11: 118 (col.), 120-1 May '52.

Duchin, Eddy. Cur. biog. p. 180 (1947).

duck decoys. Rawson: Ant. pict. bk., p. 86.

duck hunter (row boat). Holiday 24: 67 (col.) Oct '58.

duckboat (men). Natl. geog. 113: 398 (col.) Mar '58.

Duclos, Jacques. Cur. biog. p. 160 (1946).

dude ranch. Brooks: Growth of a nation, p. 296. Holiday 10: 32-3 Aug '51. Travel 104: 8-10 Jl '55.

—— (West). Amer. heri. vol. 7 no. 2 p. 8-15 (part col.) (Feb '56).

—— (camp fire). Travel 104: 6-7 Jl '55.

Dudley, Robert. Amer. heri. vol. 10 no. 3 p. 9 (Ap '59).

—— (work of). Amer. heri. vol. 9 no. 6 p. 40 (col.) (Oct '58). Natl. geog. 99: 207 (col.) Feb '51.

duel (old west). Holiday 18: 83 Nov '55.

duelers (French). Natl. geog. 100: 42 Jl '51.

Dufek, Rear Adm. George J. Cur. biog. p. 161 (1957). Natl. geog. 112: 350 (col.) Sept '57; 116: 530 Oct '59.

Duff, James H. Cur. biog. p. 164 (1948). Holiday 15: 61 Feb '54.

duffle bag, airplane. Holiday 23: 112 (col.) Je '58. Travel 113: 47 Feb '60; 114: 7 Oct '60.

Duffy, Bernard C. Cur. biog. p. 165 (1952).

Dufy, Raoul. Cur. biog. p. 169 (1951).

—— (work of). Con. 143: 1 Ap '59, XVIII May '59; 145: 1 (col.) May '60. Praeg. pict. ency., p. 474 (col.).

Duganne, Phyllis. Holiday 6: 62 Sept '49.

Duggan, Laurence H. Cur. biog. p. 181 (1947).

Duggar, Benjamin Minge. Cur. biog. p. 167 (1952).

dugout (canoe). Natl. geog. 97: 30 (col.) Jan '50.

—— (men & women). Natl. geog. 97: 237 (col.) Feb '50.

—— (Belgian Congo). Natl. geog. 112: 82-3 (col.) Jl '57.

—— (British Guiana). Natl. geog. 111: 855 Je '57.

—— (Nepal, men making). Natl. geog. 117: 378 (col.) Mar '60.

Duhamel, Georges. Holiday 21: 75 (col.) Ap '57.

Dujardin, Karel (work of). Con. 137: 194 May '56.

Du Jardin, Rosamond N. Cur. biog. p. 164 (1953).

Duke, Angier Biddle. Cur. biog. p. 113 (1962). Holiday 22: 149 Dec '57.

Duke, Patty. Cur. biog. (1963).

Duke, Vernon. Cur. biog. p. 241 (1941).

"Duke of Edinburgh" (Birley). Con. 127: 121 May '51.

Duke of York (1751). Amer. heri. vol. 11 no. 4 p. 10 (col.) (Je '60).

Duke univ. Travel 110: 17 Oct '58.

Dulac, Edmund. Jun. bk. of auth., p. 104.

dulcimer. Holiday 9: 33, 44 Mar '51. Natl. geog. 100: 113 Jl '51.

Dulles, Allen W. Cur. biog. p. 180 (1949).

Dulles, Eleanor Lansing. Cur. biog. p. 116 (1962).

Dulles, John Foster. Cur. biog. p. 181 (1944); p. 166 (1953). Travel 103: 5 Feb '55.

dumb-waiter, Chippendale. Con. 132: LXXI Nov '53.

——, Sheraton. Con. 142: inside back cover Sept '58.

dumb-waiter table (19th cent.). Con. 138: XVIII Dec '56.

Dumbarton Oaks peace conference. Natl. geog. 103: 516 Ap '53.

dumbell code, Clinton's. See Clinton's dumbell code.

Dumfries (Scotland). Natl. geog. 112: 450-1 (col.) Oct '57.

dummies in pressure suits (space). Natl. geog. 108: 240 (col.) Aug '55.

DuMont, Allen B. Cur. biog. p. 163 (1946).

Dumont, Julia. Amer. heri. vol. 2 no. 1 p. 25 (fall '50).

Dumont, Pierre (work of). Con. 133: 261 Je '54.

dump truck, Russian. See truck, Russian dump.

Dunbar, Paul B. Cur. biog. p. 181 (1949).

Dunbar, Rudolph. Cur. biog. p. 165 (1946).

Duncan, Sir Andrew Rae. Cur. biog. p. 243 (1941).

Duncan, Edward (engraving by). Con. 141: XXXI Ap '58.

Duncan, Thomas W. Cur. biog. p. 183 (1947).

Duncan, Todd. Cur. biog. p. 224 (1942).

Duncan sisters. Holiday 7: 65 Mar '50.

dunce cap (sym.). Lehner: Pict. bk. of sym., p. 85.

dune, sand. See sand dune.

—— (scooter). See sand dune scooter.

dunemobiles. Natl. geog. 112: 718-9 (col.) Nov '57.

Dunham, Franklin. Cur. biog. p. 225 (1942).

Dunham, Katherine. Cur. biog. p. 245 (1941).

Dunlap, John B. Cur. biog. p. 172 (1951).

"Dunleith" (colonial home). Jordan: Hammond's pict. atlas, p. 86 (col.).

Dunlop, John T. Cur. biog. p. 173 (1951).

Dunmore Town (Bahamas). Travel 103: 36, 38 Jan '55.

Dunn, Harvey (work of). Amer. heri. vol. 10 no. 6 p. 7-16 (col.) (Oct '59).

Dunn, James Clement. Cur. biog. p. 181 (1943).

Dunn, Loula F. Cur. biog. p. 176 (1951).

Dunne, Irene. Cur. biog. p. 161 (1945).

Dunning, John R. Cur. biog. p 166 (1948).

Dunninger, Joseph. Cur. biog. p. 184 (1944).

Dunnock, Mildred. Cur. biog. p. 176 (1955).

Dunnottar castle. Natl. geog. 112: 454-5 (col.) Oct '57.

Dunsmore, John Ward. (work of). Amer. heri. vol. 8 no. 1 p. 47 (col.) (Dec '56).

Dunton, A. Davidson. Cur. biog. p. 101 (1959).

Dunvegan castle. See castle, Dunvegan.

Duomo & Campanile, Florence. Con. 141: 236 Je '58.

Duperre, Gabriel (work of). Con. 136: XVIII (col.) Jan '56.

Duplessis, Joseph Siffred (work of). Con. 136: 33 Sept '55; 141: 248 Je '58; 143: 193 May '59.

Duplessis, Maurice. Cur. biog. p. 167 (1948).

Du Pont family. Amer. heri. vol. 4 no. 1 p. 44-5 (part col.) (fall '52).

Du Pont Winterthur museum (Wilmington, Del.). Travel 111: 22 Feb '59.

Dupre, Jules (work of). Con. ency. of ant., vol. 1, pl. 174.

Dupree, Wilmer (work of). Natl. geog. 107: 372 (col.) Mar '55.

Duquesne, Marquis. Amer. heri. vol. 5 no. 4 p. 28 (summer '54).

Durand, Asher B. (work of). Amer. heri. vol. 10 no. 1 p. 22 (col.) (Dec '58).

Durante, James (Jimmy, "big nose"). Cur. biog. p. 167 (1946). Holiday 11: 87-9 Je '52.

Duranty, Walter. Cur. biog. p. 184 (1943).

Durbin, Deanna. Cur. biog. p. 247 (1941).

Durell, Lawrence. Cur. biog. (1963).

Durer, Albrecht (self portrait). Int. gr. soc.: Arts . . . p. 89 (col.).

—— (woodcut by). Con. 133: XVI Je '54.

—— (work of). Con. ency. of ant., vol. 1, pl. 157.
Con. 133: 230 Je '54; 135: 139 Ap '55, 213 May '55; 136: 204 Dec '55; 139: 260 Je '57; 144: LXIV Sept '59.
Natl. geog. 97: 761 (col.) Je '50; 101: 94 (col.) Jan '52.
Praeg. pict. ency., p. 9, 283, 286 (col.).

"Durer" (forgery). Con. ency. of ant., vol. 3, pl. 98.

Durgin, Vice-Adm. C.T. Cur. biog p. 249 (1954).

Durham, Carl. Cur. biog. p. 163 (1957).

Durham cathedral. Holiday 18: 112 (col.) Aug '55; 23: 77 Ap '58.

—— (int.). Holiday 27: 129 Jan '60.

—— (vestibule). Praeg. pict. ency., p. 223.

Duris chalice. See chalice of Duris.

Durkin, Martin P. Cur. biog. p. 170 (1953).

Durocher, Leo. Cur. biog. p. 129 (1950).

Durrenmatt, Friedrich. Cur. biog. p. 103 (1959).

Duryea (early auto). Durant: Pict. hist. of Amer. circus, p. 156.

Dusart, Cornelius (work of). Con. 129: LXX Ap '52.
Dusenberg Phaeton auto (1930). Int. gr. soc.: Arts . . . p. 161 (col.).
D'usseau, Arnaud. Cur. biog. p. 249 (1944).
Dusseldorf, A. Normann (work of). Con. 142: XIV Sept '58.
dust storm (Mo.). Holiday 7: 40 Mar '50.
Dutch (man & child). Natl. geog. 106: 369 (col.) Sept '54.
Dutch art. See art, Dutch.
Dutch boy. See boy, Dutch.
"The Dutch buy Manhattan" (cartoon). Amer. heri. vol. 11 no. 1 p. 62-3 (Dec '59).
Dutch East India Co. warehouse (Amsterdam). Travel 110: 33 Aug '58.
"Dutch fleet" (Van de Velde). Con. 142: 258 Jan '59.
Dutch folk. See Pennsylvania Dutch country.
Dutch. See also Holland.
Dutch museum. See Zwaanendeel museum.
Dutch paintings. Con. 145: XLV Mar '60.
Dutchman. Amer. heri. vol. 10 no. 1 p. 9, 11 (col.) (Dec '58).
Holiday 6: 37 (col.) Jl '49.
—— (1640). Brooks: Growth of a nation; p. 49.
Dutra, Eurico Gaspar. Cur. biog. p. 169 (1946).
duty stamps. Con. ency. of ant., vol. 3, p. 249.
Duvalier, Francois. Cur. biog. p. 129 (1958).
Duvall, Evelyn Millis. Cur. biog. p. 185 (1947).
Duverger, T. E. (work of). Con. 141: XXVI Mar '58.
Duvieusart, Jean. Cur. biog. p. 131 (1950).
Du Vigneaud, Vincent. Cur. biog. p. 161 (1956).
Duvivier, Aimee (work of). Con. 145: LIII Mar '60.
Duvivier, Julien. Cur. biog. p. 187 (1943).
Duvoisin, Roger. Jun. bk. of auth., p. 106.
Dvorak, Antonin. Cooper: Con. ency. of music, p. 93.
dwarfs, circus. Jensen: The White House, p. 227.
dwarfs. See also circus dwarf.
dwellings. See house; home.
Dwinell, Lane. Cur. biog. p. 163 (1956).
Dworshak, Henry C. Cur. biog. p. 133 (1950).
Dyak natives. Travel 109: 49 Feb '58.
Dye, Marie. Cur. biog. p. 170 (1948).
dyepot. Rawson: Ant. pict. bk., p. 88.
Dyer-Bennet, Richard. Cur. biog. p. 186 (1944).
dyers, wool. See wool dyers.
Dykstra, Clarence A. Cur. biog. p. 249 (1941).
Dykstra, John. Cur. biog. (1963).
"Dynamite Dick". See Clifton, Dan.
dynamite explosion (desert). Natl. geog. 113: 672-3 May '58.
"Dyna-Soar" (aircraft). Readers digest 81: 97 (col.) Sept '62.
dyptych, ivory. Con. 140: 113 Nov '57.
Dzibilchaltun temple, Maya. Natl. geog. 115: 108 Jan '59.

E

Eady, Sir Crawfurd Wilfred. Cur. biog. p. 186 (1947)
eagle (U.S.A. sym.). Amer. heri. (on almost

every cover); vol. 3 no. 2 p. 2, inside back cover (col.) (winter '52).
Lehner: Pict. bk. of sym., p. 57
eagle & book (sym.). Lehner: Pict. bk. of sym., p. 37.
"Eagle dance" (Pat Goodnight). Holiday 14: 54 (col.) Dec '53.
Eagle harbor (Mich.). Travel 110: 47 Aug '58.
eagle head (from sailing vessel). Amer. heri. vol. 3 no. 2 p. 2 (col.) (winter '52).
eagle map of U.S.A. (1832). Amer. heri. vol. 8 no. 3 frontis (Ap '57).
Eagle mt. mine. Natl. geog. 112: 717 (col.) Nov. '57.
Eagle mt. water plant. Natl. geog. 112: 716 (col.) Nov '57.
Eaker, Major Gen. Ira C. Cur. biog. p. 227 (1942).
Eakins, Thomas (work of). Natl. geog. 99: 210 (col.) Feb '51.
the ear. Gray's anatomy, p.1062-88
Holiday 15: 141 May '54; 28: 34 Oct. '60, 24 Nov '60.
ear flynet. See flynet, ear (for horse).
ear marks, cow. See cow ear marks.
Earl, Ralph Eleaser Whiteside (work of). Amer. heri. vol. 12 no. 1 front cover (col.) (Dec '60).
"Earl of Essex" (Van Somer). Con. 137: XXXV (col.) Ap '56.
"Earl of Powis" (Marientreu). Con. 134: 199 Dec '54.
"Earl of Strafford" (Van Dyck). Con. 133: 14 Mar '54.
Early, Jubal A. Pakula: Cent. album, p. 117.
Early, Stephen T. Cur. biog. p. 251 (1941); p. 183 (1949).
Early, William Ashby. Cur. biog. p. 251 (1954).
Earp, James. Horan: Pict. hist. of wild west, p. 110.
Earp, Morgan. Horan: Pict. hist. of wild west, p. 111.
Earp, Virgil. Horan: Pict. hist. of wild west, p. 111.
Earp, Wyatt. Amer. heri. vol. 11 no. 5 p. 44 (Aug '60).
Brooks: Growth of a nation, p. 165.
Horan: Pict hist. of wild west, p. 103, 105, 110.
earphone test instrument. Natl. geog. 100: 766 (col.) Dec '51.
earrings. Holiday 26: 92 Sept '59.
—— (ancient). Int. gr. soc.: Arts . . . p. 29, 31 (col.).
——, African Masai. Natl. geog. 106: 492, 494, 500, 511 (part col.) Oct '54.
——, crystal star. Holiday 18: 197 Dec '55.
——, 18th cent. Con. 133: XXXV Mar '54.
——, star. Holiday 20: 212 Dec '56.
earth (80 miles up). Natl. geog. 98: 522-7 Oct '50.
—— (satellite view). Natl. geog. 118: 292-302 (part col.) Aug '60.
earth lodges, Indian. See Indian earth lodges.
earth measurements (3rd cent, B.C.). Natl. geog. 100: 753 Dec '51.
earth spirits, circle of (sym.). Lehner: Pict. bk. of sym., p. 69.
earthquake, mt. (damage, Mont.). Natl. geog. 117: 328-59 (col.) Mar '60.

earthquake waves "X-raying" the globe. Natl geog. 101: 125 Jan '52.

easel, artist's. Con. 143: 1 Ap '59.

East Corinth (Vt.). Amer. heri. vol. 6 no. 4 p. 32 (col.) (Je '55).

Easter (Holy week in Spain). See Spain (Holy week).

—— (sym.). Lehner: Pict. bk. of sym., p. 52.

Easter egg, enamel (Nuremburg, 17th cent.). Con. 134: 74 Sept '54.

——, 1st imperial (presented to Marie Fedorovna by Alexander III, 1884). Con. 135: 258 Je '55.

Easter eggs. Natl. geog. 115: 208 (col.) Feb '59.

——, Russian (19th cent.). Con. 144: 275 Jan '60.

Easter island (stone figure). Praeg. pict. ency., p. 561.

Easter Saturday (Arab Jerusalem). Natl. geog. 106: 851 (col.) Dec '54.

Easter sunrise service (Denver). Natl. geog. 106: 214 Aug '54.

Easter week (Indian, Guatemala). Natl. geog. 117: 406-9 (col.) Mar '60.

Eastlake, Sir Charles (work of). Con. 126: 137 Oct '50.

Eastland, James O. Cur. biog. p. 184 (1949).

Eastman, Joseph B. Cur. biog. p. 228 (1942).

Eastman, Seth (work of). Amer. heri. vol. 6 no. 1 p. 35 (col.) (fall '54). Con. 144: 69 Sept '59.

Eastman home, George. Amer. heri. vol. 2 no. 2 p. 59 (winter '51).

Eastman house of photography. Natl. geog. 106: 434 Sept. '54.

Eastman kodak bldg. (1892). Natl. geog. 106: 431 Sept '54.

Eastman photographic work. Natl. geog. 106: 424-38 Sept '54.

Eaton, Charles A. Cur. biog. p. 163 (1945).

Eaton, Cyrus S. Cur. biog. p. 171 (1948).

Eaton, Jeanette. Jun. bk. of auth., p. 108.

Eaton, Peggy. Jensen: The White House, p. 52.

Eaton, William (W.M.S. Doyle). Amer. heri. vol. 11 no. 2 p. 27 (Feb '60).

eaves trough hook. Rawson: Ant. pict. bk., p. 21.

Eban, Abba. Cur. biog. p. 165 (1957).

Eban, Aubrey S. Cur. biog. p. 173 (1948).

Ebbets Field (baseball). Holiday 19: 102 (col.) Mar '56.

Ebbott, Percy J. Cur. biog. p. 253 (1954).

Eberhart, Richard G. Cur. biog. p. 141 (1961).

Eberle, Irmengarde. Cur. biog. p. 171 (1946). Jun. bk. of auth., p. 109.

Eberstadt, Ferdinand. Cur. biog. p. 230 (1942).

Ebert, Carl. Cooper: Con ency. of music, p. 305.

Eccles, David. Cur. biog. p. 167 (1952).

Eccles, Marriner S. Cur. biog. p. 253 (1941).

"Ecclesia" (Strassburg cathedral). Praeg. pict. ency., p. 173.

"Ecco homo" (Rouault). Con. 145: 183 (col.) May '60.

Echols, Maj. Gen. Oliver P. Cur. biog. p. 188 (1947).

Eckardt, Felix von. Cur. biog. p. 165 (1956).

Ecker, Frederick H. Cur. biog. p. 175 (1948).

Eckstein, Gustav. Cur. biog. p. 232 (1942).

Eckstine, Billy. Cur. biog. p. 171 (1952).

eclipse marker, (1937, Canton is.). Natl. geog. 107: 121 (col.) Jan '55.

Ecole des Beaux arts (int., Paris). Holiday 17: 35 Jan '55.

"Ecstasy of St. Teresa" (altar group). Praeg. pict. ency., p. 332.

Ecuador. Holiday 20: 90-1, 95 (col.) Nov '56. Natl. geog. 97: 121-37 Jan '50. Travel 109: 44-7 Jan '58, 33-4 Mar '58.

—— (man & boy). Travel 112: 16 Sept '59.

Ecuador. See also Quito.

Ecuadorian Indian. Travel 113: 91 Ap '60.

Ecuadorians. Travel 109: 44-5 Jan '58.

ecuelle (1700). Con. 144: XLVIII Sept '59.

——, French silver. Con. ency. of ant., vol. 3, p. 66.

——, Italian silver. Con. 144: 155 Dec '59.

——, Louis XIV silver. Con. 140: 39 Sept '57.

Eddington, Sir Arthur. Cur. biog. p. 255 (1941).

Eddy, Lt. Gen. Manton S. Cur. biog. p. 177 (1951).

Eddy, Nelson. Cur. biog. p. 190 (1943).

Eddy, Roger. Holiday 27: 85 Feb '60.

Ede, James Chuter. Cur. biog. p. 172 (1946).

Edel, Leon. Cur. biog. (1963).

Edelman, Maurice. Cur. biog. p. 255 (1954).

Eden, Anthony. Cur. biog. p. 179 (1951).

Edge, Walter E. Cur. biog. p. 166 (1945).

Edinburgh, Duke of. Holiday 23: 149 Je '58. Natl. geog. 110: 333 (col.) Sept '56.

——. See also Philip, Prince.

Edinburgh, Philip, 3rd Duke of. Cur. biog. p. 190 (1947).

Edinburgh (Scotland). Natl. geog. 110: 6-7 Jl '56; 112: 460, 476-7 (part col.) Oct '57.

"Edinburgh & London mails" (Henderson). Con. 142: 122 Nov '58.

Edinburgh castle. Holiday 12: 33 (col.) Dec '52; 14: 92 (col.) Jl '53. Travel 101: 20 Je '54.

Edison, Thomas Alva. Amer. heri. vol. 9 no. 2 p. 66 (Feb '58); vol. 10 no. 6 p. 32, 41-6 (Oct '59); vol. 11 no. 3 p. 31 (Ap '60). Brooks: Growth of a nation, p. 206.

Edison carbon filament lamp. See lamp, Edison carbon filament.

Edison's home, Thomas A. Amer. heri. vol. 10 no. 6 p. 34 (Oct '59).

Edison's laboratory, Thomas A. Amer. heri. vol. 10 no. 6 p. 35, 37, 45 (Oct '59).

Edison's studio, Thomas A. Amer. heri. vol. 11 no. 3 p. 104 (Ap '60).

Edman, Irwin. Cur. biog. p. 173 (1953).

Edmonds, Walter D. Cur. biog. p. 234 (1942).

Edmonton, Alberta (night, Canada). Natl. geog. 118: 102 (col.) Jl '60.

education (sym.). Lehner: Pict. bk. of sym., p. 85.

education, patron saint for female. Lehner: Pict. bk of sym., p. 40.

"Education of Cupid" (terracotta). Con. 140: 5 Sept '57.

Edward VI, King of Gt. Brit. Amer. heri. vol. 6 no. 1 p. 43 (fall '54); vol. 10 no. 3 p. 95 Ap '59).

—— (funeral). See funeral (King Edward VI).

Edward VII, Duke. Holiday 11: 120-1 May '52.

Edward, VII, King (comedy). Holiday 24: 112-3 Dec '58.

Edward VIII (Duke of Windsor). Cur. biog. p. 738 (1944).
Holiday 14: 49 Dec '53; 18: 52 Dec '55; 23: 149 Je '58.

Edwards, G. (work of). Con. ency. of ant., vol. 3, pl. 84.

Edwards, George Wharton (bk. illus. by). Amer. heri. vol. 8 no. 1 p. 33 (col.) (Dec '56).

Edwards, India. Cur. biog. p. 186 (1949).

Edwards, Joan. Cur. biog. p. 173 (1953).

Edwards, Ralph L. Cur. biog. p. 192 (1943).

Edwards, Vincent. Cur. biog. p. 118 (1962).

Edwards, Waldo B. Cur. biog. p. 302 (1943).

Eeckhout, G. Van Den (work of). Con. 132: XII (col.) Nov '53; 143: LXV May '59.

effigies, desert Mesa (Cal.). Natl. geog. 102: 389, 394, 397-8, 403 (part col.) Sept '52.

effigy, sacred. Holiday 11: 42 (col.) Feb '52.

effort (sym.). Lehner: Pict. bk. of sym., p. 84-5.

Egan, Jack. Horan: Pict. hist. of wild west, p. 206.

Egan, William Allen. Cur. biog. p. 105 (1959).

Egbert, Sherwood H. Cur. biog. (1963).

Eger, Ernst. Cur. biog. p. 236 (1942).

Egeskov mansion. See Mansion, Egeskov.

egg (sym.). Lehner: Pict. bk. of sym., p. 78.

egg-and-dart ornament. Con. ency. of ant., vol. 1, p. 18.

egg and lotus (sym.). Lehner: Pict. bk. of sym., p. 43.

egg-and-tongue ornament. Con. ency. of ant., vol. 1, p. 18.

egg beater. Int. gr. soc.: Arts . . . p. 171 (col.).
——, **swizzle stick.** Rawson: Ant. pict. bk., p. 7.

egg boiler, silver (18th cent.). Con. 142: LVII Jan '59.

"Egg castle" (Naples). See Castel del 'Ovo.

egg cruet, Sheffield. Con. 141: XXVI Je '58.

egg-cup, antique. Con. 139: XXXV Mar '57.

egg sorting machine. Natl. geog. 104: 205 (col.) Aug '53.

Eggerth, Marta. Cur. biog. p. 194 (1943).

Eghbal, Manouchehr. Cur. biog. p. 107 (1959).

Eglevsky, Andre. Cur. biog. p. 175. (1953).

Eglisau (Switzerland). Holiday 23: 38-9 (col.) Jan '58.

Egypt. Amer. heri. vol. 11 no. 3. p. 27 (col.) (Ap '60).
Holiday 10: 116-21 (part col.) Dec '51; 27: 63-9 (col.) Mar '60.
Natl. geog. 108: 612-50 (part col.) Nov '55; 118: 358-9 (col.) Sept '60.
Travel 104: 17-9 Nov '55.
—— **(ceremonial carrier-chair, ancient).** Int. gr. soc.: Arts . . . p. 43 (col.).
—— **(map).** Natl. geog. 107: 700 May '55.
——, **ancient.** Ceram: March of arch.
Egyptian. Holiday 6: 10 Aug '49.
—— **(camel).** Amer. heri. vol. 8 no. 6 p. 107 (Oct '57); vol. 11 no. 3 p. 26 (col.) (Ap '60).
Holiday 19: 47 Mar '56.
Natl. geog. 112: 104 (col.) Jl '57.
Travel 104: 18 Nov '55.

—— **(camel driver).** Natl. geog. 100: 733 (col.) Dec '51.

Egyptian acrobats. See acrobats, Egyptian.

Egyptian architectural design. Con. 135: 243-6 Je '55.

"Egyptian book of the dead". Ceram: March of arch., p. 158-9.

Egyptian bronze cat. Con. 129: LXXVI Je '52.

Egyptian bust (Queen Nefertite). Holiday 18: 191 Dec '55.

Egyptian carving (prehistoric). Int. gr. soc.: Arts . . . p. 17 (col.)

Egyptian clay pot (man in it). Con. 142: LXXIV Jan '59.

Egyptian costumes (ancient). Int. gr. soc.: Arts . . . p. 29 (col.).

Egyptian faience cup. Con. 133: 37 (col.) Mar '54.

Egyptian games (ancient). Int. gr. soc.: Arts . . . p. 37 (col.).

Egyptian girl. Holiday 10: 120 (col.) Dec '51.

Egyptian hall in Piccadilly. Con. 135: 243 Je 55.

Egyptian head. Int. gr. soc.: Arts . . . p. 187 (col.).
Travel 112: 7 Aug '59; 113: 17 Mar '60.

"Egyptian head" (sculpture by Lachaise). Holiday 14: 61 Nov '53.

Egyptian head (woman, ancient). Int. gr. soc.: Arts . . . p. 181 (col.).
—— **(woman, 17th cent.).** Int. gr. soc.: Arts . . . p. 183 (col.).

Egyptian home (int. 3000 years ago). Int. gr. soc.: Arts . . . p. 15 (col.).

Egyptian king (5th dynasty). Int. gr. soc.: Arts . . . p. 29 (col.).

Egyptian laborers. Ceram: March. of arch., p. 151, 153-4.
Holiday 20: 63 (col.) Dec '56.

Egyptian man & woman. Holiday 10: 122 Oct '51.

Egyptian men. Travel 113: 17 Mar '60.

Egyptian monument. Natl. geog. 105: 485 (col.) Ap '54.

Egyptian murals (people, animals). Natl. geog. 112: 842-3 Dec '57.

Egyptian obelisk. See obelisk, Egyptian.

Egyptian portal (Smith). Amer. heri. vol. 7 no. no. 4 p. 39 (col.) (Je '56).

Egyptian procession (wedding). Amer. heri. vol. 11 no. 3 p. 27 (col.) (Ap '60).

"Egyptian pyramid" (circus). Durant: Pict. hist. of Amer. circus, p. 19.

Egyptian sculpture See sculpture, Egyptian.

Egyptian ship. See ship, Egyptian.

Egyptian sphinx. See Sphinx, Egyptian.

Egyptian temple (Isis). Int. gr. soc.: Arts . . . p. 13 (col).

Egyptian temple pictures (Bible times). Natl. geog. 112: 834-63 (col.) Dec '57.

Egyptian tomb carvings. Travel 106: 47 Nov '56.

Egyptian wall painting. See wall painting, Egyptian.

Egyptian zodiac. See zodiac, ancient Egyptian.

Egyptians. Natl. geog. 108: 615, 649 (col.) Nov '55.
—— **(comic).** Holiday 22: 42 Oct '57.

—— (in home, 3000 yrs. ago). Int. gr. soc.: Arts . . . p. 15 (col.).

—— (praying toward Mecca, camels). Natl. geog. 108: 612-3 (col.) Nov '55.

—— (rowing). Natl. geog. 108: 632 (col.) Nov '55.

Ehninger, John Whetton (work of). Amer. heri. vol. 7 no. 3 p. 59 (col.) (Ap '56).

Ehricke, Krafft A. Cur. biog. p. 131 (1958).

Eichelberger, Clark M. Cur. biog. p. 192 (1947).

Eichelberger, Brig. Gen. Robert L. Cur. biog. p. 197 (1943).

Eicher, Edward C. Cur. biog. p. 256 (1941).

Eicholtz, Jacob (work of). Amer. heri. vol. 7 no. 1 p. 20 (col.) (Dec '55).

Eiffel tower. Holiday 11: 122 Mar '52; 13: 13 Mar '53, 40 Ap '53, 8 May '53; 14: 23 Aug '53, 12 Oct '53; 17: 6 Jan '55, 20 Feb '55; 19: 115 Jan '56, 142 Feb '56; 21: 147 (col.) Jan '57, 33 (col.), 43 Mar '57; 22: 122 (col.) Oct '57; 25: 142 Feb '59; 26: 17 Oct '59; 27: 112, 148 Jan '60, 27 May '60; 28: 117 (col.) Sept '60.

Natl. geog. 98: 49, 59 (col.) Jl '50; 101: 775, 804 (col.) Je '52; 106: 428 Sept '54; 111: 770 (col.) Je '57; 114: 288, 302 Aug '58; 117: 766 (col.) Je '60.

Travel 101: 15 May '54; 106: 57 Oct '56; 107: 36 May '57; 110: back cover Jl '58, back cover Aug '58; 111: 6 Feb '59, 2, 5 Mar '59, 2 May '59, 2 Ap '59, 2 Je '59; 112: 7 Jl '59, 2 Aug '59, back cover Sept '59, 58 Dec '59; 113: inside cover Jan '60, inside cover Feb '60, inside cover, back cover Mar '60; 114: 7 Jl '60, inside cover Aug '60, 7 Sept '60, 13 Oct '60, 9 Dec '60.

Eilean castle (Scotland, night). Holiday 27: 73 May '60.

Finaudi, Luigi. Cur. biog. p. 178 (1948).

Einem, Gottfried von. Cur. biog. p. 177 (1953).

Einstein, Albert. Cur. biog. p. 257 (1941); p. 179 (1953).

Jensen: The White House, p. 217.

Eiseley, Loren. Cur. biog. p. 126 (1960).

Eisendrath, Maurice N. Cur. biog. p. 135 (1950).

Eisenhower, Pres. Dwight D. Amer. heri. vol. 7 no. 3 p. 33 (Ap '56).

——, Lt. Gen. Dwight D. Cur. biog. p. 238 (1942).

——, Gen. Dwight D. Cur. biog. p. 180 (1948); p. 167 (1957).

——, Pres. Dwight D. Jensen: The White House, p. 264, 268-9, 272-3, 277.

Natl. geog. 106: 125 (col.) Jl '54, 308 Sept '54; 108: 734 Dec '55; 112: 866-7 Dec '57; 114: 360 Sept '58; 115: 590 Ap '59; 116: 753 (col.) Dec '59; 117: 592, 604, 608, 610, 613, 628, 631, 644-6 (col.) May '60.

Travel 104: 3 Sept '55; 113: 32 Ap '60; 114: 58 Jl '60.

—— (Alaska statehood). Natl. geog. 116: 49 Jl '59.

—— (as a boy). Holiday 21: 90 May '57.

—— (bathynauts). Natl. geog. 118: 239 (col.) Aug '60.

—— (by Birley). Con. 134: 70 (col.) Sept '54.

—— (city key, Brasilia). Natl. geog. 117: 723 (col.) May '60.

—— (golf). Natl. geog. 105: 330 Mar '54.

—— (honorary degree, India). Natl. geog. 117: 620 (col.) May '60.

—— (presents medal to Everest climbers). Natl. geog. 106: 64 Jl '54.

—— (unknown soldier's service). Natl. geog. 114: 598, 600 (col.) Nov '58.

Eisenhower, Pres. & Mrs. Dwight. Jensen: The White House, p. 264.

Natl. geog. 106: 480 (col.) Oct '54.

Eisenhower, Mrs. Dwight D. Cur. biog. p. 181 (1953).

Jensen: The White House, p. 264, 269.

Eisenhower, John. Natl. geog. 117: 592 (col.) May '60.

Eisenhower, Mrs. John. Natl. geog. 117: 592, 619 (col.) May '60.

Eisenhower, Milton S. Cur. biog. p. 173 (1946).

Eisenhower family, Dwight. Jensen: The White House, p. 269, 272-3.

Eisenhower grandchildren, Dwight. Jensen: The White House, p. 267, 269.

Eisenhower home, Dwight. Brooks: Growth of a nation, p. 311.

Eisenhower museum. Holiday 21: 91 May '57.

Eisenhower's inauguration, Dwight. Amer. heri. vol. 4 no. 3 p. 7 (spring '53).

Eisenschiml, Otto. Cur. biog. (1963).

Eisenstein, Sergei. Cur. biog. p. 176 (1946).

Eisermann, Richard. Con. 141: XXVII Mar '58.

Eisler, Hanns. Cur. biog. p. 241 (1942).

Eklund, John M. Cur. biog. p. 188 (1949).

Eklund, Sugvard. Cur. biog. p. 120 (1962).

"Ekolsund castle" (Sweden). Con. 141: 3-4 Mar '58.

Elba (Isle of exile). Holiday 26: 118 Dec '59.

elbow chair. See chair, Hepplewhite elbow.

elbow joint. Gray's anatomy. p. 1400.

El Camino Real Mission (Cal.). Holiday 12: 12 (col.) Dec '52.

"El Capitan" (Cal.). Natl. geog. 105: 796-7 (col.) Je '54.

El Capitan rock. Jordan: Hammond's pict. atlas, p. 190 (col.).

El Castillo in Chichen Itza. Praeg. pict. ency., p. 543.

El Cortez hotel (San Diego). Travel 106: 9 Aug '56.

Elder, Albert L. Cur. biog. p. 128 (1960).

Eldora (Saskatchewan). Natl. geog. 106: 552-3 (col.) Oct '54.

Eldridge, Florence. Cur. biog. p. 495 (1943).

election, U.S. (1840). Natl. geog. 116: 102 Jl '59.

election campaign posters. See presidential campaign posters.

election campaign speaker. See campaign speaker, election.

"Election of Cardinal Albani to Pontificate". Con. 142: 165 Dec '58.

election vote record (18th cent., Va.). Amer. heri. vol. 4 no. 1 p. 7 (fall '52).

election vote (1864). Amer. heri. vol. 6 no. 4 p. 85 (Je '55).

electric fan, wall. Amer. heri. vol. 9 no. 5 frontis, (Aug '58).

electric generator. Int. gr. soc.: Arts . . . p. 173 (col.).
Natl. geog. 99: 589 (col.) May '51.

electric power alternator. Natl. geog. 98: 244 (col.) Aug '50.

electricity (sym.). Lehner: Pict. bk. of sym., p. 12.

electrochemistry (sym.). Lehner: Pict. bk. of sym., p. 12.

electronic fence (Arctic circle). Natl. geog. 114: 132-3 (col.) Jl '58.

electronic tube (sym.). Lehner: Pict. bk. of sym., p. 16.

electronics (sym.). Lehner: Pict. bk. of sym., p. 12.

elements, the four. See the four elements (sym.).

elephant (drawn by thread). Amer. heri. vol. 8 no. 6 p. 41 (col.) (Oct '57).

—— (howdah, ivory). Holiday 12: 75 (col.) Oct '52.

elephant memorial statue. See memorial statue, elephant.

elephant rock, Graniteville). Travel 105: 25 May '56.

—— (Nev.). Holiday 16: 90 (col.) Oct '54.

elephant tusks. Natl. geog. 103: 266 (col.) Feb '53.

El Escorial (Spain). Holiday 23: 116 (col.) Jan '58.
Travel 111: 32 Ap '59.

"El Espolio" (El Greco). Con. 129: 23 Ap '52.

Eleuthera island (Bahamas). Travel 105: 45-8 Mar '56.

elevation levels (men). Natl. geog. 111: 204 (col.) Feb '57.

elevator (girl). Holiday 24: 36 Nov '58.

elevator, Outside 8-story. Travel 108: 20 Aug '57.

——, street (Lisbon). Holiday 6: 101 Sept '49.

Edwards, E.G. Amer. heri. vol. 8 no. 6 p. 12 (Oct '57).

Elgar, Sir Edward. Cooper: Con. ency. of music, p. 94.

Elgin marbles. Holiday 18: 51 Sept '55.

El Greco. Int. gr. soc.: Arts . . . p. 91 (col.).

—— (crucifix). Con. 134: 176-9 Dec '54.

—— (work of). Con. 129: 23 Ap '52; 132: opp. p. 143 (col.) Jan '54; 133: 96 Ao '54; 136: 135 Nov '55; 139: 54 Mar '57; 142: 256 Jan '59; 144: 128, 135 Nov '59.
Labande: Naples, p. 111.
Natl. geog. 110: 633 (col.), 644 Nov '56.
Praeg. pict. ency., p. 314 (col.).

"Elijah fed by ravens" (Guercino). Con. 132: 12 Sept '53.

"Elijah in chariot of fire" (Blake). Con. 140: 114 Nov '57.

"Elijah taken up in a chariot of fire". Natl. geog. 101: 96 (col.) Jan '52.

Eliot, Charles. Holiday 5: 108 Feb '49.

Eliot, John. Amer. heri. vol. 9 no. 1 p. 4 (col.) (Dec '57).

—— (preaching to Indians). Amer. heri. vol. 9 no. 1 p. 118 (Dec '57).

Eliot, Martha May. Cur. biog. p. 185 (1948).

Eliot, Thomas H. Cur. biog. p. 243 (1942).

Eliot, Thomas Stearns. Amer. heri. vol. 11 no. 2 p. 8 (Feb '60).
Cur. biog. p. 122 (1962).

Eliot, T. S. Holiday 27: 75 (col.) Mar '60.

Eliot's Bible (title page). Amer. heri. vol. 9 no. 1 p. 6-7 (Dec '57).

Eliot's inscription in Bible, John. Con. 143: 102 Ap '59.

Elizabeth, Queen. Jensen: The White House, p. 240.

Elizabeth I, Queen of Gt. Brit. Amer. heri. vol. 4 no. 2 cover (col.) (winter '53) vol. 8 no. 4 p. 9 (col.) (Je '57); vol. 10 no. 3 cover (col.), p. 5 (col.) (Ap '59).
Con. 139: 6 Mar '57, 216 Je '57.

—— (Hilliard miniature). Con. ency. of ant., vol. 1, pl. 129.
Con. 145: 179 May '60.

—— (Oliver). Con. 141: 104 Ap '58.

—— (on wood). Con. 126: 207 Dec '50.

—— (16th cent.). Con. 127: 18, 20 Mar '51.

—— (theatre scene). Natl. geog. 108: 517 (col.) Oct '55.

—— (tomb). Amer. heri. vol. 11 no. 1 p. 59 (Dec '59).

—— (wedding procession). Amer. heri. vol. 10 no. 4 p. 18 (col.) (Je '59).

Elizabeth II, Queen of Gt. Brit. Con. 139: 6 Mar '57.
Cur. biog. p. 188 (1944); p. 22 (1955).
Holiday 7: 96 Mar '50; 21: 112 Mar '57; 22: cover, 62-7 (part col.) Nov '57, 89 Dec '57.
Jensen: The White House, p. 270.
Natl. geog. 113: 575 Ap '58; 115: 825-6 (part col.) Je '59.

—— (and child). Holiday 23: 71 (col.) Ap '58.

—— (coronation of). Natl. geog. 104: 292-341 (col.) Sept '53.

—— (coronation procession). Int. gr. soc.: Arts . . . p. 163 (col.).

—— (genealogy chart). Holiday 22: 88 Dec '57.

—— (in Jamaica). Natl. geog. 105: 335, 340 Mar '54.

—— (Nigerian welcome). Natl. geog. 110: 326-37 (col.) Sept '56.

—— (on horse). Natl. geog. 103: 810 (col.) Je '53.

—— (order of garter ceremony). Natl. geog. 114: 75 Jl '58.

—— (statue). Travel 113: cover Jan '60.

—— (throne). Holiday 23: 67 (col.) Jan '58.
Natl. geog. 115: 829 (col.) Je '59.

—— and family. Holiday 16: 75 Aug '54; 22: 87 (col.) Dec '57.

Elizabeth II & Prince Charles. Natl. geog. 104: 306 Sept '53.

—— (in coach). Natl. geog. 104: 333 Sept '53.

Elizabeth II & Prince Philip, Queen. Holiday 19: 53 (col.) May '56.
Natl. geog. 104: 311 (col.) Sept '53.
Elizabeth & Royal party, Queen. Holiday 20: 199 Nov '56.
Elizabeth & Margaret, Princesses. Holiday 21: 48 Jan '57.
Elizabeth, Duchess of Northumberland (Reynolds). Con. 126: 25 Aug '50.
Elizabeth, Marchioness of Tavistock (Reynolds). Con. 126: 209 Dec '50.
Elizabeth of Saxony, Princess. See "Princess Elizabeth of Saxony".
Elizabethan club, Yale. Natl. geog. 112: 328 (col.) Sept '57.
Elizabethville (Belgian Congo). Natl. geog. 101: 351 (col.) Mar '52.
Elizalde, Joaquin M. Cur. biog. p. 187 (1948).
Ellam, Patrick. Travel 101: 32 Jan '54.
Ellender, Allen J. Cur. biog. p. 178 (1946).
Ellingson, Mark. Cur. biog. p. 170 (1957).
Ellington, Buford. Cur. biog. p. 129 (1960).
Ellington, Duke. Cur. biog. p. 260 (1941). Holiday 21: 145 May '57.
Ellinor village (Ormond Beach, Fla.). Travel 101: 21-3 Mar '54.
Elliott, Bob. Cur. biog. p. 171 (1957).
Elliott, Frank. Horan: Pict. hist. of wild west, p. 196.
Elliott, Herbert. Cur. biog. p. 131 (1960).
Ellis, Elmer. Cur. biog. p. 125 (1962).
Ellis, I. C. Ceram: March of arch., p. 103.
Ellis, J. F. (work of). Con. 133: IX Je '54.
"Ellis island" immigrants. Brooks: Growth of a nation, p. 135.
Elliston, Herbert. Cur. biog. p. 189 (1949).
Ellsberg, Capt. Edward. Cur. biog. p. 245 (1942).
Ellsberg, Commander Edward. Jun. bk. of auth., p. 111.
Ellsworth, Col. Elmer E. Amer. heri. vol. 7 no. 5 p. 12 (col.) (Aug '56).
Ellsworth (1873). Horan: Pict. hist. of wild west, p. 102.
Ellyson, J. Taylor. Amer. heri. vol. 5 no. 3 p. 38 (spring '54).
El Mallakh, Kamal Cur. biog. p. 257 (1954).
Elman, Mischa. Cur. biog. p. 170 (1945). Holiday 8: 88 Dec '50.
El Misti volcano (Peru). Holiday 14: 95 Nov '53.
Elmo, Cloe (Metropolitan opera). Holiday 8: 81 Nov '50.
El Morro fortress (San Juan). Holiday 12: 64 (col.) Dec '52.
Natl. geog. 99: 420, 429 (col.) Ap '51.
El Morro national monument. Natl. geog. 112: 238-44 (part col.) Aug '57.
—— (map). Natl. geog. 112: 237 Aug '57.
Eloise (comic character). Holiday 23: 105 Jan '58, 166 Mar '58, 133 Ap '58, 26 May '58, 6 Je '58.
Elphinstone Inlet (Arabia). Natl. geog. 108: 168-9 (col.) Aug '55.
El Salto falls (San Luis Potosi). Travel 101: back cover Mar '54.
El Salvador. Travel 110: 36-40 Oct '58.

—— home (veranda). Holiday 17: 43 (col.) Mar '55.
El Sangay volcano (Andes). Natl. geog. 97: 119 Jan '50.
El Santuario de Chimayo shrine (Santa Fe). Holiday 14: 57 (col.), 58 Dec '53.
Elsheimer, Adam (work of). Con. ency. of ant., vol. 1, pl. 157.
"Elsie the cow" (Borden milk). Natl. geog. 107: 468 (col.) Ap '55.
Elvehjem, Conrad A. Cur. biog. p. 189 (1948). Holiday 27: 85 Je '60.
Ely, Gen. Paul. Cur. biog. p. 259 (1954).
Emanuel, Victor. Cur. biog. p. 183 (1951).
"Embarking on a ferry boat" (Romney). Con. 145: 114 Ap '60.
emblem. Holiday 10: 7, 23, 81 (col.) Oct '51; 11: 25 (col.) Mar '52; 12: 7 (col.) Jl '52.
emblems (sym.). Lehner: Pict. bk. of sym., p. 90-1.
——, airline. Holiday 12: 2 (col.) Oct '52; 21: 185 Ap '57.
——, auto. Holiday 12: 65 (col.) Sept '52; 19: 83 (col.) Mar '56; 21: 97 (col.) Mar '57.
——, boat. Holiday 21: 24 (col.) Feb '57.
——, Union Pacific railroad. Holiday 21: 47 (col.) Ap '57.
——, U.S. (bald eagle). Amer. heri. vol. 11 no. 6 p. 48-51 (col.) Oct '60; almost all issues (front cover).
Embree, Edwin R. Cur. biog. p. 191 (1948).
embroiderer (woman). Natl. geog. 115: 187 (col.) Feb '57.
embroiderers, Kashmir. Natl. geog. 114: 619 (col.) Nov '58.
embroideries, Calverley. Con. 145: 82-8 Ap '60, 170-7 May '60.
——, Scottish (panels). Con. 139: 197-9 May '57.
embroidery, British (16th cent.). Con. 143: 231-5 Je '59.
——, Chinese. Natl. geog. 105: 250 (col.) Feb '54.
——, Russian (17th cent.). Con. 142: 223 Jan '59.
——, Skyros island. Con. 144: 284 Jan '60.
embroidery design (antique). Con. ency. of ant. vol. 1, p. 211-16, pl. 119-21.
——, Kashmir. Natl. geog. 114: 619 (col.) Nov '58.
——, linen. Rawson: Ant. pict. bk., p. 11.
embroidery. See also needlework.
embroidery salesmen (Madeira is.). Natl. geog. 115: 393 (col.) Mar '59.
embryo. Gray's anatomy, p. 33, 36-9, 42-57.
Emeny, Brooks. Cur. biog. p. 195 (1947).
Emerald Bay (Cal.). Holiday 16: 60-1 (col.) Dec '54.
Emerald grotto. See grotto, Emerald (Amalfi).
Emerson, Faye. Cur. biog. p. 185 (1951).
Emerson, Lee E. Cur. biog. p. 183 (1953).
Emerson, Ralph Waldo. Amer. heri. vol. 8 no. 2 p. 23 (Feb '57).
Natl. geog. 97: 303 (col.) Mar '50.
—— (caricature). Amer. heri. vol. 10 no. 3 p. 61 (Ap '59).

Emery, Anne (McGuigan). Cur. biog. p. 173 (1952).

Emery, De Witt M. Cur. biog. p. 181 (1946).

Emery, Mr. & Mrs. Joseph (by Davis). Amer. heri. vol. 6 no. 2 p. 38 (col.) (winter '55).

Emery, Leslie (paintings). Natl. geog. 116: 586 (col.) Nov '59.

emigrants. Brooks: Growth of a nation, p. 192.

——, European (on ship). Amer. heri. vol. 11 no. 5 cover (col.) (Aug '60).

Emigration canyon monument (Salt Lake City). Travel 112: 34 Aug '59.

Emma (deity). Lehner: Pict. bk. of sym., p. 49.

Emmet, Evelyn. Cur. biog. p. 185 (1953).

Emmons, Lt. Gen. Delos C. Cur. biog. p. 247 (1942).

Emmons, Glenn L. Cur. biog. p. 261 (1954).

Emory, Lt. W. H. Amer. heri. vol. 11 no. 4 p. 47 (col.) (Je '60).

emotional expressions (faces). Amer. heri. vol. 4 no. 4 p. 3, 64 (summer '53).

emperor (sym.). Lehner: Pict. bk. of sym., p. 74.

——, Roman (ancient times). Int. gr. soc.: Arts . . . p. 31 (col.).

"Emperor Augustus & the Sibyl" (Hugo Van de Goes). Con. 126: 10 Aug '50.

Empie, Rev. Paul C. Cur. biog. p. 133 (1958).

Empire state bldg. Amer. heri. vol. 5 no. 1 cover (col.), 44 (fall '53).

Empire state music festival tent (Ellenville, N.Y.). Holiday 24: 45 (col.) Aug '58.

empress (sym.). Lehner: Pict. bk. of sym., p. 76.

Empress hotel (Victoria, B.C., Canada). Holiday 5: 90 (col.) Je '49; 7: 106 (col.) Ap '50.
Natl. geog. 114: 186 (col.) Aug '58.

Emrich, Duncan. Cur. biog. p. 181 (1955).

enamel box (18th cent.). Con. 142: 124 Nov '58.

——, Battersea. Con. 142: XVI Nov '58.

enamel paintings, Limoges. Con. 143: 172-4 May '59.

enamels, English painted. Con. ency. of ant., vol. 1, pl. 73-6.

"The Encantats" (Spain). Natl. geog. 109: 322 (col.) Mar '56.

Encanto park (Phoenix). Travel 113: 36 May '60.

Enchanted forest (near Frederick, Md.). Travel 105: 31-3 May '56.

Enchien, les-Bains (France). Con. 145: LV Je '60.

Enckell, Carl J.A. Cur. biog. p. 136 (1950).

encoignure, French (18th cent.). Con. 132: 62 Sept '53.

——, Louis XV. Con. 137: 126 Ap '56.

——, Louis XVI. Con. 141: 189 May '58.

end tables. See tables, end.

Endecott, John. Amer. heri. vol. 10 no. 6 p. 49 (Oct '59).

Endeley, Emmanuel M. L. Cur. biog. p. 109 (1959).

Enders, John F. Cur. biog. p. 182 (1955).

Endicott, Governor (Mass. Bay Colony). Brooks: Growth of a nation, p. 49.

Engastromenos, Sophia. See Schliemann, Sophia (Engastromenos).

Engels, Friedrich. Amer. heri. vol. 8 no. 3 p. 23 (Ap '57).

Enghien, les-Bains (France). Con. 138: LXV Jan '57; 139: LIII May '57.

engine, switch (Formosa). Natl. geog. 111: 332 Mar '57.

——, train. See train locomotive.

engine house (on rock cliff). Natl. geog. 105: 6 Jan '54.

engine pump. See pump, fuel & vacuum engine.

engineering (sym.). Lehner: Pict. bk. of sym., p. 12.

England. Con. 137: 94-100 Ap '56.
Holiday 10: 110-11 (part col.) Aug '51; 12: 67 (col.) Nov '52; 13: 95-7 Jan '53; 15: 12-3 (col.) Feb '54; 16: 28-9 (col.) Jl '54; 21: 104 (col.) Jan '57, 136 (col.) Ap '57, 181 (col.) Je '57; 23: 57-101 (col.) Ap '58; 25: 17 Jan '59; 27: 127 (col.) Feb '60, 2 (col.) May '60.
Natl. geog. 98: 173-203 (part col.) Aug '50; 103: 804-38 (part col.) Je '53; 108: 296-350 (part col.) Sept '55; 114: 46 (part col.) Jl '58.
Travel 105: 40-1 Ap '56.

England (castles). See castles (England).

—— (coronation of Elizabeth II). Natl. geog. 104: 292-341 (col.) Sept '53.

—— (costume). See English costume; costume, English; costume, British.

England (early map of southern coast). Amer. heri. vol. 10 no. 4 p. 6-7 (col.) (Je '59).

—— (Holy island). See Holy island (England).

—— (house in Wharfedale). Travel 112: 46 Aug '59.

—— (Lake district). Natl. geog. 109: 510-44 (part col.) Ap '56.

—— (Lamb Inn). Holiday 25: 17 Jan '59.

—— (map). Holiday 21: 117 Jan '57; 23: 55 Ap '58.
Natl. geog. 108: 300-1 Sept '55.

—— (map of inns location). Holiday 23: 145 Ap '58.

—— (map S.E. coast, time of Henry VIII). Amer. heri. vol. 10: no. 4 p. 6-7 (col.) Je '59.

—— (map). See also map (British Isles).

—— (Portsmouth). Natl. geog. 101: 514-43 (part col.) Ap '52.

—— (Salisbury cathedral). Amer. heri. vol. 7 no. 1 p. 7 (col.) (Dec '55).
Con. ency. of ant., vol. 1, pl. 142.
Con. 129: LXVII Je '52.
Natl. geog. 108: 347 Sept '55.

—— (Salisbury cathedral spire). Holiday 28: 31 (col.) Dec '60.

—— (village). Holiday 21: 18 (col.) Ap '57.

—— (wessex). Holiday 14: 54-5 Nov '53.

——, patron saint of. Lehner: Pict. bk. of sym., p. 39.
England royal guard. *See* royal guard, London.
England. *See* also Great Britain; London.
Engle, Clair. Cur. biog. p. 173 (1957).
Engle, Paul. Cur. biog. p. 249 (1942).
Englehart, George (miniature by). Con. ency. of ant., vol. 1, pl. 132.
Engleheart, J. C. D. (work of). Con. 145: 127 Ap '60.
English & Spanish (men at table, 1604). Amer. heri. vol. 10 no. 4 p. 16-7 (col.) (Je '59).
English architecture. *See* architecture, English; house, English.
English costume (18th cent.). Int. gr. soc.: Arts . . . p. 113 (col.).
English harbor (Antigua). Holiday 23: 41 Feb '58.
Travel 101: 34 Mar '54.
English military school. *See* Sandhurst.
"Englishman at the Moulin Rouge" (Toulouse-Lautrec). Praeg. pict. ency., p. 38 (col.).
engraver, metal (Belgian Congo). Natl. geog. 101: 329 (col.) Mar '52.
engravers, French (carve names of Amer. soldiers who died). Natl. geog. 111: 742 Je '57.
engraving, copper (nude men fighting). Praeg. pict. ency., p. 309.
——, wood & metal. Int. gr. soc.: Arts . . . p. 135 (col.).
——, wood. *See* wood engraving.
engravings. Con. 141: 98-9 Ap '58.
—— (Knight, Death & the Devil). Praeg. pict. ency., p. 283.
—— (Krol). Con. 140: 88-9 Nov '57.
—— (Wilson). Con. 139: 87-90 Ap '57.
En-Gresaille paintings. Con. 140: XLIX Sept '57.
Engstrom, Elmer W. Cur. biog. p. 187 (1951).
Enright, Elizabeth. Cur. biog. p. 196 (1947). Jun. bk. of auth., p. 113.
enseignes (15th cent.). Con. 132: 128 Nov '53.
Ensor, James (work of). Praeg. pict. ency., p. 460 (col.).
entaglement (sym.). Lehner: Pict. bk. of sym., p. 82.
Enters, Angna. Cur. biog. p. 174 (1952).
Entezam, Nasrollah. Cur. biog. p. 138 (1950).
"Enthroned Madonna with child" (Byzantine). Praeg. pict. ency., p. 182 (col.).
"The Entombment" (Garbieri). Con. 144: 22 Sept '59.
"The Entombment", Limoges reliquary. Con. 143: 199 May '59.
entrance (monastery, Singapore). Natl. geog. 103: 217 (col.) Feb '53.
entree dish (Storr, 1809). Con. 143: XXII Ap '59.
——, antique. Con. 135: XXVIII Mar '55.
——, antique silver. Con. 132: LVII Sept '53; 137: XXII Je '56; 138: X Sept '56, XXXVIII Nov '56, XVI Dec '56, XXVIII Jan '57; 139: XXVIII Mar '57; 141: XXXII Mar '58.
——, George III (silver). Con. 129: XIV Je '52; 133: VI Ap '54; 138: XVI, XXXIV Jan '57; 139: L May '57; 142: LXXI Jan '59; 143: XXVIII Mar '59, XLII May '59.

——, Georgian (silver). Con. 145: XXXVI Mar '60.
——, Sheffield (silver). Con. 144: XXIX Nov '59; 145: XXXVI Mar '60.
——, silver (18th cent.). Con. 133: III Je '54.
——, silver (19th cent.). Con. ency. of ant., vol. 1, pl. 91.
envelope. Holiday 18: 121 Oct '55.
Travel 103: inside back cover Mar '55.
envelopes, "patriotic". Amer. heri. vol. 10 no. 6 p. 90-1 (Oct '59).
envoys, Japanese. *See* Japanese envoys.
epee trophy, foil. Con. 144: 195 Dec '59.
epergne. Con. 140: LXIX Nov '57; 142: XXIV Sept '58.
——, antique silver. Con. 135: XXVII May '55; 138: III Nov '56, LV Jan '57.
——, George II silver. Con. 135: LIII May '55; 145: LXX Je '60.
——, George III silver. Con. 132: III Nov '53; 133: LXIX Je '54; 141: XX Je '58.
——, Georgian. Con. 140: VII Dec '57.
——, Georgian (Romer). Con. 145: XLII Mar '60.
——, gilt (18th cent.). Con. 133: 155 May '54.
——, Lamerie silver. Con. 144: 61 Sept '59.
——, Sheffield. Con. 144: XXXIV Jan '60.
——, silver (18th cent.). Con. 145: XVII May '60.
——, silver (Parker, 1784). Con. 145: X Ap '60.
Ephesus. Osward: Asia Minor, pl. 31-2, 34-6, 41-3, 47-8, pl. II (col.), pl. 57.
—— (library of Celsus). Natl. geog. 110: 748-9 Dec '56.
Ephrata's fair (to turn on irrigation water). Natl. geog. 102: 609 (col.) Nov '52.
Epidaurus (Greek theater). Int. gr. soc.: Arts . . . p. 35 (col.).
epilogue (sym.). Lehner: Pict. bk. of sym., p. 92.
Episcopal cross. *See* cross, Episcopal.
Epstein, Eliahu. Cur. biog. p. 193 (1948).
Epstein, Jacob. Cur. biog. p. 171 (1945).
Epstein, Sir Jacob (bronze bust). Praeg. pict. ency., p. 479.
—— (lead work). Con. 145: 277 Je '60.
equator crossing festival. *See* festival (submarine equator crossing).
equator monument. *See* monument, equator.
equilibrist, circus. Durant: Pict. hist. of Amer. circus, p. 234.
equilibrium (sym.). Lehner: Pict. bk. of sym., p. 82.
Erasmus, Desiderius. Int. gr. soc.: Arts . . . p. 93 (col.).
—— (on wood, by Holbein). Con. 127: 52-3 Mar '51.
Erato (goddess). Lehner: Pict. bk. of sym., p. 33.
Erechtheum porch. Holiday 12: 55 Sept '52.
Erencikoy (in Anatolia). Osward: Asia Minor, pl. 145.
Erhard, Ludwig. Cur. biog. p. 140 (1950). Holiday 25: 57 May '59.
Ericksen, Virgilius (work of). Con. 135: 46 Mar '55.

Erie canal (N.Y.). Amer. heri. vol. 3 no. 3 p. 8-11 (spring '52).
Holiday 15: 98-101 (part col.) Je '54.
Natl. geog. 110: 569 (col.) Nov '56.
Erie canal opening (1825). Amer. heri. vol. 8 no. 5 p. 14-5 (col.) (Aug '57).
Erikson, Leonard F. Cur. biog. p. 187 (1953).
Erkin, Feridun C. Cur. biog. p. 177 (1952).
Erlander, Tage. Cur. biog. p. 197 (1947).
"Erminia & the shepherds". Con. 145: 40 Mar '60.
—— (Diziani). Con. 135: XXXIII May '55.
Ernst, Max. Cur. biog. p. 251 (1942); p. 143 (1961).
Praeg. pict. ency., p. 453.
Ernst, Morris L. Cur. biog. p. 145 (1961).
Erskine, Lt. Gen. Sir George. Cur. biog. p. 179 (1952).
Erskine, Maj. Gen. Graves B. Cur. biog. p. 184 (1946).
Ervin, Samuel J., jr. Cur. biog. p. 185 (1955).
"Esau & Jacob" (Strozzi). Con. 144: 107 Nov '59.
Escorial (near Madrid). Holiday 27: 126 Jan '60.
—— (convent palace of Philip II). Praeg. pict. ency., p. 297.
Escosura, Ignacio Leon Y. (work of). Con. 129: XVIII (col.) Je '52.
escritoire, Louis XVI. Con. 137: XL Mar '56.
——, ormolu. Con. 144: XIX Jan '60.
——, Victorian. Con. ency. of ant., vol. 3, pl. 6.
——, Victorian sycamore marquetry. Con. ency. of ant., vol. 3, pl. 6.
escutcheon, Scotch. Holiday 27: cover (col.) May '60.
escutcheons, furniture. Rawson: Ant. pict. bk., p. 85.
Eshelman, W.W. Cur. biog. p. 132 (1960).
Eshkol, Levi. Cur. biog. (1963).
Eskimo (Alaska). Holiday 26: 40-1 (col.) Aug '59.
Natl. geog. 109: 772-3 (col.) Je '56.
Travel 101: 26-7 Feb '54.
—— (comic). Holiday 13: 9 Mar '53, 141 May '53; 14: 31 Oct '53.
—— (on caribou). Holiday 14: 19, 34 (col.) Jl '53.
Eskimo boy. Natl. geog. 110: 671 Nov '56.
—— (head). Natl. geog. 116: 42 (col.) Jl '59.
Eskimo carvings. Con. 141: 154-8 May '58.
Eskimo children. Natl. geog. 100: 471 Oct '51.
Eskimo dance. Holiday 26: 43 Aug '59.
Eskimo family. Natl. geog. 100: 473, 475, 479-80, 490-1, 507 (col.) Oct '51.
Eskimo homes. Travel 101: 26 Feb '54.
Eskimo hut (cartoon). Holiday 13: 67 Jan '53.
Eskimo igloo. See igloo, Eskimo.
Eskimo mask. Int. gr. soc.: Arts . . . p. 185 (col.).
Eskimo suits. Natl. geog. 114: 130 (col.) Jl '58.
Eskimos (Alaska). Natl. geog. 99: 551-62 Ap '51; 102: 61-86 (part col.) Jl '52; 105: 135-46 (part col.) Jan '54; 107: 558-64 (col.) Ap '55; 110: 671-87 (part col.) Nov

'56; 111: 542 (col.) Ap '57.
Travel 102: 42-3 Jl '54; 112: cover (col.) Jl '59.
—— (Canada). Natl. geog. 108: 219 (col.) Aug '55.
Eskimos (woman & child). Holiday 14: 6 Dec '53.
Eskimos & scientist (singing). Natl. geog. 110: 675 (col.) Nov '56.
esophagus. Gray's anatomy, 1188.
"Espolio" (El Greco). Praeg. pict. ency., p. 314 (col.).
Esquimo eye shield. Rawson: Ant. pict. bk., p. 60.
Essen minster golden madonna. Con. 138: 237 Jan '57.
Essenes. Natl. geog. 114: 792-3, 796 (col.) Dec '58.
Essenes community center plan. Natl. geog. 114: 791 Dec '58.
Essenes monastery. Natl. geog. 114: 786-7 (col.) Dec '58.
Essenes ritual baptism. See baptism, ritual.
"The Essex" (ship, 1813). Amer. heri. vol. 7 no. 3 p. 18 (col.) (Ap '56).
Estes, Eleanor. Cur. biog. p. 185 (1946).
Jun. bk. of auth., p. 114.
Estes, Harlow. Cur. biog. p. 263 (1941).
Estes park (Colo.). Travel 106: 13-7 Aug '56.
"Esther dining with King Xerxes". Natl. geog. 118: 848-9 (col.) Dec '60.
Estonian polka dance. Natl. geog. 118: 805 (col.) Dec '60.
Estoril castle (Portugal). Holiday 19: 29 Jan '56.
Travel 111: 33 Je '59.
"Eternal mother" (mosaic memorial chapel wall). Natl. geog. 111: 760 (col.) Je '57.
eternity (sym.). Lehner: Pict. bk. of sym., p. 28, 43, 78, 80.
Ethiopia. Natl. geog. 118: 350-1 (col.) Sept '60.
Ethiopians. Natl. geog. 118: 304-5 (col.) Sept '60.
Ethridge, Mark. Cur. biog. p. 187 (1946).
"Eton college" (by Cotman). Con. ency. of ant., vol. 1, pl. 143.
"Eton college" (by Sandby). Con. ency. of ant., vol. 1 pl. 147.
Eton college boys. Holiday 23: 70 (col.) Ap '58.
Etruscan (man & woman, ancient times). Int. gr. soc.: Arts . . . p. 31 (col.).
Etruscan mural. See mural, Etruscan.
Etruscan sculpture. Praeg. pict. ency., p. 143.
Etruscan statuette (bronze). Con. 138: XLVIII Sept '56.
Etruscan urn (500 B.C.). Int. gr. soc.: Arts . . . p. 19 (col.).
Etruscan wall painting. See wall painting, Etruscan.
Etruscan tomb exploration. Natl. geog. 116: 336-50 (part col.) Sept '59.
Etruscan warrior. Holiday 18: 6 Oct '55.
Ets, Marie Hall. Jun. bk. of auth., p. 115.
Ettinger, Richard P. Cur. biog. p. 188 (1951).
Etty, William (work of). Con. 135: XIX Mar '55, 220 Je '55; 143: 106 Ap '59; 144: 8 Sept '59.

etui case, mother of pearl & silver (Queen Anne). Con. 145: XXVIII Je '60.
Etzel, Franz. Cur. biog. p. 23 (1957).
Eucharistic congress penitents. Natl. geog. 100: 11 (col.) Jl '51.
Eucharistic service, silver-gilt (1160). Natl. geog. 97: 775 Je '50.
Eugenie, Empress. Amer. heri. vol. 11 no. 3 p. 19 (Ap '60).
Eurich, Alvin C. Cur. biog. p. 191 (1949).
Europe (map). Travel 103: 7 Ap '55.
—— (travel route map). Travel 107: 12 Ap '57.
European emigrants. See emigrants, European.
"Eurydice" (by Baratta). Con. 142: 172 Dec '58.
Eustis, Helen. Cur. biog. p. 187 (1955).
Euterpe (muse). Lehner: Pict. bk. of sym., p. 33.
"Evangeline" (statue, Grand Pre). Amer. heri. vol. 6 no. 1 p. 61 (fall '54).
Holiday 14: 100 Sept '53.
Travel 108: 12 Oct '57; 112: 32 Sept '59.
Evangeline highway. Holiday 11: 50-1 Mar '52.
Evangeline memorial. Natl. geog. 112: 169 (col.) Aug '57.
Evangeline's grave (Emmeline Labiche). Holiday 6: 55 Oct '49.
evangelist (religious meeting, 1875). Amer. heri. vol. 6 no. 5 p. 20-1 (Aug '55).
Evangelistary of Bishop Ebo (Rheim). Praeg. pict. ency., p. 185.
evangelists (preaching). Amer. heri. vol. 6 no. 5 p. 100 (Aug '55).
evangelists, the four. See the four evangelists.
evangelists & symbols (lectern woodcut, Alpirsbach). Praeg. pict. ency., p. 191 (col.).
evangelists. See also minister; preacher.
Evans, Alice C. Cur. biog. p. 199 (1943).
Evans, Arthur. Ceram: March of arch., p. 53.
Evans, Bergen. Cur. biog. p. 189 (1955).
Evans, Chris. Horan: Pict. hist. of wild west, p. 151.
Evans, Dale. See Rogers, Dale Evans.
Evans, Dame Edith. Cur. biog. p. 166 (1956).
Evans, Sir Edward R.G.R. Cur. biog. p. 265 (1941).
Evans, Herbert M. Cur. biog. p. 110 (1959).
Evans, Rev. Hugh Ivan. Cur. biog. p. 142 (1950).
Evans, J. E. (work of). Natl. geog. 99: 195 (col.) Feb '51.
Evans, Luther H. Cur. biog. p. 175 (1945).
Evans, Maurice. Cur. biog. p. 147 (1961).
Holiday 12: 90 Dec '52.
Evatt, Harriet. Cur. biog. p. 112 (1959).
Evatt, Herbert V. Cur. biog. p. 253 (1942).
"Eve" (bronze by Hering). Con. 143: 217 Je '59.
"Evening landscape" (Friedrich). Praeg. pict. ency., p. 393 (col.).
Everest, Mt. See Mt. Everest.
Everett, Edward. Amer. heri. vol. 9 no. 4 p. 33 (Je '58).
Everglades (Fla.). Holiday 10: 102-7 (part col.) Nov '51.
Travel 103: 20-3 Feb '55.

Evergood, Philip. Cur. biog. p. 191 (1944); p. 134 (1960).
"Evergreen" house, Colonial (La.). Natl. geog. 113: 545 (col.) Ap '58.
"Evergreen" plantation (La.). Amer. heri. vol. 4 no. 2 p. 26 (col.) (winter '53); vol. 7 no. 4 p. 59 (Je '56).
Eversen, A. (work of). Con. 129: LXIII Je '52.
evil, protection against (sym.). Lehner: Pict. bk. of sym., p. 26, 29, 44, 57-8.
——. See also protection.
evolution (animals). Natl. geog. 109: 370-1 Mar '56.
Ewell, Richard S. Pakula: Cent. album, p. 119.
Ewell, Tom. Cur. biog. p. 150 (1961).
ewer, antique. Con. 135: 209 May '55; 138: 273, 275 Jan '57; 140: 18 Sept '57.
——, Chinese. Con. 133: 137 Ap '54.
——, copper-gilt (Venetian, 16th cent.). Con. 144: 218 Jan '60.
——, crystal (16th cent.). Int. gr. soc.: Arts . . . p. 95 (col.).
——, Flemish (silver). Con. 129: 131 Je '52.
——, George I (silver). Con. 139: 123 Ap '57.
——, German vase type. Con. ency. of ant., vol. 3, p. 66.
——, Italian (rock crystal, 16th cent.). Con. 144: 82 Nov '59.
——, Italian (jasper, 16th cent.). Con. 144: 82 Nov '59.
——, Italian (silver). Con. 144: 153 Dec '59.
——, Louis XVI. Con. 139: 192 May '57.
——, Louis XIV (French, silver). Con. 140: 38 Sept '57.
——, medieval. Con. 137: 120 Ap '56.
——, Meissen porcelain. Con. 135: 210 May '55; 140: 60 Sept '57; 144: 70 Sept '59.
——, Ming dynasty. Con. 134: 107 Nov '54.
——, Nuremberg (16th cent.). Con. 144: 84 Nov '59.
——, porcelain (16th cent.). Con. 142: 10 Sept '58.
——, Portuguese (silver). Con. 137: 67 Mar '56.
Con. ency. of ant., vol. 3, pl. 32.
——, Portuguese (16th cent.). Con. 137: 12 Mar '56.
——, Renaissance (crystal). Con. 129: 139 Je '52.
——, Sevres. Con. ency. of ant., vol. 1, pl. 63.
——, silver (18th cent.). Con. 132: 87 Nov '53.
——, silver (17th cent.). Con. 133: 265 Je '54; 138: 273 Jan '57.
——, silver (16th cent.). Con. 141: 105 Ap '58.
——, silver-gilt (18th cent.). Con. 143: 15 Mar '59.
——, silver-gilt (Parker, 19th cent.). Con. 140: LXIII Sept '57.
——, silver-gilt (17th cent.). Con. 139: 30 Mar '57.
——, silver-gilt (12th cent.). Con. ency. of ant., vol. 3, pl. 29.
——, silver-gilt (16th cent.). Con. 144: 219 Jan '60.
——, 16th cent. Con. 136: 271 Jan '56.

ewer, Syrian (amber glass). Con. 145: 288 Je '60.

ewer & basin (antique silver). Con. 133: 151 May '54.

——, Aykered (17th cent.). Con. 143: 169 May '59.

——, Louis XV (silver). Con. 133: 292 Je '54.

——, maiolica. Con. 144: LXXVI Dec '59.

——, silver-gilt (Watts, 1717). Con. 143: 170 May '59.

ewer & dish, German gilt (18th cent.). Con. 145: XIX Ap '60.

——, silver (18th cent.). Con. 142: XXXIX Dec '58.

——, silver (18th cent., Romer). Con. 145: XLVI Ap '60.

Ewing, Maurice. Cur. biog. p. 189 (1953).

Ewing, Oscar R. Cur. biog. p. 194 (1948).

Eworth, Hans (work of). Con. 140: 111 Nov '57; 142: 25 Sept '58.

excavations (Mesopotamia). Natl. geog. 99: 43-104 (col.) Jan '51.

excavators, Syrian cave. Natl. geog. 114: 243 Aug '58.

Excelsior Palace hotel (The Lido). Holiday 24: 50 (col.) Aug '58.

excursion boat. See boat, excursion.

excursion poster (1880). Amer. heri. vol. 6 no. 4 p. 28 (Je '55).

Executive House hotel (Chicago, model). Travel 108: 43 Nov '57.

Exekias chalice. See chalice of Exekias.

exercising, girl. Holiday 10: 33 Sept '51, 132 Oct '51, 131 Nov '51, 101 Dec '51; 11: 80-3 Jan '52, 146-7 May '52, 48 (col.) Je '52.

exercising chair (18th cent.). Con. 135: LIV May '55.

Exeter cathedral (int.). Int. gr. soc.: Arts . . . p. 49 (col.).

exhibit grounds, "Center of Amer." See "Center of Amer."

exhibition, Amer. (Moscow). Natl. geog. 116: 716-21 (col.) Dec '59.

exhibition pavilion (N.C.). Travel 102: 11 Sept '54.

exhibits, state fair. Natl. geog. 106: 297, 300-32 (part col.) Sept '54.

"Exhumation of the Mastodon" (Peale). Natl. geog. 99: 188 (col.) Feb '51.

experiments, scientific. Natl. geog. 100: 762-8, 777, 780-4 (col.) Dec '51.

Explorer II balloon. Natl. geog. 110: 494 Nov '56.

explorers, Arctic. See Arctic explorers.

——, Chubb crater. Natl. geog. 101: 3-32 (part col.) Jan '52.

——, early Spanish. Amer. heri. vol. 6 no. 1 p. 91, 102, 113 (fall '54).

explosion, river blast. Natl. geog. 114: 185 Aug '58.

explosives (sym.). Lehner: Pict. bk. of sym., p. 88.

express agents (early western). Horan: Pict. hist. of wild west, p. 36.

expressions, facial. See emotional expressions.

expulsion (sym.). Lehner: Pict. bk. of sym., p. 35.

"The expulsion of Hagar" (Lorraine). Praeg. pict. ency., p. 330 (col.).

the eye. Gray's anatomy, p. 1032-47, 1052-9, 1357.

Holiday 12: 29 Oct '52; 18: 81 (col.), 82 Aug '55, 113 (col.) Oct '55, 118 Nov '55, 5 (col.) Dec '55; 19: 79 Feb '56; 21: 30 Feb '57; 26: 212 Dec '59; 27: 9 Je '60.

—— (sym.). Lehner: Pict. bk. of sym., p. 16.

——, all-seeing. See all-seeing eye.

eye & nose sign (sym.). Lehner: Pict. bk. of sym., p. 59.

eye cup. See cup, eye.

eye of God (sym.). Lehner: Pict. bk. of sym., p. 29.

eye shield (from snow blindness). Rawson: Ant. pict. bk., p. 60.

eyeglass case. Holiday 25: 131 (col.) May '59; 27: inside cover (col.) Je '60.

eyeglasses. Holiday 19: 136 (col.) Je '56; 21: 122 (col.) May '57; 25: 33 (col.) Je '59. Rawson: Ant. pict. bk., p. 60.

—— (on men & women). Holiday 14: 7, 66 Jl '53.

——, sun. See sun glasses.

eyelid blood vessels. Gray's anatomy, p. 575.

eyelid muscle. Gray's anatomy, p. 355.

eyes. Holiday 10: 14 Nov '51; 11: 93 Mar '52, 113 Je '52; 14: 17 Aug '53; 20: 43 Nov '56, 156 Dec '56; 21: 186 Ap '57; 26: 91 Sept '59; 27: 48 Ap '60, 129 Je '60; 28: 76 Sept '60, 192 Nov '60. Travel 113: 12 Mar '60.

—— (Nepal temple dome). Natl. geog. 97: 12 (col.) Jan '50.

—— (winking). Holiday 26: 91 Aug '59.

——, Black Russian. Holiday 27: 168 Je '60.

——, girls. Holiday 27: 14 Mar '60.

——, woman's. Holiday 14: 78 Oct '53; 24: 26 (col.) Nov '58. Travel 113: 12 Mar '60.

Eyre, Katherine Wigmore. Cur. biog. p. 193 (1949); p. 176 (1957).

Eyring, Henry. Cur. biog. p. 152 (1961).

Eyskens, Gaston. Cur. biog. p. 194 (1949).

Eytan, Walter. Cur. biog. p. 134 (1958).

Eyuboglu, Bedri Rahmi. Cur. biog. p. 263 (1954).

Eyup's tomb. Natl. geog. 100: 161 (col.) Aug '51.

F

Faberge, Carl (carvings). Con. 139: XXXVII May '57; 142: 197 Dec '58; 145: LXXV Je '60.

Fabian, Robert. Cur. biog. p. 265 (1954).

fable in mosaic, Roman. Natl. geog. 111: 219 Feb '57.

Fabray, Nanette. Cur. biog. p. 169 (1956).

Fabriano, Gentile da (work of). Con. 136: LXI Dec '55. Praeg. pict. ency., p. 227 (col.).

fabric, block printed. Natl. geog. 99: 577 (col.) May '51.

fabrics (designs). Int. gr. soc.: Arts . . . p. 175 (col.).

Fabritius, Carel. Praeg. pict. ency., p. 338 (col.).

—— (work of). Con. 144: 66 Sept '59.

face (profile). Natl. geog. 100: 516 Oct '51.

face muscles. Gray's anatomy, p. 354.

"Face on the barroom floor". Natl. geog. 106: 238 Aug '54.

face powder machine. See powder machine, face.

faces of the lictor (sym.). Lehner: Pict. bk. of sym., p. 95.

facial expressions. See emotional expressions.

Fackenthal, Frank D. Cur. biog. p. 195 (1949).

factories (Worcester, Mass.). Natl. geog. 107: 192, 206 (col.) Feb '55.

factory bldg. Amer. heri. vol. 9 no. 1 p. 56-7 (col.) (Dec '57).

Factory Butte (Utah). Travel 110: 27 Oct '58.

Fadiman, Clifton. Cur. biog. p. 267 (1941); p. 189 (1955).
    Holiday 13: 6 Ap '53, 6 Je '53; 14: 6 Jl '53, 6 Aug 53; 22: 8 Oct '57; 23: 11 Mar '58, 11 Ap '58, 8 May '58, 8 Je '58; 24: 6 Jl '58, 8 Aug '58, 8 Sept '58; 25: 8 Feb '59, 11 Ap '59, 8 May '59, 11 Je '59; 27: 8 May '60.

—— (comic). Holiday 26: 8 Aug '59.

Faed, Thomas (work of). Natl. geog. 112: 479 Oct '57.

Fagerholm, Karl August. Cur. biog. p. 197 (1948).

Fagg, Fred D., jr. Cur. biog. p. 171 (1956).

Fahlstrom signature. Con. 144: 97 Nov '59.

Fahy, Charles. Cur. biog. p. 255 (1942).

faience, arnhem. Con. 135: 104-5 Ap '55.

——, German (18th cent.). Con. 141: LVI Je '58.

——, Herreboe. See Herreboe faience.

——, Louis XV. Con. 133: 277 Je '54.

faience dish. Praeg. pict. ency., p. 308.

faience plate. Con. 138: 279 Jan '57.

faience relief (Robbia). Praeg. pict. ency., p. 310.

failure (sym.). Lehner: Pict. bk. of sym., p. 85.

fair (farm stunts). Natl. geog. 112: 180-1 (col.) Aug '57.

——, Brussels. See Brussels world's fair.

——, California. Natl. geog. 112: 703 (col.) Nov '57.

——, Columbian exposition. See Columbian exposition.

——, country (Cyprus is.). Natl. geog. 109: 884 Je '56.

——, Ephrata's (grand Coulee dam). Natl. geog. 102: 609 (col.) Nov '52.

——, state. Travel 114: 32-3 Aug '60.

——, state (Colo.). Natl. geog. 106: 246-7 (col.) Aug '54.

——, state (Texas). Natl. geog. 106: 294-332 (part col.) Sept '54.

——, world agricultural. See agricultural fair, world.

fair market (Guatemala). Natl. geog. 117: 410-11 (col.) Mar '60.

Fairbanks, Douglas. Holiday 22: 148 Dec '57.

Fairbanks, Douglas, jr. Cur. biog. p. 269 (1941); p. 172 (1956).
    Holiday 21: 92 Feb '57.

Fairchild, David. Cur. biog. p. 191 (1953).

Fairchild, Henry Pratt. Cur. biog. p. 256 (1942).

Fairclough, Ellen. Cur. biog. p. 177 (1957).

Fairey, rotodyne plane. Travel 111: 63 May '59.

Fairfax, Beatrice. Cur. biog. p. 194 (1944).

Fairfax, Sir. Thomas. Amer. heri. vol. 6 no. 5 p. 17 (col.) (Aug '55).

"A fair-haired boy" (Fragonard). Con. 126: cover, 2 (col.) Aug '50.

Fairless, Benjamin F. Cur. biog. p. 257 (1942); p. 179 (1957).

"Fairman Rogers four-in-hand" (Eakins). Natl. geog. 99: 210 (col.) Feb '51.

fairy tale (illus., Hans Andersen). Int. gr. soc.: Arts . . . p. 137 (col.).

Faisal II & leaders, King (Iraq). Natl. geog. 114: 456-7 (col.) Oct '58.

Faisal, Prince (Saudi Arabia). Natl. geog. 104: 35 Jl '53.

Faisal Ibn Abdul-Aziz al Saud, Prince. Cur. biog. p. 198 (1948).

faith (sym.). Lehner: Pict. bk. of sym., p. 35.

Faithorne, William (work of). Con. ency. of ant., vol. 1, pl. 136.

fakes, art. See art fakes.

falange, Spanish. Holiday 15: 46 May '54.

falangism (sym.). Lehner: Pict. bk. of sym., p. 94.

falcon (sym.). Lehner: Pict. bk. of sym., p. 26.

falconer. Holiday 21: 79 May '57.

—— (carved wood). Con. 136: LIII Sept '55. Con. ency. of ant., vol. 3, pl. 53.

——, Bedouin. Natl. geog. 110: 93 (col.) Jl '56.

Falconet, Pierre E. (work of). Con. 142: LIX Nov '58; 143: LXXI Je '59.

Falkland islands. Natl. geog. 109: 388-416 (part col.) Mar '56.

—— (map). Natl. geog. 109: 393 Mar '56.

—— (palace, Scotland). Natl. geog. 110: 14 (col.) Jl '56.

Falkner, Roland Post. Cur. biog. p. 270 (1941).

fall (sym.). Lehner: Pict. bk. of sym., p. 81.

"The fall of man" (Altdorfer). Natl. geog. 110: 626 (col.) Nov '56.

"The fallen stone" (Lehmbruck). Praeg. pict. ency., p. 491.

"Falls of Niagara" (Hicks). Amer. heri. vol. 11 no. 6 p. 2 (col.) (Oct '60).

"Falls of Terni" (More). Con. 129: 77 Je '52.

falsity (sym.). Lehner: Pict. bk. of sym., p. 58.

"Falstaff" (statue). Natl. geog. 108: 299 (col.) Sept '55.

Fama (sym.). Lehner: Pict. bk. of sym., p. 92.

fame (sym.). Lehner: Pict. bk. of sym., p. 85, 92.

the "Fame" (trading ship, 1805). Amer. heri. vol. 6 no. 2 p. 11 (col.) (winter '55).

"Fame's triumph over Death" (tapestry). Natl. geog. 97: 753 Je '50.

family (at dinner table). Holiday 5: 64 Je '49; 6: 43 (col.) Jl '49, 46 (col.) Dec '49.

—— (at prayers). Holiday 6: 47 Dec '49.

—— (picnic). Holiday 5: 15 (col.) Jan '49.

—— (playing croquet). Holiday 5: 78 Jan '49.

—— (sym.). Lehner: Pict. bk. of sym., p. 26.

"Family at home" (1900). Amer. heri. vol. 12 no. 1 p. 121 (Dec '60).
"Family compact" (Ward). Con. 142: XLVII Nov '58.
"Family dinner" (Le Nain). Con. 136: 138 Nov '55.
family group (Knight). Amer. heri. vol. 11 no. 2 p. 48-9 (col.) (Feb '60).
family life. See also man, woman & children.
family saying grace at table. Natl. geog. 113: 130 Jan '58.
"Family tree" (Peraltas). Amer. heri. vol. 7 no. 5 p. 28 (Aug '56).
Fan. Con. 133: XXXII (col.) Ap '54, XXIV (col.) May '54.
 Holiday 9: 20 Mar '51; 18: 159 Nov '55; 19: 113 (col.) Feb '56, 68 (col.) May '56.
 Natl. geog. 116: 592 (col.) Nov '59.
 Travel 110: inside cover Oct '58, 113: 7 Mar '60, inside back cover Ap '60.
—— (17th cent.). Con. 134: XXXVI (col.) Nov '54.
——, antique. Amer. heri. vol. 10 no. 1 p. 44 (col.) (Dec '58).
 Con. 135: XXXI Mar '55.
——, ceiling. Holiday 20: 64 (col.) Oct '56.
——, ceiling (antique elec.). Holiday 26: 151. Nov '59.
——, Chinese (18th cent.). Con. 134: LXII (col.) Sept '54.
——, electric. Holiday 11: 129 Je '52.
——, electric wall. See electric fan, wall.
——, fireplace. Holiday 18: 120 Jl '55.
——, paper (screen). Lehner: Pict. bk. of sym., p. 56.
——, Spanish (19th cent.). Con. 134: 43 Sept '54.
fan ornament, rising sun. Con. ency. of ant., vol. 1, p. 67.
Fane, Earl John (Romney). Con. 143: 89 Ap '59.
Faneuil Hall (Boston). Holiday 13: 25 (col.) Je '53; 14: 37 Nov '53; 26: 133 Nov '59.
Fanfani, Amintore. Cur. biog. p. 136 (1958).
fanlight (above door). Holiday 18: 73 (col.) Aug '55.
 Natl. geog. 97: 562 May '50; 98: 384 (col.) Sept '50.
fans, Korean festival. Natl. geog. 118: 202-3 (col.) Aug '60.
——, Mayan ceremonial. Natl. geog. 115: 102-3 (col.) Jan '59.
——, Nepal ceremonial. Natl. geog. 112: 143 (ocl.) Jl '57.
Fanti drummer (Africa). Natl. geog. 118: 306-7 (col.) Sept '60.
Fantin-Latour, I. Henri J. T. (work of). Con. 133: 235 Je '54; 138: XI (col.) Nov '56; 139: cover (col.) May '57; 142: XXIII (col.) Nov '58; 145: IX, 194 (col.) May '60, IX (col.) Je '60.
Fantin-Latour, Madame I. Henry J. T. Con. 143: 237 (col.) Je '59.
Farah, Empress of Iran. Jensen: The White House, p. 282.
Fargo (N.D.). Natl. geog. 100: 301 Sept '51.
Faricy, William T. Cur. biog. p. 200 (1948).
Farinelli (Carlo Broschi) (by Amigoni). Cooper: Con. ency. of music, p. 95.

Farley, James. Holiday 10: 65 Dec '51.
Farley, James A. Cur. biog. p. 197 (1944).
Farley, Walter. Cur. biog. p. 197 (1949).
 Jun. bk. of auth., p. 119.
farm. Amer. heri. vol. 6 no. 4 p. 26-7, 35 (col.) (Je '55); vol. 11 no. 5 p. 20-3 (part col.) (Aug '60).
 Face of Amer., p. 100-3, 114-5, 149, 152-3, 164-5 (col.).
 Holiday 11: 46-7 (col.) Je '52; 12: 159 (col.) Dec '52; 22: 42-3 (col.) Jl '57.
 Natl. geog. 103: 710-11 Je '53; 110: 586-7 (col.) Nov '56; 115: 482-3 (col.) Ap '57.
—— (Christmas). Amer. heri. vol. 9 no. 1 p. 16 (col.) (Dec '57).
—— (1841). Amer. heri. vol. 7 no. 3 p. 48-9, 52-3 (col.) (Ap '56).
—— (1844). Amer. heri. vol. 10 no. 3 p. 58-9 (col.) (Ap '59).
—— (1877). Amer. heri. vol. 9 no. 5 p. 40-1 (Aug '58).
—— (snow). Holiday 12: 83 Dec '52.
—— (snow, auto). Holiday 18: 184 (col.) Dec '55.
——, Africa. Holiday 25: 58-9 (col.) Ap '59.
——, Alaska. Natl. geog. 116: 61 (col.) Jl '59.
——, Balearic islands. Natl. geog. 111: 638-9 (col.) May '57.
——, Chile. Natl. geog. 117: 198-9 (col.) Feb '60.
——, Pres. Eisenhower's. Holiday 18: 109 Oct '55.
——, Israeli collective (kibbutz). Natl. geog. 114: 856-7 (col.) Dec '58.
——, Japan. Natl. geog. 118: 754 (col.) Dec '60.
——, Penn. Dutch. Holiday 12: 50 Oct '52.
——, stock. Holiday 26: 44 (col.). Sept '59.
——, Wis. Natl. geog. 111: 175 (col.) Feb '57.
farm buildings. Holiday 10: 37 Sept '51.
farm family, French (dinner). Natl. geog. 115: 607 (col.) May '59.
farm field contour planting. Natl. geog. 107: 476-7 (col.) Ap '55.
farm group meeting. Brooks: Growth of a nation, p. 255.
farm home dinner (Russian). Natl. geog. 116: 380 Sept '59.
farm house. Amer. heri. vol. 7 no. 3 p. 48, 52-3 (col.) (Ap '56).
 Brooks: Growth of a nation, p. 116.
 Face of Amer., p. 100, 115 (col.).
 Holiday 12: 83, 159 (col.) Dec '52.
 Natl. geog. 111: 603 (col.) May '57; 115: 482 (col.) Ap '59; 117: 199 (col.) Feb '60.
—— (1877). Amer. heri. vol. 9 no. 5 p. 40-1 (Aug '58).
—— (winter). Amer. heri. vol. 9 no. 1 p. 16 (col.) (Dec '57).
——, Basque. Natl. geog. 105: 184 (col.) Feb '54.
——, England. Natl. geog. 103: 818 Je '53.
——, Jamestown. Natl. geog. 111: 603 (col.) May '57.
——, southern. Brooks: Growth of a nation, p. 287.
——, Vermont. Amer. heri. vol. 6 no. 4 p. 35 (col.) (Je '55).

——, Va. Natl. geog. 111: 403, 412 (col.) Mar '57.

farm land, Tristan. Natl. geog. 97: 114 (col.) Jan '50.

farm life (1871). Amer. heri. vol. 7 no. 3 p. 42 (col.) (Ap '56).

farm tools. See tools, farm.

farm wife (sickle, Madeira is.). Natl. geog. 115: 376 (col.) Mar '59.

farm woman (Austria). Natl. geog. 118: 272 (col.) (Aug '60).

Farmer, Guy. Cur. biog. p. 192 (1955).

Farmer, James. U.S. News & world report, p. 28 Aug 31 '64.

farmer (sowing seed, Normandy). Holiday 19: 52 Jan '56.

farmer (with horse). Amer. heri. vol. 9 no. 3 p. 8 (Ap '58).

——, Alaska. Natl. geog. 116: 60 (col.) Jl '59.

——, Bali (girl). Natl. geog. 116: 807 (col.) Dec '59.

——, Cretan. Natl. geog. 104: 705 (col.) Nov '53.

——, Ethiopian. Natl. geog. 118: 304 (col.) Sept '60.

farmers. Amer. heri. vol. 11 no. 5 p. 16-7, 21 (col.) (Aug '60).

—— (cattle pasture). Holiday 25: 99 (col.) May '59.

—— (tobacco field). Natl. geog. 103: 303 (col.) Mar '53.

——, German & Denmark (ancient times). Int. gr. soc.: Arts . . . p. 31 (col.).

——, Iraq. Natl. geog. 114: 482-3 (col.) Oct '58.

——, Nepal. Natl. geog. 117: 371-2 (col.) Mar '60.

——, Nepal (grain field). Natl. geog. 117: 388 (col.) Mar '60.

——, Portugal (harvest). Natl. geog. 118: 648-9 (col.) Nov '60.

——, Turkey (head, water jar). Natl. geog. 115: 72 (col.) Jan '59.

farmer's market. See market, farm open-air.

"Farmers nooning" (Mount). Amer. heri. vol. 11 no. 5 p. 16-7 (col.) (Aug '60).

"Farmer's register", Ruffin's (title p.). Amer. heri. vol. 9 no. 1 p. 24 (Dec '57).

farmers rub down the cattle, Japan. Natl. geog. 118: 747 (col.) Dec '60.

farmers threshing wheat. Amer. heri. vol. 1 no. 2 back cover (col.) (winter '50).

Farmington canal boat (1825). Amer. heri. vol. 9 no. 2 p. 99-100 (Feb '58).

"The Farnese bull" (sculpture). Labande: Naples, p. 96.

Farnsworth, Jerry. Cur. biog. p. 267 (1954).

Farny, Henry F. (work of). Amer. heri. vol. 6 no. 1 p. 40 (fall '54).

Farouk I, King of Egypt. Cur. biog. p. 259 (1942).

Farragut, David Glasgow. Pakula: Cent. album, p. 121.

Farrar, Geraldine (as Japanese). Amer. heri. vol. 10 no. 3 p. 56 (Ap '59).

Farrar, John. Cur. biog. p. 269 (1954).

Farrar, Margaret. Cur. biog. p. 194 (1955).

Farrell, Eileen. Cur. biog. p. 153 (1961).

Farrell, James T. Cur. biog. p. 262 (1942).

Farren, Eliza. (Stuart). Con. 141: X Mar '58.

Farrington, Elizabeth Pruett. Cur. biog. p. 196 (1955).

Farrington, Joseph R. Cur. biog. p. 202 (1948).

Fascell, Dante B. Cur. biog. p. 135 (1960).

fasces (sym.). Lehner: Pict. bk. of sym., p. 83.

fascism (sym.). Lehner: Pict. bk. of sym., p. 95.

fashion, clothes (16th cent.). Amer. heri. vol. 2 no. 4 p. 11-2 (summer '51).

fashion models. See model, fashion; model, girl fashion; models, fashion.

fashion show, outdoor (Spokane). Natl. geog. 117: 486-7 (col.) Ap '60.

fashion show models (Paris). Natl. geog. 101: 791 (col.) Je '52.

fashions. Holiday 6: 118-21 Sept '49, 110-12, 114-21 (col.) Oct '49, 112-9 (part col.) Nov '49; 7: 112-4 Jan '50, 140-5 May '50; 8: 122-8 Oct '50, 110-4 (part col.) Nov '50.

—— (1902). Brooks: Growth of a nation, p. 232.

fashions. See also costume.

Fast, Howard. Cur. biog. p. 201 (1943).

fate (sym.). Lehner: Pict. bk. of sym., p. 66, 76.

Fatemi, Hossein. Cur. biog. p. 194 (1953).

Fath, Jacques. Cur. biog. p. 190 (1951). Holiday 15: 12 Jan '54.

father & baby. Travel 102: inside back cover Aug '54.

father & son. Holiday 8: 76 (col.) Dec '50.

——. See also man & boy.

Father Knickerbocker (N.Y.) (sym.). Lehner: Pict. bk. of sym., p. 93.

"Father of the Banjoe". Durant: Pict. hist. of Amer. circus, p. 47.

Father, son, Holy Spirit (sym.). Lehner: Pict. bk. of sym., p. 35.

Father Time. Lehner: Pict. bk. of sym., p. 92.

fathometer (men). Natl. geog. 111: 207 (col.) Feb '57.

Fatima Jinnah medical college. Natl. geog. 102: 674 (col.) Nov '52.

Fatu Hiva (Marquesa is.). Natl. geog. 97: 76, 84 (col.) Jan '50.

Faubus, Orval E. Cur. biog. p. 175 (1956).

faucet, water. Holiday 13: 144 Mar '53.

faucet, water. Lehner: Pict. bk. of sym., p. 91.

Faulkner, Barry (mural by). Amer. heri. vol. 3 no. 1 p. 26 (col.) (fall '51).

—— (work of). Natl. geog. 111: 69 (col.) Jan '57.

Faulkner, Nancy. Cur. biog. p. 176 (1956).

Faulkner, William. Cur. biog. p. 192 (1951). Holiday 15: 33 Ap '54.

faun (bronze, Pompeii). Labande: Naples, p. 103.

Faure, Edgar. Cur. biog. p. 180 (1952).

Faust, Clarence H. Cur. biog. p. 182 (1952).

"Faust in his study" (Rembrandt). Con. 141: 118 Ap '58.

Fauvelet, J. (work of). Con. 142: XXVII Jan '59.

Fawzi, Mahmoud. Cur. biog. p. 194 (1951).

Fay, Frank. Cur. biog. p. 177 (1945).

Fayal (Azores, map). Natl. geog. 113: 740 Je '58.

Feary, John (work of). Con. 144: XIX Nov
'59.
feast day (sym.). Lehner: Pict. bk. of sym., p.
50-6.
"Feast of Christmas in cribs" (at the Bavarian
natl. museum, Munich). Con. 132: 143-5 Jan
'54.
"Feast of the bean" (Jordaens). Natl. geog. 97:
747 (col.) Je '50.
"Feast of the circumcision procession" (Egypt).
Amer. heri. vol. 11 no. 3 p. 26 (col.) (Ap
'60).
"Feast of the Gods" (Bellini). Con. 126: 175
Dec '50.
"Feast of the visitation". See parade, "Feast of
the visitation".
feather, white (sym.). Lehner: Pict. bk. of sym.,
p. 57.
feather art work, Mexican (how made). Ceram:
March of arch., p. 261-2.
feathered serpent (relief). Ceram: March of
arch., p. 273.
Feathers hotel (Ludlow, Eng.). Holiday 23: 142
Ap '58.
Fechteler, Adm. William M. Cur. biog. p. 196
(1951).
fecundity (sym.). Lehner: Pict. bk. of sym., p.
29, 44.
Federal Hall (Bardstown, Ky.). Travel 101: 24
Feb '54.
Federal Hall (N.Y., 1789). Amer. heri. vol. 7
no. 3 p. 29 (Ap '56).
"Feeding of the five thousand". Con. 143: 267
Je '59.
"Feeding of the five thousand" (Lombard).
Con. 133: XXXVII Ap '54.
feet. Holiday 18: 194 Dec '55; 22: 254 Dec
'57; 23: 99 Jan '58.
—— (man, girl). Holiday 24: 82 (col.) Oct '58.
—— (out African hut door). Holiday 19: 3 Jan
'56.
—— (sandals, desert). Natl. geog. 113: 693
(col.) May '58.
—— (statue). Travel 112: 60 Sept '59.
—— (walking). Holiday 9: 10 (col.) Mar '51.
Fehe (sym. of love). Lehner: Pict. bk. of sym.,
p. 28.
Feiffer, Jules. Cur. biog. p. 155 (1961).
Feikema, Feike. Cur. biog. p. 143 (1950).
Feininger, Andreas. Cur. biog. p. 181 (1957).
Feininger, Lyonel. Cur. biog. p. 198 (1955).
—— (work of). Con. 145: 287 Je '60.
Praeg. pict. ency., p. 486 (col.).
Feinsinger, Nathan P. Cur. biog. p. 184 (1952).
Feis, Herbert. Cur. biog. p. 157 (1961).
Feisal II, King of Iraq. Cur. biog. p. 200
(1955).
felaheen (Egyptians). Holiday 20: 63 (col.)
Dec '56.
Felbrigg Hall (Norfolk, Eng., ext. & int.). Con.
141: 217 Je '58.
Feldmann., Markus. Cur. biog. p. 178 (1956).
Felix, Eugen (work of). Cooper: Con. ency. of
music, p. 92.
Felix, Robert H. Cur. biog. p. 182 (1957).
Feller, Abraham H. Cur. biog. p. 190 (1946).
Feller, Bob, Cur. biog. p. 271 (1941).
Fellini, Federico. Cur. biog. p. 184 (1957).

Fellows, Harold E. Cur. biog. p. 186 (1952).
Fellows, Robert. Holiday 5: 42 (col.) Jan '49.
Fels, William C. Cur. biog. p. 113 (1959).
Felsen, Gregor. Jun. bk. of auth., p. 120.
Felt, Adm. Harry D. Cur. biog. p. 115 (1959).
Feltin, Cardinal Maurice. Cur. biog. p. 271
(1954).
Felton, Cornelius Conway. Amer. heri. vol. 9
no. 4 p. 33 (Je '58).
Felton, Ralph A. Cur. biog. p. 187 (1957).
felucca (Egyptian boat). Natl. geog. 107: 722
May '55; 111: 132 Jan '57.
—— (Sudanese boat). Natl. geog. 103: 259
(col.) Feb '53.
—— (Nile river). Holiday 20: 63 (col.) Dec
'56.
"Female Hercules" (circus). Durant: Pict. hist.
of Amer. circus, p. 157.
"Femme a la Mandoline" (Braque). Con. 144:
41 Sept '59.
"Femmes des Halles". Natl. geog. 98: 64 (col.)
Jl '50.
fence, Colonial lawn. Holiday 18: 105 Nov
'55.
——, farm. Holiday 20: 27 (col.) Sept '56.
Rawson: Ant. pict. bk., p. 38-9.
——, iron. Holiday 13: 117 Jan '53; 17: 111
Jan '55; 18: 97 Aug '55; 19: 120 Jan '56;
21: 149 Jan '57; 23: 142 Jan '58.
Natl. geog. 105: 329 Mar '54.
——, lawn. Holiday 18: 41 Jl '55.
——, picket. Natl. geog. 105: 199 (col.) Feb
'54; 111: 618 (col.) May '57; 113: 189 (col.)
Feb '58; 114: 122 (col.) Jl '58; 116: 47
(col.) Jl '59.
——, plank farm (man). Natl. geog. 110: 800-
1 Dec '56.
——, plank yard. Natl. geog. 111: 603 (col.)
May '57.
——, rail. Brooks: Growth of a nation, p.
108.
Face of Amer., frontis, p. 39, 76 (col.).
Jordan: Hammond's pict. atlas, p. 139
(col.).
Rawson: Ant. pict. bk., p. 41.
——, serpentine. Natl. geog. 117: 338 Mar
'60.
——, stump. Brooks: Growth of a nation, p.
217.
——, types of early. Con. 140: 134 Nov '57.
fence & gate, iron. Con. 137: XLV Ap '56.
Holiday 21: 83 (col.) Ap '57; 25: 158 Jan
'59.
—— (ornamental antique). Con. 141: XLII-
XLIII Mar '58.
fences. Travel 105: 52 Ap '56.
fencing. Holiday 11: 109 Mar '52.
——, Chinese. Holiday 21: 76 (col.) Je '57.
——, Italian. Con. 134: 27-30 Sept '54.
——, men. Holiday 17: 107 Feb '55; 22: 193
Dec '57.
Int. gr. soc.: Arts . . . p. 107 (col.).
——, men (19th cent.). Con. 126: 114-20 Oct
'50.
fencing trophy. See épée trophy, foil.
"Fenton House" (London). Con. 137: 88 Ap
'56.
Feoh (sym. of good luck). Lehner: Pict. bk.
of sym., p. 28.

Ferber, Herbert. Cur. biog. p. 137 (1960).
Ferdinand, Archduke Franz of Austria. Amer. heri. vol. 6 no. 1 p. 47 (fall '54).
Ferdinand I, Czar of Bulgaria. Amer. heri. vol. 6 no. 1 p. 47 (fall '54).
"Ferdinand VII" (Goya). Con. 133: 15 Mar '54.
Ferguson, Mrs. C. Vaughan. Cur. biog. p. 200 (1947).
Ferguson, Elsie. Cur. biog. p. 201 (1944).
Ferguson, Garland S. Cur. biog. p. 198 (1949).
Ferguson, Harry. Cur. biog. p. 179 (1956).
Ferguson, Homer. Cur. biog. p. 203 (1943).
Ferguson, Malcolm P. Cur. biog. p. 188 (1957).
Ferguson, Major Patrick. Amer. heri. vol. 7 no. 1 p. 65 (Dec '55).
Ferguson, William Gowe (work of). Con. ency. of ant., vol. 1, pl. 170.
Ferguson, Erna. Cur. biog. p. 201 (1955).
Feriolo (Italy). Holiday 6: 10 (col.) Dec '49.
Fermi, Enrico. Cur. biog. p. 179 (1945).
Fermi, Laura. Cur. biog. p. 138 (1958).
Fermor, Patrick Leigh. Cur. biog. p. 203 (1955).
Fernandel. Cur. biog. p. 204 (1955).
Fernandes, Luis Esteves. Cur. biog. p. 144 (1950).
Fernando de Noronha island. Natl. geog. 116: 452-3 (col.) Oct '59.
Fernando Po island. Travel 109: 47-50 Mar '58.
Ferneley, John (portrait by). Con. 136: XXIX Nov '55.
—— (work of). Con. 136: XXXV (col.) Jan '56; 142: 41 Sept '58; 144: 201 Dec '59.
Fernhof, Heinrich (work of). Con. 143: 267 Je '59.
Ferrari, Defendente (work of). Con. 136: 281 Jan '56.
Ferrari, Gaudenzio (work of). Con. 138: 118 Nov '56.
Ferrari, Luca (work of). Con. 135: 58 Mar '55.
Ferrari auto. (1958). Int. gr. soc.: Arts . . . p. 160 (col.).
Ferren, John. Cur. biog. p. 139 (1958).
Ferrer, Jose. Cur. biog. p. 203 (1944).
—— (as dwarf). Holiday 13: 26 Ap '53.
Ferrier, Kathleen. Cur. biog. p. 197 (1951).
ferries (Turkey). Natl. geog. 100: 152-3 (col.) Aug '51 .
Ferris, Helen. Jun. bk. of auth., p. 121.
ferris wheel. Amer. heri. vol. 11 no. 6 p. 16 (col.) Oct '60.
Holiday 12: 97 Aug '52.
Natl. geog. 99: 765 (col.) Je '51.
—— (girls, ballons). Natl. geog. 115: 175 (col.) Feb '59.
—— (Hindu festival). Natl. geog. 117: 402 (col.) Mar '60.
Ferriss, Hugh. Cur. biog. p. 182 (1945).
Ferrucci, Francesco (work of). Con. 141: 213 Je '58.
Ferry, Elisha P. Amer. heri. vol. 4 nþ. 4 p. 54 (summer '53).
ferryboat. Amer. heri. vol. 10 no. 6 p. 26-9 (part col.) (Oct '59).
Con. 145: XLVII, 114 Ap '60, LXXIII (col.) May '60.

Holiday 11: 43 (col.) Mar '52, 53 May '52.
Jordan: Hammond's pict. atlas, p. 105 (col.).
Natl. geog. 98: 113 (col.) Jl '50; 106: 773 Dec '54.
Travel 111: 36 Je '59; 112: 31 Aug '59.
——, early sidewheel (L.T. Pratt). Amer. heri. vol. 11 no. 1, back cover (col.) (Dec '59).
——, old scow. Rawson: Ant. pict. bk., p. 51.
——, Belgian Congo. Natl. geog. 101: 356 (col.) Mar '52.
——, Calcutta. Natl. geog. 100: 738 (col.) Dec '51.
——, China. Natl. geog. 100: 726 Dec '51.
——, Lake Titicaca. Natl. geog. 98: 495 (col.) Oct '50.
——, N.Y. Natl. geog. 115: 832, 840-1 Je '59.
——, river. Natl. geog. 98: 396 (col.) Sept '50; 101: 735 (col.) Je '52.
Travel 101: 4 Jan '54.
——, river (loading, Nigeria). Natl. geog. 110: 362-3 (col.) Sept '56.
——, St. Helena. Natl. geog. 98: 270 Aug '50.
Fessenden, Reginald. Amer. heri. vol. 6 no. 5 p. 64 (Aug '55).
Festing, Maj. Gen. Francis W. Cur. biog. p. 185 (1945).
festival (submarine equator crossing). Natl. geog. 118: 592 (col.) Nov '60.
——, Angkor circus. Natl. geog. 117: 550-5 (col.) Ap '60.
——, Balearic island. Natl. geog. 111: 646-7 (col.) May '57.
——, Belgium. Natl. geog. 113: 816-9, 830 (col.) Je '58.
——, Brazil (Indian girl). Natl. geog. 116: 628-49 (part col.) Nov '59.
——, Cal. Natl. geog. 112: 703, 706-7 (col.) Nov '57.
——, Cameroon. Natl. geog. 116: 240-3 (col.) Aug '59.
——, Chile (Aiquina). Natl. geog. 117: 232, 234-5 (col.) Feb '60.
——, Corpus Christi (Canary is.). Natl. geog. 107: 491-8 (col.) Ap '55.
——, Fiji islands. Natl. geog. 114: 540-59 (col.) Oct '58.
——, Germany (Dinkelsbuhle). Natl. geog. 111: 255-68 (part col.) Feb '57.
——, Guatemala (Indian fair & passion week). Natl. geog. 117: 407-11 (col.) Mar '60.
——, Hawaii (May 1, Lei Day). Natl. geog. 118: 18 (col.) Jl '60.
——, Hindu Holi. Natl. geog. 118: 476 (col.) Oct '60.
——, India. Natl. geog. 113: 707-10 (col.) May '58.
——, Korean. See Korean festival.
——, Munich. Holiday 22: 56-7 (col.) Sept '57.
——, Polish harvest. Natl. geog. 114: 356-7 (col.) Sept '58.
——, Red China's birthday. Natl. geog. 118: 200-1 (col.) Aug '60.
——, Santa Fe. Jordan: Hammond's pict. atlas, p. 125 (col.).
——, Scandinavian music. Travel 113: 47 Ap '60.

——, **lead amorini garden.** Con. ency. of ant., vol. 3, pl. 26.

figurine. Con. 136: inside cover Sept '55.
Holiday 16: 63 Jl '54, 18 (col.) Dec '54; 25: 105 Je '59; 26: 160 Nov '59.

—— **(18th cent.).** Con. ency. of ant., vol. 1, pl. 50; 142: 11 Sept '58.

—— **("Hercules and Cerberus").** Con. 135: 14 Mar '55.

—— **(orchestral group).** Con. 135: 127 Ap '55.

—— **(wood carving).** Amer. heri. vol. 10 no. 2 frontis. (col.) (Feb '59).

——, **African.** Holiday 12: 144 Nov '52.

——, **antique.** Con. 133: XXXII Mar '54, inside cover Je '54; 134: XXXII Sept '54, XX Nov '54, inside cover Dec '54; 135: XLII Mar '55, 156-7 May '55, inside cover Je '55; 136: LVI Sept '55, LVII, XLVII Nov '55; 139: inside cover, XXII May '57, inside cover Je '57; 141: L Ap '58; 142: inside cover Nov '58.

——, **antique bronze.** Con. 132: XXV Sept '53.

——, **antique carved wood.** Con. 134: XLIX Dec '54.

——, **Astbury.** Con. 139: XXVI Je '57.

——, **Baluba wood.** Con. 145: IV Je '60.

——, **Benin bronze.** Con. 134: 60 Sept '54.

——, **Berlin.** Con. ency. of ant., vol. 1, pl. 64.
Con. 142: XLVII Dec '58.

——, **Bow.** Con. ency. of ant., vol. 1, pl. 54.
Con. 129: 123, 130, LXV Je '52; 134: XL Nov '54; 138: XXVIII Sept '56; 140: 179 Dec '57; 141: VI Mar '58, XXXIII Ap '58, 272 Je '58; 144: 3a1 Sept '59; 145: 69 Ap '60, XXIV Je '60.

——, **Bristol.** Con. ency. of ant., vol. 1, pl. 55.
Con. 137: 187 May '56; 144: 127 Nov '59; 145: XLVI May '60.

——, **bronze.** Con. 127: 46 Mar '51.

——, **Buen Retiro.** Con. 140: 182 Dec '57.

——, **Bustelli.** Con. 140: 179 Dec '57.

——, **Callot.** Con. 138: 126 Nov '56.

——, **Capodimonte.** Con. ency. of ant., vol. 1, pl. 61.
Con. 135: 19 Mar '55; 143: X May '59.

——, **carved.** Con. 136: XXIV Sept '55.

——, **Chalcedony.** Con. 145: 55 Mar '60.

——, **Chelsea.** Con. 129: XLVII Je '52; 133: XXXVI Mar '54, inside cover May '54; 134: 207 Dec '54; 134: 207 Dec '54; 137: LIII Mar '56; 138: XLIV Jan '57; 140: 179 Dec '57, inside cover, XVI Jan '58; 141: 250 Je '58; 142: XXXIII Jan '59; 143: XXVI Mar '59, LVII Ap '59; 144: inside cover, XL Sept '59, 197 Dec '59; 145: 246-51 Je '60.

——, **Chelsea (gold anchor).** Con. 135: XLIV May '55.

——, **Chelsea Derby.** Con. 142: 12 Sept '58.

——, **Chinese.** Con. ency. of ant., vol. 1, pl. 72.
Con. 133: LXIV Je '54; 141: XXXIII Ap '58; 251 Je '58.

——, **Chinese (Kwan yin).** Con. 143: V May '59.

——, **Chinese (coral).** Con. 142: 38 Sept '58.

——, **Chinese (jade).** Con. 134: XIV Dec '54.

——, **Chinese pottery.** Con. 140: LXIII Jan '58.

——, **Columbine.** Con. 135: 53 Mar '55.

——, **Copenhagen (1780).** Con. 143: inside cover Ap '59.

——, **coral.** Con. 134: XLIII Nov '54.

——, **Derby.** Con. ency. of ant., vol. 1, pl. 54-5.
Con. 140: 179 Dec '57; 141: XXXIII Ap '58; 142: XXXIII Jan '59.

——, **Dutch.** Con. 136: LX Dec '55.

——, **Etruscan bronze.** Con. 138: 214 Dec '56.

——, **"Fire & earth".** Con. 144: IV Sept '59.

——, **Frankenthal.** Con. ency. of ant., vol. 1, pl. 63.

——, **Fukien bleue-de-chine.** Con. 143: 57 Mar '59.

——, **German.** Con. 142: XXVI Sept '58.

——, **German (15th cent.).** Con. 140: 258 Jan '58.

——, **German silver-gilt (17th cent.).** Con. 135: 129 Ap '55.

——, **Hoechst.** Con. ency. of ant., vol. 1, pl. 60.

——, **Italian comedy.** Con. 142: 125 Nov '58.

——, **ivory.** Con. 136: XLIV Dec '55.

——, **jade.** Con. 136: XXX, LXVIII Jan '56. Natl. geog. 98: 796 (col.) Dec '50.

——, **Longton Hall.** Con. 138: XXXVI Dec '56; 141: XXVIII, 123 Ap '58; 142: XXIV, XXXIII Jan '59.

——, **Louis XV ormolu.** Con. 144: LVI Nov '59.

——, **Ludwigsburg.** Con. ency. of ant., vol. 1, pl. 61.

——, **Meissen.** Con. 129: 63, XXXII Ap '52; 133: 264 Je '54; 134: XX Sept '54; 135: 189 May '55; 137: 148 (col.), 150-3 May '56; 138: XXI Sept '56; 140: 59 Sept '57, 131 Nov '57; 140: inside cover, 179 Dec '57; 141: XXVIII Je '58; 142: XXXVIII Nov '58; 143: XXVI, XXX, 191 May '59; 144: 65 Sept '59, XXVI, LIII Nov '59, XI Dec '59; 145: XIV Mar '60, XLV Je '60.
Praeg. pict. ency., p. 82 (col.).

——, **Mennecy (18th cent.).** Con. 143: 138 May '59; 145: LIII Je '60.

——, **Naples.** Con. 144: LIII Nov '59.

——, **Nymphenburg.** Con. ency. of ant., vol. 1, pl. 61.
Con. 144: inside cover Jan '60.

——, **Plymouth.** Con. 142: XXXIII Jan '59.

——, **polychrome & gold wood.** Con. 134: LV Nov '54.

——, **porcelain.** Con. 135: 117 Ap '55; 136: XIV Dec '55.
Holiday 14: 146 (col.) Dec '53.

——, **pottery boxers (19th cent.).** Con. 143: XLVII Mar '59.

——, **Royal Doulton.** Holiday 28: 109 (col.) Oct '60.

——, **Russian.** Con. 144: 274 Jan '60.

——, **Russian empire.** Con. 142: 98-9 Nov '58.

——, **Sevres.** Con. ency. of ant., vol. 1, pl. 64.

figurine, Staffordshire. Con. ency. of ant., vol. 1, pl. 50.
Con. 135: 118 Ap '55.
——, Strasbourg. Con. 144: LIII Nov '59.
——, Venetian (16th cent.). Con. 142: XIV Dec '58.
——, votive. See votive figurine.
——, Zuerich. Con. ency. of ant., vol. 1, pl. 61.
figurine decanter, porcelain. Con. 134: LXI (col.) Sept '54.
figurines, antique. Con. 138: 46 Sept '56, XVI Nov '56; 143: XXXIX May '59.
——, Bow. Con. 132: XII, XXIII Sept '53; 133: inside cover Ap '54, XIV May '54.
——, Bristol. Con. 140: XVI Jan '58.
——, Bristol seasons (1775c). Con. 126: 124 Oct '50.
——, Chelsea. Con. ency. of ant., vol. 1, pl. 54.
Con. 127: 135 May '51; 138: X Sept '56.
——, Chelsea (four seasons). Con. 143: XLVI Je '59.
——, Chelsea-Derby. Con. 139: XVI Je '57.
——, Chinese. Con. 132: I Sept '53; 138: XLIII Sept '56.
——, Chinese (Ch'ien Lung). Con. 145: 129 Ap '60.
——, Chinese (T'ang). Con. 140: XIV Sept '57.
——, Doughty. Con. 144: LXV Sept '59.
——, English (18th cent.). Con. 142: XXXIII Jan '59.
——, German (carved wood). Con. 138: XLVI Jan '57.
——, Meissen. Con. 139: 10-3 Mar '57; 142: inside cover Sept '58, inside cover, 196 Dec '58; 145: 126 Ap '60.
——, Olmec (Mexico). Natl. geog. 110: 366, 373 Sept '56.
——, Plymouth. Con. 135: XLI Mar '35.
——, porcelain. Con. 137: 90-1 Ap '56.
——, Royal Doulton. Holiday 8: 26 Sept '50; 10: 122 Oct '51; 12: inside cover (col.) Oct '52; 16: 15 (col.) Nov '54; 22: 7 (col.) Oct '57; 23: 167 (col.) Ap '58; 25: 108 (col.) Ap '59; 26: 28 (col.) Dec '59.
——, "snowman". See "snowman" (figurines).
——, Staffordshire (18th cent.). Con. 138: XXVIII Jan '57.
——, terracotta (Rysbrack). Con. 140: XXI Jan '58.
——, Venetian Nubian. Con. 143: back cover Ap '59.
Fiji club (int.). Holiday 28: 162 Oct '60.
Fiji island. Holiday 7: 60-3 (col.) Je '50; 28: 57 (col.) Oct '60.
Natl. geog. 98: 122-39 Jl '50.
Travel 102: 31-3 Nov '54; 109: 54, 56 Jan '58; 111: 28-31 Mar '59; 114: 43-8 Dec '60.
—— (beach). Holiday 28: 159 (col.) Oct '60.
—— (map). Natl. geog. 98: 124 Jl '50; 114: 526, 532 Oct '58.
Fijian. Holiday 22: 104 Oct '57, 48 Dec '57; 27: 152 (col.) May '60; 28: 57, 72-97 (col.) Oct '60.

Natl. geog. 98: 135 Jl '50; 114: 528-9, 531, 538-45, 550 (col.) Oct '58.
Travel 109: 56 Jan '58; 114: 43-4 Dec '60.
—— (comic). Holiday 13: 9 Je '53.
—— (head). Holiday 22: 102 Nov '57; 23: 135 Feb '58.
—— (heads). Travel 102: 10 Nov '54.
—— (in boat). Holiday 28: 63 (col.) Oct '60.
—— (woman). Natl. geog. 98: 122 Jl '50.
Fijian dancer. Natl. geog. 107: 126 (col.) Jan '55.
Fijian dancers. Travel 102: 31 Nov '54.
Fijian homes. Holiday 7: 61 (col.) Je '50.
Fijian spear dancers. Natl. geog. 114: 528-9 (col.) Oct '58.
Fijian war chanters. Holiday 28: 104 (col.) Oct '60.
Fijian war dance. Travel 114: 38 Dec '60.
Fijian warrior. Holiday 18: 45 (col.) Aug '55; 28: 178 Oct '60.
Filho, Joao Cafe. Natl. geog. 107: 319 Mar '55.
filibuster attack by Walker. Amer. heri. vol. 9 no. 1 p. 28-9 (Dec '57).
Fillmore, Millard. Amer. heri. vol. 7 no. 3 p. 31 (Ap '56); vol. 10 no. 2 p. 94 (Feb '59).
Jensen: The White House, p. 73.
Fillmore, Parker. Jun. bk. of auth., p. 126.
film box. See kodak film box.
film strip . See movie film.
Filson, John. Amer. heri. vol. 6 no. 6 p. 10 (Oct '55).
Finch, Sir John (Lely). Con. 140: 231 Jan '58.
"Finding of Moses" (Ricci). Con. 142: 248 Jan '59.
"Finding of Moses" (Tintoretto). Con. 129: XXXIX Je '52.
Fine, Benjamin. Cur. biog. p. 159 (1961).
Fine, John S. Cur. biog. p. 200 (1951).
Finet, Paul. Cur. biog. p. 201 (1951).
finger & string (hand, sym.). Lehner: Pict. bk. of sym., p. 14.
finger bowl, Chelsea porcelain. Con. ency. of ant., vol. 1, pl. 53.
——, Irish glass. Con. ency. of ant., vol. 3, pl. 47.
Finger Lakes (N.Y.). See New York (Finger Lakes).
finger print (sym.). Lehner: Pict. bk. of sym., p. 11.
finger shield (Alaska, Indian sewing implement). Amer. heri. vol. 11 no. 3 p. 82 (Ap '60).
fingers, crossed (sym.). Lehner: Pict. bk. of sym., p. 62.
fingers, lady's. Natl. geog. 98: 798-9 (col.) Dec '50.
Fingesten, Peter. Cur. biog. p. 273 (1954).
finial, bronze (Chou). Con. 145: 277 Je '60.
——, four-headed. Con. 136: 67 Sept '55.
Finkelstein, Rabbi Louis. Cur. biog. p. 192 (1952).
Finland. Holiday 22: 104-9 Dec '57.
Natl. geog. 106: 250-80 (part col.) Aug '54.
Travel 105: 34-5 Ap '56.
—— (girl). Holiday 22: 107 (col.) Dec '57.
—— (woman). Holiday 6: 37 (col.) Jl '49.
Finletter, Thomas K. Cur. biog. p. 207 (1948).
Finley, David E. Cur. biog. p. 203 (1951).

Finley, Sam. Horan: Pict. hist. of wild west, p. 36.
Finn, Huck. See Tom Sawyer & Huck Finn.
Finnegan, Joseph F. Cur. biog. p. 118 (1959).
Finnessy, Tom. Horan: Pict. hist. of wild west, p. 125.
Finney, Albert. Cur. biog. (1963).
Finney, Gertrude E. Cur. biog. p. 190 (1957).
fins, swimming. See swimming fins.
fiord (New Zealand). Holiday 28: 108-9 (col.) Nov '60.
fiord. See also fjord.
fire (barn burning). Face of Amer., p. 36-7 (col.).
—— **(buildings burning).** Amer. heri. vol. 7 no. 1 p. 68-9 (col.) (Dec '55).
—— **(in basin).** Lehner: Pict. bk. of sym., p. 67.
—— **(log ricks).** Holiday 20: 133 Nov '56.
—— **(oil well).** Amer. heri. vol. 9 no. 4 p. 39 (Je '58).
—— **(ship).** Amer. heri. vol. 9 no. 6 p. 4-5 (col.) (Oct '58).
—— **(steamboat).** Amer. heri. vol. 8 no. 6 p. 18 (Oct '57).
—— **(sym.).** Lehner: Pict. bk. of sym., p. 28, 37.
—— **(under kettle).** Natl. geog. 107: 741 (col.) Je '55.
—— **(wall burning).** Natl. geog. 100: 764 (col.) Dec '51.
—— **(Wall St., N.Y., 1835).** Amer. heri. vol. 8 no. 5 p. 14 (col.) (Aug '57).
—— **(Wash., D.C., 1814).** Amer. heri. vol. 9 no. 5 p. 66-7 (Aug '58).
—— **(Wis., woods).** Amer. heri. vol. 7 no. 5 p. 52-3 (col.) (Aug '56).
——, **bon.** See bonfire.
——, **camp.** See camp fire.
——, **Chicago.** See Chicago fire.
——, **heavenly.** See heavenly fire (sym.).
——, **god of (sym.).** Lehner: Pict. bk. of sym., p. 49.
fire & sword (sym.). Lehner: Pict. bk. of sym., p. 87.
fire apparatus (antique). Amer .heri. vol. 7 no. 1 p. 68-9 (col.) (Dec '55).
fire basket, fishing. Rawson: Ant., pict. bk., p. 76.
fire chief. Amer. heri. vol. 10 no. 1 p. 95 (Dec '58.).
fire engine (1845). Holiday 24: 61 Sept '58.
—— **(horse drawn).** Amer. heri. vol. 7 no. 1 p. 66 (col.) (Dec '55).
——, **flying.** Natl. geog. 115: 539 Ap '59.
fire escape, The White House. Jensen: The White House, p. 196.
fire fighters (1854). Amer. heri. vol. 5 no. 1 p. 28-37 (part col.) (fall '53).
—— **(1911).** Brooks: Growth of a nation, p. 236.
——, **forest.** Natl. geog. 110: 288 (col.) Sept '56.
fire fork. Con. ency. of ant., vol. 3, p. 243.
fire hydrant. Holiday 23: 141 May '58.
fire kindling, ancient. Natl. geog. 106: 495 Oct '54.
fire mark (1830). Holiday 18: 61 (col.) Jl '55.
fire prevention sign. See "Smokey the bear".

fire screen. Holiday 22: 2 (col.) Sept '57.
——, **Chippendale.** Con. 137: XXIV Mar '56.
fire state park, Nevada. Travel 101: 36-7 Feb '54.
fire trucks, Japanese. Natl. geog. 97: 632 (col.) May '50.
fire wagon (horses). Holiday 7: 135 (col.) May '50.
firearm, antique. Con. 129: LXXV Je '52; 132: LXIV, LXVIII Nov '53, LXXIV Jan '54; 133: LXXIV Je '54.
——, **antique (18th cent.).** Con. 129: 109 Je '52.
firearms. Travel 112: 63 Dec '59.
—— **(1853).** Amer. heri. vol. 6 no. 3 p. 9, 11 (Ap '55).
—— **(Napoleonic times).** Int. gr. soc.: Arts . . . p. 115 (col.).
——, **antique.** Brooks: Growth of a nation, p. 172, 174.
   Con. 129: LXXVI Ap '52; 133: L Ap '54; 139: 246, 265 Je '57.
   Rawson: Ant. pict. bk., p. 35.
——, **antique (Scottish).** Con. 133: 71, LII Mar '54.
firearms. See also gun; pistol.
fireback (16th cent.). Con. 133: 189 May '54.
—— **(antique).** Con. ency. of ant., vol. 3, pl. 165-6
fireboat. Natl. geog. 101: 280 Mar '52; 115: 18 Jan '59, 836 Je '59.
firecracker factory, Macau (China). Natl. geog. 103: 685 (col.) May '53.
firedog, gilt (17th cent.). Con. 133: 153 May '54.
firegrate. See grate, fireplace.
fireman (rescuing woman). Amer. heri. vol. 5 no. 1 p. 17 (col.) (fall '53); vol. 7 no. 1 p. 70 (Dec '55).
fireman's certificate. Amer. heri. vol. 7 no. 1 p. 71 (col.) (Dec '55).
firemen. Holiday 12: 47 (col.) Sept '52.
—— **(Canton is).** Natl. geog. 107: 129 (col.) Jan '55.
—— **(1845).** Holiday 24: 61 Sept '58.
—— **(1850).** Amer. heri. vol. 8 no. 1 p. 54 (Dec '56).
firemen's contest. Natl. geog. 107: 783 (col.) Je '55.
Firenze, Biaggio d'Antonio da (work of). Con. 142: XLIX Sept '58.
Firenze, Michele da. See Michele da Firenze.
fireplace. Amer. heri. vol. 4 no. 2 p. 33, 35-7, 39 (part col.) (winter '53); vol. 11 no. 2 p. 48 (col.) (Feb '60).
   Con. ency. of ant., vol. 3, pl. 104-8.
   Con. 129: XXXI Ap '52; 133: XXXIII Ap '54; 135: XLIV May '55; 136: XXXV Sept '55, LIV Nov '55; 139: LIII Je '57; 140: 74, XLIII, XLVIII (part col.) Nov '57, XXXIII Dec '57; 142: back cover Dec '58; 145: 74-5 Ap '60.
   Holiday 19: 73 (col.) Jan '56, 122 (col.) May '56; 20: 2 (col.) Oct '56, 109 (col.) Nov '56; 22: 2 (col.) Sept '57, 45 Oct '57, 257 Dec '57; 26: 95 (col.) Nov '59.
   Natl. geog. 97: 577 (col.) May '50; 110: 391 (col.) Sept '56; 112: 315 (col.) Sept '57.
   Travel 112: 32 Sept '59.

fireplace (afternoon tea). Natl. geog. 110: 42 (col.) Jl '56.

fireplace (corn popping). Natl. geog. 107: 397 Mar '55.

—— **(18th cent.).** Con. 132: LI Nov '53; 142: back cover Jan '59; 143: XLI May '59; 145: LV Ap '60.
Natl. geog. 98: 600-1 (col.) Nov '50.

—— **(1825).** Natl. geog. 102: 761 (col.) Dec '52.

—— **(fire, skiers).** Natl. geog. 99: 493 (col.) Ap '53.

—— **(John Adams' home).** Natl. geog. 97: 306 (col.) Mar '50.

—— **(log cabin).** Natl. geog. 105: 193 (col.) Feb '54.

—— **(men, children).** Natl. geog. 115: 802 (col.) Je '59.

—— **(middle ages).** Int. gr. soc.: Arts . . . p. 53-4 (col.).

—— **(Mt. Vernon).** Natl. geog. 104: 662, 671 (col.) Nov '53.

—— **(Mt. Vernon, kitchen).** Natl. geog. 104: 668 (col.) Nov '53.

—— **(17th cent.).** Con. 132: XLVI Sept '53; 142: XL Jan '59.

—— **(1730).** Natl. geog. 112: 444 (col.) Oct '57.

—— **(16th cent.).** Con. 144: 4 Sept '59.
Holiday 18: 174 (col.) Dec '55.

—— **(200 years old).** Holiday 22: 202 (col.) Dec '57.

—— **(Univ. of Toronto).** Natl. geog. 104: 842 (col.) Dec '53.

——, **Adam.** Con. 135: XVI Je '55; 141: XXXI Je '58; 145: LXVII Je '60.

——, **antique.** Con. ency. of ant., vol. 3, pl. 165, 167-8.
Con. 140: XL Sept '57.
Holiday 10: 39 (col.) Nov '51.
Natl. geog. 97: 292 (col.) Mar '50.

——, **Chippendale.** Con. 139: XXXVI Mar '57.

——, **Claydon House.** Con. 142: 72 Nov '58.

——, **Colonial.** Amer. heri. vol. 1 no. 2 p. 38-9, 47 (col.) (winter '50); vol. 1 no. 4 p. 50 (col.) (summer '50); vol. 2 no. 4 p. 22-3 (col.) (summer '51); vol. 3 no. 2 p. 42-3 (col.) (winter '52).
Holiday 13: 54 Jan '53.
Natl. geog. 103: 795 (col.) Je '53; 105: 445, 457, 459, 461, 463 (col.) Ap '54; 106: 460 (col.) Oct '54; 109: 463, 480 (col.) Ap '56.

——, **Colonial bakeshop.** Natl. geog. 106: 467 (col.) Oct '54.

——, **Colonial brick kitchen.** Holiday 8: 41 (col.) Jl '50.

——, **Colonial library.** Natl. geog. 105: 453 (col.) Ap '54.

——, **Dutch (18th cent.).** Con. 144: LXI Nov '59.

——, **English.** Natl. geog. 108: 317 (col.) Sept '55.

——, **English (early).** Con. 137: LVI Je '56.

——, **English (1620).** Con. ency. of ant., vol. 3, pl. 102.

——, **French.** Holiday 27: 21 (col.) Ap '60.

——, **French (farm house).** Natl. geog. 100: 25 (col.) Jl '51.

——, **French (old).** Amer. heri. vol. 4 no. 1 p. 9 (fall '52).

——, **French Canadian.** Con. 126: 204 Dec '50.

——, **French style.** Natl. geog. 113: 549 (col.) Ap '58.

——, **hammered concrete.** Holiday 21: 94 (col.) May '57.

——, **Ireland (men, women).** Natl. geog. 108: 743 (col.) Dec '55.

——, **Italian marble.** Natl. geog. 118: 188 (col.) Aug '60.

——, **kitchen.** Amer. heri. vol. 4 no. 1 p. 9 (fall '52).
Natl. geog. 97: 288 (col.) Mar '50.

——, **kitchen (early Amer.).** Natl. geog. 100: 588 (col.) Nov '51.

——, **kitchen (15th cent.).** Natl. geog. 109: 535 (col.) Ap '56.

——, **kitchen (old).** Holiday 13: 30 Feb '53.

——, **kitchen (old, boy & dog).** Natl. geog. 101: 163 Feb '52.

——, **marble.** Con. 144: back cover Nov '59.
Natl. geog. 104: 662 (col.), 663 Nov '53.

——, **medieval.** Holiday 19: 5 (col.) Jan '56.

——, **modern.** Holiday 11: 38 (col.) Feb '52.

——, **Norway.** Con. 145: 5 Mar '60.

——, **Orkney is.** Natl. geog. 104: 523 Oct '53.

——, **outdoor barbecue.** Holiday 6: 86 (col.) Oct '49.

——, **Quonset hut.** Natl. geog. 104: 575 (col.) Oct '53.

——, **regency.** Con. 133: XLI May '54.

——, **Renaissance.** Natl. geog. 98: 603 (col.) Nov '50.

——, **Roman.** Holiday 27: 83 (col.) Ap '60.

——, **Sweden (marble).** Holiday 20: 45 (col.) Aug '56.

——, **wall (Rochester castle).** Con. ency. of ant., vol. 3, pl. 101.

fireplace fan. *See* fan, fireplace.

fireplace fittings. Con. 138: XX, XXXI Sept '56.

Firestone, Harvey. Amer. heri. vol. 10 no. 6 p. 41, 43 (Oct '59).

Firestone, Harvey S., jr. Cur. biog. p. 205 (1944).

firewalker (Greece). Travel 108: 46-7 Oct '57.

fire-walking Buddhist. *See* Buddhist (fire-walking, Japan).

firewood (on back of Katmandu man). Natl. geog. 117: 371 (col.) Mar '60.

—— **(on donkey, Mexico).** Natl. geog. 107: 233 (col.) Feb '55.

fireworks. Holiday 12: 91 (col.) Jl '52; 26: 126 (col.) Jl '59.
Natl. geog. 113: 660 (col.) May '58.
Travel 102: 52 Jl '54; 109: inside cover Mar '58.

—— **(Angkor celebration).** Natl. geog. 117: 554-6 (col.) Ap '60.

—— **(Bastile Day).** Natl. geog. 98: 44 Jl '50.

—— **(bridge opening).** Amer. heri., vol. 7 no. 6 p. 73 (col.) (Oct '56).

—— (carnival). Natl. geog. 118: 692-3 (col.) Nov '60.
—— (4th of July). Natl. geog. 111: 74 (col.) Jan '57.
—— (New Year) Natl. geog. 115: 394 Mar '59.
—— (Paris). Holiday 13: 34 (col.) Ap '53.
—— (Peking). Natl. geog. 118: 200 (col.) Aug '60.
—— (welcomes Eisenhower home). Natl. geog. 117: 648 (col.) May '60.
fireworks. *See* also rockets.
the firmament, power of. *See* power of the firmament (sym.).
firmament, seals of 7 ruling princes (sym.). Lehner: Pict. bk. of sym., p. 24.
first aid (sym.). Lehner: Pict. bk. of sym., p. 88.
"First introduction to hounds" (Harris). Con. ency. of ant., vol. 1, pl. 139.
"First Lady", U.S. *See* U.S. Presidents' wives.
"First of September" (Buss). Con. 132: 41 Sept '53.
"First state election in Detroit, Mich." Amer. heri. vol. 2 no. 4 p. 38 (col.) (summer '51).
Fischer, Bobby. Cur. biog. (1963).
Fischer, John. Cur. biog. p. 197 (1953).
Fischer, John H. Cur. biog. p. 139 (1960).
Fischer, Paul (work of). Con. 129: XLII Ap '52.
Fish, Hamilton. Amer. heri. vol. 8 no. 3 p. 53 (Ap '57).
Cur. biog. p. 279 (1941).
Fish, Hamilton, jr. Amer. heri. vol. 11 no. 2 p. 8 (Feb '60).
Fish, Marie Poland. Cur. biog. p. 280 (1941).
fish (drying). Natl. geog. 102: 64 (col.) Jl '52.
—— (sym.). Lehner: Pict. bk. of ant., p. 62.
——, smoked (girls). Natl. geog. 111: 174 (col.) Feb '57.
"fish boil", Wis. (picnic). Natl. geog. 115: 486 (col.) Ap '59.
fish curing racks. Natl. geog. 112: 184 Aug '57.
fish dish (antique). Rawson: Ant. pict. bk., p. 7.
fish factory (old). Rawson: Ant. pict. bk., p. 76.
fish globe. Natl. geog. 106: 660 (col.) Nov '54.
fish hook. Travel 109: 49 Ap '58.
—— (catching man, comic). Holiday 12: 101 Oct '52.
fish market, Iceland. Natl. geog. 100: 618-9 (col.) Nov '51.
——, Norway. Holiday 12: 93 Sept '52.
Natl. geog. 106: 160 (col.) Aug '54.
"fish men". *See* divers.
fish-net. Holiday 21: 198 Ap '57.
Natl. geog. 102: 55 Jl '52; 103: 708 Je '53; 107: 124 Jan '55.
—— (drying). Holiday 9: 56 (col.) Mar '51.
Natl. geog. 110: 742 (col.) Dec '56.
—— (man mending). Natl. geog. 111: 660 May '57.
—— (men hanging). Natl. geog. 111: 698 (col.) May '57.
—— (men mending). Natl. geog. 110: 732 (col.) Dec '56.
—— (woman). Natl. geog. 111: 36 (col.) Jan '57.
——, Bahrein. Natl. geog. 105: 509 Ap '54.
——, bamboo basket. Natl. geog. 102: 291 Sept '52.
——, butterfly. Holiday 8: 19 Sept '50.
——, dip (Ifalik). Natl. geog. 109: 571 Ap '56.
fish-net float. *See* float, Japanese fish-net.
fish-nets. (drying). Natl. geog. 115: 275 (col.) Feb '59.
Travel 110: inside back cover Sept '58.
—— (men). Natl. geog. 98: 359 (col.) Sept '50.
——(men untangle). Natl. geog. 111: 603 (col.) May '57.
—— (women mending). Natl. geog. 105: 155 (col.) Feb '54.
——, butterfly (Mexico). Natl. geog. 102: 521, 544 (col.) Oct '52.
——, Japan. Disney: People & places, p. 156 (col.).
fish racks, Norway. Travel 105: 50 Jan '56.
fish trap, basket. Natl. geog. 101: 337 (col.) Mar '52.
——, Kuwait. Natl. geog. 102: 795 (col.) Dec '52.
——, palm-rib (man weaving). Natl. geog. 113: 188 (col.) Feb '58.
——, Sarawak. Natl. geog. 109: 729 May '56.
——, Sicily. Natl. geog. 107: 10 Jan '55.
fish traps. Holiday 19: 95 (col.) Jan '56.
fish weir. Holiday 24: 57 Nov '58.
Fishback, Margaret. Cur. biog. p. 282 (1941).
Fisher, Eddie. Cur. biog. p. 275 (1954).
Fisher, Archbishop Geoffrey Francis. Cur. biog. p. 189 (1945).
Fisher, Hon. Geoffrey Francis. Holiday 23: 82 (col.) Ap '58.
Fisher, Harry L. Cur. biog. p. 277 (1954).
Fisher, John (Bishop of Rochester). Con. 139: 215 Je '57.
Fisher, Kate ("Big nose Kate"). Horan: Pict. hist. of wild west, p. 115.
Fisher, Mary F. K. Cur. biog. p. 208 (1948).
"Fisher-girl" (Hals). Praeg. pict. ency., p. 337 (col.).
"Fisher-girl & gallant" (figurine). Con. 144: 30 Sept '59.
fisherman. Holiday 6: 119, 123 (col.) Dec '49; 7: 119 Mar '50; 12: 22 Sept '52; 19: 139 (col.) Mar '56; 21: 172, 192-3 (part col.) May '57.
Natl. geog. 110: 33, 34 (col.) Jl '56, 489 Oct '56; 111: 161 (col.) Feb '57.
—— (boat). Holiday 10: 1 Nov '51; 11: 17 May '52, 138 (col.) Je '52.
—— (boat, comic). Holiday 11: 83 May '52.
—— (boat, fish). Natl. geog. 105: 352 (col.) Mar '54.
—— (comic). Holiday 10: 63 Aug '51; 21: 26 Ap '57.
—— (crab). Natl. geog. 107: 67 (col.) Jan '55.
—— (fish). Holiday 14: 101 Sept '53.
Natl. geog. 118: 574 (col.) Oct '60.
—— (fish basket). Natl. geog. 113: 821 (col.) Je '58.
—— (frozen fish). Natl. geog. 114: 865 Dec '58.

fisherman (in lake). Natl. geog. 117: 342 (col.) Mar '60.
fisherman (in ocean). Holiday 22: 11 Oct '57. Natl. geog. 105: 233 (col.) Feb '54.
—— (in rapids). Holiday 11: 47 (col.) May '52.
—— (in river). Holiday 22: 67 (col.) Sept '57. Natl. geog. 114: 71 (col.) Jl '58.
—— (in water). Holiday 10: 19 Oct '51; 12: 115, 121 (col.), 122 Jl '52; 18: 7 Jl '55; 19: 141 (col.) Feb '56, 94 (col.) May '56.
—— (in water, nets). Holiday 12: 20 (col.) Jl '52.
—— (large fish). Natl. geog. 113: 96 (col.) Jan '58.
—— (mending nets). Natl. geog. 115: 71 (col.) Jan '59.
—— (net). Labande: Naples, p. 11. Travel 102: 41 Nov '54.
—— (netting fish). Holiday 11: 101 (col.) May '52.
—— (ocean). Holiday 24: 147 (col.) Nov '58.
—— (ocean beach). Natl. geog. 112: 296 (col.) Sept '57.
—— (rowboat). Natl. geog. 111: 598 (col.) May '57.
—— (sailfish). Natl. geog. 109: 869 Je '56.
—— (salmon).) Natl. geog. 116: 57 (col.) Jl '59.
—— (snow). See man (fishing, snow).
—— (statue). Brooks: Growth of a nation, p. 99.
—— (trout). Natl. geog. 117: 208 (col.) Feb '60.
fisherman, Belgian. See Belgian fisherman.
——, boy. Holiday 19: 4 (col.) May '56.
——, Canary is. Natl. geog. 107: 522 (col.) Ap '55.
——, Filipino. Natl. geog. 118: 602-3 Nov '60.
——, Japanese. Natl. geog. 97: 618 (col.) May '50.
——, Louisiana bayou. Holiday 6: 53 Oct '49.
——, Newfoundland (boat). Natl. geog. 108: 726 (col.) Dec '55.
——, Nigeria (boat, storm). Natl. geog. 116: 250 (col.) Aug '59.
——, Portugal (harbor). Natl. geog. 108: 746 (col.) Dec '55.
——, Portugal (head). Natl. geog. 118: 623 (col.) Nov '60.
——, spear. See spear fisherman.
——, sponge. See sponge fisherman.
——, Tahiti. Natl. geog. 112: 768 (col.) Dec '57.
fisherman. See also man (fishing); man (mending fish net).
fisherman's chapel. See chapel, fisherman's (Thira).
"Fisherman's cottage" (Bonington). Con. 134: 203 (col.) Dec '54.
fisherman's fiesta. See tuna boat fiesta (Cal.).
Fisherman's wharf (Monterey, Cal.). Face of Amer., p. 84-5 (col.).
Fisherman's wharf (San Francisco). Jordan: Hammond's pict. atlas, p. 200 (col.). Natl. geog. 110: 204, 209 (col.) Aug '56.

fishermen. Disney: People & places, p. 105 (col.).
Holiday 7: 8 Ap '50; 10: 22-3 Jl '51, 60-1 (col.) Sept '51; 12: 1 Nov '52; 22: 123 (col.) Nov '57.
—— (boat). Holiday 12: 5 Jl '52, 40 (col.) Dec '52; 18: 77 (col.) Oct '55, 13 (col.) Dec '55.
Natl. geog. 107: 72 (col.) Jan '55; 115: 266 (col.) Feb '59.
—— (cast nets). Natl. geog. 105: 353 (col.) Mar '54.
—— (clams). Natl. geog. 113: 9 (col.) Jan '58.
—— (comic). Holiday 11: 153 Je '52.
—— (devilfish). Natl. geog. 116: 690-1 (col.) Nov '59.
—— (dip net). Natl. geog. 116: 58-9 (col.) Jl '59.
—— (fish). Holiday 11: 30 May '52. Natl. geog. 108: 528-9 (col.) Oct '55.
—— (haul in catch). Natl. geog. 114: 767 Dec '58.
—— (horseback, drags nets). Natl. geog. 113: 820 (col.) Je '58.
—— (ice). Natl. geog. 111: 181 (col.) Feb '57.
—— (large turtle). Holiday 21: 163 Je '57.
—— (line drawing). Holiday 10: 147 Oct '51.
—— (marlin fish). Holiday 10: 101 Nov '51.
—— (mend nets). Natl. geog. 113: 516 (col.) Ap '58.
—— (Miss.). Natl. geog. 118: 722-3 (col.) Nov '60.
—— (nets). Natl. geog. 109: 843 (col.) Je '56; 117: 454-5 (col.) Ap '60.
—— (nets, boat, night). Natl. geog. 105: 393 Mar '54.
—— (nets, sunset). Natl. geog. 114: 622-3 (col.) Nov '58.
—— (rowboat). Holiday 11: 71 May '52.
—— (seiners). Natl. geog. 114: 28 (col.) Jl '58.
——, Alaska. Natl. geog. 105: 135 (col.) Jan '54.
——, Basque. Natl. geog. 105: 151 (col.) Feb '54.
——, Brittany. Holiday 7: 99 (col.) Jan '50.
——, Cambodia. Natl. geog. 117: 526-7 (col.) Ap '60.
——, Dunkirk. Natl. geog. 101: 702 May '52.
——, France (boats). Natl. geog. 117: 729 (col.) Je '60.
——, Holland. Natl. geog. 98: 769 (col.) Dec '50.
——, ice. Natl. geog. 114: 860-72 Dec '58.
——, Ifalik (boat, nets). Natl. geog. 109: 566 (col.) Ap '56.
——, lobster. Natl. geog. 115: 286-95 Feb '59.
——, Martinique (boats). Natl. geog. 115: 275 (col.) Feb '59.
——, Naples (boat). Labande: Naples, p. 204.
——, Portugal. Holiday 6: 102-3 (col.) Sept '49; 19: 26 (col.) Jan '56. Natl. geog. 118: 640-1 Nov '60.
——, Scotland. Natl. geog. 110: 21 (col.) Jl '56.
——, shrimp. See shrimp fishermen.

——, Sweden. Natl. geog. 100: 617 (col.) Nov '51.

fishermen's memorial (Gloucester). Travel 102: 38 Jl '54; 107: 19 May '57.

fishermen's parade (Belgium). Natl. geog. 113: 824-5 (col.) Je '58.

fishermen's picnic. Natl. geog. 117: 439 (col.) Mar '60.

fishing, spear. See spear fishing.

fishing boat. See boat, fishing.

fishing equipment. Rawson: Ant. pict. bk., p. 75-80.

fishing fleet (ships). Natl. geog. 112: 172-3 (col.) Aug '57.

fishing gear shop. Natl. geog. 108: 528 (col.) Oct '55.

fishing huts, ice. Natl. geog. 113: 95 (col.) Jan '58; 114: 864-5 Dec '58.

fishing line. Travel 103: 38 Ap '55.

fishing pier. Rawson: Ant. pict. bk., p. 76.

fishing raft. See raft, fishing.

fishing reel. See reel, fishing.

fishing rod. Holiday 11: 76 (col.) Ap '52.

—— (women making). Natl. geog. 111: 161 (col.) Feb '57.

fishing team, Yale. Natl. geog. 112: 328 (col.) Sept '57.

fishing village (harbor). Holiday 16: 52 (col.) Jl '54.

fishmonger (woman, France). Natl. geog. 115: 626 (col.) May '59.

Fisk, James Brown. Cur. biog. p. 121 (1959).

Fisk, Jim. Amer. heri. vol. 8 no. 3 p. 52 (Ap '57).

fist, raised (sym.). Lehner: Pict. bk. of sym., p. 89.

Fister, George M. Cur. biog. (1963).

Fitch, Vice Adm. Aubrey. Cur. biog. p. 191 (1945).

Fitch, Robert Elliot. Cur. biog. p. 130 (1962).

Fitch Co. office (Kingston, N.Y., 1875). Amer. heri. vol. 4 no. 1 p. 15 (fall '52).

Fitch study, Clyde. Natl. geog. 97: 292 (col.) Mar '50.

Fitzgerald, Albert J. Cur. biog. p. 210 (1948).

Fitzgerald, Barry. Cur. biog. p. 193 (1945).

Fitzgerald, Edward. Cur. biog. p. 201 (1947).

Fitzgerald, Ella. Cur. biog. p. 182 (1956).

Fitzgerald, Francis Scott. Cur. biog. p. 283 (1941).

Fitz Gerald, Leslie M. Cur. biog. p. 279 (1954).

Fitzgerald, Pegeen. Cur. biog. p. 202 (1947).

Fitzpatrick, Daniel. Holiday 27: 82 May '60.

Fitzpatrick, Daniel Robert. Cur. biog. p. 284 (1941).

Fitzroy, Duke George Henry (Lawrence). Con. 143: 90 Ap '59.

Fitzwilliam, Hon. Richard (Wright). Con. 142: 193 Dec '58.

Five nations sym., Indian (5 arrows). Amer. heri. vol. 6 no. 2 p. 29 (winter '55).

"Fives court with Randall & Turner sparring". Con. ency. of ant., vol. 1, pl. 138.

fjord. Holiday 27: 57, 59 (col.) Jan '60.

——, Norway. Con. 142: XIV Sept '58.
Natl. geog. 106: 162, 164, 172 (col.) Aug '54; 111: 99-120 (part col.) Jan '57.
Travel 111: 40-1 Ap '59.

Flack, Marjorie. Jun. bk. of auth., p. 128.

flacon. See flagon.

flag (boy nailing to staff). Amer. heri. vol. 7 no. 2 back cover (col.) (Feb '56).

—— (1st raising against an enemy). Amer. heri. vol. 7 no. 2 p. 26-7 (col.) (Feb '56).

—— (girl, boy planting). Natl. geog. 104: 820 Dec '53.

—— (mourning). Lehner: Pict. bk. of sym., p. 79.

—— (on British ship). Amer. heri. vol. 9 no. 4 p. 7 (col.) (Je '58).

—— (on ship). Amer. heri. vol. 9 no. 3 p. 14 (col.) (Ap '58).

—— (raised at Ft. Moultrie). Amer. heri. vol. 6 no. 6 p. 64 (Oct '55).

—— (raised at Iwo Jima). See Iwo Jima (flag raising).

—— (raised at Seoul). Natl. geog. 99: 234 Feb '51.

—— (Russian-Amer. co.). Amer. heri. vol. 11 no. 3 p. 5 (col.) (Ap '60).

—— (sym.). Lehner: Pict. bk. of sym., p. 54.

——, African warship. Natl. geog. 108: 768 (col.) Dec '55.

——, Amer. revolution. Natl. geog. 105: 198 (col.) Feb '54.

——, Austria. Natl. geog. 99: 779 (col.) Je '51.

——, Britannia's battle. Natl. geog. 101: 540 (col.) Ap '52.

——, British. Amer. heri. vol. 6 no. 2 p. 53 (col.) (winter '55).
Holiday 18: 69 (col.) Oct '55; 24: back cover (col.) Nov '58; 25: 106 (col.) Ap '59; 26: 92 (col.) Aug '59.
Natl. geog. 101: 538 (col.) Ap '52; 105: 342 (col.) Mar '54; 110: 328-9 (col.) Sept '56; 112: 594-5 (col.) Nov '57.
Travel 112: 5 Aug '59; 113: inside cover Mar '60.

——, British royal navy. Natl. geog. 116: 91 (col.) Jl '59.

——, church. Holiday 10: 63 (col.) Dec '51.

——, Cuban. Amer. heri. vol. 8 no. 2 p. 41 (col.) (Feb '57).

——, Danish. Natl. geog. 98: 644 (col.) Nov '50.

——, divers. Natl. geog. 117: 168 (col.) Feb '60.

——, French. Holiday 18: 68 (col.) Oct '55.
Natl. geog. 111: 744, 755, 758-9 (part col.) Je '57.

——, Holland. Holiday 10: 53 (col.) Nov '51.

——, Iceland. Natl. geog. 108: 732 (col.) Dec '55.

——, Iran. Natl. geog. 117: 634 (col.) May '60.

——, Japanese. Natl. geog. 97: 604 (col.) May '50.

——, Jordan's Arab legion. Natl. geog. 98: 718 (col.) Dec '50.

——, Kuwait. Natl. geog. 102: 791 (col.) Dec '52.

——, Lebanon (Arabia). Natl. geog. 106: 830 (col.) Dec '54.

——, Maldive is. Natl. geog. 111: 830 (col.) Je '57.

——, Mexican. Natl. geog. 103: 344 (col.) Mar '53.

flag, New Zealand. Natl. geog. 112: 370 Sept '57, 595 (col.) Nov '57.

——, pirate. See pirate flag.

——, "Plan Marshall". See "Plan Marshall" flag.

——, red (sym.). Lehner: Pict. bk. of sym., p. 88, 95.

——, Red Cross. See Red Cross flag.

——, Russian navy. Amer. heri. vol. 11 no. 4 p. 38 (col.) (Je '60).

——, Swiss. Holiday 28: 42 (col.) Aug '60. Natl. geog. 98: 232 Aug '50; 111: 171 (col.) Feb '57.

——, Tasmanian. Natl. geog. 110: 796 (col.) Dec '56.

——, Turkey. Natl. geog. 100: 166 Aug '51.

——, U.S.A. Amer. heri. vol. 9 no. 5 p. 56 (col.) (Aug '58); vol. 10 no. 2 p. 35 (col.) (Feb '59); vol. 10 no. 6 p. 91 (Oct '59). Holiday 10: 63 (col.) Dec '51; 20: 97 Sept '56.
Int. gr. soc.: Arts . . . p. 163 (col.).
Natl. geog. 100: 584, 592, 594 (col.) Nov '51; 101: 622 (col.) May '52, 722 (col.) Je '52; 102: 396 (col.) Sept '52, 619 (col.) Nov '52; 103: 501 Ap '53, 741 (col.) Je '53; 105: 342 (col.) Mar '54; 107: 121 121 (col.) Jan '55; 752 (col.) Je '55; 110: 146 Aug '56 111: 768 (col.) Je '57; 112: 48 Jl '57; 397 (col.) Sept '57; 115: 489 (col.) Ap '59; 117 589, 638-9 (col.) May 60
Travel 103: 68 May '55; 104: 39 Oct '55; 113: 30 Feb '60.

——, U.S.A. (Betsy Ross). Travel 110: 31 Jl '58.

——, U.S.A. (Cal.). Natl. geog. 102: 396 (col.) Sept '52.

——, U.S.A. (changes). Natl. geog. 116: 86, 88-121 (part col.) Jl '59.

——, U.S.A. (Confederate). Amer. heri. vol. 6 no. 3 p. 34 (col.) (Ap '55).

——, U.S.A. (draped over porch). Amer. heri. vol. 11 no. 1 p. 32 (Dec '59).

——, U.S.A. ("The Grand Union," 1776). Amer. heri. vol. 7 no. 4 p. 5 (col.) (Je '56) vol. 9 no. 6 p. 58 (col.) (Oct '58). Natl. geog. 106: 440 (col.) Oct '54.

——, U.S.A. (half mast, South Pole, for Adm. Byrd). Natl. geog. 116: 114 (col.) Jl '59.

——, U.S.A. (Ill.). Travel 103: 13 Je '55.

——, U.S.A. (Iwo Jima monument). Natl. geog. 111: 76 (col.) Jan '57.

——, U.S.A. (1900). Amer. heri. vol. 7 no. 4 p. 28 (col.) (Je '56).

——, U.S.A. (N.D.). Natl. geog. 100: 291 (col.) Sept '51.

——, U.S.A. (North Pole). Natl. geog. 116: 14 (col.) Jl '59.

——, U.S.A. (patriotic pict., man holding). Amer. heri. vol. 8 no. 6 frontis (col.) (Oct '57).

——, U.S.A. (pledge). Natl. geog. 106: 810 (col.) Dec '54.

——, U.S.A. (regimental, 1860). Amer. heri. vol. 6 no. 1 p. 21 (col.) (fall '54).

——, U.S.A. (Robert E. Peary's, North Pole). Natl. geog. 106: 518, 521, 523, 531 Oct '54.

——, U.S.A. (Salem merchant's, 1835). Amer heri. vol. 6 no. 2 p. 12-4 (col.) (winter '55).

——, U.S.A. (suggested patterns for new flag). Natl. geog. 116: 99 Jl '59.

——, U.S.A. (Theo. Roosevelt presidential). Natl. geog. 112: 314 (col.) Sept '57.

——, U.S.A. (13 stars). Natl. geog. 100: 582 (col.) Nov '51.

——, U.S.A. (24 stars). Travel 113: 30 Feb '60.

——, U.S.A. (West Point cadets). Natl. geog. 101: 601 (col.) May '52.

——, U.S.A. (with eagle). Amer. heri. vol. 11 no. 6 p. 50-1 (col.) (Oct '60).

——, U.S.A. (Yankee force at Louisbourgh). Amer. heri. vol. 6 no. 2 p. 55 (winter '55).

——, U.S.A. (army, Putnam phalanx, Hartford, Conn.). Amer. heri. vol. 7 no. 5 p. 23 (Aug '56).

——, Washington's command. See Washington's command flag.

——, white (sym.). Lehner: Pict. bk. of sym., p. 86.

——, "Yellow Jack". See "Yellow Jack" flag.
flag. See also flags.
flag-bearers (Siena, Italy). Natl. geog. 100: 237-41 (col.) Aug '51.
flag pole (ship). Natl. geog. 109: 738 (col.) Je '56.
flag raising at Ft. Moultrie. Amer. heri. vol. 6 no. 6 p. 64 (Oct '55).
flag raising at Iwo Jima. See Iwo Jima (flag raising).
flag raising at Seoul. Natl. geog. 99: 234 Feb '51.
flag raising-Louisiana, 1803. Natl. geog. 116: 101 (col.) Jl '59.
flag signals. See ship flag signals.
"Flagellation of Christ" (Montegna). Con. 138: 16 Sept '56.
flagon (17th cent., Johnson). Con. 145: 244 Je '60.
——, antique. Con. 138: 124 Nov '56.
——, antique church. Con. 134: 9-11 Sept '54.
——, antique silver. Con. 133: 150 May '54.
——, antique triple. Con. 137: XLIII Je '56.
——, Charles I. Con. 129: 41 Ap '52.
——, communion. Con. 143: 169 May '59.
——, Elizabethan. Con. 136: 145 Nov '55.
——, English pewter. Con. 137: 268 Je '56.
——, old English church. Con. 126: 43 Aug '50.
——, pewter (antique). Con. 144: 125 Nov '59.
——, pewter church. Con. 126: 121-3 Oct '50.
——, silver (17th cent.). Con. 134: 160 Dec '54; 145: LXXVII May '60.
——, silver church. Con. 126: 106 Oct '50.
——, William & Mary. Con. 143: 266 Je '59.
flagons, antique silver. Con. 127: 104 May '51.
flagons. See also tankard.
flags. Amer. heri. vol. 6 no. 2 p. 61 (col.) (winter '55).
Holiday 28: 23 (col.) Jl '60, 26 (col.), 108 Aug '60.

Natl. geog. 106: 409 (col.) Sept '54.
—— (children holding). Natl. geog. 97: 72 (col.) Jan '50.
—— (on staffs). Holiday 27: 78 (col.) Feb '60.
——, Amer., Canadian. Natl. geog. 107: 551 (col.) Ap '55.
——, boat. Natl. geog. 107: 60 (col.) Jan '55.
——, Corps (U.S. Civil war). Pakula: Cent. album, pl. 8-9 (col.).
——, European. Holiday 14: 133 Dec '53.
——, hurricane. Natl. geog. 98: 535 Oct '50.
——, Mass. & Harvard. Natl. geog. 97: 309 (col.) Mar '50.
——, ship. Natl. geog. 107: 752 (col.) Je '55; 113: 778 (col.) Je '58.
——, ship (1813). Amer. heri. vol. 7 no. 3 p. 19 (col.) (Ap '56).
——, ship (1779). Amer. heri. vol. 11 no. 3 p. 13 (col.) (Ap '60).
——, Tibet (New Year). Holiday 12: 57 (col.) Dec '52.
——, United Nations. Natl. geog. 99: 221-32 (col.) Feb '51; 101: 775 (col.) Je '52.
——, U.S.A. (drape ship). Natl. geog. 107: 770 (col.) Je '55.
——, U.S.A. (1845-46). Amer. heri. vol. 9 no. 5 p. 74-5 (Aug '58).
——, U.S.A., British, Canadian. Natl. geog. 106: 710-11 (col.) Nov '54.
——, U.S.A., Civil war. Amer. heri. vol. 7 no. 6 p. 30, 66 (col.) (Oct '56).
——, U.S.A., colonial. Holiday 16: 106 (col.) Jl '54.
——, U.S. unit (World war). Natl. geog. 111: 75 (col.) Je '57.
flags. See also flag.
Flagstad, Kirsten. Cur. biog. p. 204 (1947). Holiday 8: 81 Nov '50.
—— (as Dido in "Dido & Aeneas"). Cooper: Con. ency. of music, p. 96.
Flaherty, Robert J. Amer. heri. vol. 2 no. 1 p. 70 (fall '50). Cur. biog. p. 199 (1949).
flail tying devices. Rawson: Ant. pict. bk., p. 26.
falmboyant tracery. Praeg. pict. ency., p. 248.
flame (sym.). Lehner: Pict. bk. of sym., p. 37.
flame blower (Jamaica). Travel 110: inside back cover Sept '58.
flame tree (boy picks flowers). Natl. geog. 108: 374 (col.) Sept '55.
Flamenco dancer (Spain). Holiday 19: 55 Jan '56; 26: 109 Dec '59. Int. gr. soc.: Arts . . . p. 147 (col.).
Flameng, Francois (work of). Con. 143: XXV Mar '59.
flaming sword (sym.). Lehner: Pict. bk. of sym., p. 35.
Flamingo hotel (Las Vegas). Holiday 12: 106 (col.) Dec '52.
Flanagan, Rev. Edward J. Cur. biog. p. 285 (1941).
Flanders, Helen Hartness (Mrs. R.E.). Amer. heri. vol. 2 no. 2 p. 48 (winter '51).
Flanders, Ralph E. Cur. biog. p. 213 (1948).
Flandes, Juan de (work of). Natl. geog. 110: 648 (col.) Nov '56.

Flandin, Pierre-Etienne. Cur. biog. p. 287 (1941).
Flanner, Janet. Cur. biog. p. 205 (1943).
Flannery, Harry W. Cur. biog. p. 207 (1943).
flashlight. Holiday 7: 95 May '50, 20 (col.) Je '50. Travel 112: 11 Dec '59; 114: 14 Nov '60, 11 Dec '60
—— (camera). Holiday 10: 75 Jl '51.
—— (no battery). Travel 112: 46 Dec '59; 113: 45 Jan '60, 54 May '60.
flask, Byzantine church cylindrical. Con. 135: 259 Je '55.
——, enameled glass. Holiday 18: 60 (col.) Jl '55.
——, oil & vinegar. Con. 135: 12 Mar '55.
——, Roman. Con. 145: 288 Je '60.
——, whiskey (1800's). Holiday 18: 61 (col.) Jl '55.
flasks (liquid fuels). Natl. geog. 114: 323 (col.) Sept '58.
——, historical & masonic glass. Con. ency. of ant., vol. 3, pl. 41.
flatboat. Amer. heri. vol. 2 no. 1 p. 46 (fall '50).
——, river. Natl. geog. 117: 249 (col.) Feb '60.
flatiron. Rawson: Ant. pict. bk., p. 12.
flatiron stand. Rawson: Ant. pict. bk., p. 12.
Flatman, Thomas (miniature). Con. ency. of ant, vol. 1, pl. 130.
flats, Assyrian. Con. ency. of ant., vol. 3, pl. 145.
——, German. Con. ency. of ant., vol. 3, pl. 145.
flats. See also apartment bldg.
"flatter" for smoothing iron. Rawson: Ant. pict. bk., p. 53.
flattop (airplane carrier). Natl. geog. 104: 553 (col.) Oct '53.
"Flautist" (woodcut). Praeg. pict. ency., p. 453.
Flavian amphitheatre (Rome). See Coliseum (Rome).
Flavin, Martin. Cur. biog. p. 209 (1943).
"Flawford Madonna & child". Con. ency. of ant., vol. 3, pl. 129.
flax break (1815). Rawson: Ant. pict. bk., p. 34.
"Flax-scutching bee" (Park). Natl. geog. 99: 193 (col.) Feb '51.
flax stacks (man & woman, field). Natl. geog. 115: 605 (col.) May '59.
flax swingling knife. Rawson: Ant. pict. bk., p. 33.
flax winder. Rawson: Ant. pict. bk., p. 34.
Flaxman, John (work of). Con. 144: 104-5 Nov '59.
Flea market (Paris). Natl. geog. 111: 319-26 Mar '57.
Fleck, Sir Alexander. Cur. biog. p. 183 (1956).
Fleck, Jack. Cur. biog. p. 210 (1955).
Fleeson, Doris. Cur. biog. p. 123 (1959).
Flegel, George (work of). Praeg. pict. ency., p. 71 (col.).
Fleischmann, Manly. Cur. biog. p. 206 (1951).
Fleming, Sir Alexander. Cur. biog. p. 208 (1944)
Fleming, Berry. Cur. biog. p. 199 (1953).
Fleming, Donald M. Cur. biog. p. 125 (1959).

Fleming, Ian. Holiday 26; 72 Sept '59.
Fleming, Sam M. Cur. biog. p 132 (1963).
Flemish art. See art, Flemish.
Flemish statue. (14th cent.). Con. 136: 309 Jan
  '56.
Flemming, Arthur S. Cur. biog. p. 207 (1951);
  p. 141 (1960).
Flesch, Rudolf. Cur. biog. p. 215 (1948).
Fletcher, Sir Angus. Cur. biog. p. 191 (1946).
Fletcher, Cyril Scott. Cur. biog. p. 201 (1953).
Fletcher, Henry. Jensen: The White House, p.
  216.
Fletcher, Inglis. Cur. biog. p. 206 (1947).
Fletcher, Sir James. Holiday 28: 106 Nov
  '60.
fleur-de-lis (sym.). Lehner: Pict. bk. of sym.,
  p. 78.
"Fleur du mal" (Rouault). Holiday 14: 50 (col.)
  Dec '53.
Flexner, Abraham. Cur. biog. p. 289 (1941).
flight deck (on ship). Amer. heri. vol. 7 no. 6
  p. 79 (Oct '56).
"Flight into Egypt" (Elsheimer). Con. ency. of
  ant., vol. 1 pl. 157.
"Flight into Egypt" (Giotto di Bondone).
  Praeg. pict. ency., p. 228 (col.).
"Flight into Egypt" (Poussin). Con. 143: 125
  Ap '59.
"Flight of Florimell" (Allston). Con. 141: 66
  Mar '58.
"Flight to peace" (route on globe). Natl. geog.
  117: 596-7 (col.) May '60.
Flikke, Col. Julia O. Cur. biog. p. 266: (1942).
Flin Flon, Manitoba (Canada). Holiday 6: 49
  Aug '49.
Flinck, Govaert (work of). Con. 135: XI (col.)
  Ap '55.
flint box. Rawson: Ant. pict. bk., p. 94.
float, festival (Belgium). Natl. geog. 113: 803
  (col.) Je '58.
——, festival (Japan). Natl. geog. 118: 760-1
  (col.) Dec '60.
——, flourescent nylon. Natl. geog. 116: 470
  (col.) Oct '59.
——, Japanese fish-net. Natl. geog. 117: 455
  (col.) Ap '60.
floating bridge. See bridge, floating.
floating gardens. See Xochimilco floating
  gardens.
floating market, Bangkok's. Holiday 18: 51
  Oct '55.
floating shops. See shops, floating (Siam).
floatplanes. Natl. geog. 109: 750, 753 (col.) Je
  '56.
floats (book stories parade). Natl. geog. 105:
  807-14 (col.) Je '54.
——, festival (Spain). Natl. geog. 113: 420-1
  (col.) Mar '58.
——, festival (Wis. Swiss). Natl. geog. 111:
  172-3 (col.) Feb '57.
——, Mardi Gras. Holiday 11: 57 (col.) Feb
  '52.
  Natl. geog. 103: 159-60 (col.) Feb '53.
——, Tournament of roses. Holiday 11: 94-5
  (col.) Jan '52.
  Natl. geog. 102: 584 (col.) Nov '52.
"Flodden fields" (Scotland). Natl. geog. 112:
  458-9 (col.) Oct '57.
Floherty, John J. Jun. bk. of auth., p. 129.

flood (cabins float). Natl. geog. 117: 349 (col.)
  Mar '60.
"The Flood" (tapestry from Polish collection).
  Con. 138: 2 (col.) Sept '56.
flood (wagons, people in canyon). Amer. heri.
  vol. 6 no. 1 p. 69 (fall '54).
flood, Johnstown. See Johnstown flood.
flood, Kansas. Natl. geog. 101: 484 (col.) Ap
  '52.
flood, river. See river flood.
flood control dam. Brooks: Growth of a nation, p. 280.
floodgate. Rawson: Ant. pict. bk., p. 50.
—— (1848). Natl. geog. 99: 113 Jan '51.
floor, tile. See tile floor.
floor plan (church of St. Charles, Vienna).
  Praeg. pict. ency., p. 24.
—— ("Invalides", Paris). Praeg. pict. ency., p.
  24.
—— ("Notre Dame", Paris). Praeg. pict. ency.,
  p. 24.
floor polisher. Holiday 28: 13 (col.) Dec '60.
Floors castle, Kelso (int. & ext., Scotland). Con.
  145: 70 (col.)-75 Ap '60.
"flop" (sym.). Lehner: Pict. bk. of sym., p. 85
"Flora" (sculpture). Con. 144: 179 Dec '59.
Flora (sym.). Lehner: Pict. bk. of sym., p. 33.
"Floral offering to Hymen" (Poussin). Con.
  133: 12 Mar '54.
floral street design (Canary is.). Natl. geog. 107:
  491-5 (col.) Ap '55.
Florence, Fred F. Cur. biog. p. 185 (1956).
Florence (Italy). Holiday 12: 45-7 (part col.)
  Oct '52; 15: 109 Jan '54.
  Natl. geog. 111: 794-7 (col.) Je '57.
  Travel 102: inside cover Nov '54.
—— (churches). Holiday 27: 129 Jan '60.
—— (Piazza). Natl. geog. 108: 143 Jl '55.
—— (Ponte Santa Trinita). Con. 133: XXI Je
  '54; 138: XVII Jan '57.
—— (Ponte Vecchio). Travel 114: 84 Jl '60.
Florey, Sir Howard W. Cur. biog. p. 209
  (1944).
Florida. Holiday 10: 7 (col.) Nov '51; 11: 26-
  43 (part col.) Jan '52; 13: 48-51 (part col.)
  Je '53; 14: 5 (col.) Nov '53; 18: 45-57, 136
  (part col.) Dec '55; 19: 5 (col.) Feb '56;
  20: 155 (col.) Nov '56, 66-9 (part col.)
  Dec '56; 21: 35 (col.) Je '57; 22: 5 (col.)
  Sept '57, 125 (col.) Oct '57, 173, (col.)
  Nov '57; 24: 20-1 (col.) Nov '58; 26: 83
  (col.) Sept '59, 87-91, 173 (col.) Nov '59;
  27: 38-9 (col.) Feb '60; 28: 99 (col.) Sept
  '60, 49 (col.) Nov '60.
  Jordan: Hammond's pict. atlas, p. 68-77
  (col.).
  Natl. geog. 98: 563-604 (part col.) Nov '50;
  107: 50-76 (part col.) Jan '55; 113: 44-65
  (part col.) Jan '58.
  Travel 101: 21-3 Mar '54; 102: 5-12 Jl '54;
  103: 7-23, 34-41 Feb '55; 107: 12-6 Je
  '57; 111: 32-4 Feb '59; 114: 20-37 Oct
  '60, 26-35 Dec '60.
—— (Africa U.S.A.). Travel 103: 31-2 Jan '55.
—— (beach). Holiday 23: 5 (col.) Je '58.
—— (Chokoloskee). Travel 108: 26-7 Oct '57.
—— (Dead river, fishing camp). Face of
  Amer., p. 160-1 (col.).
—— (hotels). Holiday 18: 57 (col.) Dec '55;

24: 186-7 Dec '58; 25: 156-7 Jan '59; 26: 161 Nov '59.
—— (map). Holiday 12: 21 (col.) Aug '52. Natl. geog. 110: 825 Dec '56; 115: 137 Jan '59. Travel 103: 7 Feb '55.
—— (map, 1591). Amer. heri. vol. 4 no. 2 p. 63 (winter '53).
—— (map, pictorial). Holiday 11: 7 (col.) Jan '52.
—— (St. Augustine fort). Brooks: Growth of a nation, p. 33.
—— (Seminoles). Natl. geog. 110: 820-38 (col.) Dec '56.
—— (shanty boat trip). Travel 107: 21-3 Feb '57.
—— (state parks). Travel 104: 14-7 Oct '55; 107: 12-5 Je '57.
—— (swamp). Natl. geog. 113: 98-120 (part col.) Jan '58.
——, Marineland. See Marineland, Florida.
—— "Center of America". See "Center of America (Florida).
Florida everglades. Natl. geog. 112: 512, 514 (col.) Oct '57.
Florida keys. Holiday 6: 11-125 Dec '49.
Florida overseas highways. See highway, Florida.
Florida, wild animal compound. Travel 105: 57-9 Mar '56.
Florinsky, Michael T. Cur. biog. p. 291 (1941).
florist (floating canoe). Natl. geog. 114: 628 (col.) Nov '58.
flower boxes. Natl. geog. 110: 469-71 (col.) Oct '56.
flower cart (vendor). Holiday 24: 84 (col.) Jl '58.
"flower of light" (sym.). Lehner: Pict. bk. of sym., p. 78.
flower pot, Target (18th cent.). Con. 144: 30 Sept '59.
flower preservation (woman). Natl. geog. 114: 421-7 (col.) Sept '58.
flower seller. Labande: Naples, p. 48.
"Flower seller" (Lesur). Con. 138: XXVIII Sept '56.
flower shop (man & woman). Natl. geog. 114: 169 (col.) Aug '58.
flower show. (exhibit). Natl. geog. 103: 118-9 (col.) Jan '53.
flower sprinkler. See water sprinkling can.
"The flower stall" (De Blaas). Con. 137: XXVI May '56.
flower vendor. Holiday 14: 84 (col.) Oct '53; 24: 84 (col.) Jl '58.
—— (Holland). Natl. geog. 106: 386 (col.) Sept '54.
—— (Rome). Holiday 27: 71 Ap '60.
flowers (goddess of). Lehner: Pict. bk. of sym., p. 33.
Floyd, Carlisle. Cur. biog. p. 143 (1960).
flume, mill. Amer. heri. vol. 2 no. 1 p. 11 (fall '50).
Flupart, J. J. (work of). Cooper: Con. ency. of music, p. 85.
Flushing meadow park pool. Natl. geog. 99: 309 (col.) Mar '51.
flute. Cooper: Con. ency. of music, p. 397. Int. gr. soc.: Arts . . . p. 141 (col.).

—— (medieval). Int. gr. soc.: Arts . . . p. 61 (col.).
——, bass (1501). Cooper: Con. ency. of music, p. 398.
——, bass (16th cent.). Cooper: Con. ency. of music, p. 397.
——, fipple. Natl. geog. 97: 291 (col.) Mar '50.
——, treble (16th cent.). Cooper: Con. ency. of music, p. 398.
"Flute player" (tomb painting). Praeg. pict. ency., p. 140 (col.).
flutes (ancient). Int. gr. soc.: Arts . . . p. 27 (col.).
—— (Argentine gauchos blowing). Natl. geog. 113: 332 (col.) Mar '58.
fluting ornament. Con. ency. of ant., vol. 1, p. 21.
fly, fisherman's fishing. Natl. geog. 111: 160 (col.) Feb '57.
"fly-shoer", antique. Rawson: Ant. pict. bk., p. 8.
fly-wheel. Rawson: Ant. pict. bk., p. 24.
flying, man. See man (flying).
"flying bananas". See helicopter, navy.
flying boxcars. Natl. geog. 98: 109 (col.) Jl '50; 109: 750-1 (col.) Je '56.
flying carpet. Lehner: Pict. bk. of sym., p. 64.
"Flying Dutchman" (motive). Int. gr. soc.: Arts . . . p. 123 (col.).
"Flying Dutchman & Voltiguer" (Herring). Con. 139: 68 Mar '57.
"flying jeep". See airplane "flying jeep".
flying machine, Wright. Natl. geog. 112: 267 Aug '57.
"flying pogo stick" (man). Natl. geog. 115: 537 (col.) Ap '59.
flying saucer. Holiday 18: 24 Aug '55.
flynet. Rawson: Ant. pict. bk., p. 65.
——, ear (for horse). Rawson: Ant. pict. bk., p. 65.
Flynn, Elizabeth Gurley. Cur. biog. p. 161 (1961).
Flynn, Errol. Holiday 5: 40 (col.) Jan '49.
flys, fishing (girl making). Natl. geog. 110: 41 (col.) Jl '56.
fog (N.Y. & Maine). Holiday 23: 56-9 Feb '58.
——, chemical (Africa). Natl. geog. 97: 328 Mar '50.
Fogarty, Anne. Cur. biog. p. 144 (1958).
Foggini, G. B. (sculpture by). Con. 141: 223, 225 Je '58.
foil, 1820 fencing. Con. 126: 116 Oct '50.
folding bed. Rawson: Ant. pict. bk., p. 14.
—— (cartoon, 1894). Amer. heri. vol. 11 no. 6 p. 111 (Oct '60).
Foley, Martha. Cur. biog. p. 293 (1941).
Foley, Raymond M. Cur. biog. p. 202 (1949).
Folger, U.S. ambassador & Mrs. John Clifford. Natl. geog. 113: 800 (col.) Je '58.
Folger library (Wash., D.C.). Natl. geog. 100: 412-24 Sept '51.
folk dance (Catskill country). Holiday 24: 44 (col.) Aug '58.
—— (French). Travel 104: 60 Sept '55.
—— (Portugal). Travel 107: 30-1 Ap '57.
—— (Switzerland). Disney: People & places, p. 45 (col.).
folk dancers. Holiday 11: 39 (col.) Feb '52.
folk dances. See also dancers.

Folkers, Karl. Cur. biog. p. 136 (1962).
folklore, Amer. (crafts, symbols). Holiday 18: 60-1 (col.) Jl '55.
folklore heroes. Amer. heri. vol. 1 no. 3 p. 73-9 (part col.) (spring '50).
Folliard, Edward T. Cur. biog. p. 207 (1947).
Follies' Bergere models (Paris). Natl. geog. 101: 790 (col.) Je '52.
"folly" architecture, Amer. See architecture, early Amer. "follies".
Folsom, Frank M. Cur. biog. p. 203 (1949).
Folsom, James E. Cur. biog. p. 205 (1949).
Folsom, Marion B. Cur. biog. p. 147 (1950).
Fonda, Henry. Cur. biog. p. 217 (1948).
Holiday 24: 117 Nov '58.
Fong, Hiram L. Cur. biog. p. 145 (1960).
font, Swedish silver. Con. 141: 8 Mar '58.
font canopies, English. Con. 138: 84-7 Nov '56.
Fontaine, Joan. Cur. biog. p. 211 (1944).
Fontainebleau, hotel (Fla.). Holiday 18: 57 (col.), 155 Dec '55.
Travel 103: 66 Je '55.
Fontainebleau palace, (France). Holiday 5: 123 Ap '49.
Fontainebleau school (France). Holiday 25: 117 Jan '59.
Fontana dam (Tenn.). Jordan: Hammond's pict. atlas, p. 61 (col.).
Fontana dei Fiumi (Rome). Holiday 27: 89 Ap '60.
Praeg. pict. ency., p. 318.
Fontana di Trevi fountain (Rome). Con. 141: 233 Je '58.
Holiday 27: 198 Ap '60.
Int. gr. soc.: Arts . . . p. 99 (col.).
Natl. geog. 108: 148 Jl '55.
Praeg pict. ency., p. 56.
Fontanne, Lynn. Cur. biog. p. 533 (1941).
Fontebasso, Francesco (work of). Con. 144: 191 Dec '59.
Fonteyn, Margot. Cur. biog. p. 207 (1949).
"Fonthill Abbey" (Gibb). Con. 141: 273 Je '58.
food (airplane dinner). Holiday 10: 68-9 (col.) Oct '51.
—— (cartoons). Amer. heri. vol. 8 no. 4 p. 68-9 (Je '57).
—— (cooked). Amer. heri. vol. 3 no. 4 p. 29, 32, 37 (col.) (summer '52).
Holiday 10: 64 (col.) Sept '51, 64 (col.) Nov '51; 11: 60 (col.) Ap '52, 64 (col.) Je '52; 12: 4 (col.) Sept '52; 18: 77 (col.) Nov '55, 179 (col.) Dec '55; 20: 127 (col.) Nov '56; 21: 79 (col.) Feb '57, 67 (col.) Ap '57; 22: 46-7 (col.) Sept '57.
—— (cooked, diet). Holiday 11: 72 (col.) May '52.
—— (display). Holiday 27: 23 (col.) Ap '60.
—— (on dish). Holiday 27: 207 (col.) Ap '60.
—— (on plate). Holiday 27: 10 (col.) Ap '60.
—— (on table). Holiday 20: 64 (col.) Oct '56; 25: 151, 154 (col.) May '59; 27: 147, 149, 150, 152 (part col.) Feb '60, 196 (col.) Mar '60, 125 (col.) Je '60; 28: 10 (col.) Sept '60, 202 (col.) Dec '60.
—— (on tray). Holiday 28: inside back cover (col.) Sept '60.
—— (ready to serve). Holiday 24: 111 (col.) Sept '58.

—— (ship buffet). Holiday 28: 71 (col.) Aug '60.
—— (ship table). Holiday 27: 95 (col.) Mar '60.
——, Chinese. Holiday 18: 64 (col.) Oct '55.
——, Finland. Holiday 22: 107 (col.) Dec '57
——, French restaurant. Holiday 20: 78 (col.) Aug '56.
——, Hawaiian. Holiday 22: 95 (col.) Dec '57.
——, Holland (table). Natl. geog. 98: 763 (col.) Dec '50.
——, Italian (on platters). Holiday 25: 98 (col.) Je '59.
——, Japanese. Holiday 18: 64 (col.) Jl '55.
——, molded. See molded food.
——, picnic (beach). Holiday 28: 88 (col.) Jl '60.
——, Samoan (preparation). Disney: People & places, p. 133-39 (col.).
——, Scandinavian. Holiday 10: 27 (col.) Dec '51.
——, sea. See seafood.
——, South Seas. Holiday 28: 113 (col.) Nov '60.
——, world. Holiday 20: 48 (col.) Sept '56.
food & drug (posters). Amer. heri. vol. 7 no. 5 p. 61-3, 112 (col.) (Aug '56).
food chopper (antique). Rawson: Ant. pict. bk., p. 8.
food, hutch. See hutch, food.
food market. Holiday 12: 60 (col.) Jl '52.
food preparation (Samoan). Disney: People & places, p. 133-39 (col.).
—— (Thailand). Disney: People & places, p. 165-6 (col.).
food shop. Holiday 20: 81 (col.) Oct '56.
food vessel (antique). Con. 133: 191 May '54.
——, sacrificial. See sacrificial food vessel.
food warmer (antique). Con. 134: 46 Sept '54.
food irradiated. Natl. geog. 114: 311 (col.) Sept '58.
Fool's scepter. Lehner: Pict. bk. of sym., p. 11.
Foot, Sir Hugh M. Cur. biog. p. 203 (1953).
Foot, Michael. Cur. biog. p. 149 (1950).
foot. Natl. geog. 98: 96 (col.) Jl '50.
—— (cartoon). Holiday 14: 110 Sept '53.
Holiday 12: 78 Aug '52.
—— (nervous system). Gray's anatomy, p. 993-5.
—— (skeleton). Gray's anatomy, p. 238-9, 252, 487, 490, 493-6.
——, woman's. Natl. geog. 98: 259 (col.) Aug '50.
foot log (across stream). Rawson: Ant. pict. bk., p. 50.
foot scraper. Holiday 21: 166 Mar '57.
foot stove. Rawson: Ant. pict. bk., p. 74.
——, tufted. Rawson: Ant. pict. bk., p. 9.
football. Holiday 10: 159 Dec '51; 18: 104 Dec '55.
football game. Holiday 10: 84 Nov '51.
Travel 106: 6, 61 Oct '56.
—— (comic). Holiday 12: 64 (col.) Nov '52.
football player (comic). Holiday 14: 121 (col.) Oct '53, 66 (col.) Nov '53.
football players. Holiday 6: 48 Oct '49, 72 Nov '49; 8: 67 Nov '50; 21: 71 (col.) Mar '57; 26: 164 Nov '59.

—— (1896). Amer. heri. vol. 6 no. 6 back cover (col.) (Oct '55).
—— (Harvard-Yale). Holiday 26: 64-5 Nov '59.
football stadium. Brooks: Growth of a nation. p. 306.
Holiday 10: 120 Oct '51.
—— (Ohio State Univ.). Holiday 10: 60 (col.) Nov '51.
—— (Minn. Univ.). Holiday 12: 61 (col.) Nov '52.
—— (Univ. of Cal.). Natl. geog. 105: 732-3 Je '54.
—— (Yale). Holiday 18: 38 (col.) Nov '55.
football team, Rutgers. See Rutgers Univ. football team.
football trophy "buffalo nickel" (N.D.). Natl. geog. 100: 322 (col.) Sept '51.
Foote, Andrew Hull. Pakula: Cent. album, p. 123.
footman (4-legged trivet). Con. ency. of ant., vol. 3 p. 243.
footman, Italian. Holiday 19: 46 Jan '56.
footprint. Travel 109: 47 May '58.
footprint (in sand). Holiday 28: 92 (col.) Sept '60.
footprint of Buddha. See Buddha footprints.
footstool. See stool, foot.
footwear. See shoes.
Forabosco, Girolamo (work of). Con. 144: 107 Nov '59.
Forand, Aime J. Cur. biog. p. 146 (1960).
Forbes, Allan. Holiday 14: 45 Nov '53.
Forbes, Bertie C. Cur. biog. p. 151 (1950).
Forbes, John J. Cur. biog. p. 194 (1952).
Forbes, Kathryn. Cur. biog. p. 216 (1944).
"Forbidden city" gates (China). Natl. geog. 118: 211 (col.) Aug '60.
Force, Juliana. Cur. biog. p. 295 (1941).
Forcer. Con. 134: 190-1 Dec '54.
"Forcing Hudson river passage" (Serres). Natl. geog. 99: 186 (col.) Feb '51.
Ford, Benson. Cur. biog. p. 195 (1952).
Ford, Bob (like Jesse James). Horan: Pict. hist. of wild west, p. 43.
Ford, Mrs. (mother of Bob & Charles). Horan: Pict. hist. of wild west, p. 46.
Ford, Charles. Horan: Pict. hist. of wild west, p. 46.
Ford, Mrs. Edsel. Holiday 21: 68 (col.) Je '57.
Ford, Eliakim. Amer. heri. vol. 9 no. 5 p. 40 (Aug '58).
Ford, Frederick W. Cur. biog. p. 148 (1960).
Ford, Gerald R., jr., Cur. biog. p. 164 (1961).
Ford, Glenn. Cur. biog. p. 126 (1959).
Ford, Harriet E. Amer. heri. vol. 9 no. 5 p. 41 (Aug '58).
Ford, Henry. Amer. heri. vol. 6 no. 1 p. 54-9 (fall '54); vol. 9 no. 2 p. 65 (Feb '58); vol. 10 no. 6 p. 41-3 (Oct '59).
Cur. biog. p. 217 (1944).
Holiday 21: 70-1 Je '57; 22: 61 Jl '57.
Natl. geog. 114: 104-5 (col.) Je '58.
—— (as a western badman). Amer. heri. vol. 10 no. 6 p. 42 (Oct '59).
—— (in 1st auto, 1896). Brooks: Growth of a nation, p. 224.
Ford, Henry, 2d. Cur. biog. p. 193 (1946).

Ford, John. Cur. biog. p. 297 (1941).
Holiday 5: 42 (col.) Jan '49.
Ford, Mary Theodosia. Amer. heri. vol. 9 no. 2 p. 57 (col.) (Feb '58).
Ford, Tennessee Ernie. Cur. biog. p. 145 (1958).
Ford, Whitey. Cur. biog. p.. 138 (1962).
Ford auto. See automobile, Ford.
Ford family, Henry. Holiday 21: 68-73 (col.) Je '57; 22: 60-1 Jl '57, 73, 75 Sept '57.
Ford mansion (Gen. Washington's headquarters). Natl. geog. 117: 13 Jan '60.
Ford's Dearborn museum. See Greenfield Village (Mich.).
Ford's funeral, Bob. Horan: Pict. hist. of wild west, p. 45.
Ford's theater (where Lincoln was shot). Amer. heri. vol. 3 no. 2 p. 66 (winter '52).
Natl. geog. 117: 274-5 (part col.) Feb '60.
foreign legion trainees. Natl. geog. 117: 776 (col.) Je '60.
Foreman, Clark. Cur. biog. p. 219 (1948).
"The Forest" (Blanch). Amer. heri. vol. 2 no. 4 p. 46 (col.) (summer '51).
forest, petrified. See petrified forest.
forest, rain. Natl. geog. 108: 89 (col.) Jl '55.
forest fire. Natl. geog. 110: 288, 308-9 (col.) Sept '56.
forest fire fighters. See fire fighters, forest.
forest fire prevention sign (Smokey). See "Smokey the bear".
forest rangers. See rangers, forest.
forest service crew (spray trees). Natl. geog. 110: 313 (col.) Sept '56.
Foresta hotel (Stockholm). Travel 110: 41 Jl '58.
Forester, C. S. Holiday 18: 42 Aug '55.
Forester, Friedrich Wilhelm. Cur. biog. p. 134 (1962).
forester. Natl. geog. 112: 520-1 Oct '57.
forestry (sym.). Lehner: Pict. bk. of sym., p. 12.
forests, national. Natl. geog. 110: 288-324 (part col.) Sept '56.
forge (Williamsburg). Holiday 14: 156 Dec '53.
——, horseshoe. Rawson: Ant. pict. bk., p. 55.
——, old cannon. Travel 108: 24 Oct '57.
"Forge of Vulcan" (de Velours & Van Balen Con. 134: 2 (col.) Sept '54.
forgery, art. See art fakes.
forging machines. Natl. geog. 107: 204 Feb '55.
fork, carving. Holiday 18: 4 Aug '55, 150 Dec '55; 20: 11, 164 Dec '56.
fork, hay. See hay fork.
fork, ladle (kitchen). Holiday 12: 94 Oct '52.
fork, novelty. Travel 101: 33 Ap '54.
fork, silver (table). Holiday 19: 168 May '56; 21: 115 Mar '57, 105 Je '57.
——, silver gilt (Flemish). Con. ency. of ant., vol. 3, pl. 6.
——, silver Italian (16th cent.). Con. ency. of ant., vol. 3, pl. 31.
fork & scoop, Charles II. Con. 138: 126 Nov '56.
fork & spoon (African salad set). Holiday 18: 128 Oct '55.
—— & spoons, Florentine serving. Holiday 18: 63 Nov '55.

forks (silverware). Holiday 12: 1 Oct '52; 14: 141 Jl '53.
——, pastry. Amer. heri. vol. 5 no. 3 inside cover (spring '54).
——, Towle silver. Holiday 24: 103 Nov '58.
forks. See also silverware.
formal gardens. See gardens, formal.
Formica, Mercedes (Spanish). Holiday 17: 99, 103 (col.) Feb '55.
Formosa. Natl. geog. 97: 140-76 (part col.) Feb '50; 107: 573-88 Ap '55; 109: 266-7 (col.) Feb '56; 111: 327-62 (part col.) Mar '57.
Travel 108: 36-9 Nov '57.
—— (man, bullock-silhouette). Travel 114: 6 Oct '60.
—— (man, ox). Travel 113: 10 Feb '60.
—— (map). Natl. geog. 97: 144 Feb '50; 103: 507 Ap '53; 107: 575 Ap '55; 109: 268 Feb '56; 111: 330 Mar '57.
Fornells (Spain). Travel 108: 20 Jl '57.
Forrest, Gen. Nathan B. Holiday 24: 98 (col.) Oct '58.
Pakula: Cent. album, p. 125.
Forrest, Wilbur S. Cur. biog. p. 222 (1948).
Forrestal, James V. Cur. biog. p. 267 (1942); p. 223 (1948).
Forrester, Maureen. Cur. biog. p. 140 (1962).
Forssmann, Dr. Werner. Cur. biog. p. 191 (1957).
Forsyth, William D. Cur. biog. p. 197 (1952).
fort. Amer. heri. vol. 6 no. 6 p. 97 (Oct '55).
—— (Afghanistan). Natl. geog. 98: 678 Nov '50.
—— (Canada). Holiday 19: 139 (col.) Mar '56.
—— (Chicago, 1843). Brooks: Growth of a nation, p. 116.
—— (Denmark). Natl. geog. 98: 643 (col.) Nov '50.
—— (St. Augustine, Fla.). Brooks: Growth of a nation, p. 33.
Holiday 27: 177 (col.) Je '60.
Natl. geog. 113: 42-3 (col.) Jan '58.
Travel 114: 21 Oct '60.
—— (West Indies, map). Amer. heri. vol. 10 no. 4 p. 8 (col.) (Je '59).
——, Baranov's. See Baranov's fort.
——, Cape Breton island. See Cape Breton is. fort.
——, Delhi's red. See Delhi's red fort.
——, El Morro. See El Morro fort.
——, guardians (Canada). Holiday 19: 9 May '56.
——, Gwalior. See Gwalior fort.
——, Pequot. See Pequot fort.
——, pirates'. See pirates' fort.
——, Pisac. See Pisac fort.
——, Sutter's. See Sutter's fort.
Fort Atkinson (Iowa). Travel 110: 57 Sept '58.
Fort Augusta (miniature). Natl. geog. 98: 96 (col.) Jl '50.
Fort Berthold palisade (being uncovered). Natl. geog. 103: 721 (col.) Je '53.
Fort Bragg. Holiday 6: 106-9 (col.) Oct '49.
Fort Castillo de San Marcos (rampart). Holiday 12: 99 (col.) Nov '52.
—— See also Fort Marion.

Fort Charles (Jamaica). Natl. geog. 117: 178-9 (col.) Feb '60.
Fort Christian (Virgin is.). Natl. geog. 109: 212 (col.) Feb '56.
Travel 109: 36 May '58.
Fort Conger (Arctic). Amer. heri. vol. 11 no. 4 p. 44 (col.) (Jl '60).
Fort-de-France (Martinique). Holiday 5: 108-9 (col.) Mar '49.
Natl. geog. 115: 264 Feb '59.
Travel 109: 26 May '58.
Fort Defiance (Boy Scouts, Flagstaff). Natl. geog. 107: 482 (col.) Ap '55.
Fort Delaware (Pea Patch is.). Travel 106: 22 Oct '56.
Fort Frederica (St. Simons is.). Jordan: Hammond's pict. atlas, p. 67 (col.).
Fort Greene Ville (Ohio). Amer. heri. vol. 4 no. 3 p. 34 (spring '53).
Fort Henry (Ontario, Canada). Amer. heri. vol. 3 no. 3 p. 52-5 (spring '52).
Holiday 24: 54 (col.) Nov '58.
Fort Jackson (S.C.). Natl. geog. 103: 301 (col.) Mar '53.
Fort Jefferson (Turtle is., Gulf of Mexico). Holiday 8: 60 (col.) Dec '50.
Natl. geog. 97: 52-3 (col.) Jan '50.
Fort Jesus (Mombasa, Africa). Natl. geog. 97: 336 (col.) Mar '50.
Fort Johnson (N.Y.). Amer. heri. vol. 3 no. 3 p. 24 (col.)-25 (spring '52).
—— (1759). Amer. heri. vol. 10 no. 3 p. 50 (Ap '59).
Fort Langley (Hudson's Bay Co.). Amer. heri. vol. 8 no. 4 p. 16-7 (col.) (Je '57).
Fort Laramie. Amer. heri. vol. 2 no. 2 p. 29 (winter '51); vol. 6 no. 1 p. 35 (fall '54).
Fort Laramie site. Holiday 14: 63 Jl '53.
Fort Lauderdale (Fla.). Holiday 16: 60-5 (col.) Nov '54; 18: 46-7 (col.) Dec '55.
—— (hotel). Holiday 24: 143 Oct '58; 25: 156-7 Jan '59, 202 Ap '59; 26: 118 Aug '59, 129 Sept '59; 27: 168 Jan '60.
—— (motor hotel). Holiday 27: 8 Jan '60.
—— (river). Holiday 28: 131 (col.) Dec '60.
—— (waterfront). Holiday 27: 140 (col.) Je '60.
—— (yachting center). Natl. geog. 113: 51 (col.) Jan '58.
Fort Loudoun dam. Brooks: Growth of a nation, p. 282.
Fort McHenry (Baltimore). Holiday 25: 119 Mar '59.
——, attack on. Holiday 10: 43 (col.) Nov '51.
Fort McKenzie (attack). See "Attack on Fort McKenzie".
Ft. Mackinac (Mich.). Travel 110: cover Jl '58.
Ft. Marion (entrance, St. Augustine). Travel 102: 6 Jl '54.
—— See also Fort Castillo de San Marcos.
Ft. Moultrie (attacked by British). Amer. heri. vol. 6 no. 6 p. 64 (Oct '55).
Ft. Myers beach (Fla.). Travel 107: 27 Jan '57.
Fort Necessity (1754-1954). Amer. heri. vol. 5 no. 4 p. 24-7 (part col.) (summer '54).

Fort Niagara. Amer. heri. vol. 4 no. 4 p. 32-41 (part col.) (summer '53). Travel 104: 39-41 Sept '55.

Fort of Grand Portage. Natl. geog. 108: 204-5 (col.) Aug '55.

Ft. Parker (Texas). Travel 107: 43 Mar '57.

Fort Peck dam. Natl. geog. 97: 698 Je '50.

Fort Pitt blockhouse. See blockhouse, Fort Pitt.

Fort Providentia (Formosa). Natl. geog. 97: 164 (col.) Feb '50.

Fort Raines (Columbia river). Holiday 14: 61 Jl '53.

Fort Recovery blockhouse. See blockhouse, Fort Recovery.

Fort Ross, Russian (Cal.). Amer. heri. vol. 1 no. 3 p. 46 (spring '50); vol. 11 no. 3 p. 5-6 (Ap '60). Travel 107: 48 May '57.

Ft. Sackville surrender (Ind.). Amer. heri. vol. 2 no. 1 back cover (col.) (fall '50).

Fort Ste. Marie (Ontario). Holiday 19: 93 Mar '56.

Ft. San Sebastian (Mozambique). Travel 104: 28 Nov '55.

Ft. Scott Natl. cemetery (Kan.). Face of Amer., p. 42-3 (col.).

Fort Snelling (Minn.). Amer. heri. vol. 1 no. 2 p. 7 (winter '50).

Ft. Stanwix (1777). Amer. heri. vol. 7 no. 2 p. 26-7, 31 (col.) (Feb '56).

Fort Sumter. Amer. heri. vol. 1 no. 2 p. 22 (winter '50).

—— (burning). Natl. geog. 116: 109 (col.) Jl '59.

—— (1860 model). Natl. geog. 113: 31 Jan '58.

Fort Ticonderoga (N.Y.). Amer. heri. vol. 12 no. 1 p. 11 (col.) (Dec '60). Holiday 16: 106 Jl '54. Natl. geog. 107: 746-7 (col.) Je '55. Travel 110: 16 Jl '58.

Fort Vancouver. Amer. heri. vol. 1 no. 2 p. 22 (winter '50).

Ft. Worth, Tex. (children's museum). Travel 113: 58 Jan '60.

fortress, Abyssinia. Int. gr. soc: Arts . . . p. 85 (col.).

——, Carcassonne. Natl. geog. 100: 34 (col.) Jl '51.

——, crusaders (Rhodes). Natl. geog. 114: 740 (col.) Dec '58.

——, Hopi Indian. Natl. geog. 112: 224 Aug '57.

——, Inca. See Inca fortress.

——, Karlsten. See Karlsten fortress.

——, Louisbourg. See Louisbourg fortress.

——, MacKenzie (Scotland). Holiday 8: 38 (col.) Dec '50.

——, Margat. Natl. geog. 106: 827 (col.) Dec '54.

fortress city, medieval. Holiday 25: 19 Mar '59.

fortress of Ayasluk. Osward: Asia Minor, pl. 33.

fortress of Oberhaus (Austria). Travel 103: 24 Je '55.

fortress walls (crenelated). Natl. geog. 112: 579 Oct '57.

fortresses of Tufa, rock. Osward: Asia Minor, pl. 76.

fortresses. Amer. heri. vol. 8 no. 2 p. 20-1 (Feb '57).

Fortuna (sym.). Lehner: Pict. bk. of sym., p. 31.

fortune (sym.). Lehner: Pict. bk. of sym., p. 45, 48.

fortune teller (Kashmir). Natl. geog. 114: 617 Nov '58.

"Fortune teller" (Pater). Con. 133: 259 Je '54.

fortune teller (Seoul). Holiday 18: 78 Dec '55.

——, temple. Natl. geog. 97: 219 Feb '50.

"forty niners". Holiday 24: 66-7 (col.) Aug '58.

Forum, Roman. See Roman forum.

Fosdick, Raymond B. Cur. biog. p. 195 (1945).

Foss, Joseph Jacob. Cur. biog. p. 211 (1955).

fossil, dinosaur. Natl. geog. 105: 381 (col.) Mar '54.

fossil-bearing shale (Antarctic). Natl. geog. 116: 540-1 Oct '59.

fossils. Natl. geog. 109: 364-86 (part col.) Mar '56.

—— (magnified). Natl. geog. 108: 173 Aug '55.

Foster, Genevieve. Jun. bk. of auth., p. 131.

Foster, Stephen Collins. Holiday 14: 89 Oct '53. Travel 113: 33-5 Je '60.

Foster, William C. Cur. biog. p. 152 (1950).

Foster, William Z. Cur. biog. p. 198 (1945).

Foster grave, Stephen Collins. Travel 113: 35 Je '60.

Foster home, Stephen Collins. Natl. geog. 101: 292 (col.) Mar '52.

Foster memorial, Stephen Collins. Travel 113: 34 Je '60.

Foster memorial & shrine, Stephen Collins. Holiday 14: 25 Aug '53.

Foster memorial park, Stephen Collins (Fla.). Natl. geog. 107: 74 Jan '55.

Foucou, Jean-Joseph (terracotta work). Con. 140: 4 Sept '57.

"The Foundry" (Fredenthal). Amer. heri. vol. 2 no. 4 p. 43 (col.) (summer '51).

fountain. Holiday 10: 93 Sept '51, 62 (col.) Dec '51; 12: 103 (col.) Sept '52, 49 (col.) Nov '52; 21: 119 Jan '57; 22: 69 (col.) Oct '57. Natl. geog. 104: 292-3 (col.) Sept '53; 107: 191 (col.) Feb '55.

—— (children playing). Natl. geog. 118: 800 (col.) Dec '60.

—— (lake). Natl. geog. 110: 428 (col.) Oct '56.

—— (man, woman & children). Natl. geog. 118: 175 (col.) Aug '60.

—— (pool). Natl. geog. 98: 604 (col.) Nov '50.

—— (Cairo). Natl. geog. 106: 770 (col.) Dec '54.

—— (Chicago fair). Amer. heri. vol. 11 no. 6 p. 19 (Oct '60).

—— (Edmonton, Alberta, Canada). Natl. geog. 118: 102 (col.) Jl '60.

—— (Immacolatella). Labande: Naples, p. 88.

—— (Longwood). Natl. geog. 100: 49-51 (col.) Jl '51.

fountain (Naples). Labande: Naples, p. 80.
"The Fountain" (Nilson). Con. 145: 130 Ap
'60.
fountain (Paris). Natl. geog. 101: 789 (col.)
Je '52; 114: 286 Aug '58.
—— (Peru). Holiday 27: 111 (col.) May '60.
—— (Puerto Rico). Natl. geog. 99: 456 (col.)
Ap '51.
—— (Rome). Holiday 27: 69, 103 Ap '60.
Natl. geog. 111: 456 (col.) Ap '57.
—— (royal palace). Labande: Naples, p.
130-1.
—— (Soldier's Field). Holiday 10: 47 (col.)
Oct '51.
—— (Switzerland). Natl. geog. 110: 469 (col.)
Oct '56.
—— (Turkey). Natl. geog. 100: 175 (col.) Aug
'51.
—— (Vatican). Natl. geog. 117: 595 (col.) May
'60.
—— (war memorial). Natl. geog. 111: 754
(col.) Je '57.
——, Alhambra (Spain). Natl. geog. 97: 454
(col.) Ap '50.
——, Baroque (Rome, Fontana di Trevi).
Praeg. pict. ency., p. 56.
——, Buckingham (Chicago). Natl. geog. 104:
782 (col.) Dec '53.
——, Carl Milles (St. Louis). Holiday 8: 35
(col.) Oct '50.
——, crystal. Con. 127: 101 May '51.
——, Druses at. Natl. geog. 104: 18 (col.) Jl
'53.
——, Fontana di Trevi. See Fontana di Trevi.
——, 18th cent. Con. 142: LI Dec '58.
——, garden (18th cent.). Con. 144: XXVI
Jan '60.
——, Gothic (Ulm). Praeg. pict. ency., p. 55.
——, horse water. Natl. geog. 104: 685 Nov
'53.
——, Italian model (1700). Con. 141: 121 Ap
'58.
——, Moliere. See Moliere fountain.
——, Romanesque (Goslar). Praeg. pict. ency.,
p. 55.
——, Rutger's (N.Y.). Holiday 16: 70 Sept
'54.
——, 16th cent. Con. 127: 56 Mar '51.
——, street (Denmark). Natl. geog. 108: 819
Dec '55.
——, tiled wall. Natl. geog. 107: 170 (col.)
Feb '55.
——, Trevi. See Fontana di Trevi.
——, wall. See wall fountain.
——, yard. Natl. geog. 103: 154 (col.) Feb
'53.
fountain heads, horse (Italy). Travel 102: inside cover Nov '54.
fountain of the rivers (Rome). See Fontana dei
Fiumi.
"Fountain of youth" (St. Augustine, Fla.). Holiday 12: 98 (col.) Nov '52.
fountain of youth (sym.). Lehner: Pict. bk. of
sym., p. 72.
fountains (Rome). Holiday 11: 40-1 Ap '52.
Fouquet, Jean (self portrait). Int. gr. soc.:
Arts . . . p. 89 (col.).
"The Four continents" (Rubens). Natl. geog.
97: 743 (col.) Je '50.

the four elements (sym.). Lehner: Pict. bk. of
sym., p. 15, 46.
the four evangelists (sym.). Lehner: Pict. bk. of
sym., p. 38.
"Four girls on the bridge" (Munch). Praeg.
pict. ency., p. 440 (col.).
4-H club member. Natl. geog. 101: 487 (col.)
Ap '52.
four-leaf clover. See clover, four-leaf.
four-poster bed. See bed, four-poster.
"Four Saints weeping & St. John" (Memling).
Con. 133: 13 Mar '54.
4th of July (celebration). Amer. heri. vol. 10
no. 4 p. 42-3 (Je '59).
—— (celebration, Wash., D.C.). Holiday 7:
110 (col.) Feb '50.
Fourth of July parade (early 19th cent.). Amer.
heri. vol. 6 no. 4 p. 16-7 (col.) (Je '55).
foustanella uniform (Greece). Travel 114:
cover (col.), 25, 28 Aug '60.
Fowle, Jacob (Copley). Natl. geog. 99: 184
(col.) Feb '51.
Fowler, Gene. Cur. biog. p. 222 (1944).
Holiday 25: 84 May '59.
Fowler, Henry H. Cur. biog. p. 199 (1952).
Fowler, Robert M. Cur. biog. p. 281 (1954).
"Fowling tower", Chinese. Con. ency. of ant.,
vol. 3, pl. 58.
Fox, Genevieve. Cur. biog. p. 208 (1949).
Fox, Nellie. Cur. biog. p. 150 (1960).
fox (sym.). Lehner: Pict. bk. of sym., p. 60.
fox hunt (dogs). Holiday 10: 94 (col.) Aug '51;
12: 38-9 (col.) Nov '52; 18: 29 Oct '55.
Natl. geog. 108: 327 (col.) Sept '55; 109:
515 (col.) Ap '56.
——. See also hunters (horses, dogs).
"Fox hunting" (Howitt). Con. 140: XXXV
(col.) Jan '58.
Foy, Bryan. Holiday 5: 43 (col.) Jan '49.
Foy, Eddie, jr. Holiday 17: 91 (col.) Jan '55.
Foyle, Gilbert. Cur. biog. p. 283 (1954).
Foyle, William Alfred. Cur. biog. p. 283
(1954).
Foyle, William (in library). Natl. geog. 108:
313 (col.) Sept '55.
Fracois II (Clouet). Con. 133: XV Mar '54.
Fragonard, Jean Honore. Con. 144: 67 Sept
'59.
—— (work of). Con. 126: cover, 2 (col.) Aug
'50; 129: 71 Ap '52, 132 Je '52; 135: 42,
50 Mar '55; 137: XIII (col.) May '56, 293
Je '56; 140: 54 Sept '57; 143: 208, 263
Je '59; 144: 55 Sept '59, 182 (col.) Dec
'59.
Natl. geog. 110: 654 (col.) Nov '56.
frame, picture. See picture frame.
Franca, Celia. Cur. biog. p. 187 (1956).
France. Holiday 6: 77-88 Jl '49; 10: 137 Nov
'51; 13: 125 Mar '53, 18 Ap '53; 14: back
cover (col.) Sept '53; 21: 51-95 (part col.)
Ap '57, 114 (col.) May '57.
Natl. geog. 100: 2-44 (part col.) Jl '51; 108:
531-39 (col.) Oct '55; 109: 310, 319, 326,
329, 334 (part col.) Mar '56; 111: 770-1,
809-13 (col.) Je '57; 112: 420-35 Sept '57
115: 570-88 Ap '59; 117: 727-66 (col.) Je
'60.
Travel 102: 12-3 Sept '54; 107: 52-4 Ap
'57; 108: 54-7 Jl '57; 112: 50-1 Sept '59.

—— **(boy & girl).** Holiday 13: 56-9 (part col.) Feb '53.

—— **(comic).** Holiday 11: 68-9 (col.) May '52.

—— **(costumes).** *See* costume (France).

—— **(honor insignia).** Int. gr. soc.: Arts . . . p. 167 (col.).

—— **(La Baule).** Holiday 27: 86-91 (col.) May '60.

—— **(Loire Valley).** Holiday 11: 138 (col.) Ap '52.

—— **(map).** Holiday 21: 61, 143 Ap '57; 26: 155 Nov '59.
Natl. geog. 114: 291-2 Aug '58; 115: 573 Ap '59.
Travel 107: 53 Ap '57.

—— **(Moselle Valley).** Holiday 14: 126 (col.) Oct '53.

—— **(Normandy).** Natl. geog. 115: 592-631 (part col.) May '59.

—— **(Paris).** *See* Paris.

—— **(Pont du Gard).** *See* Pont du Gard.

—— **(resorts).** Holiday 14: 90-7 (part col.) Sept '53.

—— **(The Rhone).** Holiday 27: 69-73 Jan '60.

—— **(Rocamadour).** Holiday 24: 128 (col.) Sept '58.

—— **(truffle digging).** Natl. geog. 110: 419-21 Sept '56.

—— **(Vezelay).** Natl. geog. 103: 230-46 (part col.) Feb '53.

France, Marianne. *See* Marianne, France (sym.).

France, patron saint of (sym.). Lehner: Pict. bk. of sym., p. 39.

Francesca della, Piero (work of). Con. 140: 279 Jan '58.

Francescatti, Zino. Cur. biog. p. 210 (1947).

Franceschi, Vera. Holiday 22: 121 Sept '57.

Francia, Francesco (work of). Con. 135: 137 Ap '55; 136: 119 (col.) Nov '55; 142: XVIII (col.) Dec '58.

Franciosa, Anthony. Cur. biog. p. 166 (1961).

Francis I (Titian). Con. 126: 83-5 Oct '50.

"Francis I and his sister" (Bonington). Con. 138: 55 (col.) Sept '56; 144: 127 Nov '59.

Francis, Marquess of Tavistock (Reynolds). Con. 126: 209 Dec '50.

Francis, Arlene. Cur. biog. p. 189 (1956).

Francis, Clarence. Cur. biog. p. 227 (1948).

Francis, Connie. Cur. biog. p. 142 (1962).

Francis, Frank. Cur. biog. p. 127 (1959).

Franciscan basilica. *See* basilica, Franciscan.

Franciscan priest. Natl. geog. 110: 725 (col.) Dec '56.

Francisco, Peter (legendary soldier). Amer. heri. vol. 10 no. 6 p. 22 (col.) (Oct '59).

Franck, Cesar (Rongier). Cooper: Con. ency. of music, p. 97.

Franck, James. Cur. biog. p. 193 (1957).

Franck's ceramics, Kaj. Travel 105: 37 Ap '56.

Franco, Francisco. Cur. biog. p. 269 (1942).

Franco, Gen. Francisco. Cur. biog. p. 285 (1954).

Francois, Audré (work of). Holiday 26: 90-5 (col.) Dec '59.

Francois-Poncent, Audré. Cur. biog. p. 209 (1949).

Franconi, Antoine. Durant: Pict. hist. of Amer. circus, p. 18.

Frank, Hans. Cur. biog. p. 299 (1941).

Frank, Jerome N. Cur. biog. p. 301 (1941).

Frank, Lawrence K. Cur. biog. p. 147 (1958).

Frank, Mary. Cur. biog. p. 147 (1958).

Franke, William B. Cur. biog. p. 129 (1959).

Franken, Rose. Cur. biog. p. 303 (1941); p. 212 (1947).

Frankensteen, Richard T. Cur. biog. p. 202 (1945).

Frankenthal porcelain. *See* porcelain, Frankenthal.

Frankfort (West Germany). Natl. geog. 115: 774-5 Je '59.

Frankfurter, Felix. Cur. biog. p. 305 (1941); p. 195 (1957).
Holiday 7: 78 Feb '50.

frankfurters. Nat. geog. 114: 311 (col.) Sept '58.

Franklin, Benjamin. Amer. heri. vol. 1 no. 3 p. 61 (spring '50); vol. 7 no. 2 p. 4 (col.) (Feb '56); vol. 7 no. 3 p. 67 (Ap '56); vol. 9 no. 4 p. 49 (col.) (Je '58).
Con. 129: 135 Je '52.
Holiday 11: 14 Feb '52; 19: 84 Mar '56; 21: 49 May '57; 27: 11 Mar '60.
Natl. geog. 102: 185 (col.) Aug '52; 113: 267 (col.) Feb '58.
Travel 111: 43 Mar '59; 51 Je '59; 113: 17 Jan '60; 114: 41 Jl '60, 15 Aug '60.

—— **(Peale).** Natl. geog. 99: 185 (col.) Feb '51.

—— **(bust).** Amer. heri. vol. 1 no. 2 p. 53 (winter '50).

—— **(kite & lighting).** Amer. heri. vol. 1 no. 4 p. 25 (summer '50).
Natl. geog. 97: 824 Je '50.

—— **(miniature).** Con. 140: 59 Sept '57.

—— **(playing harmonica).** Amer. heri. vol. 10 no. 4 p. 103 (Je '59).

—— **(reception at Versailles).** Amer. heri. vol. 10 no. 4 p. 41 (Je '59).

—— **(seated).** Con. ency. of ant., vol. 3, pl. 91.

Franklin, Frederic. Cur. biog. p. 213 (1943).

Franklin, Jay. Cur. biog. p. 309 (1941).

Franklin, John Hope. Cur. biog. (1963).

Franklin, John M. Cur. biog. p. 212 (1949).

Franklin, Walter S. Cur. biog. p. 155 (1950).

Franklin, William Buel. Pakula: Cent. album, p. 127.

Franklin memorial monument, Benjamin (to parents). Natl. geog. 97: 304 (col.) Mar '50.

Franks, Sir Oliver. Cur. biog. p. 229 (1948).

Franz Ferdinand. *See* Ferdinand, Archduke Franz (of Austria).

Fraser, Sir Bruce. Cur. biog. p. 215 (1943).

Fraser, Charles. Amer. heri. vol. 9 no. 2 p. 56 (col.) (Feb '58).

—— **(work of).** Amer. heri. vol. 9 no. 2 p. 53, 58-9 (col.) (Feb '58).

Fraser, Hugh Russell. Cur. biog. p. 216 (1943).

Fraser, Ian Forbes. Cur. biog. p. 288 (1954).

Fraser, James Earle. Cur. biog. p. 209 (1951).

Fraser, Peter. Cur. biog. p. 274 (1942).

Fraser, Sir. Robert. Cur. biog. p. 191 (1956).

Fraser, Sir William J. Ian. Cur. biog. p. 213 (1947).

fraternity initiations house. Holiday 24: 51 Oct '58.

fraternity ritual. Holiday 23: 94 (col.) May '58.

Frauenkirche ground plan (Dresden). Praeg. pict. ency., p. 348.

Fraunce's tavern (N.Y.). Holiday 16: 107 (col.) Jl '54; 20: 95 Sept '56.

Frazer, Joseph W. Cur. biog. p. 196 (1946).

Frazer auto. Holiday 5: 119 (col.) Jan '49; 6: 33 Aug '49, 72 Sept '49; 7: 1 (col.) May '50, 91 (col.) Je '50; 8: 19 (col.) Jl '50, 65 (col.) Aug '50.

freaks, circus. Durant: Pict. hist. of Amer. circus, p. 64.

Frear, Joseph Allen, jr. Cur. biog. p. 290 (1954).

Fred, Edwin B. Cur. biog. p. 156 (1950).

Fredenthal, David. Cur. biog. p. 276 (1942).

—— (work of). Amer. heri. vol. 2 no. 4 p. 43 (col.) (summer '51).

Frederica fort. See fort Frederica.

Frederick I, Elector of Bandenbourg (Huaut). Con. 138: 83 Nov '56.

Frederick II hunting lodge. See hunting lodge of Frederick II.

Frederick, H.R.H. Augustus (Lonsdale). Con. 143: 90 Ap '59.

Frederick, J. R. Amer. heri. vol. 11 no. 4 p. 50 (Je '60).

Frederick, Pauline. Cur. biog. p. 292 (1954).

"Frederick Prince of Wales" (Frye, 1738). Con. 133: 102 Ap '54.

Frederick, H.R.H. William (Reynolds). Con. 143: 85 Ap '59.

Frederick, H.R.H. William (Romney). Con. 143: 89 Ap '59.

Frederick Louis, Prince of Wales (on horse). Amer. heri. vol. 11 no. 4 p. 9 (col.) (Je '60).

Frederick IX, King of Denmark. Cur. biog. p. 215 (1947).

Frederick the Great, King of Prussia (bust). Praeg. pict. ency., p. 427.

Fredericks, Carlton. Travel 113: 95 Ap '60, 39 May '60.

Frederika, Queen Louise (Greece). Cur. biog. p. 213 (1955).
 Holiday 17: 58-61 (part col.) Jan '55.
 Natl. geog. 106: 472 Oct '54; 109: 42 Jan '56.

Freedley, George R. Cur. biog. p. 217 (1947).

Freedman, Benedict. Cur. biog. p. 219 (1947).

Freedman, Nancy. Cur. biog. p. 219 (1947).

freedom (sym.). Lehner: Pict. bk. of sym., p. 83.

Freedom box, George III. Con. 141: 245 Je '58.

"Freedom" statue. See statue ("Freedom").

Freedomland (N.Y., fun site). Travel 113: 12 Je '60.

Freehafer, Edward. Holiday 26: 76 Oct '59.

Freehafer, Edward G. Cur. biog. p. 216 (1955).

"Freeing of the slaves" (Baratta). Con. 142: 173 Dec '58.

Freeman, Douglas Southall. Amer. heri. vol. 7 no. 2 p. 67 (Feb '56).

Freeman, Lucy. Cur. biog. p. 205 (1953).

Freeman, Orville L. Cur. biog. p. 193 (1956).

Freemasons pay peppercorn rent to Governor (Bermuda). Natl. geog. 105: 212 Feb '54.

freezer, food. Holiday 25: 96 Je '59.

freight boat. See boat, freight.

freight car, train. Natl. geog. 99: 132 (col.) Jan '51; 110: 380 (col.) Sept '56.

freight push car (Formosa). Natl. geog. 97: 161 Feb '50.

freighter. See boat, freight.

Freitag, Walter. Cur. biog. p. 293 (1954).

Fremont, Jessie Benton. Amer. heri. vol. 7 no. 4 p. 19 (Je '56).

Fremont, John C. Pakula: Cent. album, p. 129.

Fremont, John Charles. Amer. heri. vol. 2 no. 2 p. 73 (winter '51); vol. 7 no. 4 p. 12 (col.) (Je '56).
 Brooks: Growth of a nation, p. 125.

Fremont & Indian. Amer. heri. vol. 7 no. 4 p. 106 (Je '56).

Fremont explorations, John Charles. Amer. heri. vol. 7 no. 4 p. 14-8 (part col.) (Je '56).

"Fremont Pass" (Cal.). Amer. heri. vol. 11 no. 4 frontis. (Je '60).

"Fremont Peak", Rocky Mts. Amer. heri. vol. 7 no. 4 p. 16-7 (col.) Je '56.

"Fremont planting flag on Fremont Peak". Amer. heri. vol. 7 no. 4 p. 107 (Je '56).

Fremont's men, John Charles (on march). Amer. heri. vol. 6 no. 4 p. 92 (Je '55).

French, Allen. Jun. bk. of auth., p. 133.

French, Daniel Chester. Travel 106: back cover Aug '56.

—— (sculpture by). Amer. heri. vol. 7 no. 2 p. 56-7 (Feb '56).

French, Paul Comly. Cur. biog. p. 212 (1951).

French, Robert W. Cur. biog. p. 131 (1959).

French academy member. Int. gr. soc.: Arts . . . p. 153 (col.).

French Alps. See Alps, French.

French & Indian wars (map). See Indian wars map.

French architecture. See architecture, French.

French art. See art, French.

"French comedian" (Watteau). Con. 136: 145 Nov '55.

French Congo (Negro painting). Praeg. pict. ency., p. 554 (col.).

French costumes. See costumes (French).

French dancers. See dancers, French.

"French encampment at Monterey" (Chapman). Con. 135: 251-2 Je '55.

French furniture. See furniture, French.

French literary salon (18th cent.). Int. gr. soc.: Arts . . . p. 93 (col.).

French Morocco. Natl. geog. 107: 148-88 (part col.) Feb '55.

French porcelain. See porcelain, French.

French riviera. See Riviera, French.

French West Africa (map). Natl. geog. 100: 266 Aug '51; 113: 390 Mar '58, 680 May '58.

French women. Holiday 13: 49 Ap '53.

Frenchmen (cart, horse). Holiday 25: 38 (col.) Jan '59.

Frere, Edouard (work of). Con. 142: XXVI Jan '59.

fresco. Con. 142: 154-8 Dec '58.

—— (Arena chapel, Padua). Praeg. pict. ency., p. 228 (col.).

—— (Bacchant, Pompeii). Labande: Naples, p. 106.

——(Crete). Ceram: March of arch., p. 60-1.

—— (Crete palace wall). Natl. geog. 114: 754 (col.) Dec '58.

—— (14th cent.). Labande: Naples, p. 70.

—— (hunters, by Holbein). Con. 133: 79 Ap '54.

—— (Nereid on a panther). Labande: Naples, p. 105.

—— (Raphael). Holiday 27: 90-1 (col.) Ap '60.

—— (Santa Maria del Carmine). Praeg. pict. ancy., p. 252 (col.).

—— (Santi Apostoli). Praeg. pict. ency., p. 254 (col.).

—— (Sistine chapel). Praeg. pict. ency., p. 278 (col.).

——, Gozzoli. Holiday 27: 61 Jan '60.

——, Italian (Romano). Con. 133: 139 Ap '54.

——, Memorial (Sicily-Italy campaign). Natl. geog. 111: 756-7 (col.) Je '57.

——, mud wall (Nepal). Natl. geog. 97: 21 Jan '50.

fresno on stairway (Wurzburg). Praeg. pict. ency., p. 321 (col.).

fresco painting (Francesca). Praeg. pict. ency., p. 59 (col.).

frescoes (Chinese). Natl. geog. 99: 403 (col.) Mar '51.

—— (U.S. capitol). Natl. geog. 102: 184-5 (col.) Aug '52.

——, sacred (rock-cut church). Natl. geog. 113: 142-3 Jan '58.

Fresnay, Pierre. Cur. biog. p. 133 (1959).

Freund. Philip H. Cur. biog. p. 231 (1948).

Frick, Ford C. Cur. biog. p. 205 (1945).

Frick, Whilhelm. Cur. biog. p. 278 (1942).

Friday, William. Cur. biog. p. 149 (1958).

Friday (sym.). Lehner: Pict. bk. of sym., p. 25.

fried potato wagon (Flanders). Natl. geog. 107: 638 (col.) May '55.

Friedman, Herbert. Cur. biog. (1963).

Friedrich, Caspar David (work of). Praeg. pict. ency., p. 393 (col.).

Friendly, Edwin S. Cur. biog. p. 213 (1949).

Friendly, Fred W. Cur. biog. p. 197 (1957).

Friend's meeting house (Penn.). Holiday 18: 98-9 (col.) Oct '55.

frieze, Louis XVI carved wall. Con. 133: 244 Je '54.

——, Parthenon. See Parthenon frieze.

——, Pompeian. Ceram: March of arch., p. 24.

——, tile (ancient Persian). Int. gr. soc.: Arts . . . p. 21 (col.).

frigate. Amer. heri. vol. 7 no. 3 p. 13-21 (col.) (Ap '56).

—— (ship, Chile). Natl. geog. 108: 758 (col.) Dec '55.

Frings, Ketti. Cur. biog. p 151 (1960).

Frisch, F. H. (work of). Con. ency. of ant., vol. 3, pl. 82.

Friesche, Carl A. Cur. biog. p. 144 (1962).

Frissell, Toni. Cur. biog. p. 220 (1947).

Frith, W. P. (work of). Con. 142: 83 Nov '58.

froe, iron. Rawson: Ant. pict. bk., p. 23.

Froehlich, Jack E. Cur. biog. p. 134 (1959).

frog (sym.). Lehner: Pict. bk. of sym., p. 27.

frogman (1874). Amer. heri. vol. 11 no. 3 p. 36, 92-3 (Ap '60).

Froment, Nicholas (work of). Con. 137: 166 (col.) May '56.

Frondizi, Arturo. Cur. biog. p. 150 (1958).

Frontenac, chateau. See chateau Frontenac.

frontier, western. Holiday 6: 21 (col.) Aug '49.

frontier cabin. Holiday 6: 57 Aug '49.

frontiersman. Holiday 17: 83, 115 (col.) Mar '55.

——, Amer. Int. gr. soc.: Arts . . . p. 115 (col.).

Frost, A. B. (book illus. by). Amer. heri. vol. 8 no. 1 p. 36 (Dec '56).

Frost, Frances Mary. Cur. biog. p. 158 (1950).

Frost, Leslie M. Cur. biog. p. 206 (1953).

Frost, Robert. Cur. biog. p. 279 (1942). Holiday 18: 45 Jl '55; 22: 52 (col.) Nov '57. Jensen: The White House, p. 283.

frost. See Jack Frost (sym.).

Frothingham, Channing. Cur. biog. p. 232 (1948).

Fruehauf, Roy. Cur. biog. p. 208 (1953).

fruit basket. Holiday 20: 42 (col.) Oct '56. Int. gr. soc.: Arts . . . p. 179 (col.). Natl. geog. 105: 760 (col.) Je '54. Travel 111: 52 Mar '59.

—— (bottles). Holiday 21: 139 Je '57.

—— (18th cent., silver). Con. 133: III Mar '54.

—— (Fahlstrom, 1747). Con. 144: 96 Nov '59.

—— (George II silver). Con. 133: XXIV Mar '54, X Ap '54, XVI May '54, VIII Je '54; 142: LVIII Sept '58.

—— (knives around). Travel 110: inside cover Sept '58, 41 Oct '58, inside cover Nov '58.

—— (silver). Con. 142: XI Dec '58.

—— (wicker). Con. 142: XXIV Jan '59.

fruit bowl, Irish antique. Con. 138: XLVI Nov '56.

——, Irish glass. Con. ency. of ant., vol. 3, pl. 47, 51.

——, Irish glass (antique). Con. 134: XXVIII Nov '54.

——, Kensington. Holiday 13: 124 Je '53.

fruit bowl with stand, silver-gilt. Con. 134: 132 Nov '54.

fruit cocktail. Holiday 28: 116 (col.) Sept '60.

fruit dish, antique silver. Con. 132: XIII Sept '53.

——, Irish silver. Con. 145: LVIII Je '60.

fruit stand. Amer. heri. vol. 6 no. 4 p. 48 (col.) (Je '55). Brooks: Growth of a nation, p. 290. Natl. geog. 100: 326 Sept '51.

——, silver. Holiday 26: 47 Oct '59.

frustration (sym.). Lehner: Pict. bk. of sym., p. 83.

Fry, Christopher. Cur. biog. p. 213 (1951).

Fry, Franklin Clark. Cur. biog. p. 199 (1946).

Fry, Kenneth D. Cur. biog. p. 222 (1947).

fry basket, deep (electric). Holiday 10: 127 Nov '51, 13 Dec '51.

Frye, Jack. Cur. biog. p. 208 (1945).

Frye, Thomas. Con. 133: 101 Ap '54; 144: 29 Sept '59.
—— (work of). Con. 133: 102 Ap '54.
Frye, William P. (cartoon). Amer. heri. vol. 11 no. 4 p. 77 (Je '60).
frying pan (antique). Holiday 21: 63 (col.) May '57.
Fuchs, Joseph. Cur. biog. p. 146 (1962).
Fuchs, Sir Vivian E. Cur. biog. p. 153 (1958). Natl. geog. 115: 29 (col.) Jan '59, 590 Ap '59.
Fudo (sym.). Lehner: Pict. bk. of sym., p. 49.
Fueger, Heinrich-Friedrich (miniature). Con. 138: 83 Nov '56.
Fugen (sym.). Lehner: Pict. bk. of sym., p. 48.
Fu-hsing school (China). Travel 112: 27-9 Dec '59.
Fujiyama, Aiichiro. Cur. biog. p. 155 (1958).
Fujiyama volcano. Holiday 12: 31 (col.) Aug '52.
  Natl. geog. 97: 620-1 (col.) May '50; 116: 861 (col.) Dec '59; 118: 776 (col.) Dec '60.
Fulani mother & baby (Nigeria). Natl. geog. 116: 238 (col.) Aug '59.
Fulbright, James William. Cur. biog. p. 219 (1943); p. 217 (1955).
"Full moon" (Lippold). Holiday 14: 57 (col.) Nov '53.
Fuller, Alfred C. Cur. biog. p. 159 (1950). Holiday 26: 41 Sept '59.
Fuller, Charles E. Cur. biog. p. 215 (1951).
Fuller, Isaac (work of). Con. 140: 232 Jan '58.
Fuller, John L. Cur. biog. p. 136 (1959).
Fuller, Margaret. Amer. heri. vol. 8 no. 2 p. 23, 98 (Feb '57).
Fuller, Margaret H. Cur. biog. p. 137 (1959).
Fuller, R. Buckminster. Cur. biog. p. 153 (1960).
Fuller, Samuel R., jr. Cur. biog. p. 312 (1941).
Fuller, Walter Deane. Cur. biog. p. 313 (1941).
Fulton, Edmund D. Cur. biog. p. 139 (1959).
Fulton, Robert. Amer. heri. vol. 6 no. 3 p. 44 (col.) (Ap '55).
—— (West). Amer. heri. vol. 10 no. 1 p. 16 (col.) (Dec '58).
"Fulton" steamboat. Amer. heri. vol. 10 no. 6 p. 29 (col.) (Oct '59).
Funchal (Madeira is.). Holiday 28: 63 (col.) Sept '60.
  Natl. geog. 115: 374 (col.) Mar '59.
Fundy, Bay of. See Bay of Fundy.
funeral (King Edward VI). Amer. heri. vol. 6 no. 1 p. 44 (fall '54).
——, Bali. Natl. geog. 99: 4 Jan '51; 116: 812-3 (col.) Dec '59.
——, bird (children). Amer. heri. vol. 8 no. 4 p. 43 (col.) (Je '57).
——, Hindu. See Hindu funeral.
funeral bier. Rawson: Ant. pict. bk., p. 15.
funeral bird (sym.). Lehner: Pict. bk. of sym., p. 27.
funeral ceremony (Nigeria). Natl. geog. 116: 246-7 (col.) Aug '59.
funeral dance. Natl. geog. 109: 434 (col.) Mar '56.
——, Kaleri. Natl. geog. 116: 227 Aug '59.

"Funeral of the poet Panizza" (Grosz). Praeg. pict. ency., p. 482.
funeral procession (ancient Egypt). Int. gr. soc.: Arts . . . p. 41 (col.).
—— (Lebanon). Holiday 20: 56 (col.) Dec '56.
——, Lincoln's. See Lincoln funeral, Abraham.
——, Negro. Holiday 11: 44-5 Mar '52.
funeral pyre. Natl. geog. 117: 395 Mar '60.
—— (Bali). Natl. geog. 108: 370-1 (col.) Sept '55.
  Travel 108: 14 Nov '57.
funerals, Egyptian. See Ships of the dead; tomb furnishings.
funerary steele (Ilissus, 4th cent.). Praeg. pict. ency., p. 86.
funerary steele wave. Praeg. pict. ency., p. 76.
funerary temple. See Thebes ("City of the dead").
funerary vase. See vase, Chinese funerary.
funicular cable car. See cable car.
Funk, Casimir. Cur. biog. p. 211 (1945).
Funk, Charles Earle. Cur. biog. p. 224 (1947).
Funk, Wilfred. Cur. biog. p. 220 (1955).
Funston, Gen. Frederick. Amer. heri. vol. 9 no. 2 p. 24, 29 (col.) (Feb '58).
Funston, George Keith. Cur. biog. p. 218 (1951).
Funston, Keith. Holiday 26: 59 Oct '59.
Fuoss, Robert M. Cur. biog. p. 141 (1959).
Fuqua, Maj. Gen. Stephen O. Cur. biog. p. 221 (1943).
"Fur traders" (Bingham). Praeg. pict. ency., p. 396 (col.).
fur traders (in canoe). Brooks: Growth of a nation, p. 96.
fur trappers. See trappers, fur.
Furcolo, Foster. Cur. biog. p. 155 (1958).
Furey, Warren W. Cur. biog. p. 161 (1950).
Furman, Nathaniel Howell. Cur. biog. p. 220 (1951).
furnace, solar. See solar furnace.
Furnas, Clifford Cook. Cur. biog. p. 194 (1956).
furniture. Holiday 10: 123 (col.) Oct '51, 96 Dec '51; 11: 6, 151 (col.) Ap '52, 71 (col.) Je '52; 12: 125 (col.) Nov '52, 121 Dec '52; 18: 94 Oct '55.
——, antique. Con. (all issues). Holiday 27: 28-9 (col.) Mar '60. Int. gr. soc.: Arts . . . p. 105 (col.). Rawson: Ant. pict. bk., p. 7-17.
——, antique (20th cent.). Holiday 26: 149-54 (col.) Nov '59.
——, Cescinsky. Con. 142: 19-23 Sept '58.
——, dining. Holiday 28: 93-6 (col.) Aug '60.
——, 18th cent. Con. 135: 63-70 Mar '55.
——, English. Con. 136: 78-86 Nov '55.
——, English (antique). Con. 126: 41-8 Aug '50, 91 Oct '50.
——, English (18th cent.). Con. 144: 222-4 Jan '60.
——, French. Con. 140: 23-4 Sept '57; 145: 108-10 Ap '60.
——, iron. Holiday 21: 197 May '57.
——, Italian. Con. 135: 20-8 Mar '55.

——, Italian (18th cent.). Con. ency. of ant., vol. 3, pl. 17-24.

——, lawn. Holiday 11: 168 May '52.

——, modern. Holiday 18: 56-7 (col.) Oct '55; 19: 12-3 (col.) Feb '56; 20: 134-5 Nov '56.

——, modern (room int.). Int. gr. soc.: Arts . . . p. 129 (col.).

——, Norwegian (18th cent.). Con. 145: 22-5 Mar '60.

——, Portuguese. Con. 143: 268-71 Je '59.

——, Portuguese (17th cent.). Con. 143: 195-7 May '59.

——, Rococo. Con. 137: 155-60 May '56.

——, Siamese. Con. 144: 140 (col.) Dec '59.

——, 16th cent. Int. gr. soc.: Arts . . . p. 103 (col.).

——, Stuart (restored). Con. 145: 165-8 May '60.

——, Tudor. Amer. heri. vol. 9 no. 6 p. 23 (Oct '58).

——, upholstered. Holiday 18: 173 Dec '55.

——, Victorian. Con. ency. of ant., vol. 3, pl. 1-8.

——, Viennese (18th cent.). Con. ency. of ant., vol. 3, pl. 17-24.

——, wealthy home (middle ages). Int. gr. soc.: Arts . . . p. 53-4 (col.).

——, The White House. Jensen: The White House.

——. See also name of piece wanted.

furniture ornament (antique). Con. ency. of ant., vol. 1, p. 18-35. 42-7, 59, 63.

furniture ornamental carving. Con. ency. of ant., vol. 1, pl. 3, p. 19-24.

Furse, C. W. (work of). Con. 144: 11 Sept '59.

Furtseva, Ekaterina A. Cur. biog. p. 196 (1956).

Fuseli, Heinrich (work of). Con. 144: 33 Sept '59.

Fuseli, Henry (work of). Con. 143: 93 Ap '59.
Praeg. pict. ency., p. 422.

futility (sym.). Lehner: Pict. bk. of sym., p. 83.

Fyan, Loleta D. Cur. biog. p. 221 (1951).

Fyfe, Sir David Maxwell. Cur. biog. p. 224 (1951).

Fyffe, Joseph P. Travel 106: back cover Sept '56.

Fyleman, Rose. Jun. bk. of auth., p. 134.

Fylfot-Triskele (sym.). Lehner: Pict. bk. of sym., p. 35.

G

Gabbiani, Anton Domenico (work of). Con. 138: 160 Dec '56.

Gabin, Jean. Cur. biog. p. 315 (1941).

Gable, Clark. Cur. biog. p. 213 (1945).

Gabor, Eva. Holiday 10: 64 Dec '51.

Gabor, Zsa Zsa. Holiday 12: 36 Oct '52.

Gabriel (seal of). Lehner: Pict. bk. of sym., p. 24.

Gabrielson, Guy G. Cur. biog. p. 215 (1949).

Gaddi, Agnolo (work of). Con. 126: 173 (col.) Dec '50.

gadrooning, silver (17th cent.). Con. ency. of ant., vol. 1, p. 153.

Gaer, Joseph. Cur. biog. p. 225 (1951).

gaff, mainsail. See mainsail gaff.

Gag, Wanda. Jun. bk. of auth., p. 135.

Gagarin, Yuri. Cur. biog. p. 167 (1961).

"Gailer von Kaiserberg" (Cranach). Con. ency. of ant., vol. 1, pl. 155.

Gaillard, Felix. Cur. biog. p. 157 (1958).

Gainsborough, Thomas. Con. 139: 8 Mar '57. Int. gr. soc.: Arts . . . p. 91 (col.).

—— (work of). Amer. heri. vol. 2 no. 2 inside cover (winter '51).
Con. ency. of ant., vol. 1, pl. 134, 166.
Con. 126: 125, 151 Oct '50; 127: 97 May '51; 132: 113, IX (col.) Nov '53; 133: 114 Ap '54; 134: cover, 111, 137, 142-3 (col.) Nov '54; 135: 5 Mar '55, LVIII, opp. p. 82 (col.) Ap '55, 237, 241, 286 Je 155; 136: 123 Nov '55; 137: 141 Ap '56; 139: cover (col.) Mar '57, 123 Ap '57, 165, 195 May '57, LXI Je '57; 140: 109 Nov '57, 238 Jan '58; 141: 61 Mar '58, 267 Je '58; 142: 39, 52 (col.) Sept '58, LIV, 81 Nov '58, 250 (col.) Jan '59; 143: 8, 67 Ap '59, 206-7, 273 Je '59; 144: III Dec '59, 234, 270 Jan '60; 145: III Ap '60, 162, 179, 193 (col.) May '60, V (col.), 278 Je '60.
Praeg. pict. ency., p. 374 (col.).

Gainza Paz, Alberto. Cur. biog. p. 227 (1951).

Gaither, Frances. Cur. biog. p. 162 (1950).

Gaither, Horace, jr. Cur. biog. p. 209 (1953).

Gaitskell, Hugh. Cur. biog. p. 163 (1950).

galanteries (antique). Con. 143: 137 May '59.

Galapagos is. Natl. geog. 115: 680-703 (part col.) May '59.
Travel 108: 47-9 Dec '57.

—— (map). Natl. geog. 115: 688 May '59.

Galard Terraube, Genevieve de. Cur. biog. p. 295 (1954).

Galata bridge (Istanbul). Natl. geog. 112: 110 Jl '57; 115: 84-5 (col.) Jan '59.

Galatoire's restaurant. Holiday 20: 64 (col.) Oct '56.

galaxies. Natl. geog. 110: 785 Dec '56.

galaxy. Natl. geog. 98: 410 Sept '50.

Galbraith, John Kenneth. Cur. biog. p. 143 (1959).

Galena (Ill., 1856). Amer. heri. vol. 8 no. 1 p. 15 (col.) (Dec '56).

Galilee (sea & valley). Holiday 20: 55 (col.) Dec '56.
Natl. geog. 98: 740 (col.) Dec '50; 102: 837 Dec '52; 114: 856-7 (col.) Dec '58.

—— (beach). Holiday 17: 39 (col.) Feb '55.

Galileo. Holiday 19: 87 Mar '56.

Galla woman (Ethiopia). Natl. geog. 106: 749 (col.) Dec '54.

Gallagher, Buell G. Cur. biog. p. 211 (1953).

Gallagher, William M. Cur. biog. p. 213 (1953).

Gallatin, Albert. Amer. heri. vol. 12 no. 1 p. 28 (col.) (Dec '60).

Gallego, F. (work of). Con. 133: 230 Je '54.

Gallegos, Jose (work of). Con. 133: LX May '54.

Gallegos Freire, Romulo. Cur. biog. p. 235 (1948).

galleon, Spanish. Natl. geog. 105: 537 Ap '54.

gallery, art. See art gallery.

——, palace. Holiday 27: 96-7 (col.) Ap '60.

Gallico, Paul. Cur. biog. p. 201 (1946).

Gallo, Fortune. Cur. biog. p. 216 (1949).

Gallo statue (Antwerp). Travel 103: 36 Ap '55.

Galloway, Col. Irene O. Cur. biog. p. 214 (1953).

Galloway home, Samuel (Colonial). Natl. geog. 105: 456 Ap '54.

Galloway Mazer. *See* Mazer, Galloway.

gallows (man hanging). Rawson: Ant. pict. bk., p. 42.

Gallup, George. Cur. biog. p. 201 (1952).

Galveston (Texas). Travel 103: 23-7 May '55.

Galvin, Robert W. Cur. biog. p. 155 (1960).

Galway (Ireland). Natl. geog. 104: 128 (col.) Jl '53.

Galway fair (Ireland). Natl. geog. 99: 661 May '51.

Gambia (Africa). Travel 107: 53 Jan '57.

Gambia women. Natl. geog. 112: 624-5 (col.) Nov '57.

Gambier, Lord. Amer. heri. vol. 12 no. 1 p. 28 (col.) (Dec '60).

Gamble, John Marshall. Amer. heri. vol. 10 no. 2 cover (col.) (Feb '59).

Gamble, Ralph A. Cur. biog. p. 215 (1953).

Gambling, John B. Cur. biog. p. 165 (1950).

gambling good luck. *See* good luck in gambling (sym.).

gambling room, Las Vegas. *See* Las Vegas (gambling room).

Gambrell, Enoch Smythe. Cur. biog. p. 198 (1956).

game, hornet. *See* hornussen game.

game boards (antique). Con. ency. of ant., vol. 3 pl. 140-3.

"Game of chess" (Lesrel). Con. 134: XVII (col.) Dec '54.

game table. Con. ency. of ant., vol. 3 pl. 144. Con. 142: XXXII Jan '59.

—— (antique). Con. 136: XXXI Sept '55.

——, Louis XVI Con. 145: 268 Je '60.

——, regency. Con. 133: XLIX Je '54; 142: XXI Dec '58 144: XLVII Dec '59.

——, William & Mary. Con. 142: 57 Sept '58.

game table. *See* also card table; poker table.

gamelan (Bali orchestra). Natl. geog. 116: 810 (col.) Dec '59.

games (ancient). Int. gr. soc.: Arts . . . p. 37 (col.).

—— (medieval). Int. gr. soc.: Arts . . . p. 77 (col.).

——, Olympic. *See* Olympic games.

gaming casino. *See* Monaco casino.

Gemma Augustea (stone carving). Praeg. pict. ency., p. 144.

Gamow, George. Cur. biog. p. 229 (1951).

Gandharan Bodhisattva (sculpture). Con. 134: 145 Nov '54.

Gandhi, Indira (Nehru). Cur. biog. p. 144 (1959).

Gandhi, Mohandas. Cur. biog. p. 283 (1942).

Ganges river. Natl. geog. 118: 446-95 (col.) Oct '60.
Travel 106: 12 Nov '56.

—— (bathing ghat). Travel 111: 19 Jan '59.

Gannell, Emma (work of). Amer. heri. vol. 8 no. 1 p. 77 (col.) (Dec '56).

Gannett, Frank E. Cur. biog. p. 215 (1945).

Gannett, Lewis. Cur. biog. p. 316 (1941).

Gannon, Rev. Robert I. Cur. biog. p. 219 (1945).

gantry crane. Natl. geog. 112: 790 (col.) Dec '57.

"Ganymede with eagle of Jupiter". Praeg. pict. ency., p. 392.

Garand, John C. Cur. biog. p. 222 (1945).

Garbett, Archbishop Cyril Forster. Cur. biog. p. 231 (1951).

Garbieri, Lorenzo (work of). Con. 144: 22 Sept '59.

Garbo, Greta. Cur. biog. p. 222 (1955).

Garcia, Carlos P. Cur. biog. p. 199 (1957).

"Garcon Couche" (Cezanne). Con. 142: 124 Nov '58.

garden (200 years old). Natl. geog. 103: 25 (col.) Jan '53.

——, bird refuge. Holiday 11: 58-61 (part col.) Mar '52.

——, flower. Holiday 12: 61 (col.) Sept '52.

——, formal. Holiday 10: 106 Aug '51; 11: 49 (col.) Je '52; 22: 69 (col.) Oct '57; 25: 150 (col.) Mar '59.
Natl. geog. 113: 544-5 (col.) Ap '58; 115: 706-18 (col.) May '59.

——, formal (Baltimore). Natl. geog. 109: 701-8 (col.) May '56.

——, formal (Canada). Natl. geog. 108: 211 (col.) Aug '55.

——, formal (Hampton Court). Natl. geog. 114: 82-3 (col.) Jl '58.

——, formal (Wilmington, Del.). Travel 113: cover (col.) Mar '60.

——, Japanese. Int. gr. soc.: Arts . . . p. 121 (col.).

——, Nishat Bagh (Kashmir, India). *See* Nishat Bagh garden.

——, patio. *See* patio garden.

——, rooftop. Natl. geog. 104: 798 (col.) Dec '53; 111: 480 (col.) Ap '57.

——, Villa Rufolo (concerts). Natl. geog. 116: 499 (col.) Oct '59.

——, window. *See* window garden.

——, wine. *See* wine garden.

garden fruits (goddess). Lehner: Pict. bk. of sym., p. 33.

"Garden of Eden" (Field). Amer. heri. vol. 7 no. 1 p. 56-7 (col.) (Dec '55).

Garden of Gethsemane. Natl. geog. 106: 848 (col.) Dec '54.

garden of Kelvedon Hall (formal). Int. gr. soc.: Arts . . . p. 121 (col.).

"Garden of love" (Rubens). Con. 127: 4 Mar '51.

"Garden of Pontoise" (Pissarro). Con. 142: 193 Dec '58.

"Garden of the Gods" (Colo.). Holiday 12: 34-6, 50-1 (part col.) Sept '52; 16: 47 (col.) Jl '54.
Jordan: Hammond's pict. atlas, p. 165 (col.).
Natl. geog. 106: 220 (col.) Aug '54.

garden ornaments, carved stone. Con. 144: XXVII Jan '60.

garden, palace. *See* Saray-Burnu.

garden plan, formal. Natl. geog. 117: 735 (col.) Je '60.

——, formal (English). Con. 143: 20-2 Mar '59.

——, vegetable. Holiday 23: 142 Mar '58.
garden statuary. *See* statuary, garden.
garden walk & wall. Natl. geog. 103: 797 (col.) Je '53.
gardener (picking flowers). Natl. geog. 115: 711 (col.) May '59.
—— (working flowers). Natl. geog. 114: 82 (col.) Jl '58.
——, flower. Natl. geog. 110: 611 (col.) Nov '56; 112: 468 (col.) Oct '57.
——, flower (head). Natl. geog. 117: 8 (col.) Jan '60.
gardeners. (rain suits, garden spray). Natl. geog. 117: 34 (col.) Jan '60.
gardens, Amer. public. Travel 109: 14-7 Mar '58.
——, Arles formal. Natl. geog. 109: 668-9 (col.) May '56.
——, Boboli. *See* Boboli gardens.
——, Charleston. *See* Charleston gardens.
——, floating. *See* Xochimilco.
——, formal. *See* Hampton Court; McKee jungle gardens; "Mount Vernon" (formal).
——, hanging. *See* hanging gardens.
——, rock. *See* rock gardens.
Gardner, Arthur. Cur. biog. p. 202 (1956).
Gardner, Daniel (work of). Con. 134: 76 Sept '54; 135: XXI Ap '55; 143: 7 Mar '59.
Gardner, Edward F. Cur. biog. p. 223 (1943).
Gardner, Erle Stanley. Cur. biog. p. 224 (1944).
Gardner, George Peabody. Holiday 14: 39 Nov '53.
Gardner, James G. Cur. biog. p. 201 (1956).
Gardner, John W. Cur. biog. p. 204 (1956).
Gardner, Lester D. Cur. biog. p. 226 (1947).
Gardner, Vice-Adm. Matthias B. Cur. biog. p. 203 (1952).
Gardner, Oliver Maxwell. Cur. biog. p. 227 (1947).
gardner (sym.). Lehner: Pict. bk. of sym., p. 90.
Garfield, Pres. James A. Amer. heri. vol. 2 no. 4 p. 15-6 (summer '51); vol. 7 no. 3 p. 32 (Ap '56).
Jensen: The White House, p. 120.
—— (assassination). Jensen: The White House, p. 121, 123.
—— (inauguration). Amer. heri. vol. 7 no. 1 p. 36-7 (col.) (Dec '55).
Garfield, John. Cur. biog. p. 237 (1948).
Garfield, Lucretia (Mrs. James A. Garfield). Jensen: The White House, p. 120.
Garfield's log cabin, J.A. Amer. heri. vol. 7 no. 5 p. 32 (Aug '56).
gargoyle (sym.). Lehner: Pict. bk. of sym., p. 61.
——, Notre Dame. Natl. geog. 101: 800 (col.) Je '52.
Garibaldi monument. Holiday 13: 28 Feb '53.
Garland, Judy. Cur. biog. p. 317 (1941); p. 206 (1952).
garments, to make auspicious (sym.). Lehner: Pict. bk. of sym., p. 68.
Garner, Erroll. Cur. biog. p. 146 (1959).
Garner, John N. (Cactus Jack). Horan: Pict. hist. of wild west, p. 69.

Garneray, Ambroise Louis (work of). Amer. heri. vol. 12 no. 1 p. 48-9 (col.) (Dec '60).
Natl. geog. 99: 189 (col.) Feb '51.
Garreau, Roger. Cur. biog. p. 167 (1950).
Garrett, John W. Amer. heri. vol. 8 no. 2 p. 26-7 (col.) (Feb '57).
Garrett, Pat. Horan: Pict. hist. of wild west, p. 62, 69.
Garrido, Eduardo-Leon (work of). Con. 141: XXVIII Je '58; 144: XLIV Sept '59.
Garrison, Lloyd K. Cur. biog. p. 231 (1947).
Garrison, Mrs. William Lloyd, jr. Holiday 14: 36 Nov '53.
Garrison dam (N.D.). Natl. geog. 100: 315 (col.) Sept '51 .
garrison walls, crusader. Natl. geog. 106: 816-7 (col.) Dec '54.
Garroway, Dave. Cur. biog. p. 208 (1952).
Holiday 10: 52 (col.) Oct '51.
Garson, Greer. Cur. biog. p. 290 (1942).
Holiday 5: 40 (col.) Jan '49.
Garst, Shannon. Cur. biog. p. 232 (1947).
Jun. bk. of auth., p. 137.
Garth, David. Cur. biog. p. 200 (1957).
Gary, Raymond. Cur. biog. p. 224 (1955).
gas jet, outdoor. Natl. geog. 117: 200 (col.) Feb '60.
gas mask. *See* mask, gas.
gas pipe laying (snow). Natl. geog. 114: 175 Aug '58.
gas pipe line. Natl. geog. 100: 549, 554 Oct '51.
gas scrubbers. Natl. geog. 114: 168 (col.) Aug '58.
gas station. Holiday 21: 184 (col.) Je '57.
—— (Buenos Aires). Holiday 11: 107 (col.) Mar '52.
—— (Mexican, comic). Holiday 14: 136 Dec '53.
gas station attendant. Holiday 10: inside cover (col.) Jl '51, 67 (col.) Aug '51, 79 (col.) Sept '51; 11: 29 (col.) May '52.
gas station pumps. Holiday 10: 67 (col.) Aug '51, 79 (col.) Sept '51.
gas station tanks. Holiday 10: inside cover (col.) Jl '51.
gas symbols. Holiday 16: 68 Aug '54.
"Gascoigne family" (Hayman). Con. 141: 274 Je '58.
gasoline carts (Pakistan). Natl. geog. 102: 650 (col.) Nov '52.
gasoline tank. Holiday 14: 132 Oct '53.
——, Iran. Natl. geog. 104: 711 Nov '53.
gasoline tanker. *See* boat, gasoline tanker.
Gaspe (Canada). Jordan: Hammond's pict. atlas, p. 20-1 (col.).
—— (harbor). Holiday 27: 50-1, 54 (col.) Je '60.
—— (lighthouse). *See* lighthouse, Gaspe.
Gasperi, Alcide De. Cur. biog. p. 204 (1946).
Gassel, Lucas (work of). Con. 138: 19 (col.) Sept '56.
Gasser, Herbert S. Cur. biog. p. 224 (1945).
Gassner, John. Cur. biog. p. 234 (1947).
Gast, John (work of). Amer. heri. vol. 9 no. 3 p. 4-5 (col.) (Ap '58).
gastromancy (sym.). Lehner: Pict. bk. of sym., p. 67.

gate, city (Quebec). Holiday 11: 102 (col.) Je
'52; 21: 20 Ap '57.
——, estate fence. Holiday 27: 125 (col.) Feb
'60.
——, field. Rawson: Ant. pict. bk., p. 37.
——, free-wheeling ranch. Natl. geog. 100:
196 (col.) Aug '51.
——, iron entrance. Con. 139: XLIII Ap
'57.
——, iron entrance (to salt mine). Travel 108:
29 Oct '57.
——, iron fence. Travel 103: inside cover Ap
'55.
——, iron grill. See iron grill gate.
——, iron work. Con. 137: XLV Ap '56.
Holiday 5: 52 Mar '49; 7: 60 (col.) May
'50 22: 84 Nov '57.
Natl. geog. 109: 453 (col.) Ap '56.
——, iron work (colonial palace). Natl. geog.
106: 455 (col.) Oct '54.
——, iron work (Harvard univ.). Holiday 18:
34 (col.) Nov '55.
——, medieval (St. Jean Pied de Port, France).
Natl. geog. 109: 326 (col.) Nov '56.
——, moon. See moon gate.
——, noddle pin. Rawson: Ant. pict. bk., p.
38.
——, old farm. Natl. geog. 101: 714 (col.) Je
'52.
——, Seraglio (Turkey). Natl. geog. 100: 154
(col.) Aug '51.
——, Spanish town (Salinas de Leniz). Natl.
geog. 105: 158 (col.) Feb '54.
——, trap. Rawson: Ant. pict. bk., p. 37.
——, walled-town. Natl. geog. 103: 233 Feb
'53.
gate & wall, estate (dog guard). Natl. geog.
114: 208-9 (col.) Aug '58.
"Gate keeper of Hell" (sym.). Lehner: Pict bk.
of sym., p. 49.
"Gate of complete virtue" (China). Natl. geog.
118: 220-1 (col.) Aug '60.
gate post (figures on). Rawson: Ant. pict. bk.,
p. 81.
gate to shrine (China). Natl. geog. 115: 434
Mar '59.
gatehouse. Holiday 6: 39 (col.) Sept '49.
——, Victorian. Amer. heri. vol. 6 no. 6 p.
38 (Oct '55).
gateleg table. See table, gateleg.
Gates, Doris. Jun. bk. of auth., p. 138.
Gates, Gen. Horatio (accepts Gen. Burgoyne's
sword) (Trumbull). Natl. geog. 102: 157
(col.) Aug '52.
Gates, Ralph F. Cur. biog. p. 235 (1947).
Gates, Thomas S. Natl. geog. 115: 590 Ap '59.
Gates, Thomas S., jr. Cur. biog. p. 202 (1957).
Natl. geog. 113: 13 Jan '58.
gates, farm. Rawson: Ant. pict. bk., p. 37-9.
——, city (Harar). Natl. geog. 106: 752 (col.)
Dec '54.
——, mission. Natl .geog. 116: 583 (col.) Nov
'59.
——, mud. See mud gates & wall.
gateway. Con. 140: 75 Nov '57.
——, city. Travel 101: 37 Ap '54.
——, entrance. Con. 145: 73 Ap '60.
——, Great Stupa. See Stupa gateway.
——, Jaipur (India). Travel 106: 12 Nov '56.

——, Madrid (Spain). Natl. geog. 100: 718
(col.) Dec '51.
——, Merida (Yucatan). Travel 103: 42 May
'55.
——, Moorish. Travel 104: cover Nov '55.
——, Moroccan city. Natl. geog. 107: 148
(col.) Feb '55.
Travel 102: 49 Dec '54.
——, rustic western town. Travel 108: 15 Jl
'57.
——, St. Stephen's (entrance to Jerusalem).
Natl. geog. 110: 711 (col.) Dec '56.
——, stone (Italy). Travel 106: inside cover
Aug '56.
——, Univ. of Cal. (entrance). Natl. geog.
110: 213 (col.) Aug '54.
gateway & fence, iron. Holiday 10: 141 Dec
'51.
gateway arch, rock. Travel 102: inside cover
Jl '54.
gateway to Hulne priory. Con. 142: 77 Nov
'58.
gateway to Roman fort (Cologne-Deutz). Con.
138: 234 Jan '57.
Gatling, Richard J. (and his gun). Amer. heri.
vol. 8 no. 6 p. 49 (Oct '57).
Gatti, Attilio. Jun. bk. of auth., p. 139.
Gatti-Casozza (metropolitan statue). Holiday
8: 76 Nov '50.
gaucho (Argentina cowboy). Holiday 12: 106
(col.) Oct '52; 13: 18 May '53; 26: 103
Nov '59.
——— (drinking wine). Natl. geog. 113: 322
Mar '58.
——— (horseback). Holiday 20: 54 (col.) Nov
'56.
——— (silhouettes). Holiday 20: 86-7 Nov '56.
gaucho equipment. Holiday 16: 107 (col.) Sept
'54.
gauchos (horses). Natl. geog. 113: 320-1, 324,
326-7 (col.) Mar '58.
——— (sheep). Natl. geog. 113: 340 (col.) Mar
'58.
Gauguin, Paul (work of). Con. 129: 27 Ap '52;
133: 16 Mar '54; 140: 60 Sept '57, 80 Nov
'57, 195 (col.) Dec '57; 141: 122 Ap '58;
143: 145, 198 May '59, 273 Je '59; 144:
271 Jan '60; 145: LX Ap '60.
Praeg. pict. ency., p. 438 (col.).
Gauguin's grave, Paul. See grave of Paul
Gauguin.
Gaul (warriors, ancient times). Int. gr. soc.:
Arts . . . p. 33 (col.).
Gaulle, Charles de. See de Gaulle, Charles.
gauntlet (sym.). Lehner: Pict. bk. of sym., p.
86.
——, Robert E. Lee's. Amer. heri. vol. 6 no.
3 p. 34 (col.) (Ap '55).
Gauss, Christian. Cur. biog. p. 226 (1945).
Gauss, Clarence E. Cur. biog. p. 318 (1941).
Gautier, Felisa Rincon de. Cur. biog. p. 205
(1956).
gavel (sym.). Lehner: Pict. bk. of sym., p.
94.
Gavin, Maj. Gen. James M. Cur. biog. p. 228
(1945); p. 169 (1961).
Gavin, John. Cur. biog. p. 148 (1962).
Gavrilovic, Stoyan. Cur. biog. p. 206 (1946).
Gay, Arnold C. Holiday 23: 81 Je '58.

Gaylord, E. K. Holiday 7: 116 May '50.
Gaylord, Robert. Cur. biog. p 227 (1944).
Gaynor, Janet. Holiday 10: 112 (col.) Dec '51.
Gaynor, Mitzi. Holiday 27: 131 Je '60.
gazebo (Pass Christian, Miss.). Holiday 6: 102 (col.) Nov '49.
gears (tools). Lehner: Pict. bk. of sym., p. 13.
Geary, John W. Pakula: Cent. album p. 131.
Geddes, Barbara Bel. Cur. biog. p. 239 (1948).
Gedi (Kenya, excavations). Travel 111: 57 Mar '59.
Geest, Wybrand de (work of). Con. 142: 147 Dec '58.
Gehrig, Lou. Holiday 7: 54 May '50.
Gehrmann, Donald Arthur. Cur. biog. p. 210 (1952).
Geiger, Lt. Gen. Roy S. Cur. biog. p. 231 (1945).
geiger counter. Brooks: Growth of a nation, p. 310.
   Natl. geog. 108: 210 (col.) Aug '55.
——, rolling. Natl. geog. 105: 75 Jan '54.
Geis, Bernard. Cur. biog. p. 159 (1960).
Geisel, T. S. (Seuss, Dr., pseud.). Holiday 25: 11 Ap '59.
Geisha dancers. Natl. geog. 117: 668 (col.) May '60.
Geisha girl (Japan). Natl. geog. 100: 741 (col.) Dec '51; 104: 101 Jl '53.
   Travel 113: 46 Jan '60.
—— (tea house). Natl. geog. 107: 285 Feb '55.
Geisha girl. See also costume, Japan (Geisha girl).
"Gelmeroda" (Feininger). Praeg. pict. ency., p. 486 (col.).
gem sorters (men). Natl. geog. 113: 583-5 Ap '58.
gems. Natl. geog. 98: 780-810 (part col.) Dec '50.
gems. See also diamonds.
gendarmes (Rome). Holiday 7: 110 (col.) May '50.
genealogy (born & died, sym.). Lehner: Pict. bk. of sym., p. 12.
"Gen. Doubleday crossing Potomac" (Blythe). Natl. geog. 99: 200 (col.) Feb '51.
Gen. electric plant (int.). Natl. geog. 110: 588-9 (col.) Nov '56.
Gen. Sherman tree (ring of men). Natl. geog. 113: 596, 608 (col.) May '58.
—— (base). Jordan: Hammond's pict. atlas, p. 193 (col.).
"Generall Historie", Smith's. See Smith's "Generall Historie" (page).
generators, electric. See electric generators.
Geneva. See Switzerland (Geneva).
Gengras, Mr. & Mrs. E. C. Holiday 27: 84 Feb '60.
genii (magic). Holiday 6: 97 Oct '49; 20: 84 (col.) Sept '56.
Genin, Sylvester (work of). Amer. heri. vol. 6 no. 2 p. 45 (winter '55).
the Genin family (by Genin). Amer. heri. vol. 6 no. 2 p. 45 (winter '55).
Gentileschi, Orazio (work of). Natl .geog. 110: 640 (col.) Nov '56.

gentlemen. See man.
geography (sym.). Lehner: Pict. bk. of sym., p. 9, 12.
geology (sym.). Lehner: Pict. bk. of sym., p. 12.
geomancer's compass (sym.). Lehner: Pict. bk. of sym., p. 45.
geomantic diagrams, the eight. See diagrams, geomantic.
geomantic hexagons. See the sixty-four geomantic hexagons.
geometry (sym.). Lehner: Pict. bk. of sym., p. 9.
George I, King of Gt. Brit. Amer. heri. vol. 11 no. 4 p. 8 (col.) (Je '60).
George I, King of Greece. Amer. heri. vol. 6 no. 1 p. 46 (fall '54).
George II, King of Gt. Brit. Amer. heri. vol. 11 no. 4 cover, p. 5-6, 8 (col.) (Je '60).
—— (bust, Sotheby). Con. 138: 193 Dec '56.
—— (Shackleton). Con. 135: 239 Je '55.
—— (tapestry). Con. 144: 27 (col.) Sept '59.
George II, King of Greece. Cur. biog. p. 225 (1943).
George III, King. Amer. heri. vol. 8 no. 2 p. 82. (Feb '57).
   Con. 129: 134 Je '52; 132: 148 Jan '54.
—— (Ramsay). Con. 135: 238 Je '55.
— (and family, silhouette). Amer. heri. vol. 11 no. 4 p. 97 (Je '60).
—— (as a boy). Amer. heri. vol. 11 no. 4 p. 11 (col.) (Je '60).
—— (blind). Amer. heri. vol. 11 no. 4 p. 21 (Je '60).
—— (caricature). Con. 141: 33 Mar '58.
—— (cartoon). Amer. heri. vol. 11 no. 4 p. 7, 18-9 (Je '60).
—— (statue). Amer. heri. vol. 9 no. 5 p. 62 (col.) (Aug '58).
—— (awards sword to Lord Howe, 1791). Amer. heri. vol. 11 no. 4 p. 16 (col.) (Je '60).
George III reviews London soldiers. Amer. heri. vol. 11 no. 4 p. 16 (Je '60).
George IV (Lawrence). Con. 140: LV (col.) Nov '57.
——, coronation portrait (Lawrence). Con. 143: 153 May '59.
George V, King. Holiday 22: 64 Nov '57.
George VI, King of Gt. Brit. Cur. biog. p. 294 (1942).
   Holiday 22: 65 Nov '57.
George VI on way to open Festival of Brit. Natl. geog. 100: 716 (col.) Dec '51.
George, David Lloyd. Amer. heri. vol. 9 no. 4 p. 67 (Je '58).
George, Maj. Gen. Harold L. Cur. biog. p. 293 (1942).
George, Walter F. Cur. biog. p. 229 (1943); p. 226 (1955).
   Holiday 15: 60 Feb '54.
George, Zelma W. Cur. biog. p. 172 (1961).
"George & the dragon". Con. 132: 186 Jan '54.
George Washington bridge (N.Y., night). Holiday 25: 108 (col.) Feb '59.
Georges, Elizabeth. Amer. heri. vol. 10 no. 5 p. 25 (col.) (Aug '59).

Georgetown (Wash., D.C.). Holiday 11: 75-8 Ap '52.
Natl. geog. 103: 514-44 (col.) Ap '53.
—— homes. Holiday 7: 94-7 Feb '50.
Georgetown univ. (language room). Natl. geog. 103: 541 (col.) Ap '53.
Georgia. Holiday 19: 34-45 (part col.) Je '56; 21: 25 Ap '57.
Jordan: Hammond's pict. atlas, p. 64-7 (col.).
Natl. geog. 105: 288-330 (part col.) Mar '54.
Travel 104: 14, 17 Sept '55.
—— (islands off shore). Travel 110: 48-51 Nov '58.
—— (map). Natl geog. 105: 290-1 Mar '54.
"Georgia Hall" ("Little White House", Warm Springs, Ga.). Holiday 15: 83 Feb '54.
Georgia state capitol. Holiday 16: 55 Jl '54.
Georgia state college (girls). Natl. geog. 105: 295, 300 (col.) Mar '54.
"Georgiana" (Gainsborough). Con. 140: 109 Nov '57.
"Georgiana & daughter", Duchess of Devonshire (Reynolds). Con. 141: 62 Mar '58.
Gerhard, Hubert (his bronze work). Con. 136: 1 Dec '55.
Gerhardsen, Einar. Cur. biog. p. 221 (1949).
Gericault, J.L.T. (work of). Con. 141: 248 Je '58.
Gericault, Theodore (work of). Con. ency. of ant., vol. 1, pl. 162.
Praeg. pict. ency., p. 384 (col.).
Gerini, Niccolo di Pietro (work of). Con. 136: 201 (col.) Dec '55.
German armour (medieval). Int. gr. soc.: Arts . . . p. 73 (col.).
German church (13th cent.). Int. gr. soc.: Arts . . . p. 47 (col.).
German costume (16th cent.). Int. gr. soc.: Arts . . . p. 113 (col.).
German dancers. Natl. geog. 111: 267 (col.) Feb '57; 115: 754-5 (col.) Je '59.
—— (teen age). Natl. geog. 115: 789 (col.) Je '59.
German girl (fencing). Holiday 13: 60 (col.) Feb '53.
German marine corps (1871). Natl. geog. 116: 756-7 Dec '59.
German people. Holiday 15: 48 Jan '54.
German rococo wood sculpture. Con. 145: 132 Ap '60.
German soldier. See soldiers, German.
German student. Int. gr. soc.: Arts . . . p. 153 (col.).
German woodcut, primitive (15th cent.). Con. 136: 300 Jan '56.
Germanic farmers (ancient times). Int. gr. soc.: Arts . . . p. 31 (col.).
Germanic home (Roman times). Int .gr. soc.: Arts . . . p. 11 (col.).
"Germanicus" (sculpture by della Valle). Con. 141: 224 Je '58.
Germany. Disney: People & places, p. 47-(col.)
Holiday 17: 1 Jan '55; 25: cover, 50-67 (part col.) May '59.
Natl. geog. 111: 773-80 (col.) Je '57.
—— (Baden-Baden). See Baden-Baden.

—— (castles, hotels). Travel 103: 22-4 Ap '55.
—— (farm house). Natl. geog. 108: 136 Jl '55.
—— (map, 1871-1959). Natl. geog. 115: 780 Je '59.
——, west. Natl. geog. 115: 736-90 (part col.) Je '59.
Germany, Cousin Michael. See Cousin Michael.
Gerow, Lt. Gen. Leonard T. Cur. biog. p. 233 (1945).
Gerritsz, Hendrik (work of). Con. 132: 138 Nov '53.
Gershwin, George. Int. gr. soc.: Arts . . . p. 139 (col.).
Gershwin, Ira. Cur. biog. p. 207 (1956).
Gerstacker, Carl A. Cur. biog. p. 174 (1961).
Gerstenmaier, Eugen. Cur. biog. p. 159 (1958).
Gervasi, Frank H. Cur. biog. p. 297 (1942).
Gessi, Francesco (work of). Con. 144: 22 Sept '59.
Gettysburg (Penn.). Holiday 11: 60-1 (col.) Je '52.
—— (Culp's hill). Travel 110: 20 Jl '58.
—— (Gen. Meade's headquarters). See Meade's headquarters, Gen.
—— (Pickett's charge). Amer. heri. vol. 9 no. 1 p. 30 (col.) (Dec '57).
—— (today). Amer. heri. vol. 9 no. 1 p. 49 (col.) (Dec '57).
Gettysburg battlefield. Amer. heri. vol. 2 no. 2 p. 38-9 (col.) (winter '51); vol. 5 no. 2 p. 29-37 (part col.) (winter '53-54).
U.S. News & world report vol. LV no. 1 p. 6-7 Jl '1, 1963.
—— (by Philippoteaux). Amer. heri. vol. 9 no. 1 p. 30 (col.) (Dec '57).
—— (map of). Amer. heri. vol. 9 no. 1 p. 41 (Dec '57).
Gettysburg shrine. Amer. heri. vol. 4 no. 2 back cover (winter '53).
geyser. Holiday 12: 37 Jl '52.
Jordan: Hammond's pict. atlas, p. 137 (col.).
Natl. geog. 100: 610 Nov '51; 110: 773 (col.) Dec '56.
—— (Hawaii). Natl. geog. 118: 36 (col.) Jl '60.
—— ("Old Faithful"). Holiday 21: 39 Mar '57; 22: 5 (col.) Jl '57.
Jordan: Hammond's pict. atlas, p. 137 (col.).
Natl. geog. 113: 591 (col.) May '58; 117: 358-9 (col.) Mar '60.
Ghana (Africa). Travel 108: 18-21 Oct '57.
Ghana god (Africa). Travel 113: 22 Jan '60.
Ghassulian dancers (Palestine). Natl. geog. 112: 834-5 (col.) Dec '57.
ghat, bathing (India). Natl. geog. 118: 492-5 (col.) Oct '60.
Travel 111: 19 Jan '59.
Gheeraerts, Marcus (work of). Amer. heri. vol. 10 no. 4 p. 16-8 (col.) (Je '59).
Con. 132: 37 (col.) Sept '53.
Gheerbrant, Alain. Cur. biog. p. 147 (1959).
Ghent (Belgium). Con. 129: LXIII Je '52.
Holiday 7: 6 Jan '50, 70 Feb '50.
Natl. geog. 113: 815 (col.) Je '58.
Travel 114: 12 Oct '60.
—— (1812). Amer. heri. vol. 12 no. 1 p. 86 (Dec '60).
—— (hotel, 1812). Amer. heri. vol. 12 no. 1 p. 30 (Dec '60).

Gheorghiu-Dej, Gheorghe. Cur. biog. p. 161 (1958).

Ghiberti, Lorenzo (bronze work of). Praeg. pict. ency., p. 298.

—— **(relief by).** Praeg. pict. ency., p. 18.

Ghirlandaio (work of). Con. 139: 101 Ap '57.

Ghirlandajo, Domenico (work of). Con. 134: 223 Dec '54.

Ghislandi, Vittore (work of). Con. 137: 48 Mar '56; 144: 107 Nov '59.

Ghormley, Vice-Adm. Robert L. Cur. biog. p. 299 (1942).

ghost, Halloween Lehner: Pict. bk. of sym., p. 53.

"Ghost of a flea" (Blake). Con. 144: 35 Sept '59.

ghost town. Holiday 22: 110 (col.) Oct '57.

—— **(Buena Park, Cal.).** Travel 106: 29-31 Nov '56.

—— **(gold mine).** Holiday 7: 72-3 Ap '50.

—— **(N.J.).** Travel 104: 54-5 Jl '55.

ghost-town marshal. See marshal, ghost-town

ghost towns. Travel 114: 43-5 Sept '60.

—— . See also Jerome (Ariz.); Rhyolite (Nev.).

Giacometti, Alberto. Cur. biog. p. 209 (1956).

—— **(sculpture).** Holiday 14: 59 Nov '53.

"Giacomo Doria" (Titian). Con. 126: 89 Oct '50.

Giambologna (bronze figure). Con. 143: 215 Je '59.

Gianini, Lawrence M. Cur. biog. p. 169 (1950).

Giannini, Amadeo Peter. Cur. biog. p. 238 (1947.)

giant, Cardiff. See Cardiff giant.

Giant Forest village (Natl. park). Natl. geog. 116: 178-9 (col.) Aug '59.

Giant's causeway. Holiday 27: 127 (col.) Feb '60.

Travel 108: inside cover Oct '57.

Giauque, William F. Cur. biog. p. 170 (1950).

Gibb, Robert (work of). Con. 141: 273 Je '58.

Gibbings, Robert. Natl. geog. 114: 60 Jl '58.

Gibbings, Robert John. Cur. biog. p. 241 (1948).

Gibbon, Edward. Amer. heri. vol. 8 no. 5 p. 27 (Aug '57).

Gibbon, Brig. Gen. John. Amer. heri. vol. 9 no. 1 p. 44 (Dec '57).

Gibbons, Orlando. Cooper: Con. ency. of music, p. 98.

Gibbons' limewood carvings. See Carvings, Grinling Gibbons' limewood.

Gibbs, William Francis. Cur. biog. p. 228 (1944).

Gibb's Hill lighthouse (Bermuda). Natl. geog. 113: 778 (col.) Je '58.

Gibels, Emil G. Cur. biog. p. 213 (1956).

Gibraltar. Holiday 16: 108 Nov '54.

Natl. geog. 112: 50-1 (col.) Jl '57; 113: 791 (col.) Je '58.

Gibson, Althea. Cur. biog. p. 203 (1957).

Gibson, Charles Dana. Amer. heri. vol. 10 no. 4 p. 112 (Je '59).

Gibson, Ernest W. Amer. heri. vol. 1 no. 3 p. 60 (spring '50).

Cur. biog. p. 223 (1949).

Gibson, Hugh. Cur. biog. p. 218 (1953).

Gibson, John W. Cur. biog. p. 240 (1947).

Gibson, Katharine. Jun. bk. of auth., p. 140.

Gibson girl. Amer. heri. vol. 9 no. 1 p. 81-96 (Dec '57).

Gideon on Mt. Gilboa. Natl. geog. 112: 850 (col.) Dec '57.

Gidney, Ray M. Cur. biog. p. 221 (1953).

Giegengack, Augustus E. Cur. biog. p. 231 (1944).

Gielgud, John. Cur. biog. p. 241 (1947).

Gieseking, Walter. Cur. biog. p. 211 (1956). Holiday 21: 42 Mar '57.

Giffith, David Wark. Holiday 5: 36 (col.) Jan '49.

Gifford, Chloe. Cur. biog. p. 149 (1959).

Gifford, Walter S. Cur. biog. p. 235 (1945).

gift wrapped (package). See package (gift wrapped).

gig (sails). Amer heri. vol. 2 no. 3 p. 14-5 (spring '51).

—— , **fish.** Rawson: Ant. pict. bk., p. 75.

Gigante, Giacinto (work of). Con. 140: XXV Dec '57.

Gigli, Beniamino (as Don Jose in Carmen). Cooper: Con. ency. of music, p. 99.

Gilbert, Albert (work of). Cooper: Con. ency. of music, p. 138.

Gilbert, Alfred. Con. 134: 22 Sept '54.

—— **(work of).** Con. 134: 23-6 Sept '54.

Gilbert, Sir. Humphrey. Amer. heri. vol. 10 no. 4 p. 7 (Je '59).

Gilbreth, Frank B. Cur. biog. p. 224 (1949).

Gilbreth, Lillian M. Cur. biog. p. 234 (1951).

Gilch (sym.). Lehner: Pict. bk. of sym., p. 28.

Gilchrist, Huntington. Cur. biog. p. 227 (1949).

Gilchrist, Mrs. Robert Budd. Amer. heri. vol. 9 no. 2 p. 57 (Feb '58).

Gilder, Rosamond. Cur. biog. p. 237 (1945).

Gildersleeve, Virginia C. Cur. biog. p. 319 (1941).

Giles, Lt. Gen. Barney M. Cur. biog. p. 233 (1944).

Giles, Janice Holt. Cur. biog p. 163 (1958).

Gilgamesh epic (clay tablets). Natl. geog. 99: 49-60, 73-104 (col.) Jan '51.

Gill, Eric. Cur. biog. p. 320 (1941).

gill net. See net, gill.

Gillberg, J. A. (work of). Con. 141: 20 Mar '58.

Gilles, Werner (work of). Praeg. pict. ency., p. 481.

Gillespie, Dizzy. Cur. biog. p. 205 (1957).

Gillette, Guy M. Cur. biog. p. 208 (1946).

Gillette castle (Conn.). Travel 108: 35 Aug '57.

Gillis, Rev. James M. Cur. biog. p. 215 (1956).

Gillmore, Quincy Adams. Pakula: Cent. album, p. 131.

Gilray (cartoon by). Amer. heri. vol. 11 no. 4 p. 18-9 (Je '60).

Gilmore, Eddy. Cur. biog. p. 244 (1947).

Gilmore, Voit. Cur. biog. p. 150 (1962).

Gilpin, Sawrey (work of). Con. 145: 145 May '60

Gilruth, Robert R. Cur. biog. (1963).

Gimbel, Bernard. Holiday 22: 148 Dec '57.

Gimbel, Bernard F. Cur. biog. p. 172 (1950).

Gimbel, Sophie. Holiday 26: 63 (col.) Oct '59.

Ginger, Lyman V. Cur. biog. p. 164 (1958).

ginger jar, Chinese porcelain. Con. 133: LVIII May '54; 145: LXIV Je '60.

ginger jars. Natl. geog. 105: 250 (col.) Feb '54.
ginger vase, Charles II silver. Con. 133: VII Mar '54, VII Je '54.
gingerbread man. Holiday 18: 164 Nov '55.
Gingold, Hermione. Cur. biog. p. 165 (1958).
Gingrich, Arnold. Cur. biog. p. 175 (1961).
Ginori, Carlo (bust). Con. 144: 162 Dec '59.
Ginsberg, Harry. Holiday 5: 38 (col.) Jan '49.
Giordani, Francesco. Cur. biog. p. 24 (1957).
Giordano, Luca (work of). Con. 132: 9-10 Sept '53; 136: LXIII Dec '55.
Giorgio, Francesco di. *See* di Giorgio, Francesco.
Giorgione (work of). Praeg. pict. ency., p. 229 (col.).
Giotto (work of). Con. ency. of ant., vol. 1, pl. 149.
Giotto di Bondone (work of). Praeg. pict. ency., p. 228 (col.).
Giovanni, Matteo di (work of). Cooper: Con. ency. of music, p. 430 (col.).
"Giovanni Arnolfini & his wife". *See* "Arnolfini & his wife".
Giovanni da Bologna (sculpture). Praeg. pict. ency., p. 73.
Gipson, Fred. Cur. biog. p. 207 (1957).
Gipson, Lawrence Henry. Cur. biog. p. 297 (1954)
Giral, Jose. Cur. biog. p. 211 (1946).
Giralda (Spain). Natl. geog. 97: 441 (col.) Ap '50.
Giralda bell tower. Natl. geog. 99: 500, 507 (col.) Ap '51.
——tower, cathedral (Seville). Travel 107: 21 Ap '57.
girandole, antique. Con. 133: back cover May '54; 136: 242 Jan '56; 142: VI Dec '58.
——, chippendale. Con. 136: 292 Jan '56.
——, George II. Con. 138: 127 Nov '56.
Giraud, Gen. Henri Honore. Cur. biog. p. 301 (1942).
Giraudoux, Jean (stage setting by). Int. gr. soc.: Arts . . . p. 145 (col.).
girdle, woman's. Holiday 28: 171 Oct '60, 52 Nov '60.
Girdler, Tom M. Cur. biog. p. 235 (1944).
Giresun (Turkey). Natl. geog. 115: 71 (col.) Jan '59.
girette (girl). Natl. geog. 114: 158 (col.) Aug '58.
girl. Amer. heri. vol. 2 no. 3 p. 2 (col.) (spring '51.
   Con. 143: XXI Je '59.
   Holiday 10: 77 (col.) Oct '51; 11: 24 Jan '52, 145 May '52; 13: 137-8, 156 (part col.) May '53, 102-7, 125 (part col.) Je '53; 23: 54 (col.) Jan '58; 24: 137 Jl '58, 5 Aug '58, 149 Oct '58, 37 Nov '58, 191 Dec '58; 25: 77 (col.) Mar '59, 198 Ap '59, 45 (col.) May '59; 26: 113 Aug '59, 134 Sept '59, 156, 179, 187 Oct '59, 158 Nov '59, 41 Dec '59.
   Praeg. pict. ency., p. 403 (col.).
   Travel 103: 31 Mar '55.
——(accordion). Natl. geog. 101: 801 (col.) Je '52.
—— (against lion sculpture). Holiday 27: 62 May '60, 178 Je '60.

—— (airplane hostess). Holiday 23: 129 Mar '58.
—— (ape). Natl. geog. 104: 62, 64-71, 74 Jl '53.
—— (asleep on boat). Holiday 27: 18 (col.) Feb '60, 148 (col.) May '60; 28: 111 (col.) Aug '60.
—— (at desk). Holiday 23: 142 (col.) Feb '58. Natl. geog. 108: 303 (col.) Sept '55.
—— (at table). Natl. geog. 98: 155 (col.) Aug '50;; 103: back cover (col.) Ap '53; 105: 734 (col.) Je '54.
—— (at window). Natl. geog. 97: 280 Mar '50 98: 143 Aug '50.
—— (auto). Holiday 24: 2 (col.), 72 Oct '58; 25: 76 Feb '59; 28: 22 (col.) Aug '60. Travel 108: 44-5 Aug '57.
—— (auto, laughing). Holiday 20: 6 Aug '56.
—— (back view). Holiday 27: 132 Je '60; 28: 9 Nov '60.
   Natl. geog. 97: 463 (col.) Ap '50.
   Travel 104: 41 Sept '55.
—— (back view, bathing suit). Holiday 21: 34 Mar '57.
—— (ballet). Holiday 28: 3 Nov '60.
—— (basket of grapes). Holiday 12: 110 (col.) Oct '52; 25: 34 (col.) Jan '59.
   Natl. geog. 105: 761 (col.) Je '54.
—— (bather, comic). Holiday 23: 154 Feb '58.
—— (bathing beach). Holiday 13: inside back cover (col.) Jan '53.
—— (bathing suit). Holiday 5: 23, 45, 111 (col.) Jan '49, 119 (col.), 124-5, 131 Feb '49, 103 (col.) Mar '49, 19 (col.), 161 Ap '49, 53 (col.), 83, 104, 106-12 (col.) Je '49; 6: 12, 33-4 (col.) Jl '49, 71 (col.) Dec '49; 7: 37-8 (col.), 110-11 Jan '50, 144 May '50, inside cover, 33, 93, 97, 122-32 (part col.) Je '50; 8: cover (col.) Jl '50; 10: 43, 101 Aug '51, 4 Sept '51, 83 Oct '51, 15, 53, 113 (col.) Dec '51; 11: 87 (col.) Feb '52, 79 (col.) Ap '52, 1, 41, 91 (col.) May '52, 106-11 (part col.) Je '52; 12: 91 (col.) Aug '52, 8 Sept '52, 79 Oct '52, 102 (col.) Nov '52, 124 (col.), 170 Dec '52; 13: 6, 69, 80, 126, 136, 146 (part col.) May '53, 103 (col.), 149 Je '53; 14: 12 (col.), 68, 127 Jl '53, 93 Aug '53, 5 (col.) Nov '53, 89 Dec '53; 17: 5-6, 76 (part col.) Jan '55, 16, 49 (col.), 62 Feb '55, 120 Mar '55; 18: 24, 49, 88 (part col.) Jl '55, 12, 64, 72, 110 Aug '55, 77 (col.) Oct '55, 13 (col.) Dec '55; 19: 60 (col.) Jan '56, 98, 121 Mar '56, 68-75 (col.), 96, 113, 163 May '56, 95, 106-11, 143 (part col.) Je '56; 20: 62, 65, 67 (col.) Aug '56, 9 Nov '56, 67 (col.) Dec '56; 21: 13, 55, 101 (col.) Jan '57, 4 (col.), 17 (col.), 87, 122 Feb '57, 100 Mar '57, 178 Ap '57, 23, 41, 109, 133, 164, 171 May '57, 10, 36, 39, 199 (part col.) Je '57; 22: Cover, 95 (col.) Oct '57, 140 (col.) Dec '57; 23: 127 Feb '58, 78-9 (col.), 129 Mar '58, 131, 161 Ap '58, 6, 14, 99, 103, 164, 173, 186 (part col.) May '58, 179 (col.), 182, 194 Je '58; 24: 13 Jl '58, 114, 145 Nov '58, 116, 164, 185 (col.) Dec '58; 25: 108, 134 (col.) Jan '59, 5, 100-1

(col.) Feb '59, 6, 109, 125, 172 Mar '59, 185 Ap '59, 25, 43, 115, 117, 119, 143 (part col.) May '59, 29, 31, 48, 119, 152 (part col.) Je '59; 26: 74 (col.) Jl '59, 22 (col.) Sept '59, 141 Nov '59, 236 Dec '59; 27: 12-3 (col.), 168-9 Jan '60, 167, 173-4 Feb '60, 8, 205 Mar '60, 14, 37, 166, 224 Ap '60, 148-9, 165, 167, 169, 215, 242 (part col.) May '60, 66, 141 (col.), 192 Je '60; 28: 213 Nov '60, 197 Dec '60. Natl. geog. 117: 755 (col.) Je '60; 118: 25 (col.) Jl '60.

girl (bathing suit, beach). Holiday 11: 5, 138 Je '52; 12: 21 (col.) Jl '52, 4 (col.), 82 Oct '52.
—— (bathing suit, boat). Holiday 23: 25, 144 (col.) Feb '58.
—— (bathing suit, extra modern). Holiday 26: 71 (col.) Aug '59.
—— (bathing suit, face covered). Holiday 19: 116 Je '56.
—— (bathing suit, flowers). Holiday 27: 91 (col). Mar '60.
—— (bathing suit, laughing). Holiday 11: 31 Je '52.
—— (bathing suit, old fashioned). Holiday 23: 142 (col.) Je '58.
—— (bathing suit, on float). Holiday 27: 87 (col.) May '60.
—— (bathing suit, seated). Natl. geog. 105: 346 (col.) Mar '54.
—— (bathing suit, swimming pool). Holiday 27: 4 (col.) May '60.
—— (bathing suit, waterfall). Holiday 25: 173 (col.) Ap '59.
—— bathing suit, waving). Holiday 11: 5 (col.) 142 Je '52; 27: 182 Mar '60, 173 Ap '60.
—— (bathing suit, batting ball). Natl. geog. 97: 196 Feb '50.
—— (bathing suit, beach). Holiday 20: 67 (col.) Aug '56, 7 (col.) Nov '56.
—— (bathing suit, beach robe). Holiday 25: 20 (col.). Je '59.
—— (bathing suit, beach, silhouette). Holiday 19: 151 Je '56.
—— (bicycle). Holiday 13: 106 (col.) Je '53; 15: 119 May '54; 28: 32 Aug '60. Natl. geog. 105: 173 (col.) Feb '54.
—— (biology apparatus). Natl. geog. 107: 213 (col.) Feb '55.
—— (blase). Holiday 11: 7 (col.) Feb '52.
—— (blindfolded). Holiday 18: 183 Dec '55.
—— (blindfolded, surprised). Holiday 19: 8 Feb '56.
—— (boat). Natl. geog. 98: 641 (col.) Nov '50.
—— (boat deck chair). Holiday 21: 12 (col.) Jan '57; 27: 141 (col.) Feb '60. Travel 101: 35 May '54; 104: 13 Sept '55.
—— (bowling). Holiday 28: 213 (col.) Dec '60.
—— (brown bear, museum). Natl. geog. 109: 770 (col.) Je '56.
—— (bucking horse). Holiday 19: 88 (col.) Je '56.
—— (buggy). Holiday 23: 70 (col.) Je '58.
—— (bus). Holiday 20: 131 (col.) Dec '56.
—— (bus pillows). Natl. geog. 98: 10 Jl '50.

—— (buying flowers). Holiday 28: 179 Oct '60, 51 Nov '60.
—— (buying jewelry). Natl. geog. 104: 358 (col.) Sept '53.
—— (calf). Amer. heri. vol. 11 no. 1 p. 69. (Dec '59).
—— (carrying canoe). Holiday 18: cover (col.) Aug '55.
—— (carrying child). Natl. geog. 99: 473 (col.) Ap '51.
—— (carrying peat). Natl. geog. 110: 46 (col.) Jl '56.
—— (checks for atomic contamination). Natl geog. 99: 313 Mar '51.
—— (climbing fence). Travel 103: 52 Mar '55.
—— (climbing post). Natl. geog. 101: 135 (col.) Feb '52.
—— (clothes exhibit). Holiday 11: 89-93 (col.) May '52.
—— (cocktail). Holiday 25: 144 (col.) Mar '59.
—— (comic). Holiday 5: 6 Jan '49; 11: 28, 92, 119 Mar '52, 116 Ap '52, 156 May '52; 12: 23, 66, 101, 150 Jl '52.
—— (comic, cupid). Holiday 27: 40 Feb '60.
—— (conch shell). Natl. geog. 108: 503 (col.) Oct '55.
—— (cow). Natl. geog. 111: 145 (col.) Feb '57.
—— (cricket box). Natl. geog. 104: 393 Sept '53.
—— (dancing). Con. 145: 162 May '60. Holiday 10: 22 Jl '51; 11: 1 Jan '52; 13: 18, 20, 107 (col.) Jan '53, 74 Ap '53; 19: 20 (col.) May '56; 22: 153 Nov '57; 25: 133 (col.) Mar '60.
——. See also, dancer; girls (dancing).
—— (desk). Holiday 12: 109 Sept '52.
—— (diving). Holiday 6: 121 Oct '49; 12: 118 Jl '52, 84 Aug '52, 32 (col.) Oct '52, 130 Nov '52, 108 Dec '52; 13: 73 (col.) May '53, 21, 111 Je '53; 19: 19 Feb '56; 21: 11 Ap '57; 23: 184 Ap '58; 25: 57 Mar '59; 26: 16 Jl '59, 14 Sept '59, 133 Nov '59, 51 Dec '59; 28: 81 (col.) Jl '60.
—— (dog). Holiday 6: 82 Sept '49; 11: 96 Mar '52; 13: 130 (col.) Je '53; 25: 75 (col.) Jan '59. Natl. geog. 105: 98-9, 103 (col.) Jan '54; 112: 524 (col.) Oct '57; 116: 595 (col.) Nov '59.
—— (dog jumping fence). Holiday 28: 122 (col.) Aug '60.
—— (dog, pool). Natl. geog. 118: 190 (col.) Aug '60.
—— (dog, snow on hill). Natl. geog. 103: 304 (col.) Mar '53.
—— (donkey). Holiday 24: 135 (col.) Dec '58; 27: 1 May '60.
—— (dress made of packages). Holiday 14: 26 Dec '53.
—— (dressing). Holiday 11: 22 May '52.
—— (eating). Holiday 28: 121 Aug '60.
—— (eating cherries). Natl. geog. 114: 158 (col.) Aug '58.
—— (eels, skate). Natl. geog. 112: 188-9 (col.) Aug '57.

girl (engagement ring). Holiday 22: 150 Nov '57.

girl (evening dress). Holiday 18: 172 (col.) Dec '55; 19: 61 (col.) May '56; 20: 75, 118 Nov '56; 21: 59 (col.) May '57; 22: 129 Dec '57; 25: 85 Feb '59; 26: 97 (col.) Jl '59, 82 (col.) Nov '59; 27: 206 (col.) May '60; 28: 27 (col.) Jl '60.

—— (evening dress, garden). Holiday 11: 56 (col.), 75 Feb '52.

—— (exercising). See exercising (girl).

—— (fashion model). Holiday 25: 20-1 (col.) Jan '59.

—— (fawn). Natl. geog. 99: 497 (col.) Ap '51.

—— (feeding birds). Holiday 19: 4 (col.) May '56.

—— (feeding fish). Holiday 12: 101 Nov '52.

—— (feeding giraffe). Natl. geog. 104: 127 (col.) Jl '53.

—— (feeding lamb). Natl. geog. 104: 530 Oct '53.

—— (feeding llamas). Natl. geog. 113: 311 (col.) Mar '58.

—— (feeding porpoise). Travel 102: cover Jl '54.

—— (feeding swan). Natl. geog. 114: 69 Jl '58.

—— (festival queen). Natl. geog. 103: 543 (col.) Ap '53.

—— (fish). Natl. geog. 97: 70 (col.) Jan '50; 104: 597 (col.) Nov '53.

—— (fishing). Holiday 21: 186 Ap '57; 28: 6 Sept '60.
Travel 111: 17 Feb '59.

—— (flower garden). Holiday 10: 102 (col.) Aug '51.

—— (flowers). Holiday 21: 11 May '57.
Natl. geog. 97: 483, 491 (col.) Ap '50; 100: 319 (col.) Sept '51; 109: 811, 813, 822 (col.) Je '56.
Travel 111: 18 Feb '59.

—— (flowers, desert). Holiday 19: 73 (col.) Feb '56.

—— (flying). Holiday 28: 25 Aug '60, 11 Sept '60, 182 Oct '60.

—— (flying fish). Natl. geog. 105: 395 Mar '54.

—— (flying, harp). Holiday 21: 32 Mar '57.

—— (frozen food). Natl. geog. 99: 319 (col.) Mar '51.

—— (fruit vendor). Amer. heri. vol. 6 no. 4 p. 47 (col.) (Je '55).

—— (fur coat). Holiday 22: inside cover, 143 (col.) Sept '57, 162 (col.) Dec '57; 26: 46 Oct '59.

—— (getting breakfast). Holiday 19: 46 Feb '56.

—— (gloves). Natl. geog. 100: 18 Jl '51.

—— (goat). Natl. geog. 110: 752 (col.) Dec '56.

—— (gold spike, silver hammer). Natl. geog. 110: 219 (col.) Aug '56.

—— (goose). Natl. geog. 99: 310 (col.) Mar '51.

—— (guitar). Holiday 14: 4 (col.) Dec '53; 23: 6 Je '58; 26: 67 (col.) Dec '59.

—— (gull, beach). Natl. geog. 113: 45 (col.) Jan '58.

—— (hammock). Holiday 22: 49 (col.) Jl '57; 24: cover (col.) Nov '58.

—— (handicraft). Natl. geog. 116: 673 Nov '59.

—— (happy). Holiday 18: 41 (col.) Aug '55, 148 Dec '55.

—— (happy, Christmas). Holiday 10: 18 (col.) Dec '51.

—— (harvest field). Natl. geog. 115: 767 (col.) Je '59.

—— (hat on). Praeg. pict. ency., p. 420 (col.).

—— (head). Amer. heri. vol. 2 no. 3 cover (col.) (spring '51); vol. 6 no. 2 p. 57 (col.) (winter '55).
Con. 136: XVIII (col.) Sept '55; 140: LI Sept '57, 142 Nov '57; 142: III Nov '58; 143: cover (col.) Je '59; 145: LX, 127 Ap '60, 188 May '60, L Je '60.
Holiday 10: 112 Oct '51, 14, 86 Nov '51, 87 (col.), 152 Dec '51; 12: 27, 118 (col.) Oct '52, 31, 150 Nov '52; 13: 98 (col.) Jan '53, 127 (col.), 145 Ap '53, 142 Je '53; 14: 62 Aug '53, 19, 107 Sept '53; 18: 111 Aug '55, 123 Sept '55, 120, 135 (col.) Nov '55, 158 Dec '55; 21: 21 (col.) Mar '57, 17 Ap '57, 104 May '57, 159 Je '57; 22: 102 Jl '57, 42 (col.) Sept '57, 41 (col.), 73, 123 Oct '57, 172, 178-9 Nov '57, 222 (col.), 235 (col.), 251 Dec '57; 23: 26, 149 Jan '58, 75, 114 (col.), 154 Feb '58, 71 (col.), 174 Mar '58, 185 Ap '58, 208 Je '58; 24: 130 Jl '58, 51 (col.) Aug '58, 17 Sept '58, 3 Oct '58, 8, 38, 148, 201 Nov '58, 19, 137 Dec '58; 25: 111, 173 Mar '59, 202 May '59, 120, 166 (col.), 183 Je '59; 26: 123, 137 (col.) Jl '59, 2 (col.) Aug '59, cover (col.), 19 Sept '59, 21, 97, 188 Oct '59, 24, 46 (col.), 198 Nov '59, 32, 61, 160 Dec '59; 27: 177 Feb '60, 112, 203 Mar '60, 220 Ap '60, 39, 113 (col.), 117, 141, 238 May '60, 159-60 Je '60; 28: 28 (col.), 128, 151, 156 Dec '60.
Natl. geog. 101: 89 (col.) Jan '52; 103: 124 (col.) Jan '53; 108: 736 (col.) Dec '55; 116: 83 (col.) Jl '59; 117: 326 (col.) Mar '60; 118 23 (col.) Jl '60.
Praeg. pict. ency., p. 271 (col.).
Travel 101: 47 Jan '54; 102: 51 Jl '54, 6 Oct '54; 105: 67 Feb '56, 9 May '56; 111: 4 Jan '59, 4 Mar '59, 6 Ap '59, 6 May '59; 114: 39 Aug '60.

—— (head among flowers). Natl. geog. 103: 606, 620, 622, 634 May '53.

—— (head asleep). Holiday 27: 219 May '60.

—— (head, back view). Natl. geog. 107: 198 (col.) Feb '55.

—— (head, banana tree). Natl. geog. 118: 569 (col.) Oct '60.

—— (head, bathing suit). Holiday 23: 142 (col.) Je '58.

—— (head, bathing, waving). Holiday 28: 222 Dec '60.

—— (head, bird on top). Natl. geog. 111: 790 (col.) Je '57.

—— (head, birds). Natl. geog. 106: 582 (col.) Nov '54.

—— (head, blindfolded). Holiday 21: 8 Mar '57.

—— (head, bonnet). Natl. geog. 114: 673

(col.) Nov '58.

girl (head, calling). Holiday 22: 209 Dec '57.

—— (head, camera). Holiday 28: 186 Oct '60.

—— (head, Christmas). Holiday 22: 122 (col.) Dec '57.

—— (head, cigarette). Holiday 18: 32 Jl '55.

—— (head, combing hair). Holiday 11: 11 Mar '52.

—— (head, comic). Holiday 10: 114 Sept '51, 142 Nov '51; 19: 12 Jan '56, 138 Feb '56; 20: 165 Dec '56; 21: 165 May '57; 24: 140 Nov '58; 26: 78 (col.) Sept '59; 27: 20 (col.) Feb '60, 204 (col.) Ap '60.

—— (head, Easter). Holiday 11: 12 (col.) Ap '52.

—— (head, eating). Holiday 28: 138 Oct '60. Natl. geog. 100: 309 (col.) Sept '51.

—— (head, eyeglasses). Holiday 11: 13 (col.) Je '52; 19: 126 May '56, 124 Je '56; 25: 135 May '59.

—— (head, flowers). Holiday 20: 12 Dec '56. Natl. geog. 108: 329 (col.) Sept '55, 514 (col.) Oct '55.

—— (head, frightened). Holiday 28: 22 Sept '60.

—— (head, fur stole). Holiday 18: 191 Dec '55.

—— (head, hands raised). Holiday 28: 216 Nov '60.

—— (head, hat). Holiday 27: 182 Feb '60, 136, 176 Mar '60, 48, 236 May '60; 28: 101 Sept '60, 106 Oct '60, 207 Nov '60.

—— (head, horse). Holiday 10: 38 (col.) Aug '51.

—— (head, kissing horse). Natl. geog. 106: 720 Nov '54.

—— (head, koala). Holiday 25: 20 Feb '59.

—— (head, laughing). Holiday 10: 81 (col.), 133, 141 (col.) Oct '51, 142 Dec '51; 11: 89 Ap '52, 157 Je '52; 12: 5, 120 Aug '52, cover (col.), 3, 84, 100 Sept '52, 23, 71 (col.) Oct '52, 60 (col.) Nov '52, 184 Dec '52; 18: 3, 30 Jl '55, 8, 58 Aug '55, 6 Sept '55, 118 Nov '55, 148 Dec '55; 19: 3, 18 Feb '56, 26 (col.) Mar '56, 173 May '56; 20: 20 (col.), 97 Oct '56, 9, 177 Nov '56, 120 Dec '56; 21: 138 (col.) Jan '57, 22, 103 (col.) Feb '57, 17, 164 Mar '57, 43 Ap '57, 1, 81, 129 May '57; 22: 88 Jl '57, 45 Oct '57, 134 (col.) Nov '57, 172 (col.), 236 Dec '57; 24: 148 Nov '58, 186 Dec '58; 25: 92, 98, 114 Feb '59, 20, 127 Mar '59, 138 May '59, 33, 174 (col.) Je '59; 26: 121 Oct '59, 49 Nov '59, 16 (col.), 45, 60 (col.) Dec '59; 27: 79 (col.), 160 Jan '60, 33, 41 May '60, 18 (col.), 112 Je '60; 28: 4, 41 Jl '60; 28: 2 (col.) Sept '60. Natl. geog. 108: 813 (col.) Dec '55; 112: 311 (col.) Sept '57; 117: 505 (col.) Ap '60.

—— (head, laughing, flowers). Natl. geog. 117: 209 (col.) Feb '60.

—— (head, lipstick). Holiday 26: 112 Dec '59.

—— (head, lobster). Natl. geog. 112: 311 (col.) Sept '57.

—— (head, long braids). Holiday 19: 69 (col.) May '56.

—— (head, marmot). Natl. geog. 109: 605 (col.) May '56.

—— (head, mask). Holiday 10: 38 (col.) Oct '51; 20: 38 Nov '56, 169 Dec '56 21: 162 Mar '57, 104 Ap '57, 200 May '57.

—— (head, Mexican hat). Holiday 27: 48 May '60.

—— (head, miniature). Con. ency. of ant., vol. 1, pl. 131.

—— (head, opossum). Natl. geog. 109: 438 Mar '56.

—— (head, outline). Holiday 22: 157 (col.) Nov '57.

—— (head, pelican, flower). Natl. geog. 97: 241 Feb '50.

—— (head, pineapple juice). Natl. geog. 118: 22 (col.) Jl '60.

—— (head, powder compact). Holiday 24: 101 Oct '58.

—— (head, profile). Holiday 11: 132 Je '52. Natl. geog. 98: 146, 153 (col.) Aug '50.

—— (head, scarf, kitten). Holiday 20: 137 (col.) Nov '56.

—— (head, sea urchins). Natl. geog. 116: 519 (col.) Oct '59.

—— (head, silhouette). Holiday 22: 81 (col.) Sept '57.

—— (head, skier). Holiday 28: 5 (col.) Dec '60.

—— (head, smiling). Natl. geog. 107: 244 Feb '55.

—— (head, sun glasses). Holiday 22: 236 Dec '57.

—— (head, taking pictures). Holiday 11: 18 Ap '52; 12: 137 (col.) Jl '52; 24: 134 (col.) Nov '58, 11 Dec '58; 25: 29 (col.) Jan '59; 28: 108 Aug '60.

—— (head, telephone). Holiday 19: 138 Jan '58.

—— (head, tower on top). Holiday 25: 210 Ap '59.

—— (head, waving). Holiday 28: 180 Dec '60.

—— (head, windblown). Holiday 21: 97 Ap '57.

—— (helmet on head). Natl. geog. 107: 434 Mar '55.

—— (Holland, Mich., tulip time). Travel 111: 39 Mar '59.

—— (horse). Holiday 8: cover (col.) Sept '50; 13: 117 Je '53; 16: 39 (col.) Oct '54; 24: 100 Oct '58, 1, 157 Nov '58; 26: 77 Oct '59.

—— (horse at ranch). Face of Amer., p. 39 (col.).

—— (horse in stall). Natl. geog. 108: 329 (col.) Sept '55.

—— (horse jumping). Holiday 22: 89 (col.) Jl '57. Natl. geog. 106: 701 (col.) Nov '54.

—— (horse show). Natl. geog. 106: 715 (col.) Nov '54.

—— (horseback). Holiday 10: 114 Oct '51, 98 (col.) Nov '51; 11: 94 Mar '52; 12: 50 Oct '52; 21: 172 (col.) May '57; 23: 85 Mar '58.

—— (in auto). Holiday 18: 59 Sept '55; 25: 121 (col.) Je '59; 26: 101 (col.) Jl '59; 27: 26 (col.) Feb '60, 37 May '60; 28: 12 (col.) Aug '60.

—— (in bed). Holiday 18: 77 (col.) Dec '55;

20: inside cover (col.) Dec '56; 21: 144 (col.) Jan '57, 84 (col.) May '57; 24: inside cover (col.) Sept '58, 172 Nov '58; 27: 182 Mar '60, 20 (col.) Ap '60, 31 (col.) Je '60; 28: 137 (col.) Oct '60. Natl. geog. 98: 242 (col.) Aug '50.

girl (in bed, laughing). Holiday 20: 7 (col.) Aug '56.

—— (in lake). Holiday 13: 38 (col.) Feb '53.

—— (in ocean). Holiday 13: 113 Je '53.

—— (in ship net). Holiday 26: 127 (col.) Sept '59.

—— (in tree). Holiday 26: 34 (col.) Nov '59.

—— (Indian with mask). Natl. geog. 104: 842 (col.) Dec '53.

—— (jacket). Holiday 10: 82 Oct '51; 12: 38 Dec '52.

—— (kissing prize winner man). Natl. geog. 114: 99 (col.) Jl '58.

—— (kitten). Amer. heri. vol. 6 no. 1 p. 27 (col.) (fall '54).

—— (kneeling at confession). Holiday 19: 33 Jan '56.

—— (koala bear). Holiday 24: 133 Oct '58, 167 Dec '58.

—— (ladder). Holiday 21: 40 Ap '57; 25: 164 Ap '59.

—— (ladder, painting). Holiday 25: 143 May '59; 27: 8 Mar '60.

—— (ladder, tree). Natl. geog. 114: 158 (col.) Aug '58.

—— (laughing). Holiday 10: cover (col.), 3 Jl '51, 43 Aug '51, 71 (col.) Oct '51, 47 (col.), 58 Nov '51, 18 (col.), 53 (col.) Dec '51; 11: 47 (col.) Feb '52; 18: 90 (col.) Aug '55, 4 (col.), 105 Oct '55, 62, 151 Nov '55, 111 Dec '55; 19: 127 (col.), 128 Jan '56, 58 (col.) Feb '56; 20: 2 (col.) Sept '56. Natl. geog. 104: 842 (col.) Dec '53; 112: 729 (col.) Dec '57; 113: 138 Jan '58.

—— (laughing, lamb). Holiday 18: 134 (col.) Dec '55.

—— (leading dog). Holiday 24: 74 (col.) Oct '58.

—— (library table). Natl. geog. 97: 304 (col.) Mar '50.

—— (lying on grass). Holiday 27: 143 (col.) Je '60.

—— (lying on rug). Holiday 19: 83 (col.) Je '56.

—— (maid dressing). Holiday 27: 127 Ap '60.

—— (mail box). Travel 111: 58 Jan '59.

—— (making batik). Holiday 18: 106 (col.) Sept '55.

—— (making salad)). Holiday 19: 96 (col.) Je '56.

—— (megaphone). Holiday 10: 87 Jl '51.

—— (melting hot). Holiday 10: 25 Jl '51.

—— (Mexican shirt & pants). Holiday 18: 30 Jl '55.

—— (miniature). Holiday 24: 108 Oct '58.

—— (money table). Natl. geog. 100: 132 Jl '51.

—— (mounting horse, comic). Holiday 10: 58 Jl '51.

—— (mowing lawn). Holiday 25: 172 Ap '59.

—— (mud flat). Natl. geog. 112: 157 (col.) Aug '57.

—— (nightdress & lamp). Holiday 27: 179 (col.) May '60.

—— (old loom). Natl. geog. 113: 651 (col.) May '58.

—— (on camel). Natl. geog. 107: 496 (col.) Ap '55.

—— (on couch). Holiday 24: 96 Aug '58; 26: 78 (col.) Jl '59; 27: 115 Ap '60.

—— (on couch, book, candy). Holiday 10: 71 Dec '51.

—— (on ship). Holiday 23: 145 (col.) Feb '58.

—— (operating foot water pump). Natl. geog. 111: 331 (col.) Mar '57.

—— (ostrich). Holiday 19: 10 (col.) Feb '56.

—— (painting Indian symbols). Natl. geog. 109: 220 (col.) Feb '56.

—— (painting picture). Holiday 10: 41 (col.) Aug '51; 19: 94 (col.) May '56. Natl. geog. 106: 704 (col.) Nov '54.

—— (painting, sand dunes). Natl. geog. 108: 524 (col.) Oct '55.

—— (painting wall). Holiday 21: 155 May '57.

—— (palsy victim). Travel 113: 65 Jan '60.

—— (park bench). Holiday 28: 82 (col.) Aug '60, inside cover (col.) Sept '60.

—— (parka). Holiday 19: 168 May '56.

—— (party dress). Holiday 18: 79 (col.) Nov '55; 24: 199 Dec '58; 25: 91 (col.) May '59; 26: 82 (col.), 92 Nov '59.

—— (pastry table). Natl. geog. 99: 768 (col.) Je '51.

—— (perfume shop). Natl. geog. 100: 163 (col.) Aug '51.

—— (perfume spray). Holiday 28: 178-9 Nov '60.

—— (photographers, comic). Holiday 10: 171 Dec '51.

—— (picking blueberries). Natl. geog. 107: 792 (col.) Je '55.

—— (picking breadfruit). Natl. geog. 105: 358 (col.) Mar '54.

—— (picking dates). Natl. geog. 104: 367 (col.) Sept '53.

—— (picking oranges). Holiday 14: 5 (col.) Nov '53. Travel 114: 29 Oct '60.

—— (picking tobacco). Natl. geog. 113: 827 (col.) Je '58.

—— (pigeons). Holiday 23: 116 (col.) Mar '60.

—— (play suit). Holiday 23: 144 Jan '58.

—— (playing clarinet). Holiday 12: 113 Jl '52.

—— (playing organ). Holiday 21: 105 May '57; 24: 51 Dec '58.

—— (playing piano). Amer. heri. vol. 5 no. 3 cover (col.) (spring '54). Holiday 25: 60 (col.) Feb '59. Natl. geog. 104: 125 (col.) Jl '53.

—— (playing records). Natl. geog. 97: 291 (col.) Mar '50.

—— (playing Siamese instrument). Disney: People & places, p. 173 (col.).

—— (playing with cat). Holiday 14: 1 Sept '53.

girl (playing with cricket). Natl. geog. 104: 389 Sept '53.

—— (posing for daguerreotoype). Natl. geog. 106: 427 Sept '54.

—— (pouring cocktail). Holiday 25: 28 (col.) Je '59; 26: 186 Dec '59.

—— (pouring drinks). Holiday 21: 43 (col.) Je '57; 23: 176 (col.) May '58.

—— (primitive dress). Holiday 21: 20 (col.) Ap '57.

—— (prize steer). Travel 114: 33 Aug '60.

—— (puppies). Holiday 28: 119 (col.) Aug '60.

—— (puppy). Holiday 26: cover (col.) Aug '59.

—— (raincoat). Holiday 22: 176 Nov '57.

—— (reading). Natl. geog. 97: 305, 310 (col.) Mar '50.

—— (reading, canal). Natl. geog. 117: 428 (col.) Mar '60.

—— (reading travel maps). Natl. geog. 108: 129 Jl '55.

—— (relaxing, parasol). Holiday 19: 60 (col.) May '56.

—— (riding boat boom). Natl. geog. 108: 558 Oct '55.

—— (riding donkey). Holiday 25: 31 (col.) Feb '59.

—— (riding elephant). Natl. geog. 103: 780 (col.) Je '53.

—— (riding horse, silhouette). Holiday 14: 11 Sept '53.

—— (riding rhinoceros). Natl. geog. 103: 781 (col.) Je '53.

—— (river). Natl. geog. 113: 837 (col.) Je '58.

—— (river in gorge). Natl. geog. 102: 586 (col.) Nov '52.

—— (rocky beach). Natl. geog. 101: 385 (col.) Mar '52.

—— (row boat). Con. 142: 258 Jan '59.

—— (rubber worker). Natl. geog. 102: 300 (col.) Sept '52.

—— (rug maker). Natl. geog. 114: 37 (col.) Jl '58.

—— (running). Holiday 21: cover (col.) Je '57.

—— (running, comic). Holiday 20: 61 (col.) Aug '56.

—— (running, silhouette). Holiday 13: 8 Je '53; 14: 11 Sept '53.

—— (Scottish tam). Natl. geog. 108: 202 (col.) Aug '55.

—— (seated). Holiday 14: 166 Dec '53; 18: 66 Aug '55, 27 Oct '55, 16 Nov '55; 20: 103 (col.) Sept '56; 21: 74 (col.) Mar '57; 23: 30, 76 Jan '58, cover (col.) Feb '58; 24: 49, 67 (col.) Nov '58; 25: 76 (col.), 165 Mar '59, 150, 184 Je '59; 26: 76-9 (col.) Jl '59, 151 Oct '59, 83 (col.) Nov '59, 24 Dec '59; 27: 105 Feb '60, 116 May '60; 28: 3 Jl '60. Natl. geog. 108: 796 Dec '55. Praeg. pict. ency., p. 485 (col.).

—— (seated back view). Travel 107: 17 Je '57.

—— (seated, back view, dog). Natl. geog. 97: 578 (col.) May '50.

—— (seated, dog). Holiday 28: 167 (col.) Dec '60.

—— (seated, hillside). Holiday 12: 112 Oct '52.

—— (seated, laughing). Holiday 10: 1 (col.) Sept '51.

—— (seated on balcony). Natl. geog. 103: 151 (col.) Feb '53.

—— (seated on floor). Holiday 10: 79 Aug '51; 18: 16 Nov '55, 6 Dec '55; 19: 175 Mar '56; 20: 200 Dec '56; 28: 24, 162 Dec '60.

—— (seated on grass). Natl. geog. 103: 542 (col.) Ap '53.

—— (seated on grass, back view). Natl. geog. 107: 206 (col.) Feb '55.

—— (seated on grass, dog). Natl. geog. 118: 787 (col.) Dec '60.

—— (seated on rock). Natl. geog. 98: 175 (col.) Aug '50.

—— (seated on rock wall). Holiday 18: 164 (col.) Dec '55. Natl. geog. 109: 838 (col.) Je '56.

—— (seated on stone wall). Natl. geog. 100: 35 (col.) Jl '51.

—— (seated on table, sea shore). Natl. geog. 113: 765 (col.) Je '58.

—— (seated, wicker chair). Holiday 28: 200 (col.) Nov '60.

—— (seated, winter coat). Holiday 18: 187 Dec '55.

—— (setting clock). Amer. heri. vol. 1 no. 4 p. 32 (summer '50).

—— (sewing). Con. 140: 117 (col.) Nov '57. Natl. geog. 111: 104 (col.) Jan '57.

—— (sewing table). Natl. geog. 99: 116 Jan '51.

—— (ship deck, windblown). Holiday 11: 5 (col.) May '52, 152 (col.) Je '52; 12: 64 (col.) Jl '52.

—— (shooting arrow). Holiday 19: 5 (col.) Mar '56.

—— (shopping, Rio). Natl. geog. 107: 318 Mar '55.

—— (shot from cannon). Durant: Pict. hist. of Amer. circus, p. 139 (col.).

—— (shuffleboard). Holiday 11: 147 Je '52.

—— (silkworm gut "wigs"). Natl. geog. 100: 101 (col.) Jl '51.

—— (skating). Holiday 10: 68 Dec '51; 11: 44 (col.) Jan '52; 13: 73 (col.) May '53; 14: 143 Jl '53; 25: 7 (col.) May '59; 27: 142 May '60. Travel 113: 39 Jan '60.

—— (sketching picture). Holiday 24: 106 (col.) Dec '58.

—— (ski lift). Travel 113: 21 Je '60.

—— (ski suit). Holiday 14: 26 (col.) Nov '53.

—— (skier). Hoilday 28: 91 (col.) Dec '60.

—— (skiing). Holiday 23: 19 Jan '58.

—— (snow). Amer. heri. vol. 7 no. 1 p. 19 (Dec '55).

—— (sorting apples). Natl. geog. 102: 592 Nov '52.

—— (southern costume). Holiday 13: 23 Feb '53.

—— (sport clothes). Holiday 10: 1 (col.) Sept

'51; 11: 90-1 (col.) May '52, 85 Je '52; 22: 134 Sept '57, 22-3 Oct '57.

girl (stage coach). Natl. geog. 110: 219 (col.) Aug '56.

—— (step on ship). Holiday 18: 20 (col.) Oct '55.

—— (sun bathing). Holiday 18: 171 Dec '55; 24: 137 Jl '58; 26: 38, 102 (col.) Dec '59; 28: 101 (col.) Jl '60, 46-9, 69 (part col.) Aug '60.

—— (sun glasses). Holiday 11: 90 (col.) May '52; 25: 33 (col.), 173 Je '59; 26: 71 (col.) Aug '59.

—— (sun suit). Holiday 13: 139 Ap '53, 88 (col.) May '53.

—— (sunbath in tub). Holiday 27: 117 (col.) Je '60.

—— (surfboard). Holiday 8: 114 Sept '50; 19: 133 (col.) May '56; 28: inside cover (col.) Aug '60.

—— (sweater). Holiday 24: 194, 198 Nov '58; 26: 49 Nov '59.

—— (swimmer seated). Travel 108: 60 Jl '57.

—— (swimming). Holiday 12: 108 (col.) Jl '52; 14: 90 (col.) 117 Aug '53; 18: 84 (col.) Aug '55; 23: 14 Feb '58; 25: 9 May '59; 26: 41 Nov '59, 103 (col.), 173 Dec '59; 27: 153 Jan '60, 161 Ap '60; 28: 81 (col.) Jl '60, 193 (col.) Nov '60.

—— (swing). Amer. heri. vol. 8 no. 5 p. 52 (Aug '57).

—— (swinging on moon). Holiday 6: 18 (col.) Dec '49.

—— (swinging on rope). Holiday 18: 146 Dec '55.

—— (taking picture). Holiday 13: 75 (col.) Feb '53; 14: 133 (col.) Oct '53; 19: 93 (col.) Je '56; 23: 5 (col.) Jan '58; 24: inside cover (col.) Aug '58; 26: 85 (col.) Jl '59, 213 Dec '59; 27: 132 Jan '60; 28: 22, 56 Dec '60.
Natl. geog. 106: 429 Sept '54; 115: 53 (col.) Jan '59.
Travel 110: 39 Sept '58.

—— (tea table). Natl. geog. 98: 179 (col.) Aug '50.

—— (teaches orangutan). Natl. geog. 103: 785 (col.) Je '53.

—— (telephone operator). Holiday 5: 57 (col.) Jan '49.

—— (tennis). Natl. geog. 97: 65 (col.) Jan '50.

—— (tobacco patch). Natl. geog. 107: 409 (col.) Mar '55.

—— (toe dancing). Holiday 26: 18 Aug '59.

—— (tower on head). Holiday 25: 111 Jan '59.

—— (traveling). Holiday 10: 153 (col.) Dec '51; 11: 89 (col.), 148-9, 151, 153 May '52, 69 (col.) Je '52; 14: 10 (col.) Aug '53; 19: 152 (col.) Mar '56, 135 Je '56; 22: 162 (col.) Dec '57; 23: 38 (col.) Je '58; 26: 10, 31 (col.) Sept '59, 63, 152, 171, 223 (col.) Dec '59; 28: 13 (col.) Sept '60, 144 (col.) Dec '60.

—— (tumbling). Travel 110: 60 Nov '58.

—— (Turkish bazaar). Natl. geog. 100: 159 (col.) Aug '51.

—— (umbrella). Holiday 26: 244 Dec '59.

—— (underclothes). Holiday 24: 22 Jl '58; 27: 181 Feb '60.

—— (underclothes, flying). Holiday 27: 168 Mar '60.

—— (Valentine). Holiday 21: 95 (col.) Feb '57.

—— (viperfish). Natl. geog. 104: 580 (col.) Nov '53.

—— (wading). Natl. geog. 115: 453 (col.) Ap '59.

—— (walking). Holiday 19: 88 (col.) Je '56; 28: 17 Sept '60.

—— (water skiing). Holiday 20: 113 Nov '56; 23: 28 (col.) May '58; 25: 187 (col.) Mar '59; 27: 151 Ap '60.
Travel 113: 42 May '60.

—— (waterfall). Holiday 25: 23 (col.) Mar '59.
Natl. geog. 99: 491 (col.) Ap '51.

—— (waving). Holiday 13: 129 Ap '53, 101, 146, 150 May '53, 82 Je '53.

—— (wearing jodhpur). Holiday 25: 182 Mar '59.

—— (wearing leotards). Holiday 27: 81 May '60.

—— (wearing pants). Holiday 26: 13 (col.) Sept '59; 27: 110 (col.), 142 May '60.

—— (wearing shorts). Holiday 11: 147 (col.) May '52, 47 (col.), 84 Je '52; 18: 62 Nov '55; 19: 163 Mar '56, 71, 73-5 (col.) May '56, 75 Je '56; 22: 134 Sept '57, 7 (col.) Dec '57.
Natl. geog. 98: 572 (col.) Nov '50; 118: 176 (col.) Aug '60.
Travel 104: 33 Jl '55.

—— (wearing shorts, back view). Natl. geog. 98: 152 (col.) Aug '50.

—— (wearing shorts, seated). Holiday 10: 99 (col.) Nov '51.

—— (wearing shorts, seated on ground). Natl. geog. 116: 173 (col.) Aug '59.

—— (wearing slacks). Holiday 11: 85 Je '52; 12: 91 (col.) Sept '52, 66 (col.) Oct '52; 27: 110 (col.) May '60.
Natl. geog. 99: 686 (col.) May '51.

—— (weaving tapestry). Natl. geog. 98: 354 (col.) Sept '50.

—— (wicker chair). Holiday 18: 41 Oct '55.

—— (wind blown). Holiday 22: 194 (col.) Dec '57.

—— (winter hood). Holiday 26: 225 (col.) Dec '59.

——(wolf, comic). Holiday 26: 137 (col.) Dec '59.

—— (wood on back). Natl. geog. 102: 541 (col.) Oct '52.

—— (wrapped in bath towel). Holiday 12: 96 Sept '52.

—— (writing). Holiday 21: 201 Ap '57, 191 Je '57.

girl, Andalusian (on burro). Natl. geog. 113: 417 (col.) Mar '58.

——, Argentina. Holiday 12: 110 (col.) Oct '52.

——, Attersee (head). Natl. geog. 118: 249 (col.) Aug '60.

——, Austria. Natl. geog. 99: 777 (col.) Je '51.

girl, Bali (weaving). Natl. geog. 99: 13 (col.) Jan '51.
——, Breton (head, France). Natl. geog. 117: 732 (col.) Je '60.
——, Cabaclo (Peru). Disney: People & places, p. 109 (col.).
——, Cairo (head). Natl. geog. 118: 353 (col.) Sept '60.
——, Cambodia. Natl. geog. 99: 467 (col.) Ap '51.
——, Campfire. See Campfire girl.
——, Ceylon (dancer). Holiday 27: 120 Je '60.
——, China. Holiday 26: 133 (col.) Sept '59.
——, China (basket on back). Travel 112: 17 Dec '59.
——, Colonial. Holiday 17: 104, 118 Feb '55; 23: 3 Feb '58; 26: 91 (col.) Jl '59.
——, Costa Rica. Holiday 20: 184 Dec '56.
——, Crete (weaving). Holiday 18: 39 (col.) Aug '55.
——, Cuba (poor, seated). Holiday 19: 95 (col.) Jan '56.
——, Dutch. Holiday 10: 74 (col.) Sept '51.
——, Dutch (head). Travel 106: 33 Sept '56.
——, Dyak (North Borneo). Natl. geog. 116: 785 (col.) Dec '59.
——, East Caroline island. Holiday 28: 89 (col.) Oct '60.
——, 1847. Amer. heri. vol. 10 no. 2 back cover (col.) (Feb '59).
——, 1860. Amer. heri. vol. 9 no. 3 p. 52 (col.) (Ap '58).
——, Fiji. Travel 111: 31 Mar '59.
——, Fiji (breadfruit). Natl. geog. 114: 538 (col.) Oct '58.
——, Finland (bathing). Holiday 22: 108-9 Dec '57.
——, Formosa (bicycle). Natl. geog. 97: 148 (col.) Feb '50.
——, Galapagos (backview). Natl. geog. 115: 683 (col.) May '59.
——, Gibson. See Gibson girl.
——, Greece. Natl. geog. 109: 47 Jan '56.
——, Greece (backview). Natl. geog. 103: 385 (col.) Mar '53.
——, Hawaii. See Hawaiian girl.
——, Hindu. Natl. geog. 107: 415 (col.) Mar '55.
——, Holland. See girl, Dutch.
——, India. Holiday 13: 102-3 (col.) Jan '53.
——, India (dancer). Holiday 27: 28 (col.) May '60.
——, Indian (head, laughing). Natl. geog. 116: 635 Nov '59.
——, Iraq. Natl. geog. 115: 57 (col.) Jan '59.
——, Iraq (head). Natl. geog. 114: 462 (col.) Oct '58.
——, Ireland. Holiday 19: 39 (col.) Jan '56.
——, Ireland (riding attire). Natl. geog. 104: 124 (col.) Jl '53.
——, Ischia. Natl. geog. 105: 545 (col.) Ap '54.
——, Italy. Labande: Naples, p. 182.
——, Japan. See Japanese girl.
——, Kazakh (dancing). Natl. geog. 106: 634 (col.) Nov '54.

——, Kazakh (on horse). Natl. geog. 106: 627 Nov '54.
——, Khmer (baby). Natl. geog. 117: 564 (col.) Ap '60.
——, Ladakh (head). Natl. geog. 99: 616 (col.) May '51.
——, little (laughing). Travel 113: 57 Feb '60.
——, Mardi Gras queen. Holiday 23: 83, 87 (col.) Mar '58.
——, Mexican. Natl. geog. 107: 220 (col.) Feb '55.
——, "Miss America" of 1960. Natl. geog. 118: 708 (col.) Nov '60.
——, "Miss America queen". Holiday 12: 94-5 (col.) Aug '52.
——, "Miss U.S.". Holiday 11: 86 (col.) May '52.
——, Naga (dancer, India). Natl. geog. 107: 255 (col.) Feb '55.
——, Navajo Indian (seated). Natl. geog. 114: 846 (col.) Dec '58.
——, Nepal (Cinnamon leaves on back). Natl. geog. 117: 380 (col.) Mar '60.
——, Nepal (jar on head). Natl. geog. 97: 38 (col.) Jan '50.
——, New Zealand (heads). Holiday 24: 144 Nov '58.
——, Polynesia. Natl. geog. 97: 89 (col.) Jan '50.
——, Portugal (head). Natl. geog. 118: 647 (col.) Nov '60.
——, Puerto Rico (dancing). Holiday 28: 105 Jl '60, 107 Oct '60, 220 Dec '60.
——, Russia (head laughing). Natl. geog. 116: 388 (col.) Sept '59.
——, Samoan. See Samoan girl.
——, Scandinavia. Holiday 10: 27 (col.) Dec '51; 17: 22 Feb '55, 78 Mar '55; 25: 14 Jan '59.
——, Scandinavia (head). Holiday 25: 159 Mar '59.
——, 17th cent. Con. 132: 67 Sept '53.
——, Sicily (seated). Natl. geog. 107: 29 (col.) Jan '55.
——, Spain (dancing). Holiday 10: 14 Oct '51.
——, Spain (head). Natl. geog. 118: 638 (col.) Nov '60.
——, Spain (on balcony). Natl. geog. 97: 447 (col.) Ap '50.
——, Switzerland. Holiday 25: 42 Mar '59; 28: 38 (col.) Aug '60.
——, Switzerland (dog cart). Natl. geog. 114: 569 (col.) Oct '58.
——, Tahiti. Holiday 22: 116 Jl '57; 27: 60 Ap '60; 28: 69 (col.) Oct '60. Natl. geog. 112: 729, 753 (col.) Dec '57. Travel 114: 37 Dec '60.
——, Ternate island (dancer). Natl. geog. 99: 332 Mar '51.
——, Thrace (head). Natl. geog. 109: 62 (col.) Jan '56.
——, Tibet. Natl. geog. 102: 217 Aug '52.
——, Tibet (man on Yak). Natl. geog. 108: 46 Jl '55.
——, West Indies (dancing). Holiday 13: 18 Jan '53.
——, western. Holiday 27: 142 May '60.

girl, western (head). Natl. geog. 111: 678 (col.) May '57.
Travel 102: 51 Nov '54.

——, western (head, eating). Natl. geog. 106: 301 (col.) Sept '54.

——, western (head, horse). Holiday 14: back cover (col.) Aug '53.

——, western (head, laughing). Holiday 21: 129 Je '57.

——, western (horse). Natl. geog. 100: 309 (col.) Sept '51.

——, western (horse, man). Natl. geog. 113: 622 (col.) May '58.

——, western (horseback). Holiday 12: 67 Jl '52, 36 Sept '52.

——, western (horses). Holiday 10: 33 Dec '51.

——, western (seated). Travel 103: cover Je '55.

girl & boy. See boy & girl.

girl & mule. Holiday 7: 30 Je '50.

girl & Swiss guard. Holiday 14: 7 (col.) Aug '53.

"Girl at a house door" (Rembrandt). Con. ency. of ant., vol. 1, pl. 164.

"Girl at window" (Halle). Con. 145: XLV Ap '60.

girl campers. See campers, girl.

girl dancing (wood carving). Amer. heri. vol. 12 no. 1 frontis (col.) (Dec '60).

"Girl feeding chickens" (Boucher). Con. 134: cover (col.) Sept '54.

girl graduate. See graduate, girl.

"Girl I left behind me" (early Amer. play). Amer. heri. vol. 7 no. 1 p. 33 (col.) (Dec '55).

girl of the Via Appia. Ceram: March of arch., p. 2.

"Girl peeling vegetables" (Chardin). Praeg. pict. ency., p. 359 (col.).

Girl Scout. Natl. geog. 102: 146 Aug '52.

——, Ireland (salutes). Natl. geog. 100: 613 (col.) Nov '51.

Girl Scouts, Canton island (flags). Natl. geog. 107: 128 (col.) Jan '55.

"Girl with a cardboard dog" (Kuhn). Amer. heri. vol. 7 no. 1 cover (col.) (Dec '55).

"Girl with a lute" (Melzi). Con. 127: 40 Mar '51.

"Girl with a mandoline" (Braque). Con. 144: 41 Sept '59.

"Girl with a parrot" (Courbet). Con. 144: 263 (col.) Jan '60.

"Girl with Scotch terrier" (Opie). Con. 142: cover (col.) Jan '59.

"Girl with watering can" (Renoir). Holiday 7: 106 (col.) Feb '50.

girls. Face of Amer., p. 52 (col.).
Holiday 14: 12 (col.) Nov '53; 27: 90-5 (col.), 121, 177 Feb '60; 28: 17, 72, 110 (col.), 136-7 Sept '60, 1 Nov '60.

—— (archery). Holiday 8: 53 (col.) Dec '50. Natl. geog. 106: 229 (col.) Aug '54. Travel 104: 65 Aug '55.

—— (art gallery). Natl. geog. 105: 788 (col.) Je '54.

—— (at carved doors). Natl. geog. 108: 323 (col.) Sept '55.

—— (at Eleusis, Greece). Natl. geog. 109: 53 (col.) Jan '56.

—— (at fence). Natl. geog. 97: 305 (col.) Mar '50.

—— (at lunch table). Natl. geog. 103: 14 (col.) Jan '53, 331 (col.) Mar '53.

—— (at mirror, 18th cent.). Natl. geog. 97: 565 (col.) May '50.

—— (at well). Travel 112: 40 Sept '59.

—— (Austria festival). Natl. geog. 115: 208-11 (col.) Feb '59.

—— (back view). Natl. geog. 107: 643 (col.) May '55.

—— (backview, autumn walk). Natl. geog. 99: 602 (col.) May '51.

—— (back view, harbor). Natl. geog. 104: 832 (col.) Dec '53.

—— (back view, mts.). Natl. geog. 100: 628 (col.) Nov '51.

—— (back view, river). Natl. geog. 108: 546 (col.) Oct '55.

—— (ballet dancers). See ballet dancers (girls).

—— (baseball players). Natl. geog. 99: 293 (col.) Mar '51.

—— (bathing suits). Holiday 8: 98 (col.) Sept '50, 38 (col.) Nov '50, 120 (col.) Dec '50; 14: 108-9 (col.) Jl '53; 21: 28 (col.) Jan '57; 99: 308, 323 (col.) Mar '51. Travel 102: 50 Aug '54.

—— (bathing suits, beach). Holiday 23: 92-3 (col.) Jan '58.

—— (bathing suits, boat). Natl. geog. 118: 690 (col.) Nov '60.

—— (bathing suits, "bunny ears"). Holiday 28: 83 (col.) Dec '60.

—— (bathing suits, contest). Holiday 12: 15 Sept '52.

—— (bathing suits, deck chairs). Holiday 14: 66 Jl '53.

—— (bathing suits, in ocean). Holiday 25: 31 (col.) Ap '59.

—— (bathing suits, in water). Holiday 10: 1 Nov '51; 11: 95 (col.) Ap '52; 12: 115 (col.) Aug '52.

—— (bathing suits, walking). Natl. geog. 97: 68 (col.) Jan '50.

—— (beach). Holiday 13: 76 (col.), 172 May '53, 103 (col.) Je '53; 18: 77 (col.) Oct '55, 27 Nov '55.
Natl. geog. 101: 365 Mar '52; 116: 614 (col.) Nov '59.

—— (beach, back view). Natl. geog. 101: 441 (col.) Ap '52.

—— (beauty contest). See beauty contest.

—— (beside pool). Natl. geog. 97: 561 (col.) May '50.

—— (bicycle tour). Travel 107: 21 May '57.

—— (bicycles). Holiday 8: 31 (col.) Nov '50; 11: 47 (col.) Je '52; 12: 27 Sept '52.
Natl. geog. 108: 810 (col.) Dec '55.

—— (bicycles, back view). Natl. geog. 115: 770 (col.) Je '59.

—— (bunches of dates). Natl. geog. 98: 6 Jl '50.

—— (bunk beds). Natl. geog. 107: 766 (col.) Je '55.

—— (Canadian police in chapel). Natl. geog. 108: 213 (col.) Aug '55.

girls (canoe). Holiday 11: 65 Ap '52.
Natl. geog. 98: 92 (col.) Jl '50.

—— (chairs, shipboard). Holiday 12: 91 (col.)
Dec '52.

—— ("Clooty well"). Natl. geog. 110: 12
(col.) Jl '56.

—— (clothes display). Holiday 22: 90-1 (col.)
Oct '57.

—— (clothes exhibit). Holiday 12: 102-7 (part
col.) Jl '52.

—— (Colonial dresses). Natl. geog. 100: 596
(col.) Nov '51.

—— (comic musicians). Holiday 26: 1 Nov
'59.

—— (corsets). Holiday 28: 166 Dec '60.

—— (costumes, back view). Natl. geog. 97:
206 (col.) Feb '50.

—— (crowns). Holiday 10: 69 (col.) Sept '51.

—— (curling stone game). Natl. geog. 104:
845 (col.) Dec '53.

—— (dance step). Holiday 12: 149 Dec '52.

—— (dancers). Natl. geog. 106: 366 (col.)
Sept '54.

—— (dancing). Holiday 27: 155 Jan '60, 141
May '60.

—— (dancing, Near East). Natl. geog. 107:
730 May '55.

—— (dancing, torchlight). Holiday 28: 81 Nov
'60.

—— (debutantes. Holiday 24: 62-7 (part
(col.) Nov '58.

—— (digging clams). Natl. geog. 107: 798 Je
'55.

—— (diving horses). Natl. geog. 117: 41
(col.) Jan '60.

—— (dog stunts). Natl. geog. 99: 830 Je '51.

—— (double bicycles). Holiday 26: 99 (col.)
Nov '59.

—— (drawing). Natl. geog. 97: 487 (col.) Ap
'50.

—— (embroidering). Natl. geog. 100: 407
(col.) Sept '51.

—— (evening dress). Holiday 20: 97 (col.)
Dec '56.

—— (exercising). Holiday 10: 101, 111 Dec
'51.

—— (fancy dress parade). Natl. geog. 99: 321
(col.) Mar '51.

—— (fashions). Holiday 23: 28-9 (col.) Jan
'58.

—— (feeding lamb). Natl. geog. 103: 828
(col.) Je '53.

—— (fire prevention sign). Natl. geog. 110:
307 (col.) Sept '56.

—— (fishing). Natl. geog. 105: 220 (col.) Feb
'54.

—— (fishing in boat). Travel 102: 19 Dec
'54.

—— (flower baskets). Natl. geog. 97: 308
(col.) Mar '50.

—— (frost covered trees). Natl. geog. 104:
835 (col.) Dec '53.

—— (gold panning). Natl. geog. 105: 762
(col.) Je '54.

—— (gathering grapes). Holiday 13: 120
(col.) Mar '53.

—— (grape vines). Natl. geog. 104: 816 (col.)
Dec '53.

—— (Greenfield lake, azaleas). Natl. geog.
113: 24 (col.) Jan '58.

—— (grooming prize cow). Natl. geog. 100:
298 (col.) Sept '51.

—— (hayfield). Holiday 22: 7 (col.) Dec '57.

—— (heads). Amer. heri. vol. 9 no. 1 p. 96
(Dec '57).
Con. 144: LXI (col.) Dec '59.
Natl. geog. 110: 625 Nov '56.
Travel 112: 6 Jl '59, 4 Aug '59, 6 Sept '59.

—— (heads at door). Natl. geog. 105: 432
(col.) Ap '54.

—— (heads, back view). Natl. geog. 107: 324
(col.) Mar '55.

—— (heads, group). Natl. geog. 100: 595
(col.) Nov '51.

—— (heads, horses). Natl. geog. 100 626
(col.) Nov '51.

—— (heads, outline). Travel 102: 5 Dec '54;
103: 6 Jan '55, 4 May '55, 6 Je '55; 104: 4
Jl '55, 4 Aug '55, 67 Oct '55; 105: 6 Feb '56,
8 Mar '56, 4 Ap '56, 4 May '56; 106: 4 Ap
'56, 4 Aug '56, 4 Sept '56, 4 Oct '56, 6 Nov
'56, 6 Dec '56; 107: 6 Jan '57, 4 Feb '57, 6
Mar '57, 4 Ap '57, 6 May '57, 4 Je '57; 108:
4 Jl '57, 4 Aug '57, 4 Oct '57, 4 Nov '57, 4
Dec '57; 109: 12 Jan '58, 6 Feb '58, 12 Mar
'58, 12 Ap '58, 12 Je '58; 110: 4 Jl '58, 4
Aug '58, 4 Sept '58, 4 Oct '58, 4 Nov '58;
112: 10 Dec '59; 113: 6 Jan '60, 6, 9, 57 Feb
'60, 4 Mar '60, 6 Ap '60, 4 May '60, 6 Je
'60; 114: 6 Jl '60, 6 Sept '60, 8 Dec '60.

—— (heads, singing). Holiday 25: 138 Feb
'59.

—— (hikers). Natl. geog. 100: 314 (col.) Sept
'50.

—— (hockey team). Holiday 7: 51 Ap '50; 7:
65 May '50.

—— (holding horse heads). Holiday 18: 110
(col.) Nov '55.

—— (in line, back view). Natl. geog. 99: 304
(col.) Mar '51.

—— (lace makers). Natl. geog. 100: 383 Sept
'51; 116: 492 Oct '59.

—— (lake side). Natl. geog. 109: 540 (col.)
Ap '56.

—— (large fish). Natl. geog. 99: 325 (col.) Mar
'51.

—— (lorikeets). Natl. geog. 110: 513 (col.)
Oct '56.

—— (lunch boxes). Natl. geog. 110: 194 (col.)
Aug '56.

—— (macaws). Natl. geog. 98: 592 (col.) Nov
'50.

—— (meat packing). Natl. geog. 104: 809
(col.) Dec '53.

—— (mountains). Natl. geog. 97: 719 (col.)
Je '50.

—— (office desk). Natl. geog. 111: 179 (col.)
Feb '57.

—— (old bonnets). Natl. geog. 108: 521 (col.)
Oct '55.

—— (on anchor). Travel 104: 33 Sept '55.

—— (on balcony). Holiday 25: 73, 91 (col.)
Mar '59; 27: 181 (col.) Mar '60.
Natl. geog. 103: 154-5 (col.) Feb '53; 105:
329 Mar '54.

—— (on rock wall, harbor). Natl. geog. 109:
880 Je '56.

girls (on roof garden). Natl. geog. 104: 798 (col.) Dec '53.

—— (on sailboat). Natl. geog. 112: 325 (col.) Sept '57.

—— (on scooter). Travel 110: 51 Nov '58.

girls (paint sarongs). Natl. geog. 103: 216 (col.) Feb '53.

—— (pick berries). Natl. geog. 110: 802 (col.) Dec '56.

—— (picnic, hay stacks). Natl. geog. 109: 523 (col.) Ap '56.

—— (picnic lunch). Holiday 26: 76 (col.) Aug '59.

Natl. geog. 105: 848 (col.) Je '54.

—— (playing hockey). Holiday 7: 65 (col.) May '50.

—— (playing shuffleboard). Holiday 8: 113 (col.) Oct '50.

—— (reading book). Natl. geog. 107: 458 (col.) Ap '55.

—— (reading, dog). Natl. geog. 99: 827 Je '51.

—— (reading travel maps). Natl. geog. 108: 129 Jl '55.

—— (riding horses). Holiday 6: 103 (col.) Aug '49; 8: 30 Oct '50.

Travel 103: 20 May '55.

—— (Roman princesses). Holiday 27: 94-100 (col.) Ap '60.

—— (rose exhibit). Natl. geog. 107: 470 (col.) Ap '55.

—— (rowing boat). Jordan: Hammond's pict. atlas, p. 95 (col.).

—— (San Lorenzo). Natl. geog. 102: 546 (col.) Oct '52.

—— (sand dunes). Travel 102: 53 Aug '54.

—— (Scotch highland dancers). See Scotch dancers.

—— (seated). Amer. heri. vol. 8 no. 3 p. 60 (Ap '57).

Jordan: Hammond's pict. atlas, p. 85 (col.). Natl. geog. 100: 6 Jl '51.

—— (seated, bathing suits). Natl. geog. 107: 69-79 (col.) Jan '55.

—— (seated in circle). Holiday 26: 13 (col.) Sept '59; 27: 180 (col.). Ap '60.

—— (seated on ground). Natl. geog. 105: 292 Mar '54.

—— (seated on ground, back view). Natl. geog. 103: 26 (col.) Jan '53; 104: 815 Dec '53.

—— (Shakespeare's mother's home). Natl. geog. 108: 306 (col.) Sept '55.

—— (shipboard, waving). Holiday 11: 31 Je '52.

—— (ship deck chairs). Holiday 18: 69 (col.) Nov '55.

—— (show, night club). Holiday 10: 49 (col.), 50 Sept '51.

—— (show on Coney island). Amer. heri. vol. 9 no. 4 p. 15, 93 (Je '58).

—— (show on TV). Holiday 24: 128 Nov '58.

—— (singing). Travel 108: 31 Dec '57.

—— (ski lift). Travel 111: 17 Je '59.

—— (sport clothes). Holiday 10: 100-1 Jl '51; 21: 142 (col.) May '57.

—— (strip tease). See strip tease girls.

—— (swimming pool). Holiday 27: 57 Mar '60.

—— (table, laughing). Holiday 22: 51 Sept '57.

—— (tea table). Holiday 21: 87 (col.) Jan '57.

—— (tea table. Algiers). Natl. geog. 117: 774 (col.) Je '60

—— (telephone exchange). Natl. geog. 106: 112 (col.) Jl '54.

—— (tennis). Holiday 26: 30 (col.) Sept '59.

—— (traveling, laughing). Holiday 22: 53 (col.) Sept '57.

—— (volleyball). Natl. geog. 107: 386 (col.) Mar '55.

—— (walking). Natl. geog. 103: 528 (col.) Ap '53; 107: 321 (col.) Mar '55.

—— (walking, back view). Natl. geog. 100: 34 (col.) Jl '51.

—— (watching West Point cadets). Natl. geog. 101: 602 (col.) May '52.

—— (waving). Holiday 11: 134 Ap '52; 12: 85 Aug '52.

—— (winter coats). Holiday 10: 17 Oct '51, 117 Nov '51, 146 Dec '51; 11: 24 (col.) Mar '52.

—— (youth hostel trip). Natl. geog. 101: 690 May '52.

girls, Acadian. Jordan: Hammond's pict. atlas, p. 85 (col.).

——, Angamis, India (heads). Natl. geog. 107: 258 (col.) Feb '55.

——, Bali (procession, fruit bearers to temple). Holiday 18: 56 (col.) Jl '55.

——, Bavaria (dancing). Holiday 10: 16-7 Oct '51.

——, Brazil (Indian debutante). Natl. geog. 116: 636 (col.) Nov '59.

——, Cairo (dancing). Natl. geog. 107: 730 May '55.

——, Canary islands (sewing). Natl. geog. 107: 519 (col.) Ap '55.

——, Caribbean (church ceremony). Holiday 24: 131 (col.) Nov '58.

——, China. Amer. heri. vol. 1 no. 2 p. 18 (winter '50).

Natl. geog. 103: 685 (col.) May '53; 105: 250, 253, 256, 264 (part col.) Feb '54; 110: 185 (col.) Aug '56.

——, China (pestle playing). Natl. geog. 111: 349 (col.) Mar '57.

——, chorus (dancing). Holiday 10: 95 Oct '51.

——, college. Holiday 22: 51-3 (part col.) Sept '57.

Natl. geog. 112: 410 (col.) Sept '57.

——, college (1894). Amer. heri. vol. 11 no. 6 p. 107 (Oct '60).

——, college (William & Mary college). Natl. geog. 111: 604 (col.) May '57.

——, college (Smith). Natl. geog. 97: 303 (col.) Mar '50.

——, college (studying). Natl. geog. 112: 415 (col.) Sept '57.

——, college (vacation, campfire). Natl. geog. 116: 156-7 Aug '59.

——, college (Vassar). Natl. geog. 110: 583 (col.) Nov '56.

——, college (Wis.). Natl. geog. 111: 143 (col.) Feb '57.

girls, Colonial. Holiday 25: 156 Feb '59. Travel 103: 16 May '55.

——, Crete. Natl. geog. 104: 701 (col.) Nov '53.

——, Dibai (Trucial coast). Natl. geog. 110: 88 (col.) Jl '56.

——, Dutch. Natl. geog. 106: 396 (col.) Sept '54.

——, England. Natl. geog. 108: 315 (col.) Sept '55.

——, England (dancing). Natl. geog. 98: 195 (col.) Aug '50.

——, Formosa (at plane). Natl. geog. 97: 149 (col.) Feb '50.

——, Hawaii. See Hawaiian girls.

——, Indochina. Natl. geog. 99: 471 (col.) Ap '51; 102: 295, 321 (col.) Sept '52.

——, Ireland (donkey). Natl. geog. 99: 678 May '51.

——, Ireland (folk dance). Holiday 23: 54 (col.) Je '58.

——, Japan (bowing & dancing). Natl. geog. 118: 739, 774 (col.) Dec '60.

——, Japan (fagots on head). Natl. geog. 97: 617 (col.) May '50.

——, Japan (fashion book). Natl. geog. 97: 615 May '50.

——, Japan (pick tea leaves). Natl. geog. 97: 619 (col.) May '50.

——, Japan (Wash., D.C.). Natl. geog. 111: 86 (col.) Jan '57.

——, Java (dancers). Natl. geog. 108: 353 (col.) Sept '55.

——, Java (working). Natl. geog. 108: 367 (col.) Sept '55.

——, Korea (embroidering). Natl. geog. 97: 791 Je '50.

——, Lisbon (fish trays on heads). Natl. geog. 108: 747 (col.) Dec '55.

——, Majorca (back view). Natl. geog. 111: 636-7 (col.) May '57.

——, Malaya (thresh rice). Natl. geog. 103: 218 (col.) Feb '53.

——, Maori (greeting). Holiday 25: 33 May '59.

——, Martinique. Natl. geog. 115: 262-3 (col.) Feb '59.

——, Mexico (on balcony). Natl. geog. 107: 231 (col.) Feb '55.

——, Mexico (sort tomatoes). Natl. geog. 107: 241 (col.) Feb '55.

——, Mexico (Tarascan). Natl. geog. 102: 544 (col.) Oct '52.

——, Moorish. Natl. geog. 107: 187 Feb '55.

——, Moorish (seated). Natl. geog. 112: 72 (col.) Jl '57.

——, Navajo Indian. See Indian girls, Navajo.

——, Nepal. Natl. geog. 112: 143 (col.) Jl '57.

——, New Guinea (jungle). Natl. geog. 99: 355 (col.) Mar '51.

——, New Zealand (heads). Holiday 24: 144 Nov '58.

——, Nigeria (pan of fruit on head). Natl. geog. 110: 359 (col.) Sept '56.

——, Norway. Natl. geog. 100: 714 (col.) Dec '51.

——, Norway (in boat). Natl. geog. 111: 97 (col.) Jan '57.

——, Pakistan. Natl. geog. 107: 403 (col.) Mar '55.

——, Portugal. Natl. geog. 106: 692, 694 (col.) Nov '54.

——, Portugal (casks on heads). Natl. geog. 118: 625 Nov '60.

——, Portugal (picking grapes). Disney: People & places, p. 63 (col.).

——, Puerto Rico. Natl. geog. 109: 356 (col.) Mar '56.

——, Puerto Rico (Good Friday). Natl. geog. 99: 457 (col.) Ap '51.

——, Roman police. Holiday 11: 38 (col.) Ap '52.

——, Rose queen. Natl. geog. 105: 301 (col.) Mar '54.

——, Russia (park bench). Natl. geog. 116: 402 (col.) Sept '59.

——, Russia (peasants). Holiday 18: 104 Jl '55.

——, Russia (playing). Natl. geog. 116: 352-3 (col.) Sept '59.

——, school. Natl. geog. 106: 213 (col.) Aug '54; 112: 450 (col.) Oct '57.

——, school (England). Natl. geog. 108: 308 (col.) Sept '55.

——, Scotland (dancing). Holiday 13: 131 (col.) Ap '53. Natl. geog. 110: 2-3, 36 (col.) Jl '56.

——, Sicily (wash wheat straw). Natl. geog. 107: 41 (col.) Jan '55.

——, society. Holiday 26: 99-103 (part col.) Dec '59.

——, Spain (dancing). Natl. geog. 97: 445-6 (col.) Ap '50.

——, Spain (study silkworm). Natl. geog. 100: 103 (col.) Jl '51.

——, strip-tease. Holiday 10: 105 (col.) Oct '51.

——, Switzerland (dance). Natl. geog. 111: 170-1 (col.) Feb '57.

——, Tahiti (dancing). Holiday 28: 76 (col.) Nov '60.

——, Turkey (dancing). Holiday 28: 25 Aug '60.

——, Viet Nam. Natl. geog. 102: 295 (col.), 314 Sept '52.

girls. See also boy & girl; man & girl; woman & girl.

girls dancing. See also dancer (girl); dancing, girls.

Girtin, Thomas (work of). Con. ency. of ant., vol. 1, pl. 141. Con. 145: 64 Mar '60.

Gish, Dorothy. Cur. biog. p. 240 (1944).

Gish, Lillian. Cur. biog. p. 239 (1944).

Gitlin, Irv. Holiday 21: 97 Jan '57.

gittern, 14th cent. Con. 129: 112 Je '52.

Giusti, George (work of). Holiday 25: cover (col.) Ap '59; 27: cover (col.) Ap '60; 28: cover (col.) Oct '60.

Givenchy, Hubert de. Cur. biog. p. 228 (1955).

Givens, Willard E. Cur. biog. p. 242 (1948).

giving (sym.). Lehner: Pict. bk. of sym., p. 47.

Giza pyramid. See pyramid of Giza.

glacier. Holiday 11: 55 (col.) May '52. Natl. geog. 100: 476-7 (col.) Oct '51; 101: 134 Jan '52, 457 (col.) Ap '52; 102: 199 Aug '52; 111: 535, 539 (part col.) Ap '57;

113: 346-7 (col.) Mar '58; 117: 481 (col.) Ap '60, 756 (col.) Je '60.

glacier (Alaska). Natl. geog. 116: 69 (col.) Jl '59.

—— **(Arctic).** Natl. geog. 107: 553 Ap '55.

—— **(Canada).** Natl. geog. 116: 546 (col.). Oct '59.

—— **(Chile).** Natl. geog. 108: 759-60 (col.) Dec '55.

—— **(Sierra Nevada).** Natl. geog. 105: 854 Je '54.

—— **(South Georgia).** Natl. geog. 107: 98 Jan '55.

—— **(Wis.).** Amer. heri. vol. 11 no. 3 p. 40-5 (Ap '60).

——, **blue (man).** Natl. geog. 108: 120 (col.) Jl '55.

——, **Knik.** Natl. geog. 99: 835 Je '51.

——, **Mendenhall.** Natl. geog. 109: 742 Je '56.

——, **Pasterzen.** Natl. geog. 99: 762 (col.) Je '51.

——, **Tasman.** See Tasman glacier.

glacier climbers. Natl. geog. 104: 103-14 Jl '53.

Glacier hotel (Mont.). Holiday 11: 10 (col.) Ap '52.

glacier lounge. See Cocktail lounge, glacier.

Glacier Natl. Park. Holiday 8: 38-43 (col.) Sept '60.
Natl. geog. 109: 590-636 (part col.) May '56.
Travel 104: 7 Sept '55; 113: cover (col.), 22-5 May '60.

—— **(goats).** Natl. geog. 113: 634 (col.) May '58.

—— **(hotel).** Holiday 25: 175 Mar '59; 27: 105 Feb '60.

"Glacier of the angel" (Jasper Park). Travel 103: 9 Je '55.

Galcier park. Holiday 13: 126 (col.) Ap '53.

—— **(St. Mary Lake).** Natl. geog. 97: 721 (col.) Je '50.

glacier skating rink. See skating rink, glacier.

Glacierland. See U.S.-Canadian border (Glacierland).

Gladden, Washington. Amer. heri. vol. 6 no. 3 p. 77 (Ap '55).

gladiatorial theater, Roman. Natl. geog. 98: 713 Dec '50.

gladiators (Rome). Durant. Pict. hist. of Amer. circus, p. 6.

gladiators & wild animals (Roman arena). Int. gr. soc.: Arts . . . p. 35 (col.).

Gladston, William. Holiday 19: 87 Mar '56.

Gladwin, Henry. Amer. heri. vol. 2 no. 4 p. 37 (summer '51).

glaive (16th cent. sword). Con. ency. of ant., vol. 1, pl. 109.

Glamis castle (entrance). Holiday 27: 71 (col.) May '60.

—— **(int.).** Holiday 21: 136 (col.) Ap '57.

glands, human. Gray's anatomy, p. 1328-38.

Glaoui, Thami el-Mezouari. Cur. biog. p. 299 (1954).

Glaser, Donald A. Cur. biog. p. 177 (1961).

Glasgow shipyards (Scotland). Holiday 8: 35 (col.) Dec '50.

Glass, Carter. Cur. biog. p. 321 (1941).

Glass, George. Holiday 5: 42 (col.) Jan '49.

glass. Holiday 13: 132 Mar '53; 23: 30 Feb '58, 97 Mar '58, 123 Ap '58, 17 May '58.

—— **(blackberries).** Holiday 24: 37 (col.) Dec '58; 25: 41 (col.) May '59.

—— **(fruit filled).** Holiday 24: 83 (col.) Jl '58.

—— **(raspberries).** Holiday 27: 8 (col.) Feb '60.

—— **(sym.).** Lehner: Pict. bk. of sym., p. 72.

——, **ale.** Holiday 27: 157 (col.) Mar '60.

——, **Amer. (antique).** Con. 135: 171-2 May '55.

——, **antique.** Con. 136: XL Sept '55; 138: 43 Sept '56.
Rawson: Ant. pict. bk., p. 84.

——, **Beilby.** Con. 127: 106-11 May '51.

——, **Bristol privateer.** Con. 142: XLVI Jan '59.

——, **cocktail.** See cocktail glasses.

glass. See also tumbler.

——, **Corning.** See Corning glass.

——, **18th cent.** Con. 135: XXXVII May '55.

——, **English (antique).** Con. ency. of ant., vol. 1, p. 76-83.

——, **French stained (13th cent.).** Con. 140: cover (col.) Dec '57.

——, **Hallarenglas.** Con. 142: 67 Sept '58.

——, **Hanoverian.** Con. 135: LIV Ap '55.

——, **Jacobite.** Con. 134: L Sept '54, XVI Nov '54.

——, **Jacobite drinking.** Con. 142: 127 Nov '58.

——, **Jacobite portrait.** Con. 134: XXXII Dec '54.

——, **"The luck of Edenhall".** Con. 143: 34-5 (col.) Mar '59.

——, **mint julep.** Holiday 13: 138 (col.) Je '53.

——, **molten (man).** Natl. geog. 117: 7 (col.) Jan '60.

——, **sweetmeat.** See sweetmeat glass.

——, **Venetian.** Holiday 22: 35 (col.) Nov '57.

——, **Venetian (antique).** Con. 126 52 Aug '50.

——, **Williamite.** Con. 135: XLVI Je '55.

——, **wine.** See wine glass.

glass blower. Con. 135: XLVI Mar '55.
Natl. geog. 107: 475 (col.) Ap '55.

—— **(man).** Natl. geog. 114: 125 (col.) Jl '58.

glass cameos. See cameos, glass.

glass cutter wheel (man). Natl. geog. 107: 472 Ap '55.

glass factory (Jamestown). Natl. geog. 111: 611 May '57.

glass industry. Travel 110: 29-Sept '58.

glass painting. See Chinese glass painting.

glass panel, stained (heraldic). Con. 140: 59 Sept '57.

glass window, church (15th cent.). Con. 127: 59 Mar '51.

glasses (tumbler). Holiday 13: 146 May '53, 72, 89 Je '53.

——, **ale.** Con. ency. of ant., vol. 1, p. 76.

——, **Amer. (antique).** Con. ency. of ant., vol. 3, pl. 37.

——, **antique.** Con. 142: 238-41 Jan '59.

——, **cordial.** Con. ency. of ant., vol. 1, p. 77.

——, **crystal.** Holiday 18: 135 Dec '55.
——, **dram.** Con. ency. of ant., vol. 1, p. 78.
——, **drinking (antique).** Con. ency. of ant., vol. 1, pl. 45-6.
——, **enamelled (antique).** Con. ency. of ant., vol. 1, pl. 48.
——, **Georgian.** Con. 142: XXVIII Jan '59.
——, **opera.** See opera glasses.
——, **Russian (antique).** Con. 142: 224 Jan '59.
——, **ski.** See ski glasses.
——, **sun.** See sun glasses.
glassware, Irish (antique). Con. ency. of ant., vol. 3, pl. 45-52.
——, **Sandwich.** Natl. geog. 107: 785 (col.) Je '55.
Glastonbury abbey (ruins). Natl. geog. 108: 332 (col.) Sept '55.
glazier (sym.). Lehner: Pict. bk. of sym., p. 90.
"The gleaners" (Millet). Natl. geog. 115: 603 May '59.
Gleason, Jackie. Cur. biog. p. 230 (1955).
Gleason, John S., jr. Cur. biog. p. 167 (1958).
"Glencoe valley" (Scotland). Natl. geog. 112: 486-7 (col.) Oct '57.
Glendalough, Ireland (church). Holiday 23: 65 (col.) Je '58.
Glenn, John H., jr. Cur. biog. p. 152 (1962).
Glennan, Thomas Keith. Cur. biog. p. 174 (1950).
Natl. geog. 118: 63 (col.) Jl '60.
glider. Holiday 11: 168 May '52.
Travel 107: 30 May '57.
Glindoni, H. Gillard (work of). Con. 129: XXXIX Ap '52.
Glinka, Michael Ivanovich. Cooper: Con. ency. of music, p. 100.
globe. Holiday 13: 143 (col.) Ap '53.
—— **(as man).** Holiday 14: 23 Aug '53.
—— **(comic).** Holiday 13: 19, 87 Ap '53.
—— **(face on it, comic).** Travel 114: 18 Aug '60, 21 Sept '60.
—— **(on stand).** Amer. heri. vol. 11 no. 5 p. 57 (Aug '60).
—— **(on stand).** Con. 141: LIII, 245 Je '58.
—— **(on stand), (sym.).** Lehner: Pict. bk. of sym., p. 12.
——, **antique.** Con. 142: LVI Dec '58.
——, **celestial.** Con. ency. of ant., vol. 3, pl. 164.
——, **celestial (Indo-Persian, antique).** Con. 134: 88 Nov '54.
——, **celestial (16th cent., Roll & Reinhold).** Con. 126: 167-72 Dec '50.
——, **fish.** See fish globe.
——, **water.** Natl. geog. 118: 182 (col.) Aug '60.
——, **world.** Con. 140: 181 Dec '57.
Holiday 8: 58 Oct '50; 11: 130 Mar '52; 19: 12 (col.) May '56; 21: 147 (col.) Jan '57, 43, 142 (col.) Mar '57; 23: 12 (col.) Ap '58, 42 (col.) May '58; 24: 93 (col.) Oct '58; 25: 36-7 (col.), 195 Ap '59, 55 (col.) Je '59; 27: 164-5 (col.) Ap '60.
Natl. geog. 103: 103 Jan '53, 569 May '53; 107: 154 Feb '55; 109: 288 Feb '58; 111: 127 Jan '57; 112: 735 Dec '57; 116: 834 (col.) Dec '59; 118: 563 Oct '60.

Travel 105: inside back cover May '56.
——, **world (as man's head).** Holiday 12: 134 Nov '52.
——, **world (hat on).** Holiday 13: 142 Je '53.
——, **world (map).** Natl. geog. 107: 778 (col.) Je '55.
——, **world (men, boys).** Natl. geog. 113: 800 (col.) Je '58.
——, **world (1942).** Amer. heri. vol. 7 no. 1 p. 79 (Dec '55).
——, **world (on stand).** Holiday 13: 26 (col.) Mar '53; 28: 57 Dec '60.
——, **world (satellite travels).** Natl. geog. 112: 807 Dec '57.
——, **world (U.S. Navy patrol).** Natl. geog. 116: 292-3 Sept '59.
globe cup. See cup, globe.
"Globe theater" model. Natl. geog. 100: 416 Sept '51.
globes (18-19th cent.). Con. ency. of ant., vol. 3, pl. 164.
glockenspiel. Cooper: Con. ency. of music, p. 410.
Gloria church (Rio de Janeiro). Holiday 16: inside cover (col.) Jl '54.
"Glorious victory of sloop Maria" (Feininger). Con. 145: 287 Je '60.
"Glory" (sculpture by Baratta). Con. 141: 222 Je '58.
"Glory of S. Luigi Gonzaga" (Tiepolo). Con. 135: 32 Mar '55.
"Glory Road" (Lewis & Clark). Travel 102: 11-4 Oct '54.
Gloucester, Duke of (Gainsborough). Con. 142: 39 Sept '58.
Gloucester beach (Mass.). Natl. geog. 98: 156 (col.) Aug '50.
Gloucester cathedral (cloister). Praeg. pict. ency., p. 226.
Gloucester fishermen's memorial. See fishermen's memorial (Gloucester).
glove, baseball. See baseball glove.
glove dryer. Travel 112: 15 Sept '59; 6, Dec '59; 113: 37 Jan '60, 60 Feb '60.
glove form, antique. Rawson: Ant. pict. bk., p. 7.
Glover, Brig. Gen. John. Amer. heri. vol. 11 no. 2 p. 56 (Feb '60).
——, **John (work of).** Con. 143: XIV Mar '59, XX Ap '59.
gloves. Holiday 6: 93 Oct '49, 171 Dec '49; 10: 128 Nov '51; 11: 85 (col.) Feb '52; 12: 113 Sept '52, 134 Nov '52, 84 (col.) Dec '52; 18: 190, 192 Dec '55; 19: 160 Je '56; 22: 35, 244, 247 Dec '57; 28: 137 Sept '60, 154 Nov '60.
—— **(French).** Natl. geog. 100: 18 Jl '51
——, **driving.** Holiday 26: 195 Nov '59.
——, **men's.** Holiday 10: 34 (col.) Dec '51.
——, **woman's.** Holiday 20: 136 Oct '56; 22: 135 Sept '57.
gloves. See also gauntlets.
Glubb, John Bagot. Cur. biog. p. 235 (1951).
Gluck, Christoph Willibald (Greuze). Cooper: Con. ency. of music, p. 137.
Glueck, Eleanor T. Cur. biog. p. 209 (1957).
Glueck, Nelson. Cur. biog. p. 244 (1948).
Glueck, Sheldon. Cur. biog. p. 210 (1957).

Glyndebourne. *See* opera house (Glyndebourne).

glyphs, Indian. Natl. geog. 114: 816 (col.) Dec '58.

Gmeiner, Hermann. Cur. biog. (1963).

gnosticism (sym.). Lehner: Pict. bk. of sym., p. 66.

Goa (India). Travel 113: 50, 52 Feb '60.

goad, French cattle (cowboy). Natl. geog. 109: 686 (col.) May '56.

goal post, El Pato. Holiday 20: 79 Nov '56.

goatherd. Natl. geog. 112: 60 (col.) Jl '57.

goatherd & flock. Natl. geog. 117: 100-1 (col.) Jan '60.

Gobbi, Tito. Cur. biog. p. 211 (1957).

Gobel, George. Cur. biog. p. 232 (1955).

Goblain, Antoine Louis (work of). Con. 142: XLIII Nov '58.

goblet. Holiday 14: 82 (col.) Dec '53; 18: 10 Oct '55.

—— (carved from rhinoceros horn). Amer. heri. vol. 6 no. 2 p. 17 (winter '55).

—— (Queen Eliz. II presented to French Pres.). Con. 139: 244 Je '57.

——, antique. Con. 136: 131 Nov '55, XLVIII Jan '56; 137: 292 Je '56; 142: 238-41 Jan '59.

——, antique (Whistler). Con. 139: 154-6 May '57.

——, antique (engraved). Con. 134: 97-101 Nov '54; 135: LIII Ap '55.

——, antique glass. Con. 133: X Mar '54.

——, antique gold. Con. 132: XIII Sept '53.

——, antique silver. Con. 143: LVIII Je '59.

——, Betts (18th cent.). Con. 142: 14 Sept '58.

——, ceremonial (17th cent.). Con. 140: 113 Nov '57.

——, ceremonial covered (17th cent.). Con. 141: 120 Ap '58.

——, Charles I (silver). Con. 129: 61 Ap '52.

——, Couper Beilby. Con. 145: 53 Mar '60.

——, cut glass. Daniel: Cut & engraved glass.

——, 18th cent. glass. Con. 132: XXXII Sept '53; 133: 212 May '54.

——, 18th cent. silver. Con. 139: XXXVIII Mar '57; 142: 17 Sept '58.

——, Elizabeth I silver. Con. 137: XLVI Mar '56.

——, George III. Con. 134: LI Nov '54.

——, German (Aachen) Silver gilt. Con. 135: 266 Je '55.

——, golden Greek. Ceram: March of arch., p. 51.

——, Irish antique glass. Con. ency. of ant., vol. 3, pl. 45.

——, Italian silver & glass. Con. 144: 156 Dec '59.

——, Jacobite. Con. 133: 194 May '54.

——, Laurence Whistler's (engraved). Con. 134: 97 Nov '54.

——, Nostelangen, Norwegian (Schmidt). Con. 145: 18-21 Mar '60.

——, old English & Irish glass. Con. 138: XIV Sept '56.

——, "Queen's beasts". Con. 140: LX Nov '57; 142: XXVI Sept '58; 143: XL Mar '59.

——, Radclyffe silver (St. Edmund's college ware). Con. 142: 14 Sept '58.

——, renaissance crystal covered. Con. 129: 139 Je '52.

——, rhinoceros horn. Natl. geog. 97: 750 Je '50.

——, royal oak (17th cent.). Con. 133: 67 Mar '54.

——, silver (Biennais). Con. 143: 225 Je '59.

——, Steuben glass. Con. 134: 98 Nov '54.

——, Swedish glass (antique). Con. 141: 29 Mar '58.

——, Swedish glass (18th cent.). Con. 133: 34 Mar '54.

——, Swedish silver. Con. ency. of ant., vol. 3, p. 67.

——, Venetian. Con. 136: 226 Dec '55; 142: 38 Sept '58.

——, Venetian dragon stem. Con. 142: 136 Nov '58.

——, William III. Con. 145: LVI Je '60.

——, wine. Con. 145: IX (col.) May '60.

"Goblet dance", Basque. Natl. geog. 105: 161 (col.) Feb '54.

goblets, musical (in box). *See* musical goblets, antique.

"Goblin Gulch". Natl. geog. 101: 706, 726 (col.) Je '52.

God (sym.). Lehner: Pict. bk. of sym., p. 35.

god, Asia (dancing). Holiday 27: 25 Mar '60.

——, Aztec Indian. Natl. geog. 100: 816 (col.) Dec '51.

——, demon (dancing). Natl. geog. 117: 398 (col.) Mar '60.

God, eye of. *See* eye of God (sym.).

god, Ghana. *See* Ghana god.

god, Hindu. Natl. geog. 99: 16 (col.) Jan '51.

god, Hiva Oa carved. Natl. geog. 97: 99 Jan '50.

god, New Guinea. Holiday 28: 61 (col.) Oct '60.

god, ocean. *See* ocean god.

God of happiness, Chinese. *See* Pu-tai.

God of India. Holiday 25: 104 Je '59.

"God of luck" (Bhutan). Natl. geog. 102: 730 Dec '52.

—— (Chinese statue). Natl. geog. 111: 350 (col.) May '57.

God of Siva. *See* Siva (Hindu god).

—— (Chinese statue). Natl. geog. 111: 350 (col.) Mar '57.

God of sleep. *See* Hypnos.

God of the chase, Hitite. *See* Rundas.

"God rest ye merrie gentlemen" (Lucas). Con. 132: 177 (col.) Jan '54.

Godafoss waterfall (Iceland). Holiday 23: 2 (col.) Jan '58.

goddess, Greek & Roman. Lehner: Pict. bk. of sym., p. 30-1, 33.

——, Hindu (Katmandu). Natl. geog. 112: 151 (col.) Jl '57.

——, Hitite. Osward: Asia Minor, pl. 8.

——, Kali. *See* Kali goddess.

——, snake. *See* snake goddess, Crete.

Goddess of fertility (Smyrna). Osward: Asia Minor, p. 103.

Goddess of mercy. *See* Kuan Yin.

"Goddess of Mercy", Chinese. *See* Chinese "Goddess of mercy".

"Goddess of the hunt" (Diana). Int. gr. soc.: Arts . . . p. 17 (col.).

goddesses (Neith, Isis, Selquet statues). Ceram: March of arch., p. 146.

Godey, Louis A. Amer. heri. vol. 9 no. 6 p. 22 (Oct '58).

Godey fashions. Amer. heri. vol. 9 no. 6 p. 21-7 (col.), 98-100 (Oct '58).

Godfrey, Arthur. Cur. biog. p. 246 (1948).

godowns (boats). Natl. geog. 103: 194 (col.) Feb '53.

gods, Bhutan. See deities (Bhutan).

gods, Greek & Roman (sym.). Lehner: Pict. bk. of sym., p. 30-2.

——, Hawaiian carved. Amer. heri. vol. 11 no. 2 p. 15, 18-9 (col.) (Feb '60).

——, Mexican. Ceram: March of arch., p. 265.

gods & goddesses, Greek (museum). Natl. geog. 114: 756 (col.) Dec '58.

Gods of India. See Aurobindo, Shri.

gods. See also idol.

Goebbels, Joseph. Cur. biog. p. 324 (1941).

Goering, Hermann. Cur. biog. p. 327 (1941).

Goertz, Arthemise. Cur. biog. p. 222 (1953).

Goes, Hugo Van der (work of). See Hugo Van der Goes.

Goetz, Delia. Cur. biog. p. 228 (1949).

Goetz, William. Holiday 5: 43 (col.) Jan '49.

Gog & Magog (clock strikers). Natl. geog. 104: 300 Sept '53; 114: 108 (col.) Jl '58.

Gogarty, Oliver. Cur. biog. p. 331 (1941).

Gogh, Vincent Van. See Van Gogh, Vincent.

Goheen, Robert F. Cur. biog. p. 169 (1958).

"Going to church" (Durrie). Amer. heri. vol. 7 no. 1 p. 15 (col.) (Dec '55).

"Going to school" (Webster). Con. 135: XX-XIII Mar '55.

"Going-to-the-sun" mountain (Mont.). Holiday 8: 42 (col.) Sept '50.
Travel 101: 37 Je '54.

Gold, Herbert. Cur. biog. p. 234 (1955).

gold (sym.). Lehner: Pict. bk. of sym., p. 72.

——, circle to make (sym.). Lehner: Pict. bk. of sym., p. 68.

——, molten (furnace). Natl. geog. 109: 239 (col.) Feb '56.

gold mine. Natl. geog. 101: 127 Jan '52.

gold miner. Holiday 24: 66 (col.) Aug '58.
Natl. geog. 112: 715 (col.) Nov '57.

—— (Cal.). Brooks: Growth of a nation, p. 132.

—— (1850). Amer. heri. vol. 8 no. 1 p. 56 (Dec '56).

gold-mining dredge. Natl. geog. 116: 55 (col.) Jl '59.

gold panning. Natl. geog. 106: 219 Aug '54.
Travel 104: 27-30 Sept '55.

—— (modern). Natl. geog. 105: 762 (col.) Je '54.

—— (old time western, comic). U.S. News & World report, vol. LV no. 4 p. 26 Jl 22, '63.

gold prospector. Holiday 20: 40 Oct '56.

—— (loading pack on horse). Brooks: Growth of a nation, p. 176.

—— (pack mule). Holiday 6: 89 (col.) Jl '49; 21: 138 May '57.

gold prospectors. Amer. heri. vol. 1 no. 3 p. 56 (spring '50).

"The Gold rush". Int. gr. soc.: Arts . . . p. 151 (col.).

gold rush (cartoon). See cartoon, gold rush.

gold spike (1869, C.P. & U.P. railroad). See "Golden spike" (1869 . . .).

gold vault. See safe (for gold deposits).

Goldberg, Arthur J. Cur. biog. p. 230 (1949); p. 179 (1961).
Jensen: The White House, p. 291.

Goldberg, Molly. Holiday 10: 64 Dec '51.

Goldberg, Rube. Cur. biog. p. 248 (1948).
Holiday 10: 29 Sept '51.

Golden, Clinton S. Cur. biog. p. 249 (1948).

Golden, Harry. Cur. biog. p. 151 (1959).

Golden, John. Cur. biog. p. 243 (1944).

Golden gate bridge (Cal.). Holiday 11: 22 Ap '52; 14: 40 Sept '53; 18: 125 (col.) Sept '55; 20: 34-5 (col.) Aug '56; 22: 58-9 (col.) Jl '57; 27: 166 (col.) Mar '60.
Natl. geog. 99: 736 (col.) Je '51; 105: 724-5 (col.) Je '54; 110: 182-3 (col.) Aug '56; 116: 604 (col.) Nov '59.
Travel 101: 9 Mar '54, 35 Je '54.

Golden gate park. See park, Golden gate.

"Golden Hall" (Japan). Praeg. pict. ency., p. 528.

Golden madonna (Essen minster). Con. 138: 236 Jan '57.

golden orb. Natl. geog. 104: 325 (col.) Sept '53.

——, British. Int. gr. soc.: Arts . . . p. 165 (col.).

golden pavilion (Kyoto, Japan). See Kyoto (Japan).

"golden spike" (1869, joins western C.P & U.P. railroads). Amer. heri. vol. 9 no. 2 p. 22-3 (Feb '58).
Natl. geog. 110: 219 (col.) Aug '56.

Golden temple (Amritsar, India). Travel 111: 16 Jan '59.

Goldenson, Leonard H. Cur. biog. p. 213 (1957).

Golding, P. J. (pen & ink work of). Con. 140: 110 Nov '57.

Goldman, Edwin Franko. Cur. biog. p. 303 (1942).

Goldman, Frank. Cur. biog. p. 223 (1953).

Goldman, Mrs. Olive R. Cur. biog. p. 176 (1950).

Goldmann, Nahum. Cur. biog. p. 214 (1957).

Goldmark, Peter C. Cur. biog. p. 178 (1950).

Goldovsky, Boris. Holiday 22: 121 Sept '57.

Goldsborough, Thomas Alan. Cur. biog. p. 252 (1948).

Goldsborough family, Robert (Peale). Natl. geog. 105: 447 (col.) Ap '54.

Goldstein, Rabbi Israel. Cur. biog. p. 213 (1946).

Goldwater, Barry M. Cur. biog. p. 235 (1955).

Goldwyn, Samuel. Cur. biog. p. 247 (1944).
Holiday 5: 38 (col.) Jan '49; 8: 33 Nov '50.

golf. See golfer; man (playing golf); men (golfers).

golf bag. Holiday 13: 94 May '53; 19: 11 Je '56; 22: 225 (col.) Dec '57; 27: 166 (col.) Je '60.

golf ball. Holiday 5: 165 Je '49; 7: 41 May '50; 80 Je '50; 8: 21 Jl '50, 29 Nov '50; 10: 81 Jl 51; 11: 97 May '52; 75, 117 Je '52; 13: 109 Je '53; 14: 91 Jl '53, 1 Aug '53; 18: 3 Aug '55, 125 Dec '55: 19: 133. 153

Je '56; 21: 46 May '57, 8 Je '57; 22: 93
Jl '57, 3 Sept '57; 23: 3, 32 Je '58; 24: 6,
94 Jl '58, 6 Aug '58, 96 Sept '58; 25:
8, 191 May '59, 8, 125 Je '59; 26: 99 Jl
'59, 3 Aug '59, 245 Dec '59; 27: 206 Mar
'60, 170 May '60, 172 Je '60; 28: 16 Jl
'60, 135 Sept '60, 212 Nov '60.
Travel 109: 25 Je '58.

golf club. Holiday 7: 160 May '50, 104 Je '50;
8: 75 Dec '50; 10: 126 Jl '51; 11: 161 May
'52, 29 Je '52; 13: 160 Je '53; 18: 151 Nov
'55, 104 Dec '55; 19: 93, 167, 170 (part col.)
May '56, 157 Je '56; 20: 111 Aug '56, 211
Dec '56; 21: 200 Ap '57, 105, 131 (col.), 196
May '57, 190 Je '57; 22: 3, 124 Jl '57; 88
Sept '57; 23: 133 Je '58; 27: 170, 248 May
'60, 172 Je '60.

—— **(boy).** Holiday 10: 89 Jl '51.

—— **(head).** Holiday 14: 121 Nov '53, 9 Dec
'53; 27: 178 Ap '60, 192, 202 May '60, 19,
107 Je '60.
Natl. geog. 100: 135 Jl '51.

—— **(in bag).** Holiday 24: back cover (col.)
Sept '58, 217 Dec '58; 25: 43 Je '59; 27: 200
May '60, 195 Je '60.

golf course (caddy wagons). Natl. geog. 112:
686 (col.) Nov '57.

—— **(Pine Valley, Eng.).** Holiday 15: 60 (col.)
Je '54.

—— **(tournament).** Natl. geog. 105: 297 (col.)
Mar '54.

——, **St. Andrew's.** See St. Andrew's golf
course.

golfer. Holiday 6: 4 (col.) Dec '49; 10: 7 (col.)
Nov '51, 114 Dec '51; 11: 3, 23, 95 (col.)
Ap '52, 76, 97, 118, 161 May '52, 29 Je
'52; 12: 129 (col.), 147 Jl '52; 18: 90 Jl
'55, 3 Aug '55, 113 Sept '55; 19: 133, 167
(col.) May '56, 133 Je '56; 20: 15 Sept '56,
143 Oct '56, 105 Nov '56; 21: 105 May
'57, 3, 8-9, 151 Je '57; 22: 3 Jl '57, 41,
212 Dec '57.
Natl. geog. 105: 330 Mar '54.

—— **(comic).** Holiday 11: 92 May '52.

—— **(dog pulling clubs).** Natl. geog. 114: 232
Aug '58.

—— **(woman).** Holiday 7: 65 Je '50; 10: 83
Oct '51; 11: 23 May '52, 144 (col.) Je '52;
12: 28 (col.) Jl '52, 15 (col.) Oct '52; 20:
198 Dec '56.

golfers. Holiday 7: 119 (col.) May '50, 104 Je
'50; 10: 62 Oct '51; 12: 29 Sept '52; 14:
125 Dec '53; 18: 90 Jl '55; 19: 19 Feb
'56; 21: 83 (col.) Feb '57; 24: 6 (col.) Jl
'58.
Natl. geog. 102: 115-30 Jl '52; 105: 755, 785
(col.) Je '54; 115: 316 (col.) Mar '59.

—— **(comic).** Holiday 16: 11 Sept '54.

—— **(comic, rain, umbrella).** Holiday 24: 6
(col.) Aug '58.

—— **(1888).** Amer. heri. vol. 8 no. 4 back
cover (col.) (Je '57).

—— **(girl & teacher).** Holiday 22: 93 Jl '57.

—— **(heads, laughing).** Holiday 19: 93 May
'56.

—— **(Rio).** Natl. geog. 107: 326 (col.) Mar '55.

golfers. See also man (playing golf); men
(golfers); men & women (playing golf).

"Golgotha" (Mauroy). Con. ency. of ant., vol.
1, pl. 170.

Golikov, Gen. Filip. Cur. biog. p. 234 (1943).

Gollancz, Victor. Cur. biog. (1963).

golliwog (sym.). Lehner: Pict. bk. of sym., p.
62.

Gollomb, Joseph. Jun. bk. of auth., p. 141.

Golschmann, Vladimir. Cur. biog. p. 238
(1951).

Goltzius, Hendrick (portrait). Con. 138: 14 Sept
'56.

Gomez, Laureano. Cur. biog. p. 180 (1950).

Gomez, Maximo. Amer. heri. vol. 8 no. 2 p.
39 (col.) (Feb '57).

Gomez memorial (Havana). Holiday 12: 65
(col.) Dec '52.

Gompers, Samuel. Brooks: Growth of nation,
p. 209.

Gomulka, Wladyslaw. Cur. biog. p. 217 (1957).

Goncalves, Nuno (work of). Natl. geog. 118:
621 (col.) Nov '60.

gondola (Venice). Amer. heri. vol. 6 no. 2 p.
25 (winter '55); vol. 11 no. 6 p. 16 (col.)
(Oct '60).
Con. 143: XVII Je '59.
Holiday 5: 90 Mar '49; 7: 66 (col.) Feb '50;
11: 148 Je '52; 14: 29 Oct '53; 15: 88, 98
Je '54; 17: 63 Jan '55, 13 (col.) Feb '55;
18: 42 (col.) Oct '55; 19: 130 Jan '56, 171
Mar '56; 21: 159 Mar '57; 23: 79 (col.)
Jan '58; 24: 76 Oct '58; 26: 47 Aug '59;
27: 155 Jan '60, 230 May '60; 28: 217
Nov '60.
Natl. geog. 100: 401, 408-10 (col.) Sept '51;
108: 140 Jl '55; 111: 792 (col.) Je '57.
Travel 107: inside back cover Feb '57.

—— **(comic).** Holiday 18: 18 Sept '55; 19: 36
Mar '57; 27: 214 Ap '60; 28: 96 Aug '60.

—— **(man & woman).** Holiday 23: 180 Mar
'58.

—— **(medieval).** Int. gr. soc.: Arts . . . p. 81
(col.).

gondola, ski. See ski lift.

gondolier. Holiday 28: 217 Nov '60.

—— **(Iraq).** Natl. geog. 114: 484 (col.) Oct
'58.

"Gone with the wind" house. Brooks: Growth
of a nation, p. 294.

Goneim's excavations (Egypt). Ceram: March
of arch., p. 109.

gonfalon & trumpet. See trumpet & gonfalon.

gong (sym.). Lehner: Pict. bk. of sym., p. 80.

—— **(man beating).** Holiday 28: 181 (col.) Oct
'60.

Gonzales, Richard. Cur. biog. p. 231 (1949).

Gonzalez, Cesar. Cur. biog. p. 301 (1954).

Gonzalez Videla, Gabriel. Cur. biog. p. 181
(1950).

"Good companions" (Portielje). Con. 144: XX-
XIII Nov '59.

good fortune (Oriental sym.). Lehner: Pict. bk.
of sym., p. 44.

Good Friday (sym.). Lehner: Pict. bk. of sym.,
p. 53.

good luck (sym.). Lehner: Pict. bk. of sym., p.
2, 26, 28, 47, 62-3.

good luck in gambling (sym.). Lehner: Pict. bk.
of sym., p. 44.

"Good neighbors" (Van Ostade). Con. 144: XVIII (col.) Jan '60.
"Good shepherd" (marble statuette). Praeg. pict. ency., p. 175.
good spirits, circle to attract. Lehner: Pict. bk. of sym., p. 69.
Goodloe, John Duncan. Cur. biog. p. 245 (1947).
Goodman, Benny. Cur. biog. p. 306 (1942); p. 155 (1962).
Holiday 11: 100 May '52; 21: 147 May '57; 22: 113 Jl '57, 149 Dec '57; 24: 171 (col.) Nov '58.
Goodman, Bertram. Cur. biog. p. 303 (1954).
Goodnight, Pat (in "Eagle dance"). Holiday 14: 54 (col.) Dec '53.
Goodrich, Frances. Cur. biog. p. 217 (1956).
Goodrich, Marcus. Cur. biog. p 332 (1941).
Goodspeed, Edgar J. Cur. biog. p. 216 (1946).
Goodwin, Robert C. Cur. biog p. 240 (1951).
Goodwin, Dr. W. A. R. Natl. geog. 106: 468 Oct '54.
Goodyear, Charles. Brooks: Growth of a nation, p. 197.
Googe, George L. Cur. biog. p. 246 (1947).
"Gooseberry falls" (along Lake Superior drive). Travel 102: 16 Sept '54.
Goossens, Eugene. Cur. biog. p. 239 (1945).
Gorbach, Alfons. Cur. biog. p. 182 (1961).
Gordimer, Nadine. Cur. biog. p. 152 (1959).
Gordon, Crawford, jr. Cur. biog. p. 171 (1958).
Gordon, Cyrus H. Cur. biog. (1963).
Gordon, Donald. Cur. biog. p. 184 (1950).
Gordon, Dorothy. Cur. biog. p. 237 (1955).
Gordon, John Brown. Pakula: Cent. album, p. 135.
Gordon, Kermit. Cur. biog. (1963).
Gordon, Lincoln. Cur. biog. p. 157 (1962).
Gordon, Max. Cur. biog. p. 236 (1943).
Gordon, Ruth. Cur. biog. p. 239 (1943).
Gordon, Thomas S. Cur. biog. p. 219 (1957).
Gore, Albert. Cur. biog. p. 213 (1952).
Goreme Valley (Cappadocia). Osward: Asia Minor, pl. 72-3.
Göreme Valley of Refuge. Osward: Asia Minor, pl. 77.
Goren, Charles H. Cur. biog. p. 154 (1959).
Gorey village (Normandy, France). Travel 101: 23 May '54.
gorge, river. Natl. geog. 105: 371 (col.) Mar '54.
"Gorhambury" house, England (ext. & int.). Con. 143: 2, 4 Mar '59.
Gorin, Igor. Cur. biog. p. 309 (1942).
Gork, Haydar. Cur. biog. p. 219 (1956).
Gorky, (work of). Holday 14: 61 (col.) Nov '53.
Gorman, Mike. Cur. biog. p. 221 (1956).
Gorrie, Jack. Cur. biog. p. 216 (1952).
Gosden, Freeman F. Cur. biog. p. 248 (1947).
"Goshen" (Colonial house, Va.). Natl. geog. 109: 462 (col.) Ap '56.
Goshorn, Clarence B. Cur. biog. p. 186 (1950).
gospels on wayside rocks. Rawson: Ant. pict. bk., p. 42.
Goss, Albert S. Cur. biog. p. 242 (1945).
Gossaert, Jan (work of). Con. 138: 14 Sept '56. Praeg. pict. ency., p. 271 (col.).

Gosse, Thomas (self portrait). Con. 132: 158 Jan '54.
"The Gossips" (De Blaas). Con. 137: XXVII May '56.
Gota canal (Sweden). Travel 105: 27-9 Ap '56.
Goteborg (harbor, Sweden). Natl. geog. 98: 606 Nov '50.
Götsch, Joseph (wood sculpture). Con. 145: 132 Ap '60.
Gottlieb, Adolph. Cur. biog. p. 155 (1959).
Gottwald, Element. Cur. biog. p. 254 (1948).
goucho. Holiday 22: 12 (col.) Oct '57.
Gouda (Holland). Holiday 15: 102 (col.) Jan '54.
Goudsmit, Samuel A. Cur. biog. p. 305 (1954).
Goudy, Frederic W. Cur. biog. p. 333 (1941).
Gough, Lewis. K. Cur. biog. p. 225 (1953).
Gouin, Felix. Cur. biog. p. 218 (1946).
Goujon, Jean (work of). Int. gr. soc.: Arts . . . p. 87 (col.).
Goulart, Joso Cur. biog. p. 159 (1962).
Goulburn, Henry. Amer. heri. vol. 12 no. 1 p. 30 (Dec '60).
Gould, Beatrice Blackmar. Cur. biog. p. 251 (1947).
Gould, Bruce. Cur. biog. p. 250 (1947).
Gould, Sir Charles (Gainsborough). Con. 139: 165 May '57.
Gould, Chester. Holiday 23: 135 Je '58.
Gould, Glenn. Cur. biog. p. 161 (1960).
Gould, J. (work of). Con. ency. of ant., vol. 3, pl. 88.
Gould, Jay. Amer. heri. vol. 8 no. 3 p. 52 (Ap '57).
Gould, Morton. Cur. biog. p. 244 (1945).
Gould, Ronald. Cur. biog. p. 218 (1952).
Gould, Samuel B. Cur. biog. p. 173 (1958).
Goulding, Ray. Cur. biog. p. 171 (1957).
Goulet, Robert. Cur. biog. p. 161 (1962).
Gounod, Charles (bust by Gilbert). Cooper: Con. ency. of music, p. 138.
gourd (sym.). Lehner: Pict. bk. of sym., p. 46.
gourd blowers (Belgian Congo). Natl. geog. 101: 358 (col.) Mar '52.
gourd pipe (man blowing, Pakistan). Natl. geog. 107: 417 (col.) Mar '55.
gourds, drinking. Rawson: Ant. pict. bk.
Gourielli, Prince Artchil. Holiday 14: 51 (col.) Dec '53.
Gourielli, Princess Artchil (Helena Rubinstein). Cur. biog. p. 643 (1943).
Holiday 14: 51 (col.) Dec '53; 23: 78 Feb '58.
Gove, Philip B. Cur. biog. p. 163 (1962).
Govt. land office (Neb.). Travel 109: 30 Je '58.
Governor (Bermuda). Natl. geog. 105: 212 Feb '54.
Governor's mansion (Ga.). Travel 104: 17 Sept '55.
—— (St. Helena). Travel 107: 48 Mar '57.
Gow, James. Cur. biog. p. 249 (1944).
Gower, Commander Pauline. Cur. biog. p. 241 (1943).
gowns & caps. See cap & gown, college.
Goya, Francisco (self portrait). Con. 132: 136 Nov '53; 134: 53 Sept '54.

Goya (work of). Con. 129: 130 Je '52; 133: 15 Mar '54, 230 Je '54; 134: 52-3, 62 Sept '54, cover (col.), 174-5 Dec '54; 135: 11, 36 (col.) Mar '55; 142: 257-8 Jan '59; 143: LI Ap '59; 144: 138 Nov '59; 145: 160 May '60.
Holiday 14: 43 (col.) Dec '53.
Praeg. pict. ency., p. 354 (col.).
Goya Y Lucientes, Francisco. Int. gr. soc.: Arts . . . p. 91 (col.).
Gozzoli, Benozzo (work of). Holiday 27: 61 Jan '60.
Natl. geog. 101: 97 (col.) Jan '52.
Grace, Alonzo G. Cur. biog. p. 187 (1950).
Grace, Eugene Gifford. Cur. biog. p. 336 (1941).
Grace, J. Peter. Cur. biog. p. 163 (1960).
Grace Darling's lighthouse. See lighthouse, Grace Darling's.
Graces, The Three (sym.). Lehner. Pict. bk. of sym., p. 33.
grader, land (Chile). Natl. geog. 117: 224 (col.) Feb '60.
gradual (music). See illuminated gradual (music).
graduate, girl (taking picture). Holiday 21: 7 (col.) Je '57.
——, univ. See college graduate.
graduation, West Point. Natl. geog. 101: 622 (col.) May '52.
graduation cap. See cap & gown; mortarboard.
graduation procession, Univ. of Va. Natl. geog. 97: 586 (col.) May '50.
Grady, Henry F. Cur. biog. p. 253 (1947).
Graebner, Walter. Cur. biog. p. 243 (1943).
Graf, Herbert. Cur. biog. p 310 (1942).
Graf, Urs (work of). Praeg. pict. ency., p. 284.
Gragg, Rev. J. B. Brooks: Growth of a nation, p. 312.
Graham, Billy. Holiday 23: 63 (col.), 64-5 Feb '58.
Graham, Billy (friends & wife). Holiday 23: 80-1 Mar '58.
Graham, Clarence R. Cur. biog. p. 190 (1950).
Graham, Elinor. Cur. biog. p. 220 (1952).
Graham, Evarts A. Cur. biog. p. 221 (1952).
Graham, Frank P. Cur. biog. p. 337 (1941); p. 242 (1951).
Graham, Gwethalyn. Cur. biog. p. 247 (1945).
Graham, Rev. Harry C. Cur. biog. p. 191 (1950).
Graham, John. Cur. biog. p. 165 (1962).
Graham, Martha. Cur. biog. p. 251 (1944); p. 183 (1961).
Graham, Mentor. Holiday 19: 11 May '56.
Graham, Philip L. Cur. biog. p. 257 (1948).
Graham, Shirley. Cur. biog. p. 221 (1946).
Graham, Virginia. Cur. biog. p. 222 (1956).
Graham, Brig. Gen. Wallace H. Cur. biog. p. 255 (1947).
Graham, Rev. William Franklin. Cur. biog. p. 244 (1951).
Graham, Winston. Cur. biog. p. 239 (1955).
Grahame, Gloria. Holiday 11: 52 (col.) Je '52.
Grahame—White, Claude. Amer. heri. vol. 7 no. 3 p. 5 (Aug '56).
grain elevator. Natl. geog. 103: 736 Je '53.

grain mill. See mill, grain.
grain mortar (women pounding, Nigeria). Natl. geog. 110: 353 (col.) Sept '56.
Grain pit exchange (Chicago). Natl. geog. 104: 791 Dec '53.
grain thresher (woman & ox, Cyprus). Natl. geog. 109: 878 Je '56.
Gramatky, Hardie. Jun. bk. of auth., p. 143.
Granahan, Kathryn E. Cur. biog. p. 157 (1959).
granaries, African tree branch. Natl. geog. 97: 326 (col.) Mar '50.
Grand army of the Republic (badge). Amer. heri. vol. 7 no. 6 p. 120 (Oct '56).
Grand canal (Venice). Con. 136: XX, 192 (col.) Dec '55; 138: LI Sept '56; 143: LXV Je '59; 145: 160-1 May '60.
Holiday 7: 66 (col.) Feb '50.
Natl. geog. 100: 401, 410 (col.) Sept '51; 111: 792 (col.) Je '57.
"Grand Canal, Venice" (Callow). Con. 136: XXXV (col.) Nov '55.
—— (Guardi). Con. 139: 249 (col.) Je '57.
—— (Wyld). Con. 138: XXXIX Nov '56.
Grand canyon natl. park (Ariz.). Amer. heri. vol. 10 no. 5 p. 112 (Aug '59).
Face of Amer., p. 48-9 (col.).
Holiday 12: 35 (col.) Jl '52; 13: 36-7 Jan '53; 16: 90 (col.) Aug '54; 19: 50 (col.) Mar '56; 25: 56-7 Mar '59; 26: 53 (col.) Jl '59.
Jordan: Hammond's pict. atlas, p. 175 (col.).
Natl. geog. 99: 740-1 (col.) Je '51; 107: 590-628 (col.) May '55; 113: 588-9 (col.) May '58.
Travel 102: 21 Jl '54.
—— (map). Natl. geog. 107: 596-7 May '55.
Grand central railroad station (int.). Holiday 12: 44 Dec '52.
Grand circle (Mycenae). Ceram: March of arch., p. 47.
Grand Coulee dam. Holiday 5: 39 (col.) Je '49; 13: 127 (col.) Ap '53; 27: 29 (col.) Feb '60.
Jordan: Hammond's pict. atlas, p. 142-3 (col.).
Natl. geog. 102: 603 (col.) Nov '52; 117: 446-7 (col.) Ap '60.
Grand hotel (Mackinac is.). Holiday 14: 121 Jl '53.
Grand Manan (Bay of Fundy). Travel 106: 46-8 Aug '56.
Grand Mesa (Colo.). Travel 113: 26-7 Mar '60.
"The Grand National" (Pollard). Con. 141: LII Ap '58.
grand piano. See piano, grand.
grand pianoforte. See pianoforte, grand.
Grand Pre memorial park (Nova Scotia). Natl. geog. 112: 169 (col.) Aug '57.
Travel 103: 37 Je '55; 114: 38 Jl '60.
Grand Tetons (Wyo.). Holiday 14: back cover (col.) Jl '53.
Jordan: Hammond's pict. atlas, p. 139 (col.).
Travel 101: 36 Je '54.
Grand Teton Natl. Park (map). Natl. geog. 109: 7 Jan '56.
Grand Trianon (int.). Holiday 18: 53 (col.) Aug '55.

"Grand Turk" privateer. *See* Salem privateer "Grand Turk".

Grande Corniche (France). Holiday 16: 16 Sept '54.

grandfather, great, great. . . . Holiday 19: 125 May '56.

grandfather clock. *See* clock, grandfather.

Grandi, Conte Dino. Cur. biog. p. 245 (1943).

Grandjany, Marcel. Cur. biog. p. 248 (1943).

Grandjean, Edmond Georges (work of). Con. 141: XLI (col.) Je '58.

grandmother, (lace maker). Holiday 21: 38 (col.) Jan '57.

"Grandpa's darling" (Zampighi). Con. 139: XLIL Je '57.

grandstand. Face of Amer., p. 58-9 (col.). Natl. geog. 100: 434 (col.) Oct '51.

—— **(ball game).** Face of Amer., p. 12-3 (col.).

Granger, Gordon. Pakula: Cent. album, p. 137.

Granger, Lester B. Cur. biog. p. 224 (1946).

The Grangers (1873). Amer. heri. vol. 7 no. 3 p. 42 (col.) (Ap '56).

Granik, Theodore. Cur. biog. p. 223 (1952).

granite cliffs. *See* cliffs, granite.

granite quarry. Natl. geog. 99: 581 May '51.

"Granny chair". Rawson: Ant. pict. bk., p. 16.

Grant, Cary. Cur. biog. p. 339 (1941). Holiday 23: 145 Je '58.

Grant, Mr. & Mrs. Cary. Holiday 11: 41 Feb '52.

Grant, Sir Francis (work of). Con. 135: 237, 239 Je '55.

Grant, Gordon. Cur. biog. p. 227 (1953).

Grant, Nellie (wedding). Jensen: The White House, p. 108-9.

Grant, Robert. Amer. heri. vol. 9 no. 6 p. 57 (Oct '58).

Grant, Gen. Ulysses S. Amer. heri. vol. 3 no. 2 p. 26 (winter '52); vol. 6 no. 6 p. 85 (Ap '55); vol. 7 no. 3 p. 32 (Ap '56); vol. 8 no. 3 p. 52, 57, 109 (Ap '57); vol. 11 no. 2 p. 64 (Feb '60). Jensen: The White House, p. 103. Pakula: Cent. album, p. 139.

Grant, Mrs. Ulysses S. Jensen: The White House, p. 104-5.

Grant & his generals (Balling). Amer. heri. vol. 7 no. 6 p. 30-1 (col.) (Oct '56).

Grant & Lee meet at McLean house. Brooks: Growth of a nation, p. 146.

Grant memorial, Gen. U.S. Holiday 25: 57 Je '59.

Grantham, Sir Alexander. Cur. biog. p. 307 (1954).

Grantham, Sir Guy (Malta Governor). Holiday 27: 70 (col.) Je '60.

Grant's birthplace, Gen. Ulysses S. Amer. heri. vol. 4 no. 3 p. 48 (col.) (spring '53).

Grant's home, Gen. Ulysses S. Amer. heri. vol. 7 no. 5 p. 32 (Aug '56). Travel 103: 16 Je '55.

Grant's horses, Gen. Ulysses S. Jensen: The White House, p. 107.

Granville, Earl William S. Cur. biog. p. 193 (1950).

grape harvesting. Holiday 27: 61 (col.) Ap '60.

grapefruit (in ice cup). Holiday 22: 7 (col.) Jl '57.

Grasmere (Eng.). Natl. geog. 109: 521 (col.), 530-1, 544 Ap '56.

grass cutting (by hand, Okinawa). Natl. geog. 107: 282 Feb '55.

Grasse (France). Holiday 21: 65 (col.) Ap '57.

grasshopper plague (1874). Amer. heri. vol. 11 no. 6 p. 38-41 (Oct '60).

grate, fire (Adam, antique). Con. 144: XLIX Nov '59.

——, **fireplace (18th cent.).** Con. 143: XLI May '59.

grater, Cassava. Natl. geog. 107: 345 Mar '55.

grates, dog (18th cent.). Con. 143: XLV Mar '59.

Grau, Shirley Ann. Cur. biog. p. 159 (1959).

Grau San Martin, Ramon. Cur. biog. p. 254 (1944).

Grauer, Ben. Cur. biog. p. 341 (1941); p. 161 (1959).

grave. Travel 107: 62 Mar '57.

grave of Ann Rutledge. Travel 113: 31 Feb '60.

grave of "Billy the Kid". Horan: Pict. hist. of wild west, p. 66.

grave of Jack Bennett. Horan: Pict. hist. of wild west, p. 203.

grave of John Paul Jones. Amer. heri. vol. 5 no. 4 p. 15 (summer '54).

grave of Nancy Hanks Lincoln. Natl. geog. 101: 170 (col.) Feb '52; 117: 247 (col.) Feb '60.

grave of Paul Gauguin. Natl. geog. 97: 76 Jan '50.

grave of Thomas Gray. *See* Gray's grave, Thomas.

grave of Thomas Jefferson. Natl. geog. 97: 281 Mar '50.

grave of "Wild Bill Hickok". Horan: Pict. hist. of wild west, p. 128.

grave relief (ancient Greek marble). Con. 143: LXXVI Je '59.

gravehouse (Alaska). Travel 112: 18 Jl '59.

gravel (sym.). Lehner: Pict. bk. of sym., p. 72.

Graves, Alvin C. Cur. biog. p. 225 (1952).

Graves, Morris. Cur. biog. p. 224 (1956).

—— **(work of).** Con. 145: 209 May '60.

graves (Amer. soldiers in Russia). Amer. heri. vol. 10 no. 1 p. 29 (Dec '58).

——, **Arctic.** Natl. geog. 107: 566 (col.) Ap '55.

——, **Colonial Jamestown.** Natl. geog. 111: 602 (col.) May '57.

——, **Indian.** Natl. geog. 103: 741 (col.) Je '53.

graves of Adams & Jefferson (Quincy, Mass.). Natl. geog. 97: 281 Mar '50.

graves of Ur, royal. Ceram: March of arch., p. 237.

Gravestone (Paros, 5th cent.). Con. ency. of ant. vol. 3, pl. 68.

gravestone of Hegeso (Athens, 400 A.D.). Con. ency. of ant., vol. 3, pl. 69.

graveyard. Holiday 28: 69 Jl '60.

"Graveyard of the Atlantic". Natl. geog. 108: 502-3 (col.) Oct '55.

Gravier, Charles, Comte de Vergennes. Amer. heri. vol. 7 no. 3 p. 70 (Ap '56).

gravimeter. Natl. geog. 108: 164-5 Aug '55.
Gray, Carl. R., jr. Cur. biog. p. 258 (1948).
Gray, Elizabeth Janet. Cur. biog. p. 250 (1943).
Jun. bk. of auth., p. 144.
Gray, Gordon. Cur. biog. p. 233 (1949).
Gray, Capt. Robert. Amer. heri. vol. 4 no. 4
p. 44 (summer '53); vol. 7 no. 5 p. 66 (Aug
'56).
"Gray Gables" (Grover Cleveland's home).
Amer. heri. vol. 8 no. 6 p. 103 (Oct '57).
Gray's grave, Thomas. Natl. geog. 108: 311
(col.) Sept '55.
Graziani, Rodolfo. Cur. biog. p. 342 (1941).
"Grazing flock" (Jacque). Con. 140 XXIII Dec
'57.
grease burner light. Rawson: Ant. pict. bk., p.
93.
Great barrier reef (Australia). Holiday 18: 98-
9 (col.) Nov '55.
Natl. geog. 111: 2-48 (part col.) Jan '57.
—— (map). Natl. geog. 111: 7 Jan '57.
Great basin range natl. park (Nev.). Travel
113: 32 Jan '60.
Great Britain. Holiday 17: 12-3 (col.) Mar '55.
—— (honor insignia). Int. gr. soc.: Arts . . . p.
167 (col.).
Great Britain See also England.
"Great Cascade at Tivoli" (Busiri). Con. 141:
218 J '58.
Great Falls (Mont.). Natl. geog. 97: 713 Je '50.
Great Falls (Potomac). Natl. geog. 117: 433
(col.) Mar '60.
The Great Lakes area. Natl. geog. 115: 440-
90 (part col.) Ap '59.
great master circle (sym.). Lehner: Pict. bk. of
sym., p. 69.
The "Great Mother" (rock carving). See Sun
Queen of Arinna.
"The Great Navigator in 1492". Amer. heri.
vol. 10 no. 6 frontis. (col.) (Oct '59).
Great northern railway emblem. Amer. heri.
vol. 9 no. 4 p. 99 (Je '58).
Great Salt Lake. Holiday 21: 76-7 (col.) May
'57.
Great sand dunes natl. monument (Col.). Natl.
geog. 113: 618 (col.) May '58.
Great Smoky Mts. natl. park. Natl. geog. 102:
474-502 (part col.) Oct '52.
great wall of China. Holiday 21: 81 Je '57.
Natl. geog. 118: 199 (col.) Aug '60.
"Greater George" (Leigh-Pemberton). Con.
134: 152 (col.) Dec '54.
"Greatest Mother in the World" (Red Cross
poster). Brooks: Growth of a nation p. 243.
Grebe, John Josef. Cur. biog. p. 241 (1955).
Greco, El. See El Greco.
Greco, Emilio (sculpture by). Con. 140: XX
Dec '57.
Greco, Jose. Cur. biog. p. 227 (1952).
Grede, William J. Cur. biog. p. 230 (1952).
Greece. Holiday 12: 52-7 (part col.) Sept '52;
15: 46-57 (col.) Je '54; 24: 66-71 (col.)
Sept '58; 25: 111 Feb '59; 26: 23 Sept '59.
Natl. geog. 103: 352-90 (part col.) Mar '53;
109: 38-69 (part col.) Jan '56; 110: 744-5
(col.) Dec '56; 114: 734-82 (part col.) Dec
'58; 117: 636- (col.) May '60.
Travel 113: 28, 63, 79 Ap '60; 114: 19-29
Aug '60.

—— (Arachova). Holiday 27: 187 Je '60.
—— (city, 4th cent., B.C.). Int. gr. soc.:
Arts . . . p. 13 (col.).
—— (map). Natl. geog. 109: 40 Jan '56; 114:
738 Dec '58.
Greece (Parthenon). See Parthenon (Athens).
Grecian acrobats. See acrobats (Grecian).
Grecian bride. Holiday 25: 4 Jan '59.
Grecian caique. See caique (Greek boat).
Grecian dancers. Holiday 15: 48 Je '54; 20:
31 Dec '56.
Grecian girl (flag). Natl. geog. 99: 237 Feb
'51.
Grecian men & women (500 B.C.). Int. gr.
soc.: Arts . . . p. 31 (col.).
Grecian woman. See woman, Grecian.
Greek Evzone (soldier). Int. gr. soc.: Arts . . .
p. 159 (col.).
Greek god of sleep. See Hypnos.
Greek helmet (antique). Con. 135: XXXIV
May '55.
Greek marble relief (420 B.C.). Con. 135: 143
Ap '55.
Greek monk. See monk, Greek.
Greek orthodox church cross. See cross, Greek
orthodox church.
Greek peddler (dry goods on donkey). Natl.
geog. 109: 65 (col.) Jan '56.
Greek soldier. Travel 114: cover (col.), 25, 28
Aug '60.
—— (ancient times). Int. gr. soc.: Arts . . . p.
33 (col.).
—— (King's guard). Natl. geog. 100: 730 (col.)
Dec '51.
Greek temple. See temple, Greek.
Greek theater. See theater, Greek.
Greek vase. (antique). Con. 139: LXV Je '57.
Greek vases (ancient). Int. gr. soc.: Arts . . . p.
19 (col.)
Greek vessels (ancient). Int. gr. soc.: Arts . . .
p. 19 (col.).
Greeley, Horace. Amer. heri. vol. 6 no. 2 p.
36 (winter '55); vol. 7 no. 4 p. 32 (Je '56);
vol. 8 no. 1 p. 63 (Dec '56); vol. 8 no. 3 p.
21 (Ap '57).
—— (cartoon). Amer. heri. vol. 7 no. 4 p. 29
(Je '56).
Greely, Adolphus W. Amer. heri. vol. 11 no.
4 p. 50 (Je '60).
Greely, Henrietta Nesmith. Amer. heri. vol. 11
no. 4 p. 46 (Je '60).
Green, Adolph. Cur. biog. p. 118 (1945).
Green, Constance McLaughlin. Cur. biog.
(1963).
Green, Dwight H. Cur. biog. p. 260 (1948).
Green, Edith S. Cur. biog. p 226 (1956).
Green, Howard. Cur. biog. p. 165 (1960).
Green, Martyn. Cur. biog. p 195 (1950).
Green, Theodore Francis. Cur. biog. p. 197
(1950).
Holiday 19: 86 Mar '56.
Green, William. Cur. biog. p. 313 (1942).
"Green corn dance" (Indian). Amer. heri. vol.
2 no. 1 p. 66 (fall '50).
green cross. See cross, green.
"Green head" (500 B.C.). Praeg. pict. ency., p.
156.
"Green mausoleum" (Bursa-Brussa). Osward:
Asia Minor, pl. 80.

Griscom, George C. Amer. heri. vol. 11 no. 5 p. 27 (Aug '60).
gristmill. Holiday 5: 109 (col.) Jan '49; 11: 43 (col.) Je '52.
—— (Portugal). Disney: People & places, p. 64 (col.).
—— (South Sudbury, Mass.). Travel 113: 52 Mar '60.
——, Colonial (model). Natl. geog. 106: 468 Oct '54.
——, hand turned (Morocco). Natl. geog. 107: 181 (col.) Feb '55.
Griswold, Alfred Whitney. Cur. biog. p. 201 (1950).
Griswold, Dwight P. Cur. biog. p. 265 (1947).
Griswold, Erwin N. Cur. biog. p. 232 (1956).
Griswold, Maj. Gen. Oscar W. Cur. biog. p. 253 (1943).
Gritti, Doge Andrea (Titian). Natl. geog. 110: 639 (col.) Nov '56.
Grizodubova, Valentina. Cur, biog. p. 348 (1941).
Groat, Dick. Cur. biog. p. 185 (1961).
grocery cart. See woman (grocery cart).
grocery store (int.). Natl. geog. 103: 6 Jan '53.
——, Greece (int.). Natl. geog. 114: 741 (col.) Dec '58.
Grogan, John Joseph. Cur. biog. p. 247 (1951).
Gromyko, Andrei A. Cur. biog. p. 254 (1943); p. 179 (1958).
Gronchi, Giovanni. Cur. biog. p. 246 (1965).
Groninger, Homer M. Cur. biog. p. 252 (1945).
groom & bride. See bride & groom.
Gropius, Walter. Cur. biog. p. 349 (1941).
Gross, Chaim. Cur. biog. p. 351 (1941).
Gross, Charles P. Cur. biog. p. 227 (1946).
Gross, Ernest A. Cur. biog. p. 249 (1951).
Gross, Paul Magnus. Cur. biog. (1963).
Gross, Robert E. Cur. biog. p. 233 (1956).
Grossinger, Jennie. Cur. biog. p. 236 (1956).
Grossinger's resort (Catskill mts.). Holiday 6: 99-105 Aug '49.
Grosvenor, Prof. Edwin A. (Amherst college). Natl. geog. 97: 301 Mar '50.
Grosvenor, Gilbert. Natl. geog. 112: 40 Jl '57, 583 Oct '57.
Grosvenor, Gilbert H. Cur. biog. p. 229 (1946).
Grosvenor, Dr. Melville. Natl. geog. 106: 65D, 65 G, 66 Jl '54.
Grosvenor, Melville Bell. Cur. biog. p. 172 (1960).
Natl. geog. 115: 590 Ap '59.
Grosz, George. Cur. biog. p. 317 (1942).
—— (work of). Praeg. pict. ency., p. 482.
Grotefend, Georg Friedrich (bust). Ceram: March of arch., p. 182.
grotesque, Italian (Raphael). Praeg. pict. ency., p. 62.
Grotewohl, Otto. Cur. biog. p. 203 (1950).
Groth, John. Cur. biog. p. 255 (1943).
Groton school (Mass.). Holiday 23: 56 Mar '58.
grotto (beneath 20th cent. church). Natl. geog. 110: 720 (col.) Dec '56.
—— (Christ's birthplace). Natl. geog. 98: 725 (col.) Dec '50.
—— (Paradise glacier). Natl. geog. 113: 628-9 (col.) May '58.

——, emerald (Amalfi). Natl. geog. 116: 475 (col.) Oct '59.
——, rock. Natl. geog. 113: 492 (col.) Ap '58.
Grotto of the seven sleepers (near Mt. Pion). Osward: Asia Minor, pl. 45.
"Group on seashore" (Piazzetta). Con. 143: 99 Ap '59.
"Grove Point" plantation (Ga.). Natl. geog. 105: 288 Mar '54.
Groves, Ernest R. Cur. biog. p. 257 (1943).
Groves, Gladys Hoagland. Cur. biog. p. 258 (1943).
Groves, Brig. Gen. Leslie R. Cur. biog. p. 255 (1945).
Gruber, Frank. Cur. biog. p. 353 (1941).
Gruber, Karl. Cur. biog. p. 268 (1947).
Gruen, Victor D. Cur. biog. p. 162 (1959).
Gruening, Ernest. Cur. biog. p. 232 (1946).
Gruenther, Lt. Gen. Alfred M. Cur. biog. p. 204 (1950).
Grumman, Leroy R. Cur. biog. p. 257 (1945).
Grünewald, Mathias. Int. gr. soc.: Arts . . . p. 91 (col.).
—— (work of). Con. 138: 138 Nov '56.
—— See also Neithardt, Mathis G.
Guadalajara cathedral (Mexico). Natl. geog. 114: 30 Nov '60.
Travel 101: back cover Jan '54, back cover Mar '54; 114: 30 Nov '60.
Guadalcanal. Holiday 8: 66-70 Aug '50.
Guanabara Bay (reflections, Rio). Natl. geog. 107: 323 Mar '55.
Guanajuato (Mexico). Holiday 26: 51 (col.) Nov '59.
Guano Mt., bird (Peru). Natl. geog. 115: 412 Mar '59.
guard (St. James palace). See London (St. James palace guard).
——, Canadian military. Holiday 24: 54 (col.) Nov '58.
——, English royal palace. See London (royal guard, palace).
——, Greek royal. Holiday 15: 50 Je '54. Natl. geog. 109: 47 Jan '56.
——, Irish. See Irish guards.
——, Nigerian royal. Natl. geog. 110: 326 (col.) Sept '56.
——, Roman presidential. Holiday 27: 115 Ap '60.
——, royal (comic). Holiday 19: 22 May '56.
——, Scotch. Holiday 25: 190 (col.) May '59.
——, Scotch castle. Holiday 11: 103 (col.) May '52.
——, Swiss. See Swiss guard.
guard changes, Copenhagen palace. Holiday 18: 32 Sept '55.
guardamontes (gaucho leather fenders). Natl. geog. 113: 326-7 (col.) Mar '58.
Guardi, Francesco (work of). Con. 133: 232 Je '54; 135: 6 Mar '55, X (col.) Ap '55, 278 Je '55; 136: LXV Nov '55; 137: IV Mar '56; 139: 249 (col.) Je '57; 140: 58 Sept '57, 98 Nov '57; 141: 131 Ap '58; 143: 185 May '59, 207, XXXVI-XXXVII Je '59; 144: 191 Dec '59, 239, 270 Jan '60; 145: 40 Mar '60, LXIV May '60.
Natl. geog. 97: 768 (col.) Je '50.
Praeg. pict. ency., p. 362 (col.).

Guardia, Ernesto de la, jr. Cur. biog p. 222 (1957).
guardian angel (sym.). Lehner: Pict. bk. of sym., p. 88.
guardian angels, seals of 7 (sym.). Lehner: Pict. bk. of sym., p. 24.
"guardian of the soul" (sym.). Lehner: Pict. bk. of sym., p. 48.
Guardo (Switzerland). Disney: People & places, p. 39 (col.).
guards, English life. Natl. geog. 104: 304 (col.) Sept '53.
——, English life (on horses). Holiday 17: 12 (col.) Mar '55.
——, Gangtok Maharaja. Holiday 24: 53 Sept '58.
——, Queen's. See Queen's guards.
——. See also St. Peter's cathedral guards (Vatican).
——. See also Swiss guards.
——. See also Yeoman of the guard.
——, Royal horse. See horse guards, Royal (London).
guardsman, Colonial fort. Natl. geog. 111: 584 (col.) May '57.
——, Colonial Williamsburg. Natl. geog. 106: 480-1 (col.) Oct '54.
Guarienti, Pase (by Veronese). Con. 142: 143 Dec '58.
Guarnieri, Luciano (work of). Con. 140 184 Dec '57.
Guatemala. Holiday 17: 34-5 (col.) Mar '55. Travel 108: 54, 56 Nov '57; 111: cover (col.), 23 Mar '59.
—— (Mayan ruins). Travel 108: 26-7 Dec '57.
—— (women fashions). Holiday 27: 86-7 (col.) Je '60.
Guatemala, Indian (Easter week). Natl. geog. 117: 406-11 (col.) Mar '60.
—— (map). Natl. geog. 117: 410 Mar '60.
Guayama (Puerto Rico). Natl. geog. 99: 458 (col.) Ap '51.
Guayma beach (women, horses). Holiday 10: 98 (col.) Nov '51.
Guaymas (Mexico). Holiday 10: 98-101 (part col.) Nov '51.
Gueden, Hilde. Cur. biog. p. 248 (1955).
Guerard, Albert J. Cur. biog. p 233 (1946).
Guercino (work of). Con. 132: 11-4 Sept '53, 110 Nov '53; 139: 35 Mar '57; 145: 39 Mar '60.
Gueridon (antique). Con. 136: 84 Nov '55.
——, Louis XV marquetry. Con. 140: 57 Sept '57.
——, Louis XVI. Con. 136: 75 Sept '55.
Guerin, F. (work of). Con. 143: 208 Je '59.
Guerrero, John F. Natl. geog. 113: 459 Ap '58.
Guerrero, Jose Gustavo. Cur. biog. p. 270 (1947).
Guest, Edgar A. Cur. biog. p. 354 (1941).
guesthall (Arab). See Mudhif.
Guevara, Ernesto. Cur. biog. (1963).
Guffey, Joseph F. Cur. biog. p. 259 (1944).
Guggenheim, Harry F. Cur. biog. p. 237 (1956).
Guggenheim, Minnie. Cur. biog. p. 175 (1962).
Guggenheim, Peggy. Cur. biog. p. 173 (1962).

Guggenheim museum of art (N.Y.). Int. gr. soc.: Arts . . . p. 125 (col.).
Natl. geog. 118: 808-9 (col.) Dec '60.
Guglia of Immaculata. Labande: Naples, p. 57.
guidepost (comic). Holiday 13: 153 Ap '53.
guild houses (Belgium). Holiday 23: 2 (col.) Jan '58.
guildhall (Portsmouth, Eng.). Natl. goeg. 101: 516 Ap '52.
guildhalls, trade (Brussels). Natl. geog. 113: 796-7 (col.) Je '58.
guildsman (Swiss festival). Natl. geog. 114: 576 (col.) Oct '58.
guilloche ornament. Con. ency. of ant., vol. 1, p. 19.
guillotine (sym.). Lehner: Pict. bk. of sym., p. 83.
Guinness, Alec. Cur. biog. p. 206 (1950).
Guinness, Arthur. Cur. biog. p. 262 (1948).
Guinzburg, Harold K. Cur. biog. p. 224 (1957).
Guion, Connie. Cur. biog. p. 178 (1962).
Guirma, Ambassador Frederic (& wife). Jensen: The White House, p. 289.
guitar. Holiday 18: 28 Jl '55; 20: 23 Aug '56, 172 Dec '56; 21: 140 (col.) Feb '57, 191 Ap '57; 24: 62 (col.) Aug '58, 189 Nov '58; 28: 152 Nov '60.
Natl. geog. 99: 425 Ap '51; 107: 303 (col.) Mar '55.
—— (by Panormo, 1833). Cooper: Con. ency. of music, p. 359.
—— (girl playing). Holiday 11: 36 Feb '52; 20: 64 Sept '56, 19 Oct '56; 26: 67 (col.) Dec '59.
Natl. geog. 107: 496 (col.) Ap '55.
—— (Jamaican playing). Holiday 22: 110 (col.) Nov '57.
—— (Majorcan playing). Natl. geog. 111: 647 (col.) May '57.
—— (man & girl). Holiday 12: inside cover (col.) Oct '52.
—— (man playing). Holiday 18: 56 (col.) Aug '55; 23: 40 (col.) Jan '58.
Natl. geog. 97: 534 (col.) Ap '50, 679 May '50; 100: 804 Dec '51; 101: 785 Je '52; 102: 357 (col.) Sept '52; 105: 550 Ap '51; 110: 675 (col.) Nov '56; 113: 394 (col.) Mar '58; 116: 11 Jl '59.
—— (Mexican boy). Holiday 24: 136 Nov '58.
—— (Mexican playing). Holiday 10: 99 (col.) Nov '51.
—— (Swiss man playing). Natl. geog. 111: 785 (col.) Je '57.
—— (West Indian playing). Holiday 24: 112 Oct '58.
guitar, Spanish. Con. 136: 55 Sept '55.
Guiteau, Charles (shoots Pres. Garfield). Amer. heri. vol. 2 no. 4 p. 15, 17 (summer '51).
Gulf of Mexico (map). Natl. geog. 111: 704 May '57.
Gulf of Naples (map). Natl. geog. 105: 536 Ap '54.
"Gulf stream" (Winslow Homer). Holiday 8: 53 (col.) Oct '50.
Gulick, Luther H. Cur. biog. p. 259 (1945).
Gullander, W. P. Cur. biog. (1963).
Gullion, Allen W. Cur. biog. p. 259 (1943).

"Gymnasium of the maidens". Osward: Asia Minor, pl. 40.

gypsies (Turkey). Natl. geog. 110: 735 (col.) Dec '56.

gypsy caravan. Amer. heri. vol. 9 no. p. 69 (Oct '58).

—— (Ireland). Natl. geog. 99: 670-1 (col.) May '51.

gypsy cart (oxen). Natl. geog. 100: 379 Sept '51.

gypsy cave dwellings. See cave dwellings, gypsy.

gypsy circle (sym.). Lehner: Pict. bk. of sym., p. 69.

gypsy dancer. Holiday 21: 120 Jan '57. Natl. geog. 112: 574 Oct '57.

gypsy girl (on mule). Natl. geog. 109: 878 Je '56.

gypsy wagon. See wagon, gypsy.

gyroscope (sym.). Lehner: Pict. bk. of sym., p. 82.

H

"H.M. Frigate, Seahorse" (Pocock). Con. 143: 176 May '59.

H.M.S. Trafalgar ship. Con. 144: XL Dec '59.

Haas, Bishop Francis J. Cur. biog. p. 266 (1943).

Habe, Hans. Cur. biog. p. 268 (1943).

haberdashery, animal. Rawson: Ant. pict. bk., p. 69.

Habibia college (Kabul, Afghanistan). Natl. geog. 104: 422 Sept '53.

haboob (Sudan dust storm). Natl. geog. 103: 255 Feb '53.

Habukkuk, prophet (Donatello). Praeg. pict. ency., p. 273.

Hacha, Emil. Cur. biog. p. 322 (1942).

hacienda (Mexico). Holiday 26: 54 (col.) Nov '59.

hacienda owner, Mexican (on horse). Amer. heri. vol. 9 no. 5 p. 13 (col.) (Aug '58).

Hackaart, Jan (work of). Con. 140: XXV Sept '57.

Hacker, Arthur (work of). Con. 144: 11 Sept '59.

Hackett, Albert. Cur. biog. p. 217 (1956).

Hackworth, Judge Green H. Cur. biog. p. 181 (1958).

Hadas, Moses. Cur. biog. p. 173 (1960).

Hader, Bertha. Jun. bk. of auth., p. 149.

Hader, Elmer. Jun. bk. of auth., p. 149.

Hades (sym.). Lehner: Pict. bk. of sym., p. 31.

hadjis (Mt. of Mercy). Natl. geog. 104: 46 Jl '53.

Hadley's guadrant. See quadrant, Hadley's.

Hadrian, emperor. Natl. geog. 111: 477 (col.) Ap '57.

Hadrian's arch (Antalya). Osward: Asia Minor, pl. 114-6.

Hadrian's arch (Athens). Natl. geog. 117: 637 (col.) May '60.

Hadrian's tomb (Rome). Holiday 9: 93 Mar '51; 27: 19 Ap '60. Natl. geog. 111: 474-5, 477 (col.) Ap '57.

"Hadrian's villa" (Wilson). Con. 143: 93 Ap '59.

Hadrian's villa (statuary). Holiday 27: 79 (col.) Ap '60.

"Hadrian's villa at Tivoli" (Adam). Con. 137: 78, 80 Ap '56.

Hadrian's wall (Eng.). Holiday 23: 57 (col.) Ap '58.

Hagale (sym.). Lehner: Pict. bk. of sym., p. 28.

Hagen, John P. Cur. biog. p. 226 (1957).

Hagen, Uta. Cur. biog. p. 203 (1944); (1963).

Hagerty, James C. Cur. biog. p. 229 (1953).

Hagia Sophia mosque (Istanbul). Holiday 27: 128 Jan '60, 4 Mar 60.

—— (cross section). Praeg. pict. ency., p. 231.

——, 1st Osward: Asia Minor, pl. 58.

——, 3rd (ext. & int.). Osward: Asia Minor, pl. 59-65, pl. III (col.).

—— (plan). Int. gr. soc.: Arts . . . p. 45 (col.).

Hagith (seal of). Lehner: Pict. bk. of sym., p. 25.

Hagy, Ruth Geri. Cur. biog. p. 228 (1957).

Hahn, Emily. Cur. biog. p. 325 (1942).

Hahn, Otto. Cur. biog. p. 253 (1951).

Hahn, William (work of). Natl. geog. 99: 204 (col.) Feb '51.

Hahnemann, Samuel. Holiday 19: 87 Mar '56.

Haid, J. J. (engraving by). Con. 142: 88 Nov '58.

Haig-Brown, Roderick. Cur. biog. p. 216 (1950).

Haile Selassie I, Emperor of Ethiopia. Cur. biog. p. 359 (1941); p. 316 (1954).

Hailsham, Lord Quintin. Cur. biog. p. 229 (1957).

hair (long braids). Holiday 19: 69 (col.) May '56.

hair dresser. Natl. geog. 103: 349 Mar '53.

hair dressing (Belgian Congo, primitive). Natl. geog. 101: 346 Mar '52.

—— (Morocco). Disney: People & places, p. 86 (col.).

—— (Seminole Indian). Natl. geog. 110: 830 (col.) Dec '56.

hair pins, stone age. Natl. geog. 113: 436 Mar '58.

hair style (Berber child). Natl. geog. 107: 171 Feb '55.

—— (Cretan woman, ancient). Int. gr. soc.: Arts . . . p. 29 (col.).

—— (Godey fashion). Amer. heri. vol. 9 no. 6 p. 23 (Oct '58).

—— (ancient times). Int. gr. soc.: Arts . . . p. 31 (col.).

—— (many ages & countries). Int. gr. soc.: Arts . . . p. 181 (col.).

hair styling in shop (Japan). Natl. geog. 97: 623 (col.) May '50.

Haiti. Holiday 5: 60-1 (col.), 62-3 Feb '49; 7: 98-109 (part col.) Mar '50. Travel 109: 38-9 May '58.

—— (farm workers). Holiday 5: 61 (col.) Feb '49.

—— (Hotel Castelhaiti). Travel 105: 56 May '56.

—— (man & woman, loads on head). Holiday 25: 102 Jan '59.

—— (Negro village). Holiday 10: 62-3 Nov '51.

Haiti (woman). Holiday 23: 44 Feb '58.
Haiti dancers. Holiday 16: inside cover (col.) Aug '54.
Hakenkreuz (sym). Lehner: Pict. bk. of sym., p. 95.
Hakluyt's "Principal navigations" (title page). Amer. heri. vol. 11 no. 1 p. 47 (Dec '59).
Hal Gate (Brussels, Belgium). Holiday 17: 128 Mar '55.
Halaby, Najeeb E. Cur. biog. p. 190 (1961).
Halasz, Laszlo. Cur. biog. p. 237 (1949).
halberd. Natl. geog. 112: 458 (col.) Oct '57.
—— (16th cent.). Con. ency. of ant., vol. 1, pl. 109.
Hale, Matthew. Con. 142: LIX Jan '59.
—— (Gainsborough). Con. 145: 193 (col.) May '60.
Hale, Nathan (capture of). Amer. heri. vol. 6 no. 5 p. 24 (col.) (Aug '55).
Hale, Gen. Nathan (drummed to execution). Amer. heri. vol. 6 no. 5 p. 25 (col.) (Aug '55).
Hale, Sarah Josepha. Amer. heri. vol. 9 no. 6 p. 22 (Oct '58).
Haleakala volcano crater (Hawaii). Natl. geog. 113: 633 (col.) May '58; 118: 38-9 (col.) Jl '60.
Hales, Thomas (portrait by Wolloston). Con. 138: 281 Jan '57.
Haley, Andrew G. Cur. biog. p. 251 (1955).
Haley, Sir William John. Cur. biog. p. 267 (1948).
half-timbered houses. See house, English (half-timbered).
Halicarnassus (harbor). Natl. geog. 117: 690-1 (col.) May '60.
Halim, Mustafa Ben. Cur. biog. p. 242 (1956).
Hall, Florence. Cur. biog. p. 271 (1943).
Hall, Frederick Lee. Cur. biog. p. 253 (1955).
Hall, Harry (work of). Con. 144: 113 (col.) Nov '59.
Hall, Joyce C. Cur. biog. p. 231 (1953).
Hall, Leonard W. Cur. biog. p. 232 (1953).
Hall, Marjory. Cur. biog. p. 231 (1957).
Hall, P. A. (self-portrait). Con. 141: 19 Mar '58.
Hall, Peter. Cur. biog. p. 179 (1962).
Hall, Pierre-Adolphe (miniature by). Con. 138: 83 Nov '56.
Hall, Rev. Dr. Raymond S. Cur. biog. p. 235 (1953).
Hall, William Edwin. Cur. biog. p. 318 (1954).
hall, Colonial. Natl geog. 103: 537 (col.) Ap '53; 105: 449, 454, 465 (col.) Ap '54; 113: 535 (col.) Ap '58; 118: 177 (col.) Aug '60.
——, vaulted. Holiday 21: 43 (col.) Jan '57.
Hall of liberation (Bavaria). Praeg. pict. ency., p. 423.
"Hall of State" (Dallas, Texas). See Dallas (Texas, "Hall of State").
Hallaren, Col. Mary A. Cur. biog. p. 238 (1949).
Halle, William (work of). Con. 142: XL Dec '58; 145: XLV Ap '60.
Halleck, Charles A. Cur. biog. p. 272 (1947).
Halleck, Henry Wager. Pakula: Cent. album, p. 145.
Halley, Rudolph. Cur. biog. p. 237 (1953).

Halligan, William J. Cur. biog. p. 232 (1957).
Hallinan, Vincent. Cur. biog. p. 239 (1952).
Halloween (children). Holiday 20: 130 Oct '56.
—— (sym.) Lehner: Pict. bk. of sym., p. 53.
Hallstatt (Austria). Natl. geog. 118: 257, 260- (col.) Aug '60.
Hallstein, Walter. Cur. biog. p. 239 (1953).
Hallverdiksstrand (Sweden). Travel 107: 22 May '57.
hallway. See hall.
Halpert, Edith Gregor. Cur. biog. p. 255 (1955).
Halprin, Mrs. Samuel W. Cur. biog. p. 218 (1950).
Hals, Dirk (work of). Con. 132: XXX Nov '53.
Hals, Frans (work of). Con. ency. of ant., vol. 1, pl. 163.
Con. 134: 94 Nov '54; 137: cover (col.), 115 Ap '56; 138: 278 Jan '57; 142: 42 Sept '58; 143: 62 Mar '59, 143 May '59; 144: 41 Sept '59, LXI (col.) Dec '59, XIV Jan 60; 145: 159 May '60.
Praeg. pict. ency., p. 337 (col.).
Hals, Nicolaes (Claes) (work of). Con. ency. of ant., vol. 1, pl. 171.
Halsey, Margaret. Cur. biog. p. 263 (1944).
Halsey, Adm. William F., jr. Cur. biog. p. 326 (1942).
Halsman, Philippe. Cur. biog. p. 175 (1960).
"The halt" (Brueghel the elder). Con. 135: 199 May '55, 261 (col.) Je '55.
Hamblet. Col. Julia E. Cur. biog. p. 240 (1953).
Hamburg (night, West Germany). Natl. geog. 115: 776-7 Je '59.
Hamill, Curt. Amer. heri. vol. 9 no. 4 p. 36 (Je '58).
Hamilton, Alexander. Amer. heri. vol. 6 no. 3 p. 44 (col.) (Ap '55); vol. 6 no. 4 p. 4 (Je '55); vol. 6 no. 6 p. 56 (Oct '55).
—— (statue). Natl. geog. 111: 73 Jan '57.
Hamilton, Alice. Cur. biog. p. 235 (1946).
Hamilton, Lord & Lady Claud (Kenya). Holiday 25: 85 (col.) Ap '59.
Hamilton, Edith. Cur. biog. (1963).
Hamilton, Gavin (work of). Con. 143: 245 Je '59.
Hamilton (Bermuda). Travel 111: 17 Feb '59.
Hamilton harbor (Bermuda). Holiday 23: 71 (col.) Je '58.
Hamilton's birthplace, Alexander. Amer. heri. vol. 6 no. 4 p. 6 (Je '55).
"Hamlet" (scenes). Int. gr. soc.: Arts . . . p. 107 (col.).
Hamlet's home (Kronborg castle). Holiday 18: 29 Sept '55.
Hamlin, Talbot. Cur. biog. p. 320 (1954).
Hamlin & wife, Hannibal. Jensen: The White House, p. 88.
Hammarskjold, Dag. Cur. biog. p. 241 (1953).
hammer. Holiday 19: 93 Mar '56.
Natl. geog. 103: 819 Je '53.
—— (antique). Amer. heri. vol. 7 no. 3 p. 61 (Ap '56).
—— (sym.) Lehner: Pict. bk. of sym., p. 91.
——, "head set" See "head set hammer."

——, silver headed (1869). Natl. geog. 110: 219 (col.) Aug '56.

——, sledge. *See* sledge hammer.

——, Thor's. *See* Thor's hammer.

——, Urgüp. Natl. geog. 113: 138 Je '58.

hammer & sickle (sym). Lehner: Pict. bk. of sym., p. 94.

Hammerfest (Norway). Natl. geog. 108: 738-9 (col.) Dec '55.

hammers, Mining (sym.). Lehner: Pict. bk. of sym., p. 12.

Hammerstein, Oscar, 2d. Cur. biog. p. 265 (1944).
Holiday 25: 91 Feb '59.

hammock. Holiday 20: 127 Dec '56; 21: 53 (col.) Feb '57, 197 May '57; 25: 163 (col.) Mar '59.

—— (man). Natl. geog. 107: 72 (col.) Jan '55.

—— (monkeys). Natl. geog. 102: 708 Nov '52.

—— (woman). Amer. heri. vol. 8 no. 5 p. 52 (col.) (Aug '57).
Holiday 21: cover (col.) Mar '57.

——, baby (Seminole Indian). Natl. geog. 110: 828 Dec '56.

hammocks (men & women). Holiday 11: 57 (col.) Mar '52.

Hammon, William McDowell. Cur. biog. p. 234 (1957).

Hammond, Caleb D., jr. Cur. biog. p. 244 (1956).

Hammond, Edward Cuyler. Cur. biog. p. 235 (1957).

Hammond, Godfrey. Cur. biog. p. 243 (1953).

Hammond, John Hays, jr. Cur. biog. p. 181 (1962).

Hampden, Walter. Cur. biog. p. 245 (1953).

hamper, picnic. Holiday 10: 57 Jl '51; 13: 158 May '53; 14: 17 Jl '53; 18: 60 (col.) (Aug '55; 19: cover (col.) Je '56.

Hampton, Wade. Pakula: Cent. album, p. 147.

Hampton court. Natl. geog. 114: 82-3 (col.) Jl '58.

Hampton court parterre (Marot's drawing). Con. 126: 64 Aug '50.

Hampton Roads (bridge tunnel). Natl. geog. 113: 10 Jan '58.

Hamza, J. (work of). Con. 136: LV Jan '56.

Han, Suyin. Cur. biog. p. 238 (1957).

Hancher, Virgil M. Cur. biog. p. 239 (1957).

Hancock, Florence. Cur. biog. p. 268 (1948).

Hancock, John M. Cur. biog. p. 240 (1949).

Hancock, Capt. Joy B. Cur. biog. p. 242 (1949).

Hancock, Maj. Gen. Winfield Scott. Amer. heri. vol. 9 no. 1 p. 37 (Dec '57).
Pakula: Cent. album, p. 149.

Hancock campaign card 1880. Amer. heri. vol. 11 no. 6 back cover (col.) (Oct '60).

Hand, Learned. Cur. biog. p. 219 (1950).

hand. Natl. geog. 98: 83 (col.) Jl '50.
Travel 114: back cover Jl '60.

—— (animals). Natl. geog. 111: 518-9 (col.) Ap '57.

—— (arthritis). Holiday 11: 137 May '52.

—— (auto). Holiday 12: 66 (col.) Oct '52.

—— (auto driver). Holiday 19: 24 (col.) Feb '56.

—— (baby skunk). Natl. geog. 108: 282 Aug '55.

—— (bear paw). Natl. geog. 118: 282 (col.) Aug. '60.

—— (beer glass). Holiday 21: 5 (col.) Jan '57.

—— (billfold). Holiday 10: 83 Dec '51; 20: 102 (col.) Dec '56.

—— (bone lamp, stone age). Natl. geog. 113: 429 Mar '58.

—— (book). Natl. geog. 114: 249 Aug '58.

—— (bottle). Holiday 12: 73 Nov '52; 18: 97 Nov '55, 127 Dec '55; 20: 136 (col.) Nov '56, 104 (col.) Dec '56; 21: 99 Ap '57, 160 May '57, 14 Je '57; 22: 47 Nov '57, 131 Dec '57.

—— (bottle, pouring). Holiday 22: 24 Nov '57.

—— (can). Holiday 21: 18 Je '57.

—— (card). Holiday 10: 79 (col.) Dec '51; 18: 149 (col.) Dec '55.

—— (cigarette). Holiday 18: 121 (col.) Oct '55.

—— (cigarette lighter). Holiday 22: 205 (col.) Dec '57.

—— (cocktail). Holiday 19: 74 Jan '56; 21: 192 (col.) Ap '57, 14 Je '57; 22: 141 (col.) Dec '57; 24: 80 Sept '58, 197 Dec '58; 25: 208 Ap '59, 130 Je '59; 26: 11, 121 Jl '59, 111 Sept '59, 113, 162, 175 Oct '59.

—— (corkscrew). Holiday 22: 82 Sept '57, 19 Nov '57.

—— (cosmetic can). Holiday 22: 76 Sept '57.

—— (cosmetic jar). Holiday 22: 101 Jl '57.

—— (cosmetic mixer). Holiday 22: 81 (col.) Sept '57.

—— (crab). Natl. geog. 118: 441 Sept '60.

—— (door knocker). Holiday 12: 15 (col.) Dec '52; 24: 3 Nov '58.

—— (eyeglasses). Holiday 10: 97 Oct '51.

—— (finger pointing). Holiday 27: 104 Feb '60.

—— (fingers spread). Holiday 10: 89 Aug '51.

—— (fish). Disney: People & places, p. 102 (col.).

—— (fish pole). Holiday 14: 132 Jl '53, 72 Sept '53.

—— (flowers). Natl. geog. 118: 474 (col.) Oct '60.

—— (fossil). Natl. geog. 109: 369, 372, 377, 381, 386 (part col.) Mar '56.

—— (giant beetle). Natl. geog. 115: 662 (col.) May '59.

—— (glass). Holiday 10: 73, 152 Nov '51, 12 (col.), 39 Dec '51; 11: 86 Jan '52; 12: 66 Nov '52, 17, 41 Dec '52; 18: 122 (col.) Jl '55, 90 (col.) Sept '55, 21, 93 Oct '55, 123, 146, 153 (col.) Nov '55, 70, 139, 157 (col.) Dec '55; 19: 97 Feb '56, 86 (col.) Je '56; 20: 59 (col.) Aug '56, 23, 30, 81 (col.), 84 Oct '56, 22 (col.), 110 Nov '56, 174 (col.) Dec '56; 21: 43 (col.) Je '57; 22: 91 (col.) Jl '57.

—— (glass, napkin). Holiday 19: 82 May '56.

hand (glass, pouring). Holiday 19: 137 (col.) Je '56; 20: 20 (col.) Aug '56; 21: 23 (col.) Jan '57.

—— (globe). Holiday 24: 4 Jl '58, 92 Sept '58.

—— (glove). Holiday 18: 21 Oct '55, 146, 159 Nov '55, 70 Dec '55.

—— (kiwi bird). Natl. geog. 108: 394 Sept '55.

—— (lymphatic system). Gray's anatomy, p. 712.

—— (marine vampire). Natl. geog. 115: 478 Ap '59.

—— (mice). Natl. geog. 114: 325 (col.) Sept '58.

—— (mirror, face). Holiday 12: 105 Sept '52.

—— (movie camera). Holiday 10: 2 (col.) Dec '51.

—— (mushroom). Natl. geog. 109: 818 Je '56.

—— (oil gage). Holiday 18: 83 Aug '55.

—— (on glass top). Holiday 27: 188 (col.) Mar '60.

—— (Oriental sym.). Lehner: Pict. bk. of sym., p. 43.

—— (palm reading). Lehner: Pict. bk. of sym., p. 67.

—— (pebbles). Natl. geog. 118: 425 (col.) Sept '60.

—— (pen). Holiday 12: 81 (col.) Sept '52.

—— (picture projector). Holiday 22: 77 Sept '57, 99 (col.) Nov '57.

—— (pine cone). Natl. geog. 99: 686 (col.) May '51.

—— (pine cone nuts). Natl. geog. 109: 12 (col.) Jan '56.

—— (portapaz). Natl. geog. 107: 515 (col.) Ap '55.

—— (pouring cocktail). Holiday 24: 87 (col.) Jl. '58.

—— (pouring coffee). Holiday 10: 142 Oct '51.

—— (pouring drink). Holiday 21: 19 (col.) Je '57.

—— (pouring liquor). Holiday 24: 10 (col.) Aug '58.

—— (pushing bell button). Holiday 24: 16 Oct '58.

—— (puya bloom). Natl. geog. 98: 470 (col.) Oct '50.

—— (razor). Holiday 22: 11 (col.) Dec '57.

—— (ring). Holiday 22: 207 (col.) Dec '57.

—— (sacred arm bone). Natl. geog. 110: 757 (col.) Dec '56.

—— (sculpture). Holiday 23: 112 Je '58.

—— (sea nettles). Natl. geog. 113: 8 (col.) Jan '58.

—— (shoe). Holiday 12: 2 Sept '52.

—— (skeleton). Gray's Anatomy, p. 198-9, 205, 450-1, 455, 460, 1403.

—— (snake). Natl. geog. 106: 359 Sept '54.

—— (spearheads). Natl. geog. 108: 784 Dec '55.

—— (stone age ax). Natl. geog. 113: 436 Mar '58.

—— (stone age spears). Natl. geog. 113: 434 Mar '58.

—— (sym.). Lehner: Pict. bk. of sym., p. 62, 78-9.

—— (tankard). Holiday 26: 106 (col.) Oct '59.

—— (tape measure). Holiday 22: 134 Oct '57.

—— (trade card). Amer. heri. vol. 11 no. 6 back cover (col.) (Oct '60).

—— (transistor). Holiday 19: 99 Mar '56; 21: 17 (col.) May '57; 22: 27 (col.) Jl '57.

—— (traveling bag). Holiday 19: 138 Jan '56.

—— (tray). Holiday 18: 65 Aug '55.

—— (veins). Gray's Anatomy, p. 669.

—— (watch). Natl. geog. 117: 173 (col.) Feb '60.

—— (whale tooth). Natl. geog. 114: 535 (col.) Oct '58.

hand, black (sym.). Lehner: Pict. bk. of sym., p. 83.

——, closed. Lehner: Pict. bk. of sym., p. 89.

——, Japanese (notched nails). Natl. geog. 97: 626 (col.) May '50.

——, man's. Holiday 27: 1, 41, 111 (col.) Je 60; 28: 114, 181 (col.) Oct '60. Natl. geog. 107: 43 (col.) Jan '55.

——, man's (bottle). Holiday 26: 36 Dec '59.

——, man's (cocktail). Holiday 27: 15 (col.) Jan '60, 22 Ap '60; 28: 14, 26 (col.) Nov '60.

——, mans' (fish pole). Holiday 14: 3 Aug '53.

——, man's (glove). Holiday 21: 158 Mar '57; 26: 92 Nov '59.

——, man's (pouring cocktail). Holiday 26: 190 (col.) Nov '59.

hand, raised (sym.). Lehner: Pict. bk. of sym., p. 89.

hand, woman's. Con. 140: XLIV Sept '57. Holiday 27: inside cover (col.) Feb '60.

——, woman's (glass). Holiday 21: 180 Mar '57.

hand & candle (sym.). Lehner: Pict. bk. of sym., p. 78.

hand & plant (sym.). Lehner: Pict. bk. of sym, p. 78.

hand-blocked cloth. Natl. geog. 107: 420 (col.) Mar '55.

"hand of glory" (sym.). Lehner: Pict. bk. of sym., p. 71.

hand of Lady Fatima (sym.). Lehner: Pict. bk. of sym., p. 41.

hand sign (sym.). Lehner: Pict. bk. of sym., p. 85.

hand. See also hands.

handbag. Holiday 11: 69 (col.) Je '52; 25: 200 May '59; 26: 10 (col.) Aug '59. Travel 113: 19 Ap '60.

handbill (1843, Trumbull gallery). Amer. heri. vol. 9 no. 4 p. 97 (Je '58).

handbills, circus. Durant: Pict. hist. of Amer. circus, p. 21, 25-7, 29, 31.

handcar (on tracks). Natl. geog. 97: 149 (col.), 157 Feb '50.

——, sail-powered (railroad). Natl. geog. 115: 783 (col.) Je '59.

handcuffs. Rawson: Ant. pict. bk. p. 18.

Handel, George Friedrich (Denner). Cooper: Con. ency. of music, p. 118 (col.).

Handforth, Thomas. Jun. bk. of auth., p. 151.

handicrafts. Holiday 24: 179-83 (col.) Dec '58.
——, girl making. Natl. geog. 104: 812 (col.) Dec '53.
handles, brass (furniture). Rawson: Ant. pict. bk., p. 85.
Handley, Harold W. Cur. biog. p. 177 (1960).
Handlin, Oscar. Cur. biog. p. 240 (1952).
Hands, Richard Lonsdale (work of). Con. 145: II (col.) Mar '60.
hands. Holiday 12: 97 Sept '52; 13: 1, 26 Feb 53, 141 Ap '53, inside cover (col.) May '53; 20: 32 (col.) Nov '56; 22: 100 Nov '57, 17 Dec '57; 23: 81 Jan '58. Natl. geog. 100: 105 (col.) Jl '51.
—— (auto steering wheel). Holiday 11: 83 (col.) Je '52.
—— (banding Canada goose). Natl. geog. 112: 828 (col.) Dec '57.
—— (beaver). Natl. geog. 107: 675 (col.) May '55.
—— (bottle, glass). Holiday 18: 18 Dec '55.
—— (box). Holiday 21: 23 (col.) Jan '57.
—— (broken pottery). Natl. geog. 111: 589 May '57.
—— (butterfly). Natl. geog. 112: 207 (col.) Aug '57.
—— (carving meat). Holiday 10: 64 (col.) Sept '51.
—— (carving turkey). Holiday 18: 7 (col.) Nov '55.
—— (clasped). Holiday 18: 93 Sept '55.
—— (cocktail). Holiday 19: 7 (col.) Jan '56; 24: 18 (col.) Dec '58; 25: 32 (col.) Jan '59; 27: 217 Ap '60, 132-3 (col.) Je '60.
—— (cuff links). Holiday 18: 68-9 (col.) Oct '55.
—— (cutting grapes). Holiday 26: 137 Nov '59.
—— (date flower). Natl. geog. 114: 479 (col.) Oct '58.
—— (deep sea fish). Natl. geog. 102: 462 (col.) Oct '52.
—— (diamonds). Natl. geog. 113: 573-4, 579 Ap '58.
—— (eels). Natl. geog. 116: 807 (col.) Dec '59.
—— (egg). Natl. geog. 112: 821 (col.) Dec '57.
—— (fish). Natl. geog. 101: 15 (col.) Jan '52.
—— (fixing man's tie). Holiday 18: 79 Aug '55.
—— (flowers). Natl. geog. 114: 424 (col.) Sept '58.
—— (glasses). Holiday 19: 109 Jan '56, 140 (col.) Je '56; 22: 18 Sept '57, 34 Oct '57, 235 Dec '57.
—— (lobster). Natl. geog. 115: 292 Feb '59.
—— (maps). Natl. geog. 113: 732-3 May '58.
—— (match & needle, heat). Natl. geog. 114: 315 Sept '58.
—— (Maya jar). Natl. geog. 115: 90 (col.) Jan '59.
—— (minerals). Natl. geog. 112: 136 (col.) Jl '57.
—— (mirror). Holiday 18: 21 (col.) Nov '55.
—— (music record). Holiday 18: 9 Aug '55.
—— (note paper). Holiday 12: 104 Sept '52.
—— (on ram). Natl. geog. 110: 808 (col.) Dec '56.

—— (platypus). Natl. geog. 114: 513, 521-3 Oct '58.
—— (playing cards). Holiday 27: 133 (col.) Je '60.
—— (pointing). Amer. heri. vol. 11 no. 1 p. 120 (Dec '59).
—— (pouring drink). Holiday 26: 22 (col.) Sept '59.
—— (radio). Holiday 22: 219 Dec '57.
—— (satellite chart). Natl. geog. 112: 808 Dec '57.
—— sea cucumber). Natl. geog. 111: 36 (col.) Jan '57.
—— (sheep wool). Natl. geog. 113: 349 (col.) Mar '58.
—— (smoking). Holiday 27: 133 (col.) Je '60.
—— (star fish). Natl. geog. 111: 23 (col.) Jan '57.
—— (television). Holiday 21: 1 May '57.
—— (testing baby milk). Holiday 25: 126 (col.) May '59.
—— (tree coring instrument). Natl. geog. 113: 370 (col.) Mar '58.
—— (worms). Natl. geog. 114: 518 Oct '58.
hands, clasped (sym.). Lehner: Pict. bk. of sym., p. 95.
——, folded (praying). Lehner: Pict. bk. of sym., p. 37.
——, man & woman's. Holiday 23: 103 (col.) Je '58.
——, man & woman's (cheering). Holiday 27: 139 Je '60.
——, man & woman's (meeting). Holiday 20: 3 Oct '56.
——, man's. Holiday 14: 128 Jl '53; 28: 79 (col.) Aug '60, 126 (col.), 133. 147, 193, 209 (col.) Dec '60. Travel 113: 45 Jan '60, 54 May '60.
——, man's (music conductor). Int. gr. soc.: Arts . . . p. 141 (col.).
——, man's (repairing tire). Holiday 23: 129 Je '58.
——, woman's. Holiday 20: 162 Nov '56; 21: 19 Jan '57, 168 Ap '57, 48 Je '57; 23: 132 Ap '58; 28: 209 (col.), 210 Dec '60. Natl. geog. 100: 108 (col.) Jl '51.
——, woman's (pearls). Natl. geog. 98: 789 (col.) Dec '50.
——, woman's (perfume spray). Holiday 27: 135 Ap '60.
——, woman's (work). Travel 110: inside back cover Aug '58.
hands & heart. See heart & hands.
"Hands of Godfry Mowatt" (Vasconcellos). Con. 135: 265 Je '55.
"Hands-up" poster. Horan: Pict. hist. of wild west, p. 190.
hands. See also hand.
Handy, Gen. Thomas Troy. Cur. biog. p. 254 (1951).
Handy, William C. Cur. biog. p. 361 (1941).
"The hanged man" (Hugo). Con. 143: 163 May '59.
"Hanging gardens" (Babylonian reconstruction). Int. gr. soc.: Arts . . . p. 13 (col.).
hangman (early western). Horan: Pict. hist. of wild west, p. 142.

Haniwa warrior, Japanese (sculpture, 6th cent). Con. 145: 289 Je '60.

Hanks, O. C. Horan: Pict. hist. of wild west, p. 193, 219.

Hanks' grave, Nancy. *See* grave of Nancy Hanks.

Hanna, Mark. Amer. heri. vol. 11 no. 1 p. 34 (Dec '59).

—— (cartoon). Amer. heri. vol. 11 no. 1 p. 35 (Dec '59).

Hannagan, Steve. Cur. biog. p. 267 (1944).

Hannah, John A. Cur. biog. p. 243 (1952).

"Hannah" (U.S. naval ship). Holiday 24: 57 Oct '58.

Hannegan, Robert E. Cur. biog. p. 269 (1944).

Hannibal (Mo., Tom Sawyer & Huck Finn's home town). Jordan: Hammond's pict. atlas, p. 100-1 (col.).
Natl. geog. 110: 120-40 Jl '56.

—— (scenes from "Tom Sawyer & Huck Finn"). Travel 104: 40-1 Aug '55.

Hannikainen, Tauno. Cur. biog. p. 257 (1955).

"Hans Brinker" (book illus.). Amer. heri. vol. 8 no. 1 p. 33 (col.) (Dec '56).

Hanschman, Nancy. Cur. biog. p. 183 (1962).

Hansell, Brig. Gen. Haywood S. Cur. biog. p. 263 (1945).

Hansen, Alvin H. Cur. biog. p. 265 (1945).

Hansen, Carl F. Cur. biog. p. 185 (1962).

Hansen, Hans C. Cur. biog. p. 245 (1956).

Hansen, Harry. Cur. biog. p. 329 (1942).

Hansen, Herbert L. Natl. geog. 113: 459 Ap '58.

Hansenne, Marcel. Cur. biog. p. 237 (1946).

hansom cab. *See* cab, hansom.

Hanson, Howard. Cur. biog. p. 363 (1941).

Hansson, Per Albin. Cur. biog. p. 330 (1942).

"happi" coat (Japanese). Holiday 20: 133, 135 Oct '56, 132 Dec '56.

happiness (sym.). Lehner: Pict. bk. of sym., p. 45-6.

happy coat. *See* "happi" coat (Japanese).

"Happy encounter" (Lesur). Con. 138: XXVIII Sept '56.

"Happy land" (Chavannes). Con. 142: 62 Sept '58.

Hapstad, Lawrence R. Cur. biog. p. 240 (1956).

Harbach, Otto A. Cur. biog. p. 222 (1950).

Harber, W. Elmer. Cur. biog. p. 256 (1951).

harbor. Amer. heri. vol. 9 no. 6 p. 61 (col.) (Oct '58); vol. 10 no. 3 frontis (col.) (Ap '59); vol. 10 no. 4 p. 30-1 (col.) (Je '59); vol. 10 no. 6 p. 28 (col.) (Oct '59).
Con. ency. of ant., vol. 3, pl. 90, 94-5.
Holiday 23: 12-3, 16, 38, 73 (part col.) Jan '58; 27: 183 (col.) Mar '60; 28: 19 (col.) Jl 60.
Labande: Naples.
Travel 102: 7 Oct '54, inside cover, 17 Dec '54; 103: 37 Jan '55.

—— (boats). Natl. geog. 106: 588-9 (col.) Nov '54.

—— (Colonial village). Brooks: Growth of a nation, frontis.

—— (moonlight). Travel 104: inside cover Jl '55.

—— (night). Natl. geog. 105: 266-7 (col.) Feb '54.

—— (on the Bosporus). Osward: Asia Minor, pl. 83.

—— (rocky). Holiday 19: 71 (col.) Je '56.

—— (rocky, twisted trees). Natl. geog. 105: 755, 757 (col.) Je '54.

——, Aden (Arabia). Natl. geog. 105: 506-7 (col.) Ap '54.

——, Accra (Africa). Travel 108: 18 Oct '57.

——, Alaska. Natl. geog. 109: 744-5, 788-9 (col.) Je '56.

——, Algiers. Travel 104: 14 Nov 55.

——, Amalfi (Italy). Natl. geog. 116: 504-5 (col.) Oct '59.

——, Andros is. Holiday 23: 74-5 (col.) Mar '58.

——, Antalya. Osward: Asia Minor, pl. 111.

——, Antigua. Natl. geog. 99: 364 (col.) Mar '51; 116: 449 (col.) Oct '59.

——, Antwerp. Natl. geog. 113: 808-9 Je '58.

——. Argentina. Holiday 18: 149 (col.) Nov '55.
Natl. geog. 113: 303, 313, 341, 351 (part col.) Mar '58.

——, Arles (France). Natl. geog. 109: 669 (col.) May '56.

——, Auckland. Natl. geog. 101: 430 (col.) Ap '52.

——, Azores. Natl. geog. 113: 742-3 (col.) Je '58.

——, Bahama is. Natl. geog. 113: 148-9, 160-1, 164-5, 196-7 (part col.) Feb '58.

——, Bakar (Croatia). Holiday 25: 85 (col.) Je '59.

——, Balearic is. Natl. geog. 111: 623, 626-9, 652-3 (col.) May '57.
Travel 101: 32-3 Mar '54.

——, Barbados is. Holiday 23: 40 Feb '58.
Natl. geog. 101: 368-9 (col.) Mar '52; 116: 143 (col.) Jl '59.
Travel 103: 35 Mar '55.

——, Basle (Switzerland). Natl. geog. 98: 226 (col.) Aug '50.

——, Bergen (Norway). Natl. geog. 106: 154-5 (col.) Aug '54.

——, Bermuda. Amer. heri. vol. 6 no. 5 p. 38-9 (col.) (Aug '55).
Holiday 25: 162 (col.) Je '59; 27: 170 (col.) Ap '60.
Natl. geog. 105: 204-5, 238 (col.) Feb '54; 113: 770-1 (col.) Je '58.

——, Biloxi (Miss.). Travel 109: 21 Jan '58.

——, Black Sea (Turkey). Natl. geog. 115: 70-1 (col.) Jan '59.

——, Bodo (Norway). Travel 111: 42 Ap '59.

——, Brazil. Holiday 22: 125 (col.) Sept '57.
Travel 103: cover Mar '55.

——, Buenos Aires. Natl. geog. 108: 757 (col.) Dec '55; 113: 312-3 Mar '58.

——, Calcutta. Natl. geog. 118: 502-3 (col.) Oct 60.

——, California. Face of Amer., p. 84-5 (col.).

——, Canada. Natl. geog. 104: 832 (col.) Dec '53.

——, Canton (China). Amer. heri. vol. 6 no. 2 p. 16 (col.) (winter '55).

——, **Caribbean.** Holiday 27: 136 (col.) Feb '60.

——, **Cartagena.** Holiday 24: 140 (col.) Oct '58.

——, **Charleston (S.C., 1831)** Amer. heri. vol. 9 no. 2 p. 49, 51 (col.) Feb '58.

——, **Chile.** Holiday 28: 141 (col.) Oct '60.

——, **China.** Natl. geog. 103: 682 (col.) May '53.

——. **Connecticut.** Holiday 26: 34-5 (col.) Sept '59.
Travel 104: 31-3 Sept '55.

——. **Crete.** Natl. geog. 104: 700 (col.) Nov '53.

——, **Cyprus is.** Natl. geog. 101: 660-1 (col.) May '52.

——, **Cyprus (boats, girls).** Natl. geog. **109:** 880 Je '56.

——, **Delos.** *See* Delos harbor.

——, **Denmark.** Natl. geog. 108: 810-11, 822 (col.) Dec '55.

——, **Dubrovnik.** Holiday 14: 39 (col.) Aug '53.

——, **Elanchove (Spain).** Natl. geog. 105: 154 (col.) Feb '54.

——, **England.** Holiday 27: 127 (col.) Feb '60.

——, **Estoril (Portugal).** Travel 111: 33 Je '59.

——, **Fiji.** Travel 102: 32 Nov '54.

——, **France.** Holiday 28: 5 (col.) Sept '60.
Natl. geog. 115: 612-3, 618, 623, 626-7 (part col.) May '59.

——, **Fundy Bay.** Natl. geog. 112: 154-92 (part col.) Aug '57.

——, **Gloucester (Mass.)** Natl. geog. 98: 156 (col.) Aug '50.

——, **Grand Manan.** Travel 106: 46 Aug '56.

——, **Greece.** Holiday 24: 66-7 (col.) Sept '58.
Natl. geog. 103: 371, 374 (col.) Mar '53; 109: 58 (col.) Jan '56; 114: 758 (col.) Dec '58.

——, **Hamilton (Bermuda).** Travel 111: 17 Feb '59.

——, **Hartford (Conn., 1857).** Amer. heri. vol. 7 no. 4 frontis (col.) (Je '56).

——, **Haugesund (Norway).** Natl. geog. 106: 166 (col.) Aug '54.

——, **Hawaii.** Holiday 27: 157 Feb '60.
Natl. geog. 100: 742 (col.) Dec '51.
Travel 113: 60 Mar '60.

——, **Hebrides is.** Natl. geog. 106: 572 (col.) Oct '54.

——, **Holland.** Natl. geog. 106: 391 (col.) Sept '54.

——, **Hong Kong.** Holiday 22: 131 (col.) Nov '57.
Natl. geog. 97: 383 Mar '50; 103: 509 Ap '53; 105: 240-1, 243, 246-8 (part col.) Feb '54.

——, **Hudson river (1830).** Amer. heri. vol. 10 no. 1 p. 18-9, 24-5 (col.) (Dec '58).

——, **Hudson river (1850).** Amer. heri. vol. 10 no. 1 cover, p. 4-7, 12-3 (part col.) (Dec '58).

——, **Ischia.** Natl. geog. 105: 532-3, 538-9 (col.) Ap '54.

——, **Iskenderum.** Osward: Asia Minor, pl. 21-22.

——, **Isle royal.** Jordan: Hammond's pict. atlas, p. 90 (col.).

——, **Istanbul.** Natl. geog. 100: 724 Dec '51; 112: 110-11 Jl '57; 115: 86-7 (col.) Jan '59.

——, **Italy.** Holiday 12: 125 (col.) Jl '52.
Natl. geog. 111: 806-11 (col.) Je '57.

——, **Jamaica.** Natl. geog. 105: 336-7, 357 (col.) Mar '54.

——, **Japan.** Natl. geog. 104: 644 (col.) Nov '53.

——, **Key West (storm).** Natl. geog. 111: 706 May '57.

——, **King Edward Point (South Ga.).** Natl. geog. 107: 106 Jan '55.

——, **Korea.** Natl. geog. 97: 802 (col.) Je '50; 103: 642 (col.) May '53.

——, **Lavandou (France).** Travel 108: 57 Jl '57.

——, **Lisbon.** Natl. geog. 118: 652-3 (col.) Nov '60.

——, **Long is. (N.Y.).** Holiday 24: 35, 46 (col.) Sept '58.

——, **Madeira.** Holiday 28: 62 (col.) Sept '60.

——, **Maine.** Natl. geog. 102: 352 (col.) Sept '52; 111: 616 (col.) May '57.
Travel 107: 14 Jan '57.

——, **Maine (rocky coast).** Holiday 14: 48 (col.) Aug '53.

——, **Maldive is.** Natl. geog. 111: 848 (col.) Je '57.

——, **Malta.** Travel 109: 42 Ap '58.

——, **Manta (Ecuador).** Travel 109: 47 Jan '58.

——, **Martinique.** Natl. geog. 115: 256-7, 268-9, 278-9 (col.) Feb 59.

——, **Mazatlan (Mexico).** Holiday 24: 70 (col.) Nov '58.
Travel 106: inside cover Sept '56.

——, **Memphis (Tenn.).** Natl. geog. 118: 688-9 (col.) Nov '60.

——, **Minorca.** Holiday 27: 51, 54-5 (col.) Jan '60.

——, **Mombasa (Africa).** Natl. geog. 97: 322 (col.) Mar '50.

——, **Montreal.** Natl. geog. 108: 192-3 (col.) Aug '55.

——, **Mukalla (Saudi Arabia).** Natl. geog. 108: 156-7 (col.) Aug '55; 111: 250, 253 Feb '57.

——, **Narragansett Bay.** Natl. geog. 107: 751 (col.) Je '55.

——, **New Archangel.** Amer. heri. vol. 11 no. 3 p. 7 (Ap '60).

——, **New Brunswick (sail boats).** Holiday 27: 63 (col.) May '60.

——, **New York.** *See* New York (harbor).

——, **New Zealand.** Natl. geog. 101: 446 Ap 52.

——, **Newburyport (Mass.).** Natl. geog. 99: 122 (col.) Jan '51.

——, **Norfolk is.** Natl. geog. 118: 579 (col.) Oct '60.

——, **Norway.** Natl. geog. 108: 738-9 (col.) Dec '55; 111: 98, 120 (col.) Jan '57.

——, **Nova Scotia.** Holiday 27: 131 (col.) Ap '60.
Travel 110: cover (col.) Aug '58.

harbor, Oregon. Holiday 11: 85 (col.) Ap '52; 21: 29 (col.) Feb '57.

——, **Oslo.** Natl. geog. 106: 182 Aug '54.

——, **Penang.** Natl. geog. 103: 225 Feb '53.

——, **Phoenicia.** Natl. geog. 113: 504-5 Ap '58.

——, **Piran.** Holiday 25: 89 (col.) Je '59.

——, **Pitcairn is.** Natl. geog. 112: 776-7, 779-89 (col.) Dec '57.

——, **Plymouth (Mass.).** Natl. geog. 112: 662-3 (col.) Nov '57.

——, **Port Angeles (Wash.).** Natl. geog. 117: 450-1 (col.) Ap '60.

——, **Port Mahon (Minorca).** Con. 143: XXXI Ap '59.

——, **Port royal (Jamaica).** Natl. geog. 117: 151-4 (col.) Feb '60.

——, **Portsmouth (Eng.)** Natl. geog. 101: 537 (col.) Ap '52.

——, **Portugal.** Natl. geog. 101: 570 May '52; 106: 686-7 Nov '54.

——, **Portugal (rocky).** Natl. geog. 118: 637, 645 (col.) Nov '60.

——, **Positano (Italy).** Labande: Naples, p. 200.

——, **Procida harbor.** Natl. geog. 105: 544-5 (col.) Ap '54.

——, **Puerto Rico.** Natl. geog. 99: 428 (col.) Ap 51.
Travel 111: 41 Feb '59.

——, **Rhodes.** Travel 101: 19 Je '54.

——, **Rio de Janeiro.** Holiday 10: 146 (col.) Nov '51; 18: 10 (col.) Nov '55; 19: 125 (col.) Je '56; 21: 23 (col.) Ap '57, 100-1 (col.) Nov '56; 22: 118 (col.) Jl '57, 28 (col.) Nov '57.
Natl. geog. 107: 291, 296-7 (col.) Mar '55; 108: 748 (col.) Dec '55.

——, **Rockport (Mass.).** Holiday 24: 2 (col.) Jl '58.
Natl. geog. 98: 157 (col.) Aug '50.

——, **Rotterdam.** Natl. geog. 118: 526-7, 549 (col.) Oct '60.

——, **St. George.** Holiday 23: 37 (col.) Feb '58.

——, **St. John's (Canada).** Holiday 27: 146 (col.) Mar '60.

——, **St. Lucia capitol.** Travel 109: 23 May '58.

——, **St. Mary's isle.** Travel 101: 16 Feb '54.

——, **Salem (Mass., 1805).** Amer. heri. vol. 6 no. 2 p. 10-11 (col.) (winter '55).

——, **San Diego (Cal.).** Jordan: Hammond's pict. atlas, p. 207 (col.).

——, **San Francisco.** Holiday 20: 31 (col.) Aug '56; 25: 136 (col.) Mar '59.
Natl. geog. 110: 198, 200-1, 209, 214-5 (col.) Aug '56.

——, **San Juan is.** Amer. heri. vol. 11 no. 3 p. 62 (col.) (Ap '60).

——, **San Sebastian.** Natl. geog. 105: 178-9 (col.) Feb '54.

——, **Santa Cruz.** Natl. geog. 107: 502 (col.) Ap '55.

——, **Saudi Arabia.** Natl. geog. 117: 106-7 (col.) Jan '60.

——. **Savannah (Ga.).** Natl. geog. 105: 308 Mar '54.

——, **Scotland.** Natl. geog. 110: 29 (col.) Jl '56.

——, **Scotland (sunset).** Disney: People & places, p. 35 (col.).

——, **Sevillas river.** Natl. geog. 99: 511 (col.) Ap '51.

——, **Shanghai.** Natl. geog. 103: 508 Ap '53.

——, **Shetland is.** Natl. geog. 104: 536 Oct '53.

——, **Sicily.** Amer. heri. vol. 6 no. 6 p. 16-7 (col.) (Oct '55).
Natl. geog. 107: 5, 9, 20-1, 30 (col.) Jan '55.

——, **Singapore.** Natl. geog. 103: 194-5 (col.) Feb '53.

——, **Skala (Aegean sea).** Travel 103: 42 Ap '55.

——, **Spain.** Natl. geog. 108: 68-9 (col.) Jl '55.

——, **Sweden.** Natl. geog. 98: 606, 622 Nov '50.

——, **Switzerland.** Natl. geog. 110: 469 (col.) Oct '56.

——, **Sydney (Australia).** Natl. geog. 109: 256-7 (col.) Feb '56.

——, **Tacoma (Wash.).** Face of Amer., p. 154-5 (col.).

——, **Tasmania.** Natl. geog. 110: 799, 812-3 (col.) Dec '56.

——, **Tenby (Wales).** Natl. geog. 108: 574 Oct '55.

——, **Trieste (Italy).** Natl. geog. 109: 830-1, 838-9, 855 (part col.) Je '56.

——, **Trucial Oman.** Natl. geog. 110: 96-9 (col.) Jl '56.

——, **Turkey.** Natl. geog. 110: 735 (col.) Dec '56.

——, **Valparaiso (Chile).** Natl. geog. 117: 220-1 (col.) Feb '60.

——, **Virgin is.** Natl. geog. 109: 208-9, 220-1, 223 (col.) Feb '56.

——, **West Indies.** Natl. geog. 105: 332 Mar '54.

——, **Westport (ships).** Natl. geog. 117: 478-9 (col.) Ap '60.

——, **Yugoslavia.** Holiday 25: 80 (col.) Je 59.
Natl. geog. 99: 153, 160 (col.) Feb '51.

——, **Zanzibar.** Natl. geog. 101: 274 Feb '52.

Harbord, James G. Cur. biog. p. 267 (1945).

Hardee, William Joseph. Pakula: Cent. album, p. 151.

Harden, Mrs. Cecil M. Cur. biog. p. 244 (1949).

Hardenbrook, Donald J. Cur. biog. p. 187 (1962).

Hardie, Charles Martin (work of). Natl. geog. 112: 478-9 Oct '57.

Hardie, Steven J. L. Cur. biog. p. 258 (1951).

Hardin, John Wesley. Horan: Pict. hist. of wild west, p. 117.

Harding, Chester (work of). Amer. heri. vol. 10 no. 1 p. 30 (col.) (Dec '58).

Harding, J. D. (work of). Con. 144: 93 Nov '59.

Harding, Gen. Sir John. Cur. biog. p. 244 (1952).

Harding, Margaret S. Cur. biog. p. 275 (1947).

Harding, Pres. Warren G. Amer. heri. vol. 7 no. 3 p. 33 (Ap '56); vol. 10 no. 6 p. 42-3 (Oct '59).
Jensen: The White House, p. 214, 216-7.
Harding, Mrs. Warren G. Jensen: The White House, p. 214, 219-20.
Harding's tomb, Marion. Travel 104: 19 Aug '55.
Hardwar (India). Natl. geog. 118: 450-1 (col.) Oct '60.
Hardwicke, Sir Cedric. Cur. biog. p. 245 (1949).
Hardy, Porter, jr. Cur. biog. p. 241 (1957).
Hardy, Thomas. Con. 144: 12 Sept '59.
Hare, Sir Ralph. Con. 139: 218 Je '57.
Hare, Raymond A. Cur. biog. p. 243 (1957).
"Harem scene" in art (Turkey). Natl. geog. 100: 164 (col.) Aug '51.
Hargrave, Thomas J. Cur. biog. p. 248 (1949).
Hargrove, Marion. Cur. biog. p. 239 (1946). Holiday 6: 32 Oct '49.
Harkness, Douglas S. Cur. biog. p. 192 (1961).
Harkness, Rev. Dr. Georgia. Cur. biog. p. 179 (1960).
Harkness memorial park. Travel 108: 35 Aug '57.
Harkness memorial tower (Yale univ.). Holiday 13: 61 (col.) May '53.
Natl. geog. 112: 329 (col.) Sept '57.
Travel 110: 17 Oct '58.
Harlan, Justice John Marshall. Cur. biog. p. 259 (1955).
Holiday 18: 42 (col.) Nov '55.
Harlech castle (Wales). Holiday 11: 21 (col.) Ap '52; 27: 127 (col.) Feb '60.
Praeg. pict. ency., p. 44.
Harlem (N.Y.). Holiday 5: 110, 113 Ap '49.
Harlequin columns (Tiwis). Natl. geog. 109: 435 (col.) Mar '56.
Harmodius, head of (Tyrant-slayers detail). Labande: Naples. p. 95.
Harmon, Maj. Gen. Ernest N. Cur. biog. p. 242 (1946).
Harmon, Maj. Gen. Millard F. Cur. biog. p. 333 (1942).
harmonica (18th cent.). Con. 145: XX Mar '60.
harmonics (sym.). Lehner: Pict. bk. of sym., p. 12.
harness, burro. Rawson: Ant. pict. bk., p. 65.
harness shop. Natl. geog. 100: 313 (col.) Sept '51.
harnessmaker's chair. Rawson: Ant. pict. bk., p. 58.
Harney, Brig. Gen. William S. Amer. heri. vol. 11 no. 3 p. 105 (Ap '60).
Harnwell, Gaylord P. Cur. biog. p. 247 (1956).
Harp. Rear Adm. Edward B.. jr. Cur. biog. p. 247 (1953).
harp. Holiday 9: 63 Mar '51; 11: 113 (col.) May '52; 13: 53 (col.) Jan '53; 21: 61 Mar '57.
—— (ancient). Int. gr. soc.: Arts . . . p. 27 (col.).
—— (by Erard). Cooper: Con. ency. of music, p. 358.
—— (comic). Holiday 20: 35 Nov '56.
—— (girl flying). Holiday 21: 32 Mar '57.

—— (lyre). Lehner: Pict. bk. of sym., p. 14.
—— (man playing). Holiday 12: 76 (col.) Dec '52.
—— (mouth organ). Travel 112: 11 Dec '59.
—— (19th cent.). Con. 142: IV Dec '58.
—— (13th cent.). Int. gr. soc.: Arts . . . p. 61 (col.).
—— (woman playing). Natl. geog. 102: 355 (col.) Sept '52.
——, Dital. Con. 136: 57 Sept '55.
——, Irish. Amer. heri. vol. 9 no. 5 p. 91 (Aug '58).
Holiday 12: 126 Nov '52; 13: 4 Feb '53; 19: 62 Feb '56.
——, musical watch (antique). Con. 133: 44 Mar '54.
——, Welsh. Holiday 28: 35 (col.) Sept '60.
harp-lute. Con. 136: 55 Sept '55.
—— (Wheatstone, 1810). Cooper: Con. ency. of music, p. 359.
harp of Ur. Ceram: March of arch., p. 240-1.
Harper, Marion, jr. Cur. biog. p. 194 (1961).
Harper, William R. Amer. heri. vol. 6 no. 3 p. 72 (Ap '55).
Harpers Ferry (W. Va.). Amer. heri. vol. 6 no. 2 p. 8 (winter '55).
Face of Amer., p. 124 (col.).
Natl. geog. 111: 400-15 (part col.) Mar '57.
—— (Brown's raid). Travel 112: 44-7 Jl '59.
—— (battle camp). Natl. geog. 111: 414-5 Mar '57.
Harpers Ferry region (map). Natl. geog. 111: 404-5, 410 (col.) Mar '57.
Harpignies, Henri Joseph (work of). Con. 139: 53 Mar '57; 142: IX Sept '58; 143: VII Mar '59; 145: 124 (col.) Ap '60.
Harpocrates of the lotus (sym.). Lehner: Pict. bk. of sym., p. 66.
harpooner, whale. Natl. geog. 113: 784 (col.) Je '58.
harpsichord. Holiday 28: 75 (col.) Sept '60.
—— (Cembalo). Cooper: Con. ency. of music, p. 187 (col.).
—— (18th cent.). Con. 143: 120 Ap '59.
—— (Ruckers, 1637). Cooper: Con. ency. of music, p. 353.
—— (upright, antique). Con. 138: 45 Sept '56.
Harrelson, Walter J. Cur. biog. p. 167 (1959).
Harrer, Heinrich. Cur. biog. p. 322 (1954).
Harridge, William. Cur. biog. p. 249 (1949).
Harriers meeting (Rowlandson). Con. 129: LI Ap '52.
Harriman, E. Roland. Cur. biog. p. 260 (1951).
Harriman, Mrs. J. Borden. Holiday 7: 49 (col.) Feb '50.
Harriman, William Averell. Cur. biog. p. 365 (1941); p. 243 (1946).
Harrington, Russell C. Cur. biog. p. 249 (1956).
Harris, Sir Arthur Travers. Cur. biog. p. 334 (1942).
Harris, Bernice Kelly. Cur. biog. p. 251 (1949).
Harris, Bucky. Cur. biog. p. 270 (1948).
Harris, Harwell Hamilton. Cur. biog. p. 189 (1962).
Harris, J. (work of). Con. ency. of ant., vol. 1, pl. 139.

Harris, Julie. Cur. biog. p. 251 (1956).
Harris, Mark. Cur. biog. p. 168 (1959).
Harris, Mildred. Amer. heri. vol. 9 no. 5 p. 18 (Aug 58).
Harris, Oren. Cur. biog. p. 253 (1956).
Harris, W. H. Horan: Pict. hist. of wild west, p. 105.
Harris, Walter. Cur. biog. p. 261 (1955).
Harrison, Pres. Benjamin. Amer. heri. vol. 6 no. 5 p. 58 (Aug '55); vol. 7 no. 3 p. 32 (Ap '56); vol. 7 no. 4 p. 51 (Je '56); vol. 7 no. 5 p. 102 (Aug '56); vol. 8 no. 3 p. 64 (col.) (Ap '57). Holiday 11: 83 Ap '52.
Harrison, Mrs. Benjamin. Jensen: The White House, p. 139.
Harrison V, Benjamin. Amer. heri. vol. 8 no. 3 p. 61 (col.) (Ap '57).
Harrison, Earl G. Cur. biog. p 273 (1943).
Harrison, George M. Cur. biog. p. 252 (1949).
Harrison, Gilbert A. Cur. biog. p. 254 (1949).
Harrison, James L. Cur. biog. p. 191 (1962).
Harrison, Jane Ellen. Con. 144: 13 Sept '59.
Harrison, Joan. Cur. biog. p. 273 (1944).
Harrison, Lucy. Amer. heri. vol. 8 no. 3 p. 60 (Ap '57).
Harrison, Shelby M. Cur. biog. p. 276 (1943).
Harrison, Wallace K. Cur. biog. p. 279 (1947).
Harrison, William H. Cur. biog. p. 255 (1949).
Harrison, Pres. William Henry. Amer. heri. vol. 2 no. 1 p. 16 (fall '50); vol. 4 no. 1 p. 5 (fall '52); vol. 7 no. 3 p. 31 (Ap '56); vol. 8 no. 3 p. 64 (col.) (Ap '57). Holiday 28: 10 (col.) Aug '60. Natl. geog. 100: 583 (col.) Nov '51.
—— (death of). Jensen: The White House, p. 61.
—— (silhouette). Jensen: The White House, p. 60.
Harrison, Maj. Gen. William K., jr. Cur. biog. p. 246 (1952).
Harrison & children, Mrs. Russell. Jensen: The White House, p. 148.
Harrison (Gen.) and Tecumseh. Amer. heri. vol. 4 no. 1 p. 2 (fall '52).
Harrison grandchildren, Pres. Benjamin Jensen: The White House, p. 140-47.
Harrison home, Benjamin. Natl. geog. 103: 791 (col.) Je '53.
Harrison home, William Henry. Natl. geog. 103: 791 (col.) Je '53.
Harrison's plantation (Va.). Amer. heri. vol. 8 no. 3 p. 58-63 (col.) (Ap '57).
Harrison's tomb, William Henry. Amer. heri. vol. 4 no. 3 p. 48 (col.) (spring '53).
Harron, Marion J. Cur. biog. p. 257 (1949).
harrow (horses, man). Natl. geog. 106: 573 (col.) Oct '54.
—— (man, ox work rice field). Natl. geog. 103: 664 (col.) May '53.
——, tooth. Rawson: Ant. pict. bk., p. 30.
Harry, Philip (work of). Con. 129: 69 Ap '52.
Harsch, Joseph C. Cur. biog. p. 275 (1944).
Hart, Edward J. Cur. biog. p. 248 (1953).
Hart, Merwin K. Cur. biog. p. 367 (1941).
Hart, Moss. Cur. biog. p. 181 (1960).
Hart, Pearl. Horan: Pict. hist. of wild west, p. 137.
Hart, Philip A. Cur. biog. p. 170 (1959).

Hart, Adm. Thomas C. Cur. biog. p. 336 (1942).
Hart, William S. Brooks: Growth of a nation, p. 242.
Hartford, Huntington, 2d. Cur. biog. p. 172 (1959).
Hartford (Conn.). Holiday 8: 30-7 (part col.) Jl '50; 27: 82-7 (col.) Feb '60.
—— (1857). Amer. heri. vol. 7 no. 4 frontis (col.) (Je '56).
—— (1875). Amer. heri. vol. 11 no. 1 p. 66 (Dec '59).
Hartigan, Grace. Cur. biog. p. 193 (1962).
Hartke, Vance. Cur. biog. p. 183 (1960).
Hartle, Russell P. Cur. biog. p. 337 (1942).
Hartley, Fred Allan, jr. Cur. biog. p. 281 (1947).
Hartman, Gertrude. Jun. bk. of auth., p. 152.
Hartman, Grace. Cur. biog. p. 339 (1942).
Hartman, Rev. Louis F. Cur. biog. p. 251 (1953).
Hartman, Paul. Cur. biog. p. 339 (1942).
Hartnell, Norman. Cur. biog. p. 253 (1953).
Hartnett, Rev. Robert C. Cur. biog. p. 258 (1949).
Hartung, Hans. Cur. biog. p. 183 (1958).
Hartung, Karl (bronze work). Praeg. pict. ency., p. 463.
Hartwell, John A. Cur. biog. p. 369 (1941).
Harvard, John (statue). Holiday 5: 107 Jl '59. Natl. geog. 97: 309 (col.) Mar '50.
Harvard college (1767). Amer. heri. vol. 9 no. 4 p. 30-1 (col.) (Je '58).
Harvard college presidents (1861). Amer. heri. vol. 9 no. 4 p. 33 (Je '58).
Harvard univ. Holiday 5: 106-15 (col.) Feb '49.
—— (Burgis view). Con. ency. of ant., vol. 3 pl. 89.
—— (1 bldg—a log cabin). Brooks: Growth of a nation. p. 52.
—— (Mass. Hall). Travel 110: 15 Oct '58.
Harvard univ. Hall. Natl. geog. 97: 309 (col.) Mar '50.
harvest (goddess of). Lehner: Pict. bk. of sym., p. 30.
—— (sym.). Lehner: Pict. bk. of sym., p. 55.
harvest festival (Cal.) Natl. geog. 112: 706-7 (col.) Nov '57.
Harvest festival parade (Canterbury, Eng.) Natl. geog. 103: 691 May '53.
harvest field. Amer. heri. vol. 11 no. 5 p. 16-7 (col.) (Aug '60).
harvester, corn. Natl. geog. 117: 18 (col.) Jan '60.
——, sugar cane. Natl. geog. 113: 550 (col.) Ap '58.
——, wheat. Natl. geog. 117: 742 (col.) Je '60.
harvesters & grain (on donkeys). Natl. geog. 106: 825 (col.) Dec '54.
harvesting hay (Switzerland). Disney: People & places, p. 43 (col.).
harvesting machine. 32 horse team. Amer. heri. vol. 12 no. 1 p. 124 (Dec 60).
harvesting peas (men, camels). Natl. geog. 107: 506 Ap '55.
Harvey, Charles T. Amer. heri. vol. 6 no. 3 p. 22 (Ap '55).

Harvey, Edmund Newton. Cur. biog. p. 247 (1952).
Harvey, George (work of). Amer. heri. vol. 10 no. 1 p. 18 (col.) (Dec '58). Con. 143: 276 Je '59.
Harvey, Lt. J. W. Natl. geog. 115: 7 (col.) Jan '59.
Harvey, Laurence. Cur. biog. p. 195 (1961).
Harvey, Raymond. Holiday 11: 119 Ap '52.
Harvey, Thomas. Con. 144: 232 Jan '60.
Harwood, Sir Edward (Flemish art). Con. 126: 165 Dec '50.
Hasan's mosque. See mosque, Hasan's.
Hashemite Jordan. Natl. geog. 102: 842-55 Dec '52.
Haskell, Frank Aretas. Amer. heri. vol. 9 no. 1 p. 30 (col.), 31 (Dec 57).
Haskell, Helen Eggleston. Jun. bk. of auth., p. 153.
Haskell, William N. Cur. biog. p. 285 (1947).
Haskins, Caryl P. Cur. biog. p. 185 (1958).
Haslett, Dame Caroline. Cur. biog. p. 224 (1950).
Hasluck, Paul. Cur. biog. p. 246 (1946).
Hass, Hans. Cur. biog. p. 263 (1955).
Hass, Henry B. Cur. biog. p. 254 (1956).
Hassel, Kai-uwe Von. Cur. biog. (1963).
Hastie, William H. Cur. biog. p. 278 (1944).
Hastings, Lady Selina (Reynolds). Con. 140: XLIX Nov '57.
"Hastings landing" (Harvey). Con. 143: 276 Je '59.
hat (1910). Amer. heri. vol. 11 no. 5 p. 25 (Aug '60).
——, Abe Lincoln's. Amer. heri. vol. 10 no. 2 p. 98 (Feb '59).
——, Abe Lincoln's (sym.). Lehner: Pict. bk. of sym., p. 54.
——. Bali. Natl. geog. 99: 19 Jan '51.
——, cadet full dress (19th cent.). Holiday 28: 57 Sept '60.
——, Chinese coolie. Natl. geog. 111: 337, 356-7, 360-1 (col.) Mar '57.
——, Confederate. Holiday 10: 91 (col.) Sept '51.
——, fireman's (1838). Holiday 18: 60 (col.) Jl '55.
——, Gen. Washington's (sym.). Lehner: Pict. bk. of sym., p. 55.
——, gondolier's. Holiday 24: 51 (col.) Aug '58.
——, Hawaiian. Natl. geog. 118: 24 (col.) Jl '60.
——, Jamaica straw. Holiday 25: 63 (col.) Feb '59.
——, Jefferson Davis'. Amer. heri. vol. 6 no. 3 p. 35 (col.) (Ap '55).
——, large western. Natl. geog. 111: 678 (col.) May '57.
——, lumberman's Travel 108: 30 Aug '57.
——, man's. Holiday 6: 5, 74 (col.) Nov '49; 7: 77 Mar '50; 8: 58 (col.) Nov '50; 9: 85 (col.) Mar '51. 10: inside cover, 28-9 (col.) Oct '51, 86, 133 Nov '51, 179 (col.) Dec '51; 11: 82 (col.) Mar '52, 82 (col.) Ap '52; 12: 7 (col.) Nov '52; 13: 72 (col.) Ap '53; 14: 24 (col.) Oct '53, 125 (col.) Nov '53, 173 (col.) Dec '53; 16: 118 (col.) Nov '54, 126 Dec '54; 18: 5 (col.) Nov '55; 20:

58 (col.) Sept '56, 71, 85 Oct '56, 16 Nov '56, 162 Dec '56; 21: 78 Jan '57, 11 Feb '57, 161 Mar '57, 131 Ap '57; 23: 2 (col.) Feb '58, 170 Mar '58, 120 (col.) Ap '58, 141 May '58, 147 (col.) Je '58; 24: 133 (col.) Dec '58; 25: 102 (col.) Mar '59, 18 Ap '59; 26: 28 (col.) Nov '59; 28: 37, 41, 188 (col.) Oct '60.
——, man's (Africa). Natl. geog. 118: 365 (col.) Sept '60.
——, man's (1812). Amer. heri. vol. 8 no. 3 p. 49 (col.) (Ap '57).
——, man's (on globe). Holiday 14: 23 Aug '53.
——, man's derby. Holiday 19: 29 (col.) May '56; 20: 85 Nov '56.
Int. gr. soc.: Arts . . . p. 181 (col.).
Natl. geog. 106: 425 Sept '54.
——, man's evening. Holiday 7: 153 (col.) Ap '50; 18: 18 Aug '55.
——, man's high. Int. gr. soc.: Arts . . . p. 181 (col.).
Natl. geog. 98: 337 (col.) Sept '50.
——, man's straw. Holiday 19: 40 May '56; 21: 12 (col.) Feb '57, 40 (col.) Mar '57, 21 (col.) Ap '57; 22: 83 (col.) Dec '57; 24: 9 Jl '58, 29 Sept '58.
Int. gr. soc.: Arts . . . p. 149 (col.).
Natl. geog. 99: 432 (col.) Ap '51.
——, man's straw. (Puerto Rico). Natl. geog. 99: 432 (col.) Ap '51.
——, man's "top." Holiday 11: 63 Jan '52, 97 Ap '52; 12: 134 Nov 52, 15 (col.) Dec '52; 18: 104-5 Oct '55; 25: 133 Mar '59.
——, Mexican. Holiday 14: 78 Oct '53; 17: 63 Jan '55.
Natl. geog. 103: 350 Mar '53; 105: 778 (col.) Je '54.
——, Com. Perry's. Holiday 24: 56 Oct '58.
——, Pilgrim (sym.). Lehner: Pict. bk. of sym., p. 55, 90.
——, plantation straw. Holiday 13: 143 Mar '53.
——, Robert E. Lee's. Amer. heri. vol. 6 no. 3 p. 34 (col.) (Ap '55).
——, Sarawak. Natl. geog. 109: 728 May '56.
——, soldier's (memorial). Lehner: Pict. bk. of sym., p. 54.
——, Spanish-Amer. war. Holiday 28: 57 Sept '60.
——, straw sun. Natl. geog. 105: 305 (col.) Mar '54.
——, "Uncle Sam's." Holiday 16: 75 Jl '54.
——, Gen. Wayne's army. Amer. heri. vol. 9 no. 4 p. 60 (col.) (Je '58).
——, witches Sabbath (Austria). Natl. geog. 99: 783 (col.) Je '51.
——, witches (Halloween) See witch.
——, woman's (straw). Holiday 22: 85 (col.) Oct '57.
Natl. geog. 113: 559 (col.) Ap '58.
hat badge (antique). Con. 136: 46 Sept '55.
hat, cane & gloves, man's. Holiday 27: 159 Feb '60.
hat rack. Holiday 13: 26 Je '53.
hat shop, man's (1824). Amer. heri. vol. 8 no. 3 p. 51 (col.) (Ap '57).
hat stand. Holiday 13: 120 Ap '53.

hat styles, man's (around the world). Holiday 23: 60-1 Feb 58.

hat. *See* also hats; headdress.

Hatch, Carl A. Cur. biog. p. 280 (1944).

Hatcher, Harlan. Cur. biog. p. 265 (1955).

hatchery, salmon. *See* salmon hatchery.

hatchet, Abraham Lincoln's. Travel 113: 29 Feb '60.

——, Indian. Holiday 19: 31 (col.) Feb '56.

——, Iroquois Indian. Con. 141: 34 Mar '58.

hatchet & cherries (sym). Lehner: Pict. bk. of sym., p. 55.

Hatfield, Mark O. Cur. biog. p. 173 (1959).

Hatfield house (Eng.). Holiday 19: 5 (col.) Jan '56.

Hathaway cottage, Anne. Holiday 10: 99 (col.) Jl '51.

Hathor (sym.). Lehner: Pict. bk. of sym., p. 27.

Hatoyama, Ichiro. Cur. biog. p. 268 (1955).

Hatra ruins (Iraq). Natl. geog. 115: 53 (col.) Jan '59.

hats (contest). Holiday 21: 78 (col.) Mar '57.

—— (femmes des Halles). Natl. geog. 98: 64 (col.) Jl '50.

——, bamboo. Natl. geog. 97: 148 (col.), 156 Feb '50.

——, bamboo (Formosa). Natl. geog. 107: 580-1 Ap '55.

——, Chinese women's. Natl. geog. 105: 272 Feb '54.

——, cowboy. Natl. geog. 104: 352 (col.) Sept '53.

——, Indonesia. Natl. geog. 108: 372-3 (col.) Sept '55.

——, jipijapa. Natl. geog. 105: 355 (col.) Mar '54.

——, large straw. Natl. geog. 107: 503, 517 (col.) Ap '55.

——, men's. Holiday 8: 21 (col.) Oct '50; 12: 25 (col.) Oct '52; 18: 104-5 Oct '55, 93 (col.) Nov '55; 21: 28-9 (col.) Ap '57.

——, men's (foreign). Holiday 13: 26 Je '53.

——, monk's (Tibet). Natl. geog. 108: 40-1 (col.) Jl '55.

——, Nassau (Bahama). Natl. geog. 113: 170-1 (col.) Feb '58.

——, straw (boy & girl). Holiday 24: 14 Nov '58.

——, sun. Holiday 19: 27 Mar '56.

——, U.S. Civil war soldiers. Pakula: Cent. album, pl. 20 (col.).

——, Vietnam refugees. Natl. geog. 107: 860-71 Je '55.

——, Virgin is. Natl. geog. 109: 218 (col.) Feb '56.

——, women's. Holiday 10: 16 (col.) Sept '51; 25: 32 Ap '59.

——, women's (1862). Amer. heri. vol. 10 no. 1 p. 85 (Dec '58).

hats. *See* also hat; headdress.

Hatshepsut, Queen (Karnak). Praeg. pict. ency., p. 18.

Hatshepsut's temple, Queen. Natl. geog. 105: 485 (col.) Ap '54.

Hatta, Mohammed. Cur. biog. p. 260 (1949).

hatter (sym.). Lehner: Pict. bk. of sym., p. 90.

Hatton, Sir Christopher. Amer. heri. vol. 10 no. 3 p. 9 (Ap '59).

Hauge, Gabriel. Cur. biog. p. 254 (1953).

Haughton, Percy. Holiday 26: 64 Nov '59.

"Hauling water" (Nailor). Natl. geog. 107: 372 (col.) Mar '55.

haunted sites. Travel 110: 56 Oct '58.

Hauser, Gayelord. Cur. biog. p. 270 (1955).

Haushofer, Karl. Cur. biog. p. 342 (1942).

Haussmann, E. G. (work of). Cooper: Con. ency. of music, p. 55.

Haussner's restaurant. Holiday 10: 49 (col.) Nov '51.

Hautcilly, Auguste B. du (work of). Amer. heri. vol. 1 no. 3 p. 46 (spring '50).

Havana (Cuba). Holiday 12: 64-9 (part col.) Dec '52; 26: 130 (col.) Dec '59; 27: 122 (col.), 123 Mar '60.

—— (capitol bldg.). Travel 106: 21 Dec '56.

—— (harbor). Amer. heri. vol. 8 no. 2 p. 37 (col.) (Feb '57).

Holiday 27: 59 (col.) Feb '60.

Havana dancing girls. Holiday 13: 20 Jan '53.

Havana Hilton hotel. Holiday 23: 170 (col.) Ap '58.

Havell, Edmund (work of). Con. ency. of ant., vol. 1, pl. 173.

Havell, William (work of). Con. ency. of ant., vol. 1, pl. 144.

Haven, Lord Milford. Holiday 22: 148 Dec '57.

Havener, Melvin C. Natl. geog. 113: 458 Ap '58.

Havill, Edward. Cur. biog. p. 249 (1952).

Havilland, Olivia de. Cur. biog. p. 212 (1944).

Hawaii. Amer. heri. vol. 2 no. 3 inside cover, 9-33 (part col.) (spring '51).

Holiday 10: 110 (col.) Sept '51; 11: 90 (col.) Mar '52; 12: 120 (col.) Oct '52; 13: 35 (col.) May '53; 18: 118 (col.) Oct '55; 22: 90-5 (part col.) Dec '57; 24: 129 (col.), 133 Oct '58; 25: 97 (col.) Jan '59; 26: 87 (col.) Jl '59, 34 (col.) Dec '59; 27: 157 (col.) Feb '60, 152 (col.) Ap '60; 28: 35-55 (col.) Jl '60, 118 (col.) Dec '60.

Natl. geog. 100: 742-4 (col.) Dec '51; 117: 304-27 (col.) Mar '60; 118: 2-47 (part col.) Jl '60.

Travel 105: 32-4 Feb '56; 114: 49-50 Dec '60.

—— (art by Louis Choris). Amer. heri. vol. 11 no. 2 p. 16-21 (col.) (Feb '60).

—— (beach). Holiday 14: 149 (col.) Oct '53; 20: 21 (col.) Sept '56; 25: 110 Feg '59; 26: 98 (col.) Nov '59, 175 (col.) Dec '59; 28: 4, 185 (col.) Oct '60.

Travel 112: 61 Jl '59.

—— (beach, Diamond Head). Holiday 22: 4 (col.) Nov '57.

—— (beach, fishermen). Holiday 27: 122 (col.) Feb '60.

—— (beach, Waikiki). *See* Waikiki beach (Hawaii).

—— (Capt. Cook killed). Amer. heri. vol. 11 no. 2 p. 10 (col.) (Feb '60).

—— (Diamond Head). *See* Diamond Head.

—— (harbor). Holiday 16: 126 (col.) Nov '54; 27: 6. 23 (col.) Mar '60, 122 May '60.

—— (harbor, 1848). Amer. heri. vol. 12 no. 1 p. 58 (col.) (Dec '60).

—— **(hotel).** Holiday 18: 123 Nov '55; 20: 29 Oct '56; 22: 128 Oct '57, 230 Dec '57. Travel 114: 16 Nov '60, 49 Dec '60.

—— **(hotel Princess Kaiulani).** Travel 104: 38 Aug '55.

—— **(hotel, Royal Hawaiian).** Holiday 15: 70 Jan '54.

—— **(hotels).** Holiday 17: 59 Feb '55; 18: 70 Sept '55; 19: 97 Je '56; 26: 119 Nov '59; 27: 157 (col.) Feb '60, 6 Mar '60, 122 May '60; 28: 109 Aug '60, 4 Oct '60, 118 (col.) Dec '60.

—— **(Kona beach).** Holiday 26: 98 (col.) Nov '59.

—— **(luau).** Holiday 13: 145 (col.) Mar '53, 40 May '53; 22: 95 (col.) Dec '57. Natl. geog. 118: 25 (col.) Jl '60. Travel 109: 29-31 Mar '58.

—— **(Oahu harbor).** Travel 113: 60 Mar '60.

—— **(sea life).** Natl. geog. 116: 510-24 (col.) Oct '59.

—— **(ship landing, comic).** Holiday 27: 197 Je '60.

—— **(volcano).** Natl. geog. 108: 560-3 (col.) Oct '55; 113: 633 (col.) May '58; 115: 792-823 (part col.) Je '59; 118: 38-9 (col.) Jl '60.

—— **(Waikiki beach).** *See* Waikiki beach (Hawaii).

Hawaiian. Holiday 10: 31 (col.) Oct '51; 12: 5 (col.) Sept '52; 18: 95 (col.) Nov '55; 21: 21 (col.) May '57.

—— **(Hula dress).** Holiday 21: 21 (col.) May '57.

—— **(Muumuu dress).** Holiday 23: 49 May '58. (Natl. geog. 118: 7, 24 (col.) Jl '60.

—— **(with fishing net).** Travel 106: 2 Jl '56. **Hawaiian boy (head).** Holiday 21: 134 (col.) May '57.

—— **chief's hut.** Amer. heri. vol. 11 no. 2 p. 20 (col.) (Feb '60). **Hawaiian girl.** Amer. heri. vol. 2 no. 3 p. 23-7 (part col.) (spring '51). Holiday 13: cover (col.) May '53; 16: 115 (col.) Oct '54; 17: 136 (col.) Mar '55; 18: 92 (col.) Sept '55; 19: 4 (col.) May '56; 23: 15 (col.) May '58; 24: 75 (col.) Aug '58, 129 (col.) Oct '58; 25: 106 (col.) Aug '58, 129 (col.) Oct '58; 25: 106 (col.) Mar '59; 26: 175 (col.) Dec '59. Natl. geog. 118: 40 (col.) Jl '60. Travel 102: 8 Nov '54.

—— **(fruit basket).** Holiday 18: 20 (col.) Aug '55.

—— **(head).** Holiday 21: 21 (col.) Mar '57; 22: 41 (col.) Oct '57, 235 (col.) Dec '57; 24: 53 Dec '58. Travel 113: 9 Feb '60.

—— **(head, ukelele).** Holiday 12: 70 (col.) Nov '52.

—— **(musicians).** Holiday 25: 178 (col.) Ap '59.

—— **(poi dance).** Holiday 23: 105 Mar '58.

—— **(praying).** Amer. heri. vol. 11 no. 2 p. 87 (Feb '60). **Hawaiian girls.** Holiday 13: 43 (col.) May '53.

—— **(wading).** Natl. geog. 116: 521 (col.) Oct '59.

Hawaiian "God of war" (carved). Holiday 18: 45 (col.) Aug '55.

Hawaiian Hula dancer. Holiday 12: 5 (col.) Sept '52, 70 (col.) Nov '52; 14: 149 (col.) Oct '53; 16: inside back cover (col.) Aug '54; 17: 71 (col.) Feb '55; 18: 136 Oct '55, 69 (col.) Nov '55; 19: 139 Feb '56; 21: 21 (col.) May '57; 22: 115 (col.) Oct 57, 94 (col.) Dec '57; 24: 129 (col.) Oct '58. Travel 102: 49 Sept '54; 105: 47 Jan '56, 34 Feb '56.

Hawaiian Hula dancers. Holiday 8: 120 (col.) Oct '50; 11: 90 (col.) Mar '52; 12: 120 (col.) Oct '52 18: 20 (col.) Aug '55; 22: 235 (col.) Dec '57; 23: 119 (col.) Je '58; 25: 161 Je '59; 26: 87 (col.) Jl '59. Natl. geog. 100: 743-4 (col.) Dec '51; 118: 18 (col.) Jl '60.

Hawaiian is. (map). Natl. geog. 115: 794-5 Je '59.

—— **(pictorial map).** Holiday 23: 18-9 (col.) Mar '58. **Hawaiian leis.** Holiday 10: 20 (col.) Aug '51; 19: 21 (col.) Feb '56; 24: 187 (col.) Nov '58; 28: 45 (col.) Nov '60. Natl. geog. 118: 7. 17-8 (col.) Jl '60.

Hawaiian woman. Holiday 15: 2 (col.) Feb '54.

—— **(playing guitar).** Holiday 14: 32 (col.) Nov '53. **Hawaiians.** Amer. heri. vol. 2 no. 3 p. 23-7, back cover (part col.) (spring '51). Holiday 15: 32 (col.) May '54; 18: 20 (col.) Aug '55; 20: 12-3 (col.) Oct '56.

—— **(boy & girl).** Holiday 24: 106 (col.) Oct '58.

—— **(boy & girl by pool).** Holiday 25: 86 (col.) Feb '59.

—— **(boy & girl heads).** Holiday 20: 158 (col.) Nov '56.

—— **(in boat).** Holiday 13: 36 May '53.

—— **(man & girls, beach).** Holiday 24: 187 (col.) Nov '58.

—— **(men & women).** Amer. heri. vol. 11 no. 2 p. 20-1 (col.) (Feb '60).

—— **(men & women landing).** Holiday 27: 170 (col.) Je '60.

—— **(men & women on ship board).** Holiday 24: 98 (col.) Nov '58.

—— **(musicians, beach).** Holiday 24: 53 (col.) Dec '58.

—— **(surf board).** Holiday 17: 7 (col.) Jan '55.

Hawick, Scotland. Natl. geog. 112: 458 (col.) Oct '57.

hawker, Cairo fruit juice. Holiday 25: 53 (col.) Feb '59.

hawkers (boats, Kashmir). Natl. geog. 114: 628 (col.) Nov '58.

Hawkes, Anna L. Rose. Cur. biog. p. 257 (1956).

hawking set (antique). Con. 143: 232 Je '59.

Hawkins, Erskine. Cur. biog. p. 370 (1941).

Hawkins, Harry C. Cur. biog. p. 250 (1952).

Hawkins, Jack. Cur. biog. p. 175 (1959).

Hawkins, John. Amer. heri. vol. 10 no. 3 p. 13 (col.) (Ap '59).

Hawley, Cameron. Cur. biog. p. 246 (1957).

Hawley, Maj. Gen. Paul R. Cur. biog. p. 249 (1946).

Haworth, Leland J. Cur. biog. p. 226 (1950).

Hawthorne, Hildegarde. Jun. bk. of auth., p. 154.

Hawthorne, Nathaniel. Amer. heri. vol. 8 no. 2 p. 23 (Feb '57); vol. 10 no. 1 p. 31 (col.) (Dec '58).
Natl. geog. 97: 293 (col.) Mar '50.
—— (statue). Holiday 15: 107 Mar '54.

Hawthorne, Mrs. Nathaniel. See Peabody, Sophia.

Hawthorne's home ("Old Manse"), Nathaniel. Amer. heri. vol. 10 no. 1 p. 34 (Dec '58).

Hawthorne inscriptions, Nathaniel. Amer. heri. vol. 10 no. 1 p. 114 (Dec '58).

Hay, Mrs. Dudley C. Cur. biog. p. 272 (1948).

Hay, John. Amer. heri. vol. 10 no. 5 p. 21 (Aug '59).
—— (cartoon). Amer. heri. vol. 11 no. 4 p. 76 (Je '60).

hay, drying (Norway). Natl. geog. 111: 116-7 (col.) Jan '57.

hay fork. Rawson: Ant. pict. bk., p. 26.

hay load (on mule). Natl. geog. 107: 827 (col.) Je '55.

hay stacker. Natl. geog. 97: 722 (col.) Je '50.

hay stacks (girls, picnic). Natl. geog. 109: 523 (col.) Ap 56.

Haya De La Torre, Victor Raul. Cur. biog. p. 344 (1942).

Hayakawa, Samuel I. Cur. biog. p. 177 (1959).

Hayakawa, Sessue. Cur. biog. p. 195 (1962).

Hayburn, Sam. Cur. biog. p. 501 (1949).

Haycraft, Howard. Cur. biog. p. 371 (1941); p. 324 (1954).

Hayden, Carl. Cur. biog. p. 261 (1951).

Hayden, Henri (work of). Con. 143: 92 Ap '59.

Hayden, Melissa. Cur. biog. p. 271 (1955).

Hayden, Sterling. Holiday 23: 70 (col.) May '58.

Haydn, Franz Joseph. Cooper: Con. ency. of music, p. 140.

Haydn monument (Vienna). Holiday 16: 50 Nov '54.

Hayek, Friedrich A. Cur. biog. p. 271 (1945).

Hayes, Albert J. Cur. biog. p. 257 (1953).

Hayes, Carton J. H. Cur. biog. p. 347 (1942).

Hayes, Helen. Cur. biog. p. 349 (1942); p. 259 (1956).

Hayes, Mrs. John E. Cur. biog. p. 262 (1949).

Hayes, Peter Lind. Cur. biog. p. 179 (1959).

Hayes, Roland. Cur. biog. p. 352 (1942).

Hayes, Rutherford B. Amer. heri. vol. 7 no. 3 p. 32 (Ap '56); vol. 11 no. 6 p. 4 Oct '60.

Hayes, Rutherford. Jensen: The White House, p. 111, 113-.

Hayes, Mrs. Rutherford. Jensen: The White House, p. 113-.

Hayes, Samuel P. Cur. biog. p. 326 (1954).

Hayes, Samuel P., jr. Cur. biog. p. 328 (1954).

Hayes & children, Mrs. Rutherford. Jensen: The White House, p. 112.

Hayman, Francis (work of). Con. 140: 259 Jan '58; 141: 274 Je '58; 142: XXXIII Dec '58.

Hayman is. (Australia). Travel 106: 40-1 Oct '56.

Haynes, George Edmund. Cur. biog. p. 251 (1946).

hayrack (antique). Rawson: Ant. pict. bk., p. 29.

Hays, Arthur Garfield. Cur. biog. p. 355 (1942).

Hays, Brooks. Cur. biog. p. 187 (1958).

Hays, Helen. Holiday 26: 95 (col.) Oct '59.

Hays, Will H. Cur. biog. p. 277 (1943).

Hays (Kan.). Natl. geog. 101: 462-90 (part col.) Ap '52.

haystack. Rawson: Ant. pict. bk., p. 40.

Hayter, William Stanley. Cur. biog. p. 274 (1945).

"The haywagon" (Bosch). Praeg. pict. ency., p. 272 (col.).

Hayward, Leland. Cur. biog. p. 263 (1949).

Hayward, Susan. Cur. biog. p. 258 (1953).

Haywood, Allan S. Cur. biog. p. 252 (1952).

Haywood, Carolyn. Jun. bk. of auth., p. 155.

Hayworth, Rita. Cur. biog. p. 185 (1960).

Hazard, Paul. Cur. biog. p. 373 (1941).

Hazeltine, Alan. Cur. biog. p. 273 (1948).

Hazor (ancient excavations). Natl. geog. 118: 830-1 Dec '60.

Head, Edith. Cur. biog. p. 277 (1945).
Holiday 22: 148 Dec '57.

Head, Walter W. Cur. biog. p. 279 (1945).

head. See girl (head); man (head); woman (head).

——, African (sculpture). Holiday 22: 178 Nov '57.

——, bronze (ancient). Natl. geog. 110: 348 (col.) Sept '56.

——, human (anatomy). Gray's anatomy, p. 366, 562, 1343, 1346-62.

—— (muscles). Gray's anatomy, p. 354, 362.

—— (nervous system). Gray's anatomy, p. 928, 934, 957.

—— (veins). Gray's anatomy, p. 652.

——, Peruvian pottery (before 600 AD). Holiday 18: 52 (col.) Sept '55.

"Head of a Franciscan friar" (Rubens). Con. 143: XVII Ap '59.

"Head of St. John the Baptist" (alabaster). Con. 133: opp. p. 217 (col.) Je '54.

head set hammer. Rawson: Ant. pict. bk., p. 53.

headdress (ancient). Int. gr. soc.: Arts . . . p. 31, 33 (col.).

—— (many ages & countries). Int. gr. soc.: Arts . . . p. 181 (col.).

—— (medieval). Int. gr. soc.: Arts . . . p. 69, 111, 113 (col.).

—— (Napoleonic time). Int. gr. soc.: Arts . . . p. 155 (col.).

—— (19th cent.). Int. gr. soc.: Arts . . . p. 155 (col.).

—— (various nations). Holiday 17: 17 (col.) Mar '55.

—— (woman, evening). Natl. geog. 98: 781 Dec '50.

——, African Masai. Natl. geog. 106: 509 (col.) Oct '54.

——, Aragon (medieval, Spain). Natl. geog. 109: 329 (col.) Mar '56.

——, Aztec feather. Ceram: March of arch., p. 253-4.

——, Breton lace. Holiday 27: 80 Jan '60.

——, Egyptian. Natl. geog. 108: 632 (col.) Nov '55.

——, Egyptian king (ancient). Int. gr. soc.: Arts . . . p. 29 (col.).

——, Formosa aborigines. Natl. geog. 97: 167 (col.) Feb '50.

——, Indian. See wolf headdress, Indian.

——, Israel. Holiday 26: 75 (col.) Dec '59.

——, Lama. Natl. geog. 108: 15 (col.) Jl '55.

——, Moslem women. Natl. geog. 107: 161 (col.) Feb '55.

——, Papuan feather (New Guinea). Holiday 28: 94-5 (col.) Nov '60.

——, Thrace girl. Natl. geog. 109: 62 (col.) Jan '56.

——, Tyrolian (Cambodia). Int. gr. soc.: Arts . . . p. 147 (col.).

——, Wai Wai Indian. Natl. geog. 107: 343 (col.) Mar '55.

headdress of a Queen of Ur. Ceram: March of arch, opp. p. 191 (col.).

headdresses, Africa. Natl. geog. 118: 325, 333 (col.) Sept '60.

headdress. See also hat; hats.

headhunter (Philippine). Holiday 18: 92 Aug '55.

headhunters. Natl. geog. 108: 438-86 (part col.) Oct '55.

—— (Naga, India). Natl. geog. 107: 248-9, 254-5 (col.) Feb '55.

"Headless horseman" (Sleepy Hollow). Holiday 6: 38 Sept '49, 6 Dec '49.

headlight, auto. See spotlight, auto.

Heald, Henry Townley. Cur. biog. p. 254 (1952).

"Healing of man sick of palsy." Con. 142: 191 Dec '58.

healing the sick. See "And the prayer of faith shall heal the sick."

health (goddess of). Lehner: Pict. bk. of sym., p. 30.

health (sym.). Lehner: Pict. bk. of sym., p. 27, 43, 46, 200.

health exercises (women). Amer. heri. vol. 9 no. 6 p. 26 (Oct '58).

health model, transparent woman. Natl. geog. 107: 451 (col.) Ap '55.

health resort (Bad Ems, Ger.). Travel 104: 54 Sept '55.

health resorts. See also spa resorts.

Healy, Georg P. A. (work of). Amer. heri. vol. 8 no. 3 p. 40 (col.) (Ap '57); vol. 11 no. 4 p. 55 (Je '60). Natl. geog. 99: 202 (col.) Feb '51.

(Hear no evil, speak no evil, see no evil" (carving). Natl. geog. 116: 857 (col.) Dec '59.

Hearne, John J. Cur. biog. p. 227 (1950).

hearse wagon. Rawson: Ant. pict. bk., p. 70.

Hearst, William Randolph, jr. Cur. biog. p. 273 (1955).

Hearst, Mrs. William Randolph. Holiday 14: 43 (col.) Dec '53.

Hearst home, William Randolph. Holiday 26: 87 (col.) Dec '59.

heart (artificial). Natl. geog. 104: 792 (col.) Dec '53.

heart (sym.). Lehner: Pict. bk. of sym., p. 26, 34.

heart (Valentine). Amer. heri. vol. 10 no. 4 p. 56 (col.) (Je '59). Lehner: Pict. bk. of sym., p. 55.

heart, "dream girl." Amer. heri. vol. 3 no. 4 p. 63 (summer '52).

heart, human. Gray's anatomy, p. 530-43, 552.

heart & daggers (sym.). Lehner: Pict. bk. of sym., p. 38.

heart & hands (sym.). Lehner: Pict. bk. of sym., p. 65.

heart & key (sym.). Lehner: Pict. bk. of sym., p. 65.

hearth (double-ended andirons). Con. ency. of ant., vol., 3 pl. 165.

hearth, down. See down-hearth.

hearth griddle. See griddle, hearth.

hearts & arrows (sym.). Lehner: Pict. bk. of sym., p. 65.

"Hearts content" (telegraph house, Newfoundland). Amer. heri. vol. 9 no. 6 p. 51. (col.) (Oct '58).

hearts interlocked (sym.). Lehner: Pict. bk. of sym., p. 65.

Heath, Edward. Cur. biog. p. 197 (1962).

Heaton, A. G. (work of). Con. 142: 62 Sept '58.

Heatter, Gabriel. Cur. biog. p. 374 (1941).

Heaven, sacred. See The Sacred heaven.

"Heavenly dancers," carved (Angkor Thom). Natl. geog. 117: 533 Ap '60.

heavenly fire (sym.). Lehner: Pict. bk. of sym., p. 26.

Hebe (sym.). Lehner: Pict. bk. of sym., p. 30.

Herbert, Henri (statue by). Natl. geog. 112: 169 (col.) Aug '57.

Hebgen dam. Natl. geog. 117: 354 (col.) Mar '60.

Hebrew university (Israel). Natl. geog. 115: 516-7 (col.) Ap '59.

Hebrews (ancient times). Int. gr. soc.: Arts . . . p. 31 (col.).

Hebrews. See also Israelites.

Hebrides is. Natl. geog. 106: 561-79 Oct '54.

—— (map). Natl. geog. 106: 563 Oct '54.

Hecht, Ben. Cur. biog. p. 358 (1942).

Hecht, George J. Cur. biog. p. 287 (1947). Travel 113: 26 Jan '60.

Heckart, Eileen. Cur. biog. p. 189 (1958).

Heckscher, August. Cur. biog. p. 190 (1958).

Heda, Willem Claesz (work of). Con. 144: XXXV (col.) Sept '59, LIX (col.) Dec '59.

Hedden, Worth T. Cur. biog. p. 247 (1957).

Hedgepeth, Marion. Horan: Pict. hist. of wild west, p. 149.

"Hedger & his mate" (Mote). Con. 135: cover, opp. p. 219 (col.) Je '55.

"Hedgers & ditchers" (Ayrton). Con. 132: 109 Nov '53.

Hedges, W. (work of). Con. 141: XXVI Ap '58.

Hedtoft, Hans. Cur. biog. p. 266 (1949).

Heemskerk, Martin van (work of). Con. 134: 121 Nov '54.
Heeney, Arnold D. P. Cur. biog. p. 261 (1953).
Hees, George. Cur. biog. p. 180 (1959).
Heffelfinger, Pudge. Holiday 26: 65 Nov '59.
Heflin, Van. Cur. biog. p. 282 (1943).
Heha (sym.). Lehner: Pict. bk. of sym., p. 27.
Heidelberg. Natl. geog. 115: 760-1 Je '59.
Heidelberg castle. Natl. geog. 108: 134-5 Jl '55.
—— (night flares). Natl. geog. 115: 756-7 (col.) Je '59.
Helden, Konrad. Cur. biog. p. 282 (1944).
Heidenstam, Rolf von. Cur. biog. p. 266 (1951).
Heifetz, Jascha. Cur. biog. p. 285 (1944).
Heiligenblut (Village of the Holy Blood, Austrian Tyrol). Holiday 15: 146 (col.) Ap '54.
Natl. geog. 99: 763 (col.) Je '51.
Heine, William (work of). Amer. heri. vol. 9 no. 3 p. 12-3 (col.) (Ap '58).
Heineman, Ben W. Cur. biog. p. 200 (1962). Holiday 28: 183 Dec '60.
Heinlein, Robert A. Cur. biog. p. 277 (1955).
Heintzleman, B. Frank. Cur. biog. p. 262 (1953).
Heintzelman, Samuel P. Pakula: Cent. album, p. 152.
Heinz, Henry J., 2d. Cur. biog. p. 289 (1947).
hieroglyphic tablet, Hittite. Osward: Asia Minor, pl. 71.
Heisenberg, Werner. Cur. biog. p. 249 (1957).
Heiser, Victor G. Cur. biog. p. 361 (1942).
Heiss, Carol E. Cur. biog. p. 182 (1959).
Hektoen, Ludvig. Cur. biog. p. 290 (1947).
Helburn, Theresa. Cur. biog. p. 382 (1944).
Helena (Mont., 1869). Horan: Pict. hist. of wild west, p. 102.
—— (1870). Brooks: Growth of a nation, p. 177.
Helgoland is. Travel 107: 41-3 May '57.
heliboat (man). Natl. geog. 114: 706-7 (col.) Nov '58.
helicopter. Holiday 21: 106-7 Jan '57, 1 Feb '57; 23: 138 (col.) May '58.
Natl. geog. 97: 242 (col.) Feb '50; 98: 313, 320 (col.) Sept '50, 652 Nov '50; 102: 391, 398 (col.) Sept '52, 629 Nov '52; 103: 600 (col.) May '53; 105: 505 Ap '54; 106: 144 (col.), 149 Jl '54; 109: 342 (col.) Mar '56; 110: 145, 149, 161 (col.) Aug '56, 382 (col.) Sept '56; 115: 541, 546-50, 555-7 (part col.) Ap '59; 118: 718 (col.) Nov '60.
Travel 103: 34 Ap '55; 108: 65 Oct '57; 111: 27 Feb '59.
—— (Antarctica). Natl. geog. 116: 556 (col.) Oct '59.
—— (man horseback, buffalo). Natl. geog. 115: 532 (col.) Ap '59.
—— (men, spraying field). Natl. geog. 98: 398 (col.) Sept '50.
—— (rescues man from ocean). Natl. geog. 106: 797 Dec '54.
—— (spraying cotton). Natl. geog. 103: 254 Feb '53.

—— (the White House). Jensen: The White House, p. 269.
——, army twin-turbine chinook. U.S. News . . . vol. LV no. 1 p. 23, Jl. 1 '63.
——, making a. Natl. geog. 102: 34 (col.) Jl '52.
——, navy ("flying bananas"). Natl. geog. 115: 544-5 (col.) Ap '59.
——, rescue. Natl. geog. 111: 293-4, 297 (col.) Mar '57.
——, rescue (jungle). Natl. geog. 117: 665 (col.) May '60.
——, transport (world's largest). Natl. geog. 104: 739 Dec '53.
——, Vertol (spiral landing). Natl. geog. 115: 550 (col.) Ap '59.
Helion, Jean. Cur. biog. p. 285 (1943).
Heliopolis. Natl. geog. 113: 508-9 (part col.) Ap '58.
——, temple of. Ceram: March of arch., p. 67-8.
—— See also Baalbek (temples).
Helios (sym). Lehner: Pict. bk. of sym., p. 31.
heliport. Natl. geog. 115: 557 Ap '59.
Hell, gate keeper of. See gate keeper of Hell.
"Hell cooled over." See Makoshika state park.
Heller, John R. Cur. biog. p. 268 (1949).
Heller, Walter W. Cur. biog. p. 197 (1961).
Hellinger, Mark. Cur. biog. p. 292 (1947).
Hellman, Lillian. Cur. biog. p. 375 (1941); p. 186 (1960).
Hell's canyon. Holiday 12: 102-3 (col.) Oct '52.
Natl. geog. 105: 374 (col.) Mar '54.
helmet. Holiday 20: 72 (col.) Oct '56.
—— (armour). Con. 144: 18-20 Sept '59, LXVI Jan '60.
Holiday 27: 12 Je '60.
Int. gr. soc.: Arts . . . p. 59 (col.).
—— (medieval). Int. gr. soc.: Arts . . . p. 73 (col.).
——, Bahama police. Natl. geog. 113: 157 Feb '58.
——, English. Holiday 23: 57, 61 (col.) Ap '58.
——, Greek (antique). Con. 135: XXXIV May '55.
——, Greek (bronze Corinthian). Con. 133: LXXII Je '54.
——, grenadier. Natl. geog. 104: 295 (col.) Sept '53.
——, Italian. See bascinet, Italian.
——, Lullingstone. Con. 140: 42 Sept '57.
——, steel. Natl. geog. 97: 208 (col.) Feb '50.
——, Turkish iron (16th cent.). Praeg. pict. ency., p. 519.
——, war. Amer. heri. vol. 6 no. 5 p. 18-9 (col.) (Aug '55); vol. 10 no. 6 p. 4, 7 (col.), 17 (Oct '59).
Holiday 28: 58 Sept '60.
——, war (camoflaged). Holiday 12: 128 Jl '52.
——, warrior's (Africa). Natl. geog. 118: 388 (col.) Sept '60.
——, warrior's (ancient times). Int. gr. soc.: Arts . . . p. 33 (col.).
——, winged (Nigerian ritual). Natl. geog. 116: 252 (col.) Aug '59.

helmet & cross. *See* cross & helmet.
helmet of Mars. Lehner: Pict. bk. of sym., p. 87.
helmets (antique). Con. ency. of ant., vol. 1, pl. 105, p. 191.
——, football. Natl. geog. 113: 33 (col.) Jan '58.
——, space. *See* space helmets.
Helpmann, Robert. Cur. biog. p. 229 (1950).
Helsinki (Finland). Travel 112: 50-1 Aug '59.
—— (harbor). Travel 105: 34 Ap '56.
—— ((market). Natl. geog. 98: 636 (col.) Nov '50.
Helstein, Ralph. Cur. biog. p. 275 (1948).
Helvellyn, England. Natl. geog. 109: 536-7 (col.) Ap '56.
Hemingway, Ernest. Holiday 5: 43 (col.) Feb '49; 19: 60 (col.) Feb '56.
    Int. gr. soc.: Arts . . . p. 137 (col.).
Hemingway, Mr. & Mrs. Ernest. Holiday 20: 83 Dec '56.
Hench, Philip S. Cur. biog. p. 231 (1950).
Henderson, Charles Cooper (work of). Con. 142: 122 Nov '58; 144: 254 (col.) Jan '60.
Henderson, Elmer Lee. Cur. biog. p. 232 (1950).
Henderson, "Le Grand." Jun. bk. of auth., p. 192.
Henderson, Loy W. Cur. biog. p. 277 (1948).
Hendl, Walter. Cur. biog. p. 277 (1955).
Hendrick, King (statue). *See* statue (Wm. Johnson & King Hendrick).
Hendricks, Thomas A. Amer. heri. vol. 11 no. 6 p. 5 (Oct '60).
Hendrickson, Robert C. Cur. biog. p. 257 (1952).
Heney, Francis J. Amer. heri. vol. 11 no. 1 p. 10 (Dec '59).
henhouse (Majorca). Natl. geog. 111: 637 (col.) May '57.
Henie, Sonja. Cur. biog. p. 258 (1952).
Henley boat regatta (Eng.). Natl. geog. 114: 66-7 (col.) Jl '58.
Henlopen light house (Del.). Travel 106: 21 Oct '56.
Hennell, David. Con. 136: 265 Jan '56.
Hennell, Robert. Con. 136: 262 Jan '56.
Hennings, Thomas C., jr. Cur. biog. p. 330 (1954).
Hennock, Frieda B. Cur. biog. p. 279 (1948).
Henreid, Paul. Cur. biog. p. 287 (1943).
Henrich, Tommy. Holiday 7: 50 May '50.
Henrietta Maria, Queen (wife of Charles I). Natl. geog. 98: 393 (col.) Sept '50.
—— (with her dwarf). Natl. geog. 110: 656 Nov '56.
Henry, Prince (Portugal) (by Goncalves). Natl. geog. 118: 621 (col.) Nov '60.
—— (statue). Natl. geog. 118: 627 (col.) Nov '60.
Henry, Prince of Wales (1594). Con. 139: 218 Je '57.
Henry II, King of France (16th cent., Italian). Con. 135: 1 Mar '55.
Henry VII, King. Con. 139: 213, 215 Je '57.
Henry VIII, King. Amer. heri. vol. 10 no. 3 p. 95 (Ap '59).
—— (Holbein). Con. 139: 181 May '57.

—— (Horenbout miniature). Con. 143: 102 Ap '59.
—— (miniature). Con. 144: 241 Jan '60.
Henry, Frederick. Holiday 11: 112 Jan '52.
Henry, Marguerite. Cur. biog. p. 294 (1947). Jun. bk. of auth., p. 156.
Henry monument, Prince (Portugal). Natl. geog. 118: 654 Nov '60.
Hensel, Herman Struve. Cur. biog. p. 281 (1948).
"Henshaw, Joshua" portrait (Copley). Con. 126: 54 Aug '50.
Hepburn, Audrey. Cur. biog. p. 332 (1954).
Hepburn, Katharine. Cur. biog. p. 363 (1942).
Hepburn, Mitchell F. Cur. biog. p. 377 (1941).
Hephaestus (sym.). Lehner: Pict. bk. of sym., p. 30.
heptagram (sym.). Lehner: Pict. bk. of sym., p. 66.
Hepworth, Barbara. Cur. biog. p. 250 (1957).
—— (work of). Praeg. pict. ency., p. 483.
Hera (sym.). Lehner: Pict. bk. of sym., p. 30.
Hera, temple of. *See* temple of Hera (plan).
herachord (sym.). Lehner: Pict. bk. of sym., p. 12.
Heracles (sym.). Lehner: Pict. bk. of sym., p. 32.
heraldic banner. *See* banner, heraldic.
heraldic seals. Con. 143: 187 May '59.
heraldic stained glass (Washington family). Amer. heri. vol. 8 no. 6 cover (Oct '57).
heraldic standard. Holiday 28: 95 (col.) Sept '60.
heraldic symbols. *See* coat of arms.
heraldry. *See* also coat of arms.
heralds. Natl. geog. 111: 634 (col.) May '57.
—— (with halberds, Scotland). Natl. geog. 112: 458 (col.) Oct '57.
Herat (Afghanistan). Natl. geog. 114: 23 (col.) Jl '58.
Herbert, Don. Cur. biog. p. 261 (1956).
Herbert, Edward (Oliver). Con. 141: 104 Ap '58.
Herbert, Elizabeth Sweeney. Cur. biog. p. 334 (1954).
Herbert, F. Edward. Cur. biog. p. 264 (1951).
Herbert, Sir Michael. Amer. heri. vol. 7 no. 2 p. 22 (Feb '56).
Herbster, Ben M. Cur. biog. p. 202 (1962).
Hercules (sym.). Lehner: Pict. bk. of sym., p. 32.
"Hercules" (carved wood). Con. ency. of ant., vol. 3, pl. 55.
—— (Etruscan statuette). Con. ency. of ant., vol. 3, pl. 71.
"Hercules & a dragon" (wax sculpture). Con. 126: 222 Dec '50.
"Hercules & Cacus" (bronze). Con. 142: 200 Dec '58.
"Hercules & the Nemean lion" (Baratta). Con. 142: 170 Dec '58.
herdboy, Arab buffalo. Natl. geog. 113: 215 (col.) Feb 58.
herdsman, African (cattle). Natl. geog. 118: 345 (col.) Sept '60.
——, Greece. Natl. geog. 109: 56 (col.) Jan '56.
Heribertz, Barbara. Holiday 24: 106 (col.) Dec '58.

Hering, Roy (bronze figures by). Con. 143: 217 Je '59.
Herkomer, Sir Hubert von (work of). Con. 144: 10 Sept '59.
Herlihy, James Leo. Cur. biog. p. 199 (1961).
Hermandez Martinez, Maximiliano. Cur. biog. p. 365 (1942).
Hermann, L. (work of). Con. 142: XXX Dec '58.
Hermes (sym.). Lehner: Pict. bk. of sym., p. 30.
"Hermes leading the soul" (sym.). Lehner: Pict. bk. of sym., p. 66.
"Hermes of Praxiteles," head of (statue). Con. ency. of ant., vol. 3, pl. 67.
hermetic magic (sym.). Lehner: Pict. bk. of sym., p. 72-3.
hermit (on card). Lehner: Pict. bk. of sym., p. 76.
"The Hermitage" (home of Andrew Jackson). Amer. heri. vol. 1 no. 2 p. 25 (winter '50.
Holiday 8: 46-7 (col.) Nov '50.
Travel 104: 13 Jl '55.
Hermitage building (Eng.). Con. 142: 226 Jan '59.
Hermitage castle (Scotland). Holiday 27: 68 (col.) May '60.
"Hermitage farm" (Goshen, Ky.). Holiday 11: 28 (col.) Ap '52.
Holiday 13: 21 (col.) Ap '53.
Hermitage gallery (Leningrad). Travel 109: 54 Ap '58.
"Hermitage" house (La.). Natl. geog. 113: 542 (col.) Ap '58.
"Hermitage plantation". Amer. heri. vol. 4 no. 2 p. 31 (col.) (winter '53).
Herod, William Rogers. Cur. biog. p. 268 (1951).
Herodotus. Amer. heri. vol. 8 no. 5 p. 27 (Aug '57).
heroes, folk lore. Amer. heri. vol. 1 no. 3 p. 2-3 (spring '50).
Herold, David E. Amer. heri. vol. 8 no. 2 p. 57 (Feb '57).
Herold, J. Christopher. Cur. biog. p. 184 (1959).
Herreboe faience. Con. 145: 7-11 Mar '60.
Herrera (engraving by). Amer. heri. vol. 7 no. 1 p. 86 (Dec '55).
Herrick, Elinore M. Cur. biog. p. 295 (1947).
Herrick's home, John J. (Tarrytown, N.Y.). Amer. heri. vol. 1 p. 19.
Herring, J. F. (work of). Con. 134. LII Dec '54; 139: 68 Mar '57; 144: 58 Sept '59, 109 Nov '59.
Herring, Pendleton. Cur. bioig. p. 234 (1950).
herring-bone inlay ornament. Con. ency. of ant., vol. 1, p. 19.
"The herring net" (Homer). Natl. geog. 99: 211 (col.) Feb '51.
Herriot, Edouard. Cur. biog. p. 253 (1946).
Hersey, John. Cur. biog. p. 288 (1944).
Hersey, T. F. Holiday 21: 91 May '57.
Hershey, Maj. Gen. Lewis B. Cur. biog. p. 379 (1941); p. 271 1951).
Hershey (Pa., hotel). Holiday 24: 189 Dec '58; 25: 192 May '59.
Hersholt, Jean. Cur. biog. p. 289 (1944).

Herskovits, Melville Jean. Cur. biog. p. 282 (1948).
Herter, Christian Archibald. Cur. biog. p. 298 (1947); p. 192 (1958).
Hertz, Mr. & Mrs. Edgar A. Holiday 25: 96 (col.) Ap '59.
Hertz, John D. Travel 103: 46 Je '55.
Hervey, Lord (bust by Bouchardon). Con. 141: 72 Ap '58.
Herzog, Maurice. Cur. biog. p. 264 (1953).
Herzog, Rabbi Isaac Halevi. Cur. biog. p. 185 (1959).
Herzog, Paul M. Cur. biog. p. 281 (1945).
Hesburgh, Rev. Theodore M. Cur. biog. p. 279 (1955).
Hess, Dean E. Cur. biog. p. 253 (1957).
Hess, Dr. Elmer. Cur. biog. p. 263 (1956).
Hess, Fjeril. Jun. bk. of auth., p. 158.
Hess, Max. Cur. biog. p. 201 (1961).
Hess, Dame Myra. Cur. biog. p. 290 (1943).
Hess, Rudolf. Cur. biog. p. 381 (1941).
Hess, Victor Francis. Cur. biog. (1963).
Hesse, Hermann. Cur. biog. p. 203 (1962).
Hesselgren, Kerstin. Cur. biog. p. 383 (1941).
Hesselius, Gustavus. Con. 141: 63 Mar '58.
Hesselius, John (work of). Con. 140: 141 Nov '57.
Hester, James M. Cur. biog. p. 206 (1962).
Hestia (sym.). Lehner: Pict. bk. of sym., p. 31.
Heston, Charlton. Cur. biog p. 255 (1957).
Hetherinton & Brace (hanging, 1856). Horan: Pict. hist. of wild west, p. 23.
Heusinger, Lt. Gen. Adolf. Cur. biog. p. 265 (1956).
Heuss, Theodor. Cur. biog. p. 269 (1949).
Heuven Goedhart, Gerrit J. van. Cur. biog. p. 260 (1952).
Hevesy, George C. De. Cur. biog. p. 187 (1959).
Hewes, Agnes Danforth. Jun. bk. of auth., p. 159.
Hewetson, Chistopher (sculpture by). Con. 143: 245 Je '59.
hewing dog. Rawson: Ant. pict. bk., p. 22.
Hewitt, Vice Adm. Henry K. Cur. biog. p. 292 (1943).
hex signs (Penn. Dutch). Holiday 9: 122 Mar '51; 18: 99 (col.) Oct '55.
—— (on barn). Travel 105: 22 Mar '56.
hexagons. See The sixty-four-geomantic hexagons.
Heyden, Jan Van der. See Van der Heyden, Jan (work of).
Heydler, John A. Amer. heri. vol. 11 no. 4 p. 27 (Je '60).
Heydrich, Reinhard. Cur. biog. p. 368 (1942).
Heyerdahl, Thor. Cur. biog. p. 301 (1947).
Heyliger, William. Jun. bk. of auth., p. 161.
Heym, Stefan. Cur. biog. p 293 (1943).
Heyrovsky, Jaroslav. Cur. biog. p. 203 (1961).
Heyward II, Nathaniel. Amer. heri. vol. 9 no. 2 p. 57 (col.) Feb '58.
Heywood, Joseph L. Horan: Pict. hist. of wild west, p. 38.
Hibbs, Ben. Cur. biog. p. 256 (1946).
Hickenlooper, Bourke B. Cur. biog. p. 303 (1947).
Hickerson, John D. Cur. biog. p. 236 (1950).
Hickey, Margaret A. Cur. biog p 291 (1944).
Hickman, Emily. Cur. biog. p. 282 (1945).

Hickman, Herman. Cur. biog. p 273 (1951).
Hickok, Emma (on horse, rearing). Horan: Pict. hist. of wild west, p. 55.
Hickok, "Wild Bill". Amer. heri. vol. 6 no. 4 p. 34 (Je '55); vol. 11 no. 5 p. 37 (Aug '60). Horan: Pict. hist. of wild west, p. 47, 50, 51, 53.
Hickok grave, "Wild Bill". See grave of Wild Bill Hickok.
Hicks, Beatrice A. Cur. biog. p. 256 (1957).
Hicks, Edward (work of). Amer. heri. vol. 2 no. 2 p. 45 (col.) (winter '51); vol. 6 no. 2 p. 42-3 (col.) (winter '55); vol. 8 no. 5 p. 58 (col.) (Aug '57); vol. 11 no. 6 p. 2 (col.) (Oct '60).
Hicks, Granville. Cur. biog. p. 370 (1942).
Hicks, Henry D. Cur. biog. p. 267 (1956).
Hiddeman, F. (work of). Brooks: Growth of a nation, p. 221.
Hidley, Joseph H. (work of). Amer. heri. vol. 11 no. 1 cover (col.) (Dec '59).
hieroglyphics. Travel 104: 16 Nov '55.
——, Crete. Ceram: March of arch., p. 64-5.
——, Egyptian. Ceram: March of arch., p. 88-9.
——, Mayan. See Mayan hieroglyphics.
Hieropolis. Osward: Asia Minor, pl. 134.
hi-fidelity. See record player.
Higginbotham, William A. Cur. biog. p. 305 (1947).
Higgins, Andrew J. Cur. biog. p. 295 (1943).
Higgins, Daniel Paul. Cur. biog. p. 238 (1950).
Higgins, Marguerite. Cur. biog. p. 275 (1951). Holiday 10: 64 Dec '51.
high chest, Wm. & Mary. Con. 141: 128 Ap '58.
High Savoy. Holiday 25: 72-7 (part col.) Mar '59.
High Sierras (Cal.). Travel 104: 6 Sept '55.
high tension (sym.). Lehner: Pict. bk. of sym., p. 88.
highboy, Amer. (early). Natl. geog. 117: 836 (col.) Je '60.
——, Amer. (1735). Holiday 27: 29 (col.) Mar '60.
——, Chippendale. Con. ency. of ant., vol. 1, pl. 40.
Con. 140: 56 Sept '57; 143: 66 Mar '59, 189 May '59.
——, Conn. (18th cent.). Con. 145: LII Mar '60.
——, Mass. (Queen Anne style). Con. 135: 63 Mar '55.
——, Queen Anne. Con. 140: LVIII Sept '57; 141: LVI Mar '58.
——, Wm. & Mary. Con. 144: LXXVIII Jan '60.
——, Wm. & Mary (17th cent.). Con. 142: 129 Nov '58.
highboy. See also tallboy.
"Highland fling" (Scotch dancers). Natl. geog. 110: 2-3 (col.) Jl '56.
highland fling. See also Scotch dancers.
Highmore, Joseph (portrait by). Con. 138: 123 Nov '56.
—— (work of). Con. 140: 234 Jan '58.
Hightower, John M. Cur. biog. p. 262 (1952).
highway, 1st transcontinental. Holiday 12: 12 (col.) Dec '52.

——, Florida overseas. Holiday 24: 21 (col.) Nov '58.
——, marble ceremonial (Ephesus). Osward: Asia Minor, pl. 41-2.
——. See also roadway.
Higley, Brewster. Amer. heri. vol. 1 no. 4 p. 8 (summer '50).
Higley, Harvey V. Cur. biog. p. 269 (1956).
hiker (Hawaiian gulch). Natl. geog. 118: 39 (col.) Jl '60.
hikers (boys & girls). Natl. geog. 118: 511 (col.) Oct '60.
——, (Eng.). Natl. geog. 109: 515 (col.), 528-9 Ap '56.
—— (Switzerland). Natl. geog. 110: 440 (col.) Oct '56.
——, Mt. Natl. geog. 109: 593 (col.), 618 May '56.
Hilaly, Ahmed Naguib. Cur. biog. p. 263 (1952).
Hildebrand, Jesse Richardson. Natl. geog. 101: 104 Jan '52.
Hildebrand, Joel H. Cur. biog. p. 281 (1955).
Hildebrandt, Lucas von (architecture). Praeg. pict. ency., p. 364.
Hildegarde. Cur. biog. p. 295 (1944).
Hilderbrand, Adolf von. (sculpture by). Praeg. pict. ency., p. 423.
Hildred, Sir William P. Cur. biog. p. 271 (1956).
Hildreth, Horace A. Cur. biog. p. 285 (1948).
Hill, Abram. Cur. biog. p. 283 (1945).
Hill, Ambrose. Pakula: Cent. album, p. 155.
Hill, Arthur M. Cur. biog. p. 287 (1948).
Hill, David G. Cur. biog. p. 189 (1960).
Hill, David Harvey. Pakula: Cent. album, p. 157.
Hill, George Washington. Cur. biog. p. 257 (1946).
Hill, Vice-Adm. Harry W. Cur. biog. p. 239 (1950).
Hill, James J. Amer. heri. vol. 9 no. 4 p. 10 (Je '58).
Hill, Justina Hamilton. Cur. biog. p. 385 (1941).
Hill, Lister. Cur. biog. p. 298 (1943).
Hill, Robert C. Cur. biog. p. 189 (1959).
Hill, William S. Cur. biog. p. 283 (1955).
Hillard, Moses. Amer. heri. vol. 8 no. 1 p. 40 (Dec '56).
Hillary, Sir. Edmund. Cur. biog. p. 354 (1954). Natl. geog. 115: 29 (col.) Jan '59.
Hilldring, Maj. Gen. John H. Cur. biog. p. 306 (1947).
Hilleboe, Herman E. Cur. biog. p. 285 (1955).
Hillenkoetter, Rear adm. Roscoe H. Cur. biog. p. 241 (1950).
Hiller, Wendy. Cur. biog. p. 386 (1941).
Hillestrom, Per (wok of). Con. 135: 47 Mar '55.
Hilliard, Jan. Cur. biog. p. 190 (1959).
Hilliard, Nicholas (miniature by). Con. ency. of ant., vol. 1. pl. 129.
Con. 138: 82 Nov '56; 143: 102 Ap '59; 145: 179 May '60.
—— (self portrait). Con. 142: LVI Sept '58.
—— (work of). Con. 143: 263 Je '59.
Hillings, Patrick. Cur. biog. p. 257 (1957).
Hillis, Margaret. Cur. biog. p. 273 (1956).

"Hills of enchantment". See "The Encantats".
Hillyer, V. M. Jun. bk. of auth., p. 162.
Hilsberg, Alexander. Cur. biog. p. 265 (1953).
Hilton, Conrad. Holiday 23: 42 May '58.
Hilton, Conrad N. Cur. biog. p. 271 (1949).
Hilton, Frank C. Cur. biog. p. 265 (1952).
Hilton, James. Cur. biog. p. 373 (1942).
Hilton hotel (Constantinople). Osward: Asia Minor, pl. 90.
—— (Port of Spain). Travel 109: 41 May '58.
—— (San Francisco). Travel 112: 8 Jl '59.
Hilton inn (San Francisco, airport). Travel 110: 43 Aug '58.
Himalaya mt. Holiday 24: 50-5 (part col.) Sept '58.
Natl. geog. 102: 199-234 (part col.) Aug '52; 110: 520-1 Oct '56; 114: 607-35, 640-1, 644 (col.) Nov '58.
himation (Greek man's dress, ancient). Int. gr. soc.: Arts . . . p. 31 (col.).
Himis devil dancers. See devil dancers, Himis.
Himmler, Heinrich. Cur. biog. p. 387 (1941).
Hinchliffe, John (Peters). Con. 143: 87 Ap '59.
Hindemith, Paul. Cur. biog. p. 390 (1941).
Hindu (sick man carried). Natl. geog. 110: 524 Oct '56.
Hindu dancer. Holiday 12: 41 Oct '52.
Hindu dancers (on elephant). Natl. geog. 105: 516 (col.) Ap '54.
Hindu diagrams (cosmic). Lehner: Pict. bk. of sym., p. 75.
Hindu funeral. Natl. geog. 105: 517 (col.) Ap '54.
Hindu god. See god, Hindu.
Hindu goddess. See goddess, Hindu.
Hindu holy man. See holy men.
Hindu idol. Holiday 19: 60 (col.) Je '56.
Hindu man. Holiday 6: 87 (col.) Aug '49.
Hindu mendicants. Natl. geog. 105: 518 (col.) Ap '54.
Hindu pilgrims (Ganges). See pilgrims, Hindu (Granges).
Hindu temple. Natl. geog. 103: 66 (col.) Jan '53.
—— (India). Praeg. pict. ency., p. 551.
—— (Java). Natl. geog. 108: 353 (col.) Sept '55.
——. See also Angkor Wat.
Hindu traffic police. Holiday 20: 76 Aug '56.
Hindu wedding (pray & feast). Natl. geog. 117: 394-5 (col.) Mar '60.
Hinduism (philosophies). Lehner: Pict. bk. of sym., p. 43.
Hindus (bathing in Ganges). Travel 111: 19 Jan '59.
—— (India). Holiday 6: 73 Sept '49.
Natl. geog. 107: 254-5 (col.) Feb '55.
—— (outdoor cooking). Natl. geog. 110: 523 Oct '56.
—— (pilgrimages). Natl. geog. 110: 522-35 Oct '56.
—— (tea pickers). Natl. geog. 107: 413 (col.) Mar '55.
Hindustan pavilion. Holiday 24: 47 Aug '58.
Hines, Duncan. Cur. biog. p. 260 (1946).
Hines, Frank T. Cur. biog. p. 297 (1944).
Hines, Jerome. Cur. biog. (1963).
Hingson, Robert A. Cur. biog. p. 301 (1943).

Hinshaw, Carl. Cur. biog. p. 277 (1951).
Hinshelwood, Sir Cyril. Cur. biog. p. 25 (1957).
Hinton, Sir Christopher. Cur. biog. p. 21 (1957).
Holiday 23: 94 Ap '58.
Hippocrates (Greek sculpture). Natl. geog. 103: 379 Mar '53.
hippodrome track. Durant: Pict. hist. of Amer. circus, p. 136.
"The hireling shepherd" (Hunt). Con. 140: LXV Dec '57.
Hirohito, Japanese Emperor. Cur. biog. p. 375 (1942).
Natl. geog. 97: 595 May '50.
Hiroshije (work of). Amer. heri. vol. 9 no. 3 p. 15-23 (col.) (Ap '58).
Hirschfeld, Al. Holiday 5: 32 Jan '49.
Hirschfelder, Joseph O. Cur. biog. p. 244 (1950).
Hirshfield, Morris. Cur. biog. p. 305 (1943).
Hirst, Lord Hugo. Cur. biog. p. 393 (1941).
"His eminence's choice" (Brunery). Con. 139: 147 May '57.
"His favourite opera" (Brunery). Con. 137: XL Je '56.
Hiss, Alger. Cur. biog. p. 309 (1947).
Hissarlik hill. Ceram: March of arch., p. 32.
historical markers. Amer. heri. vol. 3 no. 4 p. 76 (summer '52); vol. 5 no. 4 p. 58 (summer '54).
history (diety of). Lehner: Pict. bk. of sym., p. 33.
—— (sym.). Lehner: Pict. bk. of sym., p. 13.
Hitchcock, Alfred. Cur. biog. p. 394 (1941); p. 190 (1960).
Hitchcock, Charles B. Cur. biog. p. 335 (1954).
hitching block. Rawson: Ant. pict. bk., p. 41.
hitching post. Rawson: Ant. pict. bk., p. 44.
——, jockey (1881). Holiday 18: 61 (col.) Jl '55.
——, ox. Rawson: Ant. pict. bk., p. 53.
Hitler, Adolf. Cur. biog. p. 378 (1942).
Hitti, Philip K. Cur. biog. p. 310 (1947).
Hittite carving. Natl. geog. 115: 77 (col.) Jan '59.
Hittite chief head (1400 B.C.). Int. gr. soc.: Arts . . . p. 31 (col.).
Hittite god of the chase. See Rundas.
Hittite insignia of rank (stone carving). Osward: Asia Minor, pl. 70.
Hittite steer (rock carving). Osward: Asia Minor, pl. 2.
Hittite warrior head (ancient time). Int. gr. soc.: Arts . . . p. 31 (col.).
hive, bee. Natl. geog. 116: 201 (col.) Aug '59.
Ho Chi Minh. Cur. biog. p. 273 (1949).
Ho Ying-Chin, Gen. Cur. biog. p. 385 (1942).
Hoad, Lew. Cur. biog. p. 275 (1956).
Hoar, George F. Amer. heri. vol. 11 no. 4 p. 33 (Je '60).
Hobart, Garret A. Amer. heri. vol. 7 no. 4 p. 25 (col.) (Je '56).
Hobbema, Meindert (work of). Con. ency. of ant., vol. 1, pl. 165.
Con. 135: 164-5 May '55; 136: 45 Sept '55; 140: IX (col.) Nov '57; 145: 279 Je '60.
Praeg. pict. ency., p. 345 (col.).
hobble, animal foot. Rawson: Ant. pict. bk., p. 67.

Hobbs, Leonard S. Cur. biog. p. 337 (1954).
Hobbs, Sarah. Amer. heri. vol. 6 no. 2 p. 41 (winter '55).
Hobby, Oveta Culp. Cur. biog. p. 387 (1942); p. 267 (1953).
hobby shop (int.). Natl. geog. 103: 31 (col.) Jan '53.
hobbyhorse (antique). Rawson: Ant. pict. bk., p. 19.
"Hobbyhorse dance", Basque. Natl. geog. 105: 162-3 (part col.) Feb '54.
hobgoblin (New Guinea). Holiday 28: 71 Oct '60.
Hoboken waterfront. Holiday 16: 82 Aug '54.
Hobson, Laura Z. Cur. biog. p. 312 (1947).
Hobson, Richmond. Travel 103: back cover Feb '55.
Hochosterwitz castle. See castle Hochosterwitz.
hockey game. Holiday 25: 150 Jan '59.
   Natl. geog. 108: 666 (col.) Nov '55; 112: 604-5 Nov '57.
——, ice. Holiday 5: 15 Mar '49.
   Natl. geog. 109: 34-5 (col.) Jan '56.
hockey players. Natl. geog. 99: 135 (col.) Jan '51.
Hocking, William Ernest. Cur. biog. p. 208 1962).
Hodes, Heny I. Cur. biog. p. 191 (1959).
Hodge, Lt. Gen. John R. Cur. biog. p. 286 (1945).
Hodges, Courtney H. Cur. biog. p. 396 (1941).
Hodges, Gil. Cur. biog. p. 211 (1962).
Hodges, Luther H. Cur. biog. p. 277 (1956).
Hodgkins, Frances (work of). Con. 143: 93 Ap '59.
Hodgson, William R. Cur. biog. p. 262 (1946).
hoe. Amer. heri. vol. 7 no. 4 p. 27 (col.) (Je '56).
Hoegh, Leo A. Cur. biog. p. 279 (1956).
Hoey, Clyde R. Cur. biog. p. 275 (1949).
   Holiday 15: 58 Feb '54.
Hoey, Jane M. Cur. p. 245 (1950).
Hofbrauhaus (Munich). Holiday 22: 59 Sept '57.
Hoff, Philip H. Cur. biog. (1963).
Hoffbauer, Charles. Amer. heri. vol. 5 no. 3 p. 35 (spring '54).
—— (work of). Amer. heri. vol. 5 no. 3 p. 32-40 (part col.) (spring '54).
Hoffman, Clare E. Cur. biog. p. 276 (1949).
Hoffman, Johannes. Cur. biog. p. 247 (1950).
Hoffman: Joseph G. Cur. biog. p. 194 (1958).
Hoffman, Paul G. Cur. biog. p. 264 (1946).
Hoffmann, Johannes. Natl. geog. 105: 571 Ap '54.
Hofmann, Hans. Cur. biog. p. 196 (1958).
Hofmann, Klaus H. Cur. biog. p. 205 (1961).
Hofstadter, Richard. Cur. biog. p. 281 (1956).
Hofstadter, Robert. Cur. biog. p. 213 (1962).
hog house (int.). Rawson: Ant. pict. bk., p. 62-3.
Hogan, Ben. Cur. biog. p. 288 (1948).
Hogan, Frank S. p. 269 (1953).
Hogarth, William. Con. 141: 61 Mar '58.
—— (work of). Con. ency. of ant., vol. 1, pl. 166.
   Con. 129: 44 Ap '52; 137: 103 Ap '56; 140: LIII Nov '57, LVII Dec '57, 234.

Jan '58; 141: 72 Ap '58; 145: II (col.), XXIII May '60.
   Durant: Pict. hist. of Amer. circus, p. 14.
   Praeg. pict. ency., p. 371 (col.).
Hogben, Lancelot. Cur. biog. p. 397 (1941).
Hogenberg, Nicolaus (work of). Con. 138: 14 Sept '56.
Hoggart, Richard. Cur. biog. p. 187 (1963).
Hogner, Dorothy. Jun. bk. of auth. p. 163.
Hogner, Nils. Jun. bk. of auth., p. 163.
hogshead (barrel). Rawson: Ant. pict. bk., p. 61.
Hohenzollern castle. Disney: People & places, p. 50 (col.).
Hokkei (Japanese drawings). Con. 139: 232 Je '57.
Hokusai (work of). Praeg. pict. ency., p. 540 (col.).
Holaday, William M. Cur. biog. p. 197 (1958).
Holbein, Ambrosius (work of). Con. 133: 77 Ap '54.
Holbein, Hans. Int. gr. soc.: Arts . . . p. 91 (col.).
—— (work of). Con. ency. of ant., vol. 1, pl. 129.
   Con. 133: 75-9 Ap '54; 136: 129 Nov '55.
Holbein the elder, Hans (work of). Con. 138: 139 Nov '56.
Holbein the younger, Hans (work of). Con. 135: X (col.) Ap '55; 136: 239 Jan '56; 138: 139 Nov '56; 139: 7 Mar '57.
   Praeg. pict. ency., p. 290, 304.
Holbein, Baron Thyssen (work of). Con. 139: 181 May '57.
Holberg, Ruth. Jun. bk. of auth., p. 164.
Holberg, Ruth Langland. Cur. biog. p. 278 (1949).
Holbrook, Hal. Cur. p. 207 (1961).
Holbrook, Sabra. Cur. biog. p. 290 (1948).
Holcomb, Lt. Gen. Thomas. Cur. biog. p. 389 (1942).
Holden, William. Cur. biog. p. 339 (1954).
Holder, Ferdinand (work of). Praeg. pict. ency., p. 483.
Holder, Geoffrey. Cur. biog. p. 263 (1957).
Holderness School (boy's boarding). Holiday 18: 41 Jl '55.
Holenstein, Thomas. Cur. biog. p. 199 (1958).
holiday (sym.). Lehner: Pict. bk. of sym., p. 50-6.
Holifield, Chester E. Cur. biog. p. 287 (1955).
Holl, Elias (architecture by). Praeg. pict. ency., p. 305.
Holl, Frank (Francis M.). Con. 144: 10 Sept '59.
Holland, James (work of). Con. 143: XVII Je '59.
Holland, Kenneth. Cur. biog. p. 267 (1952).
Holland, Rupert Sargent. Jun. bk. of auth., p. 165.
Holland, Sidney G. Cur. biog. p. 249 (1950).
Holland, Spessard L. Cur. biog. p. 251 (1950).
Holland. Holiday 21: 50-9 (col.) Mar '57; 23: 56-7 Jan '58; 27: 162 Jan '60.
   Natl. geog. 98: 748-78 (part col.) Dec '50; 106: 366-412 Sept '54.
   Travel 102: inside cover Nov '54; 108: 54-7 Aug '57; 113: 51-3 Ap '60.
—— (Amsterdam). Holiday 23: 150 (col.) Feb '58.

Holland (canal & windmill). Holiday 15: 110 (col.) Jan '54.

—— (canals). Travel 113: 51-3 Ap '60.

—— (children). Holiday 19: 98-9 (part col.) Jan '56.

—— (girl). Holiday 10: 74 (col.) Sept '51.

—— (Gouda). Holiday 15: 102 Jan '54.

—— (map). Natl. geog. 98: 752 Dec '50.

—— (Reformed church, Delfshaven). Amer. heri. vol. 10 no. 6 p. 50 (col.) (Oct '59).

Holland (Mich.). Travel 106: 32 Sept '56; 114: 26 Sept '60.

—— (tulip time). Natl. geog. 101: 287-9 (col.) Mar '52.

Holleben, Baron Theodor von. Amer. heri. vol. 7 no. 2 p. 23 (Feb '56).

Hollenbeck, Don. Cur. biog. p. 279 (1951).

Holliday, D.D. S. Horan: Pict. hist. of wild west, p. 115.

Holliday, Dr. John H. Holiday 16: 69 Aug '54.

Holliday, Judy. Cur. biog. p. 280 (1951).

Holling, H. C. Jun. bk. of auth., p. 166.

Hollister, John B. Cur. biog. p. 290 (1955).

Holloway, Rear Adm. James L., jr. Cur. biog. p. 314 (1947).

Holloway, Stanley. Cur. biog. (1963).

Holm, Celeste. Cur. biog. p. 300 (1944).

Holm, Hanya. Cur. biog. p. 341 (1954).

Holman, Eugene. Cur. biog. p. 292 (1948).

Holman, Jonas W. (work of). Amer. heri. vol. 1 no. 4 p. 48 (summer '50.)

Holmes, Burton. Cur. biog. p. 303 (1944).

Holmes, Dyer Brainerd. Cur. biog. (1963).

Holmes, Rev. John Haynes. Cur. biog. p. 399 (1941).

Holmes, Brig. Gen. Julius C. Cur. biog. p. 291 (1945).

Holmes, Odetta. See Odetta.

Holmes, Oliver Wendell. Amer. heri. vol. 2 no. 2 p. 73 (winter '51); vol. 8 no. 2 p. 22 (Feb '57); vol. 11 no. 6 p. 55 (Oct '60). Holiday 7: 75 Feb '50.

Holmes, Robert D. p. 201 (1958).

Holmes, Sherlock. Int. gr. soc.: Arts . . . p. 137 (col.).

Holst, Gustav. Cooper: Con. ency. of music, p. 141.

Holt, Andrew D. Cur. biog. p. 280 (1949).

Holt, Cooper T. Cur. biog. p. 265 (1957).

Holt, Hamilton. Cur. biog. p. 315 (1947).

Holt, Isabella. Cur. biog. p. 283 (1956).

Holt, Rackham. Cur. biog. p. 304 (1944).

"Holt bridge on river Dee" (Wilson). Con. ency. of ant., vol. 1, pl. 133.

Holtz, Jackson J. Cur. biog. p. 253 (1950).

Holy blood play. See Sanguis Christi pageant.

Holy Blood village. See Heiligenblut.

Holy Cross Catholic college. Natl. geog. 107: 212 (col.) Feb '55.

Holy Cross chapel (Sedona, Ariz.). Travel 107: 60 May '57.

"The Holy family" (Cesare). Con. 138: 118 Nov '56.

"Holy family" (Poussin). Con. 143: 126 Ap '59.

"Holy family" (Raphael). Con. ency. of ant., vol. 1, pl. 150.

"Holy family" (Rembrandt). Con. 138: 30 Sept '56.

"Holy family" (Schedoni). Con. 132: 18 Sept '53.

"Holy family" (Van Cleve). Con. 138: 281 Jan '57.

"Holy family at St. Anne" (Poussin). Con. 143: VIII Ap '59.

"Holy family with a parrot". Con. 145: LXX-XVII May '60.

"Holy family with St. Catherine". Praeg. pict. ency., p. 353 (col.).

"Holy family with the infant" (Tintoretto). Con. 144: cover (col.) Dec '59.

"Holy fire" ritual. Natl. geog. 106: 850 (col.) Dec '54.

Holy island (Eng.). Natl. geog. 102: 548-69 Oct '52.

The Holy Land. Natl. geog. 98: 708-46 (part col.) Dec '50; 102: 831-40, 842-55 Dec '52; 114: 854-9 (part col.) Dec '58.

—— (map). Natl. geog. 98: 710 Dec '50; 114: 853 Dec '58; 118: 820 (col.) Dec '60.

holy man (India). Natl. geog. 118: 493 (col.) Oct '60.
Travel 106: 15 Nov '56.

—— (India, comic). Holiday 12: 11 Dec '52.

——, Hindu. Natl. geog. 110: 535 Oct '56; 114: 609 (col.) Nov '58.

——, Jain (carved in base of fort). Natl. geog. 118: 479 (col.) Oct '60.

Holy sepulchre (Jerusalem). Holiday 7: 119 (col.) Ap '50.
Travel 105: 36 Mar '56.

—— (courtyard). Natl. geog. 98: 719 (col.) Dec '50.

The Holy spirit (sym.). Lehner: Pict. bk. of sym., p. 35.

"Holy trinity" (alabaster). Con. ency. of ant., vol. 3, pl. 129.

—— (sym.). Lehner: Pict. bk. of sym., p. 35.

Holy Trinity cathedral (Addis Ababa). Natl. geog. 118: 348 (col.) Sept '60.

Holy Trinity church (Palm Beach, Fla.). Travel 105: 44 Jan '56.

—— (Stratford). Holiday 10: 98-9 (col.) Jl '51.

Holy Trinity orthodox seminary (Jordanville, near Erie Canal). Holiday 15: 101 Je '54.

Holy week (Easter, in Spain). See Spain (Holy week).

Holyoake, Keith J. Cur. biog. p. 193 (1963).

Holzer, Johann Evangelist (work of). Con. 145: 132 Ap '60.

Home, Lord Alexander F. Cur. biog. p. 203 (1958).

home (Civil war destruction). Brooks: Growth of a nation, p. 148-9.

—— (int.). See room (int.).

home, E. Ruffin ("Marlbourne"). Amer. heri. vol. 9 no. 2 p. 25 (Feb '58).

home (sym.). Lehner: Pict. bk. of sym., p. 26.

——, Abraham Lincoln's (Ill.). Natl. geog. 101: 178 (col.) Feb '52.

——, Andrew Jackson's. See "The Hermitage".

——, Annamese (Indochina). Natl. geog. 99: 473 (col.) Ap '51.

——, Betsy Ross. See Ross home, Betsy.

——, Bowditch. See Bowditch home.

home, British (Africa). Natl. geog. 97: 346 (col.) Mar '50.

——, Brittany. Holiday 27: 131 (col.) Jan '60.

——, Chase-Loyd (Annapolis). Holiday 23: 82 (col.) Je '58.

——, Colonial. Amer. heri. vol. 6 no. 3 p. 54 (Ap '55).

Face of Amer. p. 63 (col.).

Holiday 13: 93, 148 (col.) Mar '53; 14: 25 Aug '53, 25 Oct '53, 147 Nov '53, 126 (col.) Dec '53; 21: 9 Feb '57; 25: cover (col.) Je '59; 27: 120 Mar '60.

Jordan: Hammond's pict. atlas, p. 65.

——, Colonial (int.). Amer. heri. vol. 1 no. 2 p. 38-9, 47 (col.) (winter '50).

Natl. geog. 103: 793-5 (col.), 801 Je '53.

——, Colonial (Ky.). Holiday 9: inside back cover (col.) Mar '51; 10: 96 (col.) Oct '51; 11: 70 (col.) Mar '52, 28 (col.) Ap '52, 19 (col.) Je '52; 13: 138 (col.) Je '53.

——, Colonial (La. Bayou). Amer. heri. vol. 6 no. 1 p. 62 (col.) (fall '54).

——, Colonial (Long Is.). Natl. geog. 112: 308-9 (col.) Sept '57.

——, Colonial (Miss., girl). Natl. geog. 112: 537 (col.) Oct '57.

——, Colonial (Natchez). Holiday 6: Inside cover (col.) Nov '49.

——, Colonial (Newport). Holiday 6: 100 Jl '49.

——, Colonial (1735). Amer. heri. vol. 11 no. 1 p. 7 (col.) (Dec '59).

——, Colonial (southern). Holiday 10: 116 (col.) Nov '51, 48, 97 (col.) Dec '51; 12: 60 (col.) Oct '52, 38-9 (col.) Nov '52, 143 (col.) Dec '52; 19: 152 (col.) Mar '56, 34 (col.) Je '56; 20: 190 (col.) Dec '56; 22: 122 (col.) Oct '57.

Natl. geog. 118: 706-7 (col.) Nov '60.

——, Colonial (Va.). Holiday 10: 78 (col.) Nov '51; 18: 103 (col.) Nov '55, 118 (col.) Dec '55; 22: 55 (col.) Dec '57.

Natl. geog. 109: 443-84 (part col.) Ap '56.

——, Colonial (war alarm). Amer. heri. vol. 11 no. 6 p. 59 (Oct '60).

——, Colonial (women). Natl. geog. 98: 384 (col.), 386 Sept '50.

——, Colonial salt box (1700). Natl. geog. 112: 308-9 (col.) Sept '57.

——, Daniel Webster. See Webster home, Daniel.

——, Donald M. Lewis (Cal.). Holiday 14: 34-5 (col.) Sept '53.

——, Dutch Colonial (Africa). Natl. geog. 104: 168 (col.) Aug '53.

——, Dwight D. Eisenhower. Brooks: Growth of a nation, p. 311.

——, Earl of Shaftesbury (St. Giles house). Con. 144: 72 (col.) 74-7 Nov '59.

——, Egyptian. See Egyptian home (3000 yrs. ago).

——, English. See house, English.

——, farm. Amer. heri. vol. 7 no. 4 p. 27 (col.) Je '56).

——, Fiji is. governor's (int.). Holiday 28: 64-5 (col.) Oct '60.

——, Francis E. Stoner (int.). Con. 144: 212 (col.), 213-7 Jan '60.

——, Grover Cleveland. Jensen: The White house, p. 137.

——, Grover Cleveland's summer. Amer. heri. vol. 8 no. 6 p. 103 (Oct '57).

——, Hunza. Natl. geog. 104: 510 (col.) Oct '53.

——, Indian. See hut, Navajo Indian.

——, Irish. Holiday 6: 34 Dec '49; 24: 87 (col.) Dec '58.

——, Irish (ext. & int.). Con. 145: 148-55 May '60.

——, Italian villa (ext. & int.). Con. 144: 140 (col.), 141-4 Dec '59.

——, James Buchanan. Amer. heri. vol. 5 no. 3 p. 44-9 (part col.) (spring '54); vol. 7 no. 1 p. 114 Dec '55.

——, James Younger (Kearney, Mo.). Horan: Pict. hist. of wild west, p. 33.

——, Jamestown. Con. 140: 133 Nov '57.

——, Japanese (int.). Holiday 28: 26-7 (col.) Jl '60.

——, John Ringling (Fla.). Durant: Pict. hist. of Amer. circus, p. 202.

——, Joseph Smith (Mormon). Brooks: Growth of a nation, p. 127.

——, Julia & Abby Smith. Amer. heri. vol. 8 no. 4 p. 56 (Je '57).

——, King ranch (Tex.). Natl. geog. 101: 41 (col.) Jan '52.

——, Lanier (state memorial). Natl. geog. 97: 203 (col.) Feb '50.

——, "Little Women's" (int.). Holiday 27: 158 Mar '60.

——, Louisa May Alcott. See Alcott home, Louisa May.

——, Maderia. Holiday 28: 67 Sept '60.

——, "Mark Twain". See Clemen's home, Samuel Langhorne.

——, Mass. (early). Amer. heri. vol. 11 no. 4 p. 103 (Je '60).

——, Meloney (N.Y., int. & ext.). Con. 143: 134 (col.), 135-42 May '59.

——, Mennonite. Amer. heri. vol. 10 no. 5 p. 31 (Aug '59).

——, Mexican. See Mexican home.

——, Mo. Holiday 14: 111 (col.) Nov '53.

——, modern. Holiday 20: 83 Oct '56.

——, modern (int.). Holiday 14: 118-9 (col.) Dec '53.

Int. gr. soc.: Arts . . . p. 129 (col.).

——, Montenegro (int.). Holiday 25: 84 (col.) Je '59.

——, Natchez (ante-bellum). Holiday 27: 163 Feb '60.

——, New Orleans (Greek revival). Holiday 23: 86 (col.) Mar '58.

——, New Orleans (int.). Holiday 23: 84 Mar '58.

——, Normandie. Con. 145: LXXXVII Je '60.

——, Norwegian (ext. & int.). Con. 145: 2 (col.), 3-6 Mar '60.

——, Orkney is. Natl. geog. 104: 533 Oct '53.

——, P. T. Barnum. Durant: Pict. hist. of Amer. circus, p. 51, 57.

——, Pacific islander (modern). Int. gr. soc.: Arts . . . p. 15 (col.).

——, plantation (Ga.). Natl. geog. 105: 288 Mar '54.

home, plantation (La. Bayou). Holiday 6: 59 Oct '49.

——, plantation (New Orleans). Natl. geog. 103: 165 (col.), 168 Feb '53.

——, Philip Hone (1831). Amer. heri. vol. 8 no. 5 p. 13 (Aug '57).

——, Robert E. Lee. *See* "Arlington".

——, Robert Morris. Amer. heri. vol. 7 no. 6 p. 88 (Oct '56).

——, Russian (ext. & int., 19th cent.). Con. 142: 221-5 Jan '59.

——, salt box (1700). Natl. geog. 112: 308-9 (col.) Sept '57.

——, Samuel L. Clemen's. *See* Clemen's home, Samuel L.

——, Scotland. Amer. heri. vol. 11 no. 5 p. 6 (Aug '60).
Con. 145: 70 (col.), 71-5 Ap '60.

——, Shakespeare's mother's. Natl. geog. 108: 306 (col.) Sept '55.

——, S.C. Holiday 25: 131 Feb '59.

——, southern. Amer. heri. vol. 11 no. 5 p. 52 (col.) (Aug '60).

—— *See* also home, Colonial (southern).

——, Sumerian (int.). *See* Sumerian home (int.).

——, Sweden (int.). Holiday 20: 45 (col.) Aug '56.

——, thatch roof. Natl. geog. 97: 106 Jan '50.

——, thatch roof (Brittany). Con. 143: 121 Ap '59.

——, thatch roof. (Eng.). Natl. geog. 98: 178 (col.) Aug '50.

——, thatch roof (Tristan). Natl. geog. 97: 110 (col.) Jan '50.

——, Thomas Edison. Amer. heri. vol. 10 no. 6 p. 34, 112 (Oct '59).

——, Thomas Jefferson. *See* Jefferson home, Thomas.

——, Thoroughgood (oldest in Va.). Natl. geog. 109: 443 Ap '56.

——, Tudor style. Natl. geog. 103: 789 Je '53.

——, Vermont Georgian. Holiday 6: 45 Nov '49.

——, Sir Walter Raleigh. *See* Raleigh home, Sir Walter.

——, William Byrd (Va.). *See* Byrd home, William (Va.).

——, William H. McGuffey. *See* McGuffey birthplace, William Holmes.

——, William Jennings Bryan. Amer. heri. vol. 12 no. 1 p. 117 (Dec '60).

——, William McKinley. *See* McKinley home, William.

——, Col. William Somerville. Natl. geog. 105: 435 (col.) Ap '54.

——, William Sprague (R.I.). Amer. heri. vol. 7 no. 5 p. 93 (Aug '56).

——, Zerelda Samuel. *See* Samuel home, Zerelda.

home for newlyweds (Tristan). Natl. geog. 97: 112 (col.) Jan '50.

home of wealthy burgess (15th cent, int.). Int. gr. soc.: Arts . . . p. 55 (col.).

"Home, sweet home", John Howard Payne. Brooks: Growth of a nation, p. 85.

home. *See* also homes; house.

Homer (bust). Int. gr. soc.: Arts . . . p. 23 (col.).

Homer, Arthur B. Cur. biog. p. 268 (1952).

Homer, Winslow (work of). Amer. heri. vol. 3 no. 2 p. 19 (winter '52); vol. 8 no. 3 p. 30-7 (col.) (Ap '57); vol. 8 no. 5 cover, p. 44, 46-53 (col.) (Aug '57).
Con. 143: 130 Ap '59.
Holiday 7: 106 (col.) Feb '50.
Natl. geog. 99: 201, 205, 211 (col.) Feb '51.
Praeg. pict. ency., p. 432 (col.).

homes, Acadian (La.). Travel 112: 31-3 Sept '59.

——, Amer. Holiday 27: 120 (col.) May '60.

——, Amer. (early). Holiday 18: 16-7 Aug '55.

——, Amer. famous. Amer. heri. vol. 6 no. 2 p. 21 (col.), 22-3 (Feb '55); vol. 8 no. 5 p. 35 (Aug '57); vol. 10 no. 5 p. 67 (Aug '59); vol. 10 no. 6 p. 34, 64 (Oct '59).

——, Amer. historic. Travel 112: 30-8 Jl '59.

——, Batak. Natl. geog. 108: 388-9 (col.) Sept '55.

——, beach. Holiday 28: 99-106 Aug '60.

——, Breton. Holiday 27: 82-3 (col.) Jan '60.

——, Charleston (S.C.). Amer. heri. vol. 9 no. 2 p. 48, 60-1 (col.) (Feb '58).

——, Colonial. Brooks: Growth of a nation, p. 66.
Holiday 5: 52 (col.) Mar '49; 8: 41 (col.) Jl '50, 74 (col.) Oct '50, 46-7 (col.) Nov '50; 15: 106-7, inside back cover Mar '54, 140 Ap '54.
Jordan: Hammond's pict. atlas, p. 86-7, 100 (col.).

——, Colonial (Ala.). Holiday 11: 59 Feb '52.

——, Colonial (Christmas). Face of Amer., p. 174-5 (col.).

——, Colonial (Cincinnati). Holiday 8: 108 Sept '50.

——, Colonial (Del.). Amer. heri. vol. 2 no. 4 p. 22-3 (col.) (summer '51).

——, Colonial (int.). Natl. geog. 105: 445, 449-51, 453, 457, 459 (part col.) Ap '54.

——, Colonial (La.). Holiday 11: 42-7 (col.) Mar '52.
Natl. geog. 113: 532-49 (part col.) Ap '58.

——, Colonial (southern). Amer. heri. vol. 7 no. 4 p. 56-63 (Je '56).
Holiday 11: 46-7 (col.) Mar '52.
Int. gr. soc.: Arts . . . p. 101 (col.).
Travel 102: 9 Aug '54; 103: 19 May '55.

——, Colonial (Va.). Amer. heri. vol. 10 no. 5 p. 67 (Aug '59).
Holiday 8: 27 (col.) Sept '50.
Natl. geog. 111: 613 (col.) May '57.

——, English. Holiday 14: 55, 132 (col.) Nov '53.

——, English (Claydon house, int.). Con. 142: 70 (col.), 71-4 Nov '58.

——, English (16th cent.). Con. 144: 2 (col.), 3-7 Sept '59.

——, famous. Travel 103: 16 Je '55.

——, Fijian. *See* Fijian homes.

——, Fla. Holiday 7: 90-7 (part col.) Jan '50.

——, Fla. (Key West). Holiday 6: 124-5 Dec '49.

——, Ger. Holiday 25: 42-3 (col.) Jan '59.

——, Greece. Holiday 24: 69 Sept '58.

homes, Holland. Holiday 27: 162 Jan '60. Natl. geog. 98: 749 Dec '50.
——, Hudson valley (old). Holiday 6: 39, 43 (col.) Sept '49.
——, Italian. Holiday 25: 94 (col.) Mar '59.
——, Ky. See Kentucky home.
——, Md. Natl. geog. 105: 435, 442 (col.) Ap '54.
——, Mass. Holiday 28: 62-3 (col.) Aug '60.
——, Mass. (early). Holiday 24: 59 (col.) Sept '58.
——, Mexican. Holiday 25: 140 (col.) Feb '59.
——, modern (int.). Holiday 7: 90 (col.) Jan '50.
——, Panama jungle. Natl. geog. 104: 277 (col.) Aug '53.
——, plantation (La.). Travel 108: 13-4 Oct '57.
——, plantation (Va.). Natl. geog. 103: 788-801 (part col.) Je '53.
——, R. I. Holiday 27: 103, 106 (col.) May '60.
——, Shetland is. Natl. geog. 104: 536 Oct '53.
——, Swiss. Holiday 28: 31-43 (part col.) Aug '60.
——, thatch roof (Eng.). Holiday 25: 135 (col.) Feb '59.
——, Wash., D.C. Holiday 7: 94-7 Feb '50.
——, Zanzibar. Natl. geog. 101: 274 Feb '52.
homes of nobility (int., middle ages). Int. gr. soc.: Arts . . . p. 53 (col.).
homes of U.S. Presidents. Travel 114: 34-6 Sept '60.
homes of wealthy noblemen int. Middle ages. Int. gr. soc.: Arts . . . p. 53 (col.).
homes. See also home; houses; huts.
Homestead hotel (Hot Springs, Va.). Holiday 13: 96 Ap '53 21; 112 May '57.
Hondius' map of world (1590). Amer. heri. vol. 10 no. 3 p. 10-11 (Ap '59).
Hone, Nathaniel (work of). Con. 126: 193 Dec '50.
Hone, Philip. Amer. heri. vol. 8 no. 5 p. 13, 21 (col.) (Aug '57).
Hone home, Philip (1831). Amer. heri. vol. 8 no. 5 p. 13 (Aug '57).
Honegger, Arthur. Cur. biog. p. 401 (1941).
Honeyman's grave (Revolution). Amer. heri. vol. 8 no. 5 p. 60 (Aug '57).
honey-pot, earthenware (Staffordshire). Con. ency. of ant., vol. 1, pl. 50.
Honeywell, Annette. Cur. biog. p. 271 (1953).
Honfleur (France). Natl. geog. 115: 612-3 (col.) May '59.
"Honfleur" (Corot). Con. 129: 70 Ap '52.
Hong Kong (China). Holiday 6: 13 (col.) Jl '49; 8: 19-22 Nov '50; 23: 166 (col.) May '58. Natl. geog. 97: 382 Mar '50; 105: 240-72 (part col.) Feb '54; 116: 854-5 (col.) Dec '59.
Travel 113: 39-41 Feb '60.
—— (harbor). Holiday 22: 131 (col.) Nov '57; 24: 91 (col.) Aug '58.
—— (harbor, night). Natl. geog. 116: 312-3 (col.) Sept '59.
—— (junks). Natl. geog. 100: 740 (col.) Dec '51.
—— (map). Natl. geog. 105: 245 Feb '54.

—— (night). Holiday 27: inside back cover (col.) Feb '60.
Honolulu (1816). Amer. heri. vol. 11 no. 2 p. 16-7 (col.) (Feb '60).
honor, medals of. Int. gr. soc.: Arts . . . p. 167 (col.).
honor guard, Nigeria. Natl. geog. 110: 332-3 (col.) Sept '56.
Hoo, Victor. Cur. biog. p. 317 (1947).
Hooch, Pieter de. See de Hooch, Pieter.
Hood, Clifford F. Cur. biog. p. 273 (1953).
Hood, John (work of). Con. 143: 32 Mar '59.
Hood, Gen. John Bell (Civil war). Amer. heri. vol. 5 no. 3 p. 32 (col.) (spring '54); vol. 7 no. 2 p. 44 (Feb '56).
Pakula: Cent. Album, p. 159.
Hook, Sidney. Cur. biog. p. 270 (1952).
hook, eaves trough. See eaves trough hook.
——, hay loosening. Rawson: Ant. pict. bk., p. 26.
——, pot & meat. Rawson: Ant. pict. bk., p. 22.
——, reaping. Rawson: Ant. pict. bk., p. 26.
hookah (pipe). Natl. geog. 108: 157 (col.) Aug '55.
—— (man smoking). Natl. geog. 104: 19 (col.) Jl '53.
——, Egyptian. Int. gr. soc.: Arts . . . p. 177 (col.).
——. See also water pipe.
Hooker, Joseph. Pakula: Cent. album. p. 161.
hookers (Irish peat boats). Natl. geog. 108: 742 (col.) Dec '55.
hoop (boy rolling). Natl. geog. 101: 778 (col.) Je '52.
—— (boy rolling, medieval). Int. gr. soc.: Arts . . . p. 77 (col.).
—— (man rolling, ancient times). Int. gr. soc.: Arts . . . p. 37 (col.).
Hooper, Claude E. Cur. biog. p. 320 (1947).
Hoopes, Darlington. Cur. biog. p. 272 (1952).
Hoover, Pres. Herbert C. Amer. heri. vol. 7 no. 3 p. 33 (Ap '56); vol. 9 no. 4 p. 65 (Je '58); vol. 10 no. 6 p. 44 (Oct '59).
Cur. biog. p. 307 (1943).
Natl. geog. 112: 45 Jl '57.
—— (campaign poster). Amer. heri. vol. 7 no. 5 p. 104 (Aug '56).
—— (horseback). Amer. heri. vol. 6 no. 2 p. 66 (winter '55).
Hoover, Pres. & Mrs. Herbert C. Jensen: The White House, p. 231.
Hoover, Herbert, jr. Cur. biog. p. 343 (1954).
Hoover, J. Edgar. Cur. biog. p. 254 (1950).
Hoover dam (Nevada). Jordan: Hammond's pict. atlas, p. 183 (col.).
Natl. geog. 99: 729 (col.) Je '51.
"Hopalong Cassidy" (Bill Boyd). Holiday 5: 40 (col.) Jan '49.
Hope, Bob. Cur. biog. p. 403 (1941); p. 274 (1953).
Holiday 5: 47 (col.) Jan '49; 8: 24 Aug '50.
—— (service men). Natl. geog. 111: 316-7 (col.) Mar '57.
Hope, Clifford R. Cur. biog. p. 277 (1953).
Hope, Lady Jane (Romney). Con. 142: 189 (col.) Dec '58.
Hope, Stanley C. Cur. biog. p. 193 (1959).

hope (sym.). Lehner: Pict. bk. of ant., p. 35-6, 46, 77.

Hope diamond. Natl. geog. 117: 817 (col.) Je '60.

Hopetoun house (int. & ext., Scotland). Con. 139: 140 (col.), 141-3 May '57.

Hopewell village (Penn.). Travel 108: 23-4 Oct '57.

Hopkins, Arthur. Cur. biog. p. 322 (1947).

Hopkins, Ernest Martin. Cur. biog. p. 306 (1944).

Hopkins, Harry. Jensen: The White House, p. 238.

Hopkins, Harry L. Cur. biog. p. 405 (1941).

Hopkins, John Jay. Cur. biog. p. 345 (1954).

Hopkins home, James. Amer. heri. vol. 7 no. 1 p. 114 (Dec '55).

hoplite (Greek soldier, ancient times). Int. gr. soc.: Arts . . . p. 33 (col.).

Hoppe, Willie. Cur. biog. p. 323 (1947).

Hoppenot, Henri Etienne. Cur. biog. p. 308 (1944).

Hopper, Edward. Cur. biog. p. 257 (1950).
—— (work of). Amer. heri. vol. 6 no. 6 p. 34 (col.) (Oct '55).
    Holiday 14: 61 (col.) Nov '53.

Hopper, Hedda. Cur. biog. p. 391 (1942).
    Holiday 12: 37 Oct '52.

Hopper, John (work of). Con. 127: 97 May '51; 132: cover, opp. p. 3 (col.) Sept '53; 143: 88 Ap '59; 144: LXV Nov '59; 145: XXXVII Je '60.

Hopsonn, Edward (Kneller). Con. 127: 32 Mar '51.

Horace. Int. gr. soc.: Arts . . . p. 25 (col.).

Horder, Baron Thomas J. Cur. biog. p. 309 (1944).

Hore-Belisha, Leslie. Cur. biog. p. 407 (1941).

horin-rimbo (sym.). Lehner: Pict. bk. of sym., p. 47.

Hormel, Jay C. Cur. biog. p. 267 (1946).

Horn, Tom. Horan: Pict. hist. of wild west, p. 197, 242-3.

horn. Amer. heri. vol. 10 no. 1 p. 44 (col.) (Dec '58).
    Holiday 21: 15 (col.) Jan '57; 27: 142 (col.) Jan '60; 28: 24 Nov '60.
    Int. gr. soc.: Arts . . . p. 141 (col.).
—— (French pattern). Cooper: Con. ency. of music, p. 404.
—— (Korongo man). Natl. geog. 99: 264 Feb '51.
—— (man blowing, ship). Natl. geog. 100: 483 Oct '51.
—— (musical inst.). Holiday 27: 193 May '60.
—— (New Year's eve). Lehner: Pict. bk. of sym., p. 54.
——, Alpine. Holiday 19: 98 Mar '56.
——, basset. See basset horn.
——, drinking. See drinking horn.
——, hound call. Natl. geog. 99: 828 Je '51.
——, hunting. See hunting horn.
——, Malya buffalo (man blowing). Natl. geog. 103: 222 (col.) Feb '53.
——, Odin's triple. See Odin's triple horn.
——, postilion's. See postilion's horn.
——, powder. See powder horn.
——, sports car. Holiday 27: 203 Mar '60.

——, Wai Wai Indian. Natl. geog. 107: 343 (col.) Mar '55.

horn trumpet, cow (gaucho). Natl. geog. 113: 333 (col.) Mar '58.

Horne, John E. Cur. biog. p. 273 (1952).

Horne, Lena. Cur. biog. p. 311 (1944).

Horner, Hannah Mee (work of). Amer. heri. vol. 7 no. 1 p. 21 (col.) (Dec '55).

Horner, Horace Mansfield. Cur. biog. p. 292 (1955).

hornet game. See hormussen game.

Horney, Karen. Cur. biog. p. 409 (1941).

horns (moon) (sym.). Lehner: Pict. bk. of sym., p. 28.

Hornsby, Rogers. Cur. biog. p. 275 (1952).

Hornung, Paul. Cur. biog. p. 196 (1963).

Hormussen (or hornet) game (Swiss). Holiday 21: 40 (col.) May '57.

horoscope, division of. Lehner: Pict. bk. of sym., p. 22.

Horoqitz, L. S. (work of). Cooper: Con. ency. of music, p. 296.

Horowitz, Vladimir. Cur. biog. p. 313 (1943).

Horrocks, Lt. Gen. Brian G. Cur. biog. p. 294 (1945).

Horsbrugh, Florence. Cur. biog. p. 277 (1952).

horse, stick. See stick horse.

horse, white (chalk hillside etching). Natl. geog. 114: 54 Jl '58.

horse bell. Rawson: Ant. pict. bk., p. 67.

horse bits. See bits & briddle bosses, horse.

horse bog-shoe. See bog-shoe, horse.

horse briddle. See briddle bosses & bits, horse.

"The horse guards" (Scott). Con. 142: XXXV (col.) Jan '59.

Horse guards, Royal (London). Holiday 13: 12 (col.) Mar '53, 131 (col.) Ap '53, 65 (col.) May '53; 14: 67 (col.) Sept '53; 17: 61 (col.) Feb '55; 18: 116 (col.) Nov '55; 25: 190 (col.) May '59.
    Natl. geog. 100: 715 (col.) Dec '51.

Horse guards parade (London). Holiday 15: 12 (col.) Feb '54.

horse parade (State fair). Natl. geog. 104: 803 (col.) Dec '53.

horse race. Holiday 16: 9 Sept '54; 18: 185 Dec '55; 22: 129 (col.) Nov '57.
    Natl. geog. 109: 464-5 (col.) Ap '56.
—— (Falkland). Natl. geog. 109: 400-1 (col.) Mar '56.
—— (Mauritius is.). Natl. geog. 109: 94 (col.) Jan '56.
—— (New Zealand). Natl. geog. 101: 433 (col.) Ap '52.
—— (shipboard). Holiday 12: 127 (col.) Dec '52.
—— (snow). Holiday 10: 75 Oct '51.
——, Siena. See Siena palio.
——, sulky. Holiday 10: 87 Jl '51.
——, trotting. Natl. geog. 102: 22 (col.) Jl '52. Travel 106: 35 Oct '56.
——, trotting (ice). Natl. geog. 115: 334-5 (col.) Mar '59.

horse school, white. See White horse school (Vienna).

horse show. Natl. geog. 106: 698-720 (part col.) Nov '54.
—— (Dublin, Ireland). Natl. geog. 104: 120-1 (col.) Jl '53.

—— (New Zealand). Natl. geog. 101: 434 (col.) Ap '52.
horseback riders. *See* men & women (horseback).
horsemen, Nigerian ceremonial. Natl. geog. 110: 336-8 (col.) Sept '56.
"Horses fighting" (Ward). Con. ency. of ant., vol. 1, pl. 173.
"Horses going into corral" (Garcia). Natl. geog. 107: 367 (col.) Mar '55.
horseshoe. Holiday 14: 110 Sept '53; 27: 58 (col.) May '60.
—— (sym.). Lehner: Pict. bk. of sym., p. 62.
horseshoe, nail ring. Lehner: Pict. bk. of sym., p. 62.
horseshoe. *See* also bog-shoe, horse.
horseshoes. Rawson: Ant. pict. bk., p. 54, 68.
Horsfall, Frank L., jr. Cur. biog. p. 411 (1941); p. 209 (1961).
Horton, Edward Everett. Cur. biog. p. 270 (1946).
Horwich, Frances. Cur. biog. p. 280 (1953).
Horyu-ji temple. *See* temple Horyu-ji (Japan).
Hosier, Abram. Con. 139: 134 Ap '57.
Hoskins, John (miniature by). Con. ency. of ant., vol. 1, pl. 129.
Hoskins, Lewis M. Cur. biog. p. 295 (1950).
Hosmer, Craig. Cur. biog. p. 204 (1958).
hospital (Havre St. Pierre, Quebec). Travel 108: 50 Aug '57.
—— (Kuwait). Travel 103: 15 Mar '55.
—— (Ohio univ.). Natl. geog. 107: 446 (col.) Ap '55.
—— (Uganda, Africa). Natl. geog. 106: 741 (col.) Dec '54.
hostel (boys on cots). Natl. geog. 108: 144 Jl '55.
——, German. Natl. geog. 108: 132 Jl '55.
——, youth (Eng.). Natl. geog. 109: 528 Ap '56.
hostelries, English. Holiday 17: 12 (col.) Mar '55.
hostess, airplane. *See* airline hostess; stewardess, airplane.
hot dog cart. Holiday 26: 59 (col.) Oct '59.
hot dog stand. (Berlin). Natl. geog. 100: 703 Nov '51.
hot pool. Jordan: Hammond's pict. atlas, p. 137 (col.).
Hot Springs (Ark.). Holiday 16: 34 (col.) Nov '54.
Hot Springs (Va., hotel). Holiday 18: 68 Aug '57.
hot water bottle, tin. Rawson: Ant. pict. bk., p. 74.
hotel (Acapulco, Mex.). Holiday 11: 54 Mar '52.
—— (Arequipa, Peru). Holiday 14: 95 (col.) Nov '53.
—— (Ariz.). Holiday 10: 83 (col.) Nov '51. Jordan: Hammond's pict. atlas, p. 178 (col.).
—— (Aruba Caribbean). Travel 112: 49 Sept '59.
—— (Australia). Travel 102: 8 Nov '54.
—— (Banff Springs). Holiday 14: 44 Jl '53.
—— (Barbados). Natl. geog. 101: 390 (col.) Mar '52.

—— (Belgian Congo). Natl. geog. 101: 351 (col.) Mar '52.
—— (Bermuda). Holiday 26: 103 (col.) Oct '59; 28: 8 Oct '60.
—— (Biarritz, Fr.). Travel 106: 24 Oct '56.
—— (Boca Raton, Fla.). Holiday 27: 114 Jan '60; 28: 23 (col.) Nov '60.
—— (Brasilia, Brazil). Travel 111: 44 Feb '59.
—— (Cal.). Holiday 18: 78 (col.) Sept '55; 19: 73 (col.) Feb '56; 21: 81 (col.) May '57.
—— (Canada). Holiday 5: 90 (col.) Je '49; 7: 106 (col.) Ap '50; 25: 193 May '59.
—— (Cannes, Fr.). Holiday 26: 66-9 (part col.) Aug '59.
—— (Caracas, Venezuela). Holiday 26: 101 (col.) Aug '59.
—— (Carvel Hall, Annapolis). Holiday 23: 83 (col.) Je '58.
—— (Chicago). Holiday 14: 142 Oct '53.
—— (Chile). Holiday 14: 123 (col.) Oct '53.
—— (China, for Natl. minorities). Natl. geog. 118: 196 (col.) Aug '60.
—— (Colo.). Holiday 10: 77 Nov '51; 12: 26 Nov '52.
—— (Colo. Springs). Holiday 14: 85 Nov '53; 18: 38 Dec '55; 24: 59 Dec '58; 27: 23 Jan '60.
—— *See* also Broadmoor hotel.
—— (Darband, Iran). Natl. geog. 100: 449 (col.) Oct '51.
—— (Devonshire, Eng.). Travel 111: 54 Ap '59.
—— (El Panama). Holiday 13: 48-9 (col.) Jan '53.
—— (Fla.). Holiday 5: 140 Mar '49; 18: 57 (col.), 86, 155 Dec '55. Travel 103: 13 Feb '55.
—— (Ft. Lauderdale, Fla.). Holiday 24: 143 Oct '58, 165 Nov '58, 187 Dec '58; 27: 168-9 Jan '60.
—— (Glacier Natl. Park). Holiday 23: 110 (col.) Feb '58; 27: 105 Feb '60.
—— (Gsteig, Switz.). Holiday 28: 38-9 (col.) Aug '60.
—— (Havana). Holiday 25: 171 (col.) Je '59.
—— (Hawaii). Holiday 14: 166 Dec '53; 18: 70 Sept '55; 19: 66 Mar '56, 112 May '56; 20: 82 Aug '56, 29 Oct '56; 21: 19 Feb '57; 22: 91 (col.), 230 Dec '57; 26: 34 (col.) Dec '59; 27: 157 (col.) Feb '60. Travel 114: 54 Sept '60.
—— (Hershey, Pa.). Holiday 24: 189 Dec '58; 25: 204 Ap '59.
—— (Israel). Holiday 26: 71 (col.) Dec '59.
—— (Jamaica). Holiday 22: 110 (col.) Nov '57. Natl. geog. 105: 356 (col.) Mar '54.
—— (Japan). Travel 113: 19 Mar '60.
—— (Klosters, Switz.). Holiday 23: 73 Feb '58.
—— (La Quinta, Cal.). Holiday 24: 146 Nov '58.
—— (The Lido). Holiday 24: 50 (col.) Aug '58.
—— (Los Angeles). Holiday 25: 129 May '59.
—— (Miami). Travel 102: 11 Jl '54.
—— (Miami Beach). Holiday 23: 208 Je '58; 24: 186 Dec '58.

Travel 103: 44 Feb '55; 111: 51 Jan '59.
hotel (Nassau, Bahamas). Holiday 14: 6 Jl '53;
17: 97 Jan '55; 27: 74 (col.) Mar '60.
—— (New Delhi, India). Natl. geog. 116: 838
(col.) Dec '59.
—— (N. J.). Holiday 12: 98 (col.) Aug '52.
—— (Panama City). Holiday 14: 93 Dec '53.
—— (Puerto Rico). Holiday 6: 143 Dec '49;
21: 74 (col.) Mar '57.
—— (Quebec, Can.). Holiday 5: 124 (col.) Ap
'49; 11: 99 (col.) Je '52.
—— (San Francisco). Holiday 23: 164 (col.)
Je '58.
—— (San Juan, Puerto Rico). Travel 114: 44
Aug '60.
—— (Santo Domingo). Holiday 25: 41 (col.)
Ap '59.
—— (Sao Paulo, Brazil). Travel 102: 49 Aug
'54.
—— (Switz., Mt. Pilatus). Travel 102: 11 Aug
'54.
—— (Tex.). Holiday 5: 141 Mar '49; 11: 102
(col.) Ap '52.
—— (Turkey). Travel 103: 62 May '55.
—— (Venezuela). Holiday 26: 13 (col.) Jl '59.
—— (Va.). Holiday 21: 112 May '57.
—— (W. Va.). Holiday 11: 118 (col.) May
'52.
—— (White Sulphur Springs, W. Va.). Holiday
14: 103 (col.) Oct '53; 25: 165 (col.) May
'59.
—— (Yugoslavia). Holiday 10: 75 Jl '51.
hotel, Berlin Hilton. Travel 106: 49 Nov '56.
——, Biltmore (Ariz.). Holiday 8: 77 Oct '50;
10: 115 (col.) Oct '51; 12: 17 (col.) Nov '52;
17: 111 Jan '55.
——, Broadmoor (Col. Springs). Holiday 6:
119 Oct '49; 10: 146 Oct '51; 17: 126 Jan
'55; 23: 104 May '58.
——. See also Broadmoor hotel.
——, Crockett (San Antonio). Jordan: Hammond's pict. atlas, p. 118 (col.).
——, dog. See dog hotel.
——, drive-in. Travel 104: 66 Jl '55.
——, El Cortez (San Diego). Travel 106: 9
Aug '56.
——, The Empress (Victoria, B.C., Can.). Holi-
day 17: 118 (col.) Mar '55.
Natl. geog. 114: 186 (col.) Aug '58.
——, Europe's highest mt. Natl. geog. 98: 211
Aug '50.
——, floating boat (Ray is. club). Travel 106:
48 Dec '56.
——, Fontainbleau. Holiday 24: 130 Jl '58.
——, Glacier park. Natl. geog. 109: 590-1
(col.) May '56.
——, Grand hotel de n' Gor (Africa). Holiday
25: 145 Ap '59.
Natl. geog. 108: 776 (col.) Dec '55.
——, Grand Pacific (Suva, Fiji is.). Holiday
7: 61 (col.) Je '50.
——, Grand Union (Saratoga). Amer. heri.
vol. 6 no. 6 p. 37 (Oct '55).
——, Greenbrier. See Greenbrier hotel.
——, Habana Hilton. Holiday 23: 170 (col.)
Ap '58.
——, Homestead (Va.). Holiday 6: 124 Sept
'49.

——, Imperial (Copenhagen). Travel 109: 41
Ap '58.
——, Kvikne (Norway). Natl. geog. 111: 107
Jan '57.
——, Llao Llao (Argentina). Travel 102: 41
Sept '54.
——, motor (Chicago). Travel 113: 43 Feb
'60.
——, Mt. Wash. (Breton Woods, N.H.). Holi-
day 10: 40 Sept '51.
——, Mt. top (Caracas, Venezuela). Travel
107: 45 May '57.
——, Palace (Lucerne, Switz.). Con. 133: LXII
May '54.
——, Palace (St. Moritz). Holiday 27: 74-9
(col.) Feb '60.
——, Park Plaza (St. Louis). Holiday 8: 35
(col.) Oct '50.
——, Plaza (Mexico City). Natl. geog. 100:
799 (col.) Dec '51.
——, resort (model, Puerto Rico). Travel 105:
63 Jan '56.
——, resort (Three Lakes, Wis.). Holiday 28:
57 Aug '60.
——, Saxony (Miami Beach). Travel 113: 58
Ap '60.
——, Selsdon Park Mansion (London). Travel
103: 22 May '55.
——, Shelton (N.Y.). Travel 105: 56 Ap '56,
56 May '56.
——, Skyhost auto motel. Travel 114: 43 Jl
'60.
——, Statler-Hilton (Hartford, Conn.). Holi-
day 27: 82 (col.) Feb '60.
——, Surf rider inn (Santa Monica). Travel
109: 47 Feb '58.
——, Tel Aviv inn (Chicago). Travel 113: 51
Mar '60.
——, Terrace Plaza (Cincinnati). Holiday 8:
111 (col.) Sept '50.
——, Travelers (La Guardia airport). Travel
106: 46 Sept '56.
——, Venoy Park (St. Petersburg, Fla.). Holi-
day 17: 110 Jan '55.
——, Victorian style (Maine). Amer. heri. vol.
6 no. 6 p. 40 (Oct '55).
——, Virginia (Hot Springs). Holiday 5: 148
Ap '49.
——, Westbury (1st Amer. hotel built in Lon-
don). Travel 103: 45 Mar '55.
hotel. See also inn.
Hotel bill. Amer. heri. vol. 11 no. 3 p. 17 (Ap
'60).
Hotel Bel-Air (Los Angeles). Holiday 10: 98-
103 (part col.) Aug '51.
Hotel Breakers (Palm Beach, Fla.). Travel 105:
44 Jan '56.
Hotel bus (1890's). Holiday 12: 67 Sept '52.
Hotel Caracas Hilton (Caracas, Venezuela).
Travel 110: 41 Jl '58.
Hotel Caribe Hilton (San Juan, Puerto Rico).
Natl. geog. 99: 428, 449 (col.) Ap '51.
Travel 109: 41 Jan '58.
Hotel Carillon (Miami Beach). Travel 108: 43
Dec '57.
Hotel Carlsbad (Cal.). Travel 108: 47 Nov '57.
Hotel Casa Montego (Jamaica). Travel 108:
43 Aug '57.

Hotel Castelhaiti (Haiti). Travel 105: 56 May '56.

Hotel Corridor (Sahara oasis). Natl. geog. 113: 692 (col.) May '58.

Hotel Crillon (Paris, Fr.). Travel 108: 48 Jl '57.

Hotel d'Alcantara (Ghent). Amer. heri. vol. 12 no. 1 p. 30 (Dec '60).

Hotel de Sens (Paris, 15th cent.). Natl. geog. 101: 803 (col.) Je '52.

hotel dining room. Holiday 26: 15 (col.) Jl '59.

hotel dining room, Palace (San Francisco). Holiday 14: 26-7 (col.) Sept '53.

hotel doorman. Holiday 7: 95 Mar '50.

Hotel du Rhone (Geneva, Switz.). Con. 133: LXII May '54.

Hotel Europa (Denmark's tallest). Travel 103: 43 Ap '55.

Hotel Foresta (Stockholm). Travel 110: 41 Jl '58.

Hotel France et Choiseul, courtyard (Paris). Travel 110: inside back cover Aug '58.

Hotel Hahnhof (Baden-Baden). Holiday 23: 89 Je '58.

Hotel Hilton (Amsterdam). Travel 111: 53 Mar '59.

Hotel Hilton (Athens, Gr.). Travel 114: 27 Aug '60.

Hotel Hilton (Port of Spain). Travel 109: 41 May '58.

Hotel Hilton (San Francisco). Travel 112: 8 Jl '59.

Hotel Hollywood-by-the-Sea (Fla.). Travel 111: 55 Feb '59.

Hotel Kaiulani (Hawaii). Holiday 17: 59 Feb '55.

Hotel Lakeshore (Milwaukee). Travel 111: 53 Je '59.

Hotel Lexington (N.Y.). Holiday 13: 130 Ap '53, 152 May '53, 144 Je '53.
Travel 106: 45 Oct '56, 51 Dec '56; 107: 50 Feb '57, 50 Ap '57, 51 Je '57.

hotel lobby (Greenbrier hotel). Holiday 11: 123 (col.) May '52.

—— (old fashioned). Holiday 27: 24 Feb '60.

hotel model. Travel 101: 43 Je '54.

—— (Baltimore). Travel 110: 43 Sept '58.

—— (Brown's palace). Travel 107: 58 Mar '57.

—— (Executive house, Chicago). Travel 108: 43 Nov '57.

—— ("hotel of future"). Travel 104: 54 Aug '55.

—— (Isle of Pines). Travel 101: 42 Feb '54.

—— (Montreal). Travel 103: 48 Jan '55.

—— (Waikiki Beach, Hawaii). Travel 108: 43 Oct '57.

Hotel Montmartre (Miami Beach). Travel 111: 50 Ap '59.

Hotel New Japan. Travel 113: 19 Mar '60.

Hotel Normandie (San Juan, Puerto Rico). Natl. geog. 99: 428 (col.) Ap '51.

Hotel Orion (Bergen, Norway). Travel 107: 49 Ap '57.

Hotel Pennsylvania (Palm Beach, Fla.). Holiday 17: 87 Feb '55.

Hotel Portillo (Chilian Andes). Travel 113: cover (col.) Je '60.

Hotel Rondavels (Africa). Travel 104: 65 Nov '55.

Hotel Royal Caribbean (Jamaica). Travel 108: 43 Dec '57.

Hotel St. George (Algiers). Travel 104: 15 Nov '55.

Hotel Saint Georges (Beirut). Natl. geog. 113: 480 (col.) Ap '58.

Hotel Santes (Switz.). Natl. geog. 110: 457 Oct '56.

Hotel Saxony (Miami Beach). Travel 107: 37 Mar '57; 113: 58 Ap '60.

Hotel Sheraton (Dallas). Travel 107: 49 Feb '57.

Hotel Tamanaco (Caracas, Venezuela). Travel 105: 23 Feb '56; 107: 18 Mar '57.

Hotel Yankee Clipper (Ft. Lauderdale). Travel 106: 55 Jl '56.

hotels. Holiday (back of all issues).
Travel (in all issues).

—— (Dominican Republic). Holiday 23: 35 (col.) May '58.

—— (Eng.). Holiday 23: 142-7 Ap '58.

—— (Hawaii). Holiday 19: 97 Je '56; 23: 9 Feb '58, 16 Mar '58, 43 Ap '58; 24: 3 Aug '58, 85 Sept '58, 128 Oct '58; 26: 119 Nov '59; 27: 6 Mar '60, 152 (col.) Ap '60; 28: 4 Oct '60, 118 (col.) Dec '60.

hotels (Hilton around the world). Holiday 23: 42 (col.) May '58.

—— (Miami Beach). Holiday 8: 18 (col.) Dec '50.

—— (models). Travel 106: 49 Oct '56.

—— (San Juan, Puerto Rico). Travel 109: 41 Jan '58; 114: 44 Aug '60, 54 Sept '60.

——, retirement (Cal.). Travel 108: 46-8 Nov '57.

hothouse, grape. Natl. geog. 113: 827 (col.) Je '58.

Hotsprings (Va.). Holiday 24: 124 Oct '58.

Hottel, Althea Kratz. Cur. biog. p. 295 (1948).

"Hottest place on earth" (so-called). Natl. geog. 108: 168-9 (col.) Aug '55.

Houdon,, Jean Antoine (marble bust). Con. 137: 128 Ap '56.

—— (sculpture). Con. 126: 92-3 Oct '50; 144: 128 Nov '59.
Natl. geog. 110: 657 Nov '56.
Praeg. pict. ency., p. 333.

—— (terra-cotta bust). Con. 133: 236 Je '54; 140: 7 Sept '57.

—— (work of). Amer. heri. vol. 5 no. 4 p. 15 (summer '54).
Natl. geog. 113: 260-1 Feb '58.

Hough, William S. Natl. geog. 113: 459 Ap '58.

Houghton, Amory. Cur. biog. p. 325 (1947).

Houghton, Mrs. Hiram Cole. Cur. biog. p. 261 (1950).

"Houghton" (Walpole's home, Norfolk, Eng.). Con. 139: 208 (col.), 209-12 Je '57.

Houk, Ralph. Cur. biog. p. 215 (1962).

Houle, Cyril O. Cur. biog. p. 217 (1962).

"Houmas House" (plantation). Amer. heri. vol. 4 no. 2 p. 30 (col.) (winter '53).
Natl. geog. 113: 538 (col.) Ap '58.

"Hound & hunter" (Homer). Holiday 7: 106 (col.) Feb '50.

Houphouet-Boigny, Felix. Cur. biog. p. 206 (1958).

Houqua (Chinese merchant). Amer. heri. vol. 6 no. 2 p. 17 (winter '55).

hourglass, Henry VIII. Con. 136: 44 Sept '55.

hourglass, Holbein (silver gilt). Con. 134: 117 Nov '54.

——, Portuguese (16th cent.). Con. 137: 11 Mar '56.

——, winged. *See* winged hourglass.

Hours-Miedan, Magdeleine. Cur. biog. p. 210 (1961).

"Hours of Jeanne d'Evreux" (Pucelle). Con. 141: 133 Ap '58.

House, Col. Edward. Jensen: The White House, p. 205.

House, Edward Mandell. Amer. heri. vol. 9 no. 4 p. 71 (Je '58); vol. 10 no. 2 p. 62 (Feb '59).

house. Holiday 13: 123 May '53.
Natl. geog. 114: 317 (col.) Sept '58.

—— (built in exchange for 2 sheep). Brooks: Growth of a nation, p. 110.

—— (early). Con. 132: IV Nov '53.

—— (1851). Amer. heri. vol. 9 no. 6 p. 23 (Oct '58).

—— (Elizabethan type). Amer. heri. vol. 8 no. 4 p. 112 (Je '57).

—— (flooded by high water). Natl. geog. 109: 653 May '56.

—— (Indian making palm leaf roof). Natl. geog. 110: 824 Dec '56.

—— (int.). Amer. heri. vol. 4 no. 2 p. 33-9 (part col.) (winter '53).
Holiday 25: 139 (col.) Je '59; 27: 126 (col.) Ap '60.

—— (Italian villa type). Amer. heri. vol. 8 no. 4 p. 112 (Je '57).

—— (man clearing snow). Natl. geog. 110: 764 (col.) Dec '56.

—— (most eastern in U.S.). Rawson: Ant. pict. bk., p. 76.

—— (night). Holiday 26: 135 Dec '59.

—— (oldest frame house in U.S.). Holiday 11: 41 Je '52.

—— (oldest in S.C.). Natl. geog. 103: 289 (col.) Mar '53.

—— (oldest in U.S., St. Augustine). Jordan: Hammond's pict. atlas, p. 69 (col.).

—— (over waterfall). Praeg. pict. ency., p. 442.

—— (1715). Holiday 10: 38-9 (col.) Nov '51.

—— (snow). Amer. heri. vol. 9 no. 1 p. 16 (col.) (Dec '57).
Holiday 18: 201 (col.) Dec '55; 20: 11 Nov '56, 42 (col.) Dec '56; 22: 165 (col.) Dec '57.
Natl. geog. 108: 666 (col.) Nov '55.

—— (snow, getting tree). Holiday 18: 180 Dec '55.

—— (snow, lights). Holiday 18: 140 (col.) Dec '55.

—— (where Jefferson Davis was married). Brooks: Growth of a nation, p. 107.

—— (where Lincoln died). Holiday 7: 127 Feb '50.

—— (winter). Amer. heri. vol. 7 no. 1 p. 16 (col.) (Dec '55); vol. 9 no. 6 p. 51 (col.) (Oct '58).

——, adobe (El Oued, Sahara). Natl. geog. 117: 784-5 (col.) Je '60.

——, Africa. Holiday 25: 92-3 (col.) Ap '59.

——, Alabama. Natl. geog. 112: 527 (col.) Oct '57.

——, Anso (entrance, Spain). Natl. geog. 109: 305 Mar '56.

——, Antarctic (int.). Natl. geog. 112: 369, 378-9 (part col.) Sept '57.

——, Australia (on stilts). Natl. geog. 109: 242 (col.) Feb '56.

——, Austria. Disney: People & places, p. 53 (col.).
Natl. geog. 115: 205 (col.) Feb '59.

——, Bali. Natl. geog. 116: 810 (col.) Dec '59.

——, Bar Harbor (Maine). Amer. heri. vol. 6 no. 5 p. 58 (Aug '55).

——, Bayou country. Amer. heri. vol. 6 no. 1 p. 60 (col.) (fall '54).

——, Belgian. Natl. geog. 108: 548 (col.) Oct '55.

——, Bermuda. Holiday 18: 24 (col.) Sept '55, 113 (col.) Nov '55; 22: 63 (col.) Dec '57; 23: 70 (col.) Je '58; 25: 168 (col.) Ap '59.

——, building. Natl. geog. 111: 534 Ap '57.

——, building (New Guinea). Natl. geog. 100: 667 Nov '51.

——, Bursa (tiled, Turkey). Natl. geog. 100: 173-4 (col.) Aug '51.

——, butterfly type (N.C.). Holiday 19: 54-5 Mar '56.

——, Canada. Natl. geog. 98: 358 (col.) Sept '50.

——, Canada (formal garden). Natl. geog. 114: 179 (col.) Aug '58.

——, Charleston (S.C., 1714). Brooks: Growth of a nation, p. 61.

——, Chile. Natl. geog. 117: 218 (col.) Feb '60.

——, Chinese (entrance). Natl. geog. 111: 348 (col.) Mar '57.

——, Chinese (int., 18th cent.). Praeg. pict. ency., p. 542 (col.).

——, Colonial *See* architecture, Colonial; homes, Colonial.

——, Cornish miners. *See* Cornish miner's house.

——, cotton labor (south). Brooks: Growth of a nation, p. 278.

——, desert. Holiday 13: 60-3 (part col.) Mar '53.

——, dog-trot. Brooks: Growth of a nation, p. 56.

——, doll. *See* doll house.

——, Dutch. Natl. geog. 106: 372, 390-1, 412 (col.) Sept '54.

——, Dutch (int.). Natl. geog. 106: 382-3, 397, 403 (col.) Sept '54.

——, Egyptian style (int.). Con. 140: 227 Jan '58.

——, 18th cent. (Va.). Natl. geog. 109: 450 Ap '56.

——, English. Con. 138: LIII, 91 Nov '56; 141: 101 Ap '58, 193-7 May '58; 144: 232 Jan '60.

——, English (Elizabethan farm). Natl. geog. 108: 306 (col.) Sept '55.

——, English (Firle Place, int.). Con. 136: 78 (col.) Nov '55.

——, English (half-timbered). Holiday 13: 88

Ap '53; 23: cover, 37 (col.) Jan '58. Natl. geog. 111: 266-7 (col.) Feb '57; 114: 65 (col.) Jl '58.

house, English (Heveningham, int., 18th cent.). Con. 139: 71-5 (part col.) Ap '57.

——, English (int.). Con. 142: 209-11 Jan '59.

——, English (int. & ext.). Con. 139: 208 (col.), 209-12 Je '57; 141: 193-7 May '58; 143: 68 (col.), 69-73 Ap '59.

——, English (mansion). Con. 141: 68 (col.), 69-70 Ap '58.

——, English (Petworth house). Con. 132: 45 Sept '53.

——, English ("Southill", int.). Con. 129: 15-21 Ap '52.

——, English Tudor. Con. 143: 2, 4 Mar '59.

——, English. See also architecture, English.

——, farm. See farm house.

——, floating. Holiday 21: 94-5 (col.) May '57.

——, Fla. Holiday 11: 43 Jan '52.

——, French (int., woman, chickens). Natl. geog. 115: 579 Ap '59.

——, French (16th cent.). Natl. geog. 103: 242 (col.) Feb '53.

——, Ga. (plantation). Natl. geog. 112: 524 (col.) Oct '57.

——, Georgian (Va.). Natl. geog. 109: 446-7 (col.) Ap '56.

——, glass. Holiday 12: 48 (col.) Aug '52.

——, Gothic (Chicago). Holiday 10: 58-9 Oct '51.

——, Isle of Skye (Scotland). Natl. geog. 102: 101 (col.) Jl '52.

——, Jamestown (model). Natl. geog. 111: 592 May '57.

——, Japanese. See Japanese house.

——, Kitimat (Can.). Natl. geog. 110: 390-1 (col.) Sept '56.

——, lakeside. Holiday 21: 94-5 (col.) May '57.

——, Liberia jungle. Natl. geog. 100: 276 Aug '51.

——, log. Brooks: Growth of a nation, p. 52-3, 56.

——, Long Island (N.Y., 1600's). Holiday 24: 36 (col.) Sept '58.

——, Maine. Holiday 12: 79 Nov '52.

——, Maryland (1634). Brooks: Growth of a nation, p. 50.

——, Mauritius. Natl. geog. 109: 92 (col.) Jan '56.

——, modern (Cal.). Holiday 10: 98-103 (col.) Sept '51.

——, modern (int.). Holiday 18: 56-7 (col.) Oct '55; 19: 110-11 (col.) Feb '56; 20: 76 (col.) Sept '56; 21: 94 (col.) May '57; 28: 95 (col.) Dec '60.

——, modern (int. decorating). Holiday 25: 94-5 (col.) May '59.

——, mt. (N.C.). Natl. geog. 113: 857, 859 Je '58.

——, New Eng. Brooks: Growth of a nation, p. 57.

——, New Guinea (pile dwelling). Int. gr. soc.: Arts . . . p. 11 (col.).

——, N. Y. (Colonial). Natl. geog. 110: 601 (col.) Nov '56.

——, N. Y. (1840). Amer. heri. vol. 6 no. 5 p. 60 (col.) (Aug '55).

——, Normandy farm. Holiday 19: 53 Jan '56.

——, Norwegian (int.). Natl. geog. 106: 189 (col.) Aug '54.

——, Palm Springs (int.). Holiday 22: 84-5 (col.) Oct '57.

——, Pasadena (Cal.). Holiday 11: 98 (col.) Jan '52.

——, Paul Revere. See Revere home, Paul.

——, Pedregal rock city. Natl. geog. 100: 800 (col.) Dec '51.

——, Penn. (early). Natl. geog. 102: 24 (col.) Jl '52.

——, prefabricated. Natl. geog. 111: 534 Ap '57.

——, ranch. Face of Amer., p. 39 (col.).

——, reed (Arab). Natl. geog. 113: 206-11, 218-9, 224, 230 (part col.) Feb '58.

——, Rococo (int., Scotland). Con. 139: 140 (col.) May '57.

——, Roman (int.). Int. gr. soc.: Arts . . . p. 11 (col.).

——, salt-box See salt-box house.

——, sod. See sod house.

——, S. C. Holiday 23: 167 Mar '58.

——, Strausbourg (15th cent.). Holiday 23: cover (col.) Jan '58.

——, Sweden (int. & ext.). Con. 141: 3-4 Mar '58.

——, Swiss Holiday 21: 10 (col.) Je '57; 23: 137 Mar '58.
Natl. geog. 107: 832-3 (col.) Je '55.

——, Swiss (chalet). Holiday 25: 132 Ap '59.
Natl. geog. 111: 170 (col.) Feb '57.

——, Swiss (snow). Holiday 25: 126 (col.) Mar '59.

——, thatch roof. Brooks: Growth of a nation, p. 47.
Con. 141: XVI Je '58.
Holiday 21: 18 (col.) Ap '57, 26 May '57, 181 (col.) Je '57; 23: 129 (col.) Feb 58, 199 May '58; 26: 74 (col.), 137 Nov '59; 27: 2 (col.) May '60.
Natl. geog. 103: 814 (col.) Je '53; 107: 66 (col.) Jan '55.
Travel 105: 40 Ap '56; 114: 38 Sept '60.

——, thatch roof (Chinese village). Natl. geog. 111: 357 (col.) Mar '57.

——, thatch roof (Cuba). Holiday 19: 95 (col.) Jan '56.

——, thatch roof (Eng.). Holiday 25: 155 Ap '59; 26: 7 (col.) Nov '59.

——, thatch roof (Hebrides). Natl. geog. 106: 567 Oct '54.

——, thatch roof (Ireland). Con. 135: LX Ap '55.
Natl. geog. 104: 125 (col.) Jl '53.

——, thatch roof (Jamestown). Natl. geog. 111: 584 (col.) May '57.

——, thatch roof (Madeira is.). Natl. geog. 115: 382 (col.) Mar '59.

——, thatch roof. See also hut, thatch roof.

——, tree. See tree house.

——, Trojan. See Trojan house.

——, umbrella. Holiday 21: 56 (col.) Mar '56.

——, Ürgüp cliff. Natl. geog. 113: 131, 136-7 Jan '58.

house, Victorian (19th cent.). Amer. heri. vol. 6 no. 6 p. 34-41 (Oct '55).

——, Va. (17th cent.). Brooks: Growth of a nation, p. 57.

house, western Indian. Natl. geog. 112: 224, 234 Aug '57.

——, Yemen (Arabia). Natl. geog. 101: 214 Feb '52.

house & barn, thatch roof (Pyrenees mts.). Natl. geog. 109: 334 (col.) Mar '56.

house at St. Joseph (where Jesse James was killed). Horan: Pict. hist. of Wild west p. 41, 44.

"House by the railroad" (Hopper). Amer. heri. vol. 6 no. 6 p. 34 (col.) (Oct '55). Holiday 14: 61 (col.) Nov '53.

"House in the valley" (Cezanne). Con. 145: 234 Je '60.

house interior (Inigo Jones). Con. 135: XXXIX Mar '55.

house. See also home; houses.

House judiciary meeting, U.S. (1871). Amer. heri. vol. 7 no. 4 p. 47 (Je '56).

house mover trailer. Natl. geog. 115: 330 Mar '59.

House of Burgesses (Williamsburg, Va.). Natl. geog. 106: 452 (col.) Oct '54.

House of Commons (in chapel, Westminster). Amer. heri. vol. 8 no. 4 p. 95 (Je '57).

"House of Eternity" (pyramid of Giza). Natl. geog. 112: 104 (col.) Jl '57.

"House of Exiles" (Essene). See Khirbat Qumran.

"House of God". See Kaaba (Mecca).

"House of God" volcano (Africa). Natl. geog. 97: 338-9 (col.) Mar '50.

House of Representatives. See U.S. House of Representatives.

"House of Seven Gables" (Salem, Mass.). Holiday 15: 107 Mar '54. Travel 104: 39 Oct '55; 110: 21 Aug '58.

—— (int.). Natl. geog. 97: 293 (col.), 298 Mar '50.

"House of Spirits". See Tambaran house.

"House of the Moralist" (Pompeii). Ceram: March of arch., p. 25.

House of the tragic poet (Venice). Amer. heri. vol. 11 no. 3 p. 22 (col.) (Ap '60).

House of worship, Bahai (Wilmette, Ill.). Travel 106: 16 Dec '56.

house post, African. Holiday 25: 71 Ap '59.

house roof (Nigerian). Natl. geog. 110: 361 Sept '56.

house terrace (men & women). Holiday 27: 86 (col.) May '60.

house where Lincoln died. Holiday 7: 127 Feb '50.

"House that Jack built". Amer. heri. vol. 3 no. 1 p. 20 (fall '51).

house trailer, auto. Holiday 5: 31, 82 Feb '49, 23, 90 Mar '49, 16, 141 Ap '49; 6: 91 Aug '49, 5, 68 Sept '49, 136 Oct '49, 149 Nov '49, 135 Dec '49; 7: 105 Jan '50, 71 Mar '50, 11, 98 Ap '50, 132 May '50, 8, 113 Je '50; 8: 47, 68 Aug '50, 68 Sept '50, 30 Nov '50; 10: 143 Nov '51; 11: 16 Feb '52, 28 Mar '52, 145 Je '52; 12: 92 Jl '52, 18 Sept '52, 66 Nov '52; 13: 98 Ap '53, 79 May '53; 14: 144 Jl '53, 99, 149 Nov '53,

156 Dec '53; 18: 25 Nov '55; 24: 200 Nov '58; 27: 160 Jan '60, 45 May '60.

Natl. geog. 103: 112 Jan '53; 111: 773, 777, 800 (col.) Je '57; 114: 654 Nov '58; 115: 830 Je '59; 116: 443 (col.) Oct '59.

Travel 101: 36 Feb '54, 40 Mar '54, 21-3 Je '54; 102: 46 Aug '54; 103: 29-33 May '55; 107: 13, 56 May '57, 16 Je '57; 109: 24 Jan '58; 111: 32 Feb '59; 112: 61 Dec '59; 113: 23-4 Ap '60.

—— (cartoon). Travel 103: 30-4 May '55.

—— (land-water, terra-marina). Travel 114: 58 Aug '60.

—— (men & women). Travel 113: 23-4 Ap '60.

—— (plans). Travel 101: 23 Je '54.

house trailer, British auto. Travel 105: 37 Feb '56.

houseboat. Holiday 21: 114 Feb '57. Travel 106: 9 Dec '56.

—— (Fla.). Natl. geog. 107: 51, 53-4, 57, 63 (col.) Jan '55.

—— (Miss. river). Natl. geog. 114: 656-9 (part col.) Nov '58.

——, bayou. Natl. geog. 113: 556 (col.) Ap '58.

——, Indochinese. Natl. geog. 102: 290 Sept '52.

——, jungle. Natl. geog. 102: 707 Nov '52.

——, Kashmir. Natl. geog. 114: 611, 626 (part col.) Nov '58.

Houseman, John. Cur. biog. p. 195 (1959).

Houser, Theodore V. Cur. biog. p. 267 (1957).

houses (along the Amazon). Disney: People & places, p. 105, 107 (col.).

—— (burning). Amer. heri. vol. 11 no. 6 p. 22-3 (Oct '60).

—— (1858). Amer. heri. vol. 8 no. 4 p. 112 (Je '57).

—— (lighted, snow). Holiday 10: 176 (col.) Dec '51.

—— (mts., snow). Holiday 11: 108 (col.) Jan '52.

—— (moved on river barge). Natl. geog. 118: 724 (col.) Nov '60.

—— (snow covered). Natl. geog. 117: 482 (col.) Ap '60.

——, adobe (Nigeria). Natl. geog. 110: 342-3 (col.) Sept '56.

——, Alaska. Natl. geog. 109: 744, 748, 788-9 (col.) Je '56; 116: 47 (col.) Jl '59.

——, Annapolis. Natl. geog. 113: 5 (col.) Jan '58.

——, Argentina. Natl. geog. 113: 310, 338 (col.) Mar '58.

——, Avalon (N.J.). Natl. geog. 117: 38-9 (col.) Jan '60.

——, Aymara Indian (Peru). Natl. geog. 107: 142-3 Jan '55.

——, Belgian Congo. See huts, Belgian Congo.

——, Belgium. Natl. geog. 107: 635 (col.) May '55; 113: 812-3 (col.) Je '58.

——, Borneo. Natl. geog. 108: 386-7 (col.) Sept '55; 109: 712, 714, 724 May '56.

——, Boston. Holiday 11: 41 Je '52.

——, Cal. desert. Natl. geog. 112: 688, 692-3, 698 (col.) Nov '57.

——, Canton is. Natl. geog. 107: 120-1 (col.) Jan '55.

——, **English.** Natl. geog. 108: 306, 308-9, 316, 324, 326, 340 (col.) Sept '55; 114: 64-5, 76-7 (col.) Jl '58.

——, **English (half timbered).** Holiday 15: 28 (col.) Je '54.

Int. gr. soc.: Arts . . . p. 101 (col.).

——, **Falkland.** Natl. geog. 109: 392 Mar '56.

——, **Fiji is.** Natl. geog. 114: 548-9 (col.) Oct '58.

——, **Formosa.** Natl. geog. 107: 584, 586 Ap '55.

——, **French.** Natl. geog. 115: 572 Ap '59.

——, **German.** Holiday 15: 129 Ap '54; 25: 50, 54, 63, 67 (col.) May '59.

Natl. geog. 111: 258-9, 262-3, 267 (col.) Feb '57.

——, **Greece.** Natl. geog. 114: 764-5, 770-1, 776-7 (part col.) Dec '58.

——, **Harpers Ferry (Va.).** Natl. geog. 111: 406-7 (col.) Mar '57.

——, **head hunters.** Natl. geog. 108: 486 Oct '55.

——, **Hudson valley (1855-).** Amer. heri. vol. 10 no. 1 p. 20 (Dec '58).

——, **Iraq.** Natl. geog. 114: 480-1 (col.) Oct '58.

——, **Irish farm.** Natl. geog. 108: 742-3 (col.) Dec '55.

——, **Isle of Jersey.** Holiday 23: 20 Je '58.

——, **Israeli.** Natl. geog. 115: 525 Ap '54.

——, **Italian.** Natl. geog. 109: 842-3 (col.) Je '56; 116: 496-7, 509 (col.) Oct '59.

——, **Japan.** Natl. geog. 118: 734 (col.) Dec '60.

——, **Kabul.** Natl. geog. 114: 6 Jl '58.

——, **Katmandu (Nepal).** Natl. geog. 117: 396-7 (col.) Mar '60.

——, **Kurd.** Holiday 22: 30 Oct '57.

——, **Laos.** Natl. geog. 117: 69 (col.) Jan '60.

——, **log (1729).** Brooks: Growth of a nation, frontis.

——, **Madeira is.** Natl. geog. 115: 370-1 (col.) Mar '59.

——, **Mexican.** Natl. geog. 102: 537 Oct '52.

——, **mud.** Natl. geog. 104: 153, 158-9 (col.) Aug '53.

——, **Mukalla mud (Aden colony).** Natl. geog. 111: 240-1, 246, 250 Feb '57.

——, **Nagaland (India).** Natl. geog. 107: 252 Feb '55.

——, **Nepal (bamboo roof).** Natl. geog. 108: 585, 609 (col.) Nov '55.

——, **Nepal (cliff).** Natl. geog. 117: 384-5 (col.) Mar '60.

——, **Nepal (int.).** Natl. geog. 117: 386 Mar '60.

——, **Normandy (Fr.).** Natl. geog. 115: 912-3 (col.) May '59.

——, **Norway.** Holiday 27: 59 Jan '60.

——, **Pilgrim (early).** Brooks: Growth of a nation, p. 45-7.

——, **Portugal.** Holiday 19: 30-1, 35 (col.) Jan '56.

Natl. geog. 118: 628-9, 639 (col.) Nov '60.

——, **Rotterdam.** Natl. geog. 118: 543 (col.) Oct '60.

——, **Russian.** Natl. geog. 116: 744-5 (col.) Dec '59.

——, **Saint Veran (Fr.).** Natl. geog. 115: 584, 587 Ap '59.

——, **Scotland.** Natl. geog. 110: 5-9, 15, 20, 34 (part col.) Jl '56; 112: 466, 475, 488 (part col.) Oct '57.

——, **Spain.** Natl. geog. 111: 628-9 (col.) May '57.

——, **stilt (Congo river).** Natl. geog. 118: 322 (col.) Sept '60.

——, **Swiss.** Disney: People & places, p. 39 (col.).

Natl. geog. 110: 440-78 (col.) Oct '56; 114: 570 (col.) Oct '58; 116: 273 Aug '59.

——, **Tarascan (Mexico).** Natl. geog. 102: 533, 543 (part col.) Oct '52.

——, **Tibet.** Holiday 12: 57 (col.) Dec '52.

——, **Tudor.** *See* Tudor houses.

——, **Turkey.** Natl. geog. 115: 71 (col.) Jan '59.

——, **Venice.** Holiday 18: 42 (col.), 44-5, 47 (col.) Oct '55.

——, **wattle & daub (Colonial, Va.).** Travel 107: back cover May '57.

——, **West Germany.** Natl. geog. 115: 754, 763 (col.) Je '59.

houses. *See also* homes; house.

houses of parliament (London). *See* Parliament houses.

housewife (cooking). Natl. geog. 115: 577 Ap '59.

housing, Antarctic. Natl. geog. 113: 458-9 Ap '58.

Houssay, Dr. Bernardo. Holiday 20: 107 Nov '56.

Houssay, Bernardo Alberto. Cur. biog. p. 296 (1948).

Houston, Charles H. Cur. biog. p. 298 (1948).

Houston, David F. Brooks: Growth of a nation, p. 244.

Houston, Sam. Amer. heritage vol. 2 no. 3 p. 2 (col.) (spring '51).

Holiday 16: inside back cover (col.) Jl '54; 23: 73 Mar '58.

Houston, Temple. Horan: Pict. hist. of wild west, p. 116.

Houston (Texas). Holiday 11: 98-108 (part col.) Ap '52; 14: 78 Jl '53.

Houtte, Jean Van. Cur. biog. p. 279 (1952).

Hovde, Bryn J. Cur. biog. p. 272 (1946).

Hovenden, Thomas (work of). Natl. geog. 99: 197 (col.) Feb '51.

Hoving, Walter. Cur. biog. p. 274 (1946).

Howard, Lady Catherine (miniature). Con. ency. of ant., vol. 1, pl. 129.

Howard, Charles. Amer. heri. vol. 10 no. 4 p. 16 (col.) (Je '59).

Howard, Mrs. Charles P. Cur. biog. p. 281 (1953).

Howard, Elizabeth. Cur. biog. p. 282 (1951).

Howard, Henry. Amer. heri. vol. 10 no. 4 p. 16 (col.) (Je '59).

—— **(work of).** Con. 132: XI Sept '53.

Howard, Oliver Otis. Pakula: Cent. album, p. 163.

Howard, Thomas (Earl of Effingham) (by T. Hudson). Con. 142: X Sept '58.

Howard college (Negro). Holiday 7: 88 Feb '50.

howdah (on elephant). Holiday 18: 14 Jl '55.

Jensen: The White House, p. 284. Natl. geog. 112: 140-1 (col.) Jl '57.
Howe, Clarence D. Cur. biog. p. 295 (1945).
Howe, Gordie. Cur. biog. p. 219 (1962).
Howe, Helen. Cur. biog. p. 347 (1954).
Howe, James Wong. Cur. biog. p. 315 (1943).
Howe, Julia Ward. Amer. heri. vol. 8 no. 1 p. 10 (col.), 12 (Dec '56).
Howe, Louis. Jensen: The White House, p. 238.
Howe, Sir William. Amer. heri. vol. 6 no. 5 p. 24 (col.) (Aug '55).
Howell, Charles R. Cur. biog. p. 348 (1954).
Howell, Wallace E. Cur. biog. p. 262 (1950).
Howells, William Dean. Amer. heri. vol. 11 no. 1 p. 75 (Dec '59).
Howes, Seth. Durant: Pict. hist. of Amer. circus, p. 39.
Howitt, Samuel (work of). Con. 140: XXXV (col.) Jan '58.
Howland, Alfred (work of). Amer. heri. vol. 6 no. 4 p. 16-7 (col.) (Je '55).
Howorth, Lucy Somerville. Cur. biog. p. 283 (1951).
Howrey, Edward F. Cur. biog. p. 282 (1953).
Howth castle. Holiday 19: 39 (col.) Jan '56.
Hoxha, Enver. Cur. biog. p. 265 (1950).
Hoxsey, Arch. Amer. heri. vol. 7 no. 3 p. 5 (Ap '56).
Hoyle, Fred. Cur. biog. p. 192 (1960).
Hoyt, Palmer. Cur. biog. p. 318 (1943).
Hradcany castle (Prague). Holiday 21: 56, 59 (col.) Jan '57.
Hrdlicka, Ales. Cur. biog. p. 413 (1941).
Hruska, Roman Lee. Cur. biog. p. 284 (1956).
Hsiao Hisu sepulchral way. See sepulchral way, China (winged lion).
Hsiung, Gen. Shih-Fei. Cur. biog. p. 393 (1942).
Hu Shih. Cur. biog. p. 394 (1942).
huaso (Chilean rider). Natl. geog. 117: 184, 210 (col.) Feb '60.
Huaut, Les Freres (minature by). Con. 138: 83 Nov '56.
Hubbard, Father Bernard. Cur. biog. p. 321 (1943).
Hubbard, Henry (Gainsborough). Con. 143: 86 Ap '59.
Hubbard, Margaret Ann. Cur. biog. p. 207 (1958).
Hubbard medal. Natl. geog. 103: 564 Ap '53; 113: 792 Je '58.
Hubbell, Carl. Holiday 23: 84 May '58.
Huberman, Bronislaw. Cur. biog. p. 415 (1941).
Huck, Arthur. Cur. biog. p. 269 (1957).
"Huck & Tom" (bronze figures). Natl. geog. 110: 131 Jl '56.
Huckleberry Finn (Mark Twain character). Holiday 5: 59 Mar '49.
Huckleberry Finn. See also Tom Sawyer & Huckleberry Finn.
huckster (with bear & monkey). Rawson: Ant. pict. bk., p. 42.
Huddleston, Father John. Con. 144: 6 Sept '59.
Huddleston, Vice-Marshall Edmund C. Cur. biog. p. 286 (1951).
Huddleston, Bishop Trevor. Cur. biog. p. 198 (1963).
Hudner, Thomas, jr. Holiday 11: 137 Je '52.
Hudson, Henry. Holiday 6: 35 (col.) Sept '49.

—— (with Indians). Brooks: Growth of a nation, p. 40.
Hudson, Manley O. Cur. biog. p. 313 (1944).
Hudson, Robert S. Cur. biog. p. 397 (1942).
Hudson, Rock. Cur. biog. p. 212 (1961).
Hudson, Thomas (work of). Con. 132: LXII Sept '53; 140: 235 Jan '58; 142: X Sept '58, XXXV Nov '58.
Hudson auto. Holiday 5: 91 (col.) Ap '49, 30 (col.) Je '49; 6: 81 (col.) Jl '49.
Hudson Bay. Natl. geog. 110: 671-87 (part col.) Nov '56.
—— (map). Natl. geog. 110: 677 Nov '56.
Hudson Bay Co. (Ft. Langley). Amer. heri. vol. 8 no. 4 p. 16-7 (col.) (Je '57).
Hudson-Bay Co. ships. Amer. heri. vol. 10 no. 5 p. 46 (col.) (Aug '59).
Hudson Bay store locations. Natl. geog. 108: 207 (col.) Aug '55.
Hudson river. Holiday 6: 34-41 (part col.) Sept '49.
Jordan: Hammond's pict. altas, p. 36-7 (col.). Travel 107: cover Mar '57; 109: 52 Je '58.
—— (early land grants). Amer. heri. vol. 10 no. 1 p. 10 (col.) (Dec '58).
—— (1850). Amer. heri. vol. 10 no. 1 cover (col.), p. 4-5, 12-25 (col.). (Dec '58).
Hudson river valley. Amer. heri. vol. 10 no. 1 p. 104-5 (Dec '58).
Hue (Indochina). Natl. geog. 102: 306-7 (col.) Sept '52.
Huebner, Charles R. Cur. biog. p. 281 (1949).
Huet, Jean Baptiste (work of). Con. 136: LVIII Nov '55.
Huey Long statue. See statue (Huey Long).
Huger, Benjamin. Pakula: Cent. album, p. 165.
Huger II, John. Amer. heri. vol. 9 no. 2 p. 57 (col.) (Feb '58).
Hugh, Duke of Northumberland (Barry). Con. 126: 25 Aug '50.
Hugh Town (St. Mary's isle). Travel 101: 17 Feb '54.
Hughes, Archbishop John. Amer. heri. vol. 10 no. 4 p. 97 (Je '59).
Hughes, Charles Evans. Amer. heri. vol. 9 no. 1 p. 102 (Dec '57); vol. 9 no. 3 p. 25, 27 (Ap '58).
Cur. biog. p. 417 (1941).
Holiday 7: 75 Feb '50.
Hughes, Harold E. Cur. biog. p. 200 (1963).
Hughes, Howard. Cur. biog. p. 421 (1941).
Holiday 8: 83 Sept '50.
Hughes, James (work of). Amer. heri. vol. 6 no. 6 cover (col.) (Oct '55).
Hughes, Langston. Holiday 27: 75 (col.) Je '60.
Hughes, Paul. Cur. biog. p. 324 (1943).
Hughes, Richard J. Cur. biog p. 221 (1962).
Hughes, Rowland R. Cur. biog. p. 285 (1956).
Hughes, Roy O. Cur. biog. p. 266 (1950).
Hughes, Sarah T. Cur. biog. p. 268 (1950).
Hughes, Toni. Cur. biog. p. 422 (1941).
Hugo, Victor (sculpture detail). Praeg. pict. ency., p. 14.
—— (work of). Con. 143: 159-65 May '59.
Hugo Van der Goes (work of). Con. 126: 3-10, 51 Aug '50.
Praeg.: Pict. ency., p. 303.
hula dance, Tahitian. Holiday 9: 54 Mar '51.
hula dancer. See Hawaiian hula dancer.

hula hoop (children, Delhi). Natl. geog. 116: 838 (col.) Dec '59.
Hulcy, Dechard A. Cur. biog. p. 287 (1951).
Hull, Mr. & Mrs. David R. Holiday 27: inside cover (col.) Jan '60.
Hull, Isaac. Holiday 23: 77 May '58.
Hull, Gen. John E. Cur. biog. p. 350 (1954).
Hull, Josephine. Cur. biog. p. 284 (1953).
Hull house (Chicago). Amer. heri. vol. 12 no. 1 p. 15 (Dec '60).
Hulne priory (Northumberland). Con. 142: 75-9 Nov '58.
human sacrifice (buried 2000 yrs.). Natl. geog. 105: 421, 426-8 Mar '54.
Humbert, Crown Prince of Italy. Cur. biog. p. 325 (1943).
Humbolt, Baron Alexander von. Ceram: March of arch., p. 269.
Hume, Brig. Gen. Edgar Erskine. Cur. biog. p. 316 (1944).
humility in giving (sym.). Lehner: Pict. bk. of sym., p. 47.
humming bird feeder. Natl. geog. 100: 251 Aug '51.
Humperdinck, Englebert. Cooper: Con. ency. of music, p. 142.
Humphrey, Doris. Cur. biog. p. 398 (1942).
Humphrey, George M. Cur. biog. p. 286 (1953).
Humphrey, Helen F. Cur. biog. p. 280 (1952).
Humphrey, Hubert H., jr. Cur. biog. p. 283 (1949).
Humphreys, Harry E., jr. Cur. biog. p. 285 (1949).
Humpty Dumpty. Holiday 7: 160 May '50; 8: 118 Nov '50.
Hungarian refugees (flight). Natl. geog. 111: 416, 424-36 Mar '57.
Hungary. Holiday 6: 64-70 (part col.) Nov '49.
Hungary Victory memorial. Holiday 6: 64 (col.) Nov '49.
"The Hunley" (Civil war submarine). Amer. heri. vol. 9 no. 3 p. 48 (col.), 50 (Ap '58).
Hunsaker, Jerome C. Cur. biog. p. 401 (1942).
Hunt, Charles (work of). Con. ency. of ant., vol. 1, pl. 138.
Hunt, Clara Whitehill. Jun. bk. of auth., p. 167.
Hunt, Syril Benoni Holman. Con. 144: 10 Sept '59.
Hunt, Herold C. Cur. biog. p. 287 (1956).
Hunt, Sir John. Cur. biog. p. 352 (1954).
Hunt, Lester C. Cur. biog. p. 287 (1951).
Hunt, Mabel Leigh. Cur. biog. p. 291 (1951). Jun. bk. of auth., p. 169.
Hunt, Richard Morris. Amer. heri. vol. 6 no. 2 p. 20 (winter '55).
—— **(arch. of).** Amer. heri. vol. 6 no. 2 p. 21 (col.), 22-5 (winter '55).
Hunt, William Holman (work of). Con. 140: XLV Dec '57; 144: 10 Sept '59, 95 Nov '59.
Hunt, William Morris (work of). Amer. heri. vol. 8 no. 3 p. 41 (Ap '57).
hunt (goddess of). Lehner: Pict. bk. of sym., p. 32.
"hunt board". Rawson: Ant. pict. bk., p. 15.
Hunter, Croil. Cur. biog. p. 292 (1951).
Hunter, Dard. Cur. biog. p. 194 (1960).
Hunter, David. Pakula: Cent. album, p. 167.

Hunter, Evan. Cur. biog. p. 289 (1956).
Hunter, Kermit. Cur. biog. p. 197 (1959).
Hunter, Kim. Cur. biog. p. 281 (1952).
hunter. Con. 136: XLIII Dec '55.
Holiday 6: 5 (col.) Dec '49; 10: 40 (col.) Dec '51; 12: 22, 25 (col.) Sept '52, 20 Nov '52; 22: 25 Sept '57, 14 (col.) Oct '57; 23: 1 Ap '58; 26: inside cover (col.) Dec '59.
Int. gr. soc.: Arts . . . p. 153 (col.).
—— **(at car).** Holiday 24: 80 Oct '58.
—— **(bow & arrow).** Holiday 12: 53 (col.) Oct '52.
—— **(dog, gun).** Holiday 19: 39 (col.) Je '56.
—— **(dog, horse).** Con. 134: XXI Nov '54; 137: 162-3 May '56.
—— **(dogs, horse).** Holiday 18: 29 Oct '55; 20: 34 (col.) Sept '56; 21: 89 Mar '57.
Natl. geog. 114: 225, 227 (col.) Aug '58.
—— (*See* also man (hunter, dogs).
—— **(gun).** Holiday 28: 57 (col.) Nov '60.
—— **(head).** Holiday 12: 14 Sept '52.
—— **(head, Austria).** Natl. geog. 118: 273 (col.) Aug '60.
—— **(head, blowing horn).** Holiday 11: 82 (col.) Ap '52.
—— **(head, winter).** Holiday 10: 79 Nov '51.
—— **(holding wild goose).** Natl. geog. 100: 77 (col.) Jl '51.
—— **(horse).** Con. 136: 218 Dec '55; 137: XX-VI May '56.
Holiday 15: 62 Je '54.
—— **(horse, hounds).** Con. 136: XXXV (col.) Jan '56.
—— **(hounds).** Con. 136: 51 (col.) Sept '55.
"The hunter" (Ma-Pe-Wi). Natl. geog. 107: 360 (col.) Mar '55.
hunter (shooting pheasant). Holiday 26: 127 (col.) Dec '59.
——, **Iraq. canoe-bourne.** Natl. geog. 113: 216-7 (col.) Feb '58.
——, **Colonial.** Amer. heri. vol. 3 no. 1 p. 42 (col.) (fall '51).
Holiday 25: 171 Mar '59.
——, **duck.** Holiday 20: 87 (col.) Oct '56.
——, **Kenya (Africa).** Holiday 25: 147 (col.) Ap '59.
——, **Tiwi.** Natl. geog. 109: 439-40 Mar '56.
hunters, Holiday 10: 81 (col.) Oct '51; 18: 66 Jl '55; 21: 45 Jan '57; 22: 54 (col.) Nov '57; 28: 86 Sept '60.
Natl. geog. 98: 378 (col.) Sept '50.
—— **(boat, rain, comic).** Holiday 10: 180 Dec '51.
—— **(dogs).** Holiday 10: cover (col.) Nov '51; 14: 107 (col.) Nov '53.
Natl. geog. 107: 761 (col.) Je '55.
Travel 101: 26 Ap '54.
—— **(dog, bird).** Holiday 10: 179 (col.) Dec '51.
—— **(1860-).** Holiday 18: 24 Jl '55.
—— **(horses, Persian).** Praeg. pict. ency., p. 521 (col.).
—— **(hounds).** Holiday 6: 69 Nov '49, 25, 53 (col.) Dec '49; 7: 53 (col.) Ap '50; 8: 71, 107 (col.) Sept '50.
—— **(man & woman).** Natl. geog. 99: 134 (col.) Jan '51.
—— **(on elephants).** Natl. geog. 112: 492 Oct '57.

hunters, duck. Holiday 24: 20 (col.) Nov '58.
——, early English. Holiday 24: 42 (col.) Nov '58.
——, fox. *See* fox hunt.
——, ice-age. Natl. geog. 108: 782-806 (col.) Dec '55.
——, Iranian (on horses). Natl. geog. 101: 813 (col.) Je '52.
——, Moslem. *See* Moslem hunters.
——, Napore (Africa). Natl. geog. 118: 385 (col.) Sept '60.
——, Nepal. Natl. geog. 97: 15 (col.) Jan '50.
——, Roman. Natl. geog. 111: 212-3 (col.) Feb '57.
——, wild animal. Holiday 13: 11 Ap '53.
——, wild animal (ancient times). Natl. geog. 111: 220-1 (col.) Feb '57.
"hunters on horses" (Holbein). Con. 133: 79 Ap '54.
hunters. *See* also fox hunt; man hunter).
hunting club (Ala.). Holiday 27: 54 (col.) Mar '60.
hunting horn, Limoges. Con. 133: 249-51 Je '54.
hunting lodge of Frederick II. Praeg. pict. ency., p. 221.
"Hunting party" (Wouverman). Con. 144: LXI-II (col.) Dec '59.
"Hunting scene" (Turner). Con. 145: 114 Ap '60.
hunting table. *See* table, hunting.
Huntington, Anna Hyatt. Cur. biog. p. 289 (1953).
Huntington, Collis P. Amer. heri. vol. 8 no. 3 p. 52 (Ap '57).
Huntington library (Cal.). Holiday 12: 10 Sept '52.
Natl. geog. 113: 252-76 (part col.) Feb '58.
Huntley, Chet. Cur. biog. p. 290 (1956).
huntsman. *See* hunter.
Huntziger, Charles. Cur. biog. p. 423 (1941).
Hunza. Natl. geog. 104: 486-518 (part col.) Oct '53.
Hunza dancers. Natl. geog. 104: 502 (col.) Oct '53.
Hunzukut boy. Natl. geog. 117: 97 (col.) Jan '60.
Hurd, Peter. Cur. biog. p. 271 (1957).
Hurd, Richard (Gainsborough). Con. 143: 87 Ap '59.
Hurdles (boys). Natl. geog. 107: 387 (col.) Mar '55.
hurdy-gurdy man. Natl. geog. 100: 692 Nov '51.
—— (medieval). Int. gr. soc.: Arts . . . p. 61 (col.).
Hurley, Laurel. Cur. biog. p. 273 (1957).
Hurley, Maj. Gen. Patrick J. Cur. biog. p. 319 (1944).
Hurley, Roy T. Cur. biog. p. 294 (1955).
Hurok, Solomon. Cur. biog. p. 425 (1941); p. 292 (1956).
Hurrian warriors (carvings). Osward: Asia Minor, pl. 13.
hurricane (Fla., wreckage). Holiday 6: 8-13 Sept '49.
—— (map). Natl. geog. 98: 545, 557 Oct '50
—— shelter (man, woman & child). Natl. geog. 98: 544 Oct '50.
Hurston, Zora Neale. Cur. biog. p. 402 (1942).

Husain, tomb of. *See* tomb of Husain.
Husing, Ted. Cur. biog. p. 405 (1942).
hussar, Napoleon. Int. gr. soc.: Arts . . . p. 115 (col.).
Hussein I, King of Hashemite Jordan. Cur. biog. p. 296 (1955).
Natl. geog. 106: 841 (col.) Dec '54.
Hussein, Ahmed. Cur. biog. p. 294 (1956).
Hussein, Taha. Cur. biog. p. 291 (1953).
Husted, Marjorie Child. Cur. biog. p. 287 (1949).
Huston, John. Cur. biog. p. 288 (1949).
Huston, Walter. Cur. biog. p. 290 (1949).
hut, African. Int. gr. soc.: Arts . . . p. 11 (col.).
——, Amazon. Disney: People & places, p. 105, 107 (col.).
——, Amazon Tukuna Indian (Brazil). Natl. geog. 116: 634 Nov '59.
——, Fiji is. Holiday 28: 57 (col.) Oct '60.
——, Ifalik. Natl. geog. 109: 551 (col.), 552 Ap '56.
——, mat (Iraq). Natl. geog. 115: 53 (col.) Jan '59.
——, Navajo Indian. Disney: People & places, p. 121 (col.).
Natl. geog. 114: 823, 840 (col.) Dec '58.
——, Samoan (being built). Disney: People & places, p. 142-3 (col.).
——, thatch roof. Holiday 18: 115 (col.), 116 Dec '55.
Natl. geog. 97: 541 Ap '50; 107: 701 May '55.
Travel 102: 16, 33 Nov '54; 104: 6-7 Oct '55; 106: 53 Dec '56; 110: 38 Oct '58; 111: 52 Feb '59.
——, thatch roof (Australia). Travel 108: 56 Oct '57.
——, thatch roof (British Guiana). Natl. geog. 107: 330, 333 (col.) Mar '55.
——, thatch roof (Caribbean). Holiday 24: 94 (col.) Aug '58.
——, thatch roof (Fiji). Holiday 28: 81, 159 (col.) Oct '60.
——, thatch roof (Indian). Natl. geog. 115: 350, 353 (col.) Mar '59.
——, thatch roof (Indochina). Natl. geog. 102: 296 (col.) Sept '52.
——, thatch roof (Korea). Natl. geog. 97: 786, 798 (col.) Je '50.
——, thatch roof (on stilts). Travel 111: 59 Mar '59.
——, thatch roof (Paramaribo). Holiday 28: 143 Nov '60, 191 Dec '60.
——, thatch roof (Philippines). Travel 105: 26, 28 Mar '56.
——, thatch roof (pioneer). Travel 104: 41 Oct '55.
——, thatch roof (Samoa). Disney: People & places, p. 131 (col.).
——, thatch roof (South Seas). Natl. geog. 97: 92 (col.) Jan '50.
——, thatch roof (Surinam). Holiday 28: 156 Oct '60.
——, thatch roof (Suvaii). Travel 104: 25 Oct '55.
——, Valley Forge. Holiday 18: 101 Oct '55.
hutch, food (16th cent.). Con. ency. of ant., vol. 1, pl. 1.
hutch table. *See* table, hutch.

Hutcheson, James K. Horan: Pict. hist. of wild west, p. 236.
Hutcheson, William L. Cur. biog. p. 328 (1943).
Hutchings, William. Amer. heri. vol. 9 no. 3 p. 32 (Ap '58).
Hutchins, Robert Maynard. Cur. biog. p. 357 (1954).
Hutchinson, Bruce. Cur. biog. p. 296 (1956).
Hutchinson, Paul. Cur. biog. p. 293 (1949).
Hutchinson, Thomas. Amer. heri. vol. 7 no. 2 p. 107 (Feb '56).
huts, Antarctic. See huts, deepfreeze.
——, beehive (Syria). Natl. geog. 106: 822 (col.) Dec '54.
——, Belgian Congo. Natl. geog. 106: 738 (col.) Dec '54.
——, deepfreeze (Antarctica). Natl. geog. 110: 168 (col.) Aug '56.
——, Fiji is. Natl. geog. 114: 528 (col.) Oct '58.
——, ice fishermen's. See fishing huts, ice.
——, Moro (Philippines). Holiday 18: 89 Aug '55.
——, Nigeria (wrapped with straw mats). Natl. geog. 116: 253 Aug '59.
——, Nuba mud. Natl. geog. 99: 271 Feb '51.
——' palm thatched. Holiday 24: 73-4 (col.). Nov '58.
——, Panama jungle. Natl. geog. 104: 287 Aug '53.
——, pygmy (Africa). Natl. geog. 117: 282-3 Feb '60.
——, Samoa is. Holiday 28: 54-5 (col.) Oct '60.
——, South Sea island Holiday 28: 54, 57, 61 Oct '60.
——, Sudan (Azande). Natl. geog. 114: 214 (col.) Aug '58.
——, Surinam. Holiday 27: 62 May '60.
——, tarpaulin (Korea camps). Natl. geog. 103: 654 May '53.
——, thatch roof. Holiday 28: 68 Nov '60. Natl. geog. 100: 342, 361-2 (col.) Sept '51; 101: 219 Feb '52, 334 (col.) Mar '52; 107: 860-1 Je '55.
——, thatch roof (Mauritius). Natl. geog. 109: 85 (col.) Jan '56.
——, thatch roof (Nairobi). Natl. geog. 118: 346 (col.) Sept '60.
——, thatch roof (New Guinea). Natl. geog. 116: 774-5 (col.) Dec '59.
Hutterite colonies (S.D.). Travel 105: 26-9 May '56.
Hutton, Barbara. Holiday 24: 52 (col.) Aug '58.
Hutton, Betty. Cur. biog. p. 270 (1950).
Hutton, Mrs. Lee W. Cur. biog. p. 300 (1948).
"Hutton cup", Elizabeth I. Con. 141: 43 Mar '58.
Huxley, Julian. Cur. biog. p. 407 (1942).
Huxley, Sir Julian. Cur. biog. p. 202 (1963).
Hyde, H. Van Zile. Cur. biog. p. 196 (1960).
Hyde Park (18th cent.). Con. 142: XXXVI (col.) Jan '59.
—— (F. D. Roosevelt's home). Holiday 6: 43 (col.) Jan '49.
—— (town hall). Holiday 6: 45 Sept '49.
hydraulic dredge. See dredge, hydraulic.

hydraulic model (largest in world, Jackson, Miss.). Natl. geog. 118: 705 (col.) Nov '60.
hydraulic press. Natl. geog. 101: 133 Jan '52.
hydrochloric acid (sym.). Lehner: Pict. bk. of sym., p. 72.
hydrofoil ferry. Natl. geog. 111: 492-6 (part col.) Ap '57.
hydromancy (sym.). Lehner: Pict. bk. of sym., p. 67.
hydrometer. Natl. geog. 115: 152 (col.) Jan '59.
hydroplane. Natl. geog. 117: 503 (col.) Ap '60.
Hygeio (sym.). Lehner: Pict. bk. of sym., p. 30.
hygiene (sym.). Lehner: Pict. bk. of sym., p. 13.
Hylton-Foster, Sir Harry B. Cur. biog. p. 214 (1961).
Hyknos (god of sleep). Holiday 18: 52 Sept '55.

I

Iakovos, Archbishop. Cur. biog. p. 197 (1960).
Ibáñez, Gen. Carlos. Cur. biog. p. 284 (1952).
Ibbetson, J. C. (work of). Con. 138: XLVIII Nov '56; 142: XXXVI (col.) Jan '59.
Ibicencan woman (water carrier). Travel 102: 20 Oct '54.
Ibiza is. Travel 102: 19-22 Oct '54.
Ibn Saud, King of Saudi Arabia. Cur. biog. p. 331 (1943).
Ibn Tulun mosque. See mosque of Ibn Tulun.
"Icarus" (Gilbert) Con. 134: 24 Sept '54.
ice, block of. Holiday 22: inside cover Sept '57.
ice age hunters. See hunters, ice age.
ice ax. Rawson: Ant. pict. bk., p. 27.
ice bucket. Holiday 18: 187 Dec '55; 27: 56 May '60.
ice capades. Holiday 11: 44-5 (col.) Jan '52. Natl. geog. 97: 206 (col.) Feb '50.
ice cart. Amer. heri. vol. 6 no. 4 p. 49 (col.) (Je '55).
ice caves (Pyrenees). Natl. geog. 103: 392-404 Mar '53.
ice cliffs (Alaska). Natl. geog. 109: 804 (col.) Je '56.
ice cream cart (Brazil). Natl. geog. 107: 300 (col.) Mar '55.
ice cream cone. Holiday 7: cover (col.) Jan '50.
—— (boys & girl). Natl. geog. 97: 291 (col.) Mar '50.
ice crusher. Holiday 11: 30 Feb '52.
ice cube (roses in). Holiday 10: 17 (col.) Aug '51.
ice cubes. Holiday 10: 113 Oct '51; 18: 21 Aug '55, 119 (col.) Oct '55.
ice field (Greenland). Natl. geog. 100: 508, 510 (col.) Oct '51.
ice fishing. See fishermen (ice).
ice fishing "jack". See "jack", ice fishing.
ice melter, flame (Alaska). Natl. geog. 109: 765 (col.) Je '56.
ice-pail, antique silver. Con. 139: 241 Je '57.
——, Egyptian service. Con. 143: 229 Je '59.
——, George III (silver). Con. 143: XL Ap '59.
——, Sevres. Con. 127: 66 Mar '51.

ice raft (men hauling). Natl. geog. 98: 346 Sept '50.
ice revue. Int. gr. soc.: Arts . . . p. 149 (col.).
ice skaters. See skaters, ice.
ice skates. See skates.
ice statue (man on horse). Amer. heri. vol. 1 no. 4 inside back cover (summer '50).
ice tongs. Holiday 22: inside cover Sept '57. Rawson: Ant. pict. bk., p. 27.
ice yachts. Natl. geog. 117: 38-9 (col.) Jan '60.
iceberg. Amer. heri. vol. 7 no. 1 p. 50 (Dec '55).
    Natl. geog. 100: 482 Oct '51.
iceberg lake. Natl. geog. 109: 600 (col.) May '56.
iceboats. Natl. geog. 111: 184-5 (col.) Feb '57.
"icebox", natural (Etna volcano). Natl. geog. 107: 26 Jan '55.
icebreaker boat. See boat, icebreaker.
icebreaker ship. See ship, icebreaker (Navy).
Iceland. Natl. geog. 100: 601-30 (part col.) Nov '51.
—— (map). Natl. geog. 100: 604 Nov '51.
—— (Reykjavik). Holiday 23: 150 (col.) Feb '58.
Iceland coast. Natl. geog. 108: 729-34 (col.) Dec '55.
Ickes, Harold L. Cur. biog. p. 427 (1941).
Ickworth mansion (ext. & int.). Con. 141: 68 (col.), 69-70 Ap '58.
icon. Con. 142: 213-8 Jan '59; 143: 28-9 Mar '59.
—— (Greek church). Natl. geog. 114: 749 (col.) Dec '58.
—— (Madonna & child). Natl. geog. 116: 62 (col.) Jl '59.
——, Byzantine. Con. 142: 31 Sept '58.
——, Russian (18th cent.). Con. 144: 279 Jan '60.
icon of the Saviour blessing. Con. 137: XXXII Ap '56.
Iconium. See Konya (Turkey).
Idaho. Holiday 15: 34-45 (part col.) Je '54. Travel 108: 36-7 Jl '57.
—— (Redfish lake). Travel 110: 55 Aug '58.
—— (volcano lava). Natl. geog. 118: 504-25 (col.) Oct '60.
Idell, Albert E. Cur. biog. p. 334 (1943).
ideogram of letter Alpha. See letter aleph ideogram.
Idhra harbor (Greece). Natl. geog. 114: 764 (col.) Dec '58.
idol. Holiday 21: 202 May '57; 22: 103 Jl '57, 9 Sept '57; 27: 37 Feb '60, 184 Mar '60.
——, Chinese carved. Con. 134: VII Dec '54.
——, Formosa. Natl. geog. 97: 165 (col.) Feb '50.
——, Hawaiian. See Hawaiian "God of war".
——, Hindu. See Hindu idol.
——, Inca. Holiday 20: 108 (col.) Dec '56.
——, Japanese. Holiday 26: 163 Oct '59.
——, Maori. See Maori idol.
——, Mexican. Holiday 18: 31 Nov '55.
——, Oriental. Holiday 27: 151 Jan '60.
——, soapstone (Cyprus is.). Natl. geog. 109: 883 Je '56.
——, Viet Nam. Natl. geog. 102: 301 (col.) Sept '52.

idols, Toltec. See Toltec idols.
—— See also gods; Buddha.
Idriss, Senussi I., King of Libya. Cur. biog. p. 297 (1956).
Ifalik atoll (South Seas). Natl. geog. 109: 546-71 (part col.) Ap '56.
—— (map). Natl. geog. 109: 550 Ap '56.
Ifalik dancers. Natl. geog. 109: 562-3 (col.) Ap '56.
Iglehart, Austin S. Cur. biog. p. 272 (1950).
Iglesias, Roberto. Cur. biog. p. 199 (1960).
igloo (comic). Holiday 18: 139 Nov '55.
—— (sym.). Lehner: Pict. bk. of sym., p. 81.
—— (white bear). Holiday 27: 26 (col.) May '60.
——, Eskimo (Alaska). Amer. heri. vol. 12 no. 1 p. 107 (Dec '60).
Holiday 10: 109 Jl '51, 4 Aug '51, 89 Sept '51; 13: 159 May '53.
—— (U.S. service men built). Natl. geog. 103: 566, 587 May '53.
Igorots (Philippines). Holiday 18: 93 Aug '55. Travel 105: 24-8 Mar '56.
Iguassu falls (Brazil). Holiday 13: 24 Ap '53. Natl. geog. 113: 298 (col.) Mar '58. Travel 103: 8 Mar '55.
Iguazu falls. See Iguassu falls.
ihram (Mecca pilgrim dress). Natl. geog. 104: 22 (col.) Jl '53.
Ikeda, Hayato. Cur. biog. p. 216 (1961).
Ikuta shrine (Kobe, Japan). Travel 113: 48 Jan '60.
"Il Salvataggio Miracoloso" (Forabosco). Con. 144: 107 Nov '59.
"Il Silenzio" (Michelangelo). Con. 127: 56 Mar '51.
Ile de France. See Mauritius.
Ilg, Dr. Frances L. Cur. biog. p. 299 (1956).
Iliad (ancient painting). Int. gr. soc.: Arts . . . p. 23 (col.).
Ilissus (4th cent.). Praeg. pict. ency., p. 86.
Ilium's tower. Ceram: March of arch., p. 38.
Illinois. Holiday 20: 27-40 (part col.) Sept '56; 22: 63 Sept '57.
Natl. geog. 104: 782-820 (part col.) Dec '53.
Travel 103: 13-6 Je '55; 113: 55, 57 May '60.
—— (Lincoln landmarks). Travel 109: 21-7 Feb '58.
—— (map). Holiday 20: 28 Sept '56. Travel 103: 16 Je '55.
—— (old state house). Natl. geog. 101: 161 Feb '52. Travel 109: 24 Feb '58.
—— (state house, int., 1836). Holiday 20: 31 (col.) Sept '56.
Illinois central railroad (history). Amer. heri. vol. 3 no. 2 p. 58-61 (winter '52).
illuminated gradual (music). Cooper: Con. ency. of music, p. 326 (col.).
illumination, book. See book illumination; manuscript illumination.
Ilsley, James L. Cur. biog. p. 302 (1948).
Imad madonna. Con. 138: 236 Jan '57.
image (India). Holiday 26: 37 Dec '59.
Immaculata (Guglia). Labande: Naples, p. 57.
immigrant children (study English). Natl. geog. 106: 810 (col.) Dec '54.

immigrants (become citizens). Natl. geog. 109: 249 Feb '56.

—— (Ellis is.). *See* Ellis is. immigrants.

immortal, Japanese. *See* Japanese immortal.

immortality (sym.). Lehner: Pict. bk. of sym., p. 26.

"The immortals" (glazed tile, 405 B.C.). Praeg. pict. ency., p. 106 (col.).

Impeachment group of Pres. Johnson. Amer. heri. vol. 11 no. 1 p. 61 (Dec '59).

impellers, jet engine. *See* jet engine impellers.

Impellitteri, Vincent R. Cur. biog. p. 294 (1951).

Imperial dam (Colo. river). Natl. geog. 112 708-9 Nov '57.

Inperial orb, Russian. Int. gr. soc.: Arts . . . p. 165 (col.)

Imperial palace roof. Natl. geog. 118: 208 (col.) Aug '60.

"In a good cause" (Y Aranda). Con. 145: XLIII May '60.

Inary. Lehner: Pict. bk. of sym., p. 49.

Inca buildings (Peru). Praeg. pict. ency., p. 558.

Inca city. Holiday 18: 12-3 (col.) Sept '55.

Inca fortress (Peru). Disney: People & places, p. 111 (col.).
Int. gr. soc.: Arts . . . p. 13 (col.).

Inca god. Holiday 17: 84 Feb '55.

Inca highway. Amer. heri. vol. 6 no. 5 p. 32, 35 (col.) (Aug '55).

Inca ruins. *See* Machu Picchu, Peru.

Inca temples (Peru). Natl. geog. 98: 422-6 Oct '50.

Ince, Sir Godfrey. Cur. biog. p. 336 (1943).

Ince, J. M. (work of). Con. 138: XXXII Nov '56.

incense burner (copper kettle). Holiday 27: inside cover (col.) Je '60.

—— ("god of fire"). Natl. geog. 100: 816 (col.) Dec '51.

——, Buddhist. Natl. geog. 111: 350 (col.) Mar '57.

——, Chinese. Con. 132: 114 Nov '53.

——, Chinese (18th cent.). Con. 135: 128 Ap '55.

——, Chinese jade. Con. 145: XL Je '60.

——, cloisnne. Con. 143: XXVIII Ap '59.

——, jade. Con. 137: XXXVII Ap '56 LXV May '56; 144: XXI Dec '59; 145: XXI Je '60.

——, Japanese (18th cent). Con. 138: 144 Nov '56.

——, Korean (12th cent.). Con. 141: 134 Ap '58.

——, Lung, jade. Con. 138: 187 Dec '56.

——, Roman (ancient). Natl. geog 111: 212 (col.) Feb '57.

incense holder. Lehner: Pict. bk. of sym., p. 29.

incense spiral, temple. Natl. geog. 102: 302 (col.) Sept '52.

incense. *See* also censer.

inconstancy (sym.). Lehner: Pict. bk. of sym., p. 58.

Independence hall (Phila.). Amer. heri. vol. 3 no. 1 cover, 30 (col.) (fall '51); vol. 10 no. 1 p. 101 (Dec '58).
Holiday 12: 38 (col.) Jl '52; 16: 100, 106 (col.) Jl '54; 21: cover (col.) May '57.
Jordan: Hammond's pict. atlas, p. 44 (col.).
Lehner: Pict. bk. of sym., p. 53.

Natl. geog. 113: 658 (col.) May '58; 118: 157 (col.) Aug '60.
Travel 110: 29-30 Jl '58.

—— (reproduction). Natl. geog. 114: 113 (col.) Jl '58.

India. Natl. geog. 102: 197-234 (part col.) Aug '52; 109: 572-88 Ap '56; 112: 490-506 Oct '57; 116: 838-52 (part col.) Dec '59; 118: 446-503 (col.) Oct '60.
Travel 106: cover, 12-8 Nov '56; 111: cover, 16-20, 27-9 Jan '59.

—— (clerk). Holiday 18: 45 (col.) Aug '55.

—— (dancers). Holiday 26: 31 (col.) Dec '59; 27: 140 Feb '60, 28 (col.) May '60.
Natl. geog. 117: 617 (col.) May '60.

—— (girl). Holiday 27: 154 Ap '60.

—— (Goa). *See* Goa, India.

—— (golden temple of Sikhs). Holiday 26: 170 (col.) Nov '59.

—— (Himalaya). Holiday 24: 50-5 (part col.) Sept '58.

—— (Hindu temple). Praeg. pict. ency., p. 551.

—— (Kashmir). Natl. geog. 114: 606-47 (part col.) Nov '58.
Travel 105: 53-4 Feb '56.

——(Khyber Pass). Travel 107: 35 Feb '57.

—— (man, head). Holiday 13: 106 (col.) May '53.

—— (man on elephant). Natl. geog. 113: 707 (col.) May '58.
Travel 111: 17 Jan '59.

—— (man seated on bench, comic). Holiday 28: 196 Nov '60.

—— (map). Natl. geog. 110: 525 Oct '56; 112: 496 Oct '57; 118: 458-9 (col.) Oct '60.

—— (men on elephant). Jensen: The White House, p. 284.

—— (merchants). Amer. heri. vol. 6 no. 2 p. 18 (col.) (winter '55).

—— (monastery on mt.). Holiday 24: 50 (col.) Sept '58.

—— (musician, snake charmer). Int. gr. soc.: Arts . . . p. 27 (col.).

—— (Mysore festival). Natl. geog. 113: 707-10 (col.) May '58.

——(Naga Hills, headhunters). Natl. geog. 107: 248-62 (part col.) Feb '55.

—— (Naga Hills, map). Natl. geog. 107: 250 Feb '55.

—— (New Delhi, women & children). Natl. geog. 116: 838-9 (col.) Dec '59.

—— (people). Travel 101: 4 Ap 54.

—— (restaurant terrace). Holiday 27: 179 Mar '60.

—— (school boys, New Delhi). Natl. geog. 116: 838 (col.) Dec 59.

—— (stupa). Int. gr. soc.: Arts . . . p. 13 (col.).

—— (stupa & Sanchi). Praeg. pict. ency., p. 524.

—— (Taj Mahal). Praeg. pict. ency., p. 563.

—— (tea time). Holiday 27: 98 (col.) Jan '60.

—— (temple cave sculpture). Natl. geog. 103: 666-82 May '53.

—— (temple of Tanjore). Praeg. pict. ency., p. 524.

—— (welcomes Pres. Eisenhower). Natl. geog. 117: 615-31 (col.) May '60.

India (woman). Con. 144: XXXVI (col.) Dec '59.
  Holiday 17: 98 (col.) Feb '55; 22: 26 (col.) Dec '57; 23: 30 Feb '58, 160 Mar '58; 24: 100 Sept '58.
—— (woman, head). Travel 109: 4 Feb '58, 4 Mar '58, 10 May '58.
—— (women). Holiday 16: 48-9 (col.) Sept '54.
—— (women & men). Holiday 14: cover, 34-5, 42-57 (part col.) Oct. '53.
India. See also Calcutta.
Indian. Amer. heri. vol. 5 no. 2 p. 19 (winter '54).
  Holiday 16: 42 (col.) Jl '54; 19: 23 Je '56; 24: 5 (col.)) Sept 58; 25: 29 Feb '59, 158 Ap '59.
  Natl. geog. 111: 591, 595, 619 (col.) May '57.
—— (adv.). Holiday 11: 43 (col.) Je '52.
—— (at tent, comic). Travel 109: 62 Je '58.
—— (basket weaver). Brooks: Growth of a nation, p. 25.
—— (beating drum). Travel 101: 16 Jan '54; 107: inside cover Jan '57, 16 Feb '57.
—— (bow & arrow). Holiday 6: 22 (col.) Jl '49.
—— (burden on back). Holiday 17: 44 Mar '55.
'—— (canoe). Amer. heri. vol. 9 no. 5 p. 46 (col.) (Aug '58).
—— (cartoon). Holiday 26: cover,, 14 Jl '59. Travel 105: 11 Ap '56.
—— (catching horse). Amer. heri. vol. 9 no. 3 p. 11 (col.) (Ap '58).
—— (ceremonial dance). Holiday 13: 118-9 (col.) May '53.
—— (comic). Holiday 14: 68 Sept '53; 22: 132 Nov '57.
—— (earliest European drawings). Ceram: March of arch., p. 257-8.
—— (head). Amer. heri. vol. 4 no. 2 p. 43 (col.) (winter '53); vol. 4 no. 3 p. 32, 36 (col.) (spring '53).
  Natl. geog. 99: 823 Je '51; 107: 740 (col.) Je '55.
—— (head ceremonial). Int. gr. soc.: Arts . . . p. 181 (col.).
—— (horse, tepees). Natl. geog. 118: 99 (col.) Jl '60.
—— (horseback). Amer. heri. vol. 6 no. 1 p. 38, 40 (col.) (fall '54).
  Natl. geog. 114: 829 (col.) Dec '58; 116: 626 Nov '59.
—— (horseback, killing buffalo). Amer. heri. vol. 6 no. 1 cover, 37 (col.) (fall '54).
—— (molding pottery). Travel 107: 18 Feb '57.
—— (musician). Holiday 24: 40 Sept '58.
—— (on running horse). Amer. heri. vol. 6 no. 1 p. 39 (fall '54).
—— (Panama jungle). Natl. geog. 104: 289 Aug '53.
—— (peace & war sym.). Amer. heri. vol. 10 no. 6 frontis (col.) (Oct '59).
—— (rug weaver). Travel 107: 18 Feb 57.
—— (seated). Amer. heri. vol. 11 no. 1 p. 30 (col.) (Dec '59).

—— (silhouette). Amer. heri. vol. 10 no. 4 p. 112 (Je '59).
—— (South Amer., ancient times). Int. gr. soc.: Arts . . . p. 33 (col.).
—— (statue). Natl. geog. 99: 119 Jan '51.
—— (tent). Holiday 23: 158 (col.) Mar '58.
—— (war). Brooks: Growth of a nation, p. 41.
—— (war dance). Holiday 27: 5 (col.) Feb '60.
—— (weaving). Travel 110: 14 Sept '58.
——, Amer. Holiday 23: 110 (col.) Feb '58. Travel 114: cover (col.) Sept '60.
——, Arapaho. Natl. geog. 117: 809 (col.) Je '60.
——, "Babine" (Canada). Amer. heri. vol. 10 no. 5 p. 52 (col.) (Aug '59).
——, Bolivian (baby on back). Holiday 21: 12 (col.) May '57.
——, Cheyenne (head, horse). Holiday 19: 27 (col.) Feb '56.
——, cigar store. See cigar store Indian (statue).
——, Colombia. Holiday 20: 55 (col.) Nov '56.
——, Cree. Amer. heri. vol. 10 no. 5 p. 52 (col.) (Aug '59).
——, Cree (skinning fox). Holiday 6: 55 Aug '49.
——, Guatemala (making tortillas). Natl. geog. 117: 412 (col.) Mar '60.
——, Guatemala (mask maker). Natl. geog. 117: 413 (col.) Mar '60.
——, Guatemala (women, Easter). Natl. geog. 117: 407 (col.) Mar '60.
——, Huron. Amer. heri. vol. 10 no. 6 p. 59 (Oct '59).
——, Inca. Holiday 12: 19 Nov '52.
——, Jemez. Travel 105: 17 Jan '56.
——, Labrador. Natl. geog. 100: 87 (col.) Jl '51.
——, Mexican (dancing). Holiday 27: 25 Mar '60.
——, Mexican (selling pottery). Travel 114: 52 Nov '60.
——, Mohawk. Amer. heri. vol. 10 no. 3 p. 82 (Ap '59).
——, Navajo. Travel 110: 19 Sept '58.
——, Navajo (grinding corn). Disney: People & places, p. 119 (col.).
——, Nez-Perce. Amer. heri. vol. 10 no. 5 p. 52 (col.) (Aug '59).
——, Papago (Ariz.). Travel 110: 17 Sept '58.
——, San Blas (woman). Holiday 12: 57 (col.) Nov '52.
——, Seminole. Travel 110: 16 Sept '58.
——, Seminole (war canoe). Holiday 23: 127 (col.) May '58.
——, Shawnee chief. Amer. heri. vol. 2 no. 1 p. 17 (fall '50).
——, Shoshone (baby on back). Natl. geog. 103: 741 (col.) Je '53.
——, Sioux. Travel 113: 43 Mar '60.
——, Tewa. Natl. geog. 106: 244 (col.) Aug '54.
——, Yahgan (Chile). Natl. geog. 117: 205 Feb '60.

Indian actors, Mexican. Natl. geog. 107: 225 (col.) Feb '55.

Indian & westerns (hold up). Holiday 27: 190 Mar '60.

Indian area, Tukuna (Brazil, map). Natl. geog. 116: 637 Nov '59.

Indian armed force man. Natl. geog. 105: 515 (col.) Ap '54.

Indian art, Amer. See art, Amer. Indian.

——, India. Con. 139: 78-81 Ap '57.

Indian arts & crafts. Amer. heri. vol. 7 no. 6 p. 13-5 (col.) (Aug '56).

Indian attack. Durant: Pict. hist. of Amer. circus, p. 134-5.

Indian attack on fort. Brooks: Growth of a nation, p. 171.

Indian baby (cradleboard). Natl. geog. 111: 696 (col.) May '57.

Indian baby (in cradle). Amer. heri. vol. 10 no. 5 p. 52 (col.) (Aug '59).
Holiday 21: 103 (col.) Je '57.

—— (hammock, Brazil). Natl. geog. 115: 642 (col.) May '59.

Indian beaded breastplate. Amer. heri. vol. 9 no. 2 p. 42 (col.) (Feb '58).

Indian boy. Holiday 7: 84 (col.) Ap. 50; 21: 26 May '57; 24: 142 Oct '58, 166 Nov '58, 188 Dec '58; 25: 158 Jan '59, 146 Feb '59, 34 Mar '59, 203 Ap '59, 195 May '59, 190 Je '59.

—— (Amazon jungle). Natl. geog. 115: 648, 653, 663 (col.) May '59.

—— (cartoon). Holiday 23: 159 May '58; 27: 30 Mar '60.

—— (shooting arrow). Holiday 25: 163 May '59.

Indian buffalo hunt. Brooks: Growth of a nation, p. 160-1.

"Indian burial ground" (Cowlitz). Amer. heri. vol. 10 no. 5 p. 51 (col.) (Aug '59).

Indian burial mound. Amer. heri. vol. 4 no. 3 p. 52-5 (spring '53); vol. 7 no. 6 p. 10 (Oct '56).

Indian captivity. Amer. heri. vol. 9 no. 3 p. 65 (Ap '58).

Indian carvings. Natl. geog. 112: 238 Aug '57.

Indian castle church (Colonial mission). Holiday 15: 101 Je '54.

Indian ceremonial (Guatemala). Natl. geog. 117: 406-16 (col.) Mar '60.

—— (N. M.). Holiday 25: 58 (col.) Mar '59.

Indian chief. Amer. heri. vol. 8 no. 2 p. 8 (Feb '57).
Holiday 9: 87 (col.) Mar '51; 11: 19 Ap '52, 23 Je '52; 18: 32 Aug '55; 21: 176 Ap '57.
Natl. geog. 108: 480 (col.) Oct '55; 117: 477-8 (col.) Ap '60.
Travel 110: 17 Sept '58.

"Indian chief" (Catlin). Amer. heri. vol. 7 no. 2 frontis (col.) (Feb '56).

Indian chief (comic). Holiday 19: 67 (col.) Mar '56.

—— (head). Holiday 10: 31 (col.) Jl '51; 11: 85 May '52; 13: 90 (col.) Je '53.
Natl. geog. 112: 666 (col.) Nov '57.
Durant: Pict. hist. of Amer. circus, p. 243.

—— (horseback). Holiday 6: 79 (col.) Sept '49; 7: 66 (col.) Jan '50.

—— (Joseph Brant). Amer. heri. vol. 3 no. 3 cover (col.) p. 27 (spring '52).

—— (picture). Holiday 7: 119 (col.) May '50.

—— (wood carved figure). Amer. heri. vol. 2 no. 2 p. 32 (col.) (winter '51).

——, Apache. Holiday 19: 39 (col.) Feb 56.

——, Blackfeet. Natl. geog. 97: 699, 708 (col.) Je '50.

——, Casanov (Kane). Amer. heri. vol. 10 no. 5 p. 90 (Aug '59).

——, Comanche. Amer. heri. vol. 4 no. 4 p. 31 (summer '53).

——, Cree. Amer. heri. vol. 10 no. 5 p. 53 (col.) (Aug '59).

——, Crow. Holiday 19: 33 Feb '56.

——, Flathead. Holiday 19: 35 (col.) Feb '56.

——, Mandan (lodge). Holiday 19: 31 (col.) Feb '56.

——, Seneca. Amer. heri. vol. 11 no. 3 back cover (col.) (Ap '60).

——, Shoshone. Amer. heri. vol. 11 no. 2 p. 51 (Feb '60).

——, Sioux. Holiday 19: 28 Feb '56.
Natl. geog. 98: 249 Aug '50; 110: 486 (col.) Oct '56.

——, Sitka. Holiday 26: 45 (col.) Aug '59.

——, super. Holiday 10: 73 (col.) Jl '51; 18: 163 Dec '55.

Indian chief & squaw (men, radio). Natl. geog. 110: 486 (col.) Oct '56.

Indian chiefs. Amer. heri. vol. 6 no. 2 p. 27 (col.) (winter '55).

Indian child (head). Holiday 19: 150 May '56; 21: 123 Ap '57.

——, Navajo. Travel 107: 17 Feb '57.

Indian children. Natl. geog. 100: 317 (col.) Sept '51.

Indian cliff dwellings. See cliff dwellings, Indian.

Indian cliff painting. Natl. geog. 108: 406-7 Sept '55.

Indian cloak. See cloak, Indian.

Indian "corn dancers." Holiday 21: 4 (col.) Ap '57.

Indian costume. See costume (Indian ——).

Indian council (Mohawks). Amer. heri. vol. 10 no. 3 p. 48-9 (col.) (Ap '59).

Indian cove (Cal.) Holiday 12: 75 Jl '52.

Indian dance. Amer. heri. vol. 2 no. 1 p. 66 (fall '50).
Holiday 13: 90 (col.) Je '53; 27: 44 Ap '60.
Natl. geog. 106: 244 (col.) Aug '54.
Travel 106: 30 Jl '56; 108: 17 Jl '57, 37 Aug '57; 111: 31 Je '59.

—— (Bodmer). Amer. heri. vol. 7 no. 6 front cover (col.) (Oct '56).

—— (Catlin). Amer. heri. vol. 7 no. 6 p. 17 (col.) (Oct '56).

——, Cherokee. Amer. heri. vol. 5 no. 4 p. 16 (summer '54).

Indian dancer. Holiday 6: 85 Jl '49; 23: 110 Mar '58; 27: 138 Jan '60, 5 (col.) Feb '60.
Natl. geog. 112: 223, 228-9 (col.) Aug '57.
Travel 107: inside cover Jan '57; 110: 15 Sept '58.

——, Navajo. Natl. geog. 112: 722 (col.) Nov '57.

Travel 107: 16 Feb '57.

——, **Zuni.** Holiday 21: 158 (col.) May '57.

Indian dancers. Natl. geog. 107: 603 (col.) May '55.

——, **Amazon (Brazil).** Natl. geog. 116: 631 (col.) Nov '59.

——, **Bolivia.** Natl. geog. 98: 489, 493 (col.) Oct '50.

——, **Inca.** Natl. geog. 98: 433 (col.) Oct '50.

——, **Wai Wai.** Natl. geog. 107: 342 (col.) Mar '55.

Indian devil dancer. Holiday 7: 7 (col.) Ap '50.

Indian dog (pack on back). Natl. geog. 112: 257 Aug '57.

Indian drawings (fight with Custer). Amer. heri. vol. 8 no. 2 p. 4-7 (col.) (Feb '57).

Indian earth lodges (N.D.). Natl. geog. 103: 722 (col.) Je '53.

Indian encampment. Amer. heri. vol. 7 no. 4 p. 16-7 (col.) Je '56.

Indian excavations (Ohio). Amer. heri. vol. 4 no. 3 p. 52-5 (spring '53).

Indian game, Chualpay. Amer. heri. vol. 10 no. 5 p. 50 (col.) (Aug '59).

Indian girl. Natl. geog. 103: 722 (col.) Je '53.

—— **(making jewelry).** Holiday 14: 56 Dec '53.

—— **(sheep).** Holiday 25: 55 (col.) Mar '59.

——, **Amazon jungle (beetle).** Natl. geog. 115: 668 (col.) May '59.

——, **Navajo (lambs).** Natl. geog. 107: 353 (col.) Mar '55.

——, **Shuswap (horse head).** Natl. geog. 114: 165 (col.) Aug '58.

——, **Tamil.** Natl. geog. 103: 205 (col.) Feb '53.

Indian girls ("coming of age" ceremony). Disney: People & places, p. 120 (col.). Natl. geog. 116: 628-49 (part col.) Nov '59.

——, **Navajo.** Natl. geog. 114: 813 (col.) Dec '58.

Indian grave markers. Natl. geog. 103: 741 (col.) Je '53.

Indian head. Amer. heri. vol. 9 no. 4 p. 57 (Je '58).

Holiday 14: 134 (col.) Jl '53; 15: 73 Ap '54, 73 (col.) May '54; 16: 87 Nov '54; 23: 173 Ap '58; 27: 14 May '60. Travel 110: 56 Sept '58.

—— **(by Trumbull).** Amer. heri. vol. 9 no. 4 p. 43 (col.) (Je '58).

—— **(silhouette).** Holiday 7: 2 Jan '50, 64 Mar '50.

Indian headdress. Holiday 6: 88 Dec '49.

——, **Shoshone.** Amer. heri. vol. 11 no. 2 p. p. 50 (col.) (Feb '60).

Indian holy city, Inca. Holiday 12: 19 Nov '52.

Indian homes, Amer. Amer. heri. vol. 7 no. 6 p. 103-7 (Oct '56).

——, **Nevada.** Travel 101: 37 Feb '54.

Indian lodge (Davis Mts., Tex.). Jordan: Hammond's pict. atlas, p. 114 (col.).

Indian long house. Travel 106: 22 Sept '56.

Indian man (Bombay). Travel 113: 10 May '60.

—— **(candles, blessing corn seed).** Natl. geog. 117: 416 (col.) Mar '60.

Indian man & children. Natl. geog. 103: 725 (col.) Je '53.

Indian masks. See mask, Indian.

Indian massacre. Amer. heri.. vol. 8 no. 6 p. 38, 93 (Oct '57); vol. 10 no. 5 p. 87 (Aug '59).

Indian medicine mask dance, Clallam. Amer. heri. vol. 10 no. 5 p. 48-9 (col.) (Aug '59).

Indian medicine men. See medicine men, Indian.

Indian men. Holiday 7: 53 (col.) Je '50.

Indian miniature (book illus.). Praeg. pict. ency., p. 533 (col.).

Indian ocean (explorers). Natl. geog. 108: 176-82 (part col.) Aug '55.

—— **(under sea).** Natl. geog. 109: 150-200 (part col.) Feb '56.

"Indian on the lookout" (Eastman). Con. 144: 69 Sept '59.

Indian paintings (Shoshone). Amer. heri. vol. 11 no. 2 p. 52-3 (col.) (Feb '60).

Indian papoose. Travel 107: 33 Feb '57.

—— **(in cradleboard).** Disney: People & places, p. 116 (col.). Natl. geog. 101: 728 (col.) Je '52.

—— **(on mother's back).** Natl. geog. 103: 741 (col.) Je '53.

——, **Apache.** Holiday 15: 147 (col.) Je '54.

Indian parade (on horses). Travel 101: 10 Ap '54.

Indian peace pipe. Brooks: Growth of a nation, p. 182. Holiday 19: 70 (col.) Mar '56. Natl. geog. 103: 720 (col.) Je '53.

Indian pictographs (on rocks). Amer. heri. vol. 1 no. 2 p. 23 (winter '50). Natl. geog. 105: 375 (col.) Mar '54.

Indian pipe, Iroquois. Con. 141: 35 Mar '58.

Indian potter. (Bombay, India). Travel 113: 10 Jan '60.

Indian powwow. Amer. heri. vol. 9 no. 1 frontis (col.) (Dec '57).

Indian priest. See priest, Pueblo Indian high.

Indian pueblo. Amer. heri. vol. 7 no. 6 p. 103 (Oct '56). Holiday 13: 22 (col.) Je '53; 23: 16 Feb '58. Travel 110: 19 Sept '58.

——, **Taos.** Holiday 21: 31 (col.) Mar '57.

Indian racing war canoes. See canoes, Indian racing war.

Indian rain dance. Holiday 21: 75 May '57.

Indian rajah procession. Int. gr. soc.: Arts . . . p. 117 (col.).

Indian rattle. See Kolosh Indian rattle.

Indian relics. Natl. geog. 110: 546-58 (part col.) Oct '56.

"Indian religious dance" (White). Amer. heri. vol. 10 no. 4 p. 15 (col.) (Je '59).

Indian rock carvings. Natl. geog. 110: 501 (col.) Oct '56; 113: 620 May '58.

—— **(men & girl).** Natl. geog. 113: 641 (col.) May '58.

Indian ruler (riding in ratha). Holiday 7: 87 (col.) May '50.

Indian scout, Shoshone. Amer. heri. vol. 11 no. 2 p. 54 (Feb '60).

Indian settlement. Amer. heri. vol. 7 no. 2 p. 15 (col.) (Feb '56).

Indian sign carving. Natl. geog. 114: 816 (col.) Dec '58.

Indian skeletons (burial mound). Amer. heri. vol. 4 no. 3 p. 54 (spring '53).

Indian skull, Canalino. Natl. geog. 114: 266 (col.) Aug '58.

Indian squaw. Amer. heri. vol. 9 no. 5 p. 83 (Aug '58).

Indian statue. Holiday 5: 85 Jan '49.

Indian surrender, Nez Perce. Amer. heri. vol. 9 no. 2 p. 43 (col.) (Feb '58).

Indian symbols. Amer. heri. vol. 7 no. 3 p. 112 (Ap '56).

Indian temples. *See* temples, Indian.

Indian tent. *See* tent, Indian.

Indian tepee. *See* tepee, Indian.

Indian territory, Kraho (map). Natl. geog. 115: 345 Mar '59.

Indian tools. Amer. heri., vol. 11 no. 3 p. 82-3 (Ap '60).

Indian trail (to the new world). Brooks: Growth of a nation, p. 20.

Indian treaty (1795). Amer. heri. vol. 9 no. 4 p. 61 (col.) (Je '58).

Indian tribes (location). Amer. heri. vol. 7 no. 6 p. 6 (Oct '56).

—— **(location on U.S. map).** Brooks: Growth of a nation, p. 21.

—— **(work of Kane).** Amer. heri. vol. 10 no. 5 p. 45-53 (part col.) (Aug '59).

Indian turban. *See* turban, Indian.

Indian village. Amer. heri. vol. 7 no. 6 p. 11, 17 (col.) (Oct '56); vol. 8 no. 3 p. 12-3, 16-7 (col.) (Ap '57).

Brooks: Growth of a nation, p. 24.

——, **Chualpay.** Amer. heri. vol. 10 no. 5 p. 47 (col.) (Aug '59).

——, **Seminole.** Holiday 13: 43 (col.) Feb '53.

——, **Wai Wai (British Guiana).** Natl. geog. 107: 330-46 (part col.) (Mar '55).

Indian wall painting. *See* wall painting, Indian temple.

Indian warrior, Chilkat. Holiday 26: 44 (col.) Aug '59.

Indian warrior pipe. Amer. heri. vol. 7 no. 6 p. 15 (Oct '56).

Indian wars map (1790-94). Amer. heri. vol. 4 no. 3 p. 36-7 (col.) (spring '53).

Indian weapons, Iroquois. Con. 141: 34-5 Mar '58.

Indian woman (jumping). Amer. heri. vol. 7 no. 6 p. 16 (col.) (Oct '56).

—— **(seated).** Disney: People & places, p. 113 (col.).

—— **(seated spinning yarn).** Natl. geog. 98: 487 (col.) Oct '50.

—— **(sled dogs).** Natl. geog. 112: 256 (col.) Aug '57.

——, **Abernaki.** Amer. heri. vol. 10 no. 5 p. 24 (col.) (Aug '59).

——, **Amer.** Amer. heri. vol. 10 no. 5 p. 24 (col.) (Aug '59).

——, **flathead.** Amer. heri. vol. 10 no. 5 p. 52 (col.) (Aug '59).

——, **Navaho.** Holiday 19: 36 Feb '56.

Indian woman & children (corn). Natl. geog. 114: 818, 820 (part col.) Dec '58.

Indian woman & papoose. Natl. geog. 103: 730 (col.) Je '53.

—— **(Peru).** Travel 107: 33 Feb '57.

Indian woman dancing (India). Travel 113: 19 Jan '60.

Indian woman head (India). Holiday 14: 18 Aug '53.

Indian women (make bread). Natl. geog. 114: 822-3 (col.) Dec '58.

——, **Huron.** Amer. heri. vol. 10 no. 6 p. 103 (Oct '59).

——, **Zuni pueblo.** Travel 110: 17 Sept '58.

Indian. *See* also Indians.

Indiana. Amer. heri. vol. 2 no. 2 p. 8-55 (winter '51).

Holiday 8: 26-35 (part col.) Aug '50.

—— **(map).** Amer. heri. vol. 2 no. 1 p. 32 (fall '50).

Indianapolis. Holiday 8: 36-43, 80 (part col.) Aug '50, 36- Sept '50.

—— **(1854-   ).** Amer. heri. vol. 2 no. 1 p. 20-3 (fall '50).

Indians. Amer. heri. vol. 1 no. 2 p. 10 (winter '50); vol. 2 no. 4 p. 33-5 (part col.) (summer '51); vol. 4 no. 4 p. 59 (col.) (summer '53); vol. 5 no. 4 p. 32, 35 (spring '54); vol. 9 no. 3 p. 65-79 (Ap '58); vol. 9 no. 6 frontis (col.) (Oct '58); vol. 10 no. 1 p. 70-1 (Dec '58).

Brooks: Growth of a nation, p. 60.

Holiday 10: 43 (col.) Nov '51; 19: 78 Feb '56.

Natl. geog. 111: 694-6 (col.) May '57.

—— **(back view).** Amer. heri. vol. 4 no. 2 cover (col.) (winter '53).

—— **((Boy Scouts).** Natl. geog. 107: 480-1 (col.) Ap '55.

—— **(carved figures).** Amer. heri. vol. 2 no. 1 p. 51 (fall '50).

—— **(chasing buffalos).** Amer. heri. vol. 6 no. 1 p. 33 (col.) (fall '54).

—— **(comic).** Holiday 13: 120 Ap '53.

—— **(dancing).** Holiday 13: 137 (col.) May '53.

—— **(dancing, Tewa).** Natl. geog. 106: 244 (col.) Aug '54.

—— **(horseback).** Amer. heri. vol. 7 no. 3 p. 40-1 (Ap '56).

Brooks: Growth of a nation, p. 183.

Holiday 13: 31 (col.) Jan '53; 22: 41 Jl '57.

Natl. geog. 99: 176 Feb '51; 117: 476-7 (col.) Ap '60.

Travel 110: cover (col.) Sept '58.

—— **(horseback, attacking stage coach).** Amer. heri. vol. 8 no. 4 p. 26-7 (col.) (Je '57).

—— **(in canoes).** Brooks: Growth of a nation, p. 22,, 58.

—— **(in hut).** Brooks: Growth of a nation, p. 95.

—— **(in rowboat).** Holiday 7: 34-5 (col.) Mar '50.

—— **(listening to preacher).** Amer. heri. vol. 9 no. 1 p. 118 (Dec '57).

Indians (on beach). Amer. heri. vol. 8 no. 3 p. 7-19 (col.) (Ap '57).

—— (on running horse). Amer. heri. vol. 7 no. 6 p. 19 (col.) (Oct '56).

—— (painting by Winter). Amer. heri. vol. 2 no. 1 p. 35-8 (col.) (fall '50).

—— (picnic). Natl. geog. 98: 472 (col.) Oct '50.

—— (playing LaCrosse). See "LaCrosse playing among Indians."

—— (seated). Holiday 12: 140 (col.) Jl '52.

—— (selling beaver pelts). Natl. geog. 104: 826 Dec '53.

—— (smoking peace pipe). Amer. heri. vol. 11 no. 2 p. 109 (Feb '60).

—— (stealing stock, 1870). Amer. heri. vol. 9 no. 4 p. 25 (Je '58).

—— (tent). Holiday 23: 7 (col.) Mar '58.

——, Acawai. Natl. geog. 111: 862-72 Je '54.

——, Amer. Amer. heri. vol. 6 no. 1 p. 33-40 (col.) (fall '54); vol. 6 no. 2 p. 26-31 (winter '55); vol. 7 no. 6 p. 8-19 (col.) (Oct '56).
Holiday 23: 88 Feb '58.
Jordan: Hammond's pict. atlas, p. 127 (col.). Travel 102: 32-3 Dec '54.

——, Amer. (Remington). Amer. heri. vol. 12 no. 1 p. 36 (Dec '60).

——, Andes. Natl. geog. 98: 472-3 (col.) Oct '50.

——, Araucanian (Chile). Natl. geog. 117: 213 (col.) Feb '60.

——, Aymara (Peru). See Aymara Indians (Peru).

——, Blackfeet chiefs (women). Natl. geog. 109: 590 (col.) May '56.

——, Bolivian. Holiday 20: 84-5 Nov '56. Travel 104: 21 Oct '55.

——, Cherokee. Amer. heri. vol. 5 no. 4 p. 16-7 (part col.) (summer '54).

——, Colorado (Ecuadorian). Holiday 20: 90-1 (col.) Nov '56.

——, Crow (reservation). Natl. geog. 97: 731 (col.) Je '50.

——, Galibi (Brazil). Natl. geog. 115: 642-69 (part col.) May '59.

——, Hopi. Natl. geog. 110: 294 (col.) Sept '56; 112: 220-1 (col.). Aug '57.

——, Hudson's Bay. Natl. geog. 103: 115 Jan '53.

——, Inca. Natl. geog. 98: 432-3, 453, 459 (col.) Oct '50.

——, Iroquois. Brooks: Growth of a nation, p. 40.

——, Kraho (Brazil). Natl. geog. 115: 340-62 (part col.) Mar '59.

——, Kraho (running). Natl. geog. 115: 346-7 (coi.) Mar '59.

——, Kraho (weaving pouch). Natl. geog. 115: 350 (col.) Mar '59.

——, Makah (dress salmon). Natl. geog. 117: 474 (col.) Ap '60.

——, Maya. Natl. geog. 115: 96, 102-3, 105 (part col.) Jan '59.

——, Mohawk. Natl. geog. 102: 135-41 Jl '52.

——, Navajo. Disney: People & places, p. 113-28 (col.).
Natl. geog. 114: 810-46 (part col.) Dec '58.

——, Navaho (sand painters). Natl. geog. 107: 364 Mar '55.

——, New Guinea. Natl. geog. 116: 781 (col.) Dec '59.

——, New Mexico. Holiday 11: 46-7 (col.) Feb '52.

——, Nez Perce. Amer. heri. vol. 9 no. 2 p. 36-43 (part col.) (Feb '58).

——, northwest. Natl. geog. 117: 474-7 (col.) Ap '60.

——, Oklahoma. Travel 106: 28-31 Jl '56.

——, Otomi (Mexico). Travel 107: 36-7 Jan '57.

——, Peruvian. Holiday 21: 46 Ap '57.
Natl. geog. 107: 136-45 Jan '55; 109: 351-2 (col.) Mar '56.

——, Pueblo. Amer. heri. vol. 2 no. 3 p. 56-7 (spring '51).
Holiday 20: 37 Oct '56.

——, Quiche. Ceram: March of arch., p. 288.

——, Seminole. Holiday 13: 43 (col.) Feb '53; 20: 119 (col.) Oct '56; 22: 125 (col.) Oct '57; 25: 101 (col.) Jan '59.
Natl. geog. 110: 820-38 (col.) Dec '56.

——, Shuswap (at pub table). Natl. geog. 114: 165 (col.) Aug '58.

——, Sioux. Holiday 12: 36 Sept '52.
Natl. geog. 106: 124 (col.) Jl '54.

——, Sioux (at the White House). Jensen: The White House, p. 118, 226.

——, Taos. Travel 101: 14 Feb '54.

——, Tarascan. Natl. geog. 102: 523-30 (col.) Oct '52.

——, Tewa. Natl. geog. 106: 244 (col.) Aug '54.

——, treaty with (West & Hicks). Amer. heri. vol. 6 no. 2 p. 41-2 (col.) (winter '55).

——, Ute. Amer. heri. vol. 8 no. 6 p. 37, 90 (Oct '57).

——, Ute (and babies). Natl. geog. 101: 728 (col.) Je '52.

——, Ute (children). Natl. geog. 101: 739 (col.) Je '52.

——, Wai Wai. Natl. geog. 107: 330-46 (part col.) Mar '55.

——, Zuni. Natl. geog. 112: 218-36 (part col.) Aug '57.

Indians & Gen. Burgoyne. Amer. heri. vol. 7 no. 4 p. 6 (Je '56).

Indians & Puritans. See Puritans & Indians.

Indians attack a home. Amer. heri. vol. 8 no. 6 p 38 (Oct '57).

Indians sell Manhattan (cartoon). Amer. heri. vol. 11 no. 1 p. 62-3 (Dec '59).

"Indians tomahawk Jane McCrea." Amer. heri. vol. 7 no. 4 p. 7 (col.) (Je '56).

Indians weaving, Navajo. Natl. geog. 114: 844 (col.) Dec '58.

Indians. See also Indian.

Indochina. Natl. geog. 98: 499-510 Oct '50; 99: 462-98 (part col.) Ap '51; 102: 288-328 (part col.) Sept '52.

Indonesia. Holiday 18: 104-8 (part col.) Sept '55.
Natl. geog. 99: 2-39 (part col.) Jan '51; 108: 352-92 (part col.) Sept '55.

Travel 102: 20 Nov '54.

—— (map). Natl. geog. 99: 6 Jan '51; 116: 777 Dec '59.

Indonesians. Natl. geog. 108: 358, 360-92 (part col.) Sept '55.

"Indra, King of the Heavens" (temple wall painting). Praeg. pict. ency. 532 (col.).

Indra's thunderbolt. Lehner: Pict. bk. of sym. p. 43.

Industrial exhibition hall (Japan). Natl. geog. 118: 775 (col.) Dec '60.

"Industry" (Meunier). Praeg. pict. ency., p. 425.

—— (sym.). Lehner: Pict. bk. of sym., p. 58.

"Infant Hercules" (Reynolds). Con. 142: 25 Sept '58.

"Infanta Maria Theresa" (Velasquez). Natl. geog. 97: 745 (col.) Je '50

"Infanta Philip Prosper" (Velasquez). Natl. geog. 97: 755 Je '50.

Infantile paralysis sym. (1955). Holiday 17: 102 Jan '55.

infantry Honor Guard. Holiday 14: 46-7 (col.) Dec '53.

Infeld, Leopold. Cur. biog. p. 429 (1941); p. 205 (1963).

infinite cross. See cross, infinite.

Ingalls, Jeremy. Cur. biog. p. 359 (1954).

Inge, William. Cur. biog. p. 293 (1953).

Ingersoll, Adm. Royal E. Cur. biog. p. 409 (1942).

Ingles, Harry C. Cur. biog. p. 327 (1947).

ingot. See steel ingot.

Ingram, Adm. Jonas H. Cur. biog. p. 328 (1947).

Ingres, Jean Auguste Dominique (self portrait. Con. 133: 271 (col.) Je '54.

—— (work of). Con. 140: 247 Jan '58. Int. gr. soc.: Arts . . . p. 133 (col.). Praeg. pict. ency., p. 383 (col.).

Ingrid, Queen. Holiday 7: 97 Mar '50.

"ink blot" pictures. Holiday 19: 186 May '56.

ink bottle (pen). Holiday 21: 15 (col.) Je '57.

inkpot, Edward Vernon. Con. 144: 30 Sept '59.

——, Siberian jade. Con. 140: XVI Jan '58.

inkstand (antique). Con. 137: LII Ap '56.

—— (by Lamerie). Con. 139: 67 Mar '57.

——, Amer. (18th cent. silver). Con. 135: 75 Mar '55.

——, silver (antique). Con. 129: 131 Je '52; 139: 241 Je '57.

——, brass. Con. 141: 49 Mar '58.

——, bronze gilt. Con. 137: 1 Mar '56.

——, George II silver. Con. 132: XIX Nov '53; 133: VI Ap '54; 139: 193 May '57.

——, George III. Con. 129: XX Je '52; 144: XXXIV Dec '59.

——, Louis XV. Con. 138: IV Dec '56.

——, Meissen. Con. 145: inside cover Ap '60.

——, Norwegian (1765). Con. 145: 9 Mar '60.

——, Queen Anne. Con. 140: XXXVII Dec '57.

——, Sheffield silver. Con. 141: XL Je '58.

——, silver (18th cent.). Con. ency. of ant., vol. 1 pl. 89.

Con. 140: XXX Nov '57; 145: LXXXV Je '60.

ink-vase (antique). Con. 136: 219 Dec '55.

inkwell (19th cent. stoneware). Amer. heri. vol. 2 no. 2 p. 33 (col.) (winter '51).

inkwells (antique). Rawson: Ant. pict. bk., p. 91.

Inland sea (Japan). Natl. geog. 104: 623-50 (part col.) Nov '53.

Inman, Henry (miniature by). Amer. heri. vol. 7 no. 4 p. 10 (col.) (Je '56).

—— (work of). Amer. heri. vol. 10 no. 1 p. 23 (col.) (Dec '58).

inn (int., cartoon). Holiday 13: 46-7 (col.) Feb '53.

—— (int., Scotland). Natl. geog. 112: 465 (col.) Oct '57.

—— (int., Wales, 200 yrs. old). Holiday 28: 43 (col.) Sept '60.

—— (Sanibel is.). Travel 103: 26 Feb '55.

—— (Sun Valley, Idaho). Holiday 13: 5 (col.) Feb '53.

——, "The bell" (Eng., 17th cent.). Holiday 19: 143 (col.) Mar '56.

——, Colonial. Brooks: Growth of a nation, p. 84.

——, English. See Royal Oak inn.

——, Japanese. Travel 106: 16 Oct '56.

——, Oregon (snow covered). Natl. geog. 110: 303 Sept '56.

——, "The Reefs" (Bermuda). Holiday 23: 75 (col.) Je '58.

——, "Spread Eagle". See "Spread Eagle inn."

——, Wayside. See Wayside inn.

——, White horse. See "White Horse Inn."

——, Williamsburg. See Williamsburg inn.

inn. See also hotel.

inn sign (Eng.). Holiday 21: 27 Mar '57.

inn signs (1812-   ). Amer. heri. vol. 11 no. 4 p. 60-3 (col.) (Je '60).

—— (Eng.). Holiday 26: 106 (col.) Oct '59.

inner tube, auto. Holiday 10: 31 Dec '51; 11: 29 (col.) May '52, 10 Je '52.

Innes, Hammond. Cur. biog. p. 360 (1954).

Innes, Hugh. Con. 126: back of p. II Aug '50.

innocence (sym.). Lehner: Pict. bk. of sym., p. 58.

Innocenti, Ferdinando. Cur. biog. p. 198 (1959).

inns, New England. Holiday 26: 56-61 (col.) Aug '59.

——, location of (map, Eng.). Holiday 23: 145 Ap '58.

Innsbruck (Austria). Natl. geog. 99: 750 Je '51; 100: 387 (col.) Sept '51.

Inonu, Ismet. Cur. biog. p. 431 (1941).

Inouye, Daniel K. Cur. biog. p. 201 (1960).

"Inscribed cliffs" (near Hattusas). Osward: Asia Minor, pl. 1.

inscriptions, old rock (girls). Natl. geog. 112: 244 (col.) Aug '57.

Inside passage to Alaska. Natl. geog. 114: 154-5 (col.) Aug '58.

insignia of rank. Int. gr. soc.: Arts . . . p. 167 (col.).

insignia of rank, Hittite. See Hittite insignia of rank.

inspiration (sym.). Lehner: Pict. bk. of sym., p. 46.

Institute Hall (Charleston, S. C.). Amer. heri. vol. 11 no. 4 p. 56 (Je '60).

instruments, scientific. *See* scientific instruments.

Insull. Amer. heri. vol. 9 no. 5 p. 32 Aug '58.

interior decoration. *See* room interior.

"Interior of Fives Court" (Turner). Con. ency. of ant., vol. 1, pl. 138.

Interlaken (Switzerland). Travel 102: 13 Aug '54.

International bridge (Texas-Mexico). Holiday 8: 83 Dec '50.

International peace park. *See* Waterton glacier-International peace park.

intestines. Gray's anatomy, p. 1214-31.

"Invalides" floor plan (Paris). Praeg. pict. ency., p. 24.

inventions. Amer. (19th cent.). Amer. heri. vol. 9 no. 2 p. 16-7 (col.) (Feb '58).

Invercauld castle. *See* Castle of Invercauld.

Invincible Armada. Amer. heri. vol. 10 no. 3 p. 14-5 (col.) (Ap '59).

invulnerability (sym.). Lehner: Pict. bk. of sym., p. 71.

Iolani palace (throne room). Natl. geog. 118: 14 (col.) Jl '60.

Ionesco, Eugene. Cur. biog. p. 200 (1959).

Ionian is. (Greece). Holiday 24: 66-71 (col.) Sept '58.

Ionic column. *See* column, Ionic.

ionosphere station (Arctic). Natl. geog. 107: 548 (col.) Ap '55.

Iowa. Holiday 20: 42-51 (part col.) Oct '56.
—— (Christmas). Holiday 12: 83 Dec '52.
—— (lakes). Travel 110: 32 Sept '58.
—— ("Little brown church in the vale"). Brooks: Growth of a nation, p. 196.
—— (map). Travel 103: 31 Mar '55.
—— (scene by Grant Wood). Amer. heri. vol. 6 no. 1 p. 42 (col.) (fall '54).
—— (state capitol bldg.). Brooks: Growth of a nation, p. 258.
Travel 108: 18 Nov '57.

Iowa state college (1870). Brooks: Growth of a nation, p. 199.

Iowa univ. queen. Face of Amer., p. 156 (col.).

Iran, Shah of. Natl. geog. 117: 73 (col.) Jan '60.

Iran. Natl. geog. 100: 426-64 (part col.) Oct '51; 104: 708-20 Nov '53; 115: 60-3 (part col.) Jan '59.
Travel 105: 23 Jan '56; 113: 32-5 Feb '60.
—— (Kashgai). Natl. geog. 101: 806-32 (part col.) Je '52.
—— (map). Natl. geog. 98: 833 Dec '50; 117: 76-7 (col.) Jan '60.
—— (rock carvings). Natl. geog. 98: 826-42 Dec '50.
—— (welcomes Eisenhower). Natl. geog. 117: 634-5 (col.) May '60.

Iran irrigation tunnels. *See* irrigation tunnels, Iran.

"Iranistan" (home of P. T. Barnum). Durant: Pict. hist. of Amer. circus, p. 57.

Iraq. Natl. geog. 113: 204-39 (part col.) Feb '58; 114: 444-89 (part col.) Oct '58; 115: 53-63 (col.) Jan '59.

—— (map). Natl. geog. 98: 833 Dec '50; 114: 452-3 Oct '58; 117: 76 (col.) Jan '60.

Iraq desert area ("locust war"). Natl. geog. 103: 547-61 Ap '53.

Iraq women (bowls stacked on heads). Natl. geog. 114: 459 (col.) Oct '58.

Irbil (Iraq). 115: 58-9 Jan '59.

Ireland. Holiday 6: cover, 34-63 (part col.) Dec 49; 15: 65 Jan '54; 19: 38-43 (part col.) Jan '56; 22: 129 Nov '57; 23: 54-65 (col.) Je '58; 25: 88 (col.) Mar '59.
Natl. geog. 99: 654-78 (part col.) May '51; 104: 117-32 (col.) Jl '53.
Travel 101: 8, 32-3 May '54.
—— (arch.). Jensen: The White House, p. 8.
—— (coast, cliffs). Natl. geog. 108: 736 (col.) Dec '55.
—— (home). Holiday 24: 87 (col.) Dec '58.
—— (Kate Kearney's cottage). *See* Kate Kearney's cottage.
—— (Pres. Kennedy's ancestral home). U.S. News & world report vol. LV no. 1 p. 28 Jl 1, 1963.
—— (map). Holiday 21: 115 Jan '57.
Natl. geog. 99: 656 May '51.
—— (patron saint of). Lehner: Pict. bk. of sym., p. 39.
—— (Rock of Caskel). Holiday 20: 108 (col.) Aug '56.
—— Russborough house). Con. 145: 156 May '60.

Irene (Mrs. Eliot Gibbons). Cur. biog. p. 276 (1946).

Irish cart (people, donkey). Holiday 25: 91 Jan '59.

Irish glass candlesticks. Con. 145: XXXII Mar '60.

Irish glass vase. Con. 145: XXIV Ap '60.

Irish glass water jug. Con. 145: XXVI Ap '60.

Irish guards. Holiday 18: 43 Sept '55; 25: 190 (col.) May '59.

Irish people (children dancing). Holiday 17: 85 Feb '55.
—— (immigrants to Amer.). Amer. heri. vol. 9 no. 5 p. 86-9 (Aug '58).
—— (immigrants to N.Y., 1847). Amer. heri. vol. 9 no. 5 p. 22-3 (col.) (Aug '58).
—— (man seated). Holiday 26: 48 Nov '59.
—— (old lady, head). Travel 107: inside cover Jan '57.

Irish silverware. Con. 137: LI Ap '56; 145: XLIII Ap '60.
—— (antique). Con. 139: LXIX May '57.

iron. Holiday 12: 9 Sept '52; 13: 28, 81, 154 Je '53; 14: 128 Jl '53, 84 Sept '53; 20: 1 Nov '56; 21: 5 Feb '57, 138 Ap '57; 22: 7 Jl '57, 122 (col.) Dec '57; 24: 13 Dec '58; 26: 20 Dec '59.
Int. gr. soc.: Arts . . . p. 171 (col.).
—— (sym.). Lehner: Pict. bk. of sym., p. 72.
——, charcoal heated. Natl. geog. 104: 643 (col.) Nov '53.
——, flat. *See* flatiron.
——, folding. Holiday 11: 76 May '52, 128 Je '52.
——, steam. Holiday 28: 134 Jl '60, 13 (col.) Dec '60.

——, travel. Holiday 12: 113 Sept '52, 73 Nov '52, 157 Dec '52; 28: 81 Aug '60.

Iron. *See* also bonnet iron; flatiron; charcoal iron; polishing iron; sadiron; tailor's goose (iron).

"Iron brigade," death of (Gettysburg). Amer. heri. vol. 9 no. 1 p. 49 (Dec '57).

iron fence & gate. *See* fence & gate, iron.

iron filings (sym.). Lehner: Pict. bk. of sym., p. 72.

iron gate. Holiday 5: 52 Mar '49. Natl. geog. 106: 455 (col.) Oct '54.

—— (ornamental). Travel 114: cover Aug '60.

iron gate post. Travel 101: 4 Jan '54.

iron gateway. Holiday 16: 63 Aug '54.

iron grill. Brooks: Growth of a nation, p. 93. Holiday 15: 39 May '54; 16: 32 Sept '54.

iron grill gate. Holiday 10: 106 Aug '51.

iron lung (primitive). Amer. heri. vol. 8 no. 1 p. 128 (Dec '56).

iron lung patient (boards plane). Natl. geog. 111: 299 (col.) Mar '57.

"Iron man" statue (Birmingham, Ala.). Brooks: Growth of a nation, p. 290, p. 791.

"Iron mines, Ironwood" (Dehn). Amer. heri. vol. 2 no. 4 p. 67 (col.) (summer '51).

iron mining. Holiday 8: 90-7 (part col.) July 50.

iron-ore docks (freighter, Wis.). Natl. geog. 111: 164 (col.) Feb '57.

iron ore mine. Brooks: Growth of a nation, p. 219.

iron railing, wrought. Natl. geog. 103: 144 Feb '53.

iron vitriol (sym.). Lehner: Pict. bk. of sym., p. 72.

Irons, Ernest E. Cur. biog. p. 294 (1949).

irons (antique). Rawson: Ant. pict. bk., p. 12.

Ironside, Henry Allan. Cur. biog. p. 298 (1945).

Ironside, Field-Marshal Lord. Con. 145: 191 May '60.

ironworks house (Saugus, Mass.). Amer. heri. vol. 2 no. 4 p. 31 (col.) (summer '51).

Iroquois palisade. Amer. heri. vol. 6 no. 2 p. 29 (winter '55).

Iroquois witch doctor. Int. gr. soc.: Arts . . . p. 185 (col.).

irradiated foods. *See* foods, irradiated.

irradiated water *See* water, irradiated.

irrigation, desert. Natl. geog. 117: 79 (col.) Jan '60.

irrigation canals (Mesopotamia). Natl. geog. 99: 51 Jan '51.

irrigation system, field (men). Natl. geog. 100: 321 (col.) Sept '51.

irrigation tunnels, Iran. Natl. geog. 105: 510 (col.) Ap '54.

Irving, Maj. Gen. Frederick A. Cur. biog. p. 296 (1951).

Irving, Washington (& his literary friends). Amer. heri. vol. 10 no. 1 p. 22 (Dec '58).

Irving's home, Washington. Holiday 6: 39 (col.) Sept '49; 27: 120 (col.) May '60.

Irwin, Helen G. Cur. biog. p. 286 (1952).

Irwin, Margaret. Cur. biog. p. 277 (1946).

Irwin, Robert B. Cur. biog. p. 304 (1948).

Isaacs, George. Cur. biog. p. 299 (1945).

"Isabella de Bourbon," Queen (Velasquez). Con. ency. of ant., vol. 1, pl. 161. Con. 141: 239, 243 Je '58.

Isabella of Portugal. Con. 134: 189 Dec '54.

Isabella Stewart Gardner museum (courtyard). Holiday 14: 39 (col.) Nov '53.

Isabey, Jean-Baptiste (miniature by). Con. 138: 82 Nov '56.

"Isaiah" (Michelangelo). Int. gr. soc.: Arts . . . p. 89 (col.).

Ischia is. (Italy). Holiday 6: 126 Dec '49. Labande: Naples, p. 203, 206. Natl. geog. 105: 532-50 (part col.) Ap '54. Travel 103: 19-20 Ap '55.

Iselin, Columbus O'Donnell. Cur. biog. p. 305 (1948).

Isenbrandt, Adriaen (work of). Con. 145: LXVI (col.) May '60.

Isfahan. Holiday 20: 51-65 (part col.) Dec '56.

—— (mosque). Holiday 20: 52 (col.) Dec '56.

Isfahan child (rug weaver). Natl. geog. 114: 37 (col.) Jl '58.

Isfahan's Sheik Lutfallah mosque. Travel 105: 23 Jan '56.

Ishibashi, Tanzan. Cur. biog. p. 275 (1957).

Ishimoto, Tatsuo. Cur. biog. p. 302 (1956).

Ishmael tempted by Devil, site where (stone pillars). Natl. geog. 104: 36 (col.) Jl '53.

Ishtar gate (Babylon). Natl. geog. 114: 468 Oct '58.

—— (reconstruction). Ceram: March of arch., p. 229.

Ishtar gate approach (Babylon). Praeg. pict. ency., p. 113.

Isis (goddess, statue). Ceram: March of arch., p. 146.

——, buckle of. *See* buckle of Isis.

——, sistrum of. *See* sistrum of Isis.

——, temple of. *See* temple of Isis.

Iskenderun harbor. *See* harbor (Iskenderun).

Isla mujeres (Yucatan peninsula). Travel 110: 32 Nov '58.

Islam (sym.) Lehner: Pict. bk. of sym., p. 34-8.

Islamic center (Wash. D.C.). Face of Amer., p. 81 (col.). Travel 106: 13 Dec '56.

Islamic pottery. Con. 141: 190 May '58.

Islam's Dome of the rock. *See* Dome of the rock, Islam's.

island. Labande: Naples, p. 14-5.

——, Corfu. *See* Corfu island.

——, St. Stephen. *See* St. Stephen island.

"Island of birds" (St. Lawrence river). Amer. heri. vol. 10 no. 6 p. 58 (Oct '59).

island of Kizkale. Osward: Asia Minor, p. 125.

islands (Gulf of Mexico). Holiday 8: 58-63 Dec '50.

—— (St. Lawrence). Natl. geog. 115: 337 (col.) Mar '59.

——, Pacific. *See* Pacific islands.

——, South Seas (map). Holiday 28: 51 Oct '60.

——, Thousand. *See* Thousand islands.

Isle of Cyprus. Natl. geog. 100: 732 (col.) Dec '51; 101: 628-64 (part col.) May '52; 109: 873-84 (part col.) Je '56.

—— (harbor). Natl. geog. 110: 732 (col.) Dec '56.

—— (map). Natl. geog. 101: 631 May '52; 109: 873 Je '56.

—— (soapstone idol). Natl. geog 109: 883 Je '56.

—— (men & women). Natl. geog. 112: 108 (col.) Jl '57.

Isle of Jersey. Holiday 22: 2 (col.) Oct '57; 23: 20 Je '58.
Travel 101: 23 May '54.

Isle of Man (castle). Holiday 25: 19 Jan '59.

Isle of Pines (beach). Holiday 27: 194 (col.) Ap '60.

Isle of Skye. Natl geog. 102: 90-112 Jl '52; 112: 474-5 (col.) Oct '57.

—— (harbor). Holiday 27: 127 (col.) Feb '60.

—— (map). Natl. geog. 102: 88 Jl '52.

"Isle of Skye week" parade. Natl. geog. 102: 89 Jl '52.

"Isle of the Blest," Chinese jade mt. Con. 141: XV Je '58.

Isle of Wight. Holiday 27: 32 Je '60.
Travel 107: 56-8 Ap '57.

—— (map). Natl. geog. 101: 515 Ap '52.

Isle of women. See Isla mujeres.

Isle Royale (Mich.). Natl. geog. 115: 452-3 (col.) Ap '59.
Travel 102: 31-4 Jl '54.

Isles of Greece. See Greece.

Isleta mission (Albuquerque). Holiday 14: 59 Dec '53.

Ismay, Lt. Gen. Sir Hastings L. Cur. biog. p. 337 (1943).

Isnik bottle. See bottle, Isnik.

Israel. Holiday 13: 98-9 Jan '53; 17: 41-5 (part col.) Feb '55; 26: 66-76 (part col.) Dec '59.
Natl. geog. 115: 513-31 (part col.) Ap '59.

—— (harbor). Natl. geog. 110: 754 (col.) Dec '56.

—— (man & dog on beach). Holiday 26: cover (col.) Dec '59.

Israeli (map). Natl. geog. 98: 710 Dec '50.

Israeli children (playing). Natl. geog. 115: 513 (col.) Ap '59.

Israeli collective farm. Natl. geog. 114: 856-7 (col.) Dec '58.

Israeli women. Holiday 17: 45 (col.) Feb '55.

Israelites (flight to Egypt). Natl. geog. 112: 837-63 (col.) Dec '57.

Issenheim altar. See altar, Issenheim.

Istanbul. Holiday 12: 132 (col.) Nov '52.
Natl. geog. 109: 72, 74 (col.) Jan '56; 112: 110 Jl '57, 405 Sept '57; 115: 86-7 (col.) Jan '59.
Osward: Asia Minor, pl. 83-5, 86-98, pl. IV (col.).

—— (harbor). Holiday 16: 109 Nov '54.
Natl. geog. 100: 149-64 (col.) Aug '51, 724 Dec '51.

—— (mosque). Praeg. pict. ency., p. 516.

Istanbul Hilton hotel (Turkey). Travel 103: 62 May '55.

Istanbul. See also Constantinople.

Italian armour (medieval). Int. gr. soc.: Arts . . . p. 73 (col.).

Italian art. See art, Italian.

Italian carabinier. Int. gr. soc.: Arts . . . p. 159 (col.).

Italian dishes. See dishes, Italian.

Italian figure drawings. Con. 135: 274-80 Je '55.

Italian furniture. See furniture, Italian.

Italian gilt & silver, bronze objects. Con. 144: 218 Jan '60.

Italian honor insignia. Int. gr. soc.: Arts . . . p. 167 (col.).

Italian Maiolica (Ford collection). Con. 142: 148-50 Dec '58.

Italian people (children). Holiday 19: 100-3 Jan '56.

—— (man). Holiday 13: 49 (col.), 50-1 Feb '53; 27: 157 (col.) Ap '60.

—— (man, woman & children). Labande: Naples, p. 18-9, 34.

Italian porcelain. Con. 135: 12-9 Mar '55.

—— (Doccia factory). Con. 144: 157 Dec '59.

Italian Riviera. Holiday 13: 57-63 Je '53.
Natl. geog. 111: 806-7 (col.) Je '57.

Italian silverware. See silverware, Italian.

Italian tabernacle (antique, 16th cent.). Con. 135: LI May '55.

Italian town clerk (medieval). Holiday 25: 34 (col.) Jan '59.

"Italian village scenes" (tapestry). Natl. geog. 113: 255 (col.) Feb '58.

Italy. Amer. heri. vol. 11 no. 3 p. 21-3 (col.) (Ap '60).
Holiday 6: 10 (col.) Dec '49; 7: 66 (col.) Feb '50; 13: 57-63 Je '53; 16: 98-103 (col.) Sept '54; 19: 44-7 (part col.) Jan 56; 21: 22 Jan '57; 25: 90-7 (col.) Mar '59, 78-83 (col.) May '59; 26: 58-67 (col.) Sept '59; 27: 61-5 (col.) Jan '60.
Natl. geog. 100: 736-7 (col.) Dec '51; 111: 789-807 (col.) Je '57.
Travel 101: cover, 5-8 Je '54; 105: 57-9 Ap '56; 112: 39-41 Sept '59.

—— (Adriatic coast). Holiday 21: 50-5 (col.) Jan '57.

—— (Amalfi). Holiday 11: 124 (col.) Mar 52; 21: 152 (col.) Mar '57.
Natl. geog. 116: 472-509 (part col.) Oct '59.

—— (Campione). See Campione, Italy.

—— (Florence). See Florence (Italy).

—— (harbor). Holiday 28: inside back cover (col.) Aug '60.

—— (Larderello Valley). Natl. geog. 100: 711 Dec '51.

—— (Malta). Holiday 26: 88 (col.) Aug '59.

—— (map). Holiday 21: 53, 116 Jan '57; 25: 93 Mar '59.
Natl. geog. 107: 7 Jan '55; 109: 834 Je '56.

—— (Marostica). Natl. geog. 110: 659-68 (col.) Nov '56.

—— (Rome). See Rome.

—— (Siena). See Siena.

—— (Via Sacre). See Via Sacre.

——, patron saint of. Lehner: Pict. bk. of sym., p. 39.

——, southern (map). Natl. geog. 116: 477 Oct '59.

Italy's military police (honor guard). Natl. geog. 111: 755 (col.) Je '57.

Itimad-Ud-Daula (Agra). Int. gr. soc.: Arts . . . p. 85 (col.).

Ittner, Martin H. Cur. biog. p. 410 (1942).

Iturbi, Jose. Cur. biog. p. 338 (1943). Holiday 21: 42 Mar '57; 22: 121 Sept '57.

Ituri forest pygmies (Africa). Travel 113: 26-7 Jan '60.

Ituri hunter. Natl. geog. 117: 285 Feb '60.

Ivan, (Russian sym.). Lehner: Pict. bk. of sym., p. 93.

Iverson, Kenneth R. Cur. biog. p. 298 (1951).

Ives, Burl. Cur. biog. p. 279 (1946); p. 203 (1960). Holiday 19: 14 Feb '56.

Ives, Charles E. Cur. biog. p. 331 (1947).

Ives, Irving M. Cur. biog. p. 307 (1948).

Ivey, John E., jr. Cur. biog. p. 205 (1960).

ivory carving. Con. 135: 94-5 Ap '55.

—— (antique). Con. 144: 198 Dec '59.

—— (Byzantine). Con. 142: 29-30 Sept '58.

—— (Christ, 17th cent.). Con. 141: LXII-LXIII Je '58.

——, Italian. Con. 142: 269 Jan '59.

——, Scandinavian. Con. 145: 53 Mar '60.

ivory panel, Carolingian carved (9th cent.). Con. 143: 103 Ap '59.

Ivy league colleges. See Colleges, Ivy league.

Iwo Jima (U.S. Marines raising flag, 1945). Amer. heri. vol. 10 no. 2 p. 33 (Feb '59). Holiday 22: 1 Jl '57. Natl. geog. 116: 112 (col.) Jl '59.

Izac, Edouard V. Cur. biog. p. 301 (1945).

Izard, Alice De Lancey. Amer. heri. vol. 9 no. 2 p. 54 (col.) (Feb '58).

Izard, Elizabeth. Amer. heri. vol. 9 no. 2 cover (col.) (Feb '58).

Izard, Mrs. J. Allen Smith. Amer. heri. vol. 9 no. 2 p. 56 (col.) Feb '58.

Izard, Ralph. Amer. heri. vol. 9 no. 2 p. 54 (col.) (Feb '58).

Izard, Mrs. Ralph. Amer. heri. vol. 9 no. 2 p. 56 (col.) (Feb '58).

Izard children, Ralhp. Amer. heri. vol. 9 no. 2 p. 55 (col.) (Feb '58).

J

Jabara, Col. James (jet ace). Holiday 27: cover (col.) Mar '60.

Jack, Rev. Homer A. Cur. biog. p. 217 (1961).

Jack, William S. Cur. biog. p. 324 (1944).

"jack", ice fishing. Rawson: Ant. pict. bk., p. 77.

"Jack & pegs" for cording beds. Rawson: Ant. pict. bk., p. 7.

Jack frost (sym.). Lehner: Pict. bk. of sym., p. 81.

jacket, Tyrol. Holiday 28: 221 Nov '60.

Jack-o-lantern. Lehner: Pict. bk. of sym., p. 53. Natl. geog. 106: 672 (col.) Nov '54.

Jackson, Pres. Andrew. Amer. heri. vol. 6 no. 3 p. 44 (col.) (Ap '55); vol. 7 no. 3 p. 30 (Ap '56); vol. 7 no. 4 p. 8 (Je '56); vol. 12 no. 1 front cover (col.) (Dec '60). Brooks: Growth of a nation, p. 109.

Holiday 8: 35 (col.) Nov '50; 23: 77 May '58; 26: 94 (col.) Jl '59; 28: 33 (col.) Oct '60. Jensen: The White House, p. 47-9, 53, 55.

Jackson, Andrew (& James Polk). Holiday 26: 94 (col.) Jl '59.

—— (challenges Benton). Amer. heri. vol. 9 no. 2 p. 44 (Feb '58).

—— (1814). Amer. heri. vol. 8 no. 5 p. 7 (Aug '57).

—— (horseback). Amer. heri. vol. 10 no. 4 p. 63 (Je '59).

—— (punched tin). Rawson: Ant. pict. bk., p. 20.

—— (ship figurehead). Rawson: Ant. pict. bk., p. 79.

—— (stamp). Holiday 27: 63 Je '60.

—— (statue). Jensen: The White House, p. 46.

—— (statue in New Orleans). Holiday 15: 54 Mar '54.

Jackson, Charles Cur. biog. p. 326 (1944).

—— (Gainsborough). Con. 143: 87 Ap '59.

Jackson, Charles D. Cur. biog. p. 299 (1951).

Jackson, Eugene B. Cur. biog. p. 219 (1961).

Jackson, Henry M. Cur. biog. p 295 (1953).

Jackson, John (work of). Con. 144: 8 Sept '59.

Jackson, Mahalia. Cur. biog. p. 277 (1957).

Jackson, Robert H. Cur. biog. p. 273 (1950). Holiday 7: 78 Feb '50.

Jackson, T.J. "Stonewall". Holiday 12: 8 Nov '52. Pakula: Cent. album, p. 169.

Jackson, William H. Cur. biog. p. 301 (1951).

—— (work of). Amer. heri. vol. 7 no. 5 p. 39 (col.) (Aug '56); vol. 11 no. 2 p. 51 (Feb '60).

Jackson, William K. Cur. biog. p. 281 1946).

Jackson & Benton (shake hands). Amer. heri. vol. 9 no. 2 p. 46-7 (Feb '58).

Jackson Hole (Wyo.). Natl. geog. 109: 2-36 (part col.) Jan '56; 113: 624 (col.) May '58.

Jackson Hole lodge (int.). Natl. geog. 109: 21 (col.) Jan '56.

Jackson home, Andrew. See "Hermitage" (home of Andrew Jackson).

Jackson lake dam. Natl. geog. 99: 733 (col.) Je '51.

Jackson log cabin home, Andrew. Amer. heri. vol. 7 no. 5 p. 32 (Aug '56).

Jackson memorial, Andrew. Holiday 25: 63 Je '59.

Jackson reception, Andrew (Cruikshank). Jensen: The White House, p. 48.

Jacksonville (Fla.). Holiday 18: 48-51 (part col.) Jl '55. Natl. geog. 113: 38-9 (col.) Jan '58.

"Jacob & his seed" (come to Egypt). Natl. geog. 112: 837 (col.) Dec '57.

Jacob & Rachel (Hugo Van der Goes). Con. 126: 5 Aug '50.

Jacobean school of art. Con. 126: 162-5 Dec '50.

Jacobs, Rear Adm. Randall. Cur. biog. p. 411 (1942).

Jacob's well, (Nablus, Jordan, woman). Natl. geog. 110: 729 (col.) Dec '56.

Jacobson, Leon Orris. Cur. biog. p. 223 (1962).

Jacobson, Per. Cur. biog. p. 209 (1958).

Jacopi, Giulio. Cur. biog. p. 202 (1959).
Jacque, Charles Emile (work of). Con. 140: XXIII Dec '57.
jade bell-push, Siberian. Con. 142: XLIX Nov '58.
jade bowl. Con. 142: 55 Sept '58; 144: 40 Sept '59.
——, Chinese (18th cent.). Con. 143: V Mar '59.
——, white. Con. 142: LXII Nov '58.
jade buffalo, Chinese (17th cent.). Con. 145: XIX May '60.
jade burner. Con. 144: 42 Sept '59.
jade carved head. Con. 139: XIV Mar '57.
jade carving (antique). Con. 135: XXXVI Mar '55.
jade cups, Chinese. Con. 142: LXIV Jan '59.
jade elephants (antique). Con. 144: XXIV Sept '59.
——, Ming. Con. 143: LXIII May '59.
jade figures. Con. 142: 124 Nov '58.
jade group, Chinese. Con. 142: XXXVI Nov '58.
jade incense burner. Con. 144: XXI Dec '59; 145: XXI, XL Je '60.
jade koro (18th cent., Ch'ien Lung). Con. 142: XV Jan '59.
jade lantern. Con. 143: 267 Je '59.
jade objects shop. Natl. geog. 110: 197 (col.) Aug '56.
jade vase. Con. 126: back of II Aug '50; 129: LX Je '52; 137: V Mar '56; 140: XXXVIII Dec '57; 142: LII Nov '58.
—— (antique). Con. 134: 120 Nov '54.
——, Chinese (Ch'ien Lung). Con. 142: LX Jan '59; 144: XV Jan '60.
Jade vase & cover. Con. 143: XV Ap '59.
jade. See also Chinese jade.
Jagan, Cheddi. Cur. biog. (1963).
Jagendorf, Moritz. Cur. biog. p. 288 (1952).
Jahangir's tomb. See tomb, Jahangir's.
jail, 1st Cal. (Monterey). Horan: Pict. hist. of wild west, p. 21.
jail cell block (early). Horan: Pict. hist. of wild west, p. 73.
jailbird (Tibet). Holiday 12: 57 (col.) Dec '52.
Jain temple (Calcutta). Travel 101: inside cover Je '54; 111: cover Jan '59.
Jain women (India). Natl. geog. 118: 465 (col.) Oct '60.
Jaipur (India). Natl. geog. 118: 461-3 (col.) Oct '60.
Jamaica. Holiday 5: 44-7 (col.) Feb '49; 9: 98-102, 104 (part col.) Mar '51; 23: 50-1 (col.) Feb '58; 25: 58-63 (col.) Feb '59, 174 (col.) Je '59; 26: 21 (col.) Jl '59; 27: 47 (col.) Je '60.
Natl. geog. 105: 335-62 (part col.) Mar '54.
—— (beach). Holiday 20: 116 (col.) Dec '56.
—— (Casa Montego hotel). Travel 108: 43 Aug '57.
—— (dancers). Holiday 25: 118 (col.) May '59.
—— (drummer, cartoon). Holiday 23: 100 May '58; 24: 134 Jl '58.
—— (girl). Holiday 24: 93 (col.) Jl '58, 122 (col.) Aug '58.
—— (girl, bathing suit). Holiday 23: 18 (col.) Je '58.

—— (guitar). Holiday 19: 23 Je '56.
—— (harbor). Holiday 15: 48 Feb '54.
—— (hotel). Holiday 22: 110 (col.) Nov '57.
—— (Legonea mts.). Con. 143: XXXVII Ap '59.
—— (man, comic). Holiday 22: 110 (col.) Nov '57.
Travel 109: 41 May '58.
—— (musicians). Holiday 26: 169 (col.) Oct '59.
—— (musicians, comic). Holiday 24: 122 (col.) Aug '58.
—— (people on beach). Holiday 23: 18 (col.) Je '58.
—— (Royal Caribbean hotel). Travel 108: 43 Dec '57.
—— (woman). Holiday 28: 208 (col.) Nov '60.
Jamaican band. Holiday 26: 169 (col.) Oct '59, 43 (col.) Dec '59.
Jamaican House of Rep. (int.). Holiday 5: 44 (col.) Feb '49.
Jamali, Mohammed Fadhel. Cur. biog. p. 363 (1954).
James I, King of Gt. Brit. Amer. heri. vol. 8 no. 4 p. 6 (col.) (Je '57); vol. 10 no. 4 p. 19 (Je '59).
Con. 139: 217 Je '57.
Holiday 5: 61 (col.) Je '49.
James, Charles. Cur. biog. p. 303 (1956).
James, Dingus (guerrilla). Horan: Pict. hist. of wild west, p. 27.
James, Frank. Horan: Pict. hist. of wild west, p. 28, 30.
James, Frank Cyril. Cur. biog. p. 305 (1956).
James, Harry. Cur. biog. p. 341 (1943).
James, Jesse. Amer. heri. vol. 11 no 5 p. 40 (Aug '60).
Brooks: Growth of a nation, p. 155.
—— (after death). Horan: Pict. hist. of wild west, p. 41.
—— (killed in house at St. Joseph). See house at St. Joseph.
James, Mrs. Jesse. Horan: Pict. hist. of wild west, p. 33.
James, Jesse, jr. Horan: Pict. hist of wild west, p. 34.
James, Jesse W. Horan: Pict. hist. of wild west, p. 30, 42.
James, Mary (daughter of Jesse James). Horan: pict. hist. of wild west, p. 34.
James, Montague Rhodes. Con. 144: 13 Sept '59.
James, W. (work of). Con. 144: XLI Dec '59.
James, Will. Jun. bk. of auth., p. 170.
James, William (work of). Con. 142: XL Sept '58.
"James Foster" (Clipper ship). Amer. heri. vol. vol. 6 no. 6 cover (col.) (Oct '55).
"James Madison presenting constitution to Wash.". Natl. geog. 111: 69 (col.) Jan '57.
Jameson, William J. Cur. biog. p. 363 (1954).
Jamestown (St. Helena is.). Natl. geog. 98: 277 Aug '50.
Jamestown (S.D.). Travel 105: 28 May '56.
Jamestown (Va.). Jordan: Hammond's pict. atlas, p. 52 (col.).
Natl. geog. 111: 582-620 (part col.) May '57.
—— (Colonial festival). Travel 107: back cover May '57.

—— (house). Con. 140: 133 Nov '57.

—— (map, one of earliest in Va.). Con. 139: 201 May '57.

—— (1607). Brooks: Growth of a nation, p. 38.
Holiday 21: 163 (col.) Ap '57.

—— (1622). Amer. heri. vol. 8 no. 3 p. 69 (Ap '57).

Jamestown area (by Bradley Smith). Amer. heri. vol. 11 no. 1 p. 49-56 (col.) (Dec '59).

Jamestown pottery & dishes. Con. 140: 135-8 Nov '57.

Jamestown settlers. Holiday 21: 33 (col.) May '57.

Janack, Leos. Cooper: Con. ency. of music, p. 143.

Janas, Sigmund. Cur. biog. p. 276 (1950).

Jane, Calamity. See Calamity Jane.

Jane, Countess of Harrington (Reynolds). Natl. geog. 105: 788 (col.) Je '54.

Janeway, Elizabeth. Cur. biog. p. 327 (1944).

jangada (Brazilian fishing boat). Natl. geog. 108: 753-4 (col.) Dec '55.

Janinet, Francois (engravings). Con. 133: XLI Je '54.

Janis, Elsie. Holiday 7: 69 Mar '50.

Janitzio (Mexico). Travel 101: 23-5 Ap '54.

Janney, Russell. Cur. biog. p. 333 (1947).

Jansen, William. Cur. biog. p. 303 (1951).

Jansons, Cornelius (work of). Con. 140: XII (col.) Nov '57.

Janssens, Rev. John Baptist. Cur. biog. p. 203 (1959).

Janus (sym.). Lehner: Pict. bk. of sym., p. 80.

Japan. Disney: People & places, p. 147-62 (col.).
Holiday 12: 26-41 (part col.) Aug '52; 24: 91 (col.) Aug '58; 27: 66 (col.) Feb '60.
Natl. geog. 97: 595-632 (part col.) May '50; 104: 92-101 Jl '53, 620-50 (part col.) Nov '53; 116: 856-62 (col.) Dec '59; 118: 734-78 (col.) Dec '60.
Travel 106: 12-7 Oct '56; 109: 36-9 Mar '58.

—— (Ainu, head). Int. gr. soc.: Arts . . . p. 183 (col.).

—— (Americans land). See Americans land on Japan (1853).

—— (gate). Travel 102: 29 Nov '54.

—— (hotel). Travel 113: 19 Mar '60.

—— (Kwannon in temple). Praeg. pict. ency., p. 526.

—— (map). Natl. geog. 97: 597 May '50.

—— (natl. sym.). Lehner: Pict. bk. of sym., p. 47.

—— (temple pagoda). Praeg. pict. ency., p. 528.

—— (Yokohama). See Yokohama (Japan).

Japanese. Amer. heri. vol. 9 no. 3 p. 12-3 (col.) (Ap '58).
Holiday 21: 21 (col.) May '57.

—— (carrying load). Holiday 14: 76 Aug '53.

—— (carrying rice bags). Amer. heri. vol. 9 no. 3 p. 20 (col.) (Ap '58).

—— (dinner). Holiday 20: 12 Oct '56; 22: 111 (col.) Jl '57.
Int. gr. soc.: Arts . . . p. 179 (col.).

—— (eating). Disney: People & places, p. 157, 162 (col.).

—— (Geisha dance). Natl. geog. 117: 668 (col.) May '60.

—— (head). Int. gr. soc.: Arts . . . p. 185 (col.).

—— (horseback). Holiday 23: 42 Mar '58.

—— (planting rice seed). Disney: People & places, p. 148-9 (col.).

—— (woman's head). Int. gr. soc.: Arts . . . p. 181 (col.).

Japanese-American boys (playing old musical instruments). Holiday 7: 41 (col.) Jan '50.

Japanese-American girls. (seated). Holiday 7: 41 (col.) Jan '50.

Japanese animal god (for burial mound, 6th cent.). Con. 145: 289 Je '60.

Japanese armour (medieval). Int. gr. soc.: Arts . . . p. 73 (col.).

Japanese art. Con. 132: 152-7 Jan '54.

Japanese art panel. Con. 132: 65 Sept '53.

Japanese boy (playing instrument). Holiday 27: 71 Feb '60.

Japanese carved wood. Con. 139: XXX May '57.

Japanese Children. See children, Japanese.

Japanese color prints. Con. 132: 25-31 Sept '53, 90-6 Nov '53, 152-7 Jan '54.

Japanese dancer. Natl. geog. 97: 622 (col.) May '50.

Japanese dancers. Travel 112: 8 Aug '59.

Japanese dieties. See dieties, Japanese.

Japanese diplomats to Amer. (1860). Amer. heri. vol. 12 no. 1 p. 116 (Dec '60).

Japanese drawings (Taito & Hokkei). Con. 139: 157-61 May '57, 232-3 Je '57.

Japanese embassy staff (1860). Jensen: The White House, p. 80.

Japanese envoys (1st to Amer.). Jensen: The White House, p. 79.

Japanese food. Holiday 18: 64 (col.) Jl '55.

Japanese garden. Holiday 22: 196 (col.) Dec Dec '57; 26: 99 (col.) Aug '59.
Int. gr. soc.: Arts . . . p. 121 (col.).

Japanese geisha girl. See geisha girl.

Japanese gift shop. Natl. geog. 117: 508 (col.) Ap '60.

Japanese girl. Holiday 21: 137 (col.) May '57; 23: 19 (col.) Ap '58, 137 (col.) Je '58; 25: 158 Mar '59; 26: 18 Oct '59, 111 (col.) Nov '59; 27: 34 (col.), 70-1 Feb '60.

—— (feeding deer). Natl. geog. 118: 778 (col.) Dec '60.

—— (head). Holiday 26: 168 Dec '59.

—— (pearl sorter). Natl. geog. 97: 625 (col.) May '50.

—— (serving tea on airplane). Holiday 25: 105 (col.) Feb '59.

—— (stewardess). Holiday 27: 98 (col.) Feb '60.

Japanese girl & boy. Holiday 13: 52-3 Feb '53.

Japanese girls. Natl. geog. 104: 641, 643 (col.) Nov '53.

—— (Wash., D.C.). Natl. geog. 111: 86 (col.) Jan '57.

Japanese honor insignia. Int. gr. soc.: Arts . . . p. 167 (col.).

Japanese house. Travel 112: 51 Dec '59.

——, Mennecy covered porcelain. Con. ency. of ant., vol. 1, pl. 59.
——, Nuba pottery (on woman's head). Natl. geog. 99: 277 Feb '51.
——, pharmacy (Faenza maiolica). Con. 140: 162 Dec '57.
——, pottery (Cyprus is.). Natl. geog. 101: 643, 664 (col.) May '52.
——, St. Cloud. Con. 143: 140 May '59.
——, water. See water jar; water jug.
jar & cover, Longton Hall oak leaf. Con. 142: XIV Jan '59.
jar. See also jars; urn.
Jaragua hotel (Sao Paulo, Brazil). Travel 102; 49 Aug '54.
jardiniere, Chinese porcelain. Con. 139: V May '57.
——, Le Nove. Con. 135: 14 Mar '55.
——, Louis XVI. Con. 142: 109 Nov '58.
——, Marsailles faience. Con. 145: 269 Je '60.
——, Sevres. Con. 129: XLVIII Je '52.
——, Vincennes. Con. ency. of ant., vol. 1, pl. 62.
——, Vincennes porcelain. Con. 133: 5 Mar '54; 139: XVI May '57.
jarl & squad. Natl. geog. 106: 855, 860 Dec '54.
Jarman, Maj. Gen. Sanderford. Cur. biog. p. 412 (1942).
Jarring, Gunnar V. Cur. biog. p. 279 (1957).
jars. Natl. geog. 111: 639 (col.) May '57.
—— (flowers, on woman's head). Natl. geog. 117: 630 (col.) May '60.
——, glass. Natl. geog. 102: 277 Aug '52.
——, Indian. Natl. geog. 97: 239 Feb '50.
——, porous (cool water). Natl. geog. 104: 716 Nov '53.
——, Sudanese. Natl. geog. 103: 261 (col.) Feb '53.
——, wine. See wine jar.
——. See also jar; urn.
Jasmine tower (Agra's fort). Natl. geog. 116: 844 (col.) Dec '59.
"Jason & Medea". Con. ency. of ant., vol. 1, pl. 172.
Jasper, Sergeant (raising flag at Ft. Moultrie). Amer. heri. vol. 6 no. 6 p. 64 (Oct '55).
"Jasper & Newton freeing slaves" (White). Amer. heri. vol. 10 no. 1 p. 62 (col.) (Dec '58).
Jaspar Natl. Park (Rocky mts.). Holiday 16: 53 (col.) Jl '54.
Jordan: Hammond's pict. atlas, p. 133 (col.) Travel 107: 15 May '57.
jaunting cart, Irish. Holiday 25: 91 Jan '59.
Java. Holiday 18: 104-8 (part col.) Sept '55. Natl. geog. 99: 27- Jan '51; 108: 334-5 (col.) Sept '55.
—— (map). Natl. geog. 99: 6 Jan '51.
Javanese dancers. Natl. geog. 99: 2, 31 (col.) Jan '51.
Travel 102: 23 Dec '54.
Javanese musicians. Travel 102: 24 Dec '54.
Javanese woman. Travel 112: 24 Sept '59.
Javits, Jacob K. Cur. biog. p. 310 (1948); p. 210 (1958).
jaw, human. Gray's anatomy, p. 128-32.
Jawlensky, Alexej von (work of). Praeg. pict. ency., p. 485 (col.).

jazz band. Face of Amer., p. 136-7 (col.). Holiday 21: 144 May '57.
jazz orchestra, Negro. Int. gr. soc.: Arts . . . p. 143 (col.).
jazz quartet, Negro. Int. gr. soc.: Arts . . . p. 143 (col.).
Jeakes, J. (work of). Con. ency. of ant., vol. 1, pl. 140.
Jean de Bourgogne. Con. 133: 117 Ap '54.
Jeanmaire, Renee. Cur. biog. p. 289 (1952). Holiday 21: 71 (col.) Ap '57.
Jeanne d'Arc (on horse). Durant: Pict. hist. of Amer. circus, p. 181.
Travel 111: 31-3 May '59.
Jeanne d'Arc. See also St. Joan of Arc.
Jeans, Sir James Hopwood. Cur. biog. p. 434 (1941).
Jebb, Gladwyn. Cur. biog. p. 312 (1948).
Jebel Ram (Egypt). Natl. geog. 112: 107 (col.) Jl '57.
jeep. Natl. geog. 97: 128 Jan '50; 101: 718 (col.) Je '52.
—— (in desert). Natl. geog. 101: 740 (col.) Je '52.
——, airplane. See airplane "flying jeep".
——, amphibious. Natl. geog. 118: 446, 464, 484, 489, 503 (col.) Oct '60.
——, war. Amer. heri. vol. 12 no. 1 p. 39-41 (Dec '60).
jeep plane, jet. See jet jeep, plane.
Jeffers, William M. Cur. biog. p. 414 (1942).
Jefferson, Pres. Thomas. Amer. heri. vol. 1 no. 4 p. 63 (summer '50); vol. 3 no. 1 p. 27 (col.) (fall '51); vol. 6 no. 3 p. 45 (col.) (Aug '55); vol. 7 no. 3 p. 30 (Ap '56); vol. 9 no. 4 p. 49 (col.) (Je '58); vol. 9 no. 5 p. 65 (Aug '58).
Con. ency. of ant., vol. 3, pl. 91.
Con. 134: 222 Dec '54.
Holiday 12: 73 Dec '52.
—— (aquetint). Con. 133: 142 Ap '54.
—— (bust, by Houdon). Jensen: The White House, p. 13.
—— (Peale). Jensen: The White House, p. 19.
—— (architecture). Amer. heri. vol. 10 no. 5 p. 65-77 (Aug '59).
—— (Black Hills sculpt.). Natl. geog. 99: 720 (col.) Je '51.
—— (mask). Amer. heri. vol. 6 no. 4 p. 14 (Je '55).
—— (rock carving). Natl. geog. 110: 496 Oct '56.
—— (stamp). Holiday 27: 63 Je '60.
—— (statue). Natl. geog. 97: 592 (col.) May '50.
—— (Stuart). Amer. heri., vol. 9 no. 3 p. 62-3 (col.) (Ap '58).
—— (Sully). Natl. geog. 97: 556 May '50.
Jefferson home, Thomas ("Monticello"). Amer. heri. vol. 9 no. 3 p. 85 (Ap '58); vol. 10 no. 5 p. 67 (Aug '59); vol. 10 no. 6 p. 112 (Oct '59).
Brooks: Growth of a nation, p. 91.
Holiday 8: 27 (col.) Sept '50; 12: 136 Jl '52, 72 (col.) Dec '52; 18: 107 (col.) Nov '55; 20: 88 Sept '56; 21: 10 (col.) Je '57; 22: 23 (col.) Sept '57; 26: 119 (col.) Sept '59.
Natl. geog. 97: 561-8 (col.) May '50.

Praeg. pict. ency., p. 390.
Travel 112: 30 Jl '59.
Jefferson memorial, Thos. (Wash., D.C.).
Brooks: Growth of a nation, p. 15.
Face of Amer., p. 10 (col.).
Holiday 5: 103 (col.) Jan '49; 7: 39 (col.)
Feb '50; 10: inside cover (col.) Sept '51;
13: 86 May '53; 16: 55, 68 (col.) Jl '54;
19: 34 (col.) May '56; 25: 59 (col.) Je '59.
Jordan: Hammond's pict. atlas, p. 49 (col.).
Natl. geog. 111: 87 (col.) Jan '57; 113: 307
Mar '58.
Jefferson's grave, Thos. *See* graves of Adams
& Jefferson.
Jehan, Shah (feeding chipmunks). Travel 111:
29 Jan '59.
Jellinek, Elvin M. Cur. biog. p. 335 (1947).
jelly moulds (antique). Con. 132: 150 Jan '54.
Jenkins, Hayes Alan. Cur. biog. p. 307 (1956).
Jenkins, Lew. Cur. biog. p. 435 (1941).
Jenkins, Ray H. Cur. biog. p. 366 (1954).
Jenkins, Sara. Cur. biog. p. 297 (1953).
Jenkinson, Francis Henry. Con. 144: 11 Sept
'59.
Jenner, William E. Cur. biog. p. 306 (1951).
Jennings, Al. Horan: Pict. hist. of wild west,
p. 44, 244.
Jennings, Benjamin Brewster. Cur. biog. p. 307
(1951).
Jennings, John. Cur. biog. p. 296 (1949).
Jensen, Ben. F. Cur. biog. p. 207 (1960).
Jensen, Jackie. Cur. biog. p. 205 (1959).
Jensen, Oliver (work of). Amer. heri. vol. 6 no.
3 p. 40-1 (col.) (Ap '55).
Jensen, Lt. Oliver O. Cur. biog. p. 303 (1945).
Jephthah. Holiday 7: 20 Jan '50.
Jeremiah. Natl. geog. 118: 843 (col.) Dec '60.
"Jeremiah lowered into the pit" (Hogenberg).
Con. 138: 14 Sept '56.
Jericho. Natl. geog. 100: 826-43 Dec '51.
—— **(modern).** Natl. geog. 104: 860 (col.) Dec
'53.
—— **(uncovered).** Natl. geog. 104: 854-69
(part col.) Dec '53.
Jericho town wall (world's oldest). Natl. geog.
112: 848 Dec '57.
Jernegan, John D. Cur. biog. p. 207 (1959).
Jerome (Ariz., Ghost town). Travel 114: 43
Sept '60.
Jeronimos monastery (Portugal). Holiday 6: 101
Sept '49.
Jeronymites monastery *See* monastery of the
Jeronymites.
Jersey, Isle of. *See* Isle of Jersey.
"Jersey City" steamboat (1850's). Amer. heri.
vol. 10 no. 6 p. 29 (col.) (Oct '59).
Jerusalem. Holiday 7: 114-27 (part col.) Ap
'50; 17: 38 (col.) Feb '55.
Natl. geog. 98: 712-42 (part col.) Dec '50;
100: 826-43 Dec '51; 106: 844 (col.) Dec
'54; 110: 708-16 (part col.) Dec '56; 115:
492-531 (part col.) Ap '59; 118: 852 (col.)
Dec '60.
Travel 105: 33 Mar '56.
—— **(map).** Natl. geog. 115: 496 Ap '59.
Jerusalem room (ancient). Natl. geog. 112: 856-
7 (col.) Dec '57.
Jerusalem surrender to Nebuchadnezzar. Natl.
geog. 118: 843 (col.) Dec '60.

Jervas, Charles (work of). Con. 133: 180 May
'54.
Jessel, George. Cur. biog. p. 343 (1943).
Holiday 7: 69 Mar '50; 12: 77 Sept '52.
Jessup, Philip C. Cur. biog. p. 314 (1948).
Jester, Beauford H. Cur. biog. p. 317 (1948).
jester. Holiday 23: 28 (col.) Mar '58.
——, **court.** Int. gr. soc.: Arts . . . p. 71 (col.).
——, **queen's carnival.** Natl. geog. 113: 73
(col.) Jan '58.
jester head. Lehner: Pict. bk. of sym., p. 52.
Jesuits. Holiday 27: 69 Ap '60.
"Jesus Christ" (ivory carving, 17th cent.). Con.
141: LXII-LXIII Je '58.
——, **head of (Durer).** Con. 133: 230 Je '54.
Jesus of Nazareth (sym.). Lehner: Pict. bk. of
sym., p. 34.
Jesus' way to the cross. Travel 105: 34 Mar
'56.
Jesus' tomb. *See* Tomb of Jesus.
jet airplane. Travel 111: 63 Ap '59.
jet bomber. Natl. geog. 109: 764 (col.) Je
'56.
jet engine impellers. Natl. geog. 107: 205 Feb
'55.
jet fighter (man). Natl. geog. 111: 335 (col.)
Mar '57.
jet fighters. Natl. geog. 99: 320 (col.) Mar '51.
jet flyers (crash gear). Natl. geog. 109: 659
(col.) May '56.
jet jeep plane. Natl. geog. 104: 773 (col.) Dec
'53.
jet plane. Holiday 22: 12 (col.) Jl '57, 117 (col.)
Sept '57, inside cover Oct '57, 191 (col.) Dec
'57.
—— **(CPA cadets).** Natl. geog. 109: 658 (col.)
May '56.
——, **U.S. (Turkey).** Natl. geog. 115: 81 (col.)
Jan '59.
jetliner. Natl. geog. 118: 6-7 (col.) Jl '60.
—— **(Couvair).** Travel 111: 65 Mar '59.
jetliner model, swept-wing. Natl. geog. 118: 87
(col.) Jl '60.
jetliners. Natl. geog. 117: 449 (col.) Ap '60.
jets, navy Grumman. Natl. geog. 112: 700 (col.)
Nov '57.
"Jenune Femme a la Rose" (Renoir). Con. 138:
XLI Dec '56.
jewel box. Holiday 14: 123 (col.) Dec '53.
jewel cabinet, enamel. Con. 138: 111 Nov '56.
——, **Louis XV.** Con. 133: LXXVI Je '54.
jewel carving ornament. Con. ency. of ant.,
vol. 1, p. 22.
jewel case (antique). Con. 136: 34 Sept '55.
jewel cases. Holiday 20: 105 (col.) Dec '56.
jewel casket. Con. 134: 190-1 Dec '54.
—— **(14th cent.).** Con. 140: 258 Jan '58.
——, **Sevres (bronze).** Con. 133: 259 Je '54.
Jewel chest. Holiday 14: 175 (col.) Dec '53.
—— **(India).** Con. 139: 79 Ap '57.
jewel cutter (man). Natl. geog. 113: 862 Je
'58.
jeweler's shop (antique). Con. 135: LX May
'55.
jewelry. Con. 129: IX Je '52; 134 VII Dec '54;
139: XV Je '57; 141: VII Je '58.
Holiday 10: 59 (col.) Aug '51, 7 (col.) Oct
'51; 14: 123 (col.) Dec '53; 18: 79 Aug

'55, 28 Oct '55, 122 Dec '55; 19: 79 May '56; 20: 9 Aug '56, 154 Nov '56, 100 Dec '56; 21: 121 May '57; 22: 150 Nov '57, 54, 147 (col.) Dec '57; 23: 149 May '58; 24: 80 Jl '58, 6 Nov '58; 26: 92 Sept '59, 112, 184 Oct '59; 27: 123 (col.) Feb '60, 232 May '60, 103 (col.) Je '60; 28: 130 Nov '60, inside cover (col.) Dec '60.
Natl. geog. 98: 67 Jl '50, 790-1 (col.) Dec '50.

—— (ancient). Int. gr. soc.: Arts . . . p. 29, 31 (col.).

—— (brooch). Con. 135: XXV May '55; 137: VII Mar '56.

—— (diamond) Natl. geog. 113: 568-85 (part col.) Ap '58.

—— (ear-rings). Con. 135: LVII May '55; 137: XIV Ap '56.

—— (ear-rings, 18th cent.). Con. 133: XXXV Mar '54.

—— (Egyptian king's bracelets). Ceram: March of arch., p. 149.

—— (necklace). Con. 129: XXXIII Ap '52; 134: XLVII Dec '54; 135: VII, IX May '55.
Holiday 6: 5 (col.) Jl '49, 7 (col.) Sept '49; 7: 15 (col.) Mar '50, 79 (col.) May '50; 8: 63 (col.) Jl '50, 7 (col.) Sept '50, 71 (col.) Nov '50; 13: 7 (col.) May '53; 14: 31 (col.) Jl '53, 58 (col.) Aug '53, 15 (col.) Sept '53, 71 (col.) Nov '53.
Natl. geog. 117: 817 (col.) Je '60.

—— (necklace & earrings). Con. 141: 1 Ap '58.

—— (pendant, 16th cent.). Con. 132: inside cover (col.) Nov '53.

——, African (native). Natl. geog. 97: 337, 347 (col.) Mar '50.

——, African Masai. Natl. geog. 106: 492, 511 (col.) Oct '54.

——, antique. Con. ency. of ant., vol. 1, pl. 93-6.
Con. 132: 211 Jan '54; 136: 23 Sept '55, XLV Dec '55; 137: XLV May '56; 138: XXX, XXXIII Dec '56, XV, XLVI Jan '57; 142: XLV, LV, 195 Dec '58; 143: XLI Mar '59, LI May '59, VII Je '59; 144: XX Sept '59, IX, 84-5 Nov '59, VII, XLIII, 197 Dec '59, XLI Jan '60; 145: V Mar '60, XXIII, 126-7 Ap '60, III, V, XXX May '60.

——, antique (bracelet). Con. 140: 182 Dec '57.

——, antique (bracelet, 18th cent.). Con. 140: XXIV Dec '57.

——, antique (brooch & earrings). Con. 135: XXVI Ap '55.

——, antique (from Emilia). Con. 143: 8 Mar '59.

——, antique (necklace). Con. 140: 15, 61 Sept '57, LI Nov '57, 182 Dec '57.

——, antique gold collar. Con. 141: 25-6 Mar '58.

——, antique (pendant). Con. 141: 106 Ap '58.

——, antique (pin). Con. 138: V Nov '56, XX-XVI, XLVI Jan '57; 139: 55 Mar '57, XLIII Je '57.

——, India. Con. 139: 78 Ap '57.

——, Lafayette's (Amer.). Natl. geog. 112: 424 Sept '57.

——, Louis XV (necklace). Con. 138: XXV Dec '56.

——, Navajo Indian. Natl. geog. 114: 825-7, 846 (col.) Dec '58.

——, Renaissance. Con. 139: 126-32 (part col.) Ap '57.

——, Sumerian. Holiday 14: 115 Sept '53.

——, Tudor. Con. 139: 109 Ap '57.

——, Victorian. Con. 143: VII Ap '59.

jewelry making machines. Natl. geog. 112: 170-1 (col.) Aug '57.

jewels, British royal. See British royal jewels.

——, royal. Int. gr. soc.: Arts . . . p. 165 (col.).

——, Russian. See Russian state jewels.

Jewett, Frank B. Cur. biog. p. 284 (1946).

Jewish (sym.). Lehner: Pict. bk. of sym., p. 34-8.

Jewish morality pictures. See morality pictures, Jewish.

Jewish orphan children (Israeli). Natl. geog. 98: 723 (col.) Dec '50.

Jewish pilgrims (Mt. Zion). Natl. geog. 102: 840 Dec '52.

Jewish school children & teacher. Natl. geog. 110: 712-3 Dec '56.

Jewish sukkah. See sukkah, Jewish.

Jewish theological seminary. Holiday 10: 52 Sept '51.

Jews (feast day). Natl. geog. 115: 519 (col.) Ap '59.

Jhelum river. Natl. geog. 114: 612-3 (col.) Nov '58.

jigger. Holiday 21: 198 Ap '57.

——, silver. Holiday 26: 200 Nov '59.

Jiménez, Juan Ramon. Cur. biog. p. 280 (1957).

Jimerson, Earl W. Cur. biog. p. 319 (1948).

jingle bells (Christmas). Lehner: Pict. bk. of sym., p. 50.

Jinnah, Mohammed Ali. Cur. biog. p. 417 (1942).

jinricksha. See jinrikisha.

jinrikisha. Holiday 24: 91 (col.) Aug '58.

—— (Chinese). Natl. geog. 102: 288 Sept '52.

Jizo (sym.). Lehner: Pict. bk. of sym., p. 48.

Joachim, Joseph. Cooper: Con. ency. of music, p. 144.

"Joachim & Anne" (wooden figure). Con. ency. of ant., vol. 3, pl. 54.

Joan of Arc. See Jeanne d'Arc.

jockey. Holiday 14: 23 (col.). Jl '53.
Int. gr. soc.: Arts . . . p. 153 (col.).

—— (horse, comic). Holiday 22: 41 Sept '57.

—— (horse, early Eng.). Con. 137: VIII Ap '56.

—— (horse race). Holiday 23: 28 Je '58; 24: 91 Jl '58, 109 Aug '58.

—— (horse racer). Holiday 21: 38 May '57.

—— (horseback). Con. 135: XII Mar '55; 136: XXIX Nov '55; 141: XII (col.) Ap '58; 144: 113 (col.) Nov '59.
Holiday 16: cover Sept '54; 18: 65 Sept '55; 25: 196 (col.) May '59; 26: 39 (col.) Nov '59.
Natl. geog. 109: 464 (col.) Ap '56.

jockey (horseback, jumping). Face of Amer., p. 18 (col.).
Holiday 9: inside cover (col.) Mar '51.
—— (wood carved figure). Amer. heri. vol. 2 no. 2 p. 32 (col.) (winter '51).
——, Parisian. Natl. geog. 101: 799 (col.) Je '52.
jockey hitching post. *See* hitching post, jockey.
"The jockeys" (Degas). Praeg. pict. ency., p 417 (col.).
Jodoin, Claude. Cur. biog. p. 309 (1956).
Joesten, Joachim. Cur. biog. p. 419 (1942).
Jogues, Isaac (martyred). Amer. heri. vol. 10 no. 6 p. 54 (Oct '56).
"Johann Strauss" (cruise ship, Vienna). Disney: People & places, p. 56 (col.).
Johannesburg (Africa). Holiday 18: 46-51 Aug '55; 20: 69 (col.) Oct '56.
Johannesen, Grant. Cur. biog. p. 221 (1961).
Johansson, Ingemar. Cur. biog. p. 209 (1959).
John XXIII, Pope. *See* Pope John XXIII.
"John, Duke of Marlborough". Con. 145: XL-VII Mar '60.
"John, 4th earl of Sandwich" (Beach). Con. 135: 241 Je '55.
John, Augustus (work of). Con. 129: 25 Ap '52; 132: 50 Sept '53; 133: 190 May '54; 143: 105 Ap '59; 144: 12 Sept '59.
John, Augustus E. Cur. biog. p. 437 (1941).
John, John P. Cur. biog. p. 311 (1956).
John Brown's raid. *See* Brown's raid, John.
John Bull (sym., Eng.). Lehner: Pict. bk. of sym., p. 93.
—— (cartoon). Holiday 23: 64 Ap '58.
"John Simeon & King George III playing cards" (Zoffany). Con. 132: 196 (col.) Jan '54.
"John the Baptist" (Gessi). Con. 144: 22 Sept '59.
"John the Baptist as a boy" (Reynolds). Natl. geog. 108: 317 (col.) Sept '55.
John the Baptist. *See* also St. John the Baptist.
"Johnnie Walker" (Scotch). Holiday 25: 34 (col.) May '59; 26: 58 (col.) Dec '59; 28: 87 (col.) Sept '60, 180 (col.) Oct '60.
Johnny Appleseed (cartoon). Amer. heri. vol. 1 no. 3 p. 74 (spring '50).
Johnson, Alvin. Cur. biog. p. 422 (1942).
Johnson, Pres. Andrew. Amer. heri. vol. 7 no. 3 p. 32 (Ap '56); vol. 8 no. 1 p. 20 (Dec '56); vol. 9 no. 2 p. 13 (Feb '58); vol. 9 no. 6 p. 42 (Oct '58); vol. 11 no. 1 p. 60, 110 (Dec '59).
Jensen: The White House, p. 96-101.
—— (campaign poster). Amer. heri. vol. 7 no. 4 p. 26 (col.) (Je '56).
—— (cartoon). Amer. heri. vol. 8 no. 1 p. 102 (Dec '56).
Johnson, Mrs. Andrew. Jensen: The White House, p. 96.
Johnson, Arnold M. Cur. biog. p. 298 (1955).
Johnson, Ban. Amer. heri. vol. 11 no. 4 p. 27 (Je '60).
Johnson, Rev. Charles Oscar. Cur. biog. p. 321 (1948).
Johnson, Charles Spurgeon. Cur. biog. p. 286 (1946).

Johnson, Cornelius (work of). Con. 140: 231 Jan '58.
Johnson, Crockett. Cur. biog. p. 346 (1943).
Johnson, David M. Cur. biog. p. 291 (1952).
Johnson, Earl F. Natl. geog. 113: 458 Ap '58.
Johnson, Edward. Amer. heri. vol. 3 no. 2 p. 33 (winter '52).
Cur. biog. p. 347 (1943).
Holiday 8: 76 Nov '50.
Johnson, Edwin C. Cur. biog. p. 288 (1946).
Johnson, Frank Tenney (work of). Con. 144: LXXVI Dec '59.
Johnson, Guy. Amer. heri. vol. 3 no. 3 p. 20 (col.) (spring '52).
—— (work of). Amer. heri. vol. 10 no. 3 p. 50 (Ap '59).
Johnson, Hall. Cur. biog. p. 305 (1945).
Johnson, Herschel V. Cur. biog. p. 291 (1946).
Johnson, Rev. Hewlett. Cur. biog. p. 350 (1943).
Johnson, Hiram. Cur. biog. p. 439 (1941).
Johnson, Holger J. Cur. biog. p. 278 (1950).
Johnson, John Monroe. Cur. biog. p. 307 (1945).
Johnson, Joseph B. Cur. biog. p. 313 (1956).
Johnson, Joseph E. Cur. biog. p. 280 (1950).
Johnson, Joseph T. Cur. biog. p. 292 (1952).
Johnson, Leroy. Cur. biog. p. 297 (1949).
Johnson, Lt. Col. Louis. Cur. biog. p. 424 (1942).
Johnson, Sec. of defense Louis. Holiday 7: 60 (col.) Feb '50.
Johnson, Louis A. Cur. biog. p. 299 (1949).
Johnson, Lyndon B. Cur. biog. p. 309 (1951).
Holiday 15: 57 Feb '54.
—— (cartoon). U.S. news and world report p. 25 Aug 31, 1964.
—— (family). U.S. News & world report, p. 20, Aug, 31 '64.
Johnson, Malcolm. Cur. biog. p. 301 (1949).
Johnson, Margaret Sweet. Jun. bk. of auth., p. 172.
Johnson, Martha Patterson. Jensen: The White House, p. 96.
Johnson, Mordecai Wyatt. Cur. biog. p. 442 (1941).
Johnson, Nunnally. Cur. biog. p. 443 (1941).
Holiday 5: 42 (col.) Jan '49.
Johnson, Pamela Hansford. Cur. biog. p. 322 (1948).
Johnson, Philip C. Cur. biog. p. 283 (1957).
Holiday 26: 61 Oct '59.
Johnson, Rafer L. Cur. biog. p. 223 (1961).
Johnson, Robert L. Cur. biog. p. 324 (1948).
Johnson, Robert Wood. Cur. biog. p. 352 (1943).
Johnson, Row W. Cur. biog. p. 213 (1958).
Johnson, Samuel. Amer. heri. vol. 1 no. 4 p. 54 (summer '50); vol. 5 no. 1 p. 15 (fall '53).
Holiday 11: 14 Feb '52.
Johnson, Dr. Samuel (Opie). Natl. geog. 105: 453 (col.) Ap '54.
—— (Reynolds). Natl. geog. 108: 321 Sept '55.
—— (statue). Natl. geog. 98: 187 Aug '50.
Johnson, Siddie Joe. Jun. bk. of auth., p. 173.
Johnson, Thomasina Walker. Cur. biog. p. 336 (1947).

Johnson, Thor. Cur. biog. p. 304 (1949).
Johnson, Ural Alexis. Cur. biog. p. 300 (1955).
Johnson, Van. Cur. biog. p. 309 (1945).
Johnson, Walter. Amer. heri. vol. 10 no. 3 p. 22 (Ap '59).
Cur. biog. p. 284 (1957).
Johnson, Wendell A. Cur. biog. p. 212 (1959).
Johnson, William. Amer. heri. vol. 3 no. 3 p. 20 (col.) (spring '52); vol. 7 no. 1 p. 111 (Dec '55); vol. 10 no. 3 p. 46 (col.) (Ap '59).
—— (statue). Amer. heri. vol. 3 no. 3 p. 25 (spring '52).
Johnson, Wm. & King Hendrick (statue). Amer. heri. vol. 3 no. 3 p. 25 (spring '52).
Johnson, William F. Natl. geog. 113: 459 Ap '58.
Johnson, Dr. William Samuel. Con. 136: 310 Jan '56.
—— (Stuart). Con. 133: 210 May '54.
"Johnson Hall" (Johnstown, N.Y.). Amer. heri. vol. 3 no. 3 p. 21 (col.), 22-3 (spring '52); vol. 10 no. 3 p. 48-9 (col.) (Ap '59).
Johnson's home, Andrew (Raleigh, S.C.). Travel 114: 36 Sept '60.
Johnson's home, Sir. William. Amer. heri. vol. 10 no. 3 p. 48-9 (col.) (Ap '59).
Johnson's impeachment trial. Andrew. Amer. heri. vol. 8 no. 1 p. 24 (Dec '56).
Johnson's log cabin, Andrew (presidential candidate). Amer. heri. vol. 7 no. 5 p. 33 (Aug '56).
Johnson's wax admin. bldg. See wax adminis. bldg., Johnson's.
Johnston, Albert Sidney. Pakula: Cent. album, p. 171.
Johnston, Alvanley. Cur. biog. p. 293 (1946).
Johnston, Clement D. Cur. biog. p 303 (1955).
Johnston, Eric A. Cur. biog. p. 354 (1943); p. 304 (1955).
Johnston, Joseph E. Pakula: Cent. album, p. 173.
Johnston, Olin D. Cur. biog. p. 312 (1951).
Johnston, Victor. Cur. biog. p. 305 (1949).
Johnston, Wayne A. Cur. biog. p. 313 (1951).
Johnston, Ynez (painting by). Con. 142: XLI Dec '58.
Johnstone, Rev. Margaret Blair. Cur. biog. p. 307 (1955).
Johnstone, Ralph. Amer. heri. vol. 7 no. 3 p. 7 (Ap '56).
Johnstown flood. Holiday 21: 84-5 Je '57.
"Join or die" (cartoon). Amer. heri. vol. 7 no. 2 p. 7 (Feb '56).
joined stool. See stool, joined.
joints, human body. Gray's anatomy, p. 261, 292-305, 312-35.
Joli, Antonio (work of). Con. 140: 98 Nov '57; 141: XXV Mar '58; 145: XXV Je '60.
Joliot-Curie, Frederic. Cur. biog. p. 295 (1946).
"Jolly Roger" (pirate flag). Lehner: Pict. bk. of sym., p. 86.
Jolson, Al. Int. gr. soc.: Arts . . . p. 149 (col.).
Jonah's tomb. Natl. geog. 99: 47 Jan '51.
Jonasson, Hermann. Cur. biog. p. 445 (1941).
Jones, Anson. Amer. heri. vol. 4 no. 1 p. 22 (fall '52).
Jones, Arthur Creech. Cur. biog. p. 325 (1948).
Jones, Barry. Cur. biog. p. 214 (1958).
Jones, Billy. Cur. biog. p. 446 (1941).

Jones, Calven A. (work of). Con. 143 LXV Je '59.
Jones, Candy. Cur. biog. p. 225 (1961).
Jones, Elizabeth Orton. Jun. bk. of auth., p. 174.
Jones, George (work of). Con. 129: 82 Je '52.
Jones, Sir Harold Spencer. Cur. biog. p. 309 (1955).
Jones, Howard P. Cur. biog. p. 210 (1963).
Jones, Idwal. Cur. biog. p. 328 (1948).
Jones, James. Holiday 23: 48 Feb '58.
Jones, Jenkin Lloyd. Amer. heri. vol. 9 no. 2 p. 67 (Feb '58).
Jones, Jennifer. Cur. biog. p. 330 (1944).
Jones, Joe (work of). Amer. heri. vol. 2 no. 4 p. 67 (col.) (summer '51).
Jones, John Paul. Amer. heri. vol. 6 no. 3 p. 45 (col.) (Ap '55).
—— (bust). Amer. heri. vol. 5 no. 4 p. 15 (summer '54).
Jones, John Percival. Amer. heri. vol. 6 no. 1 p. 66 (fall '54).
Jones, Lewis Webster. Cur. biog. p. 215 (1958).
Jones, Marvin. Cur. biog. p. 357 (1943).
Jones, Paul. Con. 129: 135 Je '52.
Jones, Richard (work of). Con. 134: XXI Nov '54.
Jones, Robert Edmond. Cur. biog. p. 298 (1946).
Jones, Roger W. Cur. biog. p. 214 (1959).
Jones, Rufus M. Cur. biog. p. 447 (1941).
Jones, Russell. Cur. biog. p. 286 (1957).
Jones, Shirley. Cur. biog. p. 226 (1961).
Jones, William ("Canada Bill"). Horan: Pict. hist. of wild west, p. 79.
Jones beach (N.Y.). Holiday 12: 114 (col.) Jl '52.
Jones beach marine theatre. Travel 112: 10 Jl '59.
Jones' grave, John Paul. See grave of John Paul Jones.
Jonghe, Ludolf de. See De Jonghe, Ludolf.
Jongkind, J.B. (work of). Con. 135: XIII Ap '55.
"jonkeys" race. Natl. geog. 109: 228 (col.) Feb '56.
Jonsson, John Erik. Cur. biog. p. 228 (1961).
Jooste, Gerhardus P. Cur. biog. p. 315 (1951).
Jorda, Enrique. Holiday 22: 121 Sept '57.
Jordaens, Jacob (work of). Con. 129: cover (col.) Je '52; 143: 106 Ap '59, XXV Je '59.
Natl. geog. 97: 747 (col.) Je '50.
Jordan, B. Everett. Cur. biog. p. 216 (1959).
Jordan, Mildred. Cur. biog. p. 317 (1951).
Jordan, Dr. Sara M. Cur. biog. p. 368 (1954).
Jordan, Virgil. Cur. biog. p. 337 (1947).
Jordan, Wilbur K. Cur. biog. p. 311 (1955).
Jordan. Natl. geog. 102: 842-55 Dec '52.
—— (map). Natl. geog. 104: 856 Dec '53; 114: 790 Dec '58.
—— (Rose-red city of Petra). Travel 105: 22 Jan '56.
Jordan auto (1927). Int. gr. soc.: Arts . . . p. 161 (col.).
Jordan river. Holiday 17: 41 (col.) Feb '55.
Natl. geog. 102: 833 Dec '52.

Jordan valley (map). Natl. geog. 112: 838 Dec '57.

Jordana, Francisco Gomez. Cur. biog. p. 331 (1944).

Jorgenson, William (work of). Amer. heri. vol. 6 no. 5 p. 38-9 (col.) (Aug '55).

Josef, Franz, Emperor. Holiday 18: 19 Nov '55.

Joseph, Sister Mary. Cur. biog. p. 426 (1942).

"Joseph & the wife of Potiphar" (Cignani). Con. 144: 21 Sept '59.

"Joseph interpreting dreams" (Eeckhout). Con. 132: XII (col.) Nov '53.

"Joseph receiving sheaves of grain from the pyramids" (mosaic). Ceram: March of arch., p. 94.

"Joseph sold in bondage." Amer. heri. vol. 7 no. 1 p. 60 (col.) (Dec '55).

Josephine, Empress. Holiday 25: 71 Je '59.
—— (statue). Holiday 5: 109 Mar '49.

Josephs, Devereux C. Cur. biog. p. 298 (1953).

Joshua tree natl. monument. Natl. geog. 112: 721 (col.) Nov '57.

joss house, Chinese. Holiday 12: 64 (col.) Oct '52.

joss-stick holders. Con. 139: V Mar '57.
—— holders. See also Chinese biscuit joss stick holders.

Jouhaux, Leon. Cur. biog. p. 329 (1948).

Jouvet, Louis. Cur. biog. p. 307 (1949).

Jowitt, Sir William Allen. Cur. biog. p. 449 (1941).

Joxe, Louis. Cur. biog. p. 230 (1961).

Joy, Vice-Adm. C. Turner. Cur. biog. p. 318 (1951).

Joy, Thomas Musgrove (work of). Con. 129: XLVI Je '52.

joy (goddess of). Lehner: Pict. bk. of sym., p. 33.

Joyce, J. Avery. Cur. biog. p. 217 (1959).

Joyce, James. Holiday 6: 22 Aug '49.
—— (Blanche). Con. 133: 180 May '54.

Juan Carlos, Count of Barcelona. Cur. biog. p. 319 (1951).

Juarez, Benito. Amer. heri. vol. 11 no. 2 p. 103 (Feb '60).

Judaculla rock (N.C.). Travel 114: 39 Sept '60.

Judaism (sym.). Lehner: Pict. bk. of sym., p. 34-8.

Judd, Walter H. Cur. biog. p. 309 (1949).

judge (at court desk). Amer. heri. vol. 8 no. 4 p. 79 (Je '57).

"The judge" (Rouault). Con. 145: 208 May '60.

"Judge of the dead". Lehner: Pict. bk. of sym., p. 49.

"Judge to the millionaires". Amer. heri. vol. 10 no. 2 p. 6 (col.) (Feb '59).

"Judgement of Paris". Natl. geog. 110: 650-1 (col.) Nov '56.
—— (Etly). Con. 135: 220 Je '55.
—— (Rubens). Praeg. pict. ency., p. 328 (col.).
—— (Utile da Faenza). Con. 140: 184 Dec '57.

"Judgement of Solomon" (Chretien). Con. 133: opp. p. 147 (col.) May '54.

"Judith & Holofernes" (Francia). Con. 135: 137 Ap '55.

judo, Japanese. Holiday 19: 30 May '56.

judo, Japanese-Amer. Holiday 7: 41 (col.) Jan '50.

Judson, Arthur. Cur. biog. p. 311 (1945).

Judson, Clara Ingram. Cur. biog. p. 332 (1948). Jun. bk. of auth., p. 175.

Juel, Jens (work of). Con. 135: 48 Mar '55.

jug (on woman's head, desert). Natl. geog. 112: 67 (col.) Jl '57.
—— (Ürgüp woman carrying). Natl. geog. 113: 132 Jan '58.
——, alabaster wine. Natl. geog. 108: 643 (col.) Nov '55.
——, Alaja Hoyük (silver). Osward: Asia Minor, pl. 14.
——, Amer. glass. Con. 135: 172 May '55.
——, antique. Con. ency. of ant., vol. 1, pl. 169.

Con. 136: XI Jan '56; 143: 145 May '59.
——, antique on stand (Storr silver). Con. 140: XXXIII Jan '58.
——, beer (George II). Con. 136: LVI Dec '55.
——, beer (George III). Con. 140: XLVI Dec '57.
——, beer (George III silver). Con. 136: XIX Jan '56; 145: VII Ap '60.
——, beer (Irish, 18th cent.). Con. 145: XCII May '60.
——, blueware. Rawson: Ant. pict. bk., p. 87.
——, Chelsea. Con. 145: XXXVIII Je '60.
——, Chinese porcelain. Con. 139: 182 May '57.
——, cream (antique silver). Con. 136: 261 Jan '56.
——, creamware (antique). Con. 133: 48 Mar '54.
——, Danish silver (Bernadotte). Con. 134: 129 Nov '54.
——, Delft (antique). Con. 127: 21-2 Mar '51.
——, earthenware. Natl. geog. 112: 753 (col.) Dec '57.
——, Elizabethan. Con. 141: LV Mar '58.
——, Elizabethan tiger ware. Con. 134: 51 Sept '54.
——, Fahlstrom (18th cent.). Con. 144: 103 Nov '59.
——, George I (silver). Con. 140: XIII Nov '57.
——, George I (silver hot water). Con. 133: IX Ap '54.
——, George II (silver covered). Con. 141: XXXVI Mar '58.
——, George III (hot water). Con. 136: XLV Sept '55.
——, Isnik. Con. 140: 249 Jan '58.
——, Mary Tudor. Con. 139: 29 Mar '57.
——, mask. Con. 136: XIII Sept '55.
——, Meissen. Con. 138: XXXI Dec '56.
——, mushroom. Holiday 10: 19 Jl '51.
——, Persian bronze (12th cent.). Praeg. pict. ency., p. 562.
——, Portuguese (silver antique). Con. 137: 14 Mar '56.
——, pottery cow milk (antique). Con. 135: XVI Je '55.
——, Prince Hal. Con. 132: LXVIII Jan '54.

jug, Queen Anne (silver). Con. 136: XXXVII Sept '55; 137: VII Ap '56; 140: 258 Jan '58.

——, Queen Anne milk (silver). Con. 136: XXXI Dec '55.

——, Rhodian (7th cent. B.C.). Praeg. pict. ency., p. 137.

——, St. Cloud porcelain. Con. 141: 76 Ap '58.

——, shaving (18th cent silver). Con. 132: 61 Sept '53.

——, shaving See also jug & basin, shaving.

——, silver lustre. Con. 136: XXXVIII Jan '56.

——, silver. Holiday 27: 160 Je '60.

——, silver (19th cent.). Con. 134: XLV Sept '54.

——, stone (1860). Holiday 18: 61 (col.) Jl '55.

——, tigerware. Con. 140: 115 Nov '57.

——, tigerware (1560). Con. ency. of ant., vol. 1, p. 81.

——, wall period. Con. 135: XLIV Mar '55.

——, water. See water jug.

——, Wm. Penn's brew. Rawson: Ant. pict. bk., p. 87.

——, wine. See wine jug.

——, Worcester. Con. 143: LVI Je '59.

——, Worcester (18th cent.). Con. ency. of ant., vol. 1, pl. 53.

jug & basin, shaving (antique). Con. 137: 125 Ap '56.

jug & cover, silver (Louis XV). Con. 144: X-XIII Dec '59.

——, silver (Marsh, 1748). Con. 143: XLV Je '59.

"jug band". Holiday 11: 59 Feb '52.

juggernauts, steel (Antarctic). Natl. geog. 112: 396-7 (col.) Sept '57.

juggler. Holiday 21: 195 (col.) Je '57.

——, circus. Durant: Pict. hist. of Amer. circus, p. 234.

jugglers. Durant: Pict. hist. of Amer. circus, p. 8.

jugs, Antique. Rawson: Ant. pict. bk., p. 88.

——, Bennington. Rawson: Ant. pict. bk., p. 91.

——, clay. Natl. geog. 112: 850, 853 (col.) Dec '57.

——, Queen Anne (silver). Con. 134: 197 Dec '54.

——, silver. Con. 136: III Sept '55.

Juin, Gen. Alphonse. Cur. biog. p. 358 (1943).

juke box. Holiday 26: 153 Nov '59.

jukskei (African game). Holiday 21: 38 (col.) Feb '57.

Julian, Dr. Percy. Holiday 28: 80 Dec '60.

Julian, Percy L. Cur. biog. p. 339 (1947).

Juliana, Crown Princess of the Netherlands. Cur. biog. p. 334 (1944).

Juliana, Queen of Netherlands. Cur. biog. p. 313 (1955).
Holiday 10: 53-5 (part col.) Nov '51.
Natl. geog. 102: 145 Aug '52.

Juliana, Queen, & Prince Bernhard. Natl. geog. 104: 678 (col.) Nov '53.

Julien, Pierre (terracotta work). Con. 140: 7 Sept '57.

Julius Caesar. See Caesar, Julius.

jumping, high. Natl. geog. 101: 362 Mar '52.

Juneau (Alaska). Holiday 14: 104 (col.) Jl '53. Natl. geog. 109: 739 (col.) Je '56; 116: 44-5 (col.) Jl '59.

Jung, Carl Gustav. Cur. biog. p. 360 (1943); p. 300 (1953).

Jungfrau mt. Natl. geog. 108: 138 Jl '55.

jungfrauenbecher, silver. Con. ency. of ant., vol. 3, p. 67.

jungle (Angkor). Natl. geog. 117: 517-69 (part col.) Ap '60.

—— (Brazil). See Brazil (Amazon jungle).

"Jungle gardens" (Sarasota, Fla.). Holiday 15: 98 (col.) Feb '54.

Jordan: Hammond's pict. atlas, p. 70 (col.). Natl. geog. 113: 46-7 (col.) Jan '58. Travel 114: 28 Dec '60.

jungle gym, playground. Holiday 10: 88 Aug '51.

jungle people (Nigeria & Cameroons). Natl. geog. 116: 220-53 (col.) Aug '59, 781-5 (col.) Dec '59.

Junipero Serra museum. See museum, Junipero Serra.

junk, Chinese (boat). Natl. geog. 97: 381, 383-5 Mar '50; 116: 855 (col.) Dec '59.

——, Chinese (1st to visit Amer.). Amer. heri. vol. 9 no. 5 p. 23 (col.) (Aug '58).

——, Okinawa. Natl. geog. 97: 543 Ap '50.

junks, Chinese fishing. Natl. geog. 103: 683 (col.) May '53.

——, fishing. Natl. geog. 102: 308 (col.) Sept '52.

——, freight. Natl. geog. 105: 252 (col.) Feb '54.

——, Hong Kong. See Hong Kong junks.

Juno (sym.). Lehner: Pict. bk. of sym., p. 30.

"Juno" (Balestra). Con. 134: 5 Sept '54.

—— (Rembrandt). Con. 145: XIII Mar '60.

"Juno, Jupiter, Io" (Fragonard). Con. 140: 54 Sept '57.

Jupiter (magic square). Lehner: Pict. bk. of sym., p. 25.

—— (statue). Int. gr. soc.: Arts . . . p. 17 (col.).

—— (sym.). Lehner: Pict. bk. of sym., p. 30.

"Jupiter & a mare" (Stubbs). Con. 145: 142 (col.) May '60.

Jurade of St. Emilion (France). Holiday 26: 95 (col.) Aug '59.

Jurinac, Sena (as the composer in Ariadne auf Naxos). Cooper: Con. ency. of music, p. 145.

jurisprudence (sym.). Lehner: Pict. bk. of sym., p. 13.

Jusserand, Jean Jules. Amer. heri. vol. 7 no. 2 p. 23 (Feb '56).

justice (on card). Lehner: Pict. bk. of sym., p. 76.

"Justice for English Jim" (Prendergast). Amer. heri. vol. 1 no. 3 p. 45 (col.) (spring '50).

Justus, May. Jun. bk. of auth., p. 176.

jute bale. Natl. geog. 107: 401 (col.) Mar '55.

Juventas (sym.). Lehner: Pict. bk. of sym., p. 30.

K

Kaaba (Mecca). Holiday 20: 57 Dec '56. Natl. geog. 104: 26-9, 32 (col.) Jl '53.

—— ("Navel of the world"). Natl. geog. 104: 2 (col.) Jl '53.

Kabotie, Fred (work of). Natl. geog. 107: 368 (col.) Mar '55.

Kabuki actor (Japan, theater). Natl. geog. 118: 739 (col.) Dec '60.

Kabul (Afghanistan). Natl. geog. 98: 675 Nov '50; 104: 422-31 Sept '53.

—— **(market place).** Natl. geog. 114: 6 Jl '58.

Kachina, Indian. Holiday 12: 13 Jl '52. Travel 110: 16 Sept '58.

Kachinas. Natl. geog. 112: 218, 226 (col.), 235 Aug '57.

Kadar, Janos. Cur. biog. p. 288 (1957).

Kadikoy. Osward: Asia Minor, pl. IV (col.).

Kaempffert, Waldemar. Cur. biog. p. 363 (1943).

Kaganovitch, Lazar Moiseyevitch. Cur. biog. p. 428 (1942); p. 315 (1955).

Kagawa, Toyohiko. Cur. biog. p. 451 (1941).

kago, Japanese (woman riding in). Natl. geog. 104: 633 (col.) Nov '53.

Kahane, Melanie. Cur. biog. p. 219 (1959).

Kahmann, Chesley. Cur. biog. p. 293 (1952).

Kahn, Albert. Cur. biog. p. 430 (1942).

Kahn, Ely Jacques. Cur. biog. p. 314 (1945).

Kahn, Herman. Cur. biog. p. 225 (1962).

Kailasa temple (India). Natl. geog. 103: 672-3 May '53.

Kaiser, Henry J. Cur. biog. p. 433 (1942); p. 231 (1961).

Kaiser, Jakob. Cur. biog. p. 315 (1956).

Kaiser, John B. Cur. biog. p. 366 (1943).

Kaiser, Philip M. Cur. biog. p. 310 (1949).

Kaiser auto. Holiday 8: 82 (col.) Oct '50, 92 (col.) Dec '50.

Kaiser mts. (Alps). Holiday 27: 45 Jan '60.

Kaleri (Nigeria jungle tribe). Natl. geog. 116: 228-53 (part col.) Aug '59.

Kali goddess (statue). Natl. geog. 118: 501 (col.) Oct '60.

Kalinin, Mikhail. Cur. biog. p. 435 (1942).

Kallay De Nagy Kallo, Miklos. Cur. biog. p. 437 (1942).

Kallen, Horace M. Cur. biog. p. 302 (1953).

Kalmar castle. Natl. geog. 98: 640 (col.) Nov '50.

Kalmus, Herbert T. Cur. biog. p. 312 (1949).

Kaltenborn, H. V. Holiday 22: 149 Dec '57.

Kaltenbrunner, Ernest. Cur. biog. p. 367 (1943).

Kambara (Fiji is.). Holiday 28: 57 (col.) Oct '60.

Kamehameha the Great. Amer. heri. vol. 2 no. 3 p. 31 (spring '51).

Kamehameha I. Amer. heri. vol. 11 no. 2 p. 18 (col.) (Feb '60).

Kamehameha III, King of Hawaii (1825-54). Amer. heri. vol. 11 no. 2 cover (col.) (Feb '60).

Kamouraska (Canada, harbor). Natl. geog. 98: 349 Sept '50.

Kampala (Africa). Natl. geog. 106: 722- (col.) Dec '54.

"kampf" (for water). Rawson: Ant. pict. bk., p. 41.

Kampmann, Viggo. Cur. biog. p. 234 (1961).

Kanawha river (W. Va.). Holiday 14: 99 (col.) Oct '53.

Kandinsky, Wassily (work of). Con. 144: 181 (col.) Dec '59. Praeg. pict. ency., p. 488 (col.)

Kandy (Ceylon, temple). Travel 111: 23 Jan '59.

Kandy dancers. See Ceylon dancers.

Kandyan headmen). Holiday 20: 99 (col.) Aug '56; 28: 104 (col.) Oct '60.

Kane, Harnett T. Cur. biog. p. 341 (1947).

Kane, Col. John R. Holiday 27: 85 Mar '60.

Kane, Paul. Amer. heri. vol. 10 no. 5 p. 45 (Aug '59).

—— **(work of)** Amer. heri. vol. 10 no. 5 cover, 42-54 (part col.) (Aug '59).

Kangaroo is. (Kingscote harbor). Travel 112: 45 Dec '59.

Kangiten shoten. Lehner: Pict. bk. of sym., p. 49.

Kanin, Garson. Cur. biog. p. 454 (1941); p. 295 (1952).

Kannon. Lehner: Pict. bk. of sym., p. 48.

Kano (Africa). Natl. geog. 104: 147, 149, 153, 156 (col.) Aug '53.

Kansas. Natl. geog. 101: 462-90 (part col.) Ap '52.

—— **(memorial cemetery).** Face of Amer., p. 42-3 (col.).

Kansas City (Mo.). Holiday 7: 46-56 (part col.) Mar '50.

—— **(Mo., 1855).** Amer. heri. vol. 8 no. 1 p. 126 (Dec '56).

Kansas state college (Picken Hall). Natl. geog. 101: 490 (col.) Ap '52.

Kanter, Albert L. Cur. biog. p. 305 (1953).

Kanzler, Ernest C. Cur. biog. p. 438 (1942).

Kapell, William. Cur. biog. p. 333 (1948).

Kapingamarangi (Polynesia is.). Natl. geog. 97: 524-52 (part col.) Ap '50.

Kapitza, Peter L. Cur. biog. p. 318 (1955).

Kaplan, Joseph. Cur. biog. p. 317 (1956).

Kappel, Frederick R. Cur. biog. p. 290 (1957).

Kaprun dam (Alps). Natl. geog. 99: 774 Je '51.

Karachi. Natl. geog. 102: 645, 651 (col.), 662, 677 Nov '52; 117: 604-5, 609 (col.) May '60.

Karajan, Herbert von. Cur. biog. p. 319 (1956). Holiday 25: 64 (col.) Jan '59.

Karamanlis, Constantine E. Cur. biog. p. 321 (1956).

Karami, Rashid. Cur. biog. p. 221 (1959).

Karbala minaret. See minaret (Karbala).

Kardec tomb, Allan. See tomb, Allan Kardec.

Kardelj, Edvard. Cur. biog. p. 314 (1949).

Karfiol, Bernard. Cur. biog. p. 342 (1947).

Kariba dam (Rhodesia). Natl. geog. 116: 219 Aug '59; 118: 334 (col.) Sept '60.

Karloff, Boris. Cur. biog. p. 455 (1941).

Karlsten fortress (Sweden). Natl. geog. 98: 614 (col.) Nov '50.

Karnak temple of Amon. Praeg. pict. ency., p. 21.

Karnak temple pillar. See column, Karnak temple.

Karoloff, Boris. Cur. biog. p. 455 (1941).

Karp, David. Cur. biog. p. 292 (1957).

Karsh, Yousuf. Cur. biog. p. 296 (1952).

Kasavubu, Joseph. Cur. biog. p. 236 (1961).

Kase, Toshikazu. Cur. biog. p. 293 (1957).

Kashgai (Iran). Natl. geog. 101: 806-32 (part col.) Je '52.

Kashgais encampment. Natl. geog. 100: 463 (col.) Oct '51.
Kashmir (India). Holiday 14: 110 (col.) Aug '53.
  Travel 105: 53-4 Feb '56.
—— (men embroiderers). Natl. geog. 114: 619 (col.) Nov '58.
——, Valley of. Holiday 11: 18 Je '52.
  Natl. geog. 114: 606-47 (part col.) Nov '58.
——, Valley of (map). Natl. geog. 114: 615 Nov '58.
Kashmir dancer. Natl. geog. 114: 634 (col.) Nov '58.
Kashmir homes, Valley of. Holiday 24: 53, 55 (col.) Sept '58.
Kasner, Edward. Cur. biog. p. 369 (1943).
Kassem, Abdul Karim. Cur. biog. p. 223 (1959).
Kastoria (Greece). Natl. geog. 109: 57 (col.) Jan '56.
—— (harbor). Travel 114: 19, 21 Aug '60.
Katahdin (Maine, climbers). Travel 113: 31-3 May '60.
Katayama, Tetsu. Cur. biog. p. 335 (1948).
Kate Kearney's cottage (Ireland). Natl. geog. 104: 131 (col.) Jl '53.
Kathin priest. See priest, Kathin.
Katmai crater (Alaska). Natl. geog. 109: 755-9 (col.) Je '56; 113: 632 (col.) May '58.
Katmandu (Nepal). Natl. geog. 97: 32 (col.) Jan '50; 112: 138-52 (part col.) Jl '57; 117: 396 (col.) Mar '60.
Katsh, Abraham. Cur. biog. p. 227 (1962).
Katz, Label A. Cur. biog. p. 209 (1960).
Katz, Milton. Cur. biog. p. 282 (1950).
Katz castle (Rhine). Holiday 25: 67 (col.) May '59.
Katz-Suchy, Juliusz. Cur. biog. p. 322 (1951).
Kauffmann, Angelica (Benton). Con. 135: 191 (col.) May '55.
—— (work of). Con. 142: XIII Sept '58; 143: XLIV (col.) Je '59.
Kauffmann, Henrik. Cur. biog. p. 323 (1956).
Kaufman, George S. Cur. biog. p. 457 (1941).
Kaufman, Judge Irving R. Cur. biog. p. 307 (1953).
Kaukauna (Wis., paper mills). Natl. geog. 111: 166 Feb '57.
Kaur, Rajkumari Amrit. Cur. biog. p. 320 (1955).
Kavalla (Greece). Natl. geog. 109: 63 (col.) Jan '56.
Kawakami, Jotaro. Cur. biog. p. 212 (1963).
Kay, Beatrice. Cur. biog. p. 440 (1942).
Kay, Hershy. Cur. biog. p. 229 (1962).
kayak (Eskimo boat). Holiday 26: 41 (col.) Aug '59.
  Natl. geog. 109: 775 (col.) Je '56; 114: 67, 73 (col.) Jl '58.
—— (Greenland). Natl. geog. 100: 494-5, 506 (col.) Oct '51.
kayaks (Nile river). Natl. geog. 107: 697-731 May '55.
Kaye, Danny. Cur. biog. p. 460 (1941); p. 299 (1952).
  Holiday 7: 49 (col.) Je '50.
  Travel 107: 16-8 Ap '57.
—— (profile). Holiday 26: 77 Aug '59.
Kaye, Nora. Cur. biog. p. 309 (1953).
Kayseri. See Caesarea.

Kazak family (China). Natl. geog. 99: 385 Mar '51.
Kazakhs (in Kashmir). Natl. geog. 106: 622-44 (part col.) Nov '54.
Kazan, Elia. Cur. biog. p. 337 (1948).
Kazantzakis, Nikos. Cur. biog. p. 321 (1955).
Kearney cottage, Kate (Ireland). See Kate Kearney's cottage.
Kearns, Carroll D. Cur. biog. p. 325 (1956).
Kearns, Nora Lynch. Cur. biog. p. 327 (1956).
Keating, Kenneth B. Cur. biog. p. 283 (1950).
  U.S. News & world report, p. 33, Aug 31, 1964.
Keck, George Fred. Cur. biog. p. 316 (1945).
Keck, Lucile L. Cur. biog. p. 370 (1954).
Kedleston Hall (Derbyshire, dining room). Con. ency. of ant., vol. 3, pl. 9.
—— (int.). Holiday 23: 86 (col.) Ap '58.
Kee, Elizabeth. Cur. biog. p. 371 (1954).
Kee, John. Cur. biog. p. 285 (1950).
Keech, Richmond B. Cur. biog. p. 287 (1950).
keelboat. Amer. heri. vol. 2 no. 1 p. 46 (fall '50).
——, river. Natl. geog. 103: 719 (col.) Je '53.
keelboats (Madeira). Natl. geog. 115: 371 (col.) Mar '59.
Keeler, Ruby. Holiday 7: 62 Mar '50.
Keen, Dr. William W. Amer. heri. vol. 8 no. 6 p. 12 (Oct '57).
Keenan, Joseph B. Cur. biog. p. 301 (1946).
Keeney, Barnaby C. Cur. biog. p. 328 (1956).
Keeny, Spurgeon M. Cur. biog. p. 217 (1958).
Kefauver, Estes. Cur. biog. p. 316 (1949).
keg (distillery). Holiday 23: 12 (col.) Mar '58.
—— (St. Bernard dog, head). Holiday 10: 134 Oct '51, 114 Nov '51; 11: 118 Mar '52, 84 May '52.
  Natl. geog. 111: 53 (col.) Jan '57.
——, pickle. Natl. geog. 105: 314 (col.) Mar '54.
——, water (used at Erie canal opening). Amer. heri. vol. 2 no. 3 p. 63 (spring '51).
kegs, wine. Natl. geog. 115: 392 Mar '59.
Keighley, William. Cur. biog. p. 340 (1948).
Keil, Bernhart (work of). Con. 136: XXXIV Jan '56.
Keim, Georgie. Amer. heri. vol. 8 no. 3 p. 49 (col.) (Ap '57).
Keita, Modibo. Cur. biog. p. 210 (1960).
Keith, Harold. Cur. biog. p. 219 (1958).
Kekkonen, Urho K. Cur. biog. p. 288 (1950).
Keldyshi, Matislav V. Cur. biog. p. 231 (1962).
Kelheim, Bavaria (Hall of liberation). Praeg. pict. ency. p. 423.
Kellems, Vivien. Cur. biog. p. 341 (1948).
Keller, Helen. Cur. biog. p. 443 (1942).
  Natl. geog. 110: 254 Aug '56.
Keller, Rev. James. Cur. biog. p. 324 (1951).
Keller, Kaufman T. Cur. biog. p. 345 (1947).
Kellet, Col. (miniature). Con. ency. of ant., vol. 1, pl. 130.
Kelley, Augustine B. Cur. biog. p. 325 (1951).
Kelley, Benjamin F. Amer. heri. vol. 3 no. 4 p. 58 (summer '52).
Kelley, Daniel E. Amer. heri. vol. 1 no. 4 p. 9 (summer '50).
Kelley, James H. (dog). Horan: Pict. hist. of wild west, p. 108.
Kellogg, Winthrop N. Cur. biog. p. 214 (1963).

Kellogg breakfast food (cartoons). Amer. heri. vol. 8 no. 4 p. 65-85 (Je '57).
Kells, Book of. See Book of Kells.
Kelly, Edna F. Cur. biog. p. 290 (1950).
Kelly, Emmett. Cur. biog. p. 372 (1954).
Kelly, Eric P. Jun. bk. of auth., p. 177.
Kelly, Everett Lowell. Cur. biog. p. 323 (1955).
Kelly, Gene. Cur. biog. p. 318 (1945).
Kelly, Grace (Princess of Monaco). Cur. biog. p. 325 (1955).
  Holiday 24: 37 Aug '58.
Kelly, Joe. Cur. biog. p. 320 (1945).
Kelly, John (work of). Amer. heri. vol. 2 no. 3 p. 23 (col.) (spring '51).
Kelly, Judith. Cur. biog. p. 462 (1941).
Kelly, Luther. Travel 105: inside back cover Feb '56.
Kelly, Mervin J. Cur. biog. p. 329 (1956).
Kelly, Nancy. Cur. biog. p. 326 (1955).
Kelly, Lt. Oakley G. Natl. geog. 112: 279 Aug '57.
Kelly, Regina Z. Cur. biog. p. 331 (1956).
Kelly, Walt. Cur. biog. p. 333 (1956).
Kelsen, Hans. Cur. biog. p. 295 (1957).
Keltic lodge (Cape Breton, Canada). Holiday 14: 103 (col.) Sept '53.
Kelvedon Hall, garden of. See garden of Kelvedon Hall.
Kem, James P. Cur. biog. p. 292 (1950).
Kemano power development. Natl. geog. 110: 379, 381, 388-98 (part col.) Sept '56.
Kemano powerhouse (int.). Natl. geog. 110: 379 Sept '56.
Kemble, Gouverneur. Amer. heri. vol. 10 no. 1 p. 20 (col.) (Dec '58).
Kemmelmeyer, Frederick (work of). Amer. heri. vol. 9 no. 4 p. 56 (col.) (Je '58).
  Natl. geog. 99: 183 (col.) Feb '51.
Kemmerer, Edwin W. Cur. biog. p. 463 (1941).
Kemp, Hal. Cur. biog. p. 465 (1941).
Kemper, James Lawson. Pakula: Cent. album, p. 175.
Kemper, James S. Cur. biog. p. 466 (1941).
Kempner, Robert M.W. Cur. biog. p. 371 (1943).
Kemsley, Lord James Gomer. Cur. biog. p. 328 (1951).
Kenai lake (Alaska). Travel 108: 49 Jl '57.
Kendall, Amos. Amer. heri. vol. 7 no. 4 p. 103 (Je '56).
Kendall, Edward C. Cur. biog. p. 293 (1950).
Kendrew, John C. Cur. biog. p. 216 (1963).
Kendrick, Baynard H. Cur. biog. p. 303 (1946).
Kenilworth hotel (Miami Beach). Travel 103: 44 Feb '55.
Ken-L-Land (Disneyland). Travel 109: 41 Je '58.
"Kenmore". (1752 colonial mansion). Holiday 12: 60 (col.) Oct '52.
"Kenmore" (home of Washington's sister). Holiday 8: 27 (col.) Sept '50.
"Kenmore" (Fredericksburg, Va.). Travel 112: 32 Jl '59.
Kenna, Michael "Hinky Dink". Amer. heri. vol. 12 no. 1 p. 17 (Dec '60).
Kennan, George. Natl. geog. 117: 31 (col.) Jan '60.
Kennan, George F. Cur. biog. p. 347 (1947); p. 225 (1959).

Kennecott copper mill (Alaska). Natl. geog. 109: 791 (col.) Je '56.
Kennedy, Arthur. Cur. biog. p. 240 (1961).
Kennedy, Caroline. Jensen: the White House, p. 278, 280.
Kennedy, Edward M. Cur. biog. p. 218 (1963).
Kennedy, Jacqueline (Mrs. John F. Kennedy). Cur. biog. p. 238 (1961).
  Jensen: The White House, p. 278, 281-3, 286, 288.
—— (on elephant). Jensen: The White House, p. 284.
Kennedy, John. Amer. heri. vol. 10 no. 4 p. 96 (Je '59).
  Holiday 23: 149 Je '58.
Kennedy, John Arthur. Cur. biog. p. 240 (1961).
Kennedy, John B. Cur. biog. p. 337 (1944).
Kennedy, Pres. John F. Cur. biog. p. 295 (1950); p. 242 (1961).
  Jensen: The White House, p. 278, 281, 283, 287-9, 292.
  U.S. News & world rep., vol. LV no. 1 p. 27, Jl 1, '63.
Kennedy, J. F., & Khrushchev. U.S. News & world rep., vol. LV no. 4 p. 28 Jl 22, '63.
Kennedy, J. F., & Pope Paul VI. U.S. News & world rep., vol. LV no. 3 p. 37 Jl 15, '63.
Kennedy, John F., jr. Jensen: The White House, p. 280.
Kennedy, Robert. Jensen: The White House, p. 291.
Kennedy, Robert F. Cur. biog. p. 221 (1958).
Kennedy, Robert F. (picture & cartoon). U.S. News & world report, p. 28, 31-2 Aug 31 '64.
Kennedy, Stephen P. Cur. biog. p. 335 (1956).
Kennedy, Thomas. Cur. biog. p. 212 (1960).
Kennedy, William P. Cur. biog. p. 296 (1950).
Kennedy ancestral home, J.F. (Ireland). U.S. News & world report vol. LV no. 1 p. 28, Jl 1, '63.
Kennedy family, J. F. Jensen: The White House, p. 278.
"Kennedy farm" (John Brown raid plotted here). Travel 112: 47 Jl '59.
Kennelly, Ardyth. Cur. biog. p. 311 (1953).
Kennelly, Martin H. Cur. biog. p 320 (1949).
Kenney, Lt. Gen. George C. Cur. biog. p. 373 (1943).
Kennicott, Robert. Amer. heri. vol. 12 no. 1 p. 47 (Dec '60).
Kennon, Robert F. Cur. biog. p. 374 (1954).
Kenny, Sister (Polio foundation). Holiday 14: 9 Sept '53.
Kenny, Sister Elizabeth. Cur. biog. p. 445 (1942).
Kensington Runestone. Amer. heri. vol. 10 no. 3 p. 34 (Ap '59).
  Holiday 18: 33 Aug '55.
Kent, Louise Andrews. Jun. bk. of auth., p. 178.
Kent, Rockwell. Cur. biog. p. 447 (1942).
Kent, William (Dandridge). Con. 134: 3 Sept '54.
—— (work of). Con. 134: 7 Sept '54.
Kent school. Holiday 26: 45 (col.) Sept '59.
Kentucky. Travel 101: 23-5 Feb '54; 106: 29-31 Aug '56.

—— (land of the "Little Colonel"). Travel 112: 35-8 Jl '59.

—— (Lincoln's home). Face of Amer., p. 76-7 (col.).

—— (map). Natl. geog. 97: 180 Feb '50.

Kentucky arch., colonial. Holiday 11: 28 (col.) Ap '52.

Kentucky colonel. Holiday 19: 100 Mar '56.

—— (horse). Travel 113: 43 Ap '60.

—— (horse heads). Holiday 27: 8 Ap '60.

—— (horses). Holiday 27: 167 Feb '60.

Kentucky dam. Brooks: Growth of a nation, p. 281.
Travel 101: 25 Feb '54.

Kentucky home. Brooks: Growth of a nation, p. 140.
Holiday 5: 74 (col.) Je '49.

—— (colonial). Holiday 11: 70 (col.) Mar '52.

Kentucky homes. Amer. heri. vol. 11 no. 4 p. 34 (col.) (Je '60).
Holiday 7: 145 (col.) Ap '50, 26 (col.) Je '50; 8: 74 (col.) Oct '50; 13: 21 (col.) Ap '53.

—— (Bardstown). Holiday 14: 89 Oct '53.

—— (colonial). Holiday 5: 33 (col.) Ap '49; 6: inside back cover (col.) Nov '49; 8: 121 (col.) Nov '50; 9: inside back cover (col.) Mar '51.

Kentucky mt. folk. Holiday 9: 44-5 Mar '51.

Kenya, Africa. Natl. geog. 106: 730- Dec '54; 110: 537-41 (part col.) Oct '56.

Kenyatta, Jomo. Cur. biog. p. 312 (1953).

Kenyon, Dorothy. Cur. biog. p. 349 (1947).

Kenyon, Helen. Cur. biog. p. 341 (1948).

kepi (sym.). Lehner: Pict. bk. of sym., p. 54.

Keppel, Francis. Cur. biog. p. 221 (1963).

Keppler, J. (caricature by). Amer. heri. vol. 11 no. 1 p. 79 (Dec '59).

Ker, Robert. Holiday 7: 116 May '50.

"Kermesse of St. Bavon" (Balten). Con. 144: XXXVII (col.) Nov '59.

Kern, Jerome. Cur. biog. p. 450 (1942).

Kernan, Lt. Col. William F. Cur. biog. p. 452 (1942).

Kerner, Otto. Cur. biog. p. 245 (1961).

Kerouac, Jack. Cur. biog. p. 227 (1959).

Kerr, Sir Archibald Clark. Cur. biog. p. 454 (1942).

Kerr, Clark. Cur. biog. p. 246 (1961).

Kerr, Deborah. Cur. biog. p. 351 (1947).

Kerr, James W. Cur. biog. p. 228 (1959).

Kerr, Jean. Cur. biog. p. 223 (1958).

Kerr, Robert S. Cur. biog. p. 298 (1950).

Kerr, Walter F. Cur. biog. p. 315 (1953).

Kerr dam. Natl. geog. 97: 723 (col.) Je '50.

Kerst, Donald W. Cur. biog. p. 300 (1950).

Kersten, Charles J. Cur. biog. p. 302 (1952).

Kesselring, Gen. Field Marshall Albert. Cur. biog. p. 455 (1942).

Kessing, Oliver O. Cur. biog. p. 321 (1949).

Kessler, Henry H. Cur. biog. p. 297 (1957).

Kestnbaum, Meyer. Cur. biog. p. 317 (1953).

"Keswick" home (Va.). Natl. geog. 103: 796 (col.) Je '53.

ketch (boat). Natl. geog. 107: 60 (col.) Jan '55; 112: 299, 323-7 (part col.) Sept '57; 117: 700 May '60.

Ketcham, Hank. Cur. biog. p. 337 (1956).

Ketchikan (Alaska). Natl. geog. 109: 744-5 (col.) Je '56.

Ketchum, Black Jack. Horan: Pict. hist. of wild west, p. 240-1.

Kettering, Charles Franklin. Cur. biog. p. 330 (1951).
Natl. geog. 106: 65G Jl '54; 107: 467 Ap '55.

Kettle, T. (work of). Con. 139: 191 May '57.

kettle. Holiday 23: 5 (col.) Jan '58; 26: 131 Oct '59.
Rawson: Ant. pict. bk., p. 31.
Travel 113: 30 Mar '60.

—— (antique). Amer. heri. vol. 8 no. 1 p. 99 (Dec '56).
Rawson: Ant. pict. bk., p. 10.

—— (child stirring). See child (stirring kettle).

—— (18th cent.). Con. ency. of ant., vol. 3, pl. 11.

—— (outdoor fish boil). Natl. geog. 115: 486 (col.) Ap '59.

——, 1st Amer. made iron. Amer. heri. vol. 2 no. 4 p. 29 (summer '51).

——, iron. Travel 106: 31 Jl '56.

——, iron (child). Holiday 21: 139 (col.) Jan '57.

——, iron (man & woman). Natl. geog. 107: 741 (col.) Je '55.

——, syrup. See syrup kettle.

kettle-drum. See drum, kettle.

kettle stand (antique). Con. 141: VII Mar '58.

—— (Chippendale). Con. 142: 127 Nov '58.

—— (18th cent.). Con. ency. of ant., vol. 3, pl. 11.

—— (1755). Con. ency. of ant., vol. 3, pl. 11.

"kettledrummer" (Dinglinger). Con. 136: inside cover Nov '55.

kettledrums, soup & coffee. Holiday 10: 108 Aug '51.

kettles, copper beer. Natl. geog. 115: 462 (col.) Ap '59.

Kew gardens (London). Natl. geog. 97: 480-506 (part col.) Ap '50.

Kew palace "swan lake" (Eng.). Amer. heri. vol. 11 no. 4 p. 14 (col.) (Je '60).

Kewpie doll. Lehner: Pict. bk. of sym., p. 62.

Key, Francis Scott. Holiday 23: 76 May '58.

Key, Maj. Gen. William S. Cur. biog. p. 374 (1943).

key. Con. 141: 87 Ap '58.
Holiday 5: 33 Ap '49, 74 Je '49; 6: 68 Sept '49, inside back cover (col.) Nov '49, 106 Dec '49; 7: 145 (col.) Ap '50, 26 (col.) Je '50; 8: 74 (col.) Oct '50; 10: 96 (col.) Oct '51, 116 (col.) Nov '51, 84 (col.) Dec '51; 11: 28 (col.) Ap '52, 19 (col.) Je '52; 12: 142 Nov '52, 99 (col.) Dec '52; 13: 138 (col.) Je '53; 14: 11 Oct '53, 96 Nov '53; 19: 78 Jan '56, 97 Feb '56, 152 (col.) Mar '56, 168 May '56; 24: 201 Nov '58; 25: 24 Mar '59, 44 (col.) Ap '59; 26: 98 (col.) Oct '59; 28: 113 Aug '60.
Travel 111: 47 Je '59.

—— (comic). Holiday 18: 96 (col.) Jl '55.

—— (sym.). Lehner: Pict. bk. of sym., p. 89-90.

—— (to city). Holiday 23: 172 Ap '58.

key, ceremonial. Natl. geog. 101: 526 (col.) Ap '52.
——, ornamental. Holiday 13: 148 Mar '53.
key & heart. *See* heart & key.
key caddy. Holiday 22: 114 (col.) Dec '57; 24: 15 (col.) Nov '58; 25: 149 (col.) Je '59.
key case. Holiday 10: 16 Nov '51, 1 (col.) Dec '51; 11: 59 (col.) Je '52; 12: 119 (col.) Nov '52, 100 Dec '52; 14: 156 Nov '53; 27: 159 Feb '60, 248 May '60, inside cover (col.) Je '60; 28: 179 (col.) Dec '60.
Key of the years (sym.). Lehner: Pict. bk. of sym., p. 23.
key tag. Holiday 24: 61 (col.) Dec '58.
Key West. Natl. geog. 97: 43-71 (part col.) Jan '50.
—— (air view). Natl. geog. 90: 44-5 Jan '50.
Key West overseas highway. Jordan: Hammond's pict. atlas, p. 75 (col.).
keyboard, piano (sym.). Lehner: Pict. bk of sym., p. 14.
Keyes, Erasmus Darwin. Pakula: Cent. album, p. 177.
Keyhoe, Donald E. Cur. biog. p. 338 (1956).
keyhole. Natl. geog. 111: 491 Ap '57.
keyhole escutcheon, Norwegian (silver). Con. 145: 16 Mar '60.
Keynes, John Maynard. Cur. biog. p. 467 (1941).
Keys, David A. Cur. biog. p. 224 (1958).
keys. Holiday 21: 120 Mar '57, 31 May '57.
keys & tiara. *See* tiara & keys.
Keyserling, Leon H. Cur. biog. p. 354 (1947).
Khachaturian, Aram. Cur. biog. p. 344 (1948).
Khan IV, The Aga. Cur. biog. p. 1 (1960).
Khan, Prince Aly. Cur. biog. p. 9 (1960).
Khan, Begum Liaquat Ali. Cur. biog. p. 302 (1950).
Khan, Liaquat Ali. Cur. biog. p. 347 (1948).
Khartoum. Natl. geog. 103: 255-61 (part col.) Feb '53.
—— (memorial statue). Natl. geog. 103: 248 Feb '53.
khatas (Tibetan white scarf). Natl. geog. 108: 48 Jl '55.
Khirbat Qumran (Essene). Natl. geog. 114: 791-7 (part col.) Dec '58.
Khmer king (throne). Natl. geog. 117: 534-5 (col.) Ap '60.
Khmer men (writing). Natl. geog. 117: 558 (col.) Ap '60.
Khmer monuments. Holiday 19: 91 Feb '56.
Khoman, Thanat. Cur. biog. p. 226 (1958).
Khouri, Faris El. Cur. biog. p. 349 (1948).
Khoury, Bechara El. Cur. biog. p. 333 (1951).
Khrushchev, Nikita S. Cur. biog. p. 376 (1954). Natl. geog. 116: 368 Sept '59, 717 (col.) Dec '59.
—— (with Pres. Kennedy). U.S. News & world rep., vol. LV no. 4 p. 28 Jl 22, '63.
U.S. News & world report, p. 43, Aug 31, '64.
Khyber Pass (India). Holiday 23: 36 May '58. Natl. geog. 102: 654-5 (col.) Nov '52. Travel 107: 35 Feb '57.
Kiam, Omar. Cur. biog. p. 321 (1945).
Kidd, Michael. Cur. biog. p. 214 (1960).
Kidder, George W. Cur. biog. p. 323 (1949).
kidneys, human. Gray's anatomy, p. 1265-71.

Kielland, Alexander L. (statue, back view). Natl. geog. 106: 171 (col.) Aug '54.
Kiepura, Jan. Cur. biog. p. 375 (1943).
Kiesler, Frederick J. Cur. biog. p. 339 (1944).
Kilauea volcano (eruption, Hawaii). Natl. geog. 117: 305-21 (col.) Mar '60; 118: 36-7 (col.) Jl '60.
Kilauea volcano crater. Natl. geog. 117: 322-3 (col.) Mar '60.
Kilday, Paul J. Cur. biog. p. 227 (1958).
Kildebee, Mrs. (Gainsborough). Con. 142: 250 (col.) Jan '59.
Kilgallen, Dorothy. Cur. biog. p. 303 (1952).
Kilgore, Harley M. Cur. biog. p. 378 (1943).
Killarney bowling club (Africa). Holiday 25: 90 (col.) Ap '59.
Killarney Lake (Ireland). Holiday 6: 39 (col.) Dec '49.
Killian, James R., jr. Cur. biog. p. 324 (1949); p. 230 (1959).
Killion, George. Cur. biog. p. 306 (1952).
Kilp, F. (work of). Con. 138: XL Nov '56.
Kilpatrick, Ben. Horan: Pict. hist. of wild west, p. 194, 220.
Kilpatrick, Hugh Judson. Pakula: Cent. album. p. 179.
Kilpatrick, John Reed. Cur. biog. p. 351 (1948).
"Kilroy was here". Lehner: Pict. bk. of sym., p. 83.
Kimball, Abbott. Cur. biog. p. 326 (1949).
Kimball, Dan A. Cur. biog. p. 336 (1951).
Kimball, Lindsley F. Cur. biog. p. 338 (1951).
Kimble, George H. T. Cur. biog. p. 308 (1952).
Kimbrel, M. Monroe. Cur. biog. p. 223 (1963).
Kimbrough, Emily. Cur. biog. p. 342 (1944).
Kimmel, Adm. Husband E. Cur. biog. p. 457 (1942).
kimona, Japanese. Natl. geog. 104: 643 (col.) Nov '53.
Kimpton, Lawrence A. Cur. biog. p. 340 (1951).
Kinda (sym.). Lehner: Pict. bk. of sym., p. 28.
Kindelberger, James H. Cur. biog. p. 342 (1951).
Kinder, Katharine L. Cur. biog. p. 298 (1957).
kindergarten children. Natl. geog. 118: 794 Dec '60.
—— (China). Natl. geog. 118: 213 (col.) Aug '60.
Kindler, Hans. Cur. biog. p. 305 (1946).
Kiner, Ralph. Cur. biog. p. 378 (1954).
—— (baseball). Holiday 7: 51 (col.) May '50.
King, Alexander. Holiday 26: 117 Nov '59.
King, Cecil R. Cur. biog. p. 309 (1952).
King, Charles Bird (work of). Amer. heri. vol. 10 no. 3 p. 27 (col.) (Ap '59).
King, Clarence. Amer. heri. vol. 7 no. 2 p. 58, 61 (Feb '56).
King, Adm. Ernest Joseph. Cur. biog. p. 459 (1942).
King, Khmer. *See* Khmer king (throne).
King, Rev. Martin Luther, jr. Cur. biog. p. 300 (1957).
King, Muriel. Cur. biog. p. 379 (1943).
King, Samuel. (work of). Con. 141: 131 Ap '58.
King, Samuel Wilder. Cur. biog. p. 319 (1953).
king (Angkor procession). Natl. geog. 117: 544-5 (col.) Ap '60.

——, **Angkor (riding elephant).** Natl. geog. 117: 544-5 (col.) Ap '60.

——, **Babylonian (ancient).** Int. gr. soc.: Arts . . . p. 29 (col.).

——, **Egyptian (5th dynasty).** Int. gr. soc.: Arts . . . p. 29 (col.).

——, **Mesopotamian (7th cent. B.C.).** Int. gr. soc.: Arts . . . p. 29 (col.).

King Arthur (Knights of round table). See Knights of the round table.

king (bell ringing). Holiday 11: 19 Feb '52.

—— **(bell 14th cent.).** Holiday 11: 135 Ap '52.

—— **(comic).** Holiday 12: 21 (col.) Oct '52.

king & queen (Mardi Gras). Natl. geog. 118: 732 (col.) Nov '60.

—— **(throne, comic).** Holiday 22: 26 Oct '57.

——, **Nepalese.** Holiday 21: 73 (col.) May '57.

king & woman (throne, imitation). Holiday 21: 113 (col.) Jan '54.

King is. (Alaska). Natl. geog. 105: 130-46 (part col.) Jan '54.

King Neptune & Queen (Seattle). Natl. geog. 117: 503 (col.) Ap '60.

King of Bunyoro (Uganda). Natl. geog. 118: 373 (col.) Sept '60.

"King of sorrows" (Burton). Con. 139: XXII Mar '57.

"King of the mules" festival (Tenn.). Brooks: Growth of a nation, p. 290.

"King Philip's throne" (New Eng., ceremonial rock). Amer. heri. vol. 10 no. 1 p. 65 (Dec '58.

King ranch house (Texas). Natl. geog. 101: 41 (col.) Jan '52.

Kingdom, Frank. Cur. biog. p. 343 (1944).

Kingman, Dong. Cur. biog. p. 233 (1962).

King's & Clare colleges. Con. 143: 104 Ap '59.

King's chapel (Boston). Travel 112: 53 Jl '59.

King's college (N.Y.). Amer. heri. vol. 5 no. 1 p. 16 (fall '53).

King's college students (Eng.). Natl. geog. 104: 304 (col.) Sept '53.

King's Mt. monument. Holiday 16: 107 Jl '54.

Kings of Gt. Brit. Amer. heri. vol. 11 no. 4 cover, p. 7-23 (part col.) (Je '60).

King's Point (U.S. Merchant & marine acad.). Natl. geog. 108: 692-706 (part col.) Nov '55.

King's school. See Canterbury (King's school).

Kingscote harbor. See Kangaroo is.

Kingsland, Lawrence C. Cur. biog. 328 (1949).

Kingsley, Amis. Holiday 23: 93 Ap '58.

Kingsley, John Donald. Cur. biog. p. 303 (1950).

Kingsley, Myra. Cur. biog. p. 381 (1943).

Kingsley, Lt. Sidney. Cur. biog. p. 383 (1943).

Kingston (Jamaica). Holiday 9: 100 Mar '51.

—— **(coronation celebration).** Natl. geog. 105: 348-9 (col.) Mar '54.

—— **(N.Y., early days).** Amer. heri. vol. 4 no. 1 p. 12-5 (fall '52).

—— **(N.Y., 1777-).** Amer. heri. vol. 4 no. 1 p. 13-5 (fall '52).

"Kingston from Golden Hill" (1853). Amer. heri. vol. 4 no. 1 p. 12 (fall '52).

Kinkaid, Vice Adm. Thomas C. Cur. biog. p. 345 (1944).

Kinloch, Mrs. Cleland. Amer. heri. vol. 9 no. 2 p. 56 (col.) (Feb '58).

Kinnear, Judge Helen. Cur. biog. p. 301 (1957).

Kinsella, Mrs. James H. Holiday 27: 84 Feb '60.

Kinsey, Alfred C. Cur. biog. p. 380 (1954).

Kinsey, Capt. J. L. Natl. geog. 115: 7 (col.) Jan '59.

Kintner, Earl W. Cur. biog. p. 215 (1960).

Kintner, Robert E. Cur. biog. p. 306 (1950).

Kiphuth, Robert J. H. Cur. biog. p. 303 (1957).

Kipling, Rudyard. Natl. geog. 108: 350 Sept '55.

Kiplinger, Willard M. Cur. biog. p. 386 (1943); p. 235 (1962).

Kipnis, Alexander. Cur. biog. p. 388 (1943).

—— **(as Baron Ochs in "Der Rosenkavalier").** Cooper: Con. ency. of music p. 146.

Kipping, Sir Norman. Cur. biog. p. 330 (1949).

Kiprensky, Orest Adamovich. Con. 143: 31 Mar '59.

Kirby, Rollin. Cur. biog. p. 349 (1944).

Kirchner, Ernst Ludwig (work of). Praeg. pict. ency., p. 446 (col.).

Kirchner, Hans Ludwig (work of). Con. 144: 181 (col.) Dec '59.

Kirchwey, Freda. Cur. biog. p. 461 (1942).

Kirghiz man, woman & child. Natl. geog. 98: 698, 700, 705- Nov '50.

Kirk, Adm. Alan Goodrich. Cur. biog. p. 352 (1944).

Kirk, Alexander C. Cur. biog. p. 323 (1945).

Kirk, Grayson L. Cur. biog. p. 344 (1951).

Kirk, Maj. Gen. Norman T. Cur. biog. p. 353 (1944).

Kirk, Russell A. Cur. biog. p. 237 (1962).

Kirk, William T. Cur. biog. p. 217 (1960).

Kirkpatrick, Helen. Cur. biog. p. 469 (1941).

Kirkpatrick, Sir Ivone. Cur. biog. p. 307 (1950).

Kirkus, Virginia. Cur. biog. p. 471 (1941); p. 383 (1954).

Kirstein, Lincoln E. Cur. biog. p. 311 (1952).

Kirsten, Dorothy. Cur. biog. p. 353 (1948).

Kishi, Nobusuke. Cur. biog. p. 305 (1957).

Kishimojin (sym.). Lehner: Pict. bk. of sym., p. 48.

"Kiss in the rain" (Andrews). Con. 132: XXVII Sept '53.

kissing, athletes. Holiday 21: 55 Ap '57.

"kissing bridge". See bridge, kissing.

Kissinger, Henry A. Cur. biog. p. 229 (1958).

Kistiakowsky, George B. Cur. biog. p. 219 (1960).

Kit Carson's cave. See Carson's cave, Kit.

Kitchell, Iva. Cur. biog. p. 347 (1951).

kitchen. Brooks: Growth of a nation, p. 264. Holiday 14: 64 (col.) Oct '53; 18: 57 (col.) Oct '55; 22: 111 (col.) Dec '57; 23: 99 Mar '58; 29: 30 (col.) Feb '59.

—— **(after earthquake).** Natl. geog. 117: 350 (col.) Mar '60.

—— **(early Amer.).** Amer. heri. vol. 2 no. 3 p. 75 (spring '51); vol. 3 no. 4 p. 34 (summer '52).

Natl. geog. 97: 288 (col.) Mar '50; 100: 588 (col.) Nov '51.

—— **(18th cent.).** Holiday 11: 43 (col.) Je '52.

—— **(food).** Holiday 24: 218 (col.) Dec '58.

kitchen (man & woman). Holiday 27: 196 (col.) Mar '60.

——, **Baghdad (woman cooking).** Natl. geog. 114: 454 (col.) Oct '58.

——, **Colonial.** Amer. heri. vol. 3 no. 1 p. 14 (fall '51).

——, **Colonial (Negro child).** Natl. geog. 109: 447 (col.) Ap '56.

——, **Colonial (Negro cook).** Natl. geog. 113: 538 (col.) Ap '58.

——, **French.** Holiday 21: 67 (col.) Ap '57.

——, **French (18th cent.).** Holiday 21: 145 (col.) Ap '57.

——, **French (woman cooking).** Natl. geog. 115: 602 (col.) May '59.

——, **French (woman, cow).** Natl. geog. 115: 576-7 Ap '59.

——, **frontier.** Natl. geog. 101: 173, 175 (col.) Feb '52.

——, **modern.** Int. gr. soc.: Arts . . . p. 129 (col.).

——, **Mt. Vernon.** Natl. geog. 104: 668 (col.) Nov '53.

——, **Normandy (hotel).** Holiday 19: 53 Jan '56.

——, **Norway farm.** Natl. geog. 108: 741 (col.) Dec '55.

——, **Pitcairn is.** Natl. geog. 112: 743 (col.) Dec '57.

——, **Tarascan (Mexico).** Natl. geog. 102: 540 (col.) Oct '52.

——, **western.** Holiday 23: 67 (col.) Feb '58.

——, **Williamsburg.** Con. 143: 272 Je '59.

kitchen table (food). Natl. geog. 102: 510 (col.) Oct '52.

kitchen tools. Holiday 12: 94 Oct '52.

kitchen ware. *See* cooking ware.

kitchens. Holiday 24: 117-22 (part col.) Oct '58.

——, **Netherlands.** Holiday 23: 66 (col.) Feb '58.

kite (Chinese children, ancient times). Int. gr. soc.: Arts . . . p. 37 (col.).

—— **(Maldive is.).** Natl. geog. 111: 831 (col.) Je '57.

—— **(Philippine is.).** Holiday 18: 88 Aug '55.

kite-man (water skiing). Natl. geog. 114: 701, 703 (col.) Nov '58.

kite stick (India). Holiday 22: 119 (col.) Sept '57.

kites, Bell tetrahedral. Natl. geog. 110: 237-9 Aug '56.

Kitimat aluminum plant. Natl. geog. 110: 376-98 (part col.) Sept '56.

kitometer stone marker. Natl. geog. 117: 197 (col.) Feb '60.

Kitson, Harry Dexter. Cur. biog. p. 349 (1951).

Kitt, Eartha. Cur. biog. p. 328 (1955).

Kitty Hawk (Wright memorial). *See* Wright Bros. memorial (Kitty Hawk).

"Kitty Hawk flyer" airplane. Natl. geog. 104: 725 (col.), 740-1 Dec '53.

Kizkale is. *See* island of Kizkale.

Kjelgaard, Jim. Jun. bk. of auth., p. 179.

Klahre, Ethel S. Cur. biog. p. 239 (1962).

Klee, Paul (work of). Praeg. pict. ency., p. 487 (col.).

Kleffens, Eelco Van. Cur. biog. p. 356 (1947).

Klein, Julius. Cur. biog. p. 356 (1948).

Kleinberg, Ernest. Holiday 5: 32 Jan '49.

Kleine Scheidegg (Mt., Switzerland). Holiday 16: 34-5 (col.) Aug '54.

Kleinsmid, Rufus B. von. Cur. biog. p. 231 (1958).

Kleist, Col. Gen. Paul Ludwig von. Cur. biog. p. 390 (1943).

Kleitman, Nathaniel. Cur. biog. p. 307 (1957).

Klenze, Leo von (work of). Praeg. pict. ency., p. 423.

Kline, Allan B. Cur. biog. p. 358 (1948).

Kline, Clarice. Cur. biog. p. 248 (1961).

Kloehr, John J. Horan: Pict. hist. of wild west, p. 162.

Klopsteg, Paul E. Cur. biog. p. 232 (1959).

Klosters (Switzerland). Holiday 23: 70-5 (part col.) Feb '58.

Kluckhohn, Cyde. Cur. biog. p. 352 (1951).

Klumpp, Theodore G. Cur. biog. p. 233 (1958).

Knapton, George (work of). Con. 141: 268 Je '58.

Knatchbull-Hugessen, Sir Hughe. Cur. biog. p. 391 (1943).

Knaths, O. Karl. Cur. biog. p. 321 (1953).

knee joint. Gray's anatomy, p. 1416, 1419.

Kneller, Sir Godfrey (self portrait). Con. 133: 177 May '54.

—— **(work of).** Amer. heri. vol. 11 no. 1 p. 4 (col.) (Dec '59).
    Con. 127: 29-32 Mar '51; 135: 240 Je '55; 140: 232-3 Jan '58; 141: 62 Mar '58.

Knesset, Jewish. *See* parliament (Israel).

"Knickerbocker Grey" (boy in uniform). Holiday 24: 20 Aug '58.

knife, bowie or hunting. Rawson: Ant. pict. bk., p. 25.

——, **carving.** Holiday 12: 136 Nov '52, 154 Dec '52; 18: 4 Aug '55, 150 Dec '55; 20: 164 Dec '56.

——, **Case.** Rawson: Ant. pict. bk., p. 23.

——, **cheese (in cheese).** Holiday 24: 47 (col.) Dec '58.

——, **serving.** Holiday 18: 91 Nov '55.

——, **silver.** Holiday 19: 168 May '56; 21: 114 Mar '57, 105 Je '57.

——, **silver Italian (16th cent.).** Con. ency. of ant., vol. 3, pl. 31.

——, **Venetian (16th cent.).** Con. 142: 269 Jan '59.

knife box, silver (18th cent.). Con. 143: 266 Je '59.

knife, fork & spoon. Holiday 12: 1 Oct '52, 96 Nov '52; 27: 10 (col.) Ap '60.

——, **silver (19th cent.).** Con. 143: XV May '59.

—— **(sym.).** Lehner: Pict. bk. of sym., p. 90.

—— *See* also silverware.

knife rests, cut glass. Daniel: Cut & engraved glass, pl. 152.

Knight, Dame Laura (work of). Con. 135: XIV Ap '55.

Knight, Eric. Cur. biog. p. 463 (1942).

Knight, Fanny. Amer. heri. vol. 11 no. 3 p. 14 (col.) (Ap '60).

Knight, Frances. Amer. heri. vol. 11 no. 3 p. 16 (Ap '60).

Knight, Frances G. Cur. biog. p. 330 (1955).

Knight, Goodwin. Cur. biog. p. 332 (1955).

Knight, H. (work of). Amer. heri. vol. 11 no. 2 p. 48-9 (col.) (Feb '60).
Knight, John. Amer. heri. vol. 11 no. 3 p. 16 (Ap '60).
Knight, John S. Cur. biog. p. 326 (1945).
Knight, Orie A. Cur. biog. p. 314 (1952).
Knight, Ruth Adams. Cur. biog. p. 394 (1943); p. 334 (1955).
knight (armour). Holiday 16: 102-3 (col.) Sept '54; 27: 12 Je '60.
—— (armour, 15th cent.). Con. 141: LV Ap '58.
—— (armour, horseback). Int. gr. soc.: Arts . . . p. 73, 187 (col.).
—— (armour, museum). Natl. geog. 118: 806 (col.) Dec '60.
—— (armour). See also armour (knight).
—— (horseback). Holiday 12: 10, 84 (col.) Dec '52; 14: 15 (col.) Nov '53; 15: 88 Jan '54; 16: inside back cover (col.) Nov '54; 26: 177 (col.) Dec '59.
Int. gr. soc.: Arts . . . p. 67, 73, 187 (col.).
——, Scotch (horseback). Holiday 18: 135 (col.) Oct '55.
"Knight, death & the Devil" (Durer). Praeg. pict. ency., p.
Knight of the garter (Gt. Brit.). Int. gr. soc.: Arts . . . p. 167 (col.).
Knight of the order of the Ermine (Carpaccio). Con. 142: 64 Sept '58.
knight slays dragon (Austria, festival). Disney: People & places, p. 53 (col.).
knights (armour). Holiday 21: 26 (col.) Mar '57; 26: 15 (col.) Oct '59.
—— (armour, horseback). Holiday 27: 189 (col.) Ap '60.
—— (armour, medieval). Int. gr. soc.: Arts . . . p. 73 (col.).
—— (combat, horseback). Amer. heri. vol. 9 no. 6 p. 31 (Oct '58).
—— (combat, papier-mache). Natl. geog. 114: 621 (col.) Nov '58.
——, English. Amer. heri. vol. 10 no. 4 p. 18 (col.) (Je '60).
——, medieval. Disney: People & places, p. 52 (col.).
——, papier-mache. See papier-mache knights.
Knight's Hall (The Hague, Holland). Holiday 23: 56-7 Jan '58.
"Knights of labor" (1869). Brooks: Growth of a nation, p. 202.
Knights of the round table (King Arthur). Int. gr. soc.: Arts . . . p. 59 (col.).
Knights of the Tastevin, French. Holiday 21: 93 (col.) Ap '57.
"Knights of the winetasters". See wine tasters, knights of the.
Knik glacier. See glacier, Knik.
Knip, P. de C. (work of). Con. ency. of ant., vol. 3, pl. 85.
knitting machine. Natl. geog. 99: 112 Jan '51.
knives, carving. Holiday 20: 11 Dec '56.
——, steak. Holiday 20: 18 Oct '56.
knives. See also knife; silverware.
knocker, door. See door knocker.
Knoll, Hans G. Cur. biog. p. 335 (1955).
knop (on bedpost, 16th cent.). Con. ency. of ant., vol. 1 p. 19.

Knopf, Alfred A. Cur. biog. p. 396 (1943).
Knopf, Mrs. Alfred A. Cur. biog. p. 309 (1957).
Knorr, Nathan H. Cur. biog. p. 311 (1957)
Knossos. See Cnossos.
Knossos palace mural. See mural (palace, Knossos).
knot, sacred (sym.). Lehner: Pict. bk. of sym., p. 47.
——, true-love (sym.). Lehner: Pict. bk. of sym. p. 65.
Knott, Sarah Gertrude. Cur. biog., p. 358 (1947).
"Knott" flower garden (Eng.). Natl. geog. 98: 191 (col.) Aug '50.
Knowland, William F. Cur. biog. p. 359 (1947).
knowledge (sym.). Lehner: Pict. bk. of sym., p. 58.
Knowlson, James S. Cur. biog. p. 466 (1942).
Knox, Henry (horseback). Amer. heri. vol. 6 no. 3 p. 12 (col.) (Ap '56).
Knox, Maj. Gen. Jean. Cur. biog. p. 468 (1942).
Knox, John. Holiday 27: cover May '60.
Knox, Philander. Amer. heri. vol. 11 no. 6 p. 55 (Oct '60).
Knox, Msgr. Ronald. Cur. biog. p. 309 (1950).
Knox, Rose B. Jun. bk. of auth., p 181.
Knox, Mrs. Rose M. Cur. biog. p. 331 (1949).
Knox college (Ill., 1858). Natl. geog. 117: 264-5 (part col.) Feb '60.
Knox's expedition against British. Amer. heri. vol. 6 no. 3 p. 12 (col.) (Ap '55).
Knuth-Winterfeldt, Count Kield Gustav. Cur. biog. p. 233 (1959).
Knutson, Coya. Cur. biog. p. 341 (1956).
Knutson, Harold. Cur. biog. p. 362 (1947).
Kobak, Edgar. Cur. biog. p. 365 (1947).
Koch, Fred, jr. Cur. biog. p. 322 (1953).
Kock, Karin. Cur. biog. p. 359 (1948).
kodacolor prints (man drying). Natl. geog. 110: 614 (col.) Nov '56.
kodak. Holiday 23: 24, 130 Jan '58.
——. See also camera.
kodak film box. Holiday 18: 67 (col.), 89 Jl '55, 84 (col.) Aug '55, 20 (col.) Sept '55, 116 (col.) Oct '55; 20: 62 (col.) Aug '56, 75 Sept '56, 202 (col.) Dec '56; 22: 13 (col.) Dec '57; 23: 103 (col.) Mar '58, 109 (col.) Ap '58, 161 (col.) Je '58; 24: 15 (col.) Aug '58; 26: 116 (col.) Aug '59, 30 (col.) Sept '59.
kodak film roll. Holiday 18: 14 Sept '55.
Kodaly, Zoltan. Cooper: Con. ency. of music, p. 147.
Kodiak (Alaska, 1804). Amer. heri. vol. 10 no. 3 p. 64 (col.) (Ap '59).
Koekkoek, M. A. (work of). Con. 137: XXX-VII May '56.
Koellner, August (work of). Con. ency. of ant., vol. 3, pl. 95.
Koenig, Lt. Gen. Joseph-Pierre. Cur. biog. p. 356 (1944).
Koestler, Arthur. Cur. biog. p. 399 (1943); p. 241 (1962).
Kohler, Foy D. Cur. biog. p. 311 (1950).
Kohler, Walter J., jr. Cur. biog. p. 324 (1953).
Kojoji temple (Japan). Natl. geog. 104: 642 (col.) Nov '53.
Kokoschka, Oskar. Cur. biog. p. 342 (1956).
—— (work of). Praeg. pict. ency., p. 497 (col.).

Kolarov, Vassil. Cur. biog p. 333 (1949).
Kolbe, Georg (bronze statue). Praeg. pict. ency., p. 489.
Koldewey, Robert (portrait). Ceram: March of arch., p. 225.
—— (work of). Ceram: March of arch., p. 227.
Kollantay, Alexandra. Cur. biog. p. 402 (1943).
Kollmar, Dick. Cur. biog. p. 304 (1952).
Kolo dancers (Yugoslavia). Int. gr. soc.: Arts . . . p. 147 (col.).
Kolodin, Irving. Cur. biog. p. 366 (1947).
Kolosh halibut hook. Amer. heri. vol. 10 no. 3 p. 78 (Ap '59).
Kolosh Indian rattle. Amer. heri. vol. 10 no. 3 p. 68 (Ap '59).
Komarovsky, Mirra. Cur. biog. p. 326 (1953).
Kondo (Golden Hall, Japan). Praeg. pict. ency., p. 528.
Koner, Pauline. Holiday 27: 85 Feb '60.
Konev, Marshall Ivan S. Cur. biog. p. 345 (1956).
Konigslutter cathedral. Praeg. pict. ency., p. 34.
—— (cloister). Praeg. pict. ency., p. 232.
Koninginnesluis lock (Netherlands). Travel 113: 51 Ap '60.
Konstanty, Jim. Cur. biog. p. 353 (1951).
Konya (Turkey). Natl. geog. 110: 737 Dec '56.
Koo, Vi Kyuin. Cur. biog. p. 473 (1941).
Kooning, Willem de (work of). Praeg. pict. ency., p. 490.
Köprulu, Fuat. Cur. biog. p. 328 (1953).
Koran (on stand). Natl. geog. 102: 657 (col.) Nov '52.
Korda, Sir Alexander. Cur. biog. p. 308 (1946).
Kordofan (Egypt). Natl. geog. 99: 251 Feb '51.
"Kore" (Greek sculpt.). Praeg. pict. ency., p. 132.
Korea. Natl. geog. 103: 636-64 (part col.) May '53.
—— (map). Natl. geog. 97: 779 Je '50; 103: 507 Ap '53.
Korean (pack on back). Natl. geog. 103: 648 (col.) May '53.
—— (playing accordion). Natl. geog. 118: 203 (col.) Aug '60.
—— (with camera). Natl. geog. 103: 639 May '53.
Korean baby (starvation). Travel 102: 43 Sept '54.
Korean children. Holiday 17: 96 Jan '55; 23: 170 Je '58.
Korean festival (Natl. Day). Natl. geog. 118: 202-3 (col.) Aug '60.
Korean man. Holiday 18: 45 (col.) Aug '55.
Korean men (working). Natl. geog. 111: 307 (col.) Mar '57.
Korean temple (600 A.D., Japan). Int. gr. soc.: Arts . . . p. 51 (col.).
Korean women. Travel 109: inside cover Mar '58.
Korizis, Alexander. Cur. biog. p. 474 (1941).
Korn, John P. (work of). Con. 141: XVII Mar '58.
Körner, Theodore. Cur. biog. p. 355 (1951).
Korngold, Erich Wolfgang. Cur. biog. p. 405 (1943).

koro, Chinese jade. Con. 141: XXXVII Mar '58, XIII May '58.
koro & cover, Lapis lazuli. Con. 142: XXIII Dec '58.
Korongo warrior (Egypt). Natl. geog. 99: 256 Feb '51.
Korth, Fred. Cur. biog. p. 243 (1962).
Kosaka, Zentaro. Cur. biog. p. 250 (1961).
kosher food delicatessen. Holiday 10: 53 (col.) Sept '51.
Kossak, Zofia. Cur. biog. p. 358 (1944).
Kossuth, Louis. Amer. heri. vol. 8 no. 2 p. 2 (Feb '57).
Kossuth's reception (N.Y. City). Amer. heri. vol. 6 no. 2 p. 61 (col.) (winter '55).
Kostelanetz, Andre. Cur. biog. p. 470 (1942). Holiday 22: 148 Dec '57.
Kotelawala, Sir John. Cur. biog. p. 337 (1955).
Kotor (Dalmation coast). Holiday 14: 38 (col.) Aug '53.
Kotschnig, Walter M. Cur. biog. p. 316 (1952).
Kouros (Attica). Con. ency. of ant., vol. 3, pl 65.
Kouros (Greek sculpt.). Praeg. pict. ency., p. 132.
"Kouros of Melos" (6th cent. B.C.). Praeg. pict. ency., p. 11.
Kouros statuette (Athens). Con. ency. of ant., vol. 3, pl. 70.
koushi, agate. Con. 134: XXV Dec '54.
Koutoubia mosque. See mosque, Koutoubia.
Kovacs, Ernie. Cur. biog. p. 235 (1958). Holiday 24: 87 Oct '58.
kovsh, Imperial Russian. Con. 141: XXXV Je '58; 142: 271 Jan '59.
——, silver gilt. Con. 136: LXIX Jan '56.
Kowalski, Frank, jr. Cur. biog. p. 221 (1960).
Kozlenko, William. Cur. biog. p. 475 (1941).
Kozlov, Frol R. Cur. biog. p. 235 (1959).
kraal (African hut). Holiday 18: 69 Sept '55. Travel 102: 33 Aug '54.
Krafft (statue, church, Nuremberg). Praeg. pict. ency., p. 210.
Kraft, Ole Bjorn. Cur. biog. p. 330 (1953).
Krag, Jens Otto. Cur. biog. p. 245 (1962).
Kramer, Jack. Praeg. pict. ency., p. 479.
Kramer, Jake. Cur. biog. p. 368 (1947).
Kramer, Stanley. Cur. biog. p. 357 (1951). Holiday 5: 42 (col.) Jan '49.
Kramm, Joseph. Cur. biog. p. 317 (1952).
Krasna, Norman. Cur. biog. p. 320 (1952).
Kraus, Hans. P. Cur. biog. p. 223 (1960).
Kraus, Rene. Cur. biog. p. 476 (1941).
Kraushaar, Otto F. Cur. biog. p. 335 (1949).
Krauss, Clemens. Holiday 17: 33 Jan '55.
Krebs, Hans A. Cur. biog. p. 384 (1954).
Kreisky, Bruno. Cur. biog. p. 225 (1960).
Kreisler, Fritz. Cooper: Con. ency. of music, p. 148.
Cur. biog. p. 359 (1944).
Krekeler, Heinz L. Cur. biog. p. 359 (1951).
The Kremlin (Moscow). Amer. heri. vol. 11 no. 3 p. 25 (col.) (Ap '60).
Holiday 18: 102 Jl '55, 45 Nov '55. Natl. geog. 116: 352 (col.) Sept '59.
Kremlin churches & palaces. Con. 144: 277 Jan '60.
Krenek, Ernst. Cur. biog. p. 473 (1942).

Kress, Samuel H. Cur. biog. p. 339 (1955).
Krick, Irving P. Cur. biog. p. 313 (1950).
"Krishna holding up Mt. Govardhan" (bk. illus.). Praeg. pict. ency., p. 533 (col.).
Krishna Menon, V. K. Cur. biog. p. 332 (1953).
Krock, Arthur. Cur. biog. p. 408 (1943).
    Holiday 7: 101 Feb '50.
Kroeber, Alfred L. Cur. biog. p. 237 (1958).
Krohg, Per. Cur. biog. p. 386 (1954).
Krol, Abram (engravings). Con. 140: 88-9 Nov '57.
Kroll, Jack. Cur. biog. p. 311 (1946).
Kroll, Leon. Cur. biog. p. 410 (1943).
Kronborg castle. Holiday 18: 29 Sept '55.
Kronenberger, Louis. Cur. biog. p. 362 (1944).
Kross, Anna M. Cur. biog. p. 328 (1945).
Krueger, Walter. Cur. biog. p. 411 (1943).
Krug, Julius A. Cur. biog. p. 363 (1944).
Krum, Henry W. Cur. biog. p. 344 (1955).
Krupa, Gene. Cur. biog. p. 371 (1947).
Krupp, Alfried. Cur. biog. p. 341 (1955).
    Holiday 25: 56 May '59.
Krutch, Joseph Wood. Cur. biog. p. 237 (1959).
"Kuan Yin" (Chinese lacquered). Con. 142: X Nov '58.
—— (goddess of mercy). Holiday 22: 34 Nov '57.
Kubelik, Jan. Cur. biog. p. 477 (1941).
Kubelik, Rafael. Cur. biog. p. 360 (1951).
Kubitschek, Juscelino. Cur. biog. p. 347 (1956).
    Natl. geog. 117: 720, 723 (col.) May '60.
Kubly, Herbert O. Cur. biog. p. 239 (1959).
Kubrick, Stanley. Cur. biog. (1963).
Kucharski, Alexandre (work of). Con. 136: 34 Sept '55.
Kuchel, Thomas H. Cur. biog. p. 388 (1954).
Kuchler, Georg Von. Cur. biog. p. 413 (1943).
kuei, Chinese bronze. Con. 132: 208 Jan '54.
Kuekes, Edward D. Cur. biog. p. 390 (1954).
Kuhlman, Walter. Holiday 23: 69 May '58.
Kuhn, Irene. Cur. biog. p. 313 (1946).
Kuhn, Justus Engelhardt (work of). Amer. heri. vol. 7 no. 1 cover (col.) (Dec '55).
Kuiper, Gerard P. Cur. biog. p. 241 (1959).
Kulik, Gregory. Cur. biog. p. 475 (1942).
Kullmer, Ann. Cur. biog. p. 336 (1949).
Kumm, Henry W. Cur. biog. p. 344 (1955).
Kung, Hans. Cur. biog. p. 227 (1963).
Kung, Hsiang Hsi. Cur. biog. p. 415 (1943).
Kunitz, Stanley. Cur. biog. p. 243 (1959).
Kunitz, Stanley J. Cur. biog. p. 417 (1943).
Kuniyshi, Yasuo. Cur. biog. p. 478 (1941).
Kunming pilgrimage (China). Natl. geog. 97: 213-26 Feb '50.
Kunz, Alfred A. Cur. biog. p. 480 (1941).
Kupapa, The "Great Mother". See Sun Queen of Arinna.
Kurchatov, Igor V. Cur. biog. p. 313 (1957).
Kurd camel caravan. Holiday 22: 30 Oct '57.
Kurdish girl (milking). Natl. geog. 115: 62 (col.) Jan '59.
Kurdish man (harvest grain). Natl. geog. 114: 483 (col.) Oct '58.
Kurdish mother & child (horseback). Natl. geog. 115: 62 (col.) Jan '59.
Kurdish religious group. Natl. geog. 115: 48-9 Jan '59.
Kurdistan. Holiday 22: 30 Oct '57.
Kurenko, Maria. Cur. biog. p. 367 (1944).

Kurnitz, Harry. Holiday 24: 141 Dec '58.
Kursunlu Cami (Kayseri, Caesarea). Osward: Asia Minor, pl. 67.
Kurtz, Efrem. Cur. biog. p. 316 (1946).
Kurusu, Saburo. Cur. biog. p. 476 (1942).
Kusch, Polykarp. Cur. biog. p. 349 (1956).
Kustodiev, Boris Mikhailovich. (work of). Con. 143: 28 Mar '59.
Kutchuk, Fazil. Cur. biog. p. 252 (1961).
Kuter, Maj. Gen. Laurence S. Cur. biog. p. 361 (1948).
Kuusinen, Hertta E. Cur. biog. p. 338 (1949).
Kuwait (Arabian desert). Natl. geog. 102: 784-802 (part col.) Dec '52.
—— (Persian Gulf). Travel 103: 15-7 Mar '55.
—— (map). Natl. geog. 102: 787 Dec '52.
Kuwatly, Shukri Al. Cur. biog. p. 350 (1956).
Kuzmin, Josif I. Cur. biog. p. 245 (1959).
Kuznetsov, Nikolai G. Cur. biog. p. 478 (1942).
Kuznetsov, Vassili V. Cur. biog. p. 352 (1956).
Kwan Yin polychrome figure (K'ang Hsi). Con. 143: 187 May '59.
Kwannon in Chugu-ji temple (Japan). Praeg. pict. ency., p. 526.
Kyle, Anne D. Jun. bk. of auth., p. 182.
Kyoto (Japan, golden pavilion). Holiday 23: 168 (col.) Mar '58.
Kyser, Kay. Cur. biog. p. 481 (1941).

L

"La Baccelli dancing". Con. 145: 162 May '60.
"La baignade" (Seurat). Praeg. pict. ency., p. 429 (col.).
"La baigneuse" (sculpt. by Falconet). Con. 132: 42 Sept '53.
La Baule (France). Holiday 27: 86-91 (col.) May '60.
L'Abbaye de La Celle (int., France). Holiday 27: 20-1 (col.) Ap '60.
label, wine. See wine label.
Labiche, Emmeline (statue). Amer. heri. vol. 6 no. 1 p. 61 (fall '54).
Labor bureau. See U.S. Bur. of labor bldg.
Labor day (sym.). Lehner: Pict. bk. of sym., p. 53.
labor group meeting. Brooks: Growth of a nation, p. 254.
labor unions. See "Knights of labor".
laboratory (science). Natl. geog. 114: 307, 322-4, 331-2, 338, 343, 347, 353 (part col.) Sept '58.
——, experiments (aviation medicine). Natl. geog. 108: 250, 253 Aug '55.
La Borde, Jean De. Cur. biog. p. 419 (1943).
laborer (sym.). Lehner: Pict. bk. of sym., p. 53.
laborers (Brazil). Natl. geog. 117: 710, 719 (part col.) May '60.
—— (builders of early Amer.). Amer. heri. vol. 8 no. 6 p. 5 (col.) (Oct '57).
—— (building Angkor Wat). Natl. geog. 117: 528-9 (col.) Ap '60.
—— (iron workers). Natl. geog. 103: 298 (col.) Mar '53.
——, Egyptian. See Egyptian laborers.
——, Polish women. Natl. geog. 114: 364-5 Sept '58.
Labouisse, Henry R. Cur. biog. p. 254 (1961).

Labrador. Natl. geog. 100: 66-99 (part col.) Jl '51.

—— (map). Natl. geog. 101: 4 Jan '52.

"La Casa Grande" (Cal.). Natl. geog. 116: 576-7 (col.) Nov '59.

La Cava, Gregory. Cur. biog. p. 483 (1941).

La Cave, F.M. (work of). Cooper: Con. ency. of music, p. 303.

lace box (18th cent.). Con. ency. of ant., vol. 3, pl. 120.

lace maker Natl. geog. 100: 383 Sept '51.

—— (French woman). Natl. geog. 112: 427 Sept '57.

—— (woman). Natl. geog. 112: 427 Sept '57.

lace makers (children, Belgium). Natl. geog. 107: 647 (col.) May '55.

—— (France). Natl. geog. 100: 6 Jl '51.

—— (Italy). Natl. geog. 116: 492 Oct '59.

Lachaise (sculpt. by). Holiday 14: 61 Nov '53.

"La Chambre verti" (Vuillard). Con. 141: IX (col.) Ap '58.

"La Chasse au Lion" (Delacroix). Con. 143: 1 Je '59.

Lachish, sieze of. Natl. geog. 118: 834-9 (part col.) Dec '60.

Lackawanna Valley (1854). Amer. heri. vol. 9 no. 1 p. 66 (col.) (Dec '57).

Lacoste, Robert. Cur. biog. p. 314 (1957).

La Crosse (Wis.). Natl. geog. 111: 162-3 (col.) Feb '57.

lacrosse game. Holiday 20: 71 (col.) Dec '56; 21: 39 May '57.

lacrosse player. Holiday 23: 91 (col.) May '58.

"La Crosse playing among Indians" (Eastman). Amer. heri. vol. 6 no. 1 p. 35 (col.) (fall '54).

Lacy, Dan. Cur. biog. p. 392 (1954).

Ladakh (Tibet). Natl. geog. 99: 604-34 (part col.) May '51.

—— (map). Natl. geog. 99: 607 May '51.

Ladatte, Francesco (carvings by). Con. 142: 152-3 Dec '58.

Ladd, Alan. Cur. biog. p. 421 (1943).

ladder. Holiday 10: 11 Aug '51.
Natl. geog. 104: 858 (col.) Dec '53; 111: 637 (col.) May '57; 112: 511 Oct '57; 113: 411 (col.) Mar '58, 749 (col.) Je '58.

—— (burglar, police dog). Natl. geog. 114: 197 Aug '58.

—— (cat climbing). Natl. geog. 116: 493 Oct '59.

—— (double bed). Natl. geog. 98: 627 Nov '50.

—— (girl). Holiday 10: 113 (col.) Dec '51.
Natl. geog. 113: 645 (col.) May '58.

—— (girl, cherry tree). Natl. geog. 114: 158 (col.) Aug '58.

—— (man). Holiday 10: 52 (col.) Oct '51.
Natl. geog. 113: 136 Jan '58.

—— (tall date palm). Natl. geog. 112: 679 Nov '57.

"Ladder of fortune". Amer. heri. vol. 8 no. 4 p. 53 (col.) (Je '57).

"Ladder of pilgrimage of soul" (sym.). Lehner: Pict. bk. of sym., p. 78.

ladies, Colonial (lawn, tea). Holiday 22: 71 (col.) Sept '57.

——, first. *See* U.S. Presidents' wives.

ladle, silver. Con. 145: XXVI Mar '60.

——, silver (18th cent.). Con. 141: 92 Ap '58.

——, silver (shell bowl, 18th cent.). Con. 145: XIII May '60.

lady (reading to children). Natl. geog. 105: 319 (col.) Mar '54.

—— (with dog). Con. 140: LIII Nov '57.

"Lady Caroline Price" (Reynolds). Con. 126: 89 Oct '50.

"Lady Caroline Scott" (Reynolds). Con. 141: 63 Mar '58.

"Lady Cockburn & sons" (Reynolds). Praeg. pict. ency., p. 373 (col.).

"Lady Cornwallis" (Lely). Con. 126: 36 Aug '50.

Lady Fatima, hand of. *See* hand of Lady Fatima.

"Lady feeding parrot" (Van Mieris). Con. 139: XVII (col.) Ap '57.

"Lady Jane Halliday" (Reynolds). Con. 143: 207 Je '59.

"Lady reading letter" (Terborch). Con. 126: 197 (col.) Dec '50.

"Lady Sheffield" (Gainsborough). Con. 143: 207 Je '59.

"Lady Stanhope & Lady Effingham" (Cotes). Con. 142: 26 Sept '58.

"Lady with a fan" (Velasquez). Con. 127: cover, opp. p. 3 (col.) Mar '51.

lady. *See* also woman.

ladybird (sym.). Lehner: Pict. bk. of sym., p. 63.

"La famille cottet" (Bonnard). Con. 143: 146 Mar '59.

La Farge, Rev. John. Cur. biog. p. 481 (1942).

La Farge, Oliver. Cur. biog. p. 335 (1953).

Lafayette, Marquis de. Amer. heri. vol. 8 no. 1 p. 4 (col.) (Dec '56).
Con. 129: 135 Je '52.
Natl. geog. 112: 425 Sept '57.

—— (Morse). Jensen: The White House, p. 43.

—— (Paris revolution). Amer. heri. vol. 8 no. 1 p. 111 (Dec '56).

—— (statue). Natl. geog. 112: 423 Sept '57.

Lafayette & Washington (Valley Forge). Brooks: Growth of a nation, p. 77.

"Lafayette receives crown of liberty" (allegory). Amer. heri. vol. 8 no. 1 p. 6 (Feb '56).

"Lafayette visiting mount Vernon" (Mignot). Amer. heri. vol. 8 no. 1 p. 9 (col.) (Dec '56).

Lafayette's chateau, Marquis de (birthplace, France). Natl. geog. 112: 423-4 Sept '57.
Holiday 7: :33 Mar '50.
Travel 107: 53 Ap '57.

"La Feinte resistance" (Boucher). Con. 133: 261 Je '54.

La Follette, Charles M. Cur. biog. p. 315 (1950).

La Follette, Robert (statue). Holiday 6: 41 Jl '49.

La Follette, Robert M. Cur. biog. p. 369 (1944).

La Frensen the younger, Nicolas (work of). Con. 135: 47 Mar '55; 141: 22 Mar '58.

"La gamme d'amour" (Watteau). Praeg. pict. ency., p. 360 (col.).

Lagerkvist, Par. Cur. biog. p. 322 (1952).

lagoon (Los Angeles). Holiday 24: 127 (col.) Dec '58.

La Gorce, John Oliver. Natl. geog. 117: 441, 444 (part col.) Mar '60.

Lagos harbor (Nigeria). Travel 107: 41 Feb '57.

"La Halte" (Delacroix). Con. 145: L Ap '60.

Lahey, Frank H. Cur. biog. p. 485 (1941).

Lahorra, Cora (Philippine is.). Holiday 17: 56-7 Jan '55.

Lahr, Bert. Cur. biog. p. 325 (1952).

Lahrtmann, Kristian (work of). Con. 134: 206 Dec '54.

Laidler, Harry W. Cur. biog. p. 330 (1945).

Laine, Frankie. Cur. biog. p. 354 (1956).

Laing, Hugh. Cur. biog. p. 317 (1946).

Laird, Donald A. Cur. biog. p. 319 (1946).

La Jolla (Cal.). Natl. geog. 102: 756-82 (part col.) Dec '52.

La Jolla beach & tennis club. Holiday 20: 106-11 (part col.) Oct '56.

Lajos Kossuth monument (Hungary). Holiday 6: 64 (col.) Nov '49.

Lajoue, J. (work of). Con. 145: 162 May '60.

lake. Holiday 19: 121 (col.) Feb '56.

Lake Atitlan (Guatemala). Holiday 17: 35 (col.) Mar '55.

Lake Avernus (Italy). Labande: Naples, p. 145.

lake bottom, sun dried. Travel 109: inside cover Feb '58.

Lake Buenos Aires. Natl. geog. 117: 206-7 (col.) Feb '60.

Lake Caonillas (Puerto Rico). Natl. geog. 99: 430-1 (col.) Ap '51.

Lake Chelan (men & women). Natl. geog. 117: 469 (col.) Ap '60.

Lake Como (Italy). Holiday 20: 98-102 (part col.) Sept '56; 25: 94, 96 (col.) Mar '59.

Lake Constance. Holiday 27: 75 (col.), 77 Jan '60.

Lake Geneva (Switzerland). Travel 113: cover (col.) Ap '60.

Lake George (N.Y., Adirondacks). Holiday 8: 98-101 (part col.) Sept '50.

Lake Katrine. See Loch Katrine.

Lake Killarney. See Killarney lake.

Lake Louise (Canada). Holiday 12: 110 (col.) Aug '52; 21: 12 (col.) Mar '57. Travel 107: cover May '57.

Lake Lucerne (Turner). Con. 143: III Ap '59.

Lake Lugano (Alps). Holiday 26: 122 (col.) Sept '59.

Lake Maggiore. Holiday 15: 148 (col.) May '54. Natl. geog. 98: 223 (col.) Aug '50.

Lake Maracaibo (fishing village). Travel 105: 24 Feb '56.

Lake Marie (Wyo.). Travel 104: 58 Oct '55.

Lake Mead (Nev.). Jordan: Hammond's pict. atlas, p. 183 (col.).

Lake Mendota (Wis.). Natl. geog. 111: 152 (col.) Feb '57.

Lake Minnewaska (N.Y.). Holiday 24: cover (col.) Aug '58.

Lake Mohonk Mt. house (N.Y.). Holiday 24: 38-9 (col.) Aug '58.

Lake Moraine (Canada). Holiday 24: 112 (col.) Aug '58.

"Lake of Geneva" (Turner). Con. 126: 68 Aug '50.

Lake of Lugano Bussone (Switzerland). Holiday 15: 52 Jan '54.

Lake of the Ozarks (Mo.). Travel 112: cover (col.) Aug '59.

Lake Orta (Italy). Holiday 25: 90 (col.) Mar '59.

Lake Patzcuaro (Mexico). Natl. geog. 102: 526-7 (col.) Oct '52. Travel 101: 23-5 Ap '54.

Lake Placid. Travel 101: 20-1 Feb '54.

Lake Superior (sunrise, Minn.). Face of Amer., p. 168-9 (col.). Natl. geog. 115: 476-7 (col.) Ap '59.

Lake Tahoe (Cal.). Jordan: Hammond's pict. atlas, p. 188 (col.).

Lake Thun (Switzerland). Holiday 16: 26-7 (col.) Aug '54.

Lake tower motel (Chicago). Travel 111: 47 May '59.

Lake Windemere (Eng.). Con. 145: XXXIX (col.) May '60.

Lakes area, The Great. See Great Lakes area.

"La lecture" (Manet). Con. 134: 40 Sept '54.

Laleigh, Sir Walter. Amer. heri. vol. 4 no. 2 p. 46-7 (col.), 49 (winter '53).

Lalemant, Gabriel (martyred). Amer. heri. vol. 10 no. 6 p. 57 (Oct '59).

"L'Algerienne" (Renoir). Con. 132: opp. p. 107 (col.) Nov '53.

"La Liseuse" (Fragonard). Con. 129: 71 Ap '52.

Lall, Arthur S. Cur. biog. p. 356 (1956).

Lalor, Lt. William G., jr. Natl. geog. 115: 5, 7 (col.) Jan '59.

Lama. Natl. geog. 99: 611-34 (part col.) May '51.

—— (Buddhist temple). Natl. geog. 117: 33 (col.) Jan '60.

——, Bodnath (alter). Natl. geog. 117: 393 (col.) Mar '60.

——, Tibetan. See Tibetan lama.

Lama dancers. Natl. geog. 102: 748-9 (col.) Dec '52.

"La Macarena" virgin. Natl. geog. 99: 511 (col.) Ap '51.

"La Madeleine portee par les Anges" (Vouet). Con. 139: 261 Je '57.

Lamas. Natl. geog. 102: 721 (col.) Dec '52.

—— (Devil dance). Holiday 12: 56 Dec '52.

Lamayuru monastery. See monastery Lamayuru.

Lamb, Harold. Jun. bk. of auth., p. 183.

lamb (sym.). Lehner: Pict. bk. of sym., p. 58.

——, Easter. Lehner: Pict. bk. of sym., p. 52.

Lamb of God (sym.). Lehner: Pict. bk. of sym., p. 34.

Lambert, Constant (Ayrton). Cooper: Con. ency. of music, p. 149.

Lambert, Sylvester Maxwell. Cur. biog. p. 486 (1941).

Lambert, William Vincent. Cur. biog. p. 345 (1955).

Lamb, Willis E., jr. Cur. biog. p. 357 (1956).

Lambertville (music tent, N.J.). Travel 113: 26 May '60.

"Lament of death" (Gilles). Praeg. pict. ency., p. 481.

"Lamentation" (Mantegna). Praeg. pict. ency., p. 275.

"Lamentation of Christ". Con. 144: 58 Sept '59.

Lamerie silver cup. Con. 139: XXX Je '57.

"La Merienda" (Goya). Con. 133: 231 Je '54.

Lamidos palace (Rei Bouba, Cameroons). Natl. geog. 116: 240 (col.) Aug '59.

laminated wood. *See* wood, laminated.

LaMont, Corliss. Cur. biog. p. 321 (1946).

Lamont, Daniel. Amer. heri. vol. 8 no. 6 p. 11 (Oct '57).

Lamont-Hussey observatory. *See* observatory, Lamont-Hussey.

Lamorisse, Albert. Cur. biog. p. 229 (1963).

"La Mort d'Ophelie" (Delacroix). Con. 144: 198 Dec '59.

lamp (Norway). Natl. geog. 111: 104 (col.) Jan '57.

—— (Tiffany) Holiday 26: 149 (col.) Nov '59.

——, antique. Brooks: Growth of a nation, p. 207.
Con. 140: XXXIV Sept '57.
Holiday 23: 63 (col.) Mar '58; 27: 179 (col.) May '60.
Natl. geog. 99: 446 (col.) Ap '51.

——, astral (early). Daniel: Cut & engraved glass, pl. 140.

——, Betty. *See* Betty lamp.

——, carriage. Rawson: Ant. pict. bk., p. 95.

——, ceiling (antique). Holiday 20: 81 (col.) Oct '56.

——, coach. *See* coach lamp.

——, desk gooseneck. Holiday 26: 152 Nov '59.

——, Dolphin tripod (antique). Con. 132: 149 Jan '54.

——, Edison carbon filament. Amer. heri. vol. 10 no. 6 p. 40 (Oct '59).

——, 18th cent. Con. 129: back cover Ap '52.

——, electric. Holiday 27: 246 May '60.

——, electric table. Travel 101: 5 Mar '54.

——, 1st camphene. Rawson: Ant. pict. bk., p. 94.

——, 1st flat wick. Rawson: Ant. pict. bk., p. 93.

——, 1st with chimney. Rawson: Ant. pict. bk., p. 93.

——, fishing wharf. Rawson: Ant. pict. bk., p. 95.

——, floor electric. Holiday 28: 44 (col.) Oct '60, 41 (col.), 226 Nov '60.

——, globe table. Travel 104: back cover Aug '55.

——, Gen. Grant's. Holiday 28: 57 Sept '60.

——, hanging (antique). Holiday 28: 10 (col.) Sept '60.

——, magic. Holiday 19: 110 Jan '56.

——, night. *See* night light.

——, oil. Natl. geog. 112: 746 (col.) Dec '57.

——, oil (Italian silver). Con. 144: 152 Dec '59.

——, oil (sym.). Lehner: Pict. bk. of sym., p. 17.

——, reflector. Rawson: Ant. pict. bk., p. 95.

——, ship. *See* ship lamp.

——, stage coach. *See* stage coach lamps.

——, stone age bone. Natl. geog. 113: 429 Mar '58.

——, street. Amer. heri. vol. 4 no. 3 p. 1 (spring '53); vol. 4 no. 2 p. 4, 6-7 (winter '53).

Holiday 11: 51 Jan '52; 14: 115 (col.) Aug '53; 25: 5 (col.) Ap '59; 26: 145 Dec '59; 27: 75 (col.) Feb '60; 28: 109 Jl '60, 50 Nov '60.
Natl. geog. 107: 651 (col.) May '55; 114: 122 (col.) Jl '58, 444 (col.) Oct '58.
Travel 105: 15 Jan '56; 109: inside cover Jan '58, inside cover Ap '58; 112: 56 Aug '59.

——, street (Cuba). Natl. geog. 109: 647 May '56.

——, street wall. Natl. geog. 118: 655 (col.) Nov '60.

lamp, street. *See* also lamp, post.

——, sun. *See* sun lamp.

——, table. Con. 129: XXV Ap '52; 133: LIII May '54.
Holiday 10: 123 (col.) Oct '51, 2, 10 (col.) Nov '51; 11: 53 (col.) Feb '52, 151 (col.) Ap '52, 71 (col.) Je '52; 12: 125 (col.) Nov '52; 18: 25, 196 Dec '55; 22: 107 (col.) Oct '57, 24 (col.), 43 Dec '57; 24: inside cover (col.) Nov '58; 28: 27, 39 (col.) Oct '60, 145 (col.) Nov '60.
Natl. geog. 105: 453 (col.) Ap '54; 106: 666 (col.) Nov '54; 113: 176 (col.) Feb '58.

——, table (old style). Natl. geog. 107: 654 May '55.

——, table electric. Holiday 28: 64-5 (col.) Oct '60.

——, table study. Natl. geog. 112: 330 (col.) Sept '57.

——, wall. Holiday 26: 59 Aug '59.

——, whale oil glass. Natl. geog. 107: 785 (col.) Je '55.

lamp hook, gate. Rawson: Ant. pict. bk., p. 95.

lamp, post. Holiday 10: 139 Nov '51; 11: 22 Ap '52, 165 May '52; 12: 146 Jl '52, 65 (col.) Dec '52; 13: 151 May '63; 18: 37 Jl '55; 19: 24 Jan '56; 20: 76 Dec '56; 21: 117 (col.) Ap '57, 13 (col.) May '57; 28: inside back cover (col.) Oct '60.
Natl. geog. 105: 189 Feb '54; 107: 645 (col.) May '55; 113: 48 (col.) Jan '58; 114: 362 (col.) Sept '58; 117: 255 (col.) Feb '60.
Travel 101: 4, 15 Jan '54; 103: 13 May '55; 106: 60 Dec '56; 108: 29 Aug '57; 111: 25 Ap '59.

——, post (Chinese). Natl. geog. 105: 728 Je '54.

lamp room, Gen. elec. Natl. geog. 107: 453 (col.) Ap '55.

lamplighter. Amer. heri. vol. 4 no. 2 p. 4 (winter '53.

Lamprey, Louise. Jun. bk. of auth., p. 184.

lamps, antique. Rawson: Ant. pict. bk., p. 93-5.

——, gate. Natl. geog. 117: 29 (col.) Jan '60.

——, glass kerosene. Daniel: Cut & engraved glass, p. 140-1.

——, hurricane. Holiday 11: 141 Ap '52.

——, table. Natl. geog. 117: 31 (col.) Jan '60.

——, Venetian glass. Con. 138: 169 Dec '56.

——, whale oil glass. Daniel: Cut & engraved glass, pl. 139.

Lamy, Archbishop. Amer. heri. vol. 8 no. 6 p. 31 (Oct '57).

La Napoule (France). Holiday 6: 66 Nov '49.

Lancaster, Burt. Cur. biog. p. 338 (1953).
Lancaster turnpike (1795). Brooks: Growth of a nation, p. 84.
lance (ancient times). Int. gr. soc.: Arts . . . p. 33 (col.).
lancer (Bombay, India). Travel 111: 19 Jan '59.
"The lancers" (Velasquez). Holiday 25: 69 (col.) Jan '59.
Lanchester, Elsa. Cur. biog. p. 318 (1950).
Lancret, Nicholas (work of). Con. 135: 4 Mar '55; 136: cover (col.) Nov '55; 142: 6 Sept '58.
Land, Edwin H. Cur. biog. p. 340 (1953).
Land, Emory S. Cur. biog. p. 488 (1941).
land, free (poster). Amer. heri. vol. 7 no. 3 p. 51 (Ap '56).
"Land of promise: Castle garden". (Ulrich). Natl. geog. 99: 208 (col.) Feb '51.
land poster, western settlement. Amer. heri. vol. 9 no. 4 p. 12 (Je '58).
Landais, Pierre. Amer. heri. vol. 11 no. 3 p. 10 (Ap '60).
Landau, Lev. Cur. biog. p. 232 (1963).
landau (with horses). Holiday 6: 100 (col.) Dec '49.
Landers, Ann. Cur. biog. p. 316 (1957).
Landesio, Eugenio (work of). Con. 135: 251 (col.) Je '55.
Landis, James M. Cur. biog. p. 482 (1942).
Landis, Kenesaw Mountain. Amer. heri. vol. 11 no. 4 p. 27 (Je '60).
Cur. biog. p. 374 (1944).
"Landlord's story" (Bennett). Con. 135: XLIX May '55.
Landolt, Arlo U. Natl. geog. 113: 459 Ap '58.
Landon, Alf. Cur. biog. p. 377 (1944).
Landon, Margaret. Cur. biog. p. 332 (1945).
Landowska, Wanda. Cur. biog. p. 334 (1945).
Landowski, Paul (sculpt. by). Natl. geog. 107: 295 Mar '55.
Landrum, Phil M. Cur. biog. p. 227 (1960).
Land's End (Eng.). Travel 101: 17 Feb '54.
"Landscape with birds" (Savery). Natl. geog. 97: 751 Je '50.
"Landscape with the temptation of St. Anthony Abbot". Natl. geog. 101: 83 (col.) Jan '52.
landscapes. Con. 129: 77-82 Je '52.
Landseer, Sir Edwin (work of). Con. 129: XLIV Ap '52; 139: cover (col.) Je '57; 142 XXV Jan '59; 144: XX (col.) Nov '59.
Landshut (village). Disney: People & places, p. 51 (col.).
Lane, Sir Allen. Cur. biog. p. 397 (1954).
Lane, Sir Arthur Bliss. Cur. biog. p. 363 (1948).
Lane, Carl. D. Cur. biog. p. 362 (1951).
Lane, Edward William. Ceram: March of arch., p. 98, 135.
—— (work of). Ceram: March of arch., p. 135.
Lane, Harriet. Jensen: The White House, p. 78.
Lane, William Preston, jr. Cur. biog. p. 340 (1949).
Lancret, Nicolas (work of). Con. 144: LXIII Nov '59.
Lang, Al. Holiday 24: 80 Nov '58.
Lang, Archbishop Cosmo Gordon. Cur. biog. p. 491 (1941).
Lang, Fritz. Cur. biog. p. 425 (1943).

langalanga (thatch roof huts). Natl. geog. 99: 342 (col.) Mar '51.
Lange, Halvard M. Cur. biog. p. 373 (1947).
Lange, Josef (work of). Cooper: Con. ency. of music, p. 135 (col.).
Lange, Oscar. Cur. biog. p. 323 (1946).
Langenhove, Fernand van. Holiday 24: 14 Dec '58.
Langer, Lawrence. Cur. biog. p. 381 (1944).
Langer, Susanne K. Cur. biog. p. 234 (1963).
Langer, William. Cur. biog. p. 327 (1952).
Langford, Nathaniel P. Amer. heri. vol. 5 no. 3 p. 41 (spring '54).
Langley, Adria Locke. Cur. biog. p. 335 (1945).
"Langleys" (Essex, Eng., country home, int,' ext.). Con. 140: 210 (col.), 211-7 Jan '58.
Langlie, Arthur B. Cur. biog. p. 319 (1950).
Langmuir, Irving. Cur. biog. p. 322 (1950).
Holiday 7: 49 (col.) Je '50.
Langsdorff, George. Amer. heri. vol. 10 no. 3 p. 75 (Ap '59).
Langtry, Lily. Horan: Pict. hist. of wild west, p. 139.
language (Japanese letters). Travel 112: 49 Dec '59.
Languedoc (France). Natl. geog. 100: 2-44 (part col.) Jl '51.
Laniel, Joseph. Cur. biog. p. 399 (1954).
Lanin volcano. See volcano, Lanin.
Laning, Cdr. Richard B. Holiday 24: 59 (col.) Oct '58.
Lanino, Bernardino (work of). Con. 143: 93 Ap '53.
Lannung, Hermod. Cur. biog. p. 341 (1949).
Lansdowne, Lt. Com. Zachary. Amer. heri. vol. 10 no. 2 p. 18 (Feb '59).
Lansing, Marion Florence. Jun. bk. of auth., p. 185.
Lansing (Iowa). Travel 110: 55 Sept '58.
Lansing (Mich.). Natl. geog. 101: 294 (col.) Mar '52.
Lant, Dave. Horan: Pict. hist. of wild west, p. 203.
Lantana colony club (Bermuda). Travel 109: 41 Mar '58.
lantern. Amer. heri. vol. 11 no. 5 p. 32 (col.) (Aug '60).
Brooks: Growth of a nation, p. 249.
Holiday 14: 114 Aug '53; 22: 16 Dec '57.
Natl. geog. 116: 621 Nov '59.
Travel 111: inside back cover Je '59; 112: inside back cover Jl '59, inside back cover Aug '59, inside cover Sept '59.
—— (antique). Holiday 21: 164 Mar '57; 24: 136 (col.) Sept '58, 131 (col.) Dec '58.
Natl. geog. 98: 558 Oct '50; 111: 321 Mar '57.
—— (for running to fires). Rawson: Ant. pict. bk., p. 93.
—— (from tower of Old North Church, Boston). Natl. geog. 97: 310 (col.) Mar '50.
—— (man holding). Amer. heri. vol. 10 no. 3 p. 57 (Ap '59).
——, Amer. (18th cent.). Holiday 27: 181 May '60.
——, birdcage. Rawson: Ant. pict. bk., p. 94.
——, brass hall (19th cent.). Con. 145: XXVII Ap '60.

lantern, ceiling. Natl. geog. 117: 839 (col.) Je '60.

——, **ceiling ship.** Holiday 24: 12 (col.) Jl '58.

——, **Chinese.** Travel 111: 34-5 Jan '59.

——, **gate.** Natl. geog. 117: 801 (col.) Je '60.

——, **glass sugar cane.** Natl. geog. 101: 373 (col.) Mar '52.

——, **hall (Irish).** Con. 145: 152 May '60.

——, **Italian silver.** Con. 144: 152 Dec '59.

——, **jade.** *See* jade lantern.

——, **Japanese.** Holiday 13: 142 Mar '53; 20: 151 Nov '56; 21: 39 Mar '57.

Travel 104: 3 Aug '55.

——, **metal (18th cent.).** Con. ency. of ant., vol. 3, pl. 13.

——, **metal classical (18th cent.).** Con. ency. of ant., vol. 3, pl. 13.

——, **Mexican street.** Travel 114: 30 Nov '60.

——, **miners.** Natl. geog. 110: 552 (col.) Oct '56.

——, **porch.** Natl. geog. 108: 305 Sept '55.

——, **ship.** Holiday 28: 65 Jl '60.

——, **street.** Holiday 22: 68 Nov '57.

——, **temple.** *See* temple lantern.

——, **wall (Pineau, 17th cent.).** Con. 145: 108 Ap '60.

lantern lamp, Japanese. Holiday 18: 9 Sept '55, 63 Nov '55.

lantern tower (Boston, Eng.). Natl. geog. 103: 809 (col.) Je '53.

lanterns, Chinese. Holiday 16: 99 (col.) Aug '54.

——, **fishing boat.** Natl. geog. 109: 319 Mar '56.

——, **Japanese.** Holiday 17: 94 Jan '55. Natl. geog. 97: 624 (col.) May '50.

Travel 102: 39 Nov '54.

——, **wall (antique).** Natl. geog. 100: 586 (col.) Nov '51.

Laocoon group (40 B.C.). Ceram: March of arch., p. 5.

Praeg. pict. ency., p. 158.

—— **(being cleaned).** Natl. geog. 110: 644 Nov '56.

Laos. Natl. geog. 99: 478, 484-88 (part col.) Ap '51; 117: 47-69 (col.) Jan '60.

—— **(map).** Natl. geog. 117: 50 Jan '60.

—— **(royal palace).** Natl. geog. 98: 509 Oct '50.

Laotse (sym.). Lehner: Pict. bk. of sym., p. 42.

La Parguera (harbor). Travel 111: 41 Feb '59.

La Paz (Bolivia). Holiday 8: 53 (col.) Nov '50; 20: 64-5 (col.) Nov '56.

Natl. geog. 98: 488-92 (col.) Oct '50.

Travel 104: 18-9 Oct '55.

"La petite fille en rose" (Cassatt). Con. 143: X Je '59.

Lapham, Roger D. Cur. biog. p. 365 (1948).

"La Pia" (Rossetti). Con. 132: XXXIX (col.) Jan '54.

lapidary class. Natl. geog. 100: 654-5, 658 (col.) Nov '51.

lapidary work. Con. 135: XLV Ap '55.

Lapland. Disney: People & places, p. 13-24 (col.).

Natl. geog. 106: 250-80 (part col.) Aug '54.

Laplander. Holiday 18: 106-9 (part col.) Dec '55.

—— **(mother & child).** Holiday 12: 91 (col.) Sept '52.

—— **(reindeer).** Disney: People & places, p. 13 (col.).

—— **(woman).** Holiday 17: 41 Jan '55.

Laplanders. Natl. geog. 108: 741 (col.) Dec '55.

Travel 106: 35 Aug '56.

—— **(delegates to parliament).** Travel 108: 40, 42 Jl '57.

—— **(men & women).** Travel 103: 9 Ap '55.

Lapp, Ralph E. Cur. biog. p. 347 (1955).

Lapps. *See* Laplander.

"La Promenade" (Vuillard). Con. 134: 69 (col.) Sept '54.

Laramie, Fort. *See* Fort Laramie.

Lardner, John. Holiday 26: 19 Dec '59.

Lardner, Ring. Holiday 20: 6 Oct '56.

Jensen: The White House, p. 216.

Laredo (Texas). Holiday 8: 83-8 Dec '50.

Larkin, Oliver W. Cur. biog. p. 323 (1950).

La Roe, Wilbur, jr. Cur. biog. p. 367 (1948).

Laroon, Marcellus (work of). Con. 140: XXII Jan '58.

Laroon the younger, Marcellus (work of). Con. 140: 242-5 Jan '58.

Larsen, Roy E. Cur. biog. p. 325 (1950).

Larson, Arthur. Cur. biog. p. 359 (1956).

Larson, Jess. Cur. biog. p. 363 (1951).

Larson, Leonard W. Cur. biog. p. 247 (1962).

Larvie, Calvin (work of). Natl. geog. 107: 370 (col.) Mar '55.

larynx. Gray's anatomy, p. 1107-19, 1121.

La Salle. Amer. heri. vol. 2 no. 2 p. 73 (winter '51); vol. 8 no. 3 p. 71 (Ap '57).

"La Salle's expedition on the Mississippi" (Catlin). Amer. heri. vol. 8 no. 3 p. 4-19 (col.) (Ap '57).

La Salle's ship, "Griffin". *See* "Griffin" ship.

lasers. Sat. Eve. Post 237: 68-71 Oct 24, 1964.

Lasker, Albert Davis. Amer. heri. vol. 6 no. 1 p. 74 (fall '54).

Lasker, Mrs. Albert D. Cur. biog. p. 246 (1959).

Lasker, Mary Woodward. *See* Lasker, Mrs. Albert D.

Laski, Harold. Cur. biog. p 493 (1941)

Laski, Marghanita. Cur. biog. p. 365 (1951).

Lasky, Jesse L. Cur. biog. p. 374 (1947).

Las Palmas (Canary is.). Natl. geog. 107: 491-5 (col.) Ap '55.

Lassaw, Ibram. Cur. biog. p. 318 (1957).

Lassen Peak (inactive volcano, Cal.). Natl. geog. 105: 749 Je '54.

Lasser, Jacob K. Cur. biog. p. 326 (1946).

Lasswell, Harold D. Cur. biog. p. 376 (1947).

"The Last Judgment" (Dürer). Con. 144: LXIV Sept '59.

"Last Moments of John Brown" (Hovenden). Natl. geog. 99: 197 (col.) Feb '51.

"The Last of England" (Brown). Amer. heri. vol. 11 no. 5 cover (col.) (Aug '60).

"Last Supper" (Giotto). Con. ency. of ant., vol. 1, pl. 149.

"Last Supper" (Tintoretto). Con. 133: XIX Ap '54.

"Last Supper", Greek Holy week ritual. Natl. geog. 98: 721 (col.) Dec '50.

"Last Supper", pearl shell (Jerusalem). Natl. geog. 98: 743 (col.) Dec '50.

Lawrence, Ernest O. Cur. biog. p. 330 (1952).
Lawrence, Sir Geoffrey. Cur. biog. p. 330 (1946).
Lawrence, Gertrude. Cur. biog. p. 333 (1952).
Lawrence, Hilda. Cur. biog. p. 381 (1947).
Lawrence, James. Amer. heri. vol. 7 no. 3 p. 18 (col.) (Ap '56).
Holiday 23: 76 May '58.
Lawrence, Mildred. Cur. biog. p. 346 (1953).
Lawrence, Thomas. Con. 143: 90 Ap '59.
—— (work of). Amer. heri. vol. 6 no. 6 p. 4 (col.) (Oct '55).
Con. 126: 126 Oct '50; 139: 123 Ap '57; 140: LIX Sept '57, LV Nov '57, 239 Jan '58; 141: 61 Mar '58, LXI May '58; 142: 195 Dec '58;; 143: 117 Ap '59, 140, 153 May '59; 144: 76 Nov '59; 145: LVII Ap '60.
Natl. geog. 105: 788 (col.) Je '54; 113: 252-3 (col.) Feb '58.
Lawrence (Kan, 1856). Amer. heri. vol. 7 no. 5 p 5 (col.) (Aug '56).
—— (Kan., 1863, burning). Amer. heri. vol. 11 no. 6 p. 22-3 (Oct '60).
—— (Kan., 1867). Horan: Pict. hist. of wild west, p. 29.
Lawson, Edward B. Cur. biog. p. 363 (1956).
Lawson, Robert. Cur. biog. p. 499 (1941).
Jun. bk. of auth., p. 189.
Lawson, Capt. Ted. Cur. biog. p. 431 (1943).
Lawther, Sir William. Cur. biog. p. 345 (1949).
Lawton, Frederick J. Cur. biog. p. 366 (1951).
Laxness, Halldor. Cur. biog. p. 332 (1946).
Lay, Elza. Horan: Pict. hist. of wild west, p. 192.
Lay, James S., jr. Cur. biog. p. 330 (1950).
Layard, Sir Austen Henry. Ceram: March of arch., p. 211-12.
Layard's excavations at Nineveh (Sir Austen H. Layard. Ceram: March of arch., p. 213-7.
Laycock, Maj. Gen. Robert E. Cur. biog. p. 389 (1944).
Layton, Adm. Sir Geoffrey. Cur. biog. p. 487 (1942).
Layton, Mrs. Roy F. Cur. biog. p. 335 (1952).
Lazareff, Pierre. Cur. biog. p. 488 (1942).
Lea, Clarence F. Cur. biog. p. 333 (1946).
Lea, Van Antwerp. Holiday 21: 60 May '57.
Leach, Ruth M. Cur. biog. p. 373 (1948).
leach tubs. Rawson: Ant. pict. bk., p. 31.
Lead (S.D., gold mining town). Natl. geog. 110: 490 (col.) Oct '56.
lead (sym.). Lehner: Pict. bk. of sym., p. 72.
lead melting dipper. See dipper for melting lead.
lead refinery. Natl. geog. 114: 168-9 (col.) Aug '58.
lead sculpture. See sculpture, lead.
lead-sulphate (sym.). Lehner: Pict. bk. of sym., p. 72.
Leader, B.W. Con. 141: XLI May '58.
—— (work of). Con. 143: XXX Mar '59, XX-VIII Jan '60.
Leader, George M. Cur. biog. p. 364 (1956).
Leaf, Munro. Jun. bk. of auth., p. 190.
Leahy, Frank. Cur. biog. p. 501 (1941).
Leahy, William D. Cur. biog. p. 502 (1941).
Leake, Chauncey D. Cur. biog. p. 229 (1960).

Leake, Sir John (Kneller). Con. 127: 31 Mar '51.
Lean, David. Cur. biog. p. 347 (1953).
Leaning tower of Pisa. Holiday 6: 115 Aug '49, 20 Oct '49; 11: 128 Ap '52; 12: 4 Oct '52; 18: 31 Nov '55; 19: 1 Feb '56; 20: 1 Aug '56, 200 Nov '56, 176 Dec '56; 21: 105 Jan '57; 25: 135 May '59; 27: 123 Jan '60.
Natl. geog. 111: 804 (col.) Je '57.
Praeg. pict. ency., p. 218.
Travel 102: inside cover Jl '54; 113: 32 Mar '60.
Leaning tower of Soochow temple (China). Int. gr. soc.: Arts . . . p. 51 (col.).
Leao Velloso, Pedro. Cur. biog. p. 336 (1946).
leap frog game (children). Holiday 18: 7 Jl '55.
Natl. geog. 118: 540 (col.) Oct '60.
leapers, circus. Durant: Pict. hist. of Amer. circus, p. 12, 15.
Lear, Lt. Gen. Ben. Cur. biog. p. 490 (1942).
learning (sym.). Lehner: Pict. bk. of sym., p. 43.
Leary, Vice Adm. Herbert F. Cur. biog. p. 492 (1942).
Leary, Kate. Amer. heri. vol. 11 no. 1 p. 69 (Dec '59).
leather craftsman (Morocca). Natl. geog. 107: 163-5 (col.) Feb '55.
leather decorations. Rawson: Ant. pict. bk., p. 83.
leather tanning vats. Natl. geog. 112: 56-7 (col.) Jl '57.
leathernecks. See marines, U.S.
Leathers, Baron. Cur. biog. p. 503 (1941).
leaves falling (sym.). Lehner: Pict. bk. of sym., p. 81.
Leavey, Maj. Gen. Edmond H. Cur. biog. p. 368 (1951).
Lebanese figure of a god. Con. 144: 281 Jan '60.
Lebanese nomad. Natl. geog. 105: 496 (col.) Ap '54.
Lebanon. Natl. geog. 113: 480-523 (part col.) Ap '58.
—— (hillside). Natl. geog. 102: 832 Dec '52.
—— (map). Natl. geog. 113: 488 Ap '58.
Le Blanc, Alfred. Amer. heri. vol. 7 no. 3 p. 5 (Ap '56).
"Le bon bock" (Manet). Con. 134: 67 Sept '54.
"Le Boulevard des Italiens" (Grandjean). Con. 141: XLI (col.) Je '58.
"Le Bourgeosis Gentilhomme" (play). Int. gr. soc.: Arts . . . p. 107 (col.).
Le Brun, Charles (work of). Con. 136: LXIV Jan '56.
Le Brun, Mary L. E. V. (work of). Con. 135: IX (col.) Mar '55.
Lebrun, Rico. Cur. biog. p. 337 (1952).
Lebrun, Vigee (work of). Con. 136: 31-2 Sept '55; 142: 112 Nov '58.
Lech (Austria). Holiday 25: 73-7 (part col.) Jan '59.
Lech am Arlberg (Austria). Holiday 17: 112 (col.) Feb '55.
"Le Chariot d'Arras" (Corot). Con. 134: XI Nov '54; 139: XIX Je '57.

"Le Chemin de Fer" (Manet). Con. 139: 203 May '57.

Leclerc, Brig. Gen. Jacques-Philippe. Cur. biog. p. 391 (1944).

Le Clercq, Tanaquil. Cur. biog. p. 349 (1953).

Le Coq D'Or (setting for, by Gontcharova). Cooper: Con. ency. of music, p. 343 (col.).

Le Corbusier. Cur. biog. p. 383 (1947).

—— (arch. by). Int. gr. soc.: Arts . . . p. 125 (col.).

lectern (Alpirsbach). Praeg. pict. ency., p. 191 (col.).

——, Austrian. Con. 142: 40 Sept '58.

——, brass (5th cent.). Con. 129: 39 Ap '52.

lecture poster, Woodhull-Claflin. Amer. heri. vol. 7 no. 4 p. 90 (Je '56).

Lecuona, Ernesto. Cur. biog. p. 393 (1944).

Ledbetter, Bud. Horan: Pict. hist. of wild west, p. 170.

"Le de Jeuner a Berneval" (Renoir). Con. 127: 125 May '51.

Lederberg, Joshua. Cur. biog. p. 251 (1959).

lederhosen, Austrian (boy). Natl. geog. 118: 275 (col.) Aug '60.

Lederle, John W. Cur. biog. p. 259 (1961).

"L'Education Fait Tout" (Fragonard). Con. 143: 208 Je '59.

Lee, Alice Hathaway. Amer. heri. vol. 9 no. 2 p. 63 (Feb '58).

Lee, Bob. Horan: Pict. hist. of wild west, p. 195.

Lee, Canada. Cur. biog. p. 395 (1944).

Lee, Clark. Cur. biog. p. 433 (1943).

Lee, Doris. Cur. biog. p. 402 (1954).

Lee, Dorothy McCullough. Cur. biog. p. 346 (1949).

Lee, F. R. (work of). Con. 145: LXVII Ap '60.

Lee, Fitzhugh. Amer. heri. vol. 9 no. 2 p. 31 (Feb '58).
Pakula: Cent. album, p. 183.

Lee, George Washington Custis. Amer. heri. vol. 5 no. 3 p. 31 (spring '54).

Lee, Gypsy Rose. Cur. biog. p. 434 (1943).

Lee, Harper. Cur. biog. p. 261 (1961).

Lee, Major Henry. Amer. heri. vol. 8 no. 6 p. 29 (Oct '57).

Lee, J. Bracken. Cur. biog. p. 348 (1949).

Lee, Jennie. Cur. biog. p. 339 (1946).

Lee, Lt. Gen. John Clifford H. Cur. biog. p. 397 (1944).

Lee, Mrs. John G. Cur. biog. p. 332 (1950).

Lee, Laurence F. Cur. biog. p. 339 (1952).

Lee, Mary Custis. See Lee, Mrs. Robert E.

Lee, Peggy. Cur. biog. (1963).

Lee, Robert E. Amer. heri. vol. 3 no. 2 p. 17 (winter '52); vol. 4 no. 2 p. 19 (winter '53); vol. 9 no. 1 p. 37 (Dec '57).
Pakula: Cent. album, p. 185.

—— (before & after the war). Amer. heri. vol. 6 no. 3 p. 37 (Ap '55).

—— (bust). Holiday 28: 220 Nov '60.

—— (on horse after surrender). Amer. heri. vol. 8 no. 5 frontis (Aug '57).

—— (on horse, soldiers). Amer. heri. vol. 5 no. 3 p. 32-3 (col.) (spring '54).

Lee, Mrs. Robert E. Amer. heri. vol. 5 no. 3 p. 25 (col.), 27 (spring '54).

Lee, S. Smith. Amer. heri. vol. 10 no. 1 p. 51 (Dec '58).

Lee, Stephen D. Pakula: Cent. album, p. 187.

Lee, Tsung-Dao. Cur. biog. p. 240 (1958).

Lee, Vernon (Sargent). Praeg. pict. ency., p. 433.

Lee birthplace, Robert E. Holiday 11: 131 Ap '52; 28: 9 Sept '60.

Lee Bum Suk. Cur. biog. p. 350 (1949).

Lee home, Robert E. ("Arlington"). Amer. heri. vol. 1 no. 2 p. 25 (winter '50).
Holiday 13: 52-5 (part col.) Jan '53.

—— (entrance, Union Guard, 1864). Natl. geog. 103: 19 Jan '53.

Lee Kuan Yew. Cur. biog. p. 253 (1959).

"Lee surrenders to Grant". Holiday 28: 9 Sept '60.

Leech, Margaret. Cur. biog. p. 493 (1942); p. 231 (1960).

Leedom, Boyd. Cur. biog. p. 366 (1956).

Leeds castle (Kent, Eng.). Natl. geog. 108: 314 (col.) Sept '55.

Leeming, Joseph. Jun. bk. of auth., p. 191.

Lees, Charles (work of). Holiday 13: 64 (col.) Je '53.

Leese, Lt. Gen. Sir Oliver. Cur. biog. p. 400 (1944).

Lefaucheux, Marie-Helene. Cur. biog. p. 386 (1947).

Lefevre, Theodore J.A.M. Cur. biog. p. 249 (1962).

Leffingwell, Russell C. Cur. biog. p. 333 (1950).

leg. Gray's anatomy, p. 1418, 1421-4.

—— (lymphatic system). Gray's anatomy, p. 714.

—— (nervous system). Gray's anatomy, p. 983, 991-5.

—— (veins). Gray's anatomy, p. 680.

leg ornaments, African Masai. Natl. geog. 106: 501 Oct '54.

leg. See also legs.

Le Gallienne, Eva. Cur. biog. p. 495 (1942); p. 350 (1955).

"Legend of St. Anthony of Padua". See "St. Anthony of Padua".

"Legend of St. Nicholas". See "St. Nicholas", Legend of.

Leger, Alexis Saint Leger. Cur. biog. p. 263 (1961).

Leger, Fernand. Cur. biog. p. 437 (1943).

—— (work of). Con. 145: 208 May '60.
Praeg. pict. ency., p. 504 (col.).

Leger, Paul-Emile Cardinal. Cur. biog. p. 351 (1953).

Legion of honor, decoration of (France). Int. gr. soc.: Arts . . . p. 167 (col.).

legionary, Roman. See Roman legionary.

Legislature (Kingston, Jamaica). Natl. geog. 105: 340 Mar '54.

—— (interior, Ontario). Holiday 18: 38 (col.) Sept '55.

Legonea mts. (Jamaica). Con. 143: XXXVII Ap '59.

legong dancer (Bali). Natl. geog. 116: 810-11 (col.) Dec '59.

"Le Grand". See Henderson, "Le Grand".

legs, girl's. Holiday 27: 46 Mar '60.

legs, man's. Holiday 25: 104 (col.) May '59, inside cover (col.) Je '59.

——, woman's. Holiday 25: 5, 42 (col.) May '59, 10 (col.) Je '59; 26: 79 (col.) Sept '59.

legs. See also leg.

Leh (Ladakh). Natl. geog. 99: 612 (col.) May '51.

Le Havre (France). Natl. geog. 115: 608-9, 631 (part col.) May '59.

Lehman, Herbert H. Cur. biog. p. 439 (1943); p. 353 (1955).

Lehman, Lotte. Cur. biog. p. 505 (1941).

Lehmann, Inge. Cur. biog. p. 251 (1962).

Lehmann, Kurt (modern relief). Praeg. pict. ency., p. 19.

Lehmann-Haupt, Hellmut E. Cur. biog. p. 497 (1942); p. 265 (1961).

Lehmbruck, Wilhelm (sculpture by). Con. 145: 42 Mar '60.

—— (work of). Int. gr. soc.: Arts . . . p 131 (col.).

Praeg. pict. ency., p. 491.

Lehrbas, Lloyd A. Cur. biog. p. 335 (1950).

lei. Holiday 9: 57 (col.) Mar '51; 10: 31 (col.) Oct '51; 19: 21 (col.) Feb '56, 4 (col.) May '56.

—— (Hawaiian girl). Holiday 25: 106 (col.) Mar '59.

——, sponge (Fla.). Natl. geog. 107: 65 (col.) Jan '55.

Leibl, Wilhelm (work of). Praeg. pict. ency., p. 403 (col.).

Leibowitz, Samuel S. Cur. biog. p. 353 (1953).

Leigh, Robert D. Cur. biog. p. 387 (1947).

Leigh, Vivien. Cur. biog. p. 340 (1946).

Leigh, W. R. (work of). Amer. heri., vol. 4 no. 1 p. 32-3 (col.) (fall '52).

Leigh, William Colston. Cur. biog. p. 499 (1942).

"Leigh family" (Romney). Con. 143: 117 Ap '59, 133 May '59.

Leigh-Mallory, Sir Trafford. Cur. biog. p. 402 (1944).

Leigh-Pemberton, John (work of). Con. 134: 152 (col.) Dec '54.

Leighton, A. C. (work of). Con 133: 32 Mar '54.

Leighton, Margaret. Cur. biog. p. 341 (1952); p. 320 (1957).

Leinster House (Dublin, Ireland). Jensen: The White House, p. 8.

Leiper, Henry Smith. Cur. biog. p. 376 (1948).

Leira castle (Portugal). Travel 101: 8 May '54.

leis. See Hawaiian leis; lei.

Leiserson, William M. Cur. biog. p. 500 (1942).

Leith-Ross, Sir Frederick. Cur. biog. p. 502 (1942).

"Le Jeune Eveille" (Mercier). Con. 132: LI Sept '53.

Leland (dock, mich.). Travel 108: inside cover Nov '57.

"Le Lecon de Peinture" (Matisse). Con. 145: 188 May '60.

Lelong, Lucien. Cur. biog. p. 355 (1955).

Lely, Peter (work of). Con. 126: 26, 32-3, 65 Aug '50; 135: 237 Je '55; 140: back cover Dec '57, 231 Jan '58; 143: 6 Mar '59.

Lemass, Sean F. Cur. biog. p. 233 (1960).

Lemay, Maj. Gen. Curtis E. Cur. biog. p. 405 (1944); p. 404 (1954).

Natl. geog. 113: 306 Mar '58.

"L'embarquement Pourcythere" (Watteau). Con. 157: 5 Mar '51.

"Le Minuet" (Garrido). Con. 141: XXVIII Je '58.

Lemkin, Raphael. Cur. biog. p. 337 (1950).

Lemmon, Jack. Cur. biog. p. 266 (1961).

Lemnitzer, Gen. Lyman L. Cur. biog. p 357 (1955).

lemon holder, Irish glass. Con. ency. of ant., vol. 3, pl. 52.

Lemoyne, Jean-Baptiste II (sculpture by). Con. 140: 26 Sept '57.

—— (terracotta work). Con. 140: 6 Sept '57.

Le Nain, Louis (work of). Con. 133: LXIV Je '54; 141: 38 Mar '58, 198 May '58.

Le Nain, Matthieu (work of). Con. 136: 138 Nov '55.

L'Enfant memorial, Pierre Charles. Natl. geog. 103: 4 Jan '53.

L'Enfant plan for Wash., D.C. Amer. heri. vol. 2 no. 2 p. 4 (winter '51); vol. 10 no. 5 p. 76 (Aug '59).

Natl. geog. 103: 5 Jan '53.

Lengyel, Emil. Cur. biog. p. 504 (1942).

Lenin (Communist sculpt.). Holiday 13: 53 Mar '53.

Leningrad. Natl. geog. 116: 730-1 (col.) Dec '59.

—— (Hermitage gallery). Travel 109: 54 Ap '58.

—— (winter palace). Holiday 24: 56-7 Sept '58.

Lennox, Lady Sarah. Amer. heri. vol. 11 no. 4 p. 11 (col.) (Je '60).

Lennox-Boyd, Alan T. Cur. biog. p. 368 (1956).

"Lenores" monument. Amer. heri. vol. 7 no. 3 p. 97 (Ap '56).

Lenroot, Katherine F. Cur. biog. p. 338 (1950).

Lens, Bernard (miniature by). Con. ency. of ant., vol. 1, pl. 130.

lens (sym.). Lehner: Pict. bk. of sym., p. 16.

——, camera. See camera lens.

Lenski, Lois Jun. bk. of auth., p. 193.

Lent, Henry B. Jun. bk. of auth., p. 195.

Lentaigne, Maj. Gen. Walter D. A. Cur. biog. p. 407 (1944).

Lenya, Lotte. Cur. biog. p. 255 (1959).

Leonard, Bill. Cur. biog. p. 235 (1960).

Leonard, Mgr. Edward F. Cur. biog. p. 506 (1941).

Leonard, Mrs. Newton P. Cur. biog. p. 355 (1953).

Leonardo Da Vinci (work of). Con. ency. of ant., vol. 1, pl. 150.

Con. 129: 110, 116 Je '52.

Praeg. pict. ency., p. 26, 277 (col.).

Leonbruno, Lorenzo (work of). Con. 141: LV Je '58.

Leoncavallo, Ruggiero. Cooper: Con. ency. of music, p. 150.

Leonidoff, Leon. Cur. biog. p. 507 (1941).

Leopold III, King of Belgium. Cur. biog. p. 410 (1944).

Leopold, ex-king (& his wife). Holiday 5: 45 (col.) Feb '49.

Leopold, Alice K. Cur. biog. p. 359 (1955).

Leopoldville (Belgian Congo). Natl. geog. 101: 344 Mar '52; 118: 320-3 (col.) Sept '60.

"Le passage de la vierge a la Mariee". Praeg. pict. ency., p. 455.

Le Pavillon restaurant (N.Y.). Holiday 13: 82-4, 86 May '53.

"Le petit Berard" (Renoir). Con. 141: 121 Ap '58.

"Le petit Lang" (Manet). Con. 145: 207 May '60.

"Le Philosophe" (Fragonard). Con. 143: 263 Je '59.

Lepicie, Nicolas-Bernard (work of). Con. 135: 44 Mar '55 .

Le Pont Neuf (Paris). Holiday 19: 62 May '56.

"Le Pont Neuf" (Maufra). Con. 145: 114 Ap '60.

Leprince, Jean Baptiste (work of). Con. 135: XXIII Mar '55.

Le Puy (France). Natl. geog. 100: 6-11 (part col.) Jl '51; 112: 420, 433-4 Sept '57; 117: 738-9 (col.) Je '60.

"Le Quai de Louvre" (Darien). Con. 142: XLI-II Nov '58.

Lequerica, José Felix de. Cur. biog. p. 370 (1951).

Lerch, Maj. Gen. Archer L. Cur. biog. p. 345 (1945).

"Le repose de Diane" (Cranach). Con. 139: 260 Je '57.

Lerner, Alan Jay. Cur. biog. p. 242 (1958).

Lerner, Max. Cur. biog. p. 506 (1942).

Lesage, Jean. Cur. biog. p. 268 (1961).

Les Andelys, Normandy (castle). Holiday 17: 127 (col.) Mar '55.

"Les apprets pour l'école" (Chardin). Con. 133: XVIII Ap '54.

"Le Savetier" (by Pater). Con. ency. of ant., vol. 1, pl. 160.

Lescaze, William. Cur. biog. p. 507 (1942).

"Les Chenes du chateau Renard" (Harpignies). Con. 139: 53 Mar '57.

"Les Cinq Sens" (Ceccarini). Con. 135: 52 Mar '55.

Lescot, Elie. Cur. biog. p. 509 (1941).

"Le Secret de l'amour" (Corot). Con. 140: X (col.) Nov '57.

Leser, Tina. Cur. biog. p. 322 (1957).

Lesinski, John. Cur. biog. p. 351 (1949); p. 324 (1957).

Leslie, Alexander. Amer. heri. vol. 11 no. 6 p. 86 (Oct '60).

Leslie's cartoon. *See* cartoon, Leslie's.

L'Esperance, Elise. Cur. biog. p. 341 (1950).

Lesrel, A.A. (work of). Con. 134: XVII (col.) Dec '54; 136: V Sept '55.

Lesseps, Ferdinand Marie, viscount de (statue, Suez Canal). Natl. geog. 101: 114 Jan '52.

"Les trois personnages" (Leger). Con. 145: 208 May '60.

le Sueur, Eustache (work of). Con. 141: 39 Mar '58 .

Lesueur, Larry. Cur. biog. p. 440 (1943).

Lesur, V. Henry (work of). Con. 136: XLIV Nov '55; 138: XXVIII Sept '56.

Letchworth state park (N.Y.). Natl. geog. 110: 605 Nov '56.

Letourneau, Jean. Cur. biog. p. 344 (1952).

Letourneau, Robert G. Cur. biog. p. 245 (1958).

letter. Holiday 18: 121 (col.) Oct '55.

—— **(by J. P. Morgan).** Amer. heri. vol. 8 no. 4 p. 99 (Je '57).

—— **(early Egyptian).** Ceram: March of arch., p. 177, 179.

—— **(from A. Lincoln).** Amer. heri. vol. 6 no. 4 p. 82 (Je '55).

—— **(illus. by T. Roosevelt).** Amer. heri. vol. 10 no. 1 p. 128 (Dec '58).

—— **(Mrs. Lincoln to her son).** Amer. heri. vol. 6 no. 5 p. 97 (Aug '55).

letter Aleph, ideogram. Lehner: Pict. bk. of sym., p. 74.

letter case. Holiday 11: 59 (col.) Je '52.

letterheads (antique). Amer. heri. vol. 11 no. 3 p. 17 (Ap '60).

lettering (inscriptiion on early church falgons). Con. 126: 123 Oct '50.

lettering, Eng. (16th cent.). Con. 127: 18-20 Mar '51.

——, **Japanese.** Travel 112: 49 Dec '59.

letters, fan. Holiday 12: 42-3 (col.) Oct '52.

letters patent of Henry VIII. Con. ency. of ant., vol. 3, pl. 151.

Lettvin, Theodore. Holiday 22: 121 Sept '57.

Leutze, Emanuel (work of). Amer. heri. vol. 10 no. 6 p. 60 (col.) (Oct '59).

Lev, Ray. Cur. biog. p. 354 (1949).

Levant, Oscar. Cur. biog. p. 345 (1952).

the levee (New Orleans). Amer. heri. vol. 2 no. 1 p. 49, 55 (fall '50).

Levenson, Samuel. Cur. biog. p. 257 (1959).

Lever blvd. (N.Y.). Praeg. pict. ency., p. 436.

Leverone, Nathaniel. Cur. biog. p. 370 (1956).

Levi, Carlo. Cur. biog. p. 348 (1952).

Levi, Julian. Cur. biog. p. 444 (1943).

Levi-Tania, Sara. Cur. biog. p. 246 (1958).

Leviero, Anthony H. Cur. biog. p. 350 (1952).

Levine, Irving R. Cur. biog. p. 259 (1959).

Levine, Jack. Cur. biog. p. 372 (1956).

Levine, Philip. Cur. biog. p. 389 (1947).

Levis, Maurice (work of). Con. 144: LVII Jan '60.

Levitan, Isaak Ilyich (work of). Con. 143: 30 Mar '59.

Levitski, D.G. (work of). Con. 135: 7 Mar '55.

Levitsky, D. (work of). Con. 142: 223 Jan '59; 144: 276 Jan '60.

Levitt, William J. Cur. biog. p. 374 (1956).

Lewis, Alan. Holiday 28: 14 Aug '60.

Lewis, Anthony. Cur. biog. p. 361 (1955).

Lewis, Chester M. Cur. biog. p. 376 (1956).

Lewis, Clive S. Cur. biog. p. 411 (1944).

Lewis, Clyde A. Cur. biog. p. 342 (1950).

Lewis, Elizabeth Foreman. Jun. bk. of auth., p. 196.

Lewis, Fulton, jr. Cur. biog. p. 510 (1942).

Lewis, Henry (lithograph by). Amer. heri., vol. 2 no. 1 p. 48 (fall '50).

Lewis, J. F. (work of). Con. 145: 267 Je '60.

Lewis, Jerry. Cur. biog. p. 253 (1962).

Lewis, John. Cur. biog. p. 255 (1962).

Lewis, John L. Cur. biog. p. 513 (1942). Holiday 6: :45 Oct '49.

Lewis, Judith (work of). Con. 133: XVII (col.) May '54.

Lewis, Meriwether. Travel 102: 12 Oct '54.

Lewis, Norman (Negro artist). Holiday 27: 80 Je '60.

Lewis, Shari. Cur. biog. p. 248 (1958).

Lewis, Sinclair. Holiday 11: 9 Feb '52; 13: 6 Mar '53.

Lewis, Mrs. Tom. See Young, Loretta.

Lewis, Sir. Willmott. Cur. biog. p. 511 (1941).

Lewis & Clark cavern (Mont.). Natl. geog. 97: 717 (col.) Je '50.
Travel 108: 13 Jl '57.

Lewis & Clark expedition. Travel 102: 11 Oct '54.

Lewis & Clark journey (map). Travel 102: 12 Oct '54.

Lewis & Clark route west. Brooks: Growth of a nation, p. 94.

Lewis & Clark trail west. Natl. geog. 103: 708-50 (part col.) Je '53.

Lewis home, Donald M. (Cal.). Holiday 14: 34-5 (col.) Sept '53.

Lexington (commons, Mass.). Holiday 28: 63 (col.) Jl '60.

"The Lexington" boat (burning). Amer. heri. vol. 6 no. 1 p. 15 (col.) (fall '54).

Lexington hotel. See Hotel Lexington.

Ley, Willy. Cur. biog. p. 513 (1941); p. 357 (1953).

Leyburn, James G. Cur. biog. p. 446 (1943).

Lhasa. Natl. geog. 106: 65F Jl '54; 108: 2-48 (part col.) Jl '55.

—— (bride & groom). Natl. geog. 108: 5 (col.) Jl '55.

—— (map). Natl. geog. 108: 7 Jl '55.

L'Hermitte, Leon (work of). Con. 139: XXX-VIII May '57.

Lhevinne, Rosina. Cur. biog. p. 270 (1961).

Li, Choh Hao. Cur. biog. p. 242 (1963).

Liahona Tonga, Mormon college. Holiday 28: 67 Oct '60.

libation cup. See cup, bronze libation.

Libby, Frederick J. Cur. biog. p. 356 (1949).

Libby, Dr. Willard F. Cur. biog. p. 406 (1954).

Liberace, W. V. Cur. biog. p. 409 (1954).

Liberation Hall. See Hall of liberation (Bavaria).

Liberia. Holiday 13: 42-3 (col.) Mar '53.

Liberty, Miss (statue). Amer. heri. vol. 7 no. 4 p. 26 (col.) (Je '56).

Liberty bell (Phila.). Amer. heri. vol. 3 no. 1 p. 47 (col.) (fall '51); vol. 7 no. 4 p. 28 (Je '56).
Holiday 5: 69 Ap '49; 10: 11 (col.) Nov '51; 11: 19 (col.) Feb '52, 135 (col.) Ap '52.
Travel 110: 29, 31 Jl '58.

—— (sym.). Lehner: Pict. bk. of sym., p. 53.

"Liberty or Death" (church where delivered). Holiday 10: 92 Sept '51.

"Liberty pole" (1776). Brooks: Growth of a nation, p. 75.

library (int.). Con. 141: 68 (col.) Ap '58; 144: 77 Nov '59.
Holiday 14: 41 Nov '53.
Natl. geog. 108: 313 (col.) Sept '55.

—— (int., 18th cent.). Natl. geog. 113: 258-9 (col.) Feb '58.

—— (Southington, Conn.). Brooks: Growth of a nation, p. 210.

—— (study hall). Holiday 11: 60 (col.) May '52.

——, Bancroft (Cal.). Amer. heri. vol. 1 no. 3 p. 19 (spring '50).

——, Boston Athenaeum (int.). See Athenaeum library.

——, boy's club (int.). Natl. geog. 100: 578 Nov '51.

——, Brown univ. (int.). Holiday 27: 104 May '60.

——, building natl. (Pakistan). Natl. geog. 102: 651 (col.) Nov '52.

——, Cornell univ. Natl. geog. 110: 599 (col.) Nov '56.

——, Cuttyhunk island. Travel 107: 35 Je '57.

——, D.A.R. (int.). Natl. geog. 100: 568 Nov '51.

——, Folger. See Folger library.

——, Harvard univ. Holiday 11: 41 Je '52.

——, Holy Cross college. Natl. geog. 107: 212 (col.) Feb '55.

——, home. Con. 143: 4 Mar '59.
Holiday 18: 99 (col.) Aug '55; 22: 78 (col.) Dec '57.

——, home (Colonial int.). Natl. geog. 105: 453 (col.) Ap '54.

——, home (men at table). Holiday 24: 87 (col.) Nov '58.

——, home (woman). Natl. geog. 118: 185 (col.) Aug '60.

——, Huntington. See Huntington library.

——, India (man & woman). Natl. geog. 118: 456 (col.) Oct '60.

——, John Adams. Natl. geog. 97: 282 Mar '50.

——, Lamayuru (int.). Natl. geog. 99: 606 May '51.

——, Kenwood (London, Adams int.). Con. 138: 183 Dec '56.

——, Lilienfeld abbey. Natl .geog. 115: 199 (col.) Feb '57.

——, Mexico City univ. Travel 105: inside cover May '56.

——, monastic (int.). See monastic library.

——, Nairobi (Kenya, Africa). Natl. geog. 97: 312 Mar '50.

——, Natl. univ. (Mexico). Holiday 28: 181 Dec '60.

——, N.Y. public. Holiday 23: 39 Mar '58.

——, Princeton univ. Holiday 8: 101 Oct '50.

——, public (Charlotte, N.C.). Holiday 6: 83 Dec '49.

——, Radcliffe (Oxford). Praeg. pict. ency., p. 358.

——, Robert college (int.). Natl. geog. 112: 415 (col.) Sept '57.

——, Roosevelt. See Roosevelt library.

——, school (Africa). Natl. geog. 108: 774-5 (col.) Dec '55.

——, The Stone. See Stone library.

——, Tryon Place (N.C., int.). Con. 144: 135 Nov '59.

——, Univ. of Colo. Natl. geog. 106: 229 (col.) Aug '54.

——, Univ. of Ill. (entrance). Natl. geog. 104: 813 (col.) Dec '53.

——, Virgin is. Natl. geog. 109: 229 (col.) Feb '56.

library book stacks. Amer. heri. vol. 1 no. 4 p. 29 (summer '50).

library chair. *See* chair, library.

Library of Celsus (Ephesus). Natl. geog. 110: 748-9 Dec '56.
Osward: Asia Minor, pl. 39.

Library of Congress (Wash., D.C.). Holiday 19: 44 May '56.
Natl. geog. 97: 662-83 May '50.

Library of St. Gallen (int., Switzerland). Natl. geog. 110: 458-9 (col.) Oct '56.

Library of St. Mark (Venice). Praeg. pict. ency., p. 265.

library room (Mt. Vernon). Natl. geog. 104: 669 (col.) Nov '53.

library shelves (boys). Natl. geog. 102: 539 (col.) Oct '52.

library steel wall case. Natl. geog. 97: 299 Mar '50.

library step-table (1790). Con. ency. of ant., vol. 3, pl. 12.

library steps. Con. 144: XXXIII Jan '60; 145: XXVI Mar '60.

—— (18th cent.). Con. 144: 224 Jan '60.

——, folding (18th cent.). Con. ency. of ant., vol. 3, pl. 12.

——, Georgian. Con. 142: XXXIV Jan '59.

library steps-chair (1810). Con. ency. of ant., vol. 3, pl. 12.

library table. *See* table, library.

library table steps, Sheraton. Con. 142: XLVIII Jan '59.

library wall panel. Con. 144: 250 Jan '60.

Libya (Lunar landscape). Natl. geog. 118: 356 (col.) Sept '60.

"Libyan Sibyl". Praeg. pict. ency., p. 278 (col.).

license plates, auto. Holiday 11: 11 Jan '52.

Lichtenberger, Arthur Carl. Cur. biog. p. 272 (1961).

Liddel, Urner. Cur. biog. p. 371 (1951).

Liddell, Alice. *See* "Alice in Wonderland".

The Lido (near Venice). Holiday 24: 50-5 (col.) Aug '58.

Lie, Trygve. Cur. biog. p. 343 (1946).

Liebenow, Robert C. Cur. biog. p. 378 (1956).

Liebermann, Max (work of). Praeg. pict. ency., p. 430 (col.).

Liebes, Dorothy Wright. Cur. biog. p. 377 (1948).
Holiday 24: 73 Dec '58.

Liebman, Rabbi Joshua Loth. Cur. biog. p. 346 (1946).

Liebman, Max. Cur. biog. p. 359 (1953).

Liechtenstein. Holiday 6: 106-11 (part col.) Nov '49.
Travel 106: 23-7 Jl '56.

—— (Schoss Vaduz). Travel 101: 8 May '54.

Lieder, Frans (work of). Cooper: Con. ency., of music, p. 17 (col.).

Lievens, Jan (work of). Con. 139: IX May '57.

life (sym.). Lehner: Pict. bk. of sym., p. 26-7, 29, 64, 78-9.

life belt, boat. Natl. geog. 108: 703 (col.) Nov '55.

——, ship. Natl. geog. 108: 828 (col.) Dec '55.

life buoy. *See* buoy, life.

life guard (shark). Natl. geog. 98: 375 Sept '50.

——, beach. Holiday 10: 47 (col.) Nov '51.

——, English. *See* guard, English life.

life guard parade (Sydney, Australia). Travel 106: 54 Aug '56.

life preserver, boat. Holiday 23: 26 (col.) Je '58; 25: 129 (col.) Je '59.

life raft. Natl. geog. 99: 291 (col.) Mar '51.

lifeboat, French. Natl. geog. 108: 744 (col.) Dec '55.

lifesaving men & girls (Tasmania). Natl. geog. 110: 812 (col.) Dec '56.

ligament, human. Gray's anatomy, p. 264-6, 269-305, 314-35.

light, electric (office.) Int. gr. soc.: Arts . . . p. 169 (col.).

——, electric floor. *See* lamp, floor electric.

——, Rebecca shoal. *See* Rebecca shoal light.

——, road traffic. Holiday 21: 21 (col.) Ap '57.

"Light artillery" (Nast). Amer. heri. vol. 8 no. 5 back cover (col.) (Aug '57).

light beacon (Anclote Keys, Fla.). Natl. geog. 107: 54 Jan '55.

light experiment instrument. Natl. geog. 100: 765 (col.) Dec '51.

light meter. *See* meter, light.

light trails, U.S. Navy. Natl. geog. 104: 567 Oct '53.

lighter, cigarette. *See* cigarette lighter.

Lightfoot, Capt. Horan: Pict. hist. of wild west, p. 16.

lighthouse. Amer. heri. vol. 7 no. 2 p. 46 (col.) (Feb '56).
Brooks: Growth of a nation, p. 116.
Holiday 5: 107 (col.) Jan '49, 10 (col.) Mar '49, 69 (col.) Ap '49, 148 Je '49; 7: 69, 126 Mar '50, inside cover (col.), 148 May '50; 9: 127 Mar '51; 13: 28 (col.) Ap '53, 25 (col.) Je '53; 14: 89 (col.) Jl '53, 49, 52 Aug '53; 22: 5 (col.) Jl '57; 23: 119 Mar '58; 24: 119 Jl '58, cover (col.), 46 (col.) Sept '58; 25: 76 Feb '59, 123 (col.) Mar '59, 183 May '59; 27: 226 Ap '60, 244 May '60; 28: 134 Sept '60.
Jordan: Hammond's pict. atlas, p. 25, 81 (col.), 91.
Natl. geog. 102: 352 (col.) Sept '52; 106: 144 (col.) Jl '54.
Travel 103: 25 Feb '55; 111: 43 May '59; 113: 48 Je '60; 114: 36 Oct '60.

—— (sym.). Lehner: Pict. bk. of sym., p. 15.

——, Barnegat. Holiday 12: 90 (col.) Aug '52.

——, Bermuda. Natl. geog. 105: 210 (col.) Feb '54.

——, Biloxi. Natl. geog. 98: 4 Jl '50.
Travel 103: 21 May '55.

——, Boston. Amer. heri. vol. 11 no. 3 p. 11 (col.) (Ap '60).

——, Brant Point (Cape Cod). Holiday 10: 41, 44-5 (col.) Aug '51.
Travel 106: 35 Sept '56.

——, Cal. Holiday 26: 157 Nov '59.

——, Cape Fla. Natl. geog. 113: 60 (col.) Jan '58.

——, Cape Hatteras. Natl. geog. 108: 528 (col.) Oct '55; 113: 23 (col.) Jan '58.

——, Capelinhos. *See* Capelinhos lighthouse.

——, Castle Hill (R.I.). Travel 112: 40 Jl '59.

lighthouse, Currituck Beach (N.C.). Natl. geog. 108: 512 (col.) Oct '55.

——, **Duluth.** Holiday 12: 54 Aug '52.

——, **East Gloucester.** Holiday 12: 2 Aug '52.

——, **Fenwick Isle.** Travel 108: 34 Jl '57.

——, **Gaspe.** Natl. geog. 98: 358 (col.) Sept '50.

——, **Gibb's Hill (Bermuda).** *See* Gibb's Hill lighthouse.

——, **Grace Darling.** Natl. geog. 102: 564 Oct '52.

——, **Henlopen.** Travel 106: 21 Oct '56.

——, **Loon island.** Natl. geog. 98: 532 (col.) Oct '50.

——, **Los Angeles.** Holiday 12: 13 (col.) Dec '52.

——, **Maine.** Holiday 12: 79 Nov '52; 14: back cover (col.) Jl '53; 18: 47 (col.) Jl '55.

——, **Martha's Vineyard.** Natl. geog. 98: 161 (col.) Aug '50.

——, **Mass.** Travel 107: 19 May '57.

——, **Mile Rocks (Cal.).** Holiday 20: 32 Aug '56.

——, **Montauk point.** Natl. geog. 99: 322 (col.) Mar '51.

——, **Nobska (Cape Cod).** Holiday 6: 57 (col.) Sept '49.

——, **Ocracoke.** Travel 105: 66 Feb '56.

——, **Ouessant (France).** Natl. geog. 108: 745 (col.) Dec '55.

——, **Palos Verdes.** *See* Palos Verdes lighthouse.

——, **Point Arena.** Natl. geog. 116: 615 (col.) Nov '59.

——, **Point Loma.** Travel 104: 52 Oct '55.

——, **Portland (Maine).** Holiday 12: 29 (col.) Jl '52, 42, 45 (col.) Aug '52.

——, **Portland Head.** Natl. geog. 107: 789 (col.) Je '55.

——, **Ryvingen is. (Norway).** Natl. geog. 106: 181 Aug '54.

——, **St. Simon is.** Holiday 10: 57 (col.) Dec '51.

——, **Spanish (old).** Travel 103: 32 Je '55.

——, **Split Rock (Minn.).** Holiday 18: 26 (col.) Aug '55.

——, **West Quoddy (Maine).** Face of Amer., p. 106-7 (col.).

——, **Yarmouth (Canada).** Holiday 14: 102 (col.) Sept '53.

——, **Yerba Buena (Cal.).** Holiday 20: 32 Aug '56.

lighting devices (antique). Rawson: Ant. pict. bk., p. 93-5.

Lightner, Milton C. Cur. biog. p. 249 (1958).

lightning (sym.). Lehner: Pict. bk. of sym., p. 12, 15, 88.

——, **winged.** *See* winged lightning.

"Lightning" clipper ship. Amer. heri. vol. 6 no. 6 p. 15 (col.) (Oct '55).

lightning experiment instrument. Natl. geog. 100: 767 (col.) Dec '51.

lightning experiments & destruction. Natl. geog. 97: 810-28 Je '50.

lights, electric. Holiday 27: 179 (col.), 181 May '60.

——, **street (Mexico).** Holiday 10: 99 (col.) Nov '51.

——, **wall.** *See* wall sconce.

lightship (Sweden). Natl. geog. 98: 634 (col.) Nov '50.

—— **"Ambrose".** Face of America, p. 98-9 (col.).
Natl. geog. 106: 782 (col.) Dec '54.

Lilienthal, David E. Cur. biog. p. 414 (1944).

Lillie, Beatrice. Cur. biog. p. 348 (1945).

Lilly, Eli. Amer heri. vol. 2 no. 1 p. 30 (fall '50).

Lilly, John C. Cur. biog. p. 257 (1962).

Lilly drug plant, Eli. Amer. heri. vol. 2 no. 1 p. 28-31 (fall '50).

lily (sym.). Lehner: Pict. bk. of sym., p. 61.

——, **Easter (sym.).** Lehner: Pict. bk. of sym., p. 52.

"lily prince" (Stucco relief). Ceram: March of arch., p. 58-9.

Lima (Peru). Holiday 11: 106 (col.) May '52. Travel 109: 33 Mar '58.

—— **(hotel).** Holiday 15: 29 (col.) Mar '54.

Limb, Ben C. Cur. biog. p. 373 (1951).

"Limberlost" cabin. Amer. heri. vol. 2 no. 1 p. 26 (fall '50).

lime (sym.). Lehner: Pict. bk. of sym., p. 72.

limestone blocks (men cutting). Natl. geog. 105: 226 Feb '54.

Limmat river (Switzerland). Holiday 16: 30-1 (col.) Aug '54.

Limoges enamel plague (13th cent.). Con. 134: 202 Dec '54.

Limon, Jose. Cur. biog. p. 361 (1953).

Linard, Jacques (work of). Con. 142: LVII Dec '58.

Lincoln, Abraham. Amer. heri. vol. 2 no. 2 p. 36 (winter '51); vol. 4 no. 2 p. 18 (winter '53); vol. 6 no. 2 p. 48-9 (winter '55); vol. 6 no. 6 p. 83 (Oct '55); vol. 7 no. 3 p. 31-2 (Ap '56); vol. 7 no. 5 p. 33 (Aug '56); vol. 7 no. 6 p. 57 (Oct '56); vol. 9 no. 2 p. 12 (Feb '58); vol. 10 no. 2 p. 12 (col.), 15 (Feb '59); vol. 11 no. 6 p. 42, 46 (Oct '60).
Brooks: Growth of a nation, p. 147.
Holiday 28: 41 (col.) Oct '60.
Jensen: The White House, p. 82.
Natl. geog. 117: 250, 260, 268, 273 Feb '60.
Pakula: Cent. album, following pl. 20.

—— **(Borglum sculpt., Mt. Rushmere).** Natl. geog. 99: 720 (col.) Je '51; 110: 483 (col.) Oct '56 113: 644 (col.) May '58.

—— **(bust).** Natl. geog. 102: 177 Aug '52; 114: 597 Nov '58.

—— **(campaign poster).** Amer. heri. vol. 7 no. 4 p. 26 (col.) (Je '56).

—— **(cartoon).** Amer. heri. vol. 3 no. 2 p. 14-5 (winter '52); vol. 11 no. 6 p. 77 (Oct '60).

—— **(clothes he wore).** Amer. heri. vol. 8 no. 5 p. 102-3 (Aug '57).

—— **(cutting logs).** Amer. heri. vol. 3 no. 2 inside cover (winter '52).
Holiday 28: 76 (col.) Dec '60).

—— **(French sculpt.).** Amer. heri. vol. 7 no. 2 p. 56-7 (Feb '56).

—— **(greets Prince Napoleon).** Amer. heri. vol. 8 no. 5 p. 69 (Aug '57).

—— **(head).** Amer. heri. vol. 3 no. 2 p. 6 (winter '52).
Natl. geog. 101: 162 Feb '52.
Travel 103: 13 Je '55.

—— **(horseback).** Natl. geog. 117: 256 Feb '60.

—— (in Richmond). Amer. heri. vol. 6 no. 4 p. 87 (Je '55).

—— (life of). Natl. geog. 117: 241-77 (part col.) Feb '60.

—— (man shooting). Natl. geog. 117: 274 Feb '60.

—— (on train). Amer. heri. vol. 5 no. 2 p. 38 (winter '53-4).

—— (pulling baby buggy). Natl. geog. 117: 254 Feb '60.

—— (reviews troops). Jensen: The White House, p. 91.

Lincoln, Gen. Benjamin (on horse). Amer. heri. vol. 9 no. 4 p. 47 (col.) (Je '58).

Lincoln, Leroy A. Cur. biog. p. 347 (1946).

Lincoln, Mary Todd (Mrs. A Lincoln). Amer. heri. vol. 6 no. 5 p. 11 (Aug '55). Jensen: The White House, p. 84.

Lincoln, Murray D. Cur. biog. p. 363 (1953).

Lincoln, Robert. Jensen: The White House, p. 84.

—— (bust). Natl. geog. 103: 821 Je '53.

Lincoln, Robert Todd. Amer. heri. vol. 6 no. 5 p. 10 (Aug '55); vol. 11 no. 4 p. 47 (Je '60).

Lincoln, Tad. Jensen: The White House, p. 84.

Lincoln, Willie. Jensen: The White House, p. 84.

Lincoln & cabinet, Abraham. Jensen: The White House, p. 87.

Lincoln & family, Abraham. Natl. geog. 117: 246, 268 Feb '60.

Lincoln & Tad, Abraham. Jensen: The White, House, p. 85.

Lincoln assassin suspects. Amer. heri. vol. 8 no. 2 p. 57 (Feb '57).

Lincoln auto. Holiday 5: inside cover (col.) Mar '49, 79 (col.) Ap '49, 113 (col.) Je '49; 7: 15 (col.) Ap '50, inside back cover (col.) May '50; 8: 75 (col.) Jl '50, 71 (col.) Sept '50; 15: 4 (col.) Mar '54, 90 (col.) Ap '54, 64 (col.) May '54, 7 (col.) Je '54; 17: 32 (col.) Mar '55. Travel 103: 11 Jan '55.

Lincoln birthplace, Abraham. Natl. geog. 117: 244-7 (part col.) Feb '60.

Lincoln cathedral. Con. 134: 201 Dec '54.

Lincoln day (sym.). Lehner: Pict. bk. of sym., p. 54.

Lincoln debate, Abraham. Natl. geog. 101: 145 Feb '52.

Lincoln died, house where Abraham. See house where Lincoln died.

Lincoln funeral, Abraham. Amer. heri., vol. 6 no. 4 p. 24 (Je '55).

Lincoln funeral train (ghost). Holiday 6: 72 Aug '49.

Lincoln home, Abraham (Ill.). Jordan: Hammond's pict. atlas. p. 100 (col.). Natl. geog. 101: 176, 178 (col.), 182 Feb '52; 117: 254-5 (part col.) Feb '60. Travel 103: 16 Je '55; 113: 30-1 Feb '60.

—— (int.). Natl. geog. 101: 176 (col.) Feb '52. Travel 109: 27 Feb '58; 112: 31 Jl '59.

Lincoln inaugural address, Abraham. Amer. heri. vol. 6 no. 4 p. 64 (Je '55).

Lincoln inaugural reception (1865). Amer. heri. vol. 9 no. 2 p. 14 (Feb '58).

"Lincoln land", Abraham. Natl. geog. 101: 142-84 (part col.) Feb '52.

Lincoln landmarks, Abraham (Ill.). Travel 109: 21-7 Feb '58.

Lincoln log cabin, Abraham. Amer. heri. vol. 7 no. 5 p. 33 (Aug '56). Face of Amer., p. 76-7 (col.). Holiday 10: 140 (col.) Oct '51; 20: 30 (col.) Sept '56; 21: 117 (col.) Ap '57. Natl. geog. 101: 152, 168, 172 (part col.) Feb '52. Travel 114: 34 Sept '60.

Lincoln mask, Abraham. Natl. geog. 117: 241 Feb '60.

Lincoln memorial. Holiday 7: 39 (col.) Feb '50. Natl. geog. 101: 151 (col.) Feb '52.

—— (tourists). Natl. geog. 117: 243, 276-7 (col.) Feb '60.

—— (Ill. state park). Travel 103: 15 Je '55.

—— (soldier's honor service). Natl. geog. 114: 597 (col.) Nov '58.

—— (Springfield, Ill.). Travel 109: 22 Feb '58.

—— (Wash., D.C.). Amer. heri. vol. 10 no. 2 p. 101 (Feb '59). Brooks: Growth of a nation, p. 17. Holiday 14: 2 Oct '53; 19: 4 May '56. Natl. geog. 101: 184 Feb '52; 111: 77, 79 (col.) Jan '57.

Lincoln monument. Natl. geog. 101: 179-80 (col.) Feb '52. Travel 109: 22 Feb '58.

Lincoln monument, Nancy Hanks. Natl. geog. 117: 247 (col.) Feb '60.

Lincoln mourning ribbon. Amer. heri. vol. 11 no. 2 back cover (col.) (Feb '60).

Lincoln reception, Abraham. Jensen: The White House, p. 92.

Lincoln, Mrs. Abraham. Amer. heri. vol. 7 no. 5 p. 40-1 (Aug '56).

Lincoln shrine bas relief (Ind.). Natl. geog. 101: 165 (col.) Feb '52.

Lincoln statue, Abraham. Holiday 7: 117 Feb '50; 22: 1 Jl '57. Natl. geog. 101: 149 (col.) Feb '52. Travel 113: 29 Feb '60.

Lincoln theater box (where shot). Jensen: The White House, p. 93.

Lincoln travels, Abraham (map). Natl. geog. 117: 250-1 (col.) Feb '60.

Lincoln's teacher, Abraham. Holiday 19: 11 May '56.

Lincoln's grave, Nancy Hanks. See grave of Nancy Hanks Lincoln.

Lincoln's tomb, Abraham. Holiday 22: 63 Sept '57.

Lind, Jenny. Cooper: Con. ency. of music, p. 151. Holiday 28: 188 (col.) Nov '60. Durant: Pict. hist. of Amer. circus, p. 58-9, 62.

Lindbergh, Charles A. Cur. biog. p. 514 (1941); p. 411 (1954). Natl. geog. 104: 755 Dec '53.

Lindbergh, Mr. & Mrs. Charles. Jensen: The White House, p. 231.

"Lindewald" (Pres. Van Buren's home). Amer. heri. vol. 10 no. 1 p. 20 (Dec '58). Holiday 6: 39 (col.) Sept '49.

Lindfors, Elsa Viveca. Cur. biog. p. 363 (1955).
Lindisfarne. *See* Holy island (Eng.).
Lindley, Ernest K. Cur. biog. p. 447 (1943).
Lindman, Maj. Jun. bk. of auth., p. 198.
Lindsay, Howard. Cur. biog. p. 518 (1942).
Lindsay, John V. Cur. biog. p. 260 (1962).
Lindsey, Ben. Amer. heri. vol. 9 no. 2 p. 67 (Feb '58).
Lindsey house, Chelsea (Scott). Con. 144: 265 Jan '60.
Lindsley, Thayer. Cur. biog. p. 326 (1957).
Lindt, Auguste R. Cur. biog. p. 260 (1959).
linen press, Dutch. Con. 143: XIV Ap '59.
linen smoother, glass. Natl. geog. 117: 156 (col.) Feb '60.
linenfold ornament. Con. ency. of ant., vol. 1, p. 19.
Link, Adam. Amer. heri. vol. 9 no. 3 p. 30 (Ap '58).
Linkletter, Art. Cur. biog. p. 365 (1953).
Linlithgow, Victor A.J.H., 2nd Marquess. Cur. biog. p. 522 (1942).
Linnell, John. Con. 132: 102 Nov '53.
Linsley, Jesse. Horan: Pict. hist. of wild west, p. 192.
Linville, Peak, Grandfather mts. (N.C.). Travel 104: 5 Aug '55.
lion (Eng. sym.). Lehner: Pict. bk. of sym., p. '57.
lion, bronze (Art inst. entrance). Natl. geog. 104: 783 (col.) Dec '53.
——, **carved marble (18th cent.).** Con. 144: XXVII Jan '60.
——, **winged.** *See* winged lion.
Lion gate at Mycenae. Praeg. pict. ency., p. 163.
lion hunt, African Masai. Natl. geog. 106: 503-17 (col.) Oct '54.
lion trainer (in cage). Int. gr. soc.: Arts . . . p. 149 (col.)
"Lioness attacking mail coach" (Pollard). Con. 136: IV Jan '56.
Lion's gate bridge (B.C.). Jordan: Hammond's pict. atlas, p. 145 (col.).
Liotard, J. E. (work of). Con. 145: 44 Mar '60.
Lipchitz, Jacques. Cur. biog. p. 379 (1948); p. 263 (1962).
—— **(work of).** Con. 145: 209 May '60, 230 Je '60.
Holiday 14: 63 Nov '53.
Lipmann, Dr. Fritz. Cur. biog. p. 413 (1954).
Lippi, Filippino (self portrait). Con. 136: 204 Dec '55.
—— **(work of).** Con. ency. of ant., vol. 1, pl. 150.
Con. 126: 88 Oct '50; 135: 138 Ap '55; 140: 108 Nov '57.
Lippi, Fra Filippo (work of). Con. 140: 207 Dec '57.
Praeg. pict. ency., p. 253 (col.).
Lippincott, Joseph Wharton. Cur. biog. p. 365 (1955).
Lippmann, Walter. Amer. heri. vol. 11 no. 2 p. 8 (Feb '60).
Cur. biog. p. 265 (1962).
Holiday 10: 43 Jl '51.
Lippold, Richard. Cur. biog. p. 380 (1956).
—— **(work of).** Holiday 14: 57 Nov '53.
Lipsky, Eleazar. Cur. biog. p. 262 (1959).

lipstick. Holiday 18: 6 Sept '55, 18 Oct '55, 33 Nov '55; 19: 62 Jan '56, 3 Feb '56; 23: 129 (col.) Jan '58, 105 (col.) Ap '58, 153 (col.) May '58; 24: 31 (col.) Nov '58; 25: 16 (col.) Ap '59; 27: 22 (col.) May '60; 28: 33 (col.) Oct '60.
liquor chest. Holiday 28: 33 (col.) Oct '60.
liquor glass. Con. 129: XXXVII Ap '52.
Lisbon (Portugal). Holiday 6: 101 Sept '49.
Travel 108: 19-23 Aug '57.
—— **(harbor).** Natl. geog. 101: 570 May '52.
—— **(women, clothes display).** Holiday 11: 120-2, 124-5 Ap '52.
Lismore castle (Ireland). Holiday 6: 36 Dec '49.
Liszt, Franz. Cooper: Con. ency. of music, p. 152.
Li T'ai Po (figurine). Con. 142: LXXII Jan '59.
Litchfield, Edward H. Cur. biog. p. 367 (1953).
Litchfield, Paul W. Cur. biog. p. 344 (1950).
literary men. *See* authors; name of.
literature (sym.). Lehner: Pict. bk. of sym., p. 13.
lithograph (by Currier & Ives) Amer. heri. vol. 10 no. 2 p. 12 (col.) (Feb '59).
lithographs, juvenile (Santa Claus, 1821). Amer. heri. vol. 12 no. 1 p. 23-6 (col.) (Dec '60).
Lithuanian folk dancers. Amer. heri. vol. 2 no. 4 p. 52 (summer '51).
Li Tsung-Jen. Cur. biog. p. 516 (1942).
Little, Clarence C. Cur. biog. p. 417 (1944).
Little, Louis. Cur. biog. p. 351 (1945).
Little America (Antarctic, map). Natl. geog. 110: 147 Aug '56.
Little Big Horn, battle of. *See* Battle of Little Big Horn.
"Little Bo Peep" (book illus.). Amer. heri. vol. 8 no. 1 p. 26, 28 (col.) (Dec '56).
"Little Britches". Horan: Pict. hist. of wild west, p. 171.
"Little Brown Church in the Vale" (Iowa). Brooks: Growth of a nation, p. 196.
"Little Colonel's" home (Kentucky). Travel 112: 35-8 Jl '59.
"Little Draughtsman" (Lépicié). Con. 135: 44 Mar '55.
"Little Egypt" (Ill.). Travel 113: 55 May '60.
"Little Horse" (Duchamp). Praeg. pict. ency., p. 478.
little horses dance. *See* Cavallet dance.
"Little Lord Fauntleroy" (book illus.). Amer. heri. vol. 8 no. 1 p. 27 (col.), 33 (Dec '56).
Little Matterhorn mt. (Lake Odessa). Travel 106: 12 Aug '56.
"Little Mermaid" (bronze). Natl. geog. 108: 82 (col.) Jl '55.
—— **(statue, Copenhagen).** Natl. geog. 100: 709 Dec '51.
"Little Mermaid". *See* also Andersen's "Little Mermaid", Hans C.
"Little Red Boy" (Goya). Holiday 14: 43 (col.) Dec '53.
"Little Turtle" (Indian war leader). Amer. heri. vol. 4 no. 3 p. 32 (spring '53); vol. 9 no. 4 p. 57 (Je '58).

"Little White House" (Warm Springs, Ga.). Holiday 15: 83 Feb '54; 19: 133 (col.) May '56.

"Little Women" (book illus.). Amer. heri. vol. 8 no. 1 p. 30 (col.) (Dec '56).

"Little Women's home" (int.). Holiday 27: 158 Mar '60.

"Little World's Fair". See Ephrata's fair.

Littledale, Clara Savage. Cur. biog. p. 349 (1946).

Littlejohn, Robert M. Cur. biog. p. 352 (1946).

Littler, Gene. Cur. biog. p. 382 (1956).

Littleton, Mrs. Lawrence. Con. 143: 117 Ap '59.

Litvinov, Maxim. Cur. biog. p. 519 (1941).

Liu Shao-Ch'i. Cur. biog. p. 327 (1957).

liver, human. Gray's anatomy, p. 1234-43.

Liverpool, Lord Lawrence. Amer. heri. vol. 6 no. 6 p. 4 (col.) (Oct '55).

Livia, raising the statue of. See Raising the statue of Livia.

Livingston, Homer J. Cur. biog. p. 367 (1955).

Livingston, John W. Cur. biog. p. 263 (1959).

Livingston, Milton Stanley. Cur. biog. p. 368 (1955).

Livingston, Robert. Amer. heri. vol. 9 no. 4 p. 48 (col.) (Je '58); vol. 10 no. 1 p. 10 (Dec '58).

Livingston, Robert R. Amer. heri. vol. 6 no. 3 p. 27 (Ap '55).

—— **(Vanderlyn).** Con. 135: 286 Je '55.

Livingston, William. Amer. heri. vol. 5 no. 1 p. 15 (fall '53).

lizard (sym.). Lehner: Pict. bk. of sym., p. 63.

Ljungberg, Ernst Carl. Cur. biog. p. 370 (1955).

Llanfair (Wales. Abreviated town name, longest town name in world). Travel 105: 41 Ap '56.

Llao-Llao hotel, Argentina. Holiday 13: 13 (col.) Ap '53.

Lleras Camargo, Alberto. Cur. biog. p. 391 (1947).

Lloyd, Geoffrey. Cur. biog. p. 383 (1956).

Lloyd, Harold. Cur. biog. p. 357 (1949).

Lloyd, Lord. Cur. biog. p. 521 (1941).

Lloyd, Selwyn. Cur. biog. p. 352 (1952).

Lloyd, Ulrica (drawing by). Ceram: March of arch., p. 224.

Lloyd, Wesley P. Cur. biog. p. 353 (1952).

Lloyd-George, David. Amer. heri. vol. 8 no. 4 p. 25 (Je '57).
Cur. biog. p. 420 (1944).

Lloyd-George, Gwilym. Cur. biog. p. 356 (1952).

Loatian (girl). Natl. geog. 99: 479 (col.) Ap '51.

Lober, Georg J. Cur. biog. p. 329 (1957).

loberstettes (festival costume). Natl. geog. 102: 360 (col.) Sept '52.

lobster boat. Natl. geog. 115: 286-90 Feb '59.

lobster net & fish tails (steel mobile). Praeg. pict. ency., p. 464.

lobster pots. Natl. geog. 112: 172-3 (col.) Aug '57; 115: 286-7 Feb '59.
Rawson: Ant. pict. bk., p. 76.

lobster trap (man). Natl. geog. 102: 351 (col.) Sept '52.

lobster vat. Natl. geog. 107: 788 (col.) Je '55.

Loch Duich (Scotland). Holiday 27: 73 May '60.

"Loch Katrine" (Naysmith). Con. 141: 103 Ap '58.

Loch Lomond. Holiday 16: 29 (col.) Jl '54; 17: 13 (col.) Mar '55.
Natl. geog. 112: 469 (col.) Oct '57.

Lochner, Louis P. Amer. heri. vol. 9 no. 2 p. 66 (Feb '58).
Cur. biog. p. 525 (1942).

Lochner, Stefan (work of). Praeg. pict. ency., p. 229 (col.).

Lochristi (Belgium, festival). Natl. geog. 113: 816-9 (col.) Je '58.

lock. Travel 113: 17 Je '60.

—— **(Holland).** Travel 113: 51 Ap '60.

lock, door (antique style). Amer. heri. vol. 1 no. 3 p. 80 (spring '50).

—— **(18th cent.).** Con. 140: 68 Sept '57.

—— **(sym.).** Lehner: Pict. bk. of sym., p. 88, 90.

——, **gun percussion.** Con. ency. of ant., vol. 1, p. 195.

——, **river (Steubenville, Ohio).** Natl. geog. 97: 183 Feb '50.

——, **Snell.** See Snell lock.

——, **Soulanges.** See Soulanges lock.

lock Lanaye (Belgium). Natl. geog. 108: 550 (col.) Oct '55.

Locke, Alain. Cur. biog. p. 423 (1944).

Locke, Edwin A., jr. Cur. biog. p. 357 (1952).

Locke, John (Verbelst). Con. 133: 179 May '54.

Locker, Jesse D. Cur. biog. p. 371 (1955).

locket, gold antique. Rawson: Ant. pict. bk. p. 85.

Lockhart, Gene. Cur. biog. p. 347 (1950).

Lockheed planes. Natl. geog. 112: 291 Aug '57.

Lockridge, Ross F., jr. Cur. biog. p. 381 (1948).

locks, canal. See canal locks.

——, **Sault Ste. Marie.** See Sault Ste. Marie locks.

Lockwood, Margaret. Cur. biog. p. 383 (1948).

Lockwood, Rodney M. Cur. biog. p. 360 (1949).

locomotive (1856). Amer. heri. vol. 9 no. 1 cover, 56-73 (part col.) (Dec '57).

——, **electric.** Natl. geog. 110: 376 Sept '56.

——, **steam (antique toy).** Amer. heri. vol. 7 no. 1 frontis. (col.) (Dec '55).

locomotive. See also Cooper's "Tom Thumb" locomotive.

Lodge, Henry Cabot. Amer. heri. vol. 6 no. 5 p. 54-8 (Aug '55); vol. 8 no. 4 p. 23 (Je '57); vol. 11 no. 4 p. 32 (Je '60).

—— **(in play as Lady Macbeth).** Amer. heri. vol. 6 no. 5 p. 56 (Aug '55).

Lodge, Henry Cabot, jr. Cur. biog. p. 449 (1943); p. 415 (1954).

Lodge, John Davis. Cur. biog. p. 384 (1948).

lodge, Alexander Lake (Colo.). Travel 113: 27 Mar '60.

——, **Beaver Lake (Colo.).** Travel 113: 26 Mar '60.

——, **Camp Topridge.** See Camp Topridge lodge.

——, **ranch.** See ranch lodge.

——, **Yellowstone Canyon.** Natl. geog. 113: 617 May '58.

lodges, Indian earth. *See* Indian earth lodges.
Loeb, James, jr. Cur. biog. p. 267 (1962).
Loen, Alfred Van. Cur. biog. p. 467 (1961).
Loesser, Frank. Cur. biog. p. 354 (1945).
Loew home, Arthur. Holiday 24: 42 (col.) Sept '58.
Loewe, Frederick. Cur. biog. p. 243 (1958).
Loewe, Walter S. Cur. biog. p. 393 (1947).
Loewy, Raymond. Cur. biog. p. 523 (1941); p. 369 (1953).
Lofting, Hugh. Jun. bk. of auth., p. 199.
—— (book illus. by). Amer. heri. vol. 8 no. 1 p. 36 (col.) (Dec '56).
log. Natl. geog. 106: 583 (col.) Nov '54.
—— (Chinese sawing). Natl. geog. 111: 353 Mar '57.
——, yule. *See* yule log.
log boom (in lake). Natl. geog. 97: 707 (col.) Je '50; 117: 507 (col.) Ap '60.
log cabin. Amer. heri. vol. 2 no. 1 p. 44 (col.) (fall '50); vol. 8 no. 6 p. 20 (col.) (Oct '57); vol. 3 no. 1 p. 19 (fall '51); vol. 4 no. 1 p. 63 (fall '52); vol. 4 no. 2 p. 13 (winter '53); vol. 5 no. 4 p. 24 (col.) (summer '54); vol. 7 no. 3 p. 42 (col.) (Ap '56); vol. 10 no. 6 p. 66 (Oct '59).
Brooks: Growth of a nation, p. 52-3, 100.
Face of Amer., frontis, 76 (col.).
Holiday 5: 76 Feb '49; 8: 32 Aug '50; 14: 162 Dec '53; 21: 117 (col.) Ap '57.
Natl. geog. 101: 152, 168, 172 (col.) Feb '52; 108: 95 Jl '55.
Travel 101: 46 Mar '54; 109: 24-5 Feb '58, 30 Je '58.
—— (fishermen). Holiday 10: 60 (col.) Sept '51.
—— (Natl. park, boy & girl). Natl. geog. 116: 181 Aug '59.
—— (play house). Travel 113: 11 May '60.
—— (sym.). Lehner: Pict. bk. of sym., p. 54.
log cabin, Gen. Harrison's. Amer. heri. vol. 4 no. 1 p. 63 (fall '52).
——, Lincoln's. Natl. geog. 101: 152, 168 (col.) Feb '52; 117: 244-7 (part col.) Feb '60.
——, T. Roosevelt's (int.). Natl. geog. 100: 305 Sept '51.
log cabins. Natl. geog. 112: 252-3 (col.) Aug '57.
—— (famous). Amer. heri. vol. 7 no. 5 p. 32-3 (Aug '56).
——, Valley Forge. Natl. geog. 105: 192-3 (col.) Feb '54.
log driving (in river). Face of Amer., p. 28-9 (col.).
log horse (for splitting withes). Rawson: Ant. pict. bk., p. 61.
log jam (river). Natl. geog. 100: 121, 124 Jl '51.
log spinning (men). Natl. geog. 110: 314 (col.) Sept '56.
log truck. *See* truck, log.
Logan, Harlan. Cur. biog. p. 353 (1946).
Logan, Harvey (Kid Curry). Horan: Pict. hist. of wild west, p. 198, 220, 224, 228-9.
Logan, J. A. Amer. heri. vol. 11 no. 1 p. 61 (Dec '59).
Logan, John Alexander. Pakula: Cent. album, p. 189.
Logan, Joshua. Cur. biog. p. 361 (1949).

logger. Natl. geog. 100: 117: 122-3, 126-30 Jl '51; 116: 612-3 (col.) Nov '59.
—— (Pacific northwest). Amer. heri. vol. 9 no. 6 p. 10-9, 79 (Oct '58).
logging, bullteam. Amer. vol. 4 no. 4 p. 49 (col.) (summer '53).
logging camp. Rawson: Ant. pict. bk., p. 36.
logging chain. *See* chain, logging.
logging sled. Rawson: Ant. pict. bk., p. 70.
logrolling. Natl. geog. 111: 155 (col.) Feb '57.
——. *See* also birling.
logs (on truck). Natl. geog. 110: 319 (col.) Sept '56.
Lohengrin (as in Lohengrin). Cooper: Con. ency. of music, p. 192.
Loire chateaux. Travel 103: 4 Mar '55.
Loire Valley (France). Holiday 11: 138 (col.) Ap '52; 15: 50 Jan '54.
Lollobrigida, Gina. Cur. biog. p. 236 (1960). Holiday 25: 111 Je '59.
Lolonois, Francois. Amer. heri. vol. 8 no. 2 p. 19 (Feb '57).
Lomax, Alan. Cur. biog. p. 525 (1941).
Lombard, Helen. Cur. biog. p. 454 (1943).
Lombard, Lambert (work of). Con. 133: XXX-VII Ap '54.
Lombardi, Vince. Cur. biog. p. 245 (1963).
Lombardo, Guy. Cur. biog. p. 356 (1946).
London, George. Cur. biog. p. 371 (1953).
London, Julie. Cur. biog. p. 238 (1960).
London. Con. 141: 263 Je '58.
Holiday 5: 163 Je '49; 13: 18, 122 (col.) Je '53; 14: 67 (col.) Sept '53; 15: 57 Jan '54.
Natl. geog. 98: 173-203 (part col.) Aug '50; 100: 707, 715-6 (col.) Dec '51; 103: 810-13 (col.) Je '53; 114: 86-7 (col.) Jl '58.
Travel 107: 23-7 Je '57.
—— (Big Ben clock). Holiday 25: 145 Jan '59.
—— (cartoons). Holiday 27: 72-3 Mar '60.
—— (changing of the Guards). Holiday 13: inside back cover (col.) Feb '53.
—— (coronation of Elizabeth II). Natl. geog. 104: 292-341 (col.) Sept '53.
—— (18-19th cent.). Con. 139: LV Je '57.
—— (Fleet St.). Holiday 21: 26 Je '57.
—— (Houses of parliament). Praeg. pict. ency., p. 391.
—— (map). Natl. geog. 104: 296-7 Sept '53.
—— (map 1600). Natl. geog. 114: 94-5 Jl '58.
—— (Old Bailey court, cartoons). Holiday 28: 60-1 Aug '60.
—— (Royal exchange). Con. 133: 47 Mar '54.
—— (Royal festival hall). Cooper: Con. ency. of music, p. 454.
—— (Royal guard, palace). Holiday 11: 75 (col.) Mar '52, 15 (col.) May '52, 131 (col.) Je '52; 19: 10 (col.) Jan '56, 78 (col.) Mar '56; 22: 164 (col.) Dec '57; 27: 43 (col.) Ap '60.
Natl. geog. 104: 295 (col.) Sept '53; 114: 75 Jl '58.
—— (Royal horse guard). *See* horse guard, Royal (London).
—— (St. James palace guard). Holiday 23: 72 Ap '58.
—— (St. Paul's cathedral). Praeg. pict. ency., p. 380.
—— (Selsdon Park mansion). Travel 103: 22 May '55.

—— (Thames river). Con. 132: XLIV Sept '53; 137: 97 Ap '56; 140: 259 Jan '58; 144: XLVIII Jan '60.
Natl. geog. 98: 203 Aug '50; 114: 46-95 (part col.) Jl '58.
—— (Thames, early views) (Smith). Con. 133: XIX Mar '54.
—— (The Tower). Holiday 26: 84 Nov '59.
—— (Tower bridge). Holiday 14: 132 (col.) Nov '53; 23: 170 Mar '58, 190 Ap '58; 24: 136 Jl '58, 124 Aug '58, 132 Sept '58; 26: 12 Dec '59.
Natl. geog. 108: 124 Jl '55.
Travel 101: 5 May '54; 109: 7 Feb '58, 13 Mar '58, 13 Ap '58, 9 May '58, 13 Je '58; 110: 9 Jl '58, 13 Aug '58, 6 Sept '58, 40 Oct '58, 13 Nov '58.
—— (Trafalgar Square). Travel 113: 73 Ap '60.
—— (Westminster abbey chapel). Holiday 24: 116 (col.) Nov '58.
London bridge. Natl. geog. 114: 86 Jl '58.
Travel 107: 23, 26 Je '57.
London (Regent St.) (Shepherd). Con. 139: 191 May '57.
Londonderry silver. Con. 139: 240-1 Je '57.
"The loneliest isle". Natl. geog. 97: 109 (col.) Jan '50.
Long, Breckinridge. Cur. biog. p. 455 (1943).
Long, Earl K. Cur. biog. p. 348 (1950).
Long, Francis. Amer. heri. vol. 11 no. 4 p. 50 (Je '60).
Long, Huey (statue). See statue (Huey Long).
Long, Roger (Wilson). Con. 143: 86 Ap '59.
Long, Russell B. Cur. biog. p. 377 (1951).
Long, Tania. Cur. biog. p. 357 (1946).
the "long house", Indian. Amer. heri. vol. 6 no. 2 p. 26 (winter '55).
Long island (N.Y.). Holiday 24: 34-47 (part col.) Sept '58.
Natl. geog. 99: 280-326 (part col.) Mar '51.
—— (map). Holiday 24: 38-9 (col.) Sept '58.
Natl. geog. 99: 282 Mar '51; 112: 300-1 Sept '57.
"Long Jakes" (by Charles Deas). Amer. heri. vol. 6 no. 5 cover (col.) (Aug '55).
Long John silver jug. Holiday 22: 7 (col.) Oct '57.
long life (Chinese sym.). Lehner: Pict. bk. of sym., p. 44-5.
"Long live Chiang Kai-shek Hall". Natl. geog. 97: 150 (col.) Feb '50.
"The Long speech" (by Catlin). Amer. heri. vol. 9 no. 1 frontis (col.) (Dec '57).
Longbaugh, Harry (Sundance Kid). Horan: Pict. hist. of wild west, p. 194, 219-20, 227-8.
longboats (Pitcairn is.). Natl. geog. 112: 774, 779 (col.) Dec '57.
—— (rough harbor). Natl. geog. 97: 107 Jan '50.
longevity (sym.). Lehner: Pict. bk. of sym., p. 27-8, 44-8.
Longfellow, Henry W. Amer. heri. vol. 6 no. 3 p. 44 (col.) (Ap '55).
Longfellow home, H. W. Holiday 19: 53 (col.) Je '56.
—— (int.). Holiday 23: 53 Mar '58.
Longfellow memorial., H. W. Natl. geog. 112: 168 Aug '57.

Longhi, Pietro (work of). Con. 140: 259 Jan '58; 145: 267 Je '60.
longhouse, Borneo. Natl. geog. 109: 712, 714-5 May '56.
"Longleat house" (Siberechts). Con. 140: 251 (col.) Jan '58.
Longley, William P. Horan: Pict. hist. of wild west, p. 123.
Longs Peak (Colo.). Natl. geog. 106: 206 Aug '54.
Longstone lighthouse. Natl. geog. 105: 564 Oct '52.
Longstreet, Gen. James. Amer. heri. vol. 9 no. 1 p. 36 (Dec '57).
Pakula: Cent. album, p. 191.
Longton Hall figurine. See figurine, Longton Hall.
Longwood gardens (Kennett Square, Pa.). Natl. geog. 100: 45-64 (col.) Jl '51.
"Longwood" house (Natchez, Miss.). Natl. geog. 118: 707 (col.) Nov '60.
—— (exiled home of Napoleon). Travel 107: 46 Mar '57.
Longworth, Alice Roosevelt. Cur. biog. p. 457 (1943).
Lonsdale, James (work of). Con. 143: 90 Ap '59.
Lonsdale-Hands, Richard. See Hands, Richard Lonsdale.
looking glass. See mirror.
Lookout mt. Natl. geog. 105: 302 (col.) Mar '54.
lookout station, whale. Natl. geog. 113: 781 (col.) Je '58.
lookout tower. Natl. geog. 110: 222 Aug '56.
—— (Majorca). Natl. geog. 111: 632 (col.) May '57.
loom (woman weaving). Disney: People & places, p. 78 (col.).
Natl. geog. 113: 136-7 Jan '58.
——, braid weaving. Rawson: Ant. pict. bk., p. 34.
——, hand (100 year old). Natl. geog. 113: 651 (col.) May '58.
Loomis, Daniel P. Cur. biog. p. 240 (1960).
Loon is. lighthouse. Natl. geog. 98: 532 (col.) Oct '50.
loop the loop (circus). Durant: Pict. hist. of Amer. circus, p. 174-5.
Loosli, Ernest Fritz. Cur. biog. p. 527 (1942).
Lopez, Alfonso. Cur. biog. p. 529 (1942).
Lopez, Alfonso R. Cur. biog. p. 241 (1960).
Lopez, Encarnacion. See Argentinita.
Lopez, George. Holiday 20: 37 Oct '56.
Lopez, Vincent. Cur. biog. p. 243 (1960).
Lorant, Stefan. Amer. heri. vol. 6 no. 4 p. 25 (Je '55).
Lord, Milton E. Cur. biog. p. 351 (1950).
Lord, Mrs. Oswald B. Cur. biog. p. 359 (1952).
The Lord (sym.). Lehner: Pict. bk. of sym., p. 29.
"Lord Baltimore," 1st (Mytens). Con. 126: 162 Dec '50.
"Lord Baltimore & son", 2nd (Mytens). Con. 126: 162 Dec '50.
Lord Chancellor. Int. gr. soc.: Arts . . . p. 153 (col.).
"Lord Derby & wife & son" (Wilson). Con. 135: 52 Mar '55.

Lord Mayor (Australia). Natl. geog. 109: 249 Feb '56.

—— (Dublin). Holiday 19: 39 (col.) Jan '56.
—— (Plymouth, Eng.). Natl. geog. 112: 634 (col.) Nov '57.
The Lorelei (Rhine river). Holiday 15: 29 Feb '54; 23: 150 (col.) Feb '58.
Lorelei (sym.). Lehner: Pict. bk. of sym., p. 92.
Loren, Sophia. Cur. biog. p 267 (1959). Holiday 26: 87 Sept '59.
Lorenz, Konrad Z. Cur. biog. p. 373 (1955).
"Lorette" (Matisse). Con. 145: I (col.) Mar '60.
Lorge, Irving. Cur. biog. p. 268 (1959).
Lorgnette. Holiday 24: 153 Oct '58.
Lorichs, Melchior (drawings by). Con. 135: 84-92 Ap '55.
Loring, Augustus Peabody. Holiday 14: 44 Nov '53.
Lorrain, Claud de. See Claude de Lorrain.
Los Alamos (N.M.). Travel 110: 55-7 Nov '58.
Los Angeles. Holiday 7: 26-47 (part col.) Jan '50; 14: 79 Jl '53; 22: 50-67 (col.) Oct '57; 23: 26-7 (col.) Mar '58.
Jordan: Hammond's pict. atlas, p. 205 (col.).
—— (air view). Natl. geog. 105: 787 Je '54.
—— (civic center). Holiday 24: 19 Nov '58.
—— (1850). Amer. heri. vol. 9 no. 5 p. 18-9 (Aug '58).
—— (farmers market). Holiday 6: 64-70 (part col.) Aug '49.
—— (hotel). Holiday 10: 98-103 (part col.) Aug '51; 25: 17 Ap '59, 129 (col.) May '59.
Losch, Tilly. Cur. biog. p. 425 (1944).
"Lost bet" (presidential campaign). Amer. heri. vol. 7 no. 4 p. 31 (col.) (Je '56).
lost cities. See cities, lost.
"Lost colony" (pageant, Ft. Raleigh, N.C.). Jordan: Hammond's pict. atlas, p. 57 (col.).
Natl. geog. 108: 517-9, 522 (col.) Oct '55.
"Lot & his daughters". Natl. geog. 101: 94 (col.) Jan '52.
Lothar, Ernst. Cur. biog. p. 394 (1947).
lottery machine, Nicaragua. Holiday 17: 45 Mar '55.
Lotto, Lorenzo (work of). Natl. geog. 97: 771 (col.) Je '50.
Lotuka dancers (Sudan). Natl. geog. 103: 264 (col.) Feb '53.
Lotuka men & woman. Natl. geog. 103: 256-7, 264 (col.) Feb '53.
Lotuka woman smoking (baby on back). Natl. geog. 103: 252 Feb '53.
lotus (sym.). Lehner: Pict. bk. of sym., p. 27.
lotus & egg (sym.). See egg & lotus.
Louchheim, Katie. Cur. biog. p. 385 (1956).
Loudon, Alexander. Cur. biog. p. 531 (1942).
Lough, John Graham (sculpt. by). Con. 127: 105 May '51.
Loughlin, Dame Anne. Cur. biog. p. 353 (1950).
Louis IX & mother, King (in a Bible). Con. 140: 109 Nov '57.
Louis XIV. Amer. heri. vol. 8 no. 3 p. 89 (Ap '57).
Louis XIV (bust). Praeg. pict. ency., p. 334.
Louis XV (bust). Con. 143: 138 May '59.
—— (Coysevox). Con. 141: 37 Mar '58.
Louis XV, daughters of. See daughters of Louis XV.

Louis XVI. (porcelain bust). Con. 129: 73 Ap '52.
Louis XVII, Dauphin (Kucharski). Con. 136: 34 Sept '55 .
Louisbourg fortress (Nova Scotia). Holiday 25: 139 (col.) Ap '59.
—— (1758, landing of New Eng. troops). Amer. heri. vol. 6 no. 2 p. 51-3 (col.) (winter '55).
Louisbourg siege. Natl. geog. 116: 91 (col.) Jl '59.
Louise of Prussia & sister, Crown princess (sculpt.). Praeg. pict. ency., p. 397.
Louisiana. Holiday 11: 34-51 (part col.) Mar '52; 24: I Oct '58.
Jordan: Hammond's pict. atlas, p. 82-5 (col.).
Natl. geog. 113: 532-49 (part col.) Ap '58.
Travel 102: cover, 7-10 Aug '54.
—— (New Orleans). See New Orleans.
—— (state capital bldg.). Holiday 15: 78 Feb '54.
Jordan:: Hammond's pict. atlas, p. 84 (col.).
Natl. geog. 118: 710 (col.) Nov '60.
Louisiana bayou (Evangeline country). Amer. heri. vol. 6 no. 1 p. 60-3 (col.) (fall '54).
Holiday 6: 52-63 (col.) Oct '49.
Louisiana home (Colonial). Amer. heri. vol. 7 no. 4 p. 57-63 (Je '56).
Louisiana plantations. Amer. heri. vol. 4 no. 2 p. 26-31 (part col.) (winter '53); vol. 7 no. 4 p. 57-63 (Je '56); vol. 11 no. 5 p. 52 (col.) (Aug '60).
Natl. geog. 113: 532-49 (part col.) Ap '58.
Travel 108:13-4 Oct '57.
"Louisiana story" (movie scene). Int. gr. soc.: Arts . . . p. 151 (col.).
Louisville (Ky.). Holiday 21: 86-91 (col.) Je '57.
lounge, airplane. Holiday 12: 95 (col.) Oct '52.
Lourdes (France). Travel 109: 37-40 Jan '58.
—— (chapel). Holiday 23: 13 (col.) Mar '58.
Natl. geog. 109: 310 (col.) Mar '56.
Loutfi, Omar. Cur. biog. p. 331 (1957).
Loutherbourg, P. J. (work of). Con. 144: XLV Nov '59.
Louvre (Paris). Holiday 8: 81 Nov '50; 13: 110 (col.) Ap '53.
Praeg. pict. ency., p. 306.
—— (int.). Travel 106: 52-3 Nov '56.
Louw, Eric H. Cur. biog. p. 269 (1962).
Lovanium univ. (Africa). Holiday 25: 61 Ap '59.
Love, George H. Cur. biog. p. 355 (1950).
Love, James Spencer. Cur. biog. p. 333 (1957).
Love, John A. Cur. biog. p. 247 (1963).
love (sym.). Lehner: Pict. bk. of sym., p. 27-8, 65.
"Love in springtime" (Boucher). Con. 133: 108 (col.) Ap '54.
love knot. See knot, true-love.
love seat (antique). Con. 141: XXIX Ap '58.
——, George II. Con. 144: XIII Dec '59.
——, Queen Anne. Con. 138: 45 Sept '56.
lovebirds (sym.). Lehner: Pict. bk. of sym., p. 65.
Lovelace, Maud Hart. Jun. bk. of auth., p. 200.
Loveless, Herschel C. Cur. biog. p. 251 (1958).
Lovell, Bernard. Cur. biog. p. 270 (1959).
Lovell, Mansfield. Pakula: Cent. album, p. 193.
Loveman, Amy. Cur. biog. p. 460 (1943).

lovers (boy & girl on beach). Holiday 8: 49 (col.) Sept '50.
—— (on cards). Lehner: Pict. bk. of sym., p. 76.
"The lovers" (Picasso). Natl. geog. 111: 91 (col.) Jan '57.
"Love's missive" (Hunt). Con. 144: 95 Nov '59.
Lovett, Robert A. Cur. biog. p. 532 (1942); p. 380 (1951).
Lovett, Robert Morss. Cur. biog. p. 461 (1943).
loving cup. Lehner: Pict. bk. of sym., p. 65.
—— (Nottingham). Con. ency. of ant., vol. 1, pl. 51.
——, Dewey's (from school children). Amer. heri. vol. 2 no. 3 p. 53 (spring '51).
lowboy (antique). Con. 139: XLVIII Je '57.
—— (18th cent.). Con. 141: 128 Ap '58.
——, Amer. Chippendale. Con. 142: LXIX Jan '59.
——, Chippendale. Con. ency. of ant., vol. 1, pl. 41.
Con. 137: 275 Je '56.
——, Early Eng. Con. 127: 113 May '51.
——, William & Mary. Con. 141: 42 Mar '58.
Lowdermilk, Walter C. Cur. biog. p. 363 (1949).
Lowe, Jack. Cur. biog. p. 643 (1954).
Lowe, James. Horan: Pict. hist. of wild west, p. 194.
Lowe, Rowdy Joe. Horan: Pict. hist. of wild west, p. 106.
Lowell, A. Lawrence. Amer. heri. vol. 9 no. 6 p. 57 (Oct '58).
Lowell, James Russell. Amer. heri. vol. 8 no. 2 p. 22 (Feb '57).
Lowell, Ralph. Holiday 14: 47 (col.) Nov '53.
Lowell, Robert. Cur. biog. p. 395 (1947).
Lowndes, Rawlins. Amer. heri. vol. 9 no. 2 p. 57 (col.) (Feb '58).
Lowndes, Mrs. Rawlins. Amer. heri. vol. 9 no. 2 p. 56 (col.) (Feb '58).
Lownsbery, Eloise. Jun. bk. of auth., p. 201. Cur. biog. p 397 (1947).
Lowry, L. S. (work of). Con. 142: XLVIII Nov '58.
Lowther, Capt. George. Amer. heri. vol. 8 no. 2 p. 15 (Feb '57).
Loy, Myrna. Cur. biog. p. 357 (1950).
Loynd, Harry J. Cur. biog. p. 361 (1952).
Lozovsky, Solomon A. Cur. biog. p. 526 (1941).
Lozowick, Louis. Cur. biog. p. 533 (1942).
Luanda Bay. Travel 105: 45 Feb '56.
luau. See Hawaii (luau).
Lubell, Samuel. Cur. biog. p. 387 (1956).
Lubin, Isador. Cur. biog. p. 527 (1941); p. 373 (1953).
Lubke, Heinrich. Cur. biog. p 245 (1960).
"Luca da Reggio" (Ferrari). Con. 135: 58 Mar '55.
Lucas, David (work of). Con. ency. of ant., vol. 1, pl. 137.
Lucas, J. Seymour (work of). Con. 132: 177 (col.) Jan '54.
Lucas, Jannette May. Jun. bk. of auth., p. 202.
Lucas, Martha B. Cur. biog. p 398 (1947).
Lucas, Scott W. Cur. biog. p. 399 (1947).
Lucca (Italy). Travel 107: 27 Ap '57.
Luccock, Rev. Halford E. Cur. biog. p. 247 (1960).

Luce, Clare Boothe. Cur. biog. p. 375 (1953).
Luce, Henry R. Cur. biog. p. 529 (1941); p. 274 (1961).
Lucerne (Switzerland). Travel 102: 11 Aug '54.
Luchow's restaurant (int.). Holiday 18: 74 (col.) Nov '55.
Lucioni, Luigi. Cur. biog. p. 466 (1943).
—— (work of). Amer. heri. vol. 6 no. 4 p. 26-7 (col.) (Je '55).
Lucius Verus, Emperor (bust). Con. ency. of ant., vol. 3 pl. 67.
luck (goddess of). Lehner: Pict. bk. of sym., p. 31.
——, good (sym.). See good luck (sym.).
"The luck of Edenhall" glass. See glass, "The Luck of Edenhall".
Luckman, Charles. Cur. biog. p. 402 (1947).
lucky numbers triangle (sym.). Lehner: Pict. bk. of sym., p. 70.
"Lucretia" (Rembrandt). Con. 138: 32 Sept '56.
—— (stage setting for). Int. gr. soc.: Arts . . . p. 145 (col.).
—— (Veronese). Natl. geog. 97: 748 (col.) Je '50.
Ludington, Flora B. Cur. biog. p. 379 (1953).
Ludwig I, King of Bavaria. Amer. heri. vol. 6 no. 2 p. 58 (winter '55).
Lugano (Switzerland). Travel 102: 13 Aug '54.
luggage. Holiday 10: 113 Sept '51, 33 Nov '51, 7, 14, 80, 85, 144, 153 (part col.) Dec '51; 11: 2 (col.), 119 Feb '52, 162 (col.) May '52, 1, 26, 69, 149, 152, 157 (col.) Je '52; 12: 64 (col.) Jl '52, 5, 77, 92-3, 98, 148, 163 Dec '52; 13: 88 (col.) Feb '53, 30, 129 (col.) May '53, 66, 79, 92, 149 (col.) Je '53; 14: 84, 124 Jl '53, 97 Aug '53, 66 Sept '53, 18 Oct '53, 99, 171 Nov '53, 2, 28, 41, 79, 87, 133, 140, 150 (part col.) Dec '53; 18: 96, 112 (col.) Jl '55, 4, 134 (col.) Oct '55, 28-9 (col.), 118 Nov '55, 1, 28, 84-5, 96, 119, 152 (part col.) Dec '55; 19: 83 (col.) Feb '56, 152 (col.) Mar '56, 124 (col.) May '56, 74, 104-5, 132, 135 (col.) Je '56; 20: 60-1 (col.) Aug '56, 65 Sept '56, 117 (col.) Oct '56, 8-9, 97 (col.) Nov '56, 5, 36, 40-1, 142, 153, 164-5, 192 (col.) Dec '56; 21: 110 (col.) Feb '57, 180 (col.) May '57, 25, 33 (col.) Je '57; 22: 32, 82 (col.) Jl '57, 143 (col.) Sept '57, 168, 194 (col.) Nov '57, 5, 25, 116 (col.) Dec '57; 23: 5 (col.) Feb '58, 38, 103, 123 (col.) Je '58; 24: 92, 116, 141, back cover (col.) Jl '58, 123 (col.) Sept '58, 126, 158 Oct '58, 4 (col.) Nov '58, 2, 139, 153, 162-3, 165, 208 (col.) Dec '58; 25: 7 (col.) Feb '59, 208 May '59, 43, 137, 168, 185 (col.) Je '59; 26: 82, 95, back cover (col.) Jl '59, 31, 141 (col.) Sept '59, 4, 63, 125, 152, 171, 223 (col.) Dec '59; 27: 138 (col.) Feb '60, 102 (col.) Mar '60, 26, 137, 162, 166 (col.), 180 Je '60; 28: 7, back cover (col.) Jl '60, 13 (col.) Sept '60, 175, 191 (col.) Nov '60, 46, 127, 144 (col.) Dec '60.
Natl. geog. 100: 758 Dec '51; 103: 329 (col.) Mar '53.

Travel 105: 39 Feb '56; 106: 52 Jl '56; 113: 11 Jan '60, 9 May '60; 114 inside back cover Sept '60.

luggage (airplane porter). Holiday 21: 106 Jan '57.

—— **(kitten).** Holiday 27: 171 Ap '60.

luggage. See also bag; suitcase.

lugger (Australian diver's boat). Natl. geog. 111: 32-3 (col.) Jan '57.

Lujack, Johnny. Cur. biog. p. 404 (1947).

Lukas, Paul. Cur. biog. p. 535 (1942).

Luks, George (work of). Amer. heri. vol. 10 no. 6 p. 17 (col.) (Oct '59).

Lullingstone castle (Eng.). Natl. geog. 103: 692 May '53.

lumber hauling. Brooks: Growth of a nation, p. 216.

lumber raft. Amer. heri. vol. 10 no. 1 p. 18 (col.) (Dec '58).

Brooks: Growth of a nation, p. 216.

—— **(Norway).** Natl. geog. 106: 187 (col.) Aug '54.

lumber sledding. Rawson: Ant. pict. bk., p. 73.

lumberjack. Natl. geog. 100: 117, 122-3, 126-30 Jl '51.

—— **(cutting tree).** Holiday 28: 54 (col.) Aug '60.

lumberjacks (Nigerian rafts). Natl. geog. 110: 356 (col.) Sept '56.

Lumbertown (Minn.). Travel 108: 29-31 Aug '57.

Lumumba, Patrice. Cur. biog. p. 248 (1960).

Luna Park (by night, 1903). Amer heri. vol. 9 no. 4 p. 19 (Je '58).

lunar laboratory & orbiter. U.S. News & world report, p. 47, Aug, 31, 1964.

lunch, ranch buffet. Natl. geog. 104: 355 (col.) Sept '53.

lunch kit. Holiday 18: 162 Dec '55.

lunch room, outdoor (Bermuda). Holiday 23: 74 (col.) Je '58.

Lund, Wendell L. Cur. biog. p. 537 (1942).

Lundberg, Gustave (work of). Con. 135: 46 Mar '55.

Lundebery, Harry. Cur. biog. p. 363 (1952).

lunette, mosaic (19th cent.). Natl. geog. 103: 527 (col.) Ap '53.

lunette ornament. Con. ency. of ant., vol. 1, p. 20.

lungs. Gray's anatomy, p. 1122, 1129-38.

Luns, Joseph M.A. H. Cur. biog. p. 253 (1958).

Lunt, Alfred. Cur. biog. p. 532 (1941).

Lunt, Storer B. Cur. biog. p. 254 (1958).

Luny, Thomas (work of). Con. 140: VIII Jan '58; 144: 123 Nov '59.

Lupi, Miguel Angelo (work of). Con. 137: 9 Mar '56.

Lupino, Ida. Cur. biog. p. 467 (1943).

Luray cavern (Va.). Holiday 12: 37 Nov '52. Jordan: Hammond's pict. atlas, p. 51 (col.). Travel 108: 16-7 Dec '57; 109: 19 Feb '58.

Lurcat, Jean. Cur. biog. p. 386 (1948).

Lurcat tapestry. See tapestry, Jean Lurcat.

Lusitania (1907). Amer. heri. vol. 6 no. 4 p. 45 (Je '55).

—— **(sinking).** Amer. heri. vol. 6 no. 4 p. 40 (Je '55).

Lusk, Mrs. Georgia L. Cur. biog. p. 406 (1947).

lute. Con 145: 159, 203 May '60.

—— **(by Frei, 1550).** Cooper: Con. ency. of music, p. 360.

—— **(girl playing).** Natl. geog. 100: 424 Sept '51.

——, **harp.** See harp lute.

"Lute player" (Carracci). Con. 135: XXVI Je '55.

"Lute player" (Crespi). Con. 144: 24 Sept '59.

"The lute player" (Hals). Con. 145: 159 May '60.

"Lute player" (Saraceni). Con. 145: 203 May '60.

"Lute-playing angel" (Melozzo da Forli). Praeg. pict. ency., p. 254 (col.).

Lutheran church cross See cross, Lutheran.

Luthull, Albert John. Cur. biog. p. 271 (1962).

Luti, Benedetto (work of). Con. 136: 284 Jan '56.

"Luton Hoo" house. Con. 126: 86 Oct '50.

Lutyens, Sir Edwin L. Cur. biog. p. 539 (1942).

Luxembourg. Holiday 8: 31 Sept '50; 18: 128 (col.) Nov '55.

Travel 105: 23 Ap '56.

—— **(castle).** See castle, Vianden.

Luxembourg palace. Natl. geog. 98: 59 (col.) Jl '50; 101: 778 (col.) Je '52; 114: 296 Aug '58.

Luxor temple. Holiday 27: 67 (col.) Mar '60. Natl. geog. 108: 624-5 (col.) Nov '55. Praeg. pict. ency., p. 119.

—— **(colonnade).** Natl. geog. 106: 761 (col.) Dec '54.

—— **(obelisk).** Ceram: March of arch., p. 90.

Luycks, Christian (work of). Con. 142: 190 (col.) Dec '58.

Lu Yuan (work of). Praeg. pict. ency., p. 539 (col.).

Lyceum lecturer (1841). Amer. heri. vol. 8 no. 5 p. 21 (Aug '57).

Lycian stone plinth. Osward: Asia Minor, pl. 113.

Lydenberg, Harry Miller. Cur. biog. p. 535 (1941).

"Lydia Pinkham enters Heaven". Amer. heri. vol. 10 no. 3 p. 45 (col.) (Ap '59).

Lydian tombstone. See tombstone, Lydian.

lymphatic system. Gray's anatomy, p. 695-735.

Lynch, Daniel F. Cur. biog. p. 375 (1955).

Lynch, Rev. John Joseph. Cur. biog. p. 359 (1946).

Lynch, Peg. Cur. biog. p. 389 (1956).

lynching man. Natl. geog. 104: 362 Sept '53.

Lynes, Russell. Cur. biog. p. 335 (1957).

Lynn, Diana. Cur. biog. p. 380 (1953).

Lyon, Matthew. Amer. heri. vol. 6 no. 6 p. 42, 46 (Oct '55).

Lyon, Dr. W. K. Natl. geog. 115: 7 (col.) Jan '59.

Lyons, Lord. Amer. heri. vol. 8 no. 3 p. 40 (col.) (Ap '57); vol. 8 no. 5 p. 72 (Aug '57).

Lyons, Eugene. Cur. biog. p. 428 (1944).

Lyons, Harry. Cur. biog. p. 337 (1957).

lyre (chair back). Con. ency. of ant., vol. 1, p. 65.

—— **(David playing at Gibeah).** Natl. geog. 112: 853 (col.) Dec. '57.

—— **(sym.).** Lehner: Pict. bk. of sym., p. 14.

——, **Greek (ancient).** Int. gr soc.: Arts . . . p. 27 (col.).
Lysippus (Greek sculpt.). Praeg. pict. ency., p. 133.
—— **(head of Alexander the Great).** Praeg. pict. ency., p. 159.
Lyttelton, Oliver. Cur. biog. p. 537 (1941); p. 381 (1953).

M

Maani, Sitti (wife of Pietro). Ceram: March of arch., p. 166.
Maas, Maj. Gen. Melvin J. Cur. biog. p. 338 (1957).
Maass, Clara Louise. Travel 105: inside back cover Ap '56.
Mabinshe, Bope (African king). Holiday 25: 69 (col.) Ap '59.
Mabry, J. C. (Bus). Holiday 24: 80 Nov '58.
Mabuse, Jan Gossaert (work of). Con. 133: 94 Ap '54; 140: 279 Jan '58.
MacCabe, Gibson. Cur biog. p. 249 (1963).
McAfee, Lt. Com. Mildred H. Cur. biog. p. 540 (1942).
Macao (Portugul). Holiday 17: 46 Feb '55.
Macapagal, Diosdado. Cur. biog. p. 273 (1962).
MacArthur, Gen. Douglas. Amer. heri. vol. 10 no. 6 p. 13 (col.) (Oct '59). Cur. biog. p. 539 (1941); p. 389 (1948). Holiday 6: 99 Dec '49. Natl. geog. 99: 215 Feb '51.
MacArthur, Gen. & Mrs. Douglas. Natl. geog. 100: 582 (col.) Nov '51.
MacArthur, Douglas, 2d. Cur. biog. p. 419 (1954).
Macau (border to China). Natl. geog. 103: 679-88 (col.) May '53.
Macaulay, Thomas B. Amer. heri. vol. 8 no. 5 p. 27 (Aug '57).
Macauley, Mrs. Robert W. Cur. biog. p. 365 (1949).
McAuliffe, Maj. Gen. Anthony C. Cur. biog. p. 359 (1950).
Macbeth, Lady (theatre). Amer. heri. vol. 6 no. 5 p. 56 (Aug '55).
McBride, Katharine E. Cur. biog. p. 542 (1942).
McBride, Mary Margaret. Cur. biog. p. 541 (1941); p. 421 (1954).
MacBride, Sean. Cur. biog. p. 366 (1949).
McCabe, Thomas Bayard. Cur. biog. p. 393 (1948).
McCaffrey, John L. Cur. biog. p. 361 (1950).
McCain, Vice Adm. John S. Cur. biog. p. 470 (1943).
McCall, Rev. Duke K. Cur. biog. p. 271 (1959).
McCanles, David C. Horan: Pict. hist. of wild west, p. 49.
McCardell, Claire. Cur. biog. p. 423 (1954).
McCarey, Thomas Leo. Cur. biog. p. 361 (1946).
McCarran, Patrick A. Cur. biog. p. 407 (1947).
McCarthy, Charlie. Cur. biog. p. 43 (1945).
McCarthy, Clem. Cur. biog. p. 543 (1941).
McCarthy, Eugene J. Cur. biog. p. 377 (1955).
McCarthy, Col. Frank. Cur. biog. p. 356 (1945).
McCarthy, Joe. Cur. biog. p. 396 (1948). Holiday 7: 32 Ap '50; 20: 33 Oct '56.
McCarthy, Joseph R. Cur. biog. p. 362 (1950).
McCarthy, Dr. Kenneth C. Cur. biog. p. 385 (1953).

McCarthy, Leighton. Cur. biog. p. 543 (1942).
McCarthy, Mary. Cur. biog. p. 378 (1955).
McCarty, Bill. Horan: Pict. hist. of wild west, p. 205.
McCarty, Tom. Horan: Pict. hist. of wild west, p. 204.
McCarty, Daniel T., jr. Cur. biog. p. 387 (1953).
McCleery, Albert K. Cur. biog. p. 379 (1955).
McClellan, Gen. George B. (campaign poster). Amer. heri. vol. 7 no. 4 p. 26 (col.) (Je '56).
—— **(civil war).** Amer. heri. vol. 8 no. 5 p. 72 (Aug '57). Pakula: Cent. album, p. 195.
McClellan, Mrs. George B. Amer. heri. vol. 6 no. 3 p. 93 (Ap '55).
McClellan, Harold C. Cur. biog. p. 425 (1954).
McClellan, John L. Cur. biog. p. 364 (1950).
McClennan, John Hugh. Cur. biog. p. 369 (1946).
McClernand, John Alexander. Pakula: Cent. album, p. 197.
McClintic, Guthrie. Cur. biog. p. 471 (1943).
McClintock, Robert Mills. Cur. biog. p. 381 (1955).
McClinton, Katharine M. Cur. biog. p. 256 (1958).
McCloskey, Mark A. Cur. biog. p. 383 (1955).
McCloskey, Robert. Cur. biog. p. 544 (1942). Jun. bk. of auth., p. 203.
McCloy, John J. Cur. biog. p. 409 (1947); p. 276 (1961).
McClure, S. S. Amer. heri. vol. 9 no. 2 p. 66 (Feb '58).
McCobb, Paul W. Cur. biog. p. 257 (1958).
McComas, Oliver Parker. Cur. biog. p. 385 (1955).
McConachie, George W. Grant. Cur. biog. p. 259 (1958).
McCone, John A. Cur. biog. p. 273 (1959).
McConnell, Fowler B. Cur. biog. p. 366 (1952).
McConnell, Joseph H. Cur. biog. p. 366 (1950).
McConnell, Samuel K., jr. Cur. biog. p. 391 (1956).
McCook, Alexander McDowell. Pakula: Cent. album, p. 199.
McCormack, Emmet J. Cur. biog. p. 389 (1953).
McCormack, John (as Cavaradossi in Tosca). Cooper: Con. ency. of music, p. 190.
McCormack, John W. Cur. biog. p. 475 (1943); p. 276 (1962).
McCormick, Austin H. Cur. biog. p. 382 (1951).
McCormick, Cyrus. Amer. heri. vol. 7 no. 6 p. 82 (Feb '56).
McCormick, Cyrus Hall. Brooks: Growth of a nation, p. 197.
McCormick, Dr. Edward J. Cur. biog. p. 390 (1953).
McCormick, Edward T. Cur. biog. p. 383 (1951).
McCormick, Fowler. Cur. biog. p. 412 (1947).
McCormick, Jay. Cur. biog. p. 477 (1943).
McCormick, Adm. Lynde Dupuy. Cur. biog. p. 368 (1952).
McCormick, Myron. Cur. biog. p. 427 (1954).
McCormick, Robert R. Cur. biog. p. 545 (1942).
McCormick, reaper, birthplace of. Brooks: Growth of a nation, p. 103.

McCoy, Maj. Gen. Frank R. Cur. biog. p. 358 (1945).

McCoy, John J. Holiday 23: 60 Mar '58.

McCoy, Joseph C. Horan: Pict. hist. of wild west, p. 52.

McCracken, Joan. Cur. biog. p. 361 (1945).

McCracken, Harold. Cur. biog. p. 368 (1949) Jun. bk. of auth., p. 204.

McCracken, James. Cur. biog. p. 251 (1963).

McCracken, Rev. Robert James. Cur. biog. p. 370 (1949).

McCrady, Edward. Cur. biog. p. 340 (1957).

McCrary, Jinx. Cur. biog. p. 393 (1953).

McCrary, Tex. Cur. biog. p. 393 (1953).

McCrea, Jane (murdered by Indians). Amer. heri. vol. 7 no. 4 p. 7 (col.) (Je '56).

McCreery, Lt. Gen. Sir Richard L. Cur. biog. p. 362 (1945).

McCune, Francis K. Cur. biog. p. 278 (1961).

McDaniel, Glen. Cur. biog. p. 370 (1952).

McDermott, Michael J. Cur. biog. p. 386 (1951).

McDevitt, James L. Cur. biog. p. 275 (1959).

McDiarmid, Errett W. Cur. biog. p. 398 (1948).

McDonald, Betty. Cur. biog. p. 362 (1946).

McDonald, David. Cur. biog. p. 253 (1963).

McDonald, Eugene F., jr. Cur. biog. p. 372 (1949).

McDonald, James G. Cur. biog. p. 373 (1949).

McDonald, Joseph. Amer. heri. vol. 4 no. 3 p. 23 (spring '53).

McDonald, Malcolm. Cur. biog. p. 429 (1954).

McDonald, Capt. W. J. (Bill). Brooks: Growth of a nation, p. 167.

McDonnell, William A. Cur. biog. p. 276 (1959).

MacDougal, Annie. Horan: Pict. hist. of wild west: p. 171.

McDowall, Roddy. Cur. biog. p. 280 (1961).

McDowell, Irwin. Pakula: Cent. album, p. 201.

mace. Holiday 18: 38 (col.) Sept '55. Natl. geog. 105: 229 (col.) Feb '54; 113: 157 Feb '58.

—— **(sym.).** Lehner: Pict. bk. of sym., p. 94.

——, **Buddhist.** Lehner: Pict. bk. of sym., p. 42.

——, **silver-gilt.** Con. 133: 100 Ap '54.

mace head, silver. Con. 138: 250 Jan '57.

Macedonian farmer. Holiday 14: 46 Aug '53.

Macedonian warrior (ancient times). Int. gr. soc.: Arts . . . p. 33 (col.).

McElroy, Neil H. Cur. biog. p. 387 (1951).

Mcevoy, Ambrose (work of). Con. 133: 115 Ap '54; 139: 9 Mar '57.

McFarland, Ernest W. Cur. biog. p. 389 (1951).

MacFarlane, Lt. Gen. Frank N. Mason. Cur. biog. p. 479 (1943).

McGeachy, Mary Craig. Cur. biog. p. 431 (1944).

McGee, Fibber. Cur. biog. p. 544 (1941).

McGee, Gale William. Cur. biog. p. 282 (1961).

McGee, Molly. Cur. biog. p. 544 (1941).

McGhee, George C. Cur. biog. p. 368 (1950).

McGill, Ralph. Cur. biog. p. 413 (1947).

McGill univ. students. Natl. geog. 98: 354 (col.) Sept '50.

McGinley, Rev. Laurence, jr. Cur. biog. p. 375 (1949).

McGinley, Phyllis. Cur. biog. p. 545 (1941); p. 284 (1961). Jun. bk. of auth., p. 206.

McGinnis, Patrick B. Cur. biog. p. 387 (1955).

McGovern, John W. Cur. biog. p. 286 (1961).

MacGowan, Gault. Cur. biog. p. 365 (1945).

McGranery, James P. Cur. biog. p. 371 (1952).

McGrath, Earl James. Cur. biog. p. 377 (1949).

McGrath, James Howard. Cur. biog. p. 400 (1948).

McGraw, Curtis W. Cur. biog. p. 370 (1950).

McGraw, Eloise Jarvis. Cur. biog. p. 389 (1955).

McGraw, John. Amer. heri. vol. 10 no. 3 p. 23 (Ap. '59).

McGraw, John J. Holiday 23: 83 May '58.

MacGregor, Ellen. Cur. biog. p. 430 (1954).

McGregor, Gordon R. Cur. biog. p. 432 (1954).

McGregor, J. Harry. Cur. biog. p. 261 (1958).

McGuffey, William (statue). Amer. heri. vol. 8 no. 5 p. 10 (Aug '57).

McGuffey birthplace, Wm. Holmes. Brooks: Growth of a nation, p. 136.

McGuffey reader (pages from). Amer. heri. vol. 8 no. 5 p. 94-5 (Aug '57).

——. Brooks: Growth of a nation, p. 136.

McGuigan, Anne Eleanor. See Emery, Anne.

McGuigan, Cardinal James. Cur. biog. p. 372 (1950).

McGuire, Dorothy. Cur. biog. p. 547 (1941). Holiday 10: 64 Dec '51.

McHale, Kathryn. Cur. biog. p. 416 (1947).

machete. Natl. geog. 99: 433 (col.) Ap '51.

Machiavelli, Niccolo. Int. gr. soc.: Arts . . . p. 93 (col.).

Ma Chi-Chuang. Cur. biog. p. 384 (1953).

machine, carving. See carving machine.

——, **paper making.** See paper making machine.

——, **stone slicing.** See stone slicing machine.

machine gun. Natl. geog. 98: 669 Nov '50.

——, **first practical.** Amer. heri. vol. 8 no. 6 p. 49-51 (Oct '57).

——, **Gatling.** Amer. heri. vol. 8 no. 6 p. 105-7 (Oct '57).

machinery, factory (modern). Int. gr. soc.: Arts . . . p. 173 (col.).

——, **heavy.** Natl. geog. 101: 345 Mar '52.

——, **perfume-making.** See perfume-making machinery

——, **uranium.** Natl. geog. 106: 551 (col.) Oct '54.

Machold, Earle J. Cur. biog. p. 262 (1958).

Machu Picchu (Peru, lost city of Incas). Disney: People & places, p. 111 (col.). Holiday 7: 19 Je '50; 8: 13 (col.) Nov '50; 12: 19 Nov '52; 16: inside cover (col.) Oct '54, 93 Dec '54; 17: 140 Mar '55; 18: 12-3 (col.) Sept '55; 19: 28-9 (col.) Mar '56; 20: 50-1 (col.) Nov '56; 23: 152 (col.) Feb '58, 40 (col.) Ap '58. Int. gr. soc.: Arts . . . p. 51 (col.). Natl. geog. 98: 454, 456, 458 (col.) Oct '50. Praeg. pict. ency., p. 558. Travel 107: 29 Feb '57.

McIntire, Vice Adm. Ross T. Cur. biog. p. 367 (1945).

McIntosh, Millicent Carey. Cur. biog. p. 417 (1947).

Mcintyre, James Francis. Cur. biog. p. 398 (1953).

McIntyre, Thomas J. Cur. biog. p. 255 (1963).
Maciver, Loren. Cur. biog. p. 400 (1953).
McIver, Pearl. Cur. biog. p. 379 (1949).
Mack, Connie. Amer. heri. vol. 10 no. 3 p. 23 (Ap '59).
    Cur. biog. p. 434 (1944).
Mack, Lawrence L. Cur. biog. p. 342 (1957).
Mack, Nila. Cur. biog. p. 373 (1952).
Mack, Pauline Beery. Cur. biog. p. 373 (1950).
Mack, Ted. Cur. biog. p. 391 (1951).
Mack, Walter S., jr. Cur. biog. p. 364 (1946).
Mackay, Constance D'Arcy. Jun. bk. of auth., p. 207.
McKay, David O. Cur. biog. p. 393 (1951).
McKay, Douglas. Cur. biog. p. 381 (1949).
Mackay, Sir Iven Giffard. Cur. biog. p. 548 (1941).
Mackay, Rev. John A. Cur. biog. p. 375 (1952).
MacKaye, David L. Cur. biog. p. 382 (1949).
MacKaye, Julia J. Cur. biog. p. 382 (1949).
Macke, August (work of). Praeg. pict. ency., p. 449 (col.).
McKee & children, Mrs. Mary Harrison. Jensen: The White House, p. 139-43.
McKee jungle gardens. Natl. geog. 113: 46-7 (col.) Jan '58.
    Travel 105: 57-9 Mar '56.
McKeen, John E. Cur. biog. p. 288 (1961).
McKeever, Edward C. Cur. biog. p. 369 (1945).
McKeldin, Theodore R. Cur. biog. p. 378 (1952).
    Holiday 23: 80 Je '58.
McKellar, Kenneth D. Cur. biog. p. 367 (1946).
McKelway, Benjamin M. Cur. biog. p. 264 (1958).
McKenna, Siobhan. Cur. biog. p. 393 (1956).
McKenney, Ruth. Cur. biog. p. 549 (1949).
MacKenzie, Alex. Natl. geog. 108: 198 (col.) Aug '55.
Mackenzie, Alexander. Amer. heri. vol. 8 no. 6 p. 44 (Oct '57).
McKenzie, Chalmers J. Cur. biog. p. 379 (1952).
MacKenzie, Gisele. Cur. biog. p. 390 (1955).
Mackenzie, Ranald. Amer. heri. vol. 9 no. 4 p. 22 (Je '58).
Mackenzie, monument (Canada). Natl. geog. 108: 235 (col.) Aug '55.
Mackenzie's Canadian expeditions, Alexander. Amer. heri. vol. 8 no. 6 p. 47 (col.) (Oct '57).
Mackinac bridge (Mich.). Holiday 27: 25 Ap '60; 28: 6 Sept '60.
    Natl. geog. 115: 440-1, 443 (col.) Ap '59.
Mackinac island. Holiday 10: 32-3 Jl '51.
    Jordan: Hammond's pict. atlas, p. 92 (col.).
    Natl. geog. 101: 308-9 (col.) Mar '52.
    Travel 106: 40 Aug '56.
—— (hotel). Travel 114: 52 Aug '60.
McKinley, Chuck. Cur. biog. p. 257 (1963).
McKinley, William. Amer. heri. vol. 7 no. 3 p. 33 (Ap '56); vol. 7 no. 4 p. 25 (col.) (Je '56).
    Jensen: The White House, p. 172, 176, 179.
—— (cartoon). Amer. heri. vol. 11 no. 1 p. 42-3 (Dec '59).
—— (making camp. speech). Amer. heri. vol. 11 no. 1 p. 32, 38, 40 (Dec '59).
McKinley, Mrs. William. Jensen: The White House, p. 173.

McKinley home, William. Amer. heri. vol. 11 no. 1 p. 36 (Dec '59).
McKinley inauguration, William. Jensen: The White House, p. 170-1.
McKinley monument, Pres. William. See obelisk, Pres. William McKinley.
McKinley tree (sequoia). Natl. geog. 99: 690 (col.) May '51.
McKinney, Frank E. Cur. biog. p. 381 (1952).
McKinney, Robert. Cur. biog. p. 343 (1957).
McKittrick, Thomas H. Cur. biog. p. 436 (1944).
McKneally, Martin B. Cur. biog. p. 250 (1960).
Maclaine, Shirley. Cur. biog. p. 278 (1959).
McLane, Allan. Amer. heri. vol. 7 no. 6 p. 75 (col.) (Aug '56).
McLean, Alice T. Cur. biog. p. 370 (1945).
McLean, Evalyn Walsh. Cur. biog. p. 480 (1943).
McLean, Robert. Cur. biog. p. 395 (1951).
McLean house (Bull Run). Brooks: Growth of a nation, p. 146.
Macleish, Archibald. Cur. biog. p. 279 (1959).
Macleod, Iain. Cur. biog. p. 395 (1956).
MacLeod, Mrs. W. Murdoch. Cur. biog. p. 384 (1949).
Mclintock, Rear Adm. Gordon. Cur. biog. p. 402 (1953).
Macmahon, Arthur W. Cur. biog. p. 265 (1958).
McMahon, Brien. Cur. biog. p. 373 (1945).
McMath, Sidney S. Cur. biog. p. 385 (1949).
McMeekin, Clark. See McMeekin, Isabel McLennan & Clark, Dorothy Park.
McMeekin, Isabel McLennan. Cur. biog. p. 552 (1942); p. 347 (1957).
McMein, Neysa. Cur. biog. p. 549 (1941).
MacMillan, Donald Baxter. Cur. biog. p. 402 (1948).
—— (medal award). Natl. geog. 103: 563 Ap '53.
McMillan, Edwin M. Cur. biog. p. 383 (1952).
MacMillan, Sir. Ernest. Cur. biog. p. 392 (1955).
Macmillan, Harold. Cur. biog. p. 483 (1943); p. 395 (1955).
McMillan, John L. Cur. biog. p. 397 (1956).
McMinnies, Mary Jackson. Cur. biog. p. 281 (1959).
MacMitchell, Thomas Leslie. Cur. biog. p. 371 (1946).
McMurdo, Lt.-Col. Bryce. Praeg. pict. ency., p. 372 (col.).
McMurrin, Sterling M. Cur. biog. p. 290 (1961).
McMurtrie, Douglas C. Cur. biog. p. 439 (1944).
McNair, Sir. Arnold D. Cur. biog. p. 397 (1955).
McNair, Gen. Lesley J. Cur. biog. p. 553 (1942).
McNally, Andrew, 3rd. Cur. biog. p. 399 (1956).
McNamara, Patrick V. Cur. biog. p. 399 (1955).
McNamara, Robert S. Cur. biog. p. 292 (1961).
    Jensen: The White House, p. 290.
McNarney, Lt. Gen. Joseph T. Cur. biog. p. 441 (1944).
McNaughton, Lt. Gen. Andrew. Cur. biog. p. 554 (1942).
McNeely, Eugene J. Cur. biog. p. 278 (1962).

McNeely, Marian Hurd. Jun. bk. of auth., p. 208.

McNeer, May. Jun. bk. of auth., p. 209.

McNeil, Dr. D. C. Horan: Pict. hist. of wild west, p. 39.

McNeil, Hector. Cur. biog. p. 373 (1946).

McNeil, Wilfred J. Cur. biog. p. 267 1958).

McNeil, Donald T. Cur. biog. p. 387 (1949).

McNellis, Maggi. Cur. biog. p. 400 (1955).

McNicholas, Archbishop John T. Cur. biog. p. 388 (1949).

McNichols, Stephen L. R. Cur. biog. p. 269 (1958).

McParland, James. Horan: Pict. hist. of wild west, p. 209.

MacPhail, Larry. Cur. biog. p. 376 (1945).

McPharlin, Paul. Cur. biog. p. 379 (1945).

Macpherson, Guseppe. Con. 144: 66 Dec '59.

McPherson, James Birdseye. Pakula: Cent. album, 203.

McPherson, Wm. C., jr. Natl. geog. 113: 458 Ap '58.

Mcrae, John (engraving by). Amer. heri. vol. 6 no. 5, p. 30 (Aug '55).

Macready, Lt. John A. Natl. geog. 112: 279 Aug '57.

McReynolds, James C. Amer. heri. vol. 9, no. 3, p. 25 (Ap '58).

McRose, Martin. Horan: Pict. hist. of wild west, p. 125.

McSween, Sue. Horan: Pict. hist. of wild west, p. 60.

Mcswigan, Marie. Cur. biog. p. 404 (1953).

MacVeagh, Lincoln. Cur. biog. p. 550 (1941); p. 385 (1952).

McWilliams, Carey. Cur. biog. p. 485 (1943).

Macy, Mrs. Edward W. Cur. biog. p. 388 (1952).

Macy, George. Cur. biog. p. 434 (1954).

Macy, John W., jr. Cur. biog. p. 280 (1962).

"Mad Hatter" children scrubbing (statue). Natl. geog. 118: 791 (col.) Dec '60.

"Mad river". Natl. geog. 109: 9 (col.) Jan '56.

"Madame au Camus au piano" (Degas). Con. 143: 145 May '59.

"Madame de Pompadour" (Boucher). Con. 135: 41 Mar '55.

"Madame de Pompadour & Duc de Choiseul". Con. 143: 209 Je '59.

"Madame Seriziat & her son" (David). Con. ency. of ant., vol. 1, pl. 160.

"Madame Vigee Le Brun". Con. 143: 209 Je '59.

Ma'dan architecture (Iraq). Natl. geog. 113: 206-11, 218-9, 224, 228, 230 (part col.) Feb '58.

Madden, Ray J. Cur. biog. p. 405 (1953).

Maddocks, Sir Kenneth P. (Fiji island governor). Holiday 28: 65 (col.) Oct '60.

Maddox, William P. Cur. biog. p. 420 (1947).

Maddy, Joseph E. Cur. biog. p. 376 (1946).

Madeira, Jean. Cur. biog. p. 259 (1963). Holiday 25: 64 (col.) Jan '59.

Madeira island. Natl. geog. 115: 364-94 (part col.) Mar '59. Travel 104: 43-5 Nov '55.

—— (map). Natl. geog. 115: 375 Mar '59.

Madeira island dancers. Natl. geog. 115: 386 (col.) Mar '59.

The Madeleine (Paris). Natl. geog. 101: 789 (col.) Je '52. Praeg. pict. ency., p. 426.

Madeleva, Sister Mary. Cur. biog. p. 556 (1942).

Madeline island (Apostle is., Lake Superior). Travel 108: 52-3 Oct '57.

"Mademoiselle Colombe en Amour". Con. 144: 182 (col.) Dec '59.

"Madewood" plantation. Amer. heri., vol. 4 no. 2 p. 28 (winter '53).

Madison, Dolly. Amer. heri., vol. 6 no. 1 p. 52 (fall '54).

—— (Stuart). Jensen: The White, House, p. 20, 22.

Madison, James. Amer. heri. vol. 7 no. 3 p. 9 (col.), 30 (Ap '56); vol. 10 no. 6 p. 86 (Oct '59). Jensen: The White House, p. 22.

—— (cartoon, burning of Wash., D. C.). Jensen: The White House, p. 27.

—— (framer of Constitution). Amer. heri., vol. 10 no. 1 p. 58 (col.) (Dec '58).

Madison (Wis.). Holiday 27: 83-5 Je '60. Jordan: Hammond's pict. atlas, p. 94 (col.).

Madison home, Co., James (Va.). Natl. geog. 109: 464-5 (col.) Ap '56.

Madison Square Garden (N. Y.). Holiday 24: 88-91 Dec '58.

"Madness of Athanus" (marble, Flaxman). Con. 144: 231 Jan '60.

"Madonna" (Lippi). Con. 140: 207 Dec '57.

Madonna (carved ivory, 13th cent.). Con. 140: 278 Jan '58.

"Madonna adoring child" (Lippi). Praeg. pict. ency., p. 253 (col.).

"Madonna adoring child" (Verrocchio). Con. 136: 37 Sept '55.

Madonna & child. Con. 143: XX May '59.

"Madonna & child" (L. di Bicci). Con. 142: 155 Dec '58.

"Madonna & child" (Botticelli). Con. 129: 22 Ap '52.

"Madonna & child" (Caroselli). Con. 143: LIV Ap '59.

"Madonna & child" (carved polychrome, 1200). Con. 145: 213 My '60.

"Madonna & child" (carved wood). Con. 140: 54 Sept '57.

"Madonna & child" (Christus). Con. 140: 271-3, 275 (part col.) Jan '58.

"Madonna & child" (da Fabriano). Con. 145: 39 Mar '60.

"Madonna & child" (del Sarto). Con. 136: 36 Sept '55.

"Madonna & child" (della Francesca). Con. 140: 279 Jan '58.

"Madonna & child" (Dürer). Con. ency. of ant., vol. 1, pl. 157.

"Madonna & child" (18th cent.). Con. 126: 53 Aug '50.

"Madonna & child" (Firenze). Con. 142: XLIX Sept '58.

"Madonna & child" (Flemish primitive). Con. 127: 45 Mar '51.

"Madonna & child" (Florentine). Con. 141: LVII Mar '58.

"Madonna & child" (14th cent. fresco, by da Modena). Con. 129: LXXII Ap '52.

"Madonna & child" (Gentile da Fabriano). Con. 136: LXI Dec '55.
"Madonna & child" (Italian silver figure). Con. 144: 154 Dec '59.
"Madonna & child" (Lippi). Con. ency. of ant., vol. 1, p. 150.
"Madonna & child" (Monnot sculpture). Con. 141: 220 Je '58.
"Madonna & child" (needlework). Con. 142: 251 Jan '59.
"Madona & child" (polychrome statue). Con. 141: LII May '58.
"Madonna & child" (Raphael). Con. 140: 239 Jan '58.
"Madonna & child" (Russian 17th cent.). Con. 140: XXIV Nov '57.
"Madonna & child (Sirani). Con. 144: 22 Sept '59.
"Madonna & child" (16th cent polychrome). Con. 141: LXI Mar '58.
Madonna & child (statue). Natl. geog. 118: 627 (col.) Nov '60.
—— (terra-cotta). Con. 136: 137 Nov '55.
—— (13th cent. Gothic ivory). Con. 139: LI Ap '57.
—— (13th cent. Italian carved wood). Con. 142: XXI (col.) Nov '58.
"Madonna & child" (Tintoretto). Con. 140: 143 (col.) Dec '57.
Natl. geog. 110: 632 (col.) Nov '56.
"Madonna & child" (Van Orley). Con. 138: cover (col.), 253 Jan '57.
"Madonna & child" (Van Orley & Patinier). Con. 139: VIII May '57.
"Madonna & child" (Verrocchio). Con. 132: 60 Sept '53.
"Madonna & child", bronze (Wheeler). Con. 139: 259 Je '57.
"Madonna & child", ivory (14th cent.). Con. 144: 66 Sept '59.
"Madonna & child", marble (Tino da Camaino). Con. 144: IV Dec '59; 145: 53 Mar '60.
"Madonna & child with a pomegranate". Natl. geog. 110: 649 (col.) Nov '56.
"Madonna & child with angel" (Francia). Con. 136: 119 (col.) Nov '55.
"Madonna & child with angels" (Dugento). Con. 136: 228 Dec '55.
"Madonna & child with St. Anne". Con. 136: 35 Sept '55.
"Madonna & child with St. John" (Bassano). Con. 140: 165 Dec '57; 144: LXXIII Dec '59.
"Madonna & child with St. John & angels" (Pesillino). Con. 136: 136 Nov '55.
"Madonna & child with Saints" (Pessellino). Con. 129: 66 Ap '52.
Madonna & child. See also "Dangolsheim Madonna".
Madonna del Carmine festival (Rome). Holiday 11: 39 (col.) Ap '52.
"Madonna del Collo lungo" (Parmigianino). Praeg. pict. ency., p. 313 (col.).
"Madonna della Sedia (Raphael). Praeg. pict. ency., p. 279 (col.).
"Madonna enthroned" (Monaco). Con. 142: LXV Dec '58.
"Madonna of humility" (Della Robbia). Con. 139: XLV Mar '57.

"Madonna of the girdle" (Giovanni). Cooper: Con. ency. of music, p. 430 (col.).
"Madonna of the rosaries" (Michelangelo). Natl. geog. 97: 772 (col.) Je '50.
madonna relief (Michele da Firenze). Con. 140: 166 Dec '57.
"Madonna with canon van der Paele" (Van Eyck). Con. ency. of ant., vol. 1, pl. 154.
"Madonna with the basket" (Correggio). Praeg. pict. ency., p. 312 (col.).
"Madonna with cherries" (Van Cleve). Con. 133: 123 Ap '54.
"Madonna with the long neck". See "Madonna del Collo lungo".
Madonnas (Renaissance art). Natl. geog. 113: 264-5 (col.) Feb '58.
Madrid (Spain). Holiday 23: 58-65 (col.) Jan '58.
Natl. geog. 97: 444, 450 (col.) Ap '50; 100: 718 (col.) Dec '51.
Travel 101: 6 May '54.
—— (park). Travel 107: 23 Ap '57.
Madsen, Chris. Horan: Pict. hist. of wild west, p. 170.
Maenner, Theodore H. Cur. biog. p. 390 (1949).
Maes, Nicolaas (work of). Con. 135: XLV Je '55; 145: XXXVIII (col.) May '60.
Maffei, Francesco (work of). Con. 138: 119-20 Nov '56.
Magallanes, Nicholas. Cur. biog. p. 402 (1955).
Magallanes. See Punta arenas.
Magarac, Joe (folk hero). Amer. heri., vol. 1 no. 3 p. 2 (col.), 75 (spring '50).
magazine covers (1800-   ). Amer. heri. vol. 7 no. 2 p. 50-5 (col.) (Feb '56).
magazine rack. Holiday 26: 188 Oct '59.
magazine stand, street. Holiday 10: 49 (col.) Aug '51.
magazines (library table). Natl. geog. 97: 304 (col.) Mar '50.
"The Magadalen" (Francesco del Cairo). Con. 138: 119 Nov '56.
Magadalen college (Oxford). Holiday 28: 51 Dec '60.
Natl. geog. 114: 61 (col.) Jl '58.
Magdelen island (Quebec). Holiday 27: 10 (col.) Feb '60.
Magee, Elizabeth. Cur. biog. p. 375 (1950).
Magee, Frank L. Holiday 25: 86 (col.) Mar '59.
Magee, James C. Cur. biog. p. 487 (1943).
Magellan, Ferdinand. Natl. geog. 118: 614 (col.) Nov '60.
Maggi, Dr. Filippo. Holiday 23: 61 (col.) May '58.
Maggiolo, Walter A. Cur. biog. p. 389 (1952).
Maggiore, Lake. See Lake Maggiore.
Maggoty falls (Jamaica). Holiday 5: 47 (col.) Feb '49.
magic (sym.). Lehner: Pict. bk. of sym., p. 68-73.
magic carpet (man riding). Holiday 23: 27 (col.) Je '58.
"The magic flute" (setting for, by Schinkel, Berlin, 1823). Cooper: Con. ency. of music, p. 378 (col.).
"Magic Square" (Pompeii). Ceram: March of arch., p. 30.
magic squares of days of week. Lehner: Pict. bk. of sym., p. 24.

magic tricks (burlesque). Natl. geog. 97: 207 (col.) Feb '50.
Magill, Roswell. Cur. biog. p. 405 (1948).
Maglie, Sal. Cur. biog. p. 407 (1953).
Magloire, Paul E. Cur. biog. p. 390 (1952).
Magnani, Anna. Cur. biog. p. 401 (1956).
magnet (sym.). Lehner: Pict. bk. of sym., p. 13.
magnetism (sym.). Lehner: Pict. bk. of sym., p. 13.
magnifying glass. Con. 136: XLI Nov 55.
Lehner: Pict. bk. of sym., p. 11.
Natl. geog. 114: 243 Aug '58.
magnitude (sym.). Lehner: Pict. bk. of sym., p. 59.
magnolia gardens. Holiday 11: 64 (col.) Ap '52.
Natl. geog. 103: 314-7, 320 (col.) Mar '53.
Magnuson, Paul B. Cur. biog. p. 407 (1948).
Magnuson, Warren G. Cur. biog. p. 381 (1945).
Magog & Gog. See Gog & Magog.
Magruder, John Bankhead. Pakula: Cent. album, p. 205.
Magsaysay, Ramon. Cur. biog. p. 392 (1952).
maguey fiber (rug weaving). Natl. geog. 99: 455 (col.) Ap '51.
Mahabalipuram (temples, India). Travel 111: 18 Jan '59.
Mahady, Henry J. Cur. biog. p. 436 (1954).
Mahan, Alfred T. Amer. heri., vol. 11 no. 4 p. 32 (Je '60).
Mahan, John William. Cur. biog. p. 283 (1959).
Maharaja of India (on horse). Natl. geog. 113: 710 (col.) May '58.
Mahendra, King of Nepal. Cur. biog. p. 403 (1956).
Maher, Aly. Cur. biog. p. 394 (1952).
Mahler, Fritz. Holiday 27: 85 Feb '60.
Mahon, George. Cur. biog. p. 270 (1958).
Mahon, Minorca. Holiday 27: 52-5 (part col.) Jan '60.
Mahone, William. Pakula: Cent. album, p. 207.
maid (arranging bed). Holiday 25: 122 (col.) May '59.
—— (dressing woman's hair). Holiday 25: 94 (col.) Feb '59, 134 (col.) Ap '59.
—— (making bed). Holiday 28: 90 (col.) Aug '60.
Natl. geog. 110: 43 (col.) Jl '56.
——, serving. Holiday 27: 56 May '60.
maidenhood, patron saint of. Lehner: Pict. bk. of sym., p. 40.
Maiden's castle (near Mersin). Osward: Asia Minor, pl. 125.
Maier, Rev. Walter A. Cur. biog. p. 421 (1947).
mail bags, man tying. Natl. geog. 112: 771 (col.) Dec '57.
——, U. S. navy ship. Natl. geog. 116: 324 (col.) Sept '59.
mail box, rural (children). Holiday 27: 52 (col.) Ap '60.
——, street. Holiday 6: 22 (col.) Dec '49; 7: 86 (col.) Jan '50.
—— (Bermuda). Natl. geog. 105: 217 (col.) Feb '54.
——, wagon. Rawson: Ant. pict. bk., p. 74.
mail boxes, rural. Holiday 27: 52 (col.) Ap '60.
Rawson: Ant. pict. bk., p. 43.
mail carrier (on skis). Natl. geog. 111: 55 (col.) Jan '57.
——, rural cart. Brooks: Growth of a nation, p. 226.

mail coach, overland. Amer. heri., vol. 8 no. 4 p. 26-7 (col.), 29, 31 (Je '57).
mail coach. See also stagecoach.
mail delivery carts (models). Natl. geog. 106: 139 (col.) Jl '54.
mail stage. Rawson: Ant. pict. bk., p. 73.
mail truck. Natl. geog. 106: 138-9 (col.) Jl '54.
Maile, Boniface. Cur. biog. p. 396 (1951).
Mailer, Norman. Cur. biog. p. 409 (1948).
Maillol, Aristide. Cur. biog. p. 557 (1942).
—— (work of). Con. 143: 92 Ap '59; 145: 55 Mar '60.
Praeg. pict. ency., p. 492.
Main, Marjorie. Cur. biog. p. 398 (1951).
The Main line (Philadelphia). Holiday 7: 34-57 (col.) Ap '50.
Main street (rain). Holiday 13: 27 (col.) Je '53.
Mainardi, Sebastiano (work of). Natl. geog. 113: 264 (col.) Feb '58.
Mainbocher. Cur. biog. p. 559 (1942).
Maine. Jordan: Hammond's pict. atlas p. 22-3 (col.).
—— (beach). Face of Amer., p. 95 (col.).
—— (clam bake). Travel 104: 39-41 Jl '55.
—— (coast). Holiday 14: 48-9 (col.) Aug '53.
—— (harbor). Face of Amer., p. 120-1 (col.).
—— (Katahdin). See Katahdin (Maine, climbers).
—— (lighthouse). Face of Amer., p. 106-7 (col.).
—— (lobster is.). Natl. geog. 115: 284-98 Feb '59.
—— (motel at Scarboro). Travel 104: inside cover Sept '55.
The Maine (sinking of). Amer. heri., vol. 8 no. 2 p. 37 (col.) (Feb '57).
Maine coast cruise. Natl. geog. 102: 330-70 (part col.) Sept '52.
mainsail gaff & pulley. Rawson: Ant. pict. bk., p. 79.
Maintenon, Chateau de. See Chateau de Maintenon.
maiolica work (White). Con. 140: 160-3 Dec '57.
——, Italian. Con. 142: 148-50 Dec '58.
Maisky, Ivan. Cur. biog. p. 551 (1941).
Maison Carree (Roman temple, Nimes). Amer. heri., vol. 10 no. 5 p. 68 (Aug '59).
Natl. geog. 100: 3 Jl '51.
"Maison dans le Vallee" (Cezanne). Con. 145: 234 Je '60.
Maiuri, Amadeo. Ceram: March of arch., p. 31.
Majiro's illus. of the new world. Amer. heri., vol. 8 no. 1 p. 79-82, 87 (Dec '56).
"Ma Jolie" (Picasso). Holiday 14: 60 (col.) Nov '53.
"Major oak" (Sherwood forest). Natl geog. 103: 826 (col.) Je '53.
Majorca. Natl. geog. 111: 622-60 (part col.) May '57.
Majorcan (costumes). Natl. geog. 111: 646-7 (col.) May '57.
Majorcan court ladies. Natl. geog. 111: 635 (col.) May '57.
Majorcan dancers. Natl. geog. 111: 646-7 (col.) May '57.
Majorettes, Major. Natl. geog. 99: 823 Je '51.
Makarios III, Archbishop. Cur. biog. p. 405 (1956).

Makemson, Maud W. Cur. biog. p. 553 (1941).
make-up, beauty. *See* beauty make-up.
Makin, Norman J. O. Cur. biog. p. 377 (1946).
Makins, Sir Roger. Cur. biog. p. 409 (1953).
Makoshika state park. Travel 111: 41 Je '59.
Malaga (Spain). Holiday 16: 109 Nov '54.
Malahide castle (Ireland). Holiday 16: 6 Aug '54.
Malamud, Bernard. Cur. biog. p. 272 (1958).
Malan, Daniel Francois. Cur. biog. p. 391 (1949).
Malatesta, Paola (portrait by Tintoretto). Con. 138: cover (col.) Dec '56.
Malay police. Natl. geog. 103: 193 (col.) Feb '53.
Malay police (in jungle). Natl. geog. 103: 191 (col.) Feb '53.
Malaya. Natl. geog. 103: 188-228 (part col.) Feb '53.
—— (map). Natl. geog. 103: 189 Feb '53.
Malbin, Elaine. Cur. biog. p. 284 (1959).
Malbone, Edward Greene (work of). Amer. heri., vol. 9 no. 2, cover (col.) (Feb '58).
Malcolm, Judge George A. Cur. biog. p. 437 (1954).
Malden, Karl. Cur. biog. p. 350 (1957).
Malderus, Jan—Bishop of Antwerp (Van Dyck). Con. 129: 2 (col.) Ap '52.
Maldive (mosque). Travel 111: 25 Jan '59.
Maldive is. (Indian ocean). Natl. geog. 111: 830-49 (col.) Je '57.
—— (map). Natl. geog. 111: 834 Je '57.
Maledon, George (western hangman). Horan: Pict. hist. of wild west, p. 142.
maleficent spirits. *See* spirits, signs of 7 maleficent.
Malekula jungle men. Natl. geog. 99: 333, 341 (col.) Mar '51.
Malenkov, Georgi M. Cur. biog. p. 396 (1952).
Malibu colony. Holiday 11: 52-5 (part col.) Je '52.
Maligne, Lake. Holiday 5: 4 (col.) Ap '49.
Malik, Charles. Cur. biog. p. 411 (1948).
Malik, Jacob A. Cur. biog. p. 393 (1949).
Malin, Patrick Murphy. Cur. biog. p. 378 (1950).
Malinovsky, Rodion Y. Cur. biog. p. 443 (1944); p. 253 (1960).
Malinowski, Bronislaw. Cur. biog. p. 555 (1941).
Malkus, Alida Sims. Jun. bk. of auth., p. 210.
Mallet, Jean Baptiste (work of). Con. 132: LXXIV Jan '54; 134: 219 Dec '54.
mallet (sym.). Lehner: Pict. bk. of sym., p. 17. Rawson: Ant. pict. bk., p. 22.
mallet of good luck (sym.). Lehner: Pict. bk. of sym., p. 47.
Mallette, Gertrude E. Cur. biog. p. 379 (1950).
Mallorca. Holiday 15: 132 (col.) Mar '54.
Mallory, Cassius C. Cur. biog. p. 407 (1956).
Mallory, Lester D. Cur. biog. p. 255 (1960).
"Malmaison" (Napoleon's home, France). Holiday 11: 122 Mar '52; 25: 70 Je '59.
Malone, George W. Cur. biog. p. 381 (1950).
Malone, Rosser L., jr. Cur. biog. p. 286 (1959).
Maloney, Walter E. Cur. biog. p. 398 (1952).
Malott, Deane W. Cur. biog. p. 399 (1951).
Malraux, Andre. Cur. biog. p. 288 (1959).
Malsuoka, Yosuke. Cur. biog. p. 563 (1941).

Malta, Eduardo (work of). Con. 136: XVIII (col.) Sept '55, XXXVI-XXXVII (col.) Nov '55 137: 53, 61 (col.) Mar '56.
Malta (Italy). Con. 139: LXI May '57.
Holiday 26: 88 (col.) Aug '59; 27: 67-71 (col.) Je '60; 28: 12 (col.) Sept '60.
Travel 109: 42 Ap '58.
—— (beach). Holiday 27: cover (col.) Je '60.
—— (woman). Holiday 27: 156 (col.) Ap '60.
Malton, Thomas (work of). Con. 145: XL Ap '60.
Malvern, Gladys. Jun. bk. of auth., p. 211.
Malvern, Godfrey H. Cur. biog. p. 409 (1956).
Ma-Ming statuette, temple. Con. 129: LXIX Ap '52.
Mammoth cave (Ky.). Jordan: Hammond's pict. atlas, p. 104-5 (col.).
Travel 106: 29-31 Aug '56; 109: 17 Feb '58.
Mamoulian, Rouben. Cur. biog. p. 394 (1949).
man. Con. 145: 180 May '60.
Holiday 12: 13 (col.) Sept '52, 81 (col.) Oct '52; 13: 9, 123, 144, 153, 159 (col.) May '53, 24 (col.), 126, 159 Je '53; 14: 10 Oct '53, 91 (col.) Nov '53; 21: 15, 20 (col.) Ap '57, 108 May '57, 183 Je '57; 23: 26, 111 (col.) Feb '58, 154 (col.) Mar '58, 33 (col.), 155, 165 Ap '58, 20 (col.), 117, 160 (col.) May '58; 24: 40 Nov '58; 25: 31 (col.) Mar '59, 14, 20 (col.), 170 (col.), 205 Ap '59, 7, 26, 144 (col.) May '59, 100, 109 (col.) Je '59; 26: 78, 96 (col.) Oct '59, 120 Nov '59, 120, 217 Dec '59; 27: 30, 137 Feb '60, 69, 184 Ap '60, 61, 96, 160, 175 (col.), 200, inside back cover (col.) May '60, 27 Je '60; 28: 12-3 (col.) Aug '60, 2, 132 (col.), 168 (col.) Oct '60, 128 Nov '60.
Travel 101: inside back cover Ap '54; 107: 17 Ap '57.
—— (accordion, comic). Holiday 28: 171 Nov '60.
—— (air-field flag). Travel 107: 30 May '57.
—— (Alpine horn). Holiday 19: 98 Mar '56.
—— (angry). Holiday 19: 85 Feb '56.
—— (Antarctic suit). Natl. geog. 113: 457, 463, 467, 470, 474, 478 (part col.) Ap '58.
—— (antique bicycle). Amer. heri., vol. 6 no. 3 p. 98 (Ap '55).
Natl. geog. 99. 775 Je '51.
—— (Arctic dog). Natl. geog. 107: 563 (col.) Ap '55.
——(artist painting picture). *See* artist (painting picture).
—— (asleep). Holiday 18: 127 Nov '55; 28: 129 (col.) Nov '60.
—— (asleep, dreaming). Holiday 14: 58 Oct '53.
—— asleep, fishing). Holiday 25: 127 Ap '59; 27: 173 May '60.
—— (asleep in plane). Holiday 27: 7 (col.) Feb '60.
—— astride chair). Holiday 12: 6 Dec '52.
—— (at desk). Holiday 18: 35 (col.) Nov '55; 21: 13, 108 (col.) Ap '57; 22: 13, 22 (col.) Jl '57; 28: 90 (col.) Sept '60.
Natl. geog. 104: 692 Nov '53; 118: 544 (col.) Oct '60.
Travel 113: 7 May '60; 114: 7 Nov '60.

man (at desk, cartoon). Holiday 13: 78 Jan '53.

—— (at table. Holiday 13: 59 Ap '53; 23: 61, 120 Jan. '58; 24: 23 (col.), 30-1, 40 Dec '58; 25: 99 Jan '59, 42, 110 (col.) Mar '59; 26: 122 Jl '59; 27: 92 Jan '60, 159 (col.) Mar '60, 218 Ap '60; 28: 15 (col.) Sept '60.
Praeg. pict. ency., p. 290 (col.).

—— (at table, comic). Holiday 16: 32 (col.) Jl '54; 26: 228 (col.) Dec '59; 27: 35, 104 Mar '60, 120 Ap '60.

—— (at table, reading). Holiday 21: 76 Jan '57.

—— (at table, 17th cent.). Amer. heri., vol. 4 no. 2 p. 44 (winter '53).

—— (auto). Holiday 24: 7, 35, 114, 120 (part col.) Aug '58; 25: 22 Jan '59, 128, 137 (col.) Feb '59.

—— (auto, comic). Holiday 28: 113 Aug '60.

—— ("automobile plow"). Amer. heri., vol. 6 no. 1, p. 57 (fall '54).

—— (baboon). Natl. geog. 107: 701 May '55.

—— (baby on back). Natl. geog. 109: 5 (col.) Jan '56.

—— (back view). Holiday 14: 142 Nov '53; 25: 51 Mar '59, 165 Ap '59, 109 May '59, 17, 61 Je '59; 26: 11 Jl '59; 27: 121 Jan '60, 69 (col.) Feb '60, 177 Mar '60, 112, 215 May '60, 132 Je '60; 28: 20 Nov '60 140 Dec '60.
Natl. geog. 99: 136 (col.) Jan '51; 103: 553 Ap '53.
Travel 104: 25 Jl '55; 110: 24 Oct '58.

—— (back view, harbor). Natl. geog. 112: 779 (col.) Dec '57.

—— (back view, lake, birds). Natl. geog. 115: 693 (col.) May '59.

—— (back view, on ship). Natl. geog. 100: 477 (col.) Oct '51.

—— (back view, on tractor). Natl. geog. 110: 301 (col.) Sept '56.

—— (back view, overcoat). Int. gr. soc.: Arts . . . p. 157 (col.).

—— (back view, sea). Natl. geog. 114: 277 (col.) Aug '58.

—— (back view, shorts). Natl. geog. 98: 619 (col.) Nov '50.

—— (bagpipe). Holiday 19: 62 Feb '56.
Natl. geog. 114: 186 (col.) Aug '58.

—— (bale of rugs on back). Natl. geog. 102: 794 (col.) Dec '52.

—— (balloon, comic. Holiday 13: 130 May '53.

—— (bar). Holiday 27: 38 (col.) May '60.

—— (bar tender). Holiday 26: 19 Jl '59, 23 Aug '59; 27: 158 (col.) Jan '60.

—— (barber shop). Holiday 28: 80 Dec '60.

—— (barge model). Natl. geog. 117: 435 (col.) Mar '60.

—— (basket on head). Holiday 13: 25 Jan '53.
Natl. geog. 107: 409 (col.) Mar '55.

—— (bath robe). Holiday 20: 160 (col.) Dec '56.

—— (bath tub, comic). Holiday 11: 18 Feb '52.

—— (beach chair). Holiday 27: 163 Feb '60.

—— (beach, playing guitar). Holiday 21: 181 (col.) May '57.

—— (beach, waving). Holiday 18: 68 (col.) Sept '55.

—— (bear, silhouette). Holiday 16: 105 Nov '54.

——(beating drum). Travel 108: inside cover Aug '57.

—— (being executed). Horan: Pict hist. of wild west, p. 17, 23.

—— (bending down). Natl. geog. 113: 183 (col.) Feb '58.

—— (bent & tired). Travel 104: 66 Aug '55.

—— (bicycle. Holiday 23: 56-7 Jan '58.
Natl. geog. 116: 61 (col.) Jl '59.
Travel 106: 53 Je '56; 108: 32-3 Aug '57.

—— (bicycle, cartoon). Holiday 14: 8 Jl '53.

—— (bicycle, children in cart). Natl. geog. 100: 15 (col.) Jl '51.

—— (bicycle, comic). Holiday 16: 19 Aug '54.

—— (bicycle on rope). Amer. heri., vol. 9 no. 5 p. 107 (Aug '58).

—— (big fish). Holiday 24: 1 Oct '58.
Natl. geog. 99: 497 (col.) Ap '51.

—— (binoculars, silhouette). Amer. heri., vol. 9 no. 5 p. 30 (Aug '58).

—— (blind, listen to recorder). Natl. geog. 97: 676 May '50.

—— (blindfold). Holiday 18: 78 Nov '55; 25: 16 Mar '59.

—— (block printing textiles). Natl. geog. 114: 37 (col.) Jl '58.

——(blowing bone trumpet). Natl. geog. 97: 13: (col.) Jan '50.

—— (blowing fire). Natl geog. 116: 774 (col.) Dec '59.

—— (blowing glass). Natl. geog. 107: 475 (col.) Ap '55.

—— (blowing ship fog horn). Natl. geog. 100: 483 Nov '51.

—— (boat). Travel 109: 60 Mar '58.

—— (boat, comic). Holiday 28: 169 Nov '60.

—— (boat, shadow). Holiday 26: 91 (col.) Nov '59.

—— (boil fish in hot pool). Natl. geog. 109: 36 (col.) Jan '56.

—— (bottle). Holiday 25: 141 Jan '59; 26: 114 (col.) Jl '59, 105 Aug '59, 22 (col.) Oct '59.

—— (bottle, comic). Holiday 26: 96 Nov '59, 123 (col.) Dec '59; 28: 204 Nov '60.

—— (bottle, straws). Holiday 22: 111 (col.) Nov '57.

—— (bow & arrow, statue). Travel 104: 24 Nov '55.

—— (bowing). Holiday 12: 95 (col.) Oct '52; 17: 89 Mar '55.

—— (bowing, comic). Holiday 27: 95 May '60.

—— (bowing, evening dress). Holiday 18: 92 (col.) Nov '55.

—— (bowing to woman). Holiday 10: 16 Nov '51.

—— (bowing, colonial). Holiday 10: 1 Dec '51.

—— (bowling). Holiday 13: 65 Ap '53.

—— (box of groceries). Holiday 11: 136 (col.) Ap '52.

—— (branding cattle). Brooks: Growth of a nation, p. 184.

—— (bristlecone pine). Natl. geog. 113: 355, 357, 362-72 (part col.) Mar '58.

—— (brushing rhino). Natl. geog. 111: 523 Ap '57.

—— (bucking horse). Holiday 27: 44 (col.) Mar '60.
Horan: Pict. hist. of wild west, p. 96-7.

—— (buffalo chase). Amer. heri., vol. 1 no. 4 p. 7 (summer '50).

—— (building doll house). Natl. geog. 118: 770 (col.) Dec '60.

—— (building ship model). Natl. geog. 107: 749 (col.) Je '55.

—— (bull fight, comic). Holiday 13: 1 Ap '53.

—— (bundles, comic). Holiday 12: cover (col.) Dec '52.

—— (burro). Holiday 21: 70 (col.) Jan '57. Travel 114: 30 Nov '60.

—— (business paper). Holiday 20: 107 Nov '56.

—— (bust, knowledge). Holiday 27: 8 Je '60.

—— (buying shoes). Holiday 10: 84 (col.) Oct '51.

—— (buying travel ticket). Natl. geog. 98: 2 Jl '50.

—— (camera). Holiday 25: 174 May '59. Travel 108: cover Jl '57.

—— (camera, silhouette). Holiday 20: 9 Oct '56.

—— (camp cooking). See man (cooking, camp fire).

—— (camp fire). Holiday 10: 70 Nov '51.

—— (canoe). Holiday 28: 55 (col.), 56-7 Aug '60, 140 (col.) Oct '60.

—— (canoe, comic). Holiday 21: 109 Je '57.

—— (captain on ship). Holiday 23: 130 Je '58.

—— (carrying another on back). Amer. heri., vol. 8 no. 6 p. 71 (Oct '57).

—— (carrying baskets). Travel 111: 20 Mar '59.

—— (carrying canoe). Travel 112: 41 Aug '59.

—— (carrying canoe, seal). Natl. geog. 99: 554 Ap '51.

—— (carrying cross). Disney: People & places, p. 74 (col.).

—— (carrying fishnet). Natl. geog. 114: 777 (col.) Dec '58.

—— (carrying money, cartoon). Holiday 24: 88 Aug '58.

—— (cart). Labande: Naples, p. 74.

—— (cart of books). Holiday 14: 69 Dec '53.

—— (cartographer). Natl. geog. 103: 752, 755 Je '53.

—— (cartoon). See cartoon (man).

—— (carving marble). Natl. geog. 99: 597 (col.) May '51.

—— (carving totem pole). Natl. geog. 116: 78 (col.) Jl '59.

—— (carving turkey). Holiday 19: 17 Mar '56.

—— (cattle). Natl. geog. 111: 818 Je '57.

—— (caught in spider web). Holiday 18: 117 Oct '55.

—— (century plant). Natl. geog. 113: 274 (col.) Feb '58.

—— (chafing dish cooking). Holiday 25: 154 (col.) May '59.

—— (champagne bottle, comic). Amer. heri., vol. 9 no. 3 p. 59 (col.) (Ap '58).

—— (changing auto tire). Holiday 11: 20 Je '52; 14: inside back cover (col.) Jl '53.

—— (chasing woman). Holiday 23: 139 May '58.

—— (chess). Holiday 28: 35, 40 (col.) Nov '60.

—— (child hugging). Holiday 24: 144 Jl '58.

—— (child on back). Natl. geog. 97: 547 Ap '50.

—— (child on shoulder). Natl. geog. 117: 844 Je '60.

—— (child on shoulder, corn field). Natl. geog. 102: 573 Nov '52.

—— (chimney sweep). Lehner: Pict. bk. of sym., p. 62.

—— (chopping wood). Con. 143: LVI Je '59.

—— (Christmas, playing organ). Holiday 24: 171 Dec '58.

—— (cleaning airplane). Holiday 25: 122 Je '59.

—— (climbing coconut tree). Holiday 28: 84 (col.) Oct '60. Travel 108: 26 Aug '57.

—— (climbing ladder, India). Travel 111: 28 Jan '59.

—— (climbing mt.). See mt. climbing.

—— (climbing puya plant). Natl. geog. 98: 467 (col.) Oct '50.

—— (climbing tree). Natl. geog. 117: 470 (col.) Ap '60.

—— (clothes display). Holiday 23: 145-50 (part col.) Je '58.

—— (cock fight). Holiday 24: 91 Jl '58.

—— (cocktail). Holiday 19: 135 Jan '56; 23: 151 (col.) Je '58; 24: 22, 31 (col.), 56, 206 Dec '58; 25: 163 (col.), 167 Mar '59, 140 Je '59; 26: 117 Jl '59, 185 Dec '59; 27: 126 (col.) May '60, 155 Je '60.

—— (cocktail glass). Holiday 21: 126 Mar '57.

—— (cocktail table). Holiday 21: 104 (col.) Mar '57; 22: 181 (col.) Dec '57.

—— (comic). Con. 136: XXXIV Sept '55, XLII Jan '56; 137: XXVI Mar '56, XXVIII Je '56.
Holiday 5: 4, 87 Jan '49, 138-9 Mar '49, 28 Ap '49; 6: 18-21 Ap '49, 6, 14, 83-4 Oct '49, 20, 140 (col.), 153 Dec '49; 7: 79 (col.) Feb '50, 92, 121 Mar '50, 4, 30 Ap '50, 86 May '50, 141, 154 Je '50; 8: 65-6 Jl '50, 137, 159 (col.) Dec '50; 10: 14, 63 Aug '51, 27, 117 Oct '51, 4 Nov '51, 73, 180 Dec '51; 11: 64 Jan '52, 33 Feb '52, 68, 84 Mar '52, 4 Ap '52, 41 May '52, 5, 16, 24 (col.) Je '52; 12: 23, 71, 90, 92, 118, 149 Jl '52, 25, Aug '52, 30 Sept '52, 70, 101 Oct '52, 131 Nov '52; 13: 70 (col.) May '53, 67, 94 Je '53; 16: 84, 91 Oct '54; 18: 6, 21, 27, 92-3 Jl '55, 63, 67 Aug '55, 18, 37, 79, 121 Sept '55, 11, 90, 95 Oct '55, 9, 137, 139, 150, 161 Nov '55, 83, 125, 158 Dec '55; 19: 89 (col.), 125 Jan '56, 67, 72, 127, 130 Feb '56, 39, 128 Mar '56, 147, 152 May '56, 67, 134 Je '56; 20: 63 Aug '56, 23, 110 (col.) Sept '56, 30, 74, 147 Oct '56, 3, 31, 35, 47, 180 Nov '56, 23, 159, 173, 201, 208 Dec '56; 21: 109, 146, 174 Mar '57, 27, 191 Ap '57, 154, 186, 203 May '57, 6, 124, 166 Je '57; 22: 90 Jl '57, 4, 6, 48, 101 Sept '57, 89, 150, 155 Oct '57, 79-81, 112, 169, 193 Nov '57, 117, 157, 204 (col.), 234 Dec '57; 25: 131, 154 Feb '59, 1, 27, 121 Mar '59, 32, 34 Ap '59, 3, 14, 163 May '59, 6 Je '59; 26: 121 Jl '59, 12 Aug '59, 11, 20 Oct '59, 207 Dec '59; 27: 10, 121, 141, 149, 171 (part col.) Jan '60, 124 Feb '60, 19, 200, 225 Ap '60, 19, 30, 54, 93 May '60, 182 Je '60; 28: 126, 131 Jl '60, 120 Aug '60, 130, 139 Sept '60, 157 Oct '60, 192 (col.), 196 Dec '60.

Travel 109: 41 May '58.
man (comic, bowing). Holiday 27: 3 Feb '60.
—— (comic, pistol). Holiday 5: 5 Feb '49.
—— (comic running). Holiday 18: 91 Oct '55.
—— (comic soldier). Amer. heri. vol. 6 no. 2 p. 65 (col.) (winter '55).
—— (cook, comic). Holiday 27: 150 Jan '60.
—— (cooking). Holiday 10: 66 Nov '51.
—— (cooking at picnic). Holiday 23: 29 (col.) May '58.
—— (cooking at stove). Amer. heri., vol. 8 no. 4 p. 74 (Je '57).
—— (cooking, camp fire). Holiday 11: 40 Feb 52.
Natl. geog. 97: 729 (col.) Je '50.
Travel 111: 41 Je '59 114: 35 Jl '60.
—— (cooking lobsters). Natl. geog. 115: 293 Feb '59.
—— (cooking, outdoors). Holiday 24: inside cover (col.) Aug '58.
—— (corn ears). Natl. geog. 109: 316 (col.) Mar '56.
—— (cow). Amer. heri., vol. 6 no. 2 p. 70 (winter '55).
—— (cradling grain). Brooks: Growth of a nation, p. 103.
—— (craftsman). Holiday 24: 181 (col.) Dec '58.
—— (crocodile head). Natl. geog. 111: 27 (col.) Jan '57.
—— (crowned). Holiday 26: 174 Nov '59.
—— (crystal gazer, comic). Holiday 24: 22 Jl '58, 25 Aug '58, 19 Sept '58, 48 Nov '58, 40 Dec '58.
—— (curing tobacco). Natl. geog. 111: 609 (col.) May '57.
—— (cuts puya plant). Natl. geog. 98: 471 (col.) Oct 50.
—— (cutting cane). Holiday 5: 40 (col.) Feb '49.
—— (cutting flowers). Holiday 28: 133 Sept '60, 179 Oct '60, 51 Nov '60.
—— (cutting peat). Natl. geog. 99: 677 May '51.
—— (cutting tobacco). Holiday 5: 41 (col.) Feb '49.
—— (cutting tree). Holiday 28: 54 (col.) Aug '60.
—— (cutting tussock grass). Natl. geog. 109: 398 (col.) Mar '56.
—— (dancing). Holiday 19: 154 (col.) May '56; 26: 151 (col.) Dec '59; 27: 91 (col.) Jan '60, 51 Ap '60, 64, 91 (col.) May '60, 22 Je '60; 28: 26 Sept '60, 189 Nov '60, 36 Dec '60.
—— (dancing, comic). Holiday 21: 113 May '57.
—— (dancing, silhouette). Holiday 5: 94 Jan '49.
—— (decorating pottery). Natl. geog. 97: 191 (col.) Feb '50.
—— (deer). Natl. geog. 111: 174 (col.) Feb '57.
—— (designer). Natl. geog. 98: 53 (col.) Jl '50.
—— (desk, 18th cent.). Natl. geog. 97: 564 (col.) May '50.
—— (digging for sea life). Natl. geog. 112: 164 (col.) Aug '57.
—— (digging peat). Natl. geog. 104: 532 Oct '53.

—— (digging potatoes). Holiday 22: 53 (col.) Nov '57.
—— (dinner table). Holiday 20: 64, 131 (col.) Oct '56; 21: 152 (col.) Je '57; 22: 46 (col.) Oct '57.
—— (dinner, comic). Holiday 21: 32 Mar '57, 180 (col.) Ap '57.
—— (diving). Holiday 14: 71 Oct '53; 23: 136 Mar '58, 111 Ap 58; 24: 137, 155 (col.) Oct '58; 25: 41 May '59.
Natl. geog. 99: 309 (col.) Mar '51.
—— (diving, comic). Holiday 23: 45 May '58.
—— (diving in ocean). Natl. geog. 112: 652 (col.) Nov '57.
—— (diving in pool). Holiday 23: 139 (col.) Feb '58.
—— (diving with fins). Travel 113: 22 Feb '60.
—— (doctoring tapir). Natl. geog. 111: 524 Ap '57.
—— (dodo bird skeleton). Natl. geog. 109: 90 Jan '56.
—— (dog). Holiday 13: 73 Ap '53, 33 May '53, 108 Je '53; 14: 75 Oct '53; 20: 3 Dec '56.
Natl. geog. 104: 548 (col.) Oct '53.
—— (dog sled). Natl. geog. 116: 73 (col.) Jl '59.
Travel 107: 29-31 Jan '57.
—— (dogs). Holiday 18: 96 Aug '55.
—— (dogs herding sheep). Natl. geog. 114: 201 Aug '58.
—— (donkey). Holiday 5: 84 Ap '49; 20: 66 Aug '56, 118 Sept '56, 6 Oct '56, 125 Dec '56.
Natl. geog. 109: 229 (col.) Feb '56.
—— (donkey, comic). Holiday 18: 63 Aug '55; 19: 6 Jan '56.
—— (double-headed, comic). Holiday 19: 9 Feb '56.
—— (drinking cocktail). Holiday 23: 143 (col.) Jan '58.
—— (drinking from bottle). Natl. geog. 114: 232 Aug '58.
—— (drinking tea). Holiday 24: 29, 182 (col.) Nov '58.
—— (drinking at stream). Natl. geog. 111: 553 Ap '57.
—— (driving auto). Holiday 14: 127 Dec '53; 21: 131 (col.) Je '57.
—— (driving, comic). Holiday 26: 22 Aug '59.
—— (driving fire engine). Amer. heri., vol. 7 No. 1 p. 66 (col.) (Dec '55).
—— (driving funeral wagon). Holiday 6: 51 Aug '49.
—— (driving ox cart). Holiday 23: 181 Ap '58.
—— (drummer, comic). Holiday 24: 134 Jl '58.
—— (drying kodacolor prints). Natl. geog. 110: 614 (col.) Nov '56.
—— (drying sea salt). Travel 111: 42 Feb '59.
—— (duck hunting). Holiday 20: 87 (col.) Oct '56.
—— (dunce cap). Holiday 12: 126 Nov '52.
—— (eagle nest). Natl. geog. 105: 274, 285 Feb '54.
—— (earliest found). Natl. geog. 118: 435 (col.) Sept '60.
—— (eating). Holiday 10: 65 Nov '51; 27: 202 (col.) Ap '60; 28: 8 Sept '60.
—— (eating, cartoon). Holiday 28: 8 Sept '60.
—— (18th cent. writing). Natl. geog. 113: 259 (col.) Feb '58.

—— (election speaker). Amer. heri., vol. 9 no. 5 p. 112 (Aug '58).

—— (elephant, comic). Holiday 18: 150 Nov '55; 19: 136 Mar '56.

—— (elephant rifle). Natl. geog. 110: 537 Oct '56.

—— (Eng. dude, horseback, cartoon). Amer. heri., vol. 7 no. 5 p. 37 (Aug '56).

—— (evening clothes. Holiday 14: 18 Nov '53; 18: 75, 131 (col.), 159 Dec '55; 19: 97 (col.) May '56; 23: 94 Feb '58; 27: 153 Je '60.

—— (evening, clothes, bowing). Holiday 18: 125 (col.) Jl '55.

—— (examining plants). Natl. geog. 100: 297 (col.) Sept '51; 113: 273 (col.) Feb '58.

—— (examining TV). Travel 105: back cover Jan '56.

—— (exploring cave). Travel 104: 33 Oct '55.

—— (eyeglasses). Holiday 23: 119 (col.) May '58, 53 Je '58; 24: 115 Jl '58; 25: 129 (col.) Jan '59, 98 Feb '59, 47 (col.) May '59, 33 (col.) Je '59; 26: 117 Jl '59.

—— (face, comic). Holiday 19: 137 Jan '56, 33 May '56, 14 Je '56; 20: 112 Nov '56.

—— (falconer). Holiday 21: 79 May '57.

—— (fallen into ocean). Holiday 13: 14 Ap '53.

—— (falling backward). Holiday 14: 18 Nov '53.

—— (farmer, 1873). Amer. heri., vol. 7 no. 3 p. 42 (col.) (Ap '56).

—— (fat). Holiday 22: 81 Nov '57.

—— (fat, seated). Holiday 14: 93 Dec '53.

—— (fat, short). Holiday 13: 6 Je '53.

—— (fawn). Natl. geog. 109: 743 Je '56.

—— (feeding beaver). Natl. geog. 107: 680 May '55.

—— (feeding child). Holiday 10: 28 Dec '51.

—— (feeding elk herd). Natl. geog. 109: 30-1 col.) Jan '56.

—— (feeding fish). Jordan: Hammond's pict. atlas, p. 69 (col.).

—— (feeding goat). Natl. geog. 107: 848 Je '55.

—— (feeding hippopotamus). Natl. geog. 100: 696 Nov '51.

—— (feeding mule). Natl. geog. 107: 19 (col.) Jan '55.

—— (feeding porpoise). Natl. geog. 97: 67 (col.) Jan '50.

—— (fiddle). Holiday 10: 97 Aug '51.

—— (fighting shark, cartoon). Travel 112: 60 Jl '59.

—— (fish). Holiday 20: 99 Nov '56; 21: 193 May '57; 23: 37 May '58; 25: 108 Mar '59 26: 206 Dec '59; 27: 191 (col.) Ap '60; 28: 9 Sept '60.
Jordan: Hammond's pict. atlas, p. 156 (col.)
Natl. geog, 97: 433 Ap '50; 101: 436 (col.) Ap '52; 102: 523 (col.) Oct '52, 593 Nov '52; 110: 275 Aug '56.
Travel 101: 34 Mar '54, 24-5 Je '54; 105: 42 Mar '56; 106: 34 Jl '56, 44 Aug '56; 108: 24 Jl '57, 45 Oct '57; 109: 33 Je '57; 110: 55 Jl '58, 27 Sept '58; 111: 34 Mar '59.

—— (fish, comic). Holiday 27: 166 May '60.

—— (fish fry). Natl. geog. 109: 33 (col.) Jan '56.

—— (fish in boat). Travel 114: 57 Jl '60.

—— (fish on pole). Natl. geog. 99: 432 (col.) Ap '51.

—— (fisherman). Holiday 14: 5 (col.) Jl '53.
Jordan: Hammond's pict. atlas, p. 130 (col.).

—— (fisherman, comic). Holiday 14: 32 Jl '53; 16: 143 (col.) Dec '54.

—— (fisherman, head). Holiday 24: 87 (col.) Aug '58.

—— (fishing). Con. 145: LXXIII (col.) May '60.
Face of Amer., p. 60 (col.).
Holiday 5: 71 (col.) Ap '49; 6: 39 (col.) Nov '49; 7: 17 (col.) May '50; 13: 75 (col.) Feb '53, 29 (col.) Ap '53; 21: 161 Jl '57; 23: 15 (col.) May '58; 27: 4 (col.) Ap '60.
Jordan: Hammond's pict. atlas, p. 135 (col.).
Natl. geog. 108: 668 (col.) Nov '55; 118: 162 (col.) Aug '60.
Travel 101: 33 May '54; 103: 49 Je '55; 107: 17 Je '57; 108: 38 Jl '57; 113: 44 Feb '60, 56 Mar '60.

—— (fishing from house porch). Holiday 23: 71 (col.) May '58.

—— (fishing in boat). Holiday 14: 5 Aug '53.
Travel 103: 10 Feb '55; 104: 26 Aug '55; 107: 46 Jan '57.

—— (fishing, lazy). Holiday 20: 14 Sept '56.

—— (fishing, fishnet). Travel 107: 35 Ap '57.

—— (fishing in river). Natl. geog. 101: 305, 307 (col.) Mar '52.
Travel 101: 11 Mar '54.

—— (fishing in sea). Natl. geog 107: 750 (col.) Je '55.

—— (fishing in stream). Travel 102: 31-2 Sept '54; 104: 29-30 Aug '55; 107: 45-6 Jan '57; 110: 17 Aug '58; 113: 44 Feb '60.

—— (fishing, ocean beach). Natl. geog. 112: 296 (col.) Sept '57.

—— (fishing, snow). Natl. geog. 109: 33 (col.) Jan '56.

—— (fishing). See also fisherman.

—— (fishnet). Travel 106: 2 Jl '56.

—— (fishing auto tire). Holiday 23: 1 May '58.

—— (flower bouquet). Holiday 28: 21 Aug '60.

—— (flowers). Natl. geog. 97: 485-7, 490, 492 (col.) Ap '50.

—— (flying, comic). Holiday 18: 91 Oct '55; 21: 18 Feb '57.

—— (flying). Durant: Pict. hist. of Amer. circus, p. 155.

—— (food table). Holiday 19: 56 (col.) Feb '56; 28: 111 (col.) Dec '60.

—— (foot on stool). Holiday 14: 76 (col.) Nov '53.

—— (football stadium, comic). Holiday 10: 180 Dec '51.

—— (fossil). Natl. geog. 118: 420 (col.) Sept '60.

—— (gander). Natl. geog. 97: 402 Mar '50.

—— (gas station attendant). Holiday 6: 64 (col.) Sept '49.

—— (gets honey from tree). Natl. geog. 116: 215 (col.) Aug '59.

—— (giant crabs). Natl. geog. 109: 783 (col.) Je '56.

—— (gift shop). Natl. geog. 105: 235 (col.) Feb '54.

—— (girl secretary). Holiday 24: 118 (col.) Nov '58.

man (glass cutter). Natl. geog. 107: 472 Ap '55.
—— (glass in hand). Holiday 23: 92 (col.) Feb '58.
—— (goatee). Holiday 22: 45 Jl '57.
—— (goats). Natl. geog. 109: 216 Feb '56.
—— (Godey fashion). Amer. heri., vol. 9 no. 6 p. 27 (col.) (Oct '58).
—— (gold prospector). Holiday 26: 33 Aug 59. Travel 104: 33-4 Jl '55.
—— (golfer). Holiday 14: 189, 192 Dec '53; 21: 105 May '57; 23: 47 (col.) May '58.
—— (golfer, back view). Holiday 26: 129 Dec '59.
—— (golfer, silhouette). Holiday 13: 8 Je '53; 27: 8 Feb '60, 190 Mar '60, 178 Ap '60, 19 Je '60.
—— (golfers). Holiday 13: 7 (col.) Jan '53, 88 Ap '53, 32, 73 (col.), 130 May '53, 81, 109, 160 Je '53; 27: 125 (col.) Feb '60, 44, 63 (col.), 191 (col.), 202 May '60, 7 (col.), 38 Je '60; 28: 9 Sept '60, 154 (col.) Oct '60.
—— (gorillas). Natl. geog. 111: 521 Ap '57.
—— (goslings. Natl. geog. 112: 830 (col.) Dec '57.
—— (grain field). Holiday 25: 35 (col.) Feb '59.
—— (greenhouse). Natl. geog. 100: 55-6 (col.) Jl '51.
—— (grizzly bear). Natl. geog. 118: 276-91 (part col.) Aug '60.
—— (guitar). Holiday 19: 14 Feb '56; 28: 126 (col.) Nov '60.
—— (gun). Holiday 14: 150 Oct '53; 18: 74 (col.) Oct '55; 28: 57 (col.) Nov '60.
—— (hammock). Holiday 20: 179 (col.) Dec '56.
—— (hand in pocket). Holiday 10: 129 Oct '51, 11: 70 Jan '52; 12: 27 Nov '52; 20: 17, 157 Dec '56.
—— (hanged). Lehner: Pict. bk. of sym., p. 76. Rawson: Ant. pict. bk., p. 42.
—— (hanging from bridge). Natl. geog. 97: 461 Ap '50.
—— (hanging from pole). Amer. heri., vol. 10 no. 4 p. 46 (Je '59).
—— (hanging mistletoe). Holiday 14: 12 Dec '53.
—— (happy). Holiday 10: 13 (col.) Aug '51.
—— (harem girls). Holiday 20: 153 (col.) Nov '56.
—— (harrow, ox, in rice field). Natl. geog. 103: 664 (col.) May '53.
—— (harrowing field). Natl. geog. 106: 573 (col.) Oct '54.
—— (harvests lavender). Natl. geog. 117: 751 (col.) Je '60.
—— (hat & briefcase). Natl. geog. 109: 449 (col.) Ap '56.
—— (head). Con. 140: LII Dec '57; 142: LVIII Nov '58, LIV Jan '59; 144: XIV, 271 Jan '60.
Holiday 10: 86 Sept '51, 29 (col.) Oct '51; 11: 8, 87 Jan '52, 23, 70 Feb '52, 6, 26 Mar '52, 108 Ap '52, 128 May '52; 12: 23 Aug '52, 25 (col.) Oct '52, 91 Nov '52; 13: 1, 6, 29, 129, 134 Mar '53, 72 (col.), 145 Ap'53, 65 May '53, 67, 84, 92, 118 (part col.) Je '53; 14: 117, 127 Jl '53, 18, 81 Sept '53, 31 Oct '53, 67, 121, 125, 135, 142, inside back cover (col.) Nov '53, 124-5, 173

(col.), 194 Dec '53; 18: 33 Jl '55, 25 Sept '55, 5, 14 Nov '55; 19: 33 May '56, 131 Je '56; 20: 102 Aug '56, 190 Nov '56; 21: 161, 172 Mar '57; 22: 12, 146 Nov '57, 83 (col.), 112 Dec '57; 23: 80, 136 Jan '58, 115, 120 (col.) 162, 171 (col.) Ap '58, 6, 132-3, 178 (col.) May '58, 9, 106-7 (col.), 169, 187 Je '58; 24: 128 (col.) Oct '58, 40, 108 Nov '58; 25: 15 (col.), 27, 129 (col.), 171 May '59, 1, 8, 153 Je '59; 26: 8-9, 33, 131 Jl '59, 60 (col.), 114 Aug '59, 126-7 Sept '59, 108, 150 Oct '59, 28 (col.), 29, 37, 166 Nov '59, 39, 121, 132 (col.), 212, 225 (col.), 243 Dec '59; 27: 142 (col.), 153, 163 (col.) Jan '60, 58-9 (col.) Mar '60, 108 (col.), 177, 181, 206, 228 Ap '60, 7 (col.), 14, 82 May '60, 114 (col.), 165, 168-9 Je '60; 28: 142 Jl '60, 14 Aug '60, 77, 91 Sept '60, 80-1 (col.), 98, 107, 111, 196 Oct '60, 38 Nov '60, 161-2 Dec '60.
Labande: Naples, p. 109.
Natl. geog. 106: 791-2 (col.) Dec '54; 107: 515 (col.) Ap '55.
Praeg pict. ency., p. 9, 270, 280 (col.).
Travel 101: 7 Mar '54; 102: 47 Nov '54; 103: 32-3 Mar '55, 46 Je '55; 104: inside back cover Sept '55; 106: inside back cover Jl '56, inside back cover Sept '56; 107: back cover Feb '57; 110: 7 Jl '58; 111: 16 Mar '59; 112: 6 Aug '59, 19 Dec '59; 113: 7, 53 Jan '60, 42, 95 Ap '60, 39 May '60; 114: 4 Oct '60.
—— (head, Antarctic gear). Holiday 25: 135 May '59.
—— (head, beard, mustache). Holiday 20: 29 (col.) Nov '56.
—— (head, binoculars). Holiday 11: 137 Ap '52; 20: 29 (col.) Nov '56, 135 (col.) Dec '56.
—— (head, bird in hand). Natl. geog. 106: 603 (col.) Nov '54.
—— (head, blindfolded)). Holiday 20: 22 Oct '56.
—— (head, block printing). Natl. geog. 99: 577 (col.) May '51.
—— (head, blowing shell). Holiday 27: 182 Je '60; 28: 130 Jl '60, 123 Aug '60, 24 Sept '60, 187 Nov '60.
Natl. geog. 98: 86 (col.) Jl '50.
—— (head, bottles). Holiday 25: 138 Je '59.
—— (head, cartoon). Amer. heri., vol. 5 no. 1, p. 4 (fall '53).
Holiday 14: 9 Dec '53; 25: 27 Je '59; 26: 213 Dec '59.
—— (head, chalk drawing). Con. 145: LXVII-LXIX May '60.
—— (head, child on shoulder). Natl. geog. 109: 437 (col.) Mar '56.
—— (head, chimpanzee). Natl. geog. 118: 401 (col.) Sept '60.
—— (head, cocktail). Holiday 22: 226 (col.) Dec '57; 28: 104 Jl '60, 157 Dec '60.
—— (head, college cap & gown). Holiday 10: 143 Nov '51; 11: 74 Mar '52, 144 Je '52; 12: 80 Oct '52, 30 Nov '52.
—— (head, comic). Holiday 10: 82 Jl '51, 5 (col.) Sept '51, 20, 154, 163 Dec '51; 11: 105 Jan '52, 29, 63, 89 Mar '52, 159 May '52; 12: 78, 113 Aug '52, 6, 15 Sept '52, 77 Oct '52, 74 Nov '52; 13: 14 May '53; 14: 166 Dec '53; 18: 14 Jl '55, 121 Sept '55, 14 Oct

'55, 157 Dec '55; 20: 84 Aug '56, 144 Oct '56, 144 Oct '56, 107 Dec '56; 21: 157 May '57; 22: 21 Jl '57; 23: 173 Ap '58; 28: 62 Nov '60.

man (headdress). Holiday 26: 136 Nov '59.

—— (head, drinking from wineskin). Natl. geog. 97: 440 (col.) Ap '50.

—— (head, eating corn). Holiday 28: 15 (col.) Oct '60.

—— (head, eating pineapple). Natl. geog. 118: 11 (col.) Jl '60.

—— (head, 1816). Amer. heri., vol. 11 no. 2 p. 15 (Feb '60).

—— (head, eyeglasses). Holiday 10: 13 Dec '51; 11: 146 Je '52; 18: 33 Jl '55; 19: 33 May '56, 79 Je '56; 20: 141 Nov '56; 22: 6, 21, 45 Jl '57, 27 Oct '57, 111 (col.) Nov '57; 23: 35 Mar '58, 8 May '58; 27: 109 Jan '60, 30 Feb '60. Natl. geog. 112: 803 (col.) Dec '57.

—— (head, finger at mouth). Holiday 23: 132 Je '58.

—— (head, fisherman). Holiday 24: 18 (col.) Jl '58, 125 Sept '58.

—— (head, flower). Natl. geog. 113: 106 (col.) Jan '58.

—— (head, frowning). Holiday 11: 48 Mar '52; 20: 6 Dec '56. Travel 114: 19 Dec '60.

—— (head, goggles). Holiday 23: 120 Je '58.

—— (head, hand shading eyes). Holiday 10: 108 Jl '51.

—— (head, hat). Con. 144: LXXIV Jan '60. Holiday 21: 11 Feb '57; 28: 90 (col.) Sept '60, 188 (col.) Oct '60. Natl. geog. 98: 15 Jl '50.

—— (head, horse). Amer. heri., vol. 2 no. 2 p. 15 (winter '51).

—— (head, laborer). Travel 107: back cover Mar '57, inside back cover Ap '57, inside back cover May '57; 108: back cover Aug '57; 110: inside back cover Jl '58.

—— (head, laughing). Holiday 10: 3, 17 Jl '51, 30, 133, 137 Nov '51, 104, 179 (col.) Dec '51; 11: 76 Jan '52, 15 (col.), 66, 80 Feb '52, 82 (col.) Mar '52, 19, 82 (col.), 102 (col.), 117, 131 Ap '52, 142, 152 (col.) May '52, 87, 134 Je '52; 12: 22 Jl '52, 20 (col.) Aug '52, 64 Sept '52, 7 Oct '52, 3, 92, 105, 140 Dec '52; 18: 62, 79 (col.), 85 Jl '55, 1, 23, 98 (col.) Aug '55, 14, 58, 90 Oct '55, 35 Dec '55; 19: 130 Feb '56, 79 Je '56; 20: 50-1 Oct '56, 116-7 (col.) Nov '56, 12 Dec '56; 21: 78 Jan '57, 14, 33 Feb '57, 16-7, 49 Mar '57, 206 Ap '57, 9, 18, 186 May '57, 48, 107, 196 Je '57; 22: 23, 86 (col.) Jl '57, 25, 48-9 (col.) Sept '57, 116 Oct '57, 31 Nov '57, 186 (col.) Dec '57; 24: 34, 64 Dec '58; 25: 156 Jan '59, 124 Feb '59, 190 Ap '59, 111, 191 May '59; 26: 99 Jl '59, 137 Sept '59, 67 Nov '59, 59 (col.), 138 Feb '60; 27: 100 (col.) 129, 140, 184 Mar '60, 230 Ap '60, 127 May '60, 27 Je '60; 28: 120, 123 Aug '60, 104 Sept '60, 157 Oct '60. Natl. geog 116: 602 (col.) Nov '59.

—— (head, lawn rake). Holiday 28: 214 (col.) Nov '60.

—— (head, listening). Holiday 10: 77 Aug '51.

—— (head, microphone). Holiday 11: 6 Jan '52.

—— (head, mustache). Holiday 10: 130 Nov '51; 20: 117 (col.) Nov '56; 22: 146 Nov '57.

—— (head, needs shave). Holiday 22: 17 (col.) Oct '57.

—— (head, parrot). Natl. geog. 118: 544 (col.) Oct '60, 726 (col.) Nov '60.

—— (head, pipe). Holiday 18: 22 Oct '55, 96 Nov '55, 39 Dec '55; 20: 33 Oct '56, 118 Dec '56; 22: 8 Nov '57.

—— (head, pipe, laughing). Holiday 10: 40 (col.) Dec '51.

—— (head, playing clarinet). Holiday 11: 94 May '52.

—— (head, playing violin). Holiday 20: 102 Nov '56.

—— (head, profile). Holiday 11: 14 Feb '52.

—— (head, reading). Holiday 12: 23 Sept '52.

—— (head, salesman). Holiday 20: 14 Sept '56.

—— (head, sculpture). Holiday 27: 83 Ap '60.

—— (head, shadow). Holiday 12: 85 Dec '52; 22: 157 Oct '57.

—— (head, shaving). Holiday 27: 158 Je '60.

—— (head, shocked). Holiday 19: 74 Mar '56.

—— (head, silhouette). Natl. geog. 110: 724 Dec '56.

—— (head, smelling bottle). Holiday 22: 153 Dec '57.

—— (head, smelling flower). Holiday 27: 169 May '60.

—— (head, stone carved). Natl. geog. 97: 241 (col.) Feb '50.

—— (head, straw hat). Natl. geog. 108: 548 (col.) Oct '55.

—— (head, straw hat, pineapple). Natl. geog. 99: 432 (col.) Ap '51.

—— (head, sunglasses). Holiday 12: 9 Aug '52; 18: 190 Dec '55.

—— (head, taking pictures). Holiday 10: 4 (col.) Nov '51; 11: 118 Ap '52; 12: 38 Dec '52; 20: 11 Nov '56.

—— (head, teacher). Travel 109: 50 Mar '58.

—— (head, telephone). Holiday 10: 127 Dec '51; 12: 73 (col.) Sept '52; 20: 116-7 (col.) Nov '56; 27: 248 May '60. Natl. geog. 116: 446, 453 (col.) Oct '59.

—— (head, telescope). Holiday 12: 5 (col.) Nov '52.

—— (head, thinking). Holiday 20: 140 Dec '56; 21: 43 Ap '57; 22: 161 Oct '57.

—— (head, tipping hat). Holiday 27: 56 Ap '60.

—— (head, umbrella). Holiday 18: 85 Jl '55.

—— (head, winter). Holiday 10: 105 Sept '51, 148 Nov '51.

—— (head, worried). Holiday 19: 85 (col.) Feb '56. Travel 103: back cover Ap '55.

—— (head, camel). Natl. geog. 113: 511 (col.) Ap '58.

—— (heads, expressions). Holiday 27: 223 Ap '60.

—— (heads, around the world). Holiday 23: 99 Feb '58.

—— (helicopter, comic). Holiday 22: 6 Sept '57.

man (helping girl from carriage). Holiday 25: 140 May '59.
—— (high bicycle). Amer. heri., vol. 8 no. 4 p. 73 (Je '57).
—— (hiking, pack on back). Travel 113: 24 Ap '60.
—— (his shadow voice). Holiday 18: 1 Aug '55.
—— (hitching post). Holiday 14: 24 (col.) Oct '53.
—— (hoeing). Natl. geog. 101: 167 (col.) Feb '52.
—— (hoeing flowers). Natl. geog. 112: 468 (col.) Oct '57.
—— (hoeing turnip patch). Natl. geog. 102: 65 (col.) Jl '52.
—— (hog). Holiday 20: 45 Oct '65.
—— (holding box). Holiday 26: 19 Nov '59.
—— (holding corset & football helmet). Natl. geog. 98: 15 Jl '50.
—— (holding crayfish). Natl. geog. 110: 805 Dec '56.
—— (holding dog). Natl. geog. 99: 829 Je '51.
—— (holding flag, patriotic). Amer. heri. vol. 8 no. 6 frontis (col.) (Oct '57).
—— (holding frigate bird). Natl. geog. 107: 123 (col.) Jan '55.
—— (holding horse). Con. ency. of ant., vol. 1, pl. 167.
Con. 144: 113 (col.) Nov '59, 270 Jan '60.
—— (holding rooster). Natl. geog. 109: 832 (col.) Je '56.
—— (holding sick child). Travel 101: 39 Jan '54.
—— (holding sign). Holiday 11: 70 (col.) Ap '52; 12: 12 (col.) Oct '52.
—— (holding woman's wrap. Holiday 23: 132 (col.) Mar '58, inside back cover (col.) Je '58; 24: 132 (col.) Oct '58.
—— (hornbill bird). Natl. geog. 103: 786 (col.) Je '53.
—— (horse). Amer. heri., vol. 7 no. 2 p. 28 (col.) (Feb '56).
Con. 144: 200-1 Dec '59.
Face of Amer., p. 172 (col.).
Holiday 23: 4 (col.) Jan '58, 58 (col.) Je '58.
Travel 113: 43 Ap '60.
—— (horse, Bible times). Natl. geog. 112: 860 (col.) Dec '57.
—— (horse, colt). Holiday 27: 83 May '60.
—— (horse heads). Holiday 27: 8 Ap '60.
—— (horse, jumping). Holiday 10: 29 Nov '51; 17: 85 Feb '55; 24: 41 Sept '58.
Natl. geog. 109: 95 (col.) Jan '56.
—— (horse, lamb). Natl. geog. 101: 552 Ap '52.
—— (horse running). Natl. geog. 108: 212 (col.) Aug '55.
—— (horseback). Amer. heri., vol. 9 no. 1 p. 35, 39 (Dec '57); vol. 9 no. 5 cover (col.), p. 8 (col.) (Aug '58); vol. 12 no. 1 p. 19, 89 (Dec '60).
Con. 135: 46 Mar '55, XI May '55,. 253 Je '55; 136: 126 Nov '55; 140: 127 Nov '57; 141: 61 Mar '58; 142: 41 Sept '58; 145: 68 Mar '60.
Holiday 5: 40 (col.) Feb '49, 28 Mar '49, 44 (col.) Je '49; 6: 95 (col.) Nov '49; 7: 87 Ap '50, 155 (col.) May '50; 8: 44-5 Sept '50, 49 Nov '50; 10: 82 Oct '51 13: 75

(col.), 94 Jan '53, 92 Mar '53, 18 (col.) May '53; 15: 73 (col.) May '54, 62 Je '54; 16: 60 Aug '54; 18: 160 (col.) Dec '55; 19: 58 (col.) Jan '56, 33 (col.) Mar '56, 136 (col.) May '56; 20: 32 (col.) Oct '56, 109 (col.) Nov '56, 163 (col.) Dec '56; 21: 15 (col.) Mar '57; 22: 217 (col.) Dec '57; 23: 136 Mar '58, 34 (col.) May '58; 25: 126 (col.) Ap '59, 12 (col.) May '59, 108 Je '59; 27: 160 Mar '60; 28: 50-1 (col.) Jl '60, 99 (col.) Sept '60.
Horan: Pict. hist. of wild west, p. 14, 158
Jordan: Hammond's pict. atlas, p. 131 (col.).
Natl. geog. 108: 681 (col.) Nov '55; 115: 276 (col.) Feb '59.
Travel 104: 14 Sept '55.
—— (horseback, cattle). Natl. geog. 105: 307 (col.) Mar '54.
—— (horseback, Civil War). Amer. heri., vol. 6 no. 6 p. 75, 88 (Oct '55).
—— (horseback, cocktail). Holiday 21: 111 (col.) May '57; 24: 160 (col.) Dec '58.
—— (horseback, comic). Holiday 14: 17, 19 Jl '53; 18: 65 Sept '55; 19: 67, 123 Mar '56; 21: 42 Je '57.
—— (horseback, dogs). Con. 144: 109 Nov '59, 201, 203-4 Dec '59.
Holiday 13: 97 Je '53.
—— (horseback, 18th cent.). Natl. geog. 108: 332 (col.) Sept '55.
—— (horseback, hunting). Natl. geog. 97: 580-1 (col.) May '50.
—— (horseback, jumping). Face of Amer., p. 18 (col.).
—— (horseback, killing dragon). Praeg.: pict. ency., p. 402 (col.).
—— (horseback, pulling skier). Natl. geog. 115: 232-3 (col.) Feb '59.
—— (horseback, river). Natl. geog. 109: 36 (col.) Jan '56; 118: 700 (col.) Nov '60.
—— (horseback, running). Con. 139: 138 Ap '57; 143: 276 Je '59.
Holiday 10: 121 Jl '51; 13: 149 Mar '53, 151 May '53.
—— (horseback, sculpture). Labande: Naples, p. 79.
Praeg pict. ency., p .159.
—— (horseback, sculpture, 13th cent.). Praeg. pict. ency., p. 219.
—— (horseback, 1750). Amer. heri., vol. 11 no. 4 p. 9 (col.) (Je '60).
—— (horseback, silhouette). Amer. heri., vol. 11 no. 3 p. 102-3 (Ap '60).
Holiday 13: 8 Je '53.
—— (horseback, statue). Praeg. pict. ency., p. 257.
—— (horses & dog). Con. 139: 1 May '57.
—— (horses at fair). Natl. geog. 108: 342-3 (col.) Sept '55.
—— (horses, ford river). Natl. geog. 113: 612 (col.) May '58.
—— (horses, swimming lake). Natl. geog. 109: 632 (col.) May '56.
—— (hot, comic). Holiday 24: 80 Aug '58.
—— (Hudson Bay). Natl. geog. 110: 680 Nov '56.
—— (hunter). Holiday 6: 5 (col.) Nov '49; 24: 131 Sept '58; 26: 29 Aug '59, 21 Sept '59 39 Oct '59; 28: 86 Sept '60.

man (hunter, dog). Holiday 14: 23 Nov '53, 173 (col.) Dec '53.
—— (hunter, dogs). Holiday 21: 91 (col.) Je '57.
—— (hunter, gun). Holiday 14: 168 (col.) Nov '53.
—— (hunter, horseback). Con. 139: XXI Ap '57, XXXII Mar '57; 145: 146 May '60.
—— (hunter, horseback). See also hunter (dogs, horse).
—— (hunter, rowboat). Holiday 24: 67 (col.) Oct '58.
—— (hunting marine life). Natl. geog. 109: 554-7 (col.) Ap '56.
—— (hurrying to work). Holiday 20: 138 Oct '56.
—— (husky dogs). Holiday 10: 97 Dec '51.
—— (ice fishing). Natl. geog. 114: 872 Dec '58.
—— (ice fishing, comic). Holiday 14: 108 Aug '53.
—— (in auto). Holiday 12: 81 (col.) Jl '52.
—— (in auto, cartoon). Holiday 23: 184 Ap '58.
—— (in bath tub). Holiday 14: 153 Dec '53.
—— (in bear trap). Natl. geog. 118: 291 Aug '60.
—— (in bed). Holiday 13: 100 May '53.
—— (in bed, comic). Holiday 11: 33 Je '52; 23: 28 Feb '58; 24: 40 Dec '58.
—— (in bed, log, comic). Holiday 11: 80 Ap '52.
—— (in cage). Holiday 27: 11 Ap '60.
—— (in cart). Labande: Naples, p. 146.
—— (in fishnet, sculpture). Labande: Naples, p. 60.
—— (in hammock). Natl. geog. 107: 72 (col.) Jan '55.
—— (in laboratory). Travel 101: 35 Ap '54.
—— (in library). Holiday 27: 104 May '60.
—— (in stocks). Holiday 24: 118 Aug '58. Travel 104: 41 Oct '55.
—— (in swamp, catches alligator). Natl. geog. 105: 323 (col.) Mar '54.
—— (in tub, comic). Holiday 28: 9 Nov '60.
—— (injured, lowered from plane). Natl. geog. 111: 297 (col.) Mar '57.
—— (inside pipe). Natl. geog. 100: 544 Oct '51.
—— (inspecting grain). Natl. geog. 100: 297 (col.) Sept '51.
—— (Jamestown house model). Natl. geog. 111: 592 May '57.
—— (Japanese umbrella). Holiday 28: 47 Nov '60.
—— (jewel cutter). Natl. geog. 113: 862 Je '58.
—— (jumping). Holiday 27: 144 (col.) Feb '60.
—— (jumping chasm.) Natl. geog. 109: 759 (col.) Je '56.
—— (jumping for soccer ball). Holiday 18: 63 Oct '55.
—— (jungle, cooking kettle, cartoon). Holiday 21: 16 Jan '57.
—— (kissing hand). Travel 111: 39 Ap '59.
—— (kissing woman). Amer. heri. vol. 8 no. 4 p. 41 (col.) (Jl '57).
—— (kissing woman's hand). Holiday 24: 8 Nov '58.
—— (kneeling). Holiday 23: 169 (col.) May '58.

—— (kneeling, writing). Natl. geog. 112: 825 (col.) Dec '57.
—— (laboratory table). Natl. geog. 105: 84 Jan '54.
—— (lake, comic). Travel 113: 66 Feb '60.
—— (lamb). Natl. geog. 97: 460 Ap '50.
—— (lampreys). Natl. geog. 115: 480 Ap '59.
—— (large fish). Natl. geog. 113: 96 (col.) Jan '58.
—— (laughing). Holiday 10: inside cover (col.), 54, 80, 116, 148 (col.) Oct '51, 140, 156 Nov '51; 11: 132 Ap '52, 37 (col.) May '52; 19: 104 Mar '56, 137 (col.) May '56; 20: 5 Aug '56, 71 Oct '56; 21: 104 Ap '57, 173 (col.) Je '57; 22: 47 Oct '57, 124 (col.) Dec '57; 28: 16 Jl '60.
Jensen: The White House, p. 204.
—— (lawn chair). Holiday 21: 8 Jan '57.
—— (lawn mower). Holiday 27: 183 Mar '60.
—— (leading cow). Natl. geog. 115: 376 (col.) Mar '59.
—— (leading loaded donkey). Natl. geog. 113: 129 Jan '58.
—— (leaning against tree). Con. 140: XXV Nov '57.
—— (leopard around neck). Durant: Pict. hist. of Amer. circus, p. 227.
—— (Lt. Gen., 18th cent. Eng.). Con. 145: 43 (col.) Mar '60.
—— (laughing). Holiday 18: 97 Jl '55.
—— (lighting cigar). Holiday 27: 11 May '60.
—— (liquor cellar). Holiday 25: 103 Feb '59.
—— (listening). Holiday 18: 76 Sept '55, 126 Nov '55, 14 Dec '55; 19: 83 Jan '56.
—— (loading grain boat). Natl. geog. 115: 467-9 (col.) Ap '59.
—— (loading hay). Natl. geog. 112: 175 (col.) Aug '57.
—— (lobster). Natl. geog. 115: 292 Feb '59.
—— (lobster traps). Holiday 18: 34-5 (col.) Jl '55.
—— (looking at road sign). Holiday 11: 64 (col.) Feb '52.
—— (looking at statue). Natl. geog. 107: 24 (col.) Jan '55.
—— (looking for gold). Travel 112: 47 Sept '59.
—— (looking in crystal ball, comic). Holiday 23: 42 Je '58.
—— (looking in mirror). Holiday 14: 152 Dec '53.
—— (looking thru binoculars). Holiday 24: 102 Jl '58.
Natl. geog. 98: 610 Nov '50.
Travel 113: 7 Jan '60.
—— (lorikeets). Natl. geog. 110: 518 (col.) Oct '56.
—— (lounge chair). Holiday 23: 129 (col.) Mar '58.
—— (lounging robe). Holiday 18: 161 (col.) Dec '55; 22: 245 Dec '57.
—— (lovers on park bench). Holiday 16: 66 Sept '54.
—— (luggage). Holiday 13: 79 (col.) Je '53.
—— (lunch). Holiday 24: 15 (col.) Oct '58; 26: 120 Oct '59; 27: 150 Feb '60.
—— (lying down). Holiday 24: 52 (col.) Aug '58; 28: 180 (col.) Nov '60.
—— (lying down, comic). Holiday 13: 86 Je '53.

man (lying on cot). Holiday 24: 89 Aug '58.
—— **(lying on floor).** Holiday 25: 5 (col.) May '59; 28: 205 (col.) Nov '60.
man (lying on grass reading). Natl. geog. 101: 174 (col.) Feb '52.
—— **(lying on horse).** Holiday 23: 189 (col.) Je '58.
—— **(machete, cutting sugar cane).** Natl. geog. 99: 433 (col.) Ap '51.
—— **(magic carpet, comic).** Holiday 27: 165 Jan '60.
—— **(magician, comic).** Holiday 5: 24 Ap '49.
—— **(making cheese).** Natl. geog. 98: 243 (col.) Aug '50; 100: 407 (col.) Sept '51.
—— **(making enameled tray, India).** Natl. geog. 116: 842 (col.) Dec '59.
—— **(making lobster trap).** Natl. geog. 110: 804 Dec '56.
—— **(making mask).** Natl. geog. 117: 828 (col.) Je '60.
—— **(making movies).** Holiday 27: 64 Ap '60.
—— **(making rope).** Natl. geog. 98: 198 Aug '50.
—— **(making souvenirs).** Travel 110: 20 Aug '58.
—— **(making speech).** Amer. heri., vol. 10 no. 4 p. 42 (Je '59).
—— **(making sugar cane syrup).** Natl. geog. 113: 551 (col.) Ap '58.
—— **(martinis, comic).** Holiday 21: 94 Jan '57.
—— **(mechanical bell ringer).** Holiday 11: 84 (col.) Je '52; 12: 19 (col.) Aug '52.
—— **(mending fishnet).** Travel 108: 21 Jl '57.
—— **(microphone).** Holiday 19: 145 (col.) May '56.
Travel 111: 5 May '59.
—— **(milking).** Natl. geog. 98: 761 (col.) Dec '50; 107: 489 Ap '55.
—— **(milking, comic).** Holiday 13: 93 Ap '53.
—— **(mixing punch).** Natl. geog. 118: 179 (col.) Aug '60.
—— **(molten glass).** Natl. geog. 117: 7 (col.) Jan '60.
—— **(monkey cage).** Natl. geog. 109: 107, 117, 119 Jan '56.
—— **(moray eel).** Natl. geog. 116: 518 (col.) Oct '59.
—— **(motorcycle).** Holiday 27: 90 May '60.
—— **(mt. climber).** Natl. geog. 109: 97 (col.) Jan '56.
Travel 101: 18-20 May '54.
—— **(movie, comic).** Holiday 11: 121 Je '52.
—— **(mowing lawn).** Face of Amer., p. 107 (col.).
Holiday 19: 153 May '56; 21: 207 Ap '57, 154 May '57.
—— **(mule).** Holiday 7: 34 (col.) Jan '50, 123 Ap '50.
—— **(music books).** Holiday 21: 144 Mar '57.
—— **(music conductor).** Holiday 14: 159 Nov '53.
—— **(musician, shadow).** Holiday 22: 31 Nov '57.
—— **(musician, comic).** Holiday 26: 128 Nov '59.
—— **(muskrat lodge).** Natl. geog. 118: 140 Jl '60.
—— **(net fishing).** Travel 102: 35-7 Jl '54.
—— **(ocean fishing).** Holiday 24: 147 (col.) Nov '58.

—— **(offering toast).** Holiday 20: 90 Oct '56.
—— **(on auto).** Holiday 27: 42 (col.) May '60.
—— **(on bird, cartoon).** Holiday 23: 34 Mar '58.
—— **(on boat).** Holiday 28: 8 Nov '60.
—— **(on bucking horse).** Brooks: Growth of a nation, p. 80.
Holiday 5: 7 (col.) Mar '49.
Travel 101: 15 Jan '54.
—— **(on cactus, comic).** Holiday 11: 62 Mar '52.
—— **(on camel).** Holiday 13: Feb '53.
Natl. geog. 100: 733 (col.) Dec '51; 102: 123 Jl '52.
Travel 104: 18 Nov '55.
—— **(on camel, cartoon).** Travel 102: 54 Sept '54.
—— **(on horse, jumping).** Holiday 17: 117 Jan '55; 24: 157 Nov '58.
Natl. geog. 106: 699, 703 (col.), 707 Nov '54.
Travel 110: 54 Jl '58.
—— **(on horse, receiving trophy).** Natl. geog. 106: 714 (col.) Nov '54.
—— **(on horse, running).** Natl. geog. 108: 336 Sept '55.
—— **(on horse, statue).** Holiday 25: 142 (col.) Jan '59.
—— **(on ladder).** Holiday 23: 96 (col.) Jan '58; 24: 15 (col.) Dec '58; 28: 38 (col.) Oct '60.
Natl. geog. 98: 418 Sept '50; 113: 136 Jan '58.
—— **(on ladder, hanging lanterns).** Holiday 28: 58 (col.) Dec '60.
—— **(on ladder, painting).** Holiday 22: 59 Dec '57; 26: 25 (col.) Dec '59.
—— **(on ladder, painting, back view).** Holiday 28: 211 (col.) Dec '60.
—— **(on ladder, painting, comic).** Holiday 18: 8 (col.) Dec '55.
—— **(on loaded donkey).** Natl. geog. 97: 436 Ap '50.
—— **(on race horse).** Holiday 27: 191 (col.) May '60.
—— **(on race horse).** *See* also jockey (horse race).
—— **(on raft).** Travel 111: 50 Feb '59.
—— **(on ship, back view).** Natl. geog. 98: 631 (col.) Nov '50.
—— **(on skiis).** *See* skier.
—— **(on stilts).** Holiday 21: 77 (col.) Je '57; 23: 19 May '58.
—— **(on telephone pole).** Natl. geog. 109: 509 Ap '56.
—— **(on throne, laughing).** Holiday 19: 11 May '56.
—— **(orangutans).** Natl. geog. 111: 503 (col.) Ap '57.
—— **(osprey).** Holiday 21: 73 Mar '57.
—— **(ostrich chick).** Natl. geog. 118: 336 (col.) Sept '60.
—— **(outdoor cooking).** Holiday 26: 79 Aug '59; 28: 24 Aug '60.
—— **(outlaw on horse).** Horan: Pict. hist. of wild west, p. 16.
—— **(overalls).** Face of Amer., p. 43 (col.).
Holiday 16: 40 Nov '54.
—— **(office).** Holiday 22: 50 Sept '57.
—— **(office desk).** Holiday 26: 34 Oct '59.

—— (Okinawa). Natl. geog. 97: 538 Ap '50.
—— (overalls, comic). Travel 113: 10 Mar '60.
—— (overcoat). Holiday 10: 7 Sept '51, 5, 8, 112, 124 Oct '51, 71 (col.), 115, 140 Nov '51, 105 Dec '51; 11: 4, (col.), 81 Mar '52, 94 Ap '52; 12: 16 Sept '52, 12-3 (col.), 129 Oct '52, 74, 121 Nov '52, 38 134 Dec '52; 13: 168 May '53; 18: 59 Aug '55, 19 Sept '55, 14, 23 Oct '55, 65 Nov '55; 20: 73, 134, 136 Oct '56, 17, 21, 25, 111 (col.), 125, 196 Nov '56, 184 Dec '56; 21: 160 Ap '57, 23 Je '57; 22: 49 (col.) Sept '57, 29 (col.), 133 Oct '57, 106 (col.) Nov '57, 169, 201, 216, 220 Dec '57; 24: 202 Nov '58, 191 Dec '58; 25: 46, 162 Ap '59, 151 (col.), 176 May '59; 26: 181 Oct '59, 146 Nov '59, 148 Dec '59; 27: 173 Ap '60, 11, 32, 83 May '60; 28: 6 Oct '60, 167, 176 Nov '60.
—— (ox cart). Natl. geog. 100: 10 (col.) Jl '51.
—— (ox team). Natl. geog. 97: 191 (col.) Feb '50.
—— (pack horse). Natl. geog. 113: 410 (col.) Mar '58.
—— (pack horse, mts.). Natl. geog. 102: 483 (col.) Oct '52.
—— (pack on back). Natl. geog. 103: 648 (col.) May '53; 111: 854 Je '57.
—— (pack on donkeys). Natl. geog. 113: 140 Jan '58.
—— (packages). Holiday 12: 92 Dec '52; 25: 129 (col.) Jan '59.
—— (painting). Natl. geog. 102: 757 Dec '52. Travel 110: inside cover Jl '58.
—— (painting adv.). Holiday 20: 19 (col.) Nov '56.
—— (painting adv., comic). Holiday 20: 26 Dec '56.
—— (painting auto). Holiday 20: 2 (col.) Sept '56.
—— (painting boat). Natl. geog. 106: 676 Nov '54.
—— (painting bldg. sign, comic). Holiday 24: 121 (col.) Dec '58.
—— (painting miniature). See artist (painting miniature).
—— (painting picture). See artist (painting picture).
—— (painting pottery). Natl. geog. 100: 455 (col.) Oct '51.
—— (painting wall, comic). Holiday 14: 100 Dec '53.
—— (pajamas). Holiday 11: 24 (col.) Je '52; 23: 4 (col.) Feb '58; 24: 161 Dec '58.
—— (panning gold). Holiday 26: 6, 132 Nov '59.
—— (parachute). Holiday 5: 26 Feb '49. Natl. geog. 112: 21 Jl '57.
—— (party). Holiday 22: 155 (col.) Dec '57.
—— (Peary relics). Natl. geog. 104: 827 Dec '53.
—— (peddler's buggy & horses). Amer. heri., vol. 6 no. 4 p. 35 (col.) (Je '55).
—— ("pen shells"). Natl. geog. 116: 478 Oct '59.
—— (Penn. German farmer). Amer. heri., vol. 7 no. 3 p. 2 (col.) (Ap '56).
—— (penguin). Natl. geog. 109: 411 (col.) Mar '56; 112: 603 Nov '57.
—— (photographer). Travel 104: 24-5 Sept '55.

—— (photographing honey bees). Natl. geog. 116: 191 (col.) Aug '59.
—— (photographing penguins). Natl. geog. 102 412-3 Sept '52.
—— (piano, comic). Holiday 10: 11 Aug '51; 20: 208 Dec '56.
—— (picking tulips). Natl. geog. 98: 757 (col.) Dec '50.
—— (picks apples). Natl. geog. 110: 803 (col.) Dec '56.
—— (picnic). Holiday 23: inside back cover (col.) Feb '58.
—— (pipe, fisherman). Natl. geog. 98: 350 Sept '50.
—— (pipe, pajamas). Holiday 10: 37 (col.) Dec '51.
—— (plank farm fence). Natl. geog. 110: 801 Dec '56.
—— (playing accordian). Holiday 6: 80 Aug '49; 13: 140 May '53; 23: 71, 74 (col.) Feb '58.
Natl. geog. 113: 93 (col.) Jan '58; 115: 474 (col.) Ap '59.
Travel 108: 14 Dec '57.
—— (playing badminton). Holiday 14: 75 Sept '53.
—— (playing bagpipe). Disney: People & places, p. 11, 26, 27 (col.).
Holiday 18: 10 (col.) Sept '55; 25: 190 (col.) May '59.
Natl. geog. 112: 445 (col.) Oct '57.
—— (playing banjo). Holiday 28: 4 Sept '60.
—— (playing banjo, ancient). Int. gr. soc.: Arts . . . cover (col.).
—— (playing baseball). Amer. heri., vol. 11 no. 4 p. 24 (Je '60).
—— (playing cards). Holiday 28: 142 Nov '60.
—— (playing cello). Cooper: Con. ency. of music, p. 65.
Holiday 25: 42 (col.) Jan '59.
—— (playing chess). Amer. heri., vol. 11 no. 2 p. 34 (Feb '60).
—— (playing clarinet). Holiday 14: 43 Aug '53; 23: 76 Jan '58.
—— (playing golf). Holiday 14: 1, 16 Aug '53, 3, 64 Sept '53, 90 Oct '53.
Travel 103: 41 Je '55; 112: 30 Aug '59.
—— (playing golf, silhouette). Holiday 14: 11 Sept '53.
—— (playing golf). See also golfer.
—— (playing guitar). Holiday 14: 33 Sept '53; 18: 56 (col.) Aug '55; 23: 35 Feb '58; 26: 87 (col.) Oct '59; 28: 152 Nov '60, 16 Dec '60.
Natl. geog. 97: 534 (col.) Ap '50, 679 May '50; 100: 804 Dec '51; 102: 357 (col.) Sept '52; 111: 448 (col.) Ap '57; 115: 789 (col.) Je '59; 116: 11 Jl '59.
—— (playing guitar, Mardi Gras). Holiday 19: 14 Jan '56.
—— (playing guitar). See also man (beach, playing guitar).
—— (playing lute). Con. 145: 159 May '60. Cooper: Con. ency. of music, p. 447 (col.).
—— (playing musical goblets). Natl. geog. 109: 455 Ap '56.
—— (playing musical instrument). Cur. biog., p. 4 (1961).
Holiday 16: 70 (col.) Oct '54; 24: 135 Nov '58.

man (playing organ). Holiday 19: 175 May
'56; 21: 183 Ap '57; 23: 107 Ap '58.
—— (playing organ, comic). Holiday 28: 8 Jl
'60.
man (playing piano). Holiday 21: 42 Mar '57;
22: 121 Sept '57; 24: 13 (col.) 173 178
Nov '58, 96 Dec '58; 26: 138 (col.) Nov
'59 27: 102 (col.) Feb '60.
Jensen: The White House, p. 114.
Natl. geog. 117: 31, 67 (col.) Jan '60.
—— (playing piano, cartoon). Holiday 13: 22
Jan '53.
—— (playing solitaire). Natl. geog. 104: 414
(col.) Sept '53.
—— (playing tennis). Holiday 10: 108 Aug
'51; 14: 135 Jl '53; 22: 115 (col.) Jl '57;
27: 14 Je '60.
Travel 104: 45 Jl '55.
—— (playing tennis). See also tennis player.
—— (playing ukulele). Holiday 18: 69 (col.)
Nov '55.
—— (playing violin). Amer. heri., vol. 11 no.
5 p. 19 (col.) (Aug '60).
Con. 141: XXVI May '58.
Holiday 8: 15 Nov '50; 10: 97 Aug '51; 13:
131 (col.) May '53; 26: 139 Oct '59.
Natl. geog. 102: 488 Oct '52; 111: 426 Mar
'57.
Travel 101: 11 Jan '54; 104: 68-9 Oct '55;
106; 35 Aug '56.
—— (playing violin, comic). Holiday 18: 121
Sept '55.
—— (plowing). Natl. geog. 98: 194 (col.) Aug
'50; 101: 167 (col.) Feb '52.
—— (plowing, oxen). Amer. heri., vol. 7 no.
3 p. 52 (col.) (Ap '56); vol. 9 no. 3 p. 5
(col.) (Ap '58).
Natl. geog. 109: 68 (col.) Jan '56; 113: 522
(col.) Ap '58; 117: 663 (col.) May '60.
—— (plowing rice field). Natl. geog. 107: 580
Ap '55.
—— (plowing, water buffalo, silhouette). Natl.
geog. 111: 327 Mar '57.
—— (polo player). Holiday 28: 74 Jl '60.
—— (posing, auto). Holiday 21: 42 May '57.
—— (posing for sculptor). Holiday 18: 63
(col.) Sept '55.
—— (posting sign). Holiday 25: 47 Mar '59.
—— (pouring tea). Travel 107: 19 Mar '57.
—— (praying). Con. 144: VI Jan '60.
—— (pretzel seller). Amer. heri., vol. 3 no. 4
p. 38 (summer '52).
—— (professor). Holiday 13: 143 May '53.
—— (professor in cap & gown). Holiday 14:
123 Nov '53.
—— (profile, laughing). Holiday 10: 88 Oct
'51, 6 Nov '51.
—— (proposing to woman). Amer. heri., vol.
9 no. 1 p. 84 (Dec '57).
Holiday 21: 94 Feb '57.
—— (prospector riding horse). Amer. heri.,
vol. 10 no. 3 p. 36 (col.) (Ap '59).
—— (pulling balking burro). Natl. geog. 105:
857 Je '54.
—— (pulling camel, cartoon). Holiday 14: 3
Nov '53.
—— (pulling cannon, 1850). Amer. heri., vol.
10 no. 6 p. 90 (Oct '59).
—— (punch bowl, serving girl). Travel 114:
30 Sept '60.

—— (push cart). Holiday 10: 116 Oct '51.
—— (pushing food cart). Amer. heri., vol. 8
no. 4 p. 66 (Je '57).
—— (pushing wheelbarrow). Natl. geog. 112:
742-3 (col.) Dec '57.
—— (pushing woman in sled). Holiday 14: 31
Dec '53.
—— (putting chain on tire). Travel 111: 36
Feb '59.
—— (raccoon). Natl. geog. 113: 602 May '58.
—— (raccoon cage). Natl. geog. 110: 848 Dec
'56.
—— (rain, comic). Holiday 28: 20 Aug '60.
Travel 102: 22 Sept '54.
—— (rain forest). Natl. geog. 113: 846-7 Je
'58.
—— (raincoat). Holiday 10: 11 Oct '51, 138
Dec '51; 11: 35 May '52; 12: 20 Oct '52;
13: 74 Ap '53; 14: 24 Nov '53, 189 Dec '53;
21: 19 Ap '57; 23: 103 Ap '58; 26: 165, 189
Oct '59.
—— (raking leaves). Holiday 20: 20 (col.)
Nov '56.
Natl. geog 105: 456 Ap '54.
—— (reading). Holiday. 10: 122 Jl '51, 54, 70
Oct '51, 133 Nov '51; 12: 115 (col.) Aug
'52; 20: 46, 161 (col.) Dec '56; 24: 115,
145 Oct '58, 169 Nov '58, 48 Dec '58; 25:
49 (col.) Jan '59, 157 Mar '59; 26: 4 Sept
'59, 27 (col.) Oct '59, 65 Dec '59; 27: 133
Mar '60, 82 May '60; 28: 129 Sept '60,
135 Oct '60, 43, 166, 177 (col.) Nov '60,
60, 124 (col.) Dec '60.
Natl. geog. 97: 303 (col.) Mar '50, 490 (col.)
Ap '50; 99: 692 May '51, 759 (col.) Je
'51; 759 (col.) Je '51; 107: 213 (col.) Feb
'55; 112: 741 (col.) Dec '57; 115: 15 (col.)
Jan '59.
—— (reading, backview). Natl. geog. 118: 170
(col.) Aug '60.
—— (reading lake sign, comic). Travel 113: 66
Feb '60.
—— (reading, laughing). Holiday 21: 76 Jan
'57.
—— (reading magazine). Natl. geog. 111: 418
Mar '57.
—— (reading newspaper). Con. 145: X Mar
'60, XVI Ap '60, LI May '60, LX Je '60.
—— (reading old Bible). Natl. geog. 103: 833
Je '53.
—— (reading paper in rocking chair). Natl.
geog. 103: 847 Je '53.
—— (reading to children). Holiday 20: 70
Sept '56.
—— (reaper, horses). Natl. geog. 100: 33 (col.)
Jl '51.
—— (receiving key to city). Holiday 26: 98
(col.) Oct '59.
—— (reclining chair). Travel 103: 43 Ap '55.
—— (reconstructs antiques). Natl. geog. 111:
601 (col.) May '57.
—— (refinishes altar panel). Natl. geog. 110:
645 Nov '56.
—— (relaxed, chair). Holiday 19: 84 Jan '56,
150 May '56; 22: 133 (col.) Nov '57, 19
(col.), 41 Dec '57.
—— (relaxed, comic). Holiday 21: 123 (col.)
Feb '57.
—— (repairing auto). Travel 105: 57 May '56.

man (repairing figurehead). Natl. geog. 107: 749 (col.) Je '55.

—— (repairing robe). Natl. geog. 100: 159 (col.) Aug '51.

—— (repairing tire puncture). Holiday 12: 30 Jl '52.

—— (rescuing woman in ocean). Amer. heri., vol. 8 no. 4. p. 47 (Je '57)

—— (restaurant serving table). Holiday 28: 174 Oct '60.

—— (resting in chair). Holiday 26: 129 Oct '59; 27: 60 (col.) May '60; 28: 187 Nov '60.

—— (restoring mosaic). Natl. geog. 107: 23 (col.) Jan '55.

—— (rhinoceros). Natl. geog. 107: 698 May. '55.

—— (rice field). Natl. geog. 109: 694 (col.) May '56.

—— (rich, cartoon). Holiday 25: 93-5 Je '59.

—— (riding camel). Disney: People & places, p. 85 (col.).
Holiday 28: 138 (col.) Nov '60.

—— (riding camel, comic). Holiday 25: 46 May '59.

—— (riding, desert). Holiday 24: 45 (col.) Oct '58.

—— (riding donkey). Travel 101: inside cover May '54.

—— (riding elephant, circus). Durant: Pict. hist. of Amer. circus, p. 153.
Holiday 18: 92 Jl '55.

—— (riding elephant, Siam). Disney: People & places, p. 175 (col.).

—— (riding mule, man walking). Amer. heri., vol. 8 no. 6 p. 83 (Oct '57).

—— (ringing door bell). Holiday 21: 128 Je '57.

—— (river pilot). Holiday 26: 28 Aug '59.

—— (robbing safe). Holiday 11: 6 May '52.

—— (rock pinnacle). Natl. geog. 99: 667 (col.) May '51.

—— (rock whale, Antarctic). Natl. geog. 116: 544 Oct '59.

—— (rocky shore). Holiday 25: 137 (col.) Jan '59.

—— (rowboat). Holiday 23: 111 (col.) Jan '58; 24: 209 (col.) Nov '58.

—— (rowboat, night scene). Int. gr. soc.: Arts . . . p. 151 (col.).

—— (rowboat, supplies). Holiday 23: 157 (col.) Je '58.

—— (rowing boat). Holiday 18: 111 (col.) Oct '55.

—— (ruffed grouse). Natl. geog. 99: 811 Je '51.

—— (running). Holiday 12: 8 Aug '52; 27: 167 Jan '60, 25 Je '60.

—— (running after bicycle rider). Amer. heri., vol. 8 no. 4 p. 73 (Je '57).

—— (running after dog). Holiday 23: 141 May '58.

—— (running for plane). Holiday 11: 87 Ap '52; 12: 9 Jl '52.

—— (running from wife, comic). Holiday 23: 142 May '58.

—— (running horse). Holiday 28: 17 (col.) Nov '60.

—— (St. Bernard dog, mt.). Natl. geog. 110: 466 Oct '56.

—— (salesman). Holiday 11: 14 Mar '52.

—— (sawing log). Natl. geog. 110: 314 (col.) Sept '56.

—— (science experiment). Holiday 28: 156 (col.) Nov '60.

—— (scientist). Natl. geog. 99: 319 (col.) Mar '51.

—— (Scotsman). See Scotsman.

—— (sculpture). Labande: Naples, p. 77.

—— (sculpture, bust). Holiday 23: 83 Jan '58.

—— (sea coconut tree). Natl. geog. 116: 674 (col.) Nov '59.

—— (sea elephants). Natl. geog. 114: 280 (col.) Aug '58.

—— (sea stars). Natl. geog. 111: 26 (col.) Jan '57.

—— (searching for effigies). Natl. geog. 102: 402 Sept '52.

—— (seated). Amer. heri., vol. 7 no. 2 p. 67 (Feb '56).

—— (seated). Amer. heri., vol. 7 no. 3 p. 56 Ap '56); vol. 8 no. 6 p. 4 (Oct '57); vol. 9 no. 1 p. 22 (Dec '57).
Holiday 18: 25, 39 Dec '55; 21: 204 (col.) Ap '57, 31 May '57, 21 Je '57; 22: 48 Sept '57; 23: 25, 125 (col.) Jan '58, 138, 142 (col.) Feb '58, 112 (col.) May '58, 166 (col.) Je '58; 24: 37 (col.) Sept '58, 80, 206 (col.) Nov '58, 98, 122 Dec '58; 25: 82, 84 (col.) Mar '59, 135 (col.), 156 Ap '59, 92 May '59, 15 (col.) Je '59; 26: 61 (col.) Aug '59, 91, 141 (col.) Oct '59, 16-7, 48, 53-4 (col.) Nov '59, 126 (col.) Dec '59; 27: 145 (col.) Jan '60, 155, 178 Feb '60, 53, 75 (col.) Mar '60, inside back cover (col.) Ap '60, 6, 81, 88, 172 May '60, 24 Je '60; 28: 83 Aug '60, 78-9 Oct '60.
Jensen: The White House, p. 73.
Natl. geog 104: 763 (col.) Dec '53.

—— (seated at tent). Natl. geog. 97: 2, 16 (col.) Jan '50.

—— (seated, back view). Amer. heri., vol. 11 no. 5 p. 10 (Aug '60).
Holiday 24: 109 Oct '58; 97: 728 (col.) Je '50; 98: 114 (col.) Jl '50; 115: 271 Feb '59.

—— (seated, bench). Holiday 18: 98 (col.) Oct '55.

—— (seated, comic). Holiday 21: 4 (col.) Jan '57, 46 (col.) Mar '57, 133 May '57; 27: 193 May '60.

—— (seated, 1817 soldier). Amer. heri., vol. 7 no. 1 p. 24 (col.) (Dec '55).

—— (seated, 1818). Holiday 21: 98 (col.) Mar '57.

—— (seated, 1835). Amer. heri., vol. 11 no. 5 p. 61 (col.) (Aug '60).

—— (seated, 1868). Amer. heri., vol. 11 no. 1 p. 60-1 (Dec '59).

—— (seated, fireplace). Natl. geog. 109: 479 (col.) Ap '56.

—— (seated, garden). Holiday 22: 223 (col.) Dec '57.

—— (seated, happy). Holiday 27: 172 Mar '60.

—— (seated, horse show). Natl. geog. 106: 716 (col.) Nov '54.

—— (seated, lake pier). Natl. geog. 110: 474 (col.) Oct '56.

—— (seated, laughing). Holiday 18: 81 (col.) Oct '55, 152 Nov '55; 26: 135 (col.) Nov '59.

—— (seated, lawn chair). Natl. geog. 97: 405 Mar '50.

man (seated on floor). Holiday 23: 46 Mar '58; 27: 14 Je '60.

—— **(seated on grass).** Holiday 28: 69 (col.) Oct '60.

man (seated on ground). Natl. geog. 111: 660 May '57.

—— **(seated on shop floor).** Natl. geog. 102: 658 (col.) Nov '52.

—— **(seated, reading).** Holiday 18: 152 Nov '55; 23: 48 Feb '58.

—— **(seated, 1791).** Con. 145: LIII Mar '60.

—— **(seated, silhouette).** Holiday 23: 162 Mar '58.

—— **(seated, smoking).** Holiday 25: 2 (col.) Je '59; 27: 13 (col.) Je '60; 28: 203 (col.) Dec '60.

—— **(seated, thinking).** Holiday 28: 125 Nov '60.

—— **(seated, waving).** Amer. heri., vol. 9 no. 2 p. 67 (Feb '58).

—— **(seated, weighing owl).** Natl. geog. 109: 18 (col.) Jan '56.

—— **(seated with gun, 1880).** Amer. heri., vol. 11 no. 1 p. 12 (col.) (Dec '59).

—— **(secretary).** Holiday 21: 175 Mar '57.

—— **(selling apples).** Amer. heri., vol. 9 no. 5 p. 29 (Aug '58).

—— **(selling dogs).** Natl. geog. 99: 817-28 Je '51.

—— **(selling fish).** Natl. geog. 113: 96 (col.) Jan '58.

—— **(selling flowers).** Natl. geog. 116: 724 (col.) Dec '59.

—— **(selling fruit).** Holiday 24: 7 (col.) Dec '58.

—— **(Sequoia tree).** Natl. geog. 105: 799 (col.) Je '54.

—— **(serving at dinner table).** *See* waiter, dining room.

—— **(serving food).** Holiday 24: 83 (col.) Aug '58.

—— **(1715).** Amer. heri., vol. 11 no. 1 p. 4 (col.) (Dec '59).

—— **(shadow).** Holiday 13: 28 Feb '53.

—— **(sharpen scythe).** Natl. geog. 115: 588 Ap '59.

—— **(shaving).** Holiday 13: 117 Je '53.

—— **(shearing sheep).** Natl. geog. 100: 27 (col.) Jl '51.

—— **(sheep pen).** Natl. geog. 99: 659 May '51.

—— **(sheep, shop).** Natl. geog. 113: 486 (col.) Ap '58.

—— **(ship captain).** Holiday 24: 11 Jl '58.

—— **(ship model).** Natl. geog 111: 710 May '57.

—— **(shoeing horse).** Holiday 11: 43 (col.) Je '52.

Travel 113: 30 Mar '60.

—— **(shooting).** Holiday 13: 73 (col.) May '53.

—— **(shooting animals, 1836).** Amer. heri., vol. 11 no. 6 p. 36 (col.) (Oct '60).

—— **(shooting gun).** Holiday 27: 139 Jan '60, 213 (col.) Ap '60.

—— **(shooting man).** Amer. heri., vol. 7 no. 2 p. 86 (Feb '56).

—— **(shooting woman).** Amer. heri., vol. 7 no. 2 p. 117 (Feb '56).

—— **(shorts, at boat)** Holiday 28: 63 (col.) Oct '60.

—— **(shorts, sweater).** Holiday 21: 12 (col.) Feb '57.

—— **(shot by another).** Holiday 22: 97 Sept '57.

—— **(shoveling snow in Alaska).** Natl. geog. 103: 566 May '53.

—— **(show dog).** Natl. geog. 105: 99 (col.), 114 Jan '54.

—— **(shuffleboard).** Holiday 26: 113 Sept '59. Travel 103: 44 Mar '55.

—— **(sick pilgrim on back).** Natl. geog. 110: 528 Oct '56.

—— **(sick transfer at sea).** Natl. geog. 118: 595 (col.) Nov '60.

—— **(sick, xray).** Natl. geog. 114: 335 (col.) Sept '58.

—— **(sight seeing. comic).** Holiday 26: 43 Nov '59.

—— **(silhouette).** Amer. heri., vol. 6 no. 6 p. 94-6 (Oct '55).

Holiday 12: 39 Dec '52; 13: 57 (col.) May '53; 19: 72 Je '56; 20: 140 Oct '56, 151 Nov '56, 175 Dec '56; 25: 80 Mar '59; 28: 62 Oct '60.

Natl. geog. 115: 476 (col.) Ap '59, 2, 5-8 Jl '59.

—— **(singing).** Holiday 21: 124 May '57.

—— **(sitting on fence).** Holiday 20: 27 (col.) Sept '56.

—— **(skating).** Amer. heri., vol. 7 no. 1 p. 14 (col.) (Dec '55).

Holiday 5: 4 Mar '49; 26: 123 Oct '59.

—— **(skier).** Holiday 13: 19 Feb '53; 14: 82, 89 Nov '53; 23: 110 Jan '58; 26: 176 Oct '59; 27: 133 Jan '60, 171 Feb '60, 213 (col.) Ap '60.

Travel 113: cover (col.) Je '60.

—— **(skiing).** *See* also skiers.

—— **(skin diving).** Holiday 27: 54 Ap '60; 28: 177 (col.) Oct '60.

—— **(skis).** Holiday 5: 111 (col.) Jan '49; 27: 125 (col.) Mar '50.

—— **(skis, running).** Holiday 5: 10 (col.) Jan '49.

—— **(sled dogs).** Natl. geog. 110: 687 Nov '56.

—— **(sleeping).** Holiday 8: 1 Aug '50; 8: 74 Sept '50, 23 Oct '50, 135 Nov '50; 22: 118 (col.) Dec '57; 23: 9 Feb '58.

—— **(sleeping on park bench).** Natl. geog. 118: 786 (col.) Dec '60.

—— **(sleepy, window).** Natl. geog. 98: 412 Sept '50.

—— **(smoking pipe, comic).** Holiday 22: 251 Dec '57.

—— **(snake around neck).** Natl. geog. 118: 327 (col.) Sept '60.

—— **(snake charmer).** Holiday 28: 10 Jl '60.

—— **(snow making).** Travel 111: 32 Jan '59.

—— **(snow storm).** Natl. geog. 115: 294-5 Feb '59.

—— **(snowshoes, dog).** Holiday 11: 14 Jan '52.

—— **(soldier on horse).** Amer. heri., vol. 7 no. 1 p. 62 (Dec '55).

—— **(soldier on horse, cartoon.)** Amer. heri., vol. 11 no. 6 p. 57 (col.) (Oct '60).

—— **(soldier on running horse).** Horan: Pict. hist. of wild west, p. 63.

—— **(sowing seed).** Amer. heri., vol. 7 no. 4 p. 27 (col.) (Je '56).

man (sowing seed, Normandy). Holiday 19: 52 Jan '56.

—— (spading earth). Natl. geog. 107: 155 Feb '55.

—— (spinal nerves). Gray's anatomy, p. 946-7.

—— (spinning floating log). Natl. geog. 110: 314 (col.) Sept '56.

—— (sport clothes). Holiday 18: 4, 65 (col.) Sept '55, 74 (col.) Oct '55; 19: 137 (col.) May '56; 20: 16 Sept '56, 72 (col.) Oct '56, 160 (col.) Dec '56; 21: 1 Mar '57, 100, 190, 204 May '57, 5 (col.), 146 Je '57; 22: 108, 141 (col.) Sept '57.

—— (sport coat). Holiday 14: 129 Dec '53.

—— (sport jacket). Holiday 19: 66 Mar '56.

—— (sport shirt). Holiday 19: 73 (col.) Jan '56.

—— (spraying crop). Natl. geog. 109: 694 (col.) May '56.

—— (spraying elephant). Durant: Pict. hist. of Amer. circus, p. 255.

—— (standing on head). Amer. heri., vol. 12 no. 1 p. 116 (Dec '60). Holiday 11: 150 Je '52.

—— (standing, reading). Holiday 18: 67 Sept '55.

—— (steering ship). Natl. geog. 97: 96 (col.) Jan '50; 98: 164 (col.) Aug '50, 613 (col.) Nov '50.

—— (stonefish). Natl. geog. 111: 12-3 Jan '57.

—— (stooping, back view). Holiday 23: 48 May '58.

—— (stooping). Travel 104: 61 Jl '55.

—— (storm, calling). Holiday 27: 143 May '60.

—— (studies fish). Natl. geog. 113: 203 Feb '58.

—— (study table). Natl. geog. 100: 216 Aug '51.

—— (sugar cane field). Natl. geog. 109: 254 (col.) Feb '56.

—— (sugar cane, ox cart). Natl. geog. 115: 276-7 (col.) Feb '59.

—— (sun glasses). Holiday 21: 122 (col.) May '57.

—— (surf board). Holiday 5: 94 (col.) Mar '49; 28: 212 (col.) Dec '60.

—— (surprised). Holiday 24: 25 Oct '58.

—— (surveyor). Natl. geog. 97: 554 May '50; 105: 420 Mar '54.

—— (suspended in air, comic). Holiday 19: 39 Mar '59.

—— (sweater). Holiday 10: 104 Dec '51.

—— (swan). Natl. geog. 116: 567-70 Oct '59.

—— (sweeping walk). Natl. geog. 98: 40 Jl '50.

—— (swimmer pushing boat). Holiday 27: 18 (col.) Feb '60; 28: 111 (col.) Aug '60.

—— (swimming). Holiday 23: 139 (col.) Feb '58. Natl. geog. 106: 9 (col.) Jl '54. Travel 113: 22 Feb '60.

—— (swimming, comic). Holiday 23: 139 (col.) Feb '58.

—— (swimming, salt water). Holiday 12: 59 Jl '52.

—— (sword swallower, comic). Holiday 28: 32 Nov '60.

—— (taking deer picture). Natl. geog. 113: 662 May '58.

—— (taking movie picture). Travel 114: 61 Sept '60.

—— (taking nature pictures). Natl. geog. 97: 508, 511 Ap '50.

—— (taking pictures). Holiday 10: 5 Aug '51; 11: 80 May '52, 147 (col.) Oct '52; 14: 7 (col.) Aug '53, 77 (col.), 165 Nov '53, 69 Dec '53; 19: 113 (col.) Jan '56; 20: 99 (col.), 169 Dec '56; 21: 9, 15 (col.) Feb '57, 13 (col.) Mar '57, 158 (col.) Ap '57; 22: 106, 141 (col.) Sept '57, 45 (col.) Dec '57; 23: 131, 133 (col.) May '58; 24: 107 (col.) Sept '58, 114, 151 (col.) Nov '58; 26: 75 Aug '59, 167 Oct '59, 99 (col.) Nov '59; 27: 99 (col.) Feb '60, 116 (col.) Mar '60, 113, 123 Ap '60, 26 (col.) May '60; 28: 4, 11, 81 (col.) Jl '60, 8, 87 Aug '60, 43 Oct '60, 118 (col.) Nov '60. Natl. geog. 99: 645 (col.) May '51; 102: 312 Sept '52; 103: 274 Feb '53; 106: 173, 201 (col.) Aug '54; 107: 111 Jan '55; 111: 874 Je '57; 112: 56 (col.) Jl '57; 113: 407 Mar '58. Travel 109: 45 Feb '58; 114: 60 Aug '60.

—— (taking pictures, antique). Natl. geog. 106: 424-7 Sept '54.

—— (taking pictures, comic). Holiday 24: 20 Oct '58; 28: 135 Nov '60.

—— (taking pictures, 1850). Amer. heri. vol. 8 no. 1 p. 55 (Dec '56).

—— (taking pictures, Mexico). Natl. geog. 107: 241 (col.) Feb '55.

—— (taking pictures, penguins). Natl. geog. 108: 767 Dec '55.

—— (taking sea pictures). Natl. geog. 111: 18 (col) Jan '57.

—— (talking into microphone). Travel 105: inside back cover, Jan '56.

—— (talking on telephone). Amer. heri., vol. 11 no. 1 p. 8-9 (Dec '59).

—— (tall papier-mache). Natl. geog. 106: 297 (col.) Sept '54.

—— (tavern bar). Holiday 28: 218 (col.) Dec '60.

—— (tea table). Holiday 25: 119 May '59, 18 (col.) Je '59; 26: 55 (col.), 176 Oct '59.

—— (teaching bird study). Natl. geog. 106: 592 (col.) Nov '54.

—— (telephone). Holiday 10: 102 (col.) Aug '51; 18: 178 Nov '55; 20: 87 Dec '56; 27: 15 (col.) Ap '60; 28: 5 (col.) Aug '60.

—— (telephone, cartoon). Travel 112: 6 Dec '59.

—— (telephone repair). Natl. geog. 97: 824 Je '50.

—— (telescope). Holiday 20: 72 (col.) Sept '56; 24: 190 Nov '58; 25: 203 May '59. Natl. geog. 98: 822 Dec '50.

—— (tennis). Holiday 13: 163 May '53; 23: 48 May '58.

—— (tennis racquet). Holiday 23: 44 (col.) Je '58; 24: 108 (col.) Jl '58, 19 (col.) Oct '58.

—— (testing apples). Natl. geog. 110: 581 (col.) Nov '56.

—— (testing fruit juice). Travel 108: 35 Dec '57.

—— (testing monkey). Natl. geog. 108: 255 Aug '55.

—— (testing perfume). Natl. geog. 117: 750 (col.) Je '60.

—— (testing plants). Natl. geog. 104: 207, 209 (col.), 211-12 (col.) Aug '53.

man (thinking). Holiday 11: 79 Feb '52, 62 Je '52; 21: 113 Mar '57, 66 Je '57; 22: 31 (col.), 32 Dec '57.
—— **(throwing fish net).** Travel 109: 41 Feb '58.
—— **(thrown by bull).** Travel 113: 41 Mar '60.
man (thrown in water). Natl. geog. 98: 387 Sept '50.
—— **(tipping hat).** Holiday 26: 152 Oct '59; 27: 17 (col.) Jan '60; 28: 122 Nov '60.
—— **(tobacco leaf).** Holiday 23: 4 (col.) Ap '58.
Natl. geog. 109: 334 (col.) Mar '56.
—— **(topcoat).** Holiday 10: 87 (col.), 92 Oct '51, 84 Nov '51.
—— **(tortoise).** Natl. geog. 98: 266 Aug '50.
—— **(tourist, comic).** Travel 113: 43 Feb '60.
—— **(toy balloons, comic).** Holiday 24: 129 Nov '58.
—— **(traffic guide).** *See* traffic guide.
—— **(train engine, 1897).** Amer. heri., vol. 11 no. 3 p. 2 (Ap '60).
—— **(training dog).** Travel 101: 26-7 Mar '54.
—— **(travel agent).** Holiday 12: 7 (col.) Oct '52.
—— **(traveling).** Holiday 14: 128 Oct '53; 23: 21 Ap '58, 38 (col.) May '58, 21 Je '58; 24: back cover Jl '58, 9 Oct '58; 25: 33 Feb '59, 156 Mar '59; 26: 16, 165 Oct '59; 27: 6 Jan '60, 136 (col.) Ap '60; 28: 22 (col.) 179 Oct '60, 186 Dec '60.
—— **(traveling, back view).** Holiday 21: 123 (col.) Je '57.
—— **(traveling, cameras, comic).** Travel 113: 43 Feb '60.
—— **(traveling, comic).** Holiday 14: 8-9 Jl '53; 25: 208 May '59; 26: 104 Aug '59; 27: 114 Feb '60.
Travel. 113: 10 Mar '60.
—— **(tree, eagle nest).** Natl geog. 109: 17 (col.) Jan '56.
—— **(tree pollination).** Natl. geog. 110: 291 (col.) Sept '56.
—— **(trophy cup).** Holiday 22: 47 (col.) Dec '57.
Natl. geog. 111: 709 May '57.
—— **(trout fishing).** Natl. geog. 98: 529-56 (col.) Oct '50.
—— **(turtles).** Natl. geog. 113: 174 (col.) Feb '58.
—— **(two headed).** Holiday 8: 12 Aug '50.
—— **(tying girl's shoe).** Holiday 27: 1 Jan '60.
—— **(typing, outdoors).** Natl. geog. 106: 607 (col.) Nov '54.
—— **(ukulele).** Holiday 19: 139 Feb '56.
—— **(umbrella).** Holiday 23: 49 Feb '58.
Travel 103: inside cover Jan '55.
—— **(umbrella, cartoon).** Travel 102: 23 Sept '54.
—— **(umbrella, rain).** Natl. geog. 101: 554 Ap '52.
—— **(under rock bridge).** Natl. geog. 114: 55 Jl '58.
—— **(under tree).** Face of Amer., p. 34 (col.).
—— **(underwear).** Holiday 10: 180, 182 Dec '51.
—— **(underwear, resting).** Holiday 27: 4 Je '60.
—— **(U.S. outline).** Holiday 13: 107 Jan '53.

—— **(uranium search).** Travel 103: 18, 20 Mar '55.
—— **(varnishing baseball bats).** Natl. geog. 105: 299 (col.) Mar '54.
—— **(wagon, horses).** Face of Amer., p. 152 (col.).
Natl geog. 98: 113 (col.) Jl '50.
—— **(wagon, horse running).** Amer. heri., vol. 9 no. 6 p. 67 (Oct '58).
—— **(waiter, comic).** Holiday 17: 116 Mar '55.
—— **(walking).** Holiday 11: 70 (col.) Ap '52; 12: 69 (col.) Jl '52, 12-3 (col.), Oct '52, 121 Nov '52, 38, 134 Dec '52; 14: 146 Nov '53; 18: 16 (col.) Nov '55; 20: 11, 65 (col.) Aug '56, 59 Sept '56, 70 Oct '56, 101 Dec '56; 26: 50 Aug '59; 27: 234 Ap '60.
—— **(walking, comic).** Holiday 14: 134 Oct '53.
—— **(walking, overcoat).** Holiday 20: 114 Sept '56.
—— **(walking ship boom).** Natl. geog. 105: 2 (col.) Jan '54.
—— **(washing cattle).** Natl. geog. 97: 571 May '50.
—— **(washing panda).** Holiday 26: 40 Dec '59.
—— **(washing window).** Natl. geog. 107: 614 May '55.
—— **(watching T V).** Holiday 24: 93 Nov '58.
—— **(water skiing).** Holiday 22: 6 Sept '57; 23: 34 Je '58; 24: 155 (col.) Dec '58.
—— **(watering horses).** Natl. geog. 114: 186 (col.) Aug '58.
—— **(waterlily).** Natl. geog. 114: 250 Aug '58.
—— **(waving).** *See* man (beach, waving).
—— **(wearing Roman toga).** Holiday 25: 89 Ap '59.
—— **(weaving cloth).** Natl. geog. 106: 574 (col.) Oct '54.
—— **(weighing baggage).** Natl. geog. 112: 50 (col.) Jl '57.
—— **(whale, comic).** Holiday 21: 16 Feb '57.
—— **(whale oil vendor).** Amer. heri., vol. 6 no. 4 p. 47 (col.) (Je '55).
—— **(wheel chair).** Holiday 8: 9 Nov '50.
—— **(wheel chair, nurse).** Holiday 27: 164 Jan '60.
—— **(wheelbarrow).** Natl. geog. 99: 455 (col.) Ap '51.
—— **(whiskey cartoon).** Holiday 6: 48 Jl '49.
—— **(whooping crane).** Natl. geog. 116: 660 Nov '59.
—— **(wild rice field).** Holiday 18: 32 Aug '55.
—— **(winter jacket).** Holiday 12: 21 (col.) Dec '52.
—— **(with pen, cartoon).** Holiday 23: 17 May '53.
—— **(woman hugging).** Holiday 18: 162 Dec '55.
—— **(wood worker).** Amer. heri., vol. 3 no. 3 p. 33 (col.) (spring '52).
—— **(working at table).** Natl. geog. 102: 248 Aug '52; 113: 276 Feb '58.
—— **(working flower beds).** Natl. geog. 104: 681 (col.) Nov '53.
—— **(working on chart).** Natl. geog. 101: 246 Feb '52.
—— **(world globe).** Holiday 22: 1 Sept '57.
—— **(writing).** Holiday 12: 97 (col.) Oct '52, 141 (col.) Dec '52.
Natl. geog. 97 27 (col.) Jan '50; 111: 561 Ap '57.

man (writing, antique desk). Holiday 24: 30 (col.) Jl '58.

—— (writing, Civil war). Holiday 18: 24 Jl '55.

—— (writing in ledger). Natl. geog. 111: 743 Je '57.

—— (yawning). Natl. geog. 117: 844 Je '60.

——, Afghanistan. Natl. geog. 98: 677 Nov '50.

——, Afghanistan (horseback). Natl. geog. 98: 695 (col.) Nov '50.

——, Afghanistan (playing fiddle). Natl. geog. 98: 677 Nov '50.

——, African (beating drum). Travel 105: 42 Feb '56.

——, African guide (head). Natl. geog. 117: 118 (col.) Jan '60.

——, Amazon. Travel 113: 58 Feb '60.

——, Arabian. See Arabian man.

——, Argentina. Holiday 26: 103 (col.) Nov '59.

——, army (head). Holiday 28: 58 (col.) Sept '60.

——, Austria (head, whiskers). Natl. geog. 118: 273 (col.) Aug '60.

——, Basque (dancer). Holiday 27: 138 Je '60.

——, Basque (ox cart). Natl. geog. 105: 158 (col.) Feb '54.

——, Bavaria. Holiday 27: 166 Jan '60.

——, Belgian Congo. Holiday 10: 28 Sept '51.

——, Belgium (customs officer). Natl. geog. 108: 542 (col.) Oct '55.

——, Belgium (fisherman). Holiday 25: 45 Jan '59.

——, blind (factory worker). Natl. geog. 107: 473 (col.) Ap '55.

——, blind (seeing-eye dog). Natl. geog. 114: 206 Aug '58.

——, Brazil (laborer). Natl. geog. 117: 710, 719 (part col.) May '60.

——, British. Holiday 23: 147 (col.) Feb '58; 24: 120 (col.) Sept '58.

——, British Guiana (animals). Natl. geog. 111: 852-74 Je '57.

——, Caribbean (comic). Holiday 15: 127 Je '54.

——, Caribbean (playing guitar). Holiday 25: 110 (col.) May '59.

——, carnival (on stilts). Natl. geog. 109: 215 (col.) Feb '56.

——, Ceylon (boat, silhouette). Holiday 28: 133 Oct '60.

——, chef (head, comic). Holiday 14: 28 Jl '53.

——, Chile (head). Natl. geog. 117: 184 (col.) Feb '60.

——, Chile (sheep pen). Natl. geog. 108: 763 (col.) Dec '55.

——, China (head). Natl. geog. 109: 281 (col.) Feb '56.

——, China (old). Natl. geog. 118: 208, 212 (col.) Aug '60.

——, China (seated). Amer. heri., vol. 6 no. 2 p. 17 (winter '55).

——, Chinese. See also Chinese man.

——, Colonial. Holiday 14: 137 Oct '53.

——, Colonial (antique toy). Amer. heri., vol. 10 no. 1 back cover (col.) (Dec '58).

——, Colonial (at table). Amer. heri., vol. 4 no. 2 p. 34 (winter '53).

——, Colonial (head). Holiday 28: 72 Aug '60. 198 Oct '60.

——, Colonial (horseback). Brooks: Growth of a nation, p. 76.

——, Colonial (horseback, running). Amer. heri. vol., 8 no. 2 p. 69 (Feb '57).

——, Colonial (silhouette). Travel 104: 4 Nov '55; 105: 6 Jan '56.

——, Colonial (street cleaner, cartoon). Travel 106: 56 Aug '56.

——, cowboy (cartoon). Holiday 14: 11 Oct '53.

——, Crete (basket of grapes). Natl. geog. 114: 750 (col.) Dec '58.

——, Denmark (seated). Holiday 27: 8 Mar '60.

——, Dutch Holiday 23: 56 Jan '58. Natl. geog. 98: 755, 759 (col.) Dec '50.

——, Egypt (climbing tree). Natl. geog. 108: 633 (col.) Nov '55.

——, Egypt (head). Holiday 27: 129 Mar '60.

——, Egypt (head, wood painting). Praeg. pict. ency., p. 161 (col.).

——, Egypt (horse). Natl. geog. 106: 767 Dec '54.

——, England (guard on horse). Holiday 16: 28 (col.) Jl '54.

——, England (marking swan). Natl. geog. 114: 84 Jl '58.

——, Eskimo (dancing). Natl. geog. 109: 772 (col.) Je '56.

——, Fiji (dancer). Natl. geog. 107: 126 (col.) Jan '55.

——, Finland. Holiday 22: 105 Dec '57.

——, Formosa (coal carrier). Natl. geog. 111: 333 Mar '57.

——, Formosa (tea baskets on pole). Natl. geog. 107: 581 Ap '55.

——, France (farmer). Natl. geog. 100: 27 (col.) Jl '51.

——, Georgian (1700's). Natl. geog. 113: 262 (col.) Feb '58.

——, Germany. Holiday 25: 50 (col.), 60-1 May '59.

——, Greece. Natl. geog. 114: 757 Dec '58.

——, gweducs. Natl. geog. 117: 456 (col.) Ap '60.

——, Hindu (on crutches). Natl. geog. 110: 528 Oct '56.

——, hunter (head). Holiday 14: 23 Nov '53.

——, India (bowing, comic). Holiday 27: 3 Feb '60.

——, India (cobra). Con. 133: XXXVII May '54.

——, India (playing flute). Natl. geog. 98: 453 (col.) Oct '50.

——, India (playing musical instrument, Bombay). Travel 113: 10 May '60.

——, India (with carpet). Holiday 28: 33 Nov '60.

——, Indonesia (rice field). Natl. geog. 99: 35 (col.) Jan '51.

——, Iran (blows trumpet). Natl. geog. 101: 806 Je '52.

——, Iran (pack mule). Natl. geog. 101: 820 (col.) Je '52.

——, Iraq (climbing date tree). Natl. geog. 114: 479 (col.) Oct '58.

——, Iraq (donkey). Natl. geog. 114: 471 (col.) Oct '58.

man, Irish. Holiday 21: 21 (col.) Jan '57.

——, Ischia (playing guitar). Natl. geog. 105: 550 Ap '54.

——, Ischia (singing). Natl. geog. 105: 535 (col.) Ap '54.

——, Italy. Holiday 27: 157 (col.) Ap '60.

man, Italy (dinner table). Natl. geog. 116: 487, 507 (col.) Oct '59.

——, Italy (wood carver). Natl. geog. 116: 494 (col.) Oct '59.

——, Jamaica (cartoon). Holiday 9: 99 (col.) Mar '51.

——, Jamaica (donkey). Holiday 24: 122 (col.) Aug '58.

——, Japanese. See Japanese man.

——, Java (plowing rice field). Natl. geog. 108: 368-9 (col.) Sept '55.

——, Kashgai (camels). Natl. geog. 101: 828 (col.) Je '52.

——, Kashgai (horse). Natl. geog. 101: 832 Je '52.

——, Kazaph (horseback). Natl. geog. 106: 628 (col.) Nov '54.

——, Ladakh. (seated). Natl. geog. 99: 618 (col.) May '51.

——, Laos (head, turban). Natl. geog. 117: 56 (col.) Jan '60.

——, Laos (plowing ox). Natl. geog. 117: 54-5 (col.) Jan '60.

——, Malaya (blowing horn). Natl. geog. 103: 222 (col.) Feb '53.

——, Mexico (cock fight). Holiday 24: 109 Aug '58.

——, Mexico (horseback). Holiday 24: 39 (col.) Oct '58.

——, Morocco. Disney: People & places, p. 83-98 (col.).
Natl. geog. 107: 181 (col.) Feb '55.

——, Moslem (arms shop). Natl. geog. 100: 163 (col.) Aug '51.

——, mountain (laughing). Natl. geog. 113: 865 Je '58.

—— (mountain (rocking chair). Natl. geog. 113: 870 Je '58.

——, mountain (seated). Holiday 27: 185 May '60.

——, Nepal (child on back). Natl. geog. 117: 366 (col.) Mar '60.

——, Nigeria. Natl. geog. 110: 348 (col.) Sept '56.

——, Nigeria (blowing trumpet). Natl. geog. 116: 251 Aug '59.

——, Nigeria (cacao fruit tree). Natl. geog. 110: 357 (col.) Sept '56.

——, Nigeria (camel). Natl. geog. 110: 355 Sept '56.

——, Nigeria (donkey pack). Natl. geog. 104: 149, 153 (col.) Aug '53.

man, occult number diagram of. See occult number diagram of man (sym.).

——, older (head, laughing). Holiday 11: 82 (col.) May '52.

——, older (seated). Amer. heri., vol. 7 no. 6 p. 21 (Oct '56); vol. 8 no. 1 p. 33 (Dec '56).
Natl. geog. 110: 501 (col.) Oct '56.

——, older (white beard, painting). Natl. geog. 110: 733 (col.) Dec '56.

——, white beard, reading in synagogue). Natl. geog. 110: 718 (col.) Dec '56.

——, older (white hair). Natl. geog. 112: 760 (col.) Dec '57.

——, Pakistan (serving at table). Natl. geog. 107: 411 (col.) Mar '55.

——, Peru. Holiday 27: 46 Mar '60.

——, Peru (llama). Natl. geog. 98: 429, 445 (col.) Oct '50.

——, pilgrim. Amer. heri., vol. 8 no. 6 p. 86 (Oct '57).

——, policeman (shooting). Holiday 26: 8 Sept '59.

——, Puerto Rico. Natl. geog. 99: 431 (col.) Ap '51.

——, Puerto Rico (drummer). Holiday 28: 107 Oct '60.

——, ranch (horseback, roundup). Horan: Pict. hist. of wild west, p. 91 94-5, 98-9, 107.

——, Russia (grain field). Natl. geog. 116: 392 (col.) Sept '59.

——, Russia (seated). Amer. heri., vol. 11 no. 5 p. 67 (Aug '60).

——, Samoa (seated). Travel 101: 33 Jan '54.

——, Sardinia. Disney: People & places p. 69-82 (col.).

——, Scotland. Holiday 16: 124 (col.) Dec '54; 19: 119, 125 Jan '56; 23: inside back cover (col.) Je '58; 24: 12 (col.) Jl '58; 25: 131 (col.) Jan '59; 26: 132 (col.) Sept '59.

——, Scotland (caber tossing). Natl. geog. 110: 18 (col.) Jl '56.

——, Scotland (head). Holiday 27: 161 Jan '60.

——, Scotland (playing bagpipe). Holiday 15: 29 Jan '54.

——, Scotland (walking). Holiday 14: 10 (col.) Nov '53, 170 (col.) Dec '53.

——, Scotland (weight thrower). Natl. geog. 110: 17 (col.) Jl '56.

——, serving (cartoon). Holiday 17: 115 Jan '55.

——, Sicily. (painting wheel). Natl. geog. 107: 14 (col.) Jan '55.

——, Sicily (seaside). Natl. geog. 107: 5 (col.) Jan '55.

——, Spain (head). Holiday 28: 27 Oct '60.

——, Spain (head, hat). Holiday 28: 210 Dec '60.

——, Spain (horseback). Holiday 24: 110 (col.) Dec '58.

——, Spain (pack, loaded). Natl. geog. 111: 627 May '57.

——, stone-age. See Tiwi tribesmen (Australia).

——, Texas (donkey). Holiday 20: 37 Oct '56.

——, Tristan (making rope). Natl. geog. 97: 110 (col.) Jan '50.

——, Turkey. Holiday 19: 81 (col.) May '56.

——, Turkey (boatman). Natl. geog. 109: 74 (col.) Jan '56.

——, Turkey (horseback). Con. 140: 111 Nov '57.

——, Tyrol. Natl. geog. 99: 753 (col.) Je '51.

——, Uganda (carrying products on pole). Natl. geog. 106: 132 (col.) Dec '54.

——, Wai Wai Indian (fish). Natl. geog. 107: 336 (col.) Mar '55.

——, West Indies (beating drum). Holiday 13: 18 Jan '53.

——, western. Durant: Pict. hist of Amer. circus, p. 140 (col.), 222.
Holiday 19: 19 (col.) Je '56; 21: 98 (col.)

May '57; 23: 121 Je '58; 24: 128 Dec '58; 27: 125 (col.) Mar '60.

Travel 105: inside back cover Feb '56; 107: back cover Jan '57.

——, western ("bad man"). Amer. heri., vol. 6 no. 1 p. 59 (fall '54).

——, western (bucking horse). Amer. heri., vol. 6 no. 1 p. 38-9 (fall '54).

Holiday 14: 16 Jl '53; 27: 27 May '60, 27 Je '60.

——, western (bulldoging steer). Natl. geog. 97: 694 Je '50.

——, western (cart & horse). Holiday 24: 42 (col.) Oct '58.

——, western (comic). Holiday 11: 114 Je '52; 12: 106 Sept '52, 55 Nov '52.

——, western (comic). Holiday 14: 125 Jl '53.

——, western (head, comic). Holiday 10: 95 Oct '51; 21: 149 Ap '57.

——, western (head, laughing). Holiday 10: 169 Dec '51.

——, western (horseback). Amer. heri., vol. 6 no. 5, cover (col.), 109 (Oct '55).

Holiday 13: 30 Feb '53; 19: 107 (col.) Feb '56; 25: 98 Jan '59, 178 Mar '59; 27: 15 (col.) Ap '60.

Horan: Pict. hist. of wild west, p. 192, 209.

Natl. geog. 97: 469, 474 (col.) Ap '50; 101: '57, 60-4 (col.) Jan '52.

Travel 107: back cover Jan '57; 108: 11 Jl '57.

——, western (horseback, buffalo). Natl. geog. 115: 532 (col.) Ap '59.

——, western (on fence). Natl. geog. 113: 622 (col.) May '58.

——, western (relaxing). Holiday 22: 45 Sept '57.

——, western (riding steer). Holiday 14: 85 (col.) Jl '53.

——, western (roping colt). Natl. geog. 97: 734 Je '50.

——, western (roping horses in corral). Travel 110: 60 Aug '58.

——, western (seated). Amer. heri. vol .8 no. 2 p. 9 (Feb '57).

——, western (serving fruit). Holiday 28: 212 Nov '60.

——, western prospector (donkey). Holiday 27: 173 Je '60.

——, Wewak island (head). Int. gr. soc.: Arts . . . p. 183 (col.).

——, Zanzibar (donkey). Natl. geog. 101: 269 (col.) Feb '52.

——, Zulu. Holiday 27: back cover (col.) Ap '60.

man & air stewardess (at car). Holiday 25: 137 (col.) Feb '59.

man & air stewardess (bird). Natl. geog. 108: 397 Sept '55.

man & babies (comic). Holiday 11: 97 Ap '52.

man & baby. Holiday 25: 155 Feb '59.

Travel 102: inside back cover, Aug '54.

—— (comic). Holiday 25: 112 Ap '59.

—— (Indian hammock). Natl. geog. 116: 635 Nov '59.

man & boy. Holiday 14: 59 Oct '53; 19: 24 May '56; 27: 134 Jan '60.

—— (back view). Travel 112: inside cover (col.) Dec '59.

—— (bathing suits, beach). Holiday 26: 6 Jl

'59, 117, inside back cover (col.) Aug '59, 110 Sept '59.

—— (beach). Holiday 25: 127 Feb '59.

—— (book on table). Natl. geog. 113: 733 May '58.

—— (books). Natl. geog. 97: 678 May '50.

—— (cameras). Holiday 21: 156 Mar '57.

—— (comic). Holiday 10: 117 Aug '51, 26: 139 Sept '59.

—— (country store). Amer. heri., vol. 6 no. 1 p. 25 (fall '54).

—— (dog). Natl. geog. 115: 729 May '59.

—— (engineer on train). Travel 110: 30 Aug. '58.

—— (fishing) . Holiday 21: 118 (col.) Je '57; 24: 21 (col.) Nov '58; 25: 162 May '59; 27: 200 Ap '60, 109 (col.) Je '60.

—— (fishing, boat). Travel 108: 33 Nov '57; 110: 45 Aug '58.

—— (glass factory). Travel 110: 30 Sept '58.

—— (heads). Holiday 27: 16 May '60.

—— (heads, laughing). Holiday 19: 79 Jan '56.

—— (horseback). Holiday 26: 16 Nov '59.

—— (in auto). Holiday 11: 100 (col.) May '52; 19: 90 (col.) Jan '56.

—— (in barn). Amer. heri., vol. 9 no. 1 p. 18 (col.) (Dec '57).

—— (inspect undersea life). Natl. geog. 107: 807 (col.) Je '55.

—— (Japanese rooster). Natl. geog. 104: 639 (col.) Nov '53.

—— (laughing). Holiday 12: 77 Nov '52, 161 (col.) Dec '52.

—— (lily pool). Natl. geog. 108: 364 (col.) Sept '55.

—— (on boat). Holiday 27: 134 (col.) Mar '60, 55 (col.) Ap '60.

—— (pajamas). Holiday 10: 128 (col.) Oct '51; 28: 118 Sept '60.

—— (porcupine). Natl. geog. 98: 260 (col.) Aug '50.

—— (Santa Claus). Holiday 10: 61 Dec '51.

—— (seated). Holiday 14: inside cover Nov '53.

—— (snow). Holiday 20: 44 (col.) Dec '56.

—— (sport clothes alike). Holiday 12: 161 col.) Dec '52.

—— (swimming trunks). Holiday 27: 171 (col.) May '60.

—— (talking). Holiday 20: 121 Nov '56.

—— (toy train). Holiday 28: 196 Oct '60, 116 (col.) Nov '60.

—— (trap crayfish). Natl. geog. 113: 559 (col.) Ap '58.

—— (western horseback). Holiday 22: 17 Nov '57.

—— (winter). Amer. heri., vol. 9 no. 1 p. 18 (col.) (Dec '57).

Holiday 18: 79 (col.) Oct '55.

—— (winter coat). Holiday 10: 182 Dec '51; 12: 77 Nov '52.

—— (with spears). Travel 101: 43 Jan '54.

——, Greek (500 B.C.). Int. gr. soc.: Arts . . . p. 31 (col.).

man & boys. Holiday 14: 59 Oct '53; 19: 24 May '56.

—— (baseball game). Holiday 21: 106 Je '57.

—— (driving oxen). Disney: People & places, p. 79 (col.).

—— (sportsmen). Holiday 23: 141 Je '58.

man & bride (heads). Holiday 24: 88 Oct '58, 115 Nov '58.
man & child. Holiday 11: 54 Ap '52; 12: 76 (col.) Dec '52; 21: 54 Feb '57; 25: 116: May '59; 28: 65 Nov '60, 172 (col.) Dec '60.
—— **(Afghan, digging canal).** Natl. geog. 117: 79 (col.) Jan '60.
—— **(beach combing).** Natl. geog. 104: 586, 590 (col.) Nov '53.
—— **(Belgian Congo).** Natl. geog. 108: 779 Dec '55.
—— **(bird).** Natl. geog. 103: 86 (col.) Jan '53.
—— **(boat, crab hunting).** Holiday 10: 37 Nov '51.
—— **(carosel).** Holiday 25: 21 (col.) Ap '59.
—— **(feeding squirrel).** Natl. geog. 118: 556 (col.) Oct '60.
—— **(fishing).** Holiday 19: 124 (col.) Feb '56.
—— **(fishing boat).** Holiday 11: 138 (col.) Je '52.
—— **(flying kite).** Holiday 25: 107 (col.) Mar '59.
—— **(Hawaii, plants).** Natl. geog. 115: 808 (col.) Je '59.
—— **(heads).** Holiday 18: 55 Nov '55.
—— **(horseback).** Holiday 18: 33 Sept '55; 22: 65 Nov '57.
—— **(hugging).** Holiday 28: 198 Nov '60.
—— **(in car, comic).** Travel 113: 44 Ap '60.
—— **(loaded pony).** Natl. geog. 97: 88 (col.) Jan '50.
—— **(Norway).** Natl. geog. 111: 103 (col.) Jan '57.
—— **(piano).** Holiday 26: 49 Dec '59.
—— **(seated).** Travel 101: back cover Je '54.
—— **(snow drifts).** Natl. geog. 108: 86 (col.) Jl '55.
—— **(study insects).** Natl. geog. 102: 240 (col.) Aug '52.
—— **(traveler, comic).** Holiday 23: 7 (col.) Ap '58.
—— **(western, horse).** Holiday 21: 38 (col.) Mar '57.
—— **(wheel chair).** Travel 104: 52 Aug '55.
man & children. Natl. geog. 97: 179 Feb '50. Natl. geog. 105: 185 (col.) Feb '54.
—— **(antique gun shop).** Natl. geog. 114: 120 (col.) Jl '58.
—— **(aquatic nursery).** Natl. geog. 100: 221 (col.) Aug '51.
—— **(auto).** Holiday 18: 24 (col.) Nov '55.
—— **(bathing suits).** Holiday 10: 100 Aug '51; 12: 88 Aug '52.
—— **(beach, comic).** Holiday 23: 12-3 Je '58.
—— **(camping).** Natl. geog. 109: 5, 8 (col.) Jan '56.
—— **(comic).** Holiday 19: 126 Je '56.
—— **(Hawaii, coral).** Natl. geog. 116 513 (col.) Oct '59.
—— **(cutting cheese).** Travel 114: 55 Aug '60.
—— **(dog, car).** Holiday 25: 142 Mar '59.
—— **(dog, snow).** Natl. geog. 99: 551 Ap '51.
—— **(fishing).** Holiday 21: 134 (col.) Feb '57.
—— **(forest).** Natl. geog. 108: 103, 108 (col.) Jl '55.
—— **(Greenland).** Natl. geog. 111: 532 (col.) Ap '57.
—— **(in buggy).** Natl. geog. 98: 338-41 (col.) Sept '50.

—— **(nature study).** Natl. geog. 106: 647, 650, 668 (part col.) Nov '54.
—— **(nomads).** Natl. geog. 117: 80 (col.) Jan '60.
—— **(pets).** Holiday 22: 108 Nov '57.
—— **(pick ferns in woods).** Natl. geog. 99: 601 (col.) May '51.
—— **(playing, beach).** Holiday 27: 44 May '60.
—— **(roadside guide).** Natl. geog. 110: 441 (col.) Oct '56.
—— **(seated, back view, waterfall).** Natl. geog. 109: 19 (col.) Jan '56.
—— **(seated on stone steps).** Natl. geog. 110: 31 (col.) Jl '56.
—— **(tide water).** Natl. geog. 112: 167 (col.) Aug '57.
—— **(wood carver, Austria).** Natl. geog. 118: 255 (col.) Aug '60.
man & girl. Holiday 21: 100 Feb '57; 23: 123 (col.) Je '58; 24: 100 Sept '58, 117 Dec '58; 25: 95 (col.) Jan '59, 110 Feb '59, 166 May '59; 27: 1, 90, 145 (col.) Jan '60, 29, 209, 216 (col.) May '60; 28: 180 (col.) Oct '60, 21 Nov '60, 142 Dec '60.
—— **(at auto).** Holiday 25: 10 (col.) Feb '59, 10 (col.) May '59, 127 Je '59; 26: inside back cover (col.) Aug '59; 27: 141 May '60; 28: 71 (col.) Sept '60, 2 (col.) Nov '60.
—— **(at table).** Holiday 23: 15 (col.) Feb '58; 24: 157 Oct '58; 25: 142 Feb '59; 27: 13 Je '60; 28: 89 Aug '60, 218 Nov '60.
—— **(at table, lovers).** Holiday 22: 96, 127 Nov '57.
—— **(at tea cart).** Holiday 24: 30 (col.) Oct '58.
—— **(back view).** Holiday 19: 123 Mar '56.
—— **(back view, sand).** Natl. geog 98: 163 (col.) Aug '50.
—— **(back view, toboggans).** Natl. geog. 113: 70-1 (col.) Jan '58.
—— **(balcony).** Natl. geog. 103: 292 (col.) May '53.
—— **(balcony, comic).** Holiday 22: 129 Sept '57, 177 Oct '57, 162 Nov '57.
—— **(bathing suits).** Holiday 18: 37, 136 (col.) Dec '55; 21: 181 (col.) Ap '57, 48, 152 (col.) May '57; 27: 177 (col.) Je '60.
—— **(bathing beach).** Travel 111: 37, 41 Jan '59.
—— **(bathing beach, ball).** Holiday 28: 102 (col.) Sept '60.
—— **(bathing beach, lunch).** Holiday 24: 90 (col.) Sept '58.
—— **(bathing beach, moonlight).** Holiday 19: inside cover (col.) Feb '56.
—— **(bathing suits, beach).** Holiday 10: 58 Jl '51, 7 (col.) Nov '51; 11: 7 (col.) Jan '52; 12: 21 (col.) Aug '52; 21: 137 (col.) Feb '57; 24: 110 (col.) Aug '58, 141 (col.) Sept '58, 7 (col.) Nov '58, 55 (col.) Dec '58; 25: 40 (col.) Mar '59, 204 May '59, 101, 169 (col.), 188-9 Je '59; 26: 183 Oct '59, 53 (col.) Dec '59; 27: 31 Jan '60, 56 Ap '60, 48 May '60; 28: 141 (col.) Oct '60, 126 (col.) Nov '60.
Travel 114: 38 Aug '60.
—— **(bathing suits, 1888).** Travel 110: 60 Sept '58.
—— **(bathing suits, in water).** Amer. heri., vol. 1 no. 4 p. 68 (summer '50).

Holiday 12: 125 (col.) Dec '52.
—— (bathing suits, waterfalls). Holiday 27: 47 (col.) Je '60.
—— (beach). Holiday 27: 182 Feb '60, 15, 47, 189 (col.) Mar '60; 28: back cover (col.) Dec '60.
—— (beach chair). Holiday 18: 185 Dec '55.
—— (beach, running). Holiday 19: 121 May '56.
—— (beer glass). Holiday 21: 25 (col.) May '57.
—— (bicycle). Holiday 12: 69 (col.) Jl '52; 28: 211 Nov '60.
—— (boat). Holiday 14: 80 (col.) Jl '53; 19: 66 (col.) May '56; 25: 187 (col.) Mar '59; 26: 116 Jl '59; 27: 170-1 (col.) Mar '60.
—— (boat, evening). Holiday 12: 87 (col.) Sept '52.
—— (boat, fishing). Holiday 28: 177 (col.) Oct '60.
—— (boat deck, night). Holiday 23: 127 (col.) Jan '58.
—— (candle light). Holiday 27: 47 (col.) Je '60.
—— (canoe). Holiday 21: 119 Mar '57.
—— (chair lift). Natl. geog. 114: 148 (col.) Aug '58.
—— (chaise lounge). Holiday 11: 119 Je '52.
—— (Chinese dinner). Natl. geog. 110: 216 (col.) Aug '56.
—— (Christmas singing). Holiday 10: 40 (col.) Dec '51.
—— (Coca Cola). Natl. geog. 115: 788 (col.) Je '59.
—— (cocktail) Holiday 24: 169, 184 Nov '58, 99, 145 Dec '58; 25: 32 Feb '59, 174 Ap '59; 26: 84 (col.) Aug '59, 179 (col.) Dec '59; 28: 46 (col.) Oct '60, 136 (col.) Dec '60.
—— (cocktail counter). Holiday 26: 45 (col.) Oct '59.
—— (cocktail table). Holiday 24: 126 (col.) Dec '58; 27: 118 (col.) Feb '60, 63, 123 (col.) Ap '60.
—— (coffee table). Holiday 28: 186 Oct '60.
—— (colonial). Natl. geog. 118: 707 (col.) Nov '60.
—— (comic). Holiday 11: 134 May '52; 23: 109 Je '58; 24: 140 Jl '58; 26: 35 Dec '59.
—— (courtship). Holiday 21: 60-1 Mar '57.
—— (dancing). Holiday 10: 51, 76 (col.) Dec '51; 11: 96, 118 Jan '52, 39 (col.) Feb '52; 21: 118 (col.) Je '57; 27: 29 (col.) Feb '60, 125 (col.) Mar '60; 28: 150 Oct '60.
—— (dancing, comic). Holiday 18: 67 Aug '55, 121 Sept '55; 21: 126 Jan '57.
—— (dancing, Greek). Holiday 20: 31 Dec '56.
—— (drinking cocktail). Holiday 23: inside back cover (col.) Jan '58.
—— (eel hunters, Bali). Natl. geog. 116: 807 (col.) Dec '59.
—— (eloping, comic). Holiday 11: 161 May '52.
—— (evening dress). Holiday 18: 71 (col.) Nov '55; 21: 27 (col.) Je '57; 22: 33 (col.) Dec '57; 26: 136 Dec '59; 27: 103 (col.) Je '60; 28: 65 Dec '60.
—— (fishing). Holiday 26: 181 Oct '59; 28: 150 Oct '60.
—— (flower garden). Holiday 25: 123 (col.) Ap '59.

Natl. geog. 98: 191 (col.) Aug '50.
—— (football game). Holiday 12: 12 Nov '52.
—— (gift). Holiday 18: 183 Dec '55.
—— (guitar, laughing). Holiday 28: 199 (col.) Oct '60.
—— (happy). Holiday 10: 42 (col.) Dec '51.
—— (harvesting grapes). Holiday 27: 61 Ap '60.
—— (Hawaiian). Holiday 25: 86 (col.) Feb '59.
—— (heads). Holiday 20: 151 Nov '56; 24: 35, 47 (col.) Nov '58, 133 (col.), 174 Dec '58; 25: 61 May '59, 175 Je '59.
Natl. geog. 97: 564 (col.) May '50.
—— (heads, Austria). Natl. geog. 115: 211 (col.) Feb '59.
—— (heads, cocktail). Holiday 25: 148 Feb '59; 27: 205 May '60, 128 Je '60; 28: 144 Jl '60.
—— (heads, flirting). Holiday 10: 29 (col.) Dec '51.
—— (heads, hidden under umbrella). Holiday 28: 97 Aug '60.
—— (heads, in bubble). Holiday 26: 113 Dec '59.
—— (heads, laughing). Holiday 10: 12 Aug '51, 120 Nov '51, 89 (col.) Dec '51; 11: 5 (col.) Mar '52, 77 (col.) Ap '52; 12: 88 Sept '52; 18: 164 Dec '55; 21: 14, 137 Mar '57, 121 May '57, 31, 174 Je '57; 24: 93 Aug '58, 190 Nov '58; 27: 184, 186 Mar '60, 138 Ap '60, 30, 160 May '60, 128 Je '60; 28: 96 Jl '60.
—— (heads, lovers). Holiday 27: 106 Jan '60; 28: 166, 196 Oct '60, 5 (col.) Nov '60.
—— (heads, shadow). Holiday 28: 85 Aug '60, 199 Nov '60.
—— (heads, smoking). Holiday 11: 84 (col.) Ap '52.
—— (heads, western). Holiday 27: 97 Mar '60.
—— (holding hands). Holiday 12: 77 Sept '52.
Natl. geog. 100: 62, 64 (col.) Jl '51.
—— (horseback). Holiday 21: 92 Jan '57; 23: 49 Mar '58; 25: 28 Feb '59.
Natl. geog. 105: 780 (col.) Je '54.
Travel 114: 22 Jl '60.
—— (horses, dogs). Natl. geog. 113: 36 (col.) Jan '58.
—— (hotel lobby). Holiday 11: 123 (col.) May '52.
—— (hugging). Holiday 10: 6 Jl '51; 12: 15 Nov '52; 23: 125 Je '58; 24: 91 Jl '58, 24 Sept '58; 25: 96 Jan '59.
—— (in car). Holiday 23: 7 (col.) Jan 58.
—— (in heart of fruit). Holiday 13: 85 (col.) Feb '53.
—— (in old plane). Amer. heri., vol. 10 no. 4 p. 59 (col.) (Je '59).
—— (Jamaica). Holiday 24: 122 (col.) Aug '58.
—— (kissing). Holiday 12: 93 Dec '52; 25: 21 (col.) Jan '59; 27: 185 May '60, 3 Je '60.
—— (kissing, balcony scene). Holiday 12: inside cover (col.) Oct '52.
—— (laughing). Holiday 18: 15 Oct '55; 21: 32-3 Jan '57, 132 Feb '57, 148 Ap '57.
—— (lovers, cocktail table). Holiday 28: 27 col.) Nov '60.
—— (lovers, moonlight, park bench). Holiday 22: 60 Nov '57.
—— (Mexican dancer). Holiday 27: 138 Jan '60.

man & girl (movie projector). Holiday 28: 83 (col.) Sept '60.
—— (musical instruments). Natl. geog. 107: 518 (col.) Ap '55.
—— (not speaking). Amer. heri. vol. 9 no. 1 p. 89 (Dec '57).
—— (on ship). Holiday 26: 119 (col.) Jl '59, 26 (col.) Sept '59; 27: 131 Feb '60; 28: 36, 176 (col.) Oct '60.
—— (on stairway). Holiday 27: 31 (col.) Ap '60.
—— (outdoor cooking). Holiday 26: 79 Aug '59.
—— (outdoor table). Holiday 11: 25 (col.) Je '52; 26: 13 (col.) Jl '59.
—— (outdoors). Holiday 12: 71 col.) Oct '52.
—— (park). Holiday 27: 7 (col.) Mar '60.
—— (party). Holiday 19: 79 May '56.
—— (party, evening). Holiday 18: 28 Oct '55.
—— (party, festival). Holiday 24: 8 Jl '58.
—— (party table). Holiday 23: 191 Je '58.
—— (picnic). Holiday 10: 57 Jl '51.
—— (picnic, beach). Holiday 28: 88 (col.) Jl '60.
—— (playing). Holiday 11: 17 (col.) Feb '52.
—— (Rhodes harbor). Natl. geog. 103: 367 (col.) Mar '53.
—— (rickshaw). Holiday 27: 232 Ap '60.
—— (rocky shore). Holiday 19: 71 (col.) Je '56.
—— ("Romeo & Juliet", comic). Holiday 26: 25 Aug '59.
—— (Romeo, comic). Holiday 27: 40 Feb '60.
—— (rowboat). Holiday 28: 15 (col.) Aug '60.
—— (sailboat). Holiday 27: 121 (col.) Ap '60. Natl. geog. 98: 159 (col.) Aug '50.
—— (seated). Holiday 23: 9 Jan '58.
—— (seated, back view). Natl. geog. 103: 293 (col.) Mar '53.
—— (seated close on beach). Holiday 25: inside cover (col.) Feb '59; 27: 5 (col.) Mar '60; 28: 78 Nov '60.
—— (seated, 18th cent.) Con. 142: XXXIII Dec '58.
—— (seated, evening). Holiday 10: 43 Jl '51.
—— (seated, mt.). Holiday 28: 154 (col.) Oct '60.
—— (seated on floor). Holiday 19: 10 (col.), 11 Jan '56.
—— (seated on grass). Holiday 28: 12 (col.) Nov '60.
—— (seated, whispering). Holiday 28: 199 (col.) Oct '60.
—— (secrets). Holiday 21: 17 Mar '57.
—— (shadow). Holiday 20: 104 Nov '56; 26: 205 (col.) Dec '59; 27: 95 (col.) Jan '60; 28: 180 (col.) Oct '60.
—— (ship). Holiday 21: 128 (col.) Nov '57.
—— (ship deck). Holiday 23: 181 (col.) Je '58; 27: inside back cover (col.) Je '60; 28: 175 (col.) Nov '60.
—— (shipboard game). Holiday 19: 69 (col.) Jan '56.
—— (silhouette). Holiday 28: 20 Oct '60.
—— (smoking). Holiday 24: 12 (col.) Oct '58, 179 (col.) Nov '58.
—— (snow). Natl. geog. 117: 482 (col.) Ap '60.
—— (Spain). Natl. geog. 97: 424-5 (col.) Ap '50.

—— (sporting goods). Holiday 22: 91 (col.) Jl '57.
—— (sportswear). Holiday 11: 76 (col.) Ap '52; 25: 45 Feb '59; 27: 126 (col.) Je '60.
—— (sunflower). Natl. geog. 117: 191 (col.) Feb '60.
—— (sunglasses). Holiday 27: 146 May '60.
—— (swimming). Holiday 20: 193 Dec '56.
—— (swimming, pool on ship). Holiday 27: 28 (col.) Jan '60.
—— (taking pictures). Natl. geog. 102: 579 (col.) Nov '52.
—— (tea table). Holiday 25: 115 (col.) Feb '59, 200 (col.) Ap '59; 27: 58 (col.) Ap '60.
—— (telephoning). Holiday 19: 120 Mar '56.
—— (telescope). Holiday 19: 111 (col.) Mar '56.
—— (tennis). Holiday 18: 9 Jl '55; 19: 74 Feb '56.
—— (train). Holiday 20: 12 Nov '56.
—— (train dome). Holiday 18: 81 Sept '55.
—— (wading). Holiday 25: 155 Feb '59.
—— (water skiing). Holiday 10: 93 Nov '51; 11: 75 Feb '52; 25: 130 May '59.
—— (water skiing, comic). Holiday 25: 190 Je '59.
—— (western). Holiday 10: 155 Nov '51; 14: 139 (col.) Jl '53; 23: 209 Je '58; 25: 147 Feb '59.
—— (western clothes). Natl. geog. 97: 699 Je '50.
—— (western, horse). Holiday 28: 107 Oct '60.
—— (western ranch). Holiday 25: 195 May '59, 7 (col.) Je '59; 27: 207 Mar '60, 194 Je '60.
man & girls. Natl. geog. 100: 717 (col.) Dec '51.
—— (autumn park). Natl. geog. 110: 604 (col.) Nov '56.
—— (bathing beach). Holiday 12: 95 (col.) Oct '52.
—— (bathing in lake). Holiday 21: 4 (col.), 99 Feb '57, 99 (col.) Mar '57.
—— (bathing suits, beach). Holiday 18: 68 (col.) Sept '55.
—— (bathing suits, on ship). Holiday 24: 10, 94, back cover (col.) Nov '58. 29 (col.) Dec '58; 27: 28 (col.) Jan '60.
—— (beach). Holiday 24: 175 (col.) Dec '58; 25: 26 (col.) Feb '59; 26: 2 (col.) Jl '59.
—— (horseback). Holiday 11: 31 (col.) May '52.
—— (lunch). Holiday 24: 23 Aug '58.
—— (picnic, beach). Holiday 10: 20 (col.) Jl '51.
—— (skating, 1880). Amer. heri., vol. 10 no. 2 p. 112 (Feb '59).
—— (skiers resting). Holiday 27: 152 (col.) Jan '60.
—— (western, horseback). Natl. geog. 110: 493 (col.) Oct '56.
man & waitress (comic). Holiday 10: 154 Nov '51.
man & woman. Holiday 11: 104 Ap '52, 34 May '52; 14: 2 Jl '53, 79 (col.) Oct '53, 70, 134 (col.), 165 Nov '53, 105 Dec '53; 18: 140 (col.) Nov '55; 21: 4 (col.), 96 May '57, 46 (col.) Je '57; 23: 23 Jan '58, 109 Feb '58, 116 (col.) Mar '58, 175 (col.) Ap '58, 149 May '58; 25: 175, 185 (col.)

May '59, 17 Je '59; 26: 107 (col.) Jl '59, 111 (col.), 145 Oct '59, 156 (col.) Dec '59; 27: 1, 19, 26 (col.), 39 (col.) Mar '60, 101 (col.) Ap '60, 123 (col.), 147, 190 (col.) May '60, 45 Je '60; 28: 18 (col.) Sept '60, 184 (col.) Oct '60, 150, 208 (col.) Nov '60, 112, 194 (col.) Dec '60.
Natl. geog. 97: 577 (col.) May '50; 98: 87 (col.) Jl '50.
Travel 103: 4 Jan '55; 104: 34 Jl '55, 69 Oct '55; 107: cover Ap '57.

man & woman (airplane). Natl. geog. 117: 75 (col.) Jan '60.
—— **(album).** Natl. geog. 104: 686 Nov '53.
—— **(arguing).** Holiday 11: inside cover (col.) Je '52; 12: 145 (col.) Jl '52.
—— **(artists).** Natl. geog. 113: 773 (col.) Je '58.
—— **(asleep on plane).** Holiday 20: 25 (col.) Dec '56.
—— **(at home).** Holiday 23: 160 Je '58.
—— **(at table).** Holiday 13: 86 (col) Mar '53, 12, 117, 122, 135 (part col.) Ap '53, 25, 93 (col.) May '53; 14: 7, 20, 75 (part col.) Aug '53, 117 (col.) Sept '53, 22 (col.) Oct '53, 28, 126, 170, back cover (part col.) Nov '53; 19: 23 Je '56; 20: 78 Sept '56, 14 Oct '56; 23: 9 Jan '58, 117, 151, 165 (col.) Mar '58, 40 (col.), 48 Ap '58 66, back cover (col.) May '58; 24: 23, 83 (col.) Aug '58, 108 (col.) Sept '58, 77 Oct '58, 206 (col.) Nov '58, 118 (col.), 203 Dec '58; 25: 28 (col.) Jan '59, 70 (col.) Feb '59, 13, 98 (col.) Mar '59, 96, 175 (col.) Ap '59, 134 (col.) May '59, inside back cover (col.) Je '59; 26: 33 (col.) Oct '59, 101 (col.) Nov '59, 157 (col.) Dec '59; 27: 156 Jan '60; 28: 10, 36 (col.) Nov '60, 116, 202 (col.) Dec '60.
Natl. geog. 97: 285 Mar '50.
Travel 111: cover (col.) Mar '59; 113: back cover Mar '60.
—— **(at table, comic).** Holiday 14: 83 Jl '53; 22: 135 (col.) Dec '57.
—— **(at table, 18th cent.).** Con. 142: LVI Dec '58.
—— **(at table, laughing).** Holiday 21: 13 (col.) May '57.
—— **(at table, 1778).** Amer. heri., vol. 10 no. 4 p. 39 (Je '59).
—— **(at window).** Holiday 12: 122 Nov '52.
Natl. geog. 97: 293 (col.) Mar '50.
—— **(auto).** Holiday 10: 121 (col.) Oct '51; 21: 10 (col.) Jan '57; 22: 49 (col.) Sept '57; 23: 119 Mar '58, 5, 140, 172 (part col.) Ap '58, 98 May '58; 24: 5, 23 (col.) Jl '58, 82, 89 Aug '58, 103 (col.) Sept '58, 2 (col.) Oct '58, 5, 49 (col.) Nov '58, 17, 27, 178 (col.) Dec '58; 25: 90 (col.) Jan '59, 17 Mar '59, 161 May '59, 39 Je '59; 26: 83 (col.) Jl '59, 43 Oct '59, 49 Nov '59; 27: inside cover (col.) May '60, 43 (col.) Je '60; 28: 123 Sept '60, 7, 140 (col.) Nov '60, inside cover, 187 (col.) Dec '60.
—— **(baby chimpanzee).** Natl. geog. 117: 826-7 Je '60.
—— **(baby tiger).** Natl. geog. 111: 505 Ap '57.
—— **(back view).** Holiday 10: 25 (col.) Oct '51; 14: 138 Nov '53; 23: 26 (col.) Mar '58, 183 Je '58; 24: 32 Sept '58, 77 Oct

'58; 25: 29 Mar '59; 26: 177 Nov '59.
Natl. geog. 102: 365 (col.) Sept '52.
Travel 104: 41 Oct '55.
—— **(back view, flower garden).** Natl. geog. 106: 744 (col.) Dec '54.
—— **(back view, harbor).** Natl. geog. 108: 192 (col.) Aug '55.
—— **(back view, lake).** Natl. geog. 108: 684 (col.) Nov '55; 110: 448 (col.) Oct '56.
—— **(back view, lake, mts.).** Natl. geog. 109: 602 (col.) May '56.
—— **(back view, ocean).** Natl. geog. 113: 743 (col.) Je '58
—— **(back view, seated, hillside).** Natl. geog. 110: 435 (col.) Oct '56.
—— **(back view, walking).** Natl. geog. 111: 653 (col.), 655 May '57.
—— **(balcony).** Natl. geog. 113: 176 (col.) Feb '58.
—— **(balcony, evening clothes).** Holiday 22: 26 (col.) Nov '57.
—— **(balcony scene).** Holiday 14: 5 (col.) Oct '53.
—— **(ballroom).** Holiday 27: 31 (col.) Feb '60.
—— **(bar).** Travel 114: 37 Aug '60.
—— **(bathing in ocean).** Holiday 21: 109 (col.) May '57.
—— **(bathing suits).** Holiday 11: 164 May '52, 77, 91 (col.) Je '52; 18: 4, 37 (col.) Dec '55; 19: 153 (col.) Mar "56; 20: 58 (col.) Sept '56, 42 (col.) Nov '56, 186 (col.) Dec '56; 21: 4 (col.), 6, 19 Jan '57, 145 (col.) Feb '57, 46 (col.) Mar '57; 22: 65 (col.) Oct '57, 6 Dec '57; 24: 52 (col.) Aug '58; 25: 39, 106 (col.) Ap '59, 207 May '59; 27: 39 (col.) Feb '60, 232 Ap '60.
—— **(bathing suits, beach).** Holiday 27: 194 (col.) Ap 60; 28: 1 Aug '60, 23 (col.) Sept '60.
—— **(bathing suits, beach, lunch).** Holiday 28: 83 (col.) Jl '60.
—— **(bathing suits, boat).** Holiday 18: 118 (col.) Oct '55.
—— **(bathing suits, 1875).** Amer. heri., vol. 5 no. 4 p. 6 (summer '54).
—— **(bathing suits, penguins).** Natl. geog. 115: 696 (col.) May '59.
—— **(bathrobes).** Holiday 20: 208 Dec '56; 24: 188 Nov '58, 227 Dec '58; 26: 244 Dec '59; 28: 226 Dec '60.
—— **(bayou).** Natl. geog. 118: 682 (col.) Nov '60.
—— **(beach).** Holiday 10: 6 Aug '51; 11: 98 (col.) Feb '52; 14: 97 (col.), 115, 117 Jl '53; 21: 184 (col.) Ap '57, 171, 181 (col.) May '57; 22: 28 (col.) Nov '57; 27: 39 (col.), 163 Feb '60, 146 (col.) Mar '60.
Travel 109: 38 May '58; 113: 23 Ap '60.
—— **(beach, bathing).** Travel 114: 49-50 Dec '60.
—— **(beach chairs).** Holiday 13: 14 Jan '53.
—— **(beach, dog).** Holiday 19: 71 (col.) May '56.
—— **(beach, laughing).** Holiday 11: cover (col.) Jan '52; 12: 21 (col.) Aug '52.
—— **(beaver dam).** Natl. geog. 107: 670-6 (col.) May '55.
—— **(beside fountain).** Face of Amer., p. 15 (col.).

man & woman (bicycles). Travel 101: 32 Ap '54.
—— (binoculars). Natl. geog. 106: 588, 595, 602 (col.) Nov '54; 112: 808 Dec '57.
—— (boat). Holiday 11: 23 (col.) May '52.
—— (book case). Natl. geog. 97: 299 Mar '50.
—— (book stall). Holiday 11: 74 (col.) Je '52.
—— (breakfast). Holiday 20: 1 Nov '56.
—— (British caricature). Holiday 16: 11 Jl '54; 23: 123 Ap '58.
—— (building auto). Natl. geog. 115: 739 (col.) Je '59.
—— (building house). Natl. geog. 112: 698 (col.) Nov '57.
—— (buying flowers). Holiday 24: 127 Jl '58; 25: 156 (col.) May '59.
—— (buying leis, Hawaii). Holiday 28: 45 (col.) Nov '60.
—— (cactus toys). Natl. geog. 98: 11 Jl '50.
—— (camera). Holiday 13: 170 May '53.
—— (camp). Natl. geog. 106: 430 Sept '54.
—— (camp fire). Natl. geog. 112: 252 (col.) Aug '57.
—— (canoe). Holiday 10: 26 (col.) Jl 51; 12: cover (col.) Oct '52.
—— (canon). Holiday 14: 161 Nov '53.
—— (capture porcupine). Natl. geog. 98: 255-7 (col.) Aug '50.
—— (Caribbean table). Holiday 27: 106 (col.) Feb '60.
—— (carried by chair bearers, comic). Holiday 25: 181 Ap '59.
—— (cart, horse). Holiday 28: 192 (col.) Oct '60.
—— (castle steps). Natl. geog. 109: 226 (col.) Feb '56.
—— (chaise lounge). Holiday 12: 32 (col.) Jl '52, 82 Aug '52.
—— (chateau, dining table). Holiday 27: 21 (col.) Ap '60.
—— (chess). Holiday 26: 180 (col.) Oct '59; 27: 47 (col.) May '60.
—— (child on mule). Natl. geog. 107: 830 Je '55.
—— (Christmas). Holiday 20: 192 Dec '56; 26: 184 (col.) Dec '59; 28: 153 (col.) Dec '60.
—— (Christmas gift). Holiday 14: 98 Dec '53; 18: 122 Dec '55; 24: 60 (col.) Dec '58.
—— (cigarettes). Holiday 12: 107 (col.) Sept '52, 5 (col.) Oct '52.
—— (climbing hill). Holiday 28: 170 (col.) Oct '60.
—— (climbing mt.). Natl. geog. 108: 117 (col.) Jl '55.
Travel 113: 40 Mar '60.
—— (climbing stairs). Holiday 23: 23 (col.) Mar '58.
—— (coats, blanket wrapping). Holiday 18: 5 (col.) Oct '55.
—— (cocktails). Holiday 18: 86 (col.) Jl '55; 24: 109, 157 Oct '58, 17 Nov '58, 152, 164, 195 (col.), 204 Dec '58; 26: 146, 154 (col.) Oct '59, 145 Nov '59, 138 (col.), 147 Dec '59; 27: 41, 156 (col.) Feb '60, 187 Ap '60, 196 (col.) Je '60; 28: 103 (col.) Jl '60, 98 (col.) Aug '60, 75, 121, 124 (col.) Sept '60, 28 (col.), 175 Oct '60, 153, 195 (col.) Nov '60, 134 (col.) Dec '60.

—— (colonial). Holiday 14: 8 Oct '53; 23: 184 May '58.
Jordan: Hammond's pictorial atlas, 47, 57, 85.
Travel 107: 19 Jan '57.
—— (colonial bake oven). Natl. geog. 111: 600 (col.) May '57.
—— (colonial house int., dogs). Natl. geog. 109: 483 (col.) Ap '56.
—— (comic). Holiday 5: 50 Ap '49, 11, 93, 154 Je '49; 6: 33 Sept '49, 10 (col.), 126, 130 Nov '49; 7: inside cover (col.), 12, 54-5, 87 Jan '50, 16 Feb '50, 16, 58-9, 107, 111 Ap '50; 8: 101 (col.) Dec '50; 10: 20 (col.), 125 Jl '51, 12-3, 21 Aug '51, 4 Sept '51, 145 Oct '51, 73 Dec '51; 11: 23, 83 Feb '52, 81, 89 Mar '52, 129 Ap '52, 158 May '52; 12: 27, 96, 101 Jl '52, 131 Oct '52, 8, 28 Nov '52, 153 Dec '52; 13: 71, 83, 118, 120 Ap '53, 158-9 May '53, 9, 59 Je '53; 14: 122 Oct '53; 19: 8, 24, 83 Jan '56, 126 May '56; 20: 62, 116 Sept '56, 25 Oct '56; 21: 6 Je '57; 22: 14 Jl '57, 9, 30-1, 38-9 Sept '57, inside cover (col.), 125 Nov '57; 26: 127 Jl '59.
—— (complaint, cartoon). Travel 106: inside back cover Sept '56.
—— (cooking). Holiday 21: 5 (col.) Jan '57.
—— (corn field). Natl. geog. 104: 819 (col.) Dec '53.
—— (craftsman). Holiday 19: 127 (col.) Je '56.
—— (Cuban street seller). Holiday 5: 36 (col.) Feb '49.
—— (curtain). Holiday 19: 115 (col.) May '56.
—— (cut grass by hand, Okinawa). Natl. geog. 107: 282 Feb '55.
—— (daguerreotype 1850). Amer. heri., vol. 8 no. 1 p. 58 (Dec '56).
—— (dancing). Holiday 10: 33, 97 Sept '51, 42 (col.) Dec '51; 11: 54 Mar '52; 12: 33, 63, 87 (col.), 113 Sept '52, 125 (col.) Dec '52; 13: 19 (col.) Je '53; 18: 7 (col.) Jl '55, 14 Aug '55, 112 (col.) Sept '55; 19: 68 (col.) Jan '56; 20: 24, 35 (col.) Sept '56, 36 (col.), 74 Nov '56; 23: 64 Jan '58, 76 (col.) Mar '58; 25: 177 (col.) Je '59.
Natl. geog. 99: 576 (col.) May '51.
—— (dancing, comic). Holiday 20: 119 Oct '56.
—— (deck chairs). Holiday 11: 17 Ap '52.
—— (deer head). Holiday 21: 123 Ap '57.
—— (digging for treasure). Natl. geog. 97: 238, 240 (col.) Feb '50.
—— (dinner, comic). Holiday 10: 27 Oct '51.
—— (dinner, evening). Holiday 10: 25 (col.) Sept '51.
—— (dinner on train). Holiday 27: 212 (col.) Ap '60; 28: 10 (col.) Oct '60.
—— (dinner table). Amer. heri., vol. 9 no. 1 p. 90-2 (Dec '57).
Holiday 12: 57 Jl '52, 17 (col.) Sept '52, 65 Oct '52; 19: 17 (col.) Feb '56; 21: 24, 83 (col.) May '57, 153 (col.) Je '57; 22: 24 (col.), 57, 56 (col.) Nov '57; 26: 15 (col.) Jl '59.
Natl. geog. 103: 290 (col.) Mar '53; 110: 48 (col.) Jl '56.

man & woman (dinner table, beach). Natl. geog. 118: 645 (col.) Nov '60.

—— (dinner table, laughing). Holiday 19: 17 Mar '56.

—— (display Dutch food). Natl. geog. 99: 763 (col.) Dec '50.

—— (dogs). Holiday 8: 69 (col.) Dec '50; 27: 55 (col.) May '60.

—— (dog at fireplace). Natl. geog. 105: 445, 459 (col.) Ap '54.

—— (drawing room). Holiday 27: 174 (col.) Je '60.

—— (drinks). Natl. geog. 113: 324 (col.) Mar '58.

—— (eating at table). Holiday 13: 56 (col.) Jan '53, 86 (col.) Feb '53.
Natl. geog. 104: 816 (col.) Dec '53.
Travel 103: 10 Je '55.

—— (eating on boat). Holiday 27: 38 (col.) Feb '60, 145 (col.) May '60.

—— (eating on plane). Holiday 27: 153 (col.) Ap '60.

—— (elephant). Natl. geog. 111: 522 Ap '57.

—— (evening clothes). Holiday 10: 20 (col.) Oct '51, 110 (col.) Nov '51; 11: 130 (col.) May '52; 14: 35 (col.) Dec '53; 18: 41 (col.) Sept '55; 19: 15 (col.) Je '56; 23: 32 (col.) Feb '58, 2 (col.) May '58; 24: 31 (col.) Sept '58, 38 Nov '58; 25: 5 (col.) Jan '59; 26: 83 (col.) Jl '59, 18, 149 (col.) Dec '59; 27: 165 (col.) Feb '60.

—— (examine log cabin). Travel 109: 40 Je '58.

—— (examine shells). Natl. geog. 107: 429 Mar '55.

—— (farm storehouse). Natl. geog. 111: 639 (col.) May '57.

—— (feeding ducks). Holiday 27: 131 (col.) Jan '60.

—— (find shells & fish in sea). Natl. geog. 111: 2-48 (part col.) Jan '57.

—— (fireplace). Natl. geog. 97: 289 (col.) Mar '50.

—— (fish). Holiday 27: 111 (col.) Feb '60, 125 (col.) Mar '60.
Travel 108: 19-21 Dec '57.

—— (fishermen). Travel 112: 43 Sept '59.

—— (fishing). Holiday 25: 101 (col.) Ap '59; 26: 80 Sept '59; 27: 205 Mar '60.
Travel 105: 21 May '56.

—— (fishing, boat). Holiday 21: 4 (col.) Feb '57.

—— (fishing, standing in water). Holiday 12: 20 (col.) Jl '52.

—— (fishing). See also boat (man, woman fishing).

—— (flower garden). Natl. geog. 107: 192 (col.) Feb '55.

—— (flower stand). Holiday 23: 47 Je '58; 27: 2 (col.) Ap '60; 28: 133 Sept '60.

—— (food cooked). Holiday 19: 143 (col.) Mar '56.

—— (forest). Natl. geog. 108: 526 (col.) Oct '55; 113: 631 (col.) May '58.

—— (fossils). Natl. geog. 118: 100 (col.) Jl '60.

—— (fruit & lobster market). Natl. geog. 105: 211 (col.) Feb '54.

—— (gaming table). Holiday 20: 92 Nov '56; 27: 55 (col.) Feb '60.

—— (gesturing). Holiday 18: 152 Dec '55.

—— (getting furniture). Travel 106: inside cover Oct '56; 107: inside back cover Jan '57.

—— (giant yuccas). Natl. geog. 113: 640 (col.) May '58.

—— (gift). Holiday 22: 54 Dec '57.

—— (going up steps). Holiday 23: 37 (col.) Ap '58.

—— (gold-rush 49'ers). Natl. geog. 105: 762 (col.) Je '54.

—— (golfing). Holiday 13: 15 (col.) May '53; 14: 115 (col.) Aug '53.

—— (gondola). Holiday 28: 217 Nov '60.

—— (gondola, comic). Holiday 28: 96 Aug '60.

—— (gothic type). Brooks: Growth of a nation, p. 237.

—— (greenhouse). Natl. geog. 107: 465 (col.) Ap '55.

—— (greyhounds). Natl. geog. 98: 180 (col.) Aug '50.

—— (grocery bags). Holiday 12: 85 Sept '52.

—— (grotto). Natl. geog. 113: 629 (col.) May '58.

—— (hanging pictures). Holiday 25: 130 Jan '59.

—— (happy). Holiday 23: 167 Je '58.

—— (harvest grapes). Holiday 28: 159 (col.) Nov '60.

—— (heads). Holiday 13: 15 Feb '53, 12 (col.) May '53, 119 (col.) Je '53; 14: 2-3, 66 (col.) Jl '53, 25 Sept '53, 28, 97, 123 (col.) Oct '53; 18: 126 Sept '55, 75 Oct '55; 19: 11 Feb '56, 90 Je '56; 20: 71 Aug '56, 149, 153 Nov '56; 25: 139 Feb '59, 154 Mar '59, 183, 198 Ap '59 32 May '59, 170 Je '59; 26: 21 Sept '59, 191 Oct '59, 122 Nov '59, 5 Dec '59; 27: 24 Ap '60, 188, 236 May '60, 100 (col.) Je '60; 28: 6 Aug '60, 130 Sept '60, 155, 201 Dec '60.
Travel 109: back cover Mar '58, 51 Ap '58, 8 May '58; 111: 7 Je '59; 113: 17 Je '60.

—— (heads, backview). Holiday 21: 39 Mar '59.

—— (heads, buying jewelry). Holiday 11: 115 (col.) May '52.

—— (heads, cocktails). Holiday 11: 23 Feb '52; 24: 40 Nov '58; 25: 35 Mar '59, 161 May '59, 40 (col.) Je '59; 28: 71 (col.) Aug '60.

—— (heads, comic). Holiday 11: 96 May '52; 14: 149 Dec '53; 18: 101 Aug '55; 19: 125 Mar '56.

—— (heads, cowfish). Natl. geog. 115: 138 (col.) Jan '59.

—— (heads, evening dress). Holiday 10: 15 (col.) Jl '51, 20 Dec '51; 19: 113 (col.) Feb '56.

—— (heads, eyeglasses). Holiday 10: 118 Jl '51, 74 (col.) Nov '51; 12: 88 Sept '52; 19: 86 (col.) May '56, 24 (col.) Je '56.

—— (heads, forest). Natl. geog. 108: 98-9 (col.) Jl '55.

man & woman (heads, gift). Holiday 26: 154 (col.) Nov '56.
—— (heads, happy). Holiday 27: 166 Ap '60.
—— (heads, hugging). Holiday 11: 80 Feb '52, 82 (col.) Je '52.
—— (heads, in bubble). Holiday 26: 147 Nov '59.
—— (heads, kissing). Holiday 10: 27 Nov '51; 11: 21 Jan '52; 12: 3 Sept '52; 22: 166 Dec '57.
—— (heads, laughing). Holiday 10: 12 (col.) Nov '51, 89 (col.), 166 Dec '51; 11: 113 Jan '52, 12 (col.) Mar '52; 12: 89 Nov '52, 27, 75, 170 Dec '52; 18: 84 Sept '55, 19, 93 Oct '55, 8 Nov '55; 19: 13 (col.). 59 Jan '56, 143 Feb '56, 86 (col.) May '56, 23-4 (col.) Je '56; 20: 58 Aug '56, 85 Sept '56, 11 Oct '56, 154 (col.) Nov '56, 200 Dec '56; 22: 116, 118 (col.) Nov '57, 27, 132-3 (col.) Dec '57; 25: 103 (col.) Mar '59; 26: 139 Dec '59; 27: 8 Mar '60, 116 (col.) Je '60; 28: 125 Sept '60, 10 (col.), 23 (col.) Oct '60, 37 Dec '60.
—— (heads, look at state charter). Natl. geog. 98: 389 Sept '50.
—— (heads, lovers). Holiday 21: 97 Feb '57; 22: 30 Jl '57, 146 (col.) Dec '57; 28: 63 Nov '60.
—— (heads, scornful). Holiday 27: 14 Feb '60.
—— (heads, smile). Natl. geog. 109: 856 Je '56.
—— (heads, sun glasses). Holiday 12: 2 (col.), 14 Jl '52; 23: 12 Je '58; 26: 225 (col.) Dec '59.
—— (heads, travel guides). Holiday 11: 27 Mar '52.
—— (heads, waving). Holiday 22: 48 Nov '57, 137 Dec '57.
—— (heads, western). Holiday 12: 25 Dec '52.
—— (heads, worried). Holiday 27: 173 Mar '60.
—— (hikers, backview). Natl. geog. 107: 734 (col.) Je '55.
—— (honeymooners). Holiday 28: 1 Jl '60.
—— (horse). Holiday 14: 6 Oct '53.
—— (horseback). Holiday 5: 77 Jan '49, 81, 99 (col.) Feb '49; 11: 137 May '52; 13: 25 Jan '53, 31 (col.), 150, back cover (col.) Mar '53, 13, 119 (col.) Ap '53; 18: 66 Jl '55; 19: 22 Feb '56. Travel 101: cover Ap '54.
—— (horseback, cartoon). Amer. heri., vol. 11 no. 4 p. 19 (col.) (Je '60) Travel 107: 11 Ap '57.
—— (horseback, misty dream). Holiday 5: 130 (col.) Ap '49.
—— (horses, hounds). Holiday 25: 92 (col.) Ap '59.
—— (hotel balcony, comic). Holiday 25: 203 Ap '59.
—— (hugging). Holiday 11: 25 (col.) Feb '52; 23: 152 (col.) May '58; 25: 60 (col.) Feb '59.
—— (hugging, comic). Holiday 11: 58, 126 Ap '52.
—— (hunting). Natl. geog. 99: 134 (col.) Jan '51.

—— (in auto). Holiday 10: 24 (col.) Aug '51; 14: 29 Jl '53; 24: 83 Oct '58, 144 Dec '58; 25: 33, 126 (col.) Mar '59; 26: 2 (col.) Nov '59; 27: 108 (col.) Feb '60; 28: 88 Aug '60.
—— (in bed). Holiday 24: inside cover (col.) Oct '58, 102 (col.) Nov '58; 26: 31 (col.) Oct '59, 110 (col.) Nov '59.
—— (in beds, cartoon). Holiday 23: 79 Ap '58.
—— (in field). Amer. heri., vol. 8 no. 5 p. 51 (col.) (Aug '57).
—— (in flowers). Holiday 11: 143 Je '52.
—— (in kitchen). Holiday 25: 30 (col.) Feb '59; 26: 20 (col.) Jl '59; 27: 196 (col.) Mar '60.
—— (in library). Holiday 26: 76 Oct '59.
—— (in old auto). Amer. heri., vol. 10 no. 4 p. 58 (col.) Je '59.
—— (jade shop). Natl. geog. 110: 197 (col.) Aug '56.
—— (kissing). Amer. heri., vol. 9 no. 1 p. 93 (Dec '57). Holiday 10: 17 Dec '51; 13: 48 Ap '53; 15: 150 (col.) Je '54; 23: 17 Je '58; 24: 80 Jl '58, 61 Aug '58, 15 Sept '58, 27: 27 Ap '60; 28: 93 (col.) Aug '60.
—— (lake, mts., reflections). Natl. geog. 109: 626 (col.) May '56.
—— (lakeside table). Natl. geog. 106: 161 (col.) Aug '54.
—— (lakeside tea table). Holiday 22: 188 (col.) Dec '57.
—— (laughing). Holiday 10: 28 (col.) Oct '51, 22 (col.) Dec '51; 11: 4 (col.) Mar '52, 92 Ap 52; 18: 146 Dec '55; 21: 47, 48 (col.) Mar '57; 22: 91 Sept '57, 65 (col.) Oct '57, 126, 243 (col.) Dec '57. Natl. geog. 116: 841 (col.) Dec '59; 118: 430 Sept '60.
—— (laughing, evening). Holiday 10: 80 Jl '51.
—— (lawn chairs). Holiday 19: 19 Feb '56.
—— (lighting cigarettes). Holiday 21: 105 Mar '57.
—— (lion, cartoon). Travel 111: 62 Feb '59.
—— (listen to radio). Holiday 26: 1 Oct '59.
—— (looking at map). Natl. geog. 113: 67 Jan '58.
—— (lounging robes). Holiday 22: 124 (col.), 250 Dec '57.
—— (lovers). Amer. heri. vol. 8 no. 4 p. 51 (Je '57). Holiday 28: 143 Dec '60.
—— (lovers, train). Holiday 19: 146 (col.) May '56.
—— (lunch on plane). Holiday 24: 104 Oct '58.
—— (lunch on ship). Holiday 24: 135 (col.) Oct '58.
—— (lying on floor). Holiday 23: 81 Jan '58.
—— (making jewelry). Natl. geog. 112: 170-1 (col.) Aug '57.
—— (many nations). Holiday 27: 101 col.) Feb '60.
—— (market stand, Nepal). Natl. geog. 117: 381 (col.) Mar '60.
—— (mineral collectors). Natl. geog. 100: 649-50 (col.) Nov '51.

man & woman (musical instrument). Holiday 23: 124 Mar '58.

—— (Natural bridge). Travel 113: 39 Mar '60.

—— (necklace gift). Holiday 20: 9 (col.) Aug '56.

—— (newspaper). Natl. geog. 104: 852 Dec '53.

—— (1902). Brooks: Growth of a nation, p. 232.

—— (1906). Holiday 21: 40 (col.) Mar '57.

—— (old buggy). Holiday 18: 89 Sept '55.

—— (old fashioned room). Natl. geog. 118: 581 (col.) Oct '60.

—— (old, flowers). Amer. heri., vol. 9 no. 1 p. 95 (Dec '57).

—— (old, seated on lawn). Natl. geog. 97: 579 (col.) May '50.

—— (older, children). Holiday 11: 113 (col.) Feb '52.

—— (on boat). Holiday 27: 89 May '60; 28: 131 (col.) Dec '60.

—— (on boat, bathing suits). Travel 114: 57 Sept '60.

—— (on bus). Holiday 19: 4 (col.) Feb '56.

—— (on bus, comic). Travel 113: 66 Mar '60.

—— (on cloud). Holiday 12: 22 Sept '52; 26: 106 Sept '59.

—— (on cloud, cartoon). Travel 106: 63 Oct '56.

—— (on couch). Amer. heri., vol. 9 no. 1 p. 92 (Dec '57). Holiday 10: 130 Nov '51.

—— (on exercise machine). Holiday 24: 18 Aug '58.

—— (on floor, travel poster). Holiday 22: 25 (col.) Nov '57, 195 Dec '57.

—— (on garden steps). Holiday 27: 123 (col.) Feb '60.

—— (on housetop, flood, comic). Holiday 14: 9 Aug '53.

—— (on plane). Holiday 14: 95 (col.) Nov '53; 19: 15 (col.) Jan '56; 23: 131 May '58, 47 Je '58; 24: 125 (col.) Oct '58, 18 (col.) Nov '58; 27: 43 (col.) May '60; 28: 12 (col.) Jl '60.

—— (on plane, dinner). Holiday 12: 28 Oct '52.

—— (on plane, lunch). Holiday 24: 120 Dec '58; 25: 153 Ap '59, 12, 44, 112 (col.) Je '59; 26: 13 (col.) Aug '59, 93 (col.) Sept '59, 233 (col.) Dec '59; 28: 7 (col.) Oct '60.

—— (on ship). Holiday 14: 113 Oct '53.

—— (on stairs). Holiday 11: 111 (col.) Ap '52. Natl. geog. 104: 659 (col.) Nov '53; 105: 465 (col.) Ap '54; 109: 468 (col.) Ap '56.

—— (on train). Holiday 14: 139 Oct '53; 21: 147 Mar '57, 158 Ap '57; 23: 193 Ap '58, 14 Je '58; 24: 23 (col.) Sept '58; 28: 10 (col.), 42 Oct '60.

—— (organ). Holiday 22: 221 Dec '57.

—— (outdoor cooking). Holiday 27: 141 Mar '60.

—— (outdoor, table). Holiday 27: 83 (col.) Je '60; 28: 121 (col.) Sept '60, 140 (col.) Oct '60. Natl. geog. 98: 63 (col.) Jl '50.

—— (outdoor table, feeding dog). Holiday 11: 75 (col.) Mar '52.

—— (outline). Holiday 18: 17 Jl '55.

—— (painting textiles). Natl. geog. 109: 247 (col.) Feb '56.

—— (pajamas). Holiday 26: 19 (col.) Sept '59; 28: 116 (col.) Dec '60.

—— (parachute, comic). Holiday 16: 56 Aug '54.

—— (party). Holiday 26: 75 (col.) Oct '59.

—— (photographers). Natl. geog. 104: 618 Nov '53.

—— (picking berries). Holiday 5: 15 (col.) Jan '49. Natl. geog. 115: 709 (col.) May '59.

—— (picking grapes). Holiday 23: 42-3 (col.) Jan '58.

—— (picnic). Holiday 10: cover (col.) Sept '51; 19: 60 (col.) Mar '56; 20: 27 (col.) Nov '56; 22: 20 (col.) Oct '57; 24: 109 (col.) Jl '58; 25: 53 Je '59; 27: 107 (col.) Feb '60; 28: 45 (col.) Jl '60. Travel 102: 20 Dec '54; 103: 57 Je '55.

—— (picnic, beach). Holiday 26: 114, 119 (col.) Dec '59.

—— (picnic, dog). Natl. geog. 113: 490 (col.) Ap '58.

—— (picnic, river). Natl. geog. 114: 58 (col.) Jl '58.

—— (picnic, snow). Holiday 10: 68 Jl '51.

—— (pilot, plane). Natl. geog. 112: 51 (col.) Jl '57.

—— (planning trip). Travel 109: back cover Ap '58, back cover May '58.

—— (plant yard flowers). Natl. geog. 112: 312 (col.) Sept '57.

—— (playing checkers). Holiday 27: 162 (col.) Mar '60.

—— (playing organ). Holiday 19: 82 Mar '56.

—— (praying). Amer. heri., vol. 11 no. 1 p. 45 (Dec '59).

—— (prize horse). Holiday 18: 203 (col.) Dec '55.

—— (pulling sled). Holiday 27: 2 (col.) Jan '60

—— (pumpkin field). Natl. geog. 98: 379 (col.) Sept '50.

—— (puppies). Holiday 14: back cover (col.) Aug '53.

—— (raft). Holiday 25: 174 (col.) Je '59; 27: 191 (col.) May '60. Natl. geog. 105: 361 Mar '54.

—— (raining). Holiday 25: 1 Feb '59.

—— (raking hay). Natl. geog. 100: 620 (col.) Nov '51.

—— (reading). Holiday 22: 26 Oct '57; 27: 161 Mar '60.

—— (reading menu). Natl. geog. 100: 19 Jl '51.

—— (record player). Holiday 25: 103 May '59.

—— (relaxing, plane). Holiday 10: 69 (col.) Oct '51.

—— (relaxing, lawn). Holiday 22: 5 (col.) Sept '57.

—— (resort, comic). Travel 113: 65 Ap '60.

man & woman (restaurant table). Holiday 27: 198 Mar '60, 125 (col.) Je '60; 28: inside back cover (col.) Sept '60, 127 (col.) Nov '60, 129 (col.) Dec '60.

—— **(Rhine river, terrace table).** Natl. geog. 98: 227 (col.) Aug '50.

—— **(riding camels).** Natl. geog. 106: 768 (col.) Dec '54.

—— **(riding elephant).** Travel 105: 69 Feb '56.

—— **(riding horses).** *See* man & woman (horseback).

—— **(riding rocket).** Holiday 7: 74 (col.) Je '50; 8: 90 (col.) Sept '50, 2 (col.) Nov '50; 12: 17 (col.) Oct '52.

—— **(river bank).** Natl. geog. 114: 64 (col.) Jl '58.

—— **(roadside cafe).** Holiday 12: 56 Jl '52.

—— **(Roan mt., flowers).** Natl. geog. 111: 824-8 (col.) Je '57.

—— **(rock ledge, lake).** Natl. geog. 109: 629 (col.) May '56.

—— **(rocky beach).** Holiday 18: 113 (col.) Nov '55.

—— **(rose bower).** Amer. heri., vol. 8 no. 4 p. 50 (col.) (Je '57).

—— **(rowboat).** Natl. geog. 109: 202 (col.) Feb '56; 114: 62, 65 (col.) Jl '58. Travel 113: 38 Mar '60.

—— **(rug shop).** Natl. geog. 106: 831 (col.) Dec '54.

—— **(running).** Holiday 16: 24 Jl '54; 18: 23 Oct '55; 19: 75 Jan '56.

—— **(running, beach).** Travel 103: 58 May '55.

—— **(sea food shop).** Natl. geog. 105: 729 Je '54.

—— **(seated).** Amer. heri., vol. 9 no. 1 p. 81 (Dec '57).
Holiday 12: 131 Dec '52; 13: 119 Mar '53; 14: 172 (col.) Dec '53; 18: 122 Nov '55, 15 (col.), 16 Dec '55; 19: 142 Feb '56, 15 (col.) Mar '56; 23: inside cover, 112 (col.) Ap '58, 107 (col.) May '58; 24: 206 (col.) Nov '58; 25: 125 (col.) Jan '59, 115 (col.) Ap '59; 27: 154 Feb '60, 165 Mar '60; 28: 19 (col.) Jl '60, 94-5 (col.) Aug '60, 184 (col.) Oct '60, 15 (col.) Nov '60, 82 Dec '60.
Natl. geog. 98: 393 (col.) Sept '50; 106: 189 (col.) Aug '54.
Travel 102: 45 Dec '54.

—— **(seated, back to back).** Holiday 11: 54 Je '52.

—— **(seated, backview).** Holiday 27: 191 (col.) Mar '60.

—— **(seated, beer).** Holiday 11: 82 (col.) May '52.

—— **(seated by fireside).** Natl. geog. 104: 523 Oct '53.

—— **(seated, dogs).** Natl. geog. 103: 68 (col.) Jan '53.

—— **(seated in train).** Holiday 14: 63 Sept '53.

—— **(seated on bench).** Travel 106: 40 Oct '56.

—— **(seated on boat).** Travel 104: 11 Sept '55.

—— **(seated on cushions).** Travel 101: inside back cover Je '54.

—— **(seated on floor).** Holiday 10: 153 Nov '51; 19: 87 Jan '56, 78 (col.), 79 Mar '56, 177 May '56.

—— **(seated on ground).** Natl. geog. 112: 312 (col.) Sept '57.
Travel 103: 64 Je '55.

—— **(seated on ship).** Travel 109: 34 Je '58.

—— **(seated on ship floor).** Natl. geog. 99: 355 (col.) Mar '51.

—— **(seated on train).** Holiday 14: 94 Dec '53.

—— **(seated, owl).** Natl. geog. 109: 438 Mar '56.

—— **(seated, Penn., 1820).** Amer. heri. vol. 8 no. 3 p. 48-9 (col.) (Ap '57).

—— **(serving food).** Holiday 28: 10 (col.) Sept '60.

—— **(shadow).** Holiday 20: 30 Oct '56; 26: 190 (col.) Nov '59; 27: 127 (col.) Mar '60, 134,, 175 (col.) Ap '60; 28: 41 (col.) Nov '60.

—— **(ship board).** Holiday 27: 153, 161 (col.) Feb '60, 101 (col.) Mar '60.

—— **(ship concert).** Holiday 28: 117 Aug '60.

—— **(ship deck chairs).** Holiday 18: inside cover (col.) Jl '55; 19: 17 (col.) Feb '56; 20: 36 (col.) Nov '56; 22: 91 Sept '57, 48 (col.) Oct '57, 233 Dec '57.
Travel 111: 50 Jan '59.

—— **(ship dinner table).** Holiday 26: 111 (col.) Nov '59; 27: 47 (col.) Ap '60.

—— **(ship party).** Holiday 27: 34 (col.) Ap '60.

—— **(ship tea service).** Holiday 22: 259 (col.) Dec '57.

—— **(shooting at target).** Travel 101: 48 Feb '54.

—— **(shopping).** Holiday 19: 93 (col.) Feb '56; 20: 81 (col.) Oct '56.

—— **(shopping for dress).** Holiday 10: 60 Dec '51.

—— **(shorts).** Holiday 19: 71 (col.) May '56, inside cover (col.) Je '56.

—— **(shuffleboard).** Holiday 23: 151 (col.) Mar '58.

—— **(silhouette).** Holiday 20: 87 Sept '56; 25: 75 Mar '59.
Travel 104: 52 Oct '55.

—— **(silhouette, comic).** Holiday 14: 20 Oct '53.

—— **(skating).** Holiday 14: 31 Dec '53.
Travel 111: 25 Feb '59.

—— **(skytop terraces).** Natl. geog. 113: 38-9 (col.) Jan '58.

—— **(sleigh, horse).** Holiday 10: 13 (col.) Dec '51.

—— **(smoking).** Holiday 10: 16 Oct '51; 19: 71 (col.) Jan '56; 22: 8 Sept '57.

—— **(sport clothes).** Holiday 12: 94 (col.) Nov '52; 18: 25, 101 (col.) Nov '55; 20: 28 (col.) Nov '56; 21: 110 Je '57.

—— **(sports).** Holiday 19: 133 (col.) May '56.

—— **(stooping).** Natl. geog. 97: 228 Feb '50.

—— **(study plants).** Natl. geog. 98: 477 Oct '50.

—— **(study travel map).** Holiday 25: 123 (col.) May '59.

man & woman (sun bathing). Holiday 27: 202 Mar '60.

—— (sweethearts). Holiday 21: 193 Ap '57.

—— (swimming). Natl. geog. 110: 561 Oct '56.

—— (swimming pool). Holiday 13: 135 (col.) Ap '53; 14: 139 (col.) Dec '53; 24: 83 (col.) Nov '58.

—— (taking pictures). Holiday 11: 81 (col.) Feb '52, 15 (col.) May '52; 14: 87 (col.) Sept '53; 24: 5 (col.) Sept '58.

—— (tea). Holiday 26: 106, 185 (col.) Nov '59; 27: 162 (col.) Ap '60, 35 (col.) Je '60.

—— (tea table). Holiday 24: 85 (col.) Oct '58, 107 (col.) Dec '58; 25: inside back cover (col.) Mar '59, 75 (col.) May '59, 42 Je '59; 26: 38 Dec '59; 27: 35, 83 (col.) Je '60; 28: 61 Nov '60. Natl. geog. 118: 447 (col.) Oct '60. Travel 110: 40 Sept '58; 113: back cover Mar '60.

—— (tea table on porch). Holiday 27: 51, 79 (col.) Mar '60.

—— (terrace lunch table). Holiday 10: 13 (col.) Nov '51.

—— (terrace table). Holiday 26: 57 (col.) Jl '59; 27: 130 (col.) Feb '60, back cover (col.) Mar '60.

—— (tourist). Travel 113: inside cover May '60.

—— (tourist, comic). Travel 113: 65 Ap '60.

—— (train diner). Holiday 10: 4 (col.) Dec '51; 11: 7 (col.) Mar '52, 10 (col.) Ap '52; 12: 121 (col.) Jl '52; 19: 71 (col.) Feb '56; 24: 132 (col.) Dec '58; 25: 153 (col.) Feb '59.

—— (train, observation car). Holiday 27: 199 (col.) May '60.

—— (train seat). Holiday 11: 4 (col.) Je '52.

—— (train table). Holiday 27: 28 (col.) Feb '60.

—— (travel cartoon). Travel 102: 54 Oct '54.

—— (travel folder). Holiday 19: 115 Je '56.

—— (traveling). Holiday 10: 120 Sept '51, 8 Oct '51; 11: 2 (col.) Feb '52, 7 (col.) Mar '52, 20 Ap '52, 78, 103 (col.) May '52, 26 Je '52; 12: 106 Sept '52, 158 (col.) Dec '52; 13: 70 (col.), 137 Ap '53, 66 (col.) Je '53; 18: 91 Oct '55; 19: 75 Jan '56, 112, 141 (col.) Feb '56, 112 May '56, 116 Je '56; 21: 147 (col.) Jan '57, 118 Feb '57, 39, 43 (col.) Mar '57, 37, 40 Ap '57, 158 (col.) May '57, 150, 182 Je '57; 22: 92-3 Sept '57, 168 (col.), 192 Nov '57, 62, 234 Dec '57; 23: 5, 93 (col.), 103 Feb '58, 11 Mar '58, 6 Ap '58, 168 May '58, 102, 112 (col.), 210 Je '58; 24: 92 (col.) Jl '58, 4 (col.), 32, 112 Nov '58; 25: 111-13, 116 (col.) Feb '59, 28 Mar '59, 193 Ap '59, 12-3 (col.), 151 Je '59; 26: 4, 82 (col.), 131 Jl '59, 111 Aug '59, 32-3, 141 (col.) Sept '59, 147, 167 Oct '59, 38, 105, 139 (col.), 140 Nov '59, 4 Dec '59; 27: 119, 148 Jan '60, 109, 138 (col.) Feb '60, 37 Mar '60, 26 (col.), 113, 162 (col.), 178, 198 Je '60; 28: 13 (col.) Jl '60, 107 (col.) Aug '60, 103, 128 (col.) Sept '60, 51, 186 Nov '60, 46 (col.) Dec '60.

Travel 103: 44 Jan '55; 104: 69 Sept '55, 69 Nov '55; 105: 12 14- Ap '56; 107: back cover Ap '57; 111: back cover Feb '59, back cover Mar '59, 59, back cover Ap '59, back cover May '59, 43 Je '59; 112: 59 Jl '59, 59 Aug '59, 59 Sept '59; 113: 54 Je '60; 114: 61 Aug '60, 14 Sept '60.

—— (traveling, auto). Holiday 28: back cover (col.) Aug '60. Travel 110: 62 Jl '58.

—— (traveling, comic). Holiday 11: 122 Je '52; 13: 153 Je '53; 18: 93 Sept '55; 20: 12 Sept '56; 21: 110 Jan '57; 25: 181 Ap '59, 46 May '59, 135 Je '59; 26: 127 Oct '59, 48 Dec '59; 27: 106 Jan '60, 197 Je '60; 28: 122 Nov '60. Travel 111: 35 Mar '59.

—— (umbrella). Holiday 28: 146 Nov '60, 27 Dec '60.

—— (umbrella, garden). Natl. geog. 115: 717 (col.) May '59.

—— (umbrella, waterfall). Holiday 28: 124 (col.) Dec '60.

—— (under mistletoe). Holiday 24: 1 Dec '58.

—— (vacation). Holiday 21: 177 May '57; 22: 106-11 (part col.) Jl '57.

—— (Valentine day, comic). Holiday 5: 26 Feb '49.

—— (volcanic, boiling mud). Natl. geog. 108: 729 (col.) Dec '55.

—— (wading). Holiday 21: 18 Jan '57.

—— (waiter, dinner table). Natl. geog. 113: 317 (col.) Mar '58.

—— (walking). Holiday 18: 72, 96 (col.) Jl '55, 25, 84 (col.) Nov '55; 19: 23 Jan '56; 20: 73 (col.) Oct '56; 22: 4 (col.) Oct '57, 100 Nov '57.

—— (watching movie). Holiday 12: 71 (col.) Oct '52.

—— (watching picture projection). Holiday 24: 107 Oct '58.

—— (watching TV). Holiday 14: 79 (col.) Nov '53.

—— (watching volcano, comic). Travel 113: 66 Jan '60.

—— (water skiing). Holiday 18: 124 (col.) Nov '55.

—— (waving). Holiday 10: 82 Nov '51; 11: 7 (col.) Mar '52; 18: 80 Nov '55; 20: 43 Nov '56.

—— (wearing sunglasses). Holiday 27: 100 (col.) Je '60. Travel 110: 25 Nov '58; 111: 43 Jan '59, 61 Feb '59.

—— (western). Travel 104: 8 Jl '55.

—— (western, horseback). Holiday 12: 147 Jl '52; 20: 61 (col.) Sept '56.

—— (window). Holiday 27: 97 Feb '60, 135 Ap '60.

—— (window, seaside dinner). Natl geog. 112: 311 (col.) Sept '57.

—— (window table). Holiday 27: 174 (col.) Mar '60, 111, 188 (col.) Ap '60, 153 May '60.

—— (winter cartoon). Travel 111: 62 Jan '59.

man & woman (winter coats). Holiday 10: 8 Oct '51, 14 Dec '51; 11: 4 (col.) Mar '52. Natl. geog. 116: 365 (col.) Sept '59.
—— (winter underwear). Holiday 18: 124 (col.) Dec '55.
—— (world war mosaic map). Natl. geog. 111: 751 (col.) Je '57.
—— (yawning). Holiday 26: 34 Jl '59.
man & woman, Acadian (La. Bayou). Holiday 6: 57 (col.) Oct '49.
——, Africa. Natl. geog. 97: 337 (col.) Mar '50.
——, Africa (at table). Holiday 25: 87 (col.) Ap '59.
——, Alpine. Holiday 26: 74 (col.) Sept '59.
——, Arabia (tea). Natl. geog. 113: 669 May '58.
——, British West Indies. Holiday 18: 73 Oct '55.
——, Cypress is. (heads, smiling). Natl. geog. 109: 876 Je '56.
——, Egypt. Holiday 10: 122 Oct '51.
——, France (farmers). Natl. geog. 109: 334 (col.) Mar '56.
——, Holland. Con. 140: 116 Nov '57.
——, Holland (mold cheese). Natl. geog. 106: 405 (col.) Sept '54.
——, Hunza. Natl. geog. 104: 489-516 (col.) Oct '53.
——, Iceland (at table). Natl. geog. 100: 615 (col.) Nov '51.
——, India (tea time). Holiday 27: 179 Mar '60.
——, Ireland (dog). Natl. geog. 99: 655 May '51.
——, Ireland (jaunting cart). Holiday 14: 13 Aug '53.
——, Italy. Labande: Naples, p. 52.
——, Italy (at table). Natl. geog. 109: 850 (col.) Je '56
——, Japan (tea). Holiday 22: 111 (col.) Jl '57; 24: 16 (col.) Dec '58.
——, Lapland (reindeer). Natl. geog. 106: 254, 280 (col.) Aug '54.
——, Lhasa. Natl. geog. 108: 5-48 (part col.) Jl '55.
——, Lhasa (seated). Natl. geog. 108: 10 Jl '55.
——, Mexico. Travel 113: back cover Je '60.
——, Mexico (table). Natl. geog. 103: 346 Mar '53.
——, Nepal (market stand). Natl. geog. 117: 381 (col.) Mar '60.
——, Norway (holiday dress). Natl. geog. 106: 176 Aug '54.
——, Rome (shopping). Natl. geog. 111: 472 (col.) Ap '57.
——, Russia (cartoon). Holiday 14: 84 Sept '53.
——, Russia (laborers). Natl. geog. 116: 360-1 Sept '59.
——, Russia (office). Natl. geog. 116: 394 (col.) Sept '59.
——, Samoan chief. Travel 114: 40 Dec '60.
——, Scotland (hikers). Natl. geog. 110: 22 (col.) Jl '56.
——, Scotland (seated). Natl geog. 110: 19 (col.) Jl '56.
——, Spain. Travel 113: inside cover Ap '60.
——, Surinam. Travel 112: 24 Sept '59.

——, Switzerland (hay loads on backs). Natl. geog. 98: 223 (col.) Aug '50.
——, Thrace (harvest beans). Natl. geog. 109: 69 (col.) Jan '56.
——, Turkey. Osward: Asia Minor, pl. 78-9.
man, woman & baby. Holiday 5: 135 (col.) Je '49.
—— Natl. geog. 111: 305 (col.) Mar '57.
—— (comic). Holiday 11: 141 May '52.
—— (heads). Holiday 14: 84 Dec '53.
—— (on camel). Natl. geog. 107: 505 (col.) Ap '55.
—— (picnic). Holiday 14: 94 (col.) Jl '53.
—— (war mosaic). Natl. geog. 111: 765 (col.) Je '57.
man, woman & boy (fishing). Holiday 13: 69 (col.) Je '53.
—— (heads). Travel 111: 10 Mar '59.
—— (platypus). Natl geog. 114: 514-5 Oct '58.
—— (radio). Holiday 27: 45 Ap '60.
—— (raincoats). Holiday 10: 157 Dec '51.
—— (sweater suits). Holiday 14: 130 Dec '53.
—— (toy stagecoach). Natl. geog. 110: 499 (col.) Oct '56.
——, Italy (at table). Holiday 19: 103 Jan '56.
man, woman & child. Holiday 10: 119 Jl '51; 12: 115 (col.) Sept '52; 19: 91 Jan '56, 53 Mar '56, 28 Je '56; 20: 173, 220 Dec '56.
Natl. geog. 118: 516 Oct '60.
Travel 102: 43 Nov '54, 8 Dec '54; 103: 44 Jan 55, 6 Mar '55, 46 Ap '55; 107: 17 Jan '57.
—— (at harbor). Holiday 24: 2 (col.) Jl '58.
—— (auto). Holiday 20: 19-21 (col.) Nov '56; 23: 156 Mar '58, 110-11, 159 (col.) Je '58; 24: 28, 84-5, 95, 141 (col.) Jl '58, 103 Aug '58; 26: 24, 32, 90 (col.) Jl '59, 21 (col.) Nov '59; 27: 145 Mar '60, 140 (col.) Ap '60, 15, 115, 164 (col.) May '60; 28: 93 (col.) Jl '60, 84 (col.) Sept '60.
—— (auto, cartoon). Travel 111: 50 Jan '59, 54 Feb '59.
—— (back view). Holiday 23: 155 Je '58; 24: 84 (col.) Jl '58.
—— (back view, storm). Natl. geog. 107: 748 Je '55.
—— (back view, waving). Natl. geog. 112: 338 (col.) Sept '57.
—— (bathing suits). Natl. geog. 111: 623 (col.) May '57.
—— (bathing suits, beach). Holiday 10: 5, 59 (col.) Jl '51, 153 Nov '51, 56 (col.) Dec '51; 12: 136 Jl '52, 124 (col.) Dec '52; 27: 168 Jan '60, 47 (col.), 173 Feb '60, 120, 205 Mar '60, 15, 170 (col.), 225 Ap '60, 236 May '60, 38 (col.) Je '60; 28: 9 Sept '60, 150 (col.) Oct '60.
—— (bathing suits, running). Holiday 27: 17 May '60, 104 Je '60.
—— (bathing suits, comic). Holiday 27: 100 Feb '60, 121 Je '60.
—— (bathing suits, in water). Holiday 28: 5 (col.) Aug '60.
—— (beach). Holiday 13: 71 ((col.) Je '53; 14: 25 Aug '53; 19: 80 (col.) Mar '56, 128 Je '56; 20: 21 Oct '56; 21: 17 Jan '57, 143

(col.) Mar '57, 201 (col.) May '57; 23: 7, 109 (col.) Mar '58, 108 (col.), 119, 151 (col.), 192 Ap '58, 157 May '58; 24: 97 Jl '58, 20 (col.) Nov '58, 49, 155 (col.) Dec '58; 25: 10, 27 (col.) Ap '59, 178 May '59, 31, 102 (col.) Je '59; 26: 99, 122 Jl '59, 16 Aug '59.

man, woman & child (bicycle). Holiday 13: 45 Ap '53.

—— (bicycle, England). Natl. geog. 98: 186 Aug '50.

—— (birds). Holiday 26: 158 Dec '59.

—— (boat). Holiday 19: 5 (col.) Mar '56.

—— (boat, fishing). Holiday 19: 114 (col.) May '56; 20: 2 (col.) Aug '56.

—— (bowling). Holiday 28: 185 (col.) Nov '60.

—— (camp table). Natl. geog. 109: 603 (col.) May '56.

—— (Christmas). Holiday 18: inside cover (col.), 1, 88 Dec '55; 22: 115 (col.) Dec '57. Natl. geog. 108: 850-1 (col.) Dec '55.

—— (Christmas gifts). Holiday 14: 159 (col.) Dec '53.

—— (comic). Holiday 10: 4 Aug '51, 10, 84 Sept '51, 148 Oct '51; 11: 7 (col.) Je '52; 12: 85 Jl '52, 30 Sept '52; 13: 73 (col.) May '53; 27: 118 Jan '60, 140 Mar '60; 28: 102 Jl '60.

—— (cooking in kettle). Amer. heri., vol. 9 no. 3 p. 88 (Ap '58).

—— (corn field.) Holiday 28: 46 Nov '60.

—— (early train). Amer. heri., vol. 1 no. 2 p. 27 (winter '50).

—— (eating on barge). Natl. geog. 108: 534 (col.) Oct '55.

—— (feeding deer). Holiday 22: 79 (col.) Sept '57.

—— (feeding elephant). Holiday 28: 16 Sept '60.

—— (field of flowers). Natl. geog. 105: 790-1 (col.) Je '54.

—— (fishing). Holiday 22: 50 (col.) Dec '57.

—— (flower garden). Natl. geog. 97: 488-9, 492 (col.) Ap '50; 103: 314 (col.) Mar '53.

—— (going on picnic). Holiday 25: 17 Feb '59.

—— (heads). Holiday 10: 71 Jl '51, 14 Oct '51; 11: 128 Ap '52, 133 May '52; 25: 3 Je '59; 27: 9 Mar '60, 11, 23, 28-9 (col.) Je '60.

—— (heads, eyeglasses). Holiday 10: 1 Jl '51; 12: 97 Jl '52.

—— (heads, laughing). Holiday 10: 1 Jl '51, 101 Dec '51; 11: 140 Je '52; 12: 97 Jl '52; 21: 184, 205 May '57.

—— (hikers). Holiday 25: 29 Feb '59. Natl. geog. 117: 480 (col.) Ap '60.

—— (ice cream stand). Holiday 27: 184 (col.) Je '60.

—— (in lake). Holiday 25: 105 (col.) May '59.

—— (lamp exhibit). Natl. geog. 107: 453 (col.) Ap '55.

—— (laughing). Holiday 11: 8 May '52; 18: 83 Sept '55.

—— (looking at movie.) Holiday 12: 87 (col.) Jl '52.

—— (lunch). Holiday 26: 163 (col.) Dec '59.

—— (lunch counter). Holiday 26: inside back cover (col.) Sept '59.

—— (lying on grass). Holiday 28: 141 Jl '60.

—— (lying on rocky beach). Natl. geog. 116: 575 (col.) Nov '59.

—— (marine life). Natl. geog. 116: 677 (col.) Nov '59.

—— (motor boat). Holiday 27: 164 (col.) Feb '60.

—— (mt. top). Holiday 25: 31 (col.) Ap '59.

—— (musical instruments). Holiday 21: 194 May '57; 28: 4 Sept '60.

—— (Natural bridge, Ky.). Travel 113: 39 Mar '60.

—— (on plane). Holiday 27: 220 (col.) May '60.

—— (on stairway). Holiday 28: 12 (col.) Dec '60.

—— (on train). Holiday 25: 45 (col.) Mar '59; 27: 126 Feb '60, 210 May '60. Travel 113: 58 Je '60.

—— (outdoor cooking). Natl. geog. 99: 127 (col.) Jan '51.

—— (pajamas). Holiday 27: 113 (col.) Feb '60.

—— (pets). Holiday 25: 143 Je '59.

—— (picnic). Holiday 10: 47 Jl '51, 121 (col.) Nov '51; 11: 76 Mar '52; 12: 89 Jl '52, 75 (col.) Nov '52; 19: 27 (col.) Je '56; 20: 139 (col.) Dec '56; 23: 41 (col.) Mar '58, 28-9 (col.) May '58; 25: 123 (col.) Feb '59, 171 Mar '59; 27: 158 Ap '60, 225 May '60, 57 Je '60. Natl. geog. 98: 192 (col.) Aug '50; 99: 127 (col.) Jan '51.

—— (planning trip). Holiday 25: 212 Ap '59.

—— (playing in lake). Holiday 23: 155 (col.) Mar '58.

—— (reading on train). Natl. geog. 109: 236 (col.) Feb '56.

—— (refrigerator). Holiday 18: 76 (col.) Aug '55.

—— (running). Holiday 13: 91 May '53.

—— (sea food dinner). Holiday 11: 38 (col.) Je '52.

—— (seated). Holiday 23: 9 Jan '58. Travel 105: 30 Feb '56.

—— (seated, 1870). Amer. heri., vol. 9 no. 6 p. 36 (Oct '58).

—— (seaweed). Natl. geog. 112: 186 (col.) Aug '57.

—— (shopping, comic). Holiday 28: 197 Oct '60.

—— (singing & playing guitar). Holiday 28: 16 Dec '60.

—— (taking bear picture). Holiday 27: 48 Feb '60.

—— (taking pictures). Holiday 11: 9 Feb '52.

—— (tea table, outdoors). Holiday 19: 21 (col.) May '56.

—— (toy airplane). Holiday 20: 22 Oct '56.

—— (trailer camp). Travel 103: 31 May '55.

—— (train dome). Holiday 19: 80 (col.) Feb '56, 72-3 (col.) Mar '56.

—— (train,, dome, comic). Holiday 11: 2 Jan '52.

—— (traveling). Holiday 10: 18 (col.) Nov '51; 12: 24 (col.) Jl '52, 9 Sept '52. **73**

Nov '52; 14: back cover (col.) Jl '53; 19: 84 Feb '56, 97 (col.) Mar '56, 4 (col.), 25 May '56, 10 (col.) Je '56; 25: 122 Jan '59, 100, 151 Mar '59, 12-3 (col.) Ap '59; 26: 5 (col.) Aug '59, 124 Nov '59; 27: 110 Jan '60, 99 (col.), 101 Feb '60, 177 Mar '60, 128 (col.) Ap '60. Travel 103: 38 May '55, 43 Je '55; 104: 50 Oct '55.

man, woman & child (traveling by car). Holiday 27: 200 Je '60; 28: 134 Jl '60, 45 Aug '60.

—— **(traveling, cartoon).** Travel 106: 5, 38 Jl '56, 11 Aug '56, 11 Oct '56.

—— **(walking).** Natl. geog. 97: 563, 566 (col.) May '50.

—— **(watching movies).** Holiday 24: 95 (col.) Sept '58.

—— **(waving).** Holiday 19: 62 Mar '56.

—— **(western).** Holiday 10: 36 Aug '51.

——, **Amazon.** Travel 113: 58 Feb '60.

——, **Hawaii (beach).** Natl. geog. 118: 24 (col.) Jl '60.

——, **Holland.** Holiday 21: 55 (col.) Mar '57.

——, **Italy (16th cent.).** Int. gr. soc.: Arts . . . p. 111 (col.).

——, **Japan (eating at table).** Natl. geog. 118: 754 (col.) Dec '60.

——, **Korea.** Natl. geog. 97: 781-805 (col.) Je '50.

——, **Negroes (back view).** Natl. geog. 103: 55 (col.) Jan '53.

——, **Switzerland.** Holiday 24: 4 Aug '58.

——, **Switzerland (at home).** Natl. geog. 98: 242 (col.) Aug '50.

——, **Tahiti.** Holiday 28: 78-9 Nov '60.

——. *See also* family.

man, woman & children. Amer. heri., vol. 8 no. 4 p. 53 (col.) (Je '57). Holiday 13: 19, 94 (col.) Ap '53, 167 (col.) May '53; 14: 121 Nov '53; 23: 5 (col.), 133 Mar '58, 39 (col.) May '58; 25: 156, 190 Ap 59, 43 Je '59; 27: 24 (col.) Jan '60, 12 (col.) Feb '60; 28: 49 (col.) Nov '60, 206 (col.) Dec '60. Travel 103: 60 May '55, 56, 62 Je '55; 104: 5 Jl '55, 58 Aug '55; 106: 31 Nov '56.

—— **(auto).** Holiday 10: 2 (col.) Aug '51, 140 (col.) Oct '51; 24: 13 (col.) Sept '58, 29 Oct '58, 160 Nov '58; 25: 90 (col.) Feb '59, 111 (col.) Ap '59.

—— **(back view).** Natl. geog. 101: 149 (col.) Feb '52. Travel 107: 12 Je '57.

—— **(back view, waving).** Natl. geog. 107: 756 (col.) Je '55.

—— **(ball).** Natl. geog. 107: 444 Ap '55.

—— **(bathers).** Holiday 21: 97 Ap '57.

—— **(bathing suits).** Holiday 11: 126 (col.) Ap '52; 12: 142 Jl '52.

—— **(beach).** Holiday 26: 119 (col.) Sept '59; 27: 142 Feb '60. Natl. geog. 118: 690-1 (col.) Nov '60.

—— **(beach picnic).** Natl. geog. 117: 458 (col.) Ap '60.

—— **(boarding plane).** Natl. geog. 112: 313 (col.) Sept '57.

—— **(boat).** Holiday 21: 192 (col.) May '57; 27: 118 Ap '60.

—— **(boat, water skis).** Holiday 19: 140 (col.) May '56.

—— **(camp table).** Travel 110: 40 Jl '58.

—— **(camping).** Natl. geog. 111: 822 (col.) Je '57. Travel 102: 20, 22 Jl '54; 110: 56 Aug '58.

—— **(canoe).** Travel 112: 39 Aug '59.

—— **(Christmas).** Holiday 24: 171 Dec '58; 26: 47, 116-7 (col.) 128 Dec '59; 28: 42 (col.) Dec '60.

—— **(Christmas dinner).** Amer. heri., vol. 9 no. 1 p. 20 (col.) (Dec '57).

—— **(Christmas sleigh).** Amer. heri., vol. 9 no. 1 p. 16 (col.) (Dec '57).

—— **(dancing dogs).** Con. 132: IV Sept '53.

—— **(digging clams).** Natl. geog. 108: 118 Jl '55.

—— **(dinner table).** Holiday 19: 9 Feb '56.

—— **(dogs).** Natl. geog. 108: 340 (col.) Sept '55.

—— **(eating fruit).** Natl. geog. 109: 283 (col.) Feb '56.

—— **(1836).** Amer. heri., vol. 11 no. 2 p. 48-9 (col.) (Feb '60).

—— **(1853).** Amer. heri., vol. 7 no. 3 p. 59 (col.) (Ap '56).

—— **(feeding pigeons).** Natl. geog. 111: 790-1 (col.) Je '57.

—— **(fishing).** Face of Amer., p. 46 (col.).

—— **(forest).** Natl. geog. 108: 110 (col.) Jl '55.

—— **(guests arriving).** Holiday 23: 212 Je '58.

—— **(heads).** Holiday 12: 23 Jl '52. Travel 104: 58 Sept '55, 66 Oct '55, 64 Nov '55; 105: 8 Feb '56, 44 Mar '56.

—— **(heads, firefly light).** Natl. geog. 99: 699-703 May '51.

—— **(heads, laughing).** Holiday 19: 144 Feb '56.

—— **(horse).** Holiday 25: 187 (col.) Mar '59. Natl. geog. 98: 356 (col.) Sept '50.

—— **(Indian gifts).** Holiday 19: 70 (col.) Mar '56.

—— **(laughing).** Holiday 21: 174 Mar '57, 130 Ap '57, 208 May '57; 27: 24 Ap '60.

——, **(lawn fountain).** Natl. geog. 118: 175 (col.) Aug '60.

—— **(loaded donkeys).** Natl. geog. 116: 175 (col.) Aug '59.

—— **(old train).** Natl. geog. 100: 207 (col.) Aug '51.

—— **(on Hawaiian ship).** Holiday 23: 119 (col.) Je '58.

—— **(on plane).** Holiday 26: 12-3 (col.) Oct '59, 167 (col.) Nov '59; 27: 16 Jan '60, 128 (col.) Ap '60.

—— **(on train, back view).** Holiday 21: 134 Jan '57.

—— **(organ, singing).** Holiday 18: 170 Dec '55.

—— **(packing for trip).** Holiday 18: 7 Jl '55.

—— **(pajamas).** Holiday 22: 102 (col.) Oct '57; 23: 185 Je '58.

——— **(party).** Travel 114: 61 Sept '60.

——— **(picnic, comic).** Holiday 23: 76 Je '58.

—— **(picnic dinner).** Travel 107: cover Feb '57.

—— **(picnic lunch).** Travel 113: 36 Mar '60.

—— (planning vacation). Travel 111: 5 Je '59.

—— (playground, comic). Holiday 27: 156-7 (col.) May '60.

—— (pool table). Holiday 14: 139 Oct '53, 9 Nov '53, 92 Dec '53.

—— (ranch). Travel 113: 9 Mar '60.

—— (reading). Holiday 25: 209 Ap '59. Natl. geog. 111: 789 (col.) Je '57.

—— (seaside dinner table). Natl. geog. 110: 209 (col.) Aug '56.

—— (seated). Holiday 14: 74 (col.) Oct '53; 27: 121 (col.) May '60. Travel 109: 23 Je '58.

—— (shuffleboard). Holiday 21: 44 (col.) Mar '57.

—— (singing). Holiday 14: 169 Dec '53.

—— (street market). Natl. geog. 110: 453 (col.) Oct '56.

—— (table). Holiday 23: 209 Je '58; 24: 89 Jl '58; 25: 179 Mar '59.

—— (taking pictures). Holiday 23: 84 Jan '58.

—— (tourists). Natl. geog. 116: 587 (col.) Nov '59.

—— See also traveling.

—— (train). Holiday 18: 127 Nov '55.

—— (train diner). Holiday 18: 5 (col.) Aug '55, 127 Nov '55; 19: 139 (col.) Mar '56.

—— (train, private car). Holiday 20: 105 Oct '56.

—— (traveling). Holiday 21: 182 Mar '57, 8 Ap '57, 18, 27 (col.),, 187, 200 May '57.

—— (traveling, comic). Holiday 12: 27 Sept '52; 19: 147 May '56; 21: 97 May '57, 31 Je '57; 26: 241 Dec '59; 27: 22 Feb '60, 203 Ap '60, 40 May '60; 28: 189 Dec '60. Travel 102: 39 Oct '54; 108: 39 Jl '57, 9 Aug '57, 11 Oct '57.

—— (U.S. Customs office). Holiday 25: 12-3 (col.) Ap '59.

—— (walking). Holiday 10: 22 Jl '51.

—— (war memorial chapel). Natl. geog. 111: 750 (col.) Je '57.

—— (western). Holiday 19: 109 Feb '56.

—— (yard picnic). Holiday 24: inside cover (col.) Aug '58.

——, Alaska. Holiday 26: 30-1 (col.) Aug '59. Natl. geog. 99: 552-62 Ap '51.

——, Canada. Holiday 19: 2 (col.) Feb '56.

——, Chile. Natl. geog. 117: 202 (col.) Feb '60.

——, Japan (eating). Holiday 19: 102 (col.) Feb '56.

Swiss (dinner). Natl. geog. 116: 274 Aug '59.

man, woman & girl (engagement ring). Holiday 22: 150 Nov '57.

——, (fireplace). Natl. geog. 100: 25 (col.) Jl '51.

——, (at table). Natl. geog. 107: 471 (col.) Ap '55.

man, woman & girls (picnic). Travel 113: 46 Je '60.

"Man enlightened" (funeral chapel of San-gros). Labande: Naples, p. 60.

Man—God of India. See Aurobindo, Shri.

"Man in armor" (Tintoretto). Natl. geog. 97: 757 (col.) Je '50.

"Man in blue" (Titian). Con. 136: 191 (col.) Dec '55.

"Man of sorrows" (art). Holiday 11: 42 (col.) Feb '52.

—— (ceramic figure). Praeg pict. ency., p. 493.

"Man on horseback" (Rembrandt). Con. 145: 112 Ap '60.

"Man with a turban" (Van Eyck). Int. gr. soc.: Arts . . . p. 89 (col.).

"Man with musical instrument" (Van Brekel-enkam). Con. 126: 134 Oct '50.

Manáos (Peru). Disney: people & places, p. 106-9 (col.).

Manchester (river front). Natl. geog. 99: 111 Jan '51.

"Manchester" home (Lexington, Ky.). Holiday 5: 74 (col.) Je '49; 7: 26 (col.) Je '50; 13: 138 (col.) Je '53.

Manchester art exhibition bldg. (England, 1857). Con. 140: 237 Jan '58.

Manchu Picchu (Peru). Holiday 19: 28-9 (col.) Mar '56; 23: 40 (col.) Ap '58.

Mandaeans (Baghdad man). Natl. geog. 115: 51 (col.) Jan '59.

Mandarin, Chinese. See Chinese mandarin.

Madeira (Portugal). Holiday 28: 62-7 (part col.) Sept '60.

Mandelbaum gate (Jerusalem). Natl. geog. 115: 88-9 Jan '59.

mandolin (Norway). Natl. geog. 104: 687 Nov '53.

mandolin (Majorcan playing). Natl. geog. 111: 647 (col.) May '57.

mandrake (sym.). Lehner: Pict. bk. of sym., p. 71.

Manessier, Alfred. Cur. biog. p. 352 (1957).

Manet, Edouard (work of). Con. 126: 129 Oct '50; 132: 43 Sept '53; 133: 16 Mar '54, 286, 289 Je '54; 134: 40, 67 Sept '54; 139: 203 May '57; 142: 125 Nov '58, 194 Dec '58; 145: 207 May '60. Praeg. pict. ency., p. 416 (col.).

Manetti, X. (work of). Con. ency. of ant., vol. 3 pl. 83.

"Manfred on the Jungfrau" (Martin). Con. 144: 33 Sept '59.

manger, Christ's. See Christ's manger.

Manger motor inn (Charlotte, N.C.). Travel 113: 14 May '60.

Mangione, Jerre. Cur. biog., p. 489 (1943).

Mangrum, Lloyd. Cur. biog. p. 402 (1951).

Manhattan (N.Y.). See New York (Manhat-tan).

manicure set. Holiday 6: 19 Dec '49; 7: 83 Ap '50; 22: 151 (col.) Dec '57.

Manigault, Charles David (and family). Amer. heri., vol. 9 no. 2 p. 55 (col.) Feb '58.

Manigault, Gabriel. Amer. heri., vol. 9 no. 2 p. 52 (col.) Feb '58.

Manila. Travel 104: 8 Oct '55.

Manitoulin is. (Canada). Travel 114: 33-5 Jl '60.

Manjiro. Amer. heri., vol. 8 no. 1 p. 80 (Dec '56).

Mankiewicz, Joseph L. Cur. biog. p. 397 (1949).

Mankin, Helen Douglas. Cur. biog. p. 380 (1946).

Mankowitz, Cyril Wolf. Cur. biog. p. 410 (1956).

Manley, Norman W. Cur. biog. p. 289 (1959).

Mann, Cathleen (work of). Con. 145: XII Mar '60, 111 Ap '60.

Mann, Mrs. Marty. Cur. biog. p. 398 (1949).

Mann, Thomas. Cur. biog. p. 561 (1942). Int. gr. soc.: Arts . . . p. 137 (col.).

mannequin (Russian fashion model). Natl. geog. 116: 375 (col.) Sept '59.

mannequins (Macy store). Natl. geog. 114: 191 Aug '58.

Mannes, Marya. Cur. biog. p. 291 (1959).

Mannheim town plan. *See* town plan (Mannheim).

Manning, A. E. Horan: Pict. hist. of wild west, p. 38.

Manning, Ernest. Cur. biog. p. 293 (1959).

Manning, Harry. Cur. biog. p. 399 (1952).

Manning, Reg. Cur. biog. p. 404 (1951).

Manor, Renaissance (int). Holiday 20: 121 (col.) Oct '56.

Manor, Waddesdon. *See* Waddesdon manor.

Manor house (gallery, int., 17th cent.). Holiday 18: 174 (col.) Dec '55.

manor house (int.). Holiday 18: 83 (col.) Jl '55.

——, Norwegian (int. & ext.). Con. 145: 2 (col.), 6 Mar '60.

——, Russian (19th cent.). Con. 142: 219 Jan '59.

——, Sawston Hall. *See* Sawston Hall (Eng.).

——, Scotch (int.). Holiday 21: 116 (col.) Ap '57.

man's shoulder (lizards). Natl. geog. 112: 121 (col.) Jl '57.

Mansbridge, Albert. Cur. biog. p. 565 (1942).

Mansfield, Michael J. Cur. biog. p. 401 (1952).

Manship, Paul. Holiday 28: 65 Aug '60.

Mansion, Egeskov (Denmark). Holiday 18: 35 (col.) Sept '55.

Manstein, Fritz Erich von. Cur. biog. p. 567 (1942).

Mantegna, Andrea (work of). Con. ency. of ant., vol. 1, pl, 151.
Con. 138: 16 Sept '56.
Praeg. pict. ency., p. 275.

mantilla (Spanish headdress). Holiday 15: cover (col.) May '54.

mantillas (women heads). Natl. geog. 99: 513 (col.) Ap '51.

Mantle, Burns. Cur. biog. p. 445 (1944).

Mantle, Mickey. Cur. biog. p. 411 (1953).

mantle ornament, Geo. II. Con. 141: L May '58.

mantlepiece. Con. 133: XX Ap '54; 134: XXXIV, back cover Nov '54, XXXVIII, XLIII Dec '54; 136: XVI Sept '55, XXIX Dec '55; 137: X Mar '56, XXXII, XLVII May '56, XLV, LVI Je '56; 141: XXXVII May '58.
Holiday 26: 95 Nov '59; 27: 63 (col.) Ap '60.

—— (fireplace). Con. 136: XXXV, XLIX Sept '55, XLIII, XLVI Nov '55.

—— (18th cent.). Con. 137: XXXIV Mar '56; 139: LIII Je '57; 142: XXV Dec '58, XLIX Jan '59; 143: back cover May '59; 145: XLIV Je '60.

—— (17th cent.). Con. 132: LIII Nov '53.

—— (1699). Con. ency. of ant., vol. 3, pl. 103-8.

——, Adam. Con. 133: XXXIII Ap '54; 135: XXXV Mar '55, XXIV, XXXIX Ap '55; 141: X (col.) Ap '58; 144: XLIX Dec '59; 145: LXVII Je '60.

——, Adam (carved). Con. 142: XLV Nov '58.

——, Adam (18th cent.). Con. 145: XII Ap '60.

——, Adam (marble). Con. 129: XLI Je '52; 132: back cover Sept '53; 140: XXVII Sept '57; 143: XLI Ap '59; 144: XLIX Nov '59; 145: XXXVII Ap '60.

——, Adam (marble, 18th cent.). Con. 141: XXXI Je '58.

——, antique. Con. 129: 15 Ap '52; 132: XXX Nov '53; 135: back cover May '55; 143: XXXIII (col.) Je '59; 145: LX Ap '60.

——, antique (carved). Con. 140: XL Sept '57, XXXIII Dec '57.

——, carved (18th cent.). Con. 133: back cover Ap '54.

——, carved wood (18th cent.). Con. 132: XXXIX Sept '53; 138: XXXVII Jan '57; 140: XLIII Jan '58.

——, Chinese style. Con. 136: back cover Dec '55.

——, Claydon house. Con. 142: 72 Nov '58.

——, Elizabethan. Natl. geog. 107: 781 (col.) Je '55.

——, English (carved). Con. 141: XII Je '58.

——, Geo. III. Con. 139: XXI Mar '57.

——, Georgian. Con. 135: XLIII Je '55.

——, Georgian (marble). Con. 139: XLIII May '57.

——, Gothic. Con. 138: XLVII Dec '56.

——, Louis XIV. Con. 133: 242 Je '54.

——, Louis XV. Con. 135: XXXI May '55; 144: XLVII Sept '59, XLVIII Jan '60.

——, marble. Con. 137: LX May '56; 138: XXXI Sept '56, 92, XXXV, LII Nov '56, XXXIX Dec '56; 140: XLIII, LXVIII, back cover Nov '57; 142: back cover Dec '58; 144: back cover Nov '59.

——, marble (antique). Con. 129: LIV Je '52; 133: inside back cover Je '54; 145: back cover Mar '60.

——, marble (18th cent.). Con. 129: XXXI Ap '52; 132: LI Nov '53, XXXIII Jan '54; 133: XXXVII Je '54; 134: LI Sept '54; 141: XXIII, XXXV Ap '58; 142: back cover Jan '59; 143: XLI May '59; 145: LI Mar '60.

——, marble (19th cent.). Con. 143: XLV May '59.

——, old English. Con. 139: XXVI, XXIX Ap '57.

——, Palladian (carved). Con. ency. of ant., vol. 3, pl. 102.

——, regency (carved). Con. 139: XXVI Je '57.

——, regency (marble). Con. 132: XVIII Sept '53; 133: XLI May '54.

mantlepiece detail. Con. 133: back cover Mar '54.

——, Adam. Con. 141: back cover May '58.

——, detail, Adam (marble). Con. 138: XXXII Jan '57.

——, antique. Con. 129: LXI Ap '52.

——, carved. Con. 140: VI Dec '57.

——, marble. Con. 139: 144-5, back cover May '57.

——, Venetian stone. Con. 138: 214 Dec '56.

mantlepiece. See also fireplace.

Mantra of Chenrazee, Tibetan. Lehner: Pict. bk. of sym., p. 42.

Manuilsky, Dmitri Z. Cur. biog., p. 413 (1948).

manuscript, 10th cent. (woman head). Natl. geog. 114: 768 (col.) Dec '58.

manuscript illumination. Con. 132: 24 Sept '53; 133: 87-92 Ap '54; 143: 54, 56 Mar '59.

—— (Book of hours). Praeg pict. ency., p. 218 (col.).

—— (15th cent.). Con. 142: 197 Dec '58.

—— (15th cent., Ferrarese). Con. 133: 18-24 Mar '54.

—— (14th cent.). Natl. geog. 118: 815 (col.) Dec '60.

—— (Flemish, Brussels). Con. 143: 218-22 Je '59.

—— (Florentine). Con. 133: 168-72, 176 May '54.

—— (French). Con. 137: 189-91 May '56.

——, Petrarch's. Con. 143: 36 Mar '59.

manuscripts, illuminated. Con. 142: III Dec '58.

—— See also books, illumination.

Manuscripts of St. Martial, illuminated. Con. 126: 155-61 Dec '50.

Manzu, Giacomo. Cur. biog. p. 294 (1961).

Mao Tse-Tung. Cur. biog. p. 491 (1943).

Maori cave art. See cave art, Maori.

Maori cloak. Holiday 28: 107 Nov '60.

Maori girls (greeting). Holiday 25: 33 May '59.

Maori idol. Holiday 22: 105 Sept '57. Natl. geog. 101: 427 (col.) Ap '52.

Maori man (head). Int. gr. soc.: Arts . . . p. 183 (col.).

Maori ruler. Holiday 28: 77 (col.) Oct '60.

Maori women. Natl. geog. 101: 427, 440, 442 (col.) Ap '52.

Maoris. Travel 102: 19 Nov '54.

map (by Fra Mauro). Natl. geog. 118: 620-1 (col.) Nov '60.

—— (Abraham Lincoln's travels). Natl. geog. 117: 250-1 (col.) Feb '60.

—— (Aden colony). Natl. geog. 111: 234 Feb '57.

—— (Aegean). Ceram: March of arch., p. 46.

—— (Afghanistan). Natl. geog. 104: 421 Sept '53.

—— (Africa). Holiday 15: 39 (col.) Mar '54. Natl. geog. 104: 150-1 Aug '53; 106: 491 Oct '54; 110: 258 Aug '56, 330 Sept '56; 112: 586 Nov '57; 118: 422 (col.) Sept '60. Travel 104: 32 Nov '55; 106: 34 Nov '56; 113: 21, 57 Jan '60.

—— (Africa, Algeria & Sahara). Natl. geog. 113: 680 May '58.

—— (Africa, French west). Natl. geog. 113: 390 Mar '58.

—— (Africa, Nigeria). Natl. geog. 116: 232 Aug '59.

—— (Africa, northern). Natl. geog. 112: 54 Jl '57.

—— (Africa, outline). Holiday 27: back cover (col.) Ap '60.

—— (Africa, pictorial). Holiday 25: 63 Ap '59.

—— (Alaska). Holiday 26: 36 Aug '59. Natl. geog. 99: 552 Ap '51; 103: 766-7 (col.) Je '53.

—— (Alberta, Canada). Natl. geog. 118: 92 (col.) Jl '60.

—— (Algeria). Natl. geog. 113: 680 May '58; 117: 772 (col.) Je '60.

——. See also Africa, Algeria & Sahara.

—— (America, ancient civilization). Praeg. pict. ency., p. 537.

—— (America, Molineaux - Wright chart). Natl. geog. 103: 756 (col.) Je '53.

—— (Amsterdam). Travel 110: 32 Aug '58.

—— (Andalusia). Natl. geog. 112: 576 Oct '57; 113: 402 Mar '58.

—— (Andros is.). Natl. geog. 99: 639 May '51.

—— (Antarctica, Little Amer.). Natl. geog. 110: 147 Aug '56; 112: 15 Jl '57, 380-1 (col.) Sept '57; 113: 475 Ap '58; 115: 35 Jan '59; 116: 542-3 Oct '59.

—— (Arabia). Natl. geog. 114: 714-5 Nov '58.

—— (Arabia, Yemen). Natl. geog. 101: 216 Feb '52.

—— (Arctic circle). Natl. geog. 114: 136-7 Jl '58.

—— (Arctic region). Natl. geog. 103: 493 Ap '53; 107: 547 Ap '55; 111: 531 Ap '57; 115: 8-9 Jan '59; 116: 8-9 Jl '59.

—— (Arizona, products). Holiday 13: 39 (col.) Jan '54.

—— (Armenia). Holiday 19: 54 Feb '56.

—— (Australia). Natl. geog. 109: 241 Feb '56, 425 Mar '56; 110: 690 Nov '56; 112: 587 Nov '57; 114: 517 Oct '58. Travel 105: 15 Mar '56.

—— (Australia, Great Barrier Reef). Natl. geog. 111: 7 Jan '57.

—— (Austria). Holiday 19: 100 Je '56. Natl. geog. 99: 750-1 Je '51; 115: 181 Feb '59; 118: 250 (col.) Aug '60. Travel 103: 22 Je '55.

—— (Baffin is.). Natl. geog. 100: 467 Oct '51.

—— (Bahama is.). Natl. geog. 113: 152 Feb '58; 117: 170-1 (col.) Feb '60; 118: 122 (col.) Jl '60. Travel 105: 46 Mar '56.

—— (Balearic is.). Natl. geog. 111: 624 May '57.

—— (Bali). Natl. geog. 99: 6 Jan '51.

—— (Barbados is.). Natl. geog. 101: 366 Mar '52.

—— (Barbary states, 1804). Amer. heri., vol. 11 no. 2 p. 28-9 (col.) (Feb '60).

—— (battle field at Gettysburg). Amer. heri., vol. 9 no. 1 p. 41 (Dec '57).

map (battle of Island 10, Civil war). Amer. heri., vol. 10 no. 6 p. 71 (col.) Oct '59.
—— (battle of the Little Big Horn). Amer. heri., vol. 8 no. 2 p. 91 (Feb '57).
—— (battle of the Saintes, 1782). Amer. heri., vol. 9 no. 4 p. 9 (Je '58).
—— (Bay of Fundy). Natl. geog. 112: 162 Aug '57.
—— (Belgian Congo). Natl. geog. 101: 325 Mar '52; 117: 284 Feb '60.
—— (Belgium). Natl. geog. 113: 805 Je '58.
—— (Bermuda). Natl. geog. 105: 208-9 Feb '54.
—— (Bhutan). Natl. geog. 102: 716 Dec '52.
—— (Bimini is.). Natl. geog. 101: 188 Feb '52.
—— (bird routes in North & South Amer.). Natl. geog. 118: 663 (col.) Nov '60.
—— (Black Hills, S.D.). Natl. geog. 110: 485 Oct '56.
—— (Block is.). Travel 102: 21 Aug '54.
—— (Blue Ridge, N. C.). Natl. geog. 113: 860-1 Je '58.
—— (Borneo). Natl. geog. 116: 784 (col.) Dec '59.
—— (Brazil). Natl. geog. 102: 699 Nov '52; 117: 706 May '60.
—— (Brazil, Kraho Indian ter.). Natl. geog. 115: 345 Mar '59.
—— (British Columbia). Natl. geog. 114: 156-7 Aug '58.
—— (British Guiana). Natl. geog. 111: 857 Je '57.
—— (British Isles). Natl. geog. 110: 11 Jl '56.
—— (British route to New Orleans). Amer. heri., vol. 8 no. 5 p. 107 (Aug '57).
—— (Bryce canyon). Natl. geog. 114: 500-1 Oct '58.
—— (Cabeza exploration). Amer. heri., vol. 12 no. 1 p. 80 (Dec '60).
—— (Cajun country). Holiday 18: 84 Oct '55.
—— (Caldy is.). Natl. geog. 108: 567 Oct '55.
—— (California desert area). Natl. geog. 112: 680-1 Nov '57.
—— (California, 17th cent.). Natl. geog. 105: 804 Je '54.
—— (The Camargue, France). Natl. geog. 109: 670 May '56.
—— (Cambodia). Natl. geog. 117: 526 (col.) Ap '60.
—— (Canada). Natl. geog. 108: 198-9 (col.) Aug '55.
—— (Canary is.). Natl. geog. 107: 488 Ap '55.
—— (Canton is.). Natl. geog. 107: 122 Jan '55.
—— (Cappadocia). Natl. geog. 113: 129 Jan '58.
—— (Caribbean sea). Holiday 5: 35 (col.) Feb '49; 23: 34-5 (col.) Feb '58; 25: 32 Je '59.
Natl. geog. 118: 122 (col.) Jl '60.
Travel 103: 11 Mar '55.
—— (Central Amer.). Holiday 17: 36 Mar '55.
Travel 108: 24 Aug '57.

—— (Channel is., Cal.). Natl. geog. 114: 260-1 Aug '58.
—— (Charleston, S.C.). Amer. heri., vol. 9 no. 2 p. 51 (col.) (Feb '58).
—— (Chesapeake & Ohio canal). Natl. geog. 117: 424-5 (col.) Mar '60.
—— (Chicago, pictorial). Holiday 10: 49 (col.) Oct '51.
—— (Chile). Natl. geog. 117: 190 (col.) Feb '60.
—— ("Craters of the moon," Natl. monument). Natl. geog. 118: 509 (col.) Oct '60.
—— (Crete). Natl. geog. 104: 697 Nov '53.
—— (Cuba). Natl. geog. 99: 639 May '51.
Travel 106: 18 Dec '56.
—— (Cyprus is.). Natl. geog 101: 631 May '52; 109: 873 Je '56.
—— (Dalmatian coast). Travel 107: 36 Ap '57.
—— (Delaware). Natl. geog. 98: 371 Sept '50; 102: 5 Jl '52.
—— (Denmark). Travel 103: 15 May '55.
—— (desert tour). Travel 107: 34 Mar '57.
—— (Dinosaur Natl. monument). Natl. geog. 105: 364 Mar '54.
—— (discovery of Amer.). Natl. geog. 103: 756-69 (part col.) Je '53.
—— (Dodecanese). Natl. geog. 103: 358 Mar '53.
—— (Dominican Republic). Travel 103: 53 Je '55.
—— (Drake's & Cavendish's routes around the world, 1590). Amer. heri., vol. 10 no. 3 p. 10-11 (Ap '59).
—— (El Morro Natl. monument). Natl. geog. 112: 237 Aug '57.
—— (Eng.). Holiday 21: 117 Jan '57; 23: 55 Ap '58.
Natl. geog. 108: 300-1 Sept '55.
—— (Eng., inns location). Holiday 23: 145 Ap '58.
—— (Eng., south coast at time of Henry VIII). Amer. heri., vol. 10 no. 4 p. 6-7 (col.) (Je '59).
—— (England). See also map (British Isles).
—— (Europe). Travel 103: 7 Ap '55.
—— (Europe, Asia, Africa). Natl. geog. 118: 620-1 (col.) Nov '60.
—— (Falkland is.). Natl. geog. 109: 393 Mar '56.
—— (Fayal, Azores is.). Natl. geog. 113: 740 Je '58.
—— (Fiji is.). Natl. geog. 98: 124 Jl '50; 114: 526, 532 Oct '58.
Travel 102: 31 Nov '54.
—— (Florida). Natl. geog. 110: 825 Dec '56; 115: 137 Jan '59.
Travel 103: 7 Feb '55.
—— (Florida, 1591). Amer. heri., vol. 4 no. 2 p. 63 (winter '53).
—— (Florida, pictorial). Holiday 11: 7 (col.) Jan '52; 12: 21 (col.) Aug '52.
—— (Formosa is.). Natl. geog. 97: 144 Feb '50; 107: 575 Ap '55; 109: 268 Feb '56; 111: 330 Mar '57.
—— (Fort in West Indies). Amer. heri., vol. 10 no. 4 p. 8 (col.) (Je '59).

map (France). Holiday 21: 61, 143 Ap '57;
26: 155 Nov '59.
Natl. geog. 114: 291-2 Aug '58; 115: 573
Ap '59.
Travel 107: 53 Ap '57.
—— (Fremont's western explorations). Amer.
heri., vol. 7 no. 4 p. 18 (Je '56).
—— (French West Africa). Natl. geog. 100:
266 Aug '51; 113: 390 Mar '58, 680 May
'58.
—— (Galapagos is.). Natl. geog. 115: 688
May '59.
—— (Georgia). Natl. geog. 105: 290-1 Mar
'54.
—— (Germany). Holiday 25: 52 (col.) May
'59.
—— (Germany, 1871-1959). Natl. geog. 115:
780 Je '59.
—— (Grand Canyon). Natl. geog. 107: 596-
7 May '55.
—— (Grand Teton Natl. Park). Natl. geog.
109: 7 Jan '56.
—— (Greece). Natl. geog. 114: 738 Dec '58.
—— (Greenland). Natl. geog. 100: 467 Oct
'51; 106: 521 Oct '54; 109: 130-1 Jan '56.
—— (grizzly bear haunts). Natl. geog. 118:
286 (col.) Aug '60.
—— (guide to art of antiquity). Praeg. pict.
ency., p. 116.
—— (Gulf of Mexico). Natl. geog. 111: 704
May '57.
—— (Gulf of Naples). Natl. geog. 105: 536
Ap '54.
—— (Gulf of St. Lawrence). Travel 114: 26
Jl '60.
—— (Harpers Ferry region). Natl. geog. 111:
404-5 Mar '57.
—— (Hawaiian is.). Natl. geog. 115: 794-5
Je '59.
—— (Hebrides is.). Natl. geog. 106: 563 Oct
'54.
—— (Holland). Natl. geog. 98: 752 Dec '50.
—— (The Holy Land). Natl. geog. 98: 710
Dec '50; 114: 853 Dec '58; 118: 820 (col.)
Dec '60.
—— (Hong Kong). Natl. geog. 105: 245 Feb
'54.
—— (Hudson Bay). Natl. geog. 110: 677 Nov
'56.
—— (Hudson Bay stores). Natl. geog. 108:
207 (col.) Aug '55.
—— (Hudson river, land grants). Amer. heri.,
vol. 10 no. 1 p. 10 (col.) (Dec '58).
—— (Iceland). Natl. geog. 100: 604 Nov '51.
—— (Illinois). Holiday 20: 28 Sept '56.
Travel 103: 16 Je '55.
—— (India). Natl. geog. 110: 525 Oct '56;
112: 496 Oct '57; 118: 458-9 (col.) Oct '60.
—— (India, Naga Hills). Natl. geog. 107: 250
Feb '55.
—— (Indian Guatemala)). Natl. geog. 117:
410 Mar '60.
—— (Indian tribes). Amer. heri., vol. 7 no.
6 p. 6 (Oct '56).
—— (Indiana). Amer. heri., vol. 2 no. 1 p.
32 (fall '50).
—— (Indonesia). Natl. geog. 99: 6 Jan '51;
116: 777 Dec '59.
—— (Iowa). Travel 103: 31 Mar '55.

—— (Iran). Natl. geog. 98: 833 Dec '50.
—— (Iraq). Natl. geog. 98: 833 Dec '50; 114:
452-3 Oct '58.
—— (Ireland). Holiday 21: 115 Jan '57.
Natl. geog. 99: 656 May '51.
—— (Ireland, outline). Holiday 23: 132 Je
'58.
—— (Isle of Skye). Natl. geog. 102: 88 Jl
'52.
—— (Isle of Wight). Natl. geog. 101: 515 Ap
'52.
—— (Isles of Scilly). Travel 101: 15 Feb '54.
—— (Italy). Holiday 21: 53, 116 Jan '57;
25: 93 Mar '59.
Natl. geog. 107: 7 Jan '55; 109: 834 Je '56.
—— (Italy & Naples). Labande: Naples,
frontis.
—— (Italy, southern). Natl. geog. 116: 477
Oct '59.
—— (Japan). Natl. geog. 97: 597 May '50.
—— (Java). Natl. geog. 99: 6 Jan '51.
—— (Jerusalem). Natl. geog. 115: 496 Ap
'59.
—— (Jordan Valley). Natl. geog. 104: 856
Dec '53; 112: 838 Dec '57; 114: 790 Dec
'58.
—— (Kentucky). Natl. geog. 97: 180 Feb
'50.
—— (Key West). Natl. geog. 97: 43 Jan '50.
—— (Korea). Natl. geog. 97: 779 Je '50; 103:
507 Ap '53.
—— (Kuwait). Natl. geog. 102: 787 Dec '52.
—— (Labrador). Natl. geog. 101: 4 Jan '52.
—— (Ladakh). Natl. geog. 99: 607 May '51.
—— (Land of the Basques). Natl. geog. 105:
153 Feb '54.
—— (Laos). Natl. geog. 117: 50 Jan '60.
—— (Lebanon). Natl. geog. 113: 488 Ap '58.
—— (Lewis & Clark expedition). Travel 102:
12 Oct '54.
—— (Lhasa). Natl. geog. 108: 7 Jl '55.
—— (London). Natl. geog. 104: 296-7 Sept
'53.
—— (London, 1600). Natl. geog. 114: 94-5
Jl '58.
—— (Long Island, N.Y.). Holiday 24: 38-9
(col.) Sept '58.
Natl. geog. 99: 282 Mar '51; 112: 300-1
Sept '57.
—— (Mackenzies Canadian exposition). Amer.
heri., vol. 8 no. 6 p. 47 (col.) (Oct '57).
—— (Madeira is.). Natl. geog. 115: 375 Mar
'59.
—— (Malaya). Natl. geog. 103: 189 Feb '53.
—— (Maldive is.). Natl. geog. 111: 834 Je
'57.
—— (Gen. Marion's operations, Revolution).
Amer. heri., vol. 9 no. 3 p. 45 (col.) (Ap
'58).
—— (Martinique is.). Natl. geog. 115: 261
Feb '59.
—— (Maryland). Natl. geog.. 105: 438-9 (col.)
Ap '54.
—— (Mass.). Holiday 11: 36 Je '52.
—— (Mass. Bay, 1667). Amer. heri., vol. 10
no. 6 p. 79 (Oct '59).
—— (Mass. coast). Travel 107: 18 May '57.
—— (Mass. products). Holiday 17: 10 (col.)
Mar '55.

map (Mauritius is.). Natl. geog. 109: 80 Jan '56.

—— (Mayflower voyage). Natl. geog. 111: 716-7 May '57.

—— (Mediterranean sea). Ceram: March of arch., p. 171.
Natl. geog. 117: 688 (col.) May '60.
Osward: Asia Minor (back of book).

—— (Melville is.). Natl. geog. 109: 425 Mar '56.

—— (Mesa Verde Natl. Park, Colo.). Natl. geog. 116: 622 Nov '59.

—— (Mesopotamia). Natl. geog. 99: 45 Jan '51.

—— (Mexico). Amer. heri. vol. 10 no. 2 p. 81 (Feb '59).
Travel 106: 52 Oct '56.

—— (Michigan). Natl. geog. 101: 282-3 Mar '52.
Travel 103: 8 May '55.

—— (Michigan, pictorial). Holiday 10: 31 (col.) Jl '51.

—— (Mich. upper peninsula). Travel 110: 44 Aug '58. .

—— (Middle East). Holiday 20: 61 (col.) Dec '56.
Natl. geog. 105: 488-9 Ap '54; 117: 76-7 (col.) Jan '60.

—— (Miss. river, southern area). Natl. geog. 118: 683 (col.) Nov '60.

—— (Missouri). Holiday 21: 127 (col.) Ap '57.

—— (Monterey pen.). Holiday 12: 116 Dec '52.

—— (Monument Valley). Natl. geog. 114: 814-5 Dec '58.

—— (Morocco). Natl. geog. 107: 154 Feb '55.

—— (Mycenae). Ceram: March of arch., p. 48.

—— (Natl. forests). Holiday 20: 89 Aug '56.

—— (Natl. parks). Holiday 24: 44-5 (col.) Jl '58.

—— (Natl. parks, Cal.). Natl. geog. 116: 152 Aug '59.

—— (Natl. parks locations). Holiday 26: 52 Jl '59.

—— (Natl. wildlife refuge). Natl. geog. 118: 148 (col.) Jl '60.

—— (Naval war). See Naval war map.

—— (Nepal). Natl. geog. 97: 4 Jan '50; 117: 363 (col.) Mar '60.

—— (New Africa). Travel 113: 21 Jan '60.

—— (New Eng.). Natl. geog. 98: 145 Aug '50.

—— (New Eng., 1630). Amer. heri., vol. 10 no. 5 p. 107 (Aug '59).

—— (New Eng. coast, 1616). Natl. geog. 111: 614-5 May '57.

—— (New Guinea). Natl. geog. 108: 443 Oct '55; 116: 777 Dec '59.

—— (New Hampshire). Holiday 10: 36 (col.) Sept '51.

—— (New Jersey). Natl. geog. 102: 5 Jl '52; 117: 10-11 (col.) Jan '60.
Travel 102: 38 Aug '54.

—— (New Providence is.). Natl. geog. 113: 153 Feb '58.

—— (New World, 1500). Amer. heri., vol. 7 no. 1 p. 75 (Dec '55).

—— (New World, 1587). Amer. heri., vol. 7 no. 5 p. 64 (col.) (Aug '56).

—— (N.Y. City). Holiday 26: 48 (col.) Oct '59.

—— (N.Y. harbor). Natl. geog. 115: 839 Je '59.

—— (N.Y. state). Holiday 21: 103 Mar '57, 121 Ap '57, 151 May '57, 45 Je '57.

—— (N.Y. state products). Holiday 15: 113 (col.) Ap '54, 169 (col.) May '54; 17: 25 (col.) Mar '55.

—— (New Zealand). Natl. geog. 101: 423 Ap '52.

—— (Nez Perce Indian retreat). Amer. heri., vol. 9 no. 2 p. 81 (Feb '58).

—— (Nicaragua). Natl. geog. 109: 344 Mar '56.

—— (Nigeria). Natl. geog. 110: 330 Sept '56; 116: 232 Aug '59.
Travel 107: 38 Feb '57.

—— (Nomad migration routes). Natl. geog. 108: 786 Dec '55.

—— (Normandy, France). Natl. geog. 115: 600-1 May '59.

—— (North Amer., pictorial). Holiday 14: 34-5 (col.) Jl '53.

—— (North & south Amer., bird route). Natl. geog. 118: 663 (col.) Nov '60.

—— (North Carolina). Holiday 26: 12 Aug '59.

—— (North Dakota). Natl. geog. 100: 286-7 Sept '51.

—— (North Pole). Amer. heri., vol. 11 no. 3 p. 87 (Ap '60).
Natl. geog. 104: 472 Oct '53.

—— (Northwest, pictorial). Holiday 13: 29 (col.) May '53.

—— (Northwest ter.). Amer. heri., vol. 3 no. 3 p. 47 (spring '52).

—— (Nova Scotia). Holiday 14: 106 Sept '53.

—— (Ohio). Natl. geog. 107: 442-3 (col.) Ap '55.

—— (Okinawa). Natl. geog. 107: 268 Feb '55.

—— (Okla.). Travel 104: 31 Jl '55.

—— (old Testament lands). Natl. geog. 118: 821 (col.) Dec '60.

—— (Olympic natl. park). Natl. geog. 108: 90-1 Jl '55.

—— (Onondaga trail). Amer. heri., vol. 3 no. 4 p. 10 (summer '52).

—— (Orcas is., Puget Sound). Travel 105: 36 May '56.

—— (Orkney is.). Natl. geog. 104: 522 Oct '53.

—— (Pacific ocean). Holiday 25: 22 (col.) Feb '59.

—— (Pacific, early north). Amer. heri., vol. 7 no. 5 p. 73, 78 (Aug '56).

—— (Pakistan). Natl. geog. 102: 640 Nov '52; 107: 402 Mar '55.

—— (Palmer Pen.). Amer. heri., vol. 6 no. 4 p. 54 (col.) (Je '55).

—— (Panama). Holiday 12: 56 (col.) Nov '52.
Natl. geog. 97: 229 Feb '50; 104: 275 Aug '53.

—— (Paris). Travel 107: 35 May '57.

map (Paris, pictorial). Holiday 13: 53 (col.) Ap '53.

—— (Peking). Natl. geog. 118: 192 (col.) Aug '60.

—— (Persian Gulf). Travel 103: 15 Mar '55.

—— (Peru). Natl. geog. 115: 401 Mar '59.

—— (Phila., historical). Natl. geog. 118: 156-7 (col.) Aug '60.

—— (Philmont scout ranch). Natl. geog. 110: 405 Sept '56.

—— (Pitcairn is.). Natl. geog. 112: 735 Dec '57.

—— (Poland, 1914-58). Natl. geog. 114: 387 Sept '58.

—— (Portugal). Natl. geog. 106: 677 Nov '54.

—— (Pribilof is.). Natl. geog. 101: 496 Ap '52.

—— (Puerto Rico). Natl. geog. 118: 122 (col.) Jl '60.

—— (Pygmyland). Natl. geog. 117: 284 Feb '60.

—— (Pyrenees mts.). Natl. geog. 109: 308-9 Mar '56.

—— (Quebec). Natl. geog. 100: 467 Oct '51; 101: 4 Jan '52.

—— (Quebec, north shore). Travel 108: 49 Aug '57.

—— (Quemoy is.). Natl. geog. 115: 418 Mar '59.

—— (Quetico, Superior country). Amer. heri., vol. 1 no. 3 p. 48 (col.) (spring '50).

—— (Revolutionary war). Amer. heri., vol. 8 no. 2 p. 75, 86 (Feb '57).

—— (Rio Grande river). Holiday 20: 36 (col.) Oct '56.

—— (Rocky mts.). Holiday 18: 101 (col.) Jl '55.

—— (Rome, Italy). Holiday 11: 42-3 (col.) Ap '52.
Natl. geog. 111: 444-5 (col.) Ap '57.

—— (Rome, pictorial). Holiday 27: 81 Ap '60.

—— (Russia). Natl. geog. 116: 729 Dec '59; 118: 888 (col.) Dec '60.

—— (Russia, 1918-19 campaign). Amer. heri., vol. 10 no. 1 p. 27 (Dec '58).

—— (Saar). Natl. geog. 105: 564 Ap '54.

—— (Sahara). Natl. geog. 113: 680 May '58.

—— (St. Croix is.). Natl. geog. 109: 207 Feb '56.

—— (St. Helena is.). Natl. geog. 98: 271 Aug '50.

—— (St. Lawrence seaway). Natl. geog. 115: 306-7 (col.) Mar '59.

—— (San Francisco, downtown). Natl. geog. 110: 191 Aug '56.

—— (Santa Barbara is.). Natl. geog. 114: 260-1 Aug '58.

—— (Saudi Arabia). Natl. geog. 104: 9 Jl '53; 108: 160 Aug '55; 110: 71 Jl '56; 117: 76-7 (col.) Jan '60.

—— (Scotch highlands). Natl. geog. 110: 11 Jl '56.

—— (Scotland). Natl. geog. 104: 522 Oct '53; 112: 442-3 Oct '57.

—— (Seattle, Wash.). Natl. geog. 117: 500 (col.) Ap '60.

—— (Seychelles is.). Natl. geog. 116: 679 Nov '59.

—— (Seymour Narrows, Canada). Natl. geog. 114: 184 Aug '58.

—— (Shetland is.). Natl. geog. 104: 522 Oct '53.

—— (Sicily). Natl. geog. 107: 7 Jan '55.

—— (South Amer.). Holiday 20: 57 (col.) Nov '56.

—— (South Amer. outline). Holiday 27: back cover (col.) Ap '60.

—— (South Amer., pictorial). Holiday 18: 13 (col.) Jl '55.

—— (South Carolina). Natl. geog. 103: 284-5 Mar '53.

—— (South Sea is.). Holiday 28: 51 Oct '60. Natl. geog. 109: 550 Ap '56.

—— (Strait of Messina). Natl. geog. 104: 585 Nov '53.

—— (submarine voyage). Natl. geog. 118: 588, 596, 600, 608, 615 (col.) Nov '60.

—— (Sudan). Natl. geog. 103: 250 Feb '53.

—— (Susquehanna Valley). Amer. heri., vol. 3 no. 4 p. 23 (summer '52).

—— (Sweden). Natl. geog. 98: 608 Nov '50.

—— (Switzerland). Natl. geog. 98: 211 Aug '50; 110: 432-3 Oct '56.

—— (Tasmania). Natl. geog. 110: 794 Dec '56.

—— (Thailand). Natl. geog. 98: 501 Oct '50.

—— (Thompson's western North Amer.). Amer. heri., vol. 11 no. 6 p. 63 (Oct '60).

—— (Thousand is.). Travel 110: 33 Jl '58.

—— (Tibet). Natl. geog. 108: 7 Jl '55.

—— (travel route thru Europe). Travel 107: 12 Ap '57.

—— (Trinidad). Natl. geog. 103: 39 Jan '53.

—— (Trucial Oman). Natl.. geog. 110: 71 Jl '56.

—— (Turkey). Natl. geog. 100: 142-3 Aug '51; 117: 76 (col.) Jan '60.

—— (Tuscany, Italy). Travel 107: 24 Ap '57.

—— (U.S.). Brooks: Growth of a nation, p. 18, 21, 30.
Natl. geog. 98: 8-9 Jl '50; 99: 834 Je '51. Travel 105: 26 Feb '56.

—— (U.S., allied army mosaic). Natl. geog. 111: 751 (col.) Je '57.

—— (U.S., cattle trails west, 1860-90). Brooks: Growth of a nation, p. 165.

—— (U.S., Civil war). Amer. heri., vol. 7 no. 6 p. 65 (Oct '56).

—— (U.S., colonial routes). Brooks: Growth of a nation, p. 73.

—— (U.S., colonies, 1754). Amer. heri., vol. 7 no. 2 p. 6 (col.) (Feb '56).

—— (U.S., confederate states). Brooks: Growth of a nation, p. 143.

—— (U.S., early). Amer. heri., vol. 4 no. 2 p. 2 (Winter '53).

—— (U.S., European claims, 1700, 1793). Brooks: Growth of a nation, p. 62, 69.

—— (U.S., 1st hundred years, 1500-1600). Brooks: Growth of a nation, p. 30.

—— (U.S., frontier, 1790-1890). Brooks: Growth of a nation, p. 213.

—— (U.S., on globe). Amer. heri., vol. 9 no. 1 p. 72 (col.) (Dec '57).

—— (U.S., Oregon trail). Brooks: Growth of a nation, p. 123.

map (U.S., outline). Holiday 7: 7 May '50; 28: 99 Jl '60.
Travel 104: 48 Oct '55.
—— (U.S., pictorial). Holiday 12: 52-3 (col.) Jl '52.
—— (U.S., pony express, 1860). Brooks: Growth of a nation, p. 139.
—— (U.S., population, 1890). Brooks: Growth of a nation, p. 213.
—— (U.S., population, 1790-1950). Brooks: Growth of a nation, p. 261.
—— (U.S., regions). Brooks: Growth of a nation, p. 259-60.
—— (U.S., Santa Fe trail). Brooks: Growth of a nation, p. 118-9.
—— (U.S., 2nd hundred years, 1600-1700). Brooks: Growth of a nation, p. 36.
—— (U.S., southeast). Holiday 16: 34 Oct '54.
—— (U.S., territorial 1783-1853). Brooks: Growth of a nation, p. 88.
—— (U.S., 13 states). Brooks: Growth of a nation, p. 81.
—— (U.S. eagle map, 1832). Amer. heri., vol. 8 no. 3 fronti (Ap '57).
—— (Valley Forge). Natl. geog. 105: 188 Feb '54.
—— (Valley of Kashmir). Natl. geog. 114: 615 Nov '58.
—— (Viet Nam). Natl. geog. 98: 501 Oct '50; 107: 862 Je '55.
—— (Virgin is.). Natl. geog. 109: 207 Feb '56.
—— (Virginia, 1590). Amer. heri., vol. 4 no. 2 p. 50 (winter '53).
—— (Virginia, 1627). Amer. heri., vol. 9 no. 6 p. 111 (Oct '58).
—— (Waldseemuller, 1507). Amer. heri., vol. 6 no. 3 p. 18 (Ap '55).
—— (war deserter's route, John Champe's route). Amer. heri., vol. 8 no. 6 p. 26 (Oct '57) (Revolutionary war).
—— (Washington, 1889). Amer. heri., vol. 4 no. 4 p. 60 (summer '53).
—— (Wash., state). Natl. geog. 102: 576-7 Nov '52.
—— (Waterton glacier, Inter. peace park). Natl. geog. 109: 596-7 (col.) May '56.
—— (West Indies is.). Amer. heri., vol. 6 no. 4 p. 98 (Je '55). Travel 104: 62 Sept '55.
—— (West Point, 1780). Amer. heri., vol. 10 no. 1 p. 15 (Dec '58).
—— (West Virginia). Natl. geog. 97: 181 Feb '50.
—— (Wichita mts.). Natl. geog. 111: 666 May '57.
—— (Wisconsin). Natl. geog. 111: 148-9 (col.) Feb '57.
—— (Wisconsin, products). Holiday 6: 49 (col.) Jl '49.
—— (world). Holiday 7: 75 Mar '50. Natl. geog. 100: 713 (col.) Dec '51; 101: 122-3 Jan '52; 109: 294 Feb '56; 110: 150 Aug '56; 117: 828-9 (col.) Je '60.
—— (world, airplane service). Holiday 17: 120-1 (col.) Jan '55.

—— (world, 18th cent., by Nagakubo Sekisiu of Mito). Amer. heri., vol. 9 no. 3 p. 18 (col.) (Ap '58).
—— (world, livestock to Amer.). Brooks: Growth of a nation, p. 11.
—— (Yellowstone natl. park). Natl. geog. 110: 762 Dec '56.
—— (Yosemite relief, children, ranger). Natl. geog. 113: 598 (col.) May '58.
—— (Yucatan). Natl. geog. 115: 95 Jan '59.
—— (Yugoslavia). Natl. geog. 99: 144 Feb '51.
——(Yukon, Alaska). Natl. geog. 104: 400 Sept '53.
—— (Yukon river). Natl. geog. 112: 251 Aug '57.
—— (Zanzibar). Natl. geog. 101: 264 Feb '52.
—— (Zion natl. park). Natl. geog. 105: 51 Jan '54.
—— See also maps.
Ma-Pe-Wi (work of). Natl. geog. 107: 357, 360, 371 (col.) Mar '55.
maple sugar making. Amer. heri., vol. 3 no. 4 p. 35 (summer '52). Natl. geog. 105: 472-82 (col.) Ap '54.
maple-sugar making utensils. Rawson: Ant. pict. bk., p. 11.
maple syrup carts (man, horse). Natl. geog. 99: 590 (col.) May '51.
maple syrup tree tapping. Natl. geog. 108: 663 Nov '55.
mapparium (world globe). Natl. geog. 107: 778 (col.) Je '55.
maps (16-18th cent.). Con. ency. of ant., vol. 3 pl. 157-63.
—— (Spain). Natl. geog. 97: 418 Ap '50.
Maquinna (Nootka Indian chief). Amer. heri., vol. 7 no. 5 p. 76 (Aug '56).
Marais, Jean. Cur. biog. p. 285 (1962). Holiday 25: 76 (col.) Mar '59.
Maratta, Carlo (painting by). Con. 142: 165 Dec '58.
Maratti, Francesco (sculpture by). Con. 141: 222 Je '58.
marble boat. See boat, Chinese marble.
marble highway (Ephesus). Osward: Asia Minor, p. 41-2.
marble inlay (India). Natl. geog. 118: 474-5 (col.) Oct '60.
marble quarry. Amer. heri., vol. 2 no. 3 p. 34, 38-42 (part col.) (spring '51). Brooks: Growth of a nation, p. 268. Natl. geog. 107: 756 (col.) Je '55.
marble stone in honor of Emperor Augustus (on the Angora). Osward: Asia Minor, pl. 44.
Marblehead (Mass.). Holiday 24: 58-61 (part col.) Sept '58; 26: 62 Jl '59. Natl. geog. 99: 716-7 (col.) Je '51.
—— (Mass. harbor). Natl. geog. 98: 162 (col.) Aug '50.
Marc, Franz (work of). Praeg. pict. ency., p. 448 (col.).
Mar canal (Kashmir). Natl. geog. 114: 629 (col.) Nov '58.
Marcantonio, Vito. Cur. biog. p. 400 (1949).
Marceau, Marcel. Cur. biog. p. 334 (1957).

"Marcelle Lender dancing" (Toulouse Lautrec). Con. 137: 139 Ap '56.

March, Fredric. Cur. biog. p. 494 (1943).

"March of the Teutons" (Delacroix). Praeg. pict. ency., p. 385 (col.).

Marchal, Leon. Cur. biog. p. 497 (1943).

Marchand, Jean (work of). Con. 145: VI (col.) Je '60.

Marciano, Rocky. Cur. biog. p. 403 (1952).

Marcks, Gerhard (ceramic figure). Praeg. pict. ency., p. 493.

—— (work of). Praeg. pict. ency., p. 32.

Marcoule plutonium maker. See plutonium maker (Marcoule).

Marcus, Jacob R. Cur. biog. p. 256 (1960).

Marcus, Stanley. Cur. biog. p. 402 (1949).

Marcus, Aurelius (sculpture, 161 AD). Praeg. pict. ency., p. 159.

Marcy, Mary Ellen. See McClellan, Mrs. Geo. B.

Mar del Plata (Argentina). Natl. geog. 113: 302-3 Mar '58.

Travel 105: 13 Jan '56.

Mardi Gras. Holiday 11: 57 (col.) Feb '52, 34, 38-9 (col.) Mar '52.

Jordan: Hammond's pict. atlas, p. 83 (col.).

Natl. geog. 103: 159-63 (col.) Feb '53; 118: 726-32 (col.) Nov '60.

—— (Fat or Shrove Tues.). Travel 109: 30-2 Feb '58.

—— (king & queen). Holiday 23: 83 (col.) Mar '58.

—— (sym.). Lehner: Pict. bk. of sym., p. 55.

Mardi Gras characters. Holiday 17: 21 Jan '55.

Mardi Gras invitation (1860). Amer. heri., vol. 11 no. 3 p. 28 (col.) (Ap '60).

Mardi Gras parade. Holiday 19: 14 Jan '56; 25: 95 (col.) Feb '59.

Mardikian, George M. Cur. biog. p. 423 (1947).

Marealle, Thomas. Holiday 25: 70 Ap '59.

Marees, Hans von (work of). Praeg. pict. ency., p. 402 (col.).

Marek, Kurt W. Cur. biog. p. 355 (1957).

Margai, Sir Milton A. Cur. biog. p. 287 (1962).

Margaret of Austria, Queen of France (statue). Con. 133: LXXIV Je '54.

Margaret Rose, Princess (Gt. Brit.). Cur. biog. p. 413 (1953).

Holiday 21: 44 Feb '57.

—— (man, dancing). Holiday 21: 48 Jan '57.

Margat fortress. See fortress, Margat.

Margesson, David. Cur. biog. p. 557 (1941).

Margriet, Princess (Holland). Natl. geog. 98: 751 Dec '50.

Maria Anna, Grafin von Holnstein (Desmaues). Con. 142: 7 Sept '58.

Maria Anna of Austria (Velasquez). Con. 140: 142 Nov '57.

"Maria Camilla Pallavicini" (Luti). Con. 136: 285 Jan '56.

"Maria Catharina de Benzenav" (Gheeraerts). Con. 132: 37 (col.) Sept '53.

Maria Laach abbey church. Praeg. pict. ency., p. 234.

Marianna caverns. Travel 109: 16 Feb '58.

Marianne (France, sym.). Lehner: Pict. bk. of sym., p. 93.

Marie, Andre. Cur. biog. p. 414 (1948).

Marie Antoinette, Queen of France. Amer. heri., vol. 3 no. 4 p. 26 (summer '52).

Con. 136: XXI Sept '55.

—— (Lebrun). Con. 136: 31 Sept '55.

—— (bust). Con. 133: LIX Je '54.

—— (porcelain bust). Con. 129: 73 Ap '52.

"Marie Claire des Champs de Marsilly" (Nattier). Con. 136: XVII (col.) Nov '55.

"Marie von Numsen" (Peter Als). Con. 135: 48 Mar '55.

Marienburg castle (refectory). Praeg. pict. ency., p. 235.

Marientreu, Richard (work of). Con. 134: 199 Dec '54.

Marieschi, Jacopo (work of). Con. 140: 97-9 Nov '57.

Marieschi, Michele (work of). Con. 129: IX (col.) Ap '52; 138: LI Sept '56.

Marin, John. Cur. biog. p. 405 (1949).

—— (work of). Holiday 14: 61 (col.) Nov '53. Praeg. pict. ency., p. 476 (col.).

Marin, Luis Munoz. Cur. biog. p. 444 (1953).

marine barracks. See U.S. Marine barracks.

marine corp, German. See German marine corps (1871).

Marine gardens (Yaquina). Jordan: Hammond's pict. atlas, p. 157 (col.).

Marine studios (Marineland). Natl. geog. 113: 41 (col.) Jan '58.

Marineland (Cal.). Holiday 22: 59 (col.) Oct '57.

Marineland (Fla.). Natl. geog. 102: 679-94 (col.) Nov '52.

Marines, Royal British. Natl. geog. 101: 521, 538 (col.) Ap '52.

Marines, U.S. (leathernecks). See U.S. Marines.

Marines, Women. See Women marines.

Marini, Marino. Cur. biog. p. 439 (1954).

—— (wood figure). Praeg. pict. ency., p. 464.

—— (work of). Int. gr. soc.: Arts . . . p. 131 (col.).

Marion, Gen. Francis. Brooks: Growth of a nation, p. 78.

—— (by White). Amer. heri., vol. 9 no. 3 p. 40 (col.) (Ap '58).

—— (horseback). Amer. heri., vol. 9 no. 3 p. 46 (Ap '58).

Marion & his troops, Gen. Francis (Crossing river Pee Dee). Amer. heri. vol. 9 no. 3 p. 42 (col.) (Ap '58).

"Marion offers British officer food" (by White). Amer. heri. vol. 9 no. 3 p. 40 (col.) (Ap '58).

Marionettes (Sicily). Natl. geog. 107: 32 (col.) Jan '55.

Maris, Roger. Cur. biog. p. 296 (1961).

Maritain, Jacques. Cur. biog. p. 568 (1942).

maritime power (sym.). Lehner: Pict. bk. of sym., p. 95.

Marjolin, Robert. Cur. biog. p. 416 (1948).

Mark, Herman F. Cur. biog. p. 298 (1961).

Mark Twain. See Clemens, Samuel Langhorne.

Markel, Lester. Cur. biog. p. 405 (1952).

Marken (man). Natl. geog. 98: 759 (col.) Dec '50.

marker, sheep. See sheep marker; branding iron.

markers, historical. *See* historical markers.
market (Belen, Peru). Disney: People & places, p. 110 (col.).
—— **(Bolivia).** Natl. geog. 98: 488 (col.) Oct '50.
—— **(Indonesia).** Natl. geog. 99: 34, 36 (col.) Jan '51.
—— **(Mexico).** Travel 110: 20 Nov '58.
——, **camel (Egypt).** Natl. geog. 108: 646 (col.) Nov '55.
——, **city (Charleston).** Amer. heri., vol. 9 no. 2 p. 60 (col.) (Feb '58).
——, **farm open-air.** Holiday 28: 81 Sept '60.
——, **floating.** *See* floating market, Bangkok's. *See* also Xochimilco (floating gardens, Mexico).
——, **food (Indochina).** Natl. geog. 102: 302 (col.) Sept '52.
——, **food (Italian).** Holiday 11: 115 (col.) May '52.
——, **harbor (Bahama).** Natl. geog. 113: 165, 167, 171 (col.) Feb '58.
——, **hog (Poland).** Natl. geog. 114: 392-3 (col.) Sept '58.
——, **open-air (Algiers).** Holiday 5: 64 (col.) Feb '49.
——, **open-air (Fijian).** Holiday 7: 62 Je '50.
——, **open-air (Trinidad).** Natl. geog. 103: 54, 56 (col.) Jan '53.
——, **roadside.** Holiday 21: 100 (col.) Jan '57.
——, **sidewalk (France).** Holiday 21: 91 (col.) Ap '57.
——, **street (Africa).** Natl. geog. 97: 324 Mar '50.
——, **street (Arabia).** Natl. geog. 104: 866 Dec '53; 110: 69 (col.) Jl '56.
——, **street (Brussels).** Natl. geog. 101: 699 May '52.
——, **street (Copenhagen).** Natl. geog. 101: 695 May '52.
——, **street (Denmark).** Natl. geog. 108: 811, 820 (col.) Dec '55.
——, **street (El Oued).** Natl. geog. 117: 784-5 (col.) Je '60.
——, **street (Ethiopia).** Natl. geog. 106: 749 (col.) Dec '54.
——, **street (Formosa).** Natl. geog. 111: 338, 340-1 (col.) Mar '57.
——, **street (Harar).** Natl. geog. 106: 754-5 (col.) Dec '54.
——, **street (Khartoum).** Natl. geog. 103: 260-1 (col.) Feb '53.
——, **street (Korea).** Natl. geog. 103: 657 (col.) May '53.
——, **street (Lhasa).** Natl. geog. 108: 34 Jl '55.
——, **street (Mexico).** Holiday 14: 51 Jl '53. Natl. geog. 100: 797 (col.) Dec '51. Travel 114: 52-5 Nov '60.
——, **street (Naples).** Labande: Naples, p. 29.
——, **street (Nigeria).** Travel 107: 40 Feb '57.
——, **street (Peking).** Natl. geog. 118: 221 (col.) Aug '60.
——, **street (St. Lucia).** Travel 103: 12 Mar '55.
——, **street (Spain).** Natl. geog. 109: 306-7 (col.) Mar '56.

——, **street (Yemen).** Natl. geog. 101: 243 (col.) Feb '52.
——, **street fair (Guatemala).** Natl. geog. 117: 410-11 (col.) Mar '60.
——, **street food.** Amer. heri., vol. 12 no. 1 p. 14 (Dec '60). Natl. geog. 102: 25 (col.) Jl '52.
——, **street (Chinese).** Natl. geog. 99: 405 (col.) Mar '51.
——, **street French (New Orleans).** Natl. geog. 117: 248 (col.) Feb '60.
——, **street fruit (Nepal).** Natl. geog. 117: 381 (col.) Mar '60.
market boats (Madeira). Holiday 28: 65 Sept '60.
——, **floating (Chile).** Natl. geog. 117: 215 (col.) Feb '60.
—— *See* also floating market, Bangkok's. Xochimilco (floating gardens, Mexico).
"Market for hay" (Chalon). Con. 132: XVII Nov '53.
market place (Agora). *See* Agora (market place).
market room (int., Santo Domingo). Holiday 5: 57 (col.) Feb '49.
market square (Holland). Natl. geog. 106: 406-7 (col.) Sept '54.
—— **(Smyrna-Izmir).** Osward, Asia Minor, pl. 100.
"Market square, Dorchester" (Nixon). Con. 139: XLVII May '57.
market stall, vegetable (woman). Natl. geog. 111: 622 (col.) May '57.
market stand, food. Holiday 5: 61 (col.) Ap '49.
——, **outdoor (Africa).** Natl. geog. 118: 320-1 (col.) Sept '60.
——, **sidewalk (Polish).** Natl. geog. 114: 366 (col.) Sept '58.
——, **street (flower, Italy).** Natl. geog. 109: 836 (col.) Je '56.
——, **street (fruit).** Natl. geog. 109: 280 Feb '56.
——, **street (India).** Natl. geog. **118: 462** (col.) Oct '60.
——, **street (Moscow).** Natl. geog. 116: 724-5 (col.) Dec '59.
——, **street (Nigeria).** Natl. geog. 110: 359 (col.) Sept '56.
——, **street (Sicily).** Natl. geog. 107: 34-5 (col.) Jan '55.
——, **street (Turkey).** Natl. geog. 100: 180 (col.) Aug '51.
——, **street (Vientiane).** Natl. geog. 117: 60-1 (col.) Jan '60.
Markey, Mr. & Mrs. Gene. Holiday 25: 96 (col.) Ap '59.
Markham, Beryl. Cur. biog. p. 571 (1942).
Markham, William (bust). Con. 132: 118 Nov '53.
Markova, Alicia. Cur. biog. p. 498 (1943).
Mark, Lord Simon. Cur. biog. p. 289 (1962).
marks, porcelain. *See* porcelain marks.
Marland, William C. Cur. biog. p. 412 (1956).
Marlborough, Duke of. Holiday 15: 29 Je '54.
"Marlbourne" house (home of Ruffin)). Amer. heri., vol. 9 no. 1 p. 25 (Dec '57).

Marlow, William (work of). Con. 133: XXI Je '54; 136: 276 (col.) Jan '56; 141: 60 Mar '58, 236 Je '58.

Marmaduke, John Sappington. Pakula: Cent. album, p. 209.

Marmara sea. Osward: Asia Minor, pl. 160.

Maroni, Giovanni Battista (work of). Con. 142: 205 Dec '58.

Marostica (chess board, Italy). Natl. geog. 110: 659-68 (col.) Nov '56.

Marot, Daniel (drawing by). Con. 126: 64 Aug '50.

Marples, Ernest. Cur. biog. p. 258 (1960).

Marquand, Hilary A. Cur. biog. p. 405 (1951).

Marquand, John Phillips. Cur. biog. p. 573 (1942).

Marquee, Washington's (Valley Forge). Natl. geog. 105: 191 (col.) Feb '54.

Marquesa is. Natl. geog. 97: 74-104 (part col.) Jan '50.

"Marquess of Monthermer" (Mengs). Con. 135: 2 (col.) Mar '55.

Marquet, Albert (work of). Con. 145: VII (col.) Je '60.

marquetry ornament. Con. ency. of ant., vol. 1, p. 29.

Marquette & Joliet explore Miss. (sculpture). Brooks: Growth of a nation, p. 58.

"Marquis de Laborde" (Greuze). Con. 135: 43 Mar '55.

marquise seat, French directoire. Con. 139: 262 Je '57.

Marrakesh (Morocco). Disney: People & places, p. 96-7 (col.). Natl. geog. 107: 180, 182 (col.) Feb '55; 112: 53, 56-7 (col.) Jl '57.

—— **(minaret).** Int. gr. soc.: Arts . . . p. 85 (col.).

Marrel, Jacob (work of). Con. 143: 256 (col.) Je '59.

marriage (goddess of). Lehner: Pict. bk. of sym., p. 30.

—— **(Japan).** Disney: People & places, p. 154-5 (col.).

——, **Gretna Green.** See Gretna Green marriage.

marriage casket on stand, French (18th cent.). Con. 145: 286 Je '60.

"Marriage ceremony" (Nordenberg). Con. 141: XXIII Mar '58.

"Marriage of Cana." Natl. geog. 101: 99 (col.) Jan '52.

—— **(book illumination).** Con. 140: 105 Nov '57.

"Marriage of the Virgin" (Dipre). Con. 132: LXIII Nov '53.

—— **(Rubens).** Con. 141: 1 Mar '58.

marriage salver. See salver, marriage.

Marriott, Alice. Cur. biog. p. 383 (1950).

Mars (sym.). Lehner: Pict. bk. of sym., p. 24, 32.

—— **(planet).** Holiday 13: 99 (col.) Mar '53. Natl. geog. 108: 426-34 (part col.) Sept '55.

——, **helmet of.** See helmet of Mars.

"Mars & Venus" (Botticelli). Con. 139: 98 Ap '57.

—— **(Poussin).** Con. 143: 124 Ap '59.

"Marseillaise" (relief, Paris). Praeg. pict. ency., p. 428.

Marseille, Lacroix de (work of). Con. 141: 248 Je '58.

Marseille (harbor, Mediterranean). Holiday 16: 98-9 (col.) Nov '54.

Marsh, Ernest Sterling. Cur. biog. p. 260 (1960).

Marsh, Rev. John. Cur. biog. p. 262 (1960).

Marsh, Reginald. Cur. biog. p. 559 (1941).

—— **(work of).** Amer. heri., vol. 9 no. 4 p. 20-1 (col.) (Je '58).

Marshall (ghost town). Natl. geog. 112: 696 (col.) Nov '57.

Marshall, Benjamin (work of). Con. 142: 133 Nov '58; 143: 117 Ap '59; 144: 109 Nov '59, 202, 204 Dec '59, 270 Jan '60; 145: 146 May '60.

Marshall, Catherine. Cur. biog. p. 404 (1955).

Marshall, Charles Herbert, jr. Cur. biog. p. 406 (1949).

Marshall, David. Cur. biog. p. 414 (1956).

Marshall, Gen. George Catlett. Cur. biog. p. 425 (1947). Natl. geog. 106: 65B Jl '54; 111: 734, 737 Je '57; 117: 113 Jan '60.

Marshall, John. Amer. heri., vol. 6 no. 6 p. 56, 94 (Oct '55); vol. 7 no. 1 p. 10 (col.) (Dec '55). Holiday 7: 73 Feb '50.

Marshall, Lois. Cur. biog. p. 263 (1960).

Marshall, Maple Lee. Cur. biog. p. 418 (1948).

Marshall, Rev. Peter. Cur. biog. p. 420 (1948).

Marshall, Rosamond van Der Zee. Cur. biog. p. 575 (1942).

Marshall, Samuel L. A. Cur. biog. p. 416 (1953).

Marshall, Thurgood (Negro lawyer). Cur. biog. p. 441 (1954). Holiday 27: 78 Je '60.

Marshall, Verne. Cur. biog. p. 561 (1941).

Marshall, Walter P. Cur. biog. p. 384 (1950).

Marshes, Andalusian. See Andalusian marshes.

Martel, Giffard Le Quesne. Cur. biog. p. 501 (1943).

Martha's Vineyard is. Natl. geog. 98: 161, 163 (col.) Aug '50.

—— **(harbor).** Holiday 26: 16 Jl '59.

Marti, Jose (bust). Natl. geog. 97: 72 Jan '50.

Martin, Anson (work of). Con. 139: XLI May '57.

Martin, Dr. Archer J. P. Cur. biog. p. 418 (1953).

Martin, Edmund F. Cur. biog. p. 291 (1962).

Martin, Edward. Cur. biog. p. 383 (1945).

Martin, Elias (work of). Con. 135: 49 Mar '55.

Martin, Fletcher. Cur. biog. p. 273 (1958).

Martin, Glenn L. Cur. biog. p. 502 (1943).

Martin, Harry, jr. Cur. biog. p. 421 (1948).

Martin, Jackie. Cur. biog. p. 505 (1943).

Martin, John (work of). Con. 144: 33 Sept '59.

Martin, John Bartlow. Cur. biog. p. 416 (1956).

Martin, Joseph. Holiday 24: 60 Sept '58.

Martin, Joseph W., jr. Cur. biog. p. 423 (1948). Natl. geog. 102: 146 Aug '52.

Martin, Lillien J. Cur. biog. p. 576 (1942).

Martin, Mary. Cur. biog. p. 448 (1944). Holiday 20: 84 Dec '56.

Martin, Michael. See Lightfoot, Capt.

Martin, Paul. Cur. biog. p. 408 (1951).

Martin, Thomas E. Cur. biog. p. 417 (1956).

Martin, Tony. Holiday 14: 134 Dec '53.

Martin, Dr. Walter B. Cur. biog. p. 443 (1954).

Martin, Bishop William C. Cur. biog. p. 420 (1953).

Martin, William M Chesney, jr. Cur. biog. p. 410 (1951).

Martin Artajo, Alberto. Cur. biog. p. 408 (1949).

Martinelli, Giovanni. Cur. biog. p. 385 (1945).

Martinet, F. (work of). Con. ency. of ant., vol. 3, pl. 87.

Martinez, Estevan Jose (claims Nootka Sound, 1789). Amer. heri., vol. 7 no. 5 p. 81 (Aug '56).

Martinez Trueba, Andres. Cur. biog. p. 445 (1954).

Martini, Helen. Cur. biog. p. 406 (1955).

Martini, Simone (panel by). Con. 144: 193 Dec '59.

—— (work of). Praeg. pict. ency., p. 230 (col.).

Martinique is. Holiday 5: 106-10 (col.) Mar '49.
Natl. geog. 115: 256-82 (part col.) Feb '59.
Travel 114: 49-51 Oct '60.

—— (map). Natl. geog. 115: 261 Feb '59.

Martino, Gaetano. Cur. biog. p. 419 (1956).

Martinu, Bohuslav. Cur. biog. p. 449 (1944).

martyrdom (sym.). Lehner: Pict. bk. of sym., p. 36.

"Martyrdom of Christians" (Durer). Natl. geog. 97: 761 (col.) Je '50.

"Martyrdom of St. Bartholomew" (Maffei). Con. 138: 119 Nov '56.

"Martyrdom of St. Sebastian" (Tiepolo). Con. 126: 67 Aug '50.

"Martyrdom of St. Ursula" (Pasinelli). Con. 144: 22 Sept '59.

Marvel, Mrs. Archie D. Cur. biog. p. 293 (1962).

Marvin, Cloyd H. Cur. biog. p. 410 (1949).

Marx, Chico. Cur. biog. p. 426 (1948).

Marx, Groucho. Cur. biog. p. 427 (1948).
Holiday 11: 58 Ap '52; 21: 95 Jan '57.

—— (face, comic). Holiday 11: 63 Mar '52.

Marx, Harpo. Cur. biog. p. 428. (1948).

Marx, Karl. Amer. heri., vol. 8 no. 3 p. 20 (Ap '57).

Marx, Roberto Burle. Natl. geog. 107: 317 (col.) Mar '55.

The Marx brothers. Holiday 7: 62 Mar '50; 11: 59 Ap '52.

Mary, Queen of Gt. Brit. Holiday 22: 64 Nov '57.

—— (bust). Con. 132: 113 Nov '53.

Mary (Dowager Queen of Gr. Brit.), Princess Elizabeth & Margaret. Holiday 21: 48 Jan '57.

Mary, Joseph, Baby Jesus. Holiday 28: 138 Sept '60.

Mary Magdalene's church (Vezelay, France). Natl. geog. 103: 237 (col.) Feb '53.

"Mary Queen of Heaven." Natl. geog. 101: 100 (col.) Jan '52.

Mary Tudor, Queen (Scotland). Amer. heri., vol. 10 no. 3 p. 95 (Ap '59).
Holiday 5: 87 Jan '49.

"Mary Villiers" (Van Dyck). Con. 142: 255 Jan '59.

Maryland. Holiday 16: 26-34 Sept '54; 23: 78-83 (col.) Je '58.
Natl. geog. 105: 432-70 (part col.) Ap '54.
Travel 109: 21-4 Je '58.

—— (Annapolis). Holiday 23: 78-83 (col.) Je '58.

—— (Enchanted forest). Travel 105: 31-3 May '56.

—— (map). Natl. geog. 105: 438-9 (col.) Ap '54.

Maryland inn hotel. Holiday 23: 79 (col.) Je '58.

Marzotto, Count Gaetano. Cur. biog. p. 421 (1953).

Masaccio (work of). Praeg. pict. ency., p. 252 (col.).

Masai (Africa). Natl. geog. 106: 722- (col.) Dec '54.

Masai girl (Giusti). Holiday 25: cover (col.) Ap '59.

Masai tribe (Kenya, Africa). Holiday 25: 85 (col.) Ap '59.

Masai warrior (East Africa). Int. gr. soc.: Arts . . . p. 33 (col.).

Masai warriors. Natl. geog. 106: 490 Oct '54.

Masai (Africa). See also costume, Africa (Masai).

Masaryk, Jan G. Cur. biog. p. 453 (1944).

Masina, Giulietta. Cur. biog. p. 275 (1958).

Masjid-i-Shah (Great mosque, Ispahan). Int. gr. soc.: Arts . . . p. 85 (col.).
Natl. geog. 100: 452-4 (col.) Oct '51.

mask. Holiday 26: 83 (col.) Oct '59.
Natl. geog. 116: 42 (col.) Jl '59.
Travel 106: 24 Jl '56.

—— (Abraham Lincoln). See Lincoln mask, Abraham.

—— (ancient). Int. gr. soc.: Arts . . . title page cover (col.).

—— (girl). Holiday 10: 38 (col.) Oct '51; 20: 38 Nov '56; 21: 162 Mar '57.

—— (Greek). Int. gr. soc.: Arts . . . p. 35 (col.).

—— (Head hunters). Natl. geog. 108: 456-7 (col.) Oct '55.

—— (man). Amer. heri., vol. 9 no. 4 p. 15 (col.) (Je '58).

—— (Roman, ancient). Int. gr. soc.: Arts . . . p. 35 (col.).

—— (woman). Holiday 21: 132 Jan '57, 106 Feb '57.

——, African. Travel 113: 22 Jan '60.

——, ancient Egyptian marble. Con. 144: LXXX Dec '59.

——, Bakongo polychrome. Con. 145: IV Je '60.

——, Bakousou (Belgian Congo). Con. 143: 192 May '59.

——, Balinese. Holiday 24: 148 Oct '58.

——, Benin. Holiday 13: 154 Je '53.

——, Benin (16th cent.). Con. 141: 108 Ap '58.

——, Bini Africa. Holiday 18: 49 (col.) Sept '55.

——, carnival. Holiday 26: 86 (col.) Sept '59.

——, comedy. Lehner: Pict. bk. of sym., p. 11.

mask, commemorating dead man. Praeg. pict. ency., p. 556 (col.).

——, dance (French Equatorial Africa). Praeg. pict. ency., p. 548 (col.).

——, flight. Natl. geog. 108: 245 (col.) Aug '55.

——, frozen snow. Natl. geog. 113: 448 Ap '58.

——, gas. Amer. heri., vol. 10 no. 6 p. 4 (col.) (Oct '59). Natl. geog. 98: 670 Nov '50.

——, helmet dance (New Ireland). Praeg. pict. ency., p. 556 (col.).

——, Inca Indian. Natl. geog. 98: 433 (col.) Oct '50.

——, Indian. Amer. heri., vol. 6 no. 2 p. 30 (winter '55), vol. 7 no. 6 p. 15 (col.) (Oct '56). Natl. geog. 104: 842 (col.) Dec '53.

——, Indian jaguar (Brazil). Natl. geog. 116: 630 (col.) Nov '59.

——, Iroquois. Holiday 21: 52 Je '57. Natl. geog. 98: 86 (col.) Jl '50.

——, Jaguar (Mexico). Natl. geog. 110: 374 Sept '56.

——, Japanese. Holiday 18: 45 (col.) Aug '55. Travel 110: 56 Sept '58.

——, Katmandu. Holiday 25: 19 Je '59.

——. Mardi Gras. Holiday 19: 14 Jan '56. Lehner: Pict. bk. of sym., p. 55.

——, Maya. Natl. geog. 115: 125 (col.) Jan '59.

——, Mexican stone face. Con. 133: XL Ap '54.

——, Mosaic (Aztec). Praeg. pict. ency., p. 548 (col.).

——, Nigeria natives. Natl. geog. 116: 234 (col.) Aug '59.

——, Papuan. Holiday 28: 90 (col.) Nov '60.

——, scientist's. Natl. geog. 114: 679 (col.) Nov '58.

——, Tarascan Indian. Natl. geog. 102: 545 (col.) Oct '52.

——, tragedy. Lehner: Pict. bk. of sym., p. 11.

mask & breastplate, Mexican golden. Ceram: March of arch., p. 256.

mask making (man). See man (making mask).

masks. Holiday 11: 54 Je '52; 13: 109 Mar '53.

—— (foreign countries). Int. gr. soc.: Arts . . . p. 185 (col.).

—— (handicrafts) Natl. geog. 104: 812 (col.) Dec '53.

—— (man & girl). Holiday 10: 57 (col.) Oct '51.

—— (religious dance). Natl. geog. 112: 834-5 (col.) Dec '57.

——, carnival. Holiday 18: 26 Jl '55 .

——, devil. Natl. geog. 99: 783 (col.) Je '51.

——, Indian (Guatemala). Natl. geog. 117: 413 (col.) Mar '60.

——, Indian spirit. Natl. geog. 117: 810-11 (col.) Je '60.

——, Iroquois Indian spirit. Natl. geog. 117: 812 (col.) Je '60.

——, Tiwi. Natl. geog. 109: 437 (col.) Mar '56.

——, Venezuela. Holiday 20: 15 (col.) Aug '56.

Mason, George. Amer. heri., vol. 3 no. 2 p. 39 (col.) (winter '52); vol. 10 no. 1 p. 60 (Dec '58).

Mason, James. Cur. biog. p. 430 (1947).

Mason, John. Amer. heri., vol. 10 no. 1 p. 51 (Dec '58).

Mason, Lowell B. Cur. biog. p. 412 (1949).

Mason, Noah M. Cur. biog. p. 357 (1957).

Mason, Norman. Cur. biog. p. 295 (1959).

Mason, William (Reynolds). Con. 143: 85 Ap '59.

mason (sym.). Lehner: Pict. bk. of sym., p. 90.

masqueraders, Himis Monster. Natl. geog. 99: 633 (col.) May '51.

"Mass at St. Gregory" (Van der Weyden). Con. 144: 128 Nov '59.

"Mass of St. Gregory" (polychrome 15th cent.). Con. 140: LXX Jan '58.

Massachusetts. Holiday 11: 34-49 (part col.) Je '52; 23: 123 (col.) May '58; 28: 62-6 (part col.) Aug '60. Natl. geog. 97: 280-310 (part col.) Mar '50; 107: 191-214 (part col.) Feb '55, 744 (col.) Je '55. Travel 109: 27 Je '58.

—— (harbor). Holiday 24: 2 (col.) Jl '58.

—— (map). Holiday 11: 36 Je '52.

—— (state parks). Travel 108: 37-8 Oct '57.

—— (Storrowtown, W. Springfield). Travel 113: 29-31 Mar '60.

Massachusetts cemeteries (Puritan). Amer. heri., vol. 11 no. 2 p. 38-43 (Feb '60).

"Massacre of Scio" (Delacroix). Con. 137: 253 Je '56.

"Massacre of the innocents" (Brueghel). Con. 142: 26 Sept '58.

Massasoit, chief (statue). Brooks: Growth of a nation, p. 44. Jordan: Hammond's pict. atlas, p. 31 (col.).

Massey, Raymond. Cur. biog. p. 382 (1946).

Massey, Vincent. Cur. biog. p. 413 (1951).

Massigli, Rene. Cur. biog. p. 421 (1956).

Massimo, Prince & Princess. Holiday 27: 101 (col.) Ap '60.

Massys, Quentin (work of). Natl. geog. 107: 198 (col.) Feb '55.

Master, St. Bartholomew (work of). Natl. geog. 110: 627 (col.) Nov '56.

"Master Baines" (Romney). Con. 136: 247 (col.) Jan '56.

Master of Flemalle. Praeg. pict. ency., p. 307.

Master of Gilles (work of). Natl. geog. 101: 90-1 (col.) Jan '52.

Masterson, Bat. Amer. heri., vol. 11 no. 5 p. 44 (Aug '60). Brooks: Growth of a nation, p. 165. Horan: Pict. hist. of wild west, p. 105, 108.

Mastroianni, Marcello. Cur. biog. p. 261 (1963).

Mastroianni, Umberto. Cur. biog. p. 265 (1960).

matador. Holiday 11: 52-3 (col.) Jan '52 20: 80-1 (part col.) Nov '56; 21: 64-5 Jan '57, 30 (col.) May '57. Travel 107: 22 Ap '57; 114: 40-6 Nov '60.

—— (comic). Holiday 22: 37 Oct '57.

—— (test fired). Natl. geog. 111: 301 (col.) Mar '57.

matador. See also bullfighter.

Matanuska Valley (Alaska). Holiday 26: 39 (col.) Aug '59.
Matare, Ewald (bronze figure). Praeg. pict. ency., p. 494.
match books. Holiday 27: 59 Ap '60.
match box, bell shape. Con. 142: 243 Jan '59.
match box holder (Faberge). Con. 145: LXXIX May '60.
matches, crossed (sym.). Lehner: Pict. bk. of sym., p. 62.
"Matchmaker" (Rembrandt). Con. 142: 64 Sept '58.
Mateos, Adolfo Lopez. Cur. biog. (1959).
Mates, Leo. Cur. biog. p. 423 (1956).
Matham, Jacob (work of). Con. 138: 14 Sept '56.
mathematical science (sym.). Lehner: Pict. bk. of sym., p. 9.
mathematics (sym.). Lehner: Pict. bk. of sym., p. 13.
Mather, Cotton. Amer. heri., vol. 8 no. 5 p. 42 (Aug '57).
Mather, Kirtley F. Cur. biog. p. 415 (1951).
Mathew, Capt. Thomas (Gainsborough). Con. 141: 61 Mar '58.
Mathewson, Christy. Amer. heri., vol. 10 no. 3 p. 22 (Ap '59).
Holiday 23: 83 May '58.
Mathewson, Maj. Gen. Lemuel. Cur. biog. p. 407 (1952).
Mathias, Robert Bruce. Cur. biog. p. 408 (1952).
Matisse, Henri. Cur. biog. p. 507 (1943); p. 423 (1953).
—— **(work of).** Con. 133: 288 Je '54; 135: 53 Mar '55, 184 May '55; 140: 194 (col.) Dec '57; 143: 273 Je '59; 144: X Dec '59; 145: I (col.) Mar '60, 185, 188, 209 May '60, 279 Je '60.
Holiday 14: 60 (col.) Nov '53.
Praeg. pict. ency., p. 471 (col.).
Matlacha (Florida, fishing resort). Travel 107: 57 May '57.
Matskevich, Vladimir V. Cur. biog. p. 408 (1955).
Matsudaira, Koto. Cur. biog. p. 277 (1958).
Matsys, Quentin (work of). Con. 145: LXIII (col.) May '60.
Matta, Roberto A. S. Cur. biog. p. 358 (1957).
Mattei, Enrico. Cur. biog. p. 297 (1959).
Matterhorn mt. Holiday 14: 99 (col.) Aug '53 16: 37 Aug '54.
Natl. geog. 110: 438 (col.) Oct '56.
Travel 104: inside cover Nov 55; 107: 45-8 Ap '57.
—— **(shadow in lake).** Natl. geog. 98: 225 (col.) Aug '50.
Matthews, Burnita Shelton. Cur. biog. p. 386 (1950).
Matthews, Francis P. Cur. biog. p. 414 (1949).
Matthews, Harrison Freeman. Cur. biog. p. 387 (1945).
Matthews, Herbert L. Cur. biog. p. 511 (1943).
Matthews, Joseph B. Cur. biog. p. 514 (1943).
Matthews, Thomas S. Cur. biog. p. 387 (1950).
Mattingly, Garrett. Cur. biog. p. 267 (1960).
Mattocks (Arabs). Natl. geog. 113: 670 (col.) May '58.
mattress, air. Natl. geog. 98: 108 (col.) Jl '50.

mattress, concrete (to control river). Natl. geog. 118: 698-9 (col.) Nov '60.
mattress makers. Natl. geog. 100: 23 Jl '51.
Mattson, Henry. Cur. biog. p. 425 (1956).
Mature, Victor. Cur. biog. p. 417 (1951).
Mau mau, Kenya defense against. Natl. geog. 112: 98-9 (col.) Jl '57.
Maudling, Reginald. Cur. biog. p. 269 (1960).
Maufra, M. (work of). Con. 145: 114 Ap '60.
Maugham, Somerset. Cur. biog. p. 263 (1963).
Maui is. (Hawaii). Holiday 28: 42-3 (col.) Jl '60.
Travel 107: 43 Jan '57.
maul, wood. Rawson: Ant. pict, bk., p. 22.
Maulbertsch, Franz Anton (work of). Con. 145: 135 Ap '60.
Mauldin, Sgt. Bill. Cur. biog. p. 389 (1945).
Holiday 27: 82 May '60.
Maupassant's birthplace, Guy de. Holiday 19: 52 Jan '56.
Maurer, Louis (work of). Con. ency. of ant., vol. 3, pl. 96.
Mauritius is. (Indian ocean). Natl. geog. 109: 79-104 (part col.) Jan '56.
Travel 106: 33-5 Nov '56.
—— **(map).** Natl. geog. 109: 80 Jan '56.
Mauroy, P. (work of). Con. ency. of ant., vol. 1, pl. 170.
mausoleum (George III). Amer. heri., vol. 11 no. 4 p. 22 (Je '60).
—— **(King Faisel I, Baghdad).** Travel 105: 20 Jan '56.
—— **(Silifke).** Osward: Asia Minor, pl. 122.
——, **imperial (int.).** Con. 142: XLII Dec '58.
——, **thatch roof (Kampala).** Natl. geog. 106: 732 (col.) Dec '54.
——, **the turning (Döner Kümbed).** Osward: Asia Minor, pl. 68.
Mauze, Abby Rockfeller. Holiday 24: 89 Nov '58.
Mavel cave (Mo.). Travel 109: 16 Feb '58.
Maverick, Maury. Cur. biog. p. 455 (1944).
Maw, Herbert B. Cur. biog. p. 431 (1948).
Maximilian, Emperor (Mexico). Amer. heri., vol. 11 no. 2 p. 103 (Feb '60).
Maximilian's castle, Archduke (for his bride). Natl. geog. 109: 846, 848, (col.) Je '56.
Maximos, Demetrios. Cur. biog. p. 433 (1948).
Maxon, John. Holiday 28: 81 Dec '60.
Maxon, Lou R. Cur. biog. p. 517 (1943).
Maxwell, David F. Cur. biog. p. 361 (1957).
Maxwell, Elsa. Cur. biog. p. 519 (1943).
Holiday 12: 22 (col.) Oct '52; 13: 84 May '53; 14: 53 Dec '53; 26: 74 (col.) Oct '59.
Maxwell, Gen, Russell L. Cur. biog. p. 578 (1942).
Maxwell, William. Cur. biog. p. 415 (1949).
Maxwell, William D. Holiday 28: 85 Dec '60.
"Maxwelton House" (home of Annie Laurie). Natl. geog. 112: 468 (col.) Oct '57.
May, Andrew Jackson. Cur. biog. p. 565 (1941).
May, Baptist (Lily). Con. 126: 32 Aug '50.
May, Catherine. Cur. biog. p. 270 (1960).
May, Elaine. Cur. biog. p. 301 (1961).
May, Col. Geraldine P. Cur. biog. p. 416 (1949).
May (New England). Natl. geog. 99: 569 May '51.

May (Sarawak). Natl. geog. 109: 716 May '56.
May pictorial (Hawaii). Holiday 23: 18-9 (col.) Mar '58.
May of Jamestown (one of 1st in Va.). Con. 139: 201 May '57.
May pole. See Maypole.
Maya Indians. See Indians, Maya.
Mayan art ("Priestess"). Con. 135: XLIV Mar '55.
Mayan hieroglyphics. Amer. heri., vol. 11 no. 4 p. 109-11 (Je '60).
 Ceram: March of arch., p. 282.
Mayan pottery (relics). Natl. geog. 115: 90, 93, 125 (col.) Jan '59.
Mayan ruins (Guatemala). Travel 108: 25-7 Dec '57.
—— (Yucatan). Int. gr. soc.: Arts . . . p. 51 (col.).
Mayan sculpture, stone. Con. 145: LV Mar '60.
Mayan shrine (being restored). Natl. geog. 115: 97 (col.) Jan '59.
Mayan temple. Praeg. pict. ency., p. 543.
—— (Mexico). Amer. heri., vol. 7 no. 6 p. 104 (Oct '56).
Mayan temples. Natl. geog. 115: 96-108 (part col.) Jan '59.
Mayan wall painting. Ceram: March of arch., pl. XV (col.).
 Praeg. pict. ency., p. 543.
Maybank, Burnet R. Cur. biog. p. 418 (1949).
"The Maydenhead". See "Parthenia."
Mayer, Daniel. Cur. biog. p. 420 (1949).
Mayer, Jane. Cur. biog. p. 365 (1954).
Mayer, Louis B. Cur. biog. p. 521 (1943).
—— (M.G.M. studios). Holiday 5: 34 (col.) Jan '49.
Mayer, Rene. Cur. biog. p. 435 (1948).
Mayes, Mrs. Gilford. Cur. biog. p. 389 (1950).
the "Mayflower" (river steamboat). Amer. heri., vol. 8 no. 6 p. 16-7 (col.) Oct '57.
 Brooks: Growth of a nation, p. 43.
 Natl. geog. 111: 708-28 May '57.
 Travel 106: cover Jl '58.
Mayflower hotel (Wash., D.C.). Holiday 14: 28 Nov '53.
"The Mayflower" hull. Travel 106: 16 Jl '56.
"Mayflower" model. Natl. geog. 103: 808 (col.) Je '53.
"Mayflower" route to America. Travel 106: 12-7 Jl '56.
The "Mayflower" II (ship). Natl. geog. 112: 628-74 (part col.) Nov '57.
The Mayflower voyage (map). Natl. geog. 111: 716-7 May '57.
Maynard, Rev. John A. F. Cur. biog. p. 525 (1943).
Maynor, Dorothy. Cur. biog. p. 419 (1951).
Mayo, Dr. Charles W. Cur. biog. p. 567 (1941); p. 449 (1954).
Mayo clinic (Rochester, Minn.). Holiday 5: 72-8, 130 Feb '49.
Maypole (sym.). Lehner: Pict. bk. of sym., p. 54.
Maypole dance. Jensen: The White House, p. 232.
 Natl. geog. 108: 314 (col.) Sept '55.
—— (Medieval). Int. gr. soc.: Arts . . . p. 79 (col.).

Mays, Benjamin E. Cur. biog. p. 391 (1945).
Mays, Ewing W. Cur. biog. p 411 (1952).
Mays, Willie. Cur. biog. p. 410 (1955).
Maza, Jose. Cur. biog. p. 411 (1955).
Mazar-i-Sharif (tomb of Ali). Natl. geog. 114: 14-5 (col.) Jl '58.
Mazatlan (Mexico). Holiday 24: cover, 70-5 (part col.) Nov '58.
 Travel 103: 32 Jan '55; 106: inside cover Sept '56.
Mazer, Galloway. Con. 133: 201 May '54.
—— (Gray). Con. 133: XXVI Mar '54.
mazer, silver. Con. 139: 32 Mar '57.
mazer bowl, double silver & wood. Con. ency. of ant., vol. 3, p. 68.
Mazey, Emil. Cur. biog. p. 437 (1948).
mazoth & wine glass. Lehner: Pict. bk. of sym., p. 55.
Mazyck, Henry Broughton. Amer. heri., vol. 9 no. 2 p. 57 (col.) (Feb '58).
Mazyck, Mrs. Henry Broughton. Amer. heri., vol. 9 no. 2 p. 56 (col.) (Feb '58).
Mazzoni, Sebastiano (work of). Con. 144: 106 Nov '59.
Mazzuoli, Guiseppe (terracotta work). Con. 139: 34 Mar '57.
Mboya, Thomas Joseph. Cur. biog. p. 299 (1959).
Mead, George H. Cur. biog. p. 385 (1946).
Mead, James M. Cur. biog. p. 459 (1944).
Mead, Margaret. Cur. biog. p. 422 (1951).
Meade, Maj. Gen. George Gordon. Amer. heri., vol. 9 no. 1 p. 36 (Dec '57).
 Pakula: Cent. album, p. 211.
Meader, George. Cur. biog. p. 427 (1956).
Meader, Stephen W. Jun. bk. of auth., p. 213.
Meade's headquarters, Gen. (Gettysburg). Amer. heri., vol. 3 no. 4 back cover (col.) (summer '52).
Meadowcroft, Enid. Jun. bk. of auth., p. 214.
Meadowcroft, Enid La Monte. Cur. biog. p. 421 (1949).
Meadows, A. H. Cur. biog. p. 272 (1960).
Meadows, Audrey. Cur. biog. p. 279 (1958).
Meadows, Jayne. Cur. biog. p. 280 (1958).
meal grinding (women, Formosa). Natl. geog. 107: 586 Ap '55.
Means, Mrs. Alan Hay. Cur. biog. p. 386 (1946).
Means, Florence Crannell. Jun. bk. of auth., p. 215.
Meany, George. Cur. biog. p. 580 (1942); p. 451 (1954).
Mearns, David C. Cur. biog. p. 302 (1961).
Mears, Helen. Cur. biog. p. 527 (1943).
Mears, Otto. Amer. heri., vol. 8 no. 6 p. 37 (Oct '57).
measuring cup. Holiday 27: 154 Jan '60; 28: 132 Jl '60.
meat cutter. Lehner: Pict. bk. of sym., p. 90.
——, rolling. Rawson: Ant. pict. bk., p. 10.
meat dish, Georgian silver. Con. 145: XXXVII Mar '60, XXVI Ap '60.
meat packing. Natl. geog. 104: 809 (col.) Dec '53.
meat platter, Dresdon. Con. ency. of ant., vol. 3 pl., 117.
meat stand (salesman). Natl. geog. 111: 722 May '57.

meat stand & butcher. Amer. heri., vol. 6 no. 4 p. 49 (col.) (Je '55).

Mecca. Natl. geog. 104: 2-59 (part col.) Jl '53.

—— **(Mohammed).** Holiday 20: 57 Dec '56.

Mecca pilgrim. Osward: Asia Minor, pl. V (col.).

mechanics (sym). Lehner: Pict. bk. of sym., p. 13.

Mechem, Edwin L. Cur. biog. p. 453 (1954).

medal, Francis I. Con. 126: 83 Oct '50.

medal. Holiday 14: 88 (col.) Oct '53.

—— **(awarded to T. Truxtun).** Amer. heri., vol. 7 no. 2 p. 103 (Feb '56).

—— **(James II & his Queen).** Amer. heri., vol. 7 no. 3 p. 64 (Ap '56).

—— **(Politian & sister).** Con. 139: 99 Ap '57.

——, **bronze (Anne of Brittany).** Con. 142: 193 Dec '58.

——, **Grosvenor.** Natl. geog. 111: 422 Mar '57.

——, **Hubbard.** Natl. geog. 103: 564 Ap '53; 113: 792 Je '58.

——, **Mrs. Robert E. Peary's.** Natl. geog. 109: 148 Jan '56.

——, **Natl. geog. honor.** Natl. geog. 115: 589 Ap '59.

——, **Natl. geog. honor (to Prince Philip).** Natl. geog. 112: 868 Dec '57.

——, **renaissance.** Con. 142: LXII Dec '58. Natl. geog. 110: 634 Nov '56.

——, **St. Christopher.** *See* St. Christopher medal.

——, **war (1812).** Amer. heri., vol. 6 no. 3 p. 60-1 (Ap '55).

medal cabinet. Con. 138: XXIV Dec '56.

——, **broom wood.** Con. 145: 101 Ap '60.

Medal of honor, U.S. army. Int. gr. soc.: Arts . . . p. 167 (col.).

——, **war.** Holiday 10: 1 Aug '51; 11: 112 Jan '52, 137 Je '52.

medal presented to Capt. John Gill. Con. 129: VII Ap '52.

medallion, antique. Con. 132: 162 Jan '54.

——, **antique Italian.** Con. 134: 103-6 Nov '54.

——, **bronze.** Con. 140: 114 Nov '57.

——, **West Point.** Natl. geog. 101: 618 (col.) May '52.

medallions, cameo. Con. 132: 148 Jan '54.

——, **Staffordshire enamel.** Con. ency. of ant., vol. 1, pl. 75.

——, **wall (Zucchi).** Con. 141: 137-9 May '58.

"The medallist Gustaf Ljungberger" (Pasch). Con. 135: 46 Mar '55.

medals (railways). Holiday 28: 165 (col.) Dec '60.

——, **antarctic.** Natl. geog. 112: 45 Jl '57.

——, **European.** Con. 136: 43 Sept '55.

——, **"Old Crow" whiskey.** Holiday 28: 165 (col.) Dec '60.

——, **Victorian.** Con. 140: 103-4 Nov '57.

Medaris, Maj. Gen. John B. Cur. biog. p. 282 (1958).

Medary, Marjorie. Jun. bk. of auth., p. 217.

Medawar, Peter Brian. Cur. biog. p. 304 (1961).

medical history report (1775). Amer. heri., vol. 6 no. 5 p. 45 (Oct '55).

Medici, Giuliano de (Botticelli). Natl. geog. 110: 635 (col.) Nov '56.

Medici-Strozzi bridal chest. *See* chest, bridal Medici-Strozzi.

medicine (god of). Lehner: Pict. bk. of sym., p. 30.

—— **(sym.).** Lehner: Pict. bk. of sym., p. 13.

——, **patent (poster).** Amer. heri., vol. 7 no. 5 p. 58, 62-3 (col.), 95 (Aug '56).

——, **patron saint of.** Lehner: Pict. bk. of sym., p. 40.

medicine ball practice (Russia). Holiday 18: 109 Jl '55.

medicine dropper. Holiday 21: 27 Ap '57; 23: 11 Jan '58.

"Medicine man" (Indian in theatre). Natl. geog. 108: 518 (col.) Oct '55.

Medicine man, Navajo. Disney: People & places, p. 120 (col.).

Medicine men, Indian. Natl. geog. 112: 220-1 (col.) Aug '57.

Medieval fortress city. *See* fortress city, medieval.

Medina, Harold R. Cur. biog. p. 423 (1949).

Medina (Islam). Natl. geog. 104: 40 Jl '53.

Medina Angarita, Isaias. Cur. biog. p. 582 (1942).

Medina mosque. Natl. geog. 104: 35 (col.) Jl '53.

"Meditation by the sea." Amer. heri., vol. 11 no. 5 frontis (col.) (Aug '60).

Mediterranean. Natl. geog. 111: 623-60 (part col.) May '57.
Travel 102: 34-8 Sept '54.

—— **(map).** Ceram: March of arch., p. 171. Natl. geog. 117: 688 (col.) May '60. Osward: Asia Minor (at back of book).

Mediterranean area. Holiday 10: 56-8 (part col.) Sept '51; 16: 102-11 (part col.) Nov '54.

"A Mediterranean Bay" (Bonavia). Con. 139: XIII Ap '57.

Mediterranean men (at table). Holiday 23: 139 Mar '58.

Mediterranean sea (divers). Natl. geog. 105: 11-29 (col.) Jan '54.

—— **(map).** Natl. geog. 117: 688 (col.) May '60.

"Mediterranean stone" (sculpture). Praeg. pict. ency., p. 492.

"Medway" (Van Arrsens' home). Natl. geog. 103: 289 (col.) Mar '53.

Meeker, Arvilla Delight. Amer. heri., vol. 8 no. 6 p. 36 Oct '57.

Meeker, Ezra (old western man). Jensen: The White House, p. 226.

Meeker, Josie. Amer. heri., vol. 8 no. 6 p. 38 (Oct '57).

Meeker, Nathan. Amer. heri., vol. 8 no. 6 p. 36 (Oct '57).

Meenakshi temple (Madurai, India). Con. 144: XXXVI Dec '59.

Meerloo, Joost A.M. Cur. biog. p. 295 (1962).

"Meeting of the jockey club, Newmarket" (Rowlandson). Con. 129: LI Ap '52.

Meetinghouse (old New England). Amer. heri., vol. 1 no. 4 p. 38 (col.) (summer '50).

——, **Friend's (int.).** Holiday 21: 57 May '57.

Meetinghouse, Quaker. *See* Quaker meeting-house.
——. *See* also church.
Megeve (French Alps). Holiday 25: 72-3 (col.) Mar '59.
Mehaffey, Brig. Gen. Joseph C. Cur. biog. p. 440 (1948).
Mehemet I, tomb of. *See* tomb of Mehemet I.
Mehornay, Robert L. Holiday 7: 53 (col.) Mar '50.
Mehta, Gaganvihari L. Cur. biog. p. 412 (1952).
Mehta, Hansa. Cur. biog. p. 432 (1947).
Meigs, Cornelia. Jun. bk. of auth., p. 218.
Meigs, John. Amer. heri., vol. 3 no. 1 p. 58 (fall '51).
Meiling, Richard L. Cur. biog. p. 391 (1950).
Meinertzhagen, Frederick (Metsuke carvings). Con. 138: LII Jan '57.
Meissen bottle. Con. 145: XXVIII May '60, 223 Je '60.
—— bowl. Con. ency. of ant., vol. 1, pl. 57.
—— candelabra. Con. 134: 121 Nov '54.
—— candlestick. Con. 141: 251 Je '58.
—— chess set. Con. 143: 266 Je '59.
—— clock. Con. 129: LXXXII Ap '52; 138: 47 Sept '56; 145: XLIV Mar '60.
—— clock-case. Con. 139: XLV Ap '57.
—— cockatoo. Con. 142: 126 Nov '58.
—— coffee pot. Con. ency. of ant., vol. 1, pl. 58.
—— coffee pot (polychrome). Con. 145: XLI May '60.
—— coffee pot (porcelain). Con. 138: XXXIV Jan '57.
—— coffee service. Con. 145: 56 Mar '60.
—— cup & saucer. Con. ency. of ant., vol. 1, pl. 57.
Con. 132: 204 Jan '54; 144: VI Nov '59, XXXIX Jan '60; 145: XXVIII Ap '60, XXXII Je '60.
—— dish. Con. 140: XXVI Dec '57.
—— dishes. Con. 136: XXXI Jan '56; 142: inside cover Jan '59.
—— ewer. Con. 129: 62 Ap '52; 135: 210 May '55; 140: 60 Sept '57; 144: 70 Sept '59.
—— figurine. Con. ency. of ant., vol. 1, pl. 62.
Con. 133: 264 Je '54; 135: 189 May '55; 138: XXI, 46 Sept '56; 139: 57 Mar '57, 122 Ap '57; 140: 59 Sept '57, 131 Nov '57, inside cover, 179 Dec '57; 141: VI Ap '58, XXVIII Je '58; 142: inside cover Sept '58, XXXVIII Nov '58; 142: inside cover, 196 Dec '58, 255 Jan '59; 143: XXVI, XXX, LXVI, 191 May '59; 144: 65 Sept '59, XXVI, LIII Nov '59, inside cover, X Dec '59; 145: XIV Mar '60, 126 Ap '60, XLV Je '60.
Praeg. pict. ency., p. 82 (col.).
——figurines. Con. 129: XXXII, 63 Ap '52; 132: XLIII Sept '53; 139: 10-3 Mar '57.
—— figurines (ormolu). Con. 135: 146 Ap '55.
—— inkstand. Con. 145: inside cover Ap '60.
—— jar. Con. 143: XXII Je '59.
—— jug. Con. 138: XXXI Dec '56.
—— porcelain. Con. 134: inside cover Nov '54; 135: inside cover Mar '55; 137: inside

cover, XXI, XL, 128 Ap '56, 148 (col.), 150-3 May '56; 140: XII Sept '57, XVII Jan '58; 141: 123 Ap '58; 142 XXXIX Sept '58.
—— porcelain bottles. Con. 139: 231 Je '57.
—— porcelain horse. Con. 141: 187 May '58.
—— stoneware. Con. 139: XXXII May '57.
—— tankard. Con. ency. of ant., vol. 1, p. 59; 145: XIX Mar '60.
—— tankard (porcelain). Con. 142: 7 Sept '58.
—— tankard (porcelain & silver). Con. 145: 67 Mar '60.
—— tea & coffee service. Con. 142: 124 Nov '58.
—— tea caddy. Con. ency. of ant., vol. 1, pl. 59.
—— tea cup & saucer. Con. 132: 204 Jan '54.
—— tea service. Con. 138: 262 Jan '57.
—— teapot. Con. ency. of ant., vol. 1, pl. 57. Con. 141: XXIV Je '58; 145: 56 Mar '60.
—— tureen. Con. ency. of ant., vol. 1, pl. 64. Con. 140: 58 Sept '57, 183 Dec '57; 141: 42 Mar '58; 145: inside cover May '60.
—— vase. Con. ency. of ant., vol. 1, pl. 59. Con. 133: 276-7 Je '54; 139: inside cover, 14 Mar '57, 264 Je '57.
Meitner, Lise. Cur. biog. p. 394 (1945).
Melas, George V. Cur. biog. p. 429 (1956).
Melba, Nellie. Cooper: Con. ency. of music, p. 191.
Melbourne (Australia). Holiday 20: 166 (col.) Dec '56.
Natl. geog. 109: 250-1 Feb '56; 110: 688-93 Nov '59.
—— (harbor). Holiday 8: 99 (col.) Nov '50.
Melcher, Frederic G. Cur. biog. p. 395 (1945).
Melchior, Lauritz. Cur. biog. p. 569 (1941).
—— (as Lohengrin). Cooper: Con. ency. of music, p. 192.
Melchior, Mr. & Mrs. Lauritz. Natl. geog. 100: 722 Dec '51.
Melcombe home, Bingham's. *See* Bingham's Melcombe home.
Melk monastery. *See* monastery of Melk.
Mellers, Wilfrid. Cur. biog. p. 297 (1962).
Mellett, Lowell. Cur. biog. p. 584 (1942).
Mellieha (Malta, beach). Holiday 27: cover (col.) Je '60.
Mellon, Andrew. Amer. heri., vol. 9 no. 5 p. 32 (Aug '58).
Mellon, Andrew W. Holiday 25: 82 Mar '59.
Mellon, Richard B. Holiday 25: 82 Mar '59.
Mellon, Richard King (silhouette). Holiday 25: 80 (col.) Mar '59.
melodeon. Travel 113: 34 Je '60.
melon bulb ornament. Con. ency. of ant., vol. 1, p. 20.
Melozzo da Forli (work of). Praeg. pict. ency., p. 254 (col.).
Melpomene (muse). Lehner: Pict. bk. of sym., p. 33.
Melrose abbey. Natl. geog. 112: 446-7 Oct '57.
Melton, James. Cur. biog. p. 398 (1945).
Melville, Viscountess (Lady Jane Hope). Con. 142: 189 (col.) Dec '58.
Melville is. (map). Natl. geog. 109: 425 Mar '56.

Memling, Hans (work of). Con. 133: 13 Mar '54.

Natl. geog. 110: 623 (col.) Nov '56.

Memmi, Lippo (work of). Praeg.: Pict. ency., p. 230 (col.).

Memnon, Colossus of. *See* Colossus of Memnon.

memorial (Tasmania). Natl. geog. 110: 799 (col.) Dec '56.

——, **Alamo.** *See* cenotaph, Alamo memorial.

——, **Amer, Indians.** Natl. geog. 110: 487 (col.) Oct '56.

——, **D day.** *See* war memorial, D day.

——, **Gen. Gordon (Khartoum).** Natl. geog. 103: 248 Feb '53.

——, **Greek (victory over Persia).** Natl. geog. 109: 51 (col.) Jan '56.

——, **Lincoln.** *See* Lincoln memorial.

——, **Will Rogers.** *See* Roger's memorial, Will.

memorial arch. Amer. heri., vol. 6 no. 3 p. 100 (Ap '55).

—— **(Valley Forge).** Natl. geog. 105: 197 (col.) Feb '54.

memorial bell tower. *See* bell tower memorial.

memorial center, Milwaukee war. Natl. geog. 115: 474 (col.) Ap '59.

memorial church of Christ scientist. *See* Church of Christ, scientist memorial.

memorial column (Reds enter Vienna). Travel 103: 23 Je '55.

Memorial day (cemetery, Hawaii). *See* cemetery, Memorial day (Hawaii).

Memorial day (Hays, Kan.). Natl. geog. 101: 486 (col.) Ap '52.

Memorial day (sym.). Lehner: Pict. bk. of sym., p. 54.

memorial day birthplace (Columbus, Miss.). Brooks: Growth of a nation, p. 288.

memorial for men lost at sea. Natl. geog. 104: 83 (col.) Jl '53.

memorial monument (Benjamin Franklin's parents). Natl. geog. 97: 304 (col.) Mar '50.

—— **(Rome).** Travel 113: 36 Ap '60.

——, **fishermen's.** *See* Gloucester fishermen monument.

memorial park (Nova Scotia). Travel 103: 37 Je '55.

memorial statue, D.A.R. Natl. geog. 100: 586 (col.) Nov '51.

——, **elephant ("Old Bet").** Durant: Pict. hist. of Amer. circus, p. 25.

memorial study, Clyde Fitch (Amherst). Natl. geog. 97: 292 (col.) Mar '50.

memorial tablet, Greely (Ellesmere island). Natl. geog. 100: 468 Oct '51.

——, **Rev. Peter Bulkeley (Concord).** Natl. geog. 97: 301 Mar '50.

memorial to war dead (Rotterdam). Natl. geog. 118: 546 (col.) Oct '60.

memorial tower, World war I (Andover). Holiday 7: 57 (col.) Mar '50.

memorials, war. *See* war memorial.

"Memories" (by Meurer). Amer. heri., vol. 10 no. 6 p. 4 (col.) (Oct '59).

Memphis (Tenn.). Natl. geog. 118: 688-9 (col.) Nov '60.

—— **(harbor).** Holiday 5: 47 (col.) Mar '49.

Memtinc, Hans (work of). Praeg.: Pict. ency., p. 263 (col.).

men. Holiday 13: 104-6, 109, 111 (col.), 112 Mar '53, 18, 25 (col.), 50, 77, 90, 146 (col.) Ap '53; 23: 34, 192, 196 (col.) Je '58; 24: back cover (col.) Sept '58, 143, 147 Oct '58.

Travel 108: 59 Oct '57.

—— **(abalone for supper).** Natl. geog. 114: 265 Aug '58.

—— **(amused).** Holiday 19: 29 (col.) May '56; 20: 85 Oct '56.

—— **(ancient Romans playing marbles).** Int. gr. soc.: Arts . . . p. 37 (col.).

—— **(antarctic).** Natl. geog. 115: 29, 38-43, 47 (part col.) Jan '59.

—— **(antique shop).** Natl. geog. 111: 322 Mar '57.

—— **(archeologists).** Natl. geog. 115: 98, 100-6, 124-5, 127 (part col.) Jan '59.

—— **(archery, medieval).** Int. gr. soc.: Arts . . . p. 77 (col.).

—— **(architects).** Holiday 24: 130 (col.) Dec '58.

—— **(Arctic circle).** Natl. geog. 114: 130 (col.) Jl '58.

—— **(arguing).** Amer. heri., vol. 7 no. 3 p. 70 (Ap '56).

—— **(around stove in store).** Amer. heri., vol. 6 no. 1 p. 24 (fall '54).

—— **(astronomers).** Natl. geog. 110: 781, 787, 790 Dec '56.

—— **(at art exhibit).** Holiday 27: 80 May '60.

—— **(at bar).** Holiday 13: 83 (col.) Jan '53; 23: 156 Ap '58.

—— **(at bar, comic).** Holiday 11: 129 Je '52; 13: 130 Mar '53, 123 Ap '53, 74 May '53 31 Je '53.

—— **(at table).** Con. 14: XXXIII Nov '59.

Holiday 14: 21 Aug '53, 143 Nov '53; 23: 11 Ap '58, 148, 197 (col.) May '58; 24: 7 (col.) Oct '58, 87 (col.) Nov '58.

—— **(at table, comic).** Holiday 13: 141 May '53; 14: 161 Dec '53.

—— **(at table, inspect diamonds).** Natl. geog. 108: 772-3 (col.) Dec '55.

—— **(auto).** Holiday 25: 159 (col.) Ap '59. Travel 110: 38 Aug '58.

—— **(auto, early).** Amer. heri., vol. 10 no. 2 p. 40 (Feb '59).

—— **(back to back).** Holiday 18: 82 Nov '55.

—— **(backview).** Holiday 10: 90-1 Oct '51; 23: 44 Ap '58; 24: 181 Nov '58; 177 Dec '58; 25: 113 Jan '59.

Natl. geog. 106: 576 Oct '54.

Travel 104: 39 Aug '55, 41 Nov '55.

—— **(backview, birds flying).** Natl. geog. 112: 823 Dec '57.

—— **(backview, horseback).** Natl. geog. 111: 554 (col.) Ap '57.

—— **(backview, lake).** Natl. geog. 99: 674 (col.) May '51.

—— **(backview, seated, river bank).** Natl. geog. 108: 543 (col.) Oct '55.

—— **(backview, silhouettes).** Natl. geog. 109: 642 May '56.

—— **(bags of food).** Natl. geog. 118: 589 (col.) Nov '60.

—— (band parade). Amer. heri., vol. 7 no. 1 p. 36-7 (col.) (Dec '55).
—— (banding Canada geese). Natl. geog. 112: 826 Dec '57.
—— (banquet table). Amer. heri., vol. 6 no. 1 p. 28-9 (fall '54).
—— (barrel). Holiday 24: 57 Dec '58; 25: 166 (col.) Mar '59.
—— (basketball on horseback). Natl. geog. 113: 314-5 (col.) Mar '58.
—— (baskets of clams). Natl. geog. 107: 201 (col.) Feb '55.
—— (bathers, bicycles). Natl. geog. 113: 44 (col.) Jan '58.
—— (bathing camels). Natl. geog. 111: 248 Feb '57.
—— (bathing suits, beach). Holiday 28: 200 (col.) Nov '60.
—— (beach). Travel 109: 57 Je '58.
—— (beach table). Natl. geog. 114: 777 (col.) Dec '58.
—— (Bermuda parliament). Natl. geog. 105: 228 (col.) Feb '54.
—— (betting on cricket match). Natl. geog. 104: 389 Sept '53.
—— (bicycles). Natl. geog. 109: 876-7 Je '56; 118: 551-2 Oct '60.
—— (bird study). Natl. geog. 110: 108-17 Jl '56.
—— (birling match). Natl. geog. 114: 170 (col.) Aug '58.
—— (bloodhounds). Natl. geog. 113: 616 May '58.
—— (blowing Alpinhorn). Holiday 24: 4 Aug '58.
—— (boat). Travel 101: 40 May '54; 110: 26 Sept '58.
—— (boat, laughing). Holiday 11: 88 Jan '52.
—— (book, dog). Natl. geog. 106: 620 Nov '54.
—— (book makers, medieval). Int. gr. soc.: Arts . . . p. 63 (col.).
—— (boxing). Con. 129: IV Ap '52.
—— (branding cattle). Natl. geog. 118: 115 (col.) Jl '60.
—— (breakfast table). Natl. geog. 106: 103 (col.) Jl '54.
—— (brewery). Holiday 23: 12 (col.) Mar '58; 27: 176 Je '60.
—— (building house). Natl. geog. 97: 112 (col.) Jan '50.
—— (business). Holiday 27: 128 Mar '60.
—— (business meeting). Holiday 13: 19 May '53.
Natl. geog. 99: 421 Ap '21; 106: 65B Jl '54; 116: 834-5 (col.) Dec '59; 117: 113 Jan '60.
Travel 101: back cover Feb '54.
—— (business desk). Holiday 21: 143 (col.) Feb '57.
—— ("Calypso" ship). Natl. geog. 113: 374-96 (part col.) Mar '58.
—— (cameras). Holiday 13: 4 Ap '53, 119 (col.) Je '53.
Travel 111: 25-7 Je '59.
—— (camp cooking). Natl. geog. 98: 81 (col.) Jl '50; 100: 73, 79, 99 (part col.) Jl '51; 111: 103 (col.) Jan '57; 114: 166 (col.) Aug '58.

—— (camp fire). Natl. geog. 101: 555 Ap '52.
—— (camp table). Natl. geog. 103: 547 Ap '53.
—— (campers). Natl. geog. 117: 488 (col.) Ap '60.
—— (Canada goose). Natl. geog. 107: 58 Jan '55.
—— (canoe). Brooks: Growth of a nation, p. 96.
Natl. geog. 98: 82, 89, 90, 94, 112, 117 (col.) Jl '50.
Travel 107: 28-31 Mar '57.
—— (Carolina is.). Holiday 28: 72-3 (col.) Oct '60.
—— (carriage, horses & drivers). Amer. heri., vol. 6 no. 2 p. 61 (col.) (winter '55).
—— (carrots). Natl. geog. 112: 706 (col.) Nov '57.
—— (carry basket of grapes). Holiday 26: 127 (col.) Dec '59.
—— (carry baskets on pole). Natl. geog. 111: 358 (col.) Mar '57.
—— (carry cheese, Holland). Holiday 23: 57 Jan '58.
—— (carry man). Horan: Pict. hist. of wild west, p. 14.
—— (carry man in chair). Holiday 21: 72 (col.) May '57.
—— (carry molder cheese). Natl. geog. 106: 408-12 (part col.) Sept '54.
—— (carry pans of bread to village ovens). Natl. geog. 115: 587 Ap '59.
—— (carry stone, comic). Holiday 23: 3 Ap '58.
—— (carry stretcher). Natl. geog. 115: 543 (col.) Ap '59.
—— (carry trays of food). Holiday 25: 98 (col.) Je '59.
—— (cartoon). See Cartoon (men).
—— (catch turtle). Natl. geog. 97: 66 (col.) Jan '50.
—— (cattle). Natl. geog. 97: 583 (col.) May '50.
—— (cattle round-up). Holiday 24: 44 (col.) Oct '58.
Natl. geog. 101: 42 (col.), 44 Jan '52.
—— (cave explorers). Natl. geog. 113: 433 Mar '58.
—— (chart table). Natl. geog. 98: 403, 407 Sept '50, 564 Nov '50; 98: 767 (col.) Dec '50; 99: 708 Je '51.
—— (chasing dog). Holiday 26: 3 (col.) Aug '59.
—— (checkers). Holiday 18: 39 (col.) Jl '55.
—— (checking map). Natl. geog. 100: 713 (col.) Dec '51.
Travel 102: 15-8 Oct '54.
—— (chess game). Holiday 25: 23 (col.) Je '59.
Natl. geog. 116: 402 (col.) Sept '59.
—— (cleaning rug). Natl. geog. 114: 31 (col.) Jl '58.
—— (clerks in maple syrup shop). Natl. geog. 105: 482 (col.) Ap '54.
—— (cliffs). Natl. geog. 108: 400-22 (col.) Sept '55.
—— (climbing mt.). See mt. climbers.
—— (climbing pole). Natl. geog. 100: 111 Jl '51; 109: 432 (col.) Mar '56.

men (climbing steel girder). Natl. geog. 102: 140 Jl '52.

—— (climbing tree ladder). Natl. geog. 99: 689 (col.) May '51.

—— (club, talking). Holiday 18: 21 (col.) Dec '55.

—— (Coca Cola Co. meeting). Natl. geog. 105: 298 (col.) Mar '54.

—— (cocktail bar). Holiday 25: 40 (col.) Ap '59; 26: 221 (col.) Dec '59.

—— (cocktail table, comic). Holiday 22: 130 Oct '57.

—— (cocktails). Holiday 14: 74 Aug '53, 127 Nov '53; 24: 24, 81 Aug '58, 11 Sept '58, 96, 123 Oct '58, 23, 147 (col.), 175 Nov '58.

—— (cocktails, group). Holiday 24: 45, 159 (col.) Nov '58.

—— (coffee). Holiday 26: 219 Dec '59.

—— (coffee bar). Natl. geog. 107: 328 Mar '55.

—— (collect maple syrup). Natl. geog. 108: 663 Nov '55.

—— (colonial stairway). Natl. geog. 109: 481 (col.) Ap '56.

—— (comic). Holiday 5: 83-4 Feb '49; 24: 3 Jl '58, 6, 20, 28 Sept '58, 141 Nov '58, 3, 234 Dec '58; 25: 27, 91 Jan '59.

—— (conference meeting). Travel 101: back cover Feb '54.

—— (conference table). Natl. geog. 116: 834-5 (col.) Dec '59; 117: 113 Jan '60.

—— (cooking outdoors). Natl. geog. 107: 68 (col.) Jan '55.

—— (coral). Natl. geog. 111: 5 (col.) Jan '57.

—— (costume, ancient). Int. gr. soc.: Arts . . . several pages (col.).

—— (costume, medieval). Int. gr. soc.: Arts . . . p. 69, 81 (col.).

—— (costume, sports & professional). Int. gr. soc.: Arts . . . p. 153 (col.).

—— (costume, 19-20th cent.). Int. gr. soc.: Arts . . . p. 155 (col.).

—— (country fair). Amer. heri., vol. 7 no. 3 p. 48-9 (col.) (Ap '56).

—— (country store). Amer. heri., vol. 10 no. 2 p. 70 (Feb '59). Holiday 27: 55 (col.) Mar '60.

—— (crawling, cartoon). Holiday 14: 90 Nov '53.

—— (cucumber pickle plant). Natl. geog. 105: 313 (col.) Mar '54.

—— (cultivate vegetables). Natl. geog. 109: 231 (col.) Feb '56.

—— (cutting broomcorn). Natl. geog. 104: 804 (col.) Dec '53.

—— (cutting cane). Natl. geog. 103: 52 (col.) Jan '53.

—— (cutting into dolphin fish). Natl. geog. 109: 862 Je '56.

—— (cutting tall tree). Natl. geog. 110: 806 (col.) Dec '56.

—— (deep sea research). Natl. geog. 113: 375-96 (part col.) Mar '58.

—— (desert, comic). Holiday 21: 22 Mar '57.

—— (desk, business). Holiday 21: 20 (col.) May '57.

—— (digging for ancient treasures). Natl. geog. 110: 366-69 (col.) Sept '56.

—— (dinner table). Natl. geog. 101: 54 Jan '52; 117: 748-9 Je '60.

—— (dip ocean smelts). Natl. geog. 113: 630 (col.) May '58.

—— (divers on ship). Natl. geog. 102: 464 (col.) Oct '52.

—— (dividing Thames river swans). Natl. geog. 114: 85 (col.) Jl '58.

—— (diving). Holiday 5: 130 (col.) Je '49.

—— (dog). Holiday 18: 93 (col.) Nov '55.

—— (double bicycle). Natl. geog. 117: 424 (col.) Mar '60.

—— (drafting board). Holiday 27: 82 May '60.

—— (draughtsmen). Natl. geog. 107: 377 Mar '55.

—— (drinking). Holiday 13: 147 Je '53. Labande: Naples, p. 49.

—— (drinking at tables, comic). Holiday 21: 36 Je '57.

—— (drinking toasts). Holiday 10: 136 Oct '51; 13: 14 Ap '53; 17: 125 Mar '55.

—— (drummers). Holiday 28: 1 Aug '60.

—— (early Amer.). Amer. heri., vol. 6 no. 3 p. 7 (col.) (Ap '55).

—— (early auto). Amer. heri., vol. 10 no. 2 p. 40 (Feb '59).

—— (eating at floor table, Iran). Natl. geog. 101: 824-5 (col.) Je '52.

—— (eating at table). Natl. geog. 105: 25 (col.) Jan '54.

—— (eating at table, Bombay). Natl. geog. 105: 515 (col.) Ap '54.

—— (eating in Eskimo hut, cartoon). Holiday 13: 67 Jan '53.

—— (1860). Amer. heri., vol. 12 no. 1 p. 53 (Dec '60).

—— (1890). Amer. heri., vol. 6 no. 3 p. 63 (Ap '55).

—— (examine chart). Travel 107: 31 May '57.

—— (examine fossils). Natl. geog. 109: 364, 367, 372 (col.), 380 Mar '56.

—— (examine gems). Natl. geog. 98: 782, 787, 802 (col.) Dec '50.

—— (excavating in cave). Natl. geog. 110: 546-53 (col.) Oct '56.

—— (excavations, comic). Travel 113: 45 Mar '60.

—— (experiment on animals). Natl. geog. 97: 574 May '50.

—— (explorers). Natl. geog. 110: 678-9 (col.) Nov '56.

—— (family group). Holiday 21: 61 (col.) Feb '57.

—— (fat, eating). Amer. heri., vol. 8 no. 4 p. 68-9 (Je '57).

—— (fat, thin, food cartoons). Holiday 23: 161 (col.) May '58.

—— (feeding cobra snake). Natl. geog. 98: 591 (col.) Nov '50.

—— (feeding deer). Natl. geog. 110: 771 (col.) Dec '56.

—— (feeding red fox). Natl. geog. 109: 758 (col.) Je '56.

—— (fencing). Holiday 17: 107 Sept '55; 22: 193 Dec '57. Travel 105: 52 Ap '56.

men (fencing, 19th cent.). Con. 126: 114-20 Oct '50.

—— (1513). Brooks: Growth of a nation, p. 32.

—— (fighting). Amer. heri. vol. 8 no. 6 p. 7-8 (col.) (Oct '57).

—— (fighting fire). Amer. heri., vol. 7 no. 1 p. 68-9 (col.) (Dec '55).

—— (find Dead Sea scrolls). Natl. geog. 114: 784 Dec '58.

—— (fire lookouts). Natl. geog. 110: 288 (col.) Sept '56.

—— (fish). Natl. geog. 97: 31 (col.) Jan '50; 110: 388 (col.) Sept '56.
Travel 102: 36-7 Oct '54; 103: 12 Feb '55; 106: 29 Sept '56; 110: 8 Jl '58.

—— (fish nets). Natl. geog. 111: 603 (col.) May '57.
Travel 106: 12 Sept '56.

—— (fish stand). Natl. geog. 98: 344 (col.) Sept '50.

—— (fishing). Brooks: Growth of a nation, p. 284.
Holiday 13: 98 (col.) May '53; 24: 96 Sept '58; 25: 28 Feb '59, 8 Ap '59, 147 May '59; 26: 81 (col.) Sept '59.
Natl. geog. 110: 431 (col.) Oct '56.
Travel 104: 27-9 Oct '55; 105: 39 May '56; 108: 47 Aug '57; 111: 46 Feb '59.

—— (fishing in boat). Holiday 21: 34 Mar '57; 23: 2 (col.) Mar '58; 24: 143 (col.) Jl '58; 25: 109 (col.) Ap '59, 156 (col.) Je '59; 28: 49 (col.) Nov '60.
Travel 102: 42 Aug '54; 114: 31 Dec '60.

—— (fishing in river). Natl. geog. 102: 581 (col.) Nov '52.

—— (fishing in stream). Natl. geog. 97: 729 (col.) Je '50.
Travel 102: 18 Dec '54.

—— (fishing, sea). Natl. geog. 108: 528 (col.) Oct '55.

—— (fishing thru ice). Travel 109: 30 Jan '58.

—— (fishing). See also canoes (fishermen); fishermen.

—— (flamingo nests). Natl. geog. 99: 652 May '51.

—— (formal dress, 20th cent.). Int. gr. soc.: Arts . . . p. 157 (col.).

—— (frontier). Brooks: Growth of a nation, p. 100, 165.

—— (gathering pecans). Natl. geog. 112: 541 Oct '57.

—— (giant cactus). Natl. geog. 113: 635 May '58.

—— (goats). Natl. geog. 113: 145 Jan '58.

—— (golfers). Amer. heri., vol. 10 no. 1 p. 90 (Dec '58).
Holiday 14: 91 Jl '53; 23: 115 (col.) May '58, 22 (col.) Je '58; 24: 94 Jl '58, 117 (col.) Sept '58, 113 (col.) Oct '58; 25: inside back cover (col.) Feb '59, 40 (col.) Mar '59, inside back cover (col.) Ap '59; 26: 61 (col.) Jl '59, 85, 116 Sept '59, 115 Nov '59, 63 (col.) Dec '59.
Natl. geog. 118: 28 (col.) Jl '60.

—— (golfers, comic). Holiday 16: 11 Sept '54; 23: 3 (col.) Je '58; 24: 6 (col.) Aug '58; 25: 8 (col.) May '59; 26: 3 (col.) Aug '59.

—— (golfers, 1850). Holiday 13: 64 (col.) Je '53.

—— (golfers, old fashion). Holiday 23: 32 Je '58.

—— (golfers). See also golfers; man (playing golf).

—— (grape harvest). Holiday 27: 221 (col.) May '60.

—— (grape harvest, donkey). Holiday 28: 63 (col.) Dec '60.

—— (grinding coffee beans). Travel 110: 39 Oct '58.

—— (group talking). Holiday 24: 9 Jl '58, 72 Aug '58, 29 Sept '58, 127 Oct '58; 25: 96 Feb '59, 21 (col.) Je '59.

—— (guns). Holiday 26: 74 (col.) Sept '59.

—— (harvesting peas, camels). Natl. geog. 107: 506 Ap '55.

—— (harvesting rice). Natl. geog. 109: 316-7 (col.) Mar '56.

—— (harvest time). Face of Amer. p. 126-7 (col.).

—— (heads). Amer. heri., vol. 7 no. 6 p. 32 (Oct '56); vol. 8 no. 2 p. 22-3 (Feb '57).
Holiday 14: 9, 14 Jl '53; 24: 38 (col.), 73, 144 Dec '58; 25: 100 (col.), 140 Jan '59, 133 (col.), 186 Mar '59, 28, 153 Ap '59.
Int. gr. soc.: Arts . . . p. 137 (col.).
Natl. geog. 98: 86 (col.) Jl '50.
Travel 103: 5 Feb '55; 107: inside back cover Jan '57.

—— (heads, back view). Natl. geog. 98: 107 (col.) Jl '50.

—— (heads, group). Holiday 10: 39 (col.) Oct '51.

—— (heads in row). Durant: Pict. hist. of Amer. circus, p. 145.

—— (heads, look at pict.). Natl. geog. 98: 508 Oct '50.

—— (heads, reading). Natl. geog. 98: 824 Dec '50.

—— (heads, royalty cartoon). Holiday 23: 142 Jan '58.

—— (heads, talking). Holiday 24: 10 (col.) Aug '58.

—— (heads, toast). Holiday 10: 140 Nov '51, 12 (col.), 43 Dec '51; 11: 63 Jan '52, 105 May '52, 151 Je '52; 12: 26 Sept '52.

—— (helicopter). Natl. geog. 97: 242 (col.) Feb '50.

—— (hold petrel bird). Natl. geog. 105: 227 Feb '54.

—— ("hold-up"). Holiday 13: 12 Je '53.

—— (holding fish). Travel 101: 34 May '54; 106: 38 Oct '56.

—— (holding fish in boat). Travel 107: 49 May '57.

—— (horn, calling hounds). Natl. geog. 99: 828 Je '51.

—— (horse). Natl. geog. 112: 606 Nov '57.

—— (horse racing). Con. 139: 68 Mar '57; 140: XIX, 127 Nov '57.

—— (horse show). Holiday 24: 74 (col.) Dec '58.

—— (horse show, Ireland). Natl. geog. 104: 120-4 (col.) Jl '53.

men (horseback). Amer. heri., vol. 10 no. 4 p. 49 (Je '59).
Holiday 14: 81, 85 Oct '53; 21: 5 (col.) Mar '57; 23: 107 (col.) Feb '58; 24: cover (col.) Sept '58.
Labande: Naples, p. 88.
Natl. geog. 97: 132 Jan '50; 100: 602 Nov '51; 102: 324 (col.) Sept '52; 108: 326-7 (col.) Sept '55; 109: 22-3, 95 (col.) Jan '56; 112: 676-7 (col.) Nov '57; 113: 639 (col.) May '58; 114: 268 (col.) Aug '58.
Praeg. pict. ency., p. 417 (col.).
Travel 101: 15 Ap '54.
—— **(horseback, dogs).** Face of Amer., p. 96-7 (col.).
Holiday 14: 25 Oct '53.
—— **(horseback in a row).** Face of Amer., p. 49 (col.).
—— **(horseback, mt.).** Holiday 23: 41 (col.) Mar '58; 25: 123 (col.) Feb '59.
Natl. geog. 117: 483 (col.) Ap '60.
—— **(horseback, mt. trail).** Natl. geog. 109: 617 (col.) May '56; 113: 588 (col.) May '58.
—— **(horseback, Natl. park).** Natl. geog. 116: 164 (col.) Aug '59.
—— **(horseback, silhouette).** Travel 111: 53 May '59.
—— **(horseback, war).** Amer. heri., vol. 11 no. 6 p. 23 (Oct '60).
—— **(horses, running calf).** Natl. geog. 99: 518 Ap '51.
—— **(hunters).** Natl. geog. 98: 378 (col.) Sept '50.
—— **(hunters horseback, dogs).** Con. 140: XXXV (col.) Jan '58; 145: XXXIV May '60.
Holiday 26: 78 (col.) Nov '59; 27: 84 May '60.
Natl. geog. 103: 294 (col.) Mar '53.
—— **(hunting rhinoceros).** Natl. geog. 111: 394 (col.), 396, 398 Mar '57.
—— **(hurricane map).** Natl. geog. 98: 548, 550, 557 Oct '50.
—— **(iceboat).** Natl. geog. 111: 184 (col.) Feb '57.
——**(igloo, comic).** Holiday 14: 31 Oct '53.
—— **(in boat, cutting papyrus).** Natl. geog. 107: 36 (col.) Jan '55.
——**(in open tomb).** Natl. geog. 97: 244 Feb '50.
—— **(Indian rock carvings).** Natl. geog. 105: 375 (col.) Mar '54.
—— **(insect net).** Natl. geog. 100: 218 Aug '51.
—— **(inspecting auto).** Holiday 28: 13 (col.) Nov '60.
—— **(inspecting grain samples).** Natl. geog. 108: 209 (col.) Aug '55.
—— **(jockeys horseback).** Con. 138: LXXI Jan '57.
Holiday 26: 39 (col.) Nov '59.
—— **(laborers).** Natl. geog. 97: 230-1 Feb '50.
—— **(laughing).** Natl. geog. 116: 10-11 Jl '59.
—— **(launching barge).** Natl. geog. 97: 208 (col.) Feb '50.
—— **(leaning against column).** Holiday 23: 18 (col.) Ap '58.
—— **(library).** Holiday 25: 106 Feb '59.
—— **(lined up at train).** Holiday 26: 131 (col.) Nov '59.

—— **(loading camel).** Brooks: Growth of a nation, p. 138.
Natl. geog. 113: 502 (col.) Ap '58.
—— **(loading freighter).** Natl. geog. 113: 348 (col.) Mar '58.
—— **(log driving in river).** Face of Amer., p. 28 (col.).
—— **(loggers).** Amer. heri., vol. 9 no. 6 p. 14-5 (Oct '58).
—— **(logging with elephants).** Natl. geog. 112: 490-1 Oct '57.
—— **(looking at books).** Natl. geog. 97: 664 May '50.
—— **(looking at painting).** Amer. heri. vol. 11 no. 5 p. 10 (col.) (Aug '60).
—— **(looking at picture).** Con. 144: XLII Sept '59.
Natl. geog. 97: 755 Je '50; 98: 105 (col.) Jl '50.
—— **(lunch counter, comic).** Holiday 10: 88 Jl '51.
—— **(lunch on bldg. girder).** Face of Amer., p. 32-3 (col.).
—— **(making cheese).** Natl. geog. 111: 169 (col.) Feb '57.
—— **(making maple sugar).** Natl. geog. 105: 472-81 (part col.) Ap '54.
—— **(making marble inlay design).** Natl. geog. 118: 474 (col.) Oct '60.
—— **(making paper).** Natl. geog. 112: 430-1 Sept '57.
—— **(making stained glass, medieval).** Int. gr. soc.: Arts . . . p. 65 (col.).
—— **(making stick candy).** Natl. geog. 105: 299 (col.) Mar '54.
—— **(measure albatross wings).** Natl. geog. 107: 103 Jan '55.
—— **(measure tree trunk).** Natl. geog. 99: 680, 695 May '51.
—— **(mending fish nets).** Holiday 19: 26 (col.) Jan '56.
Natl. geog. 109: 843 (col.) Je '56.
—— **(microscope).** Natl. geog. 108: 173 Aug '55.
—— **(milking).** Rawson: Ant. pict. bk., p. 64.
—— **(mineral prospectors at table).** Natl. geog. 106: 545 Oct '54.
—— **(mixing egg nog).** Holiday 25: 115 Jan '59.
—— **(motor scooting).** Natl. geog. 100: 730 (col.) Dec '51.
—— **(mt. climbers).** See mt. climbers.
—— **(Mt. McKinley explorers).** Natl. geog. 104: 220-47 Aug '53.
—— **(moving office furniture, comic).** Con. 133: XLII May '54.
—— **(musical instruments).** Holiday 23: 40 (col.) Jan '58.
——**(night fishing).** Natl. geog. 107: 124 Jan '55.
—— **(19th cent.).** Amer. heri., vol. 9 no. 5 p. 14 (Aug '58).
—— **(North Pole).** Natl. geog. 115: 4-5, 7, 10, 12-3, 15 (col.) Jan '59.
—— **(office).** Holiday 22: 28 (col.) Oct '57.
—— **(office desk).** Natl. geog. 111: 420-1 Mar '57.
—— **(office table).** Natl. geog. 104: 722 (col.) Dec '53.

men (Olympic games, Ancient Greece). Int. gr. soc.: Arts . . . p. 39 (col.).
—— (on fence). Face of Amer., p. 39 (col.).
—— (on mules). Holiday 28: 37 (col.) Jl '60.
—— (overcoats). Holiday 24: 9 Oct '58.
—— (pack on back). Natl. geog. 100: 85 (col.) Jl '51.
—— (pajamas). Holiday 28: 171 Dec '60
——(parade). Amer. heri., vol. 10 no. 4 p. 43 (Je '59).
—— (park). Holiday 13: 43 (col.) Ap '53.
—— (park, snow). Natl. geog. 110: 764-5 (col.) Dec '56.
—— (picking strawberries). Natl. geog. 100: 366 (col.) Sept '51.
—— (picnic table, lawn). Natl. geog. 118: 179 (col.) Aug '60.
—— (pigs). Natl. geog. 100: 7 Jl '51.
—— (planning dam). Natl. geog. 115: 305 Mar '59.
—— (plastic rocket suits). Natl. geog. 111: 574 Ap '57.
—— (playing baseball). Amer. heri., vol. 10 no. 3 p. 21-5 (Ap '59).
Face of Amer., p. 13 (col.).
Holiday 27: 101 (col.) Je '60.
—— (playing checkers). Holiday 5: 42 (col.) Jan '49.
—— (playing chess, comic). Holiday 5: 143 Mar '49.
—— (playing cricket). Travel 104: 66 Sept '55.
—— (playing musical instruments). Holiday 5: 102 (col.) Ap '49; 24: 12-3 (col.) Nov '58.
—— (playing polo). Holiday 24: 40 Sept '58.
—— (playing skittles). Travel 105: 40 Ap '56.
—— (playing tennis, 1880). Holiday 14: 70 (col.) Sept '53.
—— (plowing with camel). Travel 110: 23 Oct '58.
—— (preaching). Amer. heri., vol. 6 no. 5 p. 100 (Aug '55).
—— (pulling boat to shore). Natl. geog. 118: 632, 640-1 (col.) Nov '60.
Travel 109: 44 Jan '58.
—— (pulling in fish net). Natl. geog. 104: 608 Nov '53.
—— (pushing auto). Natl. geog. 114: 18 (col.) Jl '58.
—— (quartet singers). Natl. geog. 118: 606 (col.) Nov '60.
—— (race horses). Travel 111: 19 May '59.
—— (rain, chickens). Holiday 13: 27 (col.) Je '53.
—— (reading). Natl. geog. 97: 304 (col.) Mar '50.
—— (reading at table). Natl. geog. 97: 296 Mar '50.
—— (reading paper). Durant: Pict. hist. of Amer. circus, p. 307.
—— (riding camels). Natl. geog. 99: 410 Mar '51; 103: 550 Ap '53.
—— (riding donkeys). Travel 101: 42 May '54.
—— (riding elephants). Natl. geog. 97: 26 (col.) Jan '50; 101: 340 (col.) Mar '52; 112: 500-2, 506 Oct '57; 118: 499 (col.) Oct '60.
Travel 111: 17 Jan '59.

—— (riding elephants in water). Natl. geog. 105: 520-1 (col.) Ap '54.
—— (riding high bicycles). Amer. her., vol. 10 no. 1 p. 90-1 (Dec '58).
—— (river lock tenders). Natl. geog. 97: 187 (col.) Feb '50.
—— (rocky beach). Holiday 26: 132 Nov '59.
—— (rolling roads, 1619). Brooks: Growth of a nation, p. 42.
—— (rounding-up wild horses, is., N.C.). Travel 107: 30- Je '57.
—— (rowboat). Natl. geog. 99: 384 Mar '51; 105: 165-7 (col.) Feb '54.
Praeg. pict. ency., p. 396 (col.).
Travel 107: cover Feb '57.
—— (rowboat, fishing, 1769) Holiday 24: inside back cover (col.) Sept '58.
—— (royal guard). Travel 111: 18-9 Ap '59.
—— (rubber raft). Natl. geog. 97: 49 (col.) Jan '50.
—— (running). Holiday 5: 76 Je '49.
—— (salesmen). Holiday 23: 182 May '58.
—— (satellite map). Natl. geog. 112: 800 (col.) Dec '57.
—— (satellite model). Natl. geog. 109: 489 (col.) Ap '56.
—— (sawing tree). Natl. geog. 100: 110 Jl '51.
—— (science work shop). Natl. geog. 113: 450, 465 (col.) Ap '58.
—— (scientific experiments). Natl. geog. 100: 762-8, 777, 780-4 (col.) Dec '51.
—— (seated). Amer. heri., vol. 6 no. 1 p. 30 (fall '54).
Holiday 10: 144-5 Oct '51; 20: 50, 71 Oct '56, 71 (col.) Dec '56; 23: 2 (col.) Feb '58; 28: 106-7, 160 Nov '60, 39, 82-5 (col.) Dec '60.
Natl. geog. 97: 115 (col.) Jan '50, 178 Feb '50.
—— (seated & lying down). Holiday 14: 43 Aug '53.
—— (seated & standing). Holiday 28: 55 (col.) Nov '60, 184 Dec '60.
—— (seated at table). Natl. geog. 98: 183 Aug '50.
—— (seated at table, birds). Natl. geog. 109: 264 Feb '56.
—— (seated at table, 1868). Amer. heri., vol. 11 no. 1 p. 68 (Dec '59).
—— (seated, tea table, maps). Natl. geog. 108: 756 (col.) Dec '55.
—— (seated, back view). Natl. geog. 97: 65 (col.) Jan '50; 100: 321 (col.) Sept '51.
—— (seated, back view, dog). Natl. geog. 116: 462 (col.) Oct '59.
—— (seated, back view, waterfall). Natl. geog. 108: 729 (col.) Dec '55.
—— (seated, cliffs). Natl. geog. 112: 736 (col.) Dec '57.
—— (seated, globe). Natl. geog. 98: 701 Nov '50.
—— (seated in home). Natl. geog. 110: 390-1 (col.) Sept '56.
—— (seated in rock canyon). Natl. geog. 105: 55 (col.) Jan '54.
—— (seated, lunch). Natl. geog. 97: 190 (col.) Feb '50.
—— (seated, map makers). Natl. geog. 109: 339 (col.) Mar '56.

men (seated, mermaid, comic). Holiday 28: 174 (col.) Nov '60.
—— (seated on bench). Amer. heri., vol. 6 no. 5 p. 57 (Aug '55).
—— (seated on ground). Natl. geog. 102: 296 (col.) Sept '52.
—— (seated on ground, back view). Natl. geog. 101: 715, 727 (col.) Je '52.
—— (seated, park plans). Natl. geog. 109: 232 Feb '56.
—— (seated, reading). Holiday 23: 8 May '58.
—— (seated, 1794). Con. ency. of ant., vol. 3, pl. 91.
—— (seated, South Seas). Natl. geog. 97: 95 (col.) Jan '50.
—— (seated, talking). Holiday 19: 92 Mar '56.
—— (shadows). Holiday 27: 228 (col.) May '60; 28: 87 (col.) Sept '60.
—— (shaking hands). Holiday 14: inside cover, 117 (col.) Nov '53; 27: 181 Mar '60.
—— (shaking hands, comic). Holiday 10: 6 Dec '51.
—— (shark). Natl. geog. 112: 328 (col.) Sept '57.
—— (shells). Natl. geog. 107: 65 (col.) Jan '55.
—— (ship). Amer. heri., vol. 9 no. 6 p. 50-1 (col.) (Oct '58).
—— (ship crew eating). Natl. geog. 97: 96 (col.) Jan '50.
—— (shorts). Holiday 11: 95, 125 Je '52.
—— (sidewalk restaurant table). Holiday 21: 171 May '57.
—— (singing). Holiday 6: 57 (col.) Jl '49; 14: 122 l '53.
Natl. geog. 118: 606 (col.) Nov '60.
—— (skeets shooting). Holiday 24: 40 Sept '58.
—— (skiing). Holiday 23: 13 Feb '58.
—— (skiis). Holiday 13: 16, 19, inside back cover (col.) Jan '53.
—— (snow, lake). Natl. geog. 113: 619 (col.) May '58.
—— (snow, survey). Natl. geog. 110: 778 (col.) Dec '56.
—— (sorting cucumbers). Natl. geog. 105: 314 (col.) Mar '54.
—— (sports). Holiday 24: 91 Jl '58.
—— (sports wear). Holiday 22: 163 (col.) Oct '57, 103, 175 (col.) Nov '57.
—— (sportsmen). Holiday 23: 44 (col.) Je '58; 25: 124 (col.) May '59.
—— (stack of pipes). Holiday 14: 105 Nov '53.
—— (stock market pens). Natl. geog. 110: 808-9 (col.) Dec '56.
—— (stone formation). Natl. geog. 114: 503 (col.) Oct '58.
—— (study maps). Natl. geog. 110: 150 Aug '56.
—— (study picture). Natl. geog. 98: 570 (col.) Nov '50.
—— (submarine, eating). Natl. geog. 102: 622 (col.) Nov '52.
—— (suit display). Holiday 21: 15, 21, 27-8 (col.) Ap '57.
—— (surveying). See surveyors.
—— (suspended concrete blocks). Natl. geog. 114: 142 Jl '58.

—— (sweeping). Travel 105: 56 Jan '56.
—— (sweeping up rice). Natl. geog. 97: 148 (col.) Feb '50.
—— (swimming). Holiday 23: 93 (col.) Feb '58.
Natl. geog. 109: 602 (col.) May '56; 118: 27 (col.) Jl '60.
—— (swimming, turtle). Natl. geog. 113: 174 (col.) Feb '58.
—— (tag seal pups). Natl. geog. 101: 505 (col.) Ap '52.
—— (take animals on ship). Natl. geog. 111: 223 (col.) Feb '57.
—— (taking pictures). Amer. heri., vol. 12 no. 1 p. 113 (Dec '60).
Face of Amer., p. 17 (col.).
Travel 111: 58 May '59.
—— (taking pictures by tube to tombs). Natl. geog. 116: 343 Sept '59.
—— (talking). Holiday 10: 81 (col.) Sept '51, 126 Oct '51; 18: 120 Sept '55; 19: 145 Mar '56; 21: 152 Ap '57; 24: 19 (col.) Oct '58, 119 (col.) Nov '58; 25: 115, 166 (col.) Mar '59; 26: 44 (col.) Oct '59; 27: 83 (col.) Feb '60; 28: 134 Oct '60.
—— (talking, bar). Holiday 19: 68 (col.) Jan '56, 96 (col.) Mar '56.
—— (talking, pistols). Holiday 18: 32 (col.) Oct '55, 131 (col.) Dec '55.
—— (tapping trees for maple syrup). Holiday 6: 42-3 (col.) Nov '49.
—— (tavern). Holiday 27: inside back cover (col.) Ap '60.
—— (tavern table). Natl. geog. 108: 321 Sept '55.
—— (telephoning). Amer. heri., vol. 9 no. 1 p. 99 (Dec '57).
—— (toasting woman). Holiday 28: 188 (col.) Nov '60.
—— (tobacco barn). Natl. geog. 105: 441 Ap '54.
—— (tractor). Natl. geog. 100: 617 (col.) Sept '51.
—— (training dogs). Natl. geog. 114: 232-3 Aug '58.
—— (training horses). Natl. geog. 102: 10 (col.) Jl '52.
—— (trapeze actors). Amer. heri., vol. 7 no. 1 p. 39 (Dec '55).
—— (trapping beaver). Natl. geog. 107: 672-80 (part col.) May '55.
—— (travel folders). Holiday 21: 80-1 Jan '57.
—— (travel guides). Holiday 21: 116-7 Mar '57.
—— (traveling, comic). Holiday 13: 81 Je '53.
—— (tree workers). Natl. geog. 97: 814 Je '50.
—— (tribesmen killing tiger). Natl. geog. 99: 474 (col.) Ap '51.
—— ("tug-of-war"). Natl. geog. 104: 210 (col.) Aug '53.
—— (turtle, large). Travel 113: 22 Feb '60.
—— (turtles & eggs). Natl. geog. 116: 682-3 (col.) Nov '59.
—— (twins). Natl. geog. 115: 616 (col.) May '59.
—— (unloading furniture from van). Travel 107: inside back cover Jan '57.

men (village post office). Natl. geog. 98: 391 Sept '50.

—— (walking). Holiday 14: 137 (col.) Nov '53, 5 (col.) Dec '53.

—— (wash clothes in stream). Natl. geog. 99: 487 Ap '51.

——(watching fire). Face of Amer., p. 36 (col.).

—— (watching pictures). Holiday 26: 99 (col.) Oct '59.

—— (weavers, 16th cent.). Int. gr. soc.: Arts . . . p. 97 (col.).

—— (weighing truffles). Natl. geog. 110: 422 Sept '56.

—— (whale). Natl. geog. 107: 115 Jan '55.

—— (whale hunting). Natl. geog. 110: 50-63 (part col.) Jl '56.

—— (whaleboat). Natl. geog. 97: 83 (col.) Jan '50.

—— (wheat field). Natl. geog. 103: 295 (col.) Mar '53; 107: 8 (col.) Jan '55.

—— (wheel chairs). Amer. heri., vol. 11 no. 6 p. 19 (Oct '60).

—— (wine tasters). See wine tasters (France).

—— (working on airplane). Natl. geog. 98: 295- (col.) Sept '50.

—— (working on tree). Natl. geog. 112: 511 Oct '57.

—— (wrestling). Natl. geog. 100: 623 (col.) Nov '51; 106: 634 (col.) Nov '54.

—— (yacht club lounge). Natl. geog. 113: 768 (col.) Je '58.

——, Afghanistan (basket on back). Natl. geog. 98: 687 (col.) Nov '50.

——, Africa. Natl. geog. 118: 304-6, 325, 332-3, 365, 388 (col.) Sept '60.

——, Africa (comic). Holiday 13: 19 May '53.

——, Africa (digging with picks). Natl. geog. 97: 320 (col.) Mar '50.

——, Africa (inoculate cow). Natl. geog. 97: 329 Mar '50.

——, Africa (rowboat). Natl. geog. 112: 62 (col.) Jl '57.

——, Africa (sorting diamonds). Natl. geog. 97: 333 Mar '50.

——, Africa (veiled). Natl. geog. 112: 68-71 (col.) Jl '57.

——, Alaska (horseback). Natl. geog. 116: 74-5 (col.) Jl '59.

——, Amazon (giant insects). Natl. geog. 115: 636-68 (part col.) May '59.

——, Antarctic. Natl. geog. 110: 146, 148-80 (part col.) Aug '56.

——, Antarctic (back view). Natl. geog. 116: 526 (col.) Oct '59.

——, Antarctic (baseball). Natl. geog. 110: 152 (col.) Aug '56.

——, Antarctic (festival dinner). Natl. geog. 113: 466 (col.) Ap '58.

——, Antarctic (salute flag). Natl. geog. 110: 166 (col.) Aug '56.

——, Antarctic (seal). Natl. geog. 112: 359 (col.) Sept '57.

——, Antarctic (silhouette). Natl. geog. 116: 549 (col.) Oct '59.

——, Antarctic (sledge). Natl. geog. 116: 532 (col.) Oct '59.

——, Arabia (seated). Int. gr. soc.: Arts . . . p. 179 (col.).

——, Arabia. See also Arabian men.

——, Austria (making pottery). Natl. geog. 115: 204 (col.) Feb '59.

——, Austria (salt mine). Natl. geog. 118: 264-5 (col.) Aug '60.

——, Austria (toasts at table). Natl. geog. 99: 782 (col.) Je '51.

——, Baffin is. Natl. geog. 100: 466-512 (part col.) Oct '51.

——, Bali (cock fight). Natl. geog. 99: 26 (col.) Jan '51.

——, Basque (France). Natl. geog. 109: 331 (col.) Mar '56.

——, Basque (dancing). Natl. geog. 105: 161-3 (part col.) Feb '54; 109: 328-9 (col.) Mar '56.

——, Basque (horseback). Natl. geog. 109: 331 (col.) Mar '56.

——, Belgium (drinking). Natl. geog. 113: 812-3 (col.) Je '58.

——, British (cartoon). Holiday 23: 43 Ap '58.

——, Cairo. Holiday 25: 50 (col.) Feb '59.

——, Caribbean (dancers). Holiday 24: 94 (col.) Aug '58.

——, Chile (horseback). Natl. geog. 117: 210 (col.) Feb '60.

——, Chile (laborers). Natl. geog. 117: 201, 216 (col.) Feb '60.

——, China See Chinese men.

——, Colonial. Amer. heri., vol. 3 no. 1 p. 26, 38-9 (col.) (fall '51).
Brooks: Growth of a nation, p. 76.
Holiday 10: 78 (col.) Nov '51, 97 (col.) Dec '51; 12: 143 (col.) Dec '52; 14: 126 (col.) Dec '53; 18: 118 (col.) Dec '55; 20: 190 (col.) Dec '56; 22: 55 (col.) Dec '57; 26: 97 Nov '59, 170 (col.) Dec '59; 28: 55 (col.) Dec '60.

——, Colonial (at table). Natl. geog. 106: 443 (col.) Oct '54.

——, Colonial (heads, back view). Amer. heri., vol. 7 no. 5 p. 97 (Aug '56).

——, Colonial (marching). Natl. geog. 107: 747 (col.) Je '55.

——, Colonial (on cliff). Amer. heri., vol. 10 no. 1 p. 22 (col.) (Dec '58).

——, Colonial (shaking hands). Holiday 23: 158 (col.) May '58.

——, Egypt. See Egyptian men.

——, English (hunters). Holiday 26: 172 (col.) Oct '59.

——, Fiji is. Holiday 28: 57, 63, 65 (col.) Oct '60.

——, forest workers. See forest service crews; forest fire fighters.

——, France (18th cent.). Int. gr. soc.: Arts . . . p. 93 (col.).

——, Greenland (cabin, int.). Natl. geog. 109: 135-7 Jan '56.

——, Hebrews (ancient time). Int. gr. soc.: Arts . . . p. 31 (col.).

——, Holland. Con. 140: LIV Sept '57; 142: XLV Sept '58.

——, Holland (carrying cheese). Natl. geog. 98: 759 (col.) Dec '50.

——, Holland (farm). Natl. geog. 106: 378 (col.) Sept '54.

——, India. (Naga Hills dancers). Natl. geog. 107: 249 (col.) Feb '55.

men, India (Sangtams, smoking pipes). Natl. geog. 107: 258 (col.) Feb '55.

——, Indonesia (carrying rice). Natl. geog. 99: 35 (col.) Jan '51.

——, Iraq (playing soccer). Natl. geog. 114: 474 (col.) Oct '58.

——, Ireland. Holiday 19: 42-3 Jan '56.

——, Ireland (fish nets). Travel 108: 46-7 Aug '57.

——, Italy (fencing). Con. 134: 27-30 Sept '54.

——, Kashmir (embroiderers). Natl. geog. 114: 619 (col.) Nov '58.

——, Kazakh (horseback). Natl. geog. 106: 643 (col.) Nov '54.

——, Kenya (cutting papyrus). Natl. geog. 106: 730 Dec '54.

——, Khmer (writing). Natl. geog. 117: 558 (col.) Ap '60.

——, Korea (voting). Natl. geog. 97: 793 Je '50.

——, Korea (yoke, carrying rock). Natl. geog. 97: 790 Je '50.

——, Ladakh (playing flute). Natl. geog. 99: 629 (col.) May '51.

——, Laos (heads). Natl. geog. 117: 57 (col.) Jan '60.

——, Lapland (herdsmen at camp fire). Disney: People & places, p. 14 (col.).

——, Lapland (in rowboat). Disney: People & places, p. 19, 22 (col.).

——, Lebanon. Natl. geog. 113: 495 (col.) Ap '58.

——, Liberia. Holiday 13: 43 Mar '53.

——, literary. See authors (name of).

——, Majorca (eating lunch). Natl. geog. 111: 658 (col.) May '57.

——, Mesopotamia (threshers). Natl. geog. 99: 58 (col.) Jan '51.

——, Morocco (weaving). Natl. geog. 107: 169 (col.) Feb '55.

——, mountain. Amer. heri., vol. 6 no. 5, cover, 4-5 (col.) (Aug '55).

——, New Hebrides. Natl. geog. 107: 79 Jan '55.

——, New Hebrides (dancing). Natl. geog. 107: 81, 83 (col.) Jan '55.

——, Nigeria (sorghum cane on head). Natl. geog. 110: 363 (col.) Sept '56.

——, Normandy (wharf). Natl. geog. 115: 613 (col.) May '59.

——, Norway (building boats). Natl. geog. 106: 175 (col.) Aug '54.

——, Pakistan (cavalry, horseback). Natl. geog. 102: 644 (col.) Nov '52.

——, Pilgrims. Amer. heri., vol. 7 no. 4 p. 92 (Aug '56); vol. 9 no. 2 p. 108 (Feb '58); vol. 10 no. 5 p. 78 (Aug '59).

——, pioneer. Holiday 24: 106 (col.) Sept '58.

——, Poland. Natl. geog. 114: 391 (col.) Sept '58.

——, primitive. Natl. geog. 108: 782-806 (part col.) Dec '55.

——, Puget Sound (back view). Natl. geog. 117: 459 (col.) Ap '60.

——, Santa Cruz (sheep). Natl. geog. 114: 273 Aug '58.

——, Saudi Arabia. Natl. geog. 105: 493 Ap '51.

——, Scotland. Natl. geog. 110: 47 (col.) Jl '56.

——, Scotland (at table). Natl. geog. 112: 478-9 Oct '57.

——, Scotsman. See also Scotsman.

——, service (holding up car). Holiday 26: 178 Nov '59.

——, ship crew. Natl. geog. 101: 577 (col.) May '52.

——, stone age. Natl. geog. 113: 426-37 Mar '58.

——, Sumeria (seated). Natl. geog. 99: 67 (col.) Jan '51.

——, Switzerland. Natl. geog. 98: 213 (col.) Aug '50.

——, Switzerland (blowing alpenhorns). Disney: People & places, p. 44 (col.).

——, Switzerland (cheese wagon). Natl. geog. 110: 467 (col.) Oct '56.

——, Switzerland (driving cow). Natl. geog. 98: 215 (col.) Aug '50.

——, Switzerland (playing instruments). Disney: People & places p. 37 (col.).

——, Tahiti (sawing lumber). Natl. geog. 112: 766 (col.) Dec '57.

——, Tibet. Natl. geog. 108: 23, 26-8 (col.) Jl '55.

——, timbermen. Holiday 14: 81 Aug '53.

——, Tiwi (dancing). Natl. geog. 109: 429 (col.) Mar '56.

——, Trinidad. Travel 109: 45 May '58.

——, Turkey (tobacco plants). Natl. geog. 115: 72 (col.) Jan '59.

——, U.S. Civil war. Amer. heri., vol. 6 no. 6 p. 67, 70, 78-9, 83-5 (Oct '55); Vol. 10 no. 1 p. 49-51 (Dec '58).

——, U.S. Navy (training). Natl. geog. 97: 46 Jan '50.

——, Venezuela (boat). Natl. geog. 97: 643 (col.) May '50.

——, western. Holiday 24: cover (col.) Oct '58.

——, western (attacking supply wagon). Amer. heri., vol. 6 no. 1 p. 39 (col.) (fall '54).

——, western (card game). Holiday 12: 38 (col.) Sept '52.

——, western (cattle). Natl. geog. 101: 54, 58, 61 (col.) Jan '52.

——, western (chuck wagon). Amer. heri., vol. 4 no. 3 p. 28 (col.) (spring '53).

——, western (dinner table, comic). Holiday 12: 103 Dec '52.

——, western (drinking from pool). Natl. geog. 101: 719 (col.) Je '52.

——, western (driving cattle). Natl. geog. 111: 674-5, 681 (col.) May '57.

——, western (early). Horan: Pict. hist. of wild west, (all thru book).

——, western (early, fighting). Horan: Pict. hist. of wild west, p. 76.

——, western (eating). Natl. geog. 101: 722 (col.) Je '52.

——, western (fighting). Holiday 24: 66 (col.) Aug '58.

——, western (fighting, horseback). Amer. heri., vol. 4 no. 1 cover (col.), p. 1 (fall '52).

——, western (guns). Natl. geog. 99: 209 (col.) Feb '51.

men, western (hold-up). Travel 104: inside back cover Sept '55.
——, **western (horse).** Natl. geog. 101: 718 (col.) Jc '52.
——, **western (horse, dog).** Natl. geog. 100: 322 (col.) Sept '51.
——, **western (horseback).** Amer. heri., vol. 4 no. 1, cover, 32-3 (col.), 48 (fall '52).
Holiday 21: 8 Jan '57; 24: 66 (col.) Aug '58.
Horan: Pict. hist. of wild west, p. 217.
Natl. geog. 101: 725 (col.) Je '52.
Travel 107: 52-4 May '57.
——, **western (horseback, cattle).** Natl. geog. 112: 539 (col.) Oct '57.
——, **western (horses on trail).** Natl. geog. 110: 324 Sept '56.
——, **western (miners).** Amer. heri., vol. 4 no. 1 p. 50-1 (fall '52).
——, **western (roping calves).** Natl. geog. 106: 247 (col.) Aug '54.
——, **western (seated, asleep).** Holiday 24: 67 (col.) Aug '58.
men & boys (marble game). Natl. geog. 98: 372 Sept '50.
men & children (camp supper). Travel 113: 29 Je '60.
—— **(maple sugar tasting).** Natl. geog. 105: 475 (col.) Ap '54.
—— **(on fence).** Face of Amer., frontis, 76 (col.).
men & girl. Natl. geog. 109: 247 (col.) Feb '56.
men & girls (back view, boat race). Natl. geog. 109: 845 (col.) Je '56.
—— **(back view, lighthouse).** Natl. geog. 113: 778 (col.) Je '58.
—— **(bar table).** Holiday 11: 55 Mar '52.
—— **(bathing suits).** Holiday 10: 82 Jl '51; 11: 77 (col.) Feb '52.
Natl. geog. 113: 299 (col.) Mar '58.
—— **(bathing suits, beach).** Holiday 23: 98 (col.) Jan '58.
—— **(beach).** Holiday 21: 111 (col.) Ap '57; 22: 134 (col.) Jl '57, 170. (col.) Dec '57.
—— **(beach, table).** Holiday 19: 117 (col.) Je '56.
—— **(bicycles).** Amer. heri., vol. 8 no. 1 p. 68-75 (Dec '56).
—— **(boat landing).** Holiday 27: 119 (col.) Ap '60.
—— **(buying flowers).** Holiday 26: 41 (col.) Oct '59.
—— **(college drama club).** Holiday 11: 64 (col.) May '52.
—— **(desk).** Holiday 21: 163 Je '57.
—— **(dinner table).** Natl. geog. 115: 248 (col.) Feb '59.
—— **(fireside group).** Natl. geog. 113: 93 (col.) Jan '58.
—— **(golfers).** Holiday 23: 17 Feb '58; 24: 6 (col.) Jl '58; 25: 167 Je '59.
—— **(heads, laughing).** Holiday 11: 86 (col.) May '52.
—— **(horseback).** Natl. geog. 105: 62, 67-8 (col.) Jan '54.
—— **(laughing).** Holiday 27: 87 (col.) Jan '60, 46 (col.) May '60.
—— **(motor boat).** Holiday 25: 101 Mar '59; 27: 134 (col.) Mar '60, 140-1 (col.) Je '60.

—— **(picnic, beach).** Holiday 25: 123 (col.) Ap '59; 28: 162 Dec '60.
Natl. geog. 105: 236 (col.) Feb '54.
—— **(picnic, canyon).** Natl. geog. 105: 58 (col.) Jan '54.
—— **(radio console).** Natl. geog. 104: 727 (col.) Dec '53.
—— **(sand dunes).** Natl. geog. 112: 124-36 (part col.) Jl '57.
—— **(shipboard).** Holiday 21: 89 (col.) Jan '57; 25: 94 Jan '59, 7 (col.), back cover (col.) Feb '59, 29, 31 (col.) Je '59.
—— **(show horses in ocean).** Natl. geog. 103: 300 (col.) Mar '53.
—— **(silversword plant).** Natl. geog. 115: 821 (col.) Je '59.
—— **(singing).** Natl. geog. 103: 291 (col.) Mar '53.
—— **(skiing).** Holiday 25: 72-7 (part col.) Jan '59.
—— **(sport clothes).** Holiday 18: 12-3 (col.) Oct '55.
—— **(swimming pool).** Holiday 25: 161 (col.) Mar '59; 27: 206 Mar '60, 190 (col.) May '60; 28: 126 Aug '60.
—— **(water skiing).** Holiday 18: 20 (col.) Sept '55.
——, **Argentina.** Natl. geog. 113: 323 Mar '58.
——, **Austria (dancing).** Natl. geog. 115: 210-11 (col.) Feb '59.
——, **German (dancers).** Natl. geog. 111: 267 (col.) Feb '57.
——, **Hawaii (ship).** Holiday 24: 98 (col.) Nov '58, 29 (col.) Dec '58.
——, **Madeira is. (dancing).** Natl. geog. 115: 386 (col.) Mar '59.
——, **Madeira is. (singing).** Natl. geog. 115: 386 (col.) Mar '59.
——, **Mexico (dancing).** Travel 114: cover (col.) Nov '60.
——, **Puerto Rico.** Natl. geog. 99: 443 (col.) Ap '51.
——, **Ukranian (dancing).** Natl. geog. 116: 388 (col.) Sept '59.
——, **West Germany (dancers).** Natl. geog. 115: 754-5 (col.) Je '59.
——, **western (on horseback).** Travel 111: 52 May '59.
men & women. Amer. heri., vol. 6 no. 2 p. 68 (winter '55).
Holiday 13: 2 (col.) Feb '53, 11-2, 15, 69 (col.) Mar '53, 3 May '53; 14: 10 (col.) Aug '53; 23: 171 (col.) Je '58; 24: 2 (col.) Oct '58, 188 Dec '58; 25: 12 (col.) Mar '59.
Travel 102: inside back cover Jl '54.
—— **(antique silhouette).** Con. 132: 34-6 Sept '53.
—— **(art exhibit).** Holiday 20: 49 (col.) Oct '56.
—— **(artists).** Holiday 25: 22 (col.) Mar '59.
—— **(at desk).** Holiday 21: 85 Ap '57.
—— **(at table).** Holiday 14: 13, 43, 45, 138-9 (col.) Dec '53; 23: 21, 40, 53, 75 (col.) Jan '58.
Natl. geog. 106: 472 Oct '54.
—— **(at table, 16th cent.).** Int. gr. soc.: Arts . . . p. 107 (col.).
—— **(back view).** Holiday 28: 151 Dec '60.

men & women (back view, boat). Natl. geog. 113: 346-7 (col.) Mar '58.

men & woman (back view, fountain). Natl. geog. 100: 49-51 (col.) Jl '51.

—— (back view, ocean). Natl. geog. 113: 18-9 (col.) Jan '58, 649 (col.) May '58.

—— (back view, snow). Natl. geog. 99: 566 May '51.

—— (back view, waterfalls). Natl. geog. 105: 796-7 (col.) Je '54.

—— (balcony). Travel 106: inside cover Oct '56.

—— (balcony table). Holiday 25: 83 (col.) May '59.

—— (baseball listeners, comic). Holiday 14: 58-9 Oct '53.

—— (bathing suits). Natl. geog. 105: 861 (col.) Je '54.

—— (bathing suits, beach, tea table). Natl. geog. 103: 72 (col.) Jan '53.

—— (bathing suits, ship deck). Holiday 14: 24 (col.) Nov '53.

—— (bathing suits, yacht). Travel 113: cover (col.) Feb '60.

—— (beach). Face of Amer., p. 95 (col.). Holiday 22: 65 (col.) Dec '57. Natl. geog. 113: 779 (col.) Je '58.

—— (beach, 1888 costume). Travel 110: 60 Sept '58.

—— (boarding airplane). Holiday 26: 18 (col.) Nov '59. Travel 109: 51 May '58; 114: 47 Aug '60.

—— (boarding bus). Travel 113: 9 Jan '60.

—— (boat deck chairs). Travel 102: 13 Nov '54.

—— (boat landing). Natl. geog. 100: 152 (col.) Aug '51.

—— (camp fire). Natl. geog. 99: 685 (col.) May '51. Travel 105: 37 Mar '56.

—— (campers). Natl. geog. 117: 331, 334 (part col.) Mar '60. Travel 103: 35 Feb '54.

—— (campers, Zion natl. park). Natl. geog. 116: 560 Oct '59.

—— (card game). Holiday 10: 2 (col.) Oct '51; 12: 80 (col.) Aug '52; 22: 68 (col.) Oct '57.

—— (card players, comic). Holiday 16: 52-3 Oct '54.

—— (castle balcony). Holiday 26: 71 (col.) Sept '59.

—— (catch & raise butterflies). Natl. geog. 112: 194-216 (part col.) Aug '57.

—— (centennial celebration). Natl. geog. 97: 200 Feb '50.

—— (climbing ship side). Natl. geog. 112: 781 (col.) Dec '57.

—— (cocktail party). Holiday 25: 195 (col.) Je '59.

—— (cocktail table). Holiday 21: 8 (col.) May '57.

—— (cocktails). Holiday 25: 71, 159 Mar '59, 35, 184 Ap '59, 106, 178 May '59, 24, 148 Je '59; 26: 18, 117 (col.) Sept '59.

—— (cocktails, 1894 cartoon). Amer. heri., vol. 11 no. 6 p. 112 (Oct '60).

—— (comic). Holiday 5: 11, 13, 60-1 (col.) Jan '49; 22: 19 Dec '57; 25: 98 May '59;

26: 170, 173 Oct '59, 79 Dec '59; 28: 50 Nov '60.

—— (costume, medieval workmen). Int. gr. soc.: Arts . . . p. 71 (col.).

—— (costume, 15-18th cent.). Int. gr. soc.: Arts . . . p. 111 (col.).

—— (crowd). Holiday 21: 204 (col.) Ap '57.

—— (crowd, traveling). Holiday 25: 43 Mar '59.

—— (cutting tobacco leaves). Natl. geog. 111: 610 May '57.

—— (dancing). Holiday 19: 17 (col.)) Feb '56.

—— (dig for clams). Natl. geog. 117: 456 (col.) Ap '60.

—— (dinner on ship deck). Holiday 25: 92-3 (col.) Jan '59.

—— (dinner table). Amer. heri., vol. 3 no. 4 p. 28 (summer '52). Holiday 10: 38 (col.) Jl '51, 103 (col.) Oct '51, 49 (col.) Nov '51; 11: 22 (col.) Mar '52; 14: 7 (col.) Nov '53; 21: 78 (col.) Feb '57. Natl. geog. 107: 436-7 (col.) Ap '55.

—— (divers' discoveries). Natl. geog. 117: 175 (col.) Feb '60.

—— (dog). Holiday 18: 10 (col.) Sept '55. Natl. geog. 114: 442 Sept '58.

—— (early California, Mexican). Amer. heri., vol. 9 no. 5 p. 11 (Aug '58).

—— (earthquake accidents). Natl. geog. 117: 335 Mar '60.

—— (eating at table). Natl. geog. 106: 403 (col.) Sept '54.

—— (eating ship deck). Holiday 14: 77 (col.) Oct '53.

—— (1865). Amer. heri., vol. 9 no. 2 p. 10-11 Feb '58.

—— (1885). Amer. heri., vol. 10 no. 1 p. 81-95 (Dec '58).

—— (evening clothes) Holiday 25: 97 (col.) Feb '59, 26 (col.) Mar '59, 139 (col.) May '59, 37 (col.) Je '59.

—— (Fair dinner). Face of Amer., p. 128-9 (col.).

—— (fish net). Natl. geog. 106: 612 (col.) Nov '54.

—— (fishing). Holiday 23: 113 Jan '58.

—— (fishing, boat). Holiday 24: 137 (col.) Oct '58 25: 169 (col.) Je '59; 28: 99 (col.), 140 Sept '60, 126 (col.) Nov '60. Travel 110: 23 Nov '58.

—— (fishing off bridge). Natl. geog. 97: 61 Jan '50.

—— (flamingoes). Natl. geog. 112: 556-7, 559, 562-5 (col.) Oct '57.

—— (flower garden). Holiday 12: 61 (col.) Sept '52.

—— (folk dance). Holiday 23: 37 (col.) Jan '58.

—— (formal dinner). Holiday 18: 56 (col.) Sept '55.

—— (fox). Natl. geog. 106: 585 (col.) Nov '54.

—— (garden table). Natl. geog. 103: 538 (col.) Ap '53.

—— (general store). Natl. geog. 118: 570-1 Oct '60.

men & women (gold panning). Natl. geog. 106: 219 Aug '54.
Travel 104: 27, 30 Sept '55.
—— (golfers). Holiday 23: 17, 101 (col.) Feb '58.
—— (grandstand). Face of Amer., p. 13, 18 (col.).
—— (harvest grapes). Holiday 26: 13 (col.) Nov '59.
—— (heads). Travel 102: 38 Sept '54; 111: 8 Feb '59.
—— (heads, comic). Holiday 25: 32 Mar '59; 28: 211 Nov '60.
—— (heads, laughing). Holiday 11: 95 Je '52; 12: 2 (col.), 14, 124 (col.) Jl '52, 20 Sept '52, 5, 69 (col.) Oct '52; 21: 182 Mar '57, 8 Ap '57, 97, 106, 199 May '57; 22: 6 Oct '57.
—— (heads, waving). Holiday 10: 76 Oct '51; 12: 10 Aug '52.
—— (hikers). Natl. geog. 110: 440 (col.) Oct '56.
—— (hill climbing). Natl. geog. 110: 500 (col.) Oct '56.
—— (holiday dinner). Holiday 22: 29 (col.) Dec '57.
—— (horse). Holiday 14: 80 Aug '53.
—— (horseback). Con. 133: XVII (col.) May '54.
Holiday 8: 5 Nov '50; 14: 42-3 (col.) Jl '53. Natl. geog. 111: 662, 678-9 (col.) May '57; 112: 439, 481 (col.) Oct '57.
Travel 110: 55 Sept '58.
—— (horses in flood). Amer. heri., vol. 6 no. 1 p. 69 (fall '54).
—— (horses on trail). Natl. geog. 109: 632-3 (col.) May '56.
—— (hunting with dogs). Holiday 14: 107 (col.) Nov '53.
—— (in auto). Holiday 23: 96 (col.) Feb '58.
—— (in church). Face of Amer., p. 170-1 (col.).
—— (in ocean). Holiday 13: 2, 7 (col.) Jan '53.
—— (in park, 18th cent.). Con. 144: XIX (col.) Nov '59.
—— (in train car). Holiday 14: 19 (col.) Oct '53.
—— (in Welch inn). Holiday 28: 43 (col.) Sept '60.
—— (inn table). Natl. geog. 99: 766 (col.) Je '51.
—— (jumping rope). Holiday 13: 126 May '53.
—— (jumping wall). Amer. heri., vol. 6 no. 5, frontis (Aug '55).
—— (laughing). Holiday 19: 101 Mar '56; 20: 97 Nov '56, 41, 185 Dec '56. Natl. geog. 109: 240 Feb '56.
—— (lawn bowling). Holiday 25: 90 (col.) Ap '59.
—— (lawn picnic). Holiday 18: 1 Jl '55.
—— (leaving plane). Holiday 10: 145 (col.) Dec '51; 20: 89 (col.) Oct '56; 28: 97 Sept '60. Natl. geog. 100: 722 Dec '51.
—— (leaving ship). Holiday 14: 86 Nov '53.
—— (listening to radio). Holiday 14: 23 Sept '53.

—— (load corn & fodder). Natl. geog. 97: 209 (col.) Feb '50.
—— (looking at painting). Holiday 23: 60 Jan '58.
—— (lunch table on boat). Natl. geog. 113: 151 (col.) Feb '58.
—— (map making). Natl. geog. 116: 411 Sept '59.
—— (marlin fish). Natl. geog. 112: 302 (col.) Sept '57.
—— (miniatures). Con. ency. of ant., vol. 1, pl. 129-32
—— (motor boat). Holiday 26: 83 (col.) Sept '59.
—— (night club). Face of Amer., p. 136-7 (col.).
—— (on exercisers). Holiday 25: 99 Feb '59, 35 Je '59.
—— (on pier). Travel 110: 19 Aug '58.
—— (on plane). Holiday 25: 7 (col.) Mar '59, 154 (col.) Je '59; 26: 115 (col.) Jl '59, 9 Aug '59, 104, 125 (col.) Oct '59; 27: 175 (col.) Mar '60; 28: 39 Nov '60.
—— (on plane, comic). Holiday 23: 67 Je '58.
—— (on stilts). See stilt walker.
—— (outdoor lunch table). Holiday 11: 122 (col.) May '52.
—— (outdoor market). Travel 106: 34 Aug '56.
—— (outdoor tea table). Holiday 11: 46, 116 (col.) Mar '52, 93, 110 (col.) Ap '52.
—— (park). Face of Amer., p. 11 (col.). Natl. geog. 118: 528 (col.) Oct '60.
—— (party). Holiday 14: 38 (col.) Sept '53; 24: 135 (col.) Jl '58.
—— (party at table). Natl. geog. 104: 284 (col.) Aug '53.
—— (party games). Holiday 24: 31 (col.) Jl '58.
—— (peasants, 16-18th cent.). Int. gr. soc.: Arts . . . p. 113 (col.).
—— (pepper strands). Natl. geog. 111: 643 (col.) May '57.
—— (perils of waltzing). Amer. heri., vol. 8 no. 5 p. 112 (Aug '57).
—— (picking oranges). Holiday 7: 34 (col.) Jan '50.
—— (picnic). Holiday 18: 49 (col.) Jl '55.
—— (picnic, beach). Travel 110: 55 Aug '58.
—— (picnic, night). Holiday 25: 60 (col.) Feb '59.
—— (playing cards). Amer. heri., vol. 9 no. 1 p. 86-7 (Dec '57).
—— (playing croquet). Amer. heri., vol. 8 no. 5 p. 52 (col.) (Aug '57).
—— (playing croquet, 1862). Amer. heri., vol. 10 no. 1 p. 83 (Dec '58).
—— (playing draughts). Natl. geog. 110: 39 (col.) Jl '56.
—— (playing golf, 1888). Amer. heri., vol. 8 no. 4 back cover (col.) (Je '57).
—— (playing golf). See also golfers.
—— (playing shuffleboard). Holiday 13: 40 Feb '53.
—— (praying). Holiday 24: 233 Dec '58.
—— (race track). Holiday 26: 19 (col.) Oct '59.
—— (restaurant lawn table). Holiday 24: 45 (col.) Sept '58.

men & women (rocks near lake). Face of Amer., p. 86 (col.).

—— (rocky beach). Natl. geog. 107: 609 (col.) May '55, 735 (col.) Je '55.

—— (roulette game). Holiday 23: 89 Je '58.

—— (running, beach). Holiday 11: 61 Jan '52.

—— (sailboat). Natl. geog. 112: 299 (col.) Sept '57.

—— (sand dunes). Natl. geog. 113: 618 (col.) May '58.

—— (seated). Con. 140: XXXIV Nov '57. Holiday 14: 21 (col.) Sept '53; 21: 101 Mar '57; 22: 43 Oct '57, 43 Nov '57. Travel 101: 14 Je '54; 106: 10 Oct '56.

—— (seated, back view). Holiday 19: 113 Mar '56. Natl. geog. 107: 646 (col.) May '55.

—— (seated, back view, harbor). Natl. geog. 105: 436 Ap '54.

—— (seated, balcony railing). Natl. geog. 100: 53-4 (col.) Jl '51.

—— (seated, Bryce canyon). Natl. geog. 114: 494 (col.) Oct '58.

—— (seated, opera group). Holiday 14: 112-6 (part col.) Dec '53.

—— (seated, party). Holiday 14: 46 (col.) Dec '53.

—— (self-serve dinner). Holiday 22: 23 Oct '57.

—— (shell collectors). Natl. geog. 115: 140 (col.) Jan '59.

—— (sheltered from rain). Holiday 25: 51 Jan '59.

—— (ship deck). Holiday 11: 98 (col.) May '52; 12: 10 (col.) Oct '52; 13: 113 (col.) Mar '53, 10, 79 (col.) Ap '53; 14: inside back cover Sept '53; 23: 127 (col.) Je '58; 24: 31 (col.) Sept '58, 123, 142, 174 (part col.) Nov '58; 25: 139 (col.) Jan '59, 23, 35 (col.) May '59, 50 (col.) Je '59. Natl. geog. 109: 738-9 (col.) Je '56; 113: 736-7 (col.) Je '58.

—— (ship deck chairs). Holiday 27: 111 Jan '60.

—— (ship, leaving harbor). Holiday 14: 167 (col.) Dec '53.

—— (ship table). Natl. geog. 108: 166 Aug '55.

—— (ship, 1856). Amer. heri., vol. 10 no. 5 p. 17 (col.) (Aug '59).

—— (ship, lunch time). Holiday 23: back cover (col.) Feb '58.

—— (ship salon). Holiday 20: 106 (col.) Nov '56.

—— (ship, silhouette). Holiday 25: inside cover Mar '59.

—— (ship sun deck). Holiday 23: 26 (col.) Ap '58.

—— (shorts). Natl. geog. 117: 469 (col.) Ap '60.

—— (shrine, Wash., D.C.). Face of Amer., p. 88-9 (col.).

—— (shuck scallop). Natl. geog. 112: 303 (col.) Sept '57.

—— (singing, T.V.). Holiday 25: 131 (col.) Mar '59.

—— (skating, comic). Amer. heri., vol. 9 no. 3 p. 61 (col.) (Ap '58).

—— (sleigh). Amer. heri., vol. 7 no. 1 p. 17-8 (col.) (Dec '55).

—— (smoking). Holiday 11: 89 (col.) Je '52.

—— (snakes). Natl. geog. 106: 334-38, 360-1 Sept '54.

—— (sort tobacco). Natl. geog. 105: 311 (col.) Mar '54.

—— (sports). Holiday 21: 13 (col.) Feb '57.

—— (sugar cane field). Natl. geog. 115: 276 (col.) Feb '59.

—— (supper club). Holiday 23: 131 (col.) Je '58.

—— (swamp land). Natl. geog. 113: 105-20 (part col.) Jan '58.

—— (swimming pool). Holiday 22: 220 (col.) Dec '57.

—— (taking allegiance to U.S.). Face of Amer., p. 26-7 (col.).

—— (talking) Holiday 10: 42 Jl '51.

—— (tea party). Holiday 24: 31 (col.) Oct '58.

—— (tea table). Natl. geog. 109: 239 (col.) Feb '56; 115: 182 (col.) Feb '59.

—— (terrace table). Holiday 11: 13 (col.) Mar '52; 12: 9 (col.) Nov '52. Natl. geog. 111: 448 (col.) Ap '57.

—— (tourists). Travel 112: 58 Dec '59; 113: 57 Ap '60.

—— (train dome). Holiday 14: 93 (col.) Nov '53; 21: 12-3 (col.) Mar '57, 116 (col.) May '57.

—— (traveling). Travel 101: 37 May '54; 104: 69 Jl '55.

—— (traveling, comic). Holiday 14: 160 Dec '53.

—— (traveling on bus). Travel 113: 9 Jan '60.

—— (tree house lunch). Holiday 26: 55 (col.) Sept '59.

—— (unearth Jericho relics). Natl. geog. 104: 857-69 (part col.) Dec '53.

—— (volcano crater). Natl. geog. 115: 818-9 (col.) Je '59.

—— (wade in ocean). Natl. geog. 105: 783 (col.) Je '54; 111: 20-1 (col.) Jan '57.

—— (walking, back view). Natl. geog. 98: 189 (col.) Aug '50.

—— (watching home movies). Holiday 11: 81 (col.) Je '52. Travel 112: 60 Jl '59.

—— (watching parade). Face of Amer., p. 50 (col.).

—— (watching volcano). Natl. geog. 117: 304, 307, 310-7 (col.) Mar '60.

—— (waving). Holiday 23: 15 (col.) Mar '58.

—— (weaving rugs). Natl. geog. 99: 455 (col.) Ap '51.

—— (wheat field). Natl. geog. 108: 214 (col.) Aug '55.

—— (work salt deposit). Natl. geog. 106: 836 (col.) Dec '54.

——, Africa. Natl. geog. 117: 116 (col.) Jan '60.

——, Africa (outdoor lunch table). Natl. geog. 110: 260 Aug '56.

——, Africa (rowboat). Travel 104: 29 Nov '55.

——, Africa (street merchant). Natl. geog. 108: 149 Jl '55.

men & women Alaska (leave plane). Natl. geog. 109: 753 (col.) Je '56.

——, Arabia. Natl. geog. 108: 159-66 (col.) Aug '55.

——, Azores is. (repair tile roof). Natl. geog. 113: 749 (col.) Je '58.

——, Basque (dancing). Holiday 23: 91 Mar '58.

——, British Guiana. Natl. geog. 107: 330-46 (part col.) Mar '55.

——, Canary is. (reforesting areas). Natl. geog. 107: 517 (col.) Ap '55.

——, Cappadocia (horseback). Osward: Asia Minor, pl. 73.

——, Caroline is. Holiday 28: 72-3 (col.) Oct '60.

——, Celtic. Int. gr. soc.: Arts . . . p. 27 (col.).

——, Colombia (jungle). Natl. geog. 102: 375, 377-82 (col.), 386 Sept '52.

——, Colonial. Amer. heri., vol. 8 no. 2 p. 107 (Feb '57); vol. 9 no. 1 p. 109 (Dec '57).
Holiday 6: 84 (col.) Jl '49; 22: 239 Dec '57.

——, Ecuador. Travel 109: 44-5 Jan '58.

——, Egypt. Int. gr. soc.: Arts . . . p. 29 (col.).

——, England (lawn bowls). Holiday 23: 70 (col.) Ap '58.

——, Fiji is. Natl. geog. 114: 540-61 (part col.) Oct '58.

——, German refugee (at table). Natl. geog. 111: 187 Feb '57.

——, Hawaii. Holiday 27: 170 (col.) Je '60.

——, Hawaii (ship). Holiday 25: 192 Ap '59.

——, Hawaii (ship rail). Holiday 23: 49 (col.) Ap '58.

——, India. Holiday 13: 102-5 Jan '53; 14: cover, 42 (col.), 44-5 Oct '53.
Int. gr. soc.: Arts . . . p. 27 (col.).

——, India (tea time). Holiday 27: 98 (col.) Jan '60.

——, Isparta (weavers). Osward: Asia Minor, pl. 140-1.

——, Italy (dinner table). Natl. geog. 100: 406 (col.) Sept '51.

——, Japan. Disney: People & places, p. 147-62 (col.).

——, Japan (at dinner). Int. gr. soc.: Arts . . . p. 179 (col.).

——, Lapland (church). Disney: People & places, p. 24 (col.).

——, Lhasa (banquet table). Natl. geog. 108: 11 Jl '55.

——, Mauritius is. Natl. geog. 109: 100-1 (col.) Jan '56.

——, Mennonites. Amer. heri., vol. 10 no. 5 p. 30 (Aug '59).

——, Nepal (back view). Natl. geog. 117: 382 (col.) Mar '60.

——, Nepal (burden on back). Natl. geog. 97: 36 (col.) Jan '50.

——, New Guinea. Natl. geog. 100: 662-5, 669-88 (col.) Nov '51; 103: 423-88 (part col.) Ap '53.

——, Panama (archaeologists). Natl. geog. 104: 282 (col.) Aug '53.

——, Paris (cafe, comic). Holiday 11: 72-3 Mar '52.

——, Paris (eating at table). Natl. geog. 101: 777 (col.) Je '52.

——, Peru. Disney: People & places, p. 99-110 (col.).

——, Peru (carry bags of guano). Natl. geog. 115: 411 Mar '59.

——, Philippines. Holiday 18: 90-1 (col.) Aug '55.

——, pioneer. Amer. heri., vol. 7 no. 3 p. 108 (Ap '56).

——, Polynesia. Holiday 9: 56 (col.) Mar '51.

——, Puritan. Amer. heri., vol. 11 no. 1 p. 113 (Dec '59).

——, Russia (crowd). Natl. geog. 116: 747-50 Dec '59.

——, Samoa. Disney: people & places, p. 132-45 (col.).

——, Spain (sorting oranges). Natl. geog. 97: 452-3 (col.) Ap '50.

——, Switzerland. Holiday 24: 20 Sept '58.

——, Tahiti. Holiday 28: 68-81 Nov '60.

——, Tiwi tribesmen (at table). Natl. geog. 109: 423 Mar '56.

——, western (cartoon). Travel 107: 11 Ap '57.

——, western (horseback). Natl. geog. 104: 354 (col.) Sept '53; 112: 546 (col.) Oct '57.

——, western (horses, comic). Holiday 21: 27 Mar '57.

men, women & boy (back view). Natl. geog. 99: 501 Ap '51.

—— (watching artist). Natl. geog. 98: 51 (col.) Jl '50.

men, women & child (airplane). Holiday 21: 106 Jan '57.

—— (Arizona). Holiday 24: 175 Nov '58.

—— (at depot). Face of Amer., p. 65 (col.).

—— (at harbor). Natl. geog. 105: 353 (col.) Mar '54.

—— (at zoo). Face of Amer., p. 66-7 (col.).

—— (baby show). Face of Amer., p. 74-5 (col.).

—— (back view, at fence). Natl. geog. 102: 10, 22 (col.) Jl '52.

—— (back view, canyon). Natl. geog. 107: 600 (col.) May '55.

—— (back view, 1893). Amer. heri., vol. 11 no. 6 p. 18 (col.) (Oct '60).

—— (back view, seated). Natl. geog. 111: 785 (col.) Je '57.

—— (back view, seated, lake). Natl. geog. 110: 597 (col.) Nov '56.

—— (beach). Holiday 18: 75 (col.) Jl '55; 21: 41 (col.) Je '57; 22: 99 (col.) Jl '57, 117 (col.) Oct '57; 23: 139 (col.) Feb '58.
Natl. geog. 98: 156 (col.) Aug '50; 104: 164-5, 167 (col.) Aug '53; 108: 502, 505 (col.) Oct '55; 109: 258-9 (col.) Feb '56; 112: 712 (col.) Nov '57.

—— (boarding plane). Holiday 18: 74 Sept '55.

—— (boat). Natl. geog. 112: 472 (col.) Oct '57.

—— (Cal. desert). Natl. geog. 112: 688, 691, 694-5, 710, 718 (part col.) Nov '57.

—— (Christmas gift). Holiday 24: 143 Dec '58.

—— (Christmas shopping). Holiday 14: 168 Dec '53.

men, women, child (city park). Natl. geog. 110: 203 (col.) Aug '56.
—— (dinner on plane). Holiday 24: 21 (col.) Aug '58.
—— (dinner table). Natl. geog. 100: 701 Nov '51; 108: 733 (col.) Dec '55.
—— (feeding pigeons). Natl. geog. 114: 378-9 (col.) Sept '58.
—— (fireplace). Natl. geog. 112: 444 (col.) Oct '57.
—— (flowers, lawn). Natl. geog. 109: 701-8 (col.) May '56.
—— (glass train dome). Holiday 22: 61 (col.) Dec '57.
—— (harvest wheat). Natl. geog. 115: 390 (col.) Mar '59.
—— (helicopter). Holiday 21: 1 Feb '57.
—— (in auto). Holiday 23: 42 (col.) Ap '58.
—— (kneeling at altar). Face of Amer., p. 30-1 (col.).
—— (large crowd). Natl. geog. 110: 514-5 (col.) Oct '56.
—— (N.C. mts.). Natl. geog. 113: 856-77 Je '58.
—— (park, sea lions). Natl. geog. 118: 803 (col.) Dec '60.
—— (picnic). Natl. geog. 100: 440 (col.) Oct '50.
—— (picnic, beach). Natl. geog. 116: 444 (col.) Oct '59.
—— (picnic, lawn). Natl. geog. 108: 522 (col.) Oct '55.
—— (rain). Natl. geog. 106: 167 (col.) Aug '54.
—— (running). Holiday 19: 136 Jan '56, 123 Feb '56.
—— (saying grace at table). Natl. geog. 112: 746 (col.) Dec '57; 113: 130 Jan '58.
—— (seated, 1773). Amer. heri., vol. 6 no. 3 p. 40-1 (col.) (Ap '55).
—— (ship deck, sailing). Holiday 18: 11 Oct '55.
—— (skating). Con. 140: cover (col.) Nov '57.
—— (swimming pool). Natl. geog. 100: 800 (col.) Dec '51.
—— (toy balloons). Holiday 25: 166 (col.) Ap '59.
—— (traveling). Holiday 21: 38 (col.) Je '57; 22: 19, 23, 144 (part col.) Sept '57.
——, Afghanistan. Natl. geog. 98: 682-705 (part col.) Nov '50.
——, Alaska. Natl. geog. 109: 753 (col.) Je '56.
——, Iranian nomad. Natl. geog. 100: 463 (col.) Oct '51.
——, Japan (bathtub). Natl. geog. 118: 752-3 (col.) Dec '60.
——, Laos (roadside table). Natl. geog. 117: 69 (col.) Jan '60.
——, Poland (dinner table). Natl. geog. 114: 370 Sept '58.
——, Poland (walkers). Natl. geog. 114: 395 (col.) Sept '58.
——, Spain. Natl. geog. 99: 523-30 (col.) Ap '51.
——, Switzerland (dinner table). Natl. geog. 110: 468 (col.) Oct '56.
men, women, child & animals (flee from fire).

Amer. heri., vol. 7 no. 5 p. 57 (Aug '56).
menat (sym.). Lehner: Pict. bk. of sym., p. 26.
Mendelsohn, Eric. Cur. biog. p. 426 (1953).
Mendelssohn, Felix. Holiday 18: 9 Aug '55.
—— (by von Schadow). Cooper: Con. ency. of music, p. 193.
Mendenhall, Thomas Corwin. Cur. biog. p. 273 (1960).
Menderes, Adman. Cur. biog. p. 455 (1954).
Mendes-France, Pierre. Cur. biog. p. 457 (1954).
Meng, John J. Cur. biog. p. 306 (1961).
Mengs, R. (work of). Con. 141: 229 Je '58.
"Menhir of Carnac." Praeg. pict. ency., p. 15.
Menjou, Adolphe. Cur. biog. p. 441 (1948).
Menlo park lab. (Edison). Amer. heri., vol. 10 no. 6 p. 37 (Oct '59).
Menninger, Karl A. Cur. biog., p. 443 (1948).
Menninger, Brig. Gen. William Claire. Cur. biog. p. 400 (1945).
Mennonites. Amer. heri., vol. 10 no. 5 p. 30-3, 102-3, 105 (Aug '59).
  Holiday 7: 78 Ap '50; 18: 102 (col.) Oct '55.
—— (heads). Durant: Pict. hist. of Amer. circus, p. 265.
Menon, Kumara P.S. Cur. biog. p. 363 (1957).
Menotti, Gian Carlo. Cooper: Con. ency of music, p. 194.
  Cur. biog. p. 434 (1947).
Menshikov, Mikhail A. Cur. biog. p. 283 (1958).
Menthon, Francois de. Cur. biog. p. 462 (1944).
Menuhin, Yehudi. Cooper: Con. ency. of music, p. 195.
  Cur. biog. p. 571 (1941).
  Holiday 15: 70 (col.) May '54.
Menuhin family, Yehudi. Holiday 22: 5 (col.) Oct '57.
Menzel, Adolf von (work of). Praeg. pict. ency., p. 404 (col.).
Menzel, Donald H. Cur. biog. p. 431 (1956).
Menzies, Robert G. Cur. biog. p. 572 (1941); p. 392 (1950).
Mephistopheles. Lehner: Pict. bk. of sym.. p. 92.
—— (as in Faust). Cooper: Con. ency. of music, p. 89.
Mercer, Johnny. Cur. biog. p. 445 (1948).
Mercer, Rev. Dr. Samuel A. B. Cur. biog. p. 429 (1953).
Merchant, Livingston T. Cur. biog. p. 433 (1956).
merchant boats. See boats, merchant.
Merchant marine academy. See U.S. Merchant marine academy.
Mercier, P. (work of). Con. 132: LI Sept '53.
Merck, George W. Cur. biog. p. 388 (1946).
Mercues chateau. See chateau Mercues.
Mercury. Lehner: Pict. bk. of sym., p. 30.
Mercury (Graeco-Roman statuette). Con. ency. of ant., vol. 3 pl. 71.
Mercury (magic square). Lehner: Pict. bk. of sym., p. 25.
Mercury auto. Travel 103: 11 Jan '55.
Mercury yardstick. See yardstick, mercury.

Mercy (deity). Lehner: Pict. bk. of sym., p. 48.
Mercy, goddess of. *See* Kuan Yin.
Merian, Matthew (work of). Praeg. pict. ency., p. 366.
Merida, Carlos. Cur. biog. p. 275 (1960).
merit, badge of. Int. gr. soc.: Arts . . . p. 167 (col.).
mermaid (on rock). Holiday 27: 37 Feb '60.
—— (sym.). Lehner: Pict. bk. of sym., p. 15, 92.
—— (statue, Copenhagen). Natl. geog. 100: 709 Dec '51.
Merman, Ethel. Cur. biog. p. 574 (1941); p. 413 (1955).
Holiday 5: 47 (col.) Ap '49.
Travel 111: 10 May '59.
Merman (jewels). Natl. geog. 117: 831 (col.) Je '60.
Merodach-Baladan (King of Babylon). Int. gr. soc.: Arts . . . p. 29 (col.).
Merriam, Charles E. Cur. biog. p. 436 (1947).
Merrick, David. Cur. biog. p. 308 (1961).
Merrick, Elliott. Cur. biog. p. 395 (1950).
Merrill, Charles E. Cur. biog. p. 435 (1956).
Merrill, Maj. Gen. Frank. Cur. biog. p. 464 (1944).
Merrill, Robert. Cur. biog. p. 415 (1952).
Merrimac (battle ship). Amer. heri., vol. 8 no. 4 p. 104 (Je '57).
Merrimac & Monitor (battle). Amer. heri., vol. 8 no. 4 p. 10-11 (col.) (Je '57).
"Merrimac & Monitor" (Riess). Natl. geog. 99: 203 (col.) Feb '51.
Merritt, Wesley. Pakula: Cent. album, 213.
"Merry company on a terrace." Con. 143: 274 Je '59.
merry-go-round (Afghanistan). Natl. geog. 104: 418 Sept '53.
—— (antique toy). Amer. heri., vol. 11 no. 1 p. 88 (col.) (Dec '59).
—— (children). Natl. geog. 97: 205 (col.) Feb '50.
Mersin. Osward: Asia Minor, p. 128-9.
Merz, Charles. Cur. biog., p. 460 (1954).
Mesa Verde (cliff dwelling). Holiday 18: 44-5 (col.) Sept '55.
—— *See* also cliff dwellings, Indian (Mesa Verde).
Mesa Verde cave city (Colo.). Natl. geog. 113: 642-3 (col.) May '58.
Mesa Verde natl. park. Holiday 12: 41 Sept '52.
Jordan: Hammond's pict. atlas, p. 166-7, 176 (col.).
—— (map). Natl. geog. 116: 622 Nov '59.
Mesabi range (Minn., iron). Holiday 8: 90-7 (part col.) Jl '50.
Natl. geog. 115: 455 (col.) Ap '59.
Mesas desert, effigies on. *See* effigies, desert Mesas.
Mesopotamia. Natl geog. 99: 43-104 (col.) Jan '51.
—— (map). Natl. geog. 99: 45 Jan '51.
—— chariots. Int. gr. soc.: Arts . . . p. 43 (col.).
—— costume (royal, ancient). Int. gr. soc.: Arts . . . p. 29 (col.).
Mesopotamian king (7th cent., B.C.). Int. gr.

soc.: Arts . . . p. 29 (col.).
—— men & women (early). Int. gr. soc.: Arts . . . p. 31 (col.).
—— warriors (ancient times). Int. gr. soc.: Arts . . . p. 33 (col.).
Messer, Thomas M. Cur. biog. p. 310 (1961).
Messersmith, George S. Cur. biog. p. 586 (1942).
Messick, Dale. Cur. biog. p. 312 (1961).
Messina, Antonello da (portrait by). Labande: Naples, p. 109.
Praeg. pict. ency., p. 270 (col.).
Messina (harbor). Natl. geog. 104: 589 Nov '53.
——, Strait of. *See* Strait of Messina.
—— cathedral. Natl. geog. 107: 33 (col.) Jan '55.
Messmer, Pierre. Cur. biog. p. 267 (1963).
Mesta, Mrs. Perle. Cur. biog. p. 424 (1949).
metal lime (sym.). Lehner: Pict. bk. of sym., p. 72.
metal planer. Int. gr. soc.: Arts . . . p. 173 (col.).
metallurgy (sym.). Lehner: Pict. bk. of sym., p. 14.
metalsmiths (at work). Amer. heri., vol. 2 no. 1 p. 66 (fall '50).
metalwork (middle ages). Int. gr. soc.: Arts p. 57 (col.).
—— (sym.). Lehner: Pict. bk. of sym., p. 91.
meteor crater (Ariz.). Natl. geog. 99: 727 Je '51.
meteorologist, air weather service. Natl. geog. 111: 303 Mar '57.
meteorologists. Natl. geog. 110: 322-2 (col.) Sept '56.
meteorology (sym.). Lehner: Pict. bk. of sym., p. 14.
meter, exposure. *See* meter, light.
meter, golf yardage. Holiday 14: 96 Dec '53.
meter, light. Holiday 10: 58, 68 Jl '51, 131 Nov '51, 6 Dec '51; 12: 15 Jl '52, 19 Dec '52; 14: 8 Jl '53, 18, 21 Oct '53, 4 Nov '53, 32, 37 Dec '53; 18: 70 Aug '55, 145 (col.) Dec '55; 20: 112 Nov '56, 177 Dec '56; 21: 44 Je '57; 22: 25 Jl '57, 30, 37 (col.) Dec '57; 28: 204 Nov '60.
Metropolitan museum (int.). Natl. geog. 118: 806-7 (col.) Dec '60.
Metropolitan museum of art (N.Y.). Holiday 16: 64-9 Dec '54.
Metropolitan opera house (N.Y.). Holiday 10: 50 Sept '51.
Metropolitan opera stars. Holiday 8: 75-81 Nov '50.
Metsu, Gabriel (work of). Con. ency. of ant., vol. 1, pl. 165.
Con. 137: 274 Je '56; 145: 159 May '60.
Metsys, Quentin (work of). Con. 133: 95 Ap '54.
Metzelthin, Pearl V. Cur. biog. p. 587 (1942).
Metzman, Gustav. Cur. biog. p. 391 (1946).
Meunier, Constantin (sculpture). Praeg. pict. ency. p. 425.
Meurer, Charles (work of). Amer. heri., vol. 10 no. 6 p. 4 (col.) (Oct '59).
Mexican. Holiday 14: 49 (col.) Jl '53.
—— (cock fight). Holiday 23: 28 Je '58.
—— (comic). Holiday 11: 79 Feb '52.

Mexican (donkey). Holiday 25: 140 (col.) Feb '59.
—— (donkey, cartoon). Holiday 14: 16 Jl '53.
—— (girl head, hat). Holiday 27: 48 May '60.
—— (head). Holiday 27: 56 Ap '60, 14 May '60.
—— (horseback). Amer. heri., vol. 9 no. 5 p. 13 (col.) (Aug '58).
  Holiday 24: 72 Nov '58.
—— (playing guitar). Holiday 10: 99 (col.), 156 Nov '51; 14: 148 Nov '53.
—— (seated). Holiday 9: 51 Mar '51; 26: 53-4 (col.) Nov '59.
—— (siesta). Holiday 15: 128 Je '54.
—— (Pre - Columbian head). Con. 129: LXXVIII Je '52.
Mexican art. Con. 135: 250-3 (part col.) Je '55.
Mexican boy. Holiday 24: 109 Aug '58, 114 Oct '58, 117 Dec '58.
—— (guitar). Holiday 24: 136 Nov '58.
Mexican boy & girl. Travel 113: back cover Je '60.
Mexican burro cart (tourist). Natl. geog. 105: 778 (col.) Je '54.
Mexican dancers. Holiday 8: 88 Dec '50; 22: 154 Nov '57; 27: 25 Mar '60.
  Travel 101: 14 Jan '54; 114: cover (col.) Nov '60.
Mexican family. Holiday 8: 79 (col.) Oct '50.
Mexican girl. Holiday 19: 13 (col.) May '56.
—— (Acapulco). Travel 110: inside back cover Sept '58.
Mexican girls (working). Travel 110: 31 Nov '58.
Mexican hacienda. Holiday 26: 54 (col.) Nov '59.
—— owner (horseback). Amer. heri., vol. 9 no. 5 p. 13 (col.) (Aug '58).
Mexican home. Travel 101: 13-6 Je '54; 104: 48 Aug '55.
——, thatch roof. Holiday 21: 26 May '57.
Mexican man (circus). Durant: Pict. hist. of Amer. circus, p. 298.
—— (walking, back view). Amer. heri., vol. 8 no. 6 p. 83 (Oct '57).
Mexican man & woman. Holiday 24: 26 Jl '58.
—— (dancing). Holiday 23: 131 (col.) Je '58.
Mexican men (camp fire). Holiday 26: cover (col.) Nov '59.
Mexican men & women. Holiday 14: 54-5 Jl '53.
Mexican mule-trolley. See mule-trolley, Mexican.
Mexican pilgrimage (Peregrinos). Travel 110: 36-40 Nov '58.
Mexican pottery. See pottery, Mexican.
Mexican sculpture (ancient). Amer. heri., vol. 10 no. 2 p. 46-57 (col.) (Feb '59).
Mexican Senor (horseback). Holiday 24: 39 (col.) Oct '58.
Mexican skull (encrusted with turquoise). Ceram: March of arch., p. 255.
Mexican woman. Holiday 11: 73 (col.) Ap '52; 28: 78-9 (col.), 105 Sept '60.
  Travel 110: 20 Nov '58.
—— (head). Holiday 14: 64 64 (col.) Nov '53.

—— (old). Travel 110: 40 Nov '58.
—— (rowing canoe). Holiday 13: cover (col.) Mar '53.
Mexicans. Natl. geog. 100: 796-824 (part col.) Dec '51; 102: 524-30 (col.) Oct '52.
  Travel 101: inside cover May '54; 110: 27, 29 Nov '58.
—— (camp meals). Travel 110: 38 Nov '58.
—— (heads). Travel 106: 37 Nov '56.
—— (seated back view). Natl. geog. 103: 350 Mar '53.
Mexico. Con. 137: 240 (col.) Je '56.
  Holiday 11: 52-7 (part col.) Mar '52, 94 May '52, 94 May '52; 13: 34-41 (part col.) Mar '53; 14: 49-57 (part col.) Jl '53; 22: 130 (col.) Sept '57; 26: 51-63 (col.) Nov '59.
  Natl. geog. 100: 786-824 (part col.) Dec '51; 102: 518-45 (part col.) Oct '52; 103: 322-50 (part col.) Mar '53; 107: 217-46 (part col.) Feb '55.
  Travel 101: 17-20, back cover Mar '54, 23 Ap '54; 103: 31-4 Jan '55; 104: 48 Aug '55; 107: 36-7 Jan '57; 110: 14-7, 19-40 Nov '58; 114: 30-55 Nov '60.
—— (Christmas procession). Holiday 16: 22 Dec '54.
—— (hotel, Taxco). Travel 114: 29 Nov '60.
—— (map). Amer. heri., vol. 10 no. 2 p. 81 (Feb '59).
  Travel 106: 52 Oct '56.
—— (Mayan area). Natl. geog. 115: 90-127 (part col.) Jan '59.
—— (San Miguel de Allende). Holiday 25: 140 (col.) Feb '59.
—— (spa resorts). Travel 107: 21-5 Mar '57.
—— (sports). Holiday 23: 28 Je '58; 24: 91 Jl '58, 109 Aug '58.
—— ("Univ. city"). Holiday 13: 35 (col.) Mar '53.
—— Xochimilco). See Xochimilco (floating gardens, Mexico).
——, U.S. war with. Amer. heri., vol. 6 no. 4 p. 21, 23 (col.) Je '55.
Mexico City. Holiday 13: 34, 38-9 (col.) Mar '53; 14: 79 Jl '53.
  Travel 101: back cover Jan '54.
—— (University city library). Travel 105: inside cover May '56.
Meyer, Agnes E. Cur. biog. p. 426 (1949).
Meyer, Albert Cardinal. Cur. biog. p. 277 (1960).
Meyer, Lt. Col. Charles R. Natl. geog. 104: 482 Oct '53.
Meyer, Cord, jr. Cur. biog. p. 447 (1948).
Meyer, Eugene. Cur. biog. p. 575 (1941).
Meyer, Jean. Cur. biog. p. 415 (1955).
Meyer, Jeremiah (miniature by). Con. ency. of ant., vol. 1, pl. 131.
Meyer, Karl F. Cur. biog. p. 417 (1952).
Meyerbeer, Giacomo. Cooper: Con. ency. of music, p. 197.
Meyerowitz, William. Cur. biog. p. 589 (1942).
Meyner, Robert B. Cur. biog. p. 417 (1955).
Mezquita mosque. See mosque, Mezquita.
Miami (Fla.). Natl. geog. 98: 563-94, 597-604 (part col.) Nov '50.
  Travel 102: 11 Jl '54; 111: 34 Feb '59.
—— (harbor). Natl. geog. 98: 538 Oct '50.

—— (hotel). Holiday 14: 157 Dec '53.

—— (Johnson's motel). Travel 109: 41 Je Je '58.

Miami Beach. Holiday 14: 26 Dec '53.
Natl. geog. 113: 54-6, 58-9 (part col.) Jan '58.
Travel 102: 11 Jl '54; 105: 47 Feb '56; 107: 37 Mar '57; 114: cover (col.) Dec '60.

—— (Beau Rivage motel). Travel 108: 43 Dec '57.

—— (Carillon hotel). Travel 108: 43 Dec '57.

—— (hotel). Holiday 23: 208 Je '58.
Travel 103: 44 Feb '55; 111: 51 Jan '59, 50 Ap '59.

—— (Hotel Saxony). Travel 113: 58 Ap '60.

Michael V, King of Rumania. Cur. biog. p. 467 (1944).

Michael (seal of). Lehner: Pict. bk. of sym., p. 24.

Michel, Claude Clodion (terracotta work of). Con. 140: 4 Sept '57; 143: 210 Je '59.

Michelangelo, Buonarroti. Holiday 19: 85 Mar '56.
Int. gr. soc.: Arts . . . p. 89 (col.).

—— (bust). Holiday 27: 86 (col.) Ap '60.

—— (sculpture by). Praeg. pict. ency., p. 273.

—— (work of). Con. 127: 56 Mar '51; 132: 191 Jan '54; 133: 147-9 May '54.
Int. gr. soc.: Arts . . . p. 87 (col.).
Natl. geog. 97: 772 (col.) Je '50; 111: 465 (col.) Ap '57.
Praeg. pict. ency., p. 7, 17, 278 (col.).

Michele da Firenze (carving). Con. 140: 166-7 Dec '57.

Michelino, Domenico de. See de Michelino, Domenico.

Michener, James A. Cur. biog. p. 449 (1948).

Michie, Allan A. Cur. biog. p. 591 (1942).

Michigan. Amer. heri., vol. 2 no. 4, cover, 33-5, 67 (part col.) (summer '51).
Holiday 10: 26-39 (part col.) Jl '51.
Jordan: Hammond's pict. atlas, p. 98- (col.).
Natl. geog. 101: 280-320 (part col.) Mar '52.
Travel 106: 41-2 Aug '56.

—— (Holland). See Holland (Michigan).

—— (map). Natl. geog. 101: 282-3 Mar '52.

—— (map, pict.). Holiday 10: 31 (col.) Jl '51.

Mich. Univ. See Univ. of Mich.

Mich. upper peninsula. Travel 110: 46-7 Aug '58.

—— (map). Travel 110: 44 Aug '58.

Mickiewicz, Adam (statue). Natl. geog. 114: 379 Sept '58.

Mickle, Kenneth. Holiday 14: 45 Dec '53.

microbiology (sym.). Lehner: Pict. bk. of sym., p. 14.

micrometer (sym.). Lehner: Pict. bk. of sym., p. 59.

microphone (sym.). Lehner: Pict. bk. of sym., p. 12.

microscope. Holiday 18: 118 Sept '55.

—— (man). Natl. geog. 103: 106 Jan '53; 113: 370 (col.) Mar '58; 118: 126 Jl '60.

—— (man head). Holiday 12: 5 (col.) Nov '52.

—— (sym.). Lehner: Pict. bk. of sym., p. 14.

—— (woman). Natl. geog. 109: 870 Je '56.

——, Alexis Magny (antique). Con. 136: 246 Jan '56.

——, antique. Con. 136: 10 Sept '55.

microscope & case, gilt bronze (Gozzi). Con. 145: 224 Je '60.

microscopes (men). Natl. geog. 108: 173 Aug '55.

"Midas bathing in river Pactolus" (Poussin). Con. 143: 124 Ap '59.

"Mid-day meal" (Chierici). Con. 138: IX (col.) Nov '56.

Middle east. Holiday 20: 51-65 (part col.) Dec '56.

—— (map). Holiday 20: 61 (col.) Dec '56.
Natl. geog. 105: 488-9 Ap '54; 117: 76-7 (col.) Jan '60.

—— (Suez to Calcutta). Natl. geog. 105: 484-522 (part col.) Ap '54.

Middle Temple Hall (int., Eng.). Natl. geog. 103: 820 Je '53.

Middlecoff, Cary. Cur. biog. 420 (1952).

Middleton, Drew. Cur. biog. p. 529 (1943).

Middleton, Thomas. Amer. heri., vol. 9 no. 2 p. 56 (col.) (Feb '58).

—— (work of). Amer. heri., vol. 9 no. 2 p. 58-9 (Feb '58).

Middleton gardens (S.C.). Face of Amer., p. 24-5 (col.).
Jordan: Hammond's pict. atlas, p. 63 (col.).
Natl. geog. 103: 318 (col.) Mar '53.

midget. Durant: Pict. hist. of Amer. circus, p. 275-83.

—— See also "Tom Thumb."

midshipmen, cadet. Natl. geog. 108: 692-706 (col.) Nov '55.

——, naval academy (on sailboat). Natl. geog. 113: 2 (col.) Jan '58.

Miers, Earl Schenck. Cur. biog. p. 428 (1949).

Mies Van Der Rohe, Ludwig. Cur. biog. p. 424 (1951).

Mifflin, Mr. & Mrs. Thomas (Copley). Amer. heri., vol. 6 no. 2 p. 39 (col.) (winter '55).

Mignon, Abraham (work of). Con. 140: 43 (col.) Sept '57; 145: XIV (col.) Je '60.

Mignone, Francisco. Cur. biog. p. 592 (1942).

Mignot, Louis (work of). Amer. heri., vol. 8 no. 1 p. 9 (col.) (Dec '56).

Mikhailov, Nikolai A. Cur. biog. p. 285 (1958).

Mikhailovitch, Gen. Draja. Cur. biog. p. 594 (1942).

Mikolajczyk, Stanislaw. Cur. biog. p. 470 (1944).

Mikoyan, Anastas I. Cur. biog. p. 420 (1955).

Milam, Carl H. Cur. biog. p. 403 (1945).

Milan cathedral (Italy). Holiday 6: 10 (col.) Dec '49.
Int. gr. soc.: Arts . . . p. 49 (col.).

Milani, Aureliano (work of). Con. 144: LXXXI Jan '60.

Milanov, Zinka. Cur. biog. p. 475 (1944).

Milbert, Jacques Gerard. Amer. heri., vol. 10 no. 4 p. 27 (col.) (Je '59).

mile-o-graph. Holiday 21: 198 May '57; 22: 124 Jl '57, 187 Nov '57.

Miles, Mary. Cur. biog. p. 597 (1942).

Milhaud, Darius. Cur. biog. p. 579 (1941); p. 314 (1961).

Milhous, Katherine. Jun. bk. of auth., p. 219.

military & civilian men (at table). Natl. geog. 104: 722 (col.) Dec '53.

military band, Jamaica. Natl. geog. 105: 343 (col.) Mar '54.

military camp. Amer. heri., vol. 7 no. 5 p. 41 (Aug '56).

military guard (Tehran). Natl. geog. 104: 718 Nov '53.

military police. Natl. geog. 99: 760 (col.) Je '51.

——, **Italy's.** See Italy's military police.

——, **Roman.** Natl. geog. 111: 482-3 (col.) Ap '57.

military school, Eng. See Sandhurst.

military school cadets. See cadets, military school.

military uniform, Canadian. Natl. geog. 104: 836 (col.) Dec '53.

militia drill (1820). Amer. heri., vol. 8 no. 3 back cover (col.) (Ap '57).

"A militia muster" (Boston, 1830). Amer. heri., vol. 7 no. 5 p. 20 (col.) (Aug '56).

milk, splash of. Brooks: Growth of a nation, p. 266.

—— **bottles (evolution of).** Amer. heri., vol. 3 no. 1 p. 25 (fall '51).

—— **cans (Holland).** Natl. geog. 98: 761 (col.) Dec '50.

—— **cart (Ireland).** Holiday 6: 47 (col.) Dec '49.

—— **crock.** Rawson: Ant. pict. bk., p. 89.

—— **gourd (Africa).** Natl. geog. 106: 494 Oct '54.

—— **pail.** Rawson: Ant. pict. bk., p. 61.

—— **pan (earthenware).** Con. 140: 136 Nov '57

—— **pot (rare).** Con. 140: LIX Jan '58.

milk story in pictures. Amer. heri., vol. 3 no. 1 p. 20-5 (part col.) (fall '51).

milking equipment. Rawson: Ant. pict. bk., p. 64.

"The milkmaid." Praeg. pict. ency., p. 27 (col.).

—— **(washing pail, Austria).** Natl. geog. 118: 271 (col.) Aug '60.

milkman. Natl. geog. 107: 468 (col.) Ap '55.

——, **Belgian (bicycle).** Natl. geog. 108: 555 Oct '55.

——, **Buenos Aires.** Holiday 11: 107 (col.) Mar '52.

milky way. Natl. geog. 98: 411 Sept '50; 110: 786 Dec '56.

mill. Travel 102: inside cover Dec '54.

——, **colonial.** Brooks: Growth of a nation, p. 55.

——, **corn.** See corn mill.

——, **cotton.** See cotton mill.

——, **grain (Mikonos, Greece).** Natl. geog. 114: 780 (col.) Dec '58.

——, **grist.** See gristmill.

——, **Mabry (Blue Ridge).** Natl. geog. 113: 651 (col.) May '58.

——, **Mennonite.** Amer. heri., vol. 10 no. 5 p. 32 (Aug '59).

——, **Old Slater (Pawtucket).** Holiday 27: 106 (col.) May '60.

——, **sugar cane.** Natl. geog. 113: 552-3 (col.) Ap '58.

——, **water.** See watermill.

——, **wind driven flour (Fayal).** Natl. geog. 113: 787 (col.) Je '58.

"The mill at Wijk" (Van Ruisdael). Praeg. pict. ency., p. 344 (col.).

mill stones. Amer. heri., vol. 2 no. 1 p. 11 (fall '50).

mill wheel. Face of Amer., p. 46 (col.).

Millais, Sir. J. E. (work of). Con. 142: 83 Nov '58.

Milland, Ray. Cur. biog. p. 395 (1946).

Millar, George R. Cur. biog. p. 429 (1949).

Millar, Kenneth. Cur. biog. p. 431 (1953).

Millar, Margaret. Cur. biog. p. 397 (1946).

Miller, Alfred Jacob (self portrait). Amer. heri., vol. 7 no. 2 p. 14 (Feb '56).

—— **(work of).** Amer. heri., vol. 6 no. 1 p. 35 (fall '54); vol. 7 no. 2 p. 8-9 (col.) (Feb '56); vol. 7 no. 6 p. 16-7 (part col.) (Oct '56).

Miller, Alice Duer. Cur biog. p. 580 (1941).

Miller, Arthur. Cur. biog. p. 439 (1947).

Miller, Douglas. Cur. biog. p. 582 (1941).

Miller, Edward G., jr. Cur. biog. p. 426 (1951).

Miller, Elizabeth Cleveland. Jun. bk. of auth., p. 220.

Miller, Frieda S. Cur. biog. p. 405 (1945).

Miller, Gilbert. Cur. biog. p. 287 (1958).

Miller, Glenn. Cur. biog. p. 598 (1942).

Miller, Harry W. Cur. biog. p. 300 (1962).

Miller, Irving. Cur. biog. p. 421 (1952).

Miller, J. Cloyd. Cur. biog. p. 428 (1951).

Miller, J. Irwin. Cur. biog. p. 316 (1961).

Miller, Jacob (work of). Amer. heri., vol. 6 no. 5 p. 9 (col.) (Aug '55).

Miller, Justin. Cur. biog. p. 441 (1947).

Miller, Lee P. Cur. biog. p. 301 (1959).

Miller, Lewis. Amer. heri., vol. 6 no. 6 p. 52 (Oct '55).

—— **(work of).** Amer. heri., vol. 6 no. 6 p. 53-5 (col.) (Oct '55).

Miller, Marshall E. Cur. biog. p. 432 (1953).

Miller, Merle. Cur. biog. p. 398 (1950).

Miller, Mildred. Cur. biog. p. 365 (1957).

Miller, Mitch. Cur. biog. p. 437 (1956).

Miller, Watson B. Cur. biog. p. 443 (1947).

Miller, William E. Cur. biog. p. 300 (1962).

Milles, Carl. Cur. biog. p. 423 (1952).

Millet, Jean Francois (work of). Con. 129: 26 Ap '52; 143: LVI Je '59; 145: LXXIV Je '60.

Natl. geog. 115: 603 May '59.

Millett, John D. Cur. biog. p. 434 (1953).

Milligan, Col. Mary Louise. Cur. biog. p. 366 (1957).

Millikan, Robert A. Cur. biog. p. 426 (1952).

Millikin, Eugene D. Cur. biog. p. 452 (1948).

Milliner, Alexander. Amer. heri., vol. 9 no. 3 p. 31 (Ap '58).

millinery shop. Holiday 26: 79 (col.) Oct '59.

millinery shop, colonial. Natl. geog. 106: 474 (col.) Oct '54.

milling machine, Whitney. Amer. heri., vol. 6 no. 3 p. 10 (Ap '55).

millionaire, America's first (E.H. Derby). Amer. heri., vol. 6 no. 2 p. 15 (col.) (winter '55).

Mills, Frederick C. Cur. biog. p. 453 (1948).

Mills, Hayley. Cur. biog. p. 269 (1963).

Mills, John. Cur. biog. p. 271 (1963).

Mills, Wilbur D. Cur. biog. p. 439 (1956).
Milne, A. A. Jun. bk. of auth., p. 222.
Milstein, Nathan. Cur. biog. p. 399 (1950).
Milton, Jeff. Horan: Pict. hist. of wild west, p. 125.
Milton, John (with daughter). Natl. geog. 108: 310 Sept '55.
Milward, Capt. John. Con. 141: 162 May '58.
Milwaukee (Wis.). Holiday 6: 54-9 Jl '49.
—— (harbor). Natl. geog. 111: 146 Feb '57.
—— (hotel). Travel 111: 53 Je '59.
minaret. Natl. geog. 101: 658 (col.) May '52; 109: 72 (col.) Jan '56; 114: 447, 450, 467 (col.) Oct '58.
   Travel 101: 18 Je '54; 111: 29 Jan '59.
—— (Aden). Natl. geog. 117: 111 (col.) Jan '60.
—— (Africa). Travel 113: 31 Jan '60.
—— (Ankara). Osward: Asia Minor, pl. 155.
—— (Cairo). Int. gr. soc.: Arts . . . p. 85 (col.).
—— (India). Travel 107: 11 Jan '57, 11 Feb '57.
—— (Isfahan). Natl. geog. 114: 2, 36 (col.) Jl '58.
—— (Karbala). Natl. geog. 104: 10 (col.) Jl '53.
—— (Marrakesh, Morocco). Int. gr. soc.: Arts . . . p. 85 (col.).
—— (Mecca). Natl. geog. 104: 29-30, 56 (col.) Jl '53.
—— (Nigeria). Natl. geog. 110: 355 Sept '56.
—— (Turkey). Natl. geog. 110: 737 Dec '56.
—— (Yemen). Natl. geog. 101: 240 (col.) Feb '52.
——, Mohammed. Natl. geog. 110: 724 (col.) Dec '56.
——, Mosul's leaning. Natl. geog. 114: 472 Oct '58.
——, Samarra's ramped. Natl. geog. 104: 15 (col.) Jl '53.
——, Seljuk. See Seljuk minaret.
Minaret of Islamic center (Wash., D.C.). Travel 106: 13 Dec '56.
Minaret of mosque (Africa). Travel 113: 31 Jan '60.
minarets. Holiday 25: 52 (col.) Feb '59.
   Int. gr. soc.: Arts . . . p. 45 (col.).
   Natl. geog. 100: 160 (col.) Aug '51, 433 (col.) Oct '51; 107: 148 (col.) Feb '55.
—— (Cairo). Natl. geog. 106: 764 (col.) Dec '54.
—— (Cyprus). Natl. geog. 109: 879 Je '56.
—— (Istanbul). Natl. geog. 115: 87 (col.) Jan '59.
—— (Medina). Natl. geog. 104: 40 Jl '53.
—— (mosque). Natl. geog. 112: 111 Jl '57.
——, Aya Sofya. Natl. geog. 112: 405 Sept '57.
mine, copper. See copper mine.
——, Eagle mt. See Eagle mt. mine.
——, iron. See iron mine.
——, open pit. Amer. heri., vol. 1 no. 2 p. 75 (winter '50).
mine driller. Natl. geog. 113: 580 Ap '58.
mine sweeper, U.S. navy. See U.S. mine sweeper.
mine-sweeping "pig." Natl. geog. 104: 568

(col.) Oct '53.
Miner, William ("Old Bill"). Horan: Pict. hist. of wild west, p. 80.
Miner, Worthington. Cur. biog. p. 436 (1953).
miner (cartoon). Holiday 23: 27 Jan '58.
—— (in cavern). Natl. geog. 97: 703 (col.) Je '50.
——, early western (Hammack). Amer. heri., vol. 6 no. 1 p. 65 (fall '54).
——, Japanese. Natl. geog. 104: 649 Nov '53.
——, Ruhr coal (cleaning up). Natl. geog. 115: 779 (col.) Je '59.
mineral collecting (men, women). Natl. geog. 100: 632-60 (col.) Nov '51.
minerals. Natl. geog. 100: 646-7, 651-3, 656-9 (col.) Nov '51; 106: 548-9 (col.) Oct '54.
—— (exhibit). Natl. geog. 117: 818-9 (col.) Je '60.
mineralogy (sym.). Lehner: Pict. bk. of sym., p. 14.
miners ("forty-niners"). Holiday 24: 66-9 (part col.) Aug '58.
—— (Mexico). Natl. geog. 107: 228 (col.) Feb '55.
——, coal. Brooks: Growth of a nation, p. 218.
——, early Texas. Amer. heri., vol. 4 no. 1 p. 50-1 (fall '52).
——, gold. See gold miner; gold prospector.
"Minerva." Con. 138: 108 Nov '56.
—— (Graeco-Roman statuette). Con. ency. of ant., vol. 3, pl. 71.
"Minerva" (Strozzi). Con. 138: 212 Dec '56.
Minerva (sym.). Lehner: Pict. bk. of sym., p. 30.
Minerva clock. Jensen: The White House, p. 32.
"Minerva pursuing Venus" (Tintoretto). Con. 136: 225 Dec '55.
Mineses, Viscount (work of). Con. 137: 2 (col.) Mar '56.
miniature (antique portrait). Con. 134: 43 Sept '54; 136: 24, 26 Sept '55; 139: 243 Je '57; 144: 138 Nov '59.
—— (18th cent.). Con. 143: XXXIII Ap '59.
—— (ivory). Con. 142: 123 Nov '58.
—— (Persian illum., 18th cent.). Con. 143: 128 Ap '59.
—— (rock crystal intaglio). Con. 145: V May '60.
—— (16th cent.). Con. 143: 174 May '59.
—— (Swedish). Con. 141: 19-20 Mar '58.
—— (by Cosway). Con. 144: XXX Sept '59.
—— (Hilliard). Con. 143: 263 Je '59.
—— (Inman). Amer. heri., vol. 7 no. 4 p. 10 (col.) (Je '56).
—— (Malbone). Amer. heri., vol. 9 no. 2 cover (col.) (Feb '58).
—— (Smart). Con. 141: 43 Mar '58.
——, Queen Elizabeth. Con. 145: 179 May '60.
——, Geo. Washington (19th cent.). Amer. heri., vol. 6 no. 2 frontis (col.) (winter '55).
——, Grassi. Praeg. pict. ency., p. 322 (col.).
——, Henry VIII. Con. 143: 103 Ap '59.
miniature mosaic, Byzantine. See mosaic, Byzantine miniature.
—— painting (evangelistary). Praeg. pict. ency., p. 181 (col.).

miniature picture frame. *See* picture frame, miniature.

miniatures. Con. 138: 82-3 Nov '56; 142: IV Dec '58; 145: 127 Ap '60.

—— (by Macpherson). Con. 144: 167 Dec '59.

—— (Trumbull). Amer. heri., vol. 9 no. 4 p. 42-3 (col.) (Je '58).

—— (English enamel). Con. ency. of ant., vol. 1, pl. 74.

—— (ivory). Amer. heri., vol. 9 no. 2 p. 56-7 (col.) (Feb '58).

—— (porcelain, man & horse). Natl. geog. 99: 755 (col.) Je '51.

—— (portrait). Con. ency. of ant., vol. 1, pl. 129-31..

Con. 132: 36 Sept '53; 136: 112 Nov '55.

—— (Royal Doulton). Holiday 14: 5 (col.) Oct '53; 24: 26 (col.) Nov '58.

—— (Russian). Con. 144: 266-7 Jan '60.

mining (Cripple Creek). Holiday 10: 90-3 (part col.) Jl '51.

—— (sym.). Lehner: Pict. bk. of sym., p. 12.

—— prospector. Amer. heri., vol. 10 no. 3 p. 39 (col.) (Ap '59).

Holiday 18: 4 (col.) Sept '55.

—— prospector (1860). Amer. heri., vol. 10 no. 3 p. 106-7 (Ap '59).

—— prospector (horseback). Amer. heri., vol. 10 no. 3 p. 36 (col.) (Ap '59).

mining town (Colo.). Natl. geog. 106: 238 Aug '54.

——, western. Amer. heri., vol. 6 no. 1 p. 64 (fall '54).

minister (being ordained). Face of Amer., p. 170-1 (col.).

—— (cartoon). Amer. heri., vol. 6 no. 3 p. 76 (Ap '55).

—— (preaching). Amer. heri., vol. 7 no. 1 p. 55 (col.) (Dec '55).

—— *See* also evangelist.

Minister of labour & welfare, & wife (Nigeria). Natl. geog. 110: 331 (col.) Sept '56.

minium (sym.) Lehner: Pict. bk. of sym., p. 72.

minna (sym.). Lehner: Pict. bk. of sym., p. 28.

Minneapolis (Minn.). Natl. geog. 114: 662-3 (col.) Nov '58.

—— (aquatennial parade). Travel 109: 18 Je '58.

Minnesota. Amer. heri., vol. 1 no. 2 p. 2-13, 75 (winter '50).

Holiday 12: 60-3 (part col.) Nov '52; 13: 28 (col.) Ap '53 18: 26-33 (part col.) Aug '55.

Travel 109: 17-8, 20 Je '58.

—— (lakes). Holiday 14: 64 (col.) Jl '53.

—— (state capitol bldg.). Natl. geog. 114: 670-1 Nov '58.

Minnewaska lake. *See* Lake Minnewaska (N.Y.).

Minoan votive axe. Con. 144: 282 Jan '60.

Minor, Robert. Cur. biog. p. 584 (1941).

Minorca is. Holiday 27: 50-5 (col.) Jan '60. Travel 101: 28-31 Mar '54.

Minos, palace of King. *See* palace of King Minos.

Minow, Newton N. Cur. biog. p. 318 (1961).

"The Minstrel" (Escosura). Con. 129: XVIII (col.) Je '52.

minstrels. Amer. heri., vol. 9 no. 3 p. 21 (col.) (Ap '58).

mint distilling vat. *See* distilling vat, mint hay.

mint julep. Holiday 10: 74 (col.) Aug '51; 11: 10 (col.) May '52, 19 (col.) Je '52; 20: 10 (col.) Sept '56; 24: 98 (col.) Jl '58, 108 (col.) Aug '58.

Minton, Sherman. Cur. biog. p. 585 (1941); p. 430 (1949).

Holiday 7: 78 Feb '50.

"The Minuet" (Millais). Con. 142: 83 Nov '58.

minute glass. Amer. heri., vol. 11 no. 5 p. 58 (Aug '60).

"Minuteman" (statue). Amer. heri., vol. 6 no. 3 frontis (Ap '55).

Holiday 16: 101, 106 Jl '54.

Natl. geog. 115: 710, 712 May '59.

Travel 110: cover Jl '58.

—— (statue, Newburgh). Holiday 6: 41 Sept '49.

Mirabell palace stairway. Praeg. pict. ency., p. 375.

"Miracle of St. Benedict." Natl. geog. 101: 95 (col.) Jan '52.

"Miracle of San Gennaro." Labande: Naples, p. 46-7.

"Miracle of the poisoned glass." Con. 143: 38 Mar '59.

Miracle play (Elche, Spain). Travel 109: 27 Ap '58.

—— (outdoor). Int. gr. soc.: Arts . . . p. 75 (col.).

Miracle rock (Glade Park, Colo.). Travel 104: 10 Oct '55.

"Miraculous draught of fishes" (Witz). Praeg. pict. ency., p. 242 (col.).

Miramare castle (Italy). Natl. geog. 109: 846-7 (col.) Je '56.

Miranda, Carmen. Cur. biog. p. 587 (1941).

Miranda, Juan Carreno de (work of). Con. 141: LII Ap '58.

Miro, Joan (work of). Praeg. pict. ency., p. 495.

Miro Cardona, Jose. Cur. biog. p. 320 (1961).

mirror. Holiday 11: 60, 113 May '52.

—— (doll). Natl. geog. 116: 830 (col.) Dec '59.

—— (embroidered frame). Con. 143: 233 Je '59.

—— (reflections). Holiday 26: 150 Oct '59.

—— (sym.). Lehner: Pict. bk. of sym., p. 60.

——, Adam. Con. 132: inside back cover Sept '53; 133: XL May '54; 140: 255 Jan '58.

——, Adam gilt. Con. 143: XXX Ap '59.

——, antique. Con. 129: XLV Ap '52; 136: 44, LIX Sept '55; 137: XX Mar '56; 139: 55 Mar '57; 141: 66 Mar '58; 143: XXIII Ap '59.

Holiday 26: 18 Aug '59.

Natl. geog. 105: 300 (col.) Mar '54.

——, antique gold. Con. 144: 76 Nov '59.

——, antique landscape. Con. 133: X May '54.

——, bronze (La Tene period). Praeg. pict. ency., p. 107.

——, Chinese. Con. 137: 107 Ap '56, 265 (col.) Je '56.

——, Chippendale. Con. 129: XL Je '52; 132: LXXI Nov '53, 208 Jan '54; 135: IV, XXI May '55; 136: VI, XLV, inside back cover Jan '56; 137: XII Ap '56, VIII Je '56; 138: VII Sept '56; 139: XXIII Mar '57, XXXIV, XLIII Ap '57; 140: XXII, XLIII Dec '57; 142: XXX, inside back cover Sept '58, 130 Nov '58, XXI Dec '58, inside back cover Jan '59; 143: X Mar '59, inside back cover May '59; 144: XXXI Sept '59, XXXVIII Jan '60; 145: XXV Ap '60.

——, Chippendale (18th cent.). Con. 144: inside back cover Sept '59.

——, Chippendale gilt. Con. 143: XXIII May '59; 144: inside back cover Dec '59; 145: XXIV, XLVII Je '60.

——, Chippendale gilt (18th cent.). Con. 145: XLIV Ap '60.

——, Chippendale gilt landscape. Con. 144: XIV Nov '59.

——, colonial (wall candle sconces). Natl. geog. 118: 173 (col.) Aug '60.

——, constitution. Con. ency. of ant., vol. 1, p. 61.

——, convex. Con. 138: XIV Dec '56.

——, convex. (18th cent.). Con. 142: inside back cover Dec '58.

——, convex gilt. Con. 144: XVI Dec '59.

——, convex gilt (18th cent.). Con. 145: XXII Mar '60.

——, convex gilt (19th cent.). Con. ency., of ant., vol. 3, pl. 112.

——, dressing. Con. 144: XXXVIII Dec '59.

——, 18th cent. Con. 132: LV Sept '53; 134: XX Sept '54; 136: XXI Nov '55, XLIII Jan '56; 138: LXV Sept '56; 139: XXXI Ap '57, XII May '57; 140: IV Sept '57, 259 Jan '58; 141: LVIII Je '58.

——, 18th cent. (gilt gesso). Con. 144: LII Jan '60.

——, 18th cent. landscape. Con. 142: XXXV Dec '58.

——, French (antique). Con. 140: 15 Sept '57.

——, Geo. I. Con. 135: XXV Je '55.

——, Geo. II. Con. 137: XXIII Je '56; 142: VIII-IX Nov '58.

——, Geo. II (gilt). Con. 145: XIII Ap '60.

——, Georgian. Con. ency. of ant., vol. 1, pl. 20. Con. 140: XXXIV Sept '57.

——, Georgian gilt. Con. 135: XXVIII Mar '55.

——, Georgian giltwood. Con. 134: XLV Nov '54.

——, Gesso gilt. Con. 132: back cover Nov '53.

——, gold wall (antique). Natl. geog. 118: 166 (col.) Aug '60.

——, Italian silver framed. Con. 144: 155 Dec '59.

——, marquetry cushion. Con. 145: XXXVIII Je '60.

——, Martelli. Con. 142: 268 Jan '59.

——, 19th cent. Con. 133: XXIV Ap '54; 142: 21 Sept '58.

——, pier glass (antique). Con. 134: XXVI-XXVII Nov '54. Natl. geog. 105: 300 (col.) Mar '54.

——, Queen Anne. Con. ency. of ant., vol. 1, pl. 20.

——, regency. Con. 133: 290 Je '54; 141: LI Mar '58.

——, Sheraton gilt. Con. 145: XXI Mar '60.

——, Stuart (pier glass). Con. 136: 241 Jan '56.

——, tall (girl). Holiday 21: 6 Mar '57.

——, tall wall. Natl. geog. 97: 565 (col.) May '50.

——, toilet. Con. ency. of ant., vol. 1, p. 35.

——, William III. Con. 142: 135 Nov '58, LX Dec '58.

——, William & Mary. Con. 133: XXVIII May '54; 138: XV Dec '56; 143: 266 Je '59.

——, William & Mary (silver). Con. 145: XXVII Je '60.

mirror & candle sconces, Chippendale. Con. 145: XXXIX Mar '60.

mirror case, enamel. Con. 143: 174 May '59.

——, French ivory (14th cent.). Con. 126: 77 Aug '50.

mirror frame (antique). Con. 141: inside back cover May '58.

Mirror lake (St. Petersburg). Holiday 24: 79 (col.) Nov '58.

Mirror of the planets (sym.). Lehner: Pict. bk. of sym., p. 22.

mirror on stand, gilt frame (18th cent.). Con. 144: 139 Dec '59.

mirror painting, Chinese (18th cent.). Con. 145: XXXV May '60.

mirror picture, Chinese. Con. 129: XLVI Ap '52; 145: 56 Mar '60.

mirrors (antique). Con. 141: XLVII Ap '58.

——, Eng. wall (antique). Con. ency. of ant., vol. 3, pl. 109-12.

Mirvish, Robert F. Cur. biog. p. 370 (1957).

Mirza, Iskander. Cur. biog. p. 441 (1956).

misfortune (sym.). Lehner: Pict. bk. of sym., p. 28.

"Miss America" contest. Natl. geog. 117: 44-5 (col.) Jan '60.

"Miss America" of 1960. Natl. geog. 118: 708 (col.) Nov '60.

Miss America queen. Holiday 12: 94-5 (col.) Aug '52.

"Miss Columbia's school" (cartoon). Amer. heri., vol. 11 no. 2 p. 12-3 (col.) (Feb '60).

"Miss Liberty." Holiday 8: 68 (col.) Nov '50.

"Miss U.S." Holiday 11: 86 (col.) May '52.

Missal, Berthold (work of). Con. 141: 131 Ap '58.

missile, Bomarc. Natl. geog. 117: 448 (col.) Ap '60.

missile, guided. Natl. geog. 112: 294 Aug '57.

——, intercontinental. Natl. geog. 116: 422, 428-9, 465 (col.) Oct '59.

——, space. Natl. geog. 118: 64-5 (col.) Jl '60.

missile range, Atlantic. Natl. geog. 116: 434-5, 438- (col.) Oct '59.

missile range boat. Natl. geog. 116: 467-8 (part col.) Oct '59.

mission (Cal.). Holiday 6: 116 (col.) Jl '49, 71 (col.) Nov '49; 7: 89 (col.) Feb '50; 15: 24 Je '54; 16: 41 Dec '54; 17: 33 Mar '55.

——, (Mexico). Travel 103: 32 Jan '55.

"The Mission" (Milani). Con. 144: LXXXI Jan '60.

mission (San Diego). Travel 108: 18 Jl '57.
——, Carmel (Cal.). Natl. geog. 116: 583 (col.) Nov '59.
Travel 113: cover (col.) Mar '60.
——, Carmel's Franciscan (Cal.). See mission, Franciscan (Cal.).
——, Franciscan (Cal.). Natl. geog. 105; 752 (col.) Je '54.
——, Indian colonial (N.Y.). Holiday 15: 101 Je '54.
——, New Mexico (1776). Amer. heri., vol. 8 no. 6 p. 101 (Oct '57).
——, San Carlo Borromeo. See San Carlo Borromeo.
——, San Gabriel (belfry). Holiday 22: 52 Oct '57.
——, San Jose. See San Jose mission.
——, San Juan Capistrano. Brooks: Growth of a nation, p. 120.
Face of Amer., p. 14-5 (col.).
——, San Xavier. See San Xavier mission.
——, San Xavier del Bac. See San Xavier del Bac.
——, Santa Barbara (Cal.). Amer. heri., vol. 1 no. 3 p. 33 (col.) (spring '50).
Holiday 5: 7 (col.) Ap '49; 6: 117 Jl '49; 14: 76 Dec '53; 16: 121 (col.) Oct '54.
Natl. geog. 105: 764 Je '54.
——, Sonoma (Cal.). Travel 101: 10 Mar '54.
——, Spanish (Cal.). Brooks: Growth of a nation, p. 120.
Holiday 12: 12 (col.) Dec '52; 13: 120 (col.) Mar '53, 91 (col.) Ap '53; 14: 12 (col.) Nov '53.
——, Spanish (entrance). Brooks: Growth of a nation, p. 74.
——, Spanish (N.M.). Holiday 13: 86 (col.) Ap '53.
——, Spanish (Santa Fe). See Spanish mission (Santa Fe).
——, Taos (N.M.). Amer. heri., vol. 8 no. 6 p. 35 (col.) (Oct '57).
mission at Acoma (N.M.). Holiday 15: 93 (col.) May '54.
mission church (Albuquerque). Holiday 14: 59 Dec '53.
—— (Cal.). Holiday 14: 76 (col.) Dec '53.
—— (Taos). Holiday 14: 58 Dec '53.
mission of Nombre de Dios (outdoor altar, St. Augustine). Face of Amer., p. 30-1 (col.).
mission of San Diego (Cal.). Jordan: Hammond's pict. atlas, p. 207 (col.).
mission of San Diego de Alcala. Travel 103: 33 Je '55.
missionaries, martyred (early Amer). Amer. heri., vol. 10 no. 6 p. 56-7 (Oct '59).
missionary home (Thule, Greenland). Natl. geog. 100: 490 (col.) Oct '51.
missions (Ariz.). Holiday 17: 18 (col.) Jan '55.
—— (Cal.). Amer. heri., vol. 1 no. 3 p. 32-5 (part col.) (spring '50).
Holiday 5: 7, 69, 117 (col.) Ap '49.
Mississippi. Holiday 5: 34-53 Mar '49; 6: 98-105 (part col.) Nov '49; 13: 63 Jan '53; 15: 34-47 (part col.) Ap '54.
Travel 103: 16-21 May '55.
—— (memorial day birthplace). Brooks:

Growth of a nation, p. 288.
—— (Ohio rivers meet). Natl. geog. 114: 698-9 Nov '58.
—— (state capitol). Travel 103: 18 May '55.
Mississippi homes. Holiday 17: 98-9 (col.) Mar '55.
Mississippi river. Amer. heri., vol. 2 no. 1 p. 41-55 (fall '50).
Holiday 5: 56-62 (part col.) Mar '49.
Natl. geog. 114: 650-99 (part col.) Nov '58; 118: 680-724 (col.). (Nov '60).
Travel 112: 24 Aug '59.
—— (marker at head). Holiday 15: 84 (col.) Ap '54.
—— traffic. Amer. heri., vol. 8 no. 6 p. 14-25 (part col.) (Oct '57).
Missouri. Holiday 14: 102-3 (col.), 104-13 Nov '53.
—— (Lake of the Ozarks). Travel 112: cover (col.) Aug '59.
—— (map). Holiday 21: 127 (col.) Ap '57.
Missouri river. Holiday 7: 34-46 (part col.) Mar '50.
—— (sketches). Amer. heri., vol. 1 no. 4 p. 18-23 (part col.) (summer '50).
"Mr. Dooley." Amer. heri., vol. 10 no. 5 p. 84 (Aug '59).
Mr. Gallagher & Mr. Shean. Holiday 7: 65 Mar '50.
mistletoe (sym.). Lehner: Pict. bk. of sym., p. 65.
Mistral, Gabriela. Cur. biog. p. 398 (1946).
"Mrs. Henry Benton" (Kauffmann). Con. 143: XLIV (col.) Je '59.
"Mrs. John Weyland & son" (Reynolds). Natl. geog. 97: 197 Feb '50.
"Mrs. Penobscot" (Amer. Indian). Amer. heri., vol. 10 no. 5 p. 24 (col.) (Aug '59).
"Mrs. Richard Yates" (Stuart). Holiday 7: 107 (col.) Feb '50.
Mitchell, Billy (in plane). Natl. geog. 112: 276 Aug '57.
Mitchell, Harry L. Cur. biog. p. 445 (1947).
Mitchell, Howard. Cur. biog. p. 428 (1952).
Mitchell, James P. Cur. biog. p. 463 (1954); p. 422 (1955).
Mitchell, John. Amer. heri., vol. 11 no. 3 p. 55 (Ap. '60).
Mitchell, Maria. Travel 108: inside back cover Aug '57.
Mitchell, Stephen A. Cur. biog. p. 430 (1952).
Mitchell, William D. Cur. biog. p. 401 (1946).
Mitchell, William L. Cur. biog. p. 302 (1959).
miter, Russian (19th cent.). Int. gr. soc.: Arts . . . p 165 (col.).
Mitla (Mexico). Travel 114: 48-9 Nov '60.
Mitropoulos, Dimitri. Cur. biog. p. 589 (1941); p. 431 (1952).
Mitscher, Vice Adm. Marc A. Cur. biog. p. 478 (1944).
mittens. Holiday 12: 140 Nov '52.
Mittersill castle. See castle Mittersill.
mixer, elec. Int. gr. soc.: Arts . . . p. 171 (col.).
——, food. Holiday 24: 49 Dec '58.
——, Waring. Holiday 21: 138 Ap '57.
Mizpah (King Asa & laborers). Natl. geog. 118: 818-9 (col.) Dec '60.
mnemonics (sym.). Lehner: Pict. bk. of sym., p. 14.

moat, castle. Holiday 18: 29 Sept '55.
Natl. geog. 107: 632 (col.) May '55.
Moats, Alice-Leone. Cur. biog. p. 531 (1943).
Mobile (Ala.). Holiday 11: 56-61 (part col.)
Feb '52.
—— **(by Calder).** Int. gr. soc.: Arts . . . p.
131 (col.).
mobile drawing. Praeg.: Pict. ency. of art, p.
464.
moccasins, Sioux Indian. Natl. geog. 98: 259
(col.) Aug '50.
Moch, Jules S. Cur. biog. p. 401 (1950).
"The mocking of Christ" (Gossaert). Con.
138: 14 Sept '56.
model, fashion. Natl. geog. 101: 493 Ap '52;
110: 218 (col.) Aug '56.
——, **girl fashion.** Holiday 10: 67 (col.) Dec
'51; 24: 72-5 (part col.) Oct '58.
——, **Shasta dam.** Natl. geog. 105: 743 (col.)
Je '54.
——, **ship.** See ship model.
models, art. Holiday 10: 52 (col.) Oct '51.
——, **fashion show.** See fashion show models.
Modersohn-Becker, Paula (work of). Praeg.:
Pict. ency., p. 445 (col.).
Modigliani, Amedeo (work of). Con. 133: 17
Mar '54; 140: 205 Dec '57; 142: 124
Nov '58; 145: 185, 188, 207 May '60,
234 Je '60.
Praeg.: Pict. ency., p. 495.
Moen, Lars. Cur. biog. p. 591 (1941).
Moffat tunnel (Colo.). Holiday 7: 76 Jan '50.
Moffo, Anna. Cur. biog. p. 322 (1961).
Mogen David (sym.). Lehner: Pict. bk. of
sym., p. 36.
Mohammed V (bodyguard). Holiday 25: 80
(col.) Ap '59.
Mohammed, Ghulam. Cur. biog. p. 465 (1954).
Mohammed Riza Pahlevi. Cur. biog. p. 403
(1950).
Mohammed Zahir Shah. Cur. biog. p. 442
(1956).
Mohammedan talismans. See talismans, Mo-
hammedan.
Mohammedans (praying). Holiday 10: 121
(col.) Dec '51.
Mohammed's tomb. Natl. geog. 104: 34 (col.)
Jl '53.
Mohawk Indian. See Indian, Mohawk.
Mohawk Valley (N.Y.). Holiday 15: 98-101
(part col.) Je '54; 21: 58-9 (col.) Je '57.
Mohawk women council. Amer. heri., vol. 6
no. 2 p. 31 (winter '55).
Moi tribe. Natl. geog. 102: 296 (col.) Sept
'52.
Moir, Phyllis. Cur. biog. p. 600 (1942).
Moiseiwitsch, Benno. Holiday 21: 42 Mar '57.
Moiseiwitsch, Tanya. Cur. biog. p. 424 (1955).
Moiseyev, Igor A. Cur. biog. p. 289 (1958).
Mola, Pier Francesco (work of). Con. 132:
15 Sept '53.
molded food. Natl. geog. 114: 311 (col.) Sept
'58.
molds, aluminum. Natl. geog. 113: 564 Ap
'58.
Molenaer, Jan Miense (work of). Con. 137:
LXVII May '56.
Moley, Raymond. Cur. biog. p. 407 (1945).
Moliere fountain (Paris). Amer. heri., vol. 11
no. 3 p. 19 (col.) (Ap '60).

"Moll Davis" (Lely). Con. 126: 37-8 Aug '50.
Mollenhoff, Clark R. Cur. biog. p. 290 (1958).
Mollet, Guy. Cur. biog. p. 405 (1950).
Molloy, Robert W. Cur. biog. p. 455 (1948).
"Molly Pitcher" at battle of Monmouth.
Amer. heri. vol. 8 no. 1 p. 47 (col.) (Dec
'56).
"Molly Stark" Cannon. See Cannon, "Molly
Stark."
Molotov, Viacheslav M. Cur. biog. p. 467
(1954).
Molyneux, Capt. Edward H. Cur. biog. p. 602
(1942).
Mombasa, Africa. Natl. geog. 97: 322 (col.)
Mar '50.
Momsen, Rear Adm. Charles B. Cur. biog. p.
403 (1946).
"Mona Lisa." Praeg.: Pict. ency., p. 26 (col.).
Monaco, Lorenzo (work of). Con. 142: LXV
Dec '58.
Monaco, Mario Del. Cur. biog. p. 371 (1957).
Monaco. Holiday 23: 2 (col.), 52 Jan '58; 24:
36-7 Aug '58; 25: 110 (col.) Je '59.
Travel 105: 65 Ap '56; 113: 30-1 Ap '60.
—— **casino (int.).** Holiday 14: 53 (col.) Nov
'53.
—— **coat of arms.** Int. gr. soc.: Arts . . . p.
67 (col.).
—— **harbor.** Travel 113: 30-1 Ap '60.
Monaghan, Maj. Frank. Cur. biog. p. 535
(1943).
Monamy, Peter (work of). Con. 136: XXXIII
Jan '56.
monarchism (sym.). Lehner: Pict. bk. of sym.,
p. 95.
monarchistic authority. See authority, monarchistic.
Monarola (Italy). Travel. 101: 6 Je '54.
monastery. Natl. geog. 106: 7 (col.) Jl '54.
—— **(Capri, Italy).** Labande: Naples, p. 215.
—— **(Lisbon, Portugal).** Holiday 6: 101 Sept
'49.
—— **(near Dead Sea).** Natl. geog. 114: 786-7
(col.) Dec '58.
——, **Buddhist (Penang).** Natl. geog. 103: 217
(col.) Feb '53.
——, **Cartegena (ruins).** Holiday 24: 140 (col.)
Oct '58.
——, **Carthusian (San Martino).** Labande:
Naples, p. 116-7.
——, **Essenes.** See Essenes monastery.
——, **Franciscan (int.).** Natl. geog. 111: 656-7
(part col.) May '57.
——, **Himis (Lama).** Natl. geog. 99: 613, 615
(col.) May '51.
——, **Jeronimos.** See Jeronimos monastery
(Lisbon).
——, **Lamayuru.** Natl. geog. 99: 634 (col.)
May '51.
——, **Pituk (Lama).** Natl. geog. 99: 628 (col.)
May '51.
——, **Russian (Mt. Athos).** Natl. geog. 114:
772, 774-5 (part col.) Dec '58.
——, **St. Bernard (Florida).** See St. Bernard
of Sacramenia monastery.
——, **"Tiger's nest" (Bhutan).** Natl. geog. 102:
735 Dec '52.
——, **Trinity (Russia).** See Trinity monastery.
—— **at Melk (Austria).** Travel 103: 25 Je '55.
—— **garden.** Labande: Naples, p. 52-3.

monastery Montserrat. Travel 104: 42-6 Aug '55.

—— of Melk (Danube). Praeg.: Pict. ency., p. 366.

—— of miracles (Russia). Natl. geog. 106: 65E Jl '54.

—— of San Francisco (Quito). Travel 101: 9 Feb '54.

—— of the Jeronymites. Natl. geog. 118: 650-1 (col.) Nov '60.

—— prayer wheels, Karr (woman). Natl. geog. 117: 391 (col.) Mar '60.

—— walls, Himis (prayer wheels). Natl. geog. 99: 609 May '51.

Monastic library (int., St. Gallen). Praeg.: Pict. ency., p. 377.

Monckton, Robert (West). Amer. heri., vol. 11 no. 1 p. 30 (col.) (Dec '59).

Monckton, Sir Walter. Cur. biog. p. 430 (1951).

Monday (sym.). Lehner: Pict. bk. of sym., p. 24.

Mondop temple. See temple, Mondop.

Mondrian, Piet (work of). Con. 139: 261 Je '57.

Praeg.: Pict. ency., p. 505 (col.).

Monet, Claude. Con. 134: 122 Nov '54.

—— (painting in boat). Praeg.: Pict. ency., p. 416 (col.).

—— (work of). Con. 129: XXXVI Je '52; 134: 122-3 Nov '54; 140: 81, XXXVII (col.) Nov '57; 142: 254 Jan '59; 144: II (col.) Nov '59.

Praeg: Pict. ency., p. 72 (col.).

money, paper (1860). See bill, $3.00 (1860).

——, paper (in barrels). Amer. heri., vol. 11 no. 1 frontis (col.) (Dec '59).

——, token (Yap is.). Natl. geog. 102: 820 Dec '52.

money. See also coins.

money bags. Lehner: Pict. bk. of sym., p. 95.

"Money tree" (Siam). Disney: People & places, p. 168-9 (col.).

Mongolian & child. Natl. geog. 99: 399, 406 (col.) Mar '51.

Monhegan is. (Maine). Natl. geog. 115: 284-98 Feb '59.

"Monitor" (ship, cross section). Amer. heri., vol. 8 no. 4 p. 102-3 (Je '57).

Monitor & Merrimac (battle). See Merrimac & Monitor.

Monk, Hank. Holiday 14: 10 Sept '53.

monk. Con. 145: 159 May '60.
Holiday 24: 24 Oct '58.
Natl. geog. 109: 66 Jan '56.

—— (filling wine pitcher). Holiday 24: 154 Dec '58.

—— (meditating in garden, silhouette). Natl. geog. 118: 762 Dec '60.

——, Buddhist (at altar). Natl. geog. 111: 350 (col.) Mar '57.

——, Carthusian. Holiday 28: 115 Sept '60.

——, Catholic (St. Bernard dog). Natl. geog. 111: 50 (col.) Jan '57.

——, Chinese. Natl. geog. 97: 216-7, 223 Feb '50.

——, Greek. Natl. geog. 102: 853 Dec '52.

——, Siamese. Disney: People & places, p. 170 (col.).

——, Siamese boy. Holiday 18: 53 (col.) Oct '55.

monk. See also Monks.

monkey dance, Balinese. See dance, Balinese monkey.

"Monkey tricks" (Schlesinger). Con. 140: XXXIX Jan '58.

monkeys, three wise. See three wise monkeys.

monks (blowing trumpets). Natl. geog. 102: 733 Dec '52.

—— (Buddhist Lama temple). Natl. geog. 118: 216-7 (col.) Aug '60.

—— (kneeling). Natl. geog. 117: 65 (col.) Jan '60.

—— (procession, Tibet). Natl. geog. 108: 24, 39-41 (col.) Jl '55.

——, Benedictine. Holiday 5: 102 (col.) Mar '49.

——, Caldy is. (work in field). Natl. geog. 108: 569 Oct '55.

——, Capuchin. Natl. geog. 98: 336 (col.) Sept '50.

——, Cistercian. Natl. geog. 115: 199 (col.) Feb '59.

——, St. Bernard. Natl. geog. 111: 52 (col.), 56, 58, 60-1 Jan '57.

——, Siamese. Holiday 18: 53 (col.) Oct '55.

——, Trappist. Holiday 6: 50 Dec '49.

monks & pilgrims (bear a cross, Way of Sorrows). Natl. geog. 115: 508 (col.) Ap '59.

monks writing, Chinese. Natl. geog. 97: 223 Feb '50.

Monnet, Jean. Cur. biog. p. 447 (1947).

Monnot, P. E. (sculpture by). Con. 141: 220 Je '58.

Monnoyer, Jean Baptiste (work of). Con. 145: LXI (col.) May '60.

monogram (Christ). Lehner: Pict. bk. of sym., p. 34.

monolith, Ba 'Albek. Natl. geog. 113: 511 (col.) Ap '58.

——, lava. Natl. geog. 118: 519 (col.) Oct '60.

——, rock. Natl. geog. 113: 127 Jan '58.

——, rock (monument canyon). Natl. geog. 101: 721 (col.) Je '52.

——, war. Natl. geog. 110: 37 (col.) Jl '56.

Monroe, Eliza Hay. Jensen: The White House, p. 37.

Monroe, James. Amer. heri., vol. 7 no. 1 p. 25 (Dec '55); vol. 7 no. 3 p. 30 (Ap '56). Jensen: The White House, p. 36.

—— (statue). Natl. geog. 97: 590 (col.) May '50.

Monroe, Mrs. James (West). Jensen: The White House, p. 37.

Monroe, Lucy. Cur. biog. p. 603 (1942).

Monroe, Marilyn. Cur. biog. p. 303 (1959). Holiday 12: 77 Sept '52, 42-3 (col.) Oct '52. Natl. geog. 107: 557 Ap '55.

Monroe, Vaughn. Cur. biog. p. 605 (1942).

Monroe home, Pres. James. Natl. geog. 109: 478 (col.) Ap '56.

"Monroe palace" (Rio). Natl. geog. 107: 321 (col.) Mar '55.

Monroney, Almer S. Mike. Cur. biog. p. 431 (1951).

Monsarrat, Nicholas J. Cur. biog. p. 407 (1950).

Monsky, Henry. Cur. biog. p. 592 (1941).

monsoon clouds (Java seas). Natl. geog. 108:

355 (col.) Sept '55.
monstrance (Portuguese). Con. ency. of ant.,
vol. 3, pl. 29.
Con. 137: 13-4 Mar '56.
—— (sym.). Lehner: Pict. bk. of sym., p. 35.
——, **copper & crystal.** Con. 138: 125 Nov
'56.
——, **Guelph (14th cent.).** Con. 144: LX Nov
'59.
——, **silver gilt (antique).** Con. 134: 60 Sept
'54.
——, **silver gilt & jewels (18th cent.).** Con.
ency. of ant., vol. 3, pl. 35.
Mont Blanc. Natl. geog. 111: 814-5 (col.) Je
'57.
Mont Orgueil, castle (Isle of Jersey). Holiday
22: 2 (col.) Oct '57; 23: 20 Je '58; 27: 2
(col.) Mar '60.
—— **(Normandy).** Travel 101: 23 May '54.
Mont Saint Michel (France). Holiday 11: 90-3
(col.) Jan '52; 13: 31 Mar '53, 18 Ap
'53; 16: 108 (col.) Aug '54; 19: 155 (col.)
Je '56; 20: 24 (col.) Nov '56, 194 (col.)
Dec '56; 21: 158 Mar '57, 95 (col.) Ap
'57.
Natl. geog. 115: 598 (col.) May '59.
Travel 101: 5 May '54.
Mont Sainte-Victoire. Praeg.: Pict. ency., p.
437 (col.).
Montagu, Charles (Kneller). Con. 140: 232
Jan '58.
Montagu, Ewen. Cur. biog. p. 444 (1956).
Montagu, Lady Mary Wortley. Amer. heri.,
vol. 8 no. 5 p. 43 (Aug '57).
Montague, Earl Edward (miniature). Con.
ency. of ant., vol. 1, pl. 130.
Montaigne. Holiday 17: 6 Jan '55.
Montana. Holiday 8: 34-51 (part col.) Sept '50.
Natl. geog. 97: 694-736 (part col.) Je '50.
Travel 108: 10-4 Jl '57.
—— **(Helena, 1870).** Brooks: Growth of a
nation, p. 177.
—— **(mts. & lake).** Face of Amer., p. 60-1
(col.).
—— **(rivers).** Travel 109: 54-5 Je '58.
Montand, Yves. Cur. biog. p. 279 (1960).
Montanez Mater Dolorosa (wood carving).
Praeg.: Pict. ency., p. 367.
Montcalm headquarters (Quebec). Holiday 11:
102 (col.) Je '52.
Monte Alban (Mexico). Amer. heri., vol. 10
no. 2 p. 51 (Feb '59).
Monte Carlo. Holiday 10: 80 Jl '51; 14: 49-
53 (col.) Nov '53; 24: 36-7 Aug '58.
—— **(casino).** Holiday 27: back cover (col.)
Ap '60.
Montecatini (Italy). Travel 105: 57 Ap '56;
113: 98 Ap '60.
—— **pavilion.** Holiday 26: 19 Nov '59.
Montego Bay (Jamaica). Holiday 5: 48-9 (col.)
Feb '49; 15: 48, 53 (col.) Feb '54.
Natl. geog. 105: 342 (col.) Mar '54.
—— **(beach).** Holiday 9: 98 (col.) Mar '51.
Montepulciano. Con. 139: 95 Ap '57.
Monterey peninsula (Cal.). Face of Amer., p.
78-9 (col.).
Holiday 12: 114-9 (part col.) Dec '52; 26:
82-7 (col.) Dec '59.
Monterey (Cal., 1863). Amer. heri., vol. 11
no. 6 p. 34 (col.) (Oct '60).

Monterey peninsula (map). Holiday 12: 116
Dec '52.
Monterey coast. Holiday 26: cover (col.) Dec
'59.
Monteux, Pierre. Cur. biog. p. 405 (1946).
Monteverdi, Claudia. Cooper: Con. ency. of
ant., p. 197 (col.).
Montevideo (beach). Travel 112: 16 Sept '59.
—— **(Plaza).** Holiday 8: 115 (col.) Jl '50.
—— **(Pocito beach, Uruguay).** Travel 103: 46
Mar '55.
Montez, Lola. Horan: Pict. hist. of wild west,
p. 23.
—— **(Stieler).** Amer. heri., vol. 6 no. 2 p. 57
(col.) (winter '55).
—— **(holding cigarette).** Amer. heri., vol. 6
no. 2 p. 59 (Feb '55).
Montezuma (meeting Cortes). Ceram: March
of arch., p. 251.
montgolfieri (sym.). Lehner: Pict. bk. of sym.,
p. 10.
Montgomery, Gen. Bernard Law. Cur. biog. p.
607 (1942).
Montgomery, Deane. Cur. biog. p. 373 (1957).
Montgomery, Elizabeth Rider. Cur. biog. p.
434 (1952).
Montgomery, George. Holiday 12: 37 Oct '52.
Montgomery, Rev. James Shera. Cur. biog. p.
456 (1948).
Montgomery, Robert. Cur. biog. p. 458 (1948).
Montgomery, Ruth. Cur. biog. p. 374 (1957).
months (allegoric representation). Lehner: Pict.
bk. of sym., p. 96.
"Monticello" (home of Thomas Jefferson).
Amer. heri., vol. 9 no. 3 p. 85 (Ap '58);
vol. 10 no. 5 p. 67 (Aug '59).
Brooks: Growth of a nation, p. 91.
Holiday 8: 27 (col.) Sept '50; 12: 136 Jl
'52, 72 (col.) Dec '52; 18: 107 (col.) Nov
'55; 20: 88 Sept '56; 21: 10 (col.) Je '57;
22: 23 (col.) Sept '57; 26: 119 (col.) Sept
'59.
Natl. geog. 97: 561-68 (col.) May '50.
Praeg.: Pict. ency., p. 390.
Travel 112: 30 Jl '59.
Montini, Archbishop Giovanni. Cur. biog. p.
446 (1956).
Montmartre. Holiday 24: 58-63 (part col.) Aug
'58.
Montmartre hotel (Miami Beach). Travel 111:
50 Ap '59.
Montmorency Falls (Canada). Holiday 16: 52
(col.) Jl '54; 24: 22 (col.) Sept '58.
Montreal (Canada). Holiday 6: 38 (col.) Aug
'49; 10: 48-55 (part col.) Aug '51; 16:
12-3 Aug '54; 26: 50-55 (part col.) Sept
'59.
Travel 105: 14 May '56.
—— **(harbor).** Natl. geog. 98: 340-1 (col.)
Sept '50; 108: 192-3 (col.) Aug '55.
—— **(night).** Natl. geog. 115: 327 (col.) Mar
'59.
—— **(St. Joseph's oratory).** Travel 105: 13
May '56.
—— **(1760).** Amer. heri., vol. 12 no. 1 p. 91
(Dec '60).
Montreux (Switzerland). Travel 113: cover
(col.) Ap '60.
Montserrat, monastery. *See* monastery Montserrat.

monument (Atlantic City, honors Greeks). Natl. geog. 109: 76 Jan '56.

—— (in church). Con. 133: 256 Je '54.

—— (Iwo Jima). Natl. geog. 111: 76 (col.) Jan '57.

—— (lost Roanoke colony). Brooks: Growth of a nation, p. 35.

——, battle (Falkland). Natl. geog. 109: 395 (col.), 397 Mar '56.

——, battle (Oriskany). Holiday 21: 53 Je '57.

——, battle (West Point). Natl. geog. 101: 620 (col.) May '52.

——, boll weevil. See boll weevil monument.

——, continental sentry (Valley Forge). Natl. geog. 105: 198 (col.) Feb '54.

——, dog (Garrard, 1806). Con. ency. of ant., vol. 3, pl. 27.

——, Egyptian. See Egyptian monument.

——, Emigration canyon. Travel 112: 34 Aug '59.

——, equator. Travel 109: 46 Jan '58.

——, funerary sketch (18th cent.). Con. 140: 2 (col.) Sept '57.

——, Lewis, Clark & Indians council. Natl. geog. 103: 718 (col.) Je '53.

——, Lincoln. See Lincoln monument, Abraham (Springfield).

——, National. See National monument (Utah).

——, Peary's Arctic circle. Natl. geog. 106: 526 Oct '54.

——, Prince Henry. See Henry monument, Prince.

——, St. Bernard. See St. Bernard monument.

——, ship. See ship monument (Tasmania).

——, Tom Sawyer & Huck Finn. Natl. geog. 110: 124 Jl '56.

——, Tri state (N.Y., Penn., N.J.). Natl. geog. 102: 25 (col.) Jl '52.

——, war (Rome). Travel 113: 36 Ap '60.

——, Will Rogers (Alaska). Natl. geog. 102: 78 (col.) Jl '52.

——, World war I dead. Natl. geog. 115: 308 Mar '59.

——, Wright Bros. See Wright Bros. memorial.

Monument canyon. Natl. geog. 101: 720-7 (col.) Je '52.

Monument of defeated Wm. Walker. Amer. heri., vol. 9 no. 1 p. 26 (Dec '57).

Monument of the discoveries (Portugal). Natl. geog. 118: 656 (col.) Nov '60.

Monument rock (Isle Royale). Travel 102: 31 Jl '54.

Monument to 5th Earl of Exeter & his wife. Con. 141: 221 Je '58.

Monument to Gregorio Capponi. Con. 143: 243 Je '59.

Monument to Lady Walpole (sculpture). Con. 144: 178 Dec '59.

Monument to Maria Odescalchi-Chigi. Con. 143: 243 Je '59.

Monument to Thomas Baldwin. Con. 143: 245 Je '54.

Monument to Sir Thomas Dereham (Italy). Con. 144: 176 Dec '59.

Monument Valley (Ariz.-Utah). Disney: People & places, p. 113-28 (col.). Holiday 13: 29 Jan '53; 16: 46 (col.) Jl '54;

22: 94 (col.) Jl '57; 24: 36-7 Jl '58.

Jordan: Hammond's pict. atlas, p. 170-1 (col.).

Natl. geog. 101: 52-3 Jan '52; 114: 810-11, 828-9, 842-44 (col.) Dec '58.

Travel 107: 35 Mar '57.

—— (map). Natl. geog. 114: 814-5 Dec '58.

Monument Valley (Ontario). Travel 103: inside cover Mar '55.

monuments (Richmond, Va.). Holiday 10: 106 Sept '51.

——, battle (in Europe & U.S., map). Natl. geog. 111: 738-68 (col.) Je '57.

Moody, Blair. Cur. biog. p. 433 (1951).

Moody, Dwight L. (evangelist meeting). Amer. heri., vol. 6 no. 5 p. 20, 23 (Aug '55).

Moody, Joseph E. Cur. biog. p. 460 (1948).

Moody, Ralph. Cur. biog. p. 426 (1955).

Moon, Bucklin. Cur. biog. p. 408 (1950).

Moon, Carl. Jun. bk. of auth., p. 224.

Moon, Grace. Jun. bk. of auth., p. 225.

the moon. Natl. geog. 113: 278-95 Feb '58; 115: 168 Feb '59.

—— (face). Holiday 12: 17 (col.) Oct '52.

—— (magic square). Lehner: Pict. bk. of sym., p. 24.

—— (sym.). Lehner: Pict. bk. of sym., p. 20.

moon gate (Chinese). Natl. geog. 105: 771 (col.) Je '54.

—— (Chinese girls). Natl. geog. 105: 264 (col.) Feb '54.

moon surface (photograph). Natl. geog. 103: 130 Jan '53.

Mooney, Cardinal Edward. Cur. biog. p. 407 (1946).

"Moonlight in Izamal" (Catherwood). Ceram: March of arch., p. 284.

Moonlight on water (auto). Holiday 10: 7 (col.) Aug '51.

Moor (with bread tray). Natl. geog. 107: 148 (col.) Feb '55.

—— See also Moors.

Moore, Anne Carroll. Jun. bk. of auth., p. 226.

Moore, Archie. Cur. biog. p. 281 (1960). Holiday 26: 133 Dec '59.

Moore, Maj. Gen. Bryant E. Cur. biog. p. 432 (1949).

Moore, Douglas. Cur. biog. p. 449 (1947).

Moore, Elisabeth Luce. Cur. biog. p. 283 (1960).

Moore, Garry. Cur. biog. p. 471 (1954).

Moore, Grace. Cur. biog. p. 481 (1944).

Moore, Henry. Cur. biog. p. 473 (1954). Holiday 23: 73 Ap '58.

—— (bronze work of). Con. 143: 92 Ap '59.

—— (sculpture). Praeg.: Pict. ency., p. 16.

—— (work of). Int. gr. soc.: Arts . . . p. 131 (col.).

Moore, John (Kneller). Con. 140: 233 Jan '58.

Moore, Marianne. Cur. biog. p. 435 (1952).

Moore, Preston J. Cur. biog. p. 306 (1959).

Moore, Ruth. Cur. biog. p. 475 (1954).

Moore, Thomas. Con. 145: 66 Mar '60.

Moore-Brabazon, J. C. T. Cur. biog. p. 594 (1941).

Moorea harbor. Holiday 9: 54 Mar '51.

Moorehead, Agnes. Cur. biog. p. 438 (1952).

Moorish arch. *See* architecture, Moorish.

Moorish dance. *See* "Morris dance" (Eng.).

Moorish girls (seated). Natl. geog. 112: 72 (col.) Jl '57.

Moorland hotel (Devonshire, Eng.). Travel 111: 54 Ap '59.

Moors (cobra entertainers). Natl. geog. 107: 153 (col.) Feb '55.

—— (desert police, camels). Natl. geog. 112: 78-9 (col.) Jl '57.

—— (horseback, parade). Natl. geog. 97: 446 (col.) Ap '50.

—— (praying to saint). Natl. geog. 107: 166-7 (col.) Feb '55.

moors (Eng.). Natl. geog. 108: 339 Sept '55.

Mor, Antonis (work of). Con. 137: LXIX May '56.

Mora, Jose A. Cur. biog. p. 448 (1956).

Moraes, Frank. Cur. biog. p. 376 (1957).

Moraine lake (Canada). Holiday 14: 118 (col.) Jl '53.

Morales, Luis (work of). Con. 144: XLI Sept '59.

Morality pictures, Jewish. Con. 134: 32-3 Sept '54.

Moran, Edward (work of). Amer. heri., vol. 10 no. 4 p. 60 (col.) (Je '59).
Natl. geog. 99: 212 (col.) Feb '51.

Morano, Albert Paul. Cur. biog. p. 440 (1952).

Morath, Max. Cur. biog. p. 274 (1963).

Moravio, Alberto. Holiday 27: 106 (col.) Ap '60.

Morcote Village (Switzerland). Natl. geog. 110: 472-3 (col.) Oct '56.

More, Sir Thomas (Holbein). Con. 136: 129 Nov '55.

"More family group" (Holbein). Con. 127: 54 Mar '51.

Moreau, Chocarne (work of). Con. 142: XXII Sept '58.

Moreell, Adm. Ben. Cur. biog. p. 410 (1946).

Morehead, Albert H. Cur. biog. p. 427 (1955).

Morgan, Anne. Cur. biog. p. 413 (1946).

Morgan, Arthur E. Cur. biog. p. 450 (1956).

Morgan, Edward P. Cur. biog. p. 435 (1951).

Morgan, Lt. Gen. Sir Frederick. Cur. biog. p. 415 (1946).

Morgan, Henry. Amer. heri., vol. 8 no. 2 p. 19 (Feb '57).
Cur. biog. p. 452 (1947).
Holiday 7: inside cover (col.) Feb '50.

Morgan, Gen. John Hunt. Holiday 24: 30 (col.) Jl '58.
Pakula: Cent. album, p. 215.

Morgan, John Pierpont. Amer. heri., vol. 8 no. 3 p. 44 (Ap '57); vol. 8 no. 4 p. 34 (Je '57).

—— (cartoon). Amer. heri., vol. 8 no. 4 p. 98 (Je '57).

Morgan, Joy Elmer. Cur. biog. p. 418 (1946).

Morgan, Lucy. Cur. biog. p. 307 (1959).

Morgan, Thomas A. Cur. biog. p. 409 (1950).

Morgan, Dr. Thomas E. Cur. biog. p. 309 (1959).

Morgenstierne, Wilhelm M. Cur. biog. p. 433 (1949).

Morgenthau, Hans J. Cur. biog. (1963).

Morin, Relman. Cur. biog. p. 291 (1958).

Morini, Erica. Cur. biog. p. 419 (1946).

Morinigo, Higinio. Cur. biog. p. 609 (1942).

Morison, Samuel Eliot. Cur. biog. p. 438 (1951); p. 303 (1962).

Morisot, Berthe (work of). Con. 134: 67 Sept '54.

Morland, George (in studio). Con. 136: 111 Nov '55.

—— (work of). Con. 136: IX Nov '55; 141: XXXIII Je '58; 142: 81 Nov '58.

Morley, Robert. Cur. biog. p. 278 (1963).

Mormon church. Jordan: Hammond's pict. atlas, p. 168 (col.).

Mormon temple (Salt Lake City). Brooks: Growth of a nation, p. 130.
Face of Amer., p. 159 (col.).
Holiday 23: 129 Ap '58; 24: 170 Dec '58; 27: 30 Mar '60.
Jordan: Hammond's pict. atlas, p. 169 (col.).
Travel 101: 36 Je '54; 106: 14 Dec '56; 112: 33 Aug '59.

—— (Logan, Utah). Holiday 23: 159 May '58.

Mormon trek westward. Brooks: Growth of a nation, p. 129.

Mormons. Amer. heri., vol. 7 no. 6 p. 20-5 (Oct '56).

—— (actors). Travel 111: 29 Je '59.

"Morning landscape" (Lorraine). Praeg.: Pict. atlas, p. 330 (col.).

Moroccan (men & women). Holiday 23: 67-71 (col.) Mar '58.

—— (woman). Holiday 8: 12 Jl '50; 23: cover (col.) Mar '58.

—— (women veiled). Holiday 25: 148 Ap '59. Travel 104: 9 Nov '55.

Moroccan band (in parade). Natl. geog. 101: 774 (col.) Je '52.

—— costume (medieval). Int. gr. soc.: Arts . . . p. 69 (col.).

—— sheik (serving tea). Holiday 20: 49 (col.) Aug '56.

Morocco. Disney: People & places, p. 83-98 (col.).
Natl. geog. 117: 646-7 (col.) May '60.
Travel 104: 9-12, 58-61 Nov '55.

—— (map). Natl. geog. 107: 154 Feb '55.

—— (mosque). Natl. geog. 107: 158 (col.) Feb '55; 112: 53 (col.) Jl '57.

——, French. *See* French Morocco.

Moron, Alonzo G. Cur. biog. p. 436 (1949).

Moroney, A. S. Holiday 15: 60 Feb '54.

Morrice, J. W. (work of). Con. 145: 180 May '60.

Morrill, James L. Cur. biog. p. 439 (1951).

Morris, Christopher. Holiday 21: 62 May '57.

Morris, George Pope. Amer. heri., vol. 10 no. 1 p. 20 (col.) (Dec '58).

Morris, Newbold. Cur. biog. p. 441 (1952).

Morris, Robert. Amer. heri., vol. 2 no. 1 p. 62 (fall '50); vol. 3 no. 4 p. 27 (summer '52); vol. 7 no. 6 p. 87 (Oct '56).

"Morris dance" (Eng.). Natl. geog. 103: 825 (col.) Je '53.

Morrison, Delesseps S. Cur. biog. p. 437 (1949).

Morrison, Herbert S. Cur. biog. p. 441 (1951).

Morrison, William Shepherd. Cur. biog. p. 444 (1952).

"Morris's folly" (home of Robert Morris).

Amer. heri., vol. 7 no. 6 p. 115 (Oct '56).

Morro castle. Travel 101: 26 Je '54.

Morro fort. Holiday 10: 180 Dec '51.

Morrow, Elizabeth Cutter. Cur. biog. p. 539 (1943).

Morsch, Lucile M. Cur. biog. p. 377 (1957).

Morse, Clarence G. Cur. biog. p. 379 (1957).

Morse, David A. Cur. biog. p. 440 (1949).

Morse, Marston. Cur. biog. p. 381 (1957).

Morse, Philip M. Cur. biog. p. 462 (1948).

Morse, Robert. Cur. biog. p. 305 (1962).

Morse, Samuel F. B. Amer. heri., vol. 9 no. 6 p. 89 (Oct '58); vol. 10 no. 2 p. 95 (Feb '59).

—— (work of). Amer. heri., vol. 7 no. 1 p. 13 (col.) (Dec '55); vol. 7 no. 5, cover (col.) (Aug '56).

Morse, Susan. Amer. heri., vol. 7 no. 5, cover, p. 2 (col.) (Aug '56).

Morse, True D. Cur. biog. p. 311 (1959).

Morse, Wayne Lyman. Cur. biog. p. 611 (1942); p. 477 (1954).

Holiday 15: 59 Feb '54.

mortar, bronze (15th cent.). Con. 132: 171-3 Jan '54.

——, Florentine (16th cent.). Con. 145: LV Mar '60.

——, grain. See grain mortar (Nigeria).

mortar & pestle (sym.). Lehner: Pict. bk. of sym., p. 16.

—— (Indian using). Natl. geog. 110: 827 (col.) Dec '56.

—— (1700's). Holiday 18: 60 (col.) Jl '55.

mortarboard (graduate's cap). Holiday 9: 132 Mar '51.

—— & diploma (sym.). Lehner: Pict. bk. of sym., p. 85.

Mortimer, Charles G., jr. Cur. biog. p. 429 (1955).

Morton, Elizabeth Homer. Cur. biog. p. 324 (1961).

Morton, Florrinell F. Cur. biog. p. 326 (1961).

Morton, John Jamieson, jr. Cur. biog. p. 431 (1955).

Morton, Levi P. Amer. heri., vol. 7 no. 5 p. 102 (Aug '56).

Morton, Thomas (Bishop of Durham). Con. 139: 218 Je '57.

Morton, Thruston B. Cur. biog. p. 383 (1957).

mortuary figures, Chinese. Con. ency. of ant., vol. 3, pl. 57-64.

—— mask, British Columbia. Int. gr. soc.: Arts . . . p. 185 (col.).

mosaic (Aztec skull). Ceram: March of arch., pl. XIII (col.).

—— (church pediment). Natl. geog. 110: 758 (col.) Dec '56.

—— (Pompeii). Labande: Naples, p. 104. Praeg.: Pict. ency., p. 149 (col.).

—— (Ravenna). Praeg.: Pict. ency., p. 179 (col.).

—— (Roman ruin, Sicily). Natl. geog. 107: 23-4 (col.) Jan '55.

—— (Ur). Ceram: March of arch., p. 242-3.

—— (The Virgin). Labande: Naples, p. 45.

——, Byzantine. Osward: Asia Minor, pl. 1 (col.), pl. 54-7, 62-3.

——, Byzantine (miniature). Con. 142: 30 Sept '58.

——, ceiling (in Kariyeh Cami). Osward: Asia Minor, pl. 52.

——, Florentine (1735). Con. 140: 177 Dec '57.

mosaic floor (Cirencester, Eng.). Natl. geog. 114: 51 Jl '58.

—— (thermal baths, Rhodes). Natl. geog. 114: 739 Dec '58.

mosaic lunette. See lunette, mosaic.

Mosaic of St. Sophia (Alexios). Con. 134: 55 Sept '54.

mosaic pavement. Holiday 11: inside cover (col.) Jan '52.

—— (Funchal, Madeira). Natl. geog. 115: 374 Mar '59.

—— (Rio de Janeiro). Holiday 19: 28 May '56; 20: 119 (col.) Dec '56; 21: 69 Jan '57.

Natl. geog. 107: 321 (col.) Mar '55.

mosaics. Natl. geog. 111: 219, 222, 228 (col.) Feb '57.

—— (man making floor). Natl. geog. 111: 224 Feb '57.

Mosbacher, Emil, jr. Cur. biog. p. 280 (1963).

Mosby, John S. Pakula: Cent. album, p. 217.

Mosconi, Willie. Cur. biog. p. 282 (1963).

Moscoso, Teodoro. Cur. biog. p. 284 (1963).

Moscow (Russia). Holiday 18: 102-5 Jl '55, 45 Nov '55.

Natl. geog. 116: 358, 370 (col.) Sept '59.

—— (night). Natl. geog. 116: 372-3 (col.) Sept '59.

Moscow university. Natl. geog. 116: 364-5 (col.) Sept '59.

Mosel, Tad. Cur. biog. p. 328 (1961).

Moselle Valley (France). Holiday 14: 126 (col.) Oct '53.

Moser, Fritz. Cur. biog. p. 432 (1955).

Moses, Anna Mary Robertson (Grandma Moses.) Cur. biog. p. 441 (1949).

Holiday 19: 86 Mar '56.

Moses, Grandma. See Moses, Anna Mary Robertson.

Moses, Harry M. Cur. biog. p. 443 (1949).

Moses, Robert. Cur. biog. p. 479 (1954).

Holiday 26: 51 (col.) Oct '59.

"Moses" (in the Chartreuse). Praeg.: Pict. ency., p. 246.

"Moses" (Michelangelo). Praeg.: Pict. ency., p. 273.

"Moses" (Ribera). Labande: Naples, p. 125.

"Moses & the burning bush" (Feti). Natl. geog. 97: 766 (col.) Je '50.

"Moses in the bulrushes." Amer. heri., vol. 7 no. 1 p. 60 (col.) (Dec '55).

Moses-Saunders power dam. Natl. geog. 115: 339 Mar '59.

Mosher, Aaron R. Cur. biog. p. 412 (1950).

Mosher, Ira. Cur. biog. p. 410 (1945).

Moslem (kissing tomb door). Natl. geog. 104: 13 (col.) Jl '53.

—— (praying). Natl. geog. 104: 7 (col.) Jl '53; 114: 729 Nov '58.

——, Kano (Nigeria). Natl. geog. 116: 235 (col.) Aug '59.

Moslem architecture. See architecture, Moslem.

—— arms (antique). Natl. geog. 100: 163 (col.) Aug '51.

—— home (int.). Holiday 25: 86 (col.) Je '59.

—— hunters (horses, dogs). Natl. geog. 114: 228-9 (col.) Aug '58.

—— man. Holiday 21: 37 Feb '57.

—— mosque. *See* mosque, Moslem.

—— mother & child. Holiday 19: 52 (col.) Feb '56.

—— pilgrims (board plane). Natl. geog. 104: 58 Jl '53.

—— professor. Holiday 25: 53 (col.) Feb '59.

—— shrine. Natl. geog. 114: 42 Jl '58.

—— worshipers. Natl. geog. 100: 161 (col.) Aug '51.

—— worshipers. *See* also Moslems (praying); Moslems (kneeling).

Moslems. Holiday 25: 76 (col.) Ap '59.
Natl. geog. 110: 331 (col.) Sept. '56; 114: 3-42 (part col.) Jl '58.

—— (bow toward Mecca). Natl. geog. 100: 143 Aug '51.

—— (goats). Natl. geog. 113: 144-5 Jan '58.

—— Kashmir). Natl. geog. 114: 606-42 (part col.) Nov '58.

—— (kneeling). Natl. geog. 98: 729 (col.) Dec '50.

—— (praying). Natl. geog. 104: 39 (col.), 41, 55 (col.) Jl '53; 114: 631 (col.) Nov '58.

—— (women veiled). Holiday 25: 148 Ap '59.

Mosley, Charles (engraving by). Con. 138: 109 Nov '56.

mosque (Arabia). Holiday 18: 59 Nov '55.
Natl. geog. 101: 224-5, 227 (col.) Feb '52.

—— (Baghdad). Natl. geog. 114: 447, 450, 467 (col.) Oct '58.

—— (Bombay, India). Travel 114: 4 Sept '60.

—— (by Sinan). Osward: Asia Minor, pl. 67.

—— (Isfahan). Holiday 20: 52-3 (col.) Dec '56.
Travel 105: 23 Jan '56; 106: inside back cover Nov '56.

—— (Istanbul). Natl. geog. 100: 724 Dec '51; 112: 111 Jl '57.
Praeg.: Pict. ency., p. 516.

—— (Jerusalem, A.D. 688). Natl. geog. 106: 844 (col.) Dec '54.

—— (Kampala). Natl. geog. 106: 722-3 (col.) Dec '54.

—— (Maldive is.). Natl. geog. 111: 839 Je '57.
Travel 111: 25 Jan '59.

—— (Mecca). Natl. geog. 104: 23 (col.) Jl '53.

—— (Morocco). Natl. geog. 107: 158 (col.) Feb '55; 112: 53 (col.) Jl '57.

—— (Nigeria). Natl. geog. 110: 350 (col.) Sept '56.

—— (Suakin is.). Travel 107: 27 Mar '57.

—— (Swat, Pakistan). Travel 108: 30 Nov '57.

—— (Tarsus). Osward: Asia Minor, pl. 130-2.

—— (Turkey). Natl. geog. 110: 737 Dec '56.

——, Acre (int.). Natl. geog. 110: 755 (col.) Dec '56.

——, Amr-ibn-el-Aas. *See* Amr-ibn-el-Aas mosque.

——, Badshahi. *See* Badshahi mosque.

——, Blue. *See* Blue mosque.

——, Cordova. *See* Cordova mosque.

——, great (courtyard, Persia). Int. gr. soc.: Arts . . . p. 85 (col.).

——, Hasan's. Natl. geog. 106: 764 (col.) Dec

'54.

——, Iranian king's. Natl. geog. 100: 452-3 (col.) Oct '51.

——, Koutoubia. Natl. geog. 112: 53 (col.) Jl '57.

——, Medina. *See* Medina mosque.

——, Mezquita (Spain). Holiday 23: 150 (col.) Feb '58.

——, Moslem (Ceylon). Travel 101: 19 Ap '54.

——, Moslem (Wash., D.C.). Face of Amer., p. 81 (col.).

——, Omayad (Syria). Travel 110: 35 Oct '58.

——, Rifai (Cairo). Natl. geog. 106: 765 (col.) Dec '54.

——, Seljuk. *See* Seljuk mosque.

——, Shah-i-Hamadan. Natl. geog. 114: 613 (col.) Nov '58.

——, Sidi Okba (Africa). Holiday 24: 20 Oct '58.

——, Suleyman. *See* Suleyman mosque.

——, Suleymaniyeh. *See* S u l e y m a n i y e h mosque.

mosque minaret. *See* minaret of mosque.

—— of Ibn Tulun. Holiday 10: 118 Dec '51.

—— of Khisrow Pasha (Aleppo). Travel 105: 21 Jan '56.

—— of Lutfallah. Travel 105: 23 Jan '56.

—— of Omar (Moslem). Holiday 7: 119 (col.) Ap '50.
Natl. geog. 98: 728 (col.) Dec '50.

—— of Suleiman (Istanbul). Int. gr. soc.: Arts . . . p. 45 (col.).

—— of Sultan Ahmed (Istanbul). Praeg.: Pict. ency., p. 516.
Travel 104: 58 Aug '55.

mosque plan (Hagia Sophia). Int. gr. soc.: Arts . . . p. 45 (col.).

—— tower, Chiappini (Africa). Travel 113: 31 Jan '60.

Moss, John E., jr. Cur. biog. p. 452 (1956).

Mossadegh, Mohammed. Cur. biog. p. 444 (1951).

Mossbauer, Rudolf L. Cur. biog. p. 307 (1962).

Mostel, Zero. Cur. biog. p. 541 (1943); (1963).

Mosul's leaning minaret. *See* minaret, Mosul's leaning.

Mote, G. W. (work of). Con. 135: cover, opp. p. 219 (col.) Je '55.

motel. Holiday 26: 24 (col.) Jl '59.

—— (Chicago). Travel 111: 47 May '59.

—— (Scarboro, Maine). Travel 104: inside cover Sept '55.

——, Beau Rivage (Miami Beach). Travel 108: 43 Dec '57.

——, Johnson (Miami). Travel 109: 41 Je '58.

——, O'Hare (world's largest). Travel 113: 47 Je '60.

——, Skyline motor inn (N.Y.). Travel 112: 64 Dec '59.

mother, Lapp (baby in cradle). Natl. geog. 106: 253 (col.) Aug '54.

mother & baby. Holiday 8: inside back cover (col.) Oct '50; 14: 96 (col.) Oct '53.

—— (Congo). Natl. geog. 118: 333 (col.) Sept '60.

—— (feeding). Natl. geog. 114: 818 Dec '58; 115: 578 Ap '59.

—— (Nigeria, Fulani). Natl. geog. 116: 238 (col.) Aug '59.

mother & baby (Thailand). Natl. geog. 116: 795 (col.) Dec '59.
—— **(war, Chinese).** Natl. geog. 115: 431 Mar '59.
Mother & child. Int. gr. soc.: Arts . . . p. 155 (col.).
Natl. geog. 115: 499 (col.) Ap '59.
Travel 101: inside back cover Mar '54, inside back cover May '54.
—— **(Berber).** Natl. geog. 117: 781 (col.) Je '60.
—— **(China).** Natl. geog. 118: 196 (col.) Aug '60.
—— **(churning, Lapland).** Natl. geog. 106: 276 (col.) Aug '54.
—— **(comic).** Travel 110: 57 Aug '58.
—— **(heads, Russian).** Natl. geog. 116: 734 (col.) Dec '59.
—— **(in chair).** Travel 107: 26 May '57.
—— **(Lapland).** Natl. geog. 106: 263 (col.) Aug '54.
—— **(scooter, France).** Natl. geog. 117: 732 (col.) Je '60.
—— *See* also woman & child.
mother & children (Portuguese). Natl. geog. 118: 633 (col.) Nov '60.
mother, baby & doctor (Turkey). Natl. geog. 115: 83 Jan '59.
mother with baby on back (Africa). Natl. geog. 118: 320 (col.) Sept '60.
—— **(Quemoy, China).** Natl. geog. 115: 414 Mar '59.
Mother's Day (gift). Holiday 11: 142 (col.) May '52.
—— **(man & woman).** Holiday 15: 95 (col.) May '54.
—— **(sym.).** Lehner: Pict. bk. of sym., p. 54.
Mothers whose sons died in World war II. Natl. geog. 114: 597 (col.) Nov '58.
Motherwell, Robert B. Cur. biog. p. 309 (1962).
"Motion in space" (bronze statue). Praeg.: Pict. ency., p. 458.
motion picture (indust.). Holiday 22: 96 Oct '57.
motion picture camera. *See* camera, Movie.
motion picture poster (Arabic). Natl. geog. 115: 500 Ap '59.
—— **(early).** Amer. heri., vol. 11 no. 3 p. 101 (Ap '60).
motion picture projector. Holiday 10: 73 Nov '51, 6, 81 (col.), 101, 135, 138 Dec '51; 11: 18, 96 Ap '52; 12: 31 Nov '52; 13: 137 Ap '53, 158 May '53, 136 Je '53; 14: 69 Jl '53, 84 Aug '53, 107 Sept '53, 11 Oct '53, 116 Nov '53, 8, 95 Dec '53; 18: 11, 67 (col.) Jl '55, 8, 23 Sept '55, 72, 93, 115, 139 Oct '55, 65, 81, 124, 137, 144 Nov '55, 15, 35, 79 (part col.) Dec '55; 20: 8, 27 Oct '56, 103 (col.) Nov '56, 8, 99, 126 (col.), 165 Dec '56; 21: 145 Feb '57, 10 (col.) Mar '57, 7 (col.) Je '57; 22: 77 (col.) Sept '57, 155 Oct '57, 17, 43, 99 (col.) Nov '57, 12, 21, 37, 126, 137, 227 (col.) Dec '57; 23: 6 Ap '58, 167 Je '58; 24: 95 (col.) Sept '58, 107 Oct '58, 26, 124, 143 Dec '58; 25: 103 (col.) Mar '59, 97 (col.) May '59; 26: 85 Jl '59, 99 (col.) Oct '59; 27: 154 Feb '60, 101 (col.) Je '60; 28: 11, 81 (col.) Jl '60, 83 (col.) Sept '60, 43 Oct '60, 56 Nov

'60, 115 (col.), 132, 139 Dec '60.
—— **(comic).** Holiday 21: 46 Mar '57, 187 Ap '57, 41 May '57; 22: 93 Sept '57, 116 Oct '57, 124 Nov '57, 208 Dec '57.
motion picture scene (being filmed). Holiday 5: 49 (col.) Jan '49.
motion picture scene ("The Robe"). Natl. geog. 105: 766-7 Je '54.
motion picture scenes. Int. gr. soc.: Arts . . . p. 151 (col.).
—— **(comic).** Holiday 5: 50-2 Jan '49.
motion picture screen. *See* screen, motion picture.
Motley, Arthur H. Cur. biog. p. 330 (1961).
motor, outboard. Holiday 11: 86 Ap '52; 12: 29 (col.) Jl '52; 13: 119 Ap '53; 18: 66 (col.) Oct '55; 19: 81 (col.) Mar '56, 140 (col.) May '56.
motor boat. *See* boat, motor.
motor hotel (Chicago). Travel 113: 43 Feb '60.
—— **(Ft. Lauderdale).** Holiday 27: 8 Jan '60.
motor lodge. Holiday 22: 18 (col.) Dec '57.
motor scooter. Travel 105: 12 Ap '56.
motor scooters (Rome). Natl. geog. 111: 442-3 Ap '57.
motor vehicle, Woods. Amer. heri., vol. 11 no. 5 p. 97 (Aug '60).
motor vehicles, Woods elec. (1900-1917). Amer. heri., vol. 11 no. 5 p. 70-3 (col.) (Aug '60).
motor yacht. Holiday 12: 72 (col.) Sept '52.
motorbus. *See* bus.
motorcycle (race). Holiday 24: 108 Dec '58.
—— **(soldier).** Natl. geog. 98: 718 (col.) Dec '50.
Mott, Frank Luther. Cur. biog. p. 596 (1941).
Mott, John R. Cur. biog. p. 454 (1947).
motto, home (colonial). Holiday 28: 71 (col.) Jl '60.
mouchette, triple. Praeg.: Pict. ency., p. 248.
moulding, roll (staircase). Praeg.: Pict. ency., p. 375.
Moulton, Forest M. Cur. biog. p. 422 (1946).
Moulton, Harold G. Cur. biog. p. 484 (1944).
Moultrie, William. Amer. heri., vol. 9 no. 2 p. 51 (col.) (Feb '58).
Mount, William Sidney. Amer. heri., vol. 11 no. 5 p. 12 (Aug '60).
—— **(work of).** Amer. heri., vol. 7 no. 3 p. 46 (col.) (Ap '56); vol. 11 no. 5 p. 10, 13-23, 92 (part col.) Aug '60.
Mt. Ararat. Natl. geog. 115: 66-7 (col.) Jan '59.
Osward: Asia Minor, pl. 146.
Mt. Athabaska. Travel 103: 11 Je '55.
Mt. Baker. Holiday 11: 44 May '52.
Mt. Cook. Natl. geog. 101: 420 Ap '52.
Mt. Everest. Holiday 13: 107-8 May '53.
Natl. geog. 106: 2-63 (part col.) Jl '54; 117: 405 (col.) Mar '60.
—— **(climbers).** Natl. geog. 108: 580-606 (part col.) Nov '55.
Mt. Hood (Ore.). Holiday 5: 105 (col.) Jan '49, 71 (col.) Mar '49; 13: 29 (col.) May '53, 34 (col.) 37 Je '53.
Jordan: Hammond's pict. atlas, p. 153, 155 (col.).
Travel 101: cover, 9 Ap '54; 111: cover May '59.

Mt. Juneau. Natl. geog. 109: 739 (col.) Je '56.

Mt. Kenya. Natl. geog. 97: 313 Mar '50.

Mt. Lassen volcano (Cal.). Jordan: Hammond's pict. atlas, p. 187 (col.).

Mt. McKinley (Alaska). Natl. geog. 109: 760 (col.) Je '56; 113: 636-7 May '58; 116: 80-1 (col.) Jl '59.

—— explorers. Natl. geog. 104: 220-47 Aug '53.

—— Natl. Park. Natl. geog. 104: 250-70 (part col.) Aug '53.

Mount Melleray chapel (Ireland). Holiday 6: 50-1 Dec '49.

Mt. Moran (Tetons). Holiday 20: 90-1 (col.) Aug '56.

Mount Nebo (Holy Land). Natl. geog. 114: 857 (col.) Dec '58.

"Mount of Mercy." Natl. geog. 104: 54 (col.) Jl '53.

Mt. of Olives. Natl. geog. 98: 715 (col.) Dec '50; 102: 834 Dec '52.

Mt. of Sodom. Natl. geog. 112: 854 Dec '57.

Mt. Olympus. Holiday 14: 27 Aug '53; 108: 114, 116 Jl '55.

Mount Osorno (Chile). Travel 101: 7 Feb '54.

Mt. Palomar observatory (Cal.). Holiday 14: 12 (col.) Nov '53; 15: 84 Feb '54, 5 (col.) Mar '54, 80-1 Ap '54, 85 May '54.
Travel 103: 34 Je '55.

Mt. Pilatus (Switzerland). Travel 102: 11 Aug '54.

"Mt. Pleasant," Beekman home (Hosier). Con. 139: 134 Ap '57.

Mt. Ranier (Wash.). Amer. heri., vol. 4 no. 4 inside cover (summer '53).
Face of Amer., p. 22 (col.).
Holiday 6: 12 (col.) Nov '49; 10: 2 (col.) Aug '51; 11: 48 May '52; 21: 29 (col.) Feb '57; 27: 12 (col.) Mar '60.
Jordan: Hammond's pict. atlas, p. 151 (col.).
Natl. geog. 117: 483-5 (col.) Ap '60.

—— (grotto). Natl. geog. 113: 628-9 (col.) May '58.

—— (pack train). Holiday 25: 123 (col.) Feb '59.

Mt. Rushmore memorial (Borglum sculpt., Black Hills, S.D.). Holiday 7: 102, 109 Je '50.

—— (President's heads, carved). Holiday 10: inside cover (col.) Sept '51; 12: 13 Aug '52; 15: 139 May '54; 16: 90 (col.) Oct '54; 18: 87, 121 Jl '55; 23: 173 Ap '58, 21 (col.) May '58, 25: 21 (col.) May '59; 27: 151 Ap '60, 27 May '60.
Jordan: Hammond's pict. atlas, p. 107 (col.).
Natl. geog. 99: 720 (col.) Je '51; 110: 483, 487, 496-7 (part col.) Oct '56.
Travel 101: 43 Ap '54; 113: 8 Mar '60.

Mt. St. Helena. Natl. geog. 102: 580 (col.) Nov '52.

"Mount St. Helens" (Kane). Amer. heri., vol. 10 no. 5 p. 46 (col.) (Aug '59).
Holiday 11: 43 (col.) May '52.

Mt. Shuksan (Wash.). Holiday 11: cover (col.) May '52; 23: 18 (col.) May '58.

Mt. Sinai. Natl. geog. 112: 844 (col.) Dec '57.

Mt. Sinyala (Grand Canyon). Natl. geog. 99: 737 (col.) Je '51.

Mt. Solaro (Capri, Italy). Labande: Naples, p. 212.

Mt. Stanley. Natl. geog. 112: 94-5 Jl '57.

"Mt. Vernon" (home of Washington). Brooks: Growth of a nation, p. 71.
Face of Amer., p. 63 (col.).
Holiday 18: 107 (col.) Nov '55; 25: cover (col.) Je '59.
Natl. geog. 97: 814 Je '50; 104: 652-82 Nov '53; 112: 511 Oct '57.
Travel 111: 29-31 Feb '59; 114: 35 Sept '60.

—— (formal gardens). Natl. geog. 104: 674-5 (col.) Nov '53.

Mt. Vesuvius. See Vesuvius.

Mt. Victoria. Natl. geog. 118: 119 (col.) Jl '60.

Mt. Washington (N.H.). Jordan: Hammond's pict. atlas, p. 26-7 (col.).

Mt. Washington hotel (Bretton Woods, N.H.). Holiday 10: 40 Sept '51.
Natl. geog. 99: 593 (col.) May '51.

Mt. Whitney. Jordan: Hammond's pict. atlas, p. 193 (col.).

Mt. Zion. Natl. geog. 102: 840 Dec '52.

Mountain campers. Natl. geog. 116: 399 (col.) Sept '59.

—— climber. Holiday 11: 55 (col.) May '52.
Natl. geog. 101: 313 (col.) Mar '52; 105: 859 (col.) Je '54; 106: 4, 13, 18-9, 22-63 (part col.) Jl '54; 110: 460-1 Oct '56; 111: 558 Ap '57; 113: 626-7 (part col.) May '58; 114: 499 Oct '58; 118: 119 (col.) Jl '60.

—— climber (comic). Holiday 18: 16 Sept '55.

—— climber (Switzerland). Natl. geog. 111: 784 Je '57.

—— climbers. Holiday 10: 48-53 (part col.) Jl '51; 13: 110 May '53; 21: 103 (col.) Ap '57; 25: 47 (col.) Feb '58.
Natl. geog. 97: 715 Je '50; 99: 571, 574, 587 (col.) May '51; 100: 189, 191, 205, 214 (col.) Aug '51; 102: 193, 204-5 Aug '52; 103: 581 (col.) May '53; 107: 844-5, 847 (col.) Je '55; 108: 580-606 (part col.) Nov '55; 109: 23 (col.) Jan '56, 518 (col.), 525 Ap '56, 608-9, 634-5 (col.) May '56; 114: 188-9 (col.) Aug '58.

—— climbers (horseback). Natl. geog. 102: 762 (col.) Dec '52.

—— climbers (Pyrenees). Natl. geog. 109: 303, 312 (col.) Mar '56.

—— climbers (Switzerland). Disney: People & places, p. 46 (col.).

—— climbers. See also man (mt. climber).

mountain cottage (Swiss type). Holiday 7: 52 (col.) Jan '50.

mountain men. See men, mountain.

"Mountain of 99 hills" (Annamese). Natl. geog. 99: 477 (col.) Ap '51.

mountain pass (Hunza). Natl. geog. 104: 496-7 (col.) Oct '53.

Mt. top hotel (Caracas, Venezuela). Travel 107: 45 May '57.

mountain trail (summer). Natl. geog. 102: 474-502 (part col.) Oct '52.

Mountain view manor (Cal.). Travel 108: 47 Nov '57.

mountaineers. Holiday 9: 44-5, 49 Mar '51.

mountains (Glacier park). Natl. geog. 109: 591-636 (part col.) May '56.

—— (snow, Alaska). Natl. geog. 109: 739-808, 817 (part col.) Je '56.

Mountbatten, Lord Louis. Cur. biog. p. 614 (1942).
mounting block. Rawson: Ant. pict. bk., p. 41.
Mourlot, Fernand. Holiday 21: 69 (col.) Ap '57.
"The mourners" sculpture (Lough). Con. 127: 105 May '51.
mourning (flag sym.). Lehner: Pict. bk. of sym., p. 79.
mourning ribbon. See Lincoln mourning ribbon.
Mouse is. (Greece). Holiday 24: 70 Sept '58.
mouse trap (antique). Rawson: Ant. pict. bk., p. 9.
Moutet, Marius. Cur. biog. p. 457 (1947).
mouth (skeleton). Gray's anatomy, p. 1152-73.
mouths (sym.). Lehner: Pict. bk. of sym., p. 96.
movie. See motion picture scene.
movie camera. See camera, movie; zoomatic movie camera.
movie film (early). Amer. heri., vol. 11 no. 3 p. 31, 33, 35 (Ap '60).
movie film strip. Holiday 21: 6 Feb '57.
movie producers & actors. Holiday 5: 34-52 (col.) Jan '49.
movie projector. See motion picture projector.
moving van. See van, moving.
mower, lawn. See lawn mower.
Mowery, Edward J. Cur. biog. p. 438 (1953).
Mowrer, Edgar Ansel. Cur. biog. p. 598 (1941); p. 311 (1962).
Mowrey, Corma. Cur. biog. p. 414 (1950).
Moya, Manuel A. De. Cur. biog. p. 385 (1957).
Moylan, Mary Ellen. Cur. biog. p. 387 (1957).
Mozambique. Travel 104: 25-8 Nov '55.
—— mask. Int. gr. soc.: Arts . . . p. 185 (col.).
Mozart, Wolfgang Amadeus (Lange). Cooper: Con. ency. of music, p. 135 (col.).
—— (age 12, at piano). Int. gr. soc.: Arts . . . p. 109 (col.).
—— (bust). Con. 138· VIII Nov '56.
Muccio, John J. Cur. biog. p. 446 (1951).
mud gates & wall, Ghazni (Afghanistan). Natl. geog. 104: 432 Sept '53.
Mudd, Emily H. Cur. biog. p. 454 (1956).
mudhif (Arab guesthall). Natl. geog. 113: 206-7, 210-11 Feb '58.
Mudmen (Goroka, New Guinea). Holiday 28: 92-3 (col.) Nov '60.
Mueller, Frederick H. Cur. biog. p. 313 (1959).
Muench, Aloisius (Cardinal). Cur. biog. p. 285 (1960).
muffineer, antique silver. Con. 138: 276 Jan '57.
mug. Holiday 10: 127 Nov '51; 28: 15 Aug '60.
Natl. geog. 97: 288 (col.) Mar '50.
—— (antique). Con. 134: XL Nov '54; 136: 97 Nov '55.
—— (antique silver). Con. 134: X Nov '54; 135: XXVIII Ap '55.
——, ale. Holiday 27: 115 (col.) Je '60.
——, beer. Holiday 28: 121 (col.) Jl '60, 119 (col.) Aug '60, 15, 146 (col.) Oct '60.
——, beer (Geo. II). Con. 136: 57 Sept '55.
——, beer (Geo. II silver). Con. 141: XI Mar '58.
——, "blackjack." Rawson: Ant. pict. bk., p. 84.

——, Bow porcelain. Con. 132: 166 Jan '54; 139: 124 Ap '57; 144: 31 Sept '59.
——, Coca Cola. Holiday 28: back cover (col.) Sept '60.
——, 18th cent. Con. 135: LIII Ap '55.
——, Liverpool pottery. Con. 132: 170 Jan '54.
——, Royal Doulton. Holiday 14: 5 (col.) Oct '53.
——, shaving. See shaving mug.
——, stoneware (Dwight, 17th cent.). Con. ency. of ant., vol. 1, pl. 5.
——, Worcester. Con. 129: XXIV Je '52; 133: XLVII Mar '54; 138: 195 Dec '56.
Muggeridge, Malcolm. Cur. biog. p. 434 (1955).
mugs. Holiday 18: 189 Dec '55.
——, pewter (antique). Natl. geog. 103: 830 (col.) Je '53.
——, silver (18th cent.). Con. ency. of ant., vol. 1, pl. 86.
Con. 141: XXIV May '58.
Muir, James. Cur. biog. p. 415 (1950).
Muir, Malcolm. Cur. biog. p. 440 (1953).
Muir, Percy. Cur. biog. p. 289 (1963).
Muir woods (Cal.). Natl. geog. 116: 610 (col.) Nov '59.
Mukalla (Saudi Arabia). Natl. geog. 108: 156-7 (col.) Aug '55.
—— (mud houses). Natl. geog. 111: 250 Feb '57.
"Mulberry Field" house. Natl. geog. 105: 435 (col.) Ap '54.
mule (sym.). Lehner: Pict. bk. of sym., p. 60.
mule chest (William III & Mary). Con. ency. of ant., vol. 3, pl. 125.
mule-trolley (Mexican). Travel 106: 50 Nov '56.
Muller, Diana Ruth. Holiday 14: 45 Dec '53.
Muller, Hermann J. Cur. biog. p 458 (1947).
Muller, Paul. Cur. biog. p. 342 (1945).
Mulligan, Gerry. Cur. biog. p. 286 (1960). Int. gr. soc.: Arts . . . p. 143 (col.).
Mulloy, Gardnar. Cur. biog. p. 389 (1957).
Mulready, William (work of). Con. 144: 94 Nov '59.
Mutiplane. Amer. heri., vol. 9 no. 5 p. 19 (Aug '58).
Multnomah falls (Ore.). Jordan: Hammond's pict. atlas, p. 154 (col.).
Travel 110: 23 Sept '58.
Mumford, Lawrence Quincy. Cur. biog. p. 482 (1954).
Mumford, Lewis. Cur. biog. p. 291 (1963).
mummers, court. Durant: Pict. hist. of Amer. circus, p. 10.
—— (Havana). Holiday 12: 68 (col.) Dec '52.
—— (Japan, medieval). Natl. geog. 104: 101 Jl '53.
—— (Penafiel, Portugal). Holiday 6: 107 (col.) Sept '49.
mummies. Ceram: March of arch., p. 112-33.
——, animal. Ceram: March of arch., p. 130-1.
mummy. Natl. geog. 117: 504 (col.) Ap '60.
——, the dancing. Ceram: March of arch., p. 113.
——, x-rayed. Ceram: March of arch., p. 128.
mummy portrait. Praeg. Pict. ency., p. 161 (col.).

Mumtaz Mahal (memorial). *See* Taj Mahal.
Munch, Charles. Cur. biog. p. 461 (1947).
　Holiday 21: 42 Mar '57; 22: 121 Sept '57.
Munch, Edvard (work of). Praeg. Pict. ency.,
　p. 440 (col.).
Mundt, Karl E. Cur. biog. p. 465 (1948).
Muni, Paul. Cur. biog. p. 485 (1944).
Munich (Ger.). Holiday 22: 56-61 (part col.)
　Sept '57.
　Natl. geog. 115: 742-8 (col.) Je '59.
—— (festival). Holiday 10: 16-9, 22 Oct '51.
—— (fountain). *See* Wittelsbach fountain.
Muniz, João Carlos. Cur. biog. p. 446 (1952).
Munn, Charles. Holiday 23: 149 Je '58.
Munn, Clarence L. Cur. biog. p. 442 (1953).
Munn, Frank. Cur. biog. p. 489 (1944).
Munnich, Ferenc. Cur. biog. p. 315 (1959).
Munnings, Sir. A. J. (work of). Con. 135: VI
　Ap '55; 136: 51 (col.) Sept '55.
Munnings, Alfred (work of). Con. 144: 123
　Nov '59.
Munoz-Marin, Luis. Cur. biog. p. 616 (1942).
Munro, Leslie Knox. Cur. biog. p. 447 (1953).
Munsel, Patrice. Cur. biog. p. 412 (1945).
Muntin furniture ornament. Con. ency of ant.,
　vol. 1, p. 20.
mural. Travel 113: 24 Je '60.
—— (Covarrubias). Natl. geog. 100: 813 (col.)
　Dec '51.
—— (Cutter, Eskimos). Natl. geog. 112: 330
　(col.) Sept '57.
—— (monastery). Natl. geog. 109: 60 (col.)
　Jan '56.
—— (nursery wall). Natl. geog. 109: 237
　(col.) Feb '56.
—— (on house). Natl. geog. 113: 111 (col.)
　Mar '58.
—— (palace, Knossos, Crete). Int. gr. soc.:
　Arts . . . p. 21 (col.).
—— (U.S. Civil war). Natl. geog. 103: 282
　Mar '53.
—— (women). Holiday 21: 92 Mar '57.
—— (Wyeth). Amer. heri., vol. 3 no. 1 p. 51
　(col.) (fall '51).
——, cave motif (Tang). Natl. geog. 99: 397
　(col.) Mar '51.
——, Etruscan (ancient). Int. gr. soc.: Arts
　. . . p. 21 (col.).
——, Fijian. Holiday 7: 60 (col.) Je '50.
——, library wall (Patzcuaro, Mexico). Natl.
　geog. 102: 539 (col.) Oct '52.
——, wall (Zuffi: Neptune's banquet). Holiday
　13: 2 (col.) Je '53.
mural crown. *See* crown, mural.
murals, Indian (on rocks). Natl. geog. 105:
　375 (col.) Mar '54.
——, U.S. capital (Brumidi). Natl. geog. 102:
　160-1, 164-6, 184-5 (col.) Aug '52.
——, Gioacchino (bust by Canoba). Con. 140:
　248 Jan '58.
Murchison falls (Africa). Natl. geog. 97: 342
　(col.) Mar '50.
Murcia dancers (Spain). Natl. geog. 97: 445
　(col.) Ap '50.
Murcia Holy week parade (Spain). Travel 107:
　21 Ap '57.
murder. Holiday 22: 97 Sept '57.
"Murdered woman & the Furies" (Fuseli).
　Con. 144: 33 Sept '59.

murders. Horan: Pict. hist. of wild west, p. 38.
Murdoch, Iris. Cur. biog. p. 293 (1958).
Murdock, George Peter. Cur. biog. p. 391
　(1957).
Murdock, Harold. Amer. heri., vol. 10 no. 5
　p. 62 (Aug '59).
Mure, Thomas (Raeburn). Con. 136: 20 Sept
　'55.
Murieta, Joaquin. Horan: Pict. hist. of wild
　west, p. 24.
Murillo, Bartolome Esteban (work of). Con.
　ency. of ant., vol. 1, pl. 162.
　Praeg: Pict. ency., p. 352 (col.).
Murphree, Eger V. Cur. biog. p. 456 (1956).
Murphy, Charles S. Cur. biog. p. 416 (1950).
Murphy, Franklin W. Cur. biog. p. 600 (1941).
Murphy, Gardner. Cur. biog. p. 288 (1960).
Murphy, Patricia. Cur. biog. p. 313 (1962).
Murphy, Robert D. Cur. biog. p. 543 (1943);
　p. 295 (1958).
Murphy, Thomas F. Cur. biog. p. 448 (1951).
Murphy, William B. Cur. biog. p. 436 (1955).
Murphy hotel (near Sequoia park, Cal.). Natl.
　geog. 99: 681 May '51.
Murray, Alfalfa Bill. Holiday 7: 116 May '50.
Murray, Arthur. Cur. biog. p. 547 (1943).
　Holiday 11: 11 Je '52.
Murray, Donald P. Cur. biog. p. 316 (1959).
Murray, Dwight H. Cur. biog. p. 392 (1957).
Murray, Frank. Horan: Pict. hist. of wild west,
　p. 209.
Murray, James E. Cur. biog. p. 414 (1945).
　Holiday 7: 36 Mar '50.
Murray, John Courtney. Cur. biog. p. 332
　(1961).
Murray, Philip. Cur. biog. p. 601 (1941); p.
　445 (1949).
　Holiday 6: 45 Oct '49.
Murray, Thomas E. Cur. biog. p. 417 (1950).
Murray, Tom. Cur. biog. p. 458 (1956).
Murray Bay. Holiday 12: 98-103 (part col.)
　Sept '52.
Murrell, Ethel Ernest. Cur. biog. p. 450 (1951).
Murrow, Edward R. Cur. biog. p. 619 (1942);
　p. 449 (1953).
Murtaugh, Daniel E. Cur. biog. p. 333 (1961).
muscles, human. Gray's anatomy, p. 343, 354-
　9, 372-3, 376, 380, 385-496.
"The muse" (by Morse, of his daughter).
　Amer. heri., vol. 7 no. 6 front cover (col.)
　(Oct '56).
muses, the nine. *See* nine muses.
museum (int.). Natl. geog. 117: 504-5 (col.)
　Ap '60.
—— (knights' armor). Natl. geog. 107: 194-7
　(col.) Feb '55.
——, Aarhus (Denmark). Travel 103: 12 May
　'55.
——, Acadian (La. Bayou). Holiday 6: 55
　Oct '49.
——, adobe. Natl. geog. 112: 118-9 Jl '57.
——, Alexander Graham Bell. Natl. geog.
　110: 231-3 (part col.) Aug '56; 116: 257
　(col.) Aug '59.
——, Arizona wildlife. Natl. geog. 113: 246
　Feb '58.
——, art. *See* also art museum.
——, British. *See* British museum.

museum, Brooklyn (int.). Holiday 7: 56 (col.) Je '50.
——, children's (Ft. Worth, Tex.). Travel 113: 58 Jan '60.
——, "Crystal palace." Amer. heri., vol. 11 no. 3 p. 17 (col.) (Ap '60).
——, Dutch Zwaanendeel. See Zwaanendeel museum.
——, Eisenhower. Holiday 21: 91 May '57.
——, Ft. Clinch (Fla.). Travel 104: 17 Oct '55.
——, history (Dresden). Con. 144: 193 Dec '59.
——, Junipero Serra (Cal.). Natl. geog. 102: 773 (col.) Dec '52.
——, Kansas City. Holiday 7: 48 Mar '50.
——, Kew Gardens (London). Natl. geog. 97: 492 (col.) Ap '50.
——, Lisbon (Spain). Con. 137: 21 Mar '56.
——, Mariners (int.). Natl. geog. 113: 17 (col.) Jan '58.
——, Mark Twain (Virginia City, Nev.). Travel 113: 48 May '60.
——, Nova Scotia. Natl. geog. 112: 169 (col.) Aug '57.
——, Red China. Natl. geog. 118: 202-3 (col.) Aug '60.
——, Ringling. See Ringling museum.
——, Taft. See Taft museum.
——, Vienna. Natl. geog. 97: 738-76 (part col.) Je '50.
——, Virginia. Holiday 28: 9 Sept '60.
——, Wilmington (Del.). Travel 111: 22 Feb '59.
museum courtyard (Boston). Holiday 14: 39 (col.) Nov '53.
museum exhibit (ship figureheads). Natl. geog. 112. 335 (col.) Sept '57.
museum of art, Guggenheim. See Guggenheim museum of art.
museum of ethnography (Ankara). Osward: Asia Minor, pl. 150, 153, 157.
museum of hist. & tech. (Wash., D.C.). Natl. geog. 117: 805 Je '60.
museum of modern art (N.Y., int.). Holiday 14: 56-63 (col.) Nov '53.
mushroom, atomic. See atomic mushroom cloud.
Musial, Stan. Cur. biog. p. 466 (1948). Holiday 25: 62 (col.) Feb '59.
music (conductor's score). Int. gr. soc.: Arts . . . p. 141 (col.).
—— (cover design, mid-19th cent.). Amer. heri., vol. 9 no. 3 p. 52-61 (col.) (Ap '58).
—— (1st printed in Amer., 1698). Amer. heri., vol. 8 no. 1 p. 117-9 (Dec '56).
—— (samples of). Cooper: Con. ency. of music, p. 481-92.
—— (sym.). Lehner: Pict. bk. of sym., p. 14-5, 33, 49.
music, illum. gradual. Cooper: Con. ency. of music, p. 326 (col.).
——, patron saint of. Lehner: Pict. bk. of sym., p. 40.
——, written (medieval). Int. gr. soc.: Arts . . . p. 61 (col.).
music academy (Assembly hall, N.Y.). Amer. heri., vol. 11 no. 4 p. 42-3 (Je '60).
—— (Salzburg, Austria). Holiday 25: 121 Jan '59.

music composers. See composers, music.
music conductor. Holiday 14: 159 Nov '53.
music festival tent (Ellenville, N.Y.). Holiday 24: 45 (col.) Aug '58.
music hall (Vienna, int.). Travel 101: 12 Jan '54.
music halls. Cooper: Con. ency. of music, p. 449-64.
"The music lesson" (Manet). Con. 126: 129 Oct '50.
"Music lesson" (Ochterveldt). Con. 136: 20 Sept '55.
music motifs (illus.). Int. gr. soc.: Arts . . . p. 139 (col.).
music note (comic). Holiday 18: 28 Jl '55; 20: 23 Aug '56.
"Music party" (Attanasio). Con. 132: LVIII Jan. '54.
—— (Netscher). Con. 142: 57 Sept '58.
—— (P. de Hooch). Con. 142: 41 Sept '58; 144: LVII (col.) Dec '59.
—— (Watteau). Cooper: Con. ency. of music, p. 447.
music rack, Thos. Jefferson. Natl. geog. 97: 568 (col.) May '50.
music record. See record, music.
music room, Royal pavillion (Brighton). Con. 126: 199 Dec '50.
music stand, Canterbury (1810). Con. ency. of ant., vol. 3, pl. 10.
——, regency. Con. 136: LXXI Jan '56.
music tent. See tent, music.
music theatre (Beverly, Mass.). Travel 113: 28 May '60.
musical goblets, antique (man playing). Natl. geog. 109: 455 Ap '56.
musical instrument (dombra). Natl. geog. 106: 634-5 (col.) Nov '54.
—— (Eskimo playing). Natl. geog. 107: 558 (col.) Ap '55.
——, Borneo. Natl. geog. 109: 718 May '56
——, Japan. Natl. geog. 118: 771 (col.) Dec '60.
——, Pescadores is. Natl. geog. 109: 282 (col.) Feb '56.
——, Siam. Disney: People & places, p. 173 (col.).
——, Tuareg. Natl. geog. 112: 71 (col.) Jl '57.
musical instruments. Cooper: Con. ency. of music.
Holiday 21: 37, 191 Ap '57; 27: 51 (col.) Mar '60.
Natl. geog. 104: 687 Nov '53.
—— (ancient). Int. gr. soc.: Arts . . . title page (col.), 27, 61 (col.).
——, Canary is. Natl. geog. 107: 518 (col.) Ap '55.
——, Ky. Rawson: Ant. pict. bk., p. 81.
——, modern symphony (orchestra). Int. gr. soc.: Arts . . . p. 141 (col.).
—— See also name of instrument.
"The musicale" (Lesrel). Con. 136: V Sept '55.
musician. Holiday 18: 35-7 Oct '55; 21: 42, 77, 144 Mar '57; 22: 113 Jl '57; 27: 195 (col.) May '60.
—— (comic). Holiday 22: 79 Nov '57.
—— (man, bagpipe). Natl. geog. 112: 445 (col.) Oct '57.

—— (man playing cello). Holiday 25: 42 (col.) Jan '59.
—— (piano, comic). Holiday 20: 208 Dec '56.
—— (playing piano). Natl. geog. 117: 31, 67 (col.) Jan '60.
—— (playing violin, comic). Holiday 18: 121 Sept '55.
—— (with violin). Travel 104: 68-9 Oct '55.
—— (woman playing guitar). Holiday 28: 16 Oct '60.
——, Basque. Natl. geog. 105: 161 (col.) Feb '54.
——, Persian. Natl. geog. 114: 39 (col.) Jl '58.
——, Puerto Rico (line drawing). Holiday 20: 85 Aug '56.
——, Santa as a. Holiday 12: 110-11 (col.) Dec '52.
musicians. Cooper: Con. ency. of music.
    Holiday 9: 62 Mar '51; 21: 194 May '57; 22: 121 Sept '57, 86 (col.) Oct '57; 24: 1 Sept '58.
    Jensen: The White House, p. 282.
—— (band). Holiday 11: 94 May '52.
—— (boy & girl, clarinets). Holiday 20: 113 Sept '56.
—— (boy & girl band). Holiday 20: 78 (col.) Dec '56.
—— (circus animals). Durant: Pict. hist. of Amer. circus, p. 157.
—— (circus band parade). Durant: Pict. hist. of Amer. circus, p. 148.
—— (comic). Holiday 20: 104 Sept '56; 21: 123, 126 Jan '57.
—— (15th cent.). Int. gr. soc.: Arts . . . p. 109 (col.).
—— (girls). Holiday 25: 188 Mar '59.
—— (girls, comic). Holiday 26: 1 Nov '59.
—— (guitars). Natl. geog. 101: 785 Je '52.
—— (home). Holiday 28: 4 Sept '60.
—— (jazz band). Holiday 18: 73 (col.) Sept '55.
—— (medieval). Int. gr. soc.: Arts . . . p. 61 (col.).
—— (middle ages). Durant: Pict. hist. of Amer. circus, p. 10.
—— (9th cent.). Durant: Pict. hist. of Amer. circus, p. 8.
—— (orchestra). Holiday 19: 78 (col.) Mar '56.
—— (playing instruments). Amer. heri., vol. 3 no. 1 p. 39 (col.) (fall '51).
    Holiday 9: 62-3 Mar '51; 24: 12-3 (col.) Nov '58.
    Natl. geog. 117: 30-1 (col.) Jan '60.
—— (shadowy). Holiday 23: 10 (col.) Ap '58.
—— (space travel cartoon). Holiday 23: 65 May '58.
—— (Toscanini). Holiday 18: 53-5 (part col.) Nov '55.
—— (violinists). Natl. geog. 117: 31 (col.) Jan '60.
—— (world group). Holiday 19: 10 (col.) Jan '56.
——, Africans. Natl. geog. 100: 270, 281 Aug '51.
——, Antarctica. Natl. geog. 116: 535 Oct '59.
——, Argentine gaucho. Natl. geog. 113: 332-3 (col.) Mar '58.
——, Bali. Natl. geog. 116: 810-11 (col.) Dec '59.

——, Bermuda. Holiday 23: 72 Je '58.
——, "Calypso" crewmen. Natl. geog. 113: 395 (col.) Mar '58.
——, Cambodia. Natl. geog. 117: 551 (col.) Ap '60.
——, Caribbean. Holiday 23: 195 (col.) Ap '58.
——, Colonial. Natl. geog. 106: 458 (col.) Oct '54.
——, Cuban (orchestra). Holiday 27: 57 Feb '60.
——, famous. Int. gr. soc.: Arts . . . p. 139 (col.)
——, French club. Holiday 28: 51 (col.) Aug '60.
——, German. Holiday 25: 8 Ap '59.
——, ghostly (Abbey theatre, Dublin). Holiday 6: 61 (col.) Dec '49.
——, Hawaii. Holiday 25: 178 (col.) Ap '59.
——, Hawaii (beach). Holiday 24: 53 (col.) Dec '58.
——, India. Natl. geog. 116: 852 (col.) Dec '59.
——, Jamaica (band). Holiday 26: 169 (col.) Oct '59.
——, Jamaica (calypso). Holiday 25: 61 (col.) Feb '59.
——, Jamaica (comic). Holiday 24: 122 (col.) Aug '58.
——, Majorca. Natl. geog. 111: 647 (col.) May '57.
——, Malaya. Natl. geog. 103: 219, 221 (col.) Feb '53.
——, mountain. Natl. geog. 102: 488 Oct '52.
——, Negro. See Negro musicians.
——, Nepal. Natl. geog. 112: 141 (col.) Jl '57.
——, night club. Holiday 21: 65 Feb '57.
——, Portugal. Disney: People & places, p. 52, 58 (col.).
——, restaurant. Holiday 20: 99 (col.) Oct '56.
——, Samoan. Disney: People & places, p. 145 (col.).
——, Switzerland. Natl. geog. 111: 785 (col.) Je '57.
——, Titanic boat. Amer. heri., vol. 7 no. 1 p. 51 (Dec '55).
——, Tyrol. Natl. geog. 100: 396 Sept '51.
——, Tyrolese miner (parade). Natl. geog. 99: 782 (col.) Je '51.
——, Vienna. Natl. geog. 115: 179, 182 (col.) Feb '59.
Musikvereinssaal (Vienna, int.). Travel 101: 12 Jan '54.
musketeer, French. Int. gr. soc.: Arts . . . p. 115 (col.).
Muskie, Edmund S. Cur. biog. p. 438 (1955).
Muslims (at prayer). Holiday 14: 56-7 Oct '53.
Mussert, Anton. Cur. biog. p. 621 (1942).
Mussolini, Benito. Cur. biog. p. 623 (1942).
Mussorgsky, Modese Petrovich (by Repin). Cooper: Con. ency. of music, p. 198.
mustache cup. See cup, mustache.
mustard box (17th cent. silver). Con. 133: III May '54.
mustard pot—porcelain (18th cent.). Con. 142: 11 Sept '58.
——, silver (1796). Con. ency. of ant., vol. 1, p. 153.

mustard pot, silver (Geo. III). Con. 141: XII Mar '58, XX Ap '58; 142: XII Sept '58, XLVI Nov '58, XII Dec '58, XXXIV Jan '59; 143: XVI May '59.
——, silver (Geo. IV). Con. 143: XLVII Mar '59, XXXIV Ap '59, XXXIV Je '59.
——, Staffordshire enamel. Con. ency. of ant., vol. 1, pl. 75.
Muttoni, Pietro (work of). Con. 144: 106 Nov '59.
muumuu (Hawaiian dress). Natl. geog. 118: 7, 24 (col.) Jl '60.
muzzle, ox. Rawson: Ant. pict. bk., p. 69.
"My fair lady" (stage setting). Int. gr. soc.: Arts . . . p. 145 (col.).
"My old Kentucky home" (Bardstown). Brooks: Growth of a nation, p. 141.
 Holiday 10: 9 Jl '51; 14: 89 Oct '53.
 Travel 101: 24 Feb '54.
Mycenae (Lion gate). See Lion gate at Mycenae.
—— (ruins & map). Ceram: March of arch., p. 41, 48.
Mycenaean artist (painting vase). Int. gr. soc.; Arts . . . p. 19 (col.).
Mydans, Carl Mayer. Cur. biog. p. 417 (1945).
Mydans, Shelley Smith. Cur. biog. p. 418 (1945).
Myer, Dillon Seymour. Cur. biog. p. 463 (1947).
Myers, Rev. C. Kilmer. Cur. biog. p. 290 (1960).
Myers, Francis J. Cur. biog. p. 448 (1949).
Myers, Reginald R. Holiday 12: 128 Jl '52.
Myerson, Mrs. Golda. Cur. biog. p. 396 (1950).
Mykonos (Greece). Holiday 15: 53 (col.) Je '54; 24: 69 Sept '58; 26: 23 Sept '59.
Myojin is. (Japan). Natl. geog. 105: 117-28 Jan '54.
Myrdal, Mrs. Alva. Cur. biog. p. 419 (1950).
Myrdal, Gunnar. Cur. biog. p. 424 (1946).
"Myron" (Athena, sculpture). Praeg.: Pict. ency., p. 133.
Mysore (India, festival parade). Natl. geog. 113: 707-10 (col.) May '58.
"Mystic marriage of Saint Catherine" (Pittoni). Con. 140: XLV Jan '58.
Mystic seaport (Conn.). Travel 104: 31 Sept '55.
mystic star (sym.). Lehner: Pict. bk. of sym., p. 66.
Mytens, Daniel (work of). Con. 126: 162-3 Dec '50.
Mytens, Jan (work of). Con. 139: 7 Mar '57.
mythology (sym.). Lehner: Pict. bk. of sym., p. 15, 26-33.

N

Naarden (island city, Holland). Natl. geog. 98: 777 Dec '50.
Nabarro, Sir Gerald. Cur. biog. p. 293 (1963).
Nabrit, James M., jr. Cur. biog. p. 335 (1961).
Nabrit, Samuel M. Cur. biog. p. 295 (1963).
Nabulsi, Suleiman. Cur. biog. p. 395 (1957).
Nadar (work of). Cooper: Con. ency. of music, p. 304.
Nade-Takara-Nusubi (sym.). Lehner: Pict. bk. of sym., p. 47.
Nadler, Marcus. Cur. biog. p. 440 (1955).
Naga folk dancers. Natl. geog. 117: 623 (col.) May '60.

Naga Hills dancers (India). Natl. geog. 107: 249 (col.) Feb '55.
Nagano, Adm. Osami. Cur. biog. p. 629 (1942).
Nagin Lake (Kashmir). Natl. geog. 114: 646-7 (col.) Nov '58.
Nag's Head (N.C., lighthouse). Travel 113: 48 Je '60.
Naguib, Mohammed. Cur. biog. p. 448 (1952).
Nahas, Mustafa. Cur. biog. p. 452 (1951).
Nahl, Arthur (work of). Amer. heri., vol. 1 no. 3 p. 47 (spring '50).
Nahl, Charles (work of). Amer. heri., vol. 10 no. 3 p. 36 (col.) (Ap '59).
 Brooks: Growth of a nation, p. 133.
Naidu, Sarojini. Cur. biog. p. 549 (1943).
Naidu funeral, Srimati Sarojini. Natl. geog. 105: 517 (col.) Ap '54.
Naigeon, Jean Claude (work of). Con. 137: XLIX Mar '56; 140: 70 Sept '57.
nail, horseshoe. Rawson: Ant. pict. bk., p. 54.
nail enamel bottle. Holiday 28: 20-1 (col.) Jl '60.
nail spike, railroad. See railroad spike.
Nailor, Gerald (work of). Natl. geog. 107: 372 (col.) Mar '55.
nails. Holiday 25: 107 May '59; 26: 15 Sept '59.
——, handwrought. Rawson: Ant. pict. bk., p. 21.
Nairobi (Kenya, Africa). Natl. geog. 97: 312 Mar '50.
—— (Government House). Holiday 25: 86 (col.) Ap '59.
Naish, Joseph Carrol. Cur. biog. p. 397 (1957).
Nakahodo dam. See dam, Nakahodo.
Nakhon-Wat (Cambodia). Int. pr. soc.: Arts . . . p. 51 (col.).
Naldini, Battista (work of). Con. 142: 197 Dec '58, 256 Jan '59.
Nam, IL. Cur. biog. p. 454 (1951).
name, town (Wales, longest in world). Travel 105: 41 Ap '56.
Nancy Hanks Lincoln monument. See Lincoln monument, Nancy Hanks.
Nandi (sacred bull). Holiday 19: 60 Je '56.
Nanking (China, winged lion). Praeg. pict. ency., p. 529.
Nantucket (Mass.). Holiday 10: 40-5 (part col.) Aug '51; 28: 12-3 (col.) Aug '60.
—— (harbor). Holiday 26: 16 Jl '59.
napkin, Colonial dinner (how used). Natl. geog. 106: 472 Oct '54.
Naples (Fla.). Holiday 20: 66 (col.) Dec '56.
Naples (Italy). Con. 145: XXV Je '60.
 Holiday 20: 98-103 (part col.) Oct '56.
 Labande: Naples, p. 37.
—— (harbor). Holiday 16: 8 Dec '54.
—— (map). Labande: Naples, frontis.
——, Bay of. Holiday 15: 29 Feb '54.
——, Gulf of. See Gulf or Naples.
Napoleon, Emperor Bonaparte. Amer. heri., vol. 7 no. 3 p. 11 (col.) (Ap '56); vol. 9 no. 2 p. 84 (Feb '58).
—— (statue). Con. 143: 227 Je '59.
 Holiday 25: 51 Jan '59.
 Travel 105: 42 Ap '56.
Napoleon, Louis. Amer. heri., vol. 11 no. 3 p. 19 (Ap '60).

Napoleon, Prince (visits Amer., Civil war). Amer. heri., vol. 8 no. 5 p. 66, 69, 79 (Aug '57).

Napoleon & Josephine's home. Holiday 11: 122 Mar '52.

"Napoleon in his study" (David). Natl. geog. 110: 647 (col.) Nov '56.

"Napoleon on board H.M.S. Bellerphon" (Eastlake). Con. 126: 137 Oct '50.

Napoleon's exile home (St. Helena). Travel 107: 46 Mar '57.

Napoleon's Waterloo memorial. Natl. geog. 113: 832 Je '58.

Napper, Richard. Con. 134: 208 Dec '54.

Narayan, Jaya Prakash. Cur. biog. p. 297 (1958).

Narcissus (sym.). Lehner: Pict. bk. of sym., p. 31.

narghile. See hookah.

Narragansett swamp fortress (attack). Amer. heri., vol. 10 no. 1 p. 75 (Dec '58).

Naseby, battle of. See battle of Naseby.

Nash, Joseph (work of). Con. 145: XL Ap '60.

Nash, Ogden. Cur. biog. p. 603 (1941).

Nash, Paul. Praeg.: Pict. ency., p. 499.

Nash, Philleo. Cur. biog. p. 315 (1962).

Nash, Walter. Cur. biog. p. 630 (1942); p. 299 (1958).

Nash auto. Holiday 15: 15 (col.) Mar '54, 30 (col.) Ap '54, 92 (col.) May '54.

Nashville (Tenn., cartoon). Holiday 9: 78 Mar '51.

—— (Parthenon). Travel 104: 14 Jl '55.

Nasmyth, Patrick (work of). Con. 126: 45 Aug '50; 132: XXII (col.) Jan '54.

Nason, John W. Cur. biog. p. 451 (1953).

Nassau (Bahama). Holiday 18: 79 (col.) Nov '55; 21: 31 (col.) Jan '57; 24: 42 (col.) Dec '58; 25: 112 (col.) May '59; 26: back cover (col.) Nov '59; 27: 39, 74-9 (col.) Mar '60, 53 (col.) May '60, 119 (col.) Je '60.
Natl. geog. 113: 158-81 (col.) Feb '58.

—— (beach). Holiday 14: 83 (col.) Nov '53; 16: 87 (col.) Dec '54; 17: back cover (col.) Mar '55; 20: 42 (col.) Nov '56; 21: 48 (col.) May '57; 23: 10 (col.) Je '58; 24: 122 (col.) Jl '58, 110 (col.) Aug '58; 26: 2 (col.) Jl '59; 28: 23 (col.) Sept '60, back cover (col.) Nov '60.

—— (beach picnic). Holiday 26: 26 (col.) Dec '59.

—— (harbor). Holiday 27: cover (col.) Mar '60.

—— (hotel).) Holiday 13: 128 Mar '53; 14: 6 Jl '53; 17: 97 Jan '55; 27: 178 Ap '60.

—— (Howard Johnson beach lodge). Holiday 25: 125 (col.) Feb '59.

—— (market scene). Holiday 26: 130 (col.) Sept '59.

—— (street). Holiday 7: 74 Feb '50; 13: 5 (col.) Jan '53.

—— (swimming pool). Holiday 17: 2 (col.) Jan '55.

Nasser, Gamal Abdel. Cur. biog. p. 484 (1954).

"Nassovy Proceres" (Delff). Con. 138: 17 Sept '56.

Nast, Peter. Holiday 15: 74 Jan '54.

Nast, Thomas (cartoon by). Amer. heri., vol.

9 no. 5 p. 90 (Aug '58).

—— (work of). Amer. heri., vol. 9 no. 4 p. 53 (Je '58).

——. See also cartoon, Thomas Nast.

Natchez, Miss. (by Audubon, 1822). Amer. heri., vol. 11 no. 1 p. 16-7 (col.) (Dec '59).

Nathan, George Jean. Cur. biog. p. 421 (1945).

Nathan, Robert R. Cur. biog. p. 605 (1941).

Nation, Carry. Amer. heri., vol. 9 no. 1 p. 52, 55 (Dec '57).

Natl. archives exhibition hall (Wash., D.C.). Natl. geog. 111: 68 (col.) Jan '57.

—— (int.). Face of Amer., p. 88-9 (col.).

Natl. Bur. of standards. Natl. geog. 100: 756-84 (part col.) Dec '51.

Natl. forests (map). Holiday 20: 89 Aug '56.

Natl. galleries of hist. & art (drawing by Smith). Amer. heri., vol. 7 no. 4 p. 40-3 (Je '56).

Natl. gallery (Wash., D.C.). Holiday 7: 106 (col.) Feb '50.

Natl. gallery of art (int.). Natl. geog. 117: 834 (col.) Je '60.

Natl. geog. soc. bldg. Natl. geog. 97: 674 May '50.

"Natl. lancers" of Boston (1855). Amer. heri., vol. 7 no. 5 p. 17 (col.) (Aug '56).

Natl. lawn tennis tournament (1880). Holiday 14: 70 (col.) Sept '53.

Natl. maritime museum (Greenwich, Eng.). Con. 132: 79 Nov '53.

Natl. monument (Utah). Natl. geog. 111: 546 (col.) Ap '57.

Natl. park (Nev.). Travel 113: 32 Jan '60.

—— (Rocky mt.). Travel 107: 52-4 Je '57.

——, Banff. See Banff natl. park.

Natl. park ranger. Travel 108: 15-7 Aug '57.

Natl. parks. Holiday 24: 36-45, 54-7 (part col.) Jl '58; 25: 38-9 (col.) Feb '59; 26: 46-52 (part col.) Jl '59.
Natl. geog. 113: 588-662 (part col.) May '58.
Travel 106: 23-5 Dec '56.

—— (Cal.). Natl. geog. 116: 148-87 (part col.) Aug '59.

—— (Cal., map). Natl. geog. 116: 152 Aug '59.

—— (Canada). Travel 107: 12-5 May '57; 114: 19 Jl '60.

——. See also Great Smoky Mt.; park.

Natl. safety council (sym.). Lehner: Pict. bk. of sym., p. 89.

Natl. wildlife refuge (map). Natl. geog. 118: 148 (col.) Jl '60.

—— (Red Rock Lakes). Natl. geog. 118: 136 (col.) Jl '60.

"The Nativity". Con. 143: VIII Mar '59.

"Nativity" (alabaster, 15th cent.). Con. 145: LXIII Ap '60.

"The Nativity" (altar panel). Praeg. pict. ency., p. 239 (col.).

Nativity (sym.). Lehner: Pict. bk. of sym., p. 50.

"The Nativity" (Bellini). Con. 145: 55 Mar '60.

—— (Botticelli). Con. ency. of ant., vol. 1, pl. 152.

—— (Bouts). Praeg. pict. ency. p. 264 (col.).

—— (David). Con. 143: 199 May '59.

"The Nativity" (de Castro, sculpture). Con. 136: 233-7 Jan '56.

"The Nativity" (di Pietro). Con. 141: 187 May '58.

—— (Durer). Praeg. pict. ency., p. 286 (col.).

—— (Flanders). Natl. geog. 110: 648 (col.) Nov '56.

—— (Goes). Praeg. pict. ency., p. 303.

—— (Sano di Pietro). Con. 141: 45 Mar '58.

—— (Santi). Con. 132: LIX Sept '53.

—— (Schongauer). Praeg. pict. ency., p. 241 (col.).

—— (Tintoretto). Con. 126: 49 Aug '50.

Nattier, Jean Marc (work of). Con. 133: 12-3 Mar '54, XXXII, 235 Je '54; 136: XVII (col.), 139 Nov '55; 138: LXXV Jan '57; 141: 41 (col.) Mar '58; 143: IV, 262, 273 Je '59.

Natural bridge (Grand Canyon). Natl. geog. 107: 618 May '55.

—— (Ky). Travel 113: 39 Mar '60.

—— (Utah). Holiday 23: 159 May '58.

—— (Va.). Holiday 6: 129 Oct '49; 12: 37 Nov '52; 13: 80 Je '53; 14: 117 Jl '53, 86 Sept '53; 15: 132 Ap '54, 93 Je '54; 16: 4 Sept '54; 18: 54 Sept '55; 20: 5 Aug '56, 83 Sept '56; 21: 164 May '57; 22: 128 Sept '57; 23: 146 May '58; 24: 118 Aug '58; 27: 120 Mar '60.

Jordan: Hammond's pict. atlas, p. 171 (col.).

—— hotel. Holiday 13: 80 Je '53; 15: 132 Ap '54, 93 Je '54.

—— natl. monument. Natl. geog. 101: 733 (col.) Je '52.

natural science (sym.). Lehner: Pict. bk. of sym., p. 15.

Naumburg cathedral (choir). Praeg. pict. ency., p. 236.

nautilus (Augsburg). Con. 145: 78 Ap '60.

nautilus cup (silver gilt shell). Con. ency. of ant., vol. 3, pl. 33.

—— (Dutch 17th cent.). Con. 133: 84 Ap '54.

—— (16th cent.). Con. 133: 151 May '54.

nautilus, eagle (Frick, 1600). Con. 145: 76-7 Ap '60.

"Nautilus", U.S.S. See U.S.S. Nautilus.

"Nautilus" submarine (North Pole). Natl. geog. 115: 2-19 (part col.) Jan '59.

Navajo bridge (Arizona). Natl. geog. 106: 542 (col.) Oct '54.

Navajo Indians. See Indians, Navajo.

Navajo natl. monument. Travel 107: 35 Mar '57.

"The Naval guests" (Flameng). Con. 143: XXV Mar '59.

naval monument (Wash., D.C.). Amer. heri., vol. 10 no. 2 p. 24 (Feb '59).

naval vessel (LST). Natl. geog. 97: 198 Feb '50.

naval war map (1812). Amer. heri., vol. 6 no. 3 p. 59 (col.) (Ap '55).

Navarre, Henri E. Cur. biog. p. 453 (1953).

navigation (sym.). Lehner: Pict. bk. of sym., p. 15.

"The Navigator" (carved wood). Amer. heri., vol. 1 no. 2 p. 69 (winter '50); vol. 2 no. 2 p. 32 (col.) (winter '51).

navigator (sights along cross-staff). Natl. geog. 110: 9 (col.) Jl '56.

navigators & charts. Natl. geog. 111: 190-1

(col.) Feb '57.

navy boat, U.S. See U.S. navy boat.

navy cadets (Denmark). See cadets, navy (Denmark).

navy floating dry dock, U.S. See U.S. navy floating dry dock.

navy men, Chinese. Natl. geog. 111: 334 (col.) Mar '57.

navy men. See also sailor; U.S. navy.

navy ships. See U.S. navy ships.

Naxos (Greece). Holiday 24: 66-7 (col.) Sept '58.

Nay, Ernst Wilhelm (work of). Praeg. pict. ency., p. 511 (col.).

Naysmith, Alexander (work of). Con. 141: 103 Ap '58.

Nazare (Portugal). Disney: People & places, p. 68 (col.).

Holiday 19: 35 (col.) Jan '56; 26: 106 (col.) Aug '59.

Natl. geog. 118: 628-9, 645 (col.) Nov '60.

Nazareth. Natl. geog. 102: 836 Dec '52.

Nazimuddin, Khwaja. Cur. biog. p. 450 (1949).

Ndebele people (Africa). Holiday 25: 122 Ap '59.

Neagle, Anna. Cur. biog. p. 424 (1945).

Nebel, Carl (work of). Amer. heri., vol. 6 no. 4 p. 21 (col.) (Je '55).

Nebo, Mount. See Mount Nebo.

Nebraska. Holiday 19: 102-11 (part col.) May '56.

Travel 106: 16 Sept '56; 109: 29-31 Je '58.

nebula. Natl. geog. 115: 674-8 (col.) May '59.

—— (sky map). Natl. geog. 98: 406, 415 Sept '50.

——, Andromeda. See Andromeda nebula.

——, crab. Natl. geog. 115: 671 (col.) May '57.

neck arteries. Gray's anatomy p. 581.

neck pad, horse. Rawson: Ant. pict. bk., p. 69.

Neckar river (near Heidelberg). Natl. geog. 115: 760-1 Je '59.

Travel 107: inside cover Je '57.

necklace. Con. 129: XXXIII Ap '52, XI, LIX Je '52; 134: XLVII Dec '54; 136: XXXIX Dec '55; 137: LVIX Je '56; 139: XXVII May '57; 141: 1 Ap '58.

Holiday 7: 79 May '50; 10: 59 (col.) Aug '51, 7 (col.) Oct '51; 11: 25 (col.) Mar '52, 7 (col.) Jl '52; 12: 65 (col.) Sept '52; 13: 7 (col.) May '53; 14: 31 (col.) Jl '53, 61 (col.) Aug '53, 15 (col.) Sept '53, 71 (col.) Nov '53; 21: 7 (col.) Jan '57, 97 (col.) Mar '57.

Natl. geog. 98: 791, 795 (col.) Dec '50.

—— (emerald). Holiday 7: 15 (col.) Mar '50; 8: 63 (col.) Jl '50.

—— (mayor's badge of office). Con. 141: 88 Ap '58.

—— (19th cent.). Con. ency. of ant., vol. 1, p. 95.

—— (pearl). Amer. heri., vol. 10 no. 3 p. 52 (col.) (Ap '59).

—— (ruby). Holiday 8: 71 (col.) Nov '50.

—— (sapphire). Holiday 6: 5 (col.) Jl '49, 7 (col.) Sept '49.

—— (18th cent.). Con. 144: XXX Sept '59.

——, antique. Con. 135: VII, IX May '55; 138: XV Jan '57; 139: 124 Ap '57; 140: 61 Sept '57, LI Nov '57, 182 Dec '57; 142: LV Dec

'58; 143: 192 May '59; 145: XXIII Ap '60.
——, antique ivory. Con. 140: 15 Sept '57.
——, ceremonial antique. Con. 144: 85 Nov '59.
——, Geo. III (diamond). Con. 145: V Mar '60, 126 Ap '60.
——, Louis XV. Con. 138: XXV Dec '56.
necklace pendant, antique. Con. 140: 115 Nov '57.
——, Italian. Con. 140: 258 Jan '58.
necromancy (Taoist sym.). Lehner: Pict. bk. of sym., p. 46, 67.
needle (sym.). Lehner: Pict. bk. of sym., p. 91.
——, carpet-rag. See carpet-rag needle.
——, fish net knitting. Rawson: Ant. pict. bk., p. 75.
needle room (Scotland). Con. 145: 70 (col.) Ap '60.
needlebook, enamel. Con. ency. of ant., vol. 1, pl. 73.
needlecase, antique. Con. 133: LV Je '54.
——, Louis XV. Con. 133: 43 Mar '54.
Needles highway (S.D.). Jordan: Hammond's pict. atlas, p. 106 (col.).
needlework, antique. Con. ency. of ant., vol. 1, p. 211-16, 219-21, pl. 119-22.
——, Elizabethan (panels). Con. 145: 141 May '60.
needlework carpet. See carpet, needlework.
needlework caskets, Stuart. Con. 145: XXXIII Ap '60.
needlework panel. See panel, needlework.
needlework picture. Con. 142: 251 Jan '59.
—— (Harrison). Con. 143: 264 Je '59.
needlework rug, antique. Con. 145: XLII May '60.
——, French (19th cent.). Con. 145: LXIV Je '60.
——, Georgian. Con. 129: LII Ap '52.
——, Queen Anne. Con. 145: XXX Mar '60.
——. See also carpet, needlework; embroidery; rug.
Neely, Matthew M. Cur. biog. p. 422 (1950).
Nef (Neuremberg, Zur Linden). Con. 145: 78 Ap '60.
Nefer (sym.). Lehner: Pict. bk., of sym., p. 26.
Nefertari, Queen (Egyptian tomb painting). Praeg. pict. ency., p. 116 (col.).
Nefertiti, Queen (Egyptian). Praeg. pict. ency., p. 122 (col.).
—— (bust). Holiday 11: 124 May '52.
"Negress au Madras Rouge" (Delacroix). Con. 133: 260 Je '54.
Negrin, Juan. Cur. biog. p. 427 (1945).
Negro (asleep, market stand). Natl. geog. 113: 167 (col.) Feb '58.
—— (at fireplace). Natl. geog. 105: 463 (col.) Ap '54.
—— (beating drum). Holiday 7: 108 Mar '50. Natl. geog. 113: 195 (col.) Feb '58.
—— (boat, fish). Natl. geog. 105: 352 (col.) Mar '54.
—— (carrying thatch). Natl. geog. 111: 611 May '57.
—— (corn field). Natl. geog. 105: 321 (col.) Mar '54.
—— (hanging from pole). Amer. heri., vol. 10 no. 4 p. 46 (Je '59).
—— (haystack). Amer. heri. vol. 11 no. 5 p.

16-7 (col.) (Aug '60).
—— (Langston Hughes) poet. Holiday 27: 75 (col.) Je '60.
—— (mule hitched to small wagon). Holiday 5: 120 (col.) Mar '49.
—— (night club). Holiday 10: 96 Sept '51.
—— (party). Holiday 10: 60-1 (col.) Oct '51.
—— (picking cotton). Brooks: Growth of a nation, p. 104.
—— (playing fiddle for dance). Amer. heri., vol. 5 no. 3 p. 13 (col.) (Aug '60).
—— (playing guitar). Holiday 25: 110 (col.) May '59.
—— (playing musical instrument). Holiday 7: 8 May '50.
—— (playing violin). Amer. heri., vol. 11 no. 5 p. 19 (col.) (Aug '60).
—— (seated, kitchen). Natl. geog. 109: 447 (col.) Ap '56.
—— (serving drinks). Holiday 22: 55 (col.) Dec '57.
—— (singing). Holiday 11: 99 May '52.
—— (tobacco field). Natl. geog. 105: 311 (col.) Mar '54.
——(washing clothes in kettle). Rawson: Ant. pict. bk., p. 13.
—— (watermelons). Natl. geog. 106: 246 (col.) Aug '54.
—— (with crab). Natl. geog. 103: 309 Mar '53.
——, Africa (rowing boat). Holiday 25: 143 (col.) Ap '59.
——, Haiti. Holiday 7: 98, 102-3 (col.) Mar '50.
——, Jamaica (basket on head). Natl. geog. 105: 361 Mar '54.
——, Jamaica (on pack mule). Natl. geog. 105: 360 Mar '54.
Negro art. Holiday 19: 115 (col.) Mar '56.
Negro artist (painting). Holiday 10: 152 Nov '51.
——, French Congo (painting). Praeg. pict. ency., p. 554 (col.).
Negro band. See band, Negro.
Negro bootblack. Natl. geog. 109: 206 Feb '56.
Negro boy. Holiday 26: 130 (col.) Sept '59.
—— (baseball game). Natl. geog. 118: 802 (col.) Dec '60.
—— (cooking outdoors). Amer. heri., vol. 9 no. 3 p. 40 (col.) (Ap '58).
—— (horse groom). Natl. geog. 106: 709 (col.) Nov '54.
—— (seated). Natl. geog. 113: 188 Feb '58.
—— (butler). Holiday 10: 39, 78 (col.) Nov '51, 97 Dec '51. Natl. geog. 109: 477 (col.) Ap '56.
—— (butler, colonial). Holiday 28: 55 (col.) Dec '60.
Negro child. Holiday 18: 51 Aug '55; 22: 48 Jl '57.
—— (doctor's office). Brooks: Growth of a nation, p. 274.
Negro cook (colonial kitchen). Natl. geog. 109: 447 (col.) Ap '56.
Negro craftsmen (at work, primitive). Int. gr. soc.: Arts . . . p. 17 (col.).
Negro funeral procession. Holiday 11: 44-5 Mar '52.

Negro girl (art). Holiday 20: 68 (col.) Sept '56.

Negro jazz orchestra. Int. gr. soc.: Arts . . . p. 143 (col.).

Negro maid. Holiday 12: 60 (col.) Oct '52.
—— (sweeps hearth). Natl. geog. 109: 463 (col.) Ap '56.

Negro man (James Farmer). U.S. News & world report, p. 28 Aug 31, 1964.
—— (Bill Robinson). Cur. biog. p. 720 (1941).
—— (Carl T. Rowan). Cur. biog. p. 371 (1958).
U.S. News & world report, p. 14 Aug. 17, 1964.
—— (Willie Smith, "The Lion"). Holiday 27: 81 Je '60.

Negro man. Natl. geog. 97: 564 (col.) May '50; 101: 156 (col.) Feb '52.
—— (carrying tray). Holiday 23: 50 (col.) Feb '58.
—— (head). Holiday 12: 103 (col.) Nov '52; 28: 81 (col.) Oct '60.
—— (head, smoking). Natl. geog. 113: 198 (col.) Feb '58.
—— (leaning against barn). Amer. heri., vol. 11 no. 5 p. 18 (col.) (Aug '60).
—— (seated). Holiday 25: 34 Ap '59.
—— (seated, eating). Natl. geog. 105: 289 Mar '54.
—— (serving at table). Natl. geog. 103: 290 (col.) Mar '53.

Negro man & woman. Brooks: Growth of a nation, p. 292.

Negro mine driller. Natl. geog. 113: 580 Ap '54.

Negro mine workers (Johannesburg). Holiday 18: 47 Aug '55.

Negro minister. Holiday 26: 41 Sept '59.

Negro musicians. Holiday 10: 61 (col.) Oct '51; 11: 44 Mar '52; 19: 40-1 Je '56; 27: 81 Je '60
Natl. geog. 103: 176 (col.) Feb '53.

Negro of Bapenda tribe (Congo). Int. gr. soc.: Arts . . . p. 183 (col.).

Negro porter. Holiday 14: 68 (col.) Aug '53.

Negro slave. See slave, negro.

Negro traffic police. Holiday 22: 171 Dec '57.

Negro voodoo. Holiday 10: 62-3 Nov '51.

Negro table waiter. Holiday 14: 19, 126 (col.) Dec '53.
Natl. geog. 103: 290 (col.) Mar '53; 113: 177, 180 (col.) Feb '58.

Negro waiter (cocktails). Holiday 10: 2 Sept '51.
—— (head, tray). Holiday 21: 112 May '57.
—— (liquor tray). Holiday 10: 81 Aug '51.
—— (service, bicycle). Natl. geog. 113: 37 Jan '58.

Negro woman. Holiday 28: 208 (col.) Nov '60.
Natl. geog. 113: 164 (col.) Feb '58.
—— (cook, children). Natl. geog. 112: 541 Oct '57.
—— (cooking). Natl. geog. 113: 538 (col.) Ap '58.
—— (grinding snuff). Holiday 18: 51 Aug '55.
—— (head). Holiday 11: 99 May '52.
—— (head, laughing). Natl. geog. 113: 198 (col.) Feb '58.
—— (in row boat). Amer. heri., vol. 11 no.

5 p. 23 (col.) (Aug '60).
—— (laughing). Holiday 18: 51 Aug '55.
——, Caribbean. Holiday 26: 159 (col.) Oct '59.

Negro woman & white child. Amer. heri., vol. 8 no. 1 p. 8 (col.) (Dec '56).

Negro women (flower arranging). Natl. geog. 103: 292 (col.) Mar '53.
—— (hat stand). Natl. geog. 113: 171 (col.) Feb '58.
—— (seated). Natl. geog. 113: 181 (col.) Feb '58.
——, Jamaica (making hats). Natl. geog. 105: 354 (col.) Mar '54.

Negroes. Brooks: Growth of a nation, p. 151-3.
Holiday 5: 48-9, 54-5, 60, 98-100 (col.) Mar '49, 111 (col.) Ap '49; 7: 84, 87-8 Feb '50.
Travel 109: 50 Jan '58.
—— (baskets on heads). Natl. geog. 113: 198 (col.) Feb '58.
—— (cotton field). Amer. heri., vol. 6 no. 3 p. 4-5 (col.) (Ap '55).
—— (dancers, comic). Holiday 16: inside cover (col.) Aug '54.
—— (dancing). Amer. heri., vol. 8 no. 6 p. 20 (col.) (Oct '57).
Holiday 23: 77 (col.) Mar '58.
—— (dancing at cabin). Amer. heri., vol. 2 no. 1 p. 44-5 (col.) (fall '50).
—— (evening dress, party). Holiday 10: 61 (col.) Oct '51.
—— (goats, on boat). Natl. geog. 113: 167 (col.) Feb '58.
—— (Harlem, N.Y.). Holiday 27: 74-81 Je '60.
—— (heads). Holiday 13: 91 (col.) Jan '53.
—— (in field). Amer. heri., vol. 7 no. 6 p. 100 (Oct '56).
—— (in war 1863). Amer. heri., vol. 9 no. 4 p. 53 (Je '58).
—— (load sugar cane). Natl. geog. 105: 355 (col.) Mar '54.
—— (playing instruments). Holiday 9: 98 (col.) Mar '51.
—— (playing instruments). See also Negro musicians.
—— (row boat). Natl. geog. 112: 62 (col.) Jl '57.
—— (running from mob). Amer. heri., vol. 10 no. 4 p. 47 (Je '59).
—— (saw limestone blocks). Natl. geog. 105: 226 Feb '54.
—— (shred sisal). Natl. geog. 105: 339 (col.) Mar '54.
—— (spongers). Natl. geog. 113: 194 (col.) Feb '58.
—— ("Uncle Tom's Cabin"). Amer. heri., vol. 6 no. 6 p. 28-33 (Oct '55).
——, Africa. Holiday 25: 64-74 (part col.) Ap '59.
——, Africa (fishermen). Natl. geog. 113: 384 (col.) Mar '58.
——, Bahamas. Natl. geog. 113: 194 (col.) Feb '58.
——, Miss. Holiday 6: 103 (col.) Nov '49.
——, Timbuktu. Natl. geog. 112: 66 (col.) Jl '57.
——, Trinidad. Natl. geog. 103: 42-3, 47-56, 65 (part col.) Jan '53.
——. See also name of Negro.

Nehru, Braj Kumar. Cur. biog. p. 297 (1963).

Nehru, Pandit Jawaharlal (India). Cur. biog. p. 606 (1941); p. 469 (1948).

Nehru, Prime minister (India). Natl. geog. 117: 620 (col.) May '60; 118: 471 (col.) Oct '60.

Neill, Alexander Sutherland. Cur. biog. p. 337 (1961).

Neill, Bishop Stephen Charles. Cur. biog. p. 291 (1960).

Neilson, Frances Fullerton. Cur. biog. p. 441 (1955).

Neith (goddess, statue). Ceram: March of arch., p. 146.

Neithardt, Mathis Gothardt (work of). Praeg. pict. ency., p. 9, 285 (col.).

"Nell Gwyn". Con. 126: 33-7 Aug '50.

Nelles, Vice Adm. Percy Walker. Cur. biog. p. 491 (1944).

Nellie Bly. See Bly, Nellie.

Nelms, G. H. Natl. geog. 115: 825 Je '59.

Nelson, Adm. Viscount (Abbott). Con. 135: 179 May '55.

Nelson, Admiral (bust). Holiday 23: 41 Feb '58.

Nelson, Byron. Cur. biog. p. 429 (1945).

Nelson, Donald M. Cur. biog. p. 609 (1941).

Nelson, Gaylord. Cur. biog. p. 293 (1960).

Nelson, Mr. & Mrs. Gaylord. Holiday 27: 84 Je '60.

Nelson, Harriet. Cur. biog. p. 452 (1949).

Nelson, Lord. Con. 142: 32-3 Sept '58. Holiday 8: 79 (col.) Dec '50.

—— (bust). Con. 142: 32 Sept '58.

—— (statue). Travel 105: 13 Feb '56.

Nelson monument (London). Travel 107: 27 Je '57.

Nelson's flagship, Admiral. See ship, Nelson's flagship.

Nelson, Ozzie. Cur. biog. p. 452 (1949).

Nenni, Pietro. Cur. biog. p. 464 (1947).

Nepal, King & Queen of (coronation). Natl. geog. 112: 138-52 (part col.) Jl '57.

Nepal. Holiday 21: 68-73 (col.) May '57. Natl. geog. 97: 3-39 (col.) Jan '50; 108: 586, 588, 590-609 (col.) Nov '55; 117: 360-405 (col.) Mar '60. Travel 106: 41-3 Sept '56.

—— (map). Natl. geog. 97: 4 Jan '50; 117: 363 (col.) Mar '60.

Nepalese bride. Natl. geog. 97: 9 (col.) Jan '50.

Nepalese man. Natl. geog. 97: 248 Feb '50.

Nepalese soldier. Holiday 24: 76 Nov '58.

Nepalese women. Natl. geog. 97: 33 (col.) Jan '50.

Nephertari's tomb (entrance). Ceram: March of arch., p. 143 (col.).

Neptune. Holiday 8: 58 Oct '50.

"Neptune" (Pajou, terracotta). Con. 140: 6 Sept '57.

Neptune (head, sculpture). Labande: Naples, p. 137.

—— (sym.). Lehner: Pict. bk. of sym., p. 31.

Neptune, Father (cartoon). Amer. heri., vol. 9 no. 6 p. 92 (Oct '58).

Neptune, King. See King Neptune & Queen.

Neptune, Temple of. See Temple of Neptune.

"Neptune & Glaucus". (Bernini, sculpture). Con. 126: 133 Oct '50.

"Neptune's banquet" (Zuffi, mural). Holiday

13: 2 (col.) Je '53.

Neptune's trident (sym.). Lehner: Pict. bk. of sym., p. 95.

"Nereid on a panther" (fresco). Labande: Naples, p. 105.

Nerina, Nadia. Cur. biog. p. 399 (1957).

Nerly, F. (work of). Con. 145: LVII Je '60.

Nervi, Pier Luigi. Cur. biog. p. 300 (1958). Holiday 27: 51 Ap '60.

nervous system. Gray's anatomy, p. 737-1015

Nesbitt, Cathleen. Cur. biog. p. 460 (1956).

Nesmeianov, Aleksandr N. Cur. biog. p. 302 (1958).

nest, bird (sym.). Lehner: Pict. bk. of sym., p. 89.

Nestingen, Ivan A. Cur. biog. p. 317 (1962).

net, camel cargo (Pushtun woman). Natl. geog. 117: 83 (col.) Jan '60.

——, fish. See fish net.

—— (, gill (fish caught). Natl. geog. 112: 157 (col.) Aug '57.

——, shad fish. Rawson: Ant. pict. bk., p. 75.

Netherlands. See Holland.

"Netley Abbey by moonlight" (Constable). Con. 133: 119 Ap '54.

Netscher, Constantine (work of). Con 142: 57 Sept '58.

Netsuke, antique Japanese. Con. 135: 151-5 May '55; 144: XXXII Nov '59.

Netsuke carvings. Con. 138: LII Jan '57; 144: XXXII Nov '59.

Neuberger, Maurine B. Cur. biog. p. 339 (1961).

Neuberger, Richard L. Cur. biog. p. 443 (1955).

Neuberger, Sen. & Mrs. Richard L. Holiday 25: 72 May '59.

the Neue Wache (Berlin). Praeg. pict. ency., p. 381.

Neuenstein (castle-hotel, Ger.). Travel 103: 24 Ap '55.

Neumann, Balthasar (architecture). Praeg. pict. ency., p. 367.

Neuschwanstein castle. See Castle Neuschwanstein.

Neutra, Richard J. Cur. biog. p. 466 (1947); p. 341 (1961).

Nevada. Holiday 17: 26-35 (part col.) Feb '55. Jordan: Hammond's pict. atlas, p. 183 (col.). Travel 101: 36-7 Feb '54.

—— (proposed natl. park). Travel 113: 32 Jan '60.

Nevill, Sir Henry. Con. 139: 7 Mar '57.

Neville, John. Cur. biog. p. 317 (1959).

Neville, Richard (Romney). Con. 134: LVII Sept '54.

Neville, Sir Robert A.R. Cur. biog. p. 455 (1953).

New Amsterdam (N.Y.). Brooks: Growth of a nation, p. 48.

—— (1653). Amer. heri., vol. 10 no. 1 p. 9 (col.) (Dec '58).

New Archangel. Amer. heri., vol. 11 no. 3 p. 7 (Ap '60).

New Canaan houses (Conn.). Holiday 12: 48-53 (col.) Aug '52.

"New Cardinal" (Brunery). Con. 139: XXXV May '57.

New Castle (Del.). Holiday 17: 104-5 Mar '55.

New Delhi (India). Natl. geog. 118: 466-7, 470-1 (col.) Oct '60.
—— **(mosque).** Travel 111: 18 Jan '59.
New England. Holiday 18: 34-47 (part col.) Jl '55.
Natl. geog. 98: 143-68 (part col.) Aug '50; 99: 564-602 (part col.) May '51; 107: 734 Je '55.
—— **(early illus. by Low).** Amer. heri., vol. 6 no. 4 p. 56-9 (Je '55).
—— **(map).** Natl. geog. 98: 145 Aug '50; 99: 569 May '51.
New England coast (map, 1616). Natl. geog. 111: 614-5 May '57.
New England primer (illus., 1727). Amer. heri., vol. 8 no. 1 p. 121 (Dec '56).
New Guinea. Holiday 8: 73, 78 Dec '50.
Natl. geog. 100: 662-88 (part col.) Nov '51; 103: 422-88 (part col.) Ap '53; 108: 438-86 (part col.) Oct '55.
—— **(jungle girls).** Natl. geog. 99: 355 (col.) Mar '51.
—— **(man, head).** Int. gr. soc.: Arts . . . p. 183 (col.).
—— **(map).** Natl. geog. 108: 443 Oct '55; 116: 777 Dec '59.
—— **(men).** Natl. geog. 97: 248-9 Feb '50.
—— **(men & women).** Natl. geog. 100: 662-5, 669-88 (col.) Nov '51; 103: 423-88 (part col.) Ap '53; 116: 774-85 (part col.) Dec '59.
—— **(native houses).** Natl. geog. 100: adv. p. 36, 686 (col.). Nov '51.
—— **(Tambaran house).** Praeg. pict. ency., p. 555 (col.).
—— **(thatched temple).** Natl. geog. 99: 351 (col.) Mar '51.
—— **(warriors).** Natl. geog. 112: 588-9 (col.) Nov '57.
New Guinea hut. Holiday 28: 61 (col.) Oct '60.
New Guinea pile-dwelling. Int. gr. soc.: Arts . . . p. 11 (col.).
New Guinea wood carving. Holiday 28: 66 (col.) Oct '60.
New Hampshire. Holiday 8: 56-9 (part col.) Sept '50; 10: 34-45 (part col.) Sept '51; 18: 41, 43 (col.) Jl '55.
Natl. geog. 107: 766-7 (col.) Je '55.
Travel 106: 33-5 Oct '56.
—— **(colonial homes).** Face of Amer., p. 174-5 (col.).
—— **(fall season).** Face of Amer., p. 110-11 (col.).
—— **(map).** Holiday 10: 36 (col.) Sept '51.
New Hebrides is. Natl. geog. 107: 78-92 (part col.) Jan '55.
—— **(dancers).** Natl. geog. 99: 353 (col.) Mar '51; 107: 81, 83 (col.) Jan '55.
New Hebrides mask. Int. gr. soc.: Arts . . . p. 185 (col.).
New Ireland masks. Praeg. pict. ency., p. 556 (col.).
New Japan hotel. See hotel, New Japan.
New Jersey. Holiday 12: 90-9 (part col.) Aug '52.
Natl. geog. 117: 2-45 (col.) Jan '60.
—— **(map).** Natl. geog. 102: 5 Jl '52; 117: 10-11 (col.) Jan '60.
Travel 102: 38 Aug '54.
New Mexico. Holiday 11: 34-47 (part col.) Feb

'52; 13: 86 (col.) Ap '53, 22 (col.) Je '53; 14: 142 (col.) Jl '53; 15: 147 (col.) Je '54; 16: 85 (col.) Sept '54.
Jordan: Hammond's pict. atlas, p. 120-27 (col.).
Natl. geog. 112: 114-36 (part col.) Jl '57.
Travel 101: 12 Feb '54; 105: 17-8 Jan '56.
—— **(state parks).** Travel 109: 19-23 Mar '58.
—— **(way station).** Face of Amer., p. 64-5 (col.).
New Orleans. Brooks: Growth of a nation, p. 93.
Holiday 9: 106 Mar '51; 23: 82-7 (part col.) Mar '58.
Jordan: Hammond's pict. atlas, p. 82-3 (col.).
Natl. geog. 103: 144-84 (part col.) Feb '53; 118: 712-16 (col.) Nov '60.
Travel 102: cover Aug '54.
—— **(aerial view).** Natl. geog. 99: 724-5 Je '51; 103: 146-7 Feb '53.
—— **(Antoine's restaurant).** Travel 110: 23 Aug '58.
—— **(French market).** Natl. geog. 117: 248 (col.) Feb '60.
—— **(harbor).** Amer. heri., vol. 16 no. 6 p. 15 (col.) (Oct '57).
—— **(Mardi Gras).** Holiday 25: 95 (col.) Feb '59.
—— **(St. Louis cathedral).** Travel 114: 27 Sept '60.
——, **battle of.** See battle of New Orleans.
New Providence Is. (map). Natl. geog. 113: 153 Feb '58.
"New Salem" state park (Ill.). Travel 103: 15 Je '55.
"New year morning in a Chelsea studio" (Munnings). Con. 144: 123 Nov '59.
New year's eve (sym.). Lehner: Pict. bk. of sym., p. 54.
"New year's love court" (Laotian). Natl. geog. 99: 485 Ap '51.
New York City. Amer. heri., vol. 5 no. 1 cover, 8-59 (part col.) (fall '53).
Holiday 5: all the issue Ap '49; 10: 46-55 (part col.) Sept '51; 13: 64-5 Mar '53; 20: 90-5 Sept '56; 23: 90-5 Je '58; 26: 48-79, 82-95 (part col.) Oct '59.
Natl. geog. 99: 714-5 (col.) Je '51; 106: 774-813 (part col.) Dec '54; 118: 780, 782-811 (col.) Dec '60.
—— **(aerial view, 1850).** Amer. heri., vol. 5 no. 1 p. 13 (fall '53); vol. 10 no. 6 p. 26-7 (col.) (Oct '59).
Natl. geog. 104: 732 (col.) Dec '53.
—— **(Bemelman's drawings).** Holiday 26: 65-71 (col.) Oct '59.
—— **(Christmas).** See Christmas (N.Y. City).
—— **(City College stadium).** Holiday 23: 94-5 Je '58.
—— **(city hall, Kossuth's reception).** Amer. heri., vol. 6 no. 2 p. 61 (col.) (winter '55).
—— **(1848).** Amer. heri., vol. 5 no. 1 p. 56 (col.) (fall '53).
—— **(1850).** Amer. heri. vol. 8 no. 5 p. 12-3 (col.) (Aug '57).
—— **(1854).** Amer. heri., vol. 8 no. 5 p. 90-1 (Aug '57).
—— **(Federal Hall).** Amer. heri., vol. 7 no. 3 p. 29 (Ap '56).

New York City. (fog). Holiday 23: 56-7 Feb '58.
—— (harbor). Natl. geog. 106: 773-813 (part col.) Dec '54; 115: 832-41 Je '59. Travel 105: 62 Feb '56.
—— (harbor, air view). Natl. geog. 111: 200-1 Feb '57.
—— (harbor, 1828-50). Amer. heri., vol. 8 no. 5 p. 16-23 (col.) (Aug '57).
—— (harbor, 1847). Amer. heri., vol. 5 no. 1 p. 18 (col.) (fall '53).
—— (harbor, 1880). Amer. heri., vol. 7 no. 6 p. 112 (Oct '56).
—— (harbor, 1890). Holiday 12: 68 Sept '52.
—— (harbor, map). Natl. geog. 115: 839 Je '59.
—— (harbor, 1905). Amer. heri., vol. 6 no. 1 p. 6-7 (col.) (fall '54).
—— (harbor, 1907). Amer. heri., vol. 6 no. 4 p. 45 (Je '55).
—— (harbor, welcome to Greely). Amer. heri., vol. 11 no. 4 p. 105 (Je '60).
—— (Lever bldg.). Praeg. pict. ency., p. 436.
—— (Manhattan, sunset). Natl. geog. 106: 793 (col.). Dec '54.
—— (Museum of modern art). See art, Museum of modern (N.Y.).
—— (night). Holiday 12: 42-52 (col.) Dec '52; 23: 15 May '58.
Natl. geog. 110: 572-3 Nov '56.
—— (park). Face of Amer., p. 86-7 (col.).
—— (playgrounds). Holiday 10: 46-7 Aug '51.
—— (Public library). Holiday 23: 39 Mar '58.
—— (restaurants). Holiday 26: 133-42 (part col.) Oct '59.
—— (1652-1700). Con. 143: XXI Ap '59.
—— (1757). Amer. heri., vol. 10 no. 1 p. 12-3 (col.) (Dec '58).
—— (skyline). Holiday 13: 7 Mar '53, 5 (col.) Je '53; 14: 77 Jl '53; 22: 21, 34-5 (col.) Sept '57 23: 157 May '58, 90-1 (col.) Je '58 26: 50-1 (col.) Oct '59.
Jordan: Hammond's pict. atlas, p. 35 (col.).
Natl. geog. 115: 832 Je '59.
Travel 105: 62 Feb '56.
—— (skyline, night). Holiday 20: 87 (col.) Sept '56.
—— (skyscrapers). Face of Amer., p. 32-3, 54-5 (col.).
—— (soldiers parade, 1851). Amer. heri., vol. 7 no. 5 p. 12-3, 15 (col.) (Aug '56).
—— ("Spook's tour"). Holiday 6: 72-5 Aug '49.
—— (N.Y. stock exchange, founding of). Amer. heri., vol. 5 no. 1 p. 10 (fall '53).
—— (tour, comic). Holiday 22: 78-81 Nov '57.
—— (twilight). Holiday 22: 154 (col.) Oct '57.
—— (Wall St., 1850). Con. 137: IV Ap '56.
—— (Yacht club banquet). Amer. heri., vol. 6 no. 1 p. 28-9 (fall '54).
New York (state). Holiday 21: 50-63 (part col.) Je '57; 23: 131 Mar '58.
Natl. geog. 110: 568-618 (part col.) Nov '56.
—— (beaches). Travel 109: 49, 52 Je '58.
—— (capitol bldg., Albany). Holiday 13: 7 Mar '53, 5 (col.) Je '53; 15: 113 (col.) Ap '54; 17: 25 (col.) Mar '55.

—— (colonial homes). Holiday 6: 39 (col.) Sept '49.
—— (Finger lakes). Travel 108: 10-2 Aug '57.
—— (Kingston, early days). See Kingston (N.Y.).
—— (map). Holiday 5: 42-3 (col.) Ap '49; 21: 103 Mar '57, 121 Ap '57, 45 Je '57.
—— (product map). Holiday 15: 113 (col.) Ap '54, 169 (col.) May '54.
—— (state seal). Natl. geog. 110: 590 (col.) Nov '56.
—— (Westchester county). Holiday 8: 112-23 (part col.) Dec '50.
"New York as Washington knew it" (1793). Con. ency. of ant., vol. 3, pl. 90.
New York-Father Knickerbocker. See Father Knickerbocker.
New York university (1850). Amer. heri., vol. 1 no. 4 p. 54 (summer '50).
New Zealand. Holiday 27: 37 (:col.) Mar '60; 28: 100-9 (col.) Nov '60.
Natl. geog. 101: 420-60 (part col.) Ap '52.
Travel 102: 17 Nov '54.
—— (fjords). Holiday 24: 176 (col.) Nov '58.
—— (girl heads). Holiday 24: 144 Nov '58.
—— (girl on beach). Holiday 24: 27 (col.) Sept '58.
—— (map). Natl. geog. 101: 423 Ap '52.
Newberry, Clare. Jun. bk. of auth., p. 227.
Newburgh (N.Y., 1820). Amer heri., vol. 10 no. 1 p. 18 (col.) (Dec '58).
Newby, Percy H. Cur. biog. p. 457 (1953).
Newcomb, Covelle. Jun. bk. of auth., p. 228.
Newcombe, Don. Cur. biog. p. 400 (1957).
Newcomer, Brig. Gen. Francis K. Cur. biog. p. 423 (1950).
Newcomer, Mabel. Cur. biog. p. 492 (1944).
Newell, Homer E., jr. Cur. biog. p. 486 (1954).
Newfoundland coast. Natl. geog. 108: 726-7 (col.) Dec '55.
Newhall, Arthur B. Cur. biog. p. 632 (1942).
Newhart, Bob. Cur. biog. p. 319 (1962).
Newhouse, Samuel I. Cur. biog. p. 343 (1961).
Newman, Bernard C. Cur. biog. p. 319 (1959).
Newman, James Wilson. Cur. biog. p. 455 (1955).
Newman, Paul. Cur. biog. p. 321 (1959).
Newmarket races (painting). Con. 142: XLIII Dec '58.
Newport. Holiday 6: 99-105 (part col.) Jl '49.
—— (beach, pier). Travel 106: 32 Jl '56.
news board (Japan, street sign). Natl. geog. 97: 599 May '50.
news stand, street. Natl. geog. 111: 80 Jan '57.
newsboy (1890). Holiday 12: 68 Sept '52.
—— (Singapore). Natl. geog. 103: 209 Feb '53.
Newsom, Carroll Vincent. Cur. biog. p. 402 (1957).
Newsom, Herschel D. Cur. biog. p. 455 (1951)
newspaper office, frontier. Brooks: Growth of a nation, p. 188.
newspaper pulp (washed, Korea). Natl. geog. 97: 801 (col.) Je '50.
Newton, Alfred. Con. 144: 11 Sept '59.
Newton, Eric. Cur. biog. p. 462 (1956).
Newton, Sir Isaac. Brooks: Growth of a nation, p. 198.

Newton, Sir Isaac (Thornbill). Con. 140: 234 Jan '58.
Newton, Sir Isaac (bust). Con. 141: 164 May '58.
Ney, Hubert. Cur. biog. p. 464 (1956).
Nez Perces Indian. *See* Indians, Nez Perces.
Ngo-Dinh-Diem. Cur. biog. p. 447 (1955).
Niagara Falls. Amer. heri., vol. 8 no. 3 p. 8 (col.) (Ap '57).
  Holiday 7: 20 (col.) Ap '50; 12: 41 Jl '52; 13: 85 (col.) May '53; 24: 52 (col.) Nov '58.
  Jordan: Hammond's pict. atlas, p. 41 (col.).
  Natl. geog. 99: 718-9 (col.) Je '51; 104: 833 (col.) Dec '53; 115: 446-7 (col.) Ap '59; 117: 258-9 (col.) Feb '60.
  Travel 104: inside cover Oct '55.
—— (night). Natl. geog. 110: 616-7 (col.) Nov '56.
—— (19th cent.). Con. 133: 207 May '54.
—— (1698). Amer. heri., vol. 8 no. 3 p. 75 (Ap '57).
Niarchos, Stavros S. Cur. biog. p. 303 (1958).
Nicaragua. Natl. geog. 109: 340-1 Mar '56.
  Travel 111: 19 Mar '59.
—— (map). Natl. geog. 109: 344 Mar '56.
Niccolo, Domenico di (work of). Con. 136: 215 Dec '55.
Nice (France). Holiday 13: 12 (col.) Mar '53.
—— (harbor). Holiday 28: 5 (col.) Sept '60.
  U.S. News & world report, p. 18 (col.) Aug 31, 1964.
Nichols, Dudley. Cur. biog. p. 611 (1941).
  Holiday 5: 42 (col.) Jan '49.
Nichols, Herbert B. Cur. biog. p. 469 (1947).
Nichols, J. C. Holiday 7: 53 (col.) Mar '50.
Nichols, Maj. Gen. Kenneth D. Cur. biog. p. 472 (1948).
Nichols, Mid. Horan: Pict. hist of wild west, p. 207.
Nichols, Mike. Cur. biog. p. 345 (1961).
Nichols, Rose Standish. Holiday 14: 42 (col.) Nov '53.
Nichols, Roy Franklin. Cur. biog. p. 454 (1949).
Nichols, William I. Cur. biog. p. 305 (1958).
Nichols, William T. Cur. biog. p. 458 (1953).
Nicholson, Ben. Cur. biog. p. 307 (1958).
Nicholson, Meredith. Amer. heri., vol. 2 no. 1 p. 24 (fall '50).
Nicholson, Sir William (work of). Con. 144: 13 Sept '59.
nickel (sym.). Lehner: Pict. bk. of sym., p. 72.
Nickerson, Albert L. Cur. biog. p. 323 (1959).
Nicklaus, Jack W. Cur. biog. p. 321 (1962).
Nicolet, Marcel. Cur. biog. p. 309 (1958).
Niebuhr, Rev. Reinhold. Cur. biog. p. 613 (1941); p. 457 (1951).
Niedzica castle (Poland). Natl. geog. 114: 391 (col.) Sept '58.
Nielsen, Arthur C. Cur. biog. p. 459 (1951).
Niemeyer, Oscar. Natl. geog. 117: 718 May '60 .
Niemeyer, Soares Oscar. Cur. biog. p. 295 (1960).
Niemoeller, Martin. Cur. biog. p. 555 (1943).
Nigeria. Natl. geog. 104: 146-52 (col.) Aug '53; 110: 326-64 (part col.) Sept '56.
  Travel 107: 37-41 Feb '57.
—— (bronze tablet, warrior). Praeg. pict. ency., p. 546.

—— (ceremonial staff). Praeg. pict. ency., p. 561.
—— (map). Natl. geog. 110: 330 Sept '56; 116: 232 Aug '59.
  Travel 107: 38 Feb '57.
—— (statue, Eliz. II, Queen). Travel 113: cover Jan '60.
—— (wood carving). Holiday 25: 146 (col.) Ap '59.
  Praeg.: pict. ency., p. 561.
Nigerian. (blowing trumpet). Natl. geog. 116: 251 Aug '59.
—— (jungle life). Natl. geog. 116: 222-53 (part col.) Aug '59.
Nigerian man. Travel 107: 41 Feb '57.
Nigerian man & child (Chameleon). Natl. geog. 116: 223 (col.) Aug '59.
Nigerian pottery. Travel 107: 40 Feb '57.
Nigerian woman. Travel 107: 37 Feb '57.
Nigerians. Natl. geog. 116: 222-53 (col.) Aug '59, 781-5 (col.) Dec '59.
Niggli, Josephina. Cur. biog. p. 456 (1949).
night club (entertainment). Holiday 10: 52 (col.) Aug '51.
—— (in cave). Holiday 10: 95 (col.) Aug '51.
—— (show). Holiday 5: 53 (col.) Ap '49.
night club model. Natl. geog. 110: 584 (col.) Nov '56.
night light, French directoire. Con. 140: 131 Nov '57.
night table, antique. Con. 135: 1 Ap '55.
—— (18th cent.). Con. ency., of ant., vol. 3, pl. 16.
Nightingale, Florence (statue). Travel 108: 25 Nov '57.
nihilism (sym.). Lehner: Pict. bk. of sym., p. 95.
Nijo palace (Kyoto). Natl. geog. 97: 608 (col.) May '50.
Nike (sym.). Lehner: Pict. bk. of sym., p. 31.
"Nike of Samothrace". Praeg. pict. ency., p. 11.
—— (sym.). Lehner: Pict. bk. of sym., p. 87.
Nikko (carved monkeys). Natl. geog. 116: 857 (col.) Dec '59.
—— (girls, umbrella). Holiday 27: 152 (col.) May '60.
Nile Hilton hotel (Cairo). Natl. geog. 118: 353 (col.) Sept '60.
Nile river. Amer. heri., vol. 11 no. 3 p. 27 (col.) (Ap '60).
  Natl. geog. 108: 636-7 (col.) Nov '55; 118: 375 (col.) Sept '60.
  Travel 104: 17 Nov '55.
Nile river boat. Amer. heri., vol. 11 no. 3 p. 27 (col.) (Ap '60).
—— (ancient). Int. gr. soc.: Arts . . . p. 43 (col.).
Nile river canal. Holiday 16: 107 (col.) Nov '54.
Nile river region. Natl. geog. 107: 697-731 May '55; 108: 636-7 (col.) Nov '55.
Niles, John Jacob. Cur. biog. p. 325 (1959).
  Holiday 9: 33 Mar '51.
Nilson, Johann Esais (work of). Con. 145: 130 Ap '60.
Nilsson, Birgit. Cur. biog. p. 297 (1960).
Nimes (France). Natl. geog. 100: 2-3 Jl '51.

—— (France, Pont du Gard). Praeg. pict. ency., p. 146.
Nimitz, Adm. Chester W. Cur. biog. p. 633 (1942).
Nin, Anais. Cur. biog. p. 493 (1944).
'"Nine gates of hell". Lehner: Pict. bk. of sym., p. 57.
"Nine heroes & heroines" (tapestry, 1385). Praeg. pict. ency., p. 216 (col.).
"Nine muses" (sym.). Lehner: Pict. bk. of sym., p. 33.
ninepins, 18th cent. Amer. heri., vol. 6 no. 3 p. 32 (Ap '55).
Nineveh (excavations). Ceram: March of arch., p. 214-9.
Nineveh relief. See alabaster relief (Nineveh).
Nineveh sculpture. See sculpture, bronze (Nineveh).
Niobid bowl (450 B.C.). Praeg pict. ency., p. 137.
nippers, fisherman's. Rawson: Ant. pict. bk., p. 76.
Nishat Bagh garden (India). Holiday 24: 55 (col.) Sept '58.
Nisida. Labande: Naples, 14-5.
nitrate plant (Chile). Natl. geog. 117: 225 Feb '60.
nitre (sym.). Lehner: Pict. bk. of sym., p. 73.
nitric acid (sym.). Lehner: Pict. bk. of sym., p. 73.
Nitze, Paul Henry. Cur. biog. p. 323 (1962).
Nixon, John. Amer. heri., vol. 3 no 1 p. 29 (fall '51).
—— (work of). Con. 139: XLVII May '57.
Nixon, Richard M. Cur. biog. p. 474 (1948); p. 311 (1958).
Natl. geog. 114: 600 (col.) Nov '58; 116: 716 (col.) Dec '59.
Travel 109: cover (col.), 16-7 May '58.
Nixon, Mrs. Richard M. Natl. geog. 116: 717, 742 (col.) Dec '59.
Nizer, Louis. Cur. biog. p. 449 (1955).
Nkrumah, Kwame. Cur. biog. p. 459 (1953).
Holiday 25: 64 Ap '59.
Natl. geog. 118: 305 (col.) Sept 60.
Noah's ark (antique toy). Amer. heri., vol. 11 no. 1 p. 81 (Dec '59).
"Noah's ark" (Hicks, 1846) Amer. heri., vol. 7 no. 1 p. 54 (col.) (Dec '55).
—— (Joseph Hidley). Amer. heri., vol. 11 no. 1 cover (col.) (Dec '59).
nobility (costume medieval). Int. gr. soc.: Arts . . . p. 71 (col.).
Noble, Comdr. Allan. Cur. biog. p. 407 (1957).
Noble, Edward J. Cur. biog. p. 496 (1944).
Noble, Gladwyn Kingsley. Cur. biog. p. 614 (1941).
Noble, James (work of). Con. 140: XXXVIII (col.) Nov '57.
"Noble train of artillery" (T. Lovell). Amer. heri., vol. 6 no. 3 p. 12 (col.). (Ap '55).
Nobs, Ernst. Cur. biog. p. 457 (1949).
"The Nocera Venus Anadyomene" (bronze). Labande: Naples, p. 102.
noctograph, Prescott's. Amer. heri., vol. 8 no. 6 p. 110 (Oct '57).
noddle pin gate. See gate, noddle pin.
nodes (sym.). Lehner: Pict. bk. of sym., p. 21.
Noel-Baker, Philip J. Cur. biog., p. 426 (1946).

Nogales (Ariz.). Travel 103: 31 Jan '55.
Nogari, Giuseppe (work of). Con. 140: 154-9 Dec '57.
Noguchi, Isamu. Cur. biog. p. 558 (1943).
Nogues, Gen. Auguste. Cur. biog. p. 559 (1943).
noise maker (wedding serenade). Rawson: Ant. pict. bk., p. 44.
—— (New Year's eve). Lehner: Pict. bk. of sym., p. 54.
Nolan, Jeannette Covert. Jun. bk. of auth., p. 230.
Nolan, Lloyd. Cur. biog. p. 466 (1956).
Nolde, Emil. (work of). Praeg. pict. ency., p. 450 (col.).
Nolde, Otto Frederick. Cur. biog. p. 471 (1947).
nomad, Arab. Holiday 20: 50-1 (col.) Dec '56.
——, Lapland. Holiday 18: 106-9 (part col.) Dec '55.
——, Lebanese. See Lebanese nomad.
nomad migration routes (map). Natl. geog. 108: 786 Dec '55.
nomad shepherd women (Greece). Natl. geog. 109: 56 (col.) Jan '56.
nomad women (spin wool). Natl. geog. 109: 71 Jan '56.
nomads. Natl. geog. 106: 622-44 (part col.) Nov '54; 108: 782-806 (part col.) Dec '55; 117: 80, 86-7, 90-1 (col.) Jan '60.
——, Amorite. See Amorite nomads.
——, desert. Natl. geog. 114: 20-1 (col.) Jl '58.
——, Kashgai. Natl. geog. 100: 447, 463 (col.) Oct '51.
——, Tibet. Natl. geog. 102: 213 (col.), 216 Aug '52.
Nomura, Kichisaburo. Cur. biog. p. 615 (1941).
Nonnius, Ludovicus (Rubens). Con. 126: 212 Dec '50.
Noon, Malik Firoz Khan. Cur. biog. p. 409 (1957).
noose, rope. See rope noose.
Norden, Carl L. Cur. biog. p. 433 (1945).
Nordenberg, Bengt (work of). Con. 141: XXIII Mar '58.
Nordhoff, Heinz. Cur. biog. p. 468 (1956).
Nordic symbols. Lehner: Pict. bk. of sym., p. 28.
Norfolk, Duke of. Holiday 23: 90 (col.) Ap '58.
Norfolk is. Natl. geog. 118: 562-84 (part col.) Oct '60.
—— church. Travel 112: 36 Dec '59.
Norkey, Tenzing. Cur. biog. p. 354 (1954).
Norman watchtower. See watchtower, Norman.
Normandy (France). Holiday 17: 126 (col.) Mar '55; 19: 52-3 Jan '56.
Natl. geog. 115: 592-631 (part col.) May '59.
Travel 111: 27-9 Ap '59.
—— (map). Natl. geog. 115: 600-1 May '59.
Normandy beaches (war landings, map). Natl. geog. 115: 595 (col.) May '59.
Normandy dancers. Natl. geog. 115: 910-11 (col.) May '59.
Norodom Sihanouk, King of Cambodia. Cur. biog. p. 488 (1954).
Norris, Bruce A. Holiday 28: 85 Dec '60.
Norris dam (Tenn.). Brooks: Growth of a nation, p. 280.
Holiday 8: 42-3 (col.) Nov '50.

Norstad, Lt. Gen. Lauris. Cur. biog. p. 476 (1948); p. 327 (1959).
North, Frederick, Lord (1770). Amer. heri., vol. 11 no. 4 p. 12 (col.) (Je '60).
North, John Ringling. Cur. biog. p. 462 (1951).
North, Levi J. Durant: Pict. hist. of Amer. circus, p. 38.
North, Sterling. Cur. biog. p. 562 (1943).
"The North" (Francesco Maffei). Con. 138: 119 Nov '56.
North America (pict. map). Holiday 14: 34-5 (col.) Jl '53.
——. See also Canada; United States.
North Carolina. Holiday 27: 7 (col.) Mar '60. Travel 106: 20-1 Aug '56.
—— (Blue Ridge). Natl. geog. 113: 856-79 Je '58.
—— (home of Vanderbilt). Amer. heri., vol. 6 no. 2 p. 21 (col.) (winter '55).
—— (Judaculla rock). Travel 114: 39 Sept '60.
—— (map). Holiday 26: 12 Aug '59.
North Carolina islands. Natl. geog. 108: 502-29 (part col.) Oct '55.
North Dakota. Natl. geog. 100: 284-322 (part col.) Sept '51.
—— (map). Natl. geog. 100: 286-7 Sept '51.
North Pole celebration cake. See cake (North Pole celebration).
North Pole. See Arctic region.
Northcote, James (work of). Con. 139: XXX-VII Je '57; 144: 8 Sept '59.
Northfield (Minn.). Horan: Pict. hist. of wild west, p. 39.
Northrop, John Howard. Cur. biog. p. 473 (1947).
Northrop, John K. Cur. biog. p. 459 (1949).
Northumberland house (Eng.). Con. 126: 39 (col.) Ap '50.
Northwest passage (cartoon). Amer. heri., vol. 3 no. 4 p. 45 (summer '52).
Northwest territory (map). Amer. heri., vol. 3 no. 3 p. 47 (spring '52).
Norton, Andre. Cur. biog. p. 411 (1957).
Norton, Howard M. Cur. biog. p. 474 (1947).
Norton, Mary T. Cur. biog. p. 501 (1944).
Norway. Holiday 12: 90-5 (part col.) Sept '52. Natl. geog. 104: 684-91 Nov '53; 106: 154-92 (part col.) Aug '54; 108: 736-41 (col.) Dec '55; 111: 97-122 (part col.) Jan '57. Travel 106: 33-7 Aug '56; 111: 40-2 Ap '59.
—— (fjord). Con. 145: XXX Mar '60. Holiday 17: 38 (col.) Jan '55; 27: 57, 59 (col.) Jan '60.
—— (stave church). Praeg. pict. ency., p. 246.
Norwegian (comic runner). Holiday 5: 10 (col.) Jan '49.
—— (playing violin). Travel 106: 35 Aug '56.
Norwegian art. Con. 145: 26-9 Mar '60.
—— & craft work. Con. 142: 104-7 Nov '58.
Norwegian boat. Brooks: Growth of a nation, p. 27.
Norwegian boys & girls. Holiday 13: 46-7 Mar '53.
Norwegian children. Natl. geog. 100: 708 Dec '51.
Norwegian faience. Con. 145: 7-11 Mar '60.
Norwegian furniture. See furniture, Norwegian.
Norwegian girl. Holiday 12: 91 (col.) Sept '52.

Norwegian girls. Natl. geog. 100: 714 (col.) Dec '51.
Norwegian glass goblet (Nostelangen). Con. 145: 18-21 Mar '60.
Norwegian man & woman. Natl. geog. 106: 176 (col.) Aug '54.
Norwegian sculpture. Con. 145: 30-3 Mar '60.
Norwegian silverware (16-19th cent.). Con. 145: 12-7 Mar '60.
Norwegian wood carvings. Con. 145: 34-7 Mar '60.
Norwegians (in home). Holiday 6: 37 (col.) Jl '49.
Norwich (Conn., 1850). Amer. heri., vol. 10 no. 4 p. 30-1 (col.) (Je '59).
Norwich paintings. Con. 138: 50 Sept '56.
nose. Gray's anatomy, p. 1025-31.
nose & eye sign. See eye & nose sign.
nose bags, horse. Rawson: Ant. pict. bk., p. 69.
nose collar, calf weaning. Rawson: Ant. pict. bk., p. 69.
nose cone, missile. Natl geog. 116: 470 (col.) Oct '59.
Noshi (sym.). Lehner: Pict. bk. of sym., p. 47.
"Nostalgia of the infinite" (art of Chirico). Holiday 14: 61 (col.) Nov '53.
Notman, James Geoffrey. Cur. biog. p. 313 (1958).
Notre Dame cathedral (Paris). Holiday 5: 123 Ap '49; 11: 77 (col.) Feb '52; 13: 46 (col.) 51 Ap '53; 20: 92-3 Dec '56; 22: 13 (col.) Nov '57.
Natl. geog. 98: 56 (col.) Jl '50; 108: 531 (col.) Oct '55.
Travel 102: 6 Dec '54; 107: inside back cover Feb '57.
—— (floor plan). Praeg. pict. ency., p. 24.
—— (int.) Praeg. pict. ency., p. 21.
—— (relief). Travel 113: 4 Je '60.
—— (towers). Natl. geog. 101: 802 (col.) Je '52.
Notre Dame church (Montreal, Canada). Holiday 6: 38 (col.) Aug '49.
Notre Dame de Portage (church). Natl. geog. 98: 338 (col.) Sept '50.
Notre Dame de Valere (church). Natl. geog. 110: 465 (col.) Oct '56.
Notre Dame du Haut (chapel). Holiday 21: 92 (col.) Ap '57.
Natl. geog. 117: 762 Je '60.
Notre Dame univ. See Univ. of Notre Dame.
Nottingham alabaster carvings. See alabaster. carvings, Nottingham.
Noue, Jehan De. Cur. biog. p. 475 (1947).
Nourse, Edwin G. Cur. biog. p. 429 (1946).
Nova Scotia (Canada). Holiday 14: 98-106 (part col.) Sept '53; 21: 151 Mar '57; 26: 84 Jl '59; 27: 21 (col.) Mar '60.
Travel 114: 37-40 Jl '60.
—— (harbor). Holiday 23: 147 (col.) Mar '58. Travel 110: cover (col.) Aug '58.
—— (rocky coast). Holiday 14: 41 Jl '53.
Novaes, Pinto Guiomar. Cur. biog. p. 46 (1953).
Novak, Kim. Cur. biog. p. 413 (1957).
novels, dime. See dime novels.
Novikov, Nikolai V. Cur. biog. p. 477 (1947).
Novotny, Antonin. Cur. biog. p. 314 (1958).

Noyes, William Albert, jr. Cur. biog. p. 479 (1947).

Nu, Thakin. Cur. biog. p. 463 (1951).

Nuba men & women (Egypt). Natl. geog. 99: 253-77 Feb '51.

Nubian figures. Con. 142: XXX Sept '58.

Nubian rock temple. Holiday 27: 64 (col.) Mar '60.

Nubian waiters. Holiday 25: 50 (col.) Feb '59.

Nuckols, Brig. Gen. William P. Cur. biog. p. 450 (1952).

nuclear ship. Natl. geog. 114: 312-3 Sept '58.

"Nude with necklace". Con. 145: 207 May '60.

Nufer, Albert F. Cur. biog. p. 451 (1955).

Nuffield, Viscount William R. Cur. biog. p. 617 (1941).

Nugent, Elliott. Cur. biog. p. 503 (1944).

numbers, lucky. See lucky numbers.

a nun. Ceram: March of arch., p. 267.

Nun, lay. Holiday 21: 38 Jan '57.

Nunez Portuondo, Emilio. Cur. biog. p. 415 (1957).

Nuns (back view). Holiday 20: 92 Dec '56.

———. See also. Catholic sisters.

Nuoro, Sardinia. Holiday 13: 26 Feb '53.

Nuovo castle. See Castle Nuovo.

Nuremberg ("The Annunciation"). Praeg. pict. ency., p. 247.

Nureyev, Rudolph. Cur. biog. p. 299 (1963).

Nuri As-Said. Cur. biog. p. 453 (1955).

nurse (feeding baby). Holiday 14: 5 Sept '53.

——— (patient). Natl. geog. 117: 780 Je '60.

——— (sym.). Lehner: Pict. bk. of sym., p. 91.

nurse, baby. Holiday 21: 199 May '57.

nursery. Natl. geog. 109: 237 (col.) Feb '56.

nursery school room, Negro. Natl. geog. 103: 74 Jan '53.

nurses. Natl. geog. 107: 446 (col.) Ap '55.

——— (Lourdes, France). Natl. geog. 109: 310 (col.) Mar '56.

———, flying. Natl. geog. 108: 266-7 (col.) Aug '55.

———, ship. Natl. geog. 104: 565 (col.) Oct '53.

———, U.S. Navy. See U.S. Navy nurses.

nut cracker. Holiday 8: 117 Oct '50.

nutmeg grater. Rawson: Ant. pict. bk., p. 7.

Nutting, Anthony. Cur. biog. p. 455 (1955).

"Nutt's Folly" (Victorian villa). Amer. heri., vol. 6 no. 6 p. 38 (Oct '55).

Nyborg, Victor H. Cur. biog. p. 491 (1954).

Nyborg castle (Funen Isle, Denmark). Travel 103: 13 May '55.

Nye, Maj. Gen. Archibald E. Cur. biog. p. 635 (1942).

Nye, Gerald P. Cur. biog. p. 619 (1941).

Nye, Russel B. Cur. biog. p. 435 (1945).

Nyerere, Julius K. Cur. biog. p. 302 (1963).

nymph (on rock). Holiday 27: 113 Mar '60.

"Nymph, satyr & cupid" (terracotta). Con. 143: 210 Je '59.

Nymphenburg palace. See Schloss Nymphen-burg.

"Nymphs & satyrs" (Rubens). Holiday 25: 70-1 (col.) Jan '59.

Nyoi-hoshu. Lehner: Pict. bk. of sym., p. 47.

Nyrop, Donald W. Cur. biog. p. 452 (1952).

Nystrom, Paul H. Cur. biog. p. 465 (1951).

O

"Oak Alley" home (Vacherie, Miss.). Holiday 17: 98-9 (col.) Mar '55.
Natl. geog. 113: 533-35 (col.) Ap '58.

"Oak Alley" plantation (La.). Amer. heri., vol. 7 no. 4 p. 57-9 (Je '56).

Oak creek canyon (Ariz.). Travel 108: 40-2 Oct '57.

"Oak Hill" (Pres. Monroe's home, Va.). Natl. geog. 109: 478 (col.) Ap '56.

Oak Ridge (Civil war battle field). Holiday 11: 60 (col.) Je '52.

Oak Ridge (Tenn.). Travel 104: 13 Jl '55.

——— houses. Holiday 8: 41 Nov '50.

Oak Ridge plant. Natl. geog. 105: 74 Jan '54.

oak tree branch (sym.). Lehner: Pict. bk. of sym., p. 87.

Oakes, Grant W. Cur. biog. p. 426 (1950).

Oakley, Annie. Horan: Pict. hist. of wild west, p 54.
Natl. geog. 107: 482 (col.) Ap '55.

Oakley plantation garden (La.). Travel 109: 15 Mar '58.

oar, rowboat. Natl. geog. 111: 548 (col.) Ap '57; 112: 748 (col.) Dec '57.

oarsmen, Basque (fisherman). Natl. geog. 105: 166-7, 170 (col.) Feb '54.

oasis (Sahara desert). Holiday 13: 70-1 Jan '53.

———, canyon (Chile). Natl. geog. 117: 230-1 (col.) Feb '60.

"Oath of the Horatii". Praeg. pict. ency., p. 398.

"Oatlands" (1802 house, Va.). Natl. geog. 109: 466-7 (col.) Ap '56.

obelisk (858-24 B.C.). Natl. geog. 118: 826 Dec '60.

——— (grave of Lt. J. Waterman). Natl. geog. 105: 196 (col.) Feb '54.

———, Argentina. Natl. geog. 113: 301 (col.) Mar '58.

———, Bunker Hill. See Bunker Hill obelisk.

———, Delaware river. Natl. geog. 102: 40 Jl '52.

———, Egyptian. Holiday 28: 193 Oct '60. Praeg. pict. ency., p. 15.

———, Egyptian (Paris). Natl. geog. 114: 286 Aug '58.

———, Ethiopian. Holiday 28: 141 Dec '60.

———, Lincoln. Natl. geog. 101: 180 (col.) Feb '52.

———, rock. Natl. geog. 114: 830-1 (col.) Dec '58.

———, Temple of Luxor. Ceram: March of arch., p. 90.

———, the black (of Salmanassar III). Ceram: March of arch., p. 216.

———, William McKinley (Pres.). Natl. geog. 110: 612 Nov '56.

———, Turkey. Osward: Asia Minor, pl. 88.

Oberhaus fortress. See fortress of Oberhaus.

Oberhofen castle (Berne, Switz.). Travel 111: 47 Je '59.

Oberlin, Russell. Cur. biog. p. 299 (1960).

Oberndorf (Austria). Travel 108: 29-31 Dec '57.

Oberon, Merle. Cur. biog. p. 622 (1941). Holiday 23: inside cover (col.) Ap '58.

Oberth, Hermann J. Cur. biog. p. 417 (1957).
oboe. Cooper: Con. ency. of music, p. 397.
Int. gr. soc.: Arts . . . p. 141 (col.).
—— (1690-1800). Cooper: Con. ency., of music, p. 399.
——, Cor Anglais. Cooper: Con. ency., of music, p. 397.
Obolensky, Serge. Cur. biog. p. 329 (1959). Holiday 23: 149 Je '58.
O'Brian, Hugh. Amer. heri., vol. 11 no. 5 p. 44 (Aug '60).
Cur. biog. 316 (1958).
O'Brien, Lawrence. Cur. biog. p. 347 (1961).
O'Brien, Leo. W. Cur. biog. p. 331 (1959).
O'Brien, Margaret. Holiday 5: 40 (col.) Jan '49; 10: 65 Dec '51; 25: 111 Mar '59.
observation hut, tetrahedral. Natl. geog. 110: 234 Aug '56.
observatory. Holiday 15: 84 Feb '54, 5 (col.) Mar '54.
—— (Switz.). Natl. geog. 98: 211 Aug '50.
——, Lamont-Hussey. Natl. geog. 108: 428 Sept '55.
——, Palomar. See Palomar observatory.
O'Byrne, Mrs. Roscoe C. Cur. biog. p. 478 (1948).
Ocampo, Victoria. Holiday 20: 108 Nov '56.
O'Casey, Sean. Cur. biog. p. 325 (1962). Holiday 6: 22 Aug '49.
occult number diagram of man (sym.). Lehner: Pict. bk. of sym., p. 70.
occupations (sym.). Lehner: Pict. bk. of sym., p. 90-1.
Ocean Falls (B.C.). Jordan: Hammond's pict. atlas, p. 145 (col.).
Ocean God (in Smyrna). Osward: Asia Minor, p. 103, 105.
ocean hole. Natl. geog. 113: 200-1 (col.) Feb '58.
oceanography (sym.). Lehner: Pict. bk. of sym., p. 15, 16.
Och (seal of). Lehner: Pict. bk. of sym., p. 24.
Ochoa, Severo. Cur. biog. p 328 (1962).
"Ochre court" (home of Goelet). Amer. heri., vol. 6 no. 2 p. 22 (winter '55).
Ochs, Adolph S. Amer. heri., vol. 3 no. 2 p. 24 (winter '52).
Ochtervelt, Jacob (work of). Con. 127: 120 May '51; 136: 20 Sept '55.
O'Connell, Cardinal William. Amer. heri., vol. 10 no. 4 p. 24 (Je '59).
Cur. biog. p. 625 (1941).
O'Connor, Basil. Cur. biog. p. 506 (1944). Holiday 23: 9 Jan '58.
O'Connor, Donald. Cur. biog. p. 457 (1955).
O'Connor, Edwin. Cur. biog. p. 305 (1963).
O'Connor, Flannery. Cur. biog. p. 317 (1958).
O'Connor, Frank. Holiday 6: 25 Aug '49.
O'Connor, Roderic (work of). Con. 139: 121 Ap '57.
O'Connor, Herbert R. Cur. biog. p. 427 (1950).
"Octagon House" (Irvington, N.Y.). Amer. heri., vol. 10 no. 1 p. 19 (Dec '58).
"Octagon House" (Wash., D.C.). Jensen: The White House, p. 29.
octagram of creation (sym.). Lehner: Pict. bk. of sym., p. 66.
octopus (sym.). Lehner: Pict. bk. of sym., p. 82.
O'Daniel, Wilbert Lee. Cur. biog. p. 481 (1947).

O'Day, Tom. Horan: Pict. hist. of wild west, p. 193, 197.
O'dense (Denmark). Travel 103: 14 May '55.
Odets, Clifford. Cur. biog. p. 627 (1941).
Odetta. Cur. biog. p. 300 (1960).
"Odin" (Fuseli). Praeg. pict. ency., p. 422.
Odin's triple horn (sym.). Lehner: Pict. bk. of sym., p. 28.
Odlum, Floyd B. Cur. biog. p. 629 (1941).
O'Donnell, Maj. Gen. Emmet, jr. Cur. biog. p. 480 (1948).
Odria, Manuel A. Cur. biog. p. 493 (1954).
O'Dwyer, William. Cur. biog. p. 632 (1941); p. 483 (1947).
Odyssey (ancient paintings). Int. gr. soc.: Arts . . . p. 23 (col.).
Oechsner, Frederick C. Cur. biog. p. 564 (1943).
Oenslager, Donald M. Cur. biog. p. 431 (1946).
Oertel, J. A. (work of). Amer. heri., vol. 6 no. 6 p. 64 (Oct '55).
Oettinger, Katherine Brownell Cur. biog. p. 419 (1957).
O'Faolain, Sean. Holiday 6: 59 Dec '49.
Offenbach, Jacques. Cooper: Con. ency., of music, p. 199.
office, modern (int.). Int. gr. soc.: Arts . . . p. 169 (col.).
O'Flaherty, Liam. Holiday 6: 24 Aug '49.
Ogburn, Charlton. Cur. biog. p. 459 (1955).
Ogburn, William F. Cur. biog. p. 461 (1955).
Ogden, Charles K. Cur. biog. p. 510 (1944).
Ogham stone (Caldy is.). Natl. geog. 108: 570 Oct '55.
Ogilvie, Elisabeth. Cur. biog. p. 467 (1951).
Ogilvy, David M. Cur. biog. p. 349 (1961).
Ogelthorpe, Gen. James Edward. Brooks: Growth of a nation, p. 67.
O'Gorman, Juan. Cur. biog. p. 470 (1956).
O'Hara, John. Cur. biog. p. 633 (1941). Holiday 24: 40 Sept '58.
O'Hara, Mary. Cur. biog. p. 513 (1944).
O'Hara, Maureen. Cur. biog. p. 463 (1953).
O'Hare inn (Chicago, O'Hare Internatl. airport). Travel 113: 47 Je '60.
O'Higgins, Patrick. Holiday 23: 147 (col.) Je '58.
Ohio. Natl. geog. 107: 436-84 (part col.) Ap '55.
Travel 104: 17-9 Aug '55.
—— (farm). Face of Amer., p. 114-5 (col.).
—— (1st state capitol). Amer. heri., vol. 4 no. 3 p. 39 (spring '53).
—— (historic sites). Amer. heri., vol. 4 no. 3 p. 34-59 (part col.) (spring '53).
—— (map). Natl. geog. 107: 442-3 (col.) Ap '55.
—— (Put-in-Bay). Travel 109: 42 Je '58.
—— (state capitol). See capitol, Ohio state.
—— (state university). Holiday 10: 56-61 (part col.) Nov '51.
Ohio-Miss. rivers meet. See Miss.-Ohio rivers meet.
Ohio river. Face of Amer., p. 34-5, 40-1 (col.). Natl. geog. 97: 179-212 (part col.) Feb '50.
Ohlin, Lloyd E. Cur. biog. p. 307 (1963).
oil & vinegar frame, Geo. II. Con. 139: 58 Mar '57.
oil & vinegar holder, Geo. II silver. Con. 139: III May '57.

oil bubble. Holiday 14: 61 Sept '53, 14 Oct '53, 70 (col.) Nov '53, 171 (col.) Dec '53.
oil can. Rawson: Ant. pict. bk., p. 61.
——, antique. Rawson: Ant. pict. bk., p. 7-8.
oil derrick. Natl. geog. 113: 567 Ap '58, 674 (col.) May '58; 116: 53 (col.) Jl '59; 118: 357 Sept '60.
—— (Canada). Natl. geog. 108: 201 Aug '55.
—— (Indonesia). Natl. geog. 108: 361 Sept '55.
oil derricks. Amer. heri., vol. 10 no. 2 p. 78 (Feb '59).
Holiday 7: 115 May '50.
Natl. geog. 105: 783 (col.) Je '54.
oil field. Holiday 13: 114-5 (col.) May '53.
—— (Algeria). Natl. geog. 117: 782 (col.) Je '60.
——, Kirkuk, (Iraq). Natl. geog. 114: 460-1 (col.) Oct '58.
——, Spindletop (Texas). Amer. heri., vol. 4 no. 1 p. 36 (col.) (fall '52).
oil gusher. Amer. heri., vol. 4 no. 1 p. 37 (fall '52).
oil lamp. Natl. geog. 112: 746 (col.) Dec '57.
—— (sym.). Lehner: Pict. bk. of sym., p. 17.
——, Italian silver. Con. 144: 152 Dec '59.
oil pipes (Iran). Natl. geog. 100: 446 Oct '51.
oil prospectors (Arabia). Natl. geog. 117: 108-9 (col.) Jan '60.
oil refinery (Edmonton). Natl. geog. 118: 110-11 (col.) Jl '60.
—— (Standard Co.). Natl. geog. 107: 445 Ap '55.
—— (Trinidad). Natl. geog. 103: 49 (col.) Jan '53.
oil storage tanks. Amer. heri., vol. 10 no. 2 p. 76 (Feb '59).
Natl. geog. 111: 146 Feb '57.
oil tank farm (Trinidad). Natl. geog. 103: 50 (col.) Jan '53.
oil tanker. See boat, oil tanker.
oil tanks. Natl. geog. 113: 566 (col.) Ap '58; 117: 6-7 (col.) Jan '60.
oil transport (early). Amer. heri., vol. 1 no. 3 p. 5 (col.) (spring '50).
oil well. Amer. heri., vol. 1 no. 2 p. 30-33 (winter '50).
—— (burning). Natl. geog. 101: 468 (col.) Ap '52.
—— (early). Amer. heri., vol. 10 no. 2 p. 73 (Feb '59).
—— (gusher). Amer. heri., vol. 9 no. 4 p. 34, 39 (Je '58).
—— (Penn. 1859). Brooks: Growth of a nation, p. 137.
oil wells. Brooks: Growth of a nation, p. 305.
—— (Texas). Amer. heri., vol. 4 no. 1 p. 36-9 (fall '52).
oilmen (plug well). Natl. geog. 118: 91 (col.) Jl '60.
Oistrakh, David. Cur. biog. p. 472 (1956).
Ojike, Mbonu. Cur. biog. p. 486 (1947).
O'Keeffe, Georgia. Cur. biog. p. 635 (1941).
Okefenokee swamp (Ga.). Face of Amer., p. 134-5 (col.).
Holiday 12: 61 (col.) Oct '52, 58-61 (part col.) Dec '52.
Jordan: Hammond's pict. atlas, p. 66 (col.).
O'Kelly, Sean Thomas. Cur. biog. p. 481 (1948).

O'Kelly, Sean T. (Pres. of Ireland). Holiday 6: 58 Dec '49.
Okinawa. Natl. geog. 97: 538-52 Ap '50; 107: 265-88 Feb '55.
—— (map). Natl. geog. 107: 268 Feb '55.
Oklahoma. Holiday 13: 114-5 (part col.) May '53.
Jordan: Hammond's pict. atlas, p. 112-3 (col.).
—— (map). Travel 104: 31 Jl '55.
Oklahoma Cherokee strip. Travel 104: 29 Jl '55.
Oklahoma city. Holiday 7: 114-9 (part col.) May '50.
"Oklahoma run" (1893). Brooks: Growth of a nation, p. 194.
O'Konski, Alvin E. Cur. biog. p. 463 (1955).
O'Laughlin, Michael. Amer. heri., vol. 8 no. 2 p. 57 (Feb '57).
Olav V, King of Norway. Cur. biog. p. 330 (1962).
—— (Norwegian sculpture). Con. 145: 30-3 Mar '60.
"Old Bet" elephant memorial statue. See Memorial statue, elephant.
"Old Bill". See Miner, William ("Old Bill").
"The old bridge". Natl. geog. 101: 81 (col.) Jan '52.
"Old curiosity shop". Natl. geog. 108: 297 (col.) Sept '55.
"Old faithful geyser". See geyser, "Old faith-ful".
"'Old Hall" East Bergholt, Suffolk. Con. 142: XVIII (col.) Jan '59.
"Old Ironsides" (ship). Amer. heri., vol. 6 no. 3 p. 57 (col.) (Ap '55).
"Old Ky. home". See "My old Kentucky home".
"Old man cave" (Ohio). Natl. geog. 107: 462-3 (col.) Ap '55.
"Old Manse" (Hawthorne's home). Amer. heri., vol. 10 no. 1 p. 34 (Dec '58).
"Old New York" (Tiffany). Natl. geog. 99: 206 (col.) Feb '51.
Old North Church. See Boston, (Old North Church.
"Old Rough & Ready". See Taylor, Zachary.
Old state house (Boston). See Boston (Old state house).
Old Sturbridge village (restored). Amer. heri., vol. 1 no. 4 p. 30-9 (part col) (summer '50).
Old Testament scenes. See Biblical scenes (Old Testament).
Oldenbroek, Jacobus H. Cur. biog. p. 430 (1950).
Older, Fremont. Amer. heri., vol. 11 no. 1 p. 10 (Dec '59).
Olds, Irving S. Cur. biog. p. 483 (1948).
Oldsmobile auto. Holiday 5: 71 (col.) Feb '49, inside back cover (col.) Ap '49, 155 (col.) Je '49; 6: 79 (col.) Aug '49, 22 (col.) Oct '49; 7: 102 (col.) Ap '50, 74 (col.) Je '50; 8: inside cover (col.) Aug '50, 90 (col.) Sept '50, 2 (col.) Nov '50; 17: 5 (col.) Feb '55.
Travel 103: 12 Jan '55.
—— (1954). Holiday 15: 74 (col.) Mar '54, 15 (col.) May '54; 16: 85 (col.) Jl '54, 65 (col.) Sept '54.

Olenin, Alexis von (work of). Ceram: March of arch., p. 190.

Oleson, Lloyd F. Cur. biog. p. 488 (1947).

Oliphant, Marcus L. Cur. biog. p. 468 (1951).

olive branch & dove (sym.). *See* dove & olive branch.

olive oil (sym.). Lehner: Pict. bk. of sym., p. 73.

Oliver, Isaac (miniatures by). Con. ency. of ant., vol. 1, pl. 129.

—— **(work of).** Con. 141: 104-5 Ap '58.

Oliver, Maj. Gen. Lunsford E. Cur. biog. p. 489 (1947).

Olivetti, Adriano. Cur. biog. p. 333 (1959).

Olivier, Laurence. Cur. biog. p. 434 (1946). Holiday 27: 119 Feb '60; 28: 83 Aug '60.

"Olivier plantation" (Persac). Natl. geog. 99: 198 (col.) Feb '51.

Ollenhauer, Erich. Cur. biog. p. 465 (1953).

Olmec buried treasures (Mexico). Natl. geog. 110: 366-74 (part col.) Sept '56.

Olmec ax, ritual (Central Amer.). Ceram: March of arch., pl. XIV (col.).

Olmedo, Alex. Cur. biog. p. 335 (1959).

Olmsted, Frederick Law. Cur. biog. p. 460 (1949).

Olson, Harry F. Cur. biog. p. 465 (1955).

Olson Rug. Co. park (Chicago, rock garden). Travel 114: 40 Sept '60.

Olympia hippodrome (London). Durant: Pict. hist. of Amer. circus, p. 154.

Olympic arena (int., Rome). Holiday 27: 51 Ap '60.

Olympic field (Melbourne, Australia). Natl. geog. 110: 688-91 Nov '56.

Olympic games, original (Greece). Int. gr. soc.: Arts . . . p. 39 (col.).

Olympic mts. Jordan: Hammond pict. atlas, p. 147 (col.).

Olympic natl. park. Natl. geog. 108: 86-123 (part col.) Jl '55.

—— **(map).** Natl. geog. 108: 90-1 Jl '55.

—— **beach (Wash.).** Face of Amer., p. 138-9 (col.).

Olympic rain forest. Holiday 26: 49 (col.) Jl '59.

Natl. geog. 117: 465 (col.) Ap '60.

"Omaha Beach". Natl. geog. 111: 744 Je '57.

O'Mahoney, Joseph C. Cur. biog. p. 436 (1945).

O'Malley, Walter F. Cur. biog. p. 495 (1954).

Oman boy. Natl. geog. 110: 67 (col.) Jl '56.

Oman men (in tobacco field). Natl. geog. 105: 506-7 (col.) Ap '54.

Omayad mosque. *See* mosque, Omayad.

O'meara, Walter. Cur. biog. p. 319 (1958).

"Omer Talon". Natl. geog. 101: 84 (col.) Jan '52.

"Om Ma-ni pad-me hum". Lehner: Pict. bk. of sym., p. 42.

omnibus (horses, 2 story, 1890's). Holiday 12: 67 Sept '52.

——. *See* also bus.

Omohundro, Texas Jack. Horan: Pict. hist. of wild west, p. 52.

"On the war trail" (sculpture). Natl. geog. 106: 237 (col.) Aug '54.

Onassis, Aristotle Socrates. Cur. biog. p. 309 (1963). Holiday 24: 114 (col.) Dec '58.

O'Neal, Edward A. Cur. biog. p. 437 (1946).

O'Neal, Frederick D. Cur. biog. p. 439 (1946).

"Oneida" (ship, sail). Amer. heri., vol. 8 no. 6 p. 13 (Oct '57).

O'Neil, Henry (work of). Con. 144: XXXV (col.) Dec '59.

O'Neil, James F. Cur. biog. p. 491 (1947).

O'Neil, Thomas F. Cur. biog. p. 467 (1955).

O'Neill, C. William. Cur. biog. p. 320 (1958).

O'Neill, Eugene F. Cur. biog. p. 311 (1963).

O'Neill, Francis A., jr. Cur. biog. p. 302 (1960).

O'Neill, John E. Cur. biog. p. 453 (1952).

Oni (sym.). Lehner: Pict. bk. of sym., p. 49.

Onis, Harriet De. Cur. biog p. 420 (1957).

onomantic circle. Lehner: Pict. bk. of sym., p. 69.

Onondaga trail (map). Amer. heri., vol. 3 no. 4 p. 10 (summer '52).

Onondaga village. Amer. heri.. vol, 6 no. 2 p. 29 (winter '55).

Onsager, Lars. Cur. biog. p. 321 (1958).

Ontario (Canada). Holiday 7: 89 (col.) Mar '50.

Natl. geog. 104: 822-52 (part col.) Dec '53.

Oosterbaan, Bennie. Cur. biog. p. 462 (1949).

opalines (19th cent.). Con. 133: 234 (col.) Je '54.

Opdyke, George. Amer. heri., vol. 10 no. 4 p. 97 (Je '59).

opera glasses. Holiday 27: back cover (col.) May '60, 139 Je '60.

opera groups. Holiday 14: 112, 116 (part col.) Dec '53.

Opera house (Bayreuth). Int. gr. soc.: Arts . . . p. 123 (col.).

—— **(Chicago, int.).** Holiday 28: 79 (col.) Dec '60.

—— **(Colo.).** Natl. geog. 106: 239 Aug '54.

—— **(Glyndebourne).** Cooper: Con. ency. of music, p. 455.

—— **(Manaos).** Disney: People & places, p. 106 (col.).

—— **(Paris). Cooper:** Con. ency. of music, p. 463.

Holiday 11: 88 Ap '52.

Natl. geog. 98: 69 Jl '50.

Praeg.: pict. ency., p. 391.

—— **(Vienna). Cooper:** Con. ency. of music, p. 464.

Disney: People & places, p. 54 (col.).

Holiday 13: 117 Mar '53; 18: 19 Nov '55.

—— **(Vienna int.).** Holiday 25: 64 (col.) Jan '59.

Natl. geog. 115: 188-91 (col.) Feb '59.

—— **(Wash., D.C., 1895).** Brooks: Growth of a nation, p. 223.

—— **(West German).** Natl. geog. 115: 736-7 (col.) Je '59.

——. *See* also theater.

opera house play posters. Amer. heri., vol. 7 no. 4 p. 97 (Je '56).

opera scene (Baths of Caracalla). Natl. geog. 111: 458 (col.) Ap '57.

—— **("The masked ball").** Holiday 8: 75 Nov '50.

operating room (surgeon, nurses). Natl. geog. 116: 404 (col.) Sept '59.

Operti, Albert (work of). Amer. heri., vol. 11 no. 4 p. 44, 47-8 (col.) (Je '60).

Ophiel (seal of). Lehner: Pict. bk. of sym., p. 25.

Opie, John (work of). Con. ency. of ant., vol. 1, pl. 172.
Con. 142: cover (col.) Jan '59; 143: 88 Ap '59.

Oppenheimer, Harry Frederick. Cur. biog. p. 351 (1961).

Oppenheimer, J. Robert. Cur. biog. p. 439 (1945).
Natl. geog. 117: 30 (col.) Jan '60.

"Optician & attendant" (Zoffany). Con. 139: 9 Mar '57.

optics (sym.). Lehner: Pict. bk. of sym., p. 16.

Oracoke is. (N.C.). Face of Amer., p. 90-1 (col.).

orange blossoms, wedding. Lehner: Pict. bk. of sym., p. 56.

orangery. Holiday 23: 84 Ap '58.

—— **("Croome court", Eng.).** Con. 132: 74 Nov '53.

—— **("Heveningham", Eng.).** Con. 139: 75 Ap '57.

oratories, church (Naples). Labande: Naples, p. 28.

oratory (muse). Lehner: Pict. bk. of sym., p. 33.

——, **Italian.** Con. 133: 116 Ap '54.

——, **St. Joseph's.** *See* St. Joseph's oratory.

orb (sym.). Lehner: Pict. bk. of sym., p. 94.

——, **British (Queen Eliz. II).** Natl. geog. 113: 575 Ap '58.

——, **golden.** *See* golden orb.

——, **imperial.** *See* Imperial orb, Russian.

"Orcagna, death & ascension of Virgin" (relief). Praeg. pict. ency., p. 209.

Orcas is. (Puget Sound). Travel 105: 34-7 May '56.

—— **(map).** Travel 105: 36 May '56.

"Orchard House" (home of Louisa May Alcott). Amer. heri., vol. 8 no. 5 p. 35 (Aug '57).

orchestra. Holiday 9: 62-7 Mar '51; 20: 25 Oct '56.

—— **(musical instruments).** Int. gr. soc.: Arts . . . p. 141 (col.).

——, **community.** Amer. heri., vol. 5 no. 2 p. 49 (winter '54).

——, **Cuban.** *See* musicians, Cuban.

——, **jazz (Negro).** Int. gr. soc.: Arts . . . p. 143 (col.).

——, **mountain.** Natl. geog. 102: 488 Oct '52.

orchestra & director, world. Holiday 19: 78 (col.) Mar '56.

Order of Holy Sepulcher (Vatican). Int. gr. soc.: Arts . . . p. 167 (col.).

Order of Lenin (U.S.S.R.)). Int. gr. soc.: Arts . . . p. 167 (col.).

Order of Leopold I (Belgium). Int. gr. soc.: Arts . . . p. 167 (col.).

Order of merit of the Republic (Italy). Int. gr. soc.: Arts . . . p. 167 (col.).

Order of San Martin the Liberator (Argentina). Int. gr. soc.: Arts . . . p. 167 (col.).

Order of the Elephant (Denmark). Int. gr. soc.: Arts . . . p. 167 (col.).

Order of the Rising Sun (Japan). Int. gr. soc.: Arts . . . p. 167 (col.).

ore boat. *See* boat, ore.

"Ore docks at Marquette" (Jones). Amer. heri.,

vol. 2 no. 4 p. 67 (col.) (summer '51).

Ore mt. (Erzberg). Natl. geog. 99: 772 Je '51.

Oregon. Holiday 5: 71 (col.) Mar '49, 167 (col.) Ap '49; 6: 101 (col.) Dec '49; 13: 115 (col.) Feb '53, 99 (col.) Ap '53, 34-47 (part col.) Je '53; 25: 48-9 (col.) Mar '59.
Travel 101: cover, 7-10 Ap '54; 102: 18-9 Aug '54; 103: 53-5 May '55; 108: 40-2 Aug '57.

—— **(Astoria, fur trading post).** Amer. heri., vol. 9 no. 5 p. 58 (col.) (Aug '58).
Brooks: Growth of a nation, p. 97.

—— **(beach).** Holiday 24: 42-3 (col.) Jl '58.

—— **(capitol bldg.).** Travel 108: 20 Nov '57.

—— **(state parks).** Travel 110: 36-9 Jl '58.

Oregon caves natl. monument. Holiday 21: 5 (col.) Mar '57; 23: 107 (col.) Feb '58.

Oregon City. Natl. geog. 102: 575 Nov '52.

Oregon trail. Holiday 14: 58-63 Jl '53.
Travel 108: 16 Jl '57.

Oregon trail marker. Travel 102: 14 Oct '54.

organ. Holiday 22: 98 (col.) Oct '57, 31 Nov '57; 23: 130 Mar '58.

—— **(man playing).** Holiday 21 183 Ap '57.

——, **Bach's.** Int. gr. soc.: Arts . . . p. 109 (col.).

——, **chamber (1627).** Cooper: Con. ency. of music., p. 239 (col.).

——, **electric.** Holiday 28: 198 Nov '60, 171 Dec '60.

——, **electric chord.** Holiday 28: 32 Nov '60.

——, **medieval (woman playing).** Int. gr. soc.: Arts . . . p. 61 (col.).

——, **modern.** Holiday 23: 4 Je '58; 24: 178 Nov '58.

——, **pipe (18th cent.).** Con. 143: 119 Ap '59.

——, **pipe (in the Wieskirche, Bavaria).** Cooper: Con. ency. of music, p. 222 (col.).

——, **pipe (Royal festival hall, London).** Cooper: Con. ency. of music, p. 411.

organ pipe natl. monument (Ariz.). Holiday 24: 57 (col.) Jl '58.

organ pipes. Lehner Pict. bk. of sym., p. 14.

"The Orgy" (Hogarth). Praeg.: pict. ency., p. 371 (col.).

Oriental authority. *See* authority, Oriental.

Oriental dancers. *See* dancers, Oriental.

Oriental philosophies & beliefs (sym.). Lehner: Pict. bk. of sym., p. 42-9.

Orion hotel (Bergen, Norway). Travel 107: 49 Ap '57.

Oriskany battle monument. *See* monument, battle (Oriskany).

Orkney is. Natl. geog. 104: 520-36 Oct '53.

—— **(map).** Natl. geog. 104: 522 Oct '53.

Orlando, Vittorio. Amer. heri., vol. 8 no. 4 p. 25 (Je '57); vol. 9 no. 4 p. 67 (Je '58).

Orlando, Vittorio E. Cur. biog. p. 515 (1944).

Orlemanski, Stanislaus. Cur. biog. p. 517 (1944).

Ormandy, Eugene. Cur. biog. p. 637 (1941).

Ormsby-Gore, Sir David. Cur. biog. p. 353 (1961).

ornament, furniture. *See* furniture ornament.

——, **Japanese.** Con. ency. of ant., vol. 1, p. 28.

——, **marquetry.** *See* marquetry ornament.

O'Rorke, Patrick Henry. Amer. heri., vol. 9 no. 2 p. 30 (Feb '58).

Orpen, William (work of). Amer. heri., vol. 8 no. 4 p. 21 (col.) (Je '57).
Con. 144: 12 Sept '59.

orphanage boys (1862). Amer. heri., vol. 10 no. 1 p. 86 (Dec '58).

"Orpheus" (statue by Baratta). Con. 142: 172 Dec '58.

"Orpheus of Hell" (Leonbruno). Con. 141: LV Je '58.

orpiment (sym.). Lehner: Pict. bk. of sym., p. 73.

Orr, Hiram Winnett. Cur. biog. p. 639 (1941).
Orr, Sir John Boyd. Cur. biog. p. 442 (1946).
Orr, Louis M. Cur. biog. p. 303 (1960).

orrery, antique portable. Con. 138: 61 Sept '56.
——, 18th cent. Con. 141: 163, 165-6 May '58.

Orsborn, Albert. Cur. biog. p. 444 (1946).

Orta, Lake. See Lake Orta.

Orton, Helen Fuller. Cur. biog. p. 640 (1941). Jun. bk. of auth., p. 233.

Orville, Capt. Howard T. Cur. biog. p. 474 (1956).

Osato, Sono. Cur. biog. p. 441 (1945).

Osborn, Fairfield. Cur. biog. p. 464 (1949).
Osborn, Frederick. Cur. biog. p. 641 (1941).
Osborn, Robert C. Cur. biog. p. 337 (1959).

Osborne, John. Cur. biog. p. 338 (1959).
Holiday 23: 92 Ap '58.

Osborne, Thomas M. Natl. geog. 113: 458 Ap '58.

Osborn's castle. Holiday 21: 51 (col.) Je '57.

an "oscar" (sym.). Lehner: Pict. bk. of sym., p. 84.

"Oscar II". See "Peace ship", Ford.

oscillography (sym.). Lehner: Pict. bk. of sym., p. 16.

oscilloscopes. Natl. geog. 111: 577 Ap '57.

Osgood,, Charles (work of). Amer. heri., vol. vol. 6 no. 2 p. 19 (col.) (winter '55); vol. 10 no. 1 p. 31 (col.) (Dec '58).
Cur. biog. p. 332 (1962).

Osiris (god, Egyptian art). Int. gr. soc.: Arts . . . p. 21 (col.).
——, tet of. See tet of Osiris.

Oslo (city map, Norway). Travel 111: 49 Je '59.

Osmanli. Osward. Asia Minor, pl. 80.

Osmena, Sergio. Cur. biog. p. 520 (1944).

ossuary (Sant' Agostino Della Zecca). Labande: Naples, p. 63.

ostensory, Voghera. Con. 142: 8 Sept '58.

Osterhaus, Peter Joseph. Pakula: Cent. album, p. 219.

Ostrade, Adrian van. See Van Ostrade, Adrian.

Ostrander, Don. R. Natl. geog. 118: 69 (col.) Jl '60.

"Otello" (setting for, by Wakhevitch). Cooper: Con. ency. of music, p. 395 (col.).

"Othello & Desdemona" (by Bonington). Con. ency. of ant., vol. 1, pl. 168.

"Other end of the world" (Walpole). Natl. geog. 109: 534-5 (col.) Ap '56.

Otis, Mr. (primitive art). Amer. heri., vol. 10 no. 3 p. 44-5 (col.) (Ap '59).

Otomi land (Mexico). Travel 107: 36-7 Jan '57.

Otsego lake. Natl. geog. 110: 596 (col.) Nov '56.

Ott, Mel. Cur. biog. p. 643 (1941).
Holiday 23: 84 May '58.

Ottawa (Canada). Holiday 18: 60-3 (part col.) Dec '55; 19: 2 (col.) Feb '56; 25: 12 (col.) Feb '59.

—— (Chateau Laurier). Holiday 5: 124 (col.) Mar '49; 14: 119 (col.) Jl '53.

—— (Natl. war memorial). Travel 106: 60 Nov '56.

—— (Parliament bldg.). Holiday 14: 45 Jl '53.
Natl. geog. 108: 195 (col.) Aug '55.
Travel 101: 4 Feb '54; 105: cover, 15 May '56; 106: 47 Nov '56.

—— (Parliament, int.). Holiday 6: 34 (col.) Aug '49.

—— (Parliament Hill). Holiday 6: 37 Aug '49.

Ottley, Roi. Cur. biog. p. 567 (1943).

Otto, Archduke of Austria. Cur. biog. p. 644 (1941).

Otuken, Adnan. Cur. biog. p. 496 (1954).

"Otwell" (Maryland home). Natl. geog. 105: 444 (col.) Ap '54.

Oudry, Jean Baptiste (work of). Con. 136: 311 Jan '56; 140: 30 Sept '57; 142: 6 Sept '58; 143: LV Je '59.

Ouless, P. J. (work of). Con. 133: XXXI (col.) Ap '54.

Oumansky, Constantine. Cur. biog. p. 646 (1942).

"Our Lady of Fatima chapel" (Brazil). Natl. geog. 117: 714-5 May '60.

"Our Lady of good voyage" (Gloucester, Mass.). Natl. geog. 104: 77 (col.) Jl '53.

"Our Lady of the angels" (alabaster carvings). Con. 139: XLIII Mar '57.

"Our Lady Pammakaristos", church of. See church of "Our Lady Pammakaristos.

Oursler, Fulton. Cur. biog. p. 637 (1942).

outboard motor. See motor, outboard.

outboard motor boat. See boat, outboard motor.

"Outer banks" (map). (N.C.). Natl. geog. 108: 507 Oct '55.

outer space life (cartoon). Holiday 14: 73 Nov '53.

"Outing on the Hudson" (1876). Amer. heri., vol. 10 no. 1 p. 20 (col.) (Dec '58).

outing set. See picnic kit.

outlaws (early western). Horan: Pict. hist. of wild west, (all thru bk.).

outrigger boats (Bora Bora). Holiday 28: 96-7 (col.) Oct '60.

—— canoe. Holiday 25: 36 (col.) Ap '59.
Natl. geog. 97: 526 Ap '50; 118: 22 (col.) Jl '60, 602 Nov '60.

—— (Hawaii). Holiday 12: 120 (col.) Oct '52.
Natl. geog. 102: 826 (col.) Dec '52.
Travel 112: 22 Dec '59.

—— (Philippines). Travel 107: 26 May '57.

outrigger sailboat. See sailboat, outrigger.

Oved, Moshed (bust). Holiday 13: 18 Jan '53.

oven, beehive. See cooking oven, French beehive.

——, clay bake. Natl. geog. 111: 600 (col.) May '57.

——, cooking. See cooking oven.

oven, elec. roasting. Holiday 23: 128 (col.) Ap '58, 4 (col.) May '58, 184 (col.) Je '58; 24: 12 (col.) Dec '58; 25: 23 (col.) Ap '59, 136 (col.) May '59; 26: 2 (col.) Oct '59, 175 (col.) Nov '59, 20 Dec '59, 27: 9 May '60, 144 Je '60.

——, Indian cooking. Natl. geog. 114: 822 (col.) Dec '58.

——, Outdoor (bread baking). Natl. geog. 98: 331 (col.) Sept '50.

——, outdoor clay. Natl. geog. 113: 222 (col.) Feb '58.

——, Terascan beehive-shaped adobe. Natl. geog. 102: 540 (col.) Oct '52.

overcoat, man's. Holiday 21: 160 (col.) Ap '57; 26: 181 Oct '59.

overcoat & hat, man's. Holiday 20: 58 (col.) Sept '56.

overcoats, men's (on rack). Natl. geog. 111: 323 Mar '57.

overcoats. See also man (overcoat).

Overholser, Winfred. Cur. biog. p. 467 (1953).

Overing house (Newport, R.I., 1777). Amer. heri., vol. 11 no. 5 p. 31 (col.) (Aug '60).

overshoe, woman's. Holiday 26: 182 Oct '59, 128 Nov '59.

Overstreet, Harry A. Cur. biog. p. 433 (1950).

ovum. Gray's anatomy, p. 21, 24, 26-8.

Owen, Arthur David K. Cur. biog. p. 445 (1946).

Owen, Robert. Amer. heri., vol. 2 no. 1 p. 12-3 (fall '50).

Owen, Ruth Bryan. Cur. biog. p. 523 (1944).

Owen, Steve. Cur. biog. p. 448 (1946).

Owen, William (work of). Con. 133: XXIII (col.) May '54.

Owen Falls dam. Natl. geog. 107: 703 May '55.

Owens, Jesse. Cur. biog. p. 476 (1956).

"Owh! in San Pao" (Davis). Praeg. pict. ency., p. 455.

owl (college cap, comic). Holiday 21: 153 Jan '57.

—— (sym.). Lehner: Pict. bk. of sym., p. 61.

ox, winged. See winged ox.

ox cart. See cart, ox.

ox hitching post. See hitching post, ox.

ox shoeing sling. Rawson: Ant. pict. bk., p. 66.

ox shoes. Rawson: Ant. pict. bk., p. 54, 68.

ox yoke. Holiday 11: 150 (col.) May '52; 15: 93 Mar '54.

—— (sym.). Lehner: Pict. bk. of sym., p. 82.

Oxford (Eng.). Holiday 25: 17 Jan '59. Natl. geog. 108: 318 Sept '55.

—— (Radcliffe library). Praeg. pict. ency., p. 358.

Oxford house motor hotel (Chicago). Travel 113: 41, 43 Feb '60.

Oxford Univ. (Eng.). Holiday 13: 97-101 Je '53; 28: 51 Dec '60. Natl. geog. 114: 61 (col.) Jl '58.

—— (Tom Tower). Holiday 17: 37 Jan '55.

oxide of antimony (sym.). Lehner: Pict. bk of sym., p. 73.

Oxnam, Bishop G. Bromley. Cur. biog. p. 526 (1944).

"Oxnard" ship. (sinking, 1848). Amer. heri., vol. 11 no. 6 p. 26 (col.) (Oct '60).

oxygen mask (air force cadets). Natl. geog. 115: 872-3 Je '59.

oyster boat (men). Natl. geog. 111: 613 (col.) May '57.

oyster stand. Amer. heri., vol. 6 no. 4 p. 49 (col.) (Je '55).

Ozarks. Holiday 10: 91-7 (part col.) Aug '51.

Ozbirn, Mrs. E. Lee. Cur. biog. p. 334 (1962).

P

Paar, Jack. Cur. biog. p. 340 (1959).

Paasikivi, Juho Kusti. Cur. biog. p. 529 (1944).

Paavo Nurmi (statue). Travel 105: 35 Ap '56.

Pacciardi, Randolfo. Cur. biog. p. 532 (1944).

Pace, Frank jr. Cur. biog. p. 436 (1950).

Pacheco E. Chaves, Joao. Cur. biog. p. 498 (1954).

Pacific island home (int.). Int. gr. soc.: Arts ... p. 15 (col.).

—— (present day). Int. gr. soc. Arts ... p. 15 (col.).

Pacific islands Holiday 28: 51- Oct '60.

Pacific ocean (map). See map (Pacific ocean).

"pack" burro. Holiday 26: 143 (col.) Dec '59.

—— (loaded). Natl. geog. 104: 51 (col.) Jl '53.

pack-saddle, cow. Rawson: Ant. pict. bk., p. 69.

pack train (New Guinea natives). Natl. geog. 103: 428 (col.) Ap '53.

package (Christmas wrapped). Holiday 23: 83 (col.) Jan '58.

—— (gift wrapped). Holiday 10: 159 Dec '51; 11: 142 (col.) May '52; 21: 122 (col.) Jan '57; 27: 135 (col.) Jan '60. Lehner: Pict. bk. of sym., p. 50.

Packard, Eleanor. Cur. biog. p. 647 (1941).

Packard, Vance. Cur. biog. p. 323 (1958).

Packard auto. Holiday 5: 15 (col.) Ap '49, 66 (col.) Je '49; 6: 31 (col.) Jl '49, inside cover (col.) Sept '49, 67 (col.) Nov '49; 9: 2 (col.) Mar '51.

—— (1954). Holiday 15: 5 (col.) May '54; 16: 77 (col.) Sept '54.

Packer, Fred L. Cur. biog. p. 455 (1952).

packet, river. See boat, river.

pacts circle (sym.). Lehner: Pict. bk. of sym., p. 70.

paddle boat. See boat, paddle.

Paddleford, Clementine. Cur. biog. p. 325 (1958).

paddles, canoe. Holiday 12: 82 (col.) Sept '52; 20: 23 Aug '56; 22: 91 (col.) Jl '57.

paddlewheel, stern. See wheel, stern paddle.

paddlewheel boat. See boat, paddlewheel.

paddlewheel ship. See ship, paddlewheel.

Paderewski, Ignaz Jan. Cooper: Con. ency. of music, p. 200.

Padilla, Ezequiel. Cur. biog. p. 638 (1942).

Padilla Nervo, Luis. Cur. biog. p. 450 (1946).

padlock (sym.). Lehner: Pict. bk. of sym., p. 88.

Padover, Saul K. Cur. biog. p. 456 (1952).

Padre island. Travel 102: 20 Dec '54.

Paepcke, Walter P. Cur. biog. p. 305 (1960).

Paestum (Italy). Labande: Naples, p. 175-81.

Paestum temples. Con. 138: 16 Sept '56.

Page, Geraldine. Cur. biog. p. 469 (1953).

Page, Joe. Cur. biog. 437 (1950).

Page, Ruth. Cur. biog. p. 336 (1962).

pageant (Bruges). See Sanguis Christi pageant.

pageant (Dinkelsbuhl. Ger.). Natl. geog. 111: 257-68 (part col.) Feb '57.

——, **Austrian historical.** Natl. geog. 100: 379 Sept '51.

——, **chess game (Marostica, Italy).** Natl. geog. 110: 659-68 (col.) Nov '56.

pageant boat (Austria). Natl. geog. 99: 779 (col.) Je '51.

pageants, outdoor. Travel 111: 28-31 Je '59.

Pagnol, Marcel. Cur. biog. p. 478 (1956).

Pago Pago harbor (Samoa). Travel 101: 33 Jan '54.

pagoda. Holiday 11: 88 (col.) Je '52; 25: 168 (col.) Mar '59; 28: 22 (col.) Jl '60. Natl. geog. 97: 500 Ap '50; 116: 856 (col.) Dec '59.

—— **(top).** Travel 111: 56 Je '59.

——, **Bali.** Travel 108: 16 Nov '57.

——, **Burma.** Natl. geog. 100: 353 (col.) Sept '51.

——, **Chinese.** Lehner: Pict. bk. of sym., p. 46.

——, **Hongkong.** Holiday 14: 118 Jl '53.

——, **Japan.** Praeg. pict. ency., p. 528.

——, **Katmandu.** Natl. geog. 117: 396-7 (col.) Mar '60.

——, **Nepal.** Travel 106: 43 Sept '56.

——, **Shwe Dagon.** Holiday 20: 45 (col.) Sept '56.

Pah-kwa and Monade. Lehner: Pict. bk. of sym., p. 44.

Pai Tsung-Hsi. Cur. biog. p. 517 (1942).

Paige, Janis. Cur. biog. p. 341 (1959).

Paige, Leroy. Cur. biog. p. 459 (1952).

Paillou, P. (work of). Con. ency. of ant., vol. 3 pl. 86.

Paine, Lewis. Amer. heri., vol. 8 no. 2 p. 57 (Feb '57).

paint brush. Holiday 11: 74 (col.) Ap '52. Travel 109: 25 Je '58.

—— **(sym.).** Lehner: Pict. bk. of sym., p. 91.

paint pallet. See pallet, paint.

painted desert. Jordan: Hammond's pict. atlas, p. 177 (col.).

painter (sym.). Lehner: Pict. bk. of sym., p. 91.

——. See also artists; man (painting).

painting (sym.). Lehner: Pict. bk. of sym., p. 16.

painting, bark. See bark painting.

——, **children's.** See art, children's.

——, **Indian sand.** See sand painting.

——, **Negro artist.** See Negro artist painting (French Congo).

——, **rock.** See rock painting.

——, **silk.** See silk painting.

——, **Yamato-e.** See Yamato-e painting.

painting on wood (Egypt 2nd cent. A.D.). Praeg. pict. ency., p. 161 (col.).

painting. See also art.

paintings, Egyptian wall. See wall paintings, Egyptian.

Paiva, Djanira. See Djanira.

pajamas (man). Holiday 10: 37 (col.) Dec '51.

——, **child's** Holiday 20: 211 Dec '56.

Pajou, Augustin (terracotta work). Con. 140: 5-6 Sept '57.

Pakenham, Gen. (1814). Amer. heri. vol. 8 no. 5 p. 6 (Aug '57).

Pakistan. Natl. geog. 102: 638-77 (part col.) Nov '52; 107: 398-425 (part col.) Mar '55; 117: 604-9 (col.) May '60. Travel 108: 29-31 Nov '57.

—— **(map).** Natl. geog. 102: 640 Nov '52; 107: 402 Mar '55.

Pakistan men. Natl. geog. 100: 747 Dec '51.

Pakistan women. Natl. geog. 100: 734 (col.) Dec '51; 111: 80 Jan '57.

Pakistan wrestlers. Natl. geog. 105: 512 (col.) Ap '54.

palace. Holiday 13: 27 Ap '53.

—— **(Africa, int.).** Holiday 25: 72-3 (col.) Ap '59.

—— **(China).** Con. 129: 99 Je '52.

—— **(Eng.).** Holiday 15: 29 Je '54.

—— **(India).** Natl. geog. 113: 710 (col.) May '58.

—— **(India, int.).** Holiday 14: 35, 46 (col.) Oct '53.

—— **(Ladakh).** Natl. geog. 99: 615 (col.) May '51.

—— **(Leningrad).** Holiday 24: 56 Sept '58.

—— **(Malta, int.).** Holiday 27: 70- (col.) Je '60.

—— **(Munich, int.).** Holiday 22: 60-1 (col.) Sept '57.

—— **(Nepal, int.).** Holiday 21: 70 May '57.

—— **(Pakistan).** Natl. geog. 107: 400 (col.) Mar '55.

—— **(Rome, int.).** Amer. heri., vol. 11 no. 3 p. 21 (col.) (Ap '60). Holiday 27: 96-7 (col.) Ap '60.

—— **(Turkey).** Natl. geog. 109; 75 (col.) Jan '56.

—— **(Venice).** Holiday 25: 186 Ap '59.

——, **Aldobrandini (near Rome).** Holiday 27: 92 (col.) Ap '60.

——, **Blenheim.** See Blenheim palace.

——, **Buckingham.** See Buckingham palace.

——, **Ceylon metal.** Int. gr. soc.: Arts . . . p. 11 (col.).

——, **Duk Soo (Korea).** Natl. geog. 97: 782 (col.) Je '50.

——, **Escorial convent.** See Escorial convent-palace.

——, **Falkland.** See Falkland palace.

——, **garden.** See Saray-Burnu palace.

——, **Governor's (Williamsburg, Va.).** Brooks: Growth of a nation, p. 64. Holiday 13: 26 Je '53. Natl. geog. 106: 455-9, 470 (col.) Oct '54.

——, **Imperial Russian.** See Russian imperial palace.

——, **Kathiri (sultan's home).** Natl. geog. 111: 246 Feb '57.

——, **Laos royal.** See Laos (royal palace).

——, **Luxembourg.** See Luxembourg palace.

——, **Mexico City natl.** Natl. geog. 100: 791 Dec '51.

——, **Monte Carlo.** Holiday 14: 52 Nov '53.

——, **Natl. (Haiti).** Holiday 7: 100 Mar '50.

——, **Nijo.** See Nijo palace.

——, **Pena.** See Pena palace.

——, **royal (Madrid, Spain).** Holiday 23: 58-63 (col.) Jan '58.

——, **royal (Naples).** Labande: Naples, p. 78.

——, **royal (Netherlands).** Holiday 10: 54-5 Nov '51.

——, royal (Stockholm). Holiday 20: 38 (col.) Aug '56.
Travel 107: 35 Ap '57.
——, royal (Stockholm, int). Con. 141: 13-7 Mar '58.
——, Russian. Holiday 18: 109 Jl '55.
——, Schonbrunn. See Schonbrunn palace.
——, Shaw Jahan. See Delhi's red fort.
——, Soestdjik. See Soestdjik palace.
——, Solomon's (int.). Natl. geog. 112: 862-3 (col.) Dec '57.
——, Sultan's. See Sultan's palace.
——, Tonga. Holiday 28: 79 Oct '60.
——, Turkish sultan's. Osward: Asia Minor, p. 93-9.
——, "Viscaya". See "Viscaya" palazzo (Miami).
——, winter (Eng.). Con. 142: 226 Jan '59.
——, Yemen (int.). Natl. geog. 101: 230 Feb '52.
——, Zanzibar. Natl. geog. 101: 266 (col.) Feb '52.
Palace & grounds of Versailles. Praeg. pict. ency., p. 326.
Palace Balbi Durazzo (Genoa, int. & ext.). Con. 142: 138-41 (part col.) Dec '58.
Palace Belvedere. See Belvedere palace.
Palace Ca'd-Ooro (Venice). Praeg. pict. ency., p. 207.
Palace Corsini. See Corsini palace (art in).
Palace dining room. Holiday 20: 204 (col.) Dec '56; 23: 59 (col.) Jan '58.
Palace hotel (Brasilia, night). Natl. geog. 117: 717 (col.) May '60.
Palace hotel (San Francisco, int.). Holiday 14: 26-7 (col.) Sept '53.
Palace of Capodimonte. Labande: Naples, p. 115.
Palace of Congress (Buenos Aires). Holiday 11: 103 (col.) Mar '52.
Palace of culture & science (Warsaw). Natl. geog. 114: 359 (col.) Sept '58.
"Palace of Dawn" (Brazil). Holiday 25: 46 Mar '59.
Palace of fine arts (Mexico City). Natl. geog. 100: 802 Dec 51.
Palace of fine arts rotunda (San Francisco). Holiday 14: 37 Sept '53.
Palace of Justice. See Palais de Justice (Paris).
Palace of King Facilidas (Abyssinia). Con. 139: XLII Ap '57.
Palace of King Minos (Knossos). Ceram: March of arch., p. 55-7.
Holiday 18: 34-5 (col.), 37 Aug '55.
Natl. geog. 114: 752-3 (col.) Dec '58.
Palace of Quelaz, royal (Portugal). Con. 139: 41 Mar '57.
Palace of Venus (Rome). Con. 129: LX Ap '52.
"Palace of the winds". Natl. geog. 118: 462-3 (col.) Oct '60.
Palace Sanssouci. See Sanssouci palace.
palace throne room, royal (Eng.). Holiday 23: 67 (col.) Jan '58.
palaces, Venetian. Natl. geog. 111: 792 (col.) Je '57.
palaces of Han (China). Praeg. pict. ency., p. 534 (col.).
Palacio de Bussaco, hotel (Portugal). Travel

111: 24 Ap '59.
Palaeolithic carving. Praeg. pict. ency., p. 172.
Palais de Justice (Paris). Natl. geog. 101: 801 (col.) Je '52.
palanquin. Amer. heri., vol. 10 no. 4 p. 18 (col.) (Je '59).
palate, human (muscles). Gray's anatomy, p. 1181.
Palamedes, Anthonie (work of). Con. 127: 123 May '51.
palanquin, African. Holiday 6: 131 (col.) Oct '49.
——, Egyptian. Holiday 6: 10 (col.) Aug '49.
——, Egyptian (camels). Holiday 8: 10 (col.) Sept '50.
Palazzo Chiericati (by Palladio). Int. gr. soc.: Arts . . . p. 83 (col.).
Palazzo dello sport (int., Rome). Holiday 27: 51 Ap '60.
Palazzo Medici, painting for (Florence, Italy). Praeg. pict. ency., p. 69 (col.).
Palazzo Reale at Turin (int.). Con. 140: 144-9, 155-6 (part col.) Dec '57.
Palazzo Ruccellai. Praeg. pict. ency., p. 265.
Palazzo Strozzi (Florence). Praeg. pict. ency., p. 265.
Palencia, Isabel de. Cur. biog. p. 649 (1941).
palenque (relief from pillar, temple city). Ceram: March of arch., p. 275, 277, 279, 297-8.
paleontologist (rock specimens). Natl. geog. 108: 171 Aug '55.
Palermo (Sicily). Natl. geog. 107: 31 (col.) Jan '55.
Palestine deity dance, shrine). Natl. geog. 112: 834-5 (col.) Dec '57.
Palestinian art. See art, Palestinian.
palette, artist's. Int. gr. soc.: Arts . . . title page (col.).
palette & brushes (art). Lehner: Pict. bk. of sym., p. 16.
Paley, William S. Cur. biog. p. 470 (1951).
Pali lookout (Hawaii). Natl. geog. 118: 28 (col.) Jl '60.
palio, Siena. See Siena palio.
palisade, Indian village. Amer. heri., vol. 6 no. 2 p. 29 (winter '55).
——, Iroquois. See Iroquois palisade.
palisade glacier (Cal.). Holiday 13: 120 (col.) Mar '53, 26 (col.) May '53.
palisades (Hudson river, 1776). Amer. heri., vol. 10 no. 1 p. 15 (col.) (Dec '58).
palla (Greek woman's dress, ancient times). Int. gr. soc.: Arts . . . p. 31 (col.).
Palladian type arch. Amer. heri., vol. 10 no. 5 p. 66 (Aug '59).
Palladian window. Natl. geog. 99: 585 May '51.
Palladio, Andrea (arch. by). Praeg.: Pict. ency., p. 309.
Palladio arch. See also arch., Palladio.
Pallavicini palace (Rome). Con. 136: 184-9, 190 (col.) Dec '55.
Pallazo dei conservatori (Rome). Praeg.: Pict. ency., p. 265.
Pallaza di Capodimonte ballroom (Naples). Con. 140: 178 Dec '57.
pallet, painter's. Con. 139: XLII May '57, back cover Je '57.

Palm Beach (Fla.). Jordan: Hammond's pict. atlas, p. 75 (col.).
Natl. geog. 113: 48 (col.) Jan '58.
Travel 105: 42-4 Jan '56.
Palm Beach towers apt. hotel. Travel 107: 49 Jan '57.
palm leaf (sym.). Lehner: Pict. bk. of sym., p. 86.
palm leaves (memorial). Lehner: Pict. bk. of sym., p. 55.
Palm Springs (Cal.). Holiday 13: 98-103 (col.) Feb '53.
Natl. geog. 112: 682-3 (col.), 684 Nov '57.
—— **(air view).** Holiday 22: 63 (col.) Oct '57.
—— **(Biltmore hotel).** Jordan: Hammond's pict. atlas, p. 196 (col.).
Palm Sunday (sym.). Lehner: Pict. bk. of sym., p. 55.
Palm Sunday parade. Natl. geog. 106: 851 (col.) Dec '54.
palm tree (sym.). Lehner: Pict. bk. of sym., p. 29.
Palma harbor (Mallorca). Holiday 15: 132 (col.) Mar '54.
Palma cathedral. Holiday 27: 128 Jan '60.
Natl. geog. 111: 622, 625 (col.) May '57.
"Palma's liberation from the Moors" (play scenes). Natl. geog. 111: 634-5 (col.) May '57.
Palmer, Arnold. Cur. biog. p. 307 (1960).
Palmer, Frances (work of). Amer. heri., vol. 6 no. 4 p. 60 (col.) (Je '55).
Palmer, Hazel. Cur. biog. p. 326 (1958).
Palmer, Lilli. Cur. biog. p. 472 (1951).
Holiday 10: 91, 136 Nov '51.
Palmer, Lynwood (work of). Con. 144: 200 Dec '59.
Palmer, N. B. Amer. heri., vol. 6 no. 4 p. 53 (Je '55).
Palmer, Thomas Waverly. Cur. biog. p. 466 (1949).
Palmer, Gen. William J. Holiday 7: 76 Jan '50.
Palmer Land (Antarctica, 1820). Amer. heri., vol. 6 no. 4 p. 51 (Je '55).
Palmer peninsula (map). Amer. heri., vol. 6 no. 4 p. 54 (col.) (Je '55).
palmistry (sym.). Lehner: Pict. bk. of sym., p. 67.
"Palmistry" (Roberts). Con. 132: 50 Sept '53.
palms (sym.). Lehner: Pict. bk. of sym., p. 84.
Palmyra (colonnade). Travel 105: 20 Jan '56.
Palmyra island. Travel 106: 10-5 Sept '56.
"Palo Duro Canyon" (Texas). Amer. heri., vol. 4 no. 1 p. 24 (fall '52).
Palo Duro state park. Travel 105: 54 Jan '56.
Palomar dome. Travel 102: 46 Jl '54.
Palomar observatory. Holiday 13: 120 (col.) Mar '53, 91 (col.) Ap '53, 26 (col.) May '53; 14: 12 (col.) Nov '53; 15: 84 Feb '54, 5 (col.) Mar '54, 80-1 Ap '54, 85 May '54.
Natl. geog. 98: 402 Sept '50.
Travel 103: 34 Je '55.
—— **(telescope).** Natl. geog. 98: 409 Sept '50.
Palos Verdes light (Los Angeles). Holiday 13: 120 (col.) Mar '53.
"Palouse Falls" (Kane). Amer. heri., vol. 10 no. 5 p. 47 (col.) (Aug '59).
Pamir Pass (Afghanistan). Natl. geog. 98: 679

Nov '50.
pamphlet, travel guide. Holiday 18: 19 Aug '55, 9 Oct '55.
pamphlets about Catholics (1836). Amer. heri., vol. 10 no. 2 p. 59 (Feb '59).
Pamukkale ("Cotton-wool castle"). Osward: Asia Minor, pl. 136-7, VIII (col.).
pan (for melting bullets). Rawson: Ant. pict. bk., p. 25.
——, **sauce.** Natl. geog. 111: 169 (col.) Feb '57.
Panama. Holiday 13: 44-9 (part col.) Jan '53.
Natl. geog. 97: 228-46 Feb '50.
—— **(hotel).** Holiday 14: 93 Dec '53.
—— **(map).** Holiday 12: 56 (col.) Nov '52.
Natl. geog. 97: 229 Feb '50; 104: 275 Aug '53.
Panama jungle. Natl. geog. 104: 272-89 (part col.) Aug '53.
"Panamint city" (Hammack). Amer. heri., vol. 6 no. 1 p. 64 (fall '54).
Panaya Kapulu (near home of Mary, Mother of Jesus). Osward: Asia Minor.
pancake rocks. Natl. geog. 101: 447 Ap '52.
pancreas. Gray's anatomy, p. 1245-49.
Pandit, Vijaya Lakshmi. Cur. biog. p. 451 (1946).
panel, courtyard (ancient Roman art). Natl. geog. 111: 218 (col.) Feb '57.
——, **needlework.** Con. 141: 105 Ap '58.
——, **wall.** Con. 133: XXXIV Mar '54; 136: XLII Dec '55; 140: 79 Nov '57; 141: 102 Ap '58; 144: 250, LIV Jan '60.
Natl. geog. 109: 463, 479 (col.) Ap '56; 111: 644 (col.) May '57.
——, **wall (Adam).** Con. 141: X-XI (col.) Ap '58.
——, **wall (antique carved).** Con. 133: 263 Je '54.
——, **wall (Canton enamel).** Con. 140: LXXII Jan '58.
——, **wall (carved, Rome).** Holiday 27: 93 (col.) Ap '60.
——, **wall (carved ivory).** Con. 143: 103 Ap '59.
——, **wall (carved, 17th cent.).** Con. 132: LIII Nov '53.
——, **wall (carved wood, "St. Hubert").** Con. 144: VI Jan '60.
——, **wall (colonial).** Holiday 13: 53 (col.) Jan '53.
——, **wall (18th cent.).** Con. 132: 67 Sept '53; 137: XXXI Mar '56.
——, **wall (Eng.).** Con. 143: 68 (col.) Ap '59.
——, **wall (Grinling Gibbons carvings).** Con. 132: 44 Sept '53.
——, **wall (India, 18th cent.).** Con. 141: back cover Mar '58.
——, **wall (Japanese art).** Con. 132: 65 Sept '53.
——, **wall (Louis XV, carved).** Con. 133: 247 Je '54.
——, **wall (Louis XVI, carved).** Con. 133: 241, 291 Je '54.
——, **wall (Pineau, 18th cent.).** Con. 145: 108 Ap '60.
——, **wall (regency carved).** Con. 133: 243 Je '54.

——, wall ("Scenes from legend of St. Nicholas"). Con. 133: 30 Mar '54.

——, wall (17th cent.). Con. 139: XII Je '57.

panels, wall (decorated drawing room). Natl. geog. 113: 547 (col.) Ap '58.

——, wall (Eng. linenfold). Con. 134: XXXI Nov '54.

——, wall (French). Con. 129: XXXV Ap '52.

——, wall (Napoleonic). Con. 145: 268 Je '60.

——, wall (17th cent.). Con. 142: XL Jan '59.

Pannell, Anne Gary. Cur. biog. p. 440 (1950).

Pannini, Giovanni Paolo (work of). Con. 136: XXXIII Dec '55; 140: 184 Dec '57; 141: 229-30 Je '58.

"Panorama of a whaling voyage around the world". Amer. heri., vol. 12 no. 1 p. 55-62 (col.) Dec '60.

pans, copper. Holiday 21: 67 (col.) Ap '57.

Pant, Govind Ballabh. Cur. biog. p. 343 (1959).

Pantaleoni, Helenka. Cur. biog. p. 480 (1956).

"Pantaloon & Columbine" (figurine). Praeg.: pict. ency., p. 82 (col.).

Pantheon (Caracas). Holiday 6: back cover (col.) Oct '49.

Pantheon (Paris). Natl. geog. 101: 787 Je '52.

Pantheon (Rome). Amer. heri., vol. 10 no. 5 p. 70 (Aug '59).
Holiday 27: 129 Jan '60.
Int. gr. soc.: Arts . . . p. 11 (col.).
Natl. geog. 111: 470-1 Ap '57.
Praeg. pict. ency., p. 142.

—— (Rome, int.). Praeg.: pict., ency., p. 164.

pants. See trousers, man's.

Panui, Priest (Hawaii). Amer. heri., vol. 2 no. 3 p. 17 (spring '51).

Panyushkin, Alexander S. Cur. biog. p. 485 (1948).

Paoli, Gen. Pascal (Bembridge). Con. 144: 264 (col.) Jan '60.

pap boat, Russian. Con. 143: XXXIII May '59.

pap boats, children's. Rawson: Ant. pict. bk., p. 83.

"Papageienallee" (Liebermann). Praeg.: pict. ency., p. 430 (col.).

Papago state park (Ariz.). Holiday 15: 103 (col.) Mar '54.

Papagos, Gen. Alexander. Cur. biog. p. 474 (1951).

Papal authority. See authority, Papal (sym.).

Papal guard, Swiss. See Swiss papal guard.

Papal rose (Rome, 1562). Con. 144: 81 Nov '59.

Papandreou, George. Cur. biog. p. 534 (1944).

Papashvily, George. Cur. biog. p. 443 (1945).

Papashvily, Helen (Waite). Cur. biog. p. 443 (1945).

Papen, Franz von. Cur. biog. p. 651 (1941).

paper craft, Japanese. Holiday 19: 103 (col.) Feb '56.

paper makers. Natl. geog. 112: 430-1 Sept '57.

paper making machine. Natl. geog. 98: 339 (col.) Sept '50; 99: 133 (col.) Jan '51.

paper mill. Natl. geog. 102: 596-7 (col.) Nov '52.

——. See also Union Bag, Camp Paper Corp. Mill.

paper-weights, glass antique. Con. 126: 138 Oct '50.

Papier-mache knights (Kashmir). Natl. geog. 114: 621 (col.) Nov '58.

papoose. See Indian papoose.

Papuan wood carving. Holiday 28: 83-97 (col.) Nov '60.

papyri, Egyptian. Ceram: March of arch., p. 158-9.

papyrus (paper making). Natl. geog. 107: 36; 39 (col.) Jan '55.

par buckle, boat. Rawson: Ant. pict. bk., p. 79.

"Parable of the Lord of the vineyard" (Feti). Con. 140: 111 Nov '57.

parachute. Natl. geog. 97: 711 Je '50; 101: 844-5 Je '52; 104: 779 (col.) Dec '53; 105: 326 (col.) Mar '54; 111: 297 (col.) Mar '57; 118: 54-5, 58 (col.) Jl '60.

—— (landing). Natl. geog. 103: 575 (col.) May '53; 109: 656 (col.) May '56.

—— (man). Holiday 5: 26 Feb '49.
Natl. geog. 112: 21 Jl '57.

—— (man & woman, comic). Holiday 16: 59 Aug '54.

parachute jumper. Holiday 27: 57 Ap '60.

—— (world's highest test). Natl. geog. 118: 855-73 (col.) Dec '60.

parachute jumpers. Natl. geog. 110: 310-11 (col.) Sept '56.

parachutist. Holiday 26: 226 Dec '59.

——, girl. Natl. geog. 101: 838-46 Je '52.

parade, Basque (France). Natl. geog. 109: 331 (col.) Mar '56.

——, Basque ("St. Peter's Day"). Natl. geog. 105: 170 (col.) Feb '54.

——, Bedouin. Natl. geog. 106: 838-9 (col.) Dec '54.

——, California. Holiday 27: 44-5 (col.) Mar '60.

——, carnival. Holiday 26: 7 (col.) Dec '59.

——, centennial. Natl. geog. 97: 204 (col.) Feb '50.

——, chess game pageant (Italy). Natl. geog. 110: 659-68 (col.) Nov '56.

——, Chinatown. Natl. geog. 110: 210-11 (col.) Aug '56.

——, circus. See circus parade.

——, dog. Natl. geog. 99: 826 Je '51.

——, El Rocio's festival. Natl. geog. 113: 420-1 (col.) Mar '58.

——, "Feast of the visitation". Natl. geog. 100: 405 (col.) Sept '51.

——, festival (Belgium). Natl. geog. 113: 830-1 (col.) Je '58.

——, festival (India). Natl. geog. 113: 707-10 (col.) May '58.

——, festival (Switzerland). Natl. geog. 107: 836 (col.) Je '55; 114: 570 (col.) Oct '58.

——, fiesta (Santa Barbara, Cal.). Natl. geog. 105: 758-9 (col.) Je '54.

——, fishermen's (Belgium). Natl. geog. 113: 824-5 (col.) Je '58.

——, French children's ("Fete of the virgins"). Natl. geog. 103: 236 (col.) Feb '53.

——, French children's (religious). Natl. geog. 103: 246 Feb '53.

parade, holiday (Mauritius). Natl. geog. 109: 87 Jan '56.

——, inauguration. Amer. heri., vol. 5 no. 1 p. 9 (col.) (fall '53).

——, London. Holiday 13: 135 (col.) Je '53.

——, Nepal coronation. See procession, Nepal coronation.

——, soldiers. See soldier's parade.

——, Spanish. Holiday 26: 2 (col.) Sept '59.

——, state fair (Colo.). Natl. geog. 106: 232 (col.) Aug '54.

——, Tirol Alps. Holiday 27: 42-3 (col.) Jan '60.

——, tournament of roses. See tournament.

——, West German (men & women). Natl. geog. 115: 755 (col.) Je '59.

"Parade de Mannequins" (Dufy). Con. 143: XVIII May '59.

parade in N.Y. (ticker tape). Int. gr. soc.: Arts . . . p. 163 (col.).

parade leader (drum major). Lehner: Pict. bk. of sym., p. 93.

parade. See also procession.

"Paradise" (Kandinsky). Con. 144: 181 (col.) Dec '59.

Paradise Falls (N.H.). Holiday 10: 43 (col.) Sept '51.

"Paradise garden" (1410). Praeg. pict. ency., p. 215 (col.).

"Paradise gateway" (15th cent., Florence). Praeg.: pict. ency., p. 18.

"Paradise gateway" (Ghiberti). Praeg.: pict. ency., p. 298.

Paradise valley (Ariz.). Holiday 25: 57 Mar '59. Natl. geog. 117: 484-5 (col.) Ap '60.

parakeets (sym.). Lehner: Pict. bk. of sym., p. 65.

parasol. Holiday 11: 118 (col.) May '52; 19: 70 (col.) Mar '56; 26: 32 Sept '59. Natl. geog. 116: 374 (col.) Sept '59. Travel 113: 7 Mar '60, inside back cover Ap '60.

—— (Burma). Holiday 20: 45 (col.) Sept '56.

—— (girl). Holiday 19: 60 (col.) May '56.

"The parasol" (Goya). Con. 135: 36 (col.) Mar '55.

parasol (over Mohammed). Holiday 25: 80 (col.) Ap '59.

—— (Siam). Holiday 18: 53 (col.) Oct '55.

parasol (thatch, beach). Natl. geog. 111: 641 (col.) May '57.

——, Japanese. See Japanese parasol.

——, royal (Vientiane temple). Natl. geog. 117: 58 (col.) Jan '60.

parasol bearer, Assyrian (ancient). Int. gr. soc.: Arts . . . p. 29 (col.).

——. See also umbrella.

paratepee. Natl. geog. 103: 576 (col.) May '53.

paratroop trainee, tower. Natl. geog. 105: 326 (col.) Mar '54.

paratrooper, British. Natl. geog. 101: 657 (col.) May '52.

"Pardon de Sainte Anne" (Concarneau, France). Holiday 7: 102 (col.) Jan '50.

"Pardon of Absalom" (Blake). Con. 129: 36 Ap '52.

"Pardon of the sea" (Concarneau, France). Holiday 7: 102 (col.) Jan '50.

Pares, Sir Bernard. Cur. biog. p. 454 (1946).

Paricutin (volcano, Mexico). Holiday 14: 49 Jl '53. Natl. geog. 102: 534 Oct '52.

Paris (France). Amer. heri., vol. 11 no. 3 p. 19 (col.) (Ap '60).

Holiday 10: 112 (col.) Jl '51; 13: entire issue (part col.) Ap '53; 16: 106-11 (col.) Oct '54, 56 (col.) Nov '54; 19: 48-9 (part col.) Jan '56, 42-3 Feb '56, 62-3 May '56; 20: 36-7 Aug '56, 88 (col.) Oct '56; 21: 62-1 (part col.) Jan '57, 134 Ap '57.

Natl. geog. 98: 44-72 (part col.) Jl '50; 100: 719 (col.) Dec '51; 101: 768-804 (part col.) Je '52; 114: 284-302 Aug '58.

Travel 107: 36-9 May '57.

—— (Arc de Triomphe). See Arc de Triomphe.

—— (book sellers row). Holiday 13: 27 Ap '53.

—— (caricatures). Holiday 28: 48-51 (part col.) Sept '60.

—— (cathedral). Natl. geog. 108: 531 (col.) Oct '55.

—— (Flea market). Natl. geog. 111: 319-26 Mar '57.

—— (Gare de Lyon, int.). Holiday 6: 110 (col.) Sept '49.

—— (harbor, night). Holiday 27: 112 (col.) Jan '60.

—— (The Louvre). Praeg.: pict. ency., p. 306.

—— (The Madeleine). Praeg.: pict. ency., p. 426.

—— (map). Travel 107: 35 May '57.

—— (map, pictorial). Holiday 13: 53 (col.) Ap '53.

—— (Montmartre st.). Holiday 23: 2 (col.) Jan '58.

—— (Notre Dame cathedral). See Notre Dame cathedral (Paris).

—— (opera). Praeg. pict. ency., p. 391.

—— (opera stairway). Travel 102: 6 Nov '54.

—— (Place de L'Etoile). Holiday 27: 38 Mar '60.

—— (street merchant). Natl. geog. 108: 153 Jl '55.

—— (Traveller's club). Holiday 16: 26 Dec '54.

Paris to Baghdad (route on map). Travel 106: 56 Oct '56.

Park, Linton (work of). Natl. geog. 99: 193 (col.) Feb '51.

Park, Matthew (work of). Amer. heri., vol. 11 no. 3 p. 11 (col.) (Ap '60).

Park, Thomas. Cur. biog. p. 313 (1963).

park. Holiday 24: 52 (col.) Nov '58.

——, Banff natl. See Banff natl. park.

——, Central (N.Y.). Natl. geog. 118: 785 (col.) Dec '60.

——, Glacier natl. See Glacier natl. park.

——, Golden gate. Natl. geog. 110: 203 (col.) Aug '56; 116: 606-7 (col.) Nov '59.

——, Grand Canyon. See Grand Canyon.

——, Harkness memorial. See Harkness memorial park.

——, Letchworth state. Natl. geog. 110: 605 (col.) Nov '56.

——, Queen Victoria. See Queen Victoria park.

——, **Yellowstone natl.** *See* Yellowstone natl. park.

park designers office (men). Natl. geog. 113: 614 May '58.

"Park of Chateau de Steen" (Rubens). Con. 127: 5 Mar '51.

Park of Vaux-le-Vicomte (France). Int. gr. soc.: Arts . . . p. 121 (col.).

park. *See* also parks.

parka, Eskimo (baby). Natl. geog. 107: 558, 561 (col.) Ap '55.

Parke-Bernet art galleries. *See* art gallery, Parke-Bernet.

Parker, Buddy. Cur. biog. p. 469 (1955).

Parker, Cola G. Cur. biog. p. 482 (1956).

Parker, Mrs. Edward. Amer. heri., vol. 9 no. 2 p. 57 (col.) (Feb '58).

Parker, Frank. Cur. biog. p. 488 (1948).

Parker, Hon. Isaac C. Horan: Pict. hist. of wild west, p. 141.

Parker, John J. Cur. biog. p. 470 (1955).

Parker, Karla V. Cur. biog. p. 493 (1947).

Parker, Chief Quanah (Comanche Indian). Amer. heri., vol. 4 no. 4 p. 31 (summer '53).

Parker, Robert. *See* Cassidy, Butch.

Parker, Maj. Gen. Roy H. Cur. biog. p. 476 (1951).

Parker, Theodore. Amer. heri., vol. 8 no. 2 p. 22 (Feb '57).

—— **(caricature).** Amer. heri., vol. 10 no. 3 p. 60 (Ap '59).

Parker home (Utah). Horan: Pict. hist. of wild west, p. 205.

Parkes, Henry Bamford. Cur. biog. p. 500 (1954).

Parkfairfax (Va.). Natl. geog. 103: 28-9 (col.) Jan '53.

parking, auto. *See* auto parking systems.

parking sign. Travel 105: inside cover Ap '56.

Parkinson, C. Northcote. Cur. biog. p. 309 (1960).

Parkinson, Thomas I. Cur. biog. p. 467 (1949).

Parkman, Francis. Amer. heri., vol. 8 no. 5 p. 27 (Aug '57).

parks, Ill. state Travel 103: 14-6 Je '55.

——, **natl.** *See* national parks.

——, **state.** *See* state parks.

——. *See* also park.

Parler, Peter (bust). Praeg. pict. ency., p. 210.

Parliament bldg., Africa (Cape Town). Natl. geog. 104: 166 (col.) Aug '53.

——, **Austria.** Travel 109: 47 Ap '58.

——, **Belgium.** Natl. geog. 113: 801 (col.) Je '58.

——, **British (London).** Amer. heri., vol. 9 no. 1 p. 13 (Dec '57).

Holiday 11: 121 (col.) Mar '52; 14: 67 (col.) Sept '53; 17: 56-61 (col.) Mar '55; 20: 29 Dec '56; 21: 33 (col.) Mar '57.

Natl. geog. 98: 203 Aug '50; 100: 715 (col.) Dec '51; 108: 127 Jl '55.

Praeg.: pict. ency., p. 391.

U.S. News & world report, vol. LV no. 1 p. 29 Jl 1, 1963.

——, **British (1775).** Amer. heri., vol. 11 no. 4 p. 13 (col.) (Je '60).

——, **British (silhouette).** Holiday 25: 154 Ap '59.

——, **Canada (Brit. Columbia).** Holiday 15: 7 Feb '54.

Natl. geog. 114: 151 (col.) Aug '58.

——, **Canada (night).** Holiday 24: 59 (col.) Nov '58.

——, **Canada (Victoria).** Travel 110: 56 Jl '58; 114: 4 Sept '60.

——, **Canada (Ottawa).** Holiday 6: 37 Aug '49; 19: 2 (col.) Feb '56.

Natl. geog. 108: 195 (col.) Aug '55; 115: 824, 829 (col.) Je '59.

Travel 101: 4 Feb '54; 114: 14 Jl '60.

——, **India.** Natl. geog. 117: 624-5 (col.) May '60.

——, **Ireland.** Holiday 6: 54 Dec '49.

——, **Israel.** Natl. geog. 115: 521 Ap '59.

Parliament room (Bermuda). Natl. geog. 105: 228 (col.) Feb '54.

parlor (19th cent.). Holiday 12: 46 (col.) Sept '52.

Parmigianino (work of). Con. 145: 39 Mar '60.

Praeg.: pict. ency., p. 313 (col.).

the Parnassus ceiling. Con. 142: 168 Dec '58.

Parnell, Mel. Holiday 7: 50 May '50.

Parnis, Mollie. Cur. biog. p. 484 (1956).

Parodi, Alexandre. Cur. biog. p. 456 (1946).

Parodi, Filippo (marble work of). Con. 139: 34 Mar '57.

—— **(sculpture by).** Con. 142: 140 Dec '58.

Parr, Albert E. Cur. biog. p. 641 (1942).

Parri, Ferruccio. Cur. biog. p. 445 (1945).

Parrish, Wayne W. Cur. biog. p. 328 (1958).

Parrott, Robert Parker. Amer. heri., vol. 10 no. 1 p. 21 (col.) (Dec '58).

Parry, Albert. Cur. biog. p. 355 (1961).

Parsons, C. (work of). Amer. heri., vol. 6 no. 6 p. 20 (col.) (Oct '55).

Parsons, Harriet. Cur. biog. p. 471 (1953).

Parsons, Talcott. Cur. biog. p. 357 (1961).

Parsons, Mrs. William Barclay. Cur. biog. p. 345 (1959).

Partch, Virgil F. Cur. biog. p. 458 (1946).

"Parthenia" (for Virginals in Eng., title page). Cooper: Con. ency. of music, p. 494.

Parthenon (Athens). Holiday 7: inside back cover (col.) Ap '50; 12: 56 (col.) Sept '52; 23: 2 (col.) Jan '58; 27: 125 Jan '60.

Natl. geog. 109: 38, 44-5 (col.) Jan '56; 110: 744 (col.) Dec '56; 117: 636 (col.) May '60.

Praeg.: pict. ency., p. 130.

Travel 101: 18 Jan '54; 106: inside cover Aug '56.

—— **(detail).** Int. gr. soc.: Arts . . . p. 17 (col.).

—— **(frieze).** Praeg.: pict. ency., p. 165.

Parthenon (Nashville, Tenn.). Travel 104: 14 Jl '55.

"Parting cheer" (O'Neil). Con. 144: XXXV (col.) Dec '59.

"Parting of David & Jonathan". (Rembrandt). Con. 138: 30 Sept '56.

partners desk, regency. *See* desk, regency partners.

Partridge, Capt. Alden. Amer. heri., vol. 7 no. 1 p. 22 (col.) (Dec '55).

Partridge, Gen Earle E. Cur. biog. p. 473 (1955).

Partridge, Eric. Cur. biog. (1963).

party (Philippine). Holiday 18: 91 (col.) Aug '55.

——, ship. Holiday 11: 130 (col.) May '52.

——. See also children's party.

Pasadena (Cal.) (Tournament of roses). Holiday 11: 94-101 (part col.) Jan '52.

Pascal, Gabriel. Cur. biog. p. 643 (1942).

Pasch, Lorenz (work of). Con. 136: 33 Sept '55.

Pasch the Younger, Lorentz (work of). Con. 135: 46 Mar '55.

Pasinelli, Lorenzo (work of). Con. 144: 22 Sept '59.

Pasini, A. (work of). Con. 138: XXXIII Jan '57.

Pasquel, Jorge. Cur. biog. p. 459 (1946).

Passau (Austria). Disney: People & places, p. 53 (col.).

"Passing storm" (Percy). Con. 129: X (col.) Ap '52.

"A passing storm" (Tissot). Con. 143: XXIX Je '59.

passion (religious sym.). Lehner: Pict. bk. of sym., p. 36-7.

Passion altar piece. See altar piece.

passion flower (sym.). Lehner: Pict. bk. of sym., p. 37.

"Passion Play" (Spearfish, S.D.). Travel 113: 42 Mar '60.

Passion play actors, Indian (Mexico). Natl. geog. 107: 225 (col.) Feb '55.

Passman, Otto E. Cur. biog. p. 311 (1960).

Passover (sym.). Lehner: Pict. bk. of sym., p. 55.

passport (foreign travel, 1859). Amer. heri., vol. 11 no. 3 p. 29 (Ap '60).

passport office (int.). Travel 111: 49 May '59.

paste jar. Holiday 12: 29 Nov '52.

Pasternak, Boris L. Cur. biog. p. 347 (1959).

Pasterzen glacier. See glacier, Pasterzen.

pastille burners, Rockingham. Con. 134: XII Sept '54.

Pastore, John O. Cur. biog. p. 474 (1953).

Pasvolsky, Leo. Cur. biog. p. 448 (1945).

Patan's' temple. See temple, Patan's.

Patch, Maj. Gen. Alexander M. Cur. biog. p. 569 (1943).

Patch, Edith M. Jun. bk. of auth., p. 237.

Patch, Thomas (work of). Con. 141: 236 Je '58.

patch box, antique silver. Con. 137: 216 May '56.

patch boxes, Bilston enamel. Con. 141: XIV Je '58.

Pate, Maurice. Cur. biog. p. 477 (1951).

Pate, Gen. Randolph M. Cur. biog. p. 329 (1958).

Pate, Walter L. Cur. biog. p. 495 (1947).

Patel, Vallabhbhai. Cur. biog. p. 489 (1948).

paten (Eucharistic service). Natl. geog. 97: 775 Je '50.

Pater, Jean-Baptiste (work of). Con. ency. of ant., vol. 1, pl. 160.
Con. 127: 27 (col.) Mar '51; 133: 259 Je '54; 142: 5 Sept '58.

"Paternal advice" (Terborch). Praeg.: pict. ency., p. 346 (col.).

Paterson, Chat. Cur. biog. p. 491 (1948).

Paterson silk strike (cartoon, 1913). Amer. heri., vol. 11 no. 2 p. 99 (Feb '60).

Patino, Simon I. Cur. biog. p. 645 (1942).

patio. Travel 103: 44 May '55.

—— (Beverly Hills). Holiday 22: 80-1 (col.) Oct '57.

patio garden. Holiday 22: 114 (col.) Sept '57.

patio. See also courtyard.

Patnam, Wright. Cur. biog. p. 462 (1946).

Paton, Alan. Cur. biog. p. 460 (1952).

patriarch, Israel. Natl. geog. 115: 523 (col.) Ap '59.

patriarch, Roman Catholic. Natl. geog. 106: 847 Dec '54.

Patrick air force missile test center. See Cape Canaveral (Fla.).

The "Patriot" (trading ship, 1809). Amer. heri., vol. 6 no. 2 p. 13 (col.) (winter '55).

patrol, camel. Natl. geog. 107: 158 (col.) Feb '55.

patrolman & dogs (training). Natl. geog. 114: 191-230 (part col.) Aug '58.

"The Patron" (Walker). Amer. heri., vol. 9 no. 5 p. 8 (col.) (Aug '58).

patron of children (sym.). Lehner: Pict. bk. of sym., p. 48.

patron saints. See saints, patron.

"Patrons of husbandry", founders of (1867). Brooks: Growth of a nation, p. 200.

Patten, Charles Lee. Jensen: The White House, p. 215.

Patterson, Alicia. Cur. biog. p. 475 (1955).

Patterson, Ernest Minor. Cur. biog. p. 469 (1949).

Patterson, Frederick Douglas. Cur. biog. p. 496 (1947).

Patterson, Floyd. Cur. biog. p. 313 (1960).

Patterson Graham. Cur. biog. p. 471 (1949).

Patterson, John. Cur. biog. p. 315 (1960).

Patterson, Joseph Medill. Cur. biog. p. 649 (1942).

Patterson Richard C., jr. Cur. biog. p. 465 (1946).
Holiday 26: 53 Oct '59.
Natl. geog. 115: 19 Jan '59.

Patterson, Robert P. Cur. biog. p. 655 (1941).

Patterson, William A. Cur. biog. p. 467 (1946).

Patti, Adelina. Cooper: Con. ency. of music, p. 201.

Patton, Frances Gray. Cur. biog. p. 477 (1955).

Patton, Gen. George S., jr. Cur. biog. p. 570 (1943).
Holiday 27: 11 Mar '60.

Patton, James G. Cur. biog. p. 451 (1945).
Holiday 7: 36 Mar '50.

Patton, Mrs. James B. Cur. biog. p. 441 (1950).

Patton, Mel. Cur. biog. p. 472 (1949).

Patzcuaro, Lake. See Lake Patzcuaro.

Pauker, Ana. Cur. biog. p. 493 (1948).

Paul I, King of the Hellenes. Cur. biog. p. 498 (1947).

Paul, King (Greece). Natl. geog. 109: 43 Jan '56.

Paul, Prince of Yugoslavia. Cur. biog. p. 657 (1941).

Paul III, Pope. See Pope Paul III.

Paul VI, Pope. See Pope Paul VI.

Paul, Alice. Cur. biog. p. 499 (1947).

Paul, Jeremiah (work of). Con. 132: 185 Jan '54.

Paul, Mrs. Josephine Bay. Holiday 26: 57 Oct '59.

Paul-Boncour, Joseph. Cur. biog. p. 454 (1945).

Paul Bunyan. See Bunyan, Paul.

Pauley, Edwin W. Cur. biog. p. 457 (1945).

Pauli, Wolfgang. Cur. biog. p. 469 (1946).

paulin (man & woman). Natl. geog. 107: 193 (col.) Feb '55.

Pauling, Dr. Linus. Jensen: The White House, p. 283.

Pauling, Linus Carl. Cur. biog. p. 474 (1949).

Paull, Grace A. Jun. bk. of auth., p. 239.

Paumgartner altar panel. Praeg.: pict. ency., p. 286 (col.).

Pavelic, Ante. Cur. biog. p. 652 (1942).

pavement, mosaic. See mosaic pavement.

pavilion, lakeside (girls & boys). Natl. geog. 98: 569 (col.) Nov '50.

——, world fair. Travel 113: 44 Ap '60.

Pavlova, Anna. Int. gr. soc.: Arts . . . p. 147 (col.).

Pawley, Edward. Cur. biog. p. 471 (1946).

pawnbroker (sym.). Lehner: Pict. bk. of sym., p. 91.

Paxinou, Katina. Cur. biog. p. 573 (1943).

Paxton, Joseph (sculpture by). Con. 127: 101 May '51.

Paxton, Robert. Cur. biog. p. 348 (1959).

"Paying the Ostler" (Morland). Con. 136: IX Nov '55.

Payne, Frederick G. Cur. biog. p. 463 (1952).

Payne, Lewis. See Powell, Lewis.

Payne, Robert. Cur. biog. p. 501 (1947).

Payne home, John Howard. Brooks: Growth of a nation, p. 85.

Payne-Gaposchkin, Cecilia. Cur. biog. p. 422 (1957).

Paz, Hipolito J. Cur. biog. p. 464 (1952).

Paz Estenssoro, Victor. Cur. biog. p. 476 (1953).

Pazzi chapel (Florence). Holiday 27: 129 Jan '60.

Peabody, Elizabeth. Amer. heri., vol. 10 no. 1 p. 32 (Dec '58).

Peabody, Joseph. Amer. heri., vol. 6 no. 2 p. 15 (winter '55).

Peabody, Sophia (Mrs. N. Hawthorne). Amer. heri., vol. 10 no. 1 p. 30 (col.) (Dec '58).

peace (amerindic sym.). Lehner: Pict. bk. of sym., p. 85.

—— (sym.). Lehner: Pict. bk. of sym., p. 44, 86-7, 92.

Peace inscription (on U.N. stairway). Travel 101: inside cover May '54.

Peace memorial monument (Put-in-Bay). Travel 104: inside back cover Aug '55.

Peace monument (victory over British). Travel 104: 19 Aug '55.

"Peace" on ship (Puck sym.). Amer. heri., vol. 11 no. 4 p. 30 (col.) (Je '60).

peace pipe. See Indian peace pipe.

Peace river canyon (Canada). Natl. geog. 108: 232-3 (col.) Aug '55.

"Peace ship", Ford. Amer. heri., vol. 9 no. 2 p. 65 (Feb '58).

—— (cartoon). Amer. heri., vol. 9 no. 2 p. 71-2, 74, 77 (Feb '58).

Peace tower (Ottawa, Canada). Holiday 19: 2

(col.) Feb '56, 94 (col.) May '56; 20: 178 Dec '56.

Natl. geog. 115: 824, 826 (col.) Je '59.

"Peaceable Kingdom" (Hicks). Amer. heri., vol. 2 no. 2 p. 45 (col.) (winter '51); vol. 6 no. 2 p. 43 (col.) (winter '55).

"The Peacemakers" (Healy). Natl. geog. 99: 202 (col.) Feb '51.

Peacham (Vermont). Jordan: Hammond's pict. atlas, p. 29 (col.).

Peacham academy (Vermont). Holiday 6: 46 (col.) Nov '49.

peacock (sym.). Lehner: Pict. bk. of sym., p. 60, 78.

Peacock throne (Tehran). Natl. geog. 104: 720 Nov '53.

Peale, Charles Wilson. Amer. heri., vol. 3 no. 1 p. 55 (fall '51); vol. 6 no. 3 p. 41 (Ap '55).

—— (self portrait). Amer. heri., vol. 6 no. 3 cover (col.) (Ap '55).

—— (work of). Amer. heri., vol. 3 no. 1 p. 54 (col.), 56 (fall '51); vol. 6 no. 3 p. 44-5, 49-(part col.) (Ap '55); vol. 9 no. 2 p. 51 (col.) (Feb '58).

Natl. geog. 99: 181, 185, 188 (col.) Feb '51; 105: 447, 463 (col.) Ap '54.

Peale, James (work of). Amer. heri., vol. 7 no. 6 p. 75 (col.) (Oct '56).

Peale, Mundy I. Cur. biog. p. 486 (1956).

Peale, Rev. Norman Vincent. Cur. biog. p. 472 (1946).

Peale, Raphaelle (work of). Amer. heri., vol. 6 no. 3 p. 51 (col.) (Ap '55).

Peale, Rembrandt (work of). Amer. heri., vol. 3 no. 2 p. 32-3 (winter '52).

Con. 135: XVII Ap '55.

Holiday 14: 46 (col.) Dec '53.

"Peale family" (by C.W. Peale). Amer. heri., vol. 6 no. 3 p. 40-3 (part col.) (Ap '55).

peanut harvesting, Chinese. Natl. geog. 111: 361 (col.) Mar '57.

Peare, Catherine Owens. Cur. biog. p. 350 (1959).

Pearkes, Maj. Gen. George R. Cur. biog. p. 423 (1957).

Pearl, Raymond. Cur. biog. p. 658 (1941).

Pearl Harbor (attack). Holiday 20: 88-91 Dec '56.

Pearl mosque (New Delhi, India). Travel 111: 18 Jan '59.

pearls. Natl. geog. 98: 788-9 (col.) Dec '50; 111: 29 (col.) Jan '57.

—— (girl sorter). Natl. geog. 97: 625 (col.) May '50.

Pearson, Chester C. Cur. biog. p. 443 (1950).

Pearson, Drew. Cur. biog. p. 659 (1941).

Holiday 7: 101 Feb '50.

Pearson, Jay F. W. Cur. biog. p. 478 (1953).

Pearson, Lester Bowles. Cur. biog. p. 502 (1947); (1963).

Peary, Josephine Diebitsch. Holiday 14: 6 Dec (1947); p. 319 (1963).

Peary, Robert Edwin. Natl. geog. 106: 520, 523 Oct '54.

Travel 104: back cover Jl '55.

Peary, Mr. & Mrs. Robert Edwin. Natl. geog. 106: 522 Oct '54.

Peary, Mrs. Robert E. & baby. Natl. geog. 106: 532 Oct '54.

Peary medal, Mrs. Robert E. Natl. geog. 109: 148 Jan '56.

Peary's Arctic circle monument. Natl. geog. 106: 526 Oct '54.

Peary's route to North Pole. Natl. geog. 104: 470-84 Oct '53.

"Peasant girl gathering faggots". Con. 145: 179 May '60.

"Peasant smoking at cottage door" (Gainsborough). Con. 134: cover, 137 (col.) Nov '54.

"The Peasant wedding" (Bruegel). Praeg. pict. ency., p. 311 (col.).

"The Peasants" (Borromini). Con. 137: 48 Mar '56.

peasants (16-18th cent., Europe). Int. gr. soc.: Arts . . . p. 113 (col.).

Pease, Howard. Jun. bk. of auth., p. 240.

Pease, Lute. Cur. biog. p. 476 (1949).

peat bog. Natl. geog. 105: 427 Mar '54.

peat cutter. Rawson: Ant. pict. bk., p. 27.

peat deposits (Ireland). Holiday 6: 47 (col.) Dec '49.

peavey, logger's. Natl. geog. 100: 117, 122 Jl '51.

Pebble Beach golf course (Cal.). Holiday 14: 85 (col.) Dec '53.

pebbles (sym.). Lehner: Pict. bk. of sym., p. 73.

Pecheux, Laurent (work of). Con. 144: 170 Dec '59.

Peck, Anne Merriman. Jun. bk. of auth., p. 241.

Peck, Gregory. Cur. biog. p. 504 (1947). Holiday 10: 77 (col.) Jl '51.

Peck, James L. H. Cur. biog. p. 654 (1942).

Pecos Bill (folk hero). Amer. heri., vol. 1 no. 3 p. 73 (col.) (spring '50).

pedal boat. Holiday 7: 82 Ap '50.

pedal catamaran boat (boy & girl). Travel 113: cover (col.) Ap '60.

"The peddler" (Holbein). Praeg. pict. ency., p. 305.

peddler (1853). Amer. heri., vol. 7 no. 3 p. 59 (col.) (Ap '56).

——, Chinese. Natl. geog. 103: 200 (col.) Feb '53.

——, German clock. Natl. geog. 111: 780 (col.) Je '57.

——, Pakistan. Natl. geog. 102: 649 (col.) Nov '52.

——, suspender. Holiday 12: 69 Sept '52.

peddlers, African (trays of bread on head). Natl. geog. 118: 316 (col.) Sept '60.

peddler's cart. See cart, peddler's.

Peden, Katherine. Cur. biog. p. 338 (1962).

pedestal. Con. 143: LVII Mar '59.

——, Adam. Con. 142: XVII Sept '58.

pedestal & urn, Adam. Con. 140: IX Dec '57; 143: LV Mar '59.

pedestal with vase, Adam. Con. 139: XLVI May '57.

pedestals, 18th cent. Con. 136: LV Nov '55.

pedicab. Natl. geog. 102: 646 (col.) Nov '52.

——, cycle-pushed (Vietnam). Natl. geog. 99: 462 Ap '51.

pedicabs, Chinese. Natl. geog. 118: 197 (col.) Aug '60.

pedometer. Holiday 10: 128 Dec '51; 11: 134 Je '52.

Peel, Roy V. Cur. biog. p. 444 (1950).

"peep show". Natl. geog. 106: 843 Dec '54.

Peerce, Jan. Cur. biog. p. 655 (1942). Holiday 9: 24 Mar '51.

"Peg leg". See Elliott, Frank.

Pegasus. Lehner: Pict. bk. of sym., p. 17.

Pei, Mario. Holiday 19: 55 Jan '56; 24: 32 Nov '58.

Peikov, Assen. Holiday 27: 104 (col.) Ap '60.

Peirce, Waldo. Cur. biog. p. 537 (1944).

Peirse, Sir Richard E. C. Cur. biog. p. 661 (1941).

Peixotto, Ernest. Cur. biog. p. 622 (1941).

Peker, Recep. Cur. biog. p. 506 (1947).

Peking (China). Natl. geog. 118: 194-223 (part col.) Aug '60.

—— (map). Natl. geog. 118: 192 (col.) Aug '60.

—— (workers' stadium). Natl. geog. 118: 204-7 (col.) Aug '60.

Pelaez, Amelia. Holiday 27: 53 Feb '60.

Pelee volcano crater. Natl. geog. 115: 280-1 (col.) Feb '59.

Pelham, Henry. Amer. heri., vol. 8 no. 1 cover (col.) (Dec '56).

Pelham, John. Amer. heri., vol. 9 no. 2 p. 31 (Feb '58).

"Pelican in piety" (earliest dated figure of a bird or animal in Eng. ceramics). Con. 144: 194 Dec '59.

Pella, Giuseppe. Cur. biog. p. 480 (1953).

Pellegrini, G. A. (work of). Con. 142: 5 Sept '58; 145: 105-7 Ap '60.

Pellegrini arms fresco (detail). Con. 143: 38 Mar '59.

Pelletier, Wilfred. Cur. biog. p. 541 (1944).

pellick. Rawson: Ant. pict. bk., p. 77.

Pellipario, Nicola (work of). Con. 142: 149 Dec '58.

pelota court (Basque). Holiday 23: 91 Mar '58.

Pelt, Adrian. Cur. biog. p. 496 (1948).

peltates (Greek soldiers, ancient times). Int. gr. soc.: Arts . . . p. 33 (col.).

Peltz, Mary Ellis. Cur. biog p. 501 (1954).

pelvis, human. Gray's anatomy, p. 213-7, 283-4, 1281, 1309.

——, (arteries). Gray's anatomy, p. 619.

——, (veins). Gray's anatomy, p. 682-8.

Pemaquid Point (Maine, lighthouse). Holiday 5: 107 (col.) Jan '49.

Pembert, Mrs. Robert (Holbein miniature). Con. ency. of ant., vol. 1, pl. 129.

Pemberton, Brock. Cur. biog. p. 461 (1945).

Pemberton, John C. Pakula: Cent. album, p. 221.

pen. Holiday 14: 77 (col.) Dec '53; 21: 15 (col.) Je '57; 25: 31 (col.) May '59; 26: 35 Oct '59.

——, fountain. Holiday 11: 2 (col.) Je '52; 12: 80 (col.) Sept '52, inside cover (col.) Dec '52; 27: 114 May '60.

——, quill. Holiday 28: 7 Sept '60. Natl. geog. 99: 185 (col.) Feb '51.

——, quill (in ink bottle). Holiday 27: 46 Feb '60.

——, quill (sym.). Lehner: Pict. bk. of sym., p. 13.

pen & ink case. Rawson: Ant. pict. bk., p. 91.

pen & pencil set. Holiday 13: inside cover (col.) May '53.

pen drawing, quill. Amer. heri., vol. 10 no. 3 back cover (col.) (Ap '59).

Pena Palace (Portugal). Holiday 19: 28 Jan '56. Travel 111: 33 Je '59.

Penang island (Indian Ocean). Travel 107: 42-5 Feb '57.

—— harbor (Prince of Wales island). Travel 112: 38 Dec '59.

Pend Oreille lake (Idaho). Holiday 15: 38-9 (col.) Je '54.

pendant (bee emblem of Napoleon). Amer. heri., vol. 6 no. 3 p. 26 (Ap '55).

——, aborigine. Holiday 21: 107 Ap '57.

——, antique (15th cent.). Con 132: 128-33 Nov '53.

——, antique (16th cent.). Con. ency. of ant., vol. 1, pl. 93-4, 96.

——, antique Spanish. Con. 139: XVI Ap '57.

——, renaissance. Con. 132: XV, inside cover (col.) Nov '53.

——, renaissance (16th cent.). Con. 132: 131 (col.) Nov '53.

——, 17th cent. Con. 143: VII Je '59.

pendants, antique. Con. 139: 127-32 (part col.) Ap '57.

Pendergast, Thomas J. Holiday 7: 50 Mar '50.

Pendleton, George H. (campaign poster). Amer. heri., vol. 7 no. 4 p. 26 (col.) (Je '56).

pendulette, Viennese. Holiday 26: 26 (col.) Nov '59.

Penfield, Wilder Graves. Cur. biog. p. 478 (1955).

Peng Teh-Huai. Cur. biog. p. 479 (1951).

"Penitent Magdalen" (Vercelli). Con. 136: 38 Sept '55.

"penitents" (Spain). Natl. geog. 99: 507 (col.) Ap '51.
——. See also Eucharistic Congress penitents.

Penn, William. Con. 129: 135 Je '52.
Holiday 21: 49 May '57.

—— (at age 12). Amer. heri., vol. 3 no. 1 p. 50 (col.) (fall '51).

—— (mural). Amer. heri., vol. 3 no. 1 p. 51 (col.) (fall '51).

—— (with Indians). See "Penn's treaty with Indians".

Penn canal landings candles. See candle, Penn canal landings.

Penn home, William. Amer. heri., vol. 1 no. 4 p. 50-1, 67 (part col) (summer '50). Holiday 18: 108 Oct '55.

Penna, Agostino (sculpture by). Con. 143: 243 Je '59.

Pennairo, Leonard J. Cur. biog. p. 351 (1959).

Pennel, John. Cur. biog. (1963).

Pennell, Lt. Joseph Stanley. Cur. biog. p. 543 (1944).

Penney, James C. Cur. biog. p. 509 (1947).

Penney, Sir William. Holiday 23: 94 Ap '58.

Penney, Sir William G. Cur. biog. p. 483 (1953).

Penn's brew jug, William. Rawson: Ant. pict. bk., p. 87.

Penn's treaty with the Indians. Brooks: Growth

of a nation, p. 60-1.
Natl. geog. 118: 152 Aug '60.

—— (Hicks). Amer. heri., vol. 6 no. 2 p. 42 (col.) (winter '55).

—— (West). Amer. heri., vol. 6 no. 2 p. 41 (col.) (winter '55).
Natl. geog. 99: 182 (col.) Feb '51.

"Pennsbury" (Wm. Penn home). See Penn home, William.

Pennsylvania. Amer. heri., vol. 3 no. 2 p. 54-7 (part col.) (winter '52).
Holiday 12: 49-58 (part col.) Oct '52; 18: 98-111 (part col.) Oct '55.
Jordan: Hammond's pict. atlas, p. 44-7 (col.).

—— (Dunkard farm). Face of Amer., p. 100-1 (col.).

—— (modern arch.). Holiday 16: 48-51 Aug '54.

Pennsylvania clothes box. Amer. heri., vol. 7 no. 3 p. 2 (col.) (Ap '56).

Pennsylvania Dutch country. Natl. geog. 102: 504-16 (part col.) Oct '52.
Travel 105: 19-23 Mar '56.

Pennsylvania Dutch design. Rawson: Ant. pict. bk., p. 17.

Penn. Dutch folk art (19th cent.). Amer. heri., vol. 9 no. 5 back cover (col.) (Aug '58).

Penn. Dutch people. Jordan: Hammond's pict. atlas, p. 47 (col.).

Penn. men & women (1812-). Amer. heri., vol. 8 no. 3 p. 48-51 (col.) (Ap '57).

Penn. state college (early). Amer. heri., vol. 6 no. 3 p. 64 (Ap '55) .

Penny, Edward (work of). Con. 144: 56 Sept '59.

penny. Holiday 27: 144 (col.) May '60.

Penobscot, Mrs. See "Mrs. Penobscot".

Pensacola (Fla.). Holiday 13: 48-51 (part col.) Je '53.

Penshurst Place (Eng.). Holiday 15: 28 (col.) Je '54; 16: 62-3 Oct '54; 17: 2 (col.) Mar '55; 23: 61 (col.) Ap '58.

pentacle (sym.). Lehner: Pict. bk. of sym., p. 22, 29.

pentacle of Venus. See Venus, pentacle of.

Pentagon. Holiday 11: 98-101 (part col.) Mar '52.
Natl. geog. 99: 706 Je '51 103: 12-5 (col.) Jan '53.

Pentecost retable (12th cent.). Con. 129: 38 Ap '52.

penthouse (int., India). Natl. geog. 118: 460 (col.) Oct '60.

Pentland, John. Durant: Pict. hist. of Amer. circus, p. 29.

"People of the sky" (Larvie). Natl. geog. 107: 370 (col.) Mar '55.

people. See also boy; girl, man, woman.

Peoria (Ill., parade). Durant: Pict. hist. of Amer. circus, p. 216-7.

"Peplos Kore" (head, Greek statue). Con. ency. of ant., vol. 3 pl. 66.

Pepper, Claude. Cur. biog. p. 663 (1941).

pepper drying (Majorca). Natl. geog. 111: 643 (col.) May '57.

pepper mill. Holiday 12: 145 Nov '52.

peppercorn rent payment (Bermuda). Natl. geog. 105: 212 Feb '54.

Pepperrell, Sir William. Amer. heri., vol. 6 no. 2 p. 50 (col.) (winter '55).

"Peppersass" train (1869). Natl. geog. 107: 764-5 (col.) Je '55.

Pepys, Samuel. Holiday 21: 137 Je '57.

Pepys' shorthand, Samuel. Con. 143: 103 Ap '59.

Pequot fort (1640). Amer. heri., vol. 6 no. 5 p. 14 (Aug '55).

Peralta land fraud (claimants in Ariz.). Amer. heri., vol. 7 no. 5 p. 28 (Aug '56).

Peranda, Sante (work of). Con. 144: 106 Nov '59.

Perce (harbor, Quebec). Holiday 14: 44 Jl '53.

Perce, rock of. *See* rock of Perce.

percolator. Holiday 25: 160 May '59.

———, **coffee.** Holiday 21: 108 Mar '57; 25: 160 May '59; 26: 191 Nov '59.

———, **Sheffield (George III).** Con. 144: 133 Nov '59.

percussion instrument, Indian. Amer. heri., vol. 11 no. 3 p. 83 (Ap '60).

——— **musical instruments.** Int. gr. soc.: Arts . . . p. 141 (col.).

Percy, Charles H. Cur. biog. p. 353 (1959).

Percy, Sydney Richard (work of). Con. 129: X (col.) Ap '52.

Perdicaris, Ion. Amer. heri., vol. 10 no. 5 p. 18 (Aug '59).

"Pere Marquette" state park (Ill.). Travel 103: 14 Je '55.

Pereda, A. (work of). Con. 133: XXV Mar '54.

Pereira, Irene Rice. Cur. biog. p. 485 (1953).

"Perette" (by Boucher). Con. ency. of ant., vol. 1, pl. 160.

Perez, Mariano Ospina. Cur. biog. p. 432 (1950).

Perez Jimenez, Marcos. Cur. biog. p. 503 (1954).

perfection (sym.). Lehner: Pict. bk. of sym., p. 37, 59.

perforated tin designs. Rawson: Ant. pict. bk., p. 20.

perfume bottle. *See* bottle, perfume.

perfume boxes, Portuguese. Con. 137: 74 Mar '56.

perfume burner, gilt-bronze Louis XV. Con. 142: 108 Nov '58.

———, **Gouthiere.** Con. 138: 221 Jan '57.

———, **jasper antique.** Con. 140: 13 Sept '57.

perfume-making machinery. Natl. geog. 99: 534-50 Ap '51.

perfume spray (1800). Con. 143: 191 May '59.

perfume vase, 18th cent. Chinese. Con. 134: 206 Dec '54.

perfumes, river of. *See* river of perfumes.

Perge, Turkey (temple ruins). Travel 106: 58 Jl '56.

Pergolesi, Giovanni. Cooper: Con. ency. of music, p. 202.

pericardium. Gray's anatomy, p. 529.

Perignon, Dom (statue). Holiday 26: 98 Aug '59.

"Perils of the sea of darkness" (by De Bry). Amer. heri., vol. 7 no. 1 p. 72 (Dec '55).

Perino, Alexander. Holiday 24: 118 (col.) Dec '58.

periscope. Natl. geog. 118: 586 Nov '60.

———, **submarine.** Natl. geog. 97: 60 Jan '50.

peritoneum. Gray's anatomy, p. 1194-1205.

Perkins, Anthony. Cur. biog. p. 317 (1960).

Perkins, Charles H. Cur. biog. p. 480 (1955).

Perkins, Dexter. Cur. biog. p. 331 (1958).

Perkins, Elliott. Holiday 14: 46 (col.) Nov '53.

Perkins, George W. Amer. heri., vol. 8 no. 3 p. 47 (Ap '57); vol. 8 no. 4 p. 34 (Je '57).
Cur. biog. p. 447 (1950).

Perkins, Lucy Fitch. Jun. bk. of auth., p. 243.

Perkins, Milo. Cur. biog. p. 658 (1942).

Perkins, Richards Marlin. Cur. biog. p. 482 (1951).

Perlman, Alfred E. Cur. biog. p. 482 (1955).

Perlman, Philip B. Cur. biog. p. 466 (1952).

Peron, Eva De. Cur. biog. p. 477 (1949).

Peron, Col. Juan. Cur. biog. p. 544 (1944).

Perrin, Francis. Cur. biog. p. 483 (1951).

Perronneau, Bacchante (work of). Con. 135: 51 Mar '55.

Perry, Com. Matthew C. Amer. heri., vol. 4 no. 4 p. 4 (summer '53).
Natl. geog. 99: 195 (col.) Feb '51.

——— **(by Japanese artist).** Amer. heri., vol. 9 no. 3, cover (col.) (Ap '58).

——— **(carved wood).** Amer. heri., vol. 9 no. 3 p. 13 (col.) (Ap '58).

——— **(in Japan).** Natl. geog. 116: 104 (col.) Jl '59.

Perry, Oliver Curtis. Horan: Pict. hist. of wild west, p. 172.

Perry, Oliver Hazard. Amer. heri., vol. 7 no. 3, cover (col.), p. 21 (col.) (Ap '56).
Holiday 23: 76 May '58.
Natl. geog. 104: 87 Jl '53.

——— **(cartoon).** Natl. geog. 104: 86 Jl '53.

Perry & Japanese banquet on ship. Natl. geog. 104: 97 Jl '53.

Perry landing in Tokyo Bay, Com. (Japan). Amer. heri., vol. 9 no. 3 p. 12-3, 17-23 (col.) (Ap '58).

"Perry on Lake Erie, 1812". Natl. geog. 102: 158 (col.) Aug '52.

Perry's advance in Japan. Natl. geog. 104: 92-3 Jl '53.

Perry's ship, "Saratoga". *See* "Saratoga".

"Perry's victory on Lake Erie" (1813). Con. ency. of ant., vol. 3, pl. 94.

Persac, Adrian (work of). Natl. geog. 99: 198 (col.) Feb '51.

Persepolis (Iran). Ceram: March of arch., p. 167-9.
Natl. geog. 100: 458-9 (col.) Oct '51; 114: 33 (col.) Jl '58; 118: 850-1 (col.) Dec '60.
Travel 113: 32, 34-5 Feb '60.

——— **(bull, sculpture).** *See* "bull of Persepolis".

"Perseus" (bronze statue). Natl. geog. 111: 797 (col.) Je '57.

——— **(sculpture by Canova).** Praeg. pict. ency., p. 411.

"Perseus & Andromeda" (Chinard terracotta). Con. 140: 7 Sept '57.

perseverance (sym.). Lehner: Pict. bk. of sym., p. 59.

Pershing, Gen. John J. Amer. heri., vol. 10 no. 6 p. 12 (Oct '59).

——— **(welcomes Eisenhower).** Natl. geog. 117: 632-3 (col.) May '60.

Persian arch. *See* architecture, Persian.

Persian banquet hall (17th cent.). Ceram: March of arch., p. 173.
Persian brocade (16th cent.). Praeg. pict. ency., p. 99 (col.).
Persian carpet (19th cent.). Praeg. pict. ency., p. 531 (col.).
Con. ency. of ant., vol. 1, p. 223, 227.
Persian chariot. See chariot, Persian.
Persian costume (ancient royal). Int. gr. soc.: Arts . . . p. 29 (col.).
Persian jug, bronze (12th cent.). Praeg. pict. ency., p. 562.
Persian minaret. See minaret, Isfahan.
Persian miniature (manuscript illum.). Praeg. pict. ency., p. 521 (col.).
Persian silversmith. See silversmith (Persia).
Persian wall painting. Praeg. pict. ency., p. 522 (col.).
Persian war chariot. See war chariot, Persian.
Persian. See also Iran.
personifications (sym.). Lehner: Pict. bk. of sym., p. 92-3.
Persons, Gordon (Gov. of Okla.). Holiday 16: 79 Aug '54.
Persons, Maj. Gen. Wilton. Cur. biog. p. 487 (1953).
Peru. Disney: People & places, p. 100-12 (col.). Holiday 12: 19-20, 24 Nov '52; 22: 158 (col.) Nov '57; 27: 189 (col.) Mar '60.
Natl. geog. 98: 422-62 (part col.) Oct '50.
Travel 101: 10 Feb '54; 112: 18 Sept '59.
—— **(Andes mts.).** Natl. geog. 107: 134-45 Jan '55.
—— **(Arequipa).** Holiday 27: 89 (col.) Jan '60.
—— **(1535-1616).** Amer. heri., vol. 6 no. 5 p. 103 (Aug '55).
—— **(game industry).** Natl. geog. 115: 396-412 (part col.) Mar '59.
—— **(Inca bldg.).** Praeg. pict. ency., p. 558.
—— **(Lima).** Travel 109: 33 Mar '58.
—— **(Machu Picchu).** See Machu Picchu (Peru).
—— **(map).** Natl. geog. 115: 401 Mar '59.
Perugia (Italy). Holiday 16: 98 (col.) Sept '54.
Perugino (work of). Con. ency. of ant., vol. 1, p. 152.
peruke maker. See wig maker.
Perutz, M. F. Cur. biog. p. 324 (1963).
Peruvian. Holiday 21: 113 (col.) Je '57.
—— **armour (medieval).** Int. gr. soc.: Arts . . . p. 73 (col.).
—— **(costume (modern).** See costume (Peru).
Peruvian child. Holiday 19: 98-101 (part col.) Feb '56.
Peruvian girl. Holiday 19: 20 (col.) May '56.
—— **Indian.** Holiday 21: 46 Ap '57.
Natl. geog. 107: 136-45 Jan '55; 109: 351-2 (col.) Mar '56.
—— **man.** Holiday 27: 46 Mar '60.
—— **man (llama).** Natl. geog. 98: 429 (col.) Oct '50.
—— **pottery.** See pottery, Peruvian.
—— **valley.** Holiday 20: 108 (col.) Dec '56.
—— **woman.** Holiday 11: 106 (col.) Mar '52.
—— **woman & papoose.** Travel 107: 33 Feb '57.
Peruvians. Holiday 6: 134 Nov '49; 19: 125

(col.) Je '56.
—— **(musicians).** Travel 112: 58 Jl '59.
Pervukhin, Mikhail G. Cur. biog. p. 488 (1956).
Pescadores island. Natl. geog. 109: 270-83 (part col.) Feb '56.
Pesellino (work of). Con. 129: 66 Ap '52.
Peshtigo fire (Wis.). Amer. heri., vol. 7 no. 5 p. 52-3 (col.), 57 (Aug '56).
Pestalozzi, Johann Heinrich. Natl. geog. 116: 269, 278-9 Aug '59.
Pestalozzi (village, Switzerland). Natl. geog. 116: 268-82 Aug '59.
pestles (Chinese girls play music). Natl. geog 111: 349 (col.) Mar '57.
Peter II, King of Yugoslavia. Cur. biog., p. 575 (1943).
Peter home, Thomas. Natl. geog. 103: 542 (col.) Ap '53.
"Peter Pan". Natl. geog. 110: 21 (col.) Jl '56.
Peter the Great, Tsar (sculpture). Natl. geog. 116: 409 Sept '59.
Peterborough cathedral (Eng.). Int. gr. soc.: Arts . . . p. 47 (col.).
"Peterkin Papers" (book illus.). Amer. heri., vol. 8 no. 1 p. 31 (col.) (Dec '56).
Peters, Matthew William (work of). Con. 143: 87 Ap '59.
Peters, Roberta. Cur. biog. p. 505 (1954).
Petersham, Maud. Jan. bk. of auth., p. 243.
Petersham, Miska. Jun. bk. of auth., p. 243.
Peterson, Esther. Cur. biog. p. 359 (1961).
Peterson, F. Raymond. Cur. biog. p. 448 (1950).
Peterson, O. F. (work of). Con. 141: 19 Mar '58.
Peterson, Roger Tory. Cur. biog. p. 355 (1959).
Peterson, Val. Cur. biog. p. 479 (1949).
Holiday 7: 36 Mar '50.
Peterson, Virgilia. Cur. biog. p. 489 (1953).
Pethick-Lawrence, Lord. Cur. biog. p. 475 (1946).
Petigru, J. L. Amer. heri., vol. 11 no. 5 p. 54 (Aug '60).
Petit, Roland. Cur. biog. p. 469 (1952).
Petitpierre, Max. Cur. biog. p. 491 (1953).
Petra (Rose-red city). Travel 105: 22 Jan '56.
—— **(entrance passage).** Natl. geog. 110: 726-7 (col.) Dec '56.
—— **(rock carvings).** Natl. geog. 108: 852-68 (part col.) Dec '55.
Petri, Egon. Cur. biog. p. 661 (1942).
Petrie, Sir William Flinders. Ceram: March of arch., p. 103-4.
petrified forest (men & women). Natl. geog. 109: 383-5 (col.) Mar '56.
petrified tree. Natl. geog. 114: 768 (col.) Dec '58.
petrified wood (Sahara). Natl. geog. 113: 698 (col.) May '58.
—— **(women).** Natl. geog. 113: 641 (col.) May '58.
petroglyphs (Panama jungle). Natl. geog. 104: 282 (col.) Aug '53.
——, **prehistoric (Colo.).** Travel 112: 36 Sept '59.
petroleum co. (poster). Amer. heri., vol. 7 no. 5 p. 112 (Aug '56).
petroleum refinery. Natl. geog. 100: 426-7 Oct '51.

Petry, Ann. Cur. biog. p. 476 (1946).
Petry, Lucile. Cur. biog. p. 546 (1944).
Petsche, Maurice. Cur. biog. p. 481 (1949).
Petter, Franz Xavier (work of). Con. 136: XVII (col.) Jan '56; 143: XXVII, 175 (col.) May '59; 144: XXXVIII (col.) Nov '59.
petticoat lamp. Rawson: Ant. pict. bk., p. 93.
Pettie, John (work of). Con. 145: XXXV Ap '60.
"petting stone" (Holy island, Eng.). Natl. geog. 102: 557 Oct '52.
Pettit, Robert. Cur. biog. p. 361 (1961).
pet-toter (dog). Holiday 11: 132 Je '52.
"Petworth house" (Eng.). Con. 132: 45 Sept '53.
Peurifoy, John E. Cur. biog. p. 482 (1949).
Pevsner, Antoine. Cur. biog. p. 357 (1959). Praeg. pict. ency., p. 463.
Pew, Joseph N., jr. Cur. biog. p. 665 (1941).
"Pewee Valley", (Ky., "Land of the Little Colonel"). Travel 112: 35-8 Jl '59.
pewter, British. Con. ency., of ant., vol. 1, pl. 77-80.
——, **early church.** Con. 126: 121-3 Oct '50.
pewter dishes. See dishes, pewter.
pewter flagons, Antique. Con. 144: 125 Nov '59.
pewter marks. Con. ency. of ant., vol. 1, p. 143.
pewterer shop. Con. 138: LVI Nov '56.
Peyrouton, Marcel. Cur. biog. p. 579 (1943).
Pfalz fortress (West Ger.). Natl. geog. 115: 764-5 (col.) Je '59.
Pflimlin, Pierre. Cur. biog. p. 484 (1955).
Pfost, Gracie. Cur. biog. p. 486 (1955).
Pfunds (Tirol, Alps). Holiday 27: 46-7 (col.) Jan '60.
phaeton (driver, horses). Natl. geog. 106: 470 (col.) Oct '54.
—— **(model).** Holiday 10: 123 Nov '51.
Phaleg (seal of). Lehner: Pict. bk. of sym., p. 24.
phanisphere, astrologic. Lehner: Pict. bk. of sym,. p. 22.
Pharaoh (statue, prehistoric). Int. gr. soc.: Arts . . . p. 17 (col.).
Pharaoh Amenophis III (statue). Ceram: March of arch., p. 80.
Pharaoh, queen & messenger (ancient). Int. gr. soc.: Arts . . . p. 29 (col.).
Pharoah's funerary temple. See Thebes "City of the Dead".
Pharoah's tombs. Ceram: March of arch., p. 95-7.
Phari Dzong (Tibet). Holiday 12: 54 (col.) Dec '52.
pharmacist (sym.). Lehner: Pict. bk. of sym., p. 91.
pharmacology (sym.). Lehner: Pict. bk. of sym., p. 16-7.
pharmacy (17th cent.). See apothecary laboratory.
—— **jar.** See jar, pharmacy.
pharynx. Gray's anatomy, p. 1183-6.
Phelan, Edward. Cur. biog. p. 511 (1947).
Phelps, William Lyon. Cur. biog. p. 583 (1943).
Philadelphia (Penn.). Amer. heri., vol. 3 no. 1 cover, p. 14-9, 30-57, 75 (col.) (fall '51).

Holiday 21: cover, 51-67 (part col.) May '57. Jordan: Hammond's pict. atlas, p. 44-5 (col.). Natl. geog. 118: 152-91 (part col.) Aug '60.
—— **(art museum).** Holiday 12: 50 Oct '52; 18: 110-11 (col.) Oct '55.
—— **(Carpenter's Hall).** Amer. heri., vol. 1 no. 2 p. 20 (winter '50).
Holiday 26: 127 Jl '59.
—— **(early map).** Amer. heri., vol. 3 no. 1 p. 13 (fall '51).
—— **(1821).** Con. ency. of ant., vol. 3, pl. 93.
—— **(historical map).** Natl. geog. 118: 156-7 (col.) Aug '60.
—— **(historical places).** Travel 110: 29-31 Jl '58.
—— **(The Main line).** Holiday 7: 34-57 (col.) Ap '50.
—— **(1793).** Amer. heri., vol. 7 no. 3 p. 54 (Ap '56).
—— **(Sheraton hotel, model).** Travel 106: 49 Oct '56.
—— **(zoo).** Face of Amer., p. 66-7 (col.).
Philae (temple of Isis). Int. gr. soc.: Arts . . . p. 13 (col.).
Philbrick, Herbert A. Cur. biog. p. 493 (1953).
Philip, King (by Paul Revere). Amer. heri., vol. 10 no. 1 p. 68 (Dec '58).
Philip II, King of Spain (bust). Natl. geog. 97: 774 Je '50.
—— **(Rubens).** Amer. heri., vol. 10 no. 3 p. 7 (col.) (Ap '59).
Philip IV (Velasquez). Con. 141: 241, 244 Je '58.
Philip, Duke of Edinburgh. Holiday 19: 52-5 (part col.) May '56.
Philip, Prince (Gt. Brit.). Holiday 19: 56-7 Je '56.
Natl. geog. 112: 583, 585, 588, 592-9, 602-20 (part col.) Nov '57; 115: 825-6, 829 (part col.) Je '59.
—— **(Order of Garter ceremony).** Natl. geog. 114: 75 Jl '58.
—— **(polo trophy).** Holiday 22: 67 (col.) Nov '57.
—— **(receives medal).** Natl. geog. 112: 866 Dec '57.
—— **(women & children).** Natl. geog. 112: 620 Nov '57.
——. See also Edinburgh, Philip III Duke of.
Philip, 5th Earl of Chesterfield (Gainsborough). Con. 144: 270 Jan '60.
Philip, Andre. Cur. biog. p. 585 (1943).
"Philippe, Duc de Chartres" (Boucher). Con. 143: 208 Je '59.
Philippi battle. See U.S. Civil war (Philippi).
Philippi ruins. Natl. geog. 109: 62 (col.) Jan '56.
Philippine cart (ox, people). Travel 113: 10 May '60.
Philippine invasion (1898). Amer. heri., vol. 12 no. 1 p. 66-77 (Dec '60).
Philippines. Holiday 18: 86-93 (part col.) Aug '55.
Travel 104: 4, 6-8 Oct '55; 105: 26-8 Mar '56.
Philippino boy (on caraboo). Travel 104: cover Oct '55.
Phillips, Thomas (work of). Con. 141: 268 Je '58.

Philip's death, King. Amer. heri., vol. 10 no. 1 p. 79 (Dec '58).

Philistines & Canaanites. *See* Canaanites & Philistines.

Phillips, Ethel Calvert. Jun. bk. of auth., p. 244.

Phillips, Harry I. Cur. biog. p. 588 (1943).

Phillips, Irna. Cur. biog. p. 590 (1943).

Phillips, John. Amer. heri., vol. 4 no. 2 p. 34 (winter '53).

Phillips, Lena Madesin. Cur. biog. p. 478 (1946).

Phillips, Morgan. Cur. biog. p. 484 (1949).

Phillips, Mrs. Robert J. Cur. biog. p. 358 (1959).

Phillips, Ruth. *See* Phillips, Mrs. Robert J.

Phillips, Thomas Hal. Cur. biog. p. 489 (1956).

Phillips, Wendell. Cur. biog. p. 333 (1958).

Phillips Andover Academy (chapel). Natl. geog. 99: 121 (col.) Jan '51.

Phillips Exeter Academy. Holiday 22: 71-3 (part col.) Dec '56.

Philmont Scout ranch. Natl. geog. 110: 400-15 (part col.) Sept '56.

—— (map). Natl. geog. 110: 405 Sept '56.

Philoff, Bogdan. Cur. biog. p. 667 (1941).

philosophies, Oriental. Lehner: Pict. bk. of sym., p. 42-3.

philosophy (sym.). Lehner: Pict. bk. of sym., p. 17.

Philpot, Glyn. (work of). Con. 129: 121 Je '52; 144: 13 Sept '59.

Phips, William. Amer. heri., vol. 7 no. 3 p. 62 (col.) (Ap '56).

Phnom Bakheng. Natl. geog. 117: 524 (col.) Ap '60.

Phnom Penh dancers. Natl. geog. 102: 305 (col.) Sept '52.

Phoenician ship (ancient). Int .gr. soc.: Arts . . . p. 43 (col.).

Phoenix (Ariz.). Jordan: Hammond's pict. atlas, p. 178 (col.).

—— (Encanto park). Travel 113: 36 May '60.

—— (sym.). Lehner: Pict. bk. of sym., p. 26, 44.

Pholein, Joseph. Cur. biog. p. 485 (1951).

phonograph. Holiday 12: 46 (col.) Sept '52.

—— (dog listening). Natl. geog. 102: 31 (col.) Jl '52.

——, Edison. Amer. heri., vol. 10 no. 6 p. 38-9 (Oct '59).

——. *See* also record player.

phosphorus (sym.). Lehner: Pict. bk. of sym., p. 73.

photographer. Holiday 18: 95 Oct '55; 22: 15 (col.) Oct '57.

—— (animals). Natl. geog. 111: 874 Je '57.

The "Photographer" (old fashioned). Con. 126: II Aug '50.
Holiday 8: 95 Oct '50; 18: 166 Dec '55; 20: 130 Dec '56.

—— (antique shop). Natl. geog. 114: 125 (col.) Jl '58.

—— (1st great woman). Holiday 12: 66 Sept '52.

—— (taking bird pictures). Natl. geog. 118: 664 (col.) Nov '60.

—— (taking picture). Holiday 11: 94 Mar '52.

Natl. geog. 109: 647 May '56; 112: 56 (col.) Jl '57.

—— (taking pictures, 1850). Amer. heri., vol. 8 no. 1 p. 55 (Dec '56).

——, Japanese (taking picture). Natl. geog. 116: 860 (col.) Dec '59.

——. *See* also men (taking pictures).

photographer's chair. *See* chair, photographer's posing.

photographer's posing stools (antique). Amer. heri., vol. 12 no. 1 p. 117 (Dec '60).

photographer's wagon. Amer. heri., vol. 12 no. 1 p. 128 (Dec '60).

photographic work, early. *See* Eastman photographic work.

photographs (earliest, 1839). Amer. heri., vol. 8 no. 1 p. 49-64 (Dec '56).

photography (sym.). Lehner: Pict. bk. of sym., p. 17.

photomicrograph. Natl. geog. 114: 322, 348 (col.) Sept '58.

photosynthesis. Natl. geog. 114: 331 (col.) Sept '58.

Phoui Sananikone. Cur. biog. p. 359 (1959).

Phrygian cap (sym.). Lehner: Pict. bk. of sym., p. 82.

Phrygian tombstones. Osward: Asia Minor, pl. 17.

Phul (seal of). Lehner: Pict. bk. of sym., p. 24.

physical training (Peking). Natl. geog. 118: 206-8 (col.) Aug '60.

physics (sym.). Lehner: Pict. bk. of sym., p. 10, 12-3, 17.

Piaf, Edith. Cur. biog. p. 450 (1950).

Piaget, Jean. Cur. biog. p. 335 (1958).

Piaggio, Father Camillo (portrait). Ceram: March of arch., p. 28.

piano. Holiday 12: 148 Oct '52; 13: 131 (col.) May '53; 18: 88 Oct '55, 114 Nov '55, 11, 153 Dec '55; 20: 14 Oct '56, 99 Nov '56; 26: 138, 151 (col.) Nov '59; 27: 102 Feb '60.

—— (1838). Natl. geog. 111: 636 May '57.

—— (man playing). Holiday 21: 42 Mar '57; 22: 121 Sept '57.

——, grand. Holiday 11: 25 May '52; 14: 89 Nov '53; 19: 162 Je '56.

——, grand (regency). Con. 144: 267 Jan '60.

——, toy. Holiday 12: 139 Nov '52.

piano keyboard. *See* keyboard, piano (sym.).

pianoforte (18th cent.). Con. 143: 131 Ap '59.

——, grand (Chappell & co., modern). Cooper: Con. ency. of music, p. 357.

——, grand (Stein, 1775). Cooper: Con. ency. of music, p. 355.

——, square (by Broadwood, 1792). Cooper: Con. ency. of music, p. 356.

Piasecki 59 K plane. Natl. geog. 115: 552 Ap '59.

Piatigorsky, Gregor. Cur. biog. p. 463 (1945).

Piazza del Campidoglio (Rome). Holiday 27: 86-7 (col.) Ap '60.

Piazza del Carmine. Labande: Naples, p. 64.

Piazza del Popolo (Rome). Con. 135: 60 Mar '55; 141: 231 Je '58.
Holiday 27: 106 (col.) Ap '60.

Piazza della Signoria (Florence, Italy). Holiday 15: 109 Jan '54.

Piazza della Signoria (fountains). Travel 102: inside cover Nov '54.

Piazza Navona (Rome, Pannini). Con. 141: 230 Je '58.

Piazza San Marco (St Mark's square, Venice). Con. 137: IV Mar '56. Holiday 27: 130 Jan '60.

Piazzetta Giovanni Battista (work of). Natl. geog. 101: 96 (col.) Jan '52.

Piazzi di Spagna. Holiday 27: 107 Ap '60.

picador (Mexico). Natl. geog. 100: 793 (col.) Dec '51.

Picasso, Pablo. Cur. biog. p. 592 (1943); p. 340 (1962).
Holiday 19: 84 Mar '56.

—— (tapestry by). Holiday 14: 51 (col.) Dec '53.

—— (work of). Amer. heri., vol. 6 no. 2 p. 41 (winter '55).
Con. 133: 16 Mar '54; 140: XVIII Dec '57; 141: 50 Mar '58; 142: 254 Jan '59; 143: LI Ap '59, 145 May '59; 145: XXVIII, 208 May '60, LXXXI, 255-7 Je '60.
Holiday 14: 58, 60 (col.) Nov '53.
Int. gr. soc.: Arts . . . p. 133 (col.).
Natl. geog. 111: 91 (col.) Jan '57.
Praeg.: Pict. ency., p. 455, 506 (col.).

Piccard, Auguste. Cur. biog. p. 516 (1947).

Piccard, Frank A. Cur. biog. p. 514 (1947).

Piccard, Jean Felix. Cur. biog. p. 517 (1947).

Piccini, Aristide. Amer. heri., vol. 2 no. 3 p. 49 (spring '51).

piccolo. Cooper: Con. ency. of music, p. 397.
Int. gr. soc.: Arts . . . p. 141 (col.).

Pichon, Stephen (of France). Amer heri., vol. 6 no. 1 p. 47 (fall '54).

Pick, Brig. Gen. Lewis Andrew. Cur. biog. p. 481 (1946).
Holiday 7: 36 Mar '50.

Pick, Vernon J. Cur. biog. p. 489 (1955).

Picken, Mary Brooks. Cur. biog. p. 507 (1954).

Pickens, Jane. Cur. biog. p. 485 (1949).

pickerel jack (carry fire). Rawson: Ant. pict. bk., p. 76.

Pickering, William H. Cur. biog. p. 337 (1958).

Pickersgill, H. W. (work of). Con. 144: 9 Sept '59.

picket fence. See fence, picket.

pickets, industrial. Holiday 7: 55 Feb '50.

Pickett, Clarence E. Cur. biog. p. 465 (1945).

Pickett, Gen. George. Amer. heri., vol. 11 no. 3 p. 106 (Ap '60).

Pickett, Maj. Gen. George Edward. Amer. heri., vol. 9 no. 1 p. 45 (Dec '57).
Pakula: Cent. album, p. 223.

Pickett, Tom. Horan: Pict. hist. of wild west, p. 64.

"Pickett's charge", Gettysburg (by Philippoteaux). Amer. heri., vol. 9 no. 1 p. 30 (col.), 42 (Dec '57).

Pickford, Mary. Cur. biog. p. 468 (1945).
Holiday 5: 36 (col.) Jan '49; 10: 65 Dec '51.

pickle dish (Geo. Washington's). Amer. heri., vol. 6 no. 5 p. 49 (col.) (Aug '55).

pickle jar, Irish glass (George IV). Con. ency. of ant., vol. 3, pl. 47.

Pickwick dam (Tenn.). Travel 104: 14 Jl '55.

picnic. Holiday 5: 15 Jan '49; 11: 81 (col.) Je '52: 18: 49 (col.) Jl '55, 60 (col.) Aug '55;

19: 113 Mar '56; 20: 107 (col.) Oct '56; 28: 164 (col.) Oct '60.

—— (around camp fire). Travel 105: 37 Mar '56.

—— (auto, bears). Holiday 10: 87 Sept '51.

—— (beach). Holiday 12: 111 (col.) Jl '52; 26: 26 (col.) Dec '59.
Natl. geog. 108: 122-3 (col.) Jl '55; 115: 445 Ap '59; 117: 458, 496 (col.) Ap '60.

—— (beach, lunch, fire). Natl. geog. 101: 314 (col.) Mar '52.

—— (beach, night). Holiday 22: 102-3 (col.) Dec '57.

—— (beach, rocky). Natl. geog. 105: 236 (col.) Feb '54.

—— (beside lake). Holiday 23: 28-9 (col.) May '58.

—— (Black Forest, Ger.). Disney: People & places, p. 49 (col.).

—— (canyon). Natl. geog. 105: 58 (col.) Jan '54.

—— (Colo.). Natl. geog. 107: 223 (col.) Feb '55.

—— (family). Holiday 22: 79 (col.) Sept '57.

—— (food). Holiday 10: 56 (col.) Jl '51.

—— (Fourth of July, 1912). Natl. geog. 116: 110-11 (col.) Jl '59.

"The picnic" (Goya). Con. 133: 231 Je '54.

picnic (horses, men). Natl. geog. 109: 24 (col.) Jan '56.

—— (Iran). Natl. geog. 100: 440 (col.) Oct '51; 104: 712 Nov '53.

—— (lawn). Holiday 10: 121 (col.) Nov '51; 12: 75 (col.) Nov '52; 20: 69 Aug '56.
Natl. geog. 108: 522 (col.) Oct '55; 117: 496 (col.) Ap '60.

—— (lunch table). Natl. geog. 117: 20-1 (col.) Jan '60.

—— (Madeira is.). Natl. geog. 115: 388 (col.) Mar '59.

—— (man & women). Natl. geog. 115: 726-7 May '59.

—— (mountain). Natl. geog. 111: 663 (col.) May '57.

—— (on boat). Natl. geog. 107: 68 (col.) Jan '55.

—— (party). Holiday 14: 62 Dec '53.

—— (river bank). Natl. geog. 98: 333 (col.) Sept '50; 114: 63 (col.) Jl '58, 656 (col.) Nov '58.

—— (sand dunes). Natl. geog. 112: 718 (col.) Nov '57.

—— (students). Natl. geog. 103: 533 Ap '53.

—— (Switzerland). Natl. geog. 107: 842 (col.) Je '55.

—— (woman & children). Natl. geog. 107: 739 (col.) Je '53.

picnic bag. Holiday 10: 12 Jl '51; 19: 70 Je '56.

picnic dinner. Holiday 21: 23 (col.) Mar '57.

picnic group. Holiday 7: 119 (col.) May '50.

picnic hamper. See hamper, picnic.

"Picnic in the Catskills" (Inman). Amer. heri., vol. 10 no. 1 p. 23 (col.) (Dec '58).

picnic kit. Holiday 10: 72 Nov '51.

"Picnic on the Hudson" (Rossiter). Amer. heri., vol. 10 no. 1 p. 20 (col.) (Dec '58).

picnic set. Holiday 11: 154 May '52.

picnic supper (at home). Holiday 14: 21 (col.) Nov '53.

picnic. See also boys & girls (picnic); man & girl; man, woman & child; men & women (picnic).

Picon, Molly. Cur. biog. p. 490 (1951).

pictorial caves. See caves, pictorial.

picture forgery. See art fakes.

picture frame. Holiday 14: 1 Nov '53.

—— (antique). Con. 135: XIX Je '55.

—— (antique gold). Amer. heri., vol. 11 no. 2 frontis. (col.) (Feb '60). Con. 142: 189 Dec '58, 250 (col.) Jan '59; 143: 67 Ap '59, cover (col.) Je '59; 144: 45 (col.) Sept '59, 76 Nov '59, XVII Dec '59; 145: LIII May '60.

—— (Faberge). Con. 143: LVIII Je '59.

—— (Faberge, miniature). Con. 139: XXXVII May '57.

—— (gilt). Con. 144: XXXV (col.) Jan '60; 145: XLVII Mar '60.

—— (Italian, Valadier). Con. 144: 153 Dec '59.

—— (miniature). Con. 141: XLVII Mar '58.

—— (miniature, antique). Con. 136: XV Sept '55; 139: XLI Ap '57, XLVII Je '57.

—— (miniature, silver). Con. 133: XXVII May '54.

picture projecture. See motion picture projector; projector, slide.

pictures, "ink blot". See "ink blot" pictures.

Pidgeon, Walter. Cur. biog. p. 663 (1942).

Pidgeon Key. Travel 103: 33 Feb '55.

pie-wheels. Rawson: Ant. pict. bk., p. 81.

Pieck, Wilhelm. Cur. biog. p. 487 (1949).

Piel, Gerard. Cur. biog. p. 361 (1959).

Pier, Arthur Stanwood. Jun. bk. of auth., p. 245.

pier (boat landing). See boat landing.

—— (Newport Beach). Travel 106: 32 Jl '56.

——, fishing. See fishing pier.

pier-glass. See mirror, pier-glass.

pier table (antique). Con. 137: 107 Ap '56.

—— (George II). Con. 129: XVII Ap '52.

Pierce, Abel Head (monument). Horan: Pict. hist. of wild west, p. 104.

Pierce, Rev. Bob. Cur. biog. p. 363 (1961).

Pierce, Franklin. Amer. heri., vol. 7 no. 3 p. 31 (Ap '56).
Jensen: The White White House, p. 74.

Pierce, J. R. Cur. biog. p. 365 (1961).

Pierce, Jane (Mrs. Franklin Pierce). Jensen: The White House, p. 75.

Pierce, John Robinson. Cur. biog. p. 365 (1961).

Pierce, Lorne. Cur. biog. p. 490 (1956).

Pierce, Mr. & Mrs. Marvin. Holiday 13: 17 Mar '53.

Pierce, Shanghai. See Pierce, Abel Head.

Pierlot, Hubert. Cur. biog. p. 595 (1943).

Pierpont, Donald E. Holiday 27: 84 Feb '60.

Pierre, Abbe. Cur. biog. p. 490 (1955).

piers, boat. See Brooklyn terminal boat piers.

Pierson, Louise Randall. Cur. biog. p. 597 (1943).

Pierson, Warren Lee. Cur. biog. p. 669 (1941); p. 509 (1954).

"Pieta" (Benvenuto). Con. 135: 55 Mar '55.

"Pieta" (bronze, by Soldani-Benzi). Con. 140: 201 Dec '57.

"Pieta" (Carracci). Con. 138: 227 Jan '57.

"Pieta" (porcelain group, Doccia). Con. 140: 196-99 (col.) Dec '57.

"Pieta" (sculpture, Von Judenburg). Con. 139: 125 Ap '57.

Pieta of Guido Mazzoni. Labande: Naples, p. 76-7.

"Pieta Rondanini". Praeg.: pict. ency., p. 17.

pietre dure cabinet. Con. 141: 215 Je '58.

pietre dure relief of Cosimo II. Con. 141: 215 Je '58.

pietre dure sculpture & arch. Con. 141: 214 Je '58.

Pietro della Valle's wife. See Maani, Sitti.

"pig" (earthenware hot-water bottle). Natl. geog. 110: 43 (col.) Jl '56.

pig, suckling (sym.). See suckling pig (sym.).

"pig killing" ceremony (New Guinea). Natl. geog. 116: 776 Dec '59.

pig molds, aluminum. Natl. geog. 115: 324 (col.) Mar '59.

pig pen. Rawson: Ant. pict. bk., p. 62-3.

pigeon house. Amer. heri., vol. 7 no. 4 p. 56 (Je '56).

pigeon nesting towers. See towers, pigeon nesting.

piggy bank. Lehner: Pict. bk. of sym., p. 59.

piggyback rider (man & child). Natl. geog. 117: 844 Je '60.

pigin. Rawson: Ant. pict. bk., p. 61.

Pike, Albert S. Pakula: Cent. album, p. 225.

Pike, Rev. James Albert. Cur. biog. p. 425 (1957).

Pike, Sumner T. Cur. biog. p. 518 (1947).

Pike, Zebulon Montgomery (horseback, surprised). Holiday 19: 8 May '56.

pike (to raise house frame). Rawson: Ant. pict. bk., p. 23.

pikeman, sergeant. See sergeant pikeman.

Pike's Peak (Colo.). Jordan: Hammond's pict. atlas, p. 165 (col.).
Natl. geog. 106: 228 (col.) Aug '54.

Pike's Peak train. Holiday 23: 104 May '58.

Pile, Lt. Gen. Sir Frederick Alfred. Cur. biog. p. 665 (1942).

Pilgrim (costume). Natl. geog. 112: 634 (col.) Nov '57.

"The Pilgrim" (river boat). Amer. heri., vol. 6 no. 1 p. 11 (col.) (fall '54).

Pilgrim (seated, reading). Holiday 18: 98 (col.) Sept '55.

——, Mecca. See Mecca pilgrim.

Pilgrim dugouts (log house). Brooks: Growth of a nation, p. 45.

"Pilgrim greeting Mecca return" (Kashmir). Natl. geog. 114: 638-9 Nov '58.

Pilgrim hat. See hat, Pilgrim.

Pilgrim march (French religious fete). Natl. geog. 117: 730-1 (col.) Je '60.

Pilgrim prostrator (Lhasa). Natl. geog. 108: 17 Jl '55.

"Pilgrim village" (at Plymouth, Mass.). Travel 107: 52-3 Mar '57.

Pilgrimage church (int.). Praeg.: pict. ency., p. 367.

Pilgrimage of the soul. See ladder of pilgrimage of soul.

pilgrimage to Glastonbury (Eng.). Natl. geog. 108: 332 (col.) Sept '55.
Pilgrims. Amer. heri. (in back of most issues). Int. gr. soc.: Arts . . . p. 113 (col.).
—— (cartoon). Holiday 15: 124 Je '54.
—— (family). Brooks: Growth of a nation, p. 47.
—— (holding parade, Israel). Natl. geog. 115: 528-9 (col.) Ap '59.
—— (lighted tapers). Natl. geog. 115: 504 (col.) Ap '59.
—— (maypole, cartoon). Amer. heri., vol. 6 no. 4 p. 101 (Je '55).
——, Andalusian festival. Natl. geog. 113: 417 (col.) Mar '58.
——, Chinese. See Chinese pilgrims.
——, Hindu (Ganges). Natl. geog. 118: 450-1, 480-3 (col.) Oct '60.
——, Japanese (temple). Natl. geog. 116: 862 (col.) Dec '59.
——, Jerusalem. Natl. geog. 102: 845 Dec '52.
——, Mecca. Natl. geog. 104: 20-59 (part col.) Jl '53.
——, Russian. Holiday 18: 110 Jl '55.
Pilgrim's landing. See Plymouth Rock.
"Pilgrims pray aboard Speedwell, 1620". Natl. geog. 102: 155 (col.) Aug '52.
"Pilgrim's progress" procession (Mass.). Holiday 11: 36 Je '52.
Pilgrim's route to Amer. Travel 106: 12-7 Jl '56.
Pilgrims to Amarnath, Hindu. Natl. geog. 110: 520-35 Oct '56.
pill tile, Delft drug (antique). Con. 127: 23-26 Mar '51.
pill tube. Con. 129: XXXVII Ap '52.
pillar, Karnak temple. See column, Karnak temple.
"Pillar of life" (sculpture). Natl. geog. 106: 192 Aug '54.
pillars, Egyptian home (int.). Int. gr. soc.: Arts . . . p. 15 (col.).
——, Roman home (int.). Int. gr. soc.: Arts . . . p. 15 (col.).
"Pillars of the sea". Con. 145: 188 May '60.
Pillement, Jean. (panels by). Con. 138: X-XI (col.) Jan '57.
pillory, public colonial. Natl. goeg. 106: 445 Oct '54.
pillow (leopard on it). Holiday 25: 146 (col.) May '59.
—— (lion on it). Holiday 25: 134 (col.) Feb '59, 41 (col.) Mar '59.
—— (tiger on it). Holiday 25: 191 (col.) Ap '59.
pillow fight (Vassar college, 1894). Amer. heri., vol. 11 no. 6 p. 107 (Oct '60).
pillows, bus. Natl. geog. 98: 10 Jl '50.
Pilon, Germain. Con. 144: XXVI Jan '60.
—— (sculpture). Natl. geog. 101: 794 (col.) Je '52.
pilot (boards boat). Natl. geog. 106: 806 Dec '54.
——, airplane. Holiday 19: 117 (col.) May '56; 20: 116 (col.) Oct '56, 144 (col.) Dec '56; 27: 155 (col.) May '60; 28: 107 (col.) Aug '60, back cover (col.) Dec '60.
Natl. geog. 100: 744 (col.) Dec '51.

Travel 103: back cover May '55.
—— (altitude garb). Natl. geog. 112: 277 Aug '57.
—— (Arctic). Natl. geog. 107: 568-9 (col.) Ap '55.
—— (elevator). Natl. geog. 108: 269 (col.) Aug '55.
—— (head). Holiday 27: 192-3 May '60.
—— (in chair descending). Natl. geog. 108: 268 (col.) Aug '55.
pilot, airplane test. Natl. geog. 104: 766, 771, 780 (col.) Dec '53.
——, boat. (Pitcairn is.). Natl. geog. 112: 774 (col.) Dec '57.
——, jet fighter. Holiday 11: 109 Ap '52.
——, U.S. air force. Holiday 27: 83, 87 (col.) Mar '60.
Natl. geog. 117: 653 (col.) May '60.
pilots, airplane (Formosa). Natl. geog. 107: 579 Ap '55.
Pilottown (near New Orleans). Travel 110: 29-31 Oct '58.
Pinay, Antoine. Cur. biog. p. 470 (1952).
pinchers (tools). Rawson: Ant. pict. bk., p. 54.
Pinchot, Gifford. Brooks: Growth of a nation, p. 228.
Pinckney, Charles. Amer. heri., vol. 10 no. 1 p. 61 (Dec '58).
Pinckney, Charles Cotesworth. Amer. heri., vol. 9 no. 2 p. 51 (Feb '58).
Pinckney, Thomas. Amer. heri., vol. 9 no. 2 p. 51 (Feb '58).
Pinckney, Thomas, jr. Amer. heri., vol. 9 no. 2 cover (col.) (Feb '58).
Pinckney, William. Amer. heri., vol. 6 no. 3 p. 45 (col.) (Ap '55).
"pincushions" (incense burners). Natl. geog. 97: 216 Feb '50.
Pine, David A. Cur. biog. p. 472 (1952).
Pine, Robert Edge (work of). Amer. heri., vol. 2 no. 2 p. 28 (winter '51).
pine cone (sym.). Lehner: Pict. bk. of sym., p. 29.
pine gum (from pine forest). Natl. geog. 105: 317 (col.) Mar '54.
pine tree pollination. Natl. geog. 110: 291 (col.) Sept '56.
pine tree shilling. See shilling, pine tree.
pineapple cup. See cup, pineapple.
Pineau, Christian. Cur. biog. p. 492 (1956).
Pinero, Jesus T. Cur. biog. p. 483 (1946).
ping pong game. Holiday 11: 53 (col.) Je '52.
Pinilla, Gustavo Rojas. Cur. biog. p. 528 (1956).
"The Pink Boy" (Master Nicholls). Con. 143: 206 Je '54.
Pinkerton, R. A. Horan: Pict. hist. of wild west, p. 197.
Pinkerton, William A. Horan: Pict. hist. of wild west, p. 36, 197, 231.
"Pinkie" (Aunt of Eliz. Barrett Browning, by Lawrence). Natl. geog. 105: 788 (col.) Je '54; 113: 252 (col.) Feb '58.
Pinner (Eng.). Travel 105: 41 Ap '56.
Pinney, Eunice (work of). Amer. heri., vol. 2 no. 2 p. 44 (col.) (winter '51).
pinocchio (book illus). Amer. heri., vol. 8 no. 1 p. 27 (col.) (Dec '56).
pins, hair. See hair pins, stone age.
Pinter, Harold. Cur. biog. p. 327 (1963).

Pinturicchio (work of). Con. 136: 59 Sept '55.
Pinxton plate. *See* plate, Pinxton.
Pinza, Ezio. Cur. biog. p. 670 (1941); p. 494 (1953).
Piombo, Sebastiano del. *See* Sebastiano del Piombo (work of).
pioneer (march west). Amer. heri., vol. 9 no. 3 p. 4-5 (col.) (Ap '58).
Pioneer column (Astoria, Ore.). Holiday 14: 61 Jl '53.
pioneer trails. *See* trails, pioneer.
Pioneer village (Neb.). Travel 109: 29 Je '58.
"Pioneer woman" (statue, Okla.). Travel 104: 29 Jl '55.
"Pioneer woman & child" (statue). Brooks: Growth of a nation, p. 195.
pioneers. Amer. heri., vol. 7 no.. 3 p. 108 (Ap '56); vol. 7 no. 5 p. 106 (Aug '56); vol. 7 no. 6 p. 98 (Oct '56); vol. 8 no. 1 p. 94 (Dec '56); vol. 8 no. 3 p. 94 (Ap '57); vol. 8 no. 4 p. 86 (Je '57); vol. 8 no. 5 p. 96 (Aug '57); vol. 9 no. 3 p. 8-9, 82 (Ap '58); vol. 9 no. 4 p. 86 (Je '58); vol. 9 no. 5 p. 108 (Aug '58); vol. 9 no. 6 p. 112 (Oct '58); vol. 10 no. 1 p. 116 (Dec '58); vol. 10 no. 2 p. 36-7, 108 Feb '59; vol. 10 no. 3 p. 108 Ap '59; vol. 10 no. 4 p. 99 Je '59.
——. *See also* pilgrims; puritans.
pipe. Holiday 6: 1 Oct '49, 132 Dec '49; 8: 151 Dec '50; 10: 12 (col.) Oct '51; 12: 173 Dec '52; 18: 22 Oct '55, 169 Nov '55, 38, 192, 198 Dec '55; 20: 33, 139 Oct '56, 118, 206 Dec '56; 22: 181 Nov '57; 23: 172 Mar '58; 24: 151 Oct '58, 224 Dec '58; 26: 248 Dec '59.
—— **(ash tray).** Holiday 22: 77 (col.) Sept '57.
—— **(sym.).** Lehner: Pict. bk. of sym., p. 91.
—— **(Vezzi porcelain, 18th cent.).** Con. 142: XIV Dec '58.
——, **Adena Indian.** *See* Adena pipe.
——, **Batta.** *See* Batta pipe.
——, **clay (antique).** Natl. geog. 109: 477 Ap '56.
——, **Indian.** *See* Indian peace pipe.
——, **Ma'di (Iraq).** Natl. geog. 113: 221 (col.) Feb '58.
——, **peace.** *See* Indian peace pipe.
——, **steatite (man head).** Natl. geog. 114: 266 (col.) Aug '58.
——, **water.** *See* water pipe.
pipe inspector (man inside). Natl. geog. 100: 544 Oct '51.
pipe-kiln. Con. ency. of ant., vol. 3 p. 244.
pipe organ. *See* organ, pipe.
Piper, John (work of). Con. 136: 40 Sept '55.
Piper, William T. Cur. biog. p. 485 (1946).
piper, Scotch. *See* Scotch bagpipe player.
pipes. Holiday 8: 124 Nov '50.
——, **churchwarden.** Natl. geog. 117: 157 (col.) Feb '60.
——, **Yale students (Elizabethan club).** Natl. geog. 112: 328 (col.) Sept '57.
pipes of Pan. Lehner: Pict. bk. of sym., p. 15.
"Pippa's Tower" (Italy). Natl. geog. 100: 407 (col.) Sept '51.
Pippin, Horace. Cur. biog. p. 471 (1945).
piracy (sym.). Lehner: Pict. bk. of sym., p. 86.
Piran (harbor). Holiday 25: 89 (col.) Je '59.
Piranesi, Giovanni Battista (work of). Con.

141: 236 Je '58.
—— **(statue).** Con. 143: 243 Je '59.
pirate. Amer. heri., vol. 8 no. 2 p. 10, 14-9 (part col.) (Feb '57).
Holiday 8: 54 Oct '50; 15: 106 Ap '54.
—— **(child as).** Holiday 22: 36 Nov '57; 23: 140 Je '58.
—— **(head).** Holiday 26: 231 Dec '59.
pirate castle. *See* castle, pirate.
pirate chest. *See* treasure chest.
pirate coast (Trucial Oman). Natl. geog. 110: 66-104 (part col.) Jl '56.
pirate flag. Amer. heri., vol. 8 no. 2 p. 13 (Feb '57).
—— **(sym.).** Lehner: Pict. bk. of sym., p. 86.
"Pirate jamboree" (N.C.). Natl. geog. 108: 506 Oct '55.
Pirate jamboree girls. Natl. geog. 113: 22 (col.) Jan '58.
pirate ship. Amer. heri., vol. 8 no. 2 p. 41 (col.) (Feb '57).
pirates, women. Amer. heri., vol. 8 no. 2 p. 14 (col.) (Feb '57).
pirates' chests. *See* treasure chest.
pirates' fort (Anamur). Osward: Asia Minor, p. 158.
Pire, Rev. Georges H. Cur. biog. p. 363 (1959).
pirogue. Amer. heri., vol. 2 no. 1 p. 46 (fall '50).
—— **(La Bayou).** Holiday 6: 59 Oct '49.
Pisa, leaning tower of. *See* Leaning tower of Pisa.
Pisa cathedral. Holiday 27: 123 Jan '60.
Int. gr. soc.: Arts . . . p. 47 (col.).
Praeg. pict. ency., p. 238.
Travel 102: inside cover Jl '54.
Pisac fort. Amer. heri., vol. 6 no. 5 p. 32 (col.) (Aug '55).
Pisac Valley (Peru). Travel 101: 10 Feb '54.
Pisani, Ferri. Amer. heri., vol. 8 no. 5 p. 72 (Aug '57).
Pisano, Giovanni (work of). Praeg.: pict. ency., p. 244.
Pisano, Nino. (sculpture by). Con. 138: 209 Dec '56.
Piscator, Erwin. Cur. biog. p. 666 (1942).
Pissarro, Camille (work of). Con. 141: 122 Ap '58, LXV (col.), 250 Je '58; 142: 61 Sept '58, 193 Dec '58; 143: 145 May '59; 144: XXX Nov '59, 1 Dec '59; 145: XXVIII, 44 Mar '60.
Praeg. pict. ency., p. 419 (col.).
pistol. Amer. heri., vol. 8 no. 2 p. 103 (Feb '57); vol. 11 no. 5 p. 32 (col.) (Aug '60).
Con. 136: 195-6 Dec '55.
Holiday 8: 157 Dec '50; 21: 125 (col.) Ap '57; 23: 171 (col.) Ap '58.
Travel 112: 63 Dec '59.
—— **(antique).** Amer. heri., vol. 2 no. 2 p. 58 (winter '51); vol. 11 no. 5 p. 82-4 (Aug '60).
Con. ency. of ant., vol. 1, pl. 110-11.
Con. 134: LVI Sept '54, LVIII, 108-9 Nov '54; 135: LXIV May '55, LIV Je '55; 136: L Jan '56.
—— **(men talking).** Holiday 18: 32 (col.) Oct '55.
—— **(silver mounted 18th cent.).** Con. 135: 174 May '55.

pistol, marines. Holiday 22: 73 Nov '57.
——, Gen. Patton's. Holiday 28: 57 Sept '60.
——, Gen. Washington's. Holiday 28: 57 Sept '60.
pistols. Holiday 8: 36 Jl '50; 18: 131 (col.) Dec '55.
—— (antique). Con. 140: 83-6 Nov '57.
——, Lafayette's (Geo. Washington's gift). Natl. geog. 112: 425 Sept '57.
——, U.S. Civil war. Pakula: Cent. album, p. 17 (col.).
——. See also revolver.
Piston, Walter. Cur. biog. p. 367 (1961).
Piston, Walter H., jr. Cur. biog. p. 497 (1948).
Pistoria silver altar. See altar, cathedral of Pistoria.
Pitcairn is. Natl. geog. 112: 732-88 (part col.) Dec '57.
—— (map). Natl. geog. 112: 734-5 Dec '57.
pitchblende mine (Africa). Natl. geog. 118: 318 (col.) Sept '60.
pitcher. Holiday 20: 37 (col.) Dec '56; 22: 222 (col.) Dec '57; 25: 201 May '59.
Natl. geog. 114: 124 (col.) Jl '58.
—— (antique). Amer. heri., vol. 9 no. 5 p. 5 (Aug '58).
Con. 136: inside cover Dec '55.
Natl. geog. 118: 262 Aug '60.
Rawson: Ant. pict. bk., p. 87.
—— (18th cent.). Amer. heri., vol. 6 no. 5 p. 52 (col.) (Aug '55).
Holiday 26: 187 Oct '59.
—— (pouring). Holiday 20: 152 Nov '56.
——, aluminum. Holiday 20: 33 Dec '56.
——, chill-it. Holiday 14: 164 Nov '53.
——, cut glass. Daniel: Cut & engraved glass, pl. 5, 23, 52, 69.
——, cyclades (700 B.C.). Int. gr. soc.: Arts . . . p. 19 (col.).
——, Derby. Con. 132: XL Sept '53.
——, Egyptian (ancient). Int. gr. soc.: Arts . . . p. 19 (col.).
——, George II. Con. 136: LI Dec '55.
——, glass. Holiday 25: 38 Je '59.
——, glass (Amer. antique). Con. ency. of ant., vol. 3, pl. 38-44.
——, gold & enamel. Con. 144: 269 Jan '60.
——, Irish glass (antique). Con. ency., of ant., vol. 3, pl. 45.
——, Islamic pottery. Con. 141: 190 May '58.
——, Kensington. Holiday 13: 124 Je '53.
——, oak. Holiday 20: 113 Sept '56.
——, pewter. Holiday 11: 125 May '52.
Natl. geog. 105: 463 (col.) Ap '54.
——, porcelain. Holiday 21: 197 May '57.
——, Rouen porcelain. Con. 141: 75 Ap '58.
——, stoneware (19th cent.). Amer. heri., vol. 2 no. 2 p. 33 (col.) (winter '51).
——, Syrian. Con. 145: 288 Je '60.
——, wood. Holiday 21: 197 May '57.
——, wooden wine. Holiday 11: 28 Feb '52.
pitcher & glasses. Holiday 10: 25 Nov '51.
pitchfork (girls, hayfield). Holiday 22: 7 (col.) Dec '57.
"Pitching quoits" (Homer). Natl. geog. 99: 201 (col.) Feb '51.
Pitkin, Walter B. Cur. biog. p. 671 (1941).
Pitman, Steuart L. Cur. biog. p. 329 (1963).
Pitt, William. Con. 129: 134 Je '52; 145: XLIV

Je '60.
Pitt, William the younger. Amer. heri., vol. 11 no. 4 p. 100 (Je '60).
Pittoni, Giovanni Battista (work of). Con. 140: XLV Jan '58; 141: 251 Je '58; 142: 40 Sept '58.
Pittsburgh. Brooks: Growth of a nation, p. 263.
Holiday 6: 34-51 (part col.) Oct '49; 25: 80-6 (col.) Mar '59.
—— (air view). Holiday 22: 6 Sept '57.
—— (early). Amer. heri., vol. 3 no. 2 p. 54-7 (part col.) (winter '52).
—— (harbor). Natl. geog. 97: 189 (col.) Feb '50.
—— (skyline). Face of Amer., p. 40-1 (col.).
Holiday 25: 81 (col.) Mar '59.
"Pittsburgh night" (Dehn). Amer. heri., vol. 3 no. 2 p. 54 (col.) (winter '52).
Pittsburgh university. See University of Pittsburgh.
Pitz river (Austria). Travel 105: 51 Ap '56.
Pitzer, Kenneth S. Cur. biog. p. 451 (1950).
Pius XII, Pope. See Pope Pius XII.
"Pizarro & priest" (by Roma de Ayala). Amer. heri., vol. 6 no. 5 p. 103 (Aug '55).
Pla y Daniel, Cardinal Enrique. Cur. biog. p. 492 (1955).
Place, Etta. Horan: Pict. hist. of wild west, p. 201, 227.
"Place of God" mountain (Iran). Natl. geog. 98: 826 Dec '50.
place symbol. Travel 113: 41 Ap '60.
"Placing Christ on the Cross" (14th cent., fresco). Labande: Naples, p. 70.
plan, floor. See floor plan.
"Plan Marshall" flag (Greek girl displays it). Natl. geog. 99: 237 Feb '51.
planetaria (Chapel Hill, N.C.). Travel 110: 45 Nov '58.
planetary crown (sym.). Lehner: Pict. bk. of sym., p. 23.
planets (photographs). Natl. geog. 103: 127-30 Jan '53.
——, configuration of the. Lehner: Pict. bk. of sym., p. 23.
——, mirror of the. See mirror of the planets (sym.).
——, sigils of (sym.). Lehner: Pict. bk. of sym., p. 24.
——. See also mars.
planisphere, Sancho Gutierrez, (1551). Amer. heri., vol. 12 no. 1 p. 34-5 (col.) (Dec '60).
plantation, Belgian Congo banana. Natl. geog. 106: 738-9 (col.) Dec '54.
——, cotton. Amer. heri., vol. 6 no. 3 p. 4-5 (col.) (Ap '55).
——, Harrison's "Berkeley Hundred". See "Berkeley Hundred."
——, Plymouth. See Plymouth plantation.
plantation home (La Bayou). Holiday 6: 59 Oct '49.
plantations, La. See Louisiana plantations.
planter, vegetable. Natl. geog. 112: 306 (col.) Sept '57.
plaster work, Eng. (int.). Con. 138: 92 Nov '56.
Plastiras, Nicholas. Cur. biog. p. 456 (1950).
plate (Phila. scene, 1824). Amer. heri., vol. 2 no. 3 p. 62 (spring '51).
—— (1600). Con. 144: III Sept '59.

plate (16th cent.). Con. 144: 126 Nov '59.
——, aluminum. Holiday 20: 33 Dec '56.
——, antique. Con. 132: 150 Jan '54.
——, antique silver. Con. 133: LXV Je '54.
——, antique silver dessert. Con. 139: 58 Mar '57.
——, antique silver dinner. Con. 145: 275 Je '60.
——, antique Betsy Ross. Amer. heri., vol. 1 no. 4 p. 56 (summer '50).
——, bleu de roi & gold. Con. 140: 58 Sept '57.
——, Bow. Con. 133: 112 Ap '54.
——, Chelsea. Con. 142: 89-94 Nov '58.
——, Chinese porcelain (K'ang Hsi). Con. 144: XXII Jan '60.
——, Copeland-Spode. Con. 133: 42 Mar '54.
——, Derby (19th cent.). Con. 145: LVIII May '60.
——, dessert. See dessert plate.
——, earthenware. Holiday 18: 61 (col.) Jl '55.
——, Egyptian service. Con. 143: 228 Je '59.
——, George I (silver). Con. 133: XXXVII Mar '54.
——, Georgian (silver). Con. 145: XXXVII Mar '60.
——, gilt (16th cent.). Con. 132: 84 Nov '53.
——, Greek (girl holding). Natl. geog. 103: 369 (col.) Mar '53.
——, Italian silver calendar. Con. 144: 153 Dec '59.
——, Meissen porcelain. Con. 142: XXXIX Sept '58.
——, painted (18th cent.). Con. 144: 99 Nov '59.
——, Persian. Int. gr. soc.: Arts . . . p. 177 (col.).
——, pewter. Con. 139: 163 May '57.
——, Pinxton. Con. 132: XXXII Nov '53.
——, porcelain ("Return of Columbus"). Holiday 12: 166 (col.) Dec '52.
——, Rouen pottery. Con. 141: 74 Ap '58.
——, Russian porcelain. Con. 144: 275 Jan '60.
——, silver (18th cent.). Con. 133: III Je '54.
——, silver-gilt (19th cent., Northcote). Con. 145: XVII Je '60.
——, stoneware (19th cent.). Amer. heri., vol. 2 no. 2 p. 33 (col.) (winter '51).
——, terra cotta. Holiday 18: 9 Sept '55.
——, Viennese porcelain. Con. 129: LVIII Ap '52.
——, Vincennes porcelain. Con. 133: 4 Mar '54.
——, William & Mary. Con. 126: 129 Oct '50.
——, Worcester. Con. 139: XII Mar '57.
——, Worcester armorial. Con. 144: 42 Sept '59.
plate chest. Con. ency. of ant., vol. 3, pl. 128.
plate pail. Con. ency., of ant., vol. 3, pl. 11.
—— (18th cent.). Con. ency. of ant., vol. 3, pl. 10.
plate warmer (antique). Con. ency. of ant., vol. 3, p. 244.
plates (dishes). Holiday 22: 222 (col.) Dec '57. Travel 111: 52 Mar '59.
——, armorial. Con. 142: 246-7 Jan '59.

——, Bow. Con. 140: XVI Jan '58.
——, Chelsea porcelain. Con. 134: 15-8 Sept '54.
——, Christmas. Holiday 10: 124 Dec '51; 12: 141 Nov '52; 22: 177 Nov '57; 24: 189 Nov '58.
——, Derby. Con. 142: XLI Nov '58.
——, dinner. Holiday 24: 159 (col.) Nov '58.
——, fruit. Travel 110: inside cover Sept '58, 41 Oct '58, inside cover Nov '58.
——, George III silver dinner. Con. 139: IX Ap '57; 143: LIV Je '59.
——, Hispano lustre pottery (early). Con. 126: 108-13 Oct '50.
——, Penn slipware & sgraffito. Rawson: Ant. pict. bk., p. 87.
——, Queen Anne silver. Con. 141: VII Ap '58.
——, Royal Doulton. Holiday 10: 122 Oct '51; 28: 109 (col.) Oct '60.
——, Russian empire. Con. 142: 102 Nov '58.
——, Salmon dinner silver (18th cent.). Con. 144: XXII Jan '60.
——, silver (antique). Con. 140: III Nov '57.
——, silver (18th cent.). Con. 141: 91 Ap '58.
——, Staffordshire. Amer. heri., vol. 6 no. 5 p. 50-1 (col.) (Aug '55).
——, Worcester. Con. 139: XVIII Mar '57; 141: XXXIII Ap '58.
——, Worcester dessert. Con. 143: LXXII Je '59.
platter, silver. Holiday 14: 117 Oct '53.
platter & cover, silver (Stoor, 19th cent.). Con. 144: XXIX Nov '59.
playhouse, tree. Holiday 19: 20 (col.) Mar '56.
Player, Gary. Cur. biog. p. 369 (1961).
playing cards (1827). Amer. heri., vol. 8 no. 4 frontis. (col.) (Je '57).
——, old Eng. Con. ency. of ant., vol. 3, pl. 140-1, p. 201.
playroom, adult. Holiday 12: 73 (col.) Aug '52.
plays (Cherokee Indian story, in N.C.). Amer. heri., vol. 5 no. 4 p. 16-23 (part col.) (summer '54).
Plaza, Galo. Cur. biog. p. 491 (1951).
Plaza hotel (Mexico City). Natl. geog. 100: 799 (col.) Dec '51.
Pleasants, Judge Henry Clay. Horan: Pict. hist. of wild west, p. 120.
Pleasonton, Alfred. Pakula: Cent. album, p. 227.
"Pleasures on the ice" (Averkamp). Con. 140: cover (col.) Nov '57.
Plesman, Albert. Cur. biog. p. 497 (1953).
"Pleurant" (Sluter). Con. 129: 37 Ap '52.
Pleven, Rene. Cur. biog. p. 458 (1950).
pliers (tools). Rawson: Ant. pict. bk., p. 54.
Plimer, Andrew (miniature by). Con. ency., of ant., vol. 1, pl. 132.
—— (work of). Con. 145: 127 Ap '60.
plinth, Lycian stone. See Lycian stone plinth.
Plisetskaya, Maya. Cur. biog. p. 331 (1963).
Plockton (Scotland). Holiday 27: 77 (col.) May '60.
plough. See plow.
plow. Amer. heri., vol. 7 no. 4 p. 27 (col.) (Je '56).
Travel 113: 31 Mar '60.

plow (boy, buffalo). Natl. geog. 102: 320 (col.) Sept '52.
—— **(man, mule).** Natl. geog. 101: 167 (col.) Feb '52.
——, **antique.** Amer. heri., vol. 7 no. 3 p. 49, 52 (col.) (Ap '56).
——, **Bucker snow train.** Amer. heri., vol. 10 no. 1 p. 54 (Dec '58).
——, **colonial.** Brooks: Growth of a nation, p. 101.
——, **French Indo China (oxen).** Travel 111: 41 Mar '59.
——, **Hunza (oxen).** Natl. geog. 104: 504-5 (col.) Oct '53.
——, **Iraq (wooden).** Natl. geog. 115: 53 (col.) Jan '59.
——, **Israeli (men, horse).** Natl. geog. 118: 828 (col.) Dec '60.
——, **Japanese rice.** Disney: People & places, p. 149 (col.).
——, **Jerusalem (mule).** Holiday 7: 126 (col.) Ap '50.
——, **Lebanon.** Natl. geog. 106: 832 (col.) Dec '54.
——, **Morocco (man, camel).** Disney: People & places, p. 94 (col.).
——, **oxen (man).** Natl. geog. 117: 663 (col.) May '60.
——, **oxen (men, ancient).** Natl. geog. 118: 828-9 (col.) Dec '60.
——, **primitive.** Rawson: Ant. pict. bk., p. 30.
——, **rotary snow train (1889-90).** Amer. heri., vol. 10 no. 1 p. 55 (Dec '58).
——, **Trinidad rice (men, cattle).** Natl. geog. 103: 46 (col.) Jan '53.
Plowden, Sir Edwin Noel. Cur. biog. p. 520 (1947).
plowman, Laos (ox). Natl. geog. 117: 54-5 (col.) Jan '60.
plum pudding. Lehner: Pict. bk. of sym., p. 51.
plumber (sym.). Lehner: Pict. bk. of sym., p. 91.
"plumed serpent" column (Mayan). Praeg.: pict. ency., p. 543.
—— **pyramid.** See Temple of Quetzalcoati.
Plumley, H. Ladd. Cur. biog. p. 333 (1963).
Plummer, Christopher. Cur. biog. p. 495 (1956).
Plura, Carlo Guiseppe (work of). Con. 138: 176-81 Dec '56.
Plura the younger, Joseph (self-portrait). Con. 138: 181 Dec '56.
Pluto. Lehner: Pict. bk. of sym., p. 31.
"Pluto carries off Proserpina" (statue). Natl. geog. 111: 485 (col.) Ap '57.
plutocracy (sym.). Lehner: Pict. bk. of sym., p. 95.
plutonium maker (Marcoule). Natl. geog. 117: 765 (col.) Je '60.
Plymouth (Mass.). Holiday 18: 98-101 (part col.) Sept '55.
Travel 107: 52-3 Mar '57.
—— **(harbor).** Natl. geog. 112: 662-3 (col.) Nov '57.
Plymouth auto. Holiday 6: 26 (col.) Sept '49, inside cover (col.) Oct '49.
Travel 103: 13 Jan '55.
Plymouth plantation (reconstruction, Mass.). Travel 114: 38 Sept '60.

Plymouth rock. Holiday 10: inside cover (col.) Sept '51; 11: 35 (col.) Je '52; 18: 101 Sept '55.
Natl. geog. 107: 740 (col.) Je '55.
Travel 106: 17 Jl '56.
poacher (fancy dress party). Natl. geog. 110: 10 Jl '56.
Paos volcano. Holiday 17: 37 Mar '55.
Pocahontas. Ameri. heri., vol. 2 no. 2 p. 27 (winter '51); vol. 9 no. 6 cover (col.) (Oct '58). ,
—— **(court dress).** Natl. geog. 111: 619 (col.) May '57.
"Pocahontas' baptism". Natl. geog. 102: 153 (col.) Aug '52.
—— **home (colonial).** Natl. geog. 111: 618 (col.) May '57.
"Pocahontas saved Capt. John Smith". Holiday 10: 43 (col.) Nov '51.
pocket books, paper back. See dime novels.
pocketbook. Holiday 6: 95 (col.) Sept '49; 14: 18 Nov '53; 18: 158 Nov '55; 27: inside (col.) Je '60.
——. See also purse; wallet.
pocketbook, man's. See wallet.
Pocock, Nicholas (work of). Con. 143: 176 May '59.
pod-auger. See auger, pod.
Poe, Edgar Allan. Amer. heri., vol. 7 no. 3 p. 22 (col.) (Ap '56).
Holiday 12: 97 Oct '52, 141 (col.) Dec '52.
Poe, John W. Horan: Pict. hist. of wild west, p. 69.
poems, heroic (muse). Lehner: Pict. bk. of sym., p. 33.
Poerson, Charles Francois (work of). Con. 140: 29 Sept '57.
poetry (sym.). Lehner: Pict. bk. of sym., p. 17.
Pogany, Willy. Jun. bk. of auth., p. 246.
Poindexter, Joseph B. Cur. biog. p. 668 (1942).
Poinso-Chapuis, Germaine. Cur. biog. p. 499 (1948).
Point Arena lighthouse. Natl. geog. 116: 615 (col.) Nov '59.
Point Barrow (Alaska). Natl. geog. 114: 128 Jl '58.
poison (sym.). Lehner: Pict. bk. of sym., p. 88.
poison making (pygmies). Natl. geog. 117: 288 Feb '60.
"Poissy-le-Pont" (Vlaminck). Con. 143: 55 Mar '59.
Poitier, Sidney. Cur. biog. p. 365 (1959).
poke, cow. Rawson: Ant. pict. bk., p. 67.
poke, sheep, geese & turkey. Rawson: Ant. pict. bk., p. 67.
poker table, Chippendale. Con. 133: XII May '54.
pokes, horse. Rawson: Ant. pict. bk., p. 67.
Poland. Natl. geog. 114: 355-98 (part col.) Sept '58.
—— **(map, 1914-1958).** Natl. geog. 114: 387 Sept '58.
——, **patron saint of.** Lehner: Pict. bk. of sym., p. 40.
"Pole cat" ceremony (North Pole). Natl. geog. 116: 17 Jl '59.
pole lathe. See lathe, pole.

polescreen, Empire wood. Con. 129: XL Ap '52.
Poletti, Lt. Col. Charles. Cur. biog. p. 599 (1943).
police (bloodhound). Natl. geog. 114: 230 (col.) Aug '58.
—— (leaning on car). Holiday 23: 159 (col.) Je '58.
——, Bahama. Natl. geog. 113: 156-7 Feb '58.
——, Barbados (harbor). Natl. geog. 101: 369 (col.) Mar '52.
——, Barbados (mounted). Natl. geog. 101: 386-7 (col.) Mar '52.
——, Canadian. Holiday 5: 19 (col.) Mar '49; 6: 36 Aug '49; 7: 115 (col.) Feb '50, 31 (col.) Mar '50, 135 (col.) Ap '50, 85, 157 (col.) May '50, 71 (col.) Je '50; 13: 123 (col.) Mar '53; 17: 7 (col.) Feb '55, 113 (col.) Mar '55; 19: 56 Jan '56, 125 (col.) Feb '56, 94 (col.) May '56, 21 Je '56; 27: 125 (col.) Mar '60.
——, Canadian (comic). Holiday 16: 90 Jl '54.
——, Canadian (comic arrest). Holiday 23: 76 Je '58.
——. See also Royal Canadian mounted police.
——, desert (camels). Natl. geog. 112: 78-9 (col.) Jl '57.
——, Egyptian traffic. Holiday 10: 120 (col.) Dec '51.
——, Iranian (holding child). Natl. geog. 100: 451 (col.) Oct '51.
——, Hindu traffic. See Hindu traffic police.
——,, Jordan desert army. Natl. geog. 112: 106 (col.) Jl '57.
——, Malay. See Malay police.
——, Mexico City traffic. Natl. geog. 100: 795 (col.) Dec '51.
——, military. See military police.
——, Nassau traffic. Holiday 23: 175 May '58.
——, Norwegian. Natl. geog. 106: 176 (col.) Aug '54.
——, Pakistan (marching). Natl. geog. 102: 645 (col.) Nov '52.
——, Quebec. Holiday 11: 99 (col.) Je '52.
——, Roman. Holiday 11: 38 (col.) Ap '52.
——, Roman military. Natl. geog. 111: 482-3 (col.) Ap '57.
——, Royal Canadian. See Royal Canadian police.
——, Spanish. Natl. geog. 97: 453 (col.) Ap '50.
——, traffic. See also Negro traffic police.
——, traffic guide. See traffic guide; traffic police.
——, Trinidad mounted. Natl. geog. 103: 63 Jan '53.
——, Vatican. Holiday 23: 58-9 (col.) May '58.
——, western (early). Horan: Pict. hist. of wild west, p. 36.
——, The White House. Jensen: The White House, p. 182.
police dog training. Natl. geog. 114: 191-230 (part col.) Aug '58.
Police Gazette (cartoons, 1894). Amer. heri., vol. 11 no. 6 p. 105-12 (Oct '60).

police guards (Omanis). Natl. geog. 110: 100 (col.) Jl '56.
police headquarters (Sarawak). Natl. geog. 109: 726 May '56.
policeman. Holiday 22: 9 Sept '57.
—— (cartoon). Holiday 27: 91 Je '60.
—— (chasing man, comic). Holiday 23: 141 May '58.
—— (child). Holiday 18: 83 (col.) Oct '55.
—— (1890). Holiday 12: 69 Sept '52.
—— (head). Holiday 25: 132 Jan '59.
—— (lets duck family pass). Natl. geog. 100: 515 Oct '51.
—— (prisoner, comic). Holiday 21: 174 May '57.
——, Canadian Royal. See Royal Canadian mounted policeman.
——, Egyptian. Travel 103: 25 Mar '55.
——, English. Holiday 23: 73 Ap '58; 28: 161 (col.) Nov '60.
Travel 102: 40 Dec '54.
——, European. Travel 109: 29-31 Ap '58.
——, European (comic). Holiday 28: 29 Sept '60, 115 Oct '60.
——, European boy. Holiday 27: 152 (col.) May '60.
——, Kingston (Jamaica). Holiday 5: 45 (col.) Feb '49.
——, Nassau. Holiday 23: 107 Ap '58.
——, Norwegian. Natl. geog. 106: 176 (col.) Aug '54.
——, Paris. Holiday 10: 62-3, 82 Sept '51. Natl. geog. 101: 783 Je '52.
——, Peru. Natl. geog. 98: 437 (col.) Oct '50.
——, Swiss. Travel 101: inside cover Je '54.
——, West Berlin. Natl. geog. 100: 699 Nov '51.
Polignac castle. Natl. geog. 100: 12 (col.) Jl '51
Poling, Rev. Daniel. Cur. biog. p. 603 (1943).
Polish bride & groom. Holiday 6: 56 (col.) Jl '49.
Polish dancers. Natl. geog. 114: 356-7 (col.) Sept '58.
Polish men. Natl. geog. 114: 391 (col.) Sept '58.
Polish mountaineer dance. Natl. geog. 111: 171 (col.) Feb '57.
Polish women (laborers). Natl. geog. 114: 364-5 Sept '58.
polishing iron. Rawson: Ant. pict. bk., p. 12.
Politi, Leo. Jun. bk. of auth., p. 247.
Politian medal (Ambrogini, Angelo). Con. 139: 99 Ap '57.
Politian with little Guiliano de Medici. Con. 139: 99 Ap '57.
Politian's birthplace. Con. 139: 96 Ap '57.
political campaign poster. See campaign poster.
political discussion (1877, cartoon). Amer. heri., vol. 11 no. 5 p. 102-3 (Aug '60).
political party symbol (cartoon). Holiday 28: 59 (col.) Jl '60.
political riots (1844). Amer. heri., vol. 10 no. 2 p. 61 (Feb '59).
politics (sym.). Lehner: Pict. bk. of sym., p. 94-5.
Politis, Athanase G. Cur. biog. p. 460 (1950).

Polk, James K. Amer. heri., vol. 7 no. 3 p. 31 (Ap '56).
Holiday 26: 94 (col.) Jl '59.
Jensen: The White House, p. 68.
Polk, Mrs. James K. Jensen: The White House, p. 69.
Polk, Leonidas. Pakula: Cent. album, p. 229.
Pollack, Jack Harrison. Cur. biog. p. 427 (1957).
Pollaiuolo, Antonio (work of). Con. 129: 72 Ap '52.
Pollard, James (work of). Con. 136: IV Jan '56; 141 LII Ap '58; 144: 203 Dec '59.
Pollard, William G. Cur. biog. p. 499 (1953).
pollination, pine tree. See pine tree pollination.
Pollitt, Harry. Cur. biog. p. 501 (1948).
Pollock, Jackson. Cur. biog. p. 497 (1956).
—— (work of). Holiday 14: 62 Nov '53.
Praeg.: Pict. ency., p. 512 (col.).
polo game. Holiday 16: 52-3 (col.) Sept '54; 28: 12 (col.) Sept '60.
polo player. Holiday 22: 127 Sept '57; 28: 65 Aug '60.
—— (on horse). Holiday 14: 88 (col.) Oct '53; 28: 74 Jl '60.
Travel 103: 55 Je '55.
—— (on horse, ancient times). Int. gr. soc.: Arts . . . p. 37 (col.).
—— (sculpture). Praeg. pict. ency. p. 509.
—— (20th cent.). Int. gr. soc. arts p. 153 (col.).
polo players. Holiday 16: 52-4 Sept '54.
Natl. geog. 99: 285 Mar '51.
—— (on horses). Holiday 25: 128 (col.) Je '59.
——, Hunzukut. Natl. geog. 117: 98-9 (col.) Jan '60.
poloist. See polo player.
Poltoratzky, Ellen Sarah (Southee). Almedingen: A very far country, following p. 150.
Poltoratzky, Serge. Almedingen: A very far country, following, p. 150.
polychrome, biscuit. Con. 138: XVIII Sept '56.
polychrome group (XVth cent.). Con. 142: XLVI Jan '59.
polychrome sculpture (15th cent.). Con. 142: LXVII Jan '59.
Polyhymnia (muse). Lehner: Pict. bk. of sym., p. 33.
Polynesia. Holiday 28: 54 Oct '60.
Natl. geog. 97: 524-52 (part col.) Ap '50.
Polynesian (cleaning fish). Natl. geog. 97: 79 Jan '50.
—— (spear-fishing). Holiday 7: 70 May '50.
—— girl. Natl. geog. 97: 89 (col.) Jan '50.
Polynesian islands & people. Holiday 9: 54-7 (part col.) Mar '51.
Polynesian women. Holiday 28: 88-93 (col.) Oct '60.
Polynesians. Disney: People & places, p. 129-45 (col.).
Holiday 7: 71 May '50; 28: 2 (col.) Oct '60.
Natl. geog. 97 74-104 (part col.) Jan '50; 99: 353 Mar '51.
polyptich, Italian (center of). Con. 145: 39 Mar '60.
polytechnic institute (Worcester). Worcester polytechnic institute.

pomade jar, Rouen porcelain. Con. 141: 74 Ap '58.
pomade pot, St. Cloud. Con. 143: 136 May '59.
pomander (16th cent.). Con. ency. of ant., vol. 1, pl. 96.
pomegranate (sym). Lehner: Pict. bk. of sym., p. 29.
Pomona. Lehner: Pict. bk. of sym., p. 33.
Pompeii. Ceram: March of arch., p. 10, 15, 20.
Labande: Naples, p. 31, 104-6, 148-73
—— (bar). Ceram: March or arch., p. 22.
—— (floor mosaic, 50 B.C.). Praeg.: Pict. ency., p. 149 (col.).
—— (House of tragic poet). Amer. heri., vol. 11 no. 3 p. 22 (col.) (Ap '60).
—— (sculpture). Ceram: March of arch., p. 21.
—— (skeletons). Ceram: March of arch., p. 18-9.
—— (theater). Ceram: March of arch., p. 16.
—— (wall paintings, 63 A.D.). Praeg.: Pict. ency., p. 162 (col.).
Pompeys pillar (monument to Clark). Natl. geog. 103: 728 (col.) Je '53.
Pompidou, Georges. Cur. biog. p. 342 (1962).
Ponape (lost city, South Pacific). Travel 108: 24, 26 Dec '57.
Ponape girl. Holiday 28: 89 (col.) Oct '60.
Ponce de Leon (seeks Fountain of Youth). Brooks: Growth of a nation, p. 32.
poncho (gaucho cloak). Natl. geog. 113: 326 (col.) Mar '58.
Poncins, Vicomte Gontran de. Cur. biog. p. 677 (1941).
pond. Holiday 27: 131 (col.) Jan '60.
Pondichery beach. Natl. geog. 105: 519 (col.) Ap '54.
Pons, Lily. Cur. biog. p. 547 (1944).
Holiday 8: 83 Sept '50; 22: 148 Dec '57; 24: 14 Dec '58; 25: 70-3 (col.) Feb '59.
Ponselle, Rosa (as Leonora in La Forza del Destino). Cooper: Con. ency. of music, p. 203.
Pont du Gard (Nimes). Natl. geog. 100: 20 Jl '51.
Praeg.: Pict. ency., p. 146.
"Ponte Lucano & tomb near Tiviole" (Busiri). Con. 141: 218 Je '58.
"Ponte Rotto, Rome" (Busiri). Con. 141: 218 Je '58.
"Ponte Santa Trinita, Florence" (Patch). Con. 138: XVII Jan '57.
Ponte Vecchio (Florence, Italy). Holiday 6: 135 (col.) Oct '49.
Natl. geog. 111: 794-5 (col.) Je '57.
Travel 114: 84 Jl '60.
Pontiac auto. Holiday 6: 21 Sept '49; 7: 2 Jan '50, 77 Feb '50, inside back cover (col.) Je '50; 8: 11 (col.) Aug '50, 93 (col.) Oct '50; 9: 79 (col.) Mar '51; 15: 10 (col.) Mar '54, 84 (col.) May '54, 2 (col.) Je '54; 16: inside cover (col.) Sept '54, inside cover (col.) Dec '54; 17: 15 (col.) Mar '55.
Travel 103: 13 Jan '55.
Pontian, Indian chief. Amer. heri., vol. 2 no. 4 p. 34-5 (col.) (summer '51).

Pontifical sedan carrier (Vatican). Holiday 23: 53 (col.) May '58.

pontoon barge. Natl. geog. 107: 682, 687 (col.) May '55.

Pontormo (self portrait). Con. 138: 58 Sept '56.

"Pony express". Brooks: Growth of a nation, p. 139.

pool, child's. Holiday 11: 132 Je '52; 12: inside cover (col.) Jl '52.

pool, garden. Natl. geog. 103: 118 (col.) Jan 53.

—— **(Iceland).** Natl. geog. 100: 620 (col.) Nov '51.

pool, Siloam. See Siloam pool.

——, **swimming.** See swimming pool.

pool game. Holiday 11: 55 Je '52.

pool table. Holiday 10: 14 Oct '51, 120 Nov '51, 163 Dec '51; 12: 23 Nov '52, 175 Dec '52.

Poole, Burnell (work of). Amer. heri., vol. 10 no. 6 p. 10 (Oct '59).

Poole, De Witt C. Cur. biog. p. 461 (1950).

Poole, Lynn. Cur. biog. p. 511 (1954).

Poor, Henry Varnum. Cur. biog. p. 669 (1942).

popcorn stand (Cypress is.). Natl. geog. 109: 877 Je '56.

Pope, Alexander (Kneller). Con. 141: 62 Mar '58.

Pope, Arthur Upham. Cur. biog. p. 522 (1947).

Pope, John. Pakula: Cent. album, p. 231.

Pope, Rev. Liston. Cur. biog. p. 499 (1956).

Pope Clement XI (bust by Baratta). Con. 142: 175 Dec '58.

Pope Clement XII (bust). Con. 138: 165 Dec '56.

—— **(statue).** Con. 138: 162 Dec '56.

Pope Clement XIV (bust). Con. 144: 228 Jan '60.

Pope John XXIII. Cur. biog. p. 211 (1959).
Holiday 27: 69 Ap '60.
Natl. geog. 117: 592 (col.) May '60.

—— **(receiving audience).** Travel 113: 38 Ap '60.

Pope Paul III (Titian). Labande: Naples, p. 110.

—— **(bust).** Holiday 27: 83 (col.) Ap '60.

"Pope Paul III Farnese" (Titian). Natl. geog. 97: 764 (col.) Je '50.

Pope Paul VI. Cur. biog. p. 317 (1963).
U.S. News & world report vol. LV no. 1 p. 43-4 July 1, 1963.

—— **(with Pres. Kennedy).** U.S. News & world report vol. LV no. 3 p. 37 July 15, 1963.

Pope Pius XII. Cur. biog. p. 673 (1941); p. 453 (1950).
Holiday 7: 107 (col.) May '50.
Natl. geog. 111: 800 (col.) Je '57.
Travel 103: 33 Ap '55.

—— **(on throne).** Holiday 23: 63 (col.) May '58.

pope (sym.). Lehner: Pict. bk. of sym., p. 76.

Popenoe, Paul. Cur. biog. p. 488 (1946).

popess (sym.). Lehner: Pict. bk. of sym., p. 76.

Popham, Sir John. Amer. heri., vol. 10 no. 5 p. 26 (col.) (Aug '59).

Popkin, Zelda. Cur. biog. p. 493 (1951).

Popocatepetl volcano. Natl. geog. 100: 815 (col.) Dec '51.

Popocic, Koca. Cur. biog. p. 429 (1957).

Popovic, Vladimir. Cur. biog. p. 474 (1952).

Popper, Karl R. Cur. biog. p. 335 (1963).

"poppet" (corn shuck doll). Holiday 9: 47 (col.) Mar '51.

population growth. U.S. (charts & book stack). Natl. geog. 116: 700-1, 710-11, 713 Nov '59.

porcelain (18th cent.). Con. 137: XXV May '56; 138: XXXI, 165 Dec '56.

——, **antique.** Con. ency. of ant., vol. 1, pl. 53-72.
Con. 135: 156-63 May '55; 137: 90-1 Ap '56; 138: inside cover Jan '56; 141: XX-XIII Ap '58; 142: 10-12 Sept '58.

——, **antique (18th cent.).** Amer. heri., vol. 6 no. 5 p. 53 (col.) (Aug '55).

——, **Bow.** Con. 144: 29-31 Sept '59.

——, **Capodimonte.** Con. 134: 147 Nov '54; 135: 117 Ap '55.

——, **Chelsea.** Con. 134: 15-21 (part col.) Sept '54; 136: 272-3 Jan '56; 138: X Sept '56, inside cover Nov '56; 139: inside cover Ap '57; 140: VI Sept '57; 141: XXXIII Ap '58, XLV Je '58; 142: 89-94 Nov '58.

——, **Chelsea figure.** Con. 140: inside cover Jan '58.

——, **Chelsea & Bow.** Con. 138: XXI Sept '56.

——, **Chinese.** See Chinese porcelain.

——, **Derby (18th cent.).** Con. 143: XVI Ap '59.

——, **English.** Con. 138: 108-9 Nov '56; 140: VI Jan '58.

——, **Frankenthal.** Con. 142: 6 Sept '58.

——, **French.** Con. 139: XVI May '57.

——, **Italian.** Con. 135: 12-9 Mar '55.

——, **Meissen.** Con. ency. of ant., vol. 1, pl. 57-64.
Con. 134: inside cover Nov '54; 135: inside cover Mar '55; 140: 58 Sept '57; 142: 7, XXXIX Sept '58.

——, **Oriental (18th cent.).** Con. 139: 1 Ap '57.

——, **Rouen.** Con. 141: 74-5 Ap '58.

——, **Russian empire.** Con. 142: 98-9, 101-3 Nov '58.

——, **St. Cloud.** Con. 141: 76 Ap '58.

——, **St. Petersburg.** Con. 142: 270 Jan '59.

——, **Worcester.** Con. 135: 269 Je '55; 139: 125 Ap '57; 141: XXXIII Ap '58.

porcelain dog, Chinese. Con. 141: XIV, XX-XIII Ap '58.

—— **figures (antique).** Con. 129: 35 Ap '52; 135: inside cover May '55.

——, **Italian.** Con. 138: XXXI Dec '56.

porcelain jar, Chinese (old). Con. 134: VIII Sept '54.

porcelain marks. Con. ency. of ant., vol. 1, p. 94-117, 126-7.
Praeg.: Pict. ency., p. 79

porcelain vase, Arita-Kakiemon. Con. 138: LXIV Jan '57.

"Porch of the maidens". See Acropolis (porch of the maidens); caryatid.

Poros (Greece). Travel 111: 37 Ap '59.

Porquerolles (harbor). Holiday 24: 14 Oct '58.

porridge pot (Scotland). Natl. geog. 98: 189 (col.) Aug '50.

porringer (antique). Con. 134: IX Sept '54, 161 Dec '54; 136: XI Sept '55; 137: 161 May '56.

——— (17th cent.). Con. 138: V Sept '56.

———, Charles II. Con. 127: 77-8, 80 May '51; 129: XXI Ap '52; 132: 137 Nov '53; 141: XX May '58.

———, James II. Con. 140: XLIII, 38 Sept '57; 143: LXVII Je '59.

———, James II (2 handled). Con. 144: 197 Dec '59.

———, pewter. Natl. geog. 117: 157 (col.) Feb '60.

———, Queen Anne (old). Con. 126: 43 Aug '50.

———, silver (antique). Con. 134: 160 Dec '54; 140: 113 Nov '57.

———, silver (1699). Con. ency. of ant., vol. 1, p. 153.

———, silver (1709). Con. 142: XIV Dec '58.

———, silver (17th cent.). Con. ency. of ant., vol. 1, pl. 83.
Con 143: 170 May '59.

———, Silver gilt (17th cent.). Con. 135: XVII Mar '55.

———, William & Mary (silver). Con. 133: XII May '54; 135: XXXII Ap '55.

———, William III (silver gilt). Con. 144: XXXIX Nov '59.

Porson, Richard (Hoppner). Con. 143: 89 Ap '59.

port. See harbor.

Port Angeles (Wash.). Natl. geog. 117: 450-1 (col.) Ap '60.

Port au Prince. Travel 106: 2 Jl '56.

Port Chalmers (New Zealand). Natl. geog. 101: 458 (col.) Ap '52.

Port Cros island (France). Travel 108: 57 Jl '57.

Port Elizabeth (Cape Providence, Africa). Natl. geog. 104: 172 (col.) Aug '53.

Port Louis (Mauritius is., Govt. House). Travel 106: 33 Nov '56.

Port of Spain. Natl. geog. 103: 37-8, 70 (col.) Jan '53.

——— (Hilton Hotel). Travel 109: 41 May '58.

Port Royal (Jamaica). Natl. geog. 117: 152-7, 162-83 (part col.) Feb '60.

——— (sunken city plan). Natl. geog. 117: 166-7 (col.) Feb '60.

Porta Maggiore. Holiday 11: 44 Ap '52.

Portal, Sir Charles. Cur. biog. p. 679 (1941).

portapoz, Catholic. Natl. geog. 107: 515 (col.) Ap '55.

Portchester castle (Eng.). Natl. geog. 101: 516 (col.) Ap '52.

"The Portello & the Brenta canal". Con. 144: 44 Sept '59.

Porter, Charles O. Cur. biog. p. 431 (1957).

Porter, Cole. Holiday 13: 84 May '53.

Porter, David. Amer. heri., vol. 7 no. 3 p. 18 (col.) (Ap '56).

Porter, David Dixon. Pakula: Cent. album, 233.

Porter, Edwin S. Amer. heri., vol. 11 no. 3 p. 33 (Ap '60).

Porter, Elizabeth K. Cur. biog. p. 476 (1952).

Porter, Fannie. Horan: Pict. hist. of wild west, p. 221.

Porter, Fitz-John. Pakula: Cent. album, p. 235.

Porter, Gen. Horace. Amer. heri., vol. 5 no. 4 p. 15 (summer '54).

Porter, Katherine Anne. Cur. biog. p. 338 (1963).

Porter, Ker (drawing by). Ceram: March of arch., p. 192-3.

Porter, Paul A. Cur. biog. p. 473 (1945).

Porter, Richard William. Cur. biog. p. 338 (1958).

Porter, Sylvia F. Cur. biog. p. 680 (1941).

Porter, Maj. Gen. William N. Cur. biog. p. 477 (1945).

porter (packages). Holiday 10: 147 Dec '51.

———, baggage. Holiday 20: 61 (col.) Aug '56.

———, hotel. See bell boy, hotel.

———, train. Holiday 6: 85 Nov '49; 10: 113 Sept '51; 19: 25 May '56; 20: 12 Nov '56; 25: 11 Mar '59; 26: 131 (col.) Nov '59; 27: 114 Feb '60.

———, train (head). Holiday 10: 7 (col.) Dec '51; 18: 127 Nov '55.

Porter home, Gene Stratton. Amer. heri., vol. 2 no. 1 p. 26 (fall '50).

Porterfield, George H. Amer. heri., vol. 3 no. 4 p. 58 (summer '52).

porters (Nepal). Natl. geog. 117: 405 (col.) Mar '60.

portfolio. Holiday 14: 36 Dec '53.

———. See also brief case.

portico. Holiday 21: 180 (col.) Je '57.

———, manor. Holiday 19: 12 (col.) Je '56.

Portinari altar panel. Praeg.: Pict. ency., p. 303.

Portland (Maine). Holiday 12: 79 Nov '52.

——— (Head lighthouse). Jordan: Hammond's pict. atlas, p. 25 (col.).

Portland (Ore.). Holiday 5: 50-4 (col.) Je '49; 23: 7 (col.) Ap '58; 25: 70-8 (part col.) May '59.
Travel 111: 18-9 May '59.

——— (night). Holiday 13: 46-7 (col.) Je '53. Natl. geog. 102: 582-3 (col.) Nov '52.

——— (rose festival). Natl. geog. 102: 584 (col.) Nov '52.

Portman, Eric. Cur. biog. p. 433 (1957).

Porto (Portugal, night). Natl. geog. 118: 624 (col.) Nov '60.

Portofino (Spain). Holiday 27: 50 (col.) Ap '60.

portrait medallion. See Wedgwood portrait medallion.

——— miniature. See miniature.

"Portrait of a Gentleman" (Hals). Con. ency. of ant., vol. 1 pl. 163.

"Portrait of a Man in Armor". Natl. geog. 101: 93 (col.) Jan '52.

"Portrait of Mrs. Tudor" (Constable). Con. 143: XVII May '59.

"Portrait of Nana Winding" (Bonnard). Con. 143: XXXIV Ap '59.

"Portrait of Sylvette" (Picasso). Con. 143: LI Ap '59.

"The Portrait Painter" (Maulpertsch). Con. 145: 135 Ap '60.

portraits (early Amer.). Amer. heri., vol. 1 no. 4 p. 46-9 (part col.) (summer '50).

Portsmouth (Eng.). Natl. geog. 101: 514-43 (part col.) Ap '52.
Portugal. Disney: People & places, p. 57-68 (col.).
  Holiday 6: 98-109 (part col.) Sept '49; 11: 110 (col.) Feb '52; 19: 26-35 (col.) Jan '56.
  Natl. geog. 106: 674-96 (part col.) Nov '54; 118: 617-56 (col.) Nov '60.
  Travel 101: 8 May '54; 111: 33 Je '59.
—— (Cistercian abbey nave). Con. 139: LX Je '57.
—— (cowboy fair). Travel 107: 29-31 Ap '57.
—— (hotel). Travel 111: 24 Ap '59.
—— (map). Natl. geog. 106: 677 Nov '54.
—— (Nazare). Holiday 26: 106 (col.) Aug '59.
—— (playground). Travel 110: 45-7 Sept '58.
—— (Royal palace of Queluz). Con. 139: 41 Mar '57.
Portugal, patron saint of. Lehner: Pict. bk. of sym., p. 40.
Portuguese (on horses). Travel 107: 29 Ap '57.
—— arms & armor. Con. 137: 22-7 Mar '56.
—— art. Con. 137: 2 (col.), 4-9, 29-31 Mar '56.
—— art (800-1800). Con. 136: 267-71 Jan '56.
—— church (int., carved work). Con. 137: 36-9 Mar '56.
—— church architecture. Con. 139: LI May '57.
—— crafts (gold & silver). Con. 137: 10-4, 66-70, 72-6 Mar '56.
—— folk dancers. Natl. geog. 118: 647 (col.) Nov '60.
  Travel 107: 30-1 Ap '57.
—— furniture. *See* furniture, Portuguese.
—— glass cameos. Con. 137: 32-4 Mar '56.
—— man & woman. Holiday 20: 37 Nov '56.
—— sailor. Natl. geog. 103: 686 (col.) May '53.
—— sculpture. Con. 137: 41-3 Mar '56.
—— women. Holiday 6: 109 Sept '49.
Poseidon. Lehner: Pict. bk. of sym., p. 31.
Poseidon & Demeter (sculpture). Osward: Asia Minor, pl. 103.
Poseidon of Smyrna (sculpture). Osward: Asia Minor, pl. 103, 105.
Poseidon's seahorse (sym.). Lehner: Pict. bk. of sym., p. 64.
Poseidon's temple. Natl. geog. 114: 761 (col.) Dec '58.
posing-stools. *See* photographer's posing-stools.
Positano (Italy). Holiday 10: 89 Sept '51; 25: 78-83 (col.) May '59; 28: inside back cover (col.) Aug '60.
  Labande: Naples, p. 200.
  Natl. geog. 116: p. 481, 492-3, 496-7, 509 (part col.) Oct '59.
posset-pot, delftware. Con. ency. of ant., vol. 1, pl. 50.
——, Ravenscroft. Con. 145: 215 Je '60.
——, Ravenscroft (17th cent.). Con. 145: 53 Mar '60.
Post, Emily. Cur. biog. p. 681 (1941).
  Holiday 19: 87 Mar '56.
Post, Frans (Hals). Con. 144: 41 Sept '59.

—— (work of). Con. 144: cover (col.) Nov '59.
post, lamp. *See* lamp post.
post box. Holiday 21: 133 Feb '57.
post office (boxes outside). Natl. geog. 112: 693 (col.) Nov '57.
—— (int.). Natl. geog. 98: 816 Dec '50; 106: 122, 127-51 (part col.) Jl '54.
—— (Dublin). Holiday 19: 41 Jan '56.
—— (Ft. Yukon, Alaska). Natl. geog. 109: 778 (col.) Je '56.
—— (Pitcairn is.). Natl. geog. 112: 771 (col.) Dec '57.
——, barrel (camp). Natl. geog. 115: 698 (col.) May '59.
——, village. Natl. geog. 98: 391 Sept '50.
post office boat, floating. Natl. geog. 114: 611 Nov '58.
postage stamp (early Amer.). Travel 109: 4 Feb '58.
—— "Cape of Good Hope". Con. 140: 58 Sept '57.
postage stamps. Con. 126: 194-5 Dec '50; 133: 45 Mar '54.
——. *See* also stamps.
poster (adv.). Travel 111: 49 Jan '59.
—— (adv. card). Amer. heri., vol. 6 no. 1 p. 27 (col.) (fall '54).
—— (bicycle riders). Amer. heri., vol. 8 no. 1 p. 71 (col.) (Dec '56).
—— (Blondin, hero of Niagara). Amer. heri., vol. 9 no. 5 p. 34 (col.) (Aug '58).
—— (boy leaving old home). Holiday 21: 6 Feb '57.
—— (cavalry, Civil war). Amer. heri., vol. 7 no. 5 p. 23 (col.) (Aug '56).
—— (early motion picture). Amer. heri., vol. 11 no. 3 p. 101 (Ap '60).
—— (1880 land offer). Brooks: Growth of a nation, p. 190-1.
—— (1834 exhibition). Amer. heri., vol. 11 no. 2 p. 83 (Feb '60).
—— (foreign travel, 1873). Amer. heri., vol. 11 no. 3 p. 112 (Ap '60).
—— (free land). Amer. heri., vol. 7 no. 3 p. 51 (Ap '56).
—— (Grangers, 1871). Amer. heri., vol. 7 no. 3 p. 42 (col.) (Ap '56).
—— ("Hands-up" poster). Horan: Pict. hist. of wild west, p. 190.
—— (Merry Christmas, 1876). Amer. heri., vol. 6 no. 1 back cover (col.) (fall '54).
—— (patent medicine). Amer. heri., vol. 7 no. 5 p. 58, 61-3, 95 (part col.) (Aug '56).
—— (sale of Clemen's home). Amer. heri., vol. 11 no. 1 p. 80 (Dec '59).
—— (smallpox). Amer. heri., vol. 8 no. 5 p. 40 (Aug '57).
—— (Temperance convention). Amer. heri., vol. 6 no. 1 p. 12 (fall '54).
—— (theater, 1815). Amer. heri., vol. 11 no. 4 p. 112 (Je '60).
—— (tourist). Amer. heri., vol. 11 no. 3 p. 18, 28 (Ap '60).
——, almanac adv. Holiday 23: 46 Ap '58.
——, antique (Christmas). Amer. heri., vol. 11 no. 2 p. 96 (Ap '60).
——, Cal. gold rush. Holiday 24: 65 Aug '58.
——, campaign. *See* campaign poster.

poster, Chinese Communist. Natl. geog. 118: 196 (col.) Aug '60.

——, Colonial festival. Natl. geog. 106: 444 Oct '54.

——, excursion (1880). Amer. heri., vol. 6 no. 4 p. 28 (Je '55).

——, Great Northern railway land settlement. Amer. heri., vol. 9 no. 4 p. 12 (Je '58).

——, inn (adv.). Amer. heri., vol. 11 no. 4 p. 60 (col.) (Je '60).

——, Mark Twain (1869). Amer. heri., vol. 11 no. 1 p. 79 (Dec '59).

——, navy recruiting. Amer. heri., vol. 10 no. 6 back cover (col.) (Oct '59).

——, peddler's patent medicine. Amer. heri., vol. 6 no. 4 p. 35 (col.) (Je '55).

——, political campaign. See campaign poster, political.

——, Red Cross. See Red Cross poster.

——, sales (antique). Rawson: Ant. pict. bk., frontis.

——, war. See war poster.

——, world travel. Holiday 23: 22-3 (col.) Ap '58.

poster requests (canal). Natl. geog. 117: 426 Mar '60.

posters (adv.). Amer. heri., vol. 4 no. 2 p. 43 (col.) (winter '53).

—— (early Amer.). Amer. heri., vol. 7 no. 1 p. 32-41 (col.) (Dec '55).

—— (merchants, salesman). Amer. heri., vol. 6 no. 1 p. 26 (fall '54).

—— (on wall). Holiday 25: 98 (col.) Mar '59.

—— (presidential campaign). See presidential campaign posters.

——, book. Amer. heri., vol. 9 no. 5 p. 38 (Aug '58).

——, British. Holiday 26 106 (col.) Oct '59.

——, cartoon. See cartoon posters.

——, circus (antique). Amer. heri., vol. 5 no. 1 p. 48 (fall '53).
Durant: Pict hist. of Amer. circus, (all thru book).

——, Civil war. See U.S. Civil war posters.

——, election campaign. See presidential campaign posters.

——, Russia (propaganda). Natl. geog. 116: 737 (col.) Dec '59.

——, state travel. Holiday 23: 114 (col.) Mar '58.

——, travel. Holiday 20: 164 (col.) Nov '56; 21: 109 (col.) Ap '57; 23: 15 (col.) May '58.

——, war. Amer. heri., vol. 10 no. 6 p. 7-17 (col.) (Oct '59).

——, war (Union dissolved). Amer. heri., vol. 9 no. 2 p. 92 (Feb '58).

——, wild west. Durant: Pict. hist. of Amer. circus, p. 136.

——, woman's rights (cartoon). Amer. heri., vol. 10 no. 6 p. 20-1 (col.), 107 (Oct '59).

——, world travel. Holiday 21: 21 (col.) Jan '57.

——. See also "Reward"! poster.

postilion's horn (sym.). Lehner: Pict. bk. of sym., p. 63.

posting inn, old Normandy. Holiday 19: 53 Jan '56.

postman. Holiday 27: 174 (col.) May '60.

Natl. geog. 106: 147 Jl '54.

—— (comic). Holiday 14: 160 Dec '53.

—— (1890). Holiday 12: 68 Sept '52.

—— (flying, comic). Holiday 21: 81 Jan '57.

—— (head). Holiday 27: 199 (col.) Ap '60.

—— (on horse). Natl. geog. 106: 132-3 (col.) Jl '54.

Poston, Tom. Cur. biog. p. 371 (1961).

posts, barnway. Rawson: Ant. pict. bk., p. 37.

pot, wooden (men carving). Natl. geog. 117: 375 (col.) Mar '60.

Potala (Tibet). Natl. geog. 108: 2, 16, 18, 22-3, 37 (part col.) Jl '55.

potash (sym.). Lehner: Pict. bk. of sym., p. 73.

potato (on plate). Natl. geog. 114: 311 (col.) Sept '58.

potato race (girls). Natl. geog. 109: 400 (col.) Mar '56.

pot-hook. Con. ency. of ant., vol. 3, p. 245.

Potofsky, Jacob S. Cur. biog. p. 489 (1946).

Potoroz (Yugoslavia). Travel 109: 32 Ap '58.

Potosi peak (Colo.). Natl. geog. 106: 210-11 (col.) Aug '54.

pot-pourri (antique porcelain, 18th cent.). Con. 133: 5 Mar '54.

—— jar, Norwegian. Con. 145: 8 Mar '60.

—— vase, Louis XV. Con. 142: 38 Sept '58.

pots, clay. See clay pots.

Potsdam (Sanssouci palace). Praeg.: Pict. ency., p. 369.

Potter, Beatrix. Jun. bk. of auth., p. 248.

Potter, Charles E. Cur. biog. p. 513 (1954).

Potter, William E. Cur. biog. p. 435 (1957).

potter (at work). Con. 136: LII Sept '55.

—— (sym.). Lehner: Pict. bk. of sym., p. 91.

Potter home, Beatrice (int.). Natl. geog. 109: 526-7 Ap '56.

potter's house (Judean, 700 B.C.). Natl. geog. 118: 832 (col.) Dec '60.

pottery (antique). Con. ency. of ant., vol. 1, pl. 49-52.
Rawson: Ant. pict. bk., p. 87-90.

—— (man decorating). Natl. geog. 97: 191 (col.) Feb '50.

——, Bedouin. Natl. geog. 108: 857 (col.) Dec '55.

——, Chinese. See Chinese pottery.

——, Danish. Travel 102: 5 Oct '54.

——, Danish & Rumania (antique). Praeg.: Pict. ency., p. 103.

——, English stoneware (antique). Con. 126: 183-5 Dec '50.

——, Etruscan (tomb). Natl. geog. 116: 341, 350 (part col.) Sept '59.

——, Hispano lustre (early). Con. 126: 108-13 Oct '50.

——, Indian (Amer.). Travel 113: 10 Jan '60.

——, Iranian. Natl. geog. 100: 455 (col.) Oct '51.

——, Liverpool (18th cent.). Amer. heri., vol. 6 no. 5 p. 52 (col.) (Aug '55).

——, Mayan. See Mayan pottery.

——, Mexican. Holiday 14: 64 (col.) Nov '53.

——, Mexican (antique). Con. 140: LI Dec '57.

——, Mexican Indian. Travel 114: 52 Nov '60.

pottery, orvieto (11th cent.). Con. 133: LXIII Je '54.

——, Peruvian. Praeg.: Pict. ency., p. 553 (col.).

——, Rouen. Con. 141: 74 Ap '58.

——, Sardinia. Disney: People & places, p. 72 (col.).

——, Sgraffito. See sgraffito pottery.

——, Staffordshire. Con. 136: XXVIII Nov '55; 140: XVI Nov '57.

——, Swedish. Con. 143: 239-40 Je '59.

——, Talaverade puebla. Con. 136: 287 Jan '56.

——, Wai Wai Indian. Natl. geog. 107: 346 Mar '55.

——, Wei dynasty (horse & rider). Con. 143: XXI Mar '59.

pottery designs, Bennington. Rawson: Ant. pict. bk., p. 90.

—— making. Natl. geog. 100: 562 Oct '51.

—— making (Austria). Natl. geog. 115: 204 (col.) Feb '59.

—— making (Chinese). Natl. geog. 110: 211 (col.) Aug '56.

—— making (girl). Natl. geog. 107: 465 (col.) Ap '55.

—— making (Indian). Disney: People & places, p. 121 (col.).

—— making (man). Natl. geog. 118: 833 Dec '60.

pottery market (Mexico). Travel 101: 19 Mar '54.

pottery marks. Con. ency. of ant., vol. 1, p. 94-6.

pottery shop, "Safi" (Morocco). Natl. geog. 107: 175 (col.) Feb '55.

pouch, tobacco. See tobacco pouch.

poudreuse, Louis XV. Con. 143: 267 Je '59.

——, (parquetry). Con. 143: 189 May '59.

Poujade, Pierre. Cur. biog. p. 501 (1956).

Pound, Sir Dudley. Cur. biog. p. 683 (1941).

Pound, Ezra. Cur. biog. p. 672 (1942); p. 341 (1963).

Pound, Roscoe. Cur. biog. p. 524 (1947).

"pounding sticks", clothes. Rawson: Ant. pict. bk., p. 13.

"Pourtales family" (Naigeon). Con. 137: XLIX Mar '56; 140: 70 Sept '57.

Poussin, Nicolas. Int. gr. soc.: Arts . . . p. 91 (col.).

—— (work of). Con. ency., of ant., vol. 1, pl. 158.

Con. 126: 179-81 Dec '50; 132: 39 Sept '53; 133: 12 Mar '54; 143: VIII Ap '59.

Praeg.: Pict. ency., p. 329 (col.).

Powahata, Indian chief. Natl. geog. 111: 596 May '57.

powder box (antique). Con. 132: 188 Jan '54.

——, Tripoli. Int. gr. soc.: Arts . . . p. 177 (col).

Powder flask. Rawson: Ant. pict. bk., p. 35.

powderhorn. Con. 144: 209 Dec '59.

Rawson: Ant. pict. bk., p. 35, 81.

—— (Daniel Boone's). Amer. heri., vol. 6 no. 6 p. 13 (Oct '55).

—— (17th cent.). Con. 135: 176 May '55.

powder machine, face. Holiday 20: 17 (col.) Sept '56.

Powdermaker, Hortense. Cur. biog. p. 372 (1961).

Powell, Adam Clayton, jr. Cur. biog. p. 675 (1942).

—— (Negro). Holiday 27: 79 (col.) Je '60.

Powell, Benjamin E. Cur. biog. p. 367 (1959).

Powell, Dick. Cur. biog. p. 503 (1948).

Powell, Lawrence Clark. Cur. biog. p. 319 (1960).

Powell, Lewis. Amer. heri., vol. 10 no. 6 p. 64-5, 98 (Oct '59).

Powell, William. Cur. biog. p. 527 (1947).

Powell, William H. (work of). Natl. geog. 102: 158 (col.) Aug '52.

Power, Donald C. Cur. biog. p. 321 (1960).

Power, Gen. Thomas S. Cur. biog. p. 340 (1958).

Power, Tyrone. Cur. biog. p. 463 (1950).

—— (as Jesse James). Amer. heri., vol. 11 no. 5 p. 40 (Aug '60).

power (sym.). Lehner: Pict. bk. of sym., p. 66, 78.

——, creative (sym.). Lehner: Pict. bk. of sym., p. 29.

——, divine (sym.). Lehner: Pict. bk. of sym., p. 28, 42.

"The power of music" (Mount). Amer. heri., vol. 11 no. 5 p. 18 (col.) (Aug '60).

power of the firmament (sym.). Lehner: Pict. bk. of sym., p. 22.

power plant. Natl. geog. 103: 175 (col.) Feb '53.

power shovel. See shovel, power.

power station (Tasmania). Natl. geog. 110: 818 (col.) Dec '56.

powerboat. Holiday 10: 34 (col.) Jl '51.

powerdam, Moses-Saunders. See Moses-Saunders powerdam.

powerhouse, Kemano. See Kemano powerhouse.

Powers, Bill. Horan: Pict. hist. of wild west, p. 163.

Powers, James E. Cur. biog. p. 343 (1963).

Powers, John. Amer. heri., vol. 12 no. 1 p. 12, 17 (Dec '60).

Powers, John Robert. Cur. biog. p. 479 (1945).

Powers, Marie. Cur. biog. p. 494 (1951).

Pozner, Vladimir. Cur. biog. p. 605 (1943).

Pozzuoli. Labande: Naples, p. 139-40.

Praeger, Frederick A. Cur. biog. p. 367 (1959).

Prague (Czechoslovakia). Holiday 21: 56-9 (col.) Jan '57; 27: 159 Ap '60.

"Prairie fire" (Bosin). Natl. geog. 107: 354-5 (col.) Mar '55.

prairie schooner (Wagon). Holiday 18: 106 (col.) Oct '55.

"Prairiesta" festival (Kansas, old costumes). Natl. geog. 101: 471-3 (col.) Ap '52.

Prambanan temple (Java). Natl. geog. 99: 27 (col.) Jan '51.

Prasad, Rajendra. Cur. biog. p. 466 (1950).

Prassinos, Mario (work of). Con. 143: 154-8 May '59.

Pratt, Edwin J. Cur. biog. p. 491 (1946).

Pratt, Fletcher. Cur. biog. p. 679 (1942).

Pratt, John Jeffreys (Lawrence). Con. 143: 90 Ap '59.

Pratt, Matthew (work of). Amer. heri., vol. 2 no. 2 p. 28 (winter '51).

Pratt, Adm. William V. Cur. biog. p. 607 (1943).

Praxiteles (Greek sculpture). Praeg.: Pict. ency., p. 133.

prayer (decade ring). Lehner: Pict. bk. of sym., p. 37.

—— **(folded hands).** Lehner: Pict. bk. of sym., p. 37.

—— **(Hawaiian).** Amer. heri., vol. 11 no. 2 p. 87 (Feb '60).

—— **(men & women).** *See* men & women (praying).

—— **(rosary).** Lehner: Pict. bk. of sym., p. 37.

prayer beads, Arab. Natl. geog. 114: 713 Nov '58; 115: 495, 510 (col.) Ap '59.

——, **Moslem.** Natl. geog. 100: 164 (col.) Aug '51.

prayer book casket. *See* casket, prayer book.

prayer boxes. Lehner: Pict. bk. of sym., p. 37.

prayer flag (Tibet). Natl. geog. 108: 22 (col.) Jl '55.

prayer lamps (India). Natl. geog. 118: 498 (col.) Oct '60.

prayer rug. Con. ency. of ant., vol. 1, pl. 126. Con. 133: 143 Ap '54; 141: XX Ap '58, XVIII Je '58.

—— **(18th cent.).** Con. 133: 143 Ap '54; 144: LXXII Jan '60.

——, **Ghiordiz (Asia Minor, 17th cent.).** Con. 145: VIII Mar '60.

——, **Ispahan.** Con. 142: X Jan '59.

——, **Kirman (Persia).** Con. 145: XXXVI May '60.

——, **Konieh.** Con. 145: XLIV May '60.

——, **Shirvan (Caucasus).** Con. 144: XVII (col.) Jan '60.

——, **Transylvanian.** Con. 143: XVI May '59.

prayer wheel (Buddhist). Natl. geog. 117: 391 (col.) Mar '60.

Pre Columbian sculpture. Con. 135: XLIV Mar '55.

preacher, "hill". Brooks: Growth of a nation, p. 312.

preachers. *See* ministers; evangelists.

precision (sym.). Lehner: Pict. bk. of sym., p. 59.

Preda, Giovanni Ambrogio (work of). Con. 133: 126 Ap '54.

predella, altar. *See* altar predella.

Preminger, Otto. Cur. biog. p. 370 (1959).

premium trade cards. *See* trade cards.

Prendergast, John (work of). Amer. heri., vol. 1 no. 3 p. 45 (col.) (spring '50).

Prescott, Jeremiah. Amer. heri., vol. 8 no. 3 p. 28 (Ap '57).

Prescott, Orville. Cur. biog. p. 437 (1957).

Prescott, William H. Amer. heri., vol. 8 no. 5 p. 27 (Aug '57); vol. 8 no. 6 p. 4 (Oct '57).

prescription, medical (sym.). Lehner: Pict. bk. of sym., p. 16.

"Presentation in the temple" (Guercino). Con. 132: 110 Nov '53.

"Presentation in the temple" (Memling). Natl. geog. 110: 623 (col.) Nov '56.

"Presentation in the temple" (Rembrandt). Con. 138: 33 Sept '56.

"Presentation of Christ child at temple" (Lochner). Praeg.: Pict. ency., p. 229 (col.).

"Presentation of the Virgin in the temple" (Burgkmair). Con. 133: 51 Mar '54.

Presepio figures (Naples, Italy). Con. 129: 28-31 Ap '52.

preserve pot, silver gilt (antique). Con. 142: 85 Nov '58.

The Preserver (sym.). Lehner: Pict. bk. of sym., p. 43.

president, U.S. *See* U.S. presidents; name of president.

presidential campaign card (1880). Amer. heri., vol. 11 no. 6, back cover (col.) (Oct '60).

presidential campaign poster. Amer. heri., vol. 7 no. 4 p. 25-33 (part col.) (Je '56); vol. 10 no. 2 p. 107 (Feb '59).

presidential campaign posters. Amer. heri., vol. 7 no. 5 p. 102-4 (Aug '56).

—— **(1840).** Amer. heri., vol. 4 no. 1 p. 2, 52 (fall '52).

—— **(Pompeian).** Ceram: March of arch., p. 23.

presidential campaign ribbon (1876). Amer. heri., vol. 11 no. 6 p. 4 (col.) (Oct '60).

presidential candidates, U.S. Amer. heri., vol. 7 no. 4 p. 25 (col.) (Je '56).

—— **(log cabin homes).** Amer. heri., vol. 7 no. 5 p. 32-3 (Aug '56).

presidential election ticket to H. of R. (vote counting 1877). Amer. heri., vol. 11 no. 6 p. 6 (Oct '60).

Presidents, U.S. *See* U.S. Presidents.

President's chair, Univ. (Princeton Univ.). Amer. heri., vol. 7 no. 5 p. 27 (Aug '56).

Presidents' wives, U.S. *See* U.S. Presidents' wives.

Presley, Elvis A. Cur. biog. p. 371 (1959).

The Press (reporters). Holiday 7: 98-101 (col.) Feb '50.

press, automobile top. Natl. geog. 102: 29 (col.) Jl '52.

press, car body stamping. Int. gr. soc.: Arts . . . p. 173 (col.).

press, clothes. *See* clothes press.

press, cupboard (antique). Con. 139: 228 Je '57.

—— **(17th cent.).** Con. ency. of ant., vol. 1, pl. 7.

——, **Jacobean.** Con. ency. of ant., vol. 1, pl. 37.

pressing board. Rawson: Ant. pict. bk., p. 12.

Pressman, Lee. Cur. biog., p. 529 (1947).

pressure suit. Natl. geog. 108: 240, 246, 248, 262 (col.) Aug '55.

Preston, Robert. Cur. biog. p. 342 (1958).

Preti, Mattia (work of). Con. 136: 282 Jan '56.

pretzel crest. Amer. heri., vol. 3 no. 4 p. 39 (summer '52).

pretzel seller. Amer. heri., vol. 3 no. 4 p. 38 (summer '52).

Previtali, Andrea (work of). Con. 138: 196 Dec '56.

"Priam's treasure". Ceram: March of arch., p. 41.

Pribichevich, Stoyan. Cur. biog. p. 549 (1944).

Pribilof islands. Natl. geog. 101: 492-512 (part col.) Ap '52.

—— **(map).** Natl. geog. 101: 496 Ap '52.

Price, Byron. Cur. biog. p. 681 (1942).

Price, Charles C. Cur. biog. p. 439 (1957).

Price, Dr. Derek J. Natl geog. 117: 31 (col.) Jan '60.
Price, Edith Ballinger. Jun. bk. of auth., p. 251.
Price, Flora Ellen. Amer. heri., vol. 8 no. 6 p. 39 (Oct '57).
Price, Gwilym A. Cur. biog. p. 489 (1949).
Price, Leontyne. Cur. biog. p. 374 (1961).
Price, Sterling. Pakula: Cent. album, p. 237.
Price, Vincent. Cur. biog. p. 503 (1956).
Pride, Vice-Adm. Alfred M. Cur. biog. p. 515 (1954).
Priest, Ivy Baker. Cur. biog. p. 477 (1952).
Priest, J. Percy. Cur. biog. p. 468 (1950).
priest. Amer. heri., vol. 8 no. 2 p. 110 (Feb '57); vol. 8 no. 3 p. 17 (col.) (Ap '57). Labande: Naples, p. 67.
Natl. geog. 106: 846-8 (part col.) Dec '54.
—— (ancient times). Int. gr. soc.: Arts . . . p. 31 (col.).
—— (St. Bernard dog). Holiday 22: 30 Dec '57.
——, Brahman. Natl. geog. 117: 535 (col.) Ap '60.
——, Catholic. See Catholic priest.
——, costumed (dancing). Natl. geog. 104: 632 (col.) Nov '53.
——, Cyprus (paints icons). Natl. geog. 110: 733 (col.) Dec '56.
——, Druid. See Druid priest.
——, Essenes (ritual baptism). Natl. geog. 114: 789 (col.) Dec '58.
——, Greek. Natl. geog. 102: 855 Dec '52; 114: 749 (col.) Dec '58.
——, Greek (altar). Natl. geog. 115: 505 (col.) Ap '59.
——, Greek orthodox. Natl. geog. 109: 879 Je '56.
——, high (Solomon's palace). Natl. geog. 112: 863 (col.) Dec '57.
——, Italian. Holiday 15: 109 Jan '54; 25: 34 (col.) Jan '59.
——, Kathin (Siam). Disney: People & places, 171 (col.).
——, Nepal. Natl. geog. 117: 369 (col.) Mar '60.
——, orthodox. Natl. geog. 116: 728 Dec '59.
——, Pueblo Indian high. Natl. geog. 112: 226 (col.) Aug '57.
——, Trinidad Hindu. Natl. geog. 103: 67 (col.) Jan '53.
priest & children (blessing bell). Natl. geog. 115: 699 (col.) May '59.
priest & followers (Madeira is.). Natl. geog. 115: 380-1 (col.) Mar '59.
priest & woman (Korean at shrine). Natl. geog. 97: 785 (col.) Je '50.
priest praying, Cambodian. Natl. geog. 102: 303 (col.) Sept '52.
priestess, Cretan (ancient). Int. gr. soc.: Arts . . . p. 29 (col.).
Priestesses of the God-King (Hitites, rock carving). Osward: Asia Minor, pl. 11.
Priestley, Joseph. Amer. heri., vol. 5 no. 3 p. 12 (spring '54).
Priestley, Sir Raymond. Natl. geog. 112: 598 (col.) Nov '57.
Priestley home, Joseph. Amer. heri., vol. 5 no. 3 p. 13-4 (spring '54).

priests ("Feast of the Dead"). Natl. geog. 99: 484 (col.) Ap '51.
priests, Angkor Wat. Natl. geog. 116: 792-3 (col.) Dec '59.
——, Greek. Natl. geog. 98: 721, 725 (col.) Dec '50.
——, Hindu (procession). Natl. geog. 112: 140 (col.) Jl '57.
——, Mayan temple. Natl. geog. 115: 102-3 (col.) Jan '59.
——, Nigeria (pagan). Natl. geog. 116: 250 (col.) Aug '59.
——, Shinto. See Shinto priests.
——, Spanish. Holiday 15: 45 May '54.
"Primavera" (Botticello). Praeg.: Pict. ency., p. 256 (col.).
primitive men. See men, primitive.
primitive village (Magdalena river, S. Amer.). Travel 106: 46 Nov '56.
Primrose, William. Cur. biog. p. 494 (1946).
Primus, Pearl. Cur. biog. p. 551 (1944).
prince, Afghanistan. Natl. geog. 98: 682 (col.) Nov '50.
——, Thailand (flying kite). Natl. geog. 116: 849 (col.) Dec '59.
"Prince Charles Edward" (Van Dyck). Con. 133: XVII (col.) Ap '54.
Prince Enrico D'Assia. See D'Assia, Prince Enrico.
Prince in the field of lilies. See "Lily prince".
Prince of Wales island. See Penang.
"Prince Rupert of the Palatinate" (Van Dyck). Natl. geog. 97: 762 (col.) Je '50.
princes (Angami warriors, India). Natl. geog. 107: 261 (col.) Feb '55.
—— (boys at school). Holiday 28: 52 Sept '60.
princes of the fermament, seals of 7 ruling. Lehner: Pict. bk. of sym., p. 24.
princess (comic on horse). Holiday 5: 28 Jan '49.
Princess Anne (engraving). Con. 145: XLIV Je '60.
"Princess Catherine Fedorovna Dolgorouka (Lebrun). Con. 142: 112 Nov '58.
"Princess de Lamballe" (Duplessis). Con. 136: 33 Sept '55.
"Princess Elizabeth of Saxony" (Cranach). Con. 138: 137 Nov '56.
Princess Kaiulani hotel (Hawaii). Travel 104: 38 Aug '55.
—— (model). Travel 102: 46 Nov '54.
Princess Marijke (Holland). Holiday 10: 55 Nov '51.
princesses, Japanese. Natl. geog. 97: 606 (col.) May '50.
Princeton Univ. Holiday 8: 98-105 (part col.) Oct '50.
—— (graduates). Holiday 18: 39 (col.) Nov '55.
—— (reunion class, 1933). Natl. geog. 117: 28 (col.) Jan '60.
—— (dormitory). Natl. geog. 117: 29 (col.) Jan '60.
"Principal navigations." Hakluvt's. See Hakluyt's "Principal navigations" (title page).
Pringle. Charles MacKenzie. Holiday 23: 43 (col.) Feb '58.
Pringle, Mrs. Julius. Amer. heri., vol. 9 no. 2 p. 57 (col.) (Feb '58).

printer (sym.). Lehner: Pict. bk. of sym., p. 91.
printer, mt. Natl. geog. 113: 869 Je '58.
printing press (1775). Natl. geog. 107: 203 (col.) Feb '55.
——, 1st Amer. Amer. heri., vol. 5 no. 3 p. 6 (spring '54).
Brooks: Growth of a nation, p. 54.
——, modern. Natl. geog. 118: 874-85 (col.) Dec '60.
printing shop (1734). Amer. heri., vol. 5 no. 1 p. 25 (col.) (fall '53).
——, colonial. Natl. geog. 106: 469 Oct '54.
——, Isaiah Thomas. Amer. heri., vol. 3 no. 4 p. 48-9 (summer '52).
Prinz, Joachim. Cur. biog. p. 345 (1963).
Prio Socarras, Carlos. Cur. biog. p. 490 (1949).
Prior, Matthew (Kneller). Con. 140: 233 Jan '58.
Prior, William Matthew (work of). Amer. heri., vol. 11 no. 3 p. 53 (col.) (Ap '60).
priory, Benedictine (Holy island). Natl. geog. 102: 553 Oct '52.
prism (sym.). Lehner: Pict. bk. of sym., p. 16.
prison, African (Fort Jesus). Natl. geog. 97: 337 (col.) Mar '50.
prison camp, Civil war. Amer. heri., vol. 10 no. 5 p. 4-13 (part col.) (Aug '59).
prison tower (San Marino, Italy). Holiday 6: 72 Oct '49.
prisoner. Holiday 21: 174 May '57.
—— (at penitentiary). Amer. heri., vol. 8 no. 2 p. 55 (Feb '57).
—— (in jail). Amer. heri., vol. 10 no. 4 p. 88 (Je '59).
——, repatriated. Natl. geog. 104: 572 (col.) Oct '53.
——, Tibet. Holiday 12: 57 (col.) Dec '52.
prisoners, Egyptian (ancient). Natl. geog. 112: 843 Dec '57.
——, German. Amer. heri., vol. 10 no. 6 p. 12-3 (col.) (Oct '59).
privateer "Grand Turk". See Salem privateer "Grand Turk".
procession (nobility, medieval). Int. gr. soc.: Arts . . . p. 79 (col.).
——, funeral. See funeral procession.
——, Nepal coronation. Natl. geog. 112: 140-52 (part col.) Jl '57.
——, Palm Sunday (Jerusalem). Natl. geog. 110: 711 (col.) Dec '56.
——, Roman triumphal (ancient). Int. gr. soc.: Arts . . . p. 41 (col.).
"Procession of the blessed sacrament" detail (Roselli). Con. 139: 100 Ap '57.
"Procession of the kings" (da Fabriano). Praeg.: Pict. ency., p. 277 (col.).
"Procession of the knights" (Canaletto). Con. 132: 195 (col.) Jan '54.
"Procession to Calvary" (Flemish tapestry). Con. 138: 59 Sept '56.
Processional way (Babylon, 580 B.C.). Praeg.: Pict. ency., p. 113.
Procida (Italy) Labande: Naples, p. 202.
—— (harbor). Labande: Naples, p. 192. Natl. geog. 105: 544-5 (col.) Ap '54.
Proctor, A. Phimister (sculpture by). Natl. geog. 106: 237 (col.) Aug '54.
Proctor, Redfield. Amer. heri., vol. 2 no. 3 p.

36 (spring '51).
Proctor, Richard. Horan: Pict. hist. of wild west, p. 242.
"Prodigal Son" (Willson). Amer. heri., vol. 7 no. 1 p. 58-9 (col.) (Decc '55).
producers, movie. See movie producers & actors.
productivity (sym.). Lehner: Pict. bk. of sym., p. 78.
professor, university. See college professor; university professor.
Profumo, John D. Cur. biog. p. 373 (1959).
progress (sym.). Lehner: Pict. bk. of sym., p. 83.
prohibition See Spirit of prohibition (sym.).
"Projectile train" (Jules Verne). Natl. geog. 113: 288 Feb '58.
projector, picture. See motion picture projector.
——, slide. Holiday 24: 156, 193 (col.) Dec '58; 28: 128 Nov '60, 148, 183 Dec '60.
Prokofiev, Sergei. Cooper: Con. ency. of music, p. 204.
Cur. biog. p. 685 (1941).
Promethean pyramid of the sun (Mexico). Holiday 13: 37 Mar '53.
"Prometheus" (Rubens). Con. 140: 238 Jan '58.
"Prometheus bound" (Rubens). Con. 127: 117 May '51.
propeller, winged (sym.). Lehner: Pict. bk. of sym., p. 10.
propellers, airplane (man & woman testing). Natl. geog. 99: 306 (col.) Mar '51.
"The Prophetess" (Boucher). Praeg.: Pict. ency., p. 361 (col.).
prospector, gold. See gold prospector.
——, mineral. See mineral prospector.
——, uranium. See uranium prospectors.
——, western. See western prospector.
prosperity (sym.). Lehner: Pict. bk. of sym., p. 44.
"Prospero" (Merlin) Con. 145: 68 Mar '60.
prostate, human. Gray's anatomy, p. 1304.
prostrator, pilgrim. See pilgrim prostrator.
protection (sym.). Lehner: Pict. bk. of sym., p. 27, 78, 88.
protection against evil. See evil, protection against.
protractor. Natl. geog. 113: 751 Je '58.
Prout, Samuel (work of). Con. ency. of ant., vol. 1, pl. 146.
Con. 144: 95 Nov '59.
Prouty, Winston L. Cur. biog. p. 323 (1960).
Provence. Holiday 26: 70-5 (col.) Nov '59.
Providence (R. I.). Holiday 11: 111-17 (part col.) May '52.
—— (state house, capitol). Travel 108: 17 Nov '57.
"The Providence" (river boat). Amer. heri., vol. 6 no. 1 p. 8 (col.) (fall '54).
Provost, Jan (work of). Con. 132: cover (col.) Jan '54; 133: LIX May '54; 134: XXXIX Sept '54.
Provost's house Dublin, Trinity College, (ext. & int.). Con. 145: 148-55 May '60.
Proxmire, William. Cur. biog. p. 344 (1958).
Prud' hon, Pierre Paul (work of). Con. 135: 44 Mar '55.

Pruden, Rev. Edward Hughes. Cur. biog. p. 469 (1950).
"Prudence" (Carpaccio). Con. 142: 206 Dec '58.
Prussian guard. Int. gr. soc.: Arts . . . p. 115 (col.).
psaltery (medieval). Int. gr. soc.: Arts . . . p. 61 (col.).
Psellino, Francesco (work of). Con. 136: 136 Nov '55.
The pseudo Seneca (sculpture). Labande: Naples, p. 101.
"Psyche carried to the ravine" (Peranda). Con. 144: 106 Nov '59.
Psyche of Capua (sculpture). Labande: Naples, p. 99.
"Psycho" (movie scene). Int. gr. soc.: Arts . . . p. 151 (col.).
Ptolemaic head of a god. Con. 144: 208 Dec '59.
"pub", English thatch roof. Holiday 26: 7 Nov '59.
——, **German (int.).** Holiday 22: 59 Sept '57.
——, **Irish.** Holiday 21: 73 Jan '57.
pub signs. See tavern sign.
"Public monument" (Ellis is.). Amer. heri., vol. 9 no. 5 frontis (Aug '58).
Pucci, Emilio. Cur. biog. p. 376 (1961).
Puccini, Giacomo. Amer. heri., vol. 10 no. 3 p. 52, 54 (Ap '59).
—— **(deathbed).** Cooper: Con. ency. of music, p. 241.
Puck cartoon. See cartoon, Puck peace.
Puckett, B. Earl. Cur. biog. p. 471 (1950).
pueblo, Indian. Amer. heri., vol. 7 no. 6 p. 103 (Oct '56).
Holiday 13: 22 (col.) Je '53; 16 Feb '58.
Travel 110: 19 Sept '58.
——, **pre-Columbian.** Natl. geog. 112: 243 (col.) Aug '57.
——, **Taos Indian.** See Taos pueblo.
Puerto de la Cruz. Travel 104: 48 Jl '55.
Puerto Nuevo (Puerto Rico). Natl. geog. 99: 438 Ap '51.
Puerto Rican (cutting sugar cane). Natl. geog. 99: 433 (col.) Ap '51.
—— **(fish on pole).** Natl. geog. 99: 432 (col.) Ap '51.
—— **(head, straw hat, pineapple).** Natl. geog. 99: 432 (col.) Ap '51.
—— **(man seated).** Holiday 23: 166 (col.) Je '58.
—— **(men & women).** Holiday 17: 56 (col.) Feb '55.
—— **(on burro).** Holiday 21: 155 Jan '57.
—— **(on donkey).** Holiday 20: 66 Aug '56.
Puerto Rican art. Holiday 20: 7 (col.) Oct '56.
Puerto Rican craftsmen. Travel 109: 30-1 May '58.
Puerto Rican dancer. Holiday 27: 110 Je '60; 28: 105 Jl '60, 134 Nov '60.
Puerto Rican dancers. Holiday 16: 128 (col.) Nov '54.
Puerto Rican folk dancers. Holiday 18: 64 (col.) Nov '55.
Puerto Rico. Holiday 5: 50-6 Feb '49; 17: 52-7 (part col.) Feb '55, 88 (col.) Mar '55; 21: 74-9 (part col.) Mar '57.

Natl. geog. 99: 420-60 Ap '51; 118: 120-8 (part col.) Jl '60.
Travel 109: 29-31 May '58; 111: 41-3 Feb '59; 114: 38-41 Oct '60.
—— **(beach).** Holiday 24: 55 (col.) Dec '58.
—— **(hotel).** Holiday 21: 74 (col.) Mar '57; 25: 122 (col.) May 59.
—— **(hotels).** Natl. geog. 99: 428, 449 (col.) Ap '51.
Travel 114: 44 Aug '60, 54 Sept '60, 18 Oct '60.
—— **(map).** Natl. geog. 118: 122 (col.) Jl '60.
Puerto Vallarts (Australia). Travel 106: 53 Oct '56.
Puerto Williams (Chile). Natl. geog. 117: 202-3 (col.) Feb '60.
puffer (Scotch boat). Disney: People & places, title page, p. 29 (col.).
Puga, Antonia (work of). Con. 139: LXVII May '57; 145: LXXVIII Je '60.
Puget, Pierre (bust by). Con. 134: 207 Dec '54.
Puget Sound (Wash.). Face of Amer., p. 154-5 (col.).
Holiday 15: 99, 101-4 (part col.) May '54.
Pugh, Rear Adm. Lamont. Cur. biog. p. 496 (1951).
pugil sticks (U.S. marines). Natl. geog. 113: 33 (col.) Jan '58.
Pugmire, Ernest I. Cur. biog. p. 481 (1945).
Pulitzer, Joseph. Holiday 7: 36 Mar '50; 8: 44 Oct '50.
Pulitzer, Joseph, 2d. Cur. biog. p. 517 (1954).
Pullman, George. Amer. heri., vol. 10 no. 5 p. 35 (Aug '59).
Pullman railroad cars, private. Amer. heri., vol. 10 no. 5 p. 34-41 (Aug '59).
pulp & paper machine (men). Natl. geog. 98: 339 (col.) Sept '50; 99: 133 (col.) Jan '51.
pulpit (Greek church). Natl. geog. 103: 376 (col.) Mar '53.
—— **(Pisa, 1260).** Praeg.: Pict. ency., p. 84.
——, **Calerno cathedral.** Labande: Naples, p. 189.
——, **Mohammedan (Minber).** Osward: Asia Minor, pl. 132.
——, **Ravello cathedral.** Labande: Naples, p. 197.
——, **Vicar & Moses (antique).** Con. 138: XXVI Sept '56.
pulpwood boat. Natl. geog. 115: 329 (col.) Mar '59.
pulpwood stack (on barge). Natl. geog. 115: 315 (col.) Mar '59.
Pulteney bridge. Holiday 26: 52 (col.) Aug '59.
pump, field foot water (Formosa). Natl. geog. 111: 331 (col.) Mar '57.
——, **fuel & vacuum engine.** Holiday 19: 69 Mar '56.
"Pump room" (Chicago, hotel). Holiday 7: 65-9 Ap '50; 10: 103 (col.) Oct '51; 22: 78 (col.) Jl '57.
pump, well. Natl. geog. 115: 205 (col.) Feb '59.
pumps, well. Rawson: Ant. pict. bk., p. 47.
punchbowl. Con. 137: 161 May '56.
Holiday 24: 210 (col.) Dec '58; 25: 15 (col.), 138 Jan '59; 26: 124 (col.) Dec '59; 28: 165 Dec '60.

punchbowl (1785, gift from Washington to Col. B. Eyre). Amer. heri., vol. 6 no. 5 p. 48-9 (col.) (Aug '55).

——, **bishop's mitre form (Norway).** Con. 145: 8 Mar '60.

——, **Chinese porcelain.** Con. 141: III Je '58.

——, **English (antique).** Con. 126: 48 Aug '50.

——, **George III (silver).** Con. 132: XXVIII Nov '53.

——, **glass.** Con. 136: XXXVIII Nov '55.

——, **James II (silver).** Con. 140: 183 Dec '57.

——, **Lambeth (18th cent.).** Con. ency. of ant., vol. 1, pl. 52.

——, **Paul Revere (silver).** Con. 135: 78 Mar '55.

——, **silver (Amer. 18th cent.).** Con. 135: 74 Mar '55.

——, **silver (18th cent.).** Con. 132: 23 Sept '53; 133: XXVII Mar '54; 141: 92 Ap '58; 144: III Nov '59; 145: XXVI Mar '60.

——, **silver (French, 18th cent.).** Con. 140: 39 Sept '57.

——, **silver (Monteith).** Con. 142: 228 Jan '59.

——, **silver (Pyne).** Con. 144: 68 Sept '59).

——, **Swedish (18th cent.).** Con. 143: 240 Je '59.

——, **William & Mary.** Con. 140: 181 Dec '57; 141: 42 Mar '58.

punchbowl & cover, Codrington (silver). Con. 145: 123 Ap '60.

punch-pot, Staffordshire. Con. ency. of ant., vol. 1, pl. 52.

"Punchinello taking leave of his companion" (Tiepolo). Con. 135: 122 Ap '55.

"Punchinello with dancing dogs" (Tiepolo). Con. 135: 276 Je '55.

Punta arenas (Chile). Travel 102: 35 Dec '54.

—— **(Jamaica).** Natl. geog. 117: 197 (col.) Feb '60.

punter (family outing). Natl. geog. 114: 62 (col.) Jl '58.

puppet. Holiday 20: 212 Dec '56.

puppet show. Holiday 13: 2 (col.) Ap '53; 14: inside cover (col.) Sept '53.

puppets. Natl. geog. 101: 779 (col.) Je '52.

—— **(masterpieces).** Con. ency. of ant., vol. 3, pl. 173-6.

—— **(Mozart play).** Natl. geog. 99: 761 (col.) Je '51.

——, **Japanese.** Natl. geog. 104: 640 (col.) Nov '53; 118: 770 (col.) Dec '60.

Purcell, Edward M. Cur. biog. p. 520 (1954).

Purcell, Henry. Amer. heri., vol. 9 no. 2 p. 59 (Feb '58).

—— **(by Clostermann).** Cooper: Con. ency. of music, p. 242.

Purcell mts. (climbers). Natl. geog. 114: 188-9 (col.) Aug '58.

purification (sym.). Lehner: Pict. bk. of sym., p. 37, 47.

purification rite (Laos). Natl. geog. 117: 65 (col.) Jan '60.

purifier, water. Natl. geog. 102: 282 Aug '52.

Puritans. Amer. heri., vol. 8 no. 1 p. 65 (Dec '56); vol. 9 no. 1 p. 109 (Dec '57); vol. 11 no. 1 p. 113 (Dec '59); vol. 11 no. 3 p. 108 (Ap '60); vol. 11 no. 5 p. 81 (Aug '60); vol. 11 no. 6 p. 88 (Oct '60); vol. 12

no. 1 p. 109 (Dec '60).
Holiday 26: 91 (col.) Jl '59.
Natl. geog. 107: 740-1 (col.) Je '55.

—— **(early drawing).** Amer. heri., vol. 6 no. 4 p. 59 (Je '55).

Puritans & Indians. Amer. heri., vol. 11 no. 2 p. 112 (Feb '60).

Purling, John (Gainsborough). Con. ency., of ant., vol. 1, pl. 166.

purse. Holiday 10: 7 (col.) Dec '51; 12: 83 Nov '52.

—— **(9th cent.).** Con. 138: 235 Jan '57.

—— **(sales counter & maker).** Natl. geog. 113: 308 (col.) Mar '58.

——, **woman's.** Holiday 21: 97 (col.) Je '57.

purses. *See* also pocketbook; wallet.

Purtell, William A. Cur. biog. p. 505 (1956).

"Purton" (colonial house, Va.). Natl. geog. 109: 452 (col.) Ap '56.

Pusey, Merlo J. Cur. biog. p. 480 (1952).

Pusey, Nathan M. Cur. biog. p. 501 (1953).

push car. *See* freight push car.

Pu-tai (Chinese god of happiness). Con. 142: XXXVIII Dec '58.

Put-in-Bay. Travel 109: 42 Je '58.

Putnam, Claude Adams. Cur. biog. p. 472 (1950).

Putnam, Roger L. Cur. biog. p. 481 (1952).

Putnam phalanx (Hartford, Conn.). Amer. heri., vol. 7 no. 5 p. 22 (Aug '56).

Putt, Donald L. Cur. biog. p. 324 (1960).

"Putti harvesting wine" (de Wit). Con. 136: XXXIX Jan '56.

"Putto drawn by dolphins" (Pompeii). Praeg.: Pict. ency., p. 162 (col.).

"Putto with a book" (carved wood). Con. ency. of ant., vol. 3, pl. 55.

"Pygmalion & Galatea" (wood relief). Con. 145: 135 Ap '60.

pygmies. Natl. geog. 101: 361 Mar '52; 106: 742-3 (col.) Dec '54; 117: 278-302 Feb '60.

——, **Africa.** Natl. geog. 112: 87, 89-92 (part col.) Jl '57.

——, **Africa (Ituri).** Travel 113: 26 Jan '60.

pygmy, Belgian Congo. Holiday 19: 14 May '56.

pygmy dance. Natl. geog. 117: 290-3 Feb '60.

Pygmyland (map). Natl. geog. 117: 284 Feb '60.

Pyle, Ernie. Cur. biog. p. 688 (1941).

Pyle, Howard. Cur. biog. p. 494 (1955).

—— **(book illus. by).** Amer. heri., vol. 8 no. 1 p. 34 (col.) (Dec '56).

pylon (Adm. Peary & North Pole). Natl. geog. 104: 470 Oct '53.

pylon commemorates the dead (Arctic). Natl. geog. 107: 567 (col.) Ap '55.

Pynchon memorial bldg. (Mass.). Amer. heri., vol. 2 no. 3 p. 54 (col.) (spring '51).

pyramid (sym.). Lehner: Pict. bk. of sym., p. 26.

—— **(Egypt).** Ceram: March of arch., p. 94-106.
Holiday 7: inside back cover (col.) Ap '50.
Int. gr. soc.: Arts . . . p. 11 (col.).
Natl. geog. 107: 728 May '55; 108: 620, 648 (col.) Nov '55.

—— **(Saqqara).** Natl. geog. 114: 236 Aug '58.

—— **(Saqqara, step).** Natl. geog. 108: 640

Nov '55.
—— (Toltec). Int. gr. soc.: Arts . . . p. 11 (col.).
pyramid of Cheops. Praeg.: Pict. ency., p. 118.
—— (cross section). Ceram: March or arch., p. 105.
—— (int.). Ceram: March of arch., p. 92-3.
pyramid of Chephren. Ceram: March of arch., p. 91.
pyramid of Cholula (Mexico). Ceram: March of arch., p. 270.
pyramid of Giza. Holiday 16: 110 (col.) Nov '54.
  Natl. geog. 112: 104 (col.) Jl '57; 118: 358-9 (col.) Sept '60.
pyramid of the sun. See Promethean pyramid of the sun (Mexico).
pyramids. Holiday 11: 25 May '52; 25: 54-5 (col.) Feb '59.
—— (Mexico). Amer. heri., vol. 10 no. 2 p. 51 (Feb '59).
pyramids at Abusir. Ceram: March of arch., p. 106-7.
"Pyramus & Thisbe" (Arnold). Con. 133: 294 Je '54.
pyre, cremation. See cremation pyre.
Pyrenees ice caves. See ice caves (Pyrenees).
Pyrenees mts. Natl. geog. 109: 300-34 (part col.) Mar '56.
—— (Basque land). Natl. geog. 105: 156-86 (part col.) Feb '54.
—— (map). Natl. geog. 109: 308-9 Mar '56.
Pyrenees route marker. Natl. geog. 109: 312 (col.) Mar '56.
pythagorean theorem. Lehner: Pict. bk. of sym., p. 13.
python rib cage (model). Natl. geog. 117: 814 Je '60.

Q

quadrant (John Paul Jones). Holiday 24: 56 Oct '58.
——, Hadley's. Amer. heri., vol. 11 no. 5 p. 85 (Aug '60).
quadrille (Spanish Embassy, New Year's Eve). Natl. geog. 111: 88-9 (col.) Jan '57.
quadross, Janio da Silva. Cur. biog. p. 378 (1961).
"Quais & institut, Paris" (Bonington). Con. ency. of ant., vol. 1, pl. 148.
Quaker. Holiday 21: 57 May '57.
Quaker meeting. Holiday 7: 56 (col.) Ap '50.
Quaker meeting house. Holiday 18: 98-9 (col.) Oct '55.
Quaker school seat. See school seat, Quaker.
qualities & virtues (sym.). Lehner: Pict. bk. of sym., p. 57-61.
quality (sym.). Lehner: Pict. bk. of sym., p. '59.
Quantrill, William Clarke. Amer. heri., vol. 11 no. 6 p. 24 (Oct '60).
quarantine (sym.). Lehner: Pict. bk. of sym., p. 88.
Quarles, Donald A. Cur. biog. p. 495 (1955).
quarry, marble. See marble quarry.
"The quarry of Optevoz" (Courbet). Praeg.: Pict. ency., p. 415 (col.).
"Quartet" (De Hooch). Con. 135: XII (col.) Ap '55.
quartet table. See table, quartet.

quartz sphere. Natl. geog. 117: 816 (col.) Je '60.
Quasimodo, Salvatore. Cur. biog. p. 326 (1960).
quatrefoil (sym.). Lehner: Pict. bk. of sym., p. 63.
  Praeg.: Pict. ency., p. 248.
Quay, Jan Eduard de. Cur. biog. p. 348 (1963).
Quebec (Canada). Holiday 11: 98-105 (part col.) Je '52; 23: 7 (col.) Mar '58; 27: 223 (col.) May '60, 58 (col.) Je '60.
  Natl. geog. 113: 70-97 (part col.) Jan '58; 115: 312-3 (col.) Mar '59.
  Travel 102: 10 Dec '54; 105: 64-5 Jan '56, 15 May '56.
—— (battle, 1759). Amer. heri., vol. 11 no. 1 p. 24-5 (col.) (Dec '59).
—— (entrance gate). Holiday 21: 20 Ap '57.
  Travel 101: 37 Ap '54.
—— (harbor). Natl. geog. 98: 324, 329 (col.) Sept '50.
—— (hotel). Holiday 14: 76 Jl '53.
—— (map). Natl. geog. 100: 467 Oct '51; 113: 74 Jan '58.
—— (19th cent.). Con. 133: 203-6 May '54.
—— (north shore map). Travel 108: 49 Aug '57.
——, (north shore). Travel 108: 50-1 Aug '57.
—— (St. Louis gate). Travel 105: 13 May '56.
—— (1759, by Richard Short). Amer. heri., vol. 11 no. 1 p. 28-9 (Dec '59).
—— (1750). Con. 129: 68 Ap '52.
Queen (Univ. of Iowa). Face of Amer., p. 156 (col.).
Queen, Assyrian (ancient). Int. gr. soc.: Arts . . . p. 29 (col.).
——, bathing beauty (Poland). Natl. geog. 114: 381 Sept '58.
——, beauty (Cal.). Natl. geog. 112: 724 Nov '57.
"Queen, Dogwood festival". Natl. geog. 103: 543 (col.) Ap '53.
Queen, rodeo. Natl. geog. 114: 165 (col.) Aug '58.
Queen Caroline of Anspach. Amer. heri., vol. 11 no. 4 p. 8 (Je '60).
"Queen Caroline", wife of George II (Gainsborough). Con. 135: 237 Je '55.
"Queen Charlotte & her baby" (Cotes). Con. 126: 27 Aug '50.
Queen Charlotte. See also Charlotte, Queen.
Queen-elect (being borne to her king). Amer. heri., vol. 7 no. 6 p. 10 (Oct '56).
Queen Elizabeth. See Elizabeth, Queen.
"Queen Elizabeth" (ship). Natl. geog. 106: 779 (col.) Dec '54.
"Queen Elizabeth" hotel (Montreal, model). Travel 103: 48 Jan '55.
"Queen Henrietta Maria with her dwarf". See Henrietta Maria, Queen (with her dwarf).
Queen Mary. See Mary, Queen.
Queen Nefertiti. See Nefertiti, Queen.
Queen of carnival. Natl. geog. 113: 73 (col.) Jan '58.
  Travel 106: 41 Nov '56.
"Queen Victoria & Duke of Wellington" (Landseer). Con. 144: XX (col.) Nov '59.
Queen Victoria. See also Victoria, Queen.

Queen Victoria Park. Natl. geog. 115: 446-7 (col.) Ap '59.
Queen's bargemaster (British). Holiday 25: 190 (col.) May '59.
Queen's guards (Eng.). Holiday 23: 70 (col.) Ap '58.
Queen's Hall (London, int. & ext.). Cooper: Con. ency. of music, p. 457.
Queens of Gt. Brit. Amer. heri., vol. 11 no. 4, p. 8, back cover (col.) (Je '60).
Queen's university (Ulster). Holiday 11: 51 Jan '52.
Queluz, Royal palace of. See Palace of Queluz.
Quemoy island (China coast). Natl. geog. 115: 414-38 Mar '59.
—— (map). Natl. geog. 115: 418 Mar '59.
Quesada, Lt. Gen. Elwood R. Cur. biog. p. 474 (1950); p. 328 (1960).
Quetico, Superior country (map). Amer. heri., vol. 1 no. 3 p. 48 (col.) (spring '50).
Quetzalcoatl, Temple of. See Temple of Quetzalcoatl.
Queuille, Henri. Cur. biog. p. 506 (1948).
Quezon, Manuel L. Cur. biog. p. 689 (1941).
Quill, Michael J. Cur. biog. p. 693 (1941); p. 503 (1953).
quill pen. See pen, quill.
quilt (antique peacock). Amer. heri., vol. 6 no. 3 p. 33 (col.) (Ap '55).
——, (applique blocks). Rawson: Ant. pict. bk., p. 12.
—— (merchant, Iran). Natl. geog. 115: 60 (col.) Jan '59.
quilting (women). Natl. geog. 102: 513 (col.) Oct '52.
"Quilting bee". Amer. heri., vol. 6 no. 2 p. 47 (col.) (winter '55).
quilting block. Rawson: Ant. pict. bk., p. 81.
Quimby, Edith H. Cur. biog. p. 493 (1949).
Quincy, Josiah. Amer. heri., vol. 9 no. 4 p. 33 (Je '58).
Quinn, Anthony. Cur. biog. p. 440 (1957).
Quinn, William F. Cur. biog. p. 346 (1958).
Quintero, Jose. Cur. biog. p. 522 (1954).
"The Quirinale". Con. 141: 231 Je '58.
Quirino, Elpidio. Cur. biog. p. 507 (1948).
Quito (Ecuador). Holiday 20: 72-3 (col.) Nov '56.
Travel 109: 33 Mar '58.
—— (cathedral). Travel 101: 9 Feb '54.
—— (church). Holiday 20: 62 (col.) Nov '56.
quixotism (sym.). Lehner: Pict. bk. of sym., p. 59.
Quiz kids (TV show). Holiday 27: 105 Jan '60.
Qumran, Khirbat. See Khirbat Qumran.
Qumran caves (Essenes). Natl. geog. 114: 854 (col.) Dec '58.
Quo Tai-Chi. Cur. biog. p. 495 (1946).
Qutb Minar tower (Delhi, India). Natl. geog. 116: 840 (col.) Dec '59.

R

RAF officers. Natl. geog. 111: 741 (col.) Je '57.
Raab, Julius. Cur. biog. p. 524 (1954).
Rab island (Dalmatia). Travel 107: 37 Ap '57.
Rabaut, Louis Charles. Cur. biog. p. 484 (1952).

rabbi (Jerusalem). Holiday 7: 125 Ap '50.
rabbit cages. Natl. geog. 103: 245 Feb '53.
rabbit's foot (sym.). Lehner: Pict. bk. of sym., p. 63.
Rabi, Isidor Isaac. Cur. biog. p. 509 (1948).
Raborn, William Francis, jr. Cur. biog. p. 347 (1958).
race, auto. See auto race.
——, trotting horse. Holiday 21: 53 Je '57; 26: 51 (col.) Sept '59.
Travel 105: 58 Ap '56.
race track, auto (Indianapolis). Holiday 27: 40 Je '60.
——, horse. Holiday 11: 37 Je '52.
——, horse (Daytona Beach, Fla.). Travel 107: 4 Mar '57.
——, horse (Fla., 1841). Con. 141: XXVI Ap '58.
——, horse (Ireland). Holiday 6: 52 (col.) Dec '49.
——, horse (jockey on horse). Holiday 25: 196 (col.) May '59.
——, horse (Puerto Rico). Holiday 5: 52 (col.) Feb '49.
race track barn (horses). Natl. geog. 101: 57 (col.) Jan '52.
racegoer. Int. gr. soc.: Arts . . . p. 153 (col.).
Rachmaninov, Sergei Vassilievich. Cooper: Con. ency. of music, p. 243.
racing car. Amer. heri., vol. 10 no. 2 p. 45 (Feb '59).
racing cup, silver (George IV). Con. 145: X-XII May '60.
"Racing on Newmarket heath" (Wootton). Con. 140: XIX Nov '57.
racing shells (Eng.). Natl. geog. 114: 66-7 (col.) Jl '58.
—— (Univ. of Wash.). Natl. geog. 117: 507 (col.) Ap '60.
Rackham, Arthur. Jun. bk. of auth., p. 252.
—— (book illus. by). Amer. heri., vol. 8 no. 1 p. 37 (col.).
Rackmil, Milton R. Cur. biog. p. 486 (1952).
racquet, tennis. See tennis racket.
Radahl, Kaare. Cur. biog. p. 525 (1956).
radar detecter. Natl. geog. 110: 609 Nov '56.
radar dome. Natl. geog. 114: 132 (col.) Jl '58.
—— (South Pole). Natl. geog. 112: 29 Jl '57.
radar island (equipment). Natl. geog. 108: 750 Dec '55.
radar reflector, signal. Natl. geog. 103: 589 (col.) May '53.
radar targets. Natl. geog. 111: 568 Ap '57.
Radcliffe, Viscount Cyril John. Cur. biog. p. 350 (1963).
Radcliffe library (Oxford). See library, Radcliffe (Oxford).
Raddall, Thomas H. Cur. biog. p. 498 (1951).
Radford, Adm. Arthur W. Cur. biog. p. 494 (1949).
Radhakrishnan, Sir Sarvepalli. Cur. biog. p. 488 (1952).
radiation (plants). Natl. geog. 114: 328-9 (col.) Sept '58.
radiation film badge. Natl. geog. 99: 313 Mar '51.

radiator, steam heat. Holiday 12: 142 Dec '52.
radio. Holiday 7: 10, 121 (col.) May '50, 27, back cover (col.) Je '50; 8: 24 Jl '50, 60 Aug '50; 12: 62 Nov '52; 13: 118 Mar '53, 17 (col.) Ap '53, 147 May '53, 15 (col.) Je '53; 14: 33 Jl '53, 7, 69 Sept '53, 31, 100, 145 Nov '53, 101, 165 (col.) Dec '53; 19: 23 (col.) May '56; 22: 1, 14, 26, 163, 170 Nov '57, 123, 172 (col.), 219 Dec '57; 23: 8-9 Mar '58, 136 Ap '58, 181 May '58, 158 Je '58; 24: 12 (col.), 211 Dec '58; 25: 85 Feb '59, 32 May '59, 198 Je '59; 26: 21 Sept '59, 1 Oct '59; 27: 36 Jan '60, 45 Ap '60, 117 May '60. Travel 104 back cover Sept '55.
—— (with ear phones). Amer. heri., vol. 6 no. 5 p. 66-7, 69, 72 (Aug '55).
——, clock. Holiday 25: 4 Ap '59; 28: 13 Dec '60.
——, crystal set. Brooks: Growth of a nation, p. 249.
——, pocket. Holiday 23: 120 Mar '58.
——, portable. Holiday 10: 113 Aug '51, 75 Dec '51; 11: 94 Ap '52; 12: 8, 138 Dec '52; 18: 141 (col.) Nov '55; 19: 88 (col.) Je '56; 21: 4 (col.) Je '57; 22: 4 (col.) Jl '57; 23: inside cover (col.) Mar '58, 29, 35 Je '58; 24: 24 Jl '58. Travel 103: back cover Je '55.
——, Zenith (1954). Holiday 15: 81 Feb '54.
radio amateur room. Natl. geog. 112: 755 Dec '57.
radio beam tower. Amer. heri., vol. 3 no. 3 p. 59 (spring '52).
radiocarbon apparatus. Natl. geog. 114: 235, 244-5, 255 Aug '58.
Radio City music hall (N.Y.). Holiday 15: 56-7 (col.) Ap '54.
radio console (air traffic operator). Natl. geog 104: 727 (col.) Dec '53.
radio equipment tester. Natl. geog. 99: 303 (col.) Mar '51.
radio loudspeaker (antique). Amer. heri., vol. 6 no. 5 p. 75, 84 (Aug '55).
radio program (crystal sets). Amer. heri., vol. 6 no. 5 p. 64-7, 69 (Aug '55).
radio sled. Natl. geog. 110: 56-7 (col.) Jl '56.
radio station (Vatican). Holiday 23: 57 May '58.
radio telescope. Natl. geog. 100: 763 (col.) Dec '51.
radio telescope (Alaska). Natl. geog. 109: 767 (col.) Je '56.
radio tower (Arctic). Natl. geog. 107: 570 (col.) Ap '55.
radio towers. Natl. geog. 112: 42 Jl '57.
radiology (sym.). Lehner: Pict. bk. of auth., p. 17.
radium receptacle (sym.). Lehner: Pict. bk. of sym., p. 17.
Radziwell, Princess Lee. Jensen: The White House, p. 284.
Raeburn, Henry (work of). Con. ency. of ant., vol. 1, pl. 166. Con. 129: 24 Ap '52; 134: 49, 61 Sept '54, 146 Nov '54; 135: LXI Ap '55; 136: 20 Sept '55, LXXV Jan '56; 137: XLIX, LXIII Ap '56; 138: LXII Nov '56; 139: 121 Ap '57; 141: 62 Mar '58; 142: L

Sept '58. Praeg.: Pict. ency., p. 372 (col.).
Raeder, Erich. Cur. biog. p. 695 (1941)|
Raedler, Dorothy. Cur. biog. p. 526 (1954).
Rafe's chasm (Mass.). Travel 107: 19 May '57.
Raft, George. Holiday 5: 40 (col.) Jan '49.
raft. Holiday 27: 76 (col.) Mar '60.
—— (boys). Natl. geog. 110: 128 Jl '56.
—— (man, woman, Cubans). Holiday 25: 171 (col.) Je '59.
—— (men). Amer. heri., vol. 1 no. 4 p. 19 (col.) (summer '50).
—— (swimmers). Holiday 11: 167 May '52.
——, bamboo. Natl. geog. 97: 168 (col.) Feb '50; 107: 418 (col.) Mar '55.
——, bamboo (Fiji). Natl. geog. 114: 553 (col.) Oct '58.
——, bamboo (Jamaica). Holiday 26: 21 (col.) Jl '59.
——, bamboo (Rio Grande). Holiday 25: 118 (col.) May '59.
——, Chinese marine rubber. Natl. geog. 111: 335 (col.) Mar '57.
——, Egyptian. Ceram: March of arch., p. 195.
——, fishing (Brazil). Natl. geog. 108: 753 (col.) Dec '55.
——, fishing (Formosa). Natl. geog. 97: 168 (col.) Feb '50.
——, life. Natl. geog. 98: 299, 313 (col.) Sept '50.
——, lumber. See lumber raft.
——, plastic play. Holiday 11: 76 (col.) Je '52.
——, rubber. Natl. geog. 97: 49 (col.) Jan '50; 109: 8 (col.) Jan '56.
——, rubber (girls display). Natl. geog. 107: 193 (col.) Feb '55.
——, rubber (men). Natl. geog. 105: 365 Mar '54.
——, rubber (men & women). Natl. geog. 111: 548 (col.) Ap '57.
——, rubber (swimmers). Holiday 7: 93 (col.) Je '50.
——, rubber life. Natl. geog. 103: 589 (col.) May '53.
"Raft of the Medusa" (Gericault). Praeg.: pict .ency., p. 384 (col.).
rafts, Assyrian. Ceram: March of arch., p. 201.
——, bamboo. Natl. geog. 105: 361 Mar '54.
——, log. Natl. geog. 116: 50 (col.) Jl '59.
——, lumber (Nigeria). Natl. geog. 110: 356-7 (col.) Sept '56.
"Raftsund" fjord (Normann). Con. 141: 263 Jl '58.
ragpickers (carts, 1890). Holiday 12: 70 Sept '52.
Rahman, Abdul (ruler of Malaya). Cur. biog. p. 442 (1957).
Rahman, Prince Abdul. Cur. biog. p. 444 (1957).
Rahotep, Prince & wife (Egyptian sculpture). Praeg.: Pict. ency., p. 115 (col.).
Rai, shrine of. See shrine of Rai.
rail fence. See fence, rail.
railcar, Free China. Travel 108: 39 Nov '57.
railing, balcony. See balconies (iron railing).

railing, stair. *See* stair railing; step railing.
railroad. Amer. heri., vol. 6 no. 1 p. 40 (fall '54).

Durant: Pict. hist. of Amer. circus, p. 147.
—— **(1897).** *See* "Annie & Mary" railroad (1897).
—— **(1st steam).** Brooks: Growth of a nation, p. 102.
—— **(map).** Amer. heri., vol. 8 no. 2 p. 28-9 (col.) (Feb '57) (time & places).
—— **(mt. side).** Amer. heri., vol. 9 no. 1 p. 70 (Dec '57).
——, **building western (1887).** Amer. heri., vol. 9 no. 4 p. 11, 13 (Je '58).
—— **car.** *See* train (private car); railway car.
railroad crossing sign. Travel 106: 56 Sept '56.
railroad depot. *See* depot, railroad; railway station.
railroad "Horseshoe curve" (Penn.). Amer. heri., vol. 5 no. 4 p. 44-7 (part col.) (summer '54).
railroad poster. *See* advertising poster (railroads).
railroad signal. Face of Amer., p. 65 (col.).
railroad spike (nail). Holiday 22: 17 Dec '57; 24: 131 Dec '58.
railroad station. *See* depot, railroad.
railroad track (1st westward). Brooks: Growth of a nation, p. 178.
railroad track laid (Canada). Natl. geog. 110: 380 (col.) Sept '56.
railroad train. *See* train.
railroads. Brooks: Growth of a nation, p. 271.
railroads join near Ogden, Utah. Amer. heri., vol. 9 no. 2 p. 21-3 (part col.) (Feb '58).
railroads of the U.S. (map). Jordan. Hammond's pict. atlas, p. 10.
railway, English (antique). Con. 133: 123 Ap '54.
——, **U.S. Senate.** Natl. geog. 102: 169 Aug '52.
railway car (int.). Holiday 11: 83, 91 Ap '52.
——, **incline (N.Y.).** Travel 114: 49 Sept '60.
—— **float.** Natl. geog. 98: 370 Sept '50.
railway coach (Winan's design). Amer. heri., vol. 9 no. 1 p. 60-1 (Dec '57).
railway crests. Con. 144: 40 Sept '59.
railway engine, cog. Travel 110: 45 Oct '58.
railway station. Amer. heri., vol. 9, no. 1 p. 65 (col.) (Dec '57).
Face of Amer., p. 64-5 (col.).
Natl. geog. 98: 78 Jl '50.
—— **(Chicago, 1881).** Amer. heri., vol. 1 no. 2 p. 26 (winter '50).
—— **(Cincinnati).** Natl. geog. 107: 448-9 (col.) Ap '55.
—— **(Ireland).** Holiday 19: 40 Jan '56.
—— **(Saar).** Natl. geog. 105: 575 Ap '54.
—— **(Stalingrad).** Travel 109: 56 Ap '58.
rain boards. (Nagaland, India). Natl. geog. 107: 263 Feb '55.
rain cape, Chinese palm fiber. Natl. geog. 111: 356 (col.) Mar '57.
rain dance (Sudan). Natl. geog. 103: 270-1 Feb '53.
rain forest. Natl. geog. 108: 89 (col.) Jl '55.
rain gauge (man & woman). Holiday 10: 37 Sept '51.
rainbow. Natl. geog. 116: 74 (col.) Jl '59; 117:

258-9 (col.) Feb '60.
rainbow bridge (Utah). Jordan: Hammond's pict. atlas, p. 171 (col.).
—— **(Natl. monument).** Natl. geog. 111: 546, 556-7, 559 (part col.) Ap '57; 113: 639 (col.) May '58; 115: 548-9 (col.) Ap '59.
raincoat, man's. Holiday 26: 165 Oct '59.
Raine, Jonathan (Hoppner). Con. 143: 88 Ap '59.
Rainey, Homer P. Cur. biog. p. 498 (1946).
Rains, Albert M. Cur. biog. p. 375 (1959).
Rains, Claude. Cur. biog. p. 496 (1949).
raised disk (sym.). Lehner: Pict. bk. of sym., p. 89.
raised fist (sym.). *See* fist, raised (sym.).
raised hand (sym.). *See* hand, raised (sym.).
"Raising of Lazarus" (Froment). Con. 137: 166 (col.) May '56.
"Raising the liberty pole" (1776). Brooks: Growth of a nation, p. 75.
"Raising the statue of Livia". Ceram: March of arch., p. 6.
Raisuli, Mulai Ahmed er. Amer. heri., vol. 10 no. 5 p. 19 (Aug '59).
Raja, Indian (on elephant). Int. gr. soc.: Arts . . . p. 115 (col.).
Raja & Rani of Bangli (Bali). Holiday 18: 57 (col.) Jl '55.
Rajagopalachari, Chakravarti. Cur. biog. p. 684 (1942).
Rajamaki church (Finland). Travel 105: 35 Ap '56.
Rajayoga (sym.). Lehner: Pict. bk. of sym., p. 43.
rake, hay. Natl. geog. 100: 630 Nov '51.
——, **leaf.** Holiday 28: 214 (col.) Nov '60.
——, **stone.** Rawson: Ant. pict. bk., p. 22, 44.
"The Rake's progress" (Hogarth). Praeg.: Pict. ency., p. 371 (col.).
Rakosi, Matyas. Cur. biog. p. 497 (1949).
Raleigh, Sir Walter. Amer. heri., vol. 4 no. 2 cover, 46-7, 49 (col.) (winter '53); vol. 8 no. 4 p. 92 (Je '57); vol. 10 no. 4 p. 4 (col.) (Je '59).
—— **(beheaded).** Amer. heri., vol. 10 no. 4 p. 19 (Je '59).
—— **(miniature).** Con. 143: 263 Je '59.
Raleigh home, Sir Walter. Holiday 23: 20 Je '58.
Raleigh (S.C.). Travel 114: 36 Sept '60.
Raleigh tavern (Williamsburg, Va.). Amer. heri., vol. 1 no. 2 p. 39 (winter '50).
Ralls, Charles C. Cur. biog. p. 499 (1951).
rally, political. Amer. heri., vol. 9 no. 1 p. 107 (Dec '57).
Ralston, William C. Amer. heri., vol. 7 no. 2 p. 63 (Feb '56).
Rama IX, King of Thailand. Cur. biog. p. 476 (1950).
Rama Rau, Santha. Cur. biog. p. 483 (1945); p. 377 (1959).
Ramadan festival (Cameroons). Natl. geog. 116: 240-3 (col.) Aug '59.
Ramadier, Paul. Cur. biog. p. 530 (1947).
Raman, Sir Venkata. Cur. biog. p. 511 (1948).
Rambler auto. Travel 103: 14 Jan '55.
Rameau, Jean Philippe (bust by Caffieri). Cooper: Con. ency. of music, p. 244.
Rameses Colossi. *See* Colossus of Rameses.

Rameses stone faces. *See* Colossus of Rameses.
Ramirez, Gen. Pedro P. Cur. biog. p. 609 (1943).
Ramo, Simon. Cur. biog. p. 348 (1958).
"Ramona's marriage place" (Cal.). Natl. geog. 102: 761 (col.) Dec '52. Travel 103: 32 Je '55.
"Rampin horseman", head (Greek statue). Con. ency. of ant., vol. 3 pl. 66.
Ramsay, Allan (statue). Natl. geog. 112: 460 (col.) Oct '57.
—— **(work of).** Con. 126: 94 Oct '50; 132: 73 Nov '53; 135: 196 May '55, 238, 249 Je '55; 138: XI Sept '56; 139: 76 Ap '57; 140: XII (col.) Nov '57, 236 Jan '58; 141: 60 Mar '58, 268 Je '58; 145: 191 May '60.
Ramsay, Vice Adm. Sir Bertram. Cur. biog. p. 544 (1944).
Ramsay, James (work of). Con. 139: XXXIII Je '57.
Ramses the Great (sculpture). Ceram: March of arch., p. 81.
Rames II temple (Abu Simbel). Holiday 27: 64-5 (col.) Mar '60.
—— **(int.).** Ceram: March of arch., p. 79.
Ramseur, S. Dodson. Amer. heri., vol. 9 no. 2 p. 31 (Feb '58).
Ramsey, Arthur Michael (archbishop). Cur. biog. p. 330 (1960).
Ramsey, Adm. Dewitt C. Cur. biog. p. 506 (1953).
Ramsey, Norman F. Cur. biog. p. 352 (1963).
"Ramsgate Harbour" (Fischer). Con. 129: XLII Ap '52.
Ramspeck, Robert C. Cur. biog. p. 501 (1951).
Rance, Sir. Hubert Elvin. Cur. biog. p. 508 (1953).
ranch. Holiday 25: 7 (col.) Je '59.
—— **(Ariz.).** Face of Amer., p. 38-9 (col.).
—— **(Cal.).** Face of Amer., p. 142-3 (col.).
—— **(Santa Cruz is.).** Natl. geog. 114: 275 (col.) Aug '58.
——, **dude.** *See* dude ranch.
ranch lodge (int.). Natl. geog. 110: 503 (col.) Oct '56.
ranch room, French (int.). Natl. geog. 109: 691 (col.), 693 May '56.
a ranchero (on horse). Amer. heri., vol. 9 no. 5, cover, p. 8 (col.) (Aug '58).
ranchmen (card game). Holiday 12: 38 (col.) Sept '52.
Rancliffe, Lord (on horse) (Ferneley). Con. 142: 41 Sept '58.
Rand, Sally. Holiday 10: 55 Oct 51.
Rand, William M. Cur. biog. p. 510 (1953).
Randall, Clarence B. Cur. biog. p. 491 (1952).
Randall, John D. Cur. biog. p. 332 (1960).
Randall, Ruth Painter. Cur. biog. p. 446 (1957).
Randall, Tony. Cur. biog. p. 381 (1961).
Randers, Gunnar. Cur. biog. p. 447 (1957).
Randolph, Asa Philip. Cur. biog. p. 503 (1951).
Randolph, Jennings. Cur. biog. p. 344 (1962).
Randolph, John. Amer. heri., vol. 3 no. 3 p. 49 (col.) (spring 52).
—— **(silhouette).** Amer. heri., vol. 6 no. 6 p. 96 (Oct '55); vol. 7 no. 5 p. 11 (Aug '56).
Randolph, Martha (Sully). Jensen: The White House, p. 19.

Randolph, Woodruff. Cur. biog. p. 513 (1948).
ranger, park. *See* Natl. park ranger.
rangers, forest (Africa). Natl. geog. 118: 335 (col.) Sept '60.
rangers, Texas. *See* Texas rangers.
Rangoon. Holiday 25: 168 (col.) Mar '59.
Ranier III, Prince of Monaco. Cur. biog. p. 498 (1955). Holiday 24: 37 Aug '58.
Rank, Joseph Arthur. Cur. biog. p. 484 (1945).
Rankin, J. Lee. Cur. biog. p. 378 (1959).
Rankin, John E. Cur. biog p. 556 (1944).
Rankin, Karl L. Cur. biog. p. 500 (1955).
Rankley, Alfred (work of). Con. 133: 40 Mar '54.
Ransome, Arthur. Jun. bk. of auth., p. 253.
Rao, Shanta. Cur. biog. p. 449 (1957).
Raoul (as in Les Huguenots). Cooper: Con. ency. of music, p. 90.
Raoux, Jean (work of). Con. 142: 7 Sept '58.
Rapacki, Adam. Cur. biog. p. 351 (1958).
"Rape of Europa" (Reni). Con. 132: 16 Sept '53.
—— **(Titian).** Con. 140: 240 Jan '58.
"Rape of Ganymede" (Preti). Con. 136: 282 Jan '56.
"Rape of the Sabine" (sculpture). Praeg.: Pict. ency., p. 273.
"Rape of the Sabine women" (Rubens). Con. 133: 31 Mar '54.
Raphael, Chaim. Cur. biog. p. 354 (1963).
Raphael (seal of). Lehner: Pict. bk. of sym., p. 25.
Raphael Santi. Int. gr. soc.: Arts . . . p. 91 (col).
—— **(bust).** Holiday 27: 91 (col.) Ap '60.
—— **(self portrait).** Praeg.: Pict. ency., p. 31.
—— **(work of).** Con. ency. of ant., vol. 1, pl. 150.
   Con. 138: 199 Dec '56; 140: 239 Jan '58.
   Holiday 27: 77 (col.) Feb '60, 90-1 (col.) Ap '60.
   Praeg.: Pict. ency., p. 46, 279 (col.).
Raphael's mural in Vatican. Holiday 7: 111 (col.) May '50.
Rappard, William E. Cur. biog. p. 505 (1951).
Rarey, John S. Amer. heri., vol. 2 no. 2 p. 15 (winter '51).
Raskob. Amer. heri., vol. 9 no. 5 p. 33 (Aug '58).
Rasminsky, Louis. Cur. biog. p. 383 (1961).
Rasmussen, Gustav. Cur. biog. p. 533 (1947).
Rassam, Hormuzd (excavations at Nineveh). Ceram: March of arch., p. 218-9.
Rassweiler, Clifford F. Cur. biog. p. 353 (1958).
ratchet loop, cow. Rawson: Ant. pict. bk., p. 69.
Ratha & sacred oxen (India). Holiday 7: 87 (col.) May '50.
"Rathaus on the Platz" (Callow). Con. ency. of ant., vol. 1, pl. 148.
Rathbone, Basil. Cur. biog. p. 507 (1951).
Rathbone, Eleanor. Cur. biog. p. 611 (1943).
Rathbone, Monroe J. Cur. biog. p. 451 (1957).
"ratlines", ship. Natl. geog. 116: 800 Dec '59.
Ratoff, Gregory. Cur. biog. p. 613 (1943).
Rattigan, Terence. Cur. biog. p. 506 (1956).

rattle, ceremonial Indian. Amer. heri., vol. 10 no. 3 p. 68 (April '59).

Rattner, Abraham. Cur. biog. p. 516 (1948).

Rau, Sir Benegal Narsing. Cur. biog. p. 510 (1951).

Rau, Sir Benegal Rama. Cur. biog. p. 499 (1949).

Rau, Dhanvanthi Rama. Cur. biog. p. 528 (1954).

Rauch, Christian Daniel (sculpture by). Praeg.: Pict. ency., p. 427.

Rauschning, Hermann. Cur. biog. p. 697 (1941).

Ravel, Maurice. Cooper: Con. ency., of music, p. 245.
Int. gr. soc.: Arts . . . p. 139 (col.).

Ravello (Italy). Labande: Naples, p. 196-8.

Ravello garden (Parsifal performance). Natl. geog. 116: 499 (col.) Oct '59.

"The Raven" (from E. A. Poe's poem). Con. 143: 154-8 May '59.

Ravenna mosaic. Praeg.: Pict. ency., p. 179 (col.).

Raver, Paul J. Cur. biog. p. 698 (1941).

Rawalt, Marguerite. Cur. biog. p. 509 (1956).

Rawanduz (Iraq). Natl. geog. 114: 480-1 (col.) Oct '58.

Rawlings, Vice Adm. Sir Bernard. Cur. biog. p. 487 (1945).

Rawlings, Marjorie Kinnan. Cur. biog. p. 687 (1942).

Rawlins, John A. Pakula: Cent. album., p. 239.

Rawlinson, Henry Creswicke (portrait). Ceram: March of arch., p. 206.

Ray, Rev. Randolph. Cur. biog. p. 489 (1945).

Ray, Satyajit. Cur. biog. p. 385 (1961).

Rayburn, Sam. Holiday 7: 62 Feb '50.
Natl. geog. 102: 146 Aug '52.

Raye, Martha. Cur. biog. p. 356 (1963).

Raymond, Henry F. Amer. heri., vol. 3 no. 2 p. 23 (winter '52).

Razmara, Ali. Cur. biog. p. 477 (1950).

razor. Holiday 27: 158 Je '60.

razor blades (antique). Rawson: Ant. pict. bk., p. 10.

Rea, Gardner. Cur. biog. p. 500 (1946).

reactor, atomic power. See atomic power reactor.

Read, Capt. See "Captain Read" (Kauffmann).

Read, Sir Herbert. Cur. biog. p. 347 (1962).

Read, Mary (pirate). Amer. heri., vol. 8 no. 2 p. 14 (col.) (Feb '57).

Read, Thomas (work of). Natl. geog. 97: 289 (col.) Mar '50.

Read house, Jehiel (N.Y.). Amer. heri., vol. 10 no. 1 p. 20 (Dec '58).

Reading, Stella (Dowager Marchioness). Cur. biog. p. 517 (1948).

"Reading Angel" (Tiepolo). Con. 143: 176 May '59.

reading stand (18th cent.). Con. 142: XXX-VIII Sept '58.

reading table (18th cent.). Con. 141: LX Mar '58.

Reagan, Ronald. Cur. biog. p. 504 (1949).

the reaper (death sym.). Lehner: Pict. bk. of sym., p. 92.

reaper, clover. See clover reaper.

reaping hook. See hook, reaping.

Reavis, James Addison. Amer. heri., vol. 7 no. 5 p. 28 (Aug '56).

rebec (medicine). Int. gr. soc.: Arts . . . p. 61 (col.).

"Rebecca at the well" (Galeotti). Con. 135: 31 Mar '55.

"Rebecca at the well" (Piazzetti). Con. 143: 99 Ap '59.

"Rebecca at the well" (Veronese). Natl. geog. 110: 637 (col.) Nov '56.

Rebecca shoal light (Gulf of Mexico). Natl. geog. 97: 58 Jan '50.

Reber, Samuel. Cur. biog. p. 505 (1949).

rebus (letters by Mathew Darly). Amer. heri., vo. 8 no. 1 p. 44-5 (col.) (Dec '56).

Rechter, Yascov. Holiday 26: 73 Dec '59.

Recife (Brazil). Natl. geog. 108: 754-5 (col.) Dec '55.

Reckford, Maj. Gen. Milton A. Cur. biog. p. 491 (1945).

record, music. Holiday 18: 9, 41 Aug '55, 199 Dec '55; 19: 128 Jan '56, 63 Mar '56, 171 May '56, 158 Je '56; 24: 1 Sept '58, 11 Nov '58.

record player. Holiday 10: 3 Nov '51, 136 Dec '51; 18: 20 (col.) Nov '55; 19: 10 (col.) Jan '56; 20: 147-49, 183 (col.) Dec '56; 21: 118 (col.) Je '57; 22: 4 (col.) Jl '57, 147 (col.) Nov '57, 23: 108 Feb '58, 42 Mar '58, 35 Je '58; 24: 9, 89 Sept '58, 5 (col.) Oct '58, 12-3, 136, 138 (col.) Nov '58, 235 Dec '58; 4, 17 Feb '59, 155, 175, 188 Mar '59, 113, 205 Ap '59, 4, 103 May '59; 26: 121 Jl '59, 24 Sept '59, 1, 179 Nov '59, 20 (col.) Dec '59; 28: 25 Sept '60, 47 (col.) Oct '60, 1 Nov '60; 49 Dec '60.

—— (antique). Natl. geog. 117: 24 Jan '60.

—— (portable). Holiday 20: 39 Nov '56; 22: 14 Dec '57; 24: 136 Oct '58.

recorder (fipple flute). Natl. geog. 97: 291 (col.) Mar '50.

——, tape. See tape recorder.

——, wax cylinder. Natl. geog. 97: 670 May '50.

——, English treble (18th cent.). Cooper: Con. ency. of music, p. 400.

——, language playing. Travel 112: 58 Dec '59; 113: inside cover Jan '60, inside cover Feb '60, inside back cover Mar '60.

rector, university. See university rector, German.

"The red boy" (Janssen). Con. 140: 216 Jan '58.

Red Cross flag (sym.). Lehner: Pict. bk. of sym., p. 88.

Red Cross poster (World war I). Brooks Growth of a nation, p. 243.

"Red haired girl with freckles" (Malta). Con. 137: 61 (col.) Mar '56.

"Red jacket" (Indian chief). Amer. heri., vol. 11 no. 3 back cover (col.) (Ap '60).

"Red jacket" clipper ship. Amer. heri., vol. 6 no. 6 p. 20 (col.) (Oct '55).

"The red path" (Macke). Praeg.: Pict. ency., p. 449 (col.).

"Red Riding Hood" (Wolf). Holiday 19: 114 Feb '56.

Red Rock Lakes. *See* Natl. wildlife refuge (Red Rock Lakes).
Red Rock Park (amphitheater, Denver, Colo.). Holiday 6: 110 (col.) Aug '49.
Red Rocks theater (Colo.). Jordan: Hammond's pict. atlas, p. 163 (col.).
Redfield, Robert. Cur. biog. p. 511 (1953).
Redgrave, Michael. Cur. biog. p. 479 (1950).
Redon, Odilon (work of). Con. 142: 108 Nov '58; 144: XXV Dec '59.
Redpath, Anne. Cur. biog. p. 452 (1957).
Redwood, Allen C. (war prisoner sketches). Amer. heri., vol. 10 no. 5 p. 6-7 (Aug '59).
redwood forest (Cal.). Face of Amer., p. 72-3 (col.).
    Travel 101: cover, 10 Mar '54.
Reece, Brazilla Carroll. Cur. biog. p. 501 (1946).
Reed, Carol. Cur. biog. p. 481 (1950).
Reed, Daniel A. Cur. biog. p. 513 (1953).
Reed, John. Amer. heri., vol. 11 no 2 p. 6 (Feb '60).
—— (cartoon). Amer. heri., vol. 11 no. 2 p. 95 (Feb '60).
Reed, John Silas. Amer. heri., vol. 11 no. 2 p. 8 (Feb '60).
Reed, Philip D. Cur. biog. p. 507 (1949).
Reed, Ralph T. Cur. biog. p. 511 (1951).
Reed, Stanley. Holiday 7: 78 Feb '50.
Reed, Stanley F. Cur. biog. p. 690 (1942).
Reed, W. Maxwell. Jun. bk. of auth., p. 255.
reeding ornament. Con. ency. of ant., vol. 1, p. 21.
reef netters. Holiday 11: 44-5 May '52.
reef of Andros. *See* Andros reef.
"The Reefs" (Bermuda inn). Holiday 23: 75 (col.) Je '58.
reel, fishing. Holiday 10: 22 Nov '51, 105 Dec '51; 11: 89 Jan '52, 72 Feb '52, 3 Mar '52, 30 May '52, 136 Je '52; 12: 14 Dec '52; 14: 32 Dec '53.
    Rawson: Ant. pict. bk., p. 75.
Rees, Edward H. Cur. biog. p. 354 (1958).
Rees, Mina S. Cur. biog. p. 454 (1957).
Reese, Everett D. Cur. biog. p. 531 (1954).
Reese, Harold. Cur. biog. p.. 483 (1950).
refectory, Marienburg castle. *See* Marienburg castle.
refectory table. *See* table, refectory.
reflections (bayou water). Natl. geog. 113: 556 (col.) Ap '58.
—— (canal). Natl. geog. 107: 650, 652 (col.) May '55; 115: 184-5 Feb '59.
—— (fjord). Natl. geog. 111: 113 (col.) Jan '57.
—— (floor). Holiday 20: 62 (col.) Nov '56.
—— (houses in lake). Holiday 27: 106-7 (col.) May '60.
—— (lake). Face of Amer., p. 24 (col.).
    Holiday 21: 23 (col.) Mar '57.
    Natl. geog. 109: 602, 626 (col.) May '56; 110: 472-3 (col.) Oct '56; 113: 304 (col.) Mar '58; 118: 90-1 (col.) Jl '60.
—— (men, canoe on water). Natl. geog. 100: 97 Jl '51.
—— (Mt. Hood). Travel 111: cover (col.) May '59.
—— (mt. in lake). Natl. geog. 116: 80-1 (col.) Jl '59.

—— (Nile river). Natl. geog. 108: 624, 634 (col.) Nov '55.
—— (ocean, ship). Natl. geog. 112: 653 (col.) Nov '57.
—— (pool). Holiday 14: 104 Sept '53.
    Natl. geog. 111: 741 (col.) Je '57; 118: 472 (col.) Oct '60.
—— (river). Natl. geog. 113: 612 (col.) May '58; 114: 657 (col.) Nov '58; 115: 614 (col.) May '59; 118: 624-5 (col.) Nov '60.
—— (water). Holiday 11: cover, 43 (col.) May '52; 12: 30-1 (col.) Aug '52, 66 Sept '52, cover (col.) Oct '52; 14: 103 (col.) Oct '53; 18: 36 Jl '55; 19: 81 (col.) Feb '56, 43 (col.) May '56, 7 (col.) Je '56; 21: 62 Ap '57, 81 (col.) May '57; 22: 54-5 (col.) Jl '57.
    Natl. geog. 108: 2-3 (col.) Jl '55, 204, 208 (col.) Aug '55; 117: 511 (col.) Ap '60.
—— (water, penguin). Natl. geog. 109 414 (col.) Mar '56.
—— (water, rock bridge). Natl. geog. 111: 559 (col.) Ap '57.
—— (water, ship, harbor). Natl. geog. 112: 336 (col.) Sept '57.
—— (woman in pool). Holiday 13: 21 May '53.
reflector towers (Arctic). Natl. geog. 114: 135 (col.) Jl '58.
refrigerator. Holiday 18: 76 (col.) Aug '55.
    Int. gr. soc.: Arts . . . p. 171 (col.).
—— (open). Holiday 21: 29 (col.) Mar '57.
refrigerator & freezer (open). Holiday 28: 58 (col.) May '60.
refuge (sym.). Lehner: Pict. bk. of auth., p. 89.
refugee, Hungarian. Holiday 21: 11 Ap '57.
refugee camp, Arab. *See* Arab refugee camp.
refugee children. Holiday 27: 196 May '60.
—— (eating). Natl. geog. 98: 723 (col.) Dec '50.
——, Chinese (at table asleep). Natl. geog. 100: 741 (col.) Dec '51.
——, Hong Kong. Natl. geog. 116: 854 (col.) Dec '59.
——, Italy. Natl. geog. 109: 832-3 (col.) Je '56.
——, Viet Nam. Natl. geog. 107: 870 Je '55.
refugee girls (learn to use silverware). Natl. geog. 109: 833 (col.) Je '56.
refugees (on ship & plane). Natl. geog. 108: 709-24 Nov '55.
——, Arab (Jerusalem). Natl. geog. 98: 728 (col.) Dec '50.
——, Korean (blizzard). Natl. geog. 103: 655 May '53.
——, Viet Nam. Natl. geog. 107: 860-74 Je '55.
refugees flight route, Hungarian (map). Natl. geog. 111: 416 Mar '57.
regatta. Holiday 10: 41 Nov '51.
"Regatta" (Monet). Praeg.: Pict. ency., p. 72 (col.).
regatta. *See* also Henley boat regatta; racing shells; rowboat, college (regatte shells); rowing regatta (Amalfi . . .).
Regnitz river (Germany). Holiday 25: 63 (col.) May '59.
"Regulus" (Pecheux). Con. 144: 170 Dec '59.

"The rehearsal" (Cipriano). Con. 143: XXXII Je '59.

Rehoboth beach (Delaware). Holiday 17: 110 (col.) Mar '55.

Reichelderfer, Francis W. Cur. biog. p. 508 (1949).

Reichstein, Tadeus. Cur. biog. p. 513 (1951).

Reid, Helen Rogers. Cur. biog. p. 700 (1941); p. 493 (1952).

Reid, Ira De A. Cur. biog. p. 504 (1946).

Reid, Ogden R. Cur. biog. p. 511 (1956).

Reid, Samuel Chester. Amer. heri., vol. 10 no. 4 cover (col.) (Je '59).

Reid, Whitelaw. Amer. heri., vol. 11 no. 4 p. 32 (Je '60).
Cur. biog. p. 532 (1954).

Reifenstein castle. See castle, Reifenstein.

Reims cathedral. Travel 112: 51 Sept '59.

Reinartz, Rev. Dr. Frederick E. Cur. biog. p. 515 (1953).

Reiner, Carl. Cur. biog. p. 387 (1961).

Reiner, Fritz. Cur. biog. p. 701 (1941); p. 517 (1953).

Reinhardt, Aurelia Henry. Cur. biog. p. 703 (1941).

Reinhold, Johannes (globes). Con. 126: 167-72 Dec '50.

Reischauer, Edwin O. Cur. biog. p. 349 (1962).

relics (divers discoveries). Natl. geog. 117: 155-7, 160, 173, 179, 183 (part col.) Feb '60.

relief (18th cent., Canova). Con. 144: 228, 231, Jan '60.

—— ("Marseillaise"). Praeg.: Pict. ency., p. 428.

—— (Michele da Firenze). Con. 140: 166 Dec '57.

—— (Notre Dame, Paris). Travel 113: 4 Je '60.

—— (palace of Assurbanipal). Ceram: March of arch., p. 217.

—— (tabernacle of San Michele). Praeg.: Pict. ency., p. 209.

——, alabaster. See alabaster relief.

——, Assyrian. Ceram: March of arch., p. 199, 202, 205.

——, Assyrian carvings. Con. 144: 198 Dec '59.

——, Assyrian limestone (668 B.C.). Con. 145: 277 Je '60.

——, carved. Praeg.: Pict. ency., p. 18.

——, Darius. See Darius relief.

——, Egyptian wall. Ceram: March of arch., p. 150.

——, marble (16th cent.). Con. 145: 53 Mar '60.

——, wood. Con. 145: 135 Ap '60.

religious (sym.). Lehner: Pict. bk. of sym., p. 34-41.

religious art (ancient life). Natl. geog. 112: 834-63 (col.) Dec '57.

religious orders (medieval costume). Int. gr. soc.: Arts . . . p. 71 (col.).

religious revival. Amer. heri., vol. 10 no. 4 p. 27 (col.) (Je '59).

—— (1875). Amer. heri., vol. 6 no. 5 p. 20-1 (Aug '55).

religious sculpture. See sculpture, Christian.

religious type (Amish). See Amish.

reliquaries, Byzantine. Con. 142: 30 Sept '58.

reliquary, Cologne (1175). Praeg.: Pict. ency., p. 194 (col.).

——, Limoges. Con. 143: 199 May '59; 144: 135 Nov '59.

——, Portuguese (17th cent.). Con. 137: 13 Mar '56.

——, Rheims. Con. 137: 51 Mar '56.

——, silver gilt antique. Con. 135: 55 Mar '55.

reliquary chasse (11th cent.). Con. 143: 131 Ap '59.

reliquary of the Holy Innocents. Con. 142: 9 Sept '58.

"Reliquary of the Holy thorn", French. Con. ency. of ant., vol. 3, pl. 29.

reliquary of the true cross. Con. 140: 175 Dec '57.

Rembrandt Van Rÿn. Con. 135: 248 Je '55; 143: 185 May '59.
Int. gr. soc. Arts . . . p. 91 (col.).
Praeg.: Pict. ency., p. 341.

—— (self-portrait). Con. 126: 221 Dec '50; 133: 15 Mar '54; 136: 120 (col.) Nov '55.

—— (work of). Con. ency. of ant., vol. 1, pl. 164.
Con. 126: 127 Oct '50, 210 Dec '50; 127: 114-5 May '51; 133: cover, opp. p. 75 (col.) Ap '54; 135: IX (col.), 137 Ap '55, 207 May '55; 138: 21-39, 69-74 Sept '56; 139: 272 Je '57; 140: 262 Jan '58; 141: 118 Ap '58; 142: 64 Sept '58, 132 Nov '58; 143: 129 Ap '59; 145: XIII Mar '60, 112, 128 Ap '60, 186 May '60, 278, 285 Je '60.
Praeg.: Pict. ency., ,p. 25 (col.), 336.

Remington, Edward W. Natl. geog. 113: 459 Ap '58.

Remington, Eliphalet II. Amer. heri., vol. 3 no. 3 p. 17 (col.) (spring '52).

Remington, Frederic (work of). Amer. heri., vol. 2 no. 4 p. 33 (summer '51); vol. 4 no. 1 cover (col.), p. 1 (fall '52); vol. 6 no. 1 p. 39 (col.) (fall '54); vol. 8 no. 2 cover (col.) (Feb '57) vol. 12 no. 1 p. 36 (Dec '60).
Natl. geog. 99: 209 (col.) Feb '51.

Remington, John W. Cur. biog. p. 333 (1960).

Remorino, Jeronimo. Cur. biog. p. 515 (1951).

Renault, Mary. Cur. biog. p. 380 (1959).

Reni, Guido (work of). Con. 132: 16 Sept '53; 138: 208 Dec '56; 143: 91 Ap '59.

Renne, Roland R. Cur. biog. p. 359 (1963).

Rennebohm, Oscar. Cur. biog. p. 484 (1950).

Renner, Karl. Cur. biog. p. 493 (1945).
Natl. geog. 99: 759 (col.) Je '51.

Reno. Frank. Horan: Pict. hist. of wild west, p. 71.

Reno, Laura Ellen. Horan: Pict. hist. of wild west, p. 73.

Reno (Nev.). Holiday 5: 98-105 Feb '49; 24: 90-1 Nov '58.
Jordan: Hammond's pict. atlas, p. 185 (col.).

Renoir, Jean (work of). Con. 132: 179 Jan '54.
Cur. biog. p. 381 (1959).

Renoir, Pierre Auguste (work of). Con. 127: 125 May '51; 132: cover, opp. p. 107 (col.) Nov '53; 133: 16 Mar '54; 136: cover (col.) Sept '55; 139: 66 Mar '57; 140: LI Sept '57, 114 Nov '57; 141: 121 Ap '58, III May '58; 142: III Nov '58; 145: XII Ap '60, 182 May '60.
Holiday 7: 106 (col.) Feb '50.
Int. gr. soc.: Arts . . . p. 133 (col.).
Praeg.: Pict. ency., p. 420 (col.).

rent table. See table, rent.

Rentzel, Delos Wilson. Cur. biog. p. 519 ((1948).

Repin, I. E. (portrait, Russian painter). Con. 138: XXXVI Sept '56.

——, Ilya Efimovich. Cooper: Con. ency. of music, p. 60, 198.

——, (work of). Con. 143: 31 Mar '59.

repousse, parcel-gilt (Schenauer). Con. 143: 121 Ap '59.

Republican party symbol (cartoon). Holiday 28: 59 (col.) Jl '60.

Republican political symbol (Turkey). Natl. geog. 100: 179 (col.) Aug '51.

rescue (Mt. climbers). Natl. geog. 109 525 Ap '56.

rescue chamber, submarine. Natl. geog. 102: 624 (col.) Nov '52.

rescue ship. See ship, rescue.

Reshevsky, Samuel. Cur. biog. p. 501 (1955).

Resnik, Regina. Cur. biog. p. 513 (1956).

Resolute air station (Arctic). Natl. geog. 107: 548-9 (col.) Ap '55.

"The Resolute" ship, British man-of-war. Amer. heri., vol. 10 no. 5 p. 14-7 (part col.) (Aug '59).

Resor, Stanley B. Cur. biog. p. 510 (1949).

resorts, U.S. Holiday 26: 56-63 (part col.) Jl '59.

respirator machine, cattle testing. Natl. geog. 104: 206 (col.) Aug '53.

"Rest on the flight to Egypt". Con. 126: 51 Aug '50; 144: 164-5 Dec '59.

"Rest on the flight to Egypt" (Cantarini). Con. 144: 22 Sept '59.

"Rest of flight into Egypt" (German woodcut, 15th cent.). Con. 136 300 Jan '56.

"Rest on the flight into Egypt" (Massys). Natl. geog. 107: 198 (col.) Feb '55.

"Rest on the flight into Egypt" (Pittoni). Con. 135: 33 Mar '55; 141: 251 Je '58; 142: 40 Sept '58.

restaurant (Gage & Tollner's). Holiday 21: 84 Mar '57.

—— (int.). Holiday 26: 133 (col.) Oct '59; 27: 149 (col.) Feb '60.

——, African (on a tripod). Natl. geog. 107: 151 (col.) Feb '55.

——, Berns (Sweden). Holiday 20: 44 (col.) Aug '56.

——, Chambord (int.). Holiday 24: 70 (col.) Oct '58.

——, Euromast tower. Natl. geog. 118: 528-30 (col.) Oct '60.

——, Florida (outdoor). Holiday 24: 82 (col.) Nov '58.

——, German. Travel 102: inside cover Sept '54.

——, Haussner's. See Haussner's restaurant.

——, Hong Kong. Natl. geog. 105: 261 (col.) Feb '54.

——, Japanese. See Japanese restaurant.

——, Le Pavillon. See Le Pavillon.

——, Luchow's. See Luchow's restaurant.

——, Nova Scotia (int.). Holiday 27: 21 (col.) Mar '60.

——, Paris (outdoor). Holiday 23: 157 (col.) Ap '58.

——, Sweet's (Manhattan, int.). Holiday 25: 78 (col.) Feb '59.

——, theatre. See theatre restaurant.

restaurant service (cartoons). Holiday 28: 107-12 Jl '60.

restaurant tables, sidewalk (French). Holiday 21: 51 Ap '57; 22: 12 (col.) Oct '57.
Natl. geog. 109: 850 (col.) Je '56.

restaurant "21" (N. Y.). Holiday 11: 64-5, 68 (part col.) Mar '52.

restaurants, European. Holiday 25: 88-9 Jan '59; 27: 93 Jan '60.

——, San Francisco. Holiday 24: 63-5 Sept '58.

restaurants. See also cafe, sidewalk; "The Colony" (N. Y.).

Reston, James B. Cur. biog. p. 616 (1943).

Restout, Jean (work of). Con. 135: 42 Mar '35.

"Resurrected Christ" (statue). Natl. geog. 101: 794 (col.) Je '52.

"The Resurrection" (15th cent.). Con. ency. of ant., vol. 3, pl. 136.

resurrection (sym.). Lehner: Pict. bk. of sym., p. 78.

"The Resurrection" (Wittingau altar). Praeg.: Pict. ency., p. 240 (col.).

"Resurrection of Christ" (Romanesque). Praeg.: Pict. ency., p. 203 (col.).

Reszke, Edouard de (as Mephistopheles in Faust). Cooper: Con. ency. of music, p. 89.

Reszke, Jean de (as Raoul in Les Huguenots). Cooper: Con. ency. of music, p. 90.

retirement city (Port Charlotte, Fla.). Travel 110: 20-2 Sept '58.

retort, chemistry. Lehner: Pict. bk. of sym., p. 11.

"Return from America" (Hiddeman). Brooks: Growth of a nation, p. 221.

"Return from Kermess" (Brueghel the younger). Con. 141: 254 (col.) Je '58.

"Return from the chase" (Rowlandson). Con. 129: LI Ap '52.

"Return from the wedding" (Andrews). Con. 132: XXVII Sept '53.

"Reunion de famille" (Mallet). Con. 134: 219 Dec '54.

Reuss, Henry S. Cur. biog. p. 383 (1959).

Reuter, Ernest. Cur. biog. p. 512 (1949).

Reuther, Victor. Cur. biog. p. 520 (1953).

Reuther, Walter. Cur. biog. p. 705 (1941); p. 514 (1949).
Holiday 26: 67-9 Nov '59, 89 Dec '59.

Revelle, Roger. Cur. biog. p. 455 (1957).

Reventlow, Count Edward. Holiday 7: 97 Mar '50.

Revercomb, Chapman. Cur. biog. p. 356 (1958).

Revere, Paul. Amer. heri., vol. 8 no. 2 p. 66, 69 (Feb '57).

Revere, Paul (art by). Amer. heri., vol. 10 no. 1 p. 68-9 (Dec '58).
—— **(on horse).** Holiday 13: 149 Mar '53, 151 May '53.
—— **(on horse, war).** Holiday 11: 124 Je '52.
—— **(silver work).** Con. 144: 70 Sept '59.
—— **(statue).** Natl. geog. 107: 743 Je '55. Travel 106: 12 Dec '56; 110: 17 Jl '58; 112: 53 Jl '59.
Revere home, Paul. Holiday 16: 106 Jl '54, 14 Oct '54; 23: 52 Mar '58.
Revere sugar urn, Paul. Con. 141: 188 May '58.
"Reveries of a bachelor". Amer. heri., vol. 12 no. 1 p. 120 (Dec '60).
Reves, Emery. Cur. biog. p. 506 (1946).
Revin (France). Natl. geog. 108: 542 (col.) Oct '55.
revivals. See religious revival.
revolution (sym.). Lehner: Pict. bk. of sym., p. 95.
Revolution, American. See American revolution.
revolution of universe (sym.). Lehner: Pict. bk. of sym., p. 47.
revolver, Colt. Con. 129: LXXVI Ap '52.
revolver. See also pistol.
revolving bookcase. See bookcase, Sheraton revolving.
"Reward" (Maryland home). Natl. geog. 105: 470 Ap '54.
"Reward" poster (robbery). Horan: Pict. hist. of wild west, p. 79, 83, 85, 134, 150, 154-5, 161, 173-4 207, 216, 218-9, 225.
Rey, H. A. Jun. bk. of auth., p. 256.
Reybold, Lt. Gen. Eugene. Cur. biog. p. 495 (1945).
Reynaud, Paul. Cur. biog. p. 486 (1950).
Reynolds, Allie. Cur. biog. p. 495 (1952).
Reynolds, Joshua (work of). Amer. heri., vol. 7 no. 4 cover (Je '56; vol. 12 no. 1 p. 4 (col.) (Dec '60).
Con. 126: 25 Aug '50, 89 Oct '50, 209 Dec '50; 133: 179 May '54; 134: 49 Sept '54; 135: 128 Ap '55, cover (col.) May '55; 136: XXIX Jan '56; 137: 222 (col.) Je '56; 138: 261 Jan '57; 139: XXVI May '57; 140: XLIX, 111 Nov '57; 141: 62 Mar '58; 142: 25 Sept '58, XXXVIII Dec '58; 143: 6 Mar '59, 84 Ap '59, 207 Je '59; 144: 76 Nov '59; 145: 179 May '60.
Natl. geog. 97: 197 Feb '50; 105: 788 (col.) Je '54; 108: 317 (col.), 321 Sept '55.
Praeg.: Pict. ency., p. 373 (col.).
Reynolds, Quentin. Cur. biog. p. 706 (1941). Holiday 11: 58 Jan '52.
Reynolds, Richard S. Cur. biog. p. 521 (1953).
Rezanov, Baron. Amer. heri., vol. 10 no. 3 p. 74 (Ap '59).
Rezanov, Nikolai Petrovich. Amer. heri., vol. 11 no. 3 p. 9 (Ap '60).
Rhee, Syngman. Cur. biog. p. 535 (1947).
Rheims cathedral. Praeg.: Pict. ency., p. 199.
—— **(visitation group).** Praeg.: Pict. ency., p. 244.
Rheims, evangelistary. See evangelistary of Bishop Ebo.
Rhine, Joseph B. Cur. biog. p. 517 (1949).
Rhine region (Germany). Holiday 25: 67 (col.)

May '59.
Rhine river. Con. 144: LIII (col.) Dec '59. Holiday 23: 37-47 (col.) Jan '58.
—— **(hotel).** Travel 103: 22 Ap '55.
Rhine Valley. Holiday 15: 29 Feb '54.
"Rhineland town en fete". Con. 145: LXXVI (col.) May '60.
Rhode island. Holiday 11: 110-17 (part col.) May '52; 27: 102-7 (col.) May '60. Natl. geog. 107: 776-7 Je '55.
—— **(capitol bldg.).** Travel 108: 17 Nov '57.
—— **(Castle Hill lighthouse).** Travel 112: 40 Jl '59.
—— **(map).** Natl. geog. 98: 145 Aug '50.
Rhodes, James A. Cur. biog. p. 519 (1949).
Rhodes' home, Cecil (Africa). Natl. geog. 104: 178 Aug '53.
Rhodes island (Greece). Natl. geog. 103: 361-9 (col.) Mar '53; 114: 737, 739-40 (part col.) Dec '58.
Travel 101: 17-9 Je '54.
—— **(ancient ruins).** Holiday 23: 132 (col.) Feb '58.
Rhodesia (Zambezi waterfall). Holiday 25: 151 (col.) Ap '59.
Rhone river (France). Holiday 27: 68-73 Jan '60.
rhumb of Heaven (sym.). Lehner: Pict. bk. of sym., p. 22.
Rhyne, Charles S. Cur. biog. p. 358 (1958).
Rhyolite (Nev. ghost town). Jordan: Hammond's pict. atlas, p. 184 (col.).
"rhythm in space" (plaster figure). Praeg.: Pict. ency., p. 467.
rhyton, Chinese white jade. Con. 135: V Mar '55.
Rialto bridge (Switzerland). Con. 141: 263 Je '58.
Rialto bridge (Venice). Con. 139: 249 Je '57; 141: 237 Je '58.
"Rialto bridge, Venice" (Canaletto). Con. 138: XXIX Jan '57.
Ribak, Louis. Holiday 14: 56 Dec '53.
Ribbentrop, Joachim von. Cur. biog. p. 707 (1941).
ribbons, horse show trophy. Natl. geog. 106: 716 (col.) Nov '54.
Ribe (Denmark). Travel 103: 15 May '55.
Ribeaupierre, Jean (Levitsky). Con. 142: 223 Jan '59.
Ribera, Jusepe de (work of). Labande: Naples, p. 125.
Natl. geog. 97: 770 (col.) Je '50.
Praeg.: Pict. ency., p. 31, 353 (col.).
Ribicoff, Abraham A. Cur. biog. p. 503 (1955). Holiday 26: 39 (col.) Sept '59.
ribs, human. Gray's anatomy, p. 102-4.
Ricci, Marco (work of). Con. 140: 184 Dec '57.
Ricci, Sebastiano (work of). Con. 142: 248 Jan '59.
Riccio, Andrea (bronze figures). Con. 143: 214 Je '59; 145: 223 Je '60.
Rice, Cecil Spring. Amer. heri., vol. 7 no. 2 p. 23 (Feb '56).
Rice, Dan (clown). Durant: Pict. hist. of Amer. circus, p. 42, 44, 46.
Rice, Elmer. Cur. biog. p. 617 (1943).

Rice, Grantland. Cur. biog. p. 710 (1941). Jensen: The White House, p. 216.

Rice, Gregory. Cur. biog. p. 711 (1941).

Rice, Paul North. Cur. biog. p. 537 (1947).

rice bearer (deity). Lehner: Pict. bk. of sym., p. 49.

rice festival (Japan). Disney: People & places, p. 149 (col.).

rice field. Natl. geog. 97: 142-3 Feb '50.

—— (men working). Natl. geog. 97: 172 Feb '50.

——, Java (man plowing). Natl. geog. 108: 368-9 (col.) Sept '59.

——, Korean (men). Natl. geog. 103: 664 (col.) May '53.

——, Sumatra. Holiday 18: 104-5 Sept '55.

rice paddies, Japan. Disney: People & places, p. 148 (col.).

rice terraces. Holiday 18: 86-7 (col.) Aug '55. Natl. geog. 118: 746-7 (col.) Dec '60.

——, Bali. Natl. geog. 116: 804-5 (col.) Dec '59.

——, Formosa. Natl. geog. 111: 328-9 (col.) Mar '57.

——, India. Natl. geog. 118: 454 (col.) Oct '60.

——, Japan. Natl. geog. 104: 625 Nov '53.

——, Nepal. Natl. geog. 108: 608-9 (col.) Nov '55.

rice threshing, Malaya. Natl. geog. 103: 218 (col.) Feb '53.

Rich, Claudius James. Ceram: March of arch., p. 187.

Rich, Daniel Catton. Cur. biog. p. 506 (1955).

Rich, Louise Dickinson. Cur. biog. p. 621 (1943).

Richard, Maurice. Cur. biog. p. 359 (1958).

"The Richard" (trading ship, 1831). Amer. heri., vol. 6 no. 2 p. 14 (col.) (winter '55).

"Richard II presented to Virgin & child" (diptych)). Praeg.: Pict. ency., p. 206 (col.).

Richards, Alfred N. Cur. biog. p. 489 (1950).

Richards, Dickinson W. Cur. biog. p. 457 (1957).

Richards, James P. Cur. biog. p. 517 (1951).

Richards, John S. Cur. biog. p. 507 (1955).

Richards, Rev. Robert E. Cur. biog. p. 459 (1957).

Richards, Vincent. Cur. biog. p. 539 (1947).

Richards, Wayne E. Cur. biog. p. 535 (1954).

Richardson, Jonathan (work of). Con. 140: 234 Jan '58.

Richardson, Sir Ralph. Cur. biog. p. 491 (1950).

Richardson, Seth W. Cur. biog. p. 521 (1948).

Richardson, Tony. Cur. biog. p. 361 (1963).

Richardson, William A. Amer. heri., vol. 8 no. 3 p. 52 (Ap '57).

Richberg, Donald R. Cur. biog. p. 520 (1949).

Richmond, George (work of). Con. 144: 9 Sept '59.

Richmond, W. B. (work of). Con. 144: 10 Sept '59.

Richmond (Va.). Amer. heri., vol. 6 no. 3 p. 39 (Ap '55). Holiday 10: 90-7 (part col.) Sept '51.

—— (capitol). Amer. heri., vol. 10 no. 5 p. 69 (Aug '59).

Richmond bridge. See bridge, Richmond.

Richter, Christian (work of). Con. 141: 19 Mar '58.

Richter, Conrad. Cur. biog. p. 520 (1951).

Richter, H. C. (work of). Con. ency. of ant., vol. 3, pl. 88.

Richter, Hans. Cooper: Con. ency. of music, p. 246.

Richter, Johan (work of). Con. 144: XLIII Jan '50.

Richter, Sviatoslav. Cur. biog. p. 389 (1961).

Rickenbacker, Capt. Eddie. Holiday 24: 73 Dec '58. Travel 103: back cover May '55.

—— (in plane). Natl. geog. 112: 274 Aug '57.

Rickenbacker, Edward Vernon. Cur. biog. p. 497 (1952).

Rickey, Branch. Cur. biog. p. 498 (1945).

Rickover, Hyman G. Cur. biog. p. 525 (1953). Natl. geog. 115: 19 Jan '59.

ricks (charcoal burning). Holiday 21: 153 May '57.

ricksha. Holiday 27: 232 Ap '60.

——, Hong Kong. Holiday 14: 68 (col.) Oct '53. Natl. geog. 115: 861 Je '59.

——, Japan. Holiday 14: 74 Aug '53.

——, Java. Holiday 18: 106 (col.) Sept '55.

ricksha man (Durban, Africa). Natl. geog. 118: 333 (col.) Sept '60.

Riddell, Robert Gerald. Cur. biog. p. 493 (1950).

"Riddle book" (illus.). Amer. heri., vol. 7 no. 1 p. 116, 118-9 (Dec '55).

Riddleberger, James W. Cur. biog. p. 461 (1957).

Rideau canal locks (Canada). Natl. geog. 104: 848 (col.) Dec '53.

Ridenour, Nina. Cur. biog. p. 521 (1951).

riders, circus bareback. Durant: Pict. hist. of Amer. circus, p. 35-6, 45, 47 138 (col.).

riders, circus horse. Durant: Pict. hist. of Amer. circus, p. 262-3, 285.

riders. See also men (horseback).

Ridgway, Lt. Gen. Matthew B. Cur. biog. p. 542 (1947).

Riding mountain natl. park (Manitoba, Canada). Travel 114: 23 Jl '60.

riding school (Eng., 1770). Durant: Pict. hist. of Amer. circus, p. 17.

Ridout IV, Orlando. Holiday 23: 81 Je '58.

Riebel, John Paul. Cur. biog. p. 463 (1957).

Riecken, Henry W. Cur. biog. p. 391 (1961).

Riedlingen (Barvaria). Disney: People & places, p. 50 (col.).

Riefler, Winfield W. Cur. biog. p. 523 (1948).

Riemenschnieder, Tilman (wood carving by). Con. ency. of ant., vol. 3, pl. 54.

—— (work of). Con. 145: 136 Ap '60. Int. gr. soc.: Arts . . . p. 87 (col.).

"Rienzi" plantation. Amer. heri., vol. 4 no. 2 29 (winter '53).

Riesenberg, Felix, jr. Cur. biog. p. 465 (1957).

Riesman, David. Cur. biog. p. 509 (1955).

Riess, C. (work of). Natl. geog. 99: 203 (col.) Feb '51.

Rieve, Emil. Cur. biog. p. 509 (1946).

Rifai mosque. See mosque, Rifai.

Rifkind, Simon H. Cur. biog. p. 510 (1946).

rifle, squirrel (antique). Rawson: Ant. pict. bk., p. 35.

rifle & powder horn, Pilgrim's. Lehner: Pict. bk. of sym., p. 55.

rifles firing, U.S. navy. Natl. geog. 104: 550 (col.) Oct '53.

rifles. See also guns.

Rift Valley (Ethiopia). Holiday 25: 52-3 Ap '59.

Rigaud, Hyacinth (work of). Con. 134: 95 Nov '54; 140: 233 Jan '58.

Rigg, Edgar T. Cur. biog. p. 392 (1961).

Riggio, Vincent. Cur. biog. p. 523 (1949).

Riggs, Robert Larimore. Cur. biog. p. 525 (1949).

Rigling, Alfred. Cur. biog. p. 713 (1941).

Riiser-Larsen, Hjalmar. Cur. biog. p. 523 (1951).

Rijeka (Yugoslavia). Natl. geog. 99: 157 (col.) Feb '51.

Riley, James Whitcomb. Amer. heri., vol. 2 no. 1 p. 24 (fall '50).

Riley, Susan B. Cur. biog. p. 527 (1953).

Riley, Lt. Gen. William E. Cur. biog. p. 525 (1951).

Riley home, James Whitcomb (Indianapolis). Holiday 8: 40-1 (part col.) Aug '50.

Rillington Place (London). Holiday 19: 36-7 Jan '56.

Rimouski (Canada). Travel 111: 22 Je '59.

Rimsky-Korsakov, Nikolai Andreievich (Serov). Cooper: Con. ency. of music, p. 247.

"Rinaldo & Armida" (Poussin). Con. 132: 39 Sept '53.

"Rinaldo in the garden of Armida" (Fragonard). Con. 135: 42 Mar '55.

Rindisbacher, Peter. Amer. heri., vol. 1 no. 2 p. 10 (winter '50).

Rinehart, Mary Roberts. Holiday 10: 43 Jl '51.

Rinehart, Stanley M., jr. Cur. biog. p. 536 (1954).

ring. Holiday 26: 184 Oct '59.
——, coronation (British). Int. gr. soc.: Arts . . . p. 165 (col.).
——, coronation "wedding". Natl. geog. 104: 325 (col.) Sept '53.
——, diamond. Holiday 26: 197 Nov '59.

Ringling, Mr. & Mrs. John. Durant: Pict. hist. of Amer. circus, p. 203.

Ringling, Robert E. Cur. biog. p. 501 (1945).

Ringling family (circus). Durant: Pict. hist. of Amer. circus, p. 149.

Ringling home, John (Fla.). Durant: Pict. hist. of Amer. circus, p. 202.
Holiday 7: 93 Jan '50.

Ringling museum of art (Sarasota). Holiday 10: 7 (col.) Nov '51; 17: 5 (col.) Jan '55; 19: 16 Mar '56.
Jordan: Hammond's pict. atlas, p. 71 (col.).
Travel 102: 7 Jl '54.

rings (jewelry). Holiday 18: 164 Nov '55; 20: 115 Sept '56; 21: 168 Mar '57, 196 May '57; 22: 175 Oct '57, 253 Dec '57; 23: 173 Mar '58; 24: 149 Oct '58; 25: 172 Mar '59.
——, wedding. Con. 145: XXXVIII Mar '60. Lehner: Pict. bk. of sym., p. 56.

rings of the sergeants-at-law (Eng.). Con. 133: 26-8 Mar '54

rings. See also ring.

Rio de Janeiro. Holiday 13: 151 (col.) Ap '53; 14: 106-111 (part col.) Dec '53; 18: 10 (col.) Nov '55; 19: 44-5 (col.) Mar '56; 20: 144 Nov '56; 24: 76-85 (col.) Dec '58.
Natl. geog. 107: 290-328 (part col.) Mar '55.
—— (harbor). Holiday 5: 137 (col.) Mar '49; 6: inside cover (col.) Sept '49; 7: 75 (col.) Jan '50; 10: 146 (col.) Nov '51; 13: 13 (col.) Ap '53; 14: 12 (col.) Jl '53; 15: 28 (col.) Mar '54; 17: 10 (col.) Feb '55; 19: 125 (col.) Je '56; 20: 100-1 (col.) Nov '56; 21: 23 (col.) Ap '57; 22: 125 (col.) Sept '57; 27: 20 (col.) Je '60.
Natl. geog. 108: 748 (col.) Dec '55.
—— (night). Holiday 20: 68-9 (col.) Nov '56.
—— (women). Holiday 25: 76-7 (col.) May '59.

Rio Grande river. Holiday 20: 34-41 (part col.) Oct '56.
—— (map). Holiday 20: 36 (col.) Oct '56.

Rio Indio (Panama). Natl. geog. 104: 287 Aug '53.

Rios, Juan Antonio. Cur. biog. p. 692 (1942).

riots, draft (1863). Amer. heri., vol. 10 no. 4 p. 44-9 (Je '59).

Rip Van Winkle. Holiday 6: 35 (col.) Sept '49.
—— (book illus.). Amer. heri., vol. 8 no. 1 p. 37 (col.) (Dec '56.
"Rip Van Winkle & dog". Natl. geog. 110: 580 (col.) Nov '56.

Rip Van Winkle country (Catskills). Holiday 24: 42-3 (col.) Aug '58.

"Rip Van Winkle" steamboat. Amer. heri. vol. 10 no. 1 p. 17 (Dec '58).

"Rip Van Winkle" retreat. Travel 102: 25 Oct '54.

"The Ripetta" (Rome). Con. 141: 230 Je '58.

Ripley, Elizabeth. Cur. biog. p. 360 (1958).

Ripley, George. Amer. heri., vol. 10 no. 3 p. 62 (Ap '59).

Ripley, Robert L. Cur. biog. p. 504 (1945).

Riquewihr (Alsace). Holiday 26: 98 Aug '59.

"Rising moon on the Staffelalp" (Kirchner). Praeg.: Pict. ency., p. 446 (col.).

the rising sun (Japan). Lehner: Pict. bk. of sym., p. 47.

rising sun (sym.). Lehner: Pict. bk. of sym., p. 36.

"rising sun of Osiris" (sym.). Lehner: Pict. bk. of sym., p. 26.

"Rita Luna" (Goya). Con. 134: cover (col.) Dec '54.

Ritchard, Cyril. Cur. biog. p. 466 (1957).

Ritchie,, Jean. Cur. biog. p. 385 (1959).

Riter, Henry G., 3d. Cur. biog. p. 511 (1955).

Ritner, Ann. Cur. biog. p. 529 (1953).

Ritner, Joseph (Gov. of Penn.). Amer. heri., vol. 7 no. 3 p. 47 (Ap '56).

Rittenhouse, Mrs. Paul. Cur. biog. p. 524 (1948).

Ritter, Thelma. Cur. biog. p. 468 (1957).

river, Ohio. See Ohio river.

river boat. See boat, river; steamboat, river.

river flood. Holiday 14: 9 Aug '53.

"River God" (bronze). Con. 140: 2 (col.) Sept '57.
—— (terracotta by Pajou). Con. 140: 5 Sept '57.

River Jordan. *See* Jordan river.
River of perfumes (Indochina). Natl. geog. 102: 290-1, 306-7 (col.) Sept '52.
Rivera, Diego. Cur. biog. p. 526 (1948). Holiday 13: 41 Mar '53.
Rivers, L. Mendel. Cur. biog. p. 335 (1960).
Rivers, Thomas M. Cur. biog. p. 337 (1960).
Riverside church (New York). Holiday 16: 16 Dec '54.
Rives, Hallie Erminie. Cur. biog. p. 514 (1956).
Riviera (Adriatic coast). Travel 109: 32, 37 Ap '58.
——, **French.** Natl. geog. 111: 810 (col.) Je '57.
——, **French (clothes exhibit).** Holiday 11: 99-103 (col.) Feb '52.
——, **French coast.** Holiday 23: 50 Jan '58.
——, **Italian.** Holiday 13: 57-63 Je '53. Natl. geog. 111: 806-7 (col.) Je '57.
Rizzuto, Philip. Holiday 28: 89 Jl '60.
Rizzuto, Philip F. Cur. biog. p. 495 (1950).
Roach, Hal. Holiday 5: 36 (col.) Jan '49.
road, mt. Natl. geog. 110: 441 (col.) Oct '56.
——, **old Roman.** Natl. geog. 100: 381 Sept '51.
road rolling (1619). Brooks: Growth of a nation, p. 42.
road signs. Holiday 10: 56, 102 Dec '51; 11: 14 Mar '52, 144 Ap '52, 104 May '52; 13: 3 Mar '53; 14: 32 Jl '53, 100 Oct '53, 30 Nov '53; 27: cover (col.) Feb '60.
Natl. geog. 98: 542 Oct '50; 107: 118 (col.) Jan '55; 108: 192, 216 (col.) Aug '55; 112: 263 (col.) Aug '57; 114: 679 (col.) Nov '58.
Rawson: Ant. pict. bk. p. 44.
Travel 102: 49 Aug '54, 45 Oct '54, 46 Nov '54; 103: 60 May '55, 4 Je '55; 104: 56 Jl '55, 57 Oct '55; 107: 21 May '57; 109: 23 Feb '58; 111: 55 Je '59; 112: 30 Aug '59.
—— (African forest). Travel 113: 26 Jan '60.
—— (Bali). Travel 108: 16 Nov '57.
—— (girl). Natl. geog. 117: 327 (col.) Mar '60.
—— (Hannibal, Mo.). Natl. geog. 110: 136 Jl '56.
—— (historical). Natl. geog. 101: 481 Ap '52.
—— (snow). Holiday 11: 64 (col.) Feb '52.
—— (Switzerland). Natl. geog. 110: 441 (col.) Oct '56.
——, carved (humor). Natl. geog. 110: 443 (col.) Oct '56.
——, Moslem. Natl. geog. 104: 8 Jl '53.
"Road to Calvary". Con. 143: LXVIII May '59.
"Road to Harlech" (Cox). Con. ency., of ant., vol. 1, pl. 144.
roads, superhighway. Brooks: Growth of a nation, p. 270.
roadside marker (Chile). Natl. geog. 117: 197 (col.) Feb '60.
roadside signs. *See* road sign.
roadway. Travel 107: 14 May '57.
——, cliff (Formosa). Natl. geog. 97: 154 (col.) Feb '50.
——, mt. Travel 104: 11 Oct '55; 107: 49 Mar '57.

——, **Prince Albert Natl. Park.** Travel 110: 14 Aug '58.
——, **Rocky mt. natl. park (Trail Ridge).** Travel 106: cover Aug '56; 107: 52 Je '57.
roadway. *See also* highway.
Roan mt. (N. C.). Travel 103: 28 May '55.
Robards, Jason N., jr. Cur. biog. p. 387 (1959).
Robarts, John P. Cur. biog. p. 351 (1962).
Robb, Inez. Cur. biog. p. 362 (1958).
robber (hold-up, comic). Holiday 7: 157 May '50.
—— (stage coach hold-up). Horan: Pict. hist. of wild west, p. 84.
—— (train hold-up). Horan: Pict. hist. of wild west, p. 89.
Natl. geog. 105: 744 Je '54.
robbery, bank. Horan: Pict. hist. of wild west, p. 35.
Robbia, Della. *See* Della Robbia, Lucca.
Robbins, Frederick C. Cur. biog. p. 183 (1955).
Robbins, Jerome. Cur. biog. p. 543 (1947).
Robbins, William J. Cur. biog. p. 516 (1956).
"The robe" (motion picture scene). Natl. geog. 105: 766-7 Je '54.
robe (outdoor blanket). Holiday 10: 120 (col.) Oct '51, 29 (col.) Nov '51, 151 (col.) Dec '51.
—— (plaid blanket). Holiday 12: 4 (col.) Dec '52.
——, auto. Holiday 14: 134 (col.) Nov '53, 143 (col.) Dec '53; 18: 126 (col.) Dec '55.
robe of St. Esprit. Con. 136: 5 Sept '55.
Rubens, Alfred. Cur. biog. p. 518 (1956).
Robert, Adm. Georges. Cur. biog. p. 623 (1943).
Robert, Hubert (work of). Con. 126: 68 Aug '50; 133: XXIII Mar '54; 135: LV Je '55; 139: XLVII, 56 Mar '57; 140: 32 Sept '57.
Natl. geog. 101: 81 (col.) Jan '52.
Robert College (Turkey). Natl. geog. 112: 400, 406, 412-3 (part col.) Sept '57.
Robert Hay expedition headquarters (Egyptian excavation). Ceram: March of arch., 134.
Robert the Bruce. Holiday 27: 23 (col.) May '60.
—— (battle dress). Holiday 27: 139 (col.) Feb '60.
—— (horse, mosaic effect). Holiday 21: 26 (col.) Mar '57.
Roberti, Ercole (work of). Con. 136: 38 Sept '55.
Roberts, Capt. Bartholomew. Amer., heri., vol. 8 no. 2 p. 15 (col.) (Feb '57).
Roberts, Charles Wesley. Cur. biog. p. 530 (1953).
Roberts, Dennis J. Cur. biog. p. 519 (1956).
Roberts, Dorothy James. Cur. biog. p. 521 (1956).
Roberts, Rev. Oral. Cur. biog. p. 339 (1960).
Roberts, Owen J. Amer. heri., vol. 9 no. 3 p. 25 (Ap '58).
Cur. biog. p. 715 (1941).
Roberts, Robin. Cur. biog. p. 532 (1953).
Roberts, Roy. Holiday 7: 53 (col.) Mar '50.
Roberts, Walter Orr. Cur. biog. p. 341 (1960).
Roberts, Will. Horan: Pict. hist. of wild west. p. 192.

Roberts, Will. (work of). Con. 132: 50 Sept '53.
Roberts, William Goodridge. Cur. biog. p. 513 (1955).
Robertson, A. Willis. Cur. biog. p. 527 (1949).
Robertson, Andrew (miniature by). Con. ency. of ant., vol. 1, pl. 132.
Robertson, Archibald & Alexander (work of). Con. ency. of ant., vol. 3, pl. 90.
Robertson, Ben, jr. Cur. biog. p. 694 (1942).
Robertson, Beverly Holcombe. Pakula: Cent. album, p. 241.
Robertson, Sir Brian. Cur. biog. p. 529 (1948).
Robertson, Constance. Cur. biog. p. 512 (1946).
Robertson, David B. Cur. biog. p. 496 (1950).
Robertson, George (work of). Con. ency. of ant., vol. 1, pl. 147.
Robertson, Norman A. Cur. biog. p. 469 (1957).
Robertson, Reuben B., jr. Cur. biog. p. 515 (1955).
Robertson, Robert B. Cur. biog. p. 471 (1957).
Robertson, Thomas E. Amer. heri., vol. 9 no. 2 p. 18 (Feb '58).
Robertson, Walter S. Cur. biog. p. 534 (1953).
Robertson, William. Amer. heri., vol. 9 no. 2 p. 56 (col.) (Feb '58).
robes (ancient royal). Int. gr. soc.: Arts . . . p. 29 (col.).
——, Chinese court. Con. 126: 11-8 Aug '50.
——, Chinese court & dragon. Con. 126: 95-105 Oct '50, 206 Dec '50.
——, coronation. See coronation robes.
robes of the Order of the Bath. Con. 134: 153-9 Dec '54.
Robeson, Eslanda Goode. Cur. biog. p. 505 (1945).
Robeson, George M. Amer. heri., vol. 8 no. 3 p. 52 (Ap '57).
Robeson, Paul. Cur. biog. p. 717 (1941).
Robey, Ralph W. Cur. biog. p. 719 (1941).
Robin Hood (book illus.). Amer. heri., vol. 8 no. 1 p. 34 (Dec '56).
—— (re-enacted). Holiday 22: 10 (col.) Nov 57.
Robin Hood's band (play). Natl. geog. 108: 330 (col.) Sept '55.
Robin Hood's Bay (Yorkshire, Eng.). Holiday 23: 74-5 (col.) Ap '58.
Robinson, Senator. Amer. heri., vol. 9 no. 3 p. 24 (Ap '58).
Robinson, Bill. Cur. biog. p. 720 (1941). Holiday 7: 65 Mar '50; 24: 17 (col.) Aug '58.
Robinson, Boardman. Cur. biog. p. 721 (1941).
Robinson, Edward G. Cur. biog. p. 498 (1950).
Robinson, Elmer E. Cur. biog. p. 517 (1955).
Robinson, H. R. (cartoon). Amer. heri., vol. 7 no. 4 p. 11 (Je '56).
Robinson, Henrietta. Amer. heri., vol. 3 no. 3 p. 13 (spring '52).
Robinson, Henry M. Amer. heri., vol. 9 no. 5 p. 33. (Aug '58).
Cur. biog. p. 500 (1950).
Robinson, Irene B. Jun. bk. of auth., p. 259.
Robinson, Jackie. Cur. biog. p. 545 (1947).
—— (baseball). Holiday 7: 50 May '50.
Robinson, Mabel Louise. Jun. bk. of auth., p. 257.
Robinson, Maurice R. Cur. biog. p. 523 (1956).

Robinson, Ray. Cur. biog. p. 528 (1951).
Robinson, Vice Adm. Samuel M. Cur. biog. p. 696 (1942).
Robinson, Spottswood W., 3d. Cur. biog. p. 353 (1962).
Robinson, Sugar Ray (Negro boxing champion). Holiday 27: 77 Je '60.
Robinson, Tom. Jun. bk. of auth., p. 258.
Robinson, William E. Cur. biog. p. 363 (1958).
robot. Holiday 11: 130 Ap '52.
—— (sym.). Lehner: Pict. bk. of sym., p. 95.
Robson, Flora. Cur. biog. p. 529 (1951).
Robus, Hugo. Cur. biog. p. 354 (1962).
Robus statue ("Girl washing hair"). Holiday 14: 58 Nov '53.
Rocamadour (France). Holiday 24: 128 (col.) Sept '58.
Rochambeau, Jean Baptiste de. Amer. heri., vol. 7 no. 2 p. 69 (Feb '56).
Roche, Josephine. Cur. biog. p. 723 (1941).
"Rochester bridge & castle" (Wheatley). Con. 129: XIII Je '52.
rock bridge. See bridge, rock.
rock carvings, ritual. Osward: Asia Minor, pl. 1.
Rock City garden (Lookout Mt.). Natl. geog. 105: 302 (col.) Mar '54.
rock cliffs (Mexico). Natl. geog. 107: 222-3 (col.) Feb '55.
rock-climbing (man). Holiday 10: 34 (col.) Aug '51.
rock crevice (men exploring). Natl. geog. 103: 278 Feb '53.
rock dwelling (near Samandag). Osward: Asia Minor, pl. 23.
rock fence (Ireland). Natl. geog. 108: 743 (col.) Dec '55.
rock formations. Natl. geog. 112: 183, 191 (col.) Aug '57.
rock gardens (Hamilton, Canada). Natl. geog. 104: 841 (col.) Dec '53.
"Rock of ages" (lighthouse). Jordan: Hammond's pict. atlas, p. 91 (col.).
Rock of Cashel (Ireland). Holiday 20: 108 (col.) Aug '56.
Rock of Gibraltar. Holiday 15: 23 Feb '54.
Rock of Perce (Gaspe, Canada). Jordan: Hammond's pict. atlas, p. 21 (col.).
rock painting (stone age). Praeg.: Pict. ency., p. 105 (col.).
rock salt (sym.). Lehner: Pict. bk. of sym., p. 73.
rock spires. See spires, rock.
rock strata. Natl. geog. 97: 708 (col.) Je '50.
Rock temple of Yazilikaya. See Yazilikaya, rock temple.
rock temple. See temple, rock.
rock wall. Holiday 23: 116 (col.) Mar '58. Natl. geog. 98: 106 (col.) Jl '50.
—— (flowers). Natl. geog. 103: 361 (col.) Mar '53.
Rockefeller, David. Cur. biog. p. 389 (1959). Holiday 24: 32 Aug '58.
Rockefeller, John D. Amer. heri., vol. 6 no. 3 p. 65 (Ap '55). Holiday 24: 73-5 Sept '58.
Rockefeller, John D., jr. Cur. biog. p. 726 (1941).

Rockefeller, John D., jr. (& his wife). Holiday 24: 53 Oct '58.

Rockefeller, John D., 3d. Cur. biog. p. 538 (1953).
Holiday 24: 29 Aug '58.

Rockefeller, Laurance. Holiday 24: 35 (col.) Aug '58.

Rockefeller, Laurance S. Cur. biog. p. 391 (1959).

Rockefeller, Nelson. Cur. biog. p. 729 (1941).
Holiday 24: 26 (col.) Aug '58.

Rockefeller, Nelson A. Cur. biog. p. 531 (1951).

Rockefeller, Winthrop. Cur. biog. p. 393 (1959).
Holiday 24: 30 (col.) Aug '58.

Rockefeller brothers (at table). Holiday 24: 87 (col.) Nov '58.

Rockefeller Center (N. Y.). Holiday 15: 52-8 (col.) Ap '54.

Rockefeller memorial chapel (int.). Holiday 28: 78 (col.) Dec '60.

rocker with baby holder (antique). Rawson: Ant. pict. bk., p. 14.

rocket. Natl. geog. 98: 513-20 (part col.) Oct '50; 109: 286 Feb '56, 490-3 (col.) Ap '56; 111: 567, 571-80 Ap '57; 116: 438 (col.) Oct '59.
Travel 114: 31-2 Oct '60.

—— (balloon borne). Natl. geog. 109: 287 Feb '56.

—— (fired by plane). Natl. geog. 104: 760 (col.) Dec '53.

—— (man & woman riding). Holiday 7: 74 (col.) Je '50; 8: 90 (col.) Sept '50, 2 (col.) Nov '50; 12: 17 (col.) Oct '52.

—— (monkey). Natl. geog. 118: 56-7 (col.) Jl '60.

—— (woman riding). Holiday 10: 24 (col.) Jl '51, 13 (col.) Sept '51, 67 (col.) Nov '51.

——, balloon. Natl. geog. 111: 567, 569 Ap '57.

rocket blasts off. Natl. geog. 112: 790 (col.) Dec '57; 117: 673 (col.) May '60.

rocket blockhouse. Natl. geog. 98: 515 (col.) Oct '50.

rocket crash (men). Natl. geog. 98: 518-20 (col.) Oct '50.

rocket explosion. Holiday 16: 34 (col.) Sept '54.

rocket "Pioneer I". Natl. geog. 115: 158-66 (part col.) Feb '59.

rocket "Pioneer II". Natl. geog. 115: 167 Feb '59.

rocket "Pioneer III" (man). Natl. geog. 115: 170 Feb '59.

rocket ship. Natl. geog. 108: 270 (col.) Aug '55.

rocket tower. See tower, rocket.

rockets. Natl. geog. 106: 110-11 (col.) Jl '54; 118: 60-3, 69-71, 81, 88-9 (col.) Jl '60, 294 (col.) Aug '60.

——, fire (for parties). Lehner: Pict. bk. of sym., p. 53.

rockets. See also fireworks.

——, sky. See sky rockets.

——, U.S. Air force. U.S. News & world report, p. 47, 56-7 Aug. 31, 1964.

rocking chair. Jensen: The White House, p 174.

—— (in which Lincoln was shot). Natl. geog. 114: 115 (col.) Jl '58.

——, child's. Holiday 12: 13 Jl '52.
Natl. geog. 106: 650 (col.) Nov '54.

rocking horse (toy). Holiday 11: 11 Je '52; 12: 174 Dec '52.

rockoon (balloon rocket). Natl. geog. 111: 568-9 Ap '57.

Rockport (Mass., harbor). Holiday 24: 2 (col.) Jl '58.
Natl. geog. 98: 157 (col.) Aug '50.
Travel 107: 18 May '57.

rocks, pancake. See pancake rocks.

Rockwell, Norman. Cur. biog. p. 507 (1945).

Rocky mts. (Colo.). Face of Amer., p. 92-3 (col.).
Holiday 12: 42-3 (col.) Sept '52; 18: 98-9 (col.) Jl '55.

—— (map). Holiday 18: 101 Jl '55.

——, Canadian. See Canadian rockies.

Rocky mt. natl. park. Natl. geog. 113: 612-3 (col.) May '58.
Travel 107: 52-4 Je '57.

rodeo. Holiday 12: 45 Sept '52.
Natl. geog. 114: 164-5 (col.) Aug '58; 117: 492 (col.) Ap '60.
Travel 105: 40 Mar '56.

—— (clown, horse). Holiday 12: 45 Sept '52.

—— (queens & cowboy rider). Natl. geog. 114: 164-4 (col.) Aug '58.

—— (riders). Holiday 16: 84 Aug '54, 8 Sept '54.

Rodgers, Richard. Cur. biog. p. 533 (1951).

Rodin, Auguste (bronze figure). Con. 143: 92 Ap '59.

—— (work of). Con. 140: VIII Sept '57; 143: XXII May '59.
Int. gr. soc.: Arts . . . p. 131 (col.).
Praeg.: Pict. ency., p. 14, 398.

Rodino, Peter W., jr. Cur. biog. p. 538 (1954).

Rodman gun. See gun, Rodman.

Rodney, Adm. Lord George Brydges. Amer. heri., vol. 9 no. 4 p. 4 (col.) (Je '58).
Holiday 8: 15 (col.) Aug '50.

Roebling, John. Amer. heri., vol. 7 no. 6 p. 68 (Oct '56).

Roebling, Mary G. Cur. biog. p. 343 (1960).

Roebling, Washington. Amer. heri., vol. 7 no. 6 p. 70 (Oct '56).

Roemer, Shuckburgh. Con. 145: 271 Je '60.

Roese, H. (work of). Amer. heri., vol. 10 no. 1 p. 24-5 (col.) (Dec '58).

Roger Williams Assoc., meeting. Holiday 11: 110 (col.) Aug '52.

Roger Williams park (R. I.). Holiday 11: 115 (col.) May '52.

Roger Williams statue. See statue (Roger Williams).

Rogers, Annie. Horan: Pict. hist. of wild west, p. 228.

Rogers, Bruce. Cur. biog. p. 513 (1946).

Rogers, Buddy. Holiday 10: 65 Dec '51.

Rogers, Carl R. Cur. biog. p. 357 (1962).

Rogers, Dale Evans. Cur. biog. p. 526 (1956).

Rogers, Edith Nourse. Cur. biog. p. 698 (1942).

Rogers, Frank B. Cur. biog. p. 359 (1962).

Rogers, Ginger. Cur. biog. p. 731 (1941). Holiday 21: 85 (col.) May '57, 179 Je '57.
Rogers, Michael. Horan: Pict. hist. of wild west, p. 71.
Rogers, Paul. Cur. biog. p. 345 (1960).
Rogers, Richard. Holiday 25: 91 Feb '59.
Rogers, Robert. Amer. heri., vol. 5 no. 2 p. 19 (winter 1953-54).
Rogers, Roy. Cur. biog. p. 532 (1948).
Rogers, Rutherford David. Cur. biog. p. 361 (1962).
Rogers, Will. Holiday 7: 65 Mar '50.
—— (head). Holiday 21: 98 Jan '57.
—— (statue). Brooks: Growth of a nation, p. 297.
Rogers, Will, jr. Cur. biog. p. 541 (1953). Holiday 12: 36 Oct '52; 20: 143 Dec '56.
Rogers, William P. Cur. biog. p. 365 (1958).
Rogers memorial, Will (Claremont, Okla.). Jordan: Hammond's pict. atlas, p. 112 (col.).
"Roger's Rock" battle. Amer. heri., vol. 6 no. 5 p. 12 (col.) (Aug '55).
Rogers shrine, Will. Holiday 21: 98 Nov '57; 23: 104 May '58.
Rogge, Oetje John. Cur. biog. p. 534 (1948).
Rognosa tower (Italy). Holiday 27: 62 (col.) Jan '60.
Rogue river. Travel 104: 22 Aug '55.
Rohr, Frank, jr. Travel 101: 33 Mar '54.
Rojankovsky, Feodor. Jun. bk. of auth., p. 261.
Rokossovsky, Konstantin. Cur. biog. p. 559 (1944).
Rolfe, A. F. (art by). Con. 138: XII Sept '56.
Roll, Georg (globes). Con. 126: 167-72 Dec '50.
roller, broom making. See broom making roller.
——, land. Rawson: Ant. pict. bk., p. 30.
——, tobacco. Rawson: Ant. pict. bk., p. 70.
roller coaster. Holiday 21: 70-1 (col.) Feb '57.
rolling chair (Atlantic City). Holiday 12: 93 Aug '52; 18: 14 Jl '55.
—— (riders). Natl. geog. 117: 42 (col.) Jan '60.
rolling pin. Rawson: Ant. pict. bk., p. 7.
Rollins, Carl Purington. Cur. biog. p. 536 (1948).
Rolls Royce auto (1959). Int. gr. soc.: Arts . . . p. 161 (col.).
Roman, Nancy G. Cur. biog. p. 346 (1960).
Roman amphitheater (Tunisia). Holiday 25: 150 (col.) Ap '59.
Roman aqueduct. Holiday 16: 111 Nov '54. Natl. geog. 97: 449 (col.) Ap '50; 111: 478 (col.) Ap '57. Travel 107: 59 Ap '57.
—— (Pont du Gard). Praeg.: Pict. ency., p. 146.
Roman arena (gladiators & wild animals). Int. gr. soc.: Arts . . . p. 35 (col.).
—— (Nimes). Holiday 7: 23 May '50.
Roman bath (Bath, Eng.). Holiday 26: 53 (col.) Aug '59.
Roman bridge. See bridge, Roman.
Roman catacomb painting (ancient). Int. gr. soc.: Arts . . . p. 21 (col.).
Roman circus. Int. gr. soc.: Arts . . . p. 35

(col.).
Roman colosseum. Durant: Pict. hist. of Amer. circus, p. 5.
Holiday 7: 10 (col.) Jan '50, 66 Feb '50; 11: 34 (col.) Ap '52; 22: 107 (col.) Nov '57; 23: 157 (col.) Ap '58; 24: 105 Oct '58; 27: 129 Jan '60.
Natl. geog. 111: 450-1 (col.) Ap '57.
Praeg.: Pict. ency., p. 142.
Roman family (eating at table). Holiday 5: 64 (col.) Je '49.
Roman fort gateway at Cologne (Deutz). Con. 138: 234 Jan '57.
Roman Forum. Con. 136: 127 Nov '55; 141: 232 Je '58.
Holiday 11: 67 Jan '52, 34-5 (col.) Ap '52; 27: 75, 222 (col.) Ap '60.
Natl. geog. 111: 455 (col.) Ap '57.
Travel 103: inside cover Jan '55.
—— (plan). Praeg.: Pict. ency. p. 155.
Roman home (int., ancient). Int. gr. soc.: Arts . . . p. 11, 15 (col.)
Roman legionary (ancient times). Int. gr. soc.: Arts . . . p. 33 (col.).
roman life (1600 year-old pictures). Natl. geog. 111: 210-28 (part col.) Feb '57.
Roman men (playing marbles, ancient times). Int. gr. soc.: Arts . . . p. 37 (col.).
"Roman picture gallery" (Pannini). Con. 141: 229 Je '58.
Roman rock dwelling (Samandag). Osward: Asia Minor, pl. 23.
Roman soldiers (ancient times). Int. gr. soc.: Arts . . . p. 33 (col.).
Roman, temple See temple, Roman.
Roman theater & arena (Arles). Natl. geog. 109: 672-3 May '56.
Roman tombs. Ceram: March of arch., p. 31.
Roman wall painting. See wall painting, Roman.
Roman woman playing cithara. Ceram: March of arch., p. 31 (col.).
Romanesque architecture. See architecture, Romanesque.
Romanesque capitals. See capitals, Romanesque.
Romanino, Girolamo (work of). Natl. geog. 101: 93 (col.) Jan '52.
Romano, Giulio (work of). Con. 133: 139 Ap '54.
Romano, Umberto. Cur. biog. p. 540 (1954).
Romanoff, Alexis L. Cur. biog. p. 543 (1953).
Romanoff, Mike. Holiday 22: 77 Oct '57.
Romans. Natl. geog. 108: 720 Nov '55.
—— (chariot). Int. gr. soc.: Arts . . . p. 43 (col.).
—— (in home, ancient). Int. gr. soc.: Arts . . . p. 15 (col.).
Romayne work (ornament). Con. ency. of ant., vol. 1, p. 21.
Rombauer, Irma. Cur. biog. p. 545 (1953).
Romberg, Sigmund. Cur. biog. p. 510 (1945).
Rome, Harold J. Cur. biog. p. 700 (1942).
Rome (Italy). Con. 141: 229-33 Je '58; 144: LXVII (col.) Jan '60.
Holiday 11: 34-57 (part col.) Ap '52; 25: 177 Ap '59; 27: 129 Jan '60, 2, 19, 67-111, 222 (part col.) Ap '60.

Natl. geog. 111: 438-91 (part col.) Ap '57; 117: 590-1, 596 (col.) May '60.
Travel 101: inside cover May '54.
Rome (airview). Holiday 28: 5 (col.) Jl '60.
—— (Arch of Constantine). Praeg.: Pict. ency., p. 141.
—— (circus). Durant: Pict. hist. of Amer. circus, p. 4-6.
—— (colosseum). See Roman colosseum.
—— (18th cent.). Con. 141: 265 Je '58; 142: 203 Dec '58.
—— (map). Holiday 11: 42-3 (col.) Ap '52. Natl. geog. 111: 444-5 (col.) Ap '57.
—— (Pallavicini palace). See Pallavicini palace.
—— (Pantheon). See Pantheon (Rome).
—— (street Trastevere). Holiday 27: 44 Ap '60.
—— (Trajan's column). See Trajan's column.
—— (triumphal procession). Int. gr. soc.: Arts . . . p. 41 (col.).
Romeo & Juliet (comic). Holiday 22: 144 Nov '57; 26: 25 Aug '59.
romer (antique glass). Con. ency. of ant., vol. 1, p. 80.
Rommel, Gen. Field Marshall Erwin. Cur. biog. p. 701 (1942).
Romney, George. Cur. biog. p. 367 (1958).
—— (work of). Con. 134: LVI, 49 Sept '54; 135: 50 Mar '55; 136: LVII Sept '55, XXVII Nov '55, 247 (col.) Jan '56; 137: 213 May '56; 142: 189 (col.) Dec '58; 143: 117, 121 Ap '59; 145: 43 (col.) Mar '60, 114 Ap '60, XXXIX, LXXXV (part col.) May '60.
Romney, John (work of). Con. 143: 88-9 Ap '59.
Romulo, Col. Carlos P. Cur. biog p. 627 (1943); p. 473 (1957).
Romulus & Remus (she wolf). Holiday 27: cover (col.) Ap '60. Natl. geog. 111: 476 Ap '57.
—— (terracotta). Con. 140: 3 Sept '57.
Ronchamp chapel. See chapel at Ronchamp.
Ronchamp church (France). See church, Ronchamp.
rondavels (Africa's tourist cabins). Natl. geog. 104: 198 Aug '53.
Rondavels hotel (Africa). Travel 104: 65 Nov '55.
Roney, Marianne. Cur. biog. p. 115 (1957).
Rongier, J. (work of). Cooper: Con. ency. of music, p. 97.
Ronne, Finn. Cur. biog. p. 538 (1948).
roof (men thatching). Natl. geog. 107: 872 Je '55.
——, house. See house roof (Nigerian).
——, thatch. See house, thatch roof.
——, tile (Azores house). Natl. geog. 113: 749 (col.) Je '58.
——, (Chinese). Con. 141: XLVI Ap '58.
——, types of. Praeg.: Pict. ency., p. 85.
roof garden. See garden, rooftop.
Rooks, Maj. Gen. Lowell W. Cur. biog. p. 548 (1947).
room (int.). Con. 139: 2-5 (part col.) Mar '57. Holiday 27: 181 (col.) Je '60; 28: 145 (col.) Nov '60.
—— (1835). Amer. heri., vol. 11 no. 5 p. 15 (col.) (Aug '60).

—— (Provincetown, Mass., 200 yrs. old). Holiday 22: 202 (col.) Dec '57.
——, bed. See bedroom.
——, colonial. Natl. geog. 109: 447, 450, 461, 463, 468, 472 477, 479-81, 483 (part col.) Ap '56.
——, D A R Mem. Cont. Hall. (int.) Natl. geog. 100: 586-93 (col.) Nov '51.
——, Eng. country home. (int.) Con. 140: 210 (col.) Jan '58.
——, Eng. Tudor (16th cent. int.) Int. gr. soc.: Arts . . . p. 103 (col.).
——, library (early style). Con. 142: 208 (col.) Jan '59.
——, Louis XV. Con. 133: 245-6 Je '54.
——, Louis XVI. Con. 133: 246, 291 Je '54.
——, Mazarine period. Con. 142: 207 Jan '59.
——, Piedmontese lacquer. Con. 138: 210 Dec '56.
——, Woburn Abbey. Con. 141: opp. p. 205 (col.), 207, 209-10 Je '58.
——, Woburn Abbey (bedroom). Con. 141: opp. p. 205 (col.) Je '58.
room panelling. Con. 138: LVII Jan '57.
Rooney, Mickey. Cur. biog. p. 705 (1942).
Roosa, Robert V. Con. biog. p. 363 (1962).
Roosevelt, Alice. Jensen: The White House, p. 182, 185, 188.
Roosevelt, Anna Eleanor. Cur. biog. p. 529 (1949).
Roosevelt, Mrs. Eleanor (Mrs. F. D.). Holiday 6: 43 (col.) Sept '49; 24: 73 Dec '58. Jensen: The White House, p. 236, 241, 244.
Roosevelt, Elliott. Cur. biog. p. 516 (1946).
Roosevelt, Pres. Franklin Delano. Amer. heri., vol. 6 no. 2 p. 66, 68, 83 (winter '55); vol. 7 no. 3 p. 33 (Ap '56); vol. 8 no. 3 p. 39 (Ap '57); vol. 10 no. 4 p. 22 (Je '59).
Cur. biog. p. 707 (1942).
Holiday 5: 22 Jan '49; 7: 36 Mar '50. Jensen: The White House, p. 234, 238-46. Natl. geog. 112: 47 Jl '57.
—— (cartoon). Amer. heri., vol. 6 no. 3 p. 109 (Ap '55); vol. 9 no. 3 p. 106 (Ap '58).
—— (convention, 1932). Holiday 10: 55 Oct '51.
—— (stamp). Holiday 27: 63 Je '60.
Roosevelt, Pres. F. D. (with Sen. Robinson). Amer. heri., vol. 9 no. 3 p. 24 (Ap '58).
Roosevelt, Mr. & Mrs. F. D. Jensen: The White House, p. 236, 241.
Roosevelt, Franklin D., jr. Cur. biog. p. 502 (1950).
Roosevelt, James. Cur. biog. p. 504 (1950).
Roosevelt, Quentin. Jensen: The White House, p. 182.
Roosevelt, Pres. Theodore. Amer. heri., vol. 4 no. 1 p. 52 (fall '52); vol. 6 no. 1 p. 43 (fall '54); vol. 6 no. 6 p. 56 (Oct '55); vol. 7 no. 2 p. 20 (Feb '56); vol. 7 no. 3 p. 33 (Ap '56); vol. 8 no. 5 p. 27 (Aug '57); vol. 9 no. 1 p. 99 (Dec '57); vol. 10 no. 5 p. 20 (Aug '59); vol. 11 no. 4 p. 32, 79 (Je '60); vol. 11 no. 6 p. 54 (Oct '60); vol. 12 no. 1 p. 117 (Dec '60).
Brooks: Growth of a nation, p. 228.
Horan: Pict. hist. of wild west, p. 69.

Jensen: The White House, p. 180, 191.
Natl. geog. 101: 147 Feb '52; 114: 573-90
Oct '58.
—— (Black Hill sculpt.). Natl. geog. 99: 720
(col.) Je '51; 110: 497 Oct '56.
—— (1878). Amer. heri., vol. 9 no. 2 p. 62
(Feb '58).
—— (campaign poster, "Teddy"). Amer. heri.,
vol. 7 no. 4 p. 27 (col.) (Je '56).
—— (cartoon, "Teddy"). Amer. heri., vol. 7
no. 2 p. 97-9 (Feb '56); vol. 11 no. 4 p. 30
(Je '60).
—— (cartoon, "Trust buster"). Amer. heri.,
vol. 11 no. 6 p. 92 (Oct '60).
Roosevelt, Mrs. Theodore. Amer. heri., vol. 6
no. 4 p. 25 (Je '55); vol. 9 no. 2 p. 63
(Feb '58).
Jensen: The White House, p. 182, 190.
Roosevelt, Theodore, jr. Jensen: The White
House, p. 182-3.
Roosevelt, Mrs. Theodore, jr. Natl. geog. 111:
745 (col.), 746 Je '57.
Roosevelt dam (Ariz.). Brooks: Growth of a
nation, p. 230.
Roosevelt family, Franklin Delano. Jensen:
The White House, p. 236.
Roosevelt family, Theodore. Jensen: The
White House, p. 182.
Roosevelt grandchildren, Franklin D. Jensen:
The White House, p. 237, 246.
Roosevelt home, Franklin D. Holiday 6: 43
(col.) Sept '49.
Roosevelt home, Theodore. Holiday 24: 41
Sept '58.
—— (int.). Natl. geog. 112: 314-5 (col.) Sept
'57.
Roosevelt library, Franklin D. Holiday 6: 46
(col.) Sept '49.
Roosevelt statue, Theodore. Natl. geog. 118:
792 (col.) Dec '60.
Roosevelt grave, Franklin D. Holiday 6: 49
(col.) Sept '49.
Roosevelt's letter to his son (illus). Amer. heri.,
vol. 10 no. 1 p. 128 (Dec '58).
rooster (sym.). Lehner: Pict. bk. of sym., p.
57, 84.
Root, Elihu. Amer. heri., vol. 6 no. 6 p. 56
(Oct '55).
Root, Oren. Cur. biog. p. 499 (1952).
Root, Waverley. Cur. biog. p. 629 (1943).
root beer cart. Amer. heri., vol. 6 no. 4 p. 46
(col.) (Je '55).
root box, Portuguese. Con. 137: 74 Mar '56.
Rootes, Sir William. Cur. biog. p. 537 (1951).
Rooth, Ivar. Cur. biog. p. 502 (1952).
rope. Holiday 24: cover (col.) Oct '58.
Natl. geog. 107: 5 (col.) Jan '55.
—— (knotted). Amer. heri., vol. 11 no. 5 p.
32 (col.) (Aug '60).
—— (3 ft. thick). Natl. geog. 107: 280 Feb
'55.
rope making. Amer. heri., vol. 3 no. 3 p. 35
(spring '52).
Natl. geog. 98: 198 Aug '50.
—— (Tristan). Natl. geog. 97: 110 (col.) Jan
'50.
rope noose. Amer. heri., vol. 7 no. 2 p. 72
(Feb '56).

rope walker (circus). Durant: Pict. hist. of
Amer. circus, p. 189, 200, 278.
—— (Cambodia). Natl. geog. 117: 550 (col.)
Ap '60.
—— (Niagra, 1859). Amer. heri., vol. 12 no.
1 p. 116 (Dec '60).
Roper, Elmo B., jr. Cur. biog. p. 513 (1945).
Ropes, George (work of). Amer. heri., vol. 6
no. 2 p. 10-11 (col.) (fall '55).
Rorimer, James J. Cur. biog. p. 519 (1955).
Rosa, Salvator (work of). Con. 142: LI Jan
'59; 145: XXXII (col.) Ap '60, XLV May
'60.
"Rosalie" (old Natchez, 1823, home model).
Natl. geog. 100: 595 (col.) Nov '51.
rosary (sym.). Lehner: Pict. bk. of sym., p. 37.
Travel 109: 23 Ap '58.
Rose, Alex. Cur. biog. p. 395 (1959).
Rose, Della. Horan: Pict. hist. of wild west,
p. 200.
Rose, Murray. Cur. biog. p. 365 (1962).
Rose, William C. Cur. biog. p. 546 (1953).
Rose, Fort (Russian, Cal.). See Fort Rose.
rose bowl (antique silver). Con. 136: XV Jan
'56.
—— (silver modern). Con. 144: 37 Sept '59.
"Rose bowl" stadium. Holiday 11: 97 Jan '52.
rose festival (Portland). Travel 101: 10 Ap
'54; 111: 19 May '50.
rose festival queen. Natl. geog. 105: 301 (col.)
Mar '54.
"Rose Hill" (Colonial house, Va.). Natl. geog.
109: 484 (col.) Ap '56.
Rose-red city of Petra. See Petra, Rose-red
city.
rose show (Cincinnati). Natl. geog. 107: 470
(col.) Ap '55.
rose window, church. Holiday 24: 131 (col.)
Nov '58.
Praeg.: Pict. ency., p. 248.
Rosecrans, Williams. Pakula: Cent. album, p.
243.
Roselli, Cosimo (fresco detail). Con. 139: 100
Ap '57.
Rosellini, Albert Dean. Cur. biog. p. 369
(1958).
Rosello, Joaquin Lugue (work of). Con. 129:
LII Je '52.
"Rosemont" home (Ala). Holiday 27: cover
(col.) Mar '60.
Rosen, Albert. Cur. biog. p. 542 (1954).
Rosenbach, Abraham S. W. Cur. biog. p. 518
(1946).
Rosenberg, Alfred. Cur. biog. p. 733 (1941).
Rosenberg, Mrs. Anna. A. Cur. biog. p. 540
(1951).
Rosenberg, Anna M. Cur. biog. p. 631 (1943).
Rosenberg, Charles G. (work of). Natl. geog.
99: 196 (col.) Feb '51.
"Rosendal" (Norwegian manor house, int. &
ext.). Con. 145: 2 (col.), 3-6 Mar '60.
Rosenfeld, Henry. Cur. biog. p. 539 (1948).
Rosenfield, Harry N. Cur. biog. p. 503 (1952).
Rosenman, Samuel I. Cur. biog. p. 715 (1942).
Rosenman, Mrs. Samuel I. Cur. biog. p. 550
(1947).
Rosenstock, Joseph. Cur. biog. p. 544 (1954).
Rosenthal, A. M. Cur. biog. p. 348 (1960).
Rosenthal, Joe. Cur. biog. p. 516 (1945).

Rosenwald, B. M. (work of). Con. 126: 51 Aug '50.
Rosenwald, Lessing J. Cur. biog. p. 552 (1947).
Rosetta stone. Ceram: March of arch., p. 87.
rosette, whorl. Praeg.: Pict. ency., p. 85.
Rosetti, Dante Gabriel (work of). Con. 132: XXXIX (col.) Jan '54.
Rosewall, Ken. Cur. biog. p. 531 (1956).
rosewater dish (antique). Con. 134: 148 Nov '54.
—— (17th cent.). Con. 135: XXXVI Ap '55.
——, Romer (18th cent.). Con. 145: XLVI Ap '60.
Rosh Hashanah (New Year). Lehner: Pict. bk. of sym., p. 55.
Rosicrucian park (San Jose, Cal.). Travel 114: 41 Sept '60.
Rosicrucian woman (head). Travel 110: 47 Nov '58.
Roslin, Alexander (work of). Con. 135: 46 Mar '55; 141: cover (col.) Mar '58.
rosquillas, Basque. Natl. geog. 105: 186 Feb '54.
Ross, Betsy (with U.S. flag). Travel 110: 31 Jl '58.
Ross, Charles. Cur. biog. p. 519 (1945).
Ross, Sir Edmund. Travel 106: back cover Oct '56.
Ross, Harold W. Cur. biog. p. 635 (1943).
Ross, Lanny. Holiday 10: 78 Jl '51, 82 Dec '51.
Ross, Malcolm. Cur. biog. p. 563 (1944).
Ross, Nancy Wilson. Cur. biog. p. 506 (1952).
Ross, Sir W. C. (miniature). Con. ency. of ant., vol. 1, pl. 132.
Ross house, Betsy. See Betsy Ross house (Phila.).
Rossel, Agda V. J. Cur. biog. p. 397 (1959).
Rosselli, Cosimo (work of). Con. 136: 37 Sept '55.
Rossellini, Roberto. Cur. biog. p. 533 (1949). Holiday 27: 127 Ap '60.
Rossen, Robert. Cur. biog. p. 507 (1950).
Rosser, Thomas Lafayette. Amer. heri., vol. 9 no. 2 p. 31 (Feb '58). Pakula: Cent. album, p. 245.
Rossetti, Dante Gabriel (work of). Con. 141: IX (col.) Je '58. Praeg.: Pict. ency., p. 399.
Rossini, Gioacchino Antonio. Cooper: Con. ency. of music, p. 248.
Rossiter, Thomas P. Amer. heri., vol. 10 no. 1 p. 20 (col.) (Dec '58).
Rostand, Jean. Cur. biog. p. 546 (1954).
Rosten, Leo C. Cur. biog. p. 718 (1942). Holiday 5: 43 (col.) Jan '49.
Rosten, Norman. Cur. biog. p. 568 (1944).
Rostow, Eugene V. Cur. biog. p. 394 (1961).
Rostow, Walt W. Cur. biog. p. 396 (1961).
rostral column. See column, rostral (sym.).
Rostrand painter's work. See dishes, Rostrand faience.
Roth, Almon E. Cur. biog. p. 521 (1946).
Rotha, Paul. Cur. biog. p. 475 (1957).
Rothenburg (Germany). Travel 107: 6 Ap '57.
Rothenburg festival costumes. See costumes, Rothenburg festival.
Rothenburg ob der Tauber (Germany). Holiday 25: 54-5 (col.) May '59.

Rothenstein, Sir John. Cur. biog. p. 477 (1957).
Rothermere, Viscount Esmond Cecil H. Cur. biog. p. 541 (1948).
Rothermere, Lord Harold S. Cur. biog. p. 736 (1941).
Rothermere silver. Con. 139: 29-32 Mar '57.
Rothery, Agnes. Cur. biog. p. 523 (1946).
Rothko, Mark. Cur. biog. p. 398 (1961).
Rothschild, Baron Ferdinand de. Con. 143: 205 Je '59.
Rothschild, James de. Con. 143: 205 Je '59.
Rothschild, Louis S. Cur. biog. p. 479 (1957).
Rothschild, Baron Phillipe de. Holiday 26: 97 Aug '59.
rotisserie. Holiday 11: 20 Jan '52.
rotocycle (man). Natl. geog. 115: 537 (col.) Ap '59.
Rotta, Antonio (work of). Con. 133: XXV Ap '54.
Rotterdam (Holland). Natl. geog. 118: 526-52 (col.) Oct '60.
—— (plan). Natl. geog. 118: 534-5 (col.) Oct '60.
Rotterdam bronze memorial. Praeg.: Pict. ency., p. 464.
Rotunda of Univ. of Virginia. See Univ. of Virginia (Rotunda).
Rouart, Helene (Degas). Con. 140: 59 Sept '57.
Rouault, Georges. Cur. biog. p. 520 (1945).
—— (work of). Con. 140: L Nov '57; 145: 183 (col.), 208 May '60. Praeg.: Pict. ency., p. 473 (col.).
Rouaults (work of). Holiday 14: 51-2 (col.) Dec '53.
Roueche, Berton. Cur. biog. p. 398 (1959).
Rouen (France). Natl. geog. 115: 618-9 (col.), 621 May '59. Praeg.: Pict. ency., p. 419 (col.).
"A rough sea" (Ruisdael). Con. 141: 125 (col.) Ap '58.
roulette game. Holiday 23: 89 Je '58.
Round tower (Ireland). Holiday 6: 37 Dec '49.
roundel, bronze relief. Con. 142: 268 Jan '59.
roundel ornament. Con. ency. of ant., vol. 1, p. 24.
Rounds, Glen. Jun. bk. of auth., p. 262.
Rountree, Martha. Cur. biog. p. 481 (1957).
Rountree, William M. Cur. biog. p. 399 (1959).
Rouss, Charles B. Amer. heri., vol. 5 no. 3 p. 34 (spring '54).
Rousseau, Henri (work of). Praeg.: Pict. ency., p. 459 (col.).
Rousseau, Jean Jacques (Houdon terracotta). Con. 140: 7 Sept '57.
—— (Ramsay). Con. 126: 94 Oct '50.
Rousseau, Theodore (work of). Con. 141: XVI Je '58. Praeg.: Pict. ency., p. 414 (col.).
Routley, T. Clarence. Cur. biog. p. 532 (1956).
Roux, Antoine (work of). Amer. heri., vol. 8 no. 1 p. 39 (col.) (Dec '56).
Rowan, Carl T. (Negro. Director of U.S. Information Agency). Cur. biog. p. 371 (1958). U.S. News & world report, p. 14 Aug. 17, 1964.

rowboat. Amer. heri., vol. 8 no. 4 p. 19 (Jl '57); vol. 8 no. 6 p. 71 (Oct '57); vol. 12 no. 1 p. 18 (col.) (Dec '60).
Holiday 8: 102 (col.) Nov '50; 11: 75 (col.) Mar '52; 15: 124, 153 Je '54; 22: 4 (col.) Nov '57; 27: 55 Jan '60.
Labande: Naples, p. 25, 89.
Natl. geog. 101: 290, 314 (col.) Mar '52, 484 (col.) Ap '52; 103: 53 (col.) Jan '53; 104: 631 (col.) Nov '53; 105: 362 Mar '54; 110: 735 (col.) Dec '56; 111: 811 (col.) Je '57; 113: 348 (col.) Mar '58.
Osward: Asia Minor, pl. 21-22.
Praeg.: Pict. ency., p. 396, 475 (col.).
Travel 105: 55 Ap '56; 108: 16 Oct '57; 109: 49 Je '58; 110: 45 Aug '58, 34 Oct '58; 112: 40 Sept '59, 23 Dec '59; 113: 26 Mar '60.
—— (boy & girl). Face of Amer., p. 21 (col.).
—— (boys). Holiday 26: 116 (col.) Aug '59.
Natl. geog. 111: 413 (col.) Mar '57.
—— (boys & girls). Holiday 23: 90-1 (col.) Je '58; 27: back cover (col.) Je '60.
—— (boys pull & push, ice). Natl. geog. 113: 88-91 (col.) Jan '58.
—— (children). Natl. geog. 106: 164 (col.) Aug '54.
—— (college crew). Holiday 5: 107 Feb '49; 26: 45 Sept '59.
—— (college, regatta shells). Natl. geog. 107: 780 (col.) Je '55.
—— (fishermen). Holiday 18: 13 (col.) Dec '55; 24: 143 (col.) Jl '58; 25: 109 (col.) Ap '59, 156, 169 (col.) Je '59.
Natl. geog. 115: 286-7 Feb '59, 687 (col.) May '59.
—— (fishermen, 1769). Holiday 24: inside back cover (col.) Sept '58.
—— (girl). Holiday 25: 159 (col.) Je '59.
Jordan: Hammond's pict. atlas, p. 95 (col.).
—— (lake). Con. 145: XXXIX (col.) May '60.
—— (man). Holiday 23: 111 (col.) Jan '58; 24: 209 (col.) Nov '58.
—— (man & girl). Natl. geog. 115: 713 (col.) May '59.
—— (man & woman). Holiday 12: 66 Sept '52.
Natl. geog. 109: 202 (col.) Feb '56; 114: 65 (col.) Jl '58; 115: 765 (col.) Je '59.
Travel 113: 38 Mar '60.
—— (man building). Natl. geog. 99: 128 (col.) Jan '51.
—— (man, supplies). Holiday 23: 157 (col.) Je '58.
—— (man, woman & child). Travel 114: 34 Jl '60.
—— (men). Holiday 12: 61 (col.) Dec '52; 23: 17 May '58, 62 (col.) Je '58; 24: 141 (col.) Sept '58, 67 (col.) Oct '58; 25: 165 Ap '59; 27: 53 (col.) Je '60.
Natl. geog. 98: 532 (col.) Oct '50; 100: 157 (col.) Aug '51; 109: 513 (col.), 516 Ap '56; 113: 785 (col.) Je '58; 114: 759 (col.) Dec '58.
—— (men & women). Holiday 18: 31 (col.) Aug '55; 20: 110 (col.) Oct '56.
Natl. geog. 106: 589 (col.) Nov '54; 107: 609, 611 (col.) May '55; 113: 562-3 (col.) Ap '58.
—— (men & women, swamp). Natl. geog. 113: 100 Jan '58.
—— (men, Arctic). Natl. geog. 100: 478 (col.) Oct '51.
—— (men catch swans). Natl. geog. 114: 85 (col.) Jl '58.
—— (men harvest wild rice). Natl. geog. 111: 154 (col.) Feb '57.
—— (men lowering horse). Natl. geog. 97: 87 (col.) Jan '50.
—— (men oyster fishing). Natl. geog. 109: 442 Ap '56.
—— (men pulling ashore). Natl. geog. 108: 325 (col.) Sept '55.
—— (men rowing). Amer. heri., vol. 8 no. 3 p. 4, 10 (col.) (Ap '57); vol. 11 no. 4 p. 65, 72 (Je '60).
Natl. geog. 97: 386 Mar '50.
—— (men, silhouettes). Rawson: Ant. pict. bk., p. 80.
—— (Negro woman & boy). Amer. heri., vol. 11 no. 5 p. 22-3 (col.) (Aug '60).
—— (night). Natl. geog. 112: 786-7 (col.) Dec '57.
—— (people, silhouettes). Natl. geog. 118: 219 (col.) Aug '60.
—— (sailor, comic). Holiday 19: 88 May '56.
—— (sailors). Holiday 23: 40 (col.) Feb '58.
Natl. geog. 108: 80 (col.) Jl '55.
—— (St. Helena). Travel 107: 48 Mar '57.
—— (silhouette). Holiday 9: 52 (col.) Mar '51.
—— (sunset). Holiday 27: 47 (col.) Feb '60.
—— (war, 1812). Amer. heri., vol. 7 no. 3 p. 21 (col.) (Ap '56).
—— (Washington's soldiers, 1776). Amer. heri., vol. 11 no. 2 p. 58 (col.) (Feb '60).
—— (whalers). Amer. heri., vol. 12 no. 1 p. 48-9 (col.) (Dec '60).
—— (woman & dog). Natl. geog. 113: 176 (col.) Feb '58.
——, Africa (men rowing). Natl. geog. 112: 62 (col.) Jl '57.
——, Aleut island. Natl. geog. 101: 497 Ap '52.
——, Arabian. Natl. geog. 105: 504 Ap '54.
——, Arabian (man & woman). Natl. geog. 118: 852 (col.) Dec '60.
——, Balearic island. Natl. geog. 111: 628 (col.) May '57.
——, Bangkok. Travel 102: 24 Nov '54.
——, Basque. Natl. geog. 105: 165-7 (col.) Feb '54.
——, Borneo. Natl. geog. 109: 711 May '56.
——, Canadian. Natl. geog. 108: 199 (col.) Aug '55.
——, Denmark (students). Natl. geog. 108: 825 (col.) Dec '55.
——, Fiji. Natl. geog. 114: 532 Oct '58.
——, Galapagos (men). Natl. geog. 115: 683 (col.) May '59.
——, Greece. Travel 114: 19 Aug '60.
——, Harvard (man studying). Holiday 26: 73 Jl '59.
——, Ireland. Natl. geog. 100: 621 (col.) Nov '51.
——, Ifalik. Natl. geog. 109: 567 (col.) Ap '56.
——, India. Holiday 14: 110 (col.) Aug '53.

rowboat, Indians (Brazil). Natl. geog. 115: 644 (col.) May '59.

——, **Ireland.** Natl. geog. 99: 669 (col.) May '51.

——, **Ischian island.** Natl. geog. 105: 542 (col.) Ap '54.

——, **Italy (Amalfi).** Natl. geog. 116: 504-5 (col.) Oct '59.

——, **Italy (men & girls).** Natl. geog. 109: 847 (col.) Je '56.

——, **Italy (Trieste).** Natl. geog. 109: 829 (col.) Je '56.

——, **Japan.** Amer. heri., vol. 9 no. 3 p. 12 (col.) (Ap '58).

Natl. geog. 97: 618 (col.) May '50.

——, **Jordan river (Holy Land).** Natl. geog. 114: 849 (col.) Dec '58.

——, **Maldive islands.** Natl. geog. 111: 845 (col.) Je '57.

——, **Mexico.** Holiday 14: 50 Jl '53.

——, **Norway.** Natl. geog. 111: 107, 114 (col.) Jan '57.

——, **Okinawa.** Natl. geog. 97: 539 Ap '50.

——, **peddler's (Holland).** Natl. geog. 98: 760 (col.) Dec '50.

——, **Pitcairn island (men).** Natl. geog. 112: 748, 750 (col.), 776, 779 Dec '57.

——, **Polynesian.** Holiday 9: 94 Mar '51.

——, **Scotland.** Natl. geog. 110: 34 (col.) Jl '56.

——, **Singapore, (Chinaman.)** Holiday 24: 120 Nov '58, 24 Dec '58.

——, **Tobago island, (men.)** Natl. geog. 114: 440 Sept '58.

——, **Trucial Oman, (men.)** Natl. geog. 110: 96-7 (col.) Jl '56.

——, **Trucial Oman (men & women).** Natl. geog. 110: 94-5 (col.) Jl '56.

rowboats. Amer. heri., vol. 7 no. 1 p. 53 (Dec '55).

—— **(fishermen).** Natl. geog. 111: 622-3 (col.) May '57.

—— **(in cave).** Natl. geog. 111: 630-1 May '57.

—— **(lake).** Natl. geog. 118: 801 (col.) Dec '60.

—— **(Marines landing).** Amer. heri., vol. 10 no. 2 p. 28 (col.) (Feb '59).

—— **(Naval acad., 8-oared shells).** Natl. geog. 107: 208 Feb '55.

——, **Aden Colony.** Natl. geog. 111: 237 Feb '57.

——, **Cambridge Univ.** Holiday 7: 118 (col.) Je '50.

——, **Ireland.** Natl. geog. 104: 132 (col.) Jl '53.

——, **Martinique.** Natl. geog. 115: 256-7 (col.) Feb '59.

——, **Sicily.** Natl. geog. 107: 9 (col.) Jan '55.

Rowe, Dorothy. Jun. bk. of auth., p. 263

Rowe, Leo S. Cur. biog. p. 824 (1945).

rowing ragatta (Amalfi, Italy). Natl. geog. 116: 504-5 (col.) Oct '59.

——. *See* also regatta.

Rowlandson, Thomas (work of). Con. ency. of ant., vol. 1, pl. 139.

Con. 137: XVII Ap '56; 140: 127 Nov '57; 141: XXXVII Ap '58; 143: 104 Ap '59.

Rowley, James J. Cur. biog. p. 363 (1963).

Roxas, Manuel. Cur. biog. p. 525 (1946).

Roy, Archbishop Maurice. Cur. biog. p. 372 (1958).

royal bargeman (Eng.). Natl. geog. 114: 90 (col.) Jl '58.

Royal Canadian mounted police. Holiday 6: cover (col.) Aug '49, 15, 79 (col.) Sept '49, 130 (col.) Oct '49, 26 (col.) Nov '49; 7: 20 (col.), 23 Ap '50; 9: 103 (col.) Mar '51; 14: 134 (col.) Jl '53; 15: 17 (col.) Feb '54, 117 (col.), 129 Ap '54, 73, 82 (col.) May '54, 5 (col.) Je '54; 19: 2 (col.) Feb '56; 21: 17 Jan '57, 175 (col.) May '57; 23: 17 Feb '58, 7, 147 (col.) Mar '58, 163 (col.) Ap '58, 115, 142 (col.) May '58; 25: 123, 161 (col.) Mar '59, 139 (col.) Ap '59; 27: 29 (col.) Feb '60.

Int. gr. soc.: Arts . . . p. 159 (col.).

Natl. geog. 98: 329, 336 (col.) Sept '50; 104: 829 (col.) Dec '53; 106: 710-13 (col.) Nov '54; 108: 212 (col.) Aug '55; 109: 631 (col.) May '56.

Travel 104: 23 Jl '55.

—— **(on running horse).** Holiday 14: 34 (col.) Jl '53.

Royal Caribbean hotel (Jamaica). Travel 108: 43 Dec '57.

Royal Doulton china. Holiday 10: 122 Oct '51.

Royal Doulton figurines. *See* figurine, Royal Doulton.

Royal Doulton jug. Holiday 25: 187 Ap '59, 100 May '59.

Royal Doulton miniature. Holiday 14: 5 (col.) Oct '53; 24: 26 (col.) Nov '58.

Royal Doulton Tobey jugs. Holiday 26: 97 Nov '59.

Royal exchange, Cornhill. Con. 139: LV Je '57.

Royal festival hall (London). *See* London (Royal festival hall).

Royal gorge (Colo.). Jordan: Hammond's pict. atlas, p. 164 (col.).

Royal guard, English. *See* London (Royal guard, palace).

——, **Greek.** *See* Greek soldiers (King's guard).

Royal Hawaiian hotel. Holiday 16: 88 Jl '54, 73 Sept '54; 18: 123 Nov '55; 19: 66 Mar '56; 21: 19 Feb '57; 25: 97 (col.) Jan '59.

Royal horse guard. *See* horse guard, Royal (London).

Royal hotel (Copenhagen). Travel 113: 58 Ap '60.

Royal Oak inn (Eng.). Holiday 21: 27 Mar '57.

Royal Pantheon (Bangkok temple). Natl. geog. 116: 848 (col.) Dec '59.

Royal Pantheon. *See* also temple, Bangkok.

Royal Scotch artillerymen. Natl. geog. 112: 462 (col.) Oct '57.

Royal Scots Grey memorial. *See* statue (Royal Scots Greys memorial).

Royall, Kenneth C. Cur. biog. p. 555 (1947).

royalty (court). Natl. geog. 100: 22 Jl '51.

—— **(Oriental sym.).** Lehner: Pict. bk. of sym., p. 44.

Royden, Agnes Maude. Cur. biog. p. 719 (1942).

Roybet, Ferdinand (work of). Con. 140: XX Nov '57.

Royen, Jan Herman Van. Cur. biog. p. 547 (1953).

Royster, Elmira. Amer. heri., vol. 7 no. 3 p. 24-5 (Ap '56).

Royster, Vermont C. Cur. biog. p. 549 (1953).

Ruanda dancers (Belgian Congo). Natl. geog. 101: 352 (col.) Mar '52.

Rubattel, Rodolphe. Cur. biog. p. 548 (1954).

rubber, crepe (African workers). Natl. geog. 118: 311 (col.) Sept '60.

rubber tree tapping. Natl. geog. 102: 300 (col.) Sept '52.

Rubens, Peter Paul. Int. gr. soc.: Arts . . . p. 91 (col.).

Natl. geog. 97: 763 (col.) Je '50.

—— (work of). Amer. heri., vol. 10 no. 3 p. 7 (col.) (Ap '59).

Con. ency. of ant., vol. 1, pl. 155.

Con. 127: 117 May '51; 133: 31 Mar '54, 97 Ap '54; 135: LIX Ap '55; 137: XLVII Mar '56; 139: 191 May '57; 140: 113 Nov '57; 141: 1 Mar '58; 142: 38 Sept '58, LVIII Nov '58; 143: XVII Ap '59; 144: 43 Sept '59, 126 Nov '59, 270 Jan '60; 145: 159 May '60, 267 Je '60.

Holiday 25: 70-1 (col.) Jan '59.

Natl. geog. 97: 743 (col.) Je '50.

Praeg.: Pict. ency., p. 328 (col.).

Rubicam, Raymon. Cur. biog. p. 638 (1943).

Rubin, Reuven. Cur. biog. p. 641 (1943).

Rubin de la Borbolla, Daniel F. Cur. biog. p. 349 (1960).

Rubinstein, Anton Gregor. Cooper. Con. ency. of music, p. 249.

Rubinstein, Arthur. Cur. biog. p. 526 (1945). Holiday 10: 131 Oct '51.

Rubinstein, Helena. See Gourielli, Princess Artchen.

Rubottom, Roy R., jr. Cur. biog. p. 401 (1959).

Ruccellai palace. See palazzo Ruccellai.

Rude, Francois (sculpture by). Praeg.: Pict. ency., p. 428.

Rudkin, Margaret F. Cur. biog. p. 403 (1959).

Rudolph, Wilma. Cur. biog. p. 400 (1961).

"Rue du Mont-Cenis a Montmartre" (Utrillo). Con. 138: XI (col.) Nov '56.

"Rue St. Honore" (Pissaro). Con. 133: 285 Je '54.

Ruef, Abraham. Amer. heri., vol. 11 no. 1 p. 8, 11 (Dec '59).

—— (cartoon). Amer. heri., vol. 11 no. 1 p. 102 (Dec '59).

Ruffin, Edmund. Amer. heri., vol. 9 no. 1 p. 22 (Dec '57).

Ruffin, William. H. Cur. biog. p. 541 (1951).

Ruffin home, Edmund ("Marlbourne"). Amer. heri., vol. 9 no. 1 p. 25 (Dec '57).

Ruffing, Charles H. Cur. biog. p. 737 (1941).

Ruffin's "Farmer's register" (title page). See "Farmer's register".

Ruffner, Mrs. Viola Knapp. Amer. heri. vol. 7 no. 1 p. 31 (Dec '55).

rug (Queen Anne design). Con. 142: XLIV Jan '59.

——, Agra. Con. 139: XLIV Je '57.

——, Aubusson. Con. 138: LV Nov '56; 140: LX Jan '58; 141: XLVII May '58; 142: XII Jan '59; 144: XVIII Nov '59, XXII Dec '59; 145: XVI Mar '60, X Ap '60.

——, Bergam (Asia Minor). Con. 143: IV May '59; 145: 192 May '60.

——, Bessarabian. Con. 132: LXIX Nov '53.

——, Caucasian. Con. 134: XLI Sept '54.

——, Caucasian Couba Cabistan. Con. 142: XLI Sept '58.

——, Indo-Ispahan. Con. 145: LXVIII Je '60.

——, Ispahan (16th cent.). Con. 132: LIV Nov '53.

——, Karastan. Holiday 28: 110 (col.) Sept '60.

——, Kashan. Con. 143: XLI May '59; 139: LIV May '57.

——, Kashgai. Natl. geog. 101: 825 (col.) Je '52.

——, Kazak (Caucasus). Con. 145: IV Ap '60.

——, Kirman (Persia). Con. 144: XXX Dec '59; 145: XLVI Je '60.

——, Louis XIV St Cyr. Con. 142: 109 Nov '58.

——, needlework. See needlework rug.

——, Persian. Con. 142: X Nov '58.

——, prayer. See prayer rug.

——, rag. Natl. geog. 98: 343 (col.) Sept '50.

——, Samarkand. Con. 138: XLVII Sept '56.

——, Shaker (Ky., 1800's). Holiday 18: 60 (col.) Jl '55.

——, Transylvania (18th cent.). Con. 144: LXIX Dec '59.

——. See also carpet; rugs.

rug cleaners (Isfahan). Natl. geog. 114: 31 (col.) Jl '58.

rug seller (Moslem). Natl. geog. 114: 5 (col.) Jl '58.

rug washers (Persian). Natl. geog. 100: 436-7 (col.) Oct '51; 117: 72 (col.) Jan '60.

rug weavers. Holiday 25: 52 (col.) Feb '59.

rug weaving, India (men). Natl. geog. 118: 486-7 (col.) Oct '60.

——, Isfahan. Holiday 20: 58 (col.) Dec '56.

——, Navajo Indian. Natl. geog. 114: 840 (col.) Dec '58.

——, Persian (women). Natl. geog. 100: 438-9 (col.) Oct '51.

Rugambwa, Laurian Cardinal. Cur. biog. p. 351 (1960).

rugby teams. Natl. geog. 105: 522 (col.) Ap '54.

rugger game (Eng.). Holiday 25: 75 Je '59.

rugs. Holiday 27: inside cover (col.) Ap '60; 28: 38 (col.) Oct '60.

——, Oriental. Con. ency. of ant., vol. 1, pl. 123-6.

Holiday 28: 176-7 (col.) Dec '60.

Natl. geog. 106: 831 (col.) Dec '54.

——. See also carpet; rug.

Ruiperez, Luis (work of). Con. 140: XXXI Nov '57.

Ruisdael, Jacob van (work of). Con. 141: 125 (col.) Ap '58.

Ruiz, Guinazu Enrique. Cur. biog. p. 721 (1942).

Rukeyser, Muriel. Cur. biog. p. 645 (1943).

rum casks. Holiday 23: 42 (col.) Feb '58.

rumba dancers. See dancers, rumba.

Rumbold, Thomas (Reynolds). Con. 135: 128 Ap '55.

Rumeli Hisar (Turkey). Natl. geog. 112: 416 (col.) Sept '57.
Ruml, Beardsley. Cur. biog. p. 647 (1943).
Rummel, Archbishop Joseph F. Cur. biog. p. 404 (1959).
rummer, toddy (antique glass). Con. ency. of ant., vol. 1, p. 80.
—— (Irish glass). Con. ency. of ant., vol. 3, pl. 50.
"Runaway horse" (1850). Amer. heri., vol. 9 no. 3 frontis (col.) (Ap '58).
Runbeck, Margaret Lee. Cur. biog. p. 508 (1952).
Runciman, John. Con. 141: 236 Je '58.
"Rundas" (Hitite god of the chase). Osward: Asia Minor, pl. 4.
Rundstedt, Karl von. Cur. biog. p. 741 (1941).
runes (sym.). Lehner: Pict. bk. of sym., p. 28.
Runestone, Kensington. See Kensington Runestone.
Runge, Philipp Otto. Praeg.: Pict. ency., p. 394 (col.).
runners, Roman women (ancient art). Natl. geog. 111: 215 (col.) Feb '57.
——, track. Holiday 5: 63 Ap '49.
"Runnymede" home (Paris, Ky.). Holiday 5: 33 (col.) Ap '49; 8: 74 (col.) Oct '50; 9: inside back cover (col.) Mar '51.
Runyon, Damon. Cur. biog. p. 723 (1942).
Runyon, Mefford R. Cur. biog. p. 534 (1949).
Ruoppolo, G. B. (work of). Con. ency., of ant., vol. 1, pl. 176.
Rusby, Henry Hurd. Cur. biog. p. 743 (1941).
Rusconi, Camillo (sculpture by). Con. 141: 223 Je '58.
Rush, Dr. Benjamin. Amer. heri., vol. 7 no. 3 p. 56 (Ap '56).
rush light. Rawson: Ant. pict. bk., p. 93.
rush candle holder. Rawson: Ant. pict. bk., p. 93.
Rushen castle (Isle of Man). Holiday 25: 19 Jan '59.
Rusk, Dean. Cur. biog. p. 536 (1949); p. 402 (1961).
Jensen: The White House, p. 291.
Rusk, Howard A. Cur. biog. p. 527 (1946).
Ruskin, John (Richmond). Con. 133: XLVI Ap '54.
Russell, Anna. Cur. biog. p. 550 (1954).
Russell, Bertrand. Cur. biog. p. 544 (1951). Holiday 23: 89 Ap '58.
Russell, Charles H. Cur. biog. p. 521 (1955).
Russell, Charles M. Amer. heri., vol. 6 no. 1 p. 40 (col.) (fall '54).
Russell, Donald J. Cur. biog. p. 368 (1962).
Russell, Harold. Cur. biog. p. 508 (1950).
Russell, James. Holiday 23: 73 Ap '58.
Russell, Adm. James S. Cur. biog. p. 370 (1962).
Russell, Jonathan. Amer. heri., vol. 12 no. 1 p. 28 (col.) (Dec '60).
Russell, Lillian. Amer. heri., vol. 7 no. 1 p. 35 (col.) (Dec '55).
Holiday 25: 78 Feb '59.
Russell, Pee Wee. Cur. biog. p. 569 (1944).
Russell, Richard B. Cur. biog. p. 537 (1949).
Russell, Rosalind. Cur. biog. p. 651 (1943).
Russell, William F. Cur. biog. p. 557 (1947).
Russia (U.S.S.R.). Amer. heri., vol. 11 no. 3 p.

25 (col.) (Ap '60).
Holiday 18: 102-11 Jl '55.
Natl. geog. 116: 352-409 (part col.) Sept '59, 716-50 (part col.) Dec '59.
Travel 109: 54-7 Ap '58.
—— (army on parade). Amer. heri., vol. 10 no. 1 p. 26-7 (Dec '58).
—— (honor insignia). Int. gr. soc.: Arts . . . p. 167 (col.).
—— (Leningrad palace). Holiday 24: 56 Sept '58.
—— (map). Natl. geog. 116: 729 Dec '59; 118: 888 (col.) Dec '60.
——, patron saint of. Lehner: Pict. bk. of sym., p. 39.
——, Ivan. See Ivan, Russia.
Russian-American company flag. Amer. heri., vol. 11 no. 3 p. 5 (col.) (Ap '60).
Russian caddies (18th cent.). Con. 143: XXVIII Je '59.
Russian cathedral. See cathedral (Sitka, Russia).
Russian children. See children, Russian.
Russian church. See church, Russian.
Russian famine, U.S. aid in. Amer. heri., vol. 11 no. 5 p. 63-7 (part col.) (Aug '60).
Russian figurines. Con. 144: 274 Jan '60.
Russian gold box. Con. 133: XXVII May '54.
Russian house furnishings (antique, 18-19th cent.). Con. 144: 272-9 Jan '60.
Russian ikon. Con. 144: 279 Jan '60.
Russian imperial palace (1809). Amer. heri., vol. 9 no. 2 p. 6 (Feb '58).
Russian manor house. See manor house, Russian.
Russian navy officers. Amer. heri., vol. 11 no. 4 p. 40-1 (Je '60).
Russian orthodox church cross. See cross, Russian orthodox church.
Russian painting (13-20th cent.). Con. 143: 28-31 Mar '59.
Russian parrot cage. Con. 145: 187 May '60.
Russian plate (Nicolas I). Con. 144: 275 Jan '60.
Russian silver (17th cent.). Con. 142: 224 Jan '59.
Russian silver tankard (1800). Con. 144: 274 Jan '60.
Russian state jewels. Int. gr. soc.: Arts . . . p. 165 (col.).
Russian tea room (N. Y.). See tea room, Russian.
Russian troops (parade, 1809). Amer. heri. vol. 9 no. 2 p. 6 (col.) (Feb '58).
Russian zone (along Danube). Travel 103: 21-6 Je '55.
Russians. Amer. heri., vol. 11 no. 5 p. 66-7 (Aug '60).
Holiday 5: 22 Jan '49.
—— (cartoon). Holiday 14: 84 Sept '53.
Russians (children). See children, Russian.
Russian man (head). Holiday 26: 8 Nov '59, 229 Dec '59.
Russisloff brig. Amer. heri., vol. 10 no. 3 p. 80 (Ap '59).
Rust, Bernhard. Cur. biog. p. 726 (1942).
Rutenborn, Rev. Gunter. Cur. biog. p. 353 (1960).
Rutgers univ. football team (1869). Brooks: Growth of a nation, p. 201.

Ruth, Babe. Amer. heri., vol. 10 no. 3 p. 23 (Ap '59).
Cur. biog. p. 572 (1944).
Ruth, George Herman (baseball). Holiday 7: 44 May '50.
Ruth (kneels before Boaz, harvest). Natl. geog. 118: 847 (col.) Dec '60.
"Ruth & Boaz" (Wheatley). Con. 142: 42 Sept '58.
Rutherford, Ernest, baron. Con. 144: 13 Sept '59.
Rutledge, Wiley. Cur. biog. p. 653 (1943).
Rutledge grave, Ann. Travel 113: 31 Feb '60.
Rutledge memorial, Ann. Travel 109: 26 Feb '58.
Rutledge tavern. Travel 113: 31 Feb '60.
Ruysch, Rachel (work of). Con. 140: XVII (col.) Sept '57.
Ruysdael, Salomon Van. See Van Ruysdael, Salomon.
Ruz, Alberto (excavations). Ceram: March of arch., p. 297-8.
Ryan, Joseph P. Cur. biog. p. 540 (1949).
Ryan, Patrick J. Cur. biog. p. 523 (1955).
Ryan, Robert. Cur. biog. p. 365 (1963).
Ryan, Thomas Fortune. Amer. heri., vol. 5 no. 3 p. 38 (spring '54).
Ryan, Tubal Claude. Cur. biog. p. 655 (1943).
Ryder, Albert Pinkham (work of). Holiday 7: 107 (col.) Feb '50.
Rye (Eng.). Holiday 16: 28 (col.) Jl '54.
Ryland (work of). Amer. heri., vol. 6 no. 1 p. 51 (Dec '54).
Ryti, Risto. Cur. biog. p. 744 (1941).

S

S. O. S. (sym., "Save our souls"). Lehner: Pict. bk. of sym., p. 88.
Saadi tomb & statue (Shiraz). Travel 105: 25 Jan '56.
Saar valley. Natl. geog. 105: 562-76 Ap '54.
—— (map). Natl. geog. 105: 564 Ap '54.
Saarinen, Aline B. Cur. biog. p. 534 (1956).
Saarinen, Eero. Cur. biog. p. 541 (1949).
Saarinen, Eliel. Cur. biog. p. 728 (1942).
Saavedra, Antonio del Castillo (work of). Con. 135: 121 Ap '55.
Saba (Caribbean). Travel 103: 13 Mar '55.
Sabath, Adolph J. Cur. biog. p. 530 (1946).
saber, cavalry (1840). Brooks: Growth of a nation, p. 173.
Sabin, Albert B. Cur. biog. p. 374 (1958).
Sabin, Edwin L. Jun. bk. of auth., p. 264.
Sabin, Florence R. Cur. biog. p. 528 (1945).
sabre, French (19th cent.). Con. 145: 110 Ap '60.
Sabrejet (airplane). Natl. geog. 104: 756, 758 (col.) Dec '53; 112: 291 Aug '57.
"Sabrina" statue (Amherst college). Natl. geog. 97: 303 (col.) Mar '50.
Sacagawea's statue. Natl. geog. 103: 725 (col.) Je '53.
Sacco, Nicola. Amer. heri., vol. 9 no. 6 p. 52, 55 (Oct '58).
Sacco-Vanzetti trial (1932). Amer. heri., vol. 9 no. 6, p. 52-7 (Oct '58).
Sachar, Abram. Cur. biog. p. 544 (1949).
Sachiel (seal of). Lehner: Pict. bk. of sym., p. 25.

Sachs, Curt. Cur. biog. p. 575 (1944).
sack (Cretan carryall). Natl. geog. 104: 705 (col.) Nov '53.
Sackett's harbor (war, 1812). Amer. heri., vol. 7 no. 3 p. 101 (Ap '56).
Sackville, Thomas. Amer. heri., vol. 10 no. 4 p. 16 (col.) (Je '59).
Sacre Coeur church (Paris). Travel 103: inside cover Je '55.
"Sacred & profane love" (Titian). Natl. geog. 111: 488-9 (col.) Ap '57.
Sacred Heart academy. See Academy of the Sacred Heart.
"The Sacred Heaven" (sym.). Lehner: Pict. bk. of sym., p. 49.
sacrifice (sym.). Lehner: Pict. bk. of sym., p. 76.
"Sacrifice of Abraham" (Empoli). Con. 136: 204 Dec '55.
sacrifices, Aztec human. Ceram: March of arch., p. 266.
sacrificial bronze vessel, Chinese. Con. 129: LXXIV Ap '52.
sacrificial food vessel (Chou). Con. 145: 64 Mar '60.
sacrificial scene (Mayan). Praeg.: Pict. ency., p. 543.
sacrificial vessel, Chinese bronze. Con. 144: 38 Sept '59.
Sadak, Necmeddin. Cur. biog. p. 510 (1950).
saddle. Holiday 7: 132 (col.) Mar '50; 21: 4 (col.) Je '57.
Natl. geog. 97: 695 Je '50.
saddle & saddle cloth, India. Con. 144: XXXVII Dec '59.
saddle bags. Rawson: Ant. pict. bk., p. 69.
Saddler, Donald. Cur. biog. p. 368 (1963).
saddler (sym.). Lehner: Pict. bk. of sym., p. 91.
saddler's seat. Rawson: Ant. pict. bk., p. 58.
Sadhu. See holy man (India).
Sa'di tomb. See Shiraz (Sa'di tomb).
sadiron. Rawson: Ant. pict. bk., p. 12.
Sadler, W. Dendy (work of). Con. 136: XXIX Sept '55.
Saenredam, Pieter Jansz (work of). Natl. geog. 110: 652 (col.) Nov '56.
safari (Belgian Congo). Natl. geog. 117: 119 (col.) Jan '60.
safe (for gold deposits). Brooks: Growth of a nation, p. 134.
safety (sym). Lehner: Pict. bk. of sym., p. 29, 88-9.
safety driving poster. Holiday 18: 82 Sept '55.
Sagadahoc fort plan (1607). Amer. heri., vol. 10 no. 5 p. 27 (Aug '59).
Sagan, Francoise. Cur. biog. p. 354 (1960).
Holiday 28: 50 (col.) Aug '60.
Sagendorph, Robb. Cur. biog. p. 536 (1956).
Sagres (Portugal). Natl. geog. 118: 636-7 (col.) Nov '60.
Sahale Falls (Ore.). Travel 101: 8 Ap '54.
Sahara desert. Natl. geog. 112: 69-78 (col.) Jl '57; 113: 665-704 (part col.) May '58.
—— (map). Natl. geog. 113: 680 May '58.
—— (oases). Holiday 13: 70-1 Jan '53.
Sahl, Mort. Cur. biog. p. 356 (1960).
sai (sym.). Lehner: Pict. bk. of sym., p. 47.
Said Bin Taimur, Sultan. Cur. biog. p. 483 (1957).

Saikko, Vaino Gabriel (work of). Natl. geog. 106: 260 (col.) Aug '54.
sail car (on railroad). Amer. heri., vol. 9 no. 1 p. 58 (Dec '57).
sailboat. Amer. heri., vol. 9 no. 2 p. 49 (col.) (Feb '58); vol. 10 no. 6 p. 31 (Oct '59).
Con. ency. of ant., vol. 3, pl. 94.
Con. 141: 125 (col.) Ap '58.
Holiday 5: 26 (col.) Jan '49, 10 (col.) Mar '49; 6: 53 (col.), 86 Jl '49, 60 (col.) Sept '49; 7: 106 Ap '50, 89 Je '50; 8: 28 Sept '50, 56 (col.) Oct '50, 38 (col.) Nov '50; 10: 41 (col.) Jl '51, 28, 150 Oct '51, 34, 41, 89 (col.) Nov '51, 15, 95 (col.) Dec '51; 11: 29 Jan '52, 13 (col.) Ap '52, 125 May '52, 37 Je '52; 12: 112, 123 Jl '52, 22, 97, 115 (col.) Aug '52, 63 Sept '52, 113 (col.) Nov '52, 12 (col.) Dec '52; 13: 123 (col.), 126 Mar '53, 29, 88, 91 (col.), 149 Ap '53, 26 (col.), 71 May '53, 9, 155 Je '53; 14: 5 Aug '53, 143 Oct '53, 12 (col.) Nov '53; 17: 4 Jan '55; 19: 56 Jan '56, 21, 52, 81 (col.) Feb '56, 23, 31, 182 (col.) May '56, 62 Je '56; 20: 75 (col.) Aug '56, 102 (col.) Sept '56, 130, 172 Nov '56; 21: 59, 83, 137 (col.) Feb '57, 141 Mar '57, 25 Ap '57, 5, 48, 114 (col.) May '57, 9, 126 (col.) Je '57; 22: 4 (col.) Nov '57, 98-9, 170 (col.) Dec '57; 23: 98 (col.) Jan '58, 10, 139 (col.) Feb '58, 18, 41, 74, 128, 135 (col.), back cover Mar '58, 106, 197 (col.) Ap '58; 24: 110 (col.) Aug '58, 62, 155 (col.) Oct '58; 25: 15, 36, 104 Feb '59, 49 (col.) Mar '59, 168 Ap '59, 26, 50 (col.) Je '59; 26: 29, 85 (col.) Jl '59, 103 (col.) Oct '59, 25, 87 (col.) Nov '59; 27: 6, 44 98 (col.) Mar '60, 121, 175 (col.) Ap '60, 122, 153, 241 May '60, 46-7 (col.), 192 Je '60; 28: 130 Jl '60, 1, 109 Aug '60, 4 Oct '60.
Labande: Naples, p. 36, 136.
Natl. geog. 98: 149, 154, 158, 161 (col.) Aug '50, 368, 382, 394 (col.) Sept '50, 629 (col.) Nov '50, 770 (col.) Dec '50; 99: 287 (col.) Mar '51, 778 (col.) Je '51; 100: 742 (col.) Dec '51; 101: 441 (col.) Ap '52; 102: 331, 366 (col.) Sept '52; 103: 26 (col.) Jan '53, 357-8 Mar '53; 104: 832 (col.) Dec '53; 105: 214, 216, 225 (col.), 218 Feb '54; 107: 478-9 (col.) Ap '55, 751, 753 (col.) Je '55; 108: 313, 337, 367 (col.) Sept '55; 110: 186-7 Aug '56, 797 (col.) Dec '56; 111: 152 (col.), 153 Feb '57; 112: 299, 312, 323-7 (col.) Sept '57; 113: 53 (col.), 58-9 Jan '58, 154-5 (col.) Feb '58; 114: 65 (col.) Jl '58, 735, 746 (col.) Dec '58; 115: 752, 831 (col.) Je '59; 116: 449 (col.) Oct '59; 117: 759 (col.) Je '60.
Praeg.: Pict. ency., p. 432, 474 (col.).
Travel 101: 31 Jan '54, 32, 35 Mar '54, 39 May '54; 102: 41 Aug '54, 7 Oct '54; 103: 15, 19 Feb '55, 40 Mar '55, 68 Je '55; 104: 62 Sept '55, 17 Nov '55; 105: inside cover Jan '56, 11, 58 Feb '56, 46, 61 Mar '56, 34 Ap '56, 19 May '56; 106: cover (col.) Jl '56, 41 Aug '56, 27 Oct '56; 107: 32 May '57; 108: 33 Jl '57, cover Aug '57; 109: 19 Mar '58, 33 May '58; 110: 32 Jl '58, 32 Sept '58; 111: 25

Jan '59, 47 Mar '59; 112: 17, 31 Aug '59; 113: 20 Feb '60.
sailboat (Arabia). Natl. geog. 110: 82, 99 (col.) Jl '56.
——— **(Arabia, toy).** Natl. geog. 110: 83 (col.) Jl '56.
——— **(at beach).** Travel 113: 19 Feb '60.
——— **(Austria).** Natl. geog. 118: 248 (col.) Aug '60.
——— **(Bermuda).** Holiday 23: 73 Je '58.
——— **(Bolivia).** Holiday 22: 122 (col.) Oct '57.
——— **(Bora Bora).** Holiday 28: 97 (col.) Oct '62.
——— **(Canary is.).** Natl. geog. 107: 486 Ap '55.
——— **(child's).** Holiday 15: 25 (col.) May '54.
——— **(clipper ship).** Brooks: Growth of a nation, p. 114.
——— **(cruiser).** Travel 112: 61 Dec '59.
——— **(Cyprus is.).** Natl. geog. 109: 881 Je '56.
——— **(Egypt).** Natl. geog. 106: 756, 758 (col.) Dec '54.
——— **(girls & boys).** Travel 112: 45 Dec '59.
——— **(Greece).** Travel 113: 79 Ap '60.
——— **(Holland).** Natl. geog. 106: 384, 391 (col.) Sept '54.
——— **(Iraq).** Natl. geog. 113: 221 (col.) Feb '58.
——— **(Italy).** Natl. geog. 109: 855 (col.) Je '56.
——— **(Majorca).** Natl. geog. 111: 659 (col.) May '57.
——— **(Maldive is.).** Natl. geog. 111: 833 (col.) Je '57.
——— **(man & woman).** Natl. geog. 98: 611 Nov '50.
——— **(men).** Amer. heri., vol. 8 no. 5 p. 46 (col.) (Aug '57).
——— **(model).** Holiday 20: 182 Nov '56; 25: 27 May '59; 28: 137 Jl '60.
Natl. geog. 107: 641 (col.) May '55; 108: 523 (col.) Oct '55.
——— **(Nile river).** Holiday 20: 63 (col.) Dec '56.
——— **(Norway).** Natl. geog. 106: 157, 172, 174 (col.) Aug '54.
——— **(Pitcairn is.).** Natl. geog. 112: 783-4 (col.) Dec '57.
——— **(sails lowered).** Holiday 8: 23 (col.) Aug '50.
——— **(small).** Jordan: Hammond's pict. atlas, p. 40 (col.).
———, **Brittany.** Holiday 7: 99 (col.) Jan '50.
———, **Dutch (old).** Holiday 20: 4 Aug '56.
———, **Egypt.** Holiday 10: 119 Dec '51.
Natl. geog. 108: 633, 636 (col.) Nov '55.
———, **Hong Kong.** Holiday 28: 93 (col.) Sept '60.
———, **Japan.** Holiday 12: 1 Aug '52.
Natl. geog. 104: 631 (col.) Nov '53.
———, **Turkey.** Holiday 19: 52 (col.) Feb '56.
———, **Pakistan (butterfly).** Natl. geog. 107: 408 (col.) Mar '55.
———, **outrigger.** Natl. geog. 111: 846-7 (col.) Je '57.
———, **outrigger (Admiralty is.).** Natl. geog. 112: 593 Nov '57.
———, **toy (boy).** Natl. geog. 113: 801 (col.) Je '58.

sailboat cabin. Natl. geog. 113: 776 (col.) Je '58.

sailboat race. Natl. geog. 113: 758-60, 766, 769-71, 790 (part col.) Jl '58.

—— (Italy). Natl. geog. 109: 845 (col.) Je '56.

sailboats. Amer. heri., vol. 8 no. 6 p. 56 (col.) (Oct '57).
Face of Amer., p. 57 (col.).
Holiday 18: 92 (col.) Sept '55, 37 (col.), 97 Dec '55.
Natl. geog. 105: 168 (col.) Feb '54, 793 (col.) Je '54; 107: 50-1, 60 (col.) Jan '55; 113: 2-3 (col.) Jan '58.
Praeg.: Pict. ency., p. 32, 72 (col.).

—— (colored sails). Holiday 24: 78 Nov '58.

—— (dinghies). Natl. geog. 107: 790 (col.) Je '55.

—— (fishing). Labande: Naples, p. 192.

—— (sails furled). Natl. geog. 105: 345 Mar '54.

——, Hudson's Bay co. Amer. heri., vol. 10 no. 5 p. 46 (col.) (Aug '59).

——, Italy. Holiday 21: 52-3 (col.) Jan '57.

——, Marquessa is. Amer. heri., vol. 12 no. 1 p. 58-9 (col.) (Dec '60).

——, Nile river. Natl. geog. 107: 722 May '55.

——, Portugal. Disney: People & places, p. 61 (col.).

——, Turkey. Natl. geog. 115: 70 (col.) Jan '59.

sailboats. See also dhow, Arab; Greek caique; junk, Chinese; ship (sails); windjammer.

sailing barges. Natl geog. 114: 92 (col.) Jl '58.

"Sailing vessel in a heavy sea" (Birch). Amer. heri., vol. 11 no. 6 cover (col.) (Oct '60).

Saillant, Louis. Cur. biog. p. 543 (1948).

Sailmaker, Isaac (work of). Con. 138: XXXV Dec '56.

sailmaker's thimble. See thimble, sailmaker's.

sailor. Holiday 13: 50 Je '53; 26: 23 (col.) Oct '59.
Natl. geog. 98: 324 Sept '50; 105: 508 Ap '54.

—— (asleep on boat deck). Natl. geog. 108: 65 (col.) Jl '55.

—— (back view). Natl. geog. 98: 642 (col.) Nov '50.

—— (binoculars). Holiday 21: 187 Je '57.

—— ("flogged like a beast"). Amer. heri., vol. 11 no. 6 p. 32 (col.) (Oct '60).

—— (head). Holiday 21: 206 May '57.

—— (horseback, 1836). Amer. heri., vol. 11 no. 6 p. 37 (col.) (Oct '60).

—— (hugs woman, cartoon, 1894). Amer. heri., vol. 11 no. 6 p. 111 (Oct '60).

—— (jungle masks). Natl. geog. 99: 341 (col.) Mar '51.

—— (peeling potatoes). Natl. geog. 116: 768 (col.) Dec '59.

—— (playing violin). Amer. heri., vol. 9 no. 6 p. 45 (col.) (Oct '58).

—— (reading). Natl. geog. 108: 67 (col.) Jl '55.

—— (salutes, back view). Natl. geog. 101: 540 (col.) Ap '52.

—— (seasick, cartoon). Amer. heri., vol. 11 no. 6 p. 33 (col.) (Oct '60).

—— (tries Jap. kimona). Natl. geog. 116: 299 (col.) Sept '59.

——, Chinese. See Chinese sailor.

——, early. Amer. heri., vol. 11 no. 5 p. 86, 90 (Aug '60).

——, Greek. Natl. geog. 109: 39 (col.) Jan '56.

sailor & family. Natl. geog. 118: 612 Nov '60.

—— (Chile). Natl. geog. 117: 202 (col.) Feb '60.

sailor & girl. Natl. geog. 97: 290 (col.) Mar '50; 101: 536 (col.) Ap '52.

—— (on boat). Natl. geog. 108: 69 (col.) Jl '55.

—— (walking). Holiday 10: 48 (col.) Aug '51.

sailor & girls (in old Scotch church). Natl. geog. 110: 9 (col.) Jl '56.

sailor & boy (Denmark). Natl. geog. 108: 813 (col.) Dec '55.

sailors. Amer. heri., vol. 8 no. 2 p. 32 (col.) (Feb '57).
Holiday 10: 46-7 (col.) Nov '51; 19: 127 (col.) Jan '56; 23: 7 Feb '58; 24: 54 (col.) Oct '58; 104: 548, 569 (col.) Oct '53.

—— (boat). Natl. geog. 114: 535 Oct '58.

—— (cooking, yacht). Natl. geog. 116: 798 (col.) Dec '59.

—— (heads). Natl. geog. 116: 313 (col.) Sept '59.

—— (heads, comic). Holiday 10: 5 Nov '51.

—— (Jap. children, dinner). Natl. geog. 116: 322 (col.) Sept '59.

—— (Negro bootblacks). Natl. geog. 109: 206 Feb '56.

—— (19th cent.). Natl. geog. 113: 17 (col.) Jan '58.

—— (shower bath on ship). Natl. geog. 108: 828 (col.) Dec '55.

——, British. Natl. geog. 101: 535 (col.) Ap '52.

——, Portuguese (drill). Natl. geog. 103: 686 (col.) May '53.

——, Tasmanian. Natl. geog. 110: 796 (col.) Dec '56.

sailors & girl. Holiday 25: 115, 117, 119 (col.) May '59.

—— (back view). Natl. geog. 101: 541 (col.) Ap '52.

—— (beach). Holiday 10: 47 (col.) Nov '51.

sailors. See also navy men.

saint, wooden (on cross). Holiday 18: 61 (col.) Jl '55.

St. Agnes (maidenhood sym.). Lehner: Pict. bk. of sym., p. 40.

"St. Agostino" (in wood by Plura). Con. 138: 177 Dec '56.

"St. Ambrose & St. Filino" (Terrari). Con. 138: 118 Nov '56.

"St. Andrew" (Saavedra). Con. 13: 121 Ap '55.

St. Andrew (sym., Scotland). Lehner: Pict. bk. of sym., p. 39.

St. Andrew's golf course (Scotland). Travel 103: 46 May '55.

St. Angelo (Bay of Naples). Travel 103: 19 Ap '55.

St. Angelo castle (Rome). Con. 145: XXXVII May '60.
Travel 101: inside cover May '54.

"St. Anne & the Virgin" (sculpture, 15th cent.). Con. 132: XXV Sept '53.

"St. Anne instructing the Virgin" (alabaster). Con. ency. of ant., vol. 3, pl. 129.

"St. Anne with Virgin & child" (statue, 15th cent.). Con. 132: LV Sept '53.

"St. Anselmo" (int., Rome). Con. 141: 178 May '58.

St. Anthony church. See church of St. Anthony.

"St. Anthony of Padua," legend of (David). Con. 144: 38 Sept '59.

Saint-Aubin-d-Ecrosville chateau. See chateau, French (Saint-Aubin-d-Ecrosville).

"St. Augustine" (Baratta). Con. 142: 177 Dec '58.

St. Augustine (Fla.). Holiday 12: 98-9 (col.) Nov '52.

—— Jordan: Hammond's pict. atlas, p. 68-9 (col.).

—— (1st school in U.S.). Travel 111: 32 Feb '59.

—— (fort). Brooks: Growth of a nation, p. 33.

Holiday 27: 177 (col.) Je '60.

Natl. geog. 113: 42-3 (col.) Jan '58.

—— (Fort Castillo de San Marcas). Travel 114: 21 Oct '60.

—— (historic views). Natl. geog. 113: 42-3 (col.) Jan '58.

—— (mission alter). Face of Amer., p. 30-1 (col.).

St. Barbara (defense). Lehner: Pict. bk. of sym., p. 40.

St. Barnabas church (Norfolk is.). Travel 112: 36 Dec '59.

'St. Bartholomew" (Baratta). Con. 142: 174 Dec '58.

"St. Bartholomew" (Rembrandt). Con. 143: 129 Ap '59.

St. Basil's cathedral (Moscow). Holiday 18: 45 Nov '55.

Natl. geog. 116: 355 (col.) Sept '59.

"St. Benedict in glory." Con. 144: 106 Nov '59.

"St. Benedict in Penitence." Con. 143: 38 Mar '59.

St. Bernard hospice (Swiss Alps). Natl. geog. 111: 56-61 Jan '57.

St. Bernard monument. Natl. geog. 111: 57 Jan '57.

St. Bernard of Sacramenia monastery. Travel 102: 25-6 Aug '54.

St. Botolph (Boston). Amer. heri., vol. 10 no. 6 p. 53 (Oct '59).

St. Catherine of Alexandria (wood sculpture, 14th cent.). Con. 140: 170 Dec '57.

St. Catherine (Italy). Lehner: Pict. bk. of sym., p. 39.

"St. Catherine" (Baratta). Con. 142: 177 Dec '58.

St. Catherine's wheel (sym.). Lehner: Pict. bk. of sym., p. 36.

St. Cecile cathedral. Natl. geog. 100: 29-32 (col.) Jl '51.

"St. Cecilia" (Cavallino). Labande: Naples, p. 112.

St. Cecilia (music sym.). Lehner: Pict. bk. of sym., p. 40.

"St. Cecilia & an angel" (Gentileschi). Natl. geog. 110: 640 (col.) Nov '56.

"St. Christopher" (carved wood). Con. 134: XLIX Dec '54.

St. Christopher medal (sym.). Lehner: Pict. bk. of sym., p. 64.

St. Clemens cathedral (Denmark). Natl. geog. 105: 423 Mar '54.

St. Cloud porcelain. See porcelain, St. Cloud.

St. Columba alter. Praeg.: Pict. ency., p. 262 (col.).

"St. Cosmas" figure (polychrome). Con. 145: 132 Ap '60.

St. Cosmo (medicine sym.). Lehner: Pict. bk. of sym., p. 40.

St. Crepin (polychrome). Con. 142: LXVII Jan '59.

St. Croix (Virgin is.). Natl. geog. 109: 228-9 (col.) Feb '56.

—— (map). Natl. geog. 109: 207 Feb '56.

—— (Nicholas Cruger's store). Amer. heri., vol. 6 no. 4 p. 7 (Je '55).

St. Cuthbert's retreat (Holy island cross). Natl. geog. 102: 561 Oct '52.

St. Damien (medicine sym.). Lehner: Pict. bk. of sym., p. 40.

St. Denis, Ruth. Cur. biog. p. 545 (1949).

St. Efisio parade (Sardinia). Holiday 23: 70 (col.) Jan '58.

St. Eloi of Nayon. Con. 138: LXI Nov '56.

St. Etienne, Caen, Normandy (choir). Praeg.: Pict. ency., p. 187.

Saint, Eva Marie. Cur. biog. p. 525 (1955).

"St. Francesca Romana," silver (Italian). Con. 144: 154 Dec '59.

'St. Francis" (Carracci). Con. 138: 228 Jan '57.

St. Francis chapel (Cal.). Natl. geog. 98: 10 Jl '50.

"St. Francis in ecstasy" (Bellini). Con. 140: 240 Jan '58.

St. Francis of Assisi (church). Holiday 16: 98 (col.) Sept '54.

"St. Francis receiving the rule" (detail, Ghirlandaio). Con. 139: 99 Ap '57.

St. Gallen (Collegiate church, int.). Praeg.: Pict. ency., p. 21.

—— (monastic library, int.). Praeg.: Pict. ency., p. 377.

Saint-Gaudens, Augustus. Amer. heri., vol. 11 no. 6 p. 11 (Oct '60).

—— (bas relief by). Amer. heri., vol. 9 no. 4 p. 55 (Je '58).

—— (work of). Amer. heri., vol. 10 no. 2 p. 11 (Feb '59).

Saint-Gaudens, Homer. Cur. biog. p. 746 (1941).

St. George, Katherine. Cur. biog. p. 560 (1947).

St. George, Sgt. Thomas R. Cur. biog. p. 577 (1944).

"St. George" (Sir Edward Burne-Jones). Con. 141: cover (col.) Je '58.

St. George (statuette). See statuette of St. George.

St. George (Eng., sym.). Lehner: Pict. bk. of sym., p. 39.

St. George hotel. See Hotel St. George (Algiers).

St. George is. (Grenada is.). Holiday 23: 37 (col.) Feb '58.

Travel 104: 42 Oct '55.

"St. George & the dragon." Natl. geog. 101: 98 (col.), 103 Jan '52.

"St. George & the dragon" (Bologna). Con. 143: 265 Je '59.

"St. George & the dragon" (Burne-Jones). Con. 142: 83 Nov '58.

"St. George & the dragon" (de Coter). Con. 143: 65 Mar '59.

"St. George & the dragon" (sym.). Lehner: Pict. bk. of sym., p. 57.

"St. George & the dragon" (Uccello). Con. 143: 107 Ap '59.

St. Gerolamo. Con. 142: LXII Jan '59.

St. Giles church (Stokes Poges). Natl. geog. 108: 311 (col.) Sept '55.

"St. Giles house" (Eng., ext. & int.). Con. 144: 72 (col.), 74-7 Nov '59.

St. Giorgio Maggiore. Con. 145: 186 May '60.

St. Gotthard Pass (Switzerland). Holiday 28: 42-3 (col.) Aug '60.

St. Guenole (Brittany). Holiday 27: 82-3 (col.) Jan '60.

"Saint Helena" (Conegliano). Natl. geog. 110: 630 (col.) Nov '56.

"St. Helena" (Havell). Con. 136: 129 Nov '55.

St. Helena is. Natl. geog. 98: 266-79 Aug '50. Travel 107: 45-8 Mar '57.

—— (map). Natl. geog. 98: 271 Aug '50.

St. Hilarion castle entrance (Cyprus is.). Natl. geog. 101: 648 (col.) May '52.

"St. Hubert" (panel, 1500). Con. 144: VI Jan '60.

St. Hubert's stag (sym.). Lehner: Pict. bk. of sym., p. 38.

"St. Hugh of Grenoble visiting the refectory" (Zurbaran). Con. 133: 125 Ap '54.

St. Irene church. See church, St. Irene.

St. James (Spain). Lehner: Pict. bk. of sym., p. 39.

"St. James" (Dali). Con. 144: 253 (col.) Jan '60.

St. James cathedral entrance (Jerusalem). Natl. geog. 98: 742 (col.) Dec '50.

St. James palace guard. See London (St. James palace guard).

"St. James supporting Virgin" (modern figure). Con. ency. of ant., vol. 3, pl. 54.

"St. James the Less" (Ger. sculpture, 13th cent.). Con. 133: 140 Ap '54.

"St. Jerome" (Durer). Con. 141: 47 Mar '58.

St. Jerome (scholars). Lehner: Pict. bk. of sym., p. 40.

"St. Jerome" (Van Eyck). Con. 138: 277 Jan '57.

"St. Jerome" (sculpture by Della Valle). Con. 144: 175 Dec '59.

"St. Jerome in his study" (Cranach). Praeg.: Pict. ency., p. 288 (col.).

"St. Jerome in Penitence" (Roberti). Con. 136: 38 Sept '55.

"St. Jerome in the wilderness" (Bellini). Con. 136: 136 Nov '55.

"St. Jerome in the wilderness" (Montegna). Con. ency. of ant., vol. 1, pl. 151.

"St. Jerome with the angels" (Domenichino). Con. 132: 8 Sept '53.

"St. Jerome with lion" (wood statue, 15th cent.). Con. 142: LXV Dec '58.

"St. Jerome writing" (Caravaggio). Con. 142: 144 Dec '58.

St. Joan of Arc (France). Lehner: Pict. bk. of sym., p. 39.

—— See also Jeanne d'arc.

St. John, Robert. Cur. biog. p. 730 (1942).

"St. John" (Marble statue). Con. 142: 9 Sept '58.

"St. John" (miniature). Con. 132: 212 Jan '54.

St. John (sym.). Lehner: Pict. bk. of sym., p. 37.

St. John (Virgin islands). Natl. geog. 109: 220-1 (col.) Feb '56.

St. John church (Wash., D.C.). Jensen: The White House, p. 31.

St. John Lateran cathedral (int., Rome). Holiday 7: 113 May '50.

"St. John on Patmos" (Poussin). Con. 143: 127 Ap '59.

"St. John the Baptist." Con. 145: 190 May '60.

"St. John the Baptist" (Florentine terracotta). Con. 145: XXXIX Mar '60.

St. John the Baptist (head on charger). Con. ency. of ant., vol. 3, pl. 136.

St. John the Baptist (Memlinc). Praeg.: Pict. ency., p. 263 (col.).

St. John the Baptist (sculpture). Labande: Naples, p. 69.

St. John the Baptist. See also John the Baptist.

"St. John the Evangelist" (Daddi). Con. 145: LXV (col.) May '60.

"St. John the Evangelist" (Niccolo). Con. 136: 215 Dec '55.

"St. John the Evangelist on Patmos." Natl. geog. 110: 636 (col.) Nov '56.

St. John's baptisterium. Osward: Asia Minor, pl. 38.

St. John's cave. See cave of St. John.

St. John's church (Canada). Holiday 27: 146 (col.) Mar '60.

St. John's church (above the Apostle's grave, Ephesus). Osward: Asia Minor, pl. 33, 48.

St. John's church (Richmond, Va.). Holiday 8: 27 (col.) Sept '50; 10: 92 Sept '51; 18: 107 (col.) Nov '55. Travel 106: cover Dec '56.

St. John's college (Cambridge). Con. 141: XXXVII Ap '58.

St. John's Latern. Travel 105: 12 Mar '56.

"St. John's vision" (El Greco). Con. 144: 135 Nov '59.

"St. Joseph" (Baratta). Con. 142: 175 Dec Dec '58.

St. Joseph's oratory (Montreal). Holiday 10: 55 Aug '51; 26: 51 (col.) Sept '59. Travel 105: 13 May '56.

"St. Katherine in prison" (Eng. 15th cent. alabaster). Con. 129: 40 Ap '52.

St. Kevin's church (Ireland). Holiday 23: 65 (col.) Je '58.

St. Kitts island. Amer. heri., vol. 6 no. 4 p. 4-5 (col.) (Je '55).

"St. Kunigunde" statue (Gunther). Con. ency. of ant., vol. 3, pl. 56.

St. Laurent, Louis. Holiday 6: 37 Aug '49.

St. Laurent, Louis S. Cur. biog. p. 545 (1948).

"St. Lawrence" (di Bicci). Con. 145: 114 Ap '60.

St. Lawrence (Memlinc). Praeg.: Pict. ency., p. 263 (col.).

"St. Lawrence" (polychrome & gilt). Con. 145: 136 Ap '60.

St. Lawrence river. Travel 110: 18-9 Aug '58.

St. Lawrence seaway. Natl. geog. 115: 300-39 (part col.) Mar '59.
Travel 106: 19-22 Nov '56.
—— (map). Natl. geog. 115: 306-7 (col.) Mar '59.
St. Leger, Barry. Amer. heri., vol. 7 no. 2 p. 28 (col.) (Feb '56).
St. Leger's orders of march. Amer. heri., vol. 7 no. 2 p. 28 (col.) (Feb '56).
St. Leonard (bust). Int. gr. soc.: Arts . . . p. 57 (col.).
"St. Leonard" (woodcut). Con. 132: 170 Jan '54.
St. Leopold (Austria). Lehner: Pict. bk. of sym., p. 39.
St. Louis (Mo.). Holiday 8: 35-49 (part col.) Oct '50; 27: 80-5 May '60.
Jordan: Hammond's pict. atlas, p. 102-3 (col.).
—— (1840). Amer. heri., vol. 2 no. 1 p. 49 (fall '50).
—— (1850). Amer. heri., vol. 8 no. 1 p. 16-7 (col.) (Dec '56).
—— (harbor). Amer. heri., vol. 8 no. 6 p. 24-5 (col.) (Oct '57).
—— (skyline). Holiday 27: 80 May '60.
—— (waterfront). Natl. geog. 114: 682-3 (col.) Nov '58.
St. Louis cathedral (New Orleans). Jordan: Hammond's Pict. atlas, p. 103 (col.).
Natl. geog. 118: 712 (col.) Nov '60.
Travel 102: 7 Aug '54; 103: 62 Je '55; 114: 27 Sept '60.
St. Louis gate (Quebec). Travel 105: 13 May '56.
St. Lucia (harbor). Travel 109: 23 May '58.
"St. Luke." Con. 143: 191 May '59.
St. Luke (sym.). Lehner: Pict. bk. of sym., p. 38.
"St. Luke writing the gospel" (12th cent.). Con. 144: 68 Sept '59.
St. Luke's tomb. See tomb of St. Luke.
"St. Malo" (Corot). Con. 142: 41 Sept '58.
"St. Margaret" (Titian). Con. 132: 48 Sept '53.
St. Marie Thrust (Martinique). Natl. geog. 115: 278-9 (col.) Feb '59.
St. Mark (sym.). Lehner: Pict. bk. of sym., p. 38.
St. Mark's church (in the Bouwerie, N.Y.). Amer. heri., vol. 5 no. 1 p. 54-5 (fall '53).
St. Mark's cathedral (Venice). Con. 145: XII Mar '60.
Natl. geog. 100: 398, 410 (col.) Sept '51; 111: 790-1 (col.) Je '57.
—— (Canaletto). Con. 142: 41 Sept '58.
—— (Guardi). Con. 140: 98 Nov '57.
—— (int.). Praeg.: Pict. ency., p. 176.
St. Mark's library. See library of St. Mark's (Venice).
St. Mark's square (Venice). Amer. heri., vol. 11 no. 3 p. 22 (col.) (Ap '60).
St. Mark's square (Venice, Del Campo). Con. 137: XXXV Mar '56.
St. Martin (sculpture). Praeg.: Pict. ency., p. 356.
"St. Martin & the beggar" (illum. page of bk.). Praeg.: Pict. ency., p. 218 (col.).
St. Martin in-the-fields church (London). Travel 113: 73 Ap '60.

St. Mary-Le-Bow (London). Holiday 27: 129 Jan '60.
"St. Mary Magdalon" (W. de Geest). Con. 142: 147 Dec '58.
"St. Mary Magdalen" (le Sueur). Con. 141: 39 Mar '58.
"St. Mary Magdalen" (Spada). Con. 142: 145 Dec '58.
St. Mary Maggiore church (Rome). Holiday 7: 112 May '50.
St. Mary's parade (Arles, France). Natl. geog. 109: 680-1 May '56.
St. Matthew (statue). Natl. geog. 100: 30 (col.) Jl '51.
St. Matthew (sym.). Lehner: Pict. bk. of sym., p. 38.
"St. Matthew writing the gospel" (Fabritius). Con. 144: 66 Sept '59.
"St. Michael" (Bermejo). Con. 126: 87 Oct '50.
"St. Michael's in Hildesheim" (int.). Praeg.: Pict. ency., p. 23.
St. Michael's mount (Cornish coast, Eng.). Holiday 15: 10 Jan '54.
St. Michel d' Aiguilhe (Le Puy, France). Holiday 14: 81 (col.) Nov '53.
St. Michel's chapel (France). Natl. geog. 100: 9 (col.) Jl '51; 117: 738 (col.) Je '60.
St. Moritz (Switzerland). Holiday 14: 60-5 (part col.) Dec '53; 27: 74-9 (col.) Feb '60; 28: 36-7 (col.) Aug '60.
Natl. geog. 98: 214 (col.) Aug '50; 110: 477 Oct '56.
Travel 105: 39-41 Feb '56.
—— (Badrutt's palace hotel). Con. 133: XLIV Mar '54, XXVI Ap '54.
St. Nicholas (Asia Minor). Amer. heri., vol. 12 no. 1 p. 23 (col.) (Dec '60).
St. Nicholas, legend of (Bari). Con. 136: 49 Sept '55.
St. Nicholas, legend of (David). Con. 133: 30 Mar '54; 144: 39 Sept '59.
St. Nicholas church (Amsterdam). Travel 105: 25 Ap '56.
St. Nicholas church (Ghent). Natl. geog. 113: 815 (col.) Je '58.
St. Nicholas day parade (Dec. 6th, Switzerland). Travel 106: 27 Dec '56.
"St. Nicholas of Tolentino" (Ferrari). Con. 136: 281 Jan '56.
St. Nicolaus (Russia). Lehner: Pict. bk. of sym., p. 39.
St. Olav. See Olav, King of Norway.
St. Panteleimon monastery (Mt. Athos). Natl. geog. 114: 772, 774-5 (part col.) Dec '58.
St. Patrick (statue, Ireland). Holiday 6: 49 Dec '49.
St. Patrick (sym., Ireland). Lehner: Pict. bk. of sym., p. 39.
St. Patrick's bell, shrine of. Holiday 23: 155 Mar '58.
St. Patrick's cathedral (N.Y.). Amer. heri., vol. 5 no. 1 p. 52 (fall '53).
Holiday 26: 227 Dec '59.
—— (int.). Holiday 10: 63 (col.) Dec '51.
St. Patrick's cathedral (red cap ceremony). Amer. heri., vol. 9 no. 5 p. 26 (col.) (Aug '58).
St. Patrick's day parade (N.Y., 1874). Amer. heri., vol. 9 no. 5 p. 27 (col.) (Aug '58).
St. Paul. Int. gr. soc.: Arts . . . p. 25 (col.).

St. Paul (statue). See statue (St. Paul).

St. Paul at Malta. *See* arrival of St. Paul at Malta.

St. Paul in stone (St. Paul without the walls). Natl. geog. 110: 758 (col.) Dec '56.

"St. Paul shipwrecked" (in Valletta). Natl. geog. 110: 756 (col.) Dec '56.

St. Paul's cathedral (London). Praeg.: Pict. ency., p. 380.

St. Paul's outside the walls (int., Rome). Holiday 7: 112 May '50.

St. Paul's tomb (supposedly). Natl. geog. 110: 759 Dec '56.

St. Paul (Minn., carnival). *See* carnival, winter (St. Paul, Minn.).

St. Paul (Minn., 1856). Amer. heri. vol. 8 no. 1 p. 18 (col.) (Dec '56).

—— (1857). Amer. heri., vol. 8 no. 1 p. 53 (Dec '56).

St. Peter (16th cent., carved oak). Con. 138: 49 Sept '56.

—— (sym.). Lehner: Pict. bk. off sym., p. 38-9.

—— (with keep, book illus., 1520). Natl. geog. 110: 459 (col.) Oct '56.

"St. Peter, Adam, St. John & King David" (Raphael's mural). Holiday 7: 111 (col.) May '50.

"St. Peter gives coins to tax collector" (Masaccio). Praeg.: Pict. ency., p. 252 (col.).

St. Peter's basilica. Holiday 23: 50 (col.) May '58.

St. Peter's cathedral (Mexico City). Travel 110: 17 Nov '58.

St. Peter's cathedral (Vatican). Holiday 5: 89 Feb '49, 91 Mar '49; 6: 33, 135 (col.) Oct '49, 127 Nov '49; 7: 106 (col.) May '50; 11: 36, 42 Ap '52; 13: 79 Feb '53; 27: 73 Ap '60.
Natl. geog. 100: 720 (col.) Dec '51; 111: 438, 462, 467, 490 (part col.) Ap '57, 800 (col.) Je '57.
Praeg.: Pict. ency., p. 315.
Travel 105: cover Ap '56.

—— (dome). Natl. geog. 111: 463 (col.) Ap '57.

—— (guards). Holiday 27: 71 Ap '60.

—— (int.). Holiday 7: 113 May '50.
Travel 113: 36-7 Ap '60.

—— (plan). Praeg.: Pict. ency., p. 313.

—— (reconstruction). Praeg.: Pict. ency., p. 40.

St. Peter's cathedral (Venice, night). Holiday 27: 124 Jan '60.

St. Peter's church (int.). Travel 103: 32 Ap '55.

St. Peter's church (Antioch). Osward: Asia Minor, pl. 25-6.

St. Peter's church (Hamilton, Bermuda). Travel 111: 17 Feb '59.

St. Peter's square (Vatican). Con. 141: 235 Je '58.

St. Petersburg (Fla). Holiday 24: 78-83 (part col.) Nov '58.
Travel 114: 25-7 Oct '60.

—— (harbor). Natl. geog. 107: 50-1 (col.) Jan '55.

St. Petersburg (Russia, 1809). Amer. heri., vol. 9 no. 2 p. 5-6 (col.) (Feb '58).

St. Petersburg porcelain. Con. 142: 270-1 Jan '59.

"St. Philip" (El Greco). Con. 142: 256 Jan '59.

St. Pierre (Martinique). Natl. geog. 115: 268-9 (col.) Feb '59.

"St. Quentin in the stocks" (15th cent. carved polychrome). Con. 140: LXIII Sept '57.

St. Regis hotel. Holiday 20: 82-7 (part col.) Dec '56.

Saint-Saens, Camille. Cooper: Con. ency. of music, p. 250.

St. Sauveur (Canada). Holiday 7: 52 (col.) Jan '50.

St. Sauveur cathedral (int., Belgium). Holiday 25: 47 (col.) Jan '59.

St. Savin church (int., France). Int. gr. soc.: Arts . . . p. 47 (col.).

"St. Sebastian" (Reni). Con. 143: 91 Ap '59.

St. Sebastian (sym. against disease). Lehner: Pict. bk. of sym., p. 40.

"St. Sebastian & holy women" (Spada). Con. 142: 146 Dec '58.

St. Severin (int.). Praeg.: Pict. ency., p. 477.

St. Sigismund (Poland). Lehner: Pict. bk. of sym., p. 40.

St. Simeon (near Quebec). Travel 110: 18 Aug '58.

St. Simon (statue). Natl. geog. 100: 30 (col.) Jl '51.

St. Simons is. (Georgia coast). Travel 110: 48-9 Oct '58.

—— (Ave. of oaks). Natl. geog. 113: 36 (col.) Jan '58.

St. Sophia cathedral. Natl. geog. 112: 405 Sept '57.

St. Sophia church (Istanbul). Natl. geog. 109: 72 (col.) Jan '56.
Travel 101: 40 May '54.

"St. Stephen" (polychrome & gilt). Con. 145: 136 Ap '60.

St. Stephen cathedral (Vienna). Natl. geog. 99: 770 Je '51; 115: 192 (col.) Feb '59.
Travel 101: 6 May '54.

St. Stephen cathedral window (Bourges, Fr.). Amer. heri., vol. 7 no. 1 p. 4 (col.) (Dec '55).

St. Stephen is. (Montenegro). Holiday 25: 87 (col.) Je '59.

St. Stephen's chapel (Westminster). Amer. heri., vol. 8 no. 4 p. 95 (Je '57).

"St. Teresa" (sculpture). Con. 144: 176 Dec '59.

St. Thomas (Portugal). Lehner: Pict. bk. of sym., p. 40.

St. Thomas (Virgin is.). Holiday 5: 116-7 (col.) Mar '49.
Travel 106: 26 Aug '56.

St. Tropez (France). Holiday 28: 46-51 (col.) Aug '60.

St. Trophine church tower. *See* church tower, St. Trophine.

"St. Ursula" (di Paolo). Con. 133: 209 May '54.

—— (fresco). Labande: Naples, p. 73.

Saint Veran (France). Natl. geog. 115: 570-88 Ap '59.

"St. Victor" (Lanino). Con. 143: 93 Ap '59.

"St. Vincent" (Goya). Con. 143: LI Ap '59.

St. Vincent procession. Holiday 7: 120 Ap '50.

St. Wenceslaus (Bohemia). Lehner: Pict. bk. of sym., p. 39.

Sainte Chapelle (int., Paris). Praeg.: Pict. ency., p. 201.

Sainte Madelaine (tympanum). Praeg.: Pict. ency., p. 249.

Saints, Patron (sym.). Lehner: Pict. bk. of sym., p. 39-40.

Sakel, Manfred. Cur. bio. p. 748 (1941).

Sakyamuni buddha (Japan). Praeg.: Pict. ency., p. 526.

Sala (Lake Como, Italy). Holiday 25: 97-8 (col.) Mar '59.

Sala di musica, decoration for (Venice). Con. 135: 38-9 Mar '55.

salad bowl & fork. Holiday 12: 13 Jl '52.

salad set, African. Holiday 18: 128 Oct '55.

Salamanassar III's black obelisk. See obelisk, the black. . . .

salamander (iron piece to brown food). Con. ency. of ant., vol. 3, p. 245.

salamander glass weight. Con. 142: 40 Sept '58.

Salant, Richard S. Cur. biog. p. 405 (1961).

Salazar, Antonio de Oliveira. Cur. biog. p. 749 (1941); p. 509 (1952).

Sale, Rhys M. Cur. biog. p. 485 (1957).

Saleh, Allah-Yar. Cur. biog. p. 552 (1953).

Salem (Mass.). Holiday 15: 106-9 (col.) Mar '54.
Travel 104: 39-41 Oct '55; 106: 29-31 Dec '56.

—— (Crowninshield wharf, 1805). Amer. heri., vol. 6 no. 2 p. 10-11 (col.) (winter '55).

Salem privateer "Grand Turk" (model). Holiday 18: 44 (col.) Aug '55.

Salermo cathedral (Italy). Labande: Naples, p. 188-9.

salesman. Holiday 22: 97 Oct '57.

—— (man head, shoes). Holiday 10: 21 (col.) Nov '51.

——, book (1890). Amer. heri., vol. 9 no. 5 p. 39 (col.) (Aug '58).

sali (Kazakh shawl). Natl. geog. 106: 636 (col.) Nov '54.

salieres, antique. Con. 143: 138 May '59.

Salinger, Pierre. Cur. biog. p. 407 (1961).
Jensen: The White House, p. 290.

Salisbury, Harrison E. Cur. biog. p. 526 (1955).

Salisbury (Rhodesia). Natl. geog. 118: 327 (col.) Sept '60.

Salisbury cathedral (Eng.). Amer. heri., vol. 7 no. 1 p. 7 (col.) (Dec '55).
Con. 129: LXVII Je '52.
Natl. geog. 108: 347 Sept '55.

"Salisbury cathedral" (Turner). Con. ency. of ant., vol. 1, pl. 142.

Salisbury cathedral spire. Holiday 28: 31 (col.) Dec '60.

Salit, Rabbi Norman. Cur. biog. p.. 528 (1955).

Salk, Dr. Jonas. Holiday 23: 9 Jan '58.

Salk, Dr. Jonas E. Cur. biog. p. 552 (1954).

salmon hatchery. Natl. geog. 102: 601 (col.) Nov '52.

Salmon river (Idaho). Holiday 15: 38 (col.) Je. '54.

"Salome awaits head of John Baptist" (mural). Natl. geog. 109: 60 (col.) Jan '56.

Salomon, Henry, jr. Cur. biog. p. 538 (1956).

Salonika (Greece). Natl. geog. 109: 58-9 (col.) Jan '56.
Travel 114: 20 Aug '60.

saloon, pioneer (int.). Horan: Pict. hist. of wild west, p. 107, 124.

saloon, western. Amer. heri. vol. 6 no. 1 p. 67 (fall '54).

Salote Tupou, Queen of Tonga. Cur. biog. p. 553 (1953).

salt, sea water evaporated. Natl. geog. 99: 455 (col.) Ap '51.

salt & pepper shakers. Holiday 24: 148 Oct '58.

——, Irish (antique). Con. 134: VII Sept '54.

salt bowl, tripod silver (antique). Con. 132: 140 Nov '53.

salt box, antique silver. Con. 132: 112 Nov '53.

——, antique silver (double). Con. 138: 273 Jan '57.

——, Elizabeth I. Con. 132: 201 Jan '54; 138: 263 Jan '57.

——, gilt (18th cent.). Con. 133: 153 May '54.

——, huntsman silver (15th cent.). Con. 132: 22 Sept '53.

——, Russian antique. Con. 140: XXXIII Nov '57.

——, sheep. Rawson: Ant. pict. bk., p. 25.

——, Stonyhurst. Con. 140: 112 Nov '57.

salt box house. Amer. heri., vol. 1 no. 4 p. 31 (col.) (summer '50); vol. 11 no. 5 p. 20 (Aug '60).

salt box house (2 centuries old). Holiday 11: 43 (col.) Je '52.

salt cellar (for Francis I). Praeg.: Pict. ency., p. 295.

——, Elizabethan. Con. 139: 30 Mar '57, 124 Ap '57.

——, George II. Con. 132: XL Sept '53; 143: XLVII Mar '59, XXXIV Ap '59, XVI May '59, XXXIV Je '59.

——, George III (by Storr). Con. 145: LIV May '60.

——, gilt bronze (Paduan, 1500). Con. 144: 220-1 Jan '60.

——, gold (Cellinis). Natl. geog. 97: 754 Je '50.

——, Irish glass. Con. ency. of ant., vol. 3, pl. 45.

——, Irish silver (antique). Con. 129: XVI Ap '52.

——, nautilus shell ship. Con. 144: 42 Sept '59.

——, silver. Holiday 10: 64 (col.) Sept '51.

——, silver (1735). Con. ency. of ant., vol. 1, p. 153.

——, silver (18th cent.). Con. 133: III Je '54; 144: XXX Nov '59, XII Dec '59, XIV Jan '60; 145: XX Mar '60, LII Ap '60, XX May '60.

——, silver (Lamerie). Con. 144: 64 Sept '59.

——, silver trencher (Queen Anne). Con. 145: XLIX Mar '60.

——, tall renaissance (Limoges, 1560). Con. 145: 79 (col.) Ap '60.

salt dish. Con. 137: LVI May '56.

——, antique silver. Con. 136: 261 Jan '56.

——, George III silver. Con. 135: X May '55.

salt holder, high silver (17th cent.). Con. ency. of ant., vol. 3, pl. 30.

——, silver (18th cent.). Con. 143: 171 May '59.

——, silver French (16th cent.). Con. ency. of ant., vol. 3, pl. 32.

——, silver gilt (Stonyhurst). Con. 143: 51 Mar '59.

——, triple. Con. 134: 193 Dec '54.

Salt Lake. See Great Salt Lake.

Salt Lake City (Utah). Holiday 14: 33 Aug '53.
Jordan: Hammond's pict. atlas, p. 168-9 (col.).
Travel 112: 33 Aug '59.
—— (early). Amer. heri. vol. 7 no. 6 p. 25 (Oct '56).
—— (Morman temple). Brooks: Growth of a nation, p. 130.
Face of Amer., p. 159 (col.).

Salt Lake Valley (Mormon). Brooks: Growth of a nation, p. 129.

salt making (Japan). Natl. geog. 104: 624 Nov '53.

salt mine (Austria). Natl. geog. 118: 264-5 (col.) Aug '60.

salt mine cathedral (Zipaquira, Colombia). Travel 108: 29-31 Oct '57.

salt pack (on yaks, Nepal). Natl. geog. 117: 377 (col.) Mar '60.

salt pan (Bahamas). Natl. geog. 113: 182-3 (col.) Feb '58.

salt plate (Russia). Con. 144: 277 Jan '60.

salt slab, desert. Natl. geog. 112: 66 (col.) Jl '57.

salt stand, copper gilt (Venetian, 1570). Con. 144: 220 Jan '60.

salt trencher (antique). Con. 132: XXXVI Nov '53.

——, silver (18th cent.). Con. ency. of ant., vol. 1, pl. 86.

salt vats. Travel 104: 41 Oct '55.

Salta (Argentina). Natl. geog. 113: 338 (col.) Mar '58.

Salter, Andrew. Cur. biog. p. 580 (1944).

Salter, Sir Arthur. Cur. biog. p. 581 (1944).

Saltonstall, Leverett. Cur. biog. p. 584 (1944); p. 540 (1956).
Holiday 14: 37 Nov '53.

Saltonstall, Richard. Amer. heri., vol. 10 no. 6 p. 49 (Oct '59).

Saltonstall, William G. Holiday 20: 71 (col.) Dec '56.

Saltzman, Charles E. Cur. biog. p. 562 (1947).

"Salute of the tongue" (Tibet). Natl. geog. 108: 45 Jl '55.

Salve Regina college. Holiday 16: 41 Aug '54.

Salvemini, Gaetano. Cur. biog. p. 658 (1943).

salver (18th cent.). Con. 141: LV Mar '58.

——, antique silver. Con. 134: XXIII Dec '54; 140: XX, XXXVI, 219 Jan '58; 141: 104 Ap '58, 200 May '58; 142: V Nov '58.

——, George I (silver). Con. 140: XXXVII Sept '57; 144: XIX Jan '60, XXXVI Nov '59.

——, George I (on stand). Con. 142: XI Jan '59.

——, George II (silver). Con. 139: 58 Mar '57, XLV May '57; 140: XII Sept '57; 141:

XII Mar '58, XX Ap '58, XXVI, 188 May '58, XVIII Je '58; 142: XII Sept '58, XLVI Nov '58, XII Dec '58, XXXIV Jan '59; 143: 55 Mar '59, XX May '59, LXVII Je '59; 144: XX Dec '59, XLII Jan '60; 145: IX Mar '60.

——, George III (silver). Con. 138: XX Nov '56; 139: LI Je '57; 140: XXXVIII Dec '57; 143: IX Ap '59, XX May '59.

——, Irish silver. Con. 139: 247 Je '57.

——, Irish silver (Daniel). Con. 145: LVIII Je '60.

——, James I (silver). Con. 139: 32 Mar '57.

——, James II. Con. 138: 142 Nov '56.

——, marriage (antique). Con. 142: 269 Jan '59.

——, Queen Anne (silver). Con. 141: III Ap '58.

——, silver. Con. 141: XVII Je '58.

——, silver (18th cent.). Con. ency. of ant., vol. 1, pl. 78.
Con. 132: XXXIII Sept '53; 133: 120 Ap '54; 137: 66 Mar '56; 143: 19 Mar '59; 144: XXXVIII Sept '59.

——, silver (19th cent.). Con. 141: XXVIII Ap '58.

——, silver (St. Edmund's college ware). Con. 142: 15 Sept '58.

——, Tazza (on stand). Con. 142: IX Jan '59.

——, William & Mary (silver). Con. 144: XV Nov '59.

——, William III (silver). Con. 145: XXXIII May '60.

salver. See also tray.

Salverson, Laura Goodman. Cur. biog. p. 486 (1957).

Salviati, Francesco (work of). Con. 136: 36 Sept '55.

Salzburg (Austria). Holiday 15: 29 Feb '54; 20: 52-5 (part col.) Aug '56.
Natl. geog. 99: 756-7 (col.), 786 Je '51.
Travel 103: 26 Ap '55; 110: 51-3 Aug '58.

Salzburg academy of music (int., Austria). Holiday 25: 121 Jan '59.

Salzburg Alps. See Alps, Salzburg.

Salzkammergut (Austrian Alpine). Natl. geog. 118: 246-75 (part col.) Aug '60.

"Sam" (Marshall). Con. 142: 133 Nov '58.

Samael (seal of). Lehner: Pict. bk. of sym., p. 24.

Samandag. Osward: Asia Minor, pl. 23-4.

Samandag beach. Osward: Asia Minor, pl. 30.

Samaritan women at well). Natl. geog. 110: 729 (col.) Dec '56.

Samaritans (in synagogue). Natl. geog. 110: 718 (col.) Dec '56.

Samarkand hotel (Santa Barbara, Cal.). Travel 108: 48 Nov '57.

Samaroff, Olga. Cur. biog. p. 532 (1946).

Samarra Barrage (Tigres river). Natl. geog. 114: 464-5 (col.) Oct '58.

samisen (Japanese musical instrument). Travel 113: 46 Jan '60.

Sammartino, Peter. Cur. biog. p. 376 (1958).

Samoa is. Disney: People & places, p. 129-46 (col.).
Holiday 28: 161 (col.) Oct '60.
Travel 101: 33-5 Jan '54; 106: 52-5 Dec '56; 114: 36 Dec '60.

—— **(huts).** Holiday 28: 54-5 (col.) Oct '60.
Samoa village. Holiday 9: 55 Mar '51.
Samoan chief. Travel 114: 40 Dec '60.
Samoan children. Disney: People & places, p. 144-45 (col.).
Travel 101: 35 Jan '54.
Samoan girl. Travel 114: 39 Dec '60.
Samoan home. Travel 102: 16 Nov '54.
Samoan man. Travel 101: 33, 35 Jan '54.
—— **(carrying banana stalk).** Disney: People & places, p. 136 (col.).
—— **(picking coconuts).** Disney: People & places, p. 137 (col.).
Samos (Temple of Hera). See Temple of Hera (plan).
samovar. Holiday 12: 133 Oct '52.
sampan (boat). Natl. geog. 105: 248-9 Feb '54.
—— **(Formosa).** Natl. geog. 109: 266 (col.) Feb '56.
—— **(Hong Kong).** Natl. geog. 104: 560 (col.) Oct '53.
—— **(Thailand).** Disney: People & places, p. 165, 176 (col.).
sampans (Bangkok). Natl. geog. 116: 788-9 (col.) Dec '59.
——, **floating market (Bangkok).** Natl. geog. 116: 847 (col.) Dec '59.
Sampson, Mrs. Edith S. Cur. biog. p. 512 (1950).
Sampson, Sam. Horan: Pict. hist. of wild west, p. 144.
"Samson & Delilah" (Brandt). Con. 145: 280 Je '60.
"Samson & Delilah" (Pellegrini). Con. 145: 107 Ap '60.
"Samson & Delilah" (Van Dyck). Natl. geog. 97: 758 (col.) Je '50.
"Samson & the lion" (figurine). Con. 129: 53 (col.) Ap '52.
"Samson & the Philistines" (da Vinci). Con. 142: 198 Dec '58.
"Samson slaying two Philistines" (sculpture by Foggini). Con. 141: 225 Je '58.
Samuel, Bernard. Cur. biog. p. 548 (1949).
Samuel, Lord Herbert Louis. Cur. biog. p. 530 (1955).
Samuel, Mrs. Zerelda (mother Jesse James). Horan: Pict. hist. of wild west, p. 29.
Samuel home, Zerelda. Horan: Pict. hist. of wild west, p. 29.
"San Andreas fault" (Cal.). Natl. geog. 101: 124 Jan '52.
San Andres is. (Caribbean). Travel 108: 24-6 Aug '57.
San Antonio (Tex.). Holiday 13: 14 Jan '53; 21: 102 Jan '57.
—— **(old west, 1876).** Horan: Pict. hist. of wild west, p. 100.
San Antonio chapel (Capri, Italy). Lebande: Naples, p. 214.
San Bernardino (wood sculpture). Con. 140: 175 Dec '57.
San Biagio (Venice). Praeg.: Pict. ency., p. 435.
Can Blas is. Holiday 12: 56-8 (part col.) Nov '52.
San Carlo Alle Quattro Fontane (ground plan, Rome). Praeg.: Pict. ency., p. 324.
San Carlo Borromeo mission (Carmel, Cal.). Travel 114: 26 Sept '60.

San Cayetano church (Mexico). Holiday 26: 50 (col.) Nov '59.
San Cristobal cathedral. Holiday 12: 65 (col.) Dec '52.
San Diego. Travel 103: 30-4 Je '55.
—— **(Balboa park).** Travel 113: 35 May '60.
—— **(harbor).** Jordan: Hammond's pict. atlas, p. 207 (col.).
—— **(mission).** Travel 108: 18 Jl '57.
San Diego de Alcala mission. See Mission San Diego de Alcala
San Domenico (altar predella). Praeg.: Pict. ency., p. 251 (col.).
San Felipe church (Albuquerque). Jordan: Hammond's pict. atlas, p. 127 (col.).
San Fernando Valley. Holiday 10: 108-15 (part col.) Dec '51; 22: 54 (col.) Oct '57.
"San Francesco della Vigna" (Venice, Canaletto). Con. 132: 123 Nov '53.
San Francisco (Cal.). Face of Amer., p. 116-7 (col.).
Holiday 14: 79 Jl '53, 27-41 (part col.) Sept '53; 25: 5 (col.) Ap '59.
Jordan: Hammond's pict. atlas, p. 200-1 (col.).
Natl. geog. 110: 182-225 (part col.) Aug '56.
—— **(Chinatown).** See Chinatown (San Francisco).
—— **(1848).** Horan: Pict. hist. of wild west, p. 22.
—— **(1849).** Durant: Pict. hist. of Amer. circus, p. 34.
—— **(1850).** Amer. heri., vol. 1 no. 3 p. 44 (col.) (spring '50).
—— **(1865).** Horan: Pict. hist. of wild west, p. 22.
—— **(harbor).** Holiday 9: 90 (col.) Mar '51; 25: 136 (col.) Mar '59.
Natl. geog. 99: 738-9 (col.) Je '51.
—— **(harbor, art).** Holiday 11: 32 (col.) Mar '52.
—— **(harbor, 1850).** Amer. heri., vol. 8 no. 1 p. 52-3 (Dec '56).
—— **(Hilton hotel).** Travel 112: 8 Jl '59.
—— **(hotel).** Holiday 23: 164 (col.) Je '58.
—— **(jazz band).** Holiday 18: 73 (col.) Sept '55.
—— **(map, downtown).** Natl. geog. 110: 191 Aug '56.
—— **(restaurant, int.).** Holiday 24: 63-5 Sept '58.
—— **(restaurants).** Holiday 19: 64-5 Je '56.
—— **(where to eat).** Holiday 11: 62-7 Feb '52.
San Francisco, church of. See church of San Francisco.
San Francisco Bay. Holiday 20: 26-35 (part col.) Aug '56.
"San Francisco blues" (Militia Co., 1856). Amer. heri., vol. 7, no. 5 back cover (col.) (Aug '56).
San Fruttuoso (Italy). Holiday 13: 60 (col.) Je '53.
San Gabriel cross. Amer. heri., vol. 2 no. 2 p. 8 (winter '51).
San Gabriel mission. Amer. heri., vol. 1 no. 3 p. 33 (col.) (spring '50).
San Gimignano (Italy). Holiday 27: 61 Jan '60.
—— **(medieval tower).** Natl. geog. 111: 798 Je '57.
Travel 111: 35 Ap '59.

"San Giorgia Maggiore" (Guardi). Con. 144: 239 Jan '60.

San Giulio is. (Italy). Holiday 25: 90 (col.) Mar '59.

San Giusto castle. See castle of San Giusto.

San Gregorio Armeno. Labande: Naples, p. 50-6.

San Jacinto (Alamo memorial, Tex.). Travel 110: 19 Jl '58.

San Jacinto monument (near Houston, Tex.). Amer. heri., vol. 2 no. 3 p. 2 (col.) (spring '51).
Holiday 11: 101 Ap '52.
Natl. geog. 99: 746 Je '51.
Travel 107: 41 Mar '57.

San Jose (Rosicrucian park, Cal.). Travel 114: 40 Sept '60.

San Jose mission (Tex.). Travel 107: 43 Mar '57.

San Juan (Puerto Rico). Holiday 5: 52 (col.) Feb '49; 25: 18 Feb '59.
Natl. geog. 99: 440 Ap '51.

—— (harbor). Holiday 5: 50 Feb '49.

—— (hotels). See hotels (San Juan).

San Juan Capistrano mission (Cal.). Brooks: growth of a nation, p. 120.
Face of Amer., p. 14-5 (col.).

San Juan is. Amer. heri., vol. 11 no. 3 p. 62 (col.) (Ap '60).

San Leo (Italy). Holiday 26: 61, 67 (col.) Sept '59.

San Luis Obispo mission (Cal.). Amer. heri., vol. 1 no. 3 p. 34 (spring '50).

San Luis Rey de Francia mission. Amer. heri., vol. 1 no. 3 p. 34 (spring '50).

San Marco piazza. Con. 136: 76 Sept '55.

San Marino (Italy). Holiday 6: 72-8 Oct '49; 18: 104 (col.) Aug '55.
Travel 109: 38 Ap '58.

San Marino's piazza della Liberta. Holiday 26: 63 (col.) Sept '59.

San Martin, Jose. Holiday 12: 111 (col.) Oct '52.

San Martino monastery. Labande: Naples, p. 116-7.

San Miguel. Travel 111: 52 Feb '59.

San Pietro, Montorio, Rome (tempietto). Praeg.: Pict. ency., p. 260.

"San Remo" (Joli). Con. 141: 189 May '58.

San Salvador (Natl. palace). Travel 110: 38 Oct '58.

San Simeon estate (Cal.). Holiday 26: 87 (col.) Dec '59.

San Solomon Spring (Balmorhea state park, Tex.). Jordan: Hammond's pict. atlas, p. 115 (col.).

San Souci palace (Haiti). Holiday 7: 99 (col.) Mar '50.

San Vitale mosaic. Praeg.: Pict. ency., p. 179 (col.).

San Xavier del Bac mission (Tucson). Jordan: Hammond's pict. atlas, p. 179 (col.).
Natl. geog. 104: 380-1 (col.) Sept '53.
Travel 106: 17 Dec '56.

San Xavier mission (Tucson). Holiday 16: 120 (col.) Oct '54; 17: 18 (col.) Jan '55; 18: 125 (col.) Nov '55; 19: 18 (col.) Jan '56; 25 63 (col.) Mar '59.
Travel 101: 15 Jan '54.

Sancta Sophia. Natl. geog. 100: 162 (col.) Aug '51.

Sand, George. Amer. heri., vol. 8 no. 2 p. 23 (Feb '57).

"sand buggy" (ocean beach). Natl. geog. 109: 661 (col.) May '56.

sand dune. Holiday 12: 90 (col.) Aug '52.
Natl. geog. 112: 114-36 (part col.) Jl '57.
Travel 102: 21 Dec '54.

sand dune scooter (men & women). Holiday 10: 35 (col.) Jl '51.

sand dunes (girl artist). Natl. geog. 108: 524 (col.) Oct '55.

sand dunes, Algodones. Natl. geog. 112: 718-9 (col.) Nov '57.

——, Cal. Natl. geog. 105: 823 Je '54.

——, Sahara. Natl. geog. 113: 684 May '58.

sand dunes. See also Great sand dunes.

sand painting, Indian. Amer. heri., vol. 7 no. 6 p. 14 (col.) (Oct '56).

——, Navajo. Disney: People & places, p. 122-3 (col.).

sandals, woman's. Holiday 15: 162 May '54; 8 Je '54; 19: 170, 172 May '56; 21: 168, 194-7 May '57; 21: 31, 191 Je '57; 22: 9 Jl '57; 23: 46 Je '58; 24: 140 Jl '58; 25: 200 May '59, 131 Je '59; 26: 118 Nov '59 27: 173, 240 May '60, 16, 195 Je '60; 28: 127 Jl '60, 181 (col.) Nov '60, 156 Dec '60.

——, Indian. Natl. geog. 114: 239 Aug '58.

——, Japanese. Holiday 11: 125 May '52.

——, sagebrush (90 centuries old). Natl. geog. 108: 796 Dec '55.

——, Tuareg (desert). Natl. geog. 113: 693 (col.) May '58.

Sandburg, Carl. Cur. biog. p. 370 (1963).
Holiday 14: 42 Sept '53; 20: 40 Sept '56; 28: 76 (col.) Dec '60.
Natl. geog. 117: 238 (col.) Feb '60.

Sandby, Paul. Con. 143: 265 Je '59.

—— (work of). Con. ency. of ant., vol. 1, pl. 147.
Con. 134: VII Nov '54; 137: 118 Ap '56; 140: IX Jan '58; 143: XXXVII May '59; 144: 123 Nov '59.

Sandby, Thomas (work of). Con. 143: LIX Je '59.

Sandeman, George. Con. 145: 96 Ap '60.

Sanders, George. Cur. biog. p. 661 (1943).
Holiday 12: 122 Oct '52.

Sandham, Henry (work of). Amer. heri., vol. 7 no. 6 p. 66 (col.) (Oct '56).

Sandhurst (Eng. military school). Holiday 23: 92-3 Mar '58.

sanding machine (man). Natl. geog. 110: 728 (col.) Dec '56.

Sandor, Gyorgy. Cur. biog. p. 563 (1947).

Sandstrom, Emil. Cur. biog. p. 545 (1951).

sandwich (bun & frankfurter). Holiday 21: 87 (col.) May '57.

Sandwich (mill pond, Cape Cod). Holiday 6: 63 Sept '49.

Sandys, Duncan. Cur. biog. p. 512 (1952).

Sandys, Sir Edwin. Amer. heri., vol. 10 no. 4 p. 11 (col.) (Je '59).

Sanford, M. M. (work of). Amer. heri., vol. 3 no. 3 p. 40 (col.) (spring '52).

Sandford, Terry. Cur. biog. p. 409 (1961).

Sanger, Margaret. Cur. biog. p. 587 (1944).

Sanguis Christi pageant (Bruges). Natl. geog. 107: 657-61, 663 (col.) May '55.

Sanibel is. Travel 103: 24-6 Feb '55.

Sanish, N. D. Natl. geog. 103: 726-7 (col.) Je '53.

Sankey, Ira D. Amer. heri., vol. 6 no. 5 p. 21, 23 (Aug '55).

Sanroma, Jesus Maria. Holiday 21: 42 Mar '57.

Sanssouci palace (Potsdam). Praeg.: Pict. ency., p. 369.

Sant' Agnese in Agone (Rome). Praeg.: Pict. ency., p. 318.

Sant' Andrea della Valle (plan, Rome). Praeg.: Pict. ency., p. 324.

Sant' Angelo, castle. See castel Sant' Angelo.

Santa Ana cathedral. See cathedral Santa Ana.

Santa Anna, Gen. Antonio Lopez de. Amer. heri., vol. 2 no. 3 p. 3-5 (spring '51).

Santa Anna, Gen. (surrender of). Holiday 23: 73 Mar '58.

Santa Barbara is. (Cal., map). Natl. geog. 114: 260-1 Aug '58.

Santa Barbara mission (Cal.). Amer. heri., vol. 1 no. 3 p. 33 (col.) (spring '50). Holiday 5: 7 (col.) Ap '49; 6: 117 Jl '49; 14: 76 Dec '53; 16: 121 (col.) Oct '54. Natl. geog. 105: 764 Je '54.

"Santa Cecilia" (Strozzi). Con. 136: LV Sept '55.

Santa Claus. Amer. heri., vol. 3 no. 2 p. 48-9 (winter '52). Holiday 10: 127, 146 Dec '51; 12: 36 Oct '52, cover, 4, 20, 26, 30, 110-11 (col.) Dec '52; 14: 2, 30, 79, 84 (col.) Dec '53. Natl. geog. 107: 288 Feb '55.

—— (asleep). Holiday 14: 143 (col.) Dec '53.

—— (cartoon). Holiday 14: 153 (col.) Nov '53.

—— (caught in chimney). Holiday 14: 37 Dec '53.

—— (charity aid). Holiday 10: 61 Dec '51.

—— (comic). Holiday 10: 41 Dec '51; 14: 117 (col.) Dec '53; 18: 85, 139, 189 (part col.) Dec '55; 20: cover, 154, 189, 203, 218-9 inside cover (part col.) Dec '56; 22: 204 (col.), 209 Dec '57; 24: 116 Dec '58; 28: 66-71 (col.) Dec '60. Travel 110: inside back cover Nov '58.

—— (crowds, comic). Holiday 24: 205 (col.) Dec '58.

—— (head). Holiday 6: 78 Oct '49; 10: 24 (col.) Dec '51; 12: 77 (col.) Dec '52; 28: 198 (col.) Dec '60.

—— (in sleigh). Lehner: Pict. bk. of sym., p. 51.

—— (lithographs, 1821). Amer. heri., vol. 12 no. 1 p. 23-6 (col.) Je '60.

—— (on bicycle, comic). Holiday 14: 132 (col.) Dec '53.

—— (reading to children). Holiday 23: 124 Jan '58.

—— (sleigh, reindeers). Natl. geog. 111: 85 (col.) Jan '57.

—— (sorting gifts). Holiday 28: 7 (col.) Dec '60.

—— (Victorian period). Amer. heri. vol. 10 no. 1 p. 40 (col.), 41 (Dec '58).

—— (with pack). Lehner: Pict. bk. of sym.,

p. 51.

——, Japanese. Natl. geog. 118: 743 (col.) Dec '60.

Santa Claus & child. Holiday 26: 199 (col.) Dec '59.

Santa Claus & man (heads, laughing). Holiday 10: 3 Dec '51.

Santa Claus. See also St. Nicholas.

Santa Cruz, Herman. Cur. biog. p. 549 (1949).

Santa Cruz (Cal.). Travel 107: 25 Feb '57.

—— (harbor). Natl. geog. 107: 502 (col.) Ap '55.

Santa Cruz (Tenerife). Travel 104: 47 Jl '55.

Santa Fe festival. Jordan: Hammond's pict. atlas, p. 125 (col.).

Santa Fe mission. See Spanish mission (Santa Fe).

Santa Fe's cathedral of St. Francis. Amer. heri., vol. 8 no. 6 p. 32 (Oct '57).

"Santa Gertrudis" (King ranch). Natl. geog. 101: 43 (col.) Jan '52.

"Santa Maria" ship (Columbus' ship). Lehner: Pict. bk. of sym., p. 52.

—— (replica). Amer. heri., vol. 11 no. 6 p. 19 (Oct '60).

Santa Maria Capua Vetere (amphitheatre). Labande: Naples, p. 134.

Santa Maria del Carmine (fresco). Praeg.: Pict. ency., p. 252 (col.).

Santa Maria del Fiore. Holiday 27: 129 Jan '60.

"Santa Maria Della Salute." Con. 140: 98 Nov '57.

"Santa Maria Della Salute" (Guardi). Con. 135: X (col.) Ap '55.

"Santa Maria Della Salute" (Marieschi). Con. 129: IX (col.) Ap '52.

Santa Maria Della Salute. Holiday 18: 47 (col.) Oct '55; 27: 129 Jan '60. Natl. geog. 111: 792 (col.) Je '57.

Santa Maria di Piedigrotta. Labande: Naples, p. 91.

Santa Maria Maggiore. Con. 141: 229 Je '58.

Santa Maria Maggiore cathedral (Rome). Holiday 16: 63 Dec '54.

Santa Maria Tonantzintla church (int., Mexico). Holiday 26: 58 (col.) Nov '59.

Santa Monica (Surf Rider Inn, Cal.). Travel 109: 47 Feb '58.

Santa Restituta (bas relief & mosaic). Labande: Naples, p. 44-5.

Santayana, George. Cur. biog. p. 590 (1944).

Santelmann, Lt. Col. William F. H. Cur. biog. p. 555 (1953).

Santi, Giovan Gioseffo (work of). Con. 144: 23 Sept '59.

Santi, Giovanni (work of). Con. 132: LIX Sept '53; 133: cover, opp. p. 3 (col.) Mar '54.

Santi Apostoli fresco (Rome). Praeg.: Pict. ency., p. 254 (col.).

Santi Maria e Donato (Murano). Travel 103: 51 May '55.

Santiago (Chile). Natl. geog. 117: 186-7 (col.) Feb '60.

Santiago (Cuba, man on cart). Holiday 5: 40 (col.) Feb '49.

Santiago de Compostela, church of. See church of Santiago de Compostela.

Santo Domingo. Holiday 5: 56-9 (col.) Feb '49.
—— (hotel). Holiday 25: 41 Ap '59.
—— (men & women). Holiday 5: 57 Feb '49.
Santo Tomas church (Chichicastenango). Natl. geog. 117: 414 (col.) Mar '60.
Santolalla, Irene Silva De. Cur. biog. p. 543 (1956).
Santorin (Greek is.). Holiday 16: 109 Nov '54.
Santorini (Greece). Holiday 15: 52 (col.) Je '54.
Santos, Rufino J., cardinal. Cur. biog. p. 358 (1960).
Santos sculpture, religious (New Mexico). Con. 140: 222-5 Jan '58.
Sanzio, Raphael (work of). Con. 145: LXXXIII May '60.
Sao Paulo (Brazil). Holiday 18: 71 (col.) Oct '55; 26: 28 Sept '59.
Natl. geog. 107: 348 Mar '55.
Travel 103: 9 Mar '55; 112: 20 Sept '59.
Sao Paulo (Musiu de arte—painting). Con. 133: 11-7 Mar '54.
sap bucket. Rawson: Ant. pict. bk., p. 61.
sap trough. Rawson: Ant. pict. bk., p. 31.
Sappington home (Arrow Rock, Mo.). Travel 105: 51 Ap '56, 58 May '56.
Saraceni (work of). Con. 145: 203 May '60.
Saracoglu, Sukru. Cur. biog. p. 732 (1942).
Saragat, Giuseppe. Cur. biog. p. 544 1956).
Sarasin, Pote. Cur. biog. p. 532 (1955).
Sarasota (Fla.). Holiday 28: 169 (col.) Dec '60.
Sarasota jungle gardens. See jungle gardens (Sarasota).
"Saratoga" (Perry's ship). Natl. geog. 104: 91 Jl '53.
Saratoga Springs (N.Y., "gay nineties"). Brooks: Growth of a nation, p. 214.
Sarawak (Borneo). Natl. geog. 109: 711-36 May '56.
Travel 109: 48-51 Feb '58.
—— (map). Natl. geog. 109: 716 May '56.
Saray-Burnu palace (ext. & int.). Osward: Asia Minor, pl. 94-9.
sarcophagus. Natl. geog. 98: 604 (col.) Nov '50.
—— (Eleusis, Greece). Natl. geog. 109: 53 (col.) Jan '53.
——, Ataturk's. See Ataturk's sarcophagus.
——, golden. Ceram: March of arch., p. 144.
——, King Sekhemkhets. Natl. geog. 108: 642 (col.) Nov '55.
sarcophagus front, Roman (1st cent.). Con. 133: 147 May '54.
sarcophagus of Alexander (detail). Osward: Asia Minor, pl. 20.
sarcophagus relief (2nd cent.). Con. ency. of ant., vol. 3, pl. 68.
Sardana dance (Spain, a Catalan dance). Holiday 26: 106 (col.) Dec '59.
Sardi, Vincent. Cur. biog. p. 488 (1957).
Sardi, Vincent, jr. Cur. biog. p. 489 (1957).
Sardinia. Disney: People & places, p. 69-82 (col.).
Sardinian (man). Holiday 13: 26 Feb '53.
—— (men & women). Holiday 23: 70-3 (part col.) Jan '58.
Sargeant, Howland H. Cur. biog. p. 514 (1952).

Sargeant, John Singer (work of). Con. 139: 9 Mar '57; 144: 11 Sept '59.
Praeg.: Pict. ency., p. 433.
Sargent, Malcolm. Cur. biog. p. 531 (1945).
Sargent, Porter. Cur. biog. p. 751 (1941).
sari (Indian woman's costume). Natl. geog. 103: 38, 66 (col.) Jan '53.
Sarnoff, David. Cur. biog. p. 547 (1951).
Sarnoff, Robert W. Cur. biog. p. 546 (1956).
Saroyan, William. Holiday 16: 89 Oct '54.
Sarto, Andrea del. See del Sarto, Andrea.
Sarton, George. Cur. biog. p. 734 (1942).
Sartorius, J. N. (work of). Con. 145: L Ap '60.
Sartre, Jean Paul. Cur. biog. p. 565 (1947).
sarungi (Afghan fiddle). Natl. geog. 98: 677 Nov '50.
Saskatchewan (early). Amer. heri., vol. 6 no. 6 p. 22-7 (Oct '55).
"Saskia carrying sick child" (Rembrandt). Con. 135: 137 Ap '55.
Sassetta (work of). Con. 132: 207 Jan '54.
Sastroamidjojo, Ali. Cur. biog. p. 513 (1950).
Satan's ram (sym.). Lehner: Pict. bk. of sym., p. 71.
Satant, Richard S. Cur. biog. p. 405 (1961).
satellite (circles globe). Natl. geog. 112: 807 Dec '57.
—— (earth view). Natl. geog. 118: 295-302 (part col.) Aug '60.
——, glass. Travel 111: 20 Feb '59.
——, project mercury. Natl. geog. 118: 49, 54-5, 83-4 (col.) Jl '60.
satellite finder (chart). Natl. geog. 112: 809 Dec '57.
satellites. Natl. geog. 112: 790-810 (col.) Dec '57.
——, space. Natl. geog. 109: 486-507 (part col.) Ap '56.
Satan (the Devil). Lehner: Pict. bk. of sym., p. 92.
"Satan's first address to Eve" (Fuseli). Con. 143: 93 Ap '59.
Satterfield, John C. Cur. biog. p. 371 (1962).
Saturday (sym.). Lehner: Pict. bk. of sym., p. 25.
Saturn (magic square). Lehner: Pict. bk. of sym., p. 25.
—— (planet). Lehner: Pict. bk. of sym., p. 10.
sauce pan. See pan, sauce.
sauce tureen (Storr). Con. 144: XXVIII Sept '59.
——, George III (silver). Con. 140: XXXVII Sept '57; 142: XXI Jan '59; 145: XV Ap '60, LIV May '60.
——, Georgian (silver). Con. 145: XXXVI Mar '60.
——, Georgian (silver, by Storr). Con. 145: XXVI Ap '60.
——, Mennecy. Con. 143: XLIX May '59.
——, silver (Bateman). Con. 144: 282 Jan '60.
——, silver (18th cent.). Con. 140: XLVIII Sept '57; 145: XIV Mar '60.
——, silver (19th cent.). Con. 144: XXIV Jan '60.
sauceboat (antique). Con. 138: XXIV Nov '56.
——, Chelsea. Con. 143: LXXV May '59.
——, double-lipped silver (George I). Con. 143: 265 Je '59.
——, Dutch silver. Con. 133: IV Mar '54, 133 Ap '54.

sauceboat, Dutch silver (18th cent.). Con. 143: LIX Mar '59.
——, gilt (18th cent.). Con. 133: 154 May '54.
——, Langton Hall. Con. 138: 195 Dec '56.
——, porcelain (antique). Con. 135: 156 May '55.
——, silver (antique). Con. 134: VI Nov '54; 135: XII Je '55.
——, silver (18th cent.). Con. ency. of ant., vol. 1, pl. 85.
Con. 139: XXXVI, XXXVIII Mar '57; 140: XLIV, 55 Sept '57.
——, silver (18th cent., Lamerie). Con. 145: XLIII Ap '60.
——, silver (George I). Con. 136: 293 Jan '56.
——, (George II). Con. 129: XXIV Ap '52; 133: LI Mar '54, IX Ap '54; 137: 128 Ap '56; 138: XLV Dec '56; 142: XVIII Nov '58; 144: XXVII Sept '59, 196 Dec '59; 145: III Mar '60, XLII Je '60.
——, silver (George II, 18th cent.). Con. 145: XIII May '60.
——, silver (George III). Con. 133: VI Ap '54; 136 LXII Jan '56; 141: XLVIII May '58; 142: LXXI Jan '59; 145: III May '60.
——, silver (Heming, 18th cent.). Con. 145: XLIII Ap '60.
——, silver (Lamerie). Con. 141: XIX May '58; 144: 64 Sept '59.
——, silver (19th cent.). Con. 145: XXXVI May '60.
——, silver (1722). Con. ency. of ant., vol. 1, p. 153.
——, silver (1792). Con. 145: XL Je '60.
——, Worcester. Con. 140: LXVI Nov '57.
saucepan, electric. Holiday 22: 122 (col.) Dec '57.
——, silver (1730). Con. ency. of ant., vol. 1, p. 153.
saucer (Martha Washington's). Amer. heri., vol. 6 no. 5 p. 49 (col.) (Aug '55).
——, Chinese porcelain (K'ang Hsi). Con. 144: V Dec '59.
——, diving. See diving saucer.
——, Venice. Con. 135: 13 Mar '55.
saucer-dish, Chinese (K'ang Hsi). Con. 142: V Dec '58.
——, Chinese porcelain. Con. 138: V Jan '57.
saucer-lipped woman. See Ubangi saucer-lipped woman.
saucer sled (child). Natl. geog. 113: 97 Jan '58.
Saud, King. Natl. geog. 114: 721 Nov '58.
Saud, King of Saudi Arabia. Cur. biog. p. 554 (1954).
Jensen: The White House, p. 272.
Saudi Arabia. Natl. geog. 117: 70, 100-1, 106 (col.) Jan '60.
—— (map). Natl. geog. 104: 9 Jl '53; 108: 160 Aug '55; 110: 71 Jl '56; 117: 76-7 (col.) Jan '60.
—— (men). Natl. geog. 105: 493 Ap '54.
Sauer, George H. Cur. biog. p. 547 (1948).
Saugus ironworks. Travel 111: 24 Feb '59.
Saulire (shi cafe, French Alps). Travel 113: 36 Jan '60.
Saulnier, Raymond J. Cur. biog. p. 491 (1957).
"Saul's conversion" (Kitto Bible, illus.). Natl. geog. 110: 722, 725 (col.) Dec '56.
Sault Ste Marie canal (Mich.). Amer. heri., vol. 6 no. 3 p. 20, 23-5 (Ap '55).

Jordan: Hammond's pict. atlas, p. 93 (col.).
Sault Ste Marie locks. Jordan: Hammond's pict. atlas, p. 93 (col.).
Natl. geog. 115: 450 (col.) Ap '59.
Travel 103: 6-10 May '55.
Sault spillway dam. Natl. geog. 115: 320-1 (col.) Mar '59.
Saund, Dalip S. Cur. biog. p. 359 (1960).
Saunders, Carl M. Cur. biog. p. 516 (1950).
Saunders, Hilary A. St. George. Cur. biog. p. 662 (1943).
Saunders, Robert. Cur. biog. p. 550 (1951).
sausage cutter (antique). Rawson: Ant. pict. bk., p. 7.
sausage packing (1906, Chicago). Amer. heri., vol. 7 no. 5 p. 61 (Aug '56).
sausage shop. Natl. geog. 99: 767 (col.) Je '51.
sausage stuffer, St. Augustine. Rawson: Ant. pict. bk., p. 9.
Sausalito (Cal.). Holiday 23: 67-71 (col.) May '58.
Sauvage, P. (work of). Con. 141: XXVI-XXVII Mar '58.
Savage, Augusta. Cur. biog. p. 753 (1941).
Savage, Edward (work of). Con. ency. of ant., vol. 3, pl. 91.
Savage, John Lucian. Cur. biog. p. 665 (1943).
Savannah (Ga.). Holiday 10: 44-51 (part col.) Dec '51.
"Savannah" ship (launching). Natl. geog. 117: 26-7 (col.) Jan '60.
"Save our souls" (S.O.S.) (sym.). Lehner: Pict. bk. of sym., p. 88.
Savery, Constance. Cur. biog. p. 548 (1948). Jun. bk. of auth., p. 266.
Savery, Roelandt (work of). Natl. geog. 97: 751 Je '50.
"The Saviour" (13th cent.). Con. 135: 55 Mar '55.
Savitt, Richard. Cur. biog. p. 516 (1952).
saw. Holiday 28: 2 (col.) Aug '60.
——, log. Amer. heri., vol. 9 no. 6 p. 14 (Oct '58).
——, pit (antique). Natl. geog. 112: 766 (col.) Dec '57.
——, stone slicing. See stone slicing machine.
sawbuck frame. Rawson: Ant. pict. bk., p. 16.
sawmill. Natl. geog. 114: 176-7 (col.) Aug '58.
"Sawmill at Baraga" (Dehn). Amer. heri., vol. 2 no. 4 p. 47 (col.) (summer '51).
Sawston Hall (Eng., 16th cent., int. & ext.). Con. 144: 2 (col.), 3-7 Sept '59.
Sawyer, Charles. Cur. biog. p. 550 (1948).
Sawyer, Eddie. Cur. biog. p. 517 (1950).
Sawyer, Helen. Cur. biog. p. 556 (1954).
Sawyer, John E. Cur. biog. p. 411 (1961).
Sawyer, Ruth. Jun. bk. of auth., p. 267.
Sawyer, Tom. See Tom Sawyer.
Saxon, James J. Cur. biog. p. 373 (1963).
Saxony hotel. See hotel Saxony.
saxophone, baritone (Negro playing). Int. gr. soc.: Arts . . . p. 143 (col.).
Saxton, Alexander. Cur. biog. p. 668 (1943).
Sayao, Bidu. Cur. biog. p. 736 (1942).
Sayegh, Fayez A. Cur. biog. p. 493 (1957).
Sayers, Frances Clarke. Jun. bk. of auth., p. 268.
Sayre, Very Rev. Francis B., jr. Cur. biog. p. 548 (1956).
Sayre, Morris. Cur. biog. p. 552 (1948).

Sayre, Mrs. Raymond. Cur. biog. p. 551 (1949).

scaffold, floating (men painting boat). Natl. geog. 106: 801 (col.) Dec '54.

Scales, Clint. Horan: Pict. hist. of wild west, p. 147.

scales (sym.). Lehner: Pict. bk. of sym., p. 13, 17, 19, 82.

——, farm (antique). Rawson: Ant. pict. bk., p. 33.

——, fruit market. Natl. geog. 105: 211 (col.) Feb '54.

——, golden (Bombay). Holiday 15: 59 May '54.

——, grocery. Holiday 20: 81 Oct '56.

——, market. Holiday 10: 48 Nov '51. Natl. geog. 99: 446 (col.) Ap '51.

——, Sutter's gold. Natl. geog. 117: 819 (col.) Je '60.

scallop shell (sym.). Lehner: Pict. bk. of sym., p. 64.

—— (18th cent.). Con. 132: 88 Nov '53.

Scandinavia. Holiday 27: 30 Jan '60. Travel 102: 31, 34 Oct '54; 107: 21-3 May '57.

Scandinavian art. Con. 135: 46-9 Mar '55.

Scandinavian ballet. See ballet dancers, Scandinavian.

"Scandinavian chariot" (medieval). Int. gr. soc.: Arts . . . p. 81 (col.).

Scandinavian dancers. Holiday 19: 114 Jan '56.

Scandinavian girl. Holiday 17: 16 Jan '55, 22 Feb '55, 78 Mar '55.

scapula. Gray's anatomy, p. 178-83.

scarabaeus (sym.). Lehner: Pict. bk. of sym., p. 27.

Scarborough, George. Horan: Pict. hist. of wild west, p. 125.

Scarbrough, Lord Lawrence Roger. Cur. biog. p. 378 (1958).

scare-crow. Rawson: Ant. pict. bk., p. 25.

scarf painting (woman). Natl. geog. 98: 239 (col.) Aug '50.

Scelba, Mario. Cur. biog. p. 557 (1953).

"Scene of Apotheosis" (Giordano). Con. 132: 9 Sept '53.

scent bottle, enamel. Con. ency. of ant., vol. 1, pl. 73.

scepter (sym.). Lehner: Pict. bk. of ant., p. 46.

——, Britain's royal. Natl. geog. 113: 575 Ap '58.

——, Hawaiian kings. Natl. geog. 118: 14 (col.) Jl '60.

——, sovereign's. See sovereign's scepter.

scepter & cross, English. Natl. geog. 104: 325 (col.) Sept '53.

Schacht, Alexander. Cur. biog. p. 535 (1946).

Schacht, Hjalmar. Cur. biog. p. 595 (1944).

Schadow, Johann Gottfried (sculpture by). Praeg.: Pict. ency., p. 397.

Schaefer, Vincent Joseph. Cur. biog. p. 553 (1948).

Schaffer, Fritz. Cur. biog. p. 558 (1953).

Schain, Josephine. Cur. biog. p. 532 (1945).

Scharf, Adolf. Cur. biog. p. 494 (1957).

Schary, Dore. Cur. biog. p. 556 (1948). Holiday 5: 38 (col.) Jan '49.

Schechter, Abel Alan. Cur. biog. p. 754 (1941).

Schedoni, Bartolomeo (work of). Con. 132: 18 Sept '53. Labande: Naples, p. 113.

Scheele, Leonard A. Cur. biog. p. 558 (1948).

Scheermaker, Peter (sculpture by). Con. 140: 54 Sept '57.

Scheiberling, Edward N. Cur. biog. p. 598 (1944).

Schell, Maria. Cur. biog. p. 412 (1961).

Schell, Maximilian. Cur. biog. p. 373 (1962).

Schellbach, Louis. Natl. geog. 107: 615 May '55.

Schenck, Robert C. Amer. heri., vol. 8 no. 3 p. 52 (Ap '57).

Schendel, P. Van (work of). Con. 135: XXXII Ap '55.

Scherer, Rev. Paul. Cur. biog. p. 755 (1941).

Scherman, Harry. Cur. biog. p. 669 (1943); p. 375 (1963).

Scherman, Thomas. Cur. biog. p. 558 (1954).

Scheveningen (Holland resort). Travel 106: inside cover Oct '56.

Schiaparelli, Elsa. Cur. biog. p. 551 (1951).

Schick, Bela. Cur. biog. p. 600 (1944).

Schildkraut, Joseph. Cur. biog. p. 550 (1956).

Schiller's "Don Carlos." Int. gr. soc.: Arts . . . p. 107 (col.).

Schindler, John A. Cur. biog. p. 552 (1956).

Schinkel, Karl Friedrich (arch. by). Praeg.: Pict. ency., p. 381, 433.

Schiotz, Aksel. Cur. biog. p. 552 (1949).

Schlauch, Margaret. Cur. biog. p. 737 (1942).

Schlein, Miriam. Cur. biog. p. 406 (1959).

Schlemmer, Oskar (work of). Praeg.: Pict. ency., p. 508.

Schlesinger, Arthur M. jr. Cur. biog. p. 537 (1946).

Schley, Commander W. S. Amer. heri., vol. 11 no. 4 p. 47 (col.) (Je '60).

Schliemann, Heinrich. Ceram: March of arch., p. 33.

Schliemann, Sophia (Engastromenos). Ceram: March of arch., p. 39.

Schliemann's diary. Ceram: March of arch., p. 37.

Schlink, Frederick John. Cur. biog. p. 757 (1941).

Schloss Nymphenburg. Holiday 22: 60-1 (col.) Sept '57.

Schluter, Andreas (sculpture by). Praeg.: Pict. ency., p. 333.

Schmidt-Rottluff, Karl (work of). Praeg.: Pict. ency., p. 447 (col.).

Schmitt, Bernadotte E. Cur. biog. p. 739 (1942).

Schmitt, Gladys. Cur. biog. p. 672 (1943).

Schmitz, Eugene. Amer. heri., vol. 11 no. 1 p. 9 (Dec '59).

Schnabel, Artur. Cooper: Con. ency. of music, p. 305. Cur. biog. p. 741 (1942).

Schneider, Alma K. Cur. biog. p. 560 (1954).

Schneider, Hannes. Cur. biog. p. 759 (1941).

Schneiderman, Rose. Cur. biog. p. 539 (1946).

Schneirla, Theodore C. Cur. biog. p. 535 (1955).

Schnurer, Carolyn. Cur. biog. p. 536 (1955).

Schoenberg, Arnold. Cur. biog. p. 743 (1942).

Schoenbrun, David. Cur. biog. p. 361 (1960).

Schoenbrunn castle (Vienna). Holiday 16: 49 (col.) Nov '54.

Schoeneman, George J. Cur. biog. p. 567 (1947).

Schoeppel, Andrew P. Cur. biog. p. 517 (1952).

Schofield, John McAllister. Pakula: Cent. album, p. 247.

scholars, patron saint of. Lehner: Pict. bk. of sym., p. 40.

Schomburg, Maj. Gen. August. Cur. biog. p. 363 (1960).

Schonbrunn palace (Vienna). Natl. geog. 99: 758 (col.) Je '51; 115: 193 (col.) Feb '59.

Schonburg castle. Natl. geog. 115: 758 (col.) Je '59.

Schonfeld, Johann Heinrich (work of). Con. 138: 140 Nov '56.

Schonguer, Martin (work of). Con. 140: 58 Sept '57.
Praeg.: Pict. ency., p. 241 (col.).

school, Amer. (cartoon). Amer. heri., vol. 11 no. 2 p. 12-3 (col.) (Feb '60).

——, boy's boarding. Holiday 18: 41 Jl '55.

——, consolidated. Brooks: Growth of a nation, p. 265.

——, country (1888). Brooks: Growth of a nation, p. 204.

——, 1st Amer. law (Phila.). Amer. heri., vol. 3 no. 1 p. 35 (col.) (fall '51).

——, Groton. See Groton school.

——, Iranian. See Chahar Bagh theological school.

——, junior high (Puerto Rico). Natl. geog. 99: 453 (col.) Ap '51.

——, Kuwait, Arabia (adults & teachers). Natl. geog. 102: 798 Dec '52.

——, rural. Holiday 10: 10 (col.) Oct '51.

——, sculpture. Natl. geog. 102: 777 (col.) Dec '52.

——, zoo animals at. Natl. geog. 110: 694-706 Nov '56.

school boy, British. Int. gr. soc.: Arts . . . p. 153 (col.).

school boys, Formosa. Natl. geog. 107: 579 Ap '55.

——, Hunza. Natl. geog. 117: 96 (col.) Jan '60.

——, Indian (New Delhi). Natl. geog. 116: 838 (col.) Dec '59.

school bus, Chinese. Natl. geog. 111: 345 (col.) Mar '57.

school child, Peking. Natl. geog. 118: 222 Aug '60.

school children (back view). Natl. geog. 110: 595 (col.) Nov '56.

—— (jumping rope). Natl. geog. 118: 16 (col.) Jl '60.

—— (leaving school). Holiday 7: 44-5 (col.) Jan '50.

——, Alaska (recess). Natl. geog. 109: 764-5 (col.) Je '56.

——, Arabia. Natl. geog. 110: 88, 95 (col.) Jl '56.

——, Berber (Algeria). Natl. geog. 117: 788 (col.) Je '60.

——, Brazil. Natl. geog. 117: 723 (col.) May '60.

——, Bhutan. Natl. geog. 102: 727 (col.) Dec '52.

——, Chile. Natl. geog. 117: 205 Feb '60.

——, China. Natl. geog. 118: 194-5 (col.) Aug '60.

——, Scotland. Natl. geog. 110: 36 (col.) Jl '56.

——, Scotland (at desk). Natl. geog. 110: 43 (col.) Jl '56.

school children & teacher, Aleut. Natl. geog. 101: 512 Ap '52.

——, Nigeria. Natl. geog. 110: 358 Sept '56.

school girls, Nigeria (back view). Natl. geog. 110: 326, 328-9 (col.) Sept '56.

school seat, Quaker. Rawson: Ant. pict. bk., p. 19.

school students (India). Natl. geog. 109: 577, 579, 586-7 Ap '56.

—— See also teacher & students.

school, outdoor (teacher & pupils, Pakistan). Natl. geog. 102: 670-1, 674 (col.) Nov '52.

schoolhouse (late 1700's). Natl. geog. 113: 42 (col.) Jan '58.

—— (one room). Holiday 12: 11 Nov '52.

——, Denver (Colo.). Natl. geog. 106: 213 (col.) Aug '54.

——, King Ranch (Tex.). Natl. geog. 101: 48 (col.) Jan '52.

——, (colonial). Travel 113: 31 Mar '60.

——, Mass. (colonial). Travel 113: 31 Mar '60.

——, Mexico City. Travel 101: back cover Jan '54.

——, St. Augustine (1st. in U.S.). Travel 111: 32 Feb '59.

——, Scotland. Natl. geog. 110: 36 (col.) Jl '56.

——, little red. Amer. heri., vol. 8 no. 5 p. 47 (col.) (Aug '57).

——, little red (where Mary took her lamb). Brooks: Growth of a nation, p. 117.

schoolhouse & children, Alaska. Natl. geog. 109: 764-5 (col.) Je '56.

——, Hawaii. Natl. geog. 118: 16 (col.) Jl '60.

——, modern (Africa, ext. & int.). Natl. geog. 108: 775 (col.) Dec '55.

schoolroom. Holiday 22: 8 Oct '57.
Natl. geog. 99: 585 May '51.

—— (1765). Amer. heri., vol. 2 no. 2 p. 28 (winter '51).

——, Australia. Natl. geog. 103: 138 Jan '53.

——, Canton is. Natl. geog. 107: 128 (col.) Jan '55.

——, China. Natl. geog. 105: 270 Feb '54.

——, country. Natl. geog. 99: 191, 205 (col.) Feb '51.

——, Del-Mar-Va. See Del-Mar-Va schoolroom.

——, Iraq. Natl. geog. 103: 561 Ap '53.

——, Trinidad. Natl. geog. 103: 74 Jan '53.

——, Turkey. Natl. geog. 100: 731 (col.) Dec '51.

——, (teacher & students). Natl. geog. 98: 416 Sept '50; 101: 467 (col.) Ap '52; 107: 207 (col.) Feb '55, 362 Mar '55.

——, Aleut. Natl. geog. 101: 512 Ap '52.

——, Australia. Natl. geog. 103: 138 Jan '53.

——, boy's (Ariz.). Natl. geog. 104: 382 (col.) Sept '53.

——, Lebanon. Natl. geog. 106: 829 (col.) Dec '54.

——, pioneer (Canada). Holiday 6: 56 (col.) Aug '49.

——, rail-borne (Canada). Natl. geog. 104: 825 Dec '53.

schoolroom, U. S. Navy. Natl. geog. 104: 572 (col.) Oct '53, 786 Dec '53.
——, West Point. Natl. geog. 101: 610, 618-9 (col.) May '52.
schooner. Holiday 23: inside cover (col.) Je '58.
Natl. geog. 101: 573-80 (col.) May '52.
Travel 105: 58 Feb '56; 114: 40 Dec '60.
—— (oldest Amer. afloat). Natl. geog. 112: 336-7 (col.) Sept '57.
schooner "America" (1851). Amer. heri., vol. 9 no. 5 p. 4 (col.) (Aug '58).
schooners (ships, Denmark). Natl. geog. 108: 810-11 (col.) Dec '55.
——, fishing. Natl. geog. 101: 566 May '52.
Schoonover, Lawrence. Cur. biog. p. 496 (1957).
Schorr, Daniel L. Cur. biog. p. 407 (1959).
Schorr, Friedrich. Cur. biog. p. 745 (1942).
Schottland, Charles I. Cur. biog. p. 553 (1956).
Schouman, Aert (work of). Con. 138: XLVII Nov '56.
Schram, Emil. Cur. biog. p. 760 (1941); p. 560 (1953).
Schreiber, Georges. Cur. biog. p. 673 (1943).
Schreiber, Walther. Cur. biog. p. 562 (1954).
Schricker, Henry F. Cur. biog. p. 519 (1950).
Schriever, Maj. Gen. Bernard. Cur. biog. p. 497 (1957).
Schroder, Gerhard. Cur. biog. p. 375 (1962).
Schroeder, Frederick R., jr. Cur. biog. p. 554 (1949).
Schroeder, Rudolph W. Cur. biog. p. 761 (1941).
Schubert, Franz. Cooper: Con. ency. of music, p. 251.
Schuck, Arthur A. Cur. biog. p. 520 (1950).
"Schuhplattler" (Austrian dance). Disney: People & places p. 53 (col.).
Schulberg, Budd. Cur. biog. p. 763 (1941); p. 554 (1951).
Holiday 5: 32 Jan '49.
Schultz, Sigrid. Cur. biog. p. 601 (1944).
Schulz, Charles M. Cur. biog. p. 364 (1960).
Schumacher, Kurt. Cur. biog. p. 561 (1948).
Schuman, Robert. Cur. biog. p. 563 (1948).
Schuman, William. Cur. biog. p. 746 (1945).
Schuman, William H. Cur. biog. p. 377 (1962).
Schumann, Clara. Cooper: Con. ency. of music, p. 253.
Schumann, Elisabeth. Cooper: Con. ency. of music, p. 252.
Schumann, Robert. Cooper: Con. ency. of music, p. 253.
Schurz, Carl. Amer. heri., vol. 11 no. 4 p. 33 (Je '60).
—— (playing piano). Jensen: The White House, p. 114.
Schussele, Christian (work of). Amer. heri., vol. 10 no. 1 p. 21 (col.) (Dec '58).
Schuster, Max Lincoln. Cur. biog. p. 795 (1941).
Schutz, Heinrich. Cooper: Con. ency. of music, p. 254.
Schuyler, Capt. Johannes (by Watson). Amer. heri., vol. 10 no. 1 p. 11 (col.) (Dec '58).
Schuyler, Mrs. Johannes (by Watson). Amer. heri., vol. 10 no. 1 p. 11 (col.) (Dec '58).
Schwab, Charles M. Amer. heri., vol. 8 no. 3 p. 44 (Ap '57).

Schwartz, Delmore. Cur. biog. p. 366 (1960).
Schwartz, Maurice. Cur. biog. p. 555 (1956).
Schwarzkopf, Elisabeth. Cur. biog. p. 538 (1955).
Schwebel, Stephen M. Cur. biog. p. 519 (1952).
Schweitzer, Albert. Cur. biog. p. 565 (1948).
Holiday 19: 84 Mar '56.
Natl. geog. 118: 324 Sept '60.
Schweitzer, Pierre-Paul. Cur biog. p 378 (1963).
Schweizerhof (Berne, Switzerland). Travel 111: 47 Je '59.
Schwellenbach, Lewis B. Cur. biog. p. 535 (1945).
Schwidetzky, Oscar. Cur. biog. p. 676 (1943).
Schwimmer, Rosika. Amer. heri., vol. 9 no. 2 p. 67 (Feb '58).
science (sym.). Lehner: Pict. bk. of sym., p. 9-22.
scientific experiments. See experiments, scientific.
scientific instruments (13th to 19th cent.). Con. 134: 85-91 Nov '54.
Scilly isles. Travel 101: 15-6 Feb '54.
Scipio (sculpture). Labande: Naples, p. 101.
scissors. Holiday 12: 104 Oct '52, 29, 131 Nov '52, 123 Dec '52; 13: 70 Feb '53; 18: 188 Dec '55; 23: 144 Mar '58; 24: 150 Dec '58.
Rawson: Ant. pict. bk., p. 12.
—— (sym.). Lehner: Pict. bk. of sym., p. 90-1.
—— antique pewter. Con. 135: XXVII Je '55.
scissors case (antique). Con. 139: 243 Je '57.
——, enamel. Con. ency. of ant., vol. 1, pl. 76.
Scobie, Lt. Gen. Ronald M. Cur. biog. p. 838 (1945).
Scofield, Paul. Cur. biog. p. 380 (1962).
Scoggin, Margaret C. Cur. biog. p. 521 (1952).
sconce (18th cent.). Con. ency. of ant., vol. 3, pl. 13.
——, cut glass (18th cent.). Con. ency. of ant., vol. 3, pl. 13.
——, gilt Chinese type (1760). Con. ency. of ant., vol. 3, pl. 13.
——, Queen Anne. Con. 138: 47 Sept '56.
——, wall. Holiday 21: 195 May '57; 24: 99 Dec '58; 28: 47 Oct '60.
——, wall (antique). Con. 143: LVI, LVIII, LXVI May '59, XIV Je '59; 144: 140 (col.) Dec '59.
——, wall (French antique). Con. 140: 14 Sept '57.
——, wall (German). Con. 141: 120 Ap '58.
——, wall (Queen Anne). Con. 142: 38 Sept '58.
——, wall (regency). Con. 144: XII Sept '59.
——, wall (17th cent.). Con. 133: 152 May '54.
——, wall candle. Holiday 26: inside cover (col.) Nov '59; 28: 29 Nov '60, 12 (col.) Dec '60.
sconces, empire ormolu. Con. 138: XXII Nov '56.
——, French ormolu. Con. 138: LIV Jan '57.
——, gilt (18th cent.). Con. ency. of ant., vol. 3, pl. 13.
——, Louis IV. Con. 138: 47 Sept '56.
scoop, double (ornament). Con. ency. of ant., vol. 1, p. 21.

——, **wooden (antique).** Rawson: Ant. pict. bk., p. 7.

scooter (girls riding). Travel 110: 51 Nov '58.

——, **motorized (forest service).** Natl. geog. 110: 289 (col.) Sept '56.

——, **sand dune.** *See* sand dune scooter.

——, **water.** *See* water scooter.

scooter bug. Holiday 19: 37 Je '56.

scorpion airplanes. Natl. geog. 109: 806 (col.) Je '56.

Scotch archer. Holiday 25: 190 (col.) May '59.

Scotch artillerymen. Natl. geog. 112: 462 (col.) (col.) Oct '57.

Scotch bagpipe player. Holiday 8: cover (col.) Dec '50; 9: inside cover (col.) Mar '51; 10: 143 (col.) Oct '51; 11: 84 (col.) Feb '52, 130 (col.) Je '52; 12: 68 (col.) Oct '52; 18: 21 (col.) Jl '55, 10 (col.) Sept '55; 20: 30 (col.) Nov '56; 21: 160 (col.) Mar '57, 136 (col.) Ap '57; 23: 134 Jan '58; 25: 190 (col.) May '59.

Natl. geog. 101: 661 (col.) May '52; 102: 93-8 (col.) Jl '52; 107: 458 (col.) Ap '55; 110: 2, 47 (col.) Jl '56; 112: 445, 463 (col.) Oct '57.

—— **parade.** Holiday 26: 84 Jl '59.

Scotch dancers. Disney: People & places, p. 32 (col.).

Holiday 8: 45 Dec '50; 13: 8, 131 (col.) Ap '53, 127 May '53, 73 Je '53; 15: 30 Mar '54, 136 Ap '54; 21: 66-7 (col.) Mar '57; 22: 123 (col.) Nov '57.

Natl. geog. 102: 108 (col.) Jl '52; 109: 103 (col.) Jan '56; 110: 2-3, 36 (col.) Jl '56; 112: 445 (col.) Oct '57.

Travel 110: 55 Jl '58; 114: 37 Jl '60.

Scotch guard. *See* guard, Scotch.

Scotch highlands (map). Natl. geog. 110: 11 Jl '56.

Scotch tape (jumbo rolls). Natl. geog. 114: 678 (col.) Nov '58.

Scotland. Disney: People & places, p. 25-36 (col.).

Holiday 8: 34-47 (col.) Dec '50; 16: 25 (col.) Jl '54, 38-45 Sept '54; 27: 67-77 (col.) May '60.

Natl. geog. 98: 182, 189 (col.) Aug '50; 102: 89-112 Jl '52; 110: 1-48 (part col.) Jl '56; 112: 438-88 (part col.) Oct '57.

—— **(castle, int.).** Holiday 26: 95 (col.) Nov '59.

—— **(eagle nests).** Natl. geog. 105: 274-85 Feb '54.

—— **(mansion).** Con. 134: XXXVII Sept '54.

—— **(map).** Natl. geog. 104: 522 Oct '53; 112: 442-3 Oct '57.

—— **(palace).** Holiday 25: 17 Jan '59.

——, **patron saint of.** Lehner: Pict. bk. of sym., p. 39.

Scotland yard. Travel 102: 40-3 Dec '54.

Scotsman. Holiday 5: 93 Ap '49, 128 (col.) Je '49; 6: 31 (col.) Sept '49, 64 (col.) Dec '49; 7: inside back cover (col.) Mar '50, 78 Je '50; 8: 109 (col.) Jl '50, 100 Aug '50, 2 (col.), 32 Sept '50, 111 (col.) Oct '50, 94 (col.) Nov '50, 35 (col.), 36 Dec '50, 68, 88, 125 (col.) Dec '50; 9: 24 Mar '51; 10: 29 Sept '51, 130 Nov '51, 82 Dec '51; 11: 8 Jan '52, 70 Feb '52, 103 (col.) May '52, 11 Je '52; 12:

122 Oct '52; 13: 122 (col.) Mar '53, 126, inside back cover Je '53; 14: 14 Jl '53, 69 (col.) Aug '53, 132 (col.) Nov '53; 15: 25 (col.) Je '54; 16: 78 (col.) Oct '54, 115 (col.) Nov '54; 17: 20 (col.), 66 (col.) Feb '55; 18: 117 (col.) Nov '55, 93 (col.), 146 Dec '55; 20: 197 (col.) Dec '56.

Natl. geog. 98: 175, 177 (col.) Aug '50.

Scotsman (tartan). Holiday 5: 29 Feb '49. U.S. News & world report. Vol. LV no. 1 back cover (col.) Jl 1, 1963.

—— **(comic runners).** Holiday 5: 10 (col.) Jan '49.

—— **(costume).** *See* costume (Scotsman).

—— **(drum major).** *See* drum major, Scotsman.

—— **(head, comic).** Holiday 11: 170 May '52.

—— **(head, toasts).** Holiday 10: 12 (col.) Dec '51.

—— **(silhouette).** Holiday 10: 85 (col.) Jl '51, 18 (col.) Oct '51, 151 (col.) Nov '51, 181 (col.) Dec '51.

—— **(walking).** Holiday 14: 170 (col.) Dec '53.

Scott, Barbara Ann. Cur. biog. p. 568 (1948).

Scott, Dred. Holiday 7: 72 Feb '50.

Scott, Sir Harold. Cur. biog. p. 522 (1950).

Scott, Hazel. Cur. biog. p. 678 (1943).

Scott, Henry L. Cur. biog. p. 556 (1949).

Scott, Hugh. Cur. biog. p. 570 (1948).

Scott, Kate Frances. Cur. biog. p. 572 (1948).

Scott, Rev Michael. Cur. biog. p. 561 (1953).

Scott, Raymond. Cur. biog. p. 764 (1941).

Scott, Capt. Robert F. (South Pole). Natl. geog. 109: 291 Feb '56.

Scott, Col. Robert L., jr. Cur. biog. p. 680 (1943).

Scott, Samuel (work of). Con. 132: XLIV Sept '53; 133: XIII Mar '54; 142: XXXV (col.), XLI Jan '59; 144: XXXV (col.), 265 Jan '60.

Scott, Thomas A. Amer. heri., vol. 8 no. 3 p. 52 (Ap '57).

Scott, Tom. Cur. biog. p. 542 (1946).

Scott, Sir Walter (15 yrs. old). Natl. geog. 112: 478 Oct '57.

—— **(reading to friends).** Natl. geog. 112: 479 Oct '57.

Scott, William Kerr. Cur. biog. p. 557 (1956).

Scott, Winfield. Amer. heri., vol. 11 no. 3 p. 107 (Ap '60).

Holiday 18: 24 Jl '55.

Pakula: Cent. album, p. 249.

Scott memorial, Sir Walter. Holiday 13: inside back cover Feb '53.

Scott's Bluff. Holiday 14: 61 (col.) Jl '53; 19: 102-3 (col.) May '56.

Scott's home, Sir Walter (Scotland). Holiday 8: 46 (col.) Dec '50.

Natl. geog. 112: 438-9, 446-7 (part col.) Oct '57.

"Scotty's castle" (Death Valley). Natl. geog. 105: 823 Je '54.

scouts, boy. *See* boy scouts.

scow. Rawson: Ant. pict. bk., p. 51.

"The scraper" (Greek sculpture). Praeg.: Pict. ency., p. 133.

screen, carved Gothic. Con. 140: XLVI Sept '57.

——, **Chinese.** Con. 145: XI May '60.

screen, Chinese (by Sesshu). Con. 132: 68 Sept '53.
——, **Chinese (17th cent.).** Con. 132: LXVI Nov '53.
——, **Chinese (coromandel lacquer).** Con. 145: VII Mar '60.
——, **Chinese jade table.** Con. 129: 97 Je '52; 145: VIII Mar '60.
——, **Chinese lacquer.** Con. 141: 42 Mar '58; 144: LXXXIV Jan '60.
Praeg.: Pict. ency., p. 542 (col.).
——, **embroidered (Calverley).** Con. 145: 170-1 May '60.
——, **Japanese (18th cent.).** Con. 143: III Je '59.
——, **Japanese paper.** Con. 144: VI Jan '60.
——, **Louis 14th (four-fold).** Con. 134: LV Sept '54.
——, **motion picture.** Holiday 20: 137 (col.) Nov '56; 26: 47 (col.) Dec '59.
——, **tall.** Holiday 28: 145 (col.) Nov '60.
——, **tripod pole (1750).** Con. ency. of ant., vol. 3, pl. 18.
scribe (at table, middle ages). Int. gr. soc.: Arts . . . p. 53 (col.).
—— **(Solomon's palace).** Natl. geog. 112: 863 (col.) Dec '57.
scribes, Jordan public. Natl. geog. 98: 744 (col.) Dec '50.
Scribner, Fred C., jr. Cur. biog. p. 380 (1958).
script, cuneiform. See cuneiform script.
The Scripture (sym.). Lehner: Pict. bk. of sym., p. 38.
scroll (sym.). Lehner: Pict. bk. of sym., p. 84.
scroll, Russian thanks to U.S. (Russian famine). Amer. heri., vol. 11 no. 5 p. 69 (Aug '60).
scrolls, Genji monogatari Emaki. Con. 134: 220 Dec '54.
scrutoire, gate-leg (Eng., 18th cent.). Con. 126: 41 Aug '50.
scuba. See diver, skin.
scull racing. Holiday 10: 66 Aug '51.
sculler. Holiday 18: 110-11 (col.) Oct '55.
sculptor. Holiday 18: 63 (col.) Sept '55.
sculptors, modern. Int. gr. soc.: Arts . . . p. 131 (col.).
sculpture. Amer. heri., vol. 8 no. 2 p. 46 (Feb '57).
Con. 142: 198-200 Dec '58.
Holiday 10: 49 (col.) Nov '51; 13: 46 Jan '53, 7, 51, 110 Ap '53, 123 May '53, 76 Je '53.
Natl. geog. 110: 487, 483 (col.), 496-7 Oct '56.
Praeg.: Pict. ency., p. 11, 14, 16, 273.
—— **(Antalya).** Osward: Asia Minor, pl. 117.
—— **(archer).** Travel 104: 24 Nov '55.
—— **(Augustus of Primaporta).** Praeg.: Pict. ency., p. 146.
—— **(Bangkok).** Travel 105: inside cover May '56.
—— **(Baratta).** Con. 142: 170-77 Dec '58.
—— **(Barlach).** Praeg.: Pict. ency., p. 457.
—— **(Berlin).** Praeg.: Pict. ency., p. 333.
—— **(Bernini).** Con. 126: 133 Oct '50.
—— **("Buddha").** Con. 145: LXIV Ap '60.
—— **(bridge, Bamberg, Ger.).** Holiday 25: 63 (col.) May '59.
—— **(bronze).** Con. 140: 206 Dec '57.
—— **(Burn's characters).** Natl. geog. 112: 457

(col.) Oct '57.
—— **(bust).** Con. 133: 183 May '54.
Holiday 21: 189 May '57; 27: 81 May '60.
—— **(bust, Ancient Roman bronze).** Con. 140: LX Dec '57.
—— **(bust by Deyde).** Con. 134: 207 Dec '54.
—— **(bust by Houdin).** Con. 126: 92-3 Oct '50; 134: 207 Dec '54.
—— **(bust, Italian reliquary).** Con. 138: 211 Dec '56.
—— **(bust, marble).** Con. 140: 26 Sept '57.
Durant: Pict. hist. of Amer. circus, p. 46.
—— **(bust, marble, Duke of Gloucester).** Con. 137: 104 Ap '56.
—— **(bust of John Paul Jones).** Amer. heri., vol. 5 no. 4 p. 15 (summer '54).
—— **(bust, Queen Mary).** Con. 132: 113 Nov '53.
—— **("Calvary Group," Sweden, 14th cent.).** Con. 145: 91-5 Ap '60.
—— **(Canova).** Con. 143: 242, 245 Je '59.
—— **(Canova, 18th cent.).** Con. 144: 226-31 Jan '60.
—— **(cathedral).** Praeg.: Pict. ency., p. 244.
—— **(cement figure).** Praeg.: Pict. ency., p. 515.
—— **(Chartres cathedral).** See Chartres cathedral (sculpture).
—— **(Chicago World's Fair).** Amer. heri., vol. 11 no. 6 p. 12 (Oct '60).
—— **(Crane, Peking).** Natl. geog. 118: 220 (col.) Aug '60.
—— **(Daniel Boone).** Brooks: Growth of a nation, p. 72.
—— **(Della Valle).** Con. 144: 172-9 Dec '59.
—— **(dog).** Holiday 25: 42 Mar '59.
—— **(early Flemish).** Con. 136: 309 Jan '56.
—— **(early Roman children).** Con. 134: 101-5 Nov '54.
—— **(Egyptian goddess).** Con. 135: LII Ap '55.
—— **(Etruscan bronze).** Con. 138: XLVIII Sept '56.
—— **(Evangeline).** Travel 112: 32 Sept '59.
—— **(Falconet).** Con. 132: 42 Sept '53; 137: 1 Ap '56.
—— **(15th cent.).** Con. 132: XXV Sept '53; 137: XLV Mar '56.
—— **(figures).** Amer. heri., vol. 11 no. 3 p. 17 (Ap '60).
—— **(Gandharan Bodhisattva).** Con. 134: 145 Nov '54.
—— **(Gilbert).** Con. 134: 23-6 Sept '54.
—— **(Greco).** Con. 140: XX Dec '57.
—— **(Gustav Vigeland, work of).** Holiday 12: 94 (col.) Sept '52.
—— **(Hans Christian Andersen).** Travel 103: 11 May '55.
—— **(head, 4th cent. B.C.).** Praeg.: Pict. ency., p. 159.
—— **("Madonna & child," 1200).** Con. 145: 213 May '60.
—— **(head).** Amer. heri., vol. 8 no. 5 p. 10 (Aug '57).
—— **(in gravel).** See effigies (desert mesas).
—— **(Indian on horse).** Natl. geog. 106: 237 (col.) Aug '54.
—— **("Iron man).** Brooks: Growth of a nation, p. 291.

sculpture (Italian museum). Labande: Naples, p. 96-103.
—— (Lebanese god). Con. 144: 281 Jan '60.
—— (Lehmbruck). Praeg.: Pict. ency., p. 491.
—— (Lenin, Tito, communist). Holiday 13: 53 Mar '53.
—— (madonna). Con. 140: 278 Jan '58.
—— (man on horse). Holiday 13: 107 Feb '53.
—— (man on horse, 13th cent.). Praeg.: Pict. ency., p. 219.
—— (man seated). Amer. heri., vol. 10 no. 2 p. 11 (Feb '59).
—— (man working). Natl. geog. 103: 326 Mar '53.
—— (middle ages). Int. gr. soc.: Arts . . . p. 57 (col.).
—— (missionary). Brooks: Growth of a nation, p. 122.
—— (nativity detail, de Castro). Con. 136: 233-7 Jan '56.
—— (N.Y. museum of modern art). Holiday 14: 58-63 Nov '53.
—— (Oved). Holiday 13: 18-9 Jan '53.
—— (Parseus, by Canova). Praeg.: Pict. ency., p 411.
—— (pioneer woman & child). Brooks: Growth of a nation, p. 195.
—— (pioneer woman & son). Travel 104: 29 Jl '55.
—— (Pluto & Proserpina). Natl. geog. 111: 485, 489 (col.) Ap '57.
—— (Parodi). Con. 142: 140 Dec '58.
—— (Traverso). Con. 142: 140 Dec '58.
—— (President's heads, Black Hills, S.D.). See Mt. Rushmore memorial. . . .
—— (priest head, 500 B.C.). Praeg.: Pict. ency., p. 156.
—— (Rodin). Con. 140: VIII Sept '57; 143: XXII May '59.
—— (Roman god). Amer. heri., vol. 6 no. 1 p. 71 (fall '54).
—— (sarcophagus detail). Osward: Asia Minor, pl. 20.
—— (Schadow). Praeg.: Pict. ency., p. 397.
—— (sea lion). Natl. geog. 113: 302 Mar '58.
—— (17th cent.). Con. 140: 54 Sept '57.
—— (Sintenis). Praeg.: Pict. ency., p. 509.
—— (650 B.C.). Praeg.: Pict. ency., p. 172.
—— (soldier & sailor). Natl. geog. 111: 755 (col.) Je '57.
—— (soldier statue, silhouette). Amer. heri., vol. 9 no. 1 p. 50 (Dec '57).
—— (statue). Natl. geog. 98: 187 Aug '50; 105: 169 Feb '54.
—— (stone lions, Delos). Natl. geog. 114: 778-9 (col.) Dec '58.
—— (sym.). Lehner: Pict. bk. of sym., p. 17.
—— (3rd cent. A.D.). Praeg.: Pict. ency., p. 175.
—— (3rd cent. B.C.). Con. 129: 46 Ap '52.
—— (13th cent. fragments of stone). Con. 135: 120 Ap '55.
—— ("The Three Graces"). Natl. geog. 116: 581 (col.) Nov '59.
—— (unveiled). Amer. heri., vol. 10 no. 2 p. 6 (Feb '59).
—— (Vasse, gilded wood). Con. 133: 258 Je '54.
—— (Vatican). Holiday 23: 61 (col.) May '58.

—— (Venus & Adonis). Holiday 26: 8 Jl '59.
—— (Verrocchio). Praeg.: Pict. ency., p. 257.
—— (Vigeland's). Natl. geog. 106: 192 Aug '54.
—— (Walker driven out of Cent. Amer.). Amer. heri., vol. 9 no. 1 p. 26-7 (Dec '57).
—— (war memorial). Natl. geog. 111: 740 Je '57.
—— (winged lion, China). Praeg.: Pict. ency., p. 529.
—— (woman). Con. 138: XXXIX Sept '56.
——, alabaster. Con. 133: 217-28 Je '54.
——, animals. Con. 140: XLI, XLIV Dec '57. Natl. geog. 113: 257 Feb '58.
——, Ankara. Osward: Asia Minor, pl. 66, 153, 156-7.
——, Assyrian. Holiday 10: 53 (col.) Oct '51.
——, Belgian Congo. Natl. geog. 101: 323 Mar '52.
——, brass. See brass sculpture.
——, bronze. See bronze figures; bronze sculpture.
——, Byzantine. Osward: Asia Minor, pl. 53.
——, Cambodia. Natl. geog. 117: 552-3 Ap '60.
——, carved stone garden. Con. 144: XXVII Jan '60.
——, carved wood. Con. 140: 54 Sept '57.
——, Chinese. See Chinese sculpture.
——, Christian (New Mexican Santos). Con. 140: 222-5 Jan '58.
——, church (London). Con. 135: 265 Je '55.
——, church (16th cent.). Con. 133: XI May '54.
——, church (Weyarn, Bavaria). Praeg.: Pict. ency., p. 332.
——, Egyptian. Con. 129: LXX Je '52.
——, Egyptian (ancient). Con. 129: LXX Je '52.
——, Egyptian (4th dynasty). Praeg.: Pict. ency., p. 115 (col.).
——, Egyptian (5th dynasty). Praeg.: Pict. ency., p. 168.
——, Egyptian (18th dynasty). Praeg.: Pict. ency., p. 122 (col.).
——, Eskimo carvings. Con. 141: 154-8 May '58.
——, Etruscan bronze. Con. 138: XLVIII Sept '56.
——, Etruscan tomb. Natl. geog. 116: 342, 349 Sept '59.
——, French. Con. 145: 282-3 Je '60.
——, French terracotta (18th cent.). Con. 140: 3-7 Sept '57.
——, German gothic (14th cent.). Con. 138: LXI Nov '56.
——, German Rhenish school. Con. 133: 140 Ap '54.
——, German wood rococo. Con. 145: 132 Ap '60.
——, Greek. Natl. geog. 103: 379 Mar '53. Osward: Asia Minor, pl. 101, 104. Praeg.: Pict. ency., p. 132-3.
——, Greek (bronze). Natl. geog. 109: 41 (col.) Jan '56.
——, Greek (early). Ceram: March of arch., p. 21.
——, Hellenistic Greek. Con. 142: 272 Jan '59.

sculpture, Indian (Mexico). Travel 114: back cover Sept '60.
——, Italian. Con. 138: 209 Dec '56; 141: 220-5 Je '58; 144: 158-9 Dec '59.
Holiday 27: 83, 85-6, 89, 91 (col.), 101, 104 Ap '60.
Labande: Naples, p. 38.
——, Italian majolica. Con. 134: 224 Dec '54.
——, ivory Gothic (16th cent.). Con. 139: LI Ap '57.
——, ivory (Japanese). Con. 142: LXIV Jan '59.
——, Japanese (wood carved figure). Con. 141: 249 Je '58.
——, Japanese wood (10th cent.). Con. 143: 201 May '59.
——, lead. Con. 145: 131 Ap '60.
——, Ma-Ming (temple statuette). Con. 129: LXIX Ap '52.
——, marble. Amer. heri., vol. 2 no. 3 p. 41 (spring '51).
——, marble (head). Con. 135: LI Mar '55.
——, marble ("St. John"). Con. 142: 9 Sept '58.
——, Mayan stone. Con. 145: LV Mar '60.
——, medieval wooden. Con. 140: 168-71 Dec '57.
——, Mexican. Holiday 13: 36, 40-1, 93 Mar '53.
——, Mexican (ancient). Amer. heri., vol. 10 no. 2 p. 46-57 (part col.) (Feb '59).
——, modern. Int. gr. soc.: Arts . . . p. 131 (col.).
——, modern (Brzeska). Con. 138: 244-7 Jan '57.
——, Nineveh. Ceram: March of arch., p. 214-5.
——, Norwegian. See Norwegian sculpture.
——, polychrome wood (15th cent.). Con. 141: XXXII Je '58.
——, polychrome figure. Ceram: March of arch., opp. p. 174 (col.).
——, Portuguese. See Portuguese sculpture.
——, prehistoric. Int. gr. soc.: Arts . . . p. 17 (col.).
——, religious. Con. 133: XXVI Je '54.
——, religious (altar piece). Con. 132: 66 Sept '53.
——, religious (15th cent.). Con. 132: LV Sept '53.
——, Renaissance. Int. gr. soc.: Arts . . . p. 87 (col.).
——, Renaissance in Augsburg. Con. 136: 238-9 Jan '56.
——, rock (Black Hills, S.D.). Jordan: Hammond's pict. atlas, p. 107 (col.).
Natl. geog. 110: 483 (col.), 496-7 Oct '56.
——, Roman. Con. 136: 190 Dec '55.
Praeg.: Pict. ency., p. 143-4.
——, Roman (cat on head). Holiday 27: 203 Ap '60.
——, Roman (161 A.D.). Praeg.: Pict. ency., p. 159.
——, Roman (2nd cent. marble bust). Con. 135: 266 Je '55.
——, Rouen faience (18th cent.). Con. 143: 261 Je '59.
——, sandstone. Con. 145: 131 Ap '60.
——, school of. See school, sculpture.
——, Sicily. Natl. geog. 107: 24 (col.) Jan '55.

——, Smyrna. Osward: Asia Minor, pl. 18.
——, stone figures (Easter is.). Praeg.: Pict. ency., p. 561.
——, Tang dynasty. Con. 135: 126-7 Ap '55.
——, terracotta. Con. 144: IV Dec '59.
——, terracotta (Bernini). Con. 145: 89 Ap '60.
——, terracotta (15th cent.). Con. 139: LXV Je '57.
——, terracotta (head by Carpeaux). Con. 135: 128 Ap '55.
——, Toltec (Mexico). Natl. geog. 100: 824 (col.) Dec '51.
——, U.S. folk art (New Mexico). Con. 140: 222-5 Jan '58.
——, Vincennes (glazed white). Con. 139: 195 May '57.
——, wood (early 14th cent. "St. Sebastin"). Con. 134: XVI Nov '54.
——, wood (figures of saints). Con. 136: LXXI Jan '56.
——, wood (San Bernardino). Con. 140: 175 Dec '57.
——, wood rococo. Con. 145: 132 Ap '60.
sculpture. See also bust; bronze sculpture; statue.
sculpture class. Natl. geog. 102: 777 (col.) Dec '52.
scythe (man). Natl. geog. 114: 371 Sept '58.
—— (man sharpens). Natl. geog. 115: 588 Ap '59.
—— (sym.). Lehner: Pict. bk. of sym., p. 79.
——, antique. Rawson: Ant. pict. bk., p. 26.
sea, god of. Lehner: Pict. bk. of sym., p. 31.
sea & air lanes, charting. Natl. geog. 111: 190-208 (part col.) Feb '57.
"Sea at Deauville" (Dufy). Praeg.: Pict. ency., p. 474 (col.).
sea divers. See divers.
sea exploration. Natl. geog. 107: 524-41 Ap '55.
Sea gull monument (Salt Lake City, Utah). Brooks: Growth of a nation, p. 130.
Travel 101: 36 Je '54.
Sea island (The Cloister). Travel 110: 49-50 Nov '58.
Sea of Galilee. Holiday 20: 55 (col.) Dec '56.
Natl. geog. 102: 837 Dec '52; 114: 856-7 (col.) Dec '58.
—— (beach). Holiday 17: 39 (col.) Feb '55.
Sea of Tiberias. See Sea of Galilee.
sea salt (sym.). Lehner: Pict. bk. of sym., p. 73.
sea scooter. See water scooter.
sea sled camera. Natl. geog. 107: 530-33 Ap '55.
"Sea voyage of Dionysos" (Chalice). Praeg.: Pict. ency., p. 151 (col.).
sea wall (Acre). Natl. geog. 110: 754 (col.) Dec '56.
sea wall (Galveston). Travel 103: 27 May '55.
Seaborg, Glenn T. Cur. biog. p. 574 (1948); p. 414 (1961).
Holiday 8: 50 Dec '50.
Seabury, David. Cur. biog. p. 766 (1941).
seafood (on plate). Holiday 27: 188 (col.) Ap '60.
seafood (restaurant). Holiday 27: 95 (col.) Je '60.

seafood barbecue. Holiday 27: 10 (col.) Ap '60.
Seago, Edward (work of). Con. 144: 265 Jan '60.
  Natl. geog. 112: 613 (col.) Nov '57.
Seagram skyscraper. Holiday 26: 61 Oct '59.
Seagrave, Gordon S. Cur. biog. p. 682 (1943).
seahorse, Poseidon's. See Poseidon's seahorse.
seal (Constitution & laws, 1826). Amer. heri., vol. 6 no. 4 p. 103 (Je '55).
——— (jade). Con. 139: XXXV Mar '57.
——— (jade ball). Con. 143: XXXIII May '59.
——— (jade hand). Con. 141: XLVII Mar '58.
———, gold hand (antique). Con. 139: XLI Ap '57.
———, hand (antique). Con. 141: XXXV Je '58; 143: XLIX Mar '59.
———, Cal. state (1862). Amer. heri., vol. 9 no. 5 p. 76 (Aug '58).
———, Chinese jade imperial. Con. 129: 95 Je '52.
———, French. Amer. heri., vol. 8 no. 3 p. 83 (Ap '57).
———, govt. (early). Amer. heri., vol. 6 no. 4 p. 89 (Je '55).
———, N.Y. state. Natl. geog. 110: 590 (col.) Nov '56.
———, Northwest territory. Amer. heri., vol. 4 no. 3 p. 38 (spring '53).
———, Ohio state. Amer. heri., vol. 4 no. 3 p. 38 (spring '53).
  Natl. geog. 107: 443 (col.) Ap '55.
———, Penn. state. Amer. heri., vol. 6 no. 3 p. 62 (col.) (Ap '55).
———, Persian (4th cent. B.C.). Natl. geog. 118: 816 (col.) Dec '60.
———, Plymouth colony. Amer. heri., vol. 10 no. 6 p. 80 (Oct '59).
———, Portsmouth City (Eng.). Natl. geog. 101: 526 (col.) Ap '52.
———, South Carolina. Amer. heri., vol. 6 no. 6 p. 61 (col.) (Oct '55).
———, Texas. Amer. heri., vol. 4 no. 1 p. 17 (col.) (fall '52).
———, U.S. Presidents. Amer. heri., vol. 10 no. 1 p. 46 (Dec '58); vol. 11 no. 5 p. 106 (Aug '60).
———, U.S. Vice Pres. Natl. geog. 102: 146 Aug '52.
seal box, Chinese. Con. 132: VIII Nov '53.
seal-case. Con. 136: 9 Sept '55.
seal of U.S. (furniture dec.). Con. ency. of ant., vol. 1, p. 63.
seals (sym.). Lehner: Pict. bk. of sym., p. 74.
——— (antique). Con. ency. of ant., vol. 3, pl. 149-51.
———, Crete. Ceram: March of arch., p. 63.
———, Dec. (on Indian pottery). Amer. heri., vol. 10 no. 2 p. 80, 82-4 (Feb '59).
———, Elizabeth I. Con. ency. of ant., vol. 3 pl. 149.
———, heraldic. Con. 143: 187 May '59.
———, state (1st 13). Amer. heri., vol. 11 no. 3 cover (col.) (Ap '60).
seals of ruling princes of fermament. Lehner: Pict. bk. of sym., p. 24.
seaman (1607). Natl. geog. 111: 585 (col.) May '57.
"Seamen's Bethel" (on Johnny Cake Hill, New Bedford). Amer. heri., vol. 4 no. 1 p. 55

(fall '52).
seaplane. Holiday 14: 64 (col.) Jl '53.
seaquarium, Miami. Natl. geog. 113: 56 (col.) Jan '58.
searchlights. Natl. geog. 109: 506-7 Ap '56.
Searle, John (work of). Natl. geog. 99: 190 (col.) Feb '51.
Searle, Ronald (cartoons by). Holiday 27: 88-93 Je '60.
Sears, Paul B. Cur. biog. p. 368 (1960).
Sears, Robert R. Cur. biog. p. 523 (1952).
Sears, Roebuck Cat. (page from 1902). Brooks: Growth of a nation, p. 232.
seashore (children, sea life). Natl. geog. 118: 436-44 Sept '60.
seasons (sym.). Lehner: Pict. bk. of sym., p. 80.
———, painting of the. Con. 140: XLIX Sept '57.
seat, Hepplewhite double sided. Con. 144: inside back cover Jan '60.
———, marble (18th cent.). Con. 138: XXXIX Sept '56.
———, Quaker school. See school seat, Quaker.
———, Regency garden. Con. ency. of ant., vol. 3 p. 55.
———, tavern wall (antique). Con. 137: LI Mar '56.
———, window. See window seat.
———. See also settle.
Seaton, Frederick A. Cur. biog. p. 559 (1956).
Seattle (Wash.). Holiday 8: 98-103 (part col.) Jl '50; 11: 50-1 (col.) May '52.
  Natl. geog. 117: 494-513 (col.) Ap '60.
——— (map). Natl. geog. 117: 500 (col.) Ap '60.
——— (skyline). Jordan: Hammond's pict. atlas, p. 148 (col.).
Sebald, William J. Cur. biog. p. 556 (1951).
Sebastian, George. Holiday 25: 89 Ap '59.
Sebastiano del Piombo (work of). Amer. heri., vol. 6 no. 6 frontispiece (col.) (Oct '55).
  Con. 127: 120 May '51; 129: 93 Je '52.
  Natl. geog. 101: 79, 92 (col.) Jan '52.
Sebrell, William Henry, jr. Cur. biog. p. 557 (1951).
Sebron, Hyppolite (work of). Amer. heri., vol. 8 no. 6 p. 14 (col.) (Oct '57).
Secrest, Edmund. Natl. geog. 107: 467 Ap '55.
Secret Chamberlain (Vatican). Holiday 23: 52 (col.) May '58.
secretaire (antique). Con. 133: 290 Je '54; 138: 221 Jan '57.
——— (17th cent.). Con. ency. of ant., vol. 3 pl. 16.
——— (18th cent.). Con. 140: 10-12 Sept '57.
———, bureau. See bureau secretaire.
———, Chippendale. Con. 133: 123 Ap '54; 136: XLIV Jan '56; 143: IV Ap '59.
———, Hepplewhite. Con. 140: XXII Dec '57.
———, Italian. Con. 135: 24, 27-8 Mar '55.
———, Italian (18th cent.). Con. 133: LXXIII Je '54.
———, Louis XV. Con. 126: 80 Aug '50; 133: XLIV Ap '54; 139: 192 May '57; 141: 42 Mar '58; 142: XLV Sept '58; 143: 189 May '59.
———, Louis XV (marquetry). Con. 139: 262 Je '57.

secretaire, Louis XVI. Con. 133: LV Mar '54; 135: 128 Ap '55; 141: 73 Ap '58; 142: LXI Sept '58; 143: 64 Mar '59.

——, Marie Antoinette. Con. 132: LIV Sept '53.

——, marquetry & parquetry (18th cent.). Con. 145: 109 Ap '60.

——, regency. Con. 140: LXVII Nov '57; 143: XX Ap '59.

——, Sheraton. Con. 140: XLVII Nov '57; 142: XIX Jan '59.

——, Viennese tall rococo (18th cent.). Con. ency. of ant., vol. 3, pl. 23.

——, William & Mary. Con. 133: LIV Je '54.

secretaire a abattant, Louis XV. Con. 143: 190 May '59.

secretaire a abattant, Louis XVI. Con. 143: 212 Je '59.

secretaire a doucine (18th cent.). Con. 145: 268 Je '60.

secretaire bookcase (antique). Con. 143: XLVI Je '59; 145: IV Ap '60.

—— (18th cent.). Con. 132: XXVIII, XXXIV Nov '53; 139: XXV Je '57; 141: XX Je '58; 142: VI Nov '58.

——, bow-fronted. Con. 140: X Jan '58.

——, Chippendale. Con. 133: LII Je '54; 142: 127 Nov '58; 145: XVI May '60.

——, Chippendale breakfront. Con. 143: XLVII May '59.

——, George II. Con. 142: 57 Sept '58.

——, Hepplewhite. Con. 137: LXIII May '56; 139: XLIII Mar '57; 142: XV Nov '58; 145: XXIII Je '60.

——, Queen Anne. Con. 143: 189 May '59.

——, regency. Con. 129: XXVII Ap '52; 133: XX Je '54.

——, Sheraton. Con. 129: XXX Ap '52; 133: XII Je '54; 135: XLII, LVII Ap '55; 139: XXV Mar '57, LXIII May '57; 144: XVII Nov '59.

——, George III. Con. 140: LIX Nov '57.

secretaire cabinet (18th cent.). Con. 142: XXXI Sept '58.

——, Adam. Con. 134: 121 Nov '54; 145: XVIII Mar '60.

——, regency. Con. 143: XIX Mar '59; 145: XXIV May '60.

——, Sheraton. Con. 137: XLIII, XLVI May '56; 140: 100 Nov '57.

secretaire chest (antique). Con. 139: IV Ap '57.

—— (18th cent.). Con. 143: 200 May '59.

secretaire commode, Chippendale. Con. 135: 256-7 Je '55.

——, Viennese (18th cent.). Con. ency. of ant., vol. 3, pl. 22.

secretary (17th cent.). Con. 142: 129 Nov '58.

—— (18th cent.). Con. 138: 279 Jan '57.

—— (18th cent. lacquer). Con. 140: 69 Sept '57.

——, Chinese style (18th cent.). Con. 143: LIV Mar '59.

——, Chippendale. Con. 138: 260 Jan '57.

——, Louis XV. Con. 142: XLVI Dec '58.

——, Louis XVI. Con. 145: LI Je '60.

——, tambour. See tambour secretary.

secretary bookcase, Chippendale. Con. 144: LXII Sept '59.

——, Georgian. Con. 144: LXXVII Dec '59.

——, Sheraton. Con. 135: XL Mar '55.

secretary-cabinet, Amer. Con. 135: LI Mar '55.

——, Chippendale. Con. 140: 56 Sept '57.

security (sym.). Lehner: Pict. bk. of sym., p. 89.

sedan (old auto). Holiday 8: back cover (col.) Jl '50.

——, electric. Holiday 6: back cover (col.) Sept '49.

sedan chair. Con. 13: 180-4 Dec '54. Holiday 6: 84 (col.) Jl '49; 8: 131 Oct '50.

—— (18th cent.). Int. gr. soc.: Arts . . . p. 119 (col.).

——, Dalai Lama's. Natl. geog. 108: 39 (col.) Jl '55.

Sedgman, Frank. Cur. biog. p. 559 (1951).

Sedgwick, John. Pakula: Cent. album, p. 251.

seduction (sym.). Lehner: Pict. bk. of sym., p. 92.

Seeger, Pete. Cur. biog. p. 380 (1963).

"seeing eye" dog (blind man). See man, blind ("seeing eye" dog).

sefirotic tree (sym.). Lehner: Pict. bk. of sym., p. 74.

senate. See U.S. senate.

Seefried, Irmgard. Cur. biog. p. 561 (1956).

Segers, Chester W. Natl. geog. 113: 458 Ap '58.

Seghers, Anna. Cur. biog. p. 749 (1942).

Seghers, Daniel (work of). Con. 144: LVIII (col.) Dec '59.

Segni, Antonio. Cur. biog. p. 540 (1955).

Segovia, Andres. Cur. biog. p. 576 (1948).

Segovia (Spain). Holiday 15: 40, 43 Jan '54; 27: 194 (col.) Mar '60.

—— (Alcazar castle). Travel 113: 69 Ap '60.

Segre, Emilio. Cur. biog. p. 369 (1960).

Segura, Francisco. Cur. biog. p. 561 (1951).

Seibert, Florence B. Cur. biog. p. 751 (1942).

Seibert, Mrs. P. A. Horan: Pict. hist. of wild west, p. 236.

Seibert, Percy. Horan: Pict. hist. of wild west, p. 232.

Seifert, Elizabeth. Cur. biog. p. 564 (1951).

Seifert, Shirley. Cur. biog. p. 565 (1951).

Seif-Ul-Islam Abdullah, Prince. Cur. biog. p. 568 (1947).

Seignac, P. (work of). Con. 142: XXVII Jan '59.

seine, fish (Ifalik). Natl. geog. 109: 570 Ap '56.

—— (Nepal). Natl. geog. 97: 25 (col.) Jan '50.

"The Seine" river (Goblain). Con. 142: XLIII Nov '58.

Seine river (Paris). Holiday 5: 68 Je '49. Natl. geog. 101: 801 (col.) Je '52; 114: 290 Aug '58; 115: 608-9, 618 (col.) May '59. Travel 101: 48 Je '54; 109: inside back cover Je '58.

seiners, Persian fish. Natl. geog. 114: 28 (col.) Jl '58.

Seitz, Frederick. Cur. biog. p. 563 (1956).

Seixas, Elias Victor, jr. Cur. biog. p. 524 (1952).

Selassie, Haile. Holiday 25: 73 (col.) Ap '59. Natl. geog. 118: 349 (col.) Sept '60.

Seldes, George. Cur. biog. p. 767 (1941).

Seler, Eduard. Ceram: March of arch., p. 293.

Self, Sir Henry. Cur. biog. p. 752 (1942).

Selfridge, Harry Gordon. Cur. biog. p. 769 (1941).
Selinko, Annemarie. Cur. biog. p. 542 (1955).
Seljuk minaret (Antalya). Osward: Asia Minor, pl. 109.
Seljuk mosque (Antalya). Osward: Asia Minor, pl. 112.
Seller monument, Isaiah. Amer. heri., vol. 2 no. 1 p. 51 (fall '50).
Sellers, Peter. Cur. biog. p. 371 (1960).
Selman, John. Horan: Pict. hist. of wild west, p. 126.
Selquet (goddess statue). Ceram: March of arch., p. 146.
Selsdon Park mansion (B.O.A.C. hotel, Eng.). Travel 103: 22 May '55.
Seltzer, Louis B. Cur. biog. p. 565 (1956).
Selwyn, George Augustus. Con. 144: 9 Sept '59.
Selye, Hans. Cur. biog. p. 565 (1953).
Selznick, David O. Cur. biog. p. 771 (1941). Holiday 5: 38 (col.) Jan '49.
semaphore signal (1830). Amer. heri., vol. 5 no. 1 p. 11 (fall '53).
Semenov, Nikolai N. Cur. biog. p. 499 (1957).
Seminole Indians. See Indians, Seminole.
Semitic sym. Lehner: Pict. bk. of sym., p. 29.
Semmes, Raphael. Pakula: Cent. Album, p. 253.
Semple, William T. (and Mrs. Semple). Ceram: March of arch., p. 43.
Sen, Binay R. Cur. biog. p. 526 (1952).
Senanayake, Don Stephen. Cur. biog. p. 524 (1950); p. 527 (1952).
senate. See U.S. senate.
Senate house (int., Conn.). Holiday 27: 87 (col.) Feb '60.
Senate house (Kingston, N.Y.). Amer. heri., vol. 4 no. 1 p. 14 (fall '52).
Sender, Toni. Cur. biog. p. 526 (1950).
Seneca (sculpture). See The pseudo Seneca (sculpture).
Seneca Indian chief. Amer. heri., vol. 11 no. 3 back cover (col.) (Ap '60).
Senghor, Leopold Sedar. Cur. biog. p. 382 (1962).
Sengstacke, John H. Cur. biog. p. 557 (1949).
Senior, Clarence. Cur. biog. p. 416 (1961).
"Sennacherib worshipping before a god" (bas relief). Ceram: March of arch., p. 213.
"Sennacherib's siege of Lachish." Natl. geog. 118: 834-9 (part col.) Dec '60.
Sennett, Mack. Holiday 5: 36 (col.) Jan '49.
"Sentinels of the moonlight" (Johnson). Con. 144: LXXVI Dec '59.
sentry, war. Amer. heri., vol. 10 no. 6 p. 11 (col.) (Oct '59).
Seoul (Korea). Holiday 18: 78 Dec '55. Natl. geog. 97: 778 Je '50.
—— **(flag raised).** See flag (raised at Seoul).
Sepik village hut. Holiday 28: 96 (col.) Nov '60.
sepulcher (Joseph of Arimathea). Natl. geog. 106: 846 Dec '56.
sepulchers (Taj Mahal). Natl. geog. 118: 475 (col.) Oct '60.
Sepulchral way, China (winged lion). Praeg.: Pict. ency., p. 529.
Sequoia Natl. park (Cal.). Holiday 13: 120 (col.) Mar '53; 24: 38-9 (col.) Jl '58.

Jordan: Hammond's pict. travel atlas, p. 192 (col.).
Natl. geog. 99: 680-95 May '51; 105: 746-7, 794-5 (col.) Je '54; 116: 148- (col.) Aug '59.
"Serapis" ship flag. Amer. heri., vol. 11 no. 3 p. 13 (col.) (Ap '60).
Serapis temple (Ephesus). Osward: Asia Minor, pl. 35-6.
Seredy, Kate. Jun. bk. of auth., p. 271.
"The Serenade" (Jordaens). Con. 143: XXV Je '59.
serfboard. Holiday 14: 32 (col.) Nov '53.
sergeant at arms (Ontario legislature). Holiday 18: 38 (col.) Sept '55.
sergeant pikeman. Holiday 25: 190 (col.) May '59.
sergeant's inn hall (Eng. 19th cent.). Con. 133: 26 Mar '54.
Sergel, Johan Tobias (work of). Con. 141: 31-3 Mar '58.
Sergio, Lisa. Cur. biog. p. 604 (1944).
"The serious conversation" (Steen). Con. 141: 178 May '58.
Serlin, Oscar. Cur. biog. p. 684 (1943).
Serling, Rod. Cur. biog. p. 409 (1959).
"Sermon on the Mount" (Stanford Univ.). Natl. geog. 110: 221 (col.) Aug '56.
Serov, Ivan A. Cur. biog. p. 567 (1956).
Serov, V. A. (work of). Cooper: Con. ency. of music, p. 247.
serpent (musical instrument). Cooper: Con. ency of music, p. 408.
—— **(sym.).** Lehner: Pict. of sym., p. 58.
——, **Amer. Indian mica.** Con. 143: 131 Ap '59.
——, **crucified.** See crucified serpent.
——, **seven-headed.** See seven-headed serpent.
——, **winged.** See winged serpent (sym.).
serpent & apple tree. Lehner: Pict. bk. of sym., p. 29.
"Serpent & creation" (sym.). Lehner: Pict. bk. of sym., p. 44.
serpent ouraboras (sym.). Lehner: Pict. bk. of sym., p. 80.
serpentine wall (brick). Natl. geog. 103: 797 (col.) Je '53.
—— **(fence at Univ. of Va.).** Natl. geog. 97: 555 May '50.
Serra museum (Cal.). Travel 103: 33 Je '55.
Serrano, Manuel (work of). Con. 135: 250, 253 Je '55.
Serratosa cibils, Joaquin. Cur. biog. p. 564 (1954).
Serres, Dominic (work of). Con. 139: XXXI Mar '57.
Serres, Dominique (work of). Natl. geog. 99: 186 (col.) Feb '51.
Serres, John Thomas (work of). Con. 144: XXXI, LXVI Dec '59.
Servan-Schreiber, Jacques. Cur. biog. p. 543 (1955).
servant, man (15th cent.). Int. gr. soc.: Arts . . . p. 69 (col.).
servants, the White House (1877). Jensen: The White House, p. 113.
service men (fish in ice). Natl. geog. 103: 584, 594 (col.) May '53.
service station attendant. See gas station attendant.

serving table. *See* table, serving.
Seton, Anya. Cur. biog. p. 567 (1953).
Seton, Ernest Thompson. Cur. biog. p. 686 (1943).
settee (antique). Con. 137: 109 Ap '56; 139: XXVIII Mar '57.
—— (17th cent.). Con. 129: XXVIII Je '52; 138: LIX Nov '56.
—— (18th cent.). Con. 142: 19-20, 23 Sept '58.
——, Adam. Con. 141: 43 Mar '58; 142: XXIX, inside back cover Sept '58.
——, Argentine colonial. Con. 144: 249 Jan '60.
——, Chippendale. Con. 138: IV Sept '56; 139: XVIII Ap '57; 140: XXVIII Nov '57; 142: LI Sept '58.
——, Colonial. Holiday 24: 149 Oct '58.
——, early Eng. cane. Con. 127: 84 May '51.
——, Eng. gilt confidante. Con. 145: 212 May '60.
——, French (18th cent.). Con. 132: 63 Sept '53; 137: 54 Mar '56.
——, French (19th cent.). Con. 140: LXVIII Jan '58.
——, George I. Con. 137: XXXIII Mar '56; 143: XXIX Ap '59.
——, gilt (18th cent.). Con. 134: back cover Sept '54.
——, gilt (Wm. Kent, 18th cent.). Con. 145: XXXI May '60.
——, Hepplewhite. Con. 129: I Je '52; 136: XXXII Nov '55; 137: XXXVI Mar '56; 140: 183 Dec '57; 141: XLVI Je '58.
——, Italian (18th cent.). Con. 135: 24 Mar '55.
——, Louis XIV. Con. 140: L Dec '57.
——, Louis XV. Con. 126: opp. II Aug '50; 144: LXXI Jan '60.
——, Louis XVI. Con. 141: XXXIX Je '58.
——, needlework (18th cent.). Con. 139: 173 (col.) May '57.
——, Norwegian (18th cent.). Con. 145: 22 Mar '60.
——, Queen Anne. Con. 126: 91 Oct '50; 129: I Ap '52; 141: LI Mar '58; 142: XXI Sept '58.
——, 2 chair back (antique). Con. 142: VI Jan '58.
——, Victorian gothic garden. Con. ency. of ant., vol. 3, pl. 28.
——, Viennese (18th cent.). Con. ency. of ant., vol. 3, pl. 20.
——, Viennese rococo (18th cent.). Con. ency. of ant., vol. 3, pl. 20.
settee. *See* also settle.
Settignano, Desiderio da (work of). Praeg.: Pict. ency., p. 296.
Settle, Mary Lee. Cur. biog. p. 411 (1959).
settle. Rawson: Ant. pict. bk., p. 16.
—— (antique). Con. 133: 255 Je '54.
——, diamond carved (17th cent.). Con. ency. of ant., vol. 1, pl. 5.
——, Victorian. Con. ency. of ant., vol. 3, pl. 1.
——, Victorian (1845). Con. ency. of ant., vol. 3, pl. 1.
settle. *See* also settee.
"Settling day at Tattersall's" (Hunt). Con. ency. of ant., vol. 1, pl. 138.

Seurat, Georges (Laurent). Con. 142: 61 Sept '58.
—— (work of). Con. 140: 81 Nov '57; 142: 59-2 Sept '58.
Praeg.: Pict. ency., p. 429 (col.).
Seuss, Dr. (pseud.). *See* Geisel, T. S.
Sevareid, Eric. Cur. biog. p. 753 (1942).
seven (sym.). Lehner: Pict. bk. of sym., p. 63.
"Seven ages of man" (Muready). Con. 144: 34 Sept '59.
seven beneficial spirits. *See* spirits, signs of 7 beneficial.
seven-branched candelabra. *See* candelabra, seven-branched.
"Seven dolls temple." *See* "Temple of the seven dolls."
"Seven Gables" (Colonial house, Va.). Natl. geog. 109: 446-7 (col.) Ap '56.
seven guardian angels. *See* guardian angels, seals of 7.
"Seven-headed beast" (Durer woodcut, Apocalypse). Con. 133: XVI Je '54.
seven-headed serpent (sym.). Lehner: Pict. bk. of sym., p. 66.
seven-league boots (sym.). Lehner: Pict. bk. of sym., p. 64.
seven maleficent spirits. *See* spirits, signs of 7 malificent.
seven-mile bridge. *See* bridge, Florida to Key West.
seven ruling princes of firmament. *See* firmament, seals of 7 ruling princes of.
"Seven sacraments" (detail). Labande: Naples, p. 33.
seven sleepers grotto. *See* Grotto of the seven sleepers.
Seville (Spain). Natl. geog. 97: 441 (col.) Ap '50; 99: 500-30 (part col.) Ap '51.
Travel 103: 12-3 Ap '55; 107: 21 Ap '57.
Seville hotel (Miami Beach, Fla., model). Travel 104: 59 Sept '55.
Sevitzky, Fabien. Cur. biog. p. 544 (1946).
Sevres dish. Con. 133: XXXV (col.) Je '54.
Sewall, Judge Samuel. Amer. heri., vol. 5 no. 3 p. 11 (spring '54).
Seward, Anna Wharton. Amer. heri., vol. 10 no. 6 p. 62 (Oct '59).
Seward, Augustus. Amer. heri., vol. 10 no. 6 p. 62 (Oct '59).
Seward, Frances Adeline. Amer. heri., vol. 10 no. 6 p. 60 (col.) (Oct '59).
Seward, Frederick William. Amer. heri., vol. 10 no. 6 p. 62 (Oct '59).
Seward, William Henry. Amer. heri., vol. 10 no. 6 p. 63 (Oct '59); vol. 11 no. 6 p. 46 (Oct '60); vol. 12 no. 1 p. 45 (Dec '60).
Seward, William Henry, jr. Amer. heri., vol. 10 no. 6 p. 62 (Oct '59).
Seward home, William Henry. Amer. heri., vol. 10 no. 6 p. 64 (Oct '59).
Sewell, Helen. Jun. bk. of auth., p. 272.
Sewell, Luke. Cur. biog. p. 607 (1944).
Sewell, Winifred. Cur. biog. p. 373 (1960).
Sewell (night, Chile). Natl. geog. 117: 226-7 (col.) Feb '60.
sewing machine, Singer (original). Amer. heri., vol. 9 no. 6 p. 103 (Oct '58).
sewing machine adv., Singer. Amer. heri., vol. 9 no. 6 p. 34, 39 (col.) (Oct '58).

sewing room. *See* needle room (Scotland).
sewing table, Martha Washington. Con. ency.
of ant., vol. 1, pl. 39.
——, Sheraton. Con. 142: 130 Nov '58.
sextant. Natl. geog. 108: 700 (col.) Nov '55.
—— (man). Natl. geog. 116: 137 (col.) Jl '59.
—— (sym.). Lehner: Pict. bk. of sym., p. 15.
——, antique. Natl. geog. 97: 290 (col.) Mar
'50.
Seychelles islands. Natl. geog. 116: 670-94
(part col.) Nov '59.
—— (map). Natl. geog. 116: 679 Nov '59.
Seyferth, Otto A. Cur. biog. p. 529 (1950).
Seymour, Charles. Cur. biog. p. 773 (1941).
Seymour, Flora Warren. Cur. biog. p. 754
(1942).
Seymour, Gov. Horatio. Amer. heri., vol. 10
no. 4 p. 97 (Je '59).
Seymour, James (work of). Con. 145: XXXIV,
144, 147 May '60.
Seymour, Whitney North. Cur. biog. p. 418
(1961).
Seymour Narrows (map, Canada). Natl. geog.
114: 184 Aug '58.
Seyss-Inquart, Artur. Cur. biog. p. 775 (1941).
Sforza, Count Carlo. Cur. biog. p. 755 (1942).
sgraffito pottery. Con. 140: 135 Nov '57.
Shabandar, Moussa. Cur. biog. p. 599 (1956).
shackles. Horan: Pict. hist. of wild west, p.
211.
Shackleton, John (work of). Con. 135: 239 Je
'55.
Shackleton memorial, Sir Ernest. Natl. geog.
112: 618 (col.) Nov '57.
shadbelly (girl wearing). Holiday 18: 105 Oct
'55.
shadow (airplane). Natl. geog. 102: 396 (col.)
Sept '52.
—— (in water, Mexico). Travel 111: 60 Jan
'59.
——, man's. Natl. geog. 98: 91 (col.) Jl '50.
——, woman's. Holiday 13: 21 (col.) May '53.
shadow puppets. *See* Chinese shadow puppets.
shadows, Children's. Travel 104: inside cover
Sept '55.
——, men's. Holiday 25: 115 Mar '59; 26: 44
(col.) Oct '59.
——, sidewalk. Travel 108: inside cover Oct
'57.
shadows. *See* also reflections.
Shafer, Paul W. Cur. biog. p. 529 (1952).
Shafik, Doria. Cur. biog. p. 545 (1955).
Holiday 17: 52-55 (part col.) Jan '55.
Shaftesbury (Eng.). Natl. geog. 108: 308 (col.)
Sept '55.
Shah (Iran). Natl. geog. 104: 718 Nov '53.
Shah Jehan. *See* Jehan, Shah.
Shah-i-Hamadan mosque. *See* mosque, Shah-i-
Hamadan.
Shahn, Benjamin. Cur. biog. p. 565 (1954).
—— (work of). Amer. heri., vol. 9 no. 6 p.
52, 54, 57 (Oct '58).
Praeg.: Pict. ency., p. 508.
Shakespeare, William. Holiday 19: 6 Je '56;
22: 135 Nov '57.
—— (bust). Holiday 10: 94 (col.) Jl '51.
—— (wood statue). Natl. geog. 108: 299 (col.)
Sept '55.
Shakespeare festival theatre (Stratford, Conn.).
Travel 113: 29 May '60.

Shakespeare illus. Con. 141: 145-9 May '58.
Shakespeare memorial theater (Stratford,
Eng.). Holiday 10: 94-7 (part col.) Jl '51.
Natl. geog. 108: 303 (col.) Sept '55.
Shakespeare's birthplace. Holiday 13: 88 Ap
'53.
Shakespeare's home (int.). Natl. geog. 108:
302 (col.) Sept '55.
Shalimar garden. Natl. geog. 114: 624-5 (col.)
Nov '58.
Shamrock hotel (Houston). Holiday 11: 102
(col.) Ap '52.
Shane, C. Donald. Holiday 8: 50 Dec '50.
Shang Chen, Gen. Cur. biog. p. 610 (1944).
Shannon, Monica. Jun. bk. of auth., p. 273.
shanty boat (Fla.). Travel 107: 21 Feb '57.
Shantz, Robert Clayton. Cur. biog. p. 568
(1953).
Shapiro, Harry L. Cur. biog. p. 531 (1952).
Shapiro, Irwin. Jun. bk. of auth., p. 273.
Shapiro, Karl. Cur. biog. p. 612 (1944).
Shapley, Harlow. Cur. biog. p. 777 (1941);
p. 534 (1952).
Shaposhnikov, Marshal Boris M. Cur. biog.
p. 757 (1942).
shark dance (Tiwi men). Natl. geog. 109: 429
(col.) Mar '56.
Shasta dam (Cal.). Jordan: Hammond's pict.
travel atlas, p. 186 (col.).
Natl. geog. 105: 743 (col.) Je '54.
Shaver, Dorothy. Cur. biog. p. 547 (1946).
Shaver, Rev. Erwin L. Cur.. biog. p. 560
(1949).
shaves, Cooper's. Rawson: Ant. pict. bk., p.
61.
shaving dish, silver (18th cent.). Con. 143: 18
Mar '59.
——, William III, silver. Con. 139: 55 Mar
'57.
shaving dish & ewer, silver (18th cent.). Con.
ency. of ant., vol. 3, p. 70.
shaving horse. Rawson: Ant. pict. bk., p. 23.
"Shaving in camp" (Civil war, by Pratt). Amer.
heri., vol. 7 no. 2 p. 119 (Feb '56).
shaving jug. *See* jug, shaving; jug & basin,
shaving.
shaving mug. Rawson: Ant. pict. bk., p. 8.
shaving set, George II, silver. Con. 141: 245
Je '58.
Shaw, Artie. Cur. biog. p. 779 (1941).
Shaw, George Bernard. Cur. biog. p. 613
(1944).
Holiday 6: 22 Aug '49.
Shaw, Irwin. Cur. biog. p. 759 (1942).
Holiday 5: 32 Jan '49; 23: 73 Feb '58.
Shaw, Lau. Cur. biog. p. 541 (1945).
Shaw, Lloyd. Cur. biog. p. 689 (1943).
Shaw, Ralph R. Cur. biog. p. 571 (1956).
Shaw, Robert. Cur. biog. p. 562 (1949).
Shaw of Iran. Natl. geog. 117: 73 (col.) Jan
'60.
Shawcross, Sir Hartley. Cur. biog. p. 543
(1945).
shawl. Natl. geog. 113: 323 Mar '58.
——, Kazakh. Natl. geog. 106: 636 (col.) Nov
'54.
——, Shetland woolen (can go thru a wed-
ding ring). Natl. geog. 104: 535 Oct '53.
Shawn, Ted. Cur. biog. p. 564 (1949).

——, **French (sheep).** Natl. geog. 115: 583 Ap '59.

——, **Nomad women.** *See* nomad shepherd women.

shepherd's dance (Kashmir). Natl. geog. 114: 634 (col.) Nov '58.

shepherd's hut (Eng.). Natl. geog. 109: 528 Ap '56.

Shepilov, Dimitri T. Cur. biog. p. 547 (1955).

Sheppard, Sir John. Holiday 23: 71 (col.) Ap '58.

Shequaga falls. *See* waterfall, Shequaga.

Sheraton furniture. Con. 138: XXXV Sept '56.

—— *See* also name of piece of furniture wanted.

Sheraton hotel (Dallas). Travel 107: 49 Feb '57.

Sheraton-Palace hotel (San Francisco). Holiday 23: 164 (col.) Je '58.

Sheraton-Tel Aviv inn (Chicago). Travel 113: 51 Mar '60.

Sherburne lake. Jordan: Hammond's pict. atlas, p. 135 (col.).

Sheridan, Philip Henry. Pakula: Cent. album, p. 255.

sheriff, early western. Horan: Pict. hist. of wild west, p. 75.

——, **Texas.** Holiday 24: 47 (col.) Oct '58.

Sherman, Vice Adm. Forrest P. Cur. biog. p. 577 (1948).

Sherman, Henry C. Cur. biog. p. 565 (1949).

Sherman, John. Amer. heri., vol. 11 no. 6 p. 53 (Oct '60).

Sherman, Roger. Amer. heri., vol. 9 no. 4 p. 48 (col.) (Je '58); vol. 10 no. 1 p. 60 (Dec '58.

Sherman, William Tecumseh (Civil war). Amer. heri., vol. 7 no. 2 p. 44 (Feb '56). Amer. heri., vol. 12 no. 1 p. 119 (Dec '60). Pakula: Cent. album, p. 257.

Sherrill, Bishop Henry Knox. Cur. biog. p. 570 (1947).

Sherrod, Robert. Cur. biog. p. 617 (1944); p. 384 (1962).

Sherry, Louis. Amer. heri., vol. 6 no. 4 p. 34 (Je '55).

Shertok, Moshe. Cur. biog. p. 580 (1948).

"Sherwood Forest" (home of Pres. Tyler). Natl. geog. 109: 456 (col.) Ap '56.

Sherwood gardens (Baltimore). Natl. geog. 109: 701-8 (col.) May '56.

Shetland & Orkney islands. Natl. geog. 104: 520-36 Oct '53.

Shetland islands (map). Natl. geog. 104: 522 Oct '53.

Shia moslems. Natl. geog. 114: 632 (col.) Nov '58.

Shibam (Saudi Arabia). Natl. geog. 114: 722-3 Nov '58.

—— **(whitewashed mud buildings).** Natl. geog. 111: 240-1 Feb '57.

Shiber, Etta. Cur. biog. p. 691 (1943).

Shickellamy (statue). Amer. heri., vol. 3 no. 4 p. 9 (summer '52).

Shidehara, Baron Kijuro. Cur. biog. p. 549 (1946).

shieks, Arabian. Natl. geog. 113: 204, 206-7, 220-1 (part col.) Feb '58.

Shield, Lansing P. Cur. biog. p. 573 (1951).

shield (sym.). Lehner: Pict. bk. of sym., p. 88.

——, **African warrior's.** Natl. geog. 106: 499, 496 (col.) Oct '54.

——, **antique armour.** Con. ency. of ant., vol. 1, pl. 107.

——, **Aztec (mosaic of feathers).** Ceram: March of arch., pl. XVI (col.).

——, **palm (Fijian).** Natl. geog. 114: 529, 531 (col.) Oct '58.

——, **U.S. (with eagle).** Amer. heri., vol. 11 no. 6 p. 48-50 (col.) (Oct '60).

——, **West Point.** Natl. geog. 101: 618 (col.) May '52.

shield & crown (sym.). Lehner: Pict. bk. of sym., p. 12.

shield bearers, Roman. Natl. geog. 111: 210 (col.) Feb '57.

Shields, James P. Cur. biog. p. 575 (1951).

shields (medieval). Int. gr. soc.: Arts . . . p. 73 (col.).

——, **warrior's (ancient times).** Int. gr. soc.: Arts . . . p. 33, 41 (col.).

——, **(Biblical times).** Natl. geog. 112: 846-7, 863 (col.) Dec '57.

Shigemitsu, Mamoru. Cur. biog. p. 693 (1943).

shikaras (boat, Kashmir). Natl. geog. 114: 627, 646 (col.) Nov '58.

Travel 105: 54 Feb '56.

shilling, pine tree. Amer. heri., vol. 4 no. 2 p. 11 (winter '53).

Shiloh (Civil War). Holiday 19: 50-1 Je '56.

Shimkin, Leon. Cur. biog. p. 567 (1954).

shingle horse. Rawson: Ant. pict. bk., p. 23.

Shinn, Everett. Cur. biog. p. 576 (1951).

Shinto (sym.). Lehner: Pict. bk. of sym., p. 47.

Shinto priests. Holiday 12: 32-3 Aug '52.

Shinto shrine (Japan). Holiday 14: 68 (col.) Oct '53.

Shinto temple. *See* temple, Shinto.

Shinwell, Emanuel. Cur. biog. p. 695 (1943).

ship. Amer. heri., vol. 6 no. 1 p. 7 (col.) (fall '54); vol. 9 no. 3 p. 54 (col.) (Ap '58).

ship ("Andrew Doria"). Amer. heri., vol. 9 no. 6 p. 61, 63 (col.) (Oct '58).

—— **(burning).** Amer. heri., vol. 9 no. 3 p. 55 (col.) (Ap '58).

—— **(burning, 1804).** Amer. heri., vol. 11 no. 2 p. 30 (Feb '60).

—— **(by Roux, 1808).** Amer. heri., vol. 8 no. 1 p. 39 (col.) (Dec '56).

—— **(by Seago).** Natl. geog. 112: 613 (col.) Nov '57.

—— **(Civil war).** Amer. heri., vol. 10 no. 1 p. 48 (col.) (Dec '58).

—— **("Constitution").** See the "Constitution" (ship).

—— **(Denmark).** Natl. geog. 108: 813, 825-7 (col.) Dec '55.

—— **(18th cent., with sails).** Int. gr. soc.: Arts . . . p. 119 (col.).

—— **(early North Pacific).** Amer. heri., vol. 7 no. 5 p. 85 (Aug '56).

—— **(early painting).** Con. 139: 242 Je '57.

—— **(1804).** Amer. heri., vol. 10 no. 3 p. 64 (col.) (Ap '59).

—— **(1830).** Holiday 23: 141 Feb '58.

—— **1831).** Amer. heri., vol. 9 no. 5 p. 42 (col.) (Aug '58).

—— **(1850).** Amer. heri., vol. 10 no. 4 p. 30 (col.) (Je '59).

ship (1860). Amer. heri., vol. 7 no. 3 p. 111 (Ap '56).

—— **(1865).** Amer. heri., vol. 9 no. 6 p. 46-51 (col.) (Oct '58).

—— **(explosion).** Amer. heri., vol. 8 no. 2 p. 37 (col.) (Feb '57).

—— **(1st on Lake Erie).** Amer. heri., vol. 8 no. 3 p. 10 (col.) (Ap '57).

—— **(in harbor).** Amer. heri., vol. 11 no. 3 p. 7, 11 (col.) (Ap '60).
Natl. geog. 97: 69 (col.) Jan '50.

—— **(Maldive is.).** Natl. geog. 111: 842-3, 846 (col.) Je '57.

—— **(Mayflower II).** *See* "Mayflower II," ship.

—— **(night).** Amer. heri., vol. 8 no. 6 p. 68 (Oct '57).

—— **("Old Ironsides").** Amer. heri., vol. 6 no. 3 p. 57 (col.) (Ap '55).

—— **(on pitcher & urn).** Amer. heri., vol. 6 no. 5 p. 52-3 (col.) (Aug '55).

—— **(on state seal).** Amer. heri., vol. 11 no. 3 cover (col.) (Ap '60).

—— **("Oneida").** Amer. heri., vol. 8 no. 6 p. 13 (Oct '57).

—— **("Pacific").** Amer. heri., vol. 11 no. 3 p. 16 (Ap '60).

—— **(sails).** Amer. heri., vol. 2 no. 4 p. 54 (summer '51); vol. 2 no. 3 p. 48 (spring '51); vol. 5 no. 3 p. 7 (spring '54); vol. 8 no. 6 p. 73 (Oct '57); vol. 10 no. 5 p. 111 (Aug '59); vol. 11 no. 5 p. 62 (col.) (Aug '60); vol. 11 no. 6 cover (col.) p. 94-7 (part col.) (Oct '60); vol. 12 no. 1 p. 6, 56-7, 60-2 (col.) (Dec '60).
Con. 134: X Sept '54, XXIV Nov '54, IX, XIV Dec '54: 135: XV, XXX Mar '55, XXXII Ap '55, XIV May '55, X Je '55; 136: IX Sept '55, XLVIII Nov '55, XXXIII Jan '56; 137: XXXIX Je '56; 140: XXXI (col.) Sept '57; 143: XIII, XXXVII Ap '59; 144: XLV Nov '59, XL, 187 Dec '59; 145: XXVII Mar '60, 203 May '60, XXXV Je '60.
Holiday 6: 57 (col.) Nov '49; 7: inside cover (col.) Feb '50, 18, 76-80 Mar '50; 8: 54-5 Oct '50; 15: back cover Mar '54, 165 (col.) Ap '54, 85, 133, 163 (col.) May '54, 135 (col.) Je '54; 16: 47, 79 Aug '54, 29 Sept '54, 86 (col.) Nov '54; 19: 11 Mar '56; 21: 9 May '57; 23: 100 (col.) Jan '58, 13, 34 (col.) Feb '58, 170 Mar '58, 111 Ap '58, 123, 183 (col.) May '58, 40, 162 (col.) Je '58; 24: 125 (col.) Jl '58, 76 (col.) Aug '58, 26 (col.) Sept '58, 10 Oct '58, 130, 191 Nov '58, 203 Dec '58; 25: 10 Jan '59, 82 (col.) Feb '59, 128 (col.) Mar '59, 28 (col.) Ap '59, 184 May '59, 136 (col.) Je '59; 26: 28 (col.) Jl '59, 102 (col.) Aug '59, 108 (col.) Sept '59, 40 (col.) Oct '59; 27: 160 (col.) Feb '60, 119 (col.) Mar '60, 208 (col.) May '60.
Natl. geog. 98: 613, 629, 632 (col.) Nov '50; 99: 336, 352, 358, 365, 368 (col.) Mar '51, 429 (col.) Ap '51; 100: 474 (col.), 500 Oct '51, 709 Dec '51; 102: 330-70 (part col.) Sept '52; 104: 91 Jl '53; 108: 62-3, 75, 79-80, 83 (col.) Jl '55; 111: 615 May '57; 112: 735, 759 Dec '57; 115: 685 (col.) May '59; 118:

587 (col.) Nov '60.
Rawson: Ant. pict. bk., p. 77.
Travel 112: 48 Jl '59, 36 Aug '59, 15 Sept '59; 113: 13 Jan '60, 9 Feb '60, 50 Mar '60, 9 Ap '60, 19 May '60; 114: 9 Sept '60, 15, 54, 57, 64 Oct '60, 9 Nov '60, 13 Dec '60.
U.S. news & world report p. 24 (col.) Aug 31, 1964.

—— **(sails, Arctic expedition, 1845).** Amer. heri., vol. 10 no. 5 p. 14-7 (part col.) Aug '59.

—— **(sails, cartoon).** Holiday 5: 28 Feb '49.

—— **(sails, cruiser).** Travel 113: 13 Jan '60, 9 Feb '60, 50 Mar '60, 8 Ap '60, 11 Je '60; 114: 10, 69 Jl '60, 12 Aug '60.

—— **(sails, 1847).** Amer. heri., vol. 5 no. 1 p. 18-9 (col.) (fall '53).

—— **(sails, 1812).** Natl. geog. 118: 185 Aug '60.

—— **(sails lowered).** Horan: Pict. hist. of wild west, p. 21.
Natl. geog. 97: 86 Jan '50; 98: 609, 618, 620, 633, 637 (col.) Nov '50.

—— **(sails lowered, "Pathfinder" govt. ship).** Natl. geog. 111: 190-1 (col.) Feb '57.

—— **(sails lowered).** Natl. geog. 117: 153 (col.) Feb '60.

—— **(sails lowered, small).** Natl. geog. 115: 681 (col.) May '59.

—— **(sails lowered, on plate).** Natl. geog. 103: 369 (col.) Mar '53.

—— **(sails, shadowy).** Int. gr. soc.: Arts . . . p. 123 (col.).

—— **(sails, 1715).** Amer. heri., vol. 11 no. 1 p. 4 (Dec '59).

—— **(sails lowered, 1673).** Amer. heri., vol. 5 no. 1 p. 8 (fall '53).

—— **sails, 1798).** Amer. heri., vol. 11 no. 2 p. 28 (Feb '60).

—— **(sails lowered, sinking, 1848).** Amer. heri., vol. 11 no. 6 p. 26 (col.) (Oct '60).
ship **(sails).** *See* also sloop, trading; sailboat.
ship **(Savannah, 1819).** Amer. heri., vol. 9 no. 4 p. 112 (Je '58).

—— **("Sea diver").** Natl. geog. 117: 159-61 (col.) Feb '60.

—— **(17th cent.).** Int. gr. soc.: Arts . . . p. 119 (col.).

—— **(sheep cargo).** Natl. geog. 97: 81 (col.) Jan '50.

—— **(silhouette).** Natl. geog. 118: 230 Aug '60.

—— **(16th cent.).** Con. 139: 136 Ap '57.

—— **(sketches, 1838-).** Amer. heri., vol. 11 no. 6 p. 30-7 (part col.) (Oct '60).

—— **(storm).** Amer. heri., vol. 6 no. 2 p. 18 (col.) (winter '55); vol. 7 no. 2 p. 18 (col.) (Feb '56); vol. 7 no. 5 p. 70 (Aug '56); vol. 9 no. 5 p. 60 (Aug '58).
Brooks: Growth of a nation, p. 99.

—— **(storm, 1609).** Amer. heri., vol. 10 no. 4 p. 10 (Je '59).

—— **(sym.).** Lehner: Pict. bk. of sym., p. 34.

—— **(tempest).** Natl. geog. 110: 756 (col.) Dec '56.

—— **(3,300 years old).** Natl. geog. 117: 688 (col.) May '60.

—— **(twilight).** Natl. geog. 111: 607 (col.) May '57.

——, "the Alliance" (with sails). Amer. heri., vol. 11 no. 3 p. 91 (Ap '60).

——, Antarctica. Natl. geog. 110: 162-71 (part col.) Aug '56.

——, Arctic circle. Natl. geog. 114: 143 Jl '58.

——, "Calypso" sea research. See "Calypso" research ship.

——, Chile frigate. Natl. geog. 108: 759 (col.) Dec '55.

——, clipper. Amer. heri., vol. 6 no. 6 p. 15-7, 20, 100-1, 112 (part col.) (Oct '55). Con. 139: 276 Je '57.

——, clipper (by James Hughes). Amer. heri., vol. 6 no. 6 cover (col.) (Oct '55).

——, clipper ("Cutty Sark"). Natl. geog. 114: 91 (col.) Jl '58.

——, Columbus'. Natl. geog. 113: 152 Feb '58.

——, convoy. See convoy ship.

——, death. See ship of the dead, Egyptian.

——, De Gama's. Natl. geog. 118: 657 Nov '60.

——, early (with sails). Amer. heri., vol. 6 no. 3 p. 103 (Ap '55); vol. 6 no. 4 p. 97 (Je '55); vol. 6 no. 5 p. 104 (Aug '55); vol. 7 no. 1 p. 72, 86, 89, 91, 120 (Dec '55).

——, Egyptian (ancient). Int. gr. soc.: Arts . . . p. 41 (col.).

——, French carrier. Natl. geog. 113: 12 (col.) Jan '58.

——, Greek. Natl. geog. 105: 2 (col.) Jan '54.

——, grounded target. Natl. geog. 97: 54 (col.) Jan '50.

——, ice breaker (navy). Natl. geog. 110: 142, 145 (col.) Aug '56.

——, La Salle's. Amer. heri., vol. 8 no. 3 p. 77 (Ap '57).

——, merchant. Natl. geog. 99: 157 (col.) Feb '51.

——, merchant (Yassi island's reef). Natl. geog. 117: 689 (col.) May '60.

——, navy training ship (Portuguese). Natl. geog. 108: 747 (col.) Dec '55.

——, Lord Nelson's. Holiday 27: 127 (col.) Feb '60.

——, Nelson's flag ship. Natl. geog. 101: 514, 542 (col.) Ap '52.

——, nuclear. See nuclear ship.

——, old navy. Holiday 24: 57 Oct '58.

——, ore carrier (German). Natl. geog. 115: 790 Je '59.

——, paddle-wheel. Travel 101: 10 May '54.

——, "Peace." See "Peace ship," Ford.

——, Perry's north pole. Natl. geog. 106: 524 Oct '54.

——, Commodore Perry's (by Hiroshige). Amer. heri., vol. 9 no. 3 p. 15, 19, 22-3 (col.) (Ap '55).

——, Perry's. Natl. geog. 104: 96 Jl '53.

——, Perry's (at Japan). Natl. geog. 116: 104 (col.) Jl '59.

——, Phoenician. See Phoenician ship.

——, pirate. Amer. heri., vol. 8 no. 1 p. 34 (col.) (Dec '56).

——, Polynesian. Natl. geog. 97: 82 (col.) Jan '50.

——, rescue. Natl. geog. 108: 830-43 Dec '55.

——, St. Lawrence. Travel 114: 26 Jl '60.

——, sea explorers. Natl. geog. 102: 449 Oct '52.

——, silver-gilt (17th cent.). Con. ency. of ant., vol. 3, pl. 33.

——, slave. Amer. heri., vol. 9 no. 6 p. 9 (Oct '58).

——, slave (plan). Amer. heri., vol. 9 no. 6 p. 6-7 (Oct '58).

——, survey. Natl. geog. 105: 126 Jan '54.

——, tanker. See tanker ship.

——, three-masted (medieval). Int. gr. soc.: Arts . . . p. 81 (col.).

—— sinking, (war). Natl. geog. 99: 349 Mar '51.

——, trading (1805). Amer. heri., vol. 6 no. 2 p. 10-11 (col.) (winter '55).

——, U.S. navy. See U.S. Navy ships.

——, U.S. Navy floating dock. See U.S. Navy floating dry dock.

——, Viking. See Viking ship.

——, war. See warship.

——, whaler. See whaler ship.

ship adv. cards, clipper. Amer. heri., vol. 6 no. 6 p. 18-9 (col.) (Oct '55).

Ship "Arbella" (colonial) (brought Gov. Winthrop to Amer.). Holiday 15: 107 (col.) Mar '54.

ship builders (Japan). Natl. geog. 118: 749 (col.) Dec '60.

ship building (Pascagoula). Holiday 6: 103 (col.) Nov '49.

ship burning, Dragon. Natl. geog. 106: 858-9 Dec '54.

ship captain. Amer. heri., vol. 7 no. 1 p. 48 (Dec '55). Natl. geog. 111: 545 Ap '57.

ship crew (Portuguese). Natl. geog. 101: 574-9 (col.) May '52.

ship departure ("Queen of Bermuda"). Natl. geog. 106: 787 (col.) Dec '54.

ship Dragon. Natl. geog. 106: 856 Dec '54.

ship figureheads. See figurehead, ship.

ship flag signals. Amer. heri., vol. 9 no. 4 p. 8 (Je '58).

ship flags. See flags, ship.

ship lamp. Holiday 24: 120 (col.) Sept '58.

ship model. Con. 136: 147 Nov '55. Holiday 8: 39 (col.) Jl '50; 21: 197 May '57, 102 Je '57. Natl. geog. 108: 697 (col.) Nov '55; 118: 560 (col.) Oct '60.

—— (church int.). Holiday 18: 30 (col.) Sept '55.

—— (De Gama). Natl. geog. 118: 650 (col.) Nov '60.

—— (French "Imperial"). Con. 133: 122 Ap '54.

—— (man). Natl. geog. 98: 351 Sept '50.

—— (sail). Natl. geog. 98: 607 Nov '50; 105: 459 (col.) Ap '54.

—— (sail, man building). Natl. geog. 107: 749 (col.) Je '55.

—— ("Mayflower"). Natl. geog. 111: 710 May '57.

—— (old). Holiday 18: 44-5 (col.) Aug '55.

ship models, Eng. antiques. Con. 132: 80-3 Nov '53.

ship monument (Tasmania). Natl. geog. 110: 813 (col.) Dec '56.

ship pilothouse eagle. Holiday 18: 61 (col.) Jl '55.

ship "Proteus" (Greenland). Natl. geog. 109: 295 Feb '56.

ship relics, old. Natl. geog. 112: 760 (col.) Dec '57.

ship sailing cards, clipper. Amer. heri., vol. 2 no. 3 p. 46-7 (part col.) (spring '51).

ship steering wheel. Natl. geog. 111: 545 Ap '57.

ship treasures, sunken. Natl. geog. 105: 9, 12, 34-5 (col.), 18 Jan '54.

ship yard (Biloxi, Miss.). Holiday 6: 98 (col.) Nov '49.

ship wheel (man steering, statue). Brooks: Growth of a nation, p. 99.

ship, "White Empress." Holiday 23: 13 (col.) Ap '58.

ship yards (Bremen). Natl. geog. 115: 769 (col.) Je '59.

shipboard (activities). Holiday 19: 69 (col.) Jan '56; 21: 85, 87 (col.) Jan '57.

Shipley, Ruth B. Cur. biog. p. 572 (1947).

Shippen, Katherine B. Cur. biog. p. 569 (1954).

"Shipping off Table Bay" (Whitcombe). Con. 145: XXXV Je '60.

Shiprock (New Mexico). Holiday 15: 157 (col.) Ap '54; 16: 85 (col.) Sept '54.
Travel 101: 12 Feb '54.

ships (Revolutionary war). Amer. heri. vol. 9 no. 4 p. 6-7 (col.) (Je '58).

—— (Capt. Smith's fleet). Natl. geog. 111: 620 May '57.

—— (1812-). Amer. heri., vol. 7 no. 3 p. 13-21 (col.) (Ap '56).

—— (1837). Amer. heri., vol. 8 no. 5 p. 16-7 (col.) (Aug '57).

—— (fishing fleet). Natl. geog. 112: 172-3 (col.) Aug '57.

—— (in harbor). Natl. geog. 101: 524 (col.) Ap '52.

—— (Iraq harbor). Natl. geog. 114: 484-5 (col.) Oct '58.

—— (Miss. river). Natl. geog. 118: 680 (col.) Nov '60.

—— (on medal). Amer. heri., vol. 6 no. 3 p. 61 (Ap '55).

—— (sails). Amer. heri., vol. 1 no. 3 p. 41 (col.) (spring '50); vol. 2 no. 2 p. 51 (col.) (winter '51); vol. 2 no. 4 p. 18 (summer '51); vol. 3 no. 4 cover (col.) (summer '52); vol. 8 no. 6 p. 15 (col.) (Oct '57); vol. 11 no. 4 p. 105 (Je '60).
Con. 126: 203 Dec '50; 143: 42 Mar '59; 144: XXXIX Sept '59.
Disney: People & places, inside cover (col.).
Durant: Pict. hist. of Amer. circus, p. 24, 34.
Natl. geog. 99: 186, 194-5 (col.) Feb '51.

—— (sails, 1849). Amer. heri., vol. 5 no. 1 p. 19 (col.) (fall '53).

—— (sails, 1775). Amer. heri., vol. 11 no. 4 p. 14 (col.) (Je '60).

—— (1758). Amer. heri., vol. 6 no. 2 p. 52-3 (col.) (winter '55).

—— (1777). Amer. heri., vol. 7 no. 3 p. 66-7 (Ap '56).

—— (1607). Natl. geog. 111: 583 (col.) May '57.

—— (1653). Amer. heri., vol. 10 no. 1 p. 9, 12-3 (col.) (Dec '58).

—— (Suez canal). Natl. geog. 111: 138 Jan '57.

—— (Turkey). Natl. geog. 110: 735 (col.) Dec '56.

—— (Westport harbor). Natl. geog. 117: 478-9 (col.) Ap '60.

ships, Antarctic. Natl. geog. 112: 348, 352 Sept '57.

——, battle. See battleships; warships.

——, Columbus'. Amer. heri., vol. 7 no. 1 p. 86, 89, 91 (Dec '55).

——, early. Amer. heri., vol. 7 no. 2 p. 46-7 (Feb '56).

——, East India traders. Amer. heri., vol. 6 no. 2 p. 11-5 (col.) (winter '55).

——, Erie canal (1825). Amer. heri., vol. 8 no. 5 p. 14-5 (col.) (Aug '57).

——, fishing (blessing). Natl. geog. 104: 80-1 (col.) (Jl '53).

——, freight. Natl. geog. 118: 314-5 (col.) Sept '60.

——, Jamestown Colony. Natl. geog. 113: 18-9 (col.) Jan '58.

——, Rhodesian. Travel 101: 17 Je '54.

——, Russian naval. Amer. heri., vol. 11 no. 4 p. 40-1 (Je '60).

——, U.S. Navy. See U.S. Navy ships.

ships. See also steamboat; steamship.

ship's launch (1789). Natl. geog. 112: 730-1 Dec '57.

ships of the dead, Egyptian. Ceram: March of arch., opp. p. 126 (col.), p. 156-7.

Shiraz (Iran). Natl. geog. 100: 445 Oct '51.

Shiraz (Sa'di tomb). Natl. geog. 114: 31 (col.) Jl '58.

Shiraz (tomb of Sa'di & statue). Travel 105: 25 Jan '56.

Shirer, William L. Cur. biog. p. 786 (1941); p. 386 (1962).

Shirley, William. Amer. heri., vol. 7 no. 2 p. 109 (Feb '56).

"Shirley Place" (Roxbury, Mass.). Amer. heri., vol. 8 no. 4 p. 36-9 (Je '57).

shirt, man's. Holiday 5: 77 Je '49; 7: 75 Je '50; 11: 2 (col.) Mar '52, 86 (col.) May '52; 13: back cover (col.) Ap '53; 14: 150 Oct '53, 36 (col.) Dec '53; 20: 171 (col.) Dec '56; 22: 16 (col.) Dec '57; 23: 132-3, 165, 178 (col.) May '58, 106-7 (col.) Je '58; 24: back cover (col.) Sept '58, 188 Nov '58; 25: 31 (col.) Mar '59, 19 Ap '59; 26: 39, 132 (col.) Dec '59; 27: 142 Jan '60; 28: 221 Nov '60.

Shivers, Allan. Cur. biog. p. 579 (1951).

Shockley, William. Cur. biog. p. 570 (1953).

shoe, button (old). Lehner: Pict. bk. of sym., p. 63.

——, Greek (500 B.C.). Int. gr. soc.: Arts . . . p. 31 (col.).

——, pewter (antique). Con. 135: XXVII Je '55.

——, woman's. Holiday 21: 127 Feb '57.

shoe horn. Holiday 24: 61 (col.) Dec '58.

shoe lasts. Rawson: Ant. pict. bk., p. 58.

shoe polisher. Holiday 25: 2 (col.) Je '59; 28: 203 (col.) Dec '60.

——, electric. Holiday 26: 96 Nov '59, 39 Dec '59; 28: 167 Nov '60.

shoe shine (row). Natl. geog. 97: 421 Ap '50.

shoe shiner. Holiday 5: 130 Jan '49.

shoe shop (Pakistan). Natl. geog. 102: 667 (col.) Nov '52.

Shoemaker, Samuel M. Cur. biog. p. 549 (1955).

shoemaker (Moroccan). Natl. geog. 107: 163 (col.) Feb '55.

—— (sym.). Lehner: Pict. bk. of sym., p. 91.

——, Colonial. Natl. geog. 106: 464 (col.) Oct '54.

shoemaker's tools. See cobbler's tools.

shoes. Holiday 15: 88, 112, 130, 143 (part col.) May '54, 26, 133 Je '54; 16: 21, 82, 96, 117 (part col.) Oct '54.

——, animal. Rawson: Ant. pict. bk., p. 68.

——, antique oriental stiltlike. Natl. geog. 104: 16 Jl '53.

——, boy's. Holiday 14: 192 Dec '53; 28: 225 Dec '60.

——, girl's. Holiday 23: 146 Jan '58.

——, Japanese (outside door). Natl. geog. 107: 276 Feb '55; 118: 774 (col.) Dec '60.

——, man's. Holiday 5: 84 Jan '49, 1, 20, 32, 116 (col.) Ap '49, 4, 124 (col.), 164 Je '49; 6: 4, 29, 84 Sept '59, 70, 83, 93 (col.) Oct '49, 4 (col.) Nov '49, 80 (col.), 172 Dec '49; 7: 118, 132 (col.) Mar '50, 68, 79, 99, 142 (col.) Ap '50, 19, 28, 122 (col.) May '50, 6, 76 (col.), 82, 90, 146 Je '50; 8: 6 Jl '50, 3 Sept '50, 4, 50-1, 81 (part col.) Oct '50, 5, 16, 120 (col.) Nov '50, 69 (col.), 140, 143 Dec '50; 9: 23, 81 Mar '51; 10: 5, 19, 25, 84-5, 112, 127 (part col.) Oct '51. Holiday 10: 21, 70 (col.), 80 Nov '51, 130 Dec '51; 11: 4, 110-11 Jan '52, 9 Mar '52, 3, 70, 133 (col.) Ap '52, 12, 23, 77, 96, 128, 137, 146 (part col.) May '52, 25, 30 (col.), 33, 153 Je '52; 12: 100, 146 Jl '52, 83 (col.), 114 Sept '52, 12-3 (col.), 127, 134 Oct '52, 4, 21, 76, 113, 121, 123, 139 Nov '52, 16, 20, 141, 168, 177-8, 181 Dec '52; 13: 16-7 Jan '53, 81 (col.), 133, 142, 144 Mar '53, 93, 134, 140 (col.), 155 Ap '53, 60, 78, 100, 127 May '53, 32, 77, 79 (col.), 89, 140 Je '53; 14: 15, 132 Jl '53, 116 Sept '53, 17 (col.), 29, 30, 67, 128 (col.) Oct '53, 90 (col.), 143, 163 Nov '53, 39 Dec '53; 16: 12 (col.), 119 (col.), 122, 133 Nov '54, 31, 137 Dec '54; 18: 76 Jl '55, 16, 73, 129 (part col.) Oct '55, 4, 16 (col.), 155 Nov '55, 147, 158, 175, 199 Dec '55; 19: 74, 118, 164 Mar '56, 144 (col.), 146, 150, 172, 176 May '56, 89 (col.), 95, 158 Je '56; 20: 15, 114 Sept '56, 4 (col.), 71, 136 Oct '56, 16, 111, 119, 125, 195, 197 (part col.) Nov '56, 4 (col.), 16, 185, 217 Dec '56; 21: 88 Jan '57, 129 Feb '57, 166-7, 179 Mar '57, 159, 198 Ap '57, 31, 99 (col.), 204 May '57, 12, 157 (col.) Je '57; 22: 125 Jl '57, 4, 103 (col.), 176 Oct '57, 5 (col.), 16, 100, 152, 180 Nov '57, 120, 185 Dec '57; 23: 136, 157, 159 Feb '58, 160, 171-3 Mar '58, 4 (col.), 39, 119 Ap '58, 5 (col.), 192 May '58, 24, 156 Je '58; 24: 136 Jl '58, 133 Sept '58, 82, 99 (col.) Oct '58, 22, 100 Nov

'58, 39, 159 Dec '58; 25: 127, 156, 184 Ap '59, 104, 179 (col.) May '59, inside cover (col.), 150 Je '59; 26: 21, 29 (col.) Sept '59, 96, 149 (col.), 161 Oct '59, 16, 29, 100 Nov '59, 135 Dec '59; 27: 180, 202 Mar '60, 17, 129 (col.), 234 Ap '60, 141, 186, 209 (col.) May '60, 16, 23 (col.), 105, 111 (col.), 137 (col.), 159 Je '60; 28: 4, 112 Aug '60, 31 (col.) Sept '60, 113, 132 (col.), 143, 169 Oct '60, 37 (col.), 64, 128, 223-4 Nov '60, 191, 204, 228 Dec '60.

Natl. geog. 108: 547 (col.) Oct '55.

Travel 102: 48 Sept '54; 108: 39 Jl '57.

shoes, medieval. Int. gr. soc.: Arts . . . p. 69, 71 (col.).

——, Mesopotamian (royal). Int. gr. soc.: Arts . . . p. 29 (col.).

——, ox. See ox shoes.

——, sport. Holiday 5: 21 Jan '49; 28: 151 (col.) Nov '60.

——, woman's. Holiday 5: 128 Mar '49; 6: 95 (col.) Sept '49, 116 (col.) Nov '49; 7: 4 (col.) Je '50; 8: 113 (col.) Nov '50; 9: 72 Mar '51; 10: 1 (col.), 19 Sept '51, 81 Oct '51; 11: 134 Mar '52, 122 Ap '52, 151-2 (col.) May '52, 30, 86 (col.), 112 Je '52; 12: 2 Sept '52; 13: 89 (col.) Mar '53, 15 Ap '53, 5 (col.), 72 (col.) May '53, 7, 33 (col.) Je '53; 14: 1 (col.) Oct '53, 82 Nov '53; 17: 21 (col.) Feb '55; 18: 27 (col.) Oct '55, 134 (col.) Nov '55, 86 Dec '55; 19: 71 (col.) Mar '56, 126, 169 May '56; 20: 14 Sept '56, 135 Oct '56, 105 Nov '56, 162 Dec '56; 21: 153 Jan '57, 167, 169 Mar '57, 164 Ap '57, 104, 128 (col.), 195 May '57, 37 Je '57; 22: 29, 134-5 Sept '57, 171 Oct '57, 177 Nov '57, 120 (col.), 245 Dec '57; 23: 125, 127 Feb '58, 179 Mar '58, 54 (col.), 189 Ap '58, 171 (col.), 191 May '58, 6 Je '58; 24: 17, 138 (col.) Sept '58, 82 (col.), 97 Oct '58, 120, 180 (col.) Nov '58, 197 (col.) Dec '58; 25: 165 (col.) Mar '59, 135 (col.) Ap '59, 5 (col.), 45, 130 (col.) May '59, 10 (col.), 38 Je '59; 26: 2, 10 (col.) Aug '59, 17, 88, 109 (col.), 134-5 Sept '59, 105 (col.), 115 Oct '59, 45 Dec '59; 27: 121 Feb '60, 122, 171 Ap '60, 29, 35 (col.) May '60 28: 2, 92 (col.), 109 Sept '60, 29, 110 Oct '60, 220 Nov '60, 204 Dec '60.

shoes. See also slippers.

Shofar (sym.). Lehner: Pict. bk. of sym., p. 55.

Sholokhov, Mikhail A. Cur. biog. p. 761 (1942); p. 375 (1960).

Shone, Terrence Allen. Cur. biog. p. 551 (1946).

Shoo-fly hat (Mexican). Holiday 10: 17 Jl '51.

"shoot the bear" coin bank (1906). Holiday 18: 61 (col.) Jl '55.

shop, textile (Pakistan). Natl. geog. 107: 420 (col.) Mar '55.

shop signs. See signs, store.

Shope, Richard E. Cur. biog. p. 385 (1963).

shopping streets, roofed over (Moscow). Holiday 18: 105 Jl '55.

shops, floating (Siam). Disney: People & places, p. 173 (col.)

Shor, Jean (Moorish dress). Natl. geog. 107: 187 Feb '55.

shoran (radar device). Natl. geog. 109: 346 Mar '56.
Shore, Dinah. Cur. biog. p. 763 (1942). Holiday 12: 37 Oct '52.
Shoriki, Matsutaro. Cur. biog. p. 385 (1958).
Short, Dewey. Cur. biog. p. 581 (1951).
Short, Hassard. Cur. biog. p. 582 (1948).
Short, Joseph. Cur. biog. p. 583 (1951).
Short, Luke. Horan: Pict. hist. of wild west, p. 105.
Short, Richard (work of). Amer. heri., vol. 11 no. 1 p. 28-9 (Dec '59) .
Short, Maj. Gen. Walter C. Cur. biog. p. 553 (1946).
shorts, man's. Holiday 18: 118 Jl '55.
Shoshone Indian. See Indian (Shoshone).
Shostakovitch, Dmitri. Cur. biog. p. 788 (1941).
Cooper: Con. ency. of music, p. 255.
shot pouch. Rawson: Ant. pict .bk., p. 35.
shotgun. See gun.
Shotten, Burton E. Cur. biog. p. 568 (1949).
Shotwell, James T. Cur. biog. p. 619 (1944).
shou (sym.). Lehner Pict. bk. of sym., p. 46.
Shoulders, Harrison H. Cur. biog. p. 555 (1946).
Shoup, Carl. Cur. biog. p. 570 (1949).
Shoup, Gen. David M. Cur. biog. p. 377 (1960).
shovel, coal. Amer. heri., vol. 11 no. 5 p. 15 (col.) (Aug '60).
——, electric. Natl. geog. 101: 345 Mar '52.
——, power. Natl. geog. 105: 341 Mar '51.
——, steam. Natl. geog. 105: 316 (col.) Mar '54.
show girls, night club. Holiday 10: 49 (col.), 50 Sept '51.
show posters (Coney island). Amer. heri., vol. 9 no. 4 p. 15 (col.) (Je '58).
show tent. Holiday 23: 142 (col.) Je '58. Natl. geog. 117: 36-7 (col.) Jan '60.
showboat. Durant: Pict. hist. of Amer. circus, p. 44, 48.
Natl. geog. 97: 179 Feb '50.
Travel 103: 39-41 Je '55.
—— (music circus). Natl. geog. 117: 36-7 (col.) Jan '60.
Shreve, Earl Owen. Cur. biog. p. 573 (1947).
Shreve, Richmond H. Cur. biog. p. 547 (1945).
Shridharani, Krishnalal. Cur. biog. p. 765 (1942).
shrimp fishermen. Natl. geog. 111: 700-7 (col.) May '57.
"Shrimp girl" (Hals). Con. 144: LXI (col.) Dec '59.
shrine (Kurdistan). Holiday 22: 30 Oct '57.
—— (on ship). Natl. geog. 104: 82 (col.) Jl '53.
—— (Tomb of Jesus). Natl. geog. 115: 502-4 (col.) Ap '59.
——, Buddha (Bhutan). Natl. geog. 102: 714 Dec '52.
——, Formosa. Natl. geog. 97: 165 (col.) Feb '50.
——, Japanese. Holiday 12: 30 (col.) Aug '52.
Travel 113: 48, 54 Jan '60.
——, Korean (worshipers). Natl. geog. 97: 785 (col.) Je '50.
——, Lama's. Natl. geog. 108: 8-9 (col.) Jl

'55.
——, Moslem. Natl. geog. 98: 831 Dec '50.
——, Philae is. Natl. geog. 107: 720-1 May '55.
——, St. Francis chapel. Natl. geog. 98: 10 Jl '50.
——, wayside. Nat. geog. 99: 788 Je '51.
——, Will Roger's. See Will Roger's shrine.
shrine gateway. Natl. geog. 104: 630 (col.) Nov '53.
Shrine of our Lady of LaLeche (St. Augustine). Travel 106: 15 Dec '56.
Shrine of Rai (Tehran). Natl. geog. 100: 450 (col.) Oct '51.
Shrine to Virgin of Montserrat. Travel 104: 43 Aug '55.
shrines, American. Travel 106: 12-7 Dec '56.
——, Japanese. See Japanese shrine.
——, Nepal. Natl. geog. 97: 10 (col.) Jan '50.
Shriver, Robert Sargent. Cur. biog. p. 423 (1961).
Shrove Tuesday (sym.). Lehner: Pict. bk. of sym., p. 55.
"Shudi family." Con. 139: 8 Mar '57.
shuffleboard (players). Holiday 8: 31 (col.) Nov '50 21: 44 (col.) Mar '57; 24: 81 Nov '58.
Natl. geog. 112: 692-3 (col.) Nov '57.
Travel 101: 52 May '54.
——, shipboard (man & girl). Natl. geog. 109: 738 (col.) Je '56.
——, shipboard (players). Holiday 8: 113 Oct '50.
Shull, Martha A. Cur. biog. p. 503 (1957).
Shull, Sarah. Horan: Pict. hist. of wild west, p. 50.
Shulman, Harry. Cur. biog. p. 541 (1952).
Shulman, Irving. Cur. biog. p. 574 (1956).
Shulman, Max. Cur. biog. p. 412 (1959).
Shuman, Charles B. Cur. biog. p. 575 (1956).
Shumlin, Herman. Cur. biog. p. 790 (1941).
Shurlock, Geoffrey M. Cur. biog. p. 388 (1962).
Shuster, George N. Cur. biog. p. 791 (1941); p. 379 (1960).
Shute, Nevil. Cur. biog. p. 768 (1942).
shutters, window. Natl. geog. 107: 651 (col.) May '55; 109: 295 Feb '56.
shuttle (for carpet weaving). Rawson: Ant. pict. bk., p. 34.
shuttlecock. Holiday 14: 75 Sept '53.
Shvernik, Nikolai. Cur. biog. p. 584 (1951).
Shwe Dagon (monument). Holiday 25: 168 (col.) Mar '59.
Shwe Dagon pagoda. See pagoda, Shwe Dagon.
Siam. Holiday 18: 49-53 (part col.) Oct '55.
Siam. See also Thailand.
Siamese architecture. See architecture, Siamese.
Siamese boy monk. See monk, Siamese boy.
Siamese dancer. See dancer, Siamese.
Siamese furniture. See furniture, Siamese.
Siamese girl. Holiday 24: 32 Sept '58.
—— (head). Holiday 18: 49 (col.) Oct '55.
Siamese twins. Durant: Pict. hist. of Amer. circus, p. 63.
Sibelius, Jean. Cooper: Con. ency. of music, p. 256.
Sibenik (Dalmatian coast). Travel 107: 38 Ap '57.

Siberian outpost. Amer. heri., vol. 10 no. 3 p. 77 (Ap '59).
Sibley, J. L. Amer. heri., vol. 9 no. 4 p. 29 (Je '58).
Sibundoy Indians. Natl. geog. 98: 473 (col.) Oct '50.
Sibyl's cave (Cumae, Italy). Labande: Naples, p. 147.
Sicard, Adm. Montgomery. Amer. heri., vol. 8 no. 2 p. 37 (col.) (Feb '57).
Sicily. Holiday 15: 114 (col.) Feb '54; 19: 46-51 (part col.) May '56.
Natl. geog. 107: 4-48 (part col.) Jan '55.
Travel 102: 19-21 Sept '54; 107: 41-2 Je '57.
—— (map). Holiday 21: 116 Jan '57.
Natl. geog. 107: 7 Jan '55.
—— (Unterberger). Con. 140: XXIX Nov '57.
sick, healing. See "And the prayer of faith shall heal the sick."
sick patient (doctor). See doctor (patient).
Sickert, Walter Richard (work of). Con. 145: LIII Ap '60, 180, 204-5 May '60.
sickle (sym.). Lehner: Pict. bk. of sym., p. 79.
sickle & hammer. See hammer & sickle (sym).
sickle of harvest (sym.). Lehner: Pict. bk. of sym., p. 20.
Sickles, Daniel Edgar. Pakula: Cent. album, p. 259.
side table. See table, side.
sideboard. Holiday 26: inside cover (col.) Nov '59.
—— (antique). Con. 127: 103 May '51; 141: 201 May '58; 143: XLIII Mar '59.
—— (18th cent.). Con. 129: LIV Je '52; 134: XXX Sept '54; 137: XVI, 290 Je '56; 142: XXXVI Sept '58.
——, Eng. (Tudor period). Int. gr. soc.: Arts . . . p. 103 (col.).
——, Hepplewhite. Con. 133: VI Mar '54; 136: IV Sept '55; 137: XLV Mar '56; 138: LIV Dec '56; 139: XLVIII Je '57.
——, Hepplewhite (serpentine front). Con. ency. of ant., vol. 1, pl. 44.
Con. 129: XXXIV Je '52; 135: XXVIII May '55; 144: LVIII Jan '60.
——, inlaid (18th cent.). Con. 144: XXV Nov '59.
——, regency. Con. 136: XLVI Sept '55, XXI Jan '56.
——, serpentine. Con. 138: XVI Sept '56.
——, serpentine (antique). Con. 133: XXXVI Ap '54; 145: LVII Je '60.
——, serpentine (18th cent.). Con. ency. of ant., vol. 1, pl. 36.
Con. 134: XXII Dec '54; 143: XLVIII May '59.
——, Sheraton. Con. 129: VI Je '52; 132: VI Sept '53; 133: VI Mar '54; 135: XLI Ap '55, XXVIII Je '55; 137: XLII, XLIV, LII May '56; 138: XXXVIII Jan '57; 140: XXXVI Dec '57; 143: IV, XXXVI Mar '59, XLIII Je '59.
——, Sheraton bowfront. Con. 133: XLV May '54; 135: XIX May '55; 142: XLVIII Dec '58.
——, Sheraton breakfront. Con. ency. of ant., vol. 1, pl. 35.
Con. 140: XLIV Jan '58.

——, Sheraton breakfront (18th cent.). Con. 145: XLII Ap '60.
——, Sheraton breakfront (serpentine). Con. 135: 1 May '55; 139: VIII Je '57; 142: XLVIII Nov '58.
——, Victorian (Talbert). Con. ency. of ant., vol. 3, pl. 3.
sideboard dish. Con. 133: XIX Je '54.
sideboard dishes (Londonderry silver). Con. 139: 240 Je '57.
sideboard table, regency. Con. 144: 268 Jan '60.
side-drum. See drum, side.
Sides, Adm. John Harold. Cur. biog. p. 425 (1961).
sidewalk, mosaic. See mosaic pavement.
sidewalk cafe. See cafe, sidewalk.
sidewalk shadows. Travel 108: inside cover Oct '57.
sidewalk tables, restaurant. See restaurant table, sidewalk.
sidewalk tea table. See tea table, sidewalk.
Sidi Mohammed, Sultan of Morocco. Cur. biog. p. 587 (1951).
Sidney, Lady Frances. Con. 139: 216 Je '57.
Sidney, Sir Philip. Amer. heri., vol. 10 no. 4 p. 6 (Je '59).
siege of Vicksburg. See Vicksburg, siege of.
"Siegfried & the Rhine maidens" (Ryder). Holiday 7: 107 (col.) Feb '50.
Siena (Italy). Holiday 16: 98-9 (col.) Sept '54.
Natl. geog. 100: 232-44 (col.) Aug '51.
—— (men, palace). Holiday 25: 34 (col.) Jan '59.
Siena cathedral. Praeg.: Pict. ency., p. 245.
Siena palio (horse race). Natl. geog. 100: 232-Aug '51.
Siena race horse (blessed in church). Natl. geog. 100: 230 Aug '51.
Sienese painting. Con. 136: 177-83 Dec '55.
Siepi, Cesare. Cur. biog. p. 551 (1955).
Sierra mts. Natl. geog. 117: 192-3 (col.) Feb '60.
Sierra Nevada range (Cal.). Holiday 24: 40-1 Jl '58.
Natl. geog. 105: 828-68 (part col.)Je '54.
Sigel, Franz. Pakula: Cent. album, p. 261.
sigil, hermetic. Lehner: Pict. bk. of sym., p. 73.
"sigil of the sun" (sym.). Lehner: Pict. bk. of sym., p. 66.
"sigil of the world" (sym.). Lehner: Pict. bk. of sym., p. 66.
sigils (sym.). Lehner: Pict. bk. of sym., p. 24.
sign, ale-house. See ale-house sign.
——, business (1700's). Holiday 18: 60 Jl '55.
——, clock shop (German). Natl. geog. 111: 780 (col.) Je '57.
——, law office (S. L. Clemens' office). Natl. geog. 110: 134 Jl '56.
——, road. See road sign.
——, tavern. See tavern sign.
——, trail. Travel 111: 33 Jan '59.
sign post, street. Natl. geog. 113: 95 (col.) Jan '58.
—— See also guidepost; road sign; signs.
Signac, Paul (work of). Con. 141: 117 Ap '58.
signal, airplane. See airplane signal.
signal light (N.Y. harbor). Natl. geog. 106: 779 (col.) Dec '54.

signal officer, airplane landing. Natl. geog. 108: 265 (col.) Aug '55.

signal torch (Turkey-Russian boundary). Natl. geog. 101: 759 Je '52.

signalers, airplane. *See* airplane signalers.

signalmen, Navy. *See* U.S. Navy signalmen.

signals, airmen ground (for help). Natl. geog. 103: 582 (col.) May '53.

signals, flag. *See* ship flag signals.

signature, Columbus. *See* Columbus signature.

——, **Fahlstrom.** *See* Fahlstrom signature.

signatures, signers of Treaty of Greene Ville. Amer. heri., vol. 4 no. 3 p. 34 (spring '53).

'Signing Declaration of Independence." Amer. heri., vol. 3 no. 2 p. 34 (col.) (winter '52). Holiday 16: 107 (col.) Jl '54. Natl. geog. 102: 156 (col.) Aug '52.

—— *See* also Declaration of independence.

Signorelli, Luca (panels by). Con. 142: 204 Dec '58.
Natl. geog. 101: 78 (col.) Jan '52.

Signoret, Simone. Cur. biog. p. 381 (1960).

signs, cave exploring. Natl. geog. 113: 430 Mar '58.

——, **store (Denmark).** Natl. geog. 108: 816-7 (col.) Dec '55.

——, **street.** *See* street signs.

——, **trade (antique).** Amer. heri., vol. 6 no. 3 p. 32 (Ap '55).

—— **(Denmark).** Natl. geog. 108: 816-7 (col.) Dec '55.

——, **zodiac.** *See* zodiac signs.

Sigsbee, Capt. Charles. Amer. heri., vol. 8 no. 2 p. 37 (col.) (Feb '57).

Sikh (bazaar). Natl. geog. 118: 453 (col.) Oct '60.

—— **(India).** Holiday 26: 170 (col.) Nov '59.

Sikorsky, Igor I. Cur. biog. p. 577 (1956).

Silandro (Alps). Holiday 27: 42-3 (col.) Jan '60.

silence (sym.). Lehner: Pict. bk. of sym., p. 83.

Siles Zuazo, Herman. Cur. biog. p. 386 (1958).

silhouette (Colonial man). Amer. heri., vol. 7 no. 5 p. 11 (Aug '56).

—— **(girl).** Holiday 21: 68 Mar '57.

—— **(King George III & family).** Amer. heri., vol. 11 no. 4 p. 97 (Je '60).

—— **(man's head).** Natl. geog. 110: 724 (col.) Dec '56.

—— **(Moslems).** Natl. geog. 114: 728 Nov '58.

—— **(war).** Amer. heri., vol. 10 no. 6 p. 8 (Oct '59).

silhouettes. Amer. heri., vol. 10 no. 4 p. 112 (Je '59).

—— **(antique).** Con. 132: 34-6 Sept '53.

—— **(boat & men).** Rawson: Ant. pict. bk., p. 80.

—— **(men's faces).** Holiday 21: 6 Jan '57.

—— **(people).** Holiday 13: 8 Je '53.

—— **(sports).** Holiday 14: 11 Sept '53.

Silifke. Osward: Asia Minor, pl. 120-23.

silk drying (Japan). Natl. geog. 118: 750-1 (col.) Dec '60.

silk making (Cyprus isle). Natl. geog. 101: 642 (col.) May '52.

silk painting (Chinese). Praeg.: Pict. ency., p. 534 (col.).

—— **(Lin Liang, 15th cent.).** Con. 143: LVIII Ap '59.

silk-screen design (fabric). Natl. geog. 104: 358 (col.) Sept '53.

silk thread reeling (Korea). Natl. geog. 97: 797 (col.) Je '50.

silkworm (breeding). Natl. geog. 100: 101-108 (col.) Jl '51.

—— **(women, men).** Natl. geog. 103: 693-701 May '53.

Sillcox, Lewis K. Cur. biog. p. 571 (1954).

silo. Amer. heri., vol. 6 no. 4 p. 26 (col.) (Je '55).
Face of Amer., p. 103, 149, 152 (col.).

—— **(barn).** Natl. geog. 115: 483 (col.) Ap '59.

Siloam pool (Holy Land). Natl. geog. 98: 722 (col.) Dec '50.

Silsbee, Nathaniel. Amer. heri., vol. 6 no. 2 p. 15 (winter '55).

Silver, Rabbi Abba Hillel. Cur. biog. p. 793 (1941); p. 387 (1963).

silver, church (Eng. antique). (The Mohawk silver). Con. 126: 106-7 Oct '50.

silver basket (antique). Con. 142: XI Dec '58.

silver case (antique). Con. 139: XI Ap '57.

silver dish, George II. Con. 126: inside cover Dec '50.

silver dishes (Paul de Lamerie). Con. 141: 130 Ap '58.

silver fruit basket, Elizabethan. Con. 126: 79 Aug '50.

silver-gilt dish, German. Con. 126: 89 Oct '50.

silver service (18th cent.). Con. 138: IV Jan '57.

silver tableware (knife, fork, spoon, etc.). *See* silverware, flat.

silver tankard, Russian (1800). Con. 144: 274 Jan '60.

Silvercruys, Baron. Holiday 24: 14, 73 Dec '58.

Silvers, Phil. Cur. biog. p. 505 (1957).

silversmith. Natl. geog. 99: 129 (col.) Jan '51.

—— **(at work).** Natl. geog. 106: 185 (col.) Aug '54.

——, **Baghdad.** Natl. geog. 115: 51 (col.) Jan '59.

——, **Navajo Indian.** Natl. geog. 114: 825-7 (col.) Dec '58.

——, **Persian.** Holiday 20: 59 (col.) Dec '56.

silverware (antique). Con. ency. of ant., vol. 1, p. 153, pl. 81-92.
Con. 134: IX Sept '54, XXXIX Nov '54; 135: L, LIII May '55, 226-7 Je '55; 136: 92-3 Nov '55; 137: XI, XXVI Je '56; 139: 29- Mar '57; 141: 90-2 Ap '58; 143: LVIII Je '59.

—— **(17th cent.).** Con. 135: XVII Mar '55.

—— **(18th cent.).** Con. 135: XL Ap '55; 142: V Sept '58.

—— **(handles).** Holiday 14: 123 Nov '53.

—— **(sym.).** Lehner: Pict. bk. of sym. p. 73.

——, **Amer. (18th cent.).** Con. 135: 72-8 Mar '55.

——, **Continental.** Con. ency. of ant., vol. 3 p. 61-71, pl. 29-36.

——, **Eng. (antique).** Con. 126: 46 Aug '50; 137: 224-9 Je '56.

——, **Eng. (modern).** Con. 138: 88-9 Nov '56; 144: 36 Sept '59.

silverware, flat. Con. 132: VIII Sept '53; 134: XXIX Nov '54; 137: XXXIV Mar '56, XLI Je '56; 139: XXIII May '57; 141: V Mar '58.
Holiday 12: 1 Oct '52; 13: 85 Ap '53, 11 May '53; 14: 141 Jl '53, 114 Oct '53, 172 Nov '53, 11 Dec '53; 19: 168 May '56; 21: 114 Mar '57, 105 Je '57; 22: 256 Dec '57; 23: inside cover May '58; 26: 180 Nov '59.
Travel 102: 5 Sept '54.

——, flat (Dutch rat-tailed table silver). Con. 140: 182 Dec '57.

——, flat (18th cent.). Con. ency. of ant., vol. 1, pl. 87.

——, flat (Faberge). Con. 139: LXIV May '57.

——, flat (Florentine). Travel 102: 5 Nov '54.

——, flat (George III). Con. 138: XXIX Dec '56; 140 VI Nov '57.

——, flat (George IV). Con. 138: LI Dec '56.

——, flat (in box). Holiday 18: 9 Dec '55.

——, flat (Italian). Con. ency. of ant., vol. 3, pl. 31.

——, flat (Queen Anne forks). Con. 144: V Nov '59.

——, flat (Towle forks). Holiday 24: 103 Nov '58.

——, French (antique, Farrer col.). Con. 140: 38-9 Sept '57.

——, George I & II. Con. 138: XLV Dec '56.

——, George III. Con. 132: VIII-IX Sept '53; 138: IX Sept '56; 145: LIV May '60.

——, George III & George IV. Con. 142: XXI Jan '59.

——, Irish. Con. 137: LI Ap '56; 145: XLIII Ap '60.

——, Irish (antique). Con. 134: VII Sept '54; 135: LV May '55; 137: LVII Je '56; 139: XLIX May '57.

——, Irish (George I). Con. 142: XLIV Jan '59.

——, Italian. Con. 144: 152--6 Dec '59.

——, Lamerie. Con. 144: 60-4 Sept '59.

——, Napoleon's. Con. 143: 225, 227 Je '59.

——, Norwegian (16-19th cent.). Con. 145: 12-7 Mar '60.

——, Russian (17th cent.). Con. 142: 224 Jan '59.

——, Scandinavian. Con. 137: 176-8 May '56.

——, Sheffield. Con. 142: XLIV Jan '59.

——, silver-gilt (antique). Con. 134: XXI Sept '54, 172 Dec '54.

——, Ulster. Con. 137: 161 May '56.
silverware chest. Con. 143: XV May '59.
Holiday 12: 165 Dec '52.
silverware shop (London). Holiday 19: 93 (col.) Feb '56.
silverware. See also name of piece wanted.
"Simeon in the temple" (Rembrandt). Con. 138: 32 Sept '56.
Simionato, Giulietta. Cur. biog. p. 383 (1960).
Simkhovitch, Mary K. Cur. biog. p. 697 (1943).
Simmons, Jean. Cur. biog. p. 542 (1952).
Simms, Hilda. Cur. biog. p. 622 (1944).
Simms, John F. Cur. biog. p. 579 (1956).
Simn, Fraz Xaver (work of). Con. 136: VIII Jan '56.
Simon, Charlie May. Cur. biog. p. 557 (1946). Jun. bk. of auth., p. 274.
Simon, Edith. Cur. biog. p. 572 (1954).

Simon, Richard L. Cur. biog. p. 794 (1941).
Simonds, Maj. Gen. Guy G. Cur. biog. p. 699 (1943).
Simonetta. Cur. biog. p. 553 (1955).
Simonini, F. (work of). Con. 135: XIX Ap '55.
Simons, Maj. David G. Cur. biog. p. 507 (1957).
Simons, Hans. Cur. biog. p. 509 (1957).
Simonson, Lee. Cur. biog. p. 576 (1947).
Simpson, Alan. Holiday 28: 78 (col.) Dec '60.
Simpson, Howard E. Cur. biog. p. 388 (1958).
Simpson, Milward L. Cur. biog. p. 511 (1957).
Simpson, Richard M. Cur. biog. p. 572 (1953).
Simpson, Lt. Gen. William H. Cur. biog. p. 549 (1945).
Sims, Hugo S., jr. Cur. biog. p. 571 (1949).
Sims, William L., 2d. Cur. biog. p. 581 (1956).
Sinan (Turkish marble statue). Osward: Asia Minor, pl. 66.
Sinatra, Frank. Cur. biog. p. 700 (1943); p. 385 (1960).
Holiday 20: 77 Aug '56, 183 Nov '56; 23: 149 Je '58.
Sinclair, Mrs. D. B. Cur. biog. p. 588 (1951).
Sinclair, Jo. Cur. biog. p. 558 (1946).
Sinclair, Upton. Cur. biog. p. 390 (1962).
Singapore. Holiday 8: 19-25 Dec '50, 16: 46 Sept '54.
Natl. geog. 103: 194-228 (part col.) Feb '53.
—— (harbor). Natl. geog. 103: 194-5 (col.) Feb '53.
—— (man, rowboat). Holiday 24: 120 Nov '58; 24: 24 Dec '58.
—— (street market). Travel 102: 39 Nov '54.
Singer, Isaac. Amer. heri., vol. 9 no. 6 p. 36 (Oct '58).
Singer, Mrs. Isaac (Isabella Boyer). Amer. heri., vol. 9 no. 6 p. 36 (Oct '58).
Singer, Kurt D. Cur. biog. p. 574 (1954).
singer, Marian Anderson. See Anderson, Marian.
Singer, Siegfried Fred. Cur. biog. p. 555 (1955).
"The Singer S' Andrade" (Slevogt). Praeg.: Pict. ency., p. 431 (col.).
Singer sewing machine in parade (Lincoln's inauguration). Amer. heri., vol. 9 no. 6 p. 104 (Oct '58).
singers, carol. See carol singers.
Singher, Martial. Cur. biog. p. 578 (1947).
"The singing tower." Holiday 26: 88 Nov '59.
"sink bed" in wall. Rawson: Ant. pict. bk., p. 14.
"Sinking of the Maine" (Havana). Amer. heri., vol. 8 no. 2 p. 37 (col.) (Feb '57).
sinners, repentant (Spain). Natl. geog. 99: 507 (col.) Ap '51.
Sinnott, Edmund W. Cur. biog. p. 584 (1948).
Sintenis, Renee (sculpture by). Praeg.: Pict. ency., p. 509.
sinuses (human). Gray's anatomy, p. 667.
Sinyala, mt. See Mount Sinyala.
Sioux Indian. Travel 113: 43 Mar '60.
"A Sioux village" (Catlin). Amer. heri., vol. 6 no. 1 p. 33 (col.) (fall '54).
Siple, Paul A. Cur. biog. p. 513 (1957).
Natl. geog. 110: 146 Aug '56; 112: 2-3, 12 (col.), 22, 30, 48 (part col.) Jl '57; 113: 444, 459 Ap '58.
—— (receiving medal). Natl. geog. 113: 793 Je '58.

Siqueiros, David Alfaro. Cur. biog. p. 413 (1959).

"Sir Lionel Walden" (Kneller). Con. 135: 240 Je '55.

"Sir William Clayton" (as a boy) (Wright). Con. 126: cover, opp. p. 83 (col.) Oct '50.

Sirani, Elisabetta (work of). Con. 144: 22 Sept '59.

siren (Figure on seaside rock). Holiday 27: 197 May '60.

Sirikit, Queen. Cur. biog. p. 387 (1960).

Siringo, Charles A. Horan: Pict. hist. of wild west, p. 209.

Siringo, Charlie. Travel 107: back cover Jan '57.

Siroky, Viliam. Cur. biog. p. 514 (1957).

Sisavang Vong, King of Laos. Cur. biog. p. 577 (1954).

Sisler, George. Amer. heri., vol. 10 no. 3 p. 23 (Ap '59).

Sisley, Alfred (work of). Con. 144: XVIII (col.) Sept '59; 145: LXXXVII (col.) Je '60. Praeg.: Pict. ency., p. 418 (col.).

sister, Catholic. *See* Catholic sister.

sisters, Ursuline. *See* Ursuline sisters.

"Sisters of charity" (Jerusalem). Holiday 7: 121 Ap '50.

Sistine chapel. Natl. geog. 111: 464-5 (part col.) Ap '57.

—— **(ceiling painting).** Praeg.: Pict. ency., p. 7.

—— **fresco (Michelangelo).** Praeg.: Pict. ency., p. 278 (col.).

Sistine library (int., Vatican). Holiday 23: 60 (col.) May '58.

"Sistine madonna" (Raphael). Holiday 27: 77 (col.) Feb '60. Praeg.: Pict. ency., p. 46.

sistrum, ivory (16th cent.). Con. 144: 68 Sept '59.

sistrum of Isis (sym.). Lehner: Pict. bk. of sym., p. 26.

Sita's bath (India, temple). Natl. geog. 103: 674-5 May '53.

Sitka (Alaska, 1804). Amer. heri., vol. 10 no. 3 p. 64 (col.) (Ap '59).

—— **(harbor).** Holiday 14: 119 (col.) Jl '53. Natl. geog. 102: 59 Jl '52.

—— **(harbor, 1860).** Amer. heri., vol. 12 no. 1 p. 44 (col.) (Dec '60).

Sitterly, Charlotte M. Cur. biog. p. 392 (1962).

Sitti Maani. *See* Maani, Sitti.

"Sitting Bull," Indian chief. Amer. heri., vol. 5 no. 4 p. 35 (summer '54). Brooks: Growth of a nation, p. 182.

sitting room (antiques). Con. 143: 139 May '59.

Siva (Hindu god). Natl. geog. 117: 521 (col.) Ap '60. Praeg.: Pict. ency., p. 526.

Siva (sym.). Lehner: Pict. bk. of sym., p. 43.

Siva shrine (India, god). Natl. geog. 103: 674-8 May '53.

Siwa oracle. Natl. geog. 108: 650 Nov '55.

Six, Jan (Rembrandt portrait). Con. 138: 29 Sept '56.

the six attributes (sym.). Lehner: Pict. bk. of sym., p. 34.

the sixty-four geomantic hexagons. Lehner: Pict. bk. of sym., p. 45.

Skala, Santorin (harbor). Travel 103: 42 Ap '55.

skate shoes. Holiday 10: 159 Dec '51.

"Skate" submarine. Natl. geog. 115: 16-7, 24 Jan '59; 116: 2-41 (part col.) Jl '59.

skater, ice. Holiday 5: 4 Mar '49. Travel 105: 41 Feb '56; 113: 39 Jan '60.

—— **(girl).** Holiday 10: 68 Dec '51.

"The skater" (Stuart). Amer. heri., vol. 7 no. 1 p. 14 (col.) (Dec '55).

skaters. Con. 144: XXXVI (col.), LXIII Jan '60. Holiday 14: 143 Jl '53, 64 (col.) Dec '53. Natl. geog. 97: 206 (col.) Feb '50.

—— **(boy & girl).** Holiday 18: 66 Jl '55.

—— **(comic).** Amer. heri., vol. 9 no. 3 p. 61 (col.) (Ap '58).

—— **(1862).** Natl. geog. 118: 798 (col.) Dec '60.

—— **(1880).** Amer. heri., vol. 10 no. 2 p. 112 (Feb '59).

—— **(Lhasa).** Natl. geog. 108: 31 Jl '55.

skaters. *See also* man (skating).

skates, ice (antique). Rawson: Ant. pict. bk., p. 18.

skating, figure. Natl. geog. 104: 814 (col.) Dec '53.

——, **figure (girl).** Travel 113: 39 Jan '60.

skating ramps (Italy). Natl. geog. 109: 856 Je '56.

skating rink. Holiday 21: 183 (col.) May '57.

——, **glacier.** Natl. geog. 98: 206 Aug '50.

"Skating scene" (Lancret). Con. 142: 6 Sept '58.

skeleton, human. Amer. heri., vol. 8 no. 5 p. 54 (Aug '57). Gray's anatomy, p. 74. Holiday 21: 69 (col.) Ap '57; 23: 204 Je '58.

skeleton, human. *See also* skeletons.

"Skeleton of washerwoman" (Pompeii). Ceram: March of arch., opp. p. 16.

skeletons, human (in car). Holiday 28: 45 Aug '60.

——, **Pompeii.** *See* Pompeii (skeletons).

skeletons. *See also* skeleton.

Skelton, Red. Cur. biog. p. 580 (1947). Holiday 12: 37 Oct '52.

"Skewbald stallion" (Ward). Con. 145: 145 May '60.

ski bums (N.H.). Natl. geog. 107: 767 (col.) Je '55.

ski chalet. Natl. goeg. 114: 220 Aug '58.

ski glasses. Holiday 21: cover (col.) Feb '57.

ski lift. Holiday 10: 40 Sept '51; 20: 35 Dec '56; 27: 156 Jan '60. Natl. geog. 97: 706 (col.) Je '50; 99: 588 (col.) May '51; 105: 740-1 (col.) Je '54; 115 228, 253 (col.) Feb '59. Travel 107: cover Jan '57; 109: 16 Jan '58, 36 Feb '58, 111: 31 Jan '59, cover (col.), 17, 19 Je '59; 113: 35 Jan '60.

—— **(French Alps).** Travel 113: 35 Jan '60.

—— **(girl).** Holiday 25: 119 Feb '59, 92 May '59. Travel 113: 21 Je '60.

—— **(skiers).** Holiday 14: 26 (col.) Nov '53, 39 Dec '53.

—— **(woman).** Holiday 25: 102 Jan '59.

ski lift. *See also* chair lift, aerial.

Skibo castle. Amer. heri., vol. 11 no. 5 p. 7 (Aug '60).

Skidmore, Louis. Cur. biog. p. 590 (1951).

Skidmore college girls. Natl. geog. 110: 590 (col.) Nov '56.

skier. Holiday 5: 111 (col.), 126 Jan '49, 7 Ap '49; 6: 40-1 Nov '49, 10 (col.) Dec '49; 7: 48-9, 68-74 (col.) Jan '50; 10: 152 Nov '51, 161 Dec '51; 11: 79 Jan '52, 22 Ap '52; 12: 15 (col.) Nov '52; 14: 82 Nov '53; 17: 66, 129 Jan '55; 18: 83 Nov '55; 22: 96 (col.) Jl '57; 28: 48, 91 (col.), 164 Dec '60.
  Natl. geog. 106: 240-1 (col.) Aug '54; 108: 691 (col.) Nov '55; 110: 305 Sept '56; 117: 482 (col.) Ap '60.
  Travel 105: inside cover, 7, 9-10 Jan '56; 107: 14, 22 Jan '57.
—— **(comic).** Holiday 5: 115 Jan '49; 10: 180 Dec '51; 14: 121 Dec '53.
—— **(girl).** Holiday 10: 101 Dec '51.
—— **(outline).** Travel 108: 38 Dec '57.
skier, clown. *See* clown skier.
skiers. Con. 140: LVI Jan '58.
  Face of Amer., p. 150-1 (col.).
  Holiday 5: 86 Feb '49, 15, 26, 91, inside back cover (col.) Mar '49; 7: 13 Feb '50, 93 (col.) Ap '50; 8: 26 Nov '50; 11: 84-5 Jan '52; 12: 105 Oct '52; 14: 167 (col.) Nov '53; 19: 117 Jan '56, cover (col.), 44-5 (col.), 47 Feb '56; 20: 45 (col.), 130, 181 Dec '56; 21: 25 Jan '57, 30, 46-9 (col.) Feb '57, 122 Mar '57; 25: 72-7 (part col.) Jan '59, 117, 121-22 (col.) Feb '59; 26: 123 Oct '59; 28: 5 (col.), 45, 142 Dec '60.
  Jordan: Hammond's pict. atlas, p. 141 (col.).
  Natl. geog. 99: 588, 595 (col.) May '51, 790 Je '51; 101: 432 (col.) Ap '52; 107: 767-8 (col.) Je '55; 109: 35 (col.) Jan '56; 113: 92-3 (col.) Jan '58; 115: 217-54 (col.) Feb '59.
  Travel 101: 40 Jan '54, 21 Feb '54; 102: cover Dec '54; 107: 15, 47, 52 Feb '57; 109: 17 Jan '58, 33-6 Feb '58, 19 Mar '58; 111: 30-1, 53-4, 62 Jan '59.
—— **(comic).** Holiday 26: 119 Nov '59.
—— **(girls).** Holiday 27: 75 (col.) Feb '60.
—— **(stop for lunch).** Natl. geog. 99: 492 (col.) Ap '51.
—— **(Switzerland).** Holiday 23: 70-5 Feb '58.
——, **children.** *See* children skiers.
——, **stunt.** Natl. geog. 115: 217, 230, 233, 242, 247, 249, 252 (part col.) Feb '59.
—— *See also* man (skiing); skiing, water.
skiff. Travel 107: cover Feb '57.
—— **(girl).** Holiday 25: back cover (col.) Mar '59.
skiing. Holiday 18: 166 Dec '55; 22: 63 (col.), 208, 229 Dec '57.
——, **sitdown.** Travel 111: 25 Feb '59.
——, **water.** Holiday 6: 60 (co.l) Sept '49; 10: 93 Nov '51; 11: 28 Jan '52; 27: 53 (col.) Ap '60.
  Natl. geog. 109: 20 (col.) Jan '56; 113: 493 (col.) Ap '58; 114: 701-11 (part col.) Nov '58; 117: 38-9 (col.) Jan '60.
  Travel 105: 47 Feb '56, 10-11 May '56.
——, **water (airborne on kite).** Natl. geog. 115: 831 Je '59.
——, **water (boy & girl).** Holiday 21: 115 (col.) Je '57.
——, **water (comic).** Holiday 18: 137 Oct '55; 22: 132 Jl '57.

——, **water (girl).** Natl. geog. 102: 766 (col.) Dec '52.
——, **water (girls).** Natl. geog. 110: 578 (col.) Nov '56.
  Travel 113: 42 May '60.
——, **water (woman).** Holiday 23: 139 (col.) Feb '58.
skillet (on tripod). Rawson: Ant. pict. bk., p. 8.
——, **electric.** Holiday 20: 1 Nov '56.
Skillin, Edward S., jr. Cur. biog. p. 573 (1949).
skimmer, brass. Natl. geog. 117: 156 (col.) Feb '60.
skimobile. Travel 105: 9 Jan '56; 109: 14 Jan '58; 111: 18 Je '59.
skin, animal (decorated). Amer. heri., vol. 6 no. 1 p. 32 (col.) (fall '54).
—— **(peace poster).** Amer. heri., vol. 8 no. 4 p. 106 (Je '57).
skin, human. Gray's anatomy, p. 1102-5.
——, **Indian painted.** Amer. heri., vol. 7 no. 6 p. 13 (col.) (Oct '56).
skin diver. *See* diver, skin.
Skinner, Cornelia Otis. Cur. biog. p. 770 (1942).
Skinner, Mrs. James M., jr. Cur. biog. p. 593 (1951).
skipper, barge. Natl. geog. 114: 93 Jl '58.
——, **boat (at wheel).** Natl. geog. 113: 776 (col.) Je '58.
——, **Yankee (George Coggeshall).** Amer. heri., vol. 8 no. 6 p. 67, 71, 76, 85 (Oct '57).
"Skirts of the wood" (Gainsborough). Con. 132: IX (col.) Nov '53.
skis. Holiday 10: 150 Dec '51; 22: 114 (col.) Nov '57; 25: 129 Mar '59.
  Travel 106: 27 Dec '56.
—— *See also* skier; skiing.
Skouras, Spyros P. Cur. biog. p. 703 (1943).
skull (sym.). Lehner: Pict. bk. of sym., p. 67.
—— **(veins).** Gray's anatomy, p. 659, 663.
——, **Aztec mosaic.** Amer. heri., vol. 10 no. 2 p. 46 (col.) (Feb '59).
——, **human.** Gray's anatomy, p. 62-5, 108-15, 118-26, 134, 362, 568, 703, 709.
  Holiday 12: 51 Oct '51.
——, **human (sym.).** Lehner: Pict. bk. of sym., p. 10.
——, **human.** Natl. geog. 108: 446 Oct '55.
——, **Indian.** *See* Indian skull.
skull & crossbones. Amer. heri., vol. 8 no. 2 p. 13 (Feb '57).
—— **(flag).** Lehner: Pict. bk. of sym., p. 86.
—— **(sym.).** Lehner: Pict. bk. of sym., p. 88.
skull & crown (sym.). Lehner: Pict. bk. of sym., p. 83.
skull & dagger (sym.). Lehner: Pict. bk. of sym., p. 89.
skull, scythe & sickle (sym.). Lehner: Pict. bk. of sym., p. 79.
skulls (fossil). Natl. geog. 118: 432 Sept '60.
—— **(prehistoric).** Natl. geog. 117: 812 (col.) Je '60.
Skutt, Vestor Joseph. Cur. biog. p. 415 (1959).
sky rockets (Bastille Day). Natl. geog. 100: 36-7 (col.) Jl '51.
sky survey. Natl. geog. 110: 781-90 Dec '56.

Skye, Isle of. *See* Isle of Skye.
skyline. Holiday 28: cover (col.) Sept '60.
——, Atlantic City. *See* Atlantic City (skyline).
——, city. Holiday 13: back cover (col.) May '53.
——, N.Y. City. *See* New York city (skyline).
——, Pittsburgh. *See* Pittsburgh (skyline).
——, St. Louis. *See* St. Louis (skyline).
Skyline motor inn (N.Y.). Travel 112: 65 Dec '59.
skyscraper (Buenos Aires). Natl. geog. 108: 757 (col.) Dec '55.
—— (Moscow). Natl. geog. 116: 359 (col.) Sept '59.
skyscrapers. Amer. heri., vol. 5 no. 1 p. 40-5 (part col.) (fall '53).
Holiday 12: 46-7 (col.) Dec '52; 24: 27 (col.) Oct '58.
Natl. geog. 106: 646 Nov '54, 773, 776 (part col.) Dec '54.
—— (Chicago). Natl. geog. 104: 785 (col.) Dec '53.
—— (Rio de Janeiro). Natl. geog. 107: 297, 305, 320 (col.) Mar '55.
——, Shibam (Aden Colony). Natl. geog. 111: 240-1 Feb '57.
"Skylark" plane. Natl. geog. 104: 773 (col.) Dec '53.
slate, school. Lehner: Pict. bk. of sym., p. 85.
Slater, John E. Cur. biog. p. 594 (1951).
Slater, Samuel. Amer. heri., vol. 9 no. 3 p. 35 (Ap '58).
Slaughter, Enos. Amer. heri., vol. 10 no. 3 p. 24 (Ap '59).
Slaughter, Frank G. Cur. biog. p. 772 (1942).
slave, Negro. Amer. heri., vol. 7 no. 1 p. 28 (Dec '55).
—— (captured). Amer. heri., vol. 7 no. 6 p. 101 (Oct '56).
—— (escaping.) Horan: Pict. hist. of wild west, p. 14.
slave block. Travel 112: 45 Jl '59.
slave house (17th cent., Va.). Natl. geog. 109: 454 Ap '56.
slave hut (Bonaire). Travel 111: 53 Feb '59.
slave quarters (Ft. George island). Travel 111: 34 Feb '59.
slave ship. *See* ship, slave.
Slavenska, Mia. Cur. biog. p. 578 (1954).
slaves. Amer. heri., vol. 6 no. 3 p. 5, 7 (col.) (Ap '55)
slaves (on ship). Amer. heri., vol. 8 no. 2 p. 63 (Feb '57).
sled. Holiday 27: 2 (col.) Jan '60.
—— (boy & girl). Holiday 6: 20 Dec '49.
—— (driver, boys, horse). Natl. geog. 113: 94-5 (col.) Jan '58.
—— (men drag). Natl. geog. 113: 463 (col.) Ap '58.
——, box. *See* box sled.
——, child's. Holiday 24: 228 Dec '58.
Natl. geog. 104: 844 (col.) Dec '53.
——, dog. Amer. heri., vol. 8 no. 3 p. 9 (col.) (Ap '57); vol. 10 no. 3 p. 79 (Ap '59).
Holiday 10: 97 Dec '51.
——, dog (Alaska). Travel 101: 23 Jan '54, 21 Feb '54.

—— (Alaska, man). Natl. geog. 116: 73, 84-5 (part col.) Jl '59.
—— (Antarctic). Natl. geog. 115: 42 Jan '59.
—— (man, tidal flats). Natl. geog. 115: 784 Je '59.
sled, dog team. Holiday 6: 141 Dec '49.
—— (man). Natl. geog. 110: 673 (col.) Nov '56.
sled, dog (race). Travel 107: 29-31 Jan '57.
——, logging. *See* logging sled.
——, maple syrup (Ver.). Holiday 6: 42-3 (col.) Nov '49.
Natl. geog. 105: 476, 479 (col.) Ap '54.
Rawson: Ant. pict. bk., p. 71.
——, mt. Rawson: Ant. pict. bk., p. 71.
——, radio. *See* radio sled.
——, saucer. *See* saucer sled.
——, ski. Holiday 19: 44 (col.) Feb '56.
sled runners (Antarctica). Natl. geog. 110: 165 (col.) Aug '56.
sledge, dog (Antarctic). Natl. geog. 112: 362, 377 (col.) Sept '57.
——, Madeira. Nat. geog. 115: 367 (col.) Mar '59.
——, ox (Madeira is.). Natl. geog. 115: 367 Mar '59.
——, radar on. Natl. geog. 112: 366 (col.) Sept '57.
——, Viking (medieval). Int. gr. soc.: Arts . . . p. 81 (col.).
sledge hammer. Natl. geog. 115: 114 Jan '59.
sleds, antique. Rawson: Ant. pict. bk., p. 72.
——, children's (park). Natl. geog. 118: 796-9 (col.) Dec '60.
——, ox. Natl. geog. 112: 180 (col.) Aug '57.
sleep, god of. *See* Hypnos.
sleepcoat, man's. Holiday 20: 216 Dec '56.
Sleeper, Ruth. Cur. biog. p. 544 (1952).
sleeping bags. Natl. geog. 98: 118 (col.) Jl '50.
"sleepin bear" dunes. Natl. geog. 101: 303 (col.) Mar '52.
Sleepy Hollow (Headless horseman). Holiday 6: 38 Sept '49.
sleeve-buttons, antique. Con. 139: 37-8, 40 Mar '57.
sleigh. Rawson: Ant. pict. bk., p. 72.
—— (drawn by doves). Amer. heri., vol. 10 no. 3 frontis. (col.) (Ap '59).
—— (1878-). Amer. heri., vol. 7 no. 6 p. 94 (col.) (Oct '56).
—— (horse). Natl. geog. 116: 263, 265 (col.) Aug '59.
—— (horses, boys). Natl. geog. 104, 834 (col.) Dec '53.
—— (horses, people). Amer. heri., vol. 3 no. 1 p. 42 (col.) (fall '51); vol. 5 no. 2 cover (col.) (winter '53-54); vol. 7 no. 1 p. 17-8 (col.) (Dec '55); vol. 9 no. 1 p. 16 (col.) (Dec '57); vol. 10 no. 1 p. 110-11, 121 (Dec '58).
Holiday 10: 13 (col.), 168 Dec '51; 13: 18 (col.) Feb '53; 22: 21 Nov '57; 26: 47 Aug '59, 20 (col.) Dec '59.
Natl. geog. 104: 744 Nov '53; 106: 240 (col.) Aug '54; 107: 738 Je '55.
—— (horses, silhouette). Travel 107: 54 Feb '57.
—— (horses, skiers). Holiday 19: 49 (col.) Feb '56.

sleigh (horses, Christmas). Amer. heri., vol. 9 no. 1 p. 16 (col.) (Dec '57).

—— (horses, Christmas, small). Holiday 26: 178, 181 Dec '59.

——, Norwegian Viking. Con. 145: 36 Mar '60.

——, Russian (horse & rider). Amer. heri., vol. 10 no. 1 p. 121 (Dec '58).

——, Swiss (horses). Holiday 14: 63 Dec '53.
sleigh bells. Holiday 10: 168 Dec '51.
Rawson: Ant. pict. bk., p. 68.
"Sleigh ride" (by Clonney). Amer. heri., vol. 8 no. 1 back cover (col.) (Dec '56).
sleigh seat. Rawson: Ant. pict. bk., p. 74.
Sleman, Charles Roy. Cur. biog. p. 582 (1956).
Slevogt, Max (work of). Praeg.: Pict. ency. p. 431 (col.).
Slezak, Walter. Cur biog. p. 557 (1955).
Slichter, Sumner Huber. Cur. biog. p. 583 (1947).
slide projector. See projector, slide.
Sleigh, Charles R. Cur. biog. p. 574 (1953).
Slim, Mongi. Cur. biog. p. 389 (1958).
Slim, Sir William Joseph. Cur. biog. p. 551 (1945).
sling shot. Natl. geog. 103: 596 (col.) May '53.
slipper, bedroom. Holiday 18: 86 Dec '55.
——, man's bedroom. Holiday 23: 145 Jan '58.
slipper case (dog carrying). Holiday 28: 14 Dec '60.
slippers, ballet. Lehner: Pict. bk. of sym., p. 11.
——, bedroom. Holiday 10: 112 Aug '51; 24: 191, 198 Nov '58; 26: 247, 252 Dec '59; 28: 17 (col.) Dec '60.
——, bedroom (man's). Holiday 18: 189 Dec '55.
——, bedroom (woman's). Holiday 24: 169 Dec '58.
slippers, Jefferson Davis' house. Amer. heri., vol. 6 no. 3 p. 35 (col.) (Ap '55).
——, lounging. Holiday 10: 112 Aug '51.
——, lounging (man's). Holiday 10: 36 (col.) Dec '51.
slippers. See also shoes.
slipware dish. Con. 138: 252 Jan '57.
Sloan, George A. Cur. biog. p. 546 (1952).
Sloan, John (work of). Amer. heri., vol. 2 no. 2 p. 75 (col.) (winter '51).
Sloan, W. G. Holiday 7: 36 Mar '50.
Sloane, Eric (sketches by). Amer. heri., vol. 7 no. 2 p. 104-5 (Feb '56).
Sloane, Everett. Cur. biog. p. 516 (1957).
Slobodkin, Louis. Cur. biog. p. 518 (1957).
Jun. bk. of auth., p. 275.
Slocum, Harvey. Cur. biog. p. 520 (1957).
Slocum, Henry Warner. Pakula: Cent. album, p. 263.
Slonimsky, Nicolas. Cur. biog. p. 559 (1955).
sloop (boat). Natl. geog. 115: 488 (col.) Ap '59.
——, Bermuda. Praeg.: Pict. ency., p. 432 (col.).
——, racing. Natl. geog. 103: 357 Mar '53.
——, trading (sails). Natl. geog. 109: 211 Feb '56.
sloop-of-war, model of navy. Con. 136: 55 Sept '55.

sloops. Holiday 10: 44-5 (col.) Jl '51, 41 Nov '51; 11: 37 Je '52.
Natl. geog. 113: 154-5, 167 (col.) Feb '58.

——, racing. Natl. geog. 116: 596-9 (col.) Nov '59.
Sluice gate, water (Sahara). Natl. geog. 113: 697 (col.) May '58.
Sluter, Claus (statue by). Con. 129: 37 Ap '52.
Sluter ("figure of Moses"). Praeg.: Pict. ency., p. 246.
slyness (sym.). Lehner: Pict. bk. of sym., p. 60.
Sma (sym.). Lehner: Pict. bk. of sym., p. 27.
smacks (boats). Face of Amer., p. 120-1 (col.).
Smadel, Joseph E. Cur. biog. p. 389 (1963).
Smallens, Alexander. Cur. biog. p. 585 (1947).
Smallwood, Joseph R. Cur. biog. p. 576 (1953).
Smallwood, Robert B. Cur. biog. p. 584 (1956).
Smart, David A. Cur. biog. p. 624 (1944).
Smart, John (miniature by). Con. ency. of ant., vol. 1, pl. 131.
—— (work of). Con. 140: 259 Jan '58; 141: 43 Mar '58; 142: IV, 196 Dec '58; 143: XXXIII Ap '59.
Smart, Richard. Holiday 28: 50 (col.) Jl '60.
Smathers, George A. Cur. biog. p. 580 (1954).
Smedberg, Rear Adm. William R. Cur. biog. p. 522 (1957).
Smedley, Agnes. Cur. biog. p. 627 (1944).
smelt run fishers (Portland). Natl. geog. 102: 600 (col.) Nov '52.
smelter plant, Alcan. See Alcan smelter.
Smetana, Bedrich (by Svabinsky). Cooper: Con. ency. of music, p. 293.
Smith, Abby. Amer. heri., vol. 8 no. 4 p. 55 (Je '57).
Smith, Al. Amer. heri., vol. 6 no. 2 p. 68 (winter '55).
Smith, Alfred E. Cur. biog. p. 630 (1944).
Smith, Austin E. Cur. biog. p. 534 (1950).
Smith, Sir Ben. Cur. biog. p. 553 (1945).
Smith, Betty. Cur. biog. p. 705 (1943).
Holiday 7: 49 (col.) Je '50.
Smith, Bill. Horan: Pict. hist. of wild west, p. 147.
Smith, Bradley (Jamestown photographs by). Amer. heri., vol. 11 no. 1 p. 49-56 (col.) (Dec '59).
Smith, Caleb B. Amer. heri., vol. 11 no. 6 p. 46 (Oct '60).
Smith, Carleton. Cur. biog. p. 427 (1961).
Smith, Carleton Sprague. Cur. biog. p. 389 (1960).
Smith, Charles Aubrey. Cur. biog. p. 634 (1944).
Smith, Courtney C. Cur. biog. p. 417 (1959).
Smith, Cyril Stanley. Cur. biog. p. 586 (1948).
Smith, Cyrus R. Cur. biog. p. 555 (1945).
Smith, David T. Cur. biog. p. 536 (1950).
Smith, Dick. Cur. biog. p. 419 (1959).
Smith, Edmund Kirby. Pakula: Cent. album, p. 265.
Smith, Capt. Edward J. Amer. heri., vol. 7 no. 1 p. 48 (Dec '55).
Smith, Elizabeth Rudel. Cur. biog. p. 429 (1961).
Smith, Francis (work of). Con. 133: XIX Mar '54.

Smith, Franklin Webster. Amer. heri., vol. 7 no. 4 p. 39 Je '56.
Smith, George (work of). Con. 143: XLVI Ap '59.
Smith, George Albert. Cur. biog. p. 587 (1947).
Smith, Gerald L. K. Cur. biog. p. 707 (1943).
Smith, Grafton Elliot (drawings by). Ceram: March of arch., p. 295.
Smith, H. Alexander. Cur. biog. p. 587 (1948).
Smith, Harold D. Cur. biog. p. 711 (1943).
Smith, Harrison. Cur. biog. p. 583 (1954).
Smith, Harry Allen. Cur. biog. p. 773 (1942).
Smith, Capt. Hervey (by West). Amer. heri., vol. 11 no. 1 p. 30 (col.) (Dec '59).
Smith, Hervey Garrett. Natl. geog. 112: 672, 674 Nov '57.
Smith, Lt. Gen. Holland M. Cur. biog. p. 557 (1945).
Smith, Howard K. Cur. biog. p. 713 (1943).
Smith, Howard W. Cur. biog. p. 798 (1941).
Smith, Capt. Humphrey. Con. 141: 161 May '58.
Smith, Ida B. Cur. biog. p. 715 (1943).
Smith, J. (work of). Con. 139: 137 Ap '57.
Smith, James H. jr. Cur. biog. p. 391 (1958).
Smith, Jessie Wilcox (book illus. by). Amer. heri. vol. 8 no. 1 p. 29-30 (col.) (Dec '56).
Smith, John. Amer. heri., vol. 9 no. 6 p. 28 (Oct '58).
Smith, John (Mormon). Brooks: Growth of a nation, p. 126.
Smith, John (by Reynolds). Con. 143: 84 Ap '59.
Smith, Capt. John. Holiday 21: 173 Ap '57. Natl. geog. 111: 587, 614 May '57.
—— (prisoner of Powatan). Natl. geog. 111: 596 May '57.
Smith, John L. Cur. biog. p. 549 (1952).
Smith, John Raphael (work of). Con. ency. of ant., vol. 1, pl. 136.
Con. 145: 237-40, 267 Je '60.
Smith, Julia. Amer. heri., vol. 8 no. 4 p. 55 (Je '57).
Smith, Lillian. Cur. biog. p. 636 (1944).
Smith, Margaret (Faithorne). Con. ency. of ant., vol. 1, pl. 136.
Smith, Margaret Chase. Cur. biog. p. 559 (1945); p. 394 (1962).
Holiday 15: 61 Feb '54.
Smith, Matthew. Con. 145: 111 Ap '60.
Smith, Oliver. Cur. biog. p. 430 (1961).
Smith, Paul C. Cur. biog. p. 717 (1943).
Smith, Raymond I. Holiday 17: 35 (col.) Feb '55.
Smith, Red. Cur. biog. p. 420 (1959).
Smith, Rex. Cur. biog. p. 775 (1942).
Smith, Robert Paul. Cur. biog. p. 393 (1958).
Smith, Samuel. Amer. heri., vol. 3 no. 2 p. 32 (winter '52).
Smith, Sidney. Cur. biog. p. 561 (1955).
Smith, Sidney L. (work of). Con. ency. of ant., vol. 3, pl. 89.
Smith, Sylvester C., jr. Cur. biog, p. 392 (1963).
Smith, Thomas J. Horan: Pict. hist. of wild west, p. 52.
Smith, Thomas V. Cur. biog. p. 586 (1956).
Smith, "Uncle Billy." Amer. heri., vol. 10 no. 2 p. 73 (Feb '59).

Smith, Lt. Gen. Walter Bedell. Cur. biog. p. 639 (1944); p. 580 (1953).
Smith, Washington G. Amer. heri., vol. 10 no. 1 p. 81 (Dec '58).
Smith, William (work of). Amer. heri., vol. 1 no. 3 p. 44 (col.) (spring '50).
Smith, Vice Adm. William Ward. Cur. biog. p. 590 (1948).
Smith, Willie "the Lion" (Negro musician). Holiday 27: 81 Je '60.
Smith & Indian prisoner, Capt. John. Natl. geog. 111: 595 May '57.
Smith College. Holiday 7: 60-7 (part col.) May '50.
Smith home, Joseph (Mormon). Brooks: Growth of a nation, p. 127.
Smith rescued by Pocahontas, Capt. John. Amer. heri., vol. 9 no. 6 p. 33 (Oct '58).
Smith's "Generall Historie" (page from). Amer. heri., vol. 11 no. 1 p. 48 (Dec '59).
Smith's "True travels" (illus.). Amer. heri., vol. 9 no. 6 p. 30-33 (Oct '58).
Smithson, James. Natl. geog. 117: 800 Je '60.
Smithsonian museum exhibits. Natl. geog. 111: 90-1 (col.) Jan '57; 117: 796-845 (part col.) Je '60.
smoke grenade. Natl. geog. 102: 393 (col.) Sept '52.
smokehouse. Holiday 6: 145 Nov '49; 7: 124 Feb '50; 10: 125 Dec '51.
Natl. geog. 97: 696 Je '50; 117: 472 (col.) Ap '60.
"Smoky the Bear" (forest fire prevention). Natl. geog. 110: 307 (col.) Sept '56.
—— (Sequoia natl. park). Natl. geog. 116: 166 (col.) Aug '59.
smoking cap. See cap, Greek smoking.
Smoky mt. natl. park. See Great Smoky mt.
smorgasbord. Holiday 23: 117 (col.) Jan '58.
"Smuggler's notch" (Stowe, Vt.). Travel 114: 42 Aug '60.
Smuts, Jan Christiaan. Cur. biog. p. 800 (1941).
Smylie, Robert E. Cur. biog. p. 588 (1956).
Smyrna sculpture. See sculpture, Smyrna.
Smyth, Henry D. Cur. biog. p. 592 (1948).
Smythe, Sir Thomas. Amer. heri., vol. 10 no. 4 p. 11 (Je '59).
snake (sym.). See serpent (sym.).
snake charmer (India). Holiday 14: 34 (col.) Oct '53; 24: 82 Jl '58; 27: 10 (col.) Jl '60.
Int. gr. soc.: Arts . . . p. 27 (col.).
Natl. geog. 112: 56 (col.) Jl '57.
—— ((comic). Holiday 11: 26 May '52.
—— (Malaya). Natl. geog. 103: 205 (col.) Feb '53.
snake-dance, street (Tokyo). Natl. geog. 118: 740 (col.) Dec '60.
snake goddess (Crete). Ceram: March of arch., p. 61-2.
Natl. geog. 114: 755 (col.) Dec '58.
snare, Indian trapper's. Natl. geog. 116: 620 Nov '59.
snares & deadfalls (for game). Natl. geog. 103: 578-9 (col.) May '53.
Snavely, Guy E. Cur. biog. p. 597 (1951).
Snayers, Pieter. Praeg.: Pict. ency., p. 335 (col.).
Snead, Sammy. Cur. biog. p. 575 (1949).

Snedeker, Caroline Dale. Jun. bk. of auth., p. 277.
Snefru's trust fund, King (on stone). Natl. geog. 108: 645 Nov '55.
Sneider, Vern. Cur. biog. p. 589 (1956).
Snell, Baron Henry. Cur. biog. p. 803 (1941).
Snell, Foster Dee. Cur. biog. p. 719 (1943).
Snell, Peter. Cur. biog. p. 397 (1962).
Snell lock (St. Lawrence river). Natl. geog. 115: 304, 322 (part col.) Mar '59.
Sneyd, Mrs. (Ramsay). Con. 145: 191 May '60.
Snider, Duke. Cur. biog. p. 591 (1956).
"The Sniper" (Dunn). Amer. heri., vol. 10 no. 6 p. 14 (col.) (Oct '59).
sno-cat sledges (Antarctica). Natl. geog. 116: 539 (col.) (Oct '59).
sno-cat truck (Antarctic). Natl. geog. 115: 27, 29 (col.) Jan '59.
sno-cats (Mt. tractors). Natl. geog. 106: 102-3 (col.) Jl '54.
snobbery (cartoon). Holiday 27: 93-5 May '60.
"The snobs" (Picasso). Con. 145: 255 Je '60.
Snodgrass, W. D. Cur. biog. p. 391 (1960).
Snofru pyramid (cross sec.). Ceram: March of arch., p. 105.
Sno-Shu chair. Holiday 10: 16 Jl '51.
Snow, Charles P. Cur. biog. p. 584 (1954); p. 432 (1961).
Snow, Edgar. Cur. biog. p. 804 (1941).
Snow, Edward Rowe. Cur. biog. p. 395 (1958).
Snow, Glenn E. Cur. biog. p. 589 (1947).
"Snow ball" (a dance, Buffalo). Holiday 18: 95 (col.) Aug '55.
snow blindness eye shield. See eye shield.
snow crystal (sym.). Lehner: Pict. bk. of sym., p. 51.
snow crystals. Holiday 18: 201 Dec '55.
—— **(polarized light).** Natl. geog. 115: 38 (col.) Jan '59.
snow sign (park). Natl. geog. 110: 778 (col.) Dec '56.
snow slide, Russia (1809). Amer. heri., vol. 9 no. 2 p. 9 (col.) (Feb '58).
snow star. See snow crystal.
snow survey (men). Natl. geog. 110: 778 (col.) Dec '56.
snow tunnel, Antarctic (man, pick). Natl. geog. 113: 446-7, 464 (col.) Ap '58.
"Snow White," Disney's (movie scene). Int. gr. soc.: Arts . . . p. 151 (col.).
snowball fight (children). Natl. geog. 105: 192 (col.) Feb '54.
snowflake. See snow crystal.
snowhouse (int., Arctic). Natl. geog. 107: 558, 560-1 (col.) Ap '55.
snowman. Holiday 13: 10 (col.) Jan '53; 18: 201 Dec '55; 19: 67 Feb '56; 22: 164 Dec '57.
Natl. geog. 104: 824 Dec '53.
Travel 109: 60 Jan '58.
—— **(child).** Natl. geog. 118: 797 (col.) Dec '60.
—— **(children).** Natl. geog. 104: 824 Dec '53.
—— **(comic).** Holiday 24: 81 Jl '58.
—— **(figurines).** Con. 139: 151-3 May '57.
—— **(flower trimmed).** Natl. geog. 114: 421 (col.) Sept '58.
—— **(Hawaii).** Natl. geog. 118: 21 (col.) Jl

'60.
—— **(on horse).** Amer. heri., vol. 1 no. 4 inside back cover (summer '50).
—— **(sym.).** Lehner: Pict. bk. of sym., p. 81.
——, **carnival.** Natl. geog. 113: 77 (col.) Jan '58.
snowmobile. Jordan: Hammond's pict. atlas, p. 131 (col.).
Natl. geog. 114: 871 Dec '58.
snowplane (rescues man). Natl. geog. 110: 765 (col.) Dec '56.
snowplow. Natl. geog. 110: 764 (col.) Dec '56.
snowshoe. Natl. geog. 103: 573 (col.) May '53.
snowshoes. Natl. geog. 109: 27 Jan '56; 110: 763 (col.) Dec '56.
—— **(man & dog).** Holiday 11: 14 Jan '52.
snowstorm. Natl. geog. 111: 788 (col.) Je '57.
snuff grinder. Holiday 18: 51 Aug '55.
snuff jar. Rawson: Ant. pict. bk., p. 88.
snuffbox. Con. 136: 9, 24 Sept '55, XXV Dec '55.
—— **(antique).** Con. 133 LV, 264 Je '54; 136: LXII Dec '55; 141: 153 May '58; 142: 242-3, 253 Jan '59; 143: XLVII Ap '59; 145: 283 Je '60.
—— **(19th cent.).** Con. 132: XXIX Jan '54.
——, **Dresden.** Con. 135: 207 May '55; 136: XLII Sept '55.
——, **Dutch gold (18th cent.).** Con. 142: XXIII Sept '58.
——, **French porcelain (antique).** Con. 135: 263 Je '55.
——, **George III gold.** Con. 144: LXII Jan '60.
——, **gold (antique).** Con. 140: XLI Sept '57.
——, **gold (18th cent.).** Con. 132: 125 Nov '53; 145; III May '60.
——, **gold (Faberge).** Con. 144: 111 Nov '59.
——, **Lafayette's.** Natl. geog. 112: 424 Sept '57.
——, **Louis XV.** Con. 141: 43 Mar '58; 144: LIII Sept '59.
——, **Louis XVI.** Con. 133: 133 Ap '54; 140: 61 Sept '57, XVI Jan '58; 144: LXI Jan '60.
——, **Russian (Nicolas I).** Con. 144: 277 Jan '60.
——, **Swiss gold.** Con. 144: VII Dec '59.
——, **carved gold (13th cent.).** Con. 144: 80 Nov '59.
snuffboxes. Natl. geog. 113: 262 (col.) Feb '58.
snuffer stand, candle. See candle snuffer stand.
snuffer tray, silver (Paul Lamerie). Con. 142: V Sept '58.
Snyder, Maj. Gen. Howard M. Cur. biog. p. 563 (1955).
Snyder, John W. Cur. biog. p. 561 (1945).
soap box, George I silver. Con. 141: XXXIV Mar '58.
——, **George II silver.** Con. 132: XVII Sept '53.
"soap box derby." Natl. geog. 107: 439 (col.), 441 Ap '55.
soap making (old style). Jordan: Hammond's pict. atlas, p. 47 (col.).
—— **(Pilgrim's kettle).** Natl. geog. 107: 741 (col.) Je '55.

Sobeloff, Simon E. Cur. biog. p. 565 (1955).

Sobolev, Arkady A. Cur. biog. p. 567 (1955).

soccer game. Holiday 11: 50 Jan '52; 18: 62 Oct '55.

Travel 104: 51 Nov '55.

—— **(Iraq).** Natl. geog. 114: 474 (col.) Oct '58.

—— **(Martinique).** Natl. geog. 115: 262-3 (col.) Feb '59.

—— **(Rio).** Natl. geog. 107: 327 (col.) Mar '55.

—— **(Rome).** Natl. geog. 111: 478 (col.) Ap '57.

—— **(Tehran vs Penn State College).** Natl. geog. 100: 434 (col.) Oct '51.

—— **(Turkey).** Natl. geog. 100: 178 (col.) Aug '51.

soccer team (Holland). Natl. geog. 106: 385 (col.) Sept '54.

socialism (sym.). Lehner: Pict. bk. of sym., p. 95.

Soc. of the Separatists of Zoar. *See* Zoar house.

sock, Christmas. Holiday 28: 207 (col.) Dec '60.

Sockman, Rev. Ralph W. Cur. biog. p. 561 (1946).

socks. Holiday 11: 13 (col.) May '52; 12: 77, 129 Oct '52, 65 Nov '52; 19: 166 Mar '56.

——, Japanese tabi. *See* tabi socks.

——, man's. Holiday 5: 5 (col.) Je '49; 6: 142 Dec '49; 7: 31 Ap '50; 10: inside cover (col.) Nov '51, 103 (col.) Dec '51; 22: 211 (col.) Dec '57.

sod house. Brooks: Growth of a nation, p. 193.

—— **(Alaska).** Natl. geog. 102: 79 (col.) Jl '52.

Soderberg, C. Richard. Cur. biog. p. 396 (1958).

Sodero, Cesare. Cur. biog. p. 720 (1943).

Sodoma (work of). Natl. geog. 101: 98 (col.) Jan '52.

Soekarno. Cur. biog. p. 590 (1947).

Soestdjik palace. Holiday 10: 52 (col.) Nov '51.

sofa (antique). Con. 129: 21 Ap '52.

—— **(brocaded).** Natl. geog. 113: 549 (col.) Ap '58.

—— **(18th cent.).** Holiday 18: 53 (col.) Aug '55.

——, Hepplewhite. Con. 127: 118 May '51; 141: 132 Ap '58; 143: X May '59.

——, Hepplewhite (camel back). Con. ency. of ant., vol. 1, p. 60.

——, Napoleon I. Con. 143: LXX May '59.

——, regency. Con. 142: 109 Nov '58.

sofa. *See* also couch.

sofa table. *See* table, sofa.

sofa writing table. *See* writing table, sofa.

Soissons (France). Natl. geog. 108: 536 (col.) Oct '55.

Sokolovsky, Vassily D. Cur. biog. p. 583 (1953).

Sokolsky, George E. Cur. biog. p. 806 (1941).

solar furnace. Natl. geog. 109: 315 Mar '56.

—— **(Algeria).** Natl. geog. 117: 793 (col.) Je '60.

solar stills. *See* water stills, solar.

Solberg, Rear Adm. Thorvald A. Cur. biog.

p. 594 (1948).

Solbert, Gen. Oscar N. Amer. heri., vol. 2 no. 2 p. 56 (winter '51).

Soldani, Massimiliano (work of). Con. 142: 159-63 Dec '58.

Soldani-Benzi (bronze "Pieta"). Con. 140: 201 Dec '57.

Soldati, Mario. Cur. biog. p. 397 (1958).

soldier. Amer. heri., vol. 10 no. 6 p. 99 (Oct '59).

Holiday 10: 40 (col.) Dec '51; 13: 119 Mar '53, 50 Je '53.

—— **(blowing taps).** Natl. geog. 111: 738 (col.) Je '57.

—— **(carrying flag).** Amer. heri., vol. 11 no. 2 p. 106 (Feb '60).

—— **(Civil war).** Amer. heri., vol. 10 no. 6 p. 98 (Oct '59).

Holiday 13: 46 (col.), 51, 55 May '53.

—— **(dreaming).** Amer. heri., vol. 8 no. 4 p. 52 (col.) (Je '57).

—— **(early Penn.).** Amer. heri., vol. 8 no. 3 p. 51 (col.) (Ap '57).

—— **(head).** Holiday 14: 119 Sept '53.

—— **(on horse).** Amer. heri., vol. 8 no. 5 p. 58 (col.) (Aug '57); vol. 9 no. 4 p. 56 (col.) (Je '58).

—— **(on horse, 1865).** Amer. heri., vol. 8 no. 5 frontis (Aug '57).

—— **(prison guard).** Amer. heri., vol. 11 no 4 p. 66 (Je '60).

—— **(running horse).** Holiday 28: 17 (col.) Nov '60.

—— **(wounded, carried on stretcher).** Amer. heri., vol. 9 no. 5 p. 96 (Aug '58).

——, Arab (motorcycle). Natl. geog. 98: 718 (col.) Dec '50.

——, Arab legion. Natl. geog. 98: 745 (col.) Dec '50.

——, Belgian (seated). Natl. geog. 108: 550 (col.) Oct '55.

——, British. Brooks: Growth of a nation, p. 78.

Holiday 26: 90 (col.) Jl '59.

——, Continental. Natl. geog. 100: 582 (col.) Nov '51.

——, early Amer. Amer. heri., vol. 8 no. 6 p. 86 (Oct '57).

——, girl (goodbye, comic). Holiday 11: 92 Ap '52.

——, Greek. Travel 114: cover (col.), 25, 28 Aug '60.

——, Greek (King's guard). Natl. geog. 100: 730 (col.) Dec '51.

——, Greek. *See* also Greek Evzone.

——, Iran (back view). Natl. geog. 100: 429 Oct '51.

——, Israeli. Holiday 26: 70 (col.) Dec '59.

——, Nepalese. *See* Nepalese soldier.

soldiers. Amer. heri., vol. 8 no. 2 cover (col.) (Feb '57).

Brooks: Growth of a nation, p. 185.

Holiday 10: 71 Aug '51.

Natl. geog. 102: 297, 299 (col.) Sept '52.

—— **(Amer. Revolution).** Amer. heri., vol. 6 no. 3 p. 12 (col.) (Ap '55); vol. 8 no. 5 p. 63 (col.) (Aug '57); vol. 9 no. 3 p. 40 (col.) (Ap '58); vol. 11 no. 6 p. 86-7 (Oct '60); vol. 12 no. 1 p. 6-7 (col.) (Dec '60).

soldiers (Amer. revolution battle field). Holiday 16: 98 (col.) Jl '54.

—— (Amer. revolution cartoon). Amer. heri., vol. 11 no. 6 p. 56-8 (part col.) (Oct '60).

—— (Amer. revolution on horses). Amer. heri., vol. 7 no. 6 p. 75 (col.) (Oct '56).

—— (Amer. revolution on rafts. Amer. heri., vol. 9 no. 3 p. 42 (col.) (Ap '58).

—— (battle, 1862). Amer. heri., vol. 9 no. 5 p. 56-7 (col.) (Aug '58).

—— (carrying machine gun). Amer. heri., vol. 8 no. 6 p. 106-7 (Oct '57).

—— (Civil war). See U.S. Civil war (soldiers).

—— (crossing river, 1899). Amer. heri., vol. 9 no. 2 p. 28-9 (col.) (Feb '58).

—— (1814). Amer. heri., vol. 6 no. 1 p. 48 (col.) (fall '54); vol. 8 no. 5 p. 9 (col.). (Aug '57).

—— (1817). Amer. heri., vol. 7 no. 1 p. 22, 24 (col.) (Dec '55).

—— (for review). Amer. heri., vol. 9 no. 4 p. 56 (col.) (Je '58).

—— (4th of July, early 19th cent.). Amer. heri., vol. 6 no. 4 p. 16-7 (col.) (Je '55).

—— (guard duty, 1840). Natl. geog. 99: 197 (col.) Feb '51.

—— (guard goat, Quebec). Natl. geog. 115: 312 (col.) Mar '59.

—— (guards, Canada). Holiday 24: 54 (col.) Nov '58.

—— (in camp). Amer. heri., vol. 9 no. 6 p. 117-20 (Oct '58).

—— (in review). Natl. geog. 99: 145 Feb '51.

—— (in trenches). Amer. heri., vol. 9 no. 2 p. 27 (Feb '58).

—— (Manila, Philippines, 1898). Amer. heri., vol. 12 no. 1 p. 66, 73-5, 77 (Dec '60).

—— (marching). Amer. heri., vol. 9 no. 1 p. 38-9, 46-7 (Dec '57); vol. 10 no. 2 p. 30 (Feb '59).
Holiday 13: 45 Ap '53; 27: 26 (col.) Feb '60.
Natl. geog. 97: 601-2 (col.) May '50.

—— (marching, 1865). Amer. heri., vol. 11 no. 2 p. 68 (Feb '60).

—— (of 3 wars). Holiday 28: 54-5 Sept '60.

—— (on foot & horseback, 1805). Amer. heri., vol. 11 no. 2 p. 32 (Feb '60).

—— (on horses). Amer. heri., vol. 6 no. 4 cover (col.) (Je '55); vol. 8 no. 4 p. 58 (col.) (Je '57).
Natl. geog. 99: 183 (col.) Feb '51.

—— (on horses, 1851). Amer. heri., vol. 7 no. 5 p. 12, 16-7 (col.) (Aug '56).

—— (on horses, 1856). Amer. heri. vol. 7 no. 5 p. 7, 16-7 (col.) (Aug '56).

—— (on horses, fighting, 1781). Amer. heri., vol. 7 no. 3 p. 34 (col.) (Ap '56).

—— (prisoners escape, 1864). Amer. heri., vol. 11 no. 4 p. 69-73 (Je '60).

—— (rebels & redcoats). Amer. heri., vol. 8 no. 2 p. 65-7, 73, 77, 89 (Feb '57).

—— (resting). Amer. heri. vol. 9 no. 1 p. 35 (Dec '57).

—— (1776). Amer. heri., vol. 11 no. 2 p. 58 (col.) (Feb '60).

—— (1795). Amer. heri. vol. 9 no. 4 p. 61 (col.) (Je '58).

—— (Spain.-Amer. war). Amer. heri. vol. 8 no. 2 p. 44-5 (col.) (Feb '57).

—— (Valley Forge). Amer. heri. vol. 6 no. 4 p. 38-9, 100 (Je '55).
Natl. geog. 105: 191, 193 (col.) Feb '54.

—— (war memorial). Natl. geog. 111: 753 (col.) Je '57.

—— (Washington's army). Amer. heri., vol. 7 no. 4 p. 74-9 (Je '56).

—— (wounded). Amer. heri., vol. 10 no. 6 p. 13 (col.) (Oct '59).

——, Afghanistan. Natl. geog. 117: 610-11 (col.) May '60.

——, Amer. (boarding plane). Natl. geog. 111: 287 (col.) Mar '57.

——, Amer. (in Japan with Com. Perry). Natl. geog. 116: 105 Jl '59.

——, Amer. (in Russia, 1918-9). Amer. heri., vol. 10 no. 1 p. 26-9 (Dec '58).

——, Amer. (in transport plane). Natl. geog. 111: 308-9 Mar '57.

——, Amer. (Korea). Natl. geog. 97: 792, 794 Je '50.

——, Amer. (medal of honor winners). Natl. geog. 111: 762-3 Je '57.

——, Amer. (officers at table). Natl. geog. 111: 287 (col.) Mar '57.

——, Amer. (1758). Amer. heri., vol. 6 no. 5 p. 12 (col.) (Aug '55).

——, Amer. (world war I). Amer. heri., vol. 10 no. 6 p. 7-17 (col.) (Oct '59).

——, Arabian. Natl. geog. 101: 239 (col.) Feb '52; 102: 790 (col.) Dec '52.

——, British (at Quebec). Amer. heri., vol. 11 no. 1 p. 30-1 (col.) (Dec '59).

——, British (in boat). Natl. geog. 116: 91 (col.) Jl '59.

——, British (Revolution). Amer. heri., vol. 10 no. 2 p. 16-7 (col.) (Feb '59).

——, British (royal guard). Natl. geog. 114: 80 (col.) Jl '58.

——, British (1645). Amer. heri., vol. 6 no. 5 p. 18-9 (col.) (Aug '55).

——, British & Amer., 1776). Amer. heri., vol. 7 no. 4 p. 4-5 (col.) (Je '56).

——, Canadian. Amer. heri., vol. 3 no. 3 p. 53 (col.) (spring '52).
Natl. geog. 98: 335 (col.) Sept '50; 115: 827 (col.) Je '59.

——, Chile (guard). Natl. geog. 117: 188 (col.) Feb '60.

——, Chinese. Natl. geog. 97: 140 Feb '50.

——, Colonial. Amer. heri., vol. 9 no. 1 p. 109 (Dec '57).
Holiday 26: 90-1 (col.) Jl '59.

——, Confederate. Amer. heri., vol. 5 no. 3 p. 32-3 (col.) (spring '54).

——, European (17th cent.). Amer. heri., vol. 6 no. 5 back cover (col.) (Aug '55).

——, Falkland (honor guard). Natl. geog. 109: 391 (col.) Mar '56.

——, Formosa (training). Natl. geog. 97: 173 Feb '50.
Natl. geog. 107: 587 Ap '55.

——, Free Chinese. Natl. geog. 111: 334-5 (col.) Mar '57.

——, German (festival). Natl. geog. 111: 258-68 (part col.) Feb '57.

——, German (1914). Travel 108: inside back cover Oct '57.

——, Greek. Natl. geog. 117: 638 (col.) May '60.

soldiers, Greek (salutes). Natl. geog. 117: 640 (col.) May '60.

——, Laos. Natl. geog. 117: 47-8 (col.) Jan '60.

——, Mexican. Natl. geog. 100: 822 (col.) Dec '51.

——, model (antique). Con. ency. of ant., vol. 3, pl. 145-8

——, Pescadores is. Natl. geog. 109: 278-9 (col.) Feb '56.

——, Scotland. Natl. geog. 112: 462 (col.) Oct '57.

——, Spanish (1803). Natl. geog. 103: 716 (col.) Je '53.

——, Turkey. Natl. geog. 100: 147 Aug '51; 101: 745, 753--5 Je '52.

——, Turkey (chart table). Natl. geog. 100: 184 Aug '51.

——, Viet Nam. Natl. geog. 102: 299, 309 (col.) Sept '52.

soldiers' & sailors' memorial (Indianapolis). Holiday 8: 36 Aug '50.

soldiers' & sailors' memorial arch (Long Island). Natl. geog. 99: 316 Mar '51.

soldiers & wives (board plane). Natl. geog. 111: 290-1 (col.) Mar '57.

"Soldiers at dice" (Van Baburen). Con. 140: 127 Nov '57.

soldiers. See also troops; warrior.

soldiers' caskets, World war. Natl. geog. 116: 113 (col.) Jl '59.

soldiers' caskets, World war II unknown. Natl. geog. 114: 594-604 (col.) Nov '58.

Soldiers Field (Chicago). Holiday 10: 47 (col.) Oct '51.

soldiers parade. Holiday 12: 58 Sept '52.

—— (London). Holiday 13: 122 (col.) Je '53.

—— (N.Y., 1851). Amer. heri., vol. 7 no. 5 p. 13, 15-23 (col.) (Aug '56).

soldier's tomb. See tomb of unknown soldier.

Solfatara (Italy, near Pozzuoli). Labande: Naples, p. 138.

Solh, Sami. Cur. biog. p. 399 (1958).

solitude (sym.). Lehner: Pict. bk. of sym., p. 38.

Solomon (on throne). Natl. geog. 112: 863 (col.) Dec '57.

Solomon, Abraham (work of). Con. 145: XVIII (col.) Ap '60.

Solomon & Sheba. See Sheba & Solomon romance.

Solomon's circle (sym.). Lehner: Pict. bk. of sym., p. 69.

Solomon's double seal (sym.). Lehner: Pict. bk. of sym., p. 74.

Solomon's palace (int.). Natl. geog. 112: 862-3 (col.) Dec '57.

Solomon's temple (Jerusalem). Natl. geog. 118: 812-3 (col.) Dec '60.

Sombrero (Chile). Natl. geog. 117: 200-1 (col.) Feb '60.

Somers, Sir George. Amer. heri., vol. 10 no. 4 p. 10 (col.) (Je '59).

Somervell, Lt. Gen. Brehon. Cur. biog. p. 777 (1942).

Somerville, Adm. Sir James. Cur. biog. p. 723 (1943).

Somerville home, Col. William. Natl. geog. 105: 435 (col.) Ap '54.

Somes, Michael. Cur. biog. p. 569 (1955).

Sommerfeld, Arnold. Cur. biog. p. 537 (1950).

Somoan girls dancing. Travel 106: 54 Dec '56.

Somoza, Anastasio. Cur. biog. p. 780 (1942).

Sonar laboratory, navy. Natl. geog. 97: 55 (col.) Jan '50.

song book (300 yrs. old). Natl. geog. 107: 515 (col.) Ap '55.

"Song of the talking wires" (Farny). Amer. heri., vol. 6 no. 1 p. 40 (fall '54).

"Song session" (skiers in Canada). Holiday 7: 53 (col.) Jan '50.

song slides. Amer. heri., vol. 10 no. 4 back cover (col.), p. 51-9 (col.) (Je '59).

Songgram, Luang Pibul. Cur. biog. p. 487 (1951).

songs (presidential campaign hits). Amer. heri., vol. 7 no. 4 p. 32-3 (Je '56).

——, love (muse of). Lehner: Pict. bk. of sym., p. 33.

Sonoma mission (Cal.). Travel 101: 10 Feb '54.

Sonora (Mexico). Natl. geog. 107: 217-46 (part col.) Feb '55. Travel 103: 31 Jan '55.

Sontag, George. Horan: Pict. hist. of wild west, p. 151.

Sontag, John. Horan: Pict. hist. of wild west, p. 151-2.

Soo canal. See Sault Ste Marie.

Soo locks. See Sault St. Marie locks.

Soochow, leaning tower of. See leaning tower of Soochow.

Soong, T. V. Cur. biog. p. 808 (1941).

soot (sym.). Lehner: Pict. bk. of sym., p. 73.

Sophia Dorothea of Celle, Queen of Gt. Brit. Amer. heri., vol. 11 no. 4 p. 8 (Je '60).

Sophoulis, Themistocles. Cur. biog. p. 593 (1947).

"Sophronia asking Caracen King. . . ." Con. 145: 40 Mar '60.

Soraya, Queen (Iran). Holiday 20: 65 Dec '56.

sorcerer (head hunters). Natl. geog. 108: 453 (col.) Oct '55.

Sordoni, Andrew J. Cur. biog. p. 592 (1956).

Sorensen, Theodore. Cur. biog. p. 435 (1961). Jensen: The White House, p. 290.

Sorensen, Virginia. Cur. biog. p. 539 (1950).

Sorokin, Pitirim A. Cur. biog. p. 782 (1942).

Sorrento (Italy). Labande: Naples, p. 185.

—— (Gigante). Con. 140: XXV Dec '57.

—— (harbor). Labande: Naples, frontis.

Soth, Lauren K. Cur. biog. p. 594 (1956).

Sothern, Ann. Cur. biog. p. 596 (1956).

Souers, Sidney W. Cur. biog. p. 577 (1949).

soul (sym.). Lehner: Pict. bk. of sym., p. 26.

soul, pilgrimage of. See ladder of pilgrimage of soul (sym.).

Soulages, Pierre. Cur. biog. p. 401 (1958).

Soulanges lock (St. Lawrence). Natl. geog. 115: 310 (col.) Mar '59.

Soule, George. Cur. biog. p. 564 (1945).

Soulen, Henry J. (work of). Natl. geog. 112: 834-63 (col.) Dec '57; 118: 812-52 (col.) Dec '60.

"Souls in torment" (war monument). Natl. geog. 111: 460 (col.) Ap '57.

soup tureen. See tureen.

"Sourdough," bronze (statue). Holiday 21: 24 Ap '57.

Sousa, John Philip. Cooper: Con. ency. of music, p. 294.
Natl. geog. 116: 756 Dec '59.
Soustelle, Jacques. Cur. biog. p. 402 (1958).
"Souter Johnie's home." Natl. geog. 112: 457 (col.) Oct '57.
South Africa. See Africa, South.
South America. Holiday 18: 76-7 (col.) Oct '55; 20: 54-95, 100-1 (col.) Nov '56; 22: 12-3 (col.) Oct '57.
Travel 111: 19-23 Mar '59; 112: 16-20 Sept '59.
—— **(map).** Holiday 20: 57 (col.) Nov '56; 27: back cover (col.) Ap '60.
—— **(pictorial map).** Holiday 18: 13 (col.) Jl '55.
South Carolina. Holiday 15: 106-7 Ap '54; 20: 75-81 (part col.) Dec '56.
Natl. geog. 103: 282-321 (part col.) Mar '53.
—— **(map).** Natl. geog. 103: 284-5 Mar '53.
—— **(Middleton gardens).** Face of Amer., p. 24-5 (col.).
South Dakota. Jordan: Hammond's pict. atlas, p. 106-7 (col.).
Travel 105: 26-9 May '56; 113: 40-3 Mar '60.
—— **(Bad lands).** Amer. heri., vol. 6 no. 3 p. 29 (Ap '55).
—— **(Black Hills).** Natl. geog. 110: 480-509 (part col.) Oct '56.
"South gate, Yarmouth" (Cotman). Con. 142: 112 Nov '58.
South Georgia island. Natl. geog. 107: 94-116 Jan '55.
South Pass City (Wyo., ghost town). Travel 114: 45 Sept '60.
South Pole. See Antarctic.
South Sea islands. Natl. geog. 97: 74-104 (part col.) Jan '50.
South Seas (map). Natl. geog. 109: 550 Ap '56.
South Seas atoll. Natl. geog. 109: 546-71 (part col.) Ap '56.
Southampton (Long Island). Holiday 8: 94-9 (part col.) Aug '50.
Southampton island (map). Natl. geog. 110: 677 Nov '56.
Southee, Ellen Sarah. See Poltoratzky, Ellen Sarah (Southee).
southern architecture. See architecture, colonial; home, colonial.
Southey, Robert (work of). Natl. geog. 109: 510 (col.) Ap '56.
"Southill" house (Bedfordshire, Eng., int.). Con. 129: 15-21 Ap '52.
"Southwark Fair" (Hogarth). Durant: Pict. hist. of Amer. circus, p. 14.
Southworth, Billy. Cur. biog. p. 641 (1944).
Southworth, James L. Cur. biog. p. 304 (1943).
Soutine, Chaim. Con. 145: 233 Je '60.
—— **(Modigliani).** Con. 145: 185 May '60.
—— **(work of).** Con. 140: XVIII (col.) Dec '57; 145: 208 May '60.
Souvanna Phouma, Prince of Laos. Cur. biog. p. 399 (1962).
"The souvenir" (Fragonard). Con. 127: cover, opp. p. 71 (col.) May '51.
souvenir shops. Travel 110: 21-3 Aug '58.
sovereign's sceptor, British. Int. gr. soc.: Arts

. . . p. 165 (col.).
Soviet-Turkey border. See Turkey-Soviet border.
Soviet Union. See Russia.
Soyer, Isaac. Cur. biog. p. 809 (1941).
Soyer, Moses. Cur. p. 810 (1941).
Soyer, Raphael. Cur. biog. p. 812 (1941).
spa (Italy). See Montecatini spa.
—— **(Pyrenees).** Natl. geog. 109: 322-3 (col.) Mar '56.
spa resorts (Mexico). Travel 107: 21-5 Mar '57.
Spaak, Paul-Henri. Cur. biog. p. 567 (1945); p. 404 (1958).
Spaatz, Maj. Gen. Carl. Cur. biog. p. 784 (1942).
space capsule (Gemini). U.S. News & world report, vol. LV no. 1 p. 69 July 1, 1963.
space helmets. Holiday 21: 6 May '57.
Natl. geog. 108: 263 (col.) Aug '55.
space missiles. See missile, space.
space satellites. See satellites, space.
space suits. Natl. geog. 108: 240, 246, 263, 275 (col.) Aug '55.
space travel (experiments). Natl. geog. 108: 242-76 (part col.) Aug '55.
Spackman, B. (work of). Con. 140: 110 Nov '57.
Spada, Leonello (work of). Con. 142: 143, 145-6 Dec '58.

spade. Amer. heri., vol. 7 no. 4 p. 27 (col.) (Je '56).
Natl. geog. 110: 307 (col.) Sept '56; 113: 321 (col.) Mar '58.
—— **(sym.).** Lehner: Pict. bk. of sym., p. 10, 90.
Spaeth, Sigmund. Cur. biog. p. 786 (1942).
Spahi. Int. gr. soc.: Arts . . . p. 159 (col.).
Spahn, Warren. Cur. biog. p. 401 (1962).
Spain, Frances Lander. Cur. biog. p. 393 (1960).
Spain. Holiday 7: 86 Ap '50; 10: 82-5 Aug '51; 13: 140 (col.) Mar '53; 15: 34-47 (part col.) May '54; 21: 149 (col.) Je '57; 23: 58-65 (col.) Jan '58; 24: 11 Oct '58, 106-111 (col.) Dec '58; 25: 116 (col.) Jan '59, 19 (col.) Feb '59; 27: 194 (col.) Mar '60.
Natl. geog. 97: 416-56 (part col.) Ap '50; 105: 154, 178-9 (col.) Feb '54; 109: 300-7, 316, 323 (part col.) Mar '56; 111: 622-60 (part col.) May '57.
Travel 103: 10-4 Ap '55; 105: 45 Ap '56; 111: 31-2 Ap '59, 37-9 May '59.
—— **(Alcazar castle).** See Alcazar castle.
—— **(Alhambra).** See Alhambra.
—— **(Andalusia).** Natl. geog. 113: 398-424 (part col.) Mar '58.
—— **(Barcelona).** Holiday 26: 104-9 (part col.) Dec '59.
—— **(castle).** Holiday 23: inside back cover Mar '58; 26: 116 (col.) Nov '59.
—— **(castle, int.).** Travel 111: 25 Ap '59.
—— **(comic).** Holiday 11: 56-7 (col.) Je '52.
—— **(Costa Brava).** Travel 108: 20-1 Jl '57.
—— **(El Escorial).** Holiday 23: 116 (col.) Jan '58.

Spain (festival). Holiday 27: 98-9 (col.) May '60.
Travel 109: 25, 27 Ap '58.
—— (harbor). Holiday 27: 50 (col.) Ap '60.
—— (Holy Week). Travel 107: 19-23 Ap '57.
—— (Holy Week procession). Holiday 15: 44 May '54.
—— (Madrid). Natl. geog. 100: 718 (col.) Dec '51.
—— (man with harrow & oxen). Holiday 23: 89 Mar '58.
—— (map). Natl. geog. 97: 418 Ap '50.
—— (Mezquita mosque). Holiday 23: 150 (col.) Feb '58.
—— (Montserat). Holiday 24: 220 (col.) Dec '58.
—— (parade). Holiday 26: 2 (col.) Sept '59.
—— (welcomes Eisenhower). Natl. geog. 117: 644 (col.) May '60.
Spain, patron saint of. Lehner: Pict. bk. of sym., p. 39.
Spain. See also Segovia (Spain).
Spalding, Albert. Cur. biog. p. 645 (1944).
Spalding, Gilbert R. "Doc." Durant: Pict. hist. of Amer. circus, p. 48.
Spang, Joseph Peter, jr. Cur. biog. p. 580 (1949).
Spangler, Edward. Amer. heri., vol. 8 no. 2 p. 57 (Feb '57).
Spangler, Harrison E. Cur. biog. p. 725 (1943).
Spaniard (on horse). Amer. heri., vol. 9 no. 5 cover, p. 8 (col.) (Aug '58).
—— (pack-loaded mule). Natl. geog. 111: 627 May '57.
—— (serenading). Holiday 8: 130 Dec '50.
Spaniards (fighting). Amer. heri., vol. 8 no. 6 p. 7-8 (col.) (Oct '57).
Spaniards & Indians (fighting). Amer. heri., vol. 8 no. 6 p. 9 (col.) (Oct '57).
Spanish-American war. Amer. heri., vol. 8 no. 2 p. 32-41 (col.) (Feb '57).
Spanish & English (men at table, 1604). Amer. heri., vol. 10 no. 4 p. 16-7 (col.) (Je '59).
Spanish costume. See costume, Spanish.
Spanish dancer. Holiday 10: 14 Oct '51; 27: 178 Je '60.
Spanish Flamenco dancers. Int. gr. soc.: Arts . . . p. 147 (col.).
Spanish horses (1st in Amer.). Brooks: Growth of a nation, p. 34.
Spanish man. Holiday 7: 66 (col.) Je '50.
Spanish man & woman. Travel 113: inside cover Ap '60.
Spanish men, women & children. Natl. geog. 99: 523-30 (col.) Ap '51.
Spanish mission (Santa Fe). Amer. heri., vol. 8 no. 6 p. 35 (col.) (Oct '57).
"Spanish shrine" (Hodgkins). Con. 143: 93 Ap '59.
"Spanish steps," Rome (Bellotto). Con. 141: 230 Je '58.
Holiday 11: 47 (col.) Ap '52.
Natl. geog. 111: 441 (col.) Ap '57.
Spanish woman (head). Travel 103: 10 Ap '55.
spark plugs, auto. Holiday 12: 26 (col.) Jl '52.
Sparkman, John J. Cur. biog. p. 540 (1950).
Holiday 27: 59 (col.) Mar '60.
Sparks, Jared. Amer. heri., vol. 9 no. 4 p. 33

(Je '58).
Sparks circus wagon carving. Amer. heri., vol. 12 no. 1 frontis. (col.) (Dec '60).
Sparling, Edward J. Cur. biog. p. 596 (1948).
Sparrowe, John (Gainsborough). Con. 143: 93 Ap '59.
Speaker, Tris. Amer. heri., vol. 10 no. 3 p. 23 (Ap '59).
speaker's chair (legislature, Canada). Holiday 18: 38 (col.) Sept '55.
spear. Travel 101: 43 Jan '54.
——, Fijian. Natl. geog. 114: 531, 550, 558-9 (col.) Oct '58.
——, fish & eel. Rawson: Ant. pict. bk., p. 75.
——, fisherman. Natl. geog. 109: 221 (col.) Feb '56.
spear fishing. Travel 101: 29 Feb '54; 104: 19-22 Sept '55.
"Spear-thrower of Polycleitus" (5th cent., B.C.). Praeg.: Pict. ency., p. 11.
Speare, Elizabeth George. Cur. biog. p. 422 (1959).
spearmen (Angkor). Natl. geog. 117: 522 (col.) Ap '60.
spears (stone age). Natl. geog. 113: 434 Mar '58.
spectacles. See eyeglasses.
Spectorsky, A. C. Cur. biog. p. 394 (1960).
spectrograph. Natl. geog. 111: 579 Ap '57.
spectrometer. Natl. geog. 111: 572 Ap '57.
speedboat. Holiday 26: 68 Aug '59.
Natl. geog. 101: 306 (col.) Mar '52; 103: 177 (col.) Feb '53.
Travel 113: 49 Mar '60.
—— (boys). Natl. geog. 112: 338 (col.) Sept '57.
—— (water skiers). Natl. geog. 111: 158 (col.) Feb '57.
speedboat racers. Natl. geog. 97: 193 (col.) Feb '50.
Speicher, Eugene E. Cur. biog. p. 595 (1947).
Speidel, Hans. Cur. biog. p. 550 (1952).
Speke Hall (Eng.). Holiday 15: 28 (col.) Je '54.
Spellman, Cardinal Francis. Cur. biog. p. 597 (1947).
Travel 105: 11-3 Mar '56.
Spence, Brent. Cur. biog. p. 551 (1952).
Spence, Capt. Hartzell. Cur. biog. p. 789 (1942).
Spence, Lowell. Horan: Pict. hist. of wild west, p. 229.
Spence, Peter. Horan: Pict. hist. of wild west, p. 113.
Spencer, Cornelia. Jun. bk. of auth., p. 278.
Spencer, Herbert. Holiday 19: 85 Mar '56.
Spencer, Percy C. Cur. biog. p. 599 (1951).
Spencer, Stanley (work of). Con. 139: 53 Mar '57.
Spender, Percy C. Cur. biog. p. 543 (1950).
"The spendthrift" (Steen). Con. 133: 97 Ap '54.
spermatozoon. Gray's anatomy, p. 22.
Sperry, Armstrong. Cur. biog. p. 813 (1941).
Jun. bk. of auth., p. 279.
Sperry, Willard L. Cur. biog. p. 554 (1952).
Speyer cathedral (nave & choir). Praeg.: Pict. ency., p. 190.
sphere, armillary. See armillary sphere.

——, **celestial.** *See* celestial sphere.
spherics (sym.). Lehner: Pict. bk. of sym., p. 9.
sphinx. Ceram: March of arch., p. 71-82.
 Holiday 6: 6 Dec '49; 8: 140 Nov '50; 10: 121 (col.), 149 Dec '51; 14: 196 Dec '53; 19: 1 Feb '56; 20: 70 Oct '56; 24: 209 Dec '58; 27: back cover (col.) Ap '60; 28: 206 Nov '60.
 Natl. geog. 100: 733 (col.) Dec '51; 106: 768 (col.) Dec '54; 108: 649 (col.) Nov '55.
 Praeg.: Pict. ency., p. 118.
 Travel 102: 37 Sept '54; 110: 15 Oct '58.
—— **(sym.).** Lehner: Pict. bk. of sym., p. 83.
——, **garden lead (18th cent.).** Con. ency. of ant., vol. 3, p. 53.
——, **lead (18th cent.).** Con. 144: XXVII Jan '60.
sphinxes (Hittite). Natl. geog. 115: 78 Jan '59.
Sphynx gateway. *See* Alaja Hoyuk (Sphynx gateway).
spice box, antique silver. Con. 138: 273 Jan '57.
——, **St. Cloud porcelain.** Con. 141: 76 Ap '58.
——, **silver (Douai, 1771).** Con. 142: 16 Sept '58.
——, **silver (Louis XIV, French).** Con. 140: 38 Sept '57.
——, **silver (Louis XV, French).** Con. 140: 38 Sept '57; 141: XXIX Je '58; 142: XI Sept '58.
——, **silver (16th cent.).** Con. 139: 31 Mar '57.
——, **trefoil-shaped.** Con. 145: 274 Je '60.
spice caster, silver (antique). Con. 138: 272 Jan '57.
——, **silver (17th cent.).** Con. 138: 272 Jan '57.
spider in web (sym.). Lehner: Pict. bk. of sym., p. 63.
Spiegel, Clara. Cur. biog. p. 365 (1954).
spike, railroad. *See* railroad spike.
spill holder (antique). Con. 142: 243 Jan '59.
spindle, corn cob. Rawson: Ant. pict. bk., p. 34.
spinet (woman playing). Natl. geog. 97: 289 (col.) Mar '50.
——, **Scottish (antique).** Con. 143: IV Mar '59.
Spink, J. G. Taylor. Holiday 27: 82 May '60.
spinning frame, Arkwright. Amer. heri., vol. 9 no. 3 p. 35, 91 (Je '58).
spinning wheel. Amer. heri., vol. 5 no. 3 p. 18 (spring '54).
 Con. ency. of ant., vol. 3, pl. 79.
 Disney: People & places, p. 30 (col.).
 Natl. geog. 97: 106 Jan '50, 288 (col.) Feb '50; 102: 24, 103 (col.) Jl '52 103: 700 May '53.
 Travel 108: 31 Aug '57 .
—— **(girl).** Natl. geog. 106: 467 (col.) Oct '54.
—— **(India).** Natl. geog. 102: 221 Aug '52.
—— **(Lapland).** Natl. geog. 106: 273 (col.) Aug '54.
—— **(1753).** Natl. geog. 100: 589 (col.) Nov '51.

—— **(woman).** Int. gr. soc.: Arts . . . p. 71 (col.).
 Natl. geog. 98: 627 Nov '50; 106: 570 (col.) Oct '54; 109: 526-7 Ap '56.
—— **(Africa).** Natl. geog. 97: 325 (col.) Mar '50.
spire, church. *See* church spire.
——, **civic center (Mont.).** Travel 108: 13 Jl '57.
——, **Ulm cathedral (world's tallest, Ger.).** Int. gr. soc.: Arts . . . p. 49 (col.).
spires, church. Natl. geog. 115: 614 (col.) May '59.
——, **rock.** Natl. geog. 101: 715-7 (col.) Je '52.
——, **rock (Bryce canyon).** Natl. geog. 114: 507-9 (col.) Oct '58.
——, **rock needle (Monument Valley).** Natl. geog. 114: 810-11 (col.) Dec '58.
——, **Univ. of Tampa.** Travel 107: inside cover Je '57.
spirit, South Seas (carved). Holiday 28: 120 Nov '60.
spirit bird sym., Dyak. Holiday 23: 32 Je '58.
"spirit house" (head-hunters). Natl. geog. 108: 446 Oct '55.
—— **(New Guinea).** Holiday 28: 83 Oct '60.
 Natl. geog. 116: 778 (col.) Dec '59.
"Spirit mound" (S.D.). Natl. geog. 103: 720 (col.) Je '53.
Spirit of prohibition (sym.). Lehner: Pict. bk. of sym., p. 93.
"Spirit of '76". Amer. heri. vol. 5 no. 2 p. 45 (winter '54).
"Spirit of 1776." Lehner: Pict. bk. of sym., p. 93.
'Spirit of '76' (Willard). Natl. geog. 107: 744 (col.) Je '55.
spirit of the sun (sym.). Lehner: Pict. bk. of sym., p. 26.
spirits, attract the (sym.). Lehner: Pict. bk. of sym., p. 68-9.
spirits, house of. *See* Tambaran house.
spirits, sign of 7 beneficial (sym.). Lehner: Pict. bk. of sym., p. 24.
spirits, signs of 7 maleficent (sym.). Lehner: Pict. bk. of sym., p. 24.
spiritualist (sym.). Lehner: Pict. bk. of sym., p. 67.
spit (mutton roasting). Int. gr. soc.: Arts . . . p. 179 (col.).
——, **dangle.** Con. ency. of ant., vol. 3 p. 242.
spittoon, brass. Amer. heri., vol. 11 no. 5 p. 32 (col.) (Aug '60).
Spitz, Leo. Holiday 5: 42 (col.) Jan '49.
Spitzer, Lyman, jr. Cur. biog. p. 396 (1960).
Spitzer, Silas. Holiday 6: 32 Sept '49.
Spitzweg, Karl (work of). Praeg.: Pict. ency., p. 401 (col.).
Spivak, Lawrence E. Cur. biog. p. 598 (1956).
"Splicing the cable" (Dudley). Natl. geog. 99: 207 (col.) Feb '51.
Split (Yugoslavia). Holiday 14: 44-5 (col.) Aug '53.
 Natl. geog. 99: 160 (col.) Feb '51.
Spock, Benjamin. Cur. biog. p. 600 (1956).
Spofford, Charles M. Cur. biog. p. 600 (1951).
Spokane (Wash.). Natl. geog. 102: 610 (col.) Nov '52.

spoke shave. Rawson: Ant. pict. bk., p. 54.
sponge fisherman. Jordan: Hammond's pict. atlas, p. 71 (col.).
sponges. Natl. geog. 115: 143 (col.) Jan '59.
—— (boat). Natl. geog. 113: 194 (col.) Feb '58.
—— (Negroes). Natl. geog. 113: 194 (col.) Feb '58.
spooling frame. Rawson: Ant. pict. bk., p. 34.
spoon. Holiday 13: 108 May '53; 21: 138 Ap '57.
—— (bird eating from). Natl. geog. 103: 78 Jan '53.
——, anointing. See anointing spoon.
——, antique silver. Con. 134: 161 Dec '54; 135: XXXII Mar '55.
——, Apostle. Con. 136: XV Nov '55; 145: 280 Je '60.
——, Apostle (Henry VII). Con. 140: XXXVIII Jan '58.
——, Apostle (Henry VIII). Con. 143: 266 Je '59.
——, Charles I slip-top silver. Con. 133: XVI Ap '54.
——, Charles II. Con. 127: 79 May '51.
——, commonwealth. Con. 135: XXIII Ap '55.
——, Dutch gold rat-tailed. Con. 140: 182 Dec '57.
——, Edward IV. Con. 140: 114 Nov '57.
——, Eng. silver (15th cent.). Con. 144: 199 Dec '59.
——, Eng. silver (15th cent. berry finial). Con. 144: 269 Jan '60.
——, Florentine silver. Travel 102: 5 Sept '54, 5 Nov '54.
——, George II. Con. 137: XXII Ap '56.
——, Gothic. Con. 141: 151 May '58.
——, Henry VIII silver. Con. 145: 127 Ap '60.
——, James I. Con. 137: XXIV Ap '56, XXIV Je '56.
——, master (17th cent.). Con. 132: 85 Nov '53.
——, medieval. Con. 137: 224 Je '56.
——, Norwich silver. Con. 134: XV Dec '54.
——, seal-top silver (17th cent.). Con. ency. of ant., vol. 1, pl. 87.
——, silver. Holiday 14: 196 Dec '53; 19: 168 May '56; 21: 114 Mar '57, 105 Je '57; 27: 117 Ap '60.
——, silver-gilt (18th cent.). Con. 134: 13 Sept '54.
——, silver-gilt (Flemish). Con. ency. of ant., vol. 3, pl. 36.
——, silver Italian (16th cent.). Con. ency. of ant., vol. 3, pl. 31.
——, souvenir. Holiday 28: 222 Nov '60.
——, tea. Holiday 12: 96 Nov '52.
——, Truro silver. Con. 134: 51 Sept '54.
spoon & fork, Florentine serving. Holiday 18: 63 Nov '55.
spoon handles, tea. Holiday 10: 24 Nov '51; 12: 131 Oct '52.
spoon rack, Dutch (18th cent.) Con. ency. of ant., vol. 1, pl. 38.
Spooner, Bourne. Amer. heri., vol. 5 no. 3 p. 18 (spring '54).
spoons. Holiday 12: 1 Oct '52; 27: 204 Mar '60; 28: back cover (col.) Sept '60.

—— (antique). Con. 137: XXIV May '56.
—— (16-17th cent.). Con. 136: III Jan '56.
—— (18th cent.). Holiday 14: 116 Sept '53.
——, pewter. Con. ency. of ant., vol. 1, pl. 79.
Natl. geog. 117: 156 (col.) Feb '60.
——, Russian silver. Con. 142: 224 Jan '59.
——, silver (17-18th cent.). Con. ency. of ant., vol. 1, pl. 87.
——, silver (18th cent.). Con. 141: 90 Ap '58.
——, tea. Holiday 18: 147 Nov '55, 9 Dec '55.
——, Towle silver. Holiday 23: 200 Je '58; 24: 95 Oct '58.
spoons. See also silverware.
Sporborg, Mrs. William Dick. Cur. biog. p. 600 (1947).
sporran, (17th cent.). Con. 135: 175 May '55.
sports. Holiday 18: 75 (col.) Jl '55.
—— (Scotland). Natl. geog. 110: 2-3, 17-9 (col.) Jl '56.
—— (vacation). Holiday 18: 7 (col.) Jl '55.
—— See also games (medieval).
sports clothes. See girl (sport clothes); men (sports wear).
——, college. Holiday 23: 91 (col.) May '58.
——, equipment. Holiday 18: 104 Dec '55.
—— goods. See name of item wanted.
—— See also name of sport.
"The sportsman's last visit" (Mount). Amer. heri., vol. 11 no. 5 p. 15 (col.) (Aug '60).
spotlight, auto. Holiday 24: 41 Nov '58, 147 Dec '58.
——, miniature. Con. 129: LXXVI Ap '52.
Spottswood, Stephen G. Cur. biog. p. 403 (1962).
Sprague, Robert C. Cur. biog. p. 602 1951).
Sprague, William. Amer. heri., vol. 7 no. 5 p. 43 (Aug '56).
spray (around ships nose). Natl. geog. 104: 542 Oct '53.
——, insect (Holland). Natl. geog. 98: 764 (col.) Dec '50.
spray machine, fruit tree. Natl. geog. 103: 302 (col.) Mar '53.
——, wine vines. Natl. geog. 109: 694 (col.) May '56.
spraying, airplane. Natl. geog. 104: 208 (col.) Aug '53.
"Spread Eagle Inn" (stage house, 1796). Amer. heri., vol. 3 no. 1 p. 42 (col.) (fall '51).
Spreckles, Rudolph. Amer. heri., vol. 11 no. 1 p. 10 (Dec '59).
Spring, Howard. Cur. biog. p. 815 (1941).
spring (sym.). Lehner: Pict. bk. of sym., p. 81.
——, sinking (near Lincoln's home). Natl. geog. 101: 153 Feb '52.
spring signs (zodiac). Lehner: Pict. bk. of sym., p. 18.
"Spring sowing" (Jacopo da Ponte, Bassano). Con. 138: 211 Dec '56.
Springer, Adele I. Cur. biog. p. 602 (1947).
springs, vehicle. Rawson: Ant. pict. bk., p. 70.
sprinkler, field water. Natl. geog. 97: 727 (col.) Je '50.
sprinkling can. Holiday 15: 163 May '54.
Sproul, Allan. Cur. biog. p. 545 (1950).
Sproul, Robert Gordon. Cur. biog. p. 569 (1945).

Spruance, Raymond Ames. Cur. biog. p. 647 (1944).
spur, rider's (Chile). Natl. geog. 117: 211 Feb '60.
Spurling, Jack (work of). Amer. heri., vol. 6 no. 6 p. 15 (col.) (Oct '55).
spurs, St. George's. Natl. geog. 104: 325 (col.) Sept '53.
Spyri, Johanna. Jun. bk. of auth., p. 280.
square dance. See dance, square.
square pianoforte. See pianoforte, square.
squares, magic (sym.). Lehner: Pict. bk. of sym., p. 68-70.
squash racquet. Holiday 23: 91 May '58.
"Squatting priest" (sculpture 650 B.C.). Praeg.: Pict. ency., p. 172.
"Squatting scribe" (Egypt, 5th dynasty). Praeg.: Pict. ency., p. 168.
Squaw dance, Navajo. Disney: People & places, p. 125-7 (col.).
Squaw Valley (Cal.). Holiday 27: 168 (col.) Feb '60.
squirrel (sym.). Lehner: Pict. bk. of sym., p. 59.
squirrel trap. Rawson: Ant. pict. bk., p. 28.
Sri Mangesh temple (Goa, India). Travel 113: 50, 52 Feb '60.
Srinagar ("Venice of the East"). Natl. geog. 114: 612-3 (col.) Nov '58.
stability (sym.). Lehner: Pict. bk. of sym., p. 26, 60.
stable, household (France). Natl. geog. 115: 576 Ap '59.
stables. Holiday 12: 100, 102 (col.) Sept '52.
—— See also barn.
Stacy, Walter P. Cur. biog. p. 563 (1946).
Stace, Walter Terence. Cur. biog. p. 437 (1961).
Stader, Maria. Cur. biog. p. 406 (1958).
stadium (Swiss festival). Natl. geog. 114: 565 (col.) Oct '58.
——, **athletic.** Holiday 18: 104-5 Jl '55.
——, **baseball.** See baseball stadium.
——, **bullfight.** Holiday 20: 80 (col.) Nov '56.
——, **football.** See football stadium.
——, **Greek.** Int. gr. soc.: Arts . . . p. 39 (col.).
——, **Melbourne (Australia).** Natl. geog. 109: 251 Feb '56.
Travel 106: 50-1 Oct '56.
——, **memorial (Sinabung).** Natl. geog. 108: 388 (col.) Sept '55.
——, **Milwaukee.** Natl. geog. 111: 150 Feb '57.
——, **National (Nicaragua).** Natl. geog. 109: 340-1 Mar '56.
——, **N.Y. City college.** See N.Y. (City college stadium).
——, **Peking.** See Peking (workers' stadium).
staff, bishop's silver (15th cent.). Con. 132: 21 Sept '53.
Stafford, Jean. Cur. biog. p. 604 (1951).
Stafford, Robert T. Cur. biog. p. 397 (1960).
Staffordshire pottery animals. Con. 129: XL Ap '52.
stag (deer), Derby ware. Con. 138: XXI Sept '56.
stag cup. See cup, stag.
stage, TV. See TV stage.

stage scenery. See theater (int., scenes).
stagecoach. Amer. heri., vol. 7 no. 1 p. 118 (Dec '55); vol. 8 no. 4 p. 29, 31 (Je '57); vol. 9 no. 3 p. 5 (col.) (Ap '58).
Brooks: Growth of a nation, p. 84, 112.
Con. 141: XXXI Ap '58; 142: 122 Nov '58.
Holiday 8: 16 Sept '50, 36 Oct '50; 15: 116 Jan '54; 22: 35 Jl '57; 25: 137 Ap '59; 26: 58 Jl '59, 29 (col.) Dec '59; 27: 107 (col.) Mar '60.
Natl. geog. 99: 210 (col.) Feb '51.
Rawson: Ant. pict. bk., p. 72.
—— **(early western).** Horan: Pict. hist. of wild west, p. 128.
—— **(people).** Amer. heri., vol. 2 no. 2 p. 29 (winter '51).
Natl. geog. 108: 296-7 (col.) Sept '55.
—— **(horses running).** Con. ency. of ant., vol. 3, pl. 96.
—— **(Indian attack).** Amer. heri., vol. 8 no. 4 p. 26-7 (col.) (Je '57).
Durant: Pict. hist. of Amer. circus, p. 135.
Holiday 27: 27 May '60.
—— **(loaded).** Con. 144: 254 (col.) Jan '60.
——, **English.** Holiday 27: 205 (col.) Ap '60; 28: 164 (col.) Nov '60.
——, **toy.** Natl. geog. 110: 499 (col.) Oct '56.
stagecoach inn. See "Spread Eagle Inn."
stagecoach lamps. Con. 142: XXXII Dec '58.
stagecoach southern route. Amer. heri., vol. 8 no. 4 p. 31 (Je '57).
Stagg, Alonzo. Cur. biog. p. 650 (1944).
"Staghound" clipper ship. Amer. heri., vol. 6 no. 6 p. 20 (col.) (Oct '55).
Stahle, Nils K. Cur. biog. p. 602 (1956).
Stahr, Elvis, jr. Cur. biog. p. 439 (1961).
Stainback, Ingram Macklin. Cur. biog. p. 603 (1947).
stained glass, medieval (men making). Int. gr. soc.: Arts . . . p. 65 (col.).
stained glass windows. See window, stained glass.
stair railing (Colonial). Natl. geog. 113: 535 (col.) Ap '58.
—— **(iron).** Holiday 27: 31 (col.) Ap '60.
staircase (17th cent. railing). Con. 144: XVI Sept '59.
——, **Chateau de Blois.** See Chateau de Blois stairway.
——, **hanging.** Natl. geog. 105: 454 (col.) Ap '54.
staircase detail, Elizabethan. Con. 133: LXVIII Je '54.
stairs (sym.). Lehner: Pict. bk. of sym., p. 27.
——, **outside house (Austria).** Natl. geog. 115: 205 (col.) Feb '59.
stairway. Con. 133: 274 Je '54.
Holiday 13: 55 Jan '53; 26: 145 Dec '59; 28: 66 (col.) Jl '60, 12 (col.) Dec '60.
—— **(carved, Grinling Gibbon).** Con. 141: 193 May '58.
—— **(Claydon house).** Con. 142: 74 Nov '58.
—— **(man & woman).** Holiday 18: 41 (col.) Sept '55.
—— **(Mirabell palace).** Praeg.: Pict. ency., p. 375.
—— **(Mt. Vernon).** Natl. geog. 104: 659 (col.) Nov '53.
—— **(Provost's house, Dublin).** Con. 145: 152 May '60.

stairway, antler. Natl. geog. 105: 449 (col.) Ap '54.

——, **church choir.** Face of Amer., p. 170-1 (col.).

——, **circular.** Amer. heri., vol. 8 no. 4 p. 38 (Je '57). Natl. geog. 103: 794 (col.) Je '53.

——, **Colonial.** Natl. geog. 103: 537 (col.) Ap '53, 793 (col.) Je '53; 105: 465 (col.) Ap '54.

——, **Colonial (children).** Natl. geog. 109: 453 (col.) Ap '56.

——, **Colonial (man & woman).** Natl. geog. 109: 449 (col.) Ap '56.

——, **Colonial (men).** Natl. geog. 109: 481 (col.) Ap '56.

——, **Colonial (Va.).** Natl. geog. 109: 468 (col.), 472 Ap '56.

——, **Colonial (woman).** Natl. geog. 118: 177 (col.) Aug '60.

——, **early Eng.** Con. 127: 127 May '51.

——, **garden.** Holiday 27: 123 (col.) Feb '60.

——, **hillside.** Holiday 6: 51 Oct '49.

——, **palace (Eng.).** Holiday 19: 5 (col.) Jan '56.

——, **secret.** Natl. geog. 97: 298 Mar '50.

——, **Spanish castle.** Travel 111: 25 Ap '59.

——, **spiral.** Holiday 25: 22 Je '59. Int. gr. soc.: Arts . . . p. 107 col.). Natl. geog. 97: 62 Jan '50; 99: 326 (col.) Mar '51.

——, **spiral (Colonial).** Natl. geog. 113: 539 (col.) Ap '58.

——, **twin (one for men, one for ladies).** Natl. geog. 109: 472 Ap '56.

Stakeman, Elvin C. Cur. biog. p. 582 (1949).

stalactites. Natl. geog. 111: 630-1 May '57.

stalagmites. Natl. geog. 111: 631 May '57.

Stalin, Joseph. Cur. biog. p. 791 (1942).

Stalin, Joseph V. Holiday 5: 27 Jan '49.

Stalingrad (Russia). Holiday 18: 106 Jl '55.

—— **(railroad station).** Travel 109: 56 Ap '58.

Stalnaker, John M. Cur. biog. p. 407 (1958).

Stamm, Bishop John S. Cur. biog. p. 583 (1949).

Stamos, Theodoros. Cur. biog. p. 423 (1959).

stamp, Eastman memorial postage. Natl. geog. 106: 438 Sept '54.

——, **U.S. (Com. 400th anniversary of discovery of Amer. by Columbus).** Con. 134: 201 Dec '54.

stamp col. shop. Natl. geog. 106: 143 (col.) Jl '54.

stamp machine. Natl. geog. 106: 137 (col.) Jl '54.

stamp shop (Paris). Natl. geog. 101: 802 (col.) Je '52.

stampede, Calgary. See Calgary stampede.

stamps (musicians). Cooper: Con. ency. of music, p. 495-6.

——, **Argentina (1862).** Con. 145: 56 Mar '60.

——, **duty.** See duty stamps.

——, **postage.** See postage stamps.

stanchion, cow. Rawson: Ant. pict. bk., p. 64.

standard-bearer (warrior, ancient times). Int. gr. soc.: Arts . . . p. 33 (col.).

Standley, Harrison (work of). Amer. heri., vol. 8 no. 5 p. 28 (col.) (Aug '57).

Standley, William H. Cur. biog. p. 797 (1942).

Stanfield, Robert L. Cur. biog. p. 409 (1958).

Stanfield, W. Clarkson (work of). Con. 134: XVIII (col.) Sept '54.

Stanford, Sir Charles Villiers. Con. 144: 12 Sept '59.

Stanford univ. (Cal.). Travel 110: cover (col.) Oct '58.

Stanford univ. memorial church. Natl. geog. 110: 221 (col.) Aug '56.

Stanky, Eddie. Cur. biog. p. 605 (1951).

Stanley, F. E. & F. O. (in auto). Amer. heri., vol. 10 no. 2 p. 40 (Feb '59).

Stanley, Kim. Cur. biog. p. 571 (1955).

Stanley, Oliver. Cur. biog. p. 727 (1943).

Stanley, Thomas B. Cur. biog. p. 572 (1955).

Stanley, Wendell M. Cur. biog. p. 605 (1947).

Stanley, Winifred. Cur. biog. p. 729 (1943).

Stanley steamer. Amer. heri., vol. 10 no. 2 p. 40-5, 87 (part col.) (Feb '59).

Stans, Maurice H. Cur. biog. p. 411 (1958).

Stansfield, Clarkson (work of). Con. 144: 93 Nov '59.

Stanton, Edwin M. Amer. heri., vol. 10 no. 6 p. 97 (Oct '59); vol. 11 no. 6 p. 46 (Oct '60).

Stanton, Elizabeth Cady. Amer. heri., vol. 7 no. 4 p. 47 (Je '56); vol. 10 no. 6 p. 19 (Oct '59).

Stanton, Frank. Cur. biog. p. 572 (1945).

Stanton Hall (Natchez, Miss.). Holiday 5: 52 (col.) Mar '49.

Stanwyck, Barbara. Cur. biog. p. 607 (1947).

Stapleton, Maureen. Cur. biog. p. 425 (1959).

Stapp, John Paul. Cur. biog. p. 426 (1959).

star, hot (cosmic smoke ring). Natl. geog. 115: 674 (col.) May '59.

——, **mystic.** See mystic star.

star & crescent. See crescent & star (sym.).

star gazing (sym.). Lehner: Pict. bk. of sym., p. 67.

Star of Bethlehem. Lehner: Pict. bk. of sym., p. 51.

Star of David (sym.). Lehner: Pict. bk. of sym., p. 36.

Star of St. George order (18th cent.). Con. 144: 85 Nov '59.

Starch, Daniel. Cur. biog. p. 394 (1963).

Stark, Louis. Cur. biog. p. 573 (1945).

Starkenborgh Stachouwer, A. W. L. T. Van. Cur. biog. p. 800 (1942).

Starker, Janos. Cur. biog. p. 396 (1963).

Starr, Belle. Amer. heri., vol. 11 no. 5 p. 41 (Aug '60). Horan: Pict. hist. of wild west, p. 132-3.

Starr, Cecile. Cur. biog. p. 574 (1955).

Starr, Chauncey. Cur. biog. p. 587 (1954).

Starr, Henry. Horan: Pict. hist. of wild west, p. 148.

Starr, Louis E. Cur. biog. p. 610 (1947).

Starr, Mark. Cur. biog. p. 565 (1946).

Starr, Pearl. Horan: Pict. hist. of wild west, p. 135.

"Starry night" (Gogh). Holiday 14: 61 (col.) Nov '53.

stars (Palomar observatory, sky survey). Natl. geog. 108: 186-9 Aug '55.

—— **(sym.).** Lehner: Pict. bk. of sym., p. 59.

stars (sym. on card). Lehner: Pict. bk. of sym., p. 77.
stars circling. Natl. geog. 101: 247 Feb '52.
"Starved Rock" park (Ill.). Travel 103: 15 Je '55.
Stassen, Harold E. Cur. biog. p. 597 1948).
state capitol. See capitol.
——. See also name of state.
"State in Schuykill" castle (Penn.). Natl. geog. 118: 157, 179 (col.) Aug '60.
state parks (Conn.). Travel 108: 32-5 Aug '57.
—— (Fla.). Travel 104: 14-7 Oct '55; 107: 12-5 Je '57.
—— (Mass.). Travel 108: 37-8 Oct '57.
—— (N.M.). Travel 109: 19-23 Mar '58.
—— (Ore.). Travel 110: 36-9 Jl '58.
—— (Tex.). Travel 105: 54 Jan '56; 107: 40-4 Mar '57.
—— (W.Va.). Travel 110: 47-9 Oct '58.
state seals. See seals, state.
statehouse, old. See Boston (Old state house).
statehouse foundations (Jamestown). Natl. geog. 111: 600-1 (col.) May '57.
states (sym.). Lehner: Pict. bk. of sym., p. 82-3.
station wagon. Holiday 5: 125 (col.) Je '49; 6: inside cover, 71 (col.) Oct '49, 7 (col.) Nov '49; 7: 15 (col.) Je '50; 19: 76 (col.) Je '56; 23: 96 (col.) Feb '58, 163 Mar '58, 13 (col.) May '58; 24: 7 (col.) Dec '58; 28: 14 (col.) Nov '60.
Natl. geog. 98: 84 (col.) Jl '50; 99: 567, 684 (col.) May '51; 109: 15 (col.) Jan '56; 117: 280 Feb '60.
—— (canoe on top). Natl. geog. 103: 740, 744 (col.) Je '53.
—— (in desert). Natl. geog. 101: 740 (col.) Je '52.
—— (1900). Natl. geog. 112: 309 (col.) Sept '57.
—— (Volkswagen). Holiday 28: 133 (col.) Nov '60.
——, experimental. Travel 112: 19 Aug '59.
stationery (writing paper). Holiday 14: 80 Sept '53.
—— (in box). Holiday 14: 146 (col.) Dec '53.
—— (samples). Holiday 13: 24 May '53.
"Statsoper" (opera house, Vienna). Disney: People & places, p. 54 (col.).
statuary. Amer. heri., vol. 11 no. 3 p. 17 (Ap '60).
——, alabaster. Con. ency. of ant., vol. 3, pl. 129.
——, garden. Con. ency. of ant., vol. 3, p. 53-5, pl. 25-6.
——, Greek & Roman. Con. ency. of ant., vol. 3, pl. 65-72.
statuary hall (Wash., D.C.). Holiday 25: 61 Je '59.
statue. Holiday 26: 100 (col.) Nov '59.
—— (Abraham Lincoln). Holiday 7: 117 Feb '50; 22: 1 Jl '57.
Natl. geog. 101 149 (col.) Feb '52.
Travel 113: 29 Feb '60.
—— (Alexander Hamilton). Natl. geog. 111: 73 Jan '56.
—— (Allan Ramsay). Natl. geog. 112: 460

(col.) Oct '57.
—— (Andrew Jackson). Jensen: The White House, p. 46.
—— ("boy sticks finger in dike"). Natl. geog. 98: 751 Dec '50.
—— (bull fight). Holiday 12: 83 Sept '52.
—— (by Canova). Con. 143: 227 Je '59.
—— (by Parodi). Con. 142: 140 Dec '58.
—— (Chinese general on vanal). Natl. geog. 103: 248 Feb '53.
—— (Christ of the Andes). See "Christ of the Andes."
—— (cowboy). Natl. geog. 100: 198 Aug '51.
—— ("Freedom"). Holiday 19: 40 May '56.
—— (George III). Amer. heri., vol. 9 no. 5 p. 62 (col.) (Aug '58).
—— (horse). Holiday 22: 53 (col.) Nov '57.
—— (Huey Long). Holiday 11: 35 Mar '52.
—— (James Monroe). Natl. geog. 97: 590 (col.) May '50.
—— (Jan Van Eyck). Natl. geog. 107: 643 (col.) May '55.
—— (John Harvard). Holiday 5: 107 Jl '59.
Natl. geog. 97: 309 (col.) Mar '50.
—— (Lord Botetourt). Natl. geog. 106: 482 (col.) Oct '54.
—— (Lafayette). Natl. geog. 112: 423 Sept '57.
—— (man in shell). Holiday 28: 44 (col.) Nov '60.
—— (man on camel). Natl. geog. 107: 716 May '55.
—— (man on horse). Holiday 26: 125 Nov '59.
—— (marble bust). Con. 140: 58 Sept '57.
—— (Mexico). Holiday 28: 167 Oct '60.
—— (Paul Revere). Natl. geog. 107: 743 Je '55.
—— (Queen Victoria). Con. 134: 26 Sept '54.
Natl. geog. 114: 151 Aug '58.
—— (Queen Victoria, Africa). Natl. geog. 104: 172 (col.) Aug '53.
—— (Queen Victoria in Parliament bldg.). Holiday 17: 59 Mar '55.
—— (Robert Burns). Natl. geog. 112: 450 (col.) Oct '57.
—— (Roger Williams). Brooks: Growth of a nation, p. 51.
Holiday 11: 110 (col.) May '52.
—— (Royal Scots Greys memorial). Natl. geog. 112: 477 Oct '57.
—— ("Sabrina"). Natl. geog. 97: 303 (col.) Mar '50.
—— (St. Paul). Natl. geog. 110: 758 (col.) Dec '56.
—— (Shakespeare). Natl. geog. 108: 299 (col.) Sept '55.
—— (Shakespeare, wood carved). Natl. geog. 108: 299 (col.) Sept '55.
—— ("sourdough"). Holiday 21: 24 Ap '57.
—— (taxidermy, humor). Holiday 26: 43 Nov '59.
—— (Thomas Jefferson). Natl. geog. 97: 592 (col.) May '50.
—— (Vulcan). Holiday 21: 186 Ap '57; 23: 128 Mar '58.
—— (warrior guard, Patzcuaro, Mexico). Natl. geog. 102: 542 (col.) Oct '52.
—— (Wm. Johnson & King Hendrick). Amer.

heri., vol. 3 no. 3 p. 25 (spring '52).

—— (woman). Jordan: Hammond's pict. atlas, p. 63.

——, bronze. Con. 145: 283 Je '60.

——, bronze (Egyptian). Con. 136: LIV Sept '55.

——, bronze (by Houdon). Natl. geog. 113: 261 Feb '58.

——, bronze (Italy). Natl. geog. 111: 797 (col.) Je '57.

——, bronze (by Kolbe). Praeg.: Pict. ency., p. 489.

——, bronze (by Maillol). Con. 145: 55 Mar '60.

——, bronze (19th cent.). Con. 145: 55 Mar '60.

——, French Burgundian. Con. 133: LXXIV Je '54.

——, Greek bronze. Con. 136: LXXXI Jan '56.

——, limestone (12th cent.). Con. 134: 72 Sept '54.

——, marble (Rome). Con. 136: 190 Dec '55.

——, minuteman. See "Minuteman" statue.

——, Polychrome wooden (India). Int. gr. soc. Arts . . . p. 57 (col.).

——, Sacagawea's. See Sacagawea's statue.

——, silver-gilt (French, 14th cent.). Con. 133: 292 Je '54.

——, terra-cotta. Natl. geog. 98: 600 (col.) Nov '50.

——, wood (1800-   ). Amer. heri., vol. 3 no. 3 p. 33, 40 (col.) (spring '52).

——, wood (15th cent.). Con. 142: LXV Dec '58.

Statue of Liberty. Amer. heri., vol. 7 no. 4 p. 28 (col.) (Je '56); vol. 7 no. 6 frontis. (Oct '56); vol. 8 no. 6 p. 40 (col.) (Oct '57).
Holiday 10: 8 Aug '51; 20: 116, 128 Nov '56; 28: 166 Oct '60.
Natl. geog. 106: 774, 776 (col.) Dec '54; 115: 549 (col.) Ap '59.

—— (by Moran). Natl. geog. 99: 212 (col.) Feb '51.

—— (Hays, Kan.). Natl. geog. 101: 483 (col.) Ap '52.

—— (head). Holiday 23: 93 Je '58.

"Statue of the Virgin" (Gloucester, Mass.). Natl. geog. 104: 84 (col.) Jl '53.

"Statue of wisdom." See "Wisdom."

statue "Summer." See "Summer."

statues (Rome). Holiday 27: 79 (col.) Ap '60.

—— (St. Cecile cathedral). Natl. geog. 100: 30 (col.) Jl '51.

——, bronze. Con. 136: 1 Dec '55.
Praeg.: Pict. ency., p. 458.

——, church (16-17th cent., ivory). Con. 133: XI May '54.

——, Swedish carved wood. Con. 141: 21-3 Mar '58.

—— See also sculpture.

statuette, Etruscan bronze. Con. 143: 103 Ap '59.

——, French ivory. Con. 126: 90 Oct '50.

statuette of St. George (gold & jewels). Con. 144: 82 Nov '59.

statuettes, Alcora (Spain). Con. 139: 60-3 Mar '57.

Statz, Hermann. Cur. biog. p. 412 (1958).

Staudinger, Dr. Hermann. Cur. biog. p. 588 (1954).

Stauffer, David (work of). Amer. heri., vol. 7 no. 1 p. 114 (Dec '55).

Stauss, Richard. Holiday 18: 9 Aug '55.

stave church. See church, stave.

Steacie, Edgar W. R. Cur. biog. p. 585 (1953).

steam jets (Italy). Natl. geog. 100: 711 Dec '51.

steam shovel. Natl. geog. 105: 316 (col.) Mar '54.

steam turbine. See turbine, steam.

steamboat. Amer. heri., vol. 6 no. 4 p. 45 (Je '55).
Face of Amer., p. 98-9 (col.).
Holiday 13: inside cover (col.), 18 Jan '53, 24 (col.), 80 Feb '53, back cover Mar '53, 100 Ap '53.
Natl. geog. 110: 796 (col.) Dec '56.
Travel 105: 49, 55 May '56; 107: 9 Ap '57, 55 Je '57; 108: 53, 65 Jl '57, 55 Oct '57; 109: 56-7 Mar '58.

—— (cabin, int.). Amer. heri., vol. 10 no. 6 p. 30 (Oct '59).

—— (1862). Amer. heri., vol. 11 no. 2 p. 75 (Feb '60).

—— (exploding). Amer. heri., vol. 7 no. 2 p. 116 (Feb '56).

—— (Falkland). Natl. geog. 109: 403, 410 (col.) Mar '56.

—— (night). Amer. heri., vol. 8 no. 6 p. 21-2 (col.) (Oct '57).

—— (people on deck). Natl. geog. 97: 210 (col.) Feb '50.

—— (Peru). Disney: People & places, p. 112 (col.).

—— (Scotland). Natl. geog. 112: 474 (col.) Oct '57.

—— (silhouette). Amer. heri., vol. 7 no. 1 p. 46 (Dec '55).

—— (sinking). Amer. heri., vol. 6 no. 4 p. 40 (Je '55).

—— ("Sultana," 1865). Amer. heri., vol. 6 no. 6 p. 50-1 (Oct '55).

—— (Switzerland). Natl. geog. 110: 429 (col.) Oct '56.

—— ("United States"). Natl. geog. 115: 836-7 Je '59.

——, Alaskan. Travel 106: 39-41 Jl '56.

——, Danube. Disney: People & places, p. 56 (col.).

——, early river (cotton loaded). Amer. heri., vol. 6 no. 3 p. 6 (Ap '55).

——, lake. Holiday 25: 68 Je '59.

——, Rhine. Natl. geog. 108: 130 Jl '55.

——, river. Amer. heri., vol. 8 no. 6 p. 16-23, 96 (part col.) (Oct '57).
Brooks: Growth of a nation, p. 105.
Holiday 11: 78 Feb '52; 12: 18, 46, 94 (col.) Jl '52, 58 Oct '52; 14: 125 Jl '53; 18: 113 Jl '55, 111 Sept '55, 137 Nov '55; 19: 151 Mar '56, 180 May '56, 121 Je '56; 20: 16 Oct '56, 185 (col.) Dec '56; 21: 138 Feb '57, 181 Mar '57; 22: 5 (col.) Sept '57, 53 (col.), 133 Nov '57, 19 Dec '57; 23: 112 May '58; 24: 1 Oct '58; 26: 215 Dec '59; 27: 115 Jan '60, 97 Feb '60, 137 Mar '60, 116 May '60;

28: 14 Jl '60.
Jordan: Hammond's pict. atlas, p. 102-3 (col.).
Natl. geog. 98: 332 (col.) Sept '50; 112: 265 Aug '57; 113: 536-7 Ap '58; 114: 674-5 (col.) Nov '58.
Travel 112: 57 Dec '59; 113: 45 May '60; 114: cover (col.) Jl '60.
——, river (Belgian Congo). Natl. geog. 101: 352-3 (col.) Mar '52.
——, river (collision). Amer. heri., vol. 2 no. 1 p. 48 (fall '50).
——, river (Delta Queen). Holiday 26: 19 Jl '59.
Travel 113: 55 May '60.
——, river (1890). Amer. heri., vol. 9 no. 2 back cover (col.) (Feb '58).
——, river (Mayflower). *See* The "Mayflower" (river steamboat).
——, river (old). Amer. heri., vol. 6 no. 3 p. 105 (Ap '55).
——, river (showboat). Durant: Pict. hist. of Amer. circus, p. 44, 48.
——, Tasmania. Natl. geog. 110: 796 (col.) Dec '56.
——, river paddle wheel. Holiday 25: 77 Feb '59, 172 Je '59.
——, sidewheeler. Amer. heri., vol. 1 no. 2 p. 54 (winter '50); vol. 2 no. 1 p. 44-5 (col.), 47 (fall '50); vol. 4 no. 4 p. 14-22 (part col.) (summer '53); vol. 5 no. 1 p. 63 (fall '53); vol. 6 no. 1 p. 6-15 (col.) (fall '54); vol. 8 no. 1 p. 89 (Dec '56); vol. 9 no. 5 p. 42-9 (col.) (Aug '58); vol. 9 no. 6 p. 46 (col.) (Oct '58; vol. 10 no. 1 p. 7 (Dec '58).
——, sidewheeler (old). Natl. geog. 107: 759 Je '55.
——, sidewheeler ("Rip Van Winkle"). Amer. heri., vol. 10 no. 1 p. 17 (Dec '58).
——, sternwheeler. Natl. geog. 101: 292 (col.) Mar '52; 110: 386 Sept '56; 114: 127 (col.) Jl '58; 118: 684-5 (col.) Nov '60.
Travel 103: 20 May '55; 108: 17 Oct '57.
——, sternwheeler (Yukon). Natl. geog. 104: 407, 410-13 (col.) Sept '53.
——, Switzerland. Natl. geog. 110: 429 (col.) Oct '56.
—— *See* also boat, river.
steamboat model, "Natchez." Natl. geog. 97: 185 Feb '50.
steamboat race, river. Amer. heri., vol. 2 no. 1 p. 48 (fall '50).
Brooks: growth of a nation, p. 154.
"steamboat rock" (Col.). Natl. geog. 105: 366, 376-8 Mar '54.
Travel 112: 37 Sept '59.
steamship. Amer. heri., vol. 8 no. 2 p. 49-53 (part col.) (Feb '57); vol. 9 no. 2 p. 65 (Feb '58); vol. 9 no. 5 p. 23 (col.) (Aug '58).
Holiday 5: 26 (col.) Jan '49, 5, 91 Mar '49, 124, 143 (col.) Ap '49; 6: 8, 13, 107-11 (col.) Jl '49, 30 (col.) Aug '49, 93 Sept '49, 33, 135 (col.) Oct '49, 55 Nov '49, 10 (col.), 154 Dec '49; 7: 75 Jan '50, 2, 7, 18 (col.) Mar '50, 24, 106 (col.) Ap '50, 91 (col.), 98 May '50; 8: 115 (col.) Jl '50, 4 (col.) Sept '50, 113 Oct '50, 68-9 (col.), 95 Nov '50, 5, 71, 129 (col.), 162

Dec '50; 9: 116 (col.), 133, 141 Mar '51; 10: 84 (col.) Jl '51, 20 Aug '51, 115 (col.) Sept '51, 2, 26 (col.), 139, 150 Oct '51, 1, 9, 31, 79 (col.), 149 Nov '51, 155, 164 Dec '51; 11: 81, 118 Jan '52, 18 Feb '52, 22, 113 (col.) Mar '52, 32, 129, 146 (col.) Ap '52, 4, 18, 20 (col.), 24, 34 May '52, 79, 88, 93 (part col.) Je '52; 12: 125 (col.) Jl '52, 1, 15, 80 (col.) Aug '52, 32, 74 (col.) Oct '52, 130 Nov '52, 2, 108, 156 (part col.) Dec '52; 13: 65, 75, back cover (part col.) May '53, 2, 30, 74, 141 (col.) Je '53; 14: 2 Jl '53, 75 (col.) Aug '53, 16, 77 Sept '53, 84, 118 (col.) Oct '53, 7, 74, 98 (part col.) Nov '53, 17, 37 (col.) Dec '53; 15: 74, 94 Jan '54, 30 Feb '54, inside cover (col.) 124 (col.), 152 Mar '54, inside back cover (col.) Ap '54, 147 May '54; 16: inside cover, 66 (col.) Jl '54, 19 Aug '54, 2, 7, 19, 32, 82 (col.), 104 Sept '54, 94, 135 Nov '54; 17: 10, 75, 99, 116 (col.) Jan '55, 23 Feb '55, 134, 146 Mar '55; 18: 19 Jl '55, inside cover (col.), 11, 25 Aug '55, 17, 112 (col.) Sept '55, 16, 138 (col.) Oct '55, 10, 69, 130 (col.) Nov '55, 82 (col.) Dec '55; 19: 69, 85 (col.) Jan '56, 112 Feb '56, 87 May '56, 113 Je '56; 20: inside cover (col.), 5, 105 Sept '56, 28, 76 (col.) Oct '56, 36, 106, 131-2 (part col.) Nov '56, 114, 177 (part col.) Dec '56; 21: 108 Feb '57, 102 (col.) Mar '57, 1, 135 Ap '57, 118 (col.), 156, 161, 179 May '57, inside cover, 99, 108 (col.) Je '57; 22: 27 (col.), 91, 105 Sept '57, 5 (col.), 101, 167 (col.) Oct '57, 105, 124 Nov '57, 26 (col.) Dec '57; 23: 9, 110 Jan '58, 1, 81 Feb '58, 106, 151 (col.) Mar '58, inside cover (col.) Ap '58, 11, 24, 150, 165 May '58, 41, 127 (col.) Je '58; 24: 10, 19 (col.) Jl '58, 22, 75, 85, 117 (col.) Aug '58, 27, 31, 35, 108, 137 (part col.) Sept '58, 27, 116, back cover (col.) Oct '58, 2, 123, 125, 152, 162, 206 (part col.) Nov '58, 14, 185 (col.) Dec '58; 25: 97, 99, 125 (part col.) Jan '59, 24, back cover (col.) Feb '59, 53, 153 (col.) Mar '59, 37, 96, 182, back cover (part col.) Ap '59, 23, 35, 101, 134, 145, 159, back cover (part col.) May '59, 126, 162 (col.) Je '59; 26: 87, 120, 138 Jl '59, 73 (col.), 80 Aug '59, 1, 7 (col.), 20, 107 Sept '59, 33 (col.), 151, 155 Oct '59, 11, 105, 127 Nov '59, 214 Dec '59; 27: 96-7, 165 (part col.) Jan '60, 120, 153, 161 (part col.) Feb '60, 48 Mar '60, 47, 164 (col.), 190, 196, back cover (col.) Ap '60, 25, 145, 217, 227 (part col.) May '60, 37, 133, 183, inside back cover (part col.) Je '60; 28: 22 (col.), 94, 133, 137 Jl '60, 16, 79 (col.) Aug '60, 15 (col.), 21, 76, 93 (col.), 119-20, 136 Sept '60, 32, 37, 100-3, 111, 120-1, 149, back cover (part col.) Oct '60, 8, 182 (col.), 184, 219 Nov '60, 35 (col.), 40, 182 (col.) Dec '60.
Natl. geog. 98: 359 (col.) Sept '50; 101: 112 Jan '52; 106: 170 (col.) Aug '54, 777-9 (col.) Dec '54; 108: 192 (col.) Aug

'55 109: 234 (col.) Feb '56; 112: 615, 619, 626 (part col.) Nov '57, 782-3 (col.) Dec '57; 113: 765 (col.) Je '58; 118: 22-3 (col.) Jl '60, 503 (col.) Oct '60.
Travel 101: 41 Ap '54, cover, 9, 10, 35 May '54, 27 Je '54; 102: 53 Oct '54, 27, 51 Nov '54, 27 Dec '54; 103: 27 Jan '55, 27 Feb '55, 27 Mar '55, 27 Ap '55, 34, 49, 56, 65 May '55, 21, 29, 59 Je '55; 104: 49 Jl '55, 19, 51 Aug '55, 73 Nov '55; 107: 9, 36 Ap '57; 109: 56-7 Mar '58; 111: 39 Je '59; 112: 37 Dec '59; 113: 81 Ap '60, 61 Je '60.
—— (being launched). Natl. geog. 102: 7 Jl '52.
—— (captain's dinner). Holiday 6: 2 (col.) Aug '49.
—— (cartoon). Holiday 23: 65 Mar '58.
—— (deck). Holiday 20: 70 (col.) Aug '56; 21: 5 (col.) Ap '57; 26: 125, 138 (col.) Sept '59; 27: inside cover (col.) Jan '60; 28: 133 (col.) Jl '60.
—— (dining room). Holiday 20: 132 (col.) Nov '56; 23: 98 (col.) Je '58.
—— (ext. & int.). Holiday 23: 31 (col.) Je '58.
—— (ext. & int., 1834). Amer. heri., vol. 11 no. 5 p. 77 (Aug '60).
—— (interior). Holiday 24: 174 (col.) Nov '58; 26: 7 (col.) Sept '59; 27: 153 (col.) Feb '60, 21 (col.) Je '60; 28: 15 (col.) Sept '60.
Natl. geog. 112: 647-49, 652, 656 (part col.) Nov '57.
—— (night). Holiday 24: 21 Sept '58, 2 (col.) Oct '58 25: 87 (col.) Feb '59, 187 (col.) May '59; 26: 15 (col.) Nov '59; 27: back cover (col.) Feb '60, 178 (col.) Mar '60, 215 Ap '60; 28: 193 (col.) Nov '60.
—— (silhouette). Holiday 19: 110 Jan '56; 26: 42 (col.) Nov '59.
—— (state room). Holiday 24: 182 (col.) Nov '58.
—— (storm at sea). Amer. heri., vol. 6 no. 2 p. 18 (col.) (Feb '55).
—— (swimming pool). Holiday 27: 28 (col.) Jan '60; 28: 133 (col.) Jl '60.
steamship "Empress of Canada." Travel 113: 65 Mar '60.
——, Italian (by Leonardo da Vinci). Travel 114: 70 Jl '60.
—— "Lusitania." Amer. heri., vol. 6 no. 4 p. 45 (Je '55).
—— "Lusitania" (sinking). Amer. heri., vol. 6 no. 4 p. 40 (Je '55).
—— "Pres. Hoover." Holiday 21: 108 (col.) Je '57.
—— "Queen of Bermuda." Natl. geog. 105: 205, 238 (col.) Feb '54.
—— "S.S. America." Natl. geog. 108: 692 (col.) Nov '55.
—— "S.S. Cleveland." Natl. geog. 105: 241 (col.) Feb '54.
—— "Savannah." See "Savannah" ship.
—— "Titanic" (silhouette). Amer. heri., vol. 7 no. 1 p. 46 (Dec '55).
—— "United States." Natl. geog. 115: 836-7 Je '59.
steamship. See also steamboat.

Steatfield, Noel. Jun. bk. of auth., p. 282.
Steber, Eleanor. Cur. biog. p. 731 (1943).
Steel, Johannes. Cur. biog. p. 817 (1941).
steel (sym.). Lehner: Pict. bk. of sym., p. 73.
——, molten. Natl. geog. 107: 314 (col.) Mar '55.
steel forge gears (workers). Natl. geog. 115: 768 (col.) Je '59.
steel ingot, fiery. Natl. geog. 114: 692 (col.) Nov '58.
steel ingots. Holiday 6: 39 (col.) Oct '49.
steel mill. Holiday 6: 46-7 (col.) Oct '49.
Natl. geog. 107: 466 Ap '55.
steel mill (int.). Amer. heri., vol. 11 no. 5 p. 6-7 (col.) (Aug '60).
Natl. geog. 106: 108 (col.) Jl '54.
steel mill ladle, molten. Natl. geog. 116: 396 Sept '59
steel plant (night). Natl. geog. 115: 458-9 (col.) Ap '59.
steel plant (Saar). See Volklingen steel plant.
steel workers. Holiday 6: 42-3 (col.) Oct '49.
steele, funerary. See funerary steele.
Steelman, John R. Cur. biog. p. 819 (1941); (1941); p. 557 (1952).
Steen, Jan (work of). Con. 133: 97 Ap '54; 134: XVI (col.) Nov '54 141: 178 May '58; 143: 274 Je '59; 144: 43 Sept '59, 232 Jan '60.
Natl. geog. 97: 746 (col.) Je '50.
Praeg.: Pict. ency., p. 60 (col.).
Steen, Marguerite. Cur. biog. p. 820 (1941).
Steenwyck, Cornelius. Amer. heri., vol. 10 no. 1 p. 8 (Dec '58).
steeple. See cupola.
steeple cup. See cup, steeple.
Steeplechase park (N.Y.). Amer. heri., vol. 9 no. 4 p. 16-7, 20-1 (col.) (Je '58).
steering wheel. See wheel, steering.
Steers, George. Amer. heri., vol. 9 no. 5 p. 7 (Aug '58).
Stefansson, Vilhjalmur. Cur. biog. p. 801 (1942).
Holiday 20: 1 Oct '56; 22: 149 Dec '57.
Steffens, Lincoln. Amer. heri., vol. 11 no. 2 p. 9 (Feb '60).
Steichen, Lt. Com. Edward. Cur. biog. p. 805 (1942).
Steig, William. Cur. biog. p. 652 (1944).
Steim am Rhein (Switzerland). Holiday 28: 32-3 Aug '60.
Travel 102: 12 Aug '54.
Stein, Gertrude. Amer. heri., vol. 6 no. 2 p. 41 (winter '55).
Stein, Nicholas. Holiday 26: 57 (col.) Jl '59.
stein. Holiday 11: 29 Feb '52.
Steinberg, Saul. Cur. biog. p. 524 (1957).
Steinberg, William. Cur. biog. p. 413 (1958).
Steincrohn, Peter J. Cur. biog. p. 526 (1957).
Steiner, Max. Cur. biog. p. 733 (1943).
Steinhardt, Laurence A. Cur. biog. p. 821 (1941).
Steinhaus, Edward A. Cur. biog. p. 576 (1955).
Steinhausen church ceiling. See ceiling, church (Wurttenberg).
Steinkraus, Herman W. Cur. biog. p. 585 (1949).
Steinman, David B. Cur. biog. p. 528 (1957).
Steins, Stand (New Mexico). Face of Amer.,

p. 64--5 (col.).
stele (Colombia). Praeg.: Pict. ency., p. 15.
——, funeral (Greek 5th cent.). Labande: Naples, p. 94.
——, Greek. Ceram: March of arch., p. 50.
——, Mayan. Ceram: March of arch., p. 282-3.
Stella, Antonietta. Cur. biog. p. 428 (1959).
Stelle, John. Cur. biog. p. 568 (1946).
Stengel, Casey. Cur. biog. p. 587 (1949). Holiday 7: 49 May '50.
Stennis, John C. Cur. biog. p. 587 (1953).
step railing, park. Holiday 27: 7 (col.) Ap '60.
step table. See table, step.
Stephanopoulos, Stephanos. Cur. biog. p. 577 (1955).
Stephen Foster memorial. See Foster memorial, Stephen.
Stephens, Henry Louis (sketches by). Amer. heri., vol. 10 no. 3 p. 106-7 (Ap '59).
Stephens, John A. Cur. biog. p. 603 (1956).
Stepinac, Cardinal Alojzije. Cur. biog. p. 589 (1953).
Stepovich, Michael A. Cur. biog. p. 415 (1958).
steps, beach. Holiday 23: back cover (col.) Mar '58.
——, house (circular entrance). Natl. geog. 103: 544 (col.) Ap '53.
——, library. See library steps.
——, porch. Holiday 10: 45 (col.) Dec '51; 28: 2 Nov '60.
steps & chair. See chair & steps.
stereoscope viewer. Amer. heri., vol. 12 no. 1 p. 113, 121, 125 (Dec '60).
Sterling, John E. Wallace. Cur. biog. p. 607 (1951).
Stern, Arthur Cecil. Cur. biog. p. 606 (1956).
Stern, Bill. Cur. biog. p. 823 (1942). Holiday 26: 202 Nov '59.
Stern, Isaac. Cur. biog. p. 589 (1949).
stern paddle wheel. See wheel, stern paddle.
Sternberg, Hermann Speck von. Amer. heri., vol. 7 no. 2 p. 22 (Feb '56).
Sterne, Hedda. Cur. biog. p. 529 (1957).
Sterne, Maurice. Cur. biog. p. 736 (1943).
sternum. Gray's anatomy, p. 98-100.
sternwheeler boat. See steamboat, sternwheeler.
Stetson, G. Henry. Holiday 22: 83 (col.) Oct '57.
Stetson, John B. Amer. heri., vol. 4 no. 3 p. 29 (spring '53).
Stevens, Alfred (work of). Con. 139: 53 Mar '57.
Stevens, Lt. Col. Ebenezer (by Trumbull). Amer. heri., vol. 9 no. 4 cover (col.) (Je '58).
Stevens, Edmund. Cur. biog. p. 547 (1950).
Stevens, Elisha. Amer. heri., vol. 6 no. 4 p. 63 (Je'55).
Stevens, George C. Cur. biog. p. 559 (1952).
Stevens, Isaac I. Amer. heri., vol. 4 no. 4 p. 57 (summer '53).
Stevens, Com. John Cox. Amer. heri., vol. 9 no. 5 p. 7 (Aug '58).
Stevens, Rise. Cur. biog. p. 824 (1941).
—— (Rose). Holiday 23: 107 Jan '58.
Stevens, Robert T. Cur. biog. p. 591 (1953).
Stevens, Roger L. Cur. biog. p. 580 (1955).
Stevens, Thaddeus. Amer. heri., vol. 6 no. 4

p. 81 (Je '55); vol. 8, no. 1 p. 23 (Dec '56); vol. 11 no. 1 p. 61 (Dec '59); vol. 12 no. 1 p. 47 (Dec '60).
—— (delivers impeachment debate). Amer. heri., vol. 11 no. 1 p. 109 (Dec '59).
Stevens, Thomas Terry Hoar. See Terry—Thomas.
Stevenson, Adlai E. Amer. heri., vol. 8 no. 6 p. 12 (Oct '57).
Cur. biog. p. 591 (1949); p. 441 (1961). Holiday 10: 58 Oct '51; 20: 27 (col.) Sept '56; 28: 81 Dec '60.
Jensen: The White House, p. 291.
—— (exercising). Holiday 26: 55 Jl '59.
Stevenson, Elizabeth. Cur. biog. p. 607 (1956).
Stevenson, George S. Cur. biog. p. 569 (1946).
Stevenson, Robert Louis. Natl. geog. 112: 467 Oct '57.
Stevenson, William E. Cur. biog. p. 738 (1943).
Steward, Joseph (work of). Amer. heri., vol. 4 no. 2 p. 34 (winter '53).
Steward, William Morris. Amer. heri., vol. 6 no. 1 p. 66 (fall '54).
steward, boat. See boat steward.
——, steamship. Holiday 26: 135 (col.) Nov '59.
stewardess, airplane. Holiday 6: 71 (col.) Sept '49, 10 (col.) Nov '49, 69 (col.) Oct '51; 12: 115 (col.) Sept '52, 95 (col.) Oct '52, 25 (col.) Nov '52; 13: 11 (col.) Mar '53, 13 (col.), 99 May '53, 15, 119, 133 (col.) Je '53; 14: 4 Jl '53, 7 (col.) Aug '53, 71, 123 (col.) Oct '53, 69 (col.) Nov '53; 16: inside back cover (col.) Oct '54; 19: 15 (col.) Jan '56; 20: 116 (col.) Oct '56, 25 (col.) Dec '56; 21: 98 Mar '57; 22: 168 Dec '57; 24: 91 (col.) Aug '58; 26: inside cover, 115 (col.) Jl '59, 133 (col.) Sept '59, 8, 125 (col.) Oct '59, 27: 16 Jan '60, 7 (col.) Feb '60, 128, 136 (col.) Ap '60, 59 (col.) May '60; 28: 107 (col.) Aug '60, 80 (col.) Sept '60, 157 Oct '60, 208 (col.) Dec '60.
Natl. geog. 99: 291 (col.) Mar '51, 709 Je '51; 104: 218 Aug '53, 724 (col.) Dec '53.
Travel 106: 7 Sept '56, 65 Nov '56.
—— (Amer., Chinese, Japanese). Holiday 27: 98 (col.) Feb '60.
—— (cocktails). Holiday 20: 109 (col.) Dec '56.
—— (Columbia). Holiday 27: 185 (col.) Je '60.
—— (comic). Holiday 23: 67 Je '58.
—— (head). Holiday 26: 93 Nov '59.
—— (Japanese). Holiday 23: 19 (col.) Ap '58.
—— (serving meal). Holiday 21: 187 May '57.
——, Irish airline. Holiday 24: 135 Oct '58, 97 Nov '58; 26: 206 Dec '59; 27: 13 Je '60.
——, Israeli airline. Holiday 26: 74 (col.) Dec '59.
——, train. Holiday 19: 9 Mar '56; 20: 15 (col.) Nov '56; 21: 121 Feb '57; 22: 106 Sept '57; 23: 44 Ap '58, 170 May '58.
——, train (head). Holiday 18: 5 (col.) Jl '55, 90 (col.) Nov '55; 25: 138 Mar '59; 27: 48 Ap '60.

Stewart, Anna Bird. Cur. biog. p. 601 (1948).
Stewart, Capt. Charles. Amer. heri., vol. 6 no. 3 p. 60 (Ap '55).
—— (by Sully). Holiday 7: 107 (col.) Feb '50.

Stewart, Donald Ogden. Cur. biog. p. 825 (1941).

Stewart, George R. Cur. biog. p. 807 (1942).

Stewart, James. Cur. biog. p. 827 (1941); p. 399 (1960). Holiday 5: 40 (col.), 47 Jan '49.

Stewart, Kenneth. Cur. biog. p. 739 (1943).

Stewart, Asso. Justice Potter. Cur. biog. p. 430 (1959).

Stewart, Robert. Amer. heri., vol. 6 no. 6 p. 7 (Oct '55).

Stewart, Sir William Drummond. Amer. heri., vol. 7 no. 2 p. 8 (Feb '56).

stewpan (by Richardson). Rawson: Ant. pict. bk., p. 83.

"stick dance" See Trinidad "Stick dance".

stick fighters, Nuba. Natl. geog. 99: 265 Feb '51.

stick horse (toy). Holiday 18: 192 Dec '55.

Stickney, Dorothy. Cur. biog. p. 519 (1942).

Stiebeling, Hazel K. Cur. biog. p. 549 (1950).

Stieler, Joseph (work of). Amer. heri., vol. 6 no. 2 p. 57 (col.) (winter '55).

Stignani, Ebe. Cur. biog. p. 592 (1949).

Stikker, Dirk U. Cur. biog. p. 550 (1950); p. 405 (1962).

stile (between fields). Rawson: Ant. pict. bk., p. 38.

Stiles, Ezra (Pres. of Yale) (by Samuel King). Con. 141: 131 Ap '58.

Still, William Grant. Cur. biog. p. 830 (1941).

still, "corn shine". Rawson: Ant. pict. bk., p. 31.

"Still life with guitar" (Hayden). Con. 143: 92 Ap '59.

stills, solar water. See water stills, solar.

stilt dancer (Nigeria). Natl. geog. 110: 340 (col.) Sept '56.

stilt walker. Holiday 15: 100 Ap '54.

—— (Belgium). Holiday 23: 19 May '58.

—— (circus). Durant: Pict. hist. of Amer. circus, p. 272.

stilt walkers. Natl. geog. 114: 287 Aug '58.

stilts (boy). Holiday 10: 130 Oct '51.

—— (carnival). Natl. geog. 109: 215 (col.) Feb '56.

Stilwell, Lt. Gen. Joseph W. Cur. biog. p. 809 (1942).

Stirnweiss, George H. Cur. biog. p. 571 (1946).

stirrup, saddle. Rawson: Ant. pict. bk., p. 65, 68.

stirrups, rider's (Chile). Natl. geog. 117: 211 Feb '60.

Stock, Joseph Whiting (work of). Amer. heri., vol. 11 no. 3 p. 53 (col.) (Ap '60).

stock brokers (cartoon). Amer. heri., vol. 9 no. 5 p. 103 (Aug '58).

stock exchange (N.Y.). Holiday 5: 90 Ap '49.

stock exchange. See also Copenhagen stock exchange.

stockade, elephants (India). Natl. geog. 112: 497-9 Oct '57.

stockade (Indian attack). Brooks: Growth of a nation, p. 171.

——, Kenya (against MauMau). Natl. geog. 112: 98-9 (col.) Jl '57.

Stockberger, Warner W. Cur. biog. p. 831 (1941).

Stockbridge, Frank Parker. Cur. biog. p. 832 (1941).

Stockholm (Sweden). Holiday 22: 107 (col.) Nov '57. Natl. geog. 98: 630 (col.) Nov '50; 101: 686 May '52. Travel 101: 8 May '54; 102: 31 Oct '54; 107: cover, 35 Ap '57; 111: 23-5 May '59.

—— (Foresta hotel). Travel 110: 41 Jl '58.

—— (map). Travel 111: 22 May '59.

—— (royal palace). Holiday 20: 38 (col.) Aug '56. Travel 107: 35 Ap '57.

—— (royal palace, int.). Con. 141: 13-7 Mar '58.

—— (town hall). Travel 104: 56 Oct '55.

stocking mill (Russian women). Natl. geog. 116: 367 Sept '59.

stockings (on forms). Natl. geog. 99: 115 Jan '51.

——, Christmas. See Christmas stockings.

stocks (man in). Holiday 24: 118 Aug '58.

stocks (men). Holiday 11: 141 Je '52.

——, antique. Rawson: Ant. pict. bk., p. 42.

——, colonial. Holiday 20: 106 Sept '56; 26: 119 Aug '59, 97 Nov '59.

——, pioneer punishment. Holiday 15: 108 Mar '54.

——, public (Williamsburg). Holiday 18: 114 Aug '55.

stockyard (Chicago). Holiday 10: 39 (col.) Oct '51.

—— (Kansas City). Holiday 7: 49 (col.) Mar '50.

—— (Oklahoma City). Holiday 7: 117 May '50.

—— (Tenn.). Holiday 8: 37 Nov '50.

Stoddard, George D. Cur. biog. p. 573 (1946).

Stoeckl, Edouard de. See deStoeckl, Edouard

Stoffels, Hendrickje (Rembrandt). Praeg.: Pict. ency., p. 336 (col.).

Stoica, Chivu. Cur. biog. p. 431 (1959).

Stoke Poges (church). Natl. geog. 108: 311 (col.) Sept '55.

Stokes, Anson Phelps, jr. Cur. biog. p. 407 (1962).

Stokes, Richard R. Cur. biog. p. 609 (1951).

Stokes, Thomas L. Cur. biog. p. 612 (1947). Holiday 7: 101 Feb '50.

Stokes, Capt. William. Holiday 21: 55 (col.) May '57.

Stokesay castle (Shropshire, Eng.). Holiday 16: 28 (col.) Jl '54; 17: 12 (col.) Mar '55.

Stokowski, Leopold. Cooper: Con. ency. of music, p. 295. Cur. biog. p. 833 (1941); p. 593 (1953).

Stolk, William C. Cur. biog. p. 596 (1953).

Stolz, Mary Slattery. Cur. biog. p. 597 (1953).

Stolz, Robert. Cur. biog. p. 741 (1943).

stomach. Gray's anatomy, p. 1206-11.

stomach. (lymphatic system). Gray's anatomy, p. 718.

stomacher, diamond. Con. 144: 197 Dec '59.

Stone, Abraham. Cur. biog. p. 561 (1952).

Stone, Barton W. Amer. heri., vol. 10 no. 4 p. 29 (Je '59).

Stone, Gen. Charles P. Amer. heri., vol. 6 no. 1 p. 16 (fall '54).

Stone, Edward D. Cur. biog. p. 417 (1958).

Stone, Harlan Fiske. Amer. heri., vol. 9 no. 3 p. 25 (Ap '58).

Cur. biog. p. 835 (1941). Holiday 7: 75 Feb '50.
Stone, Thomas. Natl. geog. 105: 464 (col.) Ap '54.
Stone, Maj. Gen. William S. Cur. biog. p. 402 (1960).
stone (sym.). Lehner: Pict. bk. of sym., p. 73.
stone age cave carvings. Natl. geog. 113: 698 (col.) May '58.
stone age cave dwellers. See cave dwellers (stone age).
stone-age man. See Tiwi tribesmen (Australia).
stone carving (Gemma Augustea). Praeg.: Pict. ency., p. 144.
——, mountain side (Lhasa). Natl. geog. Natl. geog. 108: 21 (col.) Jl '55.
"Stone City" (Grant Wood). Amer. heri., vol. 6 no. 1 p. 42 (col.) (fall '54).
stone flowers (marble inlay). Natl. geog. 118: 474-5 (col.) Oct '60.
"Stone house" (Georgetown). Natl. geog. 103: 532 Ap '53.
"Stone library" (int.). Amer. heri., vol. 10 no. 3 p. 26 (col.) (Ap '59).
Stone mountain (girls beside). Natl. geog. 105: 292 Mar '54.
stone moving contest. Natl. geog. 99: 573 (col.) May '51.
stone pillar, pre-Inca. Holiday 20: 144 Nov '56.
stone slicing machine. Natl. geog. 99: 580 May '51.
Stonehenge (Eng.). Holiday 14: 54 Nov '53; 23: 98-9 Ap '58. Natl. geog. 117:: 846-65 (part col.) Je '60. Travel 113: 5 Feb '60; 114: 3 Jl '60.
—— (map). Natl. geog. 117: 851 (col.) Je '60.
—— (reconstruction). Praeg: Pict. ency., p. 169.
Stoneleigh abbey (Eng.). Con. 141: XLVIII Je '58.
Stoneman, George. Pakula: Centennial album, p. 267.
stonemason, India. Travel 111: 28-9 Jan '59.
stonemasons, Egyptian. Ceram: March of arch., p. 153.
stool. Holiday 10: 24 Sept '51.
—— (for men). Natl. geog. 107: 344 Mar '55.
——, board back. Rawson: Ant. pict. bk., p. 16.
, box (16th cent.). Con. ency. of ant., vol. 1, pl. 2.
——, Adam. Con. 141: 43 Mar '58.
——, antique. Con. 133: 255 Je '54; 140: 149 Dec '57, 227 Jan '58.
——, antique Eng. Con. 136: 241 Jan '56.
——, antique privy. Con. 129: 89-91 Je '52.
——, antique 17th cent. Con. 141: XLIV Ap '58.
——, camel saddle. Holiday 18: 144 Nov '55.
——, cane (William III). Holiday Con. 127: 13 Mar '51.
——, captain's. Holiday 18: 187 Dec '55; 20: 114 Sept '56, 178 Nov '56; 22: 176 Oct '57, 176 Nov '57, 251 Dec '57; 24: 148 Oct '58, 201 Nov '58, 230 Dec '58; 26: 194 Nov '59, 252 Dec '59.
——, dressing (18th cent.). Con. 133: XXVIII Mar '54.
——, fireside. Holiday 18: 30 Nov '55.
——, foot. Holiday 28: 137 (col.) Nov '60.

——, foot (18th cent.). Con. 139: XLIV May '57.
——, George I. Con. 140: XXIV Dec '57.
——, George II. Con. 129: XX Je '52.
——, Georgian. Con. 138: 45 Sept '56; 143: XX Je '59.
——, joined (16th cent.). Con. 138: 183 Dec '56.
——, joined (17th cent.). Con. ency. of ant., vol. 1, pl. 2, 11.
——, Portuguese. Con. 143: 195 May '59.
——, Queen Anne. Con. 142: XLVI Nov '58.
——, Stuart. Con. 145: 168 May '60.
——, Viennese (18th cent.). Con. ency. of ant., vol. 3, pl. 24.
——, wicker. Holiday 18: 199 Dec '55.
——, William & Mary. Con. 143: XXIX Ap '59.
——, William Kent. Con. 143: XXIX Ap '59.
stools, antique group posing. Amer. heri., vol. 12 no. 1 p. 117 (Dec '60).
——, milking. Rawson: Ant. pict. bk., p. 64.
Stoopnagle, Col. Cur. biog. p. 613 (1947).
stop light. Holiday 18: 184 (col.) Dec '55.
"Stop" road sign. Holiday 21: 139 Je '57.
Stoph. Col. Gen. Willi. Cur. biog. p. 403 (1960).
stopper, glass bottle. Holiday 28: 53 Nov '60.
Storck, Abraham (work of). Con. 136: IX Sept '55; 144: XXXIX Sept '59.
store (Bolivia). Holiday 20: 84 Nov '56.
—— (maple syrup). Natl. geog. 105: 482 (col.) Ap '54.
——, Abe Lincoln's. Travel 113: 30-1 Feb '60.
——, country. Amer. heri., vol. 10 no. 2 p. 70 (Feb '59). Holiday 18: 39 (col.) Jl '55. Natl. geog. 108: 523 (col.) Oct '55. Travel 113: 31 Mar '60.
——, country (old). Amer. heri., vol. 6 no. 1 p. 22 (col.), 24-5 (fall '54).
——, country general. Natl. geog. 107: 755 (col.) Je '55.
——, early western. Horan: Pict. hist. of wild west, p. 60.
——, general (old). Holiday 21: 72 (col.) Je '57. Natl. geog. 98: 119 (col.) Jl '50.
——, general (Ala.). Holiday 27: 55 (col.) Mar '60.
——, general (1898). Brooks: Growth of a nation, p. 234.
——, general (men & women). Natl. geog. 118: 570-1 (col.) Oct '60.
——, general trading post (Canada). Natl. geog. 108: 225 Aug '55.
——, grocery (Alaska). Natl. geog. 109: 748 (col.) Je '56.
——, Japanese. Natl. geog. 118: 742 (col.) Dec '60.
——, rural hill (int.). Natl. geog. 106: 112 (col.) Jl '54.
——, village. Natl. geog. 112: 306 (col.) Sept '57.
store window (dress display). See dress display (store window).
Storey, Moorefield. Amer. heri., vol. 11 no. 4 p. 33 (Je '60).
Storey, Robert G. Cur. biog. p. 598 (1953).
stork with baby (sym.). Lehner: Pict. bk. of sym., p. 56.

Storke, Thomas M. Cur. biog. (1963).

storm (wind sym.). Lehner: Pict. bk. of sym., p. 14.

storm at sea (ship). Amer. heri., vol. 6 no. 2 p. 18 (col.) (winter '55).
Ceram: March of arch., p. 197.

"Stormalong" (folk hero). Amer. heri., vol. 1, no. 3 p. 76 (col.) (spring '50).

Storms, Harrison A., jr. Cur. biog. (1963).

Storrowtown (Mass.). Travel 113: 29-31 Mar '60.

Story, Joseph. Amer. heri., vol. 7 no. 1 p. 109 Dec '55.

storybook (scenes). Int. gr. soc.: Arts . . . p. 59 (col.).

Stoss, Viet (wood carving by). Con. ency. of ant., vol. 3, pl. 54.

Stout, Rex. Cur. biog. p. 576 (1946).

Stout, Ruth A. Cur. biog. p. 433 (1959).

Stout, Wesley Winans. Cur. biog. p. 839 (1941).

stove. Holiday 7: 81 Mar '50.

—— (Alaska). Natl. geog. 99: 556 Ap '51.

stove (country store). Amer. heri., vol. 6 no. 1 p. 24 (Dec '54); vol. 10 no. 2 p. 70 (Feb '59).
Natl. geog. 108: 523 (col.) Oct '55.

—— (Japan). Natl. geog. 118: 757 (col.) Dec '60.

—— (outdoor cooking). Natl. geog. 115: 727 May '59.

—— (woman). Holiday 26: 90 (col.) Aug '59.

——, antique. Amer. heri., vol. 3 no. 4 p. 36 (summer '52); vol. 8 no. 1 p. 99 (Dec '56); vol. 8 no. 4 p. 66, 74 (Je '57).

——, antique (general store). Holiday 27: 55 (col.) Mar '60.

——, antique Franklin. Amer. heri., vol. 1 no. 2 p. 53 (winter '50).

——, dried mud (India). Natl. geog. 109: 575 Ap '56.

——, elec. cook. Int. gr. soc.: Arts . . . p. 171 (col.).

——, gas cook. Holiday 22: 112 (col.) Oct '57, 20 (col.) Nov '57, 194 Dec '57.

——, heating (1836). Holiday 20: 31 (col.) Sept '56.

——, iron cook. Holiday 21: 5 (col.) Jan '57.

——, modern. Holiday 24: 121 (col.) Oct '58.

——, painted (18th cent.). Con. 144: 98, 101 Nov '59.

——, tile (Swiss). Natl. geog. 98: 242 (col.) Aug '50.

Stowe, Harriet Beecher. Amer. heri., vol. 4 no. 2 p. 20 (winter '53); vol. 11 no. 1 p. 68 (Dec '59).

Stowe (Vt.). Natl. geog. 99: 572 (col.) May '51.

Strachan, Paul A. Cur. biog. p. 564 (1952).

Strachey, John. Cur. biog. p. 578 (1946).

Straight, Michael. Cur. biog. p. 654 (1944).

strainer, punched. Rawson: Ant. pict. bk., p. 83.

Strait of Messina (deep sea life). Natl. geog. 104: 580-617 (part col.) Nov '53.

—— (map). Natl. geog. 104: 585 Nov '53.

Stranahan, Frank. Cur. biog. p. 611 (1951).

"Strand from Charing Cross" (by Boys). Con. ency. of ant., vol. 1, pl. 140.

Strang, Ruth. Cur. biog. p. 405 (1960).

"Strange masks" (Ensor). Praeg.: Ant. pict. bk., p. 460 (col.).

strapwork ornament. Con. ency. of ant., vol. 1, p. 22.

Strasberg, Lee. Cur. biog. p. 407 (1960).

Strasberg, Susan. Cur. biog. p. 419 (1958).

Strasbourg. Holiday 10: 54-5 Jl '51.

Strasbourg house (15th cent.). Holiday 23: cover (col.) Jan '58.

strategic air command (survival kit). Natl. geog. 103: 574 (col.) May '53.

Stratemeyer, Lt. Gen. George E. Cur. biog. p. 614 (1951).

Stratford (Conn., Shakespeare festival theatre). Travel 113: 29 May '60.

"Stratford Hall" (Colonial home of the Lees, Vir.). Brooks: Growth of a nation, p. 66. Holiday 28: 9 Sept '60.

—— (ext. & int.). Holiday 13: 52-5 Jan '53.

Stratford-on-Avon. Holiday 10: 94-9 (col.) Jl '51.

stratocruiser. Natl. geog. 99: 290 (col.) Mar '51.

stratofortress plane. Natl. geog. 112: 293 Aug '57.

stratojet (smoke). Natl. geog. 112: 289 Aug '57.

Stratton, Charles. See "Tom Thumb."

Stratton, Lt. Com. Dorothy C. Cur. biog. p. 743 (1943).

Stratton, Julius A. Cur. biog. p. 405 (1963).

Stratton, Samuel W. Amer. heri., vol. 9 no. 6 p. 57 (Oct '58).

Stratton, William G. Cur. biog. p. 601 (1953).

Straub, Johan Baptist (wood carving by). Con. ency. of ant., vol. 3, pl. 55.

Straus, Mr. and Mrs. Isidor. Amer. heri., vol. 7 no. 1 p. 51 (Dec '55).

Straus, Jack I. Cur. biog. p. 565 (1952).

Straus, Michael W. Cur. biog. p. 567 (1952).

Straus, Nathan. Cur. biog. p. 656 (1944).

Straus, Oskar. Cur. biog. p. 658 (1944).

Straus, Roger W. Cur. biog. p. 569 (1952).

Strauss, Anna Lord. Cur. biog. p. 876 (1945).

Strauss, Franz Josef. Cur. biog. p. 531 (1957).

Strauss, Jacobus G. N. Cur. biog. p. 615 (1951).

Strauss, Johann, the younger (by Horowitz). Cooper: Con. ency. of music, p. 296.

Strauss, Joseph (statue). Natl. geog. 116: 605 (col.) Nov '59.

Strauss, Levi. Amer. heri., vol. 4 no. 1 p. 49 (fall '52).

Strauss, Lewis L. Cur. biog. p. 615 (1947).

Strauss, Richard. Cooper: Con. ency. of music, p. 297.
Cur. biog. p. 660 (1944).

Stravinsky, Igor. Cur. biog. p. 602 (1953).
Int. gr. soc.: Arts . . . p. 139 (col.).

—— (by Picasso). Cooper: Con. ency. of music, p. 298.

straw hat, man's. See hat, man's straw.

strawberry dish, George I silver. Con. 142: V Sept '58.

strawberry dishes, George II silver. Con. 141: XXV Ap '58.

strawstack (on camel). Natl. geog. 113: 502 (col.) Ap '58.

student, college (studying). Holiday 11: 53 (col.) Feb '52.

——, Eton (back view). Natl. geog. 108: 348 Sept '55.

——, German. Int. gr. soc.: Arts . . . p. 153 (col.).

——, Yale. Holiday 18: 34 (col.) Nov '55.

students (boys & girls). Holiday 10: 44 (col.) Dec '51.

—— (boy's school). Holiday 18: 41 Jl '55.

—— (dancing, playing). Natl. geog. 115: 789 (col.) Je '59.

—— (examine fossils). Natl. geog. 105: 381, 383 (col.) Mar '54.

—— (girl, books, eyeglasses). Holiday 11: 62-3 May '52.

—— (girl studying). Holiday 11: 60 (col.) May '52.

—— (language classroom). Natl. geog. 103: 541 (col.) Ap '53.

—— (make geiger counters). Natl. geog. 105: 83 Jan '54.

—— (school room). Holiday 19: 97 Jan '56; 22: 8 Oct '57. Natl. geog. 116: 64 (col.) Jl '59.

—— 'sword dance.' Natl. geog. 111: 265 (col.) Feb '57.

——, Aiken Preparatory school. Holiday 19: 100-1 May '56.

——, Amer. college (Mexico). Natl. geog. 103: 325, 330, 335-49 (col.) Mar '53.

——, Andover college. Holiday 7: 61 (col.) Mar '50.

——, Auckland univ. (studying). Natl. geog. 101: 429 (col.) Ap '52.

——, Bahia univ. Holiday 20: 70 Aug '56.

——, Beirut univ. (medical). Natl. geog. 113: 482 Ap '58.

——, California univ. Natl. geog. 110: 221 (col.) Aug '56.

——, college. Natl. geog. 107: 198 (col.) Feb '55.

——, college (boys). Holiday 21: 62-3 (col.) Mar '57.

——, college (Chile). Natl. geog. 117: 219 (col.) Feb '60.

——, college (classroom). Natl. geog. 107: 207 (col.), 214 Feb '55.

——, college (Concord, N.H.). Natl. geog. 99: 123 (col.) Jan '51.

——, college (girls). Natl. geog. 105: 295, 301 (col.) Mar '54.

——, college (girls & professor, outdoor class). Holiday 11: 65 (col.) May '52.

——, college (prize steer). Natl. geog. 103: 296 (col.) Mar '53.

——, college (studying). Holiday 10: 54 Sept '51. Natl. geog. 103: 296 (col.) Mar '53.

——, Cornell univ. (party). Holiday 12: 114-5 Nov '52.

——, Dartmouth (skating). Holiday 11: 50 Feb '52.

——, Egyptian school. Natl. geog. 106: 771 (col.) Dec '54.

——, Harvard (Lampoon electors). Natl. geog. 107: 780 (col.) Je '55.

——, King's (Eng.). Natl. geog. 104: 304 (col.) Sept '53.

——, McGill univ. Natl. geog. 98: 354 (col.) Sept '50.

——, Miami univ. Natl. geog. 113: 65 Jan '58.

——, North Dakota univ. (football trophy). Natl. geog. 100: 322 (col.) Sept '51.

——, Phillips Exeter Academy. Holiday 20: 71-3 (part col.) Dec '56.

——, Robert college. Natl. geog. 112: 402-3, 406-7, 410, 414 (part col.) Sept '57.

——, Russian college (class room). Natl. geog. 116: 364 (col.) Sept '59.

——, School of design (teacher). Holiday 11: 114 (col.) May '52.

——, Syracuse univ. Natl. geog. 110: 596 (col.) Nov '56.

——, Tunisian (marching). Natl. geog. 114: 725 Nov '58.

——, Turkish air (teacher). Natl. geog. 106: 821 Dec '54.

——, university (snowshoes). Natl. geog. 109: 762 (col.) Je '56.

——, university (West Indies). Natl. geog. 105: 358 (col.) Mar '54.

——, Univ. of Va. Natl. geog. 97: 554-92 (col.) May '50.

——, Vienna (dancing). Natl. geog. 115: 178-9 (col.) Feb '59.

——, William & Mary college. Natl. geog. 106: 440-1, 483 (col.) Oct '54.

——, Yale univ. Natl. geog. 112: 328-9 (col.) Sept '57.

students. See also schoolroom (teacher & students); teacher, children; teacher & students.

students singing (Brown college). Holiday 18: 37 Nov '55.

studio, art. See art studio.

——, artist's floating. Natl. geog. 106: 808 (col.) Dec '55.

——, sculpture (int.). Holiday 26: 42 (col.) Sept '59.

studio of the Finn, Aalto. Int. gr. soc.: Arts . . . p. 125 (col.).

Stuhlinger, Ernst. Cur. biog. p. 535 (1957).

Stummvoll, Josef. Cur. biog. p. 411 (1960).

Stump, Vice adm. Felix B. Cur. biog. p. 605 (1953).

stump, Boston England. See "Boston stump" tower.

stump fence. See fence, stump.

stump puller. Rawson: Ant. pict. bk., p. 21.

stunts, state fair. Natl. geog. 106: 299-301 (col.) Sept '54.

stupa (sym.). Lehner: Pict. bk. of sym., p. 46.

—— (India). Int. gr. soc.: Arts . . . p. 13 (col.). Praeg.: Pict. ency., p. 524.

Stupa gateway (Sanchi, India). Praeg.: Pict. ency., p. 563.

Sturbridge village. See Old Sturbridge village.

Sturdee, Lt. Gen. Vernon A. H. Cur. biog. p. 812 (1942).

Sturges, Preston. Cur. biog. p. 844 (1941).

Sturgis, Lt. Gen. Samuel D., jr. Cur. biog. p. 611 (1956).

Sturzo, Luigi. Cur. biog. p. 587 (1946).

Stuyvesant, Peter. Amer. heri., vol. 5 no. 1

p. 8 (fall '53); vol. 10 no. 1 p. 8 (col.) (Dec '58).

Stuyvesant, Susan Rivington (work of). Amer. heri., vol. 10 no. 1 p. 9 (col.) (Dec '58).

Stwosz, Wit (Polish artist, work of). Natl. geog. 114: 384 (col.) Sept '58.

style show (Switzerland). Natl. geog. 110: 446-7 Oct '56.

Suakin island (Anglo-Egyptian Sudan). Travel 107: 26-7 Mar '57.

Subandrio (foreign minister of Indonesia). Cur. biog (1963).

submarine. Natl. geog. 102: 614-26, 631-6 (part col.) Nov '52; 116: 297 (col.) Sept '59.
—— (North Pole). Natl. geog. 115: 2-19 (part col.) Jan '59.
—— (int., men). Natl. geog. 97: 64 Jan '50.
——, atomic (launching). Natl. geog. 112: 333 Sept '57.
——, 1st true (1776). Amer. heri., vol. 9 no. 3 p. 109 (Ap '58).
——, guided missile. Natl. geog. 113: 12 (col.) Jan '58.
——, "Amberjack." Natl. geog. 97: 51 (col.), 59 Jan '50.
——, "Hunley" (Civil war). Amer. heri., vol. 9 no. 3 p. 48 (col.) (Ap '58).
——, "Skate." See "Skate" submarine.

submarine torpedo boat, Confederate (1863). Natl. geog. 99: 199 (col.) Feb '51.

submarine "Triton." Natl. geog. 118: 590, 598-615 (part col.) Nov '60.

submarine. See also atomic tanker.

submarines (in tank). Natl. geog. 102: 625 (col.), 630 Nov '52.

subway (Moscow). Holiday 18: 102 Jl '55. Natl. geog. 116: 727 (col.) Dec '59.

success (sym.). Lehner: Pict. bk. of sym., p. 84-5.

Suckley, Margaret (with Fala). Jensen: The White House, p. 247.

suckling pig (sym.). Lehner: Pict. bk. of sym., p. 63

Sucksdorff, Arne E. Cur. biog. p. 613 (1956).

Sucre (Bolivia). Holiday 8: 57 (col.) Nov '50.

sucriers, antique. Con. 139: LIX May '57.

Sudan. Natl. geog. 103: 248-72 (part col.) Feb '53.
—— (hunter, huts, dogs). Natl. geog. 114: 214 (col.) Aug '58.
—— (map). Natl. geog. 103: 250 Feb '53; 107: 700 May '55.

Sudanese guard. Natl. geog. 104: 47 (col.) Jl '53.

Suddaby, Rowland (work of). Con. 133: 184 May '54.

"Sudden squall in Hyde Park" (Rowlandson). Con. ency. of ant., vol. 1, pl. 139.

Sues, Ralf. Cur. biog. p. 666 (1944).

Suez canal. Natl. geog. 101: 107-15 Jan '52; 111: 124-39 Jan '57; 114: 718-9 Nov '58.

"Suffolk lock" (Constable). Con. 142: cover (col.), p. 37 Sept '58.

"Suffolk view" (Gainsborough). Con. 145: V (col.) Je '60.

suffragette (1912). Amer. heri., vol. 10 no. 6 p. 18 (Oct '59).

suffragettes (pickets, 1920). Jensen: The White House, p. 211.

sugar (sym.). Lehner: Pict. bk. of sym., p. 73.
—— (in freight cars). Natl. geog. 99: 454 (col.) Ap '51.

sugar & creamer, Luxemburg. Holiday 18: 63 Nov '55.

sugar basin (Chelsea-Derby). Con. ency. of ant., vol. 1, pl. 56.

sugar basket, cut glass & silver (Norwegian). Con. 145: 17 Mar '60.

sugar bowl. Holiday 18: 121 Oct '55.
——, Chelsea. Con. 138: 107 Nov '56.
——, Egyptian service. Con. 143: 229 Je '59.
——, Irish glass stemmed. Con. ency. of ant., vol. 3 pl. 52.
——, Portuguese. Con. 144: XLVI Dec '59.
——, silver (18th cent.). Con. 143: 275 Je '59.
——, silver (18th cent. Swedish). Con. 141: 11 Mar '58.
——, silver (George I). Con. 135: XXVI Ap '55; 140: XLVIII Nov '57.
——, silver (George II). Con. 139: XI Ap '57.
——, silver (George III). Con. 142: XXXIII Nov '58; 144: VII Nov '59.
——, silver (George IV). Con. 142: XXXVIII Nov '58.
——, silver (Louis XV). Con. 143: XXVI Je '59.
——, silver (William III). Con. 145: 187 May '60.
——, Swansea. Con. ency. of ant., vol. 1, pl. 56.

sugar box, silver (Amer., 18th cent.). Con. 135: 73 Mar '55.
——, silver (18th cent.). Con. ency. of ant., vol. 1, pl. 88.
Con. 143: XI Mar '59.
——, silver (George I). Con. 145: 187 May '60.

sugar cane mill. See mill, sugar cane.

sugar casket (Charles II). Con. 142: 256 Jan '59, 197 Dec '58.

sugar castor. See castor, sugar.

sugar dredger. Rawson: Ant. pict. bk., p. 83.
—— (George III). Con. 136: 57 Sept '55.

Sugar Loaf Rock (Rio de Janeiro). Holiday 5: 137 (col.) Mar '49; 6: inside cover (col.) Sept '49; 7: 75 (col.) Jan '50. Natl. geog. 107: 324 (col.) Mar '55; 108: 748 (col.) Dec '55. Travel 103: 7 Mar '55.
—— (South Seas). Natl. geog. 97: 86 (col.) Jan '50.

sugar making (Pakistan jungle). Natl. geog. 107: 419 (col.) Mar '55.

sugar mill. Travel 103: 41 Feb '55.
—— (Puerto Rico). Natl. geog. 99: 444 (col.) Ap '51.
——, ancient (St. Kitts). Travel 105: 12 Feb '56.

mill & plantation (Hawaii). Natl. geog. 118: 42 (col.) Jl '60.

sugar plantation (Hawaii). Amer. heri., vol. 2 no. 3 inside cover (spring '51).

sugar press, Tahitian. Nat. geog. 112: 768-9 (col.) Dec '57.

sugar spoon. Travel 101: 45 May '54.

sugar urn (Paul Revere silver). Con. 141: 188 May '58.
sugar vase. Con. 127: 46 Mar '51.
——, silver (Italian). Con. 144: 156 Dec '59.
——, silver-gilt (18th cent.). Con. ency. of ant., vol. 1, pl. 89.
Sugarbush (Vt.). Holiday 28: 90-5 (part col.) Dec '60.
sugarloaf cones (Cappadocia, Turkey). Natl. geog. 100: 186 Aug '51.
Suggia, Guilhermina (by John). Cooper: Con. ency. of music, p. 170 (col.).
Suggs, Louise. Cur. biog. p. 409 (1962).
Sugrue, Thomas. Cur. biog. p. 604 (1948).
Suhr, Otto. Cur. biog. p. 584 (1955).
Suhrawardy, Hussain S. Cur. biog. p. 537 (1957).
Suisum Valley (Cal.). Face of Amer., p. 52-3 (col.).
suitcase. Holiday 5: 18 (col.) Jan '49, 90 Feb '49, 72 Mar '49, 8, 76 Ap '49, 6, 78, 150, 159 Je '49; 6: 80 Jl '49, 93, 127 Sept '49, 82 (col.) Oct '49, 79 Nov '49, 1, 11, 29, 131 Dec '49; 7: 106, 109 Je '50; 8: 10 (col.) Jl '50, 14 Aug '50, 83 Sept '50, 72 Oct '50, 28 Nov '50, 11, 33, 89, 155 Dec '50.
    Travel 105: 39 Feb '56; 106: 52 Jl '56.
—— (man's clothes). Holiday 18: 29 (col.) Nov '55.
—— (open). Travel 101: 42 Je '54.
——, Wordsworth's (Eng.). Natl. geog. 109: 544 Ap '56.
suitcase. See also luggage.
Suits, Chauncey G. Cur. biog. p. 555 (1950).
sukiyaki, Japanese. Holiday 18: 64 (col.) Jl '55.
sukkah, Jewish. Natl. geog. 115: 519 (col.) Ap '59.
Suleyman mosque (Turkey). Travel 101: 41 May '54.
Suleymaniyeh mosque (Istanbul). Osward: Asia Minor, pl. 82.
"Sulgrave Manor" (Eng., ancestral home of Geo. Washington). Amer. heri., vol. 8 no. 6 p. 112 (Oct '57).
Sulieman mosque. See Mosque of Sulieman.
sulky (man, horse). Holiday 24: 157 Nov '58.
sulky race. Natl. geog. 106: 307 (col.) Sept '54.
Sullavan, Margaret. Cur. biog. p. 669 (1944).
Sullivan, Aloysius M. Cur. biog. p. 608 (1953).
Sullivan, Brian. Cur. biog. p. 539 (1957).
Sullivan, Ed. Cur. biog. p. 571 (1952).
Sullivan, Francis L. Cur. biog. p. 587 (1955).
Sullivan, Gael. Cur. biog. p. 619 (1947).
Sullivan, Harry Stack. Cur. biog. p. 813 (1942).
Sullivan, Henry J. Cur. biog. p. 422 (1958).
Sullivan, John L. Cur. biog. p. 606 (1948).
    Holiday 25: 78 Feb '59.
—— (boxing match). Amer. heri., vol. 10 no. 5 p. 95 (Aug '59).
Sullivan, John William. Amer. heri., vol. 10 no. 5 p. 54, 57, 59 (Aug '59).
Sullivan, Leonor K. Cur. biog. p. 590 (1954).
Sully, Thomas (work of). Amer. heri., vol. 7 no. 2 p. 64 (col.) (Feb '56).
    Holiday 7: 107 (col.) Feb '50.

Natl. geog. 97: 556 May '50.
Sully chateau. See chateau, Sully.
sulphur (sym.). Lehner: Pict. bk. of sym., p. 73.
——, liquid. Natl. geog. 118: 112-3 (col.) Jl '60.
sulphur banks (rocks, Hawaii). Natl. geog. 115: 811 (col.) Je '59.
sulphur mine (Miss.). Natl. geog. 118: 718-9 (col.) Nov '60.
Sultan (Aden colony). Natl. geog. 111: 254 Feb '57.
Sultan (Zanzibar). Natl. geog. 101: 265 (col.) Feb '52.
Sultan Ahmed, mosque of. See Mosque of Sultan Ahmed.
Sultan of the Maldives. Natl. geog. 111: 830 (col.) Je '57.
"Sultana" steamboat. See steamboat ("Sultana").
Sultan's palace (Middle East). Travel 106: 47 Nov '56.
Sultan's throne. Natl. geog. 103: 224 Feb '53.
Sulzberger, Arthur Hays. Cur. biog. p. 747 (1943).
Sulzberger, Cyrus L. Cur. biog. p. 672 (1944).
Sumac, Yma. Cur. biog. p. 588 (1955).
Sumatra. Natl. geog. 99: 33-9 (col.) Jan '51; 108: 388-92 (part col.) Sept '55.
    Travel 102: 21-2 Nov '54.
Sumatra dancers. Natl. geog. 108: 390 (col.) Sept '55.
Sumatra wedding. Natl. geog. 99: 20 Jan '51.
Sumeria. Natl. geog. 99: 64 (col.) Jan '51.
Sumerian house (int., 2850 B.C.). Int. gr. soc.: Arts . . . p. 15 (col.).
Sumerian ruler (statue). Ceram: March of arch., p. 244.
Sumerian woman (5000 yrs. ago). Int. gr. soc.: Arts . . . p. 31 (col.).
Sumerians (in home, ancient). Int. gr. soc.: Arts . . . p. 15 (col.).
"Summer" (statue of the seasons). Con. 145: 131 Ap '60.
summer (sym.). Lehner: Pict. bk. of sym., p. 81.
"Summer morning" (Lucas). Con. ency. of ant., vol. 1, pl. 137.
Summerfield, Arthur E. Cur. biog. p. 572 (1952).
Summerskill, Edith Clara. Cur. biog. p. 749 (1943).
Summerskill, Frederick H. Cur. biog. (1963).
Sumner, Charles. Amer. heri., vol. 8 no. 1 p. 22 (Dec '56); vol. 12 no. 1 p. 47 (Dec '60).
Sumner, Cid Ricketts. Cur. biog. p. 592 (1954).
Sumner, Edwin Vose. Pakula: Cent. album, p. 271.
Sumner, James B. Cur. biog. p. 621 (1947).
Sumner, Jessie. Cur. biog. p. 579 (1945).
sun (comic). Holiday 10: 78 Sept '51, 27, 95 (col.) Oct '51, 145 Nov '51, 165 Dec '51; 11: 7 (col.), 71, 104 Jan '52, 118 Mar '52, 156 May '52; 12: 1, 21 (col.) 59 Aug '52, 64 Sept '52, 79, 95 (col.) Oct '52, 30 Dec '52; 14: 7 Jl '53, 29 Aug '53; 18: 67, 125 (col.) Nov '55; 19: 114 Jan '56, 19 Feb '56, 124 Mar '56, 126, 133 (col.) May '56; 20: 107 Sept '56, 120, 143 Oct

'56, 199, 211 Dec '56; 21: 6, 19 Jan '57, 118, 145 (col.) Feb '57, 26, 190 Ap '57, 202 May '57, 182 Je '57; 22: 106 Sept '57, 103, 133, 177 Oct '57, 32 Nov '57, 19, 239 Dec '57; 23: 90 Feb '58, 52 Je '58; 24: 141 (col.) Jl '58; 25: 11 Jan '59, 109 Mar '59, 25 May '59; 26: 206, 234 Dec '59; 27: 19, 170 Jan '60, 49 Feb '60, 193 May '60; 28: 135 Sept '60, 213 Nov '60, 222 Dec '60.

Travel 105: 7 Feb '56, 10 Mar '56, 11 Ap '56; 107: 36-7 Ap '57; 113: 39 Mar '60, 53 Ap '60.

—— (god of). Lehner: Pict. bk. of sym., p. 31.

—— (magic square). Lehner: Pict. bk. of sym., p. 24.

—— (sym.). Lehner: Pict. bk. of sym., p. 24, 66, 75, 77-8, 81.

——, rising (sym.). Lehner: Pict. bk. of sym., p. 36.

——, spirit of. See spirit of the sun.

sun chariot, Trundholm. Praeg.: Pict. ency., p. 170.

Sun Fo. Cur. biog. p. 675 (1944).

Sun gate (Cartagena, Colombia). Holiday 7: back cover (col.) May '50.

sun glasses. Holiday 11: 13 (col.) Je '52; 12: 12, 97 Jl '52; 14: 7 Jl '53; 20: 65 (col.) Aug '56; 21: 10 (col.) Feb '57, 122 May '57; 26: 225, 247 Dec '59; 27: 248 May '60.

—— (girl head). Natl. geog. 108: 143 Jl '55.

—— (men & women). Holiday 14: 66 Jl '53.

—— (reflections). Natl. geog. 112: 12 (col.) Jl '57.

—— See also man & woman (heads, sun glasses).

sun-god, Chinese (on pillow). Holiday 23: 63 (col.) Mar '58.

Sun god pyramid. See Promethean Pyramid of the sun.

sun lamp. Holiday 26: 38 Dec '59.

—— (woman & baby). Holiday 27: 161 Jan '60.

sun monument (Egypt). Natl. geog. 106: 763 Dec '54.

"Sun Queen of Arinna" (Hitites). Osward: Asia Minor, pl. 8.

"Sun temple" (Mesa Verde). Jordan: Hammond's pict. atlas, p. 167 (col.).

"Sun Temple" (Mexico). Ceram: March of arch., p. 279.

Sun Valley (Idaho). Holiday 6: 91 (col.) Nov '49; 8: 26 Nov '50; 13: 90-1 (col.) Feb '53; 14: 167 (col.) Nov '53; 15: 90 (col.) May '54; 16: 4 (col.) Nov '54; 18: 120 (col.) Nov '55; 24: 204 Nov '58. Jordan: Hammond's pict. atlas, p. 141 (col.).

Travel 107: 52-4 Feb '57; 111: cover (col.) Je '59.

—— (inn). Holiday 13: 5 Feb '53. Natl. geog. 115: 248 Feb '59.

—— (ski run). Travel 109: 35 Feb '58.

sun worshiper (India). Holiday 6: 68 Jl '49.

Sun Yat-Sen, Mme. Cur. biog. p. 678 (1944).

sunbonnett. Holiday 9: 49 Mar '51. Natl. geog. 97: 200 Feb '50, 732 (col.) Je '50.

—— (girl head). Natl. geog. 114: 673 (col.) Nov '58.

—— (woman). Natl. geog. 112: 306 (col.) Sept '57.

"Sundance Kid." See Longbaugh, Harry.

Sunday, Billy. Jensen: The White House, p. 216.

"Sunday morning in the mines" (Charles Nahl). Brooks: Growth of a nation, p. 33. Holiday 24: 66-7 (col.) Aug '58.

Sunday school class. Holiday 7: 57 (col.) Ap '50.

Sunderland, Thomas E. Cur. biog. p. 411 (1962).

sundial. Con. 138: XXXIX Sept '56. Holiday 13: 144 Mar '53; 21: 76 Feb '57.

—— (sym.). Lehner: Pict. bk. of sym., p. 26, 80.

—— (column 600 years old). Natl. geog. 108: 340 (col.) Sept '55.

——, altitude (antique). Con. 134: 88 Nov '54.

——, azimuth (antique). Con. 134: 90 Nov '54.

——, Butterfield (antique). Con. 134: 89 Nov '54.

——, horizontal (antique). Con. 134: 89 Nov '54.

——, carved stone (18th cent.). Con. 144: XXVII Jan '60.

——, memorial. Natl. geog. 100: 756 Dec '51.

sundown (ocean, ship). Natl. geog. 112: 650-1 (col.) Nov '57.

"Sundown ranch" (Cal.). Face of Amer., p. 142-3 (col.).

"Sunlight gate" of Toshugu shrine (Japan). Travel 113: 54 Jan '60.

"Sunnyside" (home of Washington Irving). Holiday 6: 39 (col.) Sept '49.

suns, Antarctic. Natl. geog. 113: 452-3 (col.) Ap '58.

——, multiple (Polar). Natl. geog. 100: 492 (col.) Oct '51.

sunset. Natl. geog. 110: 322-3 (col.) Sept '56.

—— (ocean). Natl. geog. 115: 298 Feb '59.

——, Antarctic. Natl. geog. 113: 443 Ap '58.

Sunset Point (Cal., Monterey Peninsula). Face of Amer., p. 78-9 (col.).

sunspots. Natl. geog. 109: 296 Feb '56.

Superga church (Turin). Int. gr. soc.: Arts . . . p. 99 (col.).

Superion Natl. Park. Jordan: Hammond's pict. atlas, p. 91 (col.).

supermarket (int.). Brooks: growth of a nation, p. 251.

supper dish, Georgian silver. Con. 137: XXI Je '56.

Supreme court, U.S. See U.S. Supreme court.

Supreme court desk (Ill. 1836). Holiday 20: 31 (col.) Sept 56.

"Sur les boulevard" (Renoir). Con. 138: 56 (col.) Sept '56.

Surf Rider Inn (Santa Monica). Travel 109: 47 Feb '58.

surfboard. Holiday 13: 133 Mar '53.

—— (boy & girl). Holiday 12: 5 (col.) Sept '52.

surfboard (fish drawn). Natl. geog. 102: 682 Nov '52.

—— (rider). Holiday 5: 94 (col.) Mar '49, 69 (col.) Ap '49; 8: 114 Sept '50; 10: 20 (col.) Aug '51, 111 Sept '51; 13: 70 (col.) Feb '53; 15: 158 (col.) Je '54; 25: 37 Feb '59.
Natl. geog. 118: 3, 22-3 (col.) Jl '60. Travel 112: 22 Dec '59.

surfboat (Africa). Natl. geog. 100: 267 Aug '51; 118: 314-5 (col.) Sept '60.

surgeon & nurses (operating room). Natl. geog. 116: 404 (col.) Sept '59.

Surinam. Travel 102: 23-6 Dec '54; 112: 22-5 Sept '59.

—— (huts). Holiday 27: 62 May '60.

Surles, Maj. Gen. Alexander D. Cur. biog. p. 583 (1945).

Surratt, John H. Amer. heri., vol. 8 no. 2 p. 57 (Feb '57).

Surratt, Mrs. Mary E. Amer. heri., vol. 8 no. 2 p. 57 (Feb '57).

surrealist stage decor. Int. gr. soc.: Arts . . . p. 145 (col.).

surrender (sym.). Lehner: Pict. bk. of sym., p. 86.

"Surrender at Battle of Saratoga" (Trumbull). Natl. geog. 102: 157 (col.) Aug '52.

"Surrender of Cornwallis" (Trumbull). Natl. geog. 99: 187 (col.) Feb '51.

surrey. Holiday 21: 35 (col.) Je '57.

—— (horse). Holiday 9: 127 Mar '51; 10: 118 Aug '51, 15 Sept '51; 12: 67 Sept '52; 13: 5 (col.) Jan '53, 92 (col.) May '53, 119 (col.) Je '53; 24: 52 (col.), 72 Nov '58.
Natl. geog. 113: 42 (col.) Jan '58, 164, 168, 180 (col.) Feb '58; 118: 789 (col.) Dec '60.

——, Colonial (horse). Holiday 13: 151 May '53.

——, fringe on top (horse). Holiday 11: 155 (col.) May '52; 16: 84 Nov '54; 26: 53 Oct '59; 28: back cover (col.) Nov '60.

surtoute (table centerpiece). Con. 143: 83 Ap '59.

surveyors. Natl. geog. 101: 16, 31-32 (col.) Jan '52; 102: 603 (col.) Nov '52; 109: 336-63 (part col.) Mar '56; 110: 370 Sept '56.

——, Antarctic. Natl. geog. 115: 38 (col.) Jan '59.

——, early western. Amer. heri., vol. 8 no. 4 p. 109-11 (Je '57).

——, Indonesia. Natl. geog. 108: 376 Sept '55.

——, sea & air lane. Natl. geog. 111: 188-208 (part col.) Feb '57.

——, student. Natl. geog. 112: 406-7 (col.) Sept '57.

survival training. See airmen (training for emergency).

Susemihl, I. C. (work of). Con. ency. of ant., vol. 3 pl. 86.

Susini, Giovanni Francesco (sculpture by). Con. 140: 206 Dec '57.

Suslov, Mikhail A. Cur. biog. p. 540 (1957).

suspenders, man's. Holiday 10: 108 Sept '51.

Susquehanna river. Holiday 12: 52 (col.) Oct '52.

Natl. geog. 98: 74-120 (part col.) Jl '50.

Susquehannah Valley (map). Amer. heri., vol. 3 no. 4 p. 23 (summer '52).

Susskind, David. Cur. biog. p. 413 (1960).

Susten Pass (Switzerland). Travel 113: 53 Je '60.

Sutherland, George. Amer. heri., vol. 9 no. 3 p. 25 (Ap '58).

Sutherland, Graham. Cur. biog. p. 590 (1955).

—— (work of). Praeg.: Pict. ency., p. 510.

Sutherland, Joan. Cur. biog. p. 414 (1960).

Sutter, John Augustus. Amer. heri., vol. 1 no. 3 p. 39 (spring '50).

Sutter's fort (Cal.). Brooks: Growth of a nation, p. 121.

Sutton, George P. Cur. biog. p. 424 (1958).

Suva (Fiji islands). Natl. geog. 98: 123 Jl '50.

Suva clock tower (Fiji). Natl. geog. 114: 537 Oct '58.

Suva harbor. Travel 102: 32 Nov '54.

Suvaii island. Travel 104: 23-6 Oct '55.

Suzuki, Daisetz T. Cur. biog. p. 425 (1958).

Suzuki, Pat. Cur. biog. p. 417 (1960).

Svanholm, Set. Cur. biog. p. 615 (1956).

Sveda, Michael. Cur. biog. p. 593 (1954).

Svim'in, P. P. (work of). Amer. heri., vol. 2 no. 2 p. 29 (winter '51).

swag, Grinling Gibbons carved. Con. 129: XXIII Ap '52.

Swallow, Alan. Cur. biog. (1963).

swallows, three (sym.). Lehner: Pict. bk. of sym., p. 64.

"Swallow's nest castle." Natl. geog. 116: 389 (col.) Sept '59.

swamp, cypress (boat). Natl. geog. 105: 322 (col.) Mar '54.

——, Okefenokee. See Okefenokee.

"The Swamp Fox" (Francis Marion). Amer. heri., vol. 9 no. 3 p. 40 (col.) (Ap '58).

swamp land (Fla.). Natl. geog. 113: 98-120 (part col.) Jan '58.

—— (Ga.). Face of Amer., p. 134-5 (col.).

—— (La.). Holiday 6: 52 (col.) Oct '49.

swan (sym.). Lehner: Pict. bk. of sym., p. 59, 79.

swan boat. Natl. geog. 107: 772 (col.) Je '55.

—— (Boston, Mass.). Jordan: Hammond's pict. atlas, p. 31 (col.).

—— (children). Face of Amer., p. 71 (col.).

Swann, William F.G. Cur. biog. p. 847 (1941); p. 418 (1960).

Swanson, Gloria. Cur. biog. p. 557 (1950). Holiday 10: 65 Dec '51.

swape. Rawson: Ant. pict. bk., p. 51.

"Swarm of bees" (Robertson). Con. ency. of ant., vol. 1, pl. 147.

Swart, Charles R. Cur. biog. p. 420 (1960).

Swarthout, Gladys. Cur. biog. p. 683 (1944).

swastika (sym.). Lehner: Pict. bk. of sym., p. 95.

Swat (Pakistan). Travel 108: 29-31 Nov '57.

Swaythling cup (1623). Con. 129: 74 Ap '52.

sweater. Holiday 10: inside cover (col.) Nov '51; 14: 157 Nov '53; 23: 202 Je '58; 25: 173 Mar '59; 26: 186 Oct '59.

——, child's. Holiday 27: 228 Ap '60.

——, girl's. Holiday 28: 136 Sept '60.

——, man's. Holiday 10: 10 (col.) Dec '51; 11: 69 (col.) Feb '52; 12: inside cover (col.)

Nov '52, 122 (col.) Dec '52; 14: 97 Dec '53; 20: 171 (col.) Dec '56; 24: 128 (col.) Oct '58, 38 (col.) Dec '58.

——, Shetland island. Natl. geog. 104: 524 Oct '53.

sweaters (man & woman). Holiday 12: 31 (col.) Dec '52.

Sweden. Holiday 20: 38-45 (part col.) Aug '56.

Natl. geog. 98: 606-39 (part col.) Nov '50. Travel 111: 23-5 May '59.

—— (fishing village). Travel 107: 22 May '57.

—— (harbor). Travel 108: 41 Jl '57.

—— (map). Natl. geog. 98: 608 Nov '50.

—— (Stockholm, changing guard). Holiday 23: 150 (col.) Feb '58.

Swedish arch. (home, ext. & int.). Con. 141: 3-4 Mar '58.

Swedish art (miniature). Con. 141: 19-20, 31-3 Mar '58.

Swedish church (Wilmington, Del.). Con. 141: 63 Mar '58.

Swedish dining room. Holiday 24: 83 (col.) Aug '58.

Swedish pottery. See pottery, Swedish.

Swedish silver (antique). Con. 141: 8-12 Mar '58.

Sweeney, James Johnson. Cur. biog. p. 593 (1955).

Sweerts, Michiel (work of). Con. 142: 273 Jan '59.

Sweet, Abraham. Holiday 25: 78 Feb '59.

sweet shop (Damascus). Natl. geog. 106: 825 (col.) Dec '54.

sweetmeat glass, Irish. Con. ency. of ant., vol. 3, pl. 47.

Swift, Harold H. Cur. biog. p. 558 (1950). Holiday 28: 181 Dec '60.

Swift, Hildegarde Hoyt. Jun. bk. of auth., p. 284.

Swigert, Ernest G. Cur. biog. p. 543 (1957).

swim cap. Holiday 10: 4 Jl '51; 12: 108 Jl '52.

swimmer (prawns. Fiji). Natl. geog. 114: 555 (col.) Oct '58.

swimmers. Natl. geog. 114: 851 (col.) Dec '58.

—— (diving). Holiday 8: 53 (col.) Dec '50.

—— (polar rescue suits). Natl. geog. 110: 173 (col.) Aug '56.

—— (rubber rafts). Natl. geog. 112: 316-7 (col.) Sept '57.

——. See also men (swimming).

swimming fins. Holiday 23: 160 Mar '58.

swimming hole. Face of Amer., p. 82-3 (col.).

swimming pool. Holiday 5: 46 (col.) Jan '49, 43, 57 (col.) Feb '49, 65 Ap '49, 111, 113 (col.), 145 Je '49; 6: cover (col.) Jl '49, 49 Oct '49; 7: 34, 63, 91 (col.) Jan '50, 106 (col.) Ap '50; 8: 98 Dec '50; 10: 10 (col.) Jl '51, 98-9 (col.) Aug '51, 5, 53, 109 (col.) Dec '51; 11: 38-9, 99 (col.) Jan '52, 113 (col.) Feb '52, 57 (col.) Mar '52, 20 (col.) May '52, 39, 79 (col.) Je '52; 12: 50 Jl '52, 46 (col.) Oct '52, 106-7 (col.) Dec '52; 13: 7, 102 (col.) Feb '53, 135, 138, inside back cover (col.) Ap '53, 103 (col.) May '53; 14: 13 (col.) Jl

'53, 34 (col.) Sept '53; 15: 108 Je '54; 16: 110 Jl '54, 120 (col.) Oct '54, 64 (col.) Nov '54; 17: 2, 5, 18 (col.) Jan '55, cover, back cover (col.) Feb '55; 18: 125 (col.) Sept '55, 39 (col.) Oct '55, 42-3 (col.) Dec '55; 19: 18 (col.) Jan '56, 73, 81 (col.) Feb '56, 57 (col.) Mar '56, 59 Je '56; 20: 56 (col.), 77 Sept '56, 143 Oct '56, 59 (col.) Nov '56, 191 (col.) Dec '56; 21: 7 (col.) Feb '57, 7 (col.) Ap '57, 80 (col.) May '57, 168 Je '57; 22: 99 (col.) Jl '57, 130 (col.) Sept '57, 82-3, 87, 94-5 (col.) Oct '57; 23: 55 (col.) Jan '58, 51 (col) Feb '58, 7, back cover (col.) May '58, 26 (col.) Je '58; 25: 125 (col.) Feb '59; 26: 76-9, 106 (col.) Jl '59; 27: 140 (col.) Jan '60, 44 (col.), 57, 78 (col.) Mar '60, 175 (col.) Ap '60, 4, 190 (col.) May '60, 44, 175, 177 (col.) Je '60; 28: 17, 81 (col.) Jl '60, 62 Dec '60.

Natl. geog. 99: 448 (col.) Ap '51; 100: 800 (col.) Dec '51; 102: 766-7 (col.) Dec '52; 103: 197 (col.) Feb '53, 539 (col.) Ap '53; 105: 817 Je '54; 112: 689 (col.) Nov '57; 116: 580 (col.) Nov '59.

Travel 101: 36 May '54; 102: 46 Dec '54; 103: 13 Feb '55, 51 Je '55; 111: 41 Feb '59.

—— (Banff Park). Travel 106: 42 Jl '56.

—— (bathers). Natl. geog. 113: 44-5 (col.) Jan '58, 172 Feb '58.

—— (Bermuda). Travel 111: 16 Feb '59.

—— (canyon). Natl. geog. 107: 623 (col.) May '55.

—— (hotel). Jordan: Hammond's pict. atlas, p. 196 (col.).

Natl. geog. 105: 356 (col.) Mar '54.

—— (Iceland). Natl. geog. 100: 611 Nov '51.

—— (Kenya). Holiday 25: 87 (col.) Ap '59.

—— (men & girl). Holiday 25: 161 (col.) Mar '59.

—— (Mexico). Natl. geog. 107: 236 (col.) Feb '55; 115: 116 Jan '59.

—— (Miami Beach). Travel 113: 40 May '60.

—— (Sun Valley). Travel 111: 54 Jan '59.

——, children's. Travel 106: 50 Aug '56.

——, Chinese. Natl. geog. 105: 264 (col.) Feb '54.

——, indoor. Holiday 24: 83 (col.) Nov '58.

——, oceanside (largest in world). Natl. geog. 107: 151 (col.) Feb '55.

——, Romanesque. Holiday 27: 20 (col.) Ap '60.

——, ship. Holiday 5: 66 (col.) Jan '49; 7: back cover (col.) Feb '50; 11: 115 (col.) Ap '52; 12: 32, 69 (col.) Oct '52, 130 Nov '52; 14: 152 (col.) Oct '53; 15: back cover (col.) May '54; 19: 85 (col.) Jan '56, 157 (col.) Mar '56, 30 (col.) Je '56; 24: 123 Nov '58; 25: 153 (col.) Mar '59; 26: 87 (col.) Jl '59; 27: 28 (col.) Jan '60; 28: 133 (col.) Jl '60.

swimming regatta. Natl. geog. 114: 173 Aug '58.

Swing, Lt. Gen. Joseph M. Cur. biog. p. 435 (1959).

"The Swing" (Fragonard). Natl. geog. 110: 654 (col.) Nov '56.

"The Swing" (Lancret). Con. 136: cover (col.) (Nov '55).

swing, sapling (antique). Rawson: Ant. pict. bk., p. 19.

Swings, Pol. Cur. biog. p. 595 (1954).

Swirlbul, Leon A. Cur. biog. p. 609 (1953).

Swiss Alpenhorn. See Alpenhorn.

Swiss Alps. Holiday 7: 104 Jan '50; 14: 61 Dec '53; 15: 66 Jan '54.
Natl. geog. 107: 826-48 (part col.) Je '55.
Travel 113: 36 Je '60.
——. See also Alpine village.

Swiss Amer. dance. Natl. geog. 112: 706 (col.) Nov '57.

Swiss chalet. See house, Swiss (chalet).

Swiss dancers. Natl. geog. 111: 785 (col.) Je '57; 114: 568-9 (col.) Oct '58.

Swiss dancing girls. Natl. geog. 111: 170-1 (col.) Feb '57.

Swiss guard. Holiday 8: 25 Aug '50; 14: 7 (col.) Aug '53.
Travel 113: 35-7 Ap '60.
—— (salute). Travel 113: 36 Ap '60.
—— (Vatican, Rome). Holiday 7: 110 (col.) May '50; 21: 15 (col.) Feb '57; 23: cover (col.), 3, 59 (col.) May '58.
Travel 113: 35-7 Ap '60.

Swiss guards. Natl. geog. 114: 562 (col.) Oct '58.

Swiss house. See house, Swiss.

Swiss men & women. Holiday 24: 20, 77 Sept '58.

Swiss papal guard. Int. gr. soc.: Arts . . . p. 159 (col.).

Switzer, Mary E. Cur. biog. p. 413 (1962).

Switzerland. Disney: People & places, p. 37-46 (col.).
Holiday 6: 27 (col.) Oct '49; 11: 108 (col.) Jan '52; 12: 16 Dec '52; 14: 98-9 (col.) Aug '53; 16: cover (col.), 27-37 Aug '54; 23: 174 (col.) Je '58; 25: 132 Ap '59, 164 May '59; 26: 33 Sept '59; 27: 74-9 (col.) Feb '60; 28: 30-43 (col.) Aug '60.
Natl. geog. 98: 206-46 (part col.) Aug '50; 107: 826-48 (part col.) Je '55; 110: 428-78 (part col.) Oct '56; 111: 782-5 (col.) Je '57.
Travel 102: 11-4 Aug '54; 105: 39-41 Feb '56; 106: 27 Dec '56.
—— (Berne). Travel 108: 22-7 Nov '57.
—— (Castle of Chillon). Travel 109: cover Ap '58; 113: cover (col.) Ap '60.
—— (children's village). Natl. geog. 116: 268-82 Aug '59.
—— (church, woman). Holiday 25: 81 Jan '59.
—— (Geneva, Hotel du Rhone). Con. 132: XXXVIII Sept '53, XLVIII Nov '53; 133: LXII May '54.
—— (house). See house, Swiss.
—— (Lake Geneva). Travel 113: cover (col.) Ap '60.
—— (Lucerne, Palace hotel). Con. 133: LXII May '54.
—— (map). Natl. geog. 98: 210 Aug '50; 110: 432-3 Oct '56.
—— (Mt. hikers). Natl. geog. 108: 138 Jl '55.
—— (St. Moritz, Badrutt's palace hotel). Con. 132: XLVIII Nov '53.

—— (skiers). Holiday 23: 70-5 (part col.) Feb '58.
—— (Susten Pass). Travel 113: 53 Je '60.
—— (Vitznau, Park hotel on Lake Lucerne). Con. 132: XXXVIII Sept '53.

swivel gun & breech lock. Natl. geog. 117: 157 (col.) Feb '60.

Swope, Gerard. Cur. biog. p. 848 (1941).

Swope, Herbert Bayard. Cur. biog. p. 685 (1944).

Swope, John. Holiday 10: 64 Dec '51.

sword. Amer. heri., vol. 6 no. 5 p. 93 (Aug '55); vol. 11 no. 4 p. 30 (Je '60).
Holiday 26: 122 Jl '59, 173 Oct '59, 180 Nov '59; 26: 120 Dec '59; 27: 52 Mar '60.
Int. gr. soc.: Arts . . . p. 115 (col.).
—— (ancient times). Int. gr. soc.: Arts . . . p. 33 (col.).
—— (antique). Con. 129: LVIII Je '52.
—— (sym.). Lehner: Pict. bk. of sym., p. 13, 17, 55.
——, Bristol. Con. 137: 85-6 Ap '56.
——, broken (sym.). Lehner: Pict. bk. of sym., p. 86.
——, Conquistador. Amer. heri., vol. 12 no. 1 p. 32 (Dec '60).
——, Dewey's. Amer. heri., vol. 2 no. 3 p. 52 (spring '51).
——, ducal (15th cent.). Con. 144: 80 Nov '59.
——, (15th cent.). Con. 129: 104-8 Je '52.
——, flaming. See flaming sword.
——, medieval. Int. gr. soc.: Arts . . . p. 73 (col.).
——, Napoleon's. Con. 143: 224 Je '59.
——, Palatinate. Con. 144: 85 Nov '59.
——, Portuguese. Con. 137: 24. 27 Mar '56. Natl. geog. 118: 627 Nov '60.
——, Robert E. Lee's. Amer. heri., vol. 6 no. 3 p. 34 (Ap '55).
——, St. Paul. Natl. geog. 110: 758 (col.) Dec '56.
——, Samurai. Disney: People & places, p. 150-1 (col.).

sword & fire. See fire & sword (sym.)

sword. See also glaive.

sword dance, Chinese. Travel 112: 29 Dec '59.
——, German. Natl. geog. 111: 265 (col.) Feb '57.
——, Scotch girl. Natl. geog. 112: 445 (col.) Oct '57.
——, Yugoslav. Travel 113: 87 Ap '60.

sword handle (by Matzenkopf). Con. 126: 28-31 Aug '50.

sword hilt. Con. 136: 2 (col.) Sept '55.
——, antique Swedish silver. Con. 141: 27-9 Mar '58.
——, 18th cent. ("Prosperity to Scotland & no union). Con. 135: 174 May '55.
——, Wedgwood. Con. 132: 183 Jan '54.

sword holder, crusade period. Con. 134: LIII Sept '54.

sword of state, British. Int. gr. soc.: Arts . . . p. 165 (col.).

swords. Holiday 22: 73 Nov '57.
—— (antique). Con. ency. of ant., vol. 1, pl. 106-7, p. 193, 197.
—— (1840, 1860). Brooks: Growth of a nation, p. 173.

Sydney (Australia). Holiday 8: 100 Nov '50. Natl. geog. 109: 256-7 (col.) Feb '56.

——— **(air view).** Holiday 14: 4 Jl '53.

Sylvan Lake (Black Hills, S.D.). Travel 113: 40 Mar '60.

"Sylvette" (Picasso). Con. 143: LI Ap '59.

symbol, auto. *See* auto symbol.

———, **British antique dealer's assoc.** Con. 143: LXXIV May '59, LXXIV Je '59; 144: LXIV Nov '59, LXXVIII Dec '59, LXXXII Jan '60; 145: LXII Ap '60, LVIII Mar '60, LXXXIV Je '60, XC May '60.

———, **fishermen.** Holiday 24: 58 (col.) Sept '58.

———, **World's Fair.** *See* Brussels World's Fair symbol.

———, **youth hostel (on door).** Natl. geog. 109: 528 Ap '56.

symbols. Lehner: Pict. bk. of sym.

———, **airplane.** *See* airplane symbols.

———, **presidential campaign.** Holiday 27: 61, 63 (col.) Je '60.

symbols of countries. Holiday 16: 19 Aug '54.

Syme, John P. Cur. biog. p. 544 (1957).

Symes, James M. Cur. biog. p. 595 (1955).

Symington, William S. Cur. biog. p. 586 (1945); p. 616 (1956). Holiday 15: 60 Feb '54.

symphony hall. Cooper: Con. ency. of music, p. 449-64.

Synge, Richard L. M. Cur. biog. p. 611 (1953).

Syon house (Eng.). Con. 126: 19-27 Aug '50.

Syracuse univ. (students). Natl. geog. 110: 596 (col.) Nov '56.

Syria. Holiday 13: 100-1 Jan '53. Natl. geog. 106: 814- Dec '54.

syringe (sym.). Lehner: Pict. bk. of sym., p. 16.

syrup kettle. Natl. geog. 113: 542 (col.) Ap '58.

Szell, George. Cur. biog. p. 588 (1945).

Szent-Gyorgyi, Albert. Cur. biog. p. 597 (1955).

Szigeti, Joseph. Cur. biog. p. 427 (1958).

Szilard, Leo. Cur. biog. p. 623 (1947).

Szyk, Arthur. Cur. biog. p. 589 (1946).

T

TV stage. *See* television stage.

tabard (1685). Con. 143: 233 Je '59.

Taber, Gladys. Cur. biog. p. 575 (1952).

Taber, John. Cur. biog. p. 608 (1948).

Taber, Louis J. Cur. biog. p. 815 (1942).

tabernacle (church of St. Lawrence, Nuremberg). Praeg.: Pict. ency., p. 210.

——— **(Mt. Sinai).** Natl. geog. 112: 844 (col.) Dec '57.

———, **Italian (16th cent.).** Con. 135: LI May '55.

tabi socks, Japanese. Holiday 24: 62 Dec '58.

table. Holiday 19: 12 (col.) Feb '56; 23: 156 Feb '58; 28: inside cover, 1 (col.) Oct '60.

——— **(antique).** Amer. heri., vol. 6 no. 3 p. 67 (Ap '55). Con. 129: VI Ap '52.

"The Table" (Braque). Con. 145: 208 May '60. Holiday 14: 61 (col.) Nov '53.

table (18th cent.). Con. 135: LI Je '55; 136: LXI Jan. '56; 138: I Dec '56.

——— **(18th cent. & octagonal).** Con. 133: X Je '54.

——— **(18th cent. carved).** Con. 132: XLVII Nov '53.

——— **(15th cent.).** Con. 133: VI May '54.

——— **(incense burner).** Holiday 27: 93 May '60.

——— **(17th cent.).** Con. 129: LXV Ap '52; 136: LXIII Nov '55.

——— **(small).** Holiday 23: 25 Jan '58.

———, **Adam.** Con. 134: XXVII Sept '54; 136: XXX Sept '55; 143: XXXV Ap '59.

———, **alabaster (15th cent.).** Con. 133: LXXI Je '54.

———, **Amer. colonial.** Int. gr. soc.: Arts . . . p. 105 (col.).

———, **architect's.** *See* architect's table.

———, **artist's.** *See* artist's table.

———, **baroque.** Holiday 22: 60 (col.) Sept '57.

———, **bedside.** Con. 140: 99 Nov '57.

———, **breakfast (antique).** Con. 136: 242 Jan '56.

———, **(Chippendale).** Con. 132: XXXIV Sept '53; 136: XLVI Jan '56; 143: XXX Mar '59.

———, **breakfast (18th cent.).** Con. 143: 79 Ap '59.

———, **bureau.** *See* bureau table.

———, **butterfly.** Con. ency. of ant., vol. 1, pl. 39.

———, **butterfly trestle.** Rawson: Ant. pict. bk., p. 15.

———, **card.** *See* card table.

———, **Catherine the Great.** Con. 142: 222 Jan '59.

———, **Charles II.** Con. ency. of ant., vol. 1, pl. 21.

———, **cheese.** Holiday 28: 5 (col.) Oct '60.

———, **child's (17th cent.).** Con. ency. of ant., vol. 1, pl. 2.

———, **Chinese (16th cent. lacquer).** Con. 139: XII Ap '57.

———, **Chippendale.** Con. 136: LXV Dec '55; 137: VI Ap '56; 144: LX Sept '59.

———, **Chippendale centre.** Con. 141: XXIV Ap '58.

———, **Chippendale Pembroke.** Con. 134: XII Nov '54.

———, **Chippendale piecrust.** Con. 140: IV Sept '57.

———, **Chippendale serving.** Con. 136: IV Sept '55.

———, **circular (19th cent.).** Con. 140: 228 Jan '58.

———, **circular regency.** Con. 141: VIII Ap '58.

———, **cocktail.** *See* cocktail table.

———, **coffee.** Holiday 28: 145 (col.) Nov '60.

———, **console.** Con. 136: XXXVI Sept '55. Holiday 12: 92 Oct '52.

———, **console (Adam).** Con. 140: XXXIV Sept '57.

———, **console (antique).** Con. 136: XXIV Sept '55.

———, **console (antique gilt).** Con. 135: IV Mar '55.

———, **console (Chippendale).** Con. 136: VI Jan '56.

———, **console (Chippendale gilt).** Con. 145: VI Mar '60.

table, console (18th cent.). Con. 139: XIX, XL May '57; 141: XXXII Ap '58.

——, console (first empire). Con. 143: 227 Je '59.

——, console (George II gilt carved). Con. 144: XXV Jan '60.

——, console (gilt & marble, 18th cent.). Con. 144: XVI Jan '60.

——, console (Italian). Con. 135: 23, 27 Mar '55.

——, console (Japanese lacquer). Con. 145: 268 Je '60.

——, console (Kent). Con. 134: XXXVII Dec '54.

——, console (Linnell, 1760). Con. 144: 224 Jan '60.

——, console (Louis XV). Con. 137: 57 Mar '56; 142: XIV Jan '59; 144: XXIII Jan '60. Int. gr. soc.: Arts . . . p. 103 (col.).

——, console (Louis XVI). Con. 134: 75 Sept '54; 140: LXII Nov '57; 143: LIV Mar '59; 144: LXIII Nov '59.

——, console (19th cent.). Con. 140: 148 Dec '57.

——, console (Ormolu). Con. 143: XXXVI Ap '59.

——, console (regency). Con. 142: VIII-IX Nov '58; 144: XLII Jan '60.

——, console (Sheraton). Con. 141: LIV Mar '58.

——, console (William Kent). Con. 139: XXVII Mar '57.

——, credence. See credence table.

——, dining. Holiday 11: 6 Ap '52; 22: 37 Nov '57; 28: 93-5 (col.) Aug '60.

——, dining (antique). Con. 144: 72 (col.) Nov '59.

——, dining (by Matisse). Con. 140: 194 (col.) Dec '57.

——, dining (Chippendale). Con. 134: IV Sept '54.

——, dining (18th cent.). Con. 135: XIV Je '55; 140: XXIII Sept '57; 142: XLIII Sept '58.

——, dining (Fair day). Face of Amer., p. 128-9 (col.).

——, dining (food). Holiday 19: 13 (col.) Je '56.

——, dining (4 pillar). Con. 144: LI Dec '59.

——, dining (Hepplewhite). Natl. geog. 114: 114 (col.) Jl '58.

——, dining (Old Testament life). Natl. geog. 118: 848-9 (col.) Dec '60.

——, dining (regency). Con. 143: XIV May '59.

——, dining (sections, 18th cent.). Con. 143: back cover Je '59.

——, dining (ship deck). Holiday 12: 32 (col.) Nov '52.

——, dining (shipboard, people). Holiday 21: 17 (col.) Je '57.

——, dining (2 post). Con. 145: XXXI May '60.

——, dining (drawer top, antique). Con. 139: 225 Je '57.

——, dressing. See dressing table.

——, drinking. See drinking table.

——, drop-leaf. Holiday 19: 131 May '56.

——, drop-leaf (George II). Con. 144: XIV Sept '59.

——, drop-leaf (Sheraton Pembroke inlaid). Con. 144: LVIII Jan '60.

——, drum top (Sheraton). Con. 142: IV Nov '58; 145: inside back cover Mar '60.

——, drum top (Sheraton & regency). Con. ency. of ant., vol. 1, pl. 34.

——, dumb-waiter. See dumb-waiter table.

——, Elizabethan. Con. 133: VIII-IX May '54; 139: 229 Je '57.

——, empire marble top. Con. 129: LXXVI Ap '52.

——, English cane (early). Con. 127: 86-7 May '51.

——, folding (17th cent.). Con. ency. of ant., vol. 1, pl. 2.

——, French (18th cent.). Con. 140: 57 Sept '57.

——, French regency. Con. 138: I Sept '56.

——, game. See game table.

——, gateleg. Con. 140: 131 Nov '57.

——, gateleg (17th cent.). Con. ency. of ant., vol. 1, pl. 8; vol. 3, pl. 15. Con. 133: XLIII Mar '54, XXIX May '54; 142: 129 Nov '58; 144: XXVIII Sept '59.

——, George I. Con. 143: IV Mar '59.

——, George II. Con. 127: 41 Mar '51; 137: LXI Je '56; 140: IV Sept '57.

——, gilt bronze. Con. 140: 149 Dec '57.

——, Greco-Roman style. Con. 140: 228 Jan '58.

——, Greek (ancient). Int. gr. soc.: Arts . . . p. 19 (col.).

——, Hepplewhite. Con. 133: VI May '54; 136: XXXVIII Dec '55, VI Jan '56; 138: XL Jan '57.

——, Hepplewhite inlaid. Con. 140: IV Dec '57.

——, hotel dining. Holiday 21: 139 (col.) Ap '57.

——, hotel dining (terrace). Holiday 18: 47 (col.) Oct '55.

——, hunting. Con. 138: XXII Dec '56.

——, hunting (18th cent.). Con. 145: XXVIII Je '60.

——, hutch. Rawson: Ant. pict. bk., p. 16.

——, Indo-Portuguese. Con. 134: XXXIII Sept '54.

——, inlaid (18th cent.). Con. 142: LI Nov '58, LVII Dec '58.

——, Irish Chippendale. Con. 135: IV May '55.

——, iron wire (19th cent.). Con. ency. of ant., vol. 3, pl. 28.

——, Italian. Con. 135: 26-7 Mar '55.

——, Italian (antique). Con. 144: 144 Dec '59.

——, Italian (17th cent.). Con. 138: back cover Sept '56.

——, Jesuit (Topino). Con. 126: 200 Dec '50.

——, joined (17th cent.). Con. ency. of ant., vol. 1, pl. 10.

——, kidney-shaped (19th cent.). Con. 134: XIV Dec '54.

——, library (antique). Con. 143: XLVI Ap '59.

——, library (18th cent.). Con. 132: 51 Sept '53; 139: XXI May '57; 142: LVI Jan '59.

——, library (George II). Con. 142: XXXIX Sept '58.

——, library (Louis XVI). Con. 138: 45 Sept '56.

——, library (regency). Con. 139: XXXIV Je '57; 140: XXII Sept '57; 144: XLII Dec '59; 145: XXXV May '60.

——, library (Sheraton). Con. 134: XXI Dec '54; 144: inside back cover Sept '59.

——, library (Viennese). Con. ency, of ant., vol. 3, pl. 18.

——, library (Vile). Con. 140: 257 Jan '58; 145: 219 Je '60.

——, long (17th cent.). Con. ency. of ant., vol. 1, pl. 11.

——, Louis XIV. Con. 126: 59 Aug '50.

——, Louis XV. Con. 129: LXXIX Ap '52; 136: 44 Sept '55, 218 Dec '55; 138: 127 Nov '56; 139: 262 Je '57; 143: 122 Ap '59, XXVII Je '59; 144: 65 Sept '59.

——, Louis XV (kidney-shaped). Con. 143: 189 May '59; 144: 42 Sept '59.

——, Louis XV (marquetry). Con. 143: 189 May '59; 145: 129 Ap '60, 186 May '60, 278 Je '60.

——, Louis XVI (parquetry & porcelain). Con. 145: VI Ap '60.

——, Louis XVI (parquetry & Sevres). Con. 145: 129 Ap '60.

——, marble top. Natl. geog. 109: 472 Ap '56.

——, marble top (antique). Con. 139: 125 Ap '57.

——, marble top (regency). Con. 141: XVI Mar '58.

——, marble top (16th cent.). Con. 144: LXVII Sept '59.

——, Morocco (tall). Natl. geog. 107: 156 (col.) Feb '55.

——, night. See night table.

——, octagon (18th cent.). Con. 145: LIV May '60.

——, octagon (Sheraton). Con. 129: XXII Ap '52.

——, pedestal (Chippendale). Con. 136: XLVII Dec '55.

——, pedestal (empire). Con. 141: 271 Je '58.

——, pedestal (Georgian). Con. 133: 118 Ap '54.

——, pedestal (Phyfe). Con. ency. of ant., vol. 1, pl. 38.

——, pedestal (circular, 19th cent.). Con. 142: XXXI Dec '58.

——, Pembroke. Con. ency. of ant., vol. 1, pl. 39.
Con. 140: 100 Nov '57.

——, Pembroke (Sheraton). Con. 145: XXI Je '60.

——, Pembroke (18th cent.). Con. 141: XXIII Mar '58.

——, pier. See pier table.

——, Portuguese (17th cent.). Con. 143: 268 Je '59.

——, quartet (18th cent.). Con. 140: XXXIV Dec '57.

——, Queen Anne. Con. 136: XIII Nov '55; 144: XLIV Nov '59.

——, Queen Anne (gilt gesso). Con. 140 XLV Nov '57.

——, reading. See reading table.

——, refectory. Con. 143: XIV Ap '59.
Natl. geog. 98: 599 (col.) Nov '50; 116: 579 (col.) Nov '59.

——, refectory (17th cent.). Con. 132: XXXVI Sept '53; 133: XVIII Mar '54, LI Je '54.

——, regency. Con. 135: VI Je '55; 136: XVI Nov '55,, XLVI Dec '55; 140: XLI Nov '57, XXI Dec '57; 142: IV, XX, inside back cover Nov '58.

——, regency center. Con. 144: inside back cover Jan '60; 145: XXI Ap '60.

——, regency marquetry. Con. 145: LI Je '60.

——, rent (Chippendale). Con. 137: XXV Je '56.

——, rent (18th cent.). Con. 143: LII May '59.

——, rent regency. Con. 136: LVI Nov '55.

——, restaurant serving. Holiday 27: 147, 149, 152 (col.) Feb '60.

——, rococo. Natl. geog. 113: 259 (col.) Feb '58.

——, Saarinen. Holiday 26: 149 (col.) Nov '59.

——, semi-circular (18th cent.). Con. 142: XXVIII Dec '58.

——, serving. Holiday 13: 65 (col.) May '53.

——, serving (Hepplewhite). Con. 144: XIV Sept '59.

——, Sheraton. Con. 129: inside back cover Je '52; 132: XLIII Jan '54; 138: LIII Sept '56; 140: XXVI Nov '57.

——, Sheraton (18th cent.). Con. 138: XXXV Sept '56.

——, Sheraton center. Con. 145: XXI Mar '60.

——, Sheraton occasional. Con. 135: XXI Je '55.

——, side (Adam). Con. ency. of ant., vol. 1, pl. 31.
Con. 137: LX Ap '56; 140: XX Sept '57, XXXV Nov '57; 141: 120 Ap '58; 142: XIX Dec '58; 145: XIV Ap '60.

——, side (antique). Con. 129: 19 Ap '52; 136: 81, 113 Nov '55, XLVII, 242-4 Jan '56; 137: LI, 214 May '56; 142: 22 Sept '58.

——, side (Chippendale). Con. 132: VI Sept '53; 133: VI Mar '54; 135: LII May '55; 143: XXXIII Mar '59.

——, side (18th cent.). Con. 133: V Ap '54; 140: VIII Dec '57, XXV Jan '58; 141: XXXVI Je '58; 143: IV, 79 Ap '59; 144: XLIII, 1 Sept '59; 145: XXVIII Mar '60.

——, side (18th cent. serpentine). Con. 144: LVI Jan '60.

——, side (George II gilt). Con. 137: XXXV May '56.

——, side (gilt eagle). Con. 144: 75 Nov '59.

——, side (Irish Chippendale). Con. 145: 151 May '60.

——, side (Kent style). Con. ency. of ant., vol. 1, p. 24.
Con. 135: 207 May '55.

——, side (marble top). Con. 144: XXXVII Jan '60.

——, side (19th cent. gilt mounts). Con. 145: inside back cover Je '60.

——, side (regency). Con. 141: XXIV May '58.

——, side (17th cent.). Con. ency. of ant., vol. 1, pl. 10.

table, side (Sheraton). Con. 144: LIV Sept '59. XXXII Nov '59.

——, sidewalk lunch (Switzerland). Natl. geog. 111: 783 (col.) Je '57.

——, silver (19th cent.). Con. 140: XXXII Jan '58.

——, sofa (antique). Con. 142: XXXI Jan '59.

——, sofa (18th cent.). Con. 133: XXIV Ap '54; 136: XLIV Sept '55; 138: XXXIV Sept '56; 141: XVI Je '58; 142: XL Nov '58; 143: LIII Je '59.

——, sofa (Phyfe). Con. ency. of ant., vol. 1, pl. 44.

——, sofa (regency). Con. 136: IV Sept '55; 139: XXXVI May '57, XXX Je '57; 141: VII Mar '58; 142: XLII Nov '58.

——, sofa (Sheraton). Con. 132: XVI, XXXII Nov '53, 187 Jan '54; 133: XII Mar '54; 134: XXVI Sept '54; 144: LII Jan '60.

——, step. Holiday 10: 18 Jl '51, 96 Dec '51.

——, tavern. Con. ency. of ant., vol. 1, p. 69.

——, tea. See tea table.

——, terrace. Holiday 26: 132 Jl '59.

——, terrace lunch (men & women). Holiday 11: 13 (col.) Mar '52.

——, three-pillar (antique). Con. 143: XXXIX Ap '59.

——, trestle (17th cent.). Con. 142: 129 Nov '58.

——, trestle (1660). Con. ency. of ant., vol. 1, pl. 12.

——, tripod (Chippendale). Con. ency. of ant., vol. 1, pl. 34.
Con. 132: LIII Sept '53; 138: XLIII Sept '56; 140: IV Jan '58; 142: XXIII Jan '59.

——, tripod (18th cent.). Con. 142: 23 Sept '58.

——, tripod (Eng.). Con. 145: 220 Je '60.

——, tripod (pie crust, 18th cent.). Con. 142: 130 Nov '58.

——, urn. See urn table.

——, Victorian round (by Webb, 1859). Con. ency. of ant., vol. 3, pl. 1.

——, Viennese (white gold, 18th cent.). Con. ency. of ant., vol. 3, pl. 18.

——, William & Mary. Con. ency. of ant., vol. 1, pl. 22.
Con. 129: XLVI Ap '52; 138: XVII Sept '56; 141: 247 Je '58.

——, work. See work table.

——, writing. See writing table.

table a ecrire, Louis XV marquetry. Con. 145: 186 May '60.

table & chairs (1836). Holiday 20: 31 (col.) Sept '56.

——, card. See card table & chairs.

——, dining. Holiday 10: 2 (col.) Nov '51; 11: 16 Ap '52, 71 (col.) Je '52; 12: 19 (col.) Oct '52; 18: 26 Nov '55; 20: 13 (col.) Sept '56, 122 (col.) Nov '56; 22: 127 (col.) Sept '57.

——, Eng. (16th cent.). Int. gr. soc.: Arts . . . p. 103 (col.).

——, tea. Holiday 14: 115 (col.) Nov '53.

table & top, mahogany, bronze & Sevres (1806). Con. 143: 147 May '59.

table cabinet (17th cent. Chinese fret). Con. ency. of ant., vol. 1, pl. 32.

table centerpiece (18th cent.). Con. 133: 153 May '54; 143: 83 Ap '59.

——, Derby. Con. 144: XXII Nov '59.

——, Egyptian service. Con. 143: 229-30 Je '59.

——, French silver (18th cent.). Con. ency. of ant., vol. 3, pl. 31.

——, Italian (1804). Con. 145: 190 May '60.

——, Norwegian (1765). Con. 145: 9 Mar '60.

——, silver (antique). Con. 133: XXXIX Mar '54, III Ap '54.

table-chair. Con. ency. of ant., vol. 1, pl. 8.

table des grands capitaines & top, Sevres. Con. 143: 150-2 May '59.

table des Marechaux & top, Sevres (1810). Con. 143: 148 May '59.

table des saisons & top, Sevres (1806). Con. 143: 148 May '59.

table details, Eng. medieval (alabaster). Con. 135: 109-10 Ap '55.

table fountain (Swedish 18th cent.). Con. 143: 240 Je '59.

table leg, Amer. card. Con. 135: 66 Mar '55.

Table Mts. (Africa). Natl. geog. 104: 162, 166 (col.) Aug '53.

Table Mt. (Wash.). Holiday 16: 88 (col.) Aug '54.

table ornament, Italian. Con. 144: 221 Jan '60.

table service, gold & enamel (Empress Marie Louise). Con. 144: 269 Jan '60.

——, travelling (18th cent.). Con. ency. of ant., vol. 3, pl. 36.

table setting. Holiday 28: 40 Nov '60.

——, banquet. Int. gr. soc.: Arts . . . p. 179 (col.).

table silver. See silverware.

tables. Holiday 10: 18 Jl '51; 22: 159 (col.) Dec '57.

——, end. Holiday 10: 123 (col.) Oct '51; 12: 19 (col.) Oct '52.

——, middle ages. Int. gr. soc.: Arts . . . p. 53, 55 (col.).

——, nested. Con. 140: 99 Nov '57.
Holiday 10: 96 Dec '51; 12: 92 Oct '52, 125 (col.) Nov '52.

tableware. See cutlery; knife, fork & spoon; silverware.

Taboga island (Panama). Travel 106: 48-9 Sept '56.

tabouret, Louis XVI. Con. 140: 57 Sept '57.

Tac (sym.). Lehner: Pict. bk. of sym., p. 28.

Tacitus. Amer. heri., vol. 8 no. 5 p. 27 (Aug '57).

tackle box. Holiday 18: 137 Dec '55.

Tacoma (harbor, Wash.). Face of Amer., p. 154-5 (col.).

taffy candy pulling (Nigeria). Natl. geog. 110: 364 Sept '56.

Taft, Charles P. Cur. biog. p. 603 (1957).

Taft, Lorado (sculpture by). Natl. geog. 101: 183 Feb '52.

Taft, Robert A. Cur. biog. p. 611 (1948).
Holiday 11: 118 (col.) May '52.
Natl. geog. 97: 178 Feb '50; 102: 147 Aug '52.

Taft, Robert A., jr. (with his children). Natl. geog. 107: 483 Ap '55.

Taft, William. Amer. heri., vol. 7 no. 4 p. 33 (Je '56).

Taft, William Howard (Pres.). Amer. heri., vol. 6 no. 5 p. 57 (Aug '55); vol. 7 no. 3 p. 33 (Ap '56).
Holiday 8: 108 Sept '50.
Jensen: The White House, p. 193-4, 196, 198-9.
Taft, Mrs. William Howard. Jensen: The White House, p. 194.
Taft family, William Howard. Jensen: The White House, p. 194.
Taft memorial, Robert A. Natl. geog. 116: 755 (col.) Dec '59.
Taft museum (Cincinnati). Amer. heri., vol. 4 no. 3 p. 44 (spring '53).
Holiday 8: 108 Sept '50.
Tagliavini, Ferruccio. Cur. biog. p. 626 (1947).
Tahiti. Holiday 9: 55 Mar '51; 28: 68 (col.) Oct '60, 68-81 Nov '60.
Natl. geog. 112: 726-33 (col.) Dec '57.
Travel 102: 14 Nov '54; 105: 46 Jan '56.
—— **(beach).** Holiday 19: 132 (col.) Feb '56.
Tahitian dance (Hawaii). Natl. geog. 118: 18 (col.) Jl '60.
Tahitian girl. Holiday 22: 116 Jl '57; 27: 60 Ap '60; 28: 69 (col.) Oct '60.
Natl. geog. 112: 729, 753 (col.) Dec '57.
Travel 114: 37 Dec '60.
Tahitian man (blowing shell). Holiday 27: 182 Je '60.
Tahitian woman. Holiday 28: 88, 93 (col.) Oct '60.
Tahitians. Holiday 28: 68-81 (col.) Nov '60.
Tahquamenon water falls. Natl. geog. 101: 317 (col.) Mar '52.
tailor (sym.). Lehner: Pict. bk. of sym., p. 91.
tailor's goose (iron). Rawson: Ant. pict. bk., p. 12.
"Tailor's workshop" (Brekelenkam). Con. 140: 184 Dec '57.
"Tailor's workshop" (Van Slingeland). Con. 126: 135 Oct '50.
Taito (drawings by). Con. 139: 157-9 May '57, 233 Je '57.
Taiwan. See Formosa.
Taiyals (Formosa). Natl. geog. 97: 152-3 (col.), 156, 159, 176 Feb '50.
Taj Mahal (Agra, India). Con. 142: XLIV Nov '58, XXXVI Dec '58, XLI Jan '59; 143: XLIV Mar '59, XXXVIII Ap '59.
Holiday 12: 124 (col.) Jl '52; 14: 89 Sept '53, 35 (col.) Oct '53; 15: 128 May '54; 20: 59 Sept '56; 28: 126 (col.) Sept '60.
Int. gr. soc.: Arts . . . p. 85, 187 (col.).
Lehner: Pict. bk. of sym., p. 65.
Natl. geog. 100: 736 (col.) Dec '51; 116: 845 (col.) Dec '59; 117: 597, 628-9 (col.) May '60; 118: 472-5 (col.) Oct '60.
Praeg.: Pict. ency., p. 563.
Travel 101: 19 Jan '54; 111: 27-9 Jan '59.
—— **(cenotaph).** Natl. geog. 118: 475 (col.) Oct '60.
—— **(entrance).** Travel 106: 12 Nov '56.
"Taking of Jericho" (Fouquet). Int. gr. soc.: Arts . . . p. 89 (col.).
Talal. Cur. biog. p. 576 (1952).
Talbert, Billy. Cur. biog. p. 546 (1957).
Talbott, Harold E. Cur. biog. p. 614 (1953).
Talbott, Philip M. Cur. biog. p. 429 (1958).
"Taliesen West" (desert home of F. L. Wright).

Holiday 13: 34 (col.) Jan '53, 60-1 (part col.) Mar '53.
talisman of Catherine de Medici. See Catherine de Medici talisman.
talismans, Mohammedan (sym.). Lehner: Pict. bk. of sym., p. 40.
Tallamy, Bertram D. Cur. biog. p. 548 (1957).
Tallant, Robert. Cur. biog. p. 615 (1953).
tallboy (18th cent.). Con. 133: XXII Ap '54, XXXVI, 190 May '54; 134: 47 Sept '54; 142: XVI Dec '58.
——, **antique.** Con. 134: XVI Sept '54, L Nov '54; 140: 131 Nov '57.
——, **Chippendale.** Con. 135: XVI Mar '55; 139: IV Ap '57; 140: L Sept '57.
——, **George I.** Con. 135: XXII Mar '55.
——, **Georgian.** Con. ency. of ant., vol. 1, p. 19.
——, **Queen Anne.** Con. 129: LVI Ap '52; 132: VI Sept '53; 133: VI May '54; 136: XXII Nov '55; 137: VI Mar '56; 139: XLVI Ap '57; 140: LXIIII Jan '58.
——, **serpentine front.** Con. 140: XXVI Sept '57.
——, **William & Mary.** Con. 133: XLI Mar '54.
tallboy-chest (18th cent.). Con. 141: XXII Je '58.
tallboy secretaire, Chippendale. Con. 137: IV May '56.
tallboy. See also highboy.
Tallchief, Maria. Cur. biog. p. 619 (1951).
tallow making (1863). Amer. heri., vol. 11 no. 6 p. 34 (Oct '60).
tallyho. Holiday 11: 122 (col.) May '52.
Natl. geog. 114: 186 (col.) Aug '58.
——. See also stagecoach, Eng.
Talmadge, Eugene. Cur. biog. p. 851 (1941).
Talmadge, Herman E. Cur. biog. p. 627 (1947).
Tamanaco hotel. See hotel Tamanaco.
Tamayo, Rufino. Cur. biog. p. 617 (1953).
Tambaran house (New Guinea). Praeg.: Pict. ency., p. 555 (col.).
tambour bureau, Hepplewhite. Con. 138: XVII Dec '56.
tambour secretaire (18th cent.). Con. 145: LVIII Ap '60.
Tamm, Igor. Cur. biog. (1963).
Tammany Hall, N. Y. (political convention, 1868). Amer. heri., vol. 7 no. 4 p. 20-1 (Je '56).
"Tam O'Shanter & Johnie" (sculpture). Natl. geog. 112: 457 (col.) Oct '57.
"Tam O'Shanter Inn". Natl. geog. 112: 457 (col.) Oct '57.
tanbark mill. Rawson: Ant. pict. bk., p. 57.
Tandy, Jessica. Cur. biog. p. 619 (1956).
Taney, Roger Brooke. Amer. heri., vol. 7 no. 4 p. 101 (Je '56).
Holiday 7: 75 Feb '50.
Tanganyika. Travel 104: 20-2 Nov '55.
Tange, Kenso (arch. by). Int. gr. soc.: Arts . . . p. 125 (col.).
Tangier. Holiday 14: 45-9 Sept '53; 23: 66-71 (col.) Mar '58.
Tani, Masayuri. Cur. biog. p. 621 (1956).
Tanjore temple. See temple of Tanjore.

tank, Russian war. Natl. geog. 114: 375 (col.) Sept '58.

——, U.S. Holiday 21: 37 Jan '57.

——, war. Natl. geog. 102: 292 Sept '52.

tank truck. Natl. geog. 112: 713 (col.) Nov '57.

tankard. Holiday 13: 140 May '53; 21: 76 Jan '57, 55 (col.) May '57; 24: 195 Nov '58; 26: 106 (col.) Oct '59. Natl. geog. 106: 443 (col.) Oct '54.

—— (antique). Con. 132: 200 Jan '54; 134: 161 Dec '54; 136: XL, 141 Nov '55.

—— (16-17th cent.). Con. 141: 89 Ap '58.

—— (17th cent.). Con. 126: 152 Oct '50; 136: 55 Sept '55, 115 Nov '55; 140: 280 Jan '58.

——, Charles I. Con. 138: 263 Jan '57; 139: 55 Mar '57.

——, Charles II. Con. 133: 201 May '54; 138: 128 Nov '56, XLV Dec '56; 139: IX Mar '57, VII May '57; 140: XXVIII Dec '57; 141: XXXIII May '58, 246 Je '58; 142: XIV Nov '58; 143: 188, XXXIV May '59; 144: LII, LXVI Nov '59; 145: VI May '60.

——, Coburn. Con. 134: 121 Nov '54.

——, Commonwealth silver. Con. 133: 133 Ap '54.

——, Copenhagen (17th cent.). Con. 135: XVII Mar '55.

——, Cromwellian. Con. 141: LVI Ap '58.

——, Danish silver. Con. 132: 125 Nov '53.

——, Danish silver (18th cent.). Con. 133: XXI Ap '54.

——, enameled. Con. 144: 29 Sept '59.

——, Eng. (antique). Con. 136: XVI Sept '55; 138: XXIX Sept '56.

——, Eng. silver. Con. 142: 227 Jan '59.

——, "Fire of London". Con. 133: XXVII Mar '54.

——, fluted silver (18th cent.). Con. 143: 19 Mar '59.

——, George I. Con. 132: XXVI Nov '53; 133: XXIV Mar '54, X Ap '54, XVI May '54, VIII Je '54; 134: XXVI Sept '54.

——, George II. Con. 144: LII Nov '59.

——, George III. Con. 133: VI Ap '54.

——, German silver. Con. 132: LXI Nov '53.

——, gilt (17th cent.). Con. ency. of ant., vol. 3, pl. 30. Con. 142: XVII Nov '58.

——, James II. Con. 138: XLII Jan '57.

——, Lambeth Delft. Con. 145: XXVII Mar '60.

——, Leeds pottery. Con. 144: XXIV Nov '59.

——, Meissen. Con. ency. of ant., vol. 1, p. 59. Con. 142: 7 Sept '58; 145: 67, XIX Mar '60.

——, Myers silver. Con. 133: 71 Mar '54.

——, N.Y. (18th cent. silver). Con. 135: 73 Mar '55.

——, Norwegian. Con. 143: 266 Je '59.

——, Norwegian (17th cent. silver). Con. 145: 13 Mar '60.

——, parcel-gilt. Con. 137: 57 Mar '56; 142: 271 Jan '59.

——, pewter. Con. ency. of ant., vol. 1, pl. 77-80. Con. 134: XXX Nov '54, XLV Dec '54;

135: XXVII Je '55. Natl. geog. 105: 463 (col.) Ap '54.

——, Plymouth (antique). Con. 134: 192-3 Dec '54.

——, Porcelain (antique). Con. 135: 157 May '55.

——, Portobello. Con. 144: 197 Dec '59.

——, Queen Anne. Con. 136: XLV, 56 Sept '55, LI Nov '55; 144: LII Nov '59.

——, renaissance. Con. 141: 150-2 May '58.

——, Russian silver (1800). Con. 144: 274 Jan '60.

——, silver (antique). Con. 127: 112 May '51; 137: 216 May '56; 138: XXV Sept '56. Holiday 23: 188 Ap '58.

——, silver (17th cent.). Con. 132: 22 Sept '53; 139: 31 Mar '57; 145: LV Mar '60.

——, silver (17-18th cent.). Con. ency. of ant., vol. 1, pl. 82.

——, silver (1792). Con. 145: XL Je '60.

——, silver (18th cent.). Con. 137: 55 Mar '56.

——, silver-gilt (antique). Con. 127: 137 May '51.

——, silver-gilt (16th cent.). Con. 143: 168 May '59.

——, silver-gilt (17-18th cent.). Con. 145: 81 Ap '60.

——, silver (Vander Burgh). Con. 145: 138 Ap '60.

——, Swedish (antique). Con. 140: 59 Sept '57.

——, Swedish (18th cent. silver). Con. 138: XXVII Jan '57; 145: XXIX Mar '60.

——, William & Mary (silver). Con. 133: 122 Ap '54; 139: X, XXXIII May '57; 143: XXXIV May '59.

——, William III. Con. 126: inside cover Oct '50; 140: XXX Sept '57, XXX Nov '57, XII Dec '57, XII, XLVI Jan '58; 144: LII Nov '59.

——, Winslow. Con. 134: 148 Nov '54.

——, Worcester porcelain. Con. 139: 231 Je '57; 141: XLIII May '58.

——, York (silver). Con. 140: XLVIII Jan '58.

tankard & cover, German gilt (16th cent.). Con. 145: XX Je '60.

tankard-flagon, Stuart. Con. 135: XXVI Mar '55.

tankards. Holiday 14: 72 (col.) Dec '53.

—— (Belgium). Natl. geog. 113: 812-3 (col.) Je '58.

tanker (boat). Natl. geog. 109: 830-1 Je '56.

——, oil. Natl. geog. 113: 566 (col.) Ap '58.

tanker ship. Natl. geog. 102: 36 (col.) Jl '52.

tanks, war. Natl. geog. 98: 656, 665 Nov '50.

Tanner, Edward Everett, 3d. Cur. biog. p. 436 (1959).

Tanner, Vaino. Cur. biog. p. 422 (1960).

tanners, women (Greece). Natl. geog. 110: 740 Dec '56.

tannery & tools. Rawson: Ant. pict. bk., p. 57.

Tante Anna cafe (int., Dusseldorf). Holiday 23: 40 (col.) Jan '58.

Taoism founder. Lehner: Pict. bk. of sym., p. 42.

Taoist temple altar statue. Con. 129 LXXIII Je '52.
Taoist. *See* also Chinese Taoist.
Taormina. Holiday 10: 57 (col.) Sept '51.
—— **(Greek theater, Sicily).** Natl. geog. 107: 44-5 (col.) Jan '55.
Taos. Holiday 14: 54 (col.) Dec '53.
Taos Indians. Travel 101: 14 Feb '54.
Taos mission (New Mexico). Amer. heri., vol. 8 no. 6 p. 35 (col.) (Oct '57).
Taos pueblo. Holiday 11: 37, 86 Feb '52; 20: 38-9 (col.) Oct '56; 21: 31 (col.) Mar '57.
Jordan: Hammond's pict. atlas, p. 126 (col.).
Travel 108: 19 Jl '57.
tapa cloth. Disney: People & places, p. 135 (col.).
tape measure. Natl. geog. 109: 366 (col.) Mar '56.
tape recorder. Holiday 10: 130 Nov '51, 101, 188 Dec '51; 18: 181 Dec '55; 23: 152 Ap '58; 28: 114 Nov '60.
tapersticks. *See* candlesticks.
tapestry. Con. 126: II Aug '50; 134: XXXIX Dec '54; 136: XLI, 7 Sept '55.
Holiday 21: 70 (col.) Ap '57.
—— **(Polish collection).** Con. 138: 2 (col.), 4-9 Sept '56.
—— **(16th cent.).** Con. 129: 141 Je '52; 132: 135 Nov '53.
Int. gr. soc.: Arts . . . p. 97 (col.).
—— **(17th cent.).** Con 142: 107 Nov '58.
Holiday 19: 48 (col.) Jan '56.
—— **(18th cent.).** Con. 140: VI Jan '58; 141: 249 Je '58.
——, **altar (16th cent.).** Con. 129: LXIX Je '52.
——, **antique.** Con. 136: 45 Sept '55, LIV Nov '55.
Natl. geog. 97: 753 Je '50.
——, **Aubusson.** Con. 133: XLII Je '54; 142: LIII (col.) Nov '58.
——, **Aubusson (18th cent.).** Con. 132: LXV Nov '53; 143: LXI May '59.
——, **Balearic islands.** Natl. geog. 111: 644 (col.) May '57.
——, **Bayeux.** Con. 140: 8-9 Sept '57.
——, **Beauvais.** Con. 126: 55-8 Aug '50; 139: 122 Ap '57; 140: XXX Dec '57, 252 (col.) Jan '58.
Holiday 21: 78 (col.) Ap '57.
——, **Beauvais (Boucher).** Natl. geog. 113: 258 (col.) Feb '58.
——, **Boucher.** Natl. geog. 113: 255 (col.) Feb '58.
——, **Brussels.** Con. 139: 271 Je '57; 140: 54 Sept '57; 141: XXXVII Mar '58; 142: 109 Nov '58; 145: 75 Ap '60.
——, **Brussels (18th cent.).** Con. 135: 206 May '55.
——, **Brussels (medieval).** Con. 134: 112 (col.) Nov '54.
——, **Chinese.** Natl. geog. 99: 618 (col.) May '51.
——, **Demignot.** Con. 144: 148-9 Dec '59.
——, **Dini.** Con. 144: 150-1 Dec '59.
——, **"Diogenes".** Con. 143: 73 Ap '59.
——, **Elizabethan (16th cent.).** Con. 143: 56 Mar '59.
——, **English.** Con. 129: 9-14 Ap '52.

——, **Flemish.** Con. 138: 49, 59 Sept '56, 141 Nov '56; 141: LVII May '58.
——, **Flemish (16th cent.).** Con. 145: 88 Ap '60.
——, **Flemish gothic.** Con. 143: 202 May '59.
——, **Franco-Flemish.** Con. 140: LIII Dec '57.
——, **French (18th cent.).** Con. 143: XLIII Je '59.
——, **French (nine heroes & heroines).** Praeg.: Pict. ency., p. 216 (col.).
——, **French (16th cent.).** Con. 140: 67 Sept '57.
——, **German gothic.** Con. 134: LIII Dec '54.
——, **Gobelin.** Con. 133: LVII May '54; 140: 58 Sept '57.
——, **Gothic.** Con. 138: LXIII Jan '57; 140: 112 Nov '57; 142: 125 Nov '58.
——, **Gros Point (16th cent.).** Con. 141: XL Ap '58.
——, **Jean Lurcat.** Praeg.: Pict. ency., p. 100 (col.).
——, **Kashan.** Con. 142: XXVII Sept '58.
——, **Louis XIV.** Con. 141: 169-74 May '58.
——, **Morris.** Praeg.: Pict. ency., p. 408.
——, **Mortlake.** Con. 140: XL Dec '57.
——, **Norwegian folk (17th cent.).** Con. 144: 283 Jan '60.
——, **Portuguese.** Con. 137: 75-6 Mar '56.
——, **Russian (19th cent.).** Con. 144: 272 Jan '60.
——, **Sheldon.** Con. 129: XLIX Je '52.
——, **Soho.** Con. 142: 7 Sept '58.
——, **Soho chinoiserie.** Con. 144: 199 Dec '59.
——, **Soho chinoiserie (18th cent.).** Con. 144: 269 Jan '60.
——, **Soho Teniers (18th cent.).** Con. 145: 126 Ap '60.
——, **Spanish (17th cent.).** Con. 132: X-XI (col.) Nov '53.
——, **Tournai.** Con. 141: 199 May '58.
——, **Turin.** Con. 144: 146-51 Dec '59.
tapestry design (artist). Natl. geog. 113: 834 (col.) Je '58.
tapestry detail (medieval musicians). Int. gr. soc.: Arts . . . p. 61 (col.).
tapestry portrait of George II, King. Con. 144: 27 (col.) Sept '59.
tapestry weaver, Gobelin. Natl. geog. 98: 60 (col.) Jl '50.
tapestry weaving (girl). Natl. geog. 98: 354 (col.) Sept '50.
Tapies, Antonio. Holiday 26: 107 (col.) Dec '59.
taproom, Raleigh tavern. Natl. geog. 106: 443 (col.) Oct '54.
taproom equipment. Rawson: Ant. pict. bk., p. 89.
taproom whiskey barrel. Rawson: Ant. pict. bk., p. 61.
Tarantella dancers (Sicily). Natl. geog. 107: 12 (col.) Jan '55.
Tarascan Indians. *See* Indians, Tarascan.
Tarchiani, Alberto. Cur. biog. p. 562 (1950).
target & arrow. Natl. geog. 102: 494 (col.) Oct '52.
target & arrow (sym.). Lehner: Pict. bk. of sym., p. 84.

Tarkington, Booth. Amer. heri., vol. 2 no. 1 p. 24 (fall '50).

Tarleton, Lt. Col. Banastre (British). Amer. heri., vol. 9 no. 3 p. 47 (Ap '58).

—— (by Smith). Con. ency. of ant., vol. 1, pl. 136.

Tarot cards (sym.). Lehner: Pict. bk. of sym., p. 76-7.

tarpot. Rawson: Ant. pict. bk., p. 74.

Tarsus. Osward: Asia Minor, pl. 130-1.

"Tartar" (St. Petersburg porcelain). Con. 142: 270 Jan '59.

Tasman (wooden bust). Natl. geog. 110: 796 (col.) Dec '56.

Tasman glacier. Natl. geog. 101: 451 (col.) Ap '52.

Tasmania. Natl. geog. 110: 792-818 (part col.) Dec '56.
Travel 105: 14-7 Mar '56.

—— (map). Natl. geog. 110: 794 Dec '56.

tassel, window shade (antique). Amer. heri., vol. 9 no. 6 p. 23 (Oct '58).

Tassilo chalice. See chalice, Tassilo.

Tastevin. See Chevaliers du Tastevin.

Tata, J. R. D. Cur. biog. p. 431 (1958).

Tati, Jacques. Cur. biog. p. 443 (1961).
Holiday 27: 90 May '60.

Tattershall castle (Eng.). Natl. geog. 103: 836 Je '53.

tattoo (on man). Int. gr. soc.: Arts . . . p. 183 (col.).

—— (on sailor). Holiday 10: 47 (col.) Nov '51.

tattooing boy (Borneo). Natl. geog. 109: 722 May '56.

Tatum, Edward L. Cur. biog. p 438 (1959).

Tauberbischofsheim altar. Praeg.: Pict. ency., p. 285 (col.).

Taubes, Frederic. Cur. biog. p. 752 (1943).

Taubman, Hyman Howard. Cur. biog. p. 439 (1959).

Taussig, Helen B. Cur. biog. p. 52 (1946).

Tav cross. See cross, Tav.

tavern, Amer. (int.). Holiday 27: inside back cover (col.) Ap '60.

——, Belgium (old). Natl. geog. 107: 633 (col.) May '55.

——, Bump. See Bump tavern.

——, Cat & fiddle (Eng.). Holiday 25: 15 Mar '59.

——, Eagle (Vermont). Holiday 26: 60 (col.) Aug '59.

——, Ferry. Holiday 26: 58 (col.) Aug '59.

——, Great Falls (Maryland). Natl. geog. 117: 432 (col.) Mar '60.

——, Natchez trace. Brooks: Growth of a nation, p. 106, 113.

tavern interior (men). Holiday 25: 161 (col.) Ap '59.

tavern sign. Holiday 28: inside back cover (col.) Oct '60, 218 (col.) Dec '60.

—— (1808). Amer. heri., vol. 3 no. 2 inside back cover (col.) (winter '52).

—— (1813). Amer. heri., vol. 7 no. 2 p. 17 (col.) (Feb '56).

——, English. Holiday 27: 205 (col.) Ap '60.

tavern signs, English. Holiday 24: 193 Nov '58.

tavern table. See table, tavern.

taverns, New England. Amer. heri., vol. 4 no. 4 p. 24-9 (summer '53).

Tawela water tanks. Travel 105: 54 Mar '56.

Tawes, J. Millard. Cur. biog. p. 424 (1960).

Taxco (Mexico). Holiday 14: 52-3 (col.) Jl '53.
Travel 110: cover (col.) Nov '58.

taxi (comic). Holiday 26: 46 Aug '59.

——, Murcia (Spain). Natl. geog. 97: 432 Ap '50.

——, water. See water-taxi (India).

Taylor, Albert Hoyt. Cur. biog. p. 593 (1945).

Taylor, Capt. Creed. Horan: Pict. hist. of wild west, p. 119.

Taylor, Deems. Holiday 22: 19 Oct '57, 149 Dec '57.

Taylor, Elizabeth. Cur. biog. p. 614 (1948); p. 577 (1952).

Taylor, George W. Cur. biog. p. 816 (1942).

Taylor, Glen H. Cur. biog. p. 629 (1947).

Taylor, Harold A. Cur. biog. p. 591 (1946).

Taylor, Howard C., III. Natl. geog. 113: 458, 467 (col.) Ap '58.

Taylor, John W. Cur. biog. p. 597 (1954).

Taylor, Laurette. Cur. biog. p. 595 (1945).

Taylor, Maj. Gen. Maxwell D. Cur. biog. p. 594 (1946); p. 445 (1961).

Taylor, Pitkin. Horan: Pict. hist. of wild west, p. 119.

Taylor, Richard. Cur. biog. p. 853 (1941).

Taylor, Robert. Amer. heri., vol. 11 no. 5 p. 47 (Aug '60).
Cur. biog. p. 579 (1952).

Taylor, Robert Lewis. Cur. biog. p. 441 (1959).

Taylor, Susan. Horan: Pict. hist. of wild west, p. 119.

Taylor, Brig. Gen. Telford. Cur. biog. p. 615 (1948).

Taylor, William. Horan: Pict. hist. of wild west, p. 76.

Taylor, Zachary. Amer. heri., vol. 4 no. 4 p. 10 (summer '53); vol. 7 no. 3 p. 31 (Ap '56).

—— (by Brady). Jensen: The White House, p. 71.

—— (cartoons of). Amer. heri., vol. 4 no. 4 p. 11-3 (summer '53).

—— (on horse). Amer. heri., vol. 6 no. 4 p. 20 (Je '55).

tazza, Arlington (antique). Con. 132: 112 Nov '53.

——, enameled. Con. 140: 206 Dec '57.

——, George I (silver). Con. 129: XXXIV Ap '52; 139: VII Je '57.

——, gilt. Con. 145: 8 Je '60.

——, Ravenscroft (17th cent.). Con. 145: 189 May '60.

——, Venetian enameled glass (1500). Con. 144: LXXX Jan '60.

——, William & Mary (silver). Con. 132: XLVI Sept '53; 134: XIV Sept '54.

tazzas, Irish (silver). Con. 139: XLIX May '57.

Tchaikovsky, Peter Ilyich. Cooper: Con. ency. of music, p. 299.
Int. gr. soc.: Arts . . . p. 123 (col.).

Tchandi Sevou, temple of. See temple of Tchandi Sevou.

Tchelitchew, Pavel. Cur. biog. p. 753 (1943).

tea bowl, Queen Anne (silver). Con. 138: LXX Jan '57.

——, Worcester. Con. 140: XXIV Dec '57.

tea bowl & saucer, Worcester. Con. 145: XLVI Ap '60.

tea box, silver (18th cent.). Con. 132: 87 Nov '53.

tea caddies (19th cent.). Con. 132: 206 Jan '54.

——, George II (silver). Con. 139: XL Je '57; 141: XXXVIII Je '58.

——, George III (in ivory case). Con. 141: XXIII Je '58.

——, silver (antique). Con. 140: 220-1 Jan '58; 141: XXVIII May '58.

——, silver (18th cent.). Con. ency. of ant., vol. 1, pl. 88. Con. 132: 87 Nov '53.

——, silver (17th cent.). Con. 132: 88 Nov '53.

tea caddy (antique). Amer. heri., vol. 6 no. 5 p. 49 (col.) (Aug '55). Con. ency. of ant., vol. 3, p. 36-7. Con. 134: XL Nov '54.

—— (antique, rectangular, & pear-shaped). Con. ency. of ant. vol. 3, p. 36.

—— (antique silver). Con. 137: LII Ap '56.

—— (18th cent.). Con. 140: 193 (col.) Dec '57; 141: 245 Je '58.

—— (Hoff). Con. 141: 153 May '58.

—— (Paul de Lamerie). Con. 142: 6 Sept '58.

——, George II. Con. 137: 276 Je '56; 143: XIX May '59.

——, George III. Con. 135: XXXV May '55.

——, Meissen. Con. ency. of ant., vol. 1, pl. 59.

——, silver (1739). Con. ency. of ant., vol. 1, p. 153.

——, silver (18th cent.). Con. 143: 16-7 Mar '59, VII May '59.

——, silver (Norwegian, 18th cent.). Con. 145: 15 Mar '60.

——, Toleware. Holiday 18: 61 (col.) Jl '55.

——, white porcelain (antique). Con. 135: 283 Je '55.

tea can. Amer. heri., vol. 7 no. 3 p. 60 (Ap '56).

tea cart. Holiday 22: 159 (col.) Dec '57; 28: 61 Nov '60.

—— (antique). Holiday 26: 151 Nov '59.

tea ceremony (Japan). Disney: People & places, p. 153 (col.). Natl. geog. 118: 774 (col.) Dec '60.

tea chest (18th cent.). Con. 132: 88 Nov '53.

tea pavilion. Holiday 19: 56 Mar '56.

tea pickers (Java). Natl. geog. 108: 368 (col.) Sept '55.

tea plantation (Africa). Natl. geog. 97: 321 (col.) Mar '50.

tea pot. See teapot.

tea room. See tearoom.

tea service (Kashgais, Iran). Natl. geog. 101: 823 (col.) Je '52.

—— (desert warriors). Natl. geog. 112: 71 (col.) Jl '57.

——, antique silver. Con. 129: LIII Ap '52; 132: XLIII Nov '53; 141: 200 May '58.

——, Bottger porcelain. Con. 143: 267 Je '59.

——, Capodimonte. Con. 135: 17 Mar '55.

——, Chelsea Derby. Con. 144: XLIV Jan '60.

——, Dresden (in chest). Con. ency. of ant., vol. 3, pl. 117.

——, George I. Con. 134: 61 Sept '54; 145: 229 Je '60.

——, George II. Con. 133: VI Ap '54; 138: XXII Sept '56.

——, George III. Con. 132: XLII Sept '53; 133: XII Ap '54; 135: XV Ap '55; 140: XIX Jan '58; 142: XXXIII Nov '58; 144: VII Nov '59, XXXII Jan '60.

——, George IV. Con. 142: XXXVIII Nov '58.

——, Japanese. See Japanese tea service.

——, Louis XV. Con. 143: XXVI Je '59.

——, Meissen. Con. 138: 262 Jan '57; 142: 124 Nov '58.

——, Moroccan sheik. Holiday 20: 49 (col.) Aug '56.

——, Pakistan. Natl. geog. 102: 658 (col.) Nov '52.

——, porcelain (antique). Con. 132: 206 Jan '54.

——, Queen Anne (silver). Con. 134: 121 Nov '54.

——, Revere (Amer., 18th cent.). Con. 135: 78 Mar '55.

——, Sevres porcelain. Con. 135: 160 May '55.

——, silver. Holiday 28: 95 (col.) Aug '60.

——, silver (18th cent.). Con. 143: XVIII Mar '59.

——, silver (18th cent., Lisbon). Con. 145: XXXII Mar '60.

——, silver (19th cent., on stand). Con. 143: 57 Mar '59.

tea set (antique). Natl. geog. 97: 285 Mar '50.

——, Adams (silver). Con. 138: XXV Jan '57.

——, Bristol. Con. 137: XX Je '56.

——, English (19th cent.). Con. 142: XXIV Sept '58.

——, George III. Con. 134: XLII Dec '54; 136: LI Jan '56; 138: XXV Nov '56; 139: VII Ap '57, LVII Je '57; 141: XXXII Ap '58; 142: LXXI Jan '59; 144: XXIII Sept '59.

——, George IV. Con. 141: XV Ap '58.

——, Hennell (antique silver). Con. 136: 265 Jan '56.

——, Longton Hall. Con. 138: 193 Dec '56.

——, melon. Con. 138: 128 Nov '56.

——, Queen Anne (silver). Con. 138: XXXIII Nov '56.

——, Sheffield. Con. 141: XXXVIII Ap '58.

——, silver (antique). Con. 136: XX Dec '55, XXXVIII Jan '56; 137: LVII Je '56; 139: 264 Je '57; 140: XXII Sept '57.

——, silver (16th cent.). Con. 137: III Je '56.

——, silver (19th cent.). Con. 138: XI Dec '56.

——, Staffordshire (19th cent.). Amer. heri., vol. 6 no. 5 p. 52 (col.). (Aug '55).

tea shop (Pakistan). Natl. geog. 102: 658 (col.) Nov '52.

tea spoons. Holiday 11: 134 May '52.

——. See also silverware.

tea strainer, George III (silver). 141: XII Mar '58, XX Ap '58, XXVI May '58, XVIII Je '58; 142: XII Sept '58, XLVI Nov '58, XII Dec '58, XXXIII Jan '59.

tea table. Holiday 21: 87 (col.) Jan '57; 26: 120 Oct '59.

—— (18th cent.). Con. 140: 141 Nov '57; 141: 128, IV Ap '58; 143: 79 Ap '59.

——, Chippendale. Con. ency. of ant., vol. 1, pl. 33.

Con. 142: LII Sept '58.

Int. gr. soc.: Arts . . . p. 105 (col.).

——, Phila. Con. 135: 69 Mar '55.

——, regency. Con. 138: XX Sept '56.

——, Sheraton. Con. 145: LVII Ap '60.

——, sidewalk (Algiers). Natl. geog. 117: 774 (col.) Je '60.

——, sidewalk (Rome). Holiday 11: 45 Ap '52.

——, tilt-top (Georgian). Con. 145: LVII Mar '60.

tea urn (19th cent.). Con. 140: XXVIII Nov '57.

——, Amer. (silver, 18th cent.). Con. 135: 76 Mar '55.

——, George III. Con. 137: LI Ap '56; 141: XLVI May '58, 272 Je '58; 143: XXVI May '59; 145: XXXIV Ap '60.

——, Norwegian (silver, 19th cent.). Con. 145: 17 Mar '60.

——, rococo. Con. 141: 153 May '58.

——, silver (antique). Con. 140: 219 Jan '58.

tea vendor (Barbados). Natl. geog. 101: 367 (col.) Mar '52.

tearoom. Holiday 26: 57 Dec '59.

——, Russian (N.Y.). Holiday 25: 98 (col.) Mar '59.

Teach, Edward. See Blackbeard.

teacher (cap & gown). Holiday 18: 83 Nov '55.

—— (country school room). Natl. geog. 99: 191 (col.) Feb '51.

—— (dancing class). Holiday 11: 48 Je '52.

—— (Lyceum lecturer). See Lyceum lecturer (1841).

—— (men study English). Natl. geog. 109: 236 (col.) Feb '56.

—— (school room). Amer. heri., vol. 3 no. 1 p. 57 (fall '51).

Natl. geog. 99: 205 (col.) Feb '51.

——, boy's school. Holiday 18: 41 Jl '55.

——, lace school (boys & girls). Natl. geog. 115: 604 (col.) May '59.

——, Moslem. Natl. geog. 114: 630 (col.) Nov '58.

teacher & children. Natl. geog. 115: 870 (col.) Je '59; 116: 271 Aug '59.

—— (art). Natl. geog. 111: 365 Mar '57.

——, Borneo class room. Natl. geog. 108: 383 (col.) Sept '55.

—— (Hawaii). Natl. geog. 116: 866 (col.) Dec '59.

—— (kindergarten). Natl. geog. 118: 794 Dec '60.

—— (orchestra). Natl. geog. 116: 278-9 Aug '59.

—— (seated, lake). Natl. geog. 110: 443 (col.) Oct '56.

teacher & deaf children (class room). Natl. geog. 107: 378-97 (part col.) Mar '55.

teacher & marines. Natl. geog. 108: 697 (col.) Nov '55.

teacher & students. Natl. geog. 105: 319 (col.) Mar '54; 108: 539 (col.) Oct '55.

—— (Africa). Natl. geog. 108: 774-5 (col.) Dec '55.

—— (Berber, Algeria). Natl. geog. 117: 788 (col.) Je '60.

—— (Canton island). Natl. geog. 107: 128-9 (col.) Jan '55.

—— (Civil air patrol). Natl. geog. 109: 644-5 (col.) May '56.

—— (classroom). See schoolroom (teacher & students).

—— (cooking). Natl. geog. 107: 286 Feb '55.

—— (1888). Brooks: Growth of a nation, p. 204.

—— (Indians). Natl. geog. 114: 840-1 (col.) Dec '58.

—— (Japan). Natl. geog. 118: 764 (col.) Dec '60.

—— (Jewish school). Natl. geog. 110: 712-3 Dec '56.

—— (Melville is., Australia). Natl. geog. 109: 420-1 Mar '56.

—— (Mt. climbing). Natl. geog. 109: 22 (col.) Jan '56.

—— (nature study). Natl. geog. 106: 611-13, 616, 618-9 (col.) Nov '54.

—— (navigation). Natl. geog. 108: 818 Dec '55.

—— (outdoor class). Holiday 11: 65 (col.) May '52.

Natl. geog. 107: 201 (col.) Feb '55.

—— (Pakistan). Natl. geog. 102: 670-1, 674 (col.) Nov '52.

—— (Peruvian). Natl. geog. 109: 348-9 (col.) Mar '56.

—— (Russia). Natl. geog. 116: 400-1 Sept '59.

—— (school). Natl. geog. 98: 377 (col.) Sept '50.

—— (science class). Natl. geog. 114: 326 (col.) Sept '58.

—— (Tibet). Natl. geog. 108: 33 Jl '55.

—— (Univ., Israel). Natl. geog. 115: 517 (col.) Ap '59.

—— (Virgin islands). Natl. geog. 109: 218 Feb '56.

—— (Yap island). Natl. geog. 102: 822 (col.) Dec '52.

—— (zoo). Natl. geog. 110: 694-706 Nov '56.

——, Negro (classroom). Natl. geog. 103: 74 Jan '53.

teacher & tourists (park, night class). Natl. geog. 108: 94 Jl '55.

teachers (1890). Amer. heri., vol. 6 no. 3 p. 63 (Ap '55).

teacup, ball-footed (17th cent.). Con. 132: 86 Nov '53.

——, Chinese. Con. 132: 203 Jan '54.

—— See also cup & saucer.

Tead, Ordway. Cur. biog. p. 818 (1942).

Teagle, Walter C. Cur. biog. p. 819 (1942).

Teague, Olin E. Cur. biog. p. 581 (1952).

Teague, Walter Dorwin. Cur. biog. p. 822 (1942).

teahouse (Iraq). Natl. geog. 115: 56-7 (col.) Jan '59.

teakettle. Holiday 21: 5 (col.) Jan '57; 25: 173 Mar '59.
Natl. geog. 111: 573 Ap '57; 113: 321 (col.) Mar '58.

—— (children). Natl. geog. 111: 535 Ap '57.

——, antique silver. Con. 140: 219 Jan '58.

——, George I (silver). Con. 135: 267 Je '55; 136: 27 Sept '55; 139: 195 May '57; 140: 114 Nov '57.

——, George II. Con. 134: XXXIV Sept '54; 137: XXVIII Mar '56, XLVI Ap '56; 144: XXIII Nov '59.

——, Queen Anne. Con. 136: 293 Jan '56; 140: 131 Nov '57.

——, silver. Holiday 27: 24 Je '60; 28: 100 Sept '60.

——, silver (18th cent.). Con. 140: 140 Nov '57.

——, silver (Norwegian, 18th cent.). Con. 145: 16 Mar '60.

——, silver-gilt. Con. 135: 226 Je '55.

teakettle & tripod, Bowes. Con. 137: XXV Mar '56.

teakettle on stand (18th cent.). Con. 141: I May '58.

—— (enameled). Con. 129: 57 Ap '52.

——, George I (silver). Con. 129: LVII Ap '52; 133: XLVIII Ap '54; 143: XLV Ap '59.

——, George II (silver). Con. 133: XLIX Ap '54; 140: XLVII Sept '57; 141: XXXIX Mar '58; 142: XLVII Jan '59.

——, Georgian (silver). Con. 141: XII May '58.

——, Queen Anne (silver). Con. 144: LXXIII Jan '60.

——, silver (antique). Con. 143: 120 Ap '59.

——, silver (18th cent.). Con. ency. of ant., vol. 1, pl. 92; 133: XXVII Mar '54.

teakettle on tripod (1755). Con. ency. of ant., vol. 3, pl. 11.

teakettle table, Chippendale. Con. 143: XLII May '59.

teal, silver (sym.). Lehner: Pict. bk. of sym., p. 46.

Teale, Edwin Way. Cur. biog. p. 448 (1961).

Teale, Titian & Raphaelle. Amer. heri., vol. 6 no. 3 p. 46 (col.) (Ap '55).

teapot, antique. Con. 136: 55 Sept '55; 137: 188 May '56.

——, Chelsea. Con. 140: XX Nov '57; 141: inside cover May '58.

——, Chelsea-Derby porcelain. Con. 142: 12 Sept '58.

——, Chelsea porcelain. Con. 138: XXI Sept '56.

——, Chinese. Natl. geog. 99: 618 (col.) May '51.

——, Chinese (antique). Con. 134: LVIII Sept '54.

——, Chinese jade. Con. 138: XVIII Jan '57.

——, crystal (antique). Con. 132: 203 Jan '54.

——, Dutch. Holiday 10: 132 Oct '51.

——, French (18th cent.). Con. 141: 274 Je '58.

——, George I (silver). Con. 133: L Je '54; 135: 53 Mar '55; 136: 73 Sept '55; 139: XI Mar '57, XXX Ap '57; 140: LIII Sept '57; 144: V Sept '59, XV Dec '59.

——, George II (silver). Con. 132: XXIII Sept '53; 135: XXXV May '55, XXXIII Je '55; 140: XLVIII Nov '57; 141: L May '58; 142: XXII Jan '59; 144: LXXIII Jan '60.

——, George III (silver). Con. 137: XLVI Mar '56; 137: V Ap '56; 139: XXXIV Ap '57; 141: XL May '58; 142: XXII Jan '59.

——, Hennel (antique). Con. 136: 264 Jan '56.

——, Irish Bullet. Con. 140: LIII Sept '57; 142: LV Sept '58.

——, Irish (silver). Con. 136: XXVII Sept '55.

——, Italian. Con. 140: 180 Dec '57.

——, Japanese. Int. gr. soc.: Arts . . . p. 179 (col.).

——, Leeds pottery. Con. 144: XXIV Nov '59.

——, Le Nove. Con. 135: 14 Mar '55.

——, Le Nove (Venice, porcelain). Con. 140: XXIV Jan '58.

——, Meissen. Con. ency. of ant., vol. 1, pl. '57.
Con. 141: XXIV Je '58; 145: 56 Mar '60.

——, Newhall (early). Con. 134: LI Nov '54.

——, pewter (antique). Con. 140: XL Nov '57.

——, porcelain (antique). Con. 135: 156 May '55.

——, porcelain (19th cent.). Con. 132: 204 Jan '54.

——, Queen Anne (silver). Con. 134: 161, 207 Dec '54; 135: XLIII May '55; 140: 39 Sept '57.

——, Russian. Con. 142: 102 Nov '58.

——, silver (antique). Con. 132: XX Sept '53; 140 219, 221 Jan '58; 143: LVIII Je '59.

——, silver (early Scotch). Con. 140: III Sept '57.

——, silver (18th cent.). Con. ency. of ant., vol. 3, pl. 36.
Con. 129: 142 Je '52; 132: LX Nov '53; 139: XII Mar '57; 142: XXXIV Sept '58; 143: 16 Mar '59; 144: XXXVIII Sept '59.

——, silver (German, 18th cent.). Con. 144: 78 Nov '59.

——, silver (Richardson). Con. 145: 138 Ap '60.

——, silver (17th cent.). Con. 144: 16 Sept '59.

——, silver (1738). Con. 142: VII Jan '59.

——, silver (1792). Con. 145: XL Je '60.

——, Staffordshire. Con. ency. of ant., vol. 1, pl. 52.

——, Swedish (antique). Con. 141: 9 Mar '58.

——, Venice. Con. 135: 13 Mar '55.

——, Wedgwood. Con. 129: XLIII Je '52; 132: 205 Jan '54.

——, Worcester. Con. 132: 169 Jan '54; 144: XXXII Sept '59; 145: XLIV May '60.

——, Worcester porcelain (18th cent.). Con. 144: XXX Jan '60.

teapot & cups (serving). Holiday 23: 113 Mar '58.

teapot on stand, George I. Con. 140: LIII Sept '57.

teapot, George II. Con. 145: XXIX May '60.
Teatro Della Piccola Scala (int., Milan). Cooper: Con. ency. of music, p. 459.
Teatro di San Carlo (int., Naples). Cooper: Con. ency. of music, p. 460.
Teatro La Fenice (int., Venice, 1837). Cooper: Con. ency. of music, p. 291 (col.).
Teatro La Scala (ext. & int., Milan). Cooper: Con. ency. of music, p. 458.
Tebaldi, Renata. Cur. biog. p. 599 (1955).
Tebbel, John W. Cur. biog. p. 618 (1953).
technocracy (sym.). Lehner: Pict. bk. of sym., p. 95.
technology (sym.). Lehner: Pict. bk. of sym., p. 17.
Tecumseh (Indian). Amer. heri., vol. 2 no. 1 p. 17 (fall '50).
Tedder, Sir Arthur William. Cur. biog. p. 757 (1943).
teddy bear (sym.). Lehner: Pict. bk. of sym., p. 63.
Teelink, Abraham (work of). Con. 144: LXIII Jan '60.
teen-agers (comic). Holiday 24: 48-9 Sept '58.
——. See also boy & girl.
teeth, fossil. Natl. geog. 118: 430 Sept '60.
——, human. Gray's anatomy, p. 128-9, 132, 164-6, 171, 174, 363, 1026-7, 1154-6, 1158, 1163, 1166, 1172, 1178.
Teheran. Natl. geog. 100: 429, 444, 452-4 (col.) Oct '51; 104: 708-20 Nov '53.
—— (marble palace, int.). Holiday 20: 65 Dec '56.
—— (welcomes Eisenhower). Natl. geog. 117: 632-3 (col.) May '60.
Teitgen, Pierre-Henri. Cur. biog. p. 620 (1953).
'59.
Tel Aviv (Israel). Holiday 26: 71-3, 76 Dec '59.
—— (harbor). Holiday 17: 44 (col.) Feb '55.
Tel Aviv Inn (Chicago). Travel 113: 51 Mar '60.
Telegraph Creek (Alaska). Travel 106: 41 Jl '56.
Telegraph house (Heart's content, Newfoundland). Amer. heri., vol. 9 no. 6 p. 51 (col.) (Oct '58).
telegraph instrument (1851, 1951). Amer. heri., vol. 3 no 3 p. 56 (col.), 58 (spring '52).
telegraph transmitter (1853). Amer. heri., vol. 9 no. 3 p. 18 (Ap '58).
telephone. Holiday 11: 144 Ap '52; 25: 212 Ap '59.
Int. gr. soc.: Arts . . . p. 169 (col.).
—— (girl). Holiday 22: 144 Sept '57.
Natl. geog. 106: 93, 105 (col.) Jl '54.
—— (1901). Amer. heri., vol. 11 no. 1 p. 8-9 (Dec '59).
—— (old style). Amer. heri., vol. 9 no. 1 p. 99, 101 (Dec '57).
——, Bell's first. Amer. heri., vol. 3 no. 1 p. 2-5 (fall '51).
——, desk. Holiday 19: 10 (col.) Je '56.
Natl. geog. 111: 418 Mar '57.
——, wall (antique). Holiday 26: 151 Nov '59.
——, wall (1900). Brooks: Growth of a nation, p. 235.
telephone booth. Holiday 19: 10 (col.) Je '56.
——, street. Natl. geog. 116: 736 (col.) Dec '59.

telephone exchange (1888). Natl. geog. 106: 118 Jl '54.
—— (1954). Natl. geog. 106: 119 Jl '54.
telephone exchanges. Natl. geog. 106: 112 (col.) Jl '54.
telephone laboratory. Natl. geog. 106: 106-7 (col.) Jl '54.
telephone operator. Holiday 5: 57 (col.) Jan '49; 6: 47 (col.) Nov '49.
telephone pole. Travel 108: inside cover Jl '57.
—— (man repairing). Natl. geog. 106: 578 Oct '54.
telephone switchboard. Holiday 7: 55 Feb '50, 76 Je '50; 8: 32 Aug '50.
telescope. Holiday 11: 23 Mar '52; 12: 5 (col.) Nov '52; 18: 118 Sept '55, 193 Dec '55; 19: 111 (col.) Mar '56; 23: 172 Mar '58; 25: 196 Ap '59, 200 May '59, 185 Je '59.
—— (man, comic). Holiday 25: 39 May '59.
—— (man looking through). Con. ency. of ant., vol. 3, pl. 76.
—— (on stand). Amer. heri., vol. 11 no. 5 p. 56 (Aug '60).
—— (Sudan). Natl. geog. 103: 251 Feb '53.
—— (sym.). Lehner: Pict. bk. of sym., p. 10.
——, "Big Schmidt". Natl. geog. 101: 248 Feb '52.
——, observatory. Holiday 19: 36 May '56.
——, Palomar. Natl. geog. 98: 409 Sept '50.
——, Schmidt. Natl. geog. 98: 404 Sept '50.
——, surveyor's. Natl. geog. 109: 353 (col.) Mar '56.
——, World's largest (Hale). Natl. geog. 115: 670 May '59.
telesterion (Eleusis). Natl. geog. 109: 53 (col.) Jan '56.
teletalk box, barge. Natl. geog. 114: 688 (col.) Nov '58.
television. Holiday 5: 1, 14, 96 Mar '49, 133 Ap '49, 96 Je '49; 6: 10 (col.) Oct '49, 87 (col.) Nov '49; 7: 46 (col.) Ap '50; 10: 13, 118: (col.) Oct '51, 10, 74 (col.) Nov '51, 142 (col.) Dec '51; 11: 69 Mar '52, 168 May '52, 80 Je '52; 12: 79 Sept '52, 137 Nov '52, 86 Dec '52; 13: 76 Ap '53, 73 Je '53; 14: 124 Oct '53, 79 Nov '53; 18: 71 (col.), 134 Nov '55, inside cover (col.), 96 Dec '55; 19: 90 May '56; 20: 63 (col.) Sept '56, 102 Nov '56; 21: 82, 117 Feb '57, 104 Ap '57, 1, 102 (col.) May '57, 118 (col.) Je '57; 22: 31 Oct '57; 24: 5 Aug '58, 33 Sept '58, 100 Oct '58, 1, 93, 128, 133 Nov '58; 25: 131 (col.) Mar '59, 26 (col.) May '59, 4 Je '59; 26: 113 Jl '59, 14, 109 Oct '59; 28: 130 Oct '60, 29 Nov '60.
Natl. geog. 106: 93 (col.), 94 Jl '54.
—— (operation). Natl. geog. 106: 94-7, 100 (part col.) Jl '54.
television antenna. Natl. geog. 118: 746 (col.) Dec '60.
television stage. Natl. geog. 106: 90-1 (col.) Jl '54.
Telfer, Arthur J. Amer. heri., vol. 10 no. 1 p. 81 (Dec '58).
Telkes, Maria De. Cur. biog. p. 563 (1950).
Tell City (Indiana). Natl. geog. 97: 182 Feb '50.
Teller, Daniel V. Cur. biog. p. 601 (1954).

Teller, Edward. Cur. biog. p. 599 (1954).
Tello, Manuel. Cur. biog. p. 443 (1959).
"Temperance" (by Baratta). Con. 142: 174 Dec '58.
"Temperance" (terracotta). Con. 144: 174 Dec '59.
tempietto (San Pietro, Rome). Praeg. Pict. ency., p. 290.
Temple, Shirley. Cur. biog. p. 597 (1945).
Temple, Archbishop William. Cur. biog. p. 824 (1942).
temple (Cole). Amer. heri., vol. 8 no. 6 p. 53-60 (col.) (Oct '57).
temple (India). Holiday 27: 28 (col.) May '60. Natl. geog. 100: 359 (col.) Sept '51. Travel 101: inside cover Je '54; 111: cover, 16, 18 Jan '59.
—— (Indochina). Natl. geog. 99: 470 (col.) Ap '51.
—— (Jerusalem). Natl. geog. 110: 715 (col.) Dec '56.
—— (Nakhon Pathon, Thailand). Natl. geog. 116: 786-7 (col.) Dec '59.
—— (Nepal). Natl. geog. 97: 10, 12 (col.) Jan '50.
—— (Pescadores island). Natl. geog. 109: 269 (col.) Feb '56.
——, Babylonian (reconstruction, hanging gardens). Int. gr. soc.: Arts . . . p. 13 (col.).
——, Babylonian (3000 yrs. ago). Int. gr. soc.: Arts . . . p. 11 (col.).
——, Bangkok. Natl. geog. 99: 359 (col.) Mar '59.
——, Bangkok. See also Royal pantheon (Bangkok temple).
——, Borobudur. See Borobudur temple.
——, Buddhist. See Buddhist temple.
——, Confucian (Pescadores island). Natl. geog. 109: 273 (col.) Feb '56.
——, early Hawaiian. Amer. heri., vol. 11 no. 2 p. 18-9 (col.) (Feb '60).
——, elliptical (Africa). Natl. geog. 104: 196 Aug '53.
——, Formosa. Travel 108: 36 Nov '57.
——, golden (Sikhs, India). Holiday 26: 170 (col.) Nov '59.
——, Greek. Ceram: March of arch., p. 15 (col.). Holiday 13: 10 May '53; 24: 202 Dec '58.
——, Greek (Parthenon). See Parthenon.
——, Greek (Sicily). Holiday 19: 50-1 May '56. Natl. geog. 107: 22 (col.) Jan '55.
——, Hindu (India). Natl. geog. 103: 66 (col.) Jan '53. Praeg.: Pict. ency., p. 551.
——, Hindu (Java). Natl. geog. 108: 353 (col.) Sept '55.
——, Hindu. See also Angkor Wat.
——, Inca. Natl. geog. 98: 422 Oct '50.
——, Japanese. Holiday 5: 5 Mar '49; 13: 68 (col.) Mar '53. Natl. geog. 104: 642 (col.) Nov '53.
——, Japanese (medieval). Int. gr. soc.: Arts . . . p. 85 (col.).
——, Korean. See Korean temple.
——, Lama (Peking). Natl. geog. 118: 216-7 (col.) Aug '60.

——, Luxor. See Luxor temple.
——, Meenakshi. See Meenakshi temple.
——, Megalithic (Malta). Holiday 26: 88 (col.) Aug '59.
——, Mondop (Bangkok). Int. gr. soc.: Arts . . . p. 85 (col.).
——, Mormon. See Mormon temple.
——, Nimes (France). Natl. geog. 100: 3 Jl '51.
——, Patan's. Natl. geog. 112: 148-9 (col.) Jl '57.
——, Penang. Travel 107: 42 Feb '57.
——, Peruvian Indian. Travel 107: 30-2 Feb '57.
——, Prambanan. See Prambanan temple.
——, Queen Hatshepsut's. See Hatshepsut's temple, Queen.
——, Rameses II. Holiday 27: 64-7 (col.) Mar '60.
——, rock (Rameses II, Egypt). Natl. geog. 106: 756 (col.) Dec '54.
——, Roman (copy made of broom wood). Con. 145: 101 Ap '60.
——, Roman (Maison Carree). Amer. heri., vol. 10 no. 5 p. 68 (Aug '59).
——, Roman (Pantheon). See Pantheon.
——, Roman (ruins, Evora, Portugal). Travel 110: 46 Sept '58.
——, Shinto. Int. gr. soc.: Arts . . . p. 51 (col.)
——, Sri Mangesh. See Sri Mangesh temple (India).
——, Sumerian. Natl. geog. 99: 69 (col.) Jan '51.
——, thatched. Natl. geog. 99: 351 (col.) Mar '51.
——, Wat Chang (Siam). Disney: People & places, p. 170 (col.).
temple altar, Fukien. Natl. geog. 102: 302 (col.) Sept '52.
temple at Abydos of Sethos I (cornice). Ceram: March of arch., p. 79.
temple at Paestum (Italy). Holiday 12: 5 (col.) Oct '52.
temple bird, bronze (man & woman). Natl. geog. 117: 509 (col.) Ap '60.
temple carvings, Greek. Int. gr. soc.: Arts . . . p. 17 (col.).
temple colonnade, Luxor. See Luxor temple.
Temple Emanu-El (N.Y.). Travel 106: 17 Dec '56.
temple food (to gods). Natl. geog. 109: 270 Feb '56.
"Temple gateway" (winter). Praeg.: Pict. ency., p. 514.
temple guards (Vientiane). Natl. geog. 117: 58 (col.) Jan '60.
temple Horyu-ji (Japan). Praeg.: Pict. ency., p. 528.
temple lantern, Japanese. Natl. geog. 111: 86 (col.) Jan '57.
temple mound, Indian. Amer. heri., vol. 7 no. 6 p. 105 (Oct '56).
Temple of Abu Simbil (Egypt). Natl. geog. 118: 359 (col.) Sept '60.
Temple of Amon. See Karnak, Temple of Amon.
Temple of Aphaea & plan (Aegina). Praeg.: Pict. ency., p. 129.

Temple of Apollo (Pompeii). Labande: Naples, p. 151.

Temple of Athens. Natl. geog. 103: 368 (col.) Mar '53.

Temple of Augustus (Ankara, Ancyra). Osward: Asia Minor, pl. 51.

Temple of Bacchus. Ceram: March of arch., p. 67-8.

Temple of Buddha (Ceylon). Travel 101: 17 Ap '54.

Temple of Buddha (India). Travel 111: 18 Jan '59.

Temple of Buddha (int.). Natl. geog. 117: 33 (col.) Jan '60.

Temple of Buddha (Siam). Disney: People & places, p. 169-73 (col.).

Temple of Buddhagaya (India). Int. gr. soc.: Arts . . . p. 51 (col.).

Temple of Ceres (Paestum). Labande: Naples, p. 175.

Temple of Emerald Buddha. Travel 102: 23 Nov '54.

Temple of Great Buddha (China). Natl. geog. 99: 388, 391 (col.) Mar '51.

Temple of Heaven (Peking). Holiday 21: 74 Je '57.
Natl. geog. 118: 194-5 (col.) Aug '60.

Temple of Heliopolis. See Heliopolis, Temple of.

Temple of Hera plan (Samos). Praeg.: Pict. ency., p. 129.

"Temple of inscriptions" (at Palenque). Ceram: March of arch., p. 297-8.

"Temple of irrigation" (Bali). Natl. geog. 99: 25 (col.) Jan '51.

Temple of Isis (Philae). Ceram: March of arch., p. 16.
Int. gr. soc.: Arts . . . p. 13 (col.).

Temple of Isis (Pompeii). Labande: Naples, p. 152.

"Temple of love" (Island of Capri). Holiday 25: 55 Jan '59.

Temple of Luxor. See Luxor temple.

Temple of Neptune (Paestum). Labande: Naples, p. 176-81.

Temple of Queen Hatshepsut (Thebes). Con. 138: 133 Nov '56.

Temple of Queen Hatshepsut (Egypt). Natl. geog. 108: 618-9 (col.) Nov '55.

Temple of Queen Hatshepsut. Praeg: Pict. ency., p. 153.

Temple of Quetzalcoati ("Plumed serpent", Mexico). Holiday 13: 36 Mar '53.
Natl. geog. 100: 824 (col.) Dec '51.

Temple of Ramses II. See Ramses II temple.

Temple of Tanjore (India). Praeg.: Pict. ency., p. 524.

Temple of Tchandi Sevou (9th cent.). Int. gr. soc.: Arts . . . p. 51 (col.).

"Temple of the seven dolls", Mayan. Natl. geog. 115: 98, 100-06 (part col.) Jan '59.

Temple of the sun (Mexico). Travel 114: 48 Nov '60.

"Temple of the Sybil", Tivoli (Smith). Con. 126: 217 Dec '50.

Temple of the tooth (Ceylon). Travel 111: 23 Jan '59.

"Temple of trophies". See "Sun temple".

Temple of Zeus plan (Olympia). Praeg.: Pict. ency., p. 129.

Temple of Zeus relief (Olympia). Praeg.: Pict. ency., p. 18.

temple pictures. See Egyptian temple pictures.

Temple-pyramid (Chichen Itza). Praeg.: Pict. ency., p. 543.

temple scene (terra cotta model, Cyprus is.). Natl. geog. 109: 883 Je '56.

Temple Serapis. See Serapis temple (Ephesus).

Temple to goddess Kali. Natl. geog. 118: 446 (col.) Oct '60.

Temple to Juno (Tunisia). Natl. geog. 118: 355 (col.) Sept '60.

temple wall carving, Chinese. Natl. geog. 97: 221 Feb '50.

temple wall painting. See wall painting.

Templer, Gen. Sir Gerald. Cur. biog. p. 583 (1952).

temples, Ajanta cave (India). See Ajanta temples (India).

——, American. Int. gr. soc.: Arts . . . p. 51 (col.).

——, Baalbek. See Baalbek temples.

——, Chinese. Int. gr. soc.: Arts . . . p. 51 (col.).
Natl. geog. 97: 226 Feb '50.

——, Indian. Int. gr. soc.: Arts . . . p. 51 (col.).

——, Japanese. Int. gr. soc.: Arts . . . p. 51 (col.).

——, south-east Asia. Int. gr. soc.: Arts . . . p. 51 (col.).

Temples at Paestum. Con. 138: 16 Sept '56.

temptation (sym.). Lehner: Pict. book of sym., p. 29.

"Temptation of St. Anthony". Con. 145: 189 May '60.

"Temptation of St. Anthony" (Savoldo). Con. 138: 167 Dec '56.

"Temptation of St. Anthony" (Teniers). Con. 140: LVII Sept '57.

"Ten commandments" (carved oak panel). Natl. geog. 118: 559 (col.) Oct '60.

—— (Fields of the wood, Murphy, N.C.). Travel 106: 13 Dec '56.

—— (Mt. side, S.C.). Travel 103: 22 Mar '55.

—— (sym.). Lehner: Pict. bk. of sym., p. 36.

tenacity (sym.). Lehner: Pict bk. of sym., p. 60.

Tenby (Wales). Natl. geog. 108: 574 Oct '55.

Teniers, David (work of). Natl. geog. 97: 752 Je '50.

Teniers, David the younger (work of). Con. 140: LVII Sept '57; 141: cover (col.) Ap '58.

Tennant, Mrs. Julian (Malta). Con. 137: 53 Mar '56.

Tennant, Vice Adm. William G. Cur. biog. p. 600 (1945).

Tennessee. Holiday 8: 34-51 (part col.) Nov '50.
Jordan: Hammond's pict. atlas, p. 60-1 (col.). Travel 104: 11-5 Jl '55.

—— (Norris dam). Brooks: Growth of a nation, p. 280.

—— (state capitol). Holiday 8: 48 Nov '50.

tennis (girls). Holiday 10: 100-01 Jl '51.

——, deck. Travel 101: 11 May '54.

——, club. Natl. geog. 102: 776 (col.) Dec '52.

——, **club (Cal.).** Holiday 20: 106-11 (col.) Oct '56.

——, **club (Forest Hills, N.Y.).** Holiday 20: 108 (col.) Sept '56.

tennis court. Natl. geog. 99: 289 (col.) Mar '51.

tennis game. Holiday 18: 75 (col.) Jl '55.

—— **(1894).** Amer. heri., vol. 11 no. 6 p. 106 (Oct '60).

tennis player. Holiday 10: 86 Jl '51, 83 Sept '51; 12: 4 Jl '52, 18 Aug '52.

—— **(flower).** Holiday 11: 146 Je '52.

tennis players. Holiday 6: 77 (col.) Nov '49; 7: 89 Ap '50; 17: 8-9 Jan '55; 21: 76-7, 98 Mar '57.

tennis racket. Holiday 7: 13 (col.) Mar '50; 10: 100-1 Jl '51, 108 Aug '51, 159 Dec '51; 14: 114 Aug '53; 18: 104 Dec '55; 19: 94 (col.) Je '56 22: 115 (col.) Jl '57; 23: 48 May '58, 38 (col.) Je '58; 25: 43 Je '59.

—— **(girl).** Holiday 10: 83 Sept '51.

tennis rackets. Holiday 18: 9 Jl '55; 20: 111 (col.) Oct '56.

Natl. geog. 117: 16 (col.) Jan '60.

—— **(girls playing).** Natl. geog. 97: 65 (col.) Jan '50.

tennis tournament (1880). Holiday 14: 70 (col.) Sept '53.

Tennyson, Alfred, 1st baron. Con. 144: 11 Sept '59.

Tennyson, Alfred Lord. Natl. geog. 108: 333 Sept '55.

tent. Amer. heri., vol. 6 no. 2 p. 12 (winter '55); vol. 11 no. 4 p. 47 (col.) Je '60.
Holiday 15: 71 (col.) Ap '54; 22: 45 Sept '57.
Natl. geog. 100: 687 (col.) Nov '51; 102: 210-11, 213, 223 (part col.) Aug '52; 106: 424 Sept '54; 107: 698 May '55.
Travel 105: 35 May '56; 107: 23 May '57; 109: 23 Je '58; 113: 27 Je '60.

—— **(Afghanistan).** Natl. geog. 98: 690-1 (col.) Nov '50.

—— **(Antarctic).** Natl. geog. 115: 32-3 (col.) Jan '59.

—— **(boys).** Natl. geog. 110: 413 (col.) Sept '56.

—— **(camp).** Holiday 24: 78 (col.) Sept '58.
Natl. geog. 111: 822 (col.) Je '57; 113 603 (col.) May '58; 114: 167 (col.) Aug '58; 116: 148 (col.) Aug '59.
Travel 107: 30 Mar '57, 37 Je '57.

—— **(desert nomads).** Natl. geog. 114: 21 (col.) Jl '58.

—— **(man).** Natl. geog. 99: 650 (col.) May '51.

—— **(man camping).** Travel 111: 41 Je '59.

—— **(man erecting).** Natl. geog. 106: 12 (col.) Jl '54.

—— **(man erecting, Iran).** Natl. geog. 101: 818 (col.) Je '52.

—— **(man, snow).** Natl. geog. 109: 27 Jan '56.

—— **(service).** Natl. geog. 103: 573 (col.) May '53.

—— **(Mt. campers).** Natl. geog. 118 413 (col.) Sept '60.

—— **(Tibet).** Holiday 27: 64 May '60.

——, **archaeologist's (Panama jungle).** Natl. geog. 104 278, 280 (col.) Aug '53.

——, **beach.** Holiday 23: 7 (col.) May '58; 28: 20-1 (col.) Jl '60.

——, **chautauqua.** Brooks: Growth of a nation, p. 211.

——, **circus.** Durant: Pict. hist. of Amer. circus, p. 60, 173, 304.

——, **circus (setting up).** Durant: Pict. hist. of Amer. circus, p. 150.

——, **explorer's.** Natl. geog. 101: 9 (col.) Jan '52.

——, **garden.** Holiday 19: 56 (col.) Mar '56.

——, **Indian.** Amer. heri., vol. 2 no. 2 p. 29 (winter '51); vol. 4 no. 1 p. 20 (col.) (fall '52); vol. 4 no. 4 p. 59 (col.) (summer '53); vol. 9 no. 6 frontis. (col.) (Oct '58).
Holiday 18 28 Jl '55; 19: 29 Feb '56; 106: 31 Jl '56; 108: 37 Aug '57.

——, **Indian.** *See* also tepee, Indian.

——, **Lama (int.).** Natl. geog. 99: 623 May '51.

——, **music festival.** *See* music festival tent.

——, **show.** *See* show tent.

——, **Washington's (Valley Forge).** Natl. geog. 105: 191 (col.) Feb '54.

"Tenth muse of Mexico" (Christian nun). Ceram: March of arch., p. 267.

tents. Natl. geog. 97: 6 Jan '50, 466 (col.) Ap '50; 109: 746 Je '56.

—— **(camp).** Natl. geog. 111: 773 (col.) Je '57.

—— **(Mt. climbers).** Natl. geog. 108: 602-3 (col.) Nov '55.

—— **(soldiers camp, 1787).** Amer. heri., vol. 5 p. 21 (col.).

—— **(South Pole).** Natl. geog. 112: 24-5 (col.), 46 Jl '57.

——, **Arabs.** Natl. geog. 104: 862 (col.) Dec '53.

——, **Banff Park (Alberta, Canada).** Travel 114: 21 Jl '60.

——, **beach.** Holiday 27: cover (col.) Je '60; 15: 106 (col.) Jan '54.

——, **Berber.** Natl. geog. 107: 185 Feb '55.

——, **Boy Scouts jamboree (Valley Forge).** Natl. geog. 105: 194-5 (col.) Feb '54.

——, **Indian.** Amer. heri., vol. 5 no. 4 p. 39 (summer '54); vol. 8 no. 1 p. 52 (Dec '56); vol. 8 no. 3 p. 13 (col.) (Ap '57).
Natl. geog. 97: 731 (col.) Je '50.

——, **"Liberty Road" (Viet Nam).** Natl. geog. 107: 870-1 Je '55.

——, **Moslem.** Natl. geog. 104: 4-5 (col.) Jl '53.

——, **Moslem pilgrims.** Natl. geog. 104: 44, 54 (col.) Jl '53.

——, **music.** Travel 113: 26-8 May '60.

——, **Nomad.** Natl. geog. 117: 782-3 (col.) Je '60.

Teocalli of Cholula (Mexico). Ceram: March of arch., p. 270.

Teotihuacan's sculpture. Natl. geog. 100: 824 (col.) Dec '51.

tepee (Finland). Natl. geog. 106: 265 Aug '54.

——, **Arapaho Indian.** Natl. geog. 117: 809 (col.) Je '60.

——, **Indian.** Amer. heri., vol. 4 no. 1 p. 20 (col.) (fall '52); vol. 6 no. 1 p. 33-5 (col.)

(fall '54); vol. 7 no. 6 p. 106 (Oct '56); vol. 9 no. 1 frontis. (col.) (Dec '57).
Natl. geog. 111: 694 (col.) May '57.
Travel 111: 28 Je '59.

tepees. *See* also tent, Indian.

Tequendama Falls (Colombia, S.A.). Travel 112: 19 Sept '59.

Ter-Arutunian, Rouben. Cur. biog. (1963).

Ter Poorten, Lt. Gen. Hein. Cur. biog. p. 827 (1942).

Terborch, Gerard (work of). Con. 126: 197 (col.) Dec '50; 133: 97 Ap '54.
Praeg.: Pict. ency., p. 346 (col.).

Terboven, Josef. Cur. biog. p. 855 (1941).

Terbruggen, Hendrick (work of). Con. 139: 56 Mar '57.

Terechkovitch, Constantin (work of). Con. 143: XXI Je '59.

Tereshkova, Valentina. Cur. biog. (1963).

term figure, stone garden (18th cent.). Con. ency. of ant., vol. 3, pl. 25.

termite nest (Sudan). Natl. geog. 103: 268 Feb '53.

Terpsichore (muse). Lehner: Pict. bk. of sym., p. 33.

terrace, "Cotton-wool" castle. Osward: Asia Minor, pl. 136-7.

terrace, hotel. Holiday 26: 57 (col.) Jl '59.

——, house. Holiday 27: 201 May '60.

terrace table. *See* table, terrace.

terraced fields. Natl. geog. 107: 516 (col.) Ap '55.

terraced hill land, Chinese. Natl. geog. 111: 346 (col.) Mar '57.

terraced land. Natl. geog. 104: 513 (col.) Oct '53.

—— (Hunza Valley). Natl. geog. 117: 94-5 (col.) Jan '60.

—— (Madeira is.). Natl. geog. 115: 376-7 (col.) Mar '59.

terraces, rice. *See* rice terraces.

terracotta, Chinese. Con. 143: L Ap '59.

terracotta figure (17th cent.). Con. 140: XXVI Nov '57.

——, Florentine (15th cent.). Con. 145: XX-XIX Mar '60.

terracotta figures (Bernini). Con. 145: 89 Ap '60.

terracotta group (Clodion). Con. 143: 210 Je '59.

terracottas, French (18th cent.). Con. 140: 3-7 Sept '57.

terra-marina trailer, auto. Travel 114: 58 Aug '60.

Terrell, Mary Church. Cur. biog. p. 828 (1942).

terrorism (sym.). Lehner: Pict. bk. of sym., p. 83.

Terry, Bill. Holiday 23: 84 May '58.

Terry, Luther L. Cur. biog. p. 450 (1961).

Terry, Thomas. Cur. biog. p. 452 (1961).

test sphere (for rockets & radios). Natl. geog. 112: 810 Dec '57.

test tube. Travel 101: 8 Jan '54.

Testament (scenes). *See* Biblical scenes.

tet of Osiris (sym.). Lehner: Pict. bk. of sym., p. 26.

Teton Mts. Face of Amer., p. 126-7 (col.).
Natl. geog. 99: 732 (col.) Je '51; 109: 2-36

(part col.) Jan '56; 113: 624 (col.) May '58.

Tetramorph (sym.). Lehner: Pict. bk. of sym., p. 38.

Tewa Indian. *See* Indian, Tewa.

Tewksbury (Eng.) Natl. geog. 108: 316 (col.) Sept '55.

Tewson, Sir Vincent. Cur. biog. p. 585 (1952).

Texas. Amer. heri., vol. 4 no. 1 all the issue (fall '52).
Holiday 21: 52-7 (part col.) Feb '57; 24: 36-49 (part col.) Oct '58.
Jordan: Hammond's pict. atlas, p. 114-9 (col.).
Travel 105: 43-5 May '56.

—— (The Alamo). Brooks: Growth of a nation, p. 131.

—— (cowboys). Holiday 24: 35 (col.) Oct '58.

—— (early days). Amer. heri., vol. 4 no. 1 (part col.) (fall '52).

—— (Ft. Worth, children's museum). Travel 113: 58 Jan '60.

—— (Palo Duro state park). Travel 105: 54 Jan '56.

—— (state parks). Travel 105: 54 Jan '56; 107: 40-4 Mar '57.

Texas rangers (early days). Brooks: Growth of a nation, p. 167.

textile design, hand printed (India). Natl. geog. 118: 462 (col.) Oct '60.

textile designs. Con. 140 92-6 Nov '57.
Int. gr. soc.: Arts . . . p. 175 (col.).

textile dryers (Japan). Natl. geog. 118: 750 (col.) Dec '60.

textile dying (Biblical times). Natl. geog. 118: 827 (col.) Dec '60.

—— (Indonesia). Natl. geog. 108 360 Sept '55.

textile machines. Natl. geog. 107: 315 (col.) Mar '55.

—— (girls). Natl. geog. 103: 299 (col.) Mar '53.

textile printings (man). Natl. geog. 110: 455 (col.) Oct '56.

textiles, antique. Con. 136: 18 Sept '55.

——, printed cotton. Con. 143: 132 Ap '59.

——, Scottish. Natl. geog. 108: 202 (col.) Aug '55.

Teyte, Maggie. Cur. biog. p. 602 (1945).

Thach, Vice Adm. John Smith. Cur. biog. p. 426 (1960).

Thackrey, Dorothy S. Cur. biog. p. 605 (1945).

Thadden-Trieglaff, Reingold von. Cur. biog. p. 445 (1959).

Thailand. Disney: People & places, p. 163-76 (col.).

—— (map). Natl. geog. 98: 501 Oct '50.

—— (summer palace). Holiday 28: 216 (col.) Dec '60.

Thailand arch. *See* architecture, Thailand.

Thailand dancer. Travel 102: cover Nov '54.

Thailand women (carry concrete buckets). Natl. geog. 117: 669 (col.) May '60.

Thailand. *See* also Siam.

Thaler, William J. Cur. biog. p. 427 (1960).

Thalia (goddess). Lehner: Pict. bk. of sym., p. 33.

Thames river. *See* London (Thames river).

Thanksgiving (sym.). Lehner: Pict. bk. of sym., p. 51, 55.

Thant, U. Cur. biog. p. 415 (1962).

Tharp, Louise Hall. Cur. biog. p. 601 (1955).

thatch-roof house. See house, thatch roof.

thatch roof hut. See hut, thatch roof.

Thatcher house, Becky (Hannibal, Mo.). Jordan: Hammond's pict. atlas, p. 101 (col.).

Thatcher parlor, Becky. Natl. geog. 110: 133 Jl '56.

thatching roof. Natl. geog. 107: 872 Je '55.

Thaulow, Fritz (work of). Con. 139: XLIX Ap '57; 145: XXXIII Mar '60.

Thayendanegea. See Brant, Joseph.

Thayer, Col. Sylvanus. Amer. heri., vol. 7 no. 1 p. 24 (col.) (Dec '55).

Thayer, Judge (1932). Amer. heri., vol. 9 no. 6 p. 55 (Oct '58).

theater. Holiday 5: 104 Ap '49.

—— (Banff school of fine arts). Natl. geog. 118: 108 (col.) Jl '60.

—— (Dionysus, Athens — reconstruction). Praeg.: Pict. ency., p. 93.

—— (int.). Cooper: Con. ency. of music, p. 378, 395, 456-9.
Holiday 24: 127 (col.) Nov '58.

—— (int., Dock St., Charleston). Holiday 28: 72 Sept '60.

—— (int., scenes, Monterey, Cal.). Amer. heri., vol. 11 no. 6 p. 35 (col.) (Oct '60).

—— (int., scenes). Int. gr. soc.: Arts . . . p. 145 (col.).

—— (Lisbon). Travel 108: 21 Aug '57.

—— (opera stage). Holiday 8: 77 Nov '50.

—— (plays, 16th cent.). Int. gr. soc.: Arts . . . p. 107 (col.).

—— (show). Holiday 6: 85 (col.) Jl '49.
Natl. geog. 104: 839 Dec '53.

—— (stage scene). Int. gr. soc.: Arts . . . p. 149 (col.).

—— (tent show). Natl. geog. 117: 36-7 (col.) Jan '60.

——, Abbey. See Abbey theatre.

——, Cologne. See Cologne theater.

——, Ephesus (built by Claudius). Osward: Asia Minor, pl. 32.

——, Ford's. See Ford's theater.

——, French. Holiday 13: 107 (col.) Ap '53.

——, Gladiatorial (Holy Land). Natl. geog. 98: 713 Dec '50.

——, Globe. See "Globe theater" model.

——, Greek (Epidaurus). Int. gr. soc.: Arts . . . p. 35 (col.).

——, Greek (Sicily). Natl. geog. 107: 44-5 (col.) Jan '55.

——, Old bird cage (Tombstone, Ariz.). Natl. geog. 104: 356 (col.) Sept '53.

——, outdoor. Holiday 6: 110 (col.) Aug '49.

——, outdoor (Mts. in N.C.). Amer. heri., vol. 5 no. 4 p. 16-23 (part col.) (summer '54).

——, outdoor (scene). Natl. geog. 102: 355 (col.) Sept '52.

——, outdoor (Shakespeare play). Natl. geog. 118: 804-5 (col.) Dec '60.

——, palace, Rome). Holiday 27: 99 (col.) Ap '60.

——, Park (int., N.Y., 1822). Amer. heri., vol.

8 no. 5 p. 20 (col.) (Aug '57).
Natl. geog. 99: 190 (col.) Feb '51.

——, Shakespeare. See Shakespeare festival theatre (Conn.).

——, summer. Holiday 20: 9 Oct '56.

——, summer (int.). Holiday 26: 64-9 (part col.) Jl '59.

——, summer (Ogunquit). Holiday 12: 46 Aug '52.

——, Venice. See Teatro La Fenice (1837).

theater & arena, Roman. See Roman theater & arena (Arles).

theater at Pompeii. See Pompeii (theater).

theater box (1830). Holiday 21: 58 (col.) May '57.

—— (where Lincoln was shot). Jensen: The White House, p. 93.

theater bldg., summer. Holiday 20: 107 Aug '56.

Theater de Lys, (int., N.Y.). Holiday 23: 55 (col.) Mar '58.

Theater national de l'opera (Paris). Cooper: Con. ency. of music, p. 463.

theater of Delphi. See Delphi theater.

theater. See also opera house.

theater poster (early motion picture). Amer. heri., vol. 11 no. 3 p. 101 (Ap '60).

—— (early Amer.). Amer. heri., vol. 7 no. 1 p. 33-41 (col.) (Dec '55).

theater program (Lincoln's assassination). Amer. heri., vol. 3 no. 2 p. 68 (winter '52).

—— (Mark Twain book). Amer. heri., vol. 11 no. 1 p. 70 (Dec '59).

theater restaurant (Luanda). Travel 105: 42 Feb '56.

—— (Paris, France). Con. 145: LV Je '60.

theater stage. Holiday 13: 110 (col.) Mar '53; 21: 96 (col.) Ap '57.

theatre. See theater.

theatrical troup (Indochina). Natl. geog. 99: 488 Ap '51.

theatricals (Miracle play). Int. gr. soc.: Arts . . . p. 75 (col.).

"The Thebaid". Con. 136: 205 Dec '55.

Thebes ("City of the dead"). Holiday 27: 69 (col.) Mar '60.

—— (Temple of Queen Hatshepsut). Con. 138: 133 Nov '56.
Holiday 27: 69 (col.) Mar '60.

—— (tomb wall painting). Praeg.: Pict. ency., p. 116 (col.).

Thebom, Blanche. Cur. biog. p. 617 (1948).

Theiler, Max. Cur. biog. p. 586 (1952).

theocracy (sym.). Lehner: Pict. bk. of sym., p. 95.

theodolite (men). Natl. geog. 98: 517 (col.) Oct '50.

——, silver (16th cent.). Con. 132: 188 Jan '54.

Theodora, Empress (mosaic). Praeg.: Pict. ency., p. 179 (col.).

Theodoric's tomb (Ravenna). Praeg.: Pict. ency., p. 176.

Theorell, Hugo. Cur. biog. p. 623 (1956).

therma-ice (ice container). Holiday 21: 162 Je '57.

Thermae of Hieropolis. Osward: Asia, pl. 134.

thermology (sym.). Lehner: Pict. bk. of sym., p. 17.
thermometer. Holiday 10: 71 (col.) Jl '51. Natl. geog. 109: 143 Jan '56; 113: 441 Ap '58.
—— (sym.). Lehner: Pict. bk. of sym., p. 17.
——, clinical (antique jeweled). Con. 142: XLV Dec '58.
——, weather. Holiday 11: 21 Jan '52.
thermos bottle. Holiday 10: 12 Jl '51; 13: 158 May '53; 14: 17 Jl '53; 18: 162 Dec '55.
thermos bottle & cups. Holiday 12: 88 Jl '52.
thermos bottles. Holiday 10: 72 Nov '51; 14: 98 Dec '53.
——, jugs. Holiday 20: 137 (col.) Dec '56.
"Theseus & minotaur" (sculpture). Con. 144: 227 Jan '60.
Thessaloniki. See Salonika (Greece).
"They that go down to the sea in ships" (monument). Brooks: Growth of a nation p. 99.
thimble, sailmaker's. Rawson: Ant. pict. bk., p. 77.
"The thinker" (Rodin). Holiday 7: 125 May '50.
—— (head, Rodin). Int. gr. soc.: Arts . . . p. 131 (col.).
Thira harbor. Natl. geog. 114: 758 (col.) Dec '58.
Thomas, Albert. Cur. biog. p. 565 (1950).
Thomas, Charles Allen. Cur. biog. p. 567 (1950).
Thomas, Charles S. Cur. biog. p. 605 (1954).
Thomas, Danny. Cur. biog. p. 446 (1959).
Thomas, Elbert D. Cur. biog. p. 831 (1942).
Thomas, Elmer. Cur. biog. p. 600 (1949).
Thomas, George. Pakula: Cent. album, p. 273.
Thomas, Heck. Horan: Pict. hist. of wild west, p. 170.
Thomas, Isaiah. Amer. heri., vol. 3 no. 4 p. 49 (col.) (summer '52).
Thomas, John. Cur. biog. p. 429 (1960).
Thomas, John Charles. Cur. biog. p. 759 (1943).
Thomas, John Parnell. Cur. biog. p. 632 (1947).
Thomas, Lowell, Sr. Cur. biog. p. 588 (1952). Holiday 15: 12 Jan '54; 21: 1 Jan '57; 22: 149 Dec '57. Natl. geog. 108: 23 (col.) Jl '55; 112: 152 Jl '57. Travel 111: 16-7 Mar '59.
Thomas, Lowell, jr. Holiday 15: 12 Jan '54. Natl. geog. 108: 23 (col.) Jl '55; 117: 97 (col.) Jan '60.
Thomas, Mr. & Mrs. Lowell, jr. Natl. geog. 112: 50-1, 59-69, 72, 77, 86, 89, 94, 105-7, 112 (part col.) Jl '57.
Thomas, Sir Miles. Cur. biog. p. 591 (1952).
Thomas, Sir Noah (Romney). Con. 143: 88 Ap '59.
Thomas, Norman. Cur. biog. p. 689 (1944); p. 417 (1962).
—— (college reunion). Holiday 18: 43 (col.) Nov '55.
Thomas, Rolland J. Cur. biog. p. 832 (1942).
Thomas, William L., jr. Cur. biog. p. 432 (1958).
"Thomas Lane & sister" (Copley). Con. 135: 147 Ap '55.

"Thomas le Blanc of Cavenham" (Zoffany). Con. 145: LIII May '60.
Thompson, Benjamin. Amer. heri., vol. 4 no. 4 p. 6 (summer '53).
Thompson, Count Benjamin. Amer. heri., vol. 8 no. 1 p. 75 (col.) (Dec '56).
Thompson, Frank, jr. Cur. biog. p. 448 (1959).
Thompson, Homer A. Cur. biog. p. 619 (1948).
Thompson, Jacob (work of). Con. 132: 189 Jan '54.
Thompson, Kay. Cur. biog. p. 450 (1959).
Thompson, Llewellyn E., jr. Cur. biog. p. 550 (1957).
Thompson, Mary Wolfe. Cur. biog. p. 569 (1950).
Thompson, Melvin E. Cur. biog. p. 634 (1947).
Thompson, Lt. Col. Paul W. Cur. biog. p. 835 (1942).
Thompson, Roy L. Cur. biog. p. 595 (1946).
Thompson, Ruth. Cur. biog. p. 620 (1951).
Thompson home, Count Benjamin. Amer. heri., vol. 8 no. 1 p. 77 (col.) (Dec '56).
Thompson home, Benjamin F. Natl. geog. 112: 308-9 (col.) Sept '57.
Thomson, Sir George Paget. Cur. biog. p. 636 (1947).
Thomson, Henry (work of). Con. 144: 43 Sept '59.
Thomson, John Cameron. Cur. biog. p. 620 (1948).
Thomson, Sir Joseph John. Con. 144: 11 Sept '59.
Thomson, Roy. Cur. biog. p. 431 (1960).
Thomson, Vernon W. Cur. biog. p. 434 (1958).
thoracic duct. Gray's anatomy, p. 552.
thorax. Gray's anatomy. p. 95-7, 1125-6, 1369-75.
—— (veins). Gray's anatomy, p. 673-75.
Thoreau, Henry David. Amer. heri., vol. 8 no. 2 p. 22 (Feb '57). Holiday 16: 6 Sept '54.
Thoreau's rock cairn, Henry. Natl. geog. 97: 307 (col.) Mar '50.
Thorek, Max. Cur. biog. p. 622 (1951).
Thorez, Maurice. Cur. biog. p. 597 (1946).
Thorn, James. Cur. biog. p. 602 (1949).
Thorndike, Dame Sybil. Cur. biog. p. 622 (1953).
Thorndike, Edward L. Cur. biog. p. 857 (1941).
Thorne, Oakleigh. Amer. heri., vol. 8 no. 4 p. 35 (Je '57).
Thorne-Thomsen, Gudrun. Jun. bk. of auth., p. 285.
Thorneycroft, Peter. Cur. biog. p. 592 (1952).
Thornhill, Arthur H. Cur. biog. p. 436 (1958).
Thornhill, Sir James. Con. ency. of ant., vol. 1, pl. 166.
—— (work of). Con. 140: 234 Jan '58.
thorns, crown of. See crown of thorns.
Thornton, Dan. Cur. biog. p. 607 (1954).
Thornton, Dr. William. Amer. heri., vol. 9 no. 2 p. 19 (Feb '58).
Thornton's design for Natl. capitol, William. See U.S. Capitol, Wash., D.C., (Thornton's plan, 1810).
Thoroughgood, Adam (home of). Brooks: Growth of a nation, p. 57.
Thorp, Willard L. Cur. biog. p. 637 (1947).

Thorpe, Jim. Cur. biog. p. 570 (1950).
Thor's hammer (sym.). Lehner: Pict. bk. of sym., p. 28.
Thorvaldsen, Bertel (sculpture by). Praeg.: Pict. ency., p. 392.
thought concentration (sym.). Lehner: Pict. bk. of sym., p. 43.
thought symbols, winged. See winged thoughts.
thought wings. See winged thoughts.
thoughtfulness (sym.). Lehner: Pict. bk. of sym., p. 59.
Thouron, Jacques (miniature by). Con. 138: 83 Nov '53.
Thousand islands (St. Lawrence river). Holiday 14: 91-5 (part col.) Aug '53; 21: 62-3 (col.) Je '57; 24: 53 (col.) Nov '58.
Natl. geog. 98: 364-5 Sept '50.
—— (map). Travel 110: 33 Jl '58.
Thracian girl (head). Natl. geog. 109: 62 (col.) Jan '56.
thread advertising cards (1880). Amer. heri., vol. 8 no. 6 p. 40-1 (col.) (Oct '57).
threat (sym.). Lehner Pict. bk. of sym., p. 89.
"The three crosses" (Rubens). Con. 145: 267 Je '60.
"The three fruits" (sym.). Lehner: Pict. bk. of sym., p. 46.
"The three graces" (bronze figures). Con. 143: 216 Je '59.
—— (sculpture). Natl. geog. 116: 581 (col.) Nov '59.
"The three keys" to. (sym.). Lehner: Pict. bk. of sym., p. 47.
three legged toad. See toad, three-legged.
"Three Marys at the sepulchre" (Van Eyck). Con. 126: 71 Aug '50; 133: 93 Ap '54.
"Three musicians" (Picasso). Holiday 14: 58 Nov '53.
"Three of completion" (sym.). Lehner: Pict. bk. of sym., p. 80.
"Three sisters" (Monument Valley, Ont.). Travel 103: inside cover Feb '55.
"Three wise monkeys" (sym.). Lehner: Pict. bk. of sym., p. 63.
threshing barley (Bhutan). Natl. geog. 102: 726 (col.) Dec '52.
threshing wheat (Pakistan). Natl. geog. 100: 735 (col.) Dec '51.
thriftiness (sym.). Lehner: Pict. bk. of sym., p. 59.
Throckmorton, Cleon. Cur. biog. p. 761 (1943).
Throckmorton, Elizabeth. Amer. heri., vol. 10 no. 4 p. 19 (col.) (Je '59).
throne (ruler). Int. gr. soc.: Arts . . . p. 53 (col.).
—— (Vatican). Holiday 23: 63 (col.) May '58.
——, Cambodian king's. Natl. geog. 102: 304 (col.) Sept '52.
——, Eng. royal. Holiday 23: 67 (col.) Jan '58.
——, king's. See Angkor Thom (king's throne).
——, Mardi Gras. Natl. geog. 103: 162-3 (col.) Feb '53; 118: 730 (col.) Nov '60.
——, Nigerian. Natl. geog. 110: 340 (col.) Sept '56.
——, Pope John XXIII. Natl. geog. 117: 593 (col.) May '60.

——, Queen's (Canada). Natl. geog. 115: 829 (col.) Je '59.
——, Saul's. Natl. geog. 112: 853 (col.) Dec '57.
——, Solomon's. See Solomon (on throne).
——, Sultan's. See Sultan's throne.
throne & stool, Peter the Great. Con. 142: 229 Jan '59.
throne chair (Crete).) Natl. geog. 114: 754 (col.) Dec '58.
—— (Tehran). See Peacock throne.
throne of Pius VI, Venetian. Con. 135: 22 Mar '55.
throne room (African palace). Holiday 25: 73 (col.) Ap '59.
throne room, Sultan of Delis. Natl. geog. 108: 390 (col.) Sept '55.
Thucydides. Amer. heri., vol. 8 no. 5 p. 27 (Aug '57).
Thumb, Peter (arch. by). Praeg.: Pict. ency., p. 377.
Thumb, Tom. See Tom Thumb.
"thumb down" (Nay sym.). Lehner: Pict. bk. of sym., p. 79.
"thumb up" (sym.). Lehner: Pict. bk. of sym., p. 78.
"thunder people" (Bhutan). Natl. geog. 102: 747 (col.) Dec '52.
"Thunderbird", Indian. Natl. geog. 109: 741 (col.) Je '56.
Thurber, James. Cur. biog. p. 433 (1960).
thurible. See censer.
Thurman, Allen G. Amer. heri., vol. 7 no. 5 p. 103 (Aug '56).
Thurman, Rev. Howard. Cur. biog. p. 603 (1955).
Thurmond, James Strom. Cur. biog. p. 622 (1948).
thunderbolt, Indra's. Lehner: Pict. bk. of sym., p. 43.
——, Tibetan. Lehner: Pict. bk. of sym., p. 42.
Thursday (sym.). Lehner: Pict. bk. of sym., p. 25.
Thye, Edward J. Cur. biog. p. 624 (1951).
thyroid gland. Gray's anatomy, p. 1328.
tiara. Holiday 11: 115 May '52.
——, antique. Con. 145: 280 Je '60.
——, diamond. Con. 142: 256 Jan '59; 143: 120 Ap '59, 263 Je '59; 144: 42 Sept '59.
tiara & keys (sym.). Lehner: Pict. bk. of sym., p. 95.
Tibbett, Lawrence. Cur. biog. p. 607 (1945).
Tiber river (Rome). Natl. geog. 111: 474 (col.) Ap '57.
Tiberias, Israel. Holiday 17: 43 Feb '55.
Tiberias, Sea of. See Sea of Galilee.
Tibet. Holiday 12: 54-7 (col.) Dec '52.
Natl. geog. 102: 208-9 (col.) Aug '52.
—— (map). Natl. geog. 108: 7 Jl '55.
——, "Little". Natl. geog. 99: 604-34 (part col.) May '51.
Tibetan cross thunderbolt. See cross, Tibetan thunderbolt (sym.).
Tibetan girl. Natl. geog. 102: 217 Aug '52.
Tibetan lama. Natl. geog. 97: 13 (col.) Jan '50.

Tibetan lama (prayer wheel). Natl. geog. 117: 391 (col.) Mar '60.

Tibetan mantra. *See* Mantra of Chenrazee.

Tibetan wheel. *See* "Wheel of good law", Tibetan.

Tibetans. Natl. geog. 101: 408-9, 415 Mar '52; 108: 5-48 (col.) Jl '55.

Ticciati, Gerolamo (sculpture by). Con. 138: 162 Dec '56.

Tice, Merton B. Cur. biog. p. 605 (1955).

ticket (for Andrew Johnson impeachment trial). Amer. heri., vol. 8 no. 1 p. 103 (Dec '56).

ticket agent (at window). Natl. geog. 115: 833 Je '59.

ticket to Peate's museum. Amer. heri., vol. 6 no. 3 p. 48 (Ap '55).

tickets, circus. Durant: Pict. hist. of Amer. circus, p. 52, 56.

Ticonderoga, Fort. *See* Fort Ticonderoga.

"Ticonderoga" steamer. Holiday 25: 68 Je '59.

"Tidewater Hall" (Colonial home). Holiday 12: 38-9 (col.) Nov '52.

tie, man's. Holiday 11: 26 (col.) May '52; 12: 12 (col.) Sept '52, 80, 126 (col.) Oct '52; 21: 21 Je '57; 24: 35 (col.) Nov '58; 27: 142 (col.) Jan '60; 28: 23 (col.) Oct '60.

——, man's bow. Holiday 27: 170 Feb '60.

tie case. Holiday 11: 59 (col.) Je '52.

tie clasp, man's. Holiday 20: 124 Nov '56.

Tien, Cardinal Thomas. Cur. biog. p. 599 (1946).

Tiepolo, Domenico (work of). Con 135: 122 Ap '55; 144: 239 Jan '60.

Tiepolo, Giovanni Battista (work of). Con. 126: 67 Aug '50; 133: 265 Je '54; 135: 32-4, 51 Mar '55, 274-7 Je '55; 139: XL-VIII Mar '57; 140: LII Dec '57; 142: 179 (col.) Dec '58; 143: 105 Ap '59, 176 May '59.
Praeg.: Pict. ency., p. 321 (col.).

Tierney, Gene (as Belle Starr). Amer. heri., vol. 11 no. 5 p. 41 (Aug '60).

Tierra del Fuego (Yahgan island). Natl. geog. 108: 765 Dec '55.

ties, man's. Holiday 10: 23 (col.) Dec '51; 11: 2 (col.) Mar '52, 68, 71 (col.) Ap '52; 12: 28-9 (col.) Dec '52; 13: back cover (col.) Ap '53; 20: 17, 171 (col.) Dec '56; 22: 127, 164 (col.) Dec '57; 23: 34 (col.) Ap '58; 26: 5 (col.) Sept '59.

Tiffany, Louis C. (work of). Natl. geog. 99: 206 (col.) Feb '51.

Tiffin, Edward. Amer. heri., vol. 4 no. 3 p. 39 (spring '53).

tiger (Chinese sym.). Lehner: Pict. bk. of sym., p. 44, 57.

"Tiger Balm" gardens (Malaya). Natl. geog. 103: 204 (col.) Feb '53.

"Tiger's nest" monastery. *See* monastery, "Tiger's nest".

tightrope act. Holiday 22: 15 (col.) Jl '57.

tightrope walker (Cambodia). Natl. geog. 117: 550 (col.) Ap '60.

—— (Niagara, 1859). Amer. heri., vol. 12 no. 1 p. 116 (Dec '60).

——, circus). Durant: Pict. hist. of Amer. circus, p. 189, 200, 278.

Tigris river (Iraq). Natl. geog. 114: 464-5 (col.) Oct '58.

Tiki (Maori idol). Holiday 22: 105 Sept '57.

Tikopian men. Natl. geog. 99: 337 (col.) Mar '51.

Tilden, Bennie (work of). Natl. geog. 107: 365 (col.) Mar '55.

Tilden, Samuel. Amer. heri., vol. 7 no. 4 p. 33 (Je '56).

Tilden, Samuel J. Amer. heri., vol. 11 no. 6 p. 5 (Oct '60).

tile, glazed ("Immortals" 405 B.C.). Praeg.: Pict. ency., p. 106 (col.).

tile decorations, antique. Con. 137: 18-20 Mar '56.

tile floor (Egyptian, ancient). Int. gr. soc.: Arts . . . p. 15 (col.).

—— (Roman, ancient). Int. gr. soc.: Arts . . . p. 15 (col.).

tile making. Natl. geog. 107: 315 (col.) Mar '55.

tile roof. *See* roof, tile.

tiles, Delft. Natl. geog. 118: 170 (col.) Aug '60.

——, Russian (17th cent.). Con. 142: 225 Jan '59.

——, wall (Brazil). Natl. geog. 117: 714-5 May '60.

Tilghman, William. Horan: Pict. hist. of wild west, p. 169-70.

Tillemans, Peter. Con. 141: XLV Ap '58.

Tillich, Rev. Dr. Paul J. Cur. biog. p. 609 (1954).

Tillinghast, Charles C., jr. Cur. biog. p. 420 (1962).

Tillstrom, Burr. Cur. biog. p. 626 (1951).

tilting contest, canoe. *See* (tilting contest).

Tilyou, George C. Amer. heri., vol. 9 no. 4 p. 14 (Je '58).

Timberlake, Clare H. Cur. biog. p. 454 (1961).

Timberline Lodge (Mt. Hood, Ore.). Holiday 18: 140 (col.) Dec '55.

Timbuktu (Africa). Holiday 25: 129 Ap '59. Travel 104: 48 Nov '55.

time (sym.). Lehner: Pict. bk. of sym., p. 80.

Times Square (N. Y.). Holiday 10: 46 (col.) Sept '51.

Timgad (Algeria). Natl. geog. 117: 779 Je '60.

Timimoun (desert). Natl. geog. 113: 676-7 (col.) May '58.

Timmerman, George Bell, jr. Cur. biog. p. 552 (1957).

Timoshenko, Semyon. Cur. biog. p. 859 (1941).

timpani (drum). Cooper: Con. ency. of music, p. 412.

tin (sym.). Lehner: Pict. bk. of sym., p. 73.

tin ingots. Natl. geog. 103: 227 Feb '53.

tin miners (Nigeria). Natl. geog. 110: 356 (col.) Sept '56.

Tinerhir (Morocco). Natl. geog. 107: 178-9 (col.) Feb '55.

ting, bird-footed. Con. 136: 65 Sept '55.

Tinker, Maj. Gen. Clarence L. Cur. biog. p. 836 (1942).

Tinkham, George H. Cur. biog. p. 837 (1942).

Tinney, Calvin. Cur. biog. p. 763 (1943).

"Tintern Abbey" Con. 141: XLI May '58.

Tintoretto, Jacopo Robusti (work of). Con. ency. of ant., vol. 1, pl. 153 126: 49 Aug '50; 127: 116 May '51; 129: XXXIX Je '52; 133: XIX Ap '54, 200 May '54; 136: 225 Dec '55; 138: cover (col.) Dec '56; 140: 143 (col.) Dec '57; 142: 199 Dec '58; 143: 52 Mar '59; 144: cover (col.) Dec '59.
  Natl. geog. 97: 742, 757, 765 (col.) Je '50; 110: 620-1, 632 (col.) Nov '56.
  Praeg.: Pict. ency., p. 302 (col.).

tipping chart, Eng. & Europe. Travel 109: 60-1 Ap '58.

tipstaff, antique Hennell. Con. 136: 266 Jan '56.

tire, auto. See auto tire.

——, bicycle. Holiday 10: 9 Aug '51; 11: 127 Ap '52, 154 May '52, 67 Je '52; 12: 13 Aug '52.

——, heavy machine. Natl. geog. 107: 484 Ap '55.

tire measuring wheel. Rawson: Ant. pict. bk., p. 53.

tire punctured, auto. Holiday 11: 66 May '52, 20 Je '52.

Tirikatene, E. T. Holiday 28: 107 Nov '60.

"Tirpitz" ruin (Hitler's battle ship). Natl. geog. 108: 735 Dec '55.

Tiselius. Cur. biog p. 601 (1949).

Tishler, Max. Cur. biog. p. 594 (1952).

Tiso, Joseph. Cur. biog. p. 764 (1943).

Tisserant, Cardinal Eugene. Cur. biog. (1963).

Tissot, J. J. J. (work of). Con. 143: XXIX Je '59.

Tissot, James (work of). Con. 142: 258 Jan '59.

"Titanic" boat. Amer. heri., vol. 7 no. 1 p. 46-9 (Dec '55).

—— (disaster). Holiday 13: 91 Je '53.

Titian. Int. gr. soc.: Arts . . . p. 91 (col.).

Titian (Tiziano Vecellio) (work of). Con. ency. of ant., vol. 1, pl. 154.
  Con. 126: 83-5, 89 Oct '50; 132: 48 Sept '53.

Titian (work of). Con. 126: 176-9, 182 Dec '50; 133: 15 Mar '54; 136: 191 (col.) Dec '55, 307 Jan '56; 140: 207 Dec '57, 240 Jan '58; 141: 273 Je '58.
  Labande: Naples, p. 110.
  Natl. geog. 97: 744, 759, 764 (col.) Je '50; 101: 77 (col.) Jan '52; 110: 636, 638-9 (col.) Nov '56; 111: 488-9 (col.) Ap '57.
  Praeg.: Pict. ency., p. 300 (col.).

Titicaca. Natl. geog. 98: 494, 496 (col.) Oct '50.

Titicaca lake. Holiday 20: 82 (col.) Nov '56.

Tito, Marshal. Cur. biog. p. 606 (1955).
  Holiday 14: 37 Aug '53.

—— (Communist sculpture). Holiday 13: 53 Mar '53.

—— (dog, bathing). Holiday 10: 72 Jl '51.

—— (statue). Holiday 14: 40 Aug '53.

Titov, Gherman S. Cur. biog. p. 422 (1962).

Titterton, Lewis H. Cur. biog. p. 769 (1943).

Titus arch (Italy). Travel 113: 49 Ap '60.

Titusville (oil boom, 1860). Amer. heri., vol. 10 no. 2 p. 65, 70 (Feb '59).

Tivoli, Accadameia of Villa Hadriana. Ceram: March of arch., p. 15.

Tivoli fountain. Holiday 27: 103 Ap '60.

Tivoli Gardens, entrance (Copenhagen). Holiday 18: 31 (col.) Sept '55.

Tiwi dancers. Natl. geog. 109: 429, 434 (col.) Mar '56.

Tiwi mourner (being fed). Natl. geog. 109: 429 (col.) Mar '56.

Tiwi tribesmen (Australia). Natl. geog. 109: 418-40 (part col.) Mar '56.

Tizard, Sir Henry. Cur. biog. p. 605 (1949).

Toad, three-legged (sym.). Lehner: Pict. bk. of sym. p. 45.

toadstool (sym.). Lehner: Pict. bk.. of sym., p. '63.

"The toast" (Croegaert). Con. 142: XXXIX Nov '58.

"The toast" (Velten). Con. 140: XXXI Nov '57.

toaster. Holiday 13: 67 May '53, 31 Je '53; 14: 130 Jl '53, 131 Oct '53, 16 Nov '53, 75 Dec '53; 20: 1 Nov '56; 22: 122 (col.) Dec '57; 24: 13 (col.), 49 Dec '58; 26: 21 Dec '59; 28: 13 (col.) Dec '60.

toaster fork. Con. ency. of ant., vol. 3, p. 245.

tobacco barn. See barn, tobacco.

tobacco box, Louis XVI (17th cent.). Int. gr. soc.: Arts . . . p. 95 (col.).

——, silver (antique). Con. 140: XXVIII Sept '57.

tobacco jar (antique). Con. 129: 115 Je '52.

—— (delft). Int. gr. soc.: Arts . . . p. 95 (col.).

tobacco label (1755). Amer. heri., vol. 8 no. 3 p. 65 (Ap '57).

tobacco plants (men, women sorting). Natl. geog. 105: 311 (col.) Mar '54.

tobacco pouch. Holiday 10: 12 (col.) Oct '51; 14: 128 Dec '53; 18: 96 Nov '55.

tobacco racks (curing). Natl. geog. 111: 609 (col.) May '57.

tobacco tags (from plug)). Amer. heri., vol. 11 no. 5 back cover (col.) Aug '60.

tobacconist (sym.). Lehner: Pict. bk. of sym., p. 91.

Tobago island. Natl. geog. 103: 44, 68 (col.) Jan '53; 114: 430-40 (part col.) Sept '58.

—— (map). Natl. geog. 103: 39 Jan '53.

Tobey, Charles W. Cur. biog. p. 863 (1941); p. 628 (1951).

Tobey, Mark. Cur. biog. p. 553 (1957).

Tobias, Channing H. Cur. biog. p. 610 (1945).

Tobin, Daniel J. Cur. biog. p. 613 (1945).

Tobin, Frederick (work of). Amer. heri., vol. 1 no. 3 p. 44 (col.) (spring '50).

Tobin, Maurice J. Cur. biog. p. 602 (1946).

Tobin, Richard L. Cur. biog. p. 693 (1944).

toboggan, salt mine (Austria). Natl. geog. 118: 263 Aug '60.

——, street (Madeira). Holiday 28: 64 Sept '60.

toboggan slide. Travel 102: 12 Dec '54.

tobogganers. Natl. geog. 113: 70-1 (col.) Jan '58.

toby jug. Con. 143: XXXIX May '59, XVIII Je '59.
  Holiday 12: inside cover (col.) Oct '52; 24: 26 (col.) Nov '58; 26: 97 Nov '59.

——, Royal Doulton. Holiday 25: 187 Ap '59, 100 May '59.

Tocqué, Louis. Con. 135: 41 Mar '55; 142: LXXX Jan '59.

Todd, Sir Alexander. Cur. biog. p. 437 (1958).

Todd, Mike. Cur. biog. p. 609 (1955).

Todd, Richard. Cur. biog. p. 611 (1955).

"Toddsbury" (home, 1650, Va.). Natl. geog. 109: 458-9 (col.) Ap '56.

toddy rummer, glass (antique). Con. ency. of ant., vol. 1, p. 80.

——, Irish glass. Con. ency. of ant., vol. 3, pl. 50.

toga, Roman. Holiday 25: 89 Ap '59.

——, Roman (ancient). Int. gr. soc.: Arts . . . p. 31 (col.).

Togliatti, Palmiro. Cur. biog. p. 640 (1947).

"The toilet" (Netscher). Con. 142: cover (col.) Nov '58.

toilet box (antique). Con. 143: 16 Mar '59.

toilet case. Holiday 11: 59 (col.) Je '52.

toilet casket, William & Mary. Con. 139: 58 Mar '57.

toilet mirror. See mirror, toilet.

"Toilet of Venus" (Pellegrini). Con. 142: 5 Sept '58.

toilet service, silver (Paul de Lamerie). Con. 140: 38 Sept '57.

——, William & Mary. Con. 143: 266 Je '59.

toilet set, German silver (18th cent). Con. 143: XXIX May '59.

toilet tables, Tudor. Amer. heri., vol. 9 no. 6 p. 23 (Oct '58).

Tojo, Hideki. Cur. biog. p. 864 (1941).

Tokyo (Japan). Natl. geog. 97: 598, 603 May '50; 118: 736-7, 744-5 (col.) Dec '60.

—— (air view). Holiday 14: 4 Jl '53.

Tokyo Bay (1853). Amer. heri., vol. 9 no. 3 p. 12-3 (col.) (Ap '58).

Toland, Gregg. Cur. biog. p. 865 (1941).

Tolbukhin, Fedor I. Cur. biog. p. 615 (1945).

Toledane, Ralph de. Cur. biog. p. 424 (1962).

toleware maker (1850). Amer. heri., vol. 8 no. 1 p. 55 (Dec '56).

Tolkien, John R. R. Cur. biog. p. 556 (1957).

Tollefson, Thor C. Cur. biog. p. (1963).

tollgate. Rawson: Ant. pict. bk., p. 42.

Tollgate Rock (Wyo). Holiday 14: 61 (col.) Jl '53.

Tolstoy, Alexandra. Cur. biog. p. 625 (1953).

Tolstoy, Leo. Holiday 20: 6 Aug '56.

Toltec idols (Mexico). Travel 114: 47 Nov '60.

Toltec pyramid. See pyramid, Toltec.

"Tom Mollard & the hounds" (Munnings). Con. 136: 51 (col.) Sept '55.

Tom Sawyer. Holiday 5: 58 Mar '49.

Tom Sawyer & Huck Finn. Amer. heri., vol. 8 no. 1 p. 27, 32 (col.) (Dec '56).
Brooks: Growth of a nation, p. 136.
Holiday 21: 127 Ap '57; 23: 138 Mar '58.
Natl. geog. 110: 131, 135, 140 Jl '56.

Tom Sawyer & Huck Finn monument. See monument, Tom Sawyer & Huck Finn.

Tom Sawyer & Huck Finn. See also Huck Finn & Tom Sawyer.

Tom Sawyer's fence (sign). Natl. geog. 114: 696 Nov '58.

Tom Thumb. Amer. heri., vol. 5 no. 1 p. 51 (fall '53).
Durant: Pict. hist. of Amer. circus, p. 54-5.

Tom Thumb locomotive. Amer. heri., vol. 9 no. 1 p. 61 (Dec '57).
Holiday 26: 1 Jl '59.

—— (race with a horse). Amer. heri., vol. 9 no. 1 p. 60-1 (Dec '57).

Tom Thumb train, Peter Cooper's. Amer. heri., vol. 10 no. 2 p. 105 (Feb '59).

Tom Thumb, wife & baby. Durant: Pict. hist. of Amer. circus, p. 56.

Tom Thumb's wedding. Amer. heri., vol. 9 no. 3 p. 54 (col.) (Ap '58).

tom-tom (sym.). Lehner: Pict. bk. of sym., p. 87.

——, Indian. Holiday 10: 133 Dec '51.

tomahawk. Lehner: Pict. bk. of sym., p. 87.

Tomas, Rear Adm. Americo. Cur. biog. p. 439 (1958).

Tomasi, Mari. Cur. biog. p. 867 (1941).

tomb (Herbert Chapel, Wales, 1510). Praeg.: Pict. ency., p. 86.

—— (Okinawa). Natl. geog. 97: 552 Ap '50.

——, a saint's (Tibet). Natl. geog. 108: 38 (col.) Jl '55.

——, Allan Kardec. Holiday 25: 27 Jan '59.

——, Ataturk's. See Ataturk's tomb.

——, Jahangir's (Lahore). Natl. geog. 102: 657 (col.) Nov '52.

——, Jonah's. See Jonah's tomb.

——, King Cyrus. Natl. geog. 100: 464 (col.) Oct '51.

——, royal (Taj Mahal). Travel 111: 29 Jan '59.

——, Theodoric's. See Theodoric's tomb.

——, Tudor (Wales). Holiday 28: 45 (col.) Sept '60.

——, William Henry Harrison. See Harrison's tomb.

tomb carvings. See Egyptian tomb carvings.

tomb decorations, Etruscan. Natl. geog. 116: 336-42 (part col.) Sept '59.

tomb entrance, Queen Nephertari at Thebes. Ceram: March of arch., opp. p. 143 (col.).

tomb furnishings, Egyptian. Ceram: March of arch., p. 154.

tomb guardian, Chinese carved. Con. ency. of ant., vol. 3, pl. 64.

tomb interior (Egypt). Ceram: March of arch., p. 135.

Tomb of Ali. Natl. geog. 114: 14-5 (col.) Jl '58.

Tomb of Archbishop Chichele. Holiday 18: 112 (col.) Aug '55.

Tomb of Catherine of Austria. Labande: Naples, p. 68.

Tomb of Donna Dulcia & Armengol. Con. 136: 19 Sept '55.

Tomb of Elizabeth I, Queen. See Elizabeth I, Queen (tomb of).

Tomb of Husain. Natl. geog. 104: 12-3 (col.) Jl '53.

Tomb of Jesus Christ. Holiday 7: 119 (col.) Ap '50.
Natl. geog. 115: 502 (col.) Ap '59.
Travel 105: 36 Mar '56.

Tomb of Mehemet I. Osward: Asia Minor, pl. 81.

Tomb of Riza Shah Pahlevi (Iran). Natl. geog. 100: 450 (col.) Oct '51.

Tomb of Saadi (Shiraz). Travel 105: 25 Jan '56.

Tomb of St. Luke (so-called). Osward: Asia Minor, pl. 46.

Tomb of St. Sebald (Nuremberg). Praeg.: Pict. ency., p. 317.

Tomb of Shah (Teheran). Travel 105: 25 Jan '56.

Tomb of Sheikh Abdul Kadir Gilani. Natl. geog. 104: 7 (col.) Jl '53.

Tomb of the Mahdi (Sudan). Natl. geog. 107: 717 May '55.

Tomb of unknown soldier (Arlington, Va.). Holiday 24: 129 Nov '58. Natl. geog. 114: 603 (col.) Nov '58.

Tomb of unknown soldier (Paris). Natl. geog. 98: 55 (col.) Jl '50.

Tomb of Virgil. Labande: Naples, p. 90.

tomb sculpture, Julius II (Rome). Praeg.: Pict. ency., p. 273.

tomb slab, Barbia family. Natl. geog. 109: 854 Je '56.

tomb wall painting, Egyptian. Praeg.: Pict. ency., p. 116 (col.).

tomb wall painting (Leopards 480 B.C.). Praeg.: Pict. ency., p. 140 (col.).

tombs, Lamaist saints. Natl. geog. 108: 8-9 (col.) Jl '55.

tombs, Portugal carved. Con. 137: 41-3 Mar '56.

tombs, Roman. See Roman tombs.

tombs of Achaemenian kings. Natl. geog. 114: 34-5 (col.) Jl '58.

Tombstone (Ariz.). Holiday 16: 69 Aug '54. Natl. geog. 104: 356-7, 362 (part col.) Sept '53.

—— (1880). Horan: Pict. hist. of wild west, p. 109.

—— (outlaws). Horan: Pict. hist. of wild west, p. 164.

tombstone, Belle Starr. Amer. heri., vol. 11 no. no. 5 p. 41 (Aug '60).

tombstone, Lydian. Osward: Asia Minor, pl. 17.

——, William Bradford. Rawson: pict. bk., p. 92.

tombstones (Puritan). Amer. heri., vol. 11 no. 2 p. 38-43 (Feb '60).

—— (Turkey). Natl. geog. 100: 173 Aug '51.

——, Osman. Osward: Asia Minor, pl. 102.

——, Phrygian. See Phrygian tombstones.

tombstones & epitaphs (humorous). Amer. heri., vol. 9 no. 3 p. 112 (Ap '58).

tombstones (graveyard). Amer. heri., vol. 5 no. 3 p. 14 (spring '54).

tomoye (sym.). Lehner; Pict. bk. of sym., p. 47.

Tong, Hollington K. Cur. biog. p. 625 (1956).

Tonga island picnic (food table). Holiday 28: 164 (col.) Oct '60.

Tonga woman. Holiday 28: 92 (col.) Oct '60.

tongs (tools). Rawson: Ant. pict. bk., p. 54.

Tonkin road to Red China. Natl. geog. 99: 482 (col.) Ap '51.

Tooker, George. Cur. biog. p. 441 (1958).

tool kit. Travel 107: inside back cover Ap '57, inside back cover May '57; 108: back

cover Aug '57, 42 Dec '57; 110: inside back cover Jl '58.

tool making machine (men). Amer. heri., vol. 2 no. 1 p. 2 (col.) (fall '50).

tool sharpener. Int. gr. soc.: Arts . . . p. 173 (col.).

tools (18th cent.). Brooks: Growth of a nation, p. 86, 101.

—— (in case). Travel 107: back cover Mar '57.

——, agricultural (sym.). Lehner: Pict. bk. of sym., p. 10.

—— carpenter's (antique). Amer. heri., vol. 1 no. 2 p. 43 (winter '50).

——, Egyptian (ancient). Ceram: March of arch., p. 152.

—— farm. Rawson: Ant. pict. bk., p. 54-61.

——, farm (antique). Rawson: Ant. pict. bk., p. 21-35.

——, garden. Holiday 14: 158 Nov '53.

——, Louis XVI (carpenter's). Con. 133: 40 Mar '54.

——, tannery. See tannery & tools.

tooth, elephant. Amer. heri., vol. 6 no. 2 p. 17 (winter '55).

toothbrush. Travel 101: 40 Je '54; 103: 20 Je '55; 104: 66 Jl '55.

top. Holiday 12: 139 Nov '52.

——, spinning (antique). Rawson: Ant. pict. bk., p. 19.

——, spinning (sym.). Lehner: Pict. bk. of sym., p. 82.

top spinning match, Malay. Natl. geog. 103: 200 (col.) Feb '53.

topcoat (exhibit). Holiday 20: 25 (col.) Nov '56.

——. See also man (overcoat); overcoat.

Tope, John K. Cur. biog. p. 572 (1950).

tope. See stupa.

topographical instruments (antique). Con. 134: 91 Nov '54.

"topper" hat. See hat, Men's "topper".

Topping, Dr. Norman. Cur. biog. p. 451 (1959).

Topridge lodge. See Camp Topridge lodge.

torab (sym.). Lehner: Pict. bk. of sym., p. 38.

Torbert, Alfred T. A. Pakula: Cent. album, p. 275.

torch. Amer. heri., vol. 11 no. 5 p. 70 (col.) (Aug '60). Holiday 19: 122 Mar '56; 21: 102 Feb '57.

—— (on steamboat). Amer heri., vol. 8 no. 6 p. 19, 21 (col.) (Oct '57).

—— (sym.). Lehner: Pict. bk. of sym., p. 58, 60, 65, 79.

——, campaign. Amer. heri., vol. 4 no. 1 p. 52 (fall '52).

torcheres (18th cent.). Con. 142: back cover Sept '58.

——, Adam. Con. 132: XXI Sept '53; 137: 57 Mar '56; 141: XXI Je '58; 142: XXXII Nov '58.

——, Georgian. Con. 136: XLV Nov '55.

——, Georgian giltwood. Con. 145: XI Ap '60.

——, regency. Con. 142: VIII Jan '59.

——, William Masters. Con. 140: XLIX Jan '58.

toreador (bullfighter). Holiday 23: 114 Je '58; 24: 91 Jl '58.

—— (head). Travel 113: inside cover Ap '60.

——. See also bullfighter.

Torero. Natl. geog. 107: 240 (col.) Feb '55.

toreros, Portuguese. Disney: People & places, p. 67 (col.).

——, Spanish. Holiday 15: 34 (col.) May '54.

Torii (sym.). Lehner: Pict. bk. of sym., p. 47.

——, Japanese. Holiday 12: 32 Aug '52, 74 (col.) Oct '52; 21: 137 (col.) May '57; 26: 164 Nov '59.
Natl. geog. 104: 630 (col.) Nov '53.
Travel 113: 48 Jan '60.

Toronto (Canada). Holiday 6: 39 (col.) Aug '49; 18: 38-43 (part col.) Sept '55.
Travel 105: 15 May '56.

—— (airview). Natl. geog. 104: 843 (col.) Dec '53.

—— (castle Casa Loma). Travel 105: 13 May '56.

Toros Mt. (Turkey). Natl. geog. 110: 746 Dec '56.

Torp, Oscar F. Cur. biog. p. 595 (1952).

Torquay (Eng.). Holiday 14: 132 (col.) Nov '53.

—— (harbor). Holiday 15: 120 (col.) Je '54; 23: 16 Jan '58.

Torres Bodet, Jaime. Cur. biog. p. 626 (1948).

Tortilla maker, Indian (Guatemala). Natl. geog. 117: 412 (col.) Mar '60.

tortillas. Natl. geog. 102: 377 Sept '52.

tortoise (sym.). Lehner: Pict. bk. of sym., p. 45.

Tortola island. Travel 103: 17-9 Je '55.

"Torture of Saint Agnes" (Cavallini). Labande: Naples, p. 71.

Toscanini, Arturo. Cooper: Con. ency. of music, p. 300.
Cur. biog. p. 839 (1942); p. 611 (1954).
Holiday 9: 58 Mar '51; 18: 35-7 Oct '55, 53-5 (part col.) Nov '55, 59 Dec '55; 19: 51 Jan '56; 21: 1 Sept '58.

Toscanini home, Arturo. Holiday 18: 53 (col.) Nov '55.

Toshugu shrine (Japan). Travel 113: 54 Jan '60.

Tosini, Michele (work of). Natl. geog. 113: 264 (col.) Feb '58.

Tot, Amerigo. Holiday 11: 46 (col.) Ap '52; 27: 105 Ap '60.

tot-cycle. Holiday 10: 129 Nov '51.

totem masks. Natl. geog. 111: 91 (col.) Jan '57.

totem pole. Holiday 11: 18 Mar '52, 18 May '52; 14: 134 (col.) Jl '53; 15: 17 (col.), 142 May '54; 16: 131 Jl '54; 17: 86 Feb '55; 18: 95 Jl '55; 21: inside cover (col.) Mar '57, 117 (col.) Ap '57; 23: 101 (col.), 112 Feb '58; 24: 55 Nov '58; 25: 22 (col.) Feb '59, 139 (col.), 179 Ap '59; 26: 83 Aug '59, 36 Dec '59.
Int. gr. soc.: Arts . . . p. 17, 187 (col.).
Jordan: Hammond's pict. atlas, p. 144, 148 (col.).
Natl. geog. 108: 231 (col.) Aug '55; 117: 452 (col.) Ap '60.
Travel 103: 27-8 Je '55; 104: 23 Jl '55; 106: 39 Jl '56; 112: 20 Jl '59; 114: 60 Jl '60.

—— (Alaska). Holiday 14: 106-7 Jl '53.

—— (Amer. Indians). Praeg.: Pict. ency., p. 562.

—— (girl). Natl. geog. 109: 741 (col.) Je '56.

—— (man carving). Natl. geog. 116: 78-9 (part col.) Jl '59.

—— (man painting). Natl. geog. 114: 179 (col.) Aug '58.

—— (tallest in U.S.). Holiday 26: 81 Nov '59.

Toulouse-Lautrec, Henri de (work of). Con. 133: XXI, 17 Mar '54; 136: XXXIV Nov '55; 137: 139 Ap '56; 140: 60 Sept '57, 81 Nov '57, 261 Jan '58; 141: 250 Je '58; 143: XXXII May '59; 145: 231 (col.) Je '60.
Praeg.: Pict. ency., p. 38 (col.).

tour-car. See house trailer.

tour guide (maps & plans). Holiday 19: 20 Jan '56.

Tourbillon, castle of. See castle of Tourbillon.

Toure, Sekou. Cur. biog. p. 453 (1959).

Tourel, Jennie. Cur. biog. p. 642 (1947).

touring coach. See bus.

tourist cabins, Africa. See rondavels.

tourists (comic). Holiday 10: 54 Jl '51.

tourists. See also man & woman (traveling); man, woman & children (traveling).

tournament (ancient). Durant: Pict. hist. of Amer. circus, p. 10.

tournament of roses (Pasadena). Holiday 11: 94-5 (col.) Jan '52.
Natl. geog. 105: 807-14 (col.) Je '54.

Tournier, Jean-Claude (terracotta work). Con. 140: 3 Sept '57.

tours, American. See vacation tour charts, Amer.

Tousey, Sanford. Jun. bk. of auth., p. 286.

Toussaint, Jeanne. Cur. biog. p. 612 (1955).

towboat. Natl. geog. 114: 676, 683 (col.) Nov '58.

—— (on the ways). Natl. geog. 114: 694 (col.) Nov '58.

——, river. Natl. geog. 97: 183, 192 (col.) Feb '50; 103: 717 (col.) Je '53.

towels, box of. Holiday 22: 42 (col.) Nov '57.

Tower, John G. Cur. biog. p. 427 (1962).

tower (state house, Maryland). Holiday 23: 79 (col.) Je '58.

——. (sym.). Lehner: Pict. bk. of sym., p. 60.

——, Amalfi cathedral. Labande: Naples, 195.

——, bell. See belltower.

——, Brislee. Con. 142: 78 Nov '58.

——, carillon. See carillon tower.

——, clock. See clock tower.

Tower, Cuttyhunk is. (earliest Eng. settlement in Amer.). Travel 107: 34 Je '57.

——, Dublin. See Dublin tower.

——, forest ranger. Natl. geog. 108: 113 (col.) Jl '55.

——, guardian (Holland). Natl. geog. 106: 388 (col.) Sept '54.

——, Harkness (Yale). See Harkness memorial tower.

——, Ilium's. See Ilium's tower.

——, jungle. Natl. geog. 107: 78-91 (part col.) Jan '55.

——, leaning. See Leaning tower of Pisa.

——, leaning. See Leaning tower of Soochow.

Tower, London. *See* London (the Tower).

——, mosque. Natl. geog. 112: 53 (col.) Jl '57.

——, paratroop training. Natl. geog. 105: 326 (col.) Mar '54.

——, Pisa leaning. *See* Leaning tower of Pisa.

——, Qutb Minar. *See* Qutb Minar tower (Delhi).

——, rocket. Natl. geog. 115: 160-5 (col.) Feb '59.

——, round. *See* round tower.

——, Swiss (13th cent.). Natl. geog. 110: 448 (col.) Oct '56.

——, Tokyo. Natl. geog. 118: 745 (col.) Dec '60.

——, watch. *See* watchtower.

——, Westphalian. *See* Westphalian tower.

tower air traffic control, airport. Natl. geog. 104: 727 (col.) Dec '53.

Tower bridge. *See* London (Tower bridge).

Tower of Babel. Ceram: March of arch., p. 163-4.

"Tower of Babel" (Brueghel). Con. 133: 95 Ap '54.

"Tower of Babel" (Koldewey's reconstruction). Ceram: March of arch., p. 229, 231.

"Tower of Belem" (Portugal). Natl. geog. 108: 746 (col.) Dec '55; 118: 652 (col.) Nov '60. Travel 111: 33 Je '59.

"Tower of gold" (Spain, 1220). Natl. geog. 99: 511 (col.) Ap '51.

Tower of Pisa. *See* Leaning tower of Pisa.

Towers, Graham F. Cur. biog. p. 597 (1952).

Towers, John Henry. Cur. biog. p. 868 (1941).

towers, bridge. *See* bridge towers.

——, fire lookout. Natl. geog. 110: 288-9 (col.) Sept '56.

——, medieval (Italy). Travel 111: 35 Ap '59.

——, pigeon nesting. Holiday 10: 118 Dec '51.

——, rock (man & women). Natl. geog. 112: 241 (col.) Aug '57.

Towle, Col. Katherine A. Cur. biog. p. 607 (1949).

town, frontier (1885). Natl. geog. 101: 476 Ap '52.

——, pioneer. Horan: Pict. hist. of wild west, p. 92, 100-2, 106, 109, 185-6.

town crier, (ringing bell, St. George). Holiday 23: 73 Je '58.

——, African. Natl. geog. 100: 278 Aug '51.

——, Colonial. Holiday 18: 126 Jl '55; 20: 115 Aug '56.

town crier's bell (sym.). Lehner: Pict. bk. of sym., p. 84.

town hall (Augsburg). *See* Augsburg town hall.

—— (Berne, Switzerland). Travel 108: 27 Nov '57.

—— (Canary islands). Natl. geog. 107: 508 (col.) Ap '55.

—— (Conn.). Brooks: Growth of a nation, p. 258.

—— (Ebeltoft, Jutland, smallest in the world). Travel 103: 13 May '55.

—— (Oslo, Norway). Natl. geog. 106: 182 Aug '54.

—— (Stockholm). Travel 104: 56 Oct '55.

—— (Vienna). Natl. geog. 115: 196 Feb '59.

—— (Ypres). Praeg.: Pict. ency., p. 207.

town house (Storrowtown, Mass.). Travel 113: 29 Mar '60.

town name (longest in world). *See* name, town (in Wales, longest in world).

town plan (Mannheim, 1652). Praeg.: Pict. ency., p. 95.

—— (Wash., D.C., L'Enfant plan). *See* Washington, D.C. (L'Enfant plan).

town wall. *See* Jericho town wall.

Towne, Charles (work of). Con. 145: 203 May '60.

Towne, Francis (work of). Con. 138: 182 Dec '56; 143: XXXVII May '59.

Townes, Charles H. Cur. biog. (1963).

Townsend, Willard S. Cur. biog. p. 627 (1948).

Townshend, George (work of). Amer. heri., vol. 11 no. 1 p. 26 (col.) (Dec '59).

Toy, Henry, jr. Cur. biog. p. 599 (1952).

toy, antique (Colonial man). Amer. heri., vol. 10 no. 1 back cover (col.) (Dec '58).

toy animals. Holiday 28: 191 Oct '60.

Toynbee, Arnold J. Cur. biog. p. 644 (1947).

Toyokuni (work of). Praeg.: Pict. ency., p. 541 (col.).

toys. Holiday 26: 189, 191 194 (col.) Dec '59. Travel 110: inside cover Oct '58, back cover Nov '58.

—— (antique). Amer. heri., vol. 11 no. 1 p. 81-8 (col.) (Dec '59). Natl. geog. 107: 754 (col.) Je '55.

——, Egyptian (ancient). Int. gr. soc.: Arts . . . p. 37 (col.).

——, water. Holiday 12: inside cover (col.) Jl '52.

——, water (plastic). Holiday 11: 76 (col.) Je '52; 12: 82 (col.) Nov '52.

Tozzi, Giorgio. Cur. biog. p. 456 (1961).

Trabert, Tony. Cur. biog. p. 614 (1954).

trachea. Gray's anatomy, p. 1121.

track men, college (running). Natl. geog. 112: 413 (col.) Sept '57.

tractor. Natl. geog. 97: 727 (col.) Je '50; 106: 313, 322 (col.) Sept '54; 109: 69 (col.) Jan '56; 110: 542 Oct '56; 115: 457 (col.) Ap '59; 117: 108-9 (col.) Jan '60.

—— (disc). Holiday 5: 42 (col.) Je '49.

—— (hay load). Natl. geog. 112: 174 (col.) Aug '57.

——, Africa. Natl. geog. 97: 332 Mar '50.

——, amphibian. Natl. geog. 98: 658 Nov '50.

——, Antarctic. Natl. geog. 112: 385 (col.) Sept '57.

——, garden. Holiday 5: 76 Je '49.

——, diesel. Natl. geog. 107: 478 (col.) Ap '55.

——, Scotland. Natl. geog. 110: 39 (col.) Jl '56.

——, sno-cat. *See* sno-cat.

——, snow. Natl. geog. 110: 174-5 (col.) (Aug '56).

——, Turkey. Natl. geog. 101: 751 Je '52.

tractor wheels. Natl. geog. 104: 800-1 (col.) Dec '53.

tractors. Natl. geog. 100: 168, 183 Aug '51.

——, Antarctic. Natl. geog. 115: 40-1 Jan '59.

Tracy, Harry. Horan: Pict. hist. of wild west, p. 202.

Tracy, Spencer. Cur. biog. p. 771 (1943).

tracyery, architectural. Praeg.: Pict. ency., p. 248.

trade card (book sales). Amer. heri., vol. 9 no. 5 p. 39 (col.) (Aug '58).

——, **manufacturer's (18th cent.).** Con. 139: 169 May '57.

trade cards (19th cent.). Amer. heri., vol. 10 no. 5 back cover (col.) (Aug '59).

—— **(premium).** Amer. heri., vol. 8 no. 6 p. 40-1 (col.) (Oct '57).

trade guildhalls. See guildhalls, trade.

trade mark (Mayfair). Con. 142: XVI Dec '58.

——. See also pewter marks; porcelain marks; pottery marks.

trade signs. See signs, trade.

Trader Vic's restaurant (San Francisco). Holiday 8: 83-6 Aug '50.

traders, fur. See fur traders.

——, **South Seas.** Natl. geog. 97: 88 (col.) Jan '50.

trades (sym.). Lehner: Pict bk. of sym., p. 90-1.

trading post (Alaska, 1804). Amer. heri., vol. 10 no. 3 p. 64 (col.) (Ap '59).

trading sloop. See sloop, trading.

Trafalgar ship. See H.M.S. Trafalgar.

traffic guide. Holiday 19: 92 May '56; 20: 22 Sept '56, 120 Oct '56, 35 Nov '56.

—— **(Nassau).** Holiday 22: 171 Dec '57.

traffic light (Formosa). Natl. geog. 107: 578 Ap '55.

—— **(stop, go).** Holiday 22: 83 Sept '57.

traffic police. Holiday 19: 95 Je '56; 20: 177 Dec '56; 23: 99 Jan '58.

—— **(Nassau).** Holiday 23: 11 Feb '58; 27: 39 Mar '60.

—— **(Paris).** Holiday 27: 195 (col.) May '60.

—— **(Rome).** Holiday 27: 174 Ap '60.

——. See also Negro traffic police.

tragedy (muse of). Lehner: Pict. bk. of sym., p. 33.

Traies, William (work of). Con. 145: LXIX Je '60.

"Trail of tears" (painted by Elizabeth Janes). Holiday 7: 114 (col.) May '50.

"Trail of the Iron horse" (Russsell). Amer. heri., vol. 6 no. 1 p. 40 (col.) (fall '54).

trail ornament. Con. ency. of ant., vol. 1, p. 23.

trailer, auto. See house trailer, auto.

——, **fishermen's house.** Natl. geog. 114: 870-1 Dec '58.

——, **house.** See house trailer.

——, **terra-marina (auto).** Travel 114: 58 Aug '60.

trailer camp (Ky. dam). Travel 107: 38 Je '57.

trails, pioneer. Travel 108: 15-9 Jl '57.

train. Amer. heri., vol. 9 no. 3 p. 5 (col.) (Ap '58).

Face of Amer., p. 65 (col.).

Holiday 5: 13 Mar '49, 85, 120 (col.) Ap '49, 84, 91, 142 (col.) Je '49; 6: 92 (col.) Jl '49, 26, 75, 127 (col.) Aug '49, 2 (col.), 84, 126 (col.) Oct '49, 27 (col.) Dec '49; 7: 20 (col.) Jan '50, 88 (col.) Feb '50, 30 Mar '50, 33 Ap '50, 23 (col.) Je '50; 8: 101 (col.) Aug '50, 79 (col.) Sept '50; 10: 9, 114 Oct '51, 4 (col.), 73 Dec '51; 11: 2, 23, 82 Jan '52, 94 Mar '52, 16, 18 (col.),

109 May '52; 12: 47, 84 (col.), 126-7 Jl '52, 124 Oct '52, 127 (col.) Nov '52, 9 Dec '52; 13: 13 (col.) Feb '53, 32, 66, 76 (col.), 95 Mar '53, 126, 154 (col.) Ap '53, 10, 15, 28 (col.) May '53, 129 Je '53; 14: 80, 125 Oct '53, 139 (col.) Nov '53, 94, 160 Dec '53; 15: 72 Mar '54; 16: 2 Oct '54, 39 Dec '54; 17: 147 Mar '55; 18: 5, 15 (col.) Jl '55, 73 Nov '55, 89 Dec '55; 19: 131 Jan '56, 2 (col.), 84 Feb '56, 9, 72-3 (col.), 90, 129, 139 (col.) Mar '56, 138 Je '56; 20: 20 (col.) Oct '56, 15 (col.) Nov '56, 121 Dec '56; 21: 105 (col.) Feb '57, 13 (col.), 123 Mar '57; 30, 37, 171 (col.) Ap '57, 117, 172 (col.), 187, 191 May '57; 23: 136, 158 (col.) Mar '58, 13, 132 (col.) Ap '58; 25: 28-9, 84, 98 Feb '59, 177 Mar '59, 36 (col.), 183 Ap '59; 26: 131 (col.) Nov '59; 27: 30 Jan '60, 9, 97 Mar '60, 164 (col.) Ap '60; 27: 199 (col.) May '60.

Travel 101: 32 Je '54; 103: 9 Ap '55; 104: 26-7 Jl '55; 105: 39 Ap '56; 106: 56 Sept '56; 107: cover (col.)—15 Mar '57.

train (Abe Lincoln's funeral train ghost). Holiday 6: 72 Aug '49.

—— **(Chicago's 1st locomotive).** Amer. heri., vol. 1 no. 2 p. 27 (col.) (winter '50).

—— **(children riding in park).** Travel 112: 65 Jl '59.

—— **(comic).** Holiday 9: 125 Mar '51.

—— **(comic, on cloud).** Holiday 7: cover (col.) Ap '50.

—— **(dining car).** Holiday 13: 15 (col.) Mar '53, 10 (col.) Je '53; 26: 10 (col.) Sept '59.

—— **(early western).** Horan: Pict. hist of wild west, p. 72, 89.

—— **(18th cent.).** Brooks: Growth of a nation, p. 161.

—— **(1830).** Holiday 24: 131 (col.) Dec '58.

—— **(1831).** Con. 141: XXXI Ap '58.

—— **(1856).** Amer. heri., vol. 9 no. 1 p. 56-73, 127 (part col.) (Dec '57).

—— **(1870)).** Amer. heri., vol. 12 no. 1 p. 127 (Dec '60).

—— **(1881).** Amer. heri., vol. 8 no. 2 p. 27-8 (col.) (Feb '57).

—— **(1890).** Amer. heri., vol. 10 no. 1 p. 52 (col.) (Dec '58).

—— **(1898).** Amer. heri., vol. 9 no. 6 p. 71 (Oct '58).

—— **(glass dome).** Holiday 18: 12-3 (col.) Nov '55; 20: 74 Aug '56; 21: 12-3 (col.) Mar '57.

—— **(int.).** Holiday 6: 126 (col.) Oct '49; 11: 74 (col.) May '52; 13: 119 (col.) Ap '53, 29 (col.) May '53, 29 Je '53; 20: 101 Dec '56.

Travel 104: 56 Aug '55; 106: 58 Sept '56.

—— **(19th cent.).** Natl. geog. 114: 117-8 (col.) Jl '58.

—— **(observation car).** Holiday 27: 199 (col.) May '60.

—— **(old).** Holiday 21: 164 Mar '57; 22: 76-7 Jl '57; 26: 109 Sept '59.

—— **("Old Peppersass", 1869).** Natl. geog. 107: 764-5 (col.) Je '55.

—— **(old style).** Holiday 7: 77 Jan '50.

—— **(¼ size-gift from Com. Perry to Japan).** Amer. heri., vol. 9 no. 3 p. 23 (col.) (Ap '58).

—— (1729). Brooks: Growth of a nation, frontis.

—— (Virginia & Truckee). Amer. heri., vol. 4 no. 3 p. 24-7 (part col.) (spring '53).

——, Africa. Natl. geog. 97: 328 Mar '50.

——, Alpine. Natl. geog. 98: 231 Aug '50.

——, Canadian. Travel 110: 16 Aug '58.

——, Canadian (1883). Amer. heri., vol. 3 no. 4 p. 42, 44-5 (summer '52).

——, circus. Durant: Pict. hist. of Amer. circus, p. 67.

——, circus (sleeping car, int.). Durant: Pict. hist. of Amer. circus, p. 295.

——, cog-rail. Holiday 8: 58 Sept '50.

——, cog-wheel. Travel 114: 49 Sept '60.

——, cog-wheel (Mt. climber). Natl. geog. 99: 592 (col.) May '51.

——, Diesel locomotive. Int. gr. soc.: Arts . . . p. 161 (col.).

——, European. Travel 109: 24-7 Mar '58.

——, European (primitive). Amer. heri., vol. 11 no. 5 p. 76 (Aug '60).

——, Fiji. Travel 111: 29-31 Mar '59.

——, first railroad. Rawson Ant. pict. bk., p. 71.

——, first steam. Brooks: Growth of a nation, p. 102.

——, freight. Holiday 12: 127 (col.) Nov '52; 21: 90 May '57.
Natl. geog. 114: 696-7 Nov '58.

——, jungle (Guatemala). Travel 108: 54 Nov '57.

——, modern (Amer.). Int. gr. soc.: Arts . . . p. 161 (col.).

——, modern (Santa Fe). Travel 113: 57 Je '60.

——, mountain. Holiday 26: 59 Jl '59.
Travel 106: 30 Oct '56.

——, mountain (Colo.). Travel 114: 48 Sept '60.

——, Peru. Travel 107: 30 Feb '57.

——, Peter Cooper. Amer. heri., vol. 10 no. 2 p. 107 (Feb '59).

——, private car (int.). Amer. heri., vol. 7 no. 4 p. 49 (col.), 51, 82 Je '56; vol. 10 no. 5 p. 34-41 (Aug '59).
Holiday 11: 83, 91 Ap '52; 19: 123-4 (part col.) May '56.

——, scenic miniature. Natl. geog. 98: 582 Nov '50.

——, toy. Holiday 14: 38 Dec '53.
Natl. geog. 114: 324 (col.) Sept '58.

train-bus. Natl. geog. 100: 206 (col.) Aug '51.

train called "Skunk" (passengers). Natl. geog. 115: 720-34 May '59.

train conductor. Holiday 10: 7 (col.) Dec '51.

—— (1898). Amer. heri., vol. 9 no. 6 p. 72 (Oct '58).

—— (head). Natl. geog. 115: 734 May '59.

train "hold-up". Horan: Pict. hist. of wild west, p. 89.
Natl. geog. 105: 744 Je '54.

train in race with horse car (1830). Amer. heri., vol. 10 no. 2 p. 105 (Feb '59).

train "Little Tweetsie" (Blue Ridge Mts.). Travel 110: 29-31 Aug '58.

train locomotive. Holiday 27: 11 Feb '60.

—— (1856). Amer. heri., vol. 9 no. 1 cover (col.) (Dec '57).

—— (1897). Amer. heri., vol. 11 no. 3 p. 2 (Ap '60).

——, narrow gauge. Natl. geog. 100: 207 (col.) Aug '51.

train model. Travel 114: 41 Sept '60.

—— (antique). Holiday 22: 17 (col.) Dec '57.

—— (1830). Holiday 24: 136 (col.) Sept '58.

train porter. See porter, train.

train stewardess. See stewardess, train.

train washroom (old & new). Holiday 6: 27 (col.) Dec '49.

train wreck at Revere, Mass. Amer. heri., vol. 8 no. 3 p. 27 (col.), 29 (Ap '57).

trains (early). Amer. heri., vol. 1 no. 2 p. 28-9 (winter '50).

——, (Belgian (early). Int. gr. soc.: Arts . . . p. 161 (col.).

——, unique. Travel 114: 48-9 Sept '60.

"The traitor" (Pettie). Con. 145: XXXIV Ap '60.

Trajan arch. (Beneventum). Labande: Naples, p. 128.

Trajan's column (Rome). Praeg.: Pict. ency., p. 171.

tram. See mule-trolley.

a tramp. Amer. heri., vol. 4 no. 3 p. 13 (spring '53).
Horan: Pict. hist. of wild west, p. 224.

"A tramp" (Gainsborough). Con. 135: LVIII Ap '55.

Transatlantic flyers parole (1927). Natl. geog. 112: 41 Jl '57.

transcendentalism (caricatures). Amer. heri., vol. 10 no. 3 p. 60-1 (Ap '59).

transfer of man at sea. Natl. geog. 118: 595 (col.) Nov '60.

"Transfiguration" (El Greco). Con. 132: opp. p. 143 (col.) Jan '54.

transistor. Holiday 19: 99 (col.) Mar '56; 21: 118 (col.), 150 Je '57; 22: 27 (col.) Jl '57, 100, 121 Oct '57, 123 (col.), 169, 184 Dec '57; 23: 47 Mar '58, 154 May '58, 35, 52 Je '58; 24: 158 Dec '58; 25: 139 Mar '59, 52, 174 Je '59; 26: 4 Jl '59, 130, 156 Oct '59, 208 Nov '59, 64, 176 (col.) Dec '59; 27: 6 May '60, 96, 129 Je '60; 28: 134 Jl '60, 81 Aug '60, 94 Sept '60, 106 Oct '60, 59, 131 149 Nov '60, 54, 119 (col.), 196 Dec '60.

——, assembling a. Natl. geog. 117: 6 (col.) Jan '60.

transit (Robt. E. Peary). Holiday 24: 56 Oct '58.

transmigration (sym.). Lehner: Pict. bk. of sym, p. 78.

transport plane. See airplane, combat transport.

transportation (Industrial age, 20th cent.). Int. gr. soc.: Arts., p. 161 (col.).

—— (17-18th cent.). Int. gr. soc.: Arts. . . p. 119 (col.).

——, Assyrian. March of arch., p. 200-1.

——, Mexico. Travel 101: 20 Mar '54.

trap, animal. Rawson: Ant. pict. bk., p. 28.

——, grizzly bear (men). Natl. geog. 118: 278-9, 282 (col.) Aug '60.

——, pigeon (at tree top, Egypt). Natl. geog. 108: 633 (col.) Nov '55.

trap boat. See boat, trap.

trap gate. *See* gate, trap.

trapeze actors. *See* aerialists.

Traphagen, Ethel. Cur. biog. p. 629 (1948).

"The trapper" (by Charles Deas). Amer. heri., vol. 6 no. 5 cover (col.) (Aug '55).

trappers, fur (hut). Natl. geog. 100: 91 Jl '51; 113: 556 (col.) Ap '58.

trappers & house, muskrat. Natl. geog. 118: 721 (col.) Nov '60.

trapper's camp, fur (Alaska). Natl. geog. 109: 800-1 (col.) Je '56.

Traps, Joanna. Con. 139: 215 Je '57.

Trapps, Robert. Con. 139: 215 Je '57.

traps, fish. Rawson: Ant. pict. bk., p. 76.

Traubel, Helen. Cur. biog. p. 601 (1952).

Trautman, George M. Cur. biog. p. 630 (1951).

travel, safe (sym.). Lehner: Pict. bk. of sym., p. 64.

travel bags. *See* luggage.

travel bureau. Holiday 11: 40 (col.) May '52.

travel cartoon (1890). Natl. geog. 100: 750 Dec '51.

travel guides. Holiday 27: 195 Je '60.

—— (folders). Holiday 21: 142 (col.) Mar '57.

travel kit. Holiday 20: 23 Dec '56.

travel plans. *See* tour guide (maps & plans).

travelers (comic). Holiday 28: 122 Nov '60.

travelers check. Holiday 11: 7 (col.) Je '52; 19: 74 Mar '56, 63 Je '56; 21: 120 Feb '57, 34 May '57; 24: 20 Sept '58, 20 Oct '58, 129 Nov '58, 234 Dec '58; 25: 3 Jan '59, 131 Feb '59, 11, 27 Mar '59, 181 Ap '59, 3, 98 May '59, 117, 135 Je '59; 26: 14 Jl '59, 12, 104 Aug '59, 139 Sept '59, 11, 127 Oct '59, 3, 48 Dec '59; 27: 141 Jan '60, 114, 124 Feb '60, 3, 51, 210 May '60, 11, 40, 197 Je '60; 28: 102, 118 Jl '60, 26, 89, 96 Aug '60, 16, 96 Sept '60, 14 Oct '60, 189, 196 Dec '60.

traveler's club. *See* Paris (Traveler's club).

Travelers hotel (La Guardia airport). Travel 106: 46 Sept '56.

traveling bag, Holiday 21: 135 Mar '57.
Travel 114: 19 Nov '60, 25 Dec '60.

traveling table service. *See* table service, traveling.

Travell, Janet G. Cur. biog. p. 458 (1961).

Travers, Pamela. Jun. bk. of auth., p. 287.

Traverso, Nicolo (sculpture by). Con. 142: 140 Dec '58.

travois. Natl. geog. 103: 746 (col.) Je '53.

tray (cocktails). Holiday 23: inside back cover (col.) Ap '58.

—— (18th cent.). Con. 132: LXXI Jan '54.

——, brass enameled (man making, India). Natl. geog. 116: 842 (col.) Dec '59.

——, Chinese lacquer. Con. 144: XII Nov '59.

——, dinner (airplane). Holiday 10: 68-9 (col.) Oct '51.

——, George I (silver). Con. 129: XXX Ap '52; 132: XVII Sept '53; 140: 39 Sept '57, LIX Jan '58; 145: 229 Je '60.

——, George II (silver). Con. 129: inside cover, LIII Je '52; 132: XXIII Sept '53, LXI Nov '53; 141: XLIX Je '58.

——, George III (silver). Con. 129: LIX Ap '52; 132: VIII-IX LVII Sept '53; 133: XLIX Ap '54, XVIII May '54; 136: LVII Jan '56;

138: XXV, 145 Nov '56, LXI Jan '57; 139: XLIX May '57, XXII, LVII Je '57; 141: XXVIII Mar '58; 142: XIII Nov '58; 143: IX Mar '59.

——, George III tea (silver). Con. 135: XXX-VII Mar '55; 137: LI, LVII Ap '56.

——, George IV tea (silver). Con. 141: XV Ap '58.

——, Georgian (silver). Con. 145: XXXVII Mar '60.

——, Lamerie (silver). Con. 144: 63 Sept '59.

——, Norwegian (1765). Con. 145: 9 Mar '60.

——, painted (Max, 18th cent.). Con. 144: 99 Nov '59.

——, Sevres. Con. 139: 231 Je '57.

——, Sheffield (silver). Con. 138: XXVI Sept '56; 142: LXXI Jan '59.

——, silver. Con. 136: XIX Nov '55.
Holiday 27: 56 May '60.

——, silver (antique). Con. 134: IX Nov '54; 140: XXXVII Jan '58.

——, silver (1728). Con. 142: VII Jan '59.

——, silver (17th cent.). Con. 132: 87 Nov '53.

——, silver (square, 18th cent.). Con. 139: III Mar '57.

——, silver (Storr, 19th cent.). Con. 143: XX-VIII Mar '59.

——, Swedish (18th cent.). Con. 143: 239 Je '59.

tray design. Rawson: Ant. pict. bk., p. 85.

trays (antique). Rawson: Ant. pict. bk., p. 8.

——. *See* also salver.

treadmill. Rawson: Ant. pict. bk., p. 31.

——, water irrigation. Natl. geog. 102: 310 (col.) Sept '52.

treasure chest. Amer. heri., vol. 8 no. 4 p. 101 (Je '57).
Holiday 14: 175 (col.) Dec '53; 21: 131 Feb '57; 22: 36, 164, 184 Nov '57, 157 Dec '57; 23: 132 Jan '58, 182 Je '58; 24: 135 Sept '58.
Travel 113: 10 May '60.

"Treasure island" (book illus.). Amer. heri., vol. 8 no. 1 p. 35 (col.) (Dec '56).

treasure recovery, sea (divers). Natl. geog. 117: 685, 687-8, 694 (col.) May '60.

treasury of Athens (Delphi). Natl. geog. 109: 55 (col.) Jan '56.

"Treaty of Ghent" (Forestier). Amer. heri., vol. 12 no. 1 p. 28 (col.) (Dec '60).

"Treaty of Greene Ville". Amer. heri., vol. 4 no. 3 p. 35 (spring '53).

"Treaty of Greenville". Amer. heri., vol. 9 no. 4 p. 61 (col.) (Je '58).

"Treaty of peace" announcement (1812). Amer. heri., vol. 12 no. 1 p. 85 (Dec '60).

Trebizond. Holiday 19: 53 (col.) Feb '56.

Tree, Marietta. Cur. biog. p. 460 (1961).

tree petrified. *See* petrified tree.

——, sacred (life sym.). Lehner: Pict. bk. of sym., p. 29.

tree & spade (Arbor Day). Lehner: Pict. bk. of sym., p. 52.

tree felling. Natl. geog. 110: 316 (col.) Sept '56.

tree growth rings. Natl. geog. 104: 363 Sept '53.

tree house. Natl. geog. 115: 731 May '59.

—— (children). Holiday 19: 20 (col.) Mar '56.

tree identification. Natl. geog. 108: 653-91 (part col.) Nov '55.

"Tree of death". Amer. heri., vol. 9 no. 4 p. 27 (col.) (Je '58).

"Tree of life". Amer. heri., vol. 9 no. 4 p. 26 (col.) (Je '58).

"Tree of life", Billy goat at. Ceram: March of arch., opp. p. 174 (col.).

"Tree of peace", Indian. Amer. heri., vol. 6 no. 2 p. 28 (winter '55).

tree pollination, pine. See pine tree pollination.

tree root, large (men & women). Natl. geog. 116: 170 (col.) Aug '59.

tree root animals. Rawson: Ant. pict. bk., p. 86.

tree tunnel. See tunnel, tree.

treetop hotel (Africa). Natl. geog. 110: 537 Oct '56.

Trefflich, Henry. Cur. biog. p. 627 (1953).

trefoil. Praeg.: Pict. ency., p. 248.

—— (sym.). Lehner: Pict.. bk. of sym., p. 38.

Tregaskis Richard. Cur. biog. p. 773 (1943).

trencher, wheel-type (machine). Natl. geog. 100: 550 Oct '51.

Trenton iron co. plant. Amer. heri., vol. 10 no. 2 p. 9 (Feb '59).

trestle, railroad. Amer. heri., vol. 9 no. 1 p. 66-7 (Dec '57).

trestle table. See table, butterfly; table, trestle.

Trevelyan, Sir George Otto. Con. 144: 10 Sept '59.

Trevi fountain (Rome). See Fontana di Trevi fountain.

triad, cabbalistic. Lehner: Pict. bk. of sym., p. 74.

trial, frontier. Brooks: Growth of a nation, p. 166.

triangle (musical instrument). Int. gr. soc.: Arts . . . p. 141 (col.).

triangle & bob (sym.). Lehner: Pict. bk. of sym., p. 10.

triangle & halo (sym.). Lehner: Pict. bk. of sym., p. 35.

triangle of vertebrates (sym.). Lehner: Pict. bk. of sym., p. 78.

Triangle Waist Co. fire (N.Y.). Amer. heri., vol. 8 no. 5 p. 54-7 (Aug '57).

triangles (sym.). Lehner: Pict. bk. of sym., p. 13, 68-70, 74.

triangulation instrument (men). Natl. geog. 111: 202 (col.), 203 Feb '57.

tribal dance (Australia). Holiday 8: 99 (col.) Nov '50.

tribesmen, Formosa (cooking). Natl. geog. 97: 152 Feb '50.

"Tribute money" (fresco). Praeg.: Pict. ency., p. 252 (col.).

"The Tribute money" (Titian). Praeg.: Pict. ency., p. 300 (col.).

triceps (sym.). Lehner: Pict. bk. of sym., p. 28.

tric-trac, Louis XVI. Con. 143: 193 May '59.

tricycle (children riding). Holiday 7: 8 May '50.

tridarn, Welsh (17th cent.). Con. ency. of ant., vol. 1, pl. 6.

trident (design). Natl. geog. 105: 32 (col.) Jan '54.

—— (sym.). Lehner: Pict. bk. of sym., p. 95.

Trieste (Italy). Natl. geog. 109: 824-57 (part col.) Je '56.
Travel 105: 18-9 Ap '56.

—— (map). Natl. geog. 109: 834 Je '56.

Trigere, Pauline. Cur. biog. p. 435 (1960).

Trigg, Ralph S. Cur. biog. p. 574 (1950).

trigonometry, plane (sym.). Lehner: Pict. bk. of sym., p. 9.

Trimble, Vance H. Cur. biog. p. 436 (1960).

trimurti (sym.). Lehner: Pict. bk. of sym., p. 43.

Trinidad (Cuba). Holiday 5: 100-3 (col.) Mar '49; 11: 90-5 (col.) Feb '52.
Natl. geog. 103: 41-3, 46- (col.) Jan '53.
Travel 106: 20 Dec '56.

—— (carnival costume). Holiday 23: 46-7 (col.) Feb '58.

—— (carnival mask). Holiday 26: 86 (col.) Sept '59.

—— (church ceremony). Holiday 24: 131 (col.) Nov '58.

—— (map). Natl. geog. 103: 39 Jan '53.

Trinidad "Calypso Joe" singer. Holiday 5: 7-9 Jan '49.

Trinidad dancers. See dancers, Trinidad.

Trinidad jungle (butterfly hotels). Natl. geog. 112: 194-216 (part col.) Aug '57.

Trinidad men. Travel 109: 45 May '58.

Trinidad "stick dance". Holiday 18: 132 (col.) Oct '55.

Trinita dei Monti church (Rome). Holiday 11: 47 (col.) Ap '52; 27: 2 Ap '60.
Natl. geog. 111: 441 (col.) Ap '57.

"The Trinity" (in wood by Plura). Con. 138: 177 Dec '56.

trinity (sym.). Lehner: Pict. bk. of sym., p. 38.

Trinity church (Manhattan). Travel 106: 15 Dec '56.

Trinity church (N.Y.). Holiday 10: 47 Sept '51.
Natl. geog. 99: 175 Feb '51.

Trinity college (Dublin). Travel 110: 47 Jl '58.

Trinity college (Durham, N.C.). Brooks: Growth of a nation, p. 285.

Trinity college library (Cambridge). Holiday 25 76 (col.) Je '59.

Trinity island. Amer. heri., vol. 6 no. 4 p. 51 (Je '55).

Trinity monastery of St. Sergius (Russia). Natl. geog. 116: 386-7 (col.) Sept '59.

"Trinity with St. Mary Magdalene & St. John" (Botticelli). Con. 136: 38 Sept '55.

tripod, Chou. Con. 136: 69 Sept '55.

tripod kettle stand (1755). Con. ency. of ant. vol. 3, pl. 11.

tripod table. See table, tripod.

Trippe, Juan T. Cur. biog. p. 843 (1942); p. 613 (1955).

triptych. Con. 126: 3 Aug '50.
Natl. geog. 107: 646 (col.) May '55.

—— (antique). Con. 134: 186 Dec '54.

—— (carved ivory). Con. 126: 90 Oct '50.

—— (fake of early work). Con. ency. of ant., vol. 3, pl. 97.

—— (15th cent.). Con. ency. of ant., vol. 3, pl. 131.

—— (16th cent.). Con. 144: 5 Sept '59.

——, Harbaville. Con. 142: 29 Sept '58.

triptych, Limoges enamel. Con. 140: 59 Sept '57.

trishaw. Natl. geog. 103: 198 (col.) Feb '53.

triskellion (sym.). Lehner: Pict. bk. of sym., p. 83.

Tristan da Cunha (islands in Atlantic). Holiday 8: 60-1 (col.) Nov '50.
Natl. geog. 97: 109-17 (col.) Jan '50.

"Triton" submarine. See submarine "Triton".

Triton's horn shell (girl holding). Natl. geog. 114: 529 (col.) Oct '58.

Triton's horn shell (sym.). Lehner: Pict. bk. of sym., p. 64.

"Triumph of Amphitrite" (Berchem). Con. 145: 269 Je '60.

"Triumph of Amphitrite" (Boilly). Con. 135: 59 Mar '55.

"Triumph of Bacchus" (Delacroix). Con. 143: 144 May '59.

"Triumph of Bacchus" (Poussin). Con. 143: 126 Ap '59.

"Triumph of Galatea" (Raphael). Holiday 27: 90-1 (col.) Ap '60.

"Triumph of riches" (Jan de Bisschop). Con. 127: 61 Mar '51.

"Triumph of Silenus" (Poussin). Con. 126: 180 Dec '50.

Triumphal arch (Bergen, 1733). See arch., triumphal (Bergen, 1733).

triumphal arch, Hadrian's (Antalya). See Hadrian's arch.

trivet. Con. ency. of ant., vol. 3, p. 246.

——, **iron (iron stand).** Rawson: Ant. pict. bk., p. 12.

Trois Ponts crossing (1944). Amer. heri., vol. 8 no. 5 p. 28 (col.) (Aug '57).

Trojan horse. Natl. geog. 100: 115 Jl '51.

Trojan house (excavation ruins). Ceram: March of arch., p. 40-1.

trolley car. Amer. heri., vol. 10 no. 1 p. 92 (Dec '58).
Holiday 5: 52 Je '49; 12: 67 Sept '52.
Natl. geog. 107: 298 Mar '55.
Travel 114: 48 Sept '60.

—— **(comic).** Holiday 5: 126 Jan '49.

—— **(Montreal).** Holiday 10: 53 (col.) Aug '51.

—— **(Ontario).** Travel 110: 16 Aug '58.

——, **horse drawn.** Holiday 15: 14 Ap '54.

trolley. See also mule trolley.

trombone. Cooper: Con. ency. of music, p. 406.
Int. gr. soc.: Arts . . . p. 141 (col.).

troop train (leaving station). Amer. heri., vol. 10 no. 6 p. 11 (Oct '59).

troops (landing on beaches). Natl. geog. 103: 505 Ap '53.

Troost, Laurens. Cur. biog. p. 628 (1953).

trophy. Holiday 26: 174 Nov '59.

——, **fisherman's.** Natl. geog. 114: 870 Dec '58.

——, **polo team.** Holiday 22: 67 (col.) Nov '57.

——, **sailboat race (Bermuda).** Natl. geog. 113: 774 Je '58.

trophy cup. Con. 129: LXXI Ap '52.
Natl. geog. 106: 716 Nov '54.

—— **(sym.).** Lehner: Pict. bk. of sym., p. 84.

trotting races (snow, 1858). Con. ency. of ant., vol. 3, pl. 96.

troubadours. Natl. geog. 100: 22 Jl '51.

—— **(medieval).** Int. gr. soc.: Arts . . . p. 61 (col.).

trough. Rawson: Ant. pict. bk., p. 48.

——, **bread kneading.** See bread kneading trough.

Trouillebert, Paul Desire (work of). Con. 143: 53 Mar '59.

trousers. Holiday 13: back cover (col.) Ap '53.

——, **college (comic).** Holiday 21: 62-3 (col.) Mar '57.

——, **man's.** Holiday 26: 114 Oct '59, 25 Nov '59, 209 Dec '59; 27: 159 Feb '60, 14 Ap '60; 28: 21-2 Sept '60.

trowel (sym.). Lehner: Pict. bk. of sym., p. 90.

Troy (N.Y. 1820). Amer. heri., vol. 10 no. 1 p. 19 (col.) (Dec '58).

Troye, Edward (work of). Con. 145: 146 May '60.

"Truant gamblers" (Monet). Amer. heri., vol. 11 no. 5 p. 21 (col.) (Aug '60).

truce (sym.). Lehner: Pict. bk. of sym., p. 86.

Trucial Oman (map). Natl. geog. 110: 71-104 (part col.) Jl '56.

truck. Face of Amer., p. 64 (col.).
Natl. geog. 100: 292 (col.) Sept '51; 102: 391 (col.) Sept '52; 113: 672 May '58; 114: 840 (col.) Dec '58; 116; 223 (col.) Aug '59, 347 Sept '59.

—— **(Agriculture "school on wheels").** Brooks: Growth of a nation, p. 152.

—— **(Antarctic).** Natl. geog. 115: 27, 29 (col.) Jan '59.

—— **(desert).** Natl. geog. 113: 682-3 May '58.

—— **(men).** Natl. geog. 98: 535 (col.) Oct '50.

—— **(ocean beach).** Natl. geog. 108: 772 (col.) Dec '55.

—— **(Pakistan).** Natl. geog. 100: 734 (col.) Dec '51.

—— **(weapons carrier).** Natl. geog. 97: 228 Feb '50.

——, **amphibian.** Natl. geog. 98: 666 Nov '50.

——, **baggage.** Natl. geog. 111: 307 (col.) Mar '57.

——, **delivery.** Natl. geog. 112: 451 (col.) Oct '57; 115: 470 (col.) Ap '59.

——, **farm (Canada).** Natl. geog. 108: 219 (col.) Aug '55.

——, **freight.** Brooks: Growth of a nation, p. 309.

——, **library book.** Natl. geog. 97: 674 May '50.

——, **log.** Natl. geog. 98: 349 Sept '50; 105: 746 (col.) Je '54; 110: 319 (col.) Sept '56; 116: 612-3 (col.) Nov '59.

——, **Russian (women workers).** Natl. geog. 116: 733 Dec '59.

——, **Russian dump.** Natl. geog. 116: 362 (col.) Sept '59.

——, **tank.** See tank truck.

——, **war supplies.** Natl. geog. 99: 412 Mar '51.

trucks. Natl. geog. 117: 108-9 (col.) Jan '60.

—— **(sugar cane).** Natl. geog. 113: 552-3 (col.) Ap '58.

—— (tomatoes). Natl. geog. 117: 35 (col.) Jan '60.

Trudeau, Lt. Gen. Arthur G. Cur. biog. p. 442 (1958).

true-love knot. See knot, true-love (sym.).

"True travels" (illus). Amer. heri., vol. 9 no. 6 p. 30-33 Oct '58.

Truex, Ernest. Cur. biog. p. 869 (1941).

Truitt, Paul T. Cur. biog. p. 630 (1948).

Trujillo Molina, Rafael L. Cur. biog. p. 871 (1941).

Trulock, Mrs. Guy Percy. Cur. biog. p. 557 (1957).

Truman, Pres. Harry S. Amer. heri., vol. 6 no. 2 p. 67 (winter '55); vol. 7 no. 3 p. 33 (Ap '56).
Cur. biog. p. 845 (1942); p. 617 (1945).
Holiday 7: 54-5 Feb '50, 57 (col.) May '50; 23: 149 Je '58.
Jensen: The White House, p. 246-7, 250, 262.

Truman, Pres. Harry S. (with family). Holiday 7: 52 (col.) Feb '50.

Truman, Mrs. Harry S. Cur. biog. p. 647 (1947).
Jensen: The White House, p. 248.

Truman, Margaret. Cur. biog. p. 575 (1950).
Jensen: The White House, p. 248.

Trumbo, Dalton. Cur. biog. p. 873 (1941).

Trumbull, Faith (Mrs. Jonathan Trumbull, Sr.). Amer. heri., vol. 9 no. 4 p. 42 (col.) (Je '58).

Trumbull, John. Amer. heri., vol. 3 no. 2 p. 36 (winter '52); vol. 9 no. 4 p. 40 (col.) (Je '58).

—— (by Stuart). Amer. heri., vol. 9 no. 4 p. 44 (Je '58).

—— (work of). Amer. heri., vol. 7 no. 2 cover (col.) (Feb '56); vol. 7 no. 4 p. 4-5 (col.) (Je '56); vol. 9 no. 4 cover, p. 42-9 (col.) (Je '58).
Holiday 10: 42 (col.) Nov '51.
Natl. geog. 99: 187 (col.) Feb '51; 102: 156-7 (col.) Aug '52.

Trumbull, Sarah Harvey (Mrs. John Trumbull). Amer. heri., vol. 9 no. 4 p. 44 (Je '58).

Trumbull gallery handbill, John. Amer. heri., vol. 9 no. 4 p. 97 (Je '58).

trumpet. Cooper: Con. ency. of music, p. 405-6.
Int. gr. soc.: Arts . . . p. 141 (col.).

—— (human bone). Natl. geog. 97: 13 (col.) Jan '50.

—— (jazz). Int. gr. soc.: Arts . . . p. 143 (col.).

—— (medieval). Int. gr. soc.: Arts . . . p. 61 (col.).

—— (Monks, Tibet). Natl. geog. 108: 24, 37 (col.) Jl' 55.

—— (Nigerian man blowing). Natl. geog. 116: 251 Aug '59.

—— (sym.). Lehner: Pict. bk. of sym., p. 85.

——, Tukuma Indian sacred. Natl. geog. 116: 643 Nov '59.

trumpet & gonfalon (sym.). Lehner: Pict. bk. of sym., p. 85.

"The Trumpeter" (S. R. Stuyvesant). Amer. heri., vol. 10 no. 1 p. 9 (col.) (Dec '58).

trumpeter, Poland (13th cent.). Natl. geog. 114: 385 (col.) Sept '58.

trumpeter & magistrate. Natl. geog. 111: 228 (col.) Feb '57.

trumpeters, Balearic. Natl. geog. 111: 634 (col.) May '57.

——, Nigeria. Natl. geog. 110: 332 (col.) Sept '56.

trumpeters, Switzerland. Natl. geog. 114: 568 (col.) Oct '58.

trumpets, Bhutan. Natl. geog. 102: 733 Dec '52.

——, Israel (children). Natl. geog. 112: 844 (col.) Dec '57.

——, Nigeria. Natl. geog. 110: 332 (col.) Sept '56; 116: 251 Aug '59.

——, Nepal. Natl. geog. 117: 400 (col.) Mar '60.

Trundholm sun chariot. See sun chariot.

trunk. Holiday 5: 142 Ap '49; 6: 93 Sept '49; 8: 33 Dec '50; 10: 30 Oct '51, 185 Dec '51.

—— (1850). Amer. heri., vol. 11 no. 3 p. 15 (Ap '60).

——, Arabian. Natl. geog. 104: 36 (col.) Jl '53.

—— Geo. Washington's Natl. geog. 104: 664 (col.) Nov '53.

trunks (antique). Rawson: Ant. pict. bk., p. 74.

Truscott, Lt. Gen. Lucian K. Cur. biog. p. 624 (1945).

Trussell, Charles P. Cur. biog. p. 609 (1949).

"Trust memorial" (Ankara). Osward: Asia Minor, pl. 156.

"A trustworthy beast" (cartoon). Amer. heri., vol. 11 no. 5 p. 9 (Aug '60).

truth (sym.). Lehner: Pict. bk. of sym., p. 60.

Tsaldaris, Constantin. Cur. biog. p. 603 (1946).

Tsarapkin, Semyon K. Cur. biog. p. 438 (1960).

Tschirky, Oscar M. Cur. biog. p. 648 (1947).

Tse-Tung, Mao. Cur. biog. p. 289 (1962).

Tshombe, Moise. Cur. biog. p. 462 (1961).

Tsiang, Tingfu Fuller. Cur. biog. p. 632 (1948).

Tuareg (on camel). Natl. geog. 113: 691 (col.) May '58.

Tuareg cavalry man (camel). Natl. geog. 117: 783 (col.) Je '60.

Tuareg man (on horse). Natl. geog. 112: 70 (col.) Jl '57.

Tuareg man & woman. Holiday 20: 51 Aug '56.

Tuareg men. Natl. geog. 112: 68-9 (col.) Jl '57.

Tuaregs (Sahara). Natl. geog. 113: 665, 688-9, 693 (part col.) May '58.

tub, Chinese. Natl. geog. 111: 356 (col.) Mar '57.

——, forge water. See water tub, forge.

——, wash. Natl. geog. 105: 475 (col.) Ap '54.

tuba (musical instruments). Cooper: Con. ency. of music, p. 407.
Holiday 9: 63 Mar '51; 10: 16 Oct '51.
Int. gr. soc.: Arts . . . p. 141 (col.).

tube, auroral. See auroral tube.

——, inner. See inner tube, auto.

——, ointment. Holiday 28: 69 Aug '60.

——, shaving cream. Holiday 21: 41 May '57.

Tubman, William Vacanarat Shadrach. Cur.

biog. p. 617 (1955).
Holiday 25: 72 (col.) Ap '59.

tubular bells (musical instruments). Cooper: Con. ency. of music, p. 410.

Tuchman, Barbara W. Cur. biog. p. (1963).

Tuck, John, jr. Natl. geog. 113: 444, 458 Ap '58, 792 Je '58.

Tuck, William M. Cur. biog. p. 605 (1946).

Tucker, Judge Bertha Fain. Cur. biog. p. 559 (1957).

Tucker, Bishop Henry St. George. Cur. biog. p. 775 (1943).

Tucker, Richard. Cur. biog. p. 627 (1956).

Tucker, Sophie. Cur. biog. p. 627 (1945).
Holiday 7: 71 Mar '50.

Tucson (Ariz.). Holiday 16: 25 (col.) Nov '54; 18: 38-41 (part col.) Oct '55, 125 (col.) Nov '55; 19: 18 (col.) Jan '56.
Natl. geog. 104: 346-7, 351, 382 (part col.) Sept '53.
Travel 101: 13-5 Jan '54.
—— **(air view).** Holiday 25: 61 Mar '59.

Tudor, Antony. Cur. biog. p. 631 (1945).

Tudor, Tasha. Jun bk. of auth., p. 288.

Tudor architecture. See architecture, Tudor.

"Tudor Place" (home of Martha P. Custis). Natl. geog. 103: 542 (col.) Ap '53.

Tuesday (sym.). Lehner: Pict. bk. of sym., p. 24.

tug boat (India). Natl. geog. 118: 500 (col.) Oct '60.

——, **battery powered (under sea).** Natl. geog. 109: 150 Feb '56.

——, **river.** Face of Amer., p. 35 (col.).

——, **U.S. army (aground).** Natl. geog. 111: 293 Mar '57.

"Tug of Peace" (cartoon). Amer. heri., vol. 9 no. 2 p. 71 (Feb '58).

"tug of war" (sports). Natl. geog. 112: 744-5 (col.) Dec '57.

tugs (N.Y. harbor). Natl. geog. 106: 805 (col.) Dec '54.

Tugwell, Rexford. Cur. biog. p. 874 (1941); (1963).

Tulane univ. students (Tattoo alligators). Natl. geog. 103: 179 (col.) Feb '53.

Tuileries (Paris). Holiday 8: 86 (col.) Jl '50.

—— **(gardens).** Natl. geog. 98: 62 (col.) Jl '50.

"Tulip Hill" (Maryland home). Natl. geog. 105: 456 Ap '54.

Tulsa (Okla.). Holiday 16: 98-103 (col.) Oct '54.

—— **(air view).** Travel 104: 32 Jl '55.

tumbler (18th cent.). Con. 132: 163-5 Jan '54.

——, **glass.** Holiday 13: 67 Jan '53.

——, **quilting design.** Rawson: Ant. pict. bk., p. 84.

tumbler & plate. Holiday 13: 9 Ap '53.

tumblers, aluminum. Holiday 20: 33 Dec '56.

——, **cut glass.** Daniel: Cut & engraved glass.

——. See also glasses.

tuna boat fiesta (Cal.). Natl. geog. 105: 772-5 (col.) Je '54.

tuna nets (carried to beach). Disney: People & places, p. 79 (col.).

tuning fork (sym.). Lehner: Pict. bk. of sym., p. 10.

Tunis (Tunisia). Holiday 5: 65-70 Mar '49; 25:

150 (col.) Ap '59.
Travel 101: 40-1 Ap '54.

Tunisian (with donkey). Travel 101: 40 Ap '54.

Tunisian students (marching). Natl. geog. 114: 725 Nov '58.

Tunnard, Christopher. Cur. biog., p. 455 (1959).

tunnel. Natl. geog. 104: 648 Nov '58.

—— **(man on ladder).** Natl. geog. 110: 378 Sept '56.

——, **Mt.** Travel 106: back cover Nov '56.

——, **railroad.** Amer. heri., vol. 9 no. 1 p. 69 (col.) (Dec '57).

——, **road.** Holiday 21: 177 (col.) Je '57.

——, **rock (girl).** Natl. geog. 109: 634 (col.) May '56.

——, **rock (Officer's resort, near Samandag).** Osward: Asia Minor, pl. 24.

——, **snow.** See snow tunnel.

——, **tree (Cal.).** Holiday 12: 12 (col.) Dec '52. Natl. geog. 99: 689 (col.) May '51; 105: 802 (col.) Je '54.

——, **war (people, Free China).** Natl. geog. 115: 429 Mar '59.

"Tunnel of love" (comic). Holiday 11: 83 Feb '52.

Tunstall, John. Horan: Pict. hist. of wild west, p. 59.

Tuomioja, Sakari. Cur. biog. p. 616 (1954).

Tupolev, Lt. Gen. Andrei N. Cur. biog. p. 561 (1957).

turban, Indian. Holiday 27: 201 Ap '60.
Natl. geog. 105: 515 (col.) Ap '54.

turbans (Tuareg men). Natl. geog. 112: 68-71 (col.) Jl '57.

turbine, electric power. Brooks: Growth of a nation, p. 283.

——, **steam.** Natl. geog. 110: 589 (col.) Nov '56.

turbine runner. Natl. geog. 115: 338 Mar '59.

Tureck, Rosalyn. Cur. biog. p. 457 (1959).

tureen. Con. 141: XXXIX May '58.
Holiday 24: 148, 154 Oct '58.

—— **(antique).** Con. 136: LIII Jan '56, XXIII Sept '55; 138: 195 Dec '56.

——, **Arnhem.** Con. 135: 104-5 Ap '55.

——, **Chelsea.** Con. 126: 202 Dec '50; 134: 21 Sept '54, XL Dec '54; 139: XLVI Mar '57, 122 Ap '57.

——, **Chelsea pineapple.** Con. 138: XXIV Nov '56.

——, **Chinese.** Con. 136: V Jan '56.

——, **Chinese (Ch'ien Lung).** Con. 145: XVI Je '60.

——, **Chinese porcelain.** Con. 134: I Dec '54; 141: XL May '58.

——, **Copenhagen (18th cent.).** Con. 142: 12 Sept '58.

——, **Doccia.** Con. 140: LXVI Jan '58.

——, **French faience (18th cent.).** Con. 144: 208 Dec '59.

——, **George II (silver).** Con. 133: VII Ap '54; 136: V Nov '55, 219 Dec '55; 137: LI Ap '56; 139: 193 May '57; 140: VII, XLIV Jan '58; 143: LIX Mar '59; 144: V Nov '59.

——, **George III (silver).** Con. 129: XXXIV Je '52; 132: LVII Sept '53; 134: XXIII Nov '54; 135: XXI Mar '55, XIII, LIII May '55,

Turpin, Randy. Cur. biog. p. 632 (1951).
Tuscany (Italy, flag wavers of Siena). Holiday 6: 30 (col.) Aug '49.
—— (map). Travel 107: 24 Ap '57.
tusk (sym.). Lehner: Pict. bk. of sym., p. 63.
tusks, giant metal (Kenya). Natl. geog. 118: 364 Sept '60.
Tuskegee institute laboratory (old). Brooks: Growth of a nation, p. 152.
Tutankhamen (head). Ceram: March of arch., opp. p. 127 (col.), 143.
Tutankhamen's coffin, King. Praeg. Pict. ency., p. 121 (col.).
—— mask, King. Travel 104: 17 Nov '55.
—— tomb, King. Natl. geog. 108: 622 (col.) Nov '55.
Tuttle, Charles E. Cur. biog. p. 439 (1960).
Tutuila island. Travel 114: 36 Dec '60.
Twain, Mark (pseud.). See Clemens, Samuel Langhorne.
Tweed, Harrison. Cur. biog. p. 578 (1950).
Tweed, William Marcy. Amer. heri., vol. 8 no. 3 p. 52 (Ap '57).
"Twelfth night" (Steen). Praeg.: Pict. ency., p. 60 (col.).
20-mule borax team. Natl. geog. 105: 761 (col.) Je '54.
"21" restaurant. See restaurant "21" (N.Y.).
"Twenty thousand leagues under the sea" (Illus.). Int. gr. soc.: Arts . . . p. 137 (col.).
Twichell, Rev. Joseph H. Amer. heri., vol. 11 no. 1 p. 68 (Dec '59).
Twining, Gen. Nathan F. Cur. biog. p. 630 (1953).
twins, Siamese. See Siamese twins.
"Two red dancers" (Kirchner). Con. 144: 181 (col.) Dec '59.
"Two women" (Pinney). Amer. heri., vol. 2 no. 2 p. 44 (col.) (winter '51).
Twoitsie (work of). Natl. geog. 107: 360 (col.) Mar '55.
Tyche (sym.). Lehner: Pict. bk. of sym., p. 31.
Tydings, Millard E. Cur. biog. p. 633 (1945).
Tyler, John. Amer. heri., vol. 7 no. 3 p. 31 (Ap '56).
Jensen: The White House. p. 62.
Tyler, Julia Gardiner (Mrs. John Tyler). Jensen: The White House, p. 64.
—— (cartoon). Jensen: The White House, p. 66.
Tyler, Mary (fairy costume). Jensen: The White House, p. 63.
Tyler home, Pres. John. Natl. geog. 109: 456 (col.) Ap '56.
Tyman, Kenneth. Cur. biog. p. (1963).
tympanum (in St. Madelaine). Praeg.: Pict. ency., p. 249.
Typesetter, Paige. Amer. heri., vol. 11 no. 1 p. 77 (Dec '59).
typewriter. Holiday 10: 134 Dec '51; 24: 16 Sept '58.
Int. gr. soc.: Arts . . . p. 169 (col.).
—— (man). Natl. geog. 107: 557 Ap '55.
Tyr (sym.). Lehner: Pict. bk. of sym., p. 28.
Tyrol (Alps). Holiday 27: 39-47 (col.) Jan '60.
Natl. geog. 100: 387-96 (part col.) Sept '51.

—— (Austrian). Holiday 15: 146 (col.) Ap '54.
Tyrolean. Natl. geog. 99: 753 (col.) Je '51.
—— (boy). Holiday 26: 184 Oct '59.
—— (comic runner). Holiday 5: 10 (col.) Jan '49.
—— (men & girls). Holiday 21: 116 Jan '57.
Tyrolean costume. Int. gr. soc.: Arts . . . p. 147 (col.).
Natl. geog. 99: 753 (col.) Je '51.
Tyrolean schuhplatler. Int. gr. soc.: Arts . . . p. 147 (col.).
Tyrolean village. Holiday 25: 73-7 (part col.) Jan '59.

U

U.S.A.—Uncle Sam. See Uncle Sam—U.S.A.
U.S.S.R. See Russia.
Ubangi saucer-lipped woman. Durant: Pict. hist of Amer. circus, p. 213.
Uccello, Paolo (work of). Con. 127: 129 May '51; 143: 107 Ap '59.
Udall, Stewart L. Cur. biog. p. 465 (1961).
Uganda (Africa). Holiday 18: 114-17 (part col.) Dec '55.
Natl. geog. 106: 722-(col.) Dec '54.
Uganda tribesmen. Travel 113: 26-7 Jan '60.
Ugarteche, Manuel Prado. Cur. biog. p. 677 (1942).
Ugolino & his sons (wax relief). Con. 142: 200 Dec '58.
Uhlmann, Richard F. Cur. biog. p. 610 (1949).
ukelele (Hawaiian girl). Holiday 11: 90 (col.) Mar '52.
Ukranian folk dancers. Natl. geog. 116: 388 (col.) Sept '59.
Ukranian woman (bedroom). Natl. geog. 116: 395 (col.) Sept '59.
Ulanova, Galina. Cur. biog. p. 444 (1958).
Ulbricht, Walter. Cur. biog. p. 604 (1952).
Ulio, Maj. Gen. James A. Cur. biog. p. 636 (1945).
Holiday 7: 42 (col.) Feb '50.
Ullman, James R. Cur. biog. p. 638 (1945).
Ullswater (Eng.). Holiday 14: 92 (col.) Jl '53.
Natl. geog. 109: 520 (col.) Ap '56.
Ulm cathedral. Praeg.: Pict. ency., p. 248.
Ulm cathedral spire. See spire, Ulm cathedral.
Ulrich, Charles F. (work of). Natl. geog. 99: 208 (col.) Feb '51.
ultraviolet light (man). Natl. geog. 114: 322 (col.) Sept '58.
Ulu Cami (Great mosque in Tarsus). Osward: Asia Minor, pl. 130-2.
the "Ulysses" (ship in storm). Amer. heri., vol. 6 no. 2 p. 18 (col.) (winter '55).
umbilical cord. Gray's anatomy, p. 32, 52.
umbrella. Holiday 6: 131 (col.) Oct '49; 12: 45 Nov '52; 14: 6 Dec '53; 20: 21 Dec '56; 23: 43 Ap '58; 25: 19 Ap '59; 26: 110 (col.) Oct '59.
Natl. geog. 104 20-1, 49 (col.) Jl '53; 117: 250 Feb '60.
—— (child). Holiday 21: 67 May '57.
—— (market stand). Natl. geog. 113: 164-5, 170-1 (col.), 172 Feb '58.
—— (over Nepal king). Natl. geog. 117: 400 (col.) Mar '60.
——, beach. Holiday 5: 53 (col.) Jan '49, 75

Mar '49, 88 (col.) Ap '49; 6: 60 (col.)
Sept '49; 9: 133 (col.) Mar '51; 10: 44
(col.) Aug '51, 7, 47 (col.) Nov '51, 53
(col.) Dec '51; 11: inside cover, 31 (col.)
Jan '52, 12 (col.) Je '52.
Holiday 12: inside cover, 98-9 (col.) Aug
'52, 82, 95 (col.) Oct '52, 90 (col.) Nov
'52; 13: 17, 99, back cover (col.) Feb '53,
88 (col.) Mar '53, 91, 122 (col.) Ap '53,
124 May '53; 49 (col.) Je '53; 14: 96 (col.)
Jl '53, 74 (col.) Sept '53; 15: 25 (col.) May
'54; 17: 117 (col.) Feb '55, 81, 91 (col.)
Mar '55; 18: 7 (col.) Jl '55, 87 (col.) Nov
'55; 19: 5 (col.) Feb '56, 80 (col.) Mar '56,
141, 182 (col.) May '56; 20: 21 (col.) Oct
'56, 187 (col.) Dec '56, 21: 111 (col.) Ap
'57; 22: 28 (col.) Nov '57, 65, 140 (col.)
Dec '57; 23: 29, back cover (col.) May '58;
24: 52 Aug '58; 25 cover (col.) Jan '59; 27:
7, 189 (col.) Jan '60, 39 (col.) Feb '60; 28:
46 (col.) Aug '60, 169 (col.) Dec '60.
Natl. geog. 101: 306 (col.) Mar '52; 104:
165, 167 (col.) Aug '53; 105: 222-3 (col.)
Feb '54; 107: 308-9 (col.) Mar '55; 108:
524 (col.) Oct '55; 109: 203-4 (col.) Feb
'56; 113: 179 (col.) Feb '58; 116: 481
(col.) Oct '59; 117: 752-3 (col.) Je '60.
Travel 103: 51, 58 Je '55; 107: 24 Mar '57;
113: 40 May '60.
—— (bathers). Natl. geog. 113: 779 (col.) Je
'58.
—— (children, nurse). Natl. geog. 113: 27
(col.) Jan '58.
——, field. Natl. geog. 106: 833 (col.) Dec '54.
——, Hindu. Natl. geog. 105: 518 (col.) Ap
'54.
——, India. Natl. geog. 113: 710 (col.) May
'58.
——, Indonesia. Natl. geog. 108: 376 Sept
'55.
——, Japanese. See Japansese parasol.
——, lawn. Holiday 9: 43 Mar '51; 10: 98
(col.) Aug '51, 121 (col.) Nov '51, 5 (col.)
Dec '51; 11: 26 (col.) Jan '52, 116 (col.) Mar
'52, 93, 115 (col.) Ap '52, 122 (col.) May
'52; 12: 80 (col.). Aug '52, 35 (col.) Oct '52,
75 (col.) Nov '52, 106 (col.) Dec '52; 13: 69
(col.) Mar '53, 74 (col.), 77 Je '53; 14: 8 Jl
'53; 19: 81 (col.) Feb '56, 30 (col.) Je '56; 21:
52 (col.) Jan '57, 170 (col.) Ap '57; 23: 45
Jan '58.
——, lawn (beach table). Holiday 21: 28 (col.)
May '57.
——, man's. Lehner: Pict. bk. of sym., p. 54.
Natl. geog. 111: 780 (col.) Je '57.
——, palm-leaf (India). Natl. geog. 118: 492
(col.) Oct '60.
umbrella. See also parasol.
umbrella bearers (Ghana). Natl. geog. 118: 313
(col.) Sept '60.
umbrella holder (antique). Holiday 26: 151
(col.) Nov '59.
umbrella of divine power (sym.). Lehner: Pict.
bk. of sym., p. 94.
umbrella stand. Holiday 14: 147 Oct '53.
umbrellas (Angkor). Natl. geog. 117: 523,
535, 544-5, 551, 554-5 (col.) Ap '60.
—— (Cambodia priests). Natl. geog. 116: 792
(col.) Dec '59.

—— (on elephants). Natl. geog. 105: 516 (col.)
Ap '54.
—— (people, rain). Natl. geog. 106: 167 (col.)
Aug '54.
——, outdoor restaurant tables. Holiday 25:
96 (col.) Mar '59.
Natl. geog. 99: 756-7 (col.) Je '51.
umbrellas. See also parasol.
Umgeni river falls (Natal, Africa). Natl. geog.
104: 192 (col.) Aug '53.
umiak (Eskimo boat). Holiday 26: 41 (col.)
Aug '59.
Natl. geog. 102: 75 Jl '52.
Unalaska (Aleutian islands). Amer. heri., vol.
10 no. 3 p. 72 (Ap '59).
"Uncle Sam", U.S.A. Amer. heri., vol. 10 no.
6 p. 9 (col.) (Oct '59); vol. 11 no. 4 p. 31
(Je '60).
—— (cartoon). Amer. heri., vol. 9 no. 2 p. 24
(col.) (Feb '58); vol. 11 no. 5 p. 9 (Aug
'60).
Holiday 26: 127 (col.) Dec '59.
—— (comic, put new star on flag). Holiday 20:
3 Nov '56.
—— (sym.). Lehner: Pict. bk. of sym., p. 93.
"Uncle Tom's cabin" (illus.). Amer. heri., vol.
4 no. 2 p. 21-3 (winter '53).
"Uncle Tom's cabin" (page from book). Brooks:
Growth of a nation, p. 142.
"Uncle Tom's cabin" (theater scenes). Amer.
heri., vol. 6 no. 6 p. 28-33 (col.), 103 (Oct
'55).
Unden, Bo Osten. Cur. biog. p. 650 (1947).
underclothes. See woman (underclothes).
"Underground railroad", Civil war. Amer. heri
vol. 11 no. 5 p. 52 (Aug '60).
Underhill, Ruth M. Cur. biog. p. 618 (1954).
understanding (sym.). Lehner: Pict. bk. of sym.,
p. 66.
Underwood, Cecil H. Cur. biog. p. 446 (1958).
unicorn (Chinese sym.). Lehner: Pict. bk. of
sym., p. 44.
—— (sym.). Lehner: Pict. bk. of sym., p. 61.
——, Louis XIV (carved wood). Con. 133: 263
Je '54.
uniform (captain). Holiday 21: 55 (col.) May
'57.
—— (Nepal king's guard). Holiday 21: 73
(col.) May '57.
uniforms (guards & soldiers). Int. gr. soc.:
Arts . . . p. 159 (col.).
—— (warriors, 16th cent.). Int. gr. soc.: Arts
. . . p. 115 (col.).
——, British. Holiday 25: 190 (col.) May '59.
——, Quebec. Holiday 11: 98-9, 101 (part col.)
Je '52.
——, U.S. marines. Holiday 22: 74-5 (col.)
Nov '57.
——, U.S. marines (1830). Amer. heri., vol.
10 no. 2 cover (col.) (Feb '59).
——, U.S. marines (1840-). Amer. heri., vol.
10 no. 2 p. 24-35 (col.) (Feb '59).
union (sym.). Lehner: Pict. bk. of sym., p. 26-7.
Union Bag-Camp Paper Corp. Mill. Natl. geog.
113: 34-5 Jan '58.
Union college, Schenectady, N.Y. Amer. heri.,
vol. 3 no. 3 p. 29-31 (spring '52).

"Union Jack" flag, British. Natl. geog. 110: 328-9 (col.) Sept '56.

Union of Soviet Socialist Republics. *See* Russia.

Union repeating gun. *See* gun, Union repeating.

Unitas, John Cur. biog. p. 431 (1962).

United Nations bldg. Holiday 18: 124 (col.) Oct '55.

—— (N.Y. skyline reflections). Travel 101: 4 Jan '54.

—— (peace inscription on stairway). Travel 101: inside cover May '54.

United Nations flags. *See* flags, United Nations.

United Nations room (int.). Holiday 22: 50-1 (col.) Jl '57.

United States (discovery map). Natl. geog. 103: 756-69 (col.) Je '53.

—— (Eng. tour cartoons). Holiday 26: 34-45 Jl '59.

—— (highway map). U.S. News & world report, p. 44-5 Aug 31, 1964.

—— (map). Natl. geog. 98: 8-9 Jl '50; 99: 834 Je '51.
Travel 105: 26 Feb '56.

—— (map). Natl. geog. 98: 8-9 Jl '50; 99: 834 Jl '52.

——, eastern (map). Amer. heri., vol. 3 no. 3 p. 47 (spring '52).

United States airforce (communications). Natl. geog. 111: 302 (col.) Mar '57.

—— (men, planes). Natl. geog. 117: 654-7, 671 (col.) May '60.

U.S. airforce academy (Colo.). Natl. geog. 115: 844-73 (part col.) Je '59.

U.S. airforce airplane. *See* airplane, U.S. air force.

U.S. airforce & army officers (Canada). Natl. geog. 104: 836 (col.) Dec '53.

U.S. air force cadets. Natl. geog. 115: 844-73 (part col.) Je '59.

U.S. air force insignia. Natl. geog. 115: 863 (col.) Je '59.

U.S. allied army mosaic map. Natl. geog. 111: 751 (col.) Je '57.

U.S. army (honor insignia). Int. gr. soc.: Arts . . . p. 167 (col.).

U.S. army chorus. Natl. geog. 114: 600 (col.) Nov '58.

U.S. army engineer waterways experiment station (Vicksburg, model). Natl. geog. 118: 704-5 (col.) Nov '60.

U.S. army firing squad. Natl. geog. 111: 758 (col.) Je '57.

U.S. Bur. of labor bldg. (1884). Brooks: Growth of a nation, p. 203.

U.S.-Canadian border (Glacierland). Natl. geog. 109: 590-636 (part col.) May '56.

U.S. Capitol (Wash., D.C.).

——, Capitol bldg. (Wash., D.C.). Amer. heri., vol. 9 no. 1 p. 13 (Dec '57); vol. 9 no. 2 p. 10-11 (Feb '58).
Brooks: Growth of a nation, p. 14, 257.
Holiday 5: 69 (col.) Ap '49; 15: 94 May '54; 22: 21, 23 (col.) Sept '57.
Jensen: The White House.
Natl. geog. 97: 667 May '50; 111: 66-9 (col.), 83 Jan '57; 117: 257, 268-9 Feb '60.

—— (dome). Holiday 12: 42 (col.) Jl '52.

—— (1840). Amer. heri., vol. 10 no. 2 p. 24 (Feb '59).

—— (1850). Amer. heri., vol. 8 no. 1 p. 50 (Dec '56).

—— (ext. & int.). Jensen: The White House. Natl. geog. 102: 143-90 (part col.) Aug '52.

—— (Garfield inauguration). Amer. heri., vol. 7 no. 1 p. 36-7 (col.) (Dec '55).

—— (in time of John Adams). Amer. heri., vol. 6 no. 6 p. 59 (col.) (Oct '55).

—— (interior). Holiday 7: 104 Feb '50.

—— (plans). Amer. heri., vol. 10 no. 5 p. 72-7 (Aug '59).
Jensen: The White House.

—— (rotunda, soldier's casket). Natl. geog. 114: 594-5, 597 (col.) Nov '58.

—— (soldiers honor service). Natl. geog. 114: 594-6 (col.) Nov '58.

—— (temporary, 1814). Amer. heri., vol. 2 no. 2 p. 5 (winter '51).

—— (Thornton plan). Amer. heri., vol. 2 no. 2 p. 5 (winter '51).

——, The White House (plans). Jensen: The White House.

U.S. cavalry (horse running, 1875). Amer. heri., vol. 9 no. 4 p. 23 (Je '58).

U. S. cavalry. *See* also Cavalry, Colonial.

U.S. Civil war. Amer. heri., vol. 3 no. 2 p. 62-6 (winter '52); vol. 6 no. 5 p. 89-91 (Aug '55); vol. 11 no. 2 p. 64-78 (Feb '60); vol. 12 no. 1 p. 118-9 (Dec '60).

—— (battle). Amer. heri., vol. 6 no. 1 p. 18 (fall '54); vol. 6 no. 5 p. 90-1 (Aug '55).
Brooks: Growth of a nation, p. 145.
Holiday 13: 53 (col.) May '53; 22: 70-1 (col.) Jl '57.

—— (battle of Atlanta). Amer. heri., vol. 7 no. 2 p. 32-43 (col.), 119 (Feb '56).
Brooks: Growth of a nation, p. 145.
Natl. geog. 105: 309 Mar '54.

—— (battle of New Orleans). Amer. heri., vol. 8 no. 5 p. 4-5 (col.) (Aug '57).

—— (battlefield). Holiday 19: 50-1 Je '56.

—— (Clay battalion). Jensen: The White House, p. 89.

—— (Ft. Jackson). Natl. geog. 103: 301 (col.) Mar '53.

—— (Georgia). Natl. geog. 105: 309 Mar '54.

—— (Gettysburg). Amer. heri., vol. 2 no. 2 p. 38-9 (col.) (winter '51); vol. 9 no. 1 p. 30 (col.) (Dec '57).
Holiday 11: 60-1 (col.) Je '52.

—— (Lawrence, Kan.). Amer. heri., vol. 11 no. 6 p. 22-3 (Oct '60).

—— (marines). *See* U.S. Marines (Civil war).

—— (Missionary Ridge). Holiday 21: 86-7 (col.) Mar '57.

—— (mural). Natl. geog. 103: 282 Mar '53.

—— (Negroes in battle). Amer. heri., vol. 9 no. 4 p. 53 (Je '58).

—— (Philippi battle). Amer. heri., vol. 3 no. 4 p. 56-9 (summer '52).

—— (prison camp). Amer. heri., vol. 10 no. 5 p. 4-13 (part col.) (Aug '59).

—— (scenes by Hoffbauer). Amer. heri., vol. 5 no. 3 p. 32-3, 36-7 (col.) (spring '54).

—— (soldiers). Amer. heri., vol. 6 no. 1 p. 18 (fall '54); vol. 6 no. 6 p. 66-93 (Oct '55);

vol. 7 no. 6 p. 34-5, 38, 42, 45, 48-9, 61, 63 (Oct '56); vol. 8 no. 3 p. 30-7 (col.) (Ap '57); vol. 11 no. 2 p. 76 (Feb '60); 12: no. 1 p. 119 (Dec '60).

Holiday 21: 86-7 (col.) Mar '57; 22: 70-1 (col.) Jl '57.

Jensen: The White House, p. 91.

Natl. geog. 117: 271 Feb '60.

Pakula: Cent. album, (col.).

—— (soldiers in camp). Amer. heri., vol. 9 no. 1 p. 35 (Dec '57).

—— (soldiers marching). Amer. heri., vol. 7 no. 6 p. 49, 66 (col.) (Oct '56).

—— (soldiers on horses). Amer. heri., vol. 7 no. 6 p. 30-1 (col.) (Oct '56).

—— (Vicksburg). Holiday 22: 70-1 (col.) Jl '57.

U.S. Civil war bugle. Holiday 28: 57 Sept '60.

U.S. Civil war campaign map. Amer. heri., vol. 11 no. 2 p. 70-1 (Feb '60).

U.S. Civil war cartoons. See cartoons.

U.S. Civil war cemetery. Amer. heri., vol. 12 no. 1 p. 118 (Dec '60).

U.S. Civil war memorial monument (Vicksburg). Travel 103: 19 May '55; 110: 21 Jl '58.

U.S. Civil war posters. Amer. heri., vol. 7 no. 5 p. 23 (col.) (Aug '56); vol. 9 no. 6 p. 117-20 (Oct '58).

U.S. Civil war prisoners (Confederate). Amer. heri., vol. 10 no. 5 p. 97 (Aug '59).

U.S. Coast guard (hoeing flowers). Natl. geog. 114: 276 (col.) Aug '58.

U.S. Coast guard boat (square-rigger). Natl. geog. 108: 50-84 (col.) Jl '55.

U.S. Coast guard cadets (on ship). Natl. geog. 108: 57-84 (col.) Jl '55.

—— (study table). Natl. geog. 112: 330 (col.) Sept '57.

——. See also cadets.

U.S. Coast survey engineers. Natl. geog. 111: 188-208 (part col.) Feb '57.

U.S. Color guard. Natl. geog. 111: 766 (col.) Je '57.

U.S. Congress. Natl. geog. 117: 238 (col.) Feb '60.

U.S. Congressmen. See Congressmen, U.S.

U.S. destroyer boat. Natl. geog. 111: 563 Ap '57.

U.S. frigate Constitution (model). Holiday 18: 45 (col.) Aug '55.

U.S. House of representatives (int., Wash., D.C.). Amer. heri., vol. 7 no. 1 p. 13 (col.) (Dec '55).

—— (int., 1822). Amer. heri., vol. 2 no. 2 p. 26 (col.) (winter '51).

U.S. information center (Vienna). Natl. geog. 99: 760 (col.) Je '51.

U.S. insignia. Int. gr. soc.: Arts . . . p. 167 (col.).

U.S. Marine (1840). Amer. heri., vol. 10 no. 2 p. 24 (col.) (Feb '59).

—— mounting horse 1830). Amer. heri., vol. 10 no. 2 cover (col.) (Feb '59).

—— (with gun). Holiday 14: 138 Nov '53.

U.S. Marine band. Face of Amer., p. 51 (col.). Natl. geog. 116: 753, 755, 758-9, 762-65 (col.) Dec '59.

U.S. Marine barracks. Face of Amer., p. 51 (col.).

—— (drum & bugle corp.). Natl. geog. 111: 95 Jan '57.

U.S. Marine color guard (Annapolis). Holiday 23: 83 (col.) Je '58.

U.S. Marine parade. Face of Amer., p. 51 (col.).

U.S. Marines. Amer. heri., vol. 10 no. 2 p. 26-35 (col.) (Feb '59).
Holiday 22: 70-5 (col.) Nov '57.
Natl. geog. 98: 648-72 Nov '50; 116: 294 (col.) Sept '59.

—— (camouflage helmets). Natl. geog. 115: 546 (col.) Ap '59.

U.S. Marines (Civil war). Amer. heri., vol. 10 no. 2 p. 32 (Feb '59).
Pakula: Cent. album, pl. 4 (col.).

—— (landing in Mexico, 1847). Amer. heri., vol. 10 no. 2 p. 28 (col.) (Feb '59).

—— (landing on Formosa. Natl. geog. 103: 512 Ap '53.

—— (leathernecks). See Marines, U.S.

—— (marching, 1853). Amer. heri., vol. 9 no. 3 p. 18 (col.) (Ap '58).

—— Parris island, (exercises). Natl. geog. 113: 32-3 (col.) Jan '58.

—— See also uniforms (U.S. Marines).

U.S. Merchant marine academy. Natl. geog. 108: 697-706 (part col.) Nov '55.

—— (cadet-midshipmen). Natl. geog. 99: 297 Mar '51.

U.S. Natl. Bur. of Standards. See Natl. Bur. of Standards.

U.S. Naval academy. Natl. geog. 113: 2-3 (col.) Jan '58.

U.S. Navy. Holiday 24: 57-9 Oct '58.

—— (equipment). Holiday 24: 56-7 Oct '58.

—— (man). Amer. heri., vol. 10 no. 6 p. 8 (col.) (Oct '59).

—— (men). Natl. geog. 100: 730 (col.) Dec '51.

—— (men in row boat, war 1812). Amer. heri., vol. 7 no. 3 p. 21 (col.) (Ap '56).

—— (men, laboratory). Natl. geog. 97: 55 (col.) Jan '50.

U.S. Navy airplane. See airplane, U.S. Navy.

US. Navy boats. Natl. geog. 105: 258 (col.) Feb '54, 492 Ap '54, 776 (col.) Je '54; 107: 583 Ap '55.

U.S. Navy bombs. Natl. geog. 116: 306 (col.) Sept '59.

U.S. Navy floating dry docks. Natl. geog. 104: 543 Oct '53.

U.S. Navy light trails. Natl. geog. 104: 567 Oct '53.

U.S. Navy mine sweeper. Natl. geog. 117: 572 Ap '60.

U.S. Navy nurses (salute Hawaiian dead). Natl. geog. 118: 30-1 (col.) Jl '60.

U.S. Navy officers. Natl. geog. 116: 294 (col.) Sept '59.

—— (1800s). Amer. heri., vol. 8 no. 6 p. 50 (Oct '57).

—— (Monitor battleship). Amer. heri., vol. 8 no. 4 p. 12 (Je '57).

U.S. Navy poster. Amer. heri., vol. 10 no. 6 back cover (col.) (Oct '59).

U.S. Navy relief expedition (Arctic, 1884).
Amer. heri., vol. 11 no. 4 p. 47-8 (col.) (Je
'60).
U.S. Navy ship. Natl. geog. 104: 538-74 Oct
'53.
—— (bombed). Natl. geog. 112: 276 Aug '57.
—— (destroyer). Natl. geog. 116: 288-9 Sept
'59.
—— (Freedom ship). Natl. geog. 107: 858-9,
864 Je '55.
—— (sailors). Holiday 18: 7 (col.) Sept '55.
U.S. Navy signalmen. Holiday 10: 46 (col.) Nov
'51.
U.S. pavilion (Brussel's worlds fair). See Brus-
sel's worlds fair (U.S. pavilion).
U.S. Presidents. Amer. heri., vol. 6 no. 2 p.
66-8 (winter '55).
Jensen: The White House.
—— (caricatures by Berger). Amer. heri., vol.
10 no. 3 p. 88-93 (Ap '59).
U.S. Presidents & wives. Jensen: The White
House.
U.S. President's guest house. See Blair House.
U.S. President's heads. (sculpture, Black Hills).
See Mt. Rushmore memorial. . . .
U.S. President's homes. See homes of U.S.
Presidents.
U.S. Presidents memorial (Borglum sculpture).
See Mt. Rushmore memorial. . . .
U.S. President's seal. See seal, U.S. President's;
seal, U.S. Vice President's.
U.S. President's wives. Holiday 7: 53 (col.) Feb
'50.
Jensen: The White House.
—— (models). Natl. geog. 111: 90 (col.) Jan
'57; 117: 842 (col.) Je '60.
U.S. Presidents. See also name of President.
U.S.S. "Arizona" memorial (Hawaii). Natl.
geog. 118: 30 (col.) Jl '60.
U.S.S. "Chesapeake". See "Chesapeake" (ship).
U.S.S. "Housatonic" (Civil war). Amer. heri.,
vol. 9 no. 3 p. 51 (Ap '58).
U.S.S. "Nautilus" (flag draped end). Natl. geog.
107: 770 (col.) Je '55.
U.S. sailor. See sailor.
U.S. Seal. See seal of U.S., (furniture dec.).
U.S. Senate (inter.). Holiday 15: 57 (Pres. room,
col.), 63 Senate chamber Feb '54.
U.S. Senate railway. See railway, U.S. Senate.
U.S. service men (in Morocco). Natl. geog. 107:
153 (col.) Feb '55.
U.S. soldiers. See costume (U.S. soldiers);
soldiers.
U.S. State dept., old. Holiday 7: 59 Feb '50.
U.S. Supreme court (Wash., D.C.). Amer. heri.,
vol. 2 no. 1 cover (col.) (fall '50).
Brooks: Growth of a nation, p. 256.
Holiday 7: 73 Feb "50; 12: 62 Sept '52.
U.S. tank. See tank, U.S.
U.S. Vice President's seal. See seal, U.S. Vice
President's.
U.S. war cemetery (Gettysburg battlefield).
Amer. heri., vol. 9 no. 1 p. 49 (col.) (Dec
'57).
U.S. war memorial chapel. See chapel, U.S. war
memorial chapel (overseas).
U.S. White House (Wash., D.C.). Jensen: The
White House.

unity (sym.). Lehner: Pict. bk. of sym., p. 83.
universe, hermetic (sym.). Lehner: Pict. bk. of
sym., p. 75.
——, Japanese. See Japanese universe (sym.).
University, Auckland. See Auckland university
(clock tower).
University, Cambridge. See Cambridge univ.
University, Catholic. See Catholic univ. (Chile).
University, Drake. See Drake univ.
University, Hebrew. See Hebrew univ. (Israel).
University, Lovanium. See Lovanium univ.
University, Queen's. See Queen's univ.
University, Washington & Lee. See Washington
& Lee univ.
University, Yale. See Yale univ.
university bldgs. (Panama City). Holiday 13:
45 (col.) Jan '53.
"University City" (Mexico). Holiday 13: 35
(col.) Mar '53.
university graduate. See college graduate.
University of Alaska. Natl. geog. 109: 768-9
Je '56; 116: 65 Jl '59.
University of Arizona (Tucson). Travel 113: 27
Feb '60.
University of Beirut. Natl. geog. 113: 483 (col.)
Ap '58.
University of California. Holiday 8: 48-54
(part col.) Dec '50.
Natl. geog. 105: 732-3 Je '54; 110: 213 (col.)
Aug '56.
University of Chicago, chapel (int.). Holiday
28: 78 (col.) Dec '60.
University of Cincinnnati (student union). Natl.
geog. 97: 194 (col.) Feb '50.
University of Concepcion (Chile). Natl. geog.
117: 219 (col.) Feb '60.
University of Mexico. Holiday 26: 63 (col.) Nov
'59.
University of Miami (halls, students). Natl.
geog. 113: 65 Jan '58.
—— (students). Natl. geog. 98: 569, 574-6,
581, 585-9 (col.) Nov '50.
University of Michigan. Holiday 14: 68-71
Dec '53.
—— (Angell Hall). Natl. geog. 101: 291 (col.)
Mar '52.
University of North Carolina. Holiday 5: 98
(col.) Je '49.
University of Notre Dame (South Bend, Ind.).
Holiday 8: 29 Aug '50.
University of Pittsburgh. Holiday 6: 50 Oct '49.
University of Tampa (spires). Travel 107: in-
side cover Je '57.
University of Toronto (Canada). Holiday 13:
75 Mar '53.
University of Utah (student union). Travel 112:
35 Aug '59.
University of Virginia. Natl. geog. 97: 555,
572 May '50.
—— (Rotunda). Amer. heri., vol. 10 no. 5 p.
71 (Aug '59).
Brooks: Growth of a nation, p. 92.
Natl. geog. 97: 572, 585-6 (col.) May '50.
University of Washington. Natl. geog. 117: 511
(col.) Ap '60.
University of Wisconsin (campus). Natl. geog.
111: 143 (col.) Feb '57.
university. See also colleges, Ivy league.

university professor. Holiday 25: 157 Mar '59.
—— **(cap & gown).** Holiday 7: 115 (col.) Je '59; 13: 143 May '53; 25: 73 (col.) Je '59.
—— **(Moslem at Al Azhar).** Holiday 25: 53 (col.) Feb '59.
——, **German.** *See* university rector.
University rector, German. Holiday 25: 42 Jan '59.
Unknown soldier's caskets. *See* soldier's caskets, World war (honored).
Unterberger, F. R. (work of). Con. 140: XXIX Nov '57.
"Unto these hills" (outdoor theater play in NC.). Amer. heri., vol. 5 no. 4 p. 16-23 (part col.) (summer '54).
"Unveiling statue of liberty" (Moran). Natl. geog. 99: 212 (col.) Feb '51.
Unwin, Sir Stanley. Cur. biog. p. 612 (1949).
Upfield, Arthur W. Cur. biog. p. 635 (1948).
upholster (sym.). Lehner: Pict. bk. of sym., p. 91.
"upping block". Rawson: Ant. pict. bk., p. 41.
Upton, Emory. Pakula: Cent. album, p. 277.
Ur (excavations). Ceram: March of arch., p. 237-43.
Ur, "death pit" of. Ceram: March of arch., p. 239.
Ur, graves of. Ceram: March of arch., p. 237.
Ur standard (2450 B.C.). Praeg.: Pict. ency., p. 106 (col.).
Uraeus (royal serpent emblem, Egyptian). Int. gr. soc.: Arts . . . p. 29 (col.).
Urania (muse). Lehner: Pict. bk. of sym., p. 33.
uranium atoms. Natl. geog. 105: 72 Jan '54.
uranium—carbon alloy. Natl. geog. 114: 322 (col.) Sept '58.
uranium drilling. Natl. geog. 114: 834-5 Dec '58.
uranium mine. Natl. geog. 115: 471 (col.) Ap '59.
uranium prospectors. Natl. geog. 106: 535-58 (part col.) Oct '54.
Uravan (Colo.). Natl. geog. 106: 557 Oct '54.
Urey, Harold C. Cur. biog. p. 877 (1941); p. 441 (1960).
Ürgüp family (holiday dinner). Natl. geog. 113: 130 Jan '58.
urinary organs, human. Gray's anatomy, p. 1203, 1277.
urine (sym.). Lehner: Pict. bk. of sym., p. 73.
Uris, Leon Marcus. Cur. biog. p. 458 (1959).
urn. Amer. heri., vol. 6 no. 3 p. 67 (Ap '55); vol. 9 no. 1 p. 91 (Dec '57).
—— **(antique).** Con. 136: 147 Nov '55.
—— **(antique, on pedestal).** Con. 139: 275 Je '57; 140: XXXIX Sept '57.
—— **(antique on pedestal, 18th cent.).** Con. 140: IX Dec '57.
—— **(sym.).** Lehner: Pict. bk. of sym., p. 79.
——, **Adam.** Con. 145: LXXVI Je '60.
——, **Adam (on pedestal).** Con. 143: LV Mar '59.
——, **classic (1616).** Holiday 10: 38 Nov '51.
——, **coffee.** *See* coffee urn.
——, **Eng. ormolu (on stand).** Con. 143: LXVIII May '59.
——, **Etruscan (500 B.C.).** Int. gr. soc.: Arts . . . p. 19 (col.).

——, **French (1800).** Amer. heri., vol. 6 no. 5 p. 53 (col.) (Aug '55).
——, **garden (17-18th cent.).** Con. ency. of ant., vol. 3, pl. 25.
——, **garden lead (18th cent.).** Con. ency. of ant.. vol. 3, p. 54.
——, **lead (18th cent.).** Con. 144: XXVII Jan '60.
——, **mustard oil (Nepal).** Natl. geog. 97: 20 Jan '50.
——, **pottery (form of owl, antique).** Con. 141: XIV May '58.
——, **sepulchral (Austria).** Praeg.: Pict ency., p. 107.
——, **Sevres.** Con. 133: VI Je '54.
——, **silver (18th cent.).** Con. 145: 139 Ap '60.
——, **stone.** Natl. geog. 98: 178 Aug '50.
——, **stone (18th cent.).** Con. 136: LIX Jan '56.
Urn of the Deir (Petra). Natl. geog. 108: 866 (col.) Dec '55.
urn stand, Hepplewhite. Con. ency. of ant., vol. 3, pl. 11.
urn table, Sheraton. Con. 140: XIII Sept '57.
urn with lamp, George III. Con. 134: LVI Sept '54.
urns (ancient). Int. gr. soc.: Arts . . . p. 19 (col.).
—— **(18th cent.).** Con. 136: LV Nov '55.
——, **Zapotec.** Ceram: March of arch., p. 274.
Urquhart, Maj. Gen. Sir Robert E. Cur. biog. p. 697 (1944).
Urrutia, Francisco. Cur. biog. p. 447 (1958).
Urrutia Lleo, Manuel. Cur. biog. p. 459 (1959).
Ursula (female education). Lehner: Pict. bk. of sym., p. 40.
Ursuline sisters. Holiday 11: 101 Je '52.
Urumchi (China). Natl. geog. 99: 392 (col.) Mar '51.
Ushuaia (Argentina). Travel 102: 36-7 Dec '54.
Usman Ali, Nizam. Cur. biog. p. 636 (1948).
Ustinov, Peter. Cur. biog. p. 619 (1955).
Holiday 24: 99 Jl '58.
Utah. Holiday 14: 26-35 (part col.) Aug '53; 23: 159 May '58.
Jordan: Hammond's pict. atlas, p. 168-73 (col.).
Natl. geog. 101: 706-42 (part col.) Je '52; 108: 400-25 (col.) Sept '55; 111: 546-59 (part col.) Ap '57.
Travel 112: 33-5 Aug '59.
—— **(arches natl. monument).** Holiday 26: 50 Jl '59.
—— **(Mormon temple).** Face of Amer., p. 159 (col.).
Utah desert. Travel 110: 24-7 Oct '58.
Utamaro, Kitigawa (Japanese artist). Con. 138: 58 Sept '56.
Utchat (sym.). Lehner: Pict. bk. of sym., p. 27.
Ute Indian children. Natl. geog. 101: 739 (col.) Je '52.
Ute Indians. Amer. heri., vol. 8 no. 6 p. 37, 90 (Oct '57).
Ute Indians & babies. Natl. geog. 101: 728 (col.) Je '52.
uterus. Gray's anatomy, p. 31.
Utley, Freda. Cur. biog. p. 449 (1958).
Utrillo, Maurice. Cur. biog. p. 632 (1953).
—— **(work of).** Con. 133: 264 Je '54; 136:

211 Dec '55; 138: XI, 127 XLIII Nov '56; 140: 259 Jan '58; 141: 123 Ap '58; 143: 272 Je '59.

Uxmal (restoration, Yucatan). Holiday 26: 53 (col.) Nov '59.
Travel III: 20 Mar '59.

V

vacation tour charts, Amer. Holiday 18: 58-9 Jl '55.

vacuum cleaner. Holiday 22: 123 (col.) Dec '57; 24: 13 (col.) Dec '58; 26: 21 (col.) Dec '59. Int. gr. soc.: Arts . . . p. 171 (col.). Natl. geog. 112: 318 (col.) Sept '57.

vacuum jug. Natl. geog. 111: 822 (col.) Je '57.

"The Vagrants" (Morland). Con. 141: XXXIII Je '58.

Vail, Robert W. G. Cur. biog. p. 639 (1945).

"The Vailed Murderess of Troy". Amer. heri., vol. 3 no. 3 p. 13 (spring '52).

Val Kill cottage (int., Mrs. F. D. Roosevelt's home). Holiday 6: 43 (col.) Sept '49.

Velasquez (work of). Con. 140: 142 Nov '57.

Valdambrino, Francesco di (sculpture by). Con. 140: 203 Dec '57.

Vale of Kashmir. See Kashmir, Vale of

"Vale of St. John" (Towne). Con. 138: 182 Dec '56.

Valentina, Mme. Cur. biog. p. 608 (1946).

Valentine, Alan. Cur. biog. p. 579 (1950).

Valentine, Lewis J. Cur. biog. p. 609 (1946).

Valentine. Holiday 11: 107 (col.) Feb '52; 21: 95 (col.) Feb '57.

—— **(1847).** Amer. heri., vol. 10 no. 2 back cover (col.) (Feb '59).

—— **(sym.).** Lehner: Pict. bk. of sym., p. 55, 65.

Valentines (early). Amer. heri., vol. 6 no. 2 p. 62-5, back cover (col.) (winter '55).

Valentino's home, Rudolf. Holiday 5: 37 (col.) Jan '49.

valet. Holiday 14: 153 Dec '53.

Valladolid (Spain, Holy Week Procession). Travel 107: 20 Ap '57.

Valle, Filippo della. See Della Valle, Filippo.

Vallecitos laboratory. Natl. geog. 114: 308 Sept '58.

Vallee, Rudy. Cur. biog. p. 653 (1947); (1963).

Vallee, Mr. & Mrs. Rudy. Holiday 27: inside cover (col.) Jan '60.

Valley Forge. Brooks: Growth of a nation, p. 77.
Holiday 14: 162 Dec '53.
Natl. geog. 105: 189-202 (part col.) Feb '54.

—— **(army).** Holiday 16: 106 (col.) Jl '54.

—— **(hut).** See hut, Valley Forge.

—— **(map).** Natl. geog. 105: 188 Feb '54.

—— **(soldier huts).** Amer. heri., vol. 4 no. 2 back cover (winter '53).

—— **(Washington's headquarters).** Amer. heri., vol. 4 no. 1 back cover (fall '52).
Jordan: Hammond's pict. atlas, p. 45 (col.).
Natl. geog. 105: 199 (col.) Feb '54; 117: 13 Jan '60.

Valley of Goblins. Travel 107: 33 Mar '57.

"Valley of Mexico" (Chapman). Con. 137: 240 (col.) Je '56.

Valley of refuge. See Goreme valley of refuge.

"Valley of ten peaks" (Canada). Holiday 24:

112 (col.) Aug '58; 27: 223 (col.) May '60.

Valley of ten thousand smokes. Natl. geog. 109: 746 Je '56.

Valley of the tombs. Holiday 20: 54 (col.) Dec '56.

valor, medals of. Int. gr. soc.: Arts . . . p. 167 (col.).

Valparaiso. Natl. geog. 117: 220-1, 223 (col.) Feb '60.

Valtin, Jan. Cur. biog. p. 879 (1941).

van, delivery (Ischia). See delivery van.

——, **moving.** Holiday 14: 19 Jl '53.

Van Allen, James Alfred. Cur. biog. p. 461 (1959).

Van Anraadt, Pieter (work of). Con. ency. of ant., vol. 1, pl. 169.

Van Avercamp, Hendrick (work of). Con. 141: X (col.) May '58, XLII (col.) Je '58.

Van Baburen, Dirck (work of). Con. 140: 127 Nov '57.

Van Beaver, John (tapestry by). Con. 144: 27 (col.) Sept '59.

Van Beyeren, Abraham (work of). Con. 145: XIII (col.) Je '60.

Van Brekelenkam, Quiringh Gerritsz (work of). Con. 126: 134 Oct '50.

Van Buren, Abigail. Cur. biog. p. 443 (1960).

Van Buren, Angelica Singleton. Jensen: The White House, p. 59.

Van Buren, Martin (Pres.). Amer. heri., vol. 7 no. 3 p. 30 (Ap '56); vol. 7 no. 4 p. 101 (Je '56); vol. 8 no. 1 p. 63 (Dec '56).
Holiday 28: 33 (col.) Oct '60.
Jensen: The White House, p. 56.

—— **(cartoon).** Jensen: The White House, p. 57.

Van Buren's cabin home, Martin. Amer. heri., vol. 7 no. 5 p. 33 (Aug '56).

Van Buren's home, Martin. Amer. heri., vol. 10 no. 1 p. 20 (Dec '58).
Holiday 6: 39 (col.) Sept '49.

Van Cleve, Capt. James. Amer. heri., vol. 9 no. 5 p. 43 (Aug '58).

—— **(work of).** Amer. heri., vol. 9 no. 5 p. 42-9 (col.) (Aug '58).

Van Cleve, Joos (work of). Con. 133: 123 Ap '54; 138: 281 Jan '57.

Van Cliburn. See Cliburn, Van.

Van Craesbeeck, J. (work of). Con. 139: XXXVIII May '57.

Van de Velde, Esaias (work of). Con. 139: 112 Ap '57; 139: 245 Je '57; 142: 258 Jan '59.

Van de Velde the younger, Willem (work of). Con. 132: LXVII Nov '53.

Van der Ast, Balthasar (work of). Con. 145: LXXXI (col.) May '60.

Van der Donck, Adriaen. Amer. heri., vol. 10 no. 1 p. 10 (Dec '58).

Van der Goes, Hugo. See Hugo, Van der Goes.

Van der Hamen, Juan (work of). Natl. geog. 110: 641 (col.) Nov '56.

Van der Heyden, Jan (work of). Con. 141: 117 Ap '58, 177 (col.) May '58; 142: XXII (col.) Nov '58; 143: 208 Je '59.

Van der Meulen, Adam (work of). Con. 141: 39 Mar '58.

Van der Myn, Herman (work of). Con. 143: 42 Mar '59.

Van der Neer, Aert (work of). Con. 132: 199 Jan '54.

Van der Rohe, Ludwig Mies. Holiday 28: 77 (col.) Dec '60.

Van der Weyden, Rogier (work of). Con. 133: 30 Mar '54; 144: 128 Nov '59. Holiday 25: 66--7 (col.) Jan '59. Natl. geog. 113: 265 (col.) Feb '58. Praeg; Pict. ency., p. 262 (col.).

Van Devanter, Willis. Amer. heri., vol. 9 no. 3 p. 25 (Ap '58).

Van Diest, Willem (work of). Con. 145: 181 May '60.

Van Dongen, Kees. Cur. biog. p. 122 (1960).

Van Doren, Carl. Holiday 11: 9, 14 Feb '52; 21: 115 May '57.

Van Doren, Irita. Cur. biog. p. 882 (1941).

Van Dorn, Earl. Pakula: Cent. album, p. 279.

Van Druten, John. Cur. biog. p. 699 (1944).

Van Drusen, Henry P. Cur. biog. p. 581 (1950).

Van Dyck, Sir Anthony. Con. 139: 248 Je '57.
—— (self-portrait). Con. ency. of ant., vol. 1, pl. 155.
—— (terracotta figure). Con. 140: XXI Jan '58.
—— (work of). Con. 126: 208 Dec '50; 129: 2 (col.) Ap '52, opp. p. 77 (col.) Je '52; 133: 14, 31 Mar '54; 135: 248 Je '55; 136: 103-5 Nov '55, LXII Dec '55, 285 Jan '56; 137: cover (col.) May '56, LXV Je '56; 139: 54 Mar '57; 141: 206 Je '58; 142: 255, 258 Jan '59 143: 54, 57 Mar '59; 144: 265 Jan '60; 145: LVI Mar '60, 267 Je '60. Natl. geog. 97: 758, 762, 767 (col.) Je '50; 101: 86 (col.) Jan '52; 110: 656 Nov '56. Praeg.: Pict. ency., p. 335 (col.).

Van Dyke, Dick. Cur. biog. (1963).

Van Edema, Gerard (work of). Con. 143: XXI Ap '59.

Van Everdingen, Allaert (work of). Con. 126: 136 Oct '50.

Van Eyck, Jan (statue). Natl. geog. 107: 643 (col.) May '55.
—— (work of). Con. ency. of ant., vol. 1, pl. 154. Con. 126: 71 Aug '50, 213 Dec '50; 133: 93 Ap '54; 135: 144 Ap '55; 136: 13 Sept '55; 138: 277 Jan '57; 140: 274 Jan '58. Int. gr. soc.: Arts . . . p. 89 (col.). Praeg.: Pict. ency., p. 261 (col.).

Van Fleet, Lt. Gen. James A. Cur. biog. p. 642 (1948).

Van Gogh, Vincent (self-portrait). Con. 137: 137 Ap '56.
—— (work of). Con. 133: 11 Mar '54; 136: 278-9 Jan '56; 140: 53 Sept '57; 141: V May '58; 142: 125 Nov '58; 145: 232 Je '60. Holiday 14: 61 (col.) Nov '53. Int. gr. soc.: Arts . . . p. 133 (col.). Praeg.: Pict. ency., p. 32, 439 (col.).

Van Goyen, Jan (work of). Con. 133: 257 Je '54 135: XI (col.) Mar '55; 137: 195 May '56; 139: 103, 112, 121 (part col.) Ap '57, VIII, LXV (col.) May '57; 140: cover (col.) Jan '58; 141: VI, VII (col.) May '58, XLII-XLIII (col.) Je '58; 142: III (col.) Nov '58; 143: 191 May '59, XXXIX (col.) Je '59; 144:

LIII (col.) Dec '59; 145: LXVIII, LXXXIII (col.) May '60.

Van Heemskerk, Martin. See Heemskerk, Martin van.

Van Helmond, Lucas (work of). Con. 138: 19 (col.) Sept '56.

Van Honthorst, Gerard (work of). Con. 143: LVI Mar '59.

Van Hoogstraten, Samuel (work of). Con. 139: 8 Mar '57.

Van Horne, Harriet. Cur. biog. p. 622 (1954).

Van Hove, B. J. (work of). Con. 145: XX Ap '60.

Van Kessel, Jan (work of). Con. 144: LXXIX Jan '60.

Van Leyden, Lucas (work of). Con. 138: 13 Sept '56. Natl. geog. 110: 653 (col.) Nov '56.

Van Loen, Alfred. Cur. biog. p. 467 (1961).

Van Mieris, Frans (work of). Con. 135: XLIX Mar '55.

Van Mieris, Willem (work of). Con. 133: 127 (col.) Ap '54; 145 XLV Mar '60.

Van Mieris the elder, Frans (work of). Con. 139: XVII (col.) Ap '57.

Van Mook, Hubertus J. Cur. biog. p. 852 (1942).

"Van Nest murders" (paintings). Amer. heri., vol. 6 no. 5 p. 60, 63 (col.) (Aug '55).

Van Nickele, Isaak (work of). Con. 145: IX Ap '60.

Van Nieulandt, Willem (work of). Con. 139: LV May '57.

Van Nijmegen, Dionys (work of). Con. 145: LXXII-LXXIII Je '60.

Van Orley Bernard (work of). Con. 138: cover (col.), 253 Jan '57; 139: VIII May '57.

Van Os, G.J.J. (work of). Con. 142: XXIX Dec '58.

Van Os, Jan (work of). Con. 142: XVII (col.) Jan '59.

Van Ostade, Adriaen (work of). Con. ency. of ant., vol. 1, pl. 163. Con. 144: XI Nov '59, XVIII Jan '60.

Van Paassen, Pierre. Cur. biog. p. 854 (1942).

Van Pelt, John V. Cur. biog. p. 612 (1946).

Van Poelenburgh, Cornelis (work of). Con. 140: 250 Jan '58.

Van Rensselaer, Ariaantje Schuyler. Amer. heri., vol. 10 no. 1 p. 11 (col.) (Dec '58).

Van Rensselaer, Kiliaen. Amer. heri., vol. 10 no. 1 p. 10 (Dec '58).

Van Rensselaer, Philip. Holiday 26: 78 (col.) Oct '59.

Van Rijn, Rembrandt Harmensz (work of). Con. 141: 44 Mar '58.

Van Ruisdael, Jacob (work of). Praeg.: Pict. ency., p. 344 (col.).

Van Ruith, Horace (work of). Con. 133: XXXVII May '54.

Van Ruysdael, Salomon (work of). Con. 133: XVIII Je '54; 138: XXXVII Sept '56, cover (col.) Nov '56; 141: VI-VII (col.) May '58, LXIII (col.) Je '58; 143: IX May '59, XLI (col.) Je '59.

Van Ryn, Rembrandt (work of). Con. 129: LXVII Je '52.

Van Schrieck, Otto Marsens (work of). Con. ency. of ant., vol. 1, pl. 175.

Van Slingeland, Pieter (work of). Con. 126: 135 Oct '50.

Van Slyke, Donald D. Cur. biog. p. 781 (1943).

Van Somer, Paul (work of). Con. 137: XXXV (col.) Ap '56.

Van Stockum, Hilda. Jun. bk. of auth., p. 289.

Van Strij, Jac (work of). Con. 138: VIII Sept '56.

Van Sweringen, M. J. Amer. heri., vol. 9 no. 5 p. 32 (Aug '58).

Van Sweringen, O. P. Amer. heri., vol. 9 no. 5 p. 32 (Aug '58).

Van Tilborch, Ambrose (work of). Con. 141: 178 May '58.

Van Valkenborch, Lucas (work of). Con. 139: XXIV Mar '57; 141: 50 Mar '58.

Van Valkenborch, Marten (work of). Con. 145: LXXVI (col.) May '60.

Van Volkenburg, Jack L. Cur. biog. p. 621 (1955).

Van Wagoner, Murray D. Cur. biog. p. 885 (1941).

Van Waters, Miriam. Cur. biog. (1963).

Van Zandt, James E. Cur. biog. p. 584 (1950).

Vance, Cyrus R. Cur. biog. p. 435 (1962).

Vance, Harold S. Cur. biog. p. 614 (1949).

Vance, Marguerite. Cur. biog. p. 633 (1951).

Vancouver, George. Amer. heri., vol. 4 no. 4 p. 43 (summer '53).

Vancouver (Bt. Columbia, Canada). Holiday 28: 114 (col.) Aug '60.
    Natl. geog. 108: 236-7 (col.) Aug '55.
—— (harbor). Holiday 6: 39 (col.) Aug '49; 27: 125 (col.) Mar '60.

Vandegrift, Maj. Gen. Alexander Archer. Cur. biog. p. 779 (1943).

Vandenberg, Arthur. Amer. heri., vol. 11 no. 2 p. 44, 46 (Feb '60).
    Cur. biog. p. 638 (1948).

Vandenberg, Maj. Gen. Hoyt S. Cur. biog. p. 642 (1945).

Vanderbanck, J. (work of). Con. 138: XXIII Nov '56.

Vanderbilt, Amy. Cur. biog. p. 620 (1954).

Vanderbilt, Arthur T. Cur. biog. p. 655 (1947).

Vanderbilt, Cornelius. Amer. heri., vol. 8 no. 3 p. 52 (Ap '57).

Vanderbilt, Mrs. Cornelius. Holiday 6: 98, 102 (col.) Jl '49.

Vanderbilt, Mr. & Mrs. Harold S. Holiday 18: 17 (col.) Sept '55.

Vanderbilt, Jeanne Murray. Holiday 26: 75 (col.) Oct '59.

Vandercook, John W. Cur. biog. p. 851 (1942).

Vanderlyn, John. Amer. heri., vol. 4 no. 1 p. 14 (fall '52).
—— (work of). Amer. heri., vol. 7 no. 4 p. 7 (col.) (Je '56).

Vandeveer estate project (N.Y.). Natl. geog. 99: 305 (col.) Mar '51.

Vandiver, Samuel Ernest. Cur. biog. p. 435 (1962).

Vandivert, William. Cur. biog. (1963).

Vanier, George Philias. Cur. biog. p. 445 (1960).

vanity (sym.). Lehner: Pict. bk. of sym., p. 60.

vanity case, travel. Travel 113: 11 Mar '60.

Vanka, Makso (work of). Holiday 25: 84 (col.) Mar '59.

Vanocur, Sander. Cur. biog. (1963).

Vansittart, Lord Robert. Cur. biog. p. 883 (1941).

Vanzetti, Bartolomeo. Amer. heri., vol. 9 no. 6 p. 52, 55 (Oct '58).
    Holiday 27: 11 Mar '60.

vapor trails, airplane. Natl. geog. 112: 285 Aug '57.

Vaquero. Holiday 20: 38 Dec '56.

"A Vaquero" (by Walker). Amer. heri., vol. 9 no. 5 cover, p. 8 (col.) (Aug '58).

Vaqueros (capture bear). Amer. heri., vol. 9 no. 5 p. 13 (col.) (Aug '58).

Varallo, Tanzio da (work of). Con. 138: 118 Nov '56; 145: 190 May '60.

Vardaman, James K., jr. Cur. biog. p. 635 (1951).

Vargas, Getulio Dornelles. Cur. biog. p. 637 (1951).

Varian, Dorothy. Cur. biog. p. 783 (1943).

Varley, John (work of). Con. ency. of ant., vol. 1, pl. 143.

Varnay, Astrid. Cur. biog. p. 639 (1951).

Vas, Mrs. Petrus. Amer. heri., vol. 10 no. 1 p. 11 (col.) (Dec '58).

"Vasa Murrina." Con. 127: 16 Mar '51.

Vasco da Gama's passage to India (point in Africa). Natl. geog. 104: 181 Aug '53.

vase. Con. 126: 128 Oct '50.
    Holiday 10: 168 Dec '51.
    Natl. geog. 113: 264 (col.) Feb '58.
    Travel 104: back cover Nov '55.
—— (ancient). Int. gr. soc.: Arts . . . p. 177 (col.).
—— (antique). Con. 136: 73 Sept '55, 124-5, 144 Nov '55, 162 Dec '55; 141: XVI, XXXIV May '58; 144: XVI Nov '59.
—— (broken). Con. 140: XXX Sept '57, XLII Dec '57; 141: XXXVI Ap '58; 142: LIV Sept '58, XLIV Nov '58; 143: L Mar '59, XL May '59; 144: XLVIII Nov '59, LXIX Jan '60; 145: XXXVIII Mar '60, LVI May '60.
—— (flowers). Con. 140: XXXII (col.) Sept '57, XXXVIII (col.) Nov '57; 144: 24 Sept '59, LVIII (col.) Dec '59; 145: LXI, LXXI, 194 (col.) May '60, IX-XI (col.), XXXIV Je '60.
    Holiday 14: 7 (col.) Dec '53; 20: 7 (col.) Dec '56; 25: inside cover (col.) May '59.
    Natl. geog. 113: 317 (col.) Mar '58.
—— (Italian detail). Labande: Naples, p. 92.
—— (shell design). Holiday 27: 162-3 May '60.
——, Adam (2 handled). Con. 143: 15 Mar '59.
——, Amer. glass (antique). Con. ency. of ant., vol. 3, pl. 39.
——, Baluster (Faenza Maiolica). Con. 140: 162 Dec '57.
——, Bow perfume. Con. 135: 146 Ap '55.
——, Bowyer (18th cent.). Con. 141: 91 Ap '58.
——, Bristol (porcelain). Con. ency. of ant., vol. 1, pl. 55.

——, bronze (by M. Soldani). Con. 142: 159-63 Dec '58.

——, bronze garden (antique). Con. 143: 264 Je '59.

——, cameo glass (by Locke, 19th cent.). Con. 144: X Sept '59.

——, Capodimonte. Con. 135: 18 Mar '55.

——, Celtic (ancient). Int. gr. soc.: Arts . . . p. 19 (col.).

——, ceremonial. *See* ceremonial vase.

——, Chantilly. Con. ency. of ant., vol. 1, pl. 59.

——, Chelsea. Con. 127: 68 Mar '51; 140: XXX Dec '57; 141: XXI Ap '58.

——, Chelsea (porcelain). Con. ency. of ant., vol. 1, pl. 56.

——, chimes (Lowestoft). Con. 140: LII Nov '57.

——, Chinese. Con. ency. of ant., vol. 1, p. 120-4, pl. 65, 67-9.
Con. 132: XLIII Sept '53; 138: 128 Nov '56.

——, Chinese (antique). Con. 133: XXVIII Je '54; 135: 126-7, 133 Ap '55; 138: XLIII Sept '56; 139: 57 Mar '57.

——, Chinese (Chi-Lung). Con. 142: LXVI Jan '59.

——, Chinese (Ch'ien Lung, 18th cent.). Con. 145: 269 Je '60.

——, Chinese (Chou). Con. 140: LI Dec '57.

——, Chinese bronze. Con. 139: XVI Mar '57.

——, Chinese celadon. Con. 140: XXXIV Jan '58.

——, Chinese enameled. Con. 139: XII May '57.

——, Chinese funerary. Con. 138: 126 Nov '56.

——, Chinese imperial. Con. 134: LVI Nov '54.

——, Chinese jade. Con. 129: 95 Je '52; 133: 134 Ap '54; 141: VI Mar '58; 142: LII Nov '58.

——, Chinese jade (Ch'ien Lung). Con. 144: XV Jan '60.

——, Chinese mandarin. Con. 140: XXXIV Jan '58.

——, Chinese porcelain. Con. 132: V Sept '53; 137: XXVI Mar '56, XLVIII Ap '56; 138: 146 Dec '56; 139: 65 Mar '57, XXII Ap '57, I, V, VIII Je '57; 140: 249 Jan '58; 141: LX May '58, LXIV, 246 Je '58; 142: LII Jan '59; 143: XLVI Je '59.

——, Chinese porcelain (antique). Con. 143: X Je '59.

——, Chinese porcelain (K'ang Hsi). Con. 143: XXIV Mar '59; 144: XXX Jan '60.

——, Chinese porcelain (Kuan ware). Con. 143: XXX May '59.

——, Chinese porcelain baluster. Con. 145: XX May '60.

——, Chinese porcelain bottle. Con. 143: LX Je '59.

——, Chinese pottery (antique). Con. 129: VIII Je '52.

——, Chinese (Sung). Con. 145: LVI Je '60.

——, cloisonne. Con. 140: LXIV Sept '57.

——, Corning glass. Natl. geog. 110: 607 Nov '56.

——, crystal. Travel 110: 31 Sept '58.

——, crystal (18th cent.). Con. 144: LXVIII Sept '59.

——, Derby. Con. 144: LVIII Jan '60.

——, Derby porcelain. Con. 144: XX Jan '60.

——, Derbyshire. Con. 141: 187 May '58.

——, Dresden (18th cent.). Con. 144: LXII Nov '59.

——, Duplesis. Con. 133: 4 Mar '54.

——, enameled. Con. 139: XXXVIII May '57.

——, encaustic decorated. Con. 132: 149 Jan '54.

——, faience (16th cent.). Con. 134: 47 Sept '54.

——, faience (17th cent.). Int. gr. soc.: Arts . . . p. 95 (col.).

——, fishtail (antique). Con. 132: 150 Jan '54.

——, floor. Natl. geog. 100: 586 (col.) Nov '51.

——, glass. Travel 104: 3 Aug '55; 105: 60 May '56.

——, Greek. Con. 141: LIX May '58.

——, Greek (ancient). Con. 139: LXIV Je '57.

——, Greek (6th cent.). Ceram: March of arch. p. 30 (col.).

——, Handel. Con. 144: 31 Sept '59.

——, Hellenics. Holiday 28: 172 (col.) Oct '60.

——, Indochinese. Natl. geog. 98: 502 Oct '50.

——, Irish celery glass (19th cent.). Con. 145: XXIV Ap '60.

——, Irish glass. Con. 129: LXIV Je '52.

——, Italian (antique). Con. 136: 161 Dec '55.

——, Italian (Doccia factory). Con. 144: 157 Dec '59.

——, Italian (silver filigree). Con. 144: 156 Dec '59.

——, ivory. Con. 135: XXLIV May '55.

——, jade. *See* jade vase.

——, Japanese. Con. 137: 154, 203 May '56.

——, Japanese porcelain. Con. 137: V May '56.

——, lacquer (men making). Natl. geog. 111: 840 (col.) Je '57.

——, lead lawn (antique). Con. 138: XXXIX Sept '56.

——, lead garden (18th cent.). Con. ency. of ant., vol. 3, p. 54.

——, lustre glass. Con. ency. of ant., vol. 3, pl. 116.

——, Meissen. Con. 133: 276-7 Je '54; 139: inside cover Mar '57, 264 Je '57.

——, Mennecy. Con. 143: LVII Ap '59.

——, Mycenaean (man painting). Int. gr. soc.: Arts . . . p. 19 (col.).

——, Nove. Con. 140: 180 Dec '57.

——, opaline (19th cent.). Con. 133: 234 (col.) Je '54.

——, Orrefors crystal. Holiday 28: 124 Jl '60.

——, Peruvian. Praeg.: Pict. ency., p. 553 (col.).

——, porcelain. Con. 136: XII Sept '55.

——, porcelain (antique). Con. 135: 156 May '55.

——, porcelain (17th cent.). Con. 142: 11 Sept '58.

——, porcelain (18th cent.). Con. 142: 12 Sept '58.

——, porcelain imperial. Con. 135: LII Je '55.

——, Portland. Holiday 18: 53 Sept '55.

vase, Pre-Columbian clay. Con. 129: LXXI Ap '52.

——, rock-crystal (flower). Con. 145: XXIX Ap '60.

——, Rockingham. Con. 126: 46 Aug '50.

——, Roman (1st cent.). Con. 127: 16 Mar '51.

——, Russian (19th cent.). Con. 144: 277-8 Jan '60.

——, St. Cloud porcelain. Con. 141: 76 Ap '58.

——, Sandwich glass. Natl. geog. 107: 785 (col.) Je '55.

——, seashell. Holiday 28: 125 Jl '60.

——, Sevres porcelain. Con. 135: 159, 161 May '55; 145: 222 Je '60.

——, silver. Holiday 14: 14 Dec '53.

——, silver (antique). Con. 136: VII Dec '55.

——, silver gilt. Con. 144: VII Jan '60.

——, Swedish (18th cent.). Con. 143: 239 Je '59.

——, Swedish (modern stoneware). Con. 141: LXII Mar '58.

——, Syrian (800 B.C.). Int. gr. soc.: Arts . . . p. 19 (col.).

——, Tucker porcelain. Con. 140: 140 Nov '57.

——, Venetian glass. Holiday 22: 35 (col.) Nov '57.

——, Venetian silver. Con. 144: 153 Dec '59.

——, Venetian maiolica. Con. 143: XX May '59.

——, Vezzi. Con. 143: 57 Mar '59.

——, Warwick. Holiday 17: 69 (col.) Mar '55.

——, Wedgwood. Con. ency. of ant., vol. 1, pl. 51; 132: 149, 182-3 Jan '54; 138: 262 Jan '57; 139: 231 Je '57.

——, wedgwood reproduction. Daniel: Cut & engraved glass, pl. 26.

——, Worcester. Con. 129: LXII Je '52; 140: XVI, XX Jan '58 142: IV Sept '58 144: XXXIX Jan '60 145: LVIII May '60.

——, Worcester (18th cent.). Con. ency. of ant., vol. 1, pl. 53.

vase & cover, jade. Con. 143: XV Ap '59.

Vase de Nuit (18th cent.). Con. 144: 249 Jan '60.

vase on pedestal, Adam. Con. 139: XLVI May '57.

vase stand, Viennese (Boulle). Con. ency. of ant., vol. 3, pl. 17.

vase with chain, Chinese (19th cent.). Con. 141: LVII Je '58.

vases. Holiday 11: 85 Je '52.

—— (flowers). Natl. geog. 100: 22 Jl '51.

——, alabaster. Natl. geog. 108: 643 (col.) Nov '55.

——, glass bud. Holiday 18: 9 Sept '55, 63 Nov '55.

——, Morocco. Natl. geog. 107: 175 (col.) Feb '55.

——, pottery (ancient). Int. gr. soc.: Arts . . . p. 19 (col.).

Vasilevsky, Alexander M. Cur. biog. p. 784 (1943).

Vasquez, Tiburcio. Horan: Pict. hist. of wild west, p. 78.

Vassar college entrance (girls). Natl. geog. 110: 583 (col.) Nov '56.

Vatican City (Rome). Holiday 11: 36-7 Ap '52; 23: 50-63 (col.) May '58.
Natl. geog. 111: 438-9, 463-69 (col.) Ap '57, 800-1 (col.) Je '57; 117: 594-5 (col.) May '60.
Travel 103: 31-3 Ap '55; 113: 35-7 Ap '60.
U.S. News & World report, vol. LV no. 1 p. 29 Jl 1, 1963.

Vatican insignia. Int. gr. soc.: Arts . . . p. 167 (col.)

Vatican library. Natl. geog. 111: 468-9 (col.) Ap '57.

Vatican Swiss guard. Holiday 23: cover (col.), 3 May '58.
Travel 113: 35 Ap '60.

vats, cloth dye (Africa). Natl. geog. 104: 158-9 (col.) Aug '53.

——, pickle. Natl. geog. 105: 314 (col.) Mar '54.

Vaughan, Guy W. Cur. biog. p. 644 (1948).

Vaughan, Maj. Gen. Harry H. Cur. biog. p. 616 (1949).

Vaughan, Sarah. Cur. biog. p. 563 (1957).

Vaughan, Williams Ralph. Cooper: Con. ency. of music, p. 301.
Cur. biog. p. 634 (1953).

vault, burial (Okinawa). Natl. geog. 97: 552 Ap '60.

——, gold. See safe (for gold deposits).

——, medieval. Ceram: March of arch., p. 76.

vaulter, athlete pole. Natl. geog. 98: 732 Dec '50.

vaulting, Gothic ribbed. Int. gr. soc.: Arts . . . p. 49 (col.).

vaulting, Romanesque. Int. gr. soc.: Arts . . . p. 47 (col.).

——, types of. Praeg.: Pict. ency., p. 96.

Vaux-le-Vicomte, park of. See park of Vaux-le-Vicomte.

Veblen, Dr. Oswald. Natl. geog. 117: 30 (col.) Jan '60.

Vecellio, Francesco (work of). Con. 136: 165-9 Dec '55.

Veeck, Bill. Cur. biog. p. 645 (1948).
Holiday 28: 81 Dec '60.

vegetable covers, glass. Natl. geog. 98: 180 (col.) Aug '50.

vegetable dish, George III silver. Con. 143: XIII May '59.

veiled women. See women, veiled.

veins, human. Gray's anatomy, p. 651.

Velarde, Pablita (work of). Natl. geog. 107: 359, 369 (col.) Mar '55.

Velasco Ibarra, Jose Maria. Cur. biog. p. 605 (1952).

Velasquez, Diego. Int. gr. soc.: Arts . . . p. 91 (col.).

—— (work of). Con. ency. of ant., vol. 1, pl. 161.
Con. 127: opp. p. 3 (col.) Mar '51; 133: 213 May '54; 140: 238 Jan '58; 141: 72 Ap '58, 239 Je '58; 145: 102-4 Ap '60.
Holiday 25: 69 (col.) Jan '59.
Natl. geog. 97: 745, 755 (part col.) Je '50.
Praeg.: Pict. ency., p. 351 (col.).

Velde, Harold H. Cur. biog. p. 637 (1953).

Velden, Carinthia. Travel 110: 52 Aug '58.
Velikovsky, Immanuel. Cur. biog. p. 565 (1957).
Vellert, Dirk (work of). Con. 138: 13 Sept '56.
velocipede (1827). Jensen: The White House p. 45.
—— **(woman riding).** Durant: Pict. hist. of Amer. circus, p. 172.
Velten, W. (work of). Con. 140: XXXI Nov '57.
vender. *See* vendor.
vendor (fish basket on head, Portuguese). Natl. geog. 118: 653 (col.) Nov '60.
——, **flower.** *See* flower vendor.
——, **orange.** Holiday 12: 68 Sept '52.
——, **street.** Natl. geog. 108: 149, 153 Jl '55; 110: 453 (col.) Oct '56.
——, **street chestnut.** Natl. geog. 111: 326 Mar '57.
——, **water (Morocco).** Natl. geog. 107: 181 (col.) Feb '55; 112: 57 (col.) Jl '57.
vendors (Rome). Holiday 27: 71, 73 Ap '60.
——, **street (Iran).** Natl. geog. 104: 713 Nov '53.
vendors. *See* also market, street; market stands.
Venetian art (history painters). Con. 135: 30-39 Mar '55.
Venetian glass. *See* glass, Venetian.
Venetian glass tazza (1500). Con. 144: LXXX Jan '60.
Venetian painting (17th cent.). Con. 144: 106-7 Nov '59.
Venetian palace (Bigari). Con. 135: 51 Mar '55.
Veneziano, Antonio (fresco by). Con. 142: 158 Dec '58.
Veneziano, Domenico (work of). Con. 143: 104 Ap '59.
   Praeg.: Pict. ency., p. 255 (col.).
Veneziano, Paolo (work of). Con. 134: 130 Nov '54.
Venezuela. Holiday 15: 98-103 (part col.) Ap '54.
   Natl. geog. 97: 635-61 (part col.) May '50.
   Travel 105: 20-4 Feb '56.
—— **(Caracas).** *See* Caracas.
—— **(hotel).** Holiday 26: 13 (col.) Jl '59, 101 (col.) Aug '59.
Venezuelan art. Holiday 20: 15 (col.) Aug '56.
Venezuelan man. Holiday 5: inside back cover (col.) Je '49.
Venice. Amer. heri., vol. 11 no. 3 p. 22 (col.) (Ap '60).
   Con. 136: XXXV, 117 (part col.) Nov '55; 137: IV, XXXV Mar '56; 138: LI Sept '56; 141: 263 Je '58; 142: XL Sept '58; 143: XVII, LXV Je '59; 144: XLI, 191 Dec '59; 145: 160-1 May '60, LVII Je '60.
   Holiday 11: 138 (col.) May '52; 18: 42-7 (part col.) Oct '55; 19: 94 Feb '56; 20: 4 Nov '56; 21: 156 Jan '57, 49 Mar '57; 23: 79 (col.) Jan '58, 10 (col.) May '58; 25: 135 Mar '59, 100 May '59; 27: 130 Jan '60, 16 Mar '60, 155 Ap '60, 188 May '60.
   Natl. geog. 100: 398-410 (col.) Sept '51; 101: 82 (col.) Jan '52; 108: 140-1 Jl '55; 111: 790-2 (col.) Je '57.
   Travel 101: 7 May '54; 103: 50-2 May '55.
—— **(Bossuet).** Con. 133: LVI Je '54.

—— **(Ca d'Oro).** Praeg.: Pict. ency., p. 207.
—— **(canal).** Holiday 15: 98 Jan '54.
—— **(canal Cannaregio).** Praeg.: Pict. ency., p. 362 (col.).
—— **(Canaletto).** Con. 133: 232 Je '54.
—— **(comic).** Holiday 27: 214 Ap '60; 28: 96 Aug '60.
—— **(Grand Canal).** Con. 143: 185 May '59.
   Travel 111: back cover Feb '59, back cover Mar '59, back cover Ap '59, back cover May '59.
—— **(Grand Canal, by Guardi).** Con. 139: 249 (col.) Je '57.
—— **(Marieschi).** Con. 140: 97-8 Nov '57.
—— **(palace).** Holiday 25: 186 Ap '59.
—— **(piazza St. Marks).** Holiday 23: 27 May '58, 186 Je '58.
—— **(plaza).** Travel 102: inside cover Oct '54.
—— **(St. Marks).** *See* St. Marks.
—— **(San Biagio).** Praeg.: Pict. ency., p. 435.
—— **(San Francesco della Vigna).** Con. 132: 123 Nov '53.
—— **(theater, int., 1837).** Cooper: Con. ency., of music, p. 291 (col.).
—— **(Unterberger).** Con. 140: XXIX Nov '57.
—— **(Wyld).** Con. 138: XXXIX Nov '56.
—— **(Piazzetta).** Con. 139: 245 Je '57.
——, **Rialto (by Canaletto).** Con. 138: XXIX Jan '57.
—— **(Rialto bridge).** Con. 141: 237 Je '58.
Venizelos, Sophocles. Cur. biog. p. 585 (1950).
Ventris, Michael. Cur. biog. p. 567 (1957).
Venus (sym.). Lehner: Pict. bk. of sym., p. 31.
—— **(bronze figure).** Con. 143: 214-5 Je '59.
—— **(Graeco-Roman statuette).** Con. ency. of ant., vol. 3, pl. 71.
—— **(magic square).** Lehner: Pict. bk. of sym., p. 25.
—— **(sculpture).** Con. 141: 224 Je '58.
   Natl. geog. 111: 489 (col.) Ap '57.
Venus, pentacle of (sym.). Lehner: Pict. bk. of sym., p. 22.
"Venus, Adonis & Putti" (Poussin). Con. 143: 124 Ap '59.
"Venus & Adonis" (Cambiaso). Con. 138: 174 Dec '56.
"Venus & Adonis" (sculpture). Holiday 26: 8 Jl '59.
"Venus & Adonis" (statue by Scheermaker). Con. 140: 54 Sept '57.
"Venus & her satellites" (Etty). Con. 135: XIX Mar '55.
"Venus appearing to Aeneaus & Archates" (Italian porcelain). Con. 135: 15 Mar '55.
"Venus at her toilet" (Rubens). Con. ency. of ant., vol. 1, pl. 155.
"Venus au Bain" (Corot). Con. 138: XLVIII Dec '56; 139: 54 Mar '57.
"Venus au Collier" (bronze). Con. 145: 55 Mar '60.
"Venus binding eyes of Cupid." Natl. geog. 101: 77 (col.) Jan '52.
"Venus bringing arms to Aeneas" (Poussin). Con. 143: 125 Ap '59.
Venus de Milo. Holiday 22: 105 Nov '57.
   Natl. geog. 101: 771 Je '52.
"Venus drawn by doves." Amer. heri., vol. 10 no. 3 frontis. (col.) (Ap '59).

"Venus embracing Cupid" (Cossa). Con. 142: 257 Jan '59.

"Venus et l'amour" (J. F. de Troy). Con. 143: LXXI May '59.

"Venus, Mars & Vulcan" (Giordano). Con. 132: 10 Sept '53.

"Venus of Milo" (school girls examine, 1894). Amer. heri., vol. 11 no. 6 p. 107 (Oct '60).

"Venus of the East." See Srinagar.

"Venus of Willendorf" (figurine). Praeg.: Pict. ency., p. 172.

"Venus stepping from her bath" (statue, 3rd cent., B.C.). Con. 129: 46 Ap '52.

Venus. See also The Nocera Venus.

Vera-Ellen. Cur. biog. p. 463 (1959).

Verandah (El Salvador). Holiday 17: 43 (col.) Mar '55.

Verbelst, Herman (work of). Con. 133: 179 May '54.

Vercelli, Tiziano (work of). Con. 136: 38 Sept '55.

Verdi, Giuseppe. Cooper: Con. ency. of music, p. 302.

Verdon, Gwen. Cur. biog. p. 447 (1960).

Verdura, Duke Fulco di. Holiday 14: 53 Dec '53.

Verendael, Nicholas van (work of). Con. 142: XXXVII Sept '58.

"Verge a L'enfante" (Veneziano). Con. 134: 130 Nov '54.

Verge boards (from Viking ship). Amer. heri., vol. 10 no. 3 p. 103 (Ap '59).

Verheyen, J. H. (work of). Con. 142: 57 Sept '58; 144: LIX Jan '60.

Vermeer, Jan (work of). Con. 145: 158 May '60.
Holiday 7: 107 (col.) Feb '50.
Natl. geog. 97: 741 (col.) Je '50.
Praeg.: Pict. ency., p. 27 (col.).

Vermont. Amer. heri., vol. 2 no. 3 p. 34-43, 50 (col.), 51-3 (spring '51).
Holiday 6: 34-53 (part col.) Nov '49; 22: 51-9 (col.) Nov '57; 25: 66-9 (part col.) Je '59; 28: 90-5 (part col.) Dec '60.
Jordan: Hammond's pict. atlas, p. 29 (col.).
Natl. geog. 107: 737 (col.) Je '55.
Travel 108: 48-9 Oct '57.
—— (early). Amer. heri., vol. 6 no. 4 p. 26-35 (part col.) (Je '55).
—— (Fair day dinner). Face of Amer., p. 128-9 (col.).
—— (marble quarry). Brooks: Growth of a nation, p. 268.
—— (village, 1898). Amer. heri., vol. 9 no. 6 p. 65 (Oct '58).

Verne, Jules. Int. gr. soc.: Arts . . . p. 137 (col.).

Verne space illus., Jules. Natl. geog. 113: 288-9 Feb '58.

Vernet, Claude Joseph (work of). Con. 138: XLVII Jan '57; 145: LXXXVIII (col.) Je '60.

Vero Beach (wild animal compound). Travel 105: 57-9 Mar '56.

Veronese, Paolo (work of). Con. 142: 143 Dec '58.
Natl. geog. 110: 637 (col.) Nov '56.
Praeg.: Pict. ency., p. 301 (col.).

Veronese, Paul (work of). Natl. geog. 97: 748, 769 (col.) Je '50.

Veronese, Vittorino. Cur. biog. p. 465 (1959).

Verrieres (antique). Con. 135: opp. p. 151 (col.) May '55.

Verrocchio (sculpture by). Praeg.: Pict. ency., p. 257.
——, Andrea del (work of). Con. 132: 60 Sept Sept '53.
Int. gr. soc.: Arts . . . p. 87 (col.).

Versailles (France). Holiday 18: 52- (col.) Aug '55.

Versailles gardens. Natl. geog. 98: 57 (col.) Jl '50.

Versailles palace grounds. See palace & grounds of Versailles.

Vertebra. Gray's anatomy, p. 75-94.

vertebrates (sym.). See triangle of vertebrates (sym.).

Vertes, Marcel. Cur. biog. p. 469 (1961).

Verwee, Louis (work of). Con. 143: XXIX Mar '59.

Verwoerd, Hendrik F. Cur. biog. p. 467 (1959).

vesica piscis. Lehner: Pict. bk. of sym., p. 61.

Vespucius, Americus. Natl. geog. 102: 184 (col.) Aug '52.

vessel forms (antique). Praeg.: Pict. ency., p. 172.

vessels, Clay (porcelain). Int. gr. soc.: Arts . . . p. 19, 95, 177 (col.).

vest, man's. Holiday 10: 134 Dec '51; 18: 188 Dec '55; 20: 218 Dec '56; 26: 244 Dec '59; 27: 202 Mar '60; 28: 228-9 Dec '60.
——, man's sweater. Holiday 24: 230 Dec '58.

Vesta (sym.). Lehner: Pict. bk. of sym., p. 31.

Vestal virgin (statue, Rome). Travel 103: inside cover Jan '55.

Vestier, Antoine (work of). Con. 135: 56 Mar '55.

vestments (cope), Austrian. Con. 142: 7 Sept '58.

Vesuvius (volcano). Amer. heri., vol. 11 no. 3 p. 21 (col.) (Ap '60).
Labande: Naples, p. 21.

veteran (wheel chair). Natl. geog. 104: 682 Nov '53.

Vevey (Switzerland). Natl. geog. 114: 570 (col.) Oct '58.

Vezelay (France). Natl. geog. 103: 230-46 (part col.) Feb '53.

"V'geland" statue (Oslo). Travel 102: 32 Oct '54.

Via Appia, girl of. Ceram: March of arch., p. 2.

"Via Arcadia," ceremonial (Ephesus). Osward: Asia Minor, pl. 31.

Via Sacre (Italy). Travel 113: 49 Ap '60.

Viaduc de St. Germain (M. de Vlaminck). Con. 140: XXXI (col.) Sept '57.

Vian, Rear Adm. Sir Philip. Cur. biog. p. 705 (1944).

Vianden castle. See castle, Vianden.

Vicar of Bray (reading in church). Natl. geog. 98: 196 (col.) Aug '50.

vice, brace & bit, Louis XVI. Con. 133: 40 Mar '54.

Vickers, Jon. Cur. biog. p. 471 (1961).

Vickers Vanguard airplane. Travel 111: 65 Feb '59.

Vickery, Rear Adm. Howard L. Cur. biog. p. 785 (1943).

Vicksburg (Miss.). Natl. geog. 118: 703 (col.) Nov '60.

—— (1863). Amer. heri., vol. 12 no. 1 p. 20, 21 (col.) Dec '60.

—— (historical, Civil war). Amer. heri., vol. 3 no. 2 p. 27 (col.) (winter '52).

——, siege of. Holiday 22: 70-1 (col.) Jl '57.

Vicksburg memorial. Jordan: Hammond's pict. atlas, p. 87 (col.).

Vicountess Newcomen & daughters (Kauffman). Con. 142: XIII Sept '58.

Victor, Sally. Cur. biog. p. 624 (1954).

Victor Emmanuel III, King of Italy. Cur. biog. p. 787 (1943).

Victor Emmanuel monument (Rome). Holiday 27: 69 Ap '60.

Victoria, Queen of Gt. Brit. Amer. heri., vol. 9 no. 6 p. 43 (Oct '58). Holiday 16: 75 Aug '54.

—— (bust). Natl. geog. 115: 829 Je '59.

—— (statue). Natl. geog. 114: 151 Aug '58.

—— (statue, Africa). Natl. geog. 104: 172 (col.) Aug '53.

—— (statue by Gilbert). Con. 134: 26 Sept '54.

—— (statue in Parliament bldg.). Holiday 17: 59 Mar '55.

Victoria, Queen. See also "Queen Victoria & Duke of Wellington."

Victoria (B.C., Canada). Holiday 17: 105 (col.) Feb '55. Natl. geog. 114: 186 (col.) Aug '58. Travel 114: 15 Jl '60.

—— (Parliament bldg.). Travel 114: 4 Sept '60.

Victoria (sym.). Lehner: Pict. bk. of sym., p. 31.

Victoria Cross (Gt. Brit.). Int. gr. soc.: Arts . . . p. 167 (col.).

Victoria Falls (Rhodesia, Africa). Holiday 15: 49 (col.) Mar '54 25: 151 (col.) Ap '59. Natl. geog. 118: 330 (col.) Sept '60.

Victoria government house (Seychelles is.). Natl. geog. 116: 694 Nov '59.

Victoria statue (London). Travel 101: 38 May '54.

Victorian Cross. Con. 137: 213 May '56.

Victoria's memorial clock (Seychelles is.). Natl. geog. 116: 693 (col.) Nov '59.

Victory (goddess of). Lehner: Pict. bk. of sym., p. 31.

victory (sym.). Lehner: Pict. bk. of sym., p. 86-7.

——, winged. See winged victory.

Victrola (with horn). Holiday 26: 152 Nov '59.

Vidor, King. Cur. biog. p. 568 (1957).

Vieillard, Roger (engraving by). Con. 139: 87 Ap '57.

Vieira Da Silva. Cur. biog. p. 451 (1958).

Vielle (musical instrument). Travel 101: 41 May '54.

Vienna (Austria). Disney: People & places, p. 54-5 (col.). Holiday 6: 60-2 (col.) Aug '49; 16: 46-53 (part col.) Nov '54.

Natl. geog. 99: 758-70 (part col.) Je '51; 115: 176-96 (part col.) Feb '59. Travel 101: 6 May '54; 107: 41-3 Ap '57; 109: 46-7 Ap '58.

—— (Belvedere palace). Praeg.: Pict. ency., p. 364.

—— (museum collection). Natl. geog. 97: 738-76 (part col.) Je '50.

—— (opera house). Cooper: Con. ency. of music, p. 464. Holiday 13: 117 Mar '53; 18: 19 Nov '55.

—— (white horse school). See White horse school (Vienna).

Vienna concert (outdoors). Natl. geog. 99: 758 (col.) Je '51.

Vientiane market (open-air). Natl. geog. 117: 60-1 (col.) Jan '60.

Vientiane temple. Natl. geog. 117: 58 (col.) Jan '60.

Viereck, Peter. Cur. biog. p. 792 (1943).

Viet Nam. Natl. geog. 98: 504-7 Oct '50; 102: 295-328 (part col.) Sept '52; 107: 858-74 Je '55.

—— (girls). Natl. geog. 102: 295 (col.) Sept '52.

—— (map). Natl. geog. 98: 501 Oct '50; 107: 862 Je '55.

"View of the Merwede at Dordrecht" (Van Goyen). Con. 139: LXV (col.) May '57.

Vigeland, Gustav. Holiday 12: 94 (col.) Sept '52.

—— (statue by). Natl. geog. 106: 192 Aug '54. Travel 111: 49 Je '59.

vigilance (sym.). Lehner: Pict. bk. of sym., p. 61.

Vigilante headquarters (Montana). Horan: Pict. hist. of wild west, p. 25.

Vigilantes (San Francisco). Amer. heri., vol. 7 no. 2 p. 72-3, 81, 86, 91, 93 (Feb '56).

Vignola, il Gesu (Rome, int.). Praeg.: Pict. ency., p. 260.

Vik (Norway). Holiday 17: 38-9 (col.) Jan '55.

Viking. Natl. geog. 106: 853-62 Dec '54.

Viking ship. Amer. heri., vol. 10 no. 3 p. 101, 103 (Ap '59). Holiday 21: 125 May '57; 23: 134 Mar '58; 25: 14 Jan '59, 159 Mar '59; 27: 30 Jan '60, 197 May '60. Travel 110: 6 Aug '58.

—— (carving). Con. 145: 34-7 Mar '60.

Viking ship prow. Holiday 17: 43 Jan '55.

Viking sledge (medieval). Int. gr. soc.: Arts . . . p. 81 (col.).

Viking wood carvings (Norwegian). Con. 145: 34-7 Mar '60.

Vila, George R. Cur. biog. (1963).

villa (Pesaro, Italy). Holiday 21: 53 (col.) Jan '57.

—— (Porto d'Ischia). Natl. geog. 105: 546 Ap '54.

——, Italian. Natl. geog. 111: 806 (col.) Je '57.

——, Palladian type. Amer. heri., vol. 10 no. 5 p. 66 (Aug '59).

Villa Bianchi (ext. & int., Bandinelli, Italy). Con. 144: 140 (col.), 141-44 Dec '59.

Villa Cordellina (ext. & int., Italy). Con. 140: 151-3 Dec '57.

Villa D'Este. Holiday 20: 98-102 (part col.) Sept '56.

Villa d'Este fountain. Holiday 27: 102-3 Ap '60.

Villa dei Misteri, chapel (Pompeii). Ceram: March of arch., p., 26-7.

Villa Hadriana, accademia. See Accademia of Villa Hadriana.

Villa Iris (Villefranche). Holiday 23: 55 (col.) Jan '58.

Villa-Lobos, Heitor. Cur. biog. p. 645 (1945).

Villa plan, Roman imperial. Natl. geog. 111: 214 Feb '57.

Villa Rotunda, Palladio's (Vicenza, Italy). Amer. heri., vol. 10 no. 5 p. 74 (Aug '59). Jensen: The White House, p. 5. Praeg.: Pict. ency., p. 309.

villa ruins, Maximian's (1600 yrs. old). Natl. geog. 111: 216-7 Feb '57.

Villa San Michele (Capri, Italy). Labande: Naples, p. 218.

village. Amer. heri., vol. 9 no. 1 p. 58-9 (col.) (Dec '57).

—— (lighted). Natl. geog. 114: 317 (col.) Sept '58.

—— (1645). Amer. heri., vol. 6 no. 5 p. 16-7 (col.) (Aug '55).

——, Djuka. Travel 102: 26 Dec '54.

——, fishing (primitive). Travel 105: 24 Feb '56.

——, Kurd. Holiday 22: 30 Oct '57.

——, mountain. Holiday 27: 186 (col.) May '60.

——, New England. Holiday 28: 71 (col.) Jl '60.

——, thatched roof (Nairobi). Natl. geog. 118: 346 (col.) Sept '60.

——, western (early). Amer. heri., vol. 6 no. 1 p. 64 (fall '54).

——, western (1729). Brooks: Growth of a nation, frontis.

"Village church" (Rankley). Con. 133: 40 Mar '54.

village moving (India). Natl. geog. 116: 843 (col.) Dec '59.

"Village holiday" (Teniers) See "Dance of the peasants" (Teniers).

"Village of the Holy Blood." See Heiligenblut.

"Village orchestra" (Collins). Con. 132: XVIII Nov '53.

"Village school" (Molenaer). Con. 137: LXVII May '56.

Villefrenche (France). Travel 105: 31 Ap '56.

Villon, Jacques. Cur. biog. p. 629 (1956).

vinaigrettes, English (antique). Con. 138: 95-9 Nov '56.

Vinalhaven (Maine, fog). Holiday 23: 58-9 (col.) Feb '58.

Vincennes porcelain. Con. 133: 3-8 Mar '54.

Vincent, Capt. Robert Budd (Gainsborough). Con. 138: 195 Dec '56.

Vinci, Leonardo de. See de Vinci, Leonardo.

Vinci (Italy). Travel 107: 26 Ap '57.

"Vine cricket club" (Ouless). Con. 133: XXXI (col.) Ap '54.

vinegar (sym.). Lehner: Pict. bk. of sym., p. 73.

vineyard (men gathering grapes). Holiday 26: 13 (col.) Nov '59.

vineyards (Swiss). Natl. geog. 98: 237 (col.) Aug '50.

Vinson, Carl. Cur. biog. p. 857 (1942).

Vinson, Fred M. Cur. biog. p. 794 (1943). Holiday 7: 78 Feb '50.

viol (early). Int. gr. soc.: Arts . . . p. 61 (col.).

——, English (by Faye, Norman, 17th cent.). Cooper: Con. ency. of music. p. 346.

——, primitive Persian (men playing). Natl. geog. 114: 39 (col.) Jl '58.

viola (musical instrument). Cooper: Con. ency. of music, p. 345. Int. gr. soc.: Arts . . . p. 141 (col.).

Viola d' amore (German, 1700). Cooper: Con. ency. of music, p. 348.

Viola da Gamba (by Duiffobroucart, 1560). Cooper: Con. ency. of music, p. 348.

violin. Con. 136: XVIII (col.) Nov '55; 137: 213 May '56; 138: 125 Nov '56; 139: 194 May '57. Cooper: Con. ency. of music, p. 345. Holiday 8: cover Nov '50; 9: 76 Mar '51; 10: 36 Sept '51; 13: 17 Ap '53; 15: 70 (col.) May '54; 22: 120 Oct '57; 26: 5 (col.) Sept '59, 208 Nov '59; 27: 51 (col.) Mar '60. Int. gr. soc.: Arts . . . p. 141 (col.). Natl. geog. 104: 687 Nov '53; 115; 182 (col.) Feb '59. Travel 103: 26 Ap '55.

—— (boy, teacher). Natl. geog. 116: 279 Aug '59.

—— (comic). Holiday 11: 4 Mar '52.

—— (girl playing). Holiday 9: 68 Mar '51.

—— (man holding). Holiday 21: 4 (col.) May '57. Cooper: Con. ency. of music, p. 195.

—— (man playing). Holiday 10: 97 Aug '51; 18: 67 Aug '55; 20: 102 Nov '56; 22: 79 Nov '57. Natl. geog. 102: 488 Oct '52; 117: 31 (col.) Jan '60.

——, Arabian one-string. Natl. geog. 106: 840 Dec '54.

——, bass. See bass violin, double.

——, Dancla Stradivari. Con. 144: 41 Sept '59.

——, hollow-backed. Amer. heri., vol. 11 no. 5 p. 18 (Aug '60).

——, Stradivarius. Con. 143: 267 Je '59. Cooper: Con. ency. of music, p. 274 (col.).

——, Stradivarius (The "Emperor," 1715). Cooper: Con. ency. of music, p. 347 (col.).

"Violin & guitar" (Gris). Con. 145: 209 May '60.

violin maker. Natl. geog. 102: 513 (col.) Oct '52.

violins (man making). Natl. geog. 116: 760 Dec '59.

Virgil's tomb. See tomb of Virgil.

"Virgin" (carved wood, 15th cent.). Con. ency. of ant., vol. 3, pl. 54.

"The Virgin" (El Greco). Con. 139: 54 Mar '57.

"The Virgin" (Santa Restituta). Labande: Naples, p. 45.

"Virgin" (wood carving, 1300). Praeg.: Pict. ency., p. 17.

Virgin, glass enclosed (Las Lagos church). Travel 110: 40 Nov '58.

"Virgin adoring" (Matsys). Con. 145: LXIII (col.) May '60.

"Virgin & child" (alabaster image). Con. 138: 184 Dec '56.

Virgin & child (Byzantine ivory). Con. 142: 29 Sept '58.

Virgin & child (Conegliano). Con. 136: 36 Sept '55.

Virgin & child (15th cent. sculpture). Con. 137: XLV Mar '56.

Virgin & child (French statue, Amiens cathedral). Int. gr. soc.: Arts . . . p. 57 (col.).

Virgin & child (in stable). Praeg.: Pict. ency., p. 241 (col.).

Virgin & child (Lippi). Con. 126: 88 Oct '50.

Virgin & child (marble by Plura). Con. 138: 181 Dec '56.

Virgin & child (Memlinc). Con. 126: 88 Oct '50.

Virgin & child (Metsys). Con. 133: 95 Ap '54.

Virgin & child (Morales). Con. 144: XLI Sept '59.

Virgin & child (on donkey). Praeg.: Pict. ency., p. 228 (col.).

Virgin & child (Robbia). Praeg.: Pict. ency. p. 310.

Virgin & child (Russian ikon). Con. 144: 279 Jan '60.

Virgin & child (votive panel). Con. 142: 149 Dec '58.

Virgin & child (wood). Con. 136: 17 Sept '55.

Virgin & child (wood carving, late 18th cent.). Amer. heri., vol. 8 no. 1 frontis. (col.) (Dec '56).

Virgin & child (wood polychrome, Romanesque). Con. 142: 108 Nov '58.

Virgin & child (wooden sculpture, 12 & 14th cent.). Con. 140: 170 Dec '57.

"Virgin & child in glory" (Pittoni). Con. 140: XLV Jan '58.

Virgin & child statue (Rouen faience, 18th cent.). Con. 143: 261 Je '59.

"Virgin & child with St. Anne" (Provost). Con. 133: LIX May '54.

"Virgin & child with St. Dorothy" (Titian). Con. 141: 273 Je '58.

"Virgin & child with St. John the Baptist" (Castello). Con. 132: 7 Sept '53.

"Virgin & child with Saints" (Lotto). Natl. geog. 97: 771 (col.) Je '50.

"Virgin & child with Saints & a donor" (Van Eyck). Con. 135: 144 Ap '55.

"Virgin & St. John" (Hugo Van des Goes). Con. 126: 4 Aug '50.

"Virgin appearing to St. Bernard" (Perugino). Con. ency. of ant., vol. 1, p. 152.

"Virgin, child & angels" (Rosselli). Con. 136: 37 Sept '55.

"Virgin in the Louvre" (plaque). Con. 133: 157 May '54.

Virgin islands. Natl. geog. 109: 202-32 (part col.) Feb '56.

Travel 103: 6 Mar '55; 109: 33 May '58.

—— (map). Natl. geog. 109: 207 Feb '56.

Virgin islands natl. park. Natl. geog. 113: 654-5 (col.) May '58.

Virgin Mary (sym.). Lehner: Pict. bk. of sym., p. 38.

"Virgin of Candelaria." Natl. geog. 99: 503 Ap '51.

"Virgin of the rocks." Praeg.: Pict. ency., p. 277 (col.).

virginal. Con. 144: 245-8 Jan '60.

virginals (1668). Cooper: Con. ency. of music, p. 354.

Virginia. Amer. heri., vol. 1 no. 2 p. 34-41 (part col.) (winter '50).
    Holiday 8: 27 (col.) Sept '50; 12: 34-43 (part col.) Nov '52; 18: 102-11 (part col.) Nov '55; 26: 119 (col.) Sept '59.
    Natl. geog. 103: 2-32 (part col.) Jan '53; 109: 442-84 (part col.) Ap '56.

—— (architecture). Amer. heri., vol. 10 no. 5 p. 67 (Aug '59).

—— (colonial arch.). Holiday 12: 60 (col.) Oct '52.

—— (colonial home). Holiday 12: 38 (col.) Nov '52.
    Travel 112: 30, 32 Jl '59.

—— (Harpers Ferry). Natl. geog. 111: 400-15 (part col.) Mar '57.

—— (Jamestown craft shop). Holiday 28: 9 Sept '60.

—— (map, colonial). Natl. geog. 111: 590-1 May '57.

—— (map, 1590). Amer. heri., vol. 4 no. 2 p. 50 (winter '53).

—— (map, 1627). Amer. heri., vol. 9 no. 6 p. 111 (Oct '58).

—— (map, pictorial). Holiday 13: 19 Mar '53.

——, colonial. Amer. heri., vol. 5 no. 3 p. 22-3 (spring '54).

——, Univ. of. See University of Virginia.

Virginia City (ghost town, Nev.) Amer. heri., vol. 4 no. 3 p. 16-22 (spring '53).
    Holiday 7: 73-8 Je '50; 17: 31 (col.) Feb '55.

—— (crystal bar). Jordan: Hammond's pict. atlas, p. 185 (col.).

—— (ghost town restored). Holiday 8: 51 Sept '50.

Virginia military institute. Holiday 18: 106 (col.) Nov '55.

virginity (sym.). Lehner: Pict. bk. of sym., p. 61.

"Virgin's dais" (Spain). Natl. geog. 99: 508 (col.) Ap '51.

virility (sym.). Lehner: Pict. bk. of sym., p. 26.

virtues. See qualities & virtues (sym.).

Viscardi, Henry, jr. Cur. biog. p. 626 (1954).

"Viscaya" palazzo (int. & ext., Miami). Natl. geog. 98: 597-603 (col.) Nov '50.

Vischer (bronze work). Praeg.: Pict. ency., p. 317.

vise. Rawson: Ant. pict. bk., p. 24.

——, armourer's. See armourer's vise.

——, broom corn brush. Rawson: Ant. pict. bk., p. 52.

Vishnu (sym.). Lehner: Pict. bk. of sym., p. 43.

"The visitors" (Simm). Con. 136: VIII Jan '56.

Visser 'T Hooft, Rev. Willem A. Cur. biog. p. 617 (1949).

Viti, Timoteo (majolica plate by). Con. 139: 99 Ap '57.

vitrine, Louis XV. Con. 143: LI Mar '59.

Vittorio Amadeo III (bust). Con. 142: 152 Dec '58.

Vivaldi, Antonio. Int. gr. soc.: Arts . . . p. 109 (col.).

—— (by La Cave). Cooper: Con. ency. of music, p. 303.

Vlacherna island (convent). Holiday 24: 70 Sept '58.

Vlakfontein (South Africa). Natl. geog. 118: 347 (col.) Sept '60.

Vlaminck, Maurice de (work of). Con. 138: LXII Nov '56; 139: LXVI May '57; 140: XXXI (col.) Sept '57; 141: cover (col.) May '58; 143: 55 Mar '59.

Vlieger, Simon de (work of). Con. 143: LXI May '59.

Vlock, Adalbert Johann. Amer. heri., vol. 9 no. 6 p. 117-20 (Oct '58).

Vogel, Brig. Gen. Herbert D. Cur. biog. p. 628 (1954).

Vogt, William. Cur. biog. p. 639 (1953).

"Voices of silence," Palestinian carving. Con. 133: 269 Je '54.

volcanic crater (Alaska). Natl. geog. 113: 632 (col.) May '58.

—— (Bali). Natl. geog. 108: 372 (col.) Sept '55.

—— (Hawaii). Natl. geog. 113: 633 (col.) May '58.

volcanic crater pool. Natl. geog. 100: 627 (col.) Nov '51.

volcanic explosion (Myojin island). Natl. geog. 105: 117-28 Jan '54.

volcanic landscape (Canary is.). Natl. geog. 107: 510-11 (col.) Ap '55.

volcanic lava cone. See lava cone, volcanic.

volcano. Holiday 12: 31 (col.) Aug '52. Natl. geog. 99: 726 Je '51.

—— (Africa). Natl. geog. 97: 338-9 (col.) Mar '50.

—— (erupting). Holiday 7: 68 (col.) May '50; 21: 162 (col.) May '57; 28: 35 (col.) Jl '60.

—— (eruption, Fayal, Azores). Natl. geog. 113: 736-57 (part col.) Je '58.

—— (eruption, Hawaii). Natl. geog. 115: 792, 798-9, 804-5, 809, 816-9 (part col.) Je '59.

—— (Mexico). Natl. geog. 102: 804 Dec '52.

——, El Misti. See El Misti volcano.

——, Haleakala (Hawaii). Natl. geog. 113: 633 (col.) May '58; 118: 38-9 (col.) Jl '60.

——, Ischia (inactive). Natl. geog. 105: 533 (col.) Ap '54.

——, Kilauea (Hawaii). Natl. geog. 108: 560-3 (col.) Oct '55; 115: 792-819 (part col.) Je '59; 117: 305-23 (col.) Mar '60; 118: 36-7 (col.) Jl '60.

——, Lanin (Argentina). Holiday 25: 101 (col.) Ap '59.

——, Mt. Lassen (Cal.). Jordan: Hammond's pict. atlas, p. 187 (col.).

——, Osorno. Natl. geog. 117: 208, 212 (col.) Feb '60.

——, Paricutin. See Paricutin volcano.

——, Sicily. Natl. geog. 107: 41-3 (col.) Jan '55.

——, Stromboli. See Stromboli volcano.

——, Trident (Alaska). Natl. geog. 109: 752 (col.) Je '56.

volcano crater, Pelee. See Pelee volcano crater.

——, Pelee. See Pelee volcano crater.

—— (Poas). See Poas volcano.

volcano Vesuvius. See Vesuvius.

Volklingen steel plant (Saar). Natl. geog. 105: 562-3 Ap '54.

Volkswagen. Holiday 23: 148 Jan '58.

volleyball game (girls). Natl. geog. 107: 386 (col.) Mar '55.

—— (Pescadores is.). Natl. geog. 109: 273 (col.) Feb '56.

Volpe, John A. Cur. biog. p. 439 (1962).

Voltaire (sculpture). Praeg.: Pict. ency., p. 333.

"Volto Santo" (wood carving). Con. ency. of ant., vol. 3, pl. 53.

Voltz, Friedrich Johann (work of). Con. 142: 42 Sept '58.

Von Braun, Wernher. Cur. biog. p. 607 (1952). Natl. geog. 118: 69 (col.) Jl '60.

Von Hagen, Victor Wolfgang. Cur. biog. p. 859 (1942).

Von Herkomer, Sir Hubert. See Herkomer, Sir Hubert von.

Von Judenburg, Hans (sculpture by). Con. 139: 125 Ap '57.

Von Karman, Theodore. Cur. biog. p. 623 (1955).

Von Kempelen, Wolfgang. Amer. heri., vol. 11 no. 2 p. 84 (Feb '60).

Von Neumann, John. Cur. biog. p. 625 (1955).

Von Ranke. Amer. heri., vol. 8 no. 5 p. 27 (Aug '57).

Von Steuben, Baron. Amer. heri., vol. 6 no. 4 p. 37, 39 (Je '55).

Von Wicht, John. Cur. biog. (1963).

Von Zell, Harry. Cur. biog. p. 708 (1944).

voodoo, Negro. See Negro voodoo.

voodoo baptism (Haiti). Holiday 7: 109 Mar '50.

Voorhees, Donald. Cur. biog. p. 587 (1950).

Voorhees, Tracy S. Cur. biog. p. 570 (1957).

Voorhis, Jerry. Cur. biog. p. 888 (1941).

Voris, John Ralph. Cur. biog. p. 648 (1948).

Voronoff, Serge. Cur. biog. p. 889 (1941).

Voroshilov, Klementh. Cur. biog. p. 891 (1941).

Vorstermans, Johannes (work of). Con. 145: XLI Ap '60.

Vorys, John Martin. Cur. biog. p. 588 (1950).

Vota mask. Int. gr. soc.: Arts . . . p. 185 (col.).

voters, election. Natl. geog. 100: 146 Aug '51.

voting booth (Kauai, Hawaii). Natl. geog. 118: 15 (col.) Jl '60.

—— (Paris). Natl. geog. 114: 301 Aug '58.

voting polls (Kansas, early days). Amer. heri., vol. 7 no. 5 p. 89 (Aug '56).

votive ax, Minoan. Con. 144: 282 Jan '60.

votive figurines, Crete. Ceram: March of arch., p. 63.

votive panel (Faenza). Con. 142: 149 Dec '58.

Vouet, Simon (work of). Con. 139: 261 Je '57.

Vredenburgh, Mrs. Dorothy M. Cur. biog. p. 650 (1948).

Vuillard, Edouard (work of). Con. 134: LIX, 69 (col.) Sept '54; 141: IX (col.) Ap '58.

Vukmanovic-Tempo, Svetozar. Cur. biog. p. 453 (1958).

Vulcan (sym.). Lehner: Pict. bk. of sym., p. 27, 30, 79.

Vulcan (statue). Holiday 21: 186 Ap '57.

"Vulcan" (world's largest iron statue). Holiday 23: 128 Mar '58.

"Vulcan surprises Mars & Venus" (Tintoretto). Con. ency. of ant., vol. 1, pl. 153

Vulcan's forges. See solfatara.

vulture (Meissen sculpture). Con. 126: 78 Aug '50.

Vyner & family, Sir Robert (Wright). Con. 142: 24 Sept '58.

W

Wachuku, Jaja. Cur. biog. (1963).

Waddell, Capt. James. Amer. heri., vol. 10 no. 1 p. 49 (Dec '58).

Wadell, Rube. Amer. heri., vol. 10 no. 3 p. 22 (Ap '59).

Waddesdon manor, England (int.). Con. 143: 204 (col.), 211 Je '59.

Waddington, Conrad Hal. Cur. biog. p. 441 (1962).

Wade, Senator Ben. Amer. heri., vol. 6 no. 1 p. 16 (fall '54); vol. 6 no. 4 p. 78 (Je '55).

Wadsworth, Rev. Charles. Amer. heri., vol. 6 no. 3 p. 53 (Ap '55).

Wadsworth, James J. Cur. biog. p. 631 (1956).

Wadsworth, James W. Cur. biog. p. 797 (1943).

Waesche, Adm. Russell R. Cur. biog. p. 647 (1945).

Wager, Sir Charles (Kneller). Con. 127: 31 Mar '51.

wager cup. See cup, wager.

Wagman, Frederick H. Cur. biog. (1963).

Wagner, Aubrey J. Cur. biog. (1963).

Wagner, Honus. Amer. heri., vol. 10 no. 3 p. 21 (Ap '59).

Wagner, John Addington. Cur. biog. p. 633 (1956).

Wagner, Richard. Cur. biog. p. 443 (1962). Int. gr. soc.: Arts . . . p. 123 (col.).

—— (by Nadar). Cooper: Con. ency. of music, p. 304.

Wagner, Robert F. Cur. biog. p. 893 (1941).

Wagner, Robert F., jr. Cur. biog. p. 630 (1954).

wagon (hay ride, horses). Natl. geog. 112: 720 (col.) Nov '57.

—— (horse, boy). Natl. geog. 112: 158 Aug '57.

—— (horse, Holland). Natl. geog. 106: 409 (col.) Sept '54.

—— (horses). Brooks: Growth of a nation, p. 247.

—— (horses, Bursa, Turkey). Natl. geog. 100: 174 (col.) Aug '51.

—— (horses, parade). Natl. geog. 106: 232 (col.) Aug '54.

—— (horses, people). Amer. heri., vol. 7 no. 6 p. 20 (Oct '56).

—— (mules). Amer. heri., vol. 6 no. 3 p. 4 (col.) (Ap '55).

—— (mules, ducks). Holiday 21: 117 Je '57.

——, Assyrian (ancient). Ceram: March of arch., p. 200.

——, beer (horses). Holiday 8: 43 (col.) Oct '50.

——, camel (driver). Natl. geog. 102: 646 (col.) Nov '52.

——, circus. Durant: Pict. hist. of Amer. circus, p. 30, 148.

——, Conestoga. Holiday 18: 106 (col.) Oct '55; 21: 154 May '57.

——, Conestoga (horses). Amer. heri., vol. 2 no. 4 p. 2 (col.), 4-5 (summer '51). Brooks: Growth of a nation, p. 112, 118.

——, corn loaded (horses). Amer. heri., vol. 8 no. 4 p. 66 (Je '58).

——, covered. See covered wagon.

——, English (antique). Con. 136: 263 Jan '56.

——, grain loaded (men, oxen). Natl. geog. 107: 500 (col.) Ap '55.

——, gypsy. Holiday 15: 13 Mar '54.

——, hay (man, child, horse, Norway). Natl. geog. 111: 115 (col.) Jan '57.

——, hay (men, horses, Austria). Natl. geog. 118: 274-5 (col.) Aug '60.

——, hearse. See hearse wagon.

——, horse show. Natl. geog. 106: 715 (col.) Nov '54.

——, old. Travel 114: 8 Jl '60.

——, photographer's. See photographer's wagon.

——, 20-mule borax team. See 20-mule borax team.

—— See also prairie schooner.

wagon train (westward, 1866). Amer. heri., vol. 6 no. 4 p. 60 (col.) (Je '55).

wagons, bullock (festival, Spain). Natl. geog. 113: 420-1 (col.) Mar '58.

wagons-lit. See train, European.

wah mummy. Ceram: March of arch., p. 128-9.

wahine (Tahiti girl). Travel 114: 37 Dec '60.

Wahlen, Friedrich T. Cur. biog. p. 472 (1961).

Wai Wai Indians (dancing). Natl. geog. 107: 342 (col.) Mar '55.

Wai Wai village (British Guiana). Natl. geog. 107: 330-46 (part col.) Mar '55.

Waikiki beach (Hawaii). Holiday 16: 127 (col.) Nov '54; 17: 71 (col.) Feb '55; 27: 152 (col.) Ap '60; 28: 54 (col.) Jl '60, 212 (col.) Dec '60. Natl. geog. 118: 26-7 (col.) Jl '60. Travel 113: 60 Mar '60.

wailing wall (Jerusalem). Holiday 7: 118 Ap '50.

Waimea canyon (Hawaii). Natl. geog. 118: 131 (col.) Jl '60.

Wainwright, Gen. Jonathan M. Amer. heri., vol. 5 no. 4 p. 43 (summer '54). Cur. biog. p. 861 (1942).

Waitangi. See Chatham island.

Waite, Morrison Remick. Holiday 7: 75 Feb '50.

waiter. See tray; salver.

waiter (cocktails). Holiday 21: 8 May '57.

—— (drinks). Holiday 10: 64 Jl '51.

waiter (serving dinner). Holiday 27: 195 (col.) May '60.
Natl. geog. 113: 317 (col.) Mar '58.
—— **(with tray).** Holiday 28: 163 (col.) Dec '60.
—— **(dining room).** Holiday 19: 17 (col.) Feb '56 22: 41 Dec '57 25: 175 (col.) Ap '59; 27: 198 Mar '60, 58 Ap '60.
Natl. geog. 107: 436 (col.) Ap '55.
—— **(dining room, comic).** Holiday 27: 204 (col.) Ap '60.
——, **Fiji (serving food).** Holiday 28: 159 (col.) Oct '60.
——, **head (restaurant).** Holiday 21: 84 Mar '57.
——, **hotel dining room.** Holiday 24: 30 Dec '58.
——, **Negro.** *See* Negro waiter.
——, **restaurant.** Holiday 13: 54, 122 (col.) Ap '53; 21: 13 (col.) May '57; 27: 130 (col.) Je '60.
Natl. geog. 112: 311 (col.) Sept '57.
——, **restaurant (comic).** Holiday 10: 27 Oct '51; 18: 72 Aug '55; 19: 129 Mar '56; 22: 24 (col.) Jl '57, 135 (col.) Dec '57; 28: 116 Jl '60.
——, **Swedish dining room.** Holiday 24: 83 (col.) Aug '58.
——, **table.** Natl. geog. 110: 426 Sept '56.
——, **train diner.** Holiday 11: 7 (col.) Mar '52; 18: 5 (col.) Aug '55.
waiters, hotel. Holiday 26: 13, 57 (col.) Jl '59.
——, **restaurant.** Holiday 27: 150 Feb '60.
——, **restaurant (comic).** Holiday 27: 69 Mar '60.
——, **ship (trays of food).** Holiday 25: 98 (col.) Je '59.
Waitomo caves. Natl. geog. 101: 448 Ap '52.
waitress (food tray). Holiday 18: 103 Jl '55.
—— **(small).** Holiday 27: 190 Je '60.
——, **dining room.** Holiday 21: 120 Feb '57.
Waitt, Maj. Gen. Alden H. Cur. biog. p. 657 (1947).
Wakehurst, Lord John De Vere Loder. Cur. biog. p. 632 (1954).
Wakeman, Frederic. Cur. biog. p. 614 (1946).
Waksman, Selman A. Cur. biog. p. 616 (1946).
Walchensee landscape. Praeg.: Pict. ency., p. 28 (col.).
Walcott, Joe. Cur. biog. p. 619 (1949).
Walcutt, William (work of). Amer. heri., vol. 9 no. 5 p. 62 (col.) (Aug '58).
Wald, Jerry. Cur. biog. p. 610 (1952).
Holiday 5: 38 (col.) Jan '49.
Waldeck, Jo Besse McElveen. Jun. bk. of auth., p. 291.
Waldeck, Theodore J. Jun. bk. of auth., p. 292.
Walden, Amelia Elizabeth. Cur. biog. p. 635 (1956).
Walden, Sir Lionel. *See* "Sir Lionel Walden" (Kneller).
Waldo, Daniel. Amer. heri., vol. 9 no. 3 p. 32 (Ap '58).
Waldron, Kenneth L. Natl. geog. 113: 458 Ap '58.
Waldseemuller map. *See* map, Waldseemuller.
Wales. Holiday 28: 34-45 (part col.) Sept '60.

—— **(Harlech castle).** *See* Harlech castle.
—— **(lake).** Holiday 13: inside back cover (col.) Feb '53.
—— **(map).** Holiday 28: 34 (col.) Sept '60.
Wales, archdruid. *See* Archdruid of Wales.
walk, mosaic. *See* mosaic pavement.
——, **plank (above river).** Holiday 18: 89 Aug '55.
Walke, Lt. H. (work of). Con. ency. of ant., vol. 3, pl. 95.
Walker, Edward Ronald. Cur. biog. p. 636 (1956).
Walker, Eric Arthur. Cur. biog. p. 469 (1959).
Walker, James. Amer. heri., vol. 9 no. 4 p. 33 (Je '58).
—— **(work of).** Amer. heri., vol. 9 no. 5 cover, p. 8, 12-3 (col.) (Aug '58).
Walker, Jimmy. Amer. heri., vol. 10 no. 4 p. 22 (Je '59).
Walker, John. Cur. biog. p. 573 (1957).
Walker, Johnny. Holiday 10: 125 (col.) Jl '51, 81 (col.) Sept '51, 20 (col.) Nov '51, 189 (col.) Dec '51; 11: 115 (col.) Feb '52, 37 (col.) May '52; 12: 76 (col.) Jl '52, 24 (col.) Sept '52, 116 (col.) Nov '52, 94 (col.) Dec '52; 18: 10 (col.) Aug '55, 149 (col.) Dec '55; 19: 68 (col.) Feb '56; 20: 4 (col.) Sept '56, 155 (col.) Dec '56; 21: 88 (col.) Feb '57, 15 (col.) May '57; 22: 114 (col.) Jl '57, 98 (col.) Sept '57, 28 (col.) Dec '57.
Walker, Margaret. Cur. biog. p. 799 (1943).
Walker, Mildred. Cur. biog. p. 659 (1947).
Walker, Dr. Norma Ford. Cur. biog. p. 574 (1957).
Walker, Paul A. Cur. biog. p. 612 (1952).
Walker, Ralph. Cur. biog. p. 576 (1957).
Walker, Stanley. Cur. biog. p. 710 (1944).
Walker, W. A. (lithograph by). Amer. heri., vol. 2 no. 1 p. 49 (fall '50).
Walker, Lt. Gen. Walton H. Cur. biog. p. 590 (1950).
Walker, Waurine. Cur. biog. p. 627 (1955).
Walker, William. Amer. heri., vol. 9 no. 1 p. 26 (Dec '57).
—— **(monument to his filibustering defeat).** Amer. heri., vol. 9 no. 1 p. 26 (Dec '57).
—— **(filibuster attack).** Amer. heri., vol. 9 no. 1 p. 28-9 (Dec '57).
Wall, Arthur Jonathan, jr. Cur. biog. p. 471 (1959).
Wall, W. G. (work of). Amer. heri., vol. 10 no. 1 p. 18-9 (col.) (Dec '58).
wall, brick garden (dogs, frog). Natl. geog. 114: 207 (col.) Aug '58.
——, **buttressed rock.** Natl. geog. 108: 309 (col.) Sept '55.
——, **Byzantine (Nicaea, Turkey).** *See* Byzantine walls, Nicaea.
——, **Chinese.** *See* great wall of China.
——, **garden.** Natl. geog. 107: 500 (col.) Ap '55.
——, **rock.** *See* rock wall.
——, **serpentine.** *See* serpentine wall (fence).
——, **stone (Ethiopia).** Natl. geog. 106: 746 Dec '54.
——, **Tibetan.** Natl. geog. 99: 608 May '51.
——, **yard.** Holiday 16: 63 (col.) Aug '54.
wall & gate, estate. *See* gate & wall, estate.

wall bracket, Irish. Con. 145: 151 May '60.

wall brackets (candle holders, Gardner, Russia, 18th cent.). Con. 127: 42 Mar '51.

wall brackets. See also sconce.

wall carvings, Claydon house. Con. 142: 72-3 Nov '58.

wall decoration (allegorical figures). Natl. geog. 112: 444 (col.) Oct '57.

wall fountain. Con. 138: XXXIX Sept '56.

——, Norwegian faience. Con. 145: 7 Mar '60.

wall hanging (India). Con. 139: 79 Ap '57.

wall hangings (18th cent.). Con. 138: 257 (col.) Jan '57.

wall lamp. Con. 143: LXIV May '59.

wall lights (1770). Con. ency. of ant., vol. 3, pl. 115.

—— See also sconce.

Wall of Kayseri (Caesarea). Osward: Asia Minor, pl. 69.

"Wall of the missing" (Cambridge, Eng.). Natl. geog. 111: 740 Je '57.

wall painting, Egyptian home (ancient). Int. gr. soc.: Arts . . . p. 15 (col.).

——, Egyptian tomb. Ceram: March of arch., opp. p. 142 (col.). Praeg.: Pict. ency., p. 116 (col.).

——, Etruscan (480 B.C.). Praeg.: Pict. ency., p. 140 (col.).

——, Indian temple (Ajanta). Praeg.: Pict. ency., p. 532 (col.).

——, Maya. See Mayan wall painting.

——, Persian. Praeg.: Pict. ency., p. 522 (col.).

——, Roman (1st cent., B.C.). Praeg.: Pict. ency., p. 150 (col.).

——, Roman (Pompeii). Praeg.: Pict. ency., p. 162 (col.).

——, Romanesque (Resurrection of Christ). Praeg.: Pict. ency., p. 203 (col.).

——, Alexanderkirche (Germany). Con. 133: 9 Mar '54.

wall panel. See panel, wall.

wall sconce. See sconce.

"Wall Street" (Cafferty & Rosenberg). Natl. geog. 99: 196 (col.) Feb '51.

Wall Street, N.Y. (1850). Con. ency. of ant., vol. 3, pl. 95.

—— (fire 1835). Amer. heri., vol. 8 no. 5 p. 14 (col.) (Aug '57).

—— (1907 panic). Amer. heri., vol. 8 no. 4 p. 32 (Je '57).

"Walla Walla" boats (Hong Kong). Natl. geog. 104: 560 (col.) Oct '53.

Wallace, Clayton M. Cur. biog. p. 651 (1948).

Wallace, De Witt. Cur. biog. p. 637 (1956).

Wallace, George C. Cur. biog. (1963).

Wallace, Henry A. Cur. biog. p. 662 (1947).

Wallace, Lew. Amer. heri., vol. 2 no. 1 p. 27 (fall '50).

Pakula: Cent. album, p. 281.

Wallace, Governor Lew. Horan: Pict. hist. of wild west, p. 61.

Wallace, Lila Acheson. Cur. biog. p. 638 (1956).

Wallace, Mike. Cur. biog. p. 577 (1957).

Wallace, William H. Horan: Pict. hist. of wild west, p. 43.

Wallach, Eli. Cur. biog. p. 472 (1959).

walled city. Labande: Naples, p. 75. Natl. geog. 100: 34 (col.) Jl '51.

——, Acre. Travel 104: 11 Aug '55.

——, Avignon (France). Holiday 15: 101 Jan '54.

——, Avila (Spain). Natl. geog. 97: 420 Ap '50.

——, Carcassone. Travel 107: 13 Ap '57.

——, Constantinople. Osward: Asia Minor, pl. 92.

——, Jerico. Natl. geog. 112: 848 Dec '57.

——, Jerusalem. Holiday 17: 38 (col.) Feb '55.

——, Kayseri. Osward: Asia Minor, pl. 69.

——, Salinas de Leniz (Spain). Natl. geog. 105: 158 (col.) Feb '54.

——, Trogir (Yugoslavia). Travel 107: 59 May '57.

walled city gateway. Natl. geog. 101: 222 (col.) Feb '52.

walled town, (Wawel, Poland). Natl. geog. 114: 376-7 Sept '58.

Wallenstein, Alfred. Cur. biog. p. 614 (1952).

Waller, Fats. Cur. biog. p. 863 (1942).

Waller, Fred. Cur. biog. p. 642 (1953).

wallet, ladies'. Holiday 23: inside back cover (col.) May '58; 25: 131 (col.) May '59; 27: inside cover (col.) Je '60; 28: 43 (col.) Dec '60.

——, man's. Holiday 13: 68 Feb '53, 11 Je '53; 14: 11 (col.), 156 Nov '53, 137, 183 (col.), 195 Dec '53; 21: 46 (col.) Je '57; 23: 168 (col.) Je '58; 24: 15 (col.), 145 Nov '58; 25: 149 (col.) Je '59; 26: 18 (col.) Dec '59; 27: 54 Ap '60; 28: 135 Nov '60, 179 (col.) Dec '60.

——. See also billfold.

Wallgren, Monrad C. Cur. biog. p. 653 (1948).

Wallis, Hal. Holiday 5: 43 (col.) Jan '49.

Wallop, Douglass. Cur. biog. p. 640 (1956).

Wallowa Mt. (Ore.). Holiday 13: 36 Je '53. Travel 104: 8 Sept '55.

wallpaper (antique). Con. ency., of ant., vol. 3 p. 247, 252, pl. 169-72.

——, Canton (18th cent.). Con. 141: 121 Ap '58.

——, Chinese (18th cent.). Con. 142: XII Nov '58.

——, Chinese (panels). Con. 144: back cover Jan '60.

——, Eng. (antique). Con. 143: 75-7 Ap '59.

——, French (18th cent.). Con. 144: 140 (col.) Dec '59.

——, scenic (hallway). Natl. geog. 109: 461 (col.), 471 Ap '56.

walls, crenelated fortress. See fortress walls (crenelated).

——, mud-dried village (Nigeria). Natl. geog. 110: 345 (col.) Sept '56.

——, paneled. Natl. geog. 111: 644 (col.) May '57.

——, red mud village (Timimoun, Sahara). Natl. geog. 113: 694-5 (col.) May '58.

walls of Jerusalem. Holiday 17: 38 (col.) Feb '55.

walls of Tower of Babylon. Ceram: March of arch., p. 229, 231.

walls protect sea fowls (Peru). Natl. geog. 115: 408-9 (col.) Mar '59.

"Walnut Point" home. *See* "Reward" (Maryland home).

Walpole, Sir Robert (Wooton). Con. 139: 211 Je '57.

Walsh, Chad. Cur. biog. p. 445 (1962).

Walsh, John R. Holiday 7: 64 (col.) Feb '50.

Walsh, John Raymond. Cur. biog. p. 617 (1946).

Walsh, Mollie (bust). Natl. geog. 104: 396 Sept '53.

Walsh, William B. Cur. biog. p. 447 (1962).

Walsh, William Thomas. Cur. biog. p. 897 (1941).

Walsingham, Sir Francis. Amer. heri., vol. 10 no. 3 p. 9 (Ap '59).

Waltari, Mika. Cur. biog. p. 593 (1950).

Walter, Bruno. Cooper: Con. ency. of music, p. 305.
Cur. biog. p. 865 (1942).

Walter, Francis E. Cur. biog. p. 617 (1952).

Walter, Harriot (Gardner). Con. 143: 7 Mar '59.

Walters, Samuel (work of). Con. 144: XLV Nov '59.

Walton, Ernest Thomas Sinton. Cur. biog. p. 619 (1952).

Walton, Henry (work of). Con. 143: 88 Ap '59.

Walton, Sir William (Ayrton). Cooper: Con. ency. of music, p. 306.

Walworth, Arthur C. Cur. biog. p. 473 (1959).

Wambaugh, Sarah. Cur. biog. p. 620 (1946).

Wampler, Cloud. Cur. biog. p. 621 (1952).

wampum belt, Iroquois. Amer. heri., vol. 6 no. 2 p. 26 (winter '55).

Wan, Prince. Cur. biog. p. 634 (1954).

Wanamaker, Pearl A. Cur. biog. p. 621 (1946).

Wandorobo, Kenya (follow honey-guide bird). Natl. geog. 105: 560 Ap '54.

Wang, Ping-Nan. Cur. biog. p. 454 (1958).

Wang Shih-Chieh. Cur. biog. p. 651 (1945).

Wangchuk, Jigme Dorji. Cur. biog. p. 642 (1956).

Wanger, Walter. Cur. biog. p. 664 (1947).

Wank, Roland. Cur. biog. p. 801 (1943).

war (amerindic) (sym.). Lehner: Pict. bk. of sym., p. 87.

—— (god of). Lehner: Pict. bk. of sym., p. 32.

"War" (Rousseau). Praeg.: Pict. ency., p. 459 (col.).

war (sym.). Lehner: Pict. bk. of sym., p. 86-7.

war, Civil. *See* U.S. Civil war.

——, Sumerian. Natl. geog. 99: 71 (col.) Jan '51.

war canoes, Cambodia. *See* canoes, war (Khmer).

war cartoons. *See* cartoons, U.S. Civil war; cartoons, war.

war chariot, Persian (model). Ceram: March of arch., opp. p. 175 (col.).

war child (poor). Holiday 18: 180 Dec '55.

war club (man, Fiji). Natl. geog. 114: 561 Oct '58.

war dance, Hunza. Natl. geog. 104: 502 (col.) Oct '52.

war deserters route. Amer. heri., vol. 8 no. 6 p. 26 (Oct '57).

war 1812 (battleships). Holiday 23: 74-9 (col.) May '58.

—— (sea battles). Amer. heri., vol. 7 no. 3 p. 13-21 (col.) (Ap '56).

war field kit. Amer. heri., vol. 10 no. 6 p. 4 (col.) (Oct '59).

war landings (Normandy beaches, map). Natl. geog. 115: 595 (col.) May '59.

war memorial (dedication). Natl. geog. 111: 741 (col.) Je '57.

—— (overseas). Natl. geog. 111: 732-69 (col.) Je '57.

——, Auckland. *See* cenotaph, Auckland.

——, D day (Portsmouth, Eng.). Natl. geog. 101: 522 (col.) Ap '52.

——, French. Natl. geog. 111: 771 (col.) Je '57.

war memorial chapel, U.S. *See* chapel, U.S. war memorial (overseas).

war memorials, American. Travel 110: 16-21 Jl '58.

war notice (travellers, 1915). Amer. heri., vol. 6 no. 4 p. 42 (Je '55).

war I memorial, world. Natl. geog. 115: 308 Mar '59.

war orphan, crippled. Holiday 18: 138 Dec '55.

war posters. *See* posters, war.

war raids (pictured on skins, 1875). Amer. heri., vol. 11 no. 2 p. 52 (col.) (Feb '60).

war reports & rules (1776). Amer. heri., vol. 6 no. 5 p. 26-31 (Aug '55).

war ruins (Okinawa). Natl. geog. 107: 278 Feb '55.

—— (Quemoy island). Natl. geog. 115: 424-5 Mar '59.

war scene (Baltimore). Amer. heri., vol. 3 no. 2 p. 30-1 (col.) (winter '52).

—— (Custer's battlefield). Amer. heri., vol. 5 no. 4 p. 37 (col.) (summer '54).

—— (Bull Run). Amer. heri., vol. 3 no. 2 p. 62-4 (winter '52).

Warburg, Mr. & Mrs. F. M. Holiday 27: inside cover (col.) Jan '60.

Warburg, James Paul. Cur. biog. p. 655 (1948).

Warburg, Paul M. Amer. heri., vol. 9 no. 5 p. 33 (Aug '58).

Warburton, Herbert B. Cur. biog. p. 642 (1951).

Ward, Animalier James (work of). Con. 129: 119 Je '52.

Ward, Barbara. Cur. biog. p. 594 (1950).

Ward, J. (work of). Con. ency. of ant., vol. 1, pl. 173.

Ward, James (work of). Con. 142: XLVII Nov '58; 144: 109 Nov '59; 145: 145 May '60.

Ward, Mary Jane. Cur. biog. p. 623 (1946).

Ward, Paul L. Cur. biog. p. 449 (1962).

Ward, Robert. Cur. biog. (1963).

Ward, William (work of). Con. ency. of ant., vol. 1, pl. 135.

Ward-Belmont college. Holiday 8: 48 Nov '50.

"Ward Hunt family" (Wyatt). Con. 138: XIX Dec '56.

wardrobe (18th cent.). Con. 136: XXXIII Sept '55.

——, Queen Anne. Con. 141: IV Ap '58.

——, Victorian inlaid (by Heal). Con. ency. of ant., vol. 3, pl. 8.

——, **Viennese (Josef II).** Con. ency. of ant., vol. 3, pl. 23.

——, **Viennese Baroque (18th cent.).** Con. ency. of ant., vol. 3, pl. 22.

wardrobe cupboard, Dutch (16th cent.). Int. gr. soc.: Arts . . . p. 103 (col.).

warehouse. Natl. geog. 111: 307 (col.) Mar '57.

——, **stone (Majorca).** Natl. geog. 111: 642 (col.) May '57.

warehouses, Hanseatic type (Norway). Natl. geog. 106: 154 (col.) Aug '54.

Waring, Julius Waties. Cur. biog. p. 657 (1948).

Waring, Roane. Cur. biog. p. 803 (1943).

Waring blender. Holiday 21: 5 Feb '57, 138 Ap '57; 22: 7 Jl '57, 21 Oct '57, 214 Dec '57.

Waring mixer. *See* Waring blender.

Warm Springs (Georgia Hall). Holiday 15: 83 Feb '54.

warming pan cover, brass. Rawson: Ant. pict. bk., p. 85.

Warne, William E. Cur. biog. p. 623 (1952).

Warner, Albert. Cur. biog. p. 652 (1945).

Warner, Edward P. Cur. biog. p. 621 (1949).

Warner, Harry M. Cur. biog. p. 653 (1945).

Warner, Jack L. Cur. biog. p. 654 (1945).

Warner, John C. Cur. biog. p. 596 (1950).

Warner, Matt. Horan: Pict. hist. of wild west, p. 206.

Warner, Milo J. Cur. biog. p. 898 (1941).

Warner, William Lloyd. Cur. biog. p. 475 (1959).

Warren, Althea. Cur. biog. p. 868 (1942).

Warren, Avra M. Cur. biog. p. 629 (1955).

Warren, Earl. Cur. biog. p. 717 (1944).

Warren, Chief Justice Earl. Cur. biog. p. 636 (1954).

Natl. geog. 113: 793 Je '58; 114: 600 (col.) Nov '58.

Warren, Edgar L. Cur. biog. p. 667 (1947).

Warren, Fletcher. Cur. biog. p. 449 (1960).

Warren, Fuller. Cur. biog. p. 623 (1949).

Warren, Gouverneur Kemble. Pakula: Cent. album, p. 283.

Warren, Harry. Cur. biog. p. 805 (1943).

Warren, Leonard. Cur. biog. p. 644 (1953). Holiday 8: 80 Nov '50.

Warren, Lindsay C. Cur. biog. p. 624 (1949).

Warren, Shields. Cur. biog. p. 597 (1950).

Warren, William C. Cur. biog. p. 451 (1960).

Warren house, Thomas. Natl. geog. 111: 618 (col.) May '57.

warrior (Africa). Natl. geog. 118: 388 (col.) Sept '60.

—— **(Etruscan).** *See* Etruscan warrior.

—— **(Fiji).** *See* Fiji warrior.

—— **(head hunter).** Natl. geog. 108: 480, 485 (col.) Oct '55.

—— **(India, armor).** Natl. geog. 107: 196 (col.) Feb '55.

——, **Haniwa (Japanese sculpture).** *See* Haniwa warrior.

——, **Japanese.** *See* Japanese warrior.

——, **Nigeria (bronze tablet).** Praeg.: Pict. ency., p. 546.

warriors (ancient times). Int. gr. soc.: Arts . . . p. 33 (col.).

——, **African.** Holiday 15: 36, 42-3, 46-7 (col.) Mar '54.

——, **African (Masai).** Natl. geog. 106: 490 Oct '54.

——, **African (against Mau Mau).** Natl. geog. 112: 98-9 (col.) Jl '57.

——, **colonial.** Holiday 9: 77 Mar '51.

——, **India (head hunters).** Natl. geog. 107: 248, 251, 260-1 (col.) Feb '55.

——, **Highland (New Guinea).** Holiday 28: 84-5 (col.) Nov '60.

——, **Hurrian (carvings).** *See* Hurrian warriors.

——, **Israelite.** Natl. geog. 112: 847 (col.) Dec '57.

——, **Lotuka, Sudan.** Natl. geog. 103: 264 (col.) Feb '53.

——, **Watusi.** *See* Watusi warriors.

——. *See also* soldier.

Warsaw (Poland). Holiday 5: 80 Je '49.

warship. Amer. heri., vol. 9 no. 6 p. 40 (col.) (Oct '58).

"Warwick" (18th cent. house, Va.). Natl. geog. 109: 451 Ap '56.

Warwick castle (Eng.). Con. 132: 111 Nov '53. Holiday 15: 28 (col.) Je '54.

wash-hand stand, Sheraton corner. Con. 143: XXXIV Mar '59.

washbowl & pitcher. Holiday 22: 107 Sept '57.

Washburn, Gordon. Holiday 25: 84 (col.) Mar '59.

Washburn, Gordon Bailey. Cur. biog. p. 631 (1955).

washday (women use rocks in streams, Korea). Natl. geog. 103: 647 (col.) May '53.

washing (on line). Holiday 7: 46 (col.) Je '50; 8: 52 (col.) Dec '50.

washing clothes, Brittany women. Holiday 7: 98 (col.) Jan '50.

——, **women.** *See* women (washing clothes).

washing clothes in river. Natl. geog. 101: 356 (col.) Mar '52.

"washing-feet" pageant. *See* Armenian "Washing-feet" pageant.

"Washing of the feet" pageant (Jerusalem). Natl. geog. 98: 717 (col.) Dec '50.

washing stand (18th cent.). Con. ency. of ant., vol. 3, pl. 10.

Washington, Booker T. Brooks: Growth of a nation, p. 151.

Washington, Bushrod. Amer. heri., vol. 7 no. 1 p. 107 (Dec '55).

Washington, George. Amer. heri., vol. 2 no. 4 p. 9 (summer '51); vol. 7 no. 3 p. 30 (Ap '56); vol. 8 no. 1 p. 9 (col.) (Dec '56). Con. 129: 135 Je '52.

Durant: Pict. hist. of Amer. circus, p. 22. Holiday 14: 47 (col.) Nov '53.

Jensen: The White House, p. 4.

Natl. geog. 104: 662 (col.) Nov '53.

—— **(as a boy).** Amer. heri., vol. 4 no. 1 p. 60 (fall '52) .

—— **(as a Roman senator, statue).** Amer. heri., vol. 8 no. 2 p. 46 (Feb '57).

—— **(Battle of Monmouth).** Amer. heri., vol. 6 no. 4 cover (col.) (Je '55).

—— **(Black Hills sculpture).** Natl. geog. 99: 720 (col.) Je '51.

Washington, George (black Wedgwood bust). Con. 140: LV Jan '58.

—— **(bronze bust by Rush).** Con. 133: LI Mar '54.

—— **(bronze statue).** Natl. geog. 103: 32 (col.) Je '53.

—— **(bust).** Face of Amer., p. 62. Natl. geog. 104: 660 Nov '53.

—— **(by Peale).** Con. 135: XVII Ap '55. Natl. geog. 99: 181 (col.) Feb '51; 100: 591 (col.) Nov '51.

—— **(by Steuart).** Amer. heri., vol. 6 no. 5 p. 42 (col.) (Aug '55).

—— **(based on Steuart).** Amer. heri., vol. 9 no. 2 frontis (col.) (Feb '58).

—— **(by Trumbull).** Amer. heri., vol. 7 no. 2 cover (col.) (Feb '56).

—— **(dying).** Amer. heri., vol. 6 no. 5 p. 46 (Aug '55).

—— **(earliest known portrait).** Amer. heri., vol. 5 no. 4 p. 29 (summer '54); vol. 6 no. 3 p. 47 (Ap '55).

—— **(head by Peale).** Holiday 14: 46 (col.) Dec '53.

—— **(Houdon's statue).** Travel 111: 4 May '59.

—— **(inauguration).** Amer. heri., vol. 4 no. 3 p. 6 (spring '53); vol. 5 no. 1 p. 9 (col.), 10 (fall '53).

—— **(on horse).** Amer. heri., vol. 7 no. 1 p. 62 (fall '54); vol. 8 no. 5 p. 63 (col.) (Aug '57); vol. 9 no. 4 p. 56 (col.) (Je '58). Natl. geog. 116: 92, 100 (part col.) Jl '59.

—— **(on horse, by Wilson).** Amer. heri., vol. 6 no. 2 p. 44 (winter '55).

—— **(on horse, miniature).** Amer. heri., vol. 6 no. 2 frontis. (col.) (winter '55).

—— **(rock carving).** Natl. geog. 110: 496 Oct '56.

—— **(reviewing army).** Natl. geog. 99: 183 (col.) Feb '51.

——. *See also* Washington's . . .

Washington, Pres. & Mrs. George (child's drawing). Amer. heri., vol. 1 no. 3 p. 59 (spring '50).

Washington, Martha (Mrs. George Washington). Natl. geog. 100: 589 (col.) Nov '51.

Washington & family, George (Paul). Con. 132: 185 Jan '54.

—— **(Sully).** Amer. heri., vol. 7 no. 2 p. 64 (col.) (Feb '56).

Washington & Lafayette (Valley Forge). Brooks: Growth of a nation, p. 77.

Washington & Lee university. Holiday 12: 40-1 Nov '52.

Washington & Lincoln. Amer. heri., vol. 10 no. 2 p. 12 (col.) (Feb '59).

"Washington at Princeton." Amer. heri., vol. 3 no. 3 p. 40 (col.) (spring '52).

"Washington at the Delaware river." Amer. heri., vol. 8 no. 5 p. 58 (col.) (Aug '57).

"Washington at Valley Forge." Natl. geog. 102: 160 (col.) (Aug '52).

"Washington attacks Hessians" (1776). Natl. geog. 117: 12-3 (col.) Jan '60.

"Washington crossing Delaware." Amer. heri., vol. 11 no. 2 p. 58 (col.) (Feb '59).

Holiday 16: 106 (col.) Jl '54; 22: 70 (col.) Sept '57.

Natl. geog. 102: 14 (col.) Jl '52.

"Washington crossing the Delaware" (school boys enact). Natl. geog. 102: 14 (col.) Jl '52.

Washington home, Betty. *See* Washington's home, Betty.

Washington home, George. *See* Washington's home, George.

"Washington Irving & his literary friends" (Schussele). Amer. heri., vol. 10 no. 1 p. 22 (Dec '58).

"Washington welcomes Lincoln into Heaven." Amer. heri., vol. 10 no. 2 p. 15 (Feb '59).

Washington (D.C.). Amer. heri., vol. 2 no. 2 cover, 2-7, 23, 25 (part col.) (winter '51). Brooks: Growth of a nation, p. 14. Holiday 7: cover, 36-65, 102-14 (part col.) Feb '50; 11: 78 May '52; 19: 34-44 (part col.) May '56; 25: 55-63 Je '59. Natl. geog. 99: 713 (col.) Je '51; 102: 143-90 (part col.) Aug '52; 111: 64-95 (part col.) Jan '57. Travel 102: 7-9 Oct '54; 113: 24 Mar '60.

—— **(burning of).** Jensen: The White House, p. 26.

—— **(capitol bldg.).** *See* U.S. Capitol, Wash., D.C.

—— **(1800).** Jensen: The White House, p. 3.

—— **(fire).** Amer. heri. vol. 9 no. 5 p. 66-7 (Aug '58).

—— **(L'Enfant plan).** Amer. heri., vol. 2 no. 2 p. 4 (winter '51).

—— **(L'Enfant, 1791).** Amer. heri., vol. 10 no. 5 p. 76 (Aug '59). Natl. geog. 103: 5 Jan '53.

—— **(map).** Holiday 19: 38-9 May '56.

—— **(map, 1889).** Amer. heri., vol. 4 no. 4 p. 60 (summer '53).

—— **(moslem mosque).** Face of Amer., p. 81 (col.).

—— **(opera house, 1895).** Brooks: Growth of a Nation, p. 223.

—— **(Potomac river, cherry trees).** Face of Amer., p. 10-11 (col.).

—— **(riverside).** Natl. geog. 117: 422 (col.) Mar '60.

—— **(State-war-navy bldg.).** Jensen: The White House, p. 195.

—— **(street plan).** Natl. geog. 111: 70 Jan '57.

Washington, Mt. *See* Mt. Washington.

Washington cathedral (Wash. D.C.). Travel 106: 12 Dec '56.

—— **(int.).** Natl. geog. 111: 92 (col.) Jan '57.

Washington memorial chapel (Valley Forge, int.). Natl. geog. 105: 201-2 (col.) Feb '54.

Washington monument (Wash., D.C.). Amer. heri., vol. 10 no. 2 p. 100 (Feb '59). Holiday 7: 38 (col.) Feb '50, 123 May '50; 21: 93 Mar '57; 25: 109 Feb '59. Jensen: The White House, p. 145. Natl. geog. 111: 77 (col.) Jan '57; 113: 307 Mar '58, 660 (col.) May '58; 117: 649 May '60. Travel 101: inside cover Je '54.

Washington Natl. Art Gallery. Natl. geog. 110: 620-57 (part col.) Nov '56.

Washington (state). Holiday 11: 45-59 (part col.) May '52.
Natl. geog. 117: 446-92, 494-513 (col.) Ap '60.
—— **(lake & mt. Shuksan).** Holiday 23: 18 (col.) May '58.
—— **(state capitol).** Holiday 15: 151 Mar '54; 17: 129 (col.) Mar '55.
Natl. geog. 117: 460 (col.) Ap '60.
—— **(map).** Natl. geog. 102: 576-7 Nov '52.
—— **(Olympic natl. park, beach).** Face of Amer. p. 138-9.
Washington's birthday, George (sym.). Lehner: Pict. bk. of sym., p. 55.
Washington's birthplace, George (Wakefield, Va.). Holiday 17: 118 (col.) Mar '55.
Washington's command flag (Valley Forge). Amer. heri., vol. 6 no. 4 p. 36 (col.) (Je '55).
Washington's headquarters (N.Y., 1776). Con. ency. of ant., vol. 3, pl. 92.
Washington's headquarters (Valley Forge). See Valley Forge (Washington's headquarters).
Washington's home, Betty. Holiday 10: 62 Oct '51.
Washington's home, George ("Mt. Vernon"). Brooks: Growth of a nation, p. 71.
Face of Amer., p. 63 (col.).
Holiday 18: 107 (col.) Nov '55; 25: cover (col.) Je '59.
Natl. geog. 97: 814 Je '50; 104: 652-82 (part col.) Nov '53; 112: 511 Oct '57.
Travel 111: 29-31 Feb '59; 114: 35 Sept '60.
—— **(garden).** Natl. geog. 104: 674-5 (col.) Nov '53.
Washington's powder horn, George. Rawson: Ant. pict. bk., p. 35.
Washington's tomb, George. Travel 111: 31 Feb '59.
washstand (antique). Holiday 26: 61 (col.) Aug '59.
Natl. geog. 109: 454 Ap '56.
——, **corner (18th cent.).** Con. ency. of ant., vol. 1, pl. 39.
——, **Victorian (by Burges).** Con. ency. of ant., vol. 3, pl. 5.
——, **Victorian marble top.** Con. ency. of ant., vol. 3, pl. 5.
washtub. See tub, wash.
Wasilewska, Wanda. Cur. biog. p. 720 (1944).
Wason, Betty. Cur. biog. p. 807 (1943).
Wason, Robert R. Cur. biog. p. 625 (1946).
wassail bowl. Con. 132: LXVI Jan '54.
—— **(antique silver).** Con. 138: XXIV Sept '56.
Wassail cup, English. Con. 126: 43 Aug '50.
Wasserburg. Natl. geog. 115: 763 (col.) Je '59.
waste can, wire. Natl. geog. 109: 206 Feb '56.
wastebasket, brass. Holiday 24: 149 Oct '58.
Wat Chang temple (Siam). See temple, Wat Chang (Siam).
watch. Amer. heri., vol. 10 no. 3 p. 52 (Ap '59).
Holiday 6: 72 Jl '49, 128 Dec '49; 7: 78 Jan '50; 8: 27 Oct '50, 23, 102 Dec '50; 10: 104 Jl '51, 132 Oct '51, 27, 129, 131 Nov '51; 12: 79 Jl '52, 97 Sept '52, 16 Oct '52, 54, 135 Nov '52; 19: 17 Jan '56;

20: 28, 43, 100, 175 Dec '56; 21: 200 Je '57.
Natl. geog. 111: 780 (col.) Je '57.
—— **(antique).** Amer. heri., vol. 10 no. 1 p. 41 (col.) (Dec '58).
—— **(bracelet).** Holiday 24: 6 Nov '58, 236 Dec '58.
—— **(diver discovery).** Natl. geog. 117: 173 (col.) Feb '60.
—— **(man head, listening).** Holiday 18: 92 Oct '55.
—— **(street sign).** Holiday 18: 31 (col.) Sept '55.
——, **alarm.** Holiday 19: 154 May '56.
——, **astronomical (antique).** Con. 133: 43 Mar '54.
——, **astronomical (Margetts, 18th cent.).** Con. 145: LII Mar '60.
——, **brass pocket.** Natl. geog. 117: 157 (col.) Feb '60.
——, **Brequet (19th cent.).** Con. 143: 224 Je '59.
——, **chatelaine.** Con. 136: 23 Sept '55.
——, **chatelaine (closed).** Holiday 14: 147 Dec '53.
——, **ladies.** Holiday 13: 22 Je '53; 14: 31 Dec '53; 18: 202 Dec '55, 54 Dec '57; 26: 184 Oct '59.
——, **man's.** Holiday 6: 8, 89 Nov '49; 13: 9 Je '53; 14: 31, 185 Dec '53; 18: 27, 202 Nov '55; 19: 92 Je '56; 20: 118, 173 Nov '56 21: 140 Jan '57, 164 Mar '57, 9 May '57, 151 Je '57; 22: 170 Oct '57; 24: 137 Jl '58; 26: 130 Oct '59; 28: 3 Sept '60, 178 Oct '60, 50 Nov '60.
Travel 104: 68 Nov '55; 106: 37 Jl '56, 61 Sept '56, 61 Nov '56; 109: 58 Ap '58.
——, **nautical.** Holiday 20: 193 Nov '56.
——, **pistol (antique).** Con. 133: 43 Mar '54.
——, **Quaker.** Amer. heri., vol. 9 no. 3 p. 104 (Ap '58).
——, **Queen Elizabeth I.** Con. 132: 24 Sept '53.
——, **Tompion.** Con. 129: 43 Ap '52.
——, **wrist.** Con. 138: VIII Nov '56, VIII Jan '57.
Holiday 26: 113 Nov '59, 54 Dec '59.
watch & chatelaine, Louis XVI. Con. 140: 59 Sept '57.
watch bank. Holiday 18: 117 Sept '55.
watch case (antique). Con. 142: IV Dec '58.
watches. Holiday 6: 12-3, 84 Dec '49; 10: 9, 16 Dec '51; 11: 124 Je '52; 12: 1, 70, 80, 162, 179 Dec '52; 20: 12-3 (col.) Dec '56; 22: 132-3 (col.), 233 Dec '57.
—— **(antiques).** Con. ency. of ant., vol. 1, pl. 104.
——, **antique.** Con. 144: LIX Sept '59.
watchfulness (sym.). Lehner: Pict. bk. of sym., p. 66.
watchmaker. Holiday 6: 76-8, 80-2 Aug '49.
Natl. geog. 98: 246 Aug '50.
—— **(sym.).** Lehner: Pict. bk. of sym., p. 91.
watchtower. Travel 103: 25 Feb '55.
——, **Grand Canyon.** Natl. geog. 107: 621 (col.) May '55.
——, **Minorca (ancient).** Holiday 27: 50 (col.) Jan '60.

watchtower, Napoleon's (Italy). Holiday 26: 58 (col.) Sept '59.

——, **Norman.** Natl. geog. 108: 572 Oct '55.

——, **Trucial Oman.** Natl. geog. 110: 72-3 (col.) Jl '56.

Watendlath tarn (Eng.). Natl. geog. 109: 534-5 (col.) Ap '56.

water, irradiated. Natl. geog. 114: 310 (col.) Sept '58.

water baskets. See baskets, water.

water bikes. Holiday 7: 82 Ap '50.

water bottle, farm. Rawson: Ant. pict. bk., p. 61.

water carrier. Natl. geog. 109: 276 (col.) Feb '56.

—— **(man).** Rawson: Ant. pict. bk., p. 42.

water carriers (women & children, nomads). Natl. geog. 109: 71 Jan '56.

——, **Kazakh.** Natl. geog. 106: 638 Nov '54.

water control system (diagram). Brooks: Growth of a nation, p. 279.

water cycle (girls). Natl. geog. 99: 449 (col.) Ap '51.

water-fire principle (sym.). Lehner: Pict. bk. of sym., p. 66.

"water gate" (Chicago World's fair). Amer. heri., vol. 11 no. 6 p. 8 (col.) (Oct '60).

water globe. See globe, water.

water jar. Natl. geog. 99: 451 (col.) Ap '51.

—— **(Turkish farmer).** Natl. geog. 115: 72 (col.) Jan '59.

water jug (ancient). Int. gr. soc.: Arts . . . p. 177 (col.).

—— **(antique).** Con. 134: XXVIII Sept '54.

—— **(antique silver).** Con. 136: 261 Jan '56.

——, **calabash (Africa).** Natl. geog. 97: 341 (col.) Mar '50.

——, **Iraq (man drinking).** Natl. geog. 114: 454, 470 (col.) Oct '58.

——, **Irish.** Con. 136: XXVIII Jan '56.

——, **Irish glass.** Con. 145: XXIV Ap '60.

——, **Russian empire.** Con. 142: 103 Nov '58.

water jug set. Holiday 18: 162 Dec '55.

water level (antique). Con. 134: 91 Nov '54.

water log. Rawson: Ant. pict. bk., p. 51.

water main. Natl. geog. 100: 430 Oct '51.

"Water-mill, Cumberland" (by De Wint). Con. ency. of ant., vol. 1, pl. 145.

water pipe. Natl. geog. 117: 80 (col.) Jan '60; 118: 460 (col.) Oct '60.

—— **(woman smoking).** Natl. geog. 111: 836 (col.) Je '57.

——. (See also hookah.

water plant, Eagle Mt. See Eagle Mt. water plant.

water-pot, Yueh ware. Con. 143: VI Mar '59.

water purifier. See purifier, water.

water scooter (girl running). Travel 107: 9 Je '57.

water skiing. See man & girl (water skiing); man & woman (water skiing); skiing, water; surfboard (rider).

water spray system (fields). Natl. geog. 100: 321 (col.) Sept '51.

water sprinkler, grain field (Chinese). Natl. geog. 115: 434 Mar '59.

water sprinkling can (sym.). Lehner: Pict. bk. of sym., p. 90.

water sprites (boys in hydroplane). Travel 108: 29-31 Jl '57.

water stills, solar. Natl. geog. 110: 248 Aug '56.

water stills. See also stills.

water taxi (India). Holiday 11: 18 Je '52. Travel 105: 54 Feb '56.

water toys. See toys, water.

water tub, forge. Rawson: Ant. pict. bk., p. 55.

water vendor. See vendor, water.

water wheel. Amer. heri., vol. 6 no. 6 p. 106 (Oct '55). Travel 102: 2 Dec '54.

——, **Hama's.** Natl. geog. 106: 819 (col.) Dec '54.

watercourse (Madeira is.). Natl. geog. 115: 384-5 (col.) Mar '59.

watercycle (girl). Holiday 10: 19 Jl '51.

waterfall. Natl. geog. 108: 105 (col.) Jl '55; 109: 19 (col.) Jan '56.

—— **(Eng.).** Natl. geog. 109: 539 (col.) Ap '56.

—— **(fishermen, Alaska).** Natl. geog. 109: 814 Je '56.

—— **(Hawaii).** Natl. geog. 118: 32 (col.) Jl '60.

—— **(highest in France).** Natl. geog. 109: 303 (col.) Mar '56.

—— **(Iceland).** Natl. geog. 108: 729 (col.) Dec '55.

—— **(man).** Natl. geog. 114: 625 (col.) Nov '58.

—— **(man, snowshoes).** Natl. geog. 110: 763 (col.) Dec '56.

——, **Shequaga.** Natl. geog. 110: 600 (col.) Nov '56.

waterfalls. Holiday 11: 47 (col.), 75 May '52; 12: 8 Oct '52. Jordan: Hammond's pict. atlas, p. 41, 47 (col.).

—— **(basalt palisades).** Natl. geog. 109: 81 Jan '56.

—— **(N.H.).** Holiday 10: 43 (col.) Sept '51.

——, **Dingman's.** See Dingman's waterfalls.

——, **Iguazu.** Natl. geog. 113: 298-9 (col.) Mar '58.

——, **Yellowstone.** Holiday 10: 2, 31 (col.) Aug '51.

watergap. Rawson: Ant. pict. bk. p. 50.

Waterhouse, J. W. (work of). Con. 141: V Ap '58.

watering can. See sprinkling can.

watering pot (antique). Rawson: Ant. pict. bk., p. 51.

watering trough. See trough.

Waterloo memorial (Napoleon's defeat). Natl. geog. 113: 832 Je '58.

Waterman, Alan T. Cur. biog. p. 643 (1951).

Waterman obelisk, Lt. John. Natl. geog. 105: 196 (col.) Feb '54.

watermill (early). Amer. heri., vol. 6 no. 6 p. 104-7 (Oct '55).

Waters, Ethel. Cur. biog. p. 900 (1941); p. 645 (1951).

watershed, forest. Natl. geog. 110: 300-1 (col.) Sept '56.

Waterton-Glacier international peace park. Holiday 24: 50-1 (col.) Nov '58.

—— (map). Natl. geog. 109: 596-7 (col.) May '56.

Waterton Lake (Canada). Holiday 24: 50-1 Nov '58.

watertower (Israeli). Natl. geog. 98: 734 Dec '50.

waterways experiment station. *See* U.S. Army engineer waterway. . . .

Watkins, Arthur V. Cur. biog. p. 599 (1950).

Watkins, Shirley. Cur. biog. p. 456 (1958).

Watkins, Master Sergeant Travis. Holiday 10: 1 Aug '51.

Watkins, Travis. Holiday 11: 112 Jan '52.

Watkin's tavern (Versailles, Ky.). Holiday 15: 90 (col.) Mar '54.

Watkinson, Harold. Cur. biog. p. 452 (1960).

Watson, Burl S. Cur. biog. p. 579 (1957).

Watson, Donald. Cur. biog. p. 458 (1958).

Watson, James Dewey. Cur. biog. (1963).

Watson, John B. Cur. biog. p. 869 (1942).

Watson, Kate. Horan: Pict. hist. of wild west, p. 181.

Watson, Lucile. Cur. biog. p. 646 (1953).

Watson, Mark S. Cur. biog. p. 627 (1946).

Watson, Vice-Adm. R. D. Holiday 25: 86 (col.) Ap '59.

Watson, Thomas J. Cur. biog. p. 600 (1950).

Watson, Thomas, J., jr. Cur. biog. p. 643 (1956).

Watson-Watt, Sir Robert. Cur. biog. p. 657 (1945).

Watt, John Campbell. Con. 144: 13 Sept '59.

Watt, Robert J. Cur. biog. p. 658 (1945).

Watteau, Antoine. Int. gr. soc.: Arts . . . p. 91 (col.).

—— (work of). Con. 138: 111 Nov '56; 142: 5 Sept '58, 112 Nov '58.
Cooper: Con. ency. of music, p. 447 (col.).
Praeg.: Pict. ency., p. 360 (col.).

Watteau, Jean Antoine (work of). Con. 139: 123 Ap '57; 140: 109 Nov '57.

wattle & daub houses. *See* houses, wattle & daub.

Watts, Alan. Cur. biog. p. 451 (1962).

Watts, F. W. (work of). Con. 140: 127 Nov '57; 142: XXXVII Dec '58.

Watts, G. F. (work of). Con. 144: 11 Sept '59.

Watts, Lyle F. Cur. biog. p. 629 (1946).

Watusi (giant men). Natl. geog. 112: 94, 96 (col.) Jl '57.

Watusi chief (Belgian Congo). Natl. geog. 101: 353 (col.) Mar '52.

Watusi dancers (Central Africa). Int. gr. soc.: Arts . . . p. 147 (col.).

—— (Congo). Travel 104: 49-50 Nov '55.

Watusi warriors. Natl. geog. 106: 740 (col.) Dec '54.

Waugh, Samuel B. (work of). Amer. heri., vol. 5 no. 1 p. 18 (col.) (fall '53); vol. 9 no. 5 p. 22-3 (col.) (Aug '58).

Waugh, Samuel C. Cur. biog. p. 633 (1955).

Waugh, Sidney. Cur. biog. p. 659 (1948).

Wavell, Sir Archibald. Cur. biog. p. 901 (1941).

Waves (girls, world war). Natl. geog. 101: 835-46 Je '52.

waves, high (against ship). Natl. geog. 104: 577 Oct '53.

Wawel (walled town, Poland). Natl. geog. 114: 376-7 Sept '58.

wax (sym.). Lehner: Pict. bk. of sym., p. 73.

wax administration bldg., Johnson's. Natl. geog. 111: 178-9 (col.) Feb '57.

wax relief ("Ugolino & his sons"). Con. 142: 200 Dec '58.

wax sculpture. Con. 126: 222 Dec '50.

waxjack, silver (1795). Con. ency. of ant., vol. 1, p. 153.

"Way of the Cross" (carvings). Con. 133: LXXI Je '54.

Wayenberg, Daniel. Holiday 22: 121 Sept '57.

Waymack, William W. Cur. biog. p. 669 (1947).

Wayne, Anthony. Amer. heri., vol. 4 no. 3 p. 33 (col.) (spring '53); vol. 9 no. 4 p. 46 (Je '58).

Wayne, David. Cur. biog. p. 646 (1956).
Holiday 17: 94 (col.) Jan '55.

Wayne, John. Cur. biog. p. 647 (1951).

Wayne birthplace, Anthony. Amer. heri., vol. 3 no. 1 p. 15 (fall '51).

Wayne home, "Mad Anthony." Natl. geog. 118: 166 (col.) Aug '60.

"Wayside Inn" (Sudbury, Mass.). Amer. heri., vol. 4 no. 4 p. 24 (col.) (summer '53).
Holiday 11: 42 (col.) Je '52; 14: 87 (col.) Jl '53.
Travel 111: 50 Mar '59.

Weafer, Elizabeth. Cur. biog. p. 459 (1958).

wealth (sym.). Lehner: Pict. bk. of sym., p. 28, 45.

weapons, Indian. *See* Indian weapons.

weasel (Antarctic transportation). Natl. geog. 112: 362 (col.) Sept '57.

weather, good (sym.). Lehner: Pict. bk. of sym., p. 46.

weather compass, Mongolian. Lehner: Pict. bk. of sym., p. 75.

weather station (Canadian Arctic region). Natl. geog. 107: 544-71 (part col.) (Ap '55).

—— (mountain). Natl. geog. 99: 594 (col.) May '51.

weathervane. Amer. heri., vol. 2 no. 2 p. 32 (col.) (winter '51).
Con. 137: LXIV Ap '56.
Holiday 5: 24 Ap '49, 121 Je '49; 7: 79 Je '50; 10: 127 Nov '51; 20: 195 Nov '56; 21: 138 Feb '57, 207 May '57; 22: 122 Jl '57, 126 Sept '57; 23: 198, 209 Je '58; 24: 34 Nov '58, 179 Dec '58; 26: 128 Jl '59, 119 Aug '59, 120 Sept '59; 27: 201 Mar '60, 230 Ap '60, 193 Je '60.

—— (Angel Gabriel). Amer. heri., vol. 6 no. 3 p. 32 (Ap '55).

—— (antique). Amer. heri., vol. 1 no. 2 p. 67 (winter '50).

—— (sym.). Lehner: Pict. bk. of sym., p. 58.

——, bronze (12th cent.). Con. 142: 106 Nov '58.

Weaver, Robert C. Cur. biog. p. 474 (1961).

Weaver, Sylvester L., jr. Cur. biog. p. 635 (1955).

Weaver, Thomas (work of). Con. 144: 205 Dec '59.

Weaver, Warren. Cur. biog. p. 625 (1952).

weaver (antique loom). Con. 138: LXXII Jan '57.

—— (woman). Holiday 24: 183 (col.) Dec '58.

——, textile (Nigeria). Natl. geog. 110: 348 (col.) Sept '56.

weavers. Natl. geog. 110: 728 (col.) Dec '56.

——, Maori. Natl. geog. 101: 442 (col.) Ap '52.

——, Morocco. Natl. geog. 107: 169 (col.) Feb '55.

——, rug. See rug weavers.

——, Tahitian. National geog. 112: 769 (col.) Dec '57.

weaving, Bali girl. Natl. geog. 99: 13 (col.) Jan '51.

——, Japanese hand. Natl. geog. 97: 627 (col.) May '50.

——, Malay woman. Natl. geog. 103: 201 (col.) Feb '53.

——, Pakistan girls. Natl. geog. 107: 406 (col.) Mar '55.

——, woman. See woman (weaving); women (weaving).

weaving loom, braid. See loom, braid weaving.

weaving machine. Natl. geog. 106: 574 (col.) Oct '54.

weaving shop (int., weavers, 16th cent.). Int. gr. soc.: Arts . . . p. 97 (col.).

Webb, Aileen O. Cur. biog. p. 461 (1958).

Webb, Brig. Gen. Alexander Stewart. Amer. heri., vol. 9 no. 1 p. 44 (Dec '57).

Webb: Alexander Stewart. Pakula: Cent. album, p. 285.

Webb, Clifton. Cur. biog. p. 809 (1943). Holiday 23: 149 Je '58.

Webb, Jack. Cur. biog. p. 637 (1955).

Webb, James E. Cur. biog. p. 630 (1946); p. 453 (1962).

Webb, James E. (Doc). Holiday 24: 80 Nov '58.

Webb, James Watson. Amer. heri., vol. 8 no. 3 p. 52 (Ap '59).

Webb, Maurice. Cur. biog. p. 603 (1950).

Webb, Sir William Flood. Cur. biog. p. 660 (1948).

Weber, Carl Maria. Cooper: Con. ency. of music, p. 307.

Weber, Max. Cur. biog. p. 903 (1941).

—— (woodcut by). Praeg.: Pict. ency., p. 457.

Webster, Charles L. Amer. heri., vol. 11 no. 1 p. 78 (Dec '59).

Webster, Daniel. Amer. heri., vol. 6 no. 6 p. 56, 96 (Oct '55); vol. 8 no. 1 p. 63 (Dec '56); vol. 9 no. 1 p. 74, 79 (part col.) (Dec '57); vol. 11 no. 4 p. 55 (Je '60). Holiday 16: inside back cover (col.) Jl '54; 18: 24 Jl '55; 24: 106 (col.) Sept '58; 25: 15 (col.) Je '59; 26: 102 (col.) Nov '59; 27: 171 (col.) Je '60; 28: 10 (col.) Aug '60.

—— (at Crow's distillery). Holiday 16: 24 (col.) Nov '54.

—— (statue). Holiday 28: 67 Jl '60.

Webster, Sir Geoffrey (miniature). Con. 142: IV Dec '58.

Webster, George (work of). Con. 143: XXXI Ap '59.

Webster, Harold T. Cur. biog. p. 661 (1945).

Webster, Margaret. Cur. biog. p. 605 (1950).

Webster, Noah. Holiday 6: 90 Sept '49.

Webster, Thomas (work of). Con. 135: XXXIII Mar '55.

Webster, William. Cur. biog. p. 607 (1950).

Webster home, Daniel. Amer. heri., vol. 9 no. 1 p. 122 (Dec '57). Natl. geog. 99: 126 (col.) Jan '51.

Wechsberg, Joseph. Cur. biog. p. 639 (1955).

Wecter, Dixon. Amer. heri., vol. 8 no. 5 p. 24 (Aug '57). Cur. biog. p. 723 (1944).

Wedderburn, Mrs. James (portrait by Raeburn). Con. 138: LXII Nov '56; 142: L Sept '58.

wedding (sym.). Lehner: Pict. bk. of sym., p. 56.

——, Chiappini (Cape Town, Africa). Travel 113: 30 Jan '60.

——, Grover Cleveland's. Jensen: The White House, p. 136.

——, Hindu. See Hindu wedding.

——, Lapland. Disney: People & places, p. 23 (col.).

——, Malay. Natl. geog. 99: 20 Jan '51.

——, Nellie Grant's. Jensen: The White House, p. 109.

——, Russian. Holiday 23: 73 May '58.

——, Scotch. Disney: People & places, p. 26 (col.).

——, Sumatra. Natl. geog. 99: 20 Jan '51.

——, Teton Mt. (church). Holiday 10: 35 (col.) Aug '51.

——, Tom Thumb's. Amer. heri., vol. 9 no. 3 p. 54 (col.) (Ap '58).

——, Velarde. Natl. geog. 107: 369 (col.) Mar '55.

wedding banquet (Norway). Natl. geog. 111: 118 (col.) Jan '57.

wedding cake. Con. 139: XXXIII Ap '57.

—— (bride & groom, Poland). Natl. geog. 114: 398 (col.) Sept '58.

—— (sym.). Lehner: Pict. bk. of sym., p. 56.

wedding celebration (Nepal). Natl. geog. 117: 362 (col.) Mar '60.

wedding noise maker. See noise maker (wedding serenade).

"Wedding of St. George & Princess Sabra." Praeg.: Pict. ency., p. 399.

wedding party (Bhutan). Natl. geog. 102: 745-52 (col.) Dec '52.

wedding procession (Egypt). Amer. heri., vol. 11 no. 3 p. 27 (col.) (Ap '60).

"Wedding scenes" (Bruegel, Belgium). Natl. geog. 113: 806-7 (col.) Je '58.

wedding supper (France). Holiday 25: 87 (col.) Jan '59.

wedding. See also bride & groom.

Wedemeyer, Lt. Gen. Albert C. Cur. biog. p. 664 (1945).

Wedgewood, Cicely V. Cur. biog. p. 581 (1957).

Wedgewood, Sir John. Holiday 23: 71 (col.) Ap '58.

Wedgewood, Josiah. Con. 129: 133 Je '52.

Wedgewood, Baron Josiah. Cur. biog. p. 872 (1942).

Wedgewood jasper plaque. Con. 135: 255 Je '55.

Wedgewood portrait medallion. Con. 129: 133-8 Je '52.

Wedgewood teapot. Con. 132: 205 Jan '54.

Wedgewood vase. Con. 132: 149, 182-3 Jan '54.

Wedgewood ware. Con. 129: 146 Je '52.

Wednesday (sym.). Lehner: Pict. bk. of sym., p. 25.

Weede, Robert. Cur. biog. p. 583 (1957).

Weeks, Edward, jr. Cur. biog. p. 671 (1947).

Weeks, Sinclair. Cur. biog. p. 647 (1953).

Weenix, Jan (work of). Con. 143: cover (col.) May '59.

"Weeping wall" (Glacier natl. park). Travel 113: cover (col.) May '60.

Wegner, Msgr. Nicholas H. Cur. biog. p. 626 (1949).

Wei Tao-Ming. Cur. biog. p. 874 (1942).

Weidlein, Edward R. Cur. biog. p. 662 (1948).

Weidman, Charles. Cur. biog. p. 398 (1942).

Weidman, Jerome. Cur. biog. p. 876 (1942). Holiday 18: 58 Oct '55; 23: 8 May '58.

Weigel, Erhard (Muttoni). Con. 144: 106 Nov '59.

Weigle, Luther Allan. Cur. biog. p. 633 (1946).

Weigle, Richard O. Holiday 23: 80 Je '58.

Weil, Frank L. Cur. biog. p. 628 (1949).

Weil, Lisl. Cur. biog. p. 463 (1953).

Weil, Richard, jr. Cur. biog. p. 650 (1951).

Weill, Kurt. Cur. biog. p. 905 (1941).

Weir, Ernest T. Cur. biog. p. 908 (1941).

Weis, Mrs. Charles W., jr. Cur. biog. p. 477 (1959).

Weisgard, Leonard. Jun. bk. of auth., p. 293.

Weizmann, Chaim. Cur. biog. p. 878 (1942); p. 664 (1948).

Welch, Joseph N. Cur. biog. p. 639 (1954).

Welch, Leo D. Cur. biog. (1963).

Welch, Rufus. Durant: Pict. hist. of Amer. circus, p. 26.

Welch, Dr. William H. Amer. heri., vol. 8 no. 6 p. 10 (Oct '57).

"The welcome arrival" (Wright). Con. 138: XXVIII Nov '56.

welcome cup, silver (Norwegian, 17th cent.). Con. 145: 12 Mar '60.

"Welcome home" (posters at ship landing). Natl. geog. 118: 613 Nov '60.

Welitsch, Ljuba. Cur. biog. p. 629 (1949).

Welk, Lawrence. Cur. biog. p. 585 (1957).

Welker, Herman. Cur. biog. p. 641 (1955).

well (flower pictures). Natl. geog. 98: 190 (col.) Aug '50.

—— **(in palace yard).** Osward: Asia Minor, pl. 98.

—— **(well sweep).** Natl. geog. 112: 309 (col.) Sept '57.

——, **Iranian roadside.** Natl. geog. 100: 462 (col.) Oct '51.

——, **Jacob's.** See Jacob's well.

——, **kitchen.** Rawson: Ant. pict. bk., p. 47.

——, **wishing.** See wishing well.

well curbs. Rawson: Ant. pict. bk., p. 48-9.

well drum & bucket. Rawson: Ant. pict. bk., p. 49.

well head, Istrian stone. Con. 144: XXVII Jan '60.

——, **Italian.** Labande: Naples, p. 117.

well pump. See pump, well.

well shafts (Sahara). Natl. geog. 113: 697 (col.) May '58.

well stone. Rawson: Ant. pict. bk., p. 49.

well sweep. Rawson: Ant. pict. bk., p. 48.

Welland canal. Travel 106: 22 Nov '56; 109: 54-7 Mar '58.

Weller, Thomas H. Cur. biog. p. 184 (1955).

Welles, Gideon. Amer. heri., vol. 11 no. 6 p. 46 (Oct '60).

Welles, Orson. Cur. biog. p. 910 (1941).

Wellington, Duke of. See "Queen Victoria & Duke of Wellington."

Wellington harbor (New Zealand). Natl. geog. 101: 446 Ap '52.

Wellman, Frederick C. Cur. biog. p. 725 (1944).

Wellman, Manly Wade. Cur. biog. p. 643 (1955).

Wellman, Paul. Cur. biog. p. 631 (1949).

Wellman, William A. Cur. biog. p. 610 (1950).

Wells, Agnes. Cur. biog. p. 633 (1949).

Wells, Peter. Cur. biog. p. 881 (1942).

wells. Rawson: Ant. pict. bk., p. 48-9.

Wells cathedral (ext. & int.). Praeg.: Pict. ency., p. 202.

Welman, Joseph C. Cur. biog. p. 464 (1958).

Welsh, Matthew E. Cur. biog. p. 455 (1962).

Welsh family. Holiday 21: 136 (col.) Ap '57.

Welsh women. Natl. geog. 108: 566 Oct '55.

Welshman (dog, man & woman). Holiday 18: 10 (col.) Sept '55.

Welty, Eudora. Cur. biog. p. 882 (1942).

Wenner-Gren, Axel. Cur. biog. p. 883 (1942).

Wente, Carl F. Cur. biog. p. 640 (1954).

"Wentworth" (Coolidge house, N.H.). Travel 113: 22 Mar '60.

Werner, Max. Cur. biog. p. 811 (1943).

Werner, Theodore. Cur. biog. p. 466 (1958).

Wertenbaker, Charles. Holiday 6: 32 Sept '49.

Werth, Alexander. Cur. biog. p. 813 (1943).

Wertham, Fredric. Cur. biog. p. 634 (1949).

Wertmuller, Adolf Ulric (work of). Con. 141: 50 Mar '58.

Wesker, Arnold. Cur. biog. p. 457 (1962).

"weskit." See vest, man's.

Wessex (Eng.). Holiday 14: 55 Nov '53.

West, Dean Andrew F. Amer. heri., vol. 7 no. 5 p. 26 (Aug '56).

West, Benjamin (work of). Amer. heri., vol. 6 no. 2 p. 40-1 (part col.) (winter '55); vol. 10 no. 1 p. 16 (col.) (Dec '58); vol. 11 no. 1 p. 30-1 (col.) (Dec '59); vol. 11 no. 4 cover (col.) (Je '60).
Con. 135: 8 Mar '55, 223 Je '55; 141: 60 Mar '58; 144: 56 Sept '59.
Natl. geog. 99: 182 (col.) Feb '51.

West, Don. Holiday 10: 93 Aug '51.

West, Keith. Cur. biog. p. 673 (1947).

West, Levon. Cur. biog. p. 667 (1948).

West, W. Richard (work of). Natl. geog. 107: 358 (col.) Mar '55.

West, William E. (work of). Amer. heri., vol. 5 no. 3 p. 27 (spring '54).

West Indies. Holiday 5: 34-63 (part col.) Feb '49, 98-121 (col.) Mar '49.
—— (map). Amer. heri., vol. 6 no. 4 p. 98 (Je '55).
Travel 104: 62 Sept '55.
West Indies, fort in (map). *See* map (Fort in West Indies).
West Indies dancer & musician. Holiday 13: 18 Jan '53.
West Indies drummer. Holiday 18: 182 Dec '55; 19: 119 Jan '56.
West Indies regimental band. Holland 5: 44 (col.) Feb '49.
West Indies woman (comic). Holiday 5: cover (col.) Feb '49.
——, French. Travel 109: 27 May '58.
West Indies women (on donkey). Holiday 5: 34 (col.), 88 Feb '49.
West Point (1817-28). Amer. heri., vol. 7 no. 1 p. 22, 26 (col.) (Dec '55).
West Point cadet. Amer. heri., vol. 3 no. 4 p. 46 (summer '52).
West Point cadets. Holiday 28: 57 Sept '60.
Natl. geog. 101: 599-626 (part col.) May '52.
—— (girls). Natl. geog. 110: 581 (col.) Nov '56.
West Point dance (1859). Amer. heri., vol. 9 no. 2 p. 34 (Feb '58).
West Point harbor (1861). Amer. heri., vol. 9 no. 2 p. 33 (col.) (Feb '58).
West Point military academy. Amer. heri., vol. 2 no. 2 p. 68 (winter '51).
Holiday 6: 50-55 (part col.) Sept '49; 28: 57 Sept '60.
Natl. geog. 101: 598-626 (part col.) May '52.
West Virginia. Holiday 14: 98-9, 102-3 (col.) Oct '54; 27: 10 (col.) May '60.
Travel 101: 13-6 Mar '54.
—— (Harpers Ferry). Face of Amer., p. 124-5 (col.).
—— (map). Natl. geog. 97: 181 Feb '50.
—— (state parks). Travel 110: 47-9 Oct '58.
Westall, William (work of). Con. 144: 191 Dec '59.
Westbury hotel (1st Amer. built in London). Travel 103: 45 Mar '55.
western art (Indian scenes). Amer. heri., vol. 6 no. 1 p. 32-40 (col.) (Dec '54).
western lawman. *See* lawman, western.
western prospector (pack mule). Holiday 6: 89 (col.) Jl '49, inside back cover (col.) Aug '49.
Westland (Holland). Natl. geog. 98: 768 (col.) Dec '50.
Westminster Abbey (London). Travel 107: 27 Je '57.
—— (chapel). Holiday 24: 116 (col.) Nov '58.
—— (coronation, int.). Natl. geog. 104: 327 Sept '53.
Westminster bridge (18th cent.). Con. 142: XLI Jan '59.
Westminster Hall. Natl. geog. 103: 813 (col.) Je '53.
Westminster kennel club dog show (N.Y.). Natl. geog. 105: 93-115 (part col.) Jan '54.

Westminster palace (Eng.). Holiday 17: 56-61 (col.) Mar '55.
—— (night). Natl. geog. 114: 47 (col.) Jl '58.
Westmore, Perc. Cur. biog. p. 667 (1945).
Westmorland, Maj. Gen. William Childs. Cur. biog. p. 477 (1961).
"Weston sands" (by Havell). Con. ency. of ant., vol. 1, pl. 173.
"Westover" (home of Wm. Byrd II, Va.). Holiday 9: 94 Mar '51.
Natl. geog. 103: 788 Je '53.
Westphalian tower (Soest, Ger.). Holiday 15: 128 Mar '54.
Westmore, Alexander. Cur. biog. p. 669 (1948).
Wetter, Ernst. Cur. biog. p. 885 (1942).
Wewah Island man (head). Int. gr. soc.: Arts . . . p. 183 (col.).
Weyler, Valerino "Butcher." Amer. heri., vol. 8 no. 2 p. 39 (Feb '57).
"Weymouth Bay" (Constable). Praeg.: Pict. ency., p. 387 (col.).
whale (sym.). Lehner: Pict. bk. of sym., p. 59.
"Whale capture" (Garneray). Amer. heri., vol. 12 no. 1 p. 48-9 (col.) (Dec '60).
whale fishermen. Natl. geog. 100: 624-5 (col.) Nov '51.
whale weathervane (antique). Holiday 18: 61 (col.) Jl '55.
whaleboat. Natl. geog. 102: 809 Dec '52.
—— (launching). Natl. geog. 97: 83 (col.) Jan '50.
whaleboat captains (Civil war). Amer. heri., vol. 12 no. 1 p. 53 (Dec '60).
whalebone arch memorial (Falkland). Natl. geog. 109: 391 (col.) Mar '56.
Whalen, Grover A. Cur. biog. p. 728 (1944).
whaler ship. Amer. heri., vol. 8 no. 1 p. 87 (Dec '56).
Holiday 26: 35 (col.) Sept '59.
Natl. geog. 98: 150 (col.) Aug '50.
—— (last of Amer. built). Amer. heri., vol. 3 no. 4 p. 55 (summer '52).
whales bone relief "Adoration of the Magi." Con. 133: 156 May '54.
"Whaling voyage panorama." Amer. heri., vol. 12 no. 1 p. 55-62 (col.) (Dec '60).
wharf. Praeg.: Pict. ency., p. 474 (col.).
—— (Italy). Travel 101: 11 Je '54.
—— (men & women). Holiday 23: 2 (col.) Mar '58.
Wharton, Clifton R. Cur. biog. p. 467 (1958).
"What a catch"! (by Clonney). Amer. heri., vol. 9 no. 4 back cover (col.) (Je '58).
wheat (sym.). *See* sheaf of wheat.
wheat bin (Canada). Natl. geog. 108: 208 (col.) Aug '55.
wheat grinding (ancient life). Natl. geog. 112: 837 (col.) Dec '57.
"Wheatland" (home of James Buchanan). Amer. heri., vol. 5 no. 3 p. 44-49 (part col.) (spring '54).
Wheatley, Francis (work of). Con. 129: XIII Je '52; 142: 42 Sept '58, 195 Dec '58; 143: XXXVII May '59.
Wheaton, Anne. Cur. biog. p. 469 (1958).
Wheaton, Elizabeth Lee. Cur. biog. p. 887 (1942).

wheel (being retired). Natl. geog. 107: 6 Jan '55.

——, bicycle. *See* bicycle wheel.

——, boat steering. Travel 103: 39 May '55.

——, boat stern. Natl. geog. 97: 210 (col.) Feb '50.

——, cart. Labande: Naples, p. 11.

——, circus wagon. Durant: Pict. hist. of Amer. circus, p. 162-3.

——, hoisting. Holiday 11: 93 Jan '52.

——, mill. Travel 102: inside cover Dec '54.

——, St. Catherine's. *See* St. Catherine's wheel (sym.).

——, ship. Natl. geog. 100: 473 (col.) Oct '51; 108: 70, 81 (col.) Jl '55.

——, ship steering. *See* ship steering wheel.

——, solid wagon. Rawson: Ant. pict. bk., p. 70.

——, steel. Natl. geog. 98: 234 Aug '50.

——, steering (navigation). Lehner: Pict. bk. of sym., p. 15.

——, steering (steam yacht). Natl. geog. 113: 17 (col.) Jan '58.

——, stern paddle. Brooks: Growth of a nation, p. 248.

——, tire measuring. *See* tire measuring wheel.

——, wagon. Brooks: Growth of a nation, p. 118, 233.
Holiday 28: 62 Jl '60.
Natl. geog. 112: 188 (col.) Aug. '57; 115: 766 (col.) Je '59.
Travel 102: 12 Sept '54; 108: 29-30 Aug '57.

——, wagon (man repairing). Natl. geog. 112: 309 (col.) Sept '57.

——, wagon (Sicily, man painting). Natl. geog. 107: 14 (col.) Jan '55.

——, wagon (sym.). Lehner: Pict. bk. of sym., p. 63.

——, water. *See* water wheel.

——, winged. *See* winged wheel of Hermes (sym.).

wheel brake. Rawson: Ant. pict. bk., p. 74.

wheel chair, Pres. F. D. Roosevelt's. Holiday 6: 42 (col.) Sept '49.

wheel cross (sym.). Lehner: Pict. bk. of sym., p. 28.

wheel dancing, Croatian. Natl. geog. 115: 210-11 (col.) Feb '59.

wheel jack. Rawson: Ant. pict. bk., p. 53.

Wheel of fortune (sym.). Lehner: Pict. bk. of sym., p. 76.

"Wheel of good law" (Japanese sym.). Lehner: Pict. bk. of sym., p. 47.

"Wheel of good law" (Tibetan) (sym.). Lehner: Pict. bk. of sym., p. 42.

wheelbarrow. Natl. geog. 110: 553 (col.) Oct '56; 115: 286 Feb '59.

—— (flowers, glass). Holiday 10: 113 (col.) Oct '51.

—— (man, 1890). Holiday 12: 68 Sept '52.

—— (Pitcairn island). Natl. geog. 112: 743 (col.) Dec '57.

wheelbarrow race (girls). Natl. geog. 109: 401 (col.) Mar '56.

Wheeler, Henry M. Horan: Pict. hist. of wild west, p. 38.

Wheeler, Joseph. Amer. heri., vol. 9 no. 2 p. 31 (Feb '58).
Pakula: Cent. album, p. 287.

Wheeler, Mortimer. Cur. biog. p. 648 (1956).

Wheeler, Post. Cur. biog. p. 514 (1956).

Wheeler, Lt. Gen. Raymond A. Cur. biog. p. 587 (1957).

Wheeler, William A. Amer. heri., vol. 11 no. 6. p. 4 (Oct '60).

wheels, cart. Natl. geog. 99: 114 Jan '51.
Travel 111: 44 May '59.

——, wagon. Natl. geog. 101: 304 (col.) Mar '52.

Wheelwright, Jere. Cur. biog. p. 628 (1952).

wheelwrights. Natl. geog. 115: 766 (col.) Je '59.

Wherry, Kenneth S. Cur. biog. p. 635 (1946).

Whicher, George F. Natl. geog. 97: 303 (col.) Mar '50.

Whig ribbon (approved Henry Clay, 1844). Amer. heri., vol. 7 no. 4 p. 22 (col.) (Je '56).

Whipple, Fred Lawrence. Cur. biog. p. 629 (1952).

Whipple, Maurine. Cur. biog. p. 913 (1941).

whirligig (sym.). Lehner: Pict. bk. of sym., p. 58.

whisk broom (children). Natl. geog. 115: 814 (col.) Je '59.

whiskey barrel. Rawson: Ant. pict. bk., p. 61.

Whistler, James Macneill (etching). Praeg.: Pict. ency., p. 435.

Whitaker, Douglas. Cur. biog. p. 651 (1951).

Whitcomb, Richard T. Cur. biog. p. 651 (1956).

Whitcombe, Thomas (work of). Amer. heri., vol. 9 no. 4 p. 6-7 (col.) (Je '58).
Con. 145: XXXV Je '60.

White, Alexander M. Cur. biog. p. 653 (1951).

White, Byron R. Cur. biog. p. 459 (1962).

White, Charles M. Cur. biog. p. 611 (1950).

White, Eliza Orne. Jun. bk. of auth., p. 295.

White, Elwyn Brooks. Cur. biog. p. 454 (1960).

White, Francis W. Cur. biog. p. 642 (1954).

White, Frank. Cur. biog. p. 613 (1950).

White, Gilbert F. Cur. biog. p. 650 (1953).

White, Harry D. Cur. biog. p. 731 (1944).

White, Helen C. Cur. biog. p. 669 (1945).

White, Hugh L. Cur. biog. p. 645 (1955).

White, Gen. Isaac D. Cur. biog. p. 470 (1958).

White, John (work of). Amer. heri., vol. 7 no. 6 p. 10 (col.) (Oct '56); Vol. 10 no. 1 p. 62 (col.) (Dec '58); vol. 10 no. 4 p. 14-5 (col.) (Je '59).

White, John Blake (work of). Amer. heri., vol. 9 no. 3 p. 40 (col.) (Ap '58).

White, John R. Cur. biog. p. 652 (1956).

White, Josh. Cur. biog. p. 735 (1944).

White, Nelia Gardner. Cur. biog. p. 614 (1950).

White, Paul Dudley. Cur. biog. p. 646 (1955).

White, Portia. Cur. biog. p. 671 (1945).

White, Robb. Jun. bk. of auth., p. 296.

White, Maj. Robert M. Holiday 27: 87 (col.) Mar '60.

White, Robert M., 2d. Cur. biog. p. 456 (1960).

White, Lt. S. A. Natl. geog. 115: 7 (col.) Jan '59.

White, Theodore H. Cur. biog. p. 649 (1955).

White, Gen. Thomas D. Cur. biog. p. 589 (1957).

White, Wallace H., jr. Cur. biog. p. 671 (1948).

White, Walter. Cur. biog. p. 889 (1942).
White, William. Cur. biog. p. 651 (1953).
White, William L. Cur. biog. p. 817 (1943).
White, William S. Cur. biog. p. 651 (1955).
White, William Wilson. Cur. biog. p. 481 (1959).
"The White boy" (Van Dyck). Con. 136: 105 Nov '55.
White Bull, Chief. Amer. heri., vol. 8 no. 2 p. 8 (Feb '57).
"White Bull's fight with Gen. Custer". Amer. heri., vol. 8 no. 2 p. 4-7 (col.) (Feb '57).
"White Hall" (home of Cassius Clay). Amer. heri., vol. 11 no. 4 p. 35 (col.) (Je '60).
"The White horse" (Gauguin). Praeg.: Pict. ency., p. 438 (col.).
"White Horse Inn" (Austria). Natl. geog. 118: 252-3 (col.) Aug '60.
White horse school (Vienna). Natl. geog. 114: 400, 402-19 (part col.) Sept '58.
"The White House" (Wash., D.C.). Amer. heri., vol. 2 no. 1 p. 23, 25 (fall '50) vol. 9 no. 4 p. 107 (Je '58).
Brooks: Growth of a nation, p. 257.
Holiday 7: 36, 56-7 (part col.) Feb '50, 2 (col.) Ap '50; 21: 117 (col.) Ap '57; 25: 63 (col.) Je '59.
Jensen: The White House.
Natl. geog. 117: 649 (col.) May '60.
—— (burned). Amer. heri., vol. 6 no. 1 p. 53 (fall '54).
—— (changes in). Holiday 12: 48-53 (part col.) Nov '52.
—— (family quarters, 2nd floor). Jensen: The White House, p. 296.
—— (Hoban's plan). Jensen: The White House, p. 6-8.
—— (Jefferson's design). Jensen: The White House, p. 5, 12, 14.
—— (Latrobe drawing). See White House (Jefferson design).
—— (Thornton plan). Jensen: The White House, p. 5.
The White House, Confederate. See Confederate White House.
"The White House, Hampstead" (Constable). Con. 144: 35 Sept '59.
White House, The Little. See Little White House.
White House, vacation (Key West naval base). Holiday 6: 125 Dec '49.
"White Monk" (Wilson). Con. 129: XV Ap '52.
White Plains, (N.Y.). Holiday 8: 117 (col.) Dec '50.
White sands natl. monument. Holiday 11: 44 Feb '52.
Natl. geog. 112: 118-36 (part col.) Jl '57.
"White sox" baseball players (1917). Amer. heri., vol. 11 no. 4 p. 25 (Je '60).
White Sulphur Springs (W.Va., hotel). Holiday 25: 165 May '59, 129 (col.) Je '59.
"White Turbe" mausoleum (Silifke). Osward: Asia Minor, pl. 122.
"White wings" (cart, broom, shovel). Holiday 12: 69 Sept '52.
Whitefield, George. Amer. heri., vol. 7 no. 1 p. 55 (Dec '55).
"Whitehall" (Eng.). Con. 140: 262 Jan '58.
Whitehead, Don. Cur. biog. p. 654 (1953).

Whitehill, Walter Muir. Cur. biog. p. 458 (1960).
Whitelands house (Chelsea, Eng.). Con. 143: 74 Ap '59.
Whiteman, Paul. Cur. biog. p. 672 (1945).
White's home, Capt. Joseph. Amer. heri., vol. 11 no. 4 p. 103 (Je '60).
White's horse, Joel (funeral procession). Amer. heri., vol. 10 no. 1 p. 96 (Dec '58).
Whitman, Marcus. Amer. heri., vol. 10 no. 5 p. 42 (Aug '59).
—— (murdered by Indians). Amer. heri., vol. 10 no. 5 p. 87 (Aug '59).
—— (statue). Brooks: Growth of a nation, p. 122.
Whitman, Narcissa. Amer. heri., vol. 10 no. 5 p. 42 (Aug '59).
Whitman, Walt. Amer. heri., vol. 8 no. 6 p. 63 (Oct '57).
Whitman, Walter G. Cur. biog. p. 631 (1952).
Whitney, Alexander F. Cur. biog. p. 638 (1946).
Whitney, Chauncey B. Horan: Pict. hist. of wild west, p. 104.
Whitney, Maj. Gen. Courtney. Cur. biog. p. 655 (1951).
Whitney, Eli. Amer. heri., vol. 6 no. 3 p. 8 (col.) (Ap '55).
Whitney, Elinor. Jun. bk. of auth., p. 297.
Whitney, Gertrude. Cur. biog. p. 915 (1941).
Whitney, Col. John Hay. Cur. biog. p. 675 (1945).
Whitney, Phyllis A. Cur. biog. p. 674 (1948). Jun. bk. of auth., p. 298.
Whitney, Richard. Amer. heri., vol. 9 no. 5 p. 32 (Aug '58).
Whitney firearms, Eli. Amer. heri., vol. 6 no. 3 p. 11 (Ap '55).
Whittaker, Charles Evans. Cur. biog. p. 591 (1957).
Whittemore, Arthur. Cur. biog. p. 643 (1954).
Whittier, John Greenleaf. Natl. geog. 97: 288 (col.) Mar '50.
Whittle, Air Commodore Frank. Cur. biog. p. 678 (1945).
Whittle, William. Amer. heri., vol. 10 no. 1 p. 51 (Dec '58).
Whitton, Charlotte. Cur. biog. p. 655 (1953).
Whitton, Rex M. Cur. biog. p. 461 (1962).
Whitty, Dame May. Cur. biog. p. 679 (1945).
whorl ornament. Con. ency. of ant., vol. 1, p. 24.
Whyte, William H., jr. Cur. biog. p. 482 (1959).
Wichita (Kan., old west, 1873). Horan: Pict. hist. of wild west, p. 100.
Wichita Mts. Natl. geog. 111: 662-6 (col.) May '57.
—— (map). Natl. geog. 111: 666 May '57.
Wickenberg, Peter Gabriel (work of). Con. 144: 32 Sept '59.
Wickenden, Dan. Cur. biog. p. 657 (1951.)
Wickens, Aryness Joy. Cur. biog. p. 463 (1962).
Wicker, Ireene. Cur. biog. p. 819 (1943).
Widecombe Fair (Eng.). Natl. geog. 108: 332 (col.) Sept '55.
Widmark, Richard. Cur. biog. (1963).
Widow's walk (on Colonial home). Travel 108: inside back cover Aug '57.
Wiener, Alexander S. Cur. biog. p. 674 (1947).
Wiener, Norbert. Cur. biog. p. 616 (1950).
wiener shop. Natl. geog. 99: 767 (col.) Je '51.

Wies, church of. *See* church of Wies.
Wiese, Kurt. Jun. bk. of auth., p. 299.
Wiesner, Jerome B. Cur. biog. p. 478 (1961).
wig (man 1700's). Natl. geog. 113: 262 (col.) Feb '58.
wig curling iron. Rawson: Ant. pict. bk., p. 11.
wig shop, Colonial. Holiday 18: 176 Nov '55.
Wiggam, Albert Edward. Cur. biog. p. 891 (1942).
Wiggin, Albert. Amer. heri., vol. 9 no. 5 p. 33 (Aug '58).
Wigglesworth, Richard B., jr. Cur. biog. p. 484 (1959).
wigmaker, Colonial. Natl. geog. 106: 449, 474 (col.) Oct '54.
wigmaker's shop (Williamsburg, Va.). Holiday 21: 130 Feb '57; 23: 153 Feb '58.
Wignacourt, Alof de (by Caravaggio). Con. 142: 143 Dec '58.
Wigner, Eugene P. Cur. biog. p. 658 (1953).
Wigny, Pierre. Cur. biog. p. 460 (1960).
Wigstrom, Henrik (carvings by). Con. 145: 55 Mar '60.
wigwam, (Eng.). Brooks: growth of a nation, p. 46.
——, Indian. Amer. heri., vol. 7 no. 6 p. 107 (Oct '56); vol. 10 no. 5 p. 45 (Aug '59).
Wilberforce, William. Con. 144: 9 Sept '59.
Wilbur, Lt. Col. Bernice M. Cur. biog. p. 821 (1943).
Wilbur, Ray Lyman. Cur. biog. p. 676 (1947).
Wilby, Maj. Gen. Francis B. Cur. biog. p. 683 (1945).
Wilcox, Clair. Cur. biog. p. 675 (1948).
Wilcox, Francis O. Cur. biog. p. 465 (1962).
Wilcox, Herbert. Cur. biog. p. 425 (1945).
Wild, Earl. Holiday 21: 42 Mar '57.
Wild, John Casper (lithography by). Amer. heri., vol. 2 no. 1 p. 49 (fall '50).
Wilde, Frazar B. Cur. biog. p. 486 (1959).
Wilde, Capt. Louise K. Cur. biog. p. 645 (1954).
Wilder, Billy. Cur. biog. p. 658 (1951). Holiday 5: 42 (col.) Jan '49.
Wilder, Frances Farmer. Cur. biog. p. 679 (1947).
Wilder, Laura Ingalls. Cur. biog. p. 677 (1948). Jun. bk. of auth., p. 300.
Wilder, Maj. Thornton. Cur. biog. p. 822 (1943). Holiday 15: 74 Jan '54.
Wildlife project (Texas gulf coast). Travel 110: 48 Sept '58.
wildlife refuge, Natl. (swans). Natl. geog. 118: 136-50 (part col.) (Jl '60).
Wiley, Alexander. Cur. biog. p. 680 (1947).
Wilgress, Dana. Cur. biog. p. 647 (1954).
Wilhelm II, Kaiser of Ger. Amer. heri., vol. 6 no. 1 p. 46 (fall '54).
Wilkes, John. Amer. heri., vol. 11 no. 4 p. 99 (Je '60).
Wilkie, Sir David. Con. 142: 121 Nov '58.
—— (work by). Con. ency., of ant., vol. 1, pl. 135, 172. Con. 142: 121 Nov '58.
Wilkins, Maurice H. Cur. biog. (1963).
Wilkins, Sir. Hubert. Cur. biog. p. 593 (1957).
Wilkins, J. Ernest. Cur. biog. p. 649 (1954).
Wilkins, Robert W. Cur. biog. p. 472 (1958).
Wilkins, Roy. Cur. biog. p. 617 (1950).

Wilkinson, Charles. Cur. biog. p. 467 (1962).
Wilkinson, Ellen. Cur. biog. p. 917 (1941).
Will Rogers' memorial (Claremore, Okla). Jordan: Hammond's pict. atlas, p. 112 (col.).
Will Rogers' shrine. Holiday: 21: 98 Nov '57; 23: 104 May '58.
Willamette river. Natl. geog. 102: 575 Nov '52.
Wille, Pierre Alexandre (work of). Con. 145: 269 Je '60.
Willet, Henry Lee. Cur. biog. p. 682 (1947).
William III, King (Lely). Con. 126: 65 Aug '50.
William III as a child (Johnson). Con. 126: 65 Aug '50.
William & Mary college. Natl. geog. 106: 479, 482-6 (col.) Oct '54.
"William Penn's treaty with Indians" (West). *See* "Penn's treaty with Indians."
William Todd's apple (sym.). Lehner: Pict. bk. of sym., p. 84.
Williams, Alpheus Starkey. Pakula: Cent. album, p. 289.
Williams, Andy. Cur. biog. p. 461 (1960).
Williams, Camilla. Cur. biog. p. 633 (1952).
Williams, Clyde E. Cur. biog. p. 683 (1947).
Williams, Dr. Daniel Hale. Travel 106: inside back cover Jl '56.
Williams, E. C. (work of). Con. 143: XLVIII Ap '59.
Williams, Emlyn. Cur. biog. p. 919 (1941); p. 635 (1952).
Williams, Esther. Cur. biog. p. 652 (1955).
Williams, Francis. Cur. biog. p. 641 (1946).
Williams, G. Mennen. Cur. biog. p. 467 (1963).
Williams, George H. Amer. heri., vol. 8 no. 3 p. 52 (Ap '57).
Williams, Gerhard Mennen. Cur. biog. p. 637 (1949).
Williams, Gluyas. Cur. biog. p. 643 (1946).
Williams, Harrison A., jr. Cur. biog. p. 463 (1960).
Williams, Jay. Cur. biog. p. 654 (1955).
Williams, John, Arch. Bishop of York. Con. 139: 218 Je '57.
Williams, John H. Cur. biog. p. 465 (1960); p. 638 (1952).
Williams, Paul R. Cur. biog. p. 921 (1941).
Williams, Robert R. Cur. biog. p. 660 (1951).
Williams, Roger. Amer. heri., vol. 7 no. 4 p. 35 (Je '56). Holiday 25: 141 May '59.
—— (statue). Brooks: Growth of a nation, p. 51. Holiday 11: 110 (col.) May '52.
Williams, Roger J. Cur. biog. p. 595 (1957).
Williams, Ted. Cur. biog. p. 686 (1947).
Williams, Tennessee. Cur. biog. p. 645 (1946).
Williams, Thomas. Amer. heri., vol. 11 no. 1 p. 61 (Dec '59).
Williams, Tom. Cur. biog. p. 647 (1946).
Williams, W. Walter. Cur. biog. p. 678 (1948).
Williams, William Carlos. Holiday 16: 54 Nov '54.
Williams, Wythe. Cur. biog. p. 825 (1943).
Williams college (Chapin Hall). Holiday 28: 26 Sept '60.
—— (class room). Natl. geog. 99: 585 May '51.
Williams' statue, Roger. *See* Williams', Roger (statue).

Williamsburg (Va.). Amer. heri., vol. 1 no. 2 p. 34-41 (part col.) (winter '50).
Brooks: Growth of a nation, p. 64-5.
Holiday 19: 173 Mar '56, 159 May '56; 20: 148 Nov '56; 21: 176 Mar '57, 164 May '57, 170 Je '57; 22: 128 Sept '57, 162 Nov '57; 23: 175 Mar '58, 186 Ap '58; 24: 126 Sept '58, 142 Oct '58, 164 Nov '58; 25: 158 Jan '59, 147 Feb '59, 179 Mar '59, 194 May '59, 188 Je '59; 26: 129 Sept '59, 97 Nov '59.
Natl. geog. 106: 440-86 (col.) Oct '54.
—— (air view). Natl. geog. 106: 446-7 (col.) Oct '54.
—— (capitol bldg.). Amer. heri., vol. 11 no. 2 p. 81 (Feb '60).
Jordan: Hammond's pict. atlas, p. 53 (col.).
—— (Colonial arch). Holiday 16: 44-5 (col.) Aug '54.
—— (Governor's palace). Amer. heri., vol. 5 no. 3 p. 22 (spring '54).
Holiday 8: 27 (col.) Sept '50; 13: 26 Je '53.
Jordan: Hammond's pict. atlas, p. 53 (col.).
—— (inn). Holiday 22: 18 Jl '57.
—— (1900-). Amer. heri., vol. 11 no. 2 p. 22-5 (Feb '60).
—— (party). Holiday 24: 189 Dec '58.
—— (Raleigh tavern). Holiday 13: 145 Je '53.
—— (Raleigh, int.). Holiday 27: 32 Mar '60.
—— (stocks). Holiday 26: 119 Aug '59.
—— (wigmaker's shop). See wigmaker's shop.
Willis, Frances E. Cur. biog. p. 650 (1954).
Willis, Paul S. Cur. biog. p. 662 (1951).
Willison, George F. Cur. biog. p. 648 (1946).
Williston, Samuel. Cur. biog. p. 652 (1954).
Wills, Royal Barry. Cur. biog. p. 655 (1954).
Willson, Mary Ann. Amer. heri., vol. 6 no. 2 p. 44 (winter '55).
—— (work of). Amer. heri., vol. 7 no. 1 p. 58-9 (col.) (Dec '55).
Willson, Meredith. Cur. biog. p. 473 (1958).
Wilmarth, Mrs. H. M. Amer. heri., vol. 12 no. 1 p. 16 (Dec '60).
Wilson, Angus. Cur. biog. p. 488 (1959).
Wilson, Benjamin (work of). Con. 135: 52 Mar '55; 143: 86 Ap '59.
Wilson, Carroll Louis. Cur. biog. p. 688 (1947).
Wilson, Charles E. Cur. biog. p. 923 (1941); p. 827 (1943); p. 621 (1950); p. 663 (1951).
Wilson, Colin. Cur. biog. (1963).
Wilson, Donald H. Cur. biog. p. 737 (1944).
Wilson, Donald R. Cur. biog. p. 639 (1952).
Wilson, Donald V. Cur. biog. p. 656 (1954).
Wilson, Dorothy Clarke. Cur. biog. p. 667 (1951).
Wilson, Edith Galt (Mrs. Woodrow Wilson). Jensen: The White House, p. 206.
Wilson, Edmund. Cur. biog. p. 685 (1945).
Wilson, Edward Foss. Cur. biog. p. 475 (1958).
Wilson, Eleanor. Jensen: The White House, p. 200.
Wilson, Eugene E. Cur. biog. p. 688 (1945).
Wilson, Frank J. Cur. biog. p. 650 (1946).
Wilson, Halsey W. Cur. biog. p. 925 (1941); p. 680 (1948); p. 657 (1954).
Wilson, Harold. Cur. biog. (1963).
Wilson, Henry. Amer. heri., vol. 8 no. 3 p. 52 (Ap '57).

Wilson, Gen. Sir Henry Maitland. Cur. biog. p. 831 (1943).
Wilson, Hugh. Cur. biog. p. 927 (1941).
Wilson, Irving W. Cur. biog. p. 641 (1952).
Wilson, J. F. Amer. heri., vol. 11 no. 1 p. 61 (Dec '59).
Wilson, James. Amer. heri., vol. 10 no. 1 p. 59 (col.) (Dec '58).
Wilson Harold. Cur. biog. p. 683 (1948).
Wilson, James Harrison. Pakula: Cent. album, p. 291.
Wilson, Jessie. Jensen: The White House, p. 200.
Wilson, Kid. Horan: Pict. hist. of wild west, p. 148.
Wilson, Leroy A. Cur. biog. p. 685 (1948).
Wilson, Logan. Cur. biog. p. 654 (1956).
Wilson, Margaret. Jensen: The White House, p. 200.
Wilson, Richard (by Mengs). Con. 139: 82 Ap '57.
—— (work of). Con. ency. of ant., vol. 1, pl. 133.
Con. 129: XV Ap '52; 137: XIX Je '56; 138: XII (col.) Jan '57; 139: 83, 85-6 Ap '57; 140: 114 Nov '57, XXVI Dec '57; 141: 178 May '58; 142: 80 Nov '58; 143: XLIX Je '59; 144: LI Jan '60; 145: 39 Mar '60.
Wilson, Rufus H. Cur. biog. p. 655 (1955).
Wilson, Sloan. Cur. biog. p. 489 (1959).
Wilson, Volney C. Cur. biog. p. 477 (1958).
Wilson, Woodrow. Amer. heri., vol. 7 no. 3 p. 33 (Ap '56); vol. 7 no. 4 p. 26 (Je '56); vol. 8 no. 4 p. 20 (col.), 25 (Je '57); vol. 9 no. 4 p. 65, 69 (Je '58).
Jensen: The White House, p. 200-4, 212-.
—— (in cap & gown). Amer. heri., vol. 7 no. 5 p. 25 (Aug '56).
—— (stamp). Holiday 27: 63 Je '60.
Wilson, Mrs. Woodrow. Jensen: The White House, p. 200.
Wilson family, Woodrow. Jensen: The White House, p. 200.
Wilt, Fred. Cur. biog. p. 643 (1952).
Wilton diptych. See diptych, Wilton.
Wiman, Dwight Deere. Cur. biog. p. 638 (1949).
Wimble. Rawson: Ant. pict. bk., p. 21.
Wimperis, E. M. (work of). Con. 143: XXVI Ap '59.
Winant, John G. Cur. biog. p. 929 (1941).
Winchell, Walter. Cur. biog. p. 833 (1943).
Winchester, Alice. Cur. biog. p. 659 (1954).
Winckelmann, Johann Joachim (portrait). Ceram: March of arch., p. 8.
wind (sym.). Lehner: Pict. bk of sym., p. 14.
wind cave (man & woman). Natl. geog. 113: 645 (col.) May '58.
wind-god temple. See Temple of Quetzalcoatl.
wind speed indicator. Holiday 21: 194 May '57; 24: 230 Dec '58.
wind tunnel. Natl. geog. 104: 763-78 (col.) Dec '53.
——(space pilot). Natl. geog. 118: 50-1 (col.) Jl '60.
"Wind way" (Tilden). Natl. geog. 107: 365 (col.) Mar '55.

"Windemere" (by Havell). Con. ency. of ant., vol. 1, pl. 144.

Windemere (Eng.). Natl. geog. 109: 512-3, 533 (col.) Ap '56.

Windemere, Lake. *See* Lake Windemere.

windjammer boat. Travel 103: 39 May '55.

windlass & wheel, well. Rawson: Ant. pict. bk., p. 48.

windmill. Amer. heri., vol. 6 no. 5 p. 17 (col.) (Aug '55); vol. 6 no. 6 p. 104 (Oct '55).
Con. 141: 122 Ap '58; 144: LXVI Dec '59; 145: LXXV (col.) May '60.
Holiday 11: 106 Feb '52; 13: 27 Feb '53; 14: 118 (col.) Jl '53, 89 Sept '53, 12 (col.) Oct '53; 20: 11 Aug '56; 21: 71, 147 Jan '57, 7, 43, 50 (col.) Mar '57, 147 (col.) Ap '57; 22: 123 (col.) Nov '57; 23: 115 Mar '58; 25: 203 Ap '59; 27: 162 Jan '60.
Jordan: Hammond's pict. atlas, p. 33 (col.).
Natl. geog. 97: 423 (col.) Ap '50; 98: 152 (col.) Aug '50, 331 (col.) Sept '50, 624 Nov '50; 101: 390 (col.) Mar '52; 102: 126 Jl '52; 108: 313 (col.) Sept '55; 111: 638-9 (col.) May '57.
Praeg.: Pict. ency., p. 344 (col.).
Travel 112: 30 Aug '59.

—— (silhouette). Holiday 26: 22 Jl '59.

—— (sym.). Lehner: Pict. bk. of sym., p. 59.

—— (200 yr. old). Holiday 10: 44 (col.) Aug '51.

——, Cretan. Natl. geog. 104: 702 (col.) Nov '53.

——, Nantucket. Travel 106: 36 Sept '56.

——, Portugal. Travel 110: 46 Sept '58.

windmill cup. *See* cup, windmill.

windmills. Natl. geog. 103: 353 Mar '53.

——, Greece. Natl. geog. 114: 751, 780 (col.) Dec '58.

window. Holiday 24: 67 (col.) Nov '58.

—— (girl head). Natl. geog. 112: 697 (col.) Nov '57.

—— (Quaker church). Holiday 18: 98 Oct '55.

—— (Russia). Natl. geog. 116: 734 (col.) Dec '59.

—— (swimming pool). Holiday 12: 39 (col.) Sept '52.

——, cathedral. Holiday 26: 159 (col.) Dec '59.

——, Chartres cathedral. *See* Chartres cathedral window.

——, Colonial. Natl. geog. 109: 463 (col.) Ap '56.

——, grill (Delhi). Travel 106: 14 Nov '56.

—— (Moslem "Romeo & Juliet"). Natl. geog. 104: 19 (col.) Jl '53.

—— (shutters, Greece). Natl. geog. 103: 365 (col.) Mar '53.

——, house (Argentina). Natl. geog. 113: 310 (col.) Mar '58.

——, house (1666). Holiday 18: 99 (col.) Sept '55.

——, military school (stained glass). Natl. geog. 98: 355 (col.) Sept '50.

——, Palladian. Natl. geog. 99: 585 May '51.

——, rose. *See* rose window.

——, stained glass. Holiday 15: 111 (col.) Mar '54; 18: 128-9 (col.) Dec '55; 23: 70 (col.) Mar '58.

Natl. geog. 110: 462 (col.) Oct '56; 111: 157 (col.) Feb '57.

——, stained glass (antique). Con. 134: 125 Nov '54.

——, stained glass (Augsburg cathedral). Praeg.: Pict. ency., p. 204 (col.).

——, stained glass (Canterbury). Con. 143: 41 Mar '59.

——, stained glass (cathedral of St. Stephen, Bourges, Fr.). Amer. heri., vol. 7 no. 1 p. 4 (col.) (Dec '55).

——, stained glass (Jesse tree motif). Con. 141: 78-82 Ap '58.

——, stained glass (Milan cathedral). Con. 142: 8 Sept '58.

——, stained glass (St. Germain-des-Pres). Con. 140: 33-7 Sept '57.

——, stained glass (16th cent.). Con. 134: 57 Sept '54.

——, stained glass (13th cent.). Natl. geog. 107: 196 (col.) Feb '55.

——, stained glass church. Natl. geog. 98: 196 (col.) Aug '50.

——, stained glass panels. Natl. geog. 107: 647 (col.) May '55.

window drapery. Holiday 10: 111 (col.) Nov '51.

—— (18th cent.). Natl. geog. 113: 259 (col.) Feb '58.

——, Colonial. Holiday 13: 53 (col.) Jan '53. Natl. geog. 105: 300 (col.) Mar '54; 106: 461 (col.) Oct '54; 109: 479 (col.) Ap '56; 118: 155, 158 (col.) Aug '60.

window garden. Holiday 22: 109, 111 (col.) Sept '57.

window grill. Holiday 20: 49 (col.) Aug '56.

"Window rock" (Ariz.). Travel 110: 41 Aug '58.

window seat (antique). Con. 141: XXIX Ap '58.

——, Hepplewhite. Con. 129: XXV Je '52.

window stool (antique). Con. 141: XXX May '58.

windows (Morocco). Natl. geog. 107: 153 (col.) Feb '55.

—— (19th cent. curtains). Holiday 12: 46 (col.) Sept '52.

——, dormer. Natl. geog. 118: 184 (col.) Aug '60.

——, Gothic. Int. gr. soc.: Arts . . . p. 49 (col.).

——, stained glass (medieval). Int. gr. soc.: Arts . . . p. 65 (col.).

windsock (sym.). Lehner: Pict. bk. of sym., p. 14.

Windsor, Edward VII, Duke of. *See* Edward VII, Duke.

Windsor, Edward VIII, King. *See* Edward VIII, Duke of Windsor.

Windsor, Wallis Warfield, Duchess of. Cur. biog. p. 738 (1944).
Holiday 14: 48 Dec '53.

Windsor (Eng., river, boats, swans). Natl. geog. 114: 76-7 (col.) Jl '58.

Windsor castle (Eng.). Con. 135: XLII May '55; 145: XL Ap '60.
Holiday 21: 104 (col.) Jan '57.
Natl. geog. 114: 74, 80 (part col.) Jl '58.

Windsor cup trophy. Holiday 22: 67 (col.) Nov '57.

Windsor palace (1783). Amer. heri., vol. 11 no. 4 p. 15 (col.) (Je '60).

Windust, Bretaigne. Cur. biog. p. 837 (1943).

wine (god of). Lehner: Pict. bk. of sym., p. 31.

wine bottle, Chinese porcelain. Con. 136: 271 Jan '56.

——, Eng. (1660). Natl. geog. 111: 601 (col.) May '57.

wine bucket (antique). Con. 135: LV May '55.

——, George III (silver gilt). Con. 137: LIV May '56.

wine cask (on cart). Disney: people & places, p. 64 (col.).

wine cellar. Natl. geog. 103: 158 (col.) Feb '53.

wine cellarette, Chippendale. Con. 132: VI Sept '53; 137: VI Mar '56.

wine cistern, regency. Con. 138: XXIII Jan '57.

wine coaster waggons, silver (Georgian). Con. 145: XXXVI Mar '60.

wine connoisseurs meeting (Congo). Holiday 25: 91 (col.) Ap '59.

wine cooler (antique). Con. 135: LIV May '55; 136: XI Dec '55; 137: IX Ap '56.

—— (18th cent.). Con. ency. of ant., vol. 3, pl. 14.

—— (1775). Con. ency. of ant., vol. 3, pl. 14.

——, Adam. Con. 137: X Je '56.

——, Chinese porcelain (15th cent.). Con. 140: 61 Sept '57.

——, Eng. silver (18th cent.). Con. 142: 227 Jan '59.

——, Fulton. Rawson: Ant. pict. bk., p. 89.

——, George III silver. Con. 132: LVII Sept '53; 143: XL Ap '59, XLIX May '59; 144: XLXIX Jan '60.

——, Hepplewhite. Con. 137: VIII Je '56.

——, Irish silver. Con. 137: XXVII Mar '56.

——, regency. Con. 142: XII Sept '58.

——, Sheffield. Con. 141: XXVI Je '58.

——, Sheraton. Con. 142: XXI Dec '58.

——, silver (antique). Con. 139: 58 Mar '57; 137: III May '56; 139: 192 May '57; 140: XXIII Nov '57; 141: XXXVIII Mar '58.

——, silver (19th cent.). Con. 133: VII May '54; 142: 39 Sept '58.

——, silver (Storr, 19th cent.). Con. 144: XXVIII Nov '59.

——, silver-gilt. Con. 138: VII Nov '56.

wine coolers, George III (silver). Con. 139: XIX Mar '57.

——, silver. Con. 139: VII Mar '57.

wine cup (17th cent.). Con. 133: 195 May '54.

——, Bakuba wood. Con. 145: IV Je '60.

——, Charles I. Con. 134: IX Sept '54.

——, Charles II (silver). Con. 144: 58 Sept '59.

——, Edward VI (silver). Con. 127: 44 Mar '51.

——, Elizabethan (silver). Con. 132: 209 Jan '54.

——, silver (modern). Con. 144: 36 Sept '59.

——, silver (17th cent.). Con. 141: 105 Ap '58.

——, silver (1641). Con. ency. of ant., vol. 1, pl. 82.

wine ewer, Chinese Ming. Con. 141: 42 Mar '58.

——, Chinese porcelain. Con. 137: XLVI Je '56.

——, jade. Con. 134: XL Sept '54.

wine fount, silver (18th cent.). Con. 132: 89 Nov '53.

wine fountain, gilt (18th cent.). Con. 133: 153 May '54.

——, Irish glass. Con. ency. of ant., vol. 3, pl. 48.

——, silver (Lamerie). Con. 143: 15 Mar '59.

wine garden (Vienna). Disney: People & places, p. 55 (col.).

wine glass. Holiday 13: 4, 23, 81, 86 Jan '53, 73 Mar '53, 90 May '53.

—— (antique). Con. 139: 231 Je '57.

—— (18th cent.). Con. 142: LVI Jan '59; 144: XLVIII Jan '60.

——, Eng. (antique). Con. 141: XXIV Mar '58.

——, Irish. Con. ency. of ant., vol. 3, pl. 50.

——, Jacobite. Con. 138: 44 Sept '56.

——, Laurence Whistler's engraved. Con. 134: 97 Nov '54.

——, Royal Dublin artillery. Con. 143: XXX Je '59.

wine-glass cooler. See cooler, wine-glass.

wine goblet (17th cent.). Con. 135: III Mar '55.

——, silver (18th cent.). Con. 145: LXXXV Je '60.

wine jar, Chinese. Con. 138: VI Jan '57.

——, Chinese bronze. Con. 133: 258 Je '54.

——, Roman. Osward: Asia Minor, pl. 50.

——, Turkish. Osward: Asia Minor, pl. 133.

wine jars, Greek (ancient). Natl. geog. 105: 34-5 (col.) Jan '54.

wine judges, parade of (in robes). Holiday 26: 95 (col.) Aug '59.

wine jug, Georgian. Con. 137: IX Mar '56.

wine jugs, French. Natl. geog. 109: 319 (col.) Mar '56.

wine label, Battersea. Con. 143: 101 Ap '59.

——, silver. Con. 129: 83-5 Je '52.

wine pedestal, Sheraton. Con. 145: inside back cover Mar '60.

wine press. Holiday 6: 111 (col.) Nov '49.

——, French. Natl. geog. 103: 239 (col.) Feb '53.

wine shop (Japan). Natl. geog. 118: 772 (col.) Dec '60.

wine spirit (sym.). Lehner: Pict. bk. of sym., p. 73.

wine strainer, Staffordshire (enamel). Con. ency. of ant., vol. 1, pl. 75.

wine table (18th cent.). Con. 138: XXII Nov '56.

——, French (18th cent.). Con. 132: 64 Sept '53.

wine taster (17th cent.). Con. 135: XVII Mar '55.

——, Charles I and Charles II. Con. 134: IX Sept '54.

——, Charles II (silver). Con. 145: III May '60.

"Wine taster, knights of the." Natl. geog. 98: 52 (col.) Jl '50.

wine tasters, French. Natl. geog. 117: 754-5 (col.) Je '60.

wine tub, silver (Bateman, 19th cent.). Con. 145: LXXVII May '60.

wine vessel, bronze. Con. 136: 65 Sept '55.

——, Chinese (ancient). Natl. geog. 117: 833 (col.) Je '60.

——, Chinese (1766-1122, B.C.). Praeg.: Pict. ency., p. 536.

——, Chinese Broad Yu. Con. 134: 220 Dec '54.

——, Chinese bronze. Con. 139: 135 Ap '57.

——, Chou. Con. 136: 69 Sept '55.

——, silver (17th cent.). Con. 133: 85 Ap '54.

winery. Holiday 12: 102 (col.) Aug '52.

wing-cupboard. See cupboard, wing.

winged altar. See altar, winged.

winged-bull (Xerxes' gate guard). Ceram: March of arch., p. 175-6.

——, Assyrian (sculpture). Holiday 10: 53 Oct '51.

winged bulls ("Nimrod himself"). Ceram: March of arch., p. 214-5.

——, Sargon II's (Assyrian). Natl. geog. 99: 43 Jan '51.

winged hourglass (sym.). Lehner: Pict. bk. of sym., p. 80.

winged lightning (sym.). Lehner: Pict. bk. of sym., p. 94.

winged lion (Sepulchral Way, China). Praeg.: Pict. ency., p. 529.

winged lion & book (sym.). Lehner: Pict. bk. of sym., p. 38.

"Winged monster" cup. See cup, "Winged monster."

winged ox and book (sym.). Lehner: Pict. bk. of sym., p. 38.

winged propeller. See propeller, winged (sym.).

winged serpent (sym.). Lehner: Pict. bk. of sym., p. 26.

"winged thoughts" (sym.). Travel 113: 13 Feb '60, 13 Ap '60; 114: 19 Sept '60, 25 Nov '60.

"Winged Victory." Praeg.: Pict. ency., p. 11.

—— (statue). Travel 106: 52 Nov '56; 107: 38 May '57.

—— (sym.). Lehner: Pict. bk. of sym., p. 87.

"Winged Victory of Samothrace." Holiday 18: 8 Dec '55.
Natl. geog. 98: 66 Jl '50.
Travel 102: 4 Sept '54.

Winged wheel of Hermes (sym.). Lehner: Pict. bk. of sym., p. 64.

Winiarski, Bohdan S. Cur. biog. p. 469 (1962).

Winkle, Rip Van. See Rip Van Winkle.

Winnepesaukee lake (N.H.). Holiday 8: 56 (col.) Sept '50.

winnowing basket (boy, India). Natl. geog. 109: 577 Ap '56.

Winslow, Anne Goodwin. Cur. biog. p. 686 (1948).

Winslow, Edward. Amer. heri., vol. 10 no. 1 p. 67 (Dec '58); vol. 10 no. 6 p. 51 (Oct '59).

Winsor, Kathleen. Cur. biog. p. 652 (1946).

Winster, Baron Reginald T. Cur. biog. p. 653 (1946).

Winter, Ella. Cur. biog. p. 656 (1946).

Winter, Fritz. Cur. biog. p. 478 (1958).
Holiday 25: 65 May '59.

—— (work of). Praeg.: Pict. ency., p. 514.

Winter, George (work of). Amer. heri., vol. 2 no. 1 p. 35-8 (col.) (fall '50).

winter (children, snow, park). Natl. geog. 118: 796-9 (col.) Dec '60.

—— (houses, night, snow). Holiday 10: 176 (col.) Dec '51.

—— (snow, log sled). Holiday 10: 148 (col.) Dec '51.

—— (sym.). Lehner: Pict. bk. of sym., p. 81.

winter park (Russia, 1809). Amer. heri., vol. 9 no. 2 p. 9 (col.) (Feb '58).

winter scene. Amer. heri., vol. 9 no. 6 p. 51 (col.) (Oct '58).

"Winter season" (Cignani). Con. 145: XLVI Je '60.

"Winter sunshine" (Thaulow). Con. 145: XXXIII Mar '60.

Winters, Shelley. Cur. biog. p. 645 (1952).

Winthrop, Gov. John. Amer. heri., vol. 7 no. 4 p. 37 (Je '56).

Winthrop, John. Amer. heri., vol. 10 no. 6 p. 48 (col.) (Oct '59).

Winton, Mrs. Richard. Holiday 23: 69 (col.) Mar '58.

wire, barbed. See barbed wire.

wire mill. Natl. geog. 97: 736 Je '50.

wire testing machine. Natl. geog. 99: 136 (col.) Jan '51.

Wirkkala ceramics. Travel 105: 37 Ap '56.

Wirth, Conrad L. Cur. biog. p. 646 (1952).

Wirtz, William Willard. Cur. biog. p. 658 (1946); (1963).

Wisconsin. Holiday 6: 34-59 (part col.) (Jl '49); 24: 62-7 (col.) Oct '58 28: 54-9 (part col.) Aug '60.
Natl. geog. 111: 142-87 (part col.) Feb '57.

—— (map). Natl. geog. 111: 148-9 (col.) Feb '57.

—— (product map). Holiday 6: 49 (col.) Jl '49.

Wisconsin Dells. Natl. geog. 111: 158-9 (col.) Feb '57.
Travel 104: 42 Jl '55.

Wisconsin Historical Society. Amer. heri., vol. 2 no. 2 p. 16-21 (winter '51).

wisdom (Oriental sym.). Lehner: Pict. bk. of sym., p. 43.

"Wisdom" (statue by Baratta). Con. 142: 176 Dec '58.

wisdom (sym.). Lehner: Pict. bk. of sym., p. 61, 66.

Wise, James Decamp. Cur. biog. p. 661 (1954).

Wise, John. Amer. heri., vol. 6 no. 4 p. 12 (Je '55).

Wise, Rabbi Stephen S. Cur. biog. p. 931 (1941).

wishbone. Con. 144: LXIV Jan '60.

—— (sym.). Lehner: Pict. bk. of sym., p. 63.

wishing circle. Lehner: Pict. bk. of sym., p. 69.

wishing well (sym.). Lehner: Pict. bk. of sym., p. 63.

witch. Holiday 27: 112 Je '60; 28: 14 Sept '60.

—— (on broom). Lehner: Pict. bk. of sym., p. 53.

witch doctor (Columbia jungle). Natl. geog. 102: 377 (col.) Sept '52.

witch doctor mask. Int. gr. soc.: Arts . . . p. 185 (col.).

witches. Holiday 10: 133 Oct '51.

Witherington, W. F. (work of). Con. 138: L Sept '56.

Witherow, William P. Cur. biog. p. 893 (1942).

Witte, Edwin E. Cur. biog. p. 659 (1946).

Wittelsbach fountain (Munich). Praeg.: Pict. ency., p. 423.

Wittrock, Fred J. Horan: Pict. hist. of wild west, p. 152.

Witz, Conrad (work of). Praeg.: Pict. ency., p. 242 (col.).

wivern (sym.). Lehner: Pict. bk. of sym., p. 61.

wives of U.S. Presidents. See U.S. Presidents' wives.

Wizard island (Ore.). Travel 101: 9 Ap '54.

"Wizard of Oz" (characters). Travel 114: 10 Aug '60.

Woburn Abbey, Georgian (Eng.). Con. 141: XLVIII, 205-11 Je '58.

Wolchok, Samuel. Cur. biog. p. 687 (1948).

Wolcott, Frank. Horan: Pict. hist. of wild west, p. 187.

Wolcott, Jesse P. Cur. biog. p. 641 (1949).

Wolcott, Josiah (work of). Amer. heri., vol. 10 no. 3 p. 58-9 (col.) (Ap '59).

Wolf, Rabbi Alfred. Cur. biog. p. 480 (1958).

wolf headdress, Indian. Natl. geog. 117: 475 (col.) Ap '60.

Wolfe, Deborah Partridge. Cur. biog. p. 470 (1962).

Wolfe, Hugh C. Cur. biog. p. 623 (1950).

Wolfe, James. Amer. heri., vol. 11 no. 1 p. 26 (col.) (Dec '59).

—— (by Geo. Townshend). Amer. heri., vol. 11 no. 1 p. 26 (col.) (Dec '59).

——, death of (by West). Amer. heri., vol. 11 no. 1 p. 30-1 (col.) (Dec '59).

——, death of (paintings). Con. 144: 56-7 Sept '59.

Wolfe, Thomas. Holiday 10: 103 Jl. '51.

Wolfe birthplace, Thomas. Holiday 24: 13 Jl '58.

Wolfert, Ira. Cur. biog. p. 839 (1943).

Wolff, Maritta M. Cur. biog. p. 933 (1941).

Wolfgang altar. See altar, winged.

Woll, Matthew. Cur. biog. p. 841 (1943).

Wollaston, John (work of). Amer. heri., vol. 7 no. 1 p. 55 (col.) (Dec '55). Con. 138: 281 Jan '57.

Wolman, Abel. Cur. biog. p. 597 (1957).

Wolman, Leo. Cur. biog. p. 642 (1949).

Wolstenholme, D. (work of). Con. 140: XXI Sept '57.

Woltman, Frederick. Cur. biog. p. 690 (1947).

woman. Con. 142: XXXV Nov '58. Holiday 11: 13 (col.), 18 Feb '52; 13: 84, inside back cover (col.) Mar '53, 30-1, 37, 84-5 Ap '53; 14: 13 (col.), 70 Oct '53, 4 (col.) Dec '53; 21: 159 (col.) May '57, 33 (col.) Je '57; 22: 12-3 Sept '57; 23: 75-7 (part col.) Jan '58; 25: 156 Jan '59, 88, 131 (col.), Mar '59, 201 May '59, 90-1 (col.), 120 (col.), 180-1 Je '59; 26: 61 (col.) Aug '59, 143 (col.) Nov '59; 27: 46

Mar '60, 60 (col.) May '60; 28: 29 Oct '60, 61 (col.) Dec '60. Jordan: Hammond's pict. atlas, p. 131 (col.). Travel 101: inside back cover Ap '54.

woman (apple tree). Natl. geog. 117: 467 (col.) Ap '60.

—— (Arctic suit). Natl. geog. 100: 505 (col.) Oct '51.

—— (arranging flowers). Natl. geog. 105: 447 (col.) Ap '54.

—— (artist's model, nude). Holiday 12: 49 (col.) Sept '52.

—— (asleep). Holiday 7: 63 Je '50; 8: 55 Jl '50, 105 Dec '50.

—— (asleep, beach). Holiday 10: 41 Oct '51.

—— (asleep, beach chair). Holiday 18: 20 (col.) Dec '55.

—— (at desk). Natl. geog. 104: 387 Sept '53. Travel 111: 49-50 May '59.

—— (at mail box). Natl. geog. 103: 717 (col.) Je '53.

—— (at table). Amer. heri., vol. 11 no. 1 p. 104 (Dec '59). Holiday 26: 59 (col.), 85 Aug '59, 11 Oct '59; 27: 34 (col.) May '60; 28: 186 Nov '60. Natl. geog. 19: 235 (col.) Feb '50. Travel 103: 44 May '55.

—— (at table, cartoon). Holiday 14: 151 Nov '53.

—— (at table, smoking). Holiday 25: 41 Jan '59.

—— (at window). Holiday 18: 99 (col.) Sept '55.

—— (auto). Holiday 18: 32 (col.) Nov '55; 25: 43 (col.) Feb '59.

—— (baby donkey). Natl. geog. 114: 20 (col.) Jl '58.

—— (baby gorilla). Natl. geog. 117: 130-1 (col.) Jan '60.

—— (baby in cradle on head). Natl. geog. 110: 444 (col.) Oct '56.

—— (baby in crib, auto). Holiday 10: 12 Aug '51.

—— (baby on back). Natl. geog. 99: 616 (col.) May '51.

—— (back view). Holiday 25: 61 Je '59. Natl. geog. 97: 441 (col.) Ap '50.

—— (back view, desert). Natl. geog. 113: 330 (col.) Mar '58.

—— (back view, hooded). Holiday 21: 69 Jan '57.

—— (back view, painting). Natl. geog. 111: 412 (col.) Mar '57.

—— (bag on head). Holiday 24: 208 (col.) Dec '58; 26: 82 (col.) Jl '59, 4 (col.) Dec '59; 27: 138 (col.) Feb '60, 162 Je '60.

—— (balcony). Holiday 11: 57 (col.) Ap '52.

—— (balky mule). Natl. geog. 109: 625 May '56.

—— (basket of ducks on head). Holiday 12: 6 Aug '52.

—— (basket of grapes). Travel 112: 50 Sept '59.

—— (basket of twigs on back). Natl. geog. 104: 489 (col.) Oct '53.

—— (basket on head). Holiday 5: 122 Je '49; 23: 35 (col.), 44 Feb '58.

Natl. geog. 99: 164 (col.) Feb '51.
—— (baskets of tomatoes). Natl. geog. 98: 379 (col.) Sept '50.
—— (baskets on head). Holiday 7: 104 Mar '50.
—— (bath towel). Holiday 12: 72 (col.) Jl '52.
—— (bathing child in wash tub). Natl. geog. 112: 698 (col.) Nov '57.
—— (bathing suit). Holiday 9: 98 (col.) Mar '51; 10: 4, 118 Jl '51, 106-11 (part col.) Je '52; 13: 47 Jan '53, 126 May '53; 14: 91, 95 (col.) Sept '53, 158 Dec '53; 16: 51, 93 (col.) Dec '54; 18: 55 (col.) Dec '55; 19: 88, 110 (col.) Mar '56, 2 (col.) May '56, 106-11, 128 Je '56; 21: 110 Je '57; 25: 149 Ap '59, 174 (col.) Je '59; 26: 74-7 (col.) Jl '59, 22 Aug '59, 32 Sept '59; 28: 74-9 (part col.) Jl '60.
—— (bathing suit, back view). Holiday 27: 195 (col.) May '60.
—— (bathrobe). Holiday 18: 119 Jl '55.
—— (beach, comic). Holiday 13: 91 Ap '53.
—— (beach tent). Holiday 28: 20-1 (col.) Jl '60.
—— (bear hugging). Amer. heri., vol. 8 no. 4 p. 44 (col.) (Je '57).
—— (behind flowers). Natl. geog. 103: 122 (col.) Jan '53.
—— (beside statue). Natl. geog. 108: 299 (col.) Sept '55.
—— (binoculars). Natl. geog. 118: 787 (col.) Dec '60.
—— (blowing dinner horn). Amer. heri., vol. 8 no. 5 p. 50 (col.) (Aug '57).
—— (blue jeans). Travel 104: 60 Jl '55.
—— (braiding camel cargo net). Natl. geog. 117: 83 (col.) Jan '60.
—— (breakfast on balcony). Holiday 19: 57 (col.) May '56.
—— (breakfast on plane). Holiday 14: 69 (col.) Oct '53.
—— (bundle on head). Natl. geog. 100: 464 (col.) Oct '51.
—— (buying fish). Natl. geog. 113: 96 (col.) Jan '58.
—— (buying fruit). Holiday 24: 7 (col.) Dec '58.
—— (buying fur blanket). Natl. geog. 113: 335 (col.) Mar '58.
—— (buying hat). Holiday 10: 99 (col.) Oct '51; 26: 79 (col.) Oct '59.
—— (buying purse). Natl. geog. 113: 308 (col.) Mar '58.
—— (buying straw hat). Natl. geog. 113: 171 (col.) Feb '58.
—— (camels, donkey). Natl. geog. 110: 739 (col.) Dec '56.
—— (card table). Holiday 21: 190 Ap '57; 22: 17 (col.) Sept '57, 105 (col.) Nov '57.
—— (carrying child). Natl. geog. 100: 15 (col.) Jl '51; 109: 282 (col.) Feb '56.
—— (carving meat). Holiday 14: 102 (col.) Dec '53.
—— (child on back, Viet Nam). Natl. geog. 107: 868 Je '55.
—— (centennial parasol). Natl. geog. 97: 204 (col.) Feb '50.
—— (cleaning car). Travel 111: 60 Je '59.

—— (cleaning fish). Natl. geog. 107: 53 (col.) Jan '55.
—— (cleaning furniture). Travel 109: 57 Feb '58.
—— (cleaning windows). Natl. geog. 98: 765 (col.) Dec '50.
—— (climbing pyramid). Travel 103: 44 May '55.
—— (clothes exhibit). Holiday 12: 119, 121 Oct '52; 19: 60-1 (col.) Jan '56; 22: 12-3, 100 (col.) Sept '57, 90-5 (col.), Oct '57, 86-91 (part col.) Nov '57.
——. See also women (winter coats).
—— (coat, hat). Holiday 25: 25 Ap '59.
—— (cocktail). Holiday 25: inside back cover (col.) May '59; 27: 148 (col.) Mar '60; 28: 182 (col.) Nov '60.
—— (cocktail dress). Holiday 11: 53 (col.) Ap '52.
—— (coffee cup). Holiday 28: 153 (col.) Nov '60.
—— (colonial room). Natl. geog. 113: 547 (col.) Ap '58.
—— (comic). Amer. heri., vol. 6 no. 2 p. 65 (col.) (winter '55).
Holiday 11: 112 Je '52; 12: 100 Aug '52, 89 Sept '52, 139 Nov '52.
—— (comic dancer). Holiday 5: 30 Jan '49.
—— (cooking). Amer. heri., vol. 9 no. 1 p. 19 (col.) (Dec '57).
Holiday 11: 91 (col.) Jan '52; 12: 32 (col.) Sept '52; 21: 150 Mar '57, 183 May '57; 23: 101 Je '58; 25: 157 (col.) May '59.
Natl. geog. 97: 605 (col.) May '50.
—— (cooking over brazier). Natl. geog. 104: 627 (col.) Nov '53.
—— (cooking, Paris). Natl. geog. 98: 61 (col.) Jl '50.
—— (Corriedale sheep). Natl. geog. 113: 349 (col.) Mar '58.
—— (corset). Holiday 12: 119 Oct '52, 80 Nov '52; 18: 94 Nov '55; 19: 23 Feb '56, 93 May '56; 20: 123 Oct '56, 39 Nov '56.
—— (crab). Natl. geog. 97: 440 (col.) Ap '50; 98: 126 Jl '50.
—— (crawling). Holiday 14: 130 Nov '53.
—— (cutting grapes). Natl. geog. 117: 754 (col.) Je '60.
—— (dancing). Holiday 28: 21 Oct '60.
Travel 113: 19 Jan '60.
—— (dancing, cartoon, 1894). Amer. heri., vol. 11 no. 6 p. 105 (Oct '60).
—— (Puerto Rico). Holiday 28: 220 Dec '60.
—— (decorating cake). Holiday 6: 47 (col.) Nov '49.
—— (deer). Holiday 14: 34 Dec '53.
—— (dinner table). Holiday 21: 85 (col.) May '57.
—— (diving). Holiday 19: 124 Mar '56.
—— (doe, forest). Natl. geog. 113: 242 Feb '58.
—— (dog). Holiday 13: 121 Ap '53, 138 May '53; 18: 56 (col.) Nov '55; 22: 12 (col.) Sept '57; 28: 86-7, 103-4 (part col.) Dec '60.
Natl. geog. 97: 62 Jan '50.
—— (dog in basket). Natl. geog. 99: 827 Je '51.

woman (dog, stones in river). Natl. geog. 108: 345 (col.) Sept '55.

—— (dogs). Natl. geog. 118: 168 Aug '60.

—— (dolls, at table). Natl. geog. 116: 818 (col.) Dec '59.

—— (dreaming of married life). Amer. heri., vol. 9 no. 1 p. 91 (Dec '57).

—— (dress display). See woman (clothes exhibit).

—— (dress fashions). Holiday 28: 102-7 (part col.) Dec '60.

—— (dressed as man). Holiday 23: 170 Mar '58.

—— (dressing chicken). See woman (dressing fowl).

—— (dressing, comic). Holiday 14: 104 Aug '53.

—— (dressing for party). Holiday 25: 94 (col.) Feb '59.

—— (dressing fowl). Natl. geog. 104: 209 (col.) Aug '53.

—— (dressing, fowl, Middle ages). Int. gr. soc.: Arts . . . p. 53 (col.).

—— (dressing gown). Holiday 26: 135 (col.) Nov '59.

—— (dressmaker fits dress). Natl. geog. 109: 253 (col.) Feb '56.

—— (driving auto). Holiday 21: 173 (col.) May '57; 22: 7 (col.) Sept '57.

—— (dwarf corn field). Natl. geog. 107: 507 Ap '55.

—— (dying sheep fleece). Natl. geog. 106: 569 Oct '54.

—— (1864). Natl. geog. 97: 732 (col.) Je '50.

—— (1880). Amer. heri., vol. 9 no. 3 p. 8 (Ap '58).

—— (1880 costume). Travel 111: 16 May '59.

—— (evening dress). Holiday 10: 110-11, 113 (col.) Nov '51; 11: 111 (col.) Mar '52, 101 Ap '52, 93 (col.) May '52; 12: 127 (col.) Dec '52; 18: 102 (col.) Sept '55; 19: 48-9 (col.) Jan '56, 23 (col.) Mar '56, 34 (col.) Je '56; 20: 39 (col.) Aug '56, 7 (col.) Sept '56, 53 (col.), 78 Oct '56, 92-3 Nov '56; 21: 100 (col.) Jan '57, 82 (col.) Je '57; 25: 114 Jan '59, 59 (col.), 89 Mar '59, 76 (col.) May '59, 91 (col.) Je '59; 26: 7 (col.) Jl '59, 63 (col.) Aug '59, 76, 95 (col.) Oct '59; 27: inside cover, 5, 93 (col.) Ap '60, 111, 166 (col.) May '60; 28: 25, 107 (col.) Sept '60, 188 (col.) Nov '60, 79, 106-7 (col.) Dec '60.

—— (evening dress, formal). Holiday 14: 87 Oct '53. Natl. geog. 113: 547 (col.) Ap '58; 115: 176 Feb '59.

—— (evening dress, fur coat). Holiday 10: 21 (col.) Oct '51.

—— (evening wrap). Holiday 10: 110 (col.) Nov '51.

—— (exercising). Amer. heri., vol. 9 no. 6 p. 26 (Oct '58).

—— (eye glasses). Holiday 21: 49 Je '57; 22: cover (col.) Oct '57.

—— (fallen in basket, comic). Holiday 5: 21 Jan '49.

—— (falls from horse). Natl. geog. 109: 471 Ap '56.

—— (fan). Con. 133: XXIV (col.) May '54.

—— (fashions). Holiday 27: 86-7 (col.) Je '60.

—— (feeding baby animals). Natl. geog. 111: 505, 515 (col.) Ap '57.

—— (feeding chickens). Natl. geog. 97: 448 (col.) Ap '50.

—— (feeding children). Natl. geog. 109: 281 (col.) Feb '56.

—— (feeding duck). Natl. geog. 115: 204 (col.) Feb '59.

—— (feeding kangaroo). Holiday 22: 48 Dec '57; 24: 167 Dec '58. Natl. geog. 108: 491 Oct '55.

—— (feeding silkworms). Natl. geog. 103: 693 May '53.

—— (feet hurt). Holiday 26: 123 Jl '59, 117 Aug '59, 128 Sept '59, 213 Dec '59 27: 120 Jan '60, 114 Feb '60, 182 Mar '60, 215 Ap '60, 62 May '60, 165 Je '60 28: 136 Jl '60, 113 Aug '60, 101 Sept '60, 142 Oct '60, 218 Nov '60.

—— (fish). Travel 104: 30 Aug '55; 108: 34-5 Nov '57.

—— (fish in boat). Natl. geog. 112: 63 (col.) Jl '57.

—— (fish on tray). Natl. geog. 104: 593 (col.) Nov '53.

—— (fishing). Holiday 23: 102 Ap '58. Travel 104: 62 Jl '55; 114: 30 Jl '60.

—— (fishing in boat). Travel 106: 61 Sept '56.

—— (flamingo). Natl. geog. 115: 692 (col.) May '59.

—— (flower basket). Holiday 12: 99 (col.) Sept '52.

—— (flower garden). Holiday 19: 94 (col.) Mar '56.

—— (flowers). Holiday 21: 133 Ap '57. Natl. geog. 97: 348 (col.) Mar '50; 101: 166 (col.) Feb '52; 113: 797 (col.) Je '58.

—— (flowers, laughing). Holiday 19: 15 (col.) Mar '56.

—— (flying). Holiday 27: 1 Feb '60.

—— (flying, comic). Holiday 27: 93 May '60.

—— (flying, drapery). Int. gr. soc.: Arts . . . p. 123 (col.).

—— (fox). Natl. geog. 98: 366 Sept '50.

—— (fur cape). Holiday 28: 11 Nov '60.

—— (fur coat). Holiday 10: 147 Dec '51; 22: 143 (col.) Sept '57; 26: 189 Oct '59.

—— (getting bath). Holiday 27: 22 Mar '60.

—— (gifts). Holiday 12: 36 (col.) Dec '52.

—— (golf). Amer. heri., vol. 9 no. 1 p. 82 (Dec '57). Holiday 7: 65 Je '50; 14: 147 Nov '53.

—— (gondola). Holiday 23: 79 (col.) Jan '58.

—— (grocery cart). Natl. geog. 97: 545 Ap '50.

—— (ground squirrels). Natl. geog. 109: 605 (col.) May '56.

—— (harvest field). Disney: People & places, p. 71 (col.).

—— (harvest hay). Holiday 19: 53 (col.) Feb '56.

—— (head). Amer. heri., vol. 8 no. 2 p. 23 (Feb '57); vol. 11 no. 5 p. 18, 25 Aug '60. Con. 132: cover (col.), XXII, 107 (col.) Nov '53, LXXVII Jan '54; 140: 44 (col.) Sept '57, XII (col.), XLIX, LVI, LIX, 110 Nov '57, LII, 159 Dec '57; 142:

112 Nov '58; 143: 117 Ap '59, 273 Je '59; 144: XXIV, LXV Nov '59, XXIV Jan '60; 145: 127 Ap '60, XXXVII Je '60.

Holiday 12: 112 Oct '52, 16 (col.), 31 Nov '52, 39, 93 Dec '52; 13: 7 (col.), 98 Ap '53, 112 May '53, 116 Je '53; 14: 9 Jl '53, 18 Aug '53, 110 Sept '53, 1, 30, 33 Oct '53, 19, 101, 143, 160 Nov '53, 23, 42 (col.), 124-5, 192 Dec '53; 18: 135 (col.) Nov '55; 19: 14 Mar '56, 171 May '56, 78 Je '56; 20: 16, 165 Dec '56; 21: 111 Je '57; 22: 121 (col.) Jl '57, 123 Oct '57, 40, 170 Nov '57, 152 Dec '57; 23: 6, 124 Jan '58, 178 Mar '58, 47 Ap '58, 1 Je '58; 24: 142 Jl '58, 10, 105 Sept '58, 97 Oct '58, 211 Nov '58, 44, 73, 142, 152 Dec '58; 25: 125 (col.), 154 Jan '59, 63 (col.) Feb '59, 170 (col.), 176, 199 May '59; 26: 124, 129, 188 Nov '59, 98 (col.) Dec '59, 27: 176 Feb '60, 115 Mar '60; 28: 128 (col.), 129 Jl '60, 4 Aug '60, 73 Sept '60, 9, 196 Oct '60, 147 Nov '60, 121 Dec '60.

Natl. geog. 106: 614 Nov '54; 108: 102 (col.) Jl '55; 111: 456 (col.) Ap '57; 117: 71 (col.) Jan '60.

Praeg.: Pict. ency., p. 255 (col.).

Travel 101: 47, inside back cover Jan '54, 42 Mar '54; 102: back cover, 44 Sept '54, 25 Nov '54, 37 Dec '54; 103: 10, 52 Ap '55; 105: inside back cover Ap '56; 106: inside back cover Sept '56; 109: 52 Jan '58; 113: 57 Feb '60; 114: 29 Jl '60.

—— (head, aristocrat, comic). Holiday 11: 93 Mar '52; 12: 22 Sept '52.

—— (head, asleep). Holiday 18: 122 Oct '55, 160 Nov '55, 72 (col.) Dec '55; 20: 190 Nov '56.

—— (head, bag on top). Holiday 24: 4 (col.) Nov '58; 28: 46 (col.) Dec '60.

—— (head, blindfolded). Holiday 19: 73 (col.) May '56; 20: 197 Nov '56, 96 Dec '56; 21: 109 Jan '57, 196 Ap '57.

—— (head, comic). Holiday 11: 78 May '52; 12: 9 Dec '52.

—— (head, drinking). Holiday 22: 27 Dec '57.

—— (head, Easter lilies). Holiday 27: 199 (col.) Ap '60.

—— (head, 1814). Amer. heri., vol. 6 no. 1 p. 52 (fall '54).

—— (head, 1833). Amer. heri., vol. 7 no. 3 back cover (col.) (Ap '56).

—— (head, evening dress). Natl. geog. 98: 781 Dec '50.

—— (head, eyeglasses). Holiday 18: 32 Dec '55.

—— (head, flowers). Holiday 19: 59 Jan '56; 27: 174 (col.) May '60.

—— (head, goldenrod). Natl. geog. 106: 585 (col.) Nov '54.

—— (head, hat). Holiday 20: 161 (col.) Nov '56; 27: 56 Ap '60.

—— (head, hat, laughing). Natl. geog. 113: 170 (col.) Feb '58.

—— (head, holds fossil). Natl. geog. 109: 386 (col.) Mar '56.

—— (head, laughing). Holiday 10: 91, 95 Nov '51, 7 (col.) Dec '51; 11: 34 (col.) Mar

'52, 139 (col.) Je '52; 12: 85 (col.) Nov '52, 133 (col.) Dec '52; 18: 85 Aug '55, 3 Sept '55, 7 (col.), 18, 89 (col.) Oct '55, 33 Nov '55; 19: 62 Jan '56, 120 Feb '56, 73 (col.), 124 Mar '56, 175 May '56, 85 Je '56; 21: 94 Feb '57, 19 Mar '57, 104 (col.) Je '57; 22: 120 Jl '57, 132 Sept '57, 154 (col.) Oct '57, 93 Dec '57; 24: 79 Aug '58; 26: 112 Nov '59, 2 (col.) Dec '59; 27: 163 Feb '60, 107 Je '60.

Natl. geog. 101: 444 Ap '52; 116: 166 (col.) Aug '59; 117: 467 (col.) Ap '60; 118: 686 (col.) Nov '60.

—— (head, make up of face). Holiday 11: 91 Mar '52.

—— (head, marble bust). Con. 140: 26 Sept '57.

—— (head, masked, carnival). Holiday 26: 36 Dec '59.

—— (head projecting thoughts). Travel 112: 9 Jl '59, 11 Sept '59; 113: 13 Feb '60, 13 Ap '60; 114: 19 Sept '60.

—— (head, seeing double). Holiday 28: 104 Sept '60, 202 Oct '60, 154 Nov '60.

—— (head, taking picture). Holiday 11: 22 Jan '52.

—— (head, telephoning). Holiday 20: 2 (col.) Aug '56.

—— (head, thinking). Holiday 19: 141 (col.) Je '56; 22: 37 Nov '57.

—— (head, traveler). Travel 102: back cover Oct '54.

—— (head, trout). Natl. geog. 98: 536 (col.) Oct '50.

—— (head, wind sym.). Lehner: Pict. bk. of sym., p. 14.

—— (head, worried). Holiday 19: 143 May '56, 63 Je '56.

—— (health model). Natl. geog. 107: 451 (col.) Ap '55.

—— (holding parrot). Natl. geog. 102: 326 (col.) Sept '52.

—— (holding sunfish). Natl. geog. 105: 538 (col.) Ap '54.

—— (holding albatross). Natl. geog. 109: 408 (col.) Mar '56.

—— (horse). Con. 144: 108 Nov '59. Holiday 26: 62 (col.) Aug '59.

—— (horse & dog). Con. 140: LII Jan '58.

—— (horse, circus). Durant: Pict. hist. of Amer. circus, p. 186.

—— (horse head). Natl. geog. 104: 117 (col.) Jl '53.

—— (horseback). Holiday 19: 133 (col.) May '56; 21: 30, 83 (col.) Ap '57.

—— (housecoat). Holiday 27: 64 May '60.

—— (in auto). Holiday 10: 70 (col.) Aug '51, 66 (col.) Nov '51 12: 128 (col.) Oct '52.

—— (in bath tub). Holiday 25: 82 (col.) May '59.

—— (in bed). Amer. heri., vol. 8 no. 4 p. 51 (col.) (Je '57). Holiday 24: 95, 99 (col.), 100 Aug '58, 183 (col.) Nov '58; 25: 122 (col.) May '59; 26: 89 (col.) Sept '59.

—— (in bird cage, comic). Holiday 14: 129 Dec '53.

—— (in food shop). Travel 110: 22 Aug '58.

woman (in hammock). Amer. heri., vol. 8 no. 5 p. 52 (col.) (Aug '57).
Holiday 21: 53 (col.) Feb '57, cover (col.) Mar '57.

—— **(in pool).** Holiday 11: 57 (col.) Mar '52.

—— **(in ricksha).** Holiday 18: 106 (col.) Sept '55.

—— **(in surrey).** Natl. geog. 113: 180 (col.) Feb '58.

—— **(India).** Holiday 17: 98 (col.) Feb '55.

—— **(jacket).** Holiday 20: 113 Nov '56.

—— **(jug on shoulder).** Con. 145: LXXIV Je '60.

—— **(kissing man).** Holiday 25: 128 Jan '59, 132 Mar '59.

—— **(kissing snake).** Holiday 20: 44 (col.) Sept '56.

—— **(kitchen).** Holiday 24: 104 Aug '58.

—— **(kneading bread, clay figure, 9th cent.).** Natl. geog. 118: 822 Dec '60.

—— **(kneeling).** Labande: Naples, p. 63.

—— **(knitting).** Holiday 10: 96 Jl '51; 20: 70 Sept '56.
Natl. geog. 98: 242 (col.) Aug '50; 116: 781 (col.) Dec '59.

—— **(knitting, rose arbor).** Natl. geog. 109: 852-3 (col.) Je '56.

—— **(laboratory).** Natl. geog. 104: 604 (col.) Nov '53.

—— **(lamb).** Holiday 19: 116 (col.) Feb '56.

—— **(land offer poster, 1880).** Brooks: Growth of a nation, p. 191.

—— **(laughing).** Holiday 10: 102 (col.) Oct '51, 49 (col.) Nov '51; 11: 21 (col.) Feb '52 19: 21 (col.) Feb '56, 85, 130 May '56; 20: 43 Aug '56, inside cover (col.), 120 Sept '56.
Natl. geog. 101: 431 (col.) Ap '52.

—— **(laughing, lamb).** Holiday 20: 84 (col.) Sept '56.

—— **(laundry on line).** Natl. geog. 118: 629 (col.) Nov '60.

—— **(lawn chair, reading).** Holiday 10: 32 Jl '51.

—— **(leading dog).** Holiday 23: 116 May '58. Natl. geog. 107: 300 (col.) Mar '55.

—— **(lichens on tree).** Natl. geog. 113: 615 (col.) May '58.

—— **(lingerie).** Holiday 14: 115 Oct '53.

—— **(lion).** Natl. geog. 118: 369 (col.) Sept '60.

—— **(looking at antiques).** Travel 110: 57 Jl '58.

—— **(looking at books).** Natl. geog. 100: 591 (col.) Nov '51.

—— **(looking at jewelry).** Natl. geog. 98: 785, 793, 801 (part col.), 807 Dec '50.

—— **(looking in mirror).** Holiday 14: 103 Dec '53.

—— **(looking thru optical glass).** Natl. geog. 100: 761 (col.) Dec '51.

—— **(looking thru telescope).** Travel 108: inside back cover Aug '57.

—— **(lorgnette).** Holiday 23: 106 Je '58.

—— **(lounging robe).** Holiday 10: 89 (col.) Oct '51, 22 (col.) Dec '51; 21: 175 Mar '57.

—— **(lunch, western style).** Holiday 11: 150 (col.) May '52.

—— **(lying down).** Holiday 23: 10 (col.) Ap '58.
Travel 109: inside back cover Mar '58, inside back cover May '58.

—— **(lying on cot).** Holiday 24: 100 Aug '58; 25: 181 Je '59.

—— **(magazine).** Holiday 12: 76 Sept '52.

—— **(maid dressing hair).** Holiday 25: 134 (col.) Ap '59.

—— **(making bread).** Natl. geog. 107: 506 Ap '55.

—— **(making butter).** Amer. heri., vol. 3 no. 4 p. 14 (summer '52).

—— **(making camp fire).** Travel 114: 31 Jl '60.

—— **(making Christmas cookies).** Natl. geog. 108: 845-51 (col.) Dec '55.

—— **(making fish-fly).** Natl. geog. 111: 160 (col.) Feb '57.

—— **(making lace).** See lace maker (woman).

—— **(making pottery).** Travel 102: 26 Oct '54.

—— **(making pottery figures).** Natl. geog. 100: 307 (col.) Sept '51.

—— **(making terrarium).** Natl. geog. 106: 649 Nov '54.

—— **(making up bed).** Natl. geog. 108: 302 (col.) Sept '55.

—— **(map).** Natl. geog. 111: 615 May '57.

—— **(maple sugar shop).** Natl. geog. 105: 482 (col.) Ap '54.

—— **(mask).** Holiday 21: 132 Jan '57.

—— **(mending boat jib).** Natl. geog. 113: 21 (col.) Jan '58.

—— **(microphone).** Holiday 25: 98 May '59. Natl. geog. 109: 374 (col.) Mar '56, 870 Je '56.

—— **(microphone, comic).** Holiday 22: 42 Sept '57.

—— **(milking cow).** Natl. geog. 115: 593 (col.) May '59.

—— **(milking goat).** Natl. geog. 111: 110 Jan '57; 115: 580 Ap '59.

—— **(model's cloak).** Natl. geog. 98: 53 (col.) Jl '50.

—— **(mountain climber).** Holiday 10: 48 (col.) Jl '51.

—— **(Mts., snow).** Natl. geog. 109: 29 (col.) Jan '56.

—— **(mouse jumping at).** Holiday 14: 16 Oct '53.

—— **(mowing lawn).** Holiday 21: 150 May '57.

—— **(musical instrument).** Con. 141: IX (col.) Je '58.

—— **(nature eyes on films).** Natl. geog. 115: 569 Ap '59.

—— **(negligee).** Holiday 12: 81 Nov '52, 30 Dec '52; 13: 138-9 Mar '53, 109 May '53.

—— **(nightgown).** Holiday 13: 21 (col.), 87 May '53; 14: 19 Nov '53.

—— **(19th cent.).** Amer. heri., vol. 8 no. 5 p. 53 (col.) (Aug '57); vol. 9 no. 3 p. 98-9, 102-3 (Ap '58).

—— **(nude, back view).** Holiday 28: 73 (col.) Nov '60.

—— **(nude, kneeling).** Holiday 27: 219 Ap '60.

—— (nude, sun tan, seated). Holiday 28: 214 (col.) Dec '60.

—— (old style). Travel 103: inside back cover Ap '55.

—— (old telephone switchboard). Holiday 20: 51 Oct '56.

—— (on bus). Holiday 14: 4 (col.) Oct '53.

—— (on camel). Natl. geog. 112: 107 (col.) Jl '57.

—— (on couch). Amer. heri., vol. 8 no. 4 p. 52 (col.) (Je '57). Con. 143: XXIX Je '59.

—— (on donkey). Amer. heri., vol. 9 no. 3 p. 87 (Ap '58).

—— (on donkey, comic). Holiday 17: 30 Mar '55.

—— (on horse). Brooks: Growth of a nation, p. 246. Holiday 9: 46 (col.) Mar '51; 24: 99 Dec '58. Horan: Pict. hist. of wild west, p. 66. Travel 107: 31 Ap '57.

—— (on horse, Godey fashion). Amer. heri., vol. 9 no. 6 p. 27 (col.) (Oct '58).

—— (on horse, rearing). Horan: Pict. hist. of wild west, p. 55.

—— (on ladder). Holiday 10: 113 (col.) Dec '51.

—— (on ostrich). Natl. geog. 104: 171 (col.) Aug '53.

—— (on raft). Holiday 5: 109 Je '49.

—— (on ship deck). Holiday 26: 57 Oct '59.

—— (on spiral stair). Natl. geog. 113: 539 (col.) Ap '58.

—— (outdoor table). Holiday 28: 17 (col.) Jl '60.

—— (packing fish in boxes). Natl. geog. 106: 185 (col.) Aug '54.

—— (paint guide). Natl. geog. 107: 453 (col.) Ap '55.

—— (painting). Natl. geog. 112: 201 (col.) Aug '57.

—— (painting pictures). Natl. geog. 111: 729 May '57. Travel 109: 27 Je '58.

—— (papoose on back). Travel 103: 64-5 Je '55.

—— (parasol). Holiday 28: 163 Oct '60.

—— (party food). Holiday 12: 82 (col.) Dec '52.

—— (pets). Holiday 21: 120 Mar '57.

—— (photographer). Travel 104: 69 Aug '55.

——. See also woman (taking picture).

—— (picking flowers). Natl. geog. 99: 533 Ap '51; 107: 735 (col.) Je '55.

—— (picking heather). Natl. geog. 110: 24 (col.) Jl '56.

—— (playing cello). Cooper: Con. ency. of music, p. 170 (col.).

—— (playing dombra). Natl. geog. 106: 635 (col.) Nov '54.

—— (playing guitar). Holiday 28: 16 Oct '60.

—— (playing harp). Holiday 24: 133 Nov '58.

—— (playing lute). Con. 145: 203 May '60. Natl. geog. 100: 424 Sept '51.

—— (playing organ). Holiday 25: 97 Ap '59.

—— (playing piano). Cooper: Con. ency. of music, p. 151.

—— (playing spinet). Natl. geog. 97: 289 (col.) Mar '50.

—— (playing tennis). Holiday 14: 78 Oct '53.

—— (playing viola). Con. 138: LXXV Jan '57.

—— (playing violin for dancers). Holiday 23: 54 (col.) Je '58.

—— (posing for artist). Holiday 24: 63 (col.) Aug '58.

—— (pouring cocktail). Holiday 22: 230 (col.) Dec '57; 24: 18 (col.) Sept '58; 26: 17 Dec '59; 28: 117 (col.) Jl '60.

—— (pouring water from jug). Holiday 27: 22 Mar '60; 28: 2 Nov '60.

—— (pouring water from urn). Holiday 27: 219 Ap '60.

—— (powdering face). Holiday 20: 17 (col.) Sept '56.

—— (praying). Con. 145: LXIII (col.) May '60.

—— (praying in church, 16th cent.). Natl. geog. 98: 200 Aug '50.

—— (printing textile design). Natl. geog. 118: 462 (col.) Oct '60.

—— (prison dungeon). Natl. geog. 115: 282 (col.) Feb '59.

—— (pulling milk cart, dog). Natl. geog. 98: 228 (col.) Aug '50.

—— (pulling ox hay wagon). Natl. geog. 115: 206 (col.) Feb '59.

—— (pushing child in cart). Natl. geog. 113: 257 Feb '58.

—— (putting crown of leaves on man). Amer. heri., vol. 8 no. 6 frontis. (col.) (Oct '57).

—— (reading). Holiday 14: 133 Nov '53. Natl. geog. 97: 197 Feb '50.

—— (reading to children). Natl. geog. 103: 823 (col.) Je '53.

—— (reflection in water). Holiday 14: 104 Sept '53.

—— (refrigerator). Holiday 21: 28 Mar '57.

—— (relaxed, chair). Holiday 19: 70, 72 Feb '56, 145 Mar '56; 28: 150 (col.) Nov '60.

—— (relaxed, lawn chair). Holiday 20: 113 Nov '56.

—— (repairing car). Travel 111: 131 Je '59.

—— (riding ox). Natl. geog. 102: 697 Nov '52.

—— (riding rocket). Holiday 10: 67 (col.) Nov '51.

—— (robe). Holiday 11: 133 Je '52.

—— (rocking chair). Travel 101: inside back cover Ap '54.

—— (roller skating). Holiday 20: 97 Sept '56.

—— (rowing boat). Holiday 13: cover (col.) Mar '53.

—— (rubbing feet). Holiday 11: 79 Jan '52.

—— (running). Amer. heri., vol. 9 no. 3 p. 5 (col.) (Ap '58).

—— (running, comic). Holiday 11: 12 May '52.

—— (saluting). Holiday 23: 14 Mar '58.

—— (science lab.). Natl. geog. 114: 322-3 (col.) Sept '58.

—— (science lab., rats). Natl. geog. 114: 324 (col.) Sept '58.

—— (scrubbing floor). Holiday 10: 55 Nov '51.

woman (sea cucumber). Natl. geog. 111: 36 (col.) Jan '57.

—— **(sea shells).** Natl. geog. 111: 3 (col.) Jan '57.

—— **(seated).** Amer. heri., vol. 9 no. 6 p. 43 (Oct '58).
Con. 140: XII (col.) Nov '57; 142: 112 Nov '58; 143: IV, XLIV (col.) Je '59; 144: III, XVII (col.) Dec '59; 145: LIII Ap '60, LXXVIII Je '60.
Holiday 13: 91 (col.) Mar '53, 2, 79, 107 (col.) Je '53; 14: 30, 95 Jl '53, 13 (col.), 20 Oct '53, 119 (col.) Nov '53; 19: 39 (col.) Jan '56; 20: 39, 45 (col.) Aug '56; 21: 66, 78-9 (col.), 113 Ap '57, 83 Je '57; 22: 84 Nov '57; 23: 85 Mar '58; 25: 14 Ap '59; 26: 95 (col.) Oct '59; 26: inside cover (col.) Dec '59; 27: 79 (col.) Feb '60, 99 (col.) Ap '60, 89 May '60, 98 (col.), 131 Je '60; 28: 30 (col.) Oct '60, 187 Nov '60.
Natl. geog. 100: 25 (col.) Jl '51.
Praeg.: Pict. ency., p. 359 (col.).
Travel 109: 54, inside back cover Mar '58, inside back cover Ap '58, inside back cover May '58.

—— **(seated, baby in lap).** Natl. geog. 97: 38 (col.) Jan '50.

—— **(seated, back view).** Holiday 11: 113 (col.) Je '52.

—— **(seated, calf, dog).** Natl. geog. 97: 592 (col.) May '50.

—— **(seated, daguerreotype).** Amer. heri., vol. 8 no. 1 p. 59 (Dec '56).

—— **(seated, drinking).** Holiday 18: 115 (col.) Nov '55.

—— **(seated, early Amer.).** Amer. heri., vol. 7 no. 1 p. 31 (Dec '55).

—— **(seated, eating).** Natl. geog. 113: 180 (col.) Feb '58.

—— **(seated, 1884).** Amer. heri., vol. 11 no. 4 p. 46 (Je '60).

—— **(seated on couch).** Natl. geog. 108: 317 (col.) Sept '55.

—— **(seated on ground).** Holiday 20: 52 Oct '56; 27: 105 May '60.

—— **(seated on floor).** Travel 104: inside back cover Oct '55.

—— **(seated on step).** Natl. geog. 101: 430 (col.) Ap '52.

—— **(seated, rock steps).** Natl. geog. 108: 670 (col.) Nov '55.

—— **(seated with dog).** Cur. biog. p. 9 (1961).

—— **(seated, with lorgnette).** Amer. heri., vol. 6 no. 5 p. 75 (Aug '55).

—— **(selecting watch).** Holiday 18: 78 Aug '55.

—— **(serving coffee).** Holiday 22: 12 (col.) Sept '57.

—— **(1769).** Con. 145: VII (col.) May '60.

—— **(sewing).** Holiday 19: 144 Feb '56.
Natl. geog. 98: 177 (col.) Aug '50; 106: 650 (col.) Nov '54.
Praeg.: Pict. ency., p. 70 (col.).
Travel 103: 33 Mar '55.

—— **(shooting arrow).** Amer. heri., vol. 9 no. 6 p. 26 (Oct '58).

—— **(shooting pistol).** Holiday 13: 51 Mar '53.

—— **(shopping).** Holiday 20: 21, 32 (col.) Dec '56.

—— **(showing dress).** Holiday 23: 170, 172 Mar '58.

—— **(sick).** Amer. heri., vol. 7 no. 1 p. 119 (Dec '55); vol. 9 no. 1 p. 83 (Dec '57).

—— **(singing).** Holiday 28: 221 Dec '60.

—— **(16th cent.).** Con. 142: LIX Dec '58.

—— **(skating, Currier & Ives).** Amer. heri., vol. 9 no. 1 back cover (col.) (Dec '57).

—— **(smiling).** Praeg.: Pict. ency., p. 26 (col.).

——. *See* also woman (laughing).

—— **(smoking).** Holiday 21: 111 Mar '57.

—— **(smuggler).** Holiday 23: 69 Feb '58.

—— **(snails for food).** Natl. geog. 115: 624 (col.) May '59.

—— **(society, comic).** Holiday 27: 95 May '60.

—— **(sorting beans).** Natl. geog. 118: 577 (col.) Oct '60.

—— **(souvenir shop).** Holiday 10: 96 Jl '51.

—— **(sow digs truffle).** Natl. geog. 110: 419-20 Sept '56.

—— **(spinning).** Holiday 6: 56 (col.) Oct '49.
Natl. geog. 106: 571 (col.) Oct '54.
Travel 105: 26 May '56; 112: 33 Sept '59.

—— **(sport clothes).** Holiday 10: 112 Sept '51; 11: 99 (col.) Feb '52; 19: 71-5 (col.) May '56.

—— **(stringing beans).** Natl. geog. 102: 495 (col.) Oct '52.

—— **(stringing tomatoes).** Natl. geog. 111: 649 (col.) May '57.

—— **(studying fish).** Natl. geog. 109: 867 (col.), 870 Je '56.

—— **(sun bath).** Holiday 13: 17 (col.) Je '53.

—— **(swimming).** Holiday 26: 113 Oct '59.

—— **(swinging child).** Holiday 24: 86 (col.) Oct '58.

—— **(taking exercises).** Holiday 28: 143 Nov '60.

—— **(taking pack off camel).** Natl. geog. 101: 819 (col.) Je '52.

—— **(taking picture).** Natl. geog. 109: 203 (col.) Feb '56.

—— **(taking picture, cartoon).** Holiday 26: 14 Jl '59.

—— **(taking picture, Mt. cow).** Natl. geog. 110: 445 (col.) Oct '56.

—— **(taking picture of fisherman).** Holiday 23: 40 (col.) Ap '58.

—— **(taking pictures).** Holiday 22: 109 Oct '57; 25: 97 (col.) May '59; 28: 75 (col.) Aug '60, 162 Nov '60.
Natl. geog. 109: 819 Je '56.

—— **(tall & short, comic).** Holiday 16: 24 Sept '54.

—— **(tangled in dog leash).** Holiday 21: 114 Ap '57.

—— **(tea table).** Holiday 20: 41 (col.) Aug '56; 24: 51 Dec '58.

—— **(tea table, comic).** Holiday 27: 151 May '60.

—— **(teaching jungle people to type).** Natl. geog. 116: 229 (col.) Aug '59.

—— **(telephone).** Brooks: Growth of a nation, p. 235.

—— **(television).** Holiday 28: 130 Oct '60.

—— (throwing vase at man, comic). Holiday 23: 142 May '58.

—— (tomatoes hang from ceiling). Natl. geog. 109: 317 (col.) Mar '56.

—— (trading post store). Natl. geog. 108: 225 Aug '55.

—— (traveler, comic). Holiday 16: 26 Jl '54.

—— (traveling). Holiday 10: 17 (col.), 113-4 Sept '51, 108-9 Nov '51, 80 Dec '51; 11: 148-9, 151, 153 May '52, 157 Je '52; 13: 93 (col.) Je '53; 21: 126 (col.), 161, 195 May '57, 145 (col.) Je '57; 22: 143 (col.) Sept '57, 109 Oct '57, 194 (col.) Nov '57, 162 (col.) Dec '57; 23: 38 (col.) Je '58; 24: 73 Aug '58, 153 (col.) Dec '58; 25: 24 Jan '59, 158, 168 (col.), 180 Je '59; 28: 165 Nov '60.
Travel 113: 11 Jan '60.

——. See also man & woman (traveling); man, woman & child (traveling).

—— (traveling, comic). Holiday 22: 31 Jl '57.

—— (tray of sales items on head). Natl. geog. 110: 349 Sept '56.

—— (trying on hats). Natl. geog. 106: 474 (col.) Oct '54.

—— (twelve children). Holiday 8: 33 Aug '50.

—— (umbrella). Holiday 14: 6 Dec '53.

—— (umbrella, seated). Natl. geog. 97: 147 (col.) Feb '50.

—— (underclothes). Holiday 13: 8, 87 May '53; 14: 112 Oct '53, 94 Nov '53; 24: 102 Oct '58, 27 Nov '58; 25: 9 Feb '59, 47 Ap '59, 44 May '59, 132 Je '59.

—— (wading sea, comic). Holiday 24: 46 Aug '58.

—— (walking). Holiday 28: 6 Oct '60.
Natl. geog. 107: 150 (col.) Feb '55.

—— (walking, back view). Natl. geog. 105: 302 (col.) Mar '54.

—— (walking, dog). Holiday 10: 113 Nov '51.

—— (washing child's face). Natl. geog. 100: 727 Dec '51.

—— (washing hands in pan). Travel 114: 32 Jl '60.

—— water jug. Travel 102: 20 Oct '54.

—— (waving). Holiday 11: 162 (col.) May '52; 27: 50 (col.) May '60.

—— (wearing slacks). Holiday 12: 108 Sept '52.
Natl. geog. 103: 192 (col.) Feb '53.

—— (wearing shorts). Natl. geog. 111: 303 Mar '57.

—— (weaving). Holiday 24: 183 (col.) Dec '58.
Natl. geog. 97: 147 (col.) Feb '50; 98: 239 (col.) Aug '50.

—— (weaving wickerware). Holiday 28: 66 Sept '60.

—— (widow at grave). Amer. heri., vol. 8 no. 4 p. 46 (Je '57).

—— (widow, 19th cent.). Amer. heri., vol. 9 no. 3 p. 56 (Ap '58).

—— (wind blown). Holiday 22: 20 (col.) Nov '57, 194 (col.) Dec '57.

—— (winter). Amer. heri., vol. 7 no. 1 p. 41 (col.) (Dec '55).

—— (with baby chimpanzee). Natl. geog. 103: 785 (col.) Je '53.

—— (with cat). Holiday 25: 54 Jan '59.

—— (with gun facing Indians). Amer. heri., vol. 8 no. 6 p. 38 (Oct '57).

—— (with laundry). Holiday 14: 88 Sept '53.

—— (working at table). Natl. geog. 104: 278 (col.) Aug '53.

—— (writing in bed). Holiday 24: 62 (col.) Aug '58.

—— (writing letter). Con. 145: 158-9 May '60.

—— (yoke, buckets). Natl. geog. 98: 356 (col.) Sept '50.

woman, African (ancient art). Natl. geog. 111: 218 (col.) Feb '57.

——, African (banana stalk on back). Natl. geog. 97: 341 (col.) Mar '50.

——, African (calabash of water on back). Natl. geog. 97: 341 (col.) Mar '50.

——, African Masai. Natl. geog. 106: 492 Oct '54.

——, Amazon (carrying child). Disney: People & places, p. 99 (col.).

——, Andora (water jugs). Natl. geog. 106: 751 (col.) Dec '54.

——, Arabian. See Arabian woman.

——, Austrian (basket on head). Natl. geog. 115: 211 (col.) Feb '59.

——, Austrian (making pastry). Natl. geog. 115: 201 (col.) Feb '59.

——, Austrian (raking hay). Natl. geog. 115: 213 (col.) Feb '59.

——, Bavarian (harvesting). Travel 114: 8 Jl '60.

——, Belgian Congo. Natl. geog. 106: 737 (col.) Dec '54.

——, blind ("reading" face). Natl. geog. 97: 774 Je '50.

——, Bombay (head). Holiday 25: 48 May '59.

——, Cajun, La. (spinning). Travel 108: cover Oct '57.

——, Canadian. Natl. geog. 108: 207 (col.) Aug '55.

——, Caribbean. Holiday 24: 7 (col.) Sept '58; 26: 159 (col.) Oct '59.

——, Ceylon. Holiday 9: 117 Mar '51.

——, Chinese. Holiday 25: 42 Feb '59.

——, Chinese (at toilet table). Praeg.: Pict. ency., p. 541 (col.).

——, Chinese (grain field). Natl. geog. 111: 359 (col.) Mar '57.

——, Chinese (making pottery). Natl. geog. 110: 211 (col.) Aug '56.

——, circus (fat). Durant: Pict. hist. of Amer. circus, p. 294.

——, circus (horse rider). Durant: Pict. hist. of Amer. circus, p. 226.

——, circus (strong). Durant: Pict. hist. of Amer. hist., p. 157.

——, Colonial (at window). Natl. geog. 118: 191 (col.) Aug '60.

——, Colonial (writing). Holiday 14: 80 Sept '53.
Natl. geog. 113: 535 (col.) Ap '58.

——, Crete. Ceram: March of arch., p. 61-2.

woman, Crete (sorts grapes). Natl. geog. 114: 750 (col.) Dec '58.

——, Dutch. Holiday 15: 29 Jan '54.

——, Dutch (carrying child). Natl. geog. 106: 407 (col.) Sept '54.

——, Dutch (pouring milk). Natl. geog. 98: 761 (col.) Dec '50.

——, Dutch (seated). Natl. geog. 106: 382 (col.) Sept '54.

——, Egyptian (head). Praeg.: Pict. ency., p. 122 (col.).

——, Eskimo (baby on back). Natl. geog. 102: 61 (col.) Jl '52.

——, Eskimo (dish of muktuk). Natl. geog. 109: 775 (col.) Je '56.

——, Ethiopian (back view, plane). Natl. geog. 106: 751 (col.) Dec '54.

——, Etruscan (ancient times). Int. gr. soc.: Arts . . . p. 31 (col.).

——, farm (market stand). Holiday 20: 42 (col.) Oct '56.

——, Formosa. Natl. geog. 97: 145-76 (part col.) Feb '50.

——, French. Con. 143: 209 Je '59. Holiday 10: 137 Nov '51.

——, French (baking bread). Natl. geog. 115: 586 Ap '59.

——, French (cooking). Natl. geog. 115: 576 Ap '59.

——, Grecian. Int. gr. soc.: Arts . . . p. 37 (col.).

——, Grecian (at well). Natl. geog. 109: 50 (col.) Jan '56.

——, Grecian (child on donkey). Natl. geog. 109: 69 (col.) Jan '56.

——, Grecian (500 B.C.). Int. gr. soc.: Arts . . . p. 31 (col.).

——, Grecian (harvest wheat). Natl. geog. 109: 50 (col.) Jan '56.

——, Grecian (head). Ceram: March of arch., p. 39.

——, Grecian (head, 4th cent.). Int. gr. soc.: Arts . . . p. 181 (col.).

——, Grecian (knitting). Natl. geog. 114: 771 (col.) Dec '58.

——, Grecian (spinning). Natl. geog. 114: 737 (col.) Dec '58.

——, Guatemalan (basket on head). Holiday 23: 87 Jan '58.

——, Haiti. Holiday 23: 44 Feb '58.

——, India. Holiday 23: 30 Feb '58, 160 Mar '58.
Natl. geog. 103: 38 Jan '53; 117: 589, 617 (col.) May '60.
Travel 109: 4 Feb '58.

——, India (by pool). Natl. geog. 118: 472 (col.) Oct '60.

——, India (dancer). Travel 113: 19 Jan '60.

——, India (head). Con. 144: XXXVI (col.) Dec '59.
Travel 106: cover, 13 Nov '56; 109: 4 Mar '58. 10 May '58.

——, India (Naga). Natl. geog. 107: 252 Feb '55.

——, India (weaving, Angami). Natl. geog. 107: 260 (col.) Feb '55.

——, Indian (San Blas). Holiday 12: 57 (col.) Nov '52.

——, Indochina (child on back). Natl. geog. 102: 325 (col.) Sept '52.

——, Indonesia (cacao-bean pods). Natl. geog. 108: 364 (col.) Sept '55.

——, Irish. Natl. geog. 104: 132 (col.) Jl '53.

——, Irish (cart, horse). Holiday 24: 87 (col.) Dec '58.

——, Irish (head). Holiday 19: 41 Jan '56.

——, Israel. Holiday 20: 171 Nov '56.

——, Jamaica. Holiday 28: 208 (col.) Nov '60.

——, Japanese. See Japanese woman.

——, Java. Travel 112: 24 Sept '59.

——, Katmandu (cooking). Natl. geog. 117: 387 (col.) Mar '60.

——, Korean. Travel 112: 39 Dec '59.

——, Korean (child on back). Natl. geog. 103: 661 (col.) May '53.

——, Korean (cooking). Natl. geog. 97: 788 (col.) Je '50.

——, Lebanon (winnowing grain, ancient). Natl. geog. 118: 846 (col.) Dec '60.

——, Laos (rice harvest). Natl. geog. 117: 54 (col.) Jan '60.

——, Laos (head). Natl. geog. 117: 57 (col.) Jan '60.

——, Lapland. Holiday 17: 41 Jan '55.

——, Lapland (making bread). Disney: People & places, p. 18 (col.).

——, Lapland (milking reindeer). Natl. geog. 106: 255 Aug '54.

——, Lapland (spinning). Natl. geog. 106: 273 (col.) Aug '54.

——, Madeira is. (embroidering). Natl. geog. 115: 372 Mar '59.

——, Madeira is. (making lace). Travel 104: 45 Nov '55.

——, Majorcan court. Natl. geog. 111: 635 (col.) May '57.

——, Malta. Holiday 27: 122 Jan '60; 27: 156 (col.) Ap '60.

——, Mexican. Holiday 28: 105 Sept '60.

——, Mexican (head). Holiday 14: 64 (col.) Nov '53.

——, Morocco. Disney: People & places, p. 86-95 (col.).
Holiday 23: cover (col.) Mar '58.
Natl. geog. 107: 181 (col.) Feb '55.

——, Morocco (head, veiled). Natl. geog. 107: 187 Feb '55.

——, mountaineer. Brooks: Growth of a nation, p. 212.

——, Nepalese (head). Holiday 21: 70 May '57.

——, Nigeria (weaving). Natl. geog. 110: 348 (col.) Sept '56.

——, old. Holiday 10: 1 Nov '51.

——, old (18th cent.). Con. 132: 19 (col.) Sept '53.

——, old (head, grey hair). Natl. geog. 112: 753 (col.) Dec '57.

——, old (lace maker). Holiday 21: 38 (col.) Jan '57.

——, old (seated). Amer. heri., vol. 8 no. 1 p. 12 (Dec '56).
Holiday 11: 96 Feb '52; 21: 60 Je '57; 26: 73 Nov '59.

——, old (vendor). Travel 104: inside cover Oct '55.

——, old (Oriental). Holiday 26: 96 Jl '59.

——, Peruvian. Natl. geog. 98: 438-9 (col.) Oct '50.

——, Peruvian (child on back). Natl. geog. 98: 438 (col.) Oct '50.

——, Peruvian (market). Natl. geog. 98: 439 (col.) Oct '50.

——, Portuguese. Holiday 15: 128 Mar '54.

——, Puerto Rican (dancing). Holiday 28: 88 Sept '60.

——, Puritan. Amer. heri., vol. 8 no. 6 p. 86 (Oct '57).

——, Puritan (head). Natl. geog. 107: 740 (col.) Je '55.

——, Rosicrucian. Travel 113: 13 Ap '60.

——, Rosicrucian (head). Travel 113: 13 Feb '60.

——, Scottish (spinning). Holiday 8: 43 (col.) Dec '50.

——, Sherpa (Tibet). Natl. geog. 117: 403 (col.) Mar '60.

——, Shetland is. (seated). Natl. geog. 104: 534 Oct '53.

——, Siberian (head). Natl. geog. 116: 749 Dec '59.

——, Southern (comic). Holiday 26: 77 Nov '59.

——, Spanish. Holiday 15: cover (col.) May '54.

——, Spanish (canning olives). Natl. geog. 97: 429 (col.) Ap '50.

——, Spanish (dancer). Travel 111: 37 May '59.

——, Spanish (head). Natl. geog. 109: 329 (col.) Mar '56.

——, Spanish (silk worker seated). Natl. geog. 100: 104 (col.) Jl '51.

——, Spanish (seated, 16th cent.). Int. gr. soc.: Arts . . . p. 111 (col.).

——, Sumerian (5000 yrs. old). Int. gr. soc.: Arts . . . p. 31 (col.).

——, Swedish. Natl. geog. 98: 635 (col.) Nov '50.

——, Swiss. Holiday 25: 81 Jan '59.

——, Swiss (laundry at town pool). Natl. geog. 110: 452 (col.) Oct '56.

——, Swiss (making bed). Natl. geog. 110: 453 (col.) Oct '56.

——, Tahiti. Holiday 28: 93 (col.) Oct '60.

——, Thrace. Natl. geog. 109: 62-3 (col.) Jan '56.

——, Tibet. Holiday 27: 64 May '60.

——, Trinidad (with cacao pods). Natl. geog. 103: 71 (col.) Jan '53.

——, Tristan (washing clothes). Natl. geog. 97: 111 (col.) Jan '50.

——, Tyrolean (dog). Holiday 26: 75 (col.) Sept '59.

——, veiled. Natl. geog. 107: 187 Feb '55; 113: 128, 132 Jan '58; 114: 631 (col.) Nov '58.

——, veiled (head). Natl. geog. 107: 187 Feb '55; 117: 85 (col.) Jan '60.

——, veiled (spinning wool). Natl. geog. 113: 132 Jan '58.

——, veiled (weaving). Natl. geog. 113: 136-7 Jan '58.

——, West Indies. Travel 109: 27 May '58.

——, West Indies (comic). Holiday 5: cover (col.) Feb '49.

——, western (early). Horan: Pict. hist. of wild west, p. 131-3, 135, 171, 201, 221, 227-8, 236.

——, western (early, horse). Horan: Pict. hist. of wild west, p. 132, 181.

——, western (early, scout). Horan: Pict. hist. of wild west, p. 127-9.

——, western (head). Holiday 27: 16 Feb '60.

——, western (horseback). Travel 104: cover Jl '55.

woman & baby. Holiday 8: inside back cover (col.) Oct '50; 27: 67 Ap '60.
Natl. geog. 110: 46 (col.) Jl '56; 110: 735 (col.) Dec '56.

—— (asleep on plane). Holiday 26: 167 (col.) Nov '59.

—— (bathing suit). Holiday 22: 136 Jl '57.

—— (heads). Holiday 24: 97 Sept '58; 25: 21 Feb '59, 9 Mar '59, 207 Ap '59, 133 Je '59; 26: 104 (col.) Jl '59.
Natl. geog. 97: 156 Feb '50.

—— (Ma'dan). Natl. geog. 113: 233 (col.) Feb '58.

—— (on running horse). Amer. heri., vol. 7 no. 3 p. 38 (Ap '56).

——, Baghdad. Natl. geog. 114: 454 (col.) Oct '58.

——, Cocos island. Holiday 12: 72 Nov '52.

——, Iraq. Natl. geog. 114: 476-7 (col.) Oct '58.

——, Turkey. Natl. geog. 110: 751 (col.) Dec '56.

woman & boy (camping). Holiday 14: 69 Jl '53.

—— (in auto). Holiday 10: 12 (col.) Sept '51.

—— (laughing). Holiday 19: 101 May '56.
Natl. geog. 116: 269 Aug '59.

—— (laughing, dog). Holiday 20: 99 (col.) Dec '56.

—— (making fishing flys). Natl. geog. 110: 41 (col.) Jl '56.

—— (old bath tub). Amer. heri., vol. 3 no. 4 p. 3 (summer '52).

—— (statue). Travel 104: 29 Jl '55.

—— (study lessons). Natl. geog. 99: 348 Mar '51.

——, Japanese. Holiday 24: 50 Dec '58.

woman & child. Con. 132: X-XI (col.) Jan '54; 133: XXIII (col.) May '54; 145: LXXX May '60, 238-9 Je '60.
Holiday 8: 57 (col.) Nov '50 14: 19 Sept '53; 18: 83 Oct '55; 22: 241 Dec '57; 23: 114 Jan '58, 163 Mar '58, 184-5 Ap '58, 187, 193, inside back cover (col.) May '58, 23 (col.), 124 Je '58; 24: inside cover (col.) Aug '58, 154 Oct '58; 25: 89 Mar '59, 181 Je '59; 26: 63 (col.) Aug '59, 76 Oct '59; 28: 129 Sept '60, 49 Dec '60.
Natl. geog. 98: 542 Oct '50; 103: 418 Mar '53; 118: 558 (col.) Oct '60.
Travel 101: inside back cover May '54.

—— (airplane). Holiday 22: 37 Oct '57.

—— (airplane, night). Holiday 22: 260 Dec '57.

—— (arrange flowers). Natl. geog. 109: 461 (col.) Ap '56.

'56; 23: 59 (col.) Jan '58.
Labande: Naples, p. 34.
—— (antique street lamp). Natl. geog. 114: 122 (col.) Jl '58.
—— (Avon river). Natl. geog. 108: 316 (col.) Sept '55.
—— (baby skunks). Natl. geog. 108: 287 Aug '55.
—— (back view). Natl. geog. 106: 372 (col.) Sept '54; 111: 771 (col.) Je '57. Travel 103: 21 Je '55.
—— (back view, harbor). Natl. geog. 112: 160 (col.) Aug '57.
—— (back view, hikers). Natl. geog. 110: 5 (col.) Jl '56.
—— (back view, memorial). Natl. geog. 110: 37 (col.) Jl '56.
—— (bathing baby). Natl. geog. 118: 581 (col.) Oct '60.
—— (beach). Holiday 23: 189 (col.) May '58; 25: 119 Ap '59; 26: 82 (col.) Nov '59. Natl. geog. 107: 822 Je '55; 108: 776 (col.) Dec '55; 116: 596-7 (col.) Nov '59.
—— (canal locks). Natl. geog. 104: 802 (col.) Dec '53.
—— (cicada collection). Natl. geog. 104: 140 Jl '53.
—— (elephant). Durant: Pict. hist. of Amer. circus, p. 141 (col.).
—— (harbor). Amer. heri., vol. 8 no. 5 cover (col.) (Aug '57).
—— (heads, funeral boat). Natl. geog. 108: 613 (col.) Nov '55.
—— (in car). Holiday 12: 17 (col.) Jl '52; 25: 116 Ap '59; 28: 161 (col.) Nov '60.
—— (lorikeets). Natl. geog. 110: 516-7 (col.) Oct '56.
—— (making candles). Natl. geog. 114: 124 (col.) Jl '58.
—— (Mersin, on mule). Osward: Asia Minor, pl. 129.
—— (natl. park). Natl. geog. 108: 87 (col.) Jl '55.
—— (outdoor cooking). Natl. geog. 98: 331 (col.) Sept '50.
—— (reading in bed). Holiday 22: 15 (col.) Nov '57.
—— (river bank). Natl. geog. 108: 337 (col.) Sept '55.
—— (seaside). Natl. geog. 112: 154-5 (col.) Aug '57.
—— (secrets). Holiday 22: 212 Dec '57.
—— (snake). Natl. geog. 98: 565 Nov '50.
—— (snow). Holiday 27: 213 (col.) Ap '60.
—— (spinet). Natl. geog. 97: 289 (col.) Mar '50.
—— (steps, flowers). Natl. geog. 109: 205 (col.) Feb '56.
—— (study table). Natl. geog. 110: 774 (col.) Dec '56.
—— (terrarium). Natl. geog. 106: 657 (col.) Nov '54.
—— (traveling). Holiday 23: 46 (col.) May '58.
—— (traveling fun). Holiday 26: 107-8 (col.) Nov '59; 27: 166 (col.) Je '60.
—— (walking, back view). Natl. geog. 101: 802 (col.) Je '52; 110: 815 (col.) Dec '56.

——, Bali. Natl. geog. 99: 26 (col.) Jan '51.
——, Colonial. Natl. geog. 118: 180 (col.) Aug '60.
——, Dutch. Natl. geog. 108: 78 (col.) Jl '55.
—— Dutch. See also mother & baby; mother & child.
woman & conductor (dog, train seat, comic). Holiday 10: 80 Aug '51.
woman & girl. Holiday 18: 40 Jl '55.
—— (heads). Holiday 24: 102 Oct '58, 27 Nov '58.
—— (heads, whispering). Holiday 11: 112 Je '52.
—— (laughing). Holiday 18: 92 (col.) Sept '55.
—— (shoe shop). Natl. geog. 100: 140 Jl '51.
——, Angkor Thom (India). Natl. geog. 116: 850 (col.) Dec '59.
——, Lhasa. Natl. geog. 108: 14 (col.) Jl '55.
woman & girls (reading). Natl. geog. 113: 267 (col.) Feb '58.
woman & man. See man & woman; men & woman.
woman & Mexican bullfight. Holiday 23: 114 Je '58.
woman & parrot (India). Natl. geog. 103: 156 (col.) Jan '53.
woman & pygmy children. Natl. geog. 117: 281 Feb '60.
woman & toreador. Travel 113: inside cover Ap '60.
woman at well (Jordan). Natl. geog. 110: 729 (col.) Dec '56.
woman, girl & Indian (knitting). Natl. geog. 116: 781 (col.) Dec '59.
"Woman in a blue blouse" (Picasso). Praeg.: Pict. ency., p. 455.
Woman playing cithara (1st cent.). Ceram: March of arch., opp. p. 31 (col.).
woman voter, Nigeria. Natl. geog. 118: 361 Sept '60.
woman weaving, Malay. Natl. geog. 103: 201 (col.) Feb '53.
——, Peru. Natl. geog. 98: 438 (col.) Oct '50.
"Woman weighing gold" (Vermeer). Holiday 7: 107 (col.) Feb '50.
"Woman who walks through water" (Maillol). Con. 143: 92 Ap '59.
"Woman with furs" (Dubuffet). Con. 145: 207 May '60.
"Woman with gramophone." Praeg.: Pict. ency., p. 13.
woman's rights (cartoon). See posters, woman's rights.
woman. See also family; lady; man & woman.
women. Holiday 14: 108-10 Oct '53. Jordan: Hammond's pict. atlas, p. 60 (col.).
—— (actresses). Holiday 24: 113 Dec '58.
—— (at table). Holiday 14: 104 Nov '53.
—— (baby in cart). Travel 104: 38 Jl '55.
—— (back view). Natl. geog. 100: 201 Aug '51; 106: 441 Oct '54.
—— (back view, fresco). Natl. geog. 111: 756 (col.) Je '57.
—— (back view, lake). Travel 109: cover Ap '58.
—— (back view, Mts.). Natl. geog. 102: 482 (col.) Oct '52.

women (basket of fish). Natl. geog. 113: 559 (col.) Ap '58.

—— (basket on head). Natl. geog. 106: 681 Nov '54.

—— (bathing suits, 1890). Amer. heri., vol. 9 no. 1 p. 84 (Dec '57).

—— (beach, 19th cent.). Amer. heri., vol. 8 no. 5 p. 49 (col.) (Aug '57).

—— (binoculars). Holiday 21: 57 Je '57.

—— (bird house). Holiday 18: 21 (col.) Sept '55.

—— (buckets on head). Natl. geog. 101: 357 (col.) Mar '52.

—— (bus office). Natl. geog. 98: 42 Jl '50.

—— (buying evening dress). Holiday 10: 60 Dec '51.

—— (campers, Alaska). Natl. geog. 109: 816 (col.), 818 Je '56.

—— (canning truffles). Natl. geog. 110: 424 Sept '56.

—— (carding wool). Natl. geog. 97: 106 Jan '50.

—— (cherry pie making). Natl. geog. 115: 486 (col.) Ap '59.

—— (cleaning seal skins). Natl. geog. 105: 139 (col.) Jan '54.

—— (cleaning herring). Natl. geog. 106: 572 (col.) Oct '54.

—— (clothes exhibit). Holiday 10: 108-13 (part col.) Nov '51; 11: 120-2, 124-5 Ap '52; 12: 102-7 (part col.) Jl '52; 18: 60-1 (col.) Oct '55.

—— (coat display). Holiday 20: 92-3 (col.) Oct '56.

—— (cooking). Natl. geog. 102: 510-11 (col.) Oct '52.

—— (corset). Holiday 18: 26 Oct '55.

—— (costume, Colonial). Natl. geog. 105: 447 (col.) Ap '54; 113: 43 (col.) Jan '58.

—— (costume, medieval). Int. gr. soc.: Arts . . . p. 53, 55, 61, 69 (col.).

—— (crabs). Natl. geog. 114: 182 (col.) Aug '58.

—— (D.A.R.). Natl. geog. 100: 581 (col.) Nov '51.

—— (dog). Natl. geog. 112: 441 (col.) Oct '57.

—— (doing laundry in river). Disney: People & places, p. 102 (col.).

—— (dress designing). Natl. geog. 98: 238 (col.) Aug '50.

—— (drying coconuts). Natl. geog. 116: 686 Nov '59.

—— (drying fish on beach). Natl. geog. 107: 503 (col.) Ap '55.

—— (1874). Amer. heri., vol. 7 no. 4 p. 91 (Je '56).

—— (1816-). Amer. heri., vol. 1 no. 3 p. 63 (spring '50).

—— (embroidering). Holiday 28: 67 Sept '60. Natl. geog. 111: 635 (col.) May '57.

—— (fishing). Natl. geog. 110: 838 (col.) Dec '56.

—— (fishmarket). Natl. geog. 106: 160 (col.) Aug '54.

—— (Flea market, Paris). Natl. geog. 111: 319-26 Mar '57.

—— (flower garden). Natl. geog. 100: 52-3 (col.) Jl '51.

—— (flower market). Natl. geog. 109: 836 (col.) Je '56.

—— (flowers). Holiday 10: 114 Nov '51.

—— (flowers, boat). Natl. geog. 117: 215 (col.) Feb '60.

—— (formal evening dress). Holiday 14: 31 (col.) Sept '53; 21: 56-7 (col.) Feb '57. Natl. geog. 100: 581 (col.) Nov '51.

—— (French caps). Natl. geog. 117: 728 (col.) Je '60.

—— (French clothes exhibit). Holiday 11: 99-103 (col.) Feb '52.

—— (fur coats). Holiday 24: 123 (col.) Sept '58, inside back cover (col.) Nov '58.

—— (give food to Buddhist novices). Natl. geog. 117: 53 (col.) Jan '60.

—— (grain gleaners). Natl. geog. 115: 603 May '59.

—— (greeting man guest). Natl. geog. 103: 329 (col.) Mar '53.

—— (hats). Natl. geog. 99: 129 (col.) Jan '51.

—— (heads). Holiday 10: 91, 129 Nov '51, 149 Dec '51; 11: 23, 77 Jan '52, 124 Ap '52; 13: 2 (col.), 22, 29, 53 (col.), 84-5, 89 (col.), 134 Mar '53; 26: 102 Jl '59, 49 Aug '59, 124 Sept '59, 109, 186 Oct '59.

Int. gr. soc.: Arts . . . p. 133 (col.).

—— (heads, comic). Holiday 25: 169 May '59, 34 Je '59; 26: 121 Sept '59.

—— (heads, "Dove cottage"). Natl. geog. 109: 538 (col.) Ap '56.

—— (heads, hats). Holiday 10: 16 Sept '51.

—— (heads, laughing). Natl. geog. 97: 294 (col.) Mar '50.

—— (hoeing). Travel 110: 20 Oct '58.

—— (horses). Natl. geog. 112: 482-3 (col.) Oct '57.

—— (horse, back view). Natl. geog. 108: 234 (col.) Aug '55.

—— (kitchen). Holiday 10: 104-7 Aug '51. Natl. geog. 109: 535 (col.) Ap '56.

—— (laughing). Holiday 21: 83 Je '57; 22: 144 Sept '57. Natl. geog. 100: 566-7 Nov '51.

—— (library table). Natl. geog. 97: 677 May '50.

—— (looking at book). Natl. geog. 109: 445 Ap '56.

—— (lying down). Travel 10: inside back cover Ap '58.

—— (making mattress). Natl. geog. 10: 23 Jl '51.

—— (mending fishnets). Natl. geog. 105: 155 (col.) Feb '54.

—— (miniatures). Con. ency. of ant., vol. 1, pl. 129-32.

—— (models). Holiday 13: 92-5 (part col.) Feb '53. Travel 106: 11 Jl '56.

—— (Mt. top, snow). Natl. geog. 99: 594 (col.) May '51.

—— (old Testament life). Natl. geog. 118: 822-48 (part col.) Dec '60.

—— (on stairs). Natl. geog. 105: 454 (col.) Ap '54.

—— (outdoor feast, butler). Natl. geog. 113: 177 (col.) Feb '58.

—— (outdoor table). Natl. geog. 99: 448 (col.) Ap '51.

—— (pack bananas). Natl. geog. 107: 517 (col.) Ap '55.

—— (pack mule). Natl. geog. 109: 882 Je '56.

—— (party). Holiday 22: 51 Sept '57.

"Women" (Picasso tapestry). Holiday 14: 51 (col.) Dec '53.

—— (picking hops). Natl. geog. 99: 164 (col.) Feb '51.

—— (picking lilies). Natl. geog. 105: 231 (col.) Feb '54.

—— (planting rice). Natl. geog. 103: 47 (col.) Jan '53.

—— (playing chess). Amer. heri., vol. 7 no. 5 p. 2 (Aug '56).

—— (playing shuffleboard). Holiday 24: 81 Nov '58.

—— (raking hay). Natl. geog. 100: 392 (col.) Sept '51.

—— (reading paper). Natl. geog. 113: 181 (col.) Feb '58.

—— (riding airplane). Holiday 14: 66 (col.) Oct '53.

—— (rob man, 1894). Amer. heri., vol. 11 no. 6 p. 110 (Oct '60).

—— (rocks). Natl. geog. 115: 282 (col.) Feb '59.

—— (scientific experiments). Natl. geog. 100: 758, 765-6, 775, 777, 780-1, 784 (part col.) Dec '51.

—— (seated). Holiday 13: 102 (col.), 138 Mar '53, 167 (col.) May '53.

—— (seated at party). Holiday 14: 48 Dec '53.

—— (seated, back view). Natl. geog. 98: 770 (col.) Dec '50. Travel 114: 38 Dec '60.

—— (seated, 18th cent.). Int. gr. soc.: Arts . . . p. 93 (col.). Natl. geog. 113: 258 (col.) Feb '58.

—— (seated, hats on). Int. gr. soc.: Arts . . . p. 155 (col.).

—— (shaping sweater). Natl. geog. 104: 524 Oct '53.

—— (show dogs). Natl. geog. 105: 103-5, 108 (col.), 112 Jan '54.

—— (sports wear). Holiday 18: 21 (col.) Sept '55.

—— (stooping). Natl. geog. 100: 609 Nov '51.

—— (swimming). Travel 112: 34 Aug '59.

—— (table). Holiday 14: 141 Nov '53.

—— (tea table). Natl. geog. 107: 312 (col.) Mar '55; 109: 479-80 (col.) Ap '56.

—— (terrace tea table). Natl. geog. 109: 674 (col.) May '56.

—— (tie tobacco). Natl. geog. 113: 561 Ap '58.

—— (umbrellas, snow). Natl. geog. 113: 658 (col.) May '58.

—— (umbrellas, walking). Natl. geog. 106: 428 Sept '54.

—— (underclothes). Holiday 14: 145 Dec '53.

—— (washing clothes in pool). Holiday 7: 98 (col.) Jan '50.

—— (washing clothes in stream). Natl. geog. 97: 135 Jan '50.

—— (water pails on pole). Natl. geog. 109: 276 (col.) Feb '56.

—— (weaving baskets). Natl. geog. 109: 218 (col.) Feb '56.

—— (weed forest seedlings). Natl. geog. 117: 473 (col.) Ap '60.

—— (weed seedlings). Natl. geog. 110: 300-1 (col.) Sept '56.

—— (winter coats). Holiday 10: 146 Dec '51; 11: 6 Feb '52; 12: 114-17 (part col.) Oct '52.

—— (working at table). Natl. geog. 102: 103 (col.) Jl '52.

——, African. Natl. geog. 108: 774 (col.) Dec '55; 118: 332-3, 353, 361, 372, 386-7 (part col.) Sept '60.

——, African (babies on backs). Natl. geog. 101: 357 (col.) Mar '52.

——, African (trays of bread on head). Natl. geog. 118: 316, 332-3 (col.) Sept '60.

——, African (weaving). Natl. geog. 97: 325 (col.) Mar '50.

——, Algiers (veiled, shoppers). Natl. geog. 117: 771 (col.) Je '60.

——, Antioch. Osward: Asia Minor, pl. 28.

——, Arabian. See Arabian women.

——, Araucanian. Natl. geog. 117: 213 (col.) Feb '60.

——, Austria. Natl. geog. 99: 780-1 (col.) Je '51.

——, Austria (house yard). Natl. geog. 115: 205 (col.) Feb '59.

——, Baghdad (veiled). Natl. geog. 114: 40 (col.) Jl '58.

——, Bali (burden on heads). Natl. geog. 99: 25 (col.) Jan '51.

——, Bali (rice fields). Natl. geog. 99: 14 (col.) Jan '51.

——, Belgian (spinning). Natl. geog. 113: 803 (col.) Je '58.

——, Belgian (street market). Natl. geog. 108: 548 (col.) Oct '55.

——, Cambodia. Natl. geog. 117: 543 (col.) Ap '60.

——, Cameroons. Natl. geog. 116: 243 (col.) Aug '59.

——, Caribbean. Holiday 23: 38-9 (col.) Feb '58, 137 (col.) May '58.

——, Caribbean (sorting beans). Holiday 24: 144 (col.) Oct '58.

——, Chinese. See Chinese man & woman; Chinese men & women.

——, circus (on horses). Amer. heri., vol. 7 no. 1 p. 38 (col.) (Dec '55).

——, Colonial. Amer. heri., vol. 4 no. 1 p. 3 (fall '52).

——, Colonial (at tea table). Amer. heri., vol. 8 no. 1 p. 9 (col.) (Dec '56).

——, Derbyshire (Eng.). Natl. geog. 98: 176 (col.) Aug '50.

——, Dutch (heads). Natl. geog. 98: 763 (col.) Dec '50.

——, Dutch (picnic). Natl. geog. 98: 770 (col.) Dec '50.

——, Egyptian (jugs on head). Natl. geog. 108: 625 (col.) Nov '55.

women, Egyptian (19th cent.). Praeg.: Pict. ency., p. 116 (col.).

——, French (cooking). Natl. geog. 115: 602 (col.) May '59.

——, French Canadian. Natl. geog. 98: 353 (col.) Sept '50.

——, Grecian. Natl. geog. 103: 381 (col.) Mar '53; 114: 771 (col.) Dec '58.

——, Grecian (harvest wheat). Natl. geog. 109: 50 (col.) Jan '56.

——, Grecian (weeding garden). Natl. geog. 110: 739 (col.), 741 Dec '56.

——, Hawaiian. Holiday 15: 2 Feb '54.

——, Hindu. Natl. geog. 107: 413 (col.) Mar '55; 118: 481, 491 (col.) Oct '60.

——, Hunza (seated). Natl. geog. 104: 499 (col.), 501 Oct '53.

——, Hunza valley (horseback). Natl. geog. 117: 93 (col.) Jan '60.

——, Iceland. Natl. geog. 100: 615, 619 (col.) Nov '51.

——, India. Face of Amer. p. 81 (col.).

——, India (heads). Natl. geog. 117: 630-1 (col.) May '60.

——, Indian (Easter, Guatemala). Natl. geog. 117: 407 (col.) Mar '60.

——, Indian (Terascan, eating at table). Natl. geog. 102: 545 (col.) Oct '52.

——, Iranian. Natl. geog. 104: 708-20 Nov '53.

——, Iranian (washing clothes in stream). Travel 113: 35 Feb '60.

——, Iraq. (cooking). Natl. geog. 113: 222 (col.) Feb '58.

——, Jain. Natl. geog. 118: 465 (col.) Oct '60.

——, Japanese. Con. 141: VIII Je '58.

——, Japanese (sand treatment). Natl. geog. 104: 650 Nov '53.

——, Japanese (seated). Natl. geog. 97: 622 (col.) May '50.

——, Java (tea pickers). Natl. geog. 108: 368 (col.) Sept '55.

——, Karachi (baskets on head). Natl. geog. 100: 734 (col.) Dec '51.

——, Kashgai (weaving carpet). Natl. geog. 101: 826-7 (col.) Je '52.

——, Korean (silk thread reel). Natl. geog. 97: 797 (col.) Je '50.

——, Korean (washing clothes). Natl. geog. 103: 647 (col.) May '53.

——, Ladakh (winnow barley). Natl. geog. 99: 628 (col.) May '51.

——, Lapland. Disney: People & places, p. 18-23 (col.).

——, Lebanon (baking bread). Natl. geog. 113: 520-1 (col.) Ap '58.

——, Majorca (cooking). Natl. geog. 111: 651 May '57.

——, Martinique (fruit basket on head). Natl. geog. 115: 259 (col.) Feb '59.

——, Martinique (bundle on head). Natl. geog. 115: 277 (col.) Feb '59.

——, Morocco (veiled). Natl. geog. 107: 187 Feb '55.

——, Moslem. Holiday 25: 148 Ap '59. Natl. geog. 114: 29 (col.) Jl '58.

——, Moslem (child sleeping). Natl. geog. 114: 637 (col.) Nov '58.

——, Moslem (praying). Natl. geog. 114: 607 (col.) Nov '58.

——, Moslem (veiled). Natl. geog. 114: 631 (col.) Nov '58.

——, Moslem (work in field). Natl. geog. 106: 834 (col.) Dec '54.

——, Nepal (seated). Natl. geog. 97: 39 (col.) Jan '50.

——, Nigerian (baskets on heads). Natl. geog. 104: 152 (col.) Aug '53.

——, Nigerian (calabashes on heads). Natl. geog. 110: 345 (col.) Sept '56.

——, Nigerian (seated by throne). Natl. geog. 110: 340 (col.) Sept '56.

——, Nigerian (street market). Travel 107: 40 Feb '57.

——, Nomad shepherd. See Nomad shepherd women.

——, Nuba (baskets on heads). Natl. geog. 99: 257 Feb '51.

——, old (telling secrets). Con. 142: XLVII Nov '58.

——, Pakistan. Natl. geog. 111: 80 Jan '57.

——, Pakistan (at table). Natl. geog. 107: 411 (col.) Mar '55.

——, Pakistan (doing laundry). Natl. geog. 107: 414 (col.) Mar '55.

——, Pakistan (heads). Natl. geog. 117: 609 (col.) May '60.

——, Palestine (ancient). Natl. geog. 118: 840 (col.) Dec '60.

——, Palma (farm). Natl. geog. 111: 638 (col.) May '57.

——, Pennsylvania (cooking). Amer. heri., vol. 3 no. 4 p. 30 (summer '52).

——, Penn. Dutch. Jordan: Hammond's pict. atlas, p. 47 (col.).

——, Polynesian. Holiday 9: 57 (col.) Mar '51; 28: 2 (col.) Oct '60.

——, Portuguese (baskets on heads). Disney: People & places, p. 57 (col.).

——, Portuguese (sorting sardines). Disney: People & places, p. 60 (col.).

——, Portuguese (washing clothes). Holiday 6: 108 Sept '49.

——, Puerto Rican. Travel 109: 30-1 May '58.

——, Russian. Natl. geog. 116: 374 (col.) Sept '59.

——, Russian (back view). Natl. geog. 116: 741 (col.) Dec '59.

——, Russian (baskets of flowers). Natl. geog. 116: 743 (col.) Dec '59.

——, Russian (heads). Natl. geog. 116: 746 (col.) Dec '59.

——, Russian (in church). Natl. geog. 116: 385 (col.) Sept '59.

——, Russian (laborers). Natl. geog. 116: 732 Dec '59.

——, Sardinia. Disney: People & places, p. 75 (col.).

——, Sicily (picking flowers). Natl. geog. 107: 18 (col.) Jan '55.

——, South Africa. Holiday 21: 38 (col.) Feb '57.

——, Spanish. Natl. geog. 87: 439 (col.) Ap '50.

——, Spanish (heads, mantillas). Natl. geog. 99: 513 (col.) Ap '51.

——, Spanish (silk worm workers). Natl. geog. 100: 103-7 (col.) Jl '51.

——, Sumatra (baskets on heads). Natl. geog. 99: 39 (col.) Jan '51.

——, Swiss (washing clothes in trough). Natl. geog. 98: 228 (col.) Sept '50.

——, Taiyal (dancers). Natl. geog. 97: 169 (col.) Feb '50.

——, Tangier island. Travel 101: 12 Je '54.

——, Thailand (laborers). Natl. geog. 117: 669 (col.) May '60.

——, Tristan (kneeling). Natl. geog. 97: 116 (col.) Jan '50.

——, Tristan (seated, knitting). Natl. geog. 97: 116 (col.) Jan '50.

——, Turkish (seated). Natl. geog. 100: 185 Aug '51.

——, Turkish (winnowing grain). Natl. geog. 115: 66 (col.) Jan '59.

——, Ukranian. Natl. geog. 108: 226 (col.) Aug '55.

——, veiled. See woman, veiled.

——, Vienna (tea table). Natl. geog. 115: 192 (col.) Feb '59.

——, Yugoslavia. Natl. geog. 99: 149, 154-5 (col.) Feb '51.

women & babies. Travel 105: 29 May '56.

——, Russian. Natl. geog. 116: 746 (col.) Dec '59.

——. (See also woman & baby.

women & boy (Backview.) Natl. geog. 118: 327 (col.) Sept '60.

——. See also woman & boy.

women & child. Holiday 21: 31 (col.) Mar '57.

—— (dog, tea party). Natl. geog. 110: 42 (col.) Jl '56.

——, Arabia. Natl. geog. 114: 227 Nov '58.

——, Borneo. Natl. geog. 108: 387 (col.) Sept '55.

——, Kurds (camel). Natl. geog. 115: 63 (col.) Jan '59.

—— (See also woman & child.

women & children (walking, backview). Natl. geog. 114: 368 (col.) Sept '58.

——, Afghanistan (seated). Natl. geog. 98: 689 (col.) Nov '50.

——, India (New Delhi). Natl. geog. 116: 838-9 (col.) Dec '59.

——, Iran (in tent). Natl. geog. 101: 821 (col.) Je '52.

——, Japan. Natl. geog. 118: 757 (col.) Dec '60.

——, Pescadores (well). Natl. geog. 109: 272 (col.) Feb '56.

——. See also woman & children.

women & men. See men & women.

"Women bathing in a wood" (Blechen). Praeg.: Pict. ency., p. 395 (col.).

women kneeling (Catholic-Poland). Natl. geog. 114: 372-3 (col.) Sept '58.

women laborers, Polish. See laborers, Polish women.

women marines. Natl. geog. 98: 667 Nov '50.

women of the world. Holiday 16: 105-16 (part col.) Dec '54; 17: 48-62 (part col.) Jan '55.

——, famous. Holiday 17: 90 (col.), 91-103 Feb '55.

women weaving (Turkey). Natl. geog. 110: 728 (col.) Dec '56.

women. See also mother; man & woman; men & women; woman.

Wong Wen-Hao. Cur. biog. p. 690 (1948).

Wood, Barry. Holiday 26: 64 Nov '59.

Wood, Christopher (work of). Con. 136: 140 Nov '55.

Wood, Esther. Jun. bk. of auth., p. 301.

Wood, Fernando. Amer. heri., vol. 10 no. 4 p. 97 (Je '59).

Wood, Gar (work of). Brooks: Growth of a nation, p. 237.

Wood, Grant (work of). Amer. heri., vol. 6 no. 1 p. 42 (col.) (fall '54).

Wood, James. Con. 144, 8 Sept '59.

Wood, James Madison. Cur. biog. p. 691 (1947).

Wood, John (work of). Con. 135: XL Je '55.

Wood, John S. Cur. biog. p. 644 (1949).

Wood, Louise A. Cur. biog. p. 481 (1961).

Wood, Natalie. Cur. biog. p. 472 (1962).

Wood, Peggy. Cur. biog. p. 894 (1942); p. 659 (1953).

Wood, Robert E. Cur. biog. p. 934 (1941).

Wood, Sam. Cur. biog. p. 844 (1943).

wood (being carried on steamboat). Amer. heri., vol. 8 no. 6 p. 19 (col.) (Oct '57).

—— (sym.). Lehner: Pict. bk. of sym., p. 73.

——, laminated. Natl. geog. 110: 317 (col.) Sept '56.

——, petrified. See petrified wood.

wood block designs. Con. 139: 235-9 Je '57.

wood carver (Austria). Natl. geog. 118: 255 (col.) Aug '60.

—— (Japan). Disney: People & places, p. 151-2 (col.).

wood carving. Con. 127: 102-3 May '51. Natl. geog. 100: 393 (col.) Sept '51.

—— (antique). Rawson: Ant. pict. bk., p. 86.

—— (1490). Praeg.: Pict. ency., p. 205 (col.).

—— (head hunters). Natl. geog. 108: 454-5 (col.) Oct '55.

—— (Japan, 17th cent.). Natl. geog. 116: 857 (col.) Dec '59.

—— (lectern, 1150). Praeg.: Pict. ency., p. 191 (col.).

—— (man). Natl. geog. 98: 347 Sept '50.

—— (man, Italy). Natl. geog. 116: 494 (col.) Oct '59.

—— ("navigator"). Amer. heri., vol. 10 no. 2 frontis. (col.) (Feb '59).

—— (New Guinea). Holiday 28: 83-97 (col.) Nov '60.

—— (Nigeria). Holiday 25: 146 (col.) Ap '59. Praeg.: Pict. ency., p. 561.

—— (Norway). Con. 145: 34-7 Mar '60.

—— (statue). Praeg.: Pict. ency., p. 17.

—— (woman's head). Praeg.: Pict. ency., p. 367.

—— (figures). Amer. heri., vol. 2 no. 2 p. 32 (col.) (winter '51). Con. 136: LIII Sept '55.

—— (Grinling Gibbons). Con. 140: XLVII Dec '57.

wood engraving (Durer). Int. gr. soc.: Arts . . . p. 89 (col.).

wood pulp machine. Natl. geog. 99: 133 (col.) Jan '51.

wood stacked, winter. Natl. geog. 98: 219 (col.) Aug '50.

wood statue, carved (15th cent.). Con. 142: LXV Dec '58.

wood work. Amer. heri., vol. 7 no. 4 p. 99 (Je '56).

wood worker (man). Amer. heri., vol. 3 no. 3 p. 33 (col.) (spring '52).

woodcut. Amer. heri., vol. 7 no. 1 p. 83 (Dec '55).

—— (Dore, book illus.). Praeg.: Pict. ency., p. 407.

—— (Ernst). Praeg.: Pict. ency., p. 453.

—— (Holbein). Praeg.: Pict. ency., p. 304.

—— (mother & child). Praeg.: Pict. ency., p. 457.

——, German (antique). Con. 129: 143 Je '52.

woodcutters race. Natl. geog. 101: 452 (col.) Ap '52.

Woodfill, Samuel. Amer. heri., vol. 10 no. 6 p. 12 (col.) (Oct '59).

Woodford, Stewart L. Amer. heri., vol. 8 no. 2 p. 39 (Feb '57).

Woodham-Smith, Cecil. Cur. biog. p. 656 (1955).

Woodhouse, Chase Going. Cur. biog. p. 691 (1945).

Woodhull, Victoria Claflin. Amer. heri., vol. 7 no. 4 p. 45, 47 (Je '56).

Woodhull, Victoria Claflin (cartoon as Satin). Amer. heri., vol. 7 no. 4 p. 46 (Je '56).

"woodin-up" (carrying wood on steamboat). Amer. heri., vol. 8 no. 6 p. 19 (col.) (Oct '57).

"Woodpecker" (Graves). Con. 145: 209 May '60.

woodpile (Canada). Natl. geog. 118: 104-5 Jl '60.

Woodruff, George A. Amer. heri., vol. 9 no. 2 p. 30 (Feb '58).

Woodruff, Robert. Holiday 19: 39 (col.) Je '56.

Woods, Mark. Cur. biog. p. 661 (1946).

Woods, Tighe E. Cur. biog. p. 692 (1948).

Woods motor vehicles. See motor vehicles, Woods.

Woodsawyer & Apprentice (1854). Amer. heri., vol. 8 no. 1 p. 55 (Dec '56).

Woodside, John A. (work of). Amer. heri., vol. 7 no. 3 p. 48-9 (col.) (Ap '56); vol. 8 no. 6 frontis (col.) (Oct '57).

Woodsmall, Ruth F. Cur. biog. p. 646 (1949).

"Woodsman's home" (Beechey). Con. 129: 79 Je '52.

Woodson, Carter G. Cur. biog. p. 742 (1944).

Woodward, Joanne. Cur. biog. p. 482 (1958).

Woodward, Robert B. Cur. biog. p. 648 (1952)

Woodward, Robert F. Cur. biog. p. 475 (1962).

Woodward, Stanley. Cur. biog. p. 668 (1951).

woodwind musical instruments. Int. gr. soc.: Arts . . . p. 141 (col.).

wool carding comb. Rawson: Ant. pict. bk., p. 33.

wood carding comb & basket. Disney: People & places, p. 78 (col.).

wool dyers (Morocco). Natl. geog. 107: 182 (col.) Feb '55.

wool spinning (Moroccan girl). Natl. geog. 107: 181 (col.) Feb '55.

Woolridge, Dean E. Cur. biog. p. 349 (1958).

Woollcott, Alexander. Cur. biog. p. 936 (1941). Holiday 11: 9, 14 Feb '52.

Woollen, Evans, jr. Cur. biog. p. 694 (1948).

Woolley, Sir Leonard. Cur. biog. p. 663 (1954).

Woolley, Mary E. Cur. biog. p. 897 (1942).

Woolton, Lord Frederick James. Cur. biog. p. 625 (1950).

Wootton, John (work of). Con. 127: 48 Mar '51; 140: XIX Nov '57; 141: 59 Mar '58; 144: 202 Dec '59; 145: XLVII Mar '60, 146 May '60.

Worcester (Mass.). Natl. geog. 107: 191-214 (part col.) Feb '55.

Worcester academy. Natl. geog. 107: 210 (col.) Feb '55.

Worcester bowl. Con. 133: 264 Je '54.

Worcester dishes. Con. 132: 169 Jan '54.

Worcester polytechnic institute. Natl. geog. 107: 198 (col.) Feb '55.

Worcester porcelain dishes. Con. 133: LXIV Je '54; 135: 269 Je '55.

Wordsworth, William. Con. 144: 9 Sept '59.

Wordsworth's home ("Dove cottage"). Natl. geog. 109: 538 (col.) Ap '56.

Work, Martin H. Cur. biog. p. 669 (1951).

work table (18th cent.). Con. 143: XXXII Je '59.

—— (1790). Con. ency. of ant., vol. 3 pl. 14.

——, French (18th cent.). Con. ency. of ant., vol 3 pl. 14.

worker. See laborer.

workshop (McCormick reaper made here). Brooks: Growth of a nation, p. 103.

world, sigil of the. See sigil of the world.

world agricultural fair. See agricultural fair, world.

world globe (without Amer.). Amer. heri., vol. 7 no. 1 p. 79 (Dec '55).

"World upside down" (Steen). Natl. geog. 97: 746 (col.) Je '50.

world war army (in Russia). Amer. heri. vol. 10 no. 1 p. 26-9 (Dec '58).

World war memorial hall (Indianapolis). Holiday 8: 39 (col.) Aug '50.

World's agricultural fair (New Delhi, U.S. pavilion). Travel 113: 44 Ap '60.

World's fair (Chicago). See Chicago Columbian exposition.

World's fair symbol, Brussels. See Brussels world's fair symbol.

Worms cathedral. Praeg.: Pict. ency., p. 250.

Worsham, Lew. Cur. biog. p. 665 (1954).

"Worship of Venus" (Titian). Con. 126: 176 Dec '50.

Worth, Kathryn. Jun. bk. of auth., p. 302.

Wörther See, (Austria). Natl. geog. 99: 778 (col.) Je '51.

Worthington, Leslie B. Cur. biog. p. 467 (1960).

Worthington, Thomas. Amer. heri., vol. 4 no. 3 p. 46 (spring '53).

Wotruba, Fritz (work of). Praeg.: Pict. ency., p. 515.

Wouk, Herman. Cur. biog. p. 649 (1952).

Wouwerman, Philip (work of). Con. 139: 191 May '57; 144: LXIII (col.) (Dec '59).

wrappings, gift. *See* package (Christmas wrapped); package (gift wrapped).

wreath, Christmas. Holiday 8: 125, 146 (col.) Dec '50; 10: 148, 189 (col.) Dec '51.

——, **flower.** Amer. heri., vol. 8 no. 4 p. 43 (col.) (Je '57).

——, **golden wedding.** Lehner: Pict. bk. of sym., p. 56.

——, **holly.** Lehner: Pict. bk. of sym., p. 51.

——, **memorial.** Lehner: Pict. bk. of sym., p. 54.

——, **silver wedding.** Lehner: Pict. bk. of sym., p. 56.

wreath & trumpet (sym.). Lehner: Pict. bk. of sym., p. 85.

wreathes, flower. Natl. geog. 114: 600 (col.) Nov '58.

wreck, auto. *See* auto accident.

Wren, Sir Christopher (arch. by). Praeg.: Pict. ency., p. 380.

wrens, uniformed (women in war). Natl. geog. 101: 519 (col.) Ap '52.

wrestler, Mexican. Travel. 105: 52 Mar '56.

wrestlers. Natl. geog. 99: 258 Feb '51; 100: 623 (col.) Nov '51; 106: 634 (col.) Nov '54.

——, **Japanese.** Amer. heri., vol. 9 no. 3 p. 20 (col.) (Ap '58).

Natl. geog. 97: 613 May '50; 118: 768 (col.) Dec '60.

——, **Pakistan.** Natl. geog. 105: 512 (col.) Ap '54.

wrestling match. Natl. geog. 115: 860 Je '59.

Wright, Benjamin F. Cur. biog. p. 658 (1955).

Wright, Cobina, sr. Holiday 12: 36 Oct '52.

Wright, Fielding L. Cur. biog. p. 695 (1948).

Wright, Frank Lloyd. Cur. biog. p. 939 (1941); p. 652 (1952).

Holiday 19: 85 Mar '56; 23: 149 Je '58.

—— (arch. by). Int. gr. soc.: Arts . . . p. 125 (col.).

Praeg.: Pict. ency., p. 442.

Wright, Gilbert S. (work of). Con. 138: XXVIII Nov '56.

Wright, Helen. Cur. biog. p. 656 (1956).

Wright, Horatio Gouverneur. Pakula: Cent. album . . . p. 293.

Wright, Adm. Jerauld. Cur. biog. p. 661 (1955).

Wright, John J. Cur. biog. (1963).

Wright, John Michael (work of). Con. 139: 8 Mar '57.

Wright, Joseph (work of). Con. 126: cover (col.) Oct '50; 129: XIII Ap '52; 138: 188 Dec '56; 142: 193 Dec '58; 143: 176 Mar '59.

Wright, Louis B. Cur. biog. p. 628 (1950).

Wright, Loyd Earl. Cur. biog. p. 663 (1955).

Wright, Martha. Cur. biog. p. 664 (1955).

Wright, Sir Michael. Cur. biog. p. 482 (1961).

—— (work of). Con. 142: 24 Sept '58.

Wright, Orville. Amer. heri., vol. 5 no. 2 p. 42 (winter '54).

Cur. biog. p. 663 (1946).

Wright, Quincy. Cur. biog. p. 846 (1943).

Wright, Lord Robert A. Cur. biog. p. 693 (1945).

Wright, Russel. Cur. biog. p. 629 (1950).

Wright, Teresa. Cur. biog. p. 847 (1943).

Wright, Theodore P. Cur. biog. p. 695 (1945).

Wright, Wilbur. Amer. heri., vol. 5 no. 2 p. 42 (winter '54); vol. 11 no. 2 p. 60, 62 (Feb '60).

Wright architecture, Frank Lloyd. Holiday 13: 60-1 (part col.) Mar '53.

Wright Bros. memorial (Kitty Hawk, N.C.). Holiday 13: 88 Ap '53.

Jordan: Hammond's pict. atlas, p. 56 (col.). Natl. geog. 108: 509 (col.) Oct '55.

Wright Bros. work-shop (replica). Natl. geog. 108: 508 (col.) Oct '55.

Wright Bros. flying machine. *See* flying machine, Wright.

Wright home, Frank Lloyd (Ariz.). Holiday 13: 34 (col.) Jan '53.

Wright museum, Frank Lloyd (model). Natl. geog. 111: 176 (col.) Feb '57.

Wrinch, Dorothy. Cur. biog. p. 694 (1947).

Wriston, Henry M. Cur. biog. p. 655 (1952).

writer (sym.). Lehner: Pict. bk. of sym., p. 91.

writers. *See* authors.

writing, Chinese. *See* Chinese writing.

——, **Egyptian (on stone).** Natl. geog. 108: 645 Nov '55.

writing box (16th cent.). Con. ency. of ant., vol. 3, pl. 118, 121.

——, **enamel.** Con. ency. of ant., vol. 1, pl. 73.

writing bureau, Amer. Int. gr. soc.: Arts . . . p. 105 (col.).

——, **French empire.** Con. 133: VI Je '54.

writing cabinet (antique). Con. 129: 42 Ap '52; 143: LII Je '59.

—— (18th cent.). Con. 141: 83-7 Ap '58.

—— (17th cent.). Con. 143: 79 Ap '59.

——, **Charles II.** Con. 138: LVII Nov '56.

——, **Chippendale.** Con. 143: LXXI Je '59.

——, **French regency.** Con. 138: IV Sept '56.

——, **Norwegian (18th cent.).** Con. 145: 24 Mar '60.

——, **Queen Anne.** Con. 144: XXIX Dec '59.

——, **Sheraton.** Con. 135: IV Mar '55.

——, **Swedish.** Con. 133: 35 Mar '54.

writing desk (antique). Praeg.: Pict. ency., p. 347.

—— (18th cent.). Con. 133: I May '54; 142: XXXIV Nov '58.

——, **Chippendale.** Con. 141: LI Mar '58; 144: XLVIII Jan '60.

——, **marquetry (Hache).** Con. 145: LXXVII Je '60.

——, **Sheraton.** Con. 138: XXI Nov '56; 141: XXXVII Je '58; 142: XXVII Dec '58.

writing of Bernardino de Sahagun (sample). Ceram: March of arch., p. 259.

writing set & clock (18th cent.). Int. gr. soc.: Arts . . . p. 95 (col.).

writing table (antique). Con. 126: 42 Aug '50; 129: 18 Ap '52; 133: XXXIII Mar '54; 137: VI Mar '56, XXXVII Ap '56; 139: 247 Je '57; 140: 228 Jan '58.

—— (18th cent.). Con. 133: XXXV May '54; 138: XV Sept '56; 143: inside back cover Je '59; 145: XLII Je '60.

——, **back-to-back.** Con. 141: XXVII May '58.

——, **Chippendale.** Con. 135: XXXIX Je '55.

writing table, French (antique). Con. 132: VI Sept '53; 140: 40 Sept '57.

——, **gate-leg (17th cent.).** Con. ency. of ant., vol. 3, pl. 15.

——, **Gothic style.** Con. 137: 107 Ap '56.

——, **Hepplewhite.** Con. 143: inside back cover Mar '59; 145: inside back cover May '60.

——, **Hepplewhite kidney shaped.** Con. 140: XXXVIII Jan '58.

——, **kneehole (antique).** Con. 144: 42 Sept '59.

——, **Louis XV.** Con. 139: 56 Mar '57; 142: 197 Dec '58; 142: 255 Jan '59; 143: 211 Je '59; 144: LII Nov '59, LXXII Dec '59.

——, **Louis XV parquetry.** Con. 144: 269 Jan '60.

——, **marquetry (folding top).** Con. ency. of ant., vol. 3, pl. 15.

——, **marquetry & brass (18th cent.).** Con. 145: 109 Ap '60.

——, **Queen Marie Antoinette.** Con. 143: 213 Je '59.

——, **regency.** Con. 133: back cover Je '54; 136: XLI Jan '56; 138: XXIX Nov '56; 144: LVIII Jan '60; 145: XXII Ap '60.

——, **regency (18th cent.).** Con. 132: XII Sept '53.

——, **regency knee-hole.** Con. 139: XVII May '57.

——, **Rococo.** Osward: Asia Minor, pl. 99.

——, **Sheraton.** Con. 129: 129: inside back cover Ap '52; 133: VI Mar '54; 135: XII Je '55; 136: LX Nov '55, XLII Jan '56; 143: XXXV Mar '59, XII Je '59; 144: XXXVIII Sept '59.

——, **Sheraton lady's.** Con. 144: XIV Dec '59; 145: XXIV Mar '60.

——, **Sheraton pedestal.** Con. 133: XLI Ap '54.

——, **sofa (regency).** Con. 145: inside back cover Je '60.

——, **Viennese.** Con. ency. of ant., vol. 3, pl. 17.

writing table & cartonnier (Vardy, 1745). Con. 144: 223 Jan '60.

writing table & top detail (17th cent.). Con. ency. of ant., vol. 3, pl. 15.

writing table. See also bureau plat.

Wrong, Humphrey Hume. Cur. biog. p. 631 (1950).

Wu, Chien Shiung. Cur. biog. p. 491 (1959).

Wu, Kuo-Cheng. Cur. biog. p. 661 (1953).

Wu Yi-Fang. Cur. biog. p. 697 (1945).

Wurster, William Wilson. Cur. biog. p. 666 (1946).

Wurttember staatstheatre (int., Stuttgart). Cooper: Con. ency. of music, p. 459.

Wurzburg. Con. 144: 95 Nov '59.

—— **(etching).** Praeg.: Pict. ency., p. 366.

"Wuthering Heights". Natl. geog. 108: 339 Sept '55.

Wyatt, Henry (work of). Con. 138: XIX Dec '56.

Wyatt, Jane. Cur. biog. p. 599 (1957).

Wyatt, John Whitlow. Cur. biog. p. 941 (1941).

Wyatt, Wilson W. Cur. biog. p. 668 (1946).

Wye house (Maryland). Holiday 16: 31 (col.) Sept '54.

Wyeth, Andrew. Cur. biog. p. 665 (1955).

Wyeth, N.C. Jun. bk. of auth., p. 303.

—— **(book illus. by).** Amer. heri., vol. 8 no. 1 p. 35 (col.) (Dec '56).

—— **(work of).** Amer. heri., vol. 3 no. 1 p. 51 (col.) (fall '51).

Wyld, William (work of). Con. 138: XXXIX Nov '56.

Wyler, William. Cur. biog. p. 671 (1951).

Wyman, Jane. Cur. biog. p. 647 (1949).

Wynants, Jan (work of). Con. 137: XVII (col.) Je '56; 139: XLV Ap '57; 142: 249 (col.) Jan '59.

Wyndham, Sir George O'Brien (Romney). Con. 136: XXVII Nov '55.

Wynn, Ed. Cur. biog. p. 699 (1945).

Wynne, David (sculpture by). Con. 140: 129 Nov '57.

Wyoming. Holiday 10: 26-39 (part col.) Aug '51.

Natl. geog. 109: 2-36 (part col.) Jan '56. Travel 106: 19-22 Jl '56.

—— **(ghost town).** See South Pass City (Wyo.).

—— **(harvest time).** Face of Amer., p. 126-7 (col.).

Wyszynski, Cardinal Stefan. Cur. biog. p. 483 (1958).

X

Xanten, view of (Van der Heyden). Con. 141: 177 (col.) May '58.

Xerxes, King (dining with Esther). Natl. geog. 118: 848-9 (col.) Dec '60.

Xerxes' gate guard. See winged bull.

Xerxes' throne room portals. Ceram: March of arch., p. 174.

Xochimilco (floating gardens, Mexico). Holiday 11: 24 May '52; 14: 56-7 (col.) Jl '53; 22: 107 Sept '57, 34 Oct '57. Travel 101: back cover Jan '54, back cover Mar '54.

x-ray (mouse). Natl. geog. 114: 325 (col.) Sept '58.

x-ray of shells. Natl. geog. 107: 427-33 Mar '55.

x-rayed mummy. See mummy, x-rayed.

Xylophone players. Natl. geog. 99: 12 (col.) Jan '51.

Y

Y Aranda, Jose Jimenez (work of). Con. 145: XLIII May '60.

Y bridge. See bridge, Y.

yacht. Holiday 13: back cover (col.) Jan '53; 21: 115 Feb '57; 28: 86 Sep t'60. Natl. geog. 105: 337 (col.) Mar '54; 110: 393 (col.) Sept '56; 115: 488 (col.) Ap '59. Travel 113: 51 Ap '60; 114: 64 Oct '60.

—— **(Greece).** Natl. geog. 114: 746 (col.) Dec '58.

—— **(Italy).** Natl. geog. 111: 807 (col.) Je '57.

—— **(Norway).** Natl. geog. 106: 174 (col.) Aug '54.

——, **George Crowninshield's "Cleopatra's Barge" (model, 1816).** Holiday 18: 45 (col.) Aug '55.

——, **John Ringling's.** Durant: Pict. hist. of Amer. circus, p. 203.

——, **land.** Holiday 12: 100 Nov '52.

——, **motor.** Holiday 12: 72 (col.) Sept '52.

——, **"Oneida."** Amer. heri., vol. 8 no. 6 p. 13 (Oct '57).

——, **"Royal charger" (King Charles II).** Con. 138: 44 Sept '56.

——, **"Royal George" (King George III).** Amer. heri., vol. 11 no. 4 p. 14 (col.) (Je '60).

yacht basin (Florida Keys). Holiday 6: 119 (col.) Dec '49.

Yacht club (Bermuda). Natl. geog. 113: 768 (col.) Je '58.

yacht club (lunch on lawn). Holiday 10: 44 (col.) Jl '51.

yacht cruise (the "Yankee"). Natl. geog. 116: 768-814 (part col.) Dec '59.

yacht race. Natl. geog. 101: 528, 531 Ap '52.

"Yachting in the 1850's" (Butterworth). Natl. geog. 99: 194 (col.) Feb '51.

yachts. Amer. heri., vol. 9 no. 5 p. 4 (col.) (Aug '58).

Yaffe, James. Cur. biog. p. 601 (1957).

Yafi, Abdullah El. Cur. biog. p. 658 (1956).

Yale Elizabethan club. *See* Elizabethan club, Yale.

Yale fishing team. *See* fishing team, Yale.

Yale university. Holiday 13: 60-3 May '53.

—— **(Harkness tower).** *See* Harkness memorial tower (Yale).

Yamamoto, Adm. Isoroku. Cur. biog. p. 899 (1942).

Yamasaki, Minoru. Cur. biog. p. 476 (1962).

Yamato-e painting (Heian period). Praeg.: Pict. ency., p. 564.

Yamut, Gen. Nuri. Cur. biog. p. 657 (1952).

Yang, Chen Ning. Cur. biog. p. 485 (1958).

Yang, You Chan. Cur. biog. p. 663 (1953).

Yankee Cripper hotel (Ft. Lauderdale, model). Travel 106: 55 Jl '56.

"Yankee Dons." Amer. heri., vol. 9 no. 5 p. 14 (Aug '58).

"Yankee peddler" (by Ehninger). Amer. heri., vol. 7 no. 3 p. 59 (col.) (Ap '56).

Yankee skipper. *See* skipper, Yankee.

Yankee stadium (N.Y.). Holiday 5: 62 Ap '49.

"Yankee" yacht cruise. Natl. geog. 116: 768-814 (part col.) Dec '59.

Yankton Indian. Amer. heri., vol. 6 no. 1 p. 34 (fall '54).

Yap island. Natl. geog. 102: 806-28 (col.) Dec '52.

Yap girl & man. Holiday 28: 90-1 Oct '60.

Yap woman (kneeling, back view). Holiday 28: 75 Oct '60.

—— **(dancing).** Natl. geog. 102: 816-7 (col.) Dec '52.

Yarborough, Ralph W. Cur. biog. p. 469 (1960).

yardstick, mercury. Natl. geog. 100: 762 (col.) Dec '51.

yarn factory. Holiday 11: 114 (col.) May '52.

Yates, Maj. Gen. Donald N. Cur. biog. p. 487 (1958).

Yates, Elizabeth. Cur. biog. p. 697 (1948). Jun. bk. of auth., p. 304.

Yates, Herbert J. Cur. biog. p. 649 (1949). Holiday 5: 42 (col.) Jan '49.

Yates, Mrs. Richard. *See* "Mrs. Richard Yates."

yawl (boat). Natl. geog. 113: 151 (col.) Feb '58; 114: 735 (col.) Dec '58.

——, **Capt. Joshua Slocum's (model).** Holiday 18: 45 (col.) Aug '55.

Yazidis. Natl. geog. 115: 48-9 Jan '59.

Yazilikaya, rock temple (Asia Minor). Osward: Asia Minor pl. 1,9.

Ydigoras Fuentes, Miguel. Cur. biog. p. 488 (1958).

Yeager, Major Charles E. Cur. biog. p. 667 (1954).

Yeats, W. B. Holiday 6: 22 Aug '49.

Yeh, George K. C. Cur. biog. p. 665 (1953).

"Yellow Jack" flag (sym.). Lehner: Pict. bk. of sym., p. 88.

Yellowstone natl. park. Amer. heri., vol. 5 no. 3 p. 41-3 (spring '54). Brooks: Growth of a nation, p. 300. Holiday 8: 44-9 (col.) Aug '50; 10: 30-1 (col.) Aug '51; 16: 121 (col.) Oct '54. Jordan: Hammond's pict. atlas, p. 136 (col.). Natl. geog. 110: 761-78 (col.) Dec '56.

—— **(geysers).** Natl. geog. 117: 358-9 (col.) Mar '60.

—— **(map).** Natl. geog. 110: 762 Dec '56.

Yellowstone waterfalls. Holiday 10: 2, 31 (col.) Aug '51.

Yemen (Arabia). Natl. geog. 101: 214-44 (part col.) Feb '52.

—— **(map).** Natl. geog. 101: 216 Feb '52.

Yemenite. Natl. geog. 104: 43 Jl '53.

Yen, Yang Ch'u James. Cur. biog. p. 671 (1946).

Yeoman of the Guard (England). Holiday 8: 10 (col.) Nov '50; 9: 93 (col.) Mar '51; 11: 129 (col.) Ap '52; 13: 148 May '53, 26, 141 (col.) Je '53; 18: 76 (col.) Dec '55; 21: 32 (col.) Feb '57, 122, 136 (col.) Ap '57, 205 May '57, 98 Je '57; 22: 19 Jl '57, 102 Sept '57, 152 Oct '57, 32 Nov '57, 257 Dec '57; 23: 11 Feb '58, 30 (col.) Ap '58, 148 May '58; 24: 83 Sept '58, 111 Oct '58, 96 Nov '58; 25: 88 Feb '59, 37 Mar '59, 209 Ap '59, 143 May '59, 16 Je '59; 26: 106 Sept '59, 166 Oct '59, 40 Nov '59, 216 Dec '59; 27: 117 Feb '60, 150 Ap '60, 17 May '60; 28: 20 Sept '60, 108 (col.) Oct '60, 206 Nov '60, 180 Dec '60. Int. gr. soc.: Arts . . . p. 159 (col.). Natl. geog. 104: 308 Sept '53.

—— **(head).** Holiday 23: 139 Mar '58; 27: 164 Je '60.

Yerby, Frank. Cur. biog. p. 673 (1946).

Yerushalmy, Jacob. Cur. biog. p. 490 (1958).

Yesil Ture ("Green mausoleum"). Osward: Asia Minor, pl. 80.

Yevtushenko, Yevgeny. Cur. biog. (1963).

Yim, Louise. Cur. biog. p. 695 (1947).

Yin Yang (sym.). Lehner: Pict. bk. of sym., p. 45.

yodelers (Swiss). Holiday 16: 29 Aug '54.

Yoga (philosophies). Lehner: Pict. bk. of sym., p. 43.

Yogi god. *See* Aurobindo, Shri.

"Yoho lodge" (British Columbia). Travel 103: 12 Je '55.

yoke, ox. *See* ox yoke (sym.).

——, shoulder. Rawson: Ant. pict. bk., p. 10.

yokes. Rawson: Ant. pict. bk., p. 66.

Yokohama (Japan, after Perry's visit). Amer. heri., vol. 9 no. 3 p. 98-9 (Ap '58).

Yokosuka harbor. Natl. geog. 116: 310-11 Sept '59.

"Yonker Ramp & his sweetheart" (Hals). Con. 137: cover (col.), 115 Ap '56.

York, Serge. Alvin. Amer. heri., vol. 10 no. 6 p. 12 (col.) (Oct '59).

York, Herbert F. Cur. biog. p. 492 (1958).

York cathedral. Con. ency. of ant., vol. 3, pl. 78.

"York fly departing" (Cross). Con. 141: XVII May '58.

York minster. Holiday 13: 127 Mar '53. Praeg.: Pict. ency., p. 250.

—— (plan). Praeg.: Pict. ency., p. 250.

Yorkshire (Eng.). Holiday 23: 74-5 (col.) Ap '58.

Yorkshire hotel hall. Con. 135: 219 Je '55.

Yorktown (Va., Cornwallis surrender). Travel 110: 19 Jl '58.

Yorktown battlefield. Amer. heri., vol. 9 no. 4 p. 47 (Je '58).

Yorktown monument. Holiday 16: 106 Jl '54.

Yoruba wood carving (Nigeria). Praeg.: Pict. ency., p. 561.

Yosemite falls. Holiday 26: 46 (col.) Jl '59. Natl. geog. 105: 798 (col.) Je '54; 113: 600-1 (col.) May '58. Travel 102: 19 Jl '54, inside cover Oct '54.

Yosemite natl. park. Holiday 13: 120 (col.) Mar '53. Jordan: Hammond's pict. atlas, p. 190 (col.).

Yosemite valley. Natl. geog. 99: 491-98 (col.) Ap '51, 734-5 (col.) Je '51.

"Yosemite Valley" (Hahn). Natl. geog. 99: 204 (col.) Feb '51.

Yoshida, Shigeru. Cur. biog. p. 675 (1946).

Yoshimura, Junzo. Cur. biog. p. 659 (1956).

Yost, Charles W. Cur. biog. p. 493 (1959).

Youlou, Fulbert. Cur. biog. p. 478 (1962).

Youmans, Vincent. Cur. biog. p. 745 (1944).

Young, Alan. Cur. biog. p. 667 (1953).

Young, Art (cartoon by). Amer. heri., vol. 11 no. 2 p. 95 (Feb '60).

—— (poster by). Amer. heri., vol. 11 no. 2 p. 96 (Feb '60).

Young, Brigham. Amer. heri., vol. 6 no. 4 p. 34 (Je '55); vol. 7 no. 6 p. 21 (Oct '56). Brooks: Growth of a nation, p. 128.

Young, Ella. Jun. bk. of auth., p. 306.

Young, Joseph Louis. Cur. biog. p. 471 (1960).

Young, Loretta (Mrs. Tom Lewis). Cur. biog. p. 700 (1948). Holiday 5: 40 (col.) Jan '49.

Young, Marian. Cur. biog. p. 659 (1952).

Young, Milton R. Cur. biog. p. 669 (1954).

Young, Owen D. Cur. biog. p. 701 (1945).

Young, Philip. Cur. biog. p. 673 (1951).

Young, Robert. Cur. biog. p. 633 (1950).

Young, Robert R. Cur. biog. p. 697 (1947).

Young, Stanley. Cur. biog. p. 674 (1951).

Young, Stephen M. Cur. biog. p. 495 (1959).

"Young cottager's first purchase" (Collins). Con. 133: XLVII Je '54.

"Young drummer" (Couture). Con. 139: XLIX Mar '57.

Young family, Robert. Holiday 5: 46 (col.) Jan '49.

"Young fruit seller" (Bonnard). Con. 140: 91 (col.) Nov '57.

"Young fruit seller" (Murillo). Praeg.: Pict. ency., p. 352 (col.).

"Young girl lifting her veil" (Murillo). Con. 139: 54 Mar '57.

"Young girl seated" (Morisot). Con. 134: 67 Sept '54.

"Young violinist" (Schleisner). Con. 136: 45 Sept '55.

"Young widow" (Greuze). Con. 136: 45 Sept '55.

"Young woman at her toilet" (Rembrandt). Con. 138: 31 Sept '56.

Youngdahl, Luther W. Cur. biog. p. 702 (1948).

Younger, Bob. Horan: Pict. hist. of wild west, p. 31-2.

Younger, Coleman. Horan: Pict. hist. of wild west, p. 31.

Younger, James. Horan: Pict. hist. of wild west, p. 31-2.

Younger, Kenneth. Cur. biog. p. 635 (1950).

Younger, Rhetta. Horan: Pict. hist. of wild west, p. 31.

Younger home, James. *See* home, James Younger.

Youskevitch, Igor. Cur. biog. p. 661 (1956).

youth (goddess of). Lehner: Pict. bk. of sym., p. 30.

youth brigade (Yugoslavia). Natl. geog. 99: 150 (col.) Feb '51.

youth hostelers, American. Travel 107: 20-3 Je '57.

"Youth overcoming evil" (sculpture). Natl. geog. 111: 750 (col.) Je '57.

"Youth seated" (Lehmbruck). Int. gr. soc.: Arts . . . p. 131 (col.).

Ypres (cloth hall & town hall). Praeg.: Pict. ency., p. 207.

Ysaye, Eugene. Cooper: Con. ency. of music, p. 308.

Ysuchi. Lehner: Pict. bk. of sym., p. 47.

Yucatan (Maya ruins). Int. gr. soc.: Arts . . . p. 51 (col.). Travel 103: 42-5 May '55.

—— (map). Natl. geog. 115: 95 Jan '59.

Yugoslav (Kolo dancers). Int. gr. soc.: Arts . . . p. 147 (col.).

—— (sword dance). Travel 113: 87 Ap '60.

Yugoslavia. Holiday 10: 72, 74-5 Jl '51; 14: 38-47 (part col.) Aug '53; 25: 80-9 (part col.) Je '59. Natl. geog. 99: 142-71 (part col.) Feb '51.

—— (harbor). Holiday 26: 124 Jl '59. Travel 109: 35 May '58.

—— (man with ox). Holiday 13: 49 (col.) Mar '53.

—— (map). Natl. geog. 99: 144 Feb '51.

Yugoslavians. Holiday 14: 41 (col.), 42-3 Aug '53; 21: 188 May '57.

Yui, O. K. Cur. biog. p. 667 (1955).

Yukawa, Hidiki. Cur. biog. p. 636 (1950).

Yukon (Alaska, map). Natl. geog. 104: 400 Sept '53.
Yukon river (boats). Natl. geog. 112: 246-65 (part col.) Aug '57.
—— (map). Natl. geog. 112: 251 Aug '57.
Yukon trail. Natl. geog. 104: 396-416 Sept '53.
"Yukskei" (African game). Holiday 18: 50 Aug '55.
Yule log. Lehner: Pict. bk. of sym., p. 51.
Yust, Walter. Cur. biog. p. 851 (1943).

Z

Zabach, Florian. Cur. biog. p. 669 (1955).
Zablocki, Clement J. Cur. biog. p. 493 (1958).
Zacharias, Rear Adm. Ellis M. Cur. biog. p. 651 (1949).
"Zachary in the temple" (detail) (Ghirlandaio). Con. 139: 101 Ap '57.
Zadkine, Ossip. Cur. biog. p. 602 (1957).
—— (bronze memorial). Praeg.: Pict. ency., p. 464.
Int. gr. soc.: Arts . . . p 131 (col.).
Zafrullah Kahn, Mohammad Choudri. Cur. biog. p. 700 (1947).
Zagreb (Yugoslavia). Holiday 14: 47 Aug '53.
Zaharias, Babe Didrikson. Cur. biog. p. 701 (1947).
Zahedi, Fazlollah. Cur. biog. p. 671 (1954).
Zampieri, Giuseppe. Holiday 25: 64 (col.) Jan '59.
Zampighi, E. (work of). Con. 139: XLIX Je '57.
Zander, Arnold S. Cur. biog. p. 704 (1947).
Zanicho (Mexico). Holiday 14: 51 Jl '53.
Zanuck, Darryl F. Cur. biog. p. 943 (1941); p. 673 (1954).
Holiday 5: 38 (col.) Jan '49.
Zanzibar. Holiday 19: 98-9 (part col.) May '56.
Natl. geog. 99: 346 Mar '51; 101: 262-77 Feb '52.
—— (map). Natl. geog. 101: 264 Feb '52.
Zapotocky, Antonin. Cur. biog. p. 669 (1953).
Zaroubin, Georgi N. Cur. biog. p. 670 (1953).
Zatopek, Emil. Cur. biog. p. 672 (1953).
"Zechariah" (Sistine chapel ceiling, Michelangelo). Con. 132: 191 Jan '54.
Zeckendorf, William. Cur. biog. p. 661 (1952).
Zeeland, Paul Van. Cur. biog. p. 638 (1950).
Zeineddine, Farid. Cur. biog. p. 604 (1957).
Zellerbach, James D. Cur. biog. p. 704 (1948).
Zelomek, A. Wilbert. Cur. biog. p. 664 (1956).
Zenger, Peter (trial of). Amer. heri., vol. 5 no. 1 p. 25 (col.) (fall '53).
"Zephyr" clipper ship. Amer. heri., vol. 6 no. 6 p. 16-7 (col.) (Oct '55).
Zerbe, Karl. Cur. biog. p. 496 (1959).
Zermatt (Switzerland). Holiday 14: 99 (col.) Aug. '53.
Natl. geog. 110: 438-40 (col.) Oct '56.
Zernike, Frits. Cur. biog. p. 671 (1955).
Zeus. Lehner: Pict. bk. of sym., p. 30.
—— (bronze head). Natl. geog. 109: 41 (col.) Jan '56.
"Zeus abducting Ganymede" (sculpture). Ceram: March of arch., p. 14 (col.).
Zeus temple (plan). See temple of Zeus (plan).
Zevin, Benjamin D. Cur. biog. p. 853 (1943).
Zhukov, Gen. Georgi K. Cur. biog. p. 900 (1942); p. 673 (1955).
Zhukov, Georgy A. Cur. biog. p. 473 (1960).

Ziemer, Gregor. Cur. biog. p. 901 (1942).
Ziff, William B. Cur. biog p. 677 (1946).
Zilboorg, Gregory. Cur. biog. p. 945 (1941).
Zim, Herbert S. Cur. biog. p. 666 (1956).
Jun. bk. of auth., p. 307.
Zimbabwe's elliptical temple (Africa). Natl. geog. 104: 196 Aug '53.
Zimbalist, Efrem. Cur. biog p. 653 (1949).
Zimbalist, Efrem, jr. Cur. biog. p. 475 (1960).
Zimmerman, Max M. Cur. biog. p. 606 (1957).
zinc (sym.). Lehner: Pict. bk. of sym., p. 73.
Zinjanthropus. (called earliest man). Natl. geog. 118: 435 (col.) Sept '60.
Zinn, Walter H. Cur. biog. p. 675 (1955).
Zinnemann, Fred. Cur. biog. p. 673 (1953).
Zion canyon (Utah). Holiday 14: 34 Aug '53.
Zion canyon natl. park. Natl. geog. 105: 39-48, 53-70 (part col.) Jan '54.
Travel 107: 13 Feb '57.
—— (map). Natl. geog. 105: 51 Jan '54.
Zion narrows (Utah). Travel 106: 51-2 Sept '56.
Zirato, Bruno. Cur. biog. p. 498 (1959).
Zoar house (Soc. of the Separatists of Zoar). Amer. heri., vol. 4 no. 3 p. 44, 45 (col.) (spring '53).
Zobel, Benjamin (work of). Con. 135: 111-13 Ap '55.
Zocchi, Giuseppe (work of). Con. 141: 214 Je '58.
Zodiac. Holiday 28: 190 (col.) Nov '60.
—— (ancient Egyptian). Lehner: Pict. bk. of sym., p. 22.
Zodiac signs. Lehner: Pict. bk. of sym., p. 18-9.
Zoffany, Johann (work of). Con. 135: 249 Je '55; 136: 21 Sept '55; 139: 9 Mar '57; 141: 60 Mar '58.
Zoffany, John (work of). Con. 135: XLVI May '55; 141: 269 Je '58; 145: LIII May '60.
Zog I, King of Albania. Cur. biog. p. 747 (1944).
Zola, Emile (Cezanne). Con. 133: 17 Mar '54.
Zoli, Adone. Cur. biog. p. 495 (1958).
Zolotow, Maurice. Cur. biog. p. 608 (1957).
zoo (lion stunt). Natl. geog. 114: 680 (col.) Nov '58.
——, (London). Natl. geog. 103: 770-86 (part col.) Je '53.
——, (Philadelphia). Face of Amer., p. 66-7 (col.).
——, (San Diego). Natl. geog. 105: 777 (col.) Je '54.
——, Brookfield. See Brookfield zoo.
Zook, George F. Cur. biog. p. 680 (1946).
zoological park (Detroit). Jordan: Hammond's pict. atlas, p. 99 (col.).
zoomatic movie camera. Holiday 27: 64 Ap '60.
Zorach, William. Cur. biog. p. 855 (1943); p. 481 (1963).
Zorbaugh, Geraldine E. Cur. biog. p. 668 (1956).
Zorin, Valerian A. Cur. biog. p. 676 (1953).
Zorina, Vera. Cur. biog. p. 947 (1941).
Zorlu, Fatin Rustu. Cur. biog. p. 497 (1958).
Zouave cadet. Amer. heri., vol. 7 no. 5 p. 12 (col.) (Aug '56).
Zouave guard, Colonel. Holiday 11: 99 (col.) Je '52.
Zouave military band. Natl. geog. 105: 343 (col.) Mar '54.